"Nothing is perfect except your words. Oh, how I love them. I think about them all day long."
Psalm 119:96-97

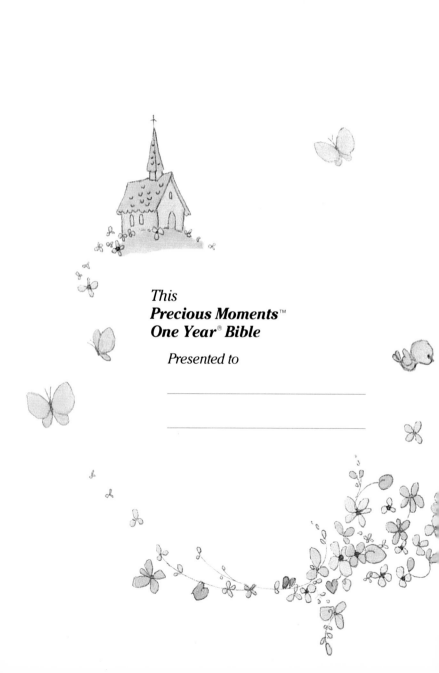

This
***Precious Moments*™**
***One Year*® Bible**

Presented to

By _____

_____

_____

Date _____

THE

PRECIOUS MOMENTS™

ONE YEAR®

BIBLE

Arranged in 365 Daily Readings

The Living Bible

Tyndale House Publishers, Inc.
WHEATON, ILLINOIS

Library of Congress Cataloging-in-Publication Data

Bible. English. Living Bible. 1992.
  The precious moments one year Bible : arranged in 365 daily
readings : the Living Bible.
    p. cm.
  ISBN 0-8423-5021-7 (hardcover). — ISBN 0-8423-5020-9 (softcover)
  1. Devotional calendars. I. Title.
BS391.2.B35   1992
220.5′208—dc20   92-22167

The One Year is a registered trademark of Tyndale House Publishers, Inc.

The Precious Moments
One Year Bible
The Living Bible

The One Year Bible copyright © 1985, 1986, 1987, 1989, 1991, 1992 by Tyndale
House Publishers, Inc., Wheaton, Illinois 60189. All rights reserved.

The Bible text used in this edition of THE ONE YEAR® BIBLE is
The Living Bible. © 1971 owned by assignment by KNT Charitable Trust. All rights
reserved.

Precious Moments illustrations, copyright © 1992 Precious Moments, Incorporated.

Printed in the United States of America

98 97 96 95 94 93 92
 8   7   6   5   4   3   2   1

INDEX
TO THE BOOKS OF THE BIBLE

ALPHABETICAL INDEX
TO THE BOOKS OF THE BIBLE

PUBLISHER'S NOTE

The One Year Bible has been prepared especially for regular Bible readers who wish to read through the entire Bible in one year.

Each day you will read a passage from the Old Testament and one from the New, along with a psalm and one or two proverbs. This gives variety and freshness to your daily reading.

Instead of following a Bible reading chart and experiencing the delay of turning from place to place, you will find the text here in sequence, ready for your quiet reading and meditation.

In this edition of *The One Year Bible* you will find bracketed noun insertions at the beginning of readings where the primary speakers and actors are only referred to by pronouns. These bracketed nouns are not part of the *The Living Bible* text, but they will ensure clarity as you begin each new day's reading.

May this year and every year be enriched as you enjoy daily portions from God's Word!

WAYS TO USE *THE ONE YEAR BIBLE*

The One Year Bible is divided into daily readings. For each day there is a portion of the Old Testament, the New Testament, Psalms, and Proverbs. These four separate daily readings are grouped on consecutive pages, giving diversity to each day's reading. This also makes it easy to use *The One Year Bible* in a variety of ways.

The One Year Bible has led thousands of readers through the Bible in one year. Its arrangement, however, is equally useful for guiding a reader through the Bible in two, or even three, years. If you feel too rushed or want to spend more time on each day's selections, here are a few other suggested reading plans:

The Revised One-Year Plan
Schedule some time in both the morning and evening. Read the New Testament and Psalms selections in the morning and the Old Testament and Proverbs selections in the evening.

The Two-Year Plan
During the first year, read only the Old Testament and Proverbs selections. Then during the second year, read the portions from the New Testament and Psalms.

The Three-Year Plan
Read the Old Testament selections the first year, the New Testament the second year, and the Psalms and Proverbs portions during the third.

Words of Praise and Wisdom in One Year
Read the Psalms and Proverbs selections for each day. This will take you through the Psalms twice and Proverbs once during the year, giving you words of praise and wisdom to live by each day.

And you need not limit yourself to these suggested plans, either. The arrangement of *The One Year Bible* makes it easy to devise any number of Bible reading plans to meet your particular needs.

JANUARY 1

GENESIS 1:1—2:25

WHEN God began creating the heavens and the earth, 2the earth was a shapeless, chaotic mass, with the Spirit of God brooding over the dark vapors.

3Then God said, "Let there be light." And light appeared. 4,5And God was pleased with it, and divided the light from the darkness. He called the light "daytime," and the darkness "nighttime." Together they formed the first day.

6And God said, "Let the vapors separate to form the sky above and the oceans below." 7,8So God made the sky, dividing the vapor above from the water below. This all happened on the second day.

9,10Then God said, "Let the water beneath the sky be gathered into oceans so that the dry land will emerge." And so it was. Then God named the dry land "earth," and the water "seas." And God was pleased. 11,12And he said, "Let the earth burst forth with every sort of grass and seed-bearing plant, and fruit trees with seeds inside the fruit, so that these seeds will produce the kinds of plants and fruits they came from." And so it

was, and God was pleased. 13This all occurred on the third day.

14,15Then God said, "Let bright lights appear in the sky to give light to the earth and to identify the day and the night; they shall bring about the seasons on the earth, and mark the days and years." And so it was. 16For God had made two huge lights, the sun and moon, to shine down upon the earth—the larger one, the sun, to preside over the day and the smaller one, the moon, to preside through the night; he had also made the stars. 17And God set them in the sky to light the earth, 18and to preside over the day and night, and to divide the light from the darkness. And God was pleased. 19This all happened on the fourth day.

20Then God said, "Let the waters teem with fish and other life, and let the skies be filled with birds of every kind." 21,22So God created great sea animals, and every sort of fish and every kind of bird. And God looked at them with pleasure, and blessed them all. "Multiply and stock the oceans," he told them, and to the birds he said, "Let your numbers increase. Fill the earth!" 23That ended the fifth day.

24And God said, "Let the earth bring

forth every kind of animal—cattle and reptiles and wildlife of every kind." And so it was. ²⁵God made all sorts of wild animals and cattle and reptiles. And God was pleased with what he had done.

²⁶Then God said, "Let us make a man—someone like ourselves, to be the master of all life upon the earth and in the skies and in the seas."

²⁷So God made man like his Maker.
Like God did God make man;
Man and maid did he make them.

²⁸And God blessed them and told them, "Multiply and fill the earth and subdue it; you are masters of the fish and birds and all the animals. ²⁹And look! I have given you the seed-bearing plants throughout the earth, and all the fruit trees for your food. ³⁰And I've given all the grass and plants to the animals and birds for their food." ³¹Then God looked over all that he had made, and it was excellent in every way. This ended the sixth day.

NOW at last the heavens and earth were successfully completed, with all that they contained. ²So on the seventh day, having finished his task, God ceased from this work he had been doing, ³and God blessed the seventh day and declared it holy, because it was the day when he ceased this work of creation.

⁴Here is a summary of the events in the creation of the heavens and earth when the Lord God made them.

⁵There were no plants or grain sprouting up across the earth at first, for the Lord God hadn't sent any rain; nor was there anyone to farm the soil. ⁶(However, water welled up from the ground at certain places and flowed across the land.)

⁷The time came when the Lord God formed a man's body from the dust of the ground and breathed into it the breath of life. And man became a living person.

⁸Then the Lord God planted a garden in Eden, to the east, and placed in the garden the man he had formed. ⁹The Lord God planted all sorts of beautiful trees there in the garden, trees producing the choicest of fruit. At the center of the garden he placed the Tree of Life, and also the Tree of Conscience, giving knowledge of Good and Bad. ¹⁰A river from the land of Eden flowed through the garden to water it; afterwards the river divided into four branches. ¹¹,¹²One of these was named the Pishon; it winds across the entire length of the land of Havilah, where nuggets of pure gold are found, also beautiful bdellium and even lapis lazuli. ¹³The second branch is called the Gihon, crossing the entire length of the land of Cush. ¹⁴The third branch is the Tigris, which flows to the east of the city of Asher. And the fourth is the Euphrates.

¹⁵The Lord God placed the man in the Garden of Eden as its gardener, to tend and care for it. ¹⁶,¹⁷But the Lord God gave the man this warning: "You may eat any fruit in the garden except fruit from the Tree of Conscience—for its fruit will open your eyes to make you aware of right and wrong, good and bad. If you eat its fruit, you will be doomed to die."

¹⁸And the Lord God said, "It isn't good for man to be alone; I will make a companion for him, a helper suited to his needs." ¹⁹,²⁰So the Lord God formed from the soil every kind of animal and bird, and brought them to the man to see what he would call them; and whatever he called them, that was their name. But still there was no proper helper for the man. ²¹Then the Lord God caused the man to fall into a deep sleep, and took one of his ribs and closed up the place from which he had removed it, ²²and made the rib into a woman, and brought her to the man.

²³"This is it!" Adam exclaimed. "She is part of my own bone and flesh! Her name is 'woman' because she was taken out of a man." ²⁴This explains why a man leaves his father and mother and is joined to his wife in such a way that the two become one person. ²⁵Now although the man and his wife were both naked, neither of them was embarrassed or ashamed.

THESE are the ancestors of Jesus Christ, a descendant of King David and of Abraham:

2 Abraham was the father of Isaac; Isaac was the father of Jacob; Jacob was the father of Judah and his brothers.

3 Judah was the father of Perez and Zerah (Tamar was their mother); Perez was the father of Hezron; Hezron was the father of Aram;

4 Aram was the father of Amminadab; Amminadab was the father of Nahshon; Nahshon was the father of Salmon;

5 Salmon was the father of Boaz (Rahab was his mother); Boaz was the father of Obed (Ruth was his mother); Obed was the father of Jesse;

6 Jesse was the father of King David. David was the father of Solomon (his mother was the widow of Uriah);

7 Solomon was the father of Rehoboam; Rehoboam was the father of Abijah; Abijah was the father of Asa;

8 Asa was the father of Jehoshaphat; Jehoshaphat was the father of Joram; Joram was the father of Uzziah;

9 Uzziah was the father of Jotham; Jotham was the father of Ahaz; Ahaz was the father of Hezekiah;

10 Hezekiah was the father of Manasseh; Manasseh was the father of Amos; Amos was the father of Josiah;

11 Josiah was the father of Jechoniah and his brothers (born at the time of the exile to Babylon).

12 After the exile:
Jechoniah was the father of Shealtiel; Shealtiel was the father of Zerubbabel;

13 Zerubbabel was the father of Abiud; Abiud was the father of Eliakim; Eliakim was the father of Azor;

14 Azor was the father of Zadok; Zadok was the father of Achim; Achim was the father of Eliud;

15 Eliud was the father of Eleazar; Eleazar was the father of Matthan; Matthan was the father of Jacob;

16 Jacob was the father of Joseph (who was the husband of Mary, the mother of Jesus Christ the Messiah).

17 These are fourteen of the generations from Abraham to King David; and fourteen from King David's time to the exile; and fourteen from the exile to Christ.

THESE are the facts concerning the birth of Jesus Christ: His mother, Mary, was engaged to be married to Joseph. But while she was still a virgin she became pregnant by the Holy Spirit. 19Then Joseph, her fiancé, being a man of stern principle, decided to break the engagement but to do it quietly, as he didn't want to publicly disgrace her.

20As he lay awake considering this, he fell into a dream, and saw an angel standing beside him. "Joseph, son of David," the angel said, "don't hesitate to take Mary as your wife! For the child within her has been conceived by the Holy Spirit. 21And she will have a Son, and you shall name him Jesus (meaning 'Savior'), for he will save his people from their sins. 22This will fulfill God's message through his prophets—

23 'Listen! The virgin shall conceive a child! She shall give birth to a Son, and he shall be called "Emmanuel" (meaning "God is with us").' "

24When Joseph awoke, he did as the angel commanded, and brought Mary home to be his wife, 25but she remained a virgin until her Son was born; and Joseph named him "Jesus."

JESUS was born in the town of Bethlehem, in Judea, during the reign of King Herod.

At about that time some astrologers from eastern lands arrived in Jerusalem, asking, 2"Where is the newborn King of the Jews? for we have seen his star in far-off eastern lands, and have come to worship him."

³King Herod was deeply disturbed by their question, and all Jerusalem was filled with rumors. ⁴He called a meeting of the Jewish religious leaders.

"Did the prophets tell us where the Messiah would be born?" he asked.

⁵"Yes, in Bethlehem," they said, "for this is what the prophet Micah wrote:

⁶'O little town of Bethlehem, you are not just an unimportant Judean village, for a Governor shall rise from you to rule my people Israel.' "

⁷Then Herod sent a private message to the astrologers, asking them to come to see him; at this meeting he found out from them the exact time when they first saw the star. Then he told them, ⁸"Go to Bethlehem and search for the child. And when you find him, come back and tell me so that I can go and worship him too!"

⁹After this interview the astrologers started out again. And look! The star appeared to them again, standing over Bethlehem. ¹⁰Their joy knew no bounds!

¹¹Entering the house where the baby and Mary his mother were, they threw themselves down before him, worshiping. Then they opened their presents and gave him gold, frankincense and myrrh. ¹²But when they returned to their own land, they didn't go through Jerusalem to report to Herod, for God had warned them in a dream to go home another way.

PSALM 1:1–6

OH, the joys of those who do not follow evil men's advice, who do not hang around with sinners, scoffing at the things of God: ²But they delight in doing everything God wants them to, and day and night are always meditating on his laws and thinking about ways to follow him more closely.

³They are like trees along a river bank bearing luscious fruit each season without fail. Their leaves shall never wither, and all they do shall prosper.

⁴But for sinners, what a different story! They blow away like chaff before the wind. ⁵They are not safe on Judgment Day; they shall not stand among the godly.

⁶For the Lord watches over all the plans and paths of godly men, but the paths of the godless lead to doom.

PROVERBS FOR TODAY/ 1:1–6

These are the proverbs of King Solomon of Israel, David's son: He wrote them to teach his people how to live—how to act in every circumstance, for he wanted them to be understanding, just and fair in everything they did. "I want to make the simple-minded wise!" he said. "I want to warn young men about some problems they will face. I want those already wise to become the wiser and become leaders by exploring the depths of meaning in these nuggets of truth."

JANUARY 2

GENESIS 3:1—4:26

THE serpent was the craftiest of all the creatures the Lord God had made. So the serpent came to the woman. "Really?" he asked. *"None* of the fruit in the garden? God says you mustn't eat *any* of it?"

2,3"Of course we may eat it," the woman told him. "It's only the fruit from the tree at the *center* of the garden that we are not to eat. God says we mustn't eat it or even touch it, or we will die."

4"That's a lie!" the serpent hissed. "You'll not die! 5God knows very well that the instant you eat it you will become like him, for your eyes will be opened—you will be able to distinguish good from evil!"

6The woman was convinced. How lovely and fresh looking it was! And it would make her so wise! So she ate some of the fruit and gave some to her husband, and he ate it too. 7And as they ate it, suddenly they became aware of their nakedness, and were embarrassed. So they strung fig leaves together to cover themselves around the hips.

8That evening they heard the sound of the Lord God walking in the garden; and they hid themselves among the trees. 9The Lord God called to Adam, "Why are you hiding?"

10And Adam replied, "I heard you coming and didn't want you to see me naked. So I hid."

11"Who told you you were naked?" the Lord God asked. "Have you eaten fruit from the tree I warned you about?"

12"Yes," Adam admitted, "but it was the woman you gave me who brought me some, and I ate it."

13Then the Lord God asked the woman, "How could you do such a thing?"

"The serpent tricked me," she replied. 14So the Lord God said to the serpent, "This is your punishment: You are singled out from among all the domestic and wild animals of the whole earth—to be cursed. You shall grovel in the dust as long as you live, crawling along on your belly. 15From now on you and the woman will be enemies, as will your offspring and hers. You will strike his heel, but he will crush his head."

16Then God said to the woman, "You shall bear children in intense pain and suffering; yet even so, you shall welcome your husband's affections, and he shall be your master."

17And to Adam, God said, "Because you listened to your wife and ate the fruit when I told you not to, I have placed a curse upon the soil. All your life you will struggle to extract a living from it. 18It will grow thorns and thistles for you, and you shall eat its grasses. 19All your life you will sweat to master it, until your dying day. Then you will return to the ground from which you came. For you were made from the ground, and to the ground you will return."

20The man named his wife Eve (meaning "The life-giving one"), for he said, "She shall become the mother of all mankind"; 21and the Lord God clothed Adam and his wife with garments made from skins of animals.

22Then the Lord said, "Now that the man has become as we are, knowing good from bad, what if he eats the fruit of the Tree of Life and lives forever?" 23So the Lord God banished him forever from the Garden of Eden, and sent him out to farm the ground from which he had been taken. 24Thus God expelled him, and placed mighty angels at the east of the Garden of Eden, with a flaming sword to guard the entrance to the Tree of Life.

THEN Adam had sexual intercourse with Eve his wife, and she conceived and gave birth to a son, Cain (meaning "I have created"). For, as she said, "With God's help, I have created a man!" 2Her next child was his brother, Abel.

Abel became a shepherd, while Cain was a farmer. 3At harvest time Cain brought the Lord a gift of his farm produce, 4and Abel brought the fatty cuts of meat from his best lambs, and presented them to the Lord. And the Lord accepted Abel's offering, 5but not Cain's. This made Cain both dejected and very angry, and his face grew dark with fury.

6"Why are you angry?" the Lord asked him. "Why is your face so dark with rage? 7It can be bright with joy if you will do what you should! But if you refuse to obey, watch out. Sin is waiting to attack you, longing to destroy you. But you can conquer it!"

8One day Cain suggested to his brother, "Let's go out into the fields." And while they were together there, Cain attacked and killed his brother.

9But afterwards the Lord asked Cain, "Where is your brother? Where is Abel?"

"How should I know?" Cain retorted. "Am I supposed to keep track of him wherever he goes?"

10But the Lord said, "Your brother's blood calls to me from the ground. What have you done? 11You are hereby banished from this ground which you have defiled with your brother's blood. 12No longer will it yield crops for you, even if you toil on it forever! From now on you will be a fugitive and a tramp upon the earth, wandering from place to place."

13Cain replied to the Lord, "My punishment is greater than I can bear. 14For you have banished me from my farm and from you, and made me a fugitive and a tramp; and everyone who sees me will try to kill me."

15The Lord replied, "They won't kill you, for I will give seven times your punishment to anyone who does." Then the Lord put an identifying mark on Cain as a warning not to kill him. 16So Cain went out from the presence of the Lord and settled in the land of Nod, east of Eden.

17Then Cain's wife conceived and presented him with a baby son named Enoch; so when Cain founded a city, he named it Enoch, after his son.

18Enoch was the father of Irad;

Irad was the father of Mehujael;

Mehujael was the father of Methusael;

Methusael was the father of Lamech;

19Lamech married two wives—Adah and Zillah. 20To Adah was born a baby named Jabal. He became the first of the cattlemen and those living in tents. 21His brother's name was Jubal, the first musician—the inventor of the harp and flute. 22To Lamech's other wife, Zillah, was born Tubal-cain. He opened the first foundry forging instruments of bronze and iron.

23One day Lamech said to Adah and Zillah, "Listen to me, my wives. I have killed a youth who attacked and wounded me. 24If anyone who kills Cain will be punished seven times, anyone taking revenge against me for killing that youth should be punished seventy-seven times!"

25Later on Eve gave birth to another son and named him Seth (meaning "Granted"); for, as Eve put it, "God has granted me another son for the one Cain killed." 26When Seth grew up, he had a son and named him Enosh. It was during his lifetime that men first began to call themselves "the Lord's people."

MATTHEW 2:13—3:6

AFTER they were gone, an angel of the Lord appeared to Joseph in a dream. "Get up and flee to Egypt with the baby and his mother," the angel said, "and stay there until I tell you to return, for King Herod is going to try to kill the child." 14That same night he left for Egypt with Mary and the baby, 15and stayed there until King Herod's death. This fulfilled the prophet's prediction,

"I have called my Son from Egypt."

16Herod was furious when he learned that the astrologers had disobeyed him. Sending soldiers to Bethlehem, he ordered them to kill every baby boy two years old and under, both in the town and on the nearby farms, for the astrologers had told him the star first appeared to them two years before. 17This brutal action of Herod's fulfilled the prophecy of Jeremiah,

18"Screams of anguish come from Ramah,
Weeping unrestrained;
Rachel weeping for her children,
Uncomforted—
For they are dead."

19When Herod died, an angel of the Lord appeared in a dream to Joseph in Egypt, and told him, 20"Get up and take the baby and his mother back to Israel, for those who were trying to kill the child are dead."

21So he returned immediately to Israel with Jesus and his mother. 22But on the way he was frightened to learn that the new king was Herod's son, Archelaus. Then, in another dream, he was warned not to go to Judea, so they went to Galilee instead, 23and lived in Nazareth. This fulfilled the prediction of the prophets concerning the Messiah,

"He shall be called a Nazarene."

WHILE they were living in Nazareth, John the Baptist began preaching out in the Judean wilderness. His constant theme was, 2"Turn from your sins . . . turn to God . . . for the Kingdom of Heaven is coming soon." 3Isaiah the prophet had told about John's ministry centuries before! He had written,

"I hear a shout from the wilderness,
'Prepare a road for the Lord—straighten out the path where he will walk.' "

4John's clothing was woven from camel's hair and he wore a leather belt; his food was locusts and wild honey. 5People from Jerusalem and from all over the Jordan Valley, and, in fact, from every section of Judea went out to the wilderness to hear him preach, 6and when they confessed their sins, he baptized them in the Jordan River.

PSALM 2:1–12

WHAT fools the nations are to rage against the Lord! How strange that men should try to outwit God! 2For a summit conference of the nations has been called to plot against the Lord and his Messiah, Christ the King. 3"Come, let us break his chains," they say, "and free ourselves from all this slavery to God."

4But God in heaven merely laughs! He is amused by all their puny plans. 5And then in fierce fury he rebukes them and fills them with fear.

6For the Lord declares, "This is the King of my choice, and I have enthroned him in Jerusalem, my holy city."

7His chosen one replies, "I will reveal the everlasting purposes of God, for the Lord has said to me, 'You are my Son. This is your Coronation Day. Today I am giving you your glory.' " 8"Only ask, and I will give you all the nations of the world. 9Rule them with an iron rod; smash them like clay pots!"

10O kings and rulers of the earth, listen while there is time. 11Serve the Lord with reverent fear; rejoice with trembling. 12Fall down before his Son and kiss his feet before his anger is roused and you perish. I am warning you—his wrath will soon begin. But oh, the joys of those who put their trust in him!

JANUARY 3

GENESIS 5:1—7:24

HERE is a list of some of the descendants of Adam—the man who was like God from the day of his creation. ²God created man and woman and blessed them, and called them Man from the start.

3,4,5*Adam:* Adam was 130 years old when his son Seth was born, the very image of his father in every way. After Seth was born, Adam lived another 800 years, producing sons and daughters, and died at the age of 930. 6,7,8*Seth:* Seth was 105 years old when his son Enosh was born. Afterwards he lived another 807 years, producing sons and daughters, and died at the age of 912. 9,10,11*Enosh:* Enosh was ninety years old when his son Kenan was born. Afterwards he lived another 815 years, producing sons and daughters, and died at the age of 905. 12,13,14*Kenan:* Kenan was seventy years old when his son Mahalalel was born. Afterwards he lived another 840 years, producing sons and daughters, and died at the age of 910. 15,16,17*Mahalalel:* Mahalalel was sixty-five years old when his son Jared was born. Afterwards he lived 830 years, producing sons and daughters, and died at the age of 895. 18,19,20*Jared:* Jared was 162 years old when his son

Enoch was born. Afterwards he lived another 800 years, producing sons and daughters, and died at the age of 962. 21-24*Enoch:* Enoch was sixty-five years old when his son Methuselah was born. Afterwards he lived another 300 years in fellowship with God, and produced sons and daughters; then, when he was 365, and in constant touch with God, he disappeared, for God took him! 25,26,27*Methuselah:* Methuselah was 187 years old when his son Lamech was born; afterwards he lived another 782 years, producing sons and daughters, and died at the age of 969. 28-31*Lamech:* Lamech was 182 years old when his son Noah was born. Lamech named him Noah (meaning "Relief") because he said, "He will bring us relief from the hard work of farming this ground which God has cursed." Afterwards Lamech lived 595 years, producing sons and daughters, and died at the age of 777. 32*Noah:* Noah was 500 years old and had three sons, Shem, Ham, and Japheth.

NOW a population explosion took place upon the earth. It was at this time that beings from the spirit world looked upon the beautiful earth women and took any they desired to be their wives. ³Then

Jehovah said, "My Spirit must not forever be disgraced in man, wholly evil as he is. I will give him 120 years to mend his ways."

4In those days, and even afterwards, when the evil beings from the spirit world were sexually involved with human women, their children became giants, of whom so many legends are told. 5When the Lord God saw the extent of human wickedness, and that the trend and direction of men's lives were only towards evil, 6he was sorry he had made them. It broke his heart.

7And he said, "I will blot out from the face of the earth all mankind that I created. Yes, and the animals too, and the reptiles and the birds. For I am sorry I made them."

8But Noah was a pleasure to the Lord. Here is the story of Noah: 9,10He was the only truly righteous man living on the earth at that time. He tried always to conduct his affairs according to God's will. And he had three sons—Shem, Ham, and Japheth.

11Meanwhile, the crime rate was rising rapidly across the earth, and, as seen by God, the world was rotten to the core. 12,13As God observed how bad it was, and saw that all mankind was vicious and depraved, he said to Noah, "I have decided to destroy all mankind; for the earth is filled with crime because of man. Yes, I will destroy mankind from the earth. 14Make a boat from resinous wood, sealing it with tar; and construct decks and stalls throughout the ship. 15Make it 450 feet long, 75 feet wide, and 45 feet high. 16Construct a skylight all the way around the ship, eighteen inches below the roof; and make three decks inside the boat— a bottom, middle, and upper deck—and put a door in the side.

17"Look! I am going to cover the earth with a flood and destroy every living being—everything in which there is the breath of life. All will die. 18But I promise to keep you safe in the ship, with your wife and your sons and their wives. 19,20Bring a pair of every animal—a male and a female—into the boat with you, to keep them alive through the flood. Bring in a pair of each kind of bird and animal and reptile. 21Store away in the boat all the food that they and you will need." 22And Noah did everything as God commanded him.

FINALLY the day came when the Lord said to Noah, "Go into the boat with all your family, for among all the people of the earth, I consider you alone to be righteous. 2Bring in the animals, too—a pair of each, except those kinds I have chosen for eating and for sacrifice: take seven pairs of each of them, 3and seven pairs of every kind of bird. Thus there will be every kind of life reproducing again after the flood has ended. 4One week from today I will begin forty days and nights of rain; and all the animals and birds and reptiles I have made will die."

5So Noah did everything the Lord commanded him. 6He was 600 years old when the flood came. 7He boarded the boat with his wife and sons and their wives, to escape the flood. 8,9With him were all the various kinds of animals— those for eating and sacrifice, and those that were not, and the birds and reptiles. They came into the boat in pairs, male and female, just as God commanded Noah.

10,11,12One week later, when Noah was 600 years, two months, and seventeen days old, the rain came down in mighty torrents from the sky, and the subterranean waters burst forth upon the earth for forty days and nights. 13But Noah had gone into the boat that very day with his wife and his sons, Shem, Ham, and Japheth, and their wives. 14,15With them in the boat were pairs of every kind of animal—domestic and wild—and reptiles and birds of every sort. 16Two by two they came, male and female, just as God had commanded. Then the Lord God closed the door and shut them in.

17For forty days the roaring floods prevailed, covering the ground and lifting the boat high above the earth. 18As the water rose higher and higher above the ground, the boat floated safely upon it; 19until finally the water covered all the high mountains under the whole heaven, 20standing twenty-two feet and more above the highest peaks. 21And all living things upon the earth perished—birds, domestic and wild animals, and reptiles and all mankind— 22everything that breathed and lived upon dry land. 23All existence on the earth was blotted out—man and animals alike, and reptiles and birds. God destroyed them all, leaving only Noah alive, and those with him in the boat. 24And the water covered the earth 150 days.

MATTHEW 3:7—4:11

BUT when he saw many Pharisees and Sadducees coming to be baptized, he denounced them.

"You sons of snakes!" he warned. "Who said that you could escape the coming wrath of God? 8Before being baptized, prove that you have turned from sin by doing worthy deeds. 9Don't try to get by as you are, thinking, 'We are safe for we are Jews—descendants of Abraham.' That proves nothing. God can change these stones here into Jews!

10"And even now the axe of God's judgment is poised to chop down every unproductive tree. They will be chopped and burned.

11"With water I baptize those who repent of their sins; but someone else is coming, far greater than I am, so great that I am not worthy to carry his shoes! He shall baptize you with the Holy Spirit and with fire. 12He will separate the chaff from the grain, burning the chaff with never-ending fire, and storing away the grain."

13Then Jesus went from Galilee to the Jordan River to be baptized there by John. 14John didn't want to do it.

"This isn't proper," he said. "I am the one who needs to be baptized by you."

15But Jesus said, "Please do it, for I must do all that is right." So then John baptized him.

16After his baptism, as soon as Jesus came up out of the water, the heavens were opened to him and he saw the Spirit of God coming down in the form of a dove. 17And a voice from heaven said, "This is my beloved Son, and I am wonderfully pleased with him."

THEN Jesus was led out into the wilderness by the Holy Spirit, to be tempted there by Satan. 2For forty days and forty nights he ate nothing and became very hungry. 3Then Satan tempted him to get food by changing stones into loaves of bread.

"It will prove you are the Son of God," he said.

4But Jesus told him, "No! For the Scriptures tell us that bread won't feed men's souls: obedience to every word of God is what we need."

5Then Satan took him to Jerusalem to the roof of the Temple. 6"Jump off," he said, "and prove you are the Son of God; for the Scriptures declare, 'God will send his angels to keep you from harm,' . . . they will prevent you from smashing on the rocks below."

7Jesus retorted, "It also says not to put the Lord your God to a foolish test!"

8Next Satan took him to the peak of a very high mountain and showed him the nations of the world and all their glory. 9"I'll give it all to you," he said, "if you will only kneel and worship me."

10"Get out of here, Satan," Jesus told him. "The Scriptures say, 'Worship only the Lord God. Obey only him.' "

11Then Satan went away, and angels came and cared for Jesus.

PSALM 3:1–8

O Lord, so many are against me. So many seek to harm me. I have so many enemies. 2So many say that God will never help me. 3But Lord, you are my shield, my glory, and my only hope. You alone can lift my head, now bowed in shame.

⁴I cried out to the Lord, and he heard me from his Temple in Jerusalem. ⁵Then I lay down and slept in peace and woke up safely, for the Lord was watching over me. ⁶And now, although ten thousand enemies surround me on every side, I am not afraid. ⁷I will cry to him, "Arise, O Lord! Save me, O my God!" And he will slap them in the face, insulting them and breaking off their teeth.

⁸For salvation comes from God. What joys he gives to all his people.

PROVERBS FOR TODAY/ 1:10–19

If young toughs tell you, "Come and join us"—turn your back on them! "We'll hide and rob and kill," they say. "Good or bad, we'll treat them all alike. And the loot we'll get! All kinds of stuff! Come on, throw in your lot with us; we'll split with you in equal shares." Don't do it, son! Stay far from men like that, for crime is their way of life, and murder is their specialty. When a bird sees a trap being set, it stays away, but not these men; they trap themselves! They lay a booby trap for their own lives. Such is the fate of all who live by violence and murder. They will die a violent death.

JANUARY 4

GENESIS 8:1—10:32

GOD didn't forget about Noah and all the animals in the boat! He sent a wind to blow across the waters, and the floods began to disappear, ²for the subterranean water sources ceased their gushing, and the torrential rains subsided. ³,⁴So the flood gradually receded until, 150 days after it began, the boat came to rest upon the mountains of Ararat. ⁵Three months later, as the waters continued to go down, other mountain peaks appeared.

⁶After another forty days, Noah opened a porthole ⁷and released a raven that flew back and forth until the earth was dry. ⁸Meanwhile he sent out a dove to see if it could find dry ground, ⁹but the dove found no place to light, and returned to Noah, for the water was still too high. So Noah held out his hand and drew the dove back into the boat.

¹⁰Seven days later Noah released the dove again, ¹¹and this time, towards evening, the bird returned to him with an olive leaf in her beak. So Noah knew that the water was almost gone. ¹²A week later he released the dove again, and this time she didn't come back.

¹³Twenty-nine days after that, Noah opened the door to look, and the water was gone. ¹⁴Eight more weeks went by. Then at last the earth was dry. ¹⁵,¹⁶Then God told Noah, "You may all go out. ¹⁷Release all the animals, birds, and reptiles, so that they will breed abundantly and reproduce in great numbers." ¹⁸,¹⁹So the boat was soon empty. Noah, his wife, and his sons and their wives all disembarked, along with all the animals, reptiles, and birds—all left the ark in pairs and groups.

20Then Noah built an altar and sacrificed on it some of the animals and birds God had designated for that purpose. 21And Jehovah was pleased with the sacrifice and said to himself, "I will never do it again—I will never again curse the earth, destroying all living things, even though man's bent is always toward evil from his earliest youth, and even though he does such wicked things. 22As long as the earth remains, there will be springtime and harvest, cold and heat, winter and summer, day and night."

GOD blessed Noah and his sons and told them to have many children and to repopulate the earth. 2,3"All wild animals and birds and fish will be afraid of you," God told him; "for I have placed them in your power, and they are yours to use for food, in addition to grain and vegetables. 4But never eat animals unless their life-blood has been drained off. 5,6And murder is forbidden. Man-killing animals must die, and any man who murders shall be killed; for to kill a man is to kill one made like God. 7Yes, have many children and repopulate the earth and subdue it."

8Then God told Noah and his sons, 9,10,11"I solemnly promise you and your children and the animals you brought with you—all these birds and cattle and wild animals—that I will never again send another flood to destroy the earth. 12And I seal this promise with this sign: 13I have placed my rainbow in the clouds as a sign of my promise until the end of time, to you and to all the earth. 14When I send clouds over the earth, the rainbow will be seen in the clouds, 15and I will remember my promise to you and to every being, that never again will the floods come and destroy all life. 16,17For I will see the rainbow in the cloud and remember my eternal promise to every living being on the earth."

18The names of Noah's three sons were Shem, Ham, and Japheth. (Ham is the ancestor of the Canaanites.) 19From these three sons of Noah came all the nations of the earth.

20,21Noah became a farmer and planted a vineyard, and he made wine. One day as he was drunk and lay naked in his tent, 22Ham, the father of Canaan, saw his father's nakedness and went outside and told his two brothers. 23Then Shem and Japheth took a robe and held it over their shoulders and, walking backwards into the tent, let it fall across their father to cover his nakedness as they looked the other way. 24,25When Noah awoke from his drunken stupor, and learned what had happened and what Ham, his younger son, had done, he cursed Ham's descendants:

"A curse upon the Canaanites," he swore.

"May they be the lowest of slaves
To the descendants of Shem and Japheth."

26,27Then he said,

"God bless Shem,
And may Canaan be his slave.
God bless Japheth,
And let him share the prosperity of Shem,
And let Canaan be his slave."

28Noah lived another 350 years after the flood, 29and was 950 years old at his death.

THESE are the families of Shem, Ham, and Japheth, who were the three sons of Noah; for sons were born to them after the flood.

2The sons of Japheth were: Gomer, Magog, Madai, Javan, Tubal, Meshech, Tiras.

3The sons of Gomer:
Ashkenaz, Riphath, Togarmah.

4The sons of Javan:
Elishah, Tarshish, Kittim, Dodanim.

5Their descendants became the maritime nations in various lands, each with a separate language. 6The sons of Ham were: Cush, Mizraim, Put, Canaan.

7The sons of Cush were: Seba, Havilah, Sabtah, Raamah, Sabteca.

The sons of Raamah were: Sheba, Dedan.

8One of the descendants of Cush was

Nimrod, who became the first of the kings. 9He was a mighty hunter, blessed of God, and his name became proverbial. People would speak of someone as being "like Nimrod—a mighty hunter, blessed of God." 10The heart of his empire included Babel, Erech, Accad, and Calneh in the land of Shinar. 11,12From there he extended his reign to Assyria. He built Nineveh, Rehoboth-Ir, Calah, and Resen (which is located between Nineveh and Calah), the main city of the empire.

13,14Mizraim was the ancestor of the people inhabiting these areas:

Ludim, Anamim, Lehabim, Naphtuhim, Pathrusim, Casluhim (from whom came the Philistines), and Caphtorim.

15-19Canaan's oldest son was Sidon, and he was also the father of Heth; from Canaan descended these nations:

Jebusites, Amorites, Girgashites, Hivites, Arkites, Sinites, Arvadites, Zemarites, Hamathites.

Eventually the descendants of Canaan spread from Sidon all the way to Gerar, in the Gaza strip; and to Sodom, Gomorrah, Admah, and Zeboiim, near Lasha.

20These, then, were the descendants of Ham, spread abroad in many lands and nations, with many languages.

21Eber descended from Shem, the oldest brother of Japheth. 22Here is a list of Shem's other descendants:

Elam, Asshur, Arpachshad, Lud, Aram.

23Aram's sons were:

Uz, Hul, Gether, Mash.

24Arpachshad's son was Shelah, and Shelah's son was Eber.

25Two sons were born to Eber:

Peleg (meaning "Division," for during his lifetime the people of the world were separated and dispersed), and Joktan (Peleg's brother).

26-30Joktan was the father of Almodad, Sheleph, Hazarmaveth, Jerah, Hadoram, Uzal, Diklah, Obal, Abima-el, Sheba, Ophir, Havi-lah, Jobab.

These descendants of Joktan lived all the way from Mesha to the eastern hills of Sephar.

31These, then, were the descendants of Shem, classified according to their political groupings, languages, and geographical locations.

32All of the men listed above descended from Noah, through many generations, living in the various nations that developed after the flood.

MATTHEW 4:12-25

WHEN Jesus heard that John had been arrested, he left Judea and returned home to Nazareth in Galilee; but soon he moved to Capernaum, beside the Lake of Galilee, close to Zebulun and Naphtali. 14This fulfilled Isaiah's prophecy:

15,16"The land of Zebulun and the land of Naphtali, beside the Lake, and the countryside beyond the Jordan River, and Upper Galilee where so many foreigners live—there the people who sat in darkness have seen a great Light; they sat in the land of death, and the Light broke through upon them."

17From then on, Jesus began to preach, "Turn from sin, and turn to God, for the Kingdom of Heaven is near."

18One day as he was walking along the beach beside the Lake of Galilee, he saw two brothers—Simon, also called Peter, and Andrew—out in a boat fishing with a net, for they were commercial fishermen.

19Jesus called out, "Come along with me and I will show you how to fish for the souls of men!" 20And they left their nets at once and went with him.

21A little farther up the beach he saw two other brothers, James and John, sitting in a boat with their father Zebedee, mending their nets; and he called to them to come too. 22At once they stopped their work and, leaving their father behind, went with him.

23Jesus traveled all through Galilee teaching in the Jewish synagogues, everywhere preaching the Good News about the Kingdom of Heaven. And he healed every kind of sickness and disease. 24The report of his miracles spread far beyond the borders of Galilee so that sick folk were soon coming to be healed from as far away as Syria. And whatever their illness and pain, or if they were possessed by demons, or were insane, or paralyzed—he healed them all. 25Enormous crowds followed him wherever he went—people from Galilee, and the Ten Cities, and Jerusalem, and from all over Judea, and even from across the Jordan River.

PSALM 4:1–8

O God, you have declared me perfect in your eyes; you have always cared for me in my distress; now hear me as I call again. Have mercy on me. Hear my prayer.

2The Lord God asks, "Sons of men, will you forever turn my glory into shame by worshiping these silly idols, when every claim that's made for them is false?"

3Mark this well: The Lord has set apart the redeemed for himself. Therefore he will listen to me and answer when I call to him. 4Stand before the Lord in awe, and do not sin against him. Lie quietly upon your bed in silent meditation. 5Put your trust in the Lord, and offer him pleasing sacrifices.

6Many say that God will never help us. Prove them wrong, O Lord, by letting the light of your face shine down upon us. 7Yes, the gladness you have given me is far greater than their joys at harvest time as they gaze at their bountiful crops. 8I will lie down in peace and sleep, for though I am alone, O Lord, you will keep me safe.

PROVERBS FOR TODAY/ 1:20–23

Wisdom shouts in the streets for a hearing. She calls out to the crowds along Main Street, and to the judges in their courts, and to everyone in all the land: "You simpletons!" she cries. "How long will you go on being fools? How long will you scoff at wisdom and fight the facts? Come here and listen to me! I'll pour out the spirit of wisdom upon you, and make you wise.

JANUARY 5

GENESIS 11:1—13:4

AT that time all mankind spoke a single language. 2As the population grew and spread eastward, a plain was discovered in the land of Babylon, and was soon thickly populated. 3,4The people who lived there began to talk about building a great city, with a temple-tower reaching to the skies—a proud, eternal monument to themselves.

"This will weld us together," they said, "and keep us from scattering all over the world." So they made great piles of hardburned brick, and collected bitumen to use as mortar.

5But when God came down to see the city and the tower mankind was making, 6he said, "Look! If they are able to accomplish all this when they have just *begun* to exploit their linguistic and political unity, just think of what they will do later! Nothing will be unattainable for them! 7Come, let us go down and give them different languages, so that they won't understand each other's words!"

8So, in that way, God scattered them all over the earth; and that ended the building of the city. 9That is why the city was called Babel (meaning "confusion"), because it was there that Jehovah confused them by giving them many languages, thus widely scattering them across the face of the earth.

10,11Shem's line of descendants included Arpachshad, born two years after the flood when Shem was 100 years old; after that he lived another 500 years, and had many sons and daughters.

12,13When Arpachshad was thirty-five years old, his son Shelah was born, and after that he lived another 403 years, and had many sons and daughters.

14,15Shelah was thirty years old when his son Eber was born, living 403 years after that, and had many sons and daughters.

16,17Eber was thirty-four years old when his son Peleg was born. He lived another 430 years afterwards, and had many sons and daughters.

18,19Peleg was thirty years old when his son Reu was born. He lived another 209 years afterwards, and had many sons and daughters.

20,21Reu was thirty-two years old when Serug was born. He lived 207 years after that, with many sons and daughters.

22,23Serug was thirty years old when his son Nahor was born. He lived 200 years afterwards, with many sons and daughters.

24,25Nahor was twenty-nine years old at the birth of his son Terah. He lived 119 years afterwards, and had sons and daughters.

26By the time Terah was seventy years old, he had three sons, Abram, Nahor, and Haran.

27And Haran had a son named Lot. 28But Haran died young, in the land where he was born (in Ur of the Chaldeans), and was survived by his father.

29Meanwhile, Abram married his half-sister Sarai, while his brother Nahor married their orphaned niece Milcah, who was the daughter of their brother Haran; and she had a brother named Iscah. 30But Sarai was barren; she had no children. 31Then Terah took his son Abram, his grandson Lot (his son Haran's child), and his daughter-in-law Sarai, and left Ur of the Chaldeans to go to the land of Canaan; but they stopped instead at the city of Haran and settled there. 32And there Terah died at the age of 205.

GOD had told Abram, "Leave your own country behind you, and your own people, and go to the land I will guide you to. 2If you do, I will cause you to become the father of a great nation; I will bless you and make your name famous, and you will be a blessing to many others. 3I will bless those who bless you and curse those who curse you; and the entire world will be blessed because of you."

4So Abram departed as the Lord had instructed him, and Lot went too; Abram was seventy-five years old at that time. 5He took his wife Sarai, his nephew Lot, and all his wealth—the cattle and slaves he had gotten in Haran—and finally arrived in Canaan. 6Traveling through Canaan, they came to a place near Shechem, and set up camp beside the oak at Moreh. (This area was inhabited by Canaanites at that time.)

7Then Jehovah appeared to Abram and said, "I am going to give this land to your descendants." And Abram built an altar there to commemorate Jehovah's visit. 8Afterwards Abram left that place and traveled southward to the hilly country between Bethel on the west and Ai on the east. There he made camp, and made an altar to the Lord and prayed to him. 9Thus he continued slowly southward to the Negeb, pausing frequently.

10There was at that time a terrible famine in the land: and so Abram went on down to Egypt to live. 11,12,13But as he was approaching the borders of Egypt, he asked Sarai his wife to tell everyone that she was his sister! "You are very beautiful," he told her, "and when the Egyptians see you they will say, 'This is his wife. Let's kill him and then we can have her!' But if you say you are my sister, then the Egyptians will treat me well because of you, and spare my life!" 14And sure enough, when they arrived in Egypt everyone spoke of her beauty. 15When the palace aides saw her, they praised her to their king, the Pharaoh, and she was taken into his harem. ¹⁶Then Pharaoh gave Abram many gifts because of her—sheep, oxen, donkeys, men and women slaves, and camels.

¹⁷But the Lord sent a terrible plague upon Pharaoh's household on account of her being there. ¹⁸Then Pharaoh called Abram before him and accused him sharply. "What is this you have done to me?" he demanded. "Why didn't you tell me she was your wife? ¹⁹Why were you willing to let me marry her, saying she was your sister? Here, take her and be gone!" ²⁰And Pharaoh sent them out of the country under armed escort—Abram, his wife, and all his household and possessions.

So they left Egypt and traveled north into the Negeb—Abram with his wife, and Lot, and all that they owned, for Abram was very rich in livestock, silver, and gold. ³,⁴Then they continued northward toward Bethel where he had camped before, between Bethel and Ai—to the place where he had built the altar. And there he again worshiped the Lord.

MATTHEW 5:1–26

ONE day as the crowds were gathering, he went up the hillside with his disciples and sat down and taught them there.

³"Humble men are very fortunate!" he told them, "for the Kingdom of Heaven is given to them. ⁴Those who mourn are fortunate! for they shall be comforted. ⁵The meek and lowly are fortunate! for the whole wide world belongs to them.

⁶"Happy are those who long to be just and good, for they shall be completely satisfied. ⁷Happy are the kind and merciful, for they shall be shown mercy. ⁸Happy are those whose hearts are pure, for they shall see God. ⁹Happy are those who strive for peace—they shall be called the sons of God. ¹⁰Happy are those who are persecuted because they are good, for the Kingdom of Heaven is theirs.

¹¹"When you are reviled and persecuted and lied about because you are my followers—wonderful! ¹²Be *happy* about it! Be *very glad!* for a *tremendous reward* awaits you up in heaven. And remember, the ancient prophets were persecuted too.

¹³"You are the world's seasoning, to make it tolerable. If you lose your flavor, what will happen to the world? And you yourselves will be thrown out and trampled underfoot as worthless. ¹⁴You are the world's light—a city on a hill, glowing in the night for all to see. ¹⁵,¹⁶Don't hide your light! Let it shine for all; let your good deeds glow for all to see, so that they will praise your heavenly Father.

¹⁷"Don't misunderstand why I have come—it isn't to cancel the laws of Moses and the warnings of the prophets. No, I came to fulfill them, and to make them all come true. ¹⁸With all the earnestness I have I say: Every law in the Book will continue until its purpose is achieved. ¹⁹And so if anyone breaks the least commandment, and teaches others to, he shall be the least in the Kingdom of Heaven. But those who teach God's laws *and obey them* shall be great in the Kingdom of Heaven.

²⁰"But I warn you—unless your goodness is greater than that of the Pharisees and other Jewish leaders, you can't get into the Kingdom of Heaven at all!

²¹"Under the laws of Moses the rule was, 'If you murder, you must die.' ²²But I have added to that rule, and tell you that if you are only *angry,* even in your own home, you are in danger of judgment! If you call your friend an idiot, you are in danger of being brought before the court. And if you curse him, you are in danger of the fires of hell.

²³"So if you are standing before the altar in the Temple, offering a sacrifice to God, and suddenly remember that a friend has something against you, ²⁴leave your sacrifice there beside the altar and go and apologize and be reconciled to him, and then come and offer your sacrifice to God. ²⁵Come to terms

quickly with your enemy before it is too late and he drags you into court and you are thrown into a debtor's cell, 26for you will stay there until you have paid the last penny.

PSALM 5:1–12

O Lord, hear me praying; listen to my plea, O God my King, for I will never pray to anyone but you. 3Each morning I will look to you in heaven and lay my requests before you, praying earnestly.

4I know you get no pleasure from wickedness and cannot tolerate the slightest sin. 5Therefore proud sinners will not survive your searching gaze, for how you hate their evil deeds. 6You will destroy them for their lies; how you abhor all murder and deception.

7But as for me, I will come into your Temple protected by your mercy and your love; I will worship you with deepest awe.

8Lord, lead me as you promised me you would; otherwise my enemies will conquer me. Tell me clearly what to do, which way to turn. 9For they cannot speak one truthful word. Their hearts are filled to the brim with wickedness. Their suggestions are full of the stench of sin and death. Their tongues are filled with flatteries to gain their wicked ends. 10O God, hold them responsible. Catch them in their own traps; let them fall beneath the weight of their own transgressions, for they rebel against you.

11But make everyone rejoice who puts his trust in you. Keep them shouting for joy because you are defending them. Fill all who love you with your happiness. 12For you bless the godly man, O Lord; you protect him with your shield of love.

PROVERBS FOR TODAY/ 1:24–28

I have called you so often but still you won't come. I have pleaded, but all in vain. For you have spurned my counsel and reproof. Some day you'll be in trouble, and I'll laugh! Mock me, will you?—I'll mock you! When a storm of terror surrounds you, and when you are engulfed by anguish and distress, then I will not answer your cry for help. It will be too late though you search for me ever so anxiously.

JANUARY 6

GENESIS 13:5—15:21

L OT too was very wealthy, with sheep and cattle and many servants. ⁶But the land could not support both Abram and Lot with all their flocks and herds. There were too many animals for the available pasture. ⁷So fights broke out between the herdsmen of Abram and Lot, despite the danger they all faced from the tribes of Canaanites and Perizzites present in the land. ⁸Then Abram talked it over with Lot. "This fighting between our men has got to stop," he said. "We can't afford to let a rift develop between our clans. Close relatives such as we are must present a united front! ⁹I'll tell you what we'll do. Take your choice of any section of the land you want, and we will separate. If you want that part over there to the east, then I'll stay here in the western section. Or, if you want the west, then I'll go over there to the east."

¹⁰Lot took a long look at the fertile plains of the Jordan River, well watered everywhere (this was before Jehovah destroyed Sodom and Gomorrah); the whole section was like the Garden of Eden, or like the beautiful countryside around Zoar in Egypt. ¹¹So that is what Lot chose—the Jordan valley to the east of them. He went there with his flocks and servants, and thus he and Abram parted company. ¹²For Abram stayed in the land of Canaan, while Lot lived among the cities of the plain, settling at a place near the city of Sodom. ¹³The men of this area were unusually wicked, and sinned greatly against Jehovah.

¹⁴After Lot was gone, the Lord said to Abram, "Look as far as you can see in every direction, ¹⁵for I am going to give it all to you and your descendants. ¹⁶And I am going to give you so many descendants that, like dust, they can't be counted! ¹⁷Hike in all directions and explore the new possessions I am giving you." ¹⁸Then Abram moved his tent to the oaks of Mamre, near Hebron, and built an altar to Jehovah there.

NOW war filled the land—
Amraphel, king of Shinar,
    Arioch, king of Ellasar,
    Ched-or-laomer, king of Elam, and
    Tidal, king of Goiim.
²Fought against:
Bera, king of Sodom,
Birsha, king of Gomorrah,
Shinab, king of Admah,
Shemeber, king of Zeboiim, and
The king of Bela (later called Zoar).
³These kings (of Sodom, Gomorrah, Admah, Zeboiim, and Bela) mobilized their armies in Siddim Valley (that is, the valley of the Dead Sea). ⁴For twelve years they had all been subject to King Ched-or-laomer, but now in the thirteenth year, they rebelled.

⁵,⁶One year later, Ched-or-laomer and his allies arrived and the slaughter began. For they were victorious over the following tribes at the places indicated:
    The Rephaim in Ashteroth-karnaim;
    The Zuzim in Ham;
    The Emim in the plain of Kiriathaim;
    The Horites in Mount Seir, as far as
        El-paran at the edge of the desert.
⁷Then they swung around to Enmishpat (later called Kadesh) and destroyed the Amalekites, and also the Amorites living in Hazazan-tamar.

⁸,⁹But now the other army, that of the kings of Sodom, Gomorrah, Admah, Zeboiim, and Bela (Zoar), unsuccessfully at-

tacked Ched-or-laomer and his allies as they were in the Dead Sea Valley (four kings against five). 10As it happened, the valley was full of asphalt pits. And as the army of the kings of Sodom and Gomorrah fled, some slipped into the pits, and the remainder fled to the mountains. 11Then the victors plundered Sodom and Gomorrah and carried off all their wealth and food, and went on their homeward way, 12taking with them Lot—Abram's nephew who lived in Sodom—and all he owned. 13One of the men who escaped came and told Abram the Hebrew, who was camping among the oaks belonging to Mamre the Amorite (brother of Eshcol and Aner, Abram's allies).

14When Abram learned that Lot had been captured, he called together the men born into his household, 318 of them in all, and chased after the retiring army as far as Dan. 15He divided his men and attacked during the night from several directions, and pursued the fleeing army to Hobah, north of Damascus, 16and recovered everything—the loot that had been taken, his relative Lot, and all of Lot's possessions, including the women and other captives.

17As Abram returned from his strike against Ched-or-laomer and the other kings at the Valley of Shaveh (later called King's Valley), the king of Sodom came out to meet him, 18and Melchizedek, the king of Salem (Jerusalem), who was a priest of the God of Highest Heaven, brought him bread and wine. 19,20Then Melchizedek blessed Abram with this blessing:

"The blessing of the supreme God, Creator of heaven and earth, be upon you, Abram; and blessed be God, who has delivered your enemies over to you."

Then Abram gave Melchizedek a tenth of all the loot.

21The king of Sodom told him, "Just give me back my people who were captured; keep for yourself the booty stolen from my city."

22But Abram replied, "I have solemnly promised Jehovah, the supreme God, Creator of heaven and earth, 23that I will not take so much as a single thread from you, lest you say, 'Abram is rich because of what I gave him!' 24All I'll accept is what these young men of mine have eaten; but give a share of the loot to Aner, Eshcol, and Mamre, my allies."

AFTERWARDS Jehovah spoke to Abram in a vision, and this is what he told him: "Don't be fearful, Abram, for I will defend you. And I will give you great blessings."

2,3But Abram replied, "O Lord Jehovah, what good are all your blessings when I have no son? For without a son, some other member of my household will inherit all my wealth."

4Then Jehovah told him, "No, no one else will be your heir, for you will have a son to inherit everything you own."

5Then God brought Abram outside beneath the nighttime sky and told him, "Look up into the heavens and count the stars if you can. Your descendants will be like that—too many to count!" 6And Abram believed God; then God considered him righteous on account of his faith.

7And he told him, "I am Jehovah who brought you out of the city of Ur of the Chaldeans, to give you this land."

8But Abram replied, "O Lord Jehovah, how can I be sure that you will give it to me?" 9Then Jehovah told him to take a three-year-old heifer, a three-year-old female goat, a three-year-old ram, a turtledove and a young pigeon, 10and to slay them and to cut them apart down the middle, and to separate the halves, but not to divide the birds. 11And when the vultures came down upon the carcasses, Abram shooed them away.

12That evening as the sun was going down, a deep sleep fell upon Abram, and a vision of terrible foreboding, darkness, and horror.

13Then Jehovah told Abram, "Your descendants will be oppressed as slaves in a foreign land for 400 years. 14But I will punish the nation that enslaves them, and at the end they will come away with great wealth. 15(But you will die in peace, at a ripe old age.) 16After four generations they will return here to this land; for the wickedness of the Amorite nations living here now will not be ready for punishment until then."

17As the sun went down and it was dark, Abram saw a smoking fire-pot and a flaming torch that passed between the halves of the carcasses. 18So that day Jehovah made this covenant with Abram: "I have given this land to your descendants from the Wadi-el-Arish to the Euphrates River. 19,20,21And I give to them these nations:

Kenites, Kenizzites, Kadmonites, Hittites, Perizzites, Rephaim, Amorites, Canaanites, Girgashites, Jebusites."

MATTHEW 5:27–48

THE laws of Moses said, 'You shall not commit adultery.' 28But I say: Anyone who even looks at a woman with lust in his eye has already committed adultery with her in his heart. 29So if your eye—even if it is your best eye!—causes you to lust, gouge it out and throw it away. Better for part of you to be destroyed than for all of you to be cast into hell. 30And if your hand—even your right hand—causes you to sin, cut it off and throw it away. Better that than find yourself in hell.

31"The law of Moses says, 'If anyone wants to be rid of his wife, he can divorce her merely by giving her a letter of dismissal.' 32But I say that a man who divorces his wife, except for fornication, causes her to commit adultery if she marries again. And he who marries her commits adultery.

33"Again, the law of Moses says, 'You shall not break your vows to God, but must fulfill them all.' 34But I say: Don't make any vows! And even to say, 'By

heavens!' is a sacred vow to God, for the heavens are God's throne. 35And if you say 'By the earth!' it is a sacred vow, for the earth is his footstool. And don't swear 'By Jerusalem!' for Jerusalem is the capital of the great King. 36Don't even swear 'By my head!' for you can't turn one hair white or black. 37Say just a simple 'Yes, I will' or 'No, I won't.' Your word is enough. To strengthen your promise with a vow shows that something is wrong.

38"The law of Moses says, 'If a man gouges out another's eye, he must pay with his own eye. If a tooth gets knocked out, knock out the tooth of the one who did it.' 39But I say: Don't resist violence! If you are slapped on one cheek, turn the other too. 40If you are ordered to court, and your shirt is taken from you, give your coat too. 41If the military demand that you carry their gear for a mile, carry it two. 42Give to those who ask, and don't turn away from those who want to borrow.

43"There is a saying, 'Love your *friends* and hate your enemies.' 44But I say: Love your *enemies!* Pray for those who *persecute* you! 45In that way you will be acting as true sons of your Father in heaven. For he gives his sunlight to both the evil and the good, and sends rain on the just and on the unjust too. 46If you love only those who love you, what good is that? Even scoundrels do that much. 47If you are friendly only to your friends, how are you different from anyone else? Even the heathen do that. 48But you are to be perfect, even as your Father in heaven is perfect.

PSALM 6:1–10

NO, Lord! Don't punish me in the heat of your anger. 2Pity me, O Lord, for I am weak. Heal me, for my body is sick, 3and I am upset and disturbed. My mind is filled with apprehension and with gloom. Oh, restore me soon.

4Come, O Lord, and make me well. In your kindness save me. 5For if I die I cannot give you glory by praising you before my friends. 6I am worn out with pain; every night my pillow is wet with tears. 7My eyes are growing old and dim with grief because of all my enemies.

8Go, leave me now, you men of evil deeds, for the Lord has heard my weeping 9and my pleading. He will answer all my prayers. 10All my enemies shall be suddenly dishonored, terror-stricken, and disgraced. God will turn them back in shame.

PROVERBS FOR TODAY/ 1:29–33

"For you closed your eyes to the facts and did not choose to reverence and trust the Lord, and you turned your back on me, spurning my advice. That is why you must eat the bitter fruit of having your own way, and experience the full terrors of the pathway you have chosen. For you turned away from me—to death; your own complacency will kill you. Fools! But all who listen to me shall live in peace and safety, unafraid."

JANUARY 7

GENESIS 16:1—18:19

BUT Sarai and Abram had no children. So Sarai took her maid, an Egyptian girl named Hagar, 2,3and gave her to Abram to be his second wife.

"Since the Lord has given me no children," Sarai said, "you may sleep with my servant girl, and her children shall be mine."

And Abram agreed. (This took place ten years after Abram had first arrived in the land of Canaan.) 4So he slept with Hagar, and she conceived; and when she realized she was pregnant, she became very proud and arrogant toward her mistress Sarai.

5Then Sarai said to Abram, "It's all your fault. For now this servant girl of mine despises me, though I myself gave her the privilege of being your wife. May the Lord judge you for doing this to me!"

6"You have my permission to punish the girl as you see fit," Abram replied. So Sarai beat her and she ran away.

7The Angel of the Lord found her beside a desert spring along the road to Shur.

8*The Angel:* "Hagar, Sarai's maid, where have you come from, and where are you going?"

Hagar: "I am running away from my mistress."

9–12*The Angel:* "Return to your mistress and act as you should, for I will make you into a great nation. Yes, you are pregnant and your baby will be a son, and you are to name him Ishmael ('God hears'), because God has heard your woes. This son of yours will be a wild one—free and untamed as a wild ass!

He will be against everyone, and everyone will feel the same tow him. But he will live near the rest of his kin."

¹³Thereafter Hagar spoke of Jehovah—for it was he who appeared to her—as "the God who looked upon me," for she thought, "I saw God and lived to tell it."

¹⁴Later that well was named "The Well of the Living One Who Sees Me." It lies between Kadesh and Bered.

¹⁵So Hagar gave Abram a son, and Abram named him Ishmael. ¹⁶(Abram was eighty-six years old at this time.)

WHEN Abram was ninety-nine years old, God appeared to him and told him, "I am the Almighty; obey me and live as you should. ²,³,⁴I will prepare a contract between us, guaranteeing to make you into a mighty nation. In fact you shall be the father of not only one nation, but a multitude of nations!" Abram fell face downward in the dust as God talked with him.

⁵"What's more," God told him, "I am changing your name. It is no longer 'Abram' ('Exalted Father'), but 'Abraham' ('Father of Nations')—for that is what you will be. I have declared it. ⁶I will give you millions of descendants who will form many nations! Kings shall be among your descendants! ⁷,⁸And I will continue this agreement between us generation after generation, forever, for it shall be between me and your children as well. It is a contract that I shall be your God and the God of your posterity. And I will give all this land of Canaan to you and them, forever. And I will be your God.

⁹,¹⁰"Your part of the contract," God told him, "is to obey its terms. You personally and all your posterity have this continual responsibility: that every male among you shall be circumcised; ¹¹the foreskin of his penis shall be cut off. This will be the proof that you and they accept this covenant. ¹²Every male shall be circumcised on the eighth day after birth. This applies to every foreign-born slave as well as to everyone born

in your household. This is a permanent part of this contract, and it applies to all your posterity. ¹³All must be circumcised. Your bodies will thus be marked as participants in my everlasting covenant. ¹⁴Anyone who refuses these terms shall be cut off from his people; for he has violated my contract."

¹⁵Then God added, "Regarding Sarai your wife—her name is no longer 'Sarai' but 'Sarah' ('Princess'). ¹⁶And I will bless her and give you a son from her! Yes, I will bless her richly, and make her the mother of nations! Many kings shall be among your posterity."

¹⁷Then Abraham threw himself down in worship before the Lord, but inside he was laughing in disbelief! "Me, be a father?" he said in amusement. "Me—100 years old? And Sarah, to have a baby at 90?"

¹⁸And Abraham said to God, "Yes, do bless Ishmael!"

¹⁹"No," God replied, "that isn't what I said. *Sarah* shall bear you a son; and you are to name him Isaac ('Laughter'), and I will sign my covenant with him forever, and with his descendants. ²⁰As for Ishmael, all right, I will bless him also, just as you have asked me to. I will cause him to multiply and become a great nation. Twelve princes shall be among his posterity. ²¹But my contract is with Isaac, who will be born to you and Sarah next year at about this time."

²²That ended the conversation and God left. ²³Then, that very day, Abraham took Ishmael his son and every other male—born in his household or bought from outside—and cut off their foreskins, just as God had told him to. ²⁴⁻²⁷Abraham was ninety-nine years old at that time, and Ishmael was thirteen. Both were circumcised the same day, along with all the other men and boys of the household, whether born there or bought as slaves.

THE Lord appeared again to Abraham while he was living in the oak grove at Mamre. This is the way it happened: One hot summer afternoon as he was sitting in the opening of his tent, 2he suddenly noticed three men coming toward him. He sprang up and ran to meet them and welcomed them.

3,4"Sirs," he said, "please don't go any further. Stop awhile and rest here in the shade of this tree while I get water to refresh your feet, 5and a bite to eat to strengthen you. Do stay awhile before continuing your journey."

"All right," they said, "do as you have said."

6Then Abraham ran back to the tent and said to Sarah, "Quick! Mix up some pancakes! Use your best flour, and make enough for the three of them!" 7Then he ran out to the herd and selected a fat calf and told a servant to hurry and butcher it. 8Soon, taking them cheese and milk and the roast veal, he set it before the men and stood beneath the trees beside them as they ate.

9"Where is Sarah, your wife?" they asked him.

"In the tent," Abraham replied.

10Then the Lord said, "Next year I will give you and Sarah a son!" (Sarah was listening from the tent door behind him.) 11Now Abraham and Sarah were both very old, and Sarah was long since past the time when she could have a baby.

12So Sarah laughed silently. "A woman my age have a baby?" she scoffed to herself. "And with a husband as old as mine?"

13Then God said to Abraham, "Why did Sarah laugh? Why did she say 'Can an old woman like me have a baby?' 14Is anything too hard for God? Next year, just as I told you, I will certainly see to it that Sarah has a son."

15But Sarah denied it. "I didn't laugh," she lied, for she was afraid.

16Then the men stood up from their meal and started on toward Sodom; and Abraham went with them part of the way.

17"Should I hide my plan from Abraham?" God asked. 18"For Abraham shall become a mighty nation, and he will be a source of blessing for all the nations of the earth. 19And I have picked him out to have godly descendants and a godly household—men who are just and good—so that I can do for him all I have promised."

MATTHEW 6:1–24

TAKE care! Don't do your good deeds publicly, to be admired, for then you will lose the reward from your Father in heaven. 2When you give a gift to a beggar, don't shout about it as the hypocrites do—blowing trumpets in the synagogues and streets to call attention to their acts of charity! I tell you in all earnestness, they have received all the reward they will ever get. 3But when you do a kindness to someone, do it secretly—don't tell your left hand what your right hand is doing. 4And your Father who knows all secrets will reward you.

5"And now about prayer. When you pray, don't be like the hypocrites who pretend piety by praying publicly on street corners and in the synagogues where everyone can see them. Truly, that is all the reward they will ever get. 6But when you pray, go away by yourself, all alone, and shut the door behind you and pray to your Father secretly, and your Father, who knows your secrets, will reward you.

7,8"Don't recite the same prayer over and over as the heathen do, who think prayers are answered only by repeating them again and again. Remember, your Father knows exactly what you need even before you ask him!

9"Pray along these lines: 'Our Father in heaven, we honor your holy name. 10We ask that your kingdom will come now. May your will be done here on earth, just as it is in heaven. 11Give us our food again today, as usual, 12and forgive us our sins, just as we have forgiven those who have sinned against us. 13Don't bring us into temptation, but de-

liver us from the Evil One. Amen.'
14,15Your heavenly Father will forgive you if you forgive those who sin against you; but if *you* refuse to forgive *them, he* will not forgive *you.*

16"And now about fasting. When you fast, declining your food for a spiritual purpose, don't do it publicly, as the hypocrites do, who try to look wan and disheveled so people will feel sorry for them. Truly, that is the only reward they will ever get. 17But when you fast, put on festive clothing, 18so that no one will suspect you are hungry, except your Father who knows every secret. And he will reward you.

19"Don't store up treasures here on earth where they can erode away or may be stolen. 20Store them in heaven where they will never lose their value, and are safe from thieves. 21If your profits are in heaven your heart will be there too.

22"If your eye is pure, there will be sunshine in your soul. 23But if your eye is clouded with evil thoughts and desires, you are in deep spiritual darkness. And oh, how deep that darkness can be!

24"You cannot serve two masters: God and money. For you will hate one and love the other, or else the other way around.

PSALM 7:1–17

I am depending on you, O Lord my God, to save me from my persecutors. 2Don't let them pounce upon me as a lion would and maul me and drag me away with no one to rescue me. 3It would be different, Lord, if I were doing evil things— 4if I were paying back evil for good or unjustly attacking those I dislike. 5Then it would be right for you to let my enemies destroy me, crush me to the ground, and trample my life in the dust.

6But Lord! Arise in anger against the anger of my enemies. Awake! Demand justice for me, Lord! 7,8Gather all peoples before you; sit high above them, judging their sins. But justify me publicly; establish my honor and truth before them all. 9End all wickedness, O Lord, and bless all who truly worship God; for you, the righteous God, look deep within the hearts of men and examine all their motives and their thoughts.

10God is my shield; he will defend me. He saves those whose hearts and lives are true and right.

11God is a judge who is perfectly fair, and he is angry with the wicked every day. 12Unless they repent, he will sharpen his sword and slay them.

He has bent and strung his bow 13and fitted it with deadly arrows made from shafts of fire.

14The wicked man conceives an evil plot, labors with its dark details, and brings to birth his treachery and lies; 15let him fall into his own trap. 16May the violence he plans for others boomerang upon himself; let him die.

17Oh, how grateful and thankful I am to the Lord because he is so good. I will sing praise to the name of the Lord who is above all lords.

PROVERBS FOR TODAY/ 2:1–5

Every young man who listens to me and obeys my instructions will be given wisdom and good sense. Yes, if you want better insight and discernment, and are searching for them as you would for lost money or hidden treasure, then wisdom will be given you, and knowledge of God himself; you will soon learn the importance of reverence for the Lord and of trusting him.

JANUARY 8

GENESIS 18:20—19:38

SO the Lord told Abraham, "I have heard that the people of Sodom and Gomorrah are utterly evil, and that everything they do is wicked. 21I am going down to see whether these reports are true or not. Then I will know.

22,23So the other two went on toward Sodom, but the Lord remained with Abraham a while. Then Abraham approached him and said, "Will you kill good and bad alike? 24Suppose you find fifty godly people there within the city—will you destroy it, and not spare it for their sakes? 25That wouldn't be right! Surely you wouldn't do such a thing, to kill the godly with the wicked! Why, you would be treating godly and wicked exactly the same! Surely you wouldn't do that! Should not the Judge of all the earth be fair?"

26And God replied, "If I find fifty godly people there, I will spare the entire city for their sake."

27Then Abraham spoke again. "Since I have begun, let me go on and speak further to the Lord, though I am but dust and ashes. 28*Suppose there are only forty-five?* Will you destroy the city for lack of five?"

And God said, "I will not destroy it if I find forty-five."

29Then Abraham went further with his request. *"Suppose there are only forty?"*

And God replied, "I won't destroy it if there are forty."

30"Please don't be angry," Abraham pleaded. "Let me speak: *suppose only thirty are found there?"*

And God replied, "I won't do it if there are thirty there."

31Then Abraham said, "Since I have dared to speak to God, let me continue—*Suppose there are only twenty?"*

And God said, "Then I won't destroy it for the sake of the twenty."

32Finally, Abraham said, "Oh, let not the Lord be angry; I will speak but this once more! *Suppose only ten are found?"*

And God said, "Then, for the sake of the ten, I won't destroy it."

33And the Lord went on his way when he had finished his conversation with Abraham. And Abraham returned to his tent.

THAT evening the two angels came to the entrance of the city of Sodom, and Lot was sitting there as they arrived. When he saw them he stood up to meet them, and welcomed them.

2"Sirs," he said, "come to my home as my guests for the night; you can get up as early as you like and be on your way again."

"Oh, no thanks," they said, "we'll just stretch out here along the street."

3But he was very urgent, until at last they went home with him, and he set a great feast before them, complete with freshly baked unleavened bread. After the meal, 4as they were preparing to retire for the night, the men of the city—yes, Sodomites, young and old from all over the city—surrounded the house 5and shouted to Lot, "Bring out those men to us so we can rape them."

6Lot stepped outside to talk to them, shutting the door behind him. 7"Please, fellows," he begged, "don't do such a wicked thing. 8Look—I have two virgin daughters, and I'll surrender them to you to do with as you wish. But leave these men alone, for they are under my protection."

9"Stand back," they yelled. "Who do you think you are? We let this fellow settle among us and now he tries to tell us what to do! We'll deal with you far worse than with those other men." And they lunged at Lot and began breaking down the door.

10But the two men reached out and pulled Lot in and bolted the door, 11and temporarily blinded the men of Sodom so that they couldn't find the door.

12"What relatives do you have here in the city?" the men asked. "Get them out of this place—sons-in-law, sons, daughters, or anyone else. 13For we will destroy the city completely. The stench of the place has reached to heaven and God has sent us to destroy it."

14So Lot rushed out to tell his daughters' fiancés, "Quick, get out of the city, for the Lord is going to destroy it." But the young men looked at him as though he had lost his senses.

15At dawn the next morning the angels became urgent. "Hurry," they said to Lot, "take your wife and your two daughters who are here and get out while you can, or you will be caught in the destruction of the city."

16When Lot still hesitated, the angels seized his hand and the hands of his wife and two daughters and rushed them to safety, outside the city, for the Lord was merciful.

17"Flee for your lives," the angels told him. *"And don't look back.* Escape to the mountains. Don't stay down here on the plain or you will die."

18,19,20"Oh no, sirs, please," Lot begged, "since you've been so kind to me and saved my life, and you've granted me such mercy, let me flee to that little village over there instead of into the mountains, for I fear disaster in the mountain. See, the village is close by and it is just a small one. Please, please, let me go there instead. Don't

you see how small it is? And my life will be saved."

21"All right," the angel said, "I accept your proposition and won't destroy that little city. 22But hurry! For I can do nothing until you are there." (From that time on that village was named Zoar, meaning "Little City.")

23The sun was rising as Lot reached the village. 24Then the Lord rained down fire and flaming tar from heaven upon Sodom and Gomorrah, 25and utterly destroyed them, along with the other cities and villages of the plain, eliminating all life—people, plants, and animals alike. 26But Lot's wife looked back as she was following along behind him, and became a pillar of salt.

27That morning Abraham was up early and hurried out to the place where he had stood before the Lord. 28He looked out across the plain to Sodom and Gomorrah and saw columns of smoke and fumes, as from a furnace, rising from the cities there. 29So God heeded Abraham's plea and kept Lot safe, removing him from the maelstrom of death that engulfed the cities.

30Afterwards Lot left Zoar, fearful of the people there, and went to live in a cave in the mountains with his two daughters. 31One day the older girl said to her sister, "There isn't a man anywhere in this entire area that our father would let us marry. And our father will soon be too old for having children. 32Come, let's fill him with wine and then we will sleep with him, so that our clan will not come to an end." 33So they got him drunk that night, and the older girl went in and had sexual intercourse with her father; but he was unaware of her lying down or getting up again.

34The next morning she said to her younger sister, "I slept with my father last night. Let's fill him with wine again tonight, and you go in and lie with him, so that our family line will continue." 35So they got him drunk again that night, and the younger girl went in and lay with him, and, as before, he didn't know that anyone was there. 36And so it was that both girls became pregnant from their father. 37The older girl's baby was named Moab; he became the ancestor of the nation of the Moabites. 38The name of the younger girl's baby was Benammi; he became the ancestor of the nation of the Ammonites.

MATTHEW 6:25—7:14

SO my counsel is: Don't worry about *things*—food, drink, and clothes. For you already have life and a body—and they are far more important than what to eat and wear. 26Look at the birds! They don't worry about what to eat—they don't need to sow or reap or store up food—for your heavenly Father feeds them. And you are far more valuable to him than they are. 27Will all your worries add a single moment to your life?

28"And why worry about your clothes? Look at the field lilies! They don't worry about theirs. 29Yet King Solomon in all his glory was not clothed as beautifully as they. 30And if God cares so wonderfully for flowers that are here today and gone tomorrow, won't he more surely care for you, O men of little faith?

31,32"So don't worry at all about having enough food and clothing. Why be like the heathen? For they take pride in all these things and are deeply concerned about them. But your heavenly Father already knows perfectly well that you need them, 33and he will give them to you if you give him first place in your life and live as he wants you to.

34"So don't be anxious about tomorrow. God will take care of your tomorrow too. Live one day at a time.

"DON'T criticize, and then you won't be criticized. 2For others will treat you as you treat them. 3And why worry about a speck in the eye of a brother when you have a board in your own? 4Should you say, 'Friend, let me help you get that speck out of your eye,' when you can't even see because of the board in your own? 5Hypocrite! First get rid of the board. Then you can see to help your brother.

6"Don't give holy things to depraved men. Don't give pearls to swine! They will trample the pearls and turn and attack you.

7"Ask, and you will be given what you ask for. Seek, and you will find. Knock, and the door will be opened. 8For everyone who asks, receives. Anyone who seeks, finds. If only you will knock, the door will open. 9If a child asks his father for a loaf of bread, will he be given a stone instead? 10If he asks for fish, will he be given a poisonous snake? Of course not! 11And if you hardhearted, sinful men know how to give good gifts to your children, won't your Father in heaven even more certainly give good gifts to those who ask him for them?

12"Do for others what you want them to do for you. This is the teaching of the laws of Moses in a nutshell.

13"Heaven can be entered only through the narrow gate! The highway to hell is broad, and its gate is wide enough for all the multitudes who choose its easy way. 14But the Gateway to Life is small, and the road is narrow, and only a few ever find it.

PSALM 8:1–9

O Lord our God, the majesty and glory of your name fills all the earth and overflows the heavens. 2You have taught the little children to praise you perfectly. May their example shame and silence your enemies!

3When I look up into the night skies and see the work of your fingers—the moon and the stars you have made—4I cannot understand how you can bother with mere puny man, to pay any attention to him!

5And yet you have made him only a little lower than the angels, and placed a crown of glory and honor upon his head.

6You have put him in charge of everything you made; everything is put under his authority: 7all sheep and oxen, and wild animals too, 8the birds and fish, and all the life in the sea. 9O Jehovah, our Lord, the majesty and glory of your name fills the earth.

PROVERBS FOR TODAY/ 2:6–15

For the Lord grants wisdom! His every word is a treasure of knowledge and understanding. He grants good sense to the godly—his saints. He is their shield, protecting them and guarding their pathway. He shows how to distinguish right from wrong, how to find the right decision every time. For wisdom and truth will enter the very center of your being, filling your life with joy. You will be given the sense to stay away from evil men who want you to be their partners in crime—men who turn from God's ways to walk down dark and evil paths, and exult in doing wrong, for they thoroughly enjoy their sins. Everything they do is crooked and wrong.

JANUARY 9

GENESIS 20:1—22:24

Now Abraham moved south to the Negeb, and settled between Kadesh and Shur. One day, when visiting the city of Gerar, 2he declared that Sarah was his sister! Then King Abimelech sent for her, and had her brought to him at his palace.

3But that night God came to him in a dream and told him, "You are a dead man, for that woman you took is married."

4But Abimelech hadn't slept with her yet, so he said, "Lord, will you slay an innocent man? 5He told me, 'She is my sister,' and she herself said, 'Yes, he is my brother.' I hadn't the slightest intention of doing anything wrong."

6"Yes, I know," the Lord replied. "That is why I held you back from sinning against me; that is why I didn't let you touch her. 7Now restore her to her husband, and he will pray for you (for he is a prophet) and you shall live. But if you don't return her to him, you are doomed to death along with all your household."

8The king was up early the next morning, and hastily called a meeting of all the palace personnel and told them what had happened. And great fear swept through the crowd.

9,10Then the king called for Abraham. "What is this you've done to us?" he demanded. "What have I done that deserves treatment like this, to make me and my kingdom guilty of this great sin? Who would suspect that you would do a thing like this to me? Whatever made you think of this vile deed?"

11,12"Well," Abraham said, "I figured this to be a godless place. 'They will want my wife and will kill me to get her,' I thought. And besides, she *is* my sister—or at least a half-sister (we both have the same father)—and I married her. 13And when God sent me traveling far from my childhood home, I told her, 'Have the kindness to mention, wherever we come, that you are my sister.'"

14Then King Abimelech took sheep and oxen and servants—both men and women—and gave them to Abraham, and returned Sarah his wife to him.

15"Look my kingdom over, and choose the place where you want to live," the king told him. 16Then he turned to Sarah. "Look," he said, "I am giving your 'brother' a thousand silver pieces as damages for what I did, to compensate for any embarrassment and to settle any claim against me regarding this matter. Now justice has been done."

17Then Abraham prayed, asking God to cure the king and queen and the other women of the household, so that they could have children; 18for God had stricken all the women with barrenness to punish Abimelech for taking Abraham's wife.

THEN God did as he had promised, and Sarah became pregnant and gave Abraham a baby son in his old age, at the time God had said; 3and Abraham named him Isaac (meaning "Laughter!"). 4,5Eight days after he was born, Abraham circumcised him, as God required. (Abraham was 100 years old at that time.)

6And Sarah declared, "God has brought me laughter! All who hear about this shall rejoice with me. 7For who would have dreamed that I would ever have a baby? Yet I have given Abraham a child in his old age!"

8Time went by and the child grew and was weaned; and Abraham gave a party to celebrate the happy occasion. 9But when Sarah noticed Ishmael—the son of Abraham and the Egyptian girl Hagar—teasing Isaac, 10she turned upon Abraham and demanded, "Get rid of that slave girl and her son. He is not going to share your property with my son. I won't have it."

11This upset Abraham very much, for after all, Ishmael too was his son.

12But God told Abraham, "Don't be upset over the boy or your slave-girl wife; do as Sarah says, for Isaac is the son through whom my promise will be fulfilled. 13And I will make a nation of the descendants of the slave-girl's son, too, because he also is yours."

14So Abraham got up early the next morning, prepared food for the journey, and strapped a canteen of water to Hagar's shoulders and sent her away with

their son. She walked out into the wilderness of Beersheba, wandering aimlessly.

15When the water was gone she left the youth in the shade of a bush 16and went off and sat down a hundred yards or so away. "I don't want to watch him die," she said, and burst into tears, sobbing wildly.

17Then God heard the boy crying, and the Angel of God called to Hagar from the sky, "Hagar, what's wrong? Don't be afraid! For God has heard the lad's cries as he is lying there. 18Go and get him and comfort him, for I will make a great nation from his descendants."

19Then God opened her eyes and she saw a well; so she refilled the canteen and gave the lad a drink. 20,21And God blessed the boy and he grew up in the wilderness of Paran, and became an expert archer. And his mother arranged a marriage for him with a girl from Egypt.

22About this time King Abimelech, and Phicol, commander of his troops, came to Abraham and said to him, "It is evident that God helps you in everything you do; 23swear to me by God's name that you won't defraud me or my son or my grandson, but that you will be on friendly terms with my country, as I have been toward you."

24Abraham replied, "All right, I swear to it!" 25Then Abraham complained to the king about a well the king's servants had taken violently away from Abraham's servants.

26"This is the first I've heard of it," the king exclaimed, "and I have no idea who is responsible. Why didn't you tell me before?"

27Then Abraham gave sheep and oxen to the king, as sacrifices to seal their pact.

28,29But when he took seven ewe lambs and set them off by themselves, the king inquired, "Why are you doing that?"

30And Abraham replied, "They are my gift to you as a public confirmation that this well is mine."

31So from that time on the well was called Beer-sheba ("Well of the Oath"), because that was the place where they made their covenant. 32Then King Abimelech, and Phicol, commander of his army, returned home again. 33And Abraham planted a tamarisk tree beside the well, and prayed there to the Lord, calling upon the Eternal God. 34And Abraham lived in the Philistine country for a long time.

LATER on, God tested Abraham's [faith and obedience].

"Abraham!" God called.

"Yes, Lord?" he replied.

2"Take with you your only son—yes, Isaac whom you love so much—and go to the land of Moriah and sacrifice him there as a burnt offering upon one of the mountains which I'll point out to you!"

3The next morning Abraham got up early, chopped wood for a fire upon the altar, saddled his donkey, and took with him his son Isaac and two young men who were his servants, and started off to the place where God had told him to go. 4On the third day of the journey Abraham saw the place in the distance. 5"Stay here with the donkey," Abraham told the young men, "and the lad and I will travel yonder and worship, and then come right back."

6Abraham placed the wood for the burnt offering upon Isaac's shoulders, while he himself carried the knife and the flint for striking a fire. So the two of them went on together.

7"Father," Isaac asked, "we have the wood and the flint to make the fire, but where is the lamb for the sacrifice?"

8"God will see to it, my son," Abraham replied. And they went on.

9When they arrived at the place where God had told Abraham to go, he built an altar and placed the wood in order, ready for the fire, and then tied Isaac and laid him on the altar over the wood. 10And Abraham took the knife and lifted it up to plunge it into his son, to slay him.

11At that moment the Angel of God shouted to him from heaven, "Abraham! Abraham!"

"Yes, Lord!" he answered.

12"Lay down the knife; don't hurt the lad in any way," the Angel said, "for I know that God is first in your life—you have not withheld even your beloved son from me."

13Then Abraham noticed a ram caught by its horns in a bush. So he took the ram and sacrificed it, instead of his son, as a burnt offering on the altar. 14Abraham named the place "Jehovah provides"—and it still goes by that name to this day.

15Then the Angel of God called again to Abraham from heaven. 16"I, the Lord, have sworn by myself that because you have obeyed me and have not withheld even your beloved son from me, 17I will bless you with incredible blessings and multiply your descendants into countless thousands and millions, like the stars above you in the sky, and like the sands along the seashore. They will conquer their enemies, 18and your offspring will be a blessing to all the nations of the earth—all because you have obeyed me."

19So they returned to his young men, and traveled home again to Beer-sheba.

20-23After this, a message arrived that Milcah, the wife of Abraham's brother Nahor, had borne him eight sons. Their names were:

Uz, the oldest, Buz, the next oldest, Kemuel (father of Aram), Chesed, Hazo, Pildash, Jidlaph, Bethuel (father of Rebekah).

24He also had four other children from his concubine, Reumah:

Tebah, Gaham, Tahash, Maacah.

MATTHEW 7:15–29

BEWARE of false teachers who come disguised as harmless sheep, but are wolves and will tear you apart. 16You can detect them by the way they act, just as you can identify a tree by its fruit. You need never confuse grapevines with thorn bushes or figs with thistles. 17Different kinds of fruit trees can quickly be identified by examining their fruit. [18]A variety that produces delicious fruit never produces an inedible kind. And a tree producing an inedible kind can't produce what is good. [19]So the trees having the inedible fruit are chopped down and thrown on the fire. [20]Yes, the way to identify a tree or a person is by the kind of fruit produced.

[21]"Not all who sound religious are really godly people. They may refer to me as 'Lord,' but still won't get to heaven. For the decisive question is whether they obey my Father in heaven. [22]At the Judgment many will tell me, 'Lord, Lord, we told others about you and used your name to cast out demons and to do many other great miracles.' [23]But I will reply, 'You have never been mine. Go away, for your deeds are evil.'

[24]"All who listen to my instructions and follow them are wise, like a man who builds his house on solid rock. [25]Though the rain comes in torrents, and the floods rise and the storm winds beat against his house, it won't collapse, for it is built on rock.

[26]"But those who hear my instructions and ignore them are foolish, like a man who builds his house on sand. [27]For when the rains and floods come, and storm winds beat against his house, it will fall with a mighty crash." [28]The crowds were amazed at Jesus' sermons, [29]for he taught as one who had great authority, and not as their Jewish leaders.

PSALM 9:1–12

O Lord, I will praise you with all my heart, and tell everyone about the marvelous things you do. [2]I will be glad, yes, filled with joy because of you. I will sing your praises, O Lord God above all gods.

[3]My enemies will fall back and perish in your presence; [4]you have vindicated me; you have endorsed my work, declaring from your throne that it is good. [5]You have rebuked the nations and destroyed the wicked, blotting out their names forever and ever. [6]O enemies of mine, you are doomed forever. The Lord will destroy your cities; even the memory of them will disappear.

[7,8]But the Lord lives on forever; he sits upon his throne to judge justly the nations of the world. [9]All who are oppressed may come to him. He is a refuge for them in their times of trouble. [10]All those who know your mercy, Lord, will count on you for help. For you have never yet forsaken those who trust in you.

[11]Oh, sing out your praises to the God who lives in Jerusalem. Tell the world about his unforgettable deeds. [12]He who avenges murder has an open ear to those who cry to him for justice. He does not ignore the prayers of men in trouble when they call to him for help.

PROVERBS FOR TODAY/ 2:16–22

Only wisdom from the Lord can save a man from the flattery of prostitutes; these girls have abandoned their husbands and flouted the laws of God. Their houses lie along the road to death and hell. The men who enter them are doomed. None of these men will ever be the same again. Follow the steps of the godly instead, and stay on the right path, for only good men enjoy life to the full; evil men lose the good things they might have had, and they themselves shall be destroyed.

GENESIS 23:1—24:51

WHEN Sarah was 127 years old, she died in Hebron in the land of Canaan; there Abraham mourned and wept for her. 3Then, standing beside her body, he said to the men of Heth:

4"Here I am, a visitor in a foreign land, with no place to bury my wife. Please sell me a piece of ground for this purpose."

5,6"Certainly," the men replied, "for you are an honored prince of God among us; it will be a privilege to have you choose the finest of our sepulchres, so that you can bury her there."

7Then Abraham bowed low before them and said, 8"Since this is your feeling in the matter, be so kind as to ask Ephron, Zohar's son, 9to sell me the cave of Mach-pelah, down at the end of his field. I will of course pay the full price for it, whatever is publicly agreed upon, and it will become a permanent cemetery for my family."

10Ephron was sitting there among the others, and now he spoke up, answering Abraham as the others listened, speaking publicly before all the citizens of the town: 11"Sir," he said to Abraham, "please listen to me. I will give you the cave and the field without any charge. Here in the presence of my people, I give it to you free. Go and bury your dead."

12Abraham bowed again to the men of Heth, 13and replied to Ephron, as all listened: "No, let me buy it from you. Let me pay the full price of the field, and then I will bury my dead."

14,15"Well, the land is worth 400 pieces of silver," Ephron said, "but what is that between friends? Go ahead and bury your dead."

16So Abraham paid Ephron the price he had suggested—400 pieces of silver, as publicly agreed. 17,18This is the land he bought: Ephron's field at Mach-pelah, near Mamre, and the cave at the end of the field, and all the trees in the field. They became his permanent possession, by agreement in the presence of the men of Heth at the city gate. 19,20So Abraham buried Sarah there, in the field and cave deeded to him by the men of Heth as a burial plot.

ABRAHAM was now a very old man, and God blessed him in every way. 2One day Abraham said to his household administrator, who was his oldest servant,

3"Swear by Jehovah, the God of heaven and earth, that you will not let my son marry one of these local girls, these Canaanites. 4Go instead to my homeland, to my relatives, and find a wife for him there."

5"But suppose I can't find a girl who will come so far from home?" the servant asked. "Then shall I take Isaac there, to live among your relatives?"

6"No!" Abraham warned. "Be careful that you don't do that under any circumstance. 7For the Lord God of heaven told me to leave that land and my people, and promised to give me and my children this land. He will send his angel on ahead of you, and he will see to it that you find a girl from there to be my son's wife. 8But if you don't succeed, then you are free from this oath; but under no circumstances are you to take my son there."

9So the servant vowed to follow Abraham's instructions.

10He took with him ten of Abraham's camels loaded with samples of the best of everything his master owned, and journeyed to Iraq, to Nahor's village. 11There he made the camels kneel down outside the town, beside a spring. It was evening, and the women of the village were coming to draw water.

12"O Jehovah, the God of my master," he prayed, "show kindness to my master Abraham and help me to accomplish the purpose of my journey. 13See, here I am, standing beside this spring, and the girls of the village are coming out to draw water. 14This is my request: When I ask one of them for a drink and she says, 'Yes, certainly, and I will water your camels too!'—let her be the one you have appointed as Isaac's wife. That is how I will know."

15,16As he was still speaking to the Lord about this, a beautiful young girl named Rebekah arrived with a water jug on her shoulder and filled it at the spring. (Her father was Bethuel the son of Nahor and his wife Milcah.) 17Running over to her, the servant asked her for a drink.

18"Certainly, sir," she said, and quickly lowered the jug for him to drink. 19Then she said, "I'll draw water for your camels, too, until they have enough!"

20So she emptied the jug into the watering trough and ran down to the spring again and kept carrying water to the camels until they had enough. 21The servant said no more, but watched her carefully to see if she would finish the job, so that he would know whether she was the one. 22Then at last, when the camels had finished drinking, he produced a quarter-ounce gold earring and two five-ounce gold bracelets for her wrists.

23"Whose daughter are you, miss?" he asked. "Would your father have any room to put us up for the night?"

24"My father is Bethuel," she replied. "My grandparents are Milcah and Nahor. 25Yes, we have plenty of straw and food for the camels, and a guest room."

26The man stood there a moment with head bowed, worshiping Jehovah. 27"Thank you, Lord God of my master Abraham," he prayed; "thank you for being so kind and true to him, and for leading me straight to the family of my master's relatives."

28The girl ran home to tell her folks, 29,30and when her brother Laban saw the ring, and the bracelets on his sister's wrists, and heard her story, he rushed out to the spring where the man was still standing beside his camels, and said to him, 31"Come and stay with us, friend; why stand here outside the city when we have a room all ready for you, and a place prepared for the camels!"

32So the man went home with Laban, and Laban gave him straw to bed down the camels, and feed for them, and water for the camel drivers to wash their feet. 33Then supper was served. But the old man said, "I don't want to eat until I have told you why I am here."

"All right," Laban said, "tell us your errand."

34"I am Abraham's servant," he explained. 35"And Jehovah has overwhelmed my master with blessings so that he is a great man among the people of his land. God has given him flocks of sheep and herds of cattle, and a fortune in silver and gold, and many slaves and camels and donkeys.

36"Now when Sarah, my master's wife, was very old, she gave birth to my master's son, and my master has given him everything he owns. 37And my master made me promise not to let Isaac marry one of the local girls, 38but to come to his relatives here in this far-off land, to his brother's family, and to bring back a girl from here to marry his son. 39'But suppose I can't find a girl who will come?' I asked him. 40'She will,' he told me—'for my Lord, in whose presence I have walked, will send his angel with you and make your mission successful. Yes, find a girl from among my relatives, from my brother's family. 41You are under oath to go and ask. If they won't send anyone, then you are freed from your promise.'

42"Well, this afternoon when I came to the spring I prayed this prayer: 'O Jehovah, the God of my master Abraham, if you are planning to make my mission a success, please guide me in this way: 43Here I am, standing beside this spring. I will say to some girl who comes out to draw water, "Please give me a drink of water!" 44And she will reply, "Certainly! And I'll water your camels too!" Let that girl be the one you have selected to be the wife of my master's son.'

45"Well, while I was still speaking

these words, Rebekah was coming along with her water jug upon her shoulder; and she went down to the spring and drew water and filled the jug. I said to her, 'Please give me a drink.' 46She quickly lifted the jug down from her shoulder so that I could drink, and told me, 'Certainly, sir, and I will water your camels too!' So she did! 47Then I asked her, 'Whose family are you from?' And she told me, 'Nahor's. My father is Bethuel, the son of Nahor and his wife Milcah.' So I gave her the ring and the bracelets. 48Then I bowed my head and worshiped and blessed Jehovah, the God of my master Abraham, because he had led me along just the right path to find a girl from the family of my master's brother. 49So tell me, yes or no. Will you or won't you be kind to my master and do what is right? When you tell me, then I'll know what my next step should be, whether to move this way or that."

50Then Laban and Bethuel replied, "The Lord has obviously brought you here, so what can we say? 51Take her and go! Yes, let her be the wife of your master's son, as Jehovah has directed."

MATTHEW 8:1–17

LARGE crowds followed Jesus as he came down the hillside.

2*Look! A leper is approaching. He kneels before him, worshiping. "Sir," the leper pleads, "if you want to, you can heal me."*

3*Jesus touches the man. "I want to," he says. "Be healed." And instantly the leprosy disappears.*

4*Then Jesus says to him, "Don't stop to talk to anyone; go right over to the priest to be examined; and take with you the offering required by Moses' law for lepers who are healed—a public testimony of your cure."*

5,6When Jesus arrived in Capernaum, a Roman army captain came and pled with him to come to his home and heal his servant boy who was in bed paralyzed and racked with pain.

7"Yes," Jesus said, "I will come and heal him."

8,9Then the officer said, "Sir, I am not worthy to have you in my home; [and it isn't necessary for you to come]. If you will only stand here and say, 'Be healed,' my servant will get well! I know, because I am under the authority of my superior officers and I have authority over my soldiers, and I say to one, 'Go,' and he goes, and to another, 'Come,' and he comes, and to my slave boy, 'Do this or that,' and he does it. And I know you have authority to tell his sickness to go— and it will go!"

10Jesus stood there amazed! Turning to the crowd he said, "I haven't seen faith like this in all the land of Israel! 11And I tell you this, that many Gentiles [like this Roman officer], shall come from all over the world and sit down in the Kingdom of Heaven with Abraham, Isaac, and Jacob. 12And many an Israelite—those for whom the Kingdom was prepared—shall be cast into outer darkness, into the place of weeping and torment."

13Then Jesus said to the Roman officer, "Go on home. What you have believed has happened!" And the boy was healed that same hour!

14When Jesus arrived at Peter's house, Peter's mother-in-law was in bed with a high fever. 15But when Jesus touched her hand, the fever left her; and she got up and prepared a meal for them!

16That evening several demon-possessed people were brought to Jesus; and when he spoke a single word, all the demons fled; and all the sick were healed. 17This fulfilled the prophecy of Isaiah, "He took our sicknesses and bore our diseases."

PSALM 9:13–20

AND now, O Lord, have mercy on me; see how I suffer at the hands of those who hate me. Lord, snatch me back from the jaws of death. 14Save me, so that I can praise you publicly before all the people at Jerusalem's gates and rejoice that you have rescued me.

¹⁵The nations fall into the pitfalls they have dug for others; the trap they set has snapped on them. ¹⁶The Lord is famous for the way he punishes the wicked in their own snares!

¹⁷The wicked shall be sent away to hell; this is the fate of all the nations forgetting the Lord. ¹⁸For the needs of the needy shall not be ignored forever; the hopes of the poor shall not always be crushed.

¹⁹O Lord, arise and judge and punish the nations; don't let them defy you! ²⁰Make them tremble in fear; put the nations in their place until at last they know they are but puny men.

PROVERBS FOR TODAY/ 3:1–6

My son, never forget the things I've taught you. If you want a long and satisfying life, closely follow my instructions. Never tire of loyalty and kindness. Hold these virtues tightly. Write them deep within your heart. If you want favor with both God and man, and a reputation for good judgment and common sense, then trust the Lord completely; don't ever trust yourself. In everything you do, put God first, and he will direct you and crown your efforts with success.

JANUARY 11

GENESIS 24:52—26:16

AT this reply, Abraham's servant fell to his knees before Jehovah. ⁵³Then he brought out jewels set in solid gold and silver for Rebekah, and lovely clothing; and he gave many valuable presents to her mother and brother. ⁵⁴Then they had supper, and the servant and the men with him stayed there overnight. But early the next morning he said, "Send me back to my master!"

⁵⁵"But we want Rebekah here at least another ten days or so!" her mother and brother exclaimed. "Then she can go."

⁵⁶But he pleaded, "Don't hinder my return; the Lord has made my mission successful, and I want to report back to my master."

⁵⁷"Well," they said, "we'll call the girl and ask her what she thinks."

⁵⁸So they called Rebekah. "Are you willing to go with this man?" they asked her.

And she replied, "Yes, I will go."

⁵⁹So they told her good-bye, sending along the woman who had been her childhood nurse, ⁶⁰and blessed her with this blessing as they parted:

"Our sister,
May you become
The mother of many millions!
May your descendants
Overcome all your enemies."

⁶¹So Rebekah and her servant girls mounted the camels and went with him.

⁶²Meanwhile, Isaac, whose home was in the Negeb, had returned to Beer-lahai-roi. ⁶³One evening as he was taking a walk out in the fields, meditating, he looked up and saw the camels coming. ⁶⁴Rebekah noticed him and quickly dismounted.

⁶⁵"Who is that man walking through the fields to meet us?" she asked the servant.

And he replied, "It is my master's son!" So she covered her face with her veil. ⁶⁶Then the servant told Isaac the whole story.

⁶⁷And Isaac brought Rebekah into his

mother's tent, and she became his wife. He loved her very much, and she was a special comfort to him after the loss of his mother.

NOW Abraham married again. Keturah was his new wife, and she bore him several children:

Zimran, Jokshan, Medan, Midian, Ishbak, Shuah.

3Jokshan's two sons were Sheba and Dedan. Dedan's sons were Asshurim, Letushim, and Leummim. 4Midian's sons were Ephah, Epher, Hanoch, Abida, and Eldaah.

5Abraham deeded everything he owned to Isaac; 6however, he gave gifts to the sons of his concubines and sent them off into the east, away from Isaac.

7,8Then Abraham died, at the ripe old age of 175, 9,10and his sons Isaac and Ishmael buried him in the cave of Machpelah near Mamre, in the field Abraham had purchased from Ephron the son of Zohar, the Hethite, where Sarah, Abraham's wife, was buried.

11After Abraham's death, God poured out rich blessings upon Isaac. (Isaac had now moved south to Beer-lahai-roi in the Negeb.)

12–15Here is a list, in the order of their births, of the descendants of Ishmael, who was the son of Abraham and Hagar the Egyptian, Sarah's slave girl:

Nebaioth, Kedar, Abdeel, Mibsam, Mishma, Dumah, Massa, Hadad, Tema, Jetur, Naphish, Kedemah.

16These twelve sons of his became the founders of twelve tribes that bore their names. 17Ishmael finally died at the age of 137, and joined his ancestors. 18These descendants of Ishmael were scattered across the country from Havilah to Shur (which is a little way to the northeast of the Egyptian border in the direction of Assyria). And they were constantly at war with one another.

19This is the story of Isaac's children: 20Isaac was forty years old when he married Rebekah, the daughter of Bethuel the Aramean from Paddam-aram. Re-

bekah was the sister of Laban. 21Isaac pleaded with Jehovah to give Rebekah a child, for even after many years of marriage she had no children. Then at last she became pregnant. 22And it seemed as though children were fighting each other inside her!

"I can't endure this," she exclaimed. So she asked the Lord about it.

23And he told her, "The sons in your womb shall become two rival nations. One will be stronger than the other; and the older shall be a servant of the younger!"

24And sure enough, she had twins. 25The first was born so covered with reddish hair that one would think he was wearing a fur coat! So they called him "Esau." 26Then the other twin was born with his hand on Esau's heel! So they called him Jacob (meaning "Grabber"). Isaac was sixty years old when the twins were born.

27As the boys grew, Esau became a skillful hunter, while Jacob was a quiet sort who liked to stay at home. 28Isaac's favorite was Esau, because of the venison he brought home, and Rebekah's favorite was Jacob.

29One day Jacob was cooking stew when Esau arrived home exhausted from the hunt.

30*Esau:* "Boy, am I starved! Give me a bite of that red stuff there!" (From this came his nickname "Edom," which means "Red Stuff.")

31*Jacob:* "All right, trade me your birthright for it!"

32*Esau:* "When a man is dying of starvation, what good is his birthright?"

33*Jacob:* "Well then, vow to God that it is mine!"

And Esau vowed, thereby selling all his eldest-son rights to his younger brother. 34Then Jacob gave Esau bread, peas, and stew; so he ate and drank and went on about his business, indifferent to the loss of the rights he had thrown away.

NOW a severe famine overshadowed the land, as had happened before, in Abraham's time, and so Isaac moved to the city of Gerar where Abimelech, king of the Philistines, lived.

2Jehovah appeared to him there and told him, "Don't go to Egypt. 3Do as I say and stay here in this land. If you do, I will be with you and bless you, and I will give all this land to you and to your descendants, just as I promised Abraham your father. 4And I will cause your descendants to become as numerous as the stars! And I will give them all of these lands; and they shall be a blessing to all the nations of the earth. 5I will do this because Abraham obeyed my commandments and laws."

6So Isaac stayed in Gerar. 7And when the men there asked him about Rebekah, he said, "She is my sister!" For he feared for his life if he told them she was his wife; he was afraid they would kill him to get her, for she was very attractive. 8But sometime later, King Abimelech, king of the Philistines, looked out of a window and saw Isaac and Rebekah making love.

9Abimelech called for Isaac and exclaimed, "She is your wife! Why did you say she is your sister?"

"Because I was afraid I would be murdered," Isaac replied. "I thought someone would kill me to get her from me."

10"How could you treat us this way?" Abimelech exclaimed. "Someone might carelessly have raped her, and we would be doomed." 11Then Abimelech made a public proclamation: "Anyone harming this man or his wife shall die."

12That year Isaac's crops were tremendous—100 times the grain he sowed. For Jehovah blessed him. 13He was soon a man of great wealth, and became richer and richer. 14He had large flocks of sheep and goats, great herds of cattle, and many servants. And the Philistines became jealous of him. 15So they filled up his wells with earth—all those dug by the servants of his father Abraham.

16And King Abimelech asked Isaac to leave the country. "Go somewhere else," he said, "for you have become too rich and powerful for us."

WHEN Jesus noticed how large the crowd was growing, he instructed his disciples to get ready to cross to the other side of the lake.

19Just then one of the Jewish religious teachers said to him, "Teacher, I will follow you no matter where you go!"

20But Jesus said, "Foxes have dens and birds have nests, but I, the Messiah, have no home of my own—no place to lay my head."

21Another of his disciples said, "Sir, when my father is dead, then I will follow you."

22But Jesus told him, "Follow me *now!* Let those who are spiritually dead care for their own dead."

23Then he got into a boat and started across the lake with his disciples. 24Suddenly a terrible storm came up, with waves higher than the boat. But Jesus was asleep.

25The disciples went to him and wakened him, shouting, "Lord, save us! We're sinking!"

26But Jesus answered, "O you men of little faith! Why are you so frightened?" Then he stood up and rebuked the wind and waves, and the storm subsided and all was calm. 27The disciples just sat there, awed! "Who is this," they asked themselves, "that even the winds and the sea obey him?"

28When they arrived on the other side of the lake, in the country of the Gadarenes, two men with demons in them met him. They lived in a cemetery and were so dangerous that no one could go through that area.

29They began screaming at him, "What do you want with us, O Son of God? You have no right to torment us yet."

30A herd of pigs was feeding in the distance, 31so the demons begged, "If you cast us out, send us into that herd of pigs."

32"All right," Jesus told them. "Begone."

And they came out of the men and

entered the pigs, and the whole herd rushed over a cliff and drowned in the water below. 33The herdsmen fled to the nearest city with the story of what had happened, 34and the entire population came rushing out to see Jesus, and begged him to go away and leave them alone.

PSALM 10:1–15

LORD, why are you standing aloof and far away? Why do you hide when I need you the most? 2Come and deal with all these proud and wicked men who viciously persecute the poor. Pour upon these men the evil they planned for others! 3For these men brag of all their evil lusts; they revile God and congratulate those the Lord abhors, whose only goal in life is money.

4These wicked men, so proud and haughty, seem to think that God is dead. They wouldn't think of looking for him! 5Yet there is success in everything they do, and their enemies fall before them. They do not see your punishment await-ing them. 6They boast that neither God nor man can ever keep them down— somehow they'll find a way!

7Their mouths are full of profanity and lies and fraud. They are always boasting of their evil plans. 8They lurk in dark alleys of the city and murder passersby. 9Like lions they crouch silently, waiting to pounce upon the poor. Like hunters they catch their victims in their traps. 10The unfortunate are overwhelmed by their superior strength and fall beneath their blows. 11"God isn't watching," they say to themselves; "he'll never know!"

12O Lord, arise! O God, crush them! Don't forget the poor or anyone else in need. 13Why do you let the wicked get away with this contempt for God? For they think that God will never call them to account. 14Lord, you see what they are doing. You have noted each evil act. You know what trouble and grief they have caused. Now punish them. O Lord, the poor man trusts himself to you; you are known as the helper of the helpless. 15Break the arms of these wicked men. Go after them until the last of them is destroyed.

PROVERBS FOR TODAY/ 3:7–8

Don't be conceited, sure of your own wisdom. Instead, trust and reverence the Lord, and turn your back on evil; when you do that, then you will be given renewed health and vitality.

JANUARY 12

GENESIS 26:17—27:46

SO Isaac moved to Gerar Valley and lived there instead. 18And Isaac redug the wells of his father Abraham, the ones the Philistines had filled after his father's death, and gave them the same names they had had be-fore, when his father had named them. 19His shepherds also dug a new well in Gerar Valley, and found a gushing under-ground spring.

20Then the local shepherds came and claimed it. "This is our land and our well," they said, and argued over it with Isaac's herdsmen. So he named the well, "The Well of Argument!" 21Isaac's men then dug another well, but again there was a fight over it. So he called it, "The Well of Anger." 22Abandoning that one, he dug again, and the local residents finally left him alone. So he called it, "The Well of Room Enough for Us at Last!" "For now at last," he said, "the Lord has made room for us and we shall thrive."

23When he went to Beer-sheba, 24Jehovah appeared to him on the night of his arrival. "I am the God of Abraham your father," he said. "Fear not, for I am with you and will bless you, and will give you so many descendants that they will become a great nation—because of my promise to Abraham, who obeyed me." 25Then Isaac built an altar and worshiped Jehovah; and he settled there, and his servants dug a well.

26One day Isaac had visitors from Gerar. King Abimelech arrived with his advisor, Ahuzzath, and also Phicol, his army commander.

27"Why have you come?" Isaac asked them. "This is obviously no friendly visit, since you kicked me out in a most uncivil way."

28"Well," they said, "we can plainly see that Jehovah is blessing you. We've decided to ask for a treaty between us. 29Promise that you will not harm us, just as we have not harmed you, and in fact, have done only good to you and have sent you away in peace; we bless you in the name of the Lord."

30So Isaac prepared a great feast for them, and they ate and drank in preparation for the treaty ceremonies. 31In the morning, as soon as they were up, they each took solemn oaths to seal a non-aggression pact. Then Isaac sent them happily home again.

32That very same day Isaac's servants came to tell him, "We have found water"—in the well they had been digging. 33So he named the well, "The Well of the Oath," and the city that grew up there was named "Oath," and is called that to this day.

34Esau, at the age of forty, married a girl named Judith, daughter of Be-eri the Hethite; and he also married Basemath, daughter of Elon the Hethite. 35But Isaac and Rebekah were bitter about his marrying them.

ONE day, in Isaac's old age when he was almost blind, he called for Esau his oldest son.

Isaac: "My son?"

Esau: "Yes, father?"

2,3,4*Isaac:* "I am an old man now, and expect every day to be my last. Take your bow and arrows out into the fields and get me some venison, and prepare it just the way I like it—savory and good—and bring it here for me to eat, and I will give you the blessings that belong to you, my first-born son, before I die."

5But Rebekah overheard the conversation. So when Esau left for the field to hunt for the venison, 6,7she called her son Jacob and told him what his father had said to his brother.

8,9,10*Rebekah:* "Now do exactly as I tell you. Go out to the flocks and bring me two young goats, and I'll prepare your father's favorite dish from them. Then take it to your father, and after he has enjoyed it he will bless *you* before his death, instead of Esau!"

11,12*Jacob:* "But mother! He won't be fooled that easily. Think how hairy Esau is, and how smooth my skin is! What if my father feels me? He'll think I'm making a fool of him, and curse me instead of blessing me!"

13*Rebekah:* "Let his curses be on me, dear son. Just do what I tell you. Go out and get the goats."

14So Jacob followed his mother's instructions, bringing the dressed kids, which she prepared in his father's favorite way. 15Then she took Esau's best clothes—they were there in the house—and instructed Jacob to put them on. 16And she made him a pair of gloves from the hairy skin of the young goats, and fastened a strip of the hide around his neck; 17then she gave him the meat, with its rich aroma, and some fresh-baked bread.

18Jacob carried the platter of food into the room where his father was lying.

Jacob: "Father?"

Isaac: "Yes? Who is it, my son—Esau or Jacob?"

19*Jacob:* "It's Esau, your oldest son. I've done as you told me to. Here is the delicious venison you wanted. Sit up and eat it, so that you will bless me with all your heart!"

20*Isaac:* "How were you able to find it so quickly, my son?"

Jacob: "Because Jehovah your God put it in my path!"

21*Isaac:* "Come over here. I want to feel you, and be sure it really is Esau!"

22(Jacob goes over to his father. He feels him!)

Isaac: (to himself) "The voice is Jacob's, but the hands are Esau's!"

23(The ruse convinces Isaac and he gives Jacob his blessings):

24*Isaac:* "Are you really Esau?"

Jacob: "Yes, of course."

25*Isaac:* "Then bring me the venison, and I will eat it and bless you with all my heart."

(Jacob takes it over to him and Isaac eats; he also drinks the wine Jacob brings him.)

26*Isaac:* "Come here and kiss me, my son!"

(Jacob goes over and kisses him on the cheek. Isaac sniffs his clothes, and finally seems convinced.)

27,28,29*Isaac:* "The smell of my son is the good smell of the earth and fields that Jehovah has blessed. May God always give you plenty of rain for your crops, and good harvests and grapes. May many nations be your slaves. Be the master of your brothers. May all your relatives bow low before you. Cursed are all who curse you, and blessed are all who bless you."

30(As soon as Isaac has blessed Jacob, and almost before Jacob leaves the room, Esau arrives, coming in from his hunting. 31He also has pre-pared his father's favorite dish and brings it to him.)

Esau: "Here I am, father, with the venison. Sit up and eat it so that you can give me your finest blessings!"

32*Isaac:* "Who is it?"

Esau: "Why, it's me, of course! Esau, your oldest son!"

33(Isaac begins to tremble noticeably.)

Isaac: "Then who is it who was just here with venison, and I have already eaten it and blessed him with irrevocable blessing?"

34(Esau begins to sob with deep and bitter sobs.)

Esau: "O my father, bless me, bless me too!"

35*Isaac:* "Your brother was here and tricked me and has carried away your blessing."

36*Esau:* (bitterly) "No wonder they call him 'The Cheater.' For he took my birthright, and now he has stolen my blessing. Oh, haven't you saved even one blessing for me?"

37*Isaac:* "I have made him your master, and have given him yourself and all of his relatives as his servants. I have guaranteed him abundance of grain and wine—what is there left to give?"

38*Esau:* "Not one blessing left for me? O my father, bless me too."

(Isaac says nothing as Esau weeps.)

39,40*Isaac:* "Yours will be no life of ease and luxury, but you shall hew your way with your sword. For a time you will serve your brother, but you will finally shake loose from him and be free."

41So Esau hated Jacob because of what he had done to him. He said to himself, "My father will soon be gone, and then I will kill Jacob." 42But someone got wind of what he was planning, and reported it to Rebekah. She sent for Jacob and told him that his life was being threatened by Esau.

43"This is what to do," she said. "Flee to your Uncle Laban in Haran. 44Stay there with him awhile until your brother's fury is spent, 45and he forgets what you have done. Then I will send for you. For why should I be bereaved of both of you in one day?"

46Then Rebekah said to Isaac, "I'm sick and tired of these local girls. I'd rather die than see Jacob marry one of them."

MATTHEW 9:1–17

SO Jesus climbed into a boat and went across the lake to Capernaum, his home town.

2Soon some men brought him a paralyzed boy on a mat. When Jesus saw their faith, he said to the sick boy, "Cheer up, son! For I have forgiven your sins!"

3"Blasphemy! This man is saying he is God!" exclaimed some of the religious leaders to themselves.

4Jesus knew what they were thinking and asked them, "Why are you thinking such evil thoughts? 5,6I, the Messiah, have the authority on earth to forgive sins. But talk is cheap—anybody could say that. So I'll prove it to you by healing this man." Then, turning to the paralyzed man, he commanded, "Pick up your stretcher and go on home, for you are healed."

7And the boy jumped up and left!

8A chill of fear swept through the crowd as they saw this happen right before their eyes. How they praised God for giving such authority to a man!

9As Jesus was going on down the road, he saw a tax collector, Matthew, sitting at a tax collection booth. "Come and be my disciple," Jesus said to him, and Matthew jumped up and went along with him.

10Later, as Jesus and his disciples were eating dinner [at Matthew's house], there were many notorious swindlers there as guests!

11The Pharisees were indignant. "Why does your teacher associate with men like that?"

12"Because people who are well don't need a doctor! It's the sick people who do!" was Jesus' reply. 13Then he added, "Now go away and learn the meaning of this verse of Scripture,

'It isn't your sacrifices and your gifts I want—I want you to be merciful.' For I have come to urge sinners, not the self-righteous, back to God."

14One day the disciples of John the Baptist came to Jesus and asked him, "Why don't your disciples fast as we do and as the Pharisees do?"

15"Should the bridegroom's friends mourn and go without food while he is with them?" Jesus asked. "But the time is coming when I will be taken from them. Time enough then for them to refuse to eat.

16"And who would patch an old garment with unshrunk cloth? For the patch would tear away and make the hole worse. 17And who would use old wineskins to store new wine? For the old skins would burst with the pressure, and the wine would be spilled and skins ruined. Only new wineskins are used to store new wine. That way both are preserved."

PSALM 10:16–18

THE Lord is King forever and forever. Those who follow other gods shall be swept from his land.

17Lord, you know the hopes of humble people. Surely you will hear their cries and comfort their hearts by helping them. 18You will be with the orphans and all who are oppressed, so that mere earthly man will terrify them no longer.

PROVERBS FOR TODAY/ 3:9–10

Honor the Lord by giving him the first part of all your income, and he will fill your barns with wheat and barley and overflow your wine vats with the finest wines.

JANUARY 13

GENESIS 28:1—29:35

SO Isaac called for Jacob and blessed him and said to him, "Don't marry one of these Canaanite girls. 2Instead, go at once to Paddan-aram, to the house of your grandfather Bethuel, and marry one of your cousins—your Uncle Laban's daughters. 3God Almighty bless you and give you many children; may you become a great nation of many tribes! 4May God pass on to you and to your descendants the mighty blessings promised to Abraham. May you own this land where we now are foreigners, for God has given it to Abraham."

5So Isaac sent Jacob away, and he went to Paddan-aram to visit his Uncle Laban, his brother's brother—the son of Bethuel the Aramean.

6,7,8Esau realized that his father despised the local girls, and that his father and mother had sent Jacob to Paddan-aram, with his father's blessing, to get a wife from there, and that they had strictly warned him against marrying a Canaanite girl, and that Jacob had agreed and had left for Paddan-aram. 9So Esau went to his Uncle Ishmael's family and married another wife from there, besides the wives he already had. Her name was Mahalath, the sister of Nebaioth, and daughter of Ishmael, Abraham's son.

10So Jacob left Beer-sheba and journeyed toward Haran. 11That night, when he stopped to camp at sundown, he found a rock for a headrest and lay down to sleep, 12and dreamed that a staircase reached from earth to heaven, and he saw the angels of God going up and down upon it.

13At the top of the stairs stood the Lord. "I am Jehovah," he said, "the God of Abraham, and of your father Isaac. The ground you are lying on is yours! I will give it to you and to your descendants. 14For you will have descendants as many as dust! They will cover the land from east to west and from north to south; and all the nations of the earth will be blessed through you and your descendants. 15What's more, I am with you, and will protect you wherever you go, and will bring you back safely to this land; I will be with you constantly until I have finished giving you all I am promising."

16,17Then Jacob woke up. "God lives here!" he exclaimed in terror. "I've stumbled into his home! This is the awesome entrance to heaven!" 18The next morning he got up very early and set his stone headrest upright as a memorial pillar, and poured olive oil over it. 19He named the place Bethel ("House of God"), though the previous name of the nearest village was Luz.

20And Jacob vowed this vow to God: "If God will help and protect me on this journey and give me food and clothes, 21and will bring me back safely to my father, then I will choose Jehovah as my God! 22And this memorial pillar shall become a place for worship; and I will give you back a tenth of everything you give me!"

JACOB traveled on, finally arriving in the land of the East. 2He saw in the distance three flocks of sheep lying beside a well in an open field, waiting to be watered. But a heavy stone covered the mouth of the well. 3(The custom was that the stone was not removed until all the flocks were there. After watering them, the stone was rolled back over the mouth of the well again.) 4Jacob went over to the shepherds and asked them where they lived.

"At Haran," they said.

5"Do you know a fellow there named Laban, the son of Nahor?"

"We sure do."

6"How is he?"

"He's well and prosperous. Look,

there comes his daughter Rachel with the sheep."

7"Why don't you water the flocks so they can get back to grazing?" Jacob asked. "They'll be hungry if you stop so early in the day!"

8"We don't roll away the stone and begin the watering until all the flocks and shepherds are here," they replied.

9As this conversation was going on, Rachel arrived with her father's sheep, for she was a shepherdess. 10And because she was his cousin—the daughter of his mother's brother—and because the sheep were his uncle's, Jacob went over to the well and rolled away the stone and watered his uncle's flock. 11Then Jacob kissed Rachel and started crying! 12,13He explained about being her cousin on her father's side, and that he was her Aunt Rebekah's son. She quickly ran and told her father, Laban, and as soon as he heard of Jacob's arrival, he rushed out to meet him and greeted him warmly and brought him home. Then Jacob told him his story.

14"Just think, my very own flesh and blood," Laban exclaimed.

After Jacob had been there about a month, 15Laban said to him one day, "Just because we are relatives is no reason for you to work for me without pay. How much do you want?" 16Now Laban had two daughters, Leah, the older, and her younger sister, Rachel. 17Leah had lovely eyes, but Rachel was shapely, and in every way a beauty. 18Well, Jacob was in love with Rachel. So he told her father, "I'll work for you seven years if you'll give me Rachel as my wife."

19"Agreed!" Laban replied. "I'd rather give her to you than to someone outside the family."

20So Jacob spent the next seven years working to pay for Rachel. But they seemed to him but a few days, he was so much in love. 21Finally the time came for him to marry her.

"I have fulfilled my contract," Jacob said to Laban. "Now give me my wife, so that I can sleep with her."

22So Laban invited all the men of the settlement to celebrate with Jacob at a big party. 23Afterwards, that night, when it was dark, Laban took Leah to Jacob, and he slept with her. 24(And Laban gave to Leah a servant girl, Zilpah, to be her maid.) 25But in the morning—it was Leah!

"What sort of trick is this?" Jacob raged at Laban. "I worked for seven years for Rachel. What do you mean by this trickery?"

26"It's not our custom to marry off a younger daughter ahead of her sister," Laban replied smoothly. 27"Wait until the bridal week is over and you can have Rachel too—if you promise to work for me another seven years!"

28So Jacob agreed to work seven more years. Then Laban gave him Rachel, too. 29And Laban gave to Rachel a servant girl, Bilhah, to be her maid. 30So Jacob slept with Rachel, too, and he loved her more than Leah, and stayed and worked the additional seven years.

31But because Jacob was slighting Leah, Jehovah let her have a child, while Rachel was barren. 32So Leah became pregnant and had a son, Reuben (meaning "God has noticed my trouble"), for she said, "Jehovah has noticed my trouble—now my husband will love me." 33She soon became pregnant again and had another son and named him Simeon (meaning "Jehovah heard"), for she said, "Jehovah heard that I was unloved, and so he has given me another son." 34Again she became pregnant and had a son, and named him Levi (meaning "Attachment") for she said, "Surely now my husband will feel affection for me, since I have given him three sons!" 35Once again she was pregnant and had a son and named him Judah (meaning "Praise"), for she said, "Now I will praise Jehovah!" And then she stopped having children.

MATTHEW 9:18–38

AS he was saying this, the rabbi of the local synagogue came and worshiped him. "My little daughter has just died," he said, "but you can bring her back to life again if you will only come and touch her."

19As Jesus and the disciples were going to the rabbi's home, 20a woman who had been sick for twelve years with internal bleeding came up behind him and touched a tassel of his robe, 21for she thought, "If I only touch him, I will be healed."

22Jesus turned around and spoke to her. "Daughter," he said, "all is well! Your faith has healed you." And the woman was well from that moment.

23When Jesus arrived at the rabbi's home and saw the noisy crowds and heard the funeral music, 24he said, "Get them out, for the little girl isn't dead; she is only sleeping!" Then how they all scoffed and sneered at him!

25When the crowd was finally outside, Jesus went in where the little girl was lying and took her by the hand, and she jumped up and was all right again! 26The report of this wonderful miracle swept the entire countryside.

27As Jesus was leaving her home, two blind men followed along behind, shouting, "O Son of King David, have mercy on us."

28They went right into the house where he was staying, and Jesus asked them, "Do you believe I can make you see?"

"Yes, Lord," they told him, "we do."

29Then he touched their eyes and said, "Because of your faith it will happen."

30And suddenly they could see! Jesus sternly warned them not to tell anyone about it, 31but instead they spread his fame all over the town.

32Leaving that place, Jesus met a man who couldn't speak because a demon was inside him. 33So Jesus cast out the demon, and instantly the man could talk.

How the crowds marveled! "Never in all our lives have we seen anything like this," they exclaimed.

34But the Pharisees said, "The reason he can cast out demons is that he is demon-possessed himself—possessed by Satan, the demon king!"

35Jesus traveled around through all the cities and villages of that area, teaching in the Jewish synagogues and announcing the Good News about the Kingdom. And wherever he went he healed people of every sort of illness. 36And what pity he felt for the crowds that came, because their problems were so great and they didn't know what to do or where to go for help. They were like sheep without a shepherd.

37"The harvest is so great, and the workers are so few," he told his disciples. 38"So pray to the one in charge of the harvesting, and ask him to recruit more workers for his harvest fields."

PSALM 11:1–7

HOW dare you tell me, "Flee to the mountains for safety," when I am trusting in the Lord?

2For the wicked have strung their bows, drawn their arrows tight against the bowstrings, and aimed from ambush at the people of God. 3"Law and order have collapsed," we are told. "What can the righteous do but flee?"

4But the Lord is still in his holy temple; he still rules from heaven. He closely watches everything that happens here on earth. 5He puts the righteous and the wicked to the test; he hates those loving violence. 6He will rain down fire and brimstone on the wicked and scorch them with his burning wind.

7For God is good, and he loves goodness; the godly shall see his face.

PROVERBS FOR TODAY/ 3:11–12

Young man, do not resent it when God chastens and corrects you, for his punishment is proof of his love. Just as a father punishes a son he delights in to make him better, so the Lord corrects you.

JANUARY 14

GENESIS 30:1—31:16

RACHEL, realizing she was barren, became envious of her sister. "Give me children or I'll die," she exclaimed to Jacob.

²Jacob flew into a rage. "Am I God?" he flared. "He is the one who is responsible for your barrenness."

³Then Rachel told him, "Sleep with my servant-girl Bilhah, and her children will be mine." ⁴So she gave him Bilhah to be his wife, and he slept with her, ⁵and she became pregnant and presented him with a son. ⁶Rachel named him Dan (meaning "Justice"), for she said, "God has given me justice, and heard my plea and given me a son." ⁷Then Bilhah, Rachel's servant-girl, became pregnant again and gave Jacob a second son. ⁸Rachel named him Naphtali (meaning "Wrestling"), for she said, "I am in a fierce contest with my sister and I am winning!"

⁹Meanwhile, when Leah realized that she wasn't getting pregnant anymore, she gave her servant-girl Zilpah to Jacob, to be his wife, ¹⁰and soon Zilpah presented him with a son. ¹¹Leah named him Gad (meaning "My luck has turned!").

¹²Then Zilpah produced a second son, ¹³and Leah named him Asher (meaning "Happy"), for she said, "What joy is mine! The other women will think me blessed indeed!"

¹⁴One day during the wheat harvest, Reuben found some mandrakes growing in a field and brought them to his mother Leah. Rachel begged Leah to give some of them to her.

¹⁵But Leah angrily replied, "Wasn't it enough to steal my husband? And now will you steal my son's mandrakes too?"

Rachel said sadly, "He will sleep with you tonight because of the mandrakes."

¹⁶That evening as Jacob was coming home from the fields, Leah went out to meet him. "You must sleep with me tonight!" she said; "for I am hiring you with some mandrakes my son has found!" So he did. ¹⁷And God answered her prayers and she became pregnant again, and gave birth to her fifth son. ¹⁸She named him Issachar (meaning "Wages"), for she said, "God has repaid me for giving my slave-girl to my husband." ¹⁹Then once again she became pregnant, with a sixth son. ²⁰She named him Zebulun (meaning "Gifts"), for she said, "God has given me good gifts for my husband. Now he will honor me, for I have given him six sons." ²¹Afterwards she gave birth to a daughter and named her Dinah.

²²Then God remembered about Rachel's plight, and answered her prayers by giving her a child. ²³,²⁴For she became pregnant and gave birth to a son. "God has removed the dark slur against my name," she said. And she named him Joseph (meaning "May I also have another!"), for she said, "May Jehovah give me another son."

²⁵Soon after the birth of Joseph to Rachel, Jacob said to Laban, "I want to go back home. ²⁶Let me take my wives and children—for I earned them from you—and be gone, for you know how fully I have paid for them with my service to you."

²⁷"Please don't leave me," Laban replied, "for a fortune-teller that I consulted told me that the many blessings I've been enjoying are all because of your being here. ²⁸How much of a raise do you need to get you to stay? Whatever it is, I'll pay it."

²⁹Jacob replied, "You know how faithfully I've served you through these many years, and how your flocks and herds have grown. ³⁰For it was little indeed you had before I came, and your wealth has increased enormously; Jehovah has blessed you from everything I do! But

now, what about me? When should I provide for my own family?"

31,32"What wages do you want?" Laban asked again.

Jacob replied, "If you will do one thing, I'll go back to work for you. Let me go out among your flocks today and remove all the goats that are speckled or spotted, and all the black sheep. Give them to me as my wages. 33Then if you ever find any white goats or sheep in my flock, you will know that I have stolen them from you!"

34"All right!" Laban replied. "It shall be as you have said!"

35,36So that very day Laban went out and formed a flock for Jacob of all the male goats that were ringed and spotted, and the females that were speckled and spotted with any white patches, and all of the black sheep. He gave them to Jacob's sons to take them three days' distance, and Jacob stayed and cared for Laban's flock. 37Then Jacob took fresh shoots from poplar, almond, and sycamore trees, and peeled white streaks in them, 38and placed these rods beside the watering troughs so that Laban's flocks would see them when they came to drink; for that is when they mated. 39,40So the flocks mated before the white-streaked rods, and their offspring were streaked and spotted, and Jacob added them to his flock. Then he divided out the ewes from Laban's flock and segregated them from the rams, and let them mate only with Jacob's black rams. Thus he built his flocks from Laban's. 41Moreover, he watched for the stronger animals to mate, and placed the peeled branches before them, 42but didn't with the feebler ones. So the less healthy lambs were Laban's and the stronger ones were Jacob's! 43As a result, Jacob's flocks increased rapidly and he became very wealthy, with many servants, camels, and donkeys.

BUT Jacob learned that Laban's sons were grumbling, "He owes everything he owns to our father. All his wealth is at our father's expense." 2Soon Jacob noticed a considerable cooling in Laban's attitude towards him.

3Jehovah now spoke to Jacob and told him, "Return to the land of your fathers, and to your relatives there; and I will be with you."

4So one day Jacob sent for Rachel and Leah to come out to the field where he was with the flocks, 5to talk things over with them.

"Your father has turned against me," he told them, "and now the God of my fathers has come and spoken to me. 6You know how hard I've worked for your father, 7but he has been completely unscrupulous and has broken his wage contract with me again and again and again. But God has not permitted him to do me any harm! 8For if he said the speckled animals would be mine, then all the flock produced speckled; and when he changed and said I could have the streaked ones, then all the lambs were streaked! 9In this way God has made me wealthy at your father's expense.

10"And at the mating season, I had a dream, and saw that the he-goats mating with the flock were streaked, speckled, and mottled. 11Then, in my dream, the Angel of God called to me 12and told me that I should mate the white female goats with streaked, speckled, and mottled male goats. 'For I have seen all that Laban has done to you,' the Angel said. 13'I am the God you met at Bethel,' he continued, 'the place where you anointed the pillar and made a vow to serve me. Now leave this country and return to the land of your birth.' "

14Rachel and Leah replied, "That's fine with us! There's nothing for us here—none of our father's wealth will come to us anyway! 15He has reduced our rights to those of foreign women; he sold us, and what he received for us has disappeared. 16The riches God has given you from our father were legally ours and our children's to begin with! So go ahead and do whatever God has told you to."

JESUS called his twelve disciples to him, and gave them authority to cast out evil spirits and to heal every kind of sickness and disease.

2,3,4Here are the names of his twelve disciples:

Simon (also called Peter),
Andrew (Peter's brother),
James (Zebedee's son),
John (James' brother),
Philip,
Bartholomew,
Thomas,
Matthew (the tax collector),
James (Alphaeus' son),
Thaddaeus,
Simon (a member of "The Zealots," a subversive political party),
Judas Iscariot (the one who betrayed him).

5Jesus sent them out with these instructions: "Don't go to the Gentiles or the Samaritans, 6but only to the people of Israel—God's lost sheep. 7Go and announce to them that the Kingdom of Heaven is near. 8Heal the sick, raise the dead, cure the lepers, and cast out demons. Give as freely as you have received!

9"Don't take any money with you; 10don't even carry a duffle bag with extra clothes and shoes, or even a walking stick; for those you help should feed and care for you. 11Whenever you enter a city or village, search for a godly man and stay in his home until you leave for the next town. 12When you ask permission to stay, be friendly, 13and if it turns out to be a godly home, give it your blessing; if not, keep the blessing. 14Any city or home that doesn't welcome you—shake off the dust of that place from your feet as you leave. 15Truly, the wicked cities of Sodom and Gomorrah will be better off at Judgment Day than they.

16"I am sending you out as sheep among wolves. Be as wary as serpents and harmless as doves. 17But beware! For you will be arrested and tried, and whipped in the synagogues. 18Yes, and you must stand trial before governors and kings for my sake. This will give you the opportunity to tell them about me, yes, to witness to the world.

19"When you are arrested, don't worry about what to say at your trial, for you will be given the right words at the right time. 20For it won't be you doing the talking—it will be the Spirit of your heavenly Father speaking through you!

21"Brother shall betray brother to death, and fathers shall betray their own children. And children shall rise against their parents and cause their deaths. 22Everyone shall hate you because you belong to me. But all of you who endure to the end shall be saved.

23"When you are persecuted in one city, flee to the next! I will return before you have reached them all!

24"A student is not greater than his teacher. A servant is not above his master. 25The student shares his teacher's fate. The servant shares his master's! And since I, the master of the household, have been called 'Satan,' how much more will you! 26But don't be afraid of those who threaten you. For the time is coming when the truth will be revealed: their secret plots will become public information.

PSALM 12:1–8

LORD! Help! Godly men are fast disappearing. Where in all the world can dependable men be found? 2Everyone deceives and flatters and lies. There is no sincerity left.

3,4But the Lord will not deal gently with people who act like that; he will destroy those proud liars who say, "We will lie to our hearts' content. Our lips are our own; who can stop us?"

5The Lord replies, "I will arise and defend the oppressed, the poor, the needy. I will rescue them as they have longed for me to do." 6The Lord's promise is sure. He speaks no careless word; all he says is purest truth, like silver seven times refined. ⁷O Lord, we know that you will forever preserve your own from the reach of evil men, ⁸although they prowl on every side and vileness is praised throughout the land.

PROVERBS FOR TODAY/ 3:13–15

The man who knows right from wrong and has good judgment and common sense is happier than the man who is immensely rich! For such wisdom is far more valuable than precious jewels. Nothing else compares with it.

JANUARY 15

GENESIS 31:17—32:12

SO one day while Laban was out shearing sheep, Jacob set his wives and sons on camels, and fled without telling Laban his intentions. He drove the flocks before him—Jacob's flocks he had gotten there at Paddan-aram—and took everything he owned and started out to return to his father Isaac in the land of Canaan. ²¹So he fled with all of his possessions (and Rachel stole her father's household gods and took them with her) and crossed the Euphrates River and headed for the territory of Gilead.

²²Laban didn't learn of their flight for three days. ²³Then, taking several men with him, he set out in hot pursuit and caught up with them seven days later, at Mount Gilead. ²⁴That night God appeared to Laban in a dream.

"Watch out what you say to Jacob," he was told. "Don't give him your blessing and don't curse him." ²⁵Laban finally caught up with Jacob as he was camped at the top of a ridge; Laban, meanwhile, camped below him in the mountains.

²⁶"What do you mean by sneaking off like this?" Laban demanded. "Are my daughters prisoners, captured in a battle, that you have rushed them away like this? ²⁷Why didn't you give me a chance to have a farewell party, with singing and orchestra and harp? ²⁸Why didn't you let

me kiss my grandchildren and tell them good-bye? This is a strange way to act. ²⁹I could crush you, but the God of your father appeared to me last night and told me, 'Be careful not to be too hard on Jacob!' ³⁰But see here—though you feel you must go, and long so intensely for your childhood home—why have you stolen my idols?"

³¹"I sneaked away because I was afraid," Jacob answered. "I said to myself, 'He'll take his daughters from me by force.' ³²But as for your household idols, a curse upon anyone who took them. Let him die! If you find a single thing we've stolen from you, I swear before all these men, I'll give it back without question." For Jacob didn't know that Rachel had taken them.

³³Laban went first into Jacob's tent to search there, then into Leah's, and then searched the two tents of the concubines, but didn't find them. Finally he went into Rachel's tent. ³⁴Rachel, remember, was the one who had stolen the idols; she had stuffed them into her camel saddle and now was sitting on them! So although Laban searched the tents thoroughly, he didn't find them.

³⁵"Forgive my not getting up, father," Rachel explained, "but I'm having my monthly period." So Laban didn't find them.

³⁶,³⁷Now Jacob got mad. "What did you

find?" he demanded of Laban. "What is my crime? You have come rushing after me as though you were chasing a criminal and have searched through everything. Now put everything I stole out here in front of us, before your men and mine, for all to see and to decide whose it is! 38Twenty years I've been with you, and all that time I cared for your ewes and goats so that they produced healthy off-spring, and I never touched one ram of yours for food. 39If any were attacked and killed by wild animals, did I show them to you and ask you to reduce the count of your flock? No, I took the loss. You made me pay for every animal stolen from the flocks, whether I could help it or not. 40I worked for you through the scorching heat of the day, and through the cold and sleepless nights. 41Yes, twenty years—fourteen of them earning your two daughters, and six years to get the flock! And you have reduced my wages ten times! 42In fact, except for the grace of God—the God of my grandfa-ther Abraham, even the glorious God of Isaac, my father—you would have sent me off without a penny to my name. But God has seen your cruelty and my hard work, and that is why he appeared to you last night."

43Laban replied, "These women are my daughters, and these children are mine, and these flocks and all that you have—all are mine. So how could I harm my own daughters and grandchildren? 44Come now and we will sign a peace pact, you and I, and will live by its terms."

45So Jacob took a stone and set it up as a monument, 46and told his men to gather stones and make a heap, and Jacob and Laban ate together beside the pile of rocks. 47,48They named it "The Wit-ness Pile"—"Jegar-sahadutha," in La-ban's language, and "Galeed" in Jacob's.

"This pile of stones will stand as a witness against us [if either of us tres-passes across this line]," Laban said. 49So it was also called "The Watchtower" (Mizpah). For Laban said, "May the Lord see to it that we keep this bargain when we are out of each other's sight. 50And if you are harsh to my daughters, or take other wives, I won't know, but God will see it. 51,52This heap," Laban continued, "stands between us as a wit-ness of our vows that I will not cross this line to attack you and you will not cross it to attack me. 53I call upon the God of Abraham and Nahor, and of their father, to destroy either one of us who does."

So Jacob took oath before the mighty God of his father Isaac, to respect the boundary line. 54Then Jacob presented a sacrifice to God there at the top of the mountain, and invited his companions to a feast, and afterwards spent the night with them on the mountain. 55Laban was up early the next morning and kissed his daughters and grandchildren, and blessed them, and returned home.

So Jacob and his household started on again. And the angels of God came to meet him. When he saw them he ex-claimed, "God lives here!" So he named the place "God's territory!"

3Jacob now sent messengers to his brother Esau in Edom, in the land of Seir, 4with this message: "Hello from Ja-cob! I have been living with Uncle Laban until recently, 5and now I own oxen, don-keys, sheep, goats, and many servants, both men and women. I have sent these messengers to inform you of my coming, hoping that you will be friendly to us."

6The messengers returned with the news that Esau was on the way to meet Jacob—with an army of 400 men! 7Jacob was frantic with fear. He divided his household, along with the flocks and herds and camels, into two groups; 8for he said, "If Esau attacks one group, perhaps the other can escape."

9Then Jacob prayed, "O God of Abra-ham my grandfather, and of my father Isaac—O Jehovah who told me to return to the land of my relatives, and said that you would do me good— 10I am not wor-thy of the least of all your lovingkind-nesses shown me again and again just as you promised me. For when I left home I owned nothing except a walking stick! And now I am two armies! 11O Lord, please deliver me from destruction at the hand of my brother Esau, for I am frightened—terribly afraid that he is coming to kill me and these mothers and my children. 12But you promised to do me good, and to multiply my descendants until they become as the sands along the shores—too many to count."

MATTHEW 10:27—11:6

WHAT I tell you now in the gloom, shout abroad when daybreak comes. What I whisper in your ears, proclaim from the housetops!

28"Don't be afraid of those who can kill only your bodies—but can't touch your souls! Fear only God who can destroy both soul and body in hell. 29Not one sparrow (What do they cost? Two for a penny?) can fall to the ground without your Father knowing it. 30And the very hairs of your head are all numbered. 31So don't worry! You are more valuable to him than many sparrows.

32"If anyone publicly acknowledges me as his friend, I will openly acknowledge him as my friend before my Father in heaven. 33But if anyone publicly denies me, I will openly deny him before my Father in heaven.

34"Don't imagine that I came to bring peace to the earth! No, rather, a sword. 35I have come to set a man against his father, and a daughter against her mother, and a daughter-in-law against her mother-in-law— 36a man's worst enemies will be right in his own home! 37If you love your father and mother more than you love me, you are not worthy of being mine; or if you love your son or daughter more than me, you are not worthy of being mine. 38If you refuse to take up your cross and follow me, you are not worthy of being mine.

39"If you cling to your life, you will lose it; but if you give it up for me, you will save it.

40"Those who welcome you are welcoming me. And when they welcome me they are welcoming God who sent me. 41If you welcome a prophet because he is a man of God, you will be given the same reward a prophet gets. And if you welcome good and godly men because of their godliness, you will be given a reward like theirs.

42"And if, as my representatives, you give even a cup of cold water to a little child, you will surely be rewarded."

WHEN Jesus had finished giving these instructions to his twelve disciples, he went off preaching in the cities where they were scheduled to go.

2John the Baptist, who was now in prison, heard about all the miracles the Messiah was doing, so he sent his disciples to ask Jesus, 3"Are you really the one we are waiting for, or shall we keep on looking?"

4Jesus told them, "Go back to John and tell him about the miracles you've seen me do— 5the blind people I've healed, and the lame people now walking without help, and the cured lepers, and the deaf who hear, and the dead raised to life; and tell him about my preaching the Good News to the poor. 6Then give him this message, 'Blessed are those who don't doubt me.' "

PSALM 13:1–6

HOW long will you forget me, Lord? Forever? How long will you look the other way when I am in need? 2How long must I be hiding daily anguish in my heart? How long shall my enemy have the upper hand?

3Answer me, O Lord my God; give me light in my darkness lest I die. 4Don't let my enemies say, "We have conquered him!" Don't let them gloat that I am down.

5But I will always trust in you and in your mercy and shall rejoice in your salvation. 6I will sing to the Lord because he has blessed me so richly.

PROVERBS FOR TODAY/ 3:16–18

Wisdom gives: A long, good life, riches, honor, pleasure, peace. Wisdom is a tree of life to those who eat her fruit; happy is the man who keeps on eating it.

JANUARY 16

GENESIS 32:13—34:31

JACOB stayed where he was for the night, and prepared a present for his brother Esau:

200 female goats,
20 male goats,
200 ewes,
20 rams,
30 milk camels, with their colts,
40 cows,
10 bulls,
20 female donkeys,
10 male donkeys.

16He instructed his servants to drive them on ahead, each group of animals by itself, separated by a distance between. 17He told the men driving the first group that when they met Esau and he asked, "Where are you going? Whose servants are you? Whose animals are these?"— 18they should reply: "These belong to your servant Jacob. They are a present for his master Esau! He is coming right behind us!"

19Jacob gave the same instructions to each driver, with the same message. 20Jacob's strategy was to appease Esau with the presents before meeting him face to face! "Perhaps," Jacob hoped, "he will be friendly to us." 21So the presents were sent on ahead, and Jacob spent that night in the camp.

22,23,24But during the night he got up and wakened his two wives and his two concubines and eleven sons, and sent them across the Jordan River at the Jabbok ford with all his possessions, then returned again to the camp and was there alone; and a Man wrestled with him until dawn. 25And when the Man saw that he couldn't win the match, he struck Jacob's hip, and knocked it out of joint at the socket.

26Then the Man said, "Let me go, for it is dawn."

But Jacob panted, "I will not let you go until you bless me."

27"What is your name?" the Man asked.

"Jacob," was the reply.

28"It isn't anymore!" the Man told him. "It is Israel—one who has power with God. Because you have been strong with God, you shall prevail with men."

29"What is *your* name?" Jacob asked him.

"No, you mustn't ask," the Man told him. And he blessed him there.

30Jacob named the place "Peniel" ("The Face of God"), for he said, "I have seen God face to face, and yet my life is spared." 31The sun rose as he started on, and he was limping because of his hip. 32(That is why even today the people of Israel don't eat meat from near the hip, in memory of what happened that night.)

THEN, far in the distance, Jacob saw Esau coming with his 400 men. 2Jacob now arranged his family into a column, with his two concubines and their children at the head, Leah and her children next, and Rachel and Joseph last. 3Then Jacob went on ahead. As he approached his brother he bowed low seven times before him. 4And then Esau ran to meet him and embraced him affectionately and kissed him; and both of them were in tears!

5Then Esau looked at the women and children and asked, "Who are these people with you?"

"My children," Jacob replied. 6Then the concubines came forward with their children, and bowed low before him. 7Next came Leah with her children, and bowed, and finally Rachel and Joseph came and made their bows.

8"And what were all the flocks and herds I met as I came?" Esau asked.

And Jacob replied, "They are my gifts, to curry your favor!"

9"Brother, I have plenty," Esau laughed. "Keep what you have."

10"No, but please accept them," Jacob said, "for what a relief it is to see your friendly smile! I was as frightened of you as though approaching God! 11Please take my gifts. For God has been very generous to me and I have enough." So Jacob insisted, and finally Esau accepted them.

12"Well, let's be going," Esau said. "My men and I will stay with you and lead the way."

13But Jacob replied, "As you can see, some of the children are small, and the flocks and herds have their young, and if they are driven too hard, they will die. 14So you go on ahead of us and we'll follow at our own pace and meet you at Seir."

15"Well," Esau said, "at least let me leave you some of my men to assist you and be your guides."

"No," Jacob insisted, "we'll get along just fine. Please do as I suggest."

16So Esau started back to Seir that same day. 17Meanwhile Jacob and his household went as far as Succoth. There he built himself a camp, with pens for his flocks and herds. (That is why the place is called Succoth, meaning "huts.") 18Then they arrived safely at Shechem, in Canaan, and camped outside the city. 19(He bought the land he camped on from the family of Hamor, Shechem's father, for 100 pieces of silver. 20And there he erected an altar and called it "El-Elohe-Israel," "The Altar to the God of Israel.")

ONE day Dinah, Leah's daughter, went out to visit some of the neighborhood girls, 2but when Shechem, son of King Hamor the Hivite, saw her, he took her and raped her. 3He fell deeply in love with her, and tried to win her affection.

4Then he spoke to his father about it. "Get this girl for me," he demanded. "I want to marry her."

5Word soon reached Jacob of what had happened, but his sons were out in the fields herding cattle, so he did nothing until their return. 6,7Meanwhile King Hamor, Shechem's father, went to talk with Jacob, arriving just as Jacob's sons came in from the fields, too shocked and angry to overlook the insult, for it was an outrage against all of them.

8Hamor told Jacob, "My son Shechem is truly in love with your daughter, and longs for her to be his wife. Please let him marry her. 9,10Moreover, we invite you folks to live here among us and to let your daughters marry our sons, and we will give our daughters as wives for your young men. And you shall live among us wherever you wish and carry on your business among us and become rich!"

11Then Shechem addressed Dinah's father and brothers. "Please be kind to me and let me have her as my wife," he begged. "I will give whatever you require. 12No matter what dowry or gift you demand, I will pay it—only give me the girl as my wife."

13Her brothers then lied to Shechem and Hamor, acting dishonorably because of what Shechem had done to their sister. 14They said, "We couldn't possibly. For you are not circumcised. It would be a disgrace for her to marry such a man. 15I'll tell you what we'll do—if every man of you will be circumcised, 16then we will intermarry with you and live here and unite with you to become one people. 17Otherwise we will take her and be on our way."

18,19Hamor and Shechem gladly agreed, and lost no time in acting upon this request, for Shechem was very much in love with Dinah, and could, he felt sure, sell the idea to the other men of the city—for he was highly respected and very popular. 20So Hamor and Shechem appeared before the city council and presented their request.

21"Those men are our friends," they said. "Let's invite them to live here among us and ply their trade. For the land is large enough to hold them, and we can intermarry with them. 22But they will only consider staying here on one condition—that every one of us men be circumcised, the same as they are. 23But if we do this, then all they have will become ours and the land will be enriched. Come on, let's agree to this so that they will settle here among us."

24So all the men agreed, and all were circumcised. 25But three days later, when their wounds were sore and sensitive to every move they made, two of Dinah's brothers, Simeon and Levi, took their swords, entered the city without opposition, and slaughtered every man there, 26including Hamor and Shechem. They rescued Dinah from Shechem's house and returned to their camp again. 27Then all of Jacob's sons went over and plundered the city because their sister had been dishonored there. 28They confiscated all the flocks and herds and donkeys—everything they could lay their hands on, both inside the city and outside in the fields, 29and took all the women and children, and wealth of every kind.

30Then Jacob said to Levi and Simeon, "You have made me stink among all the people of this land—all the Canaanites and Perizzites. We are so few that they will come and crush us, and we will all be killed."

31"Should he treat our sister like a prostitute?" they retorted.

MATTHEW 11:7–30

WHEN John's disciples had gone, Jesus began talking about him to the crowds. "When you went out into the barren wilderness to see John, what did you expect him to be like? Grass blowing in the wind? 8Or were you expecting to see a man dressed as a prince in a palace? 9Or a prophet of God? Yes, and he is more than just a prophet. 10For John is the man mentioned in the Scriptures—a messenger to precede me, to announce my coming, and prepare people to receive me.

11"Truly, of all men ever born, none shines more brightly than John the Baptist. And yet, even the lesser lights in the Kingdom of Heaven will be greater than he is! 12And from the time John the Baptist began preaching and baptizing until now, ardent multitudes have been crowding toward the Kingdom of Heaven, 13for all the laws and prophets looked forward [to the Messiah]. Then John appeared, 14and if you are willing to understand what I mean, he is Elijah, the one the prophets said would come [at the time the Kingdom begins]. 15If ever you were willing to listen, listen now!

16"What shall I say about this nation? These people are like children playing, who say to their little friends, 17'We played wedding and you weren't happy, so we played funeral but you weren't sad.' 18For John the Baptist doesn't even drink wine and often goes without food, and you say, 'He's crazy.' 19And I, the Messiah, feast and drink, and you complain that I am 'a glutton and a drinking man, and hang around with the worst sort of sinners!' But brilliant men like you can justify your every inconsistency!"

20Then he began to pour out his denunciations against the cities where he had done most of his miracles, because they hadn't turned to God.

21"Woe to you, Chorazin, and woe to you, Bethsaida! For if the miracles I did in your streets had been done in wicked Tyre and Sidon their people would have repented long ago in shame and humility. 22Truly, Tyre and Sidon will be better off on the Judgment Day than you! 23And Capernaum, though highly honored, shall go down to hell! For if the marvelous miracles I did in you had been done in Sodom, it would still be here today. ²⁴Truly, Sodom will be better off at the Judgment Day than you."

²⁵And Jesus prayed this prayer: "O Father, Lord of heaven and earth, thank you for hiding the truth from those who think themselves so wise, and for revealing it to little children. ²⁶Yes, Father, for it pleased you to do it this way! . . .

²⁷"Everything has been entrusted to me by my Father. Only the Father knows the Son, and the Father is known only by the Son and by those to whom the Son reveals him. ²⁸Come to me and I will give you rest—all of you who work so hard beneath a heavy yoke. ²⁹,³⁰Wear my yoke—for it fits perfectly—and let me teach you; for I am gentle and humble, and you shall find rest for your souls; for I give you only light burdens."

PSALM 14:1–7

THAT man is a fool who says to himself, "There is no God!" Anyone who talks like that is warped and evil and cannot really be a good person at all.

²The Lord looks down from heaven on all mankind to see if there are any who are wise, who want to please God. ³But no, all have strayed away; all are rotten with sin. Not one is good, not one! ⁴They eat my people like bread and wouldn't think of praying! Don't they really know any better?

⁵Terror shall grip them, for God is with those who love him. ⁶He is the refuge of the poor and humble when evildoers are oppressing them. ⁷Oh, that the time of their rescue were already here, that God would come from Zion now to save his people. What gladness when the Lord has rescued Israel!

PROVERBS FOR TODAY/ 3:19–20

The Lord's wisdom founded the earth; his understanding established all the universe and space. The deep fountains of the earth were broken open by his knowledge, and the skies poured down rain.

JANUARY 17

GENESIS 35:1—36:43

MOVE on to Bethel now, and settle there," God said to Jacob, "and build an altar to worship me—the God who appeared to you when you fled from your brother Esau."

²So Jacob instructed all those in his household to destroy the idols they had brought with them, and to wash themselves and to put on fresh clothing. ³"For we are going to Bethel," he told them, "and I will build an altar there to the God who answered my prayers in

the day of my distress, and was with me on my journey."

⁴So they gave Jacob all their idols and their earrings, and he buried them beneath the oak tree near Shechem. ⁵Then they started on again. And the terror of God was upon all the cities they journeyed through, so that they were not attacked. ⁶Finally they arrived at Luz (also called Bethel), in Canaan. ⁷And Jacob erected an altar there and named it "The altar to the God who met me here at Bethel" because it was there at Bethel

that God appeared to him when he was fleeing from Esau.

8Soon after this Rebekah's old nurse Deborah died and was buried beneath the oak tree in the valley below Bethel. And ever after it was called "The Oak of Weeping."

9Upon Jacob's arrival at Bethel, en route from Paddan-aram, God appeared to him once again and blessed him. 10And God said to him, "You shall no longer be called Jacob ('Grabber'), but Israel ('One who prevails with God'). 11I am God Almighty," the Lord said to him, "and I will cause you to be fertile and to multiply and to become a great nation, yes, many nations; many kings shall be among your descendants. 12And I will pass on to you the land I gave to Abraham and Isaac. Yes, I will give it to you and to your descendants."

13,14Afterwards Jacob built a stone pillar at the place where God had appeared to him; and he poured wine over it as an offering to God, and then anointed the pillar with olive oil. 15Jacob named the spot Bethel ("House of God"), because God had spoken to him there.

16Leaving Bethel, he and his household traveled on toward Ephrath (Bethlehem). But Rachel's pains of childbirth began while they were still a long way away. 17After a very hard delivery, the midwife finally exclaimed, "Wonderful—another boy!" 18And with Rachel's last breath (for she died) she named him "Ben-oni" ("Son of my sorrow"); but his father called him "Benjamin" ("Son of my right hand").

19So Rachel died, and was buried near the road to Ephrath (also called Bethlehem). 20And Jacob set up a monument of stones upon her grave, and it is there to this day.

21Then Israel journeyed on and camped beyond the Tower of Eder. 22It was while he was there that Reuben slept with Bilhah, his father's concubine, and someone told Israel about it.

Here are the names of the twelve sons of Jacob:

23The sons of Leah:
Reuben, Jacob's oldest child,
Simeon, Levi, Judah, Issachar, Zebulun.
24The sons of Rachel:
Joseph, Benjamin.
25The sons of Bilhah, Rachel's servant-girl:
Dan, Naphtali.
26The sons of Zilpah, Leah's servant-girl:
Gad, Asher.
All these were born to him at Paddanaram.

27So Jacob came at last to Isaac his father at Mamre in Kiriath-arba (now called Hebron), where Abraham too had lived. 28,29Isaac died soon afterwards, at the ripe old age of 180. And his sons Esau and Jacob buried him.

HERE is a list of the descendants of Esau (also called Edom): 2,3Esau married three local girls from Canaan:
Adah (daughter of Elon the Hethite),
Oholibamah (daughter of Anah and granddaughter of Zibeon the Hivite),
Basemath (his cousin—she was a daughter of Ishmael—the sister of Nebaioth).
4Esau and Adah had a son named Eliphaz. Esau and Basemath had a son named Reuel.
5Esau and Oholibamah had sons named Jeush, Jalam, and Korah. All these sons were born to Esau in the land of Canaan.

6,7,8Then Esau took his wives, children, household servants, cattle and flocks— all the wealth he had gained in the land of Canaan—and moved away from his brother Jacob to Mount Seir. (For there was not land enough to support them both because of all their cattle.)

9Here are the names of Esau's descendants, the Edomites, born to him in Mount Seir:
10,11,12Descended from his wife Adah, born to her son Eliphaz were:

Teman, Omar, Zepho, Gatam, Kenaz, Amalek (born to Timna, Eliphaz' concubine).

13,14Esau also had grandchildren from his wife Basemath. Born to her son Reuel were:

Nahath, Zerah, Shammah, Mizzah.

15,16Esau's grandchildren became the heads of clans, as listed here:

The clan of Teman,
The clan of Omar,
The clan of Zepho,
The clan of Kenaz,
The clan of Korah,
The clan of Gatam,
The clan of Amalek.

The above clans were the descendants of Eliphaz, the oldest son of Esau and Adah.

17The following clans were the descendants of Reuel, born to Esau and his wife Basemath while they lived in Canaan:

The clan of Nahath,
The clan of Zerah,
The clan of Shammah,
The clan of Mizzah.

18,19And these are the clans named after the sons of Esau and his wife Oholibamah (daughter of Anah):

The clan of Jeush,
The clan of Jalam,
The clan of Korah.

20,21These are the names of the tribes that descended from Seir, the Horite—one of the native families of the land of Seir:

The tribe of Lotan,
The tribe of Shobal,
The tribe of Zibeon,
The tribe of Anah,
The tribe of Dishon,
The tribe of Ezer,
The tribe of Dishan.

22The children of Lotan (the son of Seir) were Hori and Heman. (Lotan had a sister, Timna.)

23The children of Shobal: Alvan, Manahath, Ebal, Shepho, Onam.

24The children of Zibeon:

Aiah,
Anah. (This is the boy who discovered a hot springs in the wasteland while

he was grazing his father's donkeys.)

25The children of Anah:
Dishon, Oholibamah.

26The children of Dishon:
Hemdan, Eshban,
Ithran, Cheran.

27The children of Ezer:
Bilhan, Zaavan, Akan.

28,29,30The children of Dishan:
Uz, Aran.

31-39These are the names of the kings of Edom (before Israel had her first king):

King Bela (son of Beor), from Dinhabah in Edom.

Succeeded by: King Jobab (son of Zerah), from the city of Bozrah.

Succeeded by: King Husham, from the land of the Temanites.

Succeeded by: King Hadad (son of Bedad), the leader of the forces that defeated the army of Midian when it invaded Moab. His city was Avith.

Succeeded by: King Samlah, from Masrekah.

Succeeded by: King Shaul, from Rehoboth-by-the-River.

Succeeded by: King Baal-hanan (son of Achbor).

Succeeded by: King Hadad, from the city of Pau.

King Hadad's wife was Mehetabel, daughter of Matred and granddaughter of Mezahab.

40-43Here are the names of the subtribes of Esau, living in the localities named after themselves:

The clan of Timna,
The clan of Alvah,
The clan of Jetheth,
The clan of Oholibamah,
The clan of Elah,
The clan of Pinon,
The clan of Kenaz,
The clan of Teman,
The clan of Mibzar,
The clan of Magdiel,
The clan of Iram.

These, then, are the names of the subtribes of Edom, each giving its name to the area it occupied. (All were Edomites, descendants of Esau.)

MATTHEW 12:1–21

ABOUT that time, Jesus was walking one day through some grainfields with his disciples. It was on the Sabbath, the Jewish day of worship, and his disciples were hungry; so they began breaking off heads of wheat and eating the grain. 2But some Pharisees saw them do it and protested, "Your disciples are breaking the law. They are harvesting on the Sabbath."

3But Jesus said to them, "Haven't you ever read what King David did when he and his friends were hungry? 4He went into the Temple and they ate the special bread permitted to the priests alone. That was breaking the law too. 5And haven't you ever read in the law of Moses how the priests on duty in the Temple may work on the Sabbath? 6And truly, one is here who is greater than the Temple! 7But if you had known the meaning of this Scripture verse, 'I want you to be merciful more than I want your offerings,' you would not have condemned those who aren't guilty! 8For I, the Messiah, am master even of the Sabbath."

9Then he went over to the synagogue, 10and noticed there a man with a deformed hand. The Pharisees asked Jesus, "Is it legal to work by healing on the Sabbath day?" (They were, of course, hoping he would say "Yes," so they could arrest him!) 11This was his answer: "If you had just one sheep, and it fell into a well on the Sabbath, would you work to rescue it that day? Of course you would. 12And how much more valuable is a person than a sheep! Yes, it is right to do good on the Sabbath." 13Then he said to the man, "Stretch out your arm." And as he did, his hand became normal, just like the other one!

14Then the Pharisees called a meeting to plot Jesus' arrest and death.

15But he knew what they were planning, and left the synagogue, with many following him. He healed all the sick among them, 16but he cautioned them against spreading the news about his miracles. 17This fulfilled the prophecy of Isaiah concerning him:

18"Look at my Servant.
See my Chosen One.
He is my Beloved, in whom my soul delights.
I will put my Spirit upon him,
And he will judge the nations.
19He does not fight nor shout;
He does not raise his voice!
20He does not crush the weak,
Or quench the smallest hope;
He will end all conflict with his final victory,
21And his name shall be the hope
Of all the world."

PSALM 15:1–5

LORD, who may go and find refuge and shelter in your tabernacle up on your holy hill?

2Anyone who leads a blameless life and is truly sincere. 3Anyone who refuses to slander others, does not listen to gossip, never harms his neighbor, 4speaks out against sin, criticizes those committing it, commends the faithful followers of the Lord, keeps a promise even if it ruins him, 5does not crush his debtors with high interest rates, and refuses to testify against the innocent despite the bribes offered him—such a man shall stand firm forever.

PROVERBS FOR TODAY/ 3:21–26

Have two goals: wisdom—that is, knowing and doing right—and common sense. Don't let them slip away, for they fill you with living energy, and bring you honor and respect. They keep you safe from defeat and disaster and from stumbling off the trail. With them on guard you can sleep without fear; you need not be afraid of disaster or the plots of wicked men, for the Lord is with you; he protects you.

JANUARY 18

GENESIS 37:1—38:30

So Jacob settled again in the land of Canaan, where his father had lived.

2Jacob's son Joseph was now seventeen years old. His job, along with his half-brothers, the sons of his father's wives Bilhah and Zilpah, was to shepherd his father's flocks. But Joseph reported to his father some of the bad things they were doing. 3Now as it happened, Israel loved Joseph more than any of his other children, because Joseph was born to him in his old age. So one day Jacob gave him a special gift—a brightly colored coat. 4His brothers of course noticed their father's partiality, and consequently hated Joseph; they couldn't say a kind word to him. 5One night Joseph had a dream and promptly reported the details to his brothers, causing even deeper hatred.

6"Listen to this," he proudly announced. 7"We were out in the field binding sheaves, and my sheaf stood up, and your sheaves all gathered around it and bowed low before it!"

8"So you want to be our king, do you?" his brothers derided. And they hated him both for the dream and for his cocky attitude.

9Then he had another dream and told it to his brothers. "Listen to my latest dream," he boasted. "The sun, moon, and eleven stars bowed low before me!" 10This time he told his father as well as his brothers; but his father rebuked him. "What is this?" he asked. "Shall I indeed, and your mother and brothers come and bow before you?" 11His brothers were fit to be tied concerning this affair, but his father gave it quite a bit of thought and wondered what it all meant.

12One day Joseph's brothers took their father's flocks to Shechem to graze them there. 13,14A few days later Israel called for Joseph, and told him, "Your brothers are over in Shechem grazing the flocks. Go and see how they are getting along, and how it is with the flocks, and bring me word."

"Very good," Joseph replied. So he traveled to Shechem from his home at Hebron Valley. 15A man noticed him wandering in the fields.

"Who are you looking for?" he asked.

16"For my brothers and their flocks," Joseph replied. "Have you seen them?"

17"Yes," the man told him, "they are no longer here. I heard your brothers say they were going to Dothan." So Joseph followed them to Dothan and found them there. 18But when they saw him coming, recognizing him in the distance, they decided to kill him!

19,20"Here comes that masterdreamer," they exclaimed. "Come on, let's kill him and toss him into a well and tell father that a wild animal has eaten him. Then we'll see what will become of all his dreams!"

21,22But Reuben hoped to spare Joseph's life. "Let's not kill him," he said; "we'll shed no blood—let's throw him alive into this well here; that way he'll die without our touching him!" (Reuben was planning to get him out later and return him to his father.) 23So when Joseph got there, they pulled off his brightly colored robe, 24and threw him into an empty well—there was no water in it. 25Then they sat down for supper. Suddenly they noticed a string of camels coming towards them in the distance, probably Ishmaelite traders who were taking gum, spices, and herbs from Gilead to Egypt.

26,27"Look there," Judah said to the others. "Here come some Ishmaelites. Let's sell Joseph to them! Why kill him and have a guilty conscience? Let's not be responsible for his death, for, after all, he is our brother!" And his brothers agreed. 28So when the traders came by, his brothers pulled Joseph out of the well and sold him to them for twenty pieces of silver, and they took him along to Egypt. 29Some time later, Reuben (who was away when the traders came by) returned to get Joseph out of the well. When Joseph wasn't there, he ripped at his clothes in anguish and frustration. 30"The child is gone; and I, where shall I go now?" he wept to his brothers. 31Then the brothers killed a goat and spattered its blood on Joseph's coat, 32and took the coat to their father and asked him to identify it.

"We found this in the field," they told him. "Is it Joseph's coat or not?" 33Their father recognized it at once.

"Yes," he sobbed, "it is my son's coat. A wild animal has eaten him. Joseph is without doubt torn in pieces."

34Then Israel tore his garments and put on sackcloth and mourned for his son in deepest mourning for many weeks. 35His family all tried to comfort him, but it was no use.

"I will die in mourning for my son," he would say, and then break down and cry.

36Meanwhile, in Egypt, the traders sold Joseph to Potiphar, an officer of the Pharaoh—the king of Egypt. Potiphar was captain of the palace guard, the chief executioner.

ABOUT this time, Judah left home and moved to Adullam and lived there with a man named Hirah. 2There he met and married a Canaanite girl—the daughter of Shua. 3,4,5They lived at Chezib and had three sons, Er, Onan, and Shelah. These names were given to them by their mother, except for Er, who was named by his father.

6When his oldest son Er grew up, Judah arranged for him to marry a girl named Tamar. 7But Er was a wicked man, and so the Lord killed him.

8Then Judah said to Er's brother, Onan, "You must marry Tamar, as our law requires of a dead man's brother; so that her sons from you will be your brother's heirs."

9But Onan was not willing to have a child who would not be counted as his own, and so, although he married her, whenever he went in to sleep with her, he spilled the sperm on the bed to prevent her from having a baby which would be his brother's. 10So far as the Lord was concerned, it was very wrong of him [to deny a child to his deceased brother], so he killed him, too. 11Then Judah told Tamar, his daughter-in-law, not to marry again at that time, but to return to her childhood home and to her parents, and to remain a widow there until his youngest son Shelah was old enough to marry her. (But he didn't really intend for Shelah to do this, for fear God would kill him, too, just as he had his two brothers.) So Tamar went home to her parents.

12In the process of time Judah's wife died. After the time of mourning was over, Judah and his friend Hirah, the Adullamite, went to Timnah to supervise the shearing of his sheep. 13When someone told Tamar that her father-in-law had left for the sheep-shearing at Timnah, 14and realizing by now that she was not going to be permitted to marry Shelah, though he was fully grown, she laid aside her widow's clothing and covered herself with a veil to disguise herself, and sat beside the road at the entrance to the village of Enaim, which is on the way to Timnah. 15Judah noticed her as he went by and thought she was a prostitute, since her face was veiled. 16So he stopped and propositioned her to sleep with him, not realizing of course that she was his own daughter-in-law.

"How much will you pay me?" she asked.

17"I'll send you a young goat from my flock," he promised.

"What pledge will you give me, so that I can be sure you will send it?" she asked.

18"Well, what do you want?" he inquired.

"Your identification seal and your walking stick," she replied. So he gave them to her and she let him come and sleep with her; and she became pregnant as a result. 19Afterwards she resumed wearing her widow's clothing as usual. 20Judah asked his friend Hirah the Adullamite to take the young goat back to her, and to pick up the pledges he had given her, but Hirah couldn't find her!

21So he asked around of the men of the city, "Where does the prostitute live who was soliciting out beside the road at the entrance of the village?"

"But we've never had a public prostitute here," they replied. 22So he returned to Judah and told him he couldn't find her anywhere, and what the men of the place had told him.

23"Then let her keep them!" Judah exclaimed. "We tried our best. We'd be the laughingstock of the town to go back again."

24About three months later word reached Judah that Tamar, his daughter-in-law, was pregnant, obviously as a result of prostitution.

"Bring her out and burn her," Judah shouted.

25But as they were taking her out to kill her she sent this message to her father-in-law: "The man who owns this identification seal and walking stick is the father of my child. Do you recognize them?"

26Judah admitted that they were his and said, "She is more in the right than I am, because I refused to keep my promise to give her to my son Shelah." But he did not marry her.

27In due season the time of her delivery arrived and she had twin sons. 28As they were being born, the midwife tied a scarlet thread around the wrist of the child who appeared first, 29but he drew back his hand and the other baby was actually the first to be born. "Where did *you* come from!" she exclaimed. And ever after he was called Perez (meaning "Bursting Out"). 30Then, soon afterwards, the baby with the scarlet thread

on his wrist was born, and he was named Zerah.

MATTHEW 12:22–45

THEN a demon-possessed man—he was both blind and unable to talk—was brought to Jesus, and Jesus healed him so that he could both speak and see. 23The crowd was amazed. "Maybe Jesus is the Messiah!" they exclaimed.

24But when the Pharisees heard about the miracle they said, "He can cast out demons because he is Satan, king of devils."

25Jesus knew their thoughts and replied, "A divided kingdom ends in ruin. A city or home divided against itself cannot stand. 26And if Satan is casting out Satan, he is fighting himself, and destroying his own kingdom. 27And if, as you claim, I am casting out demons by invoking the powers of Satan, then what power do your own people use when they cast them out? Let them answer your accusation! 28But if I am casting out demons by the Spirit of God, then the Kingdom of God has arrived among you. 29One cannot rob Satan's kingdom without first binding Satan. Only then can his demons be cast out! 30Anyone who isn't helping me is harming me.

31,32"Even blasphemy against me or any other sin can be forgiven—all except one: speaking against the Holy Spirit shall never be forgiven, either in this world or in the world to come.

33"A tree is identified by its fruit. A tree from a select variety produces good fruit; poor varieties don't. 34You brood of snakes! How could evil men like you speak what is good and right? For a man's heart determines his speech. 35A good man's speech reveals the rich treasures within him. An evil-hearted man is filled with venom, and his speech reveals it. 36And I tell you this, that you must give account on Judgment Day for every idle word you speak. 37Your words now reflect your fate then: either you will be justified by them or you will be condemned."

38One day some of the Jewish leaders, including some Pharisees, came to Jesus asking him to show them a miracle.

39,40But Jesus replied, "Only an evil, faithless nation would ask for further proof; and none will be given except what happened to Jonah the prophet! For as Jonah was in the great fish for three days and three nights, so I, the Messiah, shall be in the heart of the earth three days and three nights. 41The men of Nineveh shall arise against this nation at the judgment and condemn you. For when Jonah preached to them, they repented and turned to God from all their evil ways. And now a greater than Jonah is here— and you refuse to believe him. 42The Queen of Sheba shall rise against this nation in the judgment, and condemn it; for she came from a distant land to hear the wisdom of Solomon; and now a greater than Solomon is here—and you refuse to believe him.

43,44,45"This evil nation is like a man possessed by a demon. For if the demon leaves, it goes into the deserts for a while, seeking rest but finding none. Then it says, 'I will return to the man I came from.' So it returns and finds the man's heart clean but empty! Then the demon finds seven other spirits more evil than itself, and all enter the man and live in him. And so he is worse off than before."

PSALM 16:1–11

SAVE me, O God, because I have come to you for refuge. 2I said to him, "You are my Lord; I have no other help but yours." 3I want the company of the godly men and women in the land; they are the true nobility. 4Those choosing other gods shall all be filled with sorrow; I will not offer the sacrifices they do or even speak the names of their gods.

5The Lord himself is my inheritance, my prize. He is my food and drink, my highest joy! He guards all that is mine. 6He sees that I am given pleasant brooks and meadows as my share! What a wonderful inheritance! 7I will bless the Lord who counsels me; he gives me wisdom in the night. He tells me what to do.

8I am always thinking of the Lord; and because he is so near, I never need to stumble or to fall.

9Heart, body, and soul are filled with joy. 10For you will not leave me among the dead; you will not allow your beloved one to rot in the grave. 11You have let me experience the joys of life and the exquisite pleasures of your own eternal presence.

PROVERBS FOR TODAY/ 3:27–32

Don't withhold repayment of your debts. Don't say "some other time," if you can pay now. Don't plot against your neighbor; he is trusting you. Don't get into needless fights. Don't envy violent men. Don't copy their ways. For such men are an abomination to the Lord, but he gives his friendship to the godly.

JANUARY 19

GENESIS 39:1—41:16

WHEN Joseph arrived in Egypt as a captive of the Ishmaelite traders, he was purchased from them by Potiphar, a member of the personal staff of Pharaoh, the king of Egypt. Now this man Potiphar was the captain of the king's bodyguard and his chief executioner. 2The Lord greatly blessed Joseph there in the home of his master, so that everything he did succeeded. ³Potiphar noticed this and realized that the Lord was with Joseph in a very special way. ⁴So Joseph naturally became quite a favorite with him. Soon he was put in charge of the administration of Potiphar's household, and all of his business affairs. ⁵At once the Lord began blessing Potiphar for Joseph's sake. All his household affairs began to run smoothly, his crops flourished and his flocks multiplied. ⁶So Potiphar gave Joseph the complete administrative responsibility over everything he owned. He hadn't a worry in the world with Joseph there, except to decide what he wanted to eat! Joseph, by the way, was a very handsome young man.

⁷One day at about this time Potiphar's wife began making eyes at Joseph, and suggested that he come and sleep with her.

⁸Joseph refused. "Look," he told her, "my master trusts me with everything in the entire household; ⁹he himself has no more authority here than I have! He has held back nothing from me except you yourself because you are his wife. How can I do such a wicked thing as this? It would be a great sin against God."

¹⁰But she kept on with her suggestions day after day, even though he refused to listen, and kept out of her way as much as possible. ¹¹Then one day as he was in the house going about his work— as it happened, no one else was around at the time— ¹²she came and grabbed him by the sleeve demanding, "Sleep with me." He tore himself away, but as he did, his jacket slipped off and she was left holding it as he fled from the house. ¹³When she saw that she had his jacket, and that he had fled, ¹⁴,¹⁵she began screaming; and when the other men around the place came running in to see what had happened, she was crying hysterically. "My husband had to bring in this Hebrew slave to insult us!" she sobbed. "He tried to rape me, but when I screamed, he ran, and forgot to take his jacket."

¹⁶She kept the jacket, and when her husband came home that night, ¹⁷she told him her story.

"That Hebrew slave you've had around here tried to rape me, ¹⁸and I was only saved by my screams. He fled, leaving his jacket behind!"

¹⁹Well, when her husband heard his wife's story, he was furious. ²⁰He threw Joseph into prison, where the king's prisoners were kept in chains. ²¹But the Lord was with Joseph there, too, and was kind to him by granting him favor with the chief jailer. ²²In fact, the jailer soon handed over the entire prison administration to Joseph, so that all the other prisoners were responsible to him. ²³The chief jailer had no more worries after that, for Joseph took care of everything, and the Lord was with him so that everything ran smoothly and well.

SOME time later it so happened that the king of Egypt became angry with both his chief baker and his chief butler, so he jailed them both in the prison where Joseph was, in the castle of Potiphar, the captain of the guard, who was the chief executioner. ⁴They remained under arrest there for quite some time, and Potiphar assigned Joseph to wait on them. ⁵One night each of them had a dream. ⁶The next morning Joseph noticed that they looked dejected and sad.

⁷"What in the world is the matter?" he asked.

⁸And they replied, "We both had dreams last night, but there is no one here to tell us what they mean."

"Interpreting dreams is God's business," Joseph replied. "Tell me what you saw."

⁹,¹⁰The butler told his dream first. "In my dream," he said, "I saw a vine with three branches that began to bud and blossom, and soon there were clusters of ripe grapes. ¹¹I was holding Pharaoh's wine cup in my hand, so I took the grapes and squeezed the juice into it, and gave it to him to drink."

¹²"I know what the dream means," Joseph said. "The three branches mean three days! ¹³Within three days Pharaoh

is going to take you out of prison and give you back your job again as his chief butler. 14And please have some pity on me when you are back in his favor, and mention me to Pharaoh, and ask him to let me out of here. 15For I was kidnapped from my homeland among the Hebrews, and now this—here I am in jail when I did nothing to deserve it."

16When the chief baker saw that the first dream had such a good meaning, he told his dream to Joseph, too.

"In my dream," he said, "there were three baskets of pastries on my head. 17In the top basket were all kinds of bakery goods for Pharaoh, but the birds came and ate them."

18,19"The three baskets mean three days," Joseph told him. "Three days from now Pharaoh will take off your head and impale your body on a pole, and the birds will come and pick off your flesh!"

20Pharaoh's birthday came three days later, and he held a party for all of his officials and household staff. He sent for his chief butler and chief baker, and they were brought to him from the prison. 21Then he restored the chief butler to his former position; 22but he sentenced the chief baker to be impaled, just as Joseph had predicted. 23Pharaoh's wine taster, however, promptly forgot all about Joseph, never giving him a thought.

ONE night two years later, Pharaoh dreamed that he was standing on the bank of the Nile River, 2when suddenly, seven sleek, fat cows came up out of the river and began grazing in the grass. 3Then seven other cows came up from the river, but they were very skinny and all their ribs stood out. They went over and stood beside the fat cows. 4Then the skinny cows ate the fat ones! At which point, Pharaoh woke up!

5Soon he fell asleep again and had a second dream. This time he saw seven heads of grain on one stalk, with every kernel well formed and plump. 6Then, suddenly, seven more heads appeared on the stalk, but these were shriveled and withered by the east wind. 7And these thin heads swallowed up the seven plump, well-formed heads! Then Pharaoh woke up again and realized it was all a dream. 8Next morning, as he thought about it, he became very concerned as to what the dreams might mean; he called for all the magicians and sages of Egypt and told them about it, but not one of them could suggest what his dreams meant. 9Then the king's wine taster spoke up. "Today I remember my sin!" he said. 10"Some time ago when you were angry with a couple of us and put me and the chief baker in jail in the castle of the captain of the guard, 11the chief baker and I each had a dream one night. 12We told the dreams to a young Hebrew fellow there who was a slave of the captain of the guard, and he told us what our dreams meant. 13And everything happened just as he said: I was restored to my position of wine taster, and the chief baker was executed, and impaled on a pole."

14Pharaoh sent at once for Joseph. He was brought hastily from the dungeon, and after a quick shave and change of clothes, came in before Pharaoh.

15"I had a dream last night," Pharaoh told him, "and none of these men can tell me what it means. But I have heard that you can interpret dreams, and that is why I have called for you."

16"I can't do it by myself," Joseph replied, "but God will tell you what it means!"

MATTHEW 12:46—13:23

AS Jesus was speaking in a crowded house his mother and brothers were outside, wanting to talk with him. When someone told him they were there, 48he remarked, "Who is my mother? Who are my brothers?" 49He pointed to his disciples. "Look!" he said, "these are my mother and brothers." 50Then he added, "Anyone who obeys my Father in heaven is my brother, sister and mother!"

LATER that same day, Jesus left the house and went down to the shore, 2,3where an immense crowd soon gathered. He got into a boat and taught from it while the people listened on the beach. He used many illustrations such as this one in his sermon:

"A farmer was sowing grain in his fields. 4As he scattered the seed across the ground, some fell beside a path, and the birds came and ate it. 5And some fell on rocky soil where there was little depth of earth; the plants sprang up quickly enough in the shallow soil, 6but the hot sun soon scorched them and they withered and died, for they had so little root. 7Other seeds fell among thorns, and the thorns choked out the tender blades. 8But some fell on good soil, and produced a crop that was thirty, sixty, and even a hundred times as much as he had planted. 9If you have ears, listen!"

10His disciples came and asked him, "Why do you always use these hard-to-understand illustrations?"

11Then he explained to them that only they were permitted to understand about the Kingdom of Heaven, and others were not.

12,13"For to him who has will more be given," he told them, "and he will have great plenty; but from him who has not, even the little he has will be taken away. That is why I use these illustrations, so people will hear and see but not understand.

14"This fulfills the prophecy of Isaiah: 'They hear, but don't understand; they look, but don't see! 15For their hearts are fat and heavy, and their ears are dull, and they have closed their eyes in sleep, 16so they won't see and hear and understand and turn to God again, and let me heal them.'

But blessed are your eyes, for they see; and your ears, for they hear. 17Many a prophet and godly man has longed to see what you have seen, and hear what you have heard, but couldn't.

18"Now here is the explanation of the story I told about the farmer planting grain: 19The hard path where some of the seeds fell represents the heart of a person who hears the Good News about the Kingdom and doesn't understand it; then Satan comes and snatches away the seeds from his heart. 20The shallow, rocky soil represents the heart of a man who hears the message and receives it with real joy, 21but he doesn't have much depth in his life, and the seeds don't root very deeply, and after a while when trouble comes, or persecution begins because of his beliefs, his enthusiasm fades, and he drops out. 22The ground covered with thistles represents a man who hears the message, but the cares of this life and his longing for money choke out God's Word, and he does less and less for God. 23The good ground represents the heart of a man who listens to the message and understands it and goes out and brings thirty, sixty, or even a hundred others into the Kingdom."

PSALM 17:1–15

I am pleading for your help, O Lord; for I have been honest and have done what is right, and you must listen to my earnest cry! 2Publicly acquit me, Lord, for you are always fair. 3You have tested me and seen that I am good. You have come even in the night and found nothing amiss and know that I have told the truth. 4I have followed your commands and have not gone along with cruel and evil men. 5My feet have not slipped from your paths.

6Why am I praying like this? Because I know you will answer me, O God! Yes, listen as I pray. 7Show me your strong love in wonderful ways, O Savior of all those seeking your help against their foes. 8Protect me as you would the pupil of your eye; hide me in the shadow of your wings as you hover over me.

9My enemies encircle me with murder in their eyes. 10They are pitiless and arrogant. Listen to their boasting. 11They close in upon me and are ready to throw me to the ground. 12They are like lions eager to tear me apart, like young lions hiding and waiting their chance.

13,14Lord, arise and stand against them. Push them back! Come and save me from these men of the world whose only concern is earthly gain—these men whom you have filled with your treasures so that their children and grandchildren are rich and prosperous.

15But as for me, my contentment is not in wealth but in seeing you and knowing all is well between us. And when I awake in heaven, I will be fully satisfied, for I will see you face to face.

PROVERBS FOR TODAY/ 3:33–35

The curse of God is on the wicked, but his blessing is on the upright. The Lord mocks at mockers, but helps the humble. The wise are promoted to honor, but fools are promoted to shame!

JANUARY 20

GENESIS 41:17—42:17

SO Pharaoh told him the dream. "I was standing upon the bank of the Nile River," he said, 18"when suddenly, seven fat, healthy-looking cows came up out of the river and began grazing along the river bank. 19But then seven other cows came up from the river, very skinny and bony—in fact, I've never seen such poor-looking specimens in all the land of Egypt. 20And these skinny cattle ate up the seven fat ones that had come out first, 21and afterwards they were still as skinny as before! Then I woke up.

22"A little later I had another dream. This time there were seven heads of grain on one stalk, and all seven heads were plump and full. 23Then, out of the same stalk, came seven withered, thin heads. 24And the thin heads swallowed up the fat ones! I told all this to my magicians, but not one of them could tell me the meaning."

25"Both dreams mean the same thing," Joseph told Pharaoh. "God was telling you what he is going to do here in the land of Egypt. 26The seven fat cows (and also the seven fat, well-formed heads of grain) mean that there are seven years of prosperity ahead. 27The seven skinny cows (and also the seven thin and with-ered heads of grain) indicate that there will be seven years of famine following the seven years of prosperity.

28"So God has showed you what he is about to do: 29The next seven years will be a period of great prosperity throughout all the land of Egypt; 30but afterwards there will be seven years of famine so great that all the prosperity will be forgotten and wiped out; famine will consume the land. 31The famine will be so terrible that even the memory of the good years will be erased. 32The double dream gives double impact, showing that what I have told you is certainly going to happen, for God has decreed it, and it is going to happen soon. 33My suggestion is that you find the wisest man in Egypt and put him in charge of administering a nation-wide farm program. 34,35Let Pharaoh divide Egypt into five administrative districts, and let the officials of these districts gather into the royal storehouses all the excess crops of the next seven years, 36so that there will be enough to eat when the seven years of famine come. Otherwise, disaster will surely strike."

37Joseph's suggestions were well received by Pharaoh and his assistants. 38As they discussed who should be appointed for the job, Pharaoh said, "Who could do it better than Joseph? For he is a man who is obviously filled with the Spirit of God." 39Turning to Joseph, Pharaoh said to him, "Since God has revealed the meaning of the dreams to you, you are the wisest man in the country! 40I am hereby appointing you to be in charge of this entire project. What you say goes, throughout all the land of Egypt. I alone will outrank you."

41,42Then Pharaoh placed his own signet ring on Joseph's finger as a token of his authority, and dressed him in beautiful clothing and placed the royal gold chain about his neck and declared, "See, I have placed you in charge of all the land of Egypt."

43Pharaoh also gave Joseph the chariot of his second-in-command, and wherever he went the shout arose, "Kneel down!" 44And Pharaoh declared to Joseph, "I, the king of Egypt, swear that you shall have complete charge over all the land of Egypt."

45Pharaoh gave him a name meaning "He has the god-like power of life and death!" And he gave him a wife, a girl named Asenath, daughter of Potiphera, priest of Heliopolis. So Joseph became famous throughout the land of Egypt. 46He was thirty years old as he entered the service of the king. Joseph went out from the presence of Pharaoh, and began traveling all across the land.

47And sure enough, for the next seven years there were bumper crops everywhere. 48During those years, Joseph requisitioned for the government a portion of all the crops grown throughout Egypt, storing them in nearby cities. 49After seven years of this, the granaries were full to overflowing, and there was so much that no one kept track of the amount.

50During this time before the arrival of the first of the famine years, two sons were born to Joseph by Asenath, the daughter of Potiphera, priest of the sun god Re of Heliopolis. 51Joseph named his oldest son Manasseh (meaning "Made to Forget"—what he meant was that God had made up to him for all the anguish of his youth, and for the loss of his father's home). 52The second boy was named Ephraim (meaning "Fruitful"— "For God has made me fruitful in this land of my slavery," he said).

53So at last the seven years of plenty came to an end. 54Then the seven years of famine began, just as Joseph had predicted. There were crop failures in all the surrounding countries too, but in Egypt there was plenty of grain in the storehouses. 55The people began to starve. They pleaded with Pharaoh for food, and he sent them to Joseph. "Do whatever he tells you to," he instructed them.

56,57So now, with severe famine all over the world, Joseph opened up the storehouses and sold grain to the Egyptians and to those from other lands who came to Egypt to buy grain from Joseph.

WHEN Jacob heard that there was grain available in Egypt he said to his sons, "Why are you standing around looking at one another? 2I have heard that there is grain available in Egypt. Go down and buy some for us before we all starve to death."

3So Joseph's ten older brothers went down to Egypt to buy grain. 4However, Jacob wouldn't let Joseph's younger brother Benjamin go with them, for fear some harm might happen to him [as it had to his brother Joseph]. 5So it was that Israel's sons arrived in Egypt along with many others from many lands to buy food, for the famine was as severe in Canaan as it was everywhere else.

6Since Joseph was governor of all Egypt, and in charge of the sale of the grain, it was to him that his brothers came, and bowed low before him, with their faces to the earth. 7Joseph recognized them instantly, but pretended he didn't.

"Where are you from?" he demanded roughly.

"From the land of Canaan," they replied. "We have come to buy grain."

8,9Then Joseph remembered the

dreams of long ago! But he said to them, "You are spies. You have come to see how destitute the famine has made our land."

10"No, no," they exclaimed. "We have come to buy food. 11We are all brothers and honest men, sir! We are not spies!"

12"Yes, you are," he insisted. "You have come to see how weak we are."

13"Sir," they said, "there are twelve of us brothers, and our father is in the land of Canaan. Our youngest brother is there with our father, and one of our brothers is dead."

14"So?" Joseph asked. "What does that prove? You are spies. 15This is the way I will test your story: I swear by the life of Pharaoh that you are not going to leave Egypt until this youngest brother comes here. 16One of you go and get your brother! I'll keep the rest of you here, bound in prison. Then we'll find out whether your story is true or not. If it turns out that you don't have a younger brother, then I'll know you are spies.

17So he threw them all into jail for three days.

MATTHEW 13:24–46

HERE is another illustration Jesus used: "The Kingdom of Heaven is like a farmer sowing good seed in his field; 25but one night as he slept, his enemy came and sowed thistles among the wheat. 26When the crop began to grow, the thistles grew too.

27"The farmer's men came and told him, 'Sir, the field where you planted that choice seed is full of thistles!'

28"An enemy has done it,' he exclaimed.

"'Shall we pull out the thistles?' they asked.

29"'No,' he replied. 'You'll hurt the wheat if you do. 30Let both grow together until the harvest, and I will tell the reapers to sort out the thistles and burn them, and put the wheat in the barn.' "

31,32Here is another of his illustrations: "The Kingdom of Heaven is like a tiny mustard seed planted in a field. It is the smallest of all seeds, but becomes the largest of all plants, and grows into a tree where birds can come and find shelter."

33He also used this example:

"The Kingdom of Heaven can be compared to a woman making bread. She takes a measure of flour and mixes in the yeast until it permeates every part of the dough."

34,35Jesus constantly used these illustrations when speaking to the crowds. In fact, because the prophets said that he would use so many, he never spoke to them without at least one illustration. For it had been prophesied, "I will talk in parables; I will explain mysteries hidden since the beginning of time."

36Then, leaving the crowds outside, he went into the house. His disciples asked him to explain to them the illustration of the thistles and the wheat.

37"All right," he said, "I am the farmer who sows the choice seed. 38The field is the world, and the seed represents the people of the Kingdom; the thistles are the people belonging to Satan. 39The enemy who sowed the thistles among the wheat is the devil; the harvest is the end of the world, and the reapers are the angels.

40"Just as in this story the thistles are separated and burned, so shall it be at the end of the world: 41I will send my angels and they will separate out of the Kingdom every temptation and all who are evil, 42and throw them into the furnace and burn them. There shall be weeping and gnashing of teeth. 43Then the godly shall shine as the sun in their Father's Kingdom. Let those with ears, listen!

44"The Kingdom of Heaven is like a treasure a man discovered in a field. In his excitement, he sold everything he owned to get enough money to buy the field—and get the treasure, too!

45"Again, the Kingdom of Heaven is like a pearl merchant on the lookout for choice pearls. 46He discovered a real bargain—a pearl of great value—and sold everything he owned to purchase it!

PSALM 18:1–15

LORD, how I love you! For you have done such tremendous things for me.

2The Lord is my fort where I can enter and be safe; no one can follow me in and slay me. He is a rugged mountain where I hide; he is my Savior, a rock where none can reach me, and a tower of safety. He is my shield. He is like the strong horn of a mighty fighting bull. 3All I need to do is cry to him—oh, praise the Lord—and I am saved from all my enemies!

4Death bound me with chains, and the floods of ungodliness mounted a massive attack against me. 5Trapped and helpless, I struggled against the ropes that drew me on to death.

6In my distress I screamed to the Lord for his help. And he heard me from heaven; my cry reached his ears. 7Then the earth rocked and reeled, and mountains shook and trembled. How they quaked! For he was angry. 8Fierce flames leaped from his mouth, setting fire to the earth; smoke blew from his nostrils. 9He bent the heavens down and came to my defense; thick darkness was beneath his feet. 10Mounted on a mighty angel, he sped swiftly to my aid with wings of wind. 11He enshrouded himself with darkness, veiling his approach with dense clouds dark as murky waters. 12Suddenly the brilliance of his presence broke through the clouds with lightning and a mighty storm of hail.

13The Lord thundered in the heavens; the God above all gods has spoken— oh, the hailstones; oh, the fire! 14He flashed his fearful arrows of lightning and routed all my enemies. See how they run! 15Then at your command, O Lord, the sea receded from the shore. At the blast of your breath the depths were laid bare.

PROVERBS FOR TODAY/ 4:1–6

Young men, listen to me as you would to your father. Listen, and grow wise, for I speak the truth—don't turn away. For I, too, was once a son, tenderly loved by my mother as an only child, and the companion of my father. He told me never to forget his words. "If you follow them," he said, "you will have a long and happy life. Learn to be wise," *he said,* "and develop good judgment and common sense! I cannot overemphasize this point." *Cling to wisdom—she will protect you. Love her—she will guard you.*

JANUARY 21

GENESIS 42:18—43:34

THE third day Joseph said to them, "I am a God-fearing man and I'm going to give you an opportunity to prove yourselves. 19I'm going to take a chance that you are honorable; only one of you shall remain in chains in jail, and the rest of you may go on home with grain for your families; 20but bring your youngest brother back to me. In this way I will know whether you are telling me the truth; and if you are, I will spare you." To this they agreed.

21Speaking among themselves, they said, "This has all happened because of what we did to Joseph long ago. We saw his terror and anguish and heard his pleadings, but we wouldn't listen."

²²"Didn't I tell you not to do it?" Reuben asked. "But you wouldn't listen. And now we are going to die because we murdered him."

²³Of course they didn't know that Joseph understood them as he was standing there, for he had been speaking to them through an interpreter. ²⁴Now he left the room and found a place where he could weep. Returning, he selected Simeon from among them and had him bound before their eyes. ²⁵Joseph then ordered his servants to fill the men's sacks with grain, but also gave secret instructions to put each brother's payment at the top of his sack! He also gave them provisions for their journey. ²⁶So they loaded up their donkeys with the grain and started for home. ²⁷But when they stopped for the night and one of them opened his sack to get some grain to feed the donkeys, there was his money in the mouth of the sack!

²⁸"Look," he exclaimed to his brothers, "my money is here in my sack." They were filled with terror. Trembling, they exclaimed to each other. "What is this that God has done to us?" ²⁹So they came to their father Jacob in the land of Canaan and told him all that had happened.

³⁰"The king's chief assistant spoke very roughly to us," they told him, "and took us for spies. ³¹'No, no,' we said, 'we are honest men, not spies. ³²We are twelve brothers, sons of one father; one is dead, and the youngest is with our father in the land of Canaan.' ³³Then the man told us, 'This is the way I will find out if you are what you claim to be. Leave one of your brothers here with me and take grain for your families and go on home, ³⁴but bring your youngest brother back to me. Then I shall know whether you are spies or honest men; if you prove to be what you say, then I will give you back your brother and you can come as often as you like to purchase grain.' "

³⁵As they emptied out the sacks, there at the top of each was the money paid for the grain! Terror gripped them, as it did their father.

³⁶Then Jacob exclaimed, "You have bereaved me of my children—Joseph didn't come back, Simeon is gone, and now you want to take Benjamin too! Everything has been against me."

³⁷Then Reuben said to his father, "Kill my two sons if I don't bring Benjamin back to you. I'll be responsible for him."

³⁸But Jacob replied, "My son shall not go down with you, for his brother Joseph is dead and he alone is left of his mother's children. If anything should happen to him, I would die."

BUT there was no relief from the terrible famine throughout the land. ²When the grain they had brought from Egypt was almost gone, their father said to them, "Go again and buy us a little food."

³,⁴,⁵But Judah told him, "The man wasn't fooling one bit when he said, 'Don't ever come back again unless your brother is with you.' We cannot go unless you let Benjamin go with us."

⁶"Why did you ever tell him you had another brother?" Israel moaned. "Why did you have to treat me like that?"

⁷"But the man specifically asked us about our family," they told him. "He wanted to know whether our father was still living and he asked us if we had another brother, so we told him. How could we know that he was going to say, 'Bring me your brother'?"

⁸Judah said to his father, "Send the lad with me and we will be on our way; otherwise we will all die of starvation—and not only we, but you and all our little ones. ⁹I guarantee his safety. If I don't bring him back to you, then let me bear the blame forever. ¹⁰For we could have gone and returned by this time if you had let him come."

¹¹So their father Israel finally said to them, "If it can't be avoided, then at least do this. Load your donkeys with the best products of the land. Take them to the man as gifts—balm, honey, spices, myrrh, pistachio nuts, and almonds. ¹²Take double money so that you can pay back what was in the mouths of your sacks, as it was probably someone's mis-

take, 13and take your brother and go. 14May God Almighty give you mercy before the man, so that he will release Simeon and return Benjamin. And if I must bear the anguish of their deaths, then so be it."

15So they took the gifts and double money and went to Egypt, and stood before Joseph. 16When Joseph saw that Benjamin was with them he said to the manager of his household, "These men will eat with me this noon. Take them home and prepare a big feast." 17So the man did as he was told and took them to Joseph's palace. 18They were badly frightened when they saw where they were being taken.

"It's because of the money returned to us in our sacks," they said. "He wants to pretend we stole it and seize us as slaves, with our donkeys."

19As they arrived at the entrance to the palace, they went over to Joseph's household manager, 20and said to him, "O sir, after our first trip to Egypt to buy food, 21as we were returning home, we stopped for the night and opened our sacks, and the money was there that we had paid for the grain. Here it is; we have brought it back again, 22along with additional money to buy more grain. We have no idea how the money got into our sacks."

23"Don't worry about it," the household manager told them; "your God, even the God of your fathers, must have put it there, for we collected your money all right."

Then he released Simeon and brought him out to them. 24They were then conducted into the palace and given water to refresh their feet; and their donkeys were fed. 25Then they got their presents ready for Joseph's arrival at noon, for they were told that they would be eating there. 26When Joseph came home they gave him their presents, bowing low before him.

27He asked how they had been getting along. "And how is your father—the old man you spoke about? Is he still alive?" 28"Yes," they replied. "He is alive and well." Then again they bowed before him.

29Looking at his brother Benjamin, he asked, "Is this your youngest brother, the one you told me about? How are you, my son? God be gracious to you." 30Then Joseph made a hasty exit, for he was overcome with love for his brother and had to go out and cry. Going into his bedroom, he wept there. 31Then he washed his face and came out, keeping himself under control. "Let's eat," he said.

32Joseph ate by himself, his brothers were served at a separate table, and the Egyptians at still another; for Egyptians despise Hebrews and never eat with them. 33He told each of them where to sit, and seated them in the order of their ages, from the oldest to the youngest, much to their amazement! 34Their food was served to them from his own table. He gave the largest serving to Benjamin—five times as much as to any of the others! They had a wonderful time bantering back and forth, and the wine flowed freely!

MATTHEW 13:47—14:13

AGAIN, the Kingdom of Heaven can be illustrated by a fisherman—he casts a net into the water and gathers in fish of every kind, valuable and worthless. When the net is full, he drags it up onto the beach and sits down and sorts out the edible ones into crates and throws the others away. 49That is the way it will be at the end of the world—the angels will come and separate the wicked people from the godly, 50casting the wicked into the fire; there shall be weeping and gnashing of teeth. 51Do you understand?"

"Yes," they said, "we do."

52Then he added, "Those experts in Jewish law who are now my disciples have double treasures—from the Old Testament as well as from the New!"

53,54When Jesus had finished giving these illustrations, he returned to his home town, Nazareth in Galilee, and taught there in the synagogue and astonished everyone with his wisdom and his miracles.

⁵⁵"How is this possible?" the people exclaimed. "He's just a carpenter's son, and we know Mary his mother and his brothers—James, Joseph, Simon, and Judas. ⁵⁶And his sisters—they all live here. How can he be so great?" ⁵⁷And they became angry with him!

Then Jesus told them, "A prophet is honored everywhere except in his own country, and among his own people!" ⁵⁸And so he did only a few great miracles there, because of their unbelief.

WHEN King Herod heard about Jesus, ²he said to his men, "This must be John the Baptist, come back to life again. That is why he can do these miracles." ³For Herod had arrested John and chained him in prison at the demand of his wife Herodias, his brother Philip's ex-wife, ⁴because John had told him it was wrong for him to marry her. ⁵He would have killed John but was afraid of a riot, for all the people believed John was a prophet.

⁶But at a birthday party for Herod, Herodias' daughter performed a dance that greatly pleased him, ⁷so he vowed to give her anything she wanted. ⁸Consequently, at her mother's urging, the girl asked for John the Baptist's head on a tray.

⁹The king was grieved, but because of his oath, and because he didn't want to back down in front of his guests, he issued the necessary orders.

¹⁰So John was beheaded in the prison, ¹¹and his head was brought on a tray and given to the girl, who took it to her mother.

¹²Then John's disciples came for his body and buried it, and came to tell Jesus what had happened.

¹³As soon as Jesus heard the news, he went off by himself in a boat to a remote area to be alone. But the crowds saw where he was headed, and followed by land from many villages.

PSALM 18:16–34

HE reached down from heaven and took me and drew me out of my great trials. He rescued me from deep waters. ¹⁷He delivered me from my strong enemy, from those who hated me—I who was helpless in their hands.

¹⁸On the day when I was weakest, they attacked. But the Lord held me steady. ¹⁹He led me to a place of safety, for he delights in me.

²⁰The Lord rewarded me for doing right and being pure. ²¹For I have followed his commands and have not sinned by turning back from following him. ²²I kept close watch on all his laws; I did not refuse a single one. ²³I did my best to keep them all, holding myself back from doing wrong. ²⁴And so the Lord has paid me with his blessings, for I have done what is right, and I am pure of heart. This he knows, for he watches my every step.

²⁵Lord, how merciful you are to those who are merciful. And you do not punish those who run from evil. ²⁶You give blessings to the pure but pain to those who leave your paths. ²⁷You deliver the humble but condemn the proud and haughty ones. ²⁸You have turned on my light! The Lord my God has made my darkness turn to light. ²⁹Now in your strength I can scale any wall, attack any troop.

³⁰What a God he is! How perfect in every way! All his promises prove true. He is a shield for everyone who hides behind him. ³¹For who is God except our Lord? Who but he is as a rock?

³²He fills me with strength and protects me wherever I go. ³³He gives me the surefootedness of a mountain goat upon the crags. He leads me safely along the top of the cliffs. ³⁴He prepares me for battle and gives me strength to draw an iron bow!

Getting wisdom is the most important thing you can do! And with your wisdom, develop common sense and good judgment. If you exalt wisdom, she will exalt you. Hold her fast and she will lead you to great honor; she will place a beautiful crown upon your head. My son, listen to me and do as I say, and you will have a long, good life.

JANUARY 22

GENESIS 44:1—45:28

WHEN his brothers were ready to leave, Joseph ordered his household manager to fill each of their sacks with as much grain as they could carry—and to put into the mouth of each man's sack the money he had paid! 2He was also told to put Joseph's own silver cup at the top of Benjamin's sack, along with the grain money. So the household manager did as he was told. 3The brothers were up at dawn and on their way with their loaded donkeys.

4But when they were barely out of the city, Joseph said to his household manager, "Chase after them and stop them and ask them why they are acting like this when their benefactor has been so kind to them? 5Ask them, 'What do you mean by stealing my lord's personal silver drinking cup, which he uses for fortune telling? What a wicked thing you have done!'" 6So he caught up with them and spoke to them along the lines he had been instructed.

7"What in the world are you talking about?" they demanded. "What kind of people do you think we are, that you accuse us of such a terrible thing as that? 8Didn't we bring back the money we found in the mouth of our sacks? Why would we steal silver or gold from your master's house? 9If you find his cup with any one of us, let that one die. And all the rest of us will be slaves forever to your master."

10"Fair enough," the man replied, "ex-cept that only the one who stole it will be a slave, and the rest of you can go free."

11They quickly took down their sacks from the backs of their donkeys and opened them. 12He began searching the oldest brother's sack, going on down the line to the youngest. And the cup was found in Benjamin's! 13They ripped their clothing in despair, loaded the donkeys again, and returned to the city. 14Joseph was still home when Judah and his brothers arrived, and they fell to the ground before him.

15"What were you trying to do?" Joseph demanded. "Didn't you know such a man as I would know who stole it?"

16And Judah said, "Oh, what shall we say to my lord? How can we plead? How can we prove our innocence? God is punishing us for our sins. Sir, we have all returned to be your slaves, both we and he in whose sack the cup was found."

17"No," Joseph said. "Only the man who stole the cup, he shall be my slave. The rest of you can go on home to your father."

18Then Judah stepped forward and said, "O sir, let me say just this one word to you. Be patient with me for a moment, for I know you can doom me in an instant, as though you were Pharaoh himself.

19"Sir, you asked us if we had a father or a brother, 20and we said, 'Yes, we have a father, an old man, and a child of his old age, a little one. And his brother is dead, and he alone is left of his mother's children, and his father loves him very much.' 21And you said to us, 'Bring him here so that I can see him.' 22But we said to you, 'Sir, the lad cannot leave his father, for his father would die.' 23But you told us, 'Don't come back here unless your youngest brother is with you.' 24So we returned to our father and told him what you had said. 25And when he said, 'Go back again and buy us a little food,' 26we replied, 'We can't, unless you let our youngest brother go with us. Only then may we come.'

27"Then my father said to us, 'You know that my wife had two sons, 28and that one of them went away and never returned—doubtless torn to pieces by some wild animal; I have never seen him since. 29And if you take away his brother from me also, and any harm befalls him, I shall die with sorrow.' 30And now, sir, if I go back to my father and the lad is not with us—seeing that our father's life is bound up in the lad's life— 31when he sees that the boy is not with us, our father will die; and we will be responsible for bringing down his gray hairs with sorrow to the grave. 32Sir, I pledged my father that I would take care of the lad. I told him, 'If I don't bring him back to you, I shall bear the blame forever.' 33Please sir, let me stay here as a slave instead of the lad, and let the lad return with his brothers. 34For how shall I return to my father if the lad is not with me? I cannot bear to see what this would do to him."

JOSEPH could stand it no longer.

"Out, all of you," he cried out to his attendants, and he was left alone with his brothers. 2Then he wept aloud. His sobs could be heard throughout the palace, and the news was quickly carried to Pharaoh's palace.

3"I am Joseph!" he said to his brothers. "Is my father still alive?" But his brothers couldn't say a word, they were so stunned with surprise.

4"Come over here," he said. So they came closer. And he said again, "I am Joseph, your brother whom you sold into Egypt! 5But don't be angry with yourselves that you did this to me, for God did it! He sent me here ahead of you to preserve your lives. 6These two years of famine will grow to seven, during which there will be neither plowing nor harvest. 7God has sent me here to keep you and your families alive, so that you will become a great nation. 8Yes, it was God who sent me here, not you! And he has made me a counselor to Pharaoh, and manager of this entire nation, ruler of all the land of Egypt.

9"Hurry, return to my father and tell him, 'Your son Joseph says, "God has made me chief of all the land of Egypt. Come down to me right away! 10You shall live in the land of Goshen so that you can be near me with all your children, your grandchildren, your flocks and herds, and all that you have. 11,12I will take care of you there" ' (you men are witnesses of my promise, and my brother Benjamin has heard me say it) ' "for there are still five years of famine ahead of us. Otherwise you will come to utter poverty along with all your household." ' 13Tell our father about all my power here in Egypt, and how everyone obeys me. And bring him to me quickly."

14Then, weeping with joy, he embraced Benjamin and Benjamin began weeping too. 15And he did the same with each of his brothers, who finally found their tongues! 16The news soon reached Pharaoh—"Joseph's brothers have come"; and Pharaoh was very happy to hear it, as were his officials.

17Then Pharaoh said to Joseph, "Tell your brothers to load their pack animals and return quickly to their homes in Canaan, 18and to bring your father and all of your families and come here to Egypt to live. Tell them, 'Pharaoh will assign to you the very best territory in the land of Egypt. You shall live off the fat of the land!' 19And tell your brothers to take wagons from Egypt to carry their wives and little ones, and to bring your father here. 20Don't worry about your property, for the best of all the land of Egypt is yours."

²¹So Joseph gave them wagons, as Pharaoh had commanded, and provisions for the journey, ²²and he gave each of them new clothes—but to Benjamin he gave five changes of clothes and three hundred pieces of silver! ²³He sent his father ten donkey-loads of the good things of Egypt, and ten donkeys loaded with grain and all kinds of other food, to eat on his journey. ²⁴So he sent his brothers off.

"Don't quarrel along the way!" was his parting shot! ²⁵And leaving, they returned to the land of Canaan, to Jacob their father.

²⁶"Joseph is alive," they shouted to him. "And he is ruler over all the land of Egypt!" But Jacob's heart was like a stone; he couldn't take it in. ²⁷But when they had given him Joseph's messages, and when he saw the wagons filled with food that Joseph had sent him, his spirit revived.

²⁸And he said, "It must be true! Joseph my son is alive! I will go and see him before I die."

MATTHEW 14:14–36

SO when Jesus came out of the wilderness, a vast crowd was waiting for him and he pitied them and healed their sick.

¹⁵That evening the disciples came to him and said, "It is already past time for supper, and there is nothing to eat here in the desert; send the crowds away so they can go to the villages and buy some food."

¹⁶But Jesus replied, "That isn't necessary—you feed them!"

¹⁷"What!" they exclaimed. "We have exactly five small loaves of bread and two fish!"

¹⁸"Bring them here," he said.

¹⁹Then he told the people to sit down on the grass; and he took the five loaves and two fish, looked up into the sky and asked God's blessing on the meal, then broke the loaves apart and gave them to the disciples to place before the people. ²⁰And everyone ate until full! And when the scraps were picked up afterwards, there were twelve basketfuls left over! ²¹(About 5,000 men were in the crowd that day, besides all the women and children.)

²²Immediately after this, Jesus told his disciples to get into their boat and cross to the other side of the lake while he stayed to get the people started home.

²³,²⁴Then afterwards he went up into the hills to pray. Night fell, and out on the lake the disciples were in trouble. For the wind had risen and they were fighting heavy seas.

²⁵About four o'clock in the morning Jesus came to them, walking on the water! ²⁶They screamed in terror, for they thought he was a ghost.

²⁷But Jesus immediately spoke to them, reassuring them. "Don't be afraid!" he said.

²⁸Then Peter called to him: "Sir, if it is really you, tell me to come over to you, walking on the water."

²⁹"All right," the Lord said, "come along!"

So Peter went over the side of the boat and walked on the water toward Jesus. ³⁰But when he looked around at the high waves, he was terrified and began to sink. "Save me, Lord!" he shouted.

³¹Instantly Jesus reached out his hand and rescued him. "O man of little faith," Jesus said. "Why did you doubt me?" ³²And when they had climbed back into the boat, the wind stopped.

³³The others sat there, awestruck. "You really are the Son of God!" they exclaimed.

³⁴They landed at Gennesaret. ³⁵The news of their arrival spread quickly throughout the city, and soon people were rushing around, telling everyone to bring in their sick to be healed. ³⁶The sick begged him to let them touch even the tassel of his robe, and all who did were healed.

PSALM 18:35–50

YOU have given me your salvation as my shield. Your right hand, O Lord, supports me; your gentleness has made me great. 36You have made wide steps beneath my feet so that I need never slip. 37I chased my enemies; I caught up with them and did not turn back until all were conquered. 38I pinned them to the ground; all were helpless before me. I placed my feet upon their necks. 39For you have armed me with strong armor for the battle. My enemies quail before me and fall defeated at my feet. 40You made them turn and run; I destroyed all who hated me. 41They shouted for help but no one dared to rescue them; they cried to the Lord, but he refused to answer them. 42So I crushed them fine as dust and cast them to the wind. I threw them away like sweepings from the floor. 43,44,45You gave me victory in every battle. The nations came and served me. Even those I didn't know before come now and bow before me. Foreigners who have never seen me submit instantly. They come trembling from their strongholds.

46God is alive! Praise him who is the great rock of protection. 47He is the God who pays back those who harm me and subdues the nations before me.

48He rescues me from my enemies; he holds me safely out of their reach and saves me from these powerful opponents. 49For this, O Lord, I will praise you among the nations. 50Many times you have miraculously rescued me, the king you appointed. You have been loving and kind to me and will be to my descendants.

PROVERBS FOR TODAY/ 4:11–13

I would have you learn this great fact: that a life of doing right is the wisest life there is. If you live that kind of life, you'll not limp or stumble as you run. Carry out my instructions; don't forget them, for they will lead you to real living.

JANUARY 23

GENESIS 46:1—47:31

SO Israel set out with all his possessions, and came to Beer-sheba, and offered sacrifices there to the God of his father Isaac. 2During the night God spoke to him in a vision.

"Jacob! Jacob!" he called.

"Yes?" Jacob answered.

3,4"I am God," the voice replied, "the God of your father. Don't be afraid to go down to Egypt, for I will see to it that you become a great nation there. And I will go down with you into Egypt and I will bring your descendants back again; but you shall die in Egypt with Joseph at your side."

5So Jacob left Beer-sheba, and his sons brought him to Egypt, along with their little ones and their wives, in the wagons Pharaoh had provided for them. 6They brought their livestock too, and all their belongings accumulated in the land of Canaan, and came to Egypt—Jacob and all his children, 7sons and daughters, grandsons and granddaughters—all his loved ones.

8–14Here are the names of his sons and grandchildren who went with him into Egypt:

Reuben, his oldest son;

Reuben's sons: Hanoch, Pallu, Hezron, and Carmi.

Simeon and his sons: Jemuel, Jamin, Ohad, Jachin, Zohar, and Shaul

(Shaul's mother was a girl from Canaan).

Levi and his sons: Gershon, Kohath, Merari.

Judah and his sons: Er, Onan, Shelah, Perez, Zerah (however, Er and Onan died while still in Canaan, before Israel went to Egypt).

The sons of Perez were Hezron and Hamul.

Issachar and his sons: Tola, Puvah, Iob, Shimron.

Zebulun and his sons: Sered, Elon, Jahleel.

15So these descendants of Jacob and Leah, not including their daughter Dinah, born to Jacob in Paddan-aram, were thirty-three in all.

16,17Also accompanying him were:

Gad and his sons: Ziphion, Haggi, Shuni,

Ezbon, Eri, Arodi, and Areli.

Asher and his sons: Imnah, Ishvah, Ishvi,

Beriah, and a sister, Serah.

Beriah's sons were Heber and Malchiel.

18These sixteen persons were the sons of Jacob and Zilpah, the slave-girl given to Leah by her father, Laban.

19-22Also in the total of Jacob's household were these fourteen sons and descendants of Jacob and Rachel:

Joseph and Benjamin;

Joseph's sons, born in the land of Egypt, were Manasseh and Ephraim (their mother was Asenath, the daughter of Potiphera, priest of Heliopolis);

Benjamin's sons: Bela, Becher, Ashbel, Gera, Naaman, Ehi, Rosh, Muppim, Huppim, and Ard.

23,24,25Also in the group were these seven sons and descendants of Jacob and Bilhah, the slave-girl given to Rachel by her father, Laban:

Dan and his son: Hushim.

Naphtali and his sons: Jahzeel, Guni, Jezer, and Shillem.

26So the total number of those going to Egypt, of his own descendants, not counting the wives of Jacob's sons, was sixty-six. 27With Joseph and his two sons included, this total of Jacob's household there in Egypt totaled seventy.

28Jacob sent Judah on ahead to tell Joseph that they were on the way, and would soon arrive in Goshen—which they did. 29Joseph jumped into his chariot and journeyed to Goshen to meet his father and they fell into each other's arms and wept a long while.

30Then Israel said to Joseph, "Now let me die, for I have seen you again and know you are alive."

31And Joseph said to his brothers and to all their households, "I'll go and tell Pharaoh that you are here, and that you have come from the land of Canaan to join me. 32And I will tell him, 'These men are shepherds. They have brought with them their flocks and herds and everything they own.' 33So when Pharaoh calls for you and asks you about your occupation, 34tell him, 'We have been shepherds from our youth, as our fathers have been for many generations.' When you tell him this, he will let you live here in the land of Goshen." For shepherds were despised and hated in other parts of Egypt.

UPON their arrival, Joseph went in to see Pharaoh.

"My father and my brothers are here from Canaan," he reported, "with all their flocks and herds and possessions. They wish to settle in the land of Goshen." 2He took five of his brothers with him, and presented them to Pharaoh. 3Pharaoh asked them, "What is your occupation?"

And they replied, "We are shepherds like our ancestors. 4We have come to live here in Egypt, for there is no pasture for our flocks in Canaan—the famine is very bitter there. We request permission to live in the land of Goshen."

5,6And Pharaoh said to Joseph, "Choose anywhere you like for them to live. Give them the best land of Egypt. The land of Goshen will be fine. And if any of them are capable, put them in charge of my flocks, too."

7Then Joseph brought his father Jacob

to Pharaoh. And Jacob blessed Pharaoh. 8"How old are you?" Pharaoh asked him.

9Jacob replied, "I have lived 130 long, hard years, and I am not nearly as old as many of my ancestors." 10Then Jacob blessed Pharaoh again before he left.

11So Joseph assigned the best land of Egypt—the land of Rameses—to his father and brothers, just as Pharaoh had commanded. 12And Joseph furnished food to them in accordance with the number of their dependents.

13The famine became worse and worse, so that all the land of Egypt and Canaan were starving. 14Joseph collected all the money in Egypt and Canaan in exchange for grain, and he brought the money to Pharaoh's treasure-houses. 15When the people were out of money, they came to Joseph crying again for food.

"Our money is gone," they said, "but give us bread; for why should we die?" 16"Well then," Joseph replied, "give me your livestock. I will trade you food in exchange."

17So they brought their cattle to Joseph in exchange for food. Soon all the horses, flocks, herds, and donkeys of Egypt were in Pharaoh's possession.

18The next year they came again and said, "Our money is gone, and our cattle are yours, and there is nothing left but our bodies and land. 19Why should we die? Buy us and our land and we will be serfs to Pharaoh. We will trade ourselves for food, then we will live, and the land won't be abandoned."

20So Joseph bought all the land of Egypt for Pharaoh; all the Egyptians sold him their fields because the famine was so severe. And the land became Pharaoh's. 21Thus all the people of Egypt became Pharaoh's serfs. 22The only land he didn't buy was that belonging to the priests, for they were assigned food from Pharaoh and didn't need to sell.

23Then Joseph said to the people, "See, I have bought you and your land for Pharaoh. Here is grain. Go and sow the land. 24And when you harvest it, a fifth of everything you get belongs to Pharaoh. Keep four parts for yourselves to be used for next year's seed, and as food for yourselves and for your households and little ones."

25"You have saved our lives," they said. "We will gladly be the serfs of Pharaoh."

26So Joseph made it a law throughout the land of Egypt—and it is still the law—that Pharaoh should have as his tax twenty percent of all the crops except those produced on the land owned by the temples.

27So Israel lived in the land of Goshen in Egypt, and soon the people of Israel began to prosper, and there was a veritable population explosion among them. 28Jacob lived seventeen years after his arrival, so that he was 147 years old at the time of his death. 29As the time drew near for him to die, he called for his son Joseph and said to him, "Swear to me most solemnly that you will honor this, my last request: do not bury me in Egypt. 30But when I am dead, take me out of Egypt and bury me beside my ancestors." And Joseph promised. 31"Swear that you will do it," Jacob insisted. And Joseph did. Soon afterwards Jacob took to his bed.

MATTHEW 15:1–28

SOME Pharisees and other Jewish leaders now arrived from Jerusalem to interview Jesus.

2"Why do your disciples disobey the ancient Jewish traditions?" they demanded. "For they ignore our ritual of ceremonial handwashing before they eat." 3He replied, "And why do your traditions violate the direct commandments of God? 4For instance, God's law is 'Honor your father and mother; anyone who reviles his parents must die.' 5,6But you say, 'Even if your parents are in need, you may give their support money to the church instead.' And so, by your man-made rule, you nullify the direct command of God to honor and care for your parents. 7You hypocrites! Well did Isaiah prophesy of you, 8"These people say they honor me, but their hearts are far away. 9Their worship is worthless, for they teach their man-made laws instead of those from God.' "

10Then Jesus called to the crowds and said, "Listen to what I say and try to understand: 11You aren't made unholy by eating non-kosher food! It is what you *say* and *think* that makes you unclean."

12Then the disciples came and told him, "You offended the Pharisees by that remark."

13,14Jesus replied, "Every plant not planted by my Father shall be rooted up, so ignore them. They are blind guides leading the blind, and both will fall into a ditch."

15Then Peter asked Jesus to explain what he meant when he said that people are not defiled by non-kosher food.

16"Don't you understand?" Jesus asked him. 17"Don't you see that any-thing you eat passes through the diges-tive tract and out again? 18But evil words come from an evil heart, and defile the man who says them. 19For from the heart come evil thoughts, murder, adultery, fornication, theft, lying and slander. 20These are what defile; but there is no spiritual defilement from eating without first going through the ritual of ceremo-nial handwashing!"

21Jesus then left that part of the coun-try and walked the fifty miles to Tyre and Sidon.

22A woman from Canaan who was liv-ing there came to him, pleading, "Have mercy on me, O Lord, King David's Son! For my daughter has a demon within her, and it torments her constantly."

23But Jesus gave her no reply—not even a word. Then his disciples urged him to send her away. "Tell her to get going," they said, "for she is bothering us with all her begging."

24Then he said to the woman, "I was sent to help the Jews—the lost sheep of Israel—not the Gentiles."

25But she came and worshiped him and pled again, "Sir, help me!"

26"It doesn't seem right to take bread from the children and throw it to the dogs," he said.

27"Yes, it is!" she replied, "for even the puppies beneath the table are permit-ted to eat the crumbs that fall."

28"Woman," Jesus told her, "your faith is large, and your request is granted." And her daughter was healed right then.

PSALM 19:1–14

THE heavens are telling the glory of God; they are a marvelous display of his craftsmanship. 2Day and night they keep on telling about God. 3,4Without a sound or word, silent in the skies, their message reaches out to all the world. The sun lives in the heavens where God placed it 5and moves out across the skies as radiant as a bride-groom going to his wedding, or as joyous as an athlete looking forward to a race! 6The sun crosses the heavens from end to end, and nothing can hide from its heat.

7,8God's laws are perfect. They protect us, make us wise, and give us joy and light. 9God's laws are pure, eternal, just. 10They are more desirable than gold. They are sweeter than honey dripping from a honeycomb. 11For they warn us away from harm and give success to those who obey them.

12But how can I ever know what sins are lurking in my heart? Cleanse me from these hidden faults. 13And keep me from deliberate wrongs; help me to stop doing them. Only then can I be free of guilt and innocent of some great crime.

14May my spoken words and unspo-ken thoughts be pleasing even to you, O Lord my Rock and my Redeemer.

PROVERBS FOR TODAY/ 4:14–19

Don't do as the wicked do. Avoid their haunts—turn away, go somewhere else, for evil men can't sleep until they've done their evil deed for the day. They can't rest unless they cause someone to stumble and fall. They eat and drink wickedness and violence! But the good man walks along in the ever-brightening light of God's favor; the dawn gives way to morning splendor, while the evil man gropes and stumbles in the dark.

JANUARY 24

GENESIS 48:1—49:33

ONE day not long after this, word came to Joseph that his father was failing rapidly. So, taking with him his two sons, Manasseh and Ephraim, he went to visit him. ²When Jacob heard that Joseph had arrived, he gathered his strength and sat up in the bed to greet him, ³and said to him,

"God Almighty appeared to me at Luz in the land of Canaan and blessed me, ⁴and said to me, 'I will make you a great nation and I will give this land of Canaan to you and to your children's children, for an everlasting possession.' ⁵And now, as to these two sons of yours, Ephraim and Manasseh, born here in the land of Egypt before I arrived, I am adopting them as my own, and they will inherit from me just as Reuben and Simeon will. ⁶But any other children born to you shall be your own, and shall inherit Ephraim's and Manasseh's portion from you. ⁷For your mother Rachel died after only two children when I came from Paddan-aram, as we were just a short distance from Ephrath, and I buried her beside the road to Bethlehem." ⁸Then Israel looked over at the two boys. "Are these the ones?" he asked.

⁹"Yes," Joseph told him, "these are my sons whom God has given me here in Egypt."

And Israel said, "Bring them over to me and I will bless them."

¹⁰Israel was half blind with age, so that he could hardly see. So Joseph brought the boys close to him and he kissed and embraced them.

¹¹And Israel said to Joseph, "I never thought that I would see you again, but now God has let me see your children too."

¹²,¹³Joseph took the boys by the hand, bowed deeply to him, and led the boys to their grandfather's knees—Ephraim at Israel's left hand and Manasseh at his right. ¹⁴But Israel crossed his arms as he stretched them out to lay his hands upon the boys' heads, so that his right hand was upon the head of Ephraim, the younger boy, and his left hand was upon the head of Manasseh, the older. He did this purposely.

¹⁵Then he blessed Joseph with this blessing: "May God, the God of my fathers Abraham and Isaac, the God who has shepherded me all my life, wonderfully bless these boys. ¹⁶He is the Angel who has kept me from all harm. May these boys be an honor to my name and to the names of my fathers Abraham and Isaac; and may they become a mighty nation."

¹⁷But Joseph was upset and displeased when he saw that his father had laid his right hand on Ephraim's head; so he lifted it to place it on Manasseh's head instead.

¹⁸"No, father," he said. "You've got your right hand on the wrong head! This one over here is the older. Put your right hand on him!"

¹⁹But his father refused. "I know what I'm doing, my son," he said. "Manasseh too shall become a great nation, but his younger brother shall become even greater."

²⁰So Jacob blessed the boys that day

with this blessing: "May the people of Israel bless each other by saying, 'God make you as prosperous as Ephraim and Manasseh.' " (Note that he put Ephraim before Manasseh.)

21Then Israel said to Joseph, "I am about to die, but God will be with you and will bring you again to Canaan, the land of your fathers. 22And I have given the choice land of Shekem to you instead of to your brothers, as your portion of that land which I took from the Amorites with my sword and with my bow."

THEN Jacob called together all his sons and said, "Gather around me and I will tell you what is going to happen to you in the days to come. 2Listen to me, O sons of Jacob; listen to Israel your father.

3"Reuben, you are my oldest son, the child of my vigorous youth. You are the head of the list in rank and in honor. 4But you are unruly as the wild waves of the sea, and you shall be first no longer. I am demoting you, for you slept with one of my wives and thus dishonored me.

5"Simeon and Levi are two of a kind. They are men of violence and injustice. 6O my soul, stay away from them. May I never be a party to their wicked plans. For in their anger they murdered a man, and maimed oxen just for fun. 7Cursed be their anger, for it is fierce and cruel. Therefore, I will scatter their descendants throughout Israel.

8"Judah, your brothers shall praise you. You shall destroy your enemies. Your father's sons shall bow before you. 9Judah is a young lion that has finished eating its prey. He has settled down as a lion—who will dare to rouse him? 10The scepter shall not depart from Judah until Shiloh comes, whom all people shall obey. 11He has chained his steed to the choicest vine, and washed his clothes in wine. 12His eyes are darker than wine and his teeth are whiter than milk.

13"Zebulun shall dwell on the shores of the sea and shall be a harbor for ships, with his borders extending to Sidon.

14"Issachar is a strong beast of burden resting among the saddle bags. 15When he saw how good the countryside was, how pleasant the land, he willingly bent his shoulder to the task and served his masters with vigor.

16"Dan shall govern his people like any other tribe in Israel. 17He shall be a serpent in the path that bites the horses' heels, so that the rider falls off. 18I trust in your salvation, Lord.

19"A marauding band shall stamp upon Gad, but he shall rob and pursue them!

20"Asher shall produce rich foods, fit for kings!

21"Naphtali is a deer let loose, producing lovely fawns.

22"Joseph is a fruitful tree beside a fountain. His branches shade the wall. 23He has been severely injured by those who shot at him and persecuted him, 24but their weapons were shattered by the Mighty One of Jacob, the Shepherd, the Rock of Israel. 25May the God of your fathers, the Almighty, bless you with blessings of heaven above and of the earth beneath—blessings of the breasts and of the womb, 26blessings of the grain and flowers, blessings reaching to the utmost bounds of the everlasting hills. These shall be the blessings upon the head of Joseph who was exiled from his brothers.

27"Benjamin is a wolf that prowls. He devours his enemies in the morning, and in the evening divides the loot."

28So these are the blessings that Israel their father blessed his twelve sons with.

29,30Then he told them, "Soon I will die. You must bury me with my fathers in the land of Canaan, in the cave in the field of Mach-pelah, facing Mamre—the field Abraham bought from Ephron the Hethite for a burial ground. 31There they buried Abraham and Sarah his wife; there they buried Isaac and Rebekah his wife; and there I buried Leah. 32It is the cave which my grandfather Abraham purchased from the sons of Heth." 33Then, when Jacob had finished his prophecies to his sons, he lay back in the bed, breathed his last, and died.

MATTHEW 15:29—16:12

JESUS now returned to the Sea of Galilee, and climbed a hill and sat there. 30And a vast crowd brought him their lame, blind, maimed, and those who couldn't speak, and many others, and laid them before Jesus, and he healed them all. 31What a spectacle it was! Those who hadn't been able to say a word before were talking excitedly, and those with missing arms and legs had new ones; the crippled were walking and jumping around, and those who had been blind were gazing about them! The crowds just marveled, and praised the God of Israel.

32Then Jesus called his disciples to him and said, "I pity these people—they've been here with me for three days now, and have nothing left to eat; I don't want to send them away hungry or they will faint along the road."

33The disciples replied, "And where would we get enough here in the desert for all this mob to eat?"

34Jesus asked them, "How much food do you have?" And they replied, "Seven loaves of bread and a few small fish!"

35Then Jesus told all of the people to sit down on the ground, 36and he took the seven loaves and the fish, and gave thanks to God for them, and divided them into pieces, and gave them to the disciples who presented them to the crowd. 37,38And everyone ate until full—4,000 men besides the women and children! And afterwards, when the scraps were picked up, there were seven basketfuls left over!

39Then Jesus sent the people home and got into the boat and crossed to Magadan.

ONE day the Pharisees and Sadducees came to test Jesus' claim of being the Messiah by asking him to show them some great demonstrations in the skies.

2,3He replied, "You are good at reading the weather signs of the skies—red sky tonight means fair weather tomorrow; red sky in the morning means foul weather all day—but you can't read the obvious signs of the times! 4This evil, unbelieving nation is asking for some strange sign in the heavens, but no further proof will be given except the miracle that happened to Jonah." Then Jesus walked out on them.

5Arriving across the lake, the disciples discovered they had forgotten to bring any food.

6"Watch out!" Jesus warned them; "beware of the yeast of the Pharisees and Sadducees."

7They thought he was saying this because they had forgotten to bring bread.

8Jesus knew what they were thinking and told them, "O men of little faith! Why are you so worried about having no food? 9Won't you ever understand? Don't you remember at all the 5,000 I fed with five loaves, and the basketfuls left over? 10Don't you remember the 4,000 I fed, and all that was left? 11How could you even think I was talking about food? But again I say, 'Beware of the yeast of the Pharisees and Sadducees.' "

12Then at last they understood that by "yeast" he meant the *wrong teaching* of the Pharisees and Sadducees.

PSALM 20:1–9

IN your day of trouble, may the Lord be with you! May the God of Jacob keep you from all harm. 2May he send you aid from his sanctuary in Zion. 3May he remember with pleasure the gifts you have given him, your sacrifices and burnt offerings. 4May he grant you your heart's desire and fulfill all your plans. 5May there be shouts of joy when we hear the news of your victory, flags flying with praise to God for all that he has done for you. May he answer all your prayers!

6"God save the king"—I know he

does! He hears me from highest heaven and sends great victories. 7Some nations boast of armies and of weaponry, but our boast is in the Lord our God.

8Those nations will collapse and perish; we will arise to stand firm and sure!

9Give victory to our king, O Lord; oh, hear our prayer.

PROVERBS FOR TODAY/ 4:20–27

Listen, son of mine, to what I say. Listen carefully. Keep these thoughts ever in mind; let them penetrate deep within your heart, for they will mean real life for you, and radiant health.

Above all else, guard your affections. For they influence everything else in your life. Spurn the careless kiss of a prostitute. Stay far from her. Look straight ahead; don't even turn your head to look. Watch your step. Stick to the path and be safe. Don't sidetrack; pull back your foot from danger.

JANUARY 25

GENESIS 50:1—EXODUS 2:10

JOSEPH threw himself upon his father's body and wept over him and kissed him. 2Afterwards he commanded his morticians to embalm the body. 3The embalming process required forty days, with a period of national mourning of seventy days. 4Then, when at last the mourning was over, Joseph approached Pharaoh's staff and requested them to speak to Pharaoh on his behalf.

5"Tell his majesty," he requested them, "that Joseph's father made Joseph swear to take his body back to the land of Canaan, to bury him there. Ask his majesty to permit me to go and bury my father; assure him that I will return promptly."

6Pharaoh agreed. "Go and bury your father, as you promised," he said.

7So Joseph went, and a great number of Pharaoh's counselors and assistants—all the senior officers of the land, 8as well as all of Joseph's people—his brothers and their families. But they left their little children and flocks and herds in the land of Goshen. 9So a very great number of chariots, cavalry, and people accompanied Joseph.

10When they arrived at Atad (meaning "Threshing Place of Brambles"), beyond the Jordan River, they held a very great and solemn funeral service, with a seven-day period of lamentation for Joseph's father. 11The local residents, the Canaanites, renamed the place Abel-mizraim (meaning "Egyptian Mourners") for they said, "It is a place of very deep mourning by these Egyptians." 12,13So his sons did as Israel commanded them, and carried his body into the land of Canaan and buried it there in the cave of Mach-pe-lah—the cave Abraham had bought in the field of Ephron the Hethite, close to Mamre.

14Then Joseph returned to Egypt with his brothers and all who had accompanied him to the funeral of his father. 15But now that their father was dead, Joseph's brothers were frightened.

"Now Joseph will pay us back for all the evil we did to him," they said. 16,17So they sent him this message: "Before he died, your father instructed us to tell you to forgive us for the great evil we did to you. We servants of the God of your father beg you to forgive us." When Joseph read the message, he broke down and cried.

18Then his brothers came and fell down before him and said, "We are your slaves."

19But Joseph told them, "Don't be afraid of me. Am I God, to judge and punish you? 20As far as I am concerned, God turned into good what you meant for evil, for he brought me to this high position I have today so that I could save the lives of many people. 21No, don't be afraid. Indeed, I myself will take care of you and your families." And he spoke very kindly to them, reassuring them.

22So Joseph and his brothers and their families continued to live in Egypt. Joseph was 110 years old when he died. 23He lived to see the birth of his son Ephraim's children, and the children of Machir, Manasseh's son, who played at his feet.

24"Soon I will die," Joseph told his brothers, "but God will surely come and get you, and bring you out of this land of Egypt and take you back to the land he promised to the descendants of Abraham, Isaac and Jacob." 25Then Joseph made his brothers promise with an oath that they would take his body back with them when they returned to Canaan. 26So Joseph died at the age of 110, and they embalmed him, and his body was placed in a coffin in Egypt.

THIS is the list of the sons of Jacob who accompanied him to Egypt, with their families:

Reuben, Simeon, Levi, Judah, Issachar, Zebulun, Benjamin, Dan, Naphtali, Gad, Asher.

5So the total number who went with him was seventy (for Joseph was already there). 6In due season Joseph and each of his brothers died, ending that generation. 7Meanwhile, their descendants were very fertile, increasing rapidly in numbers; there was a veritable population explosion so that they soon became a large nation, and they filled the land of Goshen.

8Then, eventually, a new king came to the throne of Egypt who felt no obligation to the descendants of Joseph.

9He told his people, "These Israelis are becoming dangerous to us because there are so many of them. 10Let's figure out a way to put an end to this. If we don't, and war breaks out, they will join our enemies and fight against us and escape out of the country."

11So the Egyptians made slaves of them and put brutal taskmasters over them to wear them down under heavy burdens while building the cities of Pithom and Raamses as supply centers for the king. 12But the more the Egyptians mistreated and oppressed them, the more the Israelis seemed to multiply! The Egyptians became alarmed, 13,14and made the Hebrew slavery more bitter still, forcing them to toil long and hard in the fields and to carry heavy loads of mortar and brick.

15,16Then Pharaoh, the king of Egypt, instructed the Hebrew midwives (their names were Shiphrah and Puah) to kill all Hebrew boys as soon as they were born, but to let the girls live. 17But the midwives feared God and didn't obey the king—they let the boys live too.

18The king summoned them before him and demanded, "Why have you disobeyed my command and let the baby boys live?"

19"Sir," they told him, "the Hebrew women have their babies so quickly that we can't get there in time! They are not slow like the Egyptian women!"

20And God blessed the midwives [because they were God-fearing women]. So the people of Israel continued to multiply and to become a mighty nation. 21And because the midwives revered God, he gave them children of their own. 22Then Pharaoh commanded all of his people to throw the newborn Hebrew boys into the Nile River. But the girls, he said, could live.

THERE were at this time a Hebrew fellow and girl of the tribe of Levi who married and had a family, and a baby son was born to them. When the baby's mother saw that he was an unusually beautiful baby, she hid him at home for three months. 3Then, when she could no longer hide him, she made a little boat from papyrus reeds, waterproofed it with tar, put the baby in it, and laid it among the reeds along the river's edge. 4The baby's sister watched from a distance to see what would happen to him.

5Well, this is what happened: A princess, one of Pharaoh's daughters, came down to bathe in the river, and as she and her maids were walking along the river bank, she spied the little boat among the reeds and sent one of the maids to bring it to her. 6When she opened it, there was a baby! And he was crying. This touched her heart. "He must be one of the Hebrew children!" she said.

7Then the baby's sister approached the princess and asked her, "Shall I go and find one of the Hebrew women to nurse the baby for you?"

8"Yes, do!" the princess replied. So the little girl rushed home and called her mother!

9"Take this child home and nurse him for me," the princess instructed the baby's mother, "and I will pay you well!" So she took him home and nursed him.

10Later, when he was older, she brought him back to the princess and he became her son. She named him Moses (meaning "to draw out") because she had drawn him out of the water.

MATTHEW 16:13—17:9

WHEN Jesus came to Caesarea Philippi, he asked his disciples, "Who are the people saying I am?"

14"Well," they replied, "some say John the Baptist; some, Elijah; some, Jeremiah or one of the other prophets."

15Then he asked them, "Who do *you* think I am?"

16Simon Peter answered, "The Christ, the Messiah, the Son of the living God."

17"God has blessed you, Simon, son of Jonah," Jesus said, "for my Father in heaven has personally revealed this to you—this is not from any human source. 18You are Peter, a stone; and

upon this rock I will build my church; and all the powers of hell shall not prevail against it. 19And I will give you the keys of the Kingdom of Heaven; whatever doors you lock on earth shall be locked in heaven; and whatever doors you open on earth shall be open in heaven!"

20Then he warned the disciples against telling others that he was the Messiah.

21From then on Jesus began to speak plainly to his disciples about going to Jerusalem, and what would happen to him there—that he would suffer at the hands of the Jewish leaders, that he would be killed, and that three days later he would be raised to life again.

22But Peter took him aside to remonstrate with him. "Heaven forbid, sir," he said. "This is not going to happen to you!"

23Jesus turned on Peter and said, "Get away from me, you Satan! You are a dangerous trap to me. You are thinking merely from a human point of view, and not from God's."

24Then Jesus said to the disciples, "If anyone wants to be a follower of mine, let him deny himself and take up his cross and follow me. 25For anyone who keeps his life for himself shall lose it; and anyone who loses his life for me shall find it again. 26What profit is there if you gain the whole world—and lose eternal life? What can be compared with the value of eternal life? 27For I, the Son of Mankind, shall come with my angels in the glory of my Father and judge each person according to his deeds. 28And some of you standing right here now will certainly live to see me coming in my Kingdom."

SIX days later Jesus took Peter, James, and his brother John to the top of a high and lonely hill, 2and as they watched, his appearance changed so that his face shone like the sun and his clothing became dazzling white.

3Suddenly Moses and Elijah appeared and were talking with him. 4Peter blurted out, "Sir, it's wonderful that we can be here! If you want me to, I'll make three shelters, one for you and one for Moses and one for Elijah."

5But even as he said it, a bright cloud came over them, and a voice from the cloud said, "This is my beloved Son, and I am wonderfully pleased with him. Obey him."

6At this the disciples fell face downward to the ground, terribly frightened. 7Jesus came over and touched them. "Get up," he said, "don't be afraid."

8And when they looked, only Jesus was with them.

9As they were going down the mountain, Jesus commanded them not to tell anyone what they had seen until after he had risen from the dead.

PSALM 21:1–13

How the king rejoices in your strength, O Lord! How he exults in your salvation. 2For you have given him his heart's desire, everything he asks you for!

3You welcomed him to the throne with success and prosperity. You set a royal crown of solid gold upon his head. 4He asked for a long, good life, and you have granted his request; the days of his life stretch on and on forever. 5You have given him fame and honor. You have clothed him with splendor and majesty. 6You have endowed him with eternal happiness. You have given him the unquenchable joy of your presence. 7And because the king trusts in the Lord, he will never stumble, never fall; for he depends upon the steadfast love of the God who is above all gods.

8Your hand, O Lord, will find your enemies, all who hate you. 9,10When you appear, they will be destroyed in the fierce fire of your presence. The Lord will destroy them and their children. 11For these men plot against you, Lord, but they cannot possibly succeed. 12They will turn and flee when they see your arrows aimed straight at them.

13Accept our praise, O Lord, for all your glorious power. We will write songs to celebrate your mighty acts!

PROVERBS FOR TODAY/ 5:1–6

Listen to me, my son! I know what I am saying; listen! Watch yourself, lest you be indiscreet and betray some vital information. For the lips of a prostitute are as sweet as honey, and smooth flattery is her stock in trade. But afterwards only a bitter conscience is left to you, sharp as a double-edged sword. She leads you down to death and hell. For she does not know the path to life. She staggers down a crooked trail, and doesn't even realize where it leads.

JANUARY 26

EXODUS 2:11—3:22

One day, many years later when Moses had grown up and become a man, he went out to visit his fellow Hebrews and saw the terrible conditions they were under. During his visit he saw an Egyptian knock a Hebrew to the ground—one of his own Hebrew brothers! 12Moses looked this way and that to be sure no one was watching, then killed the Egyptian and hid his body in the sand.

13The next day as he was out visiting among the Hebrews again, he saw two of them fighting. "What are you doing, hitting your own Hebrew brother like that?" he said to the one in the wrong.

14"And who are you?" the man demanded. "I suppose you think you are *our* prince and judge! And do you plan to kill me as you did that Egyptian yesterday?" When Moses realized that his deed was known, he was frightened. ¹⁵And sure enough, when Pharaoh heard about it he ordered Moses arrested and executed. But Moses ran away into the land of Midian. As he was sitting there beside a well, ¹⁶seven girls who were daughters of the priest of Midian came to draw water and fill the water troughs for their father's flocks. ¹⁷But the shepherds chased the girls away. Moses then came to their aid and rescued them from the shepherds and watered their flocks.

¹⁸When they returned to their father Reuel he asked, "How did you get the flocks watered so quickly today?"

¹⁹"An Egyptian defended us against the shepherds," they told him; "he drew water for us and watered the flocks."

²⁰"Well, where is he?" their father demanded. "Did you just leave him there? Invite him home for supper."

²¹Moses eventually decided to accept Reuel's invitation to live with them, and Reuel gave him one of the girls, Zipporah, as his wife. ²²They had a baby named Gershom (meaning "foreigner"), for he said, "I am a stranger in a foreign land."

²³Several years later the king of Egypt died. The Israelis were groaning beneath their burdens, in deep trouble because of their slavery, and weeping bitterly before the Lord. He heard their cries from heaven, ²⁴and remembered his promise to Abraham, Isaac, and Jacob [to bring their descendants back into the land of Canaan]. ²⁵Looking down upon them, he knew that the time had come for their rescue.

ONE day as Moses was tending the flock of his father-in-law Jethro, the priest of Midian, out at the edge of the desert near Horeb, the mountain of God, ²suddenly the Angel of Jehovah appeared to him as a flame of fire in a bush. When Moses saw that the bush was on fire and that it didn't burn up, ³,⁴he went over to investigate. Then God called out to him,

"Moses! Moses!"

"Who is it?" Moses asked.

⁵"Don't come any closer," God told him. "Take off your shoes, for you are standing on holy ground. ⁶I am the God of your fathers—the God of Abraham, Isaac, and Jacob." (Moses covered his face with his hands, for he was afraid to look at God.)

⁷Then the Lord told him, "I have seen the deep sorrows of my people in Egypt, and have heard their pleas for freedom from their harsh taskmasters. ⁸I have come to deliver them from the Egyptians and to take them out of Egypt into a good land, a large land, a land 'flowing with milk and honey'—the land where the Canaanites, Hittites, Amorites, Perizzites, Hivites, and Jebusites live. ⁹Yes, the wail of the people of Israel has risen to me in heaven, and I have seen the heavy tasks the Egyptians have oppressed them with. ¹⁰Now I am going to send you to Pharaoh, to demand that he let you lead my people out of Egypt."

¹¹"But I'm not the person for a job like that!" Moses exclaimed.

¹²Then God told him, "I will certainly be with you, and this is the proof that I am the one who is sending you: When you have led the people out of Egypt, you shall worship God here upon this mountain!"

¹³But Moses asked, "If I go to the people of Israel and tell them that their fathers' God has sent me, they will ask, 'Which God are you talking about?' What shall I tell them?"

¹⁴" 'The Sovereign God,' " was the reply. "Just say, 'I Am has sent me!' ¹⁵Yes, tell them, 'Jehovah, the God of your ancestors Abraham, Isaac, and Jacob, has sent me to you.' (This is my eternal name, to be used throughout all generations.)

¹⁶"Call together all the elders of Isra-

el," God instructed him, "and tell them about Jehovah appearing to you here in this burning bush and that he said to you, 'I have visited my people, and have seen what is happening to them there in Egypt. 17I promise to rescue them from the drudgery and humiliation they are undergoing, and to take them to the land now occupied by the Canaanites, Hittites, Amorites, Perizzites, Hivites, and Jebusites, a land "flowing with milk and honey." ' 18The elders of the people of Israel will accept your message. They must go with you to the king of Egypt and tell him, 'Jehovah, the God of the Hebrews, has met with us and instructed us to go three days' journey into the desert to sacrifice to him. Give us your permission.'

19"But I know that the king of Egypt will not let you go except under heavy pressure. 20So I will give him all the pressure he needs! I will destroy Egypt with my miracles, and then at last he will let you go. 21And I will see to it that the Egyptians load you down with gifts when you leave, so that you will by no means go out empty-handed! 22Every woman will ask for jewels, silver, gold, and the finest of clothes from her Egyptian master's wife and neighbors. You will clothe your sons and daughters with the best of Egypt!"

MATTHEW 17:10–27

HIS disciples asked, "Why do the Jewish leaders insist Elijah must return before the Messiah comes?"

11Jesus replied, "They are right. Elijah must come and set everything in order. 12And, in fact, he has already come, but he wasn't recognized, and was badly mistreated by many. And I, the Messiah, shall also suffer at their hands."

13Then the disciples realized he was speaking of John the Baptist.

14When they arrived at the bottom of the hill, a huge crowd was waiting for them. A man came and knelt before Jesus and said, 15"Sir, have mercy on my son, for he is mentally deranged, and in great trouble, for he often falls into the fire or into the water; 16so I brought him to your disciples, but they couldn't cure him."

17Jesus replied, "Oh, you stubborn, faithless people! How long shall I bear with you? Bring him here to me." 18Then Jesus rebuked the demon in the boy and it left him, and from that moment the boy was well.

19Afterwards the disciples asked Jesus privately, "Why couldn't we cast that demon out?"

20"Because of your little faith," Jesus told them. "For if you had faith even as small as a tiny mustard seed you could say to this mountain, 'Move!' and it would go far away. Nothing would be impossible. 21But this kind of demon won't leave unless you have prayed and gone without food."

22,23One day while they were still in Galilee, Jesus told them, "I am going to be betrayed into the power of those who will kill me, and on the third day afterwards I will be brought back to life again." And the disciples' hearts were filled with sorrow and dread.

24On their arrival in Capernaum, the Temple tax collectors came to Peter and asked him, "Doesn't your master pay taxes?"

25"Of course he does," Peter replied. Then he went into the house to talk to Jesus about it, but before he had a chance to speak, Jesus asked him, "What do you think, Peter? Do kings levy assessments against their own people, or against conquered foreigners?"

26,27"Against the foreigners," Peter replied.

"Well, then," Jesus said, "the citizens are free! However, we don't want to offend them, so go down to the shore and throw in a line, and open the mouth of the first fish you catch. You will find a coin to cover the taxes for both of us; take it and pay them."

PSALM 22:1–18

MY God, my God, why have you forsaken me? Why do you refuse to help me or even to listen to my groans? ²Day and night I keep on weeping, crying for your help, but there is no reply— ³,⁴for *you are holy.*

The praises of our fathers surrounded your throne; they trusted you and you delivered them. ⁵You heard their cries for help and saved them; they were never disappointed when they sought your aid.

⁶But I am a worm, not a man, scorned and despised by my own people and by all mankind. ⁷Everyone who sees me mocks and sneers and shrugs. ⁸"Is this the one who rolled his burden on the Lord?" they laugh. "Is this the one who claims the Lord delights in him? We'll believe it when we see God rescue him!"

⁹,¹⁰,¹¹Lord, how you have helped me before! You took me safely from my mother's womb and brought me through the years of infancy. I have depended upon you since birth; you have always been my God. Don't leave me now, for trouble is near and no one else can possibly help.

¹²I am surrounded by fearsome enemies, strong as the giant bulls from Bashan. ¹³They come at me with open jaws, like roaring lions attacking their prey. ¹⁴My strength has drained away like water, and all my bones are out of joint. My heart melts like wax; ¹⁵my strength has dried up like sun-baked clay; my tongue sticks to my mouth, for you have laid me in the dust of death. ¹⁶The enemy, this gang of evil men, circles me like a pack of dogs; they have pierced my hands and feet. ¹⁷I can count every bone in my body. See these men of evil gloat and stare; ¹⁸they divide my clothes among themselves by a toss of the dice.

PROVERBS FOR TODAY/ 5:7–14

Young men, listen to me, and never forget what I'm about to say: Run from her! Don't go near her house, *lest you fall to her temptation and lose your honor, and give the remainder of your life to the cruel and merciless; lest strangers obtain your wealth, and you become a slave of foreigners. Lest afterwards you groan in anguish and in shame, when syphilis consumes your body, and you say, "Oh, if only I had listened! If only I had not demanded my own way! Oh, why wouldn't I take advice? Why was I so stupid? For now I must face public disgrace."*

JANUARY 27

EXODUS 4:1—5:21

BUT Moses said, "They won't believe me! They won't do what *I* tell them to. They'll say, 'Jehovah never appeared to you!' "

²"What do you have there in your hand?" the Lord asked him.

And he replied, "A shepherd's rod."

³"Throw it down on the ground," the Lord told him. So he threw it down— and it became a serpent, and Moses ran from it!

⁴Then the Lord told him, "Grab it by the tail!" He did, and it became a rod in his hand again!

⁵"Do that and they will believe you!" the Lord told him. "Then they will realize that Jehovah, the God of their ancestors Abraham, Isaac, and Jacob, has really appeared to you. ⁶Now reach your hand

inside your robe, next to your chest."
And when he did, and took it out again,
it was white with leprosy! 7"Now put
it in again," Jehovah said. And when he
did, and took it out again, it was normal,
just as before!

8"If they don't believe the first miracle,
they will the second," the Lord said,
9"and if they don't accept you after these
two signs, then take water from the Nile
River and pour it upon the dry land, and
it will turn to blood."

10But Moses pleaded, "O Lord, I'm
just not a good speaker. I never have
been, and I'm not now, even after you
have spoken to me, for I have a speech
impediment."

11"Who makes mouths?" Jehovah
asked him. "Isn't it I, the Lord? Who
makes a man so that he can speak or
not speak, see or not see, hear or not
hear? 12Now go ahead and do as I tell
you, for I will help you to speak well,
and I will tell you what to say."

13But Moses said, "Lord, please! Send
someone else."

14Then the Lord became angry. "All
right," he said, "your brother Aaron is
a good speaker. And he is coming here
to look for you, and will be very happy
when he finds you. 15So I will tell you
what to tell him, and I will help both
of you to speak well, and I will tell you
what to do. 16He will be your spokesman
to the people. And you will be as God
to him, telling him what to say. 17And
be sure to take your rod along so that
you can perform the miracles I have
shown you."

18Moses returned home and talked it
over with Jethro, his father-in-law. "With
your permission," Moses said, "I will go
back to Egypt and visit my relatives. I
don't even know whether they are still
alive."

"Go with my blessing," Jethro replied.

19Before Moses left Midian, Jehovah
said to him, "Don't be afraid to return
to Egypt, for all those who wanted to
kill you are dead."

20So Moses took his wife and sons
and put them on a donkey, and returned
to the land of Egypt, holding tightly to
the "rod of God"!

21Jehovah told him, "When you arrive
back in Egypt you are to go to Pharaoh
and do the miracles I have shown you,
but I will make him stubborn so that
he will not let the people go. 22Then you
are to tell him, 'Jehovah says, "Israel is
my eldest son, 23and I have commanded
you to let him go away and worship me,
but you have refused: and now see, I
will slay your eldest son." ' "

24As Moses and his family were traveling along and had stopped for the night,
Jehovah appeared to Moses and threatened to kill him. 25,26Then Zipporah his
wife took a flint knife and cut off the
foreskin of her young son's penis, and
threw it against Moses' feet, remarking
disgustedly, "What a blood-smeared husband you've turned out to be!"

Then God let him alone.

27Now Jehovah said to Aaron, "Go into
the wilderness to meet Moses." So
Aaron traveled to Mount Horeb, the
mountain of God, and met Moses there,
and they greeted each other warmly.
28Moses told Aaron what God had said
they must do, and what they were to
say, and told him about the miracles they
must do before Pharaoh.

29So Moses and Aaron returned to
Egypt and summoned the elders of the
people of Israel to a council meeting.
30Aaron told them what Jehovah had said
to Moses, and Moses performed the miracles as they watched. 31Then the elders
believed that God had sent them, and
when they heard that Jehovah had visited
them and had seen their sorrows, and
had decided to rescue them, they all rejoiced and bowed their heads and worshiped.

AFTER this presentation to the elders,
Moses and Aaron went to see Pharaoh.
They told him, "We bring you a message
from Jehovah, the God of Israel. He says,
'Let my people go, for they must make
a holy pilgrimage out into the wilderness,
for a religious feast, to worship me
there.' "

²"Is that so?" retorted Pharaoh. "And who is Jehovah, that I should listen to him, and let Israel go? I don't know Jehovah and I will not let Israel go."

³But Aaron and Moses persisted. "The God of the Hebrews has met with us," they declared. "We must take a three days' trip into the wilderness and sacrifice there to Jehovah our God; if we don't obey him, we face death by plague or sword."

⁴,⁵"Who do you think you are," Pharaoh shouted, "distracting the people from their work? Get back to your jobs!" ⁶That same day Pharaoh sent this order to the taskmasters and officers he had set over the people of Israel: ⁷,⁸"Don't give the people any more straw for making bricks! However, don't reduce their production quotas by a single brick, for they obviously don't have enough to do or else they wouldn't be talking about going out into the wilderness and sacrificing to their God. ⁹Load them with work and make them sweat; that will teach them to listen to Moses' and Aaron's lies!"

¹⁰,¹¹So the taskmasters and officers informed the people: "Pharaoh has given orders to furnish you with no more straw. Go and find it wherever you can; but you must produce just as many bricks as before!" ¹²So the people scattered everywhere to gather straw.

¹³The taskmasters were brutal. "Fulfill your daily quota just as before," they kept demanding. ¹⁴Then they whipped the Israeli work-crew bosses. "Why haven't you fulfilled your quotas either yesterday or today?" they roared.

¹⁵These foremen went to Pharaoh and pleaded with him. "Don't treat us like this," they begged. ¹⁶"We are given no straw and told to make as many bricks as before, and we are beaten for something that isn't our fault—it is the fault of your taskmasters for making such unreasonable demands."

¹⁷But Pharaoh replied, "You don't have enough work, or else you wouldn't be saying, 'Let us go and sacrifice to Jehovah.' ¹⁸Get back to work. No straw will be given you, and you must deliver the regular quota of bricks."

¹⁹Then the foremen saw that they were indeed in a bad situation. ²⁰When they met Moses and Aaron waiting for them outside the palace, as they came out from their meeting with Pharaoh, ²¹they swore at them. "May God judge you for making us stink before Pharaoh and his people," they said, "and for giving them an excuse to kill us."

MATTHEW 18:1–22

ABOUT that time the disciples came to Jesus to ask which of them would be greatest in the Kingdom of Heaven!

²Jesus called a small child over to him and set the little fellow down among them, ³and said, "Unless you turn to God from your sins and become as little children, you will never get into the Kingdom of Heaven. ⁴Therefore anyone who humbles himself as this little child, is the greatest in the Kingdom of Heaven. ⁵And any of you who welcomes a little child like this because you are mine, is welcoming me and caring for me. ⁶But if any of you causes one of these little ones who trusts in me to lose his faith, it would be better for you to have a rock tied to your neck and be thrown into the sea.

⁷"Woe upon the world for all its evils. Temptation to do wrong is inevitable, but woe to the man who does the tempting. ⁸So if your hand or foot causes you to sin, cut it off and throw it away. Better to enter heaven crippled than to be in hell with both of your hands and feet. ⁹And if your eye causes you to sin, gouge it out and throw it away. Better to enter heaven with one eye than to be in hell with two.

¹⁰"Beware that you don't look down upon a single one of these little children. For I tell you that in heaven their angels have constant access to my Father. ¹¹And I, the Messiah, came to save the lost.

12"If a man has a hundred sheep, and one wanders away and is lost, what will he do? Won't he leave the ninety-nine others and go out into the hills to search for the lost one? 13And if he finds it, he will rejoice over it more than over the ninety-nine others safe at home! 14Just so, it is not my Father's will that even one of these little ones should perish.

15"If a brother sins against you, go to him privately and confront him with his fault. If he listens and confesses it, you have won back a brother. 16But if not, then take one or two others with you and go back to him again, proving everything you say by these witnesses. 17If he still refuses to listen, then take your case to the church, and if the church's verdict favors you, but he won't accept it, then the church should excommunicate him. 18And I tell you this—whatever you bind on earth is bound in heaven, and whatever you free on earth will be freed in heaven.

19"I also tell you this—if two of you agree down here on earth concerning anything you ask for, my Father in heaven will do it for you. 20For where two or three gather together because they are mine, I will be right there among them."

21Then Peter came to him and asked, "Sir, how often should I forgive a brother who sins against me? Seven times?"

22"No!" Jesus replied, "seventy times seven!

PSALM 22:19–31

O Lord, don't stay away. O God my Strength, hurry to my aid. 20Rescue me from death; spare my precious life from all these evil men. 21Save me from these lions' jaws and from the horns of these wild oxen. Yes, God will answer me and rescue me.

22I will praise you to all my brothers; I will stand up before the congregation and testify of the wonderful things you have done. 23"Praise the Lord, each one of you who fears him," I will say. "Each of you must fear and reverence his name. Let all Israel sing his praises, 24for he has not despised my cries of deep despair; he has not turned and walked away. When I cried to him, he heard and came."

25Yes, I will stand and praise you before all the people. I will publicly fulfill my vows in the presence of all who reverence your name.

26The poor shall eat and be satisfied; all who seek the Lord shall find him and shall praise his name. Their hearts shall rejoice with everlasting joy. 27The whole earth shall see it and return to the Lord; the people of every nation shall worship him.

28For the Lord is King and rules the nations. 29Both proud and humble together, all who are mortal—born to die—shall worship him. 30Our children too shall serve him, for they shall hear from us about the wonders of the Lord; 31generations yet unborn shall hear of all the miracles he did for us.

PROVERBS FOR TODAY/ 5:15–21

Drink from your own well, my son—be faithful and true to your wife. Why should you beget children with women of the street? Why share your children with those outside your home? Be happy, yes, rejoice in the wife of your youth. Let her breasts and tender embrace satisfy you. Let her love alone fill you with delight. Why delight yourself with prostitutes, embracing what isn't yours? For God is closely watching you, and he weighs carefully everything you do.

EXODUS 5:22—7:24

THEN Moses went back to the Lord. "Lord," he protested, "how can you mistreat your own people like this? Why did you ever send me, if you were going to do this to them? 23Ever since I gave Pharaoh your message, he has only been more and more brutal to them, and you have not delivered them at all!"

"Now you will see what I shall do to Pharaoh," the Lord told Moses. "For he must be forced to let my people go; he will not only let them go, but will *drive them out of his land!* 2,3I am Jehovah, the Almighty God who appeared to Abraham, Isaac, and Jacob—though I did not reveal my name, Jehovah, to them. 4And I entered into a solemn covenant with them; under its terms I promised to give them and their descendants the land of Canaan where they were living. 5And now I have heard the groanings of the people of Israel, in slavery now to the Egyptians, and I remember my promise.

6"Therefore tell the descendants of Israel that I will use my mighty power and perform great miracles to deliver them from slavery, and make them free. 7And I will accept them as my people and be their God. And they shall know that I am Jehovah their God who has rescued them from the Egyptians. 8,9I will bring them into the land I promised to give to Abraham, Isaac, and Jacob. It shall belong to my people."

So Moses told the people what God had said, but they wouldn't listen any more because they were too dispirited after the tragic consequence of what he had said before.

10Now the Lord spoke to Moses again and told him, 11"Go back again to Pharaoh and tell him that he *must* let the people of Israel go."

12"But look," Moses objected, "my own people won't even listen to me any more; how can I expect Pharaoh to? I'm no orator!"

13Then the Lord ordered Moses and Aaron to return to the people of Israel and to Pharaoh, king of Egypt, demanding that the people be permitted to leave.

14These are the names of the heads of the clans of the various tribes of Israel: The sons of Reuben, Israel's oldest son:

Hanoch, Pallu, Hezron, Carmi.

15The heads of the clans of the tribe of Simeon:

Jemuel, Jamin, Ohad, Jachin, Zohar, Shaul (whose mother was a Canaanite).

16These are the names of the heads of the clans of the tribe of Levi, in the order of their ages:

Gershon, Kohath, Merari. (Levi lived 137 years.)

17The sons of Gershon were:

Libni, Shime-i, (and their clans).

18The sons of Kohath:

Amram, Izhar, Hebron, Uzziel. (Kohath lived 133 years.)

19The sons of Merari:

Mahli, Mushi.

The above are the families of the Levites, listed according to their ages.

20And Amram married Jochebed, his father's sister; and Aaron and Moses were their sons.

Amram lived to the age of 137.

21The sons of Izhar:

Korah, Nepheg, Zichri.

22The sons of Uzziel:

Misha-el, Elzaphan, Sithri.

23Aaron married Elisheba, the daughter of Amminadab and sister of Nahshon. Their children were:

Nadab, Abihu, Eleazar, Ithamar.

24The sons of Korah:

Assir, Elkanah, Abiasaph.

These are the families within the clan of Korah.

25Aaron's son Eleazar married one of the daughters of Puti-el, and Phinehas was one of his children. These are all the names of the heads of the clans of the Levites, and the families within the clans.

26Aaron and Moses, included in that list, are the same Aaron and Moses to whom Jehovah said, "Lead all the people of Israel out of the land of Egypt," 27and who went to Pharaoh to ask permission to lead the people from the land, 28,29and to whom the Lord said, "I am Jehovah. Go in and give Pharaoh the message I have given you."

30This is that Moses who argued with the Lord, "I can't do it; I'm no speaker—why should Pharaoh listen to *me?*"

THEN the Lord said to Moses, "See, I have appointed you as my ambassador to Pharaoh, and your brother Aaron shall be your spokesman. 2Tell Aaron everything I say to you, and he will announce it to Pharaoh, demanding that the people of Israel be allowed to leave Egypt. 3But I will cause Pharaoh to stubbornly refuse, and I will multiply my miracles in the land of Egypt. 4Yet even then Pharaoh won't listen to you; so I will crush Egypt with a final major disaster and then lead my people out. 5The Egyptians will find out that I am indeed God when I show them my power and force them to let my people go."

6So Moses and Aaron did as the Lord commanded them. 7Moses was eighty years old and Aaron eighty-three at this time of their confrontation with Pharaoh.

8Then the Lord said to Moses and Aaron, 9"Pharaoh will demand that you show him a miracle to prove that God has sent you; when he does, Aaron is to throw down his rod, and it will become a serpent."

10So Moses and Aaron went in to see Pharaoh, and performed the miracle, as Jehovah had instructed them—Aaron threw down his rod before Pharaoh and his court, and it became a serpent. 11Then Pharaoh called in his sorcerers— the magicians of Egypt—and they were able to do the same thing with their magical arts! 12Their rods became serpents, too! But Aaron's serpent swallowed their serpents! 13Pharaoh's heart was still hard and stubborn, and he wouldn't listen, just as the Lord had predicted. 14The Lord pointed this out to Moses, that Pharaoh's heart had been unmoved, and that he would continue to refuse to let the people go.

15"Nevertheless," the Lord said, "go back to Pharaoh in the morning, to be there as he goes down to the river. Stand beside the river bank and meet him there, holding in your hand the rod that turned into a serpent. 16Say to him, 'Jehovah, the God of the Hebrews, has sent me back to demand that you let his people go to worship him in the wilderness. You wouldn't listen before, 17and now the Lord says this: "You are going to find out that I am God. For I have instructed Moses to hit the water of the Nile with his rod, and the river will turn to blood! 18The fish will die and the river will stink, so that the Egyptians will be unwilling to drink it." ' "

19Then the Lord instructed Moses: "Tell Aaron to point his rod toward the waters of Egypt: all its rivers, canals, marshes, and reservoirs, and even the water stored in bowls and pots in the homes will turn to blood."

20So Moses and Aaron did as the Lord commanded them. As Pharaoh and all of his officials watched, Aaron hit the surface of the Nile with the rod, and the river turned to blood. 21The fish died and the water became so foul that the Egyptians couldn't drink it; and there was blood throughout the land of Egypt. 22But then the magicians of Egypt used their secret arts and they, too, turned water into blood; so Pharaoh's heart remained hard and stubborn, and he wouldn't listen to Moses and Aaron, just as the Lord had predicted, 23and he returned to his palace, unimpressed. 24Then the Egyptians dug wells along the river bank to get drinking water, for they couldn't drink from the river.

THE Kingdom of Heaven can be compared to a king who decided to bring his accounts up to date. 24In the process, one of his debtors was brought in who owed him $10,000,000! 25He couldn't pay, so the king ordered him sold for the debt, also his wife and children and everything he had.

26"But the man fell down before the king, his face in the dust, and said, 'Oh, sir, be patient with me and I will pay it all.'

27"Then the king was filled with pity for him and released him and forgave his debt.

28"But when the man left the king, he went to a man who owed him $2,000 and grabbed him by the throat and demanded instant payment.

29"The man fell down before him and begged him to give him a little time. 'Be patient and I will pay it,' he pled.

30"But his creditor wouldn't wait. He had the man arrested and jailed until the debt would be paid in full.

31"Then the man's friends went to the king and told him what had happened. 32And the king called before him the man he had forgiven and said, 'You evil-hearted wretch! Here I forgave you all that tremendous debt, just because you asked me to— 33shouldn't you have mercy on others, just as I had mercy on you?'

34"Then the angry king sent the man to the torture chamber until he had paid every last penny due. 35So shall my heavenly Father do to you if you refuse to truly forgive your brothers."

AFTER Jesus had finished this address, he left Galilee and circled back to Judea from across the Jordan River. 2Vast crowds followed him, and he healed their sick. 3Some Pharisees came to interview him, and tried to trap him into saying something that would ruin him.

"Do you permit divorce?" they asked.

4"Don't you read the Scriptures?" he replied. "In them it is written that at the beginning God created man and woman, 5,6and that a man should leave his father and mother, and be forever united to his wife. The two shall become one—no longer two, but one! And no man may divorce what God has joined together."

7"Then, why," they asked, "did Moses say a man may divorce his wife by merely writing her a letter of dismissal?"

8Jesus replied, "Moses did that in recognition of your hard and evil hearts, but it was not what God had originally intended. 9And I tell you this, that anyone who divorces his wife, except for fornication, and marries another, commits adultery."

10Jesus' disciples then said to him, "If that is how it is, it is better not to marry!"

11"Not everyone can accept this statement," Jesus said. "Only those whom God helps. 12Some are born without the ability to marry, and some are disabled by men, and some refuse to marry for the sake of the Kingdom of Heaven. Let anyone who can, accept my statement."

PSALM 23:1–6

BECAUSE the Lord is my Shepherd, I have everything I need! 2,3He lets me rest in the meadow grass and leads me beside the quiet streams. He gives me new strength. He helps me do what honors him the most.

4Even when walking through the dark valley of death I will not be afraid, for you are close beside me, guarding, guiding all the way.

5You provide delicious food for me in the presence of my enemies. You have welcomed me as your guest; blessings overflow!

6Your goodness and unfailing kindness shall be with me all of my life, and afterwards I will live with you forever in your home.

The wicked man is doomed by his own sins; they are ropes that catch and hold him. He shall die because he will not listen to the truth; he has let himself be led away into incredible folly.

JANUARY 29

EXODUS 7:25—9:35

A week went by.

THEN the Lord said to Moses, "Go in again to Pharaoh and tell him, 'Jehovah says, "Let my people go and worship me. ²If you refuse, I will send vast hordes of frogs across your land from one border to the other. ³,⁴The Nile River will swarm with them, and they will come out into your houses, even into your bedrooms and right into your beds! Every home in Egypt will be filled with them. They will fill your ovens and your kneading bowls; you and your people will be immersed in them!" ' "

⁵Then the Lord said to Moses, "Instruct Aaron to point the rod toward all the rivers, streams, and pools of Egypt, so that there will be frogs in every corner of the land." ⁶Aaron did, and frogs covered the nation. ⁷But the magicians did the same with their secret arts, and they, too, caused frogs to come up upon the land.

⁸Then Pharaoh summoned Moses and Aaron and begged, "Plead with God to take the frogs away, and I will let the people go and sacrifice to him."

⁹"Be so kind as to tell me when you want them to go," Moses said, "and I will pray that the frogs will die at the time you specify, everywhere except in the river."

¹⁰"Do it tomorrow," Pharaoh said.

"All right," Moses replied, "it shall be as you have said; then you will know that there is no one like the Lord our God. ¹¹All the frogs will be destroyed, except those in the river."

¹²So Moses and Aaron went out from the presence of Pharaoh, and Moses pleaded with the Lord concerning the frogs he had sent. ¹³And the Lord did as Moses promised—dead frogs covered the countryside and filled the nation's homes. ¹⁴They were piled into great heaps, making a terrible stench throughout the land. ¹⁵But when Pharaoh saw that the frogs were gone, he hardened his heart and refused to let the people go, just as the Lord had predicted.

¹⁶Then the Lord said to Moses, "Tell Aaron to strike the dust with his rod, and it will become lice, throughout all the land of Egypt." ¹⁷So Moses and Aaron did as God commanded, and suddenly lice infested the entire nation, covering the Egyptians and their animals. ¹⁸Then the magicians tried to do the same thing with their secret arts, but this time they failed.

¹⁹"This is the finger of God," they exclaimed to Pharaoh. But Pharaoh's heart was hard and stubborn, and he wouldn't listen to them, just as the Lord had predicted.

²⁰Next the Lord told Moses, "Get up early in the morning and meet Pharaoh as he comes out to the river to bathe, and say to him, 'Jehovah says, "Let my people go and worship me. ²¹If you refuse I will send swarms of flies throughout Egypt. Your homes will be filled with them and the ground will be covered with them. ²²But it will be very different in

the land of Goshen where the Israelis live. No flies will be there; thus you will know that I am the Lord God of all the earth, 23for I will make a distinction between your people and my people. All this will happen tomorrow." ' "

24And Jehovah did as he had said, so that there were terrible swarms of flies in Pharaoh's palace and in every home in Egypt.

25Pharaoh hastily summoned Moses and Aaron and said, "All right, go ahead and sacrifice to your God, but do it here in the land. Don't go out into the wilderness."

26But Moses replied, "That won't do! Our sacrifices to God are hated by the Egyptians, and if we do this right here before their eyes, they will kill us. 27We must take a three-day trip into the wilderness and sacrifice there to Jehovah our God, as he commanded us."

28"All right, go ahead," Pharaoh replied, "but don't go too far away. Now, hurry and plead with God for me."

29"Yes," Moses said, "I will ask him to cause the swarms of flies to disappear. But I am warning you that you must never again lie to us by promising to let the people go and then changing your mind."

30So Moses went out from Pharaoh and asked the Lord to get rid of the flies. 31,32And the Lord did as Moses asked and caused the swarms to disappear, so that not one remained. But Pharaoh hardened his heart again and did not let the people go!

"Go back to Pharaoh," the Lord commanded Moses, "and tell him, 'Jehovah, the God of the Hebrews, demands that you let his people go to sacrifice to him. 2If you refuse, 3the power of God will send a deadly plague to destroy your cattle, horses, donkeys, camels, flocks, and herds. 4But the plague will affect only the cattle of Egypt; none of the Israeli herds and flocks will even be touched!' "

5The Lord announced that the plague would begin the very next day, 6and it did. The next morning all the cattle of the Egyptians began dying, but not one of the Israeli herds was even sick. 7Pharaoh sent to see whether it was true that none of the Israeli cattle were dead, yet when he found out that it was so, even then his mind remained unchanged and he refused to let the people go.

8Then Jehovah said to Moses and Aaron, "Take ashes from the kiln. Moses, toss it into the sky as Pharaoh watches. 9It will spread like fine dust over all the land of Egypt and cause boils to break out upon people and animals alike, throughout the land."

10So they took ashes from the kiln and went to Pharaoh; as he watched, Moses tossed it toward the sky, and it became boils that broke out on men and animals alike throughout all Egypt. 11And the magicians couldn't stand before Moses because of the boils, for the boils appeared upon them too. 12But Jehovah hardened Pharaoh in his stubbornness, so that he refused to listen, just as the Lord had predicted to Moses.

13Then the Lord said to Moses, "Get up early in the morning and stand before Pharaoh and tell him, 'Jehovah the God of the Hebrews says, "Let my people go to worship me. 14This time I am going to send a plague that will really speak to you and to your servants and to all the Egyptian people, and prove to you there is no other God in all the earth. 15I could have killed you all by now, 16but I didn't, for I wanted to demonstrate my power to you and to all the earth. 17So you still think you are so great, do you, and defy my power, and refuse to let my people go? 18Well, tomorrow about this time I will send a hailstorm across the nation such as there has never been since Egypt was founded! 19Quick! Bring in your cattle from the fields, for every man and animal left out in the fields will die beneath the hail!" ' "

20Some of the Egyptians, terrified by this threat, brought their cattle and slaves in from the fields; 21but those who had no regard for the word of Jehovah left them out in the storm.

22Then Jehovah said to Moses, "Point

your hand toward heaven and cause the hail to fall throughout all Egypt, upon the people, animals, and trees."

23So Moses held out his hand, and the Lord sent thunder and hail and lightning. 24It was terrible beyond description. Never in all the history of Egypt had there been a storm like that. 25All Egypt lay in ruins. Everything left in the fields, men and animals alike, was killed, and the trees were shattered and the crops were destroyed. 26The only spot in all Egypt without hail that day was the land of Goshen where the people of Israel lived.

27Then Pharaoh sent for Moses and Aaron. "I finally see my fault," he confessed. "Jehovah is right, and I and my people have been wrong all along. 28Beg God to end this terrifying thunder and hail, and I will let you go at once."

29"All right," Moses replied, "as soon as I have left the city I will spread out my hands to the Lord, and the thunder and hail will stop. This will prove to you that the earth is controlled by Jehovah. 30But as for you and your officials, I know that even yet you will not obey him." 31All the flax and barley were knocked down and destroyed (for the barley was ripe, and the flax was in bloom), 32but the wheat and the emmer were not destroyed, for they were not yet out of the ground.

33So Moses left Pharaoh and went out of the city and lifted his hands to heaven to the Lord, and the thunder and hail stopped, and the rain ceased pouring down. 34When Pharaoh saw this, he and his officials sinned yet more by their stubborn refusal to do what they had promised, 35so Pharaoh refused to let the people leave, just as the Lord had predicted to Moses.

MATTHEW 19:13–30

LITTLE children were brought for Jesus to lay his hands on them and pray. But the disciples scolded those who brought them. "Don't bother him," they said.

14But Jesus said, "Let the little children come to me, and don't prevent them. For of such is the Kingdom of Heaven." 15And he put his hands on their heads and blessed them before he left.

16Someone came to Jesus with this question: "Good master, what must I do to have eternal life?"

17"When you call me good you are calling me God," Jesus replied, "for God alone is truly good. But to answer your question, you can get to heaven if you keep the commandments."

18"Which ones?" the man asked.

And Jesus replied, "Don't kill, don't commit adultery, don't steal, don't lie, 19honor your father and mother, and love your neighbor as yourself!"

20"I've always obeyed every one of them," the youth replied. "What else must I do?"

21Jesus told him, "If you want to be perfect, go and sell everything you have and give the money to the poor, and you will have treasure in heaven; and come, follow me." 22But when the young man heard this, he went away sadly, for he was very rich.

23Then Jesus said to his disciples, "It is almost impossible for a rich man to get into the Kingdom of Heaven. 24I say it again—it is easier for a camel to go through the eye of a needle than for a rich man to enter the Kingdom of God!"

25This remark confounded the disciples. "Then who in the world can be saved?" they asked.

26Jesus looked at them intently and said, "Humanly speaking, no one. But with God, everything is possible."

27Then Peter said to him, "We left everything to follow you. What will we get out of it?"

28And Jesus replied, "When I, the Messiah, shall sit upon my glorious throne in the Kingdom, you my disciples shall certainly sit on twelve thrones judging the twelve tribes of Israel. 29And anyone who gives up his home, brothers, sisters, father, mother, wife, children, or property, to follow me, shall receive a hundred times as much in return, and shall have eternal life. 30But many who are first now will be last then; and some who are last now will be first then."

PSALM 24:1–10

THE earth belongs to God! Everything in all the world is his! 2He is the one who pushed the oceans back to let dry land appear.

3Who may climb the mountain of the Lord and enter where he lives? Who may stand before the Lord? 4Only those with pure hands and hearts, who do not practice dishonesty and lying. 5They will receive God's own goodness as their blessing from him, planted in their lives by God himself, their Savior. 6These are the ones who are allowed to stand before the Lord and worship the God of Jacob.

7Open up, O ancient gates, and let the King of Glory in. 8Who is this King of Glory? The Lord, strong and mighty, invincible in battle. 9Yes, open wide the gates and let the King of Glory in.

10Who is this King of Glory? The Commander of all of heaven's armies!

PROVERBS FOR TODAY/ 6:1–5

Son, if you endorse a note for someone you hardly know, guaranteeing his debt, you are in serious trouble. You may have trapped yourself by your agreement. Quick! Get out of it if you possibly can! Swallow your pride; don't let embarrassment stand in the way. Go and beg to have your name erased. Don't put it off. Do it now. Don't rest until you do. If you can get out of this trap you have saved yourself like a deer that escapes from a hunter, or a bird from the net.

JANUARY 30

EXODUS 10:1—12:13

THEN the Lord said to Moses, "Go back again and make your demand upon Pharaoh; but I have hardened him and his officials, so that I can do more miracles demonstrating my power. 2What stories you can tell your children and grandchildren about the incredible things I am doing in Egypt! Tell them what fools I made of the Egyptians, and how I proved to you that I am Jehovah."

3So Moses and Aaron requested another audience with Pharaoh and told him: "Jehovah, the God of the Hebrews, asks, 'How long will you refuse to submit to me? Let my people go so they can worship me. 4,5If you refuse, tomorrow I will cover the entire nation with a thick layer of locusts so that you won't even be able to see the ground, and they will finish destroying everything that escaped the hail. 6They will fill your palace, and the homes of your officials, and all the houses of Egypt. Never in the history of Egypt has there been a plague like this will be!'" Then Moses stalked out.

7The court officials now came to Pharaoh and asked him, "Are you going to destroy us completely? Don't you know even yet that all Egypt lies in ruins? Let the *men* go and serve Jehovah their God!"

8So Moses and Aaron were brought back to Pharaoh. "All right, go and serve Jehovah your God!" he said. "But just who is it you want to go?"

9"We will go with our sons and daughters, flocks and herds," Moses replied. "We will take everything with us; for we must all join in the holy pilgrimage."

¹⁰"In the name of God I will not let you take your little ones!" Pharaoh retorted. "I can see your plot! ¹¹Never! You that are men, go and serve Jehovah, for that is what you asked for." And they were driven out from Pharaoh's presence.

¹²Then the Lord said to Moses, "Hold out your hand over the land of Egypt to bring locusts—they will cover the land and eat everything the hail has left."

¹³So Moses lifted his rod and Jehovah caused an east wind to blow all that day and night; and when it was morning, the east wind had brought the locusts. ¹⁴And the locusts covered the land of Egypt from border to border; it was the worst locust plague in all Egyptian history; and there will never again be another like it. ¹⁵For the locusts covered the face of the earth and blotted out the sun so that the land was darkened; and they ate every bit of vegetation the hail had left; there remained not one green thing—not a tree, not a plant throughout all the land of Egypt.

¹⁶Then Pharaoh sent an urgent call for Moses and Aaron and said to them, "I confess my sin against Jehovah your God, and against you. ¹⁷Forgive my sin only this once, and beg Jehovah your God to take away this deadly plague. I solemnly promise that I will let you go as soon as the locusts are gone."

¹⁸So Moses went out from Pharaoh and entreated the Lord, ¹⁹and he sent a very strong west wind that blew the locusts out into the Red Sea, so that there remained not one locust in all the land of Egypt! ²⁰But the Lord hardened Pharaoh's heart and he did not let the people go.

²¹Then Jehovah said to Moses, "Lift your hands to heaven, and darkness without a ray of light will descend upon the land of Egypt." ²²So Moses did, and there was thick darkness over all the land for three days. ²³During all that time the people scarcely moved—but all the people of Israel had light as usual.

²⁴Then Pharaoh called for Moses and said, "Go and worship Jehovah—but let your flocks and herds stay here; you can even take your children with you."

²⁵"No," Moses said, "we must take our flocks and herds for sacrifices and burnt offerings to Jehovah our God. ²⁶Not a hoof shall be left behind; for we must have sacrifices for the Lord our God, and we do not know what he will choose until we get there."

²⁷So the Lord hardened Pharaoh's heart and he would not let them go.

²⁸"Get out of here and don't let me ever see you again," Pharaoh shouted at Moses. "The day you do, you shall die."

²⁹"Very well," Moses replied. "I will never see you again."

THEN the Lord said to Moses, "I will send just one more disaster on Pharaoh and his land, and after that he will let you go; in fact, he will be so anxious to get rid of you that he will practically throw you out of the country. ²Tell all the men and women of Israel to ask their Egyptian neighbors for gold and silver jewelry."

³(For God caused the Egyptians to be very favorable to the people of Israel, and Moses was a very great man in the land of Egypt and was revered by Pharaoh's officials and the Egyptian people alike.)

⁴Now Moses announced to Pharaoh, "Jehovah says, 'About midnight I will pass through Egypt. ⁵And all the oldest sons shall die in every family in Egypt, from the oldest child of Pharaoh, heir to his throne, to the oldest child of his lowliest slave; and even the firstborn of the animals. ⁶The wail of death will resound throughout the entire land of Egypt; never before has there been such anguish, and it will never be again.

⁷" 'But not a dog shall move his tongue against any of the people of Israel, nor shall any of their animals die. Then you will know that Jehovah makes a distinction between Egyptians and Israelis.' ⁸All these officials of yours will come running to me, bowing low and begging, 'Please leave at once, and take all your

people with you.' Only then will I go!" Then, red-faced with anger, Moses stomped from the palace.

9The Lord had told Moses, "Pharaoh won't listen, and this will give me the opportunity of doing mighty miracles to demonstrate my power." 10So, although Moses and Aaron did these miracles right before Pharaoh's eyes, the Lord hardened his heart so that he wouldn't let the people leave the land.

THEN the Lord said to Moses and Aaron, 2"From now on, this month will be the first and most important of the entire year. 3,4Annually, on the tenth day of this month (announce this to all the people of Israel) each family shall get a lamb (or, if a family is small, let it share the lamb with another small family in the neighborhood; whether to share in this way depends on the size of the families). 5This animal shall be a year-old male, either a sheep or a goat, without any defects.

6"On the evening of the fourteenth day of this month, all these lambs shall be killed, 7and their blood shall be placed on the two side-frames of the door of every home and on the panel above the door. Use the blood of the lamb eaten in that home. 8Everyone shall eat roast lamb that night, with unleavened bread and bitter herbs. 9The meat must not be eaten raw or boiled, but roasted, including the head, legs, heart, and liver. 10Don't eat any of it the next day; if all is not eaten that night, burn what is left.

11"Eat it with your traveling clothes on, prepared for a long journey, wearing your walking shoes and carrying your walking sticks in your hands; eat it hurriedly. This observance shall be called the Lord's Passover. 12For I will pass through the land of Egypt tonight and kill all the oldest sons and firstborn male animals in all the land of Egypt, and execute judgment upon all the gods of Egypt—for I am Jehovah. 13The blood you have placed on the doorposts will be proof that you obey me, and when I see the blood I will pass over you and I will not destroy your firstborn children when I smite the land of Egypt.

MATTHEW 20:1–28

HERE is another illustration of the Kingdom of Heaven. "The owner of an estate went out early one morning to hire workers for his harvest field. 2He agreed to pay them $20 a day and sent them out to work.

3"A couple of hours later he was passing a hiring hall and saw some men standing around waiting for jobs, 4so he sent them also into his fields, telling them he would pay them whatever was right at the end of the day. 5At noon and again around three o'clock in the afternoon he did the same thing.

6"At five o'clock that evening he was in town again and saw some more men standing around and asked them, 'Why haven't you been working today?'

7" 'Because no one hired us,' they replied.

" 'Then go on out and join the others in my fields,' he told them.

8"That evening he told the paymaster to call the men in and pay them, beginning with the last men first. 9When the men hired at five o'clock were paid, each received $20. 10So when the men hired earlier came to get theirs, they assumed they would receive much more. But they, too, were paid $20.

11,12"They protested, 'Those fellows worked only one hour, and yet you've paid them just as much as those of us who worked all day in the scorching heat.'

13" 'Friend,' he answered one of them, 'I did you no wrong! Didn't you agree to work all day for $20? 14Take it and go. It is my desire to pay all the same; 15is it against the law to give away my money if I want to? Should you be angry because I am kind?' 16And so it is that the last shall be first, and the first, last."

17As Jesus was on the way to Jerusalem, he took the twelve disciples aside, 18and talked to them about what would happen to him when they arrived.

"I will be betrayed to the chief priests and other Jewish leaders, and they will condemn me to die. ¹⁹And they will hand me over to the Roman government, and I will be mocked and crucified, and the third day I will rise to life again."

²⁰Then the mother of James and John, the sons of Zebedee, brought them to Jesus and respectfully asked a favor.

²¹"What is your request?" he asked. She replied, "In your Kingdom, will you let my two sons sit on two thrones next to yours?"

²²But Jesus told her, "You don't know what you are asking!" Then he turned to James and John and asked them, "Are you able to drink from the terrible cup I am about to drink from?"

"Yes," they replied, "we are able!"

²³"You shall indeed drink from it," he told them. "But I have no right to say who will sit on the thrones next to mine. Those places are reserved for the persons my Father selects."

²⁴The other ten disciples were indignant when they heard what James and John had asked for.

²⁵But Jesus called them together and said, "Among the heathen, kings are tyrants and each minor official lords it over those beneath him. ²⁶But among you it is quite different. Anyone wanting to be a leader among you must be your servant. ²⁷And if you want to be right at the top, you must serve like a slave.

²⁸Your attitude must be like my own, for I, the Messiah, did not come to be served, but to serve, and to give my life as a ransom for many."

PSALM 25:1–11

TO you, O Lord, I pray. ²Don't fail me, Lord, for I am trusting you. Don't let my enemies succeed. Don't give them victory over me. ³None of those who have faith in God will ever be disgraced for trusting him. But all who harm the innocent shall be defeated.

⁴Show me the path where I should go, O Lord; point out the right road for me to walk. ⁵Lead me; teach me; for you are the God who gives me salvation. I have no hope except in you. ⁶,⁷Overlook my youthful sins, O Lord! Look at me instead through eyes of mercy and forgiveness, through eyes of everlasting love and kindness.

⁸The Lord is good and glad to teach the proper path to all who go astray; ⁹he will teach the ways that are right and best to those who humbly turn to him. ¹⁰And when we obey him, every path he guides us on is fragrant with his lovingkindness and his truth.

¹¹But Lord, my sins! How many they are. Oh, pardon them for the honor of your name.

PROVERBS FOR TODAY/ 6:6–11

Take a lesson from the ants, you lazy fellow. Learn from their ways and be wise! For though they have no king to make them work, yet they labor hard all summer, gathering food for the winter. But you—all you do is sleep. When will you wake up? "Let me sleep a little longer!" Sure, just a little more! And as you sleep, poverty creeps upon you like a robber and destroys you; want attacks you in full armor.

JANUARY 31

EXODUS 12:14—13:17a

YOU shall celebrate this event each year (this is a permanent law) to remind you of this fatal night. 15The celebration shall last seven days. For that entire period you are to eat only bread made without yeast. Anyone who disobeys this rule at any time during the seven days of the celebration shall be excommunicated from Israel. 16On the first day of the celebration, and again on the seventh day, there will be special religious services for the entire congregation, and no work of any kind may be done on those days except the preparation of food.

17"This annual 'Celebration with Unleavened Bread' will cause you always to remember today as the day when I brought you out of the land of Egypt; so it is a law that you must celebrate this day annually, generation after generation. 18Only bread without yeast may be eaten from the evening of the fourteenth day of the month until the evening of the twenty-first day of the month. 19For these seven days there must be no trace of yeast in your homes; during that time anyone who eats anything that has yeast in it shall be excommunicated from the congregation of Israel. These same rules apply to foreigners who are living among you just as much as to those born in the land. 20Again I repeat, during those days you must not eat anything made with yeast; serve only yeastless bread."

21Then Moses called for all the elders of Israel and said to them, "Go and get lambs from your flocks, a lamb for one or more families depending upon the number of persons in the families, and kill the lamb so that God will pass over you and not destroy you. 22Drain the lamb's blood into a basin, and then take a cluster of hyssop branches and dip them into the lamb's blood, and strike the hyssop against the lintel above the door and against the two side panels, so that there will be blood upon them, and none of you shall go outside all night. 23"For Jehovah will pass through the land and kill the Egyptians; but when he sees the blood upon the panel at the top of the door and on the two side pieces, he will pass over that home and not permit the Destroyer to enter and kill your firstborn. 24And remember, this is a permanent law for you and your posterity. 25And when you come into the land that the Lord will give you, just as he promised, and when you are celebrating the Passover, 26and your children ask, 'What does all this mean? What is this ceremony about?' 27you will reply, 'It is the celebration of Jehovah's passing over us, for he passed over the homes of the people of Israel, though he killed the Egyptians; he passed over our houses and did not come in to destroy us.' " And all the people bowed their heads and worshiped.

28So the people of Israel did as Moses and Aaron had commanded. 29And that night, at midnight, Jehovah killed all the firstborn sons in the land of Egypt, from Pharaoh's oldest son to the oldest son of the captive in the dungeon; also all the firstborn of the cattle. 30Then Pharaoh and his officials and all the people of Egypt got up in the night; and there was bitter crying throughout all the land of Egypt, for there was not a house where there was not one dead.

31And Pharaoh summoned Moses and Aaron during the night and said, "Leave us; please go away, all of you; go and serve Jehovah as you said. 32Take your flocks and herds and be gone; and oh, give me a blessing as you go." 33And the Egyptians were urgent upon the people of Israel, to get them out of the land as quickly as possible. For they said, "We are as good as dead."

34The Israelis took with them their bread dough without yeast, and bound their kneading troughs into their spare clothes, and carried them on their shoulders. 35And the people of Israel did as Moses said and asked the Egyptians for silver and gold jewelry, and for clothing. 36And the Lord gave the Israelis favor with the Egyptians, so that they gave them whatever they wanted. And the Egyptians were practically stripped of everything they owned!

37That night the people of Israel left Rameses and started for Succoth; there were six hundred thousand of them, besides all the women and children, going on foot. 38People of various sorts went with them; and there were flocks and herds—a vast exodus of cattle. 39When they stopped to eat, they baked bread from the yeastless dough they had brought along. It was yeastless because the people were pushed out of Egypt and didn't have time to wait for bread to rise to take with them on the trip.

40,41The sons of Jacob and their descendants had lived in Egypt 430 years, and it was on the last day of the 430th year that all of Jehovah's people left the land. 42This night was selected by the Lord to bring his people out from the land of Egypt; so the same night was selected as the date of the annual celebration of God's deliverance.

43Then Jehovah said to Moses and Aaron, "These are the rules concerning the observance of the Passover. No foreigners shall eat the lamb, 44but any slave who has been purchased may eat it if he has been circumcised. 45A hired servant or a visiting foreigner may not eat of it. 46You shall, all of you who eat each lamb, eat it together in one house, and not carry it outside; and you shall not break any of its bones. 47All the congregation of Israel shall observe this memorial at the same time.

48"As to foreigners, if they are living with you and want to observe the Passover with you, let all the males be circumcised, and then they may come and celebrate with you—then they shall be just as though they had been born among you; but no uncircumcised person shall ever eat the lamb. 49The same law applies to those born in Israel and to foreigners living among you."

50So the people of Israel followed all of Jehovah's instructions to Moses and Aaron. 51That very day the Lord brought out the people of Israel from the land of Egypt, wave after wave of them crossing the border.

THE Lord instructed Moses, "Dedicate to me all of the firstborn sons of Israel, and every firstborn male animal; they are mine!"

3Then Moses said to the people, "This is a day to remember forever—the day of leaving Egypt and your slavery; for the Lord has brought you out with mighty miracles. Now remember, during the annual celebration of this event you are to use no yeast; don't even have any in your homes. 4,5Celebrate this day of your exodus, at the end of March each year, when Jehovah brings you into the land of the Canaanites, Hittites, Amorites, Hivites, and Jebusites—the land he promised your fathers, a land 'flowing with milk and honey.' 6,7For seven days you shall eat only bread without yeast, and there must be no yeast in your homes, or anywhere within the borders of your land! Then, on the seventh day, a great feast to the Lord shall be held.

8"During those celebration days each year you must explain to your children why you are celebrating—it is a celebration of what the Lord did for you when you left Egypt. 9This annual memorial week will brand you as his own unique people, just as though he had branded his mark of ownership upon your hands or your forehead.

10"So celebrate the event annually in late March. 11And remember, when the Lord brings you into the land he promised to your ancestors long ago, where the Canaanites are now living, 12all firstborn sons and firstborn male animals belong to the Lord, and you shall give them to him. 13A firstborn donkey may be purchased back from the Lord in exchange for a lamb or baby goat; but if you decide not to trade, the donkey shall be killed. However, you *must* buy back your first-born sons.

14"And in the future, when your children ask you, 'What is this all about?' you shall tell them, 'With mighty miracles Jehovah brought us out of Egypt from our slavery. 15Pharaoh wouldn't let us go, so Jehovah killed all the firstborn males throughout the land of Egypt, both of men and animals; that is why we now give all the firstborn males to the Lord—except that all the eldest sons are always bought back.' 16Again I say, this celebration shall identify you as God's people, just as much as if his brand of ownership were placed upon your foreheads. It is a reminder that the Lord brought us out of Egypt with great power."

17,18So at last Pharaoh let the people go.

MATTHEW 20:29—21:22

A S Jesus and the disciples left the city of Jericho, a vast crowd surged along behind.
30Two blind men were sitting beside the road and when they heard that Jesus was coming that way, they began shouting, "Sir, King David's Son, have mercy on us!"
31The crowd told them to be quiet, but they only yelled the louder.
32,33When Jesus came to the place where they were he stopped in the road and called, "What do you want me to do for you?"
"Sir," they said, "we want to see!"
34Jesus was moved with pity for them and touched their eyes. And instantly they could see, and followed him.

As Jesus and the disciples approached Jerusalem, and were near the town of Bethphage on the Mount of Olives, Jesus sent two of them into the village ahead.
2"Just as you enter," he said, "you will see a donkey tied there, with its colt beside it. Untie them and bring them here. 3If anyone asks you what you are

doing, just say, 'The Master needs them,' and there will be no trouble."

4This was done to fulfill the ancient prophecy, 5"Tell Jerusalem her King is coming to her, riding humbly on a donkey's colt!"

6The two disciples did as Jesus said, 7and brought the animals to him and threw their garments over the colt for him to ride on. 8And some in the crowd threw down their coats along the road ahead of him, and others cut branches from the trees and spread them out before him.

9Then the crowds surged on ahead and pressed along behind, shouting, "God bless King David's Son!" . . . "God's Man is here!" . . . Bless him, Lord!" . . . "Praise God in highest heaven!"

10The entire city of Jerusalem was stirred as he entered. "Who is this?" they asked.

11And the crowds replied, "It's Jesus, the prophet from Nazareth up in Galilee."

12Jesus went into the Temple, drove out the merchants, and knocked over the moneychangers' tables and the stalls of those selling doves.

13"The Scriptures say my Temple is a place of prayer," he declared, "but you have turned it into a den of thieves."

14And now the blind and crippled came to him and he healed them there ir the Temple. 15But when the chief priests and other Jewish leaders saw these wonderful miracles, and heard even the little children in the Temple shouting, "God bless the Son of David," they were disturbed and indignant and asked him, "Do you hear what these children are saying?"

16"Yes," Jesus replied. "Didn't you ever read the Scriptures? For they say, 'Even little babies shall praise him!' "

17Then he returned to Bethany, where he stayed overnight.

18In the morning, as he was returning to Jerusalem, he was hungry, 19and noticed a fig tree beside the road. He went over to see if there were any figs, but there were only leaves. Then he said to it, "Never bear fruit again!" And soon the fig tree withered up.

20The disciples were utterly amazed and asked, "How did the fig tree wither so quickly?"

21Then Jesus told them, "Truly, if you have faith, and don't doubt, you can do things like this and much more. You can even say to this Mount of Olives, 'Move over into the ocean,' and it will. 22You can get anything—*anything* you ask for in prayer—if you believe."

PSALM 25:12–22

WHERE is the man who fears the Lord? God will teach him how to choose the best. 13He shall live within God's circle of blessing, and his children shall inherit the earth.

14Friendship with God is reserved for those who reverence him. With them alone he shares the secrets of his promises.

15My eyes are ever looking to the Lord for help, for he alone can rescue me. 16Come, Lord, and show me your mercy, for I am helpless, overwhelmed, in deep distress; 17my problems go from bad to worse. Oh, save me from them all! 18See my sorrows; feel my pain; forgive my sins. 19See how many enemies I have and how viciously they hate me! 20Save me from them! Deliver my life from their power! Oh, let it never be said that I trusted you in vain!

21Assign me Godliness and Integrity as my bodyguards, for I expect you to protect me 22and to ransom Israel from all her troubles.

PROVERBS FOR TODAY/ 6:12–15

Let me describe for you a worthless and a wicked man; first, he is a constant liar; he signals his true intentions to his friends with eyes and feet and fingers. He is always thinking up new schemes to swindle people. He stirs up trouble everywhere. But he will be destroyed suddenly, broken beyond hope of healing.

FEBRUARY 1

EXODUS 13:17b—15:19

GOD did not lead them through the land of the Philistines, although that was the most direct route from Egypt to the Promised Land. The reason was that God felt the people might become discouraged by having to fight their way through, even though they had left Egypt armed; he thought they might return to Egypt. Instead, God led them along a route through the Red Sea wilderness.

19Moses took the bones of Joseph with them, for Joseph had made the sons of Israel vow before God that they would take his bones with them when God led them out of Egypt—as he was sure God would.

20Leaving Succoth, they camped in Etham at the edge of the wilderness. 21The Lord guided them by a pillar of cloud during the daytime, and by a pillar of fire at night. So they could travel either by day or night. 22The cloud and fire were never out of sight.

JEHOVAH now instructed Moses, 2"Tell the people to turn toward Piha-hiroth between Migdol and the sea, opposite Baal-zephon, and to camp there along the shore. 3For Pharaoh will think, 'Those Israelites are trapped now, between the desert and the sea!' 4And once again I will harden Pharaoh's heart and he will chase after you. I have planned this to gain great honor and glory over Pharaoh and all his armies, and the Egyptians shall know that I am the Lord."

So they camped where they were told.

5When word reached the king of Egypt that the Israelis were not planning to return to Egypt after three days, but to keep on going, Pharaoh and his staff became bold again. "What is this we have done, letting all these slaves get away?" they asked. 6So Pharaoh led the chase in his chariot, 7followed by the pick of Egypt's chariot corps—600 chariots in all—and other chariots driven by Egyptian officers. 8He pursued the people of Israel, for they had taken much of the wealth of Egypt with them. 9Pharaoh's entire cavalry—horses, chariots, and charioteers—was used in the chase; and the Egyptian army overtook the people of Israel as they were camped beside the shore near Piha-hiroth, across from Baal-zephon.

10As the Egyptian army approached, the people of Israel saw them far in the distance, speeding after them, and they were terribly frightened, and cried out to the Lord to help them.

11And they turned against Moses, whining, "Have you brought us out here to die in the desert because there were not enough graves for us in Egypt? Why did you make us leave Egypt? 12Isn't this what we told you, while we were slaves, to leave us alone? We said it would be better to be slaves to the Egyptians than dead in the wilderness."

13But Moses told the people, "Don't be afraid. Just stand where you are and watch, and you will see the wonderful way the Lord will rescue you today. The Egyptians you are looking at—you will never see them again. 14The Lord will fight for you, and you won't need to lift a finger!"

15Then the Lord said to Moses, "Quit praying and get the people moving! Forward, march! 16Use your rod—hold it out over the water, and the sea will open up a path before you, and all the people of Israel shall walk through on dry ground! 17I will harden the hearts of the Egyptians and they will go in after you

and you will see the honor I will get in defeating Pharaoh and all his armies, chariots, and horsemen. 18And all Egypt shall know that I am Jehovah."

19Then the Angel of God, who was leading the people of Israel, moved the cloud around behind them, 20and it stood between the people of Israel and the Egyptians. And that night, as it changed to a pillar of fire, it gave darkness to the Egyptians but light to the people of Israel! So the Egyptians couldn't find the Israelis!

21Meanwhile, Moses stretched his rod over the sea, and the Lord opened up a path through the sea, with walls of water on each side; and a strong east wind blew all that night, drying the sea bottom. 22So the people of Israel walked through the sea on dry ground! 23Then the Egyptians followed them between the walls of water along the bottom of the sea—all of Pharaoh's horses, chariots, and horsemen. 24But in the early morning Jehovah looked down from the cloud of fire upon the array of the Egyptians, and began to harass them. 25Their chariot wheels began coming off, so that their chariots scraped along the dry ground. "Let's get out of here," the Egyptians yelled. "Jehovah is fighting for them and against us."

26When all the Israelites were or the other side, the Lord said to Moses, "Stretch out your hand again over the sea, so that the waters will come back over the Egyptians and their chariots and horsemen." 27Moses did, and the sea returned to normal beneath the morning light. The Egyptians tried to flee, but the Lord drowned them in the sea. 28The water covered the path and the chariots and horsemen. And of all the army of Pharaoh that chased after Israel through the sea, not one remained alive.

29The people of Israel had walked through on dry land, and the waters had been walled up on either side of them. 30Thus Jehovah saved Israel that day from the Egyptians; and the people of Israel saw the Egyptians dead, washed up on the seashore. 31When the people of Israel saw the mighty miracle the Lord had done for them against the Egyptians, they were afraid and revered the Lord, and believed in him and in his servant Moses.

THEN Moses and the people of Israel sang this song to the Lord:
I will sing to the Lord, for he has tri-
umphed gloriously;
He has thrown both horse and rider
into the sea.
²The Lord is my strength, my song,
and my salvation.
He is my God, and I will praise him.
He is my father's God—I will exalt
him.
³The Lord is a warrior—
Yes, Jehovah is his name.
⁴He has overthrown Pharaoh's chariots and armies,
Drowning them in the sea.
The famous Egyptian captains are
dead beneath the waves.
⁵The water covers them.
They went down into the depths like
a stone.
⁶Your right hand, O Lord, is glorious
in power;
It dashes the enemy to pieces.
⁷In the greatness of your majesty
You overthrew all those who rose
against you.
You sent forth your anger, and it consumed them as fire consumes
straw.
⁸At the blast of your breath
The waters divided!
They stood as solid walls to hold the
seas apart.
⁹The enemy said, "I will chase after
them,
Catch up with them, destroy them.
I will cut them apart with my sword
And divide the captured booty."
¹⁰But God blew with his wind, and
the sea covered them.
They sank as lead in the mighty waters.
¹¹Who else is like the Lord among the
gods?
Who is glorious in holiness like him?

Who is so awesome in splendor,
A wonder-working God?
¹²You reached out your hand and the
earth swallowed them.
¹³You have led the people you redeemed.
But in your lovingkindness
You have guided them wonderfully
To your holy land.
¹⁴The nations heard what happened,
and they trembled.
Fear has gripped the people of Philistia.
¹⁵The leaders of Edom are appalled,
The mighty men of Moab tremble;
All the people of Canaan melt with
fear.
¹⁶Terror and dread have overcome
them.
O Lord, because of your great power
they won't attack us!
Your people whom you purchased
Will pass by them in safety.
¹⁷You will bring them in and plant them
on your mountain,
Your own homeland, Lord—
The sanctuary you made for them to
live in.
¹⁸Jehovah shall reign forever and forever.
¹⁹The horses of Pharaoh, his horsemen, and his chariots
Tried to follow through the sea;
But the Lord let down the walls of
water on them
While the people of Israel walked
through on dry land.

MATTHEW 21:23–46

WHEN he had returned to the Temple and was teaching, the chief priests and other Jewish leaders came up to him and demanded to know by whose authority he had thrown out the merchants the day before.

²⁴"I'll tell you if you answer one ques-tion first," Jesus replied. ²⁵"Was John the Baptist sent from God, or not?"

They talked it over among themselves. "If we say, 'From God,'" they said, "then he will ask why we didn't believe what John said. 26And if we deny that God sent him, we'll be mobbed, for the crowd all think he was a prophet." 27So they finally replied, "We don't know!"

And Jesus said, "Then I won't answer your question either.

28"But what do you think about this? A man with two sons told the older boy, 'Son, go out and work on the farm today.' 29'I won't,' he answered, but later he changed his mind and went. 30Then the father told the youngest, 'You go!' and he said, 'Yes, sir, I will.' But he didn't. 31Which of the two was obeying his father?"

They replied, "The first, of course."

Then Jesus explained his meaning: "Surely evil men and prostitutes will get into the Kingdom before you do. 32For John the Baptist told you to repent and turn to God, and you wouldn't, while very evil men and prostitutes did. And even when you saw this happening, you refused to repent, and so you couldn't believe.

33"Now listen to this story: A certain landowner planted a vineyard with a hedge around it, and built a platform for the watchman, then leased the vineyard to some farmers on a sharecrop basis, and went away to live in another country.

34"At the time of the grape harvest he sent his agents to the farmers to collect his share. 35But the farmers attacked his men, beat one, killed one and stoned another.

36"Then he sent a larger group of his men to collect for him, but the results were the same. 37Finally the owner sent his son, thinking they would surely respect him.

38"But when these farmers saw the son coming they said among themselves, 'Here comes the heir to this estate; come on, let's kill him and get it for ourselves!' 39So they dragged him out of the vineyard and killed him.

40"When the owner returns, what do you think he will do to those farmers?"

41The Jewish leaders replied, "He will put the wicked men to a horrible death, and lease the vineyard to others who will pay him promptly."

42Then Jesus asked them, "Didn't you ever read in the Scriptures: 'The stone rejected by the builders has been made the honored cornerstone; how remarkable! what an amazing thing the Lord has done'?

43"What I mean is that the Kingdom of God shall be taken away from you, and given to a nation that will give God his share of the crop. 44All who stumble on this rock of truth shall be broken, but those it falls on will be scattered as dust."

45When the chief priests and other Jewish leaders realized that Jesus was talking about them—that they were the farmers in his story— 46they wanted to get rid of him, but were afraid to try because of the crowds, for they accepted Jesus as a prophet.

PSALM 26:1–12

DISMISS all the charges against me, Lord, for I have tried to keep your laws and have trusted you without wavering. 2Cross-examine me, O Lord, and see that this is so; test my motives and affections too. 3For I have taken your lovingkindness and your truth as my ideals. 4I do not have fellowship with tricky, two-faced men; they are false and hypocritical. 5I hate the sinners' hangouts and refuse to enter them. 6I wash my hands to prove my innocence and come before your altar, 7singing a song of thanksgiving and telling about your miracles.

8Lord, I love your home, this shrine where the brilliant, dazzling splendor of your presence lives.

9,10Don't treat me as a common sinner or murderer who plots against the innocent and demands bribes.

11No, I am not like that, O Lord; I try to walk a straight and narrow path of doing what is right; therefore in mercy save me.

12I publicly praise the Lord for keeping me from slipping and falling.

PROVERBS FOR TODAY/ 6:16–19
*For there are six things the Lord hates—no, seven: haughtiness, lying, murdering,
plotting evil, eagerness to do wrong, a false witness, sowing discord among brothers.*

FEBRUARY 2

EXODUS 15:20—17:7

THEN Miriam the prophetess, the sister of Aaron, took a tambourine and led the women in dances. 21And Miriam sang this song:

Sing to the Lord, for he has triumphed gloriously.
The horse and rider have been drowned in the sea.

22Then Moses led the people of Israel on from the Red Sea, and they moved out into the wilderness of Shur and were there three days without water. 23Arriving at Marah, they couldn't drink the water because it was bitter (that is why the place was called Marah, meaning "bitter"). 24Then the people turned against Moses. "Must we die of thirst?" they demanded.

25Moses pleaded with the Lord to help them, and the Lord showed him a tree to throw into the water, and the water became sweet.

It was there at Marah that the Lord laid before them the following conditions, to test their commitment to him: 26"If you will listen to the voice of the Lord your God, and obey it, and do what is right, then I will not make you suffer the diseases I sent on the Egyptians, for I am the Lord who heals you." 27And they came to Elim where there were twelve springs and seventy palm trees; and they camped there beside the springs.

NOW they left Elim and journeyed on into the Sihn Wilderness, between Elim and Mt. Sinai, arriving there on the fif-

teenth day of the second month after leaving Egypt. 2There too, the people spoke bitterly against Moses and Aaron. 3"Oh, that we were back in Egypt," they moaned, "and that the Lord had killed us there! For there we had plenty to eat. But now you have brought us into this wilderness to kill us with starvation."

4Then the Lord said to Moses, "Look, I'm going to rain down food from heaven for them. Everyone can go out each day and gather as much food as he needs. And I will test them in this, to see whether they will follow my instructions or not. 5Tell them to gather twice as much as usual on the sixth day of each week."

6Then Moses and Aaron called a meeting of all the people of Israel and told them, "This evening you will realize that it was the Lord who brought you out of the land of Egypt. 7,8,9In the morning you will see more of his glory; for he has heard your complaints against him (for you aren't really complaining against us—who are we?). The Lord will give you meat to eat in the evening, and bread in the morning. Come now before Jehovah, and hear his reply to your complaints."

10So Aaron called them together and suddenly, out toward the wilderness, from within the guiding cloud, there appeared the awesome glory of Jehovah.

11,12And Jehovah said to Moses, "I have heard their complaints. Tell them, 'In the evening you will have meat and in the morning you will be stuffed with bread, and you shall know that I am Jehovah your God.'"

13That evening vast numbers of quail arrived and covered the camp, and in the morning the desert all around the camp was wet with dew; 14and when the dew disappeared later in the morning it left thin white flakes that covered the ground like frost. 15When the people of Israel saw it they asked each other, "What is it?"

And Moses told them, "It is the food Jehovah has given you. 16Jehovah has said for everyone to gather as much as is needed for his household—about two quarts for each person."

17So the people of Israel went out and gathered it—some getting more and some less before it melted on the ground, 18and there was just enough for everyone. Those who gathered more had nothing left over and those who gathered little had no lack! Each home had just enough.

19And Moses told them, "Don't leave it overnight."

20But of course some of them wouldn't listen, and left it until morning; and when they looked, it was full of maggots and had a terrible odor; and Moses was very angry with them. 21So they gathered the food morning by morning, each home according to its need; and when the sun became hot upon the ground, the food melted and disappeared. 22On the sixth day there was twice as much as usual on the ground—four quarts instead of two; the leaders of the people came and asked Moses why this had happened.

23And he told them, "Because the Lord has appointed tomorrow as a day of seriousness and rest, a holy Sabbath to the Lord when we must refrain from doing our daily tasks. So cook as much as you want to today, and keep what is left for tomorrow."

24And the next morning the food was wholesome and good, without maggots or odor. 25Moses said, "This is your food for today, for today is the Sabbath to Jehovah and there will be no food on the ground today. 26Gather the food for six days, but the seventh is a Sabbath, and there will be none there for you on that day."

27But some of the people went out anyway to gather food, even though it was the Sabbath, but there wasn't any.

28,29"How long will these people refuse to obey?" the Lord asked Moses. "Don't they realize that I am giving them twice as much on the sixth day, so that there will be enough for two days? For the Lord has given you the seventh day as a day of Sabbath rest; stay in your tents and don't go out to pick up food from the ground that day." 30So the people rested on the seventh day.

31And the food became known as "manna" (meaning "What is it?"); it was white, like coriander seed, and flat, and tasted like honey bread.

32Then Moses gave them this further instruction from the Lord: they were to take two quarts of it to be kept as a museum specimen forever, so that later generations could see the bread the Lord had fed them with in the wilderness, when he brought them from Egypt. 33Moses told Aaron to get a container and put two quarts of manna in it and to keep it in a sacred place from generation to generation. 34Aaron did this, just as the Lord had instructed Moses, and eventually it was kept in the Ark in the Tabernacle.

35So the people of Israel ate the manna forty years until they arrived in the land of Canaan, where there were crops to eat. 36The omer—the container used to measure the manna—held about two quarts; it is approximately a tenth of a bushel.

NOW, at God's command, the people of Israel left the Sihn desert, going by easy stages to Rephidim. But upon arrival, there was no water!

2So once more the people growled and complained to Moses. "Give us water!" they wailed.

"Quiet!" Moses commanded. "Are you trying to test God's patience with you?"

3But, tormented by thirst, they cried out, "Why did you ever take us out of Egypt? Why did you bring us here to die, with our children and cattle too?"

4Then Moses pleaded with Jehovah. "What shall I do? For they are almost ready to stone me."

5,6Then Jehovah said to Moses, "Take the elders of Israel with you and lead the people out to Mt. Horeb. I will meet you there at the rock. Strike it with your rod—the same one you struck the Nile with—and water will come pouring out, enough for everyone!" Moses did as he was told, and the water gushed out! 7Moses named the place Massah (meaning "tempting Jehovah to slay us"), and sometimes they referred to it as Meribah (meaning "argument" and "strife!")—for it was there that the people of Israel argued against God and tempted him to slay them by saying, "Is Jehovah going to take care of us or not?"

MATTHEW 22:1-32

JESUS told several other stories to show what the Kingdom of Heaven is like.

"For instance," he said, "it can be illustrated by the story of a king who prepared a great wedding dinner for his son. 3Many guests were invited, and when the banquet was ready he sent messengers to notify everyone that it was time to come. But all refused! 4So he sent other servants to tell them, 'Everything is ready and the roast is in the oven. Hurry!'

5"But the guests he had invited merely laughed and went on about their business, one to his farm, another to his store; 6others beat up his messengers and treated them shamefully, even killing some of them.

7"Then the angry king sent out his army and destroyed the murderers and burned their city. 8And he said to his servants, 'The wedding feast is ready, and the guests I invited aren't worthy of the honor. 9Now go out to the street corners and invite everyone you see.'

10"So the servants did, and brought in all they could find, good and bad alike; and the banquet hall was filled with guests. 11But when the king came in to meet the guests he noticed a man who wasn't wearing the wedding robe [provided for him].

12" 'Friend,' he asked, 'how does it happen that you are here without a wedding robe?' And the man had no reply.

13"Then the king said to his aides, 'Bind him hand and foot and throw him out into the outer darkness where there is weeping and gnashing of teeth.' 14For many are called, but few are chosen."

15Then the Pharisees met together to try to think of some way to trap Jesus into saying something for which they could arrest him. 16They decided to send some of their men along with the Herodians to ask him this question: "Sir, we know you are very honest and teach the truth regardless of the consequences, without fear or favor. 17Now tell us, is it right to pay taxes to the Roman government or not?"

18But Jesus saw what they were after. "You hypocrites!" he exclaimed. "Who are you trying to fool with your trick questions? 19Here, show me a coin." And they handed him a penny.

20"Whose picture is stamped on it?" he asked them. "And whose name is this beneath the picture?"

21"Caesar's," they replied.

"Well, then," he said, "give it to Caesar if it is his, and give God everything that belongs to God."

22His reply surprised and baffled them and they went away.

23But that same day some of the Sadducees, who say there is no resurrection after death, came to him and asked, 24"Sir, Moses said that if a man died without children, his brother should marry the widow and their children would get all the dead man's property. 25Well, we had among us a family of seven brothers.

The first of these men married and then died, without children, so his widow became the second brother's wife. 26This brother also died without children, and the wife was passed to the next brother, and so on until she had been the wife of each of them. 27And then she also died. 28So whose wife will she be in the resurrection? For she was the wife of all seven of them!"

29But Jesus said, "Your error is caused by your ignorance of the Scriptures and of God's power! 30For in the resurrection there is no marriage; everyone is as the angels in heaven. 31But now, as to whether there is a resurrection of the dead—don't you ever read the Scriptures? Don't you realize that God was speaking directly to you when he said, 32'I *am* the God of Abraham, Isaac, and Jacob'? So God is not the God of the dead, but of the *living.*"

PSALM 27:1–7

THE Lord is my light and my salvation; he protects me from danger—whom shall I fear? 2When evil men come to destroy me, they will stumble and fall! 3Yes, though a mighty army marches against me, my heart shall know no fear! I am confident that God will save me.

4The one thing I want from God, the thing I seek most of all, is the privilege of meditating in his Temple, living in his presence every day of my life, delighting in his incomparable perfections and glory. 5There I'll be when troubles come. He will hide me. He will set me on a high rock 6out of reach of all my enemies. Then I will bring him sacrifices and sing his praises with much joy.

7Listen to my pleading, Lord! Be merciful and send the help I need.

PROVERBS FOR TODAY/ 6:20–26

Young man, obey your father and your mother. Take to heart all of their advice; keep in mind everything they tell you. Every day and all night long their counsel will lead you and save you from harm; when you wake up in the morning, let their instructions guide you into the new day. For their advice is a beam of light directed into the dark corners of your mind to warn you of danger and to give you a good life. Their counsel will keep you far away from prostitutes with all their flatteries, and unfaithful wives of other men. Don't lust for their beauty. Don't let their coyness seduce you. For a prostitute will bring a man to poverty, and an adulteress may cost him his very life.

FEBRUARY 3

EXODUS 17:8—19:15

BUT now the warriors of Amalek came to fight against the people of Israel at Rephidim. 9Moses instructed Joshua to issue a call to arms to the Israelites, to fight the army of Amalek.

"Tomorrow," Moses told him, "I will stand at the top of the hill, with the rod of God in my hand!"

10So Joshua and his men went out to fight the army of Amalek. Meanwhile Moses, Aaron, and Hur went to the top of the hill. 11And as long as Moses held up the rod in his hands, Israel was winning; but whenever he rested his arms at his sides, the soldiers of Amalek were winning. 12Moses' arms finally became too tired to hold up the rod any longer; so Aaron and Hur rolled a stone for him to sit on, and they stood on each side, holding up his hands until sunset. 13As a result, Joshua and his troops crushed the army of Amalek, putting them to the sword.

14Then the Lord instructed Moses, "Write this into a permanent record, to be remembered forever, and announce to Joshua that I will utterly blot out every trace of Amalek." 15,16Moses built an altar there and called it "Jehovah-nissi" (meaning "Jehovah is my flag").

"Raise the banner of the Lord!" Moses said. "For the Lord will be at war with Amalek generation after generation."

WORD soon reached Jethro, Moses' father-in-law, the priest of Midian, about all the wonderful things God had done for his people and for Moses, and how the Lord had brought them out of Egypt.

2Then Jethro took Moses' wife, Zipporah, to him (for he had sent her home), 3along with Moses' two sons, Gershom (meaning "foreigner," for Moses said when he was born, "I have been wandering in a foreign land") 4and Eliezer (meaning "God is my help," for Moses said at his birth, "The God of my fathers was my helper, and delivered me from the sword of Pharaoh"). 5,6They arrived while Moses and the people were camped at Mt. Sinai.

"Jethro, your father-in-law, has come to visit you," Moses was told, "and he has brought your wife and your two sons."

7Moses went out to meet his father-in-law and greeted him warmly; they asked about each other's health and then went into Moses' tent to talk further. 8Moses related to his father-in-law all that had been happening and what the Lord had done to Pharaoh and the Egyptians in order to deliver Israel, and all the problems there had been along the way, and how the Lord had delivered his people from all of them. 9Jethro was very happy about everything the Lord had done for Israel, and about his bringing them out of Egypt.

10"Bless the Lord," Jethro said, "for he has saved you from the Egyptians and from Pharaoh, and has rescued Israel. 11I know now that the Lord is greater than any other god because he delivered his people from the proud and cruel Egyptians."

12Jethro offered sacrifices to God, and afterwards Aaron and the leaders of Israel came to meet Jethro, and they all ate the sacrificial meal together before the Lord.

13The next day Moses sat as usual to hear the people's complaints against each other, from morning to evening. 14When Moses' father-in-law saw how much time this was taking, he said, "Why are you trying to do all this alone, with people standing here all day long to get your help?"

15,16"Well, because the people come to me with their disputes, to ask for God's decisions," Moses told him. "I am their judge, deciding who is right and who is wrong, and instructing them in God's ways. I apply the laws of God to their particular disputes."

17"It's not right!" his father-in-law exclaimed. 18"You're going to wear yourself out—and if you do, what will happen to the people? Moses, this job is too heavy a burden for you to try to handle all by yourself. 19,20Now listen, and let me give you a word of advice, and God will bless you: Be these people's lawyer—their representative before God—bringing him their questions to decide; you will tell them his decisions, teaching them God's laws, and showing them the principles of godly living.

21"Find some capable, godly, honest men who hate bribes, and appoint them as judges, one judge for each 1000 people; he in turn will have ten judges under him, each in charge of a hundred; and under each of them will be two judges, each responsible for the affairs of fifty people; and each of these will have five judges beneath him, each counseling ten persons. 22Let these men be responsible to serve the people with justice at all times. Anything that is too important or complicated can be brought to you. But the smaller matters they can take care of themselves. That way it will be easier for you because you will share the burden with them. 23If you follow this advice, and if the Lord agrees, you will be able to endure the pressures, and there will be peace and harmony in the camp."

24Moses listened to his father-in-law's advice, and followed this suggestion. 25He chose able men from all over Israel and made them judges over the people— thousands, hundreds, fifties, and tens. 26They were constantly available to administer justice. They brought the hard cases to Moses but judged the smaller matters themselves.

27Soon afterwards Moses let his father-in-law return to his own land.

THE Israelis arrived in the Sinai peninsula three months after the night of their departure from Egypt. 2,3After breaking camp at Rephidim, they came to the base of Mt. Sinai and set up camp there. Moses climbed the rugged mountain to meet with God, and from somewhere in the mountain God called to him and said,

"Give these instructions to the people of Israel. Tell them, 4'You have seen what I did to the Egyptians, and how I brought you to myself as though on eagles' wings. 5Now if you will obey me and keep your part of my contract with you, you shall be my own little flock from among all the nations of the earth; for all the earth is mine. 6And you shall be a kingdom of priests to God, a holy nation.' "

7Moses returned from the mountain and called together the leaders of the people and told them what the Lord had said.

8They all responded in unison, "We will certainly do everything he asks of us." Moses reported the words of the people to the Lord.

9Then he said to Moses, "I am going to come to you in the form of a dark cloud, so that the people themselves can hear me when I talk with you, and then they will always believe you. 10Go down now and see that the people are ready for my visit. Sanctify them today and tomorrow, and have them wash their clothes. 11Then, the day after tomorrow, I will come down upon Mt. Sinai as all the people watch. 12Set boundary lines the people may not pass, and tell them, 'Beware! Do not go up into the mountain, or even touch its boundaries; whoever does shall die— 13no hand shall touch him, but he shall be stoned or shot to death with arrows, whether man or animal.' Stay away from the mountain entirely until you hear a ram's horn sounding one long blast; then gather at the foot of the mountain!"

14So Moses went down to the people and sanctified them and they washed their clothing.

15He told them, "Get ready for God's appearance two days from now, and do not have sexual intercourse with your wives."

MATTHEW 22:33—23:12

THE crowds were profoundly impressed by his answers— 34,35but not the Pharisees! When they heard that he had routed the Sadducees with his reply, they thought up a fresh question of their own to ask him. One of them, a lawyer, spoke up: 36"Sir, which is the most important command in the laws of Moses?"

37Jesus replied, " 'Love the Lord your God with all your heart, soul, and mind.' 38,39This is the first and greatest commandment. The second most important is similar: 'Love your neighbor as much as you love yourself.' 40All the other commandments and all the demands of the prophets stem from these two laws and are fulfilled if you obey them. Keep only these and you will find that you are obeying all the others."

41Then, surrounded by the Pharisees, he asked them a question: 42"What about the Messiah? Whose son is he?" "The son of David," they replied.

43"Then why does David, speaking under the inspiration of the Holy Spirit, call him 'Lord'?" Jesus asked. "For David said,

⁴⁴'God said to my Lord, Sit at my right hand until I put your enemies beneath your feet.'

⁴⁵Since David called him 'Lord,' how can he be merely his son?"

⁴⁶They had no answer. And after that no one dared ask him any more questions.

THEN Jesus said to the crowds, and to his disciples, ²"You would think these Jewish leaders and these Pharisees were Moses, the way they keep making up so many laws! ³And of course you should obey their every whim! It may be all right to do what they say, but above anything else, *don't follow their example.* For they don't do what they tell you to do. ⁴They load you with impossible demands that they themselves don't even try to keep.

⁵"Everything they do is done for show. They act holy by wearing on their arms little prayer boxes with Scripture verses inside, and by lengthening the memorial fringes of their robes. ⁶And how they love to sit at the head table at banquets, and in the reserved pews in the synagogue! ⁷How they enjoy the deference paid them on the streets, and to be called 'Rabbi' and 'Master'! ⁸Don't ever let anyone call you that. For only God is your Rabbi and all of you are on the same level, as brothers. ⁹And don't address anyone here on earth as 'Father,' for only God in heaven should be addressed like that. ¹⁰And don't be called 'Master,' for only one is your master, even the Messiah.

¹¹"The more lowly your service to others, the greater you are. To be the greatest, be a servant. ¹²But those who think themselves great shall be disappointed and humbled; and those who humble themselves shall be exalted.

PSALM 27:8–14

MY heart has heard you say, "Come and talk with me, O my people." And my heart responds, "Lord, I am coming."

⁹Oh, do not hide yourself when I am trying to find you. Do not angrily reject your servant. You have been my help in all my trials before; don't leave me now. Don't forsake me, O God of my salvation. ¹⁰For if my father and mother should abandon me, you would welcome and comfort me.

¹¹Tell me what to do, O Lord, and make it plain because I am surrounded by waiting enemies. ¹²Don't let them get me, Lord! Don't let me fall into their hands! For they accuse me of things I never did, and all the while are plotting cruelty. ¹³I am expecting the Lord to rescue me again, so that once again I will see his goodness to me here in the land of the living.

¹⁴Don't be impatient. Wait for the Lord, and he will come and save you! Be brave, stouthearted and courageous. Yes, wait and he will help you.

PROVERBS FOR TODAY/ 6:27–35

Can a man hold fire against his chest and not be burned? Can he walk on hot coals and not blister his feet? So it is with the man who commits adultery with another's wife. He shall not go unpunished for this sin. Excuses might even be found for a thief, if he steals when he is starving! But even so, he is fined seven times as much as he stole, though it may mean selling everything in his house to pay it back. But the man who commits adultery is an utter fool, for he destroys his own soul. Wounds and constant disgrace are his lot, for the woman's husband will be furious in his jealousy, and he will have no mercy on you in his day of vengeance. You won't be able to buy him off no matter what you offer.

FEBRUARY 4

EXODUS 19:16—21:21

ON the morning of the third day there was a terrific thunder and lightning storm, and a huge cloud came down upon the mountain, and there was a long, loud blast as from a ram's horn; and all the people trembled. 17Moses led them out from the camp to meet God, and they stood at the foot of the mountain. 18All Mt. Sinai was covered with smoke because Jehovah descended upon it in the form of fire; the smoke billowed into the sky as from a furnace, and the whole mountain shook with a violent earthquake. 19As the trumpet blast grew louder and louder, Moses spoke and God thundered his reply. 20So the Lord came down upon the top of Mt. Sinai and called Moses up to the top of the mountain, and Moses ascended to God.

21But the Lord told Moses, "Go back down and warn the people not to cross the boundaries. They must not come up here to try to see God, for if they do, many of them will die. 22Even the priests on duty must sanctify themselves, or else I will destroy them."

23"But the people won't come up into the mountain!" Moses protested. "You told them not to! You told me to set boundaries around the mountain, and to declare it off limits because it is reserved for God."

24But Jehovah said, "Go down, and bring Aaron back with you, and don't let the priests and the people break across the boundaries to try to come up here, or I will punish them."

25So Moses went down to the people and told them what God had said.

THEN God issued this edict:
2"I am Jehovah your God who liberated you from your slavery in Egypt.
3"You may worship no other god than me.

4"You shall not make yourselves any idols: no images of animals, birds, or fish. 5You must never bow or worship it in any way; for I, the Lord your God, am very possessive. I will not share your affection with any other god!

"And when I punish people for their sins, the punishment continues upon the children, grandchildren, and great-grandchildren of those who hate me; 6but I lavish my love upon thousands of those who love me and obey my commandments.

7"You shall not use the name of Jehovah your God irreverently, nor use it to swear to a falsehood. You will not escape punishment if you do.

8"Remember to observe the Sabbath as a holy day. 9Six days a week are for your daily duties and your regular work, 10but the seventh day is a day of Sabbath rest before the Lord your God. On that day you are to do no work of any kind, nor shall your son, daughter, or slaves— whether men or women—or your cattle or your house guests. 11For in six days the Lord made the heaven, earth, and sea, and everything in them, and rested the seventh day; so he blessed the Sabbath day and set it aside for rest.

12"Honor your father and mother, that you may have a long, good life in the land the Lord your God will give you.

13"You must not murder.

14"You must not commit adultery.

15"You must not steal.

16"You must not lie.

17"You must not be envious of your neighbor's house, or want to sleep with his wife, or want to own his slaves, oxen, donkeys, or anything else he has."

18All the people saw the lightning and the smoke billowing from the mountain, and heard the thunder and the long, frightening trumpet blast; and they stood at a distance, shaking with fear.

19They said to Moses, "You tell us what God says and we will obey, but don't let God speak directly to us, or it will kill us."

20"Don't be afraid," Moses told them, "for God has come in this way to show you his awesome power, so that from now on you will be afraid to sin against him!"

21As the people stood in the distance, Moses entered into the deep darkness where God was.

22And the Lord told Moses to be his spokesman to the people of Israel. "You are witnesses to the fact that I have made known my will to you from heaven. 23Remember, you must not make or worship idols made of silver or gold or of anything else!

24"The altars you make for me must be simple altars of earth. Offer upon them your sacrifices to me—your burnt offerings and peace offerings of sheep and oxen. Build altars only where I tell you to, and I will come and bless you there. 25You may also build altars from stone, but if you do, then use only uncut stones and boulders. Don't chip or shape the stones with a tool, for that would make them unfit for my altar. 26And don't make steps for the altar, or someone might look up beneath the skirts of your clothing and see your nakedness.

"HERE are other laws you must obey:

2"If you buy a Hebrew slave, he shall serve only six years and be freed in the seventh year, and need pay nothing to regain his freedom.

3"If he sold himself as a slave before he married, then if he married afterwards, only he shall be freed; but if he was married before he became a slave, then his wife shall be freed with him at the same time. 4But if his master gave him a wife while he was a slave, and they have sons or daughters, the wife and children shall still belong to the master, and he shall go out by himself free.

5"But if the man shall plainly declare, 'I prefer my master, my wife, and my children, and I would rather not go free,' 6then his master shall bring him before the judges and shall publicly bore his ear

with an awl, and after that he will be a slave forever.

7"If a man sells his daughter as a slave, she shall not be freed at the end of six years as the men are. 8If she does not please the man who bought her, then he shall let her be bought back again; but he has no power to sell her to foreigners, since he has wronged her by no longer wanting her after marrying her. 9And if he arranges an engagement between a Hebrew slave-girl and his son, then he may no longer treat her as a slave-girl, but must treat her as a daughter. 10If he himself marries her and then takes another wife, he may not reduce her food or clothing, or fail to sleep with her as his wife. 11If he fails in any of these three things, then she may leave freely without any payment.

12"Anyone who hits a man so hard that he dies shall surely be put to death. 13But if it is accidental—an act of God—and not intentional, then I will appoint a place where he can run and get protection. 14However, if a man deliberately attacks another, intending to kill him, drag him even from my altar, and kill him.

15"Anyone who strikes his father or mother shall surely be put to death.

16"A kidnapper must be killed, whether he is caught in possession of his victim or has already sold him as a slave.

17"Anyone who reviles or curses his mother or father shall surely be put to death.

18"If two men are fighting, and one hits the other with a stone or with his fist and injures him so that he must be confined to bed, but doesn't die, 19if later he is able to walk again, even with a limp, the man who hit him will be innocent except that he must pay for the loss of his time until he is thoroughly healed, and pay any medical expenses.

20"If a man beats his slave to death—whether the slave is male or female—that man shall surely be punished. 21However, if the slave does not die for a couple of days, then the man shall not be punished—for the slave is his property.

WOE to you, Pharisees, and you other religious leaders. Hypocrites! For you won't let others enter the Kingdom of Heaven, and won't go in yourselves. And you pretend to be holy, with all your long, public prayers in the streets, while you are evicting widows from their homes. Hypocrites! 15Yes, woe upon you hypocrites. For you go to all lengths to make one convert, and then turn him into twice the son of hell you are yourselves. 16Blind guides! Woe upon you! For your rule is that to swear 'By God's Temple' means nothing—you can break that oath, but to swear 'By the gold in the Temple' is binding! 17Blind fools! Which is greater, the gold, or the Temple that sanctifies the gold? 18And you say that to take an oath 'By the altar' can be broken, but to swear 'By the gifts on the altar' is binding! 19Blind! For which is greater, the gift on the altar, or the altar itself that sanctifies the gift? 20When you swear 'By the altar' you are swearing by it and everything on it, 21and when you swear 'By the Temple' you are swearing by it, and by God who lives in it. 22And when you swear 'By heavens' you are swearing by the Throne of God and by God himself.

23"Yes, woe upon you, Pharisees, and you other religious leaders—hypocrites! For you tithe down to the last mint leaf in your garden, but ignore the important things—justice and mercy and faith. Yes, you should tithe, but you shouldn't leave the more important things undone. 24Blind guides! You strain out a gnat and swallow a camel.

25"Woe to you, Pharisees, and you religious leaders—hypocrites! You are so careful to polish the outside of the cup, but the inside is foul with extortion and greed. 26Blind Pharisees! First cleanse the inside of the cup, and then the whole cup will be clean.

27"Woe to you, Pharisees, and you religious leaders! You are like beautiful mausoleums—full of dead men's bones, and of foulness and corruption. 28You try to look like saintly men, but underneath those pious robes of yours are hearts besmirched with every sort of hypocrisy and sin.

29,30"Yes, woe to you, Pharisees, and you religious leaders—hypocrites! For you build monuments to the prophets killed by your fathers and lay flowers on the graves of the godly men they destroyed, and say, 'We certainly would never have acted as our fathers did.'

31"In saying that, you are accusing yourselves of being the sons of wicked men. 32And you are following in their steps, filling up the full measure of their evil. 33Snakes! Sons of vipers! How shall you escape the judgment of hell?

34"I will send you prophets, and wise men, and inspired writers, and you will kill some by crucifixion, and rip open the backs of others with whips in your synagogues, and hound them from city to city, 35so that you will become guilty of all the blood of murdered godly men from righteous Abel to Zechariah (son of Barachiah), slain by you in the Temple between the altar and the sanctuary. 36Yes, all the accumulated judgment of the centuries shall break upon the heads of this very generation.

37"O Jerusalem, Jerusalem, the city that kills the prophets, and stones all those God sends to her! How often I have wanted to gather your children together as a hen gathers her chicks beneath her wings, but you wouldn't let me. 38And now your house is left to you, desolate. 39For I tell you this, you will never see me again until you are ready to welcome the one sent to you from God."

PSALM 28:1–9

I plead with you to help me, Lord, for you are my Rock of safety. If you refuse to answer me, I might as well give up and die. 2Lord, I lift my hands to heaven and implore your help. Oh, listen to my cry.

³Don't punish me with all the wicked ones who speak so sweetly to their neighbors while planning to murder them. ⁴Give them the punishment they so richly deserve! Measure it out to them in proportion to their wickedness; pay them back for all their evil deeds. ⁵They care nothing for God or what he has done or what he has made; therefore God will dismantle them like old buildings, never to be rebuilt again.

⁶Oh, praise the Lord, for he has listened to my pleadings! ⁷He is my strength, my shield from every danger. I trusted in him, and he helped me. Joy rises in my heart until I burst out in songs of praise to him. ⁸The Lord protects his people and gives victory to his anointed king.

⁹Defend your people, Lord; defend and bless your chosen ones. Lead them like a shepherd and carry them forever in your arms.

PROVERBS FOR TODAY/ 7:1–5

Follow my advice, my son; always keep it in mind and stick to it. Obey me and live! Guard my words as your most precious possession. Write them down, and also keep them deep within your heart. Love wisdom like a sweetheart; make her a beloved member of your family. Let her hold you back from affairs with other women—from listening to their flattery.

FEBRUARY 5

EXODUS 21:22—23:13

IF two men are fighting, and in the process hurt a pregnant woman so that she has a miscarriage, but she lives, then the man who injured her shall be fined whatever amount the woman's husband shall demand, and as the judges approve. ²³But if any harm comes to the woman and she dies, he shall be executed.

²⁴"If her eye is injured, injure his; if her tooth is knocked out, knock out his; and so on—hand for hand, foot for foot, ²⁵burn for burn, wound for wound, lash for lash.

²⁶"If a man hits his slave in the eye, whether man or woman, and the eye is blinded, then the slave shall go free because of his eye. ²⁷And if a master knocks out his slave's tooth, he shall let him go free to pay for the tooth.

²⁸"If an ox gores a man or woman to death, the ox shall be stoned and its flesh not eaten, but the owner shall not be held— ²⁹unless the ox was known to gore people in the past, and the owner had been notified and still the ox was not kept under control; in that case, if it kills someone, the ox shall be stoned and the owner also shall be killed. ³⁰But the dead man's relatives may accept a fine instead, if they wish. The judges will determine the amount.

³¹"The same law holds if the ox gores a boy or a girl. ³²But if the ox gores a slave, whether male or female, the slave's master shall be given thirty pieces of silver, and the ox shall be stoned.

³³"If a man digs a well and doesn't cover it, and an ox or a donkey falls into it, ³⁴the owner of the well shall pay full damages to the owner of the animal, and the dead animal shall belong to him.

³⁵"If a man's ox injures another, and it dies, then the two owners shall sell the live ox and divide the price between them—and each shall also own half of the dead ox. ³⁶But if the ox was known

from past experience to gore, and its owner has not kept it under control, then there will not be a division of the income; but the owner of the living ox shall pay in full for the dead ox, and the dead one shall be his.

"IF a man steals an ox or sheep and then kills or sells it, he shall pay a fine of five to one—five oxen shall be returned for each stolen ox. For sheep, the fine shall be four to one—four sheep returned for each sheep stolen.

2"If a thief is caught in the act of breaking into a house and is killed, the one who killed him is not guilty. 3But if it happens in the daylight, it must be presumed to be murder and the man who kills him is guilty.

"If a thief is captured, he must make full restitution; if he can't, then he must be sold as a slave for his debt.

4"If he is caught in the act of stealing a live ox or donkey or sheep or whatever it is, he shall pay double value as his fine.

5"If someone deliberately lets his animal loose and it gets into another man's vineyard; or if he turns it into another man's field to graze, he must pay for all damages by giving the owner of the field or vineyard an equal amount of the best of his own crop.

6"If the field is being burned off and the fire gets out of control and goes into another field so that the shocks of grain, or the standing grain, are destroyed, the one who started the fire shall make full restitution.

7"If someone gives money or goods to anyone to keep for him, and it is stolen, the thief shall pay double if he is found. 8But if no thief is found, then the man to whom the valuables were entrusted shall be brought before God to determine whether or not he himself has stolen his neighbor's property.

9"In every case in which an ox, donkey, sheep, clothing, or anything else is lost, and the owner believes he has found it in the possession of someone else who denies it, both parties to the dispute shall come before God for a decision, and the one whom God declares guilty shall pay double to the other.

10"If a man asks his neighbor to keep a donkey, ox, sheep, or any other animal for him, and it dies, or is hurt, or gets away, and there is no eyewitness to report just what happened to it, 11then the neighbor must take an oath that he has not stolen it, and the owner must accept his word, and no restitution shall be made for it. 12But if the animal or property has been stolen, the neighbor caring for it must repay the owner. 13If it was attacked by some wild animal, he shall bring the torn carcass to confirm the fact, and shall not be required to make restitution.

14"If a man borrows an animal (or anything else) from a neighbor, and it is injured or killed, and the owner is not there at the time, then the man who borrowed it must pay for it. 15But if the owner is there, he need not pay; and if it was rented, then he need not pay, because this possibility was included in the original rental fee.

16"If a man seduces a girl who is not engaged to anyone, and sleeps with her, he must pay the usual dowry and accept her as his wife. 17But if her father utterly refuses to let her marry him, then he shall pay the money anyway.

18"A sorceress shall be put to death.

19"Anyone having sexual relations with an animal shall certainly be executed.

20"Anyone sacrificing to any other god than Jehovah shall be executed.

21"You must not oppress a stranger in any way; remember, you yourselves were foreigners in the land of Egypt.

22"You must not exploit widows or orphans; 23if you do so in any way, and they cry to me for my help, I will surely give it. 24And my anger shall flame out against you, and I will kill you with enemy armies, so that your wives will be widows and your children fatherless.

25"If you lend money to a needy fellow-Hebrew, you are not to handle the transaction in an ordinary way, with interest. 26If you take his clothing as a pledge of his repayment, you must let him have it back at night. 27For it is probably his only warmth; how can he sleep without it? If you don't return it, and he cries to me for help, I will hear and be very gracious to him [at your expense], for I am very compassionate.

28"You shall not blaspheme God, nor curse government officials—your judges and your rulers.

29"You must be prompt in giving me the tithe of your crops and your wine, and the redemption payment for your oldest son.

30"As to the firstborn of the oxen and the sheep, give it to me on the eighth day, after leaving it with its mother for seven days.

31"And since you yourselves are holy—my special people—do not eat any animal that has been attacked and killed by a wild animal. Leave its carcass for the dogs to eat.

"Do not pass along untrue reports. Do not cooperate with an evil man by affirming on the witness stand something you know is false.

2,3"Don't join mobs intent on evil. When on the witness stand, don't be swayed in your testimony by the mood of the majority present, and do not slant your testimony in favor of a man just because he is poor.

4"If you come upon an enemy's ox or donkey that has strayed away, you must take it back to its owner. 5If you see your enemy trying to get his donkey onto its feet beneath a heavy load, you must not go on by, but must help him.

6"A man's poverty is no excuse for twisting justice against him.

7"Keep far away from falsely charging anyone with evil; never let an innocent person be put to death. I will not stand for this.

8"Take no bribes, for a bribe makes you unaware of what you clearly see! A bribe hurts the cause of the person who is right.

9"Do not oppress foreigners; you know what it's like to be a foreigner; remember your own experience in the land of Egypt.

10"Sow and reap your crops for six years, 11but let the land rest and lie fallow during the seventh year, and let the poor among the people harvest any volunteer crop that may come up; leave the rest for the animals to enjoy. The same rule applies to your vineyards and your olive groves.

12"Work six days only, and rest the seventh; this is to give your oxen and donkeys a rest, as well as the people of your household—your slaves and visitors.

13"Be sure to obey all of these instructions; and remember—never mention the name of any other god.

MATTHEW 24:1–28

As Jesus was leaving the Temple grounds, his disciples came along and wanted to take him on a tour of the various Temple buildings.

2But he told them, "All these buildings will be knocked down, with not one stone left on top of another!"

3"When will this happen?" the disciples asked him later, as he sat on the slopes of the Mount of Olives. "What events will signal your return, and the end of the world?"

4Jesus told them, "Don't let anyone fool you. 5For many will come claiming to be the Messiah, and will lead many astray. 6When you hear of wars beginning, this does not signal my return; these must come, but the end is not yet. 7The nations and kingdoms of the earth will rise against each other and there will be famines and earthquakes in many places. 8But all this will be only the beginning of the horrors to come.

9"Then you will be tortured and killed and hated all over the world because you are mine, 10and many of you shall fall back into sin and betray and hate each other. 11And many false prophets will appear and lead many astray. 12Sin will be rampant everywhere and will cool the love of many. 13But those enduring to the end shall be saved.

14"And the Good News about the Kingdom will be preached throughout the whole world, so that all nations will hear it, and then, finally, the end will come.

15"So, when you see the horrible thing (told about by Daniel the prophet) standing in a holy place (Note to the reader: You know what is meant!), 16then those in Judea must flee into the Judean hills. 17Those on their porches must not even go inside to pack before they flee. 18Those in the fields should not return to their homes for their clothes.

19"And woe to pregnant women and to those with babies in those days. 20And pray that your flight will not be in winter, or on the Sabbath. 21For there will be persecution such as the world has never before seen in all its history, and will never see again.

22"In fact, unless those days are shortened, all mankind will perish. But they will be shortened for the sake of God's chosen people.

23"Then if anyone tells you, 'The Messiah has arrived at such and such a place, or has appeared here or there,' don't believe it. 24For false Christs shall arise, and false prophets, and will do wonderful miracles, so that if it were possible, even God's chosen ones would be deceived. 25See, I have warned you.

26"So if someone tells you the Messiah has returned and is out in the desert, don't bother to go and look. Or, that he is hiding at a certain place, don't believe it! 27For as the lightning flashes across the sky from east to west, so shall my coming be, when I, the Messiah, return. 28And wherever the carcass is, there the vultures will gather.

PSALM 29:1–11

PRAISE the Lord, you angels of his; praise his glory and his strength. 2Praise him for his majestic glory, the glory of his name. Come before him clothed in sacred garments.

3The voice of the Lord echoes from the clouds. The God of glory thunders through the skies. 4So powerful is his voice; so full of majesty. 5,6It breaks down the cedars. It splits the giant trees of Lebanon. It shakes Mount Lebanon and Mount Sirion. They leap and skip before him like young calves! 7The voice of the Lord thunders through the lightning. 8It resounds through the deserts and shakes the wilderness of Kadesh. 9The voice of the Lord spins and topples the mighty oaks. It strips the forests bare. They whirl and sway beneath the blast. But in his temple all are praising, "Glory, glory to the Lord."

10At the Flood, the Lord showed his control of all creation. Now he continues to unveil his power. 11He will give his people strength. He will bless them with peace.

PROVERBS FOR TODAY/ 7:6–23

I was looking out the window of my house one day, and saw a simple-minded lad, a young man lacking common sense, walking at twilight down the street to the house of this wayward girl, a prostitute. She approached him, saucy and pert, and dressed seductively. She was the brash, coarse type, seen often in the streets and markets, soliciting at every corner for men to be her lovers. She put her arms around him and kissed him, and with a saucy look she said, "I was just coming to look for you and here you are! Come home with me and I'll fix you a wonderful dinner, and after that—well, my bed is spread with lovely, colored sheets of finest linen imported from Egypt, perfumed with myrrh, aloes and cinnamon. Come on, let's take our fill of love until morning, for my husband is away on a long trip. He has taken a wallet full of money with him, and won't return for several days." So she seduced him with her pretty speech, her coaxing and her wheedling, until he yielded to her. He couldn't resist her flattery. He followed her as an ox

"You are to go into all the world and preach the Good News to everyone, everywhere."
Mark 16:15

"Work hard and cheerfully at all you do, just as though you were working for the Lord."
Colossians 3:23

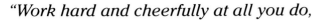

going to the butcher, or as a stag that is trapped, waiting to be killed with an arrow through its heart. He was as a bird flying into a snare, not knowing the fate awaiting it there.

FEBRUARY 6

EXODUS 23:14—25:40

THERE are three annual religious pilgrimages you must make. 15"The first is the Pilgrimage of Unleavened Bread, when for seven days you are not to eat bread with yeast, just as I commanded you before. This celebration is to be an annual event at the regular time in March, the month you left Egypt; everyone must bring me a sacrifice at that time. 16Then there is the Harvest Pilgrimage, when you must bring to me the first of your crops. And, finally, the Pilgrimage of Ingathering at the end of the harvest season. 17At these three times each year, every man in Israel shall appear before the Lord God.

18"No sacrificial blood shall be offered with leavened bread; no sacrificial fat shall be left unoffered until the next morning.

19"As you reap each of your crops, bring me the choicest sample of the first day's harvest; it shall be offered to the Lord your God.

"Do not boil a young goat in its mother's milk.

20"See, I am sending an Angel before you to lead you safely to the land I have prepared for you. 21Reverence him and obey all of his instructions; do not rebel against him, for he will not pardon your transgression; he is my representative—he bears my name. 22But if you are careful to obey him, following all my instructions, then I will be an enemy to your enemies. 23For my Angel shall go before you and bring you into the land of the Amorites, Hittites, Perizzites, Canaanites, Hivites, and Jebusites, to live there.

And I will destroy those people before you.

24"You must not worship the gods of these other nations, nor sacrifice to them in any way, and you must not follow the evil example of these heathen people; you must utterly conquer them and break down their shameful idols.

25"You shall serve the Lord your God only; then I will bless you with food and with water, and I will take away sickness from among you. 26There will be no miscarriages nor barrenness throughout your land, and you will live out the full quota of the days of your life.

27"The terror of the Lord shall fall upon all the people whose land you invade, and they will flee before you; 28and I will send hornets to drive out the Hivites, Canaanites, and Hittites from before you. 29I will not do it all in one year, for the land would become a wilderness, and the wild animals would become too many to control. 30But I will drive them out a little at a time, until your population has increased enough to fill the land. 31And I will set your enlarged boundaries from the Red Sea to the Philistine coast, and from the southern deserts as far as the Euphrates River; and I will cause you to defeat the people now living in the land, and you will drive them out ahead of you.

32"You must make no covenant with them, nor have anything to do with their gods. 33Don't let them live among you! For I know that they will infect you with their sin of worshiping false gods, and that would be an utter disaster to you."

THE Lord now instructed Moses, "Come up here with Aaron, Nadab, Abihu, and seventy of the elders of Israel. All of you except Moses are to worship at a distance. 2Moses alone shall come near to the Lord; and remember, none of the ordinary people are permitted to come up into the mountain at all."

3Then Moses announced to the people all the laws and regulations God had given him; and the people answered in unison, "We will obey them all."

4Moses wrote down the laws; and early the next morning he built an altar at the foot of the mountain, with twelve pillars around the altar because there were twelve tribes of Israel. 5Then he sent some of the young men to sacrifice the burnt offerings and peace offerings to the Lord. 6Moses took half of the blood of these animals, and drew it off into basins. The other half he splashed against the altar.

7And he read to the people the Book he had written—the Book of the Covenant—containing God's directions and laws. And the people said again, "We solemnly promise to obey every one of these rules."

8Then Moses threw the blood from the basins towards the people and said, "This blood confirms and seals the covenant the Lord has made with you in giving you these laws."

9Then Moses, Aaron, Nadab, Abihu, and seventy of the elders of Israel went up into the mountain. 10And they saw the God of Israel; under his feet there seemed to be a pavement of brilliant sapphire stones, as clear as the heavens. 11Yet, even though the elders saw God, he did not destroy them; and they had a meal together before the Lord.

12And the Lord said to Moses, "Come up to me into the mountain, and remain until I give you the laws and commandments I have written on tablets of stone, so that you can teach the people from them." 13So Moses and Joshua, his assistant, went up into the mountain of God.

14He told the elders, "Stay here and wait for us until we come back; if there are any problems while I am gone, consult with Aaron and Hur."

15Then Moses went up the mountain and disappeared into the cloud at the top. 16And the glory of the Lord rested upon Mt. Sinai and the cloud covered it six days; the seventh day he called to Moses from the cloud. 17Those at the bottom of the mountain saw the awesome sight: the glory of the Lord on the mountain top looked like a raging fire. 18And Moses disappeared into the cloud-covered mountain top, and was there for forty days and forty nights.

JEHOVAH said to Moses, "Tell the people of Israel that everyone who wants to may bring me an offering from this list:

gold, silver, bronze, blue cloth, purple cloth, scarlet cloth, fine linen, goats' hair, red-dyed rams' skins, goat-skins, acacia wood, olive oil for the lamps, spices for the anointing oil and for the fragrant incense, onyx stones, stones to be set in the ephod and in the breastplate.

8"For I want the people of Israel to make me a sacred Temple where I can live among them.

9"This home of mine shall be a tent pavilion—a Tabernacle. I will give you a drawing of the construction plan, and the details of each furnishing.

10"Using acacia wood, make an Ark 3¾ feet long, 2¼ feet wide, and 2¼ feet high. 11Overlay it inside and outside with pure gold, with a molding of gold all around it. 12Cast four rings of gold for it and attach them to the four lower corners, two rings on each side. 13,14Make poles from acacia wood overlaid with gold, and fit the poles into the rings at the sides of the Ark, to carry it. 15These carrying poles shall never be taken from the rings, but are to be left there permanently. 16When the Ark is finished, place inside it the tablets of stone I will give you, with the Ten Commandments engraved on them.

17"And make a lid of pure gold, 3¾ feet long and 2¼ feet wide. This is the place of mercy for your sins. 18Then make two statues of Guardian Angels using beaten gold, and place them at the two ends of the lid of the Ark. 19They shall be one piece with the mercy place, one at each end. 20The Guardian Angels shall be facing each other, looking down upon the place of mercy, and shall have wings spread out above the gold lid. 21Install the lid upon the Ark, and place within the Ark the tablets of stone I shall give you. 22And I will meet with you there and talk with you from above the place of mercy between the Guardian Angels; and the Ark will contain the laws of my covenant. There I will tell you my commandments for the people of Israel.

23"Then make a table of acacia wood three feet long, 1½ feet wide, and 2¼ feet high. 24Overlay it with pure gold, and run a rib of gold around it. 25Put a molding four inches wide around the edge of the top, and a gold ridge along the molding, all around. 26,27Make four gold rings and put the rings at the outside corner of the four legs, close to the top; these are rings for the poles that will be used to carry the table. 28Make the poles from acacia wood overlaid with gold. 29And make gold dishes, spoons, pitchers, and flagons; 30and always keep the special Bread of the Presence on the table before me.

31"Make a lampstand of pure, beaten gold. The entire lampstand and its decorations shall be one piece—the base, shaft, lamps, and blossoms. 32,33It will have three branches going out from each side of the center shaft, each branch decorated with three almond flowers. 34,35The central shaft itself will be decorated with four almond flowers—one placed between each set of branches; also, there will be one flower above the top set of branches and one below the bottom set. 36These decorations and branches and the shaft are all to be one piece of pure, beaten gold. 37Then make seven lamps for the lampstand, and set them so that they reflect their light forward. 38The snuffers and trays are to be made of pure gold. 39You will need about 107 pounds of pure gold for the lampstand and its accessories.

40"Be sure that everything you make follows the pattern I am showing you here on the mountain.

MATTHEW 24:29–51

IMMEDIATELY after the persecution of those days the sun will be darkened, and the moon will not give light, and the stars will seem to fall from the heavens, and the powers overshadowing the earth will be convulsed.

30"And then at last the signal of my coming will appear in the heavens and there will be deep mourning all around the earth. And the nations of the world will see me arrive in the clouds of heaven, with power and great glory. 31And I shall send forth my angels with the sound of a mighty trumpet blast, and they shall gather my chosen ones from the farthest ends of the earth and heaven.

32"Now learn a lesson from the fig tree. When her branch is tender and the leaves begin to sprout, you know that summer is almost here. 33Just so, when you see all these things beginning to happen, you can know that my return is near, even at the doors. 34Then at last this age will come to its close.

35"Heaven and earth will disappear, but my words remain forever. 36But no one knows the date and hour when the end will be—not even the angels. No, nor even God's Son. Only the Father knows.

37,38"The world will be at ease—banquets and parties and weddings—just as it was in Noah's time before the sudden coming of the flood; 39people wouldn't believe what was going to happen until the flood actually arrived and took them all away. So shall my coming be.

40"Two men will be working together in the fields, and one will be taken, the other left. 41Two women will be going about their household tasks; one will be taken, the other left.

42"So be prepared, for you don't know what day your Lord is coming.

43"Just as a man can prevent trouble from thieves by keeping watch for them, 44so you can avoid trouble by always being ready for my unannounced return.

45"Are you a wise and faithful servant of the Lord? Have I given you the task of managing my household, to feed my children day by day? 46Blessings on you if I return and find you faithfully doing your work. 47I will put such faithful ones in charge of everything I own!

48"But if you are evil and say to yourself, 'My Lord won't be coming for a while,' 49and begin oppressing your fellow servants, partying and getting drunk, 50your Lord will arrive unannounced and unexpected, 51and severely whip you and send you off to the judgment of the hypocrites; there will be weeping and gnashing of teeth.

PSALM 30:1–12

I will praise you, Lord, for you have saved me from my enemies. You refuse to let them triumph over me. 2O Lord my God, I pleaded with you, and you gave me my health again. 3You brought me back from the brink of the grave, from death itself, and here I am alive!

4Oh, sing to him, you saints of his; give thanks to his holy name. 5His anger lasts a moment; his favor lasts for life! Weeping may go on all night, but in the morning there is joy.

6,7In my prosperity I said, "This is forever; nothing can stop me now! The Lord has shown me his favor. He has made me steady as a mountain." Then, Lord, you turned your face away from me and cut off your river of blessings. Suddenly my courage was gone; I was terrified and panic-stricken. 8I cried to you, O Lord; oh, how I pled: 9"What will you gain, O Lord, from killing me? How can I praise you then to all my friends? How can my dust in the grave speak out and tell the world about your faithfulness? 10Hear me, Lord; oh, have pity and help me." 11Then he turned my sorrow into joy! He took away my clothes of mourning and clothed me with joy 12so that I might sing glad praises to the Lord instead of lying in silence in the grave. O Lord my God, I will keep on thanking you forever!

PROVERBS FOR TODAY/ 7:24–27

Listen to me, young men, and not only listen but obey; don't let your desires get out of hand; don't let yourself think about her. Don't go near her; stay away from where she walks, lest she tempt you and seduce you. For she has been the ruin of multitudes—a vast host of men have been her victims. If you want to find the road to hell, look for her house.

FEBRUARY 7

EXODUS 26:1—27:21

MAKE the tabernacle-tent from ten colored sheets of fine linen, forty-two feet long and six feet wide, dyed blue, purple, and scarlet, with figures of Guardian Angels embroidered on them. 3Join five sheets end to end for each side of the tent, forming two long pieces, one for each side. 4,5Use loops at the edges to join these two long pieces together side by side. There are to be fifty loops on each side, opposite each other. 6Then make fifty gold clasps to fasten the loops together, so that the Tabernacle, the dwelling place of God, becomes a single unit.

7,8"The roof of the Tabernacle is made of goat's hair tarpaulins. There are to be eleven of these tarpaulins, each forty-five feet across and six feet wide. 9Connect five of these tarpaulins into one wide section; and use the other six for another wide section. (The sixth tarpaulin will hang down to form a curtain across the front of the sacred tent.) 10,11Use fifty loops along the edges of each of these two wide pieces, to join them together with fifty bronze clasps. Thus the two widths become one. 12There will be a 1½-foot length of this roof-covering hanging down from the back of the tent, 13and a 1½-foot length at the front. 14On top of these blankets is placed a layer of rams' skins, dyed red, and over them a top layer of goatskins. This completes the roof-covering.

15,16"The framework of the sacred tent shall be made from acacia wood, each frame-piece being fifteen feet high and 2¼ feet wide, standing upright, 17with grooves on each side to mortise into the next upright piece. 18,19Twenty of these frames will form the south side of the sacred tent, with forty silver bases for the frames to fit into—two bases under each piece of the frame. 20On the north side there will also be twenty of these frames, 21with their forty silver bases, two bases for each frame, one under each edge. 22On the west side there will be six frames, 23and two frames at each corner. 24These corner frames will be connected at the bottom and top with clasps. 25So, in all, there will be eight frames on that end of the building with sixteen silver bases for the frames—two bases under each frame.

26,27"Make bars of acacia wood to run across the frames, five bars on each side of the Tabernacle. Also five bars for the rear of the building, facing westward. 28The middle bar, halfway up the frames, runs all the way from end to end of the Tabernacle. 29Overlay the frames with gold, and make gold rings to hold the bars; and also overlay the bars with gold. 30Set up this Tabernacle-tent in the manner I showed you on the mountain.

31"[Inside the Tabernacle], make a curtain from fine linen, with blue, purple, and scarlet Guardian Angels embroidered into the cloth. 32Hang this curtain on gold hooks set into four pillars made from acacia wood overlaid with gold. The pillars are to be set in silver bases. 33Behind this curtain place the Ark containing the stone tablets engraved with God's laws. The curtain will separate the Holy Place and the Most Holy Place.

34"Now install the mercy place—the golden lid of the Ark—in the Most Holy Place. 35Place the table and lampstand across the room from each other on the outer side of the veil, the lampstand on the south and the table on the north.

36"As a screen for the door of the sacred tent, make another curtain from fine linen, skillfully embroidered in blue, purple, and scarlet. 37Hang this curtain on gold hooks set into posts made from acacia wood overlaid with gold. The posts are to rest on bronze bases.

"USING acacia wood, make a square altar 7½ feet wide, and 4½ feet high. 2Make horns for the four corners of the altar, attach them firmly, and overlay everything with bronze. 3The ash buckets, shovels, basins, carcass-hooks, and fire pans are all to be made of bronze. 4Make a bronze grating, with a metal ring at each corner, 5and fit the grating halfway down into the fire box, resting it upon the ledge built there. 6For moving the altar, make poles from acacia wood overlaid with bronze. 7To carry it, put the poles into the rings at each side of the altar. 8The altar is to be hollow, made from planks, just as was shown you on the mountain.

9,10"Then make a courtyard for the Tabernacle, enclosed with curtains made from fine-twined linen. On the south side the curtains will stretch for 150 feet, and be held up by twenty posts, fitting into twenty bronze post holders. The curtains will be held up with silver hooks attached to silver rods, attached to the posts. ¹¹It will be the same on the north side of the court—150 feet of curtains held up by twenty posts fitted into bronze sockets, with silver hooks and rods. ¹²The west side of the court will be seventy-five feet wide, with ten posts and ten sockets. ¹³The east side will also be seventy-five feet. ¹⁴,¹⁵On each side of the entrance there will be 22½ feet of curtain, held up by three posts imbedded in three sockets.

¹⁶"The entrance to the court will be a thirty-foot-wide curtain, made of beautifully embroidered blue, purple, and scarlet fine-twined linen, and attached to four posts imbedded in their four sockets. ¹⁷All the posts around the court are to be connected by silver rods, using silver hooks, the posts being imbedded in solid bronze bases. ¹⁸So the entire court will be 150 feet long, and 75 feet wide, with curtain walls 7½ feet high, made from fine-twined linen.

¹⁹"All utensils used in the work of the Tabernacle, including all the pins and pegs for hanging the utensils on the walls, will be made of bronze.

²⁰"Instruct the people of Israel to bring you pure olive oil to use in the lamps of the Tabernacle, to burn there continually. ²¹Aaron and his sons shall place this eternal flame in the outer holy room, tending it day and night before the Lord, so that it never goes out. This is a permanent rule for the people of Israel.

MATTHEW 25:1-30

THE Kingdom of Heaven can be illustrated by the story of ten bridesmaids who took their lamps and went to meet the bridegroom. ²,³,⁴But only five of them were wise enough to fill their lamps with oil, while the other five were foolish and forgot. ⁵,⁶"So, when the bridegroom was delayed, they lay down to rest until midnight, when they were roused by the shout, 'The bridegroom is coming! Come out and welcome him!'

⁷,⁸"All the girls jumped up and trimmed their lamps. Then the five who hadn't any oil begged the others to share with them, for their lamps were going out.

⁹"But the others replied, 'We haven't enough. Go instead to the shops and buy some for yourselves.'

¹⁰"But while they were gone, the bridegroom came, and those who were ready went in with him to the marriage feast, and the door was locked.

¹¹"Later, when the other five returned, they stood outside, calling, 'Sir, open the door for us!'

¹²"But he called back, 'Go away! It is too late!'

¹³"So stay awake and be prepared, for you do not know the date or moment of my return.

¹⁴"Again, the Kingdom of Heaven can be illustrated by the story of a man going into another country, who called together his servants and loaned them money to invest for him while he was gone.

¹⁵"He gave $5,000 to one, $2,000 to another, and $1,000 to the last—dividing it in proportion to their abilities—and then left on his trip. ¹⁶The man who received the $5,000 began immediately to buy and sell with it and soon earned another $5,000. ¹⁷The man with $2,000 went right to work, too, and earned another $2,000.

¹⁸"But the man who received the $1,000 dug a hole in the ground and hid the money for safekeeping.

¹⁹"After a long time their master returned from his trip and called them to him to account for his money. ²⁰The man to whom he had entrusted the $5,000 brought him $10,000.

²¹"His master praised him for good work. 'You have been faithful in handling this small amount,' he told him, 'so now I will give you many more responsibilities. Begin the joyous tasks I have assigned to you.'

²²"Next came the man who had received the $2,000, with the report, 'Sir,

you gave me $2,000 to use, and I have doubled it.'

23" 'Good work,' his master said. 'You are a good and faithful servant. You have been faithful over this small amount, so now I will give you much more.'

24,25"Then the man with the $1,000 came and said, 'Sir, I knew you were a hard man, and I was afraid you would rob me of what I earned, so I hid your money in the earth and here it is!'

26"But his master replied, 'Wicked man! Lazy slave! Since you knew I would demand your profit, 27you should at least have put my money into the bank so I could have some interest. 28Take the money from this man and give it to the man with the $10,000. 29For the man who uses well what he is given shall be given more, and he shall have abundance. But from the man who is unfaithful, even what little responsibility he has shall be taken from him. 30And throw the useless servant out into outer darkness: there shall be weeping and gnashing of teeth.'

PSALM 31:1–8

LORD, I trust in you alone. Don't let my enemies defeat me. Rescue me because you are the God who always does what is right. 2Answer quickly when I cry to you; bend low and hear my whispered plea. Be for me a great Rock of safety from my foes. 3Yes, you are my Rock and my fortress; honor your name by leading me out of this peril. 4Pull me from the trap my enemies have set for me. For you alone are strong enough. 5,6Into your hand I commit my spirit.

You have rescued me, O God who keeps his promises. I worship only you; how you hate all those who worship idols, those imitation gods. 7I am radiant with joy because of your mercy, for you have listened to my troubles and have seen the crisis in my soul. 8You have not handed me over to my enemy, but have given me open ground in which to maneuver.

PROVERBS FOR TODAY/ 8:1–11

Can't you hear the voice of wisdom? She is standing at the city gates and at every fork in the road, and at the door of every house. Listen to what she says: "Listen, men!" she calls. "How foolish and naive you are! Let me give you understanding. O foolish ones, let me show you common sense! Listen to me! For I have important information for you. Everything I say is right and true, for I hate lies and every kind of deception. My advice is wholesome and good. There is nothing of evil in it. My words are plain and clear to anyone with half a mind—if it is only open! My instruction is far more valuable than silver or gold." For the value of wisdom is far above rubies; nothing can be compared with it.

FEBRUARY 8

EXODUS 28:1–43

CONSECRATE Aaron your brother, and his sons Nadab, Abihu, Eleazar, and Ithamar, to be priests, to minister to me. 2Make special clothes for Aaron, to indicate his separation to God—beautiful garments that will lend dignity to his work. 3Instruct those to whom I have given special skill as tailors to make the garments that will set him apart from others, so that he may minister to me in the priest's office. 4This is the wardrobe they shall make: a chestpiece, an ephod, a robe, an embroidered shirt, a turban, and a sash. They shall also make special garments for Aaron's sons.

5,6"The ephod shall be made by the

most skilled of the workmen, using gold, blue, purple, and scarlet threads of fine linen. 7It will consist of two pieces, front and back, joined at the shoulders. 8And the sash shall be made of the same material—threads of gold, blue, purple, and scarlet fine-twined linen. 9Take two onyx stones, and engrave on them the names of the tribes of Israel. 10Six names shall be on each stone, so that all the tribes are named in the order of their births. 11When engraving these names, use the same technique as in making a seal; and mount the stones in gold settings. 12Fasten the two stones upon the shoulders of the ephod, as memorial stones for the people of Israel: Aaron will carry their names before the Lord as a constant reminder. 13,14Two chains of pure, twisted gold shall be made and attached to gold clasps on the shoulder of the ephod.

15"Then, using the most careful workmanship, make a chestpiece to be used as God's oracle; use the same gold, blue, purple, and scarlet threads of fine-twined linen as you did in the ephod. 16This chestpiece is to be of two folds of cloth, forming a pouch nine inches square. 17Attach to it four rows of stones: A ruby, a topaz, and an emerald shall be in the first row. 18The second row will be carbuncle, a sapphire, and a diamond. 19The third row will be an amber, an agate, and an amethyst. 20The fourth row will be an onyx, a beryl, and a jasper— all set in gold settings. 21Each stone will represent one of the tribes of Israel and the name of that tribe will be engraved upon it like a seal.

22,23,24"Attach the top of the chestpiece to the ephod by means of two twisted cords of pure gold. One end of each cord is attached to gold rings placed at the outer top edge of the chestpiece. 25The other ends of the two cords are attached to the front edges of the two settings of the onyx stones on the shoulder of the ephod. 26Then make two more gold rings and place them on the two lower, inside edges of the chestpiece; 27also make two other gold rings for the bottom front edge of the ephod at the sash. 28Now attach the bottom of the chestpiece to the bottom rings of the ephod by means of blue ribbons; this will prevent the chestpiece from coming loose from the ephod. 29In this way Aaron shall carry the names of the tribes of Israel on the chestpiece over his heart (it is God's oracle) when he goes in to the Holy Place; thus Jehovah will be reminded of them continually. 30,31Insert into the pocket of the chestpiece the Urim and Thummim, to be carried over Aaron's heart when he goes in before Jehovah. Thus Aaron shall always be carrying the oracle over his heart when he goes in before the Lord.

"The ephod shall be made of blue cloth, 32with an opening for Aaron's head. It shall have a woven band around this opening, just as on the neck of a coat of mail, so that it will not fray. 33,34The bottom edge of the ephod shall be embroidered with blue, purple, and scarlet pomegranates, alternated with gold bells. 35Aaron shall wear the ephod whenever he goes in to minister to the Lord; the bells will tinkle as he goes in and out of the presence of the Lord in the Holy Place, so that he will not die.

36"Next, make a plate of pure gold and engrave on it, just as you would upon a seal, 'Consecrated to Jehovah.' 37,38This plate is to be attached by means of a blue ribbon to the front of Aaron's turban. In this way Aaron will be wearing it upon his forehead, and thus bear the guilt connected with any errors regarding the offerings of the people of Israel. It shall always be worn when he goes into the presence of the Lord, so that the people will be accepted and forgiven.

39"Weave Aaron's embroidered shirt from fine-twined linen, using a checkerboard pattern; make the turban, too, of this linen; and make him an embroidered sash.

40"Then, for Aaron's sons, make robes, sashes, and turbans to give them honor and respect. 41Clothe Aaron and his sons with these garments, and then dedicate these men to their ministry by anointing their heads with olive oil, thus sanctifying them as the priests, my ministers. 42Also make linen undershorts for them, to be worn beneath their robes next to their bodies, reaching from hips to knees. 43These are to be worn whenever Aaron and his sons go into the Tabernacle or to the altar in the Holy Place, lest they be guilty and die. This is a permanent ordinance for Aaron and his sons.

MATTHEW 25:31—26:13

BUT when I, the Messiah, shall come in my glory, and all the angels with me, then I shall sit upon my throne of glory. 32And all the nations shall be gathered before me. And I will separate the people as a shepherd separates the sheep from the goats, 33and place the sheep at my right hand, and the goats at my left.

34"Then I, the King, shall say to those at my right, 'Come, blessed of my Father, into the Kingdom prepared for you from the founding of the world. 35For I was hungry and you fed me; I was thirsty and you gave me water; I was a stranger and you invited me into your homes; 36naked and you clothed me; sick and in prison, and you visited me.'

37"Then these righteous ones will reply, 'Sir, when did we ever see you hungry and feed you? Or thirsty and give you anything to drink? 38Or a stranger, and help you? Or naked, and clothe you? 39When did we ever see you sick or in prison, and visit you?'

40"And I, the King, will tell them, 'When you did it to these my brothers you were doing it to me!' 41Then I will turn to those on my left and say, 'Away with you, you cursed ones, into the eternal fire prepared for the devil and his demons. 42For I was hungry and you wouldn't feed me; thirsty, and you wouldn't give me anything to drink; 43a stranger, and you refused me hospitality; naked, and you wouldn't clothe me; sick, and in prison, and you didn't visit me.'

44"Then they will reply, 'Lord, when did we ever see you hungry or thirsty or a stranger or naked or sick or in prison, and not help you?'

45"And I will answer, 'When you refused to help the least of these my brothers, you were refusing help to me.'

46"And they shall go away into eternal punishment; but the righteous into everlasting life."

WHEN Jesus had finished this talk with his disciples, he told them,

2"As you know, the Passover celebration begins in two days, and I shall be betrayed and crucified."

3At that very moment the chief priests and other Jewish officials were meeting at the residence of Caiaphas the High Priest, 4to discuss ways of capturing Jesus quietly, and killing him. 5"But not during the Passover celebration," they agreed, "for there would be a riot."

6Jesus now proceeded to Bethany, to the home of Simon the leper. 7While he was eating, a woman came in with a bottle of very expensive perfume, and poured it over his head.

8,9The disciples were indignant. "What a waste of good money," they said. "Why, she could have sold it for a fortune and given it to the poor."

10Jesus knew what they were thinking, and said, "Why are you criticizing her? For she has done a good thing to me. 11You will always have the poor among you, but you won't always have me. 12She has poured this perfume on me to prepare my body for burial. 13And she will always be remembered for this deed. The story of what she has done will be told throughout the whole world, wherever the Good News is preached."

PSALM 31:9–18

O Lord, have mercy on me in my anguish. My eyes are red from weeping; my health is broken from sorrow. I am pining away with grief; my years are shortened, drained away because of sadness. My sins have sapped my strength; I stoop with sorrow and with shame. ¹¹I am scorned by all my enemies and even more by my neighbors and friends. They dread meeting me and look the other way when I go by. ¹²I am forgotten like a dead man, like a broken and discarded pot. ¹³I heard the lies about me, the slanders of my enemies. Everywhere I looked I was afraid, for they were plotting against my life.

¹⁴,¹⁵But I am trusting you, O Lord. I said, "You alone are my God; my times are in your hands. Rescue me from those who hunt me down relentlessly. ¹⁶Let your favor shine again upon your servant; save me just because you are so kind! ¹⁷Don't disgrace me, Lord, by not replying when I call to you for aid. But let the wicked be shamed by what they trust in; let them lie silently in their graves, ¹⁸their lying lips quieted at last—the lips of these arrogant men who are accusing honest men of evil deeds."

PROVERBS FOR TODAY/ 8:12–13

Wisdom and good judgment live together, for wisdom knows where to discover knowledge and understanding. If anyone respects and fears God, he will hate evil. For wisdom hates pride, arrogance, corruption and deceit of every kind.

FEBRUARY 9

EXODUS 29:1—30:10

THIS is the ceremony for the dedication of Aaron and his sons as priests: get a young bull and two rams with no defects, ²and bread made without yeast, and thin sheets of sweetened bread mingled with oil, and unleavened wafers with oil poured over them. (The various kinds of bread shall be made with finely ground wheat flour.) ³,⁴Place the bread in a basket and bring it to the entrance of the Tabernacle, along with the young bull and the two rams.

"Bathe Aaron and his sons there at the entrance. ⁵Then put Aaron's robe on him, and the embroidered shirt, ephod, chestpiece, and sash, ⁶and place on his head the turban with the gold plate. ⁷Then take the anointing oil and pour it upon his head. ⁸Next, dress his sons in their robes, ⁹with their woven sashes, and place caps on their heads. They will then be priests forever; thus you shall consecrate Aaron and his sons.

¹⁰"Then bring the young bull to the Tabernacle, and Aaron and his sons shall lay their hands upon its head; ¹¹and you shall kill it before the Lord, at the entrance of the Tabernacle. ¹²Place its blood upon the horns of the altar, smearing it on with your finger, and pour the rest at the base of the altar. ¹³Then take all the fat that covers the inner parts, also the gall bladder and two kidneys, and the fat on them, and burn them upon the altar. ¹⁴Then take the body, including the skin and the dung, outside the camp and burn it as a sin offering.

¹⁵,¹⁶"Next, Aaron and his sons shall lay their hands upon the head of one of the rams as it is killed. Its blood shall also be collected and sprinkled upon the altar. ¹⁷Cut up the ram and wash off the entrails and the legs; place them with the head and the other pieces of the body, ¹⁸and burn it all upon the altar; it is a burnt offering to the Lord, and very pleasant to him.

¹⁹,²⁰"Now take the other ram, and

Aaron and his sons shall lay their hands upon its head as it is killed. Collect the blood and place some of it upon the tip of the right ear of Aaron and his sons, and upon their right thumbs and the big toes of their right feet; sprinkle the rest of the blood over the altar. 21Then scrape off some of the blood from the altar and mix it with some of the anointing oil and sprinkle it upon Aaron and his sons and upon their clothes; and they and their clothing shall be sanctified to the Lord.

22"Then take the fat of the ram, including the fat tail and the fat that covers the insides, also the gall bladder and the two kidneys and the fat surrounding them, and the right thigh—for this is the ram for ordination of Aaron and his sons— 23and one loaf of bread, one cake of shortening bread, and one wafer from the basket of unleavened bread that was placed before the Lord: 24Place these in the hands of Aaron and his sons, to wave them in a gesture of offering to the Lord. 25Afterwards, take them from their hands and burn them on the altar as a fragrant burnt offering to him. 26Then take the breast of Aaron's ordination ram and wave it before the Lord in a gesture of offering; afterwards, keep it for yourself.

27"Give the breast and thigh of the consecration ram 28to Aaron and his sons. The people of Israel must always contribute this portion of their sacrifices—whether peace offerings or thanksgiving offerings—as their contribution to the Lord.

29"These sacred garments of Aaron shall be preserved for the consecration of his son who succeeds him, from generation to generation, for his anointing ceremony. 30Whoever is the next High Priest after Aaron shall wear these clothes for seven days before beginning to minister in the Tabernacle and the Holy Place.

31"Take the ram of consecration—the ram used in the ordination ceremony—and boil its meat in a sacred area. 32Aaron and his sons shall eat the meat, also the bread in the basket, at the door of the Tabernacle. 33They alone shall eat those items used in their atonement (that is, in their consecration ceremony). The ordinary people shall not eat them, for these things are set apart and holy. 34If any of the meat or bread remains until the morning, burn it; it shall not be eaten, for it is holy.

35"This, then, is the way you shall ordain Aaron and his sons to their offices. This ordination shall go on for seven days. 36Every day you shall sacrifice a young bull as a sin offering for atonement; afterwards, purge the altar by making atonement for it; pour olive oil upon it to sanctify it. 37Make atonement for the altar and consecrate it to God every day for seven days. After this the altar shall be exceedingly holy, so that whatever touches it shall be set apart for God.

38"Each day offer two yearling lambs upon the altar, 39one in the morning and the other in the evening. 40With one of them offer three quarts of finely ground flour mixed with 2½ pints of oil, pressed from olives; also 2½ pints of wine, as an offering.

41Offer the other lamb in the evening, along with the flour and the wine as in the morning, for a fragrant offering to the Lord, an offering made to the Lord by fire.

42"This shall be a perpetual daily offering at the door of the Tabernacle before the Lord, where I will meet with you and speak with you. 43And I will meet with the people of Israel there, and the Tabernacle shall be sanctified by my glory. 44Yes, I will sanctify the Tabernacle and the altar and Aaron and his sons who are my ministers, the priests. 45And I will live among the people of Israel and be their God, 46and they shall know that I am the Lord their God. I brought them out of Egypt so that I could live among them. I am Jehovah their God.

"THEN make a small altar for burning incense. It shall be made from acacia wood. 2It is to be eighteen inches square and three feet high, with horns carved from the wood of the altar—they are not to be merely separate parts that are attached. 3Overlay the top, sides, and horns of the altar with pure gold, and run a gold molding around the entire altar. 4Beneath the molding, on each of two sides, construct two gold rings to hold the carrying poles. 5The poles are to be made of acacia wood overlaid with gold. 6Place the altar just outside the veil, near the place of mercy that is above the Ark containing the Ten Commandments. I will meet with you there.

7"Every morning when Aaron trims the lamps, he shall burn sweet spices on the altar, 8and each evening when he lights the lamps he shall burn the incense before the Lord, and this shall go on from generation to generation. 9Offer no unauthorized incense, burnt offerings, meal offerings, or wine offerings.

10"Once a year Aaron must sanctify the altar, placing upon its horns the blood of the sin offering for atonement. This shall be a regular, annual event from generation to generation, for this is the Lord's supremely holy altar."

MATTHEW 26:14–46

THEN Judas Iscariot, one of the twelve apostles, went to the chief priests, 15and asked, "How much will you pay me to get Jesus into your hands?" And they gave him thirty silver coins. 16From that time on, Judas watched for an opportunity to betray Jesus to them.

17On the first day of the Passover ceremonies, when bread made with yeast was purged from every Jewish home, the disciples came to Jesus and asked, "Where shall we plan to eat the Passover?"

18He replied, "Go into the city and see Mr. So-and-So, and tell him, 'Our Master says, my time has come, and I will eat the Passover meal with my disciples at your house.'" 19So the disciples did as he told them, and prepared the supper there.

20,21That evening as he sat eating with the Twelve, he said, "One of you will betray me."

22Sorrow chilled their hearts, and each one asked, "Am I the one?"

23He replied, "It is the one I served first. 24For I must die just as was prophesied, but woe to the man by whom I am betrayed. Far better for that one if he had never been born."

25Judas, too, had asked him, "Rabbi, am I the one?" And Jesus had told him, "Yes."

26As they were eating, Jesus took a small loaf of bread and blessed it and broke it apart and gave it to the disciples and said, "Take it and eat it, for this is my body."

27And he took a cup of wine and gave thanks for it and gave it to them and said, "Each one drink from it, 28for this is my blood, sealing the New Covenant. It is poured out to forgive the sins of multitudes. 29Mark my words—I will not drink this wine again until the day I drink it new with you in my Father's Kingdom."

30And when they had sung a hymn, they went out to the Mount of Olives.

31Then Jesus said to them, "Tonight you will all desert me. For it is written in the Scriptures that God will smite the Shepherd, and the sheep of the flock will be scattered. 32But after I have been brought back to life again I will go to Galilee, and meet you there."

33Peter declared, "If everyone else deserts you, I won't."

34Jesus told him, "The truth is that this very night, before the cock crows at dawn, you will deny me three times!"

35"I would die first!" Peter insisted. And all the other disciples said the same thing.

36Then Jesus brought them to a garden grove, Gethsemane, and told them to sit down and wait while he went on ahead to pray. 37He took Peter with him and Zebedee's two sons James and John, and began to be filled with anguish and despair.

38Then he told them, "My soul is crushed with horror and sadness to the point of death . . . stay here . . . stay awake with me."

39He went forward a little, and fell face downward on the ground, and prayed, "My Father! If it is possible, let this cup be taken away from me. But I want your will, not mine."

40Then he returned to the three disciples and found them asleep. "Peter," he called, "couldn't you even stay awake with me one hour? 41Keep alert and pray. Otherwise temptation will overpower you. For the spirit indeed is willing, but how weak the body is!"

42Again he left them and prayed, "My Father! If this cup cannot go away until I drink it all, your will be done."

43He returned to them again and found them sleeping, for their eyes were heavy, 44so he went back to prayer the third time, saying the same things again.

45Then he came to the disciples and said, "Sleep on now and take your rest . . . but no! The time has come! I am betrayed into the hands of evil men! 46Up! Let's be going! Look! Here comes the man who is betraying me!"

PSALM 31:19–24

OH, how great is your goodness to those who publicly declare that you will rescue them. For you have stored up great blessings for those who trust and reverence you.

20Hide your loved ones in the shelter of your presence, safe beneath your hand, safe from all conspiring men. 21Blessed is the Lord, for he has shown me that his never-failing love protects me like the walls of a fort! 22I spoke too hastily when I said, "The Lord has deserted me," for you listened to my plea and answered me.

23Oh, love the Lord, all of you who are his people; for the Lord protects those who are loyal to him, but harshly punishes all who haughtily reject him. 24So cheer up! Take courage if you are depending on the Lord.

PROVERBS FOR TODAY/ 8:14–26

"I, Wisdom, give good advice and common sense. Because of my strength, kings reign in power, and rulers make just laws. I love all who love me. Those who search for me shall surely find me. Unending riches, honor, justice and righteousness are mine to distribute. My gifts are better than the purest gold or sterling silver! My paths are those of justice and right. Those who love and follow me are indeed wealthy. I fill their treasuries. The Lord formed me in the beginning, before he created anything else. From ages past, I am. I existed before the earth began. I lived before the oceans were created, before the springs bubbled forth their waters onto the earth; before the mountains and the hills were made. Yes, I was born before God made the earth and fields, and the first handfuls of soil.

FEBRUARY 10

EXODUS 30:11—31:18

AND Jehovah said to Moses, "Whenever you take a census of the people of Israel, each man who is numbered shall give a ransom to the Lord for his soul, so that there will be no plague among the people when you number them. 13His payment shall be half a dollar. 14All who have reached their twentieth birthday shall give this offering. 15The rich shall not give more and the poor shall not give less, for it is an offering to the Lord to make atonement for yourselves. 16Use this money for the care of the Tabernacle; it is to bring you, the people of Israel, to the Lord's attention, and to make atonement for you."

17,18And the Lord said to Moses, "Make a bronze basin with a bronze pedestal. Put it between the Tabernacle and the altar, and fill it with water. 19Aaron and his sons shall wash their hands and feet there, 20when they go into the Tabernacle to appear before the Lord, or when they approach the altar to burn offerings to the Lord. They must always wash before doing so, or they will die. 21These are instructions to Aaron and his sons from generation to generation."

22,23Then the Lord told Moses to collect the choicest of spices—eighteen pounds of pure myrrh; half as much of cinnamon and of sweet cane; 24the same amount of cassia as of myrrh; and 1½ gallons of olive oil. 25The Lord instructed skilled perfumemakers to compound all this into a holy anointing oil.

26,27"Use this," he said, "to anoint the Tabernacle, the Ark, the table and all its instruments, the lampstand and all its utensils, the incense altar, 28the burnt offering altar with all its instruments, and the washbasin and its pedestal. 29Sanctify them, to make them holy; whatever touches them shall become holy. 30Use it to anoint Aaron and his sons, sanctifying them so that they can minister to me as priests. 31And say to the people of Israel, 'This shall always be my holy anointing oil. 32It must never be poured upon an ordinary person, and you shall never make any of it yourselves, for it is holy, and it shall be treated by you as holy. 33Anyone who compounds any incense like it or puts any of it upon someone who is not a priest shall be excommunicated.' "

34These were the Lord's directions to Moses concerning the incense: "Use sweet spices—stacte, onycha, galbanum, and pure frankincense, weighing out the same amounts of each, 35using the usual techniques of the incensemaker, and sea-soning it with salt; it shall be a pure and holy incense. 36Beat some of it very fine and put some of it in front of the Ark where I meet with you in the Tabernacle; this incense is most holy. 37Never make it for yourselves, for it is reserved for the Lord and you must treat it as holy. 38Anyone making it for himself shall be excommunicated."

THE Lord also said to Moses, "See, I have appointed Bezalel (son of Uri, and grandson of Hur, of the tribe of Judah), 3and have filled him with the Spirit of God, giving him great wisdom, ability, and skill in constructing the Tabernacle and everything it contains. 4He is highly capable as an artistic designer of objects made of gold, silver, and bronze. 5He is skilled, too, as a jeweler and in carving wood.

6"And I have appointed Oholiab (son of Ahisamach of the tribe of Dan) to be his assistant; moreover, I have given special skill to all who are known as experts, so that they can make all the things I have instructed you to make: 7the Tabernacle; the Ark with the place of mercy upon it; all the furnishings of the Tabernacle; 8the table and its instruments; the pure gold lampstand with its instruments; the altar of incense; 9the burnt offering altar with its instruments; the laver and its pedestal; 10the beautifully made, holy garments for Aaron the priest, and the garments for his sons, so that they can minister as priests; 11the anointing oil; and the sweet-spice incense for the Holy Place. They are to follow exactly the directions I gave you."

12,13The Lord then gave these further instructions to Moses: "Tell the people of Israel to rest on my Sabbath day, for the Sabbath is a reminder of the covenant between me and you forever; it helps you to remember that I am Jehovah who makes you holy. 14,15Yes, rest on the Sabbath, for it is holy. Anyone who does not obey this command must die; anyone who does any work on that day shall be killed. 16,17Work six days only, for the seventh day is a special day to remind you of my covenant—a weekly reminder forever of my promises to the people of Israel. For in six days the Lord made heaven and earth, and rested on the seventh day, and was refreshed."

18Then, as God finished speaking with Moses on Mount Sinai, he gave him the two tablets of stone on which the Ten Commandments were written with the finger of God.

MATTHEW 26:47–68

AT that very moment while he was still speaking, Judas, one of the Twelve, arrived with a great crowd armed with swords and clubs, sent by the Jewish leaders. 48Judas had told them to arrest the man he greeted, for that would be the one they were after. 49So now Judas came straight to Jesus and said, "Hello, Master!" and embraced him in friendly fashion.

50Jesus said, "My friend, go ahead and do what you have come for." Then the others grabbed him.

51One of the men with Jesus pulled out a sword and slashed off the ear of the High Priest's servant.

52"Put away your sword," Jesus told him. "Those using swords will get killed. 53Don't you realize that I could ask my Father for thousands of angels to protect us, and he would send them instantly? 54But if I did, how would the Scriptures be fulfilled that describe what is happening now?" 55Then Jesus spoke to the crowd. "Am I some dangerous criminal," he asked, "that you had to arm yourselves with swords and clubs before you could arrest me? I was with you teaching daily in the Temple and you didn't stop me then. 56But this is all happening to fulfill the words of the prophets as recorded in the Scriptures."

At that point, all the disciples deserted him and fled.

57Then the mob led him to the home of Caiaphas the High Priest, where all the Jewish leaders were gathering. 58Meanwhile, Peter was following far to the rear, and came to the courtyard of the High Priest's house and went in and sat with the soldiers, and waited to see what was going to be done to Jesus.

59The chief priests and, in fact, the entire Jewish Supreme Court assembled there and looked for witnesses who would lie about Jesus, in order to build a case against him that would result in a death sentence. 60,61But even though they found many who agreed to be false witnesses, these always contradicted each other.

Finally two men were found who declared, "This man said, 'I am able to destroy the Temple of God and rebuild it in three days.'"

62Then the High Priest stood up and said to Jesus, "Well, what about it? Did you say that, or didn't you?" 63But Jesus remained silent.

Then the High Priest said to him, "I demand in the name of the living God that you tell us whether you claim to be the Messiah, the Son of God."

64"Yes," Jesus said, "I am. And in the future you will see me, the Messiah, sitting at the right hand of God and returning on the clouds of heaven."

65,66Then the High Priest tore at his own clothing, shouting, "Blasphemy! What need have we for other witnesses? You have all heard him say it! What is your verdict?"

They shouted, "Death!—Death!—Death!"

67Then they spat in his face and struck him and some slapped him, 68saying, "Prophesy to us, you Messiah! Who struck you that time?"

PSALM 32:1–11

WHAT happiness for those whose guilt has been forgiven! What joys when sins are covered over! What relief for those who have confessed their sins and God has cleared their record.

3There was a time when I wouldn't admit what a sinner I was. But my dishonesty made me miserable and filled my days with frustration. 4All day and all night your hand was heavy on me. My strength evaporated like water on a sunny day ⁵until I finally admitted all my sins to you and stopped trying to hide them. I said to myself, "I will confess them to the Lord." And you forgave me! All my guilt is gone.

⁶Now I say that each believer should confess his sins to God when he is aware of them, while there is time to be forgiven. Judgment will not touch him if he does.

⁷You are my hiding place from every storm of life; you even keep me from getting into trouble! You surround me with songs of victory. ⁸I will instruct you (says the Lord) and guide you along the best pathway for your life; I will advise you and watch your progress. ⁹Don't be like a senseless horse or mule that has to have a bit in its mouth to keep it in line!

¹⁰Many sorrows come to the wicked, but abiding love surrounds those who trust in the Lord. ¹¹So rejoice in him, all those who are his, and shout for joy, all those who try to obey him.

PROVERBS FOR TODAY/ 8:27–32

"I was there when he established the heavens and formed the great springs in the depths of the oceans. I was there when he set the limits of the seas and gave them his instructions not to spread beyond their boundaries. I was there when he made the blueprint for the earth and oceans. I was the craftsman at his side. I was his constant delight, rejoicing always in his presence. And how happy I was with what he created—his wide world and all his family of mankind! And so, young men, listen to me, for how happy are all who follow my instructions.

FEBRUARY 11

EXODUS 32:1—33:23

WHEN Moses didn't come back down the mountain right away, the people went to Aaron. "Look," they said, "make us a god to lead us, for this fellow Moses who brought us here from Egypt has disappeared; something must have happened to him."

²,³"Give me your gold earrings," Aaron replied.

So they all did—men and women, boys and girls. ⁴Aaron melted the gold, then molded and tooled it into the form of a calf. The people exclaimed, "O Israel, this is the god that brought you out of Egypt!"

⁵When Aaron saw how happy the people were about it, he built an altar before the calf and announced, "Tomorrow there will be a feast to Jehovah!"

⁶So they were up early the next morning and began offering burnt offerings and peace offerings to the calf-idol; afterwards they sat down to feast and drink at a wild party, followed by sexual immorality.

⁷Then the Lord told Moses, "Quick! Go on down, for your people that you brought from Egypt have defiled themselves, ⁸and have quickly abandoned all my laws. They have molded themselves a calf, and worshiped it, and sacrificed to it, and said, 'This is your god, O Israel, that brought you out of Egypt.' "

⁹Then the Lord said, "I have seen what a stubborn, rebellious lot these people are. ¹⁰Now let me alone and my anger shall blaze out against them and destroy them all; and I will make you, Moses, into a great nation instead of them."

¹¹But Moses begged God not to do

it. "Lord," he pleaded, "why is your anger so hot against your own people whom you brought from the land of Egypt with such great power and mighty miracles? 12Do you want the Egyptians to say, 'God tricked them into coming to the mountains so that he could slay them, destroying them from off the face of the earth'? Turn back from your fierce wrath. Turn away from this terrible evil you are planning against your people! 13Remember your promise to your servants—to Abraham, Isaac, and Israel. For you swore by your own self, 'I will multiply your posterity as the stars of heaven, and I will give them all of this land I have promised to your descendants, and they shall inherit it forever.' "

14So the Lord changed his mind and spared them.

15Then Moses went down the mountain, holding in his hands the Ten Commandments written on both sides of two stone tablets. 16(God himself had written the commandments on the tablets.)

17When Joshua heard the noise below them, of all the people shouting, he exclaimed to Moses, "It sounds as if they are preparing for war!"

18But Moses replied, "No, it's not a cry of victory or defeat, but singing."

19When they came near the camp, Moses saw the calf and the dancing, and in terrible anger he threw the tablets to the ground and they lay broken at the foot of the mountain. 20He took the calf and melted it in the fire, and when the metal cooled, he ground it into powder and spread it upon the water and made the people drink it.

21Then he turned to Aaron. "What in the world did the people do to you," he demanded, "to make you bring such a terrible sin upon them?"

22"Don't get so upset," Aaron replied. "You know these people and what a wicked bunch they are. 23They said to me, 'Make us a god to lead us, for something has happened to this fellow Moses who led us out of Egypt.' 24Well, I told them, 'Bring me your gold earrings.' So they brought them to me and I threw them into the fire, and . . . well . . . this calf came out!"

25When Moses saw that the people had been committing adultery—at Aaron's encouragement, and much to the amusement of their enemies— 26he stood at the camp entrance and shouted, "All of you who are on the Lord's side, come over here and join me." And all the Levites came.

27He told them, "Jehovah the God of Israel says, 'Get your swords and go back and forth from one end of the camp to the other and kill even your brothers, friends, and neighbors.' " 28So they did, and about three thousand men died that day.

29Then Moses told the Levites, "Today you have ordained yourselves for the service of the Lord, for you obeyed him even though it meant killing your own sons and brothers; now he will give you a great blessing."

30The next day Moses said to the people, "You have sinned a great sin, but I will return to the Lord on the mountain—perhaps I will be able to obtain his forgiveness for you."

31So Moses returned to the Lord and said, "Oh, these people have sinned a great sin, and have made themselves gods of gold. 32Yet now if you will only forgive their sin—and if not, then blot *me* out of the book you have written."

33And the Lord replied to Moses, "Whoever has sinned against me will be blotted out of my book. 34And now go, lead the people to the place I told you about, and I assure you that my Angel shall travel on ahead of you; however, when I come to visit these people, I will punish them for their sins."

35And the Lord sent a great plague upon the people because they had worshiped Aaron's calf.

THE Lord said to Moses, "Lead these people you brought from Egypt to the land I promised Abraham, Isaac, and Jacob; for I said, 'I will give this land to your descendants.' 2I will send an Angel before you to drive out the Canaanites,

Amorites, Hittites, Perizzites, Hivites, and Jebusites. 3It is a land 'flowing with milk and honey'; but I will not travel among you, for you are a stubborn, unruly people, and I would be tempted to destroy you along the way."

4When the people heard these stern words, they went into mourning and stripped themselves of their jewelry and ornaments.

5For the Lord had told Moses to tell them, "You are an unruly, stubborn people. If I were there among you for even a moment, I would exterminate you. Remove your jewelry and ornaments until I decide what to do with you." 6So, after that, they wore no jewelry.

7Moses always erected the sacred tent (the "Tent for Meeting with God," he called it) far outside the camp, and everyone who wanted to consult with Jehovah went out there.

8Whenever Moses went to the Tabernacle, all the people, when they saw it, stood and would rise and stand in their tent doors. 9As he entered, the pillar of cloud would come down and stand at the door while the Lord spoke with Moses. 10Then all the people worshiped from their tent doors, bowing low to the pillar of cloud. 11Inside the tent the Lord spoke to Moses face to face, as a man speaks to his friend. Afterwards Moses would return to the camp, but the young man who assisted him, Joshua (son of Nun), stayed behind in the Tabernacle.

12Moses talked there with the Lord and said to him, "You have been telling me, 'Take these people to the Promised Land,' but you haven't told me whom you will send with me. You say you are my friend, and that I have found favor before you; 13please, if this is really so, guide me clearly along the way you want me to travel so that I will understand you and walk acceptably before you. For don't forget that this nation is your people."

14And the Lord replied, "I myself will go with you and give you success."

15For Moses had said, "If you aren't going with us, don't let us move a step from this place. 16If you don't go with us, who will ever know that I and my people have found favor with you, and that we are different from any other people upon the face of the earth?"

17And the Lord had replied to Moses, "Yes, I will do what you have asked, for you have certainly found favor with me, and you are my friend."

18Then Moses asked to see God's glory.

19The Lord replied, "I will make my goodness pass before you, and I will announce to you the meaning of my name Jehovah, the Lord. I show kindness and mercy to anyone I want to. 20But you may not see the glory of my face, for man may not see me and live. 21However, stand here on this rock beside me. 22And when my glory goes by, I will put you in the cleft of the rock and cover you with my hand until I have passed. 23Then I will remove my hand and you shall see my back, but not my face."

MATTHEW 26:69—27:14

MEANWHILE, as Peter was sitting in the courtyard a girl came over and said to him, "You were with Jesus, for both of you are from Galilee."

70But Peter denied it loudly. "I don't even know what you are talking about," he angrily declared.

71Later, out by the gate, another girl noticed him and said to those standing around, "This man was with Jesus—from Nazareth."

72Again Peter denied it, this time with an oath. "I don't even know the man," he said.

73But after a while the men who had been standing there came over to him and said, "We know you are one of his disciples, for we can tell by your Galilean accent."

74Peter began to curse and swear. "I don't even know the man," he said.

And immediately the cock crowed. 75Then Peter remembered what Jesus had said, "Before the cock crows, you will deny me three times." And he went away, crying bitterly.

WHEN it was morning, the chief priests and Jewish leaders met again to discuss how to induce the Roman government to sentence Jesus to death. 2Then they sent him in chains to Pilate, the Roman governor.

3About that time Judas, who betrayed him, when he saw that Jesus had been condemned to die, changed his mind and deeply regretted what he had done, and brought back the money to the chief priests and other Jewish leaders.

4"I have sinned," he declared, "for I have betrayed an innocent man."

"That's your problem," they retorted. 5Then he threw the money onto the floor of the Temple and went out and hanged himself. 6The chief priests picked the money up. "We can't put it in the collection," they said, "since it's against our laws to accept money paid for murder."

7They talked it over and finally decided to buy a certain field where the clay was used by potters, and to make it into a cemetery for foreigners who died in Jerusalem. 8That is why the cemetery is still called "The Field of Blood."

9This fulfilled the prophecy of Jeremiah which says,

"They took the thirty pieces of silver—the price at which he was valued by the people of Israel— 10and purchased a field from the potters as the Lord directed me."

11Now Jesus was standing before Pilate, the Roman governor. "Are you the Jews' Messiah?" the governor asked him. "Yes," Jesus replied.

12But when the chief priests and other Jewish leaders made their many accusations against him, Jesus remained silent. 13"Don't you hear what they are saying?" Pilate demanded.

14But Jesus said nothing, much to the governor's surprise.

PSALM 33:1–11

LET all the joys of the godly well up in praise to the Lord, for it is right to praise him. 2Play joyous melodies of praise upon the lyre and on the harp. 3Compose new songs of praise to him, accompanied skillfully on the harp; sing joyfully.

4For all God's words are right, and everything he does is worthy of our trust. 5He loves whatever is just and good; the earth is filled with his tender love. 6He merely spoke, and the heavens were formed, and all the galaxies of stars. 7He made the oceans, pouring them into his vast reservoirs.

8Let everyone in all the world—men, women and children—fear the Lord and stand in awe of him. 9For when he but spoke, the world began! It appeared at his command! 10And with a breath he can scatter the plans of all the nations who oppose him, 11but his own plan stands forever. His intentions are the same for every generation.

PROVERBS FOR TODAY/ 8:33–36

"Listen to my counsel—oh, don't refuse it—and be wise. Happy is the man who is so anxious to be with me that he watches for me daily at my gates, or waits for me outside my home! For whoever finds me finds life and wins approval from the Lord. But the one who misses me has injured himself irreparably. Those who refuse me show that they love death."

FEBRUARY 12

EXODUS 34:1—35:9

THE Lord told Moses, "Prepare two stone tablets like the first ones and I will write upon them the same commands that were on the tablets you broke. 2Be ready in the morning to come up into Mount Sinai and present yourself to me on the top of the mountain. 3No one shall come with you and no one must be anywhere on the mountain. Do not let the flocks or herds feed close to the mountain."

4So Moses took two tablets of stone like the first ones, and was up early and climbed Mount Sinai, as the Lord had told him to, taking the two stone tablets in his hands.

5,6Then the Lord descended in the form of a pillar of cloud and stood there with him, and passed in front of him and announced the meaning of his name. "I am Jehovah, the merciful and gracious God," he said, "slow to anger and rich in steadfast love and truth. 7I, Jehovah, show this steadfast love to many thousands by forgiving their sins; or else I refuse to clear the guilty, and require that a father's sins be punished in the sons and grandsons, and even later generations."

8Moses fell down before the Lord and worshiped. 9And he said, "If it is true that I have found favor in your sight, O Lord, then please go with us to the Promised Land; yes, it is an unruly, stubborn people, but pardon our iniquity and our sins, and accept us as your own."

10The Lord replied, "All right, this is the contract I am going to make with you. I will do miracles such as have never been done before anywhere in all the earth, and all the people of Israel shall see the power of the Lord—the terrible power I will display through you. 11Your part of the agreement is to obey all of my commandments; then I will drive out from before you the Amorites, Canaanites, Hittites, Perizzites, Hivites, and Jebusites.

12"Be very, very careful never to compromise with the people there in the land where you are going, for if you do, you will soon be following their evil ways. 13Instead, you must break down their heathen altars, smash the obelisks they worship, and cut down their shameful idols. 14For you must worship no other gods, but only Jehovah, for he is a God who claims absolute loyalty and exclusive devotion.

15"No, do not make a peace treaty of any kind with the people living in the land, for they are spiritual prostitutes, committing adultery against me by sacrificing to their gods. If you become friendly with them and one of them invites you to go with him and worship his idol, you are apt to do it. 16And you would accept their daughters, who worship other gods, as wives for your sons—and then your sons would commit adultery against me by worshiping their wives' gods. 17You must have nothing to do with idols.

18"Be sure to celebrate the Feast of Unleavened Bread for seven days, just as I instructed you, at the dates appointed each year in March; that was the month you left Egypt.

19"Every firstborn male is mine—cattle, sheep, and goats. 20The firstborn colt of a donkey may be redeemed by giving a lamb in its place. If you decide not to redeem it, then its neck must be broken. But your sons must all be redeemed. And no one shall appear before me without a gift.

21"Even during plowing and harvest times, work only six days, and rest on the seventh.

22"And you must remember to celebrate these three annual religious festivals: the Festival of Weeks, the Festival of the First Wheat, and the Harvest Festival. 23On each of these three occasions all the men and boys of Israel shall appear before the Lord. 24No one will attack and conquer your land when you go up to appear before the Lord your God those three times each year. For I will drive out the nations from before you and enlarge your boundaries.

25"You must not use leavened bread with your sacrifices to me, and none of the meat of the Passover lamb may be kept over until the following morning. 26And you must bring the best of the first of each year's crop to the Tabernacle of the Lord your God. You must not cook a young goat in its mother's milk."

27And the Lord said to Moses, "Write down these laws that I have given you, for they represent the terms of my covenant with you and with Israel."

28Moses was up on the mountain with the Lord for forty days and forty nights, and in all that time he neither ate nor drank. At that time God wrote out the Covenant—the Ten Commandments—on the stone tablets.

29Moses didn't realize as he came back down the mountain with the tablets that his face glowed from being in the presence of God. 30Because of this radiance upon his face, Aaron and the people of Israel were afraid to come near him. 31But Moses called them over to him, and Aaron and the leaders of the congregation came and talked with him. 32Afterwards, all the people came to him, and he gave them the commandments the Lord had given him upon the mountain. 33When Moses had finished speaking with them, he put a veil over his face; 34but whenever he went into the Tabernacle to speak with the Lord, he removed the veil until he came out again; then he would pass on to the people whatever instructions God had given him, 35and the people would see his face aglow. Afterwards he would put the veil on again until he returned to speak with God.

NOW Moses called a meeting of all the people and told them, "These are the laws of Jehovah you must obey.

2"Work six days only; the seventh day is a day of solemn rest, a holy day to be used to worship Jehovah; anyone working on that day must die. 3Don't even light the fires in your homes that day."

4Then Moses said to all the people, "This is what the Lord has commanded: 5-9All of you who wish to, all those with generous hearts, may bring these offerings to Jehovah:

Gold, silver, and bronze;

Blue, purple, and scarlet cloth, made of fine-twined linen or of goat's hair;

Tanned rams' skins and specially treated goatskins;

Acacia wood;

Olive oil for the lamps;

Spices for the anointing oil and for the incense;

Onyx stones and stones to be used for the ephod and chestpiece.

MATTHEW 27:15–34

NOW the governor's custom was to release one Jewish prisoner each year during the Passover celebration—anyone they wanted. 16This year there was a particularly notorious criminal in jail named Barabbas, 17and as the crowds gathered before Pilate's house that morning he asked them, "Which shall I release to you—Barabbas, or Jesus your Messiah?" 18For he knew very well that the Jewish leaders had arrested Jesus out of envy because of his popularity with the people.

19Just then, as he was presiding over the court, Pilate's wife sent him this message: "Leave that good man alone; for I had a terrible nightmare concerning him last night."

20Meanwhile the chief priests and Jewish officials persuaded the crowds to ask for Barabbas' release, and for Jesus' death. 21So when the governor asked again, "Which of these two shall I release to you?" the crowd shouted back their reply: "Barabbas!"

22"Then what shall I do with Jesus, your Messiah?" Pilate asked.

And they shouted, "Crucify him!" 23"Why?" Pilate demanded. "What has he done wrong?" But they kept shouting, "Crucify! Crucify!"

24When Pilate saw that he wasn't getting anywhere, and that a riot was developing, he sent for a bowl of water and washed his hands before the crowd, saying, "I am innocent of the blood of this good man. The responsibility is yours!"

25And the mob yelled back, "His blood be on us and on our children!"

26Then Pilate released Barabbas to them. And after he had whipped Jesus, he gave him to the Roman soldiers to take away and crucify.

27But first they took him into the armory and called out the entire contingent. 28They stripped him and put a scarlet robe on him, 29and made a crown from long thorns and put it on his head, and placed a stick in his right hand as a scepter and knelt before him in mockery. "Hail, King of the Jews," they yelled. 30And they spat on him and grabbed the stick and beat him on the head with it.

31After the mockery, they took off the robe and put his own garment on him again, and took him out to crucify him.

32As they were on the way to the execution grounds they came across a man from Cyrene, in Africa—Simon was his name—and forced him to carry Jesus' cross. 33Then they went out to an area known as Golgotha, that is, "Skull Hill," 34where the soldiers gave him drugged wine to drink; but when he had tasted it, he refused.

PSALM 33:12–22

BLESSED is the nation whose God is the Lord, whose people he has chosen as his own. 13,14,15The Lord gazes down upon mankind from heaven where he lives. He has made their hearts and closely watches everything they do.

16,17The best-equipped army cannot save a king—for great strength is not enough to save anyone. A war horse is a poor risk for winning victories—it is strong but it cannot save.

18,19But the eyes of the Lord are watching over those who fear him, who rely upon his steady love. He will keep them from death even in times of famine! 20We depend upon the Lord alone to save us. Only he can help us; he protects us like a shield. 21No wonder we are happy in the Lord! For we are trusting him. We trust his holy name. 22Yes, Lord, let your constant love surround us, for our hopes are in you alone.

PROVERBS FOR TODAY/ 9:1–6

Wisdom has built a palace supported on seven pillars, and has prepared a great banquet, and mixed the wines, and sent out her maidens inviting all to come. She calls from the busiest intersections in the city, "Come, you simple ones without good judgment; come to wisdom's banquet and drink the wines that I have mixed. Leave behind your foolishness and begin to live; learn how to be wise."

FEBRUARY 13

EXODUS 35:10—36:38

COME, all of you who are skilled craftsmen having special talents, and construct what God has commanded us:

The Tabernacle tent, and its coverings, clasps, frames, bars, pillars, and bases;
The Ark and its poles;
The place of mercy;

The curtain to enclose the Holy Place;
The table, its carrying poles, and all of its utensils;
The Bread of the Presence;
Lamp holders, with lamps and oil;
The incense altar and its carrying poles;
The anointing oil and sweet incense;
The curtain for the door of the Tabernacle;
The altar for the burnt offerings;
The bronze grating of the altar, and its carrying poles and utensils;
The basin with its pedestal;
The drapes for the walls of the court;
The pillars and their bases;
Drapes for the entrance to the court;
The posts of the Tabernacle court, and their cords;
The beautiful clothing for the priests, to be used when ministering in the Holy Place;
The holy garments for Aaron the priest, and for his sons."

20So all the people went to their tents to prepare their gifts. 21Those whose hearts were stirred by God's Spirit returned with their offerings of materials for the Tabernacle, its equipment, and for the holy garments. 22Both men and women came, all who were willinghearted. They brought to the Lord their offerings of gold, jewelry—earrings, rings from their fingers, necklaces—and gold objects of every kind. 23Others brought blue, purple, and scarlet cloth made from the fine-twined linen or goat's hair; and ram skins dyed red, and specially treated goatskins. 24Others brought silver and bronze as their offering to the Lord; and some brought the acacia wood needed in the construction.

25The women skilled in sewing and spinning prepared blue, purple, and scarlet thread and cloth, and fine-twined linen, and brought them in. 26Some other women gladly used their special skill to spin the goat's hair into cloth. 27The leaders brought onyx stones to be used for the ephod and the chestpiece; 28and spices, and oil—for the light, and for compounding the anointing oil and the sweet incense. 29So the people of Israel—every man and woman who wanted to assist in the work given to them by the Lord's command to Moses—brought their freewill offerings to him.

30,31And Moses told them, "Jehovah has specifically appointed Bezalel (the son of Uri and grandson of Hur of the tribe of Judah) as general superintendent of the project. 32He will be able to create beautiful workmanship from gold, silver, and bronze; 33he can cut and set stones like a jeweler, and can do beautiful carving; in fact, he has every needed skill. 34And God has made him and Oholiab gifted teachers of their skills to others. (Oholiab is the son of Ahisamach, of the tribe of Dan.) 35God has filled them both with unusual skills as jewelers, carpenters, embroidery designers in blue, purple, and scarlet on linen backgrounds, and as weavers—they excel in all the crafts we will be needing in the work.

"ALL the other craftsmen with God-given abilities are to assist Bezalel and Oholiab in constructing and furnishing the Tabernacle." So Moses told Bezalel and Oholiab and all others who felt called to the work to begin. 3Moses gave them the materials donated by the people and additional gifts were received each morning.

4-7But finally the workmen all left their task to meet with Moses and told him, "We have more than enough materials on hand now to complete the job!" So Moses sent a message throughout the camp announcing that no more donations were needed. Then at last the people were restrained from bringing more!

8,9The skilled weavers first made ten sheets from fine linen, then embroidered into them blue, purple, and scarlet Guardian Angels. Each sheet was forty-two feet long and six feet wide. 10Five of these sheets were attached end to end, then five others similarly attached, forming two long roofsheets. 11,12Fifty blue ribbons were looped along the edges of these two long sheets, each loop being opposite its mate on the other long sheet. 13Then fifty clasps of gold were made to connect the loops, thus tying the two long sheets together to form the ceiling of the Tabernacle.

14,15Above the ceiling was a second layer formed by eleven draperies made of goat's hair (uniformly forty-five feet long and six feet wide). 16Bezalel coupled five of these draperies together to make one long piece, and six others to make another long piece. 17Then he made fifty loops along the end of each, 18and fifty small bronze clasps to couple the loops so that the draperies were firmly attached to each other.

19The top layer of the roof was made of rams' skins, dyed red, and tanned goat skins.

20For the sides of the Tabernacle he used frames of acacia wood standing on end. 21The height of each frame was fifteen feet and the width 2¼ feet. 22Each frame had two clasps joining it to the next. 23There were twenty frames on the south side, 24with the bottoms fitting into forty silver bases. Each frame was connected to its base by two clasps. 25,26There were also twenty frames on the north side of the Tabernacle, with forty silver bases, two for each frame. 27The west side of the Tabernacle, which was its rear, was made from six frames, 28plus another at each corner. 29These frames, including those at the corners, were linked to each other at both top and bottom by rings. 30So, on the west side, there were a total of eight frames with sixteen silver bases beneath them, two for each frame.

31,32Then he made five sets of bars from acacia wood to tie the frames together along the sides, five for each side of the Tabernacle. 33The middle bar of the five was halfway up the frames, along each side, running from one end to the other. 34The frames and bars were all overlaid with gold, and the rings were pure gold.

35The blue, purple, and scarlet inner curtain was made from woven linen, with Guardian Angels skillfully embroidered into it. 36The curtain was then attached to four gold hooks set into four posts of acacia wood, overlaid with gold and set into four silver bases.

37Then he made a drapery for the entrance to the Tabernacle; it was woven from finespun linen, embroidered with blue, purple, and scarlet. 38This drapery was connected by five hooks to five posts. The posts and their capitals and rods were overlaid with gold; their five bases were molded from bronze.

MATTHEW 27:35–66

AFTER the crucifixion, the soldiers threw dice to divide up his clothes among themselves. 36Then they sat around and watched him as he hung there. 37And they put a sign above his head, "This is Jesus, the King of the Jews."

38Two robbers were also crucified there that morning, one on either side of him. 39And the people passing by hurled abuse, shaking their heads at him and saying, 40"So! You can destroy the Temple and build it again in three days, can you? Well, then, come on down from the cross if you are the Son of God!"

41,42,43And the chief priests and Jewish leaders also mocked him. "He saved others," they scoffed, "but he can't save himself! So you are the King of Israel, are you? Come down from the cross and we'll believe you! He trusted God—let God show his approval by delivering him! Didn't he say, 'I am God's Son'?"

44And the robbers also threw the same in his teeth.

45That afternoon, the whole earth was covered with darkness for three hours, from noon until three o'clock.

46About three o'clock, Jesus shouted, "Eli, Eli, lama sabachthani?" which means, "My God, my God, why have you forsaken me?"

47Some of the bystanders misunderstood and thought he was calling for Elijah. 48One of them ran and filled a sponge with sour wine and put it on a stick and held it up to him to drink. 49But the rest said, "Leave him alone. Let's see whether Elijah will come and save him."

50Then Jesus shouted out again, dismissed his spirit, and died.

51And look! The curtain secluding the Holiest Place in the Temple was split apart from top to bottom; and the earth shook, and rocks broke, 52and tombs opened, and many godly men and women who had died came back to life again. 53After Jesus' resurrection, they left the cemetery and went into Jerusalem, and appeared to many people there.

54The soldiers at the crucifixion and their sergeant were terribly frightened by the earthquake and all that happened. They exclaimed, "Surely this was God's Son."

55And many women who had come down from Galilee with Jesus to care for him were watching from a distance. 56Among them were Mary Magdalene and Mary the mother of James and Joseph, and the mother of James and John (the sons of Zebedee).

57When evening came, a rich man from Arimathea named Joseph, one of Jesus' followers, 58went to Pilate and asked for Jesus' body. And Pilate issued an order to release it to him. 59Joseph took the body and wrapped it in a clean linen cloth, 60and placed it in his own new rock-hewn tomb, and rolled a great stone across the entrance as he left. 61Both Mary Magdalene and the other Mary were sitting nearby watching.

62The next day—at the close of the first day of the Passover ceremonies—the chief priests and Pharisees went to Pilate, 63and told him, "Sir, that liar once said, 'After three days I will come back to life again.' 64So we request an order from you sealing the tomb until the third day, to prevent his disciples from coming and stealing his body and then telling everyone he came back to life! If that happens we'll be worse off than we were at first."

65"Use your own Temple police," Pilate told them. "They can guard it safely enough."

66So they sealed the stone and posted guards to protect it from intrusion.

PSALM 34:1–10

I will praise the Lord no matter what happens. I will constantly speak of his glories and grace. 2I will boast of all his kindness to me. Let all who are discouraged take heart. 3Let us praise the Lord together, and exalt his name.

4For I cried to him and he answered me! He freed me from all my fears. 5Others too were radiant at what he did for them. Theirs was no downcast look of rejection! 6This poor man cried to the Lord—and the Lord heard him and saved him out of his troubles. 7For the Angel of the Lord guards and rescues all who reverence him.

8Oh, put God to the test and see how kind he is! See for yourself the way his mercies shower down on all who trust in him. 9If you belong to the Lord, reverence him; for everyone who does this has everything he needs. 10Even strong young lions sometimes go hungry, but those of us who reverence the Lord will never lack any good thing.

PROVERBS FOR TODAY/ 9:7–8

If you rebuke a mocker, you will only get a smart retort; yes, he will snarl at you. So don't bother with him; he will only hate you for trying to help him. But a wise man, when rebuked, will love you all the more.

FEBRUARY 14

EXODUS 37:1—38:31

NEXT Bezalel made the Ark. This was constructed of acacia wood and was 3¾ feet long, 2¼ feet wide, and 2¼ feet high. ²It was plated with pure gold inside and out, and had a molding of gold all the way around the sides. ³There were four gold rings fastened into its four feet, two rings at each end. ⁴Then he made poles from acacia wood, and overlaid them with gold, ⁵and put the poles into the rings at the sides of the Ark, to carry it.

⁶Then, from pure gold, he made a lid called "the place of mercy"; it was 3¾ feet long and 2¼ feet wide. ⁷He made two statues of Guardian Angels of beaten gold, and placed them at the two ends of the gold lid. ⁸They were molded so that they were actually a part of the gold lid—it was all one piece. ⁹The Guardian Angels faced each other, with outstretched wings that overshadowed the place of mercy, looking down upon it.

¹⁰Then he made a table, using acacia wood, three feet long, 1½ feet wide and 2¼ feet high. ¹¹It was overlaid with pure gold, with a gold molding all around the edge. ¹²A rim four inches high was constructed around the edges of the table, with a gold molding along the rim. ¹³Then he cast four rings of gold and placed them into the four table legs, ¹⁴close to the molding, to hold the carrying poles in place. ¹⁵He made the carrying poles of acacia wood covered with gold. ¹⁶Next, using pure gold, he made the bowls, flagons, dishes, and spoons to be placed upon this table.

¹⁷Then he made the lampstand, again using pure, beaten gold. Its base, shaft, lamp-holders, and decorations of almond flowers were all of one piece. ¹⁸The lampstand had six branches, three from each side. ¹⁹Each of the branches was decorated with identical carvings of blossoms. ²⁰,²¹The main stem of the lampstand was similarly decorated with almond blossoms, a flower on the stem beneath each pair of branches; also a flower below the bottom pair and above the top pair, four in all. ²²The decorations and branches were all one piece of pure, beaten gold. ²³,²⁴Then he made the seven lamps at the ends of the branches, the snuffers, and the ashtrays, all of pure gold. The entire lampstand weighed 107 pounds, all pure gold.

²⁵The incense altar was made of acacia wood. It was eighteen inches square and three feet high, with its corner-horns made as part of the altar so that it was all one piece. ²⁶He overlaid it all with pure gold and ran a gold molding around the edge. ²⁷Two gold rings were placed on each side, beneath this molding, to hold the carrying poles. ²⁸The carrying poles were gold-plated acacia wood. ²⁹Then, from sweet spices, he made the sacred oil for anointing the priests, and the pure incense, using the techniques of the most skilled perfumers.

THE burnt-offering altar was also constructed of acacia wood; it was 7½ feet square at the top, and 4½ feet high. ²There were four horns at the four corners, all of one piece with the rest. This altar was overlaid with bronze. ³Then he made bronze utensils to be used with the altar—the pots, shovels, basins, meat hooks, and fire pans. ⁴Next he made a bronze grating that rested upon a ledge about halfway up [in the fire box]. ⁵Four rings were cast for each side of the grating, to insert the carrying poles. ⁶The carrying poles themselves were made of acacia wood, overlaid with bronze. ⁷The carrying poles were inserted into the rings at the side of the altar. The altar was hollow, with plank siding.

⁸The bronze washbasin and its bronze pedestal were cast from the solid bronze

mirrors donated by the women who assembled at the entrance to the Tabernacle.

9Then he constructed the courtyard. The south wall was 150 feet long; it consisted of drapes woven from fine-twined linen thread. 10There were twenty posts to hold drapes, with bases of bronze and with silver hooks and rods. 11The north wall was also 150 feet long, with twenty bronze posts and bases and with silver hooks and rods. 12The west side was seventy-five feet wide; the walls were made from drapes supported by ten posts and bases, and with silver hooks and rods. 13The east side was also seventy-five feet wide.

14,15The drapes at either side of the entrance were 22½ feet wide, each with three posts and three bases. 16All the drapes making up the walls of the court were woven of fine-twined linen. 17Each post had a bronze base, and all the hooks and rods were silver; the tops of the posts were overlaid with silver, and the rods to hold up the drapes were solid silver.

18The drapery covering the entrance to the court was made of fine-twined linen, beautifully embroidered with blue, purple, and scarlet thread.

It was thirty feet long and 7½ feet wide, just the same as the drapes composing the walls of the court. 19It was supported by four posts, with four bronze bases, and with silver hooks and rods; the tops of the posts were also silver.

20All the nails used in constructing the Tabernacle and court were bronze.

21This summarizes the various steps in building the Tabernacle to house the Ark, so that the Levites could carry on their ministry. All was done in the order designated by Moses and was supervised by Ithamar, son of Aaron the priest. 22Bezalel (son of Uri and grandson of Hur, of the tribe of Judah) was the master craftsman, 23assisted by Oholiab (son of Ahisamach of the tribe of Dan); he too was a skilled craftsman and also an expert at engraving, weaving, and at embroidering blue, purple, and scarlet threads into fine linen cloth.

24The people brought gifts of 3,140 pounds of gold, all of which was used throughout the Tabernacle.

25,26The amount of silver used was 9,575 pounds, which came from the fifty-cent head tax collected from all those registered in the census who were twenty years old or older, a total of 603,550 men. 27The bases for the frames of the sanctuary walls and for the posts supporting the veil required 9,500 pounds of silver, ninety-five pounds for each socket. 28The silver left over was used for the posts and to overlay their tops, and for the rods and hooks.

29,30,31The people brought 7,540 pounds of bronze, which was used for casting the bases for the posts at the entrance to the Tabernacle, and for the bronze altar, the bronze grating, the altar utensils, the bases for the posts supporting the drapes enclosing the court, and for all the nails used in the construction of the Tabernacle and the court.

MATTHEW 28:1–20

EARLY on Sunday morning, as the new day was dawning, Mary Magdalene and the other Mary went out to the tomb.

2Suddenly there was a great earthquake; for an angel of the Lord came down from heaven and rolled aside the stone and sat on it. 3His face shone like lightning and his clothing was a brilliant white. 4The guards shook with fear when they saw him, and fell into a dead faint.

5Then the angel spoke to the women. "Don't be frightened!" he said. "I know you are looking for Jesus, who was crucified, 6but he isn't here! For he has come back to life again, just as he said he would. Come in and see where his body was lying. . . . 7And now, go quickly and tell his disciples that he has risen from the dead, and that he is going to Galilee to meet them there. That is my message to them."

8The women ran from the tomb, badly frightened, but also filled with joy, and rushed to find the disciples to give them the angel's message. 9And as they were running, suddenly Jesus was there in front of them!

"Good morning!" he said. And they fell to the ground before him, holding his feet and worshiping him.

10Then Jesus said to them, "Don't be frightened! Go tell my brothers to leave at once for Galilee, to meet me there."

11As the women were on the way into the city, some of the Temple police who had been guarding the tomb went to the chief priests and told them what had happened. 12,13A meeting of all the Jewish leaders was called, and it was decided to bribe the police to say they had all been asleep when Jesus' disciples came during the night and stole his body.

14"If the governor hears about it," the Council promised, "we'll stand up for you and everything will be all right."

15So the police accepted the bribe and said what they were told to. Their story spread widely among the Jews, and is still believed by them to this very day.

16Then the eleven disciples left for Galilee, going to the mountain where Jesus had said they would find him. 17There they met him and worshiped him—but some of them weren't sure it really was Jesus!

18He told his disciples, "I have been given all authority in heaven and earth. 19Therefore go and make disciples in all the nations, baptizing them into the name of the Father and of the Son and of the Holy Spirit, 20and then teach these new disciples to obey all the commands I have given you; and be sure of this—that I am with you always, even to the end of the world."

PSALM 34:11–22

SONS and daughters, come and listen and let me teach you the importance of trusting and fearing the Lord. 12Do you want a long, good life? 13Then watch your tongue! Keep your lips from lying. 14Turn from all known sin and spend your time in doing good. Try to live in peace with everyone; work hard at it.

15For the eyes of the Lord are intently watching all who live good lives, and he gives attention when they cry to him. 16But the Lord has made up his mind to wipe out even the memory of evil men from the earth. 17Yes, the Lord hears the good man when he calls to him for help, and saves him out of all his troubles.

18The Lord is close to those whose hearts are breaking; he rescues those who are humbly sorry for their sins. 19The good man does not escape all troubles—he has them too. But the Lord helps him in each and every one. 20Not one of his bones is broken.

21Calamity will surely overtake the wicked; heavy penalties are meted out to those who hate the good. 22But as for those who serve the Lord, he will redeem them; everyone who takes refuge in him will be freely pardoned.

PROVERBS FOR TODAY/ 9:9–10

Teach a wise man, and he will be the wiser; teach a good man, and he will learn more. For the reverence and fear of God are basic to all wisdom. Knowing God results in every other kind of understanding.

FEBRUARY 15

EXODUS 39:1—40:38

THEN, for the priests, the people made beautiful garments of blue, purple, and scarlet cloth—garments to be used while ministering in the Holy Place. This same cloth was used for Aaron's sacred garments, in accordance with the Lord's instructions to Moses. 2The ephod was made from this cloth too, woven from fine-twined linen thread. 3Bezalel beat gold into thin plates and cut it into wire threads, to work into the blue, purple, and scarlet linen; it was a skillful and beautiful piece of workmanship when finished.

4,5The ephod was held together by shoulder straps at the top, and was tied down by an elaborate one-piece woven sash made of the same gold, blue, purple, and scarlet cloth cut from fine-twined linen thread, just as God had directed Moses. 6,7The [two] onyx stones, attached to the [two] shoulder straps of the ephod, were set in gold, and the stones were engraved with the names of the tribes of Israel, just as initials are engraved upon a ring. These stones were reminders to Jehovah concerning the people of Israel; all this was done in accordance with the Lord's instructions to Moses.

8The chestpiece was a beautiful piece of work, just like the ephod, made from the finest gold, blue, purple, and scarlet linen. 9It was a piece nine inches square, doubled over to form a pouch; 10there were four rows of stones across it. In the first row were a sardius, a topaz, and a carbuncle; 11in the second row were an emerald, a sapphire, and a diamond. 12In the third row were a jacinth, an agate, and an amethyst. 13In the fourth row, a beryl, an onyx, and a jasper—all set in gold filigree. 14The stones were engraved like a seal, with the names of the twelve tribes of Israel.

15-18[To attach the chestpiece to the ephod], a gold ring was placed at the top of each shoulder strap of the ephod, and from these gold rings, two strands of twined gold attached to gold clasps on the top corners of the chestpiece. 19Two gold rings were also set at the lower edge of the chestpiece, on the under side, next to the ephod. 20Two other gold rings were placed low on the shoulder straps of the ephod, close to where the ephod joined its beautifully woven sash. 21The chestpiece was held securely above the beautifully woven sash of the ephod by tying the rings of the chestpiece to the rings of the ephod, with a blue ribbon.

All this was commanded to Moses by the Lord.

22The main part of the ephod was woven, all of blue, 23and there was a hole at the center just as in a coat of mail, for the head to go through, reinforced around the edge so that it would not tear. 24Pomegranates were attached to the bottom edge of the robe; these were made of linen cloth, embroidered with blue, purple, and scarlet. 25,26Bells of pure gold were placed between the pomegranates along the bottom edge of the skirt, with bells and pomegranates alternating all around the edge. This robe was worn when Aaron ministered to the Lord, just as the Lord had commanded Moses.

27Robes were now made for Aaron and his sons from fine-twined linen thread. 28,29The chestpiece, the beautiful turbans, and the caps and the underclothes were all made of this linen, and the linen belt was beautifully embroidered with blue, purple, and scarlet threads, just as Jehovah had commanded Moses. 30Finally they made the holy plate of pure gold to wear on the front of the turban, engraved with the words, "Consecrated to Jehovah." 31It was tied to the turban with a blue cord, just as the Lord had instructed.

32And so at last the Tabernacle was

finished, following all of the Lord's instructions to Moses.

33-40Then they brought the entire Tabernacle to Moses:

Furniture; clasps; frames; bars;

Posts; bases; layers of covering for the roof and sides—the rams' skins dyed red, the specially tanned goat skins, and the entrance drape; the Ark with the Ten Commandments in it;

The carrying poles;

The place of mercy;

The table and all its utensils;

The Bread of the Presence;

The pure [gold] lampstand with its lamps, utensils, and oil;

The gold altar;

The anointing oil;

The sweet incense;

The curtain-door of the Tabernacle;

The bronze altar;

The bronze grating;

The poles and the utensils;

The washbasin and its base;

The drapes for the walls of the court and the posts holding them up;

The bases and the drapes at the gate of the court;

The cords and nails;

All the utensils used there in the work of the Tabernacle.

41They also brought for his inspection the beautifully tailored garments to be worn while ministering in the Holy Place, and the holy garments for Aaron the priest and those for his sons, to be worn when on duty.

42So the people of Israel followed all the Lord's instructions to Moses. 43And Moses inspected all their work and blessed them because it was all as the Lord had instructed him.

THE Lord now said to Moses, 2"Put together the Tabernacle on the first day of the first month. 3In it, place the Ark containing the Ten Commandments; and install the veil to enclose the Ark within the Holy of Holies. 4Then bring in the table and place the utensils on it, and bring in the lampstand and light the lamps.

5"Place the gold altar for the incense in front of the Ark. Set up the drapes at the entrance of the Tabernacle, 6and place the altar for burnt offerings in front of the entrance. 7Set the washbasin between the Tabernacle-tent and the altar, and fill it with water. 8Then make the courtyard around the outside of the tent, and hang the curtain-door at the entrance to the courtyard.

9"Take the anointing oil and sprinkle it here and there upon the Tabernacle and everything in it, upon all of its utensils and parts, and all the furniture, to hallow it; and it shall become holy. 10Sprinkle the anointing oil upon the altar of burnt offering and its utensils, sanctifying it; for the altar shall then become most holy. 11Then anoint the washbasin and its pedestal, sanctifying it.

12"Now bring Aaron and his sons to the entrance of the Tabernacle and wash them with water; 13and clothe Aaron with the holy garments and anoint him, sanctifying him to minister to me as a priest. 14Then bring his sons and put their robes upon them, 15and anoint them as you did their father, that they may minister to me as priests; their anointing shall be permanent from generation to generation: all their children and children's children shall forever be my priests."

16So Moses proceeded to do all as the Lord had commanded him. 17On the first day of the first month, in the second year, the Tabernacle was put together. 18Moses erected it by setting its frames into their bases and attaching the bars. 19Then he spread the coverings over the framework, and put on the top layers, just as the Lord had commanded him.

20Inside the Ark he placed the stones with the Ten Commandments engraved on them, and attached the carrying poles to the Ark and installed the gold lid, the place of mercy. 21Then he brought the Ark into the Tabernacle and set up the curtain to screen it, just as the Lord had commanded.

22Next he placed the table at the north side of the room outside the curtain, 23and set the Bread of the Presence upon the table before the Lord, just as the Lord had commanded.

24And he placed the lampstand next to the table, on the south side of the Tabernacle. 25Then he lighted the lamps before the Lord, following all the instructions, 26and placed the gold altar in the Tabernacle next to the curtain, 27and burned upon it the incense made from sweet spices, just as the Lord had commanded.

28He attached the curtain at the entrance of the Tabernacle, 29and placed the outside altar for the burnt offerings near the entrance, and offered upon it a burnt offering and a meal offering, just as the Lord had commanded him.

30Next he placed the washbasin between the tent and the altar, and filled it with water so that the priests could use it for washing. 31Moses and Aaron and Aaron's sons washed their hands and feet there. 32Whenever they walked past the altar to enter the Tabernacle, they stopped and washed, just as the Lord had commanded Moses.

33Then he erected the enclosure surrounding the tent and the altar, and set up the curtain-door at the entrance of the enclosure. So at last Moses finished the work.

34Then the cloud covered the Tabernacle and the glory of the Lord filled it. 35Moses was not able to enter because the cloud was standing there, and the glory of the Lord filled the Tabernacle. 36Whenever the cloud lifted and moved, the people of Israel journeyed onward, following it. 37But if the cloud stayed, they stayed until it moved. 38The cloud rested upon the Tabernacle during the daytime, and at night there was fire in the cloud so that all the people of Israel could see it.

This continued throughout all their journeys.

MARK 1:1–28

HERE begins the wonderful story of Jesus the Messiah, the Son of God.

2In the book written by the prophet Isaiah, God announced that he would send his Son to earth, and that a special messenger would arrive first to prepare the world for his coming.

3"This messenger will live out in the barren wilderness," Isaiah said, "and will proclaim that everyone must straighten out his life to be ready for the Lord's arrival."

4This messenger was John the Baptist. He lived in the wilderness and taught that all should be baptized as a public announcement of their decision to turn their backs on sin, so that God could forgive them. 5People from Jerusalem and from all over Judea traveled out into the Judean wastelands to see and hear John, and when they confessed their sins he baptized them in the Jordan River. 6His clothes were woven from camel's hair and he wore a leather belt; locusts and wild honey were his food. 7Here is a sample of his preaching:

"Someone is coming soon who is far greater than I am, so much greater that I am not even worthy to be his slave. 8I baptize you with water but he will baptize you with God's Holy Spirit!"

9Then one day Jesus came from Nazareth in Galilee, and was baptized by John there in the Jordan River. 10The moment Jesus came up out of the water, he saw the heavens open and the Holy Spirit in the form of a dove descending on him, 11and a voice from heaven said, "You are my beloved Son; you are my Delight."

12,13Immediately the Holy Spirit urged Jesus into the desert. There, for forty days, alone except for desert animals, he was subjected to Satan's temptations to sin. And afterwards the angels came and cared for him.

¹⁴Later on, after John was arrested by King Herod, Jesus went to Galilee to preach God's Good News.

¹⁵"At last the time has come!" he announced. "God's Kingdom is near! Turn from your sins and act on this glorious news!"

¹⁶One day as Jesus was walking along the shores of the Sea of Galilee, he saw Simon and his brother Andrew fishing with nets, for they were commercial fishermen.

¹⁷Jesus called out to them, "Come, follow me! And I will make you fishermen for the souls of men!" ¹⁸At once they left their nets and went along with him.

¹⁹A little farther up the beach, he saw Zebedee's sons, James and John, in a boat mending their nets. ²⁰He called them too, and immediately they left their father Zebedee in the boat with the hired men and went with him.

²¹Jesus and his companions now arrived at the town of Capernaum and on Saturday morning went into the Jewish place of worship—the synagogue—where he preached. ²²The congregation was surprised at his sermon because he spoke as an authority, and didn't try to prove his points by quoting others—quite unlike what they were used to hearing!

²³A man possessed by a demon was present and began shouting, ²⁴"Why are you bothering us, Jesus of Nazareth—have you come to destroy us demons? I know who you are—the holy Son of God!"

²⁵Jesus curtly commanded the demon to say no more and to come out of the man. ²⁶At that the evil spirit screamed and convulsed the man violently and left him. ²⁷Amazement gripped the audience and they began discussing what had happened.

"What sort of new religion is this?" they asked excitedly. "Why, even evil spirits obey his orders!"

²⁸The news of what he had done spread quickly through that entire area of Galilee.

PSALM 35:1–16

O Lord, fight those fighting me; declare war on them for their attacks on me. ²Put on your armor, take your shield and protect me by standing in front. ³Lift your spear in my defense, for my pursuers are getting very close. Let me hear you say that you will save me from them. ⁴Dishonor those who are trying to kill me. Turn them back and confuse them. ⁵Blow them away like chaff in the wind—wind sent by the Angel of the Lord. ⁶Make their path dark and slippery before them, with the Angel of the Lord pursuing them. ⁷For though I did them no wrong, yet they laid a trap for me and dug a pitfall in my path. ⁸Let them be overtaken by sudden ruin, caught in their own net, and destroyed.

⁹But I will rejoice in the Lord. He shall rescue me! ¹⁰From the bottom of my heart praise rises to him. Where is his equal in all of heaven and earth? Who else protects the weak and helpless from the strong, and the poor and needy from those who would rob them?

¹¹These evil men swear to a lie. They accuse me of things I have never even heard about. ¹²I do them good, but they return me harm. I am sinking down to death. ¹³When they were ill, I mourned before the Lord in sackcloth, asking him to make them well; I refused to eat; I prayed for them with utmost earnestness, but God did not listen. ¹⁴I went about sadly as though it were my mother, friend or brother who was sick and nearing death. ¹⁵But now that I am in trouble they are glad; they come together in meetings filled with slander against me—I didn't even know some of those who were there. ¹⁶For they gather with the worthless fellows of the town and spend their time cursing me.

FEBRUARY 16

LEVITICUS 1:1—3:17

THE Lord now spoke to Moses from the Tabernacle, 2,3and commanded him to give the following instructions to the people of Israel: "When you sacrifice to the Lord, use animals from your herds and flocks.

"If your sacrifice is to be an ox given as a burnt offering, use only a bull with no physical defects. Bring the animal to the entrance of the Tabernacle where the priests will accept your gift for the Lord. 4The person bringing it is to lay his hand upon its head, and it then becomes his substitute: the death of the animal will be accepted by God instead of the death of the man who brings it, as the penalty for his sins. 5The man shall then kill the animal there before the Lord, and Aaron's sons, the priests, will present the blood before the Lord, sprinkling it upon all sides of the altar at the entrance of the Tabernacle. 6,7Then the priests will skin the animal and quarter it, and build a wood fire upon the altar, 8and put the sections of the animal and its head and fat upon the wood. 9The internal organs and the legs are to be washed, then the priests will burn them upon the altar, and they will be an acceptable burnt offering with which the Lord is pleased.

10"If the animal used as a burnt offering is a sheep or a goat, it too must be a male, and without any blemishes. 11The man who brings it will kill it before the Lord on the north side of the altar, and Aaron's sons, the priests, will sprinkle its blood back and forth upon the altar. 12Then the man will quarter it, and the priests will lay the pieces, with the head and the fat, on top of the wood on the altar. 13But the internal organs and the legs shall first be washed with water. Then the priests shall burn it all upon the altar as an offering to the Lord; for burnt offerings give much pleasure to the Lord.

14"If anyone wishes to use a bird as his burnt offering, he may choose either turtledoves or young pigeons. 15,16,17A priest will take the bird to the altar and wring off its head, and the blood shall be drained out at the side of the altar. Then the priest will remove the crop and the feathers and throw them on the east side of the altar with the ashes. Then, grasping it by the wings, he shall tear it apart, but not completely. And the priest shall burn it upon the altar, and the Lord will have pleasure in this sacrifice.

"ANYONE who wishes to sacrifice a grain offering to the Lord is to bring fine flour and is to pour olive oil and incense upon it. 2Then he is to take a handful, representing the entire amount, to one of the priests to burn, and the Lord will be fully pleased. 3The remainder of the flour is to be given to Aaron and his sons as their food; but all of it is counted as a holy burnt offering to the Lord.

4"If bread baked in the oven is brought as an offering to the Lord, it must be made from finely ground flour, baked with olive oil but without yeast. Wafers made without yeast and spread with olive oil may also be used as an offering.

5If the offering is something from the griddle, it shall be made of finely ground flour without yeast, and mingled with olive oil. 6Break it into pieces and pour oil upon it—it is a form of grain offering. 7If your offering is cooked in a pan, it too shall be made of fine flour mixed with olive oil.

8"However it is prepared—whether baked, fried, or grilled—you are to bring this grain offering to the priest and he shall take it to the altar to present it to the Lord.

9"The priests are to burn only a representative portion of the offering, but all of it will be fully appreciated by the Lord. 10The remainder belongs to the priests for their own use, but it is all counted as a holy burnt offering to the Lord.

11"Use no yeast with your offerings of flour; for no yeast or honey is permitted in burnt offerings to the Lord. 12You may offer yeast bread and honey as thanksgiving offerings at harvest time, but not as burnt offerings.

13"Every offering must be seasoned with salt, because the salt is a reminder of God's covenant.

14"If you are offering from the first of your harvest, remove the kernels from a fresh ear, crush and roast them, then offer them to the Lord. 15Put olive oil and incense on the offering, for it is a grain offering. 16Then the priests shall burn part of the bruised grain mixed with oil and all of the incense as a representative portion before the Lord.

"WHEN anyone wants to give an offering of thanksgiving to the Lord, he may use either a bull or a cow, but the animal must be entirely without defect if it is to be offered to the Lord! 2The man who brings the animal shall lay his hand upon its head and kill it at the door of the Tabernacle. Then Aaron's sons shall throw the blood against the sides of the altar, 3,4,5and shall burn before the Lord the fat that covers the inward parts, the two kidneys and the loin-fat on them, and the gall bladder. And it will give the Lord much pleasure.

6"If a goat or sheep is used as a thank-offering to the Lord, it must have no defect and may be either a male or female.

7,8"If it is a lamb, the man who brings it shall lay his hand upon its head and kill it at the entrance of the Tabernacle; the priests shall throw the blood against the sides of the altar, 9,10,11and shall offer upon the altar the fat, the tail removed close to the backbone, the fat covering the internal organs, the two kidneys with the loin-fat on them, and the gall bladder, as a burnt offering to the Lord.

12"If anyone brings a goat as his offering to the Lord, 13he shall lay his hand upon its head and kill it at the entrance of the Tabernacle. The priest shall throw its blood against the sides of the altar, 14and shall offer upon the altar, as a burnt offering to the Lord, the fat which covers the insides, 15,16the two kidneys and the loin-fat on them, and the gall bladder. This burnt offering is very pleasing to the Lord. All the fat is Jehovah's. 17This is a permanent law throughout your land, that you shall eat neither fat nor blood."

MARK 1:29—2:12

THEN, leaving the synagogue, he and his disciples went over to Simon and Andrew's home, where they found Simon's mother-in-law sick in bed with a high fever. They told Jesus about her right away. 31He went to her bedside, and as he took her by the hand and helped her to sit up, the fever suddenly left, and she got up and prepared dinner for them!

32,33By sunset the courtyard was filled with the sick and demon-possessed, brought to him for healing; and a huge crowd of people from all over the city of Capernaum gathered outside the door to watch. 34So Jesus healed great numbers of sick folk that evening and ordered many demons to come out of their victims. (But he refused to allow the demons to speak, because they knew who he was.)

35The next morning he was up long before daybreak and went out alone into the wilderness to pray.

36,37Later, Simon and the others went out to find him, and told him, "Everyone is asking for you."

38But he replied, "We must go on to other towns as well, and give my message to them too, for that is why I came."

39So he traveled throughout the province of Galilee, preaching in the synagogues and releasing many from the power of demons.

40Once a leper came and knelt in front of him and begged to be healed. "If you want to, you can make me well again," he pled.

41And Jesus, moved with pity, touched him and said, "I want to! Be healed!" 42Immediately the leprosy was gone—the man was healed!

43,44Jesus then told him sternly, "Go and be examined immediately by the Jewish priest. Don't stop to speak to anyone along the way. Take along the offering prescribed by Moses for a leper who is healed, so that everyone will have proof that you are well again."

45But as the man went on his way he began to shout the good news that he was healed; as a result, such throngs soon surrounded Jesus that he couldn't publicly enter a city anywhere, but had to stay out in the barren wastelands. And people from everywhere came to him there.

SEVERAL days later he returned to Capernaum, and the news of his arrival spread quickly through the city. 2Soon the house where he was staying was so packed with visitors that there wasn't room for a single person more, not even outside the door. And he preached the Word to them. 3Four men arrived carrying a paralyzed man on a stretcher. 4They couldn't get to Jesus through the crowd, so they dug through the clay roof above his head and lowered the sick man on his stretcher, right down in front of Jesus.

5When Jesus saw how strongly they believed that he would help, Jesus said to the sick man, "Son, your sins are forgiven!"

6But some of the Jewish religious leaders said to themselves as they sat there, 7"What? This is blasphemy! Does he think he is God? For only God can forgive sins."

8Jesus could read their minds and said to them at once, "Why does this bother you? 9,10,11I, the Messiah, have the authority on earth to forgive sins. But talk is cheap—anybody could say that. So I'll prove it to you by healing this man." Then, turning to the paralyzed man, he commanded, "Pick up your stretcher and go on home, for you are healed!"

12The man jumped up, took the stretcher, and pushed his way through the stunned onlookers! Then how they praised God. "We've never seen anything like this before!" they all exclaimed.

PSALM 35:17–28

LORD, how long will you stand there, doing nothing? Act now and rescue me, for I have but one life and these young lions are out to get it. 18Save me, and I will thank you publicly before the entire congregation, before the largest crowd I can find.

19Don't give victory to those who fight me without any reason! Don't let them rejoice at my fall—let them die. 20They don't talk of peace and doing good, but of plots against innocent men who are minding their own business. 21They shout that they have seen *me* doing wrong! "Aha!" they say. "With our own eyes we saw him do it." 22Lord, you know all about it. Don't stay silent! Don't desert me now!

23Rise up, O Lord my God; vindicate me. 24Declare me "not guilty," for you are just. Don't let my enemies rejoice over me in my troubles. 25Don't let them say, "Aha! Our dearest wish against him will soon be fulfilled!" and, "At last we have him!" 26Shame them; let these who boast against me and who rejoice at my troubles be themselves overcome by misfortune that strips them bare of everything they own. Bare them to dishonor. 27But give great joy to all who wish me well. Let them shout with delight, "Great is the Lord who enjoys helping his child!" 28And I will tell everyone how great and good you are; I will praise you all day long.

PROVERBS FOR TODAY/ 9:13–18

A prostitute is loud and brash, and never has enough of lust and shame. She sits at the door of her house or stands at the street corners of the city, whispering to men going by, and to those minding their own business. "Come home with me," she urges simpletons. "Stolen melons are the sweetest; stolen apples taste the best!" But they don't realize that her former guests are now citizens of hell.

FEBRUARY 17

LEVITICUS 4:1—5:19

THEN the Lord gave these further instructions to Moses:

2"Tell the people of Israel that these are the laws concerning anyone who unintentionally breaks any of my commandments. 3If a priest sins unintentionally, and so brings guilt upon the people, he must offer a young bull without defect as a sin offering to the Lord. 4He shall bring it to the door of the Tabernacle, and shall lay his hand upon its head and kill it there before Jehovah. 5Then the priest shall take the animal's blood into the Tabernacle, 6and shall dip his finger in the blood and sprinkle it seven times before the Lord in front of the veil that bars the way to the Holy of Holies. 7Then the priest shall put some of the blood upon the horns of the incense altar before the Lord in the Tabernacle; the remainder of the blood shall be poured out at the base of the altar for burnt offerings, at the entrance to the Tabernacle. 8Then he shall take all the fat on the entrails, 9the two kidneys and the loin-fat on them, and the gall bladder, 10and shall burn them on the altar of burnt offering, just as in the case of a bull or cow sacrificed as a thank-offering.

11,12But the remainder of the young bull—the skin, meat, head, legs, internal organs, and intestines—shall be carried to a ceremonially clean place outside the camp—a place where the ashes are brought from the altar—and burned there on a wood fire.

13"If the entire nation of Israel sins without realizing it, and does something that Jehovah has said not to do, all the people are guilty. 14When they realize it, they shall offer a young bull for a sin offering, bringing it to the Tabernacle 15where the leaders of the nation shall lay their hands upon the animal's head and kill it before the Lord. 16Then the priest shall bring its blood into the Tabernacle, 17and shall dip his finger in the blood and sprinkle it seven times before the Lord, in front of the veil. 18Then he shall put blood upon the horns of the altar there in the Tabernacle before the Lord, and all the remainder of the blood shall be poured out at the base of the burnt offering altar, at the entrance to the Tabernacle. 19All the fat shall be removed and burned upon the altar. 20He shall follow the same procedure as for a sin offering; in this way the priest shall make atonement for the nation, and everyone will be forgiven. 21The priest shall then cart the young bull outside the camp and burn it there, just as though it were a sin offering for an individual, only this time it is a sin offering for the entire nation.

22"If one of the leaders sins without realizing it and is guilty of disobeying one of God's laws, 23as soon as it is called to his attention he must bring as his sacrifice a male goat without any physical defect. 24He shall lay his hand upon its head and kill it at the place where the burnt offerings are killed, and present it to the Lord. This is his sin offering. 25Then the priest shall take some of the blood of this sin offering and place it with his finger upon the horns of the altar of burnt offerings, and the rest of the blood shall be poured out at the base of the altar. 26All the fat shall be burned upon the altar, just as if it were the fat of the sacrifice of a thank-offering; thus the priest shall make atonement for the leader concerning his sin, and he shall be forgiven.

27"If any one of the common people sins and doesn't realize it, he is guilty. 28But as soon as he does realize it, he is to bring as his sacrifice a female goat without defect to atone for his sin. 29He shall bring it to the place where the animals for burnt offerings are killed, and there lay his hand upon the head of the sin offering and kill it. 30And the priest shall take some of the blood with his finger and smear it upon the horns of the burnt offering altar. Then the priest shall pour out the remainder of the blood at the base of the altar. 31All the fat shall be taken off, just as in the procedure for the thank-offering sacrifice, and the priest shall burn it upon the altar; and the Lord will appreciate it. Thus the priest shall make atonement for that man, and he shall be forgiven.

32"However, if he chooses to bring a lamb as his sin offering, it must be a female without physical defect. 33He shall bring it to the place where the burnt offerings are killed, and lay his hand upon its head and kill it there as a sin offering.

34The priest shall take some of the blood with his finger and smear it upon the horns of the burnt offering altar, and all the rest of the blood shall be poured out at the base of the altar. 35The fat shall be used just as in the case of a thank-offering lamb—the priest shall burn the fat on the altar as in any other sacrifice made to Jehovah by fire; and the priest shall make atonement for the man, and his sin shall be forgiven.

"ANYONE refusing to give testimony concerning what he knows about a crime is guilty.

2"Anyone touching anything ceremonially unclean—such as the dead body of an animal forbidden for food, wild or domesticated, or the dead body of some forbidden insect—is guilty, even though he wasn't aware of touching it. 3Or if he touches human discharge of any kind, he becomes guilty as soon as he realizes that he has touched it.

4"If anyone makes a rash vow, whether the vow is good or bad, when he realizes what a foolish vow he has taken, he is guilty.

5"In any of these cases, he shall confess his sin 6and bring his guilt offering to the Lord, a female lamb or goat, and the priest shall make atonement for him, and he shall be freed from his sin, and need not fulfill the vow.

7"If he is too poor to bring a lamb to the Lord, then he shall bring two turtledoves or two young pigeons as his guilt offering; one of the birds shall be his sin offering and the other his burnt offering. 8The priest shall offer as the sin sacrifice whichever bird is handed to him first, breaking its neck, but not severing its head from its body. 9Then he shall sprinkle some of the blood at the side of the altar and the rest shall be drained out at the base of the altar; this is the sin offering. 10He shall offer the second bird as a burnt offering, following the customary procedures that have been set forth; so the priest shall make atonement for him concerning his sin and he shall be forgiven.

11"If he is too poor to bring turtle-doves or young pigeons as his sin offering, then he shall bring a tenth of a bushel of fine flour. He must not mix it with olive oil or put any incense on it, because it is a sin offering. 12He shall bring it to the priest and the priest shall take out a handful as a representative portion, and burn it on the altar just as any other offering to Jehovah made by fire; this shall be his sin offering. 13In this way the priest shall make atonement for him for any sin of this kind, and he shall be forgiven. The rest of the flour shall belong to the priest, just as was the case with the grain offering."

14And the Lord said to Moses, 15"If anyone sins by unintentionally defiling what is holy, then he shall bring a ram without defect, worth whatever fine you charge against him, as his guilt offering to the Lord. 16And he shall make restitution for the holy thing he has defiled, or the tithe omitted, by paying for the loss, plus a twenty percent penalty; he shall bring it to the priest, and the priest shall make atonement for him with the ram of the guilt offering, and he shall be forgiven.

17,18"Anyone who disobeys some law of God without realizing it is guilty anyway, and must bring his sacrifice of a value determined by Moses. This sacrifice shall be a ram without blemish taken to the priest as a guilt offering; with it the priest shall make atonement for him, so that he will be forgiven for whatever it is he has done without realizing it. 19It must be offered as a guilt offering, for he is certainly guilty before the Lord."

MARK 2:13—3:6

THEN Jesus went out to the seashore again, and preached to the crowds that gathered around him. 14As he was walking up the beach he saw Levi, the son of Alphaeus, sitting at his tax collection booth. "Come with me," Jesus told him. "Come be my disciple."

And Levi jumped to his feet and went along.

15That night Levi invited his fellow tax collectors and many other notorious sinners to be his dinner guests so that they could meet Jesus and his disciples. (There were many men of this type among the crowds that followed him.) 16But when some of the Jewish religious leaders saw him eating with these men of ill repute, they said to his disciples, "How can he stand it, to eat with such scum?"

17When Jesus heard what they were saying, he told them, "Sick people need the doctor, not healthy ones! I haven't come to tell good people to repent, but the bad ones."

18John's disciples and the Jewish leaders sometimes fasted, that is, went without food as part of their religion. One day some people came to Jesus and asked why his disciples didn't do this too.

19Jesus replied, "Do friends of the bridegroom refuse to eat at the wedding feast? Should they be sad while he is with them? 20But some day he will be taken away from them, and then they will mourn. 21[Besides, going without food is part of the old way of doing things.] It is like patching an old garment with unshrunk cloth! What happens? The patch pulls away and leaves the hole worse than before. 22You know better than to put new wine into old wineskins. They would burst. The wine would be spilled out and the wineskins ruined. New wine needs fresh wineskins."

23Another time, on a Sabbath day as Jesus and his disciples were walking through the fields, the disciples were breaking off heads of wheat and eating the grain.

24Some of the Jewish religious leaders said to Jesus, "They shouldn't be doing that! It's against our laws to work by harvesting grain on the Sabbath."

25,26But Jesus replied, "Didn't you ever

hear about the time King David and his companions were hungry, and he went into the house of God—Abiathar was High Priest then—and they ate the special bread only priests were allowed to eat? That was against the law too. 27But the Sabbath was made to benefit man, and not man to benefit the Sabbath. 28And I, the Messiah, have authority even to decide what men can do on Sabbath days!"

WHILE in Capernaum Jesus went over to the synagogue again, and noticed a man there with a deformed hand.

2Since it was the Sabbath, Jesus' enemies watched him closely. Would he heal the man's hand? If he did, they planned to arrest him!

3Jesus asked the man to come and stand in front of the congregation. 4Then turning to his enemies he asked, "Is it all right to do kind deeds on Sabbath days? Or is this a day for doing harm? Is it a day to save lives or to destroy them?" But they wouldn't answer him. 5Looking around at them angrily, for he was deeply disturbed by their indifference to human need, he said to the man, "Reach out your hand." He did, and instantly his hand was healed!

6At once the Pharisees went away and met with the Herodians to discuss plans for killing Jesus.

PSALM 36:1–12

SIN lurks deep in the hearts of the wicked, forever urging them on to evil deeds. They have no fear of God to hold them back. 2Instead, in their conceit, they think they can hide their evil deeds and not get caught. 3Everything they say is crooked and deceitful; they are no longer wise and good. 4They lie awake at night to hatch their evil plots, instead of planning how to keep away from wrong.

5Your steadfast love, O Lord, is as great as all the heavens. Your faithfulness reaches beyond the clouds. 6Your justice is as solid as God's mountains. Your decisions are as full of wisdom as the oceans are with water. You are concerned for men and animals alike. 7How precious is your constant love, O God! All humanity takes refuge in the shadow of your wings. 8You feed them with blessings from your own table and let them drink from your rivers of delight.

9For you are the Fountain of life; our light is from your Light. 10Pour out your unfailing love on those who know you! Never stop giving your blessings to those who long to do your will.

11Don't let these proud men trample me. Don't let their wicked hands push me around. 12Look! They have fallen. They are thrown down and will not rise again.

PROVERBS FOR TODAY/ 10:1–2

Happy is the man with a level-headed son; sad the mother of a rebel. Ill-gotten gain brings no lasting happiness; right living does.

FEBRUARY 18

LEVITICUS 6:1—7:27

AND the Lord said to Moses, 2"If anyone sins against me by refusing to return a deposit on something borrowed or rented, or by re- fusing to return something entrusted to him, or by robbery, or by oppressing his neighbor, 3or by finding a lost article and lying about it, swearing that he doesn't have it— 4,5on the day he is found guilty of any such sin, he shall restore what he took, adding a twenty percent fine, and give it to the one he has harmed; and on the same day he shall bring his guilt offering to the Tabernacle. 6His guilt offering shall be a ram without defect, and must be worth whatever value you demand. He shall bring it to the priest, 7and the priest shall make atonement for him before the Lord, and he shall be forgiven."

8Then the Lord said to Moses, 9*"Give Aaron and his sons these regulations concerning the burnt offering:*

"The burnt offering shall be left upon the hearth of the altar all night, with the altar fire kept burning. 10(The next morning) the priest shall put on his linen undergarments and his linen outer garments and clean out the ashes of the burnt offering and put them beside the altar. 11Then he shall change his clothes and carry the ashes outside the camp to a place that is ceremonially clean. 12Meanwhile, the fire on the altar must be kept burning—it must not go out. The priest shall put on fresh wood each morning, and lay the daily burnt offering on it, and burn the fat of the daily peace offering. 13The fire must be kept burning upon the altar continually. It must never go out.

14*"These are the regulations concerning the grain offering:*

"Aaron's sons shall stand in front of the altar to offer it before the Lord. 15The priest shall then take out a handful of the finely ground flour with the olive oil and the incense mixed into it, and burn it upon the altar as a representative portion for the Lord; and it will be received with pleasure by the Lord. 16After taking out this handful, the remainder of the flour will belong to Aaron and his sons for their food; it shall be eaten without yeast in the courtyard of the Tabernacle. 17(Stress this instruction, that if it is baked it must be without yeast.) I have given to the priests this part of the burnt offerings made to me. However, all of it is most holy, just as is the entire sin offering and the entire

guilt offering. 18It may be eaten by any male descendant of Aaron, any priest, generation after generation. But only the priests may eat these offerings made by fire to the Lord."

19,20And Jehovah said to Moses, "On the day Aaron and his sons are anointed and inducted into the priesthood, they shall bring to the Lord a regular grain offering—a tenth of a bushel of fine flour, half to be offered in the morning and half in the evening. 21It shall be cooked on a griddle, using olive oil, and should be well cooked, then brought to the Lord as an offering that pleases him very much. 22,23As the sons of the priests replace their fathers, they shall be inducted into office by offering this same sacrifice on the day of their anointing. This is a perpetual law. These offerings shall be entirely burned up before the Lord; none of it shall be eaten."

24Then the Lord said to Moses, 25*"Tell Aaron and his sons that these are the instructions concerning the sin offering:*

"This sacrifice is most holy, and shall be killed before the Lord at the place where the burnt offerings are killed. 26The priest who performs the ceremony shall eat it in the courtyard of the Tabernacle. 27Only those who are sanctified— the priests—may touch this meat; if any blood sprinkles onto their clothing, it must be washed in a holy place. 28Then the clay pot in which the clothing is boiled shall be broken; or if a bronze kettle is used, it must be scoured and rinsed out thoroughly. 29Every male among the priests may eat this offering, but only they, for it is most holy. 30No sin offering may be eaten by the priests if any of its blood is taken into the Tabernacle, to make atonement in the Holy Place. That carcass must be entirely burned with fire before the Lord.

"HERE are the *instructions concerning the most holy offering for guilt:*

2"The sacrificial animal shall be killed at the place where the burnt offering sacrifices are slain, and its blood shall be sprinkled back and forth upon the altar. 3The priest will offer upon the altar all its fat, including the tail, the fat that covers the insides, 4the two kidneys and the loin-fat, and the gall bladder—all shall be set aside for sacrificing. 5The priests will burn them upon the altar as a guilt offering to the Lord. 6Only males among the priests may then eat the carcass, and it must be eaten in a holy place, for this is a most holy sacrifice.

7"The same instructions apply to both the sin offering and the guilt offering— the carcass shall be given to the priest who is in charge of the atonement ceremony, for his food. 8(When the offering is a burnt sacrifice, the priest who is in charge shall also be given the animal's hide.) 9The priests who present the people's grain offerings to the Lord shall be given whatever remains of the sacrifice after the ceremony is completed. This rule applies whether the sacrifice is baked, fried, or grilled. 10All other grain offerings, whether mixed with olive oil or dry, are the common property of all sons of Aaron.

11 *Here are the instructions concerning the sacrifices given to the Lord as special peace offerings:*

12"If it is an offering of thanksgiving, unleavened short bread shall be included with the sacrifice, along with unleavened wafers spread with olive oil and loaves from a batter of flour mixed with olive oil. 13This thanksgiving peace offering shall be accompanied with loaves of leavened bread. 14Part of this sacrifice shall be presented to the Lord by a gesture of waving it before the altar, then it shall be given to the assisting priest, the one who sprinkles the blood of the animal presented for the sacrifice. 15After the animal has been sacrificed and presented to the Lord as a peace offering to show special appreciation and thanksgiving to him, its meat is to be eaten that same day, and none left to be eaten the next day.

16"However, if someone brings a sacrifice that is not for thanksgiving, but is because of a vow or is simply a voluntary offering to the Lord, any portion of the sacrifice that is not eaten the day it is sacrificed may be eaten the next day. 17,18But anything left over until the third day shall be burned. For if any of it is eaten on the third day, the Lord will not accept it; it will have no value as a sacrifice, and there will be no credit to the one who brought it to be offered; and the priest who eats it shall be guilty, for it is detestable to the Lord, and the person who eats it must answer for his sin.

19"Any meat that comes into contact with anything that is ceremonially unclean shall not be eaten, but burned; and as for the meat that may be eaten, it may be eaten only by a person who is ceremonially clean. 20Any priest who is ceremonially unclean but eats the thanksgiving offering anyway, shall be cut off from his people, for he has defiled what is sacred. 21Anyone who touches anything that is ceremonially unclean, whether it is uncleanness from man or beast, and then eats the peace offering, shall be cut off from his people, for he has defiled what is holy."

22Then the Lord said to Moses, 23"Tell the people of Israel never to eat fat, whether from oxen, sheep, or goats. 24The fat of an animal that dies of disease, or is attacked and killed by wild animals, may be used for other purposes, but never eaten. 25Anyone who eats fat from an offering sacrificed by fire to the Lord shall be outlawed from his people.

26,27"Never eat blood, whether of birds or animals. Anyone who does shall be excommunicated from his people."

MARK 3:7–30

MEANWHILE, Jesus and his disciples withdrew to the beach, followed by a huge crowd from all over Galilee, Judea, Jerusalem, Idumea, from beyond the Jordan River, and even from as far away as Tyre and Sidon. For the news about his miracles had spread far and wide and vast numbers came to see him for themselves.

9He instructed his disciples to bring around a boat and to have it standing ready to rescue him in case he was crowded off the beach. 10For there had been many healings that day and as a result great numbers of sick people were crowding around him, trying to touch him.

11And whenever those possessed by demons caught sight of him they would fall down before him shrieking, "You are the Son of God!" 12But he strictly warned them not to make him known.

13Afterwards he went up into the hills and summoned certain ones he chose, inviting them to come and join him there; and they did. 14,15Then he selected twelve of them to be his regular companions and to go out to preach and to cast out demons. 16-19These are the names of the twelve he chose:

Simon (he renamed him "Peter"),

James and John (the sons of Zebedee, but Jesus called them "Sons of Thunder"),

Andrew,

Philip,

Bartholomew,

Matthew,

Thomas,

James (the son of Alphaeus),

Thaddaeus,

Simon (a member of a political party advocating violent overthrow of the Roman government),

Judas Iscariot (who later betrayed him).

20When he returned to the house where he was staying, the crowds began to gather again, and soon it was so full of visitors that he couldn't even find time to eat. 21When his friends heard what was happening they came to try to take him home with them.

"He's out of his mind," they said.

22But the Jewish teachers of religion who had arrived from Jerusalem said, "His trouble is that he's possessed by Satan, king of demons. That's why demons obey him."

23Jesus summoned these men and asked them (using proverbs they all understood), "How can Satan cast out Satan? 24A kingdom divided against itself will collapse. 25A home filled with strife and division destroys itself. 26And if Satan is fighting against himself, how can he accomplish anything? He would never survive. 27[Satan must be bound before his demons are cast out], just as a strong man must be tied up before his house can be ransacked and his property robbed.

28"I solemnly declare that any sin of man can be forgiven, even blasphemy against me; 29but blasphemy against the Holy Spirit can never be forgiven. It is an eternal sin."

30He told them this because they were saying he did his miracles by Satan's power [instead of acknowledging it was by the Holy Spirit's power].

PSALM 37:1–11

NEVER envy the wicked! 2Soon they fade away like grass and disappear. 3Trust in the Lord instead. Be kind and good to others; then you will live safely here in the land and prosper, feeding in safety.

4Be delighted with the Lord. Then he will give you all your heart's desires. 5Commit everything you do to the Lord. Trust him to help you do it and he will. 6Your innocence will be clear to everyone. He will vindicate you with the blazing light of justice shining down as from the noonday sun.

7Rest in the Lord; wait patiently for him to act. Don't be envious of evil men who prosper.

8Stop your anger! Turn off your wrath. Don't fret and worry—it only leads to harm. 9For the wicked shall be destroyed, but those who trust the Lord shall be given every blessing. 10Only a little while and the wicked shall disappear. You will look for them in vain. 11But all who humble themselves before the Lord shall be given every blessing, and shall have wonderful peace.

FEBRUARY 19

LEVITICUS 7:28—9:6

AND the Lord said to Moses, 29"Tell the people of Israel that anyone bringing a thanksgiving offering to the Lord must bring it personally with his own hands. 30He shall bring the offering of the fat and breast, which is to be presented to the Lord by waving it before the altar. 31Then the priest shall burn the fat upon the altar, but the breast shall belong to Aaron and his sons, 32,33while the right thigh shall be given to the officiating priest. 34For I have designated the breast and thigh as donations from the people of Israel to the sons of Aaron. Aaron and his sons must always be given this portion of the sacrifice. 35This is their pay! It is to be set apart from the burnt offerings, and given to all who have been appointed to minister to the Lord as priests—to Aaron and to his sons. 36For on the day the Lord anointed them, he commanded that the people of Israel give these portions to them; it is their right forever throughout all their generations."

37These were the instructions concerning the burnt offering, grain offering, sin offering, and guilt offering, and concerning the consecration offering and the peace offering; 38these instructions were given to Moses by the Lord on Mount Sinai, to be passed on to the people of Israel so that they would know how to offer their sacrifices to God in the Sinai desert.

THE Lord said to Moses, "Now bring Aaron and his sons to the entrance of the Tabernacle, together with their gar-

ments, the anointing oil, the young bull for the sin offering, the two rams, and the basket of bread made without yeast; and summon all Israel to a meeting there."

4So all the people assembled, 5and Moses said to them, "What I am now going to do has been commanded by Jehovah."

6Then he took Aaron and his sons and washed them with water, 7and he clothed Aaron with the special coat, sash, robe, and the ephod-jacket with its beautifully woven belt. 8Then he put on him the chestpiece and deposited the Urim and the Thummim inside its pouch; 9and placed on Aaron's head the turban with the sacred gold plate at its front—the holy crown—as the Lord had commanded Moses.

10Then Moses took the anointing oil and sprinkled it upon the Tabernacle itself and on each item in it, sanctifying them. 11When he came to the altar he sprinkled it seven times, and also sprinkled the utensils of the altar and the washbasin and its pedestal, to sanctify them. 12Then he poured the anointing oil upon Aaron's head, thus setting him apart for his work. 13Next Moses placed the robes on Aaron's sons, with the belts and caps, as the Lord had commanded him.

14Then he took the young bull for the sin offering, and Aaron and his sons laid their hands upon its head 15,16as Moses killed it. He smeared some of the blood with his finger upon the four horns of the altar, and upon the altar itself, to sanctify it, and poured out the rest of the blood at the base of the altar; thus he sanctified the altar, making atonement for it. He took all the fat covering the entrails, the fatty mass above the liver, and the two kidneys and their fat, and burned them all on the altar. 17The carcass of the young bull, with its hide and dung, was burned outside the camp, as the Lord had commanded Moses.

18Then he presented to the Lord the ram for the burnt offering. Aaron and his sons laid their hands upon its head, 19and Moses killed it and sprinkled the blood back and forth upon the altar. 20Next he quartered the ram and burned the pieces, the head and the fat. 21He then washed the insides and the legs with water, and burned them upon the altar, so that the entire ram was consumed before the Lord; it was a burnt offering that pleased the Lord very much, for Jehovah's directions to Moses were followed in every detail.

22Then Moses presented the other ram, the ram of consecration; Aaron and his sons laid their hands upon its head. 23Moses killed it and took some of its blood and smeared it upon the lobe of Aaron's right ear and the thumb of his right hand and upon the big toe of his right foot. 24Next he smeared some of the blood upon Aaron's sons—upon the lobes of their right ears, upon their right thumbs, and upon the big toes of their right feet. The rest of the blood he sprinkled back and forth upon the altar.

25Then he took the fat, the tail, the fat upon the inner organs, the gall bladder, the two kidneys with their fat, and the right shoulder, 26and placed on top of these one unleavened wafer, one wafer spread with olive oil, and a slice of bread, all taken from the basket which had been placed there before the Lord. 27All this was placed in the hands of Aaron and his sons to present to the Lord by a gesture of waving them before the altar. 28Moses then took it all back from them and burned it upon the altar, along with the burnt offering to the Lord; and Jehovah was pleased by the offering. 29Now Moses took the breast and pre-sented it to the Lord by waving it before the altar; this was Moses' portion of the ram of consecration, just as the Lord had instructed him.

30Next he took some of the anointing oil and some of the blood that had been sprinkled upon the altar, and sprinkled it upon Aaron and upon his clothes and upon his sons and upon their clothes, thus consecrating to the Lord's use Aaron and his sons and their clothes.

31Then Moses said to Aaron and his sons, "Boil the meat at the entrance of the Tabernacle, and eat it along with the bread that is in the basket of consecration, just as I instructed you to do. 32Anything left of the meat and bread must be burned."

33Next he told them not to leave the Tabernacle entrance for seven days, after which time their consecration would be completed—for it takes seven days. 34Then Moses stated again that all he had done that day had been commanded by the Lord in order to make atonement for them. 35And again he warned Aaron and his sons to stay at the entrance of the Tabernacle day and night for seven days. "If you leave," he told them, "you will die—this is what the Lord has said."

36So Aaron and his sons did all that the Lord had commanded Moses.

ON the eighth day (of the consecration ceremonies), Moses summoned Aaron and Aaron's sons and the elders of Israel, 2and told Aaron to take a bull calf from the herd for a sin offering, and a ram without bodily defect for a burnt offering, and to offer them before the Lord.

3"And tell the people of Israel," Moses instructed, "to select a male goat for their sin offering, also a yearling calf and a yearling lamb, all without bodily defect, for their burnt offering. 4In addition, the people are to bring to the Lord a peace offering sacrifice—an ox and a ram, and a grain offering—flour mingled with olive oil. For today," Moses said, "Jehovah will appear to them."

⁵So they brought all these things to the entrance of the Tabernacle, as Moses had commanded, and the people came and stood there before the Lord.

⁶Moses told them, "When you have followed the Lord's instructions, his glory will appear to you."

MARK 3:31—4:25

Now his mother and brothers arrived at the crowded house where he was teaching, and they sent word for him to come out and talk with them. "Your mother and brothers are outside and want to see you," he was told.

³³He replied, "Who is my mother? Who are my brothers?" ³⁴Looking at those around him he said, "These are my mother and brothers! ³⁵Anyone who does God's will is my brother, and my sister, and my mother."

ONCE again an immense crowd gathered around him on the beach as he was teaching, so he got into a boat and sat down and talked from there. ²His usual method of teaching was to tell the people stories. One of them went like this:

³"Listen! A farmer decided to sow some grain. As he scattered it across his field, ⁴some of it fell on a path, and the birds came and picked it off the hard ground and ate it. ⁵,⁶Some fell on thin soil with underlying rock. It grew up quickly enough, but soon wilted beneath the hot sun and died because the roots had no nourishment in the shallow soil. ⁷Other seeds fell among thorns that shot up and crowded the young plants so that they produced no grain. ⁸But some of the seeds fell into good soil and yielded thirty times as much as he had planted—some of it even sixty or a hundred times as much! ⁹If you have ears, listen!"

¹⁰Afterwards, when he was alone with the twelve and with his other disciples,

they asked him, "What does your story mean?"

¹¹,¹²He replied, "You are permitted to know some truths about the kingdom of God that are hidden to those outside the kingdom:

'Though they see and hear, they will not understand or turn to God, or be forgiven for their sins.'

¹³But if you can't understand *this* simple illustration, what will you do about all the others I am going to tell?

¹⁴"The farmer I talked about is anyone who brings God's message to others, trying to plant good seed within their lives. ¹⁵The hard pathway, where some of the seed fell, represents the hard hearts of some of those who hear God's message; Satan comes at once to try to make them forget it. ¹⁶The rocky soil represents the hearts of those who hear the message with joy, ¹⁷but, like young plants in such soil, their roots don't go very deep, and though at first they get along fine, as soon as persecution begins, they wilt.

¹⁸"The thorny ground represents the hearts of people who listen to the Good News and receive it, ¹⁹but all too quickly the attractions of this world and the delights of wealth, and the search for success and lure of nice things come in and crowd out God's message from their hearts, so that no crop is produced.

²⁰"But the good soil represents the hearts of those who truly accept God's message and produce a plentiful harvest for God—thirty, sixty, or even a hundred times as much as was planted in their hearts." ²¹Then he asked them, "When someone lights a lamp, does he put a box over it to shut out the light? Of course not! The light couldn't be seen or used. A lamp is placed on a stand to shine and be useful.

²²"All that is now hidden will someday come to light. ²³If you have ears, listen! ²⁴And be sure to put into practice what you hear. The more you do this, the more you will understand what I tell you. ²⁵To him who has shall be given; from him who has not shall be taken away even what he has.

THE Lord is laughing at those who plot against the godly, for he knows their judgment day is coming. 14Evil men take aim to slay the poor; they are ready to butcher those who do right. 15But their swords will be plunged into their own hearts and all their weapons will be broken.

16It is better to have little and be godly than to own an evil man's wealth; 17for the strength of evil men shall be broken, but the Lord takes care of those he has forgiven.

18Day by day the Lord observes the good deeds done by godly men, and gives them eternal rewards. 19He cares for them when times are hard; even in famine, they will have enough. 20But evil men shall perish. These enemies of God will wither like grass, and disappear like smoke. 21Evil men borrow and "cannot pay it back"! But the good man returns what he owes with some extra besides. 22Those blessed by the Lord shall inherit the earth, but those cursed by him shall die.

23The steps of good men are directed by the Lord. He delights in each step they take. 24If they fall it isn't fatal, for the Lord holds them with his hand.

25I have been young and now I am old. And in all my years I have never seen the Lord forsake a man who loves him; nor have I seen the children of the godly go hungry. 26Instead, the godly are able to be generous with their gifts and loans to others, and their children are a blessing.

27So if you want an eternal home, leave your evil, low-down ways and live good lives. 28For the Lord loves justice and fairness; he will never abandon his people. They will be kept safe forever; but all who love wickedness shall perish.

PROVERBS FOR TODAY/ 10:5

A wise youth makes hay while the sun shines, but what a shame to see a lad who sleeps away his hour of opportunity.

FEBRUARY 20

LEVITICUS 9:7—10:20

MOSES then told Aaron to proceed to the altar and to offer the sin offering and the burnt offering, making atonement for himself first, and then for the people, as the Lord had commanded. 8So Aaron went up to the altar and killed the calf as a sacrifice for his own sin; 9his sons caught the blood for him, and he dipped his finger in it and smeared it upon the horns of the altar, and poured out the rest at the base of the altar. 10Then he burned upon the altar the fat, kidneys, and gall bladder from this sin offering, as the Lord had commanded Moses, 11but he burned the meat and hide outside the camp.

12Next he killed the burnt offering animal, and his sons caught the blood and he sprinkled it back and forth upon the altar; 13they brought the animal to him piece by piece, including the head, and he burned each part upon the altar. 14Then he washed the insides and the legs, and offered these also upon the altar as a burnt offering.

15Next he sacrificed the people's offering; he killed the goat and offered it in just the same way as he had the sin offering for himself. 16Thus he sacrificed their burnt offering to the Lord, in accordance with the instructions God had given.

17Then he presented the grain offering, taking a handful and burning it upon the altar in addition to the regular morning offering.

18Next he killed the ox and ram—the people's peace offering sacrifice; and Aaron's sons brought the blood to him and he sprinkled it back and forth upon the altar. 19Then he collected the fat of the ox and the ram—the fat from their tails and the fat covering the inner organs— and the kidneys and gall bladders. 20The fat was placed upon the breasts of these animals, and Aaron burned it upon the altar; 21but he waved the breasts and right shoulders slowly before the Lord as a gesture of offering it to him, just as Moses had commanded.

22Then, with hands spread out towards the people, Aaron blessed them and came down from the altar. 23Moses and Aaron went into the Tabernacle, and when they came out again they blessed the people; and the glory of the Lord appeared to the whole assembly. 24Then fire came from the Lord and consumed the burnt offering and fat on the altar; and when the people saw it, they all shouted and fell flat upon the ground before the Lord.

BUT Nadab and Abihu, the sons of Aaron, placed unholy fire in their censers, laid incense on the fire, and offered the incense before the Lord—contrary to what the Lord had just commanded them! 2So fire blazed forth from the presence of the Lord and destroyed them.

3Then Moses said to Aaron, "This is what the Lord meant when he said, 'I will show myself holy among those who approach me, and I will be glorified before all the people.' " And Aaron was speechless.

4Then Moses called for Misha-el and Elzaphon, Aaron's cousins, the sons of Uzziel, and told them, "Go and get the charred bodies from before the Tabernacle, and carry them outside the camp."

5So they went over and got them, and carried them out in their coats as Moses had told them to.

6Then Moses said to Aaron and his sons Eleazar and Ithamar, "Do not mourn—do not let your hair hang loose as a sign of your mourning, and do not tear your clothes. If you do, God will strike you dead too, and his wrath will come upon all the people of Israel. But the rest of the people of Israel may lament the death of Nadab and Abihu, and mourn because of the terrible fire the Lord has sent. 7But you are not to leave the Tabernacle under penalty of death, for the anointing oil of Jehovah is upon you." And they did as Moses commanded.

8,9Now the Lord instructed Aaron, "Never drink wine or strong drink when you go into the Tabernacle, lest you die; and this rule applies to your sons and to all your descendants from generation to generation. 10Your duties will be to arbitrate for the people, to teach them the difference between what is holy and what is ordinary, what is pure and what is impure; 11and to teach them all the laws Jehovah has given through Moses."

12Then Moses said to Aaron and to his sons who were left, Eleazar and Ithamar, "Take the grain offering—the food that remains after the handful has been offered to the Lord by burning it on the altar—make sure there is no leaven in it, and eat it beside the altar. The offering is most holy; 13therefore you must eat it in the sanctuary, in a holy place. It belongs to you and to your sons, from the offerings to Jehovah made by fire; for so I am commanded. 14But the breast and the thigh, which have been offered to the Lord by the gesture of waving it before him, may be eaten in any holy place. It belongs to you and to your sons and daughters for your food. It is your portion of the peace offering sacrifices of the people of Israel.

15The people are to bring the thigh that was set aside, along with the breast that was offered when the fat was burned, and they shall be presented before the Lord by the gesture of waving them. And afterwards they shall belong to you and your family, for the Lord has commanded this."

16Then Moses searched everywhere for the goat of the sin offering and discovered that it had been burned! He was very angry about this with Eleazar and Ithamar, the remaining sons of Aaron.

17"Why haven't you eaten the sin offering in the sanctuary, since it is most holy, and God has given it to you to take away the iniquity and guilt of the people, to make atonement for them before the Lord?" he demanded. 18"Since its blood was not taken inside the sanctuary, you should certainly have eaten it there, as I ordered you."

19But Aaron interceded with Moses. "They offered their sin offering and burnt offering before the Lord," he said, "but if I had eaten the sin offering on such a day as this, would it have pleased the Lord?" 20And when Moses heard that, he was satisfied.

MARK 4:26—5:20

HERE is another story illustrating what the Kingdom of God is like:

"A farmer sowed his field, 27and went away, and as the days went by, the seeds grew and grew without his help. 28For the soil made the seeds grow. First a leaf-blade pushed through, and later the wheat-heads formed and finally the grain ripened, 29and then the farmer came at once with his sickle and harvested it."

30Jesus asked, "How can I describe the Kingdom of God? What story shall I use to illustrate it? 31,32It is like a tiny mustard seed! Though this is one of the smallest of seeds, yet it grows to become one of the largest of plants, with long branches where birds can build their nests and be sheltered."

33He used many such illustrations to teach the people as much as they were ready to understand. 34In fact, he taught only by illustrations in his public teaching, but afterwards, when he was alone

with his disciples, he would explain his meaning to them.

35As evening fell, Jesus said to his disciples, "Let's cross to the other side of the lake." 36So they took him just as he was and started out, leaving the crowds behind (though other boats followed). 37But soon a terrible storm arose. High waves began to break into the boat until it was nearly full of water and about to sink. 38Jesus was asleep at the back of the boat with his head on a cushion. Frantically they wakened him, shouting, "Teacher, don't you even care that we are all about to drown?"

39Then he rebuked the wind and said to the sea, "Quiet down!" And the wind fell, and there was a great calm!

40And he asked them, "Why were you so fearful? Don't you even yet have confidence in me?"

41And they were filled with awe and said among themselves, "Who is this man, that even the winds and seas obey him?"

WHEN they arrived at the other side of the lake a demon-possessed man ran out from a graveyard, just as Jesus was climbing from the boat.

3,4This man lived among the gravestones, and had such strength that whenever he was put into handcuffs and shackles—as he often was—he snapped the handcuffs from his wrists and smashed the shackles and walked away. No one was strong enough to control him. 5All day long and through the night he would wander among the tombs and in the wild hills, screaming and cutting himself with sharp pieces of stone.

6When Jesus was still far out on the water, the man had seen him and had run to meet him, and fell down before him.

7,8Then Jesus spoke to the demon within the man and said, "Come out, you evil spirit."

It gave a terrible scream, shrieking, "What are you going to do to me, Jesus, Son of the Most High God? For God's sake, don't torture me!"

9"What is your name?" Jesus asked, and the demon replied, "Legion, for there are many of us here within this man."

10Then the demons begged him again and again not to send them to some distant land.

11Now as it happened there was a huge herd of hogs rooting around on the hill above the lake. 12"Send us into those hogs," the demons begged.

13And Jesus gave them permission. Then the evil spirits came out of the man and entered the hogs, and the entire herd plunged down the steep hillside into the lake and drowned.

14The herdsmen fled to the nearby towns and countryside, spreading the news as they ran. Everyone rushed out to see for themselves. 15And a large crowd soon gathered where Jesus was; but as they saw the man sitting there, fully clothed and perfectly sane, they were frightened. 16Those who saw what happened were telling everyone about it, 17and the crowd began pleading with Jesus to go away and leave them alone! 18So he got back into the boat. The man who had been possessed by the demons begged Jesus to let him go along. 19But Jesus said no.

"Go home to your friends," he told him, "and tell them what wonderful things God has done for you; and how merciful he has been."

20So the man started off to visit the Ten Towns of that region and began to tell everyone about the great things Jesus had done for him; and they were awestruck by his story.

PSALM 37:29–40

THE godly shall be firmly planted in the land, and live there forever. 30,31The godly man is a good counselor because he is just and fair and knows right from wrong.

32Evil men spy on the godly, waiting for an excuse to accuse them and then demanding their death. 33But the Lord will not let these evil men succeed, nor let the godly be condemned when they are brought before the judge.

34Don't be impatient for the Lord to act! Keep traveling steadily along his pathway and in due season he will honor you with every blessing, and you will see the wicked destroyed. 35,36I myself have seen it happen: a proud and evil man, towering like a cedar of Lebanon, but when I looked again, he was gone! I searched but could not find him! 37But the good man—what a different story! For the good man—the blameless, the upright, the man of peace—he has a wonderful future ahead of him. For him there is a happy ending. 38But evil men shall be destroyed, and their posterity shall be cut off.

39The Lord saves the godly! He is their salvation and their refuge when trouble comes. 40Because they trust in him, he helps them and delivers them from the plots of evil men.

PROVERBS FOR TODAY/ 10:6–7

The good man is covered with blessings from head to foot, but an evil man inwardly curses his luck. We all have happy memories of good men gone to their reward, but the names of wicked men stink after them.

FEBRUARY 21

LEVITICUS 11:1—12:8

THEN the Lord said to Moses and Aaron, 2,3"Tell the people of Israel that the animals which may be used for food include any animal with cloven hooves which chews its cud. 4-7This means that the following may *not* be eaten:

The camel (it chews the cud but does not have cloven hooves);

The coney, or rock badger (because although it chews the cud, it does not have cloven hooves);

The hare (because although it chews the cud, it does not have cloven hooves);

The swine (because although it has cloven hooves, it does not chew the cud).

8You may not eat their meat or even touch their dead bodies; they are forbidden foods for you.

9"As to fish, you may eat whatever has fins and scales, whether taken from rivers or from the sea; 10but all other water creatures are strictly forbidden to you. 11You mustn't eat their meat or even touch their dead bodies. 12I'll repeat it again—any water creature that does not have fins or scales is forbidden to you.

13-19"Among the birds, these are the ones you may *not* eat:

The eagle, the metire, the osprey,

The falcon (all kinds), the kite,

The raven (all kinds), the ostrich,

The nighthawk, the seagull,

The hawk (all kinds), the owl,

The cormorant, the ibis,

The marsh hen,

The pelican,

The vulture, the stork,

The heron (all kinds),

The hoopoe, the bat.

20"No insects may be eaten, 21,22with the exception of those that jump; locusts of all varieties—ordinary locusts, bald locusts, crickets, and grasshoppers—may be eaten. 23All insects that fly and walk or crawl are forbidden to you.

24"Anyone touching their dead bodies shall be defiled until the evening, 25and must wash his clothes immediately. He must also quarantine himself until nightfall, as being ceremonially defiled.

26"You are also defiled by touching any animal with only semi-parted hoofs, or any animal that does not chew the cud. 27Any animal that walks on paws is forbidden to you as food. Anyone touching the dead body of such an animal shall be defiled until evening. 28Anyone carrying away the carcass shall wash his clothes and be ceremonially defiled until evening; for it is forbidden to you.

29,30"These are the forbidden small animals which scurry about your feet or crawl upon the ground:

The mole, the rat,

The great lizard, the gecko,

The mouse, the lizard,

The snail, the chameleon.

31Anyone touching their dead bodies shall be defiled until evening, 32and anything upon which the carcass falls shall be defiled—any article of wood, or of clothing, a rug, or a sack; anything it touches must be put into water, and is defiled until evening. After that it may be used again. 33If it falls into a pottery bowl, anything in the bowl is defiled, and you shall smash the bowl. 34If the water used to cleanse the defiled article touches any food, all of it is defiled. Any drink which is in the defiled bowl is also contaminated.

35"If the dead body of such an animal touches any clay oven, it is defiled and must be smashed. 36If the body falls into a spring or cistern where there is water, that water is not defiled; yet anyone who pulls out the carcass is defiled. 37And if the carcass touches grain to be sown in the field, it is not contaminated; 38but if the seeds are wet and the carcass falls upon it, the seed is defiled.

39"If an animal which you are permitted to eat dies of disease, anyone touching the carcass shall be defiled until evening. 40Also, anyone eating its meat or carrying away its carcass shall wash his clothes and be defiled until evening.

41,42"Animals that crawl shall not be eaten. This includes all reptiles that slither along upon their bellies as well as those that have legs. No crawling thing with many feet may be eaten, for it is defiled. 43Do not defile yourselves by touching it.

44"I am the Lord your God. Keep yourselves pure concerning these things, and be holy, for I am holy; therefore do not defile yourselves by touching any of these things that crawl upon the earth. 45For I am the Lord who brought you out of the land of Egypt to be your God. You must therefore be holy, for I am holy." 46These are the laws concerning animals, birds, and whatever swims in the water or crawls upon the ground. 47These are the distinctions between what is ceremonially clean and may be eaten, and what is ceremonially defiled and may not be eaten, among all animal life upon the earth.

THE Lord told Moses to give these instructions to the people of Israel:

2"When a baby boy is born, the mother shall be ceremonially defiled for seven days, and under the same restrictions as during her monthly menstrual periods. 3On the eighth day, her son must be circumcised. 4Then, for the next thirty-three days, while she is recovering from her ceremonial impurity, she must not touch anything sacred, nor enter the Tabernacle.

5"When a baby girl is born, the mother's ceremonial impurity shall last two weeks, during which time she will be under the same restrictions as during menstruation. Then for a further sixty-six days she shall continue her recovery.

6"When these days of purification are ended (the following instructions are applicable whether her baby is a boy or girl), she must bring a yearling lamb as a burnt offering, and a young pigeon or a turtledove for a sin offering.

She must take them to the door of the Tabernacle to the priest; 7and the priest will offer them before the Lord and make atonement for her; then she will be ceremonially clean again after her bleeding at childbirth.

"These then, are the procedures after childbirth. 8But if she is too poor to bring a lamb, then she must bring two turtledoves or two young pigeons. One will be for a burnt offering and the other for a sin offering. The priest will make atonement for her with these, so that she will be ceremonially pure again."

MARK 5:21–43

WHEN Jesus had gone across by boat to the other side of the lake, a vast crowd gathered around him on the shore.

22The leader of the local synagogue, whose name was Jairus, came and fell down before him, 23pleading with him to heal his little daughter.

"She is at the point of death," he said in desperation. "Please come and place your hands on her and make her live."

24Jesus went with him, and the crowd thronged behind. 25In the crowd was a woman who had been sick for twelve years with a hemorrhage. 26She had suffered much from many doctors through the years and had become poor from paying them, and was no better but, in fact, was worse. 27She had heard all about the wonderful miracles Jesus did, and that is why she came up behind him through the crowd and touched his clothes.

28For she thought to herself, "If I can just touch his clothing, I will be healed." 29And sure enough, as soon as she had touched him, the bleeding stopped and she knew she was well!

30Jesus realized at once that healing power had gone out from him, so he turned around in the crowd and asked, "Who touched my clothes?"

31His disciples said to him, "All this crowd pressing around you, and you ask who touched you?"

32But he kept on looking around to see who it was who had done it. 33Then the frightened woman, trembling at the realization of what had happened to her, came and fell at his feet and told him what she had done. 34And he said to her, "Daughter, your faith has made you well; go in peace, healed of your disease."

35While he was still talking to her, messengers arrived from Jairus' home with the news that it was too late—his daughter was dead and there was no point in Jesus' coming now. 36But Jesus ignored their comments and said to Jairus, "Don't be afraid. Just trust me."

37Then Jesus halted the crowd and wouldn't let anyone go on with him to Jairus' home except Peter and James and John. 38When they arrived, Jesus saw that all was in great confusion, with unrestrained weeping and wailing. 39He went inside and spoke to the people.

"Why all this weeping and commotion?" he asked. "The child isn't dead; she is only asleep!"

40They laughed at him in bitter derision, but he told them all to leave, and taking the little girl's father and mother and his three disciples, he went into the room where she was lying.

41,42Taking her by the hand he said to her, "Get up, little girl!" (She was twelve years old.) And she jumped up and walked around! Her parents just couldn't get over it. 43Jesus instructed them very earnestly not to tell what had happened, and told them to give her something to eat.

PSALM 38:1–22

O Lord, don't punish me while you are angry! 2Your arrows have struck deep; your blows are crushing me. 3,4Because of your anger my body is sick, my health is broken beneath my sins. They are like a flood, higher than my head; they are a burden too heavy to bear. 5,6My wounds are festering and full of pus. Because of my sins I am bent and racked with pain. My days are filled with anguish. 7My loins burn with inflammation and my whole body is diseased. 8I am exhausted and crushed; I groan in despair.

9Lord, you know how I long for my health once more. You hear my every sigh. 10My heart beats wildly, my strength fails, and I am going blind. 11My loved ones and friends stay away, fearing my disease. Even my own family stands at a distance.

12Meanwhile my enemies are trying to kill me. They plot my ruin and spend all their waking hours planning treachery. 13,14But I am deaf to all their threats; I am silent before them as a man who cannot speak. I have nothing to say. 15For I am waiting for you, O Lord my God. Come and protect me. 16Put an end to their arrogance, these who gloat when I am cast down!

17How constantly I find myself upon the verge of sin; this source of sorrow always stares me in the face. 18I confess my sins; I am sorry for what I have done. 19But my enemies persecute with vigor, and continue to hate me—though I have done nothing against them to deserve it. 20They repay me evil for good and hate me for standing for the right.

21Don't leave me, Lord; don't go away! 22Come quickly! Help me, O my Savior.

PROVERBS FOR TODAY/ 10:8–9

The wise man is glad to be instructed, but a self-sufficient fool falls flat on his face. A good man has firm footing, but a crook will slip and fall.

FEBRUARY 22

LEVITICUS 13:1–59

THE Lord said to Moses and Aaron, "If anyone notices a swelling in his skin, or a scab or boil or pimple with transparent skin, leprosy is to be suspected. He must be brought to Aaron the priest or to one of his sons 3for the spot to be examined. If the hair in this spot turns white, and if the spot looks to be more than skin-deep, it is leprosy, and the priest must declare him a leper.

4"But if the white spot in the skin does not seem to be deeper than the skin, and the hair in the spot has not turned white, the priest shall quarantine him for seven days. 5At the end of that time, on the seventh day, the priest will examine him again, and if the spot has not changed and has not spread in the skin, then the priest must quarantine him seven days more. 6Again on the seventh day the priest will examine him, and if the marks of the disease have become fainter and have not spread, then the priest shall pronounce him cured; it was only a scab, and the man need only wash his clothes and everything will be normal again. 7But if the spot spreads in the skin after he has come to the priest to be examined, he must come back to the priest again, 8and the priest shall look again, and if the spot has spread, then the priest must pronounce him a leper.

9,10"When anyone suspected of having leprosy is brought to the priest, the priest is to look to see if there is a white swelling in the skin with white hairs in the spot, and an ulcer developing. 11If he finds these symptoms, it is an established case of leprosy, and the priest must pronounce him defiled. The man is not to be quarantined for further observation, for he is definitely diseased. 12But if the priest sees that the leprosy has erupted and spread all over his body from head to foot wherever he looks, 13then the priest shall pronounce him cured of lep-

rosy, for it has all turned white; he is cured. 14,15But if there is raw flesh anywhere, the man shall be declared a leper. It is proved by the raw flesh. 16,17But if the raw flesh later changes to white, the leper will return to the priest to be examined again. If the spot has indeed turned completely white, then the priest will pronounce him cured.

18"In the case of a man who has a boil in his skin which heals, 19but which leaves a white swelling or a bright spot, sort of reddish white, the man must go to the priest for examination. 20If the priest sees that the trouble seems to be down under the skin, and if the hair at the spot has turned white, then the priest shall declare him defiled, for leprosy has broken out from the boil. 21But if the priest sees that there are no white hairs in this spot, and the spot does not appear to be deeper than the skin, and if the color is gray, then the priest shall quarantine him for seven days. 22If during that time the spot spreads, the priest must declare him a leper. 23But if the bright spot grows no larger and does not spread, it is merely the scar from the boil, and the priest shall declare that all is well.

24"If a man is burned in some way, and the burned place becomes bright reddish white or white, 25then the priest must examine the spot. If the hair in the bright spot turns white, and the problem seems to be more than skin-deep, it is leprosy that has broken out from the burn, and the priest must pronounce him a leper. 26But if the priest sees that there are no white hairs in the bright spot, and the brightness appears to be no deeper than the skin and is fading, the priest shall quarantine him for seven days, 27and examine him again the seventh day. If the spot spreads in the skin, the priest must pronounce him a leper. 28But if the bright spot does not move or spread in the skin, and is fading, it is simply a scar from the burn, and the priest shall declare that he does not have leprosy.

29,30"If a man or woman has a sore on the head or chin, the priest must examine him; if the infection seems to be below the skin and yellow hair is found in the sore, the priest must pronounce him a leper. 31But if the priest's examination reveals that the spot seems to be only in the skin but there is healthy hair in it, then he shall be quarantined for seven days, 32and examined again on the seventh day. If the spot has not spread and no yellow hair has appeared, and if the infection does not seem to be deeper than the skin, 33he shall shave off all the hair around the spot (but not on the spot itself) and the priest shall quarantine him for another seven days. 34He shall be examined again on the seventh day, and if the spot has not spread, and it appears to be no deeper than the skin, the priest shall pronounce him well, and after washing his clothes, he is free. 35But if, later on, this spot begins to spread, 36then the priest must examine him again and, without waiting to see if any yellow hair develops, declare him a leper. 37But if it appears that the spreading has stopped and black hairs are found in the spot, then he is healed and is not a leper, and the priest shall declare him healed.

38"If a man or a woman has white, transparent areas in the skin, 39but these spots are growing dimmer, this is not leprosy, but an ordinary infection that has broken out in the skin.

40"If a man's hair is gone, this does not make him a leper even though he is bald! 41If the hair is gone from the front part of his head, he simply has a bald forehead, but this is not leprosy. 42However, if in the baldness there is a reddish white spot, it may be leprosy breaking out. 43In that case the priest shall examine him, and if there is a reddish white lump that looks like leprosy, 44then he is a leper, and the priest must pronounce him such.

45"Anyone who is discovered to have leprosy must tear his clothes and let his hair grow in wild disarray, and cover his upper lip and call out as he goes, "I am a leper, I am a leper." 46As long as the disease lasts, he is defiled and must live outside the camp.

47,48"If leprosy is suspected in a woolen or linen garment or fabric, or in a piece of leather or leather-work, 49and there is a greenish or a reddish spot in it, it is probably leprosy, and must be taken to the priest to be examined. 50The priest will put it away for seven days 51and look at it again on the seventh day. If the spot has spread, it is a contagious leprosy, 52and he must burn the clothing, fabric, linen or woolen covering, or leather article, for it is contagious and must be destroyed by fire.

53"But if when he examines it again on the seventh day the spot has not spread, 54the priest shall order the suspected article to be washed, then isolated for seven more days. 55If after that time the spot has not changed its color, even though it has not spread, it is leprosy and shall be burned, for the article is infected through and through. 56But if the priest sees that the spot has faded after the washing, then he shall cut it out from the garment or leather goods or whatever it is in. 57However, if it then reappears, it is leprosy and he must burn it. 58But if after washing it there is no further trouble, it can be put back into service after another washing."

59These are the regulations concerning leprosy in a garment or anything made of skin or leather, indicating whether to pronounce it leprous or not.

MARK 6:1–29

SOON afterwards he left that section of the country and returned with his disciples to Nazareth, his home town. 2,3The next Sabbath he went to the synagogue to teach, and the people were astonished at his wisdom and his miracles because he was just a local man like themselves.

"He's no better than we are," they

said. "He's just a carpenter, Mary's boy, and a brother of James and Joseph, Judas and Simon. And his sisters live right here among us." And they were offended!

⁴Then Jesus told them, "A prophet is honored everywhere except in his home town and among his relatives and by his own family." ⁵And because of their unbelief he couldn't do any mighty miracles among them except to place his hands on a few sick people and heal them. ⁶And he could hardly accept the fact that they wouldn't believe in him.

Then he went out among the villages, teaching.

⁷And he called his twelve disciples together and sent them out two by two, with power to cast out demons. ⁸,⁹He told them to take nothing with them except their walking sticks—no food, no knapsack, no money, not even an extra pair of shoes or a change of clothes.

¹⁰"Stay at one home in each village—don't shift around from house to house while you are there," he said. ¹¹"And whenever a village won't accept you or listen to you, shake off the dust from your feet as you leave; it is a sign that you have abandoned it to its fate."

¹²So the disciples went out, telling everyone they met to turn from sin. ¹³And they cast out many demons, and healed many sick people, anointing them with olive oil.

¹⁴King Herod soon heard about Jesus, for his miracles were talked about everywhere. The king thought Jesus was John the Baptist come back to life again. So the people were saying, "No wonder he can do such miracles." ¹⁵Others thought Jesus was Elijah the ancient prophet, now returned to life again; still others claimed he was a new prophet like the great ones of the past.

¹⁶"No," Herod said, "it is John, the man I beheaded. He has come back from the dead."

¹⁷,¹⁸For Herod had sent soldiers to arrest and imprison John because he kept saying it was wrong for the king to marry Herodias, his brother Philip's wife.

¹⁹Herodias wanted John killed in revenge, but without Herod's approval she was powerless. ²⁰And Herod respected John, knowing that he was a good and holy man, and so he kept him under his protection. Herod was disturbed whenever he talked with John, but even so he liked to listen to him.

²¹Herodias' chance finally came. It was Herod's birthday and he gave a stag party for his palace aides, army officers, and the leading citizens of Galilee. ²²,²³Then Herodias' daughter came in and danced before them and greatly pleased them all.

"Ask me for anything you like," the king vowed, "even half of my kingdom, and I will give it to you!"

²⁴She went out and consulted her mother, who told her, "Ask for John the Baptist's head!"

²⁵So she hurried back to the king and told him, "I want the head of John the Baptist—right now—on a tray!"

²⁶Then the king was sorry, but he was embarrassed to break his oath in front of his guests. ²⁷So he sent one of his bodyguards to the prison to cut off John's head and bring it to him. The soldier killed John in the prison, ²⁸and brought back his head on a tray, and gave it to the girl and she took it to her mother.

²⁹When John's disciples heard what had happened, they came for his body and buried it in a tomb.

PSALM 39:1–13

I said to myself, I'm going to quit complaining! I'll keep quiet, especially when the ungodly are around me. ²,³But as I stood there silently the turmoil within me grew to the bursting point. The more I mused, the hotter the fires inside. Then at last I spoke, and pled with God: ⁴Lord, help me to realize how brief my time on earth will be. Help me to know that I am here for but a moment more. ⁵,⁶My life is no longer than my hand! My whole lifetime is but a moment to you. Proud man! Frail as breath! A shadow! And all his busy rushing ends in nothing. He heaps up riches for someone else to spend. 7And so, Lord, my only hope is in you.

8Save me from being overpowered by my sins, for even fools will mock me then.

9Lord, I am speechless before you. I will not open my mouth to speak one word of complaint, for my punishment is from you.

10Lord, don't hit me anymore—I am exhausted beneath your hand. 11When you punish a man for his sins, he is destroyed, for he is as fragile as a moth-infested cloth; yes, man is frail as breath.

12Hear my prayer, O Lord; listen to my cry! Don't sit back, unmindful of my tears. For I am your guest. I am a traveler passing through the earth, as all my fathers were.

13Spare me, Lord! Let me recover and be filled with happiness again before my death.

PROVERBS FOR TODAY/ 10:10

Winking at sin leads to sorrow; bold reproof leads to peace.

FEBRUARY 23

LEVITICUS 14:1–57

AND the Lord gave Moses these regulations concerning a person whose leprosy disappears:

3"The priest shall go out of the camp to examine him. If the priest sees that the leprosy is gone, 4he shall require two living birds of a kind permitted for food, and shall take some cedar wood, a scarlet string, and some hyssop branches, to be used for the purification ceremony of the one who is healed. 5The priest shall then order one of the birds killed in an earthenware pot held above running water. 6The other bird, still living, shall be dipped in the blood, along with the cedar wood, the scarlet thread, and the hyssop branch. 7Then the priest shall sprinkle the blood seven times upon the man cured of his leprosy, and the priest shall pronounce him cured, and shall let the living bird fly into the open field.

8"Then the man who is cured shall wash his clothes, shave off all his hair, and bathe himself, and return to live inside the camp; however, he must stay outside his tent for seven days. 9The seventh day he shall again shave all the hair from his head, beard, and eyebrows, and wash his clothes and bathe, and shall then be declared fully cured of his leprosy.

10"The next day, the eighth day, he shall take two male lambs without physical defect, one yearling ewe-lamb without physical defect, ten quarts of finely ground flour mixed with olive oil, and a pint of olive oil; 11then the priest who examines him shall place the man and his offerings before the Lord at the entrance of the Tabernacle. 12The priest shall take one of the lambs and the pint of olive oil and offer them to the Lord as a guilt offering by the gesture of waving them before the altar. 13Then he shall kill the lamb at the place where sin offerings and burnt offerings are killed, there at the Tabernacle; this guilt offering shall then be given to the priest for food, as in the case of a sin offering. It is a most holy offering. 14The priest shall take the blood from this guilt offering and smear some of it upon the tip of the right ear of the man being cleansed, and upon the thumb of his right hand, and upon the big toe of his right foot.

15"Then the priest shall take the olive oil and pour it into the palm of his left hand, 16and dip his right finger into it, and sprinkle it with his finger seven times before the Lord. 17Some of the oil remaining in his left hand shall then be placed by the priest upon the tip of the man's right ear and the thumb of his right hand and the big toe of his right foot—just as he did with the blood of the guilt offering. 18The remainder of the oil in his hand shall be used to anoint the man's head. Thus the priest shall make atonement for him before the Lord.

19"Then the priest must offer the sin offering and again perform the rite of atonement for the person being cleansed from his leprosy; and afterwards the priest shall kill the burnt offering, 20and offer it along with the grain offering upon the altar, making atonement for the man, who shall then be pronounced finally cleansed.

21"If he is so poor that he cannot afford two lambs, then he shall bring only one, a male lamb for the guilt offering, to be presented to the Lord in the rite of atonement by waving it before the altar; and only three quarts of fine white flour, mixed with olive oil, for a grain offering, and a pint of olive oil.

22"He shall also bring two turtledoves or two young pigeons—whichever he is able to afford—and use one of the pair for a sin offering and the other for a burnt offering. 23He shall bring them to the priest at the entrance of the Tabernacle on the eighth day, for his ceremony of cleansing before the Lord. 24The priest shall take the lamb for the guilt offering, and the pint of oil, and wave them before the altar as a gesture of offering to the Lord. 25Then he shall kill the lamb for the guilt offering and smear some of its blood upon the tip of the man's right ear—the man on whose behalf the ceremony is being performed—and upon the thumb of his right hand and on the big toe of his right foot.

26"The priest shall then pour the olive oil into the palm of his own left hand, 27and with his right finger he is to sprinkle some of it seven times before the Lord. 28Then he must put some of the olive oil from his hand upon the tip of the man's right ear, and upon the thumb of his right hand, and upon the big toe of his right foot, just as he did with the blood of the guilt offering. 29The remaining oil in his hand shall be placed upon the head of the man being cleansed, to make atonement for him before the Lord.

30"Then he must offer the two turtledoves or two young pigeons (whichever pair he is able to afford). 31One of the pair is for a sin offering and the other for a burnt offering, to be sacrificed along with the grain offering; and the priest shall make atonement for the man before the Lord."

32These, then, are the laws concerning those who are cleansed of leprosy but are not able to bring the sacrifices normally required for the ceremony of cleansing.

33,34Then the Lord said to Moses and Aaron, "When you arrive in the land of Canaan which I have given you, and I place leprosy in some house there, 35then the owner of the house shall come and report to the priest, 'It seems to me that there may be leprosy in my house!'

36"The priest shall order the house to be emptied before he examines it, so that everything in the house will not be declared contaminated if he decides that there is leprosy there. 37If he finds greenish or reddish streaks in the walls of the house which seem to be beneath the surface of the wall, 38he shall close up the house for seven days, 39and return the seventh day to look at it again. If the spots have spread in the wall, 40then the priest shall order the removal of the spotted section of wall, and the material must be thrown into a defiled place outside the city. 41Then he shall order the inside walls of the house scraped thoroughly, and the scrapings dumped in a defiled place outside the city. 42Other stones shall be brought to replace those that have been removed, new mortar used, and the house replastered.

⁴³"But if the spots appear again, ⁴⁴the priest shall come again and look, and if he sees that the spots have spread, it is leprosy, and the house is defiled. ⁴⁵Then he shall order the destruction of the house—all its stones, timbers, and mortar shall be carried out of the city to a defiled place. ⁴⁶Anyone entering the house while it is closed shall be defiled until evening. ⁴⁷Anyone who lies down or eats in the house shall wash his clothing.

⁴⁸"But if, when the priest comes again to look, the spots have not reappeared after the fresh plastering, then he will pronounce the house cleansed, and declare the leprosy gone. ⁴⁹He shall also perform the ceremony of cleansing, using two birds, cedar wood, scarlet thread, and hyssop branches. ⁵⁰He shall kill one of the birds over fresh water in an earthenware bowl, ⁵¹,⁵²and dip the cedar wood, hyssop branch, and scarlet thread, as well as the living bird, into the blood of the bird that was killed over the fresh water, and shall sprinkle the house seven times. In this way the house shall be cleansed. ⁵³Then he shall let the live bird fly away into an open field outside the city. This is the method for making atonement for the house and cleansing it."

⁵⁴These, then, are the laws concerning the various places where leprosy may appear: ⁵⁵in a garment or in a house, ⁵⁶or in any swelling in one's skin, or a scab from a burn, or a bright spot. ⁵⁷In this way you will know whether or not it is actually leprosy. That is why these laws are given.

MARK 6:30–56

THE apostles now returned to Jesus from their tour and told him all they had done and what they had said to the people they visited.

³¹Then Jesus suggested, "Let's get away from the crowds for a while and rest." For so many people were coming and going that they scarcely had time to eat. ³²So they left by boat for a quieter spot. ³³But many people saw them leaving and ran on ahead along the shore and met them as they landed. ³⁴So the usual vast crowd was there as he stepped from the boat; and he had pity on them because they were like sheep without a shepherd, and he taught them many things they needed to know.

³⁵,³⁶Late in the afternoon his disciples came to him and said, "Tell the people to go away to the nearby villages and farms and buy themselves some food, for there is nothing to eat here in this desolate spot, and it is getting late."

³⁷But Jesus said, *"You* feed them."

"With what?" they asked. "It would take a fortune to buy food for all this crowd!"

³⁸"How much food do we have?" he asked. "Go and find out."

They came back to report that there were five loaves of bread and two fish. ³⁹,⁴⁰Then Jesus told the crowd to sit down, and soon colorful groups of fifty or a hundred each were sitting on the green grass.

⁴¹He took the five loaves and two fish and looking up to heaven, gave thanks for the food. Breaking the loaves into pieces, he gave some of the bread and fish to each disciple to place before the people. ⁴²And the crowd ate until they could hold no more!

⁴³,⁴⁴There were about 5,000 men there for that meal, and afterwards twelve basketfuls of scraps were picked up off the grass!

⁴⁵Immediately after this Jesus instructed his disciples to get back into the boat and strike out across the lake to Bethsaida, where he would join them later. He himself would stay and tell the crowds good-bye and get them started home.

⁴⁶Afterwards he went up into the hills to pray. ⁴⁷During the night, as the disciples in their boat were out in the middle of the lake, and he was alone on land, ⁴⁸he saw that they were in serious trouble, rowing hard and struggling against the wind and waves.

About three o'clock in the morning

he walked out to them on the water. He started past them, 49but when they saw something walking along beside them they screamed in terror, thinking it was a ghost, 50for they all saw him.

But he spoke to them at once. "It's all right," he said. "It is I! Don't be afraid." 51Then he climbed into the boat and the wind stopped!

They just sat there, unable to take it in! 52For they still didn't realize who he was, even after the miracle the evening before! For they didn't want to believe!

53When they arrived at Gennesaret on the other side of the lake they moored the boat, 54and climbed out.

The people standing around there recognized him at once, 55and ran throughout the whole area to spread the news of his arrival, and began carrying sick folks to him on mats and stretchers. 56Wherever he went—in villages and cities, and out on the farms—they laid the sick in the market plazas and streets, and begged him to let them at least touch the fringes of his clothes; and as many as touched him were healed.

PSALM 40:1–10

I waited patiently for God to help me; then he listened and heard my cry. 2He lifted me out of the pit of despair, out from the bog and the mire, and set my feet on a hard, firm path and steadied me as I walked along. 3He has given me a new song to sing, of praises to our God. Now many will hear of the glorious things he did for me, and stand in awe before the Lord, and put their trust in him. 4Many blessings are given to those who trust the Lord, and have no confidence in those who are proud, or who trust in idols.

5O Lord my God, many and many a time you have done great miracles for us and we are ever in your thoughts. Who else can do such glorious things? No one else can be compared with you. There isn't time to tell of all your wonderful deeds.

6It isn't sacrifices and offerings which you really want from your people. Burnt animals bring no special joy to your heart. But you have accepted the offer of my life-long service. 7Then I said, "See, I have come, just as all the prophets foretold. 8And I delight to do your will, my God, for your law is written upon my heart!"

9I have told everyone the Good News that you forgive people's sins. I have not been timid about it, as you well know, O Lord. 10I have not kept this Good News hidden in my heart, but have proclaimed your lovingkindness and truth to all the congregation.

PROVERBS FOR TODAY/ 10:11–12

There is living truth in what a good man says, but the mouth of the evil man is filled with curses. Hatred stirs old quarrels, but love overlooks insults.

FEBRUARY 24

LEVITICUS 15:1—16:28

THE Lord told Moses and Aaron to give the people of Israel these further instructions:

"Any man who has a genital discharge is ceremonially defiled. 3This applies not only while the discharge is active, but also for a time after it heals. 4Any bed he lies on and anything he sits on is contaminated: 5so anyone touching the man's bed is ceremonially defiled until evening, and must wash his clothes and bathe himself. 6Anyone sitting on a seat the man has sat upon while defiled is himself ceremonially impure until evening, and must wash his clothes and bathe himself. 7The same instructions apply to anyone touching him. 8Anyone he spits on is ceremonially impure until evening, and must wash his clothes and bathe himself. 9Any saddle he rides on is defiled. 10Anyone touching or carrying anything else that was beneath him shall be defiled until evening, and must wash his clothes and bathe himself. 11If the defiled man touches anyone without first rinsing his hands, that person must wash his clothes and bathe himself and be defiled until evening. 12Any earthen pot touched by the defiled man must be broken, and every wooden utensil must be rinsed in water.

13"When the discharge stops, he shall begin a seven-day cleansing ceremony by washing his clothes and bathing in running water. 14On the eighth day he shall take two turtledoves or two young pigeons and come before the Lord at the entrance of the Tabernacle, and give them to the priest. 15The priest shall sacrifice them there, one for a sin offering and the other for a burnt offering; thus the priest shall make atonement before the Lord for the man because of his discharge.

16"Whenever a man's semen goes out from him, he shall take a complete bath and be ceremonially impure until the evening. 17Any clothing or bedding the semen spills on must be washed and remain ceremonially defiled until evening. 18After sexual intercourse, the woman as well as the man must bathe, and they are ceremonially defiled until the next evening.

19"Whenever a woman menstruates, she shall be in a state of ceremonial defilement for seven days afterwards, and during that time anyone touching her shall be defiled until evening. 20Anything she lies on or sits on during that time shall be defiled. 21,22,23Anyone touching her bed or anything she sits upon shall wash his clothes and bathe himself and be ceremonially defiled until evening. 24A man having sexual intercourse with her during this time is ceremonially defiled for seven days, and every bed he lies upon shall be defiled.

25"If the menstrual flow continues after the normal time, or at some irregular time during the month, the same rules apply as indicated above, 26so that anything she lies upon during that time is defiled, just as it would be during her normal menstrual period, and everything she sits on is in a similar state of defilement. 27Anyone touching her bed or anything she sits on shall be defiled, and shall wash his clothes and bathe and be defiled until evening. 28Seven days after the menstruating stops, she is no longer ceremonially defiled.

29"On the eighth day, she shall take two turtledoves or two young pigeons and bring them to the priest at the entrance of the Tabernacle, 30and the priest shall offer one for a sin offering and the other for a burnt offering, and make atonement for her before the Lord, for her menstrual defilement. 31In this way you shall cleanse the people of Israel from their defilement, lest they die because of defiling my Tabernacle that is among them."

32This, then, is the law for the man who is defiled by a genital disease or by a seminal emission; 33and for a woman's menstrual period; and for anyone who has sexual intercourse with her while she is in her period of defilement afterwards.

AFTER Aaron's two sons died before the Lord, the Lord said to Moses, "Warn your brother Aaron not to enter into the Holy Place behind the veil, where the Ark and the place of mercy are, just whenever he chooses. The penalty for intrusion is death. For I myself am present in the cloud above the place of mercy.

3"Here are the conditions for his entering there: He must bring a young bull for a sin offering, and a ram for a burnt offering. 4He must bathe himself and put on the sacred linen coat, shorts, belt, and turban. 5The people of Israel shall then bring him two male goats for their sin offering, and a ram for their burnt offering. 6First he shall present to the Lord the young bull as a sin offering for himself, making atonement for himself and his family. 7Then he shall bring the two goats before the Lord at the entrance of the Tabernacle, 8and cast lots to determine which is the Lord's and which is to be sent away. 9The goat allotted to the Lord shall then be sacrificed by Aaron as a sin offering. 10The other goat shall be kept alive and placed before the Lord. The rite of atonement shall be performed over it, and it shall then be sent out into the desert as a scapegoat.

11"After Aaron has sacrificed the young bull as a sin offering for himself and his family, 12he shall take a censer full of live coals from the altar of the Lord, and fill his hands with sweet incense beaten into fine powder, and bring it inside the veil. 13There before the Lord he shall put the incense upon the coals, so that a cloud of incense will cover the mercy place above the Ark (containing the stone tablets of the Ten Commandments); thus he will not die. 14And he shall bring some of the blood of the young bull and sprinkle it with his finger upon the east side of the mercy place, and then seven times in front of it.

15"Then he must go out and sacrifice the people's sin offering goat, and bring its blood within the veil, and sprinkle it upon the place of mercy and in front of it, just as he did with the blood of the young bull. 16Thus he shall make atonement for the holy place because it is defiled by the sins of the people of Israel, and for the Tabernacle, located right among them and surrounded by their defilement. 17Not another soul shall be inside the Tabernacle when Aaron enters to make atonement in the Holy Place—not until after he comes out again and has made atonement for himself and his household and for all the people of Israel. 18Then he shall go out to the altar

before the Lord and make atonement for it. He must smear the blood of the young bull and the goat on the horns of the altar, 19and sprinkle blood upon the altar seven times with his finger, thus cleansing it from the sinfulness of Israel, and making it holy.

20"When he has completed the rite of atonement for the Holy Place, the entire Tabernacle, and the altar, he shall bring the live goat and, 21laying both hands upon its head, confess over it all the sins of the people of Israel. He shall lay all their sins upon the head of the goat and send it into the desert, led by a man appointed for the task. 22So the goat shall carry all the sins of the people into a land where no one lives, and the man shall let it loose in the wilderness.

23"Then Aaron shall go into the Tabernacle again and take off the linen garments he wore when he went behind the veil, and leave them there in the Tabernacle. 24Then he shall bathe in a sacred place, put on his clothes again, and go out and sacrifice his own burnt offering for the people, making atonement for himself and for them. 25He shall also burn upon the altar the fat for the sin offering.

26"(The man who took the goat out into the desert shall afterwards wash his clothes and bathe himself and then come back into the camp.) 27And the young bull and the goat used for the sin offering (their blood was taken into the Holy Place by Aaron, to make atonement) shall be carried outside the camp and burned, including the hides and internal organs. 28Afterwards, the person doing the burning shall wash his clothes and bathe himself and then return to camp.

MARK 7:1–23

ONE day some Jewish religious leaders arrived from Jerusalem to investigate him, 2and noticed that some of his disciples failed to follow the usual Jewish rituals before eating. 3(For the Jews, especially the Pharisees, will never eat until they have sprinkled their arms to the elbows, as required by their ancient traditions. 4So when they come home from the market they must always sprinkle themselves in this way before touching any food. This is but one of many examples of laws and regulations they have clung to for centuries, and still follow, such as their ceremony of cleansing for pots, pans and dishes.)

5So the religious leaders asked him, "Why don't your disciples follow our age-old customs? For they eat without first performing the washing ceremony."

6,7Jesus replied, "You bunch of hypocrites! Isaiah the prophet described you very well when he said, 'These people speak very prettily about the Lord but they have no love for him at all. Their worship is a farce, for they claim that God commands the people to obey their petty rules.' How right Isaiah was! 8For you ignore God's specific orders and substitute your own traditions. 9You are simply rejecting God's laws and trampling them under your feet for the sake of tradition.

10"For instance, Moses gave you this law from God: 'Honor your father and mother.' And he said that anyone who speaks against his father or mother must die. 11But you say it is perfectly all right for a man to disregard his needy parents, telling them, 'Sorry, I can't help you! For I have given to God what I could have given to you.' 12,13And so you break the law of God in order to protect your man-made tradition. And this is only one example. There are many, many others."

14Then Jesus called to the crowd to come and hear. "All of you listen," he said, "and try to understand. 15,16Your souls aren't harmed by what you eat, but by what you think and say!"

17Then he went into a house to get away from the crowds, and his disciples asked him what he meant by the statement he had just made.

18"Don't you understand either?" he asked. "Can't you see that what you eat won't harm your soul? 19For food doesn't come in contact with your heart, but only passes through the digestive system." (By saying this he showed that every kind of food is kosher.)

20And then he added, "It is the thought-life that pollutes. 21For from within, out of men's hearts, come evil thoughts of lust, theft, murder, adultery, 22wanting what belongs to others, wickedness, deceit, lewdness, envy, slander, pride, and all other folly. 23All these vile things come from within; they are what pollute you and make you unfit for God."

PSALM 40:11–17

O Lord, don't hold back your tender mercies from me! My only hope is in your love and faithfulness. 12Otherwise I perish, for problems far too big for me to solve are piled higher than my head. Meanwhile my sins, too many to count, have all caught up with me and I am ashamed to look up. My heart quails within me.

13Please, Lord, rescue me! Quick! Come and help me! 14,15Confuse them! Turn them around and send them sprawling—all these who are trying to destroy me. Disgrace these scoffers with their utter failure!

16But may the joy of the Lord be given to everyone who loves him and his salvation. May they constantly exclaim, "How great God is!"

17I am poor and weak, yet the Lord is thinking about me right now! O my God, you are my helper. You are my Savior; come quickly, and save me. Please don't delay!

PROVERBS FOR TODAY/ 10:13–14

Men with common sense are admired as counselors; those without it are beaten as servants. A wise man holds his tongue. Only a fool blurts out everything he knows; that only leads to sorrow and trouble.

FEBRUARY 25

LEVITICUS 16:29—18:30

THIS is a permanent law: You must do no work on the twenty-fifth day of September, but must spend the day in self-examination and humility. This applies whether you are born in the land or are a foreigner living among the people of Israel; for this is the day commemorating the atonement, cleansing you in the Lord's eyes from all of your sins. 31It is a Sabbath of solemn rest for you, and you shall spend the day in quiet humility; this is a permanent law. 32This ceremony, in later generations, shall be performed by the anointed High Priest, consecrated in place of his ancestor Aaron; he shall be the one to put on the holy linen garments, 33and make atonement for the holy sanctuary, the Tabernacle, the altar, the priests, and the people. 34This shall be an everlasting law for you, to make atonement for the people of Israel once each year, because of their sins."

And Aaron followed all these instructions that the Lord gave to Moses.

THE Lord gave to Moses these additional instructions for Aaron and the priests and for all the people of Israel:

3,4"Any Israelite who sacrifices an ox, lamb, or goat anywhere except at the Tabernacle is guilty of murder and shall be excommunicated from his nation. 5The purpose of this law is to stop the people of Israel from sacrificing in the open fields, and to cause them to bring their sacrifices to the priest at the entrance of the Tabernacle, and to burn the fat as a savor the Lord will appreciate and enjoy— 6for in this way the priest will be able to sprinkle the blood upon the altar of the Lord at the entrance of the Tabernacle, and to burn the fat as a savor the Lord will appreciate and enjoy— 7instead of the people's sacrificing to evil spirits out in the fields. This shall

be a permanent law for you, from generation to generation. 8,9I repeat: Anyone, whether an Israelite or a foreigner living among you who offers a burnt offering or a sacrifice anywhere other than at the entrance of the Tabernacle, where it will be sacrificed to the Lord, shall be excommunicated.

10"And I will turn my face against anyone, whether an Israelite or a foreigner living among you, who eats blood in any form. I will excommunicate him from his people. 11For the life of the flesh is in the blood, and I have given you the blood to sprinkle upon the altar as an atonement for your souls; it is the blood that makes atonement, because it is the life. 12That is the reasoning behind my decree to the people of Israel, that neither they, nor any foreigner living among them, may eat blood. 13Anyone, whether an Israelite or a foreigner living among you, who goes hunting and kills an animal or bird of a kind permitted for food, must pour out the blood and cover it with dust, 14for the blood is the life. That is why I told the people of Israel never to eat it, for the life of every bird and animal is its blood. Therefore, anyone who eats blood must be excommunicated.

15"And anyone—native born or foreigner—who eats the dead body of an animal that dies a natural death, or is killed by wild animals, must wash his clothes and bathe himself and be defiled until evening; after that he shall be declared cleansed. 16But if he does not wash his clothes and bathe, he shall suffer the consequence."

THE Lord then told Moses to tell the people of Israel,

"I am Jehovah your God, 3so don't act like heathen—like the people of Egypt where you lived so long, or the people of Canaan where I am going to take you. 4,5You must obey only my laws, and you must carry them out in detail, for I am the Lord your God. If you obey them you shall live. I am the Lord.

6"None of you shall marry a near relative, for I am the Lord. 7Do not disgrace your father by having intercourse with your mother, 8nor any other of your father's wives. 9Do not have intercourse with your sister or half-sister, whether the daughter of your father or your mother, whether brought up in the same household or elsewhere.

10"You shall not have intercourse with your granddaughter—the daughter of either your son or your daughter—for she is a close relative. 11You may not have intercourse with a half-sister—your father's wife's daughter; 12nor your aunt—your father's sister—because she is so closely related to your father; 13nor your aunt—your mother's sister—because she is a close relative of your mother; 14nor your aunt—the wife of your father's brother.

15"You may not marry your daughter-in-law—your son's wife; 16nor your brother's wife, for she is your brother's. 17You may not marry both a woman and her daughter or granddaughter, for they are near relatives, and to do so is horrible wickedness. 18You shall not marry two sisters, for they will be rivals. However, if your wife dies, then it is all right to marry her sister.

19"There must be no sexual relationship with a woman who is menstruating; 20nor with anyone else's wife, to defile yourself with her.

21"You shall not give any of your children to Molech, burning them upon his altar; never profane the name of your God, for I am Jehovah.

22"Homosexuality is absolutely forbidden, for it is an enormous sin. 23A man shall have no sexual intercourse with any female animal, thus defiling himself; and a woman must never give herself to a male animal, to mate with it; this is a terrible perversion.

24"Do not defile yourselves in any of these ways, for these are the things the heathen do; and because they do them

I am going to cast them out from the land into which you are going. 25That entire country is defiled with this kind of activity; that is why I am punishing the people living there, and will throw them out of the land. 26You must strictly obey all of my laws and ordinances, and you must not do any of these abominable things; these laws apply both to you who are born in the nation of Israel and to foreigners living among you.

27"Yes, all these abominations have been done continually by the people of the land where I am taking you, and the land is defiled. 28Do not do these things or I will throw you out of the land, just as I will throw out the nations that live there now. 29,30Whoever does any of these terrible deeds shall be excommunicated from this nation. So be very sure to obey my laws, and do not practice any of these horrible customs. Do not defile yourselves with the evil deeds of those living in the land where you are going. For I am Jehovah your God."

MARK 7:24—8:9

THEN he left Galilee and went to the region of Tyre and Sidon, and tried to keep it a secret that he was there, but couldn't. For as usual the news of his arrival spread fast.

25Right away a woman came to him whose little girl was possessed by a demon. She had heard about Jesus and now she came and fell at his feet, 26and pled with him to release her child from the demon's control. (But she was Syrophoenician—a "despised Gentile!")

27Jesus told her, "First I should help my own family—the Jews. It isn't right to take the children's food and throw it to the dogs."

28She replied, "That's true, sir, but even the puppies under the table are given some scraps from the children's plates."

29"Good!" he said, "You have answered well—so well that I have healed your little girl. Go on home, for the demon has left her!"

"Look at the birds! They don't worry about what to eat . . . for your heavenly Father feeds them. And you are far more valuable to him than they are."
  Matthew 6:26

"This is the day the Lord has made. We will rejoice and be glad in it."
   Psalm 118:24

30And when she arrived home, her little girl was lying quietly in bed, and the demon was gone.

31From Tyre he went to Sidon, then back to the Sea of Galilee by way of the Ten Towns. 32A deaf man with a speech impediment was brought to him, and everyone begged Jesus to lay his hands on the man and heal him.

33Jesus led him away from the crowd and put his fingers into the man's ears, then spat and touched the man's tongue with the spittle. 34Then, looking up to heaven, he sighed and commanded, "Open!" 35Instantly the man could hear perfectly and speak plainly!

36Jesus told the crowd not to spread the news, but the more he forbade them, the more they made it known, 37for they were overcome with utter amazement. Again and again they said, "Everything he does is wonderful; he even corrects deafness and stammering!"

ONE day about this time as another great crowd gathered, the people ran out of food again. Jesus called his disciples to discuss the situation.

"I pity these people," he said, "for they have been here three days, and have nothing left to eat. 3And if I send them home without feeding them, they will faint along the road! For some of them have come a long distance."

4"Are we supposed to find food for them here in the desert?" his disciples scoffed.

5"How many loaves of bread do you have?" he asked.

"Seven," they replied. 6So he told the crowd to sit down on the ground. Then he took the seven loaves, thanked God for them, broke them into pieces and passed them to his disciples; and the disciples placed them before the people. 7A few small fish were found, too, so

Jesus also blessed these and told the disciples to serve them.

8,9And the whole crowd ate until they were full, and afterwards he sent them home. There were about 4,000 people in the crowd that day and when the scraps were picked up after the meal, there were seven very large basketfuls left over!

PSALM 41:1–13

GOD blesses those who are kind to the poor. He helps them out of their troubles. 2He protects them and keeps them alive; he publicly honors them and destroys the power of their enemies. 3He nurses them when they are sick, and soothes their pains and worries.

4"O Lord," I prayed, "be kind and heal me, for I have confessed my sins." 5But my enemies say, "May he soon die and be forgotten!" 6They act so friendly when they come to visit me while I am sick; but all the time they hate me and are glad that I am lying there upon my bed of pain. And when they leave, they laugh and mock. 7They whisper together about what they will do when I am dead. 8"It's fatal, whatever it is," they say. "He'll never get out of that bed!"

9Even my best friend has turned against me—a man I completely trusted; how often we ate together. 10Lord, don't you desert me! Be gracious, Lord, and make me well again so I can pay them back! 11I know you are pleased with me because you haven't let my enemies triumph over me. 12You have preserved me because I was honest; you have admitted me forever to your presence.

13Bless the Lord, the God of Israel, who exists from everlasting ages past— and on into everlasting eternity ahead. Amen and amen!

PROVERBS FOR TODAY/ 10:15–16

The rich man's wealth is his only strength. The poor man's poverty is his only curse. The good man's earnings advance the cause of righteousness. The evil man squanders his on sin.

FEBRUARY 26

LEVITICUS 19:1—20:21

THE Lord also told Moses to tell the people of Israel, "You must be holy because I, the Lord your God, am holy. You must respect your mothers and fathers, and obey my Sabbath law, for I am the Lord your God. 3,4Do not make or worship idols, for I am Jehovah your God.

5"When you sacrifice a peace offering to the Lord, offer it correctly so that it will be accepted: 6Eat it the same day you offer it, or the next day at the latest; any remaining until the third day must be burned. 7For any of it eaten on the third day is repulsive to me, and will not be accepted. 8If you eat it on the third day you are guilty, for you profane the holiness of Jehovah, and you shall be excommunicated from Jehovah's people.

9"When you harvest your crops, don't reap the corners of your fields, and don't pick up stray grains of wheat from the ground. 10It is the same with your grape crop—don't strip every last piece of fruit from the vines, and don't pick up the grapes that fall to the ground. Leave them for the poor and for those traveling through, for I am Jehovah your God.

11"You must not steal nor lie nor defraud. 12You must not swear to a falsehood, thus bringing reproach upon the name of your God, for I am Jehovah.

13"You shall not rob nor oppress anyone, and you shall pay your hired workers promptly. If something is due them, don't even keep it overnight.

14"You must not curse the deaf nor trip up a blind man as he walks. Fear your God; I am Jehovah!

15"Judges must always be just in their sentences, not noticing whether a person is poor or rich; they must always be perfectly fair.

16"Don't gossip. Don't falsely accuse your neighbor of some crime, for I am Jehovah.

17"Don't hate your brother. Rebuke anyone who sins; don't let him get away with it, or you will be equally guilty. 18Don't seek vengeance. Don't bear a grudge; but love your neighbor as yourself, for I am Jehovah.

19"Obey my laws: Do not mate your cattle with a different kind; don't sow your field with two kinds of seed; don't wear clothes made of half wool and half linen.

20"If a man seduces a slave girl who is engaged to be married, they shall be tried in a court but not put to death, because she is not free. 21The man involved shall bring his guilt offering to the Lord at the entrance of the Tabernacle; the offering shall be a ram. 22The priest shall make atonement with the ram for the sin the man has committed, and it shall be forgiven him.

23"When you enter the land and have planted all kinds of fruit trees, do not eat the first three crops, for they are considered ceremonially defiled. 24And the fourth year the entire crop shall be devoted to the Lord, and shall be given to the Lord in praise to him. 25Finally, in the fifth year, the crop is yours.

26"I am Jehovah your God! You must not eat meat with undrained blood nor use fortune telling or witchcraft.

27"You must not trim off your hair on your temples or clip the edges of your beard, as the heathen do. 28You shall not cut yourselves nor put tattoo marks upon yourselves in connection with funeral rites; I am the Lord.

29"Do not violate your daughter's sanctity by making her a prostitute, lest the land become full of enormous wickedness.

30"Keep my Sabbath laws and reverence my Tabernacle, for I am the Lord.

31"Do not defile yourselves by consulting mediums and wizards, for I am Jehovah your God.

32"You shall give due honor and respect to the elderly, in the fear of God. I am Jehovah.

33"Do not take advantage of foreigners in your land; do not wrong them. 34They must be treated like any other citizen; love them as yourself, for remember that you too were foreigners in the land of Egypt. I am Jehovah your God.

35,36"You must be impartial in judgment. Use accurate measurements—lengths, weights, and volumes—and give full measure, for I am Jehovah your God who brought you from the land of Egypt. 37You must heed all of my commandments and ordinances, carefully obeying them, for I am Jehovah."

THE Lord gave Moses these further instructions for the people of Israel:

"Anyone—whether an Israelite or a foreigner living among you—who sacrifices his child as a burnt offering to Molech shall without fail be stoned by his peers. 3And I myself will turn against that man and cut him off from all his people, because he has given his child to Molech, thus making my Tabernacle unfit for me to live in, and insulting my holy name. 4And if the people of the land pretend they do not know what the man has done, and refuse to put him to death, 5then I myself will set my face against that man and his family and cut him off, along with all others who turn to other gods than me.

6"I will set my face against anyone who consults mediums and wizards instead of me and I will cut that person off from his people. 7So sanctify yourselves and be holy, for I am the Lord your God. 8You must obey all of my commandments, for I am the Lord who sanctifies you.

9"Anyone who curses his father or mother shall surely be put to death—for he has cursed his own flesh and blood.

10"If a man commits adultery with another man's wife, both the man and woman shall be put to death. 11If a man sleeps with his father's wife, he has defiled what is his father's; both the man and the woman must die, for it is their own fault. 12And if a man has sexual intercourse with his daughter-in-law, both shall be executed: they have brought it upon themselves by defiling each other. 13The penalty for homosexual acts is death to both parties. They have brought it upon themselves. 14If a man has sexual intercourse with a woman and with her mother, it is a great evil. All three shall be burned alive to wipe out wickedness from among you.

15"If a man has sexual intercourse with an animal, he shall be executed and the animal killed. 16If a woman has sexual intercourse with an animal, kill the woman and the animal, for they deserve their punishment.

17"If a man has sexual intercourse with his sister, whether the daughter of his father or of his mother, it is a shameful thing, and they shall publicly be cut off from the people of Israel. He shall bear his guilt. 18If a man has sexual intercourse with a woman during her period of menstruation, both shall be excommunicated, for he has uncovered the source of her flow, and she has permitted it.

19"Sexual intercourse is outlawed between a man and his maiden aunt—whether the sister of his mother or of his father—for they are near of kin; they shall bear their guilt. 20If a man has intercourse with his uncle's wife, he has taken what belongs to his uncle; their punishment is that they shall bear their sin and die childless. 21If a man marries his brother's wife, this is impurity; for he has taken what belongs to his brother, and they shall be childless.

MARK 8:10–38

IMMEDIATELY after this he got into a boat with his disciples and came to the region of Dalmanutha.

11When the local Jewish leaders learned of his arrival they came to argue with him.

"Do a miracle for us," they said. "Make something happen in the sky. Then we will believe in you."

¹²He sighed deeply when he heard this and he said, "Certainly not. How many more miracles do you people need?"

¹³So he got back into the boat and left them, and crossed to the other side of the lake. ¹⁴But the disciples had forgotten to stock up on food before they left, and had only one loaf of bread in the boat.

¹⁵As they were crossing, Jesus said to them very solemnly, "Beware of the yeast of King Herod and of the Pharisees."

¹⁶"What does he mean?" the disciples asked each other. They finally decided that he must be talking about their forgetting to bring bread.

¹⁷Jesus realized what they were discussing and said, "No, that isn't it at all! Can't you understand? Are your hearts too hard to take it in? ¹⁸'Your eyes are to see with—why don't you look? Why don't you open your ears and listen?' Don't you remember anything at all?

¹⁹"What about the 5,000 men I fed with five loaves of bread? How many basketfuls of scraps did you pick up afterwards?"

"Twelve," they said.

²⁰"And when I fed the 4,000 with seven loaves, how much was left?"

"Seven basketfuls," they said.

²¹"And yet you think I'm worried that we have no bread?"

²²When they arrived at Bethsaida, some people brought a blind man to him and begged him to touch and heal him. ²³Jesus took the blind man by the hand and led him out of the village, and spat upon his eyes, and laid his hands over them.

"Can you see anything now?" Jesus asked him.

²⁴The man looked around. "Yes!" he said, "I see men! But I can't see them very clearly; they look like tree trunks walking around!"

²⁵Then Jesus placed his hands over the man's eyes again and as the man stared intently, his sight was completely restored, and he saw everything clearly, drinking in the sights around him.

²⁶Jesus sent him home to his family. "Don't even go back to the village first," he said.

²⁷Jesus and his disciples now left Galilee and went out to the villages of Caesarea Philippi. As they were walking along he asked them, "Who do the people think I am? What are they saying about me?"

²⁸"Some of them think you are John the Baptist," the disciples replied, "and others say you are Elijah or some other ancient prophet come back to life again."

²⁹Then he asked, "Who do you think I am?" Peter replied, "You are the Messiah." ³⁰But Jesus warned them not to tell anyone!

³¹Then he began to tell them about the terrible things he would suffer, and that he would be rejected by the elders and the Chief Priests and the other Jewish leaders—and be killed, and that he would rise again three days afterwards. ³²He talked about it quite frankly with them, so Peter took him aside and chided him. "You shouldn't say things like that," he told Jesus.

³³Jesus turned and looked at his disciples and then said to Peter very sternly, "Satan, get behind me! You are looking at this only from a human point of view and not from God's."

³⁴Then he called his disciples and the crowds to come over and listen. "If any of you wants to be my follower," he told them, "you must put aside your own pleasures and shoulder your cross, and follow me closely. ³⁵If you insist on saving your life, you will lose it. Only those who throw away their lives for my sake and for the sake of the Good News will ever know what it means to really live.

³⁶"And how does a man benefit if he gains the whole world and loses his soul in the process? ³⁷For is anything worth more than his soul? ³⁸And anyone who is ashamed of me and my message in these days of unbelief and sin, I, the Messiah, will be ashamed of him when I return in the glory of my Father, with the holy angels."

PSALM 42:1–11

As the deer pants for water, so I long for you, O God. ²I thirst for God, the living God. Where can I find him to come and stand before him? ³Day and night I weep for his help, and all the while my enemies taunt me. "Where is this God of yours?" they scoff.

⁴,⁵Take courage, my soul! Do you remember those times (but how could you ever forget them!) when you led a great procession to the Temple on festival days, singing with joy, praising the Lord? Why then be downcast? Why be discouraged and sad? Hope in God! I shall yet praise him again. Yes, I shall again praise him for his help.

⁶Yet I am standing here depressed and gloomy, but I will meditate upon your kindness to this lovely land where the Jordan River flows and where Mount Hermon and Mount Mizar stand. ⁷All your waves and billows have gone over me, and floods of sorrow pour upon me like a thundering cataract.

⁸Yet day by day the Lord also pours out his steadfast love upon me, and through the night I sing his songs and pray to God who gives me life.

⁹"O God my Rock," I cry, "why have you forsaken me? Why must I suffer these attacks from my enemies?" ¹⁰Their taunts pierce me like a fatal wound; again and again they scoff, "Where is that God of yours?" ¹¹But O my soul, don't be discouraged. Don't be upset. Expect God to act! For I know that I shall again have plenty of reason to praise him for all that he will do. He is my help! He is my God!

PROVERBS FOR TODAY/ 10:17

Anyone willing to be corrected is on the pathway to life. Anyone refusing has lost his chance.

FEBRUARY 27

LEVITICUS 20:22—22:20

You must obey all of my laws and ordinances so that I will not throw you out of your new land. ²³You must not follow the customs of the nations I cast out before you, for they do all these things I have warned you against; that is the reason I abhor them. ²⁴I have promised you their land; I will give it to you to possess it. It is a land 'flowing with milk and honey.' I am the Lord your God who has made a distinction between you and the people of other nations.

²⁵"You shall therefore make a distinction between the birds and animals I have given you permission to eat and those you may not eat. You shall not contaminate yourselves and make yourselves hateful to me by eating any animal or bird which I have forbidden, though the land teem with them. ²⁶You shall be holy to me, for I the Lord am holy, and I have set you apart from all other peoples, to be mine.

²⁷"A medium or a wizard—whether man or woman—shall surely be stoned to death. They have caused their own doom."

The Lord said to Moses: "Tell the priests never to defile themselves by touching a dead person, ²,³unless it is a near relative—a mother, father, son, daughter, brother, or unmarried sister for whom he has special responsibility since she has no husband. 4For the priest is a leader among his people and he may not ceremonially defile himself as an ordinary person can.

5"The priests shall not clip bald spots in their hair or beards, nor cut their flesh. 6They shall be holy unto their God, and shall not dishonor and profane his name; otherwise they will be unfit to make food offerings by fire to the Lord their God. 7A priest shall not marry a prostitute, nor a woman of another tribe, and he shall not marry a divorced woman, for he is a holy man of God. 8The priest is set apart to offer the sacrifices of your God; he is holy, for I, the Lord who sanctifies you, am holy. 9The daughter of any priest who becomes a prostitute, thus violating her father's holiness as well as her own, shall be burned alive.

10"The High Priest—anointed with the special anointing oil and wearing the special garments—must not let his hair hang loose in mourning, nor tear his clothing, 11nor be in the presence of any dead person—not even his father or mother. 12He shall not leave the sanctuary [when on duty], nor treat my Tabernacle like an ordinary house, for the consecration of the anointing oil of his God is upon him; I am Jehovah. 13He must marry a virgin. 14,15He may not marry a widow, nor a woman who is divorced, nor a prostitute. She must be a virgin from his own tribe, for he must not be the father of children of mixed blood—half priestly and half ordinary."

16,17And the Lord said to Moses, "Tell Aaron that any of his descendants from generation to generation who have any bodily defect may not offer the sacrifices to God. 18For instance, if a man is blind or lame, or has a broken nose or any extra fingers or toes, 19or has a broken foot or hand, 20or has a humped back, or is a dwarf, or has a defect in his eye, or has pimples or scabby skin, or has imperfect testicles— 21although he is a descendant of Aaron—he is not permitted to offer the fire sacrifices to the Lord because of his physical defect. 22However, he shall be fed with the food of the priests from the offerings sacrificed to God, both from the holy and most holy offerings. 23But he shall not go in behind the veil, nor come near the altar, because of the physical defect; this would defile my sanctuary, for it is Jehovah who sanctifies it."

24So Moses gave these instructions to Aaron and his sons and to all the people of Israel.

THE Lord told Moses, "Instruct Aaron and his sons to be very careful not to defile my holy name by desecrating the people's sacred gifts; for I am Jehovah. 3From now on and forever, if a priest who is ceremonially defiled sacrifices the animals brought by the people or handles the gifts dedicated to Jehovah, he shall be discharged from the priesthood. For I am Jehovah!

4"No priest who is a leper or who has a running sore may eat the holy sacrifices until healed. And any priest who touches a dead person, or who is defiled by a seminal emission, 5or who touches any reptile or other forbidden thing, or who touches anyone who is ceremonially defiled for any reason— 6that priest shall be defiled until evening, and shall not eat of the holy sacrifices until after he has bathed that evening. 7When the sun is down, then he shall be purified again and may eat the holy food, for it is his source of life. 8He may not eat any animal that dies of itself or is torn by wild animals, for this will defile him. I am Jehovah. 9Warn the priests to follow these instructions carefully, lest they be declared guilty and die for violating these rules. I am the Lord who sanctifies them.

10"No one may eat of the holy sacrifices unless he is a priest; no one visiting the priest, for instance, nor a hired servant, may eat this food. 11However, there is one exception—if the priest buys a slave with his own money, that slave may eat it, and any slave children born in his household may eat it. 12If a priest's daughter is married outside the tribe, she may not eat the sacred offerings. 13But if she is a widow or divorced and has no son to support her, and has returned home to her father's household, she may eat of her father's food again. But otherwise, no one who is not in the priestly families may eat this food.

14"If someone should eat of the holy sacrifices without realizing it, he shall return to the priest the amount he has used, with twenty percent added; 15for the holy sacrifices brought by the people of Israel must not be defiled by being eaten by unauthorized persons, for these sacrifices have been offered to the Lord. 16Anyone who violates this law is guilty and is in great danger because he has eaten the sacred offerings; for I am Jehovah who sanctifies the offerings."

17,18And the Lord said to Moses, "Tell Aaron and his sons and all the people of Israel that if an Israelite or other person living among you offers a burnt offering sacrifice to the Lord—whether it is to fulfill a promise or is a spontaneous free will offering— 19it will only be acceptable to the Lord if it is a male animal without defect; it must be a young bull or a sheep or a goat. 20Anything that has a defect must not be offered, for it will not be accepted.

MARK 9:1–29

JESUS went on to say to his disciples, "Some of you who are standing here right now will live to see the Kingdom of God arrive in great power!"

2Six days later Jesus took Peter, James and John to the top of a mountain. No one else was there.

Suddenly his face began to shine with glory, 3and his clothing became dazzling white, far more glorious than any earthly process could ever make it! 4Then Elijah and Moses appeared and began talking with Jesus!

5"Teacher, this is wonderful!" Peter exclaimed. "We will make three shelters here, one for each of you. . . . "

6He said this just to be talking, for he didn't know what else to say and they were all terribly frightened.

7But while he was still speaking these words, a cloud covered them, blotting out the sun, and a voice from the cloud said, "*This* is my beloved Son. Listen to *him*."

8Then suddenly they looked around and Moses and Elijah were gone, and only Jesus was with them.

9As they descended the mountainside he told them never to mention what they had seen until after he had risen from the dead. 10So they kept it to themselves, but often talked about it, and wondered what he meant by "rising from the dead."

11Now they began asking him about something the Jewish religious leaders often spoke of, that Elijah must return [before the Messiah could come]. 12,13Jesus agreed that Elijah must come first and prepare the way—and that he had, in fact, already come! And that he had been terribly mistreated, just as the prophets had predicted. Then Jesus asked them what the prophets could have been talking about when they predicted that the Messiah would suffer and be treated with utter contempt.

14At the bottom of the mountain they found a great crowd surrounding the other nine disciples, as some Jewish leaders argued with them. 15The crowd watched Jesus in awe as he came toward them, and then ran to greet him. 16"What's all the argument about?" he asked.

17One of the men in the crowd spoke up and said, "Teacher, I brought my son for you to heal—he can't talk because he is possessed by a demon. 18And whenever the demon is in control of him it dashes him to the ground and makes him foam at the mouth and grind his teeth and become rigid. So I begged your disciples to cast out the demon, but they couldn't do it."

19Jesus said [to his disciples], "Oh, what tiny faith you have; how much longer must I be with you until you believe? How much longer must I be patient with you? Bring the boy to me."

20So they brought the boy, but when

he saw Jesus the demon convulsed the child horribly, and he fell to the ground writhing and foaming at the mouth.

21"How long has he been this way?" Jesus asked the father.

And he replied, "Since he was very small, 22and the demon often makes him fall into the fire or into water to kill him. Oh, have mercy on us and do something if you can."

23"If I can?" Jesus asked. *"Anything is possible if you have faith."*

24The father instantly replied, "I *do* have faith; oh, help me to have *more!"*

25When Jesus saw the crowd was growing he rebuked the demon.

"O demon of deafness and dumbness," he said, "I command you to come out of this child and enter him no more!"

26Then the demon screamed terribly and convulsed the boy again and left him; and the boy lay there limp and motionless, to all appearance dead. A murmur ran through the crowd—"He is dead."

27But Jesus took him by the hand and helped him to his feet and he stood up and was all right! 28Afterwards, when Jesus was alone in the house with his disciples, they asked him, "Why couldn't we cast that demon out?"

29Jesus replied, "Cases like this require prayer."

PSALM 43:1–5

O God, defend me from the charges of these merciless, deceitful men. 2For you are God, my only place of refuge. Why have you tossed me aside? Why must I mourn at the oppression of my enemies?

3Oh, send out your light and your truth—let them lead me. Let them lead me to your Temple on your holy mountain, Zion. 4There I will go to the altar of God my exceeding joy, and praise him with my harp. O God—my God! 5O my soul, why be so gloomy and discouraged? Trust in God! I shall again praise him for his wondrous help; he will make me smile again, *for he is my God!*

PROVERBS FOR TODAY/ 10:18

To hide hatred is to be a liar; to slander is to be a fool.

FEBRUARY 28

LEVITICUS 22:21—23:44

A NYONE sacrificing a peace offering to the Lord from the herd or flock, whether to fulfill a vow or as a voluntary offering, must sacrifice an animal that has no defect, or it will not be accepted: 22An animal that is blind or disabled or mutilated, or which has sores or itch or any other skin disease, must not be offered to the Lord; it is not a fit burnt offering for the altar of the Lord. 23If the young bull or lamb presented to the Lord has anything superfluous or lacking in its body parts, it may be offered as a free will offering, but not for a vow. 24An animal that has injured genitals—crushed or castrated—shall not be offered to the Lord at any time. 25This restriction applies to the sacrifices made by foreigners among you as well as those made by yourselves, for no defective animal is acceptable for this sacrifice."

26,27And the Lord said to Moses, "When a bullock, sheep, or goat is born, it shall be left with its mother for seven days, but from the eighth day onward it is acceptable as a sacrifice by fire to the Lord. 28You shall not slaughter a mother animal and her offspring the same day, whether she is a cow or ewe. 29,30When you offer the Lord a sacrifice of thanksgiving, you must do it in the right way, eating the sacrificial animal the same day it is slain. Leave none of it for the following day. I am the Lord.

31"You must keep all of my commandments, for I am the Lord. 32,33You must not treat me as common and ordinary. Revere me and hallow me, for I, the Lord, made you holy to myself and rescued you from Egypt to be my own people! I am Jehovah!"

THE Lord said to Moses, "Announce to the people of Israel that they are to celebrate several annual festivals of the Lord—times when all Israel will assemble and worship me. 3(These are in addition to your Sabbaths—the seventh day of every week—which are always days of rest in every home, times for assembling to worship, and for resting from the normal business of the week.)

4These are the holy festivals which are to be observed each year:

5 *"The Passover of the Lord:* This is to be celebrated on the first day of April, beginning at sundown.

6 *"The Festival of Unleavened Bread:* This is to be celebrated beginning the day following the Passover, and for seven days you must not eat any bread made with yeast. 7On the first day of this festival, you shall gather the people for worship, and all ordinary work shall cease. 8You shall do the same on the seventh day of the festival. On each of the intervening days you shall make an offering by fire to the Lord.

9,10,11 *"The Festival of First Fruits:* When you arrive in the land I will give you, and you reap your first harvest, bring the first sheaf of the harvest to the priest on the day after the Sabbath. He shall wave it before the Lord in a gesture of offering, and it will be accepted by the Lord as your gift. 12That same day you shall sacrifice to the Lord a male yearling lamb without defect as a burnt offering. 13A grain offering shall accompany it, consisting of a fifth of a bushel of finely ground flour mixed with olive oil, to be offered by fire to the Lord; this will be very pleasant to him. Also offer a drink offering consisting of three pints of wine. 14Until this is done you must not eat any of the harvest for yourselves—neither fresh kernels nor bread nor parched grain. This is a permanent law throughout your nation.

15,16 *"The Harvest Festival (Festival of Pentecost):* Fifty days later you shall bring to the Lord an offering of a sample of the new grain of your later crops. 17This shall consist of two loaves of bread from your homes to be waved before the Lord in a gesture of offering. Bake this bread from a fifth of a bushel of fine flour containing yeast. It is an offering to the Lord of the first sampling of your later crops. 18Along with the bread and the wine, you shall sacrifice as burnt offerings to the Lord seven yearling lambs without defects, one young bull, and two rams. All are fire offerings, very acceptable to Jehovah. 19And you shall offer one male goat for a sin offering, and two male yearling lambs for a peace offering.

20"The priests shall wave these offerings before the Lord along with the loaves representing the first sampling of your later crops. They are holy to the Lord, and will be given to the priests as food. 21That day shall be announced as a time of sacred convocation of all the people; don't do any work that day. This is a law to be honored from generation to generation. 22(When you reap your harvests, you must not thoroughly reap all the corners of the fields, nor pick up the fallen grain; leave it for the poor and for foreigners living among you who have no land of their own; I am Jehovah your God!)

23,24 *"The Festival of Trumpets:* Mid-September is a time for all the people to meet together for worship; it is a time of remembrance, and is to be announced by loud blowing of trumpets. 25Don't do any hard work on that day, but offer a sacrifice by fire to the Lord.

26,27 *"The Day of Atonement* follows nine days later: All the people are to come together before the Lord, saddened by their sin; and they shall offer sacrifices by fire to the Lord. 28Don't do any work that day, for it is a special day for making atonement before the Lord your God. 29Anyone who does not spend the day in repentance and sorrow for sin shall be excommunicated from his people. 30,31And I will put to death anyone who does any kind of work that day. This is a law of Israel from generation to generation. 32For this is a Sabbath of rest, and in it you shall go without food and be filled with sorrow; this time for atonement begins in the evening and continues through the next day.

33,34 *"The Festival of Shelters:* Five days later, on the last day of September, is the Festival of Shelters to be celebrated before the Lord for seven days. 35On the first day there will be a sacred assembly of all the people; don't do any hard work that day. 36On each of the seven days of the festival you are to sacrifice an offering by fire to the Lord. The eighth day requires another sacred convocation of all the people, at which time there will again be an offering by fire to the Lord. It is the closing assembly, and no regular work is permitted.

37"(These, then, are the regular annual festivals—sacred convocations of all people—when offerings to the Lord are to be made by fire. 38These annual festivals are in addition to your regular Sabbaths—the weekly days of holy rest. The sacrifices made during the festivals are to be in addition to your regular giving and normal fulfillment of your vows.)

39"This last day of September, at the end of your harvesting, is the time to begin to celebrate this seven-day festival before the Lord. Remember that the first and last days of the festival are special days of rest. 40On the first day, take boughs of fruit trees laden with fruit, and palm fronds, and the boughs of leafy trees—such as willows that grow by the brooks—and [build shelters with them], rejoicing before the Lord your God for seven days. 41This seven-day annual feast is a law from generation to generation. 42During those seven days, all of you who are native Israelites are to live in these shelters. 43The purpose of this is to remind the people of Israel, generation after generation, that I rescued you from Egypt, and caused you to live in shelters. I am Jehovah your God."

44So Moses announced these annual festivals of the Lord to the people of Israel.

MARK 9:30—10:12

LEAVING that region they traveled through Galilee where he tried to avoid all publicity in order to spend more time with his disciples, teaching them. He would say to them, "I, the Messiah, am going to be betrayed and killed and three days later I will return to life again."

32But they didn't understand and were afraid to ask him what he meant.

33And so they arrived at Capernaum. When they were settled in the house where they were to stay he asked them, "What were you discussing out on the road?"

34But they were ashamed to answer, for they had been arguing about which of them was the greatest!

35He sat down and called them around him and said, "Anyone wanting to be the greatest must be the least—the servant of all!"

36Then he placed a little child among them; and taking the child in his arms he said to them, 37"Anyone who welcomes a little child like this in my name is welcoming me, and anyone who welcomes me is welcoming my Father who sent me!"

38One of his disciples, John, told him one day, "Teacher, we saw a man using your name to cast out demons; but we told him not to, for he isn't one of our group."

39"Don't forbid him!" Jesus said. "For no one doing miracles in my name will quickly turn against me. 40Anyone who isn't against us is for us. 41If anyone so much as gives you a cup of water because you are Christ's—I say this solemnly—he won't lose his reward. 42But if someone causes one of these little ones who believe in me to lose faith—it would be better for that man if a huge millstone were tied around his neck and he were thrown into the sea.

43,44"If your hand does wrong, cut it off. Better live forever with one hand than be thrown into the unquenchable fires of hell with two! 45,46If your foot carries you toward evil, cut it off! Better be lame and live forever than have two feet that carry you to hell.

47"And if your eye is sinful, gouge it out. Better enter the Kingdom of God half blind than have two eyes and see the fires of hell, 48where the worm never dies, and the fire never goes out—49where all are salted with fire.

50"Good salt is worthless if it loses its saltiness; it can't season anything. So don't lose your flavor! Live in peace with each other."

THEN he left Capernaum and went southward to the Judean borders and into the area east of the Jordan River. And as always there were the crowds; and as usual he taught them.

2Some Pharisees came and asked him, "Do you permit divorce?" Of course they were trying to trap him.

3"What did Moses say about divorce?" Jesus asked them.

4"He said it was all right," they replied. "He said that all a man has to do is write his wife a letter of dismissal."

5"And why did he say that?" Jesus asked. "I'll tell you why—it was a concession to your hardhearted wickedness. 6,7But it certainly isn't God's way. For from the very first he made man and woman to be joined together permanently in marriage; therefore a man is to leave his father and mother, 8and he and his wife are united so that they are no longer two, but one. 9And no man may separate what God has joined together."

10Later, when he was alone with his disciples in the house, they brought up the subject again.

11He told them, "When a man divorces his wife to marry someone else, he commits adultery against her. 12And if a wife divorces her husband and remarries, she, too, commits adultery."

PSALM 44:1–7

O God, we have heard of the glorious miracles you did in the days of long ago. Our forefathers have told us how you drove the heathen nations from this land and gave it all to us, spreading Israel from one end of the country to the other. 3They did not conquer by their own strength and skill, but by your mighty power and because you smiled upon them and favored them.

4You are my King and my God. Decree victories for your people. 5For it is only by your power and through your name that we tread down our enemies; 6I do not trust my weapons. They could never save me. 7Only you can give us the victory over those who hate us.

PROVERBS FOR TODAY/ 10:19

Don't talk so much. You keep putting your foot in your mouth. Be sensible and turn off the flow!

MARCH 1

LEVITICUS 24:1—25:46

THE Lord said to Moses, "Tell the people of Israel to bring you pure olive oil for an eternal flame 3,4in the lampstand of pure gold which stands outside the veil that secludes the Holy of Holies. Each morning and evening Aaron shall supply it with fresh oil and trim the wicks. It will be an eternal flame before the Lord from generation to generation.

5-8"Every Sabbath day the High Priest shall place twelve loaves of bread in two rows upon the gold table that stands before the Lord. These loaves shall be baked from finely ground flour, using a fifth of a bushel for each. Pure frankincense shall be sprinkled along each row. This will be a memorial offering made by fire to the Lord, in memory of his everlasting covenant with the people of Israel. 9The bread shall be eaten by Aaron and his sons, in a place set apart for the purpose. For these are offerings made by fire to the Lord under a permanent law of God, and are most holy."

10Out in the camp one day, a young man whose mother was an Israelite and whose father was an Egyptian, got into a fight with one of the men of Israel. 11During the fight the Egyptian man's son cursed God, and was brought to Moses for judgment. (His mother's name was Shelomith, daughter of Dibri of the tribe of Dan.) 12He was put in jail until the Lord would indicate what to do with him.

13,14And the Lord said to Moses, "Take him outside the camp and tell all who heard him to lay their hands upon his head; then all the people are to execute him by stoning. 15,16And tell the people of Israel that anyone who curses his God must pay the penalty: he must die. All the congregation shall stone him; this law applies to the foreigner as well as to the Israelite who blasphemes the name of Jehovah. He must die.

17"Also, all murderers must be executed. 18Anyone who kills an animal [that isn't his] shall replace it. 19The penalty for injuring anyone is to be injured in exactly the same way: 20fracture for fracture, eye for eye, tooth for tooth. Whatever anyone does to another shall be done to him.

21"To repeat, whoever kills an animal must replace it, and whoever kills a man must die. 22You shall have the same law for the foreigner as for the home-born citizen, for I am Jehovah your God."

23So they took the youth out of the camp and stoned him until he died, as Jehovah had commanded Moses.

WHILE Moses was on Mount Sinai, the Lord gave him these instructions for the people of Israel:

"When you come into the land I am going to give you, you must let the land rest before the Lord every seventh year. 3For six years you may sow your field and prune your vineyards and harvest your crops, 4but during the seventh year the land is to lie fallow before the Lord, uncultivated. Don't sow your crops and don't prune your vineyards during that entire year. 5Don't even reap for yourself the volunteer crops that come up, and don't gather the grapes for yourself; for it is a year of rest for the land. 6,7Any crops that do grow that year shall be free to all—for you, your servants, your slaves, and any foreigners living among you. Cattle and wild animals alike shall be allowed to graze there.

8"Every fiftieth year, 9on the Day of Atonement, let the trumpets blow loud and long throughout the land. 10For the fiftieth year shall be holy, a time to proclaim liberty throughout the land to all enslaved debtors, and a time for the canceling of all public and private debts. It shall be a year when all the family estates sold to others shall be returned to the original owners or their heirs.

11"What a happy year it will be! In it you shall not sow, nor gather crops nor grapes; 12for it is a holy Year of Jubilee for you. That year your food shall be the volunteer crops that grow wild in the fields. 13Yes, during the Year of Jubilee everyone shall return home to his original family possession; if he has sold it, it shall be his again! 14,15,16Because of this, if the land is sold or bought during the preceding forty-nine years, a fair price shall be arrived at by counting the number of years until the Jubilee. If the Jubilee is many years away, the price will be high; if few years, the price will be low; for what you are really doing is selling the number of crops the new owner will get from the land before it is returned to you.

17,18"You must fear your God and not overcharge! For I am Jehovah. Obey my laws if you want to live safely in the land. 19When you obey, the land will yield bumper crops and you can eat your fill in safety. 20But you will ask, 'What shall we eat the seventh year, since we are not allowed to plant or harvest crops that year?' 21,22The answer is, 'I will bless you with bumper crops the sixth year that will last you until the crops of the eighth year are harvested!' 23And remember, the land is mine, so you may not sell it permanently. You are merely my tenants and sharecroppers!

24"In every contract of sale there must be a stipulation that the land can be redeemed at any time by the seller. 25If anyone becomes poor and sells some of his land, then his nearest relatives may redeem it. 26If there is no one else to redeem it, and he himself gets together enough money, 27then he may always buy it back at a price proportionate to the number of harvests until the Jubilee, and the owner must accept the money and return the land to him. 28But if the original owner is not able to redeem it, then it shall belong to the new owner until the Year of Jubilee; but at the Jubilee year it must be returned again.

29"If a man sells a house in the city, he has up to one year to redeem it, with full right of redemption during that time. 30But if it is not redeemed within the year, then it will belong permanently to the new owner—it does not return to the original owner in the Year of Jubilee. 31But village houses—a village is a settlement without fortifying walls around it—are like farmland, redeemable at any time, and are always returned to the original owner in the Year of Jubilee.

32"There is one exception: The homes of the Levites, even though in walled cities, may be redeemed at any time, 33and must be returned to the original owners in the Year of Jubilee; for the Levites will not be given farmland like the other tribes, but will receive only houses in their cities, and the surrounding fields. 34The Levites are not permitted to sell the fields of common land surrounding their cities, for these are their permanent possession, and they must belong to no one else.

35"If your brother becomes poor, you are responsible to help him; invite him to live with you as a guest in your home. 36Fear your God and let your brother live with you; and don't charge him interest on the money you lend him. 37Remember—no interest; and give him what he needs, at your cost: don't try to make a profit! 38For I, the Lord your God, brought you out of the land of Egypt to *give* you the land of Canaan, and to be your God.

39"If a fellow Israelite becomes poor and sells himself to you, you must not treat him as an ordinary slave, 40but rather as a hired servant or as a guest; and he shall serve you only until the Year of Jubilee. 41At that time he can leave with his children, and return to his own family and possessions. 42For I brought you from the land of Egypt, and you are my servants; so you may not be sold as ordinary slaves, 43or treated harshly; fear your God.

44"However, you may purchase slaves from the foreign nations living around you, 45and you may purchase the children of the foreigners living among you, even though they have been born in your land.

46They will be permanent slaves for you to pass on to your children after you; but your brothers, the people of Israel, shall not be treated so.

MARK 10:13–31

ONCE when some mothers were bringing their children to Jesus to bless them, the disciples shooed them away, telling them not to bother him.

14But when Jesus saw what was happening he was very much displeased with his disciples and said to them, "Let the children come to me, for the Kingdom of God belongs to such as they. Don't send them away! 15I tell you as seriously as I know how that anyone who refuses to come to God as a little child will never be allowed into his Kingdom."

16Then he took the children into his arms and placed his hands on their heads and he blessed them.

17As he was starting out on a trip, a man came running to him and knelt down and asked, "Good Teacher, what must I do to get to heaven?"

18"Why do you call me good?" Jesus asked. "Only God is truly good! 19But as for your question—you know the commandments: don't kill, don't commit adultery, don't steal, don't lie, don't cheat, respect your father and mother."

20"Teacher," the man replied, "I've never once broken a single one of those laws."

21Jesus felt genuine love for this man as he looked at him. "You lack only one thing," he told him; "go and sell all you have and give the money to the poor—and you shall have treasure in heaven—and come, follow me."

22Then the man's face fell, and he went sadly away, for he was very rich.

23Jesus watched him go, then turned around and said to his disciples, "It's almost impossible for the rich to get into the Kingdom of God!"

24This amazed them. So Jesus said it again: "Dear children, how hard it is for those who trust in riches to enter the Kingdom of God. 25It is easier for a camel to go through the eye of a needle than for a rich man to enter the Kingdom of God."

26The disciples were incredulous! "Then who in the world can be saved, if not a rich man?" they asked.

27Jesus looked at them intently, then said, "Without God, it is utterly impossible. But with God everything is possible."

28Then Peter began to mention all that he and the other disciples had left behind. "We've given up everything to follow you," he said.

29And Jesus replied, "Let me assure you that no one has ever given up anything—home, brothers, sisters, mother, father, children, or property—for love of me and to tell others the Good News, 30who won't be given back, a hundred times over, homes, brothers, sisters, mothers, children, and land—with persecutions!

"All these will be his here on earth, and in the world to come he shall have eternal life. 31But many people who seem to be important now will be the least important then; and many who are considered least here shall be greatest there."

PSALM 44:8–26

MY constant boast is God. I can never thank you enough! 9And yet for a time, O Lord, you have tossed us aside in dishonor, and have not helped us in our battles. 10You have actually fought against us and defeated us before our foes. Our enemies have invaded our land and pillaged the countryside. 11You have treated us like sheep in a slaughter pen, and scattered us among the nations. 12You sold us for a pittance. You valued us at nothing at all. 13The neighboring nations laugh and mock at us because of all the evil you have sent. 14You have made the word "Jew" a byword of contempt and shame among the nations, disliked by all. 15,16I am constantly despised, mocked, taunted and cursed by my vengeful enemies.

17And all this has happened, Lord, despite our loyalty to you. We have not violated your covenant. 18Our hearts have not deserted you! We have not left your path by a single step. 19If we had, we could understand your punishing us in the barren wilderness and sending us into darkness and death. 20If we had turned away from worshiping our God, and were worshiping idols, 21would God not know it? Yes, he knows the secrets of every heart. 22But that is not our case. For we are facing death threats constantly because of serving you! We are like sheep awaiting slaughter.

23Waken! Rouse yourself! Don't sleep, O Lord! Are we cast off forever? 24Why do you look the other way? Why do you ignore our sorrows and oppression? 25We lie face downward in the dust. 26Rise up, O Lord, and come and help us. Save us by your constant love.

PROVERBS FOR TODAY/ 10:20–21

When a good man speaks, he is worth listening to, but the words of fools are a dime a dozen. A godly man gives good advice, but a rebel is destroyed by lack of common sense.

MARCH 2

LEVITICUS 25:47—27:13

IF a foreigner living among you becomes rich, and an Israelite becomes poor and sells himself to the foreigner or to the foreigner's family, 48he may be redeemed by one of his brothers, 49his uncle, nephew, or anyone else who is a near relative. He may also redeem himself if he can find the money. 50The price of his freedom shall be in proportion to the number of years left before the Year of Jubilee—whatever it would cost to hire a servant for that number of years. 51If there are still many years until the Jubilee, he shall pay almost the amount he received when he sold himself; 52if the years have passed and only a few remain until the Jubilee, then he will repay only a small part of the amount he received when he sold himself. 53If he sells himself to a foreigner, the foreigner must treat him as a hired servant rather than as a slave or as property. 54If he has not been redeemed by the time the Year of Jubilee arrives, then he and his children shall be freed at that time. 55For the people of Israel are *my* servants; I brought them from the land of Egypt; I am the Lord your God.

"YOU must have no idols; you must never worship carved images, obelisks, or shaped stones, for I am the Lord your God. 2You must obey my Sabbath laws of rest, and reverence my Tabernacle, for I am the Lord.

3"If you obey all of my commandments, 4,5I will give you regular rains, and the land will yield bumper crops, and the trees will be loaded with fruit long after the normal time! And grapes will still be ripening when sowing time comes again. You shall eat your fill, and live safely in the land, 6for I will give you peace, and you will go to sleep without fear. I will chase away the dangerous animals. 7You will chase your enemies; they will die beneath your swords. 8Five of you will chase a hundred, and a hundred of you, ten thousand! You will defeat all of your enemies. 9I will look after you, and multiply you, and fulfill my covenant with you. 10You will have such a surplus of crops that you won't know what to do with them when the new harvest is ready! ¹¹And I will live among you, and not despise you. ¹²I will walk among you and be your God, and you shall be my people. ¹³For I am the Lord your God who brought you out of the land of Egypt, so that you would be slaves no longer; I have broken your chains so that you can walk with dignity.

¹⁴"But if you will not listen to me or obey me, ¹⁵but reject my laws, ¹⁶this is what I will do to you: I will punish you with sudden terrors and panic, and with tuberculosis and burning fever; your eyes shall be consumed and your life shall ebb away; you will sow your crops in vain, for your enemies will eat them. ¹⁷I will set my face against you and you will flee before your attackers; those who hate you will rule you; you will even run when no one is chasing you!

¹⁸"And if you still disobey me, I will punish you seven times more severely for your sins. ¹⁹I will break your proud power and make your heavens as iron, and your earth as bronze. ²⁰Your strength shall be spent in vain; for your land shall not yield its crops, nor your trees their fruit.

²¹"And if even then you will not obey me and listen to me, I will send you seven times more plagues because of your sins. ²²I will send wild animals to kill your children and destroy your cattle and reduce your numbers so that your roads will be deserted.

²³"And if even this will not reform you, but you continue to walk against my wishes, ²⁴then I will walk against your wishes, and I, even I, will personally smite you seven times for your sin. ²⁵I will revenge the breaking of my covenant by bringing war against you. You will flee to your cities, and I will send a plague among you there; and you will be conquered by your enemies. ²⁶I will destroy your food supply so that one oven will be large enough to bake all the bread available for ten entire families; and you will still be hungry after your pittance has been doled out to you.

²⁷"And if you still won't listen to me or obey me, ²⁸then I will let loose my great anger and send you seven times greater punishment for your sins. ²⁹You shall eat your own sons and daughters, ³⁰and I will destroy the altars on the hills where you worship your idols, and I will cut down your incense altars, leaving your dead bodies to rot among your idols; and I will abhor you. ³¹I will make your cities desolate, and destroy your places of worship, and will not respond to your incense offerings. ³²Yes, I will desolate your land; your enemies shall live in it, utterly amazed at what I have done to you.

³³"I will scatter you out among the nations, destroying you with war as you go. Your land shall be desolate and your cities destroyed. ³⁴,³⁵Then at last the land will rest and make up for the many years you refused to let it lie idle; for it will lie desolate all the years that you are captives in enemy lands. Yes, then the land will rest and enjoy its Sabbaths! It will make up for the rest you didn't give it every seventh year when you lived upon it.

³⁶"And for those who are left alive, I will cause them to be dragged away to distant lands as prisoners of war, and slaves. There they will live in constant fear. The sound of a leaf driven in the wind will send them fleeing as though chased by a man with a sword; they shall fall when no one is pursuing them. ³⁷Yes, though none pursue they shall stumble over each other in flight, as though fleeing in battle, with no power to stand before their enemies. ³⁸You shall perish among the nations and be destroyed among your enemies. ³⁹Those left shall pine away in enemy lands because of their sins, the same sins as those of their fathers.

⁴⁰,⁴¹"But at last they shall confess their sins and their fathers' sins of treachery against me. (Because they were against me, I was against them, and brought them into the land of their enemies.) When at last their evil hearts are humbled and they accept the punishment I send them for their sins, ⁴²then I will remem-

ber again my promises to Abraham, Isaac, and Jacob, and I will remember the land (and its desolation). 43For the land shall enjoy its Sabbaths as it lies desolate. But then at last they shall accept their punishment for rejecting my laws and for despising my rule. 44But despite all they have done, I will not utterly destroy them and my covenant with them, for I am Jehovah their God. 45For their sakes I will remember my promises to their ancestors, to be their God. For I brought their forefathers out of Egypt as all the nations watched in wonder. I am Jehovah."

46These were the laws, ordinances, and instructions that Jehovah gave to the people of Israel, through Moses, on Mount Sinai.

THE Lord said to Moses, "Tell the people of Israel that when a person makes a special vow to give himself to the Lord, he shall give these payments instead: 3A man from the age of twenty to sixty shall pay twenty-five dollars; 4a woman from the age of twenty to sixty shall pay fifteen dollars; 5a boy from five to twenty shall pay ten dollars; a girl, five dollars. 6A boy one month to five years old shall have paid for him two and a half dollars; a girl, one and a half dollars. 7A man over sixty shall pay seven and a half dollars; a woman, five dollars. 8But if the person is too poor to pay this amount, he shall be brought to the priest and the priest shall talk it over with him, and he shall pay as the priest shall decide.

9"But if it is an animal that is vowed to be given to the Lord as a sacrifice, it must be given. 10The vow may not be changed; the donor may neither change his mind about giving it to the Lord, nor substitute good for bad or bad for good; if he does, both the first and the second shall belong to the Lord! 11,12But if the animal given to the Lord is not a kind that is permitted as a sacrifice, the owner shall bring it to the priest to value it, and he shall be told how much to pay instead. 13If the animal is a kind that may be offered as a sacrifice, but

the man wants to redeem it, then he shall pay twenty percent more than the value set by the priest.

MARK 10:32–52

NOW they were on the way to Jerusalem, and Jesus was walking along ahead; and as the disciples were following they were filled with terror and dread.

Taking them aside, Jesus once more began describing all that was going to happen to him when they arrived at Jerusalem.

33"When we get there," he told them, "I, the Messiah, will be arrested and taken before the chief priests and the Jewish leaders, who will sentence me to die and hand me over to the Romans to be killed. 34They will mock me and spit on me and flog me with their whips and kill me; but after three days I will come back to life again."

35Then James and John, the sons of Zebedee, came over and spoke to him in a low voice. "Master," they said, "we want you to do us a favor."

36"What is it?" he asked.

37"We want to sit on the thrones next to yours in your kingdom," they said, "one at your right and the other at your left!"

38But Jesus answered, "You don't know what you are asking! Are you able to drink from the bitter cup of sorrow I must drink from? Or to be baptized with the baptism of suffering I must be baptized with?"

39"Oh, yes," they said, "we are!"

And Jesus said, "You shall indeed drink from my cup and be baptized with my baptism, 40but I do not have the right to place you on thrones next to mine. Those appointments have already been made."

41When the other disciples discovered what James and John had asked, they were very indignant. 42So Jesus called them to him and said, "As you know, the kings and great men of the earth lord it over the people; 43but among you it is different. Whoever wants to be great among you must be your servant. 44And whoever wants to be greatest of all must be the slave of all. 45For even I, the Messiah, am not here to be served, but to help others, and to give my life as a ransom for many."

46And so they reached Jericho. Later, as they left town, a great crowd was following. Now it happened that a blind beggar named Bartimaeus (the son of Timaeus) was sitting beside the road as Jesus was going by.

47When Bartimaeus heard that Jesus from Nazareth was near, he began to shout out, "Jesus, Son of David, have mercy on me!"

48"Shut up!" some of the people yelled at him.

But he only shouted the louder, again and again, "O Son of David, have mercy on me!"

49When Jesus heard him he stopped there in the road and said, "Tell him to come here."

So they called the blind man. "You lucky fellow," they said, "come on, he's calling you!" 50Bartimaeus yanked off his old coat and flung it aside, jumped up and came to Jesus.

51"What do you want me to do for you?" Jesus asked.

"O Teacher," the blind man said, "I want to see!"

52And Jesus said to him, "All right, it's done. Your faith has healed you." And instantly the blind man could see, and followed Jesus down the road!

PSALM 45:1–17

MY heart is overflowing with a beautiful thought! I will write a lovely poem to the King, for I am as full of words as the speediest writer pouring out his story.

2You are the fairest of all; Your words are filled with grace; God himself is blessing you forever. 3Arm yourself, O Mighty One, So glorious, so majestic! 4And in your majesty Go on to victory, Defending truth, humility, and justice. Go forth to awe-inspiring deeds! 5Your arrows are sharp In your enemies' hearts; They fall before you. 6Your throne, O God, endures forever. Justice is your royal scepter. 7You love what is good And hate what is wrong. Therefore God, your God, Has given you more gladness Than anyone else.

8Your robes are perfumed with myrrh, aloes and cassia. In your palaces of inlaid ivory, lovely music is being played for your enjoyment. 9Kings' daughters are among your concubines. Standing beside you is the queen, wearing jewelry of finest gold from Ophir.

10,11"I advise you, O daughter, not to fret about your parents in your homeland far away. Your royal husband delights in your beauty. Reverence him, for he is your lord. 12The people of Tyre, the richest people of our day, will shower you with gifts and entreat your favors."

13The bride, a princess, waits within her chamber, robed in beautiful clothing woven with gold. 14Lovely she is, led beside her maids of honor to the king! 15What a joyful, glad procession as they enter in the palace gates! 16"Your sons will some day be kings like their father. They shall sit on thrones around the world!

17"I will cause your name to be honored in all generations; the nations of the earth will praise you forever."

PROVERBS FOR TODAY/ 10:22

The Lord's blessing is our greatest wealth. All our work adds nothing to it!

MARCH 3

IF someone donates his home to the Lord and then wishes to redeem it, the priest will decide its value and the man shall pay that amount plus twenty percent, and the house will be his again.

16"If a man dedicates any part of his field to the Lord, value it in proportion to its size, as indicated by the amount of seed required to sow it. A section of land that requires ten bushels of barley seed for sowing is valued at twenty-five dollars. 17If a man dedicates his field in the Year of Jubilee, then the whole estimate shall stand; 18but if it is after the Year of Jubilee, then the value shall be in proportion to the number of years remaining until the next Year of Jubilee. 19If the man decides to redeem the field, he shall pay twenty percent in addition to the priest's valuation, and the field will be his again. 20But if he decides not to redeem the field, or if he has sold the field to someone else [and has given to the Lord his rights to it at the Year of Jubilee], it shall not be returned to him again. 21When it is freed in the Year of Jubilee, it shall belong to the Lord as a field devoted to him, and it shall be given to the priests.

22"If a man dedicates to the Lord a field he has bought, but which is not part of his family possession, 23the priest shall estimate the value until the Year of Jubilee, and he shall immediately give that estimated value to the Lord, 24and in the Year of Jubilee the field shall return to the original owner from whom it was bought. 25All the valuations shall be stated in standard money.

26"You may not dedicate to the Lord the firstborn of any ox or sheep, for it is already his. 27But if it is the firstborn of an animal that cannot be sacrificed because it is not on the list of those acceptable to the Lord, then the owner shall pay the priest's estimate of its worth, plus twenty percent; or if the owner does not redeem it, the priest may sell it to someone else. 28However, anything utterly devoted to the Lord—people, animals, or inherited fields—shall not be sold or redeemed, for they are most holy to the Lord. 29No one sentenced by the courts to die may pay a fine instead; he shall surely be put to death.

30"A tenth of the produce of the land, whether grain or fruit, is the Lord's, and is holy. 31If anyone wants to buy back this fruit or grain, he must add a fifth to its value. 32And the Lord owns every tenth animal of your herds and flocks and other domestic animals, as they pass by for counting. 33The tenth given to the Lord shall not be selected on the basis of whether it is good or bad, and there shall be no substitutions; for if there is any change made, then both the original and the substitution shall belong to the Lord, and may not be bought back!"

34These are the commandments the Lord gave to Moses for the people of Israel on Mount Sinai.

IT was on the fifteenth day of April of the second year after the Israelis left Egypt that the Lord issued the following instructions to Moses. (He was in the Tabernacle at the camp of Israel on the Sinai peninsula at the time.) 2-15"Take a census of all the men twenty years old and older who are able to go to war, indicating their tribe and family. You and Aaron are to direct the project, assisted by these leaders from each tribe:"

Tribe	Leader
Reuben	Elizur (son of Shedeur)
Simeon	Shelumi-el (son of Zurishaddai)
Judah	Nahshon (son of Amminadab)
Issachar	Nethanel (son of Zuar)
Zebulun	Eliab (son of Helon)

Tribe	Leader
Ephraim (son of Joseph)	Elishama (son of Ammihud
Manasseh (son of Joseph)	Gamaliel (son of Pedahzur)
Benjamin	Abidan (son of Gideoni)
Dan	Ahiezer (son of Ammishaddai)
Asher	Pagiel (son of Ochran)
Gad	Eliasaph (son of Deuel)
Naphtali	Ahira (son of Enan)

16These were the tribal leaders elected from among the people.

17,18,19On the same day Moses and Aaron and the above-named leaders summoned all the men of Israel who were twenty years old or older to come and register, each man indicating his tribe and family, as the Lord had commanded Moses. 20-46Here is the final tabulation:

Tribe	Total
Reuben (the oldest son of Jacob)	46,500
Simeon	59,300
Gad	45,650
Judah	74,600
Issachar	54,400
Zebulun	57,400
Joseph: Ephraim (son of Joseph)	40,500
Joseph: Manasseh (son of Joseph)	32,200
Benjamin	35,400
Dan	62,700
Asher	41,500
Naphtali	53,400

Grand Total: 603,550

47,48,49This total does not include the Levites, for the Lord had said to Moses, "Exempt the entire tribe of Levi from the draft, and do not include their number in the census. 50For the Levites are assigned for the work connected with the Tabernacle and its transportation. They are to live near the Tabernacle, 51and whenever the Tabernacle is moved, the Levites are to take it down and set it up again; anyone else touching it shall be executed. 52Each tribe of Israel shall have a separate camping area with its own flag. 53The Levites' tents shall be clustered around the Tabernacle as a wall between the people of Israel and God's wrath—to protect them from his fierce anger against their sins."

54So all these instructions of the Lord to Moses were put into effect.

MARK 11:1-25

AS they neared Bethphage and Bethany on the outskirts of Jerusalem and came to the Mount of Olives, Jesus sent two of his disciples on ahead.

2"Go into that village over there," he told them, "and just as you enter you will see a colt tied up that has never been ridden. Untie him and bring him here. 3And if anyone asks you what you are doing, just say, 'Our Master needs him and will return him soon.'"

4,5Off went the two men and found the colt standing in the street, tied outside a house. As they were untying it, some who were standing there demanded, "What are you doing, untying that colt?"

6So they said what Jesus had told them to, and then the men agreed.

7So the colt was brought to Jesus and the disciples threw their cloaks across its back for him to ride on. 8Then many in the crowd spread out their coats along the road before him, while others threw down leafy branches from the fields.

9He was in the center of the procession with crowds ahead and behind, and all of them shouting, "Hail to the King!" "Praise God for him who comes in the name of the Lord!" . . . 10"Praise God for the return of our father David's kingdom . . . " "Hail to the King of the universe!"

11And so he entered Jerusalem and went into the Temple. He looked around carefully at everything and then left—for now it was late in the afternoon—and went out to Bethany with the twelve disciples.

12The next morning as they left Bethany, he felt hungry. 13A little way off he noticed a fig tree in full leaf, so he went over to see if he could find any figs on it. But no, there were only leaves, for it was too early in the season for fruit.

14Then Jesus said to the tree, "You shall never bear fruit again!" And the disciples heard him say it.

15When they arrived back to Jerusalem he went to the Temple and began to drive out the merchants and their customers, and knocked over the tables of the moneychangers and the stalls of those selling doves, 16and stopped everyone from bringing in loads of merchandise.

17He told them, "It is written in the Scriptures, 'My Temple is to be a place of prayer for all nations,' but you have turned it into a den of robbers."

18When the chief priests and other Jewish leaders heard what he had done they began planning how best to get rid of him. Their problem was their fear of riots because the people were so enthusiastic about Jesus' teaching.

19That evening as usual they left the city.

20Next morning, as the disciples passed the fig tree he had cursed, they saw that it was withered from the roots! 21Then Peter remembered what Jesus had said to the tree on the previous day, and exclaimed, "Look, Teacher! The fig tree you cursed has withered!"

22,23In reply Jesus said to the disciples, "If you only have faith in God—this is the absolute truth—you can say to this Mount of Olives, 'Rise up and fall into the Mediterranean,' and your command will be obeyed. All that's required is that you really believe and have no doubt! 24Listen to me! You can pray for *any-thing,* and *if you believe, you have it;* it's yours! 25But when you are praying, first forgive anyone you are holding a grudge against, so that your Father in heaven will forgive you your sins too."

PSALM 46:1–11

GOD is our refuge and strength, a tested help in times of trouble. 2And so we need not fear even if the world blows up, and the mountains crumble into the sea. 3Let the oceans roar and foam; let the mountains tremble!

4There is a river of joy flowing through the City of our God—the sacred home of the God above all gods. 5God himself is living in that City; therefore it stands unmoved despite the turmoil everywhere. He will not delay his help. 6The nations rant and rave in anger—but when God speaks, the earth melts in submission and kingdoms totter into ruin.

7The Commander of the armies of heaven is here among us. He, the God of Jacob, has come to rescue us.

8Come, see the glorious things that our God does, how he brings ruin upon the world, 9and causes wars to end throughout the earth, breaking and burning every weapon. 10"Stand silent! Know that I am God! I will be honored by every nation in the world!"

11The Commander of the heavenly armies is here among *us!* He, the God of Jacob, has come to rescue *us!*

PROVERBS FOR TODAY/ 10:23
A fool's fun is being bad; a wise man's fun is being wise!

MARCH 4

NUMBERS 2:1—3:51

THE Lord gave these further instructions to Moses and Aaron: "Each tribe will have its own tent area, with its flagpole and tribal banner; and at the center of these tribal compounds will be the Tabernacle." 3-31Here are the tribal locations:

Tribe:	Leader:	Location:	Census:
Judah	Nahshon (son of Amminadab)	East side of the Tabernacle	74,600
Issachar	Nethanel (son of Zuar)	Next to Judah	54,400
Zebulun	Eliab (son of Helon)	Next to Issachar	57,400

So the total of all those on Judah's side of the camp was 186,400. These three tribes led the way whenever the Israelites traveled to a new campsite.

Reuben	Elizur (son of Shedeur)	South side of the Tabernacle	46,500
Simeon	Shelumi-el (son of Zurishaddai)	Next to Reuben	59,300
Gad	Eliasaph (son of Reuel)	Next to Simeon	45,650

So the total of the Reuben side of the camp was 151,450. These three tribes were next in line whenever the Israelis traveled.

Next in the line of march was the Tabernacle, with the Levites. When traveling, each tribe stayed together under its own flag, just as each was separate from the others in camp.

Ephraim	Elishama (son of Ammihud)	West side of Tabernacle	40,500
Manasseh	Gamaliel (son of Pedahzur)	Next to Ephraim	32,200
Benjamin	Abidan (son of Gideoni)	Next to Manasseh	35,400

So the total on the Ephraim side of the camp was 108,100, and they were next in the line of march.

Dan	Ahiezer (son of Ammishaddai)	North side of Tabernacle	62,700
Asher	Pagiel (son of Ochran)	Next to Dan	41,500
Naphtali	Ahira (son of Enan)	Next to Asher	53,400

So the total on Dan's side of the camp was 157,600. They brought up the rear whenever Israel traveled. 32,33In summary, the armies of Israel totaled 603,550 (not including the Levites, who were exempted by Jehovah's commandment to Moses). 34So the people of Israel set up their camps, each tribe under its own banner, in the locations indicated by the Lord to Moses.

AT the time when the Lord spoke to Moses on Mount Sinai, 2Aaron's sons were:

Nadab (his oldest), Abihu, Eleazar, Ithamar.

3All were anointed as priests and set apart to minister at the Tabernacle. 4But Nadab and Abihu died before the Lord in the wilderness of Sinai when they used unholy fire. And since they had no children, this left only Eleazar and Ithamar to assist their father Aaron.

5Then the Lord said to Moses, 6"Summon the tribe of Levi and present them to Aaron as his assistants. 7,8,9They will follow his instructions and perform the sacred duties at the Tabernacle on behalf of all the people of Israel. For they are assigned to him as representatives of all the people of Israel. They are in charge of all the furnishings and maintenance of the Tabernacle. [10]However, only Aaron and his sons may carry out the duties of the priesthood; anyone else who presumes to assume this office shall be executed."

[11,12]And the Lord said to Moses, "I have accepted the Levites in substitution for all the oldest sons of the people of Israel. The Levites are mine [13]in exchange for all the oldest sons. From the day I killed all the oldest sons of the Egyptians, I took for myself all the firstborn in Israel of both men and animals! They are mine; I am Jehovah."

[14,15]The Lord now spoke again to Moses at the Sinai peninsula, telling him, "Take a census of the tribe of Levi, indicating each person's clan; count every male down to one month old." [16-24]So Moses did:

Levi's son	Levi's grandsons (clan names)	Census	Leader	Camp Location
Gershon	Libni Shime-i	7,500	Elisaph (son of Lael)	West side of Tabernacle

[25-30]*Responsibilities:*

The responsibility of these two clans of Levites was the care of the Tabernacle: its coverings, its entry drapes, the drapes covering the fence surrounding the courtyard, the screen at the entrance of the courtyard surrounding the Tabernacle, the altar, and all the ropes used in tying the Tabernacle together.

Levi's son	Levi's grandsons (clan names)	Census	Leader	Camp Location
Kohath	Amran Izhar Hebron Uzziel	8,600	Elizaphan (son of Uzziel)	Southside of the Tabernacle

[31-35]*Responsibilities:*

The responsibility of these four clans of Levites was the care of the Ark, the table, the lampstand, the altars, the various utensils used in the Tabernacle, the veil, and any repairs needed on any of these items. (Note: Eleazar, Aaron's son, shall be the chief administrator over the leaders of the Levites, with special responsibility for the oversight of the sanctuary.)

Levi's son	Levi's grandsons (clan names)	Census	Leader	Camp Location
Merari	Mahli Mushi	6,200	Zuriel (son of Abihail)	North side of Tabernacle

[36,37]*Responsibilities:*

The responsibility of these two clans was the care of the frames of the Tabernacle building; the posts; the bases for the posts, and all of the equipment needed for their use; the posts around the courtyard and their bases, pegs, and ropes.

[38]The area east of the Tabernacle was reserved for the tents of Moses and of Aaron and his sons, who had the final responsibility for the Tabernacle on behalf of the people of Israel. (Anyone who was not a priest or Levite, but came into the Tabernacle, was to be executed.)

[39]So all the Levites, as numbered by Moses and Aaron at the command of the Lord, were 22,000 males one month old and older.

[40]Then the Lord said to Moses, "Now take a census of all the eldest sons in Israel who are one month old and older, and register each name. [41]The Levites shall be mine (I am Jehovah) as substitutes for the eldest sons of Israel; and the Levites' cattle are mine as substitutes for the firstborn cattle of the whole nation."

[42]So Moses took a census of the eldest sons of the people of Israel, as the Lord had commanded, [43]and found the total number of eldest sons one month old and older to be 22,273.

[44]Now the Lord said to Moses, [45]"Give me the Levites instead of the eldest sons of the people of Israel; and give me the cattle of the Levites instead of the firstborn cattle of the people of Israel; yes, the Levites shall be mine; I am Jehovah. [46]To redeem the 273 eldest sons in excess of the number of Levites,

^{47,48}pay five dollars for each one to Aaron and his sons."

⁴⁹So Moses received redemption money for the 273 eldest sons of Israel who were in excess of the number of Levites. (All the others were redeemed because the Levites had been given to the Lord in their place.) ⁵⁰The money collected came to a total of $1,365. ⁵¹And Moses gave it to Aaron and his sons as the Lord had commanded.

MARK 11:26—12:17

BY this time they had arrived in Jerusalem again, and as he was walking through the Temple area, the chief priests and other Jewish leaders came up to him demanding, "What's going on here? Who gave you the authority to drive out the merchants?"

²⁹Jesus replied, "I'll tell you if you answer one question! ³⁰What about John the Baptist? Was he sent by God, or not? Answer me!"

³¹They talked it over among themselves. "If we reply that God sent him, then he will say, 'All right, why didn't you accept him?' ³²But if we say God didn't send him, then the people will start a riot." (For the people all believed strongly that John was a prophet.)

³³So they said, "We can't answer. We don't know."

To which Jesus replied, "Then I won't answer your question either!"

HERE are some of the story-illustrations Jesus gave to the people at that time:

"A man planted a vineyard and built a wall around it and dug a pit for pressing out the grape juice, and built a watchman's tower. Then he leased the farm to tenant farmers and moved to another country. ²At grape-picking time he sent one of his men to collect his share of the crop. ³But the farmers beat up the man and sent him back empty-handed. ⁴"The owner then sent another of his men, who received the same treatment, only worse, for his head was seriously injured. ⁵The next man he sent was killed; and later, others were either beaten or killed, until ⁶there was only one left— his only son. He finally sent him, thinking they would surely give him their full respect.

⁷"But when the farmers saw him coming they said, 'He will own the farm when his father dies. Come on, let's kill him— and then the farm will be ours!' ⁸So they caught him and murdered him and threw his body out of the vineyard.

⁹"What do you suppose the owner will do when he hears what happened? He will come and kill them all, and lease the vineyard to others. ¹⁰Don't you remember reading this verse in the Scriptures? 'The Rock the builders threw away became the cornerstone, the most honored stone in the building! ¹¹This is the Lord's doing and it is an amazing thing to see.'"

¹²The Jewish leaders wanted to arrest him then and there for using this illustration, for they knew he was pointing at them—they were the wicked farmers in his story. But they were afraid to touch him for fear of a mob. So they left him and went away.

¹³But they sent other religious and political leaders to talk with him and try to trap him into saying something he could be arrested for.

¹⁴"Teacher," these spies said, "we know you tell the truth no matter what! You aren't influenced by the opinions and desires of men, but sincerely teach the ways of God. Now tell us, is it right to pay taxes to Rome, or not?"

¹⁵Jesus saw their trick and said, "Show me a coin and I'll tell you."

¹⁶When they handed it to him he asked, "Whose picture and title is this on the coin?" They replied, "The emperor's."

¹⁷"All right," he said, "if it is his, give it to him. But everything that belongs to God must be given to God!" And they scratched their heads in bafflement at his reply.

COME, everyone, and clap for joy! Shout triumphant praises to the Lord! ²For the Lord, the God above all gods, is awesome beyond words; he is the great King of all the earth. ³He subdues the nations before us, ⁴and will personally select his choicest blessings for his Jewish people—the very best for those he loves.

⁵God has ascended with a mighty shout, with trumpets blaring. ⁶,⁷Sing out your praises to our God, our King. Yes, sing your highest praises to our King, the King of all the earth. Sing thoughtful praises! ⁸He reigns above the nations, sitting on his holy throne. ⁹The Gentile rulers of the world have joined with us in praising him—praising the God of Abraham—for the battle shields of all the armies of the world are his trophies. He is highly honored everywhere.

PROVERBS FOR TODAY/ 10:24–25

The wicked man's fears will all come true, and so will the good man's hopes. Disaster strikes like a cyclone and the wicked are whirled away. But the good man has a strong anchor.

MARCH 5

NUMBERS 4:1—5:31

THEN the Lord said to Moses and Aaron, "Take a census of the Kohath division of the Levite tribe. ³This census will be of all males from ages thirty to fifty who are able to work in the Tabernacle. ⁴These are their sacred duties:

⁵"When the camp moves, Aaron and his sons will enter the Tabernacle first and take down the veil and cover the Ark with it. ⁶Then they will cover the veil with goatskin leather, cover the goatskins with a blue cloth, and place the carrying poles of the Ark in their rings.

⁷"Next they must spread a blue cloth over the table where the Bread of the Presence is displayed, and place the dishes, spoons, bowls, cups, and the Bread upon the cloth. ⁸They will spread a scarlet cloth over that, and finally a covering of goatskin leather on top of the scarlet cloth. Then they shall insert the carrying poles into the table.

⁹"Next they must cover with a blue cloth the lampstand, the lamps, snuffers, trays, and the reservoir of olive oil. ¹⁰This entire group of objects shall then be covered with goatskin leather, and the bundle shall be placed upon a carrying frame.

¹¹"They must then spread a blue cloth over the gold altar, cover it with a covering of goatskin leather, and insert the carrying poles into the altar. ¹²All of the remaining utensils of the Tabernacle are to be wrapped in a blue cloth, covered with goatskin leather, and placed on the carrying frame.

¹³"The ashes are to be removed from the altar, and the altar shall be covered with a purple cloth. ¹⁴All of the altar utensils are to be placed upon the cloth—the firepans, hooks, shovels, basins, and other containers—and a cover of goatskin leather will be spread over them. Finally, the carrying poles are to be put in place. ¹⁵When Aaron and his sons have finished packing the sanctuary and all the utensils, the clan of Kohath shall come and carry the units to wherever the camp is traveling; but they must not touch the holy items, lest they die. This, then,

is the sacred work of the sons of Kohath.

16"Aaron's son Eleazar shall be responsible for the oil for the light, the sweet incense, the daily grain offering, and the anointing oil—in fact, the supervision of the entire Tabernacle and everything in it will be his responsibility."

17,18,19Then the Lord said to Moses and Aaron, "Don't let the families of Kohath destroy themselves! This is what you must do so that they will not die when they carry the most holy things: Aaron and his sons shall go in with them and point out what each is to carry. 20Otherwise they must never enter the sanctuary for even a moment, lest they look at the sacred objects there and die."

21,22,23And the Lord said to Moses, "Take a census of the Gershonite division of the tribe of Levi, all of the men between the ages of thirty and fifty who are eligible for the sacred work of the Tabernacle. 24These will be their duties:

25"They will carry the curtains of the Tabernacle, the Tabernacle itself with its coverings, the goatskin leather roof, and the curtain for the Tabernacle entrance. 26They are also to carry the drapes covering the courtyard fence, and the curtain across the entrance to the courtyard that surrounds the altar and the Tabernacle. They will also carry the altar, the ropes, and all of the accessories. They are fully responsible for the transportation of these items. 27Aaron or any of his sons may assign the Gershonites' tasks to them, 28but the Gershonites will be directly responsible to Aaron's son Ithamar.

29"Now take a census of the Merari division of the Levite tribe, all of the men from thirty to fifty who are eligible for the Tabernacle service. 30,31When the Tabernacle is moved, they are to carry the frames of the Tabernacle, the bars, the bases, 32the frames for the courtyard fence with their bases, pegs, cords, and everything else connected with their use and repair.

"Assign duties to each man by name. 33The Merari division will also report to Aaron's son Ithamar."

34So Moses and Aaron and the other leaders took a census of the Kohath division, 35including all of the men thirty to fifty years of age who were eligible for the Tabernacle service, 36and found that the total number was 2,750. 37All this was done to carry out the Lord's instructions to Moses. 38-41A similar census of the Gershon division totaled 2,630. 42-45And of the Merari division, 3,200. 46,47,48Thus Moses and Aaron and the leaders of Israel found that the total of all the Levites who were thirty to fifty years old and who were eligible for the Tabernacle service and transportation, was 8,580. 49This census was taken in response to the Lord's instructions to Moses.

THESE are further instructions from the Lord to Moses: "Inform the people of Israel that they must expel all lepers from the camp, and all who have open sores, or who have been defiled by touching a dead person. 3This applies to men and women alike. Remove them so that they will not defile the camp where I live among you." 4These instructions were put into effect.

5,6Then the Lord said to Moses, "Tell the people of Israel that when anyone, man or woman, betrays the Lord by betraying a trust, it is sin. 7He must confess his sin and make full repayment for what he has stolen, adding twenty percent and returning it to the person he took it from. 8But if the person he wronged is dead, and there is no near relative to whom the payment can be made, it must be given to the priest, along with a lamb for atonement. 9,10When the people of Israel bring a gift to the Lord it shall go to the priests."

11,12And the Lord said to Moses, "Tell the people of Israel that if a man's wife commits adultery, 13but there is no proof, there being no witness, 14and he is jealous and suspicious, 15the man shall bring his wife to the priest with an offering for her of a tenth of a bushel of barley meal without oil or frankincense mingled with it—for it is a suspicion offering—to bring out the truth as to whether or not she is guilty.

16"The priest shall bring her before the Lord, 17and take holy water in a clay jar and mix into it dust from the floor of the Tabernacle. 18He shall unbind her hair and place the suspicion offering in her hands to determine whether or not her husband's suspicions are justified. The priest shall stand before her holding the jar of bitter water that brings a curse. 19He shall require her to swear that she is innocent, and then he shall say to her, 'If no man has slept with you except your husband, be free from the effects of this bitter water that causes the curse. 20But if you have committed adultery, 21,22then Jehovah shall make you a curse among your people, for he will make your thigh rot away and your body swell.' And the woman shall be required to say, 'Yes, let it be so.' 23Then the priest shall write these curses in a book and wash them off into the bitter water. 24(When he requires the woman to drink the water, it becomes bitter within her [if she is guilty].)

25"Then the priest shall take the suspicion offering from the woman's hand and wave it before Jehovah, and carry it to the altar. 26He shall take a handful, representing all of it, and burn the handful upon the altar, and then require the woman to drink the water. 27If she has been defiled, having committed adultery against her husband, the water will become bitter within her, and her body will swell and her thigh will rot, and she shall be a curse among her people. 28But if she is pure and has not committed adultery, she shall be unharmed and will soon become pregnant.

29"This, then, is the law concerning a wayward wife—or a husband's suspicions against his wife— 30to determine whether or not she has been unfaithful to him. He shall bring her before the Lord and the priest shall handle the situation as outlined above. 31Her husband shall not be brought to trial for causing her horrible disease, for she is responsible."

MARK 12:18-37

THEN the Sadducees stepped forward—a group of men who say there is no resurrection. Here was their question:

19"Teacher, Moses gave us a law that when a man dies without children, the man's brother should marry his widow and have children in his brother's name. 20,21,22Well, there were seven brothers and the oldest married and died, and left no children. So the second brother married the widow, but soon he died too, and left no children. Then the next brother married her, and died without children, and so on until all were dead, and still there were no children; and last of all, the woman died too.

23"What we want to know is this: In the resurrection, whose wife will she be, for she had been the wife of each of them?"

24Jesus replied, "Your trouble is that you don't know the Scriptures, and don't know the power of God. 25For when these seven brothers and the woman rise from the dead, they won't be married—they will be like the angels.

26"But now as to whether there will be a resurrection—have you never read in the book of Exodus about Moses and the burning bush? God said to Moses, 'I *am* the God of Abraham, and I *am* the God of Isaac, and I *am* the God of Jacob.'

27"God was telling Moses that these men, though dead for hundreds of years, were still very much alive, for he would not have said, 'I *am* the God' of those who don't exist! You have made a serious error."

28One of the teachers of religion who was standing there listening to the discussion realized that Jesus had answered well. So he asked, "Of all the commandments, which is the most important?"

29Jesus replied, "The one that says, 'Hear, O Israel! The Lord our God is the one and only God. 30And you must love him with all your heart and soul and mind and strength.'

31"The second is: 'You must love others as much as yourself.' No other commandments are greater than these."

32The teacher of religion replied, "Sir, you have spoken a true word in saying that there is only one God and no other. 33And I know it is far more important to love him with all my heart and understanding and strength, and to love others as myself, than to offer all kinds of sacrifices on the altar of the Temple."

34Realizing this man's understanding, Jesus said to him, "You are not far from the Kingdom of God." And after that, no one dared ask him any more questions.

35Later, as Jesus was teaching the people in the Temple area, he asked them this question:

"Why do your religious teachers claim that the Messiah must be a descendant of King David? 36For David himself said—and the Holy Spirit was speaking through him when he said it—'God said to my Lord, sit at my right hand until I make your enemies your footstool.' 37Since David called him his Lord, how can he be his *son?*"

(This sort of reasoning delighted the crowd and they listened to him with great interest.)

PSALM 48:1–14

HOW great is the Lord! How much we should praise him. He lives upon Mount Zion in Jerusalem. 2What a glorious sight! See Mount Zion rising north of the city high above the plains for all to see—Mount Zion, joy of all the earth, the residence of the great King.

3God himself is the defender of Jerusalem. 4The kings of the earth have arrived together to inspect the city. 5They marvel at the sight and hurry home again, 6afraid of what they have seen; they are filled with panic like a woman in travail! 7For God destroys the mightiest warships with a breath of wind. 8We have heard of the city's glory—the city of our God, the Commander of the armies of heaven. And now we see it for ourselves! God has established Jerusalem forever.

9Lord, here in your Temple we meditate upon your kindness and your love. 10Your name is known throughout the earth, O God. You are praised everywhere for the salvation you have scattered throughout the world. 11O Jerusalem, rejoice! O people of Judah, rejoice! For God will see to it that you are finally treated fairly. 12Go, inspect the city! Walk around and count her many towers! 13Note her walls and tour her palaces, so that you can tell your children.

14For this great God is our God forever and ever. He will be our guide until we die.

PROVERBS FOR TODAY/ 10:26

A lazy fellow is a pain to his employers—like smoke in their eyes or vinegar that sets the teeth on edge.

MARCH 6

NUMBERS 6:1—7:89

THE Lord gave Moses these further instructions for the people of Israel: "When either a man or a woman takes the special vow of a Nazirite, consecrating himself to the Lord in a special way, 3,4he must not thereafter, during the entire period of his special consecration to the Lord, taste strong drink or wine or even fresh wine, grape juice, grapes, or raisins! He may eat nothing that comes from grape vines, not even the seeds or skins!

5"Throughout that time he must never cut his hair, for he is holy and consecrated to the Lord; that is why he must let his hair grow.

6,7"And he may not go near any dead body during the entire period of his vow, even if it is the body of his father, mother, brother, or sister; for his vow of consecration remains in effect, 8and he is consecrated to the Lord throughout the entire period. 9If he is defiled by having someone fall dead beside him, then seven days later he shall shave his defiled head; he will then be cleansed from the contamination of being in the presence of death. 10The next day, the eighth day, he must bring two turtledoves or two young pigeons to the priest at the entrance of the Tabernacle. 11The priest shall offer one of the birds for a sin offering, and the other for a burnt offering, and make atonement for his defilement. And he must renew his vows that day and let his hair begin to grow again. 12The days of his vow that were fulfilled before his defilement no longer count. He must begin all over again with a new vow, and must bring a male lamb a year old for a guilt offering.

13"At the conclusion of the period of his vow of separation to the Lord, he must go to the entrance of the Tabernacle 14and offer a burnt sacrifice to the Lord, a year-old lamb without defect. He must also offer a sin offering, a yearling ewe

lamb without defect; a peace offering, a ram without defect; 15a basket of bread made without yeast; pancakes made of fine flour mixed with olive oil; unleavened wafers spread with oil; and the accompanying grain offering and drink offerings. 16The priest shall present these offerings before the Lord: first the sin offering and the burnt offering; 17then the ram for a peace offering, along with the basket of bread made without yeast; and finally the grain offering along with the drink offering.

18"Then the Nazirite shall shave his long hair—the sign of his vow of separation. This shall be done at the entrance of the Tabernacle, after which the hair shall be put in the fire under the peace offering sacrifice. 19After the man's head has been shaved, the priest shall take the roasted shoulder of the lamb, one of the pancakes (made without yeast), and one of the wafers (also made without yeast), and put them all into the man's hands. 20The priest shall then wave it all back and forth before the Lord in a gesture of offering; all of it is a holy portion for the priest, as are the rib piece and shoulder that were waved before the Lord. After that the Nazirite may again drink wine, for he is freed from his vow.

21"These are the regulations concerning a Nazirite and his sacrifices at the conclusion of his period of special dedication. In addition to these sacrifices he must bring any further offering he promised at the time he took his vow to become a Nazirite."

22,23Now the Lord said to Moses, "Tell Aaron and his sons that they are to give this special blessing to the people of Israel: 24,25,26'May the Lord bless and protect you; may the Lord's face radiate with joy because of you; may he be gracious to you, show you his favor, and give you his peace.' 27This is how Aaron and his sons shall call down my blessings upon the people of Israel; and I myself will personally bless them."

MOSES anointed and sanctified each part of the Tabernacle, including the altar and its utensils, on the day he finished setting it up. 2Then the leaders of Israel—the chiefs of the tribes, the men who had organized the census—brought their offerings. 3They brought six covered wagons, each drawn by two oxen—a wagon for every two leaders and an ox for each one; and they presented them to the Lord in front of the Tabernacle.

4,5"Accept their gifts," the Lord told Moses, "and use these wagons for the work of the Tabernacle. Give them to the Levites for whatever needs they may have."

6So Moses presented the wagons and the oxen to the Levites. 7Two wagons and four oxen were given to the Gershon division for their use, 8and four wagons and eight oxen were given to the Merari division, which was under the leadership of Ithamar, Aaron's son. 9None of the wagons or teams was given to the Kohath division, for they were required to carry their portion of the Tabernacle upon their shoulders.

10The leaders also presented dedication gifts on the day the altar was anointed, placing them before the altar. 11The Lord said to Moses, "Let each of them bring his gift on a different day for the dedication of the altar."

12So Nahshon, the son of Amminadab of the tribe of Judah, brought his gift the first day. 13It consisted of a silver platter weighing three pounds and a silver bowl of about two pounds, both filled with grain offerings of fine flour mixed with oil. 14He also brought a tiny gold box of incense which weighed only about four ounces. 15He brought a young bull, a ram, and a male yearling lamb as burnt offerings; 16a male goat for a sin offering; 17and for the peace offerings two oxen, five rams, five male goats, and five male yearling lambs.

18-23The next day Nethanel, the son of Zuar, chief of the tribe of Issachar, brought his gifts and offerings. They were exactly the same as Nahshon had presented on the previous day.

24-29On the third day Eliab, the son of Helon, chief of the tribe of Zebulun, came with his offerings—the same as those presented on the previous days.

30-35On the fourth day the gifts were presented by Elizur, son of Shedeur, chief of the tribe of Reuben; his gifts and offerings were the same as those given on the previous days.

36-41On the fifth day came Shelumi-el, the son of Zuri-shaddai, chief of the tribe of Simeon, with the same gifts.

42-47The next day it was Eliasaph's turn, son of Deuel, chief of the tribe of Gad. He, too, offered the same gifts and sacrifices.

48-53On the seventh day, Elishama, the son of Ammihud, chief of the tribe of Ephraim, brought his gifts, the same as those presented on the previous days.

54-59Gamaliel, son of Pedahzur, prince of the tribe of Manasseh, came the eighth day with the same offerings.

60-65On the ninth day it was Abidan the son of Gideoni, chief of the tribe of Benjamin, with his gifts, the same as those offered by the others.

66-71Ahiezer, the son of Ammishaddai, brought his gifts on the tenth day. He was the chief of the tribe of Dan and his offerings were the same as those on the previous days.

72-77Pagiel, son of Ochran, chief of the tribe of Asher, brought his gifts on the eleventh day—the same gifts and offerings as the others.

78-83On the twelfth day came Ahira, son of Enan, chief of the tribe of Naphtali, with his offerings; they were identical to those brought by the others.

84,85,86So, beginning the day the altar was anointed, it was dedicated by these gifts from the chiefs of the tribes of Israel. Their combined offerings were as follows:

12 silver platters (each weighing about three pounds);

12 silver bowls (each weighing about two pounds); (so the total weight of the silver was about sixty pounds);

12 gold trays (the trays weighing about four ounces apiece); (so the total weight of gold was about three pounds).

87For the burnt offerings they brought: 12 bulls, 12 rams,

12 yearling male goats (with the grain offerings that accompanied them).

For sin offerings they brought:

12 male goats.

88For the peace offerings they brought: 24 young bulls,

60 rams, 60 male goats,

60 male lambs one year old.

89When Moses went into the Tabernacle to speak with God, he heard the Voice speaking to him from above the place of mercy over the Ark, between the statues of the two Guardian Angels.

MARK 12:38—13:13

HERE are some of the other things he taught them at this time:

"Beware of the teachers of religion! For they love to wear the robes of the rich and scholarly, and to have everyone bow to them as they walk through the markets. 39They love to sit in the best seats in the synagogues, and at the places of honor at banquets— 40but they shamelessly cheat widows out of their homes and then, to cover up the kind of men they really are, they pretend to be pious by praying long prayers in public. Because of this, their punishment will be the greater."

41Then he went over to the collection boxes in the Temple and sat and watched as the crowds dropped in their money. Some who were rich put in large amounts. 42Then a poor widow came and dropped in two pennies.

43,44He called his disciples to him and remarked, "That poor widow has given more than all those rich men put together! For they gave a little of their extra fat, while she gave up her last penny."

As he was leaving the Temple that day, one of his disciples said, "Teacher, what beautiful buildings these are! Look at the decorated stonework on the walls."

2Jesus replied, "Yes, look! For not one stone will be left upon another, except as ruins."

3,4And as he sat on the slopes of the Mount of Olives across the valley from Jerusalem, Peter, James, John, and Andrew got alone with him and asked him, "Just when is all this going to happen to the Temple? Will there be some warning ahead of time?"

5So Jesus launched into an extended reply. "Don't let anyone mislead you," he said, 6"for many will come declaring themselves to be your Messiah, and will lead many astray. 7And wars will break out near and far, but this is not the signal of the end-time.

8"For nations and kingdoms will proclaim war against each other, and there will be earthquakes in many lands, and famines. These herald only the early stages of the anguish ahead. 9But when these things begin to happen, watch out! For you will be in great danger. You will be dragged before the courts, and beaten in the synagogues, and accused before governors and kings of being my followers. This is your opportunity to tell them the Good News. 10And the Good News must first be made known in every nation before the end-time finally comes. 11But when you are arrested and stand trial, don't worry about what to say in your defense. Just say what God tells you to. Then you will not be speaking, but the Holy Spirit will.

12"Brothers will betray each other to death, fathers will betray their own children, and children will betray their parents to be killed. 13And everyone will hate you because you are mine. But all who endure to the end without renouncing me shall be saved.

L ISTEN, everyone! High and low, rich and poor, all around the world—listen to my words, 3for they are wise and filled with insight.

4I will tell in song accompanied by harps the answer to one of life's most perplexing problems:

5*There is no need to fear when times of trouble come,* even though surrounded by enemies! 6They trust in their wealth and boast about how rich they are, 7yet not one of them, though rich as kings, can ransom his own brother from the penalty of sin! For God's forgiveness does not come that way. 8,9For a soul is far too precious to be ransomed by mere earthly wealth. There is not enough of it in all the earth to buy eternal life for just one soul, to keep it out of hell.

10Rich man! Proud man! Wise man! You must die like all the rest! You have no greater lease on life than foolish, stupid men. You must leave your wealth to others. 11You name your estates after yourselves as though your lands could be forever yours, and you could live on them eternally. 12But man with all his pomp must die like any animal. 13Such is the folly of these men, though after they die they will be quoted as having great wisdom.

14Death is the shepherd of all mankind. And "in the morning" those who are evil will be the slaves of those who are good. For the power of their wealth is gone when they die; they cannot take it with them.

15But as for me, God will redeem my soul from the power of death, for he will receive me. 16So do not be dismayed when evil men grow rich and build their lovely homes. 17For when they die they carry nothing with them! Their honors will not follow them. 18Though a man calls himself happy all through his life— and the world loudly applauds success— 19yet in the end he dies like everyone else, and enters eternal darkness.

20For man with all his pomp must die like any animal.

PROVERBS FOR TODAY/ 10:27–28

Reverence for God adds hours to each day; so how can the wicked expect a long, good life? The hope of good men is eternal happiness; the hopes of evil men are all in vain.

MARCH 7

NUMBERS 8:1—9:23

T HE Lord said to Moses, 2"Tell Aaron that when he lights the seven lamps in the lampstand, he is to set them so that they will throw their light forward."

3So Aaron did this. 4The lampstand, including the floral decorations on the base and branches, was made entirely of beaten gold. It was constructed according to the exact design the Lord had shown Moses.

5,6Then the Lord said to Moses, "Now set apart the Levites from the other people of Israel. 7Do this by sprinkling water of purification upon them, then having them shave their entire bodies and wash their clothing and themselves. 8Have them bring a young bull and a grain offering of fine flour mingled with oil, along with another young bull for a sin offering. 9Then bring the Levites to the door of the Tabernacle as all the people watch. 10There the leaders of the tribes shall lay their hands upon them, [11]and Aaron, with a gesture of offering, shall present them to the Lord as a gift from the entire nation of Israel. The Levites will represent all the people in serving the Lord.

[12]"Next, the Levite leaders shall lay their hands upon the heads of the young bulls and offer them before the Lord; one for a sin offering and the other for a burnt offering, to make atonement for the Levites. [13]Then the Levites are to be presented to Aaron and his sons, just as any other gift to the Lord is given to the priests! [14]In this way you will dedicate the Levites from among the rest of the people of Israel, and the Levites shall be mine. [15]After you have sanctified them and presented them in this way, they shall go in and out of the Tabernacle to do their work.

[16]"They are mine from among all the people of Israel, and I have accepted them in place of all the firstborn children of the Israelites: I have taken the Levites as their substitutes. [17]For all the firstborn among the people of Israel are mine, both men and animals; I claimed them for myself the night I killed all the firstborn Egyptians. [18]Yes, I have accepted the Levites in place of all the eldest sons of Israel. [19]And I will give the Levites as a gift to Aaron and his sons. The Levites will carry out the sacred duties required of the people of Israel in the Tabernacle, and will offer the people's sacrifices, making atonement for them. There will be no plague among the Israelites—as there would be if the ordinary people entered the Tabernacle."

[20]So Moses and Aaron and all the people of Israel dedicated the Levites, carefully following Jehovah's instructions to Moses. [21]The Levites purified themselves and washed their clothes, and Aaron presented them to the Lord in a gesture of offering. He then performed the rite of atonement over them to purify them. [22]After that they went into the Tabernacle as assistants to Aaron and his sons; everything was done just as the Lord had commanded Moses.

[23,24]The Lord also instructed Moses, "The Levites are to begin serving in the Tabernacle at the age of twenty-five, and are to retire at the age of fifty. [25,26]After retirement they can assist with various light duties in the Tabernacle, but will have no regular responsibilities."

JEHOVAH gave these instructions to Moses while he and the rest of the Israelis were on the Sinai peninsula, during the first month of the second year after leaving Egypt:

[2,3]"The people of Israel must celebrate the Passover annually on April first, beginning in the evening. Be sure to follow all of my instructions concerning this celebration."

[4,5]So Moses announced that the Passover celebration would begin on the evening of April first, there in the Sinai peninsula, just as the Lord had commanded. [6,7]But as it happened, some of the men had just attended a funeral, and were ceremonially defiled by having touched the dead, so they couldn't eat the Passover lamb that night. They came to Moses and Aaron and explained their problem and protested at being forbidden from offering their sacrifice to the Lord at the time he had appointed.

[8]Moses said he would ask the Lord about it, [9]and this was God's reply:

[10]"If any of the people of Israel, now or in the generations to come, are defiled at Passover time because of touching a dead body, or if they are on a journey and cannot be present, they may still celebrate the Passover, but one month later, [11]on May first, beginning in the evening. They are to eat the lamb at that time, with unleavened bread and bitter herbs. [12]They must not leave any of it until the next morning, and must not break a bone of it, and must follow all the regular instructions concerning the Passover.

[13]"But anyone who is not defiled, and anyone who is not away on a trip, and yet refuses to celebrate the Passover at the regular time, shall be excommunicated from the people of Israel for refusing to sacrifice to Jehovah at the proper time; he must bear his guilt. [14]And if a

foreigner is living among you and wants to celebrate the Passover to the Lord, he shall follow all these same instructions. There is one law for all."

15On the day the Tabernacle was raised, the Cloud covered it; and that evening the Cloud changed to the appearance of fire, and stayed that way throughout the night. 16It was always so—the daytime Cloud changing to the appearance of fire at night. 17When the Cloud lifted, the people of Israel moved on to wherever it stopped, and camped there. 18In this way they journeyed at the command of the Lord and stopped when he told them to, then remained there as long as the Cloud stayed. 19If it stayed a long time, then they stayed a long time. But if it stayed only a few days, then they remained only a few days; for so the Lord had instructed them. 20,21Sometimes the fire-cloud stayed only during the night and moved on the next morning. But day or night, when it moved, the people broke camp and followed. 22If the Cloud stayed above the Tabernacle two days, a month, or a year, that is how long the people of Israel stayed; but as soon as it moved, they moved. 23So it was that they camped or traveled at the commandment of the Lord; and whatever the Lord told Moses they should do, they did.

MARK 13:14–37

WHEN you see the horrible thing standing in the Temple—reader, pay attention!—flee, if you can, to the Judean hills. 15,16Hurry! If you are on your rooftop porch, don't even go back into the house. If you are out in the fields, don't even return for your money or clothes.

17"Woe to pregnant women in those days, and to mothers nursing their children. 18And pray that your flight will not be in winter. 19For those will be days of such horror as have never been since the beginning of God's creation, nor will ever be again. 20And unless the Lord

shortens that time of calamity, not a soul in all the earth will survive. But for the sake of his chosen ones he will limit those days.

21"And then if anyone tells you, 'This is the Messiah,' or, 'That one is,' don't pay any attention. 22For there will be many false Messiahs and false prophets who will do wonderful miracles that would deceive, if possible, even God's own children. 23Take care! I have warned you!

24"After the tribulation ends, then the sun will grow dim and the moon will not shine, 25and the stars will fall—the heavens will convulse.

26"Then all mankind will see me, the Messiah, coming in the clouds with great power and glory. 27And I will send out the angels to gather together my chosen ones from all over the world—from the farthest bounds of earth and heaven.

28"Now, here is a lesson from a fig tree. When its buds become tender and its leaves begin to sprout, you know that spring has come. 29And when you see these things happening that I've described, you can be sure that my return is very near, that I am right at the door.

30"Yes, these are the events that will signal the end of the age. 31Heaven and earth shall disappear, but my words stand sure forever.

32"However, no one, not even the angels in heaven, nor I myself, knows the day or hour when these things will happen; only the Father knows. 33And since you don't know when it will happen, stay alert. Be on the watch [for my return].

34"My coming can be compared with that of a man who went on a trip to another country. He laid out his employees' work for them to do while he was gone, and told the gatekeeper to watch for his return.

35,36,37"Keep a sharp lookout! For you do not know when I will come, at evening, at midnight, early dawn or late daybreak. Don't let me find you sleeping. *Watch for my return!* This is my message to you and to everyone else."

PSALM 50:1–23

THE mighty God, the Lord, has summoned all mankind from east to west!

2God's glory-light shines from the beautiful Temple on Mount Zion. 3He comes with the noise of thunder, surrounded by devastating fire; a great storm rages round about him. 4He has come to judge his people. To heaven and earth he shouts, 5"Gather together my own people who by their sacrifice upon my altar have promised to obey me." 6God will judge them with complete fairness, for all heaven declares that he is just.

7O my people, listen! For I am your God. Listen! Here are my charges against you: 8I have no complaint about the sacrifices you bring to my altar, for you bring them regularly. 9But it isn't sacrificial bullocks and goats that I really want from you. 10,11For all the animals of field and forest are mine! The cattle on a thousand hills! And all the birds upon the mountains! 12If I were hungry, I would not mention it to you—for all the world is mine, and everything in it. 13No, I don't need your sacrifices of flesh and blood. 14,15What I want from you is your true thanks; I want your promises fulfilled. *I want you to trust me in your times of trouble, so I can rescue you, and you can give me glory.*

16But God says to evil men: Recite my laws no longer, and stop claiming my promises, 17for you have refused my discipline, disregarding my laws. 18You see a thief and help him, and spend your time with evil and immoral men. 19You curse and lie, and vile language streams from your mouths. 20You slander your own brother. 21I remained silent—you thought I didn't care—but now your time of punishment has come, and I list all the above charges against you. 22This is the last chance for all of you who have forgotten God, before I tear you apart—and no one can help you then.

23But true praise is a worthy sacrifice; this really honors me. Those who walk my paths will receive salvation from the Lord.

PROVERBS FOR TODAY/ 10:29–30

God protects the upright but destroys the wicked. The good shall never lose God's blessings, but the wicked shall lose everything.

MARCH 8

NUMBERS 10:1—11:23

NOW the Lord said to Moses, "Make two trumpets of beaten silver to be used for summoning the people to assemble and for signaling the breaking of camp. 3When both trumpets are blown, the people will know that they are to gather at the entrance of the Tabernacle. 4But if only one is blown, then only the chiefs of the tribes of Israel shall come to you.

5,6,7"Different trumpet blasts will be necessary to distinguish between the summons to assemble and the signal to break camp and move onward. When the travel signal is blown, the tribes camped on the east side of the Tabernacle shall leave first; at the second signal, the tribes on the south shall go. 8Only the priests are permitted to blow the trumpets. This is a permanent instruction to be followed from generation to generation.

9"When you arrive in the Promised Land and go to war against your enemies, God will hear you and save you from your enemies when you sound the alarm with these trumpets. [10]Use the trumpets in times of gladness, too, blowing them at your annual festivals and at the beginning of each month to rejoice over your burnt offerings and peace offerings. And God will be reminded of his covenant with you. For I am Jehovah, your God."

[11]The Cloud lifted from the Tabernacle on the twentieth day of the second month of the second year of Israel's leaving Egypt; [12]so the Israelites left the Sinai wilderness, and followed the Cloud until it stopped in the wilderness of Paran. [13]This was their first journey after having received the Lord's travel instructions to Moses.

[14]At the head of the march was the tribe of Judah grouped behind its flag, and led by Nahshon, the son of Amminadab. [15]Next came the tribe of Issachar, led by Nethanel, the son of Zuar, [16]and the tribe of Zebulun, led by Eliab, the son of Helon.

[17]The Tabernacle was taken down and the men of the Gershon and Merari divisions of the tribe of Levi were next in the line of march, carrying the Tabernacle upon their shoulders. [18]Then came the flag of the camp of Reuben, with Elizur the son of Shedeur leading his people. [19]Next was the tribe of Simeon headed by Shelumi-el, the son of Zuri-shaddai; [20]and the tribe of Gad led by Eliasaph, the son of Deuel.

[21]Next came the Kohathites carrying the items from the inner sanctuary. (The Tabernacle was already erected in its new location by the time they arrived.) [22]Next in line was the tribe of Ephraim behind its flag, led by Elishama, the son of Ammihud; [23]and the tribe of Manasseh led by Gamaliel the son of Pedahzur; [24]and the tribe of Benjamin, led by Abidan the son of Gideoni. [25]Last of all were the tribes headed by the flag of the tribe of Dan under the leadership of Ahiezer, the son of Ammishaddai; [26]the tribe of Asher, led by Pagiel, the son of Ochran; [27]and the tribe of Naphtali, led by Ahira, the son of Enan. [28]That was the order in which the tribes traveled.

[29]One day Moses said to his brother-in-law Hobab (son of Reuel, the Midianite), "At last we are on our way to the Promised Land. Come with us and we will do you good; for the Lord has given wonderful promises to Israel!"

[30]But his brother-in-law replied, "No, I must return to my own land and kinfolk."

[31]"Stay with us," Moses pleaded, "for you know the ways of the wilderness and will be a great help to us. [32]If you come, you will share in all the good things the Lord does for us."

[33]They traveled for three days after leaving Mount Sinai, with the Ark at the front of the column to choose a place for them to stop. [34]It was daytime when they left, with the Cloud moving along ahead of them as they began their march. [35]As the Ark was carried forward, Moses cried out, "Arise, O Lord, and scatter your enemies; let them flee before you." [36]And when the Ark was set down he said, "Return, O Lord, to the millions of Israel."

THE people were soon complaining about all their misfortunes, and the Lord heard them. His anger flared out against them because of their complaints, so the fire of the Lord began destroying those at the far end of the camp. [2]They screamed to Moses for help, and when he prayed for them the fire stopped. [3]Ever after, the area was known as "The Place of Burning," because the fire from the Lord burned among them there.

[4,5]Then the Egyptians who had come with them began to long for the good things of Egypt. This added to the discontent of the people of Israel and they wept, "Oh, for a few bites of meat! Oh, that we had some of the delicious fish we enjoyed so much in Egypt, and the wonderful cucumbers and melons, leeks, onions, and garlic! [6]But now our strength is gone, and day after day we have to face this manna!"

[7]The manna was the size of small seeds, whitish yellow in color. [8]The people gathered it from the ground and pounded it into flour, then boiled it, and

then made pancakes from it—they tasted like pancakes fried in vegetable oil. 9The manna fell with the dew during the night.

10Moses heard all the families standing around their tent doors weeping, and the anger of the Lord grew hot; Moses too was highly displeased.

11Moses said to the Lord, "Why pick on me, to give me the burden of a people like this? 12Are they *my* children? Am I their father? Is that why you have given me the job of nursing them along like babies until we get to the land you promised their ancestors? 13Where am I supposed to get meat for all these people? For they weep to me saying, 'Give us meat!' 14I can't carry this nation by myself! The load is far too heavy! 15If you are going to treat me like this, please kill me right now; it will be a kindness! Let me out of this impossible situation!"

16Then the Lord said to Moses, "Summon before me seventy of the leaders of Israel; bring them to the Tabernacle, to stand there with you. 17I will come down and talk with you there and I will take of the Spirit which is on you and will put it upon them also; they shall bear the burden of the people along with you, so that you will not have the task alone.

18"And tell the people to purify themselves, for tomorrow they shall have meat to eat. Tell them, 'The Lord has heard your tearful complaints about all you left behind in Egypt, and he is going to give you meat. You shall eat it, 19,20not for just a day or two, or five or ten or even twenty! For one whole month you will have meat until you vomit it from your noses; for you have rejected the Lord who is here among you, and you have wept for Egypt.'"

21But Moses said, "There are 600,000 men alone [besides all the women and children], and yet you promise them meat for a whole month! 22If we butcher all our flocks and herds it won't be enough! We would have to catch every fish in the ocean to fulfill your promise!"

23Then the Lord said to Moses, "When did I become weak? Now you shall see whether my word comes true or not!"

MARK 14:1–21

THE Passover observance began two days later—an annual Jewish holiday when no bread made with yeast was eaten. The chief priests and other Jewish leaders were still looking for an opportunity to arrest Jesus secretly and put him to death.

2"But we can't do it during the Passover," they said, "or there will be a riot."

3Meanwhile Jesus was in Bethany, at the home of Simon the leper; during supper a woman came in with a beautiful flask of expensive perfume. Then, breaking the seal, she poured it over his head.

4,5Some of those at the table were indignant among themselves about this "waste," as they called it.

"Why, she could have sold that perfume for a fortune and given the money to the poor!" they snarled.

6But Jesus said, "Let her alone; why berate her for doing a good thing? 7You always have the poor among you, and they badly need your help, and you can aid them whenever you want to; but I won't be here much longer.

8"She has done what she could, and has anointed my body ahead of time for burial. 9And I tell you this in solemn truth, that wherever the Good News is preached throughout the world, this woman's deed will be remembered and praised."

10Then Judas Iscariot, one of his disciples, went to the chief priests to arrange to betray Jesus to them.

11When the chief priests heard why he had come, they were excited and happy and promised him a reward. So he began looking for the right time and place to betray Jesus.

12On the first day of the Passover, the day the lambs were sacrificed, his disciples asked him where he wanted to go to eat the traditional Passover supper. 13He sent two of them into Jerusalem to make the arrangements.

"As you are walking along," he told them, "you will see a man coming toward you carrying a pot of water. Follow him. 14At the house he enters, tell the man in charge, 'Our Master sent us to see the room you have ready for us, where we will eat the Passover supper this evening!' 15He will take you upstairs to a large room all set up. Prepare our supper there."

16So the two disciples went on ahead into the city and found everything as Jesus had said, and prepared the Passover.

17In the evening Jesus arrived with the other disciples, 18and as they were sitting around the table eating, Jesus said, "I solemnly declare that one of you will betray me, one of you who is here eating with me."

19A great sadness swept over them, and one by one they asked him, "Am I the one?"

20He replied, "It is one of you twelve eating with me now. 21I must die, as the prophets declared long ago; but, oh, the misery ahead for the man by whom I am betrayed. Oh, that he had never been born!"

PSALM 51:1–19

O loving and kind God, have mercy. Have pity upon me and take away the awful stain of my transgressions. 2Oh, wash me, cleanse me from this guilt. Let me be pure again. 3For I admit my shameful deed—it haunts me day and night. 4It is against you and you alone I sinned, and did this terrible thing. You saw it all, and your sentence against me is just. 5But I was born a sinner, yes, from the moment my mother conceived me. 6You deserve honesty from the heart; yes, utter sincerity and truthfulness. Oh, give me this wisdom.

7Sprinkle me with the cleansing blood and I shall be clean again. Wash me and I shall be whiter than snow. 8And after you have punished me, give me back my joy again. 9Don't keep looking at my sins—erase them from your sight. 10Create in me a new, clean heart, O God, filled with clean thoughts and right desires. 11Don't toss me aside, banished forever from your presence. Don't take your Holy Spirit from me. 12Restore to me again the joy of your salvation, and make me willing to obey you. 13Then I will teach your ways to other sinners, and they—guilty like me—will repent and return to you. 14,15Don't sentence me to death. O my God, you alone can rescue me. Then I will sing of your forgiveness, for my lips will be unsealed—oh, how I will praise you.

16You don't want penance; if you did, how gladly I would do it! You aren't interested in offerings burned before you on the altar. 17It is a broken spirit you want—remorse and penitence. A broken and a contrite heart, O God, you will not ignore.

18And Lord, don't punish Israel for my sins—help your people and protect Jerusalem.

19And when my heart is right, then you will rejoice in the good that I do and in the bullocks I bring to sacrifice upon your altar.

PROVERBS FOR TODAY/ 10:31–32

The good man gives wise advice, but the liar's counsel is shunned. The upright speak what is helpful; the wicked speak rebellion.

MARCH 9

NUMBERS 11:24—13:33

SO Moses left the Tabernacle and reported Jehovah's words to the people; and he gathered the seventy elders and placed them around the Tabernacle. 25And the Lord came down in the Cloud and talked with Moses, and the Lord took of the Spirit that was upon Moses and put it upon the seventy elders; and when the Spirit rested upon them, they prophesied for some time.

26But two of the seventy—Eldad and Medad—were still in the camp, and when the Spirit rested upon them, they prophesied there. 27Some young men ran and told Moses what was happening, 28and Joshua (the son of Nun), one of Moses' personally chosen assistants, protested, "Sir, make them stop!"

29But Moses replied, "Are you jealous for my sake? I only wish that all of the Lord's people were prophets, and that the Lord would put his Spirit upon them all!" 30Then Moses returned to the camp with the elders of Israel.

31The Lord sent a wind that brought quail from the sea, and let them fall into the camp and all around it! As far as one could walk in a day in any direction, there were quail flying three or four feet above the ground. 32So the people caught and killed quail all that day and through the night and all the next day too! The least anyone gathered was 100 bushels! Quail were spread out all around the camp. 33But as everyone began eating the meat, the anger of the Lord rose against the people and he killed large numbers of them with a plague. 34So the name of that place was called, "The Place of the Graves Caused by Lust," because they buried the people there who had lusted for meat and for Egypt. 35And from that place they journeyed to Hazeroth, where they stayed awhile.

ONE day Miriam and Aaron were criticizing Moses because his wife was a Cushite woman, 2and they said, "Has the Lord spoken only through Moses? Hasn't he spoken through us, too?"

But the Lord heard them. 3,4Immediately he summoned Moses, Aaron, and Miriam to the Tabernacle: "Come here, you three," he commanded. So they stood before the Lord. (Now Moses was the humblest man on earth.)

5Then the Lord descended in the Cloud and stood at the entrance of the Tabernacle. "Aaron and Miriam, step forward," he commanded; and they did. 6And the Lord said to them, "Even with a prophet, I would communicate by visions and dreams; 7,8but that is not how I communicate with my servant Moses. He is completely at home in my house! With him I speak face to face! And he shall see the very form of God! Why then were you not afraid to criticize him?"

9Then the anger of the Lord grew hot against them, and he departed. 10As the Cloud moved from above the Tabernacle, Miriam suddenly became white with leprosy. When Aaron saw what had happened, 11he cried out to Moses, "Oh, sir, do not punish us for this sin; we were fools to do such a thing. 12Don't let her be as one dead, whose body is half rotted away at birth."

13And Moses cried out to the Lord, "Heal her, O God, I beg you!"

14And the Lord said to Moses, "If her father had but spit in her face she would be defiled seven days. Let her be banished from the camp for seven days, and after that she can come back again."

15So Miriam was excluded from the camp for seven days, and the people waited until she was brought back in before they traveled again. 16Afterwards they left Hazeroth and camped in the wilderness of Paran.

JEHOVAH now instructed Moses, 2"Send spies into the land of Canaan—the land

I am giving to Israel; send one leader from each tribe."

3-15(The Israelis were camped in the wilderness of Paran at the time.) Moses did as the Lord had commanded and sent these twelve tribal leaders:

Shammu-a, son of Zaccur, from the tribe of Reuben;

Shaphat, son of Hori, from the tribe of Simeon;

Caleb, son of Jephunneh, from the tribe of Judah;

Igal, son of Joseph, from the tribe of Issachar;

Hoshea, son of Nun, from the half-tribe of Ephraim;

Palti, son of Raphu, from the tribe of Benjamin;

Gaddiel, son of Sodi, from the tribe of Zebulun;

Gaddi, son of Susi, from the tribe of Joseph (actually, the half-tribe of Manasseh);

Ammiel, son of Gemalli, from the tribe of Dan;

Sethur, son of Michael, from the tribe of Asher;

Nahbi, son of Vophsi, from the tribe of Naphtali;

Geuel, son of Machi, from the tribe of Gad.

16It was at this time that Moses changed Hoshea's name to Joshua.

17Moses sent them out with these instructions: "Go northward into the hill country of the Negeb, 18and see what the land is like; see also what the people are like who live there, whether they are strong or weak, many or few; 19and whether the land is fertile or not; and what cities there are, and whether they are villages or are fortified; 20whether the land is rich or poor, and whether there are many trees. Don't be afraid, and bring back some samples of the crops you see." (The first of the grapes were being harvested at that time.)

21So they spied out the land all the way from the wilderness of Zin to Rehob near Hamath. 22Going northward, they passed first through the Negeb and arrived at Hebron. There they saw the Ahimanites, Sheshites, and Talmites, all families descended from Anak. (By the way, Hebron was very ancient, having been founded seven years before Tanis in Egypt). 23Then they came to what is now known as the Valley of Eshcol where they cut down a single cluster of grapes so large that it took two of them to carry it on a pole between them! They also took some samples of the pomegranates and figs. 24The Israelis named the valley "Eshcol" at that time (meaning "Cluster") because of the cluster of grapes they found!

25After forty days of exploration they returned from their tour. 26They made their report to Moses, Aaron, and all the people of Israel in the wilderness of Paran at Kadesh, and they showed the fruit they had brought with them.

27This was their report: "We arrived in the land you sent us to see, and it is indeed a magnificent country—a land 'flowing with milk and honey.' Here is some fruit we have brought as proof. 28But the people living there are powerful, and their cities are fortified and very large; and what's more, we saw Anakim giants there! 29The Amalekites live in the south, while in the hill country there are the Hittites, Jebusites, and Amorites; down along the coast of the Mediterranean Sea and in the Jordan River valley are the Canaanites."

30But Caleb reassured the people as they stood before Moses. "Let us go up at once and possess it," he said, "for we are well able to conquer it!"

31"Not against people as strong as they are!" the other spies said. "They would crush us!"

32So the majority report of the spies was negative: "The land is full of warriors, the people are powerfully built, 33and we saw some of the Anakim there, descendants of the ancient race of giants. We felt like grasshoppers before them, they were so tall!"

A
S they were eating, Jesus took bread and asked God's blessing on it and broke it in pieces and gave it to them and said, "Eat it—this is my body."

23Then he took a cup of wine and gave thanks to God for it and gave it to them; and they all drank from it. 24And he said to them, "This is my blood, poured out for many, sealing the new agreement between God and man. 25I solemnly declare that I shall never again taste wine until the day I drink a different kind in the Kingdom of God."

26Then they sang a hymn and went out to the Mount of Olives.

27"All of you will desert me," Jesus told them, "for God has declared through the prophets, 'I will kill the Shepherd, and the sheep will scatter.' 28But after I am raised to life again, I will go to Galilee and meet you there."

29Peter said to him, "I will never desert you no matter what the others do!"

30"Peter," Jesus said, "before the cock crows a second time tomorrow morning you will deny me three times."

31"No!" Peter exploded. "Not even if I have to die with you! I'll *never* deny you!" And all the others vowed the same.

32And now they came to an olive grove called the Garden of Gethsemane, and he instructed his disciples, "Sit here, while I go and pray."

33He took Peter, James and John with him and began to be filled with horror and deepest distress. 34And he said to them, "My soul is crushed by sorrow to the point of death; stay here and watch with me."

35He went on a little further and fell to the ground and prayed that if it were possible the awful hour awaiting him might never come.

36"Father, Father," he said, "everything is possible for you. Take away this cup from me. Yet I want your will, not mine."

37Then he returned to the three disciples and found them asleep.

"Simon!" he said. "Asleep? Couldn't you watch with me even one hour? 38Watch with me and pray lest the Tempter overpower you. For though the spirit is willing enough, the body is weak."

39And he went away again and prayed, repeating his pleadings. 40Again he returned to them and found them sleeping, for they were very tired. And they didn't know what to say.

41The third time when he returned to them he said, "Sleep on; get your rest! But no! The time for sleep has ended! Look! I am betrayed into the hands of wicked men. 42Come! Get up! We must go! Look! My betrayer is here!"

43And immediately, while he was still speaking, Judas (one of his disciples) arrived with a mob equipped with swords and clubs, sent out by the chief priests and other Jewish leaders.

44Judas had told them, "You will know which one to arrest when I go over and greet him. Then you can take him easily." 45So as soon as they arrived he walked up to Jesus. "Master!" he exclaimed, and embraced him with a great show of friendliness. 46Then the mob arrested Jesus and held him fast. 47But someone pulled a sword and slashed at the High Priest's servant, cutting off his ear.

48Jesus asked them, "Am I some dangerous robber, that you come like this, armed to the teeth to capture me? 49Why didn't you arrest me in the Temple? I was there teaching every day. But these things are happening to fulfill the prophecies about me."

50Meanwhile, all his disciples had fled. 51,52There was, however, a young man following along behind, clothed only in a linen nightshirt. When the mob tried to grab him, he escaped, though his clothes were torn off in the process, so that he ran away completely naked.

PSALM 52:1–9

Y
OU call yourself a *hero,* do you? You *boast* about this evil deed of yours against God's people. 2You are sharp as a tack in plotting your

evil tricks. ³How you love wickedness—far more than good! And lying more than truth! ⁴You love to slander—you love to say anything that will do harm, O man with the lying tongue.

⁵But God will strike you down and pull you from your home, and drag you away from the land of the living. ⁶The followers of God will see it happen. They will watch in awe. Then they will laugh and say, ⁷"See what happens to those who despise God and trust in their wealth, and become ever more bold in their wickedness."

⁸But I am like a sheltered olive tree protected by the Lord himself. I trust in the mercy of God forever and ever. ⁹O Lord, I will praise you forever and ever for your punishment. And I will wait for your mercies—for everyone knows what a merciful God you are.

PROVERBS FOR TODAY/ 11:1–3

The Lord hates cheating and delights in honesty. Proud men end in shame, but the meek become wise. A good man is guided by his honesty; the evil man is destroyed by his dishonesty.

MARCH 10

NUMBERS 14:1—15:16

THEN all the people began weeping aloud, and they carried on all night. ²Their voices rose in a great chorus of complaint against Moses and Aaron.

"We wish we had died in Egypt," they wailed, "or even here in the wilderness, ³rather than be taken into this country ahead of us. Jehovah will kill us there, and our wives and little ones will become slaves. Let's get out of here and return to Egypt!" ⁴The idea swept the camp. "Let's elect a leader to take us back to Egypt!" they shouted.

⁵Then Moses and Aaron fell face downward on the ground before the people of Israel. ⁶Two of the spies, Joshua (the son of Nun), and Caleb (the son of Jephunneh), ripped their clothing ⁷and said to all the people, "It is a wonderful country ahead, ⁸and the Lord loves us. He will bring us safely into the land and give it to us. It is *very* fertile, a land 'flowing with milk and honey'! ⁹Oh, do not rebel against the Lord, and do not fear the people of the land. For they are but bread for us to eat! The Lord is with us and he has removed his protection from them! Don't be afraid of them!"

¹⁰,¹¹But the only response of the people was to talk of stoning them. Then the glory of the Lord appeared, and the Lord said to Moses, "How long will these people despise me? Will they *never* believe me, even after all the miracles I have done among them? ¹²I will disinherit them and destroy them with a plague, and I will make you into a nation far greater and mightier than they are!"

¹³"But what will the Egyptians think when they hear about it?" Moses pleaded with the Lord. "They know full well the power you displayed in rescuing your people. ¹⁴They have told this to the inhabitants of this land, who are well aware that you are with Israel and that you talk with her face to face. They see the pillar of cloud and fire standing above us, and they know that you lead and protect us day and night. ¹⁵Now if you kill all your people, the nations that have heard your fame will say, ¹⁶'The Lord had to kill them because he wasn't able

to take care of them in the wilderness. He wasn't strong enough to bring them into the land he swore he would give them.'

17,18"Oh, please, show the great power [of your patience] by forgiving our sins and showing us your steadfast love. Forgive us, even though you have said that you don't let sin go unpunished, and that you punish the father's fault in the children to the third and fourth generation. 19Oh, I plead with you, pardon the sins of this people because of your magnificent, steadfast love, just as you have forgiven them all the time from when we left Egypt until now."

20,21Then the Lord said, "All right, I will pardon them as you have requested. But I vow by my own name that just as it is true that all the earth shall be filled with the glory of the Lord, 22so it is true that not one of the men who has seen my glory and the miracles I did both in Egypt and in the wilderness—and ten times refused to trust me and obey me— 23shall even see the land I promised to this people's ancestors. 24But my servant Caleb is a different kind of man—he has obeyed me fully. I will bring him into the land he entered as a spy, and his descendants shall have their full share in it. 25But now, since the people of Israel are so afraid of the Amalekites and the Canaanites living in the valleys, tomorrow you must turn back into the wilderness in the direction of the Red Sea."

26,27Then the Lord said to Moses and to Aaron, "How long will this wicked nation complain about me? For I have heard all that they have been saying. 28Tell them, 'The Lord vows to do to you what you feared: 29You will all die here in this wilderness! Not a single one of you twenty years old and older, who has complained against me, 30shall enter the Promised Land. Only Caleb (son of Jephunneh) and Joshua (son of Nun) are permitted to enter it.

31" 'You said your children would become slaves of the people of the land. Well, instead I will bring *them* safely into the land and they shall inherit what you have despised. 32But as for you, your dead bodies shall fall in this wilderness. 33You must wander in the desert like nomads for forty years. In this way you will pay for your faithlessness, until the last of you lies dead in the desert.

34,35" 'Since the spies were in the land for forty days, you must wander in the wilderness for forty years—a year for each day, bearing the burden of your sins. I will teach you what it means to reject me. I, Jehovah, have spoken. Every one of you who has conspired against me shall die here in this wilderness.' "

36,37,38Then the ten spies who had incited the rebellion against Jehovah by striking fear into the hearts of the people were struck dead before the Lord. Of all the spies, only Joshua and Caleb remained alive. 39What sorrow there was throughout the camp when Moses reported God's words to the people!

40They were up early the next morning, and started towards the Promised Land.

"Here we are!" they said. "We realize that we have sinned, but now we are ready to go on into the land the Lord has promised us."

41But Moses said, "It's too late. Now you are disobeying the Lord's orders to return to the wilderness. 42Don't go ahead with your plan or you will be crushed by your enemies, for the Lord is not with you. 43Don't you remember? The Amalekites and the Canaanites are there! You have deserted the Lord, and now he will desert you."

44But they went ahead into the hill country, despite the fact that neither the Ark nor Moses left the camp. 45Then the Amalekites and the Canaanites who lived in the hills came down and attacked them and chased them to Hormah.

THE Lord told Moses to give these instructions to the people of Israel: "When your children finally live in the land I am going to give them, 3,4and they want to please the Lord with a burnt offering or any other offering by fire, their sacrifice must be an animal from their flocks of sheep and goats, or from their herds of cattle. Each sacrifice—whether an ordinary one, or a sacrifice to fulfill a vow, or a free-will offering, or a special sacrifice at any of the annual festivals—must be accompanied by a grain offering. If a lamb is being sacrificed, use three quarts of fine flour mixed with three pints of oil, 5accompanied by three pints of wine for a drink offering.

6"If the sacrifice is a ram, use six quarts of fine flour mixed with four pints of oil, 7and four pints of wine for a drink offering. This will be a sacrifice that is a pleasing fragrance to the Lord.

8,9"If the sacrifice is a young bull, then the grain offering accompanying it must consist of nine quarts of fine flour mixed with three quarts of oil, 10plus three quarts of wine for the drink offering. This shall be offered by fire as a pleasing fragrance to the Lord.

11,12"These are the instructions for what is to accompany each sacrificial bull, ram, lamb, or young goat. 13,14These instructions apply both to native-born Israelis and to foreigners living among you who want to please the Lord with sacrifices offered by fire; 15,16for there is the same law for all, native-born or foreigner, and this shall be true forever from generation to generation; all are the same before the Lord. Yes, one law for all!"

MARK 14:53–72

J ESUS was led to the High Priest's home where all of the chief priests and other Jewish leaders soon gathered. 54Peter followed far behind and then slipped inside the gates of the High Priest's residence and crouched beside a fire among the servants.

55Inside, the chief priests and the whole Jewish Supreme Court were trying to find something against Jesus that would be sufficient to condemn him to death. But their efforts were in vain. 56Many false witnesses volunteered, but they contradicted each other.

57Finally some men stood up to lie about him and said, 58"We heard him say, 'I will destroy this Temple made with human hands and in three days I will build another, made without human hands!' " 59But even then they didn't get their stories straight!

60Then the High Priest stood up before the Court and asked Jesus, "Do you refuse to answer this charge? What do you have to say for yourself?"

61To this Jesus made no reply.

Then the High Priest asked him. "Are you the Messiah, the Son of God?"

62Jesus said, "I am, and you will see me sitting at the right hand of God, and returning to earth in the clouds of heaven."

63,64Then the High Priest tore at his clothes and said, "What more do we need? Why wait for witnesses? You have heard his blasphemy. What is your verdict?" And the vote for the death sentence was unanimous.

65Then some of them began to spit at him, and they blindfolded him and began to hammer his face with their fists.

"Who hit you that time, you prophet?" they jeered. And even the bailiffs were using their fists on him as they led him away.

66,67Meanwhile Peter was below in the courtyard. One of the maids who worked for the High Priest noticed Peter warming himself at the fire.

She looked at him closely and then announced, *"You* were with Jesus, the Nazarene."

68Peter denied it. "I don't know what you're talking about!" he said, and walked over to the edge of the courtyard.

Just then, a rooster crowed.

69The maid saw him standing there and began telling the others, "There he is! There's that disciple of Jesus!"

70Peter denied it again.

A little later others standing around the fire began saying to Peter, "You are, too, one of them, for you are from Galilee!"

71He began to curse and swear. "I don't even know this fellow you are talking about," he said.

72And immediately the rooster crowed the second time. Suddenly Jesus' words flashed through Peter's mind: "Before the cock crows twice, you will deny me three times." And he began to cry.

PSALM 53:1–6

ONLY a fool would say to himself, "There is no God." And why does he say it? Because of his wicked heart, his dark and evil deeds. His life is corroded with sin.

2God looks down from heaven, searching among all mankind to see if there is a single one who does right and really seeks for God. 3But all have turned their backs on him; they are filthy with sin—corrupt and rotten through and through. Not one is good, not one! 4How can this be? Can't they understand anything? For they devour my people like bread and refuse to come to God. 5But soon unheard-of terror will fall on them. God will scatter the bones of these, your enemies. They are doomed, for God has rejected them.

6Oh, that God would come from Zion now and save Israel! Only when the Lord himself restores them can they ever be really happy again.

PROVERBS FOR TODAY/ 11:4

Your riches won't help you on Judgment Day; only righteousness counts then.

MARCH 11

NUMBERS 15:17—16:40

THE Lord also said to Moses at this time, "Instruct the people of Israel that when they arrive in the land that I am going to give them, 19,20,21they must present to the Lord a sample of each year's new crops by making a loaf, using coarse flour from the first grain that is cut each year. This loaf must be waved back and forth before the altar in a gesture of offering to the Lord. It is an annual offering from your threshing floor, and must be observed from generation to generation.

22"If by mistake you or future generations fail to carry out all of these regulations which the Lord has given you over the years through Moses, 23,24then when the people realize their error, they must offer one young bull for a burnt offering. It will be a pleasant odor before the Lord, and must be offered along with the usual grain offering and drink offering, and one male goat for a sin offering. 25And the priest shall make atonement for all of the people of Israel and they shall be forgiven; for it was an error, and they have corrected it with their sacrifice made by fire before the Lord, and by their sin offering. 26All the people shall be forgiven, including the foreigners living among them, for the entire population is involved in such error and forgiveness.

27"If the error is made by a single individual, then he shall sacrifice a one-year-old female goat for a sin offering, 28and the priest shall make atonement for him before the Lord, and he shall be forgiven. 29This same law applies to individual foreigners who are living among you.

30"But anyone who deliberately makes the 'mistake,' whether he is a native Israeli or a foreigner, is blaspheming Jehovah, and shall be cut off from among his people. 31For he has despised the commandment of the Lord and deliberately failed to obey his law; he must be executed, and die in his sin."

32One day while the people of Israel

were in the wilderness, one of them was caught gathering wood on the Sabbath day. [33]He was arrested and taken before Moses and Aaron and the other judges. [34]They jailed him until they could find out the Lord's mind concerning him.

[35]Then the Lord said to Moses, "The man must die—all the people shall stone him to death outside the camp."

[36]So they took him outside the camp and killed him as the Lord had commanded.

[37,38]The Lord said to Moses, "Tell the people of Israel to make tassels for the hems of their clothes (this is a permanent regulation from generation to generation) and to attach the tassels to their clothes with a blue cord. [39]The purpose of this regulation is to remind you, whenever you notice the tassels, of the commandments of the Lord, and that you are to obey his laws instead of following your own desires and going your own ways, as you used to do in serving other gods. [40]It will remind you to be holy to your God. [41]For I am Jehovah your God who brought you out of the land of Egypt; yes, I am the Lord, your God."

ONE day Korah (son of Izhar, grandson of Kohath, and a descendant of Levi) conspired with Dathan and Abiram (the sons of Eliab) and On (the son of Peleth), all three from the tribe of Reuben, [2]to incite a rebellion against Moses. Two hundred and fifty popular leaders, all members of the Assembly, were involved.

[3]They went to Moses and Aaron and said, "We have had enough of your presumption; you are no better than anyone else; everyone in Israel has been chosen of the Lord, and he is with all of us. What right do you have to put yourselves forward, claiming that we must obey you, and acting as though you were greater than anyone else among all these people of the Lord?"

[4]When Moses heard what they were saying he fell face downward to the ground. [5]Then he said to Korah and to those who were with him, "In the morning the Lord will show you who are his,

and who is holy, and whom he has chosen as his priest. [6,7]Do this: You, Korah, and all those with you, take censers tomorrow and light them, and put incense upon them before the Lord, and we will find out whom the Lord has chosen. You are the presumptuous ones, you sons of Levi."

[8,9]Then Moses spoke again to Korah: "Does it seem a small thing to you that the God of Israel has chosen you from among all the people of Israel to be near to himself as you work in the Tabernacle of Jehovah, and to stand before the people to minister to them? [10]Is it nothing to you that he has given this task to only you Levites? And now are you demanding the priesthood also? [11,12]That is what you are really after! That is why you are revolting against Jehovah. And what has Aaron done, that you are dissatisfied with him?" Then Moses summoned Dathan and Abiram (the sons of Eliab), but they refused to come.

[13]"Is it a small thing," they mimicked, "that you brought us out of lovely Egypt to kill us here in this terrible wilderness, and that now you want to make yourself our king? [14]What's more, you haven't brought us into the wonderful country you promised, nor given us fields and vineyards. Whom are you trying to fool? We refuse to come."

[15]Then Moses was very angry and said to the Lord, "Do not accept their sacrifices! I have never stolen so much as a donkey from them, and have not hurt one of them."

[16]And Moses said to Korah, "Come here tomorrow before the Lord with all your friends; Aaron will be here too. [17]Be sure to bring your censers with incense on them; a censer for each man, 250 in all; and Aaron will also be here with his."

[18]So they did. They came with their censers and lit them and placed the incense on them, and stood at the entrance of the Tabernacle with Moses and Aaron. [19]Meanwhile, Korah had stirred up the entire nation against Moses and Aaron, and they all assembled to watch. Then

the glory of Jehovah appeared to all the people, 20and Jehovah said to Moses and Aaron, 21"Get away from these people so that I may instantly destroy them."

22But Moses and Aaron fell face downward to the ground before the Lord. "O God, the God of all mankind," they pleaded, "must you be angry with all the people when one man sins?"

23,24And the Lord said to Moses, "Then tell the people to get away from the tents of Korah, Dathan, and Abiram."

25So Moses rushed over to the tents of Dathan and Abiram, followed closely by the 250 Israeli leaders. 26"Quick!" he told the people, "get away from the tents of these wicked men, and don't touch anything that belongs to them, lest you be included in their sins [and be destroyed with them]."

27So all the people stood back from the tents of Korah, Dathan, and Abiram. And Dathan and Abiram came out and stood at the entrances of their tents with their wives and sons and little ones.

28And Moses said, "By this you shall know that Jehovah has sent me to do all these things that I have done—for I have not done them on my own. 29If these men die a natural death or from some ordinary accident or disease, then Jehovah has not sent me. 30But if the Lord does a miracle and the ground opens up and swallows them and everything that belongs to them, and they go down alive into Sheol, then you will know that these men have despised the Lord."

31He had hardly finished speaking the words when the ground suddenly split open beneath them, 32and a great fissure swallowed them up, along with their tents and families and the friends who were standing with them, and everything they owned. 33So they went down alive into Sheol and the earth closed upon them, and they perished. 34All of the people of Israel fled at their screams, fearing that the earth would swallow them too. 35Then fire came from Jehovah and burned up the 250 men who were offering incense.

36,37And the Lord said to Moses, "Tell Eleazar the son of Aaron the priest to pull those censers from the fire; for they are holy, dedicated to the Lord. He must also scatter the burning incense 38from the censers of these men who have sinned at the cost of their lives. He shall then beat the metal into a sheet as a covering for the altar, for these censers are holy because they were used before the Lord; and the altar sheet shall be a reminder to the people of Israel."

39So Eleazar the priest took the 250 bronze censers and beat them out into a sheet of metal to cover the altar, 40to be a reminder to the people of Israel that no unauthorized person—no one who is not a descendant of Aaron—may come before the Lord to burn incense, lest the same thing happen to him as happened to Korah and his associates. Thus the Lord's directions to Moses were carried out.

MARK 15:1–47

EARLY in the morning the chief priests, elders and teachers of religion—the entire Supreme Court—met to discuss their next steps. Their decision was to send Jesus under armed guard to Pilate, the Roman governor.

2Pilate asked him, "Are you the King of the Jews?"

"Yes," Jesus replied, "it is as you say."

3,4Then the chief priests accused him of many crimes, and Pilate asked him, "Why don't you say something? What about all these charges against you?"

5But Jesus said no more, much to Pilate's amazement.

6Now, it was Pilate's custom to release one Jewish prisoner each year at Passover time—any prisoner the people requested. 7One of the prisoners at that time was Barabbas, convicted along with others for murder during an insurrection.

8Now a mob began to crowd in toward Pilate, asking him to release a prisoner as usual.

9"How about giving you the 'King of Jews'?" Pilate asked. "Is he the one you want released?" 10(For he realized by now that this was a frameup, backed by the chief priests because they envied Jesus' popularity.)

11But at this point the chief priests whipped up the mob to demand the release of Barabbas instead of Jesus.

12"But if I release Barabbas," Pilate asked them, "what shall I do with this man you call your king?"

13They shouted back, "Crucify him!"

14"But why?" Pilate demanded. "What has he done wrong?" They only roared the louder, "Crucify him!"

15Then Pilate, afraid of a riot and anxious to please the people, released Barabbas to them. And he ordered Jesus flogged with a leaded whip, and handed him over to be crucified.

16,17Then the Roman soldiers took him into the barracks of the palace, called out the entire palace guard, dressed him in a purple robe, and made a crown of long, sharp thorns and put it on his head. 18Then they saluted, yelling, "Yea! King of the Jews!" 19And they beat him on the head with a cane, and spat on him and went down on their knees to "worship" him.

20When they finally tired of their sport, they took off the purple robe and put his own clothes on him again, and led him away to be crucified.

21Simon of Cyrene, who was coming in from the country just then, was pressed into service to carry Jesus' cross. (Simon is the father of Alexander and Rufus.)

22And they brought Jesus to a place called Golgotha. (Golgotha means skull.) 23Wine drugged with bitter herbs was offered to him there, but he refused it. 24And then they crucified him—and threw dice for his clothes.

25It was about nine o'clock in the morning when the crucifixion took place.

26A signboard was fastened to the cross above his head, announcing his crime. It read, "The King of the Jews."

27Two robbers were also crucified that morning, their crosses on either side of his. 28And so the Scripture was fulfilled that said, "He was counted among evil men."

29,30The people jeered at him as they walked by, and wagged their heads in mockery.

"Ha! Look at you now!" they yelled at him. "Sure, you can destroy the Temple and rebuild it in three days! If you're so wonderful, save yourself and come down from the cross."

31The chief priests and religious leaders were also standing around joking about Jesus.

"He's quite clever at 'saving' others," they said, "but he can't save himself!"

32"Hey there, Messiah!" they yelled at him. "You 'King of Israel'! Come on down from the cross and we'll believe you!"

And even the two robbers dying with him, cursed him.

33About noon, darkness fell across the entire land, lasting until three o'clock that afternoon.

34Then Jesus called out with a loud voice, "Eli, Eli, lama sabachthani?" ("My God, my God, why have you deserted me?")

35Some of the people standing there thought he was calling for the prophet Elijah. 36So one man ran and got a sponge and filled it with sour wine and held it up to him on a stick.

"Let's see if Elijah will come and take him down!" he said.

37Then Jesus uttered another loud cry, and dismissed his spirit.

38And the curtain in the Temple was split apart from top to bottom.

39When the Roman officer standing beside his cross saw how he dismissed his spirit, he exclaimed, "Truly, this was the Son of God!"

40Some women were there watching from a distance—Mary Magdalene, Mary (the mother of James the Younger and of Joses), Salome, and others. 41They and many other Galilean women who were his followers had ministered to him when he was up in Galilee, and had come with him to Jerusalem.

42,43This all happened the day before the Sabbath. Late that afternoon Joseph from Arimathea, an honored member of the Jewish Supreme Court (who personally was eagerly expecting the arrival of God's Kingdom), gathered his courage and went to Pilate and asked for Jesus' body.

44Pilate couldn't believe that Jesus was already dead so he called for the Roman officer in charge and asked him. 45The officer confirmed the fact, and Pilate told Joseph he could have the body.

46Joseph bought a long sheet of linen cloth and, taking Jesus' body down from the cross, wound it in the cloth and laid it in a rock-hewn tomb, and rolled a stone in front of the entrance.

47(Mary Magdalene and Mary the mother of Joses were watching as Jesus was laid away.)

PSALM 54:1–7

COME with great power, O God, and save me! Defend me with your might! 2Oh, listen to my prayer. 3For violent men have risen against me—ruthless men who care nothing for God are seeking my life.

4But God is my helper. He is a friend of mine! 5He will cause the evil deeds of my enemies to boomerang upon them. Do as you promised and put an end to these wicked men, O God. 6Gladly I bring my sacrifices to you; I will praise your name, O Lord, for it is good.

7God has rescued me from all my trouble, and triumphed over my enemies.

PROVERBS FOR TODAY/ 11:5–6

Good people are directed by their honesty; the wicked shall fall beneath their load of sins. The good man's goodness delivers him; the evil man's treachery is his undoing.

MARCH 12

NUMBERS 16:41—18:32

BUT the very next morning all the people began muttering again against Moses and Aaron, saying, "You have killed the Lord's people."

42Soon a great, sullen mob formed; suddenly, as they looked toward the Tabernacle, the Cloud appeared and the awesome glory of the Lord was seen. 43,44Moses and Aaron came and stood at the entrance of the Tabernacle, and the Lord said to Moses,

45"Get away from these people so that I can instantly destroy them." But Moses and Aaron fell face downward to the earth before the Lord.

46And Moses said to Aaron, "Quick, take a censer and place fire in it from the altar; lay incense on it, and carry it quickly among the people and make atonement for them; for God's anger has gone out among them—the plague has already begun."

47Aaron did as Moses had told him to, and ran among the people, for the plague had indeed already begun; and he put on the incense and made atonement for them. 48And he stood between the living and the dead, and the plague was stopped, 49but not before 14,700 people had died (in addition to those who had died the previous day with Korah).

50Then Aaron returned to Moses at the entrance of the Tabernacle; and so the plague was stopped.

THEN the Lord said to Moses, "Tell the people of Israel that each of their tribal chiefs is to bring you a wooden rod with his name inscribed upon it. Aaron's name is to be on the rod of the tribe of Levi. 4Put these rods in the inner room of the Tabernacle where I meet with you, in front of the Ark. 5I will use these rods to identify the man I have chosen: for buds will grow on his rod! Then at last this murmuring and complaining against you will stop!"

6So Moses gave the instructions to the people, and each of the twelve chiefs (including Aaron) brought him a rod. 7He put them before the Lord in the inner room of the Tabernacle, 8and when he went in the next day, he found that Aaron's rod, representing the tribe of Levi, had budded and was blossoming, and had ripe almonds hanging from it!

9When Moses brought them out to show the others, they stared in disbelief! Then each man except Aaron claimed his rod. 10The Lord told Moses to place Aaron's rod permanently beside the Ark as a reminder of this rebellion. He was to [bring it out and show it to the people again] if there were any further complaints about Aaron's authority; this would ward off further catastrophe to the people. 11So Moses did as the Lord commanded him.

12,13But the people of Israel only grumbled the more. "We are as good as dead," they whined. "Everyone who even comes close to the Tabernacle dies. Must we all perish?"

THE Lord now spoke to Aaron: "You and your sons and your family are responsible for any desecration of the sanctuary," he said, "and will be held liable for any impropriety in your priestly work.

2,3"Your kinsmen, the tribe of Levi, are your assistants; but only you and your sons may perform the sacred duties in the Tabernacle itself. The Levites must be careful not to touch any of the sacred articles or the altar, lest I destroy both them and you. 4No one who is not a member of the tribe of Levi shall assist you in any way. 5Remember, only the priests are to perform the sacred duties within the sanctuary and at the altar. If you follow these instructions the wrath of God will never again fall upon any of the people of Israel for violating this law. 6I say it again—your kinsmen the Levites are your assistants for the work of the Tabernacle. They are a gift to you from the Lord. 7But you and your sons, the priests, shall personally handle all the sacred service, including the altar and all that is within the veil, for the priesthood is your special gift of service. Anyone else who attempts to perform these duties shall die."

8The Lord gave these further instructions to Aaron: "I have given the priests all the gifts which are brought to the Lord by the people; all these offerings presented to the Lord by the gesture of waving them before the altar belong to you and your sons, by permanent law. 9The grain offerings, the sin offerings, and the guilt offerings are yours, except for the sample presented to the Lord by burning upon the altar. All these are most holy offerings. 10They are to be eaten only in a most holy place, and only by males. 11All other gifts presented to me by the gesture of waving them before the altar are for you and your families, sons and daughters alike. For all the members of your families may eat these unless anyone is ceremonially impure at the time.

12"Yours also are the first-of-the-harvest gifts the people bring as offerings to the Lord—the best of the olive oil, wine, grain, 13and every other crop. Your families may eat these unless they are ceremonially defiled at the time. 14,15So everything that is dedicated to the Lord shall be yours, including the firstborn sons of the people of Israel, and the firstborn of their animals. 16However, you may never accept the firstborn sons, nor the firstborn of any animals that I do not permit for food. Instead, there must be a payment of two and a half dollars made for each firstborn child. It is to be brought when he is one month old.

17"However, the firstborn of cows, sheep, or goats may not be bought back; they must be sacrificed to the Lord. Their blood is to be sprinkled upon the altar, and their fat shall be burned as a fire offering; it is very pleasant to the Lord. 18The meat of these animals shall be yours, including the breast and right thigh that are presented to the Lord by the gesture of waving before the altar. 19Yes, I have given to you all of these 'wave offerings' brought by the people of Israel to the Lord; they are for you and your families as food; this is a permanent contract between the Lord and you and your descendants.

20"You priests may own no property, nor have any other income, for I am all that you need.

21"As for the tribe of Levi, your relatives, they shall be paid for their service with the tithes from the entire land of Israel.

22"From now on, Israelites other than the priests and Levites shall not enter the sanctuary, lest they be judged guilty and die. 23Only the Levites shall do the work there, and they shall be guilty if they fail. This is a permanent law among you, that the Levites shall own no property in Israel, 24for the people's tithes, offered to the Lord by the gesture of waving before the altar, shall belong to the Levites; these are their inheritance, and so they have no need for property."

25,26The Lord also said to Moses, "Tell the Levites to give to the Lord a tenth of the tithes they receive—a tithe of the tithe, to be presented to the Lord by the gesture of waving before the altar. 27The Lord will consider this as your first-of-the-harvest offering to him of grain and wine, as though it were from your own property. 28,29This tithe of the tithe shall be selected from the choicest part of the tithes you receive as the Lord's portion, and shall be given to Aaron the priest. 30It shall be credited to you just as though it were from your own threshing floor and wine press. 31Aaron and his sons and their families may eat it in their homes or anywhere they wish, for it is their compensation for their service in the Tabernacle. 32You Levites will not be held guilty for accepting the Lord's tithes if you then give the best tenth to the priests. But beware that you do not treat the holy gifts of the people of Israel as though they were common, lest you die."

MARK 16:1–20

THE next evening, when the Sabbath ended, Mary Magdalene and Salome and Mary the mother of James went out and purchased embalming spices.

Early the following morning, just at sunrise, they carried them out to the tomb. 3On the way they were discussing how they could ever roll aside the huge stone from the entrance.

4But when they arrived they looked up and saw that the stone—a *very* heavy one—was already moved away and the entrance was open! 5So they entered the tomb—and there on the right sat a young man clothed in white. The women were startled, 6but the angel said, "Don't be so surprised. Aren't you looking for Jesus, the Nazarene who was crucified? He isn't here! He has come back to life! Look, that's where his body was lying. 7Now go and give this message to his disciples including Peter:

" 'Jesus is going ahead of you to Galilee. You will see him there, just as he told you before he died!' "

8The women fled from the tomb, trembling and bewildered, too frightened to talk.

9It was early on Sunday morning when Jesus came back to life, and the first person who saw him was Mary Magdalene—the woman from whom he had cast out seven demons. 10,11She found the disciples wet-eyed with grief and exclaimed that she had seen Jesus, and he was alive! But they didn't believe her!

12Later that day he appeared to two who were walking from Jerusalem into the country, but they didn't recognize him at first because he had changed his appearance. 13When they finally realized who he was, they rushed back to Jerusalem to tell the others, but no one believed them.

14Still later he appeared to the eleven disciples as they were eating together. He rebuked them for their unbelief—their stubborn refusal to believe those who had seen him alive from the dead.

15And then he told them, "You are to go into all the world and preach the Good News to everyone, everywhere. 16Those who believe and are baptized will be saved. But those who refuse to believe will be condemned.

17"And those who believe shall use my authority to cast out demons, and they shall speak new languages. 18They will be able even to handle snakes with safety, and if they drink anything poisonous, it won't hurt them; and they will be able to place their hands on the sick and heal them."

19When the Lord Jesus had finished talking with them, he was taken up into heaven and sat down at God's right hand.

20And the disciples went everywhere preaching, and the Lord was with them and confirmed what they said by the miracles that followed their messages.

PSALM 55:1–23

LISTEN to my prayer, O God; don't hide yourself when I cry to you. 2Hear me, Lord! Listen to me! For I groan and weep beneath my burden of woe.

3My enemies shout against me and threaten me with death. They surround me with terror and plot to kill me. Their fury and hatred rise to engulf me.

4My heart is in anguish within me. Stark fear overpowers me. 5Trembling and horror overwhelm me. 6Oh, for wings like a dove, to fly away and rest! 7I would fly to the far-off deserts and stay there. 8I would flee to some refuge from all this storm.

9O Lord, make these enemies begin to quarrel among themselves—destroy them with their own violence and strife. 10Though they patrol their walls night and day against invaders, their real problem is internal—wickedness and dishonesty are entrenched in the heart of the city. 11There is murder and robbery there, and cheating in the markets and wherever you look.

12It was not an enemy who taunted me—then I could have borne it; I could have hidden and escaped. 13But it was you, a man like myself, my companion and my friend. 14What fellowship we had, what wonderful discussions as we walked together to the Temple of the Lord on holy days.

15Let death seize them and cut them down in their prime, for there is sin in their homes, and they are polluted to the depths of their souls.

16But I will call upon the Lord to save me—and he will. 17I will pray morning, noon, and night, pleading aloud with God; and he will hear and answer. 18Though the tide of battle runs strongly against me, for so many are fighting me, yet he will rescue me. 19God himself—God from everlasting ages past—will answer them! For they refuse to fear him or even honor his commands.

20This friend of mine betrayed me—I who was at peace with him. He broke his promises. 21His words were oily smooth, but in his heart was war. His words were sweet, but underneath were daggers.

22Give your burdens to the Lord. He will carry them. He will not permit the godly to slip or fall. 23He will send my enemies to the pit of destruction. Murderers and liars will not live out half their days. But I am trusting you to save me.

When an evil man dies, his hopes all perish, for they are based upon this earthly life.

MARCH 13

NUMBERS 19:1—20:29

THE Lord said to Moses and Aaron, "Here is another of my laws:

"Tell the people of Israel to bring you a red heifer without defect, one that has never been yoked. Give her to Eleazar the priest and he shall take her outside the camp and someone shall kill her as he watches. 4Eleazar shall take some of her blood upon his finger and sprinkle it seven times towards the front of the Tabernacle. 5Then someone shall burn the heifer as he watches—her hide, meat, blood, and dung. 6Eleazar shall take cedar wood and hyssop branches and scarlet thread, and throw them into the burning pile.

7"Then he must wash his clothes, and bathe, and afterwards return to the camp and be ceremonially defiled until the evening. 8And the one who burns the animal must wash his clothes, and bathe, and he too shall be defiled until evening. 9Then someone who is not ceremonially defiled shall gather up the ashes of the heifer and place them in some purified place outside the camp, where they shall be kept for the people of Israel as a source of water for the purification ceremonies, for removal of sin. 10And the one who gathers up the ashes of the heifer must wash his clothes and be defiled until evening; this is a permanent law for the benefit of the people of Israel and any foreigners living among them.

11"Anyone who touches a dead human body shall be defiled for seven days, 12and must purify himself the third and seventh days with water [run through the ashes of the red heifer]; then he will

be purified; but if he does not do this on the third day, he will continue to be defiled even after the seventh day. 13Anyone who touches a dead person and does not purify himself in the manner specified, has defiled the Tabernacle of the Lord, and shall be excommunicated from Israel. The cleansing water was not sprinkled upon him, so the defilement continues.

14"When a man dies in a tent, these are the various regulations: Everyone who enters the tent, and those who are in it at the time, shall be defiled seven days. 15Any container in the tent without a lid over it is defiled.

16"If someone out in a field touches the corpse of someone who has been killed in battle, or who has died in any other way, or if he even touches a bone or a grave, he shall be defiled seven days. 17To become purified again, ashes from the red heifer sin offering are to be added to spring water in a kettle. 18Then a person who is not defiled shall take hyssop branches and dip them into the water and sprinkle the water upon the tent and upon all the pots and pans in the tent, and upon anyone who has been defiled by being in the tent, or by touching a bone, or touching someone who has been killed or is otherwise dead, or has touched a grave. 19This shall take place on the third and seventh days; then the defiled person must wash his clothes and bathe himself, and that evening he will be out from under the defilement.

20"But anyone who is defiled and doesn't purify himself shall be excommunicated, for he has defiled the sanctuary of the Lord, and the water to cleanse him has not been sprinkled upon him; so he remains defiled. 21This is a permanent law. The man who sprinkles the water must afterwards wash his clothes; and anyone touching the water shall be defiled until evening. 22And anything a defiled person touches shall be defiled until evening."

THE people of Israel arrived in the wilderness of Zin in April and camped at Kadesh, where Miriam died and was buried. 2There was not enough water to drink at that place, so the people again rebelled against Moses and Aaron. A great mob formed, 3and they held a protest meeting.

"Would that we too had died with our dear brothers the Lord killed!" they shouted at Moses. 4"You have deliberately brought us into this wilderness to get rid of us, along with our flocks and herds. 5Why did you ever make us leave Egypt and bring us here to this evil place? Where is the fertile land of wonderful crops—the figs, vines, and pomegranates you told us about? Why, there isn't even water enough to drink!"

6Moses and Aaron turned away and went to the entrance of the Tabernacle, where they fell face downward before the Lord; and the glory of Jehovah appeared to them.

7And he said to Moses, 8"Get Aaron's rod; then you and Aaron must summon the people. As they watch, speak to that rock over there and tell it to pour out its water! You will give them water from a rock, enough for all the people and all their cattle!"

9So Moses did as instructed. He took the rod from the place where it was kept before the Lord; 10then Moses and Aaron summoned the people to come and gather at the rock; and he said to them, "Listen, you rebels! Must we bring you water from this rock?"

11Then Moses lifted the rod and struck the rock twice, and water gushed out; and the people and their cattle drank.

12But the Lord said to Moses and Aaron, "Because you did not believe me and did not sanctify me in the eyes of the people of Israel, you shall not bring them into the land I have promised them!"

13This place was named Meribah (meaning "Rebel Waters"), because it was where the people of Israel fought against Jehovah, and where he showed himself to be holy before them.

14While Moses was at Kadesh he sent messengers to the king of Edom: "We are the descendants of your brother Israel," he declared. "You know our sad history, 15how our ancestors went down to visit Egypt and stayed there so long, and became slaves of the Egyptians. 16But when we cried to the Lord he heard us and sent an Angel who brought us out of Egypt, and now we are here at Kadesh, encamped on the borders of your land. 17Please let us pass through your country. We will be careful not to go through your planted fields, nor through your vineyards; we won't even drink water from your wells, but will stay on the main road and not leave it until we have crossed your border on the other side."

18But the king of Edom said, "Stay out! If you attempt to enter my land I will meet you with an army!"

19"But, sir," protested the Israeli ambassadors, "we will stay on the main road and will not even drink your water unless we pay whatever you demand for it. We only want to pass through, and nothing else."

20But the king of Edom was adamant. "Stay out!" he warned, and, mobilizing his army, he marched to the frontier with a great force. 21,22Because Edom refused to allow Israel to pass through their country, Israel turned back and journeyed from Kadesh to Mount Hor.

23Then the Lord said to Moses and Aaron at the border of the land of Edom, 24"The time has come for Aaron to die—for he shall not enter the land I have given the people of Israel, for the two of you rebelled against my instructions concerning the water at Meribah. 25Now take Aaron and his son Eleazar and lead them up onto Mount Hor. 26There you shall remove Aaron's priestly garments from him and put them on Eleazar his son; and Aaron shall die there."

27So Moses did as the Lord commanded him. The three of them went up together into Mount Hor as all the people watched. 28When they reached the summit, Moses removed the priestly garments from Aaron and put them on his son Eleazar; and Aaron died on the top of the mountain. Moses and Eleazar returned, 29and when the people were informed of Aaron's death, they mourned for him for thirty days.

LUKE 1:1–25

DEAR friend who loves God: 1,2Several biographies of Christ have already been written using as their source material the reports circulating among us from the early disciples and other eyewitnesses. 3However, it occurred to me that it would be well to recheck all these accounts from first to last and after thorough investigation to pass this summary on to you, 4to reassure you of the truth of all you were taught.

5My story begins with a Jewish priest, Zacharias, who lived when Herod was king of Judea. Zacharias was a member of the Abijah division of the Temple service corps. (His wife Elizabeth was, like himself, a member of the priest tribe of the Jews, a descendant of Aaron.) 6Zacharias and Elizabeth were godly folk, careful to obey all of God's laws in spirit as well as in letter. 7But they had no children, for Elizabeth was barren; and now they were both very old.

8,9One day as Zacharias was going about his work in the Temple—for his division was on duty that week—the honor fell to him by lot to enter the inner sanctuary and burn incense before the Lord. 10Meanwhile, a great crowd stood outside in the Temple court, praying as they always did during that part of the service when the incense was being burned.

11,12Zacharias was in the sanctuary when suddenly an angel appeared, standing to the right of the altar of incense! Zacharias was startled and terrified.

13But the angel said, "Don't be afraid, Zacharias! For I have come to tell you that God has heard your prayer, and your wife Elizabeth will bear you a son! And you are to name him John. 14You will both have great joy and gladness at his birth, and many will rejoice with you. 15For he will be one of the Lord's great men. He must never touch wine or hard liquor—and he will be filled with the Holy Spirit, even from before his birth! 16And he will persuade many a Jew to turn to the Lord his God. 17He will be a man of rugged spirit and power like Elijah, the prophet of old; and he will precede the coming of the Messiah, preparing the people for his arrival. He will soften adult hearts to become like little children's, and will change disobedient minds to the wisdom of faith."

18Zacharias said to the angel, "But this is impossible! I'm an old man now, and my wife is also well along in years."

19Then the angel said, "I am Gabriel! I stand in the very presence of God. It was he who sent me to you with this good news! 20And now, because you haven't believed me, you are to be stricken silent, unable to speak until the child is born. For my words will certainly come true at the proper time."

21Meanwhile the crowds outside were waiting for Zacharias to appear and wondered why he was taking so long. 22When he finally came out, he couldn't speak to them, and they realized from his gestures that he must have seen a vision in the Temple. 23He stayed on at the Temple for the remaining days of his Temple duties and then returned home. 24Soon afterwards Elizabeth his wife became pregnant and went into seclusion for five months.

25"How kind the Lord is," she exclaimed, "to take away my disgrace of having no children!"

PSALM 56:1-13

LORD, have mercy on me; all day long the enemy troops press in. So many are proud to fight against me; how they long to conquer me.

3,4But when I am afraid, I will put my confidence in you. Yes, I will trust the promises of God. And since I am trusting him, what can mere man do to me? 5They are always twisting what I say. All their thoughts are how to harm me. 6They meet together to perfect their plans; they hide beside the trail, listening for my steps, waiting to kill me. 7They expect to get away with it. Don't let them, Lord. In anger cast them to the ground.

8You have seen me tossing and turning through the night. You have collected all my tears and preserved them in your bottle! You have recorded every one in your book.

9The very day I call for help, the tide of battle turns. My enemies flee! This one thing I *know: God is for me!* 10,11I am trusting God—oh, praise his promises! I am not afraid of anything mere man can do to me! Yes, praise his promises. 12I will surely do what I have promised, Lord, and thank you for your help. 13For you have saved me from death and my feet from slipping, so that I can walk before the Lord in the land of the living.

PROVERBS FOR TODAY/ 11:8

God rescues good men from danger while letting the wicked fall into it.

MARCH 14

NUMBERS 21:1—22:20

WHEN the king of Arad heard that the Israelis were approaching (for they were traveling the same route as the spies), he mobilized his army and attacked Israel, taking some of the men as prisoners. 2Then the people of Israel vowed to the Lord that if he would help them conquer the king of Arad and his people, they would completely annihilate all the cities of that area. 3The Lord heeded their request and defeated the Canaanites; and the Israelis completely destroyed them and their cities. The name of the region was thereafter called Hormah (meaning "Utterly Destroyed").

4Then the people of Israel returned to Mount Hor, and from there continued southward along the road to the Red Sea in order to go around the land of Edom. The people were very discouraged;

5they began to murmur against God and to complain against Moses. "Why have you brought us out of Egypt to die here in the wilderness?" they whined. "There is nothing to eat here, and nothing to drink, and we hate this insipid manna."

6So the Lord sent poisonous snakes among them to punish them, and many of them were bitten and died.

7Then the people came to Moses and cried out, "We have sinned, for we have spoken against Jehovah and against you. Pray to him to take away the snakes." So Moses prayed for the people.

8Then the Lord told him, "Make a bronze replica of one of these snakes and attach it to the top of a pole; anyone who is bitten shall live if he simply looks at it!"

9So Moses made the replica, and whenever anyone who had been bitten looked at the bronze snake, he recovered!

¹⁰Israel journeyed next to Oboth and camped there. ¹¹Then they went on to Iyeabarim, in the wilderness, a short distance east of Moab, ¹²and from there they traveled to the valley of the brook Zared and set up camp. ¹³Then they moved to the far side of the Arnon River, near the borders of the Amorites. (The Arnon River is the boundary line between the Moabites and the Amorites. ¹⁴This fact is mentioned in *The Book of the Wars of Jehovah,* where it is stated that the valley of the Arnon River, and the city of Waheb, ¹⁵lie between the Amorites and the people of Moab.)

¹⁶Then Israel traveled to Beer (meaning "A Well"). This is the place where the Lord told Moses, "Summon the people, and I will give them water." ¹⁷,¹⁸What happened is described in this song the people sang:

Spring up, O well!
Sing of the water!
This is a well
The leaders dug.
It was hollowed
With their staves
And shovels.

Then they left the desert and proceeded on through Mattanah, ¹⁹Naha-liel, and Bamoth; ²⁰then to the valley in the plateau of Moab, which overlooks the desert with Mount Pisgah in the distance.

²¹Israel now sent ambassadors to King Sihon of the Amorites.

²²"Let us travel through your land," they requested. "We will not leave the road until we have passed beyond your borders. We won't trample your fields or touch your vineyards or drink your water."

²³But King Sihon refused. Instead he mobilized his army and attacked Israel in the wilderness, battling them at Jahaz. ²⁴But Israel slaughtered them and occupied their land from the Arnon River to the Jabbok River, as far as the borders of the Ammonites; but they were stopped there by the rugged terrain.

²⁵,²⁶So Israel captured all the cities of the Amorites and lived in them, including the city of Heshbon, which had been King

Sihon's capital. ²⁷⁻³⁰The ancient poets had referred to King Sihon in this poem:

Come to Heshbon,
King Sihon's capital,
For a fire has flamed forth
And devoured
The city of Ar in Moab,
On the heights of the Arnon River.
Woe to Moab!
You are finished,
O people of Chemosh;
Your sons have fled,
And your daughters are captured
By King Sihon of the Amorites.
He has destroyed
The little children
And the men and women
As far as Dibon, Nophah, and Medeba.

³¹,³²While Israel was there in the Amorite country, Moses sent spies to look over the Jazer area; he followed up with an armed attack, capturing all of the towns and driving out the Amorites. ³³They next turned their attention to the city of Bashan, but King Og of Bashan met them with his army at Edrei. ³⁴The Lord told Moses not to fear—that the enemy was already conquered! "The same thing will happen to King Og as happened to King Sihon at Heshbon," the Lord assured him. ³⁵And sure enough, Israel was victorious and killed King Og, his sons, and his subjects, so that not a single survivor remained; and Israel occupied the land.

THE people of Israel now traveled to the plains of Moab and camped east of the Jordan River opposite Jericho. ²,³When King Balak of Moab (the son of Zippor) realized how many of them there were, and when he learned what they had done to the Amorites, he and his people were terrified. ⁴They quickly consulted with the leaders of Midian.

"This mob will eat us like an ox eats grass," they exclaimed.

So King Balak ⁵,⁶sent messengers to Balaam (son of Beor) who was living in his native land of Pethor, near the Euphrates River. He begged Balaam to come and help him.

"A vast horde of people has arrived from Egypt, and they cover the face of the earth and are headed toward me," he frantically explained. "Please come and curse them for me, so that I can drive them out of my land; for I know what fantastic blessings fall on those whom you bless, and I also know that those whom you curse are doomed."

7The messengers he sent were some of the top leaders of Moab and Midian. They went to Balaam with money in hand, and urgently explained to him what Balak wanted.

8"Stay here overnight," Balaam said, "and I'll tell you in the morning whatever the Lord directs me to say." So they did.

9That night God came to Balaam and asked him, "Who are these men?"

10"They have come from King Balak of Moab," he replied. 11"The king says that a vast horde of people from Egypt has arrived at his border, and he wants me to go at once and curse them, in the hope that he can battle them successfully."

12"Don't do it!" God told him. "You are not to curse them, for I have blessed them!"

13The next morning Balaam told the men, "Go on home! The Lord won't let me do it."

14So King Balak's ambassadors returned without him and reported his refusal. 15Balak tried again. This time he sent a larger number of even more distinguished ambassadors than the former group. 16,17They came to Balaam with this message:

"King Balak pleads with you to come. He promises you great honors plus any payment you ask. Name your own figure! Only come and curse these people for us."

18But Balaam replied, "If he were to give me a palace filled with silver and gold, I could do nothing contrary to the command of the Lord my God. 19However, stay here tonight so that I can find out whether the Lord will add anything to what he said before."

20That night God told Balaam, "You may get up and go with these men, but be sure to say only what I tell you to."

LUKE 1:26–56

THE following month God sent the angel Gabriel to Nazareth, a village in Galilee, 27to a virgin, Mary, engaged to be married to a man named Joseph, a descendant of King David.

28Gabriel appeared to her and said, "Congratulations, favored lady! The Lord is with you!"

29Confused and disturbed, Mary tried to think what the angel could mean.

30"Don't be frightened, Mary," the angel told her, "for God has decided to wonderfully bless you! 31Very soon now, you will become pregnant and have a baby boy, and you are to name him 'Jesus.' 32He shall be very great and shall be called the Son of God. And the Lord God shall give him the throne of his ancestor David. 33And he shall reign over Israel forever; his Kingdom shall never end!"

34Mary asked the angel, "But how can I have a baby? I am a virgin."

35The angel replied, "The Holy Spirit shall come upon you, and the power of God shall overshadow you; so the baby born to you will be utterly holy—the Son of God. 36Furthermore, six months ago your Aunt Elizabeth—'the barren one,' they called her—became pregnant in her old age! 37For every promise from God shall surely come true."

38Mary said, "I am the Lord's servant, and I am willing to do whatever he wants. May everything you said come true." And then the angel disappeared.

39,40A few days later Mary hurried to the highlands of Judea to the town where Zacharias lived, to visit Elizabeth.

41At the sound of Mary's greeting, Elizabeth's child leaped within her and she was filled with the Holy Spirit.

42She gave a glad cry and exclaimed to Mary, "You are favored by God above all other women, and your child is destined for God's mightiest praise. 43What an honor this is, that the mother of my Lord should visit me! 44When you came in and greeted me, the instant I heard your voice, my baby moved in me for joy! 45You believed that God would do what he said; that is why he has given you this wonderful blessing."

46Mary responded, "Oh, how I praise the Lord. 47How I rejoice in God my Savior! 48For he took notice of his lowly servant girl, and now generation after generation forever shall call me blest of God. 49For he, the mighty Holy One, has done great things to me. 50His mercy goes on from generation to generation, to all who reverence him.

51"How powerful is his mighty arm! How he scatters the proud and haughty ones! 52He has torn princes from their thrones and exalted the lowly. 53He has satisfied the hungry hearts and sent the rich away with empty hands. 54And how he has helped his servant Israel! He has not forgotten his promise to be merciful. 55For he promised our fathers—Abraham and his children—to be merciful to them forever."

56Mary stayed with Elizabeth about three months and then went back to her own home.

PSALM 57:1–11

O God, have pity, for I am trusting you! I will hide beneath the shadow of your wings until this storm is past. 2I will cry to the God of heaven who does such wonders for me. 3He will send down help from heaven to save me, because of his love and his faithfulness. He will rescue me from these liars who are so intent upon destroying me. 4I am surrounded by fierce lions—hotheads whose teeth are sharp as spears and arrows. Their tongues are like swords. 5Lord, be exalted above the highest heavens! Show your glory high above the earth. 6My enemies have set a trap for me. Frantic fear grips me. They have dug a pitfall in my path. But look! They themselves have fallen into it!

7O God, my heart is quiet and confident. No wonder I can sing your praises! 8Rouse yourself, my soul! Arise, O harp and lyre! Let us greet the dawn with song! 9I will thank you publicly throughout the land. I will sing your praises among the nations. 10Your kindness and love are as vast as the heavens. Your faithfulness is higher than the skies.

11Yes, be exalted, O God, above the heavens. May your glory shine throughout the earth.

PROVERBS FOR TODAY/ 11:9–11

Evil words destroy. Godly skill rebuilds. The whole city celebrates a good man's success—and also the godless man's death. The good influence of godly citizens causes a city to prosper, but the moral decay of the wicked drives it downhill.

MARCH 15

NUMBERS 22:21—23:30

SO the next morning he saddled his donkey and started off with them. 22,23But God was angry about Balaam's eager attitude, so he sent an angel to stand in the road to kill him. As Balaam and two servants were riding along, Balaam's donkey suddenly saw the angel of the Lord standing in the road with a drawn sword. She bolted off the road into a field, but Balaam beat her back onto the road. 24Now the angel of the Lord stood at a place where the road went between two vineyard walls.

25When the donkey saw him standing there, she squirmed past by pressing against the wall, crushing Balaam's foot in the process. So he beat her again. 26Then the angel of the Lord moved farther down the road and stood in a place so narrow that the donkey couldn't get by at all.

27So she lay down in the road! In a great fit of temper Balaam beat her again with his staff.

28Then the Lord caused the donkey to speak! "What have I done that deserves your beating me these three times?" she asked.

29"Because you have made me look like a fool!" Balaam shouted. "I wish I had a sword with me, for I would kill you."

30"Have I ever done anything like this before in my entire life?" the donkey asked.

"No," he admitted.

31Then the Lord opened Balaam's eyes and he saw the angel standing in the roadway with drawn sword, and he fell flat on the ground before him.

32"Why did you beat your donkey those three times?" the angel demanded. "I have come to stop you because you are headed for destruction. 33Three times the donkey saw me and shied away from me; otherwise I would certainly have killed you by now, and spared her."

34Then Balaam confessed, "I have sinned. I didn't realize you were there. I will go back home if you don't want me to go on."

35But the angel told him, "Go with the men, but say only what I tell you to say." So Balaam went on with them. 36When King Balak heard that Balaam was on the way, he left the capital and went out to meet him at the Arnon River, at the border of his land.

37"Why did you delay so long?" he asked Balaam. "Didn't you believe me when I said I would give you great honors?"

38Balaam replied, "I have come, but I have no power to say anything except what God tells me to say; and that is what I shall speak." 39Balaam accompanied the king to Kiriathhuzoth, 40where King Balak sacrificed oxen and sheep, and gave animals to Balaam and the ambassadors for their sacrifices. 41The next morning Balak took Balaam to the top of Mount Bamoth-baal, from which he could see the people of Israel spread out before him.

BALAAM said to the king, "Build seven altars here, and prepare seven young bulls and seven rams for sacrifice."

2Balak followed his instructions, and a young bull and a ram were sacrificed on each altar.

3,4Then Balaam said to the king, "Stand here by your burnt offerings and I will see if the Lord will meet me; and I will tell you what he says to me." So he went up to a barren height, and God met him there. Balaam told the Lord, "I have prepared seven altars, and have sacrificed a young bull and a ram on each." 5Then the Lord gave Balaam a message for King Balak.

6When Balaam returned, the king was standing beside the burnt offerings with all the princes of Moab. 7-10This was Balaam's message:

"King Balak, king of Moab, has brought me
From the land of Aram,
From the eastern mountains.
'Come,' he told me, 'curse Jacob for me!
Let your anger rise on Israel.'
But how can I curse
What God has not cursed?
How can I denounce
A people God has not denounced?
I see them from the cliff tops,
I watch them from the hills.
They live alone,
And prefer to remain distinct
From every other nation.
They are as numerous as dust!
They are beyond numbering.
If only I could die as happy as an Israelite!
Oh, that my end might be like theirs!"

11"What have you done to me?" demanded King Balak. "I told you to curse my enemies, and now you have blessed them!"

¹²But Balaam replied, "Can I say anything except what Jehovah tells me to?"

¹³Then Balak told him, "Come with me to another place; there you will see only a portion of the nation of Israel. Curse at least that many!"

¹⁴So King Balak took Balaam into the fields of Zophim at the top of Mount Pisgah, and built seven altars there; and he offered up a young bull and a ram on each altar.

¹⁵Then Balaam said to the king, "Stand here by your burnt offering while I go to meet the Lord." ¹⁶And the Lord met Balaam and told him what to say. ¹⁷So he returned to where the king and the princes of Moab were standing beside their burnt offerings.

"What has Jehovah said?" the king eagerly inquired.

¹⁸⁻²⁴And he replied,

"Rise up, Balak, and hear:
Listen to me, you son of Zippor.
God is not a man, that he should lie;
He doesn't change his mind like humans do.
Has he ever promised,
Without doing what he said?
Look! I have received a command to bless them,
For God has blessed them,
And I cannot reverse it!
He has not seen sin in Jacob.
He will not trouble Israel!
Jehovah their God is with them.
He is their king!
God has brought them out of Egypt.
Israel has the strength of a wild ox.
No curse can be placed on Jacob,
And no magic shall be done against him.
For now it shall be said of Israel,
'What wonders God has done for them!'
These people rise up as a lion;
They shall not lie down
Until they have eaten what they capture
And have drunk the blood of the slain!"

²⁵"If you aren't going to curse them, at least don't *bless* them!" the king exclaimed to Balaam.

²⁶But Balaam replied, "Didn't I tell you that I must say whatever Jehovah tells me to?"

²⁷Then the king said to Balaam, "I will take you to yet another place. Perhaps it will please God to let you curse them from there."

²⁸So King Balak took Balaam to the top of Mount Peor, overlooking the desert. ²⁹Balaam again told the king to build seven altars, and to prepare seven young bulls and seven rams for the sacrifice. ³⁰The king did as Balaam said, and offered a young bull and ram on every altar.

LUKE 1:57–80

BY now Elizabeth's waiting was over, for the time had come for the baby to be born—and it was a boy. ⁵⁸The word spread quickly to her neighbors and relatives of how kind the Lord had been to her, and everyone rejoiced.

⁵⁹When the baby was eight days old, all the relatives and friends came for the circumcision ceremony. They all assumed the baby's name would be Zacharias, after his father.

⁶⁰But Elizabeth said, "No! He must be named John!"

⁶¹"What?" they exclaimed. "There is no one in all your family by that name."

⁶²So they asked the baby's father, talking to him by gestures.

⁶³He motioned for a piece of paper and to everyone's surprise wrote, "His name is *John!*" ⁶⁴Instantly Zacharias could speak again, and he began praising God.

⁶⁵Wonder fell upon the whole neighborhood, and the news of what had happened spread through the Judean hills. ⁶⁶And everyone who heard about it thought long thoughts and asked, "I wonder what this child will turn out to be? For the hand of the Lord is surely upon him in some special way."

⁶⁷Then his father Zacharias was filled with the Holy Spirit and gave this prophecy:

⁶⁸"Praise the Lord, the God of Israel, for he has come to visit his people and has redeemed them. ⁶⁹He is sending us a Mighty Savior from the royal line of his servant David, ⁷⁰just as he promised through his holy prophets long ago— ⁷¹someone to save us from our enemies, from all who hate us.

⁷²,⁷³"He has been merciful to our ancestors, yes, to Abraham himself, by remembering his sacred promise to him, ⁷⁴and by granting us the privilege of serving God fearlessly, freed from our enemies, ⁷⁵and by making us holy and acceptable, ready to stand in his presence forever.

⁷⁶"And you, my little son, shall be called the prophet of the glorious God, for you will prepare the way for the Messiah. ⁷⁷You will tell his people how to find salvation through forgiveness of their sins. ⁷⁸All this will be because the mercy of our God is very tender, and heaven's dawn is about to break upon us, ⁷⁹to give light to those who sit in darkness and death's shadow, and to guide us to the path of peace."

⁸⁰The little boy greatly loved God and when he grew up he lived out in the lonely wilderness until he began his public ministry to Israel.

PSALM 58:1–11

JUSTICE? You high and mighty politicians don't even know the meaning of the word! Fairness? Which of you has any left? Not one! All your dealings are crooked: you give "justice" in exchange for bribes. ³These men are born sinners, lying from their earliest words! ⁴,⁵They are poisonous as deadly snakes, cobras that close their ears to the most expert of charmers.

⁶O God, break off their fangs. Tear out the teeth of these young lions, Lord. ⁷Let them disappear like water into thirsty ground. Make their weapons useless in their hands. ⁸Let them be as snails that dissolve into slime; and as those who die at birth, who never see the sun. ⁹God will sweep away both old and young. He will destroy them more quickly than a cooking pot can feel the blazing fire of thorns beneath it.

¹⁰The godly shall rejoice in the triumph of right; they shall walk the blood-stained fields of slaughtered, wicked men. ¹¹Then at last everyone will know that good is rewarded, and that there is a God who judges justly here on earth.

PROVERBS FOR TODAY/ 11:12–13

To quarrel with a neighbor is foolish; a man with good sense holds his tongue. A gossip goes around spreading rumors, while a trustworthy man tries to quiet them.

MARCH 16

NUMBERS 24:1—25:18

BALAAM realized by now that Jehovah planned to bless Israel, so he didn't even go to meet the Lord as he had earlier. Instead, he went at once and looked out toward the camp of Israel ²which stretched away across the plains, divided by tribal areas.

Then the Spirit of God came upon him, ³⁻⁹and he spoke this prophecy concerning them:

"Balaam the son of Beor says—
The man whose eyes are open says—
'I have listened to the word of God,
I have seen what God Almighty showed me;

I fell, and my eyes were opened:
Oh, the joys awaiting Israel,
Joys in the homes of Jacob.
I see them spread before me as green valleys,
And fruitful gardens by the riverside;
As aloes planted by the Lord himself;
As cedar trees beside the waters.
They shall be blessed with an abundance of water,
And they shall live in many places.
Their king will be greater than Agag;
Their kingdom is exalted.
God has brought them from Egypt.
Israel has the strength of a wild ox,
And shall eat up the nations that oppose him;
He shall break their bones in pieces,
And shall shoot them with many arrows.
Israel sleeps as a lion or a lioness—
Who dares arouse him?
Blessed is everyone who blesses you, O Israel,
And curses shall fall upon everyone who curses you.' "

¹⁰King Balak was livid with rage by now. Striking his hands together in anger and disgust he shouted, "I called you to curse my enemies and instead you have blessed them three times. ¹¹Get out of here! Go back home! I had planned to promote you to great honor, but Jehovah has kept you from it!"

¹²Balaam replied, "Didn't I tell your messengers ¹³that even if you gave me a palace filled with silver and gold, I could not go beyond the words of Jehovah, and could not say a word of my own? I said that I would say only what Jehovah says! ¹⁴Yes, I shall return now to my own people. But first, let me tell you what the Israelites are going to do to your people!"

¹⁵⁻¹⁹So he spoke this prophecy to him:
"Balaam the son of Beor is the man
Whose eyes are open!
He hears the words of God
And has knowledge from the Most High;
He sees what Almighty God has shown him;

He fell, and his eyes were opened:
I see in the future of Israel,
Far down the distant trail,
That there shall come a star from Jacob!
This ruler of Israel
Shall smite the people of Moab,
And destroy the sons of Sheth.
Israel shall possess all Edom and Seir.
They shall overcome their enemies.
Jacob shall arise in power
And shall destroy many cities."

²⁰Then Balaam looked over at the homes of the people of Amalek and prophesied:
"Amalek was the first of the nations,
But its destiny is destruction!"

²¹,²²Then he looked over at the Kenites:
"Yes, you are strongly situated,
Your nest is set in the rocks!
But the Kenites shall be destroyed,
And the mighty army of the king of Assyria shall deport you from this land!"

²³,²⁴He concluded his prophecies by saying:
"Alas, who can live when God does this?
Ships shall come from the coasts of Cyprus,
And shall oppress both Eber and Assyria.
They too must be destroyed."

²⁵So Balaam and Balak returned to their homes.

WHILE Israel was camped at Acacia, some of the young men began going to wild parties with the local Moabite girls. ²These girls also invited them to attend the sacrifices to their gods, and soon the men were not only attending the feasts, but also bowing down and worshiping the idols. ³Before long all Israel was joining freely in the worship of Baal, the god of Moab; and the anger of the Lord was hot against his people.

⁴He issued the following command to Moses:

"Execute all the tribal leaders of Israel. Hang them up before the Lord in broad daylight, so that his fierce anger will turn away from the people."

⁵So Moses ordered the judges to execute all who had worshiped Baal.

⁶But one of the Israeli men insolently brought a Midianite girl into the camp, right before the eyes of Moses and all the people, as they were weeping at the door of the Tabernacle. ⁷When Phinehas (son of Eleazar and grandson of Aaron the priest) saw this, he jumped up, grabbed a spear, ⁸and rushed after the man into his tent, where he had taken the girl. He thrust the spear all the way through the man's body and into her stomach. So the plague was stopped, ⁹but only after 24,000 people had already died.

¹⁰,¹¹Then the Lord said to Moses, "Phinehas (son of Eleazar and grandson of Aaron the priest) has turned away my anger for he was angry with my anger, and would not tolerate the worship of any God but me. So I have stopped destroying all Israel as I had intended. ¹²,¹³Now because of what he has done—because of his zeal for his God, and because he has made atonement for the people of Israel by what he did—I promise that he and his descendants shall be priests forever."

¹⁴The name of the man who was killed with the Midianite girl was Zimri, son of Salu, a leader of the tribe of Simeon. ¹⁵The girl's name was Cozbi, daughter of Zur, a Midianite prince.

¹⁶,¹⁷Then the Lord said to Moses, "Destroy the Midianites, ¹⁸for they are destroying you with their wiles. They are causing you to worship Baal, and they are leading you astray, as you have just seen by the death of Cozbi."

LUKE 2:1–35

ABOUT this time Caesar Augustus, the Roman Emperor, decreed that a census should be taken throughout the nation. ²(This census was taken when Quirinius was governor of Syria.)

³Everyone was required to return to his ancestral home for this registration. ⁴And because Joseph was a member of the royal line, he had to go to Bethlehem in Judea, King David's ancient home—journeying there from the Galilean village of Nazareth. ⁵He took with him Mary, his fiancée, who was obviously pregnant by this time.

⁶And while they were there, the time came for her baby to be born; ⁷and she gave birth to her first child, a son. She wrapped him in a blanket and laid him in a manger, because there was no room for them in the village inn.

⁸That night some shepherds were in the fields outside the village, guarding their flocks of sheep. ⁹Suddenly an angel appeared among them, and the landscape shone bright with the glory of the Lord. They were badly frightened, ¹⁰but the angel reassured them.

"Don't be afraid!" he said. "I bring you the most joyful news ever announced, and it is for everyone! ¹¹The Savior—yes, the Messiah, the Lord—has been born tonight in Bethlehem! ¹²How will you recognize him? You will find a baby wrapped in a blanket, lying in a manger!"

¹³Suddenly, the angel was joined by a vast host of others—the armies of heaven—praising God:

¹⁴"Glory to God in the highest heaven," they sang, "and peace on earth for all those pleasing him."

¹⁵When this great army of angels had returned again to heaven, the shepherds said to each other, "Come on! Let's go to Bethlehem! Let's see this wonderful thing that has happened, which the Lord has told us about."

¹⁶They ran to the village and found their way to Mary and Joseph. And there was the baby, lying in the manger. ¹⁷The shepherds told everyone what had happened and what the angel had said to them about this child. ¹⁸All who heard the shepherds' story expressed astonishment, ¹⁹but Mary quietly treasured these

things in her heart and often thought about them.

²⁰Then the shepherds went back again to their fields and flocks, praising God for the visit of the angels, and because they had seen the child, just as the angel had told them.

²¹Eight days later, at the baby's circumcision ceremony, he was named Jesus, the name given him by the angel before he was even conceived.

²²When the time came for Mary's purification offering at the Temple, as required by the laws of Moses after the birth of a child, his parents took him to Jerusalem to present him to the Lord; ²³for in these laws God had said, "If a woman's first child is a boy, he shall be dedicated to the Lord."

²⁴At that time Jesus' parents also offered their sacrifice for purification—"either a pair of turtledoves or two young pigeons" was the legal requirement. ²⁵That day a man named Simeon, a Jerusalem resident, was in the Temple. He was a good man, very devout, filled with the Holy Spirit and constantly expecting the Messiah to come soon. ²⁶For the Holy Spirit had revealed to him that he would not die until he had seen him—God's anointed King. ²⁷The Holy Spirit had impelled him to go to the Temple that day; and so, when Mary and Joseph arrived to present the baby Jesus to the Lord in obedience to the law, ²⁸Simeon was there and took the child in his arms, praising God.

^{29,30,31}"Lord," he said, "now I can die content! For I have seen him as you promised me I would. I have seen the Savior you have given to the world. ³²He is the Light that will shine upon the nations, and he will be the glory of your people Israel!"

³³Joseph and Mary just stood there, marveling at what was being said about Jesus.

^{34,35}Simeon blessed them but then said to Mary, "A sword shall pierce your soul, for this child shall be rejected by many in Israel, and this to their undoing. But he will be the greatest joy of many others. And the deepest thoughts of many hearts shall be revealed."

PSALM 59:1–17

O my God, save me from my enemies. Protect me from these who have come to destroy me. ²Preserve me from these criminals, these murderers. ³They lurk in ambush for my life. Strong men are out there waiting. And not, O Lord, because I've done them wrong. ⁴Yet they prepare to kill me. Lord, waken! See what is happening! Help me! ⁵(And O Jehovah, God of heaven's armies, God of Israel, arise and punish the heathen nations surrounding us.) Do not spare these evil, treacherous men. ⁶At evening they come to spy, slinking around like dogs that prowl the city. ⁷I hear them shouting insults and cursing God, for "No one will hear us," they think. ⁸Lord, laugh at them! (And scoff at these surrounding nations too.)

⁹O God my Strength! I will sing your praises, for you are my place of safety. ¹⁰My God is changeless in his love for me and he will come and help me. He will let me see my wish come true upon my enemies. ¹¹Don't kill them—for my people soon forget such lessons—but stagger them with your power and bring them to their knees. Bring them to the dust, O Lord our shield. ^{12,13}They are proud, cursing liars. Angrily destroy them. Wipe them out. (And let the nations find out too that God rules in Israel and will reign throughout the world.) ^{14,15}Let these evil men slink back at evening, and prowl the city all night before they are satisfied, howling like dogs and searching for food.

¹⁶But as for me, I will sing each morning about your power and mercy. For you have been my high tower of refuge, a place of safety in the day of my distress. ¹⁷O my Strength, to you I sing my praises; for you are my high tower of safety, my God of mercy.

MARCH 17

NUMBERS 26:1–51

AFTER the plague had ended, Jehovah said to Moses and to Eleazar (son of Aaron the priest), 2"Take a census of all the men of Israel who are twenty years old or older, to find out how many of each tribe and clan are able to go to war."

3,4So Moses and Eleazar issued census instructions to the leaders of Israel. (The entire nation was camped in the plains of Moab beside the Jordan River, opposite Jericho.) Here are the results of the census:

5–11*The tribe of Reuben:* 43,730.

(Reuben was Israel's oldest son.) In this tribe were the following clans, named after Reuben's sons:

The Hanochites, named after their ancestor Hanoch.

The Palluites, named after their ancestor Pallu. (In the sub-clan of Eliab—who was one of the sons of Pallu—were the families of Nemu-el, Abiram, and Dathan. This Dathan and Abiram were the two leaders who conspired with Korah against Moses and Aaron, and in fact challenged the very authority of God! But the earth opened and swallowed them; and 250 men were destroyed by fire from the Lord that day, as a warning to the entire nation.)

The Hezronites, named after their ancestor Hezron.

The Carmites, named after their ancestor Carmi.

12,13,14*The tribe of Simeon:* 22,200.

In this tribe were the following clans, founded by Simeon's sons:

The Nemu-elites, named after their ancestor Nemu-el.

The Jaminites, named after their ancestor Jamin.

The Jachinites, named after their ancestor Jachin.

The Zerahites, named after their ancestor Zerah.

The Shaulites, named after their ancestor Shaul.

15–18*The tribe of Gad:* 40,500.

In this tribe were the following clans founded by the sons of Gad:

The Zephonites, named after their ancestor Zephon.

The Haggites, named after their ancestor Haggi.

The Shunites, named after their ancestor Shuni.

The Oznites, named after their ancestor Ozni.

The Erites, named after their ancestor Eri.

The Arodites, named after their ancestor Arod.

The Arelites, named after their ancestor Areli.

19–22*The tribe of Judah:* 76,500

In this tribe were the following clans named after the sons of Judah—but not including Er and Onan who died in the land of Canaan:

The Shelanites, named after their ancestor Shelah.

The Perezites, named after their ancestor Perez.

The Zerahites, named after their ancestor Zerah.

This census also included the subclans of Perez: The Hezronites, named after their ancestor Hezron. The Hamulites, named after their ancestor Hamul.

23,24,25 *The tribe of Issachar:* 64,300.

In this tribe were the following clans named after the sons of Issachar:

The Tolaites, named after their ancestor Tola.

The Punites, named after their ancestor Puvah.

The Jashubites, named after their ancestor Jashub.

The Shimronites, named after their ancestor Shimron.

26,27 *The tribe of Zebulun:* 60,500.

In this tribe were the following clans named after the sons of Zebulun:

The Seredites, named after their ancestor Sered.

The Elonites, named after their ancestor Elon.

The Jahleelites, named after their ancestor Jahleel.

28–37 *The tribe of Joseph:* 32,500 *in the half-tribe of Ephraim; and* 52,700 *in the half-tribe of Manasseh.*

In the half-tribe of Manasseh was the following clan of Machirites, named after their ancestor Machir.

The sub-clan of the Machirites was the Gileadites, named after their ancestor Gilead.

The tribes of the Gileadites: The Jezerites, named after their ancestor Jezer. The Helekites, named after their ancestor Helek. The Asrielites, named after their ancestor Asriel. The Shechemites, named after their ancestor Shechem. The Shemidaites, named after their ancestor Shemida. The Hepherites, named after their ancestor Hepher. (Hepher's son, Zelophehad, had no sons. Here are the names of his daughters: Mahlah, Noah, Hoglah, Milcah, Tirzah.

The 32,500 registered in the half-tribe of Ephraim included the following clans, named after the sons of Ephraim:

The Shuthelahites, named after their ancestor Shuthelah. (A sub-clan of the Shuthelahites was the Eranites, named after their ancestor Eran, a son of Shuthelah.)

The Becherites, named after their ancestor Becher.

The Tahanites, named after their ancestor Tahan.

38–41 *The tribe of Benjamin:* 45,600.

In this tribe were the following clans named after the sons of Benjamin:

The Bela-ites, named after their ancestor Bela.

Sub-clans named after sons of Bela were: The Ardites, named after their ancestor Ard. The Naamites, named after their ancestor Naaman. The Ashbelites, named after their ancestor Ashbel. The Ahiramites, named after their ancestor Ahiram. The Shuphamites, named after their ancestor Shephupham. The Huphamites, named after their ancestor Hupham.

42,43 *The tribe of Dan:* 64,400.

In this tribe was the clan of the Shuhamites, named after Shuham, the son of Dan.

44–47 *The tribe of Asher:* 53,400.

In this tribe were the following clans named after the sons of Asher:

The Imnites, named after their ancestor Imnah.

The Ishvites, named after their ancestor Ishvi.

The Beriites, named after their ancestor Beriah.

Sub-clans named after the sons of Beriah were: The Heberites, named after their ancestor Heber. The Malchi-elites, named after their ancestor Malchi-el.

Asher also had a daughter named Serah.

48,49,50 *The tribe of Naphtali:* 45,400.

In this tribe were the following clans, named after the sons of Naphtali:

The Jahzeelites, named after their ancestor Jahzeel.

The Gunites, named after their ancestor Guni.

The Jezerites, named after their ancestor Jezer.

The Shillemites, named after their ancestor Shillem.

51So the total number of the men of draft age throughout Israel was 601,730.

LUKE 2:36–52

ANNA, a prophetess, was also there in the Temple that day. She was the daughter of Phanuel, of the Jewish tribe of Asher, and was very old, for she had been a widow for eighty-four years following seven years of marriage. She never left the Temple but stayed there night and day, worshiping God by praying and often fasting. 38She came along just as Simeon was talking with Mary and Joseph, and she also began thanking God and telling everyone in Jerusalem who had been awaiting the coming of the Savior that the Messiah had finally arrived.

39When Jesus' parents had fulfilled all the requirements of the Law of God they returned home to Nazareth in Galilee. 40There the child became a strong, robust lad, and was known for wisdom beyond his years; and God poured out his blessings on him.

41,42When Jesus was twelve years old he accompanied his parents to Jerusalem for the annual Passover Festival, which they attended each year. 43After the celebration was over they started home to Nazareth, but Jesus stayed behind in Jerusalem. His parents didn't miss him the first day, 44for they assumed he was with friends among the other travelers. But when he didn't show up that evening, they started to look for him among their relatives and friends; 45and when they couldn't find him, they went back to Jerusalem to search for him there.

46,47Three days later they finally discovered him. He was in the Temple, sitting among the teachers of Law, discussing deep questions with them and amazing everyone with his understanding and answers.

48His parents didn't know what to think. "Son!" his mother said to him. "Why have you done this to us? Your father and I have been frantic, searching for you everywhere."

49"But why did you need to search?" he asked. "Didn't you realize that I would be here at the Temple, in my Father's House?" 50But they didn't understand what he meant.

51Then he returned to Nazareth with them and was obedient to them; and his mother stored away all these things in her heart. 52So Jesus grew both tall and wise, and was loved by God and man.

PSALM 60:1–12

O God, you have rejected us and broken our defenses; you have become angry and deserted us. Lord, restore us again to your favor. 2You have caused this nation to tremble in fear; you have torn it apart. Lord, heal it now, for it is shaken to its depths. 3You have been very hard on us and made us reel beneath your blows.

4,5But you have given us a banner to rally to; all who love truth will rally to it; then you can deliver your beloved people. Use your strong right arm to rescue us. 6,7God has promised to help us. He has vowed it by his holiness! No wonder I exult! "Shechem, Succoth, Gilead, Manasseh—still are mine!" he says. "Judah shall continue to produce kings, and Ephraim great warriors. 8Moab shall become my lowly servant, and Edom my slave. And I will shout in triumph over the Philistines."

9,10Who will bring me in triumph into Edom's strong cities? God will! He who cast us off! He who abandoned us to our foes! 11Yes, Lord, help us against our enemies, for man's help is useless.

12With God's help we shall do mighty things, for he will trample down our foes.

PROVERBS FOR TODAY/ 11:15

Be sure you know a person well before you vouch for his credit! Better refuse than suffer later.

MARCH 18

NUMBERS 26:52—28:14

THEN the Lord told Moses to divide the land among the tribes in proportion to their population, as indicated by the census— 54the larger tribes to be given more land, the smaller tribes less land.

55,56"Let the representatives of the larger tribes have a lottery, drawing for the larger sections," the Lord instructed, "and let the smaller tribes draw for the smaller sections."

57These are the clans of the Levites numbered in the census:

The Gershonites, named after their ancestor Gershon.

The Kohathites, named after their ancestor Kohath.

The Merarites, named after their ancestor Merari.

58,59These are the families of the tribe of Levi:

The Libnites, the Hebronites,

The Mahlites, the Mushites,

The Korahites.

While Levi was in Egypt, a daughter, Jochebed, was born to him and she became the wife of Amram, son of Kohath. They were the parents of Aaron, Moses, and Miriam. 60To Aaron were born Nadab, Abihu, Eleazar, and Ithamar. 61But Nadab and Abihu died when they offered unauthorized incense before the Lord.

62 *The total number of Levites in the census* was 23,000, counting all the males a month old and upward. But the Levites were not included in the total census figure of the people of Israel, for the Levites were given no land when it was divided among the tribes.

63So these are the census figures as prepared by Moses and Eleazar the priest, in the plains of Moab beside the Jordan River, across from Jericho. 64,65Not one person in this entire census had been counted in the previous census taken in the wilderness of Sinai! For all who had been counted then had died, as the Lord had decreed when he said of them, "They shall die in the wilderness." The only exceptions were Caleb (son of Jephunneh) and Joshua (son of Nun).

ONE day the daughters of Zelophehad came to the entrance of the Tabernacle to give a petition to Moses, Eleazar the priest, the tribal leaders, and others who were there. The names of these women were Mahlah, Noah, Hoglah, Milcah and Tirzah. They were members of the half-tribe of Manasseh (a son of Joseph). Their ancestor was Machir, son of Manasseh. Manasseh's son Gilead was their great-grandfather, his son Hepher was their grandfather, and his son Zelophehad was their father.

3,4"Our father died in the wilderness," they said, "and he was not one of those who perished in Korah's revolt against the Lord—it was a natural death, but he had no sons. Why should the name of our father disappear just because he had no son? We feel that we should be given property along with our father's brothers."

5So Moses brought their case before the Lord.

6,7And the Lord replied to Moses, "The daughters of Zelophehad are correct. Give them land along with their uncles; give them the property that would have been given to their father if he had lived. 8Moreover, this is a general law among you, that if a man dies and has no sons, then his inheritance shall be passed on to his daughters. 9And if he has no daughter, it shall belong to his brothers. 10And if he has no brother, then it shall go to his uncles. 11But if he has no uncles, then it shall go to the nearest relative."

12One day the Lord said to Moses, "Go up into Mount Abarim and look across the river to the land I have given to the people of Israel. 13After you have seen it, you shall die as Aaron your brother did, 14for you rebelled against my instructions in the wilderness of Zin. When the people of Israel rebelled, you did not glorify me before them by following my instructions to order water to come out of the rock." He was referring to the incident at the waters of Meribah ("Place of Strife") in Kadesh, in the wilderness of Zin.

15Then Moses said to the Lord, 16"O Jehovah, the God of the spirits of all mankind, [before I am taken away] please appoint a new leader for the people, 17a man who will lead them into battle and care for them, so that the people of the Lord will not be as sheep without a shepherd."

18The Lord replied, "Go and get Joshua (son of Nun), who has the Spirit in him, 19and take him to Eleazar the priest, and as all the people watch, charge him with the responsibility of leading the people. 20Publicly give him your authority so that all the people of Israel will obey him. 21He shall be the one to consult with Eleazar the priest in order to get directions from the Lord. The Lord will speak to Eleazar through the use of the Urim, and Eleazar will pass on these instructions to Joshua and the people. In this way the Lord will continue to give them guidance."

22So Moses did as Jehovah commanded, and took Joshua to Eleazar the priest. As the people watched, 23Moses laid his hands upon him and dedicated him to his responsibilities, as the Lord had commanded.

THE Lord gave Moses these instructions to give to the people of Israel: "The offerings which you burn on the altar for me are my food, and are a pleasure to me; so see to it that they are brought regularly and are offered as I have instructed you.

3"When you make offerings by fire, you shall use yearling male lambs—each without defect. Two of them shall be offered each day as a regular burnt offering.

4One lamb shall be sacrificed in the morning, the other in the evening. 5With them shall be offered a grain offering of three quarts of finely ground flour mixed with three pints of oil. 6This is the burnt offering ordained at Mount Sinai, to be regularly offered as a fragrant odor, an offering made by fire to the Lord. 7Along with it shall be the drink offering, consisting of three pints of strong wine with each lamb, poured out in the holy place before the Lord. 8Offer the second lamb in the evening with the same grain offering and drink offering. It too is a fragrant odor to the Lord, an offering made by fire.

9,10"On the Sabbath day, sacrifice two yearling male lambs—both without defect—in addition to the regular offerings. They are to be accompanied by a grain offering of six quarts of fine flour mixed with oil, and the usual drink offering.

11"Also, on the first day of each month there shall be an extra burnt offering to the Lord of two young bulls, one ram, and seven male yearling lambs—all without defect. 12Accompany them with nine quarts of finely ground flour mixed with oil as a grain offering with each bull; and six quarts of finely ground flour mixed with oil as a grain offering for the ram; 13and for each lamb, three quarts of finely ground flour mixed with oil for a grain offering. This burnt offering shall be presented by fire, and will please the Lord very much. 14Along with each sacrifice shall be a drink offering—six pints of wine with each bull, four pints for a ram, and three pints for a lamb. This, then, will be the burnt offering each month throughout the year.

LUKE 3:1–22

IN the fifteenth year of the reign of Emperor Tiberius Caesar, a message came from God to John (the son of Zacharias), as he was living out in the deserts. (Pilate was governor over Judea at that time; Herod, over Galilee; his brother Philip, over Iturea and Trachonitis; Lysanias, over Abilene; and

Annas and Caiaphas were High Priests.) ³Then John went from place to place on both sides of the Jordan River, preaching that people should be baptized to show that they had turned to God and away from their sins, in order to be forgiven.

⁴In the words of Isaiah the prophet, John was "a voice shouting from the barren wilderness, 'Prepare a road for the Lord to travel on! Widen the pathway before him! ⁵Level the mountains! Fill up the valleys! Straighten the curves! Smooth out the ruts! ⁶And then all mankind shall see the Savior sent from God.' "

⁷Here is a sample of John's preaching to the crowds that came for baptism: "You brood of snakes! You are trying to escape hell without truly turning to God! That is why you want to be baptized! ⁸First go and prove by the way you live that you really have repented. And don't think you are safe because you are descendants of Abraham. That isn't enough. God can produce children of Abraham from these desert stones! ⁹The axe of his judgment is poised over you, ready to sever your roots and cut you down. Yes, every tree that does not produce good fruit will be chopped down and thrown into the fire."

¹⁰The crowd replied, "What do you want us to do?"

¹¹"If you have two coats," he replied, "give one to the poor. If you have extra food, give it away to those who are hungry."

¹²Even tax collectors—notorious for their corruption—came to be baptized and asked, "How shall we prove to you that we have abandoned our sins?"

¹³"By your honesty," he replied. "Make sure you collect no more taxes than the Roman government requires you to."

¹⁴"And us," asked some soldiers, "what about us?"

John replied, "Don't extort money by threats and violence; don't accuse anyone of what you know he didn't do; and be content with your pay!"

¹⁵Everyone was expecting the Messiah to come soon, and eager to know whether or not John was he. This was the question of the hour, and was being discussed everywhere.

¹⁶John answered the question by saying, "I baptize only with water; but someone is coming soon who has far higher authority than mine; in fact, I am not even worthy of being his slave. He will baptize you with fire—with the Holy Spirit. ¹⁷He will separate chaff from grain, and burn up the chaff with eternal fire and store away the grain." ¹⁸He used many such warnings as he announced the Good News to the people.

¹⁹,²⁰(But after John had publicly criticized Herod, governor of Galilee, for marrying Herodias, his brother's wife, and for many other wrongs he had done, Herod put John in prison, thus adding this sin to all his many others.)

²¹Then one day, after the crowds had been baptized, Jesus himself was baptized; and as he was praying, the heavens opened, ²²and the Holy Spirit in the form of a dove settled upon him, and a voice from heaven said, "You are my much loved Son, yes, my delight."

PSALM 61:1–8

O God, listen to me! Hear my prayer! ²For wherever I am, though far away at the ends of the earth, I will cry to you for help. When my heart is faint and overwhelmed, lead me to the mighty, towering Rock of safety. ³For you are my refuge, a high tower where my enemies can never reach me. ⁴I shall live forever in your tabernacle; oh, to be safe beneath the shelter of your wings! ⁵For you have heard my vows, O God, to praise you every day, and you have given me the blessings you reserve for those who reverence your name.

⁶You will give me added years of life, as rich and full as those of many generations, all packed into one. ⁷And I shall live before the Lord forever. Oh, send

your lovingkindness and truth to guard and watch over me, 8and I will praise your name continually, fulfilling my vow of praising you each day.

PROVERBS FOR TODAY/ 11:16–17

Honor goes to kind and gracious women, mere money to cruel men. Your own soul is nourished when you are kind; it is destroyed when you are cruel.

MARCH 19

NUMBERS 28:15—29:40

ALSO on the first day of each month you shall offer one male goat for a sin offering to the Lord. This is in addition to the regular daily burnt offering and its drink offering.

16"On April first, you shall celebrate the Passover—[when the death angel passed over the oldest sons of the Israelites in Egypt, leaving them unharmed]. 17On the following day, a great, joyous seven-day festival will begin, but no leavened bread shall be served. 18On the first day of the festival all the people shall be called together before the Lord. No hard work shall be done on that day. 19You shall offer as burnt sacrifices to the Lord two young bulls, one ram, and seven yearling male lambs—all without defect. 20,21With each bull there shall be a grain offering of nine quarts of fine flour mixed with oil; with the ram there shall be six quarts; and with each of the seven lambs there shall be three quarts of fine flour. 22You must also offer a male goat as a sin offering, to make atonement for yourselves. 23These offerings shall be in addition to the usual daily sacrifices. 24This same sacrifice shall be offered on each of the seven days of the feast; they will be very pleasant to the Lord. 25On the seventh day there shall again be a holy and solemn assembly of all the people, and during that day you may do no hard work.

26"On the first day of the Harvest Festival, all the people must come before the Lord for a special, solemn assembly to celebrate the new harvest. On that day you are to present the first of the new crop of grain as a grain offering to the Lord; there is to be no regular work by anyone on that day. 27A special burnt offering, very pleasant to the Lord, shall be offered that day. It shall consist of two young bulls, one ram, and seven yearling male lambs. 28,29These shall be accompanied by your grain offering of nine quarts of fine flour mixed with oil with each bull, six quarts with the ram, and three quarts with each of the seven lambs. 30Also offer one male goat to make atonement for yourselves. 31These special offerings are in addition to the regular daily burnt offerings and grain offerings and drink offerings. Make sure that the animals you sacrifice are without defect.

THE Festival of Trumpets shall be celebrated on the fifteenth day of September each year; there shall be a solemn assembly of all the people on that day, and no hard work may be done. 2On that day you shall offer a burnt sacrifice consisting of one young bull, one ram, and seven yearling male lambs—all without defect. These are sacrifices which the Lord will appreciate and enjoy. 3,4A grain offering of nine quarts of fine flour mingled with oil shall be offered with the bull, six quarts with the ram, and three quarts with each of the seven lambs.

5In addition, there shall be a male goat sacrificed as a sin offering, to make atonement for you. 6These special sacrifices are in addition to the regular monthly burnt offering for that day, and also in addition to the regular daily burnt sacrifices, which are to be offered with the respective grain offerings and drink offerings, as specified by the ordinances governing them.

7"Ten days later another convocation of all the people shall be held. This will be a day of solemn humility before the Lord, and no work of any kind may be done. 8On that day you shall offer a burnt sacrifice to the Lord—it will be very pleasant to him—of one young bull, one ram, seven yearling male lambs—each without defect— 9,10and their accompanying grain offerings. Nine quarts of fine flour mixed with oil are to be offered with the bull; six with the ram; and three with each of the seven lambs. 11You are also to sacrifice one male goat for a sin offering. This is in addition to the sin offering of the Day of Atonement [offered annually on that day], and in addition to the regular daily burnt sacrifices, grain offerings, and drink offerings.

12"Five days later there shall be yet another assembly of all the people, and on that day no hard work shall be done; it is the beginning of a seven-day festival before the Lord. 13Your special burnt sacrifice that day, which will give much pleasure to the Lord, shall be thirteen young bulls, two rams, and fourteen male yearling lambs—each without defect— 14accompanied by the usual grain offerings—nine quarts of fine flour mingled with oil for each of the thirteen young bulls; six quarts for each of the two rams; 15and three quarts for each of the fourteen lambs. 16There must also be a male goat sacrificed for a sin offering, in addition to the regular daily burnt sacrifice with its accompanying grain offerings and drink offerings.

17"On the second day of this seven-day festival you shall sacrifice twelve young bulls, two rams, and fourteen male yearling lambs—each without defect— 18accompanied by the usual grain offerings and drink offerings. 19Also, in addition to the regular daily burnt sacrifice, you are to sacrifice a male goat with its accompanying grain offering and drink offering for a sin offering.

20"On the third day of the festival, offer eleven young bulls, two rams, fourteen male yearling lambs—each without defect— 21and the usual grain offering and drink offering with each sacrifice. 22And in addition to the regular daily burnt sacrifices, sacrifice a male goat for a sin offering, with its accompanying grain offering and drink offering.

23"On the fourth day of the festival, you are to sacrifice ten young bulls, two rams, and fourteen male yearling lambs—each without defect— 24each with its accompanying grain offering and drink offering; 25also a male goat as a sin offering (along with the usual grain and drink offerings) in addition to the regular daily sacrifices.

26,27"On the fifth day of the festival, sacrifice nine young bulls, two rams, and fourteen male yearling lambs—each without defect—accompanied by the usual grain offerings and drink offerings; 28also sacrifice a male goat with the usual grain and drink offerings, as a special sin offering, in addition to the usual daily sacrifices.

29"On the sixth day of the festival, you must sacrifice eight young bulls, two rams, and fourteen male yearling lambs—each without defect— 30along with their usual grain and drink offerings. 31In addition to the usual daily sacrifices, sacrifice a male goat and the usual grain and drink offerings as a sin offering.

32"On the seventh day of the festival, sacrifice seven young bulls, two rams, and fourteen male yearling lambs—each without defect— 33each with its customary grain and drink offerings; 34also sacrifice an extra sin offering of one male goat, with the usual grain and drink offerings, in addition to the regular daily sacrifices.

35"On the eighth day summon the people to another solemn assembly; you must do no hard work that day. 36Sacrifice a burnt offering—they are very pleasant to the Lord—of one young bull, one ram, seven male yearling lambs—each without defect— 37and the customary grain and drink offerings. 38Sacrifice also one male goat with the usual grain and drink offerings for a sin offering, in addition to the regular daily sacrifices. 39These offerings are compulsory at the times of your annual feasts, and are in addition to sacrifices and offerings you present in connection with vows, or as free-will offerings, burnt sacrifices, grain offerings, drink offerings, or peace offerings."

40So Moses gave all of these instructions to the people of Israel.

LUKE 3:23–38

JESUS was about thirty years old when he began his public ministry.

Jesus was known as the son of Joseph.
Joseph's father was Heli;
Heli's father was Matthat;
Matthat's father was Levi;
Levi's father was Melchi;
Melchi's father was Jannai;
Jannai's father was Joseph;
Joseph's father was Mattathias;
Mattathias' father was Amos;
Amos' father was Nahum;
Nahum's father was Esli;
Esli's father was Naggai;
Naggai's father was Maath;
Maath's father was Mattathias;
Mattathias' father was Semein;
Semein's father was Josech;
Josech's father was Joda;
Joda's father was Joanan;
Joanan's father was Rhesa;
Rhesa's father was Zerubbabel;
Zerubbabel's father was Shealtiel;
Shealtiel's father was Neri;
Neri's father was Melchi;
Melchi's father was Addi;
Addi's father was Cosam;
Cosam's father was Elmadam;
Elmadam's father was Er;
Er's father was Joshua;
Joshua's father was Eliezer;
Eliezer's father was Jorim;
Jorim's father was Matthat;
Matthat's father was Levi;
Levi's father was Simeon;
Simeon's father was Judah;
Judah's father was Joseph;
Joseph's father was Jonam;
Jonam's father was Eliakim;
Eliakim's father was Melea;
Melea's father was Menna;
Menna's father was Mattatha;
Mattatha's father was Nathan;
Nathan's father was David;
David's father was Jesse;
Jesse's father was Obed;
Obed's father was Boaz;
Boaz' father was Salmon;
Salmon's father was Nahshon;
Nahshon's father was Amminadab;
Amminadab's father was Admin;
Admin's father was Arni;
Arni's father was Hezron;
Hezron's father was Perez;
Perez' father was Judah;
Judah's father was Jacob;
Jacob's father was Isaac;
Isaac's father was Abraham;
Abraham's father was Terah;
Terah's father was Nahor;
Nahor's father was Serug;
Serug's father was Reu;
Reu's father was Peleg;
Peleg's father was Eber;
Eber's father was Shelah;
Shelah's father was Cainan;
Cainan's father was Arphaxad;
Arphaxad's father was Shem;
Shem's father was Noah;
Noah's father was Lamech;
Lamech's father was Methuselah;
Methuselah's father was Enoch;
Enoch's father was Jared;
Jared's father was Mahalaleel;
Mahalaleel's father was Cainan;
Cainan's father was Enos;
Enos' father was Seth;
Seth's father was Adam;
Adam's father was God.

PSALM 62:1–12

I stand silently before the Lord, waiting for him to rescue me. For salvation comes from him alone. ²Yes, he alone is my Rock, my rescuer, defense and fortress. Why then should I be tense with fear when troubles come?

³,⁴But what is this? They pick on me at a time when my throne is tottering; they plot my death and use lies and deceit to try to force me from the throne. They are so friendly to my face while cursing in their hearts!

⁵But I stand silently before the Lord, waiting for him to rescue me. For salvation comes from him alone. ⁶Yes, he alone is my Rock, my rescuer, defense and fortress—why then should I be tense with fear when troubles come?

⁷My protection and success come from God alone. He is my refuge, a Rock where no enemy can reach me. ⁸O my people, trust him all the time. Pour out your longings before him, for he can help! ⁹The greatest of men, or the lowest—both alike are nothing in his sight. They weigh less than air on scales.

¹⁰⁻¹²Don't become rich by extortion and robbery; if your riches increase, don't be proud. God has said it many times, that power belongs to him; (and also, O Lord, steadfast love belongs to you). He rewards each one of us according to what our works deserve.

PROVERBS FOR TODAY/ 11:18–19

The evil man gets rich for the moment, but the good man's reward lasts forever. The good man finds life; the evil man, death.

MARCH 20

NUMBERS 30:1—31:54

Now Moses summoned the leaders of the tribes and told them, "The Lord has commanded that when anyone makes a promise to the Lord, either to do something or to quit doing something, that vow must not be broken: the person making the vow must do exactly as he has promised.

³"If a woman promises the Lord to do or not do something, and she is still a girl at home in her father's home, ⁴and her father hears that she has made a vow with penalties, but says nothing, then her vow shall stand. ⁵But if her father refuses to let her make the vow, or feels that the penalties she has agreed to are too harsh, then her promise will automatically become invalid. Her father must state his disagreement on the first day he hears about it; and then Jehovah will forgive her because her father would not let her do it.

⁶"If she takes a vow or makes a foolish pledge, and later marries, ⁷and her husband learns of her vow and says nothing on the day he hears of it, her vow shall stand. ⁸But if her husband refuses to accept her vow or foolish pledge, his disagreement makes it void, and Jehovah will forgive her.

⁹"But if the woman is a widow or is divorced, she must fulfill her vow.

¹⁰"If she is married and living in her husband's home when she makes the vow, ¹¹and her husband hears of it and does nothing, the vow shall stand; ¹²but if he refuses to allow it on the first day he hears of it, her vow is void and Jehovah will forgive her. ¹³So her husband may either confirm or nullify her vow, ¹⁴but if he says nothing for a day, then he has already agreed to it. ¹⁵If he waits more than a day and then refuses to permit the vow, whatever penalties to which she agreed shall come

upon him—he shall be responsible."

16These, then, are the commandments the Lord gave Moses concerning relationships between a man and his wife and between a father and his daughter who is living at home.

THEN the Lord said to Moses, "Take vengeance on the Midianites for leading you into idolatry, and then you must die."

3Moses said to the people, "Some of you must take arms to wage Jehovah's war against Midian. 4,5Conscript 1,000 men from each tribe." So this was done; and out of the many thousands of Israel, 12,000 armed men were sent to battle by Moses. 6Phinehas (son of Eleazar the priest) led them into battle, accompanied by the Ark, with trumpets blaring. 7And every man of Midian was killed. 8Among those killed were all five of the Midianite kings—Evi, Rekem, Zur, Hur, and Reba. Balaam, the son of Beor, was also killed.

9,10,11Then the Israeli army took as captives all the women and children, and seized the cattle and flocks and a lot of miscellaneous booty. All of the cities, towns, and villages of Midian were then burned. 12The captives and other war loot were brought to Moses and Eleazar the priest, and to the rest of the people of Israel who were camped on the plains of Moab beside the Jordan River, across from Jericho. 13Moses and Eleazar the priest and all the leaders of the people went out to meet the victorious army, 14but Moses was very angry with the army officers and battalion leaders.

15"Why have you let all the women live?" he demanded. 16"These are the very ones who followed Balaam's advice and caused the people of Israel to worship idols on Mount Peor, and they are the cause of the plague that destroyed us. 17Now kill all the boys and all the women who have had sexual intercourse. 18Only the little girls may live; you may keep them for yourselves. 19Now stay outside of the camp for seven days, all of you who have killed anyone or touched

a dead body. Then purify yourselves and your captives on the third and seventh days. 20Remember also to purify all your garments and everything made of leather, goat's hair, or wood."

21Then Eleazar the priest said to the men who were in the battle, "This is the commandment Jehovah has given Moses: 22'Anything that will stand heat—such as gold, silver, bronze, iron, tin, or lead— 23shall be passed through fire in order to be made ceremonially pure; it must then be further purified with the purification water. But anything that won't stand heat shall be purified by the water alone.' 24On the seventh day you must wash your clothes and be purified, and then you may come back into the camp."

25And the Lord said to Moses, 26"You and Eleazar the priest and the leaders of the tribes are to make a list of all the loot, including the people and animals; 27then divide it into two parts. Half of it is for the men who were in the battle, and the other half is to be given to the people of Israel. 28But first, the Lord gets a share of all the captives, oxen, donkeys, and flocks kept by the army. His share is one out of every five hundred. 29Give this share to Eleazar the priest to be presented to the Lord by the gesture of waving before the altar. 30Also levy a two percent tribute of all the captives, flocks, and cattle that are given to the people of Israel. Present this to the Levites in charge of the Tabernacle, for it is the Lord's portion."

31So Moses and Eleazar the priest did as the Lord commanded. 32–35The total booty (besides the jewelry, clothing, etc., which the soldiers kept for themselves) was 675,000 sheep; 72,000 oxen; 61,000 donkeys; and 32,000 young girls.

36–40So the half given to the army totaled:

337,500 sheep (of which 675 were given to the Lord);

36,000 oxen (of which 72 were given to the Lord);

30,500 donkeys (of which 61 were given to the Lord);

16,000 girls (of whom 32 went to the Levites).

41All of the Lord's portion was given to Eleazar the priest, as the Lord had directed Moses.

42-46The half of the booty assigned to the people of Israel—Moses had separated it from the half belonging to the warriors—amounted to:

337,500 sheep,
36,000 oxen,
30,500 donkeys, and
16,000 girls

47In accordance with the Lord's directions, Moses gave two percent of these to the Levites.

48,49Then the officers and battalion leaders came to Moses and said, "We have accounted for all the men who went out to battle, and not one of us is missing! 50So we have brought a special thank-offering to the Lord from our loot—gold jewelry, bracelets, anklets, rings, earrings, and necklaces. This is to make atonement for our souls before the Lord."

51,52Moses and Eleazar the priest received this special offering from the captains and battalion leaders and company commanders, and found its total value to be more than $300,000. 53(The soldiers had also kept personal loot for themselves.) 54The offering was taken into the Tabernacle and kept there before the Lord as a memorial of the people of Israel.

LUKE 4:1–30

THEN Jesus, full of the Holy Spirit, left the Jordan River, being urged by the Spirit out into the barren wastelands of Judea, where Satan tempted him for forty days. He ate nothing all that time, and was very hungry.

3Satan said, "If you are God's Son, tell this stone to become a loaf of bread."

4But Jesus replied, "It is written in the Scriptures, 'Other things in life are much more important than bread!' "

5Then Satan took him up and revealed to him all the kingdoms of the world in a moment of time; 6,7and the devil told him, "I will give you all these splendid kingdoms and their glory—for they are mine to give to anyone I wish—if you will only get down on your knees and worship me."

8Jesus replied, "We must worship God, and him alone. So it is written in the Scriptures."

9,10,11Then Satan took him to Jerusalem to a high roof of the Temple and said, "If you are the Son of God, jump off! For the Scriptures say that God will send his angels to guard you and to keep you from crashing to the pavement below!"

12Jesus replied, "The Scriptures also say, 'Do not put the Lord your God to a foolish test.' "

13When the devil had ended all the temptations, he left Jesus for a while and went away.

14Then Jesus returned to Galilee, full of the Holy Spirit's power. Soon he became well known throughout all that region 15for his sermons in the synagogues; everyone praised him.

16When he came to the village of Nazareth, his boyhood home, he went as usual to the synagogue on Saturday, and stood up to read the Scriptures. 17The book of Isaiah the prophet was handed to him, and he opened it to the place where it says:

18,19"The Spirit of the Lord is upon me; he has appointed me to preach Good News to the poor; he has sent me to heal the brokenhearted and to announce that captives shall be released and the blind shall see, that the downtrodden shall be freed from their oppressors, and that God is ready to give blessings to all who come to him."

20He closed the book and handed it back to the attendant and sat down, while everyone in the synagogue gazed at him intently. 21Then he added, "These Scriptures came true today!"

22All who were there spoke well of him and were amazed by the beautiful words that fell from his lips. "How can this be?" they asked. "Isn't this Joseph's son?"

23Then he said, "Probably you will quote me that proverb, 'Physician, heal yourself'—meaning, 'Why don't you do miracles here in your home town like those you did in Capernaum?' 24But I solemnly declare to you that no prophet is accepted in his own home town! 25,26For example, remember how Elijah the prophet used a miracle to help the widow of Zarephath—a foreigner from the land of Sidon. There were many Jewish widows needing help in those days of famine, for there had been no rain for three and one-half years, and hunger stalked the land; yet Elijah was not sent to them. 27Or think of the prophet Elisha, who healed Naaman, a Syrian, rather than the many Jewish lepers needing help."

28These remarks stung them to fury; 29and jumping up, they mobbed him and took him to the edge of the hill on which the city was built, to push him over the cliff. 30But he walked away through the crowd and left them.

PSALM 63:1–11

O God, my God! How I search for you! How I thirst for you in this parched and weary land where there is no water. How I long to find you! 2How I wish I could go into your sanctuary to see your strength and glory, 3for your love and kindness are better to me than life itself. How I praise you! 4I will bless you as long as I live, lifting up my hands to you in prayer. 5At last I shall be fully satisfied; I will praise you with great joy.

6I lie awake at night thinking of you— 7of how much you have helped me—and how I rejoice through the night beneath the protecting shadow of your wings. 8I follow close behind you, protected by your strong right arm. 9But those plotting to destroy me shall go down to the depths of hell. 10They are doomed to die by the sword, to become the food of jackals. 11But I will rejoice in God. All who trust in him exult, while liars shall be silenced.

PROVERBS FOR TODAY/ 11:20–21

The Lord hates the stubborn but delights in those who are good. You can be very sure the evil man will not go unpunished forever. And you can also be very sure God will rescue the children of the godly.

MARCH 21

NUMBERS 32:1—33:39

WHEN Israel arrived in the land of Jazar and Gilead, the tribes of Reuben and Gad (who had large flocks of sheep) noticed what wonderful sheep country it was. 2So they came to Moses and Eleazar the priest and the other tribal leaders and said, 3,4"The Lord has used Israel to destroy the population of this whole countryside—Ataroth, Dibon, Jazer, Nimrah, Heshbon, Elealeh, Sebam, Nebo, and

Beon. And it is all wonderful sheep country, ideal for our flocks. 5Please let us have this land as our portion instead of the land on the other side of the Jordan River."

6"You mean you want to sit here while your brothers go across and do all the fighting?" Moses demanded. 7"Are you trying to discourage the rest of the people from going across to the land that the Lord has given them? 8This is the same kind of thing your fathers did! I sent them from Kadesh-barnea to spy out the land, 9but when they finished their survey and returned from the valley of Eshcol, they discouraged the people from going on into the Promised Land. 10,11And the Lord's anger was hot against them, and he swore that of all those he had rescued from Egypt, no one over twenty years of age would ever see the land he promised Abraham, Isaac, and Jacob, for they had refused to do what he wanted them to.

12"The only exceptions were Caleb (son of Jephunneh the Kenizzite) and Joshua (son of Nun)—for they wholeheartedly followed the Lord and urged the people to go on into the Promised Land.

13"The Lord made us wander back and forth in the wilderness for forty years until all that evil generation died. 14But here you are, a brood of sinners doing exactly the same thing! Only there are more of you, so Jehovah's anger against Israel will be even fiercer this time. 15If you turn away from God like this, he will make the people stay even longer in the wilderness, and you will be responsible for destroying his people and bringing disaster to this entire nation!"

16"Not at all!" they explained. "We will build sheepfolds for our flocks and cities for our little ones, 17but we ourselves will go over armed, ahead of the rest of the people of Israel, until we have brought them safely to their inheritance. But first we will need to build walled cities here for our families, to keep them safe from attack by the local inhabitants. 18We will not settle down here until all the people of Israel have received their inheritance. 19We don't want land on the other side of the Jordan; we would rather have it on this side, on the east."

20Then Moses said, "All right, if you will do what you have said and arm yourselves for Jehovah's war, 21and keep your troops across the Jordan until the Lord has driven out his enemies, 22then, when the land is finally subdued before the Lord, you may return. Then you will have discharged your duty to the Lord and to the rest of the people of Israel. And the land on the eastern side shall be your possession from the Lord. 23But if you don't do as you have said, then you will have sinned against the Lord, and you may be sure that your sin will catch up with you. 24Go ahead and build cities for your families and sheepfolds for your sheep, and do all you have said."

25"We will follow your instructions exactly," the people of Gad and Reuben replied. 26"Our children, wives, flocks, and cattle shall stay here in the cities of Gilead. 27But all of us who are conscripted will go over to battle for the Lord, just as you have said."

28So Moses gave his approval by saying to Eleazar, Joshua, and the tribal leaders of Israel, 29"If all the men of the tribes of Gad and Reuben who are conscripted for the Lord's battles go with you over Jordan, then, when the land is conquered, you must give them the land of Gilead; 30but if they refuse, then they must accept land among the rest of you in the land of Canaan."

31The tribes of Gad and Reuben said again, "As the Lord has commanded, so we will do— 32we will follow the Lord fully armed into Canaan, but our own land shall be here on this side of the Jordan."

33So Moses assigned the territory of King Sihon of the Amorites, and of King Og of Bashan—all the land and cities— to the tribes of Gad, Reuben, and the half-tribe of Manasseh (son of Joseph).

34,35,36The people of Gad built these cities:

Dibon, Ataroth, Aroer, Atroth-shophan, Jazer, Jogbehah, Beth-nimrah, Beth-haran.

They were all fortified cities with sheepfolds.

37,38The children of Reuben built the following cities:

Heshbon, Elealeh, Kiriathaim, Nebo, Baal-meon, Sibmah.

(The Israelites later changed the names of some of these cities they had conquered and rebuilt.)

39Then the clan of Machir of the tribe of Manasseh went to Gilead and conquered it, and drove out the Amorites who were living there. 40So Moses gave Gilead to the Machirites, and they lived there. 41The men of Jair, another clan of the tribe of Manasseh, occupied many of the towns in Gilead, and changed the name of their area to Havroth-jair. 42Meanwhile, a man named Nobah led an army to Kenath and its surrounding villages, and occupied them, and he called the area Nobah, after his own name.

THIS is the itinerary of the nation of Israel from the time Moses and Aaron led them out of Egypt. 2Moses had written down their movements as the Lord had instructed him. 3,4They left the city of Rameses, Egypt, on the first day of April, the day after the night of the Passover. They left proudly, hurried along by the Egyptians who were burying all their eldest sons, killed by the Lord the night before. The Lord had certainly defeated all the gods of Egypt that night!

5,6After leaving Rameses, they stayed in Succoth, Etham (at the edge of the wilderness), and 7Pihahiroth (near Baal-zephon, where they camped at the foot of Mount Migdol). 8From there they went through the middle of the Red Sea and on for three days into the Etham wilderness, camping at Marah.

9Leaving Marah, they came to Elim, where there are twelve springs of water and seventy palm trees; they stayed there for quite a long time.

10Leaving Elim, they camped beside the Red Sea, 11and then in the wilderness of Sihn.

12Next was Dophkah, 13and then Alush; 14then on to Rephidim (where there was no water for the people to drink).

15-37From Rephidim they went to the wilderness of Sinai; from the wilderness of Sinai to Kibroth-hattaavah;

From Kibroth-hattaavah to Hazeroth;
From Hazeroth to Rithmah;
From Rithmah to Rimmon-parez;
From Rimmon-parez to Libnah;
From Libnah to Rissah;
From Rissah to Kehelathah;
From Kehelathah to Mount Shepher;
From Mount Shepher to Haradah;
From Haradah to Makheloth;
From Makheloth to Tahath;
From Tahath to Terah;
From Terah to Mithkah;
From Mithkah to Hashmonah;
From Hashmonah to Moseroth;
From Moseroth to Bene-jaakan;
From Bene-jaakan to Hor-haggidgad;
From Hor-haggidgad to Jotbathah;
From Jotbathah to Abronah;
From Abronah to Ezion-geber;
From Ezion-geber to Kadesh (in the wilderness of Zin);
From Kadesh to Mount Hor (at the edge of the land of Edom).

38,39While they were at the foot of Mount Hor, Aaron the priest was directed by the Lord to go up into the mountain, and there he died. This occurred during the fortieth year after the people of Israel had left Egypt. The date of his death was July 15, when he was 123 years old.

LUKE 4:31—5:11

THEN he returned to Capernaum, a city in Galilee, and preached there in the synagogue every Saturday. 32Here, too, the people were amazed at the things he said. For he spoke as one who knew the truth, instead of merely quoting the opinions of others as his authority.

33Once as he was teaching in the synagogue, a man possessed by a demon began shouting at Jesus, 34"Go away! We want nothing to do with you, Jesus from Nazareth. You have come to destroy us. I know who you are—the Holy Son of God."

35Jesus cut him short. "Be silent!" he told the demon. "Come out!" The demon threw the man to the floor as the crowd watched, and then left him without hurting him further.

36Amazed, the people asked, "What is in this man's words that even demons obey him?" 37The story of what he had done spread like wildfire throughout the whole region.

38After leaving the synagogue that day, he went to Simon's home where he found Simon's mother-in-law very sick with a high fever. "Please heal her," everyone begged.

39Standing at her bedside he spoke to the fever, rebuking it, and immediately her temperature returned to normal and she got up and prepared a meal for them!

40As the sun went down that evening, all the villagers who had any sick people in their homes, no matter what their diseases were, brought them to Jesus; and the touch of his hands healed every one! 41Some were possessed by demons; and the demons came out at his command, shouting, "You are the Son of God." But because they knew he was the Christ, he stopped them and told them to be silent.

42Early the next morning he went out into the desert. The crowds searched everywhere for him and when they finally found him they begged him not to leave them, but to stay at Capernaum. 43But he replied, "I must preach the Good News of the Kingdom of God in other places too, for that is why I was sent." 44So he continued to travel around preaching in synagogues throughout Judea.

ONE day as he was preaching on the shore of Lake Gennesaret, great crowds pressed in on him to listen to the Word of God. 2He noticed two empty boats standing at the water's edge while the fishermen washed their nets. 3Stepping into one of the boats, Jesus asked Simon, its owner, to push out a little into the water, so that he could sit in the boat and speak to the crowds from there.

4When he had finished speaking, he said to Simon, "Now go out where it is deeper and let down your nets and you will catch a lot of fish!"

5"Sir," Simon replied, "we worked hard all last night and didn't catch a thing. But if you say so, we'll try again."

6And this time their nets were so full that they began to tear! 7A shout for help brought their partners in the other boat and soon both boats were filled with fish and on the verge of sinking.

8When Simon Peter realized what had happened, he fell to his knees before Jesus and said, "Oh, sir, please leave us— I'm too much of a sinner for you to have around." 9For he was awestruck by the size of their catch, as were the others with him, 10and his partners too—James and John, the sons of Zebedee. Jesus replied, "Don't be afraid! From now on you'll be fishing for the souls of men!"

11And as soon as they landed, they left everything and went with him.

PSALM 64:1–10

LORD, listen to my complaint: Oh, preserve my life from the conspiracy of these wicked men, these gangs of criminals. 3They cut me down with sharpened tongues; they aim their bitter words like arrows straight at my heart. 4They shoot from ambush at the innocent. Suddenly the deed is done, yet they are not afraid. 5They encourage each other to do evil. They meet in secret to set their traps. "He will never notice them here," they say. 6They keep a sharp lookout for opportunities of crime. They spend long hours with all their endless evil thoughts and plans.

7But God himself will shoot them down. Suddenly his arrow will pierce them. 8They will stagger backward, destroyed by those they spoke against. All who see it happening will scoff at them. 9Then everyone shall stand in awe and confess the greatness of the miracles of God; at last they will realize what amazing things he does. 10And the godly shall rejoice in the Lord, and trust and praise him.

A beautiful woman lacking discretion and modesty is like a fine gold ring in a pig's snout.

MARCH 22

NUMBERS 33:40—35:34

IT was then that the Canaanite king of Arad, who lived in the Negeb, in the land of Canaan, heard that the people of Israel were approaching his land. 41After dealing with him, the Israelis journeyed from Mount Hor and camped in Zalmonah, 42then at Punon, 43then at Oboth, 44then Iyeabarim (at the border of Moab). 45From there they went to Dibon-gad, 46and then to Almon-diblathaim, 47and on into the mountains of Abarim, near Mount Nebo, 48and finally to the plains of Moab beside the river Jordan, opposite Jericho. 49While in that area they camped at various places along the Jordan River, from Bethjeshimoth as far as Abel-shittim, on the plains of Moab.

50,51It was while they were camped there that the Lord told Moses to tell the people of Israel, "When you pass across the Jordan River into the land of Canaan, 52you must drive out all the people living there and destroy all their idols—their carved stones, molten images, and the open-air sanctuaries in the hills where they worship their idols. 53I have given the land to you; take it and live there. 54You will be given land in proportion to the size of your tribes. The larger sections of land will be divided by lot among the larger tribes, and the smaller sections will be allotted to the smaller tribes. 55But if you refuse to drive out the people living there, those who remain will be as cinders in your eyes and thorns in your sides. 56And I will destroy you as I had planned for you to destroy them."

THE Lord told Moses to tell the people of Israel, "When you come into the land of Canaan (I am giving you the entire land as your homeland), 3the southern portion of the country will be the wilderness of Zin, along the edge of Edom. The southern boundary will begin at the Dead Sea, 4and will continue south past Scorpion Pass in the direction of Zin. Its southernmost point will be Kadesh-barnea, from which it will go to Hazarad-dar, and on to Azmon. 5From Azmon the boundary will follow the Brook of Egypt down to the Mediterranean Sea.

6"Your western boundary will be the coastline of the Mediterranean Sea.

7,8,9"Your northern border will begin at the Mediterranean Sea and will proceed eastward to Mount Hor, then to Lebo-Hamath, and on through Zedad and Ziphron to Hazar-enan.

10,11"The eastern border will be from Hazar-enan south to Shepham, then on to Riblah at the east side of Ain. From there it will make a large half-circle, first going south and then westward until it touches the southernmost tip of the Sea of Galilee, 12and then along the Jordan River, ending at the Dead Sea."

13"This is the territory you are to apportion among yourselves by lot," Moses said. "It is to be divided up among the nine and one-half tribes, 14,15for the tribes of Reuben and Gad and the half-tribe of Manasseh have already been assigned land on the east side of the Jordan, opposite Jericho."

16-28And the Lord said to Moses, "These are the names of the men I have appointed to handle the dividing up of the land: Eleazar the priest, Joshua (son of Nun), and one leader from each tribe, as listed below:

Tribe	Leader
Judah	Caleb (son of Jephunneh)
Simeon	Shemuel (son of Ammihud)
Benjamin	Elidad (son of Chislon)
Dan	Bukki (son of Jogli)
Manasseh	Hanniel (son of Ephod)
Ephraim	Kemuel (son of Shiphtan)
Zebulun	Elizaphan (son of Parnach)
Issachar	Paltiel (son of Azzan)
Asher	Ahihud (son of Shelomi)
Naphtali	Pedahel (son of Ammihud)

29These are the names of the men I have appointed to oversee the dividing of the land among the tribes."

WHILE Israel was camped beside the Jordan on the plains of Moab, opposite Jericho, the Lord said to Moses, 2"Instruct the people of Israel to give to the Levites as their inheritance certain cities and surrounding pasture lands. 3These cities are for their homes, and the surrounding lands for their cattle, flocks, and other livestock. 4,5Their gardens and vineyards shall extend 1500 feet out from the city walls in each direction, with an additional 1500 feet beyond that for pastureland.

6"You shall give the Levites the six Cities of Refuge where a person who has accidentally killed someone can run and be safe, and forty-two other cities besides. 7In all, there shall be forty-eight cities with the surrounding pastureland given to the Levites. 8These cities shall be in various parts of the nation; the larger tribes with many cities will give several to the Levites, while the smaller tribes will give fewer."

9,10And the Lord said to Moses, "Tell the people that when they arrive in the land, 11Cities of Refuge shall be designated for anyone to flee into if he has killed someone accidentally. 12These Cities will be places of protection from the dead man's relatives who want to avenge his death; for the slayer must not be killed unless a fair trial establishes his guilt.

13,14Three of these six Cities of Refuge are to be located in the land of Canaan, and three on the east side of the Jordan River. 15These are not only for the protection of Israelites, but also for foreigners and travelers.

16"But if someone is struck and killed by a piece of iron, it must be presumed to be murder, and the murderer must be executed. 17Or if the slain man was struck down with a large stone, it is murder, and the murderer shall die. 18The same is true if he is killed with a wooden weapon. 19The avenger of his death shall personally kill the murderer when he meets him. 20So, if anyone kills another out of hatred by throwing something at him, or ambushing him, 21or angrily striking him with his fist so that he dies, he is a murderer; and the murderer shall be executed by the avenger.

22,23"But if it is an accident—a case in which something is thrown unintentionally, or in which a stone is thrown without anger, without realizing it will hit anyone, and without wanting to harm an enemy—yet the man dies, 24then the people shall judge whether or not it was an accident, and whether or not to hand the killer over to the avenger of the dead man. 25If it is decided that it was accidental, then the people shall save the killer from the avenger; the killer shall be permitted to stay in the City of Refuge; and he must live there until the death of the High Priest.

26"If the slayer leaves the City, 27and the avenger finds him outside and kills him, it is not murder, 28for the man should have stayed inside the City until the death of the High Priest. But after the death of the High Priest, the man may return to his own land and home. 29These are permanent laws for all Israel from generation to generation.

30"All murderers must be executed, but only if there is more than one witness; no man shall die with only one person testifying against him. 31Whenever anyone is judged guilty of murder, he must die—no ransom may be accepted for him. 32Nor may a payment be accepted from a refugee in a City of Refuge, permitting him to return to his home before the death of the High Priest. [33]In this way the land will not be polluted, for murder pollutes the land, and no atonement can be made for murder except by the execution of the murderer. [34]You shall not defile the land where you are going to live, for I, Jehovah, will be living there."

LUKE 5:12–28

ONE day in a certain village he was visiting, there was a man with an advanced case of leprosy. When he saw Jesus he fell to the ground before him, face downward in the dust, begging to be healed.

"Sir," he said, "if you only will, you can clear me of every trace of my disease."

[13]Jesus reached out and touched the man and said, "Of course I will. Be healed." And the leprosy left him instantly! [14]Then Jesus instructed him to go at once without telling anyone what had happened and be examined by the Jewish priest. "Offer the sacrifice Moses' law requires for lepers who are healed," he said. "This will prove to everyone that you are well." [15]Now the report of his power spread even faster and vast crowds came to hear him preach and to be healed of their diseases. [16]But he often withdrew to the wilderness for prayer.

[17]One day while he was teaching, some Jewish religious leaders and teachers of the Law were sitting nearby. (It seemed that these men showed up from every village in all Galilee and Judea, as well as from Jerusalem.) And the Lord's healing power was upon him.

[18,19]Then—look! Some men came carrying a paralyzed man on a sleeping mat. They tried to push through the crowd to Jesus but couldn't reach him. So they went up on the roof above him, took off some tiles and lowered the sick man down into the crowd, still on his sleeping mat, right in front of Jesus.

[20]Seeing their faith, Jesus said to the man, "My friend, your sins are forgiven!"

[21]"Who does this fellow think he is?" the Pharisees and teachers of the Law exclaimed among themselves. "This is blasphemy! Who but God can forgive sins?"

[22]Jesus knew what they were thinking, and he replied, "Why is it blasphemy? [23,24]I, the Messiah, have the authority on earth to forgive sins. But talk is cheap—anybody could say that. So I'll prove it to you by healing this man." Then, turning to the paralyzed man, he commanded, "Pick up your stretcher and go on home, for you are healed!"

[25]And immediately, as everyone watched, the man jumped to his feet, picked up his mat and went home praising God! [26]Everyone present was gripped with awe and fear. And they praised God, remarking over and over again, "We have seen strange things today."

[27]Later on as Jesus left the town he saw a tax collector—with the usual reputation for cheating—sitting at a tax collection booth. The man's name was Levi. Jesus said to him, "Come and be one of my disciples!" [28]So Levi left everything, sprang up and went with him.

PSALM 65:1–13

O God in Zion, we wait before you in silent praise, and thus fulfill our vow. And because you answer prayer, all mankind will come to you with their requests. [3]Though sins fill our hearts, you forgive them all. [4]How greatly to be envied are those you have chosen to come and live with you within the holy tabernacle courts! What joys await us among all the good things there. [5]With dread deeds and awesome power you will defend us from our enemies, O God who saves us. You are the only hope of all mankind throughout the world and far away upon the sea.

[6]He formed the mountains by his mighty strength. [7]He quiets the raging oceans and all the world's clamor. [8]In the farthest corners of the earth the

glorious acts of God shall startle everyone. The dawn and sunset shout for joy! 9He waters the earth to make it fertile. The rivers of God will not run dry! He prepares the earth for his people and sends them rich harvests of grain. 10He waters the furrows with abundant rain. Showers soften the earth, melting the clods and causing seeds to sprout across the land. 11,12Then he crowns it all with green, lush pastures in the wilderness; hillsides blossom with joy. 13The pastures are filled with flocks of sheep, and the valleys are carpeted with grain. All the world shouts with joy, and sings.

PROVERBS FOR TODAY/ 11:23

The good man can look forward to happiness, while the wicked can expect only wrath.

MARCH 23

NUMBERS 36:1—DEUTERONOMY 1:46

THEN the heads of the sub-clan of Gilead (of the clan of Machir, of the tribe of Manasseh, one of the sons of Joseph) came to Moses and the leaders of Israel with a petition: "The Lord instructed you to divide the land by lot among the people of Israel," they reminded Moses, "and to give the inheritance of our brother Zelophehad to his daughters. 3But if they marry into another tribe, their land will go with them to the tribe into which they marry. In this way the total area of our tribe will be reduced, 4and will not be returned at the Year of Jubilee."

5Then Moses replied publicly, giving them these instructions from the Lord: "The men of the tribe of Joseph have a proper complaint. 6This is what the Lord has further commanded concerning the daughters of Zelophehad: 'Let them be married to anyone they like, so long as it is within their own tribe. 7In this way none of the land of the tribe will shift to any other tribe, for the inheritance of every tribe is to remain permanently as it was first allotted. 8The girls throughout the tribes of Israel who are heiresses must marry within their own tribe, so that their land won't leave the tribe. 9In this way no inheritance shall move from one tribe to another.' "

10The daughters of Zelophehad did as the Lord commanded Moses. 11,12These girls, Mahlah, Tirzah, Hoglah, Milcah, and Noah, were married to men in their own tribe of Manasseh (son of Joseph); so their inheritance remained in their tribe.

13These are the commandments and ordinances which the Lord gave to the people of Israel through Moses, while they were camped on the plains of Moab beside the Jordan River, across from Jericho.

THIS book records Moses' address to the people of Israel when they were camped in the valley of the Arabah in the wilderness of Moab, east of the Jordan River. (Cities in the area included Suph, Paran, Tophel, Laban, Hazeroth, and Dizahab.) The speech was given on February 15, forty years after the people of Israel left Mount Horeb—though it takes only eleven days to travel by foot from Mount Horeb to Kadesh-barnea, going by way of Mount Seir! At the time of this address, King Sihon of the Amorites had already been defeated at Heshbon, and King Og of Bashan had been defeated at Ashtaroth, near Edre-i. Here, then, is Moses' address to Israel, stating all the laws God had commanded him to pass on to them:

6"It was forty years ago, at Mount Horeb, that Jehovah our God told us, 'You have stayed here long enough. 7Now go and occupy the hill country of the Amorites, the valley of the Arabah, and the Negeb, and all the land of Canaan and Lebanon—the entire area from the shores of the Mediterranean Sea to the Euphrates River. 8I am giving all of it to you! Go in and possess it, for it is the land the Lord promised to your ancestors Abraham, Isaac, and Jacob, and all of their descendants.'

9"At that time I told the people, 'I need help! You are a great burden for me to carry all by myself, 10for the Lord has multiplied you to become as many as the stars! 11And may he multiply you a thousand times more, and bless you as he promised, 12but what can one man do to settle all your quarrels and problems? 13So choose some men from each tribe who are wise, experienced, and understanding, and I will appoint them as your leaders.'

14"They agreed to this; 15I took the men they selected, some from every tribe, and appointed them as administrative assistants in charge of thousands, hundreds, fifties, and tens to decide their quarrels and assist them in every way. 16I instructed them to be perfectly fair at all times, even to foreigners. 17'When giving your decisions,' I told them, 'never favor a man because he is rich; be fair to great and small alike. Don't fear their displeasure, for you are judging in the place of God. Bring me any cases too difficult for you, and I will handle them.' 18And I gave them other instructions at that time, also.

19,20,21"Then we left Mount Horeb and traveled through the great and terrible desert, finally arriving among the Amorite hills to which the Lord our God had directed us. We were then at Kadesh-barnea [on the border of the Promised Land] and I said to the people, 'The Lord God has given us this land. Go and possess it as he told us to. Don't be afraid! Don't even doubt!'

22"But they replied, 'First let's send out spies to discover the best route of entry, and to decide which cities we should capture first.'

23"This seemed like a good idea, so I chose twelve spies, one from each tribe. 24,25They crossed into the hills and came to the Valley of Eshcol, and returned with samples of the local fruit. One look was enough to convince us that it was indeed a good land the Lord our God had given us. 26But the people refused to go in, and rebelled against the Lord's command.

27"They murmured and complained in their tents and said, 'The Lord must hate us, bringing us here from Egypt to be slaughtered by these Amorites. 28What are we getting into? Our brothers who spied out the land have frightened us with their report. They say that the people of the land are tall and powerful, and that the walls of their cities rise high into the sky! They have even seen giants there—the descendants of the Anakim!'

29"But I said to them, 'Don't be afraid! 30The Lord God is your leader, and he will fight for you with his mighty miracles, just as you saw him do in Egypt. 31And you know how he has cared for you again and again here in the wilderness, just as a father cares for his child!' 32But nothing I said did any good.

"They refused to believe the Lord our God 33who had led them all the way, and had selected the best places for them to camp, and had guided them by a pillar of fire at night and a pillar of cloud during the day.

34,35"Well, the Lord heard their complaining and was very angry. He vowed that not one person in that entire generation would live to see the good land he had promised their fathers, 36except Caleb (the son of Jephunneh), who, because he had wholly followed the Lord, would receive as his personal inheritance some of the land he had walked over.

37"And the Lord was even angry with

me because of them and said to me, 'You shall not enter the Promised Land! 38Instead, your assistant, Joshua (the son of Nun), shall lead the people. Encourage him as he prepares to take over the leadership. 39I will give the land to the children they said would die in the wilderness. 40But as for you of the older generation, turn around now and go on back across the desert toward the Red Sea.'

41"Then they confessed, 'We have sinned! We will go into the land and fight for it as the Lord our God has told us to.' So they strapped on their weapons and thought it would be easy to conquer the whole area.

42"But the Lord said to me, 'Tell them not to do it, for I will not go with them; they will be struck down before their enemies.'

43"I told them, but they wouldn't listen. Instead, they rebelled again against the Lord's commandment and went on up into the hill country to fight. 44But the Amorites who lived there came out against them, and chased them like bees and killed them from Seir to Hormah. 45Then they returned and wept before the Lord, but he wouldn't listen. 46So they stayed there at Kadesh for a long time.

LUKE 5:29—6:11

SOON Levi held a reception in his home with Jesus as the guest of honor. Many of Levi's fellow tax collectors and other guests were there.

30But the Pharisees and teachers of the Law complained bitterly to Jesus' disciples about his eating with such notorious sinners.

31Jesus answered them, "It is the sick who need a doctor, not those in good health. 32My purpose is to invite sinners to turn from their sins, not to spend my time with those who think themselves already good enough."

33Their next complaint was that Jesus' disciples were feasting instead of fasting. "John the Baptist's disciples are con-

stantly going without food, and praying," they declared, "and so do the disciples of the Pharisees. Why are yours wining and dining?"

34Jesus asked, "Do happy men fast? Do wedding guests go hungry while celebrating with the groom? 35But the time will come when the bridegroom will be killed; then they won't want to eat."

36Then Jesus used this illustration: "No one tears off a piece of a new garment to make a patch for an old one. Not only will the new garment be ruined, but the old garment will look worse with a new patch on it! 37And no one puts new wine into old wineskins, for the new wine bursts the old skins, ruining the skins and spilling the wine. 38New wine must be put into new wineskins. 39But no one after drinking the old wine seems to want the fresh and the new. 'The old ways are best,' they say."

ONE Sabbath as Jesus and his disciples were walking through some grainfields, they were breaking off the heads of wheat, rubbing off the husks in their hands and eating the grains.

2But some Pharisees said, "That's illegal! Your disciples are harvesting grain, and it's against the Jewish law to work on the Sabbath."

3Jesus replied, "Don't you read the Scriptures? Haven't you ever read what King David did when he and his men were hungry? 4He went into the Temple and took the shewbread, the special bread that was placed before the Lord, and ate it—illegal as this was—and shared it with others." 5And Jesus added, "I am master even of the Sabbath."

6On another Sabbath he was in the synagogue teaching, and a man was present whose right hand was deformed. 7The teachers of the Law and the Pharisees watched closely to see whether he would heal the man that day, since it was the Sabbath. For they were eager to find some charge to bring against him.

8How well he knew their thoughts! But he said to the man with the deformed hand, "Come and stand here where everyone can see." So he did.

9Then Jesus said to the Pharisees and teachers of the Law, "I have a question for you. Is it right to do good on the Sabbath day, or to do harm? To save life, or to destroy it?"

10He looked around at them one by one and then said to the man, "Reach out your hand." And as he did, it became completely normal again. 11At this, the enemies of Jesus were wild with rage, and began to plot his murder.

PSALM 66:1–20

SING to the Lord, all the earth! 2Sing of his glorious name! Tell the world how wonderful he is. 3How awe-inspiring are your deeds, O God! How great your power! No wonder your enemies surrender! 4All the earth shall worship you and sing of your glories. 5Come, see the glorious things God has done. What marvelous miracles happen to his people! 6He made a dry road through the sea for them. They went across on foot. What excitement and joy there was that day!

7Because of his great power he rules forever. He watches every movement of the nations. O rebel lands, he will deflate your pride.

8Let everyone bless God and sing his praises, 9for he holds our lives in his hands. And he holds our feet to the path. 10You have purified us with fire, O Lord, like silver in a crucible. 11You captured us in your net and laid great burdens on our backs. 12You sent troops to ride across our broken bodies. We went through fire and flood. But in the end, you brought us into wealth and great abundance.

13Now I have come to your Temple with burnt offerings to pay my vows. 14For when I was in trouble I promised you many offerings. 15That is why I am bringing you these fat male goats, rams and calves. The smoke of their sacrifice shall rise before you.

16Come and hear, all of you who reverence the Lord, and I will tell you what he did for me: 17For I cried to him for help, with praises ready on my tongue. 18He would not have listened if I had not confessed my sins. 19But he listened! He heard my prayer! He paid attention to it!

20Blessed be God who didn't turn away when I was praying, and didn't refuse me his kindness and love.

PROVERBS FOR TODAY/ 11:24–26

It is possible to give away and become richer! It is also possible to hold on too tightly and lose everything. Yes, the liberal man shall be rich! By watering others, he waters himself. People curse the man who holds his grain for higher prices, but they bless the man who sells it to them in their time of need.

MARCH 24

DEUTERONOMY 2:1—3:29

THEN we turned back across the wilderness toward the Red Sea, for so the Lord had instructed me. For many years we wandered around in the area of Mount Seir. 2Then at last the Lord said,

3" 'You have stayed here long enough. Turn northward. 4Inform the people that they will be passing through the country belonging to their brothers the Edomites, the descendants of Esau who live in Seir; the Edomites will be nervous, so be careful. 5Don't start a fight! For I have given them all the Mount Seir hill country as their permanent possession, and I will not give you even a tiny piece of their land. 6Pay them for whatever food or water you use. 7The Lord your God has watched over you and blessed you every step of the way for all these forty years as you have wandered around in this great wilderness; and you have lacked nothing in all that time.'

8"So we passed through Edom where our brothers lived, crossing the Arabah Road that goes south to Elath and Ezi-on-geber, and traveling northward toward the Moab desert.

9"Then the Lord warned us, 'Don't attack the Moabites either, for I will not give you any of their land; I have given it to the descendants of Lot.'

10"(The Emim used to live in that area, a very large tribe, tall as the giants of Anakim; 11both the Emim and the Anakim are often referred to as the Rephaim, but the Moabites call them Emim. 12In earlier days the Horites lived in Seir, but they were driven out and displaced by the Edomites, the descendants of Esau, just as Israel would displace the peoples of Canaan, whose land had been assigned to Israel by the Lord.)

13" 'Now cross Zered Brook,' the Lord said; and we did.

14,15"So it took us thirty-eight years to finally get across Zered Brook from Kadesh! For the Lord had decreed that this could not happen until all the men, who thirty-eight years earlier were old enough to bear arms, had died. Yes, the hand of the Lord was against them until finally all were dead.

16,17"Then at last the Lord said to me, 18" 'Today Israel shall cross the borders of Moab at Ar, 19into the land of the Ammonites. But do not attack them, for I will not give you any of their land. I have given it to the descendants of Lot.'

20"(That area, too, used to be inhabited by the Rephaim, called 'Zamzummim' by the Ammonites. 21They were a large and powerful tribe, as tall as the Anakim; but Jehovah destroyed them as the Ammonites came in, and the Ammonites lived

there in their place. 22The Lord had similarly helped the descendants of Esau at Mount Seir, for he destroyed the Horites who were living there before them. 23Another similar situation occurred when the people of Caphtor invaded and destroyed the tribe of Avvim living in villages scattered across the countryside as far away as Gaza.)

24"Then the Lord said, 'Cross the Arnon River into the land of King Sihon the Amorite, king of Heshbon. War against him and begin to take possession of his land. 25Beginning today I will make people throughout the whole earth tremble with fear because of you, and dread your arrival.'

26"Then from the wilderness of Kedemoth I sent ambassadors to King Sihon of Heshbon with a proposal of peace. 27'Let us pass through your land,' we said. 'We will stay on the main road and won't turn off into the fields on either side. 28We will not steal food as we go, but will purchase every bite we eat and everything we drink; all we want is permission to pass through. 29The Edomites at Seir allowed us to go through their country, and so did the Moabites, whose capital is at Ar. We are on our way across the Jordan into the land the Lord our God has given us.'

30"But King Sihon refused because Jehovah your God made him obstinate, so that he could destroy Sihon by the hands of Israel, as has now been done.

31"Then the Lord said to me, 'I have begun to give you the land of King Sihon; when you possess it, it shall belong to Israel forever.'

32"King Sihon then declared war on us and mobilized his forces at Jahaz. 33,34But the Lord our God crushed him, and we conquered all his cities, and utterly destroyed everything, including the women and babies. We left nothing alive 35,36except the cattle, which we took as our reward, along with the booty gained from ransacking the cities we had taken. We conquered everything from Aroer to Gilead—from the edge of the Arnon River valley, and including all the cities in the valley. Not one city was too strong for us, for the Lord our God gave all of them to us. 37However, we stayed away from the people of Ammon and from the Jabbok River and the hill country cities, the places Jehovah our God had forbidden us to enter.

"NEXT we turned toward King Og's land of Bashan. He immediately mobilized his army and attacked us at Edre-i. But the Lord told me not to be afraid of him. 'All his people and his land are yours,' the Lord told me. 'You will do to him as you did to King Sihon of the Amorites, at Heshbon.' 3So the Lord helped us fight against King Og and his people, and we killed them all. 4We conquered all sixty of his cities, the entire Argob region of Bashan. 5These were well-fortified cities with high walls and barred gates. Of course we also took all of the unwalled towns. 6We utterly destroyed the kingdom of Bashan just as we had destroyed King Sihon's kingdom at Heshbon, killing the entire population—men, women, and children alike. 7But we kept the cattle and loot for ourselves.

8"We now possessed all the land of the two kings of the Amorites east of the Jordan River—all the land from the valley of the Arnon to Mount Hermon. 9(The Sidonians called Mount Hermon 'Sirion,' while the Amorites called it 'Senir.') 10We had now conquered all the cities on the plateau, and all of Gilead and Bashan as far as the cities of Salecah and Edre-i.

11"Incidentally, King Og of Bashan was the last of the giant Rephaim. His iron bedstead is kept in a museum at Rabbah, one of the cities of the Ammonites, and measures thirteen and a half feet long by six feet wide.

12"At that time I gave the conquered land to the tribes of Reuben, Gad, and the half-tribe of Manasseh. To the tribes of Reuben and Gad I gave the area beginning at Aroer on the Arnon River, plus half of Mount Gilead, including its cities. 13The half-tribe of Manasseh received the remainder of Gilead and all of the former

kingdom of King Og, the Argob region. (Bashan is sometimes called 'The Land of the Rephaim.') 14The clan of Jair, of the tribe of Manasseh, took over the whole Argob region (Bashan) to the borders of the Geshurites and Ma-acathites. They renamed their country after themselves, calling it Havvoth-jair (meaning 'Jair's Villages') as it is still known today. 15Then I gave Gilead to the clan of Machir. 16The tribes of Reuben and Gad received the area extending from the Jabbok River in Gilead (which was the Ammonite frontier) to the middle of the valley of the Arnon River. 17They also received the Arabah (or, wasteland), bounded by the Jordan River on the west, from Chinnereth to Mount Pisgah and the Dead Sea (also called the Sea of the Arabah).

18"At that time I reminded the tribes of Reuben and Gad and the half-tribe of Manasseh, that although the Lord had given them the land, they could not begin settling down until their armed men led the other tribes across the Jordan to the land the Lord was giving them.

19" 'But your wives and children,' I told them, 'may live here in the cities the Lord has given you, caring for your many cattle 20until you return after the Lord has given victory to the other tribes, too. When they conquer the land the Lord your God has given them across the Jordan River, then you may return here to your own land.'

21"Then I said to Joshua, 'You have seen what the Lord your God has done to those two kings. You will do the same to all the kingdoms on the other side of the Jordan. 22Don't be afraid of the nations there, for the Lord your God will fight for you.'

23,24,25"At that time I made this plea to God: 'O Lord God, please let me cross over into the Promised Land—the good land beyond the Jordan River with its rolling hills—and Lebanon. I want to see the result of all the greatness and power you have been showing us; for what God in all of heaven or earth can do what you have done for us?'

26"But the Lord was angry with me because of you, and would not let me cross over. 'Speak of it no more,' he ordered, 27'but go to the top of Mount Pisgah where you can look out in every direction, and there you will see the land in the distance. But you shall not cross the Jordan River. 28Commission Joshua to replace you, and then encourage him, for he shall lead the people across to conquer the land you will see from the mountaintop.'

29"So we remained in the valley near Beth-peor.

LUKE 6:12–38

ONE day soon afterwards he went out into the mountains to pray, and prayed all night. 13At daybreak he called together his followers and chose twelve of them to be the inner circle of his disciples. (They were appointed as his "apostles," or "missionaries.") 14,15,16Here are their names:

Simon (he also called him Peter),
Andrew (Simon's brother),
James,
John,
Philip,
Bartholomew,
Matthew,
Thomas,
James (the son of Alphaeus),
Simon (a member of the Zealots, a subversive political party),
Judas (son of James),
Judas Iscariot (who later betrayed him).

17,18When they came down the slopes of the mountain, they stood with Jesus on a large, level area, surrounded by many of his followers who, in turn, were surrounded by the crowds. For people from all over Judea and from Jerusalem and from as far north as the seacoasts of Tyre and Sidon had come to hear him or to be healed. And he cast out many demons. 19Everyone was trying to touch him, for when they did healing power went out from him and they were cured.

20Then he turned to his disciples and said, "What happiness there is for you who are poor, for the Kingdom of God is yours! 21What happiness there is for you who are now hungry, for you are going to be satisfied! What happiness there is for you who weep, for the time will come when you shall laugh with joy! 22What happiness it is when others hate you and exclude you and insult you and smear your name because you are mine! 23When that happens, rejoice! Yes, leap for joy! For you will have a great reward awaiting you in heaven. And you will be in good company—the ancient prophets were treated that way too!

24"But, oh, the sorrows that await the rich. For they have their only happiness down here. 25They are fat and prosperous now, but a time of awful hunger is before them. Their careless laughter now means sorrow then. 26And what sadness is ahead for those praised by the crowds—for *false* prophets have *always* been praised.

27"Listen, all of you. Love your *enemies*. Do *good* to those who *hate* you. 28Pray for the happiness of those who *curse* you; implore God's blessing on those who *hurt* you.

29"If someone slaps you on one cheek, let him slap the other too! If someone demands your coat, give him your shirt besides. 30Give what you have to anyone who asks you for it; and when things are taken away from you, don't worry about getting them back. 31Treat others as you want them to treat you.

32"Do you think you deserve credit for merely loving those who love you? Even the godless do that! 33And if you do good only to those who do you good—is that so wonderful? Even sinners do that much! 34And if you lend money only to those who can repay you, what good is that? Even the most wicked will lend to their own kind for full return!

35"Love your *enemies!* Do good to *them!* Lend to *them!* And don't be concerned about the fact that they won't repay. Then your reward from heaven will be very great, and you will truly be acting as sons of God: for he is kind to the *unthankful* and to those who are *very wicked.*

³⁶"Try to show as much compassion as your Father does.

³⁷"Never criticize or condemn—or it will all come back on you. Go easy on others; then they will do the same for you. ³⁸For if you give, you will get! Your gift will return to you in full and overflowing measure, pressed down, shaken together to make room for more, and running over. Whatever measure you use to give—large or small—will be used to measure what is given back to you."

PSALM 67:1–7

O God, in mercy bless us; let your face beam with joy as you look down at us.

²Send us around the world with the news of your saving power and your eternal plan for all mankind. ³How everyone throughout the earth will praise the Lord! ⁴How glad the nations will be, singing for joy because you are their King and will give true justice to their people! ⁵Praise God, O world! May all the peoples of the earth give thanks to you. ⁶,⁷For the earth has yielded abundant harvests. God, even our own God, will bless us. And peoples from remotest lands will worship him.

PROVERBS FOR TODAY/ 11:27

If you search for good you will find God's favor; if you search for evil you will find his curse.

MARCH 25

DEUTERONOMY 4:1–49

AND now, O Israel, listen carefully to these laws I teach you, and obey them if you want to live and enter into and possess the land given you by the Lord God of your ancestors. ²Do not add other laws or subtract from these; just obey them, for they are from the Lord your God. ³You have seen what the Lord did to you at Baalpeor, where he destroyed many people for worshiping idols. ⁴But all of you who were faithful to the Lord your God are still alive today.

⁵"These are the laws for you to obey when you arrive in the land where you will live. They are from the Lord our God. He has given them to me to pass on to you. ⁶If you obey them they will give you a reputation for wisdom and intelligence. When the surrounding nations hear these laws they will exclaim,

'What other nation is as wise and prudent as Israel!' ⁷For what other nation, great or small, has God among them, as the Lord our God is here among us whenever we call upon him? ⁸And what nation, no matter how great, has laws as fair as these I am giving you today?

⁹"But watch out! Be very careful never to forget what you have seen God doing for you. May his miracles have a deep and permanent effect upon your lives! Tell your children and your grandchildren about the glorious miracles he did. ¹⁰Tell them especially about the day you stood before the Lord at Mount Horeb, and he told me, 'Summon the people before me and I will instruct them, so that they will learn always to reverence me, and so that they can teach my laws to their children.' ¹¹You stood at the foot of the mountain, and the mountain burned with fire; flames shot far into the

sky, surrounded by black clouds and deep darkness. 12And the Lord spoke to you from the fire; you heard his words but didn't see him. 13He proclaimed the laws you must obey—the Ten Commandments—and wrote them on two stone tablets. 14Yes, it was at that time that the Lord commanded me to issue the laws you must obey when you arrive in the Promised Land.

15"But beware! You didn't see the form of God that day as he spoke to you from the fire at Mount Horeb, 16,17so do not defile yourselves by trying to make a statue of God—an idol in any form, whether of a man, woman, animal, bird, 18a small animal that runs along the ground, or a fish. 19And do not look up into the sky to worship the sun, moon, or stars. The Lord may permit other nations to get away with this, but not you. 20The Lord has rescued you from prison—Egypt—to be his special people, his own inheritance; this is what you are today. 21,22But he was angry with me because of you; he vowed that I could not go over the Jordan River into the good land he has given you as your inheritance. I must die here on this side of the river. 23Beware lest you break the contract the Lord your God has made with you! You will break it if you make any idols, for the Lord your God has utterly forbidden this. 24He is a devouring fire, a jealous God.

25"In the future, when your children and grandchildren are born and you have been in the land a long time, and you have defiled yourselves by making idols, and the Lord your God is very angry because of your sin, 26heaven and earth are witnesses that you shall be quickly destroyed from the land. Soon, now, you will cross the Jordan River and conquer that land. But your days there will be brief; you will then be utterly destroyed. 27For the Lord will scatter you among the nations, and you will be but few in number. 28There, far away, you will worship idols made from wood and stone, idols that neither see nor hear nor eat nor smell.

29"But you will also begin to search again for Jehovah your God, and you shall find him when you search for him with all your hearts and souls. 30When those bitter days have come upon you in the latter times, you will finally return to the Lord your God and listen to what he tells you. 31For the Lord your God is merciful—he will not abandon you nor destroy you nor forget the promises he has made to your ancestors.

32"In all history, going back to the time when God created man upon the earth, search from one end of the heavens to the other to see if you can find anything like this: 33An entire nation heard the voice of God speaking to it from fire, as you did, and lived! 34Where else will you ever find another example of God's removing a nation from its slavery by sending terrible plagues, mighty miracles, war, and terror? Yet that is what the Lord your God did for you in Egypt, right before your very eyes. 35He did these things so you would realize that Jehovah is God, and that there is no one else like him. 36He let you hear his voice instructing you from heaven, and he let you see his great pillar of fire upon the earth; you even heard his words from the center of the fire.

37"It was because he loved your ancestors and chose to bless their descendants that he personally brought you out from Egypt with a great display of power. 38He drove away other nations greater by far than you, and gave you their land as an inheritance, as it is today. 39This is your wonderful thought for the day: Jehovah is God both in heaven and down here upon the earth; and there is no God other than him! 40You must obey these laws that I will tell you today, so that all will be well with you and your children, and so that you will live forever in the land the Lord your God is giving you."

41Then Moses instructed the people of Israel to set apart three cities east of the Jordan River, 42where anyone who accidentally killed someone could flee for safety. 43These cities were Bezer, on the plateau in the wilderness, for the tribe of Reuben; Ramoth, in Gilead, for the tribe of Gad; and Golan, in Bashan, for the tribe of Manasseh.

44,45,46Listed below are the laws Moses issued to the people of Israel when they left Egypt, and as they were camped east of the Jordan River near the city of Beth-peor. (This was the land formerly occupied by the Amorites under King Sihon, whose capital was Heshbon; he and his people were destroyed by Moses and the Israelis. 47Israel conquered his land and that of King Og of Bashan—they were two Amorite kings east of the Jordan. 48Israel also conquered all the area from Aroer at the edge of the Arnon River valley to Mount Sirion, or Mount Hermon, as it is sometimes called; 49and all the Arabah east of the Jordan River over to the Dead Sea, below the slopes of Mount Pisgah.)

LUKE 6:39—7:10

HERE are some of the story-illustrations Jesus used in his sermons: "What good is it for one blind man to lead another? He will fall into a ditch and pull the other down with him. 40How can a student know more than his teacher? But if he works hard, he may learn as much.

41"And why quibble about the speck in someone else's eye—his little fault—when a board is in your own? 42How can you think of saying to him, 'Brother, let me help you get rid of that speck in your eye,' when you can't see past the board in yours? Hypocrite! First get rid of the board, and then perhaps you can see well enough to deal with his speck!

43"A tree from good stock doesn't produce scrub fruit nor do trees from poor stock produce choice fruit. 44A tree is identified by the kind of fruit it produces. Figs never grow on thorns, or grapes on bramble bushes. 45A good man produces good deeds from a good heart. And an evil man produces evil deeds from his hidden wickedness. Whatever is in the heart overflows into speech.

46"So why do you call me 'Lord' when you won't obey me? 47,48But all those who come and listen and obey me are like a man who builds a house on a strong foundation laid upon the underlying rock. When the floodwaters rise and break against the house, it stands firm, for it is strongly built.

49"But those who listen and don't obey are like a man who builds a house without a foundation. When the floods sweep down against that house, it crumbles into a heap of ruins."

WHEN Jesus had finished his sermon he went back into the city of Capernaum.

2Just at that time the highly prized slave of a Roman army captain was sick and near death. 3When the captain heard about Jesus, he sent some respected Jewish elders to ask him to come and heal his slave. 4So they began pleading earnestly with Jesus to come with them and help the man. They told him what a wonderful person the captain was.

"If anyone deserves your help, it is he," they said, 5"for he loves the Jews and even paid personally to build us a synagogue!"

6,7,8Jesus went with them; but just before arriving at the house, the captain sent some friends to say, "Sir, don't inconvenience yourself by coming to my home, for I am not worthy of any such honor or even to come and meet you. Just speak a word from where you are, and my servant boy will be healed! I know, because I am under the authority of my superior officers, and I have authority over my men. I only need to say 'Go!' and they go; or 'Come!' and they come; and to my slave, 'Do this or that,' and he does it. So just say, 'Be healed!' and my servant will be well again!"

9Jesus was amazed. Turning to the crowd he said, "Never among all the Jews in Israel have I met a man with faith like this."

10And when the captain's friends returned to his house, they found the slave completely healed.

PSALM 68:1–18

ARISE, O God, and scatter all your enemies! Chase them away! ²Drive them off like smoke before the wind; melt them like wax in fire! So let the wicked perish at the presence of God.

³But may the godly man exult. May he rejoice and be merry. ⁴Sing praises to the Lord! Raise your voice in song to him who rides upon the clouds! Jehovah is his name—oh, rejoice in his presence. ⁵He is a father to the fatherless; he gives justice to the widows, for he is holy. ⁶He gives families to the lonely, and releases prisoners from jail, singing with joy! But for rebels there is famine and distress.

⁷O God, when you led your people through the wilderness, ⁸the earth trembled and the heavens shook. Mount Sinai quailed before you—the God of Israel. ⁹,¹⁰You sent abundant rain upon your land, O God, to refresh it in its weariness!

There your people lived, for you gave them this home when they were destitute.

¹¹,¹²,¹³The Lord speaks. The enemy flees. The women at home cry out the happy news: "The armies that came to destroy us have fled!" Now all the women of Israel are dividing the booty. See them sparkle with jewels of silver and gold, covered all over as wings cover doves! ¹⁴God scattered their enemies like snowflakes melting in the forests of Zalmon.

¹⁵,¹⁶O mighty mountains in Bashan! O splendid many-peaked ranges! Well may you look with envy at Mount Zion, the mount where God has chosen to live forever. ¹⁷Surrounded by unnumbered chariots, the Lord moves on from Mount Sinai and comes to his holy temple high upon Mount Zion. ¹⁸He ascends the heights, leading many captives in his train. He receives gifts for men, even those who once were rebels. God will live among us here.

PROVERBS FOR TODAY/ 11:28

Trust in your money and down you go! Trust in God and flourish as a tree!

MARCH 26

DEUTERONOMY 5:1—6:25

MOSES continued speaking to the people of Israel and said, "Listen carefully now to all these laws God has given you; learn them, and be sure to obey them!

²,³The Lord our God made a contract with you at Mount Horeb—*not with your ancestors, but with you who are here alive today.* ⁴He spoke with you face to face from the center of the fire, there at the mountain. ⁵I stood as an intermediary between you and Jehovah, for you were

afraid of the fire and did not go up to him on the mountain. He spoke to me and I passed on his laws to you. This is what he said:

⁶" 'I am Jehovah your God who rescued you from slavery in Egypt.

⁷" 'Never worship any god but me.

⁸" 'Never make idols; don't worship images, whether of birds, animals, or fish. ⁹,¹⁰You shall not bow down to any images nor worship them in any way, for I am the Lord your God. I am a jealous God, and I will bring the curse of a father's

sins upon even the third and fourth generation of the children of those who hate me; but I will show kindness to a thousand generations of those who love me and keep my commandments.

11"'You must never use my name to make a vow you don't intend to keep. I will not overlook that.

12"'Keep the Sabbath day holy. This is my command. 13Work the other six days, 14but the seventh day is the Sabbath of the Lord your God; no work shall be done that day by you or by any of your household—your sons, daughters, servants, oxen, donkeys, or cattle; even foreigners living among you must obey this law. Everybody must rest as you do. 15Why should you keep the Sabbath? It is because you were slaves in Egypt, and the Lord your God brought you out with a great display of miracles.

16"'Honor your father and mother (remember, this is a commandment of the Lord your God); if you do so, you shall have a long, prosperous life in the land he is giving you.

17"'You must not murder.

18"'You must not commit adultery.

19"'You must not steal.

20"'You must not tell lies.

21"'You must not burn with desire for another man's wife, nor envy him for his home, land, servants, oxen, donkeys, nor anything else he owns.'

22"The Lord has given these laws to each one of you from the heart of the fire, surrounded by the clouds and thick darkness that engulfed Mount Sinai. Those were the only commandments he gave you at that time, and he wrote them out on two stone tablets and gave them to me. 23But when you heard the loud voice from the darkness, and saw the terrible fire at the top of the mountain, all your tribal leaders came to me 24and pleaded, 'Today the Lord our God has shown us his glory and greatness; we have even heard his voice from the heart of the fire. Now we know that a man may speak to God and not die; 25but we will surely die if he speaks to

us again. This awesome fire will consume us. 26,27What man can hear, as we have, the voice of the living God speaking from the heart of the fire, and live? You go and listen to all that God says, then come and tell us, and we will listen and obey.'

28"And the Lord agreed to your request, and said to me, 'I have heard what the people have said to you, and I agree. 29Oh, that they would always have such a heart for me, wanting to obey my commandments. Then all would go well with them in the future, and with their children throughout all generations! 30Go and tell them to return to their tents. 31Then you come back and stand here beside me, and I will give you all my commandments, and you shall teach them to the people; and they will obey them in the land I am giving to them.'"

32So Moses told the people, "You must obey all the commandments of the Lord your God, following his directions in every detail, going the whole way he has laid out for you; 33only then will you live long and prosperous lives in the land you are to enter and possess.

"THE Lord your God told me to give you all these commandments which you are to obey in the land you will soon be entering, where you will live. 2The purpose of these laws is to cause you, your sons, and your grandsons to reverence the Lord your God by obeying all of his instructions as long as you live; if you do, you will have long, prosperous years ahead of you. 3Therefore, O Israel, listen closely to each command and be careful to obey it, so that all will go well with you, and so that you will have many children. If you obey these commands you will become a great nation in a glorious land 'flowing with milk and honey,' even as the God of your fathers promised you.

4"O Israel, listen: Jehovah is our God, Jehovah alone. 5You must love him with *all* your heart, soul, and might. 6And you must think constantly about these commandments I am giving you today. ⁷You must teach them to your children and talk about them when you are at home or out for a walk; at bedtime and the first thing in the morning. ⁸Tie them on your finger, wear them on your forehead, ⁹and write them on the doorposts of your house!

¹⁰,¹¹,¹²"When the Lord your God has brought you into the land he promised your ancestors, Abraham, Isaac, and Jacob, and when he has given you great cities full of good things—cities you didn't build, wells you didn't dig, and vineyards and olive trees you didn't plant—and when you have eaten until you can hold no more, then beware lest you forget the Lord who brought you out of the land of Egypt, the land of slavery. ¹³When you are full, don't forget to be reverent to him and to serve him and to use *his* name alone to endorse your promises.

¹⁴"You must not worship the gods of the neighboring nations, ¹⁵for Jehovah your God who lives among you is a jealous God, and his anger may rise quickly against you, and wipe you off the face of the earth. ¹⁶You must not provoke him and try his patience as you did when you complained against him at Massah. ¹⁷You must actively obey him in everything he commands. ¹⁸Only then will you be doing what is right and good in the Lord's eyes. If you obey him, all will go well for you, and you will be able to go in and possess the good land which the Lord promised your ancestors. ¹⁹You will also be able to throw out all the enemies living in your land, as the Lord agreed to help you do.

²⁰"In the years to come when your son asks you, 'What is the purpose of these laws which the Lord our God has given us?' ²¹you must tell him, 'We were Pharaoh's slaves in Egypt, and the Lord brought us out of Egypt with great power ²²and mighty miracles—with terrible blows against Egypt and Pharaoh and all his people. We saw it all with our own eyes. ²³He brought us out of Egypt so that he could give us this land he had promised to our ancestors. ²⁴And he has commanded us to obey all of these laws and to reverence him so that he can preserve us alive as he has until now. ²⁵For it always goes well with us when we obey all the laws of the Lord our God.'

LUKE 7:11-35

NOT long afterwards Jesus went with his disciples to the village of Nain, with the usual great crowd at his heels. ¹²A funeral procession was coming out as he approached the village gate. The boy who had died was the only son of his widowed mother, and many mourners from the village were with her.

¹³When the Lord saw her, his heart overflowed with sympathy. "Don't cry!" he said. ¹⁴Then he walked over to the coffin and touched it, and the bearers stopped. "Laddie," he said, "come back to life again."

¹⁵Then the boy sat up and began to talk to those around him! And Jesus gave him back to his mother.

¹⁶A great fear swept the crowd, and they exclaimed with praises to God, "A mighty prophet has risen among us," and, "We have seen the hand of God at work today."

¹⁷The report of what he did that day raced from end to end of Judea and even out across the borders.

¹⁸The disciples of John the Baptist soon heard of all that Jesus was doing. When they told John about it, ¹⁹he sent two of his disciples to Jesus to ask him, "Are you really the Messiah? Or shall we keep on looking for him?"

²⁰,²¹,²²The two disciples found Jesus while he was curing many sick people of their various diseases—healing the lame and the blind and casting out evil spirits. When they asked him John's question, this was his reply: "Go back to John and tell him all you have seen and heard here today: how those who

were blind can see. The lame are walking without a limp. The lepers are completely healed. The deaf can hear again. The dead come back to life. And the poor are hearing the Good News. 23And tell him, 'Blessed is the one who does not lose his faith in me.'"

24After they left, Jesus talked to the crowd about John. "Who is this man you went out into the Judean wilderness to see?" he asked. "Did you find him weak as grass, moved by every breath of wind? 25Did you find him dressed in expensive clothes? No! Men who live in luxury are found in palaces, not out in the wilderness. 26But did you find a prophet? Yes! And more than a prophet. 27He is the one to whom the Scriptures refer when they say, 'Look! I am sending my messenger ahead of you, to prepare the way before you.' 28In all humanity there is no one greater than John. And yet the least citizen of the Kingdom of God is greater than he."

29And all who heard John preach— even the most wicked of them—agreed that God's requirements were right, and they were baptized by him. 30All, that is, except the Pharisees and teachers of Moses' Law. They rejected God's plan for them and refused John's baptism.

31"What can I say about such men?" Jesus asked. "With what shall I compare them? 32They are like a group of children who complain to their friends, 'You don't like it if we play "wedding" and you don't like it if we play "funeral" '! 33For John the Baptist used to go without food and never took a drop of liquor all his life, and you said, 'He must be crazy!' 34But I eat my food and drink my wine, and you say, 'What a glutton Jesus is! And he drinks! And has the lowest sort of friends!' 35But I am sure you can always justify your inconsistencies."

WHAT a glorious Lord! He who daily bears our burdens also gives us our salvation.

20He frees us! He rescues us from death. 21But he will crush his enemies, for they refuse to leave their guilty, stubborn ways. 22The Lord says, "Come," to all his people's enemies; they are hiding on Mount Hermon's highest slopes and deep within the sea! 23His people must destroy them. Cover your feet with their blood; dogs will eat them.

24The procession of God my King moves onward to the sanctuary— 25singers in front, musicians behind, girls playing the timbrels in between. 26Let all the people of Israel praise the Lord, who is Israel's fountain. 27The little tribe of Benjamin leads the way. The princes and elders of Judah, and the princes of Zebulun and Naphtali are right behind. 28Summon your might; display your strength, O God, for you have done such mighty things for us.

29The kings of the earth are bringing their gifts to your temple in Jerusalem. 30Rebuke our enemies, O Lord. Bring them—submissive, tax in hand. Scatter all who delight in war. 31Egypt will send gifts of precious metals. Ethiopia will stretch out her hands to God in adoration. 32Sing to the Lord, O kingdoms of the earth—sing praises to the Lord, 33to him who rides upon the ancient heavens, whose mighty voice thunders from the sky.

34Power belongs to God! His majesty shines down on Israel; his strength is mighty in the heavens. 35What awe we feel, kneeling here before him in the sanctuary. The God of Israel gives strength and mighty power to his people. Blessed be God!

PROVERBS FOR TODAY/ 11:29–31

The fool who provokes his family to anger and resentment will finally have nothing worthwhile left. He shall be the servant of a wiser man. Godly men are growing a tree that bears life-giving fruit, and all who win souls are wise. Even the godly shall be rewarded here on earth; how much more the wicked!

MARCH 27

DEUTERONOMY 7:1—8:20

WHEN the Lord brings you into the Promised Land, as he soon will, he will destroy the following seven nations, all greater and mightier than you are:

The Hittites, the Girgashites,
The Amorites, the Canaanites,
The Perizzites, the Hivites,
The Jebusites.

2"When the Lord your God delivers them over to you to be destroyed, do a complete job of it—don't make any treaties or show them mercy; utterly wipe them out. 3Do not intermarry with them, nor let your sons and daughters marry their sons and daughters. 4That would surely result in your young people's beginning to worship their gods. Then the anger of the Lord would be hot against you and he would surely destroy you.

5"You must break down the heathen altars and shatter the obelisks and cut up the shameful images and burn the idols.

6"For you are a holy people, dedicated to the Lord your God. He has chosen you from all the people on the face of the whole earth to be his own chosen ones. 7He didn't choose you and pour out his love upon you because you were a larger nation than any other, for you were the smallest of all! 8It was just because he loves you, and because he kept his promise to your ancestors. That is why he brought you out of slavery in Egypt with such amazing power and mighty miracles.

9"Understand, therefore, that the Lord your God is the faithful God who for a thousand generations keeps his promises and constantly loves those who love him and who obey his commands. 10But those who hate him shall be punished publicly and destroyed. He will deal with them personally. 11Therefore, obey all these commandments I am giving you today.

12Because of your obedience, the Lord your God will keep his part of the contract which, in his tender love, he made with your fathers. 13And he will love you and bless you and make you into a great nation. He will make you fertile and give fertility to your ground and to your animals, so that you will have large crops of grain, grapes, and olives, and great flocks of cattle, sheep, and goats when you arrive in the land he promised your fathers to give you. 14You will be blessed above all the nations of the earth; not one of you, whether male or female, shall be barren, not even your cattle. 15And the Lord will take away all your sickness and will not let you suffer any of the diseases of Egypt you remember so well; he will give them all to your enemies!

16"You must destroy all the nations which the Lord your God delivers into your hands. Have no pity, and do not worship their gods; if you do, it will be a sad day for you. 17Perhaps you will think to yourself, 'How can we ever conquer these nations that are so much more powerful than we are?' 18But don't be afraid of them! Just remember what the Lord your God did to Pharoah and to all the land of Egypt. 19Do you remember the terrors the Lord sent upon them—your parents saw it with their own eyes—and the mighty miracles and wonders, and the power and strength of Almighty God which he used to bring you out of Egypt? Well, the Lord your God will use this same might against the people you fear. 20Moreover, the Lord your God will send hornets to drive out those who hide from you!

21"No, do not be afraid of those nations, for the Lord your God is among you, and he is a great and awesome God. 22He will cast them out a little at a time; he will not do it all at once, for if he did, the wild animals would multiply too quickly and become dangerous. 23He will do it gradually, and you will move in against those nations and destroy them. [24]He will deliver their kings into your hands, and you will erase their names from the face of the earth. No one will be able to stand against you.

[25]"Burn their idols and do not touch the silver or gold they are made of. Do not take it or it will be a snare to you, for it is horrible to the Lord your God. [26]Do not bring an idol into your home and worship it, for then your doom is sealed. Utterly detest it, for it is a cursed thing.

"YOU must obey all the commandments I give you today. If you do, you will not only live, you will multiply and will go in and take over the land promised to your fathers by the Lord. [2]Do you remember how the Lord led you through the wilderness for all those forty years, humbling you and testing you to find out how you would respond, and whether or not you would really obey him? [3]Yes, he humbled you by letting you go hungry and then feeding you with manna, a food previously unknown to both you and your ancestors. He did it to help you realize that food isn't everything, and that real life comes by obeying every command of God. [4]For all these forty years your clothes haven't grown old, and your feet haven't been blistered or swollen. [5]So you should realize that, as a man punishes his son, the Lord punishes you to help you.

[6]"Obey the laws of the Lord your God. Walk in his ways and fear him. [7]For the Lord your God is bringing you into a good land of brooks, pools, gushing springs, valleys, and hills; [8]it is a land of wheat and barley, of grape vines, fig trees, pomegranates, olives, and honey; [9]it is a land where food is plentiful, and nothing is lacking; it is a land where iron is as common as stone, and copper is abundant in the hills. [10]When you have eaten your fill, bless the Lord your God for the good land he has given you.

[11]"But that is the time to be careful!

Beware that in your plenty you don't forget the Lord your God and begin to disobey him. [12,13]For when you have become full and prosperous and have built fine homes to live in, and when your flocks and herds have become very large, and your silver and gold have multiplied, [14]that is the time to watch out that you don't become proud, and forget the Lord your God who brought you out of your slavery in the land of Egypt. [15]Beware that you don't forget the God who led you through the great and terrible wilderness with the dangerous snakes and scorpions, where it was so hot and dry. He gave you water from the rock! [16]He fed you with manna in the wilderness (it was a kind of bread unknown before) so that you would become humble and so that your trust in him would grow, and he could do you good. [17]He did it so that you would never feel that it was your own power and might that made you wealthy. [18]Always remember that it is the Lord your God who gives you power to become rich, and he does it to fulfill his promise to your ancestors.

[19]"But if you forget about the Lord your God and worship other gods instead, and follow evil ways, you shall certainly perish, [20]just as the Lord has caused other nations in the past to perish. That will be your fate, too, if you don't obey the Lord your God.

LUKE 7:36—8:3

ONE of the Pharisees asked Jesus to come to his home for lunch and Jesus accepted the invitation. As they sat down to eat, [37]a woman of the streets—a prostitute—heard he was there and brought an exquisite flask filled with expensive perfume. [38]Going in, she knelt behind him at his feet, weeping, with her tears falling down upon his feet; and she wiped them off with her hair and kissed them and poured the perfume on them.

[39]When Jesus' host, a Pharisee, saw what was happening and who the woman

was, he said to himself, "This proves that Jesus is no prophet, for if God had really sent him, he would know what kind of woman this one is!"

⁴⁰Then Jesus spoke up and answered his thoughts. "Simon," he said to the Pharisee, "I have something to say to you."

"All right, Teacher," Simon replied, "go ahead."

⁴¹Then Jesus told him this story: "A man loaned money to two people— $5,000 to one and $500 to the other. ⁴²But neither of them could pay him back, so he kindly forgave them both, letting them keep the money! Which do you suppose loved him most after that?"

⁴³"I suppose the one who had owed him the most," Simon answered.

"Correct," Jesus agreed.

⁴⁴Then he turned to the woman and said to Simon, "Look! See this woman kneeling here! When I entered your home, you didn't bother to offer me water to wash the dust from my feet, but she has washed them with her tears and wiped them with her hair. ⁴⁵You refused me the customary kiss of greeting, but she has kissed my feet again and again from the time I first came in. ⁴⁶You neglected the usual courtesy of olive oil to anoint my head, but she has covered my feet with rare perfume. ⁴⁷Therefore her sins—and they are many—are forgiven, for she loved me much; but one who is forgiven little, shows little love."

⁴⁸And he said to her, "Your sins are forgiven."

⁴⁹Then the men at the table said to themselves, "Who does this man think he is, going around forgiving sins?"

⁵⁰And Jesus said to the woman, "Your faith has saved you; go in peace."

Nᴏᴛ long afterwards he began a tour of the cities and villages of Galilee to announce the coming of the Kingdom of God, and took his twelve disciples with him. ²Some women went along, from whom he had cast out demons or whom he had healed; among them were Mary Magdalene (Jesus had cast out seven demons from her), ³Joanna, Chuza's wife (Chuza was King Herod's business manager and was in charge of his palace and domestic affairs), Susanna, and many others who were contributing from their private means to the support of Jesus and his disciples.

PSALM 69:1–14

Sᴀᴠᴇ me, O my God. The floods have risen. Deeper and deeper I sink in the mire; the waters rise around me. ³I have wept until I am exhausted; my throat is dry and hoarse; my eyes are swollen with weeping, waiting for my God to act. ⁴I cannot even count all those who hate me without cause. They are influential men, these who plot to kill me though I am innocent. They demand that I be punished for what I didn't do.

⁵O God, you know so well how stupid I am, and you know all my sins. ⁶O Lord God of the armies of heaven, don't let me be a stumbling block to those who trust in you. O God of Israel, don't let me cause them to be confused, ⁷though I am mocked and cursed and shamed for your sake. ⁸Even my own brothers pretend they don't know me! ⁹My zeal for God and his work burns hot within me. And because I advocate your cause, your enemies insult me even as they insult you. ¹⁰How they scoff and mock me when I mourn and fast before the Lord! ¹¹How they talk about me when I wear sackcloth to show my humiliation and sorrow for my sins! ¹²I am the talk of the town and the song of the drunkards. ¹³But I keep right on praying to you, Lord. For now is the time—you are bending down to hear! You are ready with a plentiful supply of love and kindness. Now answer my prayer and rescue me as you promised. ¹⁴Pull me out of this mire. Don't let me sink in. Rescue me from those who hate me, and from these deep waters I am in.

PROVERBS FOR TODAY/ 12:1

To learn, you must want to be taught. To refuse reproof is stupid.

MARCH 28

DEUTERONOMY 9:1—10:22

O Israel, listen! Today you are to cross the Jordan River and begin to dispossess the nations on the other side. Those nations are much greater and more powerful than you are! They live in high walled cities. Among them are the famed Anak giants, against whom none can stand! ³But the Lord your God will go before you as a devouring fire to destroy them, so that you will quickly conquer them and drive them out.

⁴"Then, when the Lord has done this for you, don't say to yourselves, 'The Lord has helped us because we are so good!' No, it is because of the wickedness of the other nations that he is doing it. ⁵It is not at all because you are such fine, upright people that the Lord will drive them out from before you! I say it again, it is only because of the wickedness of the other nations, and because of his promises to your ancestors, Abraham, Isaac, and Jacob, that he will do it. ⁶I say it yet again: *Jehovah your God is not giving you this good land because you are good, for you are not*—you are a wicked, stubborn people.

⁷"Don't you remember (oh, never forget it!) how continually angry you made the Lord your God out in the wilderness, from the day you left Egypt until now? For all this time you have constantly rebelled against him.

⁸"Don't you remember how angry you made him at Mount Horeb? He was ready to destroy you. ⁹I was on the mountain at the time, receiving the contract which Jehovah had made with you—the stone tablets with the laws inscribed upon

them. I was there for forty days and forty nights, and all that time I ate nothing. I didn't even take a drink of water. ¹⁰,¹¹At the end of those forty days and nights the Lord gave me the contract, the tablets on which he had written the commandments he had spoken from the fire-covered mountain while the people had watched below. ¹²He told me to go down quickly because the people I had led out of Egypt had defiled themselves, quickly turning away from the laws of God, and had made an idol from molten metal.

¹³,¹⁴" 'Let me alone that I may destroy this evil, stubborn people!' the Lord told me, 'and I will blot out their name from under heaven, and I will make a mighty nation of you, mightier and greater than they are.'

¹⁵"I came down from the burning mountain, holding in my hands the two tablets inscribed with the laws of God. ¹⁶There below me I could see the calf you had made in your terrible sin against the Lord your God. How quickly you turned away from him! ¹⁷I lifted the tablets high above my head and dashed them to the ground! I smashed them before your eyes! ¹⁸Then, for another forty days and nights I lay before the Lord, neither eating bread nor drinking water, for you had done what the Lord hated most, thus provoking him to great anger. ¹⁹How I feared for you—for the Lord was ready to destroy you. But that time, too, he listened to me. ²⁰Aaron was in great danger because the Lord was so angry with him; but I prayed, and the Lord spared him. ²¹I took your sin—the calf you had made—and burned it and ground it into

fine dust, and threw it into the stream that cascaded out of the mountain.

22"Again at Taberah and once again at Massah you angered the Lord, and yet again at Kibroth-hattaavah. 23At Kadesh-barnea, when the Lord told you to enter the land he had given you, you rebelled and wouldn't believe that he would help you; you refused to obey him. 24Yes, you have been rebellious against the Lord from the first day I knew you. 25That is why I fell down before him for forty days and nights when the Lord was ready to destroy you.

26"I prayed to him, 'O Lord God, don't destroy your own people. They are your inheritance saved from Egypt by your mighty power and glorious strength. 27Don't notice the rebellion and stubbornness of these people, but remember instead your promises to your servants Abraham, Isaac, and Jacob. Oh, please overlook the awful wickedness and sin of these people. 28For if you destroy them the Egyptians will say, "It is because the Lord wasn't able to bring them to the land he promised them," or "He destroyed them because he hated them: he brought them into the wilderness to slay them." 29They are your people and your inheritance which you brought from Egypt by your great power and your mighty arm.'

"AT that time the Lord told me to cut two more stone tablets like the first ones, and to make a wooden Ark to keep them in, and to return to God on the mountain. 2He said he would rewrite on the tablets the same commandments that were on the tablets I had smashed, and that I should place them in the Ark. 3So I made an Ark of acacia wood and hewed out two stone tablets like the first two, and took the tablets up on the mountain to God. 4He again wrote the Ten Commandments on them and gave them to me. (They were the same commandments he had given you from the heart of the fire on the mountain as you all watched below.) 5Then I came down and placed the tablets in the Ark I had made, where they are to this day, just as the Lord commanded me.

6"The people of Israel then journeyed from Be-eroth of Bene-jaakan to Moserah, where Aaron died and was buried. His son Eleazar became the next priest.

7"Then they journeyed to Gudgodah, and from there to Jotbathah, a land of brooks and water. 8It was there that Jehovah set apart the tribe of Levi to carry the Ark containing the Ten Commandments of Jehovah, and to stand before the Lord and to do his work and to bless his name, just as is done today. 9(That is why the tribe of Levi does not have a portion of land reserved for it in the Promised Land, as their brother tribes do; for as the Lord told them, he himself is their inheritance.)

10"As I said before, I stayed on the mountain before the Lord for forty days and nights the second time, just as I had the first, and the Lord again yielded to my pleas and didn't destroy you.

11"But he said to me, 'Arise and lead the people to the land I promised their fathers. It is time to go in and possess it.'

12,13"And now, Israel, what does the Lord your God require of you except to listen carefully to all he says to you, and to obey for your own good the commandments I am giving you today, and to love him, and to worship him with all your hearts and souls? 14Earth and highest heaven belong to the Lord your God. 15And yet he rejoiced in your fathers and loved them so much that he chose you, their children, to be above every other nation, as is evident today. 16Therefore, cleanse your sinful hearts and stop your stubbornness.

17"Jehovah your God is God of gods and Lord of lords. He is the great and mighty God, the God of terror who shows no partiality and takes no bribes. 18He gives justice to the fatherless and widows. He loves foreigners and gives them food and clothing. 19(You too must love foreigners, for you yourselves were foreigners in the land of Egypt.) 20You must fear the Lord your God and worship him and cling to him and take oaths by his name alone. 21He is your praise and he is your God, the one who has done mighty miracles you yourselves have seen. 22When your ancestors went down into Egypt there were only seventy of them, but now the Lord your God has made you as many as the stars in the sky!

LUKE 8:4–21

ONE day he gave this illustration to a large crowd that was gathering to hear him—while many others were still on the way, coming from other towns.

5"A farmer went out to his field to sow grain. As he scattered the seed on the ground, some of it fell on a footpath and was trampled on; and the birds came and ate it as it lay exposed. 6Other seed fell on shallow soil with rock beneath. This seed began to grow, but soon withered and died for lack of moisture. 7Other seed landed in thistle patches, and the young grain stalks were soon choked out. 8Still other fell on fertile soil; this seed grew and produced a crop one hundred times as large as he had planted." (As he was giving this illustration he said, "If anyone has listening ears, use them now!")

9His apostles asked him what the story meant.

10He replied, "God has granted you to know the meaning of these parables, for they tell a great deal about the Kingdom of God. But these crowds hear the words and do not understand, just as the ancient prophets predicted.

11"This is its meaning: The seed is God's message to men. 12The hard path where some seed fell represents the hard hearts of those who hear the words of God, but then the devil comes and steals the words away and prevents people from believing and being saved. 13The stony ground represents those who enjoy listening to sermons, but somehow the message never really gets through to them and doesn't take root and grow.

They know the message is true, and sort of believe for awhile; but when the hot winds of persecution blow, they lose interest. 14The seed among the thorns represents those who listen and believe God's words but whose faith afterwards is choked out by worry and riches and the responsibilities and pleasures of life. And so they are never able to help anyone else to believe the Good News.

15"But the good soil represents honest, good-hearted people. They listen to God's words and cling to them and steadily spread them to others who also soon believe."

16[Another time he asked,] "Who ever heard of someone lighting a lamp and then covering it up to keep it from shining? No, lamps are mounted in the open where they can be seen. 17This illustrates the fact that someday everything [in men's hearts] shall be brought to light and made plain to all. 18So be careful how you listen; for whoever has, to him shall be given more; and whoever does not have, even what he thinks he has shall be taken away from him."

19Once when his mother and brothers came to see him, they couldn't get into the house where he was teaching, because of the crowds. 20When Jesus heard they were standing outside and wanted to see him, 21he remarked, "My mother and my brothers are all those who hear the message of God and obey it."

PSALM 69:15–36

DON'T let the floods overwhelm me, or the ocean swallow me; save me from the pit that threatens me. 16O Jehovah, answer my prayers, for your lovingkindness is wonderful; your mercy is so plentiful, so tender and so kind. 17Don't hide from me, for I am in deep trouble. Quick! Come and save me. 18Come, Lord, and rescue me. Ransom me from all my enemies. 19You know how they talk about me, and how they so shamefully dishonor me. You see them all and know what each has said.

20Their contempt has broken my heart; my spirit is heavy within me. If even one would showsome pity, if even one would comfort me! 21For food they gave me gall; for my awful thirst they offered vinegar. 22Let their joys turn to ashes and their peace disappear; 23let darkness, blindness and great feebleness be theirs. 24Pour out your fury upon them; consume them with the fierceness of your anger. 25Let their homes be desolate and abandoned. 26For they persecute the one you have smitten, and scoff at the pain of the one you have pierced. 27Pile their sins high and do not overlook them. 28Let these men be blotted from the list of the living; do not give them the joys of life with the righteous.

29But rescue me, O God, from my poverty and pain. 30Then I will praise God with my singing! My thanks will be his praise— 31that will please him more than sacrificing a bullock or an ox. 32The humble shall see their God at work for them. No wonder they will be so glad! All who seek for God shall live in joy. 33For Jehovah hears the cries of his needy ones, and does not look the other way.

34Praise him, all heaven and earth! Praise him, all the seas and everything in them! 35For God will save Jerusalem; he rebuilds the cities of Judah. His people shall live in them and not be dispossessed. 36Their children shall inherit the land; all who love his name shall live there safely.

PROVERBS FOR TODAY/ 12:2–3

The Lord blesses good men and condemns the wicked. Wickedness never brings real success; only the godly have that.

MARCH 29

DEUTERONOMY 11:1—12:32

YOU must love the Lord your God and obey every one of his commands. 2Listen! I am not talking now to your children who have never experienced the Lord's punishments or seen his greatness and his awesome power. 3They weren't there to see the miracles he did in Egypt against Pharaoh and all his land. 4They didn't see what God did to the armies of Egypt and to their horses and chariots—how he drowned them in the Red Sea as they were chasing you, and how the Lord has kept them powerless against you until this very day! 5They didn't see how the Lord cared for you time and again through all the years you were wandering in the wilderness, until your arrival here. 6They weren't there when Dathan and Abiram (the sons of Eliab, descendants

of Reuben) sinned, and the earth opened up and swallowed them, with their households and tents and all their belongings, as all Israel watched!

7"But *you* have seen these mighty miracles! 8How carefully, then, you should obey these commandments I am going to give you today, so that you may have the strength to go in and possess the land you are about to enter. 9If you obey the commandments, you will have a long and good life in the land the Lord promised to your ancestors and to you, their descendants—a wonderful land 'flowing with milk and honey'! 10For the land you are about to enter and possess is not like the land of Egypt where you have come from, where irrigation is necessary. 11It is a land of hills and valleys with plenty of rain— 12a land that the Lord your God personally cares for! His eyes are always upon it, day after day throughout the year!

13"And if you will carefully obey all of his commandments that I am going to give you today, and if you will love the Lord your God with all your hearts and souls, and will worship him, 14then he will continue to send both the early and late rains that will produce wonderful crops of grain, grapes for your wine, and olive oil. 15He will give you lush pastureland for your cattle to graze in, and you yourselves shall have plenty to eat and be fully content.

16"But beware that your hearts do not turn from God to worship other gods. 17For if you do, the anger of the Lord will be hot against you, and he will shut the heavens—there will be no rain and no harvest, and you will quickly perish from the good land the Lord has given you. 18So keep these commandments carefully in mind. Tie them to your hand to remind you to obey them, and tie them to your forehead between your eyes! 19Teach them to your children. Talk about them when you are sitting at home, when you are out walking, at bedtime, and before breakfast! 20Write them upon the doors of your houses and upon your gates, 21so that as long as there is sky above the earth, you and your children will enjoy the good life awaiting you in the land the Lord has promised you.

22"If you carefully obey all the commandments I give you, loving the Lord your God, walking in all his ways, and clinging to him, 23then the Lord will drive out all the nations in your land, no matter how much greater and stronger than you they might be. 24Wherever you go, the land is yours. Your frontiers will stretch from the southern Negeb to Lebanon, and from the Euphrates River to the Mediterranean Sea. 25No one will be able to stand against you, for the Lord your God will send fear and dread ahead of you wherever you go, just as he has promised.

26"I am giving you the choice today between God's blessing or God's curse! 27There will be blessing if you obey the commandments of the Lord your God which I am giving you today, 28and a curse if you refuse them and worship the gods of these other nations. 29When the Lord your God brings you into the land to possess it, a blessing shall be proclaimed from Mount Gerizim, and a curse from Mount Ebal! 30(Gerizim and Ebal are mountains west of the Jordan River, where the Canaanites live, in the wasteland near Gilgal, where the oaks of Moreh are.) 31For you are to cross the Jordan and live in the land the Lord is giving you. 32But you must obey all the laws I am giving you today.

"THESE are the laws you must obey when you arrive in the land which Jehovah, the God of your fathers, has given you forever:

2"You must destroy all the heathen altars wherever you find them—high in the mountains, up in the hills, or under the trees. 3Break the altars, smash the obelisks, burn the shameful images, cut down the metal idols, and leave nothing even to remind you of them!

4,5"You must not make sacrifices to your God just anywhere, as the heathen sacrifice to their gods. Rather, you must build a sanctuary for him at a place he himself will select as his home. 6There you shall bring to the Lord your burnt offerings and other sacrifices—your tithes, your offerings presented by the gesture of waving before the altar, your offerings to fulfill your vows, your freewill offerings, and your offerings of the firstborn animals of your flocks and herds. 7There you and your families shall feast before the Lord your God, and shall rejoice in all he has done for you.

8"You will no longer go your own way as you do now, everyone doing whatever he thinks is right; 9(for these laws don't go into effect until you arrive in the place of rest the Lord will give to you). 10But when you cross the Jordan River and live in the Promised Land, and the Lord gives you rest and keeps you safe from all your enemies, 11then you must bring all your burnt sacrifices and other offerings to his sanctuary, the place he will choose as his home. 12You shall rejoice there before the Lord with your sons and daughters and servants; and remember to invite the Levites to feast with you, for they have no land of their own.

13"You are not to sacrifice your burnt offerings just anywhere; 14you may only do so in the place the Lord will choose. He will pick a place in the territory allotted to one of the tribes. Only there may you offer your sacrifices and bring your offerings. 15However, the meat you eat may be butchered anywhere, just as you do now with gazelle and deer. Eat as much of this meat as you wish and as often as you are able to obtain it, because the Lord has prospered you. Those who are ceremonially defiled may eat it, too. 16The only restriction is that you are not to eat the blood—pour it out on the ground, like water.

17"But none of the offerings may be eaten at home. Neither the tithe of your grain and new wine and olive oil, nor the firstborn of your flocks and herds, nor anything you have vowed to give the Lord, nor your freewill offerings, nor the offerings to be presented to the Lord by waving them before his altar. 18All these must be brought to the central altar where you, your children, and the Levites shall eat them before the Lord your God. He will tell you where this altar must be located. Rejoice before the Lord your God in everything you do. 19(By the way, be very careful not to forget about the Levites. Share with them.)

20-23"If, when the Lord enlarges your borders, the central altar is too far away from you, then your flocks and herds may be butchered on your own farms, just as you do now with gazelle and deer. And even persons who are ceremonially defiled may eat them. The only restriction is never to eat the blood, for the blood is the life, and you shall not eat the life with the meat. 24,25Instead, pour the blood out upon the earth. If you do, all will be well with you and your chil-

dren. 26,27Only your gifts to the Lord, and the offerings you have promised in your vows, and your burnt offerings need be taken to the central altar. These may only be sacrificed upon the altar of the Lord your God. The blood will be poured out upon the altar, and you will eat the meat.

28"Be careful to obey all of these commandments. If you do what is right in the eyes of the Lord your God, all will go well with you and your children forever. 29When he destroys the nations in the land where you will live, 30don't follow their example in worshiping their gods. Do not ask, 'How do these nations worship their gods?' and then go and worship as they do! 31You must not insult the Lord your God like that! These nations have done horrible things that he hates, all in the name of their religion. They have even roasted their sons and daughters in front of their gods. 32Obey all the commandments I give you. Do not add to or subtract from them.

LUKE 8:22-40

ONE day about that time, as he and his disciples were out in a boat, he suggested that they cross to the other side of the lake. 23On the way across he lay down for a nap, and while he was sleeping the wind began to rise. A fierce storm developed that threatened to swamp them, and they were in real danger.

24They rushed over and woke him up. "Master, Master, we are sinking!" they screamed.

So he spoke to the storm: "Quiet down," he said, and the wind and waves subsided and all was calm! 25Then he asked them, "Where is your faith?"

And they were filled with awe and fear of him and said to one another, "Who is this man, that even the winds and waves obey him?"

26So they arrived at the other side, in the Gerasene country across the lake from Galilee. 27As he was climbing out of the boat a man from the city of Gadara came to meet him, a man who had been demon-possessed for a long time. Homeless and naked, he lived in a cemetery among the tombs. 28As soon as he saw Jesus he shrieked and fell to the ground before him, screaming, "What do you want with me, Jesus, Son of God Most High? Please, I beg you, oh, don't torment me!"

29For Jesus was already commanding the demon to leave him. This demon had often taken control of the man so that even when shackled with chains he simply broke them and rushed out into the desert, completely under the demon's power. 30"What is your name?" Jesus asked the demon. "Legion," they replied—for the man was filled with thousands of them! 31They kept begging Jesus not to order them into the Bottomless Pit.

32A herd of pigs was feeding on the mountainside nearby, and the demons pled with him to let them enter into the pigs. And Jesus said they could. 33So they left the man and went into the pigs, and immediately the whole herd rushed down the mountainside and fell over a cliff into the lake below, where they drowned. 34The herdsmen rushed away to the nearby city, spreading the news as they ran.

35Soon a crowd came out to see for themselves what had happened and saw the man who had been demon-possessed sitting quietly at Jesus' feet, clothed and sane! And the whole crowd was badly frightened. 36Then those who had seen it happen told how the demon-possessed man had been healed. 37And everyone begged Jesus to go away and leave them alone (for a deep wave of fear had swept over them). So he returned to the boat and left, crossing back to the other side of the lake.

38The man who had been demon-possessed begged to go too, but Jesus said no.

39"Go back to your family," he told him, "and tell them what a wonderful thing God has done for you."

So he went all through the city telling everyone about Jesus' mighty miracle.

40On the other side of the lake the crowds received him with open arms, for they had been waiting for him.

PSALM 70:1–5

RESCUE me, O God! Lord, hurry to my aid! 2,3They are after my life, and delight in hurting me. Confuse them! Shame them! Stop them! Don't let them keep on mocking me! 4But fill the followers of God with joy. Let those who love your salvation exclaim, "What a wonderful God he is!" 5But I am in deep trouble. Rush to my aid, for only you can help and save me. O Lord, don't delay.

PROVERBS FOR TODAY/ 12:4

A worthy wife is her husband's joy and crown; the other kind corrodes his strength and tears down everything he does.

MARCH 30

DEUTERONOMY 13:1—15:23

IF there is a prophet among you, or one who claims to foretell the future by dreams, 2and if his predictions come true but he says, 'Come, let us worship the gods of the other nations,' 3don't listen to him. For the Lord is testing you to find out whether or not you really love him with all your heart and soul. 4You must *never* worship any God but Jehovah; obey only his commands and cling to him.

⁵"The prophet who tries to lead you astray must be executed, for he has attempted to foment rebellion against the Lord your God who brought you out of slavery in the land of Egypt. By executing him you will clear out the evil from among you.

⁶,⁷If your nearest relative or closest friend, even a brother, son, daughter, or beloved wife whispers to you to come and worship these foreign gods, ⁸do not consent nor listen, and have no pity: Do not spare that person from the penalty; don't conceal his horrible suggestion. ⁹Execute him! Your own hand shall be the first upon him to put him to death, then the hands of all the people. ¹⁰Stone him to death because he has tried to draw you away from the Lord your God who brought you from the land of Egypt, the place of slavery. ¹¹Then all Israel will hear about his evil deed, and will fear such wickedness as this among you.

¹²,¹³,¹⁴"If you ever hear it said about one of the cities of Israel that some worthless rabble have led their fellow citizens astray with the suggestion that they worship foreign gods, first check the facts to see if the rumor is true. If you find that it is, that it is certain that such a horrible thing is happening among you in one of the cities the Lord has given you, ¹⁵you must without fail declare war against that city and utterly destroy all of its inhabitants, and even all of the cattle. ¹⁶Afterwards you must pile all the booty into the middle of the street and burn it, then put the entire city to the torch, as a burnt offering to Jehovah your God. That city shall forever remain a lifeless mound and may never be rebuilt. ¹⁷Keep none of the booty! Then the Lord will turn from his fierce anger and be merciful to you, and have compassion upon you, and make you a great nation just as he promised your ancestors.

¹⁸"Of course, the Lord your God will be merciful only if you have been obedient to him and to his commandments which I am giving you today, and if you have been doing that which is right in the eyes of the Lord.

"SINCE you are the people of God, never cut yourselves [as the heathen do when they worship their idols] nor shave the front halves of your heads for funerals. ²You belong exclusively to the Lord your God, and he has chosen you to be his own possession, more so than any other nation on the face of the earth.

³,⁴,⁵"You are not to eat any animal I have declared to be ceremonially defiled. These are the animals you may eat:

The ox, the sheep, the goat,
The deer, the gazelle, the roebuck,
The wild goat, the ibex,
The antelope, and the mountain sheep.

⁶"Any animal that has cloven hooves and chews the cud may be eaten, ⁷but if the animal doesn't have both, it may not be eaten. So you may not eat the camel, the hare, or the coney.

"They chew the cud but do not have cloven hooves. ⁸Pigs may not be eaten because, although they have cloven hooves, they don't chew the cud. You may not even touch the dead bodies of such animals.

⁹"Only sea animals with fins and scales may be eaten; ¹⁰all other kinds are ceremonially defiled.

¹¹⁻¹⁸"You may eat any bird except the following:

The eagle, the vulture,
The osprey, the buzzard,
The falcon (any variety),
The raven (any variety),
The ostrich, the nighthawk,
The sea gull, the hawk (any variety),
The screech owl, the great owl,
The horned owl, the pelican,
The vulture, the cormorant,
The stork, the heron (any variety),
The hoopoe, the bat.

¹⁹,²⁰"With certain exceptions, insects are a defilement to you and may not be eaten.

²¹"Don't eat anything that has died a natural death. However, a foreigner among you may eat it. You may give it

or sell it to him, but don't eat it yourself, for you are holy to the Lord your God.

"You must not boil a young goat in its mother's milk.

22"You must tithe all of your crops every year. 23Bring this tithe to eat before the Lord your God at the place he shall choose as his sanctuary; this applies to your tithes of grain, new wine, olive oil, and the firstborn of your flocks and herds. The purpose of tithing is to teach you always to put God first in your lives. 24If the place the Lord chooses for his sanctuary is so far away that it isn't convenient to carry your tithes to that place, 25then you may sell the tithe portion of your crops and herds and take the money to the Lord's sanctuary. 26When you arrive, use the money to buy an ox, a sheep, some wine, or beer, to feast there before the Lord your God, and to rejoice with your household.

27"Don't forget to share your income with the Levites in your community, for they have no property or crops as you do.

28"Every third year you are to use your entire tithe for local welfare programs: 29Give it to the Levites who have no inheritance among you, or to foreigners, or to widows and orphans within your city, so that they can eat and be satisfied; and then Jehovah your God will bless you and your work.

"AT the end of every seventh year there is to be a canceling of all debts! 2Every creditor shall write 'Paid in full' on any promissory note he holds against a fellow Israelite, for the Lord has released everyone from his obligation. 3(This release does not apply to foreigners.) 4,5No one will become poor because of this, for the Lord will greatly bless you in the land he is giving you if you obey this command. The only prerequisite for his blessing is that you carefully heed all the commands of the Lord your God that I am giving you today. 6He will bless you as he has promised. You shall lend money to many nations but will never need to

borrow! You shall rule many nations, but they shall not rule over you!

7"But if, when you arrive in the land the Lord will give you, there are any among you who are poor, you must not shut your heart or hand against them; 8you must lend them as much as they need. 9Beware! Don't refuse a loan because the year of debt cancellation is close at hand! If you refuse to make the loan and the needy man cries out to the Lord, it will be counted against you as a sin. 10You must lend him what he needs, and don't moan about it either! For the Lord will prosper you in everything you do because of this! 11There will always be some among you who are poor; that is why this commandment is necessary. You must lend to them liberally.

12"If you buy a Hebrew slave, whether a man or woman, you must free him at the end of the sixth year you have owned him, 13and don't send him away empty-handed! 14Give him a large farewell present from your flock, your olive press, and your wine press. Share with him in proportion as the Lord your God has blessed you. 15Remember that you were slaves in the land of Egypt and the Lord your God rescued you! That is why I am giving you this command.

16"But if your Hebrew slave doesn't want to leave—if he says he loves you and enjoys your pleasant home and gets along well with you— 17then take an awl and pierce his ear into the door, and after that he shall be your slave forever. Do the same with your women slaves. 18But when you free a slave you must not feel bad, for remember that for six years he has cost you less than half the price of a hired hand! And the Lord your God will prosper all you do because you have released him!

19"You shall set aside for God all the firstborn males from your flocks and herds. Do not use the firstborn of your herds to work your fields, and do not shear the firstborn of your flocks of sheep and goats. 20Instead, you and your family shall eat these animals before the Lord your God each year at his sanctuary. 21However, if this firstborn animal has any defect such as being lame or blind, or if anything else is wrong with it, you shall not sacrifice it. 22Instead, use it for food for your family at home. Anyone, even if ceremonially defiled at the time, may eat it, just as anyone may eat a gazelle or deer. 23But don't eat the blood; pour it out upon the ground like water.

LUKE 8:41—9:6

AND now a man named Jairus, a leader of a Jewish synagogue, came and fell down at Jesus' feet and begged him to come home with him, 42for his only child was dying, a little girl twelve years old. Jesus went with him, pushing through the crowds.

43,44As they went a woman who wanted to be healed came up behind and touched him, for she had been slowly bleeding for twelve years, and could find no cure (though she had spent everything she had on doctors). But the instant she touched the edge of his robe, the bleeding stopped.

45"Who touched me?" Jesus asked.

Everyone denied it, and Peter said, "Master, so many are crowding against you. . . ."

46But Jesus told him, "No, it was someone who deliberately touched me, for I felt healing power go out from me."

47When the woman realized that Jesus knew, she began to tremble and fell to her knees before him and told why she had touched him and that now she was well.

48"Daughter," he said to her, "your faith has healed you. Go in peace."

49While he was still speaking to her, a messenger arrived from the Jairus' home with the news that the little girl was dead. "She's gone," he told her father; "there's no use troubling the Teacher now."

50But when Jesus heard what had happened, he said to the father, "Don't be afraid! Just trust me, and she'll be all right."

51When they arrived at the house Jesus wouldn't let anyone into the room except Peter, James, John, and the little girl's father and mother. 52The home was filled with mourning people, but he said, "Stop the weeping! She isn't dead; she is only asleep!" 53This brought scoffing and laughter, for they all knew she was dead.

54Then he took her by the hand and called, "Get up, little girl!" 55And at that moment her life returned and she jumped up! "Give her something to eat!" he said. 56Her parents were overcome with happiness, but Jesus insisted that they not tell anyone the details of what had happened.

ONE day Jesus called together his twelve apostles and gave them authority over all demons—power to cast them out—and to heal all diseases. 2Then he sent them away to tell everyone about the coming of the Kingdom of God and to heal the sick.

3"Don't even take along a walking stick," he instructed them, "nor a beggar's bag, nor food, nor money. Not even an extra coat. 4Be a guest in only one home at each village.

5"If the people of a town won't listen to you when you enter it, turn around and leave, demonstrating God's anger against it by shaking its dust from your feet as you go."

6So they began their circuit of the villages, preaching the Good News and healing the sick.

PSALM 71:1–24

LORD, you are my refuge! Don't let me down! 2Save me from my enemies, for you are just! Rescue me! Bend down your ear and listen to my plea and save me. 3Be to me a great protecting Rock, where I am always welcome, safe from all attacks. For you have issued the order to save me. 4Rescue me, O God, from these unjust and cruel men. 5O Lord, you alone are my hope; I've trusted you from childhood. 6Yes, you have been with me from birth and have helped me constantly—no wonder I am always praising you! 7My success—at which so many stand amazed—is because you are my mighty protector. 8All day long I'll praise and honor you, O God, for all that you have done for me.

9And now, in my old age, don't set me aside. Don't forsake me now when my strength is failing. 10My enemies are whispering, 11"God has forsaken him! Now we can get him. There is no one to help him now!" 12O God, don't stay away! Come quickly! Help! 13Destroy them! Cover them with failure and disgrace—these enemies of mine.

14I will keep on expecting you to help me. I praise you more and more. 15I cannot count the times when you have faithfully rescued me from danger. I will tell everyone how good you are, and of your constant, daily care. 16I walk in the strength of the Lord God. I tell everyone that you alone are just and good. 17O God, you have helped me from my earliest childhood—and I have constantly testified to others of the wonderful things you do. 18And now that I am old and gray, don't forsake me. Give me time to tell this new generation (and their children too) about all your mighty miracles. 19Your power and goodness, Lord, reach to the highest heavens. You have done such wonderful things. Where is there another God like you? 20You have let me sink down deep in desperate problems. But you will bring me back to life again, up from the depths of the earth. 21You will give me greater honor than before, and turn again and comfort me.

22I will praise you with music, telling of your faithfulness to all your promises, O Holy One of Israel. 23I will shout and sing your praises for redeeming me. 24I will talk to others all day long about your justice and your goodness. For all who tried to hurt me have been disgraced and dishonored.

PROVERBS FOR TODAY/ 12:5–7

A good man's mind is filled with honest thoughts; an evil man's mind is crammed with lies. The wicked accuse; the godly defend. The wicked shall perish; the godly shall stand.

MARCH 31

DEUTERONOMY 16:1—17:20

ALWAYS remember to celebrate the Passover during the month of April, for that was when Jehovah your God brought you out of Egypt by night. 2Your Passover sacrifice shall be either a lamb or an ox, sacrificed to the Lord your God at his sanctuary. 3Eat the sacrifice with unleavened bread. Eat unleavened bread for seven days as a reminder of the bread you ate as you escaped from Egypt. This is to remind you that you left Egypt in such a hurry that there was no time for the bread to rise. Remember that day all the rest of your lives! 4For seven days no trace of yeast shall be in your homes, and none of the Passover lamb shall be left until the next morning.

5"The Passover is not to be eaten in your homes. 6It must be eaten at the place the Lord shall choose as his sanctuary. Sacrifice it there on the anniversary evening just as the sun goes down. 7Roast the lamb and eat it, then start back to your homes the next morning. 8For the following six days you shall eat no bread made with yeast. On the seventh day there shall be a quiet gathering of the people of each city before the Lord your God. Don't do any work that day.

9"Seven weeks after the harvest begins, 10there shall be another festival before the Lord your God called the Festival of Weeks. At that time bring to him a free-will offering proportionate in size to his blessing upon you as judged by the amount of your harvest. 11It is a time to rejoice before the Lord with your family and household. And don't forget to include the local Levites, foreigners, widows, and orphans. Invite them to accompany you to the celebration at the sanctuary. 12Remember! You were a slave in Egypt, so be sure to carry out this command.

13"Another celebration, the Festival of Shelters, must be observed for seven days at the end of the harvest season, after the grain is threshed and the grapes have been pressed. 14This will be a happy time of rejoicing together with your family and servants. And don't forget to include the Levites, foreigners, orphans, and widows of your town.

15"This feast will be held at the sanctuary, which will be located at the place the Lord will designate. It is a time of deep thanksgiving to the Lord for blessing you with a good harvest and in so many other ways; it shall be a time of great joy.

16"Every man in Israel shall appear before the Lord your God three times a year at the sanctuary for these festivals:

The Festival of Unleavened Bread,

The Festival of Weeks,

The Festival of Shelters.

"On each of these occasions bring a gift to the Lord. 17Give as you are able, according as the Lord has blessed you.

18"Appoint judges and administrative officials for all the cities the Lord your God is giving you. They will administer justice in every part of the land. 19Never twist justice to benefit a rich man, and never accept bribes. For bribes blind the eyes of the wisest and corrupt their decisions. 20Justice must prevail.

"That is the only way you will be successful in the land which the Lord your God is giving you.

21"Never, under any circumstances, are you to erect shameful images beside the altar of the Lord your God. 22And never set up stone pillars to worship them, for the Lord hates them!

"NEVER sacrifice a sick or defective ox or sheep to the Lord your God. He doesn't feel honored by such gifts!

2,3"If anyone, whether man or woman, in any village throughout your land violates your covenant with God by worshiping other gods, the sun, moon, or stars—which I have strictly forbidden—4first check the rumor very carefully; if there is no doubt it is true, 5then that man or woman shall be taken outside the city and shall be stoned to death. 6However, never put a man to death on the testimony of only one witness; there must be at least two or three. 7The witnesses shall throw the first stones, and then all the people shall join in. In this way you will purge all evil from among you.

8"If a case arises that is too hard for you to decide—for instance, whether someone is guilty of murder when there is insufficient evidence, or whether someone's rights have been violated—you shall take the case to the sanctuary of the Lord your God, 9to the priests and Levites, and the chief judge on duty at the time will make the decision. 10His decision is without appeal and is to be followed to the letter. 11The sentence he imposes is to be fully executed. 12If the defendant refuses to accept the decision of the priest or judge appointed by God for this purpose, the penalty is death. Such sinners must be purged from Israel. 13Then everyone will hear about what happened to the man who refused God's verdict, and they will be afraid to defy a court's judgment.

14"When you arrive in the land the Lord your God will give you, and have conquered it, and begin to think, 'We ought to have a king like the other nations around us'— 15be sure that you select as king the man the Lord your God shall choose. He must be an Israelite, not a foreigner. 16Be sure that he doesn't build up a large stable of horses for himself, nor send his men to Egypt to raise horses for him there, for the Lord has told you, 'Never return to Egypt again.' 17He must not have too many wives, lest his heart be turned away from the Lord, neither shall he be excessively rich.

18"And when he has been crowned and sits upon his throne as king, then he must copy these laws from the book kept by the Levite-priests. 19That copy of the laws shall be his constant companion. He must read from it every day of his life so that he will learn to respect the Lord his God by obeying all of his commands. 20This regular reading of God's laws will prevent him from feeling that he is better than his fellow citizens. It will also prevent him from turning away from God's laws in the slightest respect, and will ensure his having a long, good reign. His sons will then follow him upon the throne.

LUKE 9:7–27

WHEN reports of Jesus' miracles reached Herod, the governor, he was worried and puzzled, for some were saying, "This is John the Baptist come back to life again"; 8and others, "It is Elijah or some other ancient prophet risen from the dead." These rumors were circulating all over the land.

9"I beheaded John," Herod said, "so who is this man about whom I hear such strange stories?" And he tried to see him.

10After the apostles returned to Jesus and reported what they had done, he slipped quietly away with them toward the city of Bethsaida. 11But the crowds found out where he was going, and followed. And he welcomed them, teaching them again about the Kingdom of God and curing those who were ill.

12Late in the afternoon all twelve of the disciples came and urged him to send the people away to the nearby villages and farms, to find food and lodging for the night. "For there is nothing to eat here in this deserted spot," they said.

13But Jesus replied, *"You feed them!"*

"Why, we have only five loaves of bread and two fish among the lot of us," they protested; "or are you expecting us to go and buy enough for this whole mob?" 14For there were about 5,000 men there!

"Just tell them to sit down on the ground in groups of about fifty each," Jesus replied. 15So they did.

16Jesus took the five loaves and two fish and looked up into the sky and gave thanks; then he broke off pieces for his disciples to set before the crowd. 17And everyone ate and ate; still, twelve basketfuls of scraps were picked up afterwards!

18One day as he was alone, praying, with his disciples nearby, he came over and asked them, "Who are the people saying I am?"

19"John the Baptist," they told him, "or perhaps Elijah or one of the other ancient prophets risen from the dead."

20Then he asked them, "Who do you think I am?"

Peter replied, "The Messiah—the Christ of God!"

21He gave them strict orders not to speak of this to anyone. 22"For I, the Messiah, must suffer much," he said, "and be rejected by the Jewish leaders— the elders, chief priests, and teachers of the Law—and be killed; and three days later I will come back to life again!"

23Then he said to all, "Anyone who wants to follow me must put aside his own desires and conveniences and carry his cross with him every day and *keep close to me!* 24Whoever loses his life for my sake will save it, but whoever insists on keeping his life will lose it; 25and what profit is there in gaining the whole world when it means forfeiting one's self?

26"When I, the Messiah, come in my glory and in the glory of the Father and the holy angels, I will be ashamed then of all who are ashamed of me and of my words now. 27But this is the simple truth—some of you who are standing here right now will not die until you have seen the Kingdom of God."

PSALM 72:1–20

O God, help the king to judge as you would, and help his son to walk in godliness. 2Help him to give justice to your people, even to the poor. 3May the mountains and hills flourish in prosperity because of his good reign. 4Help him to defend the poor and needy and to crush their oppressors. 5May the poor and needy revere you constantly, as long as sun and moon continue in the skies! Yes, forever!

6May the reign of this son of mine be as gentle and fruitful as the springtime rains upon the grass—like showers that water the earth! 7May all good men flourish in his reign, with abundance of peace to the end of time.

8Let him reign from sea to sea, and from the Euphrates River to the ends of the earth. 9The desert nomads shall bow before him; his enemies shall fall face downward in the dust. 10Kings along the Mediterranean coast—the kings of Tarshish and the islands—and those from Sheba and from Seba—all will bring their gifts. 11Yes, kings from everywhere! All will bow before him! All will serve him!

12He will take care of the helpless and poor when they cry to him; for they have no one else to defend them. 13He feels pity for the weak and needy, and will rescue them. 14He will save them from oppression and from violence, for their lives are precious to him.

15And he shall live; and to him will be given the gold of Sheba, and there will be constant praise for him. His people will bless him all day long. 16Bless us with abundant crops throughout the land, even on the highland plains; may there be fruit like that of Lebanon; may the cities be as full of people as the fields are of grass. 17His name will be honored forever; it will continue as the sun; and all will be blessed in him; all nations will praise him.

18Blessed be Jehovah God, the God of Israel, who only does wonderful things! 19Blessed be his glorious name forever! Let the whole earth be filled with his glory. Amen, and amen!

20(This ends the psalms of David, son of Jesse.)

PROVERBS FOR TODAY/ 12:8–9

Everyone admires a man with good sense, but a man with a warped mind is despised. It is better to get your hands dirty—and eat, than to be too proud to work—and starve.

APRIL 1

DEUTERONOMY 18:1—20:20

REMEMBER that the priests and all the other members of the Levite tribe will not be given property like the other tribes. So the priests and Levites are to be supported by the sacrifices brought to the altar of the Lord and by the other offerings the people bring to him. 2They don't need to own property, for the Lord is their property! That is what he promised them! 3The shoulder, the cheeks, and the stomach of every ox or sheep brought for sacrifice must be given to the priests.

4In addition, the priests shall receive the harvest samples brought in thanksgiving to the Lord—the first of the grain, the new wine, the olive oil, and of the fleece at shearing time. 5For the Lord your God has chosen the tribe of Levi, of all the tribes, to minister to the Lord from generation to generation.

6,7"Any Levite, no matter where he lives in the land of Israel, has the right to come to the sanctuary at any time and minister in the name of the Lord, just like his brother Levites who work there regularly. 8He shall be given his share of the sacrifices and offerings as his right, not just if he is in need.

9"When you arrive in the Promised Land you must be very careful lest you be corrupted by the horrible customs of the nations now living there. 10For example, any Israeli who presents his child to be burned to death as a sacrifice to heathen gods, must be killed. No Israeli may practice black magic, or call on the evil spirits for aid, or be a fortune teller, 11or be a serpent charmer, medium, or wizard, or call forth the spirits of the dead. 12Anyone doing these things is an object of horror and disgust to the Lord, and it is because the nations do these things that the Lord your God will displace them. 13You must walk blamelessly before the Lord your God. 14The nations you replace all do these evil things, but the Lord your God will not permit you to do such things.

15"Instead, he will raise up for you a Prophet like me, an Israeli, a man to whom you must listen and whom you must obey. 16For this is what you yourselves begged of God at Mount Horeb. There at the foot of the mountain you begged that you might not have to listen to the terrifying voice of God again, or see the awesome fire on the mountain, lest you die.

17" 'All right,' the Lord said to me, 'I will do as they have requested. 18I will raise up from among them a Prophet, an Israeli like you. I will tell him what to say, and he shall be my spokesman to the people. 19I will personally deal with anyone who will not listen to him and heed his messages from me. 20But any prophet who falsely claims that his message is from me, shall die. And any prophet who claims to give a message from other gods must die.' 21If you wonder, 'How shall we know whether the prophecy is from the Lord or not?' 22this is the way to know: If the thing he prophesies doesn't happen, it is not the Lord who has given him the message; he has made it up himself. You have nothing to fear from him.

"WHEN the Lord your God has destroyed the nations you will displace, and when you are living in their cities and homes, 2,3you must set apart three Cities of Refuge so that anyone who accidentally kills someone may flee to safety. Divide the country into three districts, with one of these cities in each district; and keep the roads to these cities in good repair.

4"Here is an example of the purpose of these cities: 5If a man goes into the forest with his neighbor to chop wood, and the axe head flies off the handle and kills the man's neighbor, he may flee to one of those cities and be safe. 6,7Anyone seeking to avenge the death will not be able to. These cities must be scattered so that one of them will be reasonably close to everyone; otherwise the angry avenger might catch and kill the innocent slayer, even though he should not have died since he had not killed deliberately.

8"If the Lord enlarges your boundaries as he promised your ancestors, and gives you all the land he promised 9(whether he does this depends on your obedience to all these commandments I am giving you today—loving the Lord your God and walking his paths), then you must designate three additional Cities of Refuge. 10In this way you will be able to avoid the death of innocent people, and you will not be held responsible for unjustified bloodshed.

11"But if anyone hates his neighbor and springs out of hiding and kills him, and then flees into one of the Cities of

Refuge, 12the elders of his home town shall send for him and shall bring him home and deliver him over to the dead man's avenger, to kill him. 13Don't pity him! Purge all murderers from Israel! Only then will all go well with you.

14"When you arrive in the land the Lord your God is giving you, remember that you must never steal a man's land by moving the boundary marker.

15"Never convict anyone on the testimony of one witness. There must be at least two, and three is even better. 16If anyone gives false witness, claiming he has seen someone do wrong when he hasn't, 17both men shall be brought before the priests and judges on duty before the Lord at the time. 18They must be closely questioned, and if the witness is lying, 19his penalty shall be the punishment he thought the other man would get. In this way you will purge out evil from among you. 20Then those who hear about it will be afraid to tell lies on the witness stand. 21You shall not show pity to a false witness. Life for life, eye for eye, tooth for tooth, hand for hand, foot for foot; this is your rule in such cases.

"WHEN you go to war and see before you vast numbers of horses and chariots, an army far greater than yours, don't be frightened! The Lord your God is with you—the same God who brought you safely out of Egypt! 2Before you begin the battle, a priest shall stand before the Israeli army and say,

3" 'Listen to me, all you men of Israel! Don't be afraid as you go out to fight today! 4For the Lord your God is going with you! He will fight for you against your enemies, and he will give you the victory!'

5"Then the officers of the army shall address the men in this manner: 'Has anyone just built a new house, but not yet dedicated it? If so, go home! For you might be killed in the battle, and someone else would dedicate it! 6Has anyone just planted a vineyard but not yet eaten any of its fruit? If so, go home! You might die in battle and someone else would eat

it! 7Has anyone just become engaged? Well, go home and get married! For you might die in the battle, and someone else would marry your fiancée. 8And now, is anyone afraid? If you are, go home before you frighten the rest of us!' 9When the officers have finished saying this to their men, they will announce the names of the battalion leaders.

10"As you approach a city to fight against it, first offer it a truce. 11If it accepts the truce and opens its gates to you, then all its people shall become your servants. 12But if it refuses and won't make peace with you, you must besiege it. 13When the Lord your God has given it to you, kill every male in the city; 14but you may keep for yourselves all the women, children, cattle, and booty. 15These instructions apply only to distant cities, not to those in the Promised Land itself.

16"For in the cities within the boundaries of the Promised Land you are to save no one; destroy every living thing. 17Utterly destroy the Hittites, the Amorites, the Canaanites, the Perizzites, the Hivites, and the Jebusites. This is the commandment of the Lord your God. 18The purpose of this command is to prevent the people of the land from luring you into idol worship and into participation in their loathsome customs, thus sinning deeply against the Lord your God.

19"When you besiege a city, don't destroy the fruit trees. Eat all the fruit you wish; just don't cut down the trees. They aren't enemies who need to be slaughtered! 20But you may cut down trees that aren't valuable for food. Use them for the siege [to make ladders, portable towers, and battering rams].

LUKE 9:28-50

EIGHT days later he took Peter, James, and John with him into the hills to pray. 29And as he was praying, his face began to shine, and his clothes became dazzling white and blazed with light. 30Then two men appeared and began talking with him—Moses and Elijah! 31They were splendid in appearance, glorious to see; and they were speaking of his death at Jerusalem, to be carried out in accordance with God's plan.

32Peter and the others had been very drowsy and had fallen asleep. Now they woke up and saw Jesus covered with brightness and glory, and the two men standing with him. 33As Moses and Elijah were starting to leave, Peter, all confused and not even knowing what he was saying, blurted out, "Master, this is wonderful! We'll put up three shelters—one for you and one for Moses and one for Elijah!"

34But even as he was saying this, a bright cloud formed above them; and terror gripped them as it covered them. 35And a voice from the cloud said, *"This is my Son, my Chosen One; listen to him."*

36Then, as the voice died away, Jesus was there alone with his disciples. They didn't tell anyone what they had seen until long afterwards.

37The next day as they descended from the hill, a huge crowd met him, 38and a man in the crowd called out to him, "Teacher, this boy here is my only son, 39and a demon keeps seizing him, making him scream; and it throws him into convulsions so that he foams at the mouth; it is always hitting him and hardly ever leaves him alone. 40I begged your disciples to cast the demon out, but they couldn't."

41"O you stubborn faithless people," Jesus said [to his disciples], "how long should I put up with you? Bring him here."

42As the boy was coming the demon knocked him to the ground and threw him into a violent convulsion. But Jesus ordered the demon to come out, and healed the boy and handed him over to his father.

43Awe gripped the people as they saw this display of the power of God.

Meanwhile, as they were exclaiming over all the wonderful things he was doing, Jesus said to his disciples, 44"Listen to me and remember what I say. I, the Messiah, am going to be betrayed."

45But the disciples didn't know what he meant, for their minds had been sealed and they were afraid to ask him.

46Now came an argument among them as to which of them would be greatest [in the coming Kingdom]! 47But Jesus knew their thoughts, so he stood a little child beside him 48and said to them, "Anyone who takes care of a little child like this is caring for me! And whoever cares for me is caring for God who sent me. Your care for others is the measure of your greatness." 49His disciple John came to him and said, "Master, we saw someone using your name to cast out demons. And we told him not to. After all, he isn't in our group."

50But Jesus said, "You shouldn't have done that! For anyone who is not against you is for you."

PSALM 73:1–28

How good God is to Israel—to those whose hearts are pure. 2But as for me, I came *so* close to the edge of the cliff! My feet were slipping and I was almost gone. 3For I was envious of the prosperity of the proud and wicked. 4Yes, all through life their road is smooth! They grow sleek and fat. 5They aren't always in trouble and plagued with problems like everyone else, 6so their pride sparkles like a jeweled necklace, and their clothing is woven of cruelty! 7These fat cats have everything their hearts could ever wish for! 8They scoff at God and threaten his people. How proudly they speak! 9They boast against the very heavens, and their words strut through the earth.

10And so God's people are dismayed and confused, and drink it all in. 11"Does God realize what is going on?" they ask. 12"Look at these men of arrogance; they never have to lift a finger— theirs is a life of ease; and all the time their riches multiply."

13Have I been wasting my time? Why take the trouble to be pure? 14All I get out of it is trouble and woe—every day and all day long! 15If I had really said that, I would have been a traitor to your people. 16Yet it is so hard to explain it—this prosperity of those who hate the Lord. 17Then one day I went into God's sanctuary to meditate, and thought about the future of these evil men. 18What a slippery path they are on—suddenly God will send them sliding over the edge of the cliff and down to their destruction: 19an instant end to all their happiness, an eternity of terror. 20Their present life is only a dream! They will awaken to the truth as one awakens from a dream of things that never really were!

21When I saw this, what turmoil filled my heart! 22I saw myself so stupid and so ignorant; I must seem like an animal to you, O God. 23But even so you love me! You are holding my right hand! 24You will keep on guiding me all my life with your wisdom and counsel; and afterwards receive me into the glories of heaven! 25Whom have I in heaven but you? And I desire no one on earth as much as you! 26My health fails; my spirits droop, yet God remains! He is the strength of my heart; he is mine forever!

27But those refusing to worship God will perish, for he destroys those serving other gods.

28But as for me, I get as close to him as I can! I have chosen him and I will tell everyone about the wonderful ways he rescues me.

PROVERBS FOR TODAY/ 12:10

A good man is concerned for the welfare of his animals, but even the kindness of godless men is cruel.

APRIL 2

DEUTERONOMY 21:1—22:30

IF, when you arrive in the Promised Land, a murder victim is found lying in a field and no one has seen the murder, 2the elders and judges shall measure from the body to the nearest city. 3Then the elders of that city shall take a heifer that has never been yoked, 4and lead it to a valley where there is running water—a valley neither plowed nor sowed—and there break its neck. 5"Then the priests shall come (for the Lord your God has chosen them to minister before him and to pronounce his blessings and decide lawsuits and punishments), 6and shall wash their hands over the heifer, 7and say, 'Our hands have not shed this blood, neither have our eyes seen it. 8O Lord, forgive your people Israel whom you have redeemed, and do not charge them with murdering an inno-cent man. Forgive us the guilt of this man's blood.' 9In this way you will put away the guilt from among you by following the Lord's directions.

10"When you go to war and the Lord your God delivers your enemies to you, 11and you see among the captives a beautiful girl you want as your wife, 12take her home with you. She must shave her head and pare her nails 13and change her clothing, laying aside that which she was wearing when she was captured, then remain in your home in mourning for her father and mother for a full month. After that you may marry her. 14However, if after marrying her you decide you don't like her, you must let her go free—you may not sell her or treat her as a slave, for you have humiliated her.

15"If a man has two wives but loves one and not the other, and both have borne him children, and the mother of his oldest son is the wife he doesn't love, 16he may not give a larger inheritance to his younger son, the son of the wife he loves. 17He must give the customary double portion to his oldest son, who is the beginning of his strength and who owns the rights of a firstborn son, even though he is the son of the wife his father doesn't love.

18"If a man has a stubborn, rebellious son who will not obey his father or mother, even though they punish him, 19then his father and mother shall take him before the elders of the city 20and declare, 'This son of ours is stubborn and rebellious and won't obey; he is a worthless drunkard.' 21Then the men of the city shall stone him to death. In this way you shall put away this evil from among you, and all the young men of Israel will hear about what happened and will be afraid.

22"If a man has committed a crime worthy of death, and is executed and then hanged on a tree, 23his body shall not remain on the tree overnight. You must bury him the same day, for anyone hanging on a tree is cursed of God. Don't defile the land the Lord your God has given you.

"IF you see someone's ox or sheep wandering away, don't pretend you didn't see it; take it back to its owner. 2If you don't know who the owner is, take it to your farm and keep it there until the owner comes looking for it, and then give it to him. 3The same applies to donkeys, clothing, or anything else you find. Keep it for its owner.

4"If you see someone trying to get an ox or donkey onto its feet when it has slipped beneath its load, don't look the other way. Go and help!

5"A woman must not wear men's clothing, and a man must not wear women's clothing. This is abhorrent to the Lord your God.

6"If a bird's nest is lying on the ground, or if you spy one in a tree, and there are young ones or eggs in it with the mother sitting in the nest, don't take the mother with the young. 7Let her go, and take only the young. The Lord will bless you for it.

8"Every new house must have a guardrail around the edge of the flat rooftop to prevent anyone from falling off and bring guilt to both the house and its owner.

9"Do not sow other crops in the rows of your vineyard. If you do, both the crops and the grapes shall be confiscated by the priests.

10"Don't plow with an ox and a donkey harnessed together.

11"Don't wear clothing woven from two kinds of thread: for instance, wool and linen.

12"You must sew tassels on the four corners of your cloaks.

13,14"If a man marries a girl, then after sleeping with her accuses her of having had premarital intercourse with another man, saying, 'She was not a virgin when I married her,' 15then the girl's father and mother shall bring the proof of her virginity to the city judges.

16"Her father shall tell them, 'I gave my daughter to this man to be his wife, and now he despises her, 17,18and has accused her of shameful things, claiming that she was not a virgin when she married; yet here is the proof.' And they shall spread before the judges the bloodstained sheet from her marriage bed. The judges shall sentence the man to be whipped, 19and fine him one hundred dollars to be given to the girl's father, for he has falsely accused a virgin of Israel. She shall remain his wife and he may never divorce her. 20But if the man's accusations are true, and she was not a virgin, 21the judges shall take the girl to the door of her father's home where the men of the city shall stone her to death. She has defiled Israel by flagrant crime, being a prostitute while living at home with her parents; and such evil must be cleansed from among you.

22"If a man is discovered committing adultery, both he and the other man's wife must be killed; in this way evil will be cleansed from Israel. 23,24If a girl who is engaged is seduced within the walls of a city, both she and the man who seduced her shall be taken outside the gates and stoned to death—the girl because she didn't scream for help, and the man because he has violated the virginity of another man's fiancée. 25,26,27In this way you will reduce crime among you. But if this deed takes place out in the country, only the man shall die. The girl is as innocent as a murder victim; for it must be assumed that she screamed, but there was no one to hear and rescue her out in the field. 28,29If a man rapes a girl who is not engaged, and is caught in the act, he must pay a fine to the girl's father and marry her; he may never divorce her. 30A man shall not sleep with his father's widow since she belonged to his father.

LUKE 9:51—10:12

As the time drew near for his return to heaven, he moved steadily onward toward Jerusalem with an iron will.

52One day he sent messengers ahead to reserve rooms for them in a Samaritan village. 53But they were turned away! The people of the village refused to have anything to do with them because they were headed for Jerusalem.

54When word came back of what had happened, James and John said to Jesus, "Master, shall we order fire down from heaven to burn them up?" 55But Jesus turned and rebuked them, 56and they went on to another village.

57As they were walking along someone said to Jesus, "I will always follow you no matter where you go."

58But Jesus replied, "Remember, I don't even own a place to lay my head. Foxes have dens to live in, and birds have nests, but I, the Messiah, have no earthly home at all."

59Another time, when he invited a man to come with him and to be his disciple, the man agreed—but wanted to wait until his father's death.

60Jesus replied, "Let those without eternal life concern themselves with things like that. Your duty is to come and preach the coming of the Kingdom of God to all the world."

61Another said, "Yes, Lord, I will come, but first let me ask permission of those at home."

62But Jesus told him, "Anyone who lets himself be distracted from the work I plan for him is not fit for the Kingdom of God."

THE Lord now chose seventy other disciples and sent them on ahead in pairs to all the towns and villages he planned to visit later.

2These were his instructions to them: "Plead with the Lord of the harvest to send out more laborers to help you, for the harvest is so plentiful and the workers so few. 3Go now, and remember that I am sending you out as lambs among wolves. 4Don't take any money with you, or a beggar's bag, or even an extra pair of shoes. And don't waste time along the way.

5"Whenever you enter a home, give it your blessing. 6If it is worthy of the blessing, the blessing will stand; if not, the blessing will return to you.

7"When you enter a village, don't shift around from home to home, but stay in one place, eating and drinking without question whatever is set before you. And don't hesitate to accept hospitality, for the workman is worthy of his wages!

8,9"If a town welcomes you, follow these two rules:

(1) Eat whatever is set before you.

(2) Heal the sick; and as you heal them, say, 'The Kingdom of God is very near you now.'

10"But if a town refuses you, go out into its streets and say, 11'We wipe the dust of your town from our feet as a public announcement of your doom. Never forget how close you were to the Kingdom of God!' 12Even wicked Sodom will be better off than such a city on the Judgment Day.

PSALM 74:1–23

O God, why have you cast us away forever? Why is your anger hot against us—the sheep of your own pasture? ²Remember that we are your people—the ones you chose in ancient times from slavery and made the choicest of your possessions. You chose Jerusalem as your home on earth!

³Walk through the awful ruins of the city, and see what the enemy has done to your sanctuary. ⁴There they shouted their battle cry and erected their idols to flaunt their victory. ⁵,⁶Everything lies in shambles like a forest chopped to the ground. They came with their axes and sledgehammers and smashed and chopped the carved paneling, ⁷and set the sanctuary on fire, and razed it to the ground—your sanctuary, Lord. ⁸"Let's wipe out every trace of God," they said, and went through the entire country burning down the assembly places where we worshiped you.

⁹,¹⁰There is nothing left to show that we are your people. The prophets are gone, and who can say when it all will end? How long, O God, will you allow our enemies to dishonor your name? Will you let them get away with this forever? ¹¹Why do you delay? Why hold back your power? Unleash your fist and give them a final blow.

¹²God is my King from ages past; you have been actively helping me everywhere throughout the land. ¹³,¹⁴You divided the Red Sea with your strength; you crushed the sea-god's heads! You gave him to the desert tribes to eat! ¹⁵At your command the springs burst forth to give your people water; and then you dried a path for them across the ever-flowing Jordan. ¹⁶Day and night alike belong to you; you made the starlight and the sun. ¹⁷All nature is within your hands; you make the summer and the winter too. ¹⁸Lord, see how these enemies scoff at you. O Jehovah, an arrogant nation has blasphemed your name.

¹⁹O Lord, save me! Protect your turtledove from the hawks. Save your beloved people from these beasts. ²⁰Remember your promise! For the land is full of darkness and cruel men. ²¹O Lord, don't let your downtrodden people be constantly insulted. Give cause for these poor and needy ones to praise your name! ²²Arise, O God, and state your case against our enemies. Remember the insults these rebels have hurled against you all day long. ²³Don't overlook the cursing of these enemies of yours; it grows louder and louder.

PROVERBS FOR TODAY/ 12:11
Hard work means prosperity; only a fool idles away his time.

APRIL 3

DEUTERONOMY 23:1—25:19

IF a man's testicles are crushed or his penis cut off, he shall not enter the sanctuary. ²A bastard may not enter the sanctuary, nor any of his descendants for ten generations.

³"No Ammonite or Moabite may ever enter the sanctuary, even after the tenth generation. ⁴The reason for this law is that these nations did not welcome you with food and water when you came out of Egypt; they even tried to hire Balaam, the son of Beor from Pethor, Mesopotamia, to curse you. ⁵But the Lord wouldn't listen to Balaam; instead, he turned the intended curse into a blessing for you,

because the Lord loves you. 6You must never, as long as you live, try to help the Ammonites or the Moabites in any way. 7But don't look down on the Edomites and the Egyptians; the Edomites are your brothers and you lived among the Egyptians. 8The grandchildren of the Egyptians who came with you from Egypt may enter the sanctuary of the Lord.

9,10"When you are at war, the men in the camps must stay away from all evil. Any man who becomes ceremonially defiled because of a seminal emission during the night must leave the camp, 11and stay outside until the evening; then he shall bathe himself and return at sunset. 12The toilet area shall be outside the camp. 13Each man must have a spade as part of his equipment; after every bowel movement he must dig a hole with the spade and cover the excrement. 14The camp must be holy, for the Lord walks among you to protect you and to cause your enemies to fall before you; and the Lord does not want to see anything indecent lest he turn away from you.

15,16"If a slave escapes from his master, you must not force him to return; let him live among you in whatever town he shall choose, and do not oppress him.

17,18"No prostitutes are permitted in Israel, either men or women; you must not bring to the Lord any offering from the earnings of a prostitute or a homosexual, for both are detestable to the Lord your God.

19"Don't demand interest on loans you make to a brother Israelite, whether it is in the form of money, food, or anything else. 20You may take interest from a foreigner, but not from an Israeli. For if you take interest from a brother, an Israeli, the Lord your God won't bless you when you arrive in the Promised Land.

21"When you make a vow to the Lord, be prompt in doing whatever it is you promised him, for the Lord demands that you promptly fulfill your vows; it is a sin if you don't. 22(But it is not a sin if you refrain from vowing!) 23Once you make the vow, you must be careful to do as you have said, for it was your own choice, and you have vowed to the Lord your God.

24"You may eat your fill of the grapes from another man's vineyard, but do not take any away in a container. 25It is the same with someone else's grain—you may eat a few handfuls of it, but don't use a sickle.

"If a man doesn't like something about his wife, he may write a letter stating that he has divorced her, give her the letter, and send her away. 2If she then remarries, 3and the second husband also divorces her, or dies, 4the former husband may not marry her again, for she has been defiled; this would bring guilt upon the land the Lord your God is giving you.

5"A newly married man is not to be drafted into the army nor given any other special responsibilities; for a year he shall be free to be at home, happy with his wife.

6"It is illegal to take a millstone as a pledge, for it is a tool by which its owner gains his livelihood. 7If anyone kidnaps a brother Israelite, and treats him as a slave or sells him, the kidnapper must die, in order to purge the evil from among you.

8"Be very careful to follow the instructions of the priest in cases of leprosy, for I have given him rules and guidelines you must obey to the letter: 9Remember what the Lord your God did to Miriam as you were coming from Egypt.

10"If you lend anything to another man, you must not enter his house to get his security. 11Stand outside! The owner will bring it out to you. 12,13If the man is poor and gives you his cloak as security, you are not to sleep in it. Take it back to him at sundown so that he can use it through the night and bless you; and the Lord your God will count it as righteousness for you.

14,15"Never oppress a poor hired man, whether a fellow Israelite or a foreigner living in your town. Pay him his wage each day before sunset, for since he is poor he needs it right away; otherwise he may cry out to the Lord against you and it would be counted as a sin against you.

16"Fathers shall not be put to death for the sins of their sons nor the sons for the sins of their fathers; every man worthy of death shall be executed for his own crime.

17"Justice must be given to migrants and orphans and you must never accept a widow's garment in pledge of her debt. 18Always remember that you were slaves in Egypt, and that the Lord your God rescued you; that is why I have given you this command. 19If, when reaping your harvest, you forget to bring in a sheaf from the field, don't go back after it. Leave it for the migrants, orphans, and widows; then the Lord your God will bless and prosper all you do. 20When you beat the olives from your olive trees, don't go over the boughs twice; leave anything remaining for the migrants, orphans, and widows. 21It is the same for the grapes in your vineyard; don't glean the vines after they are picked, but leave what's left for those in need. 22Remember that you were slaves in the land of Egypt—that is why I am giving you this command.

"IF a man is guilty of a crime, and the penalty is a beating, the judge shall command him to lie down and be beaten in his presence with up to forty stripes in proportion to the seriousness of the crime; but no more than forty stripes may be given lest the punishment seem too severe, and your brother be degraded in your eyes.

4"Don't muzzle an ox as it treads out the grain.

5"If a man's brother dies without a son, his widow must not marry outside the family; instead, her husband's brother must marry her and sleep with her. 6The first son she bears to him shall be counted as the son of the dead brother, so that his name will not be forgotten. 7But if the dead man's brother refuses to do his duty in this matter, refusing to marry the widow, then she shall go to the city elders and say to them, 'My husband's brother refuses to let his brother's name continue—he refuses to marry me.' 8The elders of the city will then summon him and talk it over with him, and if he still refuses, 9the widow shall walk over to him in the presence of the elders, pull his sandal from his foot and spit in his face. She shall then say, 'This is what happens to a man who refuses to build his brother's house.' 10And ever afterwards his house shall be referred to as 'the home of the man who had his sandal pulled off!'

11"If two men are fighting and the wife of one intervenes to help her husband by grabbing the testicles of the other man, 12her hand shall be cut off without pity.

13,14,15"In all your transactions you must use accurate scales and honest measurements, so that you will have a long, good life in the land the Lord your God is giving you. 16All who cheat with unjust weights and measurements are detestable to the Lord your God.

17"You must never forget what the people of Amalek did to you as you came from Egypt. 18Remember that they fought with you and struck down those who were faint and weary and lagging behind, with no respect or fear of God. 19Therefore, when the Lord your God has given you rest from all your enemies in the Promised Land, you are utterly to destroy the name of Amalek from under heaven. Never forget this.

LUKE 10:13–37

WHAT horrors await you, you cities of Chorazin and Bethsaida! For if the miracles I did for you had been done in the cities of Tyre and Sidon, their people would have sat in deep repentance long ago, clothed in sackcloth and throwing ashes on their heads to show their remorse. 14Yes, Tyre and Sidon will receive less punishment on the Judgment Day than you. 15And you people of Capernaum, what shall I say about you? Will you be exalted to heaven? No, you shall be brought down to hell."

¹⁶Then he said to the disciples, "Those who welcome you are welcoming me. And those who reject you are rejecting me. And those who reject me are rejecting God who sent me."

¹⁷When the seventy disciples returned, they joyfully reported to him, "Even the demons obey us when we use your name."

¹⁸"Yes," he told them, "I saw Satan falling from heaven as a flash of lightning! ¹⁹And I have given you authority over all the power of the Enemy, and to walk among serpents and scorpions and to crush them. Nothing shall injure you! ²⁰However, the important thing is not that demons obey you, but that your names are registered as citizens of heaven."

²¹Then he was filled with the joy of the Holy Spirit and said, "I praise you, O Father, Lord of heaven and earth, for hiding these things from the intellectuals and worldly wise and for revealing them to those who are as trusting as little children. Yes, thank you, Father, for that is the way you wanted it. ²²I am the Agent of my Father in everything; and no one really knows the Son except the Father, and no one really knows the Father except the Son and those to whom the Son chooses to reveal him."

²³Then, turning to the twelve disciples, he said quietly, "How privileged you are to see what you have seen. ²⁴Many a prophet and king of old has longed for these days, to see and hear what you have seen and heard!"

²⁵One day an expert on Moses' laws came to test Jesus' orthodoxy by asking him this question: "Teacher, what does a man need to do to live forever in heaven?"

²⁶Jesus replied, "What does Moses' law say about it?"

²⁷"It says," he replied, "that you must love the Lord your God with all your heart, and with all your soul, and with all your strength, and with all your mind. And you must love your neighbor just as much as you love yourself."

²⁸"Right!" Jesus told him. *"Do* this and *you* shall live!"

²⁹The man wanted to justify (his lack of love for some kinds of people), so he asked, "Which neighbors?"

³⁰Jesus replied with an illustration: "A Jew going on a trip from Jerusalem to Jericho was attacked by bandits. They stripped him of his clothes and money and beat him up and left him lying half dead beside the road.

³¹"By chance a Jewish priest came along; and when he saw the man lying there, he crossed to the other side of the road and passed him by. ³²A Jewish Temple-assistant walked over and looked at him lying there, but then went on.

³³"But a despised Samaritan came along, and when he saw him, he felt deep pity. ³⁴Kneeling beside him the Samaritan soothed his wounds with medicine and bandaged them. Then he put the man on his donkey and walked along beside him till they came to an inn, where he nursed him through the night. ³⁵The next day he handed the innkeeper two twenty-dollar bills and told him to take care of the man. 'If his bill runs higher than that,' he said, 'I'll pay the difference the next time I am here.'

³⁶"Now which of these three would you say was a neighbor to the bandits' victim?"

³⁷The man replied, "The one who showed him some pity."

Then Jesus said, "Yes, now go and do the same."

PSALM 75:1–10

HOW we thank you, Lord! Your mighty miracles give proof that you care.

²"Yes," the Lord replies, "and when I am ready, I will punish the wicked! ³Though the earth shakes and all its people live in turmoil, yet its pillars are firm, for I have set them in place!"

4I warned the proud to cease their arrogance! I told the wicked to lower their insolent gaze, 5and to stop being stubborn and proud. 6,7For promotion and power come from nowhere on earth, but only from God. He promotes one and deposes another. 8In Jehovah's hand there is a cup of pale and sparkling wine. It is his judgment, poured out upon the wicked of the earth. They must drain that cup to the dregs.

9But as for me, I shall forever declare the praises of the God of Jacob. 10"I will cut off the strength of evil men," says the Lord, "and increase the power of good men in their place."

PROVERBS FOR TODAY/ 12:12–14

Crooks are jealous of each other's loot, while good men long to help each other. Lies will get any man into trouble, but honesty is its own defense. Telling the truth gives a man great satisfaction, and hard work returns many blessings to him.

APRIL 4

DEUTERONOMY 26:1—27:26

WHEN you arrive in the land and have conquered it and are living there, 2,3you must present to the Lord at his sanctuary the first sample from each annual harvest. Bring it in a basket and hand it to the priest on duty and say to him, 'This gift is my acknowledgment that the Lord my God has brought me to the land he promised our ancestors.' 4The priest will then take the basket from your hand and set it before the altar. 5You shall then say before the Lord your God, 'My ancestors were migrant Arameans who went to Egypt for refuge. They were few in number, but in Egypt they became a mighty nation. 6,7The Egyptians mistreated us and we cried to the Lord God. He heard us and saw our hardship, toil, and oppression, 8and brought us out of Egypt with mighty miracles and a powerful hand. He did great and awesome miracles before the Egyptians, 9and has brought us to this place and given us this land "flowing with milk and honey!" 10And now, O Lord, see, I have brought you a token of the first of the crops from the ground you have given me.' Then place the sample before the Lord your God, and worship him. 11Afterwards, go and feast on all the good things he has given you. Celebrate with your family and with any Levites or migrants living among you.

12"Every third year is a year of special tithing. That year you are to give all your tithes to the Levites, migrants, orphans, and widows, so that they will be well fed. 13Then you shall declare before the Lord your God, 'I have given all of my tithes to the Levites, the migrants, the orphans, and the widows, just as you commanded me; I have not violated or forgotten any of your rules. 14I have not touched the tithe while I was ceremonially defiled (for instance, while I was in mourning), nor have I offered any of it to the dead. I have obeyed the Lord my God and have done everything you commanded me. 15Look down from your holy home in heaven and bless your people and the land you have given us, as you promised our ancestors; make it a land "flowing with milk and honey"!'

16"You must wholeheartedly obey all of these commandments and ordinances which the Lord your God is giving you today. 17You have declared today that he is your God, and you have promised to obey and keep his laws and ordinances, and to heed all he tells you to do. 18And the Lord has declared today that you are his very own people, just as he promised, and that you must obey all of his laws. 19If you do, he will make you greater than any other nation, allowing you to receive praise, honor, and renown; but to attain this honor and renown you must be a holy people to the Lord your God, as he requires."

THEN Moses and the elders of Israel gave the people these further instructions to obey:

2,3,4"When you cross the Jordan River and go into the Promised Land—a land 'flowing with milk and honey'—take out boulders from the river bottom and immediately pile them into a monument on the other side, at Mount Ebal. Face the stones with a coating of lime and then write the laws of God in the lime. 5,6And build an altar there to the Lord your God. Use uncut boulders, and on the altar offer burnt offerings to the Lord your God. 7Sacrifice peace offerings upon it also, and feast there with great joy before the Lord your God. 8Write all of these laws plainly [upon the monument]."

9Then Moses and the Levite-priests addressed all Israel as follows: "O Israel, listen! Today you have become the people of the Lord your God, 10so today you must begin to obey all of these commandments I have given you."

11That same day Moses gave this charge to the people:

12"When you cross into the Promised Land, the tribes of Simeon, Levi, Judah, Issachar, Joseph, and Benjamin shall stand upon Mount Gerizim to proclaim a blessing, 13and the tribes of Reuben, Gad, Asher, Zebulun, Dan, and Naphtali shall stand upon Mount Ebal to proclaim a curse. 14Then the Levites standing between them shall shout to all Israel,

15" 'The curse of God be upon anyone who makes and worships an idol, even in secret, whether carved of wood or made from molten metal—for these handmade gods are hated by the Lord.' And all the people shall reply, 'Amen.'

16" 'Cursed is anyone who despises his father or mother.' And all the people shall reply, 'Amen.'

17" 'Cursed is he who moves the boundary marker between his land and his neighbor's.' And all the people shall reply, 'Amen.'

18" 'Cursed is he who takes advantage of a blind man.' And all the people shall reply, 'Amen.'

19" 'Cursed is he who is unjust to the foreigner, the orphan, and the widow.' And all the people shall reply, 'Amen.'

20" 'Cursed is he who commits adultery with one of his father's wives, for she belongs to his father.' And all the people shall reply, 'Amen.'

21" 'Cursed is he who has sexual intercourse with an animal.' And all the people shall reply, 'Amen.'

22" 'Cursed is he who has sexual intercourse with his sister, whether she be a full sister or a half-sister.' And all the people shall reply, 'Amen.'

23" 'Cursed is he who has sexual intercourse with his widowed mother-in-law.' And all the people shall reply, 'Amen.'

24" 'Cursed is he who secretly slays another.' And all the people shall reply, 'Amen.'

25" 'Cursed is he who accepts a bribe to kill an innocent person.' And all the people shall reply, 'Amen.'

26" 'Cursed is anyone who does not obey these laws.' And all the people shall reply, 'Amen.'

LUKE 10:38—11:13

AS Jesus and the disciples continued on their way to Jerusalem they came to a village where a woman named Martha welcomed them into her home. 39Her sister Mary sat on the floor, listening to Jesus as he talked.

40But Martha was the jittery type, and was worrying over the big dinner she was preparing.

She came to Jesus and said, "Sir, doesn't it seem unfair to you that my sister just sits here while I do all the work? Tell her to come and help me."

⁴¹But the Lord said to her, "Martha, dear friend, you are so upset over all these details! ⁴²There is really only one thing worth being concerned about. Mary has discovered it—and I won't take it away from her!"

ONCE when Jesus had been out praying, one of his disciples came to him as he finished and said, "Lord, teach us a prayer to recite just as John taught one to his disciples."

²And this is the prayer he taught them: "Father, may your name be honored for its holiness; send your Kingdom soon. ³Give us our food day by day. ⁴And forgive our sins—for we have forgiven those who sinned against us. And don't allow us to be tempted."

⁵,⁶Then, teaching them more about prayer, he used this illustration: "Suppose you went to a friend's house at midnight, wanting to borrow three loaves of bread. You would shout up to him, 'A friend of mine has just arrived for a visit and I've nothing to give him to eat.' ⁷He would call down from his bedroom, 'Please don't ask me to get up. The door is locked for the night and we are all in bed. I just can't help you this time.' ⁸"But I'll tell you this—though he won't do it as a friend, if you keep knocking long enough he will get up and give you everything you want—just because of your persistence. ⁹And so it is with prayer—keep on asking and you will keep on getting; keep on looking and you will keep on finding; knock and the door will be opened. ¹⁰Everyone who asks, receives; all who seek, find; and the door is opened to everyone who knocks.

¹¹"You men who are fathers—if your boy asks for bread, do you give him a stone? If he asks for fish, do you give him a snake? ¹²If he asks for an egg, do you give him a scorpion? [Of course not!]

¹³"And if even sinful persons like yourselves give children what they need, don't you realize that your heavenly Father will do at least as much, and give the Holy Spirit to those who ask for him?"

PSALM 76:1–12

GOD'S reputation is very great in Judah and in Israel. ²His home is in Jerusalem. He lives upon Mount Zion. ³There he breaks the weapons of our enemies.

⁴The everlasting mountains cannot compare with you in glory! ⁵The mightiest of our enemies are conquered. They lie before us in the sleep of death; not one can lift a hand against us. ⁶When you rebuked them, God of Jacob, steeds and riders fell. ⁷No wonder you are greatly feared! Who can stand before an angry God? ⁸You pronounce sentence on them from heaven; the earth trembles and stands silently before you. ⁹You stand up to punish the evil-doers and to defend the meek of the earth. ¹⁰Man's futile wrath will bring you glory. You will use it as an ornament!

¹¹Fulfill all your vows that you have made to Jehovah your God. Let everyone bring him presents. He should be reverenced and feared, ¹²for he cuts down princes and does awesome things to the kings of the earth.

PROVERBS FOR TODAY/ 12:15–17

A fool thinks he needs no advice, but a wise man listens to others. A fool is quick-tempered; a wise man stays cool when insulted. A good man is known by his truthfulness; a false man by deceit and lies.

"The meek will be filled with fresh joy from the Lord, and the poor shall exult in the Holy One of Israel."
Isaiah 29:19

*"As for me and my family,
we will serve the Lord."*
Joshua 24:15

"May the Lord bless and protect you; may the Lord's face radiate with joy because of you."
Numbers 6:24-26

APRIL 5

DEUTERONOMY 28:1–68

I F you fully obey all of these commandments of the Lord your God, the laws I am declaring to you today, God will transform you into the greatest nation in the world. 2–6These are the blessings that will come upon you:

Blessings in the city,
Blessings in the field;
Many children,
Ample crops,
Large flocks and herds;
Blessings of fruit and bread;
Blessings when you come in,
Blessings when you go out.

7"The Lord will defeat your enemies before you; they will march out together against you but scatter before you in seven directions! 8The Lord will bless you with good crops and healthy cattle, and prosper everything you do when you arrive in the land the Lord your God is giving you. 9He will change you into a holy people dedicated to himself; this he has promised to do if you will only obey him and walk in his ways. 10All the nations in the world shall see that you belong to the Lord, and they will stand in awe.

11"The Lord will give you an abundance of good things in the land, just as he promised: many children, many cattle, and abundant crops. 12He will open to you his wonderful treasury of rain in the heavens, to give you fine crops every season. He will bless everything you do; and you shall lend to many nations, but shall not borrow from them. 13If you will only listen and obey the commandments of the Lord your God that I am giving you today, he will make you the head and not the tail, and you shall always have the upper hand. 14But each of these blessings depends on your not turning aside in any way from the laws I have given you; and you must never worship other gods.

15–19"If you won't listen to the Lord your God and won't obey these laws I am giving you today, then all of these curses shall come upon you:

Curses in the city,
Curses in the fields,
Curses on your fruit and bread,
The curse of barren wombs,
Curses upon your crops,
Curses upon the fertility of your cattle and flocks,
Curses when you come in,
Curses when you go out.

20"For the Lord himself will send his personal curse upon you. You will be confused and a failure in everything you do, until at last you are destroyed because of the sin of forsaking him. 21He will send disease among you until you are destroyed from the face of the land which you are about to enter and possess. 22He will send tuberculosis, fever, infections, plague, and war. He will blight your crops, covering them with mildew. All these devastations shall pursue you until you perish.

23"The heavens above you will be as unyielding as bronze, and the earth beneath will be as iron. 24The land will become as dry as dust for lack of rain, and dust storms shall destroy you.

25"The Lord will cause you to be defeated by your enemies. You will march out to battle gloriously, but flee before your enemies in utter confusion; and you will be tossed to and fro among all the nations of the earth. 26Your dead bodies will be food to the birds and wild animals, and no one will be there to chase them away.

27"He will send upon you Egyptian boils, tumors, scurvy, and itch, for none of which will there be a remedy. 28He will send madness, blindness, fear, and panic upon you. 29You shall grope in the bright sunlight just as the blind man gropes in darkness. You shall not prosper in anything you do; you will be oppressed and robbed continually, and nothing will save you.

30"Someone else will marry your fiancée; someone else will live in the house you build; someone else will eat the fruit of the vineyard you plant. 31Your oxen shall be butchered before your eyes, but you won't get a single bite of the meat. Your donkeys will be driven away as you watch, and will never return to you again. Your sheep will be given to your enemies. And there will be no one to protect you. 32You will watch as your sons and daughters are taken away as slaves. Your heart will break with longing for them, but you will not be able to help them. 33A foreign nation you have not even heard of will eat the crops you will have worked so hard to grow. You will always be oppressed and crushed. 34You will go mad because of all the tragedy you see around you. 35The Lord will cover you with boils from head to foot.

36"He will exile you and the king you will choose, to a nation to whom neither you nor your ancestors gave a second thought; and while in exile you shall worship gods of wood and stone! 37You will become an object of horror, a proverb and a byword among all the nations, for the Lord will thrust you away.

38"You will sow much but reap little, for the locusts will eat your crops. 39You will plant vineyards and care for them, but you won't eat the grapes or drink the wine, for worms will destroy the vines. 40Olive trees will be growing everywhere, but there won't be enough olive oil to anoint yourselves! For the trees will drop their fruit before it is matured. 41Your sons and daughters will be snatched away from you as slaves. 42The locusts shall destroy your trees and vines. 43Foreigners living among you shall become richer and richer while you become poorer and poorer. 44They shall lend to you, not you to them! They shall be the head and you shall be the tail!

45"All these curses shall pursue and overtake you until you are destroyed—all because you refuse to listen to the Lord your God. 46These horrors shall befall you and your descendants as a warning: 47,48You will become slaves to your enemies because of your failure to praise God for all that he has given you. The Lord will send your enemies against you, and you will be hungry, thirsty, naked, and in want of everything. A yoke of iron shall be placed around your neck until you are destroyed!

49"The Lord will bring a distant nation against you, swooping down upon you like an eagle; a nation whose language you don't understand— 50a nation of fierce and angry men who will have no mercy upon young or old. 51They will eat you out of house and home until your cattle and crops are gone. Your grain, new wine, olive oil, calves, and lambs will all disappear. 52That nation will lay siege to your cities and knock down your highest walls—the walls you will trust to protect you. 53You will even eat the flesh of your own sons and daughters in the terrible days of siege that lie ahead. 54The most tenderhearted man among you will be utterly callous toward his own brother and his beloved wife and his children who are still alive. 55He will refuse to give them a share of the flesh he is devouring—the flesh of his own children—because he is starving in the midst of the siege of your cities. 56,57The most tender and delicate woman among you—the one who would not so much as touch her feet to the ground—will refuse to share with her beloved husband, son, and daughter. She will hide from them the afterbirth and the new baby she has borne, so that she herself can eat them: so terrible will be the hunger during the siege and the awful distress caused by your enemies at your gates.

58,59"If you refuse to obey all the laws written in this book, thus refusing reverence to the glorious and fearful name of Jehovah your God, then Jehovah will send perpetual plagues upon you and upon your children. 60He will bring upon you all the diseases of Egypt which you feared so much, and they shall plague the land. 61And that is not all! The Lord will bring upon you every sickness and plague there is, even those not mentioned in this book, until you are destroyed. 62There will be few of you left, though before you were as numerous as stars. All this if you do not listen to the Lord your God.

63"Just as the Lord has rejoiced over you and has done such wonderful things for you and has multiplied you, so the Lord at that time will rejoice in destroying you; and you shall disappear from the land. 64For the Lord will scatter you among all the nations from one end of the earth to the other. There you will worship heathen gods that neither you nor your ancestors have known, gods made of wood and stone! 65There among those nations you shall find no rest, but the Lord will give you trembling hearts, darkness, and bodies wasted from sorrow and fear. 66Your lives will hang in doubt. You will live night and day in fear, and will have no reason to believe that you will see the morning light. 67In the morning you will say, 'Oh, that night were here!' And in the evening you will say, 'Oh, that morning were here!' You will say this because of the awesome horrors surrounding you. 68Then the Lord will send you back to Egypt in ships, a journey I promised you would never need to make again; and there you will offer to sell yourselves to your enemies as slaves—but no one will even want to buy you."

LUKE 11:14–36

ONCE, when Jesus cast out a demon from a man who couldn't speak, his voice returned to him. The crowd was excited and enthusiastic, 15but some said, "No wonder he can cast them out. He gets his power from Satan, the king of demons!" 16Others asked for something to happen in the sky to prove his claim of being the Messiah.

17He knew the thoughts of each of them, so he said, "Any kingdom filled with civil war is doomed; so is a home filled with argument and strife. 18Therefore, if what you say is true, that Satan

is fighting against himself by empowering me to cast out his demons, how can his kingdom survive? 19And if I am empowered by Satan, what about your own followers? For they cast out demons! Do you think this proves they are possessed by Satan? Ask *them* if you are right! 20But if I am casting out demons because of power from God, it proves that the Kingdom of God has arrived.

21"For when Satan, strong and fully armed, guards his palace, it is safe— 22until someone stronger and better-armed attacks and overcomes him and strips him of his weapons and carries off his belongings.

23"Anyone who is not for me is against me; if he isn't helping me, he is hurting my cause.

24"When a demon is cast out of a man, it goes to the deserts, searching there for rest; but finding none, it returns to the person it left, 25and finds that its former home is all swept and clean. 26Then it goes and gets seven other demons more evil than itself, and they all enter the man. And so the poor fellow is seven times worse off than he was before."

27As he was speaking, a woman in the crowd called out, "God bless your mother—the womb from which you came, and the breasts that gave you suck!"

28He replied, "Yes, but even more blessed are all who hear the Word of God and put it into practice."

29,30As the crowd pressed in upon him, he preached them this sermon: "These are evil times, with evil people. They keep asking for some strange happening in the skies [to prove I am the Messiah], but the only proof I will give them is a miracle like that of Jonah, whose experiences proved to the people of Nineveh that God had sent him. My similar experience will prove that God has sent me to these people.

31"And at the Judgment Day the Queen of Sheba shall arise and point her finger at this generation, condemning it, for she went on a long, hard journey to listen to the wisdom of Solomon; but one far greater than Solomon is here [and few pay any attention].

32"The men of Nineveh, too, shall arise and condemn this nation, for they repented at the preaching of Jonah; and someone far greater than Jonah is here [but this nation won't listen].

33"No one lights a lamp and hides it! Instead, he puts it on a lampstand to give light to all who enter the room. 34Your eyes light up your inward being. A pure eye lets sunshine into your soul. A lustful eye shuts out the light and plunges you into darkness. 35So watch out that the sunshine isn't blotted out. 36If you are filled with light within, with no dark corners, then your face will be radiant too, as though a floodlight is beamed upon you."

PSALM 77:1–20

I cry to the Lord; I call and call to him. Oh, that he would listen. 2I am in deep trouble and I need his help so much. All night long I pray, lifting my hands to heaven, pleading. There can be no joy for me until he acts. 3I think of God and moan, overwhelmed with longing for his help. 4I cannot sleep until you act. I am too distressed even to pray!

5I keep thinking of the good old days of the past, long since ended. 6Then my nights were filled with joyous songs. I search my soul and meditate upon the difference now. 7Has the Lord rejected me forever? Will he never again be favorable? 8Is his lovingkindness gone forever? Has his promise failed? 9Has he forgotten to be kind to one so undeserving? Has he slammed the door in anger on his love? 10And I said: This is my fate, that the blessings of God have changed to hate. 11I recall the many miracles he did for me so long ago. 12Those wonderful deeds are constantly in my thoughts. I cannot stop thinking about them.

13O God, your ways are holy. Where is there any other as mighty as you? 14You are the God of miracles and wonders! You still demonstrate your awesome power.

15You have redeemed us who are the sons of Jacob and of Joseph by your might. 16When the Red Sea saw you, how it feared! It trembled to its depths! 17The clouds poured down their rain, the thunder rolled and crackled in the sky. Your lightning flashed. 18There was thunder in the whirlwind; the lightning lighted up the world! The earth trembled and shook.

19Your road led by a pathway through the sea—a pathway no one knew was there! 20You led your people along that road like a flock of sheep, with Moses and Aaron as their shepherds.

PROVERBS FOR TODAY/ 12:18
Some people like to make cutting remarks, but the words of the wise soothe and heal.

APRIL 6

DEUTERONOMY 29:1—30:20

I T was on the plains of Moab that Moses restated the covenant which the Lord had made with the people of Israel at Mount Horeb. 2,3He sum- moned all Israel before him and told them,

"You have seen with your own eyes the great plagues and mighty miracles that the Lord brought upon Pharaoh and his people in the land of Egypt. 4But even yet the Lord hasn't given you hearts that understand or eyes that see or ears that hear! 5For forty years God has led you through the wilderness, yet your clothes haven't become old, and your shoes haven't worn out! 6The reason he hasn't let you settle down to grow grain for bread or grapes for wine and strong drink, is so that you would realize that it is the Lord your God who has been caring for you.

7"When we came here, King Sihon of Heshbon and King Og of Bashan came out against us in battle, but we destroyed them, 8and took their land and gave it to the tribes of Reuben and Gad and to the half-tribe of Manasseh as their inheritance. 9Therefore, obey the terms of this covenant so that you will prosper in everything you do. 10All of you—your leaders, the people, your judges, and your administrative officers—are standing today before the Lord your God, 11along with your little ones and your wives and the foreigners that are among you— those who chop your wood and carry your water. 12You are standing here to enter into a contract with Jehovah your God, a contract he is making with you today. 13He wants to confirm you today as his people, and to confirm that he is your God, just as he promised your ancestors, Abraham, Isaac, and Jacob. 14,15This contract is not with you alone as you stand before him today, but with all future generations of Israel as well.

16"Surely you remember how we lived in the land of Egypt, and how as we left, we came safely through the territory of enemy nations. 17And you have seen their heathen idols made of wood, stone, silver, and gold. 18The day that any of you—man or woman, family or tribe of Israel—begins to turn away from the Lord our God and desires to worship these gods of other nations, that day a root will be planted that will grow bitter and poisonous fruit.

19"Let no one blithely think, when he hears the warnings of this curse, 'I shall prosper even though I walk in my own stubborn way!' 20For the Lord will not pardon! His anger and jealousy will be hot against that man. And all the curses written in this book shall lie heavily upon him, and the Lord will blot out his name from under heaven. 21The Lord will separate that man from all the tribes of Israel, to pour out upon him all the curses (which are recorded in this book) that befall those who break this contract. 22Then your children and the generations to come and the foreigners that pass by from distant lands shall see the devastation of the land and the diseases the Lord will have sent upon it. 23They will see that the whole land is alkali and salt, a burned over wasteland, unsown, without crops, without a shred of vegetation— just like Sodom and Gomorrah and Admah and Zeboiim, destroyed by the Lord in his anger.

24" 'Why has the Lord done this to his land?' the nations will ask. 'Why was he so angry?'

25"And they will be told, 'Because the people of the land broke the contract made with them by Jehovah, the God of their ancestors, when he brought them out of the land of Egypt. 26For they worshiped other gods, violating his express command. 27That is why the anger of the Lord was hot against this land, so that all his curses (which are recorded in this book) broke forth upon them. 28In great anger the Lord rooted them out of their land and threw them away into another land, where they still live today!'

29"There are secrets the Lord your God has not revealed to us, but these words which he has revealed are for us and our children to obey forever.

"WHEN all these things have happened to you—the blessings and the curses I have listed—you will meditate upon them as you are living among the nations where the Lord your God will have driven you. 2If at that time you want to return to the Lord your God, and you and your children have begun wholeheartedly to obey all of the commandments I have given you today, ³then the Lord your God will rescue you from your captivity! He will have mercy upon you and come and gather you out of all the nations where he will have scattered you. ⁴Though you are at the ends of the earth, he will go and find you and bring you back again ⁵to the land of your ancestors. You shall possess the land again, and he will do you good and bless you even more than he did your ancestors! ⁶He will cleanse your hearts and the hearts of your children and of your children's children so that you will love the Lord your God with all your hearts and souls, and Israel shall come alive again!

⁷,⁸"If you return to the Lord and obey all the commandments that I command you today, the Lord your God will take his curses and turn them against your enemies—against those who hate you and persecute you. ⁹The Lord your God will prosper everything you do and give you many children and much cattle and wonderful crops; for the Lord will again rejoice over you as he did over your fathers. ¹⁰He will rejoice if you but obey the commandments written in this book of the law, and if you turn to the Lord your God with all your hearts and souls.

¹¹"Obeying these commandments is not something beyond your strength and reach; ¹²for these laws are not in the far heavens, so distant that you can't hear and obey them, and with no one to bring them down to you; ¹³nor are they beyond the ocean, so far that no one can bring you their message; ¹⁴but they are very close at hand—in your hearts and on your lips—so obey them.

¹⁵"Look, today I have set before you life and death, depending on whether you obey or disobey. ¹⁶I have commanded you today to love the Lord your God and to follow his paths and to keep his laws, so that you will live and become a great nation, and so that the Lord your God will bless you and the land you are about to possess. ¹⁷But if your hearts turn away and you won't listen—if you are drawn away to worship other gods— ¹⁸then I declare to you this day that you

shall surely perish; you will not have a long, good life in the land you are going in to possess.

¹⁹"I call heaven and earth to witness against you that today I have set before you life or death, blessing or curse. Oh, that you would choose life; that you and your children might live! ²⁰Choose to love the Lord your God and to obey him and to cling to him, for he is your life and the length of your days. You will then be able to live safely in the land the Lord promised your ancestors, Abraham, Isaac, and Jacob."

LUKE 11:37—12:7

As he was speaking, one of the Pharisees asked him home for a meal. When Jesus arrived, he sat down to eat without first performing the ceremonial washing required by Jewish custom. This greatly surprised his host.

³⁹Then Jesus said to him, "You Pharisees wash the outside, but inside you are still dirty—full of greed and wickedness! ⁴⁰Fools! Didn't God make the inside as well as the outside? ⁴¹Purity is best demonstrated by generosity.

⁴²"But woe to you Pharisees! For though you are careful to tithe even the smallest part of your income, you completely forget about justice and the love of God. You should tithe, yes, but you should not leave these other things undone.

⁴³"Woe to you Pharisees! For how you love the seats of honor in the synagogues and the respectful greetings from everyone as you walk through the markets! ⁴⁴Yes, awesome judgment is awaiting you. For you are like hidden graves in a field. Men go by you with no knowledge of the corruption they are passing."

⁴⁵"Sir," said an expert in religious law who was standing there, "you have insulted my profession, too, in what you just said."

⁴⁶"Yes," said Jesus, "the same horrors await you! For you crush men beneath impossible religious demands—demands that you yourselves would never think

of trying to keep. [47]Woe to you! For you are exactly like your ancestors who killed the prophets long ago. [48]Murderers! You agree with your fathers that what they did was right—you would have done the same yourselves.

[49]"This is what God says about you: 'I will send prophets and apostles to you, and you will kill some of them and chase away the others.'

[50]"And you of this generation will be held responsible for the murder of God's servants from the founding of the world— [51]from the murder of Abel to the murder of Zechariah who perished between the altar and the sanctuary. Yes, it will surely be charged against you.

[52]"Woe to you experts in religion! For you hide the truth from the people. You won't accept it for yourselves, and you prevent others from having a chance to believe it."

[53,54]The Pharisees and legal experts were furious; and from that time on they plied him fiercely with a host of questions, trying to trap him into saying something for which they could have him arrested.

MEANWHILE the crowds grew until thousands upon thousands were milling about and crushing each other. He turned now to his disciples and warned them, "More than anything else, beware of these Pharisees and the way they pretend to be good when they aren't. But such hypocrisy cannot be hidden forever. [2]It will become as evident as yeast in dough. [3]Whatever they have said in the dark shall be heard in the light, and what you have whispered in the inner rooms shall be broadcast from the housetops for all to hear!

[4]"Dear friends, don't be afraid of these who want to murder you. They can only kill the body; they have no power over your souls. [5]But I'll tell you whom to fear—fear God who has the power to kill and then cast into hell.

[6]"What is the price of five sparrows? A couple of pennies? Not much more than that. Yet God does not forget a single one of them. [7]And he knows the number of hairs on your head! Never fear, you are far more valuable to him than a whole flock of sparrows.

PSALM 78:1–25

O my people, listen to my teaching. Open your ears to what I am saying. [2,3]For I will show you lessons from our history, stories handed down to us from former generations. [4]I will reveal these truths to you so that you can describe these glorious deeds of Jehovah to your children, and tell them about the mighty miracles he did. [5]For he gave his laws to Israel, and commanded our fathers to teach them to their children, [6]so that they in turn could teach their children too. Thus his laws pass down from generation to generation. [7]In this way each generation has been able to obey his laws and to set its hope anew on God and not forget his glorious miracles. [8]Thus they did not need to be as their fathers were—stubborn, rebellious, unfaithful, refusing to give their hearts to God.

[9]The people of Ephraim, though fully armed, turned their backs and fled when the day of battle came, [10]because they didn't obey his laws. They refused to follow his ways. [11,12]And they forgot about the wonderful miracles God had done for them, and for their fathers in Egypt. [13]For he divided the sea before them and led them through! The water stood banked up along both sides of them! [14]In the daytime he led them by a cloud, and at night by a pillar of fire. [15]He split open the rocks in the wilderness to give them plenty of water, as though gushing from a spring. [16]Streams poured from the rock, flowing like a river!

[17]Yet they kept on with their rebellion, sinning against the God who is above all gods. [18]They murmured and complained, demanding other food than God was giving them. [19,20]They even spoke against God himself. "Why can't he give us decent food as well as water?" they grumbled. [21]Jehovah heard them and was

angry; the fire of his wrath burned against Israel, 22because they didn't believe in God or trust in him to care for them, 23even though he commanded the skies to open—he opened the windows of heaven— 24and rained down manna for their food. He gave them bread from heaven! 25They ate angels' food! He gave them all they could hold.

PROVERBS FOR TODAY/ 12:19–20

Truth stands the test of time; lies are soon exposed. Deceit fills hearts that are plotting for evil; joy fills hearts that are planning for good!

APRIL 7

DEUTERONOMY 31:1—32:29

AFTER Moses had said all these things to the people of Israel, 2he told them, "I am now 120 years old! I am no longer able to lead you, for the Lord has told me that I shall not cross the Jordan River. 3But the Lord himself will lead you, and will destroy the nations living there, and you shall overcome them. Joshua is your new commander, as the Lord has instructed. 4The Lord will destroy the nations living in the land, just as he destroyed Sihon and Og, the kings of the Amorites. 5The Lord will deliver over to you the people living there, and you shall destroy them as I have commanded you. 6Be strong! Be courageous! Do not be afraid of them! For the Lord your God will be with you. He will neither fail you nor forsake you."

7Then Moses called for Joshua and said to him, as all Israel watched, "Be strong! Be courageous! For you shall lead these people into the land promised by the Lord to their ancestors; see to it that they conquer it. 8Don't be afraid, for the Lord will go before you and will be with you; he will not fail nor forsake you."

9Then Moses wrote out the laws he had already delivered to the people and gave them to the priests, the sons of Levi, who carried the Ark containing the Ten Commandments of the Lord. Moses also gave copies of the laws to the elders of Israel. 10,11The Lord commanded that these laws be read to all the people at the end of every seventh year—the Year of Release—at the Festival of Tabernacles, when all Israel would assemble before the Lord at the sanctuary.

12"Call them all together," the Lord instructed, "—men, women, children, and foreigners living among you—to hear the laws of God and to learn his will, so that you will reverence the Lord your God and obey his laws. 13Do this so that your little children who have not known these laws will hear them and learn how to revere the Lord your God as long as you live in the Promised Land."

14Then the Lord said to Moses, "The time has come when you must die. Summon Joshua and come into the Tabernacle where I can give him his instructions." So Moses and Joshua came and stood before the Lord.

15He appeared to them in a great cloud at the Tabernacle entrance, 16and said to Moses, "You shall die and join your ancestors. After you are gone, these people will begin worshiping foreign gods in the Promised Land. They will forget about me and break the contract I have made with them. 17Then my anger will flame out against them and I will abandon them, hiding my face from them, and they shall be destroyed. Terrible trouble will come upon them, so that they will say, 'God is no longer among us!' 18I will turn away from them because of their sins in worshiping other gods.

19"Now write down the words of this song, and teach it to the people of Israel as my warning to them. 20When I have brought them into the land I promised their ancestors—a land 'flowing with milk and honey'—and when they have become fat and prosperous, and worship other gods and despise me and break my contract, 21and great disasters come upon them, then this song will remind them of the reason for their woes. (For this song will live from generation to generation.) I know now, even before they enter the land, what these people are like."

22So, on that very day, Moses wrote down the words of the song and taught it to the Israelites. 23Then he charged Joshua (son of Nun) to be strong and courageous, and said to him, "You must bring the people of Israel into the land the Lord promised them; for the Lord says, 'I will be with you.'"

24When Moses had finished writing down all the laws that are recorded in this book, 25he instructed the Levites who carried the Ark containing the Ten Commandments 26to put this book of the law beside the Ark, as a solemn warning to the people of Israel.

27"For I know how rebellious and stubborn you are," Moses told them. "If even today, while I am still here with you, you are defiant rebels against the Lord, how much more rebellious will you be after my death! 28Now summon all the elders and officers of your tribes so that I can speak to them, and call heaven and earth to witness against them. 29I know that after my death you will utterly defile yourselves and turn away from God and his commands; and in the days to come evil will crush you for you will do what the Lord says is evil, making him very angry."

30So Moses recited this entire song to the whole assembly of Israel:

"LISTEN, O heavens and earth!
Listen to what I say!
2My words shall fall upon you
Like the gentle rain and dew,
Like rain upon the tender grass,
Like showers on the hillside.
3I will proclaim the greatness of the Lord.
How glorious he is!
4He is the Rock. His work is perfect.
Everything he does is just and fair.
He is faithful, without sin.
5But Israel has become corrupt,
Smeared with sin. They are no longer his;
They are a stubborn, twisted generation.
6Is this the way you treat Jehovah?
O foolish people,
Is not God your Father?
Has he not created you?
Has he not established you and made you strong?
7Remember the days of long ago!
(Ask your father and the aged men;
They will tell you all about it.)
8When God divided up the world among the nations,
He gave each of them a supervising angel!
9But he appointed none for Israel;
For Israel was God's own personal possession!
10God protected them in the howling wilderness
As though they were the apple of his eye.
11He spreads his wings over them,
Even as an eagle overspreads her young.
She carries them upon her wings—
As does the Lord his people!
12When the Lord alone was leading them,
And they lived without foreign gods,
13God gave them fertile hilltops,
Rolling, fertile fields,
Honey from the rock,
And olive oil from stony ground!
14He gave them milk and meat—
Choice Bashan rams, and goats—
And the finest of the wheat;

They drank the sparkling wine.
15But Israel was soon overfed;
Yes, fat and bloated;
Then, in plenty, they forsook their
God.
They shrugged away the Rock of their
salvation.
16Israel began to follow foreign gods,
And Jehovah was very angry;
He was jealous of his people.
17They sacrificed to heathen gods,
To new gods never before worshiped.
18They spurned the Rock who had
made them,
Forgetting it was God who had given
them birth.
19God saw what they were doing,
And detested them!
His sons and daughters were insulting
him.
20He said, 'I will abandon them;
See what happens to them then!
For they are a stubborn, faithless generation.
21They have made me very jealous of
their idols,
Which are not gods at all.
Now I, in turn, will make them jealous
By giving my affections
To the foolish Gentile nations of the
world.
22For my anger has kindled a fire
That burns to the depths of the under-
world,
Consuming the earth and all of its
crops,
And setting its mountains on fire.
23I will heap evils upon them
And shoot them down with my ar-
rows.
24I will waste them with hunger,
Burning fever, and fatal disease.
I will devour them! I will set wild
beasts upon them,
To rip them apart with their teeth;
And deadly serpents
Crawling in the dust.
25Outside, the enemies' sword—
Inside, the plague—
Shall terrorize young men and girls
alike;
The baby nursing at the breast,

And aged men.
26I had decided to scatter them to dis-
tant lands,
So that even the memory of them
Would disappear.
27But then I thought,
"My enemies will boast,
'Israel is destroyed by our own might;
It was not the Lord
Who did it!' "'
28Israel is a stupid nation;
Foolish, without understanding.
29Oh, that they were wise!
Oh, that they could understand!
Oh, that they would know what they
are getting into!

LUKE 12:8–34

AND I assure you of this: I, the
Messiah, will publicly honor you
in the presence of God's angels
if you publicly acknowledge me here on
earth as your Friend. 9But I will deny
before the angels those who deny me
here among men. 10(Yet those who speak
against me may be forgiven—while those
who speak against the Holy Spirit shall
never be forgiven.)

11"And when you are brought to trial
before these Jewish rulers and authorities
in the synagogues, don't be concerned
about what to say in your defense,
12for the Holy Spirit will give you the
right words even as you are standing
there."

13Then someone called from the
crowd, "Sir, please tell my brother to
divide my father's estate with me."

14But Jesus replied, "Man, who made
me a judge over you to decide such
things as that? 15Beware! Don't always
be wishing for what you don't have. For
real life and real living are not related
to how rich we are."

16Then he gave an illustration: "A rich
man had a fertile farm that produced fine
crops. 17In fact, his barns were full to
overflowing—he couldn't get everything
in. He thought about his problem,

18and finally exclaimed, 'I know—I'll tear down my barns and build bigger ones! Then I'll have room enough. 19And I'll sit back and say to myself, "Friend, you have enough stored away for years to come. Now take it easy! Wine, women, and song for you!" '

20"But God said to him, 'Fool! Tonight you die. Then who will get it all?'

21"Yes, every man is a fool who gets rich on earth but not in heaven."

22Then turning to his disciples he said, "Don't worry about whether you have enough food to eat or clothes to wear. 23For life consists of far more than food and clothes. 24Look at the ravens—they don't plant or harvest or have barns to store away their food, and yet they get along all right—for God feeds them. And you are far more valuable to him than any birds!

25"And besides, what's the use of worrying? What good does it do? Will it add a single day to your life? Of course not! 26And if worry can't even do such little things as that, what's the use of worrying over bigger things?

27"Look at the lilies! They don't toil and spin, and yet Solomon in all his glory was not robed as well as they are. 28And if God provides clothing for the flowers that are here today and gone tomorrow, don't you suppose that he will provide clothing for you, you doubters? 29And don't worry about food—what to eat and drink; don't worry at all that God will provide it for you. 30All mankind scratches for its daily bread, but your heavenly Father knows your needs. 31He will always give you all you need from day to day if you will make the Kingdom of God your primary concern.

32"So don't be afraid, little flock. For it gives your Father great happiness to give you the Kingdom. 33Sell what you have and give to those in need. This will fatten your purses in heaven! And the purses of heaven have no rips or holes in them. Your treasures there will never disappear; no thief can steal them; no moth can destroy them. 34Wherever your treasure is, there your heart and thoughts will also be.

PSALM 78:26–45

AND he led forth the east wind and guided the south wind by his mighty power. 27He rained down birds as thick as dust, clouds of them like sands along the shore! 28He caused the birds to fall to the ground among the tents. 29The people ate their fill. He gave them what they asked for. 30But they had hardly finished eating, and the meat was yet in their mouths, 31when the anger of the Lord rose against them and killed the finest of Israel's young men. 32Yet even so the people kept on sinning and refused to believe in miracles. 33So he cut their lives short and gave them years of terror and disaster.

34Then at last, when he had ruined them, they walked awhile behind him; how earnestly they turned around and followed him! 35Then they remembered that God was their Rock—that their Savior was the God above all gods. 36But it was only with their words they followed him, not with their hearts; 37their hearts were far away. They did not keep their promises. 38Yet he was merciful and forgave their sins and didn't destroy them all. Many and many a time he held back his anger. 39For he remembered that they were merely mortal men, gone in a moment like a breath of wind.

40Oh, how often they rebelled against him in those desert years and grieved his heart. 41Again and again they turned away and tempted God to kill them, and limited the Holy One of Israel from giving them his blessings. 42They forgot his power and love, and how he had rescued them from their enemies; 43they forgot the plagues he sent upon the Egyptians in Tanis— 44how he turned their rivers into blood, so that no one could drink, 45and how he sent vast swarms of flies to fill the land, and how the frogs had covered all of Egypt!

No real harm befalls the good, but there is constant trouble for the wicked. God delights in those who keep their promises, and abhors those who don't. A wise man doesn't display his knowledge, but a fool displays his foolishness.

APRIL 8

DEUTERONOMY 32:30–52

How could one single enemy chase a thousand of them,

And two put ten thousand to flight,
Unless their Rock had abandoned them,
Unless the Lord had destroyed them?
31But the rock of other nations
Is not like our Rock;
Prayers to their gods are valueless.
32They act like men of Sodom and Gomorrah:
Their deeds are bitter with poison;
33They drink the wine of serpent venom.
34But Israel is my special people,
Sealed as jewels within my treasury.
35Vengeance is mine,
And I decree the punishment of all her enemies:
Their doom is sealed.
36The Lord will see his people righted,
And will have compassion on them when they slip.
He will watch their power ebb away,
Both slave and free.
37Then God will ask,
'Where are their gods—
The rocks they claimed to be their refuge?
38Where are these gods now,
To whom they sacrificed their fat and wine?
Let those gods arise,
And help them!
39Don't you see that I alone am God?
I kill and make live.
I wound and heal—
No one delivers from my power.

40,41I raise my hand to heaven
And vow by my existence,
That I will whet the lightning of my sword!
And hurl my punishments upon my enemies!
42My arrows shall be drunk with blood!
My sword devours the flesh and blood
Of all the slain and captives.
The heads of the enemy
Are gory with blood.'
43Praise his people,
Gentile nations,
For he will avenge his people,
Taking vengeance on his enemies,
Purifying his land
And his people."

44,45When Moses and Joshua had recited all the words of this song to the people, 46Moses made these comments: "Meditate upon all the laws I have given you today, and pass them on to your children. 47These laws are not mere words—they are your life! Through obeying them you will live long, plentiful lives in the land you are going to possess across the Jordan River."

48That same day, the Lord said to Moses, 49"Go to Mount Nebo in the Abarim mountains, in the land of Moab across from Jericho. Climb to its heights, and look out across the land of Canaan, the land I am giving to the people of Israel. 50After you see the land you must die and join your ancestors, just as Aaron your brother died in Mount Hor and joined them. 51For you dishonored me among the people of Israel at the springs of Meribah-kadesh, in the wilderness of

Zin. ⁵²You will see spread out before you the land I am giving the people of Israel, but you will not enter it."

LUKE 12:35–59

BE prepared—all dressed and ready— ³⁶for your Lord's return from the wedding feast. Then you will be ready to open the door and let him in the moment he arrives and knocks. ³⁷There will be great joy for those who are ready and waiting for his return. He himself will seat them and put on a waiter's uniform and serve them as they sit and eat! ³⁸He may come at nine o'clock at night—or even at midnight. But whenever he comes there will be joy for his servants who are ready!

³⁹"Everyone would be ready for him if they knew the exact hour of his return—just as they would be ready for a thief if they knew when he was coming. ⁴⁰So be ready all the time. For I, the Messiah, will come when least expected."

⁴¹Peter asked, "Lord, are you talking just to us or to everyone?"

⁴²,⁴³,⁴⁴And the Lord replied, "I'm talking to any faithful, sensible man whose master gives him the responsibility of feeding the other servants. If his master returns and finds that he has done a good job, there will be a reward—his master will put him in charge of all he owns.

⁴⁵"But if the man begins to think, 'My Lord won't be back for a long time,' and begins to whip the men and women he is supposed to protect, and to spend his time at drinking parties and in drunkenness— ⁴⁶well, his master will return without notice and remove him from his position of trust and assign him to the place of the unfaithful. ⁴⁷He will be severely punished, for though he knew his duty he refused to do it.

⁴⁸"But anyone who is not aware that he is doing wrong will be punished only lightly. Much is required from those to whom much is given, for their responsibility is greater.

⁴⁹"I have come to bring fire to the earth, and, oh, that my task were completed! ⁵⁰There is a terrible baptism ahead of me, and how I am pent up until it is accomplished!

⁵¹"Do you think I have come to give peace to the earth? *No!* Rather, strife and division! ⁵²From now on families will be split apart, three in favor of me, and two against—or perhaps the other way around. ⁵³A father will decide one way about me; his son, the other; mother and daughter will disagree; and the decision of an honored mother-in-law will be spurned by her daughter-in-law."

⁵⁴Then he turned to the crowd and said, "When you see clouds beginning to form in the west, you say, 'Here comes a shower.' And you are right.

⁵⁵"When the south wind blows you say, 'Today will be a scorcher.' And it is. ⁵⁶Hypocrites! You interpret the sky well enough, but you refuse to notice the warnings all around you about the crisis ahead. ⁵⁷Why do you refuse to see for yourselves what is right?

⁵⁸"If you meet your accuser on the way to court, try to settle the matter before it reaches the judge, lest he sentence you to jail; ⁵⁹for if that happens you won't be free again until the last penny is paid in full."

PSALM 78:46–58

HE gave their crops to caterpillars. Their harvest was consumed by locusts. ⁴⁷He destroyed their grapevines and their sycamores with hail. ⁴⁸Their cattle died in the fields, mortally wounded by huge hailstones from heaven. Their sheep were killed by lightning. ⁴⁹He loosed on them the fierceness of his anger, sending sorrow and trouble. He dispatched against them a band of destroying angels. ⁵⁰He gave free course to his anger and did not spare the Egyptians' lives, but handed them over to plagues and sickness. ⁵¹Then he killed the eldest son in each Egyptian family—he who was the beginning of its strength and joy. ⁵²But he led forth his own people like a flock, guiding them safely through the wilderness. ⁵³He kept them safe, so they were not afraid. But the Sea closed in upon their enemies and overwhelmed them. ⁵⁴He brought them to the border of his land of blessing, to this land of hills he made for them. ⁵⁵He drove out the nations occupying the land, and gave each tribe of Israel its apportioned place as its home.

⁵⁶Yet though he did all this for them, they still rebelled against the God above all gods, and refused to follow his commands. ⁵⁷They turned back from entering the Promised Land and disobeyed as their fathers had. Like a crooked arrow, they missed the target of God's will. ⁵⁸They made him angry by erecting idols and altars to other gods.

PROVERBS FOR TODAY/ 12:24

Work hard and become a leader; be lazy and never succeed.

APRIL 9

DEUTERONOMY 33:1–29

THIS is the blessing Moses, the man of God, gave to the people of Israel before his death:

²"The Lord came to us at Mount Sinai,
And dawned upon us from Mount Seir;
He shone from Mount Paran,
Surrounded by ten thousands of holy angels,
And with flaming fire at his right hand.
³How he loves his people—
His holy ones are in his hands.
They followed in your steps, O Lord.
They have received their directions from you.
⁴The laws I have given
Are your precious possession.
⁵The Lord became king in Jerusalem,
Elected by a convocation of the leaders of the tribes!
⁶Let Reuben live forever
And may his tribe increase!"
⁷And Moses said of Judah:
"O Lord, hear the cry of Judah
And unite him with Israel;
Fight for him against his enemies."
⁸Then Moses said concerning the tribe of Levi:
"Give to godly Levi
Your Urim and your Thummim.

You tested Levi at Massah and at Meribah;
⁹He obeyed your instructions
[and destroyed many sinners],
Even his own children, brothers, fathers, and mothers.
¹⁰The Levites shall teach God's laws to Israel
And shall work before you at the incense altar
And the altar of burnt offering.
¹¹O Lord, prosper the Levites
And accept the work they do for you.
Crush those who are their enemies;
Don't let them rise again."
¹²Concerning the tribe of Benjamin, Moses said:
"He is beloved of God
And lives in safety beside him.
God surrounds him with his loving care,
And preserves him from every harm."
¹³Concerning the tribe of Joseph, he said:
"May his land be blessed by God
With the choicest gifts of heaven
And of the earth that lies below.
¹⁴May he be blessed
With the best of what the sun makes grow;
Growing richly month by month,

15With the finest of mountain crops
And of the everlasting hills.
16May he be blessed with the best gifts
Of the earth and its fullness,
And with the favor of God who appeared
In the burning bush.
Let all these blessings come upon Joseph,
The prince among his brothers.
17He is a young bull in strength and splendor,
With the strong horns of a wild ox
To push against the nations everywhere;
This is my blessing on the multitudes of Ephraim
And the thousands of Manasseh."
18Of the tribe of Zebulun, Moses said:
"Rejoice, O Zebulun, you outdoorsmen,
And Issachar, you lovers of your tents;
19They shall summon the people
To celebrate their sacrifices with them.
Lo, they taste the riches of the sea
And the treasures of the sand."
20Concerning the tribe of Gad, Moses said:
"A blessing upon those who help Gad.
He crouches like a lion,
With savage arm and face and head.
21He chose the best of the land for himself
Because it is reserved for a leader.
He led the people
Because he carried out God's penalties for Israel."
22Of the tribe of Dan, Moses said:
"Dan is like a lion's cub
Leaping out from Bashan."
23Of the tribe of Naphtali, Moses said:
"O Naphtali, you are satisfied
With all the blessings of the Lord;
The Mediterranean coast and the Negeb
Are your home."
24Of the tribe of Asher:
"Asher is a favorite son,
Esteemed above his brothers;
He bathes his feet in oil.
25May you be protected with strong bolts
Of iron and bronze,
And may your strength match the length of your days!
26There is none like the God of Jerusalem—
He descends from the heavens
In majestic splendor to help you.
27The eternal God is your Refuge,
And underneath are the everlasting arms.
He thrusts out your enemies before you;
It is he who cries, 'Destroy them!'
28So Israel dwells safely,
Prospering in a land of corn and wine,
While the gentle rains descend from heaven.
29What blessings are yours, O Israel!
Who else has been saved by the Lord?
He is your shield and your helper!
He is your excellent sword!
Your enemies shall bow low before you,
And you shall trample on their backs!"

LUKE 13:1–22

ABOUT this time he was informed that Pilate had butchered some Jews from Galilee as they were sacrificing at the Temple in Jerusalem. 2"Do you think they were worse sinners than other men from Galilee?" he asked. "Is that why they suffered? 3Not at all! And don't you realize that you also will perish unless you leave your evil ways and turn to God?

4"And what about the eighteen men who died when the Tower of Siloam fell on them? Were they the worst sinners in Jerusalem? 5Not at all! And you, too, will perish unless you repent."

6Then he used this illustration: "A man planted a fig tree in his garden and came again and again to see if he could find any fruit on it, but he was always disappointed. 7Finally he told his gardener to cut it down. 'I've waited three years and there hasn't been a single fig!' he said. 'Why bother with it any longer? It's taking up space we can use for something else.'

8" 'Give it one more chance,' the gardener answered. 'Leave it another year, and I'll give it special attention and plenty of fertilizer. 9If we get figs next year, fine; if not, I'll cut it down.' "

10One Sabbath as he was teaching in a synagogue, 11he saw a seriously handicapped woman who had been bent double for eighteen years and was unable to straighten herself.

12Calling her over to him Jesus said, "Woman, you are healed of your sickness!" 13He touched her, and instantly she could stand straight. How she praised and thanked God!

14But the local Jewish leader in charge of the synagogue was very angry about it because Jesus had healed her on the Sabbath day. "There are six days of the week to work," he shouted to the crowd. "Those are the days to come for healing, not on the Sabbath!"

15But the Lord replied, "You hypocrite! You work on the Sabbath! Don't you untie your cattle from their stalls on the Sabbath and lead them out for water? 16And is it wrong for me, just because it is the Sabbath day, to free this Jewish woman from the bondage in which Satan has held her for eighteen years?"

17This shamed his enemies. And all the people rejoiced at the wonderful things he did.

18Now he began teaching them again about the Kingdom of God: "What is the Kingdom like?" he asked. "How can I illustrate it? 19It is like a tiny mustard seed planted in a garden; soon it grows into a tall bush and the birds live among its branches.

20,21"It is like yeast kneaded into dough, which works unseen until it has risen high and light."

22He went from city to city and village to village, teaching as he went, always pressing onward toward Jerusalem.

PSALM 78:59–72

WHEN God saw their deeds, his wrath was strong and he despised his people. 60Then he abandoned his Tabernacle at Shiloh, where he had lived among mankind, 61and allowed his Ark to be captured; he surrendered his glory into enemy hands. 62He caused his people to be butchered because his anger was intense. 63Their young men were killed by fire and their girls died before they were old enough to sing their wedding songs. 64The priests were slaughtered and their widows died before they could even begin their lament. 65Then the Lord rose up as though awakening from sleep, and like a mighty man aroused by wine, 66he routed his enemies and drove them back and sent them to eternal shame. 67But he rejected Joseph's family, the tribe of Ephraim, 68and chose the tribe of Judah—and Mount Zion which he loved. 69There he built his towering temple, solid and enduring as the heavens and the earth. 70He chose his servant David, taking him from feeding sheep, 71,72and from following the ewes with lambs; God presented David to his people as their shepherd and he cared for them with a true heart and skillful hands.

PROVERBS FOR TODAY/ 12:25
Anxious hearts are very heavy but a word of encouragement does wonders!

APRIL 10

DEUTERONOMY 34:1—JOSHUA 2:24

THEN Moses climbed from the plains of Moab to Pisgah Peak in Mount Nebo, across from Jericho. And the Lord pointed out to him the Promised Land, as they gazed out across Gilead as far as Dan: 2"There is Naphtali; and there is Ephraim and Manasseh; and across there, Judah, extending to the Mediterranean Sea; 3there is the Negeb; and the Jordan Valley; and Jericho, the city of palm trees; and Zoar," the Lord told him.

4"It is the Promised Land," the Lord told Moses. "I promised Abraham, Isaac, and Jacob that I would give it to their descendants. Now you have seen it, but you will not enter it."

5So Moses, the disciple of the Lord, died in the land of Moab as the Lord had said. 6The Lord buried him in a valley near Beth-Peor in Moab, but no one knows the exact place.

7Moses was 120 years old when he died, yet his eyesight was perfect and he was as strong as a young man. 8The people of Israel mourned for him for thirty days on the plains of Moab.

9Joshua (son of Nun) was full of the spirit of wisdom, for Moses had laid his hands upon him; so the people of Israel obeyed him, and followed the commandments the Lord had given to Moses.

10There has never been another prophet like Moses, for the Lord talked to him face to face. 11,12And at God's command he performed amazing miracles which have never been equaled.

AFTER the death of Moses, the Lord's disciple, God spoke to Moses' assistant, whose name was Joshua (the son of Nun), and said to him,

2"Now that my disciple is dead, [you are the new leader of Israel]. Lead my people across the Jordan River into the Promised Land. 3I say to you what I said to Moses: 'Wherever you go will be part of the land of Israel— 4all the way from Negeb desert in the south to the Lebanon mountains in the north, and from the Mediterranean Sea in the west to the Euphrates River in the east, including all the land of the Hittites.' 5No one will be able to oppose you as long as you live, for I will be with you just as I was with Moses; I will not abandon you or fail to help you.

6"Be strong and brave, for you will be a successful leader of my people; and they shall conquer all the land I promised to their ancestors. 7You need only to be strong and courageous and to obey to the letter every law Moses gave you, for if you are careful to obey every one of them you will be successful in everything you do. 8Constantly remind the people about these laws, and you yourself must think about them every day and every night so that you will be sure to obey all of them. For only then will you succeed. 9Yes, be bold and strong! Banish fear and doubt! For remember, the Lord your God is with you wherever you go."

10,11Then Joshua issued instructions to the leaders of Israel to tell the people to get ready to cross the Jordan River. "In three days we will go across and conquer and live in the land which God has given us!" he told them.

12,13Then he summoned the leaders of the tribes of Reuben, Gad, and the half-tribe of Manasseh and reminded them of their agreement with Moses: "The Lord your God has given you a homeland here on the east side of the Jordan River," Moses had told them, 14"so your wives and children and cattle may remain here, but your troops, fully armed, must lead the other tribes across the Jordan River to help them conquer their territory on the other side; 15stay with them until they complete the conquest. Only then may you settle down here on the east side of the Jordan."

16To this they fully agreed, and pledged themselves to obey Joshua as their commander-in-chief.

17,18"We will obey you just as we obeyed Moses," they assured him, "and may the Lord your God be with you as he was with Moses. If anyone, no matter who, rebels against your commands, he shall die. So lead on with courage and strength!"

THEN Joshua sent two spies from the Israeli camp at Acacia to cross the river and check out the situation on the other side, especially at Jericho. They arrived at an inn operated by a woman named Rahab, who was a prostitute. They were planning to spend the night there, 2but someone informed the king of Jericho that two Israelis who were suspected of being spies had arrived in the city that evening. 3He dispatched a police squadron to Rahab's home, demanding that she surrender them.

"They are spies," he explained. "They have been sent by the Israeli leaders to discover the best way to attack us."

4But she had hidden them, so she told the officer in charge, "The men were here earlier, but I didn't know they were spies. 5They left the city at dusk as the city gates were about to close, and I don't know where they went. If you hurry you can probably catch up with them!"

6But actually she had taken them up to the roof and hidden them beneath piles of flax that were drying there. 7So the constable and his men went all the way to the Jordan River looking for them; meanwhile, the city gates were kept shut. 8Rahab went up to talk to the men before they retired for the night.

9"I know perfectly well that your God is going to give my country to you," she told them. "We are all afraid of you; everyone is terrified if the word *Israel* is even mentioned. 10For we have heard how the Lord made a path through the Red Sea for you when you left Egypt! And we know what you did to Sihon and Og, the two Amorite kings east of the Jordan, and how you ruined their land and completely destroyed their people. 11No wonder we are afraid of you! No one has any fight left in him after hearing things like that, for your God is the supreme God of heaven, not just an ordinary god. 12,13Now I beg for this one thing: Swear to me by the sacred name of your God that when Jericho is conquered you will let me live, along with my father and mother, my brothers and sisters, and all their families. This is only fair after the way I have helped you."

14The men agreed. "If you won't betray us, we'll see to it that you and your family aren't harmed," they promised. 15"We'll defend you with our lives." Then, since her house was on top of the city wall, she let them down by a rope from a window.

16"Escape to the mountains," she told them. "Hide there for three days until the men who are searching for you have returned; then go on your way."

17,18But before they left, the men had said to her, "We cannot be responsible for what happens to you unless this rope is hanging from this window and unless all your relatives—your father, mother, brothers, and anyone else—are here inside the house. 19If they go out into the street we assume no responsibility whatsoever; but we swear that no one inside this house will be killed or injured. 20However, if you betray us, then this oath will no longer bind us in any way."

21"I accept your terms," she replied. And she left the scarlet rope hanging from the window.

22The spies went up into the mountains and stayed there three days, until the men who were chasing them had returned to the city after searching everywhere along the road without success. 23Then the two spies came down from the mountain and crossed the river and reported to Joshua all that had happened to them.

24"The Lord will certainly give us the entire land," they said, "for all the people over there are scared to death of us."

SOMEONE asked him, "Will only a few be saved?"

And he replied, 24,25"The door to heaven is narrow. Work hard to get in, for the truth is that many will try to enter but when the head of the house has locked the door, it will be too late. Then if you stand outside knocking, and pleading, 'Lord, open the door for us,' he will reply, 'I do not know you.'

26" 'But we ate with you, and you taught in our streets,' you will say.

27"And he will reply, 'I tell you, I don't know you. You can't come in here, guilty as you are. Go away.'

28"And there will be great weeping and gnashing of teeth as you stand outside and see Abraham, Isaac, Jacob, and all the prophets within the Kingdom of God— 29for people will come from all over the world to take their places there. 30And note this: some who are despised now will be greatly honored then; and some who are highly thought of now will be least important then."

31A few minutes later some Pharisees said to him, "Get out of here if you want to live, for King Herod is after you!"

32Jesus replied, "Go tell that fox that I will keep on casting out demons and doing miracles of healing today and tomorrow; and the third day I will reach my destination. 33Yes, today, tomorrow, and the next day! For it wouldn't do for a prophet of God to be killed except in Jerusalem!

34"O Jerusalem, Jerusalem! The city that murders the prophets. The city that stones those sent to help her. How often I have wanted to gather your children together even as a hen protects her brood under her wings, but you wouldn't let me. 35And now—now your house is left desolate. And you will never again see me until you say, 'Welcome to him who comes in the name of the Lord.' "

ONE Sabbath as he was in the home of a member of the Jewish Council, the Pharisees were watching him like hawks to see if he would heal a man who was present who was suffering from dropsy.

3Jesus said to the Pharisees and legal experts standing around, "Well, is it within the Law to heal a man on the Sabbath day, or not?"

4And when they refused to answer, Jesus took the sick man by the hand and healed him and sent him away.

5Then he turned to them: "Which of you doesn't work on the Sabbath?" he asked. "If your cow falls into a pit, don't you proceed at once to get it out?"

6Again they had no answer.

PSALM 79:1–13

O God, your land has been conquered by the heathen nations. Your Temple is defiled and Jerusalem is a heap of ruins. 2The bodies of your people lie exposed—food for birds and animals. 3The enemy has butchered the entire population of Jerusalem; blood has flowed like water. No one is left even to bury them. 4The nations all around us scoff. They heap contempt on us.

5O Jehovah, how long will you be angry with us? Forever? Will your jealousy burn till every hope is gone? 6Pour out your wrath upon the godless nations, not on us! And on kingdoms that refuse to pray, that will not call upon your name! 7For they have destroyed your people Israel, invading every home. 8Oh, do not hold us guilty for our former sins! Let your tenderhearted mercies meet our needs, for we are brought low to the dust. 9Help us, God of our salvation! Help us for the honor of your name. Oh, save us and forgive our sins. 10Why should the heathen nations be allowed to scoff, "Where is their God?" Publicly avenge this slaughter of your people! 11Listen to the sighing of the prisoners and those condemned to die. Demonstrate the greatness of your power by saving them. 12O Lord, take sevenfold vengeance on these nations scorning you.

13Then we your people, the sheep of your pasture, will thank you forever and forever, praising your greatness from generation to generation.

PROVERBS FOR TODAY/ 12:26

The good man asks advice from friends; the wicked plunge ahead—and fall.

APRIL 11

JOSHUA 3:1—4:24

EARLY the next morning Joshua and all the people of Israel left Acacia, and arrived that evening at the banks of the Jordan River, where they camped for a few days before crossing.

2,3,4On the third day, officers went through the camp giving these instructions: "When you see the priests carrying the Ark of God, follow them. You have never before been where we are going now, so they will guide you. However, stay about a half mile behind, with a clear space between you and the Ark; be sure that you don't get any closer."

5Then Joshua told the people to purify themselves. "For tomorrow," he said, "the Lord will do a great miracle."

6In the morning Joshua ordered the priests, "Take up the Ark and lead us across the river!" And so they started out.

7"Today," the Lord told Joshua, "I will give you great honor, so that all Israel will know that I am with you just as I was with Moses. 8Instruct the priests who are carrying the Ark to stop at the edge of the river."

9Then Joshua summoned all the people and told them, "Come and listen to what the Lord your God has said. 10Today you are going to know for sure that the living God is among you and that he will, without fail, drive out the Canaanites, Hittites, Hivites, Perizzites, Girgashites, Amorites, and Jebusites—all the people who now live in the land you will soon occupy.

11Think of it! The Ark of God, who is Lord of the whole earth, will lead you across the river!

12"Now select twelve men, one from each tribe, for a special task. 13,14When the priests who are carrying the Ark touch the water with their feet, the river will stop flowing as though held back by a dam, and will pile up as though against an invisible wall!" Now it was the harvest season and the Jordan was overflowing all its banks; but as the people set out to cross the river and as the feet of the priests who were carrying the Ark touched the water at the river's edge, 15,16suddenly, far up the river at the city of Adam, near Zarethan, the water began piling up as though against a dam! And the water below that point flowed on to the Dead Sea until the riverbed was empty. Then all the people crossed at a spot where the river was close to the city of Jericho, 17and the priests who were carrying the Ark stood on dry ground in the middle of the Jordan and waited as all the people passed by.

WHEN all the people were safely across, the Lord said to Joshua,

2,3"Tell the twelve men chosen for a special task, one from each tribe, each to take a stone from where the priests are standing in the middle of the Jordan, and to carry them out and pile them up as a monument at the place where you camp tonight."

4So Joshua summoned the twelve men, 5and told them, "Go out into the middle of the Jordan where the Ark is. Each of you is to carry out a stone on your shoulder—twelve stones in all, one for each of the twelve tribes. 6We will use them to build a monument so that in the future, when your children ask, 'What is this monument for?' 7you can tell them, 'It is to remind us that the Jordan River stopped flowing when the Ark of God went across!' The monument will be a permanent reminder to the people of Israel of this amazing miracle."

8So the men did as Joshua told them. They took twelve stones from the middle of the Jordan river—one for each tribe, just as the Lord had commanded Joshua. They carried them to the place where they were camped for the night and constructed a monument there. 9Joshua also built another monument of twelve stones in the middle of the river, at the place where the priests were standing; and it is there to this day. 10The priests who were carrying the Ark stood in the middle of the river until all these instructions of the Lord, which had been given to Joshua by Moses, had been carried out. Meanwhile, the people had hurried across the riverbed, 11and when everyone was over, the people watched the priests carry the Ark out of the riverbed.

12,13The troops of Reuben, Gad, and the half-tribe of Manasseh—fully armed as Moses had instructed, and forty thousand strong—led the other tribes of the Lord's army across to the plains of Jericho.

14It was a tremendous day for Joshua! The Lord made him great in the eyes of all the people of Israel, and they revered him as much as they had Moses, and respected him deeply all the rest of his life. 15,16For it was Joshua who, at the Lord's command, issued the orders to the priests carrying the Ark.

"Come up from the riverbed," the Lord now told him to command them.

17So Joshua issued the order. 18And as soon as the priests came out, the water poured down again as usual and overflowed the banks of the river as before! 19This miracle occurred on the 25th of March. That day the entire nation crossed the Jordan River and camped in Gilgal at the eastern edge of the city of Jericho; 20and there the twelve stones from the Jordan were piled up as a monument.

21Then Joshua explained again the purpose of the stones: "In the future," he said, "when your children ask you why these stones are here and what they mean, 22you are to tell them that these stones are a reminder of this amazing miracle—that the nation of Israel crossed the Jordan River on dry ground! 23Tell them how the Lord our God dried up the river right before our eyes, and then kept it dry until we were all across! It is the same thing the Lord did forty years ago at the Red Sea! 24He did this so that all the nations of the earth will realize that Jehovah is the mighty God, and so that all of you will worship him forever."

LUKE 14:7–35

WHEN he noticed that all who came to the dinner were trying to sit near the head of the table, he gave them this advice: 8"If you are invited to a wedding feast, don't always head for the best seat. For if someone more respected than you shows up, 9the host will bring him over to where you are sitting and say, 'Let this man sit here instead.' And you, embarrassed, will have to take whatever seat is left at the foot of the table!

10"Do this instead—start at the foot; and when your host sees you he will come and say, 'Friend, we have a better place than this for you!' Thus you will be honored in front of all the other guests. 11For everyone who tries to honor himself shall be humbled; and he who humbles himself shall be honored."

12Then he turned to his host. "When you put on a dinner," he said, "don't invite friends, brothers, relatives, and rich neighbors! For they will return the invitation. 13Instead, invite the poor, the crippled, the lame, and the blind. 14Then at the resurrection of the godly, God will reward you for inviting those who can't repay you."

15Hearing this, a man sitting at the table with Jesus exclaimed, "What a privilege it would be to get into the Kingdom of God!"

16Jesus replied with this illustration: "A man prepared a great feast and sent out many invitations. 17When all was ready, he sent his servant around to notify the guests that it was time for them to arrive. 18But they all began making excuses. One said he had just bought a field and wanted to inspect it, and asked to be excused. 19Another said he had just bought five pair of oxen and wanted to try them out. 20Another had just been married and for that reason couldn't come.

21"The servant returned and reported to his master what they had said. His master was angry and told him to go quickly into the streets and alleys of the city and to invite the beggars, crippled, lame, and blind. 22But even then, there was still room.

23" 'Well, then,' said his master, 'go out into the country lanes and out behind the hedges and urge anyone you find to come, so that the house will be full. 24For none of those I invited first will get even the smallest taste of what I had prepared for them.' "

25Great crowds were following him. He turned around and addressed them as follows: 26"Anyone who wants to be my follower must love me far more than he does his own father, mother, wife, children, brothers, or sisters—yes, more than his own life—otherwise he cannot be my disciple. 27And no one can be my disciple who does not carry his own cross and follow me.

28"But don't begin until you count the cost. For who would begin construction of a building without first getting estimates and then checking to see if he has enough money to pay the bills? 29Otherwise he might complete only the foundation before running out of funds. And then how everyone would laugh!

30" 'See that fellow there?' they would mock. 'He started that building and ran out of money before it was finished!'

31"Or what king would ever dream of going to war without first sitting down with his counselors and discussing whether his army of 10,000 is strong enough to defeat the 20,000 men who are marching against him?

32"If the decision is negative, then while the enemy troops are still far away, he will send a truce team to discuss terms of peace. 33So no one can become my disciple unless he first sits down and counts his blessings—and then renounces them all for me.

34"What good is salt that has lost its saltiness? 35Flavorless salt is fit for nothing—not even for fertilizer. It is worthless and must be thrown out. Listen well, if you would understand my meaning."

PSALM 80:1–19

O Shepherd of Israel who leads Israel like a flock; O God enthroned above the Guardian Angels, bend down your ear and listen as I plead. Display your power and radiant glory. 2Let Ephraim, Benjamin and Manasseh see you rouse yourself and use your mighty power to rescue us.

3Turn us again to yourself, O God. Look down on us in joy and love; only then shall we be saved.

4O Jehovah, God of heaven's armies, how long will you be angry and reject our prayers? 5You have fed us with sorrow and tears, 6and have made us the scorn of the neighboring nations. They laugh among themselves.

7Turn us again to yourself, O God of Hosts. Look down on us in joy and love; only then shall we be saved. 8You brought us from Egypt as though we were a tender vine and drove away the heathen from your land and planted us. 9You cleared the ground and tilled the soil and we took root and filled the land. 10The mountains were covered with our shadow; we were like the mighty cedar trees, [11]covering the entire land from the Mediterranean Sea to the Euphrates River. [12]But now you have broken down our walls, leaving us without protection. [13]The boar from the forest roots around us, and the wild animals feed on us.

[14]Come back, we beg of you, O God of the armies of heaven, and bless us. Look down from heaven and see our plight and care for this your vine! [15]Protect what you yourself have planted, this son you have raised for yourself. [16]For we are chopped and burned by our enemies. May they perish at your frown. [17]Strengthen the man you love, the son of your choice, [18]and we will never forsake you again. Revive us to trust in you.

[19]Turn us again to yourself, O God of the armies of heaven. Look down on us, your face aglow with joy and love— only then shall we be saved.

PROVERBS FOR TODAY/ 12:27–28

A lazy man won't even dress the game he gets while hunting, but the diligent man makes good use of everything he finds. The path of the godly leads to life. So why fear death?

APRIL 12

JOSHUA 5:1—7:15

WHEN the nations west of the Jordan River—the Amorites and Canaanites who lived along the Mediterranean coast—heard that the Lord had dried up the Jordan River so the people of Israel could cross, their courage melted away completely and they were paralyzed with fear.

[2,3]The Lord then told Joshua to set aside a day to circumcise the entire male population of Israel. (It was the second time in Israel's history that this was done.) The Lord instructed them to manufacture flint knives for this purpose. The place where the circumcision rite took place was named "The Hill of the Foreskins." [4,5]The reason for this second circumcision ceremony was that although when Israel left Egypt all of the men who had been old enough to bear arms had been circumcised, that entire generation had died during the years in the wilderness, and none of the boys born since that time had been circumcised. [6]For the nation of Israel had traveled back and forth across the wilderness for forty years until all the men who had been old enough to bear arms when they left Egypt were dead; they had not obeyed the Lord, and he vowed that he wouldn't let them enter the land he had promised to Israel—a land that "flowed with milk and honey." [7]So now Joshua circumcised their children—the men who had grown up to take their fathers' places.

[8,9]And the Lord said to Joshua, "Today I have ended your shame of not being circumcised." So the place where this was done was called Gilgal (meaning, "to end"), and is still called that today. After the ceremony the entire nation rested in camp until the raw flesh of their wounds had been healed.

[10]While they were camped at Gilgal on the plains of Jericho, they celebrated the Passover during the evening of April first. [11,12]The next day they began to eat from the gardens and grain fields which they invaded, and they made unleavened bread. The following day no manna fell, and it was never seen again! So from that time on they lived on the crops of Canaan.

¹³As Joshua was sizing up the city of Jericho, a man appeared nearby with a drawn sword. Joshua strode over to him and demanded, "Are you friend or foe?"

¹⁴"I am the Commander-in-Chief of the Lord's army," he replied.

Joshua fell to the ground before him and worshiped him and said, "Give me your commands."

¹⁵"Take off your shoes," the Commander told him, "for this is holy ground." And Joshua did.

THE gates of Jericho were kept tightly shut because the people were afraid of the Israelis; no one was allowed to go in or out.

²But the Lord said to Joshua, "Jericho and its king and all its mighty warriors are already defeated, for I have given them to you! ³,⁴Your entire army is to walk around the city once a day for six days, followed by seven priests walking ahead of the Ark, each carrying a trumpet made from a ram's horn. On the seventh day you are to walk around the city seven times, with the priests blowing their trumpets. ⁵Then, when they give one long, loud blast, all the people are to give a mighty shout and the walls of the city will fall down; then move in upon the city from every direction."

⁶⁻⁹So Joshua summoned the priests and gave them their instructions: the armed men would lead the procession followed by seven priests blowing continually on their trumpets. Behind them would come the priests carrying the Ark, followed by a rear guard.

¹⁰"Let there be complete silence except for the trumpets," Joshua commanded. "Not a single word from any of you until I tell you to shout; then *shout!*"

¹¹The Ark was carried around the city once that day, after which everyone returned to the camp again and spent the night there. ¹²,¹³,¹⁴At dawn the next morning they went around again, and returned again to the camp. They followed this pattern for six days.

¹⁵At dawn of the seventh day they started out again, but this time they went around the city not once, but seven times. ¹⁶The seventh time, as the priests blew a long, loud trumpet blast, Joshua yelled to the people, *"Shout!* The Lord has given us the city!"

¹⁷(He had told them previously, "Kill everyone except Rahab the prostitute and anyone in her house, for she protected our spies. ¹⁸Don't take any loot, for everything is to be destroyed. If it isn't, disaster will fall upon the entire nation of Israel. ¹⁹But all the silver and gold and the utensils of bronze and iron will be dedicated to the Lord, and must be brought into his treasury.")

²⁰So when the people heard the trumpet blast, they shouted as loud as they could. And suddenly the walls of Jericho crumbled and fell before them, and the people of Israel poured into the city from every side and captured it! ²¹They destroyed everything in it—men and women, young and old; oxen; sheep; donkeys—everything.

²²Meanwhile Joshua had said to the two spies, "Keep your promise. Go and rescue the prostitute and everyone with her."

²³The young men found her and rescued her, along with her father, mother, brothers, and other relatives who were with her. Arrangements were made for them to live outside the camp of Israel. ²⁴Then the Israelis burned the city and everything in it except that the silver and gold and the bronze and iron utensils were kept for the Lord's treasury. ²⁵Thus Joshua saved Rahab the prostitute and her relatives who were with her in the house, and they still live among the Israelites because she hid the spies sent to Jericho by Joshua.

²⁶Then Joshua declared a terrible curse upon anyone who might rebuild Jericho, warning that when the foundation was laid, the builder's oldest son would die, and when the gates were set up, his youngest son would die.

²⁷So the Lord was with Joshua, and his name became famous everywhere.

BUT there was sin among the Israelis. God's command to destroy everything except that which was reserved for the Lord's treasury was disobeyed. For Achan (the son of Carmi, grandson of Zabdi, and great-grandson of Zerah, of the tribe of Judah) took some loot for himself, and the Lord was very angry with the entire nation of Israel because of this.

²Soon after Jericho's defeat, Joshua sent some of his men to spy on the city of Ai, east of Bethel.

³Upon their return they told Joshua, "It's a small city and it won't take more than two or three thousand of us to destroy it; there's no point in all of us going there."

⁴So approximately three thousand soldiers were sent—and they were soundly defeated. ⁵About thirty-six of the Israelis were killed during the attack, and many others died while being chased by the men of Ai as far as the quarries. The Israeli army was paralyzed with fear at this turn of events. ⁶Joshua and the elders of Israel tore their clothing and lay prostrate before the Ark of the Lord until evening, with dust on their heads.

⁷Joshua cried out to the Lord, "O Jehovah, why have you brought us over the Jordan River if you are going to let the Amorites kill us? Why weren't we content with what we had? Why didn't we stay on the other side? ⁸O Lord, what am I to do now that Israel has fled from her enemies! ⁹For when the Canaanites and the other nearby nations hear about it, they will surround us and attack us and wipe us out. And then what will happen to the honor of your great name?"

¹⁰,¹¹But the Lord said to Joshua, "Get up off your face! Israel has sinned and disobeyed my commandment and has taken loot when I said it was not to be taken; and they have not only taken it, they have lied about it and have hidden it among their belongings. ¹²That is why the people of Israel are being defeated. That is why your men are running from their enemies—for they are cursed. I will

not stay with you any longer unless you completely rid yourselves of this sin.

¹³"Get up! Tell the people, 'Each of you must undergo purification rites in preparation for tomorrow, for the Lord your God of Israel says that someone has stolen from him, and you cannot defeat your enemies until you deal with this sin. ¹⁴In the morning you must come by tribes, and the Lord will point out the tribe to which the guilty man belongs. And that tribe must come by its clans and the Lord will point out the guilty clan; and the clan must come by its families, and then each member of the guilty family must come one by one. ¹⁵And the one who has stolen that which belongs to the Lord shall be burned with fire, along with everything he has, for he has violated the covenant of the Lord and has brought calamity upon all of Israel.' "

LUKE 15:1–32

DISHONEST tax collectors and other notorious sinners often came to listen to Jesus' sermons; ²but this caused complaints from the Jewish religious leaders and the experts on Jewish law because he was associating with such despicable people—even eating with them!

³,⁴So Jesus used this illustration: "If you had a hundred sheep and one of them strayed away and was lost in the wilderness, wouldn't you leave the ninety-nine others to go and search for the lost one until you found it? ⁵And then you would joyfully carry it home on your shoulders. ⁶When you arrived you would call together your friends and neighbors to rejoice with you because your lost sheep was found.

⁷"Well, in the same way heaven will be happier over one lost sinner who returns to God than over ninety-nine others who haven't strayed away!

⁸"Or take another illustration: A woman has ten valuable silver coins and loses one. Won't she light a lamp and look in every corner of the house and sweep every nook and cranny until she

finds it? 9And then won't she call in her friends and neighbors to rejoice with her? 10In the same way there is joy in the presence of the angels of God when one sinner repents."

11To further illustrate the point, he told them this story: "A man had two sons. 12When the younger told his father, 'I want my share of your estate now, instead of waiting until you die!' his father agreed to divide his wealth between his sons.

13"A few days later this younger son packed all his belongings and took a trip to a distant land, and there wasted all his money on parties and prostitutes. 14About the time his money was gone a great famine swept over the land, and he began to starve. 15He persuaded a local farmer to hire him to feed his pigs. 16The boy became so hungry that even the pods he was feeding the swine looked good to him. And no one gave him anything.

17"When he finally came to his senses, he said to himself, 'At home even the hired men have food enough and to spare, and here I am, dying of hunger! 18I will go home to my father and say, "Father, I have sinned against both heaven and you, 19and am no longer worthy of being called your son. Please take me on as a hired man." '

20"So he returned home to his father. And while he was still a long distance away, his father saw him coming, and was filled with loving pity and ran and embraced him and kissed him.

21"His son said to him, 'Father, I have sinned against heaven and you, and am not worthy of being called your son—'

22"But his father said to the slaves, 'Quick! Bring the finest robe in the house and put it on him. And a jeweled ring for his finger; and shoes! 23And kill the calf we have in the fattening pen. We must celebrate with a feast, 24for this son of mine was dead and has returned to life. He was lost and is found.' So the party began.

25"Meanwhile, the older son was in the fields working; when he returned home, he heard dance music coming from the house, 26and he asked one of the servants what was going on.

27" 'Your brother is back,' he was told, 'and your father has killed the calf we were fattening and has prepared a great feast to celebrate his coming home again unharmed.'

28"The older brother was angry and wouldn't go in. His father came out and begged him, 29but he replied, 'All these years I've worked hard for you and never once refused to do a single thing you told me to; and in all that time you never gave me even one young goat for a feast with my friends. 30Yet when this son of yours comes back after spending your money on prostitutes, you celebrate by killing the finest calf we have on the place.'

31" 'Look, dear son,' his father said to him, 'you and I are very close, and everything I have is yours. 32But it is right to celebrate. For he is your brother; and he was dead and has come back to life! He was lost and is found!' "

PSALM 81:1–16

THE Lord makes us strong! Sing praises! Sing to Israel's God!
2Sing, accompanied by drums; pluck the sweet lyre and harp. 3Sound the trumpet! Come to the joyous celebrations at full moon, new moon and all the other holidays. 4For God has given us these times of joy; they are scheduled in the laws of Israel. 5He gave them as reminders of his war against Egypt where we were slaves on foreign soil.

I heard an unknown voice that said, 6"Now I will relieve your shoulder of its burden; I will free your hands from their heavy tasks." 7He said, "You cried to me in trouble and I saved you; I answered from Mount Sinai where the thunder hides. I tested your faith at Meribah, when you complained there was no water. 8Listen to me, O my people, while I give you stern warnings. O Israel, if you will only listen! 9*You must never worship any other god,* nor ever have an idol in your home. 10For it was I, Jehovah your God, who brought you out of the land of Egypt. Only test me! Open your mouth wide and see if I won't fill it. You will receive every blessing you can use!

11"But no, my people won't listen. Israel doesn't want me around. 12So I am letting them go their blind and stubborn way, living according to their own desires.

13"But oh, that my people would listen to me! Oh, that Israel would follow me, walking in my paths! 14How quickly then I would subdue her enemies! How soon my hands would be upon her foes! 15Those who hate the Lord would cringe before him; their desolation would last forever. 16But he would feed you with the choicest foods. He would satisfy you with honey for the taking."

PROVERBS FOR TODAY/ 13:1

A wise youth accepts his father's rebuke; a young mocker doesn't.

APRIL 13

JOSHUA 7:16—9:2

SO, early the next morning, Joshua brought the tribes of Israel before the Lord, and the tribe of Judah was indicated. 17Then he brought the clans of Judah, and the clan of Zerah was singled out. Then the families of that clan were brought before the Lord and the family of Zabdi was indicated. 18Zabdi's family was brought man by man, and his grandson Achan was found to be the guilty one.

19Joshua said to Achan, "My son, give glory to the God of Israel and make your confession. Tell me what you have done."

20Achan replied, "I have sinned against the Lord, the God of Israel. 21For I saw a beautiful robe imported from Babylon, and some silver worth $200, and a bar of gold worth $500. I wanted them so much that I took them, and they are hidden in the ground beneath my tent, with the silver buried deeper than the rest."

22So Joshua sent some men to search for the loot. They ran to the tent and found the stolen goods hidden there just as Achan had said, with the silver buried beneath the rest. 23They brought it all to Joshua and laid it on the ground in front of him. 24Then Joshua and all the Israelites took Achan, the silver, the robe, the wedge of gold, his sons, his daughters, his oxen, donkeys, sheep, his tent, and everything he had, and brought them to the valley of Achor.

25Then Joshua said to Achan, "Why have you brought calamity upon us? The Lord will now bring calamity upon you."

And the men of Israel stoned them to death and burned their bodies, 26and piled a great heap of stones upon them. The stones are still there to this day, and even today that place is called "The Valley of Calamity." And so the fierce anger of the Lord was ended.

THEN the Lord said to Joshua, "Don't be afraid or discouraged; take the entire army and go to Ai, for it is now yours to conquer. I have given the king of Ai and all of his people to you. 2You shall do to them as you did to Jericho and her king; but this time you may keep the loot and the cattle for yourselves. Set an ambush behind the city."

3,4Before the main army left for Ai, Joshua sent thirty thousand of his bravest troops to hide in ambush close behind the city, alert for action.

5"This is the plan," he explained to them. "When our main army attacks, the men of Ai will come out to fight as they did before, and we will run away. 6We will let them chase us until they have all left the city; for they will say, 'The Israelis are running away again just as they did before!' 7Then you will jump up from your ambush and enter the city, for the Lord will give it to you. 8Set the city on fire, as the Lord has commanded. You now have your instructions."

9So they left that night and lay in ambush between Bethel and the west side of Ai; but Joshua and the rest of the army remained in the camp at Jericho. 10Early the next morning Joshua roused his men and started toward Ai, accompanied by the elders of Israel, 11,12,13and stopped at the edge of a valley north of the city. That night Joshua sent another five thousand men to join the troops in ambush on the west side of the city. He himself spent the night in the valley.

14The King of Ai, seeing the Israelis across the valley, went out early the next morning and attacked at the Plain of Arabah. But of course he didn't realize that there was an ambush behind the city. 15Joshua and the Israeli army fled across the wilderness as though badly beaten, 16and all the soldiers in the city were called out to chase after them; so the city was left defenseless; 17there was not a soldier left in Ai or Bethel and the city gates were left wide open.

18Then the Lord said to Joshua, "Point your spear toward Ai, for I will give you the city." Joshua did. 19And when the men in ambush saw his signal, they jumped up and poured into the city and set it on fire. 20,21When the men of Ai looked behind them, smoke from the city was filling the sky, and they had nowhere to go. When Joshua and the troops who were with him saw the smoke, they knew that their men who had been in ambush were inside the city, so they turned upon their pursuers and began killing them.

22Then the Israelis who were inside the city came out and began destroying the enemy from the rear. So the men of Ai were caught in a trap and all of them died; not one man survived or escaped, 23except for the king of Ai, who was captured and brought to Joshua.

24When the army of Israel had finished slaughtering all the men outside the city, they went back and finished off everyone left inside. 25So the entire population of Ai, twelve thousand in all, was wiped out that day. 26For Joshua kept his spear pointed toward Ai until the last person was dead. 27Only the cattle and the loot were not destroyed, for the armies of Israel kept these for themselves. (The Lord had told Joshua they could.) 28So Ai became a desolate mound of refuse, as it still is today.

29Joshua hanged the king of Ai on a tree until evening, but as the sun was going down, he took down the body and threw it in front of the city gate. There he piled a great heap of stones over it, which can still be seen.

30Then Joshua built an altar to the Lord God of Israel at Mount Ebal, 31as Moses had commanded in the book of his laws: "Make me an altar of boulders that have neither been broken nor carved," the Lord had said concerning Mount Ebal. Then the priests offered burnt sacrifices and peace offerings to the Lord on the altar. 32And as the people of Israel watched, Joshua carved upon the stones of the altar each of the Ten Commandments.

33Then all the people of Israel—including the elders, officers, judges, and the foreigners living among them—divided into two groups, half of them standing at the foot of Mount Gerizim and half at the foot of Mount Ebal. Between them stood the priests with the Ark, ready to pronounce their blessing. (This was all done in accordance with the instructions given long before by Moses.) 34Joshua then read to them all of the statements of blessing and curses that Moses had written in the book of God's laws. 35Every commandment Moses had ever given was read before the entire assembly, including the women and children and the foreigners who lived among the Israelis.

WHEN the kings of the surrounding area heard what had happened to Jericho, they quickly combined their armies to fight for their lives against Joshua and the Israelis. These were the kings of the nations west of the Jordan River, along the shores of the Mediterranean as far north as the Lebanon mountains—the Hittites, Amorites, Canaanites, Perizzites, Hivites, and Jebusites.

LUKE 16:1–18

JESUS now told this story to his disciples: "A rich man hired an accountant to handle his affairs, but soon a rumor went around that the accountant was thoroughly dishonest.

2"So his employer called him in and said, 'What's this I hear about your stealing from me? Get your report in order, for you are to be dismissed.'

3"The accountant thought to himself, 'Now what? I'm through here, and I haven't the strength to go out and dig ditches, and I'm too proud to beg. 4I know just the thing! And then I'll have plenty of friends to take care of me when I leave!'

5,6"So he invited each one who owed money to his employer to come and discuss the situation. He asked the first one, 'How much do you owe him?' 'My debt is 850 gallons of olive oil,' the man replied. 'Yes, here is the contract you signed,' the accountant told him. 'Tear it up and write another one for half that much!'

7"'And how much do you owe him?' he asked the next man. 'A thousand bushels of wheat,' was the reply. 'Here,' the accountant said, 'take your note and replace it with one for only 800 bushels!'

8"The rich man had to admire the rascal for being so shrewd. And it is true that the citizens of this world are more clever [in dishonesty!] than the godly are.

9But shall I tell *you* to act that way, to buy friendship through cheating? Will this ensure your entry into an everlasting home in heaven? 10*No!* For unless you are honest in small matters, you won't be in large ones. If you cheat even a little, you won't be honest with greater responsibilities. 11And if you are untrustworthy about worldly wealth, who will trust you with the true riches of heaven? 12And if you are not faithful with other people's money, why should you be entrusted with money of your own?

13"For neither you nor anyone else can serve two masters. You will hate one and show loyalty to the other, or else the other way around—you will be enthusiastic about one and despise the other. You cannot serve both God and money."

14The Pharisees, who dearly loved their money, naturally scoffed at all this.

15Then he said to them, "You wear a noble, pious expression in public, but God knows your evil hearts. Your pretense brings you honor from the people, but it is an abomination in the sight of God. 16Until John the Baptist began to preach, the laws of Moses and the messages of the prophets were your guides. But John introduced the Good News that the Kingdom of God would come soon. And now eager multitudes are pressing in. 17But that doesn't mean that the Law has lost its force in even the smallest point. It is as strong and unshakable as heaven and earth.

18"So anyone who divorces his wife and marries someone else commits adultery, and anyone who marries a divorced woman commits adultery."

PSALM 82:1–8

GOD stands up to open heaven's court. He pronounces judgment on the judges. 2How long will you judges refuse to listen to the evidence? How long will you shower special favors on the wicked? 3Give fair judgment to the poor man, the afflicted, the fatherless, the destitute. 4Rescue the poor and helpless from the grasp of evil men.

⁵But you are so foolish and so ignorant! Because you are in darkness, all the foundations of society are shaken to the core. ⁶I have called you all "gods" and "sons of the Most High." ⁷But in death you are mere men. You will fall as any prince—for all must die.

⁸Stand up, O God, and judge the earth. For all of it belongs to you. All nations are in your hands.

PROVERBS FOR TODAY/ 13:2–3

The good man wins his case by careful argument; the evil-minded only wants to fight. Self-control means controlling the tongue! A quick retort can ruin everything.

APRIL 14

JOSHUA 9:3—10:43

BUT when the people of Gibeon heard what had happened to Jericho and Ai, they resorted to trickery to save themselves. They sent ambassadors to Joshua wearing worn-out clothing, as though from a long journey, with patched shoes, weatherworn saddlebags on their donkeys, old, patched wineskins and dry, moldy bread. ⁶When they arrived at the camp of Israel at Gilgal, they told Joshua and the men of Israel, "We have come from a distant land to ask for a peace treaty with you."

⁷The Israelis replied to these Hivites, "How do we know you don't live nearby? For if you do, we cannot make a treaty with you."

⁸They replied, "We will be your slaves."

"But who are you?" Joshua demanded. "Where do you come from?"

⁹And they told him, "We are from a very distant country; we have heard of the might of the Lord your God and of all that he did in Egypt, ¹⁰and what you did to the two kings of the Amorites—Sihon, king of Heshbon, and Og, king of Bashan. ¹¹So our elders and our people instructed us, 'Prepare for a long journey; go to the people of Israel and declare our nation to be their servants, and ask for peace.' ¹²This bread was hot from the ovens when we left, but now as you see, it is dry and moldy; ¹³these wineskins were new, but now they are old and cracked; our clothing and shoes have become worn out from our long, hard trip."

¹⁴,¹⁵Joshua and the other leaders finally believed them. They did not bother to ask the Lord, but went ahead and signed a peace treaty. And the leaders of Israel ratified the agreement with a binding oath.

¹⁶Three days later the facts came out—these men were close neighbors. ¹⁷The Israeli army set out at once to investigate, and reached their cities in three days. (The names of the cities were Gibeon, Chephirah, Be-eroth, and Kiriath-jearim.) ¹⁸But the cities were not harmed because of the vow which the leaders of Israel had made before the Lord God. The people of Israel were angry with their leaders because of the peace treaty.

¹⁹But the leaders replied, "We have sworn before the Lord God of Israel that we will not touch them, and we won't ²⁰We must let them live, for if we break our oath the wrath of Jehovah will be upon us."

²¹So they became servants of the Israelis, chopping their wood and carrying their water.

²²Joshua summoned their leaders and demanded, "Why have you lied to us by

saying that you lived in a distant land, when you were actually living right here among us? 23Now a curse shall be upon you! From this moment you must always furnish us with servants to chop wood and carry water for the service of our God."

24They replied, "We did it because we were told that Jehovah instructed his disciple Moses to conquer this entire land and destroy all the people living in it. So we feared for our lives because of you; that is why we have done it. 25But now we are in your hands; you may do with us as you wish."

26So Joshua would not allow the people of Israel to kill them, 27but they became wood-choppers and water-carriers for the people of Israel and for the altar of the Lord—wherever it would be built (for the Lord hadn't yet told them where to build it). This arrangement is still in force at the time of this writing.

WHEN Adoni-zedek, the king of Jerusalem, heard how Joshua had captured and destroyed Ai and had killed its king, the same as he had done at Jericho, and how the people of Gibeon had made peace with Israel and were now their allies, 2he was very frightened. For Gibeon was a great city—as great as the royal cities and much larger than Ai—and its men were known as hard fighters. 3So King Adoni-zedek of Jerusalem sent messengers to several other kings:

King Hoham of Hebron,
King Piram of Jarmuth,
King Japhia of Lachish,
King Debir of Eglon.

4"Come and help me destroy Gibeon," he urged them, "for they have made peace with Joshua and the people of Israel."

5So these five Amorite kings combined their armies for a united attack on Gibeon. 6The men of Gibeon hurriedly sent messengers to Joshua at Gilgal.

"Come and help your servants!" they demanded. "Come quickly and save us! For all the kings of the Amorites who live in the hills are here with their armies."

7So Joshua and the Israeli army left Gilgal and went to rescue Gibeon.

8"Don't be afraid of them," the Lord said to Joshua, "for they are already defeated! I have given them to you to destroy. Not a single one of them will be able to stand up to you."

9Joshua traveled all night from Gilgal and took the enemy armies by surprise. 10Then the Lord threw them into a panic so that the army of Israel slaughtered great numbers of them at Gibeon and chased the others all the way to Beth-horon and Azekah and Makkedah, killing them along the way. 11And as the enemy was racing down the hill to Beth-horon, the Lord destroyed them with a great hailstorm that continued all the way to Azekah; in fact, more men died from the hail than by the swords of the Israelis.

12As the men of Israel were pursuing and harassing the foe, Joshua prayed aloud, "Let the sun stand still over Gibeon, and let the moon stand in its place over the valley of Aijalon!"

13And the sun and the moon didn't move until the Israeli army had finished the destruction of its enemies! This is described in greater detail in *The Book of Jashar.* So the sun stopped in the heavens and stayed there for almost twenty-four hours! 14There had never been such a day before, and there has never been another since, when the Lord stopped the sun and moon—all because of the prayer of one man. But the Lord was fighting for Israel. 15(Afterwards Joshua and the Israeli army returned to Gilgal.)

16During the battle the five kings escaped and hid in a cave at Makkedah. 17When the news was brought to Joshua that they had been found, 18he issued a command that a great stone be rolled against the mouth of the cave and that guards be placed there to keep the kings inside.

19Then Joshua commanded the rest of the army, "Go on chasing the enemy and cut them down from the rear. Don't let them get back to their cities, for the

Lord will help you to completely destroy them."

20So Joshua and the Israeli army continued the slaughter and wiped out the five armies except for a tiny remnant that managed to reach their fortified cities. 21Then the Israelis returned to their camp at Makkedah without having lost a single man! And after that no one dared to attack Israel.

22,23Joshua now instructed his men to remove the stone from the mouth of the cave and to bring out the five kings—of Jerusalem, Hebron, Jarmuth, Lachish, and Eglon. 24Joshua told the captains of his army to put their feet on the kings' necks.

25"Don't ever be afraid or discouraged," Joshua said to his men. "Be strong and courageous, for the Lord is going to do this to all of your enemies."

26With that, Joshua plunged his sword into each of the five kings, killing them. He then hanged them on five trees until evening.

27As the sun was going down, Joshua instructed that their bodies be taken down and thrown into the cave where they had been hiding; and a great pile of stones was placed at the mouth of the cave. (The pile is still there today.)

28On that same day Joshua destroyed the city of Makkedah and killed its king and everyone in it. Not one person in the entire city was left alive. 29Then the Israelis went to Libnah. 30There, too, the Lord gave them the city and its king. Every last person was slaughtered, just as at Jericho.

31From Libnah they went to Lachish and attacked it. 32And the Lord gave it to them on the second day; here, too, the entire population was slaughtered, just as at Libnah.

33During the attack on Lachish, King Horam of Gezer arrived with his army to try to help defend the city, but Joshua's men killed him and destroyed his entire army.

34,35The Israeli army then captured Eglon on the first day and, as at Lachish, they killed everyone in the city. 36After leaving Eglon they went to Hebron, 37and captured it and all of its surrounding villages, slaughtering the entire population. Not one person was left alive. 38Then they turned back to Debir, 39which they quickly captured with all of its outlying villages. And they killed everyone just as they had at Libnah.

40So Joshua and his army conquered the whole country—the nations and kings of the hill country, the Negeb, the lowlands, and the mountain slopes. They destroyed everyone in the land, just as the Lord God of Israel had commanded, 41slaughtering them from Kadesh-barnea to Gaza, and from Goshen to Gibeon. 42This was all accomplished in one campaign, for the Lord God of Israel was fighting for his people. 43Then Joshua and his army returned to their camp at Gilgal.

LUKE 16:19—17:10

THERE was a certain rich man," Jesus said, "who was splendidly clothed and lived each day in mirth and luxury. 20One day Lazarus, a diseased beggar, was laid at his door. 21As he lay there longing for scraps from the rich man's table, the dogs would come and lick his open sores. 22Finally the beggar died and was carried by the angels to be with Abraham in the place of the righteous dead. The rich man also died and was buried, 23and his soul went into hell. There, in torment, he saw Lazarus in the far distance with Abraham.

24" 'Father Abraham,' he shouted, 'have some pity! Send Lazarus over here if only to dip the tip of his finger in water and cool my tongue, for I am in anguish in these flames.'

25"But Abraham said to him, 'Son, remember that during your lifetime you had everything you wanted, and Lazarus had nothing. So now he is here being comforted and you are in anguish. 26And besides, there is a great chasm separating us, and anyone wanting to come to you from here is stopped at its edge; and no one over there can cross to us.'

27"Then the rich man said, 'O Father Abraham, then please send him to my father's home— 28for I have five brothers—to warn them about this place of torment lest they come here when they die.'

29"But Abraham said, 'The Scriptures have warned them again and again. Your brothers can read them any time they want to.'

30"The rich man replied, 'No, Father Abraham, they won't bother to read them. But if someone is sent to them from the dead, then they will turn from their sins.'

31"But Abraham said, 'If they won't listen to Moses and the prophets, they won't listen even though someone rises from the dead.' "

"THERE will always be temptations to sin," Jesus said one day to his disciples, "but woe to the man who does the tempting. 2,3If he were thrown into the sea with a huge rock tied to his neck, he would be far better off than facing the punishment in store for those who harm these little children's souls. I am warning you!

"Rebuke your brother if he sins, and forgive him if he is sorry. 4Even if he wrongs you seven times a day and each time turns again and asks forgiveness, forgive him."

5One day the apostles said to the Lord, "We need more faith; tell us how to get it."

6"If your faith were only the size of a mustard seed," Jesus answered, "it would be large enough to uproot that mulberry tree over there and send it hurtling into the sea! Your command would bring immediate results! 7,8,9When a servant comes in from plowing or taking care of sheep, he doesn't just sit down and eat, but first prepares his master's meal and serves him his supper before he eats his own. And he is not even thanked, for he is merely doing what he

is supposed to do. 10Just so, if you merely obey me, you should not consider yourselves worthy of praise. For you have simply done your duty!"

PSALM 83:1–18

O God, don't sit idly by, silent and inactive when we pray. Answer us! Deliver us!

2Don't you hear the tumult and commotion of your enemies? Don't you see what they are doing, these proud men who hate the Lord? 3They are full of craftiness and plot against your people, laying plans to slay your precious ones. 4"Come," they say, "and let us wipe out Israel as a nation—we will destroy the very memory of her existence." 5This was their unanimous decision at their summit conference—they signed a treaty to ally themselves against Almighty God— 6these Ishmaelites and Edomites and Moabites and Hagrites; 7people from the lands of Gebal, Ammon, Amalek, Philistia and Tyre; 8Assyria has joined them too, and is allied with the descendants of Lot.

9Do to them as once you did to Midian, or as you did to Sisera and Jabin at the river Kishon, 10and as you did to your enemies at Endor, whose decaying corpses fertilized the soil. 11Make their mighty nobles die as Oreb did, and Zeeb; let all their princes die like Zebah and Zalmunna, 12who said, "Let us seize for our own use these pasturelands of God!"

13O my God, blow them away like dust; like chaff before the wind— 14as a forest fire that roars across a mountain. 15Chase them with your fiery storms, tempests and tornados. 16Utterly disgrace them until they recognize your power and name, O Lord. 17Make them failures in everything they do; let them be ashamed and terrified 18until they learn that you alone, Jehovah, are the God above all gods in supreme charge of all the earth.

PROVERBS FOR TODAY/ 13:4
Lazy people want much but get little, while the diligent are prospering.

APRIL 15

JOSHUA 11:1—12:24

WHEN King Jabin of Hazor heard what had happened, he sent urgent messages to the following kings:

King Jobab of Madon;

The king of Shimron;

The king of Achshaph;

All the kings of the northern hill country;

The kings in the Arabah, south of Chinneroth;

Those in the lowland;

The kings in the mountain areas of Dor, on the west;

The kings of Canaan, both east and west;

The kings of the Amorites;

The kings of the Hittites;

The kings of the Perizzites;

The kings in the Jebusite hill country;

The Hivite kings in the cities on the slopes of Mount Hermon, in the land of Mizpah.

4All these kings responded by mobilizing their armies, and uniting to crush Israel. Their combined troops, along with a vast array of horses and chariots, covered the landscape around the Springs of Merom as far as one could see; 5for they established their camp at the Springs of Merom.

6But the Lord said to Joshua, "Don't be afraid of them, for by this time tomorrow they will all be dead! Hamstring their horses and burn their chariots." 7Joshua and his troops arrived suddenly at the Springs of Merom and attacked. 8And the Lord gave all that vast army to the Israelis, who chased them as far as Great Sidon and a place called the Salt Pits, and eastward into the valley of Mizpah; so not one enemy troop survived the battle. 9Then Joshua and his men did as the Lord had instructed, for they hamstrung the horses and burned all the chariots.

10On the way back, Joshua captured Hazor and killed its king. (Hazor had at one time been the capital of the federation of all those kingdoms.) 11Every person there was killed and the city was burned.

12Then he attacked and destroyed all the other cities of those kings. All the people were slaughtered, just as Moses had commanded long before. 13(However, Joshua did not burn any of the cities built on mounds except for Hazor.) 14All the loot and cattle of the ravaged cities were taken by the Israelis for themselves, but they killed all the people. 15For so the Lord had commanded his disciple Moses; and Moses had passed the commandment on to Joshua, who did as he had been told: he carefully obeyed all of the Lord's instructions to Moses.

16So Joshua conquered the entire land—the hill country, the Negeb, the land of Goshen, the lowlands, the Arabah, and the hills and lowlands of Israel. 17The Israeli territory now extended all the way from Mount Halak, near Seir, to Baal-gad in the valley of Lebanon, at the foot of Mount Hermon. And Joshua killed all the kings of those territories. 18It took seven years of war to accomplish all of this. 19None of the cities was given a peace treaty except the Hivites of Gibeon; all of the others were destroyed. 20For the Lord made the enemy kings want to fight the Israelis instead of asking for peace; so they were mercilessly killed, as the Lord had commanded Moses.

21During this period Joshua routed all of the giants—the descendants of Anak who lived in the hill country in Hebron, Debir, Anab, Judah, and Israel; he killed them all and completely destroyed their cities. 22None was left in all the land of Israel, though some still remained in Gaza, Gath, and Ashdod.

23So Joshua took the entire land just as the Lord had instructed Moses; and he gave it to the people of Israel as their inheritance, dividing the land among the tribes. So the land finally rested from its war.

HERE is the list of the kings on the east side of the Jordan River whose cities were destroyed by the Israelis: (The area involved stretched all the way from the valley of the Arnon River to Mount Hermon, including the cities of the eastern desert.)

2King Sihon of the Amorites, who lived in Heshbon. His kingdom extended from Aroer, on the edge of the Arnon Valley, and from the middle of the valley of the Arnon River to the Jabbok River, which is the boundary of the Ammonites. This includes half of the present area of Gilead, which lies north of the Jabbok River. 3Sihon also controlled the Jordan River valley as far north as the western shores of the Lake of Galilee; and as far south as the Dead Sea and the slopes of Mount Pisgah.

4King Og of Bashan, the last of the Rephaim, who lived at Ashtaroth and Edre-i: 5He ruled a territory stretching from Mount Hermon in the north to Salecah on Mount Bashan in the east, and on the west, extending to the boundary of the kingdoms of Geshur and Ma-acah. His kingdom also stretched south to include the northern half of Gilead where the boundary touched the border of the kingdom of Sihon, king of Heshbon. 6Moses and the people of Israel had destroyed these people, and Moses gave the land to the tribes of Reuben and the half-tribe of Manasseh.

7Here is a list of the kings destroyed by Joshua and the armies of Israel on the west side of the Jordan. (This land which lay between Baal-gad in the Valley of Lebanon and Mount Halak, west of Mount Seir, was allotted by Joshua to the other tribes of Israel. 8-24The area included the hill country, the lowlands, the Arabah, the mountain slopes, the Judean Desert, and the Negeb. The people who lived there were the Hittites, the Amorites, the Canaanites, the Perizzites, the Hivites, and the Jebusites):

The king of Jericho;
The king of Ai, near Bethel;
The king of Jerusalem;
The king of Hebron;
The king of Jarmuth;
The king of Lachish;
The king of Eglon;
The king of Gezer;
The king of Debir;
The king of Geder;
The king of Hormah;
The king of Arad;
The king of Libnah;
The king of Adullam;
The king of Makkedah;
The king of Bethel;
The king of Tappu-ah;
The king of Hepher;
The king of Aphek;
The king of Lasharon;
The king of Madon;
The king of Hazor;
The king of Shimron-meron;
The king of Achshaph;
The king of Taanach;
The king of Megiddo;
The king of Kedesh;
The king of Jokne-am, in Carmel;
The king of Dor in the city of Naphath-dor;
The king of Goiim in Gilgal;
The king of Tirzah.
So in all, thirty-one kings and their cities were destroyed.

LUKE 17:11–37

AS they continued onward toward Jerusalem, they reached the border between Galilee and Samaria, 12and as they entered a village there, ten lepers stood at a distance, 13crying out, "Jesus, sir, have mercy on us!"

14He looked at them and said, "Go to the Jewish priest and show him that you are healed!" And as they were going, their leprosy disappeared.

15One of them came back to Jesus, shouting, "Glory to God, I'm healed!"

16He fell flat on the ground in front of Jesus, face downward in the dust, thanking him for what he had done. This man was a despised Samaritan.

17Jesus asked, "Didn't I heal ten men? Where are the nine? 18Does only this foreigner return to give glory to God?"

19And Jesus said to the man, "Stand up and go; your faith has made you well."

20One day the Pharisees asked Jesus, "When will the Kingdom of God begin?" Jesus replied, "The Kingdom of God isn't ushered in with visible signs. 21You won't be able to say, 'It has begun here in this place or there in that part of the country.' For the Kingdom of God is within you."

22Later he talked again about this with his disciples. "The time is coming when you will long for me to be with you even for a single day, but I won't be here," he said. 23"Reports will reach you that I have returned and that I am in this place or that; don't believe it or go out to look for me. 24For when I return, you will know it beyond all doubt. It will be as evident as the lightning that flashes across the skies. 25But first I must suffer terribly and be rejected by this whole nation.

26"[When I return] the world will be [as indifferent to the things of God] as the people were in Noah's day. 27They ate and drank and married—everything just as usual right up to the day when Noah went into the ark and the flood came and destroyed them all.

28"And the world will be as it was in the days of Lot: people went about their daily business—eating and drinking, buying and selling, farming and building— 29until the morning Lot left Sodom. Then fire and brimstone rained down from heaven and destroyed them all. 30Yes, it will be 'business as usual' right up to the hour of my return.

31"Those away from home that day must not return to pack; those in the fields must not return to town— 32remember what happened to Lot's wife! 33Whoever clings to his life shall lose it, and whoever loses his life shall save it. 34That night two men will be asleep in the same room, and one will be taken away, the other left. 35,36Two women will be working together at household tasks; one will be taken, the other left; and so it will be with men working side by side in the fields."

37"Lord, where will they be taken?" the disciples asked.

Jesus replied, "Where the body is, the vultures gather!"

PSALM 84:1–12

How lovely is your Temple, O Lord of the armies of heaven. 2I long, yes, faint with longing to be able to enter your courtyard and come near to the Living God. 3Even the sparrows and swallows are welcome to come and nest among your altars and there have their young, O Lord of heaven's armies, my King and my God! 4How happy are those who can live in your Temple, singing your praises.

5Happy are those who are strong in the Lord, who want above all else to follow your steps. 6When they walk through the Valley of Weeping it will become a place of springs where pools of blessing and refreshment collect after rains! 7They will grow constantly in strength and each of them is invited to meet with the Lord in Zion.

8O Jehovah, God of the heavenly armies, hear my prayer! Listen, God of Israel. 9O God, our Defender and our Shield, have mercy on the one you have anointed as your king.

10A single day spent in your Temple is better than a thousand anywhere else! I would rather be a doorman of the Temple of my God than live in palaces of wickedness. 11For Jehovah God is our Light and our Protector. He gives us grace and glory. No good thing will he withhold from those who walk along his paths.

12O Lord of the armies of heaven, blessed are those who trust in you.

A good man hates lies; wicked men lie constantly and come to shame. A man's goodness helps him all through life, while evil men are being destroyed by their wickedness.

APRIL 16

JOSHUA 13:1—14:15

J OSHUA was now an old man. "You are growing old," the Lord said to him, "and there are still many nations to be conquered. 2-7Here is a list of the areas still to be occupied:

All the land of the Philistines;

The land of the Geshurites;

The territory now belonging to the Canaanites from the brook of Egypt to the southern boundary of Ekron;

Five cities of the Philistines: Gaza, Ashdod, Ashkelon, Gath, Ekron;

The land of the Avvim in the south;

In the north, all the land of the Canaanites, including Me-arah (which belongs to the Sidonians), stretching northward to Aphek at the boundary of the Amorites;

The land of the Gebalites on the coast and all of the Lebanon mountain area from Baal-gad beneath Mount Hermon in the south to the entrance of Hamath in the north;

All the hill country from Lebanon to Misrephoth-maim, including all the land of the Sidonians.

I am ready to drive these people out from before the nation of Israel, so include all this territory when you divide the land among the nine tribes and the half-tribe of Manasseh as I have commanded you."

8The other half of the tribe of Manasseh, and the tribes of Reuben and Gad, had already received their inheritance on the east side of the Jordan, for Moses had previously assigned this land to them. 9Their territory ran from Aroer, on the edge of the valley of the Arnon River, included the city in the valley, and crossed the tableland of Medeba to Dibon; 10it also included all the cities of King Sihon of the Amorites, who reigned in Heshbon, and extended as far as the borders of Ammon. 11It included Gilead; the territory of the Geshurites and the Ma-acathites; all of Mount Hermon; Mount Bashan with its city of Salecah; 12and all the territory of King Og of Bashan, who had reigned in Ashtaroth and Edre-i. (He was the last of the Rephaim, for Moses had attacked them and driven them out. 13However, the people of Israel had not driven out the Geshurites or the Ma-acathites, who still live there among the Israelites to this day.)

14The Territorial Assignments

The Land Given to the Tribe of Levi:
Moses hadn't assigned any land to the tribe of Levi: instead, they were given the offerings brought to the Lord.

15*The Land Given to the Tribe of Reuben:*

Fitting the size of its territory to its size of population, Moses had assigned the following area to the tribe of Reuben: 16Their land extended from Aroer on the edge of the valley of the Arnon River, past the city of Arnon in the middle of the valley, to beyond the tableland near Medeba. 17It included Heshbon and the other cities on the plain—Dibon, Bamoth-baal, Beth-baal-meon, 18Jahaz, Kedemoth, Mepha-ath, 19Kiriathaim, Sibmah, Zereth-shahar on the mountain above the valley, 20Beth-peor, Beth-jeshimoth, and the slopes of Mount Pisgah.

²¹The land of Reuben also included the cities of the tableland and the kingdom of Sihon. Sihon was the king who had lived in Heshbon and was killed by Moses along with the other chiefs of Midian—Evi, Rekem, Zur, Hur, and Reba. ²²The people of Israel also killed Balaam the magician, the son of Beor. ²³The Jordan River was the western boundary of the tribe of Reuben.

²⁴ *The Land Given to the Tribe of Gad:*
Moses also assigned land to the tribe of Gad in proportion to its population. ²⁵This territory included Jazer, all the cities of Gilead and half of the land of Ammon as far as Aroer near Rabbah. ²⁶It also extended from Heshbon to Ramath-mizpeh and Betonim, and from Mahanaim to Lodebar. ²⁷,²⁸In the valley were Beth-haram, and Beth-nimrah, Succoth, Zaphon, and the rest of the kingdom of King Sihon of Heshbon. The Jordan River was the western border, extending as far as the Lake of Galilee; then the border turned east from the Jordan River.

²⁹ *The Land Given to the Half-Tribe of Manasseh:*
Moses had assigned the following territory to the half-tribe of Manasseh in proportion to its needs: ³⁰Their territory extended north from Mahanaim, included all of Bashan, the former kingdom of King Og, and the sixty cities of Jair in Bashan. ³¹Half of Gilead and King Og's royal cities of Ashtaroth and Edre-i were given to half of the clan Machir, who was Manasseh's son.

³²That was how Moses divided the land east of the Jordan River where the people were camped at that time across from Jericho. ³³But Moses had given no land to the tribe of Levi for, as he had explained to them, the Lord God was their inheritance. He was all they needed. He would take care of them in other ways.

THE conquered lands of Canaan were allotted to the remaining nine and a half tribes of Israel. The decision as to which tribe would receive which area was decided by throwing dice before the Lord, and he caused them to turn up in the ways he wanted. Eleazar the priest, Joshua, and the tribal leaders supervised the lottery.

³,⁴(Moses had already given land to the two and a half tribes on the east side of the Jordan River. The tribe of Joseph had become two separate tribes, Manasseh and Ephraim, and the Levites were given no land at all, except cities in which to live and the surrounding pasturelands for their cattle. ⁵So the distribution of the land was in strict accordance with the Lord's directions to Moses.)

⁶ *The Land Given to Caleb:*
A delegation from the tribe of Judah, led by Caleb, came to Joshua in Gilgal. "Remember what the Lord said to Moses about you and me when we were at Kadesh-barnea?" Caleb asked Joshua. ⁷"I was forty years old at the time, and Moses had sent us from Kadesh-barnea to spy out the land of Canaan. I reported what I felt was the truth, ⁸but our brothers who went with us frightened the people and discouraged them from entering the Promised Land. But since I had followed the Lord my God, ⁹Moses told me, 'The section of Canaan you were just in shall belong to you and your descendants forever.'

¹⁰"Now, as you see, from that time until now the Lord has kept me alive and well for all these forty-five years since crisscrossing the wilderness, and today I am eighty-five years old. ¹¹I am as strong now as I was when Moses sent us on that journey, and I can still travel and fight as well as I could then! ¹²So I'm asking that you give me the hill country which the Lord promised me. You will remember that as spies we found the Anakim living there in great, walled cities, but if the Lord is with me I shall drive them out of the land."

¹³,¹⁴So Joshua blessed him and gave him Hebron as a permanent inheritance because he had followed the Lord God of Israel. ¹⁵(Before that time Hebron had been called Kiriath-arba, after a great hero of the Anakim.)

And there was no resistance from the

local populations as the Israelis resettled the land.

LUKE 18:1–17

ONE day Jesus told his disciples a story to illustrate their need for constant prayer and to show them that they must keep praying until the answer comes.

2"There was a city judge," he said, "a very godless man who had great contempt for everyone. 3A widow of that city came to him frequently to appeal for justice against a man who had harmed her. 4,5The judge ignored her for a while, but eventually she got on his nerves.

" 'I fear neither God nor man,' he said to himself, 'but this woman bothers me. I'm going to see that she gets justice, for she is wearing me out with her constant coming!' "

6Then the Lord said, "If even an evil judge can be worn down like that, 7don't you think that God will surely give justice to his people who plead with him day and night? 8Yes! He will answer them quickly! But the question is: When I, the Messiah, return, how many will I find who have faith [and are praying]?"

9Then he told this story to some who boasted of their virtue and scorned everyone else:

10"Two men went to the Temple to pray. One was a proud, self-righteous Pharisee, and the other a cheating tax collector. 11The proud Pharisee 'prayed' this prayer: 'Thank God, I am not a sinner like everyone else, especially like that tax collector over there! For I never cheat, I don't commit adultery, 12I go without food twice a week, and I give to God a tenth of everything I earn.'

13"But the corrupt tax collector stood at a distance and dared not even lift his eyes to heaven as he prayed, but beat upon his chest in sorrow, exclaiming, 'God, be merciful to me, a sinner.'

14I tell you, this sinner, not the Pharisee, returned home forgiven! For the proud shall be humbled, but the humble shall be honored."

15One day some mothers brought their babies to him to touch and bless. But the disciples told them to go away.

16,17Then Jesus called the children over to him and said to the disciples, "Let the little children come to me! Never send them away! For the Kingdom of God belongs to men who have hearts as trusting as these little children's. And anyone who doesn't have their kind of faith will never get within the Kingdom's gates."

PSALM 85:1–13

LORD, you have poured out amazing blessings on this land! You have restored the fortunes of Israel, 2and forgiven the sins of your people—yes, covered over each one, 3so that all your wrath, your blazing anger, is now ended.

4Now bring us back to loving you, O Lord, so that your anger will never need rise against us again. 5(Or will you be always angry—on and on to distant generations?) 6Oh, revive us! Then your people can rejoice in you again. 7Pour out your love and kindness on us, Lord, and grant us your salvation.

8I am listening carefully to all the Lord is saying—for he speaks peace to his people, his saints, if they will only stop their sinning. 9Surely his salvation is near to those who reverence him; our land will be filled with his glory.

10Mercy and truth have met together. Grim justice and peace have kissed! 11Truth rises from the earth and righteousness smiles down from heaven.

12Yes, the Lord pours down his blessings on the land and it yields its bountiful crops. 13Justice goes before him to make a pathway for his steps.

PROVERBS FOR TODAY/ 13:7–8

Some rich people are poor, and some poor people have great wealth! Being kidnapped and held for ransom never worries the poor man!

JOSHUA 15:1–63

THE land given *to the Tribe of Judah* (as assigned by sacred lot): Judah's southern boundary began at the northern border of Edom, crossed the Wilderness of Zin, and ended at the northern edge of the Negeb. 2,3,4More specifically, this boundary began at the south bay of the Dead Sea, ran along the road going south of Mount Akrabbim, on into the Wilderness of Zin to Hezron (south of Kadesh-barnea), and then up through Karka and Azmon, until it finally reached the Brook of Egypt, and along that to the Mediterranean Sea.

5The eastern boundary extended along the Dead Sea to the mouth of the Jordan River.

The northern boundary began at the bay where the Jordan River empties into the Salt Sea, 6crossed to Beth-hoglah, then proceeded north of Beth-arabah to the stone of Bohan (son of Reuben). 7From that point it went through the Valley of Achor to Debir, where it turned northwest toward Gilgal, opposite the slopes of Adummim on the south side of the valley. From there the border extended to the springs at Enshemesh and on to En-rogel. 8The boundary then passed through the Valley of Hinnom, along the southern shoulder of Jebus (where the city of Jerusalem is located), then west to the top of the mountain above the Valley of Hinnom and on up to the northern end of the Valley of Rephaim. 9From there the border extended from the top of the mountain to the spring of Nephtoah, and from there to the cities of Mount Ephron before it turned northward to circle around Baalah (which is another name for Kiriath-jearim). 10,11Then the border circled west of Baalah to Mount Seir, passed along to the town of Chesalon on the northern shoulder of Mount Jearim, and went down to Beth-shemesh. Turning north-

west again, the boundary line proceeded past the south of Timnah to the shoulder of the hill north of Ekron, where it bent to the left, passing south of Shikkeron and Mount Baalah. Turning again to the north, it passed Jabneel and ended at the Mediterranean Sea.

12The western border was the shoreline of the Mediterranean.

13*The Land Given to Caleb:*

The Lord instructed Joshua to assign some of Judah's territory to Caleb (son of Jephunneh), so he was given the city of Arba (also called Hebron), which had been named after Anak's father. 14Caleb drove out the descendants of the three sons of Anak: Talmai, Sheshai, and Ahiman. 15Then he fought against the people living in the city of Debir (formerly called Kiriath-sepher).

16Caleb said that he would give his daughter Achsah to be the wife of anyone who would go and capture Kiriath-sepher. 17Othni-el (son of Kenaz), Caleb's nephew, was the one who conquered it, so Achsah became Othni-el's wife. 18,19As she was leaving with him, she urged him to ask her father for an additional field as a wedding present. She got off her donkey to speak to Caleb about this.

"What is it? What can I do for you?" he asked.

And she replied, "Give me another present! For the land you gave me is a desert. Give us some springs, too!" Then he gave her the upper and lower springs.

20So this was the assignment of land to the tribe of Judah:

21-32The cities of Judah which were situated along the borders of Edom in the Negeb, namely:

Kabzeel, Eder, Jagur, Kinah,
Dimonah, Adadah, Kedesh, Hazor,
Ithnan, Ziph, Telem, Be-aloth,
Hazor-hadattah, Keri-oth-hezron
(or, Hazor), Amam, Shema,

Moladah, Hazar-gaddah, Heshmon,
Beth-pelet, Hazar-shual,
Beer-sheba, Biziothiah, Baalah, Iim,
Ezem, Eltolad, Chesil, Hormah,
Ziklag, Madmannah, Sansannah,
Lebaoth, Shilhim, Ain, and
Rimmon.

In all, there were twenty-nine of these cities with their surrounding villages.

33-36The following cities situated in the lowlands were also given to Judah:
Eshtaol, Zorah, Ashnah, Zanoah,
En-gannim, Tappu-ah, Enam,
Jarmuth, Adullam, Socoh, Azekah,
Sha-araim, Adithaim, Gederah, and
Gederothaim.

In all, there were fourteen of these cities with their surrounding villages.

37-44The tribe of Judah also inherited twenty-five other cities with their villages:
Zenan, Hadashah, Migdal-gad,
Dilean, Mizpeh, Jokthe-el, Lachish,
Bozkath, Eglon, Cabbon, Lahmam,
Chitlish, Gederoth, Beth-dagon,
Naamah, Makkedah, Libnah,
Ether, Ashan, Iphtah, Ashnah,
Nezib, Keilah, Achzib, and
Mareshah.

45The territory of the tribe of Judah also included all the towns and villages of Ekron. 46From Ekron the boundary extended to the Mediterranean, and included the cities along the borders of Ashdod with their nearby villages; 47also the city of Ashdod with its villages, and Gaza with its villages as far as the Brook of Egypt; also the entire Mediterranean coast from the mouth of the Brook of Egypt on the south, to Tyre on the north.

48-62Judah also received these forty-four cities in the hill country with their surrounding villages:
Shamir, Jattir, Socoh, Dannah,
Kiriath-sannah (or Debir), Anab,
Eshtemoh, Anim, Goshen, Holon,
Giloh, Arab, Dumah, Eshan,
Janim, Beth-tappu-ah, Aphekah,
Humtah, Kiriath-arba (or, Hebron),
Zior, Maon, Carmel, Ziph, Juttah,
Jezreel, Jokde-am, Zanoah, Kain,
Gibe-ah, Timnah, Halhul, Beth-zur,
Gedor, Maarath, Beth-anoth,
Eltekon, Kiriath-baal (also known
as Kiriath-jearim), Rabbah,
Beth-arabah, Middin, Secacah,
Nibshan, The City of Salt, and En-gedi.

63But the tribe of Judah could not drive out the Jebusites who lived in the city of Jerusalem, so the Jebusites live there among the people of Judah to this day.

LUKE 18:18-43

ONCE a Jewish religious leader asked him this question: "Good sir, what shall I do to get to heaven?"

19"Do you realize what you are saying when you call me 'good'?" Jesus asked him. "Only God is truly good, and no one else.

20"But as to your question, you know what the ten commandments say—don't commit adultery, don't murder, don't steal, don't lie, honor your parents, and so on." 21The man replied, "I've obeyed every one of these laws since I was a small child."

22"There is still one thing you lack," Jesus said. "Sell all you have and give the money to the poor—it will become treasure for you in heaven—and come, follow me."

23But when the man heard this he went sadly away, for he was very rich.

24Jesus watched him go and then said to his disciples, "How hard it is for the rich to enter the Kingdom of God! 25It is easier for a camel to go through the eye of a needle than for a rich man to enter the Kingdom of God."

26Those who heard him say this exclaimed, "If it is that hard, how can *anyone* be saved?"

27He replied, "God can do what men can't!"

28And Peter said, "We have left our homes and followed you."

29"Yes," Jesus replied, "and everyone who has done as you have, leaving home, wife, brothers, parents, or children for the sake of the Kingdom of God, 30will be repaid many times over now, as well as receiving eternal life in the world to come."

31Gathering the Twelve around him he told them, "As you know, we are going to Jerusalem. And when we get there, all the predictions of the ancient prophets concerning me will come true. 32I will be handed over to the Gentiles to be mocked and treated shamefully and spat upon, 33and lashed and killed. And the third day I will rise again."

34But they didn't understand a thing he said. He seemed to be talking in riddles.

35As they approached Jericho, a blind man was sitting beside the road, begging from travelers. 36When he heard the noise of a crowd going past, he asked what was happening. 37He was told that Jesus from Nazareth was going by, 38so he began shouting, "Jesus, Son of David, have mercy on me!"

39The crowds ahead of Jesus tried to hush the man, but he only yelled the louder, "Son of David, have mercy on me!"

40When Jesus arrived at the spot, he stopped. "Bring the blind man over here," he said. 41Then Jesus asked the man, "What do you want?"

"Lord," he pleaded, "I want to see!"

42And Jesus said, "All right, begin seeing! Your faith has healed you."

43And instantly the man could see, and followed Jesus, praising God. And all who saw it happen praised God too.

PSALM 86:1–17

BEND down and hear my prayer, O Lord, and answer me, for I am deep in trouble.

2Protect me from death, for I try to follow all your laws. Save me, for I am serving you and trusting you. 3Be merciful, O Lord, for I am looking up to you in constant hope. 4Give me happiness, O Lord, for I worship only you. 5O Lord, you are so good and kind, so ready to forgive; so full of mercy for all who ask your aid.

6Listen closely to my prayer, O God. Hear my urgent cry. 7I will call to you whenever trouble strikes, and you will help me.

8Where among the heathen gods is there a god like you? Where are their miracles? 9All the nations—and you made each one—will come and bow before you, Lord, and praise your great and holy name. 10For you are great, and do great miracles. You alone are God.

11Tell me where you want me to go and I will go there. May every fiber of my being unite in reverence to your name. 12With all my heart I will praise you. I will give glory to your name forever, 13for you love me so much! You are constantly so kind! You have rescued me from deepest hell.

14O God, proud and insolent men defy me; violent, godless men are trying to kill me. 15But you are merciful and gentle, Lord, slow in getting angry, full of constant lovingkindness and of truth; 16so look down in pity and grant strength to your servant and save me. 17Send me a sign of your favor. When those who hate me see it they will lose face because you help and comfort me.

PROVERBS FOR TODAY/ 13:9–10

The good man's life is full of light. The sinner's road is dark and gloomy. Pride leads to arguments; be humble, take advice and become wise.

APRIL 18

JOSHUA 16:1—18:28

THE southern boundary *of the Tribes of Joseph* (Ephraim and the half-tribe of Manasseh):

This boundary extended from the Jordan River at Jericho through the wilderness and the hill country to Bethel. It then went from Bethel to Luz, then on to Ataroth, in the territory of the Archites; and west to the border of the Japhletites as far as Lower Beth-horon, then to Gezer and on over to the Mediterranean.

5,6 *The Land Given to the Tribe of Ephraim:* The eastern boundary began at Ataroth-addar. From there it ran to Upper Beth-horon, then on to the Mediterranean Sea. The northern boundary began at the Sea, ran east past Michmethath, then continued on past Taanath-shiloh and Janoah. 7From Janoah it turned southward to Ataroth and Naarah, and touched Jericho, and ended at the Jordan River. 8[The western half of the northern boundary] went from Tappu-ah, and followed along Kanah Brook to the Mediterranean Sea. 9Ephraim was also given some of the cities in the territory of the half-tribe of Manasseh. 10The Canaanites living in Gezer were never driven out, so they still live as slaves among the people of Ephraim.

THE land given *to the Half-tribe of Manasseh* (Joseph's oldest son):

The clan of Machir (Manasseh's oldest son who was the father of Gilead) had already been given the land of Gilead and Bashan [on the east side of the Jordan River], for they were great warriors. 2So now, land on the west side of the Jordan was given to the clans of Abiezer, Helek, Asri-el, Shechem, Shemida, and Hepher.

3However, Hepher's son Zelophehad (grandson of Gilead, great-grandson of Machir, and great-great-grandson of Manasseh) had no sons. He had only five daughters whose names were Mahlah, Noah, Hoglah, Milcah, and Tirzah. 4These women came to Eleazar the priest and to Joshua and the Israeli leaders and reminded them,

"The Lord told Moses that we were to receive as much property as the men of our tribe."

5,6So, as the Lord had commanded through Moses, these five women were given an inheritance along with their five great-uncles, and the total inheritance came to ten sections of land (in addition to the land of Gilead and Bashan across the Jordan River).

7The northern boundary of the tribe of Manasseh extended southward from the border of Asher to Michmethath, which is east of Shechem. On the south the boundary went from Michmethath to the Spring of Tappu-ah. 8(The land of Tappu-ah belonged to Manasseh, but the city of Tappu-ah, on the border of Manasseh's land, belonged to the tribe of Ephraim.) 9From the spring of Tappu-ah the border of Manasseh followed the north bank of the Brook of Kanah to the Mediterranean Sea. (Several cities south of the brook belonged to the tribe of Ephraim, though they were located in Manasseh's territory.) 10The land south of the brook and as far west as the Mediterranean Sea was assigned to Ephraim, and the land north of the brook and east of the sea went to Manasseh. Manasseh's northern boundary was the territory of Asher and the eastern boundary was the territory of Issachar.

11The half-tribe of Manasseh was also given the following cities which were situated in the areas assigned to Issachar and Asher: Beth-shean, Ible-am, Dor, En-dor, Taanach, Megiddo (where there are the three cliffs), with their respective villages. 12But since the descendants of Manasseh could not drive out the people who lived in those cities, the Canaanites remained. 13Later on, however, when the

Israelis became strong enough, they forced the Canaanites to work as slaves.

14Then the two tribes of Joseph came to Joshua and asked, "Why have you given us only one portion of land when the Lord has given us such large populations?"

15"If the hill country of Ephraim is not large enough for you," Joshua replied, "and if you are able to do it, you may clear out the forest land where the Perizzites and Rephaim live."

16,17,18"Fine," said the tribes of Joseph, "for the Canaanites in the lowlands around Beth-shean and the Valley of Jezreel have iron chariots and are too strong for us."

"Then you shall have the mountain forests," Joshua replied, "and since you are such a large, strong tribe you will surely be able to clear it all and live there. And I'm sure you can drive out the Canaanites from the valleys, too, even though they are strong and have iron chariots."

AFTER the conquest—although seven of the tribes of Israel had not yet entered and conquered the land God had given them—all Israel gathered at Shiloh to set up the Tabernacle.

3Then Joshua asked them, "How long are you going to wait before clearing out the people living in the land which the Lord your God has given to you? 4Select three men from each tribe and I will send them to scout the unconquered territory and bring back a report of its size and natural divisions so that I can divide it for you. 5,6The scouts will map it into seven sections, and then I will throw the sacred dice to decide which section will be assigned to each tribe. 7However, remember that the Levites won't receive any land; they are priests of the Lord. That is their wonderful heritage. And of course the tribes of Gad and Reuben and the half-tribe of Manasseh won't receive any more, for they already have land on the east side of the Jordan where Moses promised them that they could settle."

8So the scouts went out to map the country and to bring back their report to Joshua. Then the Lord could assign the sections of land to the tribes by the throw of the sacred dice. 9The men did as they were told and divided the entire territory into seven sections, listing the cities in each section. Then they returned to Joshua and the camp at Shiloh. 10There at the Tabernacle at Shiloh the Lord showed Joshua by the sacred lottery which tribe should have each section:

11 *The Land Given to the Tribe of Benjamin:*

The section of land assigned to the families of the tribe of Benjamin lay between the territory previously assigned to the tribes of Judah and Joseph.

12The northern boundary began at the Jordan River, went north of Jericho, then west through the hill country and the Wilderness of Beth-aven. 13From there the boundary went south to Luz (also called Bethel) and proceeded down to Ataroth-addar in the hill country south of Lower Beth-horon. 14There the border turned south, passing the mountain near Beth-horon and ending at the village of Kiriath-baal (sometimes called Kiriath-jearim), one of the cities of the tribe of Judah. This was the western boundary.

15The southern border ran from the edge of Kiriath-baal, over Mount Ephron to the spring of Naphtoah, 16and down to the base of the mountain beside the valley of Hinnom, north of the valley of Rephaim. From there it continued across the valley of Hinnom, crossed south of the old city of Jerusalem where the Jebusites lived, and continued down to En-rogel. 17From En-rogel the boundary proceeded northeast to En-shemesh and on to Geliloth (which is opposite the slope of Adummim). Then it went down to the Stone of Bohan (who was a son of Reuben), 18where it passed along the north edge of the Arabah. The border then went down into the Arabah, 19ran south past Beth-hoglah, and ended at the north bay of the Dead Sea—which is the southern end of the Jordan River.

20The eastern border was the Jordan River. This was the land assigned to the tribe of Benjamin. 21–28These twenty-six cities were included in the land given to the tribe of Benjamin:

Jericho, Beth-hoglah, Emek-keziz, Beth-arabah, Zimaraim, Bethel, Avvim, Parah, Ophrah, Chephar-ammoni, Ophni, Geba, Gibeon, Ramah, Be-er-oth, Mizpeh, Chephirah, Mozah, Rekem, Irpeel, Taralah, Zela, Ha-eleph, Jebus (or Jerusalem), Gibe-ah, and Kiriath-jearim.

All of these cities and their surrounding villages were given to the tribe of Benjamin.

LUKE 19:1–27

AS Jesus was passing through Jericho, a man named Zacchaeus, one of the most influential Jews in the Roman tax-collecting business (and, of course, a very rich man), 3tried to get a look at Jesus, but he was too short to see over the crowds. 4So he ran ahead and climbed into a sycamore tree beside the road, to watch from there.

5When Jesus came by he looked up at Zacchaeus and called him by name! "Zacchaeus!" he said. "Quick! Come down! For I am going to be a guest in your home today!"

6Zacchaeus hurriedly climbed down and took Jesus to his house in great excitement and joy.

7But the crowds were displeased. "He has gone to be the guest of a notorious sinner," they grumbled.

8Meanwhile, Zacchaeus stood before the Lord and said, "Sir, from now on I will give half my wealth to the poor, and if I find I have overcharged anyone on his taxes, I will penalize myself by giving him back four times as much!"

9,10Jesus told him, "This shows that salvation has come to this home today. This man was one of the lost sons of Abraham, and I, the Messiah, have come to search for and to save such souls as his."

11And because Jesus was nearing Jerusalem, he told a story to correct the impression that the Kingdom of God would begin right away.

12"A nobleman living in a certain province was called away to the distant capital of the empire to be crowned king of his province. 13Before he left he called together ten assistants and gave them each $2,000 to invest while he was gone. 14But some of his people hated him and sent him their declaration of independence, stating that they had rebelled and would not acknowledge him as their king.

15"Upon his return he called in the men to whom he had given the money, to find out what they had done with it, and what their profits were.

16"The first man reported a tremendous gain—ten times as much as the original amount!

17" 'Fine!' the king exclaimed. 'You are a good man. You have been faithful with the little I entrusted to you, and as your reward, you shall be governor of ten cities.'

18"The next man also reported a splendid gain—five times the original amount.

19" 'All right!' his master said. 'You can be governor over five cities.'

20"But the third man brought back only the money he had started with. 'I've kept it safe,' he said, 21'because I was afraid [you would demand my profits], for you are a hard man to deal with, taking what isn't yours and even confiscating the crops that others plant.' 22'You vile and wicked slave,' the king roared. 'Hard, am I? That's exactly how I'll be toward you! If you knew so much about me and how tough I am, 23then why didn't you deposit the money in the bank so that I could at least get some interest on it?'

24"Then turning to the others standing by he ordered, 'Take the money away from him and give it to the man who earned the most.'

25" 'But, sir,' they said, 'he has enough already!'

26" 'Yes,' the king replied, 'but it is always true that those who have, get more, and those who have little, soon lose even that. 27And now about these enemies of mine who revolted—bring them in and execute them before me.' "

PSALM 87:1–7

HIGH on his holy mountain stands Jerusalem, the city of God, the city he loves more than any other!

3O city of God, what wondrous tales are told of you! 4Nowadays when I mention among my friends the names of Egypt and Babylonia, Philistia and Tyre, or even distant Ethiopia, someone boasts that he was born in one or another of those countries. 5But someday the highest honor will be to be a native of Jerusalem! For the God above all gods will personally bless this city. 6When he registers her citizens he will place a checkmark beside the names of those who were born here. 7And in the festivals they'll sing, "All my heart is in Jerusalem."

PROVERBS FOR TODAY/ 13:11

Wealth from gambling quickly disappears; wealth from hard work grows.

APRIL 19

JOSHUA 19:1—20:9

THE land given *to the Tribe of Simeon:*

The tribe of Simeon received the next assignment of land—including part of the land previously assigned to Judah. 2–7Their inheritance included these seventeen cities with their respective villages:

Beer-sheba, Sheba, Moladah, Hazar-shual, Balah, Ezem, Eltolad, Bethul, Hormah, Ziklag, Beth-marcaboth, Hazar-susah, Beth-lebaoth, Sharuhen, En-rimmon, Ether, and Ashan.

8The cities as far south as Baalath-beer (also known as Ramah-in-the-Negeb) were also given to the tribe of Simeon. 9So the Simeon tribe's inheritance came from what had earlier been given to Judah, for Judah's section had been too large for them.

10 *The Land Given to the Tribe of Zebulun:*

The third tribe to receive its assignment of land was Zebulun. Its boundary started on the south side of Sarid. 11From there it circled to the west, going near Mareal and Dabbesheth until it reached the brook east of Jeokne-am. 12In the other direction, the boundary line went east to the border of Chisloth-tabor, and from there to Daberath and Japhia; 13then it continued east of Gath-hepher, Ethkazin, and Rimmon and turned toward Neah. 14The northern boundary of Zebulun passed Hannathon and ended at the Valley of Iphtahel. 15,16The cities in these areas, besides those already mentioned, included Kattath, Nahalal, Shimron, Idalah, Bethlehem, and each of their surrounding villages. Altogether there were twelve of these cities.

17–23 *The Land Given to the Tribe of Issachar:*

The fourth tribe to be assigned its land was Issachar. Its boundaries included the following cities:

Jezreel, Chesulloth, Shunem, Hapharaim, Shion, Anaharath, Rabbith, Kishion, Ebez, Remeth, En-gannim, En-haddah, Beth-pazzez, Tabor, Shahazumah, and Beth-shemesh—

sixteen cities in all, each with its surrounding villages. The boundary of Issachar ended at the Jordan River.

The Land Given to the Tribe of Asher:

The fifth tribe to be assigned its land was Asher. The boundaries included these cities:

Helkath, Hali, Beten, Achshaph, Allammelech, Amad, and Mishal.

The boundary on the west side went from Carmel to Shihor-libnath, 27turned east toward Beth-dagon, and ran as far as Zebulun in the Valley of Iphtahel, running north of Beth-emek and Neiel. It then passed to the east of Kabul, 28Ebron, Rehob, Hammon, Kanah, and Greater Sidon. 29Then the boundary turned toward Ramah and the fortified city of Tyre and came to the Mediterranean Sea at Hosah. The territory also included Mahalab, Achzib, 30,31Ummah, Aphek, and Rehob—an overall total of twenty-two cities and their surrounding villages.

32 *The Land Given to the Tribe of Naphtali:*

The sixth tribe to receive its assignment was the tribe of Naphtali. 33Its boundary began at Judah, at the oak in Zaanannim, and extended across to Adami-nekeb, Jabneel, and Lakkum, ending at the Jordan River. 34The western boundary began near Heleph and ran past Aznoth-tabor, then to Hukkok, and coincided with the Zebulun boundary in the south, and with the boundary of Asher on the west, and with the Jordan River at the east. 35-39The fortified cities included in this territory were:

Ziddim, Zer, Hammath, Rakkath, Chinnereth, Adamah, Ramah, Hazor, Kedesh, Edre-i, Enhazor, Yiron, Migdalel, Horem, Beth-anath, and Beth-shemesh.

So altogether the territory included nineteen cities with their surrounding villages.

40 *The Land Given to the Tribe of Dan:*

The last tribe to be assigned its land was Dan. 41-46The cities within its area included:

Zorah, Eshta-ol, Ir-shemesh, Sha-alabbin, Aijalon, Ithlah, Elon, Timnah, Ekron, Eltekeh, Gibbethon, Baalath, Jehud, Bene-berak, Gath-rimmon, Mejarkon, and Rakkon, also the territory near Joppa.

47,48But some of this territory proved impossible to conquer, so the tribe of Dan captured the city of Leshem, slaughtered its people, and lived there; and they called the city "Dan," naming it after their ancestor.

49So all the land was divided among the tribes, with the boundaries indicated; and the nation of Israel gave a special piece of land to Joshua, 50for the Lord had said that he could have any city he wanted. He chose Timnath-serah in the hill country of Ephraim; he rebuilt it and lived there.

51Eleazar the priest, Joshua, and the leaders of the tribes of Israel supervised the sacred lottery to divide the land among the tribes. This was done in the Lord's presence at the entrance of the Tabernacle at Shiloh.

THE Lord said to Joshua,

2"Tell the people of Israel to designate now the Cities of Refuge, as I instructed Moses. 3If a man is guilty of killing someone unintentionally, he can run to one of these cities and be protected from the relatives of the dead man, who may try to kill him in revenge. 4When the innocent killer reaches any of these cities, he will meet with the city council and explain what happened, and they must let him come in and must give him a place to live among them. 5If a relative of the dead man comes to kill him in revenge, the innocent slayer must not be released to him for the death was accidental. 6The man who caused the accidental death must stay in that city until he has been tried by the judges and found innocent, and must live there until the death of the High Priest who was in office at the time of the accident. But then he is free to return to his own city and home."

7The cities chosen as Cities of Refuge were Kedesh of Galilee in the hill country of Naphtali; Shechem, in the hill country of Ephraim; and Kiriath-arba (also known as Hebron) in the hill country of Judah. 8The Lord also instructed that three cities be set aside for this purpose on the east side of the Jordan River, across from Jericho. They were Bezer, in the wilderness of the land of the tribe of Reuben; Ramoth of Gilead, in the territory of the tribe of Gad; and Golan of Bashan, in the land of the tribe of Manasseh. 9These Cities of Refuge were for foreigners living in Israel as well as for the Israelis themselves, so that anyone who accidentally killed another man could run to that place for a trial, and not be killed in revenge.

LUKE 19:28–48

AFTER telling this story, Jesus went on toward Jerusalem, walking along ahead of his disciples. 29As they came to the towns of Bethphage and Bethany, on the Mount of Olives, he sent two disciples ahead, 30with instructions to go to the next village, and as they entered they were to look for a donkey tied beside the road. It would be a colt, not yet broken for riding.

"Untie him," Jesus said, "and bring him here. 31And if anyone asks you what you are doing, just say, 'The Lord needs him.' "

32They found the colt as Jesus said, 33and sure enough, as they were untying it, the owners demanded an explanation.

"What are you doing?" they asked. "Why are you untying our colt?"

34And the disciples simply replied, "The Lord needs him!" 35So they brought the colt to Jesus and threw some of their clothing across its back for Jesus to sit on.

36,37Then the crowds spread out their robes along the road ahead of him, and as they reached the place where the road started down from the Mount of Olives, the whole procession began to shout and sing as they walked along, praising God for all the wonderful miracles Jesus had done.

38"God has given us a King!" they exulted. "Long live the King! Let all heaven rejoice! Glory to God in the highest heavens!"

39But some of the Pharisees among the crowd said, "Sir, rebuke your followers for saying things like that!"

40He replied, "If they keep quiet, the stones along the road will burst into cheers!"

41But as they came closer to Jerusalem and he saw the city ahead, he began to cry. 42"Eternal peace was within your reach and you turned it down," he wept, "and now it is too late. 43Your enemies will pile up earth against your walls and encircle you and close in on you, 44and crush you to the ground, and your children within you; your enemies will not leave one stone upon another—for you have rejected the opportunity God offered you."

45Then he entered the Temple and began to drive out the merchants from their stalls, 46saying to them, "The Scriptures declare, 'My Temple is a place of prayer; but you have turned it into a den of thieves.' "

47After that he taught daily in the Temple, but the chief priests and other religious leaders and the business community were trying to find some way to get rid of him. 48But they could think of nothing, for he was a hero to the people—they hung on every word he said.

PSALM 88:1–18

O Jehovah, God of my salvation, I have wept before you day and night. 2Now hear my prayers; oh, listen to my cry, 3for my life is full of troubles, and death draws near. 4They say my life is ebbing out—a hopeless case. 5They have left me here to die, like those slain on battlefields, from whom your mercies are removed.

6You have thrust me down to the darkest depths. 7Your wrath lies heavy on me; wave after wave engulfs me. 8You have made my friends to loathe me, and they have gone away. I am in a trap with no way out. 9My eyes grow dim with weeping. Each day I beg your help; O Lord, I reach my pleading hands to you for mercy.

10Soon it will be too late! Of what use are your miracles when I am in the grave? How can I praise you then? 11Can those in the grave declare your lovingkindness? Can they proclaim your faithfulness? 12Can the darkness speak of your miracles? Can anyone in the Land of Forgetfulness talk about your help?

13O Lord, I plead for my life and will keep on pleading day by day. 14O Jehovah, why have you thrown my life away? Why are you turning your face from me, and looking the other way?

15From my youth I have been sickly and ready to die. I stand helpless before your terrors. 16Your fierce wrath has overwhelmed me. Your terrors have cut me off. 17They flow around me all day long. 18Lover, friend, acquaintance—all are gone. There is only darkness everywhere.

PROVERBS FOR TODAY/ 13:12–14

Hope deferred makes the heart sick; but when dreams come true at last, there is life and joy. Despise God's Word and find yourself in trouble. Obey it and succeed. The advice of a wise man refreshes like water from a mountain spring. Those accepting it become aware of the pitfalls on ahead.

APRIL 20

JOSHUA 21:1—22:20

THEN the leaders of the tribe of Levi came to Shiloh to consult with Eleazar the priest and with Joshua and the leaders of the various tribes.

2"The Lord instructed Moses to give cities to us Levites for our homes, and pastureland for our cattle," they said.

3So they were given some of the recently conquered cities with their pasturelands. 4Thirteen of these cities had been assigned originally to the tribes of Judah, Simeon, and Benjamin. These were given to some of the priests of the Kohath division (of the tribe of Levi, descendants of Aaron). 5The other families of the Kohath division were given ten cities from the territories of Ephraim, Dan, and the half-tribe of Manasseh. 6The Gershon division received thirteen cities, selected by sacred lot in the area of Bashan. These cities were given by the tribes of Issachar, Asher, Naphtali, and the half-tribe of Manasseh. 7The Merari division received twelve cities from the tribes of Reuben, Gad, and Zebulun. 8So the Lord's command to Moses was obeyed, and the cities and pasturelands were assigned by the toss of the sacred dice.

9–16First to receive their assignment were the priests—the descendants of Aaron, who was a member of the Kohath division of the Levites. The tribes of Judah and Simeon gave them the nine cities listed below, with their surrounding pasturelands:

Hebron, in the Judean hills, as a City of Refuge—it was also called Kiriatharba (Arba was the father of Anak)—although the fields beyond the city and the surrounding villages were given to Caleb, the son of Jephunneh;

Libnah, Jattir, Eshtemoa, Holon, Debir, Ain, Juttah, and Beth-shemesh. 17,18The tribe of Benjamin gave them these four cities and their pasturelands:

Gibeon, Gaba, Anathoth, and Almon. 19So in all, thirteen cities were given to the priests—the descendants of Aaron.

20,21,22The other families of the Kohath division received four cities and pasturelands from the tribe of Ephraim:

Shechem (a City of Refuge), Gezer, Kibza-im, and Beth-horon.

23,24The following four cities and pasturelands were given by the tribe of Dan:

Elteke, Gibbethon, Aijalon, and Gath-rimmon.

25The half-tribe of Manasseh gave the cities of Taanach and Gath-rimmon with their surrounding pasturelands. 26So the total number of cities and pasturelands given to the remainder of the Kohath division was ten.

27The descendants of Gershon, another division of the Levites, received two cities and pasturelands from the half-tribe of Manasseh:

Golan, in Bashan (a City of Refuge), and Be-eshterah.

28,29The tribe of Issachar gave four cities:

Kishion, Daberath, Jarmuth, and En-gannim.

30,31The tribe of Asher gave four cities and pasturelands:

Mishal, Abdon, Helkath, and Rehob.

32The tribe of Naphtali gave:

Kedesh, in Galilee (a City of Refuge), Hammoth-dor, and Kartan.

33So thirteen cities with their pasturelands were assigned to the division of Gershon.

34,35The remainder of the Levites—the Merari division—were given four cities by the tribe of Zebulun:

Jokne-am, Kartah, Dimnah, and Nahalal.

36,37Reuben gave them:

Bezer, Jahaz, Kedemoth, and Mephaath.

38,39Gad gave them four cities with pasturelands:

Ramoth (a City of Refuge), Mahanaim, Heshbon, and Jazer.

40So the Merari division of the Levites was given twelve cities in all.

41,42The total number of cities and pasturelands given to the Levites came to forty-eight.

43So in this way the Lord gave to Israel all the land he had promised to their ancestors, and they went in and conquered it and lived there. 44And the Lord gave them peace, just as he had promised, and no one could stand against them; the Lord helped them destroy all their enemies. 45Every good thing the Lord had promised them came true.

JOSHUA now called together the troops from the tribes of Reuben, Gad, and the half-tribe of Manasseh, 2,3and addressed them as follows:

"You have done as the Lord's disciple Moses commanded you, and have obeyed every order I have given you—every order of the Lord your God. You have not deserted your brother tribes, even though the campaign has lasted for such a long time. 4And now the Lord our God has given us success and rest as he promised he would. So go home now to the land given you by the Lord's servant Moses, on the other side of the Jordan River. 5Be sure to continue to obey all of the commandments Moses gave you. Love the Lord and follow his plan for your lives. Cling to him and serve him enthusiastically."

6So Joshua blessed them and sent them home. 7,8(Moses had assigned the land of Bashan to the half-tribe of Manasseh, although the other half of the tribe was given land on the west side of the Jordan.) As Joshua sent away these troops, he blessed them and told them to share their great wealth with their relatives back home—their loot of cattle, silver, gold, bronze, iron, and clothing.

9So the troops of Reuben, Gad, and the half-tribe of Manasseh left the army of Israel at Shiloh in Canaan and crossed the Jordan River to their own homeland of Gilead. 10Before they went across, while they were still in Canaan, they built a large monument for everyone to see, in the shape of an altar.

11But when the rest of Israel heard about what they had done, 12they mustered an army at Shiloh and prepared to go to war against their brother tribes. 13First, however, they sent a delegation led by Phinehas, the son of Eleazar the priest. They crossed the river and talked to the tribes of Reuben, Gad, and Manasseh. ¹⁴In this delegation were ten high officials of Israel, one from each of the ten tribes, and each a clan leader. ¹⁵When they arrived in the land of Gilead they said to the tribes of Reuben, Gad, and the half-tribe of Manasseh,

¹⁶"The whole congregation of the Lord demands to know why you are sinning against the God of Israel by turning away from him and building an altar of rebellion against the Lord. ¹⁷,¹⁸Was our guilt at Peor—from which we have not even yet been cleansed despite the plague that tormented us—so little that you must rebel again? For you know that if you rebel today the Lord will be angry with all of us tomorrow. ¹⁹If you need the altar because your land is defiled, then join us on our side of the river where the Lord lives among us in his Tabernacle, and we will share our land with you. But do not rebel against the Lord by building another altar in addition to the only true altar of our God. ²⁰Don't you remember that when Achan, the son of Zerah, sinned against the Lord, the entire nation was punished in addition to the one man who had sinned?"

LUKE 20:1–26

On one of those days when he was teaching and preaching the Good News in the Temple, he was confronted by the chief priests and other religious leaders and councilmen. ²They demanded to know by what authority he had driven out the merchants from the Temple.

³"I'll ask you a question before I answer," he replied. ⁴"Was John sent by God, or was he merely acting under his own authority?"

⁵They talked it over among themselves. "If we say his message was from heaven, then we are trapped because he will ask, 'Then why didn't you believe him?' ⁶But if we say John was not sent from God, the people will mob us, for they are convinced that he was a prophet." ⁷Finally they replied, "We don't know!"

⁸And Jesus responded, "Then I won't answer your question either."

⁹Now he turned to the people again and told them this story: "A man planted a vineyard and rented it out to some farmers, and went away to a distant land to live for several years. ¹⁰When harvest time came, he sent one of his men to the farm to collect his share of the crops. But the tenants beat him up and sent him back empty-handed. ¹¹Then he sent another, but the same thing happened; he was beaten up and insulted and sent away without collecting. ¹²A third man was sent and the same thing happened. He, too, was wounded and chased away.

¹³" 'What shall I do?' the owner asked himself. 'I know! I'll send my cherished son. Surely they will show respect for him.'

¹⁴"But when the tenants saw his son, they said, 'This is our chance! This fellow will inherit all the land when his father dies. Come on. Let's kill him, and then it will be ours.' ¹⁵So they dragged him out of the vineyard and killed him.

"What do you think the owner will do? ¹⁶I'll tell you—he will come and kill them and rent the vineyard to others."

"But they would never do a thing like that," his listeners protested.

¹⁷Jesus looked at them and said, "Then what does the Scripture mean where it says, 'The Stone rejected by the builders was made the cornerstone'?" ¹⁸And he added, "Whoever stumbles over that Stone shall be broken; and those on whom it falls will be crushed to dust."

¹⁹When the chief priests and religious leaders heard about this story he had told, they wanted him arrested immediately, for they realized that he was talking about them. They were the wicked tenants in his illustration. But they were afraid that if they themselves arrested him there would be a riot. So they tried to get him to say something that could be reported to the Roman governor as reason for arrest by him.

20Watching their opportunity, they sent secret agents pretending to be honest men. 21They said to Jesus, "Sir, we know what an honest teacher you are. You always tell the truth and don't budge an inch in the face of what others think, but teach the ways of God. 22Now tell us—is it right to pay taxes to the Roman government or not?"

23He saw through their trickery and said, 24"Show me a coin. Whose portrait is this on it? And whose name?"

They replied, "Caesar's—the Roman emperor's."

25He said, "Then give the emperor all that is his—and give to God all that is his!"

26Thus their attempt to outwit him before the people failed; and marveling at his answer, they were silent.

PSALM 89:1–13

FOREVER and ever I will sing about the tender kindness of the Lord! Young and old shall hear about your blessings. 2Your love and kindness are forever; your truth is as enduring as the heavens.

3,4The Lord God says, "I have made a solemn agreement with my chosen servant David. I have taken an oath to establish his descendants as kings forever on his throne, from now until eternity!"

5All heaven shall praise your miracles, O Lord; myriads of angels will praise you for your faithfulness. 6For who in all of heaven can be compared with God? What mightiest angel is anything like him? 7The highest of angelic powers stand in dread and awe of him. Who is as revered as he by those surrounding him? 8O Jehovah, Commander of the heavenly armies, where is there any other Mighty One like you? Faithfulness is your very character.

9You rule the oceans when their waves arise in fearful storms; you speak, and they lie still. 10You have cut haughty Egypt to pieces. Your enemies are scattered by your awesome power. 11The heavens are yours, the world, everything—for you created them all. 12You created north and south! Mount Tabor and Mount Hermon rejoice to be signed by your name as their maker! 13Strong is your arm! Strong is your hand! Your right hand is lifted high in glorious strength.

PROVERBS FOR TODAY/ 13:15–16

A man with good sense is appreciated. A treacherous man must walk a rocky road. A wise man thinks ahead; a fool doesn't, and even brags about it!

APRIL 21

JOSHUA 22:21—23:16

THIS was the reply of the people of Reuben, Gad, and the half-tribe of Manasseh to these high officials:

22,23"We swear by Jehovah, the God of gods, that we have not built the altar in rebellion against the Lord. He knows (and let all Israel know it too) that we have not built the altar to sacrifice burnt offerings or grain offerings or peace offerings—may the curse of God be on us if we did. 24,25We have done it because we love the Lord and because we fear that in the future your children will say to ours, 'What right do you have to worship the Lord God of Israel? The Lord has placed the Jordan River as a barrier between our people and your people! You have no part in the Lord.' And your children may make our children stop worshiping him. 26,27So we decided to build the altar as a symbol to show our children and your children that we, too, may worship the Lord with our burnt offerings and peace offerings and sacrifices, and your children will not be able to say to ours, 'You have no part in the Lord our God.' 28If they say this, our children can reply, 'Look at the altar of the Lord which our fathers made, patterned after the altar of Jehovah. It is not for burnt offerings or sacrifices but is a symbol of the relationship with God that both of us have.' 29Far be it from us to turn away from the Lord or to rebel against him by building our own altar for burnt offerings, grain offerings, or sacrifices. Only the altar in front of the Tabernacle may be used for that."

30When Phinehas the priest and the high officials heard this from the tribes of Reuben, Gad, and Manasseh, they were very happy.

31Phinehas replied to them, "Today we know that the Lord is among us because you have not sinned against the Lord as we thought; instead, you have saved us from destruction!"

32Then Phinehas and the ten ambassadors went back to the people of Israel and told them what had happened, 33and all Israel rejoiced and praised God and spoke no more of war against Reuben and Gad. 34The people of Reuben and Gad named the altar "The Altar of Witness," for they said, "It is a witness between us and them that Jehovah is our God, too."

LONG after this, when the Lord had given success to the people of Israel against their enemies and when Joshua was very old, 2he called for the leaders of Israel— the elders, judges, and officers—and said to them, "I am an old man now, 3and you have seen all that the Lord your God has done for you during my lifetime. He has fought for you against your enemies and has given you their land. 4,5And I have divided to you the land of the nations yet unconquered as well

as the land of those you have already destroyed. All the land from the Jordan River to the Mediterranean Sea shall be yours, for the Lord your God will drive out all the people living there now, and you will live there instead, just as he has promised you.

6"But be very sure to follow all the instructions written in the book of the laws of Moses; do not deviate from them the least little bit. 7Be sure that you do not mix with the heathen people still remaining in the land; do not even mention the names of their gods, much less swear by them or worship them. 8But follow the Lord your God just as you have until now. 9He has driven out great, strong nations from before you, and no one has been able to defeat you. 10Each one of you has put to flight a thousand of the enemy, for the Lord your God fights for you, just as he has promised. 11So be very careful to keep on loving him.

12"If you don't, and if you begin to intermarry with the nations around you, 13then know for a certainty that the Lord your God will no longer chase those nations from your land. Instead, they will be a snare and a trap to you, a pain in your side and a thorn in your eyes, and you will disappear from this good land which the Lord your God has given you.

14"Soon I will be going the way of all the earth—I am going to die.

"You know very well that God's promises to you have all come true. 15,16But as certainly as the Lord has given you the good things he promised, just as certainly he will bring evil upon you if you disobey him. For if you worship other gods he will completely wipe you out from this good land which the Lord has given you. His anger will rise hot against you, and you will quickly perish."

LUKE 20:27–47

THEN some Sadducees—men who believed that death is the end of existence, that there is no resurrection— 28came to Jesus with this:

"The laws of Moses state that if a

man dies without children, the man's brother shall marry the widow and their children will legally belong to the dead man, to carry on his name. ²⁹We know of a family of seven brothers. The oldest married and then died without any children. ³⁰His brother married the widow and he, too, died. Still no children. ³¹And so it went, one after the other, until each of the seven had married her and died, leaving no children. ³²Finally the woman died also. ³³Now here is our question: Whose wife will she be in the resurrection? For all of them were married to her!"

³⁴,³⁵Jesus replied, "Marriage is for people here on earth, but when those who are counted worthy of being raised from the dead get to heaven, they do not marry. ³⁶And they never die again; in these respects they are like angels, and are sons of God, for they are raised up in new life from the dead.

³⁷,³⁸"But as to your real question— whether or not there is a resurrection— why, even the writings of Moses himself prove this. For when he describes how God appeared to him in the burning bush, he speaks of God as 'the God of Abraham, the God of Isaac, and the God of Jacob.' To say that the Lord *is* some person's God means that person is *alive,* not dead! So from God's point of view, all men are living."

³⁹"Well said, sir!" remarked some of the experts in the Jewish law who were standing there. ⁴⁰And that ended their questions, for they dared ask no more!

⁴¹Then he presented *them* with a question. "Why is it," he asked, "that Christ, the Messiah, is said to be a descendant of King David? ⁴²,⁴³For David himself wrote in the book of Psalms: 'God said to my Lord, the Messiah, "Sit at my right hand until I place your enemies beneath your feet." ' ⁴⁴How can the Messiah be both David's son and David's God at the same time?"

⁴⁵Then, with the crowds listening, he turned to his disciples and said, ⁴⁶"Beware of these experts in religion, for they love to parade in dignified robes and to be bowed to by the people as they walk along the street. And how they love the seats of honor in the synagogues and at religious festivals! ⁴⁷But even while they are praying long prayers with great outward piety, they are planning schemes to cheat widows out of their property. Therefore God's heaviest sentence awaits these men."

PSALM 89:14-37

YOUR throne is founded on two strong pillars—the one is Justice and the other Righteousness. Mercy and Truth walk before you as your attendants. Blessed are those who hear the joyful blast of the trumpet, for they shall walk in the light of your presence. ¹⁶They rejoice all day long in your wonderful reputation and in your perfect righteousness. ¹⁷You are their strength. What glory! Our power is based on your favor! ¹⁸Yes, our protection is from the Lord himself and he, the Holy One of Israel, has given us our king.

¹⁹In a vision you spoke to your prophet and said, "I have chosen a splendid young man from the common people to be the king— ²⁰he is my servant David! I have anointed him with my holy oil. ²¹I will steady him and make him strong. ²²His enemies shall not outwit him, nor shall the wicked overpower him. ²³I will beat down his adversaries before him, and destroy those who hate him. ²⁴I will protect and bless him constantly and surround him with my love; he will be great because of me. ²⁵He will hold sway from the Euphrates River to the Mediterranean Sea. ²⁶And he will cry to me, 'You are my Father, my God, and my Rock of Salvation.'

²⁷"I will treat him as my firstborn son, and make him the mightiest king in all the earth. ²⁸I will love him forever, and be kind to him always; my covenant with him will never end. ²⁹He will always have an heir; his throne will be as endless as the days of heaven. ³⁰,³¹,³²If his children forsake my laws and don't obey them, then I will punish them, ³³but I

will never completely take away my lovingkindness from them, nor let my promise fail. ³⁴No, I will not break my covenant; I will not take back one word of what I said. ³⁵,³⁶For I have sworn to David (and a holy God can never lie), that his dynasty will go on forever, and his throne will continue to the end of time. ³⁷It shall be eternal as the moon, my faithful witness in the sky!"

PROVERBS FOR TODAY/ 13:17–19

An unreliable messenger can cause a lot of trouble. Reliable communication permits progress. □ *If you refuse criticism you will end in poverty and disgrace; if you accept criticism you are on the road to fame.* □ *It is pleasant to see plans develop. That is why fools refuse to give them up even when they are wrong.*

APRIL 22

JOSHUA 24:1–33

THEN Joshua summoned all the people of Israel to him at Shechem, along with their leaders—the elders, officers, and judges. So they came and presented themselves before God.

²Then Joshua addressed them as follows: "The Lord God of Israel says, 'Your ancestors, including Terah the father of Abraham and Nahor, lived east of the Euphrates River; and they worshiped other gods. ³But I took your father Abraham from that land across the river and led him into the land of Canaan and gave him many descendants through Isaac his son. ⁴Isaac's children, whom I gave him, were Jacob and Esau. To Esau I gave the area around Mount Seir while Jacob and his children went into Egypt.

⁵"'Then I sent Moses and Aaron to bring terrible plagues upon Egypt; and afterwards I brought my people out as free men. ⁶But when they arrived at the Red Sea, the Egyptians chased after them with chariots and cavalry. ⁷Then Israel cried out to me and I put darkness between them and the Egyptians; and I brought the sea crashing in upon the Egyptians, drowning them. You saw what I did. Then Israel lived in the wilderness for many years.

⁸"'Finally I brought you into the land of the Amorites on the other side of the Jordan; and they fought against you, but I destroyed them and gave you their land. ⁹Then King Balak of Moab started a war against Israel, and he asked Balaam, the son of Beor, to curse you. ¹⁰But I wouldn't listen to him. Instead I made him bless you; and so I delivered Israel from him.

¹¹"'Then you crossed the Jordan River and came to Jericho. The men of Jericho fought against you, and so did many others—the Perizzites, the Canaanites, the Hittites, the Girgashites, the Hivites, and the Jebusites. Each in turn fought against you but I destroyed them all. ¹²And I sent hornets ahead of you to drive out the two kings of the Amorites and their people. It was not your swords or bows that brought you victory! ¹³I gave you land you had not worked for and cities you did not build—these cities where you are now living. I gave you vineyards and olive groves for food, though you did not plant them.'

¹⁴"So revere Jehovah and serve him in sincerity and truth. Put away forever the idols your ancestors worshiped when they lived beyond the Euphrates River and in Egypt. Worship the Lord alone. ¹⁵But if you are unwilling to obey the

Lord, then decide today whom you will obey. Will it be the gods of your ancestors beyond the Euphrates or the gods of the Amorites here in this land? But as for me and my family, we will serve the Lord." 16And the people replied, "We would never forsake the Lord and worship other gods! 17For the Lord our God is the one who rescued our fathers from their slavery in the land of Egypt. He is the God who did mighty miracles before the eyes of Israel, as we traveled through the wilderness, and preserved us from our enemies when we passed through their land. 18It was the Lord who drove out the Amorites and the other nations living here in the land. Yes, we choose the Lord, for he alone is our God."

19But Joshua replied to the people, "You can't worship the Lord God, for he is holy and jealous; he will not forgive your rebellion and sins. 20If you forsake him and worship other gods, he will turn upon you and destroy you, even though he has taken care of you for such a long time."

21But the people answered, "We choose the Lord!"

22"You have heard yourselves say it," Joshua said—"you have chosen to obey the Lord."

"Yes," they replied, "we are witnesses."

23"All right," he said, "then you must destroy all the idols you now own, and you must obey the Lord God of Israel."

24The people replied to Joshua, "Yes, we will worship and obey the Lord alone."

25So Joshua made a covenant with them that day at Shechem, committing them to a permanent and binding contract between themselves and God. 26Joshua recorded the people's reply in the book of the laws of God, and took a huge stone as a reminder and rolled it beneath the oak tree that was beside the Tabernacle.

27Then Joshua said to all the people, "This stone has heard everything the Lord said, so it will be a witness to testify against you if you go back on your word."

28Then Joshua sent the people away to their own sections of the country.

29Soon after this he died at the age of 110. 30He was buried on his own estate at Timnath-serah, in the hill country of Ephraim, on the north side of the mountains of Gaash.

31Israel obeyed the Lord throughout the lifetimes of Joshua and the other old men who had personally witnessed the amazing deeds the Lord had done for Israel.

32The bones of Joseph, the people of Israel had brought them along when they left Egypt—were buried in Shechem, in the parcel of ground Jacob had bought from the sons of Hamor. (The land was located in the territory assigned to the tribes of Joseph.)

33Eleazar, the son of Aaron, also died; he was buried in the hill country of Ephraim, at Gibe-ah, the city which had been given to his son Phinehas.

LUKE 21:1–28

As he stood in the Temple, he was watching the rich tossing their gifts into the collection box. 2Then a poor widow came by and dropped in two small copper coins.

3"Really," he remarked, "this poor widow has given more than all the rest of them combined. 4For they have given a little of what they didn't need, but she, poor as she is, has given everything she has."

5Some of his disciples began talking about the beautiful stonework of the Temple and the memorial decorations on the walls.

6But Jesus said, "The time is coming when all these things you are admiring will be knocked down, and not one stone will be left on top of another; all will become one vast heap of rubble."

7"Master!" they exclaimed. "When? And will there be any warning ahead of time?"

8He replied, "Don't let anyone mislead you. For many will come announcing themselves as the Messiah, and saying,

'The time has come.' But don't believe them! ⁹And when you hear of wars and insurrections beginning, don't panic. True, wars must come, but the end won't follow immediately— ¹⁰for nation shall rise against nation and kingdom against kingdom, ¹¹and there will be great earthquakes, and famines in many lands, and epidemics, and terrifying things happening in the heavens.

¹²"But before all this occurs, there will be a time of special persecution, and you will be dragged into synagogues and prisons and before kings and governors for my name's sake. ¹³But as a result, the Messiah will be widely known and honored. ¹⁴Therefore, don't be concerned about how to answer the charges against you, ¹⁵for I will give you the right words and such logic that none of your opponents will be able to reply! ¹⁶Even those closest to you—your parents, brothers, relatives, and friends will betray you and have you arrested; and some of you will be killed. ¹⁷And everyone will hate you because you are mine and are called by my name. ¹⁸But not a hair of your head will perish! ¹⁹For if you stand firm, you will win your souls.

²⁰"But when you see Jerusalem surrounded by armies, then you will know that the time of its destruction has arrived. ²¹Then let the people of Judea flee to the hills. Let those in Jerusalem try to escape, and those outside the city must not attempt to return. ²²For those will be days of God's judgment, and the words of the ancient Scriptures written by the prophets will be abundantly fulfilled. ²³Woe to expectant mothers in those days, and those with tiny babies. For there will be great distress upon this nation and wrath upon this people. ²⁴They will be brutally killed by enemy weapons, or sent away as exiles and captives to all the nations of the world; and Jerusalem shall be conquered and trampled down by the Gentiles until the period of Gentile triumph ends in God's good time.

²⁵"Then there will be strange events in the skies—warnings, evil omens and portents in the sun, moon and stars; and down here on earth the nations will be in turmoil, perplexed by the roaring seas and strange tides. ²⁶The courage of many people will falter because of the fearful fate they see coming upon the earth, for the stability of the very heavens will be broken up. ²⁷Then the peoples of the earth shall see me, the Messiah, coming in a cloud with power and great glory. ²⁸So when all these things begin to happen, stand straight and look up! For your salvation is near."

PSALM 89:38–52

THEN why cast me off, rejected? Why be so angry with the one you chose as king? ³⁹Have you renounced your covenant with him? For you have thrown his crown in the dust. ⁴⁰You have broken down the walls protecting him and laid in ruins every fort defending him. ⁴¹Everyone who comes along has robbed him while his neighbors mock. ⁴²You have strengthened his enemies against him and made them rejoice. ⁴³You have struck down his sword and refused to help him in battle. ⁴⁴You have ended his splendor and overturned his throne. ⁴⁵You have made him old before his time and publicly disgraced him.

⁴⁶O Jehovah, how long will this go on? Will you hide yourself from me forever? How long will your wrath burn like fire? ⁴⁷Oh, remember how short you have made man's lifespan. Is it an empty, futile life you give the sons of men? ⁴⁸No man can live forever. All will die. Who can rescue his life from the power of the grave?

⁴⁹Lord, where is the love you used to have for me? Where is your kindness that you promised to David with a faithful pledge? ⁵⁰Lord, see how all the people are despising me. ⁵¹Your enemies joke about me, the one you anointed as their king.

⁵²And yet—blessed be the Lord forever! Amen and amen!

APRIL 23

JUDGES 1:1—2:9

AFTER Joshua died, the nation of Israel went to the Lord to receive his instructions.

"Which of our tribes should be the first to go to war against the Canaanites?" they inquired.

²God's answer came, "Judah. And I will give them a great victory."

³The leaders of the tribe of Judah, however, asked help from the tribe of Simeon. "Join us in clearing out the people living in the territory allotted to us," they said, "and then we will help you conquer yours." So the army of Simeon went with the army of Judah. ⁴,⁵,⁶And the Lord helped them defeat the Canaanites and Perizzites, so that ten thousand of the enemy were slain at Bezek. King Adoni-bezek escaped, but the Israeli army soon captured him and cut off his thumbs and big toes.

⁷"I have treated seventy kings in this same manner and have fed them the scraps under my table!" King Adoni-bezek said. "Now God has paid me back." He was taken to Jerusalem, and died there.

⁸(Judah had conquered Jerusalem, and massacred its people, setting the city on fire.) ⁹Afterward the army of Judah fought the Canaanites in the hill country and in the Negeb, as well as on the coastal plains. ¹⁰Then Judah marched against the Canaanites in Hebron (formerly called Kiriath-arba), destroying the cities of Sheshai, Ahiman, and Talmai. ¹¹Later they attacked the city of Debir (formerly called Kiriath-sepher).

¹²"Who will lead the attack against Debir?" Caleb challenged them. "Whoever conquers it shall have my daughter Achsah as his wife!"

¹³Caleb's nephew, Othni-el, son of his younger brother Kenaz, volunteered to lead the attack; and he conquered the city and won Achsah as his bride. ¹⁴As they were leaving for their new home, she urged him to ask her father for an additional piece of land. She dismounted from her donkey to speak to Caleb about it.

"What do you wish?" he asked.

¹⁵And she replied, "You have been kind enough to give me land in the Negeb, but please give us springs of water too."

So Caleb gave her the upper and lower springs.

¹⁶When the tribe of Judah moved into its new land in the Negeb wilderness south of Arad, the descendants of Moses' father-in-law—members of the Kenite tribe—accompanied them. They left their homes in Jericho, "The City of Palm Trees," and the two tribes lived together after that. ¹⁷Afterwards the army of Judah joined Simeon's and they fought the Canaanites at the city of Zephath and massacred all its people. So now the city is named Hormah (meaning, "massacred"). ¹⁸The army of Judah also conquered the cities of Gaza, Ashkelon, and Ekron, with their surrounding villages. ¹⁹The Lord

helped the tribe of Judah exterminate the people of the hill country, though they failed in their attempt to conquer the people of the valley, who had iron chariots.

20The city of Hebron was given to Caleb as the Lord had promised; so Caleb drove out the inhabitants of the city; they were descendants of the three sons of Anak.

21The tribe of Benjamin failed to exterminate the Jebusites living in their part of the city of Jerusalem, so they still live there today, mingled with the Israelis.

22,23As for the tribe of Joseph, they attacked the city of Bethel, formerly known as Luz, and the Lord was with them. First they sent scouts, 24who captured a man coming out of the city. They offered to spare his life and that of his family if he would show them the entrance passage through the wall. 25So he showed them how to get in, and they massacred the entire population except for this man and his family. 26Later the man moved to Syria and founded a city there, naming it Luz, too, as it is still known today.

27The tribe of Manasseh failed to drive out the people living in Beth-shean, Taanach, Dor, Ibleam, Megiddo, with their surrounding towns; so the Canaanites stayed there. 28In later years when the Israelis were stronger they put the Canaanites to work as slaves, but never did force them to leave the country. 29This was also true of the Canaanites living in Gezer; they still live among the tribe of Ephraim.

30And the tribe of Zebulun did not massacre the people of Kitron or Nahalol, but made them their slaves; 31,32nor did the tribe of Asher drive out the residents of Acco, Sidon, Ahlab, Achzib, Helbah, Aphik, or Rehob; so the Israelis still live among the Canaanites, who were the original people of that land. 33And the tribe of Naphtali did not drive out the people of Beth-shemesh or of Beth-anath, so these people continue to live among them as servants.

34As for the tribe of Dan, the Amorites forced them into the hill country and wouldn't let them come down into the valley; 35but when the Amorites later spread into Mount Heres, Aijalon, and Sha-albim, the tribe of Joseph conquered them and made them their slaves. 36The boundary of the Amorites begins at the ascent of Scorpion Pass, runs to a spot called The Rock, and continues upward from there.

ONE day the Angel of the Lord arrived at Bochim, coming from Gilgal, and announced to the people of Israel, "I brought you out of Egypt into this land which I promised to your ancestors, and I said that I would never break my covenant with you, 2if you, on your part, would make no peace treaties with the people living in this land; I told you to destroy their heathen altars. Why have you not obeyed? 3And now since you have broken the contract, it is no longer in effect, and I no longer promise to destroy the nations living in your land; rather, they shall be thorns in your sides, and their gods will be a constant temptation to you."

4The people broke into tears as the Angel finished speaking; 5so the name of that place was called "Bochim" (meaning, "the place where people wept"). Then they offered sacrifices to the Lord.

6When Joshua finally disbanded the armies of Israel, the tribes moved into their new territories and took possession of the land. 7,8,9Joshua, the man of God, died at the age of 110, and was buried at the edge of his property in Timnath-heres, in the hill country of Ephraim, north of Mount Gaash. The people had remained true to the Lord throughout Joshua's lifetime, and as long afterward as the old men of his generation were still living— those who had seen the mighty miracles the Lord had done for Israel.

LUKE 21:29—22:13

THEN he gave them this illustration: "Notice the fig tree, or any other tree. 30When the leaves come out, you know without being told that summer is near. 31In the same way, when you see the events taking place that I've described you can be just as sure that the Kingdom of God is near.

32"I solemnly declare to you that when these things happen, the end of this age has come. 33And though all heaven and earth shall pass away, yet my words remain forever true.

34,35"Watch out! Don't let my sudden coming catch you unawares; don't let me find you living in careless ease, carousing and drinking, and occupied with the problems of this life, like all the rest of the world. 36Keep a constant watch. And pray that if possible you may arrive in my presence without having to experience these horrors."

37,38Every day Jesus went to the Temple to teach, and the crowds began gathering early in the morning to hear him. And each evening he returned to spend the night on the Mount of Olives.

AND now the Passover celebration was drawing near—the Jewish festival when only bread made without yeast was used. 2The chief priests and other religious leaders were actively plotting Jesus' murder, trying to find a way to kill him without starting a riot—a possibility they greatly feared.

3Then Satan entered into Judas Iscariot, who was one of the twelve disciples, 4and he went over to the chief priests and captains of the Temple guards to discuss the best way to betray Jesus to them. 5They were, of course, delighted to know that he was ready to help them and promised him a reward. 6So he began to look for an opportunity for them to arrest Jesus quietly when the crowds weren't around.

7Now the day of the Passover celebration arrived, when the Passover lamb was killed and eaten with the unleavened bread. 8Jesus sent Peter and John ahead to find a place to prepare their Passover meal.

9"Where do you want us to go?" they asked.

10And he replied, "As soon as you en-

ter Jerusalem, you will see a man walking along carrying a pitcher of water. Follow him into the house he enters, 11and say to the man who lives there, 'Our Teacher says for you to show us the guest room where he can eat the Passover meal with his disciples.' 12He will take you upstairs to a large room all ready for us. That is the place. Go ahead and prepare the meal there."

13They went off to the city and found everything just as Jesus had said, and prepared the Passover supper.

PSALM 90:1—91:16

LORD, through all the generations you have been our home! 2Before the mountains were created, before the earth was formed, you are God without beginning or end.

3You speak, and man turns back to dust. 4A thousand years are but as yesterday to you! They are like a single hour! 5,6We glide along the tides of time as swiftly as a racing river, and vanish as quickly as a dream. We are like grass that is green in the morning but mowed down and withered before the evening shadows fall. 7We die beneath your anger; we are overwhelmed by your wrath. 8You spread out our sins before you— our secret sins—and see them all. 9No wonder the years are long and heavy here beneath your wrath. All our days are filled with sighing.

10Seventy years are given us! And some may even live to eighty. But even the best of these years are often emptiness and pain; soon they disappear, and we are gone. 11Who can realize the terrors of your anger? Which of us can fear you as he should?

12Teach us to number our days and recognize how few they are; help us to spend them as we should.

13O Jehovah, come and bless us! How long will you delay? Turn away your anger from us. 14Satisfy us in our earliest youth with your lovingkindness, giving us constant joy to the end of our lives. 15Give us gladness in proportion to our former misery! Replace the evil years with good. 16Let us see your miracles again; let our children see glorious things, the kind you used to do, 17and let the Lord our God favor us and give us success. May he give permanence to all we do.

WE live within the shadow of the Almighty, sheltered by the God who is above all gods. 2This I declare, that he alone is my refuge, my place of safety; he is my God, and I am trusting him. 3For he rescues you from every trap, and protects you from the fatal plague. 4He will shield you with his wings! They will shelter you. His faithful promises are your armor. 5Now you don't need to be afraid of the dark any more, nor fear the dangers of the day; 6nor dread the plagues of darkness, nor disasters in the morning.

7Though a thousand fall at my side, though ten thousand are dying around me, the evil will not touch me. 8I will see how the wicked are punished but I will not share it. 9For Jehovah is my refuge! I choose the God above all gods to shelter me. 10How then can evil overtake me or any plague come near? 11For he orders his angels to protect you wherever you go. 12They will steady you with their hands to keep you from stumbling against the rocks on the trail. 13You can safely meet a lion or step on poisonous snakes, yes, even trample them beneath your feet!

14For the Lord says, "Because he loves me, I will rescue him; I will make him great because he trusts in my name. 15When he calls on me I will answer; I will be with him in trouble, and rescue him and honor him. 16I will satisfy him with a full life and give him my salvation."

PROVERBS FOR TODAY/ 13:24–25

If you refuse to discipline your son, it proves you don't love him; for if you love him you will be prompt to punish him. The good man eats to live, while the evil man lives to eat.

APRIL 24

JUDGES 2:10—3:31

BUT finally all that generation died; and the next generation did not worship Jehovah as their God, and did not care about the mighty miracles he had done for Israel. 11They did many things which the Lord had expressly forbidden, including the worshiping of heathen gods. 12,13,14They abandoned Jehovah, the God loved and worshiped by their ancestors—the God who had brought them out of Egypt. Instead, they were worshiping and bowing low before the idols of the neighboring nations. So the anger of the Lord flamed out against all Israel. He left them to

the mercy of their enemies, for they had departed from Jehovah and were worshiping Baal and the Ashtaroth idols.

15So now when the nation of Israel went out to battle against its enemies, the Lord blocked their path. He had warned them about this, and in fact had vowed that he would do it. But when the people were in this terrible plight, 16the Lord raised up judges to save them from their enemies.

17Yet even then Israel would not listen to the judges, but broke faith with Jehovah by worshiping other gods instead. How quickly they turned away from the true faith of their ancestors, for they refused to obey God's commands. [18]Each judge rescued the people of Israel from their enemies throughout his lifetime, for the Lord was moved to pity by the groaning of his people under their crushing oppressions; so he helped them as long as that judge lived. [19]But when the judge died, the people turned from doing right and behaved even worse than their ancestors had. They prayed to heathen gods again, throwing themselves to the ground in humble worship. They stubbornly returned to the evil customs of the nations around them.

[20]Then the anger of the Lord would flame out against Israel again. He declared, "Because these people have violated the treaty I made with their ancestors, [21]I will no longer drive out the nations left unconquered by Joshua when he died. [22]Instead, I will use these nations to test my people, to see whether or not they will obey the Lord as their ancestors did."

[23]So the Lord left those nations in the land and did not drive them out, nor let Israel destroy them.

HERE is a list of the nations the Lord left in the land to test the new generation of Israel who had not experienced the wars of Canaan. For God wanted to give opportunity to the youth of Israel to exercise faith and obedience in conquering their enemies:

The Philistines (five cities),
The Canaanites,
The Sidonians,
The Hivites living in Mount Lebanon, from Baal-hermon to the entrance of Hamath.

[4]These people were a test to the new generation of Israel, to see whether they would obey the commandments the Lord had given to them through Moses.

[5]So Israel lived among the Canaanites, Hittites, Hivites, Perizzites, Amorites, and Jebusites. [6]But instead of destroying them, the people of Israel intermarried with them. The young men of Israel took their girls as wives, and the Israeli girls married their men. And soon Israel was worshiping their gods. [7]So the people of Israel were very evil in God's sight, for they turned against Jehovah their God and worshiped Baal and the Asheroth idols.

[8]Then the anger of the Lord flamed out against Israel, and he let King Cushan-rishathaim of eastern Syria conquer them. They were under his rule for eight years. [9]But when Israel cried out to the Lord, he gave them Caleb's nephew, Othni-el (son of Kenaz, Caleb's younger brother) to save them. [10]The Spirit of the Lord took control of him and he reformed and purged Israel so that when he led the forces of Israel against the army of King Cushan-rishathaim, the Lord helped Israel conquer him completely.

[11]Then, for forty years under Othni-el, there was peace in the land. But when Othni-el died, [12]the people of Israel turned once again to their sinful ways, so God helped King Eglon of Moab to conquer part of Israel at that time. [13]Allied with him were the armies of the Ammonites and the Amalekites. These forces defeated the Israelis and took possession of Jericho, often called "The City of Palm Trees." [14]For the next eighteen years the people of Israel were required to pay crushing taxes to King Eglon.

[15]But when they cried to the Lord, he sent them a savior, Ehud (son of Gera, a Benjaminite), who was left-handed. Ehud was the man chosen to carry Israel's annual tax money to the Moabite capital. [16]Before he went on this journey he made himself a double-edged dagger eighteen inches long and hid it in his clothing, strapped against his right thigh. [17,18,19]After delivering the money to King Eglon (who, by the way, was very fat!) he started home again. But outside the city, at the quarries of Gilgal, he sent his companions on and returned alone to the king.

"I have a secret message for you," he told him.

The king immediately dismissed all those who were with him so that he could have a private interview. [20]Ehud walked over to him as he was sitting in a cool upstairs room and said to him, "It is a message from God!"

King Eglon stood up at once to receive it, 21whereupon Ehud reached beneath his robe with his strong left hand, pulled out the double-bladed dagger strapped against his right thigh, and plunged it deep into the king's belly. 22,23The hilt of the dagger disappeared beneath the flesh, and the fat closed over it as the entrails oozed out. Leaving the dagger there, Ehud locked the doors behind him and escaped across an upstairs porch.

24When the king's servants returned and saw that the doors were locked, they waited, thinking that perhaps he was using the bathroom. 25But when, after a long time, he still didn't come out, they became concerned and got a key. And when they opened the door, they found their master dead on the floor.

26Meanwhile Ehud had escaped past the quarries to Se-irah. 27When he arrived in the hill country of Ephraim, he blew a trumpet as a call to arms and mustered an army under his own command.

28"Follow me," he told them, "for the Lord has put your enemies, the Moabites, at your mercy!"

The army then proceeded to seize the fords of the Jordan River near Moab, preventing anyone from crossing. 29Then they attacked the Moabites and killed about ten thousand of the strongest and most skillful of their fighting men, letting not one escape. 30So Moab was conquered by Israel that day, and the land was at peace for the next eighty years.

31The next judge after Ehud was Shamgar (son of Anath). He once killed six hundred Philistines with an ox goad, thereby saving Israel from disaster.

LUKE 22:14–34

THEN Jesus and the others arrived, and at the proper time all sat down together at the table; 15and he said, "I have looked forward to this hour with deep longing, anxious to eat this Passover meal with you before my suffering begins. 16For I tell you now that I won't eat it again until what it represents has occurred in the Kingdom of God."

17Then he took a glass of wine, and when he had given thanks for it, he said, "Take this and share it among yourselves. 18For I will not drink wine again until the Kingdom of God has come."

19Then he took a loaf of bread; and when he had thanked God for it, he broke it apart and gave it to them, saying, "This is my body, given for you. Eat it in remembrance of me."

20After supper he gave them another glass of wine, saying, "This wine is the token of God's new agreement to save you—an agreement sealed with the blood I shall pour out to purchase back your souls. 21But here at this table, sitting among us as a friend, is the man who will betray me. 22I must die. It is part of God's plan. But, oh, the horror awaiting that man who betrays me."

23Then the disciples wondered among themselves which of them would ever do such a thing.

24And they began to argue among themselves as to who would have the highest rank [in the coming Kingdom].

25Jesus told them, "In this world the kings and great men order their slaves around, and the slaves have no choice but to like it! 26But among you, the one who serves you best will be your leader. 27Out in the world the master sits at the table and is served by his servants. But not here! For I am your servant. 28Nevertheless, because you have stood true to me in these terrible days, 29and because my Father has granted me a Kingdom, I, here and now, grant you the right 30to eat and drink at my table in that Kingdom; and you will sit on thrones judging the twelve tribes of Israel.

31"Simon, Simon, Satan has asked to have you, to sift you like wheat, 32but I have pleaded in prayer for you that your faith should not completely fail. So when you have repented and turned to me again, strengthen and build up the faith of your brothers."

33Simon said, "Lord, I am ready to go to jail with you, and even to die with you."

34But Jesus said, "Peter, let me tell you something. Between now and tomorrow morning when the rooster crows, you will deny me three times, declaring that you don't even know me."

PSALM 92:1—93:5

IT is good to say, "Thank you" to the Lord, to sing praises to the God who is above all gods.

2Every morning tell him, "Thank you for your kindness," and every evening rejoice in all his faithfulness. 3Sing his praises, accompanied by music from the harp and lute and lyre. 4You have done so much for me, O Lord. No wonder I am glad! I sing for joy.

5O Lord, what miracles you do! And how deep are your thoughts! 6Unthinking people do not understand them! No fool can comprehend this: 7that although the wicked flourish like weeds, there is only eternal destruction ahead of them. 8But the Lord continues forever, exalted in the heavens, 9while his enemies—all evil-doers—shall be scattered.

10But you have made me as strong as a wild bull. How refreshed I am by your blessings! 11I have heard the doom of my enemies announced and seen them destroyed. 12But the godly shall flourish like palm trees, and grow tall as the cedars of Lebanon. 13For they are transplanted into the Lord's own garden, and are under his personal care. 14Even in old age they will still produce fruit and be vital and green. 15This honors the Lord, and exhibits his faithful care. He is my shelter. There is nothing but goodness in him!

JEHOVAH is King! He is robed in majesty and strength. The world is his throne.

2O Lord, you have reigned from prehistoric times, from the everlasting past. 3The mighty oceans thunder your praise. 4You are mightier than all the breakers pounding on the seashores of the world! 5Your royal decrees cannot be changed. Holiness is forever the keynote of your reign.

PROVERBS FOR TODAY/ 14:1-2

A wise woman builds her house, while a foolish woman tears hers down by her own efforts. To do right honors God; to sin is to despise him.

APRIL 25

JUDGES 4:1—5:31

AFTER Ehud's death the people of Israel again sinned against the Lord, 2,3so the Lord let them be conquered by King Jabin of Hazor, in Canaan. The commander-in-chief of his army was Sisera, who lived in Harosheth-ha-goiim. He had nine hundred iron chariots, and made life unbearable for the Israelis for twenty years. But finally they begged the Lord for help.

4Israel's leader at that time, the one who was responsible for bringing the people back to God, was Deborah, a prophetess, the wife of Lappidoth. 5She held court at a place now called "Deborah's Palm Tree," between Ramah and Bethel, in the hill country of Ephraim; and the Israelites came to her to decide their disputes.

6One day she summoned Barak (son of Abinoam), who lived in Kedesh, in

"We are one in Christ Jesus."
    Galatians 3:28

*"Her children stand
and bless her."*
Proverbs 31:28

the land of Naphtali, and said to him, "The Lord God of Israel has commanded you to mobilize ten thousand men from the tribes of Naphtali and Zebulun. Lead them to Mount Tabor, 7to fight King Jabin's mighty army with all his chariots, under General Sisera's command. The Lord says, 'I will draw them to the Kishon River, and you will defeat them there.'"

8"I'll go, but only if you go with me!" Barak told her.

9"All right," she replied, "I'll go with you; but I'm warning you now that the honor of conquering Sisera will go to a woman instead of to you!" So she went with him to Kedesh.

10When Barak summoned the men of Zebulun and Naphtali to mobilize at Kedesh, ten thousand men volunteered. And Deborah marched with them. 11(Heber, the Kenite—the Kenites were the descendants of Moses' father-in-law Hobab—had moved away from the rest of his clan, and had been living in various places as far away as the Oak of Za-anan-nim, near Kedesh.) 12When General Sisera was told that Barak and his army were camped at Mount Tabor 13he mobilized his entire army, including the nine hundred iron chariots, and marched from Harosheth-ha-goiim to the Kishon River.

14Then Deborah said to Barak, "Now is the time for action! The Lord leads on! He has already delivered Sisera into your hand!"

So Barak led his ten thousand men down the slopes of Mount Tabor into battle.

15Then the Lord threw the enemy into a panic, both the soldiers and the charioteers, and Sisera leaped from his chariot and escaped on foot. 16Barak and his men chased the enemy and the chariots as far as Harosheth-ha-goiim, until all of Sisera's army was destroyed; not one man was left alive. 17Meanwhile, Sisera had escaped to the tent of Jael, the wife of Heber the Kenite, for there was a mutual-assistance agreement between King Jabin of Hazor and the clan of Heber.

18Jael went out to meet Sisera and said to him, "Come into my tent, sir. You will be safe here in our protection. Don't be afraid." So he went into her tent and she covered him with a blanket.

19"Please give me some water," he said, "for I am very thirsty." So she gave him some milk and covered him again.

20"Stand in the door of the tent," he told her, "and if anyone comes by, looking for me, tell them that no one is here."

21Then Jael took a sharp tent peg and a hammer and, quietly creeping up to him as he slept, she drove the peg through his temples and into the ground; and so he died, for he was fast asleep from weariness.

22When Barak came by looking for Sisera, Jael went out to meet him and said, "Come, and I will show you the man you are looking for."

So he followed her into the tent and found Sisera lying there dead, with the tent peg through his temples. 23So that day the Lord used Israel to subdue King Jabin of Canaan. 24And from that time on Israel became stronger and stronger against King Jabin, until he and all his people were destroyed.

THEN Deborah and Barak sang this song about the wonderful victory:
2"Praise the Lord!
Israel's leaders bravely led;
The people gladly followed!
Yes, bless the Lord!
3Listen, O you kings and princes,
For I shall sing about the Lord,
The God of Israel.
4When you led us out from Seir,
Out across the fields of Edom,
The earth trembled
And the sky poured down its rain.
5Yes, even Mount Sinai quaked
At the presence of the God of Israel!
6In the days of Shamgar and of Jael,
The main roads were deserted.
Travelers used the narrow, crooked side paths.
7Israel's population dwindled,
Until Deborah became a mother to Israel.
8When Israel chose new gods,

Everything collapsed.
Our masters would not let us have
A shield or spear.
Among forty thousand men of Israel,
Not a weapon could be found!
9How I rejoice
In the leaders of Israel
Who offered themselves so willingly!
Praise the Lord!
10Let all Israel, rich and poor,
Join in his praises—
Those who ride on white donkeys
And sit on rich carpets,
And those who are poor and must
   walk.
11The village musicians
Gather at the village well
To sing of the triumphs of the Lord.
Again and again they sing the ballad
Of how the Lord saved Israel
With an army of peasants!
The people of the Lord
Marched through the gates!
12Awake, O Deborah, and sing!
Arise, O Barak!
O son of Abino-am, lead away your
   captives!
13,14Down from Mount Tabor marched
   the noble remnant.
The people of the Lord
Marched down against great odds.
They came from Ephraim and Benja-
   min,
From Machir and from Zebulun.
15Down into the valley
Went the princes of Issachar
With Deborah and Barak.
At God's command they rushed into
   the valley.
(But the tribe of Reuben didn't go.
16Why did you sit at home among the
   sheepfolds,
Playing your shepherd pipes?
Yes, the tribe of Reuben has an uneasy
   conscience.
17Why did Gilead remain across the
   Jordan,
And why did Dan remain with his
   ships?
And why did Asher sit unmoved
Upon the seashore,
At ease beside his harbors?)

18But the tribes of Zebulun and Naph-
   tali
Dared to die upon the fields of battle.
19The kings of Canaan fought in Taa-
   nach
By Megiddo's springs,
But did not win the victory.
20The very stars of heaven
Fought Sisera.
21The rushing Kishon River
Swept them away.
March on, my soul, with strength!
22Hear the stamping
Of the horsehoofs of the enemy!
See the prancing of his steeds!
23But the Angel of Jehovah
Put a curse on Meroz.
'Curse them bitterly,' he said,
'Because they did not come to help
   the Lord
Against his enemies.'
24Blessed be Jael,
The wife of Heber the Kenite—
Yes, may she be blessed
Above all women who live in tents.
25He asked for water
And she gave him milk in a beautiful
   cup!
26Then she took a tent pin and a work-
   man's hammer
And pierced Sisera's temples,
Crushing his head.
She pounded the tent pin through his
   head.
27He sank, he fell, he lay dead at her
   feet.
28The mother of Sisera watched
   through the window
For his return.
'Why is his chariot so long in coming?
Why don't we hear the sound of the
   wheels?'
29But her ladies-in-waiting—and she
   herself—replied,
30'There is much loot to be divided,
And it takes time.
Each man receives a girl or two;
And Sisera will get gorgeous robes,
And he will bring home
Many gifts for me.'
31O Lord, may all your enemies
Perish as Sisera did,

But may those who love the Lord
Shine as the sun!"

After that there was peace in the land
for forty years.

LUKE 22:35–54

T HEN Jesus asked them, "When I
sent you out to preach the Good
News and you were without
money, duffle bag, or extra clothing, how
did you get along?"

"Fine," they replied.

36"But now," he said, "take a duffle
bag if you have one, and your money.
And if you don't have a sword, better
sell your clothes and buy one! 37For the
time has come for this prophecy about
me to come true: 'He will be condemned
as a criminal!' Yes, everything written
about me by the prophets will come
true."

38"Master," they replied, "we have
two swords among us."

"Enough!" he said.

39Then, accompanied by the disciples,
he left the upstairs room and went as
usual to the Mount of Olives. 40There
he told them, "Pray God that you will
not be overcome by temptation."

41,42He walked away, perhaps a stone's
throw, and knelt down and prayed this
prayer: "Father, if you are willing, please
take away this cup of horror from
me. But I want your will, not mine."
43Then an angel from heaven appeared
and strengthened him, 44for he was in
such agony of spirit that he broke into
a sweat of blood, with great drops falling
to the ground as he prayed more and
more earnestly. 45At last he stood up
again and returned to the disciples—only
to find them asleep, exhausted from
grief.

46"Asleep!" he said. "Get up! Pray God
that you will not fall when you are
tempted."

47But even as he said this, a mob approached, led by Judas, one of his twelve
disciples. Judas walked over to Jesus and
kissed him on the cheek in friendly greeting.

48But Jesus said, "Judas, how can you
do this—betray the Messiah with a
kiss?"

49When the other disciples saw what
was about to happen, they exclaimed,
"Master, shall we fight? We brought
along the swords!" 50And one of them
slashed at the High Priest's servant, and
cut off his right ear.

51But Jesus said, "Don't resist any
more." And he touched the place where
the man's ear had been and restored it.
52Then Jesus addressed the chief priests
and captains of the Temple guards and
the religious leaders who headed the
mob. "Am I a robber," he asked, "that
you have come armed with swords and
clubs to get me? 53Why didn't you arrest
me in the Temple? I was there every
day. But this is your moment—the time
when Satan's power reigns supreme."

54So they seized him and led him to
the High Priest's residence, and Peter
followed at a distance.

PSALM 94:1–23

L ORD God, to whom vengeance belongs, let your glory shine out.
Arise and judge the earth; sentence the proud to the penalties they deserve. 3Lord, how long shall the wicked
be allowed to triumph and exult?
4Hear their insolence! See their arrogance! How these men of evil boast!
5See them oppressing your people, O
Lord, afflicting those you love. 6,7They
murder widows, immigrants, and orphans, for "The Lord isn't looking,"
they say, "and besides, he doesn't
care."

8Fools! 9Is God deaf and blind—he
who makes ears and eyes? 10He punishes
the nations—won't he also punish you?
He knows everything—doesn't he also
know what you are doing?

11The Lord is fully aware of how limited and futile the thoughts of mankind
are, 12,13so he helps us by punishing us.
This makes us follow his paths, and gives
us respite from our enemies while God
traps them and destroys them. 14The

Lord will not forsake his people, for they are his prize. 15Judgment will again be just and all the upright will rejoice.

16Who will protect me from the wicked? Who will be my shield? 17I would have died unless the Lord had helped me. 18I screamed, "I'm slipping, Lord!" and he was kind and saved me.

19Lord, when doubts fill my mind, when my heart is in turmoil, quiet me and give me renewed hope and cheer.

20Will you permit a corrupt government to rule under your protection—a government permitting wrong to defeat right? 21,22Do you approve of those who condemn the innocent to death? No! The Lord my God is my fortress—the mighty Rock where I can hide. 23God has made the sins of evil men to boomerang upon them! He will destroy them by their own plans. Jehovah our God will cut them off.

PROVERBS FOR TODAY/ 14:3–4

A rebel's foolish talk should prick his own pride! But the wise man's speech is respected. An empty stable stays clean—but there is no income from an empty stable.

APRIL 26

JUDGES 6:1–40

THEN the people of Israel began once again to worship other gods, and once again the Lord let their enemies harass them. This time it was by the people of Midian, for seven years. 2The Midianites were so cruel that the Israelis took to the mountains, living in caves and dens. 3,4When they planted their seed, marauders from Midian, Amalek, and other neighboring nations came and destroyed their crops and plundered the countryside as far away as Gaza, leaving nothing to eat, and taking away all their sheep, oxen, and donkeys. 5These enemy hordes arrived on droves of camels too numerous to count and stayed until the land was completely stripped and devastated. 6,7So Israel was reduced to abject poverty because of the Midianites. Then at last the people of Israel began to cry out to the Lord for help.

8However, the Lord's reply through the prophet he sent to them was this: "The Lord God of Israel brought you out of slavery in Egypt, 9and rescued you from the Egyptians and from all who were cruel to you, and drove out your enemies before you, and gave you their land. 10He told you he is the Lord your God, and you must not worship the gods of the Amorites who live around you on every side. But you have not listened to him."

11But one day the Angel of the Lord came and sat beneath the oak tree at Ophrah, on the farm of Joash the Abiezrite. Joash's son, Gideon, had been threshing wheat by hand in the bottom of a grape press—a pit where grapes were pressed to make wine—for he was hiding from the Midianites.

12The Angel of the Lord appeared to him and said, "Mighty soldier, the Lord is with you!"

13"Stranger," Gideon replied, "if the Lord is with us, why has all this happened to us? And where are all the miracles our ancestors have told us about—such as when God brought them out of Egypt? Now the Lord has thrown us away and has let the Midianites completely ruin us."

14Then the Lord turned to him and

said, "I will make you strong! Go and save Israel from the Midianites! I am sending you!"

15But Gideon replied, "Sir, how can *I* save Israel? My family is the poorest in the whole tribe of Manasseh, and I am the least thought of in the entire family!"

16Whereupon the Lord said to him, "But I, Jehovah, will be with you! And you shall quickly destroy the Midianite hordes!"

17Gideon replied, "If it is really true that you are going to help me like that, then do some miracle to prove it! Prove that it is really Jehovah who is talking to me! 18But stay here until I go and get a present for you."

"All right," the Angel agreed. "I'll stay here until you return."

19Gideon hurried home and roasted a young goat, and baked some unleavened bread from a bushel of flour. Then, carrying the meat in a basket and broth in a pot, he took it out to the Angel, who was beneath the oak tree, and presented it to him.

20The Angel said to him, "Place the meat and the bread upon that rock over there, and pour the broth over it."

When Gideon had followed these instructions, 21the Angel touched the meat and bread with his staff, and fire flamed up from the rock and consumed them! And suddenly the Angel was gone!

22When Gideon realized that it had indeed been the Angel of the Lord, he cried out, "Alas, O Lord God, for I have seen the Angel of the Lord face to face!"

23"It's all right," the Lord replied. "Don't be afraid! You shall not die."

24And Gideon built an altar there and named it "The Altar of Peace with Jehovah." (The altar is still there in Ophrah in the land of the Abiezrites.) 25That night the Lord told Gideon to hitch his father's best ox to the family altar of Baal, and pull it down, and to cut down the wooden idol of the goddess Asherah that stood nearby.

26"Replace it with an altar for the Lord your God, built here on this hill, laying the stones carefully. Then sacrifice the ox as a burnt offering to the Lord, using the wooden idol as wood for the fire on the altar."

27So Gideon took ten of his servants and did as the Lord had commanded. But he did it at night for fear of the other members of his father's household, and for fear of the men of the city; for he knew what would happen if they found out who did it! 28Early the next morning, as the city began to stir, someone discovered that the altar of Baal was knocked apart, the idol beside it was gone, and a new altar had been built instead, with the remains of a sacrifice on it.

29"Who did this?" everyone demanded. Finally they learned that it was Gideon, the son of Joash.

30"Bring out your son," they shouted to Joash. "He must die for insulting the altar of Baal, and for cutting down the Asherah idol."

31But Joash retorted to the whole mob, "Does Baal need *your* help? What an insult to a god! You are the ones who should die for insulting Baal! If Baal is really a god, let him take care of himself and destroy the one who broke apart his altar!"

32From then on Gideon was called "Jerubbaal," a nickname meaning "Let Baal take care of himself!"

33Soon afterward the armies of Midian, Amalek, and other neighboring nations united in one vast alliance against Israel. They crossed the Jordan and camped in the valley of Jezreel. 34Then the Spirit of the Lord came upon Gideon, and he blew a trumpet as a call to arms, and the men of Abiezer came to him. 35He also sent messengers throughout Manasseh, Asher, Zebulun, and Naphtali, summoning their fighting forces, and all of them responded.

36Then Gideon said to God, "If you are really going to use me to save Israel as you promised, 37prove it to me in this way: I'll put some wool on the threshing floor tonight, and if, in the morning, the fleece is wet and the ground is dry, I will know you are going to help me!"

38And it happened just that way! When he got up the next morning he pressed the fleece together and wrung out a whole bowlful of water!

39Then Gideon said to the Lord, "Please don't be angry with me, but let me make one more test: this time let the fleece remain dry while the ground around it is wet!"

40So the Lord did as he asked; that night the fleece stayed dry, but the ground was covered with dew!

LUKE 22:55—23:10

THE soldiers lit a fire in the courtyard and sat around it for warmth, and Peter joined them there.

56A servant girl noticed him in the firelight and began staring at him. Finally she spoke: "This man was with Jesus!"

57Peter denied it. "Woman," he said, "I don't even know the man!"

58After a while someone else looked at him and said, "You must be one of them!"

"No sir, I am not!" Peter replied.

59About an hour later someone else flatly stated, "I know this fellow is one of Jesus' disciples, for both are from Galilee."

60But Peter said, "Man, I don't know what you are talking about." And as he said the words, a rooster crowed.

61At that moment Jesus turned and looked at Peter. Then Peter remembered what he had said—"Before the rooster crows tomorrow morning, you will deny me three times." 62And Peter walked out of the courtyard, crying bitterly.

63,64Now the guards in charge of Jesus began mocking him. They blindfolded him and hit him with their fists and asked, "Who hit you that time, prophet?" 65And they threw all sorts of other insults at him.

66Early the next morning at daybreak the Jewish Supreme Court assembled, including the chief priests and all the top religious authorities of the nation. Jesus was led before this Council, 67,68and instructed to state whether or not he claimed to be the Messiah.

But he replied, "If I tell you, you won't believe me or let me present my case. 69But the time is soon coming when I, the Messiah, shall be enthroned beside Almighty God."

70They all shouted, "Then you claim you are the Son of God?"

And he replied, "Yes, I am."

71"What need do we have for other witnesses?" they shouted. "For we ourselves have heard him say it."

THEN the entire Council took Jesus over to Pilate, the governor. 2They began at once accusing him: "This fellow has been leading our people to ruin by telling them not to pay their taxes to the Roman government and by claiming he is our Messiah—a King."

3So Pilate asked him, "Are you their Messiah—their King?"

"Yes," Jesus replied, "it is as you say."

4Then Pilate turned to the chief priests and to the mob and said, "So? That isn't a crime!"

5Then they became desperate. "But he is causing riots against the government everywhere he goes, all over Judea, from Galilee to Jerusalem!"

6"Is he then a Galilean?" Pilate asked.

7When they told him yes, Pilate said to take him to King Herod, for Galilee was under Herod's jurisdiction; and Herod happened to be in Jerusalem at the time. 8Herod was delighted at the opportunity to see Jesus, for he had heard a lot about him and had been hoping to see him perform a miracle.

9He asked Jesus question after question, but there was no reply. 10Meanwhile, the chief priests and the other religious leaders stood there shouting their accusations.

PSALM 95:1—96:13

OH, come, let us sing to the Lord! Give a joyous shout in honor of the Rock of our salvation! 2Come before him with thankful hearts. Let us sing him psalms of praise. 3For the Lord is a great God, the great King of all gods. 4He controls the formation of the depths of the earth and the mightiest mountains; all are his. 5He made the sea and formed the land; they too are his. 6Come, kneel before the Lord our Maker, 7for he is our God. We are his sheep and he is our Shepherd. Oh, that you would hear him calling you today and come to him!

8Don't harden your hearts as Israel did in the wilderness at Meribah and Massah. 9For there your fathers doubted me, though they had seen so many of my miracles before. My patience was severely tried by their complaints. 10"For forty years I watched them in disgust," the Lord God says. "They were a nation whose thoughts and heart were far away from me. They refused to accept my laws. 11Therefore in mighty wrath I swore that they would never enter the Promised Land, the place of rest I planned for them."

SING a new song to the Lord! Sing it everywhere around the world! 2Sing out his praises! Bless his name. Each day tell someone that he saves.

3Publish his glorious acts throughout the earth. Tell everyone about the amazing things he does. 4For the Lord is great beyond description, and greatly to be praised. Worship only him among the gods! 5For the gods of other nations are merely idols, but our God made the heavens! 6Honor and majesty surround him; strength and beauty are in his Temple.

7O nations of the world, confess that God alone is glorious and strong. 8Give him the glory he deserves! Bring your offering and come to worship him. 9Worship the Lord with the beauty of holy lives. Let the earth tremble before him. 10Tell the nations that Jehovah reigns! He rules the world. His power can never be overthrown. He will judge all nations fairly.

11Let the heavens be glad, the earth rejoice; let the vastness of the roaring seas demonstrate his glory. 12Praise him for the growing fields, for they display his greatness. Let the trees of the forest rustle with praise. 13For the Lord is coming to judge the earth; he will judge the nations fairly and with truth!

PROVERBS FOR TODAY/ 14:5–6

A truthful witness never lies; a false witness always lies. A mocker never finds the wisdom he claims he is looking for, yet it comes easily to the man with common sense.

APRIL 27

JUDGES 7:1—8:16

JERUBBAAL (that is, Gideon—his other name) and his army got an early start and went as far as the spring of Harod. The armies of Midian were camped north of them, down in the valley beside the hill of Moreh.

2The Lord then said to Gideon, "There are too many of you! I can't let all of you fight the Midianites, for then the people of Israel will boast to me that they saved themselves by their own strength! 3Send home any of your men who are timid and frightened."

So twenty-two thousand of them left, and only ten thousand remained who were willing to fight.

4But the Lord told Gideon, "There are

still too many! Bring them down to the spring and I'll show you which ones shall go with you and which ones shall not."

5,6So Gideon assembled them at the water. There the Lord told him, "Divide them into two groups decided by the way they drink. In Group 1 will be all the men who cup the water in their hands to get it to their mouths and lap it like dogs. In Group 2 will be those who kneel, with their mouths in the stream."

Only three hundred of the men drank from their hands; all the others drank with their mouths to the stream.

7"I'll conquer the Midianites with these three hundred!" the Lord told Gideon. "Send all the others home!"

8,9So after Gideon had collected all the clay jars and trumpets they had among them, he sent them home, leaving only three hundred men with him.

During the night, with the Midianites camped in the valley just below, the Lord said to Gideon, "Get up! Take your troops and attack the Midianites, for I will cause you to defeat them! 10But if you are afraid, first go down to the camp alone—take along your servant Purah if you like— 11and listen to what they are saying down there! You will be greatly encouraged and be eager to attack!"

So he took Purah and crept down through the darkness to the outposts of the enemy camp. 12,13The vast armies of Midian, Amalek, and the other nations of the Mideast were crowded across the valley like locusts—yes, like the sand upon the seashore—and there were too many camels even to count! Gideon crept up to one of the tents just as a man inside had wakened from a nightmare and was telling his tent-mate about it.

"I had this strange dream," he was saying, "and there was this huge loaf of barley bread that came tumbling down into our camp. It hit our tent and knocked it flat!"

14The other soldier replied, "Your dream can mean only one thing! Gideon, the son of Joash, the Israeli, is going to come and massacre all the allied forces of Midian!"

15When Gideon heard the dream and the interpretation, all he could do was just stand there worshiping God! Then he returned to his men and shouted, "Get up! For the Lord is going to use you to conquer all the vast armies of Midian!"

16He divided the three hundred men into three groups and gave each man a trumpet and a clay jar with a torch in it. 17Then he explained his plan.

"When we arrive at the outer guard-posts of the camp," he told them, "do just as I do. 18As soon as I and the men in my group blow our trumpets, you blow yours on all sides of the camp and shout, 'We fight for God and for Gideon!'"

19,20It was just after midnight and the change of guards when Gideon and the hundred men with him crept to the outer edge of the camp of Midian.

Suddenly they blew their trumpets and broke their clay jars so that their torches blazed into the night. Then the other two hundred of his men did the same, blowing the trumpets in their right hands, and holding the flaming torches in their left hands, all shouting, "For the Lord and for Gideon!"

21Then they just stood and watched as the whole vast enemy army began rushing around in a panic, shouting and running away. 22For in the confusion the Lord caused the enemy troops to begin fighting and killing each other from one end of the camp to the other, and they fled into the night to places as far away as Beth-shittah near Zererah, and to the border of Abel-meholah near Tabbath.

23Then Gideon sent for the troops of Naphtali, Asher, and Manasseh and told them to come and chase and destroy the fleeing army of Midian. 24Gideon also sent messengers throughout the hill country of Ephraim summoning troops who seized the fords of the Jordan River at Beth-barah, thus preventing the Midianites from escaping by going across. 25Oreb and Zeeb, the two generals of Midian, were captured. Oreb was killed at the rock now known by his name, and Zeeb at the winepress of Zeeb, as it is now called; and the Israelis took the heads of Oreb and Zeeb across the Jordan to Gideon.

BUT the tribal leaders of Ephraim were violently angry with Gideon.

"Why didn't you send for us when you first went out to fight the Midianites?" they demanded.

2,3But Gideon replied, "God let you capture Oreb and Zeeb, the generals of the army of Midian. What have I done in comparison with that? Your actions at the end of the battle were more important than ours at the beginning!" So they calmed down.

4Gideon now crossed the Jordan River with his three hundred men. They were very tired, but still chasing the enemy. 5He asked the men of Succoth for food. "We are weary from chasing after Zebah and Zalmunna, the kings of Midian," he said.

6But the leaders of Succoth replied, "You haven't caught them yet! If we feed you and you fail, they'll return and destroy us."

7Then Gideon warned them, "When the Lord has delivered them to us, I will return and tear your flesh with the thorns and briars of the wilderness."

8Then he went up to Penuel and asked for food there, but got the same answer. 9And he said to them also, "When this is all over, I will return and break down this tower."

10By this time King Zebah and King Zalmunna with a remnant of fifteen thousand troops were in Karkor. That was all that was left of the allied armies of the east; for one hundred twenty thousand had already been killed. 11Then Gideon circled around by the caravan route east of Nobah and Jogbehah, striking at the Midianite army in surprise raids. 12The two kings fled, but Gideon chased and captured them, routing their entire force. 13Later, Gideon returned by way of Heres Pass. 14There he captured a young fellow from Succoth and demanded that he write down the names of all the seventy-seven political and religious leaders of the city.

15He then returned to Succoth. "You taunted me that I would never catch King Zebah and King Zalmunna, and you refused to give us food when we were tired and hungry," he said. "Well, here they are!"

16Then he took the leaders of the city and scraped them to death with wild thorns and briars.

LUKE 23:11–43

NOW Herod and his soldiers began mocking and ridiculing Jesus; and putting a kingly robe on him, they sent him back to Pilate. 12That day Herod and Pilate—enemies before—became fast friends.

13Then Pilate called together the chief priests and other Jewish leaders, along with the people, 14and announced his verdict:

"You brought this man to me, accusing him of leading a revolt against the Roman government. I have examined him thoroughly on this point and find him innocent. 15Herod came to the same conclusion and sent him back to us—nothing this man has done calls for the death penalty. 16I will therefore have him scourged with leaded thongs, and release him."

17,18But now a mighty roar rose from the crowd as with one voice they shouted. "Kill him, and release Barabbas to us!" 19(Barabbas was in prison for starting an insurrection in Jerusalem against the government, and for murder.) 20Pilate argued with them, for he wanted to release Jesus. 21But they shouted, "Crucify him! Crucify him!"

22Once more, for the third time, he demanded, "Why? What crime has he committed? I have found no reason to sentence him to death. I will therefore scourge him and let him go." 23But they shouted louder and louder for Jesus' death, and their voices prevailed.

24So Pilate sentenced Jesus to die as they demanded. 25And he released Barabbas, the man in prison for insurrection and murder, at their request. But he delivered Jesus over to them to do with as they would.

26As the crowd led Jesus away to his death, Simon of Cyrene, who was just coming into Jerusalem from the country, was forced to follow, carrying Jesus' cross. 27Great crowds trailed along behind, and many grief-stricken women.

28But Jesus turned and said to them, "Daughters of Jerusalem, don't weep for me, but for yourselves and for your children. 29For the days are coming when the women who have no children will be counted fortunate indeed. 30Mankind will beg the mountains to fall on them and crush them, and the hills to bury them. 31For if such things as this are done to me, the Living Tree, what will they do to you?"

32,33Two others, criminals, were led out to be executed with him at a place called "The Skull." There all three were crucified—Jesus on the center cross, and the two criminals on either side.

34"Father, forgive these people," Jesus said, "for they don't know what they are doing."

And the soldiers gambled for his clothing, throwing dice for each piece. 35The crowd watched. And the Jewish leaders laughed and scoffed. "He was so good at helping others," they said, "let's see him save himself if he is really God's Chosen One, the Messiah."

36The soldiers mocked him, too, by offering him a drink—of sour wine. 37And they called to him, "If you are the King of the Jews, save yourself!"

38A signboard was nailed to the cross above him with these words: "This is the King of the Jews."

39One of the criminals hanging beside him scoffed, "So you're the Messiah, are you? Prove it by saving yourself—and us, too, while you're at it!"

40,41But the other criminal protested. "Don't you even fear God when you are dying? We deserve to die for our evil deeds, but this man hasn't done one thing wrong." 42Then he said, "Jesus, remember me when you come into your Kingdom."

43And Jesus replied, "Today you will be with me in Paradise. This is a solemn promise."

PSALM 97:1—98:9

JEHOVAH is King! Let all the earth rejoice! Tell the farthest islands to be glad.

2Clouds and darkness surround him. Righteousness and justice are the foundation of his throne. 3Fire goes forth before him and burns up all his foes. 4His lightning flashes out across the world. The earth sees and trembles. 5The mountains melt like wax before the Lord of all the earth. 6The heavens declare his perfect righteousness; every nation sees his glory.

7Let those who worship idols be disgraced—all who brag about their worthless gods—for every god must bow to him! 8,9Jerusalem and all the cities of Judah have heard of your justice, Lord, and are glad that you reign in majesty over the entire earth and are far greater than these other gods.

10The Lord loves those who hate evil; he protects the lives of his people, and rescues them from the wicked. 11Light is sown for the godly and joy for the good. 12May all who are godly be happy in the Lord and crown him, our holy God.

SING a new song to the Lord telling about his mighty deeds! For he has won a mighty victory by his power and holiness. 2,3He has announced this victory and revealed it to every nation by fulfilling his promise to be kind to Israel. The whole earth has seen God's salvation of his people. 4That is why the earth breaks out in praise to God, and sings for utter joy!

5Sing your praise accompanied by music from the harp. 6Let the cornets and trumpets shout! Make a joyful symphony before the Lord, the King! 7Let the sea in all its vastness roar with praise! Let the earth and all those living on it shout, "Glory to the Lord."

PROVERBS FOR TODAY/ 14:7–8

If you are looking for advice, stay away from fools. The wise man looks ahead. The fool attempts to fool himself and won't face facts.

APRIL 28

JUDGES 8:17—9:21

HE also went to Penuel and knocked down the city tower and killed the entire male population.

18Then Gideon asked King Zebah and King Zalmunna, "The men you killed at Tabor—what were they like?"

They replied, "They were dressed just like you—like sons of kings!"

19"They must have been my brothers!" Gideon exclaimed. "I swear that if you hadn't killed them I wouldn't kill you."

20Then, turning to Jether, his oldest son, he instructed him to kill them. But the boy was only a lad and was afraid to.

21Then Zebah and Zalmunna said to Gideon, "You do it; we'd rather be killed by a man!" So Gideon killed them and took the ornaments from their camels' necks.

22Now the men of Israel said to Gideon, "Be our king! You and your sons and all your descendants shall be our rulers, for you have saved us from Midian."

23,24But Gideon replied, "I will not be your king, nor shall my son; the Lord is your King! However, I have one request. Give me all the earrings collected from your fallen foes,"—for the troops of Midian, being Ishmaelites, all wore gold earrings.

25"Gladly!" they replied, and spread out a sheet for everyone to throw in the gold earrings he had gathered. 26Their value was estimated at $25,000, not in-cluding the crescents and pendants or the royal clothing of the kings, or the chains around the camels' necks. 27Gideon made an ephod from the gold and put it in Ophrah, his home town. But all Israel soon began worshiping it, so it became an evil deed that Gideon and his family did.

28That is the true account of how Midian was subdued by Israel. Midian never recovered, and the land was at peace for forty years—all during Gideon's lifetime. 29He returned home, 30and eventually had seventy sons, for he married many wives. 31He also had a concubine in Shechem, who presented him with a son named Abimelech. 32Gideon finally died, an old, old man, and was buried in the sepulcher of his father Joash in Ophrah, in the land of the Abiezrites.

33But as soon as Gideon was dead, the Israelis began to worship the idols Baal and Baal-berith. 34They no longer considered the Lord as their God, though he had rescued them from all their enemies on every side. 35Nor did they show any kindness to the family of Gideon despite all he had done for them.

ONE day Gideon's son Abimelech visited his uncles—his mother's brothers—in Shechem.

2"Go and talk to the leaders of Shechem," he requested, "and ask them whether they want to be ruled by seventy kings—Gideon's seventy sons—or by one man—meaning me, your own flesh and blood!"

3So his uncles went to the leaders of the city and proposed Abimelech's scheme; and they decided that since his mother was a native of their town they would go along with it. 4They gave him money from the temple offerings of the idol Baal-berith, which he used to hire some worthless loafers who agreed to do whatever he told them to. 5He took them to his father's home at Ophrah and there, upon one stone, they slaughtered all seventy of his half-brothers, except for the youngest, Jotham, who escaped and hid. 6Then the citizens of Shechem and Beth-millo called a meeting under the oak beside the garrison at Shechem, and Abimelech was acclaimed king of Israel.

7When Jotham heard about this, he stood at the top of Mount Gerizim and shouted across to the men of Shechem, "If you want God's blessing, listen to me! 8Once upon a time the trees decided to elect a king. First they asked the olive tree, 9but it refused.

" 'Should I quit producing the olive oil that blesses God and man, just to wave to and fro over the other trees?' it asked.

10"Then they said to the fig tree, 'You be our king!'

11"But the fig tree also refused. 'Should I quit producing sweetness and fruit just to lift my head above all the other trees?' it asked.

12"Then they said to the grapevine, 'You reign over us!'

13"But the grapevine replied, 'Shall I quit producing the wine that cheers both God and man, just to be mightier than all the other trees?'

14"Then all the trees finally turned to the thorn bush. 'You be our king!' they explained.

15"And the thorn bush replied, 'If you really want me, come and humble yourselves beneath my shade! If you refuse, let fire flame forth from me and burn down the great cedars of Lebanon!'

16"Now make sure that you have done the right thing in making Abimelech your king, that you have done right by Gideon and all of his descendants. 17For my father fought for you and risked his life and delivered you from the Midianites, 18yet you have revolted against him and killed his seventy sons upon one stone. And now you have chosen his slave girl's son, Abimelech, to be your king just because he is your relative. 19If you are sure that you have done right by Gideon and his descendants, then may you and Abimelech have a long and happy life together. 20But if you have not been fair to Gideon, then may Abimelech destroy the citizens of Shechem and Beth-millo; and may they destroy Abimelech!"

21Then Jotham escaped and lived in Beer for fear of his brother Abimelech.

LUKE 23:44—24:12

BY now it was noon, and darkness fell across the whole land for three hours, until three o'clock. 45The light from the sun was gone—and suddenly the thick veil hanging in the Temple split apart.

46Then Jesus shouted, "Father, I commit my spirit to you," and with those words he died.

47When the captain of the Roman military unit handling the executions saw what had happened, he was stricken with awe before God and said, "Surely this man was innocent."

48And when the crowd that came to see the crucifixion saw that Jesus was dead they went home in deep sorrow. 49Meanwhile, Jesus' friends, including the women who had followed him down from Galilee, stood in the distance watching.

50,51,52Then a man named Joseph, a member of the Jewish Supreme Court, from the city of Arimathea in Judea, went to Pilate and asked for the body of Jesus. He was a godly man who had been expecting the Messiah's coming and had not agreed with the decision and actions of the other Jewish leaders. 53So he took down Jesus' body and wrapped it in a long linen cloth and laid it in a new, unused tomb hewn into the rock [at the side of a hill]. 54This was done late on Friday afternoon, the day of preparation for the Sabbath.

55As the body was taken away, the women from Galilee followed and saw it carried into the tomb. 56Then they went home and prepared spices and ointments to embalm him; but by the time they were finished it was the Sabbath, so they rested all that day as required by the Jewish law.

BUT very early on Sunday morning they took the ointments to the tomb— 2and found that the huge stone covering the entrance had been rolled aside. 3So they went in—but the Lord Jesus' body was gone.

4They stood there puzzled, trying to think what could have happened to it. Suddenly two men appeared before them, clothed in shining robes so bright their eyes were dazzled. 5The women were terrified and bowed low before them.

Then the men asked, "Why are you looking in a tomb for someone who is alive? 6,7He isn't here! He has come back to life again! Don't you remember what he told you back in Galilee—that the Messiah must be betrayed into the power of evil men and be crucified and that he would rise again the third day?"

8Then they remembered, 9and rushed back to Jerusalem to tell his eleven disciples—and everyone else—what had happened. 10(The women who went to the tomb were Mary Magdalene and Joanna and Mary the mother of James, and several others.) 11But the story sounded like a fairy tale to the men—they didn't believe it.

12However, Peter ran to the tomb to look. Stooping, he peered in and saw the empty linen wrappings; and then he went back home again, wondering what had happened.

PSALM 99:1–9

JEHOVAH is King! Let the nations tremble! He is enthroned between the Guardian Angels. Let the whole earth shake.

2Jehovah sits in majesty in Zion, supreme above all rulers of the earth. 3Let them reverence your great and holy name.

4This mighty King is determined to give justice. Fairness is the touchstone of everything he does. He gives justice throughout Israel. 5Exalt the Lord our holy God! Bow low before his feet.

6When Moses and Aaron and Samuel, his prophet, cried to him for help, he answered them. 7He spoke to them from the pillar of cloud and they followed his instructions. 8O Jehovah our God! You answered them and forgave their sins, yet punished them when they went wrong.

9Exalt the Lord our God, and worship at his holy mountain in Jerusalem, for he is holy.

PROVERBS FOR TODAY/ 14:9–10

The common bond of rebels is their guilt. The common bond of godly people is good will. Only the person involved can know his own bitterness or joy—no one else can really share it.

APRIL 29

JUDGES 9:22—10:18

THREE years later God stirred up trouble between King Abimelech and the citizens of Shechem, and they revolted. 24In the events that followed, both Abimelech and the citizens of Shechem who aided him in butchering Gideon's seventy sons were given their just punishment for these murders. 25For the men of Shechem set an ambush for Abimelech along the trail at the top of the mountain. (While they were waiting for him to come along, they robbed everyone else who passed that way.) But someone warned Abimelech about their plot.

26At that time Gaal (the son of Ebed) moved to Shechem with his brothers, and he became one of the leading citizens. 27During the harvest feast at Shechem that year, held in the temple of the local god, the wine flowed freely and everyone began cursing Abimelech.

28"Who is Abimelech," Gaal shouted, "and why should he be our king? Why should we be his servants? He and his friend Zebul should be *our* servants. Down with Abimelech! 29Make me your king and you'll soon see what happens to Abimelech! I'll tell Abimelech, 'Get up an army and come on out and fight!'"

30But when Zebul, the mayor of the city, heard what Gaal was saying, he was furious. 31He sent messengers to Abimelech in Arumah telling him, "Gaal, son of Ebed, and his relatives have come to live in Shechem, and now they are arousing the city to rebellion against you. 32Come by night with an army and hide out in the fields; 33and in the morning, as soon as it is daylight, storm the city. When he and those who are with him come out against you, you can do with them as you wish!"

34So Abimelech and his men marched through the night and split into four groups, stationing themselves around the city. 35The next morning as Gaal sat at the city gates, discussing various issues with the local leaders, Abimelech and his men began their march upon the city.

36When Gaal saw them, he exclaimed to Zebul, "Look over at that mountain! Doesn't it look like people coming down?"

"No!" Zebul said. "You're just seeing shadows that look like men!"

37"No, look over there," Gaal said. "I'm sure I see people coming towards us. And look! There are others coming along the road past the oak of Meonenim!"

38Then Zebul turned on him triumphantly. "Now where is that big mouth of yours?" he demanded. "Who was it who said, 'Who is Abimelech, and why should he be our king?' The men you taunted and cursed are right outside the city! Go on out and fight!"

39So Gaal led the men of Shechem into the battle and fought with Abimelech, 40but was defeated, and many of the men of Shechem were left wounded all the way to the city gate. 41Abimelech was living at Arumah at this time, and Zebul drove Gaal and his relatives out of Shechem, and wouldn't let them live there any longer.

42The next day the men of Shechem went out to battle again. However, someone had told Abimelech about their plans, 43so he had divided his men into three groups hiding in the fields. And when the men of the city went out to attack, he and his men jumped up from their hiding places and began killing them. 44Abimelech stormed the city gate to keep the men of Shechem from getting back in, while his other two groups cut them down in the fields. 45The battle went on all day before Abimelech finally captured the city, killed its people, and leveled it to the ground. 46The people at the nearby town of Migdal saw what was happening and took refuge in the fort next to the temple of Baal-berith.

47,48When Abimelech learned of this, he led his forces to Mount Zalmon where he began chopping a bundle of firewood, and placed it upon his shoulder. "Do as I have done," he told his men. 49So each of them quickly cut a bundle and carried it back to the town where, following Abimelech's example, the bundles were piled against the walls of the fort and set on fire. So all the people inside died, about a thousand men and women.

50Abimelech next attacked the city of Thebez, and captured it. 51However, there was a fort inside the city and the entire population fled into it, barricaded the gates, and climbed to the top of the roof to watch. 52But as Abimelech was preparing to burn it, 53a woman on the roof threw down a millstone. It landed on Abimelech's head, crushing his skull.

54"Kill me!" he groaned to his youthful armor bearer. "Never let it be said that a woman killed Abimelech!"

So the young man pierced him with his sword, and he died. 55When his men saw that he was dead, they disbanded and returned to their homes. 56,57Thus God punished both Abimelech and the men of Shechem for their sin of murdering Gideon's seventy sons. So the curse of Jotham, Gideon's son, came true.

AFTER Abimelech's death, the next judge of Israel was Tola (son of Puah and grandson of Dodo). He was from the tribe of Issachar, but lived in the city of Shamir in the hill country of Ephraim. 2He was Israel's judge for twenty-three years. When he died, he was buried in Shamir, 3and was succeeded by Jair, a man from Gilead, who judged Israel for twenty-two years. 4His thirty sons rode around together on thirty donkeys, and they owned thirty cities in the land of Gilead which are still called "The Cities of Jair." 5When Jair died he was buried in Kamon.

6Then the people of Israel turned away from the Lord again, and worshiped the heathen gods Baal and Ashtaroth, and the gods of Syria, Sidon, Moab, Ammon and Philistia. Not only this, but they no longer worshiped Jehovah at all. 7,8This made Jehovah very angry with his people, so he immediately permitted the Philistines and the Ammonites to begin tormenting them. These attacks took place east of the Jordan River in the land of the Amorites (that is, in Gilead), 9and also in Judah, Benjamin, and Ephraim. For the Ammonites crossed the Jordan to attack the Israelis. This went on for eighteen years. 10Finally the Israelis turned to Jehovah again and begged him to save them.

"We have sinned against you and have forsaken you as our God and have worshiped idols," they confessed.

11But the Lord replied, "Didn't I save you from the Egyptians, the Amorites, the Ammonites, the Philistines, 12the Sidonians, the Amalekites, and the Maonites? Has there ever been a time when you cried out to me that I haven't rescued you? 13Yet you continue to abandon me and to worship other gods. So go away; I won't save you any more. 14Go and cry to the new gods you have chosen! Let them save you in your hour of distress!"

15But they pleaded with him again and said, "We have sinned. Punish us in any way you think best, only save us once more from our enemies."

16Then they destroyed their foreign gods and worshiped only the Lord; and he was grieved by their misery. 17The armies of Ammon were mobilized in Gilead at that time, preparing to attack Israel's army at Mizpah.

18"Who will lead our forces against the Ammonites?" the leaders of Gilead asked each other. "Whoever volunteers shall be our king!"

LUKE 24:13–53

THAT same day, Sunday, two of Jesus' followers were walking to the village of Emmaus, seven miles out of Jerusalem. 14As they walked along they were talking of Jesus' death, 15when suddenly Jesus himself came along and joined them and began walking beside them. 16But they didn't recognize him, for God kept them from it.

17"You seem to be in a deep discussion about something," he said. "What are you so concerned about?" They stopped short, sadness written across their faces. 18And one of them, Cleopas, replied, "You must be the only person in Jerusalem who hasn't heard about the terrible things that happened there last week."

19"What things?" Jesus asked.

"The things that happened to Jesus, the Man from Nazareth," they said. "He was a Prophet who did incredible miracles and was a mighty Teacher, highly regarded by both God and man. 20But the chief priests and our religious leaders arrested him and handed him over to the Roman government to be condemned to death, and they crucified him. 21We had thought he was the glorious Messiah and that he had come to rescue Israel.

"And now, besides all this—which happened three days ago— 22,23some women from our group of his followers were at his tomb early this morning and came back with an amazing report that his body was missing, and that they had seen some angels there who told them Jesus is alive! 24Some of our men ran out to see, and sure enough, Jesus' body was gone, just as the women had said."

25Then Jesus said to them, "You are such foolish, foolish people! You find it so hard to believe all that the prophets wrote in the Scriptures! 26Wasn't it clearly predicted by the prophets that the Messiah would have to suffer all these things before entering his time of glory?"

27Then Jesus quoted them passage after passage from the writings of the prophets, beginning with the book of Genesis and going right on through the Scriptures, explaining what the passages meant and what they said about himself.

28By this time they were nearing Emmaus and the end of their journey. Jesus would have gone on, 29but they begged him to stay the night with them, as it was getting late. So he went home with them. 30As they sat down to eat, he asked God's blessing on the food and then took a small loaf of bread and broke it and was passing it over to them, 31when suddenly—it was though their eyes were opened—they recognized him! And at that moment he disappeared!

32They began telling each other how their hearts had felt strangely warm as he talked with them and explained the Scriptures during the walk down the road. 33,34Within the hour they were on their way back to Jerusalem, where the eleven disciples and the other followers of Jesus greeted them with these words, "The Lord has really risen! He appeared to Peter!"

35Then the two from Emmaus told their story of how Jesus had appeared to them as they were walking along the road and how they had recognized him as he was breaking the bread.

36And just as they were telling about it, Jesus himself was suddenly standing there among them, and greeted them. 37But the whole group was terribly frightened, thinking they were seeing a ghost!

38"Why are you frightened?" he asked. "Why do you doubt that it is really I? 39Look at my hands! Look at my feet! You can see that it is I, myself! Touch me and make sure that I am not a ghost! For ghosts don't have bodies, as you see that I do!" 40As he spoke, he held out his hands for them to see [the marks of the nails], and showed them [the wounds in] his feet.

41Still they stood there undecided, filled with joy and doubt.

Then he asked them, "Do you have anything here to eat?"

42They gave him a piece of broiled fish, 43and he ate it as they watched!

44Then he said, "When I was with you before, don't you remember my telling you that everything written about me by Moses and the prophets and in the Psalms must all come true?" 45Then he opened their minds to understand at last these many Scriptures! 46And he said, "Yes, it was written long ago that the

Messiah must suffer and die and rise again from the dead on the third day; [47]and that this message of salvation should be taken from Jerusalem to all the nations: *There is forgiveness of sins for all who turn to me.* [48]You have seen these prophecies come true.

[49]"And now I will send the Holy Spirit upon you, just as my Father promised. Don't begin telling others yet—stay here in the city until the Holy Spirit comes and fills you with power from heaven."

[50]Then Jesus led them out along the road to Bethany, and lifting his hands to heaven, he blessed them, [51]and then began rising into the sky, and went on to heaven. [52]And they worshiped him, and returned to Jerusalem filled with mighty joy, [53]and were continually in the Temple, praising God.

PSALM 100:1–5

SHOUT with joy before the Lord, O earth! [2]Obey him gladly; come before him, singing with joy.

[3]Try to realize what this means—the Lord is God! He made us—we are his people, the sheep of his pasture.

[4]Go through his open gates with great thanksgiving; enter his courts with praise. Give thanks to him and bless his name. [5]For the Lord is always good. He is always loving and kind, and his faithfulness goes on and on to each succeeding generation.

PROVERBS FOR TODAY/ 14:11–12

The work of the wicked will perish; the work of the godly will flourish. Before every man there lies a wide and pleasant road that seems right but ends in death.

APRIL 30

JUDGES 11:1—12:15

NOW Jephthah was a great warrior from the land of Gilead, but his mother was a prostitute. His father (whose name was Gilead) had several other sons by his legitimate wife, and when these half brothers grew up, they chased Jephthah out of the country.

"You son of a whore!" they said. "You'll not get any of our father's estate."

[3]So Jephthah fled from his father's home and lived in the land of Tob. Soon he had quite a band of malcontents as his followers, living off the land as bandits. [4]It was about this time that the Ammonites began their war against Israel. [5]The leaders of Gilead sent for Jephthah, [6]begging him to come and lead their army against the Ammonites.

[7]But Jephthah said to them, "Why do you come to me when you hate me and have driven me out of my father's house? Why come now when you're in trouble?"

[8]"Because we need you," they replied. "If you will be our commander-in-chief against the Ammonites, we will make you the king of Gilead."

[9]"Sure!" Jephthah exclaimed. "Do you expect me to believe that?"

[10]"We swear it," they replied. "We promise with a solemn oath."

[11]So Jephthah accepted the commission and was made commander-in-chief and king. The contract was ratified before the Lord in Mizpah at a general assembly of all the people. [12]Then Jephthah sent messengers to the king of Ammon, demanding to know why Israel was being attacked. [13]The king of Ammon replied

that the land belonged to the people of Ammon; it had been stolen from them, he said, when the Israelis came from Egypt; the whole territory from the Arnon River to the Jabbok and the Jordan was his, he claimed.

"Give us back our land peaceably," he demanded.

14,15Jephthah replied, "Israel did not steal the land. 16What happened was this: When the people of Israel arrived at Kadesh, on their journey from Egypt after crossing the Red Sea, 17they sent a message to the king of Edom asking permission to pass through his land. But their petition was denied. Then they asked the king of Moab for similar permission. It was the same story there, so the people of Israel stayed in Kadesh.

18"Finally they went around Edom and Moab through the wilderness, and traveled along the eastern border until at last they arrived beyond the boundary of Moab at the Arnon River; but they never once crossed into Moab. 19Then Israel sent messengers to King Sihon of the Amorites, who lived in Heshbon, and asked permission to cross through his land to get to their destination.

20"But King Sihon didn't trust Israel, so he mobilized an army at Jahaz and attacked them. 21,22But the Lord our God helped Israel defeat King Sihon and all your people, so Israel took over all of your land from the Arnon River to the Jabbok, and from the wilderness to the Jordan River.

23"So you see, it was the Lord God of Israel who took away the land from the Amorites and gave it to Israel. Why, then, should we return it to you? 24You keep whatever your god Chemosh gives you, and we will keep whatever Jehovah our God gives us! 25And besides, just who do you think you are? Are you better than King Balak, the king of Moab? Did he try to recover his land after Israel defeated him? No, of course not. 26But now after three hundred years you make an issue of this! Israel has been living here for all that time, spread across the land from Heshbon to Aroer, and all along the Arnon River. Why have you made no effort to recover it before now? 27No, I have not sinned against you; rather, you have wronged me by coming to war against me; but Jehovah the Judge will soon show which of us is right—Israel or Ammon."

28But the king of Ammon paid no attention to Jephthah's message.

29At that time the Spirit of the Lord came upon Jephthah and he led his army across the land of Gilead and Manasseh, past Mizpah in Gilead, and attacked the army of Ammon. 30,31Meanwhile Jephthah had vowed to the Lord that if God would help Israel conquer the Ammonites, then when he returned home in peace, the first person coming out of his house to meet him would be sacrificed as a burnt offering to the Lord!

32So Jephthah led his army against the Ammonites, and the Lord gave him the victory. 33He destroyed the Ammonites with a terrible slaughter all the way from Aroer to Minnith, including twenty cities, and as far away as Vineyard Meadow. Thus the Ammonites were subdued by the people of Israel.

34When Jephthah returned home his daughter—his only child—ran out to meet him, playing on a tambourine and dancing for joy. 35When he saw her he tore his clothes in anguish.

"Alas, my daughter!" he cried out. "You have brought me to the dust. For I have made a vow to the Lord and I cannot take it back."

36And she said, "Father, you must do whatever you promised the Lord, for he has given you a great victory over your enemies, the Ammonites. 37But first let me go up into the hills and roam with my girl friends for two months, weeping because I'll never marry."

38"Yes," he said. "Go."

And so she did, bewailing her fate with her friends for two months. 39Then she returned to her father, who did as he had vowed. So she was never married. And after that it became a custom in Israel, 40that the young girls went away for four days each year to lament the fate of Jephthah's daughter.

THEN the tribe of Ephraim mobilized its army at Zaphon and sent this message to Jephthah: "Why didn't you call for us to help you fight against Ammon? We are going to burn down your house, with you in it!"

2"I summoned you, but you refused to come!" Jephthah retorted. "You failed to help us in our time of need, 3so I risked my life and went to battle without you, and the Lord helped me to conquer the enemy. Is that anything for you to fight us about?"

4Then Jephthah, furious at the taunt of Ephraim that the men of Gilead were mere outcasts and the scum of the earth, mobilized his army and attacked the army of Ephraim. 5He captured the fords of the Jordan behind the army of Ephraim, and whenever a fugitive from Ephraim tried to cross the river, the Gilead guards challenged him.

"Are you a member of the tribe of Ephraim?" they asked. If the man replied that he was not, 6then they demanded, "Say 'Shibboleth.' " But if he couldn't pronounce the H and said, "Sibboleth" instead of "Shibboleth," he was dragged away and killed. So forty-two thousand people of Ephraim died there at that time.

7Jephthah was Israel's judge for six years. At his death he was buried in one of the cities of Gilead.

8The next judge was Ibzan, who lived in Bethlehem. 9,10He had thirty sons and thirty daughters. He married his daughters to men outside his clan, and brought in thirty girls to marry his sons. He judged Israel for seven years before he died, and was buried at Bethlehem.

11,12The next judge was Elon from Zebulun. He judged Israel for ten years and was buried at Aijalon in Zebulun.

13Next was Abdon (son of Hillel) from Pirathon. 14He had forty sons and thirty grandsons, who rode on seventy donkeys. He was Israel's judge for eight years. 15Then he died and was buried in Pirathon, in Ephraim, in the hill country of the Amalekites.

JOHN 1:1–28

BEFORE anything else existed, there was Christ, with God. He has always been alive and is himself God. 3He created everything there is—nothing exists that he didn't make. 4Eternal life is in him, and this life gives light to all mankind. 5His life is the light that shines through the darkness—and the darkness can never extinguish it.

6,7God sent John the Baptist as a witness to the fact that Jesus Christ is the true Light. 8John himself was not the Light; he was only a witness to identify it.

9Later on, the one who is the true Light arrived to shine on everyone coming into the world.

10But although he made the world, the world didn't recognize him when he came. 11,12Even in his own land and among his own people, the Jews, he was not accepted. Only a few would welcome and receive him. But to all who received him, he gave the right to become children of God. All they needed to do was to trust him to save them. 13All those who believe this are reborn!—not a physical rebirth resulting from human passion or plan—but from the will of God.

14And Christ became a human being and lived here on earth among us and was full of loving forgiveness and truth. And some of us have seen his glory— the glory of the only Son of the heavenly Father!

15John pointed him out to the people, telling the crowds, "This is the one I was talking about when I said, 'Someone is coming who is greater by far than I am—for he existed long before I did!' " 16We have all benefited from the rich blessings he brought to us—blessing upon blessing heaped upon us! 17For Moses gave us only the Law with its rigid demands and merciless justice, while Jesus Christ brought us loving forgiveness as well. 18No one has ever actually seen

God, but, of course, his only Son has, for he is the companion of the Father and has told us all about him.

19The Jewish leaders sent priests and assistant priests from Jerusalem to ask John whether he claimed to be the Messiah.

20He denied it flatly. "I am not the Christ," he said.

21"Well then, who are you?" they asked. "Are you Elijah?"

"No," he replied.

"Are you the Prophet?"

"No."

22"Then who are you? Tell us, so we can give an answer to those who sent us. What do you have to say for yourself?"

23He replied, "I am a voice from the barren wilderness, shouting as Isaiah prophesied, 'Get ready for the coming of the Lord!'"

24,25Then those who were sent by the Pharisees asked him, "If you aren't the Messiah or Elijah or the Prophet, what right do you have to baptize?"

26John told them, "I merely baptize with water, but right here in the crowd is someone you have never met, 27who will soon begin his ministry among you, and I am not even fit to be his slave."

28This incident took place at Bethany, a village on the other side of the Jordan River where John was baptizing.

PSALM 101:1–8

I will sing about your lovingkindness and your justice, Lord. I will sing your praises!

2I will try to walk a blameless path, but how I need your help, especially in my own home, where I long to act as I should.

3Help me to refuse the low and vulgar things; help me to abhor all crooked deals of every kind, to have no part in them. 4I will reject all selfishness and stay away from every evil. 5I will not tolerate anyone who secretly slanders his neighbors; I will not permit conceit and pride. 6I will make the godly of the land my heroes, and invite them to my home. Only those who are truly good shall be my servants. 7But I will not allow those who deceive and lie to stay in my house. 8My daily task will be to ferret out criminals and free the city of God from their grip.

PROVERBS FOR TODAY/ 14:13–14

Laughter cannot mask a heavy heart. When the laughter ends, the grief remains. The backslider gets bored with himself; the godly man's life is exciting.

MAY 1

JUDGES 13:1—14:20

ONCE again Israel sinned by worshiping other gods, so the Lord let them be conquered by the Philistines, who kept them in subjection for forty years.

2,3Then one day the Angel of the Lord appeared to the wife of Manoah, of the tribe of Dan, who lived in the city of Zorah. She had no children, but the Angel said to her, "Even though you have been barren so long, you will soon conceive and have a son! 4Don't drink any wine or beer, and don't eat any food that isn't kosher. 5Your son's hair must never be cut, for he shall be a Nazirite, a special servant of God from the time of his birth; and he will begin to rescue Israel from the Philistines."

6The woman ran and told her husband,

"A man from God appeared to me and I think he must be the Angel of the Lord, for he was almost too glorious to look at. I didn't ask where he was from, and he didn't tell me his name, 7but he told me, 'You are going to have a baby boy!' And he told me not to drink any wine or beer, and not to eat food that isn't kosher, for the baby is going to be a Nazirite—he will be dedicated to God from the moment of his birth until the day of his death!"

8Then Manoah prayed, "O Lord, please let the man from God come back to us again and give us more instructions about the child you are going to give us." 9The Lord answered his prayer, and the Angel of God appeared once again to his wife as she was sitting in the field. But again she was alone—Manoah was not with her— 10so she quickly ran and found her husband and told him, "The same man is here again!"

11Manoah ran back with his wife and asked, "Are you the man who talked to my wife the other day?"

"Yes," he replied, "I am."

12So Manoah asked him, "Can you give us any special instructions about how we should raise the baby after he is born?"

13,14And the Angel replied, "Be sure that your wife follows the instructions I gave her. She must not eat grapes or raisins, or drink any wine or beer, or eat anything that isn't kosher."

15Then Manoah said to the Angel, "Please stay here until we can get you something to eat."

16"I'll stay," the Angel replied, "but I'll not eat anything. However, if you wish to bring something, bring an offering to sacrifice to the Lord." (Manoah didn't yet realize that he was the Angel of the Lord.)

17Then Manoah asked him for his name. "When all this comes true and the baby is born," he said to the Angel, "we will certainly want to tell everyone that you predicted it!"

18"Don't even ask my name," the Angel replied, "for it is a secret."

19Then Manoah took a young goat and a grain offering and offered it as a sacrifice to the Lord; and the Angel did a strange and wonderful thing, 20for as the flames from the altar were leaping up toward the sky, and as Manoah and his wife watched, the Angel ascended in the fire! Manoah and his wife fell face downward to the ground, 21and that was the last they ever saw of him. It was then that Manoah finally realized that it had been the Angel of the Lord.

22"We will die," Manoah cried out to his wife, "for we have seen God!"

23But his wife said, "If the Lord were going to kill us he wouldn't have accepted our burnt offerings and wouldn't have appeared to us and told us this wonderful thing and done these miracles."

24When her son was born they named him Samson, and the Lord blessed him as he grew up. 25And the Spirit of the Lord began to excite him whenever he visited the parade grounds of the army of the tribe of Dan, located between the cities of Zorah and Eshta-ol.

ONE day when Samson was in Timnah, he noticed a certain Philistine girl, 2and when he got home he told his father and mother that he wanted to marry her. 3They objected strenuously.

"Why don't you marry a Jewish girl?" they asked. "Why must you go and get a wife from these heathen Philistines? Isn't there one girl among all the people of Israel you could marry?"

But Samson told his father, "She is the one I want. Get her for me."

4His father and mother didn't realize that the Lord was behind the request, for God was setting a trap for the Philistines, who at that time were the rulers of Israel.

5As Samson and his parents were going to Timnah, a young lion attacked Samson in the vineyards on the outskirts of the town. 6At that moment the Spirit of the Lord came mightily upon him and since he had no weapon, he ripped the lion's jaws apart, and did it as easily as though it were a young goat! But he didn't tell his father or mother about it.

7Upon arriving at Timnah he talked with the girl and found her to be just what he wanted, so the arrangements were made.

8When he returned for the wedding, he turned off the path to look at the carcass of the lion. And he found a swarm of bees in it, and some honey! 9He took some of the honey with him, eating as he went, and gave some of it to his father and mother. But he didn't tell them where he had gotten it.

10,11As his father was making final arrangements for the marriage, Samson threw a party for thirty young men of the village, as was the custom of the day. 12When Samson asked if they would like to hear a riddle, they replied that they would.

"If you solve my riddle during these seven days of the celebration," he said, "I'll give you thirty plain robes and thirty fancy robes. 13But if you can't solve it, then you must give the robes to me!"

"All right," they agreed, "let's hear it."

14This was his riddle: "Food came out of the eater, and sweetness from the strong!" Three days later they were still trying to figure it out.

15On the fourth day they said to his new wife, "Get the answer from your husband, or we'll burn down your father's house with you in it. Were we invited to this party just to make us poor?"

16So Samson's wife broke down in tears before him and said, "You don't love me at all; you hate me, for you have told a riddle to my people and haven't told me the answer!"

"I haven't even told it to my father or mother; why should I tell you?" he replied.

17So she cried whenever she was with him and kept it up for the remainder of the celebration. At last, on the seventh day, he told her the answer and she, of course, gave the answer to the young men. 18So before sunset of the seventh day they gave him their reply.

"What is sweeter than honey?" they asked, "and what is stronger than a lion?"

"If you hadn't plowed with my heifer, you wouldn't have found the answer to my riddle!" he retorted.

19Then the Spirit of the Lord came upon him and he went to the city of Ashkelon, killed thirty men, took their clothing, and gave it to the young men who had told him the answer to his riddle. But he was furious about it and abandoned his wife and went back home to live with his father and mother. 20So his wife was married instead to the fellow who had been best man at Samson's wedding.

JOHN 1:29–51

THE next day John saw Jesus coming toward him and said, "Look! There is the Lamb of God who takes away the world's sin! 30He is the one I was talking about when I said, 'Soon a man far greater than I am is coming, who existed long before me!' 31I didn't know he was the one, but I am here baptizing with water in order to point him out to the nation of Israel."

32Then John told about seeing the Holy Spirit in the form of a dove descending from heaven and resting upon Jesus.

33"I didn't know he was the one," John said again, "but at the time God sent me to baptize he told me, 'When you see the Holy Spirit descending and resting upon someone—he is the one you are looking for. He is the one who baptizes with the Holy Spirit.' 34I saw it happen to this man, and I therefore testify that he is the Son of God."

35The following day as John was standing with two of his disciples, 36Jesus walked by. John looked at him intently and then declared, "See! There is the Lamb of God!"

37Then John's two disciples turned and followed Jesus.

38Jesus looked around and saw them following. "What do you want?" he asked them.

"Sir," they replied, "where do you live?"

39"Come and see," he said. So they went with him to the place where he was staying and were with him from about four o'clock that afternoon until the evening. 40(One of these men was Andrew, Simon Peter's brother.)

41Andrew then went to find his brother Peter and told him, "We have found the Messiah!" 42And he brought Peter to meet Jesus.

Jesus looked intently at Peter for a moment and then said, "You are Simon, John's son—but you shall be called Peter, the rock!"

43The next day Jesus decided to go to Galilee. He found Philip and told him, "Come with me." 44(Philip was from Bethsaida, Andrew and Peter's home town.)

45Philip now went off to look for Nathanael and told him, "We have found the Messiah!—the very person Moses and the prophets told about! His name is Jesus, the son of Joseph from Nazareth!"

46"Nazareth!" exclaimed Nathanael. "Can anything good come from there?"

"Just come and see for yourself," Philip declared.

47As they approached, Jesus said, "Here comes an honest man—a true son of Israel."

48"How do you know what I am like?" Nathanael demanded.

And Jesus replied, "I could see you under the fig tree before Philip found you."

49Nathanael replied, "Sir, you are the Son of God—the King of Israel!"

50Jesus asked him, "Do you believe all this just because I told you I had seen you under the fig tree? You will see greater proofs than this. 51You will even see heaven open and the angels of God coming back and forth to me, the Messiah."

PSALM 102:1–28

LORD, hear my prayer! Listen to my plea! 2Don't turn away from me in this time of my distress. Bend down your ear and give me speedy answers, 3,4for my days disappear like smoke. My health is broken and my heart is sick; it is trampled like grass and is withered. My food is tasteless, and I have lost my appetite. 5I am reduced to skin and bones because of all my groaning and despair. 6I am like a vulture in a far-off wilderness, or like an owl alone in the desert. 7I lie awake, lonely as a solitary sparrow on the roof.

8My enemies taunt me day after day and curse at me. 9,10I eat ashes instead of bread. My tears run down into my drink because of your anger against me, because of your wrath. For you have rejected me and thrown me out. 11My life is passing swiftly as the evening shadows. I am withering like grass, 12while you, Lord, are a famous King forever. Your fame will endure to every generation.

13I know that you will come and have mercy on Jerusalem—and now is the time to pity her—the time you promised help. 14For your people love every stone in her walls and feel sympathy for every grain of dust in her streets. 15Now let the nations and their rulers tremble before the Lord, before his glory. 16For Jehovah will rebuild Jerusalem! He will appear in his glory!

17He will listen to the prayers of the destitute, for he is never too busy to heed their requests. 18I am recording this so that future generations will also praise the Lord for all that he has done. And a people that shall be created shall praise the Lord. 19Tell them that God looked down from his temple in heaven, 20and heard the groans of his people in slavery—they were children of death—and released them, 21,22so that multitudes would stream to the Temple in Jerusalem to praise him, and his praises were sung throughout the city; and many rulers throughout the earth came to worship him.

23He has cut me down in middle life, shortening my days. 24But I cried to him, "O God, you live forever and forever! Don't let me die half through my years!

25In ages past you laid the foundations of the earth, and made the heavens with your hands! 26They shall perish, but you go on forever. They will grow old, like worn-out clothing, and you will change them like a man putting on a new shirt and throwing away the old one! 27But you yourself never grow old. You are forever, and your years never end.

28"But our families will continue; generation after generation will be preserved by your protection."

PROVERBS FOR TODAY/ 14:15–16

Only a simpleton believes everything he's told! A prudent man understands the need for proof. A wise man is cautious and avoids danger; a fool plunges ahead with great confidence.

MAY 2

JUDGES 15:1—16:31

LATER on, during the wheat harvest, Samson took a young goat as a present to his wife, intending to sleep with her; but her father wouldn't let him in.

2"I really thought you hated her," he explained, "so I married her to your best man. But look, her sister is prettier than she is. Marry her instead."

3Samson was furious. "You can't blame me for whatever happens now," he shouted.

4So he went out and caught three hundred foxes and tied their tails together in pairs, with a torch between each pair. 5Then he lit the torches and let the foxes run through the fields of the Philistines, burning the grain to the ground along with all the sheaves and shocks of grain, and destroying the olive trees.

6"Who did this?" the Philistines demanded.

"Samson," was the reply, "because his wife's father gave her to another man." So the Philistines came and got the girl and her father and burned them alive.

7"Now my vengeance will strike again!" Samson vowed. 8So he attacked them with great fury and killed many of them. Then he went to live in a cave in the rock of Etam. 9The Philistines in turn sent a huge posse into Judah and raided Lehi.

10"Why have you come here?" the men of Judah asked.

And the Philistines replied, "To capture Samson and do to him as he has done to us."

11So three thousand men of Judah went down to get Samson at the cave in the rock of Etam.

"What are you doing to us?" they demanded of him. "Don't you realize that the Philistines are our rulers?"

But Samson replied, "I only paid them back for what they did to me."

12,13"We have come to capture you and take you to the Philistines," the men of Judah told him.

"All right," Samson said, "but promise me that you won't kill me yourselves."

"No," they replied, "we won't do that."

So they tied him with two new ropes and led him away. 14As Samson and his captors arrived at Lehi, the Philistines shouted with glee; but then the strength of the Lord came upon Samson, and the ropes with which he was tied snapped like thread and fell from his wrists! 15Then he picked up a donkey's jawbone that was lying on the ground and killed a thousand Philistines with it. 16,17Tossing away the jawbone, he remarked,

"Heaps upon heaps,
All with a donkey's jaw!
I've killed a thousand men,
All with a donkey's jaw!"

(The place has been called "Jawbone Hill" ever since.)

18But now he was very thirsty and he prayed to the Lord and said, "You have given Israel such a wonderful deliverance through me today! Must I now die of thirst, and fall to the mercy of these heathen?" 19So the Lord caused water to gush out from a hollow in the ground and Samson's spirit was revived as he drank. Then he named the place "The Spring of the Man Who Prayed," and the spring is still there today.

20Samson was Israel's leader for the next twenty years, but the Philistines still controlled the land.

ONE day Samson went to the Philistine city of Gaza and spent the night with a prostitute. 2Word soon spread that he had been seen in the city, so the police were alerted and many men of the city lay in wait all night at the city gate to capture him if he tried to leave.

"In the morning," they thought, "when there is enough light, we'll find him and kill him."

3Samson stayed in bed with the girl until midnight, then went out to the city gates and lifted them, with the two gateposts, right out of the ground. He put them on his shoulders and carried them to the top of the mountain across from Hebron!

4Later on he fell in love with a girl named Delilah over in the valley of Sorek. 5The five heads of the Philistine nation went personally to her and demanded that she find out from Samson what made him so strong, so that they would know how to overpower and subdue him and put him in chains.

"Each of us will give you a thousand dollars for this job," they promised.

6So Delilah begged Samson to tell her his secret. *"Please* tell me, Samson, why you are so strong," she pleaded. "I don't think anyone could ever capture you!"

7"Well," Samson replied, "if I were tied with seven raw-leather bowstrings, I would become as weak as anyone else."

8So they brought her the seven bowstrings, and while he slept she tied him with them. 9Some men were hiding in the next room, so as soon as she had tied him up she exclaimed,

"Samson! The Philistines are here!"

Then he snapped the bowstrings like cotton thread, and so his secret was not discovered.

10Afterward Delilah said to him, "You are making fun of me! You told me a lie! *Please* tell me how you can be captured!"

11"Well," he said, "if I am tied with brand new ropes which have never been used, I will be as weak as other men."

12So that time, as he slept, Delilah took new ropes and tied him with them. The men were hiding in the next room, as before. Again Delilah exclaimed,

"Samson! The Philistines have come to capture you!"

But he broke the ropes from his arms like spiderwebs!

13"You have mocked me again, and told me more lies!" Delilah complained. "Now tell me how you can *really* be captured."

"Well," he said, "if you weave my hair into your loom . . . !"

14So while he slept, she did just that and then screamed, "The Philistines have come, Samson!" And he woke up and yanked his hair away, breaking the loom.

15"How can you say you love me when you don't confide in me?" she whined. "You've made fun of me three times now, and you still haven't told me what makes you so strong!"

16,17She nagged at him every day until he couldn't stand it any longer and finally told her his secret.

"My hair has never been cut," he confessed, "for I've been a Nazirite to God since before my birth. If my hair were cut, my strength would leave me, and I would become as weak as anyone else."

18Delilah realized that he had finally told her the truth, so she sent for the five Philistine leaders.

"Come just this once more," she said, "for this time he has told me everything."

So they brought the money with them. 19She lulled him to sleep with his head in her lap, and they brought in a barber and cut off his hair. Delilah began to hit him, but she could see that his strength was leaving him.

20Then she screamed, "The Philistines are here to capture you, Samson!" And he woke up and thought, "I will do as before; I'll just shake myself free." But he didn't realize that the Lord had left him. 21So the Philistines captured him and gouged out his eyes and took him to Gaza, where he was bound with bronze chains and made to grind grain in the prison. 22But before long his hair began to grow again.

23,24The Philistine leaders declared a great festival to celebrate the capture of Samson. The people made sacrifices to their god Dagon and excitedly praised him.

"Our god has delivered our enemy Samson to us!" they gloated as they saw him there in chains. "The scourge of our nation who killed so many of us is now in our power!" 25,26Half drunk by now, the people demanded, "Bring out Samson so we can have some fun with him!"

So he was brought from the prison and made to stand at the center of the temple, between the two pillars supporting the roof. Samson said to the boy who was leading him by the hand, "Place my hands against the two pillars. I want to rest against them."

27By then the temple was completely filled with people. The five Philistine leaders were there as well as three thousand people in the balconies who were watching Samson and making fun of him.

28Then Samson prayed to the Lord and said, "O Lord Jehovah, remember me again—please strengthen me one more time, so that I may pay back the Philistines for the loss of at least one of my eyes."

29Then Samson pushed against the pillars with all his might.

30"Let me die with the Philistines," he prayed.

And the temple crashed down upon the Philistine leaders and all the people. So those he killed at the moment of his death were more than those he had killed during his entire lifetime. 31Later, his brothers and other relatives came down to get his body, and they brought him back home and buried him between Zorah and Eshta-ol, where his father, Manoah, was buried. He had led Israel for twenty years.

JOHN 2:1–25

TWO days later Jesus' mother was a guest at a wedding in the village of Cana in Galilee, 2and Jesus and his disciples were invited too. 3The wine supply ran out during the festivities, and Jesus' mother came to him with the problem.

4"I can't help you now," he said. "It isn't yet my time for miracles."

5But his mother told the servants, "Do whatever he tells you to."

6Six stone waterpots were standing there; they were used for Jewish ceremonial purposes and held perhaps twenty to thirty gallons each. 7,8Then Jesus told the servants to fill them to the brim with water. When this was done he said, "Dip some out and take it to the master of ceremonies."

9When the master of ceremonies tasted the water that was now wine, not knowing where it had come from (though, of course, the servants did), he called the bridegroom over.

10"This is wonderful stuff!" he said. "You're different from most. Usually a host uses the best wine first, and afterwards, when everyone is full and doesn't care, then he brings out the less expensive brands. But you have kept the best for the last!"

11This miracle at Cana in Galilee was

Jesus' first public demonstration of his heaven-sent power. And his disciples believed that he really was the Messiah.

12After the wedding he left for Capernaum for a few days with his mother, brothers, and disciples.

13Then it was time for the annual Jewish Passover celebration, and Jesus went to Jerusalem.

14In the Temple area he saw merchants selling cattle, sheep, and doves for sacrifices, and moneychangers behind their counters. 15Jesus made a whip from some ropes and chased them all out, and drove out the sheep and oxen, scattering the moneychangers' coins over the floor and turning over their tables! 16Then, going over to the men selling doves, he told them, "Get these things out of here. Don't turn my Father's House into a market!"

17Then his disciples remembered this prophecy from the Scriptures: "Concern for God's House will be my undoing."

18"What right have you to order them out?" the Jewish leaders demanded. "If you have this authority from God, show us a miracle to prove it."

19"All right," Jesus replied, "this is the miracle I will do for you: Destroy this sanctuary and in three days I will raise it up!"

20"What!" they exclaimed. "It took forty-six years to build this Temple, and you can do it in three days?" 21But by "this sanctuary" he meant his body. 22After he came back to life again, the disciples remembered his saying this and realized that what he had quoted from the Scriptures really did refer to him, and had all come true!

23Because of the miracles he did in Jerusalem at the Passover celebration, many people were convinced that he was indeed the Messiah. 24,25But Jesus didn't trust them, for he knew mankind to the core. No one needed to tell him how changeable human nature is!

PSALM 103:1–22

I bless the holy name of God with all my heart. 2Yes, I will bless the Lord and not forget the glorious things he does for me.

3He forgives all my sins. He heals me. 4He ransoms me from hell. He surrounds me with lovingkindness and tender mercies. 5He fills my life with good things! My youth is renewed like the eagle's! 6He gives justice to all who are treated unfairly. 7He revealed his will and nature to Moses and the people of Israel.

8He is merciful and tender toward those who don't deserve it; he is slow to get angry and full of kindness and love. 9He never bears a grudge, nor remains angry forever. 10He has not punished us as we deserve for all our sins, 11for his mercy toward those who fear and honor him is as great as the height of the heavens above the earth. 12He has removed our sins as far away from us as the east is from the west. 13He is like a father to us, tender and sympathetic to those who reverence him. 14For he knows we are but dust, 15and that our days are few and brief, like grass, like flowers, 16blown by the wind and gone forever.

17,18But the lovingkindness of the Lord is from everlasting to everlasting, to those who reverence him; his salvation is to children's children of those who are faithful to his covenant and remember to obey him!

19The Lord has made the heavens his throne; from there he rules over everything there is. 20Bless the Lord, you mighty angels of his who carry out his orders, listening for each of his commands. 21Yes, bless the Lord, you armies of his angels who serve him constantly.

22Let everything everywhere bless the Lord. And how I bless him too!

PROVERBS FOR TODAY/ 14:17–19

A short-tempered man is a fool. He hates the man who is patient. The simpleton is crowned with folly; the wise man is crowned with knowledge. Evil men shall bow before the godly.

MAY 3

JUDGES 17:1—18:31

IN the hill country of Ephraim lived a man named Micah.

2One day he said to his mother, "That thousand dollars you thought was stolen from you, and you were cursing about—well, I stole it!"

"God bless you for confessing it," his mother replied. 3So he returned the money to her.

"I am going to give it to the Lord as a credit for your account," she declared. "I'll have an idol carved for you and plate it with the silver."

4,5So his mother took a fifth of it to a silversmith, and the idol he made from it was placed in Micah's shrine. Micah had many idols in his collection, also an ephod and some teraphim, and he installed one of his sons as the priest. 6(For in those days Israel had no king, so everyone did whatever he wanted to—whatever seemed right in his own eyes.)

7,8One day a young priest from the town of Bethlehem, in Judah, arrived in that area of Ephraim, looking for a good place to live. He happened to stop at Micah's house as he was traveling through.

9"Where are you from?" Micah asked him.

And he replied, "I am a priest from Bethlehem, in Judah, and I am looking for a place to live."

10,11"Well, stay here with me," Micah said, "and you can be my priest. I will give you one hundred dollars a year plus a new suit and your board and room." The young man agreed to this, and became as one of Micah's sons. 12So Micah consecrated him as his personal priest.

13"I know the Lord will really bless me now," Micah exclaimed, "because now I have a genuine priest working for me!"

As has already been stated, there was no king in Israel at that time. The tribe of Dan was trying to find a place to settle, for they had not yet driven out the people living in the land assigned to them. 2So the men of Dan chose five army heroes from the cities of Zorah and Eshta-ol as scouts to go and spy out the land they were supposed to settle in. Arriving in the hill country of Ephraim, they stayed at Micah's home. 3Noticing the young Levite's accent, they took him aside and asked him, "What are you doing here? Why did you come?" 4He told them about his contract with Micah, and that he was his personal priest.

5"Well, then," they said, "ask God whether or not our trip will be successful."

6"Yes," the priest replied, "all is well. The Lord is taking care of you."

7So the five men went on to the town of Laish, and noticed how secure everyone felt. Their manner of life was Phoenician, and they were wealthy. They lived quietly, and were unprepared for an attack, for there were no tribes in the area strong enough to try it. They lived a great distance from their relatives in Sidon, and had little or no contact with the nearby villages. 8So the spies returned to their people in Zorah and Eshta-ol.

"What about it?" they were asked. "What did you find?"

9,10And the men replied, "Let's attack! We have seen the land and it is ours for the taking—a broad, fertile, wonderful place—a real paradise. The people aren't even prepared to defend themselves! Come on, let's go! For God has given it to us!"

11So six hundred armed troops of the tribe of Dan set out from Zorah and Eshtaol. 12They camped first at a place west of Kiriath-jearim in Judah (which is still called "The Camp of Dan"), 13then they went on up into the hill country of Ephraim.

As they passed the home of Micah,

¹⁴the five spies told the others. "There is a shrine in there with an ephod, some teraphim, and many plated idols. It's obvious what we ought to do!"

¹⁵,¹⁶So the five men went over to the house and with all of the armed men standing just outside the gate, they talked to the young priest, and asked him how he was getting along. ¹⁷Then the five spies entered the shrine and took the idols, the ephod, and the teraphim.

¹⁸"What are you doing?" the young priest demanded when he saw them carrying them out.

¹⁹"Be quiet and come with us," they said. "Be a priest to all of us. Isn't it better for you to be a priest to a whole tribe in Israel instead of just to one man in his private home?"

²⁰The young priest was then quite happy to go with them, and he took along the ephod, the teraphim, and the idols. ²¹They started on their way again, placing their children, cattle, and household goods at the front of the column. ²²When they were quite a distance from Micah's home, Micah and some of his neighbors came chasing after them, ²³yelling at them to stop.

"What do you want, chasing after us like this?" the men of Dan demanded.

²⁴"What do you mean, 'What do I want'!" Micah retorted. "You've taken away all my gods and my priest, and I have nothing left!"

²⁵"Be careful how you talk, mister," the men of Dan replied. "Somebody's apt to get angry and kill every one of you."

²⁶So the men of Dan kept going. When Micah saw that there were too many of them for him to handle, he turned back home.

²⁷Then, with Micah's idols and the priest, the men of Dan arrived at the city of Laish. There weren't even any guards, so they went in and slaughtered all the people and burned the city to the ground. ²⁸There was no one to help the inhabitants, for they were too far away from Sidon, and they had no local allies, for they had no dealings with anyone.

This happened in the valley next to Beth-rehob. Then the people of the tribe of Dan rebuilt the city and lived there. ²⁹The city was named "Dan" after their ancestor, Israel's son, but it had originally been called Laish.

³⁰Then they set up the idols and appointed a man named Jonathan (son of Gershom and grandson of Moses!) and his sons as their priests. This family continued as priests until the city was finally conquered by its enemies. ³¹So Micah's idols were worshiped by the tribe of Dan as long as the Tabernacle remained at Shiloh.

JOHN 3:1–22

AFTER dark one night a Jewish religious leader named Nicodemus, a member of the sect of the Pharisees, came for an interview with Jesus. "Sir," he said, "we all know that God has sent you to teach us. Your miracles are proof enough of this."

³Jesus replied, "With all the earnestness I possess I tell you this: Unless you are born again, you can never get into the Kingdom of God."

⁴"Born again!" exclaimed Nicodemus. "What do you mean? How can an old man go back into his mother's womb and be born again?"

⁵Jesus replied, "What I am telling you so earnestly is this: Unless one is born of water and the Spirit, he cannot enter the Kingdom of God. ⁶Men can only reproduce human life, but the Holy Spirit gives new life from heaven; ⁷so don't be surprised at my statement that you must be born again! ⁸Just as you can hear the wind but can't tell where it comes from or where it will go next, so it is with the Spirit. We do not know on whom he will next bestow this life from heaven."

⁹"What do you mean?" Nicodemus asked.

¹⁰,¹¹Jesus replied, "You, a respected Jewish teacher, and yet you don't understand these things? I am telling you what I know and have seen—and yet you

won't believe me. 12But if you don't even believe me when I tell you about such things as these that happen here among men, how can you possibly believe if I tell you what is going on in heaven? 13For only I, the Messiah, have come to earth and will return to heaven again. 14And as Moses in the wilderness lifted up the bronze image of a serpent on a pole, even so I must be lifted up upon a pole, 15so that anyone who believes in me will have eternal life. 16For God loved the world so much that he gave his only Son so that anyone who believes in him shall not perish but have eternal life. 17God did not send his Son into the world to condemn it, but to save it.

18"There is no eternal doom awaiting those who trust him to save them. But those who don't trust him have already been tried and condemned for not believing in the only Son of God. 19Their sentence is based on this fact: that the Light from heaven came into the world, but they loved the darkness more than the Light, for their deeds were evil. 20They hated the heavenly Light because they wanted to sin in the darkness. They stayed away from that Light for fear their sins would be exposed and they would be punished. 21But those doing right come gladly to the Light to let everyone see that they are doing what God wants them to."

22Afterwards Jesus and his disciples left Jerusalem and stayed for a while in Judea and baptized there.

PSALM 104:1–24

I bless the Lord: O Lord my God, how great you are! You are robed with honor and with majesty and light! You stretched out the starry curtain of the heavens, 3and hollowed out the surface of the earth to form the seas. The clouds are his chariots. He rides upon the wings of the wind. 4The angels are his messengers—his servants of fire!

5You bound the world together so that it would never fall apart. 6You clothed the earth with floods of waters covering up the mountains. 7,8You spoke, and at the sound of your shout the water collected into its vast ocean beds, and mountains rose and valleys sank to the levels you decreed. 9And then you set a boundary for the seas, so that they would never again cover the earth.

10He placed springs in the valleys, and streams that gush from the mountains. 11They give water for all the animals to drink. There the wild donkeys quench their thirst, 12and the birds nest beside the streams and sing among the branches of the trees. 13He sends rain upon the mountains and fills the earth with fruit. 14The tender grass grows up at his command to feed the cattle, and there are fruit trees, vegetables and grain for man to cultivate, 15and wine to make him glad, and olive oil as lotion for his skin, and bread to give him strength. 16The Lord planted the cedars of Lebanon. They are tall and flourishing. 17There the birds make their nests, the storks in the firs. 18High in the mountains are pastures for the wild goats, and rock-badgers burrow in among the rocks and find protection there.

19He assigned the moon to mark the months, and the sun to mark the days. 20He sends the night and darkness, when all the forest folk come out. 21Then the young lions roar for their food, but they are dependent on the Lord. 22At dawn they slink back into their dens to rest, 23and men go off to work until the evening shadows fall again. 24O Lord, what a variety you have made! And in wisdom you have made them all! The earth is full of your riches.

PROVERBS FOR TODAY/ 14:20–21

Even his own neighbors despise the poor man, while the rich have many "friends." But to despise the poor is to sin. Blessed are those who help them.

MAY 4

JUDGES 19:1—20:48

A T this time before Israel had a
king, there was a man of the tribe
of Levi living on the far side of
the hill country of Ephraim, who brought
home a girl from Bethlehem in Judah to
be his concubine. 2But she became angry
with him and ran away, and returned to
her father's home in Bethlehem, and was
there about four months. 3Then her husband, taking along a servant and an extra
donkey, went to see her to try to win
her back again. When he arrived at her
home, she let him in and introduced him
to her father, who was delighted to meet
him. 4Her father urged him to stay
awhile, so he stayed three days, and they
all had a very pleasant time.

5On the fourth day they were up early,
ready to leave, but the girl's father insisted on their having breakfast first.
6Then he pleaded with him to stay one
more day, as they were having such a
good time. 7At first the man refused, but
his father-in-law kept urging him until
finally he gave in. 8The next morning
they were up early again, and again the
girl's father pleaded, "Stay just today and
leave sometime this evening." So they
had another day of feasting.

9That afternoon as he and his wife and
servant were preparing to leave, his father-in-law said, "Look, it's getting late.
Stay just tonight, and we will have a
pleasant evening together and tomorrow
you can get up early and be on your
way."

10But this time the man was adamant,
so they left, getting as far as Jerusalem
(also called Jebus) before dark.

11His servant said to him, "It's getting
too late to travel; let's stay here tonight."
12,13"No," his master said, "we can't
stay in this heathen city where there are
no Israelites—we will go on to Gibe-ah,
or possibly Ramah."

14So they went on. The sun was setting just as they came to Gibe-ah, a village

of the tribe of Benjamin, 15so they went
there for the night. But as no one invited
them in, they camped in the village
square. 16Just then an old man came by
on his way home from his work in the
fields. (He was originally from the hill
country of Ephraim, but was living now
in Gibe-ah, even though it was in the
territory of Benjamin.) 17When he saw
the travelers camped in the square, he
asked them where they were from, and
where they were going.

18"We're on the way home from Bethlehem, in Judah," the man replied. "I live
on the far edge of the Ephraim hill country, near Shiloh. But no one has taken
us in for the night, 19even though we
have fodder for our donkeys, and plenty
of food and wine for ourselves."

20"Don't worry," the old man said, "be
my guests; for you mustn't stay here
in the square. It's too dangerous."

21So he took them home with him.
He fed their donkeys while they rested,
and afterward they had supper together.
22Just as they were beginning to warm
to the occasion, a gang of sex perverts
gathered around the house and began
beating at the door and yelling at the
old man to bring out the man who was
staying with him, so they could rape him.
23The old man stepped outside to talk
to them.

"No, my brothers, don't do such a
dastardly act," he begged, "for he is my
guest. 24Here, take my virgin daughter
and this man's wife. I'll bring them out
and you can do whatever you like to
them—but don't do such a thing to this
man."

25But they wouldn't listen to him. Then
the girl's husband pushed her out to
them, and they abused her all night, taking turns raping her until morning. Finally, just at dawn, they let her go.
26She fell down at the door of the house
and lay there until it was light. 27When
her husband opened the door to be on

his way, he found her there, fallen down in front of the door with her hands digging into the threshold.

28"Well, come on," he said. "Let's get going."

But there was no answer, for she was dead; so he threw her across the donkey's back and took her home. 29When he got there he took a knife and cut her body into twelve parts and sent one piece to each tribe of Israel. 30Then the entire nation was roused to action against the men of Benjamin because of this awful deed.

"There hasn't been such a horrible crime since Israel left Egypt," everyone said. "We've got to do something about it."

THEN the entire nation of Israel sent their leaders and 450,000 troops to assemble with one mind before the Lord at Mizpah. They came from as far away as Dan and Beersheba, and everywhere between, and from across the Jordan in the land of Gilead. 3(Word of the mobilization of the Israeli forces at Mizpah soon reached the land of Benjamin.) The chiefs of Israel now called for the murdered woman's husband and asked him just what had happened.

4"We arrived one evening at Gibe-ah, a village in Benjamin," he began. 5"That night the men of Gibe-ah surrounded the house, planning to kill me, and they raped my wife until she was dead. 6So I cut her body into twelve pieces and sent the pieces throughout the land of Israel, for these men have committed a terrible crime. 7Now then, sons of Israel, express your mind and give me your counsel!"

8,9,10And as one man they replied, "Not one of us will return home until we have punished the village of Gibe-ah. A tenth of the army will be selected by lot as a supply line to bring us food, and the rest of us will destroy Gibe-ah for this horrible deed."

11So the whole nation united in this task.

12Then messengers were sent to the tribe of Benjamin, asking, "Did you know about the terrible thing that was done among you? 13Give up these evil men from the city of Gibe-ah so that we can execute them and purge Israel of her evil." But the people of Benjamin wouldn't listen. 14,15Instead, twenty-six thousand of them arrived in Gibe-ah to join the seven hundred local men in their defense against the rest of Israel. 16(Among all these there were seven hundred men who were left-handed sharpshooters. They could hit a target within a hair's breadth, never missing!) 17The army of Israel, not counting the men of Benjamin, numbered 400,000 men.

18Before the battle the Israeli army went to Bethel first to ask counsel from God. "Which tribe shall lead us against the people of Benjamin?" they asked.

And the Lord replied, "Judah shall go first."

19,20So the entire army left early the next morning to go to Gibe-ah, to attack the men of Benjamin. 21But the men defending the village stormed out and killed twenty-two thousand Israelis that day. 22,23,24Then the Israeli army wept before the Lord until evening and asked him, "Shall we fight further against our brother Benjamin?"

And the Lord said, "Yes." So the men of Israel took courage and went out again the next day to fight at the same place. 25And that day they lost another eighteen thousand men, all experienced swordsmen.

26Then the entire army went up to Bethel and wept before the Lord and fasted until evening, offering burnt sacrifices and peace offerings. 27,28(The Ark of God was in Bethel in those days. Phinehas, the son of Eleazar and grandson of Aaron, was the priest.)

The men of Israel asked the Lord, "Shall we go out again and fight against our brother Benjamin, or shall we stop?"

And the Lord said, "Go, for tomorrow I will see to it that you defeat the men of Benjamin."

29So the Israeli army set an ambush all around the village, 30and went out again on the third day and set themselves in their usual battle formation. 31When the army of Benjamin came out of the town to attack, the Israeli forces retreated and Benjamin was drawn away from the town as they chased after Israel. And as they had done previously, Benjamin began to kill the men of Israel along the roadway running between Bethel and Gibe-ah, so that about thirty of them died.

32Then the army of Benjamin shouted, "We're defeating them again!" But the armies of Israel had agreed in advance to run away so that the army of Benjamin would chase them and be drawn away from the town. 33But when the main army of Israel reached Baal-tamar, it turned and attacked, and the ten thousand men in ambush west of Geba jumped up from where they were, 34and advanced against the rear of the army of Benjamin, who still didn't realize the impending disaster. 35-39So the Lord helped Israel defeat Benjamin, and the Israeli army killed 25,100 men of Benjamin that day, leaving but a tiny remnant of their forces.

Summary of the Battle:

The army of Israel retreated from the men of Benjamin in order to give the ambush more room for maneuvering. When the men of Benjamin had killed about thirty of the Israelis, they were confident of a massive slaughter just as on the previous days. But then the men in ambush rushed into the village and slaughtered everyone in it, and set it on fire. The great cloud of smoke pouring into the sky was the signal for the Israeli army to turn around and attack the army of Benjamin, 40,41who now looked behind them and were terrified to discover that their city was on fire, and that they were in serious trouble. 42So they ran toward the wilderness, but the Israelis chased after them, and the men who had set the ambush came out and joined the slaughter from the rear. 43They encircled the army of Benjamin east of Gibe-ah, and killed most of them there. 44Eighteen thousand of the Benjamin troops died in that day's battle. 45The rest of the army fled into the wilderness toward the rock

of Rimmon, but five thousand were killed along the way, and two thousand more near Gidom.

46,47So the tribe of Benjamin lost twenty-five thousand brave warriors that day, leaving only six hundred men who escaped to the rock of Rimmon, where they lived for four months. 48Then the Israeli army returned and slaughtered the entire population of the tribe of Benjamin—men, women, children, and cattle—and burned down every city and village in the entire land.

JOHN 3:23—4:3

AT this time John the Baptist was not yet in prison. He was baptizing at Aenon, near Salim, because there was plenty of water there. 25One day someone began an argument with John's disciples, telling them that Jesus' baptism was best. 26So they came to John and said, "Master, the man you met on the other side of the Jordan River—the one you said was the Messiah—he is baptizing too, and everybody is going over there instead of coming here to us."

27John replied, "God in heaven appoints each man's work. 28My work is to prepare the way for that man so that everyone will go to him. You yourselves know how plainly I told you that I am not the Messiah. I am here to prepare the way for him—that is all. 29The crowds will naturally go to the main attraction—the bride will go where the bridegroom is! A bridegroom's friends rejoice with him. I am the Bridegroom's friend, and I am filled with joy at his success. 30He must become greater and greater, and I must become less and less.

31"He has come from heaven and is greater than anyone else. I am of the earth, and my understanding is limited to the things of earth. 32He tells what he has seen and heard, but how few believe what he tells them! 33,34Those who believe him discover that God is a fountain of truth. For this one—sent by God—speaks God's words, for God's

Spirit is upon him without measure or limit. 35The Father loves this man because he is his Son, and God has given him everything there is. 36And all who trust him—God's Son—to save them have eternal life; those who don't believe and obey him shall never see heaven, but the wrath of God remains upon them."

WHEN the Lord knew that the Pharisees had heard about the greater crowds coming to him than to John to be baptized and to become his disciples—(though Jesus himself didn't baptize them, but his disciples did)— 3he left Judea and returned to the province of Galilee.

PSALM 104:25–35

THERE before me lies the mighty ocean, teeming with life of every kind, both great and small. 26And look! See the ships! And over there, the whale you made to play in the sea. 27Every one of these depends on you to give them daily food. 28You supply it, and they gather it. You open wide your hand to feed them and they are satisfied with all your bountiful provision.

29But if you turn away from them, then all is lost. And when you gather up their breath, they die and turn again to dust.

30Then you send your Spirit, and new life is born to replenish all the living of the earth. 31Praise God forever! How he must rejoice in all his work! 32The earth trembles at his glance; the mountains burst into flame at his touch.

33I will sing to the Lord as long as I live. I will praise God to my last breath! 34May he be pleased by all these thoughts about him, for he is the source of all my joy. 35Let all sinners perish—all who refuse to praise him. But I will praise him. Hallelujah!

PROVERBS FOR TODAY/ 14:22–24

Those who plot evil shall wander away and be lost, but those who plan good shall be granted mercy and quietness. Work brings profit; talk brings poverty! Wise men are praised for their wisdom; fools are despised for their folly.

MAY 5

JUDGES 21:1—RUTH 1:22

THE leaders of Israel had vowed at Mizpah never to let their daughters marry a man from the tribe of Benjamin. 2And now the Israeli leaders met at Bethel and sat before God until evening, weeping bitterly.

3"O Lord God of Israel," they cried out, "why has this happened, that now one of our tribes is missing?"

4The next morning they were up early and built an altar, and offered sacrifices and peace offerings on it. 5And they said among themselves, "Was any tribe of Israel not represented when we held our council before the Lord at Mizpah?" For at that time it was agreed by solemn oath that anyone who refused to come must die. 6There was deep sadness throughout all Israel for the loss of their brother tribe, Benjamin.

"Gone," they kept saying to themselves, "gone—an entire tribe of Israel has been cut off, and is gone. 7And how shall we get wives for the few who remain, since we have sworn by the Lord that we will not give them our daughters?"

8,9Then they thought again of their oath to kill anyone who refused to come to Mizpah, and discovered that no one had attended from Jabesh-gilead. 10,11,12So they sent twelve thousand of their best soldiers to destroy the people of Jabesh-gilead. All the men, married women, and children were slain, but the young virgins of marriageable age were saved. There were four hundred of these, and they were brought to the camp at Shiloh.

13Then Israel sent a peace delegation to the little remnant of the men of Benjamin at Rimmon Rock. 14The four hundred girls were given to them as wives, and they returned to their homes; but there were not enough of these girls for all of them. 15(What a sad time it was in Israel in those days, because the Lord had made a breach in the tribes of Israel.)

16"What shall we do for wives for the others, since all the women of the tribe of Benjamin are dead?" the leaders of Israel asked. 17"There must be some way to get wives for them, so that an entire tribe of Israel will not be lost forever. 18But we can't give them our own daughters. We have sworn with a solemn oath that anyone who does this shall be cursed of God."

19Suddenly someone thought of the annual religious festival held in the fields of Shiloh, between Lebonah and Bethel, along the east side of the road that goes from Bethel to Shechem.

20They told the men of Benjamin who still needed wives, "Go and hide in the vineyards, 21and when the girls of Shiloh come out for their dances, rush out and catch them and take them home with you to be your wives! 22And when their fathers and brothers come to us in protest, we will tell them, 'Please be understanding and let them have your daughters, for we didn't find enough wives for them when we destroyed Jabesh-gilead, and you couldn't have given your daughters to them without being guilty.' "

23So the men of Benjamin did as they were told and kidnapped the girls who took part in the celebration, and carried them off to their own land. Then they rebuilt their cities and lived in them. 24So the people of Israel returned to their homes.

25(There was no king in Israel in those days, and every man did whatever he thought was right.)

LONG ago when judges ruled in Israel, a man named Elimelech, from Bethlehem, left the country because of a famine and moved to the land of Moab. With him were his wife, Naomi, and his two sons, Mahlon and Chilion. 3During the time of their residence there, Elimelech died and Naomi was left with her two sons.

4,5These young men, Mahlon and Chilion, married girls of Moab, Orpah and Ruth. But later, both men died, so that Naomi was left alone, without her husband or sons. 6,7She decided to return to Israel with her daughters-in-law, for she had heard that the Lord had blessed his people by giving them good crops again.

8But after they had begun their homeward journey, she changed her mind and said to her two daughters-in-law, "Why don't you return to your parents' homes instead of coming with me? And may the Lord reward you for your faithfulness to your husbands and to me. 9And may he bless you with another happy marriage." Then she kissed them and they all broke down and cried.

10"No," they said. "We want to go with you to your people."

11But Naomi replied, "It is better for you to return to your own people. Do I have younger sons who could grow up to be your husbands? 12No, my daughters, return to your parents' homes, for I am too old to have a husband. And even if that were possible, and I became pregnant tonight, and bore sons, 13would you wait for them to grow up? No, of course not, my daughters; oh, how I grieve for you that the Lord has punished me in a way that injures you."

14And again they cried together, and

Orpah kissed her mother-in-law good-bye, and returned to her childhood home; but Ruth insisted on staying with Naomi.

15"See," Naomi said to her, "your sister-in-law has gone back to her people and to her gods; you should do the same."

16But Ruth replied, "Don't make me leave you, for I want to go wherever you go, and to live wherever you live; your people shall be my people, and your God shall be my God; 17I want to die where you die, and be buried there. May the Lord do terrible things to me if I allow anything but death to separate us."

18And when Naomi saw that Ruth had made up her mind and could not be persuaded otherwise, she stopped urging her. 19So they both came to Bethlehem and the entire village was stirred by their arrival.

"Is it really Naomi?" the women asked.

20But she told them, "Don't call me Naomi. Call me Mara," (Naomi means "pleasant"; Mara means "bitter") "for Almighty God has dealt me bitter blows. 21I went out full and the Lord has brought me home empty; why should you call me Naomi when the Lord has turned his back on me and sent such calamity!"

22(Their return from Moab and arrival in Bethlehem was at the beginning of the barley harvest.)

JOHN 4:4–42

JESUS had to go through Samaria on the way, 5,6and around noon as he approached the village of Sychar, he came to Jacob's Well, located on the parcel of ground Jacob gave to his son Joseph. Jesus was tired from the long walk in the hot sun and sat wearily beside the well.

7Soon a Samaritan woman came to draw water, and Jesus asked her for a drink. 8He was alone at the time as his disciples had gone into the village to buy some food. 9The woman was surprised that a Jew would ask a "despised Samaritan" for anything—usually they wouldn't

even speak to them!—and she remarked about this to Jesus.

10He replied, "If you only knew what a wonderful gift God has for you, and who I am, you would ask me for some *living* water!"

11"But you don't have a rope or a bucket," she said, "and this is a very deep well! Where would you get this living water? 12And besides, are you greater than our ancestor Jacob? How can you offer better water than this which he and his sons and cattle enjoyed?"

13Jesus replied that people soon became thirsty again after drinking this water. 14"But the water I give them," he said, "becomes a perpetual spring within them, watering them forever with eternal life."

15"Please, sir," the woman said, "give me some of that water! Then I'll never be thirsty again and won't have to make this long trip out here every day."

16"Go and get your husband," Jesus told her.

17,18"But I'm not married," the woman replied.

"All too true!" Jesus said. "For you have had five husbands, and you aren't even married to the man you're living with now."

19"Sir," the woman said, "you must be a prophet. 20But say, tell me, why is it that you Jews insist that Jerusalem is the only place of worship, while we Samaritans claim it is here [at Mount Gerizim], where our ancestors worshiped?"

21-24Jesus replied, "The time is coming, ma'am, when we will no longer be concerned about whether to worship the Father here or in Jerusalem. For it's not *where* we worship that counts, but *how* we worship—is our worship spiritual and real? Do we have the Holy Spirit's help? For God is Spirit, and we must have his help to worship as we should. The Father wants this kind of worship from us. But you Samaritans know so little about him, worshiping blindly, while we Jews know all about him, for salvation comes to the world through the Jews."

25The woman said, "Well, at least I know that the Messiah will come—the one they call Christ—and when he does, he will explain everything to us."

26Then Jesus told her, "I am the Messiah!"

27Just then his disciples arrived. They were surprised to find him talking to a woman, but none of them asked him why, or what they had been discussing.

28,29Then the woman left her waterpot beside the well and went back to the village and told everyone, "Come and meet a man who told me everything I ever did! Can this be the Messiah?" 30So the people came streaming from the village to see him.

31Meanwhile, the disciples were urging Jesus to eat. 32"No," he said, "I have some food you don't know about."

33"Who brought it to him?" the disciples asked each other.

34Then Jesus explained: "My nourishment comes from doing the will of God who sent me, and from finishing his work. 35Do you think the work of harvesting will not begin until the summer ends four months from now? Look around you! Vast fields of human souls are ripening all around us, and are ready now for reaping. 36The reapers will be paid good wages and will be gathering eternal souls into the granaries of heaven! What joys await the sower and the reaper, both together! 37For it is true that one sows and someone else reaps. 38I sent you to reap where you didn't sow; others did the work, and you received the harvest."

39Many from the Samaritan village believed he was the Messiah because of the woman's report: "He told me everything I ever did!" 40,41When they came out to see him at the well, they begged him to stay at their village; and he did, for two days, long enough for many of them to believe in him after hearing him. 42Then they said to the woman, "Now we believe because we have heard him ourselves, not just because of what you told us. He is indeed the Savior of the world."

PSALM 105:1–15

THANK the Lord for all the glorious things he does; proclaim them to the nations. 2Sing his praises and tell everyone about his miracles. 3Glory in the Lord; O worshipers of God, rejoice.

4Search for him and for his strength, and keep on searching!

5,6Think of the mighty deeds he did for us, his chosen ones—descendants of God's servant Abraham, and of Jacob. Remember how he destroyed our enemies. 7He is the Lord our God. His goodness is seen everywhere throughout the land. 8,9Though a thousand generations pass he never forgets his promise, his covenant with Abraham and Isaac, 10,11and confirmed with Jacob. This is his never-ending treaty with the people of Israel: *I will give you the land of Canaan as your inheritance.* 12He said this when they were but few in number, very few, and were only visitors in Canaan. 13Later they were dispersed among the nations, and were driven from one kingdom to another; 14but through it all he would not let one thing be done to them apart from his decision. He destroyed many a king who tried! 15"Touch not these chosen ones of mine," he warned, "and do not hurt my prophets."

PROVERBS FOR TODAY/ 14:25

A witness who tells the truth saves good men from being sentenced to death, but a false witness is a traitor.

RUTH 2:1—4:22

N ow Naomi had an in-law there in Bethlehem who was a very wealthy man. His name was Boaz.

2One day Ruth said to Naomi, "Perhaps I can go out into the fields of some kind man to glean the free grain behind his reapers."

And Naomi said, "All right, dear daughter. Go ahead."

3So she did. And as it happened, the field where she found herself belonged to Boaz, this relative of Naomi's husband.

4,5Boaz arrived from the city while she was there. After exchanging greetings with the reapers he said to his foreman, "Hey, who's that girl over there?"

6And the foreman replied, "It's that girl from the land of Moab who came back with Naomi. 7She asked me this morning if she could pick up the grains dropped by the reapers, and she has been at it ever since except for a few minutes' rest over there in the shade."

8,9Boaz went over and talked to her. "Listen, my child," he said to her. "Stay right here with us to glean; don't think of going to any other fields. Stay right behind my women workers; I have warned the young men not to bother you; when you are thirsty, go and help yourself to the water."

10,11She thanked him warmly. "How can you be so kind to me?" she asked. "You must know I am only a foreigner."

"Yes, I know," Boaz replied, "and I also know about all the love and kindness you have shown your mother-in-law since the death of your husband, and how you left your father and mother in your own land and have come here to live among strangers. 12May the Lord God of Israel, under whose wings you have come to take refuge, bless you for it."

13"Oh, thank you, sir," she replied. "You are so good to me, and I'm not even one of your workers!"

14At lunch time Boaz called to her, "Come and eat with us."

So she sat with his reapers and he gave her food, more than she could eat. 15And when she went back to work again, Boaz told his young men to let her glean right among the sheaves without stopping her, 16and to snap off some heads of barley and drop them on purpose for her to glean, and not to make any remarks. 17So she worked there all day, and in the evening when she had beaten out the barley she had gleaned, it came to a whole bushel! 18She carried it back into the city and gave it to her mother-in-law, with what was left of her lunch.

19"So much!" Naomi exclaimed. "Where in the world did you glean today? Praise the Lord for whoever was so kind to you." So Ruth told her mother-in-law all about it, and mentioned that the owner of the field was Boaz.

20"Praise the Lord for a man like that! God has continued his kindness to us as well as to your dead husband!" Naomi cried excitedly. "Why, that man is one of our closest relatives!"

21"Well," Ruth told her, "he said to come back and stay close behind his reapers until the entire field is harvested."

22"This is wonderful!" Naomi exclaimed. "Do as he has said. Stay with his girls right through the whole harvest; you will be safer there than in any other field!"

23So Ruth did, and gleaned with them until the end of the barley harvest, and then the wheat harvest, too.

ONE day Naomi said to Ruth, "My dear, isn't it time that I try to find a husband for you, and get you happily married again? 2The man I'm thinking of is Boaz! He has been so kind to us, and is a close relative. I happen to know that he will be winnowing barley tonight out on the threshing-floor. 3Now do what I tell you—bathe and put on some perfume and some nice clothes and go on down to the threshing-floor, but don't let him see you until he has finished his supper. 4Notice where he lies down to sleep; then go and lift the cover off his feet and lie down there, and he will tell you what to do concerning marriage."

5And Ruth replied, "All right. I'll do whatever you say."

6,7So she went down to the threshing-floor that night and followed her mother-in-law's instructions. After Boaz had finished a good meal, he lay down very contentedly beside a heap of grain and went to sleep. Then Ruth came quietly and lifted the covering off his feet and lay there. 8Suddenly, around midnight, he wakened and sat up, startled. There was a woman lying at his feet!

9"Who are you?" he demanded.

"It's I, sir—Ruth," she replied. "Make me your wife according to God's law, for you are my close relative."

10"Thank God for a girl like you!" he exclaimed. "For you are being even kinder to Naomi now than before. Naturally you'd prefer a younger man, even though poor. But you have put aside your personal desires. 11Now don't worry about a thing, my child; I'll handle all the details, for everyone knows what a wonderful person you are. 12But there is one problem. It's true that I am a close relative, but there is someone else who is more closely related to you than I am. 13Stay here tonight, and in the morning I'll talk to him, and if he will marry you, fine; let him do his duty; but if he won't, then I will, I swear by Jehovah; lie down until the morning."

14So she lay at his feet until the morning and was up early, before daybreak, for he had said to her, "Don't let it be known that a woman was here at the threshing-floor."

15-18"Bring your shawl," he told her. Then he tied up a bushel and a half of barley in it as a present for her mother-in-law, and laid it on her back. Then she returned to the city.

"Well, what happened, dear?" Naomi asked her when she arrived home. She told Naomi everything and gave her the barley from Boaz, and mentioned his remark that she mustn't go home without a present.

Then Naomi said to her, "Just be patient until we hear what happens, for Boaz won't rest until he has followed through on this. He'll settle it today."

So Boaz went down to the marketplace and found the relative he had mentioned. "Say, come over here," he called to him. "I want to talk to you a minute."

So they sat down together. 2Then Boaz called for ten of the chief men of the village, and asked them to sit as witnesses.

3Boaz said to his relative, "You know Naomi, who came back to us from Moab. She is selling our brother Elimelech's property. 4I felt that I should speak to you about it so that you can buy it if you wish, with these respected men as witnesses. If you want it, let me know right away, for if you don't take it, I will. You have the first right to purchase it and I am next."

The man replied, "All right, I'll buy it."

5Then Boaz told him, "Your purchase of the land from Naomi requires your marriage to Ruth so that she can have children to carry on her husband's name, and to inherit the land."

6"Then I can't do it," the man replied. "For her son would become an heir to my property, too; you buy it."

7In those days it was the custom in Israel for a man transferring a right of purchase to pull off his sandal and hand it to the other party; this publicly validated the transaction. 8So, as the man said to Boaz, "You buy it for yourself," he drew off his sandal.

9Then Boaz said to the witnesses and to the crowd standing around, "You have seen that today I have bought all the property of Elimelech, Chilion, and Mahlon, from Naomi, 10and that with it I have purchased Ruth the Moabitess, the widow of Mahlon, to be my wife, so that she can have a son to carry on the family name of her dead husband."

11And all the people standing there, and the witnesses replied, "We are witnesses. May the Lord make this woman, who has now come into your home, as fertile as Rachel and Leah, from whom all the nation of Israel descended! May you be a great and successful man in Bethlehem, 12and may the descendants the Lord will give you from this young woman be as numerous and honorable as those of our ancestor Perez, the son of Tamar and Judah."

13So Boaz married Ruth, and when he slept with her, the Lord gave her a son.

14And the women of the city said to Naomi, "Bless the Lord who has given you this little grandson; may he be famous in Israel. 15May he restore your youth and take care of you in your old age; for he is the son of your daughter-in-law who loves you so much, and who has been kinder to you than seven sons!"

16,17Naomi took care of the baby, and the neighbor women said, "Now at last Naomi has a son again!"

And they named him Obed. He was the father of Jesse and grandfather of King David.

18-22This is the family tree of Boaz, beginning with his ancestor Perez:

Perez, Hezron, Ram, Amminadab, Nashon, Salmon, Boaz, Obed, Jesse, David.

JOHN 4:43–54

A T the end of the two days' stay he went on into Galilee. Jesus used to say, "A prophet is honored everywhere except in his own country!" 45But the Galileans welcomed him with open arms, for they had been in Jerusalem at the Passover celebration and had seen some of his miracles.

46,47In the course of his journey through Galilee he arrived at the town of Cana, where he had turned the water into wine. While he was there, a man in the city of Capernaum, a government official, whose son was very sick, heard that Jesus had come from Judea and was traveling in Galilee. This man went over to Cana, found Jesus, and begged him to come to Capernaum with him and heal his son, who was now at death's door.

48Jesus asked, "Won't any of you believe in me unless I do more and more miracles?"

49The official pled, "Sir, please come now before my child dies."

50Then Jesus told him, "Go back home. Your son is healed!" And the man believed Jesus and started home. 51While he was on his way, some of his servants met him with the news that all was well—his son had recovered. 52He asked them when the lad had begun to feel better, and they replied, "Yesterday afternoon at about one o'clock his fever suddenly disappeared!" 53Then the father realized it was the same moment that Jesus had told him, "Your son is healed." And the officer and his entire household believed that Jesus was the Messiah.

54This was Jesus' second miracle in Galilee after coming from Judea.

PSALM 105:16–38

H E called for a famine on the land of Canaan, cutting off its food supply. 17Then he sent Joseph as a slave to Egypt to save his people from starvation. 18There in prison they hurt his feet with fetters, and placed his neck in an iron collar, 19until God's time finally came—how God tested his patience! 20Then the king sent for him and set him free. 21He was put in charge of all the king's possessions. 22At his pleasure he could imprison the king's aides and teach the king's advisors.

23Then Jacob (Israel) arrived in Egypt and lived there with his sons. 24In the years that followed, the people of Israel multiplied explosively, until they were a greater nation than their rulers. 25At that point God turned the Egyptians against the Israelis; they hated and enslaved them.

26But God sent Moses as his representative, and Aaron with him, 27to call down miracles of terror upon the land of Egypt. 28They followed his instructions and he sent thick darkness through the land, 29and turned the nation's water into blood, poisoning the fish. 30Then frogs invaded in enormous numbers; they were found even in the king's private rooms. 31When Moses spoke, the flies and other insects swarmed in vast clouds from one end of Egypt to the other. 32Instead of rain he sent down murderous hail, and lightning flashes overwhelmed the na-tion. 33Their grape vines and fig trees were ruined; all the trees lay broken on the ground. 34He spoke, and hordes of locusts came, 35and ate up everything green, destroying all the crops. 36Then he killed the oldest child in each Egyptian home, their pride and joy— 37and brought his people safely out from Egypt, loaded with silver and gold; there were no sick and feeble folk among them then. 38Egypt was glad when they were gone, for the dread of them was great.

PROVERBS FOR TODAY/ 14:26–27

Reverence for God gives a man deep strength; his children have a place of refuge and security. Reverence for the Lord is a fountain of life; its waters keep a man from death.

MAY 7

1 SAMUEL 1:1—2:21

THIS is the story of Elkanah, a man of the tribe of Ephraim who lived in Ramathaim-zophim, in the hills of Ephraim.

His father's name was Jeroham,
His grandfather was Elihu,
His great-grandfather was Tohu,
His great-great-grandfather was Zuph.

2He had two wives, Hannah and Penin-nah. Peninnah had some children, but Hannah didn't.

3Each year Elkanah and his families journeyed to the Tabernacle at Shiloh to worship the Lord of the heavens and to sacrifice to him. (The priests on duty at that time were the two sons of Eli— Hophni and Phinehas.) 4On the day he presented his sacrifice, Elkanah would celebrate the happy occasion by giving presents to Peninnah and her children; 5but although he loved Hannah very much, he could give her only one present, for the Lord had sealed her womb; so she had no children to give presents to. 6Peninnah made matters worse by taunt-ing Hannah because of her barrenness. 7Every year it was the same—Peninnah scoffing and laughing at her as they went to Shiloh, making her cry so much she couldn't eat.

8"What's the matter, Hannah?" Elka-nah would exclaim. "Why aren't you eat-ing? Why make such a fuss over having no children? Isn't having me better than having ten sons?"

9One evening after supper, when they were at Shiloh, Hannah went over to the Tabernacle. Eli the priest was sitting at his customary place beside the entrance. 10She was in deep anguish and was crying bitterly as she prayed to the Lord. 11And she made this vow: "O Lord of heaven, if you will look down upon my sorrow and answer my prayer and give me a son, then I will give him back to you, and he'll be yours for his entire lifetime, and his hair shall never be cut."

12,13Eli noticed her mouth moving as she was praying silently and, hearing no sound, thought she had been drinking. 14"Must you come here drunk?" he demanded. "Throw away your bottle."

15,16"Oh, no, sir!" she replied, "I'm not drunk! But I am very sad and I was pouring out my heart to the Lord. Please don't think that I am just some drunken bum!"

17"In that case," Eli said, "cheer up! May the Lord of Israel grant you your petition, whatever it is!"

18"Oh, thank you, sir!" she exclaimed, and went happily back, and began to take her meals again.

19,20The entire family was up early the next morning and went to the Tabernacle to worship the Lord once more. Then they returned home to Ramah, and when Elkanah slept with Hannah, the Lord remembered her petition; in the process of time, a baby boy was born to her. She named him Samuel (meaning "asked of God") because, as she said, "I asked the Lord for him."

21,22The next year Elkanah and Peninnah and her children went on the annual trip to the Tabernacle without Hannah, for she told her husband, "Wait until the baby is weaned, and then I will take him to the Tabernacle and leave him there."

23"Well, whatever you think best," Elkanah agreed. "May the Lord's will be done."

So she stayed home until the baby was weaned. 24Then, though he was still so small, they took him to the Tabernacle in Shiloh, along with a three-year-old bull for the sacrifice, and a bushel of flour and some wine. 25After the sacrifice they took the child to Eli.

26"Sir, do you remember me?" Hannah asked him. "I am the woman who stood here that time praying to the Lord! 27I asked him to give me this child, and he has given me my request; 28and now I am giving him to the Lord for as long as he lives." So she left him there at the Tabernacle for the Lord to use.

THIS was Hannah's prayer:
"How I rejoice in the Lord!
    How he has blessed me!
    Now I have an answer for my enemies,
    For the Lord has solved my problem.
    How I rejoice!

2No one is as holy as the Lord!
There is no other God,
Nor any Rock like our God.

3Quit acting so proud and arrogant!
The Lord knows what you have done,
And he will judge your deeds.

4Those who were mighty are mighty
    no more!
Those who were weak are now strong.

5Those who were well are now starving;
Those who were starving are fed.
The barren woman now has seven
    children;
She with many children has no more!

6The Lord kills,
The Lord gives life.

7Some he causes to be poor
And others to be rich.
He cuts one down
And lifts another up.

8He lifts the poor from the dust—
Yes, from a pile of ashes—
And treats them as princes
Sitting in the seats of honor.
For all the earth is the Lord's
And he has set the world in order.

9He will protect his godly ones,
But the wicked shall be silenced in
    darkness.
No one shall succeed by strength
    alone.

10Those who fight against the Lord
    shall be broken;
He thunders against them from
    heaven.
He judges throughout the earth.
He gives mighty strength to his King,
And gives great glory to his anointed
    one."

11So they returned home to Ramah without Samuel; and the child became the Lord's helper, for he assisted Eli the priest.

12Now the sons of Eli were evil men who didn't love the Lord. 13,14It was their regular practice to send out a servant whenever anyone was offering a sacrifice, and while the flesh of the sacrificed animal was boiling, the servant would put a three-pronged fleshhook into the pot and demand that whatever it brought up be given to Eli's sons. They treated all of the Israelites in this way when they came to Shiloh to worship. 15Sometimes the servant would come even before the rite of burning the fat on the altar had been performed, and he would demand raw meat before it was boiled, so that it could be used for roasting.

16If the man offering the sacrifice replied, "Take as much as you want, but the fat must first be burned," [as the law requires], then the servant would say,

"No, give it to me now or I'll take it by force."

17So the sin of these young men was very great in the eyes of the Lord; for they treated the people's offerings to the Lord with contempt.

18Samuel, though only a child, was the Lord's helper and wore a little linen robe just like the priest's. 19Each year his mother made a little coat for him and brought it to him when she came with her husband for the sacrifice. 20Before they returned home Eli would bless Elkanah and Hannah and ask God to give them other children to take the place of this one they had given to the Lord. 21And the Lord gave Hannah three sons and two daughters. Meanwhile Samuel grew up in the service of the Lord.

JOHN 5:1–23

AFTERWARDS Jesus returned to Jerusalem for one of the Jewish religious holidays. 2Inside the city, near the Sheep Gate, was Bethesda Pool, with five covered platforms or porches surrounding it. 3Crowds of sick folks—lame, blind, or with paralyzed limbs—lay on the platforms (waiting for a certain movement of the water, 4for an angel of the Lord came from time to time and disturbed the water, and the first person to step down into it afterwards was healed).

5One of the men lying there had been sick for thirty-eight years. 6When Jesus saw him and knew how long he had been ill, he asked him, "Would you like to get well?"

7"I can't," the sick man said, "for I have no one to help me into the pool at the movement of the water. While I am trying to get there, someone else always gets in ahead of me."

8Jesus told him, "Stand up, roll up your sleeping mat and go on home!"

9Instantly, the man was healed! He rolled up the mat and began walking!

But it was on the Sabbath when this miracle was done. 10So the Jewish leaders objected. They said to the man who was cured, "You can't work on the Sabbath! It's illegal to carry that sleeping mat!"

11"The man who healed me told me to," was his reply.

12"Who said such a thing as that?" they demanded.

13The man didn't know, and Jesus had disappeared into the crowd. 14But afterwards Jesus found him in the Temple and told him, "Now you are well; don't sin as you did before, or something even worse may happen to you."

15Then the man went to find the Jewish leaders and told them it was Jesus who had healed him.

16So they began harassing Jesus as a Sabbath breaker.

17But Jesus replied, "My Father constantly does good, and I'm following his example."

18Then the Jewish leaders were all the more eager to kill him because in addition to disobeying their Sabbath laws, he had spoken of God as his Father, thereby making himself equal with God.

19Jesus replied, "The Son can do nothing by himself. He does only what he sees the Father doing, and in the same way. 20For the Father loves the Son, and tells him everything he is doing; and the Son will do far more awesome miracles than this man's healing. 21He will even raise from the dead anyone he wants to, just as the Father does. 22And the Father leaves all judgment of sin to his Son, 23so that everyone will honor the Son, just as they honor the Father. But if you refuse to honor God's Son, whom he sent to you, then you are certainly not honoring the Father.

PSALM 105:39–45

HE spread out a cloud above them to shield them from the burning sun, and gave them a pillar of flame at night to give them light. 40They asked for meat and he sent them quail, and gave them manna—bread from heaven. 41He opened up a rock, and water gushed out to form a river through the dry and barren land; 42for he remembered his sacred promises to Abraham his servant.

43So he brought his chosen ones singing into the Promised Land. 44He gave them the lands of the Gentiles, complete with their growing crops; they ate what others planted. 45This was done to make them faithful and obedient to his laws. Hallelujah!

PROVERBS FOR TODAY/ 14:28–29

A growing population is a king's glory; a dwindling nation is his doom. A wise man controls his temper. He knows that anger causes mistakes.

MAY 8

1 SAMUEL 2:22—4:22

ELI was now very old, but he was aware of what was going on around him. He knew, for instance, that his sons were seducing the young women who assisted at the entrance of the Tabernacle.

23,24,25"I have been hearing terrible reports from the Lord's people about what you are doing," Eli told his sons. "It is an awful thing to make the Lord's people sin. Ordinary sin receives heavy punishment, but how much more this sin of yours which has been committed against the Lord!" But they wouldn't listen to their father, for the Lord was already planning to kill them.

26Little Samuel was growing in two ways—he was getting taller, and he was becoming everyone's favorite (and he was a favorite of the Lord's, too!).

27One day a prophet came to Eli and gave him this message from the Lord: "Didn't I demonstrate my power when the people of Israel were slaves in Egypt? 28Didn't I choose your ancestor Levi from among all his brothers to be my priest, and to sacrifice upon my altar, and to burn incense, and to wear a priestly robe as he served me? And didn't I assign the sacrificial offerings to you priests? 29Then why are you so greedy for all the other offerings which are brought to me? Why have you honored your sons more than me—for you and they have become fat from the best of the offerings of my people!

30"Therefore, I, the Lord God of Israel, declare that although I promised that your branch of the tribe of Levi could always be my priests, it is ridiculous to think that what you are doing can continue. I will honor only those who honor me, and I will despise those who despise me. 31I will put an end to your family, so that it will no longer serve as priests. Every member will die before his time. None shall live to be old. 32You will envy the prosperity I will give my people, but you and your family will be in distress and need. Not one of them will live out his days. 33Those who are left alive will live in sadness and grief; and their children shall die by the sword. 34And to prove that what I have said will come true, I will cause your two sons, Hophni and Phinehas, to die on the same day! ³⁵"Then I will raise up a faithful priest who will serve me and do whatever I tell him to do. I will bless his descendants, and his family shall be priests to my kings forever. ³⁶Then all of your descendants shall bow before him, begging for money and food. 'Please,' they will say, 'give me a job among the priests so that I will have enough to eat.'"

MEANWHILE little Samuel was helping the Lord by assisting Eli. Messages from the Lord were very rare in those days, ²,³but one night after Eli had gone to bed (he was almost blind with age by now), and Samuel was sleeping in the Temple near the Ark, ⁴,⁵the Lord called out, "Samuel! Samuel!"

"Yes?" Samuel replied. "What is it?" He jumped up and ran to Eli. "Here I am. What do you want?" he asked.

"I didn't call you," Eli said. "Go on back to bed." So he did. ⁶Then the Lord called again, "Samuel!" And again Samuel jumped up and ran to Eli.

"Yes?" he asked. "What do you need?"

"No, I didn't call you, my son," Eli said. "Go on back to bed."

⁷(Samuel had never had a message from Jehovah before.) ⁸So now the Lord called the third time, and once more Samuel jumped up and ran to Eli.

"Yes?" he asked. "What do you need?"

Then Eli realized it was the Lord who had spoken to the child. ⁹So he said to Samuel, "Go and lie down again, and if he calls again, say, 'Yes, Lord, I'm listening.'" So Samuel went back to bed.

¹⁰And the Lord came and called as before, "Samuel! Samuel!"

And Samuel replied, "Yes, I'm listening."

¹¹Then the Lord said to Samuel, "I am going to do a shocking thing in Israel. ¹²I am going to do all of the dreadful things I warned Eli about. ¹³I have continually threatened him and his entire family with punishment because his sons are blaspheming God, and he doesn't stop

them. ¹⁴So I have vowed that the sins of Eli and of his sons shall never be forgiven by sacrifices and offerings."

¹⁵Samuel stayed in bed until morning, then opened the doors of the Temple as usual, for he was afraid to tell Eli what the Lord had said to him. ¹⁶,¹⁷But Eli called him.

"My son," he said, "what did the Lord say to you? Tell me everything. And may God punish you if you hide anything from me!"

¹⁸So Samuel told him what the Lord had said.

"It is the Lord's will," Eli replied; "let him do what he thinks best."

¹⁹As Samuel grew, the Lord was with him and people listened carefully to his advice. ²⁰And all Israel from one end of the land to the other knew that Samuel was going to be a prophet of the Lord. ²¹,⁴:¹Then the Lord began to give messages to him there at the Tabernacle in Shiloh, and he passed them on to the people of Israel.

AT that time Israel was at war with the Philistines. The Israeli army was camped near Ebenezer, the Philistines at Aphek. ²And the Philistines defeated Israel, killing four thousand of them. ³After the battle was over, the army of Israel returned to their camp and their leaders discussed why the Lord had let them be defeated.

"Let's bring the Ark here from Shiloh," they said. "If we carry it into battle with us, the Lord will be among us and he will surely save us from our enemies."

⁴So they sent for the Ark of the Lord of heaven who is enthroned above the angels. Hophni and Phinehas, the sons of Eli, accompanied it into the battle. ⁵When the Israelis saw the Ark coming, their shout of joy was so loud that it almost made the ground shake!

⁶"What's going on?" the Philistines asked. "What's all the shouting about over in the camp of the Hebrews?"

When they were told it was because the Ark of the Lord had arrived, ⁷they panicked.

"God has come into their camp!" they cried out. "Woe upon us, for we have never had to face anything like this before! 8Who can save us from these mighty gods of Israel? They are the same gods who destroyed the Egyptians with plagues when Israel was in the wilderness. 9Fight as you never have before, O Philistines, or we will become their slaves just as they have been ours."

10So the Philistines fought desperately and Israel was defeated again. Thirty thousand men of Israel died that day and the remainder fled to their tents. 11And the Ark of God was captured and Hophni and Phinehas were killed.

12A man from the tribe of Benjamin ran from the battle and arrived at Shiloh the same day with his clothes torn and dirt on his head. 13Eli was waiting beside the road to hear the news of the battle, for his heart trembled for the safety of the Ark of God. As the messenger from the battlefront arrived and told what had happened, a great cry arose throughout the city.

14"What is all the noise about?" Eli asked. And the messenger rushed over to Eli and told him what had happened. 15(Eli was ninety-eight years old and was blind.)

16"I have just come from the battle— I was there today," he told Eli, 17"and Israel has been defeated and thousands of the Israeli troops are dead on the battlefield. Hophni and Phinehas were killed too, and the Ark has been captured."

18When the messenger mentioned what had happened to the Ark, Eli fell backward from his seat beside the gate and his neck was broken by the fall and he died (for he was old and fat). He had judged Israel for forty years.

19When Eli's daughter-in-law, Phinehas's wife, who was pregnant, heard that the Ark had been captured and that her husband and father-in-law were dead, her labor pains suddenly began. 20Just before she died, the women who were attending her told her that everything was all right and that the baby was a boy. But she did not reply or respond in any way. 21,22Then she murmured, "Name the child 'Ichabod,' for Israel's glory is gone." (Ichabod means "there is no glory." She named him this because the Ark of God had been captured and because her husband and her father-in-law were dead.)

JOHN 5:24–47

I say emphatically that anyone who listens to my message and believes in God who sent me has eternal life, and will never be damned for his sins, but has already passed out of death into life.

25"And I solemnly declare that the time is coming, in fact, it is here, when the dead shall hear my voice—the voice of the Son of God—and those who listen shall live. 26The Father has life in himself, and has granted his Son to have life in himself, 27and to judge the sins of all mankind because he is the Son of Man. 28Don't be so surprised! Indeed the time is coming when all the dead in their graves shall hear the voice of God's Son, 29and shall rise again—those who have done good, to eternal life; and those who have continued in evil, to judgment.

30"But I pass no judgment without consulting the Father. I judge as I am told. And my judgment is absolutely fair and just, for it is according to the will of God who sent me and is not merely my own.

31"When I make claims about myself they aren't believed, 32,33but someone else, yes, John the Baptist, is making these claims for me too. You have gone out to listen to his preaching, and I can assure you that all he says about me is true! 34But the truest witness I have is not from a man, though I have reminded you about John's witness so that you will believe in me and be saved. 35John shone brightly for a while, and you benefited and rejoiced, 36but I have a greater witness than John. I refer to the miracles I do; these have been assigned me by the Father, and they prove that the Father has sent me. 37And the Father himself has also testified about me, though not appearing to you personally, or speaking to you directly. 38But you are not listening to him, for you refuse to believe me—the one sent to you with God's message.

39"You search the Scriptures, for you believe they give you eternal life. And the Scriptures point to me! 40Yet you won't come to me so that I can give you this life eternal!

41,42"Your approval or disapproval means nothing to me, for as I know so well, you don't have God's love within you. 43I know, because I have come to you representing my Father and you refuse to welcome me, though you readily enough receive those who aren't sent from him, but represent only themselves! 44No wonder you can't believe! For you gladly honor each other, but you don't care about the honor that comes from the only God!

45"Yet it is not I who will accuse you of this to the Father—Moses will! Moses, on whose laws you set your hopes of heaven. 46For you have refused to believe Moses. He wrote about me, but you refuse to believe him, so you refuse to believe in me. 47And since you don't believe what he wrote, no wonder you don't believe me either."

PSALM 106:1–12

HALLELUJAH! Thank you, Lord! How good you are! Your love for us continues on forever. 2Who can ever list the glorious miracles of God? Who can ever praise him half enough?

3Happiness comes to those who are fair to others and are always just and good.

4Remember me too, O Lord, while you are blessing and saving your people. 5Let me share in your chosen ones' prosperity and rejoice in all their joys, and receive the glory you give to them.

6Both we and our fathers have sinned so much. 7They weren't impressed by the wonder of your miracles in Egypt, and soon forgot your many acts of kindness to them. Instead they rebelled against you at the Red Sea. 8Even so you saved them—to defend the honor of your name and demonstrate your power to all the world. 9You commanded the Red Sea to divide, forming a dry road across its bottom. Yes, as dry as any desert! 10Thus you rescued them from their enemies. 11Then the water returned and covered the road and drowned their foes; not one survived.

12Then at last his people believed him. Then they finally sang his praise.

PROVERBS FOR TODAY/ 14:30–31

A relaxed attitude lengthens a man's life; jealousy rots it away. Anyone who oppresses the poor is insulting God who made them. To help the poor is to honor God.

MAY 9

1 SAMUEL 5:1—7:17

THE Philistines took the captured Ark of God from the battleground at Ebenezer to the temple of their idol Dagon in the city of Ashdod. 3But when the local citizens went to see it the next morning, Dagon had fallen with his face to the ground before the Ark of Jehovah! They set him up again, 4but the next morning the same thing had happened—the idol had fallen face down before the Ark of the Lord again. This time his head and hands had been cut off and were lying in the doorway;

only the trunk of his body was left intact. 5(That is why to this day neither the priests of Dagon nor his worshipers will walk on the threshold of the temple of Dagon in Ashdod.)

6Then the Lord began to destroy the people of Ashdod and the nearby villages with bubonic plague. 7When the people realized what was happening, they exclaimed, "We can't keep the Ark of the God of Israel here any longer. We will all perish along with our god Dagon."

8So they called a conference of the mayors of the five cities of the Philistines to decide how to dispose of the Ark. The decision was to take it to Gath. 9But when the Ark arrived at Gath, the Lord began destroying its people, young and old, with the plague, and there was a great panic. 10So they sent the Ark to Ekron, but when the people of Ekron saw it coming they cried out, "They are bringing the Ark of the God of Israel here to kill us too!"

11So they summoned the mayors again and begged them to send the Ark back to its own country, lest the entire city die. For the plague had already begun and great fear was sweeping across the city. 12Those who didn't die were deathly ill; and there was weeping everywhere.

THE Ark remained in the Philistine country for seven months in all. 2Then the Philistines called for their priests and diviners and asked them, "What shall we do about the Ark of God? What sort of gift shall we send with it when we return it to its own land?"

3"Yes, send it back with a gift," they were told. "Send a guilt offering so that the plague will stop. Then, if it doesn't, you will know God didn't send the plague upon you after all."

4,5"What guilt offering shall we send?" they asked.

And they were told, "Send five gold models of the tumor caused by the plague, and five gold models of the rats that have ravaged the whole land—the capital cities and villages alike. If you send these gifts and then praise the God of Israel, perhaps he will stop persecuting you and your god. 6Don't be stubborn and rebellious as Pharaoh and the Egyptians were. They wouldn't let Israel go until God had destroyed them with dreadful plagues. 7Now build a new cart and hitch to it two cows that have just had calves—cows that never before have been yoked—and shut their calves away from them in the barn. 8Place the Ark of God on the cart beside a chest containing the gold models of the rats and tumors, and let the cows go wherever they want to. 9If they cross the border of our land and go into Beth-shemesh, then you will know that it was God who brought this great evil upon us; if they don't, [but return to their calves,] then we will know that the plague was simply a coincidence and was not sent by God at all."

10So these instructions were carried out. Two cows with newborn calves were hitched to the cart and their calves were shut up in the barn. 11Then the Ark of the Lord and the chest containing the gold rats and tumors were placed upon the cart. 12And sure enough, the cows went straight along the road toward Beth-shemesh, lowing as they went; and the Philistine mayors followed them as far as the border of Beth-shemesh. 13The people of Beth-shemesh were reaping wheat in the valley, and when they saw the Ark they went wild with joy!

14The cart came into the field of a man named Joshua and stopped beside a large rock. So the people broke up the wood of the cart for a fire and killed the cows and sacrificed them to the Lord as a burnt offering. 15Several men of the tribe of Levi lifted the Ark and the chest containing the gold rats and tumors from the cart and laid them on the rock. And many burnt offerings and sacrifices were offered to the Lord that day by the men of Beth-shemesh.

16After the five Philistine mayors had watched for awhile, they returned to Ekron that same day. 17The five gold models of tumors which had been sent by the Philistines as a guilt offering to the Lord were gifts from the mayors of the capital cities, Ashdod, Gaza, Ashkelon, Gath, and Ekron. 18The gold rats were to placate God for the other Philistine cities, both the fortified cities and the country villages controlled by the five capitals. (By the way, that large rock at Beth-shemesh can still be seen in the field of Joshua.) 19But the Lord killed seventy of the men of Beth-shemesh because they looked into the Ark. And the people mourned because of the many people whom the Lord had killed.

20"Who is able to stand before Jehovah, this holy God?" they cried out. "Where can we send the Ark from here?"

21So they sent messengers to the people at Kiriath-jearim and told them that the Philistines had brought back the Ark of the Lord.

"Come and get it!" they begged.

So the men of Kiriath-jearim came and took the Ark to the hillside home of Abinadab; and installed his son Eleazar to be in charge of it. 2The Ark remained there for twenty years, and during that time all Israel was in sorrow because the Lord had seemingly abandoned them.

3At that time Samuel said to them, "If you are really serious about wanting to return to the Lord, get rid of your foreign gods and your Ashtaroth idols. Determine to obey only the Lord; then he will rescue you from the Philistines."

4So they destroyed their idols of Baal and Ashtaroth and worshiped only the Lord.

5Then Samuel told them, "Come to Mizpah, all of you, and I will pray to the Lord for you."

6So they gathered there and, in a great ceremony, drew water from the well and poured it out before the Lord. They also went without food all day as a sign of sorrow for their sins. So it was at Mizpah that Samuel became Israel's judge.

7When the Philistine leaders heard about the great crowds at Mizpah, they mobilized their army and advanced. The Israelis were badly frightened when they learned that the Philistines were approaching.

8"Plead with God to save us!" they begged Samuel.

9So Samuel took a suckling lamb and offered it to the Lord as a whole burnt offering and pleaded with him to help Israel. And the Lord responded. 10Just as Samuel was sacrificing the burnt offering, the Philistines arrived for battle, but the Lord spoke with a mighty voice of thunder from heaven, and they were thrown into confusion, and the Israelis routed them, 11and chased them from Mizpah to Beth-car, killing them all along the way. 12Samuel then took a stone and placed it between Mizpah and Jeshanah and named it Ebenezer (meaning, "the Stone of Help"), for he said, "The Lord has certainly helped us!" 13So the Philistines were subdued and didn't invade Israel again at that time, because the Lord was against them throughout the remainder of Samuel's lifetime. 14The Israeli cities between Ekron and Gath, which had been conquered by the Philistines, were now returned to Israel, for the Israeli army rescued them from their Philistine captors. And there was peace between Israel and the Amorites in those days.

15Samuel continued as Israel's judge for the remainder of his life. 16He rode circuit annually, setting up his court first at Bethel, then Gilgal, and then Mizpah, and cases of dispute were brought to him in each of those three cities from all the surrounding territory. 17Then he would come back to Ramah, for his home was there, and he would hear cases there, too. And he built an altar to the Lord at Ramah.

JOHN 6:1–21

AFTER this, Jesus crossed over the Sea of Galilee, also known as the Sea of Tiberias. 2-5And a huge crowd, many of them pilgrims on their way to Jerusalem for the annual Passover celebration, were following him wherever he went, to watch him heal the sick. So when Jesus went up into the hills and sat down with his disciples around him, he soon saw a great multitude of people climbing the hill, looking for him.

Turning to Philip he asked, "Philip, where can we buy bread to feed all these people?" 6(He was testing Philip, for he already knew what he was going to do.)

7Philip replied, "It would take a fortune to begin to do it!"

8,9Then Andrew, Simon Peter's brother, spoke up. "There's a youngster here with five barley loaves and a couple of fish! But what good is that with all this mob?"

10"Tell everyone to sit down," Jesus ordered. And all of them—the approximate count of the men only was 5,000—sat down on the grassy slopes. 11Then Jesus took the loaves and gave thanks to God and passed them out to the people. Afterwards he did the same with the fish. And everyone ate until full!

12"Now gather the scraps," Jesus told his disciples, "so that nothing is wasted." 13And twelve baskets were filled with the leftovers!

14When the people realized what a great miracle had happened, they exclaimed, "Surely, he is the Prophet we have been expecting!"

15Jesus saw that they were ready to take him by force and make him their king, so he went higher into the mountains alone.

16That evening his disciples went down to the shore to wait for him. 17But as darkness fell and Jesus still hadn't come back, they got into the boat and headed out across the lake toward Capernaum. 18,19But soon a gale swept down upon them as they rowed, and the sea grew very rough. They were three or four miles out when suddenly they saw Jesus walking toward the boat! They were terrified, 20but he called out to them and told them not to be afraid. 21Then

they were willing to let him in, and immediately the boat was where they were going!

PSALM 106:13–31

YET how quickly they forgot again! They wouldn't wait for him to act, 14but demanded better food, testing God's patience to the breaking point. 15So he gave them their demands, but sent them leanness in their souls. 16They were envious of Moses; yes, and Aaron, too, the man anointed by God as his priest. 17Because of this the earth opened and swallowed Dathan, Abiram and his friends; 18and fire fell from heaven to consume these wicked men. 19,20For they preferred a statue of an ox that eats grass, to the glorious presence of God himself. 21,22Thus they despised their Savior who had done such mighty miracles in Egypt and at the Sea. 23So the Lord declared he would destroy them. But Moses, his chosen one, stepped into the breach between the people and their God and begged him to turn from his wrath, and not destroy them.

24They refused to enter the Promised Land, for they wouldn't believe his solemn oath to care for them. 25Instead, they pouted in their tents and mourned and despised his command. 26Therefore he swore that he would kill them in the wilderness 27and send their children away to distant lands as exiles. 28Then our fathers joined the worshipers of Baal at Peor and even offered sacrifices to the dead! 29With all these things they angered him—and so a plague broke out upon them 30and continued until Phineas executed those whose sins had caused the plague to start. 31(For this good deed Phineas will be remembered forever.)

PROVERBS FOR TODAY/ 14:32–33

The godly have a refuge when they die, but the wicked are crushed by their sins. Wisdom is enshrined in the hearts of men of common sense, but it must shout loudly before fools will hear it.

1 SAMUEL 8:1—9:27

IN his old age, Samuel retired and appointed his sons as judges in his place. 2Joel and Abijah, his oldest sons, held court in Beer-sheba; 3but they were not like their father, for they were greedy for money. They accepted bribes and were very corrupt in the administration of justice. 4Finally the leaders of Israel met in Ramah to discuss the matter with Samuel. 5They told him that since his retirement things hadn't been the same, for his sons were not good men.

"Give us a king like all the other nations have," they pleaded. 6Samuel was terribly upset and went to the Lord for advice.

7"Do as they say," the Lord replied, "for I am the one they are rejecting, not you—they don't want me to be their king any longer. 8Ever since I brought them from Egypt they have continually forsaken me and followed other gods. And now they are giving you the same treatment. 9Do as they ask, but warn them about what it will be like to have a king!"

10So Samuel told the people what the Lord had said:

11"If you insist on having a king, he will conscript your sons and make them run before his chariots; 12some will be made to lead his troops into battle, while others will be slave laborers; they will be forced to plow in the royal fields, and harvest his crops without pay; and make his weapons and chariot equipment. 13He will take your daughters from you and force them to cook and bake and make perfumes for him. 14He will take away the best of your fields and vineyards and olive groves and give them to his friends. 15He will take a tenth of your harvest and distribute it to his favorites. 16He will demand your slaves and the finest of your youth and will use your animals for his personal gain. 17He will

demand a tenth of your flocks, and you shall be his slaves. 18You will shed bitter tears because of this king you are demanding, but the Lord will not help you."

19But the people refused to listen to Samuel's warning.

"Even so, we still want a king," they said, 20"for we want to be like the nations around us. He will govern us and lead us to battle."

21So Samuel told the Lord what the people had said, 22and the Lord replied again, "Then do as they say and give them a king."

So Samuel agreed and sent the men home again.

KISH was a rich, influential man from the tribe of Benjamin. He was the son of Abiel, grandson of Zeror, great-grandson of Becorath, and great-great-grandson of Aphiah. 2His son Saul was the most handsome man in Israel. And he was head and shoulders taller than anyone else in the land!

3One day Kish's donkeys strayed away, so he sent Saul and a servant to look for them. 4They traveled all through the hill country of Ephraim, the land of Shalisha, the Shaalim area, and the entire land of Benjamin, but couldn't find them anywhere. 5Finally, after searching in the land of Zuph, Saul said to the servant, "Let's go home; by now my father will be more worried about us than about the donkeys!"

6But the servant said, "I've just thought of something! There is a prophet who lives here in this city; he is held in high honor by all the people because everything he says comes true; let's go and find him and perhaps he can tell us where the donkeys are."

7"But we don't have anything to pay him with," Saul replied. "Even our food is gone and we don't have a thing to give him."

8"Well," the servant said, "I have a dollar! We can at least offer it to him and see what happens!"

9,10,11"All right," Saul agreed, "let's try it!"

So they started into the city where the prophet lived. As they were climbing a hill toward the city, they saw some young girls going out to draw water and asked them if they knew whether the seer was in town. (In those days prophets were called seers. "Let's go and ask the seer," people would say, rather than, "Let's go and ask the prophet," as we would say now.)

12,13"Yes," they replied, "stay right on this road. He lives just inside the city gates. He has just arrived back from a trip to take part in a public sacrifice up on the hill. So hurry, because he'll probably be leaving about the time you get there; the guests can't eat until he arrives and blesses the food."

14So they went into the city, and as they were entering the gates they saw Samuel coming out toward them to go up the hill. 15The Lord had told Samuel the previous day,

16"About this time tomorrow I will send you a man from the land of Benjamin. You are to anoint him as the leader of my people. He will save them from the Philistines, for I have looked down on them in mercy and have heard their cry."

17When Samuel saw Saul the Lord said, "That's the man I told you about! He will rule my people."

18Just then Saul approached Samuel and asked, "Can you please tell me where the seer's house is?"

19"I am the seer!" Samuel replied. "Go on up the hill ahead of me and we'll eat together; in the morning I will tell you what you want to know and send you on your way. 20And don't worry about those donkeys that were lost three days ago, for they have been found. And anyway, you own all the wealth of Israel now!"

21"Pardon me, sir," Saul replied. "I'm from the tribe of Benjamin, the smallest in Israel, and my family is the least important of all the families of the tribe! You must have the wrong man!"

22Then Samuel took Saul and his servant into the great hall and placed them at the head of the table, honoring them above the thirty special guests. 23Samuel then instructed the chef to bring Saul the choicest cut of meat, the piece that had been set aside for the guest of honor. 24So the chef brought it in and placed it before Saul.

"Go ahead and eat it," Samuel said, "for I was saving it for you, even before I invited these others!"

So Saul ate with Samuel. 25After the feast, when they had returned to the city, Samuel took Saul up to the porch on the roof and talked with him there. 26,27At daybreak the next morning, Samuel called up to him, "Get up; it's time you were on your way!"

So Saul got up and Samuel accompanied him to the edge of the city. When they reached the city walls Samuel told Saul to send the servant on ahead. Then he told him, "I have received a special message for you from the Lord."

JOHN 6:22–46

THE next morning, back across the lake, crowds began gathering on the shore [waiting to see Jesus]. For they knew that he and his disciples had come over together and that the disciples had gone off in their boat, leaving him behind. Several small boats from Tiberias were nearby, 24so when the people saw that Jesus wasn't there, nor his disciples, they got into the boats and went across to Capernaum to look for him.

25When they arrived and found him, they said, "Sir, how did you get here?" 26Jesus replied, "The truth of the matter is that you want to be with me because I fed you, not because you believe in me. 27But you shouldn't be so concerned about perishable things like food. No, spend your energy seeking the eternal life that I, the Messiah, can give you. For God the Father has sent me for this very purpose."

28They replied, "What should we do to satisfy God?"

29Jesus told them, "This is the will of God, that you believe in the one he has sent."

30,31They replied, "You must show us more miracles if you want us to believe you are the Messiah. Give us free bread every day, like our fathers had while they journeyed through the wilderness! As the Scriptures say, 'Moses gave them bread from heaven.'"

32Jesus said, "Moses didn't give it to them. My Father did. And now he offers you true Bread from heaven. 33The true Bread is a Person—the one sent by God from heaven, and he gives life to the world."

34"Sir," they said, "give us that bread every day of our lives!"

35Jesus replied, "I am the Bread of Life. No one coming to me will ever be hungry again. Those believing in me will never thirst. 36But the trouble is, as I have told you before, you haven't believed even though you have seen me. 37But some will come to me—those the Father has given me—and I will never, never reject them. 38For I have come here from heaven to do the will of God who sent me, not to have my own way. 39And this is the will of God, that I should not lose even one of all those he has given me, but that I should raise them to eternal life at the Last Day. 40For it is my Father's will that everyone who sees his Son and believes on him should have eternal life—that I should raise him at the Last Day."

41Then the Jews began to murmur against him because he claimed to be the Bread from heaven.

42"What?" they exclaimed. "Why, he is merely Jesus the son of Joseph, whose father and mother we know. What is this he is saying, that he came down from heaven?"

43But Jesus replied, "Don't murmur among yourselves about my saying that.

44For no one can come to me unless the Father who sent me draws him to me, and at the Last Day I will cause all such to rise again from the dead. 45As it is written in the Scriptures, 'They shall all be taught of God.' Those the Father speaks to, who learn the truth from him, will be attracted to me. 46(Not that anyone actually sees the Father, for only I have seen him.)

PSALM 106:32-48

AT Meribah, too, Israel angered God, causing Moses serious trouble, 33for he became angry and spoke foolishly.

34Nor did Israel destroy the nations in the land as God had told them to, 35but mingled in among the heathen and learned their evil ways, 36sacrificing to their idols, and were led away from God. 37,38They even sacrificed their little children to the demons—the idols of Canaan—shedding innocent blood and polluting the land with murder. 39Their evil deeds defiled them, for their love of idols was adultery in the sight of God. 40That is why Jehovah's anger burned against his people, and he abhorred them. 41,42That is why he let the heathen nations crush them. They were ruled by those who hated them and oppressed by their enemies.

43Again and again he delivered them from their slavery, but they continued to rebel against him, and were finally destroyed by their sin. 44Yet, even so, he listened to their cries and heeded their distress; 45he remembered his promises to them and relented because of his great love, 46and caused even their enemies who captured them to pity them.

47O Lord God, save us! Regather us from the nations so we can thank your holy name and rejoice and praise you.

48Blessed be the Lord, the God of Israel, from everlasting to everlasting. Let all the people say, "Amen!" Hallelujah!

MAY 11

1 SAMUEL 10:1—11:15

THEN Samuel took a flask of olive oil and poured it over Saul's head and kissed him on the cheek and said,

"I am doing this because the Lord has appointed you to be the king of his people, Israel! 2When you leave me, you will see two men beside Rachel's tomb at Zelzah, in the land of Benjamin; they will tell you that the donkeys have been found and that your father is worried about you and is asking, 'How am I to find my son?' 3And when you get to the oak of Tabor you will see three men coming toward you who are on their way to worship God at the altar at Bethel; one will be bringing three young goats, another will have three loaves of bread, and the third will have a bottle of wine. 4They will greet you and offer you two of the loaves, which you are to accept. 5After that you will come to Gibeath-elohim, also known as "God's Hill," where the garrison of the Philistines is. As you arrive there you will meet a band of prophets coming down the hill playing a psaltery, a timbrel, a flute, and a harp, and prophesying as they come.

6"At that time the Spirit of the Lord will come mightily upon you, and you will prophesy with them and you will feel and act like a different person. 7From that time on your decisions should be based on whatever seems best under the circumstances, for the Lord will guide you. 8Go to Gilgal and wait there seven days for me, for I will be coming to sacrifice burnt offerings and peace offerings.

I will give you further instructions when I arrive."

9As Saul said good-bye and started to go, God gave him a new attitude, and all of Samuel's prophecies came true that day. 10When Saul and the servant arrived at the Hill of God they saw the prophets coming toward them, and the Spirit of God came upon him, and he too began to prophesy.

11When his friends heard about it, they exclaimed, "What? Saul a prophet?" 12And one of the neighbors added, "With a father like his?" So that is the origin of the proverb, "Is Saul a prophet, too?"

13When Saul had finished prophesying he climbed the hill to the altar.

14"Where in the world did you go?" Saul's uncle asked him.

And Saul replied, "We went to look for the donkeys, but we couldn't find them; so we went to the prophet Samuel to ask him where they were."

15"Oh? And what did he say?" his uncle asked.

16"He said the donkeys had been found!" Saul replied. (But he didn't tell him that he had been anointed as king!)

17Samuel now called a convocation of all Israel at Mizpah, 18,19and gave them this message from the Lord God: "I brought you from Egypt and rescued you from the Egyptians and from all of the nations that were torturing you. But although I have done so much for you, you have rejected me and have said, 'We want a king instead!' All right, then, present yourselves before the Lord by tribes and clans."

²⁰So Samuel called the tribal leaders together before the Lord, and the tribe of Benjamin was chosen by sacred lot. ²¹Then he brought each family of the tribe of Benjamin before the Lord, and the family of the Matrites was chosen. And finally, the sacred lot selected Saul, the son of Kish. But when they looked for him, he had disappeared!

²²So they asked the Lord, "Where is he? Is he here among us?"

And the Lord replied, "He is hiding in the baggage."

²³So they found him and brought him out, and he stood head and shoulders above anyone else.

²⁴Then Samuel said to all the people, "This is the man the Lord has chosen as your king. There isn't his equal in all of Israel!"

And all the people shouted, "Long live the king!"

²⁵Then Samuel told the people again what the rights and duties of a king were; he wrote them in a book and put it in a special place before the Lord. Then Samuel sent the people home again.

²⁶When Saul returned to his home at Gibe-ah, a band of men whose hearts the Lord had touched became his constant companions. ²⁷There were, however, some bums and loafers who exclaimed, "How can this man save us?" And they despised him and refused to bring him presents, but he took no notice.

AT this time Nahash led the army of the Ammonites against the Israeli city of Jabesh-gilead. But the citizens of Jabesh asked for peace. "Leave us alone and we will be your servants," they pleaded.

²"All right," Nahash said, "but only on one condition: I will gouge out the right eye of every one of you as a disgrace upon all Israel!"

³"Give us seven days to see if we can get some help!" replied the elders of Jabesh. "If none of our brothers will come and save us, we will agree to your terms."

⁴When a messenger came to Gibe-ah, Saul's home town, and told the people about their plight, everyone broke into tears.

⁵Saul was plowing in the field, and when he returned to town he asked, "What's the matter? Why is everyone crying?"

So they told him about the message from Jabesh. ⁶Then the Spirit of God came strongly upon Saul and he became very angry. ⁷He took two oxen and cut them into pieces and sent messengers to carry them throughout all Israel.

"This is what will happen to the oxen of anyone who refuses to follow Saul and Samuel to battle!" he announced. And God caused the people to be afraid of Saul's anger, and they came to him as one man. ⁸He counted them in Bezek and found that there were three hundred thousand of them in addition to thirty thousand from Judah.

⁹So he sent the messengers back to Jabesh-gilead to say, "We will rescue you before tomorrow noon!" What joy there was throughout the city when that message arrived!

¹⁰The men of Jabesh then told their enemies, "We surrender. Tomorrow we will come out to you and you can do to us as you wish."

¹¹But early the next morning Saul arrived, having divided his army into three detachments, and launched a surprise attack against the Ammonites and slaughtered them all morning. The remnant of their army was so badly scattered that no two of them were left together.

¹²Then the people exclaimed to Samuel, "Where are those men who said that Saul shouldn't be our king? Bring them here and we will kill them!"

¹³But Saul replied, "No one will be executed today; for today the Lord has rescued Israel!"

¹⁴Then Samuel said to the people, "Come, let us all go to Gilgal and reconfirm Saul as our king."

¹⁵So they went to Gilgal and in a solemn ceremony before the Lord they crowned him king. Then they offered

peace offerings to the Lord, and Saul and all Israel were very happy.

JOHN 6:47–71

How earnestly I tell you this—anyone who believes in me already has eternal life! 48-51Yes, I am the Bread of Life! When your fathers in the wilderness ate bread from the skies, they all died. But the Bread from heaven gives eternal life to everyone who eats it. I am that Living Bread that came down out of heaven. Anyone eating this Bread shall live forever; this Bread is my flesh given to redeem humanity."

52Then the Jews began arguing with each other about what he meant. "How can this man give us his flesh to eat?" they asked.

53So Jesus said it again, "With all the earnestness I possess I tell you this: Unless you eat the flesh of the Messiah and drink his blood, you cannot have eternal life within you. 54But anyone who does eat my flesh and drink my blood has eternal life, and I will raise him at the Last Day. 55For my flesh is the true food, and my blood is the true drink. 56Everyone who eats my flesh and drinks my blood is in me, and I in him. 57I live by the power of the living Father who sent me, and in the same way those who partake of me shall live because of me! 58I am the true Bread from heaven; and anyone who eats this Bread shall live forever, and not die as your fathers did—though they ate bread from heaven." 59(He preached this sermon in the synagogue in Capernaum.)

60Even his disciples said, "This is very hard to understand. Who can tell what he means?"

61Jesus knew within himself that his disciples were complaining and said to them, "Does *this* offend you? 62Then what will you think if you see me, the Messiah, return to heaven again? 63Only the Holy Spirit gives eternal life. Those born only once, with physical birth, will never receive this gift. But now I have told you how to get this true spiritual life. 64But some of you don't believe me." (For Jesus knew from the beginning who didn't believe and knew the one who would betray him.)

65And he remarked, "That is what I meant when I said that no one can come to me unless the Father attracts him to me."

66At this point many of his disciples turned away and deserted him.

67Then Jesus turned to the Twelve and asked, "Are you going too?"

68Simon Peter replied, "Master, to whom shall we go? You alone have the words that give eternal life, 69and we believe them and know you are the holy Son of God."

70Then Jesus said, "I chose the twelve of you, and one is a devil." 71He was speaking of Judas, son of Simon Iscariot, one of the Twelve, who would betray him.

PSALM 107:1–43

Say "Thank you" to the Lord for being so good, for always being so loving and kind. 2Has the Lord redeemed you? Then speak out! Tell others he has saved you from your enemies.

3He brought the exiles back from the farthest corners of the earth. 4They were wandering homeless in the desert, 5hungry and thirsty and faint. 6"Lord, help!" they cried, and he did! 7He led them straight to safety and a place to live. 8Oh, that these men would praise the Lord for his loving-kindness, and for all of his wonderful deeds! 9For he satisfies the thirsty soul and fills the hungry soul with good.

10Who are these who sit in darkness, in the shadow of death, crushed by misery and slavery? 11They rebelled against the Lord, scorning him who is the God above all gods. 12That is why he broke them with hard labor; they fell and none could help them rise again. 13Then they cried to the Lord in their troubles, and he rescued them! 14He led them from the darkness and shadow of death and snapped their chains. 15Oh, that these men would praise the Lord for his loving-kindness and for all of his wonderful deeds! 16For he broke down their prison gates of brass and cut apart their iron bars.

17Others, the fools, were ill because of their sinful ways. 18Their appetites were gone and death was near. 19Then they cried to the Lord in their troubles, and he helped them and delivered them. 20He spoke, and they were healed—snatched from the door of death. 21Oh, that these men would praise the Lord for his lovingkindness and for all of his wonderful deeds! 22Let them tell him "Thank you" as their sacrifice, and sing about his glorious deeds.

23And then there are the sailors sailing the seven seas, plying the trade routes of the world. 24They, too, observe the power of God in action. 25He calls to the storm winds; the waves rise high. 26Their ships are tossed to the heavens and sink again to the depths; the sailors cringe in terror. 27They reel and stagger like drunkards and are at their wit's end. 28Then they cry to the Lord in their trouble, and he saves them. 29He calms the storm and stills the waves. 30What a blessing is that stillness, as he brings them safely into harbor! 31Oh, that these men would praise the Lord for his loving-kindness and for all of his wonderful deeds! 32Let them praise him publicly before the congregation, and before the leaders of the nation.

33He dries up rivers, 34and turns the good land of the wicked into deserts of salt. 35Again, he turns deserts into fertile, watered valleys. 36He brings the hungry to settle there and build their cities, 37to sow their fields and plant their vineyards, and reap their bumper crops! 38How he blesses them! They raise big families there, and many cattle.

39But others become poor through oppression, trouble and sorrow. 40For God pours contempt upon the haughty and causes princes to wander among ruins; 41but he rescues the poor who are godly and gives them many children and much prosperity. 42Good men everywhere will see it and be glad, while evil men are stricken silent.

43Listen, if you are wise, to what I am saying. Think about the lovingkindness of the Lord!

PROVERBS FOR TODAY/ 15:1–3

A gentle answer turns away wrath, but harsh words cause quarrels. A wise teacher makes learning a joy; a rebellious teacher spouts foolishness. The Lord is watching everywhere and keeps his eye on both the evil and the good.

MAY 12

1 SAMUEL 12:1—13:23

THEN Samuel addressed the people again:

"Look," he said, "I have done as you asked. I have given you a king. 2I have selected him ahead of my own sons and now I stand here, an old, grey-haired man who has been in public service from the time he was a lad. 3Now tell me as I stand before the Lord and before his anointed king—whose ox or donkey have I stolen? Have I ever defrauded you? Have I ever oppressed you? Have I ever taken a bribe? Tell me and I will make right whatever I have done wrong."

4"No," they replied, "you have never defrauded or oppressed us in any way and you have never taken even one single bribe."

⁵"The Lord and his anointed king are my witnesses," Samuel declared, "that you can never accuse me of robbing you."

"Yes, it is true," they replied.

⁶"It was the Lord who appointed Moses and Aaron," Samuel continued. "He brought your ancestors out of the land of Egypt.

⁷"Now stand here quietly before the Lord as I remind you of all the good things he has done for you and for your ancestors:

⁸"When the Israelites were in Egypt and cried out to the Lord, he sent Moses and Aaron to bring them into this land. ⁹But they soon forgot about the Lord their God, so he let them be conquered by Sisera, the general of King Hazor's army, and by the Philistines and the king of Moab.

¹⁰"Then they cried to the Lord again and confessed that they had sinned by turning away from him and worshiping the Baal and Ashtaroth idols. And they pleaded, 'We will worship you and you alone if you will only rescue us from our enemies.' ¹¹Then the Lord sent Gideon, Barak, Jephthah, and Samuel to save you, and you lived in safety.

¹²"But when you were afraid of Nahash, the king of Ammon, you came to me and said that you wanted a king to reign over you. But the Lord your God was already your King, for he has always been your King. ¹³All right, here is the king you have chosen. Look him over. You have asked for him, and the Lord has answered your request.

¹⁴"Now if you will fear and worship the Lord and listen to his commandments and not rebel against the Lord, and if both you and your king follow the Lord your God, then all will be well. ¹⁵But if you rebel against the Lord's commandments and refuse to listen to him, then his hand will be as heavy upon you as it was upon your ancestors.

¹⁶"Now watch as the Lord does great miracles. ¹⁷You know that it does not rain at this time of the year, during the wheat harvest; I will pray for the Lord to send thunder and rain today, so that you will realize the extent of your wickedness in asking for a king!"

¹⁸So Samuel called to the Lord, and the Lord sent thunder and rain; and all the people were very much afraid of the Lord and of Samuel.

¹⁹"Pray for us lest we die!" they cried out to Samuel. "For now we have added to all our other sins by asking for a king."

²⁰"Don't be frightened," Samuel reassured them. "You have certainly done wrong, but make sure now that you worship the Lord with true enthusiasm, and that you don't turn your back on him in any way. ²¹Other gods can't help you. ²²The Lord will not abandon his chosen people, for that would dishonor his great name. He made you a special nation for himself—just because he wanted to!

²³"As for me, I will certainly not sin against the Lord by ending my prayers for you; and I will continue to teach you those things which are good and right.

²⁴"Trust the Lord and sincerely worship him; think of all the tremendous things he has done for you. ²⁵But if you continue to sin, you and your king will be destroyed."

BY this time Saul had reigned for one year. In the second year of his reign, ²he selected three thousand special troops and took two thousand of them with him to Michmash and Mount Bethel while the other thousand remained with Jonathan, Saul's son, in Gibe-ah in the land of Benjamin. The rest of the army was sent home. ³,⁴Then Jonathan attacked and destroyed the garrison of the Philistines at Geba. The news spread quickly throughout the land of the Philistines, and Saul sounded the call to arms throughout Israel. He announced that he had destroyed the Philistine garrison and warned his men that the army of Israel stank to high heaven as far as the Philistines were concerned. So the entire Israeli army mobilized again and joined at Gilgal. ⁵The Philistines recruited a mighty army of three thousand chariots, six thousand horsemen, and so many soldiers that they were as thick as sand along the seashore; and they camped at Michmash east of Beth-aven.

6When the men of Israel saw the vast mass of enemy troops, they lost their nerve entirely and tried to hide in caves, thickets, coverts, among the rocks, and even in tombs and cisterns. 7Some of them crossed the Jordan River and escaped to the land of Gad and Gilead. Meanwhile, Saul stayed at Gilgal, and those who were with him trembled with fear at what awaited them. 8Samuel had told Saul earlier to wait seven days for his arrival, but when he still didn't come, and Saul's troops were rapidly slipping away, 9he decided to sacrifice the burnt offering and the peace offerings himself. 10But just as he was finishing, Samuel arrived. Saul went out to meet him and to receive his blessing, 11but Samuel said, "What is this you have done?"

"Well," Saul replied, "when I saw that my men were scattering from me, and that you hadn't arrived by the time you said you would, and that the Philistines were at Michmash, ready for battle, 12I said, 'The Philistines are ready to march against us and I haven't even asked for the Lord's help!' So I reluctantly offered the burnt offering without waiting for you to arrive."

13"You fool!" Samuel exclaimed. "You have disobeyed the commandment of the Lord your God. He was planning to make you and your descendants kings of Israel forever, 14but now your dynasty must end; for the Lord wants a man who will obey him. And he has discovered the man he wants and has already appointed him as king over his people; for you have not obeyed the Lord's commandment."

15Samuel then left Gilgal and went to Gibe-ah in the land of Benjamin.

When Saul counted the soldiers who were still with him, he found only six hundred left! 16Saul and Jonathan and these six hundred men set up their camp in Geba in the land of Benjamin; but the Philistines stayed at Michmash. 17Three companies of raiders soon left the camp of the Philistines; one went toward Ophrah in the land of Shual, 18another went to Beth-horon, and the third moved toward the border above the valley of Zeboim near the desert.

19There were no blacksmiths at all in the land of Israel in those days, for the Philistines wouldn't allow them for fear of their making swords and spears for the Hebrews. 20So whenever the Israelites needed to sharpen their plowshares, discs, axes, or sickles, they had to take them to a Philistine blacksmith. 21(The schedule of charges was as follows:

For sharpening a plow point, 60¢

For sharpening a disc, 60¢

For sharpening an axe, 30¢

For sharpening a sickle, 30¢

For sharpening an ox goad, 30¢)

22So there was not a single sword or spear in the entire "army" of Israel that day, except for Saul's and Jonathan's. 23The mountain pass at Michmash had meanwhile been secured by a contingent of the Philistine army.

JOHN 7:1–30

AFTER this, Jesus went to Galilee, going from village to village, for he wanted to stay out of Judea where the Jewish leaders were plotting his death. 2But soon it was time for the Tabernacle Ceremonies, one of the annual Jewish holidays, 3and Jesus' brothers urged him to go to Judea for the celebration.

"Go where more people can see your miracles!" they scoffed. 4"You can't be famous when you hide like this! If you're so great, prove it to the world!" 5For even his brothers didn't believe in him.

6Jesus replied, "It is not the right time for me to go now. But you can go anytime and it will make no difference, 7for the world can't hate you; but it does hate me, because I accuse it of sin and evil. 8You go on, and I'll come later when it is the right time." 9So he remained in Galilee.

10But after his brothers had left for the celebration, then he went too, though secretly, staying out of the public eye. 11The Jewish leaders tried to find him at the celebration and kept asking if anyone had seen him. 12There was a lot of discussion about him among the crowds. Some said, "He's a wonderful man," while others said, "No, he's duping the public." 13But no one had the courage to speak out for him in public for fear of reprisals from the Jewish leaders.

14Then, midway through the festival, Jesus went up to the Temple and preached openly. 15The Jewish leaders were surprised when they heard him. "How can he know so much when he's never been to our schools?" they asked.

16So Jesus told them, "I'm not teaching you my own thoughts, but those of God who sent me. 17If any of you really determines to do God's will, then you will certainly know whether my teaching is from God or is merely my own. 18Anyone presenting his own ideas is looking for praise for himself, but anyone seeking to honor the one who sent him is a good and true person. 19None of *you* obeys the laws of Moses! So why pick on *me* for breaking them? Why kill *me* for this?"

20The crowd replied, "You're out of your mind! Who's trying to kill you?"

21,22,23Jesus replied, "I worked on the Sabbath by healing a man, and you were surprised. But you work on the Sabbath, too, whenever you obey Moses' law of circumcision (actually, however, this tradition of circumcision is older than the Mosaic law); for if the correct time for circumcising your children falls on the Sabbath, you go ahead and do it, as you should. So why should I be condemned for making a man completely well on the Sabbath? 24Think this through and you will see that I am right."

25Some of the people who lived there in Jerusalem said among themselves, "Isn't this the man they are trying to kill? 26But here he is preaching in public, and they say nothing to him. Can it be

that our leaders have learned, after all, that he really is the Messiah? 27But how could he be? For we know where this man was born; when Christ comes, he will just appear and no one will know where he comes from."

28So Jesus, in a sermon in the Temple, called out, "Yes, you know me and where I was born and raised, but I am the representative of one you don't know, and he is Truth. 29I know him because I was with him, and he sent me to you."

30Then the Jewish leaders sought to arrest him; but no hand was laid on him, for God's time had not yet come.

PSALM 108:1–13

O God, my heart is ready to praise you! I will sing and rejoice before you.

2Wake up, O harp and lyre! We will meet the dawn with song. 3I will praise you everywhere around the world, in every nation. 4For your lovingkindness is great beyond measure, high as the heavens. Your faithfulness reaches the skies. 5His glory is far more vast than the heavens. It towers above the earth. 6Hear the cry of your beloved child—come with mighty power and rescue me.

7God has given sacred promises; no wonder I exult! He has promised to give us all the land of Shechem, and also Succoth Valley. 8"Gilead is mine to give to you," he says, "and Manasseh as well; the land of Ephraim is the helmet on my head. Judah is my scepter. 9But Moab and Edom are despised; and I will shout in triumph over the Philistines."

10Who but God can give me strength to conquer these fortified cities? Who else can lead me into Edom?

11Lord, have you thrown us away? Have you deserted our army? 12Oh, help us fight against our enemies, for men are useless allies. 13But with the help of God we shall do mighty acts of valor. For he treads down our foes.

PROVERBS FOR TODAY/ 15:4

Gentle words cause life and health; griping brings discouragement.

MAY 13

1 SAMUEL 14:1–52

A day or so later, Prince Jonathan said to his young bodyguard, "Come on, let's cross the valley to the garrison of the Philistines." But he didn't tell his father that he was leaving.

²Saul and his six hundred men were camped at the edge of Gibe-ah, around the pomegranate tree at Migron. ³Among his men was Ahijah the priest (the son of Ahitub, Ichabod's brother; Ahitub was the son of Phinehas and the grandson of Eli, the priest of the Lord in Shiloh).

No one realized that Jonathan had gone. ⁴To reach the Philistine garrison, Jonathan had to go over a narrow pass between two rocky crags which had been named Bozez and Seneh. ⁵The crag on the north was in front of Michmash and the southern one was in front of Geba.

⁶"Yes, let's go across to those heathen," Jonathan had said to his bodyguard. "Perhaps the Lord will do a miracle for us. For it makes no difference to him how many enemy troops there are!"

⁷"Fine!" the youth replied. "Do as you think best; I'm with you heart and soul, whatever you decide."

⁸"All right, then this is what we'll do," Jonathan told him. ⁹"When they see us, if they say, 'Stay where you are or we'll kill you!' then we will stop and wait for them. ¹⁰But if they say, 'Come on up and fight!' then we will do just that; for it will be God's signal that he will help us defeat them!"

¹¹When the Philistines saw them coming they shouted, "Look! The Israelis are crawling out of their holes!" ¹²Then they shouted to Jonathan, "Come on up here and we'll show you how to fight!"

"Come on, climb right behind me," Jonathan exclaimed to his bodyguard, "for the Lord will help us defeat them!"

¹³So they clambered up on their hands and knees, and the Philistines fell back as Jonathan and the lad killed them right and left, ¹⁴about twenty men in all, and their bodies were scattered over about half an acre of land. ¹⁵Suddenly panic broke out throughout the entire Philistine army, and even among the raiders. And just then there was a great earthquake, increasing the terror.

¹⁶Saul's lookouts in Gibe-ah saw a strange sight—the vast army of the Philistines began to melt away in all directions.

¹⁷"Find out who isn't here," Saul ordered. And when they had checked, they found that Jonathan and his bodyguard were gone. ¹⁸"Bring the Ark of God," Saul shouted to Ahijah. (For the Ark was among the people of Israel at that time.) ¹⁹But while Saul was talking to the priest, the shouting and the tumult in the camp of the Philistines grew louder and louder. "Quick! What does God say?" Saul demanded.

²⁰Then Saul and his six hundred men rushed out to the battle and found the Philistines killing each other, and there was terrible confusion everywhere. ²¹And now the Hebrews who had been drafted into the Philistine army revolted and joined with the Israelis. ²²Finally even the men hiding in the hills joined the chase when they saw that the Philistines were running away. ²³So the Lord saved Israel that day, and the battle continued out beyond Beth-aven.

²⁴,²⁵Saul had declared, "A curse upon anyone who eats anything before evening—before I have full revenge on my enemies." So no one ate anything all day, even though they found honeycomb on the ground in the forest, ²⁶for they all feared Saul's curse. ²⁷Jonathan, however, had not heard his father's command; so he dipped a stick into a honeycomb, and when he had eaten the honey he felt much better. ²⁸Then someone told him that his father had laid a curse upon any-

one who ate food that day, and everyone was weary and faint as a result.

29"That's ridiculous!" Jonathan exclaimed. "A command like that only hurts us. See how much better I feel now that I have eaten this little bit of honey. 30If the people had been allowed to eat freely from the food they found among our enemies, think how many more we could have slaughtered!"

31But hungry as they were, they chased and killed the Philistines all day from Michmash to Aijalon, growing more and more faint. 32That evening they flew upon the battle loot and butchered the sheep, oxen, and calves, and ate the raw, bloody meat. 33Someone reported to Saul what was happening, that the people were sinning against the Lord by eating blood.

"That is very wrong," Saul said. "Roll a great stone over here, 34and go out among the troops and tell them to bring the oxen and sheep here to kill and drain them, and not to sin against the Lord by eating the blood." So that is what they did.

35And Saul built an altar to the Lord— his first.

36Afterwards Saul said, "Let's chase the Philistines all night and destroy every last one of them."

"Fine!" his men replied. "Do as you think best."

But the priest said, "Let's ask God first."

37So Saul asked God, "Shall we go after the Philistines? Will you help us defeat them?" But the Lord made no reply all night.

38Then Saul said to the leaders, "Something's wrong! We must find out what sin was committed today. 39I vow by the name of the God who saved Israel that though the sinner be my own son Jonathan, he shall surely die!" But no one would tell him what the trouble was.

40Then Saul proposed, "Jonathan and I will stand over here, and all of you stand over there." And the people agreed.

41Then Saul said, "O Lord God of Israel, why haven't you answered my question? What is wrong? Are Jonathan and I guilty, or is the sin among the others? O Lord God, show us who is guilty." And Jonathan and Saul were chosen by sacred lot as the guilty ones, and the people were declared innocent.

42Then Saul said, "Now draw lots between me and Jonathan." And Jonathan was chosen as the guilty one.

43"Tell me what you've done," Saul demanded of Jonathan.

"I tasted a little honey," Jonathan admitted. "It was only a little bit on the end of a stick; but now I must die."

44"Yes, Jonathan," Saul said, "you must die; may God strike me dead if you are not executed for this."

45But the troops retorted, "Jonathan, who saved Israel today, shall die? Far from it! We vow by the life of God that not one hair on his head will be touched, for he has been used of God to do a mighty miracle today." So the people rescued Jonathan.

46Then Saul called back the army, and the Philistines returned home. 47And now, since he was securely in the saddle as king of Israel, Saul sent the Israeli army out in every direction against Moab, Ammon, Edom, the kings of Zobah, and the Philistines. And wherever he turned, he was successful. 48He did great deeds and conquered the Amalekites and saved Israel from all those who had been their conquerors.

49Saul had three sons, Jonathan, Ishvi, and Malchishua; and two daughters, Merab and Michal. 50,51Saul's wife was Ahino-am, the daughter of Ahima-az. And the general-in-chief of his army was his cousin Abner, his uncle Ner's son. (Abner's father, Ner, and Saul's father, Kish, were brothers; both were the sons of Abiel.)

52The Israelis fought constantly with the Philistines throughout Saul's lifetime. And whenever Saul saw any brave, strong young man, he conscripted him into his army.

MANY among the crowds at the Temple believed on him. "After all," they said, "what miracles do you expect the Messiah to do that this man hasn't done?"

32When the Pharisees heard that the crowds were in this mood, they and the chief priests sent officers to arrest Jesus. 33But Jesus told them, "[Not yet!] I am to be here a little longer. Then I shall return to the one who sent me. 34You will search for me but not find me. And you won't be able to come where I am!"

35The Jewish leaders were puzzled by this statement. "Where is he planning to go?" they asked. "Maybe he is thinking of leaving the country and going as a missionary among the Jews in other lands, or maybe even to the Gentiles! 36What does he mean about our looking for him and not being able to find him, and, 'You won't be able to come where I am'?"

37On the last day, the climax of the holidays, Jesus shouted to the crowds, "If anyone is thirsty, let him come to me and drink. 38For the Scriptures declare that rivers of living water shall flow from the inmost being of anyone who believes in me." 39(He was speaking of the Holy Spirit, who would be given to everyone believing in him; but the Spirit had not yet been given, because Jesus had not yet returned to his glory in heaven.)

40When the crowds heard him say this, some of them declared, "This man surely is the prophet who will come just before the Messiah." 41,42Others said, "He *is* the Messiah." Still others, "But he *can't* be! Will the Messiah come from *Galilee?* For the Scriptures clearly state that the Messiah will be born of the royal line of David, in *Bethlehem,* the village where David was born." 43So the crowd was divided about him. 44And some wanted him arrested, but no one touched him.

45The Temple police who had been sent to arrest him returned to the chief priests and Pharisees. "Why didn't you bring him in?" they demanded.

46"He says such wonderful things!" they mumbled. "We've never heard anything like it."

47"So you also have been led astray?" the Pharisees mocked. 48"Is there a single one of us Jewish rulers or Pharisees who believes he is the Messiah? 49These stupid crowds do, yes; but what do they know about it? A curse upon them anyway!"

50Then Nicodemus spoke up. (Remember him? He was the Jewish leader who came secretly to interview Jesus.) 51"Is it legal to convict a man before he is even tried?" he asked.

52They replied, "Are you a wretched Galilean too? Search the Scriptures and see for yourself—no prophets will come from Galilee!"

53Then the meeting broke up and everybody went home.

PSALM 109:1–31

O God of my praise, don't stand silent and aloof 2while the wicked slander me and tell their lies. 3They have no reason to hate and fight me, yet they do! 4I love them, but even while I am praying for them, they are trying to destroy me. 5They return evil for good, and hatred for love.

6Show him how it feels! Let lies be told about him, and bring him to court before an unfair judge. 7When his case is called for judgment, let him be pronounced guilty. Count his prayers as sins. 8Let his years be few and brief; let others step forward to replace him. 9,10May his children become fatherless and his wife a widow; may they be evicted from the ruins of their home. 11May creditors seize his entire estate and strangers take all he has earned. 12,13Let no one be kind to him; let no one pity his fatherless children. May they die. May his family name be blotted out in a single generation. 14Punish the sins of his father and mother. Don't overlook them. 15Think constantly about the evil things he has done, and cut off his name from the memory of man.

16For he refused all kindness to others, and persecuted those in need, and hounded brokenhearted ones to death. 17He loved to curse others; now you curse him. He never blessed others; now don't you bless him. 18Cursing is as much a part of him as his clothing, or as the water he drinks, or the rich food he eats.

19Now may those curses return and cling to him like his clothing or his belt. 20This is the Lord's punishment upon my enemies who tell lies about me and threaten me with death.

21But as for me, O Lord, deal with me as your child, as one who bears your name! Because you are so kind, O Lord, deliver me.

22,23I am slipping down the hill to death; I am shaken off from life as easily as a man brushes a grasshopper from his arm. 24My knees are weak from fasting and I am skin and bones. 25I am a symbol of failure to all mankind; when they see me they shake their heads.

26Help me, O Lord my God! Save me because you are loving and kind. 27Do it publicly, so all will see that you yourself have done it. 28Then let them curse me if they like—I won't mind that if you are blessing me! For then all their efforts to destroy me will fail, and I shall go right on rejoicing!

29Make them fail in everything they do. Clothe them with disgrace. 30But I will give repeated thanks to the Lord, praising him to everyone. 31For he stands beside the poor and hungry to save them from their enemies.

PROVERBS FOR TODAY/ 15:5–7

Only a fool despises his father's advice; a wise son considers each suggestion. There is treasure in being good, but trouble dogs the wicked. Only the good can give good advice. Rebels can't.

MAY 14

1 SAMUEL 15:1—16:23

ONE day Samuel said to Saul, "I crowned you king of Israel because God told me to. Now be sure that you obey him. 2Here is his commandment to you: 'I have decided to settle accounts with the nation of Amalek for refusing to allow my people to cross their territory when Israel came from Egypt. 3Now go and completely destroy the entire Amalek nation—men, women, babies, little children, oxen, sheep, camels, and donkeys.' "

4So Saul mobilized his army at Telaim. There were two hundred thousand troops in addition to ten thousand men from Judah. 5The Amalekites were camped in the valley below them.

6Saul sent a message to the Kenites, telling them to get out from among the Amalekites or else die with them. "For you were kind to the people of Israel when they came out of the land of Egypt," he explained. So the Kenites packed up and left.

7Then Saul butchered the Amalekites from Havilah all the way to Shur, east of Egypt. 8He captured Agag, the king of the Amalekites, but killed everyone else. 9However, Saul and his men kept the best of the sheep and oxen and the fattest of the lambs—everything, in fact, that appealed to them. They destroyed only what was worthless or of poor quality.

10Then the Lord said to Samuel,

11"I am sorry that I ever made Saul king, for he has again refused to obey me."

Samuel was so deeply moved when he heard what God was saying, that he cried to the Lord all night. 12Early the next morning he went out to find Saul. Someone said that he had gone to Mount Carmel to erect a monument to himself, and had then gone on to Gilgal. 13When Samuel finally found him, Saul greeted him cheerfully.

"Hello there," he said. "Well, I have carried out the Lord's command!"

14"Then what was all the bleating of sheep and lowing of oxen I heard?" Samuel demanded.

15"It's true that the army spared the best of the sheep and oxen," Saul admitted, "but they are going to sacrifice them to the Lord your God; and we have destroyed everything else."

16Then Samuel said to Saul, "Stop! Listen to what the Lord told me last night!"

"What was it?" Saul asked.

17And Samuel told him, "When you didn't think much of yourself, God made you king of Israel. 18And he sent you on an errand and told you, 'Go and completely destroy the sinners, the Amalekites, until they are all dead.' 19Then why didn't you obey the Lord? Why did you rush for the loot and do exactly what God said not to?"

20"But I *have* obeyed the Lord," Saul insisted. "I did what he told me to; and I brought King Agag but killed everyone else. 21And it was only when my troops demanded it that I let them keep the best of the sheep and oxen and loot to sacrifice to the Lord."

22Samuel replied, "Has the Lord as much pleasure in your burnt offerings and sacrifices as in your obedience? Obedience is far better than sacrifice. He is much more interested in your listening to him than in your offering the fat of rams to him. 23For rebellion is as bad as the sin of witchcraft, and stubbornness is as bad as worshiping idols. And now because you have rejected the word of Jehovah, he has rejected you from being king."

24"I have sinned," Saul finally admitted. "Yes, I have disobeyed your instructions and the command of the Lord, for I was afraid of the people and did what they demanded. 25Oh, please pardon my sin now and go with me to worship the Lord."

26But Samuel replied, "It's no use! Since you have rejected the commandment of the Lord, he has rejected you from being the king of Israel."

27As Samuel turned to go, Saul grabbed at him to try to hold him back, and tore his robe.

28And Samuel said to him, "See? The Lord has torn the kingdom of Israel from you today and has given it to a countryman of yours who is better than you are. 29And he who is the glory of Israel is not lying, nor will he change his mind, for he is not a man!"

30Then Saul pleaded again, "I have sinned; but oh, at least honor me before the leaders and before my people by going with me to worship the Lord your God."

31So Samuel finally agreed and went with him.

32Then Samuel said, "Bring King Agag to me." Agag arrived all full of smiles, for he thought, "Surely the worst is over and I have been spared!" 33But Samuel said, "As your sword has killed the sons of many mothers, now your mother shall be childless." And Samuel chopped him in pieces before the Lord at Gilgal. 34Then Samuel went home to Ramah, and Saul returned to Gibe-ah. 35Samuel never saw Saul again, but he mourned constantly for him; and the Lord was sorry that he had ever made Saul king of Israel.

FINALLY the Lord said to Samuel, "You have mourned long enough for Saul, for I have rejected him as king of Israel. Now take a vial of olive oil and go to Bethlehem and find a man named Jesse, for I have selected one of his sons to be the new king."

2But Samuel asked, "How can I do

that? If Saul hears about it, he will kill me."

"Take a heifer with you," the Lord replied, "and say that you have come to make a sacrifice to the Lord. ³Then call Jesse to the sacrifice and I will show you which of his sons to anoint."

⁴So Samuel did as the Lord had told him to. When he arrived at Bethlehem, the elders of the city came trembling to meet him.

"What is wrong?" they asked. "Why have you come?"

⁵But he replied, "All is well. I have come to sacrifice to the Lord. Purify yourselves and come with me to the sacrifice."

And he performed the purification rite on Jesse and his sons, and invited them too. ⁶When they arrived, Samuel took one look at Eliab and thought, "Surely this is the man the Lord has chosen!"

⁷But the Lord said to Samuel, "Don't judge by a man's face or height, for this is not the one. I don't make decisions the way you do! Men judge by outward appearance, but I look at a man's thoughts and intentions."

⁸Then Jesse told his son Abinadab to step forward and walk in front of Samuel. But the Lord said, "This is not the right man either."

⁹Next Jesse summoned Shammah, but the Lord said, "No, this is not the one." In the same way all seven of his sons presented themselves to Samuel and were rejected.

¹⁰,¹¹"The Lord has not chosen any of them," Samuel told Jesse. "Are these all there are?"

"Well, there is the youngest," Jesse replied. "But he's out in the fields watching the sheep."

"Send for him at once," Samuel said, "for we will not sit down to eat until he arrives."

¹²So Jesse sent for him. He was a fine looking boy, ruddy-faced, and with pleasant eyes. And the Lord said, "This is the one; anoint him."

¹³So as David stood there among his brothers, Samuel took the olive oil he had brought and poured it upon David's head; and the Spirit of Jehovah came upon him and gave him great power from that day onward. Then Samuel returned to Ramah.

¹⁴But the Spirit of the Lord had left Saul, and instead, the Lord had sent a tormenting spirit that filled him with depression and fear. ¹⁵,¹⁶Some of Saul's aides suggested a cure.

"We'll find a good harpist to play for you whenever the tormenting spirit is bothering you," they said. "The harp music will quiet you and you'll soon be well again."

¹⁷"All right," Saul said. "Find me a harpist."

¹⁸One of them said he knew a young fellow in Bethlehem, the son of a man named Jesse, who was not only a talented harp player, but was handsome, brave, and strong, and had good, solid judgment. "What's more," he added, "the Lord is with him."

¹⁹So Saul sent messengers to Jesse, asking that he send his son David the shepherd. ²⁰Jesse responded by sending not only David but a young goat and a donkey carrying a load of food and wine. ²¹From the instant he saw David, Saul admired and loved him; and David became his bodyguard.

²²Then Saul wrote to Jesse, "Please let David join my staff, for I am very fond of him."

²³And whenever the tormenting spirit from God troubled Saul, David would play the harp and Saul would feel better, and the evil spirit would go away.

JOHN 8:1–20

JESUS returned to the Mount of Olives, ²but early the next morning he was back again at the Temple. A crowd soon gathered, and he sat down and talked to them. ³As he was speaking, the Jewish leaders and Pharisees brought a woman caught in adultery and placed her out in front of the staring crowd.

⁴"Teacher," they said to Jesus, "this woman was caught in the very act of

adultery. 5Moses' law says to kill her. What about it?"

6They were trying to trap him into saying something they could use against him, but Jesus stooped down and wrote in the dust with his finger. 7They kept demanding an answer, so he stood up again and said, "All right, hurl the stones at her until she dies. But only he who never sinned may throw the first!"

8Then he stooped down again and wrote some more in the dust. 9And the Jewish leaders slipped away one by one, beginning with the eldest, until only Jesus was left in front of the crowd with the woman.

10Then Jesus stood up again and said to her, "Where are your accusers? Didn't even one of them condemn you?"

11"No, sir," she said.

And Jesus said, "Neither do I. Go and sin no more."

12Later, in one of his talks, Jesus said to the people, "I am the Light of the world. So if you follow me, you won't be stumbling through the darkness, for living light will flood your path."

13The Pharisees replied, "You are boasting—and lying!"

14Jesus told them, "These claims are true even though I make them concerning myself. For I know where I came from and where I am going, but you don't know this about me. 15You pass judgment on me without knowing the facts. I am not judging you now; 16but if I were, it would be an absolutely correct judgment

in every respect, for I have with me the Father who sent me. 17Your laws say that if two men agree on something that has happened, their witness is accepted as fact. 18Well, I am one witness, and my Father who sent me is the other."

19"Where is your father?" they asked.

Jesus answered, "You don't know who I am, so you don't know who my Father is. If you knew me, then you would know him too."

20Jesus made these statements while in the section of the Temple known as the Treasury. But he was not arrested, for his time had not yet run out.

PSALM 110:1–7

JEHOVAH said to my Lord the Messiah, "Rule as my regent—I will subdue your enemies and make them bow low before you."

2Jehovah has established your throne in Jerusalem to rule over your enemies. 3In that day of your power your people shall come to you willingly, dressed in holy altar robes. And your strength shall be renewed day by day like morning dew. 4Jehovah has taken oath, and will not rescind his vow, that you are a priest forever like Melchizedek. 5God stands beside you to protect you. He will strike down many kings in the day of his anger. 6He will punish the nations, and fill them with their dead. He will crush many heads. 7But he himself shall be refreshed from springs along the way.

PROVERBS FOR TODAY/ 15:8–10

The Lord hates the gifts of the wicked, but delights in the prayers of his people. The Lord despises the deeds of the wicked, but loves those who try to be good. If they stop trying, the Lord will punish them; if they rebel against that punishment, they will die.

MAY 15

1 SAMUEL 17:1—18:4a

THE Philistines now mustered their army for battle and camped between Socoh in Judah and Azekah in Ephes-dammim. 2Saul countered with a buildup of forces at Elah Valley. 3So the Philistines and Israelis faced each other on opposite hills, with the valley between them.

4-7Then Goliath, a Philistine champion from Gath, came out of the Philistine ranks to face the forces of Israel. He was a giant of a man, measuring over nine feet tall! He wore a bronze helmet, a two-hundred-pound coat of mail, bronze leggings, and carried a bronze javelin several inches thick, tipped with a twenty-five-pound iron spearhead, and his armor bearer walked ahead of him with a huge shield.

8He stood and shouted across to the Israelis, "Do you need a whole army to settle this? I will represent the Philistines, and you choose someone to represent you, and we will settle this in single combat! 9If your man is able to kill me, then we will be your slaves. But if I kill him, then you must be our slaves! 10I defy the armies of Israel! Send me a man who will fight with me!"

11When Saul and the Israeli army heard this, they were dismayed and frightened. 12David (the son of aging Jesse, a member of the tribe of Judah who lived in Bethlehem) had seven older brothers. 13The three oldest—Eliab, Abinadab, and Shammah—had already volunteered for Saul's army to fight the Philistines. 14,15David was the youngest son, and was on Saul's staff on a part-time basis. He went back and forth to Bethlehem to help his father with the sheep. 16For forty days, twice a day, morning and evening the Philistine giant strutted before the armies of Israel.

17One day Jesse said to David, "Take this bushel of roasted grain and these ten loaves of bread to your brothers. 18Give this cheese to their captain and see how the boys are getting along; and bring us back a letter from them!"

19(Saul and the Israeli army were camped at the valley of Elah.)

20So David left the sheep with another shepherd and took off early the next morning with the gifts. He arrived at the outskirts of the camp just as the Israeli army was leaving for the battlefield with shouts and battle cries. 21Soon the Israeli and Philistine forces stood facing each other, army against army. 22David left his luggage with a baggage officer and hurried out to the ranks to find his brothers. 23As he was talking with them, he saw Goliath the giant step out from the Philistine troops and shout his challenge to the army of Israel. 24As soon as they saw him the Israeli army began to run away in fright.

25"Have you seen the giant?" the soldiers were asking. "He has insulted the entire army of Israel. And have you heard about the huge reward the king has offered to anyone who kills him? And the king will give him one of his daughters for a wife, and his whole family will be exempted from paying taxes!"

26David talked to some others standing there to verify the report. "What will a man get for killing this Philistine and ending his insults to Israel?" he asked them. "Who is this heathen Philistine, anyway, that he is allowed to defy the armies of the living God?" 27And he received the same reply as before.

28But when David's oldest brother, Eliab, heard David talking like that, he was angry. "What are you doing around here, anyway?" he demanded. "What about the sheep you're supposed to be taking care of? I know what a cocky brat you are; you just want to see the battle!"

29"What have I done now?" David replied. "I was only asking a question!"

30And he walked over to some others and asked them the same thing and received the same answer. 31When it was finally realized what David meant, someone told King Saul, and the king sent for him.

32"Don't worry about a thing," David told him. "I'll take care of this Philistine!"

33"Don't be ridiculous!" Saul replied. "How can a kid like you fight with a man like him? You are only a boy and he has been in the army *since* he was a boy!"

34But David persisted. "When I am taking care of my father's sheep," he said, "and a lion or a bear comes and grabs a lamb from the flock, 35I go after it with a club and take the lamb from its mouth. If it turns on me I catch it by the jaw and club it to death. 36I have done this to both lions and bears, and I'll do it to this heathen Philistine too, for he has defied the armies of the living God! 37The Lord who saved me from the claws and teeth of the lion and the bear will save me from this Philistine!"

Saul finally consented, "All right, go ahead," he said, "and may the Lord be with you!"

38,39Then Saul gave David his own armor—a bronze helmet and a coat of mail. David put it on, strapped the sword over it, and took a step or two to see what it was like, for he had never worn such things before. "I can hardly move!" he exclaimed, and took them off again. 40Then he picked up five smooth stones from a stream and put them in his shepherd's bag and, armed only with his shepherd's staff and sling, started across to Goliath. 41,42Goliath walked out towards David with his shield bearer ahead of him, sneering in contempt at this nice little red-cheeked boy!

43"Am I a dog," he roared at David, "that you come at me with a stick?" And he cursed David by the names of his gods. 44"Come over here and I'll give your flesh to the birds and wild animals," Goliath yelled.

45David shouted in reply, "You come to me with a sword and a spear, but I come to you in the name of the Lord of the armies of heaven and of Israel— the very God whom you have defied. 46Today the Lord will conquer you and I will kill you and cut off your head; and then I will give the dead bodies of *your* men to the birds and wild animals, and the whole world will know that there is a God in Israel! 47And Israel will learn that the Lord does not depend on weapons to fulfill his plans—he works without regard to human means! He will give you to us!"

48,49As Goliath approached, David ran out to meet him and, reaching into his shepherd's bag, took out a stone, hurled it from his sling, and hit the Philistine in the forehead. The stone sank in, and the man fell on his face to the ground. 50,51So David conquered the Philistine giant with a sling and a stone. Since he had no sword, he ran over and pulled Goliath's from its sheath and killed him with it, and then cut off his head. When the Philistines saw that their champion was dead, they turned and ran.

52Then the Israelis gave a great shout of triumph and rushed after the Philistines, chasing them as far as Gath and the gates of Ekron. The bodies of the dead and wounded Philistines were strewn all along the road to Shaaraim. 53Then the Israeli army returned and plundered the deserted Philistine camp.

54(Later David took Goliath's head to Jerusalem, but stored his armor in his tent.)

55As Saul was watching David go out to fight Goliath, he asked Abner, the general of his army, "Abner, what sort of family does this young fellow come from?"

"I really don't know," Abner said.

56"Well, find out!" the king told him.

57After David had killed Goliath, Abner brought him to Saul with the Philistine's head still in his hand.

58"Tell me about your father, my boy," Saul said.

And David replied, "His name is Jesse and we live in Bethlehem."

AFTER King Saul had finished his conversation with David, David met Jonathan, the king's son, and there was an immediate bond of love between them. Jonathan swore to be his blood brother, 4and sealed the pact by giving him his robe, sword, bow, and belt.

JOHN 8:21–31

LATER he said to them again, "I am going away; and you will search for me, and die in your sins. And you cannot come where I am going."

22The Jews asked, "Is he planning suicide? What does he mean, 'You cannot come where I am going'?"

23Then he said to them, "You are from below; I am from above. You are of this world; I am not. 24That is why I said that you will die in your sins; for unless you believe that I am the Messiah, the Son of God, you will die in your sins."

25"Tell us who you are," they demanded.

He replied, "I am the one I have always claimed to be. 26I could condemn you for much and teach you much, but I won't, for I say only what I am told to by the one who sent me; and he is Truth." 27But they still didn't understand that he was talking to them about God.

28So Jesus said, "When you have killed the Messiah, then you will realize that I am he and that I have not been telling you my own ideas, but have spoken what the Father taught me. 29And he who sent me is with me—he has not deserted me—for I always do those things that are pleasing to him."

30,31Then many of the Jewish leaders who heard him say these things began believing him to be the Messiah.

PSALM 111:1–10

HALLELUJAH! I want to express publicly before his people my heartfelt thanks to God for his mighty miracles. All who are thankful should ponder them with me. 3For his miracles demonstrate his honor, majesty, and eternal goodness.

4Who can forget the wonders he performs—deeds of mercy and of grace? 5He gives food to those who trust him; he never forgets his promises. 6He has shown his great power to his people by giving them the land of Israel, though it was the home of many nations living there. 7All he does is just and good, and all his laws are right, 8for they are formed from truth and goodness, and stand firm forever. 9He has paid a full ransom for his people; now they are always free to come to Jehovah (what a holy, awe-inspiring name that is).

10How can men be wise? The only way to begin is by reverence for God. For growth in wisdom comes from obeying his laws. Praise his name forever.

PROVERBS FOR TODAY/ 15:11

The depths of hell are open to God's knowledge. How much more the hearts of all mankind!

MAY 16

1 SAMUEL 18:4b—19:24

KING Saul now kept David with him and wouldn't let him return home any more.

5He was Saul's special assistant, and he always carried out his assignments successfully. So Saul made him commander of his troops, an appointment which was applauded by the army and general public alike. 6But something had happened when the victorious Israeli army was returning home after David had killed Goliath. Women came out from all the towns along the way to celebrate and to cheer for King Saul, and were singing and dancing for joy with tambourines and cymbals.

7However, this was their song: "Saul has slain his thousands, and David his ten thousands!"

8Of course Saul was very angry. "What's this?" he said to himself. "They credit David with ten thousands and me with only thousands. Next they'll be making him their king!"

9So from that time on King Saul kept a jealous watch on David. 10The very next day, in fact, a tormenting spirit from God overwhelmed Saul, and he began to rave like a madman. David began to soothe him by playing the harp, as he did whenever this happened. But Saul, who was fiddling with his spear, 11,12suddenly hurled it at David, intending to pin him to the wall. But David jumped aside and escaped. This happened another time, too, for Saul was afraid of him and jealous because the Lord had left him and was now with David. 13Finally Saul banned him from his presence and demoted him to the rank of captain. But the controversy put David more than ever in the public eye.

14David continued to succeed in everything he undertook, for the Lord was with him. 15,16When King Saul saw this, he became even more afraid of him; but all Israel and Judah loved him, for he was as one of them.

17One day Saul said to David, "I am ready to give you my oldest daughter Merab as your wife. But first you must prove yourself to be a real soldier by fighting the Lord's battles." For Saul thought to himself, "I'll send him out against the Philistines and let them kill him rather than doing it myself."

18"Who am I that I should be the king's son-in-law?" David exclaimed. "My father's family is nothing!"

19But when the time arrived for the wedding, Saul married her to Adriel, a man from Meholath, instead. 20In the meantime Saul's daughter Michal had fallen in love with David, and Saul was delighted when he heard about it.

21"Here's another opportunity to see him killed by the Philistines!" Saul said to himself. But to David he said, "You can be my son-in-law after all, for I will give you my youngest daughter."

22Then Saul instructed his men to say confidentially to David that the king really liked him a lot, and that they all loved him and thought he should accept the king's proposition and become his son-in-law.

23But David replied, "How can a poor man like me from an unknown family find enough dowry to marry the daughter of a king?"

24When Saul's men reported this back to him, 25he told them, "Tell David that the only dowry I need is one hundred dead Philistines! Vengeance on my enemies is all I want." But what Saul had in mind was that David would be killed in the fight.

26David was delighted to accept the offer. So, before the time limit expired, 27he and his men went out and killed two hundred Philistines and presented their foreskins to King Saul. So Saul gave Michal to him.

28When the king realized how much the Lord was with David and how immensely popular he was with all the people, 29he became even more afraid of him, and grew to hate him more with every passing day. 30Whenever the Philistine army attacked, David was more successful against them than all the rest of Saul's officers. So David's name became very famous throughout the land.

SAUL now urged his aides and his son Jonathan to assassinate David. But Jonathan, because of his close friendship with David, 2told him what his father was planning. "Tomorrow morning," he warned him, "you must find a hiding place out in the fields. 3I'll ask my father to go out there with me, and I'll talk to him about you; then I'll tell you everything I can find out."

4The next morning as Jonathan and his father were talking together, he spoke well of David and begged him not to be against David.

"He's never done anything to harm you," Jonathan pleaded. "He has always helped you in any way he could. 5Have you forgotten about the time he risked his life to kill Goliath, and how the Lord brought a great victory to Israel as a result? You were certainly happy about it then. Why should you now murder an innocent man? There is no reason for it at all!"

6Finally Saul agreed, and vowed, "As the Lord lives, he shall not be killed."

7Afterwards Jonathan called David and told him what had happened. Then he took David to Saul and everything was as it had been before. 8War broke out shortly after that and David led his troops against the Philistines and slaughtered many of them, and put to flight their entire army.

9,10But one day as Saul was sitting at home, listening to David playing the harp, suddenly the tormenting spirit from the Lord attacked him. He had his spear in his hand, and hurled it at David in an attempt to kill him. But David dodged out of the way and fled into the night, leaving the spear imbedded in the timber of the wall. 11Saul sent troops to watch David's house and kill him when he came out in the morning.

"If you don't get away tonight," Michal warned him, "you'll be dead by morning."

12So she helped him get down to the ground through a window. 13Then she took an idol and put it in his bed, and covered it with blankets, with its head on a pillow of goat's hair. 14When the soldiers came to arrest David and take him to Saul, she told them he was sick and couldn't get out of bed. 15Saul said to bring him in his bed, then, so that he could kill him. 16But when they came to carry him out, they discovered that it was only an idol!

17"Why have you deceived me and let my enemy escape?" Saul demanded of Michal.

"I had to," Michal replied. "He threatened to kill me if I didn't help him."

18In that way David got away and went to Ramah to see Samuel, and told him all that Saul had done to him. So Samuel took David with him to live at Naioth. 19When the report reached Saul that David was at Naioth in Ramah, 20he sent soldiers to capture him; but when they arrived and saw Samuel and the other prophets prophesying, the Spirit of God came upon them and they also began to prophesy. 21When Saul heard what had happened, he sent other soldiers, but they too prophesied! The same thing happened a third time! 22Then Saul himself went to Ramah and arrived at the great well in Secu.

"Where are Samuel and David?" he demanded.

Someone told him they were at Naioth. 23But on the way to Naioth the Spirit of God came upon Saul, and he too began to prophesy! 24He tore off his clothes and lay naked all day and all night, prophesying with Samuel's prophets. Saul's men were incredulous!

"What!" they exclaimed. "Is Saul a prophet, too?"

JESUS said to them, "You are truly my disciples if you live as I tell you to, and you will know the truth, and the truth will set you free."

33"But we are descendants of Abraham," they said, "and have never been slaves to any man on earth! What do you mean, 'set free'?"

34Jesus replied, "You are slaves of sin, every one of you. 35And slaves don't have rights, but the Son has every right there is! 36So if the Son sets you free, you will indeed be free— 37(Yes, I realize that you are descendants of Abraham!) And yet some of you are trying to kill me because my message does not find a home within your hearts. 38I am telling you what I saw when I was with my Father. But you are following the advice of *your* father."

39"Our father is Abraham," they declared.

"No!" Jesus replied, "for if he were, you would follow his good example. 40But instead you are trying to kill me— and all because I told you the truth I heard from God. Abraham wouldn't do a thing like that! 41No, you are obeying your *real* father when you act that way."

They replied, "We were not born out of wedlock—our true Father is God himself."

42Jesus told them, "If that were so, then you would love me, for I have come to you from God. I am not here on my own, but he sent me. 43Why can't you understand what I am saying? It is because you are prevented from doing so! 44For you are the children of your father the devil and you love to do the evil things he does. He was a murderer from the beginning and a hater of truth—there is not an iota of truth in him. When he lies, it is perfectly normal; for he is the father of liars. 45And so when I tell the truth, you just naturally don't believe it!

46"Which of you can truthfully accuse me of one single sin? [No one!] And since I am telling you the truth, why don't you believe me? 47Anyone whose Father is God listens gladly to the words of God. Since you don't, it proves you aren't his children."

48"You Samaritan! Foreigner! Devil!" the Jewish leaders snarled. "Didn't we say all along you were possessed by a demon?"

49"No," Jesus said, "I have no demon in me. For I honor my Father—and you dishonor me. 50And though I have no wish to make myself great, God wants this for me and judges [those who reject me]. 51With all the earnestness I have I tell you this—no one who obeys me shall ever die!"

52The leaders of the Jews said, "Now we know you are possessed by a demon. Even Abraham and the mightiest prophets died, and yet you say that obeying you will keep a man from dying! 53So you are greater than our father Abraham, who died? And greater than the prophets, who died? Who do you think you are?" 54Then Jesus told them this: "If I am merely boasting about myself, it doesn't count. But it is my Father— and you claim him as your God—who is saying these glorious things about me. 55But you do not even know him. I do. If I said otherwise, I would be as great a liar as you! But it is true—I know him and fully obey him. 56Your father Abraham rejoiced to see my day. He knew I was coming and was glad."

57*The Jewish leaders:* "You aren't even fifty years old—sure, you've seen Abraham!"

58*Jesus:* "The absolute truth is that I was in existence before Abraham was ever born!"

59At that point the Jewish leaders picked up stones to kill him. But Jesus was hidden from them, and walked past them and left the Temple.

PSALM 112:1–10

PRAISE the Lord! For all who fear God and trust in him are blessed beyond expression. Yes, happy is the man who delights in doing his commands.

²His children shall be honored everywhere, for good men's sons have a special heritage. ³He himself shall be wealthy, and his good deeds will never be forgotten. ⁴When darkness overtakes him, light will come bursting in. He is kind and merciful— ⁵and all goes well for the generous man who conducts his business fairly.

⁶Such a man will not be overthrown by evil circumstances. God's constant care of him will make a deep impression on all who see it. ⁷He does not fear bad news, nor live in dread of what may happen. For he is settled in his mind that Jehovah will take care of him. ⁸That is why he is not afraid, but can calmly face his foes. ⁹He gives generously to those in need. His deeds will never be forgotten. He shall have influence and honor.

¹⁰Evil-minded men will be infuriated when they see all this; they will gnash their teeth in anger and slink away, their hopes thwarted.

PROVERBS FOR TODAY/ 15:12–14

A mocker stays away from wise men because he hates to be scolded. A happy face means a glad heart; a sad face means a breaking heart. A wise man is hungry for truth, while the mocker feeds on trash.

MAY 17

1 SAMUEL 20:1—21:15

DAVID now fled from Naioth in Ramah, and found Jonathan.

"What have I done?" he exclaimed. "Why is your father so determined to kill me?"

²"That's not true!" Jonathan protested. "I'm sure he's not planning any such thing, for he always tells me everything he's going to do, even little things, and I know he wouldn't hide something like this from me. It just isn't so."

³"Of course you don't know about it!" David fumed. "Your father knows perfectly well about our friendship, so he has said to himself, 'I'll not tell Jonathan—why should I hurt him?' But the truth is that I am only a step away from death! I swear it by the Lord and by your own soul!"

⁴"Tell me what I can do," Jonathan begged.

⁵And David replied, "Tomorrow is the beginning of the celebration of the new moon. Always before, I've been with your father for this occasion, but tomorrow I'll hide in the field and stay there until the evening of the third day. ⁶If your father asks where I am, tell him that I asked permission to go home to Bethlehem for an annual family reunion. ⁷If he says, 'Fine!' then I'll know that all is well. But if he is angry, then I'll know that he is planning to kill me. ⁸Do this for me as my sworn brother. Or else kill me yourself if I have sinned against your father, but don't betray me to him!"

⁹"Of course not!" Jonathan exclaimed. "Look, wouldn't I say so if I knew that my father was planning to kill you?"

¹⁰Then David asked, "How will I know whether or not your father is angry?"

¹¹"Come out to the field with me," Jonathan replied. And they went out there together.

¹²Then Jonathan told David, "I promise by the Lord God of Israel that about this time tomorrow, or the next day at the latest, I will talk to my father about you and let you know at once how he feels about you. ¹³If he is angry and wants you killed, then may the Lord kill me if I don't tell you, so you can escape and

live. May the Lord be with you as he used to be with my father. 14And remember, you must demonstrate the love and kindness of the Lord not only to me during my own lifetime, 15but also to my children after the Lord has destroyed all of your enemies."

16So Jonathan made a covenant with the family of David, and David swore to it with a terrible curse against himself and his descendants, should he be unfaithful to his promise. 17But Jonathan made David swear to it again, this time by his love for him, for he loved him as much as he loved himself.

18Then Jonathan said, "Yes, they will miss you tomorrow when your place at the table is empty. 19By the day after tomorrow, everyone will be asking about you, so be at the hideout where you were before, over by the stone pile. 20I will come out and shoot three arrows in front of the pile as though I were shooting at a target. 21Then I'll send a lad to bring the arrows back. If you hear me tell him, 'They're on this side,' then you will know that all is well and that there is no trouble. 22But if I tell him, 'Go farther—the arrows are still ahead of you,' then it will mean that you must leave immediately. 23And may the Lord make us keep our promises to each other, for he has witnessed them."

24,25So David hid himself in the field. When the new moon celebration began, the king sat down to eat at his usual place against the wall. Jonathan sat opposite him and Abner was sitting beside Saul, but David's place was empty. 26Saul didn't say anything about it that day, for he supposed that something had happened so that David was ceremonially impure. Yes, surely that must be it! 27But when his place was still empty the next day, Saul asked Jonathan, "Why hasn't David been here for dinner either yesterday or today?"

28,29"He asked me if he could go to Bethlehem to take part in a family celebration," Jonathan replied. "His brother demanded that he be there, so I told him to go ahead."

30Saul boiled with rage. "You fool!" he yelled at him. "Do you think I don't know that you want this son of a nobody to be king in your place, shaming yourself and your mother? 31As long as that fellow is alive, you'll never be king. Now go and get him so I can kill him!"

32"But what has he done?" Jonathan demanded. "Why should he be put to death?"

33Then Saul hurled his spear at Jonathan, intending to kill him; so at last Jonathan realized that his father really meant it when he said David must die. 34Jonathan left the table in fierce anger and refused to eat all that day, for he was crushed by his father's shameful behavior toward David.

35The next morning, as agreed, Jonathan went out into the field and took a young boy with him to gather his arrows.

36"Start running," he told the boy, "so that you can find the arrows as I shoot them." So the boy ran and Jonathan shot an arrow beyond him. 37When the boy had almost reached the arrow, Jonathan shouted, "The arrow is still ahead of you. 38Hurry, hurry, don't wait." So the boy quickly gathered up the arrows and ran back to his master. 39He, of course, didn't understand what Jonathan meant; only Jonathan and David knew. 40Then Jonathan gave his bow and arrows to the boy and told him to take them back to the city.

41As soon as he was gone, David came out from where he had been hiding near the south edge of the field. Both of them were crying as they said goodbye, especially David. 42At last Jonathan said to David, "Cheer up, for we have entrusted each other and each other's children into God's hands forever." So they parted, David going away and Jonathan returning to the city.

DAVID went to the city of Nob to see Ahimelech, the priest. Ahimelech trembled when he saw him.

"Why are you alone?" he asked. "Why is no one with you?"

2"The king has sent me on a private

matter," David lied. "He told me not to tell anybody why I am here. I have told my men where to meet me later. 3Now, what is there to eat? Give me five loaves of bread, or anything else you can."

4"We don't have any regular bread," the priest replied, "but there is the holy bread, which I guess you can have if only your young men have not slept with any women for awhile."

5"Rest assured," David replied. "I never let my men run wild when they are on an expedition, and since they stay clean even on ordinary trips, how much more so on this one!"

6So, since there was no other food available, the priest gave him the holy bread—the Bread of the Presence that was placed before the Lord in the Tabernacle. It had just been replaced that day with fresh bread.

7(Incidentally, Doeg the Edomite, Saul's chief herdsman, was there at that time for ceremonial purification.)

8David asked Ahimelech if he had a spear or sword he could use. "The king's business required such haste, and I left in such a rush that I came away without a weapon!" David explained.

9"Well," the priest replied, "I have the sword of Goliath, the Philistine—the fellow you killed in the valley of Elah. It is wrapped in a cloth in the clothes closet. Take that if you want it, for there is nothing else here."

"Just the thing!" David replied. "Give it to me!"

10Then David hurried on, for he was fearful of Saul, and went to King Achish of Gath. 11But Achish's officers weren't happy about his being there. "Isn't he the top leader of Israel?" they asked.

"Isn't he the one the people honor at their dances, singing, 'Saul has slain his thousands and David his ten thousands'?"

12David heard these comments and was afraid of what King Achish might do to him, 13so he pretended to be insane! He scratched on doors and let his spittle flow down his beard, 14,15until finally King Achish said to his men.

"Must you bring me a madman? We already have enough of them around here! Should such a fellow as this be my guest?"

JOHN 9:1–41

AS he was walking along, he saw a man blind from birth.

2"Master," his disciples asked him, "why was this man born blind? Was it a result of his own sins or those of his parents?"

3"Neither," Jesus answered. "But to demonstrate the power of God. 4All of us must quickly carry out the tasks assigned us by the one who sent me, for there is little time left before the night falls and all work comes to an end. 5But while I am still here in the world, I give it my light."

6Then he spat on the ground and made mud from the spittle and smoothed the mud over the blind man's eyes, 7and told him, "Go and wash in the Pool of Siloam" (the word "Siloam" means "Sent"). So the man went where he was sent and washed and came back seeing!

8His neighbors and others who knew him as a blind beggar asked each other, "Is this the same fellow—that beggar?"

9Some said yes, and some said no. "It can't be the same man," they thought, "but he surely looks like him!"

And the beggar said, "I *am* the same man!"

10Then they asked him how in the world he could see. What had happened?

11And he told them, "A man they call Jesus made mud and smoothed it over my eyes and told me to go to the Pool of Siloam and wash off the mud. I did, and I can see!"

12"Where is he now?" they asked.

"I don't know," he replied.

13Then they took the man to the Pharisees. 14Now as it happened, this all occurred on a Sabbath. 15Then the Pharisees asked him all about it. So he told them how Jesus had smoothed the mud over his eyes, and when it was washed away, he could see!

16Some of them said, "Then this fellow Jesus is not from God, because he is working on the Sabbath."

Others said, "But how could an ordinary sinner do such miracles?" So there was a deep division of opinion among them.

17Then the Pharisees turned on the man who had been blind and demanded, "This man who opened your eyes—who do you say he is?"

"I think he must be a prophet sent from God," the man replied.

18The Jewish leaders wouldn't believe he had been blind, until they called in his parents 19and asked them, "Is this your son? Was he born blind? If so, how can he see?"

20His parents replied, "We know this is our son and that he was born blind, 21but we don't know what happened to make him see, or who did it. He is old enough to speak for himself. Ask him."

22,23They said this in fear of the Jewish leaders who had announced that anyone saying Jesus was the Messiah would be excommunicated.

24So for the second time they called in the man who had been blind and told him, "Give the glory to God, not to Jesus, for we know Jesus is an evil person."

25"I don't know whether he is good or bad," the man replied, "but I know this: *I was blind, and now I see!*"

26"But what did he do?" they asked. "How did he heal you?"

27"Look!" the man exclaimed. "I told you once; didn't you listen? Why do you want to hear it again? Do you want to become his disciples too?"

28Then they cursed him and said, "You are his disciple, but we are disciples of Moses. 29We know God has spoken to Moses, but as for this fellow, we don't know anything about him."

30"Why, that's very strange!" the man replied. "He can heal blind men, and yet you don't know anything about him! 31Well, God doesn't listen to evil men, but he has open ears to those who worship him and do his will. 32Since the world began there has never been anyone who could open the eyes of someone born blind. 33If this man were not from God, he couldn't do it."

34"You illegitimate bastard, you!" they shouted. "Are you trying to teach *us?*" And they threw him out.

35When Jesus heard what had happened, he found the man and said, "Do you believe in the Messiah?"

36The man answered, "Who is he, sir, for I want to."

37"You have seen him," Jesus said, "and he is speaking to you!"

38"Yes, Lord," the man said, "I believe!" And he worshiped Jesus.

39Then Jesus told him, "I have come into the world to give sight to those who are spiritually blind and to show those who think they see that they are blind."

40The Pharisees who were standing there asked, "Are you saying we are blind?"

41"If you were blind, you wouldn't be guilty," Jesus replied. "But your guilt remains because you claim to know what you are doing.

PSALM 113:1—114:8

HALLELUJAH! O servants of Jehovah, praise his name. 2Blessed is his name forever and forever. 3Praise him from sunrise to sunset! 4For he is high above the nations; his glory is far greater than the heavens.

5Who can be compared with God enthroned on high? 6Far below him are the heavens and the earth; he stoops to look, 7and lifts the poor from the dirt, and the hungry from the garbage dump, 8and sets them among princes! 9He gives children to the childless wife, so that she becomes a happy mother.

Hallelujah! Praise the Lord.

LONG ago when the Israelis escaped from Egypt, from that land of foreign tongue, 2then the lands of Judah and of Israel became God's new home and kingdom.

3The Red Sea saw them coming and

quickly broke apart before them. The Jordan River opened up a path for them to cross. 4The mountains skipped like rams, the little hills like lambs! 5What's wrong, Red Sea, that made you cut yourself in two? What happened, Jordan River, to your waters? Why were they held back? 6Why, mountains, did you skip like rams? Why, little hills, like lambs?

7Tremble, O earth, at the presence of the Lord, the God of Jacob. 8For he caused gushing streams to burst from flinty rock.

PROVERBS FOR TODAY/ 15:15–17

When a man is gloomy, everything seems to go wrong; when he is cheerful, everything seems right! Better a little with reverence for God, than great treasure and trouble with it. It is better to eat soup with someone you love than steak with someone you hate.

MAY 18

1 SAMUEL 22:1—23:29

So David left Gath and escaped to the cave of Adullam, where his brothers and other relatives soon joined him. 2Then others began coming—those who were in any kind of trouble, such as being in debt, or merely discontented—until David was the leader of about four hundred men.

3(Later David went to Mizpeh in Moab to ask permission of the king for his father and mother to live there under royal protection until David knew what God was going to do for him. 4They stayed in Moab during the entire period when David was living in the cave.)

5One day the prophet Gad told David to leave the cave and return to the land of Judah. So David went to the forest of Hereth. 6The news of his arrival in Judah soon reached Saul. He was in Gibe-ah at the time, sitting beneath an oak tree playing with his spear, surrounded by his officers.

7"Listen here, you men of Benjamin!" Saul exclaimed when he heard the news. "Has David promised you fields and vineyards and commissions in his army? 8Is that why you are against me? For not one of you has ever told me that my own son is on David's side. You're not even sorry for me. Think of it! My own son—encouraging David to come and kill me!"

9,10Then Doeg the Edomite, who was standing there with Saul's men, spoke up. "When I was at Nob," he said, "I saw David talking to Ahimelech the priest. Ahimelech consulted the Lord to find out what David should do, and then gave him food and the sword of Goliath the Philistine."

11,12King Saul immediately summoned Ahimelech and all his family and all the other priests at Nob. When they arrived Saul shouted at him, "Listen to me, you son of Ahitub!"

"What is it?" quavered Ahimelech.

13"Why have you and David conspired against me?" Saul demanded. "Why did you give him food and a sword and talk to God for him? Why did you encourage him to revolt against me and to come here and attack me?"

14"But sir," Ahimelech replied, "is there anyone among all your servants who is as faithful as David your son-in-law? Why, he is the captain of your bodyguard and a highly honored member of your own household! 15This was certainly not the first time I had consulted God for him! It's unfair for you to accuse me and my family in this matter, for we knew nothing of any plot against you."

16"You shall die, Ahimelech, along with your entire family!" the king shouted. 17He ordered his bodyguards, "Kill these priests, for they are allies and conspirators with David; they knew he was running away from me, but they didn't tell me!"

But the soldiers refused to harm the clergy.

18Then the king said to Doeg, "You do it."

So Doeg turned on them and killed them, eighty-five priests in all, all wearing their priestly robes. 19Then he went to Nob, the city of the priests, and killed the priests' families—men, women, children, and babies, and also all the oxen, donkeys, and sheep. 20Only Abiathar, one of the sons of Ahimelech, escaped and fled to David.

21When he told him what Saul had done, 22David exclaimed, "I knew it! When I saw Doeg there, I knew he would tell Saul. Now I have caused the death of all of your father's family. 23Stay here with me, and I'll protect you with my own life. Any harm to you will be over my dead body."

ONE day news came to David that the Philistines were at Keilah robbing the threshing floors.

2David asked the Lord, "Shall I go and attack them?"

"Yes, go and save Keilah," the Lord told him.

3But David's men said, "We're afraid even here in Judah; we certainly don't want to go to Keilah to fight the whole Philistine army!"

4David asked the Lord again, and the Lord again replied, "Go down to Keilah, for I will help you conquer the Philistines."

5They went to Keilah and slaughtered the Philistines and confiscated their cattle, and so the people of Keilah were saved. 6(Abiathar the priest went to Keilah with David, taking his ephod with him to get answers for David from the Lord.) 7Saul soon learned that David was at Keilah.

"Good!" he exclaimed. "We've got him now! God has delivered him to me, for he has trapped himself in a walled city!"

8So Saul mobilized his entire army to march to Keilah and besiege David and his men. 9But David learned of Saul's plan and told Abiathar the priest to bring the ephod and to ask the Lord what he should do.

10"O Lord God of Israel," David said, "I have heard that Saul is planning to come and destroy Keilah because I am here. 11Will the men of Keilah surrender me to him? And will Saul actually come, as I have heard? O Lord God of Israel, please tell me."

And the Lord said, "He will come."

12"And will these men of Keilah betray me to Saul?" David persisted.

And the Lord replied, "Yes, they will betray you."

13So David and his men—about six hundred of them now—left Keilah and began roaming the countryside. Word soon reached Saul that David had escaped, so he didn't go there after all. 14,15David now lived in the wilderness caves in the hill country of Ziph. One day near Horesh he received the news that Saul was on the way to Ziph to search for him and kill him. Saul hunted him day after day, but the Lord didn't let him find him.

16(Prince Jonathan now went to find David; he met him at Horesh and encouraged him in his faith in God.

17"Don't be afraid," Jonathan reassured him. "My father will never find you! You are going to be the king of Israel and I will be next to you, as my father is well aware." 18So the two of them renewed their pact of friendship; and David stayed at Horesh while Jonathan returned home.)

19But now the men of Ziph went to Saul in Gibe-ah and betrayed David to him.

"We know where he is hiding," they said. "He is in the caves of Horesh on Hachilah Hill, down in the southern part of the wilderness. ²⁰Come on down, sir, and we will catch him for you and your fondest wish will be fulfilled!"

²¹"Well, praise the Lord!" Saul said. "At last someone has had pity on me! ²²Go and check again to be sure of where he is staying and who has seen him there, for I know that he is very crafty. ²³Discover his hiding places and then come back and give me a more definite report. Then I'll go with you. And if he is in the area at all, I'll find him if I have to search every inch of the entire land!"

²⁴,²⁵So the men of Ziph returned home. But when David heard that Saul was on his way to Ziph, he and his men went even further into the wilderness of Maon in the south of the desert. But Saul followed them there. ²⁶He and David were now on opposite sides of a mountain. As Saul and his men began to close in, David tried his best to escape, but it was no use. ²⁷But just then a message reached Saul that the Philistines were raiding Israel again, ²⁸so Saul quit the chase and returned to fight the Philistines. Ever since that time the place where David was camped has been called, "The Rock of Escape!" ²⁹David then went to live in the caves of Engedi.

JOHN 10:1–21

ANYONE refusing to walk through the gate into a sheepfold, who sneaks over the wall, must surely be a thief! ²For a shepherd comes through the gate. ³The gatekeeper opens the gate for him, and the sheep hear his voice and come to him; and he calls his own sheep by name and leads them out. ⁴He walks ahead of them; and they follow him, for they recognize his voice. ⁵They won't follow a stranger but will run from him, for they don't recognize his voice."

⁶Those who heard Jesus use this illustration didn't understand what he meant, ⁷so he explained it to them.

"I am the Gate for the sheep," he said. ⁸"All others who came before me were thieves and robbers. But the true sheep did not listen to them. ⁹Yes, I am the Gate. Those who come in by way of the Gate will be saved and will go in and out and find green pastures. ¹⁰The thief's purpose is to steal, kill and destroy. My purpose is to give life in all its fullness.

¹¹"I am the Good Shepherd. The Good Shepherd lays down his life for the sheep. ¹²A hired man will run when he sees a wolf coming and will leave the sheep, for they aren't his and he isn't their shepherd. And so the wolf leaps on them and scatters the flock. ¹³The hired man runs because he is hired and has no real concern for the sheep.

¹⁴"I am the Good Shepherd and know my own sheep, and they know me, ¹⁵just as my Father knows me and I know the Father; and I lay down my life for the sheep. ¹⁶I have other sheep, too, in another fold. I must bring them also, and they will heed my voice; and there will be one flock with one Shepherd.

¹⁷"The Father loves me because I lay down my life that I may have it back again. ¹⁸No one can kill me without my consent—I lay down my life voluntarily. For I have the right and power to lay it down when I want to and also the right and power to take it again. For the Father has given me this right."

¹⁹When he said these things, the Jewish leaders were again divided in their opinions about him. ²⁰Some of them said, "He has a demon or else is crazy. Why listen to a man like that?"

²¹Others said, "This doesn't sound to us like a man possessed by a demon! Can a demon open the eyes of blind men?"

PSALM 115:1–18

GLORIFY your name, not ours, O Lord! Cause everyone to praise your lovingkindness and your truth. ²Why let the nations say, "Their God is dead!"

3For he is in the heavens, and does as he wishes. 4Their gods are merely manmade things of silver and of gold. 5They can't talk or see, despite their eyes and mouths! 6Nor can they hear, nor smell, 7nor use their hands or feet! Nor speak! 8And those who make and worship them are just as foolish as their idols are.

9O Israel, trust the Lord! He is your helper. He is your shield. 10O priests of Aaron, trust the Lord! He is your helper; he is your shield. 11All of you, his people, trust in him. He is your helper; he is your shield.

12Jehovah is constantly thinking about us and he will surely bless us. He will bless the people of Israel and the priests of Aaron, 13and all, both great and small, who reverence him.

14May the Lord richly bless both you and your children. 15Yes, Jehovah who made heaven and earth will personally bless you! 16The heavens belong to the Lord, but he has given the earth to all mankind.

17The dead cannot sing praises to Jehovah here on earth, 18but we can! We praise him forever! Hallelujah! Praise the Lord!

PROVERBS FOR TODAY/ 15:18–19

A quick-tempered man starts fights; a cool-tempered man tries to stop them. A lazy fellow has trouble all through life; the good man's path is easy!

MAY 19

1 SAMUEL 24:1—25:44

AFTER Saul's return from his battle with the Philistines, he was told that David had gone into the wilderness of Engedi; 2so he took three thousand special troops and went to search for him among the rocks and wild goats of the desert. 3At the place where the road passes some sheepfolds, Saul went into a cave to go to the bathroom, but as it happened, David and his men were hiding in the cave!

4"Now's your time!" David's men whispered to him. "Today is the day the Lord was talking about when he said, 'I will certainly put Saul into your power, to do with as you wish'!" Then David crept forward and quietly slit off the bottom of Saul's robe! 5But then his conscience began bothering him.

6"I shouldn't have done it," he said to his men. "It is a serious sin to attack God's chosen king in any way."

7,8These words of David persuaded his men not to kill Saul.

After Saul had left the cave and gone on his way, David came out and shouted after him, "My lord the king!" And when Saul looked around, David bowed low before him.

9,10Then he shouted to Saul, "Why do you listen to the people who say I am trying to harm you? This very day you have seen it isn't true. For the Lord placed you at my mercy back there in the cave and some of my men told me to kill you, but I spared you. For I said, 'I will never harm him—he is the Lord's chosen king.' 11See what I have in my hand? It is the hem of your robe! I cut it off, but I didn't kill you! Doesn't this convince you that I am not trying to harm you and that I have not sinned against you, even though you have been hunting for my life?

12"The Lord will decide between us.

Perhaps he will kill you for what you are trying to do to me, but I will never harm you. 13As that old proverb says, 'Wicked is as wicked does,' but despite your wickedness, I'll not touch you. 14And who is the king of Israel trying to catch, anyway? Should he spend his time chasing one who is as worthless as a dead dog or a flea? 15May the Lord judge as to which of us is right and punish whichever one of us is guilty. He is my lawyer and defender, and he will rescue me from your power!"

16Saul called back, "Is it really you, my son David?" Then he began to cry. 17And he said to David, "You are a better man than I am, for you have repaid me good for evil. 18Yes, you have been wonderfully kind to me today, for when the Lord delivered me into your hand, you didn't kill me. 19Who else in all the world would let his enemy get away when he had him in his power? May the Lord reward you well for the kindness you have shown me today. 20And now I realize that you are surely going to be king, and Israel shall be yours to rule. 21Oh, swear to me by the Lord that when that happens you will not kill my family and destroy my line of descendants!"

22So David promised, and Saul went home, but David and his men went back to their cave.

SHORTLY afterwards, Samuel died and all Israel gathered for his funeral and buried him in his family plot at Ramah.

Meanwhile David went down to the wilderness of Paran. 2A wealthy man from Maon owned a sheep ranch there, near the village of Carmel. He had three thousand sheep and a thousand goats, and was at his ranch at this time for the sheep shearing. 3His name was Nabal and his wife, a beautiful and very intelligent woman, was named Abigail. But the man, who was a descendant of Caleb, was uncouth, churlish, stubborn, and ill-mannered.

4When David heard that Nabal was shearing his sheep, 5he sent ten of his young men to Carmel to give him this message: 6"May God prosper you and your family and multiply everything you own. 7I am told that you are shearing your sheep and goats. While your shepherds have lived among us, we have never harmed them, nor stolen anything from them the whole time they have been in Carmel. 8Ask your young men and they will tell you whether or not this is true. Now I have sent my men to ask for a little contribution from you, for we have come at a happy time of holiday. Please give us a present of whatever is at hand."

9The young men gave David's message to Nabal and waited for his reply.

10"Who is this fellow David?" he sneered. "Who does this son of Jesse think he is? There are lots of servants these days who run away from their masters. 11Should I take my bread and my water and my meat that I've slaughtered for my shearers and give it to a gang who comes from God knows where?"

12So David's messengers returned and told him what Nabal had said.

13"Get your swords!" was David's reply as he strapped on his own. Four hundred of them started off with David and two hundred remained behind to guard their gear.

14Meanwhile, one of Nabal's men went and told Abigail, "David sent men from the wilderness to talk to our master, but he insulted them and railed at them. 15,16But David's men were very good to us and we never suffered any harm from them; in fact, day and night they were like a wall of protection to us and the sheep, and nothing was stolen from us the whole time they were with us. 17You'd better think fast, for there is going to be trouble for our master and his whole family—he's such a stubborn lout that no one can even talk to him!"

18Then Abigail hurriedly took two hundred loaves of bread, two barrels of wine, five dressed sheep, two bushels of roasted grain, one hundred raisin cakes, and two hundred fig cakes, and packed them onto donkeys.

19"Go on ahead," she said to her young

men, "and I will follow." But she didn't tell her husband what she was doing. 20As she was riding down the trail on her donkey, she met David coming towards her.

21David had been saying to himself, "A lot of good it did us to help this fellow. We protected his flocks in the wilderness so that not one thing was lost or stolen, but he has repaid me bad for good. All that I get for my trouble is insults. 22May God curse me if even one of his men remains alive by tomorrow morning!"

23When Abigail saw David, she quickly dismounted and bowed low before him. 24"I accept all blame in this matter, my lord," she said. "Please listen to what I want to say. 25Nabal is a bad-tempered boor, but please don't pay any attention to what he said. He is a fool—just like his name means. But I didn't see the messengers you sent. 26Sir, since the Lord has kept you from murdering and taking vengeance into your own hands, I pray by the life of God, and by your own life too, that all your enemies shall be as cursed as Nabal is. 27And now, here is a present I have brought to you and your young men. 28Forgive me for my boldness in coming out here. The Lord will surely reward you with eternal royalty for your descendants, for you are fighting his battles; and you will never do wrong throughout your entire life. 29Even when you are chased by those who seek your life, you are safe in the care of the Lord your God, just as though you were safe inside his purse! But the lives of your enemies shall disappear like stones from a sling! 30,31When the Lord has done all the good things he promised you and has made you king of Israel, you won't want the conscience of a murderer who took the law into his own hands! And when the Lord has done these great things for you, please remember me!"

32David replied to Abigail, "Bless the Lord God of Israel who has sent you to meet me today! 33Thank God for your good sense! Bless you for keeping me from murdering the man and carrying out vengeance with my own hands. 34For I swear by the Lord, the God of Israel who has kept me from hurting you, that if you had not come out to meet me, not one of Nabal's men would be alive tomorrow morning."

35Then David accepted her gifts and told her to return home without fear, for he would not kill her husband. 36When she arrived home she found that Nabal had thrown a big party. He was roaring drunk, so she didn't tell him anything about her meeting with David until the next morning. 37,38By that time he was sober, and when his wife told him what had happened, he had a stroke and lay paralyzed for about ten days, then died, for the Lord killed him.

39When David heard that Nabal was dead, he said, "Praise the Lord! God has paid back Nabal and kept me from doing it myself; he has received his punishment for his sin."

Then David wasted no time in sending messengers to Abigail to ask her to become his wife. 40When the messengers arrived at Carmel and told her why they had come, 41she readily agreed to his request. 42Quickly getting ready, she took along five of her serving girls as attendants, mounted her donkey, and followed the men back to David. So she became his wife.

43David also married Ahino-am from Jezreel. 44King Saul, meanwhile, had forced David's wife Michal, Saul's daughter, to marry a man from Gallim named Palti (the son of Laish).

JOHN 10:22–42

IT was winter, and Jesus was in Jerusalem at the time of the Dedication Celebration. He was at the Temple, walking through the section known as Solomon's Hall. 24The Jewish leaders surrounded him and asked, "How long are you going to keep us in suspense? If you are the Messiah, tell us plainly."

25"I have already told you, and you don't believe me," Jesus replied. "The proof is in the miracles I do in the name of my Father. 26But you don't believe me because you are not part of my flock. 27My sheep recognize my voice, and I know them, and they follow me. 28I give them eternal life and they shall never perish. No one shall snatch them away from me, 29for my Father has given them to me, and he is more powerful than anyone else, so no one can kidnap them from me. 30I and the Father are one."

31Then again the Jewish leaders picked up stones to kill him.

32Jesus said, "At God's direction I have done many a miracle to help the people. For which one are you killing me?"

33They replied, "Not for any good work, but for blasphemy; you, a mere man, have declared yourself to be God."

34,35,36"In your own Law it says that men are gods!" he replied. "So if the Scripture, which cannot be untrue, speaks of those as gods to whom the message of God came, do you call it blasphemy when the one sanctified and sent into the world by the Father says, 'I am the Son of God'? 37Don't believe me unless I do miracles of God. 38But if I do, believe them even if you don't believe me. Then you will become convinced that the Father is in me, and I in the Father."

39Once again they started to arrest him. But he walked away and left them, 40and went beyond the Jordan River to stay near the place where John was first baptizing. 41And many followed him.

"John didn't do miracles," they remarked to one another, "but all his predictions concerning this man have come true." 42And many came to the decision that he was the Messiah.

PSALM 116:1–19

I love the Lord because he hears my prayers and answers them. 2Because he bends down and listens, I will pray as long as I breathe! 3Death stared me in the face—I was frightened and sad. 4Then I cried, "Lord, save me!" 5How kind he is! How good he is! So merciful, this God of ours! 6The Lord protects the simple and the childlike; I was facing death and then he saved me. 7Now I can relax. For the Lord has done this wonderful miracle for me. 8He has saved me from death, my eyes from tears, my feet from stumbling. 9I shall live! Yes, in his presence—here on earth!

10,11In my discouragement I thought, "They are lying when they say I will recover." 12But now what can I offer Jehovah for all he has done for me? 13I will bring him an offering of wine and praise his name for saving me. 14I will publicly bring him the sacrifice I vowed I would. 15His loved ones are very precious to him and he does not lightly let them die.

16O Lord, you have freed me from my bonds and I will serve you forever. 17I will worship you and offer you a sacrifice of thanksgiving. 18,19Here in the courts of the Temple in Jerusalem, before all the people, I will pay everything I vowed to the Lord. Praise the Lord.

PROVERBS FOR TODAY/ 15:20–21

A sensible son gladdens his father. A rebellious son saddens his mother. If a man enjoys folly, something is wrong! The sensible stay on the pathways of right.

1 SAMUEL 26:1—28:25

NOW the men from Ziph came back to Saul at Gibe-ah to tell him that David had returned to the wilderness and was hiding on Hachilah Hill. ²So Saul took his elite corps of three thousand troops and went to hunt him down. ³,⁴Saul camped along the road at the edge of the wilderness where David was hiding, but David knew of Saul's arrival and sent out spies to watch his movements.

⁵,⁶,⁷David slipped over to Saul's camp one night to look around. King Saul and General Abner were sleeping inside a ring formed by the slumbering soldiers.

"Any volunteers to go down there with me?" David asked Ahimelech (the Hittite) and Abishai (Joab's brother and the son of Zeruiah).

"I'll go with you," Abishai replied. So David and Abishai went to Saul's camp and found him asleep, with his spear in the ground beside his head.

⁸"God has put your enemy within your power this time for sure," Abishai whispered to David. "Let me go and put that spear through him. I'll pin him to the earth with it—I'll not need to strike a second time!"

⁹"No," David said. "Don't kill him, for who can remain innocent after attacking the Lord's chosen king? ¹⁰Surely God will strike him down some day, or he will die in battle or of old age. ¹¹But God forbid that I should kill the man he has chosen to be king! But I'll tell you what— we'll take his spear and his jug of water and then get out of here!"

¹²So David took the spear and jug of water, and they got away without anyone seeing them or even waking up, because the Lord had put them sound asleep. ¹³They climbed the mountain slope opposite the camp until they were at a safe distance.

¹⁴Then David shouted down to Abner and Saul, "Wake up, Abner!"

"Who is it?" Abner demanded.

¹⁵"Well, Abner, you're a great fellow, aren't you?" David taunted. "Where in all Israel is there anyone as wonderful? So why haven't you guarded your master the king when someone came to kill him? ¹⁶This isn't good at all! I swear by the Lord that you ought to die for your carelessness. Where is the king's spear and the jug of water that was beside his head? Look and see!"

¹⁷,¹⁸Saul recognized David's voice and said, "Is that you, my son David?"

And David replied, "Yes, sir, it is. Why are you chasing me? What have I done? What is my crime? ¹⁹If the Lord has stirred you up against me, then let him accept my peace offering. But if this is simply the scheme of a man, then may he be cursed by God. For you have driven me out of my home so that I can't be with the Lord's people, and you have sent me away to worship heathen gods. ²⁰Must I die on foreign soil, far from the presence of Jehovah? Why should the king of Israel come out to hunt my life like a partridge on the mountains?"

²¹Then Saul confessed, "I have done wrong. Come back home, my son, and I'll no longer try to harm you; for you saved my life today. I have been a fool, and very, very wrong."

²²"Here is your spear, sir," David replied. "Let one of your young men come over and get it. ²³The Lord gives his own reward for doing good and for being loyal, and I refused to kill you even when the Lord placed you in my power. ²⁴Now may the Lord save my life, even as I have saved yours today. May he rescue me from all my troubles."

²⁵And Saul said to David, "Blessings on you, my son David. You shall do heroic deeds and be a great conqueror."

Then David went away and Saul returned home.

BUT David kept thinking to himself, "Some day Saul is going to get me. I'll try my luck among the Philistines until Saul gives up and quits hunting for me; then I will finally be safe again."

2,3So David took his six hundred men and their families to live at Gath under the protection of King Achish. He had his two wives with him—Ahino-am of Jezreel and Abigail of Carmel, Nabal's widow. 4Word soon reached Saul that David had fled to Gath, so he quit hunting for him.

5One day David said to Achish, "My lord, if it is all right with you, we would rather live in one of the country towns instead of here in the royal city."

6So Achish gave him Ziklag (which still belongs to the kings of Judah to this day), 7and they lived there among the Philistines for a year and four months. 8He and his men spent their time raiding the Geshurites, the Girzites, and the Amalekites—people who had lived near Shur along the road to Egypt ever since ancient times. 9They didn't leave one person alive in the villages they hit, and took for themselves the sheep, oxen, donkeys, camels, and clothing before returning to their homes.

10"Where did you make your raid today?" Achish would ask.

And David would reply, "Against the south of Judah and the people of Jerahmeel and the Kenites."

11No one was left alive to come to Gath and tell where he had really been. This happened again and again while he was living among the Philistines. 12Achish believed David and thought that the people of Israel must hate him bitterly by now. "Now he will have to stay here and serve me forever!" the king thought.

ABOUT that time the Philistines mustered their armies for another war with Israel.

"Come and help us fight," King Achish said to David and his men.

2"Good," David agreed. "You will soon see what a help we can be to you."

"If you are, you shall be my personal bodyguard for life," Achish told him.

3(Meanwhile, Samuel had died and all Israel had mourned for him. He was buried in Ramah, his home town. King Saul had banned all mediums and wizards from the land of Israel.)

4The Philistines set up their camp at Shunem, and Saul and the armies of Israel were at Gilboa. 5,6When Saul saw the vast army of the Philistines, he was frantic with fear and asked the Lord what he should do. But the Lord refused to answer him, either by dreams, or by Urim, or by the prophets. 7,8Saul then instructed his aides to try to find a medium so that he could ask her what to do, and they found one at Endor. Saul disguised himself by wearing ordinary clothing instead of his royal robes. He went to the woman's home at night, accompanied by two of his men.

"I've got to talk to a dead man," he pleaded. "Will you bring his spirit up?"

9"Are you trying to get me killed?" the woman demanded. "You know that Saul has had all of the mediums and fortune-tellers executed. You are spying on me."

10But Saul took a solemn oath that he wouldn't betray her.

11Finally the woman said, "Well, whom do you want me to bring up?"

"Bring me Samuel," Saul replied.

12When the woman saw Samuel, she screamed, "You've deceived me! You are Saul!"

13"Don't be frightened!" the king told her. "What do you see?"

"I see a specter coming up out of the earth," she said.

14"What does he look like?"

"He is an old man wrapped in a robe."

Saul realized that it was Samuel and bowed low before him.

15"Why have you disturbed me by bringing me back?" Samuel asked Saul.

"Because I am in deep trouble," he replied. "The Philistines are at war with us, and God has left me and won't reply by prophets or dreams; so I have called for you to ask you what to do."

16But Samuel replied, "Why ask me if the Lord has left you and has become your enemy? 17He has done just as he said he would and has taken the kingdom from you and given it to your rival, David. 18All this has come upon you because you did not obey the Lord's instructions when he was so angry with Amalek. 19What's more, the entire Israeli army will be routed and destroyed by the Philistines tomorrow, and you and your sons will be here with me."

20Saul now fell full length upon the ground, paralyzed with fright because of Samuel's words. He was also faint with hunger, for he had eaten nothing all day. 21When the woman saw how distraught he was, she said, "Sir, I obeyed your command at the risk of my life. 22Now do what I say, and let me give you something to eat so you'll regain your strength for the trip back."

23But he refused. The men who were with him added their pleas to that of the woman until he finally yielded and got up and sat on the bed. 24The woman had been fattening a calf, so she hurried out and killed it and kneaded dough and baked unleavened bread. 25She brought the meal to the king and his men, and they ate it. Then they went out into the night.

JOHN 11:1–53

DO you remember Mary, who poured the costly perfume on Jesus' feet and wiped them with her hair? Well, her brother Lazarus, who lived in Bethany with Mary and her sister Martha, was sick. 3So the two sisters sent a message to Jesus telling him, "Sir, your good friend is very, very sick."

4But when Jesus heard about it he said, "The purpose of his illness is not death, but for the glory of God. I, the Son of God, will receive glory from this situation."

5Although Jesus was very fond of Martha, Mary, and Lazarus, 6he stayed where he was for the next two days and made no move to go to them. 7Finally, after

the two days, he said to his disciples, "Let's go to Judea."

8But his disciples objected. "Master," they said, "only a few days ago the Jewish leaders in Judea were trying to kill you. Are you going there again?"

9Jesus replied, "There are twelve hours of daylight every day, and during every hour of it a man can walk safely and not stumble. 10Only at night is there danger of a wrong step, because of the dark." 11Then he said, "Our friend Lazarus has gone to sleep, but now I will go and waken him!"

12,13The disciples, thinking Jesus meant Lazarus was having a good night's rest, said, "That means he is getting better!" But Jesus meant Lazarus had died.

14Then he told them plainly, "Lazarus is dead. 15And for your sake, I am glad I wasn't there, for this will give you another opportunity to believe in me. Come, let's go to him."

16Thomas, nicknamed "The Twin," said to his fellow disciples, "Let's go too—and die with him."

17When they arrived at Bethany, they were told that Lazarus had already been in his tomb for four days. 18Bethany was only a couple of miles down the road from Jerusalem, 19and many of the Jewish leaders had come to pay their respects and to console Martha and Mary on their loss. 20When Martha got word that Jesus was coming, she went to meet him. But Mary stayed at home.

21Martha said to Jesus, "Sir, if you had been here, my brother wouldn't have died. 22And even now it's not too late, for I know that God will bring my brother back to life again, if you will only ask him to."

23Jesus told her, "Your brother will come back to life again."

24"Yes," Martha said, "when everyone else does, on Resurrection Day."

25Jesus told her, "I am the one who raises the dead and gives them life again. Anyone who believes in me, even though he dies like anyone else, shall live again. 26He is given eternal life for believing in me and shall never perish. Do you believe this, Martha?"

27"Yes, Master," she told him. "I believe you are the Messiah, the Son of God, the one we have so long awaited."

28Then she left him and returned to Mary and, calling her aside from the mourners, told her, "He is here and wants to see you." 29So Mary went to him at once.

30Now Jesus had stayed outside the village, at the place where Martha met him. 31When the Jewish leaders who were at the house trying to console Mary saw her leave so hastily, they assumed she was going to Lazarus' tomb to weep; so they followed her.

32When Mary arrived where Jesus was, she fell down at his feet, saying, "Sir, if you had been here, my brother would still be alive."

33When Jesus saw her weeping and the Jewish leaders wailing with her, he was moved with indignation and deeply troubled. 34"Where is he buried?" he asked them.

They told him, "Come and see." 35Tears came to Jesus' eyes.

36"They were close friends," the Jewish leaders said. "See how much he loved him."

37,38But some said, "This fellow healed a blind man—why couldn't he keep Lazarus from dying?"

And again Jesus was moved with deep anger. Then they came to the tomb. It was a cave with a heavy stone rolled across its door.

39"Roll the stone aside," Jesus told them.

But Martha, the dead man's sister, said, "By now the smell will be terrible, for he has been dead four days."

40"But didn't I tell you that you will see a wonderful miracle from God if you believe?" Jesus asked her.

41So they rolled the stone aside. Then Jesus looked up to heaven and said, "Father, thank you for hearing me. 42(You always hear me, of course, but I said it because of all these people standing here, so that they will believe you sent me.)"

43Then he shouted, "Lazarus, come out!"

44And Lazarus came—bound up in the gravecloth, his face muffled in a head swath. Jesus told them, "Unwrap him and let him go!"

45And so at last many of the Jewish leaders who were with Mary and saw it happen, finally believed on him. 46But some went away to the Pharisees and reported it to them.

47Then the chief priests and Pharisees convened a council to discuss the situation.

"What are we going to do?" they asked each other. "For this man certainly does miracles. 48If we let him alone the whole nation will follow him—and then the Roman army will come and kill us and take over the Jewish government."

49And one of them, Caiaphas, who was High Priest that year, said, "You stupid idiots— 50let this one man die for the people—why should the whole nation perish?"

51This prophecy that Jesus should die for the entire nation came from Caiaphas in his position as High Priest—he didn't think of it by himself, but was inspired to say it. 52It was a prediction that Jesus' death would not be for Israel only, but for all the children of God scattered around the world. 53So from that time on the Jewish leaders began plotting Jesus' death.

PSALM 117:1–2

PRAISE the Lord, all nations everywhere. Praise him, all the peoples of the earth. 2For he loves us very dearly, and his truth endures. Praise the Lord.

PROVERBS FOR TODAY/ 15:22–23

Plans go wrong with too few counselors; many counselors bring success. Everyone enjoys giving good advice, and how wonderful it is to be able to say the right thing at the right time!

1 SAMUEL 29:1—31:13

THE Philistine army now mobilized at Aphek, and the Israelis camped at the springs in Jezreel. ²As the Philistine captains were leading out their troops by battalions and companies, David and his men marched at the rear with King Achish.

³But the Philistine commanders demanded, "What are these Israelis doing here?"

And King Achish told them, "This is David, the runaway servant of King Saul of Israel. He's been with me for years, and I've never found one fault in him since he arrived."

⁴But the Philistine leaders were angry. "Send them back!" they demanded. "They aren't going into the battle with us—they'll turn against us. Is there any better way for him to reconcile himself with his master than by turning against us in the battle? ⁵This is the same man the women of Israel sang about in their dances: 'Saul has slain his thousands and David his ten thousands!' "

⁶So Achish finally summoned David and his men.

"I swear by the Lord," he told them, "you are some of the finest men I've ever met, and I think you should go with us, but my commanders say no. ⁷Please don't upset them, but go back quietly."

⁸"What have I done to deserve this treatment?" David demanded. "Why can't I fight your enemies?"

⁹But Achish insisted, "As far as I'm concerned, you're as perfect as an angel of God. But my commanders are afraid to have you with them in the battle. ¹⁰Now get up early in the morning and leave as soon as it is light."

¹¹So David headed back into the land of the Philistines while the Philistine army went on to Jezreel.

THREE days later, when David and his men arrived home at their city of Ziklag, they found that the Amalekites had raided the city and burned it to the ground, ²carrying off all the women and children. ³As David and his men looked at the ruins and realized what had happened to their families, ⁴they wept until they could weep no more. ⁵(David's two wives, Ahino-am and Abigail, were among those who had been captured.) ⁶David was seriously worried, for in their bitter grief for their children, his men began talking of killing him. But David took strength from the Lord.

⁷Then he said to Abiathar the priest, "Bring me the oracle!" So Abiathar brought it.

⁸David asked the Lord, "Shall I chase them? Will I catch them?"

And the Lord told him, "Yes, go after them; you will recover everything that was taken from you!"

⁹,¹⁰So David and his six hundred men set out after the Amalekites. When they reached Besor Brook, two hundred of the men were too exhausted to cross, but the other four hundred kept going. ¹¹,¹²Along the way they found an Egyptian youth in a field and brought him to David. He had not had anything to eat or drink for three days and nights, so they gave him part of a fig cake, two clusters of raisins, and some water, and his strength soon returned.

¹³"Who are you and where do you come from?" David asked him.

"I am an Egyptian—the servant of an Amalekite," he replied. "My master left me behind three days ago because I was sick. ¹⁴We were on our way back from raiding the Cherethites in the Negeb, and had raided the south of Judah and the land of Caleb, and had burned Ziklag."

¹⁵"Can you tell me where they went?" David asked.

The young man replied, "If you swear by God's name that you will not kill me or give me back to my master, then I will guide you to them."

16So he led them to the Amalekite encampment. They were spread out across the fields, eating and drinking and dancing with joy because of the vast amount of loot they had taken from the Philistines and from the men of Judah. 17David and his men rushed in among them and slaughtered them all that night and the entire next day until evening. No one escaped except four hundred young men who fled on camels. 18,19David got back everything they had taken. The men recovered their families and all of their belongings, and David rescued his two wives. 20His troops rounded up all the flocks and herds and drove them on ahead of them. "These are all yours personally, as your reward!" they told David.

21When they reached Besor Brook and the two hundred men who had been too exhausted to go on, David greeted them joyfully. 22But some of the ruffians among David's men declared, "They didn't go with us, so they can't have any of the loot. Give them their wives and their children and tell them to be gone."

23But David said, "No, my brothers! The Lord has kept us safe and helped us defeat the enemy. 24Do you think that anyone will listen to you when you talk like this? We share and share alike—those who go to battle and those who guard the equipment."

25From then on David made this a law for all of Israel, and it is still followed.

26When he arrived at Ziklag, he sent part of the loot to the elders of Judah. "Here is a present for you, taken from the Lord's enemies," he wrote them. 27-31The gifts were sent to the elders in the following cities where David and his men had been: Bethel, South Ramoth, Jattir, Aroer, Siphmoth, Eshtemoa, Racal, the cities of the Jerahmeelites, the cities of the Kenites, Hormah, Borashan, Athach, Hebron.

MEANWHILE the Philistines had begun the battle against Israel, and the Israelis fled from them and were slaughtered wholesale on Mount Gilboa. 2The Philistines closed in on Saul, and killed his sons Jonathan, Abinidab, and Malchishua.

3,4Then the archers overtook Saul and wounded him badly. He groaned to his armor bearer, "Kill me with your sword before these heathen Philistines capture me and torture me." But his armor bearer was afraid to, so Saul took his own sword and fell upon the point of the blade, and it pierced him through. 5When his armor bearer saw that he was dead, he also fell upon his sword and died with him. 6So Saul, his armor bearer, his three sons, and his troops died together that same day.

7When the Israelis on the other side of the valley and beyond the Jordan heard that their comrades had fled and that Saul and his sons were dead, they abandoned their cities; and the Philistines lived in them.

8The next day when the Philistines went out to strip the dead, they found the bodies of Saul and his three sons on Mount Gilboa. 9They cut off Saul's head and stripped off his armor and sent the wonderful news of Saul's death to their idols and to the people throughout their land.

10His armor was placed in the temple of Ashtaroth, and his body was fastened to the wall of Beth-shan.

11But when the people of Jabesh-gilead heard what the Philistines had done, 12warriors from that town traveled all night to Beth-shan and took down the bodies of Saul and his sons from the wall and brought them to Jabesh, where they cremated them. 13Then they buried their remains beneath the oak tree at Jabesh and fasted for seven days.

JOHN 11:54—12:19

JESUS now stopped his public ministry and left Jerusalem; he went to the edge of the desert, to the village of Ephraim, and stayed there with his disciples.

55The Passover, a Jewish holy day, was near, and many country people arrived in Jerusalem several days early so that they could go through the cleansing ceremony before the Passover began. 56They wanted to see Jesus, and as they gossiped in the Temple, they asked each other, "What do you think? Will he come for the Passover?" 57Meanwhile the chief priests and Pharisees had publicly announced that anyone seeing Jesus must report him immediately so that they could arrest him.

SIX days before the Passover ceremonies began, Jesus arrived in Bethany where Lazarus was—the man he had brought back to life. 2A banquet was prepared in Jesus' honor. Martha served, and Lazarus sat at the table with him. 3Then Mary took a jar of costly perfume made from essence of nard, and anointed Jesus' feet with it and wiped them with her hair. And the house was filled with fragrance.

4But Judas Iscariot, one of his disciples—the one who would betray him—said, 5"That perfume was worth a fortune. It should have been sold and the money given to the poor." 6Not that he cared for the poor, but he was in charge of the disciples' funds and often dipped into them for his own use!

7Jesus replied, "Let her alone. She did it in preparation for my burial. 8You can always help the poor, but I won't be with you very long."

9When the ordinary people of Jerusalem heard of his arrival, they flocked to see him and also to see Lazarus—the man who had come back to life again. 10Then the chief priests decided to kill Lazarus too, 11for it was because of him that many of the Jewish leaders had deserted and believed in Jesus as their Messiah.

12The next day, the news that Jesus was on the way to Jerusalem swept through the city, and a huge crowd of Passover visitors 13took palm branches and went down the road to meet him, shouting, "The Savior! God bless the King of Israel! Hail to God's Ambassador!"

14Jesus rode along on a young donkey, fulfilling the prophecy that said: 15"Don't be afraid of your King, people of Israel, for he will come to you meekly, sitting on a donkey's colt!"

16(His disciples didn't realize at the time that this was a fulfillment of prophecy; but after Jesus returned to his glory in heaven, then they noticed how many prophecies of Scripture had come true before their eyes.)

17And those in the crowd who had seen Jesus call Lazarus back to life were telling all about it. 18That was the main reason why so many went out to meet him—because they had heard about this mighty miracle.

19Then the Pharisees said to each other, "We've lost. Look—the whole world has gone after him!"

PSALM 118:1–18

O H, thank the Lord, for he's so good! His lovingkindness is forever.

2Let the congregation of Israel praise him with these same words: "His lovingkindness is forever." 3And let the priests of Aaron chant, "His lovingkindness is forever." 4Let the Gentile converts chant, "His lovingkindness is forever."

5In my distress I prayed to the Lord and he answered me and rescued me. 6He is for me! How can I be afraid? What can mere man do to me? 7The Lord is on my side, he will help me. Let those who hate me beware.

8It is better to trust the Lord than to put confidence in men. 9It is better to take refuge in him than in the mightiest king!

10Though all the nations of the world attack me, I will march out behind his banner and destroy them. 11Yes, they surround and attack me; but with his flag flying above me I will cut them off. 12They swarm around me like bees; they blaze against me like a roaring flame. Yet beneath his flag I shall destroy them. 13You did your best to kill me, O my enemy, but the Lord helped me. 14He is my strength and song in the heat of battle, and now he has given me the victory. 15,16Songs of joy at the news of our rescue are sung in the homes of the godly. The strong arm of the Lord has done glorious things! 17I shall not die, but live to tell of all his deeds. 18The Lord has punished me, but not handed me over to death.

PROVERBS FOR TODAY/ 15:24–26

The road of the godly leads upward, leaving hell behind. The Lord destroys the possessions of the proud but cares for widows. The Lord hates the thoughts of the wicked but delights in kind words.

MAY 22

2 SAMUEL 1:1—2:11

SAUL was dead and David had returned to Ziklag after slaughtering the Amalekites. Three days later a man arrived from the Israeli army with his clothes torn and with dirt on his head as a sign of mourning. He fell to the ground before David in deep respect.

3"Where do you come from?" David asked.

"From the Israeli army," he replied.

4"What happened?" David demanded. "Tell me how the battle went."

And the man replied, "Our entire army fled. Thousands of men are dead and wounded on the field, and Saul and his son Jonathan have been killed."

5"How do you know they are dead?"

6"Because I was on Mount Gilboa and saw Saul leaning against his spear with the enemy chariots closing in upon him. 7When he saw me he cried out for me to come to him.

8" 'Who are you?' he asked.

" 'An Amalekite,' I replied.

9" 'Come and put me out of my misery,' he begged, 'for I am in terrible pain but life lingers on.'

10"So I killed him, for I knew he couldn't live. Then I took his crown and one of his bracelets to bring to you, my lord."

11David and his men tore their clothes in sorrow when they heard the news. 12They mourned and wept and fasted all day for Saul and his son Jonathan, and for the Lord's people, and for the men of Israel who had died that day.

13Then David said to the young man who had brought the news, "Where are you from?"

And he replied, "I am an Amalekite."

14"Why did you kill God's chosen king?" David demanded.

15Then he said to one of his young men, "Kill him!" So he ran him through with his sword and he died.

16"You die self-condemned," David said, "for you yourself confessed that you killed God's appointed king."

17,18Then David composed a dirge for Saul and Jonathan and afterward commanded that it be sung throughout Israel. It is quoted here from the book, *Heroic Ballads.*

19O Israel, your pride and joy lies dead
    upon the hills;
Mighty heroes have fallen.
20Don't tell the Philistines, lest they
    rejoice.
Hide it from the cities of Gath and
    Ashkelon,
Lest the heathen nations laugh in tri-
    umph.
21O Mount Gilboa,
Let there be no dew nor rain upon
    you,
Let no crops of grain grow on your
    slopes.
For there the mighty Saul has died;

He is God's appointed king no more.
²²Both Saul and Jonathan slew their strongest foes,
And did not return from battle empty-handed.
²³How much they were loved, how wonderful they were—
Both Saul and Jonathan!
They were together in life and in death.
They were swifter than eagles, stronger than lions.
²⁴But now, O women of Israel, weep for Saul;
He enriched you
With fine clothing and gold ornaments.
²⁵These mighty heroes have fallen in the midst of the battle.
Jonathan is slain upon the hills.
²⁶How I weep for you, my brother Jonathan;
How much I loved you!
And your love for me was deeper
Than the love of women!
²⁷The mighty ones have fallen,
Stripped of their weapons, and dead.

DAVID then asked the Lord, "Shall I move back to Judah?"

And the Lord replied, "Yes."

"Which city shall I go to?"

And the Lord replied, "Hebron."

²So David and his wives—Ahino-am from Jezreel and Abigail the widow of Nabal from Carmel— ³and his men and their families all moved to Hebron. ⁴Then the leaders of Judah came to David and crowned him king of the Judean confederacy.

When David heard that the men of Jabesh-gilead had buried Saul, ⁵he sent them this message: "May the Lord bless you for being so loyal to your king and giving him a decent burial. ⁶May the Lord be loyal to you in return, and reward you with many demonstrations of his love! And I too will be kind to you because of what you have done. ⁷And now I ask you to be my strong and loyal subjects, now that Saul is dead. Be like the tribe of Judah who have appointed me as their new king."

⁸But Abner, Saul's commander-in-chief, had gone to Mahanaim to crown Saul's son Ish-bosheth as king. ⁹His territory included Gilead, Ashuri, Jezreel, Ephraim, the tribe of Benjamin, and all the rest of Israel. ¹⁰,¹¹Ish-bosheth was forty years old at the time. He reigned in Mahanaim for two years; meanwhile, David was reigning in Hebron and was king of the Judean confederacy for seven and one-half years.

JOHN 12:20–50

SOME Greeks who had come to Jerusalem to attend the Passover ²¹paid a visit to Philip, who was from Bethsaida, and said, "Sir, we want to meet Jesus." ²²Philip told Andrew about it, and they went together to ask Jesus.

²³,²⁴Jesus replied that the time had come for him to return to his glory in heaven, and that "I must fall and die like a kernel of wheat that falls into the furrows of the earth. Unless I die I will be alone—a single seed. But my death will produce many new wheat kernels—a plentiful harvest of new lives. ²⁵If you love your life down here—you will lose it. If you despise your life down here—you will exchange it for eternal glory.

²⁶"If these Greeks want to be my disciples, tell them to come and follow me, for my servants must be where I am. And if they follow me, the Father will honor them. ²⁷Now my soul is deeply troubled. Shall I pray, 'Father, save me from what lies ahead'? But that is the very reason why I came! ²⁸Father, bring glory and honor to your name."

Then a voice spoke from heaven saying, "I have already done this, and I will do it again." ²⁹When the crowd heard the voice, some of them thought it was thunder, while others declared an angel had spoken to him.

³⁰Then Jesus told them, "The voice was for your benefit, not mine. ³¹The time of judgment for the world has come—and the time when Satan, the prince of this world, shall be cast out. ³²And when I am lifted up [on the cross],

I will draw everyone to me." 33He said this to indicate how he was going to die.

34"Die?" asked the crowd. "We understood that the Messiah would live forever and never die. Why are you saying he will die? What Messiah are you talking about?"

35Jesus replied, "My light will shine out for you just a little while longer. Walk in it while you can, and go where you want to go before the darkness falls, for then it will be too late for you to find your way. 36Make use of the Light while there is still time; then you will become light bearers."

After saying these things, Jesus went away and was hidden from them.

37But despite all the miracles he had done, most of the people would not believe he was the Messiah. 38This is exactly what Isaiah the prophet had predicted: "Lord, who will believe us? Who will accept God's mighty miracles as proof?" 39But they couldn't believe, for as Isaiah also said: 40"God has blinded their eyes and hardened their hearts so that they can neither see nor understand nor turn to me to heal them." 41Isaiah was referring to Jesus when he made this prediction, for he had seen a vision of the Messiah's glory.

42However, even many of the Jewish leaders believed him to be the Messiah but wouldn't admit it to anyone because of their fear that the Pharisees would excommunicate them from the synagogue; 43for they loved the praise of men more than the praise of God.

44Jesus shouted to the crowds, "If you trust me, you are really trusting God. 45For when you see me, you are seeing the one who sent me. 46I have come as a Light to shine in this dark world, so that all who put their trust in me will no longer wander in the darkness. 47If anyone hears me and doesn't obey me, I am not his judge—for I have come to save the world and not to judge it. 48But all who reject me and my message will be judged at the Day of Judgment by the truths I have spoken. 49For these are not my own ideas, but I have told you what the Father said to tell you. 50And I know his instructions lead to eternal life; so whatever he tells me to say, I say!"

PSALM 118:19–29

OPEN the gates of the Temple—I will go in and give him my thanks. 20Those gates are the way into the presence of the Lord, and the godly enter there. 21O Lord, thank you so much for answering my prayer and saving me.

22The stone rejected by the builders has now become the capstone of the arch! 23This is the Lord's doing, and it is marvelous to see! 24This is the day the Lord has made. We will rejoice and be glad in it. 25O Lord, please help us. Save us. Give us success. 26Blessed is the one who is coming, the one sent by the Lord. We bless you from the Temple.

27,28Jehovah God is our light. I present to him my sacrifice upon the altar, for you are my God, and I shall give you this thanks and this praise. 29Oh, give thanks to the Lord, for he is so good! For his lovingkindness is forever.

PROVERBS FOR TODAY/ 15:27–28

Dishonest money brings grief to all the family, but hating bribes brings happiness. A good man thinks before he speaks; the evil man pours out his evil words without a thought.

MAY 23

2 SAMUEL 2:12—3:39

ONE day General Abner led some of Ishbosheth's troops to Gibeon from Mahanaim, 13and General Joab (the son of Zeruiah) led David's troops out to meet them. They met at the pool of Gibeon, where they sat facing each other on opposite sides of the pool. 14Then Abner suggested to Joab, "Let's watch some sword play between our young men!"

Joab agreed, 15so twelve men were chosen from each side to fight in mortal combat. 16Each one grabbed his opponent by the hair and thrust his sword into the other's side, so that all of them died. The place has been known ever since as Sword Field.

17The two armies then began to fight each other, and by the end of the day Abner and the men of Israel had been defeated by Joab and the forces of David. 18Joab's brothers, Abishai and Asahel, were also in the battle. Asahel could run like a deer, 19and he began chasing Abner. He wouldn't stop for anything, but kept on, singleminded, after Abner alone.

20When Abner looked behind and saw him coming, he called out to him, "Is that you, Asahel?"

"Yes," he called back, "it is."

21"Go after someone else!" Abner warned. But Asahel refused and kept on coming.

22Again Abner shouted to him, "Get away from here. I could never face your brother Joab if I have to kill you!"

23But he refused to turn away, so Abner pierced him through the belly with the butt end of his spear. It went right through his body and came out his back. He stumbled to the ground and died there, and everyone stopped when they came to the place where he lay.

24Now Joab and Abishai set out after Abner. The sun was just going down as they arrived at Ammah Hill near Giah, along the road into the Gibeon desert.

25Abner's troops from the tribe of Benjamin regrouped there at the top of the hill, 26and Abner shouted down to Joab, "Must our swords continue to kill each other forever? How long will it be before you call off your people from chasing their brothers?"

27Joab shouted back, "I swear by God that even if you hadn't spoken, we would all have gone home tomorrow morning." 28Then he blew his trumpet and his men stopped chasing the troops of Israel.

29That night Abner and his men retreated across the Jordan Valley, crossed the river, and traveled all the next morning until they arrived at Mahanaim. 30Joab and the men who were with him returned home too, and when he counted his casualties, he learned that only nineteen men were missing, in addition to Asahel. 31But three hundred and sixty of Abner's men (all from the tribe of Benjamin) were dead. 32Joab and his men took Asahel's body to Bethlehem and buried him beside his father; then they traveled all night and reached Hebron at daybreak.

THAT was the beginning of a long war between the followers of Saul and of David. David's position now became stronger and stronger, while Saul's dynasty became weaker and weaker.

2Several sons were born to David while he was at Hebron. The oldest was Amnon, born to his wife Ahino-am. 3His second son, Chileab, was born to Abigail, the widow of Nabal of Carmel. The third was Absalom, born to Maacah, the daughter of King Talmai of Geshur. 4The fourth was Adonijah, who was born to Haggith. Then Shephatiah was born to Abital, and 5Ithream was born to Eglah.

6As the war went on, Abner became a very powerful political leader among the followers of Saul. 7He took advantage of his position by sleeping with one of

Saul's concubines, a girl named Rizpah. But when Ish-bosheth accused Abner of this, 8Abner was furious.

"Am I a Judean dog to be kicked around like this?" he shouted. "After all I have done for you and for your father by not betraying you to David, is this my reward—to find fault with me about some woman? 9,10May God curse me if I don't do everything I can to take away the entire kingdom from you, all the way from Dan to Beersheba, and give it to David, just as the Lord predicted."

11Ish-bosheth made no reply, for he was afraid of Abner.

12Then Abner sent messengers to David to discuss a deal—to surrender the kingdom of Israel to him in exchange for becoming commander-in-chief of the combined armies of Israel and Judah.

13"All right," David replied, "but I will not negotiate with you unless you bring me my wife Michal, Saul's daughter." 14David then sent this message to Ish-bosheth: "Give me back my wife Michal, for I bought her with the lives of one hundred Philistines."

15So Ish-bosheth took her away from her husband Palti. 16He followed along behind her as far as Behurim, weeping as he went. Then Abner told him, "Go on home now." So he returned.

17Meanwhile, Abner consulted with the leaders of Israel and reminded them that for a long time they had wanted David as their king.

18"Now is the time!" he told them. "For the Lord has said, 'It is David by whom I will save my people from the Philistines and from all their other enemies.'"

19Abner also talked to the leaders of the tribe of Benjamin; then he went to Hebron and reported to David his progress with the people of Israel and Benjamin. 20Twenty men accompanied him, and David entertained them with a feast.

21As Abner left, he promised David, "When I get back I will call a convention of all the people of Israel, and they will elect you as their king, as you've so long desired." So David let Abner return in safety.

22But just after Abner left, Joab and some of David's troops returned from a raid, bringing much loot with them. 23When Joab was told that Abner had just been there visiting the king and had been sent away in peace, 24,25he rushed to the king, demanding, "What have you done? What do you mean by letting him get away? You know perfectly well that he came to spy on us and that he plans to return and attack us!"

26Then Joab sent messengers to catch up with Abner and tell him to come back. They found him at the well of Sirah and he returned with them; but David knew nothing about it. 27When Abner arrived at Hebron, Joab took him aside at the city gate as if to speak with him privately; but then he pulled out a dagger and killed him in revenge for the death of his brother Asahel.

28When David heard about it he declared, "I vow by the Lord that I and my people are innocent of this crime against Abner. 29Joab and his family are the guilty ones. May each of his children be victims of cancer, or be lepers, or be sterile, or die of starvation, or be killed by the sword!"

30So Joab and his brother Abishai killed Abner because of the death of their brother Asahel at the battle of Gibeon.

31Then David said to Joab and to all those who were with him, "Go into deep mourning for Abner." And King David accompanied the bier to the cemetery. 32They buried Abner in Hebron. And the king and all the people wept at the graveside.

33,34"Should Abner have died like a fool?" the king lamented.

"Your hands were not bound,
Your feet were not tied—
You were murdered—
The victim of a wicked plot."

And all the people wept again for him. 35,36David had refused to eat anything the day of the funeral, and now everyone begged him to take a bite of supper. But David vowed that he would eat nothing until sundown. This pleased his people, just as everything else he did pleased them! ³⁷Thus the whole nation, both Judah and Israel, understood from David's actions that he was in no way responsible for Abner's death.

³⁸And David said to his people, "A great leader and a great man has fallen today in Israel; ³⁹and even though I am God's chosen king, I can do nothing with these two sons of Zeruiah. May the Lord repay wicked men for their wicked deeds."

JOHN 13:1–30

JESUS knew on the evening of Passover Day that it would be his last night on earth before returning to his Father. During supper the devil had already suggested to Judas Iscariot, Simon's son, that this was the night to carry out his plan to betray Jesus. Jesus knew that the Father had given him everything and that he had come from God and would return to God. And how he loved his disciples! ⁴So he got up from the supper table, took off his robe, wrapped a towel around his loins, ⁵poured water into a basin, and began to wash the disciples' feet and to wipe them with the towel he had around him.

⁶When he came to Simon Peter, Peter said to him, "Master, you shouldn't be washing our feet like this!"

⁷Jesus replied, "You don't understand now why I am doing it; some day you will."

⁸"No," Peter protested, "you shall never wash my feet!"

"But if I don't, you can't be my partner," Jesus replied.

⁹Simon Peter exclaimed, "Then wash my hands and head as well—not just my feet!"

¹⁰Jesus replied, "One who has bathed all over needs only to have his feet washed to be entirely clean. Now you are clean—but that isn't true of everyone here." ¹¹For Jesus knew who would betray him. That is what he meant when he said, "Not all of you are clean."

¹²After washing their feet he put on his robe again and sat down and asked, "Do you understand what I was doing? ¹³You call me 'Master' and 'Lord,' and you do well to say it, for it is true. ¹⁴And since I, the Lord and Teacher, have washed your feet, you ought to wash each other's feet. ¹⁵I have given you an example to follow: do as I have done to you. ¹⁶How true it is that a servant is not greater than his master. Nor is the messenger more important than the one who sends him. ¹⁷You know these things—now do them! That is the path of blessing.

¹⁸"I am not saying these things to all of you; I know so well each one of you I chose. The Scripture declares, 'One who eats supper with me will betray me,' and this will soon come true. ¹⁹I tell you this now so that when it happens, you will believe on me.

²⁰"Truly, anyone welcoming my messenger is welcoming me. And to welcome me is to welcome the Father who sent me."

²¹Now Jesus was in great anguish of spirit and exclaimed, "Yes, it is true— one of you will betray me." ²²The disciples looked at each other, wondering whom he could mean. ²³Since I was sitting next to Jesus at the table, being his closest friend, ²⁴Simon Peter motioned to me to ask him who it was who would do this terrible deed.

²⁵So I turned and asked him, "Lord, who is it?"

²⁶He told me, "It is the one I honor by giving the bread dipped in the sauce."

And when he had dipped it, he gave it to Judas, son of Simon Iscariot.

²⁷As soon as Judas had eaten it, Satan entered into him. Then Jesus told him, "Hurry—do it now."

²⁸None of the others at the table knew what Jesus meant. ²⁹Some thought that since Judas was their treasurer, Jesus was telling him to go and pay for the food or to give some money to the poor. ³⁰Judas left at once, going out into the night.

PSALM 119:1–16

HAPPY are all who perfectly follow the laws of God. ²Happy are all who search for God, and always do his will, ³rejecting compromise with evil, and walking only in his paths. ⁴You have given us your laws to obey— ⁵oh, how I want to follow them consistently. ⁶Then I will not be disgraced, for I will have a clean record.

⁷After you have corrected me I will thank you by living as I should! ⁸I *will* obey! Oh, don't forsake me and let me slip back into sin again.

⁹How can a young man stay pure? By reading your Word and following its rules. ¹⁰I have tried my best to find you— don't let me wander off from your instructions. ¹¹I have thought much about your words, and stored them in my heart so that they would hold me back from sin.

¹²Blessed Lord, teach me your rules. ¹³I have recited your laws, ¹⁴and rejoiced in them more than in riches. ¹⁵I will meditate upon them and give them my full respect. ¹⁶I will delight in them and not forget them.

PROVERBS FOR TODAY/ 15:29–30

The Lord is far from the wicked, but he hears the prayers of the righteous. Pleasant sights and good reports give happiness and health.

MAY 24

2 SAMUEL 4:1—6:23

WHEN King Ish-bosheth heard about Abner's death at Hebron, he was paralyzed with fear, and his people too were badly frightened. ²,³The command of the Israeli troops then fell to two brothers, Baanah and Rechab, who were captains of King Ish-bosheth's raiding bands. They were the sons of Rimmon, who was from Be-eroth in Benjamin. (People from Be-eroth are counted as Benjaminites even though they fled to Gittaim, where they now live.)

⁴(There was a little lame grandson of King Saul's named Mephibosheth, who was the son of Prince Jonathan. He was five years old at the time Saul and Jonathan were killed at the battle of Jezreel. When the news of the outcome of the battle reached the capital, the child's nurse grabbed him and fled, but she fell and dropped him as she was running, and he became lame.)

⁵Rechab and Baanah arrived at King Ish-bosheth's home one noon as he was taking a nap. ⁶,⁷They walked into the kitchen as though to get a sack of wheat, but then sneaked into his bedroom and murdered him and cut off his head. Taking his head with them, they fled across the desert that night and escaped. ⁸They presented the head to David at Hebron.

"Look!" they exclaimed. "Here is the head of Ish-bosheth, the son of your enemy Saul who tried to kill you. Today the Lord has given you revenge upon Saul and upon his entire family!"

⁹But David replied, "I swear by the Lord who saved me from my enemies, ¹⁰that when someone told me, 'Saul is dead,' thinking he was bringing me good news, I killed him; that is how I rewarded him for his 'glad tidings.' ¹¹And how much more shall I do to wicked men who kill a good man in his own house and on his bed! Shall I not demand your lives?"

¹²So David ordered his young men to

kill them, and they did. They cut off their hands and feet and hanged their bodies beside the pool in Hebron. And they took Ish-bosheth's head and buried it in Abner's tomb in Hebron.

REPRESENTATIVES of all the tribes of Israel now came to David at Hebron and gave him their pledge of loyalty.

"We are your blood brothers," they said. 2"And even when Saul was our king you were our real leader. The Lord has said that you should be the shepherd and leader of his people."

3So David made a contract before the Lord with the leaders of Israel there at Hebron, and they crowned him king of Israel. 4,5(He had already been the king of Judah for seven years, since the age of thirty. He then ruled thirty-three years in Jerusalem as king of both Israel and Judah; so he reigned for forty years altogether.)

6David now led his troops to Jerusalem to fight against the Jebusites who lived there.

"You'll never come in here," they told him. "Even the blind and lame could keep you out!" For they thought they were safe. 7But David and his troops defeated them and captured the stronghold of Zion, now called the City of David.

8When the insulting message from the defenders of the city reached David, he told his troops, "Go up through the water tunnel into the city and destroy those 'lame' and 'blind' Jebusites. How I hate them." (That is the origin of the saying, "Even the blind and the lame could conquer you!")

9So David made the stronghold of Zion (also called the City of David) his headquarters. Then, beginning at the old Millo section of the city, he built northward toward the present city center. 10So David became greater and greater, for the Lord God of heaven was with him.

11Then King Hiram of Tyre sent cedar lumber, carpenters, and masons to build a palace for David. 12David now realized why the Lord had made him the king and blessed his kingdom so greatly—it was because God wanted to pour out his kindness on Israel, his chosen people.

13After moving from Hebron to Jerusalem, David married additional wives and concubines, and had many sons and daughters. 14,15,16These are his children who were born at Jerusalem:

Shammu-a, Shobab, Nathan, Solomon, Ibhar, Elishu-a, Nepheg, Japhia, Elishama, Eliada, Eliphelet.

17When the Philistines heard that David had been crowned king of Israel, they tried to capture him; but David was told that they were coming and went into the stronghold. 18The Philistines arrived and spread out across the valley of Rephaim.

19Then David asked the Lord, "Shall I go out and fight against them? Will you defeat them for me?"

And the Lord replied, "Yes, go ahead, for I will give them to you."

20So David went out and fought with them at Baal-perazim, and defeated them. "The Lord did it!" he exclaimed. "He burst through my enemies like a raging flood." So he named the place "Bursting." 21At that time David and his troops confiscated many idols which had been abandoned by the Philistines. 22But the Philistines returned and again spread out across the valley of Rephaim.

23When David asked the Lord what to do, he replied, "Don't make a frontal attack. Go behind them and come out by the balsam trees. 24When you hear a sound like marching feet in the tops of the balsam trees, attack! For it will signify that the Lord has prepared the way for you and will destroy them."

25So David did as the Lord had instructed him and destroyed the Philistines all the way from Geba to Gezer.

THEN David mobilized thirty thousand special troops and led them to Baal-judah to bring home the Ark of the Lord of heaven who is en-throned above the Guardian Angels. 3The Ark was placed upon a new cart and taken from the hillside home of Abinadab. It was driven by Abinadab's sons, Uzzah and Ahio. 4Ahio was walking in front, 5and was followed by David and the other leaders of Israel, who were joyously waving branches of juniper trees and playing every sort of musical instrument before the Lord—lyres, harps, tambourines, castanets, and cymbals.

6But when they arrived at the threshing floor of Nacon, the oxen stumbled and Uzzah put out his hand to steady the Ark. 7Then the anger of the Lord flared out against Uzzah and he killed him for doing this, so he died there beside the Ark. 8David was angry at what the Lord had done, and named the spot "The Place of Wrath upon Uzzah" (which it is still called to this day).

9David was now afraid of the Lord and asked, "How can I ever bring the Ark home?" 10So he decided against taking it into the City of David, but carried it instead to the home of Obed-edom, who had come from Gath. 11It remained there for three months, and the Lord blessed Obed-edom and all his household.

12When David heard this, he brought the Ark to the City of David with a great celebration. 13After the men who were carrying it had gone six paces, they stopped and waited so that he could sacrifice an ox and a fat lamb. 14And David danced before the Lord with all his might, and was wearing priests' clothing. 15So Israel brought home the Ark of the Lord with much shouting and blowing of trumpets.

16(But as the procession came into the city, Michal, Saul's daughter, watched from a window and saw King David leaping and dancing before the Lord; and she was filled with contempt for him.)

17The Ark was placed inside the tent which David had prepared for it; and he sacrificed burnt offerings and peace offerings to the Lord. 18Then he blessed the people in the name of the Lord of heaven, 19and gave a present to everyone—men and women alike—of a loaf of bread, some wine, and a cake of raisins. When it was all over, and everyone had gone home, 20David returned to bless his family.

But Michal came out to meet him and exclaimed in disgust, "How glorious the king of Israel looked today! He exposed himself to the girls along the street like a common pervert!"

21David retorted, "I was dancing before the Lord who chose me above your father and his family and who appointed me as leader of Israel, the people of the Lord! So I am willing to act like a fool in order to show my joy in the Lord. 22Yes, and I am willing to look even more foolish than this, but I will be respected by the girls of whom you spoke!"

23So Michal was childless throughout her life.

JOHN 13:31—14:14

As soon as Judas left the room, Jesus said, "My time has come; the glory of God will soon surround me—and God shall receive great praise because of all that happens to me. 32And God shall give me his own glory, and this so very soon. 33Dear, dear children, how brief are these moments before I must go away and leave you! Then, though you search for me, you cannot come to me—just as I told the Jewish leaders.

34"And so I am giving a new commandment to you now—love each other just as much as I love you. 35Your strong love for each other will prove to the world that you are my disciples."

36Simon Peter said, "Master, where are you going?"

And Jesus replied, "You can't go with me now; but you will follow me later."

37"But why can't I come now?" he asked, "for I am ready to die for you."

38Jesus answered, "Die for me? No—three times before the cock crows tomorrow morning, you will deny that you even know me!

"Let not your heart be troubled. You are trusting God, now trust in me. 2,3There are many homes up there where my Father lives, and I am going to prepare them for your coming. When everything is ready, then I will come and get you, so that you can always be with me where I am. If this weren't so, I would tell you plainly. 4And you know where I am going and how to get there."

5"No, we don't," Thomas said. "We haven't any idea where you are going, so how can we know the way?"

6Jesus told him, "I am the Way—yes, and the Truth and the Life. No one can get to the Father except by means of me. 7If you had known who I am, then you would have known who my Father is. From now on you know him—and have seen him!"

8Philip said, "Sir, show us the Father and we will be satisfied."

9Jesus replied, "Don't you even yet know who I am, Philip, even after all this time I have been with you? Anyone who has seen me has seen the Father! So why are you asking to see him? 10Don't you believe that I am in the Father and the Father is in me? The words I say are not my own but are from my Father who lives in me. And he does his work through me. 11Just believe it—that I am in the Father and the Father is in me. Or else believe it because of the mighty miracles you have seen me do.

12,13"In solemn truth I tell you, anyone believing in me shall do the same miracles I have done, and even greater ones, because I am going to be with the Father. You can ask him for *anything,* using my name, and I will do it, for this will bring praise to the Father because of what I, the Son, will do for you. 14Yes, ask *anything,* using my name, and I will do it!

PSALM 119:17–35

BLESS me with life so that I can continue to obey you. 18Open my eyes to see wonderful things in your Word. 19I am but a pilgrim here on earth: how I need a map—and your commands are my chart and guide. 20I long for your instructions more than I can tell.

21You rebuke those cursed proud ones who refuse your commands— 22don't let them scorn me for obeying you. 23For even princes sit and talk against me, but I will continue in your plans. 24Your laws are both my light and my counselors.

25I am completely discouraged—I lie in the dust. Revive me by your Word. 26I told you my plans and you replied. Now give me your instructions. 27Make me understand what you want; for then I shall see your miracles.

28I weep with grief; my heart is heavy with sorrow; encourage and cheer me with your words. 29,30Keep me far from every wrong; help me, undeserving as I am, to obey your laws, for I have chosen to do right. 31I cling to your commands and follow them as closely as I can. Lord, don't let me make a mess of things. 32If you will only help me to want your will, then I will follow your laws even more closely.

33,34Just tell me what to do and I will do it, Lord. As long as I live I'll wholeheartedly obey. 35Make me walk along the right paths for I know how delightful they really are.

PROVERBS FOR TODAY/ 15:31–32

If you profit from constructive criticism you will be elected to the wise men's hall of fame. But to reject criticism is to harm yourself and your own best interests.

MAY 25

2 SAMUEL 7:1—8:18

WHEN the Lord finally sent peace upon the land, and Israel was no longer at war with the surrounding nations, 2David said to Nathan the prophet, "Look! Here I am living in this beautiful cedar palace while the Ark of God is out in a tent!"

3"Go ahead with what you have in mind," Nathan replied, "for the Lord is with you."

4But that night the Lord said to Nathan, 5"Tell my servant David not to do it! 6For I have never lived in a temple. My home has been a tent ever since the time I brought Israel out of Egypt. 7And I have never once complained to Israel's leaders, the shepherds of my people. Have I ever asked them, 'Why haven't you built me a beautiful cedar temple?'

8"Now go and give this message to David from the Lord of heaven: 'I chose you to be the leader of my people Israel when you were a mere shepherd, tending your sheep in the pastureland. 9I have been with you wherever you have gone and have destroyed your enemies. And I will make your name greater yet, so that you will be one of the most famous men in the world! 10,11I have selected a homeland for my people from which they will never have to move. It will be their own land where the heathen nations won't bother them as they did when the judges ruled my people. There will be no more wars against you; and your descendants shall rule this land for generations to come! 12For when you die, I will put one of your sons upon your throne and I will make his kingdom strong. 13He is the one who shall build me a temple. And I will continue his kingdom into eternity. 14I will be his father and he shall be my son. If he sins, I will use other nations to punish him, 15but my love and kindness shall not leave him as I took it from Saul, your

predecessor. 16Your family shall rule my kingdom forever.' "

17So Nathan went back to David and told him everything the Lord had said.

18Then David went into the Tabernacle and sat before the Lord and prayed, "O Lord God, why have you showered your blessings on such an insignificant person as I am? 19And now, in addition to everything else, you speak of giving me an eternal dynasty! Such generosity is far beyond any human standard! Oh, Lord God! 20What can I say? For you know what I am like! 21You are doing all these things just because you promised to and because you want to! 22How great you are, Lord God! We have never heard of any other god like you. And there is no other god. 23What other nation in all the earth has received such blessings as Israel, your people? For you have rescued your chosen nation in order to bring glory to your name. You have done great miracles to destroy Egypt and its gods. 24You chose Israel to be your people forever, and you became our God.

25"And now, Lord God, do as you have promised concerning me and my family. 26And may you be eternally honored when you have established Israel as your people and have established my dynasty before you. 27For you have revealed to me, O Lord of heaven, God of Israel, that I am the first of a dynasty which will rule your people forever; that is why I have been bold enough to pray this prayer of acceptance. 28For you are indeed God, and your words are truth; and you have promised me these good things— 29so do as you have promised! Bless me and my family forever! May our dynasty continue on and on before you; for you, Lord God, have promised it."

AFTER this David subdued and humbled the Philistines by conquering Gath, their largest city. 2He also devastated the land of Moab. He divided his victims by making them lie down side by side in rows. Two-thirds of each row, as measured with a tape, were butchered, and one-third were spared to become David's servants—they paid him tribute each year.

3He also destroyed the forces of King Hadadezer (son of Rehob) of Zobah in a battle at the Euphrates River, for Hadadezer had attempted to regain his power. 4David captured seventeen hundred cavalry and twenty thousand infantry; then he lamed all of the chariot horses except for one hundred teams. 5He also slaughtered twenty-two thousand Syrians from Damascus when they came to help Hadadezer. 6David placed several army garrisons in Damascus, and the Syrians became David's subjects and brought him annual tribute money. So the Lord gave him victories wherever he turned. 7David brought the gold shields to Jerusalem which King Hadadezer's officers had used. 8He also carried back to Jerusalem a very large amount of bronze from Hadadezer's cities of Betah and Berothai.

9When King Toi of Hamath heard about David's victory over the army of Hadadezer, 10he sent his son Joram to congratulate him, for Hadadezer and Toi were enemies. He gave David presents made from silver, gold, and bronze. 11,12David dedicated all of these to the Lord, along with the silver and gold he had taken from Syria, Moab, Ammon, the Philistines, Amalek, and King Hadadezer.

13So David became very famous. After his return he destroyed eighteen thousand Edomites at the Valley of Salt, 14and then placed garrisons throughout Edom, so that the entire nation was forced to pay tribute to Israel—another example of the way the Lord made him victorious wherever he went.

15David reigned with justice over Israel and was fair to everyone. 16The general of his army was Joab (son of Zeruiah), and his secretary of state was Jehoshaphat (son of Ahilud). 17Zadok (son of Ahitub) and Ahimelech (son of Abiathar) were the High Priests, and Seraiah was the king's private secretary. 18Benaiah (son of Jehoiada) was captain of his bodyguard, and David's sons were his assistants.

JOHN 14:15–31

IF you love me, obey me; and I will ask the Father and he will give you another Comforter, and he will never leave you. 17He is the Holy Spirit, the Spirit who leads into all truth. The world at large cannot receive him, for it isn't looking for him and doesn't recognize him. But you do, for he lives with you now and some day shall be in you. 18No, I will not abandon you or leave you as orphans in the storm—I will come to you. 19In just a little while I will be gone from the world, but I will still be present with you. For I will live again— and you will too. 20When I come back to life again, you will know that I am in my Father, and you in me, and I in you. 21The one who obeys me is the one who loves me; and because he loves me, my Father will love him; and I will too, and I will reveal myself to him."

22Judas (not Judas Iscariot, but his other disciple with that name) said to him, "Sir, why are you going to reveal yourself only to us disciples and not to the world at large?"

23Jesus replied, "Because I will only reveal myself to those who love me and obey me. The Father will love them too, and we will come to them and live with them. 24Anyone who doesn't obey me doesn't love me. And remember, I am not making up this answer to your question! It is the answer given by the Father who sent me.

25"I am telling you these things now while I am still with you. 26But when the Father sends the Comforter instead of me—and by the Comforter I mean the Holy Spirit—he will teach you much, as well as remind you of everything I myself have told you.

27"I am leaving you with a gift—peace of mind and heart! And the peace I give isn't fragile like the peace the world gives.

So don't be troubled or afraid. 28Remember what I told you—I am going away, but I will come back to you again. If you really love me, you will be very happy for me, for now I can go to the Father, who is greater than I am. 29I have told you these things before they happen so that when they do, you will believe [in me].

30"I don't have much more time to talk to you, for the evil prince of this world approaches. He has no power over me, 31but I will freely do what the Father requires of me so that the world will know that I love the Father. Come, let's be going.

PSALM 119:36–52

HELP me to prefer obedience to making money! 37Turn me away from wanting any other plan than yours. Revive my heart toward you. 38Reassure me that your promises are for me, for I trust and revere you.

39How I dread being mocked for obey-ing, for your laws are right and good. 40,41,42I long to obey them! Therefore in fairness renew my life, for this was your promise—yes, Lord, to save me! Now spare me by your kindness and your love. Then I will have an answer for those who taunt me, for I trust your promises.

43May I never forget your words; for they are my only hope. 44,45,46Therefore I will keep on obeying you forever and forever, free within the limits of your laws. I will speak to kings about their value, and they will listen with interest and respect.

47How I love your laws! How I enjoy your commands! 48"Come, come to me," I call to them, for I love them and will let them fill my life.

49,50Never forget your promises to me your servant, for they are my only hope. They give me strength in all my troubles; how they refresh and revive me! 51Proud men hold me in contempt for obedience to God, but I stand unmoved. 52From my earliest youth I have tried to obey you; your Word has been my comfort.

PROVERBS FOR TODAY/ 15:33
Humility and reverence for the Lord will make you both wise and honored.

MAY 26

2 SAMUEL 9:1—11:27

ONE day David began wondering if any of Saul's family was still living, for he wanted to be kind to them, as he had promised Prince Jonathan. 2He heard about a man named Ziba who had been one of Saul's servants, and summoned him.

"Are you Ziba?" the king asked.

"Yes, sir, I am," he replied.

3The king then asked him, "Is anyone left from Saul's family? If so, I want to fulfill a sacred vow by being kind to him."

"Yes," Ziba replied, "Jonathan's lame son is still alive."

4"Where is he?" the king asked.

"In Lo-debar," Ziba told him. "At the home of Machir."

5,6So King David sent for Mephibosheth—Jonathan's son and Saul's grandson. Mephibosheth arrived in great fear and greeted the king in deep humility, bowing low before him.

7But David said, "Don't be afraid! I've asked you to come so that I can be kind to you because of my vow to your father

Jonathan. I will restore to you all the land of your grandfather Saul, and you shall live here at the palace!"

8Mephibosheth fell to the ground before the king. "Should the king show kindness to a dead dog like me?" he exclaimed.

9Then the king summoned Saul's servant Ziba. "I have given your master's grandson everything that belonged to Saul and his family," he said. 10,11"You and your sons and servants are to farm the land for him, to produce food for his family; but he will live here with me."

Ziba, who had fifteen sons and twenty servants, replied, "Sir, I will do all you have commanded."

And from that time on, Mephibosheth ate regularly with King David, as though he were one of his own sons. 12Mephibosheth had a young son, Mica. All the household of Ziba became Mephibosheth's servants, 13but Mephibosheth (who was lame in both feet) moved to Jerusalem to live at the palace.

SOME time after this the Ammonite king died and his son Hanun replaced him. 2"I am going to show special respect for him," David said, "because his father Nahash was always so loyal and kind to me." So David sent ambassadors to express regrets to Hanun about his father's death.

3But Hanun's officers told him, "These men aren't here to honor your father! David has sent them to spy out the city before attacking it!"

4So Hanun took David's men and shaved off half their beards and cut their robes off at the buttocks and sent them home half naked. 5When David heard what had happened he told them to stay at Jericho until their beards grew out; for the men were very embarrassed over their appearance.

6Now the people of Ammon realized how seriously they had angered David, so they hired twenty thousand Syrian mercenaries from the lands of Rehob and Zobah, one thousand from the king of Maacah, and ten thousand from the land

of Tob. 7,8When David heard about this, he sent Joab and the entire Israeli army to attack them. The Ammonites defended the gates of their city while the Syrians from Zobah, Rehob, Tob, and Maacah fought in the fields. 9When Joab realized that he would have to fight on two fronts, he selected the best fighters in his army, placed them under his personal command, and took them out to fight the Syrians in the fields. 10He left the rest of the army to his brother Abishai, who was to attack the city.

11"If I need assistance against the Syrians, come out and help me," Joab instructed him. "And if the Ammonites are too strong for you, I will come and help you. 12Courage! We must really act like men today if we are going to save our people and the cities of our God. May the Lord's will be done."

13And when Joab and his troops attacked, the Syrians began to run away. 14Then, when the Ammonites saw the Syrians running, they ran too, and retreated into the city. Afterwards Joab returned to Jerusalem. 15,16The Syrians now realized that they were no match for Israel. So when they regrouped, they were joined by additional Syrian troops summoned by Hadadezer from the other side of the Euphrates River. These troops arrived at Helam under the command of Shobach, the commander-in-chief of all of Hadadezer's forces.

17When David heard what was happening, he personally led the Israeli army to Helam, where the Syrians attacked him. 18But again the Syrians fled from the Israelis, this time leaving seven hundred charioteers dead on the field, also forty thousand cavalrymen, including General Shobach. 19When Hadadezer's allies saw that the Syrians had been defeated, they surrendered to David and became his servants. And the Syrians were afraid to help the Ammonites anymore after that.

IN the spring of the following year, at the time when wars begin, David sent Joab and the Israeli army to destroy the

Ammonites. They began by laying siege to the city of Rabbah. But David stayed in Jerusalem.

2One night he couldn't get to sleep and went for a stroll on the roof of the palace. As he looked out over the city, he noticed a woman of unusual beauty taking her evening bath. 3He sent to find out who she was and was told that she was Bath-sheba, the daughter of Eliam and the wife of Uriah. 4Then David sent for her and when she came he slept with her. (She had just completed the purification rites after menstruation.) Then she returned home. 5When she found that he had gotten her pregnant she sent a message to inform him.

6So David dispatched a memo to Joab: "Send me Uriah the Hittite." 7When he arrived, David asked him how Joab and the army were getting along and how the war was prospering. 8Then he told him to go home and relax, and he sent a present to him at his home. 9But Uriah didn't go there. He stayed that night at the gateway of the palace with the other servants of the king.

10When David heard what Uriah had done, he summoned him and asked him, "What's the matter with you? Why didn't you go home to your wife last night after being away for so long?"

11Uriah replied, "The Ark and the armies and the general and his officers are camping out in open fields, and should I go home to wine and dine and sleep with my wife? I swear that I will never be guilty of acting like that."

12"Well, stay here tonight," David told him, "and tomorrow you may return to the army."

So Uriah stayed around the palace. 13David invited him to dinner and got him drunk; but even so he didn't go home that night, but again he slept at the entry to the palace.

14Finally the next morning David wrote a letter to Joab and gave it to Uriah to deliver. 15The letter instructed Joab to put Uriah at the front of the hottest part of the battle—and then pull back and leave him there to die! 16So Joab

assigned Uriah to a spot close to the besieged city where he knew that the enemies' best men were fighting; 17and Uriah was killed along with several other Israeli soldiers.

18When Joab sent a report to David of how the battle was going, 19,20,21he told his messenger, "If the king is angry and asks, 'Why did the troops go so close to the city? Didn't they know there would be shooting from the walls? Wasn't Abimelech killed at Thebez by a woman who threw down a millstone on him?'—then tell him, 'Uriah was killed, too.'"

22So the messenger arrived at Jerusalem, and gave the report to David.

23"The enemy came out against us," he said, "and as we chased them back to the city gates, 24the men on the wall attacked us; and some of our men were killed, and Uriah the Hittite is dead too."

25"Well, tell Joab not to be discouraged," David said. "The sword kills one as well as another! Fight harder next time, and conquer the city; tell him he is doing well."

26When Bath-sheba heard that her husband was dead, she mourned for him; 27then, when the period of mourning was over, David sent for her and brought her to the palace and she became one of his wives; and she gave birth to his son. But the Lord was very displeased with what David had done.

JOHN 15:1–27

I am the true Vine, and my Father is the Gardener. 2He lops off every branch that doesn't produce. And he prunes those branches that bear fruit for even larger crops. 3He has already tended you by pruning you back for greater strength and usefulness by means of the commands I gave you. 4Take care to live in me, and let me live in you. For a branch can't produce fruit when severed from the vine. Nor can you be fruitful apart from me.

5"Yes, I am the Vine; you are the branches. Whoever lives in me and I in him shall produce a large crop of fruit. For apart from me you can't do a thing. 6If anyone separates from me, he is thrown away like a useless branch, withers, and is gathered into a pile with all the others and burned. 7But if you stay in me and obey my commands, you may ask any request you like, and it will be granted! 8My true disciples produce bountiful harvests. This brings great glory to my Father.

9"I have loved you even as the Father has loved me. Live within my love. 10When you obey me you are living in my love, just as I obey my Father and live in his love. 11I have told you this so that you will be filled with my joy. Yes, your cup of joy will overflow! 12I demand that you love each other as much as I love you. 13And here is how to measure it—the greatest love is shown when a person lays down his life for his friends; 14and you are my friends if you obey me. 15I no longer call you slaves, for a master doesn't confide in his slaves; now you are my friends, proved by the fact that I have told you everything the Father told me.

16"You didn't choose me! I chose you! I appointed you to go and produce lovely fruit always, so that no matter what you ask for from the Father, using my name, he will give it to you. 17I demand that you love each other, 18for you get enough hate from the world! But then, it hated me before it hated you. 19The world would love you if you belonged to it; but you don't—for I chose you to come out of the world, and so it hates you. 20Do you remember what I told you? 'A slave isn't greater than his master!' So since they persecuted me, naturally they will persecute you. And if they had listened to me, they would listen to you! 21The people of the world will persecute you because you belong to me, for they don't know God who sent me.

22"They would not be guilty if I had not come and spoken to them. But now they have no excuse for their sin.

23Anyone hating me is also hating my Father. 24If I hadn't done such mighty miracles among them they would not be counted guilty. But as it is, they saw these miracles and yet they hated both of us—me and my Father. 25This has fulfilled what the prophets said concerning the Messiah, 'They hated me without reason.'

26"But I will send you the Comforter— the Holy Spirit, the source of all truth. He will come to you from the Father and will tell you all about me. 27And you also must tell everyone about me, because you have been with me from the beginning.

PSALM 119:53–70

I am very angry with those who spurn your commands. 54For these laws of yours have been my source of joy and singing through all these years of my earthly pilgrimage. 55I obey them even at night and keep my thoughts, O Lord, on you. 56What a blessing this has been to me—to constantly obey.

57Jehovah is mine! And I promise to obey! 58With all my heart I want your blessings. Be merciful just as you promised. 59,60I thought about the wrong direction in which I was headed, and turned around and came running back to you. 61Evil men have tried to drag me into sin, but I am firmly anchored to your laws.

62At midnight I will rise to give my thanks to you for your good laws. 63Anyone is my brother who fears and trusts the Lord and obeys him. 64O Lord, the earth is full of your lovingkindness! Teach me your good paths.

65Lord, I am overflowing with your blessings, just as you promised. 66Now teach me good judgment as well as knowledge. For your laws are my guide. 67I used to wander off until you punished me; now I closely follow all you say. 68You are good and do only good; make me follow your lead.

69Proud men have made up lies about

me, but the truth is that I obey your laws with all my heart. 70Their minds are dull and stupid, but I have sense enough to follow you.

PROVERBS FOR TODAY/ 16:1–3

We can make our plans, but the final outcome is in God's hands. We can always "prove" that we are right, but is the Lord convinced? Commit your work to the Lord, then it will succeed.

MAY 27

2 SAMUEL 12:1–31

So the Lord sent the prophet Nathan to tell David this story:

"There were two men in a certain city, one very rich, owning many flocks of sheep and herds of goats; 3and the other very poor, owning nothing but a little lamb he had managed to buy. It was his children's pet and he fed it from his own plate and let it drink from his own cup; he cuddled it in his arms like a baby daughter. 4Recently a guest arrived at the home of the rich man. But instead of killing a lamb from his own flocks for food for the traveler, he took the poor man's lamb and roasted it and served it."

5David was furious. "I swear by the living God," he vowed, "any man who would do a thing like that should be put to death; 6he shall repay four lambs to the poor man for the one he stole, and for having no pity."

7Then Nathan said to David, *"You* are that rich man! The Lord God of Israel says, 'I made you king of Israel and saved you from the power of Saul. 8I gave you his palace and his wives and the kingdoms of Israel and Judah; and if that had not been enough, I would have given you much, much more. 9Why, then, have you despised the laws of God and done this horrible deed? For you have murdered Uriah and stolen his wife. 10Therefore murder shall be a constant threat in your family from this time on, because you have insulted me by taking

Uriah's wife. 11I vow that because of what you have done I will cause your own household to rebel against you. I will give your wives to another man, and he will go to bed with them in public view. 12You did it secretly, but I will do this to you openly, in the sight of all Israel.' "

13"I have sinned against the Lord," David confessed to Nathan.

Then Nathan replied, "Yes, but the Lord has forgiven you, and you won't die for this sin. 14But you have given great opportunity to the enemies of the Lord to despise and blaspheme him, so your child shall die."

15Then Nathan returned to his home. And the Lord made Bath-sheba's baby deathly sick. 16David begged him to spare the child, and went without food and lay all night before the Lord on the bare earth. 17The leaders of the nation pleaded with him to get up and eat with them, but he refused. 18Then, on the seventh day, the baby died. David's aides were afraid to tell him.

"He was so broken up about the baby being sick," they said, "what will he do to himself when we tell him the child is dead?"

19But when David saw them whispering, he realized what had happened.

"Is the baby dead?" he asked.

"Yes," they replied, "he is." 20Then David got up off the ground, washed himself, brushed his hair, changed his clothes, and went into the Tabernacle and worshiped the Lord. Then he returned to the palace and ate. [21]His aides were amazed.

"We don't understand you," they told him. "While the baby was still living, you wept and refused to eat; but now that the baby is dead, you have stopped your mourning and are eating again."

[22]David replied, "I fasted and wept while the child was alive, for I said, 'Perhaps the Lord will be gracious to me and let the child live.' [23]But why should I fast when he is dead? Can I bring him back again? I shall go to him, but he shall not return to me."

[24]Then David comforted Bath-sheba; and when he slept with her, she conceived and gave birth to a son and named him Solomon. And the Lord loved the baby, [25]and sent congratulations and blessings through Nathan the prophet. David nicknamed the baby Jedidiah (meaning, "Beloved of Jehovah") because of the Lord's interest. [26,27]Meanwhile Joab and the Israeli army were successfully ending their siege of Rabbah the capital of Ammon. Joab sent messengers to tell David, "Rabbah and its beautiful harbor are ours! [28]Now bring the rest of the army and finish the job, so that you will get the credit for the victory instead of me."

[29,30]So David led his army to Rabbah and captured it. Tremendous amounts of loot were carried back to Jerusalem, and David took the king of Rabbah's crown—a $50,000 treasure made from solid gold set with gems—and placed it on his own head. [31]He made slaves of the people of the city and made them labor with saws, picks, and axes and work in the brick kilns; that is the way he treated all of the cities of the Ammonites. Then David and the army returned to Jerusalem.

JOHN 16:1–33

I have told you these things so that you won't be staggered [by all that lies ahead.] [2]For you will be excommunicated from the synagogues, and indeed the time is coming when those who kill you will think they are doing God a service. [3]This is because they have never known the Father or me. [4]Yes, I'm telling you these things now so that when they happen you will remember I warned you. I didn't tell you earlier because I was going to be with you for a while longer.

[5]"But now I am going away to the one who sent me; and none of you seems interested in the purpose of my going; none wonders why. [6]Instead you are only filled with sorrow. [7]But the fact of the matter is that it is best for you that I go away, for if I don't, the Comforter won't come. If I do, he will—for I will send him to you.

[8]"And when he has come he will convince the world of its sin, and of the availability of God's goodness, and of deliverance from judgment. [9]The world's sin is unbelief in me; [10]there is righteousness available because I go to the Father and you shall see me no more; [11]there is deliverance from judgment because the prince of this world has already been judged.

[12]"Oh, there is so much more I want to tell you, but you can't understand it now. [13]When the Holy Spirit, who is truth, comes, he shall guide you into all truth, for he will not be presenting his own ideas, but will be passing on to you what he has heard. He will tell you about the future. [14]He shall praise me and bring me great honor by showing you my glory. [15]All the Father's glory is mine; this is what I mean when I say that he will show you my glory.

[16]"In just a little while I will be gone, and you will see me no more; but just a little while after that, and you will see me again!"

[17,18]"Whatever is he saying?" some of his disciples asked. "What is this about 'going to the Father'? We don't know what he means."

[19]Jesus realized they wanted to ask him so he said, "Are you asking yourselves what I mean? [20]The world will greatly rejoice over what is going to happen to me, and you will weep. But your weeping

shall suddenly be turned to wonderful joy [when you see me again]. 21It will be the same joy as that of a woman in labor when her child is born—her anguish gives place to rapturous joy and the pain is forgotten. 22You have sorrow now, but I will see you again and then you will rejoice; and no one can rob you of that joy. 23At that time you won't need to ask me for anything, for you can go directly to the Father and ask him, and he will give you what you ask for because you use my name. 24You haven't tried this before, [but begin now]. Ask, using my name, and you will receive, and your cup of joy will overflow.

25"I have spoken of these matters very guardedly, but the time will come when this will not be necessary and I will tell you plainly all about the Father. 26Then you will present your petitions over my signature! And I won't need to ask the Father to grant you these requests, 27for the Father himself loves you dearly because you love me and believe that I came from the Father. 28Yes, I came from the Father into the world and will leave the world and return to the Father."

29"At last you are speaking plainly," his disciples said, "and not in riddles. 30Now we understand that you know everything and don't need anyone to tell you anything. From this we believe that you came from God."

31"Do you finally believe this?" Jesus asked. 32"But the time is coming—in fact, it is here—when you will be scattered, each one returning to his own home, leaving me alone. Yet I will not be alone, for the Father is with me. 33I have told you all this so that you will have peace of heart and mind. Here on earth you will have many trials and sorrows; but cheer up, for I have overcome the world."

PSALM 119:71–80

THE punishment you gave me was the best thing that could have happened to me, for it taught me to pay attention to your laws. They are more valuable to me than millions in silver and gold!

73You made my body, Lord; now give me sense to heed your laws. 74All those who fear and trust in you will welcome me because I too am trusting in your Word.

75,76,77I know, O Lord, that your decisions are right and that your punishment was right and did me good. Now let your lovingkindness comfort me, just as you promised. Surround me with your tender mercies, that I may live. For your law is my delight.

78Let the proud be disgraced, for they have cut me down with all their lies. But I will concentrate my thoughts upon your laws.

79Let all others join me, who trust and fear you, and we will discuss your laws. 80Help me to love your every wish; then I will never have to be ashamed of myself.

PROVERBS FOR TODAY/ 16:4–5

The Lord has made everything for his own purposes—even the wicked, for punishment. Pride disgusts the Lord. Take my word for it—proud men shall be punished.

MAY 28

2 SAMUEL 13:1–39

PRINCE Absalom, David's son, had a beautiful sister named Tamar. And Prince Amnon (her half brother) fell desperately in love with her. 2Amnon became so tormented by his love for her that he became ill. He had no way of talking to her, for the girls and young men were kept strictly apart. 3But Amnon had a very crafty friend—his cousin Jonadab (the son of David's brother Shime-ah).

4One day Jonadab said to Amnon, "What's the trouble? Why should the son of a king look so haggard morning after morning?"

So Amnon told him, "I am in love with Tamar, my half sister."

5"Well," Jonadab said, "I'll tell you what to do. Go back to bed and pretend you are sick; when your father comes to see you, ask him to let Tamar come and prepare some food for you. Tell him you'll feel better if she feeds you."

6So Amnon did. And when the king came to see him, Amnon asked him for this favor—that his sister Tamar be permitted to come and cook a little something for him to eat. 7David agreed, and sent word to Tamar to go to Amnon's quarters and prepare some food for him. 8So she did, and went into his bedroom so that he could watch her mix some dough; then she baked some special bread for him. 9But when she set the serving tray before him, he refused to eat!

"Everyone get out of here," he told his servants; so they all left the apartment.

10Then he said to Tamar, "Now bring me the food again here in my bedroom and feed it to me." So Tamar took it to him. 11But as she was standing there before him, he grabbed her and demanded, "Come to bed with me, my darling."

12"Oh, Amnon," she cried. "Don't be foolish! Don't do this to me! You know what a serious crime it is in Israel. 13Where could I go in my shame? And you would be called one of the greatest fools in Israel. Please, just speak to the king about it, for he will let you marry me."

14But he wouldn't listen to her; and since he was stronger than she, he forced her. 15Then suddenly his love turned to hate, and now he hated her more than he had loved her.

"Get out of here!" he snarled at her.

16"No, no!" she cried. "To reject me now is a greater crime than the other you did to me."

But he wouldn't listen to her. 17,18He shouted for his valet and demanded, "Throw this woman out and lock the door behind her."

So he put her out. She was wearing a long robe with sleeves, as was the custom in those days for virgin daughters of the king. 19Now she tore the robe and put ashes on her head and with her head in her hands went away crying.

20Her brother Absalom asked her, "Is it true that Amnon raped you? Don't be so upset, since it's all in the family anyway. It's not anything to worry about!"

So Tamar lived as a desolate woman in her brother Absalom's quarters.

21-24When King David heard what had happened, he was very angry, but Absalom said nothing one way or the other about this to Amnon. However, he hated him with a deep hatred because of what he had done to his sister. Then, two years later, when Absalom's sheep were being sheared at Baal-hazor in Ephraim, Absalom invited his father and all his brothers to come to a feast to celebrate the occasion.

25The king replied, "No, my boy; if we all came, we would be too much of a burden on you."

Absalom pressed him, but he wouldn't come, though he sent his thanks.

²⁶"Well, then," Absalom said, "if you can't come, how about sending my brother Amnon instead?"

"Why Amnon?" the king asked.

²⁷Absalom kept on urging the matter until finally the king agreed, and let all of his sons attend, including Amnon.

²⁸Absalom told his men, "Wait until Amnon gets drunk, then, at my signal, kill him! Don't be afraid. I'm the one who gives the orders around here, and this is a command. Take courage and do it!"

^{29,30}So they murdered Amnon. Then the other sons of the king jumped on their mules and fled. As they were on the way back to Jerusalem, the report reached David: "Absalom has killed all of your sons, and not one is left alive!"

³¹The king jumped up, ripped off his robe, and fell prostrate to the ground. His aides also tore their clothes in horror and sorrow.

^{32,33}But just then Jonadab (the son of David's brother Shime-ah) arrived and said, "No, not all have been killed! It was only Amnon! Absalom has been plotting this ever since Amnon raped Tamar. No, no! Your sons aren't all dead! It was only Amnon."

³⁴Meanwhile Absalom escaped. Now the watchman on the Jerusalem wall saw a great crowd coming toward the city along the road at the side of the hill.

³⁵"See!" Jonadab told the king. "There they are now! Your sons are coming, just as I said."

³⁶They soon arrived, weeping and sobbing, and the king and his officials wept with them. ^{37,38,39}Absalom fled to King Talmai of Geshur (the son of Ammihud) and stayed there three years. Meanwhile David, now reconciled to Amnon's death, longed day after day for fellowship with his son Absalom.

JOHN 17:1–26

WHEN Jesus had finished saying all these things he looked up to heaven and said, "Father, the time has come. Reveal the glory of your Son so that he can give the glory back to you. ²For you have given him authority over every man and woman in all the earth. He gives eternal life to each one you have given him. ³And this is the way to have eternal life—by knowing you, the only true God, and Jesus Christ, the one you sent to earth! ⁴I brought glory to you here on earth by doing everything you told me to. ⁵And now, Father, reveal my glory as I stand in your presence, the glory we shared before the world began.

⁶"I have told these men all about you. They were in the world, but then you gave them to me. Actually, they were always yours, and you gave them to me; and they have obeyed you. ⁷Now they know that everything I have is a gift from you, ⁸for I have passed on to them the commands you gave me; and they accepted them and know of a certainty that I came down to earth from you, and they believe you sent me.

⁹"My plea is not for the world but for those you have given me because they belong to you. ¹⁰And all of them, since they are mine, belong to you; and you have given them back to me with everything else of yours, and so *they are my glory!* ¹¹Now I am leaving the world, and leaving them behind, and coming to you. Holy Father, keep them in your own care—all those you have given me—so that they will be united just as we are, with none missing. ¹²During my time here I have kept safe within your family all of these you gave me. I guarded them so that not one perished, except the son of hell, as the Scriptures foretold.

¹³"And now I am coming to you. I have told them many things while I was with them so that they would be filled with my joy. ¹⁴I have given them your commands. And the world hates them because they don't fit in with it, just as I don't. ¹⁵I'm not asking you to take them out of the world, but to keep them safe from Satan's power. ¹⁶They are not part of this world any more than I am.

17Make them pure and holy through teaching them your words of truth. 18As you sent me into the world, I am sending them into the world, 19and I consecrate myself to meet their need for growth in truth and holiness.

20"I am not praying for these alone but also for the future believers who will come to me because of the testimony of these. 21My prayer for all of them is that they will be of one heart and mind, just as you and I are, Father—that just as you are in me and I am in you, so they will be in us, and the world will believe you sent me.

22"I have given them the glory you gave me—the glorious unity of being one, as we are— 23I in them and you in me, all being perfected into one—so that the world will know you sent me and will understand that you love them as much as you love me. 24Father, I want them with me—these you've given me— so that they can see my glory. You gave me the glory because you loved me before the world began!

25"O righteous Father, the world doesn't know you, but I do; and these disciples know you sent me. 26And I have revealed you to them, and will keep on revealing you so that the mighty love you have for me may be in them, and I in them."

PSALM 119:81–95

I faint for your salvation; but I expect your help, for you have promised it. 82My eyes are straining to see your promises come true. When will you comfort me with your help? 83I am shriveled like a wineskin in the smoke, exhausted with waiting. But still I cling to your laws and obey them. 84How long must I wait before you punish those who persecute me? 85,86These proud men who hate your truth and laws have dug deep pits for me to fall in. Their lies have brought me into deep trouble. Help me, for you love only truth. 87They had almost finished me off, yet I refused to yield and disobey your laws. 88In your kindness, spare my life; then I can continue to obey you.

89Forever, O Lord, your Word stands firm in heaven. 90,91Your faithfulness extends to every generation, like the earth you created; it endures by your decree, for everything serves your plans.

92I would have despaired and perished unless your laws had been my deepest delight. 93I will never lay aside your laws, for you have used them to restore my joy and health. 94I am yours! Save me! For I have tried to live according to your desires. 95Though the wicked hide along the way to kill me, I will quietly keep my mind upon your promises.

PROVERBS FOR TODAY/ 16:6–7

Iniquity is atoned for by mercy and truth; evil is avoided by reverence for God. When a man is trying to please God, God makes even his worst enemies to be at peace with him.

MAY 29

2 SAMUEL 14:1—15:22

WHEN General Joab realized how much the king was longing to see Absalom, 2,3he sent for a woman of Tekoa who had a reputation for great wisdom and told her to ask for an appointment with the king. He told her what to say to him.

"Pretend you are in mourning," Joab instructed her. "Wear mourning clothes, and dishevel your hair as though you have been in deep sorrow for a long time."

⁴When the woman approached the king, she fell face downward on the floor in front of him, and cried out, "O king! Help me!"

⁵,⁶"What's the trouble?" he asked.

"I am a widow," she replied, "and my two sons had a fight out in the field, and since no one was there to part them, one of them was killed. ⁷Now the rest of the family is demanding that I surrender my other son to them to be executed for murdering his brother. But if I do that, I will have no one left, and my husband's name will be destroyed from the face of the earth."

⁸"Leave it with me," the king told her, "I'll see to it that no one touches him."

⁹"Oh, thank you, my lord," she replied. "And I'll take the responsibility if you are criticized for helping me like this."

¹⁰"Don't worry about that!" the king replied. "If anyone objects, bring him to me; I can assure you he will never complain again!"

¹¹Then she said, "Please swear to me by God that you won't let anyone harm my son. I want no more bloodshed."

"I vow by God," he replied, "that not a hair of your son's head shall be disturbed!"

¹²"Please let me ask one more thing of you!" she said.

"Go ahead," he replied. "Speak!"

¹³"Why don't you do as much for all the people of God as you have promised to do for me?" she asked. "You have convicted yourself in making this decision, because you have refused to bring home your own banished son. ¹⁴All of us must die eventually; our lives are like water that is poured out on the ground— it can't be gathered up again. But God will bless you with a longer life if you will find a way to bring your son back from his exile. ¹⁵,¹⁶But I have come to plead with you for my son because my life and my son's life have been threatened, and I said to myself, 'Perhaps the king will listen to me and rescue us from those who would end our existence in Israel. ¹⁷Yes, the king will give us peace again.' I know that you are like the angel of God and can discern good from evil. May God be with you."

¹⁸"I want to know one thing," the king replied.

"Yes, my lord?" she asked.

¹⁹"Did Joab send you here?"

And the woman replied, "How can I deny it? Yes, Joab sent me and told me what to say. ²⁰He did it in order to place the matter before you in a different light. But you are as wise as an angel of God, and you know everything that happens!"

²¹So the king sent for Joab and told him, "All right, go and bring back Absalom."

²²Joab fell to the ground before the king and blessed him and said, "At last I know that you like me! For you have granted me this request!"

²³Then Joab went to Geshur and brought Absalom back to Jerusalem.

²⁴"He may go to his own quarters," the king ordered, "but he must never come here. I refuse to see him."

²⁵Now no one in Israel was such a handsome specimen of manhood as Absalom, and no one else received such praise. ²⁶He cut his hair only once a year—and then only because it weighed three pounds and was too much of a load to carry around! ²⁷He had three sons and one daughter, Tamar, who was a very beautiful girl.

²⁸After Absalom had been in Jerusalem for two years and had not yet seen the king, ²⁹he sent for Joab to ask him to intercede for him; but Joab wouldn't come. Absalom sent for him again, but again he refused to come.

³⁰So Absalom said to his servants, "Go and set fire to that barley field of Joab's next to mine," and they did.

³¹Then Joab came to Absalom and demanded, "Why did your servants set my field on fire?"

³²And Absalom replied, "Because I wanted you to ask the king why he brought me back from Geshur if he didn't intend to see me. I might as well have

stayed there. Let me have an interview with the king; then if he finds that I am guilty of murder, let him execute me."

33So Joab told the king what Absalom had said. Then at last David summoned Absalom, and he came and bowed low before the king, and David kissed him.

ABSALOM then bought a magnificent chariot and chariot horses, and hired fifty footmen to run ahead of him. 2He got up early every morning and went out to the gate of the city; and when anyone came to bring a case to the king for trial, Absalom called him over and expressed interest in his problem.

3He would say, "I can see that you are right in this matter; it's unfortunate that the king doesn't have anyone to assist him in hearing these cases. 4I surely wish I were the judge; then anyone with a lawsuit could come to me, and I would give him justice!"

5And when anyone came to bow to him, Absalom wouldn't let him, but shook his hand instead! 6So in this way Absalom stole the hearts of all the people of Israel.

7,8After four years, Absalom said to the king, "Let me go to Hebron to sacrifice to the Lord in fulfillment of a vow I made to him while I was at Geshur— that if he would bring me back to Jerusalem, I would sacrifice to him."

9"All right," the king told him, "go and fulfill your vow."

So Absalom went to Hebron. 10But while he was there, he sent spies to every part of Israel to incite rebellion against the king. "As soon as you hear the trumpets," his message read, "you will know that Absalom has been crowned in Hebron." 11He took two hundred men from Jerusalem with him as guests, but they knew nothing of his intentions. 12While he was offering the sacrifice, he sent for Ahithophel, one of David's counselors who lived in Giloh. Ahithophel declared for Absalom, as did more and more others. So the conspiracy became very strong.

13A messenger soon arrived in Jerusalem to tell King David, "All Israel has joined Absalom in a conspiracy against you!"

14"Then we must flee at once or it will be too late!" was David's instant response to his men. "If we get out of the city before he arrives, both we and the city of Jerusalem will be saved."

15"We are with you," his aides replied. "Do as you think best."

16So the king and his household set out at once. He left no one behind except ten of his young wives to keep the palace in order. 17,18David paused at the edge of the city to let his troops move past him to lead the way—six hundred Gittites who had come with him from Gath, and the Cherethites and Pelethites.

19,20But suddenly the king turned to Ittai, the captain of the six hundred Gittites, and said to him, "What are you doing here? Go on back with your men to Jerusalem, to your king, for you are a guest in Israel, a foreigner in exile. It seems but yesterday that you arrived, and now today should I force you to wander with us, who knows where? Go on back and take your troops with you, and may the Lord be merciful to you."

21But Ittai replied, "I vow by God and by your own life that wherever you go, I will go, no matter what happens— whether it means life or death."

22So David replied, "All right, come with us." Then Ittai and his six hundred men and their families went along.

JOHN 18:1–24

AFTER saying these things Jesus crossed the Kidron ravine with his disciples and entered a grove of olive trees. 2Judas, the betrayer, knew this place, for Jesus had gone there many times with his disciples.

3The chief priests and Pharisees had given Judas a squad of soldiers and police to accompany him. Now with blazing torches, lanterns, and weapons they arrived at the olive grove.

4,5Jesus fully realized all that was going

to happen to him. Stepping forward to meet them he asked, "Whom are you looking for?"

"Jesus of Nazareth," they replied.

"I am he," Jesus said. 6And as he said it, they all fell backwards to the ground!

7Once more he asked them, "Whom are you searching for?"

And again they replied, "Jesus of Nazareth."

8"I told you I am he," Jesus said; "and since I am the one you are after, let these others go." 9He did this to carry out the prophecy he had just made, "I have not lost a single one of those you gave me. . . ."

10Then Simon Peter drew a sword and slashed off the right ear of Malchus, the High Priest's servant.

11But Jesus said to Peter, "Put your sword away. Shall I not drink from the cup the Father has given me?"

12So the Jewish police, with the soldiers and their lieutenant, arrested Jesus and tied him. 13First they took him to Annas, the father-in-law of Caiaphas, the High Priest that year. 14Caiaphas was the one who told the other Jewish leaders, "Better that one should die for all."

15Simon Peter followed along behind, as did another of the disciples who was acquainted with the High Priest. So that other disciple was permitted into the courtyard along with Jesus, 16while Peter stood outside the gate. Then the other disciple spoke to the girl watching at the gate, and she let Peter in. 17The girl asked Peter, "Aren't you one of Jesus' disciples?"

"No," he said, "I am not!"

18The police and the household servants were standing around a fire they had made, for it was cold. And Peter stood there with them, warming himself.

19Inside, the High Priest began asking Jesus about his followers and what he had been teaching them.

20Jesus replied, "What I teach is widely known, for I have preached regularly in the synagogue and Temple; I have been heard by all the Jewish leaders and teach nothing in private that I have not said in public. 21Why are you asking me this question? Ask those who heard me. You have some of them here. They know what I said."

22One of the soldiers standing there struck Jesus with his fist. "Is that the way to answer the High Priest?" he demanded.

23"If I lied, prove it," Jesus replied. "Should you hit a man for telling the truth?"

24Then Annas sent Jesus, bound, to Caiaphas the High Priest.

PSALM 119:96–112

NOTHING is perfect except your words. 97Oh, how I love them. I think about them all day long. 98They make me wiser than my enemies, because they are my constant guide. 99Yes, wiser than my teachers, for I am ever thinking of your rules. 100They make me even wiser than the aged.

101I have refused to walk the paths of evil for I will remain obedient to your Word. 102,103No, I haven't turned away from what you taught me; your words are sweeter than honey. 104And since only your rules can give me wisdom and understanding, no wonder I hate every false teaching.

105Your words are a flashlight to light the path ahead of me, and keep me from stumbling. 106I've said it once and I'll say it again and again: I will obey these wonderful laws of yours.

107I am close to death at the hands of my enemies; oh, give me back my life again, just as you promised me. 108Accept my grateful thanks and teach me your desires. 109My life hangs in the balance, but I will not give up obedience to your laws. 110The wicked have set their traps for me along your path, but I will not turn aside. 111Your laws are my joyous treasure forever. 112I am determined to obey you until I die.

*A little, gained honestly, is better than great wealth gotten by dishonest means.
We should make plans—counting on God to direct us.*

MAY 30

2 SAMUEL 15:23—16:23

THERE was deep sadness throughout the city as the king and his retinue passed by, crossed Kidron Brook, and went out into the country. 24Abiathar and Zadok and the Levites took the Ark of the Covenant of God and set it down beside the road until everyone had passed. 25,26Then, following David's instructions, Zadok took the Ark back into the city. "If the Lord sees fit," David said, "he will bring me back to see the Ark and the Tabernacle again. But if he is through with me, well, let him do what seems best to him."

27Then the king told Zadok, "Look, here is my plan. Return quietly to the city with your son Ahima-az and Abiathar's son Jonathan. 28I will stop at the ford of the Jordan River and wait there for a message from you. Let me know what happens in Jerusalem before I disappear into the wilderness."

29So Zadok and Abiathar carried the Ark of God back into the city and stayed there.

30David walked up the road that led to the Mount of Olives, weeping as he went. His head was covered and his feet were bare as a sign of mourning. And the people who were with him covered their heads and wept as they climbed the mountain. 31When someone told David that Ahithophel, his advisor, was backing Absalom, David prayed, "O Lord, please make Ahithophel give Absalom foolish advice!" 32As they reached the spot at the top of the Mount of Olives where people worshiped God, David found Hushai the Archite waiting for him

with torn clothing and earth upon his head.

33,34But David told him, "If you go with me, you will only be a burden; return to Jerusalem and tell Absalom, 'I will counsel you as I did your father.' Then you can frustrate and counter Ahithophel's advice. 35,36Zadok and Abiathar, the priests, are there. Tell them the plans that are being made to capture me, and they will send their sons Ahima-az and Jonathan to find me and tell me what is going on."

37So David's friend Hushai returned to the city, getting there just as Absalom arrived.

DAVID was just past the top of the hill when Ziba, the manager of Mephibosheth's household, caught up with him. He was leading two donkeys loaded with two hundred loaves of bread, one hundred clusters of raisins, one hundred bunches of grapes, and a small barrel of wine.

2"What are these for?" the king asked Ziba.

And Ziba replied, "The donkeys are for your people to ride on, and the bread and summer fruit are for the young men to eat; the wine is to be taken with you into the wilderness for any who become faint."

3"And where is Mephibosheth?" the king asked him.

"He stayed at Jerusalem," Ziba replied. "He said, 'Now I'll get to be king! Today I will get back the kingdom of my father, Saul.'"

4"In that case," the king told Ziba, "I give you everything he owns."

"Thank you, thank you, sir," Ziba replied.

5As David and his party passed Bahurim, a man came out of the village cursing them. It was Shime-i, the son of Gera, a member of Saul's family. 6He threw stones at the king and the king's officers and all the mighty warriors who surrounded them!

7,8"Get out of here, you murderer, you scoundrel!" he shouted at David. "The Lord is paying you back for murdering King Saul and his family; you stole his throne and now the Lord has given it to your son Absalom! At last you will taste some of your own medicine, you murderer!"

9"Why should this dead dog curse my lord the king?" Abishai demanded. "Let me go over and strike off his head!"

10"No!" the king said. "If the Lord has told him to curse me, who am I to say no? 11My own son is trying to kill me, and this Benjaminite is merely cursing me. Let him alone, for no doubt the Lord has told him to do it. 12And perhaps the Lord will see that I am being wronged and will bless me because of these curses."

13So David and his men continued on, and Shime-i kept pace with them on a nearby hillside, cursing as he went and throwing stones at David and tossing dust into the air. 14The king and all those who were with him were weary by the time they reached Bahurim, so they stayed there awhile and rested.

15Meanwhile, Absalom and his men arrived at Jerusalem, accompanied by Ahithophel. 16When David's friend, Hushai the Archite, arrived, he went immediately to see Absalom.

"Long live the king!" he exclaimed. "Long live the king!"

17"Is this the way to treat your friend David?" Absalom asked him. "Why aren't you with him?"

18"Because I work for the man who is chosen by the Lord and by Israel," Hushai replied. 19"And anyway, why shouldn't I? I helped your father and now I will help you!"

20Then Absalom turned to Ahithophel and asked him, "What shall I do next?"

21Ahithophel told him, "Go and sleep with your father's wives, for he has left them here to keep the house. Then all Israel will know that you have insulted him beyond the possibility of reconciliation, and they will all close ranks behind you."

22So a tent was erected on the roof of the palace where everybody could see it, and Absalom went into the tent to lie with his father's wives. 23(Absalom did whatever Ahithophel told him to, just as David had; for every word Ahithophel spoke seemed as wise as though it had come directly from the mouth of God.)

JOHN 18:25—19:22

MEANWHILE, as Simon Peter was standing by the fire, he was asked again, "Aren't you one of his disciples?"

"Of course not," he replied.

26But one of the household slaves of the High Priest—a relative of the man whose ear Peter had cut off—asked, "Didn't I see you out there in the olive grove with Jesus?"

27Again Peter denied it. And immediately a rooster crowed.

28Jesus' trial before Caiaphas ended in the early hours of the morning. Next he was taken to the palace of the Roman governor. His accusers wouldn't go in themselves for that would "defile" them, they said, and they wouldn't be allowed to eat the Passover lamb. 29So Pilate, the governor, went out to them and asked, "What is your charge against this man? What are you accusing him of doing?"

30"We wouldn't have arrested him if he weren't a criminal!" they retorted.

31"Then take him away and judge him yourselves by your own laws," Pilate told them.

"But we want him crucified," they demanded, "and your approval is required." 32This fulfilled Jesus' prediction concerning the method of his execution.

33Then Pilate went back into the palace and called for Jesus to be brought to him. "Are you the King of the Jews?" he asked him.

34" 'King' as *you* use the word or as the *Jews* use it?" Jesus asked.

35"Am I a Jew?" Pilate retorted. "Your own people and their chief priests brought you here. Why? What have you done?"

36Then Jesus answered, "I am not an earthly king. If I were, my followers would have fought when I was arrested by the Jewish leaders. But my Kingdom is not of the world."

37Pilate replied, "But you are a king then?"

"Yes," Jesus said. "I was born for that purpose. And I came to bring truth to the world. All who love the truth are my followers."

38"What is truth?" Pilate exclaimed. Then he went out again to the people and told them, "He is not guilty of any crime. 39But you have a custom of asking me to release someone from prison each year at Passover. So if you want me to, I'll release the 'King of the Jews.' "

40But they screamed back. "No! Not this man, but Barabbas!" Barabbas was a robber.

THEN Pilate laid open Jesus' back with a leaded whip, 2and the soldiers made a crown of thorns and placed it on his head and robed him in royal purple. 3"Hail, 'King of the Jews!' " they mocked, and struck him with their fists.

4Pilate went outside again and said to the Jews, "I am going to bring him out to you now, but understand clearly that I find him *not guilty.*"

5Then Jesus came out wearing the crown of thorns and the purple robe. And Pilate said, "Behold the man!"

6At sight of him the chief priests and Jewish officials began yelling, "Crucify! Crucify!"

"*You* crucify him," Pilate said. "I find him *not guilty.*"

7They replied, "By our laws he ought to die because he called himself the Son of God."

8When Pilate heard this, he was more frightened than ever. 9He took Jesus back into the palace again and asked him, "Where are you from?" but Jesus gave no answer.

10"You won't talk to me?" Pilate demanded. "Don't you realize that I have the power to release you or to crucify you?"

11Then Jesus said, "You would have no power at all over me unless it were given to you from above. So those who brought me to you have the greater sin."

12Then Pilate tried to release him, but the Jewish leaders told him, "If you release this man, you are no friend of Caesar's. Anyone who declares himself a king is a rebel against Caesar."

13At these words Pilate brought Jesus out to them again and sat down at the judgment bench on the stone-paved platform. 14It was now about noon of the day before Passover.

And Pilate said to the Jews, "Here is your king!"

15"Away with him," they yelled. "Away with him—crucify him!"

"What? Crucify your king?" Pilate asked.

"We have no king but Caesar," the chief priests shouted back.

16Then Pilate gave Jesus to them to be crucified.

17So they had him at last, and he was taken out of the city, carrying his cross to the place known as "The Skull," in Hebrew, "Golgotha." 18There they crucified him and two others with him, one on either side, with Jesus between them. 19And Pilate posted a sign over him reading, "Jesus of Nazareth, the King of the Jews." 20The place where Jesus was crucified was near the city; and the signboard was written in Hebrew, Latin, and Greek, so that many people read it.

21Then the chief priests said to Pilate, "Change it from 'The King of the Jews' to 'He said, I am King of the Jews.' "

22Pilate replied, "What I have written, I have written. It stays exactly as it is."

PSALM 119:113–131

I hate those who are undecided whether or not to obey you; but my choice is clear—I love your law. 114You are my refuge and my shield, and your promises are my only source of hope. 115Begone, you evil-minded men. Don't try to stop me from obeying God's commands. 116Lord, you promised to let me live! Never let it be said that God failed me. 117Hold me safe above the heads of all my enemies; then I can continue to obey your laws.

118But you have rejected all who reject your laws. They are only fooling themselves. 119The wicked are the scum you skim off and throw away; no wonder I love to obey your laws! 120I tremble in fear of you; I fear your punishments.

121Don't leave me to the mercy of my enemies, for I have done what is right; I've been perfectly fair. 122Commit yourself to bless me! Don't let the proud oppress me! 123My eyes grow dim with longing for you to fulfill your wonderful promise to rescue me. 124Lord, deal with me in lovingkindness, and teach me, your servant, to obey; 125for I am your servant; therefore give me common sense to apply your rules to everything I do.

126Lord, it is time for you to act. For these evil men have violated your laws, 127while I love your commandments more than the finest gold. 128Every law of God is right, whatever it concerns. I hate every other way.

129Your laws are wonderful; no wonder I obey them. 130As your plan unfolds, even the simple can understand it. 131No wonder I wait expectantly for each of your commands.

PROVERBS FOR TODAY/ 16:10–11

God will help the king to judge the people fairly; there need be no mistakes. The Lord demands fairness in every business deal. He established this principle.

MAY 31

2 SAMUEL 17:1–29

Now," Ahithophel said, "give me twelve thousand men to start out after David tonight. 2,3I will come upon him while he is weary and discouraged, and he and his troops will be thrown into a panic and everyone will run away; and I will kill only the king, and let all those who are with him live, and restore them to you."

4Absalom and all the elders of Israel approved of the plan, 5but Absalom said, "Ask Hushai the Archite what he thinks about this."

6When Hushai arrived, Absalom told him what Ahithophel had said.

"What is your opinion?" Absalom asked him. "Should we follow Ahithophel's advice? If not, speak up."

7"Well," Hushai replied, "this time I think Ahithophel has made a mistake. 8You know your father and his men; they are mighty warriors and are probably as upset as a mother bear who has been robbed of her cubs. And your father is an old soldier and isn't going to be spending the night among the troops; 9he has probably already hidden in some pit or cave. And when he comes out and attacks and a few of your men fall, there will be panic among your troops and everyone will start shouting that your men are being slaughtered. 10Then even the bravest of them, though they have hearts of lions, will be paralyzed with fear; for all Israel knows what a mighty man your father is and how courageous his soldiers are.

11"What I suggest is that you mobilize the entire army of Israel, bringing them from as far away as Dan and Beer-sheba, so that you will have a huge force. And I think that you should personally lead the troops. 12Then when we find him we can destroy his entire army so that not one of them is left alive. 13And if David has escaped into some city, you will have the entire army of Israel there at your command, and we can take ropes and drag the walls of the city into the nearest valley until every stone is torn down."

14Then Absalom and all the men of Israel said, "Hushai's advice is better than Ahithophel's." For the Lord had arranged to defeat the counsel of Ahithophel, which really was the better plan, so that he could bring disaster upon Absalom! 15Then Hushai reported to Zadok and Abiathar, the priests, what Ahithophel had said and what he himself had suggested instead.

16"Quick!" he told them. "Find David and urge him not to stay at the ford of the Jordan River tonight. He must go across at once into the wilderness beyond; otherwise he will die, and his entire army with him."

17Jonathan and Ahima-az had been staying at En-rogel so as not to be seen entering and leaving the city. Arrangements had been made for a servant girl to carry to them the messages they were to take to King David. 18But a boy saw them leaving En-rogel to go to David, and he told Absalom about it. Meanwhile, they escaped to Bahurim where a man hid them inside a well in his backyard. 19The man's wife put a cloth over the top of the well with grain on it to dry in the sun; so no one suspected they were there.

20When Absalom's men arrived and asked her if she had seen Ahima-az and Jonathan, she said they had crossed the brook and were gone. They looked for them without success and returned to Jerusalem. 21Then the two men crawled out of the well and hurried on to King David. "Quick!" they told him, "cross the Jordan tonight!" And they told him how Ahithophel had advised that he be captured and killed. 22So David and all the people with him went across during the night and were all on the other bank before dawn.

23Meanwhile, Ahithophel—publicly disgraced when Absalom refused his advice—saddled his donkey, went to his home town, set his affairs in order, and hanged himself; so he died and was buried beside his father.

24David soon arrived at Mahanaim. Meanwhile, Absalom had mobilized the entire army of Israel and was leading the men across the Jordan River. 25Absalom had appointed Amasa as general of the army, replacing Joab. (Amasa was Joab's second cousin; his father was Ithra, an Ishmaelite, and his mother was Abigail, the daughter of Nahash, who was the sister of Joab's mother Zeruiah.) 26Absalom and the Israeli army now camped in the land of Gilead.

27When David arrived at Mahanaim, he was warmly greeted by Shobi (son of Nahash of Rabbah, an Ammonite) and Machir (son of Ammiel of Lodebar) and Barzillai (a Gileadite of Rogelim). 28,29They brought him and those who were with him mats to sleep on, cooking pots, serving bowls, wheat and barley flour, parched grain, beans, lentils, honey, butter, and cheese. For they said, "You must be very tired and hungry and thirsty after your long march through the wilderness."

JOHN 19:23–42

WHEN the soldiers had crucified Jesus, they put his garments into four piles, one for each of them. But they said, "Let's not tear up his robe," for it was seamless. "Let's throw dice to see who gets it." This fulfilled the Scripture that says,

"They divided my clothes among them, and cast lots for my robe." 25So that is what they did.

Standing near the cross were Jesus' mother, Mary, his aunt, the wife of Cleopas, and Mary Magdalene. 26When Jesus saw his mother standing there beside me, his close friend, he said to her, "He is your son."

27And to me he said, "She is your mother!" And from then on I took her into my home.

28Jesus knew that everything was now finished, and to fulfill the Scriptures said, "I'm thirsty." 29A jar of sour wine was sitting there, so a sponge was soaked in it and put on a hyssop branch and held up to his lips.

30When Jesus had tasted it, he said, "It is finished," and bowed his head and dismissed his spirit.

31The Jewish leaders didn't want the victims hanging there the next day, which was the Sabbath (and a very special Sabbath at that, for it was the Passover), so they asked Pilate to order the legs of the men broken to hasten death; then their bodies could be taken down. 32So the soldiers came and broke the legs of the two men crucified with Jesus; 33but when they came to him, they saw that he was dead already, so they didn't break his. 34However, one of the soldiers pierced his side with a spear, and blood and water flowed out. 35I saw all this myself and have given an accurate report so that you also can believe. 36,37The soldiers did this in fulfillment of the Scripture that says, "Not one of his bones shall be broken," and, "They shall look on him whom they pierced."

38Afterwards Joseph of Arimathea, who had been a secret disciple of Jesus for fear of the Jewish leaders, boldly asked Pilate for permission to take Jesus' body down; and Pilate told him to go ahead. So he came and took it away. 39Nicodemus, the man who had come to Jesus at night, came too, bringing a hundred pounds of embalming ointment made from myrrh and aloes. 40Together they wrapped Jesus' body in a long linen cloth saturated with the spices, as is the Jewish custom of burial. 41The place of crucifixion was near a grove of trees, where there was a new tomb, never used before. 42And so, because of the need for haste before the Sabbath, and because the tomb was close at hand, they laid him there.

PSALM 119:132–155

COME and have mercy on me as is your way with those who love you. 133Guide me with your laws so that I will not be overcome by evil. 134Rescue me from the oppression of evil men; then I can obey you. 135Look down in love upon me and teach me all your laws. 136I weep because your laws are disobeyed.

137O Lord, you are just and your punishments are fair. 138Your demands are just and right. 139I am indignant and angry because of the way my enemies have disregarded your laws. 140I have thoroughly tested your promises and that is why I love them so much. 141I am worthless and despised, but I don't despise your laws.

142Your justice is eternal for your laws are perfectly fair. 143In my distress and anguish, your commandments comfort me. 144Your laws are always fair; help me to understand them and I shall live.

145I am praying with great earnestness; answer me, O Lord, and I will obey your laws. 146"Save me," I cry, "for I am obeying." 147Early in the morning, before the sun is up, I am praying and pointing out how much I trust in you. 148I stay awake through the night to think about your promises. 149Because you are so loving and kind, listen to me and make me well again.

150Here come these lawless men to attack me; 151but you are near, O Lord; all your commandments are based on truth. 152I have known from earliest days that your will never changes.

153Look down upon my sorrows and rescue me, for I am obeying your commands. 154Yes, rescue me and give me back my life again just as you have promised. 155The wicked are far from salvation for they do not care for your laws.

It is a horrible thing for a king to do evil. His right to rule depends upon his fairness. The king rejoices when his people are truthful and fair.

JUNE 1

2 SAMUEL 18:1—19:10a

D AVID now appointed regimental colonels and company commanders over his troops. ²A third were placed under Joab's brother, Abishai (the son of Zeruiah); and a third under Ittai, the Gittite. The king planned to lead the army himself, but his men objected strongly.

³"You mustn't do it," they said, "for if we have to turn and run, and half of us die, it will make no difference to them—they will be looking only for you. You are worth ten thousand of us, and it is better that you stay here in the city and send us help if we need it."

⁴"Well, whatever you think best," the king finally replied. So he stood at the gate of the city as all the troops passed by.

⁵And the king commanded Joab, Abishai, and Ittai, "For my sake, deal gently with young Absalom." And all the troops heard the king give them this charge.

⁶So the battle began in the forest of Ephraim, ⁷and the Israeli troops were beaten back by David's men. There was a great slaughter and twenty thousand men laid down their lives that day. ⁸The battle raged all across the countryside, and more men disappeared in the forest than were killed. ⁹During the battle Absalom came upon some of David's men and as he fled on his mule, it went beneath the thick boughs of a great oak tree, and his hair caught in the branches. His mule went on, leaving him dangling in the air. ¹⁰One of David's men saw him and told Joab.

¹¹"What? You saw him there and didn't kill him?" Joab demanded. "I would have rewarded you handsomely and made you a commissioned officer."

¹²"For a million dollars I wouldn't do it," the man replied. "We all heard the king say to you and Abishai and Ittai, 'For my sake, please don't harm young Absalom.' ¹³And if I had betrayed the king by killing his son (and the king would certainly find out who did it), you yourself would be the first to accuse me."

¹⁴"Enough of this nonsense," Joab said. Then he took three daggers and plunged them into the heart of Absalom as he dangled alive from the oak. ¹⁵Ten of Joab's young armor bearers then surrounded Absalom and finished him off. ¹⁶Then Joab blew the trumpet, and his men returned from chasing the army of Israel. ¹⁷They threw Absalom's body into a deep pit in the forest and piled a great heap of stones over it. And the army of Israel fled to their homes.

¹⁸(Absalom had built a monument to himself in the King's Valley, for he said, "I have no sons to carry on my name." He called it "Absalom's Monument," as it is still known today.)

¹⁹Then Zadok's son Ahima-az said, "Let me run to King David with the good news that the Lord has saved him from his enemy Absalom."

²⁰"No," Joab told him, "it wouldn't be good news to the king that his son is dead. You can be my messenger some other time."

²¹Then Joab said to a man from Cush, "Go tell the king what you have seen." The man bowed and ran off.

²²But Ahima-az pleaded with Joab, "Please let me go, too."

"No, we don't need you now, my boy." Joab replied. "There is no further news to send."

23"Yes, but let me go anyway," he begged.

And Joab finally said, "All right, go ahead." Then Ahima-az took a short cut across the plain and got there ahead of the man from Cush. 24David was sitting at the gate of the city. When the watchman climbed the stairs to his post at the top of the wall, he saw a lone man running towards them.

25He shouted the news down to David, and the king replied, "If he is alone, he has news."

As the messenger came closer, 26the watchman saw another man running towards them. He shouted down, "Here comes another one."

And the king replied, "He will have more news."

27"The first man looks like Ahima-az, the son of Zadok," the watchman said.

"He is a good man and comes with good news," the king replied.

28Then Ahima-az cried out to the king, "All is well!" He bowed low with his face to the ground and said, "Blessed be the Lord your God who has destroyed the rebels who dared to stand against you."

29"What of young Absalom?" the king demanded. "Is he all right?"

"When Joab told me to come, there was a lot of shouting; but I didn't know what was happening," Ahima-az answered.

30"Wait here," the king told him. So Ahima-az stepped aside.

31Then the man from Cush arrived and said, "I have good news for my lord the king. Today Jehovah has rescued you from all those who rebelled against you."

32"What about young Absalom? Is he all right?" the king demanded.

And the man replied, "May all of your enemies be as that young man is!"

33Then the king broke into tears, and went up to his room over the gate, crying as he went. "O my son Absalom, my son, my son Absalom. If only I could have died for you! O Absalom, my son, my son."

WORD soon reached Joab that the king was weeping and mourning for Absalom. 2As the people heard of the king's deep grief for his son, the joy of that day's wonderful victory was turned into deep sadness. 3The entire army crept back into the city as though they were ashamed and had been beaten in battle.

4The king covered his face with his hands and kept on weeping, "O my son Absalom! O Absalom my son, my son!"

5Then Joab went to the king's room and said to him, "We saved your life today and the lives of your sons, your daughters, your wives and concubines; and yet you act like this, making us feel ashamed, as though we had done something wrong. 6You seem to love those who hate you, and hate those who love you. Apparently we don't mean anything to you; if Absalom had lived and all of us had died, you would be happy. 7Now go out there and congratulate the troops, for I swear by Jehovah that if you don't, not a single one of them will remain here during the night; then you will be worse off than you have ever been in your entire life."

8,9,10So the king went out and sat at the city gates, and as the news spread throughout the city that he was there, everyone went to him.

JOHN 20:1-31

EARLY Sunday morning, while it was still dark, Mary Magdalene came to the tomb and found that the stone was rolled aside from the entrance.

2She ran and found Simon Peter and me and said, "They have taken the Lord's body out of the tomb, and I don't know where they have put him!"

3,4We ran to the tomb to see; I outran Peter and got there first, 5and stooped and looked in and saw the linen cloth lying there, but I didn't go in. 6Then Simon Peter arrived and went on inside. He also noticed the cloth lying there, [7]while the swath that had covered Jesus' head was rolled up in a bundle and was lying at the side. [8]Then I went in too, and saw, and believed [that he had risen]— [9]for until then we hadn't realized that the Scriptures said he would come to life again!

[10]We went on home, [11]and by that time Mary had returned to the tomb and was standing outside crying. And as she wept, she stooped and looked in [12]and saw two white-robed angels sitting at the head and foot of the place where the body of Jesus had been lying.

[13]"Why are you crying?" the angels asked her.

"Because they have taken away my Lord," she replied, "and I don't know where they have put him."

[14]She glanced over her shoulder and saw someone standing behind her. It was Jesus, but she didn't recognize him!

[15]"Why are you crying?" he asked her. "Whom are you looking for?"

She thought he was the gardener. "Sir," she said, "if you have taken him away, tell me where you have put him, and I will go and get him."

[16]"Mary!" Jesus said. She turned toward him.

"Master!" she exclaimed.

[17]"Don't touch me," he cautioned, "for I haven't yet ascended to the Father. But go find my brothers and tell them that I ascend to my Father and your Father, my God and your God."

[18]Mary Magdalene found the disciples and told them, "I have seen the Lord!" Then she gave them his message.

[19]That evening the disciples were meeting behind locked doors, in fear of the Jewish leaders, when suddenly Jesus was standing there among them! After greeting them, [20]he showed them his hands and side. And how wonderful was their joy as they saw their Lord!

[21]He spoke to them again and said, "As the Father has sent me, even so I am sending you." [22]Then he breathed on them and told them, "Receive the Holy Spirit. [23]If you forgive anyone's sins, they are forgiven. If you refuse to forgive them, they are unforgiven."

[24]One of the disciples, Thomas, "The Twin," was not there at the time with the others. [25]When they kept telling him, "We have seen the Lord," he replied, "I won't believe it unless I see the nail wounds in his hands—and put my fingers into them—and place my hand into his side."

[26]Eight days later the disciples were together again, and this time Thomas was with them. The doors were locked; but suddenly, as before, Jesus was standing among them and greeting them.

[27]Then he said to Thomas, "Put your finger into my hands. Put your hand into my side. Don't be faithless any longer. Believe!"

[28]"My Lord and my God!" Thomas said.

[29]Then Jesus told him, "You believe because you have seen me. But blessed are those who haven't seen me and believe anyway."

[30,31]Jesus' disciples saw him do many other miracles besides the ones told about in this book, but these are recorded so that you will believe that he is the Messiah, the Son of God, and that believing in him you will have life.

PSALM 119:156–176

LORD, how great is your mercy; oh, give me back my life again. [157]My enemies are so many. They try to make me disobey, but I have not swerved from your will. [158]I loathed these traitors because they care nothing for your laws. [159]Lord, see how much I really love your demands. Now give me back my life and health because you are so kind. [160]There is utter truth in all your laws; your decrees are eternal.

[161]Great men have persecuted me, though they have no reason to, but I stand in awe of only your words. [162]I rejoice in your laws like one who finds a great treasure. [163]How I hate all falsehood but how I love your laws.

164I will praise you seven times a day because of your wonderful laws.

165Those who love your laws have great peace of heart and mind and do not stumble. 166I long for your salvation, Lord, and so I have obeyed your laws. 167I have looked for your commandments and I love them very much; 168yes, I have searched for them. You know this because everything I do is known to you.

169O Lord, listen to my prayers; give me the common sense you promised.

170Hear my prayers; rescue me as you said you would. 171I praise you for letting me learn your laws. 172I will sing about their wonder, for each of them is just. 173Stand ready to help me because I have chosen to follow your will. 174O Lord, I have longed for your salvation, and your law is my delight. 175If you will let me live, I will praise you; let your laws assist me.

176I have wandered away like a lost sheep; come and find me for I have not turned away from your commandments.

PROVERBS FOR TODAY/ 16:14–15

The anger of the king is a messenger of death and a wise man will appease it. Many favors are showered on those who please the king.

JUNE 2

2 SAMUEL 19:10b—20:13

MEANWHILE, there was much discussion and argument going on all across the nation: "Why aren't we talking about bringing the king back?" was the great topic everywhere. "For he saved us from our enemies, the Philistines; and Absalom, whom we made our king instead, chased him out of the country, but now Absalom is dead. Let's ask David to return and be our king again."

11,12Then David sent Zadok and Abiathar the priests to say to the elders of Judah, "Why are you the last ones to reinstate the king? For all Israel is ready, and only you are holding out. Yet you are my own brothers, my own tribe, my own flesh and blood!"

13And he told them to tell Amasa, "Since you are my nephew, may God strike me dead if I do not appoint you as commander-in-chief of my army in place of Joab." 14Then Amasa convinced all the leaders of Judah, and they responded as one man. They sent word to the king, "Return to us and bring back all those who are with you."

15So the king started back to Jerusalem. And when he arrived at the Jordan River, it seemed as if everyone in Judah had come to Gilgal to meet him and escort him across the river! 16Then Shime-i (the son of Gera the Benjaminite), the man from Bahurim, hurried across with the men of Judah to welcome King David. 17A thousand men from the tribe of Benjamin were with him, including Ziba, the servant of Saul, and Ziba's fifteen sons and twenty servants; they rushed down to the Jordan to arrive ahead of the king. 18They all worked hard ferrying the king's household and troops across, and helped them in every way they could.

As the king was crossing, Shime-i fell down before him, 19and pleaded, "My lord the king, please forgive me and forget the terrible thing I did when you left Jerusalem; 20for I know very well how much I sinned. That is why I have come here today, the very first person in all the tribe of Joseph to greet you."

²¹Abishai asked, "Shall not Shime-i die, for he cursed the Lord's chosen king!"

²²"Don't talk to me like that!" David exclaimed. "This is not a day for execution but for celebration! I am once more king of Israel!"

²³Then, turning to Shime-i, he vowed, "Your life is spared."

²⁴,²⁵Now Mephibosheth, Saul's grandson, arrived from Jerusalem to meet the king. He had not washed his feet or clothes nor trimmed his beard since the day the king left Jerusalem.

"Why didn't you come with me, Mephibosheth?" the king asked him.

²⁶And he replied, "My lord, O king, my servant Ziba deceived me. I told him, 'Saddle my donkey so that I can go with the king.' For as you know I am lame. ²⁷But Ziba has slandered me by saying that I refused to come. But I know that you are as an angel of God, so do what you think best. ²⁸I and all my relatives could expect only death from you, but instead you have honored me among all those who eat at your own table! So how can I complain?"

²⁹"All right," David replied. "My decision is that you and Ziba will divide the land equally between you."

³⁰"Give him all of it," Mephibosheth said. "I am content just to have you back again!"

³¹,³²Barzillai, who had fed the king and his army during their exile in Mahanaim, arrived from Rogelim to conduct the king across the river. He was very old now, about eighty, and very wealthy.

³³"Come across with me and live in Jerusalem," the king said to Barzillai. "I will take care of you there."

³⁴"No," he replied, "I am far too old for that. ³⁵I am eighty years old today, and life has lost its excitement. Food and wine are no longer tasty, and entertainment is not much fun; I would only be a burden to my lord the king. ³⁶Just to go across the river with you is all the honor I need! ³⁷Then let me return again to die in my own city, where my father and mother are buried. But here is Chimham. Let him go with you and receive whatever good things you want to give him."

³⁸"Good," the king agreed. "Chimham shall go with me, and I will do for him whatever I would have done for you."

³⁹So all the people crossed the Jordan with the king; and after David had kissed and blessed Barzillai, he returned home. ⁴⁰The king then went on to Gilgal, taking Chimham with him. And most of Judah and half of Israel were there to greet him. ⁴¹But the men of Israel complained to the king because only men from Judah had ferried him and his household across the Jordan.

⁴²"Why not?" the men of Judah replied. "The king is one of our own tribe. Why should this make you angry? We have charged him nothing—he hasn't fed us or given us gifts!"

⁴³"But there are ten tribes in Israel," the others replied, "so we have ten times as much right in the king as you do; why didn't you invite the rest of us? And, remember, we were the first to speak of bringing him back to be our king again."

The argument continued back and forth, and the men of Judah were very rough in their replies.

THEN a hot-head whose name was Sheba (son of Bichri, a Benjaminite) blew a trumpet and yelled, "We want nothing to do with David. Come on, you men of Israel, let's get out of here. He's not our king!"

²So all except Judah and Benjamin turned around and deserted David and followed Sheba! But the men of Judah stayed with their king, accompanying him from the Jordan to Jerusalem. ³When he arrived at his palace in Jerusalem, the king instructed that his ten wives he had left to keep house should be placed in seclusion. Their needs were to be cared for, he said, but he would no longer sleep with them as his wives. So they remained in virtual widowhood until their deaths.

⁴Then the king instructed Amasa to mobilize the army of Judah within three days and to report back at that time.

5So Amasa went out to notify the troops, but it took him longer than the three days he had been given.

6Then David said to Abishai, "That fellow Sheba is going to hurt us more than Absalom did. Quick, take my bodyguard and chase after him before he gets into a fortified city where we can't reach him."

7So Abishai and Joab set out after Sheba with an elite guard from Joab's army and the king's own bodyguard. 8,9,10As they arrived at the great stone in Gibeon, they came face to face with Amasa. Joab was wearing his uniform with a dagger strapped to his side. As he stepped forward to greet Amasa, he stealthily slipped the dagger from its sheath. "I'm glad to see you, my brother," Joab said, and took him by the beard with his right hand as though to kiss him. Amasa didn't notice the dagger in his left hand, and Joab stabbed him in the stomach with it, so that his bowels gushed out onto the ground. He did not need to strike again, and he died there. Joab and his brother Abishai left him lying there and continued after Sheba.

11One of Joab's young officers shouted to Amasa's troops, "If you are for David, come and follow Joab."

12But Amasa lay in his blood in the middle of the road, and when Joab's young officers saw that a crowd was gathering around to stare at him, they dragged him off the road into a field and threw a garment over him. 13With the body out of the way, everyone went on with Joab to capture Sheba.

JOHN 21:1–25

LATER Jesus appeared again to the disciples beside the Lake of Galilee. This is how it happened:

2A group of us were there—Simon Peter, Thomas, "The Twin," Nathanael from Cana in Galilee, my brother James and I and two other disciples.

3Simon Peter said, "I'm going fishing."

"We'll come too," we all said. We did, but caught nothing all night. 4At dawn we saw a man standing on the beach but couldn't see who he was.

5He called, "Any fish, boys?"

"No," we replied.

6Then he said, "Throw out your net on the right-hand side of the boat, and you'll get plenty of them!" So we did, and couldn't draw in the net because of the weight of the fish, there were so many!

7Then I said to Peter, "It is the Lord!" At that, Simon Peter put on his tunic (for he was stripped to the waist) and jumped into the water [and swam ashore]. 8The rest of us stayed in the boat and pulled the loaded net to the beach, about 300 feet away. 9When we got there, we saw that a fire was kindled and fish were frying over it, and there was bread.

10"Bring some of the fish you've just caught," Jesus said. 11So Simon Peter went out and dragged the net ashore. By his count there were 153 large fish; and yet the net hadn't torn.

12"Now come and have some breakfast!" Jesus said; and none of us dared ask him if he really was the Lord, for we were quite sure of it. 13Then Jesus went around serving us the bread and fish.

14This was the third time Jesus had appeared to us since his return from the dead.

15After breakfast Jesus said to Simon Peter, "Simon, son of John, do you love me more than these others?"

"Yes," Peter replied, "You know I am your friend."

"Then feed my lambs," Jesus told him.

16Jesus repeated the question: "Simon, son of John, do you *really* love me?"

"Yes, Lord," Peter said, "you know I am your friend."

"Then take care of my sheep," Jesus said.

17Once more he asked him, "Simon, son of John, are you even my friend?"

Peter was grieved at the way Jesus asked the question this third time. "Lord, you know my heart; you know I am," he said.

"He will never let me stumble, slip, or fall. For he is always watching, never sleeping."

Psalm 121:3-4

*"If God cares so wonderfully for flowers
that are here today and gone tomorrow,
won't he more surely care for you?"*
   Matthew 6:30

Jesus said, "Then feed my little sheep. 18When you were young, you were able to do as you liked and go wherever you wanted to; but when you are old, you will stretch out your hands and others will direct you and take you where you don't want to go." 19Jesus said this to let him know what kind of death he would die to glorify God. Then Jesus told him, "Follow me."

20Peter turned around and saw the disciple Jesus loved following, the one who had leaned around at supper that time to ask Jesus, "Master, which of us will betray you?" 21Peter asked Jesus, "What about him, Lord? What sort of death will he die?"

22Jesus replied, "If I want him to live until I return, what is that to you? *You* follow me."

23So the rumor spread among the brotherhood that that disciple wouldn't die! But that isn't what Jesus said at all! He only said, "If I want him to live until I come, what is that to you?"

24*I am that disciple!* I saw these events and have recorded them here. And we all know that my account of these things is accurate.

25And I suppose that if all the other events in Jesus' life were written, the whole world could hardly contain the books!

PSALM 120:1–7

I N my troubles I pled with God to help me and he did!
2Deliver me, O Lord, from liars. 3O lying tongue, what shall be your fate? 4You shall be pierced with sharp arrows and burned with glowing coals.

5,6My troubles pile high among these haters of the Lord, these men of Meshech and Kedar. I am tired of being here among these men who hate peace. 7I am for peace, but they are for war, and my voice goes unheeded in their councils.

PROVERBS FOR TODAY/ 16:16–17

How much better is wisdom than gold, and understanding than silver! The path of the godly leads away from evil; he who follows that path is safe.

JUNE 3

2 SAMUEL 20:14—22:20

M EANWHILE Sheba had traveled across Israel to mobilize his own clan of Bichri at the city of Abel in Beth-maacah. 15When Joab's forces arrived, they besieged Abel and built a mound to the top of the city wall and began battering it down.

16But a wise woman in the city called out to Joab, "Listen to me, Joab. Come over here so I can talk to you."

17As he approached, the woman asked, "Are you Joab?"

And he replied, "I am."

18So she told him, "There used to be a saying, 'If you want to settle an argument, ask advice at Abel.' For we always give wise counsel. 19You are destroying an ancient, peace-loving city, loyal to Israel. Should you destroy what is the Lord's?"

20And Joab replied, "That isn't it at all. 21All I want is a man named Sheba from the hill country of Ephraim, who has revolted against King David. If you will deliver him to me, we will leave the city in peace."

"All right," the woman replied, "we will throw his head over the wall to you."

22Then the woman went to the people

with her wise advice, and they cut off Sheba's head and threw it out to Joab. And he blew the trumpet and called his troops back from the attack, and they returned to the king at Jerusalem.

23Joab was commander-in-chief of the army, and Benaiah was in charge of the king's bodyguard. 24Adoram was in charge of the forced labor battalions, and Jehoshaphat was the historian who kept the records. 25Sheva was the secretary, and Zadok and Abiathar were the chief priests. 26Ira the Jairite was David's personal chaplain.

THERE was a famine during David's reign that lasted year after year for three years, and David spent much time in prayer about it. Then the Lord said, "The famine is because of the guilt of Saul and his family, for they murdered the Gibeonites."

2So King David summoned the Gibeonites. They were not part of Israel, but were what was left of the nation of the Amorites. Israel had sworn not to kill them; but Saul, in his nationalistic zeal, had tried to wipe them out.

3David asked them, "What can I do for you, to rid ourselves of this guilt and to induce you to ask God to bless us?"

4"Well, money won't do it," the Gibeonites replied, "and we don't want to see Israelites executed in revenge."

"What can I do, then?" David asked. "Just tell me and I will do it for you."

5,6"Well, then," they replied, "give us seven of Saul's sons—the sons of the man who did his best to destroy us. We will hang them before the Lord in Gibeon, the city of King Saul."

"All right," the king said, "I will do it."

7He spared Jonathan's son Mephibosheth, who was Saul's grandson, because of the oath between himself and Jonathan. 8But he gave them Saul's two sons Armoni and Mephibosheth, whose mother was Rizpah, the daughter of Aiah. He also gave them the five adopted sons of Michal that she brought up for Saul's daughter Merab, the wife of Adri-el.

9The men of Gibeon impaled them in the mountain before the Lord. So all seven of them died together at the beginning of the barley harvest.

10Then Rizpah, the mother of two of the men, spread sackcloth upon a rock and stayed there through the entire harvest season to prevent the vultures from tearing at their bodies during the day and the wild animals from eating them at night. 11When David learned what she had done, 12,13,14he arranged for the men's bones to be buried in the grave of Saul's father, Kish. At the same time he sent a request to the men of Jabesh-gilead, asking them to bring him the bones of Saul and Jonathan. They had stolen their bodies from the public square at Beth-shan where the Philistines had impaled them after they had died in battle on Mount Gilboa. So their bones were brought to him. Then at last God answered prayer and ended the famine.

15Once when the Philistines were at war with Israel, and David and his men were in the thick of the battle, David became weak and exhausted. 16Ishbi-be-nob, a giant whose speartip weighed more than twelve pounds and who was sporting a new suit of armor, closed in on David and was about to kill him. 17But Abishai the son of Zeruiah came to his rescue and killed the Philistine. After that David's men declared, "You are not going out to battle again! Why should we risk snuffing out the light of Israel?"

18Later, during a war with the Philistines at Gob, Sibbecai the Hushathite killed Saph, another giant. 19At still another time and at the same place, Elhanan killed the brother of Goliath the Gittite, whose spearhandle was as huge as a weaver's beam! 20,21And once when the Philistines and the Israelis were fighting at Gath, a giant with six fingers on each hand and six toes on each foot defied Israel, and David's nephew Jonathan—the son of David's brother Shime-i—killed him. 22These four were from the tribe of giants in Gath, and were killed by David's troops.

DAVID sang this song to the Lord after he had rescued him from Saul and from all his other enemies:

2"Jehovah is my rock,
My fortress and my Savior.
3I will hide in God,
Who is my rock and my refuge.
He is my shield
And my salvation,
My refuge and high tower.
Thank you, O my Savior,
For saving me from all my enemies.
4I will call upon the Lord,
Who is worthy to be praised;
He will save me from all my enemies.
5The waves of death surrounded me;
Floods of evil burst upon me;
6I was trapped, and bound
By hell and death;
7But I called upon the Lord in my distress,
And he heard me from his Temple.
My cry reached his ears.
8Then the earth shook and trembled;
The foundations of the heavens quaked
Because of his wrath.
9Smoke poured from his nostrils;
Fire leaped from his mouth
And burned up all before him,
Setting fire to the world.
10He bent the heavens down and came to earth;
He walked upon dark clouds.
11He rode upon the glorious—
On the wings of the wind.
12Darkness surrounded him,
And clouds were thick around him;
13The earth was radiant with his brightness.
14The Lord thundered from heaven;
The God above all gods gave out a mighty shout.
15He shot forth his arrows of lightning
And routed his enemies.
16By the blast of his breath
Was the sea split in two.
The bottom of the sea appeared.
17From above, he rescued me.
He drew me out from the waters;
18He saved me from powerful enemies,
From those who hated me
And from those who were too strong for me.
19They came upon me
In the day of my calamity,
But the Lord was my salvation.
20He set me free and rescued me,
For I was his delight.

ACTS 1:1–26

DEAR friend who loves God:
In my first letter I told you about Jesus' life and teachings and how he returned to heaven after giving his chosen apostles further instructions from the Holy Spirit. 3During the forty days after his crucifixion he appeared to the apostles from time to time, actually alive, and proved to them in many ways that it was really he himself they were seeing. And on these occasions he talked to them about the Kingdom of God.

4In one of these meetings he told them not to leave Jerusalem until the Holy Spirit came upon them in fulfillment of the Father's promise, a matter he had previously discussed with them.

5"John baptized you with water," he reminded them, "but you shall be baptized with the Holy Spirit in just a few days."

6And another time when he appeared to them, they asked him, "Lord, are you going to free Israel [from Rome] now and restore us as an independent nation?"

7"The Father sets those dates," he replied, "and they are not for you to know. 8But when the Holy Spirit has come upon you, you will receive power to testify about me with great effect, to the people in Jerusalem, throughout Judea, in Samaria, and to the ends of the earth, about my death and resurrection."

9It was not long afterwards that he rose into the sky and disappeared into a cloud, leaving them staring after him. 10As they were straining their eyes for another glimpse, suddenly two white-robed men were standing there among them, 11and said, "Men of Galilee, why are you standing here staring at the sky?

Jesus has gone away to heaven, and some day, just as he went, he will return!"

12They were at the Mount of Olives when this happened, so now they walked the half mile back to Jerusalem 13and held a prayer meeting in an upstairs room of the house where they were staying.

14Here is the list of those who were present at the meeting:

Peter,
John, James,
Andrew,
Philip, Thomas,
Bartholomew,
Matthew,
James (son of Alphaeus),
Simon (also called "The Zealot"),
Judas (son of James),
and the brothers of Jesus.
Several women, including Jesus' mother, were also there.

15This prayer meeting went on for several days. During this time, on a day when about 120 people were present, Peter stood up and addressed them as follows:

16"Brothers, it was necessary for the Scriptures to come true concerning Judas, who betrayed Jesus by guiding the mob to him, for this was predicted long ago by the Holy Spirit, speaking through King David. 17Judas was one of us, chosen to be an apostle just as we were. 18He bought a field with the money he received for his treachery and falling headlong there, he burst open, spilling out his bowels. 19The news of his death spread rapidly among all the people of Jerusalem, and they named the place 'The Field of Blood.' 20King David's prediction

of this appears in the Book of Psalms, where he says, 'Let his home become desolate with no one living in it.' And again, 'Let his work be given to someone else to do.'

21,22"So now we must choose someone else to take Judas' place and to join us as witnesses of Jesus' resurrection. Let us select someone who has been with us constantly from our first association with the Lord—from the time he was baptized by John until the day he was taken from us into heaven."

23The assembly nominated two men: Joseph Justus (also called Barsabbas) and Matthias. 24,25Then they all prayed for the right man to be chosen. "O Lord," they said, "you know every heart; show us which of these men you have chosen as an apostle to replace Judas the traitor, who has gone on to his proper place."

26Then they drew straws, and in this manner Matthias was chosen and became an apostle with the other eleven.

PSALM 121:1–8

SHALL I look to the mountain gods for help? 2No! My help is from Jehovah who made the mountains! And the heavens too! 3,4He will never let me stumble, slip or fall. For he is always watching, never sleeping.

5Jehovah himself is caring for you! He is your defender. 6He protects you day and night. 7He keeps you from all evil, and preserves your life. 8He keeps his eye upon you as you come and go, and always guards you.

PROVERBS FOR TODAY/ 16:18

Pride goes before destruction and haughtiness before a fall.

JUNE 4

2 SAMUEL 22:21—23:23

T HE Lord rewarded me for my
goodness,
For my hands were clean;
22And I have not departed from my
God.
23I knew his laws,
And I obeyed them.
24I was perfect in obedience
And kept myself from sin.
25That is why the Lord has done so
much for me,
For he sees that I am clean.
26You are merciful to the merciful;
You show your perfections
To the blameless.
27To those who are pure,
You show yourself pure;
But you destroy those who are evil.
28You will save those in trouble,
But you bring down the haughty;
For you watch their every move.
29O Lord, you are my light!
You make my darkness bright.
30By your power I can crush an army;
By your strength I leap over a wall.
31As for God, his way is perfect;
The word of the Lord is true.
He shields all who hide behind him.
32Our Lord alone is God;
We have no other Savior.
33God is my strong fortress;
He has made me safe.
34He causes the good to walk a steady
tread
Like mountain goats upon the rocks.
35He gives me skill in war
And strength to bend a bow of bronze.
36You have given me the shield of your
salvation;
Your gentleness has made me great.
37You have made wide steps for my
feet,
To keep them from slipping.
38I have chased my enemies
And destroyed them.
I did not stop till all were gone.
39I have destroyed them

So that none can rise again.
They have fallen beneath my feet.
40For you have given me strength for
the battle
And have caused me to subdue
All those who rose against me.
41You have made my enemies
Turn and run away;
I have destroyed them all.
42They looked in vain for help;
They cried to God,
But he refused to answer.
43I beat them into dust;
I crushed and scattered them
Like dust along the streets.
44You have preserved me
From the rebels of my people;
You have preserved me
As the head of the nations.
Foreigners shall serve me
45And shall quickly submit to me
When they hear of my power.
46They shall lose heart
And come, trembling,
From their hiding places.
47The Lord lives.
Blessed be my Rock.
Praise to him—
The Rock of my salvation.
48Blessed be God
Who destroys those who oppose me
49And rescues me from my enemies.
Yes, you hold me safe above their
heads.
You deliver me from violence.
50No wonder I give thanks to you,
O Lord, among the nations,
And sing praises to your name.
51He gives wonderful deliverance to
his king,
And shows mercy to his anointed—
To David and his family,
Forever."

THESE are the last words of David:
"David, the son of Jesse, speaks.

David, the man to whom God gave such wonderful success;

David, the anointed of the God of Jacob;

David, sweet psalmist of Israel:

2The Spirit of the Lord spoke by me, And his word was on my tongue.

3The Rock of Israel said to me: 'One shall come who rules righteously, Who rules in the fear of God.

4He shall be as the light of the morning;

A cloudless sunrise

When the tender grass

Springs forth upon the earth;

As sunshine after rain.'

5And it is my family

He has chosen!

Yes, God has made

An everlasting covenant with me;

His agreement is eternal, final, sealed.

He will constantly look after

My safety and success.

6But the godless are as thorns to be thrown away,

For they tear the hand that touches them.

7One must be armed to chop them down;

They shall be burned."

8These are the names of the Top Three—the most heroic men in David's army: the first was Josheb-basshebeth from Tah-chemon, known also as Adino, the Eznite. He once killed eight hundred men in one battle.

9Next in rank was Eleazar, the son of Dodo and grandson of Ahohi. He was one of the three men who, with David, held back the Philistines that time when the rest of the Israeli army fled. 10He killed the Philistines until his hand was too tired to hold his sword; and the Lord gave him a great victory. (The rest of the army did not return until it was time to collect the loot!)

11,12After him was Shammah, the son of Agee from Harar. Once during a Philistine attack, when all his men deserted him and fled, he stood alone at the center of a field of lentils and beat back the Philistines; and God gave him a great victory.

13One time when David was living in the cave of Adullam and the invading Philistines were at the valley of Rephaim, three of The Thirty—the top-ranking officers of the Israeli army—went down at harvest time to visit him. 14David was in the stronghold at the time, for Philistine marauders had occupied the nearby city of Bethlehem.

15David remarked, "How thirsty I am for some of that good water in the city well!" (The well was near the city gate.)

16So the three men broke through the Philistine ranks and drew water from the well and brought it to David. But he refused to drink it! Instead, he poured it out before the Lord.

17"No, my God," he exclaimed, "I cannot do it! This is the blood of these men who have risked their lives."

18,19Of those three men, Abishai, the brother of Joab (son of Zeruiah), was the greatest. Once he took on three hundred of the enemy singlehanded and killed them all. It was by such feats that he earned a reputation equal to The Three, though he was not actually one of them. But he was the greatest of The Thirty—the top-ranking officers of the army—and was their leader.

20There was also Benaiah (son of Jehoiada), a heroic soldier from Kabzeel. Benaiah killed two giants, sons of Ariel of Moab. Another time he went down into a pit and, despite the slippery snow on the ground, took on a lion that was caught there and killed it. 21Another time, armed only with a staff, he killed an Egyptian warrior who was armed with a spear; he wrenched the spear from the Egyptian's hand and killed him with it. 22These were some of the deeds that gave Benaiah almost as much renown as the Top Three. 23He was one of the greatest of The Thirty, but was not actually one of the Top Three. And David made him chief of his bodyguard.

SEVEN weeks had gone by since Jesus' death and resurrection, and the Day of Pentecost had now arrived. As the believers met together that day, 2suddenly there was a sound like the roaring of a mighty windstorm in the skies above them and it filled the house where they were meeting. 3Then, what looked like flames or tongues of fire appeared and settled on their heads. 4And everyone present was filled with the Holy Spirit and began speaking in languages they didn't know, for the Holy Spirit gave them this ability.

5Many godly Jews were in Jerusalem that day for the religious celebrations, having arrived from many nations. 6And when they heard the roaring in the sky above the house, crowds came running to see what it was all about, and were stunned to hear their own languages being spoken by the disciples.

7"How can this be?" they exclaimed. "For these men are all from Galilee, 8and yet we hear them speaking all the native languages of the lands where we were born! 9Here we are—Parthians, Medes, Elamites, men from Mesopotamia, Judea, Cappadocia, Pontus, Asia Minor, 10Phrygia, Pamphylia, Egypt, the Cyrene language areas of Libya, visitors from Rome—both Jews and Jewish converts— 11Cretans, and Arabians. And we all hear these men telling in our own languages about the mighty miracles of God!"

12They stood there amazed and perplexed. "What can this mean?" they asked each other.

13But others in the crowd were mocking. "They're drunk, that's all!" they said.

14Then Peter stepped forward with the eleven apostles, and shouted to the crowd, "Listen, all of you, visitors and residents of Jerusalem alike! 15Some of you are saying these men are drunk! It isn't true! It's much too early for that! People don't get drunk by 9 A.M.! 16No! What you see this morning was predicted centuries ago by the prophet Joel—17'In the last days,' God said, 'I will pour out my Holy Spirit upon all mankind, and your sons and daughters shall prophesy, and your young men shall see visions, and your old men dream dreams. 18Yes, the Holy Spirit shall come upon all my servants, men and women alike, and they shall prophesy. 19And I will cause strange demonstrations in the heavens and on the earth—blood and fire and clouds of smoke; 20the sun shall turn black and the moon blood-red before that awesome Day of the Lord arrives. 21But anyone who asks for mercy from the Lord shall have it and shall be saved.'

22"O men of Israel, listen! God publicly endorsed Jesus of Nazareth by doing tremendous miracles through him, as you well know. 23But God, following his prearranged plan, let you use the Roman government to nail him to the cross and murder him. 24Then God released him from the horrors of death and brought him back to life again, for death could not keep this man within its grip.

25"King David quoted Jesus as saying: 'I know the Lord is always with me. He is helping me. God's mighty power supports me.

26'No wonder my heart is filled with joy and my tongue shouts his praises! For I know all will be well with me in death—

27'You will not leave my soul in hell or let the body of your Holy Son decay.

28'You will give me back my life, and give me wonderful joy in your presence.'

29"Dear brothers, think! David wasn't referring to himself when he spoke these words I have quoted, for he died and was buried, and his tomb is still here among us. 30But he was a prophet, and knew God had promised with an unbreakable oath that one of David's own descendants would [be the Messiah and] sit on David's throne. 31David was looking far into the future and predicting the Messiah's resurrection, and saying that the Messiah's soul would not be left in hell and his body would not decay. 32He was speaking of Jesus, and we all are witnesses that Jesus rose from the dead.

33"And now he sits on the throne of highest honor in heaven, next to God. And just as promised, the Father gave him the authority to send the Holy Spirit—with the results you are seeing and hearing today.

34"[No, David was not speaking of himself in these words of his I have quoted], for he never ascended into the skies. Moreover, he further stated, 'God spoke to my Lord, the Messiah, and said to him, Sit here in honor beside me 35until I bring your enemies into complete subjection.'

36"Therefore I clearly state to everyone in Israel that God has made this Jesus you crucified to be the Lord, the Messiah!"

37These words of Peter's moved them deeply, and they said to him and to the other apostles, "Brothers, what should we do?"

38And Peter replied, "Each one of you must turn from sin, return to God, and be baptized in the name of Jesus Christ for the forgiveness of your sins; then you also shall receive this gift, the Holy Spirit. 39For Christ promised him to each one of you who has been called by the Lord our God, and to your children and even to those in distant lands!"

40Then Peter preached a long sermon, telling about Jesus and strongly urging all his listeners to save themselves from the evils of their nation. 41And those who believed Peter were baptized—about 3,000 in all! 42They joined with the other believers in regular attendance at the apostles' teaching sessions and at the Communion services and prayer meetings.

43A deep sense of awe was on them all, and the apostles did many miracles.

44And all the believers met together constantly and shared everything with each other, 45selling their possessions and dividing with those in need. 46They worshiped together regularly at the Temple each day, met in small groups in homes for Communion, and shared their meals with great joy and thankfulness, 47praising God. The whole city was favorable to them, and each day God added to them all who were being saved.

PSALM 122:1–9

I was glad for the suggestion of going to Jerusalem, to the Temple of the Lord. 2,3Now we are standing here inside the crowded city. 4All Israel—Jehovah's people—have come to worship as the law requires, to thank and praise the Lord. 5Look! There are the judges holding court beside the city gates, deciding all the people's arguments.

6Pray for the peace of Jerusalem. May all who love this city prosper. 7O Jerusalem, may there be peace within your walls and prosperity in your palaces. 8This I ask for the sake of all my brothers and my friends who live here; 9and may there be peace as a protection to the Temple of the Lord.

PROVERBS FOR TODAY/ 16:19–20

Better poor and humble than proud and rich. God blesses those who obey him; happy the man who puts his trust in the Lord.

JUNE 5

2 SAMUEL 23:24—24:25

ASAHEL, the brother of Joab, was also one of The Thirty. Others were:

Elhanan (son of Dodo) from Bethlehem;

Shammah from Harod;

Elika from Harod;

Helez from Palti;

Ira (son of Ikkesh) from Tekoa;

Abi-ezer from Anathoth;

Mebunnai from Hushath;

Zalmon from Ahoh;

Maharai from Netophah;

Heleb (son of Baanah) from Netophah;

Ittai (son of Ribai) from Gibe-ah, of the tribe of Benjamin;

Benaiah of Pirathon;

Hiddai from the brooks of Gaash;

Abi-albon from Arbath;

Azmaveth from Bahurim;

Eliahba from Sha-albon;

The sons of Jashen;

Jonathan;

Shammah from Harar;

Ahiam (the son of Sharar) from Harar;

Eliphelet (son of Ahasbai) from Maacah;

Eliam (the son of Ahithophel) from Gilo;

Hezro from Carmel;

Paarai from Arba;

Igal (son of Nathan) from Zobah;

Bani from Gad;

Zelek from Ammon;

Naharai from Be-eroth, the armor bearer of Joab (son of Zeruiah);

Ira from Ithra;

Gareb from Ithra;

Uriah the Hittite—thirty-seven in all.

ONCE again the anger of the Lord flared against Israel, and he caused David to harm them by taking a national census. "Go and count the people of Israel and Judah," the Lord told him.

²So the king said to Joab, commander-in-chief of his army, "Take a census of all the people from one end of the nation to the other, so that I will know how many of them there are."

³But Joab replied, "God grant that you will live to see the day when there will be a hundred times as many people in your kingdom as there are now! But you have no right to rejoice in their strength."

⁴But the king's command overcame Joab's remonstrance; so Joab and the other army officers went out to count the people of Israel. ⁵First they crossed the Jordan and camped at Aroer, south of the city that lies in the middle of the valley of Gad, near Jazer; ⁶then they went to Gilead in the land of Tahtim-hodshi and to Dan-jaan and around to Sidon; ⁷and then to the stronghold of Tyre, and all the cities of the Hivites and Canaanites, and south to Judah as far as Beersheba. ⁸Having gone through the entire land, they completed their task in nine months and twenty days. ⁹And Joab reported the number of the people to the king—800,000 men of conscription age in Israel and 500,000 in Judah.

¹⁰But after he had taken the census, David's conscience began to bother him, and he said to the Lord, "What I did was very wrong. Please forgive this foolish wickedness of mine."

¹¹The next morning the word of the Lord came to the prophet Gad, who was David's contact with God.

The Lord said to Gad, ¹²"Tell David that I will give him three choices."

¹³So Gad came to David and asked him, "Will you choose seven years of famine across the land, or to flee for three months before your enemies, or to submit to three days of plague? Think this over and let me know what answer to give to God."

¹⁴"This is a hard decision," David replied, "but it is better to fall into the hand of the Lord (for his mercy is great) than into the hands of men."

¹⁵So the Lord sent a plague upon Israel

that morning, and it lasted for three days; and seventy thousand men died throughout the nation. 16But as the death angel was preparing to destroy Jerusalem, the Lord was sorry for what was happening and told him to stop. He was by the threshing floor of Araunah the Jebusite at the time.

17When David saw the angel, he said to the Lord, "Look, I am the one who has sinned! What have these sheep done? Let your anger be only against me and my family."

18That day Gad came to David and said to him, "Go and build an altar to the Lord on the threshing floor of Araunah the Jebusite." 19So David went to do what the Lord had commanded him. 20When Araunah saw the king and his men coming towards him, he came forward and fell flat on the ground with his face in the dust.

21"Why have you come?" Araunah asked.

And David replied, "To buy your threshing floor, so that I can build an altar to the Lord, and he will stop the plague."

22"Use anything you like," Araunah told the king. "Here are oxen for the burnt offering, and you can use the threshing instruments and ox yokes for wood to build a fire on the altar. 23I will give it all to you, and may the Lord God accept your sacrifice."

24But the king said to Araunah, "No, I will not have it as a gift. I will buy it, for I don't want to offer to the Lord my God burnt offerings that have cost me nothing."

So David paid him for the threshing floor and the oxen. 25And David built an altar there to the Lord and offered burnt offerings and peace offerings. And the Lord answered his prayer, and the plague was stopped.

ACTS 3:1–26

PETER and John went to the Temple one afternoon to take part in the three o'clock daily prayer meeting. 2As they approached the Temple, they saw a man lame from birth carried along the street and laid beside the Temple gate—the one called The Beautiful Gate—as was his custom every day. 3As Peter and John were passing by, he asked them for some money.

4They looked at him intently, and then Peter said, "Look here!"

5The lame man looked at them eagerly, expecting a gift.

6But Peter said, "We don't have any money for you! But I'll give you something else! I command you in the name of Jesus Christ of Nazareth, *walk!*"

7,8Then Peter took the lame man by the hand and pulled him to his feet. And as he did, the man's feet and ankle-bones were healed and strengthened so that he came up with a leap, stood there a moment and began walking! Then, walking, leaping, and praising God, he went into the Temple with them.

9When the people inside saw him walking and heard him praising God, 10and realized he was the lame beggar they had seen so often at The Beautiful Gate, they were inexpressibly surprised! 11They all rushed out to Solomon's Hall, where he was holding tightly to Peter and John! Everyone stood there awed by the wonderful thing that had happened.

12Peter saw his opportunity and addressed the crowd. "Men of Israel," he said, "what is so surprising about this? And why look at us as though we by our own power and godliness had made this man walk? 13For it is the God of Abraham, Isaac, Jacob and of all our ancestors who has brought glory to his servant Jesus by doing this. I refer to the Jesus whom you rejected before Pilate, despite Pilate's determination to release him. 14You didn't want him freed—this holy, righteous one. Instead you demanded the release of a murderer. 15And you killed the Author of Life; but God brought him back to life again. And John and I are witnesses of this fact, for after you killed him we saw him alive!

16"Jesus' name has healed this man—and you know how lame he was before.

Faith in Jesus' name—faith given us from God—has caused this perfect healing.

17"Dear brothers, I realize that what you did to Jesus was done in ignorance; and the same can be said of your leaders. 18But God was fulfilling the prophecies that the Messiah must suffer all these things. 19Now change your mind and attitude to God and turn to him so he can cleanse away your sins and send you wonderful times of refreshment from the presence of the Lord 20and send Jesus your Messiah back to you again. 21,22For he must remain in heaven until the final recovery of all things from sin, as prophesied from ancient times. Moses, for instance, said long ago, 'The Lord God will raise up a Prophet among you, who will resemble me! Listen carefully to everything he tells you. 23Anyone who will not listen to him shall be utterly destroyed.'

24"Samuel and every prophet since have all spoken about what is going on today. 25You are the children of those prophets; and you are included in God's promise to your ancestors to bless the entire world through the Jewish race— that is the promise God gave to Abraham. 26And as soon as God had brought his servant to life again, he sent him first of all to you men of Israel, to bless you by turning you back from your sins."

PSALM 123:1–4

O God enthroned in heaven, I lift my eyes to you. 2We look to Jehovah our God for his mercy and kindness just as a servant keeps his eyes upon his master or a slave girl watches her mistress for the slightest signal.

3,4Have mercy on us, Lord, have mercy. For we have had our fill of contempt and of the scoffing of the rich and proud.

PROVERBS FOR TODAY/ 16:21–23

The wise man is known by his common sense, and a pleasant teacher is the best. Wisdom is a fountain of life to those possessing it, but a fool's burden is his folly. From a wise mind comes careful and persuasive speech.

JUNE 6

1 KINGS 1:1–53

IN his old age King David was confined to his bed; but no matter how many blankets were heaped upon him, he was always cold.

2"The cure for this," his aides told him, "is to find a young virgin to be your concubine and nurse. She will lie in your arms and keep you warm."

3,4So they searched the country from one end to the other to find the most beautiful girl in all the land. Abishag, from Shunam, was finally selected. They brought her to the king and she lay in his arms to warm him (but he had no sexual relations with her).

5At about that time, David's son Adonijah (his mother was Haggith) decided to crown himself king in place of his aged father. So he hired chariots and drivers and recruited fifty men to run down the streets before him as royal footmen. 6Now his father, King David, had never disciplined him at any time—not so much as by a single scolding! He was a very handsome man, and was Absalom's younger brother. 7He took General Joab and Abiathar the priest into his confidence, and they agreed to help him become king. 8But among those who remained loyal to King David and refused to endorse Adonijah were the priests Zadok and Benaiah, the prophet Nathan, Shime-i, Rei, and David's army chiefs.

9Adonijah went to En-rogel where he sacrificed sheep, oxen, and fat young goats at the Serpent's Stone. Then he summoned all of his brothers—the other sons of King David—and all the royal officials of Judah, requesting that they come to his coronation. 10But he didn't invite Nathan the prophet, Benaiah, the loyal army officers, or his brother Solomon.

11Then Nathan the prophet went to Bath-sheba, Solomon's mother, and asked her, "Do you realize that Haggith's son, Adonijah, is now the king and that our lord David doesn't even know about it? 12If you want to save your own life and the life of your son Solomon—do exactly as I say! 13Go at once to King David and ask him, 'My lord, didn't you promise me that my son Solomon would be the next king and would sit upon your throne? Then why is Adonijah reigning?' 14And while you are still talking with him, I'll come and confirm everything you've said."

15So Bath-sheba went into the king's bedroom. He was an old, old man now, and Abishag was caring for him. 16Bath-sheba bowed low before him.

"What do you want?" he asked her.

17She replied, "My lord, you vowed to me by the Lord your God that my son Solomon would be the next king and would sit upon your throne. 18But instead, Adonijah is the new king, and you don't even know about it. 19He has celebrated his coronation by sacrificing oxen, fat goats, and many sheep and has invited all your sons and Abiathar the priest and General Joab. But he didn't invite Solomon. 20And now, my lord the king, all Israel is waiting for your decision as to whether Adonijah is the one you have chosen to succeed you. 21If you don't act, my son Solomon and I will be arrested and executed as criminals as soon as you are dead."

22,23While she was speaking, the king's aides told him, "Nathan the prophet is here to see you."

Nathan came in and bowed low before the king, 24and asked, "My lord, have you appointed Adonijah to be the next king? Is he the one you have selected to sit upon your throne? 25Today he celebrated his coronation by sacrificing oxen and fat goats and many sheep, and has invited your sons to attend the festivities. He also invited General Joab and Abiathar the priest; and they are feasting and drinking with him and shouting, 'Long live King Adonijah!' 26But Zadok the priest and Benaiah and Solomon and I weren't invited. 27Has this been done with your knowledge? For you haven't said a word as to which of your sons you have chosen to be the next king."

28"Call Bath-sheba," David said. So she came back in and stood before the king.

29And the king vowed, "As the Lord lives who has rescued me from every danger, 30I decree that your son Solomon shall be the next king and shall sit upon my throne, just as I swore to you before by the Lord God of Israel."

31Then Bath-sheba bowed low before him again and exclaimed, "Oh, thank you, sir. May my lord the king live forever!"

32"Call Zadok the priest," the king ordered, "and Nathan the prophet, and Benaiah."

When they arrived, 33he said to them, "Take Solomon and my officers to Gihon. Solomon is to ride on my personal mule, 34and Zadok the priest and Nathan the prophet are to anoint him there as king of Israel. Then blow the trumpets and shout, 'Long live King Solomon!' 35When you bring him back here, place him upon my throne as the new king; for I have appointed him king of Israel and Judah."

36"Amen! Praise God!" replied Benaiah, and added, 37"May the Lord be with Solomon as he has been with you, and may God make Solomon's reign even greater than yours!"

³⁸So Zadok the priest, Nathan the prophet, Benaiah, and David's bodyguard took Solomon to Gihon, riding on King David's own mule. ³⁹At Gihon, Zadok took a flask of sacred oil from the Tabernacle and poured it over Solomon; and the trumpets were blown and all the people shouted, "Long live King Solomon!"

⁴⁰Then they all returned with him to Jerusalem, making a joyous and noisy celebration all along the way.

⁴¹Adonijah and his guests heard the commotion and shouting just as they were finishing their banquet.

"What's going on?" Joab demanded. "Why is the city in such an uproar?"

⁴²And while he was still speaking, Jonathan, the son of Abiathar the priest, rushed in.

"Come in," Adonijah said to him, "for you are a good man; you must have good news."

⁴³"Our lord King David has declared Solomon as king!" Jonathan shouted. ⁴⁴,⁴⁵"The king sent him to Gihon with Zadok the priest and Nathan the prophet and Benaiah, protected by the king's own bodyguard; and he rode on the king's own mule. And Zadok and Nathan have anointed him as the new king! They have just returned, and the whole city is celebrating and rejoicing. That's what all the noise is. ⁴⁶,⁴⁷Solomon is sitting on the throne, and all the people are congratulating King David, saying, 'May God bless you even more through Solomon than he has blessed you personally! May God make Solomon's reign even greater than yours!' And the king is lying in bed, acknowledging their blessings. ⁴⁸He is saying, 'Blessed be the Lord God of Israel who has selected one of my sons to sit upon my throne while I am still alive to see it.'"

⁴⁹,⁵⁰Then Adonijah and his guests jumped up from the banquet table and fled in panic; for they were fearful for their lives. Adonijah rushed into the Tabernacle and caught hold of the horns of the sacred altar. ⁵¹When word reached Solomon that Adonijah was claiming sanctuary in the Tabernacle, and pleading for clemency, ⁵²Solomon replied, "If he behaves himself, he will not be harmed; but if he does not, he shall die." ⁵³So King Solomon summoned him, and they brought him down from the altar. He came to bow low before the king; and then Solomon curtly dismissed him.

"Go on home," he said.

ACTS 4:1–37

WHILE they were talking to the people, the chief priests, the captain of the Temple police, and some of the Sadducees came over to them, ²very disturbed that Peter and John were claiming that Jesus had risen from the dead. ³They arrested them and since it was already evening, jailed them overnight. ⁴But many of the people who heard their message believed it, so that the number of believers now reached a new high of about 5,000 men!

⁵The next day it happened that the Council of all the Jewish leaders was in session in Jerusalem— ⁶Annas the High Priest was there, and Caiaphas, John, Alexander, and others of the High Priest's relatives. ⁷So the two disciples were brought in before them.

"By what power, or by whose authority have you done this?" the Council demanded.

⁸Then Peter, filled with the Holy Spirit, said to them, "Honorable leaders and elders of our nation, ⁹if you mean the good deed done to the cripple, and how he was healed, ¹⁰let me clearly state to you and to all the people of Israel that it was done in the name and power of Jesus from Nazareth, the Messiah, the man you crucified—but God raised back to life again. It is by his authority that this man stands here healed! ¹¹For Jesus the Messiah is (the one referred to in the Scriptures when they speak of) a 'stone discarded by the builders which became the capstone of the arch.' ¹²There is salvation in no one else! Under all heaven there is no other name for men to call upon to save them."

¹³When the Council saw the boldness

of Peter and John, and could see that they were obviously uneducated non-professionals, they were amazed and realized what being with Jesus had done for them! 14And the Council could hardly discredit the healing when the man they had healed was standing right there beside them! 15So they sent them out of the Council chamber and conferred among themselves.

16"What shall we do with these men?" they asked each other. "We can't deny that they have done a tremendous miracle, and everybody in Jerusalem knows about it. 17But perhaps we can stop them from spreading their propaganda. We'll tell them that if they do it again we'll really throw the book at them." 18So they called them back in, and told them never again to speak about Jesus.

19But Peter and John replied, "You decide whether God wants us to obey you instead of him! 20We cannot stop telling about the wonderful things we saw Jesus do and heard him say."

21The Council then threatened them further, and finally let them go because they didn't know how to punish them without starting a riot. For everyone was praising God for this wonderful miracle— 22the healing of a man who had been lame for forty years.

23As soon as they were freed, Peter and John found the other disciples and told them what the Council had said.

24Then all the believers united in this prayer:

"O Lord, Creator of heaven and earth and of the sea and everything in them— 25,26you spoke long ago by the Holy Spirit through our ancestor King David, your servant, saying, 'Why do the heathen rage against the Lord, and the foolish nations plan their little plots against Almighty God? The kings of the earth unite to fight against him, and against the anointed Son of God!'

27"That is what is happening here in this city today! For Herod the king, and Pontius Pilate the governor, and all the Romans—as well as the people of Israel—are united against Jesus, your anointed Son, your holy servant. 28They won't stop at anything that you in your wise power will let them do. 29And now, O Lord, hear their threats, and grant to your servants great boldness in their preaching, 30and send your healing power, and may miracles and wonders be done by the name of your holy servant Jesus."

31After this prayer, the building where they were meeting shook and they were all filled with the Holy Spirit and boldly preached God's message.

32All the believers were of one heart and mind, and no one felt that what he owned was his own; everyone was sharing. 33And the apostles preached powerful sermons about the resurrection of the Lord Jesus, and there was warm fellowship among all the believers, 34,35and no poverty—for all who owned land or houses sold them and brought the money to the apostles to give to others in need.

36For instance, there was Joseph (the one the apostles nicknamed "Barnabas, the encourager." He was of the tribe of Levi, from the island of Cyprus). 37He was one of those who sold a field he owned and brought the money to the apostles for distribution to those in need.

PSALM 124:1-8

IF the Lord had not been on our side (let all Israel admit it), if the Lord had not been on our side, 2,3we would have been swallowed alive by our enemies, destroyed by their anger. 4,5We would have drowned beneath the flood of these men's fury and pride.

6Blessed be Jehovah who has not let them devour us. 7We have escaped with our lives as a bird from a hunter's snare. The snare is broken and we are free!

8Our help is from the Lord who made heaven and earth.

PROVERBS FOR TODAY/ 16:24

Kind words are like honey—enjoyable and healthful.

JUNE 7

1 KINGS 2:1—3:2

As the time of King David's death approached, he gave this charge to his son Solomon:

2"I am going where every man on earth must some day go. I am counting on you to be a strong and worthy successor. 3Obey the laws of God and follow all his ways; keep each of his commands written in the law of Moses so that you will prosper in everything you do, wherever you turn. 4If you do this, then the Lord will fulfill the promise he gave me, that if my children and their descendants watch their step and are faithful to God, one of them shall always be the king of Israel—my dynasty will never end.

5"Now listen to my instructions. You know that Joab murdered my two generals, Abner and Amasa. He pretended that it was an act of war, but it was done in a time of peace. 6You are a wise man and will know what to do—don't let him die in peace. 7But be kind to the sons of Barzillai the Gileadite. Make them permanent guests of the king, for they took care of me when I fled from your brother Absalom. 8And do you remember Shime-i, the son of Gera the Benjaminite from Bahurim? He cursed me with a terrible curse as I was going to Mahanaim; but when he came down to meet me at the Jordan River I promised I wouldn't kill him. 9But that promise doesn't bind you! You are a wise man, and you will know how to arrange a bloody death for him."

10Then David died and was buried in Jerusalem. 11He had reigned over Israel for forty years, seven of them in Hebron and thirty-three in Jerusalem. 12And Solomon became the new king, replacing his father David; and his kingdom prospered.

13One day Adonijah the son of Haggith came to see Solomon's mother, Bathsheba.

"Have you come to make trouble?" she asked him.

"No," he replied, "I come in peace. 14As a matter of fact, I have a favor to ask of you."

"What is it?" she asked.

15"Everything was going well for me," he said, "and the kingdom was mine: everyone expected me to be the next king. But the tables are turned, and everything went to my brother instead; for that is the way the Lord wanted it. 16But now I have just a small favor to ask of you; please don't turn me down."

"What is it?" she asked.

17He replied, "Speak to King Solomon on my behalf (for I know he will do anything you request) and ask him to give me Abishag, the Shunammite, as my wife."

18"All right," Bath-sheba replied, "I'll ask him."

19So she went to ask the favor of King Solomon. The king stood up from his throne as she entered and bowed low to her. He ordered that a throne for his mother be placed beside his; so she sat at his right hand.

20"I have one small request to make of you," she said. "I hope you won't turn me down."

"What is it, my mother?" he asked. "You know I won't refuse you."

21"Then let your brother Adonijah marry Abishag," she replied.

22"Are you crazy?" he demanded. "If I were to give him Abishag, I would be giving him the kingdom too! For he is my older brother! He and Abiathar the priest and General Joab would take over!" 23,24Then King Solomon swore with a great oath, "May God strike me dead if Adonijah does not die this very day for this plot against me! I swear it by the living God who has given me the throne of my father David and this kingdom he promised me."

25So King Solomon sent Benaiah to execute him, and he killed him with a sword.

26Then the king said to Abiathar the priest, "Go back to your home in Anathoth. You should be killed, too, but I won't do it now. For you carried the Ark of the Lord during my father's reign, and you suffered right along with him in all of his troubles."

27So Solomon forced Abiathar to give up his position as the priest of the Lord, thereby fulfilling the decree of Jehovah at Shiloh concerning the descendants of Eli.

28When Joab heard about Adonijah's death (Joab had joined Adonijah's revolt, though not Absalom's) he ran to the Tabernacle for sanctuary and caught hold of the horns of the altar. 29When news of this reached King Solomon, he sent Benaiah to execute him.

30Benaiah went into the Tabernacle and said to Joab, "The king says to come out!"

"No," he said, "I'll die here."

So Benaiah returned to the king for further instructions.

31"Do as he says," the king replied. "Kill him there beside the altar and bury him. This will remove the guilt of his senseless murders from me and from my father's family. 32Then Jehovah will hold him personally responsible for the murders of two men who were better than he. For my father was no party to the deaths of General Abner, commander-in-chief of the army of Israel, and General Amasa, commander-in-chief of the army of Judah. 33May Joab and his descendants be forever guilty of these murders, and may the Lord declare David and his descendants guiltless concerning their deaths."

34So Benaiah returned to the Tabernacle and killed Joab; and he was buried beside his house in the desert.

35Then the king appointed Benaiah as commander-in-chief, and Zadok as priest instead of Abiathar.

36,37The king now sent for Shime-i and told him, "Build a house here in Jerusalem, and don't step outside the city on pain of death. The moment you go beyond Kidron Brook, you die; and it will be your own fault."

38"All right," Shime-i replied, "whatever you say." So he lived in Jerusalem for a long time.

39But three years later two of Shime-i's slaves escaped to King Achish of Gath. When Shime-i learned where they were, 40he saddled a donkey and went to Gath to visit the king. And when he had found his slaves, he took them back to Jerusalem.

41When Solomon heard that Shime-i had left Jerusalem and had gone to Gath and returned, 42he sent for him and demanded, "Didn't I command you in the name of God to stay in Jerusalem or die? You replied, 'Very well, I will do as you say.' 43Then why have you not kept your agreement and obeyed my commandment? 44And what about all the wicked things you did to my father, King David? May the Lord take revenge on you, 45but may I receive God's rich blessings, and may one of David's descendants always sit upon this throne."

46Then, at the king's command, Benaiah took Shime-i outside and killed him.

So Solomon's grip upon the kingdom became secure.

SOLOMON made an alliance with Pharoah, the king of Egypt, and married one of his daughters. He brought her to Jerusalem to live in the City of David until he could finish building his palace and the Temple and the wall around the city.

2At that time the people of Israel sacrificed their offerings on altars in the hills, for the Temple of the Lord hadn't yet been built.

ACTS 5:1–42

BUT there was a man named Ananias (with his wife Sapphira) who sold some property, 2and brought only part of the money, claiming it was the full price. (His wife had agreed to this deception.)

3But Peter said, "Ananias, Satan has filled your heart. When you claimed this was the full price, you were lying to the Holy Spirit. 4The property was yours to sell or not, as you wished. And after selling it, it was yours to decide how much to give. How could you do a thing like this? You weren't lying to us, but to God."

5As soon as Ananias heard these words, he fell to the floor, dead! Everyone was terrified, 6and the younger men covered him with a sheet and took him out and buried him.

7About three hours later his wife came in, not knowing what had happened. 8Peter asked her, "Did you people sell your land for such and such a price?"

"Yes," she replied, "we did."

9And Peter said, "How could you and your husband even think of doing a thing like this—conspiring together to test the Spirit of God's ability to know what is going on? Just outside that door are the young men who buried your husband, and they will carry you out too."

10Instantly she fell to the floor, dead, and the young men came in and, seeing that she was dead, carried her out and buried her beside her husband. 11Terror gripped the entire church and all others who heard what had happened.

12Meanwhile, the apostles were meeting regularly at the Temple in the area known as Solomon's Hall, and they did many remarkable miracles among the people. 13The other believers didn't dare join them, though, but all had the highest regard for them. 14And more and more believers were added to the Lord, crowds both of men and women. 15Sick people were brought out into the streets on beds and mats so that at least Peter's shadow would fall across some of them as he went by! 16And crowds came in from the Jerusalem suburbs, bringing their sick folk and those possessed by demons; and every one of them was healed.

17The High Priest and his relatives and friends among the Sadducees reacted with violent jealousy 18and arrested the apostles, and put them in the public jail. 19But an angel of the Lord came at night, opened the gates of the jail and

brought them out. Then he told them, 20"Go over to the Temple and preach about this Life!"

21They arrived at the Temple about daybreak, and immediately began preaching! Later that morning the High Priest and his courtiers arrived at the Temple, and, convening the Jewish Council and the entire Senate, they sent for the apostles to be brought for trial. 22But when the police arrived at the jail, the men weren't there, so they returned to the Council and reported, 23"The jail doors were locked, and the guards were standing outside, but when we opened the gates, no one was there!"

24When the police captain and the chief priests heard this, they were frantic, wondering what would happen next and where all this would end! 25Then someone arrived with the news that the men they had jailed were out in the Temple, preaching to the people!

26,27The police captain went with his officers and arrested them (without violence, for they were afraid the people would kill them if they roughed up the disciples) and brought them in before the Council.

28"Didn't we tell you never again to preach about this Jesus?" the High Priest demanded. "And instead you have filled all Jerusalem with your teaching and intend to bring the blame for this man's death on us!"

29But Peter and the apostles replied, "We must obey God rather than men. 30The God of our ancestors brought Jesus back to life again after you had killed him by hanging him on a cross. 31Then, with mighty power, God exalted him to be a Prince and Savior, so that the people of Israel would have an opportunity for repentance, and for their sins to be forgiven. 32And we are witnesses of these things, and so is the Holy Spirit, who is given by God to all who obey him."

33At this, the Council was furious, and decided to kill them. 34But one of their members, a Pharisee named Gamaliel (an expert on religious law and very popular with the people), stood up and requested that the apostles be sent outside the Council chamber while he talked.

35Then he addressed his colleagues as follows:

"Men of Israel, take care what you are planning to do to these men! 36Some time ago there was that fellow Theudas, who pretended to be someone great. About 400 others joined him, but he was killed, and his followers were harmlessly dispersed.

37"After him, at the time of the taxation, there was Judas of Galilee. He drew away some people as disciples, but he also died, and his followers scattered.

38"And so my advice is, leave these men alone. If what they teach and do is merely on their own, it will soon be overthrown. 39But if it is of God, you will not be able to stop them, lest you find yourselves fighting even against God."

40The Council accepted his advice, called in the apostles, had them beaten, and then told them never again to speak in the name of Jesus, and finally let them go. 41They left the Council chamber rejoicing that God had counted them worthy to suffer dishonor for his name. 42And every day, in the Temple and in their home Bible classes, they continued to teach and preach that Jesus is the Messiah.

PSALM 125:1–5

THOSE who trust in the Lord are steady as Mount Zion, unmoved by any circumstance.

2Just as the mountains surround and protect Jerusalem, so the Lord surrounds and protects his people. 3For the wicked shall not rule the godly, lest the godly be forced to do wrong. 4O Lord, do good to those who are good, whose hearts are right with the Lord; 5but lead evil men to execution. And let Israel have quietness and peace.

PROVERBS FOR TODAY/ 16:25

Before every man there lies a wide and pleasant road he thinks is right, but it ends in death.

JUNE 8

1 KINGS 3:3—4:34

SOLOMON loved the Lord and followed all of his father David's instructions except that he continued to sacrifice in the hills and to offer incense there.) 4The most famous of the hilltop altars was at Gibeon and now the king went there and sacrificed one thousand burnt offerings! 5The Lord appeared to him in a dream that night and told him to ask for anything he wanted, and it would be given to him!

6Solomon replied, "You were wonderfully kind to my father David because he was honest and true and faithful to you, and obeyed your commands. And you have continued your kindness to him by giving him a son to succeed him. 7O Lord my God, now you have made me the king instead of my father David, but I am as a little child who doesn't know his way around. 8And here I am among your own chosen people, a nation so great that there are almost too many people to count! 9Give me an understanding mind so that I can govern your people well and know the difference between what is right and what is wrong. For who by himself is able to carry such a heavy responsibility?"

10The Lord was pleased with his reply and was glad that Solomon had asked for wisdom. 11So he replied, "Because you have asked for wisdom in governing my people, and haven't asked for a long life or riches for yourself, or the defeat of your enemies— 12yes, I'll give you what you asked for! I will give you a wiser mind than anyone else has ever had or ever will have! 13And I will also give you what you didn't ask for—riches and honor! And no one in all the world will be as rich and famous as you for the rest of your life! 14And I will give you a long life if you follow me and obey my laws as your father David did."

15Then Solomon woke up and realized it had been a dream. He returned to Jerusalem and went into the Tabernacle. And as he stood before the Ark of the Covenant of the Lord, he sacrificed burnt offerings and peace offerings. Then he invited all of his officials to a great banquet.

16Soon afterwards two young prostitutes came to the king to have an argument settled.

17,18"Sir," one of them began, "we live in the same house, just the two of us, and recently I had a baby. When it was three days old, this woman's baby was born too. 19But her baby died during the night when she rolled over on it in her sleep and smothered it. 20Then she got up in the night and took my son from beside me while I was asleep, and laid her dead child in my arms and took mine to sleep beside her. 21And in the morning when I tried to feed my baby it was dead! But when it became light outside, I saw that it wasn't my son at all."

22Then the other woman interrupted, "It certainly was her son, and the living child is mine."

"No," the first woman said, "the dead one is yours and the living one is mine." And so they argued back and forth before the king.

23Then the king said, "Let's get the facts straight: both of you claim the living child, and each says that the dead child belongs to the other. 24All right, bring me a sword." So a sword was brought to the king. 25Then he said, "Divide the living child in two and give half to each of these women!"

26Then the woman who really was the mother of the child, and who loved him very much, cried out, "Oh, no, sir! Give her the child—don't kill him!"

But the other woman said, "All right, it will be neither yours nor mine; divide it between us!"

27Then the king said, "Give the baby to the woman who wants him to live, for she is the mother!"

28Word of the king's decision spread quickly throughout the entire nation, and all the people were awed as they realized the great wisdom God had given him.

HERE is a list of King Solomon's cabinet members:

Azariah (son of Zadok) was the High Priest;

Elihoreph and Ahijah (sons of Shisha) were secretaries;

Jehoshaphat (son of Ahilud) was the official historian and in charge of the archives;

Benaiah (son of Jehoiada) was commander-in-chief of the army;

Zadok and Abiathar were priests;

Azariah (son of Nathan) was secretary of state;

Zabud (son of Nathan) was the king's personal priest and special friend;

Ahishar was manager of palace affairs;

Adoniram (son of Abda) was superintendent of public works.

7There were also twelve officials of Solomon's court—one man from each tribe—responsible for requisitioning food from the people for the king's household. Each of them arranged provisions for one month of the year.

8–19The names of these twelve officers were:

Ben-hur, whose area for this taxation was the hill country of Ephraim;

Ben-deker, whose area was Makaz, Sha-albim, Beth-shemesh, and Elon-beth-hanan;

Ben-hesed, whose area was Arubboth,

including Socoh and all the land of Hepher;

Ben-abinadab (who married Solomon's daughter, the princess Taphath), whose area was the highlands of Dor;

Baana (son of Ahilud), whose area was Taanach and Megiddo, all of Beth-shean near Zarethan below Jezreel, and all the territory from Beth-shean to Abel-meholah and over to Jokmeam;

Ben-geber, whose area was Ramoth-gilead, including the villages of Jair (the son of Manasseh) in Gilead; and the region of Argob in Bashan, including sixty walled cities with bronze gates;

Ahinadab (the son of Iddo), whose area was Mahanaim;

Ahima-az (who married Princess Basemath, another of Solomon's daughters), whose area was Naph-tali;

Baana (son of Hushai), whose areas were Asher and Bealoth;

Jehoshaphat (son of Paruah), whose area was Issachar;

Shime-i (son of Ela), whose area was Benjamin;

Geber (son of Uri), whose area was Gilead, including the territories of King Sihon of the Amorites and King Og of Bashan.

A general manager supervised these officials and their work.

20Israel and Judah were a wealthy, populous, contented nation at this time. 21King Solomon ruled the whole area from the Euphrates River to the land of the Philistines, and down to the borders of Egypt. The conquered peoples of those lands sent taxes to Solomon and continued to serve him throughout his lifetime.

22The daily food requirements for the palace were 195 bushels of fine flour, 390 bushels of meal, 23 10 oxen from the fattening pens, 20 pasture-fed cattle, 100 sheep, and, from time to time, deer, gazelles, roebucks, and plump fowl.

24His dominion extended over all the kingdoms west of the Euphrates River, from Tiphsah to Gaza. And there was peace throughout the land.

25Throughout the lifetime of Solomon, all of Judah and Israel lived in peace and safety; and each family had its own home and garden.

26Solomon owned forty thousand chariot horses and employed twelve thousand charioteers. 27Each month the tax officials provided food for King Solomon and his court; 28also the barley and straw for the royal horses in the stables.

29God gave Solomon great wisdom and understanding, and a mind with broad interests. 30In fact, his wisdom excelled that of any of the wise men of the East, including those in Egypt. 31He was wiser than Ethan the Ezrahite and Heman, Calcol, and Darda, the sons of Mahol; and he was famous among all the surrounding nations. 32He was the author of 3,000 proverbs and wrote 1,005 songs. 33He was a great naturalist, with interest in animals, birds, snakes, fish, and trees—from the great cedars of Lebanon down to the tiny hyssop which grows in cracks in the wall. 34And kings from many lands sent their ambassadors to him for his advice.

ACTS 6:1–15

BUT with the believers multiplying rapidly, there were rumblings of discontent. Those who spoke only Greek complained that their widows were being discriminated against, that they were not being given as much food, in the daily distribution, as the widows who spoke Hebrew. 2So the Twelve called a meeting of all the believers.

"We should spend our time preaching, not administering a feeding program," they said. 3"Now look around among yourselves, dear brothers, and select seven men, wise and full of the Holy Spirit, who are well thought of by everyone; and we will put them in charge of this business. 4Then we can spend our time in prayer, preaching, and teaching."

5This sounded reasonable to the

whole assembly, and they elected the following:

Stephen (a man unusually full of faith and the Holy Spirit),
Philip,
Prochorus,
Nicanor,
Timon,
Parmenas,
Nicolaus of Antioch (a Gentile convert to the Jewish faith, who had become a Christian).

6These seven were presented to the apostles, who prayed for them and laid their hands on them in blessing.

7God's message was preached in ever-widening circles, and the number of disciples increased vastly in Jerusalem; and many of the Jewish priests were converted too.

8Stephen, the man so full of faith and the Holy Spirit's power, did spectacular miracles among the people.

9But one day some of the men from the Jewish cult of "The Freedmen" started an argument with him, and they were soon joined by Jews from Cyrene, Alexandria in Egypt, and the Turkish provinces of Cilicia, and Asia Minor. 10But none of them was able to stand against Stephen's wisdom and spirit.

11So they brought in some men to lie about him, claiming they had heard Stephen curse Moses, and even God.

12This accusation roused the crowds to fury against Stephen, and the Jewish leaders arrested him and brought him before the Council. 13The lying witnesses testified again that Stephen was constantly speaking against the Temple and against the laws of Moses.

14They declared, "We have heard him say that this fellow Jesus of Nazareth will destroy the Temple, and throw out all of Moses' laws." 15At this point everyone in the Council chamber saw Stephen's face become as radiant as an angel's!

PSALM 126:1–6

WHEN Jehovah brought back his exiles to Jerusalem, it was like a dream! 2How we laughed and sang for joy. And the other nations said, "What amazing things the Lord has done for them."

3Yes, glorious things! What wonder! What joy! 4May we be refreshed as by streams in the desert.

5Those who sow tears shall reap joy. 6Yes, they go out weeping, carrying seed for sowing, and return singing, carrying their sheaves.

PROVERBS FOR TODAY/ 16:26–27

Hunger is good—if it makes you work to satisfy it! Idle hands are the devil's workshop; idle lips are his mouthpiece.

JUNE 9

1 KINGS 5:1—6:38

KING Hiram of Tyre had always been a great admirer of David, so when he learned that David's son Solomon was the new king of Israel, he sent ambassadors to extend congratulations and good wishes. 2,3Solomon replied with a proposal about the Temple of the Lord he wanted to build. His father David, Solomon pointed out to Hiram, had not been able to build it because of the numerous wars going on, and he had been waiting for the Lord to give him peace.

⁴"But now," Solomon said to Hiram, "the Lord my God has given Israel peace on every side; I have no foreign enemies or internal rebellions. ⁵So I am planning to build a Temple for the Lord my God, just as he instructed my father that I should do. For the Lord told him, 'Your son, whom I will place upon your throne, shall build me a Temple.' ⁶Now please assist me with this project. Send your woodsmen to the mountains of Lebanon to cut cedar timber for me, and I will send my men to work beside them, and I will pay your men whatever wages you ask; for as you know, no one in Israel can cut timber like you Sidonians!"

⁷Hiram was very pleased with the message from Solomon. "Praise God for giving David a wise son to be king of the great nation of Israel," he said. ⁸Then he sent this reply to Solomon: "I have received your message and I will do as you have asked concerning the timber. I can supply both cedar and cypress. ⁹My men will bring the logs from the Lebanon mountains to the Mediterranean Sea and build them into rafts. We will float them along the coast to wherever you need them; then we will break the rafts apart and deliver the timber to you. You can pay me with food for my household."

¹⁰So Hiram produced for Solomon as much cedar and cypress timber as he desired, ¹¹and in return Solomon sent him an annual payment of 125,000 bushels of wheat for his household and 96 gallons of pure olive oil. ¹²So the Lord gave great wisdom to Solomon just as he had promised. And Hiram and Solomon made a formal alliance of peace.

¹³Then Solomon drafted thirty thousand laborers from all over Israel, ¹⁴and rotated them to Lebanon, ten thousand a month, so that each man was a month in Lebanon and two months at home. Adoniram was the general superintendent of this labor camp. ¹⁵Solomon also had seventy thousand additional laborers, eighty thousand stonecutters in the hill country, ¹⁶and thirty-three hundred foremen. ¹⁷The stonecutters quarried and shaped huge blocks of stone—a very expensive job—for the foundation of the Temple. ¹⁸Men from Gebal helped Solomon's and Hiram's builders in cutting the timber and making the boards, and in preparing the stone for the Temple.

It was in the spring of the fourth year of Solomon's reign that he began the actual construction of the Temple. (This was 480 years after the people of Israel left their slavery in Egypt.) ²The Temple was ninety feet long, thirty feet wide, and forty-five feet high. ³All along the front of the Temple was a porch thirty feet long and fifteen feet deep. ⁴Narrow windows were used throughout.

⁵An annex of rooms was built along the full length of both sides of the Temple against the outer walls. ⁶These rooms were three stories high, the lower floor being 7½ feet wide, the second floor 9 feet wide, and the upper floor 10½ feet wide. The rooms were connected to the walls of the Temple by beams resting on blocks built out from the wall—so the beams were not inserted into the walls themselves.

⁷The stones used in the construction of the Temple were prefinished at the quarry, so the entire structure was built without the sound of hammer, axe, or any other tool at the building site.

⁸The bottom floor of the side rooms was entered from the right side of the Temple, and there were winding stairs going up to the second floor; another flight of stairs led from the second to the third. ⁹After completing the Temple, Solomon paneled it all, including the beams and pillars, with cedar. ¹⁰As already stated, there was an annex on each side of the building, attached to the Temple walls by cedar timbers. Each story of the annex was 7½ feet high.

¹¹,¹²Then the Lord sent this message to Solomon concerning the Temple he was building: "If you do as I tell you to and follow all of my commandments and instructions, I will do what I told your father David I would do: ¹³I will

live among the people of Israel and never forsake them."

14At last the Temple was finished. 15The entire inside, from floor to ceiling, was paneled with cedar, and the floors were made of cypress boards. 16The thirty-foot inner room at the far end of the Temple—the Most Holy Place—was also paneled from the floor to the ceiling with cedar boards. 17The remainder of the Temple—other than the Most Holy Place—was sixty feet long. 18Throughout the Temple the cedar paneling laid over the stone walls was carved with designs of rosebuds and open flowers.

19The inner room was where the Ark of the Covenant of the Lord was placed. 20This inner sanctuary was thirty feet long, thirty feet wide, and thirty feet high. Its walls and ceiling were overlaid with pure gold, and Solomon made a cedarwood altar for this room. 21,22Then he overlaid the interior of the remainder of the Temple—including the cedar altar—with pure gold; and he made gold chains to protect the entrance to the Most Holy Place.

23-28Within the inner sanctuary Solomon placed two statues of Guardian Angels made from olive wood, each fifteen feet high. They were placed so that their outspread wings reached from wall to wall, while their inner wings touched each other at the center of the room; each wing was 7½ feet long, so each angel measured fifteen feet from wing tip to wing tip. The two angels were identical in all dimensions, and each was overlaid with gold.

29Figures of angels, palm trees, and open flowers were carved on all the walls of both rooms of the Temple, 30and the floor of both rooms was overlaid with gold.

31The doorway to the inner sanctuary was a five-sided opening, 32and its two olive-wood doors were carved with Guardian Angels, palm trees, and open flowers, all overlaid with gold.

33Then he made square doorposts of olive wood for the entrance to the Temple. 34There were two folding doors of cypress wood, and each door was hinged to fold back upon itself. 35Angels, palm trees, and open flowers were carved on these doors and carefully overlaid with gold.

36The wall of the inner court had three layers of hewn stone and one layer of cedar beams.

37The foundation of the Temple was laid in the month of May in the fourth year of Solomon's reign, 38and the entire building was completed in every detail in November of the eleventh year of his reign. So it took seven years to build.

ACTS 7:1–29

THEN the High Priest asked him, "Are these accusations true?"

2This was Stephen's lengthy reply: "The glorious God appeared to our ancestor Abraham in Iraq before he moved to Syria, 3and told him to leave his native land, to say good-bye to his relatives and to start out for a country that God would direct him to. 4So he left the land of the Chaldeans and lived in Haran, in Syria, until his father died. Then God brought him here to the land of Israel, 5but gave him no property of his own, not one little tract of land.

"However, God promised that eventually the whole country would belong to him and his descendants—though as yet he had no children! 6But God also told him that these descendants of his would leave the land and live in a foreign country and there become slaves for 400 years. 7'But I will punish the nation that enslaves them,' God told him, 'and afterwards my people will return to this land of Israel and worship me here.'

8"God also gave Abraham the ceremony of circumcision at that time, as evidence of the covenant between God and the people of Abraham. And so Isaac, Abraham's son, was circumcised when he was eight days old. Isaac became the father of Jacob, and Jacob was the father of the twelve patriarchs of the Jewish nation. 9These men were very jealous of Joseph and sold him to be a slave in

Egypt. But God was with him, 10and delivered him out of all of his anguish, and gave him favor before Pharaoh, king of Egypt. God also gave Joseph unusual wisdom, so that Pharaoh appointed him governor over all Egypt, as well as putting him in charge of all the affairs of the palace.

11"But a famine developed in Egypt and Canaan and there was great misery for our ancestors. When their food was gone, 12Jacob heard that there was still grain in Egypt, so he sent his sons to buy some. 13The second time they went, Joseph revealed his identity to his brothers, and they were introduced to Pharaoh. 14Then Joseph sent for his father Jacob and all his brothers' families to come to Egypt, seventy-five persons in all. 15So Jacob came to Egypt, where he died, and all his sons. 16All of them were taken to Shechem and buried in the tomb Abraham bought from the sons of Hamor, Shechem's father.

17,18"As the time drew near when God would fulfill his promise to Abraham to free his descendants from slavery, the Jewish people greatly multiplied in Egypt; but then a king was crowned who had no respect for Joseph's memory. 19This king plotted against our race, forcing parents to abandon their children in the fields.

20"About that time Moses was born—a child of divine beauty. His parents hid him at home for three months, 21and when at last they could no longer keep him hidden, and had to abandon him, Pharaoh's daughter found him and adopted him as her own son, 22and taught him all the wisdom of the Egyptians, and

he became a mighty prince and orator.

23"One day as he was nearing his fortieth birthday, it came into his mind to visit his brothers, the people of Israel. 24During this visit he saw an Egyptian mistreating a man of Israel. So Moses killed the Egyptian. 25Moses supposed his brothers would realize that God had sent him to help them, but they didn't.

26"The next day he visited them again and saw two men of Israel fighting. He tried to be a peacemaker. 'Gentlemen,' he said, 'you are brothers and shouldn't be fighting like this! It is wrong!'

27"But the man in the wrong told Moses to mind his own business. 'Who made *you* a ruler and judge over us?' he asked. 28'Are you going to kill me as you killed that Egyptian yesterday?'

29"At this, Moses fled the country, and lived in the land of Midian, where his two sons were born.

PSALM 127:1–5

UNLESS the Lord builds a house, the builders' work is useless. Unless the Lord protects a city, sentries do no good. 2It is senseless for you to work so hard from early morning until late at night, fearing you will starve to death; for God wants his loved ones to get their proper rest.

3Children are a gift from God; they are his reward. 4Children born to a young man are like sharp arrows to defend him.

5Happy is the man who has his quiver full of them. That man shall have the help he needs when arguing with his enemies.

PROVERBS FOR TODAY/ 16:28–30

An evil man sows strife; gossip separates the best of friends. Wickedness loves company—and leads others into sin. The wicked man stares into space with pursed lips, deep in thought, planning his evil deeds.

JUNE 10

1 KINGS 7:1–51

THEN Solomon built his own palace, which took thirteen years to construct.

²One of the rooms in the palace was called the Hall of the Forest of Lebanon. It was huge—measuring 150 feet long, 75 feet wide, and 45 feet high. The great cedar ceiling beams rested upon four rows of cedar pillars. ³,⁴There were forty-five windows in the hall, set in three tiers, one tier above the other, five to a tier, facing each other from three walls. ⁵Each of the doorways and windows had a square frame.

⁶Another room was called the Hall of Pillars. It was 75 feet long and 45 feet wide, with a porch in front covered by a canopy which was supported by pillars.

⁷There was also the Throne Room or Judgment Hall, where Solomon sat to hear legal matters; it was paneled with cedar from the floor to the rafters.

⁸His cedar-paneled living quarters surrounded a courtyard behind this hall. (He designed similar living quarters, the same size, in the palace which he built for Pharaoh's daughter—one of his wives.) ⁹These buildings were constructed entirely from huge, expensive stones, cut to measure. ¹⁰The foundation stones were 12 to 15 feet across. ¹¹The huge stones in the walls were also cut to measure, and were topped with cedar beams. ¹²The Great Court had three courses of hewn stone in its walls, topped with cedar beams, just like the inner court of the Temple and the porch of the palace.

¹³King Solomon then asked for a man named Hiram to come from Tyre, for he was a skilled craftsman in bronze work. ¹⁴He was half Jewish, being the son of a widow of the tribe of Naphtali, and his father had been a foundry worker from Tyre. So he came to work for King Solomon.

¹⁵He cast two hollow bronze pillars, each 27 feet high and 18 feet around, with three-inch-thick walls. ¹⁶⁻²²At the tops of the pillars he made two lily-shaped capitals from molten bronze, each 7½ feet high. The upper part of each capital was shaped like a lily 6 feet high. Each capital was decorated with seven sets of bronze, chain-designed lattices and four hundred pomegranates in two rows. Hiram set these pillars at the entrance of the Temple. The one on the south was named the Jachin Pillar, and the one on the north, the Boaz Pillar.

²³Then Hiram cast a round bronze tank, 7½ feet high and 15 feet from brim to brim; 45 feet in circumference. ²⁴On the underside of the rim were two rows of ornaments an inch or two apart, which were cast along with the tank. ²⁵It rested on twelve bronze oxen standing tail to tail, three facing north, three west, three south, and three east. ²⁶The sides of the tank were four inches thick; its brim was shaped like a goblet, and it had a twelve thousand gallon capacity.

²⁷⁻³⁰Then he made ten four-wheeled movable stands, each 6 feet square and 4½ feet high. They were constructed with undercarriages braced with square crosspieces. These crosspieces were decorated with carved lions, oxen, and angels. Above and below the lions and oxen were wreath decorations. Each of these movable stands had four bronze wheels and bronze axles, and at each corner of the stands were supporting posts made of bronze and decorated with wreaths on each side. ³¹The top of each stand was a round piece 1½ feet high. Its center was concave, 2¼ feet deep, decorated on the outside with wreaths. Its panels were square, not round.

³²The stands rode on four wheels which were connected to axles that had been cast as part of the stands. The wheels were twenty-seven inches high,

33and were similar to chariot wheels. All the parts of the stands were cast from molten bronze, including the axles, spokes, rims, and hubs. 34There were supports at each of the four corners of the stands, and these, too, were cast with the stands. 35A nine-inch rim surrounded the tip of each stand, banded with lugs. All was cast as one unit with the stand. 36Guardian Angels, lions, and palm trees surrounded by wreaths were engraved on the borders of the band wherever there was room. 37All ten stands were the same size and were made alike, for each was cast from the same mold.

38Then he made ten brass vats, and placed them on the stands. Each vat was six feet square and contained 240 gallons of water. 39Five of these vats were arranged on the left and five on the right-hand side of the room. The tank was in the southeast corner, on the right-hand side of the room. 40Hiram also made the necessary pots, shovels, and basins and at last completed the work in the Temple of the Lord which had been assigned to him by King Solomon.

41-46Here is a list of the items he made:
Two pillars;
A capital at the top of each pillar;
Latticework covering the bases of the capitals of each pillar;
Four hundred pomegranates in two rows on the latticework, to cover the bases of the two capitals;
Ten movable stands holding ten vats;
One large tank and twelve oxen supporting it;
Pots;
Shovels;
Basins.

All these items were made of burnished bronze, and were cast at the plains of the Jordan River between Succoth and Zarethan. 47The total weight of these pieces was not known because they were too heavy to weigh!

48All the utensils and furniture used in the Temple were made of solid gold. This included the altar, the table where the Bread of the Presence of God was displayed, 49the lampstands (five on the right-hand side and five on the left, in front of the Most Holy Place), the flowers, lamps, tongs, 50cups, snuffers, basins, spoons, firepans, the hinges of the doors to the Most Holy Place, and the main entrance doors of the Temple. Each of these was made of solid gold.

51When the Temple was finally finished, Solomon took into the treasury of the Temple the silver, the gold, and all the vessels dedicated for that purpose by his father David.

ACTS 7:30–50

FORTY years later, in the desert near Mount Sinai, an Angel appeared to him in a flame of fire in a bush. 31Moses saw it and wondered what it was, and as he ran to see, the voice of the Lord called out to him, 32'I am the God of your ancestors—of Abraham, Isaac and Jacob.' Moses shook with terror and dared not look.

33"And the Lord said to him, 'Take off your shoes, for you are standing on holy ground. 34I have seen the anguish of my people in Egypt and have heard their cries. I have come down to deliver them. Come, I will send you to Egypt.' 35And so God sent back the same man his people had previously rejected by demanding, 'Who made you a ruler and judge over us?' Moses was sent to be their ruler and savior. 36And by means of many remarkable miracles he led them out of Egypt and through the Red Sea, and back and forth through the wilderness for forty years.

37"Moses himself told the people of Israel, 'God will raise up a Prophet much like me from among your brothers.' 38How true this proved to be, for in the wilderness, Moses was the go-between—the mediator between the people of Israel and the Angel who gave them the Law of God—the Living Word—on Mount Sinai.

39"But our fathers rejected Moses and wanted to return to Egypt. 40They told Aaron, 'Make idols for us, so that we will have gods to lead us back; for we don't know what has become of this Moses, who brought us out of Egypt.' ⁴¹So they made a calf-idol and sacrificed to it, and rejoiced in this thing they had made.

⁴²"Then God turned away from them and gave them up, and let them serve the sun, moon and stars as their gods! In the book of Amos' prophecies the Lord God asks, 'Was it to me you were sacrificing during those forty years in the desert, Israel? ⁴³No, your real interest was in your heathen gods—Sakkuth, and the star god Kaiway, and in all the images you made. So I will send you into captivity far away beyond Babylon.'

⁴⁴"Our ancestors carried along with them a portable Temple, or Tabernacle, through the wilderness. In it they kept the stone tablets with the Ten Commandments written on them. This building was constructed in exact accordance with the plan shown to Moses by the Angel. ⁴⁵Years later, when Joshua led the battles against the Gentile nations, this Tabernacle was taken with them into their new territory, and used until the time of King David.

⁴⁶"God blessed David greatly, and David asked for the privilege of building a permanent Temple for the God of Jacob. ⁴⁷But it was Solomon who actually built it. ⁴⁸,⁴⁹However, God doesn't live in temples made by human hands. 'The heaven is my throne,' says the Lord through his prophets, 'and earth is my footstool. What kind of home could you build?' asks the Lord. 'Would I stay in it? ⁵⁰Didn't I make both heaven and earth?'

PSALM 128:1–6

BLESSINGS on all who reverence and trust the Lord—on all who obey him! ²Their reward shall be prosperity and happiness. ³Your wife shall be contented in your home. And look at all those children! There they sit around the dinner table as vigorous and healthy as young olive trees. ⁴That is God's reward to those who reverence and trust him.

⁵May the Lord continually bless you with heaven's blessings as well as with human joys. ⁶May you live to enjoy your grandchildren! And may God bless Israel!

PROVERBS FOR TODAY/ 16:31–33

White hair is a crown of glory and is seen most among the godly. It is better to be slow-tempered than famous; it is better to have self-control than to control an army. We toss the coin, but it is the Lord who controls its decision.

JUNE 11

1 KINGS 8:1–66

THEN Solomon called a convocation at Jerusalem of all the leaders of Israel—the heads of the tribes and clans—to observe the transferring of the Ark of the Covenant of the Lord from the Tabernacle in Zion, the City of David, to the Temple. ²This celebration occurred at the time of the Tabernacle Festival in the month of October. ³,⁴During the festivities the priests carried the Ark to the Temple, along with all the sacred vessels which had previously been in the Tabernacle. ⁵King Solomon and all the people gathered before the Ark, sacrificing uncounted sheep and oxen.

⁶Then the priests took the Ark into

the inner sanctuary of the Temple—the Most Holy Place—and placed it under the wings of the statues of the mighty angels. 7The angels had been constructed in such a manner that their wings spread out over the spot where the Ark would be placed; so now their wings overshadowed the Ark and its carrying poles. 8The poles were so long that they stuck out past the angels and could be seen from the next room, but not from the outer court; and they remain there to this day. 9There was nothing in the Ark at that time except the two stone tablets which Moses had placed there at Mount Horeb at the time the Lord made his covenant with the people of Israel after they left Egypt.

10*Look! As the priests are returning from the inner sanctuary, a bright cloud fills the Temple!* 11*The priests have to go outside because the glory of the Lord is filling the entire building!*

12,13Now King Solomon prayed this invocation:

"The Lord has said that he would live in the thick darkness;
But, O Lord, I have built you a lovely home on earth, a place for you to live forever."

14Then the king turned around and faced the people as they stood before him, and blessed them.

15"Blessed be the Lord God of Israel," he said, "who has done today what he promised my father David: 16for he said to him, 'When I brought my people from Egypt, I didn't appoint a place for my Temple, but I appointed a man to be my people's leader.' 17This man was my father, David. He wanted to build a Temple for the Lord God of Israel, 18but the Lord told him not to. 'I am glad you want to do it,' he said, 19'but your son is the one who shall build my Temple.' 20And now the Lord has done what he promised; for I have followed my father as king of Israel, and now this Temple has been built for the Lord God of Israel. 21And I have prepared a place in the Temple for the Ark which contains the covenant made by the Lord with our fathers, at the time that he brought them out of the land of Egypt."

22,23Then, as all the people watched, Solomon stood before the altar of the Lord with his hands spread out towards heaven and said, "O Lord God of Israel, there is no god like you in heaven or earth, for you are loving and kind and you keep your promises to your people if they do their best to do your will. 24Today you have fulfilled your promise to my father David, who was your servant; 25and now, O Lord God of Israel, fulfill your further promise to him: that if his descendants follow your ways and try to do your will as he did, one of them shall always sit upon the throne of Israel. 26Yes, O God of Israel, fulfill this promise too.

27"But is it possible that God would really live on earth? Why, even the skies and the highest heavens cannot contain you, much less this Temple I have built! 28And yet, O Lord my God, you have heard and answered my request: 29Please watch over this Temple night and day—this place you have promised to live in—and as I face toward the Temple and pray, whether by night or by day, please listen to me and answer my requests. 30Listen to every plea of the people of Israel whenever they face this place to pray; yes, hear in heaven where you live, and when you hear, forgive.

31"If a man is accused of doing something wrong and then, standing here before your altar, swears that he didn't do it, 32hear him in heaven and do what is right; judge whether or not he did it.

33,34"And when your people sin and their enemies defeat them, hear them from heaven and forgive them if they turn to you again and confess that you are their God. Bring them back again to this land which you have given to their fathers.

35,36"And when the skies are shut up and there is no rain because of their sin, hear them from heaven and forgive them when they pray toward this place and confess your name. And after you have punished them, help them to follow the good ways in which they should walk, and send rain upon the land which you have given your people.

37"If there is a famine in the land caused by plant disease or locusts or caterpillars, or if Israel's enemies besiege one of her cities, or if the people are struck by an epidemic or plague—or whatever the problem is— 38then when the people realize their sin and pray toward this Temple, 39hear them from heaven and forgive and answer all who have made an honest confession; for you know each heart. 40In this way they will always learn to reverence you as they continue to live in this land which you have given their fathers.

41,42"And when foreigners hear of your great name and come from distant lands to worship you (for they shall hear of your great name and mighty miracles) and pray toward this Temple, 43hear them from heaven and answer their prayers. And all the nations of the earth will know and fear your name just as your own people Israel do; and all the earth will know that this is your Temple.

44"When you send your people out to battle against their enemies and they pray to you, looking toward your chosen city of Jerusalem and toward this Temple which I have built in your name, 45hear their prayer and help them.

46"If they sin against you (and who doesn't?) and you become angry with them and let their enemies lead them away as captives to some foreign land, whether far or near, 47and they come to their senses and turn to you and cry to you saying, 'We have sinned, we have done wrong'; 48if they honestly return to you and pray toward this land which you have given their fathers, and toward this city of Jerusalem which you have chosen, and toward this Temple, which I have built for your name, 49hear their prayers and pleadings from heaven where you live, and come to their assistance.

50"Forgive your people for all of their evil deeds, and make their captors merciful to them; 51for they are your people—

your inheritance that you brought out from the Egyptian furnace. 52May your eyes be open and your ears listening to their pleas. O Lord, hear and answer them whenever they cry out to you, 53for when you brought our fathers out of the land of Egypt, you told your servant Moses that you had chosen Israel from among all the nations of the earth to be your own special people."

54,55Solomon had been kneeling with his hands outstretched toward heaven. As he finished this prayer, he rose from before the altar of Jehovah and cried out this blessing upon all the people of Israel:

56"Blessed be the Lord who has fulfilled his promise and given rest to his people Israel; not one word has failed of all the wonderful promises proclaimed by his servant Moses. 57May the Lord our God be with us as he was with our fathers; may he never forsake us. 58May he give us the desire to do his will in everything, and to obey all the commandments and instructions he has given our ancestors. 59And may these words of my prayer be constantly before him day and night, so that he helps me and all of Israel in accordance with our daily needs. 60May people all over the earth know that the Lord is God, and that there is no other god at all. 61O my people, may you live good and perfect lives before the Lord our God; may you always obey his laws and commandments, just as you are doing today."

62,63Then the king and all the people dedicated the Temple by sacrificing peace offerings to the Lord—a total of 22,000 oxen and 120,000 sheep and goats! 64As a temporary measure the king sanctified the court in front of the Temple for the burnt offerings, grain offerings, and the fat of the peace offerings: for the bronze altar was too small to handle so much. 65The celebration lasted for fourteen days, and a great crowd came from one end of the land to the other. 66Afterwards Solomon sent the people home, happy for all the goodness that the Lord had shown to his servant David and to his people Israel. And they blessed the king.

ACTS 7:51—8:13

Y OU stiff-necked heathen! Must you forever resist the Holy Spirit? But your fathers did, and so do you! 52Name one prophet your ancestors didn't persecute! They even killed the ones who predicted the coming of the Righteous One—the Messiah whom you betrayed and murdered. 53Yes, and you deliberately destroyed God's Laws, though you received them from the hands of angels."

54The Jewish leaders were stung to fury by Stephen's accusation, and ground their teeth in rage. 55But Stephen, full of the Holy Spirit, gazed steadily upward into heaven and saw the glory of God and Jesus standing at God's right hand. 56And he told them, "Look, I see the heavens opened and Jesus the Messiah standing beside God, at his right hand!"

57Then they mobbed him, putting their hands over their ears, and drowning out his voice with their shouts, 58and dragged him out of the city to stone him. The official witnesses—the executioners— took off their coats and laid them at the feet of a young man named Paul.

59And as the murderous stones came hurtling at him, Stephen prayed, "Lord Jesus, receive my spirit." 60And he fell to his knees, shouting, "Lord, don't charge them with this sin!" and with that, he died.

PAUL was in complete agreement with the killing of Stephen.

And a great wave of persecution of the believers began that day, sweeping over the church in Jerusalem, and everyone except the apostles fled into Judea and Samaria. 2(But some godly Jews came and with great sorrow buried Stephen.) 3Paul was like a wild man, going everywhere to devastate the believers, even entering private homes and dragging out men and women alike and jailing them.

4But the believers who had fled Jerusalem went everywhere preaching the Good News about Jesus! 5Philip, for instance, went to the city of Samaria and told the people there about Christ. 6Crowds listened intently to what he had to say because of the miracles he did. 7Many evil spirits were cast out, screaming as they left their victims, and many who were paralyzed or lame were healed, 8so there was much joy in that city!

9,10,11A man named Simon had formerly been a sorcerer there for many years; he was a very influential, proud man because of the amazing things he could do—in fact, the Samaritan people often spoke of him as the Messiah. 12But now they believed Philip's message that Jesus was the Messiah, and his words concerning the Kingdom of God; and many men and women were baptized. 13Then Simon himself believed and was baptized and began following Philip wherever he went, and was amazed by the miracles he did.

PSALM 129:1–8

P ERSECUTED from my earliest youth (Israel is speaking), 2and faced with never-ending discrimination—but not destroyed! My enemies have never been able to finish me off!

3,4Though my back is cut to ribbons with their whips, the Lord is good. For he has snapped the chains that evil men had bound me with.

5May all who hate the Jews be brought to ignominious defeat. 6,7May they be as grass in shallow soil, turning sere and yellow when half grown, ignored by the reaper, despised by the binder. 8And may those passing by refuse to bless them by saying, "Jehovah's blessings be upon you; we bless you in Jehovah's name."

A dry crust eaten in peace is better than steak every day along with argument and strife.

JUNE 12

1 KINGS 9:1—10:29

WHEN Solomon had finished building the Temple and the palace and all the other buildings he had always wanted, 2,3the Lord appeared to him the second time (the first time had been at Gibeon) and said to him,

"I have heard your prayer. I have hallowed this Temple which you have built and have put my name here forever. I will constantly watch over it and rejoice in it. 4And if you live in honesty and truth as your father David did, always obeying me, 5then I will cause your descendants to be the kings of Israel forever, just as I promised your father David when I told him, 'One of your sons shall always be upon the throne of Israel.'

6"However, if you or your children turn away from me and worship other gods and do not obey my laws, 7then I will take away the people of Israel from this land which I have given them. I will take them from this Temple which I have hallowed for my name and I will cast them out of my sight; and Israel will become a joke to the nations and an example and proverb of sudden disaster. 8This Temple will become a heap of ruins, and everyone passing by will be amazed and will whistle with astonishment, asking, 'Why has the Lord done such things to this land and this Temple?' 9And the answer will be, 'The people of Israel abandoned the Lord their God who brought them out of the land of Egypt; they worshiped other gods instead. That is why the Lord has brought this evil upon them.' "

10At the end of the twenty years during which Solomon built the Temple and the palace, 11,12he gave twenty cities in the land of Galilee to King Hiram of Tyre as payment for all the cedar and cypress lumber and gold he had furnished for the construction of the palace and Temple. Hiram came from Tyre to see the cities, but he wasn't at all pleased with them.

13"What sort of deal is this, my brother?" he asked. "These cities are a wasteland!" (And they are still known as "The Wasteland" today.) 14For Hiram had sent gold to Solomon valued at $3,500,000!

15Solomon had conscripted forced labor to build the Temple, his palace, Fort Millo, the wall of Jerusalem, and the cities of Hazor, Megiddo, and Gezer. 16Gezer was the city the king of Egypt conquered and burned, killing the Canaanite population; later he had given the city to his daughter as a dowry—she was one of Solomon's wives. 17,18So now Solomon rebuilt Gezer along with Lower Bethhoron, Baalath, and Tamar, a desert city. 19He also built cities for grain storage, cities in which to keep his chariots, cities for homes for his cavalry and chariot drivers, and resort cities near Jerusalem and in the Lebanon mountains and elsewhere throughout the land.

20,21Solomon conscripted his labor forces from those who survived in the nations he conquered—the Amorites, Hittites, Perizzites, Hivites, and Jebusites. For the people of Israel had not been able to wipe them out completely at the time of the invasion and conquest of Israel, and they continue as slaves even today. 22Solomon didn't conscript any Israelis for this work, although they became soldiers, officials, army officers, chariot commanders, and cavalrymen. 23And there were 550 men of Israel who were overseers of the labor forces.

Miscellaneous Notes:

24King Solomon moved Pharaoh's daughter from the City of David—the old sector of Jerusalem—to the new quarters he had built for her in the palace. Then he built Fort Millo.

25After the Temple was completed, Solomon offered burnt offerings and peace offerings three times a year on the altar he had built. And he also burned incense upon it.

26King Solomon had a shipyard in Ezion-geber near Eloth on the Red Sea in the land of Edom, where he built a fleet of ships. 27,28King Hiram supplied experienced sailors to accompany Solomon's crews. They used to sail back and forth from Ophir, bringing gold to King Solomon, the total value of which was several million dollars each trip.

WHEN the Queen of Sheba heard how wonderfully the Lord had blessed Solomon with wisdom, she decided to test him with some hard questions. 2She arrived in Jerusalem with a long train of camels carrying spices, gold, and jewels; and she told him all her problems. 3Solomon answered all her questions; nothing was too difficult for him, for the Lord gave him the right answers every time. 4She soon realized that everything she had ever heard about his great wisdom was true. She also saw the beautiful palace he had built, 5and when she saw the wonderful foods on his table, the great number of servants and aides who stood around in splendid uniforms, his cupbearers, and the many offerings he sacrificed by fire to the Lord—well, there was no more spirit in her!

6She exclaimed to him, "Everything I heard in my own country about your wisdom and about the wonderful things going on here is all true. 7I didn't believe it until I came, but now I have seen it

for myself! And really! The half had not been told me! Your wisdom and prosperity are far greater than anything I've ever heard of! 8Your people are happy and your palace aides are content—but how could it be otherwise, for they stand here day after day listening to your wisdom! 9Blessed be the Lord your God who chose you and set you on the throne of Israel. How the Lord must love Israel—for he gave you to them as their king! And you give your people a just, good government!"

10Then she gave the king a gift of $3,500,000 in gold, along with a huge quantity of spices and precious gems; in fact, it was the largest single gift of spices King Solomon had ever received.

11(And when King Hiram's ships brought gold to Solomon from Ophir, they also brought along a great supply of algum trees and gems. 12Solomon used the algum wood to make pillars for the Temple and the palace, and for harps and harpsichords for his choirs. Never before or since has there been such a supply of beautiful wood.)

13In exchange for the gifts from the queen of Sheba, King Solomon gave her everything she asked him for, besides the presents he had already planned. Then she and her servants returned to their own land.

14Each year Solomon received gold worth a quarter of a billion, 15besides sales taxes and profits from trade with the kings of Arabia and the other surrounding territories. 16,17Solomon had some of the gold beaten into two hundred pieces of armor (gold worth $6,000 went into each piece) and three hundred shields ($1,800 worth of gold in each). And he kept them in his palace in the Hall of the Forest of Lebanon.

18He also made a huge ivory throne and overlaid it with pure gold. 19It had six steps and a rounded back, with arm rests; and a lion standing on each side. 20And there were two lions on each step—twelve in all. There was no other throne in all the world so splendid as that one.

²¹All of King Solomon's cups were of solid gold, and in the Hall of the Forest of Lebanon his entire dining service was made of solid gold. (Silver wasn't used because it wasn't considered to be of much value!)

²²King Solomon's merchant fleet was in partnership with King Hiram's, and once every three years a great load of gold, silver, ivory, apes, and peacocks arrived at the Israeli ports.

²³So King Solomon was richer and wiser than all the kings of the earth. ²⁴Great men from many lands came to interview him and listen to his God-given wisdom. ²⁵They brought him annual tribute of silver and gold dishes, beautiful cloth, myrrh, spices, horses, and mules.

²⁶Solomon built up a great stable of horses with a vast number of chariots and cavalry—1,400 chariots in all, and 12,000 cavalrymen who lived in the chariot cities and with the king at Jerusalem. ²⁷Silver was as common as stones in Jerusalem in those days, and cedar was of no greater value than the common sycamore! ²⁸Solomon's horses were brought to him from Egypt and southern Turkey, where his agents purchased them at wholesale prices. ²⁹An Egyptian chariot delivered to Jerusalem cost $400, and the horses were valued at $150 each. Many of these were then resold to the Hittite and Syrian kings.

ACTS 8:14–40

WHEN the apostles back in Jerusalem heard that the people of Samaria had accepted God's message, they sent down Peter and John. ¹⁵As soon as they arrived, they began praying for these new Christians to receive the Holy Spirit, ¹⁶for as yet he had not come upon any of them. For they had only been baptized in the name of the Lord Jesus. ¹⁷Then Peter and John laid their hands upon these believers, and they received the Holy Spirit.

¹⁸When Simon saw this—that the Holy Spirit was given when the apostles placed their hands upon people's heads—he offered money to buy this power.

¹⁹"Let me have this power too," he exclaimed, "so that when I lay my hands on people, they will receive the Holy Spirit!"

²⁰But Peter replied, "Your money perish with you for thinking God's gift can be bought! ²¹You can have no part in this, for your heart is not right before God. ²²Turn from this great wickedness and pray. Perhaps God will yet forgive your evil thoughts— ²³for I can see that there is jealousy and sin in your heart."

²⁴"Pray for me," Simon exclaimed, "that these terrible things won't happen to me."

²⁵After testifying and preaching in Samaria, Peter and John returned to Jerusalem, stopping at several Samaritan villages along the way to preach the Good News to them too.

²⁶But as for Philip, an angel of the Lord said to him, "Go over to the road that runs from Jerusalem through the Gaza Desert, arriving around noon." ²⁷So he did, and who should be coming down the road but the Treasurer of Ethiopia, a eunuch of great authority under Candace the queen. He had gone to Jerusalem to worship, ²⁸and was now returning in his chariot, reading aloud from the book of the prophet Isaiah.

²⁹The Holy Spirit said to Philip, "Go over and walk along beside the chariot."

³⁰Philip ran over and heard what he was reading and asked, "Do you understand it?"

³¹"Of course not!" the man replied. "How can I when there is no one to instruct me?" And he begged Philip to come up into the chariot and sit with him.

³²The passage of Scripture he had been reading from was this:

"He was led as a sheep to the slaughter, and as a lamb is silent before the shearers, so he opened not his mouth; ³³in his humiliation, justice was denied him; and who can express the wickedness of the people of his generation?

For his life is taken from the earth."

34The eunuch asked Philip, "Was Isaiah talking about himself or someone else?"

35So Philip began with this same Scripture and then used many others to tell him about Jesus.

36As they rode along, they came to a small body of water, and the eunuch said, "Look! Water! Why can't I be baptized?"

37"You can," Philip answered, "if you believe with all your heart."

And the eunuch replied, "I believe that Jesus Christ is the Son of God."

38He stopped the chariot, and they went down into the water and Philip baptized him. 39And when they came up out of the water, the Spirit of the Lord caught away Philip, and the eunuch never saw him again, but went on his way rejoicing. 40Meanwhile, Philip found himself at Azo-tus! He preached the Good News there and in every city along the way, as he traveled to Caesarea.

PSALM 130:1–8

O Lord, from the depths of despair I cry for your help: 2"Hear me! Answer! Help me!"

3,4Lord, if you keep in mind our sins then who can ever get an answer to his prayers? But you forgive! What an awesome thing this is! 5That is why I wait expectantly, trusting God to help, for he has promised. 6I long for him more than sentinels long for the dawn.

7O Israel, hope in the Lord; for he is loving and kind, and comes to us with armloads of salvation. 8He himself shall ransom Israel from her slavery to sin.

PROVERBS FOR TODAY/ 17:2–3

A wise slave will rule his master's wicked sons and share their estate. Silver and gold are purified by fire, but God purifies hearts.

JUNE 13

1 KINGS 11:1—12:19

KING Solomon married many other girls besides the Egyptian princess. Many of them came from nations where idols were worshiped—Moab, Ammon, Edom, Sidon, and from the Hittites— 2even though the Lord had clearly instructed his people not to marry into those nations, because the women they married would get them started worshiping their gods. Yet Solomon did it anyway. 3He had seven hundred wives and three hundred concubines; and sure enough, they turned his heart away from the Lord, 4especially in his old age. They encouraged him to worship their gods instead of trusting completely in the Lord as his father David had done. 5Solomon worshiped Ashtoreth, the goddess of the Sidonians, and Milcom, the horrible god of the Ammonites. 6Thus Solomon did what was clearly wrong and refused to follow the Lord as his father David did. 7He even built a temple on the Mount of Olives, across the valley from Jerusalem, for Chemosh, the depraved god of Moab, and another for Molech, the unutterably vile god of the Ammonites. 8Solomon built temples for these foreign wives to use for burning incense and sacrificing to their gods.

9,10Jehovah was very angry with Solomon about this, for now Solomon was no longer interested in the Lord God of Israel who had appeared to him twice to warn him specifically against worshiping other gods. But he hadn't listened, [11]so now the Lord said to him, "Since you have not kept our agreement and have not obeyed my laws, I will tear the kingdom away from you and your family and give it to someone else. [12,13]However, for the sake of your father David, I won't do this while you are still alive. I will take the kingdom away from your son. And even so I will let him be king of one tribe, for David's sake and for the sake of Jerusalem, my chosen city."

[14]So the Lord caused Hadad the Edomite to grow in power. And Solomon became apprehensive, for Hadad was a member of the royal family of Edom. [15]Years before, when David had been in Edom with Joab to arrange for the burial of some Israeli soldiers who had died in battle, the Israeli army had killed nearly every male in the entire country. [16,17,18]It took six months to accomplish this, but they finally killed all except Hadad and a few royal officials who took him to Egypt (he was a very small child at the time). They slipped out of Midian and went to Paran, where others joined them and accompanied them to Egypt, and Pharaoh had given them homes and food.

[19]Hadad became one of Pharaoh's closest friends, and he gave him a wife—the sister of Queen Tahpenes. [20]She presented him with a son, Genubath, who was brought up in Pharaoh's palace among Pharaoh's own sons. [21]When Hadad, there in Egypt, heard that David and Joab were both dead, he asked Pharaoh for permission to return to Edom.

[22]"Why?" Pharaoh asked him. "What do you lack here? How have we disappointed you?"

"Everything is wonderful," he replied "but even so, I'd like to go back home."

[23]Another of Solomon's enemies whom God raised to power was Rezon, one of the officials of King Hadad-ezer of Zobah who had deserted his post and fled the country. [24]He had become the leader of a gang of bandits—men who fled with him to Damascus (where he later became king) when David destroyed Zobah. [25]During Solomon's entire lifetime, Rezon and Hadad were his enemies, for they hated Israel intensely.

[26]Another rebel leader was Jeroboam (the son of Nebat), who came from the city of Zeredah in Ephraim; his mother was Zeruah, a widow. [27,28]Here is the story back of his rebellion: Solomon was rebuilding Fort Millo, repairing the walls of this city his father had built. Jeroboam was very able, and when Solomon saw how industrious he was, he put him in charge of his labor battalions from the tribe of Joseph.

[29]One day as Jeroboam was leaving Jerusalem, the prophet Ahijah from Shiloh (who had put on a new robe for the occasion) met him and called him aside to talk to him. And as the two of them were alone in the field, [30]Ahijah tore his new robe into twelve parts, [31]and said to Jeroboam, "Take ten of these pieces, for the Lord God of Israel says, 'I will tear the kingdom from the hand of Solomon and give ten of the tribes to you! [32]But I will leave him one tribe for the sake of my servant David and for the sake of Jerusalem, which I have chosen above all the other cities of Israel. [33]For Solomon has forsaken me and worships Ashtoreth, the goddess of the Sidonians; and Chemosh, the god of Moab; and Milcom, the god of the Ammonites. He has not followed my paths and has not done what I consider right; he has not kept my laws and instructions as his father David did. [34]I will not take the kingdom from him now, however; for the sake of my servant David, my chosen one who obeyed my commandments, I will let Solomon reign for the rest of his life.

[35]" 'But I will take away the kingdom from his son and give ten of the tribes to you. [36]His son shall have the other one so that the descendants of David will continue to reign in Jerusalem, the city I have chosen to be the place for my name to be enshrined. [37]And I will place you on the throne of Israel, and give you absolute power. [38]If you listen

to what I tell you and walk in my path and do whatever I consider right, obeying my commandments as my servant David did, then I will bless you; and your descendants shall rule Israel forever. (I once made this same promise to David. 39But because of Solomon's sin I will punish the descendants of David—though not forever.)' "

40Solomon tried to kill Jeroboam, but he fled to King Shishak of Egypt and stayed there until the death of Solomon. 41The rest of what Solomon did and said is written in the book *The Acts of Solomon.* 42He ruled in Jerusalem for forty years, 43and then died and was buried in the city of his father David; and his son Rehoboam reigned in his place.

REHOBOAM'S inauguration was at Shechem, and all Israel came for the coronation ceremony. 2,3,4Jeroboam, who was still in Egypt where he had fled from King Solomon, heard about the plans from his friends. They urged him to attend, so he joined the rest of Israel at Shechem, and was the ringleader in getting the people to make certain demands upon Rehoboam.

"Your father was a hard master," they told Rehoboam. "We don't want you as our king unless you promise to treat us better than he did."

5"Give me three days to think this over," Rehoboam replied. "Come back then for my answer." So the people left.

6Rehoboam talked it over with the old men who had counseled his father Solomon.

"What do you think I should do?" he asked them.

7And they replied, "If you give them a pleasant reply and agree to be good to them and serve them well, you can be their king forever."

8But Rehoboam refused the old men's counsel and called in the young men with whom he had grown up.

9"What do you think I should do?" he asked them.

10And the young men replied, "Tell them, 'If you think my father was hard on you, well, I'll be harder! 11Yes, my father was harsh, but I'll be even harsher! My father used whips on you, but I'll use scorpions!' "

12So when Jeroboam and the people returned three days later, 13,14the new king answered them roughly. He ignored the old men's advice and followed that of the young men; 15so the king refused the people's demands. (But the Lord's hand was in it—he caused the new king to do this in order to fulfill his promise to Jeroboam, made through Ahijah, the prophet from Shiloh.)

16,17When the people realized that the king meant what he said and was refusing to listen to them, they began shouting, "Down with David and all his relatives! Let's go home! Let Rehoboam be king of his own family!"

And they all deserted him except for the tribe of Judah, who remained loyal and accepted Rehoboam as their king. 18When King Rehoboam sent Adoram (who was in charge of the draft) to conscript men from the other tribes, a great mob stoned him to death. But King Rehoboam escaped by chariot and fled to Jerusalem. 19And Israel has been in rebellion against the dynasty of David to this day.

ACTS 9:1–25

BUT Paul, threatening with every breath and eager to destroy every Christian, went to the High Priest in Jerusalem. 2He requested a letter addressed to synagogues in Damascus, requiring their cooperation in the persecution of any believers he found there, both men and women, so that he could bring them in chains to Jerusalem.

3As he was nearing Damascus on this mission, suddenly a brilliant light from heaven spotted down upon him! 4He fell to the ground and heard a voice saying to him, "Paul! Paul! Why are you persecuting me?"

5"Who is speaking, sir?" Paul asked.

And the voice replied, "I am Jesus,

the one you are persecuting! 6Now get up and go into the city and await my further instructions."

7The men with Paul stood speechless with surprise, for they heard the sound of someone's voice but saw no one! 8,9As Paul picked himself up off the ground, he found that he was blind. He had to be led into Damascus and was there three days, blind, going without food and water all that time.

10Now there was in Damascus a believer named Ananias. The Lord spoke to him in a vision, calling, "Ananias!"

"Yes, Lord!" he replied.

11And the Lord said, "Go over to Straight Street and find the house of a man named Judas and ask there for Paul of Tarsus. He is praying to me right now, for 12I have shown him a vision of a man named Ananias coming in and laying his hands on him so that he can see again!"

13"But Lord," exclaimed Ananias, "I have heard about the terrible things this man has done to the believers in Jerusalem! 14And we hear that he has arrest warrants with him from the chief priests, authorizing him to arrest every believer in Damascus!"

15But the Lord said, "Go and do what I say. For Paul is my chosen instrument to take my message to the nations and before kings, as well as to the people of Israel. 16And I will show him how much he must suffer for me."

17So Ananias went over and found Paul and laid his hands on him and said, "Brother Paul, the Lord Jesus, who appeared to you on the road, has sent me so that you may be filled with the Holy Spirit and get your sight back."

18Instantly (it was as though scales fell from his eyes) Paul could see, and was immediately baptized. 19Then he ate and was strengthened.

He stayed with the believers in Damascus for a few days 20and went at once to the synagogue to tell everyone there the Good News about Jesus—that he is indeed the Son of God!

21All who heard him were amazed. "Isn't this the same man who persecuted Jesus' followers so bitterly in Jerusalem?" they asked. "And we understand that he came here to arrest them all and take them in chains to the chief priests."

22Paul became more and more fervent in his preaching, and the Damascus Jews couldn't withstand his proofs that Jesus was indeed the Christ.

23After a while the Jewish leaders determined to kill him. 24But Paul was told about their plans, that they were watching the gates of the city day and night prepared to murder him. 25So during the night some of his converts let him down in a basket through an opening in the city wall!

PSALM 131:1–3

LORD, I am not proud and haughty. I don't think myself better than others. I don't pretend to "know it all." 2I am quiet now before the Lord, just as a child who is weaned from the breast. Yes, my begging has been stilled.

3O Israel, you too should quietly trust in the Lord—now, and always.

PROVERBS FOR TODAY/ 17:4–5

The wicked enjoy fellowship with others who are wicked; liars enjoy liars. Mocking the poor is mocking the God who made them. He will punish those who rejoice at others' misfortunes.

JUNE 14

1 KINGS 12:20—13:34

WHEN the people of Israel learned of Jeroboam's return from Egypt, he was asked to come before an open meeting of all the people; and there he was made king of Israel. Only the tribe of Judah continued under the kingship of the family of David.

21When King Rehoboam arrived in Jerusalem, he summoned his army—all the able-bodied men of Judah and Benjamin: 180,000 special troops—to force the rest of Israel to acknowledge him as their king. 22But God sent this message to Shemaiah, the prophet:

23,24"Tell Rehoboam the son of Solomon, king of Judah, and all the people of Judah and Benjamin that they must not fight against their brothers, the people of Israel. Tell them to disband and go home, for what has happened to Rehoboam is according to my wish." So the army went home as the Lord had commanded.

25Jeroboam now built the city of Shechem in the hill country of Ephraim, and it became his capital. Later he built Penuel. 26Jeroboam thought, "Unless I'm careful, the people will want a descendant of David as their king. 27When they go to Jerusalem to offer sacrifices at the Temple, they will become friendly with King Rehoboam; then they will kill me and ask him to be their king instead."

28So on the advice of his counselors, the king had two gold calf-idols made and told the people, "It's too much trouble to go to Jerusalem to worship; from now on these will be your gods—they rescued you from your captivity in Egypt!"

29One of these calf-idols was placed in Bethel and the other in Dan. 30This was of course a great sin, for the people worshiped them. 31He also made shrines on the hills and ordained priests from the rank and file of the people—even those who were not from the priest-tribe

of Levi. 32,33Jeroboam also announced that the annual Tabernacle Festival would be held at Bethel on the first of November (a date he decided upon himself), similar to the annual festival at Jerusalem; he himself offered sacrifices upon the altar to the calves at Bethel, and burned incense to them. And it was there at Bethel that he ordained priests for the shrines on the hills.

As Jeroboam approached the altar to burn incense to the gold calf-idol, a prophet of the Lord from Judah walked up to him. 2Then, at the Lord's command, the prophet shouted, "O altar, the Lord says that a child named Josiah shall be born into the family line of David, and he shall sacrifice upon you the priests from the shrines on the hills who come here to burn incense; and men's bones shall be burned upon you."

3Then he gave this proof that his message was from the Lord: "This altar will split apart, and the ashes on it will spill to the ground."

4The king was very angry with the prophet for saying this. He shouted to his guards, "Arrest that man!" and shook his fist at him. Instantly the king's arm became paralyzed in that position; he couldn't pull it back again! 5At the same moment a wide crack appeared in the altar and the ashes poured out, just as the prophet had said would happen. For this was the prophet's proof that God had been speaking through him.

6"Oh, please, please," the king cried out to the prophet, "beg the Lord your God to restore my arm again."

So he prayed to the Lord, and the king's arm became normal again.

7Then the king said to the prophet, "Come to the palace with me and rest awhile and have some food; and I'll give you a reward because you healed my arm."

8But the prophet said to the king,

"Even if you gave me half your palace, I wouldn't go into it; nor would I eat or drink even water in this place! ⁹For the Lord has given me strict orders not to eat anything or drink any water while I'm here, and not to return to Judah by the road I came on."

¹⁰So he went back another way.

¹¹As it happened, there was an old prophet living in Bethel, and his sons went home and told him what the prophet from Judah had done and what he had said to the king.

¹²"Which way did he go?" the old prophet asked. So they told him.

¹³"Quick, saddle the donkey," the old man said. And when they had saddled the donkey for him, ¹⁴he rode after the prophet and found him sitting under an oak tree.

"Are you the prophet who came from Judah?" he asked him.

"Yes," he replied, "I am."

¹⁵Then the old man said to the prophet, "Come home with me and eat."

¹⁶,¹⁷"No," he replied, "I can't; for I am not allowed to eat anything or to drink any water at Bethel. The Lord strictly warned me against it; and he also told me not to return home by the same road I came on."

¹⁸But the old man said, "I am a prophet too, just as you are; and an angel gave me a message from the Lord. I am to take you home with me and give you food and water."

But the old man was lying to him. ¹⁹So they went back together, and the prophet ate some food and drank some water at the old man's home.

²⁰Then, suddenly, while they were sitting at the table, a message from the Lord came to the old man, ²¹,²²and he shouted at the prophet from Judah, "The Lord says that because you have been disobedient to his clear command, and have come here, and have eaten and drunk water in the place he told you not to, therefore your body shall not be buried in the grave of your fathers."

²³After finishing the meal, the old man saddled the prophet's donkey, ²⁴,²⁵and the prophet started off again. But as he was traveling along, a lion came out and killed him. His body lay there on the road, with the donkey and the lion standing beside it. Those who came by and saw the body lying in the road and the lion standing quietly beside it, reported it in Bethel where the old prophet lived.

²⁶When he heard what had happened he exclaimed, "It is the prophet who disobeyed the Lord's command; the Lord fulfilled his warning by causing the lion to kill him."

²⁷Then he said to his sons, "Saddle my donkey!" And they did.

²⁸He found the prophet's body lying in the road; and the donkey and lion were still standing there beside it, for the lion had not eaten the body nor attacked the donkey. ²⁹So the prophet laid the body upon the donkey and took it back to the city to mourn over it and bury it.

³⁰He laid the body in his own grave, exclaiming, "Alas, my brother!"

³¹Afterwards he said to his sons, "When I die, bury me in the grave where the prophet is buried. Lay my bones beside his bones. ³²For the Lord told him to shout against the altar in Bethel, and his curse against the shrines in the cities of Samaria shall surely be fulfilled."

³³Despite the prophet's warning, Jeroboam did not turn away from his evil ways; instead, he made more priests than ever from the common people, to offer sacrifices to idols in the shrines on the hills. Anyone who wanted to could be a priest. ³⁴This was a great sin, and resulted in the destruction of Jeroboam's kingdom and the death of all of his family.

ACTS 9:26–43

UPON arrival in Jerusalem he tried to meet with the believers, but they were all afraid of him. They thought he was faking! ²⁷Then Barnabas brought him to the apostles and told them how Paul had seen the Lord on the way to Damascus, what the Lord had said to him, and all about his powerful preaching in the name of Jesus. ²⁸Then they accepted him, and after that he was constantly with the believers 29and preached boldly in the name of the Lord. But then some Greek-speaking Jews with whom he had argued plotted to murder him. 30However, when the other believers heard about his danger, they took him to Caesarea and then sent him to his home in Tarsus.

31Meanwhile, the church had peace throughout Judea, Galilee and Samaria, and grew in strength and numbers. The believers learned how to walk in the fear of the Lord and in the comfort of the Holy Spirit.

32Peter traveled from place to place to visit them, and in his travels came to the believers in the town of Lydda. 33There he met a man named Aeneas, paralyzed and bedridden for eight years. 34Peter said to him, "Aeneas! Jesus Christ has healed you! Get up and make your bed." And he was healed instantly. 35Then the whole population of Lydda and Sharon turned to the Lord when they saw Aeneas walking around.

36In the city of Joppa there was a woman named Dorcas ("Gazelle"), a believer who was always doing kind things for others, especially for the poor. 37About this time she became ill and died. Her friends prepared her for burial and laid her in an upstairs room. 38But when they learned that Peter was nearby at Lydda, they sent two men to beg him to return with them to Joppa. 39This he did; as soon as he arrived, they took him upstairs where Dorcas lay. The room was filled with weeping widows who were showing one another the coats and other garments Dorcas had made for them. 40But Peter asked them all to leave the room; then he knelt and prayed. Turning to the body he said, "Get up, Dorcas," and she opened her eyes! And when she saw Peter, she sat up! 41He gave her his hand and helped her up and called in the believers and widows, presenting her to them.

42The news raced through the town, and many believed in the Lord. 43And Peter stayed a long time in Joppa, living with Simon, the tanner.

PSALM 132:1–18

LORD, do you remember that time when my heart was so filled with turmoil? 2-5I couldn't rest, I couldn't sleep, thinking how I ought to build a permanent home for the Ark of the Lord, a Temple for the mighty one of Israel. Then I vowed that I would do it; I made a solemn promise to the Lord.

6First the Ark was in Ephrathah, then in the distant countryside of Jaar. 7But now it will be settled in the Temple, in God's permanent home here on earth. That is where we will go to worship him. 8Arise, O Lord, and enter your Temple with the Ark, the symbol of your power.

9We will clothe the priests in white, the symbol of all purity. May our nation shout for joy.

10Do not reject your servant David—the king you chose for your people. 11For you promised me that my son would sit on my throne and succeed me. And surely you will never go back on a promise! 12You also promised that if my descendants will obey the terms of your contract with me, then the dynasty of David shall never end.

13O Lord, you have chosen Jerusalem as your home: 14"This is my permanent home where I shall live," you said, "for I have always wanted it this way. 15I will make this city prosperous and satisfy her poor with food. 16I will clothe her priests with salvation; her saints shall shout for joy. 17David's power shall grow, for I have decreed for him a mighty Son. 18I'll clothe his enemies with shame, but he shall be a glorious King."

PROVERBS FOR TODAY/ 17:6

An old man's grandchildren are his crowning glory. A child's glory is his father.

JUNE 15

JEROBOAM'S son Abijah now became very sick. ²Jeroboam told his wife, "Disguise yourself so that no one will recognize you as the queen, and go to Ahijah the prophet at Shiloh—the man who told me that I would become king. ³Take him a gift of ten loaves of bread, some fig bars, and a jar of honey and ask him whether the boy will recover."

⁴So his wife went to Ahijah's home at Shiloh. He was an old man now, and could no longer see. ⁵But the Lord told him that the queen, pretending to be someone else, would come to ask about her son, for he was very sick. And the Lord told him what to tell her.

⁶So when Ahijah heard her at the door, he called out, "Come in, wife of Jeroboam! Why are you pretending to be someone else?" Then he told her, "I have sad news for you. ⁷Give your husband this message from the Lord God of Israel: 'I promoted you from the ranks of the common people and made you king of Israel. ⁸I ripped the kingdom away from the family of David and gave it to you, but you have not obeyed my commandments as my servant David did. His heart's desire was always to obey me and to do whatever I wanted him to. ⁹But you have done more evil than all the other kings before you; you have made other gods and have made me furious with your gold calves. And since you have refused to acknowledge me, ¹⁰I will bring disaster upon your home and will destroy all of your sons—this boy who is sick and all those who are well. I will sweep away your family as a stable hand shovels out manure. ¹¹I vow that those of your family who die in the city shall be eaten by dogs, and those who die in the field shall be eaten by birds.' "

¹²Then Ahijah said to Jeroboam's wife, "Go on home, and when you step into the city, the child will die. ¹³All of Israel will mourn for him and bury him, but he is the only member of your family who will come to a quiet end. For this child is the only good thing which the Lord God of Israel sees in the entire family of Jeroboam. ¹⁴And the Lord will raise up a king over Israel who will destroy the family of Jeroboam. ¹⁵Then the Lord will shake Israel like a reed whipped about in a stream; he will uproot the people of Israel from this good land of their fathers and scatter them beyond the Euphrates River, for they have angered the Lord by worshiping idol-gods. ¹⁶He will abandon Israel because Jeroboam sinned and made all of Israel sin along with him."

¹⁷So Jeroboam's wife returned to Tirzah; and the child died just as she walked through the door of her home. ¹⁸And there was mourning for him throughout the land, just as the Lord had predicted through Ahijah.

¹⁹The rest of Jeroboam's activities—his wars and the other events of his reign—are recorded in *The Annals of the Kings of Israel*. ²⁰Jeroboam reigned twenty-two years, and when he died, his son Nadab took the throne.

²¹Meanwhile, Rehoboam the son of Solomon was king in Judah. He was forty-one years old when he began to reign, and he was on the throne seventeen years in Jerusalem, the city which, among all the cities of Israel, the Lord had chosen to live in. (Rehoboam's mother was Naamah, an Ammonite woman.) ²²During his reign the people of Judah, like those in Israel, did wrong and angered the Lord with their sin, for it was even worse than that of their ancestors. ²³They built shrines and obelisks and idols on every high hill and under every green tree. ²⁴There was homosexuality throughout the land, and the people of Judah became as depraved as the heathen nations which the Lord drove out to make room for his people.

25In the fifth year of Rehoboam's reign, King Shishak of Egypt attacked and conquered Jerusalem. 26He ransacked the Temple and the palace and stole everything, including all the gold shields Solomon had made. 27Afterwards Rehoboam made bronze shields as substitutes, and the palace guards used these instead. 28Whenever the king went to the Temple, the guards paraded before him and then took the shields back to the guard chamber.

29The other events in Rehoboam's reign are written in *The Annals of the Kings of Judah.* 30There was constant war between Rehoboam and Jeroboam. 31When Rehoboam died—his mother was Naamah the Ammonitess—he was buried among his ancestors in Jerusalem, and his son Abijam took the throne.

ABIJAM began his three-year reign as king of Judah in Jerusalem during the eighteenth year of Jeroboam's reign in Israel. (Abijam's mother was Maacah, the daughter of Abishalom.) 3He was as great a sinner as his father was, and his heart was not right with God, as King David's was. 4But despite Abijam's sin, the Lord remembered David's love and did not end the line of David's royal descendants. 5For David had obeyed God during his entire life except for the affair concerning Uriah the Hittite. 6During Abijam's reign there was constant war between Israel and Judah. 7The rest of Abijam's history is recorded in *The Annals of the Kings of Judah.* 8When he died he was buried in Jerusalem, and his son Asa reigned in his place.

9Asa became king of Judah, in Jerusalem, in the twentieth year of the reign of Jeroboam over Israel, 10and reigned forty-one years. (His grandmother was Maacah, the daughter of Abishalom.) 11He pleased the Lord like his ancestor King David. 12He executed the male prostitutes and removed all the idols his father had made. 13He deposed his grandmother Maacah as queen-mother because she had made an idol—which he cut down

and burned at Kidron Brook. 14However, the shrines on the hills were not removed, for Asa did not realize that these were wrong. 15He made permanent exhibits in the Temple of the bronze shields his grandfather had dedicated, along with the silver and gold vessels he himself had donated.

16There was lifelong war between King Asa of Judah and King Baasha of Israel. 17King Baasha built the fortress city of Ramah in an attempt to cut off all trade with Jerusalem. 18Then Asa took all the silver and gold left in the Temple treasury and all the treasures of the palace, and gave them to his officials to take to Damascus, to King Ben-hadad of Syria, with this message:

19"Let us be allies just as our fathers were. I am sending you a present of gold and silver. Now break your alliance with King Baasha of Israel so that he will leave me alone."

20Ben-hadad agreed and sent his armies against some of the cities of Israel; and he destroyed Ijon, Dan, Abel-beth-maacah, all of Chinneroth, and all the cities in the land of Naphtali. 21When Baasha received word of the attack, he discontinued building the city of Ramah and returned to Tirzah. 22Then King Asa made a proclamation to all Judah, asking every able-bodied man to help demolish Ramah and haul away its stones and timbers. And King Asa used these materials to build the city of Geba in Benjamin and the city of Mizpah.

23The rest of Asa's biography—his conquests and deeds and the names of the cities he built—is found in *The Annals of the Kings of Judah.* In his old age his feet became diseased, 24and when he died he was buried in the royal cemetery in Jerusalem. Then his son Jehoshaphat became the new king of Judah.

ACTS 10:1-23

IN Caesarea there lived a Roman army officer, Cornelius, a captain of an Italian regiment. 2He was a godly man, deeply reverent, as was his entire household. He gave generously to charity and was a man of prayer. 3While wide awake one afternoon he had a vision—it was about three o'clock—and in this vision he saw an angel of God coming toward him.

"Cornelius!" the angel said.

4Cornelius stared at him in terror. "What do you want, sir?" he asked the angel.

And the angel replied, "Your prayers and charities have not gone unnoticed by God! 5,6Now send some men to Joppa to find a man named Simon Peter, who is staying with Simon, the tanner, down by the shore, and ask him to come and visit you."

7As soon as the angel was gone, Cornelius called two of his household servants and a godly soldier, one of his personal bodyguard, 8and told them what had happened and sent them off to Joppa.

9,10The next day, as they were nearing the city, Peter went up on the flat roof of his house to pray. It was noon and he was hungry, but while lunch was being prepared, he fell into a trance. 11He saw the sky open, and a great canvas sheet, suspended by its four corners, settle to the ground. 12In the sheet were all sorts of animals, snakes and birds [forbidden to the Jews for food].

13Then a voice said to him, "Go kill and eat any of them you wish."

14"Never, Lord," Peter declared, "I have never in all my life eaten such creatures, for they are forbidden by our Jewish laws."

15The voice spoke again, "Don't contradict God! If he says something is kosher, then it is."

16The same vision was repeated three times. Then the sheet was pulled up again to heaven.

17Peter was very perplexed. What could the vision mean? What was he supposed to do?

Just then the men sent by Cornelius had found the house and were standing outside at the gate, 18inquiring whether this was the place where Simon Peter lived!

19Meanwhile, as Peter was puzzling over the vision, the Holy Spirit said to him, "Three men have come to see you. 20Go down and meet them and go with them. All is well, I have sent them."

21So Peter went down. "I'm the man you're looking for," he said. "Now what is it you want?"

22Then they told him about Cornelius the Roman officer, a good and godly man, well thought of by the Jews, and how an angel had instructed him to send for Peter to come and tell him what God wanted him to do.

23So Peter invited them in and lodged them overnight.

The next day he went with them, accompanied by some other believers from Joppa.

PSALM 133:1–3

How wonderful it is, how pleasant, when brothers live in harmony! 2For harmony is as precious as the fragrant anointing oil that was poured over Aaron's head, and ran down onto his beard, and onto the border of his robe. 3Harmony is as refreshing as the dew on Mount Hermon, on the mountains of Israel. And God has pronounced this eternal blessing on Jerusalem, even life forevermore.

PROVERBS FOR TODAY/ 17:7–8

Truth from a rebel or lies from a king are both unexpected. A bribe works like magic. Whoever uses it will prosper!

JUNE 16

1 KINGS 15:25—17:24

MEANWHILE, over in Israel, Nadab the son of Jeroboam had become king. He reigned two years, beginning in the second year of the reign of King Asa of Judah. 26But he was not a good king; like his father, he worshiped many idols and led all of Israel into sin.

27Then Baasha (the son of Ahijah, from the tribe of Issachar) plotted against him and assassinated him while he was with the Israeli army laying siege to the Philistine city of Gibbethon. 28So Baasha replaced Nadab as the king of Israel in Tirzah, during the third year of the reign of King Asa of Judah. 29He immediately killed all of the descendants of King Jeroboam, so that not one of the royal family was left, just as the Lord had said would happen when he spoke through Ahijah, the prophet from Shiloh. 30This was done because Jeroboam had angered the Lord God of Israel by sinning and leading the rest of Israel into sin.

31Further details of Baasha's reign are recorded in *The Annals of the Kings of Israel.*

32,33There was continuous warfare between King Asa of Judah and King Baasha of Israel. Baasha reigned for twenty-four years, 34but all that time he continually disobeyed the Lord. He followed the evil paths of Jeroboam, for he led the people of Israel into the sin of worshiping idols.

A message of condemnation from the Lord was delivered to King Baasha at this time by the prophet Jehu:

2"I lifted you out of the dust," the message said, "to make you king of my people Israel; but you have walked in the evil paths of Jeroboam. You have made my people sin, and I am angry! 3So now I will destroy you and your family, just as I did the descendants of Jeroboam. 4-7Those of your family who die in the

city will be eaten by dogs, and those who die in the fields will be eaten by the birds."

The message was sent to Baasha and his family because he had angered the Lord by all his evil deeds. He was as evil as Jeroboam despite the fact that the Lord had destroyed all of Jeroboam's descendants for their sins.

The rest of Baasha's biography—his deeds and conquests—are written in *The Annals of the Kings of Israel.*

8Elah, Baasha's son, began reigning during the twenty-sixth year of the reign of King Asa of Judah, but he reigned only two years. 9Then General Zimri, who had charge of half the royal chariot troops, plotted against him. One day King Elah was half drunk at the home of Arza, the superintendent of the palace, in the capital city of Tirzah. 10Zimri simply walked in and struck him down and killed him. (This occurred during the twenty-seventh year of the reign of King Asa of Judah.) Then Zimri declared himself to be the new king of Israel.

11He immediately killed the entire royal family—leaving not a single male child. He even destroyed distant relatives and friends. 12This destruction of the descendants of Baasha was in line with what the Lord had predicted through the prophet Jehu. 13The tragedy occurred because of the sins of Baasha and his son Elah; for they had led Israel into worshiping idols and the Lord was very angry about it. 14The rest of the history of Elah's reign is written in *The Annals of the Kings of Israel.*

15,16But Zimri lasted only seven days; for when the army of Israel, which was then engaged in attacking the Philistine city of Gibbethon, heard that Zimri had assassinated the king, they decided on General Omri, commander-in-chief of the army, as their new ruler. 17So Omri led the army of Gibbethon to besiege Tirzah, Israel's capital. 18When Zimri saw that the city had been taken, he went into the palace and burned it over him and died in the flames. 19For he, too, had sinned like Jeroboam; he had worshiped idols and had led the people of Israel to sin with him. 20The rest of the story of Zimri and his treason are written in *The Annals of the Kings of Israel.*

21But now the kingdom of Israel was split in two; half the people were loyal to General Omri, and the other half followed Tibni, the son of Ginath. 22But General Omri won and Tibni was killed; so Omri reigned without opposition.

23King Asa of Judah had been on the throne thirty-one years when Omri began his reign over Israel, which lasted twelve years, six of them in Tirzah. 24Then Omri bought the hill now known as Samaria from its owner, Shemer, for $4,000 and built a city on it, calling it Samaria in honor of Shemer. 25But Omri was worse than any of the kings before him; 26he worshiped idols as Jeroboam had, and led Israel into this same sin. So God was very angry. 27The rest of Omri's history is recorded in *The Annals of the Kings of Israel.* 28When Omri died he was buried in Samaria, and his son Ahab became king in his place.

29King Asa of Judah had been on the throne thirty-eight years when Ahab became the king of Israel; and Ahab reigned for twenty-two years. 30But he was even more wicked than his father Omri; he was worse than any other king of Israel! 31And as though that were not enough, he married Jezebel, the daughter of King Ethbaal of the Sidonians, and then began worshiping Baal. 32First he built a temple and an altar for Baal in Samaria. 33Then he made other idols and did more to anger the Lord God of Israel than any of the other kings of Israel before him.

34(It was during his reign that Hiel, a man from Bethel, rebuilt Jericho. When he laid the foundations, his oldest son, Abiram, died; and when he finally completed it by setting up the gates, his youngest son, Segub, died. For this was the Lord's curse upon Jericho as declared by Joshua, the son of Nun.)

THEN Elijah, the prophet from Tishbe in Gilead, told King Ahab, "As surely as the Lord God of Israel lives—the God whom I worship and serve—there won't be any dew or rain for several years until I say the word!"

2Then the Lord said to Elijah, 3"Go to the east and hide by Cherith Brook at a place east of where it enters the Jordan River. 4Drink from the brook and eat what the ravens bring you, for I have commanded them to feed you."

5So he did as the Lord had told him to, and camped beside the brook. 6The ravens brought him bread and meat each morning and evening, and he drank from the brook. 7But after awhile the brook dried up, for there was no rainfall anywhere in the land.

8,9Then the Lord said to him, "Go and live in the village of Zarephath, near the city of Sidon. There is a widow there who will feed you. I have given her my instructions."

10So he went to Zarephath. As he arrived at the gates of the city he saw a widow gathering sticks; and he asked her for a cup of water.

11As she was going to get it, he called to her, "Bring me a bite of bread, too."

12But she said, "I swear by the Lord your God that I haven't a single piece of bread in the house. And I have only a handful of flour left and a little cooking oil in the bottom of the jar. I was just gathering a few sticks to cook this last meal, and then my son and I must die of starvation."

13But Elijah said to her, "Don't be afraid! Go ahead and cook that 'last meal,' but bake me a little loaf of bread first; and afterwards there will still be enough food for you and your son. 14For the Lord God of Israel says that there will always be plenty of flour and oil left in your containers until the time when the Lord sends rain, and the crops grow again!"

15So she did as Elijah said, and she and Elijah and her son continued to eat from her supply of flour and oil as long as it was needed. 16For no matter how much they used, there was always plenty left in the containers, just as the Lord had promised through Elijah!

17But one day the woman's son became sick and died.

18"O man of God," she cried, "what have you done to me? Have you come here to punish my sins by killing my son?"

19"Give him to me," Elijah replied. And he took the boy's body from her and carried it upstairs to the guest room where he lived, and laid the body on his bed, 20and then cried out to the Lord, "O Lord my God, why have you killed the son of this widow with whom I am staying?"

21And he stretched himself upon the child three times, and cried out to the Lord, "O Lord my God, please let this child's spirit return to him."

22And the Lord heard Elijah's prayer; and the spirit of the child returned, and he became alive again! 23Then Elijah took him downstairs and gave him to his mother.

"See! He's alive!" he beamed.

24"Now I know for sure that you are a prophet," she told him afterward, "and that whatever you say is from the Lord!"

ACTS 10:24–48

THEY arrived in Caesarea the following day, and Cornelius was waiting for him, and had called together his relatives and close friends to meet Peter. 25As Peter entered his home, Cornelius fell to the floor before him in worship.

26But Peter said, "Stand up! I'm not a god!"

27So he got up and they talked together for a while and then went in where the others were assembled.

28Peter told them, "You know it is against the Jewish laws for me to come into a Gentile home like this. But God has shown me in a vision that I should never think of anyone as inferior.

29So I came as soon as I was sent for. Now tell me what you want."

30Cornelius replied, "Four days ago I was praying as usual at this time of the afternoon, when suddenly a man was standing before me clothed in a radiant robe! 31He told me, 'Cornelius, your prayers are heard and your charities have been noticed by God! 32Now send some men to Joppa and summon Simon Peter, who is staying in the home of Simon, a tanner, down by the shore.' 33So I sent for you at once, and you have done well to come so soon. Now here we are, waiting before the Lord, anxious to hear what he has told you to tell us!"

34Then Peter replied, "I see very clearly that the Jews are not God's only favorites! 35In every nation he has those who worship him and do good deeds and are acceptable to him. 36,37I'm sure you have heard about the Good News for the people of Israel—that there is peace with God through Jesus, the Messiah, who is Lord of all creation. This message has spread all through Judea, beginning with John the Baptist in Galilee. 38And you no doubt know that Jesus of Nazareth was anointed by God with the Holy Spirit and with power, and he went around doing good and healing all who were possessed by demons, for God was with him.

39"And we apostles are witnesses of all he did throughout Israel and in Jerusalem, where he was murdered on a cross. 40,41But God brought him back to life again three days later and showed him to certain witnesses God had selected beforehand—not to the general public, but to us who ate and drank with him after he rose from the dead. 42And he sent us to preach the Good News everywhere and to testify that Jesus is ordained of God to be the Judge of all—living and dead. 43And all the prophets have written about him, saying that everyone who believes in him will have their sins forgiven through his name."

44Even as Peter was saying these things, the Holy Spirit fell upon all those listening! 45The Jews who came with Peter were amazed that the gift of the Holy Spirit would be given to Gentiles too! 46,47But there could be no doubt about it, for they heard them speaking in tongues and praising God.

Peter asked, "Can anyone object to my baptizing them, now that they have received the Holy Spirit just as we did?" 48So he did, baptizing them in the name of Jesus, the Messiah. Afterwards Cornelius begged him to stay with them for several days.

PSALM 134:1–3

OH, bless the Lord, you who serve him as watchmen in the Temple every night. 2Lift your hands in holiness and bless the Lord.

3The Lord bless you from Zion—the Lord who made heaven and earth.

PROVERBS FOR TODAY/ 17:9–11

Love forgets mistakes; nagging about them parts the best of friends. A rebuke to a man of common sense is more effective than a hundred lashes on the back of a rebel. The wicked live for rebellion; they shall be severely punished.

JUNE 17

1 KINGS 18:1–46

IT was three years later that the Lord said to Elijah, "Go and tell King Ahab that I will soon send rain again!"

2So Elijah went to tell him. Meanwhile the famine had become very severe in Samaria.

3,4The man in charge of Ahab's household affairs was Obadiah, who was a devoted follower of the Lord. Once when Queen Jezebel had tried to kill all of the Lord's prophets, Obadiah had hidden one hundred of them in two caves—fifty in each—and had fed them with bread and water.

5That same day, while Elijah was on the way to see King Ahab, the king said to Obadiah, "We must check every stream and brook to see if we can find enough grass to save at least some of my horses and mules. You go one way and I'll go the other, and we will search the entire land."

6So they did, each going alone. 7Suddenly Obadiah saw Elijah coming toward him! Obadiah recognized him at once and fell to the ground before him.

"Is it really you, my lord Elijah?" he asked.

8"Yes, it is," Elijah replied. "Now go and tell the king I am here."

9"Oh, sir," Obadiah protested, "what harm have I done to you that you are sending me to my death? 10For I swear by God that the king has searched every nation and kingdom on earth from end to end to find you. And each time when he was told 'Elijah isn't here,' King Ahab forced the king of that nation to swear to the truth of his claim. 11And now you say, 'Go and tell him Elijah is here'! 12But as soon as I leave you, the Spirit of the Lord will carry you away, who knows where, and when Ahab comes and can't find you, he will kill me; yet I have been a true servant of the Lord all my life. 13Has no one told you about the time when Queen Jezebel was trying to kill the Lord's prophets, and I hid a hundred of them in two caves and fed them with bread and water? 14And now you say, 'Go tell the king that Elijah is here'! Sir, if I do that, I'm dead!"

15But Elijah said, "I swear by the Lord God of the armies of heaven, in whose presence I stand, that I will present myself to Ahab today."

16So Obadiah went to tell Ahab that Elijah had come; and Ahab went out to meet him.

17"So it's you, is it?—the man who brought this disaster upon Israel!" Ahab exclaimed when he saw him.

18"You're talking about yourself," Elijah answered. "For you and your family have refused to obey the Lord, and have worshiped Baal instead. 19Now bring all the people of Israel to Mount Carmel, with all 450 prophets of Baal and the 400 prophets of Asherah who are supported by Jezebel."

20So Ahab summoned all the people and the prophets to Mount Carmel.

21Then Elijah talked to them. "How long are you going to waver between two opinions?" he asked the people. "If the Lord is God, *follow* him! But if Baal is God, then follow *him!*"

22Then Elijah spoke again. "I am the only prophet of the Lord who is left," he told them, "but Baal has 450 prophets. 23Now bring two young bulls. The prophets of Baal may choose whichever one they wish and cut it into pieces and lay it on the wood of their altar, but without putting any fire under the wood; and I will prepare the other young bull and lay it on the wood on the Lord's altar, with no fire under it. 24Then pray to your god, and I will pray to the Lord; and the god who answers by sending fire to light the wood is the true God!" And all the people agreed to this test.

25Then Elijah turned to the prophets of Baal. "You first," he said, "for there are many of you; choose one of the bulls and prepare it and call to your god; but don't put any fire under the wood."

26So they prepared one of the young bulls and placed it on the altar; and they called to Baal all morning, shouting, "O Baal, hear us!" But there was no reply of any kind. Then they began to dance around the altar. 27About noontime, Elijah began mocking them.

"You'll have to shout louder than that," he scoffed, "to catch the attention of your god! Perhaps he is talking to someone, or is out sitting on the toilet, or maybe he is away on a trip, or is asleep and needs to be wakened!"

28So they shouted louder and, as was their custom, cut themselves with knives and swords until the blood gushed out. 29They raved all afternoon until the time of the evening sacrifice, but there was no reply, no voice, no answer.

30Then Elijah called to the people, "Come over here."

And they all crowded around him as he repaired the altar of the Lord which had been torn down. 31He took twelve stones, one to represent each of the tribes of Israel, 32and used the stones to rebuild the Lord's altar. Then he dug a trench about three feet wide around the altar. 33He piled wood upon the altar and cut the young bull into pieces and laid the pieces on the wood.

"Fill four barrels with water," he said, "and pour the water over the carcass and the wood."

After they had done this he said, 34"Do it again." And they did.

"Now, do it once more!" And they did; 35and the water ran off the altar and filled the trench.

36At the customary time for offering the evening sacrifice, Elijah walked up to the altar and prayed, "O Lord God of Abraham, Isaac, and Israel, prove today that you are the God of Israel and that I am your servant; prove that I have done all this at your command. 37O Lord, answer me! Answer me so these people will know that you are God and that you have brought them back to yourself."

38Then, suddenly, fire flashed down from heaven and burned up the young bull, the wood, the stones, the dust, and even evaporated all the water in the ditch!

39And when the people saw it, they fell to their faces upon the ground shouting, "Jehovah is God! Jehovah is God!"

40Then Elijah told them to grab the prophets of Baal. "Don't let a single one escape," he commanded.

So they seized them all, and Elijah took them to Kishon Brook and killed them there.

⁴¹Then Elijah said to Ahab, "Go and enjoy a good meal! For I hear a mighty rainstorm coming!"

⁴²So Ahab prepared a feast. But Elijah climbed to the top of Mount Carmel and got down on his knees, with his face between his knees, ⁴³and said to his servant, "Go and look out toward the sea."

He did, but returned to Elijah and told him, "I didn't see anything."

Then Elijah told him, "Go again, and again, and again, seven times!"

⁴⁴Finally, the seventh time, his servant told him, "I saw a little cloud about the size of a man's hand rising from the sea."

Then Elijah shouted, "Hurry to Ahab and tell him to get into his chariot and get down the mountain, or he'll be stopped by the rain!"

⁴⁵And sure enough, the sky was soon black with clouds, and a heavy wind brought a terrific rainstorm. Ahab left hastily for Jezreel, ⁴⁶and the Lord gave special strength to Elijah so that he was able to run ahead of Ahab's chariot to the entrance of the city!

ACTS 11:1–30

SOON the news reached the apostles and other brothers in Judea that Gentiles also were being converted! ²But when Peter arrived back in Jerusalem, the Jewish believers argued with him.

³"You fellowshiped with Gentiles and even ate with them," they accused.

⁴Then Peter told them the whole story. ⁵"One day in Joppa," he said, "while I was praying, I saw a vision— a huge sheet, let down by its four corners from the sky. ⁶Inside the sheet were all sorts of animals, reptiles and birds [which we are not to eat]. ⁷And I heard a voice say, 'Kill and eat whatever you wish.'

⁸" 'Never, Lord,' I replied. 'For I have never yet eaten anything forbidden by our Jewish laws!'

⁹"But the voice came again, 'Don't say it isn't right when God declares it is!'

¹⁰"This happened *three times* before the sheet and all it contained disappeared into heaven. ¹¹Just then three men who had come to take me with them to Caesarea arrived at the house where I was staying! ¹²The Holy Spirit told me to go with them and not to worry about their being Gentiles! These six brothers here accompanied me, and we soon arrived at the home of the man who had sent the messengers. ¹³He told us how an angel had appeared to him and told him to send messengers to Joppa to find Simon Peter! ¹⁴'He will tell you how you and all your household can be saved!' the angel had told him.

¹⁵"Well, I began telling them the Good News, but just as I was getting started with my sermon, the Holy Spirit fell on them, just as he fell on us at the beginning! ¹⁶Then I thought of the Lord's words when he said, 'Yes, John baptized with water, but you shall be baptized with the Holy Spirit.' ¹⁷And since it was *God* who gave these Gentiles the same gift he gave us when we believed on the Lord Jesus Christ, who was I to argue?"

¹⁸When the others heard this, all their objections were answered and they began praising God! "Yes," they said, "God has given to the Gentiles, too, the privilege of turning to him and receiving eternal life!"

¹⁹Meanwhile, the believers who fled from Jerusalem during the persecution after Stephen's death traveled as far as Phoenicia, Cyprus, and Antioch, scattering the Good News, but only to Jews. ²⁰However, some of the believers who went to Antioch from Cyprus and Cyrene also gave their message about the Lord Jesus to some Greeks. ²¹And the Lord honored this effort so that large numbers of these Gentiles became believers.

²²When the church at Jerusalem heard what had happened, they sent Barnabas to Antioch to help the new converts. ²³When he arrived and saw the wonderful things God was doing, he was filled with excitement and joy, and encouraged the believers to stay close to the Lord, what-

ever the cost. 24Barnabas was a kindly person, full of the Holy Spirit and strong in faith. As a result large numbers of people were added to the Lord.

25Then Barnabas went on to Tarsus to hunt for Paul. 26When he found him, he brought him back to Antioch; and both of them stayed there for a full year, teaching the many new converts. (It was there at Antioch that the believers were first called "Christians.")

27During this time some prophets came down from Jerusalem to Antioch, 28and one of them, named Agabus, stood up in one of the meetings to predict by the Spirit that a great famine was coming upon the land of Israel. (This was fulfilled during the reign of Claudius.) 29So the believers decided to send relief to the Christians in Judea, each giving as much as he could. 30This they did, consigning their gifts to Barnabas and Paul to take to the elders of the church in Jerusalem.

PSALM 135:1–21

HALLELUJAH! 2Yes, let his people praise him as they stand in his Temple courts. 3Praise the Lord because he is so good; sing to his wonderful name. 4For the Lord has chosen Israel as his personal possession.

5I know the greatness of the Lord— that he is greater far than any other god.

6He does whatever pleases him throughout all of heaven and earth, and in the deepest seas. 7He makes mists rise throughout the earth and sends the lightning to bring down the rain; and sends the winds from his treasuries. 8He destroyed the eldest child in each Egyptian home, along with the firstborn of the flocks. 9He did great miracles in Egypt before Pharaoh and all his people. 10He smote great nations, slaying mighty kings— 11Sihon, king of Amorites; and Og, the king of Bashan; and the kings of Canaan— 12and gave their land as an eternal gift to his people Israel.

13O Jehovah, your name endures forever; your fame is known to every generation. 14For Jehovah will vindicate his people, and have compassion on his servants.

15The heathen worship idols of gold and silver, made by men— 16idols with speechless mouths and sightless eyes 17and ears that cannot hear; they cannot even breathe. 18Those who make them become like them! And so do all who trust in them!

19O Israel, bless Jehovah! High priests of Aaron, bless his name. 20O Levite priests, bless the Lord Jehovah! Oh, bless his name, all of you who trust and reverence him. 21All people of Jerusalem, praise the Lord, for he lives here in Jerusalem. Hallelujah!

PROVERBS FOR TODAY/ 17:12–13

It is safer to meet a bear robbed of her cubs than a fool caught in his folly. If you repay evil for good, a curse is upon your home.

JUNE 18

1 KINGS 19:1–21

WHEN Ahab told Queen Jezebel what Elijah had done, and that he had slaughtered the prophets of Baal, 2she sent this message to Elijah: "You killed my prophets, and now I swear by the gods that I am going to kill you by this time tomorrow night."

3So Elijah fled for his life; he went to Beer-sheba, a city of Judah, and left his servant there. 4Then he went on alone into the wilderness, traveling all day, and sat down under a broom bush and prayed that he might die.

"I've had enough," he told the Lord. "Take away my life. I've got to die sometime, and it might as well be now."

5Then he lay down and slept beneath the broom bush. But as he was sleeping, an angel touched him and told him to get up and eat! 6He looked around and saw some bread baking on hot stones, and a jar of water! So he ate and drank and lay down again.

7Then the angel of the Lord came again and touched him and said, "Get up and eat some more, for there is a long journey ahead of you."

8So he got up and ate and drank, and the food gave him enough strength to travel forty days and forty nights to Mount Horeb, the mountain of God, 9where he lived in a cave.

But the Lord said to him, "What are you doing here, Elijah?"

10He replied, "I have worked very hard for the Lord God of the heavens; but the people of Israel have broken their covenant with you and torn down your altars and killed your prophets, and only I am left; and now they are trying to kill me, too."

11"Go out and stand before me on the mountain," the Lord told him. And as Elijah stood there the Lord passed by, and a mighty windstorm hit the mountain; it was such a terrible blast that the rocks were torn loose, but the Lord was not in the wind. After the wind, there was an earthquake, but the Lord was not in the earthquake. 12And after the earthquake, there was a fire, but the Lord was not in the fire. And after the fire, there was the sound of a gentle whisper. 13When Elijah heard it, he wrapped his face in his scarf and went out and stood at the entrance of the cave.

And a voice said, "Why are you here, Elijah?"

14He replied again, "I have been working very hard for the Lord God of the armies of heaven, but the people have broken their covenant and have torn down your altars; they have killed every one of your prophets except me; and now they are trying to kill me, too."

15Then the Lord told him, "Go back by the desert road to Damascus, and when you arrive, anoint Hazael to be king of Syria. 16Then anoint Jehu (son of Nimshi) to be king of Israel, and anoint Elisha (the son of Shaphat of Abel-meholah) to replace you as my prophet. 17Anyone who escapes from Hazael shall be killed by Jehu, and those who escape Jehu shall be killed by Elisha! 18And incidentally, there are 7,000 men in Israel who have never bowed to Baal nor kissed him!"

19So Elijah went and found Elisha who was plowing a field with eleven other teams ahead of him; he was at the end of the line with the last team. Elijah went over to him and threw his coat across his shoulders and walked away again.

20Elisha left the oxen standing there and ran after Elijah and said to him, "First let me go and say good-bye to my father and mother, and then I'll go with you!"

Elijah replied, "Go on back! Why all the excitement?"

21Elisha then returned to his oxen, killed them, and used wood from the plow to build a fire to roast their flesh. He passed around the meat to the other plowmen, and they all had a great feast. Then he went with Elijah, as his assistant.

ACTS 12:1–23

ABOUT that time King Herod moved against some of the believers, 2and killed the apostle James (John's brother). 3When Herod saw how much this pleased the Jewish leaders, he arrested Peter during the Passover celebration 4and imprisoned him, placing him under the guard of sixteen soldiers. Herod's intention was to deliver Peter to the Jews for execution after the Passover. 5But earnest prayer was going up to God from the church for his safety all the time he was in prison.

6The night before he was to be executed, he was asleep, double-chained between two soldiers with others standing guard before the prison gate, 7when suddenly there was a light in the cell and an angel of the Lord stood beside Peter! The angel slapped him on the side to awaken him and said, "Quick! Get up!" And the chains fell off his wrists! 8Then the angel told him, "Get dressed and put on your shoes." And he did. "Now put on your coat and follow me!" the angel ordered.

9So Peter left the cell, following the angel. But all the time he thought it was a dream or vision, and didn't believe it was really happening. 10They passed the first and second cell blocks and came to the iron gate to the street, and this opened to them of its own accord! So they passed through and walked along together for a block, and then the angel left him.

11Peter finally realized what had happened! "It's really true!" he said to himself. "The Lord has sent his angel and saved me from Herod and from what the Jews were hoping to do to me!"

12After a little thought he went to the home of Mary, mother of John Mark, where many were gathered for a prayer meeting.

13He knocked at the door in the gate, and a girl named Rhoda came to open it. 14When she recognized Peter's voice, she was so overjoyed that she ran back inside to tell everyone that Peter was standing outside in the street. 15They didn't believe her. "You're out of your mind," they said. When she insisted they decided, "It must be his angel. [They must have killed him.]"

16Meanwhile Peter continued knocking. When they finally went out and opened the door, their surprise knew no bounds. 17He motioned for them to quiet down and told them what had happened and how the Lord had brought him out of jail. "Tell James and the others what happened," he said—and left for safer quarters.

18At dawn, the jail was in great commotion. What had happened to Peter? 19When Herod sent for him and found that he wasn't there, he had the sixteen guards arrested, court-martialed and sentenced to death. Afterwards he left to live in Caesarea for a while.

20While he was in Caesarea, a delegation from Tyre and Sidon arrived to see him. He was highly displeased with the people of those two cities, but the delegates made friends with Blastus, the royal secretary, and asked for peace, for their cities were economically dependent upon trade with Herod's country. 21An appointment with Herod was granted, and when the day arrived he put on his royal robes, sat on his throne and made a speech to them. 22At its conclusion the people gave him a great ovation, shouting, "It is the voice of a god and not of a man!"

23Instantly, an angel of the Lord struck Herod with a sickness so that he was filled with maggots and died—because he accepted the people's worship instead of giving the glory to God.

PSALM 136:1–26

OH, give thanks to the Lord, for he is good; his lovingkindness continues forever.

2Give thanks to the God of gods, for his lovingkindness continues forever. 3Give thanks to the Lord of lords, for his lovingkindness continues forever. 4Praise him who alone does mighty miracles, for his lovingkindness continues forever. 5Praise him who made the heavens, for his lovingkindness continues forever. 6Praise him who planted the water within the earth, for his lovingkindness continues forever. 7Praise him who made the heavenly lights, for his lovingkindness continues forever: 8the sun to rule the day, for his lovingkindness continues forever; 9and the moon and stars at night, for his lovingkindness continues forever. 10Praise the God who smote the firstborn of Egypt, for his lovingkindness to Israel continues forever.

11,12He brought them out with mighty power and upraised fist to strike their enemies, for his lovingkindness to Israel continues forever. 13Praise the Lord who opened the Red Sea to make a path before them, for his lovingkindness continues forever, 14and led them safely through, for his lovingkindness continues forever— 15but drowned Pharaoh's army in the sea, for his lovingkindness to Israel continues forever.

16Praise him who led his people through the wilderness, for his lovingkindness continues forever. 17Praise him who saved his people from the power of mighty kings, for his lovingkindness continues forever, 18and killed famous kings who were their enemies, for his lovingkindness to Israel continues forever: 19Sihon, king of Amorites—for God's lovingkindness to Israel continues forever— 20and Og, king of Bashan—for his lovingkindness to Israel continues forever. 21God gave the land of these kings to Israel as a gift forever, for his lovingkindness to Israel continues forever; 22yes, a permanent gift to his servant Israel, for his lovingkindness continues forever.

23He remembered our utter weakness, for his lovingkindness continues forever. 24And saved us from our foes, for his lovingkindness continues forever.

25He gives food to every living thing, for his lovingkindness continues forever. 26Oh, give thanks to the God of heaven, for his lovingkindness continues forever.

PROVERBS FOR TODAY/ 17:14–15

It is hard to stop a quarrel once it starts, so don't let it begin. The Lord despises those who say that bad is good, and good is bad.

JUNE 19

1 KINGS 20:1—21:29

KING Ben-hadad of Syria now mobilized his army and, with thirty-two allied nations and their hordes of chariots and horses, besieged Samaria, the Israeli capital. 2,3He sent this message into the city to King Ahab of Israel: "Your silver and gold are mine, as are your prettiest wives and the best of your children!"

4"All right, my lord," Ahab replied. "All that I have is yours!"

5,6Soon Ben-hadad's messengers returned again with another message: "You must not only give me your silver, gold, wives, and children, but about this time tomorrow I will send my men to search your palace and the homes of your people, and they will take away whatever they like!"

7Then Ahab summoned his advisors. "Look what this man is doing," he complained to them. "He is stirring up trouble despite the fact that I have already told him he could have my wives and children and silver and gold, just as he demanded."

8"Don't give him anything more," the elders advised.

9So he told the messengers from Ben-hadad, "Tell my lord the king, 'I will give you everything you asked for the first time, but your men may not search the palace and the homes of the people.'" So the messengers returned to Ben-hadad.

10Then the Syrian king sent this message to Ahab: "May the gods do more to me than I am going to do to you if I don't turn Samaria into handfuls of dust!"

11The king of Israel retorted, "Don't count your chickens before they hatch!"

12This reply of Ahab's reached Ben-hadad and the other kings as they were drinking in their tents.

"Prepare to attack!" Ben-hadad commanded his officers.

13Then a prophet came to see King Ahab and gave him this message from the Lord: "Do you see all these enemy forces? I will deliver them all to you today. Then at last you will know that I am the Lord."

14Ahab asked, "How will he do it?"

And the prophet replied, "The Lord says, 'By the troops from the provinces.'"

"Shall we attack first?" Ahab asked.

"Yes," the prophet answered.

15So he mustered the troops from the provinces, 232 of them, then the rest of his army of 7,000 men. 16About noontime, as Ben-hadad and the thirty-two allied kings were still drinking themselves drunk, the first of Ahab's troops marched out of the city.

17As they approached, Ben-hadad's scouts reported to him, "Some troops are coming!"

18"Take them alive," Ben-hadad commanded, "whether they have come for truce or for war."

19By now Ahab's entire army had joined the attack. 20Each one killed a Syrian soldier, and suddenly the entire Syrian army panicked and fled. The Israelis chased them, but King Ben-hadad and a few others escaped on horses. 21However, the great bulk of the horses and chariots were captured, and most of the Syrian army was killed in a great slaughter.

22Then the prophet approached King Ahab and said, "Get ready for another attack by the king of Syria."

23For after their defeat, Ben-hadad's officers said to him, "The Israeli God is a god of the hills; that is why they won. But we can beat them easily on the plains. 24Only this time replace the kings with generals! 25Recruit another army like the one you lost; give us the same number of horses, chariots, and men, and we will fight against them in the plains; there's not a shadow of a doubt that we will beat them." So King Ben-hadad did as they suggested. 26The following year he called up the Syrian army and marched out against Israel again, this time at Aphek. 27Israel then mustered its army, set up supply lines, and moved into the battle; but the Israeli army looked like two little flocks of baby goats in comparison to the vast Syrian forces that filled the countryside!

28Then a prophet went to the king of Israel with this message from the Lord: "Because the Syrians have declared, 'The Lord is a God of the hills and not of the plains,' I will help you defeat this vast army, and you shall know that I am indeed the Lord."

29The two armies camped opposite each other for seven days, and on the seventh day the battle began. And the Israelis killed 100,000 Syrian infantrymen that first day. 30The rest fled behind the walls of Aphek, but the wall fell on them and killed another 27,000. Ben-hadad fled into the city and hid in the inner room of one of the houses.

31"Sir," his officers said to him, "we have heard that the kings of Israel are very merciful. Let us wear sackcloth and put ropes on our heads and go out to King Ahab to see if he will let you live."

32So they went to the king of Israel and begged, "Your servant Ben-hadad pleads, 'Let me live!'"

"Oh, is he still alive?" the king of Israel asked. "He is my brother!"

33The men were quick to grab this straw of hope and hurried to clinch the matter by exclaiming, "Yes, your brother Ben-hadad!"

"Go and get him," the king of Israel told them. And when Ben-hadad arrived, he invited him up into his chariot!

34Ben-hadad told him, "I will restore the cities my father took from your father, and you may establish trading posts in Damascus, as my father did in Samaria."

35Meanwhile, the Lord instructed one of the prophets to say to another man, "Strike me with your sword!" But the man refused.

36Then the prophet told him, "Because you have not obeyed the voice of the Lord, a lion shall kill you as soon as you leave me." And sure enough, as he turned to go a lion attacked and killed him.

37Then the prophet turned to another man and said, "Strike me with your sword." And he did, wounding him.

38The prophet waited for the king beside the road, having placed a bandage over his eyes to disguise himself.

39As the king passed by, the prophet called out to him, "Sir, I was in the battle, and a man brought me a prisoner and said, 'Keep this man; if he gets away, you must die, or else pay me $2,000!' 40But while I was busy doing something else, the prisoner disappeared!"

"Well, it's your own fault," the king replied. "You'll have to pay."

41Then the prophet yanked off the bandage from his eyes, and the king recognized him as one of the prophets. 42Then the prophet told him, "The Lord says, 'Because you have spared the man I said must die, now you must die in his place, and your people shall perish instead of his.' "

43So the king of Israel went home to Samaria angry and sullen.

NABOTH, a man from Jezreel, had a vineyard on the outskirts of the city near King Ahab's palace. 2One day the king talked to him about selling him this land.

"I want it for a garden," the king explained, "because it's so convenient to the palace." He offered cash or, if Naboth preferred, a piece of better land in trade.

3But Naboth replied, "Not on your life! That land has been in my family for generations."

4So Ahab went back to the palace angry and sullen. He refused to eat and went to bed with his face to the wall!

5"What in the world is the matter?" his wife, Jezebel, asked him. "Why aren't you eating? What has made you so upset and angry?"

6"I asked Naboth to sell me his vineyard, or to trade it, and he refused!" Ahab told her.

7"Are you the king of Israel or not?" Jezebel demanded. "Get up and eat and don't worry about it. I'll get you Naboth's vineyard!"

8So she wrote letters in Ahab's name, sealed them with his seal, and addressed them to the civic leaders of Jezreel, where Naboth lived. 9In her letter she commanded: "Call the citizens together for fasting and prayer. Then summon Naboth, 10and find two scoundrels who will accuse him of cursing God and the king. Then take him out and execute him."

11The city fathers followed the queen's instructions. 12They called the meeting and put Naboth on trial. 13Then two men who had no conscience accused him of cursing God and the king; and he was dragged outside the city and stoned to death. 14The city officials then sent word to Jezebel that Naboth was dead.

15When Jezebel heard the news, she said to Ahab, "You know the vineyard Naboth wouldn't sell you? Well, you can have it now! He's dead!"

16So Ahab went down to the vineyard to claim it.

17But the Lord said to Elijah, 18"Go to Samaria to meet King Ahab. He will be at Naboth's vineyard, taking possession of it. 19Give him this message from me: 'Isn't killing Naboth bad enough? Must you rob him, too? Because you have done this, dogs shall lick your blood outside the city just as they licked the blood of Naboth!' "

20"So my enemy has found me!" Ahab exclaimed to Elijah.

"Yes," Elijah answered, "I have come to place God's curse upon you because you have sold yourself to the devil. 21The Lord is going to bring great harm to you and sweep you away; he will not let a single one of your male descendants survive! 22He is going to destroy your family as he did the family of King Jeroboam and the family of King Baasha, for you have made him very angry and have led all of Israel into sin. 23The Lord has also told me that the dogs of Jezreel shall tear apart the body of your wife, Jezebel. 24The members of your family who die in the city shall be eaten by dogs and those who die in the country shall be eaten by vultures."

25No one else was so completely sold out to the devil as Ahab, for his wife Jezebel encouraged him to do every sort of evil. 26He was especially guilty because he worshiped idols just as the Amorites did—the people whom the Lord had chased out of the land to make room for the people of Israel. 27When Ahab heard these prophecies, he tore his clothing, put on rags, fasted, slept in sackcloth, and went about in deep humility.

28Then another message came to Elijah: 29"Do you see how Ahab has humbled himself before me? Because he has done this, I will not do what I promised during his lifetime; it will happen to his sons; I will destroy his descendants."

ACTS 12:24—13:15

GOD'S Good News was spreading rapidly and there were many new believers.
25Barnabas and Paul now visited Jerusalem and, as soon as they had finished their business, returned to Antioch, taking John Mark with them.

AMONG the prophets and teachers of the church at Antioch were Barnabas and Symeon (also called "The Black Man"), Lucius (from Cyrene), Manaen (the foster-brother of King Herod), and Paul. 2One day as these men were worshiping and fasting the Holy Spirit said, "Dedicate Barnabas and Paul for a special job I have for them." 3So after more fasting and prayer, the men laid their hands on them—and sent them on their way.

4Directed by the Holy Spirit they went to Seleucia and then sailed for Cyprus. 5There, in the town of Salamis, they went to the Jewish synagogue and preached. (John Mark went with them as their assistant.)

6,7Afterwards they preached from town to town across the entire island until finally they reached Paphos where they met a Jewish sorcerer, a fake prophet named Bar-Jesus. He had attached himself to the governor, Sergius Paulus, a man of considerable insight and understanding. The governor invited Barnabas and Paul to visit him, for he wanted to hear their message from God. 8But the sorcerer, Elymas (his name in Greek), interfered and urged the governor to pay no attention to what Paul and Barnabas said, trying to keep him from trusting the Lord.

9Then Paul, filled with the Holy Spirit, glared angrily at the sorcerer and said, 10"You son of the devil, full of every sort of trickery and villainy, enemy of all that is good, will you never end your opposition to the Lord? 11And now God has laid his hand of punishment upon you, and you will be stricken awhile with blindness."

Instantly mist and darkness fell upon him, and he began wandering around begging for someone to take his hand and lead him. 12When the governor saw what happened he believed and was astonished at the power of God's message.

13Now Paul and those with him left Paphos by ship for Turkey, landing at the port town of Perga. There John deserted them and returned to Jerusalem. 14But Barnabas and Paul went on to Antioch, a city in the province of Pisidia.

On the Sabbath they went into the synagogue for the services. 15After the usual readings from the Books of Moses and from the Prophets, those in charge of the service sent them this message: "Brothers, if you have any word of instruction for us come and give it!"

PSALM 137:1–9

WEEPING, we sat beside the rivers of Babylon thinking of Jerusalem. 2We have put away our lyres, hanging them upon the branches of the willow trees, 3,4for how can we sing? Yet our captors, our tormentors, demand that we sing for them the happy songs of Zion! 5,6If I forget you, O Jerusalem, let my right hand forget its skill upon the harp. If I fail to love her more than my highest joy, let me never sing again.

⁷O Jehovah, do not forget what these Edomites did on that day when the armies of Babylon captured Jerusalem. "Raze her to the ground!" they yelled.

⁸O Babylon, evil beast, you shall be destroyed. Blessed is the man who destroys you as you have destroyed us. ⁹Blessed is the man who takes your babies and smashes them against the rocks!

PROVERBS FOR TODAY/ 17:16

It is senseless to pay tuition to educate a rebel who has no heart for truth.

JUNE 20

1 KINGS 22:1–53

FOR three years there was no war between Syria and Israel. ²But during the third year, while King Jehoshaphat of Judah was visiting King Ahab of Israel, ³Ahab said to his officials, "Do you realize that the Syrians are still occupying our city of Ramoth-gilead? And we're sitting here without doing a thing about it!"

⁴Then he turned to Jehoshaphat and asked him, "Will you send your army with mine to recover Ramoth-gilead?"

And King Jehoshaphat of Judah replied, "Of course! You and I are brothers; my people are yours to command, and my horses are at your service. ⁵But," he added, "we should ask the Lord first, to be sure of what he wants us to do."

⁶So King Ahab summoned his four hundred heathen prophets and asked them, "Shall I attack Ramoth-gilead, or not?"

And they all said, "Yes, go ahead, for God will help you conquer it."

⁷But Jehoshaphat asked, "Isn't there a prophet of the Lord here? I'd like to ask him, too."

⁸"Well, there's one," King Ahab replied, "but I hate him, for he never prophesies anything good. He always has something gloomy to say. His name is Micaiah, the son of Imlah."

"Oh, come now!" Jehoshaphat replied. "Don't talk like that!"

⁹So King Ahab called to one of his aides, "Go get Micaiah. Hurry!"

¹⁰Meanwhile, all the prophets continued prophesying before the two kings, who were dressed in their royal robes and were sitting on thrones placed on the threshing floor near the city gate. ¹¹One of the prophets, Zedekiah (son of Chenaanah), made some iron horns and declared, "The Lord promises that you will push the Syrians around with these horns until they are destroyed."

¹²And all the others agreed. "Go ahead and attack Ramoth-gilead," they said, "for the Lord will cause you to triumph!"

¹³The messenger who went to get Micaiah told him what the other prophets were saying, and urged him to say the same thing.

¹⁴But Micaiah told him, "This I vow, that I will say only what the Lord tells me to!"

¹⁵When he arrived, the king asked him, "Micaiah, shall we attack Ramoth-gilead, or not?"

"Why, of course! Go right ahead!" Micaiah told him. "You will have a great victory, for the Lord will cause you to conquer!"

¹⁶"How many times must I tell you to speak only what the Lord tells you to?" the king demanded.

¹⁷Then Micaiah told him, "I saw all Israel scattered upon the mountains as sheep without a shepherd. And the Lord

said, 'Their king is dead; send them to their homes.' "

18Turning to Jehoshaphat, Ahab complained, "Didn't I tell you this would happen? He *never* tells me anything good. It's *always* bad."

19Then Micaiah said, "Listen to this further word from the Lord. I saw the Lord sitting on his throne, and the armies of heaven stood around him.

20"Then the Lord said, 'Who will entice Ahab to go and die at Ramoth-gilead?'

"Various suggestions were made, 21until one angel approached the Lord and said, 'I'll do it!'

22" 'How?' the Lord asked.

"And he replied, 'I will go as a lying spirit in the mouths of all his prophets.'

"And the Lord said, 'That will do it; you will succeed. Go ahead.'

23"Don't you see? The Lord has put a lying spirit in the mouths of all these prophets, but the fact of the matter is that the Lord has decreed disaster upon you."

24Then Zedekiah (son of Chenaanah) walked over and slapped Micaiah on the face.

"When did the Spirit of the Lord leave me and speak to you?" he demanded.

25And Micaiah replied, "You will have the answer to your question when you find yourself hiding in an inner room."

26Then King Ahab ordered Micaiah's arrest.

"Take him to Amon, the mayor of the city, and to my son Joash. 27Tell them, 'The king says to put this fellow in jail and feed him with bread and water—and only enough to keep him alive—until I return in peace.' "

28"If you return in peace," Micaiah replied, "it will prove that the Lord has not spoken through me." Then he turned to the people standing nearby and said, "Take note of what I've said."

29So King Ahab of Israel and King Jehoshaphat of Judah led their armies to Ramoth-gilead.

30Ahab said to Jehoshaphat, "You wear your royal robes, but I'll not wear mine!" So Ahab went into the battle disguised in an ordinary soldier's uniform. 31For the king of Syria had commanded his thirty-two chariot captains to fight no one except King Ahab himself. 32,33When they saw King Jehoshaphat in his royal robes, they thought, "That's the man we're after." So they wheeled around to attack him. But when Jehoshaphat shouted out to identify himself, they turned back! 34However, someone shot an arrow at random and it struck King Ahab between the joints of his armor.

"Take me out of the battle, for I am badly wounded," he groaned to his chariot driver.

35The battle became more and more intense as the day wore on, and King Ahab went back in, propped up in his chariot with the blood from his wound running down onto the floorboards. Finally, toward evening, he died. 36,37Just as the sun was going down the cry ran through his troops. "It's all over—return home! The king is dead!"

And his body was taken to Samaria and buried there. 38When his chariot and armor were washed beside the pool of Samaria, where the prostitutes bathed, dogs came and licked the king's blood just as the Lord had said would happen.

39The rest of Ahab's history—including the story of the ivory palace and the cities he built—is written in *The Annals of the Kings of Israel.* 40So Ahab was buried among his ancestors, and Ahaziah his son became the new king of Israel.

41Meanwhile, over in Judah, Jehoshaphat the son of Asa had become king during the fourth year of the reign of King Ahab of Israel. 42Jehoshaphat was thirty-five years old when he ascended the throne, and he reigned in Jerusalem for twenty-five years. His mother was Azubah, the daughter of Shilhi. 43He did as his father Asa had done, obeying the Lord in all but one thing: he did not destroy the shrines on the hills, so the people sacrificed and burned incense there. 44He also made peace with Ahab, the king of Israel. 45The rest of the deeds of Jehoshaphat and his heroic achievements and his wars are described in *The Annals of the Kings of Judah.*

⁴⁶He also closed all the houses of male prostitution that still continued from the days of his father Asa. ⁴⁷(There was no king in Edom at that time, only a deputy.)

⁴⁸King Jehoshaphat built great freighters to sail to Ophir for gold; but they never arrived, for they were wrecked at Eziongeber. ⁴⁹Ahaziah, King Ahab's son and successor, had proposed to Jehoshaphat that his men go too, but Jehoshaphat had refused the offer.

⁵⁰When King Jehoshaphat died he was buried with his ancestors in Jerusalem, the city of his forefather David; and his son Jehoram took the throne. ⁵¹It was during the seventeenth year of the reign of King Jehoshaphat of Judah that Ahaziah, Ahab's son, began to reign over Israel in Samaria; and he reigned two years. ⁵²,⁵³But he was not a good king, for he followed in the footsteps of his father and mother and of Jeroboam, who had led Israel into the sin of worshiping idols. So Ahaziah made the Lord God of Israel very angry.

ACTS 13:16–41

SO Paul stood, waved a greeting to them and began. "Men of Israel," he said, "and all others here who reverence God, [let me begin my remarks with a bit of history].

¹⁷"The God of this nation Israel chose our ancestors and honored them in Egypt by gloriously leading them out of their slavery. ¹⁸And he nursed them through forty years of wandering around in the wilderness. ¹⁹,²⁰Then he destroyed seven nations in Canaan, and gave Israel their land as an inheritance. Judges ruled for about 450 years, and were followed by Samuel the prophet.

²¹"Then the people begged for a king, and God gave them Saul (son of Kish), a man of the tribe of Benjamin, who reigned for forty years. ²²But God removed him and replaced him with David as king, a man about whom God said, 'David (son of Jesse) is a man after my

own heart, for he will obey me.' ²³And it is one of King David's descendants, Jesus, who is God's promised Savior of Israel!

²⁴"But before he came, John the Baptist preached the need for everyone in Israel to turn from sin to God. ²⁵As John was finishing his work he asked, 'Do you think I am the Messiah? No! But he is coming soon—and in comparison with him, I am utterly worthless.'

²⁶"Brothers—you sons of Abraham, and also all of you Gentiles here who reverence God—this salvation is for all of us! ²⁷The Jews in Jerusalem and their leaders fulfilled prophecy by killing Jesus; for they didn't recognize him, or realize that he is the one the prophets had written about, though they heard the prophets' words read every Sabbath. ²⁸They found no just cause to execute him, but asked Pilate to have him killed anyway. ²⁹When they had fulfilled all the prophecies concerning his death, he was taken from the cross and placed in a tomb.

³⁰"But God brought him back to life again! ³¹And he was seen many times during the next few days by the men who had accompanied him to Jerusalem from Galilee—these men have constantly testified to this in public witness.

³²,³³"And now Barnabas and I are here to bring you this Good News—that God's promise to our ancestors has come true in our own time, in that God brought Jesus back to life again. This is what the second Psalm is talking about when it says concerning Jesus, 'Today I have honored you as my Son.'

³⁴"For God had promised to bring him back to life again, no more to die. This is stated in the Scripture that says, 'I will do for you the wonderful thing I promised David.' ³⁵In another Psalm he explained more fully, saying, 'God will not let his Holy One decay.' ³⁶This was not a reference to David, for after David had served his generation according to the will of God, he died and was buried, and his body decayed. ³⁷[No, it was a reference to another]—someone God brought back to life, whose body was

not touched at all by the ravages of death.

³⁸"Brothers! Listen! In this man Jesus, there is forgiveness for your sins! ³⁹Everyone who trusts in him is freed from all guilt and declared righteous— something the Jewish law could never do. ⁴⁰Oh, be careful! Don't let the prophets' words apply to you. For they said, ⁴¹'Look and perish, you despisers [of the truth], for I am doing something in your day—something that you won't believe when you hear it announced.'"

PSALM 138:1–8

LORD, with all my heart I thank you. I will sing your praises before the armies of angels. ²I face your Temple as I worship, giving thanks to you for all your lovingkindness and your faithfulness, for your promises are backed by all the honor of your name. ³When I pray, you answer me, and encourage me by giving me the strength I need.

⁴Every king in all the earth shall give you thanks, O Lord, for all of them shall hear your voice. ⁵Yes, they shall sing about Jehovah's glorious ways, for his glory is very great. ⁶Yet though he is so great, he respects the humble, but proud men must keep their distance. ⁷Though I am surrounded by troubles, you will bring me safely through them. You will clench your fist against my angry enemies! Your power will save me. ⁸The Lord will work out his plans for my life—for your lovingkindness, Lord, continues forever. Don't abandon me— for you made me.

PROVERBS FOR TODAY/ 17:17–18

A true friend is always loyal, and a brother is born to help in time of need. It is poor judgment to countersign another's note, to become responsible for his debts.

JUNE 21

2 KINGS 1:1—2:25

AFTER King Ahab's death the nation of Moab declared its independence and refused to pay tribute to Israel any longer.

²Israel's new king, Ahaziah, had fallen off the upstairs porch of his palace at Samaria and was seriously injured. He sent messengers to the temple of the god Baal-zebub at Ekron to ask whether he would recover.

³But an angel of the Lord told Elijah the prophet, "Go and meet the messengers and ask them, 'Is it true that there is no God in Israel? Is that why you are going to Baal-zebub, the god of Ekron, to ask whether the king will get well? ⁴,⁵Because King Ahaziah has done this, the Lord says that he will never leave the bed he is lying on; he will surely die.'"

When Elijah told the messengers this, they returned immediately to the king.

"Why have you returned so soon?" he asked them.

⁶"A man came up to us," they said, "and told us to go back to the king and tell him, 'The Lord wants to know why you are asking questions of Baal-zebub, the god of Ekron. Is it because there is no God in Israel? Now, since you have done this, you will not leave the bed you are lying on; you will surely die.'"

⁷"Who was this fellow?" the king demanded. "What did he look like?"

⁸"He was a hairy man," they replied, "with a wide leather belt."

"It was Elijah the prophet!" the king

exclaimed. ⁹Then he sent an army captain with fifty soldiers to arrest him. They found him sitting on top of a hill. The captain said to him, "O man of God, the king has commanded you to come along with us."

¹⁰But Elijah replied, "If I am a man of God, let fire come down from heaven and destroy you and your fifty men!" Then lightning struck them and killed them all!

¹¹So the king sent another captain with fifty men to demand, "O man of God, the king says that you must come down right away."

¹²Elijah replied, "If I am a man of God, let fire come down from heaven and destroy you and your fifty men." And again the fire from God burned them up.

¹³Once more the king sent fifty men, but this time the captain fell to his knees before Elijah and pleaded with him, "O man of God, please spare my life and the lives of these, your fifty servants. ¹⁴Have mercy on us! Don't destroy us as you did the others."

¹⁵Then the angel of the Lord said to Elijah, "Don't be afraid. Go with him." So Elijah went to the king.

¹⁶"Why did you send messengers to Baal-zebub, the god of Ekron, to ask about your sickness?" Elijah demanded. "Is it because there is no God in Israel to ask? Because you have done this, you shall not leave this bed; you will surely die."

¹⁷So Ahaziah died as the Lord had predicted through Elijah, and his brother Joram became the new king—for Ahaziah did not have a son to succeed him. This occurred in the second year of the reign of King Jehoram (son of Jehoshaphat) of Judah. ¹⁸The rest of the history of Ahaziah's reign is recorded in *The Annals of the Kings of Israel.*

Now the time came for the Lord to take Elijah to heaven—by means of a whirlwind! Elijah said to Elisha as they left Gilgal, "Stay here, for the Lord has told me to go to Bethel."

But Elisha replied, "I swear to God that I won't leave you!"

So they went on together to Bethel. ³There the young prophets of Bethel Seminary came out to meet them and asked Elisha, "Did you know that the Lord is going to take Elijah away from you today?"

"Quiet!" Elisha snapped. "Of course I know it."

⁴Then Elijah said to Elisha, "Please stay here in Bethel, for the Lord has sent me to Jericho."

But Elisha replied again, "I swear to God that I won't leave you." So they went on together to Jericho.

⁵Then the students at Jericho Seminary came to Elisha and asked him, "Do you know that the Lord is going to take away your master today?"

"Will you please be quiet?" he commanded. "Of course I know it!"

⁶,⁷Then Elijah said to Elisha, "Please stay here, for the Lord has sent me to the Jordan River."

But Elisha replied as before, "I swear to God that I won't leave you."

So they went on together and stood beside the Jordan River as fifty of the young prophets watched from a distance. ⁸Then Elijah folded his cloak together and struck the water with it; and the river divided and they went across on dry ground!

⁹When they arrived on the other side Elijah said to Elisha, "What wish shall I grant you before I am taken away?"

And Elisha replied, "Please grant me twice as much prophetic power as you have had."

¹⁰"You have asked a hard thing," Elijah replied. "If you see me when I am taken from you, then you will get your request. But if not, then you won't."

¹¹As they were walking along, talking, suddenly a chariot of fire, drawn by horses of fire, appeared and drove between them, separating them, and Elijah was carried by a whirlwind into heaven.

¹²Elisha saw it and cried out, "My father! My father! The Chariot of Israel and the charioteers!"

As they disappeared from sight he tore his robe. 13,14Then he picked up Elijah's cloak and returned to the bank of the Jordan River, and struck the water with it.

"Where is the Lord God of Elijah?" he cried out. And the water parted and Elisha went across!

15When the young prophets of Jericho saw what had happened, they exclaimed, "The spirit of Elijah rests upon Elisha!" And they went to meet him and greeted him respectfully.

16"Sir," they said, "just say the word and fifty of our best athletes will search the wilderness for your master; perhaps the Spirit of the Lord has left him on some mountain or in some ravine."

"No," Elisha said, "don't bother."

17But they kept urging until he was embarrassed, and finally said, "All right, go ahead." Then fifty men searched for three days, but didn't find him.

18Elisha was still at Jericho when they returned. "Didn't I tell you not to go?" he growled.

19Now a delegation of the city officials of Jericho visited Elisha. "We have a problem," they told him. "This city is located in beautiful natural surroundings, as you can see; but the water is bad, and causes our women to have miscarriages."

20"Well," he said, "bring me a new bowl filled with salt." So they brought it to him.

21Then he went out to the city well and threw the salt in and declared, "The Lord has healed these waters. They shall no longer cause death or miscarriage."

22And sure enough! The water was purified, just as Elisha had said.

23From Jericho he went to Bethel. As he was walking along the road, a gang of young men from the city began mocking and making fun of him because of his bald head. 24He turned around and cursed them in the name of the Lord; and two female bears came out of the woods and tore forty-two of them. 25Then he went to Mount Carmel and finally returned to Samaria.

AS the people left the synagogue that day, they asked Paul to return and speak to them again the next week. 43And many Jews and godly Gentiles who worshiped at the synagogue followed Paul and Barnabas down the street as the two men urged them to accept the mercies God was offering. 44The following week almost the entire city turned out to hear them preach the Word of God.

45But when the Jewish leaders saw the crowds, they were jealous, and cursed and argued against whatever Paul said.

46Then Paul and Barnabas spoke out boldly and declared, "It was necessary that this Good News from God should be given first to you Jews. But since you have rejected it, and shown yourselves unworthy of eternal life—well, we will offer it to Gentiles. 47For this is as the Lord commanded when he said, 'I have made you a light to the Gentiles, to lead them from the farthest corners of the earth to my salvation.'"

48When the Gentiles heard this, they were very glad and rejoiced in Paul's message; and as many as wanted eternal life, believed. 49So God's message spread all through that region.

50Then the Jewish leaders stirred up both the godly women and the civic leaders of the city and incited a mob against Paul and Barnabas, and ran them out of town. 51But they shook off the dust of their feet against the town and went on to the city of Iconium. 52And their converts were filled with joy and with the Holy Spirit.

AT Iconium, Paul and Barnabas went together to the synagogue and preached with such power that many—both Jews and Gentiles—believed.

2But the Jews who spurned God's message stirred up distrust among the Gentiles against Paul and Barnabas, saying all sorts of evil things about them. 3Nevertheless, they stayed there a long time, preaching boldly, and the Lord proved their message was from him by giving them power to do great miracles. ⁴But the people of the city were divided in their opinion about them. Some agreed with the Jewish leaders, and some backed the apostles.

5,6When Paul and Barnabas learned of a plot to incite a mob of Gentiles, Jews, and Jewish leaders to attack and stone them, they fled for their lives, going to the cities of Lycaonia, Lystra, Derbe, and the surrounding area, ⁷and preaching the Good News there.

PSALM 139:1–24

O Lord, you have examined my heart and know everything about me. ²You know when I sit or stand. When far away you know my every thought. ³You chart the path ahead of me, and tell me where to stop and rest. Every moment, you know where I am. ⁴You know what I am going to say before I even say it. ⁵You both precede and follow me, and place your hand of blessing on my head.

⁶This is too glorious, too wonderful to believe! ⁷I can *never* be lost to your Spirit! I can *never* get away from my God! ⁸If I go up to heaven, you are there; if I go down to the place of the dead, you are there. ⁹If I ride the morning winds to the farthest oceans, ¹⁰even there your hand will guide me, your strength will support me. ¹¹If I try to hide in the darkness, the night becomes light around me. ¹²For even darkness cannot hide from God; to you the night shines as bright as day. Darkness and light are both alike to you.

¹³You made all the delicate, inner parts of my body, and knit them together in my mother's womb. ¹⁴Thank you for making me so wonderfully complex! It is amazing to think about. Your workmanship is marvelous—and how well I know it. ¹⁵You were there while I was being formed in utter seclusion! ¹⁶You saw me before I was born and scheduled each day of my life before I began to breathe. Every day was recorded in your Book!

17,18How precious it is, Lord, to realize that you are thinking about me constantly! I can't even count how many times a day your thoughts turn towards me. And when I waken in the morning, you are still thinking of me!

¹⁹Surely you will slay the wicked, Lord! Away, bloodthirsty men! Begone! ²⁰They blaspheme your name and stand in arrogance against you—how silly can they be? ²¹O Lord, shouldn't I hate those who hate you? Shouldn't I be grieved with them? ²²Yes, I hate them, for your enemies are my enemies too.

²³Search me, O God, and know my heart; test my thoughts. ²⁴Point out anything you find in me that makes you sad, and lead me along the path of everlasting life.

PROVERBS FOR TODAY/ 17:19–21

Sinners love to fight; boasting is looking for trouble. An evil man is suspicious of everyone and tumbles into constant trouble. It's no fun to be a rebel's father.

JUNE 22

2 KINGS 3:1—4:17

A HAB'S son Joram began his reign over Israel during the eighteenth year of the reign of King Jehoshaphat of Judah; and he reigned twelve years. His capital was Samaria. ²He was a very evil man, but not as wicked as his father and mother had been, for he at least tore down the pillar to Baal that his father had made. ³Nevertheless he still clung to the great sin of Jeroboam (the son of Nebat), who had led the people of Israel into the worship of idols.

⁴King Mesha of Moab and his people were sheep ranchers. They paid Israel an annual tribute of 100,000 lambs and the wool of 100,000 rams; ⁵but after Ahab's death, the king of Moab rebelled against Israel. ⁶⁻⁸So King Joram mustered the Israeli army and sent this message to King Jehoshaphat of Judah:

"The king of Moab has rebelled against me. Will you help me fight him?"

"Of course I will," Jehoshaphat replied. "My people and horses are yours to command. What are your battle plans?"

"We'll attack from the wilderness of Edom," Jehoram replied.

⁹So their two armies, now joined also by troops from Edom, moved along a roundabout route through the wilderness for seven days; but there was no water for the men or their pack animals.

¹⁰"Oh, what shall we do?" the king of Israel cried out. "The Lord has brought us here to let the king of Moab defeat us."

¹¹But Jehoshaphat, the king of Judah, asked, "Isn't there a prophet of the Lord with us? If so, we can find out what to do!"

"Elisha is here," one of the king of Israel's officers replied. Then he added, "He was Elijah's assistant."

¹²"Fine," Jehoshaphat said. "He's just the man we want." So the kings of Israel, Judah, and Edom went to consult Elisha.

¹³"I want no part of you," Elisha snarled at King Jehoram of Israel. "Go to the false prophets of your father and mother!"

But King Jehoram replied, "No! For it is the Lord who has called us here to be destroyed by the king of Moab!"

¹⁴"I swear by the Lord God that I wouldn't bother with you except for the presence of King Jehoshaphat of Judah," Elisha replied. ¹⁵"Now bring me someone to play the lute." And as the lute was played, the message of the Lord came to Elisha:

¹⁶"The Lord says to fill this dry valley with trenches to hold the water he will send. ¹⁷You won't see wind nor rain, but this valley will be filled with water, and you will have plenty for yourselves and for your animals! ¹⁸But this is only the beginning, for the Lord will make you victorious over the army of Moab! ¹⁹You will conquer the best of their cities—even those that are fortified—and ruin all the good land with stones."

²⁰And sure enough, the next day at about the time when the morning sacrifice was offered—look! Water! It was flowing from the direction of Edom, and soon there was water everywhere.

²¹Meanwhile, when the people of Moab heard about the three armies marching against them, they mobilized every man who could fight, old and young, and stationed themselves along their frontier. ²²But early the next morning the sun looked red as it shone across the water!

²³"Blood!" they exclaimed. "The three armies have attacked and killed each other! Let's go and collect the loot!"

²⁴But when they arrived at the Israeli camp, the army of Israel rushed out and began killing them; and the army of Moab fled. Then the men of Israel moved forward into the land of Moab, destroying everything as they went. ²⁵They de-

stroyed the cities, threw stones on every good piece of land, stopped up the wells, and felled the fruit trees; finally, only Fort Kir-hareseth was left, but even that finally fell to them.

26When the king of Moab saw that the battle had been lost, he led 700 of his swordsmen in a last desperate attempt to break through to the king of Edom; but he failed. 27Then he took his oldest son, who was to have been the next king, and to the horror of the Israeli army, killed him and sacrificed him as a burnt offering upon the wall. So the army of Israel turned back in disgust to their own land.

ONE day the wife of one of the seminary students came to Elisha to tell him of her husband's death. He was a man who had loved God, she said. But he had owed some money when he died, and now the creditor was demanding it back. If she didn't pay, he said he would take her two sons as his slaves.

2"What shall I do?" Elisha asked. "How much food do you have in the house?"

"Nothing at all, except a jar of olive oil," she replied.

3"Then borrow many pots and pans from your friends and neighbors!" he instructed. 4"Go into your house with your sons and shut the door behind you. Then pour olive oil from your jar into the pots and pans, setting them aside as they are filled!"

5So she did. Her sons brought the pots and pans to her, and she filled one after another! 6Soon every container was full to the brim!

"Bring me another jar," she said to her sons.

"There aren't any more!" they told her. And then the oil stopped flowing!

7When she told the prophet what had happened, he said to her, "Go and sell the oil and pay your debt, and there will be enough money left for you and your sons to live on!"

8One day Elisha went to Shunem. A prominent woman of the city invited him in to eat, and afterwards, whenever he passed that way, he stopped for dinner.

9She said to her husband, "I'm sure this man who stops in from time to time is a holy prophet. 10Let's make a little room for him on the roof; we can put in a bed, a table, a chair, and a lamp, and he will have a place to stay whenever he comes by."

11,12Once when he was resting in the room he said to his servant Gehazi, "Tell the woman I want to speak to her."

When she came, 13he said to Gehazi, "Tell her that we appreciate her kindness to us. Now ask her what we can do for her. Does she want me to put in a good word for her to the king or to the general of the army?"

"No," she replied, "I am perfectly content."

14"What can we do for her?" he asked Gehazi afterwards.

He suggested, "She doesn't have a son, and her husband is an old man."

15,16"Call her back again," Elisha told him.

When she returned, he talked to her as she stood in the doorway. "Next year at about this time you shall have a son!"

"O man of God," she exclaimed, "don't lie to me like that!"

17But it was true; the woman soon conceived and had a baby boy the following year, just as Elisha had predicted.

ACTS 14:8–28

WHILE they were at Lystra, they came upon a man with crippled feet who had been that way from birth, so he had never walked. 9He was listening as Paul preached, and Paul noticed him and realized he had faith to be healed. 10So Paul called to him, "Stand up!" and the man leaped to his feet and started walking!

11When the listening crowd saw what Paul had done, they shouted (in their local dialect, of course), "These men are gods in human bodies!" 12They decided that Barnabas was the Greek god Jupiter, and that Paul, because he was the chief speaker, was Mercury! 13The local priest of the Temple of Jupiter, located on the outskirts of the city, brought them cartloads of flowers and prepared to sacrifice oxen to them at the city gates before the crowds.

14But when Barnabas and Paul saw what was happening they ripped at their clothing in dismay and ran out among the people, shouting, 15"Men! What are you doing? We are merely human beings like yourselves! We have come to bring you the Good News that you are invited to turn from the worship of these foolish things and to pray instead to the living God who made heaven and earth and sea and everything in them. 16In bygone days he permitted the nations to go their own ways, 17but he never left himself without a witness; there were always his reminders—the kind things he did such as sending you rain and good crops and giving you food and gladness."

18But even so, Paul and Barnabas could scarcely restrain the people from sacrificing to them!

19Yet only a few days later, some Jews arrived from Antioch and Iconium and turned the crowds into a murderous mob that stoned Paul and dragged him out of the city, apparently dead. 20But as the believers stood around him, he got up and went back into the city!

The next day he left with Barnabas for Derbe. 21After preaching the Good News there and making many disciples, they returned again to Lystra, Iconium and Antioch, 22where they helped the believers to grow in love for God and each other. They encouraged them to continue in the faith in spite of all the persecution, reminding them that they must enter into the Kingdom of God through many tribulations. 23Paul and Barnabas also appointed elders in every church and prayed for them with fasting, turning them over to the care of the Lord in whom they trusted.

24Then they traveled back through Pisidia to Pamphylia, 25preached again in Perga, and went on to Attalia. 26Finally they returned by ship to Antioch, where their journey had begun, and where they had been committed to God for the work now completed.

27Upon arrival they called together the believers and reported on their trip, telling how God had opened the door of faith to the Gentiles too. 28And they stayed there with the believers at Antioch for a long while.

PSALM 140:1–13

O Lord, deliver me from evil men. Preserve me from the violent, 2who plot and stir up trouble all day long. 3Their words sting like poisonous snakes. 4Keep me out of their power. Preserve me from their violence, for they are plotting against me. 5These proud men have set a trap to catch me, a noose to yank me up and leave me dangling in the air; they wait in ambush with a net to throw over and hold me helpless in its meshes.

6,7,8O Jehovah, my Lord and Savior, my God and my shield—hear me as I pray! Don't let these wicked men succeed; don't let them prosper and be proud. 9Let their plots boomerang! Let them be destroyed by the very evil they have planned for me. 10Let burning coals fall down upon their heads, or throw them into the fire, or into deep pits from which they can't escape.

11Don't let liars prosper here in our land; quickly punish them. 12But the Lord will surely help those they persecute; he will maintain the rights of the poor. 13Surely the godly are thanking you, for they shall live in your presence.

PROVERBS FOR TODAY/ 17:22

A cheerful heart does good like medicine, but a broken spirit makes one sick.

JUNE 23

2 KINGS 4:18—5:27

ONE day when her child was older, he went out to visit his father, who was working with the reapers. 19He complained about a headache, and soon was moaning in pain. His father said to one of the servants, "Carry him home to his mother."

20So he took him home, and his mother held him on her lap; but around noontime he died. 21She carried him up to the bed of the prophet and shut the door; 22then she sent a message to her husband: "Send one of the servants and a donkey so that I can hurry to the prophet and come right back."

23"Why today?" he asked. "This isn't a religious holiday."

But she said, "It's important. I must go."

24So she saddled the donkey and said to the servant, "Hurry! Don't slow down for my comfort unless I tell you to."

25As she approached Mount Carmel, Elisha saw her in the distance and said to Gehazi, "Look, that woman from Shunem is coming. 26Run and meet her and ask her what the trouble is. See if her husband is all right and if the child is well."

"Yes," she told Gehazi, "everything is fine."

27But when she came to Elisha at the mountain she fell to the ground before him and caught hold of his feet. Gehazi began to push her away, but the prophet said, "Let her alone; something is deeply troubling her and the Lord hasn't told me what it is."

28Then she said, "It was you who said I'd have a son. And I begged you not to lie to me!"

29Then he said to Gehazi, "Quick, take my staff! Don't talk to anyone along the way. Hurry! Lay the staff upon the child's face."

30But the boy's mother said, "I swear to God that I won't go home without you." So Elisha returned with her.

31Gehazi went on ahead and laid the staff upon the child's face, but nothing happened. There was no sign of life. He returned to meet Elisha and told him, "The child is still dead."

32When Elisha arrived, the child was indeed dead, lying there upon the prophet's bed. 33He went in and shut the door behind him and prayed to the Lord. 34Then he lay upon the child's body, placing his mouth upon the child's mouth, and his eyes upon the child's eyes, and his hands upon the child's hands. And the child's body began to grow warm again! 35Then the prophet went down and walked back and forth in the house a few times; returning upstairs, he stretched himself again upon the child. This time the little boy sneezed seven times and opened his eyes!

36Then the prophet summoned Gehazi. "Call her!" he said. And when she came in, he said, "Here's your son!"

37She fell to the floor at his feet and then picked up her son and went out.

38Elisha now returned to Gilgal, but there was a famine in the land. One day as he was teaching the young prophets, he said to Gehazi, "Make some stew for supper for these men."

39One of the young men went out into the field to gather vegetables and came back with some wild gourds. He shredded them and put them into a kettle without realizing that they were poisonous. 40But after the men had eaten a bite or two they cried out, "Oh, sir, there's poison in this stew!"

41"Bring me some meal," Elisha said. He threw it into the kettle and said, "Now it's all right! Go ahead and eat!" And then it didn't harm them.

42One day a man from Baal-shalishah brought Elisha a sack of fresh corn and twenty individual loaves of barley bread made from the first grain of his harvest.

Elisha told Gehazi to use it to feed the young prophets.

43"What?" Gehazi exclaimed. "Feed one hundred men with only this?"

But Elisha said, "Go ahead, for the Lord says there will be plenty for all, and some will even be left over!"

44And sure enough, there was, just as the Lord had said!

THE king of Syria had high admiration for Naaman, the commander-in-chief of his army, for he had led his troops to many glorious victories. So he was a great hero, but he was a leper. 2Bands of Syrians had invaded the land of Israel and among their captives was a little girl who had been given to Naaman's wife as a maid.

3One day the little girl said to her mistress, "I wish my master would go to see the prophet in Samaria. He would heal him of his leprosy!"

4Naaman told the king what the little girl had said.

5"Go and visit the prophet," the king told him. "I will send a letter of introduction for you to carry to the king of Israel."

So Naaman started out, taking gifts of $20,000 in silver, $60,000 in gold, and ten suits of clothing. 6The letter to the king of Israel said: "The man bringing this letter is my servant Naaman; I want you to heal him of his leprosy."

7When the king of Israel read it, he tore his clothes and said, "This man sends me a leper to heal! Am I God, that I can kill and give life? He is only trying to get an excuse to invade us again."

8But when Elisha the prophet heard about the king of Israel's plight, he sent this message to him: "Why are you so upset? Send Naaman to me, and he will learn that there is a true prophet of God here in Israel."

9So Naaman arrived with his horses and chariots and stood at the door of Elisha's home. 10Elisha sent a messenger out to tell him to go and wash in the Jordan River seven times and he would be healed of every trace of his leprosy! 11But Naaman was angry and stalked away.

"Look," he said, "I thought at least he would come out and talk to me! I expected him to wave his hand over the leprosy and call upon the name of the Lord his God, and heal me! 12Aren't the Abana River and Pharpar River of Damascus better than all the rivers of Israel put together? If it's rivers I need, I'll wash at home and get rid of my leprosy." So he went away in a rage.

13But his officers tried to reason with him and said, "If the prophet had told you to do some great thing, wouldn't you have done it? So you should certainly obey him when he says simply to go and wash and be cured!"

14So Naaman went down to the Jordan River and dipped himself seven times, as the prophet had told him to. And his flesh became as healthy as a little child's, and he was healed! 15Then he and his entire party went back to find the prophet; they stood humbly before him and Naaman said, "I know at last that there is no God in all the world except in Israel; now please accept my gifts."

16But Elisha replied, "I swear by Jehovah my God that I will not accept them."

Naaman urged him to take them, but he absolutely refused. 17"Well," Naaman said, "all right. But please give me two muleloads of earth to take back with me, for from now on I will never again offer any burnt offerings or sacrifices to any other God except the Lord. 18However, may the Lord pardon me this one thing—when my master the king goes into the temple of the god Rimmon to worship there and leans on my arm, may the Lord pardon me when I bow too."

19"All right," Elisha said. So Naaman started home again.

20But Gehazi, Elisha's servant, said to himself, "My master shouldn't have let this fellow get away without taking his gifts. I will chase after him and get something from him."

21So Gehazi caught up with him. When Naaman saw him coming, he jumped down from his chariot and ran to meet him.

"Is everything all right?" he asked.

22"Yes," he said, "but my master has sent me to tell you that two young prophets from the hills of Ephraim have just arrived, and he would like $2,000 in silver and two suits to give to them."

23"Take $4,000," Naaman insisted. He gave him two expensive robes, tied up the money in two bags, and gave them to two of his servants to carry back with Gehazi. 24But when they arrived at the hill where Elisha lived, Gehazi took the bags from the servants and sent the men back. Then he hid the money in his house.

25When he went in to his master, Elisha asked him, "Where have you been, Gehazi?"

"I haven't been anywhere," he replied.

26But Elisha asked him, "Don't you realize that I was there in thought when Naaman stepped down from his chariot to meet you? Is this the time to receive money and clothing and olive farms and vineyards and sheep and oxen and servants? 27Because you have done this, Naaman's leprosy shall be upon you and upon your children and your children's children forever."

And Gehazi walked from the room a leper, his skin as white as snow.

ACTS 15:1–31

WHILE Paul and Barnabas were at Antioch, some men from Judea arrived and began to teach the believers that unless they adhered to the ancient Jewish custom of circumcision, they could not be saved. 2Paul and Barnabas argued and discussed this with them at length, and finally the believers sent them to Jerusalem, accompanied by some local men, to talk to the apostles and elders there about this question. 3After the entire congregation had escorted them out of the city the delegates went on to Jerusalem, stopping along the way in the cities of Phoenicia and Samaria to visit the believers, telling them—much to everyone's joy—that the Gentiles, too, were being converted.

4Arriving in Jerusalem, they met with the church leaders—all the apostles and elders were present—and Paul and Barnabas reported on what God had been doing through their ministry. 5But then some of the men who had been Pharisees before their conversion stood to their feet and declared that all Gentile converts must be circumcised and required to follow all the Jewish customs and ceremonies.

6So the apostles and church elders set a further meeting to decide this question.

7At the meeting, after long discussion, Peter stood and addressed them as follows: "Brothers, you all know that God chose me from among you long ago to preach the Good News to the Gentiles, so that they also could believe. 8God, who knows men's hearts, confirmed the fact that he accepts Gentiles by giving them the Holy Spirit, just as he gave him to us. 9He made no distinction between them and us, for he cleansed their lives through faith, just as he did ours. 10And now are you going to correct God by burdening the Gentiles with a yoke that neither we nor our fathers were able to bear? 11Don't you believe that all are saved the same way, by the free gift of the Lord Jesus?"

12There was no further discussion, and everyone now listened as Barnabas and Paul told about the miracles God had done through them among the Gentiles.

13When they had finished, James took the floor. "Brothers," he said, "listen to me. 14Peter has told you about the time God first visited the Gentiles to take from them a people to bring honor to his name. 15And this fact of Gentile conversion agrees with what the prophets predicted. For instance, listen to this passage from the prophet Amos:

16'Afterwards' [says the Lord], 'I will return and renew the broken contract with David, 17so that Gentiles, too, will find the Lord—all those marked with my name.'

18That is what the Lord says, who reveals his plans made from the beginning.

19"And so my judgment is that we should not insist that the Gentiles who turn to God must obey our Jewish laws, 20except that we should write to them to refrain from eating meat sacrificed to idols, from all fornication, and also from eating unbled meat of strangled animals. 21For these things have been preached against in Jewish synagogues in every city on every Sabbath for many generations."

22Then the apostles and elders and the whole congregation voted to send delegates to Antioch with Paul and Barnabas, to report on this decision. The men chosen were two of the church leaders— Judas (also called Barsabbas) and Silas.

23This is the letter they took along with them:

"*From:* The apostles, elders and brothers at Jerusalem.

"*To:* The Gentile brothers in Antioch, Syria and Cilicia. Greetings!

24"We understand that some believers from here have upset you and questioned your salvation, but they had no such instructions from us. 25So it seemed wise to us, having unanimously agreed on our decision, to send to you these two official representatives, along with our beloved Barnabas and Paul. 26These men—Judas and Silas, who have risked their lives for the sake of our Lord Jesus Christ— will confirm orally what we have decided concerning your question.

27,28,29"For it seemed good to the Holy Spirit and to us to lay no greater burden of Jewish laws on you than to abstain from eating food offered to idols and from unbled meat of strangled animals, and, of course, from fornication. If you do this, it is enough. Farewell."

30The four messengers went at once to Antioch, where they called a general meeting of the Christians and gave them the letter. 31And there was great joy throughout the church that day as they read it.

PSALM 141:1–10

QUICK, Lord, answer me—for I have prayed. Listen when I cry to you for help! 2Regard my prayer as my evening sacrifice and as incense wafting up to you.

3Help me, Lord, to keep my mouth shut and my lips sealed. 4Take away my lust for evil things; don't let me want to be with sinners, doing what they do, sharing their delicacies. 5Let the godly smite me! It will be a kindness! If they reprove me, it is medicine! Don't let me refuse it. But I am in constant prayer against the wicked and their deeds. 6,7When their leaders are condemned, and their bones are strewn across the ground, then these men will finally listen to me and know that I am trying to help them.

8I look to you for help, O Lord God. You are my refuge. Don't let them slay me. 9Keep me out of their traps. 10Let them fall into their own snares, while I escape.

PROVERBS FOR TODAY/ 17:23

It is wrong to accept a bribe to twist justice.

JUNE 24

2 KINGS 6:1—7:20

ONE day the seminary students came to Elisha and told him, "As you can see, our dormitory is too small. Tell us, as our president, whether we can build a new one down beside the Jordan River, where there are plenty of logs."

"All right," he told them, "go ahead."

3"Please, sir, come with us," someone suggested.

"I will," he said.

4When they arrived at the Jordan, they began cutting down trees; 5but as one of them was chopping, his axhead fell into the river.

"Oh, sir," he cried, "it was borrowed!"

6"Where did it fall?" the prophet asked. The youth showed him the place, and Elisha cut a stick and threw it into the water; and the axhead rose to the surface and floated! 7"Grab it," Elisha said to him; and he did.

8Once when the king of Syria was at war with Israel, he said to his officers, "We will mobilize our forces at ____" (naming the place).

9Immediately Elisha warned the king of Israel, "Don't go near ____" (naming the same place) "for the Syrians are planning to mobilize their troops there!"

10The king sent a scout to see if Elisha was right, and sure enough, he had saved him from disaster. This happened several times.

11The king of Syria was puzzled. He called together his officers and demanded, "Which of you is the traitor? Who has been informing the king of Israel about my plans?"

12"It's not us, sir," one of the officers replied. "Elisha, the prophet, tells the king of Israel even the words you speak in the privacy of your bedroom!"

13"Go and find out where he is, and we'll send troops to seize him," the king exclaimed.

And the report came back, "Elisha is at Dothan."

14So one night the king of Syria sent a great army with many chariots and horses to surround the city. 15When the prophet's servant got up early the next morning and went outside, there were troops, horses, and chariots everywhere.

"Alas, my master, what shall we do now?" he cried out to Elisha.

16"Don't be afraid!" Elisha told him. "For our army is bigger than theirs!"

17Then Elisha prayed, "Lord, open his eyes and let him see!" And the Lord opened the young man's eyes so that he could see horses of fire and chariots of fire everywhere upon the mountain!

18As the Syrian army advanced upon them, Elisha prayed, "Lord, please make them blind." And he did.

19Then Elisha went out and told them, "You've come the wrong way! This isn't the right city! Follow me and I will take you to the man you're looking for." And he led them to Samaria!

20As soon as they arrived Elisha prayed, "Lord, now open their eyes and let them see." And the Lord did, and they discovered that they were in Samaria, the capital city of Israel!

21When the king of Israel saw them, he shouted to Elisha, "Oh, sir, shall I kill them? Shall I kill them?"

22"Of course not!" Elisha told him. "Do we kill prisoners of war? Give them food and drink and send them home again."

23So the king made a great feast for them, and then sent them home to their king. And after that the Syrian raiders stayed away from the land of Israel.

24Later on, however, King Ben-hadad of Syria mustered his entire army and besieged Samaria. 25As a result there was a great famine in the city, and after a long while even a donkey's head sold for fifty dollars and a pint of dove's dung brought three dollars!

26-30One day as the king of Israel was walking along the wall of the city, a woman called to him, "Help, my lord the king!"

"If the Lord doesn't help you, what can I do?" he retorted. "I have neither food nor wine to give you. However, what's the matter?"

She replied, "This woman proposed that we eat my son one day and her son the next. So we boiled my son and ate him, but the next day when I said, 'Kill your son so we can eat him,' she hid him."

When the king heard this he tore his clothes. (The people watching noticed through the rip in them that he was wearing an inner robe made of sackcloth next to his flesh.)

31"May God kill me if I don't execute Elisha this very day," the king vowed.

32Elisha was sitting in his house at a meeting with the elders of Israel when the king sent a messenger to summon him. But before the messenger arrived Elisha said to the elders, "This murderer has sent a man to kill me. When he arrives, shut the door and keep him out, for his master will soon follow him."

33While Elisha was still saying this, the messenger arrived [followed by the king].

"The Lord has caused this mess," the king stormed. "Why should I expect any help from him?"

ELISHA replied, "The Lord says that by this time tomorrow two gallons of flour or four gallons of barley grain will be sold in the markets of Samaria for a dollar!"

2The officer assisting the king said, "That couldn't happen if the Lord made windows in the sky!"

But Elisha replied, "You will see it happen, but you won't be able to buy any of it!"

3Now there were four lepers sitting outside the city gates.

"Why sit here until we die?" they asked each other. 4"We will starve if we stay here and we will starve if we go back into the city; so we might as well go out and surrender to the Syrian army. If they let us live, so much the better; but if they kill us, we would have died anyway."

5So that evening they went out to the camp of the Syrians, but there was no one there! 6(For the Lord had made the whole Syrian army hear the clatter of speeding chariots and a loud galloping of horses and the sounds of a great army approaching. "The king of Israel has hired the Hittites and Egyptians to attack us," they cried out. 7So they panicked and fled into the night, abandoning their tents, horses, donkeys, and everything else.)

8When the lepers arrived at the edge of the camp they went into one tent after another, eating, drinking wine, and carrying out silver and gold and clothing and hiding it. 9Finally they said to each other, "This isn't right. This is wonderful news, and we aren't sharing it with anyone! Even if we wait until morning, some terrible calamity will certainly fall upon us; come on, let's go back and tell the people at the palace."

10So they went back to the city and told the watchmen what had happened— they had gone out to the Syrian camp and no one was there! The horses and donkeys were tethered and the tents were all in order, but there was not a soul around. 11Then the watchmen shouted the news to those in the palace.

12The king got out of bed and told his officers, "I know what has happened. The Syrians know we are starving, so they have left their camp and have hidden in the fields, thinking that we will be lured out of the city. Then they will attack us and make slaves of us and get in."

13One of his officers replied, "We'd better send out scouts to see. Let them take five of the remaining horses—if something happens to the animals it won't be any greater loss than if they stay here and die with the rest of us!"

14Four chariot-horses were found and the king sent out two charioteers to see where the Syrians had gone. 15They followed a trail of clothing and equipment all the way to the Jordan River—thrown away by the Syrians in their haste. The scouts returned and told the king, 16and the people of Samaria rushed out and plundered the camp of the Syrians. So it was true that two gallons of flour and four gallons of barley were sold that day for one dollar, just as the Lord had said!

17The king appointed his special assistant to control the traffic at the gate, but he was knocked down and trampled and killed as the people rushed out. This is what Elisha had predicted on the previous day when the king had come to arrest him, 18and the prophet had told the king that flour and barley would sell for so little on the following day.

19The king's officer had replied, "That couldn't happen even if the Lord opened the windows of heaven!"

And the prophet had said, "You will see it happen, but you won't be able to buy any of it!"

20And he couldn't, for the people trampled him to death at the gate!

ACTS 15:32—16:15

THEN Judas and Silas, both being gifted speakers, preached long sermons to the believers, strengthening their faith. 33They stayed several days, and then Judas and Silas returned to Jerusalem taking greetings and appreciation to those who had sent them. 34,35Paul and Barnabas stayed on at Antioch to assist several others who were preaching and teaching there.

36Several days later Paul suggested to Barnabas that they return again to Turkey, and visit each city where they had preached before, to see how the new converts were getting along. 37Barnabas agreed, and wanted to take along John Mark. 38But Paul didn't like that idea at all, since John had deserted them in Pamphylia. 39Their disagreement over this was so sharp that they separated. Barnabas took Mark with him and sailed for Cyprus, 40,41while Paul chose Silas and,

with the blessing of the believers, left for Syria and Cilicia, to encourage the churches there.

PAUL and Silas went first to Derbe and then on to Lystra where they met Timothy, a believer whose mother was a Christian Jewess but his father a Greek. 2Timothy was well thought of by the brothers in Lystra and Iconium, 3so Paul asked him to join them on their journey. In deference to the Jews of the area, he circumcised Timothy before they left, for everyone knew that his father was a Greek [and hadn't permitted this before]. 4Then they went from city to city, making known the decision concerning the Gentiles, as decided by the apostles and elders in Jerusalem. 5So the church grew daily in faith and numbers.

6Next they traveled through Phrygia and Galatia because the Holy Spirit had told them not to go into the Turkish province of Asia Minor at that time. 7Then going along the borders of Mysia they headed north for the province of Bithynia, but again the Spirit of Jesus said no. 8So instead they went on through Mysia province to the city of Troas.

9That night Paul had a vision. In his dream he saw a man over in Macedonia, Greece, pleading with him, "Come over here and help us." 10Well, that settled it. We would go to Macedonia, for we could only conclude that God was sending us to preach the Good News there.

11We went aboard a boat at Troas, and sailed straight across to Samothrace, and the next day on to Neapolis, 12and finally reached Philippi, a Roman colony just inside the Macedonian border, and stayed there several days.

13On the Sabbath, we went a little way outside the city to a river bank where we understood some people met for prayer; and we taught the Scriptures to some women who came. 14One of them was Lydia, a saleswoman from Thyatira, a merchant of purple cloth. She was already a worshiper of God and, as she listened to us, the Lord opened her heart and she accepted all that Paul was saying.

¹⁵She was baptized along with all her household and asked us to be her guests. "If you agree that I am faithful to the Lord," she said, "come and stay at my home." And she urged us until we did.

PSALM 142:1–7

How I plead with God, how I implore his mercy, pouring out my troubles before him. ³For I am overwhelmed and desperate, and you alone know which way I ought to turn to miss the traps my enemies have set for me. ⁴(There's one—just over there to the right!) No one gives me a passing thought. No one will help me; no one cares a bit what happens to me. ⁵Then I prayed to Jehovah. "Lord," I pled, "you are my only place of refuge. Only you can keep me safe.

⁶"Hear my cry, for I am very low. Rescue me from my persecutors, for they are too strong for me. ⁷Bring me out of prison, so that I can thank you. The godly will rejoice with me for all your help."

PROVERBS FOR TODAY/ 17:24–25

Wisdom is the main pursuit of sensible men, but a fool's goals are at the ends of the earth! A rebellious son is a grief to his father and a bitter blow to his mother.

JUNE 25

2 KINGS 8:1—9:15a

ELISHA had told the woman whose son he had brought back to life, "Take your family and move to some other country, for the Lord has called down a famine on Israel that will last for seven years."

²So the woman took her family and lived in the land of the Philistines for seven years. ³After the famine ended, she returned to the land of Israel and went to see the king about getting back her house and land. ⁴Just as she came in, the king was talking with Gehazi, Elisha's servant, and saying, "Tell me some stories of the great things Elisha has done." ⁵And Gehazi was telling the king about the time when Elisha brought a little boy back to life. At that very moment, the mother of the boy walked in!

"Oh, sir!" Gehazi exclaimed. "Here is the woman now, and this is her son— the very one Elisha brought back to life!"

⁶"Is this true?" the king asked her. And she told him that it was. So he directed one of his officials to see to it that everything she had owned was restored to her, plus the value of any crops that had been harvested during her absence.

⁷Afterwards Elisha went to Damascus (the capital of Syria), where King Benhadad lay sick. Someone told the king that the prophet had come.

⁸,⁹When the king heard the news, he said to Hazael, "Take a present to the man of God and tell him to ask the Lord whether I will get well again."

So Hazael took forty camel-loads of the best produce of the land as presents for Elisha and said to him, "Your son Ben-hadad, the king of Syria, has sent me to ask you whether he will recover."

¹⁰And Elisha replied, "Tell him, 'Yes.' But the Lord has shown me that he will surely die!"

¹¹Elisha stared at Hazael until he became embarrassed, and then Elisha started crying.

[12]"What's the matter, sir?" Hazael asked him.

Elisha replied, "I know the terrible things you will do to the people of Israel: you will burn their forts, kill the young men, dash their babies against the rocks, and rip open the bellies of the pregnant women!"

[13]"Am I a dog?" Hazael asked him. "I would *never* do that sort of thing."

But Elisha replied, "The Lord has shown me that you are going to be the king of Syria."

[14]When Hazael went back, the king asked him, "What did he tell you?"

And Hazael replied, "He told me that you would recover."

[15]But the next day Hazael took a blanket and dipped it in water and held it over the king's face until he smothered to death. And Hazael became king instead.

[16]King Jehoram, the son of King Jehoshaphat of Judah, began his reign during the fifth year of the reign of King Joram of Israel, the son of Ahab. [17]Jehoram was thirty-two years old when he became king, and he reigned in Jerusalem for eight years. [18]But he was as wicked as Ahab and the other kings of Israel; he even married one of Ahab's daughters. [19]Nevertheless, because God had promised his servant David that he would watch over and guide his descendants, he did not destroy Judah.

[20]During Jehoram's reign, the people in Edom revolted from Judah and appointed their own king. [21]King Jehoram tried unsuccessfully to crush the rebellion: he crossed the Jordan River and attacked the city of Zair, but was quickly surrounded by the army of Edom. Under cover of night he broke through their ranks, but his army deserted him and fled. [22]So Edom has maintained its independence to this day. Libnah also rebelled at that time.

[23]The rest of the history of King Jehoram is written in *The Annals of the Kings of Judah*. [24,25]He died and was buried in the royal cemetery in the City of David—the old section of Jerusalem.

Then his son Ahaziah became the new king during the twelfth year of the reign of King Joram of Israel, the son of Ahab. [26]Ahaziah was twenty-two years old when he began to reign but he reigned only one year, in Jerusalem. His mother was Athaliah, the granddaughter of King Omri of Israel. [27]He was an evil king, just as all of King Ahab's descendants were—for he was related to Ahab by marriage.

[28]He joined King Joram of Israel (son of Ahab) in his war against Hazael, the king of Syria, at Ramoth-gilead. King Joram was wounded in the battle, [29]so he went to Jezreel to rest and recover from his wounds. While he was there, King Ahaziah of Judah (son of Jehoram) came to visit him.

MEANWHILE Elisha had summoned one of the young prophets.

"Get ready to go to Ramoth-gilead," he told him. "Take this vial of oil with you, [2]and find Jehu (the son of Jehoshaphat, the son of Nimshi). Call him into a private room away from his friends, [3]and pour the oil over his head. Tell him that the Lord has anointed him to be the king of Israel; then run for your life!"

[4]So the young prophet did as he was told. When he arrived in Ramoth-gilead, [5]he found Jehu sitting around with the other army officers.

"I have a message for you, sir," he said.

"For which one of us?" Jehu asked.

"For you," he replied.

[6]So Jehu left the others and went into the house, and the young man poured the oil over his head and said, "The Lord God of Israel says, 'I anoint you king of the Lord's people, Israel. [7]You are to destroy the family of Ahab; you will avenge the murder of my prophets and of all my other people who were killed by Jezebel. [8]The entire family of Ahab must be wiped out—every male, no matter who. [9]I will destroy the family of Ahab as I destroyed the families of Jeroboam (son of Nebat) and of Baasha (son of Ahijah). [10]Dogs shall eat Ahab's wife Jez-

ebel at Jezreel, and no one will bury her.'"

Then he opened the door and ran.

11Jehu went back to his friends and one of them asked him, "What did that crazy fellow want? Is everything all right?"

"You know very well who he was and what he wanted," Jehu replied.

12"No, we don't," they said. "Tell us."

So he told them what the man had said and that he had been anointed king of Israel!

13They quickly carpeted the bare steps with their coats and blew a trumpet, shouting, "Jehu is king!"

14That is how Jehu (son of Jehoshaphat, son of Nimshi) rebelled against King Joram. (King Joram had been with the army at Ramoth-gilead, defending Israel against the forces of King Hazael of Syria. 15But he had returned to Jezreel to recover from his wounds.)

ACTS 16:16–40

ONE day as we were going down to the place of prayer beside the river, we met a demon-possessed slave girl who was a fortune-teller, and earned much money for her masters. 17She followed along behind us shouting, "These men are servants of God and they have come to tell you how to have your sins forgiven."

18This went on day after day until Paul, in great distress, turned and spoke to the demon within her. "I command you in the name of Jesus Christ to come out of her," he said. And instantly it left her.

19Her masters' hopes of wealth were now shattered; they grabbed Paul and Silas and dragged them before the judges at the marketplace.

20,21"These Jews are corrupting our city," they shouted. "They are teaching the people to do things that are against the Roman laws."

22A mob was quickly formed against Paul and Silas, and the judges ordered them stripped and beaten with wooden whips. 23Again and again the rods slashed down across their bared backs; and afterwards they were thrown into prison. The jailer was threatened with death if they escaped, 24so he took no chances, but put them into the inner dungeon and clamped their feet into the stocks.

25Around midnight, as Paul and Silas were praying and singing hymns to the Lord—and the other prisoners were listening— 26suddenly there was a great earthquake; the prison was shaken to its foundations, all the doors flew open—and the chains of every prisoner fell off! 27The jailer wakened to see the prison doors wide open, and assuming the prisoners had escaped, he drew his sword to kill himself.

28But Paul yelled to him, "Don't do it! We are all here!"

29Trembling with fear, the jailer called for lights and ran to the dungeon and fell down before Paul and Silas. 30He brought them out and begged them, "Sirs, what must I do to be saved?"

31They replied, "Believe on the Lord Jesus and you will be saved, and your entire household."

32Then they told him and all his household the Good News from the Lord. 33That same hour he washed their stripes and he and all his family were baptized. 34Then he brought them up into his house and set a meal before them. How he and his household rejoiced because all were now believers! 35The next morning the judges sent police officers over to tell the jailer, "Let those men go!" 36So the jailer told Paul they were free to leave.

37But Paul replied, "Oh, no they don't! They have publicly beaten us without trial and jailed us—and we are Roman citizens! So now they want us to leave secretly? Never! Let them come themselves and release us!"

38The police officers reported to the judges, who feared for their lives when they heard Paul and Silas were Roman citizens. 39So they came to the jail and begged them to go, and brought them out and pled with them to leave the city.

⁴⁰Paul and Silas then returned to the home of Lydia where they met with the believers and preached to them once more before leaving town.

PSALM 143:1–12

HEAR my prayer, O Lord; answer my plea, because you are faithful to your promises. ²Don't bring me to trial! For as compared with you, no one is perfect.

³My enemies chased and caught me. They have knocked me to the ground. They force me to live in the darkness like those in the grave. ⁴I am losing all hope; I am paralyzed with fear.

⁵I remember the glorious miracles you did in days of long ago. ⁶I reach out for you. I thirst for you as parched land thirsts for rain. ⁷Come quickly, Lord, and answer me, for my depression deepens; don't turn away from me or I shall die. ⁸Let me see your kindness to me in the morning, for I am trusting you. Show me where to walk, for my prayer is sincere. ⁹Save me from my enemies. O Lord, I run to you to hide me. ¹⁰Help me to do your will, for you are my God. Lead me in good paths, for your Spirit is good.

¹¹Lord, saving me will bring glory to your name. Bring me out of all this trouble because you are true to your promises. ¹²And because you are loving and kind to me, cut off all my enemies and destroy those who are trying to harm me; for I am your servant.

PROVERBS FOR TODAY/ 17:26

How short-sighted to fine the godly for being good! And to punish nobles for being honest!

JUNE 26

2 KINGS 9:15b—10:31

SINCE you want me to be king," Jehu told the men who were with him, "don't let anyone escape to Jezreel to report what we have done."

¹⁶Then Jehu jumped into a chariot and rode to Jezreel himself to find King Joram, who was lying there wounded. (King Ahaziah of Judah was there too, for he had gone to visit him.) ¹⁷The watchman on the Tower of Jezreel saw Jehu and his company approaching and shouted, "Someone is coming."

"Send out a rider and find out if he is friend or foe," King Joram shouted back. ¹⁸So a soldier rode out to meet Jehu.

"The king wants to know whether you are friend or foe," he demanded. "Do you come in peace?"

Jehu replied, "What do you know about peace? Get behind me!"

The watchman called out to the king that the messenger had met them but was not returning. ¹⁹So the king sent out a second rider. He rode up to them and demanded in the name of the king to know whether their intentions were friendly or not.

Jehu answered, "What do you know about friendliness? Get behind me!"

²⁰"He isn't returning either!" the watchman exclaimed. "It must be Jehu, for he is driving so furiously."

²¹"Quick! Get my chariot ready!" King Joram commanded.

Then he and King Ahaziah of Judah

rode out to meet Jehu. They met him at the field of Naboth, 22and King Joram demanded, "Do you come as a friend, Jehu?"

Jehu replied, "How can there be friendship as long as the evils of your mother Jezebel are all around us?"

23Then King Joram reined the chariot-horses around and fled, shouting to King Ahaziah, "There is treachery, Ahaziah! Treason!"

24Then Jehu drew his bow with his full strength and shot Joram between the shoulders; and the arrow pierced his heart, and he sank down dead in his chariot.

25Jehu said to Bidkar, his assistant, "Throw him into the field of Naboth, for once when you and I were riding along behind his father Ahab, the Lord revealed this prophecy to me: 26'I will repay him here on Naboth's property for the murder of Naboth and his sons.' So throw him out on Naboth's field, just as the Lord said."

27Meanwhile, King Ahaziah of Judah had fled along the road to Beth-haggan. Jehu rode after him, shouting, "Shoot him, too."

So they shot him in his chariot at the place where the road climbs to Gur, near Ibleam. He was able to go on as far as Megiddo, but died there. 28His officials took him by chariot to Jerusalem where they buried him in the royal cemetery. 29(Ahaziah's reign over Judah had begun in the twelfth year of the reign of King Joram of Israel.)

30When Jezebel heard that Jehu had come to Jezreel, she painted her eyelids and fixed her hair and sat at a window. 31When Jehu entered the gate of the palace, she shouted at him, "How are you today, you murderer! You son of a Zimri who murdered his master!"

32He looked up and saw her at the window and shouted, "Who is on my side?" And two or three eunuchs looked out at him.

33"Throw her down!" he yelled.

So they threw her out the window, and her blood spattered against the wall and on the horses; and she was trampled by the horses' hoofs.

34Then Jehu went into the palace for lunch. Afterwards he said, "Someone go and bury this cursed woman, for she is the daughter of a king."

35But when they went out to bury her, they found only her skull, her feet, and her hands.

36When they returned and told him, he remarked, "That is just what the Lord said would happen. He told Elijah the prophet that dogs would eat her flesh 37and that her body would be scattered like manure upon the field, so that no one could tell whose it was."

THEN Jehu wrote a letter to the city council of Samaria and to the guardians of Ahab's seventy sons—all of whom were living there.

2,3"Upon receipt of this letter, select the best one of Ahab's sons to be your king, and prepare to fight for his throne. For you have chariots and horses and a fortified city and an armory."

4But they were too frightened to do it. "Two kings couldn't stand against this man! What can we do?" they said.

5So the manager of palace affairs and the city manager, together with the city council and the guardians of Ahab's sons, sent him this message:

"Jehu, we are your servants and will do anything you tell us to. We have decided that you should be our king instead of one of Ahab's sons."

6Jehu responded with this message: "If you are on my side and are going to obey me, bring the heads of your master's sons to me at Jezreel at about this time tomorrow."

(These seventy sons of King Ahab were living in the homes of the chief men of the city, where they had been raised since childhood.) 7When the letter arrived, all seventy of them were murdered, and their heads were packed into baskets and presented to Jehu at Jezreel. 8When a messenger told Jehu that the heads of the king's sons had arrived, he said to pile them in two heaps at the entrance of the city gate, and to leave them there until the next morning.

9,10In the morning he went out and spoke to the crowd that had gathered around them. "You aren't to blame," he told them. "I conspired against my master and killed him, but I didn't kill his sons! The Lord has done that, for everything he says comes true. He declared through his servant Elijah that this would happen to Ahab's descendants."

11Jehu then killed all the rest of the members of the family of Ahab who were in Jezreel, as well as all of his important officials, personal friends, and private chaplains. Finally, no one was left who had been close to him in any way. 12Then he set out for Samaria, and stayed overnight at a shepherd's inn along the way. 13While he was there he met the brothers of King Ahaziah of Judah.

"Who are you?" he asked them.

And they replied, "We are brothers of King Ahaziah. We are going to Samaria to visit the sons of King Ahab and of the Queen Mother, Jezebel."

14"Grab them!" Jehu shouted to his men. And he took them out to the cistern and killed all forty-two of them.

15As he left the inn, he met Jehonadab, the son of Rechab, who was coming to meet him. After they had greeted each other, Jehu said to him, "Are you as loyal to me as I am to you?"

"Yes," Jehonadab replied.

"Then give me your hand," Jehu said, and he helped him into the royal chariot.

16"Now come along with me," Jehu said, "and see how much I have done for the Lord." So Jehonadab rode along with him. 17When he arrived in Samaria he butchered all of Ahab's friends and relatives, just as Elijah, speaking for the Lord, had predicted.

Then Jehu called a meeting of all the people of the city and said to them, "Ahab hardly worshiped Baal at all in comparison to the way I am going to! 18,19Summon all the prophets and priests of Baal, and call together all his worshipers. See to it that every one of them comes, for we worshipers of Baal are going to have a great celebration to praise him. Any of Baal's worshipers who don't come will be put to death."

But Jehu's plan was to exterminate them. 20,21He sent messengers throughout all Israel summoning those who worshiped Baal; and they all came and filled the temple of Baal from one end to the other. 22He instructed the head of the robing room, "Be sure that every worshiper wears one of the special robes."

23Then Jehu and Jehonadab (son of Rechab) went into the temple to address the people: "Check to be sure that only those who worship Baal are here; don't let anyone in who worships the Lord!"

24As the priests of Baal began offering sacrifices and burnt offerings, Jehu surrounded the building with eighty of his men and told them, "If you let anyone escape, you'll pay for it with your own life."

25As soon as he had finished sacrificing the burnt offering, Jehu went out and told his officers and men, "Go in and kill the whole bunch of them. Don't let a single one escape."

So they slaughtered them all and dragged their bodies outside. Then Jehu's men went into the inner temple, 26dragged out the pillar used for the worship of Baal, and burned it. 27They wrecked the temple and converted it into a public toilet, which it still is today. 28Thus Jehu destroyed every trace of Baal from Israel. 29However, he didn't destroy the gold calves at Bethel and Dan—this was the great sin of Jeroboam (son of Nebat), for it resulted in all Israel sinning.

30Afterwards the Lord said to Jehu, "You have done well in following my instructions to destroy the dynasty of Ahab. Because of this I will cause your son, your grandson, and your great-grandson to be the kings of Israel."

31But Jehu didn't follow the Lord God of Israel with all his heart, for he continued to worship Jeroboam's gold calves that had been the cause of such great sin in Israel.

NOW they traveled through the cities of Amphipolis and Apollonia and came to Thessalonica, where there was a Jewish synagogue. 2As was Paul's custom, he went there to preach, and for three Sabbaths in a row he opened the Scriptures to the people, 3explaining the prophecies about the sufferings of the Messiah and his coming back to life, and proving that Jesus is the Messiah. 4Some who listened were persuaded and became converts—including a large number of godly Greek men, and also many important women of the city.

5But the Jewish leaders were jealous and incited some worthless fellows from the streets to form a mob and start a riot. They attacked the home of Jason, planning to take Paul and Silas to the City Council for punishment.

6Not finding them there, they dragged out Jason and some of the other believers, and took them before the Council instead. "Paul and Silas have turned the rest of the world upside down, and now they are here disturbing our city," they shouted, 7"and Jason has let them into his home. They are all guilty of treason, for they claim another king, Jesus, instead of Caesar."

8,9The people of the city, as well as the judges, were concerned at these reports and let them go only after they had posted bail.

10That night the Christians hurried Paul and Silas to Beroea, and, as usual, they went to the synagogue to preach. 11But the people of Beroea were more open-minded than those in Thessalonica, and gladly listened to the message. They searched the Scriptures day by day to check up on Paul and Silas' statements to see if they were really so. 12As a result, many of them believed, including several prominent Greek women and many men also.

13But when the Jews in Thessalonica learned that Paul was preaching in Beroea, they went over and stirred up trouble. 14The believers acted at once, sending Paul on to the coast, while Silas and Timothy remained behind. 15Those accompanying Paul went on with him to Athens, and then returned to Beroea with a message for Silas and Timothy to hurry and join him.

16While Paul was waiting for them in Athens, he was deeply troubled by all the idols he saw everywhere throughout the city. 17He went to the synagogue for discussions with the Jews and the devout Gentiles, and spoke daily in the public square to all who happened to be there.

18He also had an encounter with some of the Epicurean and Stoic philosophers. Their reaction, when he told them about Jesus and his resurrection, was, "He's a dreamer," or, "He's pushing some foreign religion."

19But they invited him to the forum at Mars Hill. "Come and tell us more about this new religion," they said, 20"for you are saying some rather startling things and we want to hear more." 21(I should explain that all the Athenians as well as the foreigners in Athens seemed to spend all their time discussing the latest new ideas!)

22So Paul, standing before them at the Mars Hill forum, addressed them as follows:

"Men of Athens, I notice that you are very religious, 23for as I was out walking I saw your many altars, and one of them had this inscription on it—'To the Unknown God.' You have been worshiping him without knowing who he is, and now I wish to tell you about him.

24"He made the world and everything in it, and since he is Lord of heaven and earth, he doesn't live in man-made temples; 25and human hands can't minister to his needs—for he has no needs! He himself gives life and breath to everything, and satisfies every need there is. 26He created all the people of the world from one man, Adam, and scattered the nations across the face of the earth. He decided beforehand which should rise and fall, and when. He determined their boundaries.

²⁷"His purpose in all of this is that they should seek after God, and perhaps feel their way toward him and find him—though he is not far from any one of us. ²⁸For in him we live and move and are! As one of your own poets says it, 'We are the sons of God.' ²⁹If this is true, we shouldn't think of God as an idol made by men from gold or silver or chipped from stone. ³⁰God tolerated man's past ignorance about these things, but now he commands everyone to put away idols and worship only him. ³¹For he has set a day for justly judging the world by the man he has appointed, and has pointed him out by bringing him back to life again."

³²When they heard Paul speak of the resurrection of a person who had been dead, some laughed, but others said, "We want to hear more about this later." ³³That ended Paul's discussion with them, ³⁴but a few joined him and became believers. Among them was Dionysius, a member of the City Council, and a woman named Damaris, and others.

PSALM 144:1-15

BLESS the Lord who is my immovable Rock. He gives me strength and skill in battle. ²He is always kind and loving to me; he is my fortress, my tower of strength and safety, my deliverer. He stands before me as a shield. He subdues my people under me.

³O Lord, what is man that you even notice him? Why bother at all with the human race? ⁴For man is but a breath; his days are like a passing shadow.

⁵Bend down the heavens, Lord, and come. The mountains smoke beneath your touch.

⁶Let loose your lightning bolts, your arrows, Lord, upon your enemies, and scatter them.

⁷Reach down from heaven and rescue me; deliver me from deep waters, from the power of my enemies. ⁸Their mouths are filled with lies; they swear to the truth of what is false.

⁹I will sing you a new song, O God, with a ten-stringed harp. ¹⁰For you grant victory to kings! You are the one who will rescue your servant David from the fatal sword. ¹¹Save me! Deliver me from these enemies, these liars, these treacherous men.

¹²⁻¹⁵Here is my description of a truly happy land where Jehovah is God:

Sons vigorous and tall as growing plants.

Daughters of graceful beauty like the pillars of a palace wall.

Barns full to the brim with crops of every kind.

Sheep by the thousands out in our fields.

Oxen loaded down with produce.

No enemy attacking the walls, but peace everywhere.

No crime in our streets.

Yes, happy are those whose God is Jehovah.

PROVERBS FOR TODAY/ 17:27-28

The man of few words and settled mind is wise; therefore, even a fool is thought to be wise when he is silent. It pays him to keep his mouth shut.

JUNE 27

2 KINGS 10:32—12:21

AT about that time the Lord began to whittle down the size of Israel. King Hazael conquered several sections of the country east of the Jordan River, as well as all of Gilead, Gad, and Reuben; he also conquered parts of Manasseh from the Aroer River in the valley of the Arnon as far as Gilead and Bashan.

34The rest of Jehu's activities are recorded in *The Annals of the Kings of Israel.* 35When Jehu died, he was buried in Samaria; and his son Jehoahaz became the new king. 36In all, Jehu reigned as king of Israel, in Samaria, for twenty-eight years.

WHEN Athaliah, the mother of King Ahaziah of Judah, learned that her son was dead, she killed all of his children, 2,3except for his year-old son Joash. Joash was rescued by his Aunt Jehosheba, who was a sister of King Ahaziah (for she was a daughter of King Jehoram, Ahaziah's father). She stole him away from among the rest of the king's children who were waiting to be slain, and hid him and his nurse in a storeroom of the Temple. They lived there for six years while Athaliah reigned as queen.

4In the seventh year of Queen Athaliah's reign, Jehoiada the priest summoned the officers of the palace guard and the queen's bodyguard. He met them in the Temple, swore them to secrecy, and showed them the king's son.

5Then he gave them their instructions: "A third of those who are on duty on the Sabbath are to guard the palace. 6,7,8The other two-thirds shall stand guard at the Temple; surround the king, weapons in hand, and kill anyone who tries to break through. Stay with the king at all times."

9So the officers followed Jehoiada's instructions. They brought to Jehoiada the men who were going off duty on the Sabbath and those who were coming on duty, 10and he armed them from the Temple's supply of spears and shields that had belonged to King David. 11The guards, with weapons ready, stood across the front of the sanctuary, and surrounded the altar, which was near Joash's hideaway.

12Then Jehoiada brought out the young prince and put the crown upon his head and gave him a copy of the Ten Commandments, and anointed him as king. Then everyone clapped and shouted, "Long live the king!"

13,14When Athaliah heard all the noise, she ran into the Temple and saw the new king standing beside the pillar, as was the custom at times of coronation, surrounded by her bodyguard and many trumpeters; and everyone was rejoicing and blowing trumpets.

"Treason! Treason!" she screamed, and began to tear her clothes.

15"Get her out of here," shouted Jehoiada to the officers of the guard. "Don't kill her here in the Temple. But kill anyone who tries to come to her rescue."

16So they dragged her to the palace stables and killed her there.

17Jehoiada made a treaty between the Lord, the king, and the people, that they would be the Lord's people. He also made a contract between the king and the people. 18Everyone went over to the temple of Baal and tore it down, breaking the altars and images and killing Mattan, the priest of Baal, in front of the altar. And Jehoiada set guards at the Temple of the Lord. 19Then he and the officers and the guard and all the people led the king from the Temple, past the guardhouse, and into the palace. And he sat upon the king's throne.

20So everyone was happy, and the city settled back into quietness after Athaliah's death. 21Joash was seven years old when he became king.

IT was seven years after Jehu had become the king of Israel that Joash became king of Judah. He reigned in Jerusalem for forty years. (His mother was Zibiah, from Beer-sheba.) 2All his life Joash did what was right because Jehoiada the High Priest instructed him. 3Yet even so he didn't destroy the shrines on the hills—the people still sacrificed and burned incense there.

4,5One day King Joash said to Jehoiada, "The Temple building needs repairing. Whenever anyone brings a contribution to the Lord, whether it is a regular assessment or some special gift, use it to pay for whatever repairs are needed."

6But in the twenty-third year of his reign the Temple was still in disrepair. 7So Joash called for Jehoiada and the other priests and asked them, "Why haven't you done anything about the Temple? Now don't use any more money for your own needs; from now on it must all be spent on getting the Temple into good condition."

8So the priests agreed to set up a special repair fund that would not go through their hands, lest it be diverted to care for their personal needs. 9Jehoiada the priest bored a hole in the lid of a large chest and set it on the right-hand side of the altar at the Temple entrance. The doorkeepers put all of the people's contributions into it. 10Whenever the chest became full, the king's financial secretary and the High Priest counted it, put it into bags, 11,12and gave it to the construction superintendents to pay the carpenters, stonemasons, quarrymen, timber dealers, and stone merchants, and to buy the other materials needed to repair the Temple of the Lord. 13,14It was not used to buy silver cups, gold snuffers, bowls, trumpets, or similar articles, but only for repairs to the building. 15No accounting was required from the construction superintendents, for they were honest and faithful men. 16However, the money that was contributed for guilt offerings and sin offerings was given to the priests for their own use. It was not put into the chest.

17About this time, King Hazael of Syria went to war against Gath and captured it; then he moved on toward Jerusalem to attack it. 18King Joash took all the sacred objects that his ancestors—Jehoshaphat, Jehoram, and Ahaziah, the kings of Judah—had dedicated, along with what he himself had dedicated, and all the gold in the treasuries of the Temple and the palace, and sent it to Hazael. So Hazael called off the attack.

19The rest of the history of Joash is recorded in *The Annals of the Kings of Judah.* 20But his officers plotted against him and assassinated him in his royal residence at Millo on the road to Silla. 21The assassins were Jozachar, the son of Shimeath, and Jehozabad, the son of Shomer—both trusted aides. He was buried in the royal cemetery in Jerusalem, and his son Amaziah became the new king.

ACTS 18:1–21

THEN Paul left Athens and went to Corinth. 2,3There he became acquainted with a Jew named Aquila, born in Pontus, who had recently arrived from Italy with his wife, Priscilla. They had been expelled from Italy as a result of Claudius Caesar's order to deport all Jews from Rome. Paul lived and worked with them, for they were tentmakers just as he was.

4Each Sabbath found Paul at the synagogue, trying to convince the Jews and Greeks alike. 5And after the arrival of Silas and Timothy from Macedonia, Paul spent his full time preaching and testifying to the Jews that Jesus is the Messiah. 6But when the Jews opposed him and blasphemed, hurling abuse at Jesus, Paul shook off the dust from his robe and said, "Your blood be upon your own heads—I am innocent—from now on I will preach to the Gentiles."

7After that he stayed with Titus Justus, a Gentile who worshiped God and lived next door to the synagogue. 8However, Crispus, the leader of the synagogue, and all his household believed in the Lord and were baptized—as were many others in Corinth.

9One night the Lord spoke to Paul in a vision and told him, "Don't be afraid! Speak out! Don't quit! 10For I am with you and no one can harm you. Many people here in this city belong to me." 11So Paul stayed there the next year and a half, teaching the truths of God.

12But when Gallio became governor of Achaia, the Jews rose in concerted action against Paul and brought him before the governor for judgment. 13They accused Paul of "persuading men to worship God in ways that are contrary to Roman law." 14But just as Paul started to make his defense, Gallio turned to his accusers and said, "Listen, you Jews, if this were a case involving some crime, I would be obliged to listen to you, 15but since it is merely a bunch of questions of semantics and personalities and your silly Jewish laws, you take care of it. I'm not interested and I'm not touching it." 16And he drove them out of the courtroom.

17Then the mob grabbed Sosthenes, the new leader of the synagogue, and beat him outside the courtroom. But Gallio couldn't have cared less.

18Paul stayed in the city several days after that and then said good-bye to the Christians and sailed for the coast of Syria, taking Priscilla and Aquila with him. At Cenchreae, Paul had his head shaved according to Jewish custom, for he had taken a vow. 19Arriving at the port of Ephesus, he left us aboard ship while he went over to the synagogue for a discussion with the Jews. 20They asked him to stay for a few days, but he felt that he had no time to lose.

21"I must by all means be at Jerusalem for the holiday," he said. But he promised to return to Ephesus later if God permitted; and so he set sail again.

PSALM 145:1–21

I will praise you, my God and King, and bless your name each day and forever.

3Great is Jehovah! Greatly praise him! His greatness is beyond discovery! 4Let each generation tell its children what glorious things he does. 5I will meditate about your glory, splendor, majesty and miracles. 6Your awe-inspiring deeds shall be on every tongue; I will proclaim your greatness. 7Everyone will tell about how good you are, and sing about your righteousness.

8Jehovah is kind and merciful, slow to get angry, full of love. 9He is good to everyone, and his compassion is intertwined with everything he does. 10All living things shall thank you, Lord, and your people will bless you. 11They will talk together about the glory of your kingdom and mention examples of your power. 12They will tell about your miracles and about the majesty and glory of your reign. 13For your kingdom never ends. You rule generation after generation.

14The Lord lifts the fallen and those bent beneath their loads. 15The eyes of all mankind look up to you for help; you give them their food as they need it. 16You constantly satisfy the hunger and thirst of every living thing.

17The Lord is fair in everything he does, and full of kindness. 18He is close to all who call on him sincerely. 19He fulfills the desires of those who reverence and trust him; he hears their cries for help and rescues them. 20He protects all those who love him, but destroys the wicked.

21I will praise the Lord and call on all men everywhere to bless his holy name forever and forever.

PROVERBS FOR TODAY/ 18:1
The selfish man quarrels against every sound principle of conduct by demanding his own way.

JUNE 28

2 KINGS 13:1—14:29

JEHOAHAZ (the son of Jehu) began a seventeen-year reign over Israel during the twenty-third year of the reign of King Joash of Judah. ²But he was an evil king, and he followed the wicked paths of Jeroboam, who had caused Israel to sin. ³So the Lord was very angry with Israel, and he continually allowed King Hazael of Syria and his son Ben-hadad to conquer them.

⁴But Jehoahaz prayed for the Lord's help, and the Lord listened to him; for the Lord saw how terribly the king of Syria was oppressing Israel. ⁵So the Lord raised up leaders among the Israelis to rescue them from the tyranny of the Syrians; and then Israel lived in safety again as they had in former days. ⁶But they continued to sin, following the evil ways of Jeroboam; and they continued to worship the goddess Asherah at Samaria. ⁷Finally the Lord reduced Jehoahaz's army to fifty mounted troops, ten chariots, and ten thousand infantry; for the king of Syria had destroyed the others as though they were dust beneath his feet.

⁸The rest of the history of Jehoahaz is recorded in *The Annals of the Kings of Israel.*

⁹,¹⁰Jehoahaz died and was buried in Samaria, and his son Joash reigned in Samaria for sixteen years. He came to the throne in the thirty-seventh year of the reign of King Joash of Judah. ¹¹But he was an evil man, for, like Jeroboam, he encouraged the people to worship idols and led them into sin. ¹²The rest of the history of the reign of Joash, including his wars against King Amaziah of Judah, are written in *The Annals of the Kings of Israel.* ¹³Joash died and was buried in Samaria with the other kings of Israel; and Jeroboam II became the new king.

¹⁴When Elisha was in his last illness, King Joash visited him and wept over him.

"My father! My father! You are the strength of Israel!" he cried.

¹⁵Elisha told him, "Get a bow and some arrows," and he did.

¹⁶,¹⁷"Open that eastern window," he instructed.

Then he told the king to put his hand upon the bow, and Elisha laid his own hands upon the king's hands.

"Shoot!" Elisha commanded, and he did.

Then Elisha proclaimed, "This is the Lord's arrow, full of victory over Syria; for you will completely conquer the Syrians at Aphek. ¹⁸Now pick up the other arrows and strike them against the floor."

So the king picked them up and struck the floor three times. ¹⁹But the prophet was angry with him. "You should have struck the floor five or six times," he exclaimed, "for then you would have beaten Syria until they were entirely destroyed; now you will be victorious only three times."

²⁰,²¹So Elisha died and was buried.

In those days bandit gangs of Moabites used to invade the land each spring. Once some men who were burying a friend spied these marauders so they hastily threw his body into the tomb of Elisha. And as soon as the body touched Elisha's bones, the dead man revived and jumped to his feet!

²²King Hazael of Syria had oppressed Israel during the entire reign of King Jehoahaz. ²³But the Lord was gracious to the people of Israel, and they were not totally destroyed. For God pitied them, and also he was honoring his contract with Abraham, Isaac, and Jacob. And this is still true. ²⁴Then King Hazael of Syria died, and his son Ben-hadad reigned in his place.

²⁵King Joash of Israel (the son of Jehoahaz) was successful on three occasions in reconquering the cities that his father had lost to Ben-hadad.

DURING the second year of the reign of King Joash of Israel, King Amaziah began his reign over Judah. ²Amaziah was twenty-five years old at the time, and he reigned in Jerusalem for twenty-nine years. (His mother was Jeho-addin, a native of Jerusalem.) ³He was a good king in the Lord's sight, though not quite like his ancestor David; but he was as good a king as his father Joash. ⁴However, he didn't destroy the shrines on the hills, so the people still sacrificed and burned incense there.

⁵As soon as he had a firm grip on the kingdom, he killed the men who had assassinated his father; ⁶but he didn't kill their children, for the Lord had commanded through the law of Moses that fathers shall not be killed for their children, nor children for the sins of their fathers: everyone must pay the penalty for his own sins. ⁷Once Amaziah killed ten thousand Edomites in Salt Valley; he also conquered Sela and changed its name to Jokthe-el, as it is called to this day.

⁸One day he sent a message to King Joash of Israel (the son of Jehoahaz and the grandson of Jehu), daring him to mobilize his army and come out and fight.

⁹But King Joash replied, "The thistle of Lebanon demanded of the mighty cedar tree, 'Give your daughter to be a wife for my son.' But just then a wild animal passed by and stepped on the thistle and trod it into the ground! ¹⁰You have destroyed Edom and are very proud about it; but my advice to you is, be content with your glory and stay home! Why provoke disaster for both yourself and Judah?"

¹¹But Amaziah refused to listen, so King Joash of Israel mustered his army. The battle began at Beth-shemesh, one of the cities of Judah, ¹²and Judah was defeated and the army fled home. ¹³King Amaziah was captured, and the army of Israel marched on Jerusalem and broke down its wall from the Gate of Ephraim to the Corner Gate, a distance of about six hundred feet. ¹⁴King Joash took many hostages and all the gold and silver from the Temple and palace treasury, also the gold cups. Then he returned to Samaria.

¹⁵The rest of the history of Joash and his war with King Amaziah of Judah are recorded in *The Annals of the Kings of Israel.* ¹⁶When Joash died, he was buried in Samaria with the other kings of Israel. And his son Jeroboam became the new king.

¹⁷Amaziah lived fifteen years longer than Joash, ¹⁸and the rest of his biography is recorded in *The Annals of the Kings of Judah.* ¹⁹There was a plot against his life in Jerusalem, and he fled to Lachish; but his enemies sent assassins and killed him there. ²⁰His body was returned on horses, and he was buried in the royal cemetery, in the City of David section of Jerusalem.

²¹Then his son Azariah became the new king at the age of sixteen. ²²After his father's death he built Elath and restored it to Judah.

²³Meanwhile, over in Israel, Jeroboam II had become king during the fifteenth year of the reign of King Amaziah of Judah. Jeroboam's reign lasted forty-one years. ²⁴But he was as evil as Jeroboam I (the son of Nebat), who had led Israel into the sin of worshiping idols. ²⁵Jeroboam II recovered the lost territories of Israel between Hamath and the Dead Sea, just as the Lord God of Israel had predicted through Jonah (son of Amittai) the prophet from Gatthhepher. ²⁶For the Lord saw the bitter plight of Israel—she had no one to help her. ²⁷And he had not said that he would blot out the name of Israel, so he used King Jeroboam II to save her.

²⁸The rest of Jeroboam's biography—all that he did, and his great power, and his wars, and how he recovered Damascus and Hamath (which had been captured by Judah)—is recorded in *The Annals of the Kings of Israel.* ²⁹When Jeroboam II died he was buried with the other kings of Israel, and his son Zechariah became the new king of Israel.

THE next stop was at the port of Caesarea from where Paul visited the church [at Jerusalem] and then sailed on to Antioch. 23After spending some time there, he left for Turkey again, going through Galatia and Phrygia visiting all the believers, encouraging them and helping them grow in the Lord.

24As it happened, a Jew named Apollos, a wonderful Bible teacher and preacher, had just arrived in Ephesus from Alexandria in Egypt. 25,26While he was in Egypt, someone had told him about John the Baptist and what John had said about Jesus, but that is all he knew. He had never heard the rest of the story! So he was preaching boldly and enthusiastically in the synagogue, "The Messiah is coming! Get ready to receive him!" Priscilla and Aquila were there and heard him—and it was a powerful sermon. Afterwards they met with him and explained what had happened to Jesus since the time of John, and all that it meant!

27Apollos had been thinking about going to Greece, and the believers encouraged him in this. They wrote to their fellow-believers there, telling them to welcome him. And upon his arrival in Greece, he was greatly used of God to strengthen the church, 28for he powerfully refuted all the Jewish arguments in public debate, showing by the Scriptures that Jesus is indeed the Messiah.

WHILE Apollos was in Corinth, Paul traveled through Turkey and arrived in Ephesus, where he found several disciples. 2"Did you receive the Holy Spirit when you believed?" he asked them.

"No," they replied, "we don't know what you mean. What is the Holy Spirit?"

3"Then what beliefs did you acknowledge at your baptism?" he asked.

And they replied, "What John the Baptist taught."

4Then Paul pointed out to them that John's baptism was to demonstrate a desire to turn from sin to God and that those receiving his baptism must then go on to believe in Jesus, the one John said would come later.

5As soon as they heard this, they were baptized in the name of the Lord Jesus. 6Then, when Paul laid his hands upon their heads, the Holy Spirit came on them, and they spoke in other languages and prophesied. 7The men involved were about twelve in number.

8Then Paul went to the synagogue and preached boldly each Sabbath day for three months, telling what he believed and why, and persuading many to believe in Jesus. 9But some rejected his message and publicly spoke against Christ, so he left, refusing to preach to them again. Pulling out the believers, he began a separate meeting at the lecture hall of Tyrannus and preached there daily. 10This went on for the next two years, so that everyone in the Turkish province of Asia Minor—both Jews and Greeks—heard the Lord's message.

11And God gave Paul the power to do unusual miracles, 12so that even when his handkerchiefs or parts of his clothing were placed upon sick people, they were healed, and any demons within them came out.

PSALM 146:1–10

PRAISE the Lord! Yes, really praise him! 2I will praise him as long as I live, yes, even with my dying breath.

3Don't look to men for help; their greatest leaders fail; 4for every man must die. His breathing stops, life ends, and in a moment all he planned for himself is ended. 5But happy is the man who has the God of Jacob as his helper, whose hope is in the Lord his God— 6the God who made both earth and heaven, the seas and everything in them. He is the God who keeps every promise, 7and gives justice to the poor and oppressed, and food to the hungry. He frees the prisoners, 8and opens the eyes of the blind; he lifts the burdens from those bent down beneath their loads. For the

Lord loves good men. 9He protects the immigrants, and cares for the orphans and widows. But he turns topsy-turvy the plans of the wicked.

10The Lord will reign forever. O Jerusalem, your God is King in every generation! Hallelujah! Praise the Lord!

PROVERBS FOR TODAY/ 18:2–3
A rebel doesn't care about the facts. All he wants to do is yell. Sin brings disgrace.

JUNE 29

2 KINGS 15:1—16:20

NEW king of Judah: Azariah
Name of his father: Amaziah, the former king
Name of his mother: Jecoliah of Jerusalem
Length of his reign: 52 years, in Jerusalem
His age at the beginning of his reign: 16 years old
Reigning in Israel at this time: King Jeroboam, who had been the king there for 27 years.

3Azariah was a good king, and he pleased the Lord just as his father Amaziah had. 4But like his predecessors, he didn't destroy the shrines on the hills where the people sacrificed and burned incense. 5Because of this the Lord struck him with leprosy, which lasted until the day of his death; so he lived in a house by himself. And his son Jotham was the acting king. 6The rest of the history of Azariah is recorded in *The Annals of the Kings of Judah.* 7When Azariah died, he was buried with his ancestors in the City of David, and his son Jotham became king.

8New king of Israel: Zechariah
Name of his father: Jeroboam
Length of reign: 6 months
Reigning in Judah at that time: King Azariah, who had been the king there for 38 years

9But Zechariah was an evil king in the Lord's sight, just like his ancestors. Like Jeroboam I (the son of Nebat), he encouraged Israel in the sin of worshiping idols. 10Then Shallum (the son of Jabesh) conspired against him and assassinated him at Ibleam and took the crown himself. 11The rest of the history of Zechariah's reign is found in *The Annals of the Kings of Israel.* 12(So the Lord's statement to Jehu came true, that Jehu's son, grandson, and great-grandson would be kings of Israel.)

13New king of Israel: Shallum
Father's name: Jabesh
Length of reign: 1 month
Reigning in Judah at that time: King Uzziah, who had been the king there for 39 years

14One month after Shallum became king, Menahem (the son of Gadi) came to Samaria from Tirzah and assassinated him and took the throne. 15Additional details about King Shallum and his conspiracy are recorded in *The Annals of the Kings of Israel.*

16Menahem destroyed the city of Tappuah and the surrounding countryside, for its citizens refused to accept him as their king; he killed the entire population and ripped open the pregnant women.

17Name of new king of Israel: Menahem
Length of reign: 10 years, in Samaria
Concurrent with: King Azariah of Judah who had been the king there for 39 years

18But Menahem was an evil king. He

worshiped idols, as King Jeroboam I had done so long before, and he led the people of Israel into grievous sin. 19,20Then King Pul of Assyria invaded the land; but King Menahem bought him off with a gift of $2,000,000, so he turned around and returned home. Menahem extorted the money from the rich, assessing each one $2,000 in the form of a special tax. 21The rest of the history of King Menahem is written in *The Annals of the Kings of Israel.* 22When he died, his son Pekahiah became the new king.

23Name of new king of Israel: Pekahiah
Father's name: King Menahem
Length of reign: 2 years, in Samaria
Concurrent with: King Azariah of Judah, who had been the king there for 50 years

24But Pekahiah was an evil king, and he continued the idol-worship begun by Jeroboam I (son of Nebat) who led Israel down that evil trail.

25Then Pekah (son of Remaliah), the commanding general of his army, conspired against him with fifty men from Gilead, and assassinated him in the palace at Samaria (Argob and Arieh were also slain in the revolt). So Pekah became the new king. 26The rest of the history of King Pekahiah is recorded in *The Annals of the Kings of Israel.*

27New king of Israel: Pekah
Father's name: Remaliah
Length of reign: 20 years, in Samaria
Concurrent with: King Azariah of Judah, who had been the king there for 52 years

28Pekah, too, was an evil king, and he continued in the example of Jeroboam I (son of Nebat), who led all of Israel into the sin of worshiping idols. 29It was during his reign that King Tiglathpileser led an attack against Israel. He captured the cities of Ijon, Abel-beth-maacah, Janoah, Kedesh, Hazor, Gilead, Galilee, and all the land of Naphtali; and he took the people away to Assyria as captives. 30Then Hoshea (the son of Elah) plotted against Pekah and assassinated him; and he took the throne for himself.

New king of Israel: Hoshea

Concurrent with: Jotham (son of Uzziah) king of Judah, who had been the king there for 20 years

31The rest of the history of Pekah's reign is recorded in *The Annals of the Kings of Israel.* 32,33New king of Judah: Jotham
Father's name: King Uzziah
His age when he became king: 25 years old
Duration of his reign: 16 years, in Jerusalem
Mother's name: Jerusha (daughter of Zadok)
Reigning in Israel at this time: Pekah (son of Remaliah), who had been the king there for 2 years

34,35Generally speaking, Jotham was a good king. Like his father Uzziah, he followed the Lord. But he didn't destroy the shrines on the hills where the people sacrificed and burned incense. It was during King Jotham's reign that the upper gate of the Temple of the Lord was built. 36The rest of Jotham's history is written in *The Annals of the Kings of Judah.* 37In those days the Lord caused King Rezin of Syria and King Pekah of Israel to attack Judah. 38When Jotham died he was buried with the other kings of Judah in the royal cemetery, in the City of David section of Jerusalem. Then his son Ahaz became the new king.

NEW king of Judah: Ahaz
Father's name: Jotham
Age: 20 years old
Duration of reign: 16 years, in Jerusalem
Character of his reign: evil
Reigning in Israel at this time: King Pekah (son of Remaliah) who had been the king there for 17 years

2But he did not follow the Lord as his ancestor David had; 3he was as wicked as the kings of Israel. He even killed his own son by offering him as a burnt sacrifice to the gods, following heathen customs of the nations around Judah—nations which the Lord destroyed when the people of Israel entered the land. 4He also sacrificed and burned incense at the shrines on the hills and at the numerous altars in the groves of trees.

5Then King Rezin of Syria and King Pekah (son of Remaliah) of Israel declared war on Ahaz and besieged Jerusalem; but they did not conquer it. 6However, at that time King Rezin of Syria recovered the city of Elath for Syria; he drove out the Jews and sent Syrians to live there, as they do to this day. 7King Ahaz sent a messenger to King Tiglath-pileser of Assyria, begging him to help him fight the attacking armies of Syria and Israel. 8Ahaz took the silver and gold from the Temple and from the royal vaults and sent it as a payment to the Assyrian king. 9So the Assyrians attacked Damascus, the capital of Syria. They took away the population of the city as captives, resettling them in Kir, and King Rezin of Syria was killed.

10King Ahaz now went to Damascus to meet with King Tiglath-pileser, and while he was there he noticed an unusual altar in a heathen temple. He jotted down its dimensions and made a sketch and sent it back to Uriah the priest with a detailed description. 11,12Uriah built one just like it by following these directions and had it ready for the king, who, upon his return from Damascus, inaugurated it with an offering. 13The king presented a burnt offering and a grain offering, poured a drink offering over it, and sprinkled the blood of peace offerings upon it. 14Then he removed the old bronze altar from the front of the Temple (it had stood between the Temple entrance and the new altar), and placed it on the north side of the new altar. 15He instructed Uriah the priest to use the new altar for the sacrifices of burnt offering, the evening grain offering, the king's burnt offering and grain offering, and the offerings of the people, including their drink offerings. The blood from the burnt offerings and sacrifices was also to be sprinkled over the new altar. So the old altar was used only for purposes of divination.

"The old bronze altar," he said, "will be only for my personal use."

16Uriah the priest did as King Ahaz instructed him. 17Then the king dismantled the wheeled stands in the Temple, removed their crosspieces and the water vats they supported, and removed the great tank from the backs of the bronze oxen and placed it upon the stone pavement. 18In deference to the king of Assyria he also removed the festive passageway he had constructed between the palace and the Temple.

19The rest of the history of the reign of King Ahaz is recorded in *The Annals of the Kings of Judah.* 20When Ahaz died he was buried in the royal cemetery, in the City of David sector of Jerusalem, and his son Hezekiah became the new king.

ACTS 19:13–41

A team of itinerant Jews who were traveling from town to town casting out demons planned to experiment by using the name of the Lord Jesus. The incantation they decided on was this: "I adjure you by Jesus, whom Paul preaches, to come out!" 14Seven sons of Sceva, a Jewish priest, were doing this. 15But when they tried it on a man possessed by a demon, the demon replied, "I know Jesus and I know Paul, but who are you?" 16And he leaped on two of them and beat them up, so that they fled out of his house naked and badly injured.

17The story of what happened spread quickly all through Ephesus, to Jews and Greeks alike; and a solemn fear descended on the city, and the name of the Lord Jesus was greatly honored. 18,19Many of the believers who had been practicing black magic confessed their deeds and brought their incantation books and charms and burned them at a public bonfire. (Someone estimated the value of the books at $10,000.) 20This indicates how deeply the whole area was stirred by God's message.

21Afterwards, Paul felt impelled by the

Holy Spirit to go across to Greece before returning to Jerusalem. "And after that," he said, "I must go on to Rome!" 22He sent his two assistants, Timothy and Erastus, on ahead to Greece while he stayed awhile longer in Asia Minor.

23But about that time, a big blowup developed in Ephesus concerning the Christians. 24It began with Demetrius, a silversmith who employed many craftsmen to manufacture silver shrines of the Greek goddess Diana. 25He called a meeting of his men, together with others employed in related trades, and addressed them as follows:

"Gentlemen, this business is our income. 26As you know so well from what you've seen and heard, this man Paul has persuaded many, many people that handmade gods aren't gods at all. As a result, our sales volume is going down! And this trend is evident not only here in Ephesus, but throughout the entire province! 27Of course, I am not only talking about the business aspects of this situation and our loss of income, but also of the possibility that the temple of the great goddess Diana will lose its influence, and that Diana—this magnificent goddess worshiped not only throughout this part of Turkey but all around the world—will be forgotten!"

28At this their anger boiled and they began shouting, "Great is Diana of the Ephesians!"

29A crowd began to gather and soon the city was filled with confusion. Everyone rushed to the amphitheater, dragging along Gaius and Aristarchus, Paul's traveling companions, for trial. 30Paul wanted to go in, but the disciples wouldn't let him. 31Some of the Roman officers of the province, friends of Paul, also sent a message to him, begging him not to risk his life by entering.

32Inside, the people were all shouting, some one thing and some another—everything was in confusion. In fact, most of them didn't even know why they were there.

33Alexander was spotted among the crowd by some of the Jews and dragged forward. He motioned for silence and tried to speak. 34But when the crowd realized he was a Jew, they started shouting again and kept it up for two hours: "Great is Diana of the Ephesians! Great is Diana of the Ephesians!"

35At last the mayor was able to quiet them down enough to speak. "Men of Ephesus," he said, "everyone knows that Ephesus is the center of the religion of the great Diana, whose image fell down to us from heaven. 36Since this is an indisputable fact, you shouldn't be disturbed no matter what is said, and should do nothing rash. 37Yet you have brought these men here who have stolen nothing from her temple and have not defamed her. 38If Demetrius and the craftsmen have a case against them, the courts are currently in session and the judges can take the case at once. Let them go through legal channels. 39And if there are complaints about other matters, they can be settled at the regular City Council meetings; 40for we are in danger of being called to account by the Roman government for today's riot, since there is no cause for it. And if Rome demands an explanation, I won't know what to say."

41Then he dismissed them, and they dispersed.

PSALM 147:1–20

HALLELUJAH! Yes, praise the Lord! How good it is to sing his praises! How delightful, and how right!

2He is rebuilding Jerusalem and bringing back the exiles. 3He heals the brokenhearted, binding up their wounds. 4He counts the stars and calls them all by name. 5How great he is! His power is absolute! His understanding is unlimited. 6The Lord supports the humble, but brings the wicked into the dust.

7Sing out your thanks to him; sing praises to our God, accompanied by harps. 8He covers the heavens with clouds, sends down the showers and makes the green grass grow in mountain pastures. 9He feeds the wild animals and the young ravens cry to him for food. ¹⁰The speed of a horse is nothing to him. How puny in his sight is the strength of a man. ¹¹But his joy is in those who reverence him, those who expect him to be loving and kind.

¹²Praise him, O Jerusalem! Praise your God, O Zion! ¹³For he has fortified your gates against all enemies, and blessed your children. ¹⁴He sends peace across your nation, and fills your barns with plenty of the finest wheat. ¹⁵He sends his orders to the world. How swiftly his word flies. ¹⁶He sends the snow in all its lovely whiteness, and scatters the frost upon the ground, ¹⁷and hurls the hail upon the earth. Who can stand before his freezing cold? ¹⁸But then he calls for warmer weather, and the spring winds blow and all the river ice is broken. ¹⁹He has made known his laws and ceremonies of worship to Israel— ²⁰something he has not done with any other nation; they have not known his commands.

Hallelujah! Yes, praise the Lord!

PROVERBS FOR TODAY/ 18:4–5

A wise man's words express deep streams of thought. It is wrong for a judge to favor the wicked and condemn the innocent.

JUNE 30

2 KINGS 17:1—18:12

NEW king of Israel: Hoshea
Father's name: Elah

Length of his reign: 9 years, in Samaria
Character of his reign: evil—but not as bad as some of the other kings of Israel
Reigning in Judah at this time: King Ahaz, who had been the king there for 12 years

³King Shalmaneser of Assyria attacked and defeated King Hoshea, so Israel had to pay heavy annual taxes to Assyria. ⁴Then Hoshea conspired against the king of Assyria by asking King So of Egypt to help him shake free of Assyria's power, but this treachery was discovered. At the same time he refused to pay the annual tribute to Assyria. So the king of Assyria put him in prison and in chains for his rebellion.

⁵Now the land of Israel was filled with Assyrian troops for three years besieging Samaria, the capital city of Israel. ⁶Finally, in the ninth year of King Hoshea's reign, Samaria fell and the people of Israel were exiled to Assyria. They were placed in colonies in the city of Halah and along the banks of the Habor River in Gozan, and among the cities of the Medes.

⁷This disaster came upon the nation of Israel because the people worshiped other gods, thus sinning against the Lord their God who had brought them safely out of their slavery in Egypt. ⁸They had followed the evil customs of the nations which the Lord had cast out from before them. ⁹The people of Israel had also secretly done many things that were wrong, and they had built altars to other gods throughout the land. ¹⁰They had placed obelisks and idols at the top of every hill and under every green tree; ¹¹and they had burned incense to the gods of the very nations which the Lord had cleared out of the land when Israel came in. So the people of Israel had done many evil things, and the Lord was very angry. ¹²Yes, they worshiped idols, despite the Lord's specific and repeated warnings.

13Again and again the Lord had sent prophets to warn both Israel and Judah to turn from their evil ways; he had warned them to obey his commandments which he had given to their ancestors through these prophets, 14but Israel wouldn't listen. The people were as stubborn as their ancestors and refused to believe in the Lord their God. 15They rejected his laws and the covenant he had made with their ancestors, and despised all his warnings. In their foolishness they worshiped heathen idols despite the Lord's stern warnings. 16They defied all the commandments of the Lord their God and made two calves from molten gold. They made detestable, shameful idols and worshiped Baal and the sun, moon, and stars. 17They even burned their own sons and daughters to death on the altars of Molech; they consulted fortune-tellers and used magic and sold themselves to evil. So the Lord was very angry. 18He swept them from his sight until only the tribe of Judah remained in the land.

19But even Judah refused to obey the commandments of the Lord their God; they too walked in the same evil paths as Israel had. 20So the Lord rejected all the descendants of Jacob. He punished them by delivering them to their attackers until they were destroyed. 21For Israel split off from the kingdom of David and chose Jeroboam I (the son of Nebat) as its king. Then Jeroboam drew Israel away from following the Lord. He made them sin a great sin, 22and the people of Israel never quit doing the evil things that Jeroboam led them into, 23until the Lord finally swept them away, just as all his prophets had warned would happen. So Israel was carried off to the land of Assyria where they remain to this day.

24And the king of Assyria transported colonies of people from Babylon, Cuthah, Avva, Hamath, and Sepharvaim and resettled them in the cities of Samaria, replacing the people of Israel. So the Assyrians took over Samaria and the other cities of Israel. 25But since these Assyrian colonists did not worship the Lord when they first arrived, the Lord sent lions among them to kill some of them.

26Then they sent a message to the king of Assyria: "We colonists here in Israel don't know the laws of the god of the land, and he has sent lions among us to destroy us because we have not worshiped him."

27,28The king of Assyria then decreed that one of the exiled priests from Samaria should return to Israel and teach the new residents the laws of the god of the land. So one of them returned to Bethel and taught the colonists from Babylon how to worship the Lord.

29But these foreigners also worshiped their own gods. They placed them in the shrines on the hills near their cities. 30Those from Babylon worshiped idols of their god Succoth-benoth; those from Cuth worshiped their god Nergal; and the men of Hamath worshiped Ashima. 31The gods Nibhaz and Tartak were worshiped by the Avvites, and the people from Sephar even burned their own children on the altars of their gods Adrammelech and Anammelech.

32They also worshiped the Lord, and they appointed from among themselves priests to sacrifice to the Lord on the hilltop altars. 33But they continued to follow the religious customs of the nations from which they came. 34And this is still going on among them today—they follow their former practices instead of truly worshiping the Lord or obeying the laws he gave to the descendants of Jacob (whose name was later changed to Israel). 35,36For the Lord had made a contract with them—that they were never to worship or make sacrifices to any heathen gods. They were to worship only the Lord who had brought them out of the land of Egypt with such tremendous miracles and power. 37The descendants of Jacob were to obey all of God's laws and *never* worship other gods.

38For God had said, *"You must never forget the covenant I made with you; never worship other gods. 39You must worship only the Lord; he will save you from all your enemies."*

40But Israel didn't listen, and the people continued to worship other gods. 41These colonists from Babylon worshiped the Lord, yes—but they also worshiped their idols. And to this day their descendants do the same thing.

NEW king of Judah: Hezekiah
Father's name: Ahaz
   Length of his reign: 29 years, in Jerusalem
   His age at the beginning of his reign: 25 years old
   His mother's name: Abi (daughter of Zechariah)
   Character of his reign: good (similar to that of his ancestor David)
   Reigning in Israel at this time: King Hoshea (son of Elah), who had been the king there for 3 years

4He removed the shrines on the hills, broke down the obelisks, knocked down the shameful idols of Asherah, and broke up the bronze serpent that Moses had made, because the people of Israel had begun to worship it by burning incense to it; even though, as King Hezekiah pointed out to them, it was merely a piece of bronze. 5He trusted very strongly in the Lord God of Israel. In fact, none of the kings before or after him were as close to God as he was. 6For he followed the Lord in everything, and carefully obeyed all of God's commands to Moses. 7So the Lord was with him and prospered everything he did. Then he rebelled against the king of Assyria and refused to pay tribute any longer. 8He also conquered the Philistines as far distant as Gaza and its suburbs, destroying cities both large and small.

9It was during the fourth year of his reign (which was the seventh year of the reign of King Hoshea in Israel) that King Shalmaneser of Assyria attacked Israel and began a siege on the city of Samaria. 10Three years later (during the sixth year of the reign of King Hezekiah and the ninth year of the reign of King Hoshea of Israel) Samaria fell. 11It was

at that time that the king of Assyria transported the Israelis to Assyria and put them in colonies in the city of Halath and along the banks of the Habor River in Gozan, and in the cities of the Medes. 12For they had refused to listen to the Lord their God or to do what he wanted them to do. Instead, they had transgressed his covenant and disobeyed all the laws given to them by Moses the servant of the Lord.

ACTS 20:1–38

WHEN it was all over, Paul sent for the disciples, preached a farewell message to them, said good-bye and left for Macedonia, 2preaching to the believers along the way, in all the cities he passed through. 3He was in Greece three months and was preparing to sail for Syria when he discovered a plot by the Jews against his life, so he decided to go north to Macedonia first.

4Several men were traveling with him, going as far as Turkey; they were Sopater of Beroea, the son of Pyrrhus; Aristarchus and Secundus, from Thessalonica; Gaius, from Derbe; and Timothy; and Tychicus and Trophimus, who were returning to their homes in Turkey, 5and had gone on ahead and were waiting for us at Troas. 6As soon as the Passover ceremonies ended, we boarded ship at Philippi in northern Greece and five days later arrived in Troas, Turkey, where we stayed a week.

7On Sunday, we gathered for a communion service, with Paul preaching. And since he was leaving the next day, he talked until midnight! 8The upstairs room where we met was lighted with many flickering lamps; 9and as Paul spoke on and on, a young man named Eutychus, sitting on the window sill, went fast asleep and fell three stories to his death below. 10,11,12Paul went down and took him into his arms. "Don't worry," he said, "he's all right!" And he was! What a wave of awesome joy swept through the crowd! They all went back upstairs and ate the Lord's Supper together; then

Paul preached another long sermon—so it was dawn when he finally left them!

¹³Paul was going by land to Assos, and we went on ahead by ship. ¹⁴He joined us there and we sailed together to Mitylene; ¹⁵the next day we passed Chios; the next, we touched at Samos; and a day later we arrived at Miletus.

¹⁶Paul had decided against stopping at Ephesus this time, as he was hurrying to get to Jerusalem, if possible, for the celebration of Pentecost.

¹⁷But when we landed at Miletus, he sent a message to the elders of the church at Ephesus asking them to come down to the boat to meet him.

¹⁸When they arrived he told them, "You men know that from the day I set foot in Turkey until now ¹⁹I have done the Lord's work humbly—yes, and with tears—and have faced grave danger from the plots of the Jews against my life. ²⁰Yet I never shrank from telling you the truth, either publicly or in your homes. ²¹I have had one message for Jews and Gentiles alike—the necessity of turning from sin to God through faith in our Lord Jesus Christ.

²²"And now I am going to Jerusalem, drawn there irresistibly by the Holy Spirit, not knowing what awaits me, ²³except that the Holy Spirit has told me in city after city that jail and suffering lie ahead. ²⁴But life is worth nothing unless I use it for doing the work assigned me by the Lord Jesus—the work of telling others the Good News about God's mighty kindness and love.

²⁵"And now I know that none of you among whom I went about teaching the Kingdom will ever see me again. ²⁶Let me say plainly that no man's blood can be laid at my door, ²⁷for I didn't shrink from declaring all God's message to you.

²⁸"And now beware! Be sure that you feed and shepherd God's flock—his church, purchased with his blood—for the Holy Spirit is holding you responsible as overseers. ²⁹I know full well that after I leave you, false teachers, like vicious wolves, will appear among you, not spar-

ing the flock. ³⁰Some of you yourselves will distort the truth in order to draw a following. ³¹Watch out! Remember the three years I was with you—my constant watchcare over you night and day and my many tears for you.

³²"And now I entrust you to God and his care and to his wonderful words which are able to build your faith and give you all the inheritance of those who are set apart for himself.

³³"I have never been hungry for money or fine clothing— ³⁴you know that these hands of mine worked to pay my own way and even to supply the needs of those who were with me. ³⁵And I was a constant example to you in helping the poor; for I remembered the words of the Lord Jesus, 'It is more blessed to give than to receive.' "

³⁶When he had finished speaking, he knelt and prayed with them, ³⁷and they wept aloud as they embraced him in farewell, ³⁸sorrowing most of all because he said that he would never see them again. Then they accompanied him down to the ship.

PSALM 148:1–14

PRAISE the Lord, O heavens! Praise him from the skies! ²Praise him, all his angels, all the armies of heaven. ³Praise him, sun and moon, and all you twinkling stars. ⁴Praise him, skies above. Praise him, vapors high above the clouds.

⁵Let everything he has made give praise to him. For he issued his command, and they came into being; ⁶he established them forever and forever. His orders will never be revoked.

⁷And praise him down here on earth, you creatures of the ocean depths. ⁸Let fire and hail, snow, rain, wind and weather, all obey. ⁹Let the mountains and hills, the fruit trees and cedars, ¹⁰the wild animals and cattle, the snakes and birds, ¹¹the kings and all the people with their rulers and their judges, ¹²young men and maidens, old men and children— ¹³all praise the Lord together. For he

alone is worthy. His glory is far greater than all of earth and heaven. [14]He has made his people strong, honoring his godly ones—the people of Israel, the people closest to him.

Hallelujah! Yes, praise the Lord!

PROVERBS FOR TODAY/ 18:6—7

A fool gets into constant fights. His mouth is his undoing! His words endanger him.

JULY 1

2 KINGS 18:13—19:37

L ATER, during the fourteenth year of the reign of King Hezekiah, King Sennacherib of Assyria besieged and captured all the fortified cities of Judah. [14]King Hezekiah sued for peace and sent this message to the king of Assyria at Lachish: "I have done wrong. I will pay whatever tribute you demand if you will only go away." The king of Assyria then demanded a settlement of $1,500,000. [15]To gather this amount, King Hezekiah used all the silver stored in the Temple and in the palace treasury. [16]He even stripped off the gold from the Temple doors, and from the doorposts he had overlaid with gold, and gave it all to the Assyrian king.

[17]Nevertheless the king of Assyria sent his field marshal, his chief treasurer, and his chief of staff from Lachish with a great army; and they camped along the highway beside the field where cloth was bleached, near the conduit of the upper pool. [18]They demanded that King Hezekiah come out to speak to them, but instead he sent a truce delegation of the following men: Eliakim, his business manager; Shebnah, his secretary; and Joah, his royal historian.

[19]Then the Assyrian general sent this message to King Hezekiah: "The great King of Assyria says, 'No one can save you from my power! [20,21]You need more than mere promises of help before rebelling against me. But which of your allies will give you more than words? Egypt? If you lean on Egypt, you will find her to be a stick that breaks beneath your weight and pierces your hand. The Egyptian Pharaoh is totally unreliable! [22]And if you say, "We're trusting the Lord to rescue us"—just remember that he is the very one whose hilltop altars you've destroyed. For you require everyone to worship at the altar in Jerusalem!' [23]I'll tell you what: Make a bet with my master, the king of Assyria! If you have two thousand men left who can ride horses, we'll furnish the horses! [24]And with an army as small as yours, you are no threat to even the least lieutenant in charge of the smallest contingent in my master's army. Even if Egypt supplies you with horses and chariots, it will do no good. [25]And do you think we have come here on our own? No! The Lord sent us and told us, 'Go and destroy this nation!' "

[26]Then Eliakim, Shebnah, and Joah said to them, "Please speak in Aramaic, for we understand it. Don't use Hebrew, for the people standing on the walls will hear you."

[27]But the Assyrian general replied, "Has my master sent me to speak only to you and to your master? Hasn't he sent me to the people on the walls too? For they are doomed with you to eat their own excrement and drink their own urine!"

[28]Then the Assyrian ambassador shouted in Hebrew to the people on the

wall, "Listen to the great king of Assyria! 29'Don't let King Hezekiah fool you. He will never be able to save you from my power. 30Don't let him fool you into trusting in the Lord to rescue you. 31,32Don't listen to King Hezekiah. Surrender! You can live in peace here in your own land until I take you to another land just like this one—with plentiful crops, grain, grapes, olive trees, and honey. All of this instead of death! Don't listen to King Hezekiah when he tries to persuade you that the Lord will deliver you. 33Have any of the gods of the other nations ever delivered their people from the king of Assyria? 34What happened to the gods of Hamath, Arpad, Sepharvaim, Hena, and Ivvah? Did they rescue Samaria? 35What god has ever been able to save any nation from my power? So what makes you think the Lord can save Jerusalem?' "

36But the people on the wall remained silent, for the king had instructed them to say nothing. 37Then Eliakim (son of Hilkiah) the business manager, and Shebnah the king's secretary, and Joah (son of Asaph) the historian went to King Hezekiah with their clothes torn and told him what the Assyrian general had said.

WHEN King Hezekiah heard their report he tore his clothes and put on sackcloth and went into the Temple to pray. 2Then he told Eliakim, Shebnah, and some of the older priests to clothe themselves in sackcloth and to go to Isaiah (son of Amoz), the prophet, with this message:

3"King Hezekiah says, 'This is a day of trouble, insult, and dishonor. It is as when a child is ready to be born, but the mother has no strength to deliver it. 4Yet perhaps the Lord your God has heard the Assyrian general defying the living God, and will rebuke him. Oh, pray for the few of us who are left.' "

5,6Isaiah replied, "The Lord says, 'Tell your master not to be troubled by the sneers these Assyrians have made against me.' 7For the king of Assyria will receive bad news from home and will decide to return; and the Lord will see to it that he is killed when he arrives there."

8Then the Assyrian general returned to his king at Libnah (for he received word that he had left Lachish). 9Soon afterwards news reached the king that King Tirhakah of Ethiopia was coming to attack him. Before leaving to meet the attack, he sent back this message to King Hezekiah:

10"Don't be fooled by that god you trust in. Don't believe it when he says that I won't conquer Jerusalem. 11You know perfectly well what the kings of Assyria have done wherever they have gone; they have completely destroyed everything. Why would you be any different? 12Have the gods of the other nations delivered them—such nations as Gozan, Haran, Rezeph, and Eden in the land of Telassar? The former kings of Assyria destroyed them all! 13What happened to the king of Hamoth and the king of Arpad? What happened to the kings of Sepharvaim, Hena, and Ivvah?"

14Hezekiah took the letter from the messengers, read it, and went over to the Temple and spread it out before the Lord. 15Then he prayed this prayer:

"O Lord God of Israel, sitting on your throne high above the angels, you alone are the God of all the kingdoms of the earth. You created the heavens and the earth. 16Bend low, O Lord, and listen. Open your eyes, O Lord, and see. Listen to this man's defiance of the living God. 17Lord, it is true that the kings of Assyria have destroyed all those nations, 18and have burned their idol-gods. But they weren't gods at all; they were destroyed because they were only things that men had made of wood and stone. 19O Lord our God, we plead with you to save us from his power; then all the kingdoms of the earth will know that you alone are God."

20Then Isaiah sent this message to Hezekiah: "The Lord God of Israel says, 'I have heard you! 21And this is my reply to King Sennacherib: The virgin daughter of Zion isn't afraid of you! The daughter of Jerusalem scorns and mocks at you. 22Whom have you defied and blasphemed? And toward whom have you felt so cocky? It is the Holy One of Israel!

23" 'You have boasted, "My chariots have conquered the highest mountains, yes, the peaks of Lebanon. I have cut down the tallest cedars and choicest cypress trees and have conquered the farthest borders. 24I have been refreshed at many conquered wells, and I destroyed the strength of Egypt just by walking by!"

25" 'Why haven't you realized long before this that it is I, the Lord, who lets you do these things? I decreed your conquest of all those fortified cities! 26So of course the nations you conquered had no power against you! They were like grass shriveling beneath the hot sun, and like grain blighted before it is half grown. 27I know everything about you. I know all your plans and where you are going next; and I also know the evil things you have said about me. 28And because of your arrogance against me I am going to put a hook in your nose and a bridle in your mouth and turn you back on the road by which you came. 29And this is the proof that I will do as I have promised: This year my people will eat the volunteer wheat, and use it as seed for next year's crop; and in the third year they will have a bountiful harvest.

30" 'O my people Judah, those of you who have escaped the ravages of the siege shall become a great nation again; you shall be rooted deeply in the soil and bear fruit for God. 31A remnant of my people shall become strong in Jerusalem. The Lord is eager to cause this to happen.

32" 'And my command concerning the king of Assyria is that he shall not enter this city. He shall not stand before it with a shield, nor build a ramp against its wall, nor even shoot an arrow into it. 33He shall return by the road he came, 34for I will defend and save this city for the sake of my own name and for the sake of my servant David.' "

35That very night the angel of the Lord killed 185,000 Assyrian troops, and dead bodies were seen all across the landscape in the morning.

36Then King Sennacherib returned to Nineveh; 37and as he was worshiping in the temple of his god Nisroch, his sons Adrammelech and Sharezer killed him. They escaped into eastern Turkey—the land of Ararat—and his son Esarhaddon became the new king.

ACTS 21:1–17

AFTER parting from the Ephesian elders, we sailed straight to Cos. The next day we reached Rhodes and then went to Patara. 2There we boarded a ship sailing for the Syrian province of Phoenicia. 3We sighted the island of Cyprus, passed it on our left and landed at the harbor of Tyre, in Syria, where the ship unloaded. 4We went ashore, found the local believers and stayed with them a week. These disciples warned Paul—the Holy Spirit prophesying through them—not to go on to Jerusalem. 5At the end of the week when we returned to the ship, the entire congregation including wives and children walked down to the beach with us where we prayed and said our farewells. 6Then we went aboard and they returned home.

7The next stop after leaving Tyre was Ptolemais where we greeted the believers, but stayed only one day. 8Then we went on to Caesarea and stayed at the home of Philip the Evangelist, one of the first seven deacons. 9He had four unmarried daughters who had the gift of prophecy.

10During our stay of several days, a man named Agabus, who also had the gift of prophecy, arrived from Judea 11and visited us. He took Paul's belt, bound his own feet and hands with it and said, "The Holy Spirit declares, 'So shall the owner of this belt be bound by the Jews in Jerusalem and turned over to the Romans.' " 12Hearing this, all of us—the local believers and his traveling companions—begged Paul not to go on to Jerusalem.

13But he said, "Why all this weeping? You are breaking my heart! For I am ready not only to be jailed at Jerusalem, but also to die for the sake of the Lord Jesus." 14When it was clear that he wouldn't be dissuaded, we gave up and said, "The will of the Lord be done."

15So shortly afterwards, we packed our things and left for Jerusalem. 16Some disciples from Caesarea accompanied us, and on arrival we were guests at the home of Mnason, originally from Cyprus, one of the early believers; 17and all the believers at Jerusalem welcomed us cordially.

PSALM 149:1–9

HALLELUJAH! Yes, praise the Lord! Sing him a new song. Sing his praises, all his people.

2O Israel, rejoice in your Maker. O people of Jerusalem, exult in your King. 3Praise his name with dancing, accompanied by drums and lyre.

4,5For Jehovah enjoys his people; he will save the humble. Let his people rejoice in this honor. Let them sing for joy as they lie upon their beds.

6,7Adore him, O his people! And take a double-edged sword to execute his punishment upon the nations. 8Bind their kings and leaders with iron chains, 9and execute their sentences.

He is the glory of his people. Hallelujah! Praise him!

PROVERBS FOR TODAY/ 18:8

What dainty morsels rumors are. They are eaten with great relish!

JULY 2

2 KINGS 20:1—22:3

HEZEKIAH now became deathly sick, and Isaiah the prophet went to visit him.

"Set your affairs in order and prepare to die," Isaiah told him. "The Lord says you won't recover."

2Hezekiah turned his face to the wall. 3"O Lord," he pleaded, "remember how I've always tried to obey you and to please you in everything I do. . . . " Then he broke down and cried.

4So before Isaiah had left the courtyard, the Lord spoke to him again.

5"Go back to Hezekiah, the leader of my people, and tell him that the Lord God of his ancestor David has heard his prayer and seen his tears. I will heal him, and three days from now he will be out of bed and at the Temple! 6I will add fifteen years to his life and save him and

this city from the king of Assyria. And it will all be done for the glory of my own name and for the sake of my servant David."

7Isaiah then instructed Hezekiah to boil some dried figs and to make a paste of them and spread it on the boil. And he recovered!

8Meanwhile, King Hezekiah had said to Isaiah, "Do a miracle to prove to me that the Lord will heal me and that I will be able to go to the Temple again three days from now."

9"All right, the Lord will give you a proof," Isaiah told him. "Do you want the shadow on the sundial to go forward ten points or backward ten points?"

10"The shadow always moves forward," Hezekiah replied; "make it go backward."

11So Isaiah asked the Lord to do this,

and he caused the shadow to move ten points backward on the sundial of Ahaz!

12At that time Merodach-baladan (the son of King Baladan of Babylon) sent ambassadors with greetings and a present to Hezekiah, for he had learned of his sickness. 13Hezekiah welcomed them and showed them all his treasures—the silver, gold, spices, aromatic oils, the armory—everything.

14Then Isaiah went to King Hezekiah and asked him, "What did these men want? Where are they from?"

"From far away in Babylon," Hezekiah replied.

15"What have they seen in your palace?" Isaiah asked.

And Hezekiah replied, "Everything. I showed them all my treasures."

16Then Isaiah said to Hezekiah, "Listen to the word of the Lord: 17The time will come when everything in this palace shall be carried to Babylon. All the treasures of your ancestors will be taken—nothing shall be left. 18Some of your own sons will be taken away and made into eunuchs who will serve in the palace of the king of Babylon."

19"All right," Hezekiah replied, "if this is what the Lord wants, it is good." But he was really thinking, "At least there will be peace and security during the remainder of my own life!"

20The rest of the history of Hezekiah and his great deeds—including the pool and conduit he made and how he brought water into the city—are recorded in *The Annals of the Kings of Judah.* 21When he died, his son Manasseh became the new king.

NEW king of Judah: Manasseh

His age at beginning of his reign: 12 years

Length of his reign: 55 years, in Jerusalem

Name of his mother: Hephzibah

Character of his reign: evil. He did the same things the nations had done that were thrown out of the land to make room for the people of Israel

3,4,5He rebuilt the hilltop shrines which his father Hezekiah had destroyed. He built altars for Baal and made a shameful Asherah idol, just as Ahab the king of Israel had done. Heathen altars to the sun god, moon god, and the gods of the stars were placed even in the Temple of the Lord—in the very city and building which the Lord had selected to honor his own name. 6And he sacrificed one of his sons as a burnt offering on a heathen altar. He practiced black magic and used fortune-telling, and patronized mediums and wizards. So the Lord was very angry, for Manasseh was an evil man, in God's sight. 7Manasseh even set up a shameful Asherah-idol in the Temple—the very place which the Lord had spoken to David and Solomon about when he said, "I will place my name forever in this Temple, and in Jerusalem—the city I have chosen from among all the cities of the tribes of Israel. 8If the people of Israel will only follow the instructions I gave them through Moses, I will never again expel them from this land of their fathers."

9But the people did not listen to the Lord, and Manasseh enticed them to do even more evil than the surrounding nations had done, even though Jehovah had destroyed those nations for their evil ways when the people of Israel entered the land.

10Then the Lord declared through the prophets,

11"Because King Manasseh has done these evil things and is even more wicked than the Amorites who were in this land long ago, and because he has led the people of Judah into idolatry: 12I will bring such evil upon Jerusalem and Judah that the ears of those who hear about it will tingle with horror. 13I will punish Jerusalem as I did Samaria, and as I did King Ahab of Israel and his descendants. I will wipe away the people of Jerusalem as a man wipes a dish and turns it upside down to dry. 14Then I will reject even those few of my people who are left, and I will hand them over to their enemies. 15For they have done great evil and have angered me ever since I brought their ancestors from Egypt."

16In addition to the idolatry which God hated and into which Manasseh led the people of Judah, he murdered great numbers of innocent people. And Jerusalem was filled from one end to the other with the bodies of his victims.

17The rest of the history of Manasseh's sinful reign is recorded in *The Annals of the Kings of Judah.* 18When he died he was buried in the garden of his palace at Uzza, and his son Amon became the new king. 19,20Name of the new king of Judah: Amon

His age at the beginning of his reign: 22 years old

Length of his reign: 2 years, in Jerusalem

His mother's name: Meshullemeth (daughter of Haruz, of Jotbah)

Character of his reign: evil

21He did all the evil things his father had done: he worshiped the same idols, 22and turned his back on the Lord God of his ancestors. He refused to listen to God's instructions. 23But his aides conspired against him and killed him in the palace. 24Then a posse of civilians killed all the assassins and placed Amon's son Josiah upon the throne. 25The rest of Amon's biography is recorded in *The Annals of the Kings of Judah.* 26He was buried in a crypt in the garden of Uzza, and his son Josiah became the new king.

NEW king of Judah: Josiah

His age at the beginning of his reign: 8 years old

Duration of his reign: 31 years in Jerusalem

Name of his mother: Jedidah (daughter of Adaiah of Bozkath)

Character of his reign: good; for he followed in the steps of his ancestor King David, obeying the Lord completely

3In the eighteenth year of his reign, King Josiah sent his secretary Shaphan (son of Azaliah, son of Meshullam) to the Temple to give instruction to Hilkiah, the High Priest:

THE second day Paul took us with him to meet with James and the elders of the Jerusalem church. 19After greetings were exchanged, Paul recounted the many things God had accomplished among the Gentiles through his work.

20They praised God but then said, "You know, dear brother, how many thousands of Jews have also believed, and they are all very insistent that Jewish believers must continue to follow the Jewish traditions and customs. 21Our Jewish Christians here at Jerusalem have been told that you are against the laws of Moses, against our Jewish customs, and that you forbid the circumcision of their children. 22Now what can be done? For they will certainly hear that you have come.

23"We suggest this: We have four men here who are preparing to shave their heads and take some vows. 24Go with them to the Temple and have your head shaved too—and pay for theirs to be shaved.

"Then everyone will know that you approve of this custom for the Hebrew Christians and that you yourself obey the Jewish laws and are in line with our thinking in these matters.

25"As for the Gentile Christians, we aren't asking them to follow these Jewish customs at all—except for the ones we wrote to them about: not to eat food offered to idols, not to eat unbled meat from strangled animals, and not to commit fornication."

26,27So Paul agreed to their request and the next day went with the men to the Temple for the ceremony, thus publicizing his vow to offer a sacrifice seven days later with the others.

The seven days were almost ended when some Jews from Turkey saw him in the Temple and roused a mob against him. They grabbed him, 28yelling, "Men of Israel! Help! Help! This is the man who preaches against our people and tells everybody to disobey the Jewish laws.

He even talks against the Temple and defiles it by bringing Gentiles in!" 29(For down in the city earlier that day, they had seen him with Trophimus, a Gentile from Ephesus in Turkey, and assumed that Paul had taken him into the Temple.)

30The whole population of the city was electrified by these accusations and a great riot followed. Paul was dragged out of the Temple, and immediately the gates were closed behind him. 31As they were killing him, word reached the commander of the Roman garrison that all Jerusalem was in an uproar. 32He quickly ordered out his soldiers and officers and ran down among the crowd. When the mob saw the troops coming, they quit beating Paul. 33The commander arrested him and ordered him bound with double chains. Then he asked the crowd who he was and what he had done. 34Some shouted one thing and some another. When he couldn't find out anything in all the uproar and confusion, he ordered Paul to be taken to the armory. 35As they reached the stairs, the mob grew so violent that the soldiers lifted Paul to their shoulders to protect him, 36and the crowd surged behind shouting, "Away with him, away with him!"

PSALM 150:1–6

HALLELUJAH! Yes, praise the Lord! Praise him in his Temple, and in the heavens he made with mighty power. 2Praise him for his mighty works. Praise his unequaled greatness. 3Praise him with the trumpet and with lute and harp. 4Praise him with the drums and dancing. Praise him with stringed instruments and horns. 5Praise him with the cymbals, yes, loud clanging cymbals.

6Let everything alive give praises to the Lord! *You* praise him!

Hallelujah!

PROVERBS FOR TODAY/ 18:9–10

A lazy man is brother to the saboteur. The Lord is a strong fortress. The godly run to him and are safe.

JULY 3

2 KINGS 22:4—23:30

COLLECT the money given to the priests at the door of the Temple when the people come to worship. 5,6Give this money to the building superintendents so that they can hire carpenters and masons to repair the Temple, and to buy lumber and stone."

7(The building superintendents were not required to keep account of their expenditures, for they were honest men.)

8One day Hilkiah the High Priest went to Shaphan the secretary and exclaimed, "I have discovered a scroll in the Temple, with God's laws written on it!"

He gave the scroll to Shaphan to read. 9,10When Shaphan reported to the king about the progress of the repairs at the Temple, he also mentioned the scroll found by Hilkiah. Then Shaphan read it to the king. 11When the king heard what was written in it, he tore his clothes in terror. 12,13He commanded Hilkiah the priest, and Shaphan, and Asaiah, the king's assistant, and Ahikam (Shaphan's son), and Achbor (Michaiah's son) to ask the Lord, "What shall we do? For we have not been following the instructions of this book: you must be very angry with us, for neither we nor our ancestors have followed your commands."

14So Hilkiah the priest, and Ahikam, and Achbor, and Shaphan, and Asaiah went to the Mishneh section of Jerusalem to find Huldah the prophetess. (She was the wife of Shallum—son of Tikvah, son of Harhas—who was in charge of the palace tailor shop.) 15,16She gave them this message from the Lord God of Israel:

"Tell the man who sent you to me, that I am going to destroy this city and its people, just as I stated in that book you read. 17For the people of Judah have thrown me aside and have worshiped other gods and have made me very angry; and my anger can't be stopped. 18,19But because you were sorry and concerned and humbled yourself before the Lord when you read the book and its warnings that this land would be cursed and become desolate, and because you have torn your clothing and wept before me in contrition, I will listen to your plea. 20The death of this nation will not occur until after you die—you will not see the evil which I will bring upon this place."

So they took the message to the king.

THEN the king sent for the elders and other leaders of Judah and Jerusalem to go to the Temple with him. So all the priests and prophets and the people, small and great, of Jerusalem and Judah gathered there at the Temple so that the king could read to them the entire book of God's laws which had been discovered in the Temple. 3He stood beside the pillar in front of the people, and he and they made a solemn promise to the Lord to obey him at all times and to do everything the book commanded.

4Then the king instructed Hilkiah the High Priest and the rest of the priests and the guards of the Temple to destroy all the equipment used in the worship of Baal, Asherah, and the sun, moon, and stars. The king had it all burned in the fields of the Kidron Valley outside Jerusalem, and he carried the ashes to Bethel. 5He killed the heathen priests who had been appointed by the previous kings of Judah, for they had burned incense in the shrines on the hills throughout Judah and even in Jerusalem. They had also offered incense to Baal and to the sun, moon, stars, and planets. 6He removed the shameful idol of Asherah from the Temple and took it outside Jerusalem to Kidron Brook; there he burned it and beat it to dust and threw the dust on the graves of the common people. 7He also tore down the houses of male prostitution around the Temple, where the women wove robes for the Asherah-idol.

8He brought back to Jerusalem the priests of the Lord, who were living in other cities of Judah, and tore down all the shrines on the hills where they had burned incense, even those as far away as Geba and Beersheba. He also destroyed the shrines at the entrance of the palace of Joshua, the former mayor of Jerusalem, located on the left side as one enters the city gate. 9However, these priests did not serve at the altar of the Lord in Jerusalem, even though they ate with the other priests.

10Then the king destroyed the altar of Topheth in the Valley of the Sons of Hinnom, so that no one could ever again use it to burn his son or daughter to death as a sacrifice to Molech. 11He tore down the statues of horses and chariots located near the entrance of the Temple, next to the quarters of Nathan-melech the eunuch. These had been dedicated by former kings of Judah to the sun god. 12Then he tore down the altars which the kings of Judah had built on the palace roof above the Ahaz Room. He also destroyed the altars which Manasseh had built in the two courts of the Temple; he smashed them to bits and scattered the pieces in Kidron Valley.

13Next he removed the shrines on the hills east of Jerusalem and south of Destruction Mountain. (Solomon had built these shrines for Ashtoreth, the evil goddess of the Sidonians; and for Chemosh, the evil god of Moab; and for Milcom, the evil god of the Ammonites.) 14He smashed the obelisks and cut down the shameful idols of Asherah; then he defiled these places by scattering human bones over them. ¹⁵He also tore down the altar and shrine at Bethel which Jeroboam I had made when he led Israel into sin. He crushed the stones to dust and burned the shameful idol of Asherah.

¹⁶As Josiah was looking around, he noticed several graves in the side of the mountain. He ordered his men to bring out the bones in them and to burn them there upon the altar at Bethel to defile it, just as the Lord's prophet had declared would happen to Jeroboam's altar.

¹⁷"What is that monument over there?" he asked.

And the men of the city told him, "It is the grave of the prophet who came from Judah and proclaimed that what you have just done would happen here at the altar at Bethel!"

¹⁸So King Josiah replied, "Leave it alone. Don't disturb his bones."

So they didn't burn his bones or those of the prophet from Samaria.

¹⁹Josiah demolished the shrines on the hills in all of Samaria. They had been built by the various kings of Israel and had made the Lord very angry. But now he crushed them into dust, just as he had done at Bethel. ²⁰He executed the priests of the heathen shrines upon their own altars, and he burned human bones upon the altars to defile them. Finally he returned to Jerusalem.

²¹The king then issued orders for his people to observe the Passover ceremonies as recorded by the Lord their God in *The Book of the Covenant.* ²²There had not been a Passover celebration like that since the days of the judges of Israel, and there was never another like it in all the years of the kings of Israel and Judah. ²³This Passover was in the eighteenth year of the reign of King Josiah, and it was celebrated in Jerusalem.

²⁴Josiah also exterminated the mediums and wizards, and every kind of idol worship, both in Jerusalem and throughout the land. For Josiah wanted to follow all the laws which were written in the book that Hilkiah the priest had found in the Temple. ²⁵There was no other king

who so completely turned to the Lord and followed all the laws of Moses; and no king since the time of Josiah has approached his record of obedience.

²⁶But the Lord still did not hold back his great anger against Judah, caused by the evils of King Manasseh. ²⁷For the Lord had said, "I will destroy Judah just as I have destroyed Israel; and I will discard my chosen city of Jerusalem and the Temple that I said was mine."

²⁸The rest of the biography of Josiah is written in *The Annals of the Kings of Judah.* ²⁹In those days King Neco of Egypt went out to help the king of Assyria at the Euphrates River. Then King Josiah went out with his troops to fight King Neco; but King Neco withstood him at Meggido and killed him. ³⁰His officers took his body back in a chariot from Megiddo to Jerusalem and buried him in the grave he had selected. And his son Jehoahaz was chosen by the nation as its new king.

ACTS 21:37—22:16

AS Paul was about to be taken inside, he said to the commander, "May I have a word with you?"

"Do you know Greek?" the commander asked, surprised. "Aren't you that Egyptian who led a rebellion a few years ago and took 4,000 members of the Assassins with him into the desert?"

³⁹"No," Paul replied, "I am a Jew from Tarsus in Cilicia which is no small town. I request permission to talk to these people."

⁴⁰The commander agreed, so Paul stood on the stairs and motioned to the people to be quiet; soon a deep silence enveloped the crowd, and he addressed them in Hebrew as follows:

"BROTHERS and fathers, listen to me as I offer my defense." ²(When they heard him speaking in Hebrew, the silence was even greater.) ³"I am a Jew," he said, "born in Tarsus, a city in Cilicia, but educated here in Jerusalem under Gamaliel, at whose feet I learned to follow our Jewish laws and customs very carefully.

I became very anxious to honor God in everything I did, just as you have tried to do today. 4And I persecuted the Christians, hounding them to death, binding and delivering both men and women to prison. 5The High Priest or any member of the Council can testify that this is so. For I asked them for letters to the Jewish leaders in Damascus, with instructions to let me bring any Christians I found to Jerusalem in chains to be punished.

6"As I was on the road, nearing Damascus, suddenly about noon a very bright light from heaven shone around me. 7And I fell to the ground and heard a voice saying to me, 'Paul, Paul, why are you persecuting me?'

8" 'Who is it speaking to me, sir?' I asked. And he replied, 'I am Jesus of Nazareth, the one you are persecuting.' 9The men with me saw the light but didn't understand what was said.

10"And I said, 'What shall I do, Lord?'

"And the Lord told me, 'Get up and go into Damascus, and there you will be told what awaits you in the years ahead.'

11"I was blinded by the intense light, and had to be led into Damascus by my companions. 12There a man named Ananias, as godly a man as you could find for obeying the law, and well thought of by all the Jews of Damascus, 13came to me, and standing beside me said,

'Brother Paul, receive your sight!' And that very hour I could see him!

14"Then he told me, 'The God of our fathers has chosen you to know his will and to see the Messiah and hear him speak. 15You are to take his message everywhere, telling what you have seen and heard. 16And now, why delay? Go and be baptized, and be cleansed from your sins, calling on the name of the Lord.'

PSALM 1:1–6

OH, the joys of those who do not follow evil men's advice, who do not hang around with sinners, scoffing at the things of God: 2But they delight in doing everything God wants them to, and day and night are always meditating on his laws and thinking about ways to follow him more closely.

3They are like trees along a river bank bearing luscious fruit each season without fail. Their leaves shall never wither, and all they do shall prosper.

4But for sinners, what a different story! They blow away like chaff before the wind. 5They are not safe on Judgment Day; they shall not stand among the godly.

6For the Lord watches over all the plans and paths of godly men, but the paths of the godless lead to doom.

PROVERBS FOR TODAY/ 18:11–12

The rich man thinks of his wealth as an impregnable defense, a high wall of safety. What a dreamer! Pride ends in destruction; humility ends in honor.

JULY 4

2 KINGS 23:31—25:30

NEW king of Judah: Jehoahaz
   His age when he became king: 23 years old
Length of his reign: 3 months, in Jerusalem

His mother's name: Hamutal (the daughter of Jeremiah of Libnah)
Character of his reign: evil, like the other kings who had preceded him
33Pharaoh-Neco jailed him at Riblah in Hamath to prevent his reigning in Jerusa-

lem, and he levied a tax against Judah totaling $230,000. 34The Egyptian king then chose Eliakim, another of Josiah's sons, to reign in Jerusalem; and he changed his name to Jehoiakim. Then he took King Jehoahaz to Egypt, where he died. 35Jehoiakim taxed the people to get the money that the Pharaoh had demanded.

36,37New king of Judah: Jehoiakim

His age when he became king: 25 years old

Length of his reign: 11 years, in Jerusalem

His mother's name: Zebidah (daughter of Pedaiah of Rumah)

Character of his reign: evil, like the other kings who had preceded him

DURING the reign of King Jehoiakim, King Nebuchadnezzar of Babylon attacked Jerusalem. Jehoiakim surrendered and paid him tribute for three years, but then rebelled. 2And the Lord sent bands of Chaldeans, Syrians, Moabites, and Ammonites against Judah in order to destroy the nation, just as the Lord had warned through his prophets that he would. 3,4It is clear that these disasters befell Judah at the direct command of the Lord. He had decided to wipe Judah out of his sight because of the many sins of Manasseh, for he had filled Jerusalem with blood, and the Lord would not pardon it.

5The rest of the history of the life of Jehoiakim is recorded in *The Annals of the Kings of Judah.* 6When he died, his son Jehoiachin became the new king. 7(The Egyptian Pharaoh never returned after that, for the king of Babylon occupied the entire area claimed by Egypt— all of Judah from the Brook of Egypt to the Euphrates River.)

8,9New king of Judah, Jehoiachin

His age at the beginning of his reign: 18 years old

Length of his reign: 3 months, in Jerusalem

Name of his mother: Nehushta (daughter of Elnathan, a citizen of Jerusalem)

10During his reign the armies of King Nebuchadnezzar of Babylon besieged the city of Jerusalem. 11Nebuchadnezzar himself arrived during the siege, 12and King Jehoiachin, all of his officials, and the queen mother surrendered to him. The surrender was accepted, and Jehoiachin was imprisoned in Babylon during the eighth year of Nebuchadnezzar's reign.

13The Babylonians carried home all the treasures from the Temple and the royal palace; and they cut apart all the gold bowls which King Solomon of Israel had placed in the Temple at the Lord's directions. 14King Nebuchadnezzar took ten thousand captives from Jerusalem, including all the princes and the best of the soldiers, craftsmen, and smiths. So only the poorest and least skilled people were left in the land. 15Nebuchadnezzar took King Jehoiachin, his wives and officials, and the queen mother, to Babylon. 16He also took seven thousand of the best troops and one thousand craftsmen and smiths, all of whom were strong and fit for war. 17Then the king of Babylon appointed King Jehoiachin's great-uncle, Mattaniah, to be the next king; and he changed his name to Zedekiah.

18,19New king of Judah: Zedekiah

His age when he became king: 21 years old

Length of his reign: 11 years, in Jerusalem

His mother's name: Hamutal (daughter of Jeremiah of Libnah)

Character of his reign: evil, like that of Jehoiakim

20So the Lord finally, in his anger, destroyed the people of Jerusalem and Judah. But now King Zedekiah rebelled against the king of Babylon.

THEN King Nebuchadnezzar of Babylon mobilized his entire army and laid siege to Jerusalem, arriving on March 25 of the ninth year of the reign of King Zedekiah of Judah. 2The siege continued into the eleventh year of his reign.

3The last food in the city was eaten on July 24, 4,5and that night the king and his troops made a hole in the inner wall and fled out toward the Arabah through a gate that lay between the double walls near the king's garden. The Babylonian troops surrounding the city took out after him and captured him in the plains of Jericho, and all his men scattered. 6He was taken to Riblah, where he was tried and sentenced before the king of Babylon. 7He was forced to watch as his sons were killed before his eyes; then his eyes were put out and he was bound with chains and taken away to Babylon.

8General Nebuzaradan, the captain of the royal bodyguard, arrived at Jerusalem from Babylon on July 22 of the nineteenth year of the reign of King Nebuchadnezzar. 9He burned down the Temple, the palace, and all the other houses of any worth. 10He then supervised the Babylonian army in tearing down the walls of Jerusalem. 11The remainder of the people in the city and the Jewish deserters who had declared their allegiance to the king of Babylon were all taken as exiles to Babylon. 12But the poorest of the people were left to farm the land.

13The Babylonians broke up the bronze pillars of the Temple and the bronze tank and its bases and carried all the bronze to Babylon. 14,15They also took all the pots, shovels, firepans, snuffers, spoons, and other bronze instruments used for the sacrifices. The gold and silver bowls, with all the rest of the gold and silver, were melted down to bullion. 16It was impossible to estimate the weight of the two pillars and the great tank and its bases—all made for the Temple by King Solomon—because they were so heavy. 17Each pillar was twenty-seven feet high, with an intricate bronze network of pomegranates decorating the 4½-foot capitals at the tops of the pillars.

18The general took Seraiah, the chief priest, his assistant Zephaniah, and the three Temple guards to Babylon as captives. 19A commander of the army of Judah, the chief recruiting officer, five of the king's counselors, and sixty farmers, all of whom were discovered hiding in the city, 20were taken by General Nebu-zaradan to the king of Babylon at Riblah, 21where they were put to the sword and died.

So Judah was exiled from its land.

22Then King Nebuchadnezzar appointed Gedaliah (the son of Ahikam and grandson of Shaphan) as governor over the people left in Judah. 23When the Israeli guerrilla forces learned that the king of Babylon had appointed Gedaliah as governor, some of these underground leaders and their men joined him at Mizpah. These included Ishmael, the son of Nethaniah; Johanan, the son of Kareah; Seraiah, the son of Tanhumeth the Netophathite; and Jaazaniah, son of Maachathite, and their men.

24Gedaliah vowed that if they would give themselves up and submit to the Babylonians, they would be allowed to live in the land and would not be exiled. 25But seven months later, Ishmael, who was a member of the royal line, went to Mizpah with ten men and killed Gedaliah and his court—both the Jews and the Babylonians.

26Then all the men of Judah and the guerrilla leaders fled in panic to Egypt, for they were afraid of what the Babylonians would do to them.

27King Jehoiachin was released from prison on the twenty-seventh day of the last month of the thirty-seventh year of his captivity.

This occurred during the first year of the reign of King Evil-merodach of Babylon. 28He treated Jehoiachin kindly and gave him preferential treatment over all the other kings who were being held as prisoners in Babylon. 29Jehoiachin was given civilian clothing to replace his prison garb, and for as long as he lived, he ate regularly at the king's table. 30The king also gave him a daily cash allowance for the rest of his life.

ACTS 22:17—23:10

ONE day after my return to Jerusalem, while I was praying in the Temple, I fell into a trance and saw a vision of God saying to me, 'Hurry!

Leave Jerusalem, for the people here won't believe you when you give them my message.'

19" 'But Lord,' I argued, 'they certainly know that I imprisoned and beat those in every synagogue who believed on you. 20And when your witness Stephen was killed, I was standing there agreeing— keeping the coats they laid aside as they stoned him.'

21"But God said to me, 'Leave Jerusalem, for I will send you far away to the *Gentiles!*' "

22The crowd listened until Paul came to that word, then with one voice they shouted, "Away with such a fellow! Kill him! He isn't fit to live!" 23They yelled and threw their coats in the air and tossed up handfuls of dust.

24So the commander brought him inside and ordered him lashed with whips to make him confess his crime. He wanted to find out why the crowd had become so furious!

25As they tied Paul down to lash him, Paul said to an officer standing there, "Is it legal for you to whip a Roman citizen who hasn't even been tried?"

26The officer went to the commander and asked, "What are you doing? This man is a Roman citizen!"

27So the commander went over and asked Paul, "Tell me, are you a Roman citizen?"

"Yes, I certainly am."

28"I am too," the commander muttered, "and it cost me plenty!"

"But I am a citizen by birth!"

29The soldiers standing ready to lash him, quickly disappeared when they heard Paul was a Roman citizen, and the commander was frightened because he had ordered him bound and whipped.

30The next day the commander freed him from his chains and ordered the chief priests into session with the Jewish Council. He had Paul brought in before them to try to find out what the trouble was all about.

GAZING intently at the Council, Paul began:

"Brothers, I have always lived before God in all good conscience!"

2Instantly Ananias the High Priest commanded those close to Paul to slap him on the mouth.

3Paul said to him, "God shall slap you, you whitewashed pigpen. What kind of judge are you to break the law yourself by ordering me struck like that?"

4Those standing near Paul said to him, "Is that the way to talk to God's High Priest?"

5"I didn't realize he was the High Priest, brothers," Paul replied, "for the Scriptures say, 'Never speak evil of any of your rulers.' "

6Then Paul thought of something! Part of the Council were Sadducees, and part were Pharisees! So he shouted, "Brothers, I am a Pharisee, as were all my ancestors! And I am being tried here today because I believe in the resurrection of the dead!"

7This divided the Council right down the middle—the Pharisees against the Sadducees— 8for the Sadducees say there is no resurrection or angels or even eternal spirit within us, but the Pharisees believe in all of these.

9So a great clamor arose. Some of the Jewish leaders jumped up to argue that Paul was all right. "We see nothing wrong with him," they shouted. "Perhaps a spirit or angel spoke to him [there on the Damascus road]."

10The shouting grew louder and louder, and the men were tugging at Paul from both sides, pulling him this way and that. Finally the commander, fearing they would tear him apart, ordered his soldiers to take him away from them by force and bring him back to the armory.

PSALM 2:1-12

WHAT fools the nations are to rage against the Lord! How strange that men should try to outwit God! 2For a summit conference of the nations has been called to plot against the Lord and his Messiah, Christ the King. ³"Come, let us break his chains," they say, "and free ourselves from all this slavery to God."

⁴But God in heaven merely laughs! He is amused by all their puny plans. ⁵And then in fierce fury he rebukes them and fills them with fear.

⁶For the Lord declares, "This is the King of my choice, and I have enthroned him in Jerusalem, my holy city."

⁷His chosen one replies, "I will reveal the everlasting purposes of God, for the Lord has said to me, 'You are my Son. This is your Coronation Day. Today I am giving you your glory.'" ⁸"Only ask, and I will give you all the nations of the world. ⁹Rule them with an iron rod; smash them like clay pots!"

¹⁰O kings and rulers of the earth, listen while there is time. ¹¹Serve the Lord with reverent fear; rejoice with trembling. ¹²Fall down before his Son and kiss his feet before his anger is roused and you perish. I am warning you—his wrath will soon begin. But oh, the joys of those who put their trust in him!

PROVERBS FOR TODAY/ 18:13
What a shame—yes, how stupid!—to decide before knowing the facts!

JULY 5

1 CHRONICLES 1:1—2:17

THESE are the earliest generations of mankind:

Adam, Seth, Enosh, Kenan, Mahalalel, Jared, Enoch, Methuselah, Lamech, Noah, **Shem, Ham,** and **Japheth.**

⁵⁻⁹The sons of *Japheth* were:

Gomer, Magog, Madai, **Javan,** Tubal, Meshech, and Tiras.

The sons of *Gomer:*

Ashkenaz, Diphath, and Togarmah.

The sons of *Javan:*

Elishah, Tarshish, Kittim, and Rodanim.

The sons of *Ham:*

Cush, Misream, Canaan, and **Put.**

The sons of *Cush* were:

Seba, Havilah, Sabta, Raama, and Sabteca.

The sons of Raama were Sheba and Dedan.

¹⁰Another of the sons of *Cush* was Nimrod, who became a great hero.

¹¹,¹²The clans named after the sons of *Misream* were:

the Ludim, the Anamim, the Lehabim, the Naphtuhim, the Pathrusim, the Caphtorim, and the Casluhim (the ancestors of the Philistines).

¹³⁻¹⁶Among *Canaan's* sons were:

Sidon (his firstborn) and Heth.

Canaan was also the ancestor of the Jebusites, Amorites, Girgashites, Hivites, Arkites, Sinites, Arvadites, Zemarites, and Hamathites.

¹⁷The sons of *Shem:*

Elam, Asshur, **Arpachshad,** Lud, Aram, Uz, Hul, Gether, and Meshech.

¹⁸*Arpachshad's* son was **Shelah,** and *Shelah's* son was **Eber.**

¹⁹*Eber* had two sons: Peleg (which means "Divided," for it was during his lifetime that the people of the earth were divided into different language groups), and Joktan.

²⁰⁻²³The sons of Joktan:

Almodad, Sheleph, Hazarmaveth, Jerah, Hadoram, Uzal, Diklah, Ebal, Abima-el, Sheba, Ophir, Havilah, and Jobab.

²⁴⁻²⁷So the son of *Shem* was Arpachshad, the son of Arpachshad was Shelah,

The son of Shelah was Eber,

The son of Eber was Peleg,

The son of Peleg was Reu,
The son of Reu was Serug,
The son of Serug was Nahor,
The son of Nahor was Terah,
The son of Terah was Abram (later
known as Abraham).

28-31Abraham's sons were Isaac and
Ishmael.

The sons of *Ishmael:*
Nabaioth (the oldest), Kedar, Adbeel,
Mibsam, Mishma, Dumah, Massa, Hadad, Tema, Jetur, Naphish, and Kedemah.

32Abraham also had sons by his concubine Keturah:
Zimram, **Jokshan,** Medan, **Midian,**
Ishbak, and Shuah.

Jokshan's sons were Sheba and Dedan.

33The sons of *Midian:*
Ephah, Epher, Hanoch, Abida, and
Eldaah. These were the descendants of Abraham by his concubine
Keturah.

34Abraham's son *Isaac* had two sons,
Esau and Israel.

35The sons of *Esau:*
Eliphaz, Reuel, Jeush, Jalam, and
Korah.

36The sons of *Eliphaz:*
Teman, Omar, Zephi, Gatam, Kenaz,
Timna, and Amalek.

37The sons of *Reuel:*
Nahath, Zerah, Shammah, and Mizzah.

38,39The sons of *Esau* also included
Lotan, Shobal, Zibeon, Anah, **Dishon, Ezer,** and **Dishan;** and Esau's
daughter was named Timna.

Lotan's sons: Hori and Homam.

40The sons of *Shobal:* Alian, Manahath,
Ebal, Shephi, and Onam.

Zibeon's sons were Aiah and **Anah.**

41*Anah's* son was **Dishon:**
The sons of *Dishon:* Hamran, Eshban,
Ithran, and Cheran.

42The sons of *Ezer:* Bilhan, Zaavan,
and Jaakan.

Dishan's sons were Uz and Aran.

43Here is a list of the names of the
kings of Edom who reigned before the
kingdom of Israel began:
Bela (the son of Beor), who lived in
the city of Dinhabah.

44When Bela died, Jobab the son of
Zerah from Bozrah became the new king.

45When Jobab died, Husham from the
country of the Temanites became the
king.

46When Husham died, Hadad the son
of Bedad—the one who destroyed the
army of Midian in the fields of Moab—
became king and ruled from the city of
Avith.

47When Hadad died, Samlah from the
city of Masrekah came to the throne.

48When Samlah died, Shaul from the
river town of Rehoboth became the new
king.

49When Shaul died, Baal-hanan the son
of Achbor became king.

50When Baal-hanan died, Hadad became king and ruled from the city of Pai
(his wife was Mehetabel, the daughter
of Matred and granddaughter of Mezahab).

51-54At the time of Hadad's death, the
kings of Edom were:
Chief Timna, Chief Aliah, Chief Jetheth, Chief Oholibamah, Chief Elah,
Chief Pinon, Chief Kenaz, Chief Teman, Chief Mibzar, Chief Magdi-el,
Chief Iram.

THE sons of Israel were:
Reuben, Simeon, Levi, Judah, Issachar,
Zebulun, Dan, Joseph, Benjamin, Naphtali, Gad, Asher.

3Judah had three sons by Bath-shua,
a girl from Canaan: **Er,** Onan, and Shelah.
But the oldest son, *Er,* was so wicked
that the Lord killed him.

4Then Er's widow, Tamar, and her father-in-law, Judah, became the parents
of twin sons, **Perez** and **Zerah.** So Judah had five sons.

5The sons of *Perez* were Hezron and
Hamul.

6The sons of *Zerah* were:
Zimri, **Ethan,** Heman, Calcol, and
Dara.

7(Achan, the son of Carmi, was the
man who robbed God and was such a
troublemaker for his nation.)

8*Ethan's* son was Azariah.

9The sons of *Hezron* were Jerahmeel, Ram, and Chelubai.

10Ram was the father of Amminadab, and Amminadab was the father of Nahshon, a leader of Israel.

11Nahshon was the father of Salma, and Salma was the father of Boaz.

12Boaz was the father of Obed, and Obed was the father of Jesse.

13*Jesse's* first son was Eliab, his second was Abinadab, his third was Shimea, 14his fourth was Nethanel, his fifth was Raddai, 15his sixth was Ozem, and his seventh was David. 16He also had two girls (by the same wife) named **Zeruiah** and **Abigail.**

Zeruiah's sons were Abishai, Joab, and Asahel.

17*Abigail,* whose husband was Jether from the land of Ishmael, had a son named Amasa.

ACTS 23:11–35

THAT night the Lord stood beside Paul and said, "Don't worry, Paul; just as you have told the people about me here in Jerusalem, so you must also in Rome."

12,13The next morning some forty or more of the Jews got together and bound themselves by a curse neither to eat nor drink until they had killed Paul! 14Then they went to the chief priests and elders and told them what they had done. 15"Ask the commander to bring Paul back to the Council again," they requested. "Pretend you want to ask a few more questions. We will kill him on the way."

16But Paul's nephew got wind of their plan and came to the armory and told Paul.

17Paul called one of the officers and said, "Take this boy to the commander. He has something important to tell him."

18So the officer did, explaining, "Paul, the prisoner, called me over and asked me to bring this young man to you to tell you something."

19The commander took the boy by the hand, and leading him aside asked, "What is it you want to tell me, lad?"

20"Tomorrow," he told him, "the Jews are going to ask you to bring Paul before the Council again, pretending they want to get some more information. 21But don't do it! There are more than forty men hiding along the road ready to jump him and kill him. They have bound themselves under a curse to neither eat nor drink till he is dead. They are out there now, expecting you to agree to their request."

22"Don't let a soul know you told me this," the commander warned the boy as he left. 23,24Then the commander called two of his officers and ordered, "Get 200 soldiers ready to leave for Caesarea at nine o'clock tonight! Take 200 spearmen and 70 mounted cavalry. Give Paul a horse to ride and get him safely to Governor Felix."

25Then he wrote this letter to the governor:

26"*From:* Claudius Lysias

"*To:* His Excellency, Governor Felix. "Greetings!

27"This man was seized by the Jews and they were killing him when I sent the soldiers to rescue him, for I learned that he was a Roman citizen. 28Then I took him to their Council to try to find out what he had done. 29I soon discovered it was something about their Jewish beliefs, certainly nothing worthy of imprisonment or death. 30But when I was informed of a plot to kill him, I decided to send him on to you and will tell his accusers to bring their charges before you."

31So that night, as ordered, the soldiers took Paul to Antipatris. 32They returned to the armory the next morning, leaving him with the cavalry to take him on to Caesarea.

33When they arrived in Caesarea, they presented Paul and the letter to the governor. 34He read it and then asked Paul where he was from.

"Cilicia," Paul answered.

35"I will hear your case fully when your accusers arrive," the governor told him, and ordered him kept in the prison at King Herod's palace.

PSALM 3:1–8

O Lord, so many are against me. So many seek to harm me. I have so many enemies. ²So many say that God will never help me. ³But Lord, you are my shield, my glory, and my only hope. You alone can lift my head, now bowed in shame.

⁴I cried out to the Lord, and he heard me from his Temple in Jerusalem.

⁵Then I lay down and slept in peace and woke up safely, for the Lord was watching over me. ⁶And now, although ten thousand enemies surround me on every side, I am not afraid. ⁷I will cry to him, "Arise, O Lord! Save me, O my God!" And he will slap them in the face, insulting them and breaking off their teeth.

⁸For salvation comes from God. What joys he gives to all his people.

PROVERBS FOR TODAY/ 18:14–15

A man's courage can sustain his broken body, but when courage dies, what hope is left? The intelligent man is always open to new ideas. In fact, he looks for them.

JULY 6

1 CHRONICLES 2:18—4:4

CALEB (the son of **Hezron**) had two wives, **Azubah** and Jerioth. These are the children of *Azubah:* Jesher, Shobab, and Ardon.

¹⁹After Azubah's death, Caleb married Ephrath, who presented him with a son, **Hur.**

²⁰*Hur's* son was **Uri,** and *Uri's* son was Bezalel.

²¹**Hezron** married Machir's daughter at the age of sixty, and she presented him with a son, **Segub.** (Machir was also the father of Gilead.)

²²*Segub* was the father of Jair, who ruled twenty-three cities in the land of Gilead. ²³But Geshur and Aram wrested these cities from him and also took Kenath and its sixty surrounding villages.

²⁴Soon after his father *Hezron's* death, Caleb married Ephrathah, his father's widow, and she gave birth to Ashhur, the father of Tekoa.

²⁵These are the sons of **Jerahmeel** (the oldest son of *Hezron*):

Ram (the oldest), Bunah, Oren, Ozem, and Ahijah.

²⁶*Jerahmeel's* second wife Atarah was the mother of **Onam.**

²⁷The sons of *Ram:*

Maaz, Jamin, and Eker.

²⁸*Onam's* sons were **Shammai** and Jada.

Shammai's sons were **Nadab** and **Abishur.**

²⁹The sons of *Abishur* and his wife Abihail were Ahban and Molid.

³⁰*Nadab's* sons were **Seled** and **Appa-im.** *Seled* died without children, ³¹but *Appa-im* had a son named **Ishi;** *Ishi's* son was **Sheshan;** and *Sheshan's* son was Ahlai.

³²*Shammai's* brother Jada had two sons, **Jether** and **Jonathan.** *Jether* died without children, ³³but *Jonathan* had two sons named Peleth and Zaza.

³⁴,³⁵*Sheshan* had no sons, although he had several daughters. He gave one of his daughters to be the wife of Jarha, his Egyptian servant. And they had a son whom they named **Attai.**

³⁶Attai's son was Nathan; Nathan's was Zabad; ³⁷Zabad's son was Ephlal; Ephlal's son was Obed; ³⁸Obed's son was

Jehu; Jehu's son was Azariah; 39Azariah's son was Helez; Helez's son was Ele-asah; 40Ele-asah's son was Sismai; Sismai's son was Shallum; 41Shallum's son was Jekamiah; Jekamiah's son was Eli-shama.

42The oldest son of **Caleb** (Jerah-meel's brother) was Mesha; he was the father of Ziph, who was father of Mareshah, who was the father of **Hebron.**

43The sons of *Hebron:* Korah, Tap-puah, **Rekem,** and **Shema.**

44*Shema* was the father of Raham, who was the father of Jorke-am.

Rekem was the father of **Shammai.** 45*Shammai's* son was Maon, the fa-ther of Bethzur.

46*Caleb's* concubine Ephah bore him **Haran,** Moza, and Gazez; *Haran* had a son named Gazez.

47The sons of Jahdai: Regem, Jotham, Geshan, Pelet, Ephah, and Shaaph.

48,49Another of *Caleb's* concubines, Maacah, bore him Sheber, Tirhanah, Shaaph (the father of Madmannah), and Sheva (the father of Machbenah and of Gibe-a). *Caleb* also had a daughter, whose name was Achsah.

50The sons of Hur (who was the oldest son of *Caleb* and Ephrathah) were **Shobal** (the father of Kiriath-jearim), 51**Salma** (the father of Bethlehem), and Hareph (the father of Beth-gader).

52**Shobal's** sons included **Kiriath-jearim** and Haroeh, the ancestor of half of the Menuhoth tribe.

53The families of *Kiriath-jearim* were the Ithrites, the Puthites, the Shuma-thites, and the Mishraites (from whom descended the Zorathites and Eshta-olites).

54The descendants of Salma were his son Bethlehem, the Netophathites, Atrothbeth-joab, half the Manahathites, and the Zorites; 55they also included the families of the writers living at Jabez—the Tirathites, Shime-athites, and Suca-thites. All these are Kenites who de-scended from Hammath, the founder of the family of Rechab.

KING David's oldest son was Amnon, who was born to his wife, Ahino-am of Jezreel.

The second was Daniel, whose mother was Abigail from Carmel.

2The third was Absalom, the son of his wife Maacah, who was the daughter of King Talmai of Geshur.

The fourth was Adonijah, the son of Haggith.

3The fifth was Shephatiah, the son of Abital.

The sixth was Ithream, the son of his wife Eglah.

4These six were born to him in He-bron, where he reigned seven and one-half years. Then he moved the capital to Jerusalem, where he reigned another thirty-three years.

5While he was in Jerusalem, his wife Bathsheba (the daughter of Ammi-el) be-came the mother of his sons Shime-a, Shobab, Nathan, and **Solomon.**

6,7,8David also had nine other sons: Ibhar, Elishama, Eliphelet, Nogah, Nepheg, Japhia, Elishama, Eliada, and Eliphelet.

9(This list does not include the sons of his concubines.) David also had a daughter Tamar.

10–14These are the descendants of King *Solomon:*

Rehoboam, Abijah, Asa, Jehoshaphat, Joram, Ahaziah, Joash, Amaziah, Aza-riah, Jotham, Ahaz, Hezekiah, Manas-seh, Amon, Josiah.

15The sons of *Josiah* were: Johanan, **Jehoiakim,** Zedekiah, Shal-lum.

16The sons of *Jehoiakim:* **Jeconiah,** Zedekiah.

17,18These are the sons who were born to King *Jeconiah* during the years that he was under house arrest: Shealtiel, Malchiram, **Pedaiah,** Shen-azzar, Jekamiah, Hoshama, Nedabiah.

19,20*Pedaiah* was the father of **Zerub-babel** and Shime-i.

Zerubbabel's children were: Meshullam, **Hananiah,** Hashubah, Ohel, Berechiah, Hasadiah, Jushab-hesed, Shelomith (a daughter).

21,22*Hananiah's* sons were Pelatiah and Jeshaiah;

Jeshaiah's son was Rephaiah; Rephaiah's son was Arnan; Arnan's son was Obadiah; Obadiah's son was Shecaniah. Shecaniah's son was Shemaiah; Shemaiah had six sons, including Hattush, Igal, Bariah, **Neariah,** and Shaphat.

23*Neariah* had three sons:

Eli-o-enai, Hizkiah, Azrikam.

24*Eli-o-enai* had seven sons:

Hodaviah, Eliashib, Pelaiah, Akkub, Johanan, Delaiah, Anani.

THESE are the sons of Judah:

Perez, Hezron, Carmi, Hur, **Shobal.**

2*Shobal's* son Re-aiah was the father of Jahath, the ancestor of Ahumai and Lahad. These were known as the Zorathite clans.

3,4The descendants of Etam:

Jezreel, Ishma, Idbash,

Hazzelelponi (his daughter),

Penuel (the ancestor of Gedor),

Ezer (the ancestor of Hushah),

The son of Hur, the oldest son of Ephrathah, who was the father of Bethlehem.

ACTS 24:1–27

FIVE days later Ananias the High Priest arrived with some of the Jewish leaders and the lawyer Tertullus, to make their accusations against Paul. 2When Tertullus was called forward, he laid charges against Paul in the following address to the governor:

"Your Excellency, you have given quietness and peace to us Jews and have greatly reduced the discrimination against us. 3And for this we are very, very grateful to you. 4But lest I bore you, kindly give me your attention for only a moment as I briefly outline our case against this man. 5For we have found him to be a troublemaker, a man who is constantly inciting the Jews throughout the entire world to riots and rebellions against the Roman government. He is a ringleader of the sect known as the Nazarenes. 6Moreover, he was trying to defile the Temple when we arrested him.

"We would have given him what he justly deserves, 7but Lysias, the commander of the garrison, came and took him violently away from us, 8demanding that he be tried by Roman law. You can find out the truth of our accusations by examining him yourself."

9Then all the other Jews chimed in, declaring that everything Tertullus said was true.

10Now it was Paul's turn. The governor motioned for him to rise and speak.

Paul began: "I know, sir, that you have been a judge of Jewish affairs for many years, and this gives me confidence as I make my defense. 11You can quickly discover that it was no more than twelve days ago that I arrived in Jerusalem to worship at the Temple, 12and you will discover that I have never incited a riot in any synagogue or on the streets of any city; 13and these men certainly cannot prove the things they accuse me of doing.

14"But one thing I do confess, that I believe in the way of salvation, which they refer to as a sect; I follow that system of serving the God of our ancestors; I firmly believe in the Jewish law and everything written in the books of prophecy; 15and I believe, just as these men do, that there will be a resurrection of both the righteous and ungodly. 16Because of this I try with all my strength to always maintain a clear conscience before God and man.

17"After several years away, I returned to Jerusalem with money to aid the Jews, and to offer a sacrifice to God. 18My accusers saw me in the Temple as I was presenting my thank offering. I had shaved my head as their laws required, and there was no crowd around me, and no rioting! But some Jews from Turkey were there 19(who ought to be here if they have anything against me)— 20but look! Ask these men right here what wrongdoing their Council found in me, 21except that I said one thing I shouldn't when I shouted out, 'I am here before the Council to defend myself for believing that the dead will rise again!' "

22Felix, who knew Christians didn't go around starting riots, told the Jews to wait for the arrival of Lysias, the garrison commander, and then he would decide the case. 23He ordered Paul to prison but instructed the guards to treat him gently and not to forbid any of his friends from visiting him or bringing him gifts to make his stay more comfortable.

24A few days later Felix came with Drusilla, his legal wife, a Jewess. Sending for Paul, they listened as he told them about faith in Christ Jesus. 25And as he reasoned with them about righteousness and self-control and the judgment to come, Felix was terrified.

"Go away for now," he replied, "and when I have a more convenient time, I'll call for you again."

26He also hoped that Paul would bribe him, so he sent for him from time to time and talked with him. 27Two years went by in this way; then Felix was succeeded by Porcius Festus. And because Felix wanted to gain favor with the Jews, he left Paul in chains.

PSALM 4:1–8

O God, you have declared me perfect in your eyes; you have always cared for me in my distress; now hear me as I call again. Have mercy on me. Hear my prayer.

2The Lord God asks, "Sons of men, will you forever turn my glory into shame by worshiping these silly idols, when every claim that's made for them is false?"

3Mark this well: The Lord has set apart the redeemed for himself. Therefore he will listen to me and answer when I call to him. 4Stand before the Lord in awe, and do not sin against him. Lie quietly upon your bed in silent meditation. 5Put your trust in the Lord, and offer him pleasing sacrifices.

6Many say that God will never help us. Prove them wrong, O Lord, by letting the light of your face shine down upon us. 7Yes, the gladness you have given me is far greater than their joys at harvest time as they gaze at their bountiful crops. 8I will lie down in peace and sleep, for though I am alone, O Lord, you will keep me safe.

PROVERBS FOR TODAY/ 18:16–18

A gift does wonders; it will bring you before men of importance! Any story sounds true until someone tells the other side and sets the record straight. A coin toss ends arguments and settles disputes between powerful opponents.

JULY 7

1 CHRONICLES 4:5—5:17

ASHHUR, the father of Tekoa, had two wives—**Helah,** and **Naarah.**

6*Naarah* bore him Ahuzzam, Hepher, Temeni, and Haahashtari; 7and *Helah* bore him Zereth, Izhar, and Ethnan.

8Koz was the father of Anub and Zobebah; he was also the ancestor of the clan named after Aharhel, the son of Harum.

9Jabez was more distinguished than any of his brothers. His mother named him Jabez because she had such a hard time at his birth (Jabez means "Distress").

10He was the one who prayed to the God of Israel, "Oh, that you would wonderfully bless me and help me in my work; please be with me in all that I do, and keep me from all evil and disaster!" And God granted him his request.

11,12The descendants of Recah were: Chelub (the brother of Shuhah), whose son was Mahir, the father of **Eshton;**

Eshton was the father of Bethrapha, Paseah, and Tehinnah;

Tehinnah was the father of Irnahash.

13The sons of Kenaz were **Othni-el** and **Seraiah.**

Othni-el's sons were Hathath and **Meonothai;**

14*Meonothai* was the father of Ophrah;

Seraiah was the father of Joab, the ancestor of the inhabitants of Craftsman Valley (called that because many craftsmen lived there).

15The sons of Caleb (the son of Jephunneh):

Iru, **Elah,** Naam.

The sons of *Elah* included Kenaz.

16Jehallelel's sons were:

Ziph, Ziphah, Tiri-a, Asarel.

17Ezrah's sons were:

Jether, **Mered,** Epher, Jalon.

Mered married Bithi-ah, an Egyptian princess. She was the mother of Miriam, Shammai, and Ishbah—an ancestor of **Eshtemoa.**

18*Eshtemoa's* wife was a Jewess; she was the mother of Jered, Heber, and Jekuthiel, who were, respectively, the ancestors of the Gedorites, Socoites, and Zanoahites.

19Hodiah's wife was the sister of Naham. One of her sons was the father of Keilah the Garmite, and another was the father of Eshtemoa the Maacathite.

20The sons of Shimon:

Amnon, Rinnah, Ben-hanan, Tilon.

The sons of Ishi:

Zoheth, Ben-zoheth.

21,22The sons of Shelah (the son of Judah):

Er (the father of Lecah),

Laadah (the father of Mareshah),

The families of the linen workers who worked at Beth-ashbea,

Jokim,

The clans of Cozeba,

Joash,

Saraph (who was a ruler in Moab before he returned to Lehem).

These names all come from very ancient records.

23These clans were noted for their pottery, gardening, and planting; they all worked for the king:

24The sons of Simeon:

Nemu-el, Jamin, Jarib, Zerah, **Shaul.**

25*Shaul's* son was Shallum, his grandson was Mibsam, and his great-grandson was **Mishma.**

26*Mishma's* sons included Hammu-el (the father of Zaccur and grandfather of **Shime-i**).

27*Shime-i* had sixteen sons and six daughters, but none of his brothers had large families—they all had fewer children than was normal in Judah.

28They lived at Beer-sheba, Moladah, Hazar-shual, 29Bilhah, Ezem, Tolad, 30Bethuel, Hormah, Ziklag, 31Beth-marcaboth, Hazar-susim, Beth-biri, and Shaaraim. These cities were under their control until the time of David.

32,33Their descendants also lived in or near Etam, Ain, Rimmon, Tochen, and Ashan; some were as far away as Baal. (These facts are recorded in their genealogies.)

34-39These are the names of some of the princes of wealthy clans who traveled to the east side of Gedor Valley in search of pasture for their flocks:

Meshobab, Jamlech, Joshah, Joel, Jehu, Eli-o-enai, Ja-akobah, Jeshohaiah, Asaiah, Adi-el, Jesimi-el, Benaiah, Ziza (the son of Shiphi, son of Allon, son of Jedaiah, son of Shimri, son of Shemaiah).

40,41They found good pastures, and everything was quiet and peaceful; but the land belonged to the descendants of Ham.

So during the reign of King Hezekiah of Judah these princes invaded the land and struck down the tents and houses of the descendants of Ham; they killed the inhabitants of the land and took possession of it for themselves.

42Later, five hundred of these invaders from the tribe of Simeon went to Mount Seir. (Their leaders were Pelatiah, Neariah, Rephaiah, and Uzziel—all sons of Ishi.)

43There they destroyed the few surviving members of the tribe of Amalek. And they have lived there ever since.

THE oldest son of Israel was Reuben, but since he dishonored his father by sleeping with one of his father's wives, his birthright was given to his half brother, Joseph. So the official genealogy doesn't name Reuben as the oldest son. 2Although Joseph received the birthright, yet Judah was a powerful and influential tribe in Israel, and from Judah came a Prince.

3The sons of Reuben, Israel's son, were:

Hanoch, Pallu, Hezron, Carmi.

4Joel's descendants were his son Shemaiah, his grandson Gog, and his great-grandson **Shime-i.**

5*Shime-i's* son was Micah; his grandson was Reaiah; and his great-grandson was **Baal.**

6*Baal's* son was Beerah. He was a prince of the tribe of Reuben and was taken into captivity by King Tilgath-pilneser of Assyria.

7,8His relatives became heads of clans and were included in the official genealogy:

Je-iel, Zechariah, Bela (the son of Azaz, grandson of Shema, and great-grandson of **Joel**).

These Reubenites lived in Aroer and as far distant as Mount Nebo and Baalmeon.

9Joel was a cattle man, and he pastured his animals eastward to the edge of the desert and to the Euphrates River, for there were many cattle in the land of Gilead.

10During the reign of King Saul, the men of Reuben defeated the Hagrites in war and moved into their tents on the eastern edge of Gilead. 11Across from them, in the land of Bashan, lived the descendants of Gad, who were spread as far as Salecah.

12Joel was the greatest and was followed by Shapham, also Janai and Shaphat. 13Their relatives, the heads of the seven clans, were Michael, Meshullam, Sheba, Jorai, Jacan, Zia, and Eber.

14The descendants of Buz, in the order of their generations, were:

Jahdo, Jeshishai, Michael, Gilead, Jaroah, Huri, Abihail.

15Ahi, the son of Abdi-el and grandson of Guni, was the leader of the clan. 16The clan lived in and around Gilead (in the land of Bashan) and throughout the entire pasture country of Sharon. 17All were included in the official genealogy at the time of King Jotham of Judah and King Jeroboam of Israel.

ACTS 25:1–27

THREE days after Festus arrived in Caesarea to take over his new responsibilities, he left for Jerusalem, 2where the chief priests and other Jewish leaders got hold of him and gave him their story about Paul. 3They begged him to bring Paul to Jerusalem at once. (Their plan was to waylay and kill him.) 4But Festus replied that since Paul was at Caesarea and he himself was returning there soon, 5those with authority in this affair should return with him for the trial.

6Eight or ten days later he returned to Caesarea and the following day opened Paul's trial.

7On Paul's arrival in court the Jews from Jerusalem gathered around, hurling many serious accusations which they couldn't prove. 8Paul denied the charges: "I am not guilty," he said. "I have not opposed the Jewish laws or desecrated the Temple or rebelled against the Roman government."

9Then Festus, anxious to please the Jews, asked him, "Are you willing to go to Jerusalem and stand trial before me?"

10,11But Paul replied, "No! I demand my privilege of a hearing before the Emperor himself. You know very well I am not guilty. If I have done something worthy of death, I don't refuse to die! But if I am innocent, neither you nor anyone else has a right to turn me over to these men to kill me. *I appeal to Caesar.*"

12Festus conferred with his advisors

and then replied, "Very well! You have appealed to Caesar, and to Caesar you shall go!"

13A few days later King Agrippa arrived with Bernice for a visit with Festus. 14During their stay of several days Festus discussed Paul's case with the king. "There is a prisoner here," he told him, "whose case was left for me by Felix. 15When I was in Jerusalem, the chief priests and other Jewish leaders gave me their side of the story and asked me to have him killed. 16Of course I quickly pointed out to them that Roman law does not convict a man before he is tried. He is given an opportunity to defend himself face to face with his accusers.

17"When they came here for the trial, I called the case the very next day and ordered Paul brought in. 18But the accusations made against him weren't at all what I supposed they would be. 19It was something about their religion, and about someone called Jesus who died, but Paul insists is alive! 20I was perplexed as to how to decide a case of this kind and asked him whether he would be willing to stand trial on these charges in Jerusalem. 21But Paul appealed to Caesar! So I ordered him back to jail until I could arrange to get him to the Emperor."

22"I'd like to hear the man myself," Agrippa said.

And Festus replied, "You shall—tomorrow!"

23So the next day, after the king and Bernice had arrived at the courtroom with great pomp, accompanied by military officers and prominent men of the city, Festus ordered Paul brought in.

24Then Festus addressed the audience: "King Agrippa and all present," he said, "this is the man whose death is demanded both by the local Jews and by those in Jerusalem! 25But in my opinion he has done nothing worthy of death. However, he appealed his case to Caesar, and I have no alternative but to send him. 26But what shall I write the Emperor? For there is no real charge against him! So I have brought him before you all, and especially you, King Agrippa, to examine him and then tell me what to write. 27For it doesn't seem reasonable to send a prisoner to the Emperor without any charges against him!"

PSALM 5:1–12

O Lord, hear me praying; listen to my plea, O God my King, for I will never pray to anyone but you. 3Each morning I will look to you in heaven and lay my requests before you, praying earnestly.

4I know you get no pleasure from wickedness and cannot tolerate the slightest sin. 5Therefore proud sinners will not survive your searching gaze, for how you hate their evil deeds. 6You will destroy them for their lies; how you abhor all murder and deception.

7But as for me, I will come into your Temple protected by your mercy and your love; I will worship you with deepest awe.

8Lord, lead me as you promised me you would; otherwise my enemies will conquer me. Tell me clearly what to do, which way to turn. 9For they cannot speak one truthful word. Their hearts are filled to the brim with wickedness. Their suggestions are full of the stench of sin and death. Their tongues are filled with flatteries to gain their wicked ends. 10O God, hold them responsible. Catch them in their own traps; let them fall beneath the weight of their own transgressions, for they rebel against you.

11But make everyone rejoice who puts his trust in you. Keep them shouting for joy because you are defending them. Fill all who love you with your happiness. 12For you bless the godly man, O Lord; you protect him with your shield of love.

PROVERBS FOR TODAY/ 18:19

It is harder to win back the friendship of an offended brother than to capture a fortified city. His anger shuts you out like iron bars.

JULY 8

1 CHRONICLES 5:18—6:81

THERE were 44,760 armed, trained, and brave troops in the army of Reuben, Gad, and the half-tribe of Manasseh. ¹⁹They declared war on the Hagrites, the Jeturites, the Naphishites, and the Nodabites. ²⁰They cried out to God to help them, and he did, for they trusted in him. So the Hagrites and all their allies were defeated. ²¹The booty included 50,000 camels, 250,000 sheep, 2,000 donkeys, and 100,000 captives. ²²A great number of the enemy also died in the battle, for God was fighting against them. So the Reubenites lived in the territory of the Hagrites until the time of the exile.

²³The half-tribe of Manasseh spread through the land from Bashan to Baal-hermon, Senir, and Mount Hermon. They too were very numerous.

²⁴The chiefs of their clans were the following:

Epher, Ishi, Eliel, Azri-el, Jeremiah, Hodaviah, Jahdi-el.

Each of these men had a great reputation as a warrior and leader. ²⁵But they were not true to the God of their fathers; instead they worshiped the idols of the people whom God had destroyed. ²⁶So God caused King Pul of Assyria (also known as Tilgath-pilneser III) to invade the land and deport the men of Reuben, Gad, and the half-tribe of Manasseh. They took them to Halah, Habor, Hara, and the Gozan River, where they remain to this day.

THESE are the names of the sons of Levi: **Gershom, Kohath, Merari.**

²*Kohath's* sons were:

Amram, Izhar, Hebron, Uzziel.

³*Amram's* descendants included:

Aaron, Moses, Miriam.

Aaron's sons were:

Nadab, Abihu, Eleazar, Ithamar.

⁴⁻¹⁵The oldest sons of the successive generations of Aaron were as follows:

Eleazar, the father of

Phinehas, the father of

Abishua, the father of

Bukki, the father of

Uzzi, the father of

Zerahiah, the father of

Meraioth, the father of

Amariah, the father of

Ahitub, the father of

Zadok, the father of

Ahima-az, the father of

Azariah, the father of

Johanan, the father of

Azariah (the High Priest in Solomon's Temple at Jerusalem), the father of

Amariah, the father of

Ahitub, the father of

Zadok, the father of

Shallum, the father of

Hilkiah, the father of

Azariah, the father of

Seraiah, the father of

Jehozadak (who went into exile when the Lord sent the people of Judah and Jerusalem into captivity under Nebuchadnezzar).

¹⁶As previously stated, the sons of Levi were:

Gershom, Kohath, Merari.

¹⁷The sons of *Gershom* were:

Libni, Shime-i.

¹⁸The sons of *Kohath* were:

Amram, Izhar, Hebron, Uzziel.

¹⁹,²⁰,²¹The sons of *Merari* were:

Mahli, Mushi.

The subclans of the Levites were:

In the Gershom clan:

Libni, Jahath, Zimmah, Joah, Iddo, Zerah, Jeatherai.

²²,²³,²⁴In the Kohath clan:

Amminadab, Korah, Assir, **Elkanah,** Ebiasaph, Assir, Tahath, Uriel, Uzziah, Shaul.

²⁵,²⁶,²⁷The subclan of *Elkanah* was further divided into the families of his sons:

Amasai, Ahimoth, Elkanah, Zophai, Nahath, Eliab, Jeroham, Elkanah.

28The families of the subclan of Samuel were headed by Samuel's sons:

Joel, the oldest;

Abijah, the second.

29,30The subclans of the clan of Merari were headed by his sons:

Mahli, Libni, Shime-i, Uzzah, Shime-a, Haggiah, Asaiah.

31King David appointed songleaders and choirs to praise God in the Tabernacle after he had placed the Ark in it. 32Then, when Solomon built the Temple at Jerusalem, the choirs carried on their work there.

33-38These are the names and ancestries of choir leaders: Heman the Cantor was from the clan of Kohath; his genealogy was traced back through:

Joel, Samuel, Elkanah III, Jeroham, Eliel, Toah, Zuph, Elkanah II, Mahath, Amasai, Elkanah I, Joel, Azariah, Zephaniah, Tahath, Assir, Ebiasaph, Korah, Izhar, Kohath, Levi, Israel.

39-43Heman's assistant was his colleague Asaph, whose genealogy was traced back through:

Berechiah, Shime-a, Michael, Baaseiah, Malchijah, Ethni, Zerah, Adaiah, Ethan, Zimmah, Shime-i, Jahath, Gershom, Levi.

44-47Heman's second assistant was Ethan, a representative from the clan of Merari, who stood on his left. Merari's ancestry was traced back through:

Kishi, Abdi, Malluch, Hashabiah, Amaziah, Hilkiah, Amzi, Bani, Shemer, Mahli, Mushi, Merari, Levi.

48Their relatives—all the other Levites—were appointed to various other tasks in the Tabernacle. 49But only Aaron and his descendants were the priests. Their duties included sacrificing burnt offerings and incense, handling all the tasks relating to the inner sanctuary—the Holy of Holies—and the tasks relating to the annual Day of Atonement for Israel. They saw to it that all the details commanded by Moses the servant of God were strictly followed.

50-53The descendants of Aaron were: Eleazar, Phinehas, Abishua, Bukki,

Uzzi, Zerahiah, Meraioth, Amariah, Ahitub, Zadok, Ahima-az.

54This is a record of the cities and land assigned by lot to the descendants of Aaron, all of whom were members of the Kohath clan:

55,56,57Hebron and its surrounding pasturelands in Judah (although the fields and suburbs were given to Caleb the son of Jephunneh), 58,59and the following Cities of Refuge with their surrounding pasturelands:

Libnah, Jattir, Eshtemoa, Hilen, Debir, Ashan, Beth-shemesh.

60Thirteen other cities with surrounding pastures—including Geba, Alemeth, and Anathoth—were given to the priests by the tribe of Benjamin. 61Lots were then drawn to assign land to the remaining descendants of Kohath, and they received ten cities in the territory of the half-tribe of Manasseh.

62The subclans of the Gershom clan received by lot thirteen cities in the Bashan area from the tribes of Issachar, Asher, Naphtali, and Manasseh.

63The subclans of Merari received by lot twelve cities from the tribes of Reuben, Gad, and Zebulun.

64,65Cities and pasturelands were also assigned by lot to the Levites (and then renamed) from the tribes of Judah, Simeon, and Benjamin.

66-69The tribe of Ephraim gave these Cities of Refuge with the surrounding pasturelands to the subclans of Kohath:

Shechem, in Mount Ephraim; Gezer; Jokme-am; Beth-horon; Aijalon; Gath-rimmon.

70The following Cities of Refuge and their pasturelands were given to the subclans of the Kohathites by the half-tribe of Manasseh:

Aner, Bile-am.

71Cities of Refuge and pastureland given to the clan of Gershom by the half-tribe of Manasseh were:

Golan, in Bashan; Ashtaroth.

72The tribe of Issachar gave them Kedesh, Daberath, 73Ramoth, and Anem, and the surrounding pastureland of each.

74The tribe of Asher gave them Abdon,

Mashal, 75Hukok, and Rehob, with their pasturelands.

76The tribe of Naphtali gave them Kedesh in Galilee, Hammon, and Kiriathaim with pasturelands.

77The tribe of Zebulun gave Rimmono and Tabor to the Merari clan as Cities of Refuge.

78,79And across the Jordan River, opposite Jericho, the tribe of Reuben gave them Bezer (a desert town), Jahzah, Kedemoth and Mepha-ath, along with their pasturelands.

80The tribe of Gad gave them Ramoth in Gilead, Mahanaim, 81Heshbon, and Jazer, each with their surrounding pasturelands.

ACTS 26:1–32

THEN Agrippa said to Paul, "Go ahead. Tell us your story."

So Paul, with many gestures, presented his defense:

2"I am fortunate, King Agrippa," he began, "to be able to present my answer before you, 3for I know you are an expert on Jewish laws and customs. Now please listen patiently!

4"As the Jews are well aware, I was given a thorough Jewish training from my earliest childhood in Tarsus and later at Jerusalem, and I lived accordingly. 5If they would admit it, they know that I have always been the strictest of Pharisees when it comes to obedience to Jewish laws and customs. 6But the real reason behind their accusations is something else—it is because I am looking forward to the fulfillment of God's promise made to our ancestors. 7The twelve tribes of Israel strive night and day to attain this same hope I have! Yet, O King, for me it is a crime, they say! 8But is it a crime to believe in the resurrection of the dead? Does it seem incredible to you that God can bring men back to life again?

9"I used to believe that I ought to do many horrible things to the followers of Jesus of Nazareth. 10I imprisoned many of the saints in Jerusalem, as authorized by the High Priests; and when they were condemned to death, I cast my vote against them. 11I used torture to try to make Christians everywhere curse Christ. I was so violently opposed to them that I even hounded them in distant cities in foreign lands.

12"I was on such a mission to Damascus, armed with the authority and commission of the chief priests, 13when one day about noon, sir, a light from heaven brighter than the sun shone down on me and my companions. 14We all fell down, and I heard a voice speaking to me in Hebrew, 'Paul, Paul, why are you persecuting me? You are only hurting yourself.'

15" 'Who are you, sir?' I asked.

"And the Lord replied, 'I am Jesus, the one you are persecuting. 16Now stand up! For I have appeared to you to appoint you as my servant and my witness. You are to tell the world about this experience and about the many other occasions when I shall appear to you. 17And I will protect you from both your own people and the Gentiles. Yes, I am going to send you to the Gentiles 18to open their eyes to their true condition so that they may repent and live in the light of God instead of in Satan's darkness, so that they may receive forgiveness for their sins and God's inheritance along with all people everywhere whose sins are cleansed away, who are set apart by faith in me.'

19"And so, O King Agrippa, I was not disobedient to that vision from heaven! 20I preached first to those in Damascus, then in Jerusalem and through Judea, and also to the Gentiles that all must forsake their sins and turn to God—and prove their repentance by doing good deeds. 21The Jews arrested me in the Temple for preaching this, and tried to kill me, 22but God protected me so that I am still alive today to tell these facts to everyone, both great and small. I teach nothing except what the prophets and Moses said— 23that the Messiah would suffer, and be the First to rise from the dead, to bring light to Jews and Gentiles alike."

24Suddenly Festus shouted, "Paul, you are insane. Your long studying has broken your mind!"

25But Paul replied, "I am not insane, Most Excellent Festus. I speak words of sober truth. 26And King Agrippa knows about these things. I speak frankly for I am sure these events are all familiar to him, for they were not done in a corner! 27King Agrippa, do you believe the prophets? But I know you do—"

28Agrippa interrupted him. "With trivial proofs like these, you expect me to become a Christian?"

29And Paul replied, "Would to God that whether my arguments are trivial or strong, both you and everyone here in this audience might become the same as I am, except for these chains."

30Then the king, the governor, Bernice, and all the others stood and left. 31As they talked it over afterwards they agreed, "This man hasn't done anything worthy of death or imprisonment."

32And Agrippa said to Festus, "He could be set free if he hadn't appealed to Caesar!"

PSALM 6:1–10

No, Lord! Don't punish me in the heat of your anger. 2Pity me, O Lord, for I am weak. Heal me, for my body is sick, 3and I am upset and disturbed. My mind is filled with apprehension and with gloom. Oh, restore me soon.

4Come, O Lord, and make me well. In your kindness save me. 5For if I die I cannot give you glory by praising you before my friends. 6I am worn out with pain; every night my pillow is wet with tears. 7My eyes are growing old and dim with grief because of all my enemies.

8Go, leave me now, you men of evil deeds, for the Lord has heard my weeping 9and my pleading. He will answer all my prayers. 10All my enemies shall be suddenly dishonored, terror-stricken, and disgraced. God will turn them back in shame.

PROVERBS FOR TODAY/ 18:20–21

Ability to give wise advice satisfies like a good meal! Those who love to talk will suffer the consequences. Men have died for saying the wrong thing!

JULY 9

1 CHRONICLES 7:1—8:40

THE sons of Issachar:
Tola, Puah, Jashub, Shimron.
2The sons of *Tola,* each of whom was the head of a subclan:
Uzzi, Rephaiah, Jeri-el, Jahmai, Ibsam, Shemuel.

At the time of King David, the total number of men of war from these families totaled 22,600.

3*Uzzi's* son was Izrahiah among whose five sons were Michael, Obadiah, Joel, and Isshiah, all chiefs of subclans. 4Their descendants, at the time of King David, numbered 36,000 troops; for all five of them had several wives and many sons. 5The total number of men available for military service from all the clans of the tribe of Issachar numbered 87,000 stouthearted warriors, all included in the official genealogy.

6The sons of Benjamin were:
Bela, Becher, Jedia-el.
7The sons of *Bela:*
Ezbon, Uzzi, Uzziel, Jerimoth, Iri.

These five mighty warriors were chiefs of subclans and were the leaders of 22,034 troops (all of whom were recorded in the official genealogies).

⁸The sons of *Becher* were: Zemirah, Joash, Eliezer, Eli-o-enai, Omri, Jeremoth, Abijah, Anathoth, Alemeth.

⁹At the time of David there were 20,200 mighty warriors among their descendants; and they were led by their clan chiefs.

¹⁰The son of *Jedia-el* was **Bilhan.**

The sons of *Bilhan* were:

Jeush, Benjamin, Ehud, Chenaanah, Zethan, Tarshish, Ahishahar.

¹¹They were the chiefs of the subclans of *Jedia-el,* and their descendants included 17,200 warriors at the time of King David.

¹²The sons of Ir were Shuppim and Huppim. Hushim was one of the sons of Aher.

¹³The sons of Naphtali (descendants of Jacob's wife Bilhah) were:

Jahzi-el, Guni, Jezer, Shallum.

¹⁴The sons of Manasseh, born to his Aramaean concubine, were Asri-el and Machir (who became the father of Gilead).

¹⁵It was Machir who found wives for Huppim and Shuppim. Machir's sister was Maacah. Another descendant was Zelophehad, who had only daughters.

¹⁶Machir's wife, also named Maacah, bore him a son whom she named Peresh; his brother's name was Sheresh, and he had sons named Ulam and Rakem.

¹⁷Ulam's son was Bedan. So these were the sons of Gilead, the grandsons of Machir, and the great-grandsons of Manasseh.

¹⁸Hammolecheth, Machir's sister, bore Ishhod, Abiezer, and Mahlah.

¹⁹The sons of Shemida were Ahian, Shechem, Likhi, and Aniam.

²⁰,²¹The sons of Ephraim:

Shuthelah, Bered, Tahath, Eleadah, Tahath, Zabad, Shuthelah, **Ezer, El-e-ad.**

Ele-ad and *Ezer* attempted to rustle cattle at Gath, but they were killed by the local farmers. ²²Their father Ephraim mourned for them a long time, and his brothers tried to comfort him. ²³After-

wards, his wife conceived and bore a son whom he called Beriah (meaning "a tragedy") because of what had happened.

²⁴Ephraim's daughter's name was Sheerah. She built Lower and Upper Beth-horon and Uzzen-sheerah.

²⁵,²⁶,²⁷This is Ephraim's line of descent:

Rephah, the father of
Resheph, the father of
Telah, the father of
Tahan, the father of
Ladan, the father of
Ammihud, the father of
Elishama, the father of
Nun, the father of
Joshua.

²⁸They lived in an area bounded on one side by Bethel and its surrounding towns, on the east by Naaran, on the west by Gezer and its villages, and finally by Shechem and its surrounding villages as far as Ayyah and its towns.

²⁹The tribe of Manasseh, descendants of Joseph the son of Israel, controlled the following cities and their surrounding areas: Beth-shean, Taanach, Megiddo, and Dor.

³⁰The children of Asher:

Imnah, Ishvah, Ishvi, **Beriah,** Serah (their sister).

³¹The sons of *Beriah* were:

Heber, Malchi-el (the father of Birzaith).

³²*Heber's* children were:

Japhlet, Shomer, Hotham, Shua (their sister).

³³*Japhlet's* sons were:

Pasach, Bimhal, Ashvath.

³⁴His brother *Shomer's* sons were:

Rohgah, Jehubbah, Aram.

³⁵The sons of his brother *Hotham* were:

Zophah, Imna, Shelesh, Amal.

³⁶,³⁷The sons of *Zophah* were:

Suah, Harnepher, Shual, Beri, Imrah, Bezer, Hod, Shamma, Shilshah, **Ithran,** Be-era.

³⁸The sons of *Ithran* were:

Jephunneh, Pispa, Ara.

³⁹The sons of Ulla were:

Arah, Hanniel, Rizia.

⁴⁰These descendants of Asher were

heads of subclans and were all skilled warriors and chiefs. Their descendants in the official genealogy numbered 36,000 men of war.

THE sons of Benjamin, according to age, were:
Bela, the first,
Ashbel, the second,
Aharah, the third,
Nohah, the fourth,
Rapha, the fifth.

3,4,5The sons of *Bela* were:
Addar, Gera, Abihud, Abishua, Naaman, Ahoah, Gera, Shephuphan, Huram.

6,7The sons of Ehud, chiefs of the subclans living at Geba, were captured in war and exiled to Manahath. They were:
Naaman, Ahijah, Gera (also called Heglam), the father of Uzza and Ahihud.

8,9,10Shaharaim divorced his wives **Hushim** and Baara, but he had children in the land of Moab by Hodesh, his new wife:
Jobab, Zibia, Mesha, Malcam, Jeuz, Sachia, Mirmah.
These sons all became chiefs of subclans.

11His wife *Hushim* had borne him Abitub and **Elpaal.**

12The sons of *Elpaal* were:
Eber, Misham, Shemed (who built Ono and Lod and their surrounding villages).

13His other sons were **Beriah** and Shema, chiefs of subclans living in Aijalon; they chased out the inhabitants of Gath.

14*Elpaal's* sons also included:
Ahio, **Shashak,** Jeremoth.

15,16The sons of *Beriah* were:
Zebadiah, Arad, Eder, Michael, Ishpah, Joha.

17,18The sons of *Elpaal* also included:
Zebadiah, Meshullam, Hizki, Heber, Ishmerai, Izliah, Jobab.

19,20,21The sons of Shime-i were:
Jakim, Zichri, Zabdi, Eli-enai, Zille-thai, Eliel, Adaiah, Beraiah, Shimrath.

22-25The sons of *Shashak* were:

Ishpan, Eber, Eliel, Abdon, Zichri, Hanan, Hananiah, Elam, Anthothijah, Iphdeiah, Penuel.

26,27The sons of Jeroham were:
Shamsherai, Shehariah, Athaliah, Jaareshiah, Elijah, Zichri.

28These were the chiefs of the subclans living at Jerusalem.

29Je-iel, the father of Gibeon, lived at Gibeon; and his wife's name was Maacah.
30,31,32His oldest son was named Abdon, followed by:
Zur, Kish, Baal, Nadab, Gedor, Ahio, Zecher, Mikloth who was the father of Shimeah.
All of these families lived together near Jerusalem.

33Ner was the father of Kish, and Kish was the father of Saul;
Saul's sons included:
Jonathan, Malchishua, Abinadab, Eshbaal.

34The son of *Jonathan* was Mephibosheth;
The son of Mephibosheth was Micah.

35The sons of Micah:
Pithon, Melech, Tarea, Ahaz.

36Ahaz was the father of Jehoaddah, Jehoaddah was the father of:
Alemeth, Azmaveth, Zimri.
Zimri's son was Moza.

37Moza was the father of Bine-a, whose sons were:
Raphah, Eleasah, Azel.

38Azel had six sons:
Azrikam, Bocheru, Ishmael, She-ariah, Obadiah, Hanan.

39Azel's brother Eshek had three sons:
Ulam, the first, Jeush, the second, Eliphelet, the third.

40*Ulam's* sons were prominent warriors who were expert marksmen with their bows. These men had 150 sons and grandsons, and they were all from the tribe of Benjamin.

ACTS 27:1–20

ARRANGEMENTS were finally made to start us on our way to Rome by ship; so Paul and several other prisoners were placed in the custody of an officer named Julius, a member of the imperial guard. 2We left on a boat which was scheduled to make several stops along the Turkish coast. I should add that Aristarchus, a Greek from Thessalonica, was with us.

3The next day when we docked at Sidon, Julius was very kind to Paul and let him go ashore to visit with friends and receive their hospitality. 4Putting to sea from there, we encountered headwinds that made it difficult to keep the ship on course, so we sailed north of Cyprus between the island and the mainland, 5and passed along the coast of the provinces of Cilicia and Pamphylia, landing at Myra, in the province of Lycia. 6There our officer found an Egyptian ship from Alexandria, bound for Italy, and put us aboard.

7,8We had several days of rough sailing, and finally neared Cnidus; but the winds had become too strong, so we ran across to Crete, passing the port of Salome. Beating into the wind with great difficulty and moving slowly along the southern coast, we arrived at Fair Havens, near the city of Lasea. 9There we stayed for several days. The weather was becoming dangerous for long voyages by then, because it was late in the year, and Paul spoke to the ship's officers about it.

10"Sirs," he said, "I believe there is trouble ahead if we go on—perhaps shipwreck, loss of cargo, injuries, and death." 11But the officers in charge of the prisoners listened more to the ship's captain and the owner than to Paul. 12And since Fair Havens was an exposed harbor—a poor place to spend the winter—most of the crew advised trying to go further up the coast to Phoenix, in order to winter there; Phoenix was a good harbor with only a northwest and southwest exposure.

13Just then a light wind began blowing from the south, and it looked like a perfect day for the trip; so they pulled up anchor and sailed along close to shore. 14,15But shortly afterwards, the weather changed abruptly and a heavy wind of typhoon strength (a "northeaster," they called it) caught the ship and blew it out to sea. They tried at first to face back to shore but couldn't, so they gave up and let the ship run before the gale.

16We finally sailed behind a small island named Clauda, where with great difficulty we hoisted aboard the lifeboat that was being towed behind us, 17and then banded the ship with ropes to strengthen the hull. The sailors were afraid of being driven across to the quicksands of the African coast, so they lowered the topsails and were thus driven before the wind.

18The next day as the seas grew higher, the crew began throwing the cargo overboard. 19The following day they threw out the tackle and anything else they could lay their hands on. 20The terrible storm raged unabated many days, until at last all hope was gone.

PSALM 7:1–17

I am depending on you, O Lord my God, to save me from my persecutors. 2Don't let them pounce upon me as a lion would and maul me and drag me away with no one to rescue me. 3It would be different, Lord, if I were doing evil things— 4if I were paying back evil for good or unjustly attacking those I dislike. 5Then it would be right for you to let my enemies destroy me, crush me to the ground, and trample my life in the dust.

6But Lord! Arise in anger against the anger of my enemies. Awake! Demand justice for me, Lord! 7,8Gather all peoples before you; sit high above them, judging their sins. But justify me publicly; establish my honor and truth before them all. 9End all wickedness, O Lord, and bless all who truly worship God; for you, the righteous God, look deep within the hearts of men and examine all their motives and their thoughts.

10God is my shield; he will defend me. He saves those whose hearts and lives are true and right.

11God is a judge who is perfectly fair,

and he is angry with the wicked every day. 12Unless they repent, he will sharpen his sword and slay them.

He has bent and strung his bow 13and fitted it with deadly arrows made from shafts of fire.

14The wicked man conceives an evil plot, labors with its dark details, and brings to birth his treachery and lies; 15let him fall into his own trap. 16May the violence he plans for others boomerang upon himself; let him die.

17Oh, how grateful and thankful I am to the Lord because he is so good. I will sing praise to the name of the Lord who is above all lords.

PROVERBS FOR TODAY/ 18:22

The man who finds a wife finds a good thing; she is a blessing to him from the Lord.

JULY 10

1 CHRONICLES 9:1—10:14

THE family tree of every person in Israel was carefully recorded in *The Annals of the Kings of Israel.*

Judah was exiled to Babylon because the people worshiped idols.

2The first to return and live again in their former cities were families from the tribes of Israel, and also the priests, the Levites, and the Temple assistants.

3Then some families from the tribes of Judah, Benjamin, Ephraim, and Manasseh arrived in Jerusalem:

4One family was that of Uthai (the son of Ammihud, son of Omri, son of Imri, son of Bani) of the clan of Perez (son of Judah).

5The Shilonites were another family to return, including Asaiah (Shilon's oldest son) and his sons; 6there were also the sons of Zerah, including Jeuel and his relatives: 690 in all.

7,8Among the members of the tribe of Benjamin who returned were these:

Sallu (the son of Meshullam, the son of Hodaviah, the son of Hassenuah);
Ibneiah (the son of Jeroham);
Elah (the son of Uzzi, the son of Michri);
Meshullam (the son of Shephatiah, the son of Reuel, the son of Ibnijah).

9These men were all chiefs of subclans. A total of 956 Benjaminites returned.

10,11The priests who returned were:
Jedaiah, Jehoiarib, Jachin,
Azariah (the son of Hilkiah, son of Meshullam, son of Zadok, son of Meraioth, son of Ahitub). He was the chief custodian of the Temple.

12Another of the returning priests was Adaiah (son of Jeroham, son of Pashhur, son of Malchijah).

Another priest was Maasai (son of Adi-el, son of Jahzerah, son of Meshullam, son of Meshillemith, son of Immer).

13In all, 1,760 priests returned.

14Among the Levites who returned was Shemaiah (son of Hasshub, son of Azrikam, son of Hashabiah, who was a descendant of Merari).

15,16Other Levites who returned included:
Bakbakkar, Heresh, Galal,
Mattaniah (the son of Mica, who was the son of Zichri, who was the son of Asaph).
Obadiah (the son of Shemaiah, son of Galal, son of Jeduthun).
Berechiah (the son of Asa, son of Elkanah, who lived in the area of the Netophathites).

17,18The gatekeepers were Shallum

(the chief gatekeeper), Akkub, Talmon, and Ahiman—all Levites. They are still responsible for the eastern royal gate. 19Shallum's ancestry went back through Kore and Ebiasaph to Korah. He and his close relatives the Korahites were in charge of the sacrifices and the protection of the sanctuary, just as their ancestors had supervised and guarded the Tabernacle. 20Phinehas, the son of Eleazar, was the first director of this division in ancient times. And the Lord was with him.

21At that time Zechariah, the son of Meshelemiah, had been responsible for the protection of the entrance to the Tabernacle. 22There were 212 doorkeepers in those days. They were chosen from their villages on the basis of their genealogies, and they were appointed by David and Samuel because of their reliability. 23They and their descendants were in charge of the Lord's Tabernacle. 24They were assigned to each of the four sides: east, west, north, and south. 25And their relatives in the villages were assigned to help them from time to time, for seven days at a time.

26The four head gatekeepers, all Levites, were in an office of great trust, for they were responsible for the rooms and treasuries in the Tabernacle of God. 27Because of their important positions they lived near the Tabernacle, and they opened the gates each morning. 28Some of them were assigned to care for the various vessels used in the sacrifices and worship; they checked them in and out to avoid loss. 29Others were responsible for the furniture, the items in the sanctuary, and the supplies such as fine flour, wine, incense, and spices.

30Other priests prepared the spices and incense.

31And Mattithiah (a Levite and the oldest son of Shallum the Korahite) was entrusted with making the flat cakes for grain offerings.

32Some members of the Kohath clan were in charge of the preparation of the special bread each Sabbath.

33,34The cantors were all prominent Levites. They lived in Jerusalem at the Temple and were on duty at all hours. They were free from other responsibilities and were selected by their genealogies.

35,36,37Jeiel (whose wife was Maacah) lived in Gibeon. He had many sons, including:

Gibeon, Abdon (the oldest), Zur, Kish, Baal, **Ner,** Nadab, Gedor, Ahio, Zechariah, Mikloth.

38Mikloth lived with his son Shime-am in Jerusalem near his relatives.

39Ner was the father of Kish, Kish was the father of Saul, Saul was the father of Jonathan, Malchishua, Abinadab, and Eshbaal.

40Jonathan was the father of Mephibosheth;

Mephibosheth was the father of Micah;

41Micah was the father of Pithon, Melech, Tahre-a, and Ahaz;

42Ahaz was the father of Jarah;

Jarah was the father of Alemeth, Azmaveth, and Zimri;

Zimri was the father of Moza.

43Moza was the father of Bine-a, Rephaiah, Eleasah, and Azel.

44Azel had six sons:

Azrikam, Bocheru, Ishmael, She-ariah, Obadiah, Hanan.

THE Philistines attacked and defeated the Israeli troops, who turned and fled and were slaughtered on the slopes of Mount Gilboa. 2They caught up with Saul and his three sons, Jonathan, Abinadab, and Malchishua, and killed them all. 3Saul had been hard pressed with heavy fighting all around him, when the Philistine archers shot and wounded him.

4He cried out to his bodyguard, "Quick, kill me with your sword before these uncircumcised heathen capture and torture me."

But the man was afraid to do it, so Saul took his own sword and fell against its point; and it pierced his body. 5Then his bodyguard, seeing that Saul was dead, killed himself in the same way. 6So Saul and his three sons died together;

the entire family was wiped out in one day.

7When the Israelis in the valley below the mountain heard that their troops had been routed and that Saul and his sons were dead, they abandoned their cities and fled. And the Philistines came and lived in them. 8When the Philistines went back the next day to strip the bodies of the men killed in action and to gather the booty from the battlefield, they found the bodies of Saul and his sons. 9So they stripped off Saul's armor and cut off his head; then they displayed them throughout the nation and celebrated the wonderful news before their idols. 10They fastened his armor to the walls of the Temple of the Gods and nailed his head to the wall of Dagon's temple.

11But when the people of Jabesh-gilead heard what the Philistines had done to Saul, 12their heroic warriors went out to the battlefield and brought back his body and the bodies of his three sons. Then they buried them beneath the oak tree at Jabesh and mourned and fasted for seven days.

13Saul died for his disobedience to the Lord and because he had consulted a medium, 14and did not ask the Lord for guidance. So the Lord killed him and gave the kingdom to David, the son of Jesse.

ACTS 27:21–44

NO one had eaten for a long time, but finally Paul called the crew together and said, "Men, you should have listened to me in the first place and not left Fair Havens—you would have avoided all this injury and loss! 22But cheer up! Not one of us will lose our lives, even though the ship will go down.

23"For last night an angel of the God to whom I belong and whom I serve stood beside me, 24and said, 'Don't be afraid, Paul—for you will surely stand trial before Caesar! What's more, God has granted your request and will save the lives of all those sailing with you.' 25So take courage! For I believe God!

It will be just as he said! 26But we will be shipwrecked on an island."

27About midnight on the fourteenth night of the storm, as we were being driven to and fro on the Adriatic Sea, the sailors suspected land was near. 28They sounded, and found 120 feet of water below them. A little later they sounded again, and found only ninety feet. 29At this rate they knew they would soon be driven ashore; and fearing rocks along the coast, they threw out four anchors from the stern and prayed for daylight.

30Some of the sailors planned to abandon the ship, and lowered the emergency boat as though they were going to put out anchors from the prow. 31But Paul said to the soldiers and commanding officer, "You will all die unless everyone stays aboard." 32So the soldiers cut the ropes and let the boat fall off.

33As the darkness gave way to the early morning light, Paul begged everyone to eat. "You haven't touched food for two weeks," he said. 34"Please eat something now for your own good! For not a hair of your heads shall perish!"

35Then he took some hardtack and gave thanks to God before them all, and broke off a piece and ate it. 36Suddenly everyone felt better and began eating, 37all two hundred seventy-six of us—for that is the number we had aboard. 38After eating, the crew lightened the ship further by throwing all the wheat overboard.

39When it was day, they didn't recognize the coastline, but noticed a bay with a beach and wondered whether they could get between the rocks and be driven up onto the beach. 40They finally decided to try. Cutting off the anchors and leaving them in the sea, they lowered the rudders, raised the foresail and headed ashore. 41But the ship hit a sandbar and ran aground. The bow of the ship stuck fast, while the stern was exposed to the violence of the waves and began to break apart.

42The soldiers advised their commanding officer to let them kill the prisoners

"He will wipe away all tears from their eyes."
  Revelation 21:4

*"Therefore go and make
disciples in all the
nations."*
  Matthew 28:19

the subclan of Ahoh. 13He was with David in the battle against the Philistines at Pasdammim. The Israeli army was in a barley field and had begun to run away, 14but he held his ground in the middle of the field, and recovered it and slaughtered the Philistines; and the Lord saved them with a great victory.

15Another time, three of The Thirty went to David while he was hiding in the cave of Adullam. The Philistines were camped in the Valley of Rephaim, 16and David was in the stronghold at the time; an outpost of the Philistines had occupied Bethlehem. 17David wanted a drink from the Bethlehem well beside the gate, and when he mentioned this to his men, 18,19these three broke through to the Philistine camp, drew some water from the well, and brought it back to David. But he refused to drink it! Instead he poured it out as an offering to the Lord and said, "God forbid that I should drink it! It is the very blood of these men who risked their lives to get it."

20Abishai, Joab's brother, was commander of The Thirty. He had gained his place among The Thirty by killing 300 men at one time with his spear. 21He was the chief and the most famous of The Thirty, but he was not as great as The Three.

22Benaiah, whose father was a mighty warrior from Kabzeel, killed the two famous giants from Moab. He also killed a lion in a slippery pit when there was snow on the ground. 23Once he killed an Egyptian who was seven and one-half feet tall, whose spear was as thick as a weaver's beam. But Benaiah went up to him with only a club in his hand and pulled the spear away from him and used it to kill him. 24,25He was nearly as great as The Three, and he was very famous among The Thirty. David made him captain of his bodyguard.

26–47Other famous warriors among David's men were:

Asahel (Joab's brother);

Elhanan, the son of Dodo from Bethlehem;

Shammoth from Harod;

Helez from Pelon;

Ira (son of Ikkesh) from Tekoa;

Abi-ezer from Anathoth;

Sibbecai from Hushath;

Ilai from Ahoh;

Maharai from Netophah;

Heled (son of Baanah) from Netophah;

Ithai (son of Ribai) a Benjaminite from Gibe-ah;

Benaiah from Pirathon;

Hurai from near the brooks of Gaash;

Abiel from Arbath;

Azmaveth from Baharum;

Eliahba from Sha-albon;

The sons of Hashem from Gizon;

Jonathan (son of Shagee) from Harar;

Ahiam (son of Sacher) from Harar;

Eliphal (son of Ur);

Hepher from Mecherath;

Ahijah from Pelon;

Hezro from Carmel;

Naarai (son of Ezbai);

Joel (brother of Nathan);

Mibhar (son of Hagri);

Zelek from Ammon;

Naharai from Be-eroth—he was General Joab's armorbearer;

Ira from Ithra;

Gareb from Ithra;

Uriah the Hittite;

Zabad (son of Ahlai);

Adina (son of Shiza) from the tribe of Reuben—he was among the thirty-one leaders of the tribe of Reuben;

Hanan (son of Maacah);

Joshaphat from Mithna;

Uzzia from Ashterath;

Shama and Je-iel (sons of Hotham) from Aroer;

Jedia-el (son of Shimri);

Joha (his brother) from Tiza;

Eliel from Mahavi;

Jeribai and Joshaviah (sons of Elna-am);

Ithmah from Moab;

Eliel; Obed; Ja-asiel from Mezoba.

THESE are the names of the famous warriors who joined David at Ziklag while he was hiding from King Saul. 2All of them were expert archers and slingers, lest any of them swim ashore and escape. 43But Julius wanted to spare Paul, so he told them no. Then he ordered all who could swim to jump overboard and make for land, 44and the rest to try for it on planks and debris from the broken ship. So everyone escaped safely ashore!

PSALM 8:1–9

O Lord our God, the majesty and glory of your name fills all the earth and overflows the heavens. 2You have taught the little children to praise you perfectly. May their example shame and silence your enemies!

3When I look up into the night skies and see the work of your fingers—the moon and the stars you have made— 4I cannot understand how you can bother with mere puny man, to pay any attention to him!

5And yet you have made him only a little lower than the angels, and placed a crown of glory and honor upon his head.

6You have put him in charge of everything you made; everything is put under his authority: 7all sheep and oxen, and wild animals too, 8the birds and fish, and all the life in the sea. 9O Jehovah, our Lord, the majesty and glory of your name fills the earth.

PROVERBS FOR TODAY/ 18:23–24

The poor man pleads and the rich man answers with insults. There are "friends" who pretend to be friends, but there is a friend who sticks closer than a brother.

JULY 11

1 CHRONICLES 11:1—12:18

THEN the leaders of Israel went to David at Hebron and told him, "We are your relatives, 2and even when Saul was king, you were the one who led our armies to battle and brought them safely back again. And the Lord your God has told you, 'You shall be the shepherd of my people Israel. You shall be their king.' "

3So David made a contract with them before the Lord, and they anointed him as king of Israel, just as the Lord had told Samuel. 4Then David and the leaders went to Jerusalem (or Jebus, as it used to be called) where the Jebusites—the original inhabitants of the land—lived. 5,6But the people of Jebus refused to let them enter the city. So David captured the fortress of Zion, later called the City of David, and said to his men, "The first man to kill a Jebusite shall be made com-

mander-in-chief!" Joab, the son of Zeruiah, was the first, so he became the general of David's army. 7David lived in the fortress and that is why that area of Jerusalem is called the City of David. 8He extended the city out around the fortress while Joab rebuilt the rest of Jerusalem. 9And David became more and more famous and powerful, for the Lord of the heavens was with him.

10These are the names of some of the bravest of David's warriors (who also encouraged the leaders of Israel to make David their king, as the Lord had said would happen):

11Jashobeam (the son of a man from Hachmon) was the leader of The Top Three—the three greatest heroes among David's men. He once killed 300 men with his spear.

12The second of The Top Three was Eleazar, the son of Dodo, a member of and they could use their left hands as readily as their right! Like King Saul, they were all of the tribe of Benjamin.

3-7 Their chief was Ahi-ezer, son of Shemaah from Gibe-ah. The others were: His brother Joash; Jezi-el and Pelet, sons of Azmaveth; Beracah; Jehu from Anathoth; Ishmaiah from Gibeon (a brave warrior rated as high or higher than The Thirty); Jeremiah; Jahaziel; Johanan; Jozabad from Gederah; Eluzai; Jerimoth; Bealiah; Shemariah; Shephatiah from Haruph; Elkanah, Jesiah, Azarel, Jo-ezer, Jashobe-am—all Korahites; Jo-elah and Zebadiah (sons of Jeroham from Gedor).

8-13Great and brave warriors from the tribe of Gad also went to David in the wilderness. They were experts with both shield and spear and were "lion-faced men, swift as deer upon the mountains."
Ezer was the chief;
Obadiah was second in command;
Eliab was third in command;
Mishmannah was fourth in command;
Jeremiah was fifth in command;
Attai was sixth in command;
Eliel was seventh in command;
Johanan was eighth in command;
Elzabad was ninth in command;
Jeremiah was tenth in command;
Machbannai was eleventh in command.

14These men were army officers; the weakest was worth a hundred normal troops, and the greatest was worth a thousand! 15They crossed the Jordan River during its seasonal flooding and conquered the lowlands on both the east and west banks.

16Others came to David from Benjamin and Judah. 17David went out to meet them and said, "If you have come to help me, we are friends; but if you have come to betray me to my enemies when I am innocent, then may the God of our fathers see and judge you."

18Then the Holy Spirit came upon them, and Amasai, a leader of The Thirty, replied,

"We are yours, David;
We are on your side, son of Jesse.

Peace, peace be unto you,
And peace to all who aid you;
For your God is with you."

So David let them join him, and he made them captains of his army.

ACTS 28:1–31

WE soon learned that we were on the island of Malta. The people of the island were very kind to us, building a bonfire on the beach to welcome and warm us in the rain and cold.

3As Paul gathered an armful of sticks to lay on the fire, a poisonous snake, driven out by the heat, fastened itself onto his hand! 4The people of the island saw it hanging there and said to each other, "A murderer, no doubt! Though he escaped the sea, justice will not permit him to live!"

5But Paul shook off the snake into the fire and was unharmed. 6The people waited for him to begin swelling or suddenly fall dead; but when they had waited a long time and no harm came to him, they changed their minds and decided he was a god.

7Near the shore where we landed was an estate belonging to Publius, the governor of the island. He welcomed us courteously and fed us for three days. 8As it happened, Publius' father was ill with fever and dysentery. Paul went in and prayed for him, and laying his hands on him, healed him! 9Then all the other sick people in the island came and were cured. 10As a result we were showered with gifts, and when the time came to sail, people put on board all sorts of things we would need for the trip.

11It was three months after the shipwreck before we set sail again, and this time it was in *The Twin Brothers* of Alexandria, a ship that had wintered at the island. 12Our first stop was Syracuse, where we stayed three days. 13From there we circled around to Rhegium; a day later a south wind began blowing, so the following day we arrived at Puteoli, 14where we found some believers!

They begged us to stay with them seven days. Then we went on to Rome.

15The brothers in Rome had heard we were coming and came to meet us at the Forum on the Appian Way. Others joined us at The Three Taverns. When Paul saw them, he thanked God and took courage.

16When we arrived in Rome, Paul was permitted to live wherever he wanted to, though guarded by a soldier.

17Three days after his arrival, he called together the local Jewish leaders and spoke to them as follows:

"Brothers, I was arrested by the Jews in Jerusalem and handed over to the Roman government for prosecution, even though I had harmed no one nor violated the customs of our ancestors. 18The Romans gave me a trial and wanted to release me, for they found no cause for the death sentence demanded by the Jewish leaders. 19But when the Jews protested the decision, I felt it necessary, with no malice against them, to appeal to Caesar. 20I asked you to come here today so we could get acquainted and I could tell you that it is because I believe the Messiah has come that I am bound with this chain."

21They replied, "We have heard nothing against you! We have had no letters from Judea or reports from those arriving from Jerusalem. 22But we want to hear what you believe, for the only thing we know about these Christians is that they are denounced everywhere!"

23So a time was set and on that day large numbers came to his house. He told them about the Kingdom of God and taught them about Jesus from the Scriptures—from the five books of Moses and the books of prophecy. He began lecturing in the morning and went on into the evening!

24Some believed, and some didn't. 25But after they had argued back and forth among themselves, they left with this final word from Paul ringing in their ears: "The Holy Spirit was right when he said through Isaiah the prophet,

26" 'Say to the Jews, "You will hear and see but not understand, 27for your hearts are too fat and your ears don't listen and you have closed your eyes against understanding, for you don't want to see and hear and understand and turn to me to heal you." ' 28,29So I want you to realize that this salvation from God is available to the Gentiles too, and they will accept it."

30Paul lived for the next two years in his rented house and welcomed all who visited him, 31telling them with all boldness about the Kingdom of God and about the Lord Jesus Christ; and no one tried to stop him.

PSALM 9:1–12

O Lord, I will praise you with all my heart, and tell everyone about the marvelous things you do. 2I will be glad, yes, filled with joy because of you. I will sing your praises, O Lord God above all gods.

3My enemies will fall back and perish in your presence; 4you have vindicated me; you have endorsed my work, declaring from your throne that it is good. 5You have rebuked the nations and destroyed the wicked, blotting out their names forever and ever. 6O enemies of mine, you are doomed forever. The Lord will destroy your cities; even the memory of them will disappear.

7,8But the Lord lives on forever; he sits upon his throne to judge justly the nations of the world. 9All who are oppressed may come to him. He is a refuge for them in their times of trouble. 10All those who know your mercy, Lord, will count on you for help. For you have never yet forsaken those who trust in you.

11Oh, sing out your praises to the God who lives in Jerusalem. Tell the world about his unforgettable deeds. 12He who avenges murder has an open ear to those who cry to him for justice. He does not ignore the prayers of men in trouble when they call to him for help.

JULY 12

1 CHRONICLES 12:19—14:17

SOME men from Manasseh deserted the Israeli army and joined David just as he was going into battle with the Philistines against King Saul. But as it turned out, the Philistine generals refused to let David and his men go with them. After much discussion they sent them back, for they were afraid that David and his men would imperil them by deserting to King Saul.

20Here is a list of the men from Manasseh who deserted to David as he was en route to Ziklag:

Adnah, Jozabad, Jedia-el, Michael, Jozabad, Elihu, Zillethai.

Each was a high-ranking officer of Manasseh's troops. 21They were brave and able warriors, and they assisted David when he fought against the Amalek raiders at Ziklag.

22More men joined David almost every day until he had a tremendous army—the army of God. 23Here is the registry of recruits who joined David at Hebron. They were all anxious to see David become king instead of Saul, just as the Lord had said would happen.

24-37From Judah, 6,800 troops armed with shields and spears.

From the tribe of Simeon, 7,100 outstanding warriors.

From the Levites, 4,600.

From the priests—descendants of Aaron—there were 3,700 troops under the command of Zadok, a young man of unusual courage, and Jehoiada. (He and twenty-two members of his family were officers of the fighting priests.)

From the tribe of Benjamin, the same tribe Saul was from, there were 3,000. (Most of that tribe retained its allegiance to Saul.)

From the tribe of Ephraim, 20,800 mighty warriors, each famous in his respective clan.

From the half-tribe of Manasseh, 18,000 were sent for the express purpose of helping David become king.

From the tribe of Issachar there were 200 leaders of the tribe with their relatives—all men who understood the temper of the times and knew the best course for Israel to take.

From the tribe of Zebulun there were 50,000 trained warriors; they were fully armed and totally loyal to David.

From Naphtali there were 1,000 officers and 37,000 troops equipped with shields and spears.

From the tribe of Dan there were 28,600 troops, all of them prepared for war.

From the tribe of Asher, there were 40,000 trained and ready troops.

From the other side of the Jordan River—where the tribes of Reuben and Gad and the half-tribe of Manasseh lived—there were 120,000 troops equipped with every kind of weapon.

38All these men came in battle array to Hebron with the single purpose of making David the king of Israel. In fact, all of Israel was ready for this change. 39They feasted and drank with David for three days, for preparations had been made for their arrival. ⁴⁰People from nearby and from as far away as Issachar, Zebulun, and Naphtali brought food on donkeys, camels, mules, and oxen. Vast supplies of flour, fig cakes, raisins, wine, oil, cattle, and sheep were brought to the celebration, for joy had spread throughout the land.

AFTER David had consulted with all of his army officers, ²he addressed the assembled men of Israel as follows:

"Since you think that I should be your king, and since the Lord our God has given his approval, let us send messages to our brothers throughout the land of Israel, including the priests and Levites, inviting them to come and join us. ³And let us bring back the Ark of our God, for we have been neglecting it ever since Saul became king."

⁴There was unanimous consent, for everyone agreed with him. ⁵So David summoned the people of Israel from all across the nation so that they could be present when the Ark of God was brought from Kiriath-jearim.

⁶Then David and all Israel went to Baalah (i.e., Kiriath-jearim) in Judah to bring back the Ark of the Lord God enthroned above the angels. ⁷It was taken from the house of Abinadab on a new cart. Uzza and Ahio drove the oxen. ⁸Then David and all the people danced before the Lord with great enthusiasm, accompanied by singing and by zithers, harps, tambourines, cymbals, and trumpets. ⁹But as they arrived at the threshing-floor of Chidon, the oxen stumbled and Uzza reached out his hand to steady the Ark. ¹⁰Then the anger of the Lord blazed out against Uzza, and killed him because he had touched the Ark. And so he died there before God. ¹¹David was angry at the Lord for what he had done to Uzza, and he named the place "The Outbreak Against Uzza." And it is still called that today.

¹²Now David was afraid of God and asked, "How shall I ever get the Ark of God home?"

¹³Finally he decided to take it to the home of Obed-edom the Gittite instead of bringing it to the City of David. ¹⁴The Ark remained there with the family of Obed-edom for three months, and the Lord blessed him and his family.

KING Hiram of Tyre sent masons and carpenters to help build David's palace and he supplied him with much cedar lumber. ²David now realized why the Lord had made him king and why he had made his kingdom so great; it was for a special reason—to give joy to God's people!

³After David moved to Jerusalem, he married additional wives and became the father of many sons and daughters.

⁴⁻⁷These are the names of the sons born to him in Jerusalem:

Shammua, Shobab, Nathan, Solomon, Ibhar, Elishu-a, Elpelet, Nogah, Nepheg, Japhia, Elishama, Beeliada, Eliphelet.

⁸When the Philistines heard that David was Israel's new king, they mobilized their forces to capture him. But David learned that they were on the way, so he called together his army. ⁹The Philistines were raiding the Valley of Rephaim, ¹⁰and David asked the Lord, "If I go out and fight them, will you give me the victory?"

And the Lord replied, "Yes, I will."

¹¹So he attacked them at Baal-perazim and wiped them out. He exulted, "God has used me to sweep away my enemies like water bursting through a dam!" That is why the place has been known as Baal-perazim ever since (meaning, "The Place of Breaking Through").

¹²After the battle the Israelis picked up many idols left by the Philistines, but David ordered them burned.

¹³Later the Philistines raided the valley again, ¹⁴and again David asked God what to do.

The Lord replied, "Go around by the mulberry trees and attack from there. ¹⁵When you hear a sound like marching in the tops of the mulberry trees, that is your signal to attack, for God will go before you and destroy the enemy."

16So David did as the Lord commanded him; and he cut down the army of the Philistines all the way from Gibeon to Gezer. 17David's fame spread everywhere, and the Lord caused all the nations to fear him.

ROMANS 1:1–17

DEAR friends in Rome: 1This letter is from Paul, Jesus Christ's slave, chosen to be a missionary, and sent out to preach God's Good News. 2This Good News was promised long ago by God's prophets in the Old Testament. 3It is the Good News about his Son, Jesus Christ our Lord, who came as a human baby, born into King David's royal family line; 4and by being raised from the dead he was proved to be the mighty Son of God, with the holy nature of God himself.

5And now, through Christ, all the kindness of God has been poured out upon us undeserving sinners; and now he is sending us out around the world to tell all people everywhere the great things God has done for them, so that they, too, will believe and obey him.

6,7And you, dear friends in Rome, are among those he dearly loves; you, too, are invited by Jesus Christ to be God's very own—yes, his holy people. May all God's mercies and peace be yours from God our Father and from Jesus Christ our Lord.

8Let me say first of all that wherever I go I hear you being talked about! For your faith in God is becoming known around the world. How I thank God through Jesus Christ for this good report, and for each one of you. 9God knows how often I pray for you. Day and night I bring you and your needs in prayer to the one I serve with all my might, telling others the Good News about his Son.

10And one of the things I keep on praying for is the opportunity, God willing, to come at last to see you and, if possible, that I will have a safe trip. 11,12For I long to visit you so that I can impart to you the faith that will help your church grow strong in the Lord. Then, too, I need your help, for I want not only to share my faith with you but to be encouraged by yours: Each of us will be a blessing to the other.

13I want you to know, dear brothers, that I planned to come many times before (but was prevented) so that I could work among you and see good results, just as I have among the other Gentile churches. 14For I owe a great debt to you and to everyone else, both to civilized people and uncivilized alike; yes, to the educated and uneducated alike. 15So, to the fullest extent of my ability, I am ready to come also to you in Rome to preach God's Good News.

16For I am not ashamed of this Good News about Christ. It is God's powerful method of bringing all who believe it to heaven. This message was preached first to the Jews alone, but now everyone is invited to come to God in this same way. 17This Good News tells us that God makes us ready for heaven—makes us right in God's sight—when we put our faith and trust in Christ to save us. This is accomplished from start to finish by faith. As the Scripture says it, "The man who finds life will find it through trusting God."

PSALM 9:13–20

AND now, O Lord, have mercy on me; see how I suffer at the hands of those who hate me. Lord, snatch me back from the jaws of death. 14Save me, so that I can praise you publicly before all the people at Jerusalem's gates and rejoice that you have rescued me.

15The nations fall into the pitfalls they have dug for others; the trap they set has snapped on them. 16The Lord is famous for the way he punishes the wicked in their own snares!

17The wicked shall be sent away to hell; this is the fate of all the nations forgetting the Lord. 18For the needs of the needy shall not be ignored forever;

the hopes of the poor shall not always be crushed.

19O Lord, arise and judge and punish the nations; don't let them defy you! 20Make them tremble in fear; put the nations in their place until at last they know they are but puny men.

PROVERBS FOR TODAY/ 19:4–5

A wealthy man has many "friends"; the poor man has none left. Punish false witnesses. Track down liars.

JULY 13

1 CHRONICLES 15:1—16:36

DAVID now built several palaces for himself in Jerusalem, and he also built a new Tabernacle to house the Ark of God, 2and issued these instructions: "[When we transfer the Ark to its new home], no one except the Levites may carry it, for God has chosen them for this purpose; they are to minister to him forever."

3Then David summoned all Israel to Jerusalem to celebrate the bringing of the Ark into the new Tabernacle. 4–10These were the priests and Levites present:

120 from the clan of Kohath; with Uriel as their leader;

220 from the clan of Merari; with Asaiah as their leader;

130 from the clan of Gershom; with Joel as their leader;

200 from the subclan of Elizaphan; with Shemaiah as their leader;

80 from the subclan of Hebron; with Eliel as their leader;

112 from the subclan of Uzziel; with Amminadab as their leader.

11Then David called for Zadok and Abiathar, the High Priests, and for the Levite leaders: Uriel, Asaiah, Joel, Shemaiah, Eliel, and Amminadab.

12"You are the leaders of the clans of the Levites," he told them. "Now sanctify yourselves with all your brothers so that you may bring the Ark of Jehovah, the God of Israel, to the place I have pre- pared for it. 13The Lord destroyed us before because we handled the matter improperly—you were not carrying it."

14So the priests and the Levites underwent the ceremonies of sanctification in preparation for bringing home the Ark of Jehovah, the God of Israel. 15Then the Levites carried the Ark on their shoulders with its carrying poles, just as the Lord had instructed Moses.

16King David also ordered the Levite leaders to organize the singers into an orchestra, and they played loudly and joyously upon psalteries, harps, and cymbals. 17Heman (son of Joel), Asaph (son of Berechiah), and Ethan (son of Kushaiah) from the clan of Merari were the heads of the musicians.

18The following men were chosen as their assistants:

Zechariah, Ja-aziel, Shemiramoth, Jehiel, Unni, Eliab, Benaiah, Ma-asseiah, Mattithiah, Eliphelehu, Mikneiah, Obed-edom and Je-iel, the door keepers.

19Heman, Asaph, and Ethan were chosen to sound the bronze cymbals; 20and Zechariah, Azi-el, Shemiramoth, Jehiel, Unni, Eliab, Ma-aseiah, and Benaiah comprised an octet accompanied by harps. 21Mattithiah, Eliphelehu, Mikneiah, Obed-edom, Je-iel, and Azaziah were the harpists. 22The song leader was Chenaniah, the chief of the Levites, who was selected for his skill. 23Berechiah and Elkanah were guards for the Ark.

²⁴Shebaniah, Joshaphat, Nethanel, Amasai, Zechariah, Benaiah, and Eliezer—all of whom were priests—formed a bugle corps to march at the head of the procession. And Obed-edom and Jehiah guarded the Ark.

²⁵Then David and the elders of Israel and the high officers of the army went with great joy to the home of Obed-edom to take the Ark to Jerusalem. ²⁶And because God didn't destroy the Levites who were carrying the Ark, they sacrificed seven bulls and seven lambs. ²⁷David, the Levites carrying the Ark, the singers, and Chenaniah the song leader were all dressed in linen robes. David also wore a linen ephod. ²⁸So the leaders of Israel took the Ark to Jerusalem with shouts of joy, the blowing of horns and trumpets, the crashing of cymbals, and loud playing on the harps and zithers.

²⁹(But as the Ark arrived in Jerusalem, David's wife Michal, the daughter of King Saul, felt a deep disgust for David as she watched from the window and saw him dancing like a madman.)

So they brought the Ark of God into the special tent that David had prepared for it, and the leaders of Israel sacrificed burnt offerings and peace offerings before God. ²At the conclusion of these offerings David blessed the people in the name of the Lord; ³then he gave every person present (men and women alike) a loaf of bread, some wine, and a cake of raisins.

⁴He appointed certain of the Levites to minister before the Ark by giving constant praise and thanks to the Lord God of Israel and by asking for his blessings upon his people. These are the names of those given this assignment: ⁵Asaph, the leader of this detail, sounded the cymbals. His associates were Zechariah, Je-iel, Shemiramoth, Jehiel, Mattithiah, Eliab, Benaiah, Obededom, and Je-iel; they played the harps and zithers. ⁶The priests Benaiah and Jahaziel played their trumpets regularly before the Ark.

⁷At that time David began the custom of using choirs in the Tabernacle to sing thanksgiving to the Lord. Asaph was the director of this choral group of priests.

⁸"Oh, give thanks to the Lord and pray to him," they sang.

"Tell the peoples of the world
About his mighty doings.
⁹Sing to him; yes, sing his praises
And tell of his marvelous works.
¹⁰Glory in his holy name;
Let all rejoice who seek the Lord.
¹¹Seek the Lord; yes, seek his strength
And seek his face untiringly.
^{12,13}O descendants of his servant Abraham,
O chosen sons of Jacob,
Remember his mighty miracles
And his marvelous miracles
And his authority!
¹⁴He is the Lord our God!
His authority is seen throughout the earth.
¹⁵Remember his covenant forever—
The words he commanded
To a thousand generations:
¹⁶His agreement with Abraham,
And his oath to Isaac,
¹⁷And his confirmation to Jacob.
He promised Israel
With an everlasting promise:
¹⁸'I will give you the land of Canaan
As your inheritance.'
¹⁹When Israel was few in number—
oh, so few—
And merely strangers in the Promised Land;
²⁰When they wandered from country to country,
From one kingdom to another—
²¹God didn't let anyone harm them.
Even kings were killed who sought to hurt them.
²²'Don't harm my chosen people,' he declared.
'These are my prophets—touch them not.'
²³Sing to the Lord, O earth,
Declare each day that he is the one who saves!
²⁴Show his glory to the nations!
Tell everyone about his miracles.
²⁵For the Lord is great, and should be highly praised;

He is to be held in awe above all gods.
26The other so-called gods are demons,
But the Lord made the heavens.
27Majesty and honor march before him,
Strength and gladness walk beside him.
28O people of all nations of the earth,
Ascribe great strength and glory to his name!
29Yes, ascribe to the Lord
The glory due his name!
Bring an offering and come before him;
Worship the Lord when clothed with holiness!
30Tremble before him, all the earth!
The world stands unmoved.
31Let the heavens be glad, the earth rejoice;
Let all the nations say, 'It is the Lord who reigns.'
32Let the vast seas roar,
Let the countryside and everything in it rejoice!
33Let the trees in the woods sing for joy before the Lord,
For he comes to judge the earth.
34Oh, give thanks to the Lord, for he is good;
His love and his kindness go on forever.
35Cry out to him, 'Oh, save us, God of our salvation;
Bring us safely back from among the nations.
Then we will thank your holy name,
And triumph in your praise.'
36Blessed be Jehovah, God of Israel,
Forever and forevermore."
And all the people shouted "Amen!" and praised the Lord.

ROMANS 1:18–32

BUT God shows his anger from heaven against all sinful, evil men who push away the truth from them. 19For the truth about God is known to them instinctively; God has put this knowledge in their hearts. 20Since earliest times men have seen the earth and sky and all God made, and have known of his existence and great eternal power. So they will have no excuse [when they stand before God at Judgment Day].

21Yes, they knew about him all right, but they wouldn't admit it or worship him or even thank him for all his daily care. And after awhile they began to think up silly ideas of what God was like and what he wanted them to do. The result was that their foolish minds became dark and confused. 22Claiming themselves to be wise without God, they became utter fools instead. 23And then, instead of worshiping the glorious, ever-living God, they took wood and stone and made idols for themselves, carving them to look like mere birds and animals and snakes and puny men.

24So God let them go ahead into every sort of sex sin, and do whatever they wanted to—yes, vile and sinful things with each other's bodies. 25Instead of believing what they knew was the truth about God, they deliberately chose to believe lies. So they prayed to the things God made, but wouldn't obey the blessed God who made these things.

26That is why God let go of them and let them do all these evil things, so that even their women turned against God's natural plan for them and indulged in sex sin with each other. 27And the men, instead of having a normal sex relationship with women, burned with lust for each other, men doing shameful things with other men and, as a result, getting paid within their own souls with the penalty they so richly deserved.

28So it was that when they gave God up and would not even acknowledge him, God gave them up to doing everything their evil minds could think of. 29Their lives became full of every kind of wickedness and sin, of greed and hate, envy, murder, fighting, lying, bitterness, and gossip.

30They were backbiters, haters of God, insolent, proud braggarts, always thinking of new ways of sinning and continually being disobedient to their parents. ³¹They tried to misunderstand, broke their promises, and were heartless—without pity. ³²They were fully aware of God's death penalty for these crimes, yet they went right ahead and did them anyway, and encouraged others to do them, too.

PSALM 10:1–15

LORD, why are you standing aloof and far away? Why do you hide when I need you the most? ²Come and deal with all these proud and wicked men who viciously persecute the poor. Pour upon these men the evil they planned for others! ³For these men brag of all their evil lusts; they revile God and congratulate those the Lord abhors, whose only goal in life is money.

⁴These wicked men, so proud and haughty, seem to think that God is dead. They wouldn't think of looking for him! ⁵Yet there is success in everything they do, and their enemies fall before them. They do not see your punishment awaiting them. ⁶They boast that neither God nor man can ever keep them down—somehow they'll find a way!

⁷Their mouths are full of profanity and lies and fraud. They are always boasting of their evil plans. ⁸They lurk in dark alleys of the city and murder passersby. ⁹Like lions they crouch silently, waiting to pounce upon the poor. Like hunters they catch their victims in their traps. ¹⁰The unfortunate are overwhelmed by their superior strength and fall beneath their blows. ¹¹"God isn't watching," they say to themselves; "he'll never know!"

¹²O Lord, arise! O God, crush them! Don't forget the poor or anyone else in need. ¹³Why do you let the wicked get away with this contempt for God? For they think that God will never call them to account. ¹⁴Lord, you see what they are doing. You have noted each evil act. You know what trouble and grief they have caused. Now punish them. O Lord, the poor man trusts himself to you; you are known as the helper of the helpless. ¹⁵Break the arms of these wicked men. Go after them until the last of them is destroyed.

PROVERBS FOR TODAY/ 19:6–7

Many beg favors from a man who is generous; everyone is his friend! A poor man's own brothers turn away from him in embarrassment; how much more his friends! He calls after them, but they are gone.

JULY 14

1 CHRONICLES 16:37—18:17

DAVID arranged for Asaph and his fellow Levites to minister regularly at the Tabernacle, doing each day whatever needed to be done. ³⁸This group included Obed-edom (the son of Jeduthun), Hosah and sixty-eight of their colleagues as guards.

³⁹Meanwhile the old Tabernacle of the Lord on the hill of Gibeon continued to be active. David left Zadok the priest and his fellow-priests to minister to the Lord there. ⁴⁰They sacrificed burnt offerings to the Lord each morning and evening upon the altar set aside for that purpose, just as the Lord had commanded Israel. ⁴¹David also appointed Heman, Jeduthun, and several others who were chosen by name to give thanks to the Lord for his constant love and mercy. ⁴²They used their trumpets and cymbals to accompany the singers with loud praises to

God. And Jeduthun's sons were appointed as guards.

43At last the celebration ended and the people returned to their homes, and David returned to bless his own household.

AFTER David had been living in his new palace for some time he said to Nathan the prophet, "Look! I'm living here in a cedar-paneled home while the Ark of the Covenant of God is out there in a tent!"

2And Nathan replied, "Carry out your plan in every detail, for it is the will of the Lord."

3But that same night God said to Nathan, 4"Go and give my servant David this message: 'You are not to build my temple! 5I've gone from tent to tent as my home from the time I brought Israel out of Egypt. 6In all that time I never suggested to any of the leaders of Israel—the shepherds I appointed to care for my people—that they should build me a cedar-lined temple.'

7"Tell my servant David, 'The Lord of heaven says to you, I took you from being a shepherd and made you the king of my people. 8And I have been with you everywhere you've gone; I have destroyed your enemies, and I will make your name as great as the greatest of the earth. 9And I will give a permanent home to my people Israel, and will plant them in their land. They will not be disturbed again; the wicked nations won't conquer them as they did before, 10when the judges ruled them. I will subdue all of your enemies. And I now declare that I will cause your descendants to be kings of Israel just as you are.

11" 'When your time here on earth is over and you die, I will place one of your sons upon your throne; and I will make his kingdom strong. 12He is the one who shall build me a temple, and I will establish his royal line of descent forever. 13I will be his father, and he shall be my son; I will never remove my mercy and love from him as I did from Saul. 14I will place him over my people and over the kingdom of Israel forever—and

his descendants will always be kings.' "

15So Nathan told King David everything the Lord had said.

16Then King David went in and sat before the Lord and said, "Who am I, O Lord God, and what is my family that you have given me all this? 17For all the great things you have already done for me are nothing in comparison to what you have promised to do in the future! For now, O Lord God, you are speaking of future generations of my children being kings too! You speak as though I were someone very great. 18What else can I say? You know that I am but a dog, yet you have decided to honor me! 19O Lord, you have given me these wonderful promises just because you want to be kind to me, because of your own great heart. 20O Lord, there is no one like you—there is no other God. In fact, we have never even heard of another god like you!

21"And what other nation in all the earth is like Israel? You have made a unique nation and have redeemed it from Egypt so that the people could be your people. And you made a great name for yourself when you did glorious miracles in driving out the nations from before your people. 22You have declared that your people Israel belong to you forever, and you have become their God.

23"And now I accept your promise, Lord, that I and my children will always rule this nation. 24And may this bring eternal honor to your name as everyone realizes that you always do what you say. They will exclaim, 'The Lord of heaven is indeed the God of Israel!' And Israel shall always be ruled by my children and their posterity! 25Now I have the courage to pray to you, for you have revealed this to me. 26God himself has promised this good thing to me! 27May this blessing rest upon my children forever, for when you grant a blessing, Lord, it is an eternal blessing!"

DAVID finally subdued the Philistines and conquered Gath and its surrounding towns. 2He also conquered Moab and required its people to send him a large sum of money every year. ³He conquered the dominion of King Hadadezer of Zobah (as far as Hamath) at the time Hadadezer went to tighten his grip along the Euphrates River. ⁴David captured a thousand of his chariots, seven thousand cavalry, and twenty thousand troops. He crippled all the chariot teams except a hundred that he kept for his own use.

⁵When the Syrians arrived from Damascus to help King Hadadezer, David killed twenty-two thousand of them; ⁶then he placed a garrison of his troops in Damascus, the Syrian capital. So the Syrians, too, were forced to send him large amounts of money every year. And the Lord gave David victory everywhere he went. ⁷He brought the gold shields of King Hadadezer's officers to Jerusalem, ⁸as well as a great amount of bronze from Hadadezer's cities of Tibhath and Cun. (King Solomon later melted the bronze and used it for the Temple. He molded it into the bronze tank, the pillars, and the instruments used in offering sacrifices on the altar.)

⁹When King Tou of Hamath learned that King David had destroyed Hadadezer's army, ¹⁰he sent his son Hadoram to greet and congratulate King David on his success and to present him with many gifts of gold, silver, and bronze, seeking an alliance. For Hadadezer and Tou had been enemies and there had been many wars between them. ¹¹King David dedicated these gifts to the Lord, as he did the silver and gold he took from the nations of Edom, Moab, Ammon, Amalek, and the Philistines.

¹²Abishai (son of Zeruiah) then destroyed eighteen thousand Edomites in the Valley of Salt. ¹³He put garrisons in Edom and forced the Edomites to pay large sums of money annually to David. This is just another example of how the Lord gave David victory after victory. ¹⁴David reigned over all of Israel and was a just ruler.

¹⁵Joab (son of Zeruiah) was commander-in-chief of the army; Jehoshaphat (son of Ahilud) was the historian; ¹⁶Zadok (son of Ahitub) and Ahimelech (son of Abiathar) were the head priests; Shavsha was the king's special assistant; ¹⁷Benaiah (son of Jehoiada) was in charge of the king's bodyguard—the Cherethites and Pelethites—and David's sons were his chief aides.

ROMANS 2:1–23

W ELL," you may be saying, "what terrible people you have been talking about!" But wait a minute! You are just as bad. When you say they are wicked and should be punished, you are talking about yourselves, for you do these very same things. ²And we know that God, in justice, will punish anyone who does such things as these. ³Do you think that God will judge and condemn others for doing them and overlook you when you do them, too? ⁴Don't you realize how patient he is being with you? Or don't you care? Can't you see that he has been waiting all this time without punishing you, to give you time to turn from your sin? His kindness is meant to lead you to repentance.

⁵But no, you won't listen; and so you are saving up terrible punishment for yourselves because of your stubbornness in refusing to turn from your sin; for there is going to come a day of wrath when God will be the just Judge of all the world. ⁶He will give each one whatever his deeds deserve. ⁷He will give eternal life to those who patiently do the will of God, seeking for the unseen glory and honor and eternal life that he offers. ⁸But he will terribly punish those who fight against the truth of God and walk in evil ways—God's anger will be poured out upon them. ⁹There will be sorrow and suffering for Jews and Gentiles alike who keep on sinning. ¹⁰But there will be glory and honor and peace from God for all who obey him, whether they are Jews or Gentiles. ¹¹For God treats everyone the same.

¹²⁻¹⁵He will punish sin wherever it is found. He will punish the heathen when they sin, even though they never had

God's written laws, for down in their hearts they know right from wrong. God's laws are written within them; their own conscience accuses them, or sometimes excuses them. And God will punish the Jews for sinning because they have his written laws but don't obey them. They know what is right but don't do it. After all, salvation is not given to those who know what to do, unless they do it. 16The day will surely come when at God's command Jesus Christ will judge the secret lives of everyone, their inmost thoughts and motives; this is all part of God's great plan which I proclaim.

17You Jews think all is well between yourselves and God because he gave his laws to you; you brag that you are his special friends. 18Yes, you know what he wants; you know right from wrong and favor the right because you have been taught his laws from earliest youth. 19You are so sure of the way to God that you could point it out to a blind man. You think of yourselves as beacon lights, directing men who are lost in dark-ness to God. 20You think that you can guide the simple and teach even children the affairs of God, for you really know his laws, which are full of all knowledge and truth.

21Yes, you teach others—then why don't you teach yourselves? You tell others not to steal—do *you* steal? 22You say it is wrong to commit adultery—do *you* do it? You say, "Don't pray to idols," and then make money your god instead.

23You are so proud of knowing God's laws, *but you dishonor him by breaking them.*

PSALM 10:16–18

THE Lord is King forever and forever. Those who follow other gods shall be swept from his land. 17Lord, you know the hopes of humble people. Surely you will hear their cries and comfort their hearts by helping them. 18You will be with the orphans and all who are oppressed, so that mere earthly man will terrify them no longer.

PROVERBS FOR TODAY/ 19:8–9

He who loves wisdom loves his own best interest and will be a success. A false witness shall be punished and a liar shall be caught.

JULY 15

1 CHRONICLES 19:1—21:30

WHEN King Nahash of Ammon died, his son Hanun became the new king.

2,3Then David declared, "I am going to show friendship to Hanun because of all the kind things his father did for me."

So David sent a message of sympathy to Hanun for the death of his father. But when David's ambassadors arrived, King Hanun's counselors warned him, "Don't fool yourself that David has sent these men to honor your father! They are here to spy out the land so that they can come in and conquer it!"

4So King Hanun insulted King David's ambassadors by shaving their beards and cutting their robes off at the middle to expose their buttocks; then he sent them back to David in shame. 5When David heard what had happened, he sent a message to his embarrassed emissaries, telling them to stay at Jericho until their beards had grown out again. 6When King Hanun realized his mistake he sent $2,000,000 to enlist mercenary troops, chariots, and cavalry from Mesopotamia, Aram-maacah, and Zobah. 7He hired thirty-two thousand chariots, as well as the support of the king of Maacah and his entire army. These forces camped at Medeba where they were joined by the troops King Hanun had recruited from his cities.

8When David learned of this, he sent Joab and the mightiest warriors of Israel. 9The army of Ammon went out to meet them and began the battle at the gates of the city of Medeba. Meanwhile, the mercenary forces were out in the field. 10When Joab realized that the enemy forces were both in front and behind him, he divided his army and sent one group to engage the Syrians. 11The other group, under the command of his brother Abishai, moved against the Ammonites.

12"If the Syrians are too strong for me, come and help me," Joab told his brother; "and if the Ammonites are too strong for you, I'll come and help you. 13Be courageous and let us act like men to save our people and the cities of our God. And may the Lord do what is best."

14So Joab and his troops attacked the Syrians, and the Syrians turned and fled. 15When the Ammonites, under attack by Abishai's troops, saw that the Syrians were retreating, they fled into the city. Then Joab returned to Jerusalem.

16After their defeat, the Syrians summoned additional troops from east of the Euphrates River, led personally by Shophach, King Hadadezer's commander-in-chief. 17,18When this news reached David, he mobilized all Israel, crossed the Jordan River, and engaged the enemy troops in battle. But the Syrians again fled from David, and he killed seven thousand charioteers and forty thousand of their troops. He also killed Shophach, the commander-in-chief of the Syrian army. 19Then King Hadadezer's troops surrendered to King David and became his subjects. And never again did the Syrians aid the Ammonites in their battles.

THE following spring (spring was the season when wars usually began) Joab led the Israeli army in successful attacks against the cities and villages of the people of Ammon. After destroying them, he laid siege to Rabbah and conquered it. Meanwhile, David had stayed in Jerusalem. 2When David arrived on the scene, he removed the crown from the head of King Milcom of Rabbah and placed it upon his own head. It was made of gold inlaid with gems and weighed seventy-five pounds! David also took great amounts of plunder from the city. 3He drove the people from the city and set them to work with saws, iron picks, and axes, as was his custom with all the conquered Ammonite peoples. Then David and all his army returned to Jerusalem.

4The next war was against the Philistines again, at Gezer. But Sibbecai, a man from Hushath, killed one of the sons of the giant, Sippai, and so the Philistines surrendered. 5During another war with the Philistines, Elhanan (the son of Jair) killed Lahmi, the brother of Goliath the giant; the handle of his spear was like a weaver's beam! 6,7During another battle, at Gath, a giant with six fingers on each hand and six toes on each foot (his father was also a giant) defied and taunted Israel; but he was killed by David's nephew Jonathan, the son of David's brother Shimea. 8These giants were descendants of the giants of Gath, and they were killed by David and his soldiers.

THEN Satan brought disaster upon Israel, for he made David decide to take a census.

2"Take a complete census throughout the land and bring me the totals," he told Joab and the other leaders.

3But Joab objected. "If the Lord were to multiply his people a hundred times, would they not all be yours? So why are you asking us to do this? Why must you cause Israel to sin?"

4But the king won the argument, and Joab did as he was told; he traveled all through Israel and returned to Jerusalem. 5The total population figure which he gave came to 1,100,000 men of military age in Israel and 470,000 in Judah. 6But he didn't include the tribes of Levi and Benjamin in his figures because he was so distressed at what the king had made him do.

7And God, too, was displeased with the census and punished Israel for it.

8But David said to God, "I am the one who has sinned. Please forgive me, for I realize now how wrong I was to do this."

9Then the Lord said to Gad, David's personal prophet, 10,11"Go and tell David, 'The Lord has offered you three choices. Which will you choose? 12You may have three years of famine, or three months of destruction by the enemies of Israel, or three days of deadly plague as the angel of the Lord brings destruction to the land. Think it over and let me know what answer to return to the one who sent me.' "

13"This is a terrible decision to make," David replied, "but let me fall into the hands of the Lord rather than into the power of men, for God's mercies are very great."

14So the Lord sent a plague upon Israel and 70,000 men died as a result. 15During the plague God sent an angel to destroy Jerusalem; but then he felt such compassion that he changed his mind and commanded the destroying angel, "Stop! It is enough!" (The angel of the Lord was standing at the time by the threshing-floor of Ornan the Jebusite.) 16When David saw the angel of the Lord standing between heaven and earth with his sword drawn, pointing toward Jerusalem, he and the elders of Israel clothed themselves in sackcloth and fell to the ground before the Lord.

17And David said to God, "I am the one who sinned by ordering the census. But what have these sheep done? O Lord my God, destroy me and my family, but do not destroy your people."

18Then the angel of the Lord told Gad to instruct David to build an altar to the Lord at the threshing-floor of Ornan the Jebusite. 19,20So David went to see Ornan, who was threshing wheat at the time.

Ornan saw the angel as he turned, and his four sons ran and hid. 21Then Ornan saw the king approaching. So he left the threshing-floor and bowed to the ground before King David.

22David said to Ornan, "Let me buy this threshing-floor from you at its full price; then I will build an altar to the Lord and the plague will stop."

23"Take it, my lord, and use it as you wish," Ornan said to David. "Take the oxen, too, for burnt offerings; use the threshing instruments for wood for the fire and use the wheat for the grain offering. I give it all to you."

24"No," the king replied, "I will buy it for the full price; I cannot take what is yours and give it to the Lord. I will not offer a burnt offering that has cost me nothing!"

25So David paid Ornan $4,300 in gold, 26and built an altar to the Lord there, and sacrificed burnt offerings and peace offerings upon it; and he called out to the Lord, who answered by sending down fire from heaven to burn up the offering on the altar. 27Then the Lord commanded the angel to put back his sword into its sheath; 28and when David saw that the Lord had answered his plea, he sacrificed to him again. 29The Tabernacle and altar made by Moses in the wilderness were on the hill of Gibeon, 30but David didn't have time to go there to plead before the Lord, for he was terrified by the drawn sword of the angel of Jehovah.

ROMANS 2:24—3:8

NO wonder the Scriptures say that the world speaks evil of God because of you.

25Being a Jew is worth something if you obey God's laws; but if you don't, then you are no better off than the heathen. 26And if the heathen obey God's laws, won't God give them all the rights and honors he planned to give the Jews? 27In fact, those heathen will be much better off than you Jews who know so much about God and have his promises but don't obey his laws.

28For you are not real Jews just because you were born of Jewish parents or because you have gone through the Jewish initiation ceremony of circumcision. 29No, a real Jew is anyone whose heart is right with God. For God is not looking for those who cut their bodies in actual body circumcision, but he is looking for those with changed hearts and minds. Whoever has that kind of change in his life will get his praise from God, even if not from you.

THEN what's the use of being a Jew? Are there any special benefits for them from God? Is there any value in the Jewish circumcision ceremony? 2Yes, being a Jew has many advantages.

First of all, God trusted them with his laws [so that they could know and do his will]. 3True, some of them were unfaithful, but just because they broke their promises to God, does that mean God will break his promises? 4Of course not! Though everyone else in the world is a liar, God is not. Do you remember what the book of Psalms says about this? That God's words will always prove true and right, no matter who questions them.

5"But," some say, "our breaking faith with God is good, our sins serve a good purpose, for people will notice how good God is when they see how bad we are. Is it fair, then, for him to punish us when our sins are helping him?" (That is the way some people talk.) 6God forbid! Then what kind of God would he be, to overlook sin? How could he ever condemn anyone? 7For he could not judge and condemn me as a sinner if my dishonesty brought him glory by pointing up his honesty in contrast to my lies. 8If you follow through with that idea you come to this: the worse we are, the better God likes it! But the damnation of those who say such things is just. Yet some claim that this is what I preach!

PSALM 11:1–7

HOW dare you tell me, "Flee to the mountains for safety," when I am trusting in the Lord?

2For the wicked have strung their bows, drawn their arrows tight against the bowstrings, and aimed from ambush at the people of God. 3"Law and order have collapsed," we are told. "What can the righteous do but flee?"

4But the Lord is still in his holy temple; he still rules from heaven. He closely watches everything that happens here on earth. 5He puts the righteous and the wicked to the test; he hates those loving violence. 6He will rain down fire and brimstone on the wicked and scorch them with his burning wind.

7For God is good, and he loves goodness; the godly shall see his face.

PROVERBS FOR TODAY/ 19:10–12

It doesn't seem right for a fool to succeed or for a slave to rule over princes! A wise man restrains his anger and overlooks insults. This is to his credit. The king's anger is as dangerous as a lion's. But his approval is as refreshing as the dew on grass.

JULY 16

1 CHRONICLES 22:1—23:32

THEN David said, "Right here at Ornan's threshing-floor is˜ the place where I'll build the Temple of the Lord and construct the altar for Israel's burnt offering!"

2David now drafted all the resident aliens in Israel to prepare blocks of squared stone for the Temple. 3They also manufactured iron into the great quantity of nails needed for the doors in the gates and for the clamps; and they smelted so much bronze that it was too much to weigh. 4The men of Tyre and Sidon brought great rafts of cedar logs to David.

5"Solomon my son is young and tender," David said, "and the Temple of the Lord must be a marvelous structure, famous and glorious throughout the world; so I will begin the preparations for it now."

So David collected the construction materials before his death. 6He now commanded his son Solomon to build a temple for the Lord God of Israel.

7"I wanted to build it myself," David told him, 8"but the Lord said not to do it. 'You have killed too many men in great wars,' he told me. 'You have reddened the ground before me with blood: so you are not to build my Temple. 9But I will give you a son,' he told me, 'who will be a man of peace, for I will give him peace with his enemies in the surrounding lands. His name shall be Solomon (meaning "Peaceful"), and I will give peace and quietness to Israel during his reign. 10He shall build my temple, and he shall be as my own son and I will be his father; and I will cause his sons and his descendants to reign over every generation of Israel.'

11"So now, my son, may the Lord be with you and prosper you as you do what he told you to do and build the Temple of the Lord. 12And may the Lord give you the good judgment to follow all his laws when he makes you king of Israel. 13For if you carefully obey the rules and regulations which he gave to Israel through Moses, you will prosper. Be strong and courageous, fearless and enthusiastic!

14"By hard work I have collected several billion dollars worth of gold bullion, millions in silver, and so much iron and bronze that I haven't even weighed it; I have also gathered timber and stone for the walls. This is at least a beginning, something with which to start. 15And you have many skilled stonemasons and carpenters and craftsmen of every kind. 16They are expert gold and silver smiths and bronze and iron workers. So get to work, and may the Lord be with you!"

17Then David ordered all the leaders of Israel to assist his son in this project.

18"The Lord your God is with you," he declared. "He has given you peace with the surrounding nations, for I have conquered them in the name of the Lord and for his people. 19Now try with every fiber of your being to obey the Lord your God, and you will soon be bringing the Ark and the other holy articles of worship into the Temple of the Lord!"

BY this time David was an old, old man, so he stepped down from the throne and appointed his son Solomon as the new king of Israel. 2He summoned all the political and religious leaders of Israel for the coronation ceremony. 3At this time a census was taken of the men of the tribe of Levi who were thirty years or older. The total came to 38,000.

4,5"Twenty-four thousand of them will supervise the work at the Temple," David instructed, "six thousand are to be bailiffs and judges, four thousand will be temple guards, and four thousand will praise the Lord with the musical instruments I have made."

6Then David divided them into three

main divisions named after the sons of Levi—the Gershom division, the Kohath division and the Merari division.

7Subdivisions of the *Gershom* corps were named after his sons Ladan and Shime-i. 8,9These subdivisions were still further divided into six groups named after the sons of *Ladan:* Jehiel the leader, Zetham, Joel; and the sons of *Shime-i*—Shelomoth, Haziel, and Haran.

10,11The subclans of *Shime-i* were named after his four sons: Jahath was greatest, Zizah was next, and Jeush and Beriah were combined into a single subclan because neither had many sons.

12The division of Kohath was subdivided into four groups named after his sons Amram, Izhar, Hebron, and Uzziel.

13*Amram* was the ancestor of Aaron and Moses. Aaron and his sons were set apart for the holy service of sacrificing the people's offerings to the Lord. He served the Lord constantly and pronounced blessings in his name at all times.

14,15As for Moses, the man of God, his sons Gershom and Eliezer were included with the tribe of Levi. 16*Gershom's* sons were led by Shebuel, 17and *Eliezer's* only son, Rehabiah, was the leader of his clan, for he had many children.

18The sons of *Izhar* were led by Shelomith.

19The sons of *Hebron* were led by Jeriah. Amariah was second in command, Jahaziel was third, and Jekameam was fourth.

20The sons of *Uzziel* were led by Micah, and Isshiah was the second in command.

21The sons of *Merari* were Mahli and Mushi. The sons of *Mahli* were Eleazar and Kish. 22*Eleazar* died without any sons, and his daughters were married to their cousins, the sons of *Kish*. 23*Mushi's* sons were Mahli, Eder, and Jeremoth.

24In the census, all the men of Levi who were twenty years old or older were classified under the names of these clans and subclans; and they were all assigned to the ministry at the Temple. 25For David said, "The Lord God of Israel has given us peace, and he will always live in Jerusalem. 26Now the Levites will no longer need to carry the Tabernacle and its instruments from place to place."

27(This census of the tribe of Levi was one of the last things David did before his death.) 28The work of the Levites was to assist the priests—the descendants of Aaron—in the sacrifices at the Temple; they also did the custodial work and helped perform the ceremonies of purification. 29They provided the Bread of the Presence, the flour for the grain offerings, and the wafers made without yeast (either fried or mixed with olive oil); they also checked all the weights and measures. 30Each morning and evening they stood before the Lord to sing thanks and praise to him. 31They assisted in the special sacrifices of burnt offerings, the Sabbath sacrifices, the new moon celebrations, and at all the festivals. There were always as many Levites present as were required for the occasion. 32And they took care of the Tabernacle and the Temple and assisted the priests in whatever way they were needed.

ROMANS 3:9–31

WELL, then, are we Jews *better* than others? No, not at all, for we have already shown that all men alike are sinners, whether Jews or Gentiles. 10As the Scriptures say,

"No one is good—no one in all the world is innocent."

11No one has ever really followed God's paths, or even truly wanted to.

12Every one has turned away; all have gone wrong. No one anywhere has kept on doing what is right; not one.

13Their talk is foul and filthy like the stench from an open grave. Their tongues are loaded with lies. Everything they say has in it the sting and poison of deadly snakes.

¹⁴Their mouths are full of cursing and bitterness.

¹⁵They are quick to kill, hating anyone who disagrees with them.

¹⁶Wherever they go they leave misery and trouble behind them, ¹⁷and they have never known what it is to feel secure or enjoy God's blessing.

¹⁸They care nothing about God nor what he thinks of them.

¹⁹So the judgment of God lies very heavily upon the Jews, for they are responsible to keep God's laws instead of doing all these evil things; not one of them has any excuse; in fact, all the world stands hushed and guilty before Almighty God.

²⁰Now do you see it? No one can ever be made right in God's sight by doing what the law commands. For the more we know of God's laws, the clearer it becomes that we aren't obeying them; his laws serve only to make us see that we are sinners.

²¹,²²But now God has shown us a different way to heaven—not by "being good enough" and trying to keep his laws, but by a new way (though not new, really, for the Scriptures told about it long ago). Now God says he will accept and acquit us—declare us "not guilty"—if we trust Jesus Christ to take away our sins. And we all can be saved in this same way, by coming to Christ, no matter who we are or what we have been like. ²³Yes, all have sinned; all fall short of God's glorious ideal; ²⁴yet now God declares us "not guilty" of offending him if we trust in Jesus Christ, who in his kindness freely takes away our sins.

²⁵For God sent Christ Jesus to take the punishment for our sins and to end all God's anger against us. He used Christ's blood and our faith as the means of saving us from his wrath. In this way he was being entirely fair, even though he did not punish those who sinned in former times. For he was looking forward to the time when Christ would come and take away those sins. ²⁶And now in these days also

he can receive sinners in this same way, because Jesus took away their sins.

But isn't this unfair for God to let criminals go free, and say that they are innocent? No, for he does it on the basis of their trust in Jesus who took away their sins.

²⁷Then what can we boast about doing, to earn our salvation? Nothing at all. Why? Because our acquittal is not based on our good deeds; it is based on what Christ has done and our faith in him. ²⁸So it is that we are saved by faith in Christ and not by the good things we do.

²⁹And does God save only the Jews in this way? No, the Gentiles, too, may come to him in this same manner. ³⁰God treats us all the same; all, whether Jews or Gentiles, are acquitted if they have faith. ³¹Well then, if we are saved by faith, does this mean that we no longer need obey God's laws? Just the opposite! In fact, only when we trust Jesus can we truly obey him.

PSALM 12:1–8

LORD! Help! Godly men are fast disappearing. Where in all the world can dependable men be found? ²Everyone deceives and flatters and lies. There is no sincerity left.

³,⁴But the Lord will not deal gently with people who act like that; he will destroy those proud liars who say, "We will lie to our hearts' content. Our lips are our own; who can stop us?"

⁵The Lord replies, "I will arise and defend the oppressed, the poor, the needy. I will rescue them as they have longed for me to do." ⁶The Lord's promise is sure. He speaks no careless word; all he says is purest truth, like silver seven times refined. ⁷O Lord, we know that you will forever preserve your own from the reach of evil men, ⁸although they prowl on every side and vileness is praised throughout the land.

A rebellious son is a calamity to his father, and a nagging wife annoys like constant dripping. A father can give his sons homes and riches, but only the Lord can give them understanding wives.

JULY 17

1 CHRONICLES 24:1—26:11

THE priests (the descendants of Aaron) were placed into two divisions named after Aaron's sons, Eleazar and Ithamar.

Nadab and Abihu were also sons of Aaron, but they died before their father did and had no children; so only Eleazar and Ithamar were left to carry on. ³David consulted with Zadok, who represented the Eleazar clan, and with Ahimelech, who represented the Ithamar clan; then he divided Aaron's descendants into many groups to serve at various times. ⁴*Eleazar's* descendants were divided into sixteen groups and *Ithamar's* into eight (for there was more leadership ability among the descendants of Eleazar).

⁵All tasks were assigned to the various groups by coin-toss so that there would be no preference, for there were many famous men and high officials of the Temple in each division. ⁶Shemaiah, a Levite and the son of Nethanel, acted as recording secretary and wrote down the names and assignments in the presence of the king and of these leaders: Zadok the priest, Ahimelech the son of Abiathar, and the heads of the priests and Levites. Two groups from the division of Eleazar and one from the division of Ithamar were assigned to each task.

⁷⁻¹⁸The work was assigned (by coin-toss) in this order:

First, the group led by Jehoiarib;
Second, the group led by Jedaiah;
Third, the group led by Harim;

Fourth, the group led by Se-orim;
Fifth, the group led by Malchijah;
Sixth, the group led by Mijamin;
Seventh, the group led by Hakkoz;
Eighth, the group led by Ahijah;
Ninth, the group led by Jeshua;
Tenth, the group led by Shecaniah;
Eleventh, the group led by Eliashib;
Twelfth, the group led by Jakim;
Thirteenth, the group led by Huppah;
Fourteenth, the group led by Jeshebeab;
Fifteenth, the group led by Bilgah;
Sixteenth, the group led by Immer;
Seventeenth, the group led by Hezir;
Eighteenth, the group led by Happizzez;
Nineteenth, the group led by Pethahiah;
Twentieth, the group led by Jehezkel;
Twenty-first, the group led by Jachin;
Twenty-second, the group led by Gamul;
Twenty-third, the group led by Delaiah;
Twenty-fourth, the group led by Maaziah.

¹⁹Each group carried out the Temple duties as originally assigned by God through their ancestor Aaron.

²⁰These were the other descendants of Levi: Amram; his descendant Shuba-el; and Shuba-el's descendant Jehdeiah; ²¹the Rehabiah group, led by his oldest son Isshiah; ²²the Izhar group, consisting of Shelamoth and his descendant Jahath. ²³The Hebron group:

Jeriah, Hebron's oldest son;

Amariah, his second son;
Jahaziel, his third son;
Jekameam, his fourth son.

24,25The Uzziel group was led by his son Micah and his grandsons Shamir and Isshiah, and by Isshiah's son Zechariah.

26,27The Merari group was led by his sons: Mahli and Mushi. (Ja-aziah's group, led by his son Beno, included his brothers Shoham, Zaccur, and Ibri.) 28*Mahli's* descendants were Eleazar, who had no sons, 29and Kish, among whose sons was Jerahmeel. 30The sons of *Mushi* were Mahli, Eder, and Jerimoth.

These were the descendants of Levi in their various clans. 31Like the descendants of Aaron, they were assigned to their duties by coin-toss without distinction as to age or rank. It was done in the presence of King David, Zadok, Ahimelech, and the leaders of the priests and the Levites.

DAVID and the officials of the Tabernacle then appointed men to prophesy to the accompaniment of zithers, harps, and cymbals. These men were from the groups of Asaph, Heman, and Jeduthun. Here is a list of their names and their work:

2Under the leadership of Asaph, the king's private prophet, were his sons Zaccur, Joseph, Nethaniah, and Asharelah.

3Under Jeduthun, who led in giving thanks and praising the Lord (while accompanied by the zither), were his six sons: Gedaliah, Zeri, Jeshaiah, Shime-i, Hashabiah, and Mattithiah.

4,5Under the direction of Heman, the king's private chaplain, were his sons: Bukkiah, Mattaniah, Uzziel, Shebuel, Jerimoth, Hananiah, Hanani, Eliathah, Geddalti, Romamti-ezer, Joshbekashah, Mallothi, Hothir, and Mahazi-oth. (For God had honored him with fourteen sons and three daughters.) 6,7Their music ministry included the playing of cymbals, harps, and zithers; all were under the direction of their father as they performed this ministry in the Tabernacle.

Asaph, Jeduthun, and Heman reported directly to the king. They and their families were all trained in singing praises to the Lord; each one—288 of them in all—was a master musician. 8The singers were appointed to their particular term of service by coin-toss, without regard to age or reputation.

9-31The first toss indicated Joseph of the Asaph clan;

The second, Gedaliah, along with twelve of his sons and brothers;

The third, Zaccur and twelve of his sons and brothers;

The fourth, Izri and twelve of his sons and brothers;

Fifth, Nethaniah and twelve of his sons and brothers;

Sixth, Bukkiah and twelve of his sons and brothers;

Seventh, Jesharelah and twelve of his sons and brothers;

Eighth, Jeshaiah and twelve of his sons and brothers;

Ninth, Mattaniah and twelve of his sons and brothers;

Tenth, Shime-i and twelve of his sons and brothers;

Eleventh, Azarel and twelve of his sons and brothers;

Twelfth, Hashabiah and twelve of his sons and brothers;

Thirteenth, Shuba-el and twelve of his sons and brothers;

Fourteenth, Mattithiah and twelve of his sons and brothers;

Fifteenth, Jeremoth and twelve of his sons and brothers;

Sixteenth, Hananiah and twelve of his sons and brothers;

Seventeenth, Joshbekasha and twelve of his sons and brothers;

Eighteenth, Hanani and twelve of his sons and brothers;

Nineteenth, Mallothi and twelve of his sons and brothers;

Twentieth, Eliathah and twelve of his sons and brothers;

Twenty-first, Hothir and twelve of his sons and brothers;

Twenty-second, Giddalti and twelve of his sons and brothers;

Twenty-third, Mahazi-oth and twelve of his sons and brothers;

Twenty-fourth, Romamti-ezer and twelve of his sons and brothers.

THE temple guards were from the Asaph division of the Korah clan. The captain of the guard was Meshelemiah, the son of Kore.

2,3His sergeants were his sons:

Zechariah (the oldest),

Jedia-el (the second),

Zebadiah (the third),

Jathni-el (the fourth),

Elam (the fifth),

Jeho-hanan (the sixth),

Elie-ho-enai (the seventh).

4,5The sons of Obed-edom were also appointed as Temple guards:

Shemaiah (the oldest),

Jehozabad (the second),

Joah (the third),

Sacar (the fourth),

Nethanel (the fifth),

Ammi-el (the sixth),

Issachar (the seventh),

Pe-ullethai (the eighth).

What a blessing God gave him with all those sons!

6,7Shemaiah's sons were all outstanding men, and had positions of great authority in their clan. Their names were:

Othni, Repha-el, Obed, Elzabad.

Their brave brothers, Elihu and Semachiah, were also very able men.

8All of these sons and grandsons of Obed-edom—all sixty-two of them—were outstanding men who were particularly well qualified for their work. 9Meshelemiah's eighteen sons and brothers, too, were real leaders. 10Hosah, one of the Merari group, appointed Shimri as the leader among his sons, though he was not the oldest. 11The names of some of his other sons were:

Hilkiah, the second;

Tebaliah, the third;

Zechariah, the fourth.

Hosah's sons and brothers numbered thirteen in all.

ROMANS 4:1–13

ABRAHAM was, humanly speaking, the founder of our Jewish nation. What were his experiences concerning this question of being saved by faith? Was it because of his good deeds that God accepted him? If so, then he would have something to boast about. But from God's point of view Abraham had no basis at all for pride. 3For the Scriptures tell us Abraham *believed God,* and that is why God canceled his sins and declared him "not guilty."

4,5But didn't he earn his right to heaven by all the good things he did? No, for being saved is a gift; if a person could earn it by being good, then it wouldn't be free—but it is! It is *given* to those who do *not* work for it. For God declares sinners to be good in his sight if they have faith in Christ to save them from God's wrath.

6King David spoke of this, describing the happiness of an undeserving sinner who is declared "not guilty" by God. 7"Blessed, and to be envied," he said, "are those whose sins are forgiven and put out of sight. 8Yes, what joy there is for anyone whose sins are no longer counted against him by the Lord."

9Now then, the question: Is this blessing given only to those who have faith in Christ but also keep the Jewish laws, or is the blessing also given to those who do not keep the Jewish rules, but only trust in Christ? Well, what about Abraham? We say that he received these blessings through his faith. Was it by faith alone? Or because he also kept the Jewish rules?

10For the answer to that question, answer this one: *When* did God give this blessing to Abraham? It was *before he became a Jew*—before he went through the Jewish initiation ceremony of circumcision.

11It wasn't until later on, *after* God had promised to bless him *because of his faith,* that he was circumcised. The circumcision ceremony was a sign that Abraham already had faith and that God had already accepted him and declared him just and good in his sight—before the ceremony took place. So Abraham is the spiritual father of those who believe and are saved without obeying Jewish laws. We see, then, that those who do not keep these rules are justified by God through faith. 12And Abraham is also the spiritual father of those Jews who have been circumcised. They can see from his example that it is not this ceremony that saves them, for Abraham found favor with God by faith alone, *before he was circumcised.*

13It is clear, then, that God's promise to give the whole earth to Abraham and his descendants was not because Abraham obeyed God's laws but because he trusted God to keep his promise.

PSALM 13:1–6

HOW long will you forget me, Lord? Forever? How long will you look the other way when I am in need? 2How long must I be hiding daily anguish in my heart? How long shall my enemy have the upper hand?

3Answer me, O Lord my God; give me light in my darkness lest I die. 4Don't let my enemies say, "We have conquered him!" Don't let them gloat that I am down.

5But I will always trust in you and in your mercy and shall rejoice in your salvation. 6I will sing to the Lord because he has blessed me so richly.

PROVERBS FOR TODAY/ 19:15–16

A lazy man sleeps soundly—and he goes hungry! Keep the commandments and keep your life; despising them means death.

JULY 18

1 CHRONICLES 26:12—27:34

THE divisions of the Temple guards were named after the leaders. Like the other Levites, they were responsible to minister at the Temple. 13They were assigned guard duty at the various gates without regard to the reputation of their families, for it was all done by coin-toss. 14,15The responsibility of the east gate went to Shelemiah and his group; of the north gate to his son Zechariah, a man of unusual wisdom; of the south gate to Obed-edom and his group (his sons were given charge of the storehouses); 16of the west gate and the Shallecheth Gate on the upper road, to Shuppim and Hosah. 17Six guards were assigned daily to the east gate, four to the north gate, four to the south gate, and two to each of the storehouses.

18Six guards were assigned each day to the west gate, four to the upper road, and two to the nearby areas. 19The Temple guards were chosen from the clans of Korah and Merari.

20,21,22Other Levites, led by Ahijah, were given the care of the gifts brought to the Lord and placed in the Temple treasury. These men of the Ladan subclan from the clan of Gershom included Zetham and Joel, the sons of Jehieli. 23,24Shebuel, son of Gershom and grandson of Moses, was the chief officer of the treasury. He was in charge of the divisions named after Amram, Izhar, Hebron, and Uzziel.

25The line of descendants from Eliezer went through Rehabiah, Jesha-iah, Joram, Zichri, and Shelomoth. 26Shelomoth and his brothers were appointed to care for the gifts given to the Lord by King David and the other leaders of the nation such as the officers and generals of the army. 27For these men dedicated their war loot to support the operating expenses of the Temple. 28Shelomoth and his brothers were also responsible for the care of the items dedicated to the Lord by Samuel the prophet, Saul the son of Kish, Abner the son of Ner, Joab the son of Zeruiah, and anyone else of distinction who brought gifts to the Lord.

29Chenaniah and his sons (from the subclan of Izhar) were appointed public administrators and judges. 30Hashabiah and 1,700 of his clansmen from Hebron, all outstanding men, were placed in charge of the territory of Israel west of the Jordan River; they were responsible for the religious affairs and public administration of that area. 31,32Twenty-seven hundred outstanding men of the clan of the Hebronites, under the supervision of Jerijah, were appointed to control the religious and public affairs of the tribes of Reuben, Gad, and the half-tribe of Manasseh. These men, all of whom had excellent qualifications, were appointed on the basis of their ancestry and ability at Jazer in Gilead in the fortieth year of King David's reign.

THE Israeli army was divided into twelve regiments, each with 24,000 troops, including officers and administrative staff. These units were called up for active duty one month each year. Here is the list of the units and their regimental commanders:

2,3The commander of the First Division was Jashobeam. He had charge of 24,000 troops who were on duty the first month of each year.

4The commander of the Second Division was Dodai (a descendant of Ahohi). He had charge of 24,000 troops who were on duty the second month of each year. Mikloth was his executive officer.

5,6The commander of the Third Division was Benaiah. His 24,000 men were on duty the third month of each year. (He was the son of Jehoiada the High Priest, and was the chief of the thirty highest-ranking officers in David's army.) His son Ammizabad succeeded him as division commander.

7The commander of the Fourth Division was Asahel (the brother of Joab), who was later replaced by his son Zebadiah. He had 24,000 men on duty the fourth month of each year.

8The commander of the Fifth Division was Shamuth from Izrah, with 24,000 men on duty the fifth month of each year.

9The commander of the Sixth Division was Ira, the son of Ikkesh from Tekoa; he had 24,000 men on duty the sixth month of each year.

10The commander of the Seventh Division was Helez from Pelona in Ephraim, with 24,000 men on duty the seventh month of each year.

11The commander of the Eighth Division was Sibbecai of the Hushite subclan from Zerah, who had 24,000 men on duty the eighth month of each year.

12The commander of the Ninth Division was Abi-ezer (from Anathoth in the tribe of Benjamin), who commanded 24,000 troops during the ninth month of each year.

13The commander of the Tenth Division was Maharai from Netophah in Zerah, with 24,000 men on duty the tenth month of each year.

14The commander of the Eleventh Division was Benaiah from Pirathon in Ephraim, with 24,000 men on duty during the eleventh month of each year.

15The commander of the Twelfth Division was Heldai from Netophah in the area of Othni-el, who commanded 24,000 men on duty during the twelfth month of each year.

16-22The top political officers of the tribes of Israel were as follows:

Over Reuben, Eliezer (son of Zichri);
Over Simeon, Shephatiah (son of Maacah);
Over Levi, Hashabiah (son of Kemuel);
Over the descendants of Aaron, Zadok;
Over Judah, Elihu (a brother of King David);

Over Issachar, Omri (son of Michael);

Over Zebulun, Ishmaiah (son of Obadiah);

Over Naphtali, Jeremoth (son of Azriel);

Over Ephraim, Hoshea (son of Azaziah);

Over the half-tribe of Manasseh, Joel (son of Pedaiah);

Over the other half of Manasseh, in Gilead, Iddo (son of Zechariah);

Over Benjamin, Ja-asiel (son of Abner);

Over Dan, Azarel (son of Jeroham).

23When David took his census he didn't include the twenty-year-olds, or those younger, for the Lord had promised a population explosion for his people. 24Joab began the census, but he never finished it, for the anger of God broke out upon Israel; the final total was never put into the annals of King David.

25Azmaveth (son of Adi-el) was the chief financial officer in charge of the palace treasuries, and Jonathan (son of Uzziah) was chief of the regional treasuries throughout the cities, villages, and fortresses of Israel.

26Ezri (son of Chelub) was manager of the laborers on the king's estates. 27And Shime-i from Ramath had the oversight of the king's vineyards; and Zabdi from Shiphma was responsible for his wine production and storage. 28Baal-hanan from Gedera was responsible for the king's olive yards and sycamore trees in the lowlands bordering Philistine territory, while Joash had charge of the supplies of olive oil.

29Shitrai from Sharon was in charge of the cattle on the Plains of Sharon, and Shaphat (son of Adlai) had charge of those in the valleys. 30Obil, from the territory of Ishmael, had charge of the camels, and Jehdeiah from Meronoth had charge of the donkeys. 31The sheep were under the care of Jaziz the Hagrite. These men were King David's overseers.

32The attendant to the king's sons was Jonathan, David's uncle, a wise counselor and an educated man. Jehiel (the son of Hachmoni) was their tutor.

33Ahithophel was the king's official counselor and Hushai the Archite was his personal advisor. 34Ahithophel was assisted by Jehoiada (the son of Benaiah) and by Abiathar. Joab was commander-in-chief of the Israeli army.

ROMANS 4:14—5:2

SO if you still claim that God's blessings go to those who are "good enough," then you are saying that God's promises to those who have faith are meaningless, and faith is foolish. 15But the fact of the matter is this: when we try to gain God's blessing and salvation by keeping his laws we always end up under his anger, for we always fail to keep them. The only way we can keep from breaking laws is not to have any to break!

16So God's blessings are given to us by faith, as a free gift; we are certain to get them whether or not we follow Jewish customs if we have faith like Abraham's, for Abraham is the father of us all when it comes to these matters of faith. 17That is what the Scriptures mean when they say that God made Abraham the father of many nations. God will accept all people in every nation who trust God as Abraham did. And this promise is from God himself, who makes the dead live again and speaks of future events with as much certainty as though they were already past.

18So, when God told Abraham that he would give him a son who would have many descendants and become a great nation, Abraham believed God even though such a promise just couldn't come to pass! 19And because his faith was strong, he didn't worry about the fact that he was too old to be a father, at the age of one hundred, and that Sarah his wife, at ninety, was also much too old to have a baby.

20But Abraham never doubted. He believed God, for his faith and trust grew ever stronger, and he praised God for this blessing even before it happened.

21He was completely sure that God was well able to do anything he promised. 22And because of Abraham's faith God forgave his sins and declared him "not guilty."

23Now this wonderful statement—that he was accepted and approved through his faith—wasn't just for Abraham's benefit. 24It was for us, too, assuring us that God will accept us in the same way he accepted Abraham—when we believe the promises of God who brought back Jesus our Lord from the dead. 25He died for our sins and rose again to make us right with God, filling us with God's goodness.

So now, since we have been made right in God's sight by faith in his promises, we can have real peace with him because of what Jesus Christ our Lord has done for us. 2For because of our faith, he has brought us into this place of highest privilege where we now stand, and we confidently and joyfully look forward to actually becoming all that God has had in mind for us to be.

PSALM 14:1–7

THAT man is a fool who says to himself, "There is no God!" Anyone who talks like that is warped and evil and cannot really be a good person at all.

2The Lord looks down from heaven on all mankind to see if there are any who are wise, who want to please God. 3But no, all have strayed away; all are rotten with sin. Not one is good, not one! 4They eat my people like bread and wouldn't think of praying! Don't they really know any better?

5Terror shall grip them, for God is with those who love him. 6He is the refuge of the poor and humble when evildoers are oppressing them. 7Oh, that the time of their rescue were already here, that God would come from Zion now to save his people. What gladness when the Lord has rescued Israel!

PROVERBS FOR TODAY/ 19:17

When you help the poor you are lending to the Lord—and he pays wonderful interest on your loan!

JULY 19

1 CHRONICLES 28:1—29:30

DAVID now summoned all of his officials to Jerusalem—the political leaders, the commanders of the twelve army divisions, the other army officers, those in charge of his property and livestock and all the other men of authority in his kingdom. 2He rose and stood before them and addressed them as follows:

"My brothers and my people! It was my desire to build a temple in which the Ark of the Covenant of the Lord could rest—a place for our God to live in. I have now collected everything that is necessary for the building, 3but God has told me, 'You are not to build my temple, for you are a warrior and have shed much blood.'

4"Nevertheless, the Lord God of Israel has chosen me from among all my father's family to begin a dynasty that will rule Israel forever; he has chosen the tribe of Judah, and from among the families of Judah, my father's family; and from among his sons, the Lord took pleasure in me and has made me king over all Israel. 5And from among my sons—the Lord has given me many children—he has chosen Solomon to succeed me on the throne of his Kingdom of Israel. 6He has told me, 'Your son Solomon shall build my temple; for I have chosen him as my son and I will be his father. 7And if he continues to obey my commandments and instructions as he has until now, I will make his kingdom last forever.' "

8Then David turned to Solomon and said:

"Here before the leaders of Israel, the people of God, and in the sight of our God, I am instructing you to search out every commandment of the Lord so that you may continue to rule this good land and leave it to your children to rule forever. 9Solomon, my son, get to know the God of your fathers. Worship and serve him with a clean heart and a willing mind, for the Lord sees every heart and understands and knows every thought. If you seek him, you will find him; but if you forsake him, he will permanently throw you aside. 10So be very careful, for the Lord has chosen you to build his holy temple. Be strong and do as he commands."

11Then David gave Solomon the blueprint of the Temple and its surroundings—the treasuries, the upstairs rooms, the inside rooms, and the sanctuary for the place of mercy. 12He also gave Solomon his plans for the outer court, the outside rooms, the Temple storage areas, and the treasuries for the gifts dedicated by famous persons. For the Holy Spirit had given David all these plans. 13The king also passed on to Solomon the instructions concerning the work of the various groups of priests and Levites; and he gave specifications for each item in the Temple which was to be used for worship and sacrifice.

14David weighed out enough gold and silver to make these various items, 15as well as the specific amount of gold needed for the lampstands and lamps. He also weighed out enough silver for the silver candlesticks and lamps, each according to its use. 16He weighed out the gold for the table on which the Bread of the Presence would be placed and for the other gold tables, and he weighed the silver for the silver tables. 17Then he weighed out the gold for the solid gold hooks used in handling the sacrificial meat and for the basins, cups, and bowls of gold and silver. 18Finally, he weighed out the refined gold for the altar of incense and for the gold angels whose wings were stretched over the Ark of the Covenant of the Lord.

19"Every part of this blueprint," David told Solomon, "was given to me in writing from the hand of the Lord." 20Then he continued, "Be strong and courageous and get to work. Don't be frightened by the size of the task, for the Lord my God is with you; he will not forsake you. He will see to it that everything is finished correctly. 21And these various groups of priests and Levites will serve in the Temple. Others with skills of every kind will volunteer, and the army and the entire nation are at your command."

THEN King David turned to the entire assembly and said: "My son Solomon, whom God has chosen to be the next king of Israel, is still young and inexperienced, and the work ahead of him is enormous; for the temple he will build is not just another building—it is for the Lord God himself! 2Using every resource at my command, I have gathered as much as I could for building it—enough gold, silver, bronze, iron, wood, and great quantities of onyx, other precious stones, costly jewels, and marble. 3And now, because of my devotion to the Temple of God, I am giving all of my own private treasures to aid in the construction. This is in addition to the building materials I have already collected. 4,5These personal contributions consist of millions of dollars of gold from Ophir and huge amounts of silver to be used for overlaying the walls of the buildings. It will also be used for the articles made of gold and silver and for the artistic decorations. Now then, who will follow my example? Who will give himself and all that he has to the Lord?"

6,7Then the clan leaders, the heads of the tribes, the army officers, and the administrative officers of the king pledged huge sums of gold, silver and foreign currency, also 675 tons of bronze; and 3,750 tons of iron. 8They also contributed great amounts of jewelry, which were deposited at the Temple treasury with Jehiel (a descendant of Gershom). 9Everyone was excited and happy for this opportunity of service, and King David was moved with deep joy.

10While still in the presence of the whole assembly, David expressed his praises to the Lord: "O Lord God of our father Israel, praise your name for ever and ever! 11Yours is the mighty power and glory and victory and majesty. Everything in the heavens and earth is yours, O Lord, and this is your kingdom. We adore you as being in control of everything. 12Riches and honor come from you alone, and you are the Ruler of all mankind; your hand controls power and might, and it is at your discretion that men are made great and given strength. 13O our God, we thank you and praise your glorious name, 14but who am I and who are my people that we should be permitted to give anything to you? Everything we have has come from you, and we only give you what is yours already! 15For we are here for but a moment, strangers in the land as our fathers were before us; our days on earth are like a shadow, gone so soon, without a trace. 16O Lord our God, all of this material that we have gathered to build a temple for your holy name comes from you! It all belongs to you! 17I know, my God, that you test men to see if they are good; for you enjoy good men. I have done all this with good motives, and I have watched your people offer their gifts willingly and joyously.

18"O Lord God of our fathers: Abraham, Isaac, and Israel! Make your people always want to obey you, and see to it that their love for you never changes.

19Give my son Solomon a good heart toward God, so that he will want to obey you in the smallest detail, and will look forward eagerly to finishing the building of your temple, for which I have made all of these preparations."

20Then David said to all the people, "Give praise to the Lord your God!" And they did, bowing low before the Lord and the king.

21The next day they brought a thousand young bulls, a thousand rams, and a thousand lambs as burnt offerings to the Lord; they also offered drink offerings and many other sacrifices on behalf of all Israel. 22Then they feasted and drank before the Lord with great joy.

And again they crowned King David's son Solomon as their king. They anointed him before the Lord as their leader, and they anointed Zadok as their priest. 23So God appointed Solomon to take the throne of his father David; and he prospered greatly, and all Israel obeyed him. 24The national leaders, the army officers, and his brothers all pledged their allegiance to King Solomon. 25And the Lord gave him great popularity with all the people of Israel, and he amassed even greater wealth and honor than his father.

26,27David was king of the land of Israel for forty years; seven of them during his reign in Hebron and thirty-three in Jerusalem. 28He died at an old age, wealthy and honored; and his son Solomon reigned in his place. 29Detailed biographies of King David have been written in the history of Samuel the prophet, the history written by Nathan the prophet, and in the history written by the prophet Gad. 30These accounts tell of his reign and of his might and all that happened to him and to Israel and to the kings of the nearby nations.

ROMANS 5:3–21

WE can rejoice, too, when we run into problems and trials for we know that they are good for us—they help us learn to be patient. 4And patience develops strength of character in us and helps us trust God more each time we use it until finally our hope and faith are strong and steady. 5Then, when that happens, we are able to hold our heads high no matter what happens and know that all is well, for we know how dearly God loves us, and we feel this warm love everywhere within us because God has given us the Holy Spirit to fill our hearts with his love.

6When we were utterly helpless with no way of escape, Christ came at just the right time and died for us sinners who had no use for him. 7Even if we were good, we really wouldn't expect anyone to die for us, though, of course, that might be barely possible. 8But God showed his great love for us by sending Christ to die for us while we were still sinners. 9And since by his blood he did all this for us as sinners, how much more will he do for us now that he has declared us not guilty? Now he will save us from all of God's wrath to come. 10And since, when we were his enemies, we were brought back to God by the death of his Son, what blessings he must have for us now that we are his friends, and he is living within us!

11Now we rejoice in our wonderful new relationship with God—all because of what our Lord Jesus Christ has done in dying for our sins—making us friends of God.

12When Adam sinned, sin entered the entire human race. His sin spread death throughout all the world, so everything began to grow old and die, for all sinned. 13[We know that it was Adam's sin that caused this] because although, of course, people were sinning from the time of Adam until Moses, God did not in those days judge them guilty of death for breaking his laws—because he had not yet given his laws to them, nor told them what he wanted them to do. 14So when their bodies died it was not for their own sins since they themselves had never disobeyed God's special law against eating the forbidden fruit, as Adam had.

What a contrast between Adam and Christ who was yet to come! 15And what a difference between man's sin and God's forgiveness!

For this one man, Adam, brought death to many through his *sin.* But this one man, Jesus Christ, brought forgiveness to many through God's *mercy.* 16Adam's *one* sin brought the penalty of death to many, while Christ freely takes away *many* sins and gives glorious life instead. 17The sin of this one man, Adam, caused *death to be king over all,* but all who will take God's gift of forgiveness and acquittal are *kings of life* because of this one man, Jesus Christ. 18Yes, Adam's *sin* brought *punishment* to all, but Christ's *righteousness* makes men *right with God,* so that they can live. 19Adam caused many to be sinners because he *disobeyed* God, and Christ caused many to be made acceptable to God because he *obeyed.*

20The Ten Commandments were given so that all could see the extent of their failure to obey God's laws. But the more we see our sinfulness, the more we see God's abounding grace forgiving us. 21Before, sin ruled over all men and brought them to death, but now God's kindness rules instead, giving us right standing with God and resulting in eternal life through Jesus Christ our Lord.

PSALM 15:1–5

LORD, who may go and find refuge and shelter in your tabernacle up on your holy hill?

2Anyone who leads a blameless life and is truly sincere. 3Anyone who refuses to slander others, does not listen to gossip, never harms his neighbor, 4speaks out against sin, criticizes those committing it, commends the faithful followers of the Lord, keeps a promise even if it ruins him, 5does not crush his debtors with high interest rates, and refuses to testify against the innocent despite the bribes offered him—such a man shall stand firm forever.

Discipline your son in his early years while there is hope. If you don't you will ruin his life. A short-tempered man must bear his own penalty; you can't do much to help him. If you try once you must try a dozen times!

JULY 20

2 CHRONICLES 1:1—3:17

KING David's son Solomon was now the undisputed ruler of Israel, for the Lord his God had made him a powerful monarch. 2,3He summoned all the army officers and judges to Gibeon as well as all the political and religious leaders of Israel. He led them up to the hill to the old Tabernacle constructed by Moses, the Lord's assistant, while he was in the wilderness. 4(There was a later Tabernacle in Jerusalem, built by King David for the Ark of God when he removed it from Kiriathjearim.) 5,6The bronze altar made by Bezalel (son of Uri, son of Hur) still stood in front of the old Tabernacle, and now Solomon and those he had invited assembled themselves before it, as he sacrificed upon it 1,000 burnt offerings to the Lord.

7That night God appeared to Solomon and told him, "Ask me for anything, and I will give it to you!"

8Solomon replied, "O God, you have been so kind and good to my father David, and now you have given me the kingdom— 9this is all I want! For you have fulfilled your promise to David my father and have made me king over a nation as full of people as the earth is full of dust! 10Now give me wisdom and knowledge to rule them properly, for who is able to govern by himself such a great nation as this one of yours?"

11God replied, "Because your greatest desire is to help your people, and you haven't asked for personal wealth and honor, and you haven't asked me to curse your enemies, and you haven't asked for a long life, but for wisdom and knowledge to properly guide my people— 12yes, I am giving you the wisdom and knowledge you asked for! And I am also giving you such riches, wealth, and honor as no other king has ever had before you! And there will never again be so great a king in all the world!"

13Solomon then left the Tabernacle, returned down the hill, and went back to Jerusalem to rule Israel. 14He built up a huge force of 1,400 chariots and recruited 12,000 cavalry to guard the cities where the chariots were garaged, though some, of course, were stationed at Jerusalem near the king. 15During Solomon's reign, silver and gold were as plentiful in Jerusalem as rocks on the road! And expensive cedar lumber was used like common sycamore! 16Solomon sent horse-traders to Egypt to purchase entire herds at wholesale prices. 17At that time Egyptian chariots sold for $400 each and horses for $100, delivered at Jerusalem. Many of these were then resold to the kings of the Hittites and Syria.

SOLOMON now decided that the time had come to build a temple for the Lord and a palace for himself. 2This required a force of 70,000 laborers, 80,000 stonecutters in the hills, and 3,600 foremen. 3Solomon sent an ambassador to King Hiram at Tyre, requesting shipments of cedar lumber such as Hiram had supplied to David when he was building his palace.

4"I am about to build a temple for the Lord my God," Solomon told Hiram. "It will be a place where I can burn incense and sweet spices before God, and display the special sacrificial bread, and sacrifice burnt offerings each morning and evening, and on the Sabbaths, and at the new moon celebration and other regular festivals of the Lord our God. For God wants Israel always to celebrate these special occasions. 5It is going to be a wonderful temple because he is a great God, greater than any other. 6But who can ever build him a worthy home? Not even the highest heaven would be beautiful enough! And who am I to be allowed to build a temple for God? But it will be a place to worship him.

7"So send me skilled craftsmen—goldsmiths and silversmiths, brass and iron workers; and send me weavers to make purple, crimson, and blue cloth; and skilled engravers to work beside the craftsmen of Judah and Jerusalem who were selected by my father David. 8Also send me cedar trees, fir trees, and algum trees from the Forests of Lebanon, for your men are without equal as lumbermen, and I will send my men to help them. 9An immense amount of lumber will be needed, for the temple I am going to build will be large and incredibly beautiful. 10As to the financial arrangements, I will pay your men 20,000 sacks of crushed wheat, 20,000 barrels of barley, 20,000 barrels of wine, and 20,000 barrels of olive oil."

11King Hiram replied to King Solomon: "It is because the Lord loves his people that he has made you their king! 12Blessed be the Lord God of Israel who made the heavens and the earth and who has given to David such a wise, intelligent, and understanding son to build God's Temple, and a royal palace for himself.

13"I am sending you a master craftsman—my famous Huramabi! He is a brilliant man, 14the son of a Jewish woman from Dan in Israel; his father is from here in Tyre. He is a skillful goldsmith and silversmith, and also does exquisite work with brass and iron, and knows all about stonework, carpentry, and weaving; and he is an expert in the dyeing of purple and blue linen and crimson cloth. He is an engraver besides, and an inventor! He will work with your craftsmen and those appointed by my lord David, your father. 15So send along the wheat, barley, olive oil, and wine you mentioned, 16and we will begin cutting wood from the Lebanon mountains, as much as you need, and bring it to you in log floats across the sea to Joppa, and from there you can take them inland to Jerusalem."

17Solomon now took a census of all foreigners in the country (just as his father David had done) and found that there were 153,600 of them. 18He indentured 70,000 as common laborers, 80,000 as loggers and 3,600 as foremen.

FINALLY the actual construction of the Temple began. Its location was in Jerusalem at the top of Mount Moriah, where the Lord had appeared to Solomon's father, King David, and where the threshing-floor of Ornan the Jebusite had been. David had selected it as the site for the Temple. 2The actual construction began on the seventeenth day of April in the fourth year of King Solomon's reign.

3The foundation was ninety feet long and thirty feet wide. 4A covered porch ran along the entire thirty-foot width of the Temple, with the inner walls and ceiling overlaid with pure gold! The roof was 180 feet high.

5The main part of the Temple was paneled with cypress wood, plated with pure gold, and engraved with palm trees and chains. 6Beautiful jewels were inlaid into the walls to add to the beauty; the gold, by the way, was of the best, from Parvaim. 7All the walls, beams, doors, and thresholds throughout the Temple were plated with gold, with angels engraved on the walls.

8Within the Temple, at one end, was the most sacred room—the Holy of Holies—thirty feet square. This too was overlaid with the finest gold, valued at millions of dollars. 9Twenty-six-ounce gold nails were used. The upper rooms were also plated with pure gold.

¹⁰Within the innermost room, the Holy of Holies, Solomon placed two sculptured statues of angels, and plated them with gold. ¹¹,¹²,¹³They stood on the floor facing the outer room, with wings stretched wingtip to wingtip across the room, from wall to wall. ¹⁴Across the entrance to this room he placed a veil of blue and crimson finespun linen, decorated with angels.

¹⁵At the front of the Temple were two pillars 52½ feet high, topped by a 7½-foot capital flaring out to the roof. ¹⁶He made chains and placed them on top of the pillars, with 100 pomegranates attached to the chains. ¹⁷Then he set up the pillars at the front of the Temple, one on the right and the other on the left. And he gave them names: Jachin (the one on the right), and Boaz (the one on the left).

ROMANS 6:1–23

WELL then, shall we keep on sinning so that God can keep on showing us more and more kindness and forgiveness?

²,³Of course not! Should we keep on sinning when we don't have to? For sin's power over us was broken when we became Christians and were baptized to become a part of Jesus Christ; through his death the power of your sinful nature was shattered. ⁴Your old sin-loving nature was buried with him by baptism when he died, and when God the Father, with glorious power, brought him back to life again, you were given his wonderful new life to enjoy.

⁵For you have become a part of him, and so you died with him, so to speak, when he died; and now you share his new life, and shall rise as he did. ⁶Your old evil desires were nailed to the cross with him; that part of you that loves to sin was crushed and fatally wounded, so that your sin-loving body is no longer under sin's control, no longer needs to be a slave to sin; ⁷for when you are deadened to sin you are freed from all its allure and its power over you. ⁸And since

your old sin-loving nature "died" with Christ, we know that you will share his new life. ⁹Christ rose from the dead and will never die again. Death no longer has any power over him. ¹⁰He died once for all to end sin's power, but now he lives forever in unbroken fellowship with God. ¹¹So look upon your old sin nature as dead and unresponsive to sin, and instead be alive to God, alert to him, through Jesus Christ our Lord.

¹²Do not let sin control your puny body any longer; do not give in to its sinful desires. ¹³Do not let any part of your bodies become tools of wickedness, to be used for sinning; but give yourselves completely to God—every part of you—for you are back from death and you want to be tools in the hands of God, to be used for his good purposes. ¹⁴Sin need never again be your master, for now you are no longer tied to the law where sin enslaves you, but you are free under God's favor and mercy.

¹⁵Does this mean that now we can go ahead and sin and not worry about it? (For our salvation does not depend on keeping the law, but on receiving God's grace!) Of course not!

¹⁶Don't you realize that you can choose your own master? You can choose sin (with death) or else obedience (with acquittal). The one to whom you offer yourself—he will take you and be your master and you will be his slave. ¹⁷Thank God that though you once chose to be slaves of sin, now you have obeyed with all your heart the teaching to which God has committed you. ¹⁸And now you are free from your old master, sin; and you have become slaves to your new master, righteousness.

¹⁹I speak this way, using the illustration of slaves and masters, because it is easy to understand: just as you used to be slaves to all kinds of sin, so now you must let yourselves be slaves to all that is right and holy.

²⁰In those days when you were slaves of sin you didn't bother much with goodness. ²¹And what was the result? Evidently not good, since you are ashamed

now even to think about those things you used to do, for all of them end in eternal doom. 22But now you are free from the power of sin and are slaves of God, and his benefits to you include holiness and everlasting life. 23For the wages of sin is death, but the free gift of God is eternal life through Jesus Christ our Lord.

PSALM 16:1–11

SAVE me, O God, because I have come to you for refuge. 2I said to him, "You are my Lord; I have no other help but yours." 3I want the company of the godly men and women in the land; they are the true nobility. 4Those choosing other gods shall all be filled with sorrow; I will not offer the sacrifices they do or even speak the names of their gods.

5The Lord himself is my inheritance, my prize. He is my food and drink, my highest joy! He guards all that is mine. 6He sees that I am given pleasant brooks and meadows as my share! What a wonderful inheritance! 7I will bless the Lord who counsels me; he gives me wisdom in the night. He tells me what to do.

8I am always thinking of the Lord; and because he is so near, I never need to stumble or to fall.

9Heart, body, and soul are filled with joy. 10For you will not leave me among the dead; you will not allow your beloved one to rot in the grave. 11You have let me experience the joys of life and the exquisite pleasures of your own eternal presence.

PROVERBS FOR TODAY/ 19:20–21

Get all the advice you can and be wise the rest of your life. Man proposes, but God disposes.

JULY 21

2 CHRONICLES 4:1—6:13a

HE also made a bronze altar thirty feet long, thirty feet wide, and fifteen feet high. 2Then he forged a huge round tank fifteen feet across from rim to rim. The rim stood 7½ feet above the floor, and was forty-five feet around. 3The tank was encircled at its base by two rows of gourd designs, cast as part of the tank. 4The tank stood on twelve metal oxen facing outward; three faced north, three faced west, three faced south, and three faced east. 5The walls of the tank were five inches thick, flaring out like the cup of a lily. It held 3,000 barrels of water.

6He also constructed ten vats for water to wash the offerings, five to the right of the huge tank and five to the left. The priests used the tank, and not the vats, for their own washing.

7Carefully following God's instructions, he then cast ten gold lampstands and placed them in the Temple, five against each wall; 8he also built ten tables and placed five against each wall on the right and left. And he molded 100 solid gold bowls. 9Then he constructed a court for the priests, also the public court, and overlaid the doors of these courts with bronze. 10The huge tank was in the southeast corner of the outer room of the Temple. 11Huramabi also made the necessary pots, shovels, and basins for use in connection with the sacrifices.

So at last he completed the work assigned to him by King Solomon:

12-16The construction of the two pillars,

The two flared capitals on the tops of the pillars,

The two sets of chains on the capitals,

The 400 pomegranates hanging from the two sets of chains on the capitals,

The bases for the vats, and the vats themselves,

The huge tank and the twelve oxen under it,

The pots, shovels, and fleshhooks.

This skillful craftsman, Huramabi, made all of the above-mentioned items for King Solomon, using polished bronze. 17,18The king did the casting at the claybanks of the Jordan valley between Succoth and Zeredah. Great quantities of bronze were used, too heavy to weigh.

19Solomon commanded that all of the furnishings of the Temple—the utensils, the altar, and the table for the Bread of the Presence must be made of gold; 20also the lamps and lampstands, 21the floral decorations, tongs, 22lamp snuffers, basins, spoons, and firepans—all were made of solid gold. Even the doorway of the Temple, the main door, and the inner doors to the Holy of Holies were overlaid with gold.

So the Temple was finally finished. Then Solomon brought in the gifts dedicated to the Lord by his father, King David. They were stored in the Temple treasuries.

2Solomon now summoned to Jerusalem all of the leaders of Israel—the heads of the tribes and clans—for the ceremony of transferring the Ark from the [Tabernacle in the] City of David, also known as Zion, [to its new home in the Temple]. 3This celebration took place in October at the annual Festival of Tabernacles. 4,5As the leaders of Israel watched, the Levites lifted the Ark and carried it out of the Tabernacle, along with all the other sacred vessels. 6King Solomon and the others sacrificed sheep and oxen before the Ark in such numbers that no one tried to keep count!

7,8Then the priests carried the Ark into the inner room of the Temple—the Holy of Holies—and placed it beneath the angels' wings; their wings spread over the Ark and its carrying poles. 9These carrying poles were so long that their ends could be seen from the outer room, but not from the outside doorway.

The Ark is still there at the time of this writing. 10Nothing was in the Ark except the two stone tablets which Moses had put there at Mount Horeb, when the Lord made a covenant with the people of Israel as they were leaving Egypt.

11,12When the priests had undergone the purification rites for themselves, they all took part in the ceremonies without regard to their normal duties. And how the Levites were praising the Lord as the priests came out of the Holy of Holies! The singers were Asaph, Heman, Jeduthun and all their sons and brothers, dressed in finespun linen robes and standing at the east side of the altar. The choir was accompanied by 120 priests who were trumpeters, while others played the cymbals, lyres, and harps. 13,14The band and chorus united as one to praise and thank the Lord; their selections were interspersed with trumpet obbligatos, the clashing of cymbals, and the loud playing of other musical instruments—all praising and thanking the Lord. Their theme was "He is so good! His lovingkindness lasts forever!"

And at that moment the glory of the Lord, coming as a bright cloud, filled the Temple so that the priests could not continue their work.

This is the prayer prayed by Solomon on that occasion:

"The Lord has said that he would live in the thick darkness,

But I have made a Temple for you, O Lord, to live in forever!"

3Then the king turned around to the people and they stood to receive his blessing:

4"Blessed be the Lord God of Israel," he said to them, "—the God who talked personally to my father David and has now fulfilled the promise he made to him. For he told him, 5,6'I have never before, since bringing my people from the land of Egypt, chosen a city anywhere in Israel as the location of my Temple where my name will be glorified; and never before have I chosen a king for my people Israel. But now I have chosen Jerusalem as that city, and David as that king.'

7"My father David wanted to build this Temple, 8but the Lord said not to. It was good to have the desire, the Lord told him, 9but he was not the one to build it: his son was chosen for that task. 10And now the Lord has done what he promised, for I have become king in my father's place, and I have built the Temple for the Name of the Lord God of Israel, 11and placed the Ark there. And in the Ark is the Covenant between the Lord and his people Israel."

12,13As he spoke, Solomon was standing before the people on a platform in the center of the outer court, in front of the altar of the Lord. The platform was made of bronze, 7½ feet square and 4½ feet high.

ROMANS 7:1–14

DON'T you understand yet, dear Jewish brothers in Christ, that when a person dies the law no longer holds him in its power?

2Let me illustrate: when a woman marries, the law binds her to her husband as long as he is alive. But if he dies, she is no longer bound to him; the laws of marriage no longer apply to her. 3Then she can marry someone else if she wants to. That would be wrong while he was alive, but it is perfectly all right after he dies.

4Your "husband," your master, used to be the Jewish law; but you "died," as it were, with Christ on the cross; and since you are "dead," you are no longer "married to the law," and it has no more control over you. Then you came back to life again when Christ did, and are a new person. And now you are "married," so to speak, to the one who rose from the dead, so that you can produce good fruit, that is, good deeds for God. 5When your old nature was still active, sinful desires were at work within you, making you want to do whatever God said not to, and producing sinful deeds, the rotting fruit of death. 6But now you need no longer worry about the Jewish laws and customs because you "died" while in their captivity, and now you can really serve God; not in the old way, mechanically obeying a set of rules, but in the new way, [with all of your hearts and minds].

7Well then, am I suggesting that these laws of God are evil? Of course not! No, the law is not sinful but it was the law that showed me my sin. I would never have known the sin in my heart—the evil desires that are hidden there—if the law had not said, "You must not have evil desires in your heart." 8But sin used this law against evil desires by reminding me that such desires are wrong and arousing all kinds of forbidden desires within me! Only if there were no laws to break would there be no sinning.

9That is why I felt fine so long as I did not understand what the law really demanded. But when I learned the truth, I realized that I had broken the law and was a sinner, doomed to die. 10So as far as I was concerned, the good law which was supposed to show me the way of life resulted instead in my being given the death penalty. 11Sin fooled me by taking the good laws of God and using them to make me guilty of death. 12But still, you see, the law itself was wholly right and good.

13But how can that be? Didn't the law cause my doom? How then can it be good? No, it was sin, devilish stuff that it is, that used what was good to bring about my condemnation. So you can see how cunning and deadly and damnable it is. For it uses God's good laws for its own evil purposes.

14The law is good, then, and the trouble is not there but with *me*, because I am sold into slavery with Sin as my owner.

PSALM 17:1–15

I am pleading for your help, O Lord; for I have been honest and have done what is right, and you must listen to my earnest cry! ²Publicly acquit me, Lord, for you are always fair. ³You have tested me and seen that I am good. You have come even in the night and found nothing amiss and know that I have told the truth. ⁴I have followed your commands and have not gone along with cruel and evil men. ⁵My feet have not slipped from your paths.

⁶Why am I praying like this? Because I know you will answer me, O God! Yes, listen as I pray. ⁷Show me your strong love in wonderful ways, O Savior of all those seeking your help against their foes. ⁸Protect me as you would the pupil of your eye; hide me in the shadow of your wings as you hover over me.

⁹My enemies encircle me with murder in their eyes. ¹⁰They are pitiless and arrogant. Listen to their boasting. ¹¹They close in upon me and are ready to throw me to the ground. ¹²They are like lions eager to tear me apart, like young lions hiding and waiting their chance.

¹³,¹⁴Lord, arise and stand against them. Push them back! Come and save me from these men of the world whose only concern is earthly gain—these men whom you have filled with your treasures so that their children and grandchildren are rich and prosperous.

¹⁵But as for me, my contentment is not in wealth but in seeing you and knowing all is well between us. And when I awake in heaven, I will be fully satisfied, for I will see you face to face.

PROVERBS FOR TODAY/ 19:22–23

Kindness makes a man attractive. And it is better to be poor than dishonest. Reverence for God gives life, happiness, and protection from harm.

JULY 22

2 CHRONICLES 6:13b—8:10

Now, as all the people watched, he knelt down, reached out his arms toward heaven, and prayed this prayer:

¹⁴O Lord God of Israel, there is no God like you in all of heaven and earth. You are the God who keeps his kind promises to all those who obey you, and who are anxious to do your will. ¹⁵And you have kept your promise to my father David, as is evident today. ¹⁶And now, O God of Israel, carry out your further promise to him that 'your descendants shall always reign over Israel if they will obey my laws as you have.' ¹⁷Yes, Lord God of Israel, please fulfill this promise too. ¹⁸But will God really live upon the earth with men? Why, even the heaven and the heaven of heavens cannot contain you—how much less this Temple which I have built!

¹⁹"How I pray that you will heed my prayers, O Lord my God! Listen to my prayer that I am praying to you now! ²⁰,²¹Look down with favor day and night upon this Temple—upon this place where you have said that you would put your name. May you always hear and answer the prayers I will pray to you as I face toward this place. Listen to my prayers and to those of your people Israel when they pray toward this Temple; yes, hear us from heaven, and when you hear, forgive.

²²"Whenever someone commits a

crime, and is required to swear to his innocence before this altar, 23then hear from heaven and punish him if he is lying, or else declare him innocent.

24"If your people Israel are destroyed before their enemies because they have sinned against you, and if they turn to you and call themselves your people, and pray to you here in this Temple, 25then listen to them from heaven and forgive their sins and give them back this land you gave to their fathers.

26"When the skies are shut and there is no rain because of our sins, and then we pray toward this Temple and claim you as our God, and turn from our sins because you have punished us, 27then listen from heaven and forgive the sins of your people, and teach them what is right; and send rain upon this land which you have given to your people as their own property.

28"If there is a famine in the land, or plagues, or crop disease, or attacks of locusts or caterpillars, or if your people's enemies are in the land besieging our cities—whatever the trouble is— 29listen to every individual's prayer concerning his private sorrow, as well as all the public prayers. 30Hear from heaven where you live, and forgive, and give each one whatever he deserves, for you know the hearts of all mankind. 31Then they will reverence you forever, and will continually walk where you tell them to go.

32"And when foreigners hear of your power, and come from distant lands to worship your great name, and to pray toward this Temple, 33hear them from heaven where you live, and do what they request of you. Then all the peoples of the earth will hear of your fame and will reverence you, just as your people Israel do; and they too will know that this Temple I have built is truly yours.

34"If your people go out at your command to fight their enemies, and they pray toward this city of Jerusalem which you have chosen, and this Temple which I have built for your name, 35then hear their prayers from heaven and give them success.

36"If they sin against you (and who has never sinned?) and you become angry with them, and you let their enemies defeat them and take them away as captives to some foreign nation near or far, 37,38and if in that land of exile they turn to you again, and face toward this land you gave their fathers, and this city and your Temple I have built, and plead with you with all their hearts to forgive them, 39then hear from heaven where you live and help them and forgive your people who have sinned against you.

40"Yes, O my God, be wide awake and attentive to all the prayers made to you in this place. 41And now, O Lord God, arise and enter this resting place of yours where the Ark of your strength has been placed. Let your priests, O Lord God, be clothed with salvation, and let your people rejoice in your kind deeds. 42O Lord God, do not ignore me—do not turn your face away from me, your anointed one. Oh, remember your love for David and your kindness to him."

As Solomon finished praying, fire flashed down from heaven and burned up the sacrifices! And the glory of the Lord filled the Temple, so that the priests couldn't enter! 3All the people had been watching and now they fell flat on the pavement, and worshiped and thanked the Lord.

"How good he is!" they exclaimed. "He is always so loving and kind."

4,5Then the king and all the people dedicated the Temple by sacrificing burnt offerings to the Lord. King Solomon's contribution for this purpose was 22,000 oxen and 120,000 sheep. 6The priests were standing at their posts of duty, and the Levites were playing their thanksgiving song, "His Lovingkindness Is Forever," using the musical instruments King David himself had made and had used to praise the Lord. Then, when the priests blew the trumpets, all the people stood again. 7Solomon consecrated the inner court of the Temple for use that day as a place of sacrifice, because there were too many sacrifices for the bronze altar to accommodate.

8For the next seven days, they celebrated the Tabernacle Festival, with large crowds coming in from all over Israel; they arrived from as far away as Hamath at one end of the country to the brook of Egypt at the other. 9A final religious service was held on the eighth day. 10Then, on October 7, he sent the people home, joyful and happy because the Lord had been so good to David and Solomon and to his people Israel.

11So Solomon finished building the Temple as well as his own palace. He completed what he had planned to do.

12One night the Lord appeared to Solomon and told him, "I have heard your prayer and have chosen this Temple as the place where I want you to sacrifice to me. 13If I shut up the heavens so that there is no rain, or if I command the locust swarms to eat up all of your crops, or if I send an epidemic among you, 14then if my people will humble themselves and pray, and search for me, and turn from their wicked ways, I will hear them from heaven and forgive their sins and heal their land. 15I will listen, wide awake, to every prayer made in this place. 16For I have chosen this Temple and sanctified it to be my home forever; my eyes and my heart shall always be here.

17"As for yourself, if you follow me as your father David did, 18then I will see to it that you and your descendants will always be the kings of Israel; 19but if you don't follow me, if you refuse the laws I have given you, and worship idols, 20then I will destroy my people from this land of mine which I have given them, and this Temple shall be destroyed even though I have sanctified it for myself. Instead, I will make it a public horror and disgrace. 21Instead of its being famous, all who pass by will be incredulous.

" 'Why has the Lord done such a terrible thing to this land and to this Temple?' they will ask.

22"And the answer will be, 'Because his people abandoned the Lord God of their fathers, the God who brought them out of the land of Egypt, and they worshiped other gods instead. That is why he has done all this to them.' "

IT was now twenty years since Solomon had become king, and the great building projects of the Lord's Temple and his own royal palace were completed. 2He now turned his energies to rebuilding the cities which King Hiram of Tyre had given to him, and he relocated some of the people of Israel into them. 3It was at this time, too, that Solomon fought against the city of Hamath-zobah and conquered it. 4He built Tadmor in the desert, and built cities in Hamath as supply centers. 5He fortified the cities of upper Beth-horon and lower Beth-horon, both being supply centers, building their walls and installing barred gates. 6He also built Baalath and other supply centers at this time, and constructed cities where his chariots and horses were kept. He built to his heart's desire in Jerusalem and Lebanon and throughout the entire realm.

7,8He began the practice that still continues of conscripting as slave laborers the Hittites, Amorites, Perizzites, Hivites, and Jebusites—the descendants of those nations which the Israelis had not completely wiped out. 9However, he didn't make slaves of any of the Israeli citizens, but used them as soldiers, officers, charioteers, and cavalrymen; 10also, two hundred fifty of them were government officials who administered all public affairs.

ROMANS 7:15—8:8

I don't understand myself at all, for I really want to do what is right, but I can't. I do what I don't want to—what I hate. 16I know perfectly well that what I am doing is wrong, and my bad conscience proves that I agree with these laws I am breaking. 17But I can't help myself, because I'm no longer doing it. It is sin inside me that is stronger than I am that makes me do these evil things.

18I know I am rotten through and

through so far as my old sinful nature is concerned. No matter which way I turn I can't make myself do right. I want to but I can't. 19When I want to do good, I don't; and when I try not to do wrong, I do it anyway. 20Now if I am doing what I don't want to, it is plain where the trouble is: sin still has me in its evil grasp.

21It seems to be a fact of life that when I want to do what is right, I inevitably do what is wrong. 22I love to do God's will so far as my new nature is concerned; 23,24,25but there is something else deep within me, in my lower nature, that is at war with my mind and wins the fight and makes me a slave to the sin that is still within me. In my mind I want to be God's willing servant but instead I find myself still enslaved to sin.

So you see how it is: my new life tells me to do right, but the old nature that is still inside me loves to sin. Oh, what a terrible predicament I'm in! Who will free me from my slavery to this deadly lower nature? Thank God! It has been done by Jesus Christ our Lord. He has set me free.

So there is now no condemnation awaiting those who belong to Christ Jesus. 2For the power of the life-giving Spirit— and this power is mine through Christ Jesus—has freed me from the vicious circle of sin and death. 3We aren't saved from sin's grasp by knowing the commandments of God, because we can't and don't keep them, but God put into effect a different plan to save us. He sent his own Son in a human body like ours— except that ours are sinful—and destroyed sin's control over us by giving himself as a sacrifice for our sins. 4So now we can obey God's laws if we follow after the Holy Spirit and no longer obey the old evil nature within us.

5Those who let themselves be controlled by their lower natures live only to please themselves, but those who follow after the Holy Spirit find themselves doing those things that please God. 6Following after the Holy Spirit leads to life and peace, but following after the old nature leads to death, 7because the old sinful nature within us is against God. It never did obey God's laws and it never will. 8That's why those who are still under the control of their old sinful selves, bent on following their old evil desires, can never please God.

PSALM 18:1–15

LORD, how I love you! For you have done such tremendous things for me.

2The Lord is my fort where I can enter and be safe; no one can follow me in and slay me. He is a rugged mountain where I hide; he is my Savior, a rock where none can reach me, and a tower of safety. He is my shield. He is like the strong horn of a mighty fighting bull. 3All I need to do is cry to him—oh, praise the Lord—and I am saved from all my enemies!

4Death bound me with chains, and the floods of ungodliness mounted a massive attack against me. 5Trapped and helpless, I struggled against the ropes that drew me on to death.

6In my distress I screamed to the Lord for his help. And he heard me from heaven; my cry reached his ears. 7Then the earth rocked and reeled, and mountains shook and trembled. How they quaked! For he was angry. 8Fierce flames leaped from his mouth, setting fire to the earth; smoke blew from his nostrils. 9He bent the heavens down and came to my defense; thick darkness was beneath his feet. 10Mounted on a mighty angel, he sped swiftly to my aid with wings of wind. 11He enshrouded himself with darkness, veiling his approach with dense clouds dark as murky waters. 12Suddenly the brilliance of his presence broke through the clouds with lightning and a mighty storm of hail.

13The Lord thundered in the heavens; the God above all gods has spoken— oh, the hailstones; oh, the fire! 14He flashed his fearful arrows of lightning and routed all my enemies. See how they run! ¹⁵Then at your command, O Lord, the sea receded from the shore. At the blast of your breath the depths were laid bare.

PROVERBS FOR TODAY/ 19:24–25

Some men are so lazy they won't even feed themselves! Punish a mocker and others will learn from his example. Reprove a wise man and he will be the wiser.

JULY 23

2 CHRONICLES 8:11—10:19

SOLOMON now moved his wife (she was Pharaoh's daughter) from the City of David sector of Jerusalem to the new palace he had built for her. For he said, "She must not live in King David's palace, for the Ark of the Lord was there and it is holy ground."

¹²Then Solomon sacrificed burnt offerings to the Lord on the altar he had built in front of the porch of the Temple. ¹³The number of sacrifices differed from day to day in accordance with the instructions Moses had given; there were extra sacrifices on the Sabbaths, on new moon festivals, and at the three annual festivals—the Passover celebration, the Festival of Weeks, and the Festival of Tabernacles. ¹⁴In assigning the priests to their posts of duty he followed the organizational chart prepared by his father David; he also assigned the Levites to their work of praise and of helping the priests in each day's duties; and he assigned the gatekeepers to their gates. ¹⁵Solomon did not deviate in any way from David's instructions concerning these matters and concerning the treasury personnel. ¹⁶Thus Solomon successfully completed the construction of the Temple.

¹⁷,¹⁸Then he went to the seaport towns of Eziongeber and Eloth, in Edom, to launch a fleet presented to him by King Hiram. These ships, with King Hiram's experienced crews working alongside Solomon's men, went to Ophir and brought back to him several million dollars worth of gold on each trip!

WHEN the Queen of Sheba heard of Solomon's fabled wisdom, she came to Jerusalem to test him with hard questions. A very great retinue of aides and servants accompanied her, including camel-loads of spices, gold, and jewels. ²And Solomon answered all her problems. Nothing was hidden from him; he could explain everything to her. ³When she discovered how wise he really was, and how breathtaking the beauty of his palace, ⁴and how wonderful the food at his tables, and how many servants and aides he had, and when she saw their spectacular uniforms and his stewards in full regalia, and saw the size of the men in his bodyguard, she could scarcely believe it!

⁵Finally she exclaimed to the king, "Everything I heard about you in my own country is true! ⁶I didn't believe it until I got here and saw it with my own eyes. Your wisdom is far greater than I could ever have imagined. ⁷What a privilege for these men of yours to stand here and listen to you talk! ⁸Blessed be the Lord your God! How he must love Israel to give them a just king like you! He wants them to be a great, strong nation forever."

⁹She gave the king a gift of over a million dollars in gold, and great quantities of spices of incomparable quality, and many, many jewels.

¹⁰King Hiram's and King Solomon's

crews brought gold from Ophir, also sandalwood and jewels. ¹¹The king used the sandalwood to make terraced steps for the Temple and the palace, and to construct harps and lyres for the choir. Never before had there been such beautiful instruments in all the land of Judah.

¹²King Solomon gave the Queen of Sheba gifts of the same value as she had brought to him, plus everything else she asked for! Then she and her retinue returned to their own land.

¹³,¹⁴Solomon received a quarter of a billion dollars worth of gold each year from the kings of Arabia and many other lands that paid annual tribute to him. In addition, there was a trade balance from the exports of his merchants. ¹⁵He used some of the gold to make 200 large shields, each worth $100,000, ¹⁶and 300 smaller shields, each worth $50,000. The king placed these in the Forest of Lebanon Room in his palace. ¹⁷He also made a huge ivory throne overlaid with pure gold. ¹⁸It had six gold steps and a footstool of gold; also gold armrests, each flanked by a gold lion. ¹⁹Gold lions also stood at each side of each step. No other throne in all the world could be compared with it! ²⁰All of King Solomon's cups were solid gold, as were all the furnishings in the Forest of Lebanon Room. Silver was too cheap to count for much in those days!

²¹Every three years the king sent his ships to Tarshish, using sailors supplied by King Hiram, to bring back gold, silver, ivory, apes, and peacocks.

²²So King Solomon was richer and wiser than any other king in all the earth. ²³Kings from every nation came to visit him, and to hear the wisdom God had put into his heart. ²⁴Each brought him annual tribute of silver and gold bowls, clothing, armor, spices, horses, and mules.

²⁵In addition, Solomon had 4,000 stalls of horses and chariots, and 12,000 cavalrymen stationed in the chariot cities, as well as in Jerusalem to protect the king. ²⁶He ruled over all kings and kingdoms from the Euphrates River to the land of the Philistines and as far away as the border of Egypt. ²⁷He made silver become as plentiful in Jerusalem as stones in the road! And cedar was used as though it were common sycamore. ²⁸Horses were brought to him from Egypt and other countries.

²⁹The rest of Solomon's biography is written in the history of Nathan the prophet and in the prophecy of Ahijah the Shilonite, and also in the visions of Iddo the seer concerning Jeroboam the son of Nebat.

³⁰So Solomon reigned in Jerusalem over all of Israel for forty years. ³¹Then he died and was buried in Jerusalem, and his son Rehoboam became the new king.

ALL the leaders of Israel came to Shechem for Rehoboam's coronation. ²,³Meanwhile, friends of Jeroboam (son of Nebat) sent word to him of Solomon's death. He was in Egypt at the time, where he had gone to escape from King Solomon. He now quickly returned, and was present at the coronation, and led the people's demands on Rehoboam:

⁴"Your father was a hard master," they said. "Be easier on us than he was, and we will let you be our king!"

⁵Rehoboam told them to return in three days for his decision. ⁶He discussed their demand with the old men who had counseled his father Solomon.

"What shall I tell them?" he asked.

⁷"If you want to be their king," they replied, "you will have to give them a favorable reply and treat them with kindness."

⁸,⁹But he rejected their advice and asked the opinion of the young men who had grown up with him. "What do you fellows think I should do?" he asked. "Shall I be easier on them than my father was?"

¹⁰"No!" they replied. "Tell them, 'If you think my father was hard on you, just wait and see what I'll be like!' Tell them, 'My little finger is thicker than my father's loins! ¹¹I am going to be tougher

on you, not easier! My father used whips on you, but I'll use scorpions!' "

12So when Jeroboam and the people returned in three days to hear King Rehoboam's decision, 13he spoke roughly to them; for he refused the advice of the old men, 14and followed the counsel of the younger ones.

"My father gave you heavy burdens but I will give you heavier!" he told them. "My father punished you with whips, but I will punish you with scorpions!"

15So the king turned down the people's demands. (God caused him to do it in order to fulfill his prediction spoken to Jeroboam by Ahijah, the Shilonite.) 16When the people realized what the king was saying they turned their backs and deserted him.

"Forget David and his dynasty!" they shouted angrily. "We'll get someone else to be our king. Let Rehoboam rule his own tribe of Judah! Let's go home!" So they did.

17The people of the tribe of Judah, however, remained loyal to Rehoboam. 18Afterwards, when King Rehoboam sent Hadoram to draft forced labor from the other tribes of Israel, the people stoned him to death. When this news reached King Rehoboam he jumped into his chariot and fled to Jerusalem. 19And Israel has refused to be ruled by a descendant of David to this day.

ROMANS 8:9–23

BUT you are not like that. You are controlled by your new nature if you have the Spirit of God living in you. (And remember that if anyone doesn't have the Spirit of Christ living in him, he is not a Christian at all.) 10Yet, even though Christ lives within you, your body will die because of sin; but your spirit will live, for Christ has pardoned it. 11And if the Spirit of God, who raised up Jesus from the dead, lives in you, he will make your dying bodies live again after you die, by means of this same Holy Spirit living within you.

12So, dear brothers, you have no obligations whatever to your old sinful nature to do what it begs you to do. 13For if you keep on following it you are lost and will perish, but if through the power of the Holy Spirit you crush it and its evil deeds, you shall live. 14For all who are led by the Spirit of God are sons of God.

15And so we should not be like cringing, fearful slaves, but we should behave like God's very own children, adopted into the bosom of his family, and calling to him, "Father, Father." 16For his Holy Spirit speaks to us deep in our hearts, and tells us that we really are God's children. 17And since we are his children, we will share his treasures—for all God gives to his Son Jesus is now ours too. But if we are to share his glory, we must also share his suffering.

18Yet what we suffer now is nothing compared to the glory he will give us later. 19For all creation is waiting patiently and hopefully for that future day when God will resurrect his children. 20,21For on that day thorns and thistles, sin, death, and decay—the things that overcame the world against its will at God's command—will all disappear, and the world around us will share in the glorious freedom from sin which God's children enjoy.

22For we know that even the things of nature, like animals and plants, suffer in sickness and death as they await this great event. 23And even we Christians, although we have the Holy Spirit within us as a foretaste of future glory, also groan to be released from pain and suffering. We, too, wait anxiously for that day when God will give us our full rights as his children, including the new bodies he has promised us—bodies that will never be sick again and will never die.

PSALM 18:16–34

HE reached down from heaven and took me and drew me out of my great trials. He rescued me from deep waters. 17He delivered me from my strong enemy, from those who hated me—I who was helpless in their hands.

18On the day when I was weakest, they attacked. But the Lord held me steady. 19He led me to a place of safety, for he delights in me.

20The Lord rewarded me for doing right and being pure. 21For I have followed his commands and have not sinned by turning back from following him. 22I kept close watch on all his laws; I did not refuse a single one. 23I did my best to keep them all, holding myself back from doing wrong. 24And so the Lord has paid me with his blessings, for I have done what is right, and I am pure of heart. This he knows, for he watches my every step.

25Lord, how merciful you are to those who are merciful. And you do not punish those who run from evil. 26You give blessings to the pure but pain to those who leave your paths. 27You deliver the humble but condemn the proud and haughty ones. 28You have turned on my light! The Lord my God has made my darkness turn to light. 29Now in your strength I can scale any wall, attack any troop.

30What a God he is! How perfect in every way! All his promises prove true. He is a shield for everyone who hides behind him. 31For who is God except our Lord? Who but he is as a rock?

32He fills me with strength and protects me wherever I go. 33He gives me the surefootedness of a mountain goat upon the crags. He leads me safely along the top of the cliffs. 34He prepares me for battle and gives me strength to draw an iron bow!

PROVERBS FOR TODAY/ 19:26
A son who mistreats his father or mother is a public disgrace.

JULY 24

2 CHRONICLES 11:1—13:22

UPON arrival at Jerusalem, Rehoboam mobilized the armies of Judah and Benjamin, 180,000 strong, and declared war against the rest of Israel in an attempt to reunite the kingdom.

2But the Lord told Shemaiah the prophet,

3"Go and say to King Rehoboam of Judah, Solomon's son, and to the people of Judah and of Benjamin:

4" 'The Lord says, Do not fight against your brothers. Go home, for I am behind their rebellion.' " So they obeyed the Lord and refused to fight against Jeroboam.

5-10Rehoboam stayed in Jerusalem and fortified these cities of Judah with walls and gates to protect himself:

Bethlehem, Etam, Tekoa, Beth-zur, Soco, Adullam, Gath, Mareshah, Ziph, Adoraim, Lachish, Azekah, Zorah, Aijalon, and Hebron.

11He also rebuilt and strengthened the forts, and manned them with companies of soldiers under their officers, and stored them with food, olive oil, and wine. 12Shields and spears were placed in armories in every city as a further safety measure. For only Judah and Benjamin remained loyal to him.

13,14However, the priests and Levites from the other tribes now abandoned their homes and moved to Judah and Jerusalem, for King Jeroboam had fired them, telling them to stop being priests of the Lord. 15He had appointed other priests instead who encouraged the people to worship idols instead of God, and to sacrifice to carved statues of goats and calves which he placed on the hills.

16Laymen, too, from all over Israel began moving to Jerusalem where they could freely worship the Lord God of their fathers, and sacrifice to him. 17This strengthened the kingdom of Judah, so King Rehoboam survived for three years without difficulty; for during those years there was an earnest effort to obey the Lord as King David and King Solomon had done.

18Rehoboam married his cousin Mahalath. She was the daughter of David's son Jerimoth and of Abihail, the daughter of David's brother Eliab. 19Three sons were born from this marriage—Jeush, Shemariah, and Zaham.

20Later he married Maacah, the daughter of Absalom. The children she bore him were Abijah, Attai, Ziza, and Shelomith. 21He loved Maacah more than any of his other wives and concubines (he had eighteen wives and sixty concubines—with twenty-eight sons and sixty daughters). 22Maacah's son Abijah was his favorite, and he intended to make him the next king. 23He very wisely scattered his other sons in the fortified cities throughout the land of Judah and Benjamin, and gave them large allowances and arranged for them to have several wives apiece.

BUT just when Rehoboam was at the height of his popularity and power he abandoned the Lord, and the people followed him in this sin. 2As a result, King Shishak of Egypt attacked Jerusalem in the fifth year of King Rehoboam's reign, 3with twelve hundred chariots, sixty thousand cavalrymen and an unnumbered host of infantrymen—Egyptians, Libyans, Sukkiim, and Ethiopians. 4He quickly conquered Judah's fortified cities and soon arrived at Jerusalem.

5The prophet Shemaiah now met with Rehoboam and the Judean leaders from every part of the nation (they had fled to Jerusalem for safety), and told them, "The Lord says, 'You have forsaken me, so I have forsaken you and abandoned you to Shishak.'"

6Then the king and the leaders of Israel confessed their sins and exclaimed, "The Lord is right in doing this to us!"

7And when the Lord saw them humble themselves he sent Shemaiah to tell them, "Because you have humbled yourselves, I will not completely destroy you; some will escape. I will not use Shishak to pour out my anger upon Jerusalem. 8But you must pay annual tribute to him. Then you will realize how much better it is to serve me than to serve him!"

9So King Shishak of Egypt conquered Jerusalem and took away all the treasures of the Temple and of the palace, also all of Solomon's gold shields. 10King Rehoboam replaced them with bronze shields and committed them to the care of the captain of his bodyguard. 11Whenever the king went to the Temple, the guards would carry them, and afterwards return them to the armory. 12When the king humbled himself, the Lord's anger was turned aside and he didn't send total destruction; in fact, even after Shishak's invasion, the economy of Judah remained strong.

13King Rehoboam reigned seventeen years in Jerusalem, the city God had chosen as his residence after considering all the other cities of Israel. He had become king at the age of forty-one, and his mother's name was Naamah the Ammonitess. 14But he was an evil king, for he never did decide really to please the Lord. 15The complete biography of Rehoboam is recorded in the histories written by Shemaiah the prophet and by Iddo the seer, and in *The Genealogical Register.*

There were continual wars between Rehoboam and Jeroboam. 16When Rehoboam died he was buried in Jerusalem, and his son Abijah became the new king.

ABIJAH became the new king of Judah, in Jerusalem, in the eighteenth year of the reign of King Jeroboam of Israel. He lasted three years. His mother's name was Micaiah (daughter of Uriel of Gibeah).

Early in his reign war broke out between Judah and Israel. 3Judah, led by King Abijah, fielded 400,000 seasoned warriors against twice as many Israeli troops—strong, courageous men led by King Jeroboam. 4When the army of Judah arrived at Mount Zemaraim, in the hill country of Ephraim, King Abijah shouted to King Jeroboam and the Israeli army:

5"Listen! Don't you realize that the Lord God of Israel swore that David's descendants would always be the kings of Israel? 6Your King Jeroboam is a mere servant of David's son, and was a traitor to his master. 7Then a whole gang of worthless rebels joined him, defying Solomon's son Rehoboam, for he was young and frightened and couldn't stand up to them. 8Do you really think you can defeat the kingdom of the Lord that is led by a descendant of David? Your army is twice as large as mine, but you are cursed with those gold calves you have with you, that Jeroboam made for you—he calls them your gods! 9And you have driven away the priests of the Lord and the Levites, and have appointed heathen priests instead. Just like the people of other lands, you accept as priests anybody who comes along with a young bullock and seven rams for consecration. Anyone at all can be a priest of these no-gods of yours!

10"But as for us, the Lord is our God and we have not forsaken him. Only the descendants of Aaron are our priests, and the Levites alone may help them in their work. 11They burn sacrifices to the Lord every morning and evening—burnt offerings and sweet incense; and they place the Bread of the Presence upon the holy table. The gold lampstand is lighted every night, for we are careful to follow the instructions of the Lord our God; but you have forsaken him. 12So you see, God is with us; he is our Leader. His priests, trumpeting as they go, will lead us into battle against you. O people of Israel, do not fight against the Lord God of your fathers, for you will not succeed!"

13,14Meanwhile, Jeroboam had secretly sent part of his army around behind the men of Judah to ambush them; so Judah was surrounded, with the enemy before and behind them. Then they cried out to the Lord for mercy, and the priests blew the trumpets. 15,16The men of Judah began to shout. And as they shouted, God used King Abijah and the men of Judah to turn the tide of battle against King Jeroboam and the army of Israel, 17and they slaughtered 500,000 elite troops of Israel that day.

18,19So Judah, depending upon the Lord God of their fathers, defeated Israel, and chased King Jeroboam's troops, and captured some of his cities—Bethel, Jeshanah, Ephron, and their suburbs. 20King Jeroboam of Israel never regained his power during Abijah's lifetime, and eventually the Lord struck him and he died.

21Meanwhile, King Abijah of Judah became very strong. He married fourteen wives and had twenty-two sons and sixteen daughters. 22His complete biography and speeches are recorded in the prophet Iddo's *History of Judah*.

ROMANS 8:24–39

WE are saved by trusting. And trusting means looking forward to getting something we don't yet have—for a man who already has something doesn't need to hope and trust that he will get it. 25But if we must keep trusting God for something that hasn't happened yet, it teaches us to wait patiently and confidently.

26And in the same way—by our faith— the Holy Spirit helps us with our daily problems and in our praying. For we don't even know what we should pray for, nor how to pray as we should; but the Holy Spirit prays for us with such feeling that it cannot be expressed in words. 27And the Father who knows all hearts knows, of course, what the Spirit is saying as he pleads for us in harmony with God's own will. 28And we know that all that happens to us is working for our good if we love God and are fitting into his plans.

29For from the very beginning God

decided that those who came to him—and all along he knew who would—should become like his Son, so that his Son would be the First, with many brothers. ³⁰And having chosen us, he called us to come to him; and when we came, he declared us "not guilty," filled us with Christ's goodness, gave us right standing with himself, and promised us his glory.

³¹What can we ever say to such wonderful things as these? If God is on our side, who can ever be against us? ³²Since he did not spare even his own Son for us but gave him up for us all, won't he also surely give us everything else?

³³Who dares accuse us whom God has chosen for his own? Will God? No! He is the one who has forgiven us and given us right standing with himself.

³⁴Who then will condemn us? Will Christ? *No!* For he is the one who died for us and came back to life again for us and is sitting at the place of highest honor next to God, pleading for us there in heaven.

³⁵Who then can ever keep Christ's love from us? When we have trouble or calamity, when we are hunted down or destroyed, is it because he doesn't love us anymore? And if we are hungry, or penniless, or in danger, or threatened with death, has God deserted us?

³⁶No, for the Scriptures tell us that for his sake we must be ready to face death at every moment of the day—we are like sheep awaiting slaughter; ³⁷but despite all this, overwhelming victory is ours through Christ who loved us enough to die for us. ³⁸For I am convinced that nothing can ever separate us from his love. Death can't, and life can't. The angels won't, and all the powers of hell itself cannot keep God's love away. Our fears for today, our worries about tomorrow, ³⁹or where we are—high above the sky, or in the deepest ocean—nothing will ever be able to separate us from the love of God demonstrated by our Lord Jesus Christ when he died for us.

PSALM 18:35–50

YOU have given me your salvation as my shield. Your right hand, O Lord, supports me; your gentleness has made me great. ³⁶You have made wide steps beneath my feet so that I need never slip. ³⁷I chased my enemies; I caught up with them and did not turn back until all were conquered. ³⁸I pinned them to the ground; all were helpless before me. I placed my feet upon their necks. ³⁹For you have armed me with strong armor for the battle. My enemies quail before me and fall defeated at my feet. ⁴⁰You made them turn and run; I destroyed all who hated me. ⁴¹They shouted for help but no one dared to rescue them; they cried to the Lord, but he refused to answer them. ⁴²So I crushed them fine as dust and cast them to the wind. I threw them away like sweepings from the floor. ⁴³,⁴⁴,⁴⁵You gave me victory in every battle. The nations came and served me. Even those I didn't know before come now and bow before me. Foreigners who have never seen me submit instantly. They come trembling from their strongholds.

⁴⁶God is alive! Praise him who is the great rock of protection. ⁴⁷He is the God who pays back those who harm me and subdues the nations before me.

⁴⁸He rescues me from my enemies; he holds me safely out of their reach and saves me from these powerful opponents. ⁴⁹For this, O Lord, I will praise you among the nations. ⁵⁰Many times you have miraculously rescued me, the king you appointed. You have been loving and kind to me and will be to my descendants.

PROVERBS FOR TODAY/ 19:27–29

Stop listening to teaching that contradicts what you know is right. A worthless witness cares nothing for truth—he enjoys his sinning too much. Mockers and rebels shall be severely punished.

JULY 25

2 CHRONICLES 14:1—16:14

KING Abijah was buried in Jerusalem. Then his son Asa became the new king of Judah, and there was peace in the land for the first ten years of his reign, 2for Asa was careful to obey the Lord his God. 3He demolished the heathen altars on the hills, and broke down the obelisks, and chopped down the shameful Asherim-idols, 4and demanded that the entire nation obey the commandments of the Lord God of their ancestors. 5Also, he removed the sun-images from the hills, and the incense altars from every one of Judah's cities. That is why God gave his kingdom peace. 6This made it possible for him to build walled cities throughout Judah.

7"Now is the time to do it, while the Lord is blessing us with peace because of our obedience to him," he told his people. "Let us build and fortify cities now, with walls, towers, gates, and bars." So they went ahead with these projects very successfully.

8King Asa's Judean army was 300,000 strong, equipped with light shields and spears. His army of Benjaminites numbered 280,000, armed with large shields and bows. Both armies were composed of well-trained, brave men.

9,10But now he was attacked by an army of 1,000,000 troops from Ethiopia with 300 chariots, under the leadership of General Zerah. They advanced to the city of Mareshah, in the valley of Zephathah, and King Asa sent his troops to battle with them there.

11"O Lord," he cried out to God, "no one else can help us! Here we are, powerless against this mighty army. Oh, help us, Lord our God! For we trust in you alone to rescue us, and in your name we attack this vast horde. Don't let mere men defeat you!"

12Then the Lord defeated the Ethiopians, and Asa and the army of Judah triumphed as the Ethiopians fled. 13They

chased them as far as Gerar, and the entire Ethiopian army was wiped out so that not one man remained; for the Lord and his army destroyed them all. Then the army of Judah carried off vast quantities of plunder. 14While they were at Gerar they attacked all the cities in that area, and terror from the Lord came upon the residents. As a result, additional vast quantities of plunder were collected from these cities too. 15They not only plundered the cities, but destroyed the cattle tents and captured great herds of sheep and camels before finally returning to Jerusalem.

THEN the Spirit of God came upon Azariah (son of Oded), 2and he went out to meet King Asa as he was returning from the battle.

"Listen to me, Asa! Listen, armies of Judah and Benjamin!" he shouted. "The Lord will stay with you as long as you stay with him! Whenever you look for him, you will find him. But if you forsake him, he will forsake you. 3For a long time now, over in Israel, the people haven't worshiped the true God, and have not had a true priest to teach them. They have lived without God's laws. 4But whenever they have turned again to the Lord God of Israel in their distress, and searched for him, he has helped them. 5In their times of rebellion against God there was no peace. Problems troubled the nation on every hand. Crime was on the increase everywhere. 6There were external wars, and internal fighting of city against city, for God was plaguing them with all sorts of trouble. 7But you men of Judah, keep up the good work and don't get discouraged, for you will be rewarded."

8When King Asa heard this message from God, he took courage and destroyed all the idols in the land of Judah and Benjamin, and in the cities he had captured in the hill country of Ephraim, and he rebuilt the altar of the Lord in front of the Temple.

9Then he summoned all the people of Judah and Benjamin, and the immigrants from Israel (for many had come from the territories of Ephraim, Manasseh, and Simeon, in Israel, when they saw that the Lord God was with King Asa). 10They all came to Jerusalem in June of the fifteenth year of King Asa's reign, 11and sacrificed to the Lord seven hundred oxen and seven thousand sheep— it was part of the plunder they had captured in the battle. 12Then they entered into a contract to worship only the Lord God of their fathers, 13and agreed that anyone who refused to do this must die—whether old or young, man or woman. 14They shouted out their oath of loyalty to God with trumpets blaring and horns sounding. 15All were happy for this covenant with God, for they had entered into it with all their hearts and wills, and wanted him above everything else, and they found him! And he gave them peace throughout the nation.

16King Asa even removed his mother Maacah from being the queen mother because she made an Asherah-idol; he cut down the idol and crushed and burned it at Kidron Brook. 17Over in Israel the idol-temples were not removed. But here in Judah and Benjamin the heart of King Asa was perfect before God throughout his lifetime. 18He brought back into the Temple the silver and gold bowls which he and his father had dedicated to the Lord. 19So there was no more war until the thirty-fifth year of King Asa's reign.

IN the thirty-sixth year of King Asa's reign, King Baasha of Israel declared war on him and built the fortress of Ramah in order to control the road to Judah. 2Asa's response was to take the silver and gold from the Temple and from the palace, and to send it to King Ben-hadad of Syria, at Damascus, with this message:

3"Let us renew the mutual security pact that there was between your father and my father. See, here is silver and gold to induce you to break your alliance with King Baasha of Israel, so that he will leave me alone."

4Ben-hadad agreed to King Asa's request and mobilized his armies to attack Israel. They destroyed the cities of Ijon, Dan, Abel-maim and all of the supply centers in Naphtali. 5As soon as King Baasha of Israel heard what was happening, he discontinued building Ramah and gave up his plan to attack Judah. 6Then King Asa and the people of Judah went out to Ramah and carried away the building stones and timbers and used them to build Geba and Mizpah instead.

7About that time the prophet Hanani came to King Asa and told him, "Because you have put your trust in the king of Syria instead of in the Lord your God, the army of the king of Syria has escaped from you. 8Don't you remember what happened to the Ethiopians and Libyans and their vast army, with all of their chariots and cavalrymen? But you relied then on the Lord, and he delivered them all into your hand. 9For the eyes of the Lord search back and forth across the whole earth, looking for people whose hearts are perfect toward him, so that he can show his great power in helping them. What a fool you have been! From now on you shall have wars."

10Asa was so angry with the prophet for saying this that he threw him into jail. And Asa oppressed all the people at that time.

11The rest of the biography of Asa is written in *The Annals of the Kings of Israel and Judah.* 12In the thirty-ninth year of his reign, Asa became seriously diseased in his feet but he didn't go to the Lord with the problem, but to the doctors. 13,14So he died in the forty-first year of his reign, and was buried in his own vault that he had hewn out for himself in Jerusalem. He was laid on a bed perfumed with sweet spices and ointments, and his people made a very great burning of incense for him at his funeral.

OH, Israel, my people! Oh, my Jewish brothers! How I long for you to come to Christ. My heart is heavy within me and I grieve bitterly day and night because of you. Christ knows and the Holy Spirit knows that it is no mere pretense when I say that I would be willing to be forever damned if that would save you. 4God has given you so much, but still you will not listen to him. He took you as his own special, chosen people and led you along with a bright cloud of glory and told you how very much he wanted to bless you. He gave you his rules for daily life so you would know what he wanted you to do. He let you worship him, and gave you mighty promises. 5Great men of God were your fathers, and Christ himself was one of you, a Jew so far as his human nature is concerned, he who now rules over all things. Praise God forever!

6Well then, has God failed to fulfill his promises to the Jews? No! [For these promises are only to those who are truly Jews.] And not everyone born into a Jewish family is truly a Jew! 7Just the fact that they come from Abraham doesn't make them truly Abraham's children. For the Scriptures say that the promises apply only to Abraham's son Isaac and Isaac's descendants, though Abraham had other children too. 8This means that not all of Abraham's children are children of God, but only those who believe the promise of salvation which he made to Abraham.

9For God had promised, "Next year I will give you and Sarah a son." 10–13And years later, when this son, Isaac, was grown up and married, and Rebecca his wife was about to bear him twin children, God told her that Esau, the child born first, would be a servant to Jacob, his twin brother. In the words of the Scripture, "I chose to bless Jacob, but not Esau." And God said this before the children were even born, before they had done anything either good or bad. This proves that God was doing what he had decided from the beginning; it was not because of what the children did but because of what God wanted and chose.

14Was God being unfair? Of course not. 15For God had said to Moses, "If I want to be kind to someone, I will. And I will take pity on anyone I want to." 16And so God's blessings are not given just because someone decides to have them or works hard to get them. They are given because God takes pity on those he wants to.

17Pharaoh, king of Egypt, was an example of this fact. For God told him he had given him the kingdom of Egypt for the very purpose of displaying the awesome power of God against him: so that all the world would hear about God's glorious name. 18So you see, God is kind to some just because he wants to be, and he makes some refuse to listen.

19Well then, why does God blame them for not listening? Haven't they done what he made them do?

20No, don't say that. Who are you to criticize God? Should the thing made say to the one who made it, "Why have you made me like this?" 21When a man makes a jar out of clay, doesn't he have a right to use the same lump of clay to make one jar beautiful, to be used for holding flowers, and another to throw garbage into? 22Does not God have a perfect right to show his fury and power against those who are fit only for destruction, those he has been patient with for all this time? 23,24And he has a right to take others such as ourselves, who have been made for pouring the riches of his glory into, whether we are Jews or Gentiles, and to be kind to us so that everyone can see how very great his glory is.

PSALM 19:1–14

THE heavens are telling the glory of God; they are a marvelous display of his craftsmanship. 2Day and night they keep on telling about God. 3,4Without a sound or word, silent in the skies, their message reaches out to all the world. The sun lives in the heavens where God placed it 5and moves out across the skies as radiant as a bridegroom going to his wedding, or as joyous as an athlete looking forward to a race! 6The sun crosses the heavens from end to end, and nothing can hide from its heat.

7,8God's laws are perfect. They protect us, make us wise, and give us joy and light. 9God's laws are pure, eternal, just. 10They are more desirable than gold. They are sweeter than honey dripping from a honeycomb. 11For they warn us away from harm and give success to those who obey them.

12But how can I ever know what sins are lurking in my heart? Cleanse me from these hidden faults. 13And keep me from deliberate wrongs; help me to stop doing them. Only then can I be free of guilt and innocent of some great crime.

14May my spoken words and unspoken thoughts be pleasing even to you, O Lord my Rock and my Redeemer.

PROVERBS FOR TODAY/ 20:1

Wine gives false courage; hard liquor leads to brawls; what fools men are to let it master them, making them reel drunkenly down the street!

JULY 26

2 CHRONICLES 17:1—18:34

THEN his son Jehoshaphat became the king and mobilized for war against Israel. 2He placed garrisons in all of the fortified cities of Judah, in various other places throughout the country, and in the cities of Ephraim that his father had conquered.

3The Lord was with Jehoshaphat because he followed in the good footsteps of his father's early years, and did not worship idols. 4He obeyed the commandments of his father's God—quite unlike the people across the border in the land of Israel. 5So the Lord strengthened his position as king of Judah. All the people of Judah cooperated by paying their taxes, so he became very wealthy as well as being very popular. 6He boldly followed the paths of God—even knocking down the heathen altars on the hills, and destroying the Asherim idols.

7,8,9In the third year of his reign he began a nationwide religious education program. He sent out top government officials as teachers in all the cities of Judah. These men included Ben-hail, Oba-diah, Zechariah, Nethanel, and Micaiah. He also used the Levites for this purpose, including Shemaiah, Nethaniah, Zebadiah, Asahel, Shemiramoth, Jehonathan, Adonijah, Tobijah, and Tobadonijah; also the priests, Elishama and Jehoram. They took copies of *The Book of the Law of the Lord* to all the cities of Judah, to teach the Scriptures to the people.

10Then the fear of the Lord fell upon all the surrounding kingdoms so that none of them declared war on King Jehoshaphat.

11Even some of the Philistines brought him presents and annual tribute, and the Arabs donated 7,700 rams and 7,700 male goats. 12So Jehoshaphat became very strong, and built fortresses and supply cities throughout Judah.

13His public works program was also extensive, and he had a huge army stationed at Jerusalem, his capital. 14,15Three hundred thousand Judean troops were there under General Adnah. Next in command was Jeho-hanan with an army of 280,000 men. 16Next was Amasiah (son of Zichri), a man of unusual piety, with 200,000 troops. 17Benjamin supplied 200,000 men equipped with bows and shields under the command of Eliada, a great general. 18His second in command was Jehozabad, with 180,000 trained men. 19These were the troops in Jerusalem in addition to those placed by the king in the fortified cities throughout the nation.

BUT rich, popular King Jehoshaphat of Judah made a marriage alliance [for his son] with [the daughter of] King Ahab of Israel. 2A few years later he went down to Samaria to visit King Ahab, and King Ahab gave a great party for him and his aides, butchering great numbers of sheep and oxen for the feast. Then he asked King Jehoshaphat to join forces with him against Ramoth-gilead.

3,4,5"Why, of course!" King Jehoshaphat replied. "I'm with you all the way. My troops are at your command! However, let's check with the Lord first."

So King Ahab summoned 400 of his heathen prophets and asked them, "Shall we go to war with Ramoth-gilead or not?"

And they replied, "Go ahead, for God will give you a great victory!"

6,7But Jehoshaphat wasn't satisfied. "Isn't there some prophet of the Lord around here too?" he asked. "I'd like to ask him the same question."

"Well," Ahab told him, "there is one, but I hate him, for he never prophesies anything but evil! His name is Micaiah (son of Imlah)."

"Oh, come now, don't talk like that!" Jehoshaphat exclaimed. "Let's hear what he has to say."

8So the king of Israel called one of his aides. "Quick! Go and get Micaiah (son of Imlah)," he ordered.

9The two kings were sitting on thrones in full regalia at an open place near the Samaria gate, and all the "prophets" were prophesying before them. 10One of them, Zedekiah (son of Chenaanah), made some iron horns for the occasion and proclaimed, "The Lord says you will gore the Syrians to death with these!"

11And all the others agreed. "Yes," they chorused, "go up to Ramoth-gilead and prosper, for the Lord will cause you to conquer."

12The man who went to get Micaiah told him what was happening, and what all the prophets were saying—that the war would end in triumph for the king.

"I hope you will agree with them and give the king a favorable reading," the man ventured.

13But Micaiah replied, "I vow by God that whatever God says is what I will say."

14When he arrived before the king, the king asked him, "Micaiah, shall we go to war against Ramoth-gilead or not?"

And Micaiah replied, "Sure, go ahead! It will be a glorious victory!"

15"Look here," the king said sharply, "how many times must I tell you to speak nothing except what the Lord tells you to?"

16Then Micaiah told him, "In my vision I saw all Israel scattered upon the mountain as sheep without a shepherd. And the Lord said, 'Their master has been killed. Send them home.' "

17"Didn't I tell you?" the king of Israel exclaimed to Jehoshaphat. "He does it every time. He *never* prophesies *anything* but evil against me."

18"Listen to what else the Lord has told me," Micaiah continued. "I saw him upon his throne surrounded by vast throngs of angels.

19,20"And the Lord said, 'Who can get King Ahab to go to battle against Ramoth-gilead and be killed there?'

"There were many suggestions, but finally a spirit stepped forward before the Lord and said, 'I can do it!'

" 'How?' the Lord asked him.

21"He replied, 'I will be a lying spirit in the mouths of all of the king's prophets!'

" 'It will work,' the Lord said; 'go and do it.'

22"So you see, the Lord has put a lying spirit in the mouths of these prophets of yours, when actually he has determined just the opposite of what they are telling you!"

²³Then Zedekiah (son of Chenaanah) walked up to Micaiah and slapped him across the face. "You liar!" he yelled. "When did the Spirit of the Lord leave me and enter you?"

²⁴"You'll find out soon enough," Micaiah replied, "—when you are hiding in an inner room!"

²⁵"Arrest this man and take him back to Governor Amon and to my son Joash," the king of Israel ordered. ²⁶"Tell them, 'The king says to put this fellow in prison and feed him with bread and water until I return safely from the battle!'"

²⁷Micaiah replied, "If you return safely, the Lord has not spoken through me." Then, turning to those around them, he remarked, "Take note of what I have said."

²⁸So the king of Israel and the king of Judah led their armies to Ramoth-gilead.

²⁹The king of Israel said to Jehoshaphat, "I'll disguise myself so that no one will recognize me, but you put on your royal robes!" So that is what they did.

³⁰Now the king of Syria had issued these instructions to his charioteers: "Ignore everyone but the king of Israel!"

³¹So when the Syrian charioteers saw King Jehoshaphat of Judah in his royal robes, they went for him, supposing that he was the man they were after. But Jehoshaphat cried out to the Lord to save him, and the Lord made the charioteers see their mistake and leave him. ³²For as soon as they realized he was not the king of Israel, they stopped chasing him. ³³But one of the Syrian soldiers shot an arrow haphazardly at the Israeli troops, and it struck the king of Israel at the opening where the lower armor and the breastplate meet. "Get me out of here," he groaned to the driver of his chariot, "for I am badly wounded." ³⁴The battle grew hotter and hotter all that day, and King Ahab went back in, propped up in his chariot, to fight the Syrians, but just as the sun sank into the western skies, he died.

REMEMBER what the prophecy of Hosea says? There God says that he will find other children for himself (who are not from his Jewish family) and will love them, though no one had ever loved them before. ²⁶And the heathen, of whom it once was said, "You are not my people," shall be called "sons of the Living God."

²⁷Isaiah the prophet cried out concerning the Jews that though there would be millions of them, only a small number would ever be saved. ²⁸"For the Lord will execute his sentence upon the earth, quickly ending his dealings, justly cutting them short."

²⁹And Isaiah says in another place that except for God's mercy all the Jews would be destroyed—all of them—just as everyone in the cities of Sodom and Gomorrah perished.

³⁰Well then, what shall we say about these things? Just this, that God has given the Gentiles the opportunity to be acquitted by faith, even though they had not been really seeking God. ³¹But the Jews, who tried so hard to get right with God by keeping his laws, never succeeded. ³²Why not? Because they were trying to be saved by keeping the law and being good instead of by depending on faith. They have stumbled over the great stumbling stone. ³³God warned them of this in the Scriptures when he said, "I have put a Rock in the path of the Jews, and many will stumble over him (Jesus). Those who believe in him will never be disappointed."

DEAR brothers, the longing of my heart and my prayer is that the Jewish people might be saved. ²I know what enthusiasm they have for the honor of God, but it is misdirected zeal. ³For they don't understand that Christ has died to make them right with God. Instead they are trying to make themselves good enough to gain God's favor by keeping the Jewish laws and customs, but that is not God's way of salvation. ⁴They don't understand that Christ gives to those who trust in him everything they are trying to get by keeping his laws. He ends all of that.

5For Moses wrote that if a person could be perfectly good and hold out against temptation all his life and never sin once, only then could he be pardoned and saved. 6But the salvation that comes through faith says, "You don't need to search the heavens to find Christ and bring him down to help you," and, 7"You don't need to go among the dead to bring Christ back to life again."

8For salvation that comes from trusting Christ—which is what we preach— is already within easy reach of each of us; in fact, it is as near as our own hearts and mouths. 9For if you tell others with your own mouth that Jesus Christ is your Lord, and believe in your own heart that God has raised him from the dead, you will be saved. 10For it is by believing in his heart that a man becomes right with God; and with his mouth he tells others of his faith, confirming his salvation.

11For the Scriptures tell us that no one who believes in Christ will ever be disappointed. 12Jew and Gentile are the same in this respect: they all have the same Lord who generously gives his riches to all those who ask him for them.

PSALM 20:1–9

IN your day of trouble, may the Lord be with you! May the God of Jacob keep you from all harm. 2May he send you aid from his sanctuary in Zion. 3May he remember with pleasure the gifts you have given him, your sacrifices and burnt offerings. 4May he grant you your heart's desire and fulfill all your plans. 5May there be shouts of joy when we hear the news of your victory, flags flying with praise to God for all that he has done for you. May he answer all your prayers!

6"God save the king"—I know he does! He hears me from highest heaven and sends great victories. 7Some nations boast of armies and of weaponry, but our boast is in the Lord our God. 8Those nations will collapse and perish; we will arise to stand firm and sure!

9Give victory to our king, O Lord; oh, hear our prayer.

PROVERBS FOR TODAY/ 20:2–3

The king's fury is like that of a roaring lion; to rouse his anger is to risk your life. It is an honor for a man to stay out of a fight. Only fools insist on quarreling.

JULY 27

2 CHRONICLES 19:1—20:37

AS King Jehoshaphat of Judah returned home, uninjured, 2the prophet Jehu (son of Hanani) went out to meet him.

"Should you be helping the wicked, and loving those who hate the Lord?" he asked him. "Because of what you have done, God's wrath is upon you. 3But there are some good things about you, in that you got rid of the shame-idols throughout the land, and you have tried to be faithful to God."

4So Jehoshaphat made no more trips to Israel after that, but remained quietly at Jerusalem. Later he went out again among the people, traveling from Beersheba to the hill country of Ephraim to encourage them to worship the God of their ancestors. 5He appointed judges throughout the nation in all the larger cities, 6and instructed them:

"Watch your step—I have not appointed you—God has; and he will stand beside you and help you give justice in each case that comes before you. 7Be very much afraid to give any other decision than what God tells you to. For there must be no injustice among God's judges, no partiality, no taking of bribes."

8Jehoshaphat set up courts in Jerusalem, too, with the Levites and priests and clan leaders and judges. 9These were his instructions to them: "You are to act always in the fear of God, with honest hearts. 10Whenever a case is referred to you by the judges out in the provinces, whether murder cases or other violations of the laws and ordinances of God, you are to clarify the evidence for them and help them to decide justly, lest the wrath of God come down upon you and them; if you do this, you will discharge your responsibility."

11Then he appointed Amariah, the High Priest, to be the court of final appeal in cases involving violation of sacred affairs; and Zebadiah (son of Ishmael), a ruler in Judah, as the court of final appeal in all civil cases; with the Levites as their assistants. "Be fearless in your stand for truth and honesty. And may God use you to defend the innocent," was his final word to them.

LATER on, the armies of the kings of Moab, Ammon, and of the Meunites declared war on Jehoshaphat and the people of Judah. 2Word reached Jehoshaphat that "a vast army is marching against you from beyond the Dead Sea, from Syria. It is already at Hazazon-tamar" (also called Engedi). 3Jehoshaphat was badly shaken by this news and determined to beg for help from the Lord; so he announced that all the people of Judah should go without food for a time, in penitence and intercession before God. 4People from all across the nation came to Jerusalem to plead unitedly with him. 5Jehoshaphat stood among them as they gathered at the new court of the Temple, and prayed this prayer:

6"O Lord God of our fathers—the only God in all the heavens, the Ruler of all the kingdoms of the earth—you are so powerful, so mighty. Who can stand against you? 7O our God, didn't you drive out the heathen who lived in this land when your people arrived? And didn't you give this land forever to the descendants of your friend Abraham? 8Your people settled here and built this Temple for you, 9truly believing that in a time like this—whenever we are faced with any calamity such as war, disease, or famine—we can stand here before this Temple and before you—for you are here in this Temple—and cry out to you to save us; and that you will hear us and rescue us.

10"And now see what the armies of Ammon, Moab, and Mount Seir are doing. You wouldn't let our ancestors invade those nations when Israel left Egypt, so we went around and didn't destroy them. 11Now see how they reward us! For they have come to throw us out of your land which you have given us. 12O our God, won't you stop them? We have no way to protect ourselves against this mighty army. We don't know what to do, but we are looking to you."

13As the people from every part of Judah stood before the Lord with their little ones, wives, and children, 14the Spirit of the Lord came upon one of the men standing there—Jahaziel (son of Zechariah, son of Benaiah, son of Je-iel, son of Mattaniah the Levite, who was one of the sons of Asaph).

15"Listen to me, all you people of Judah and Jerusalem, and you, O king Jehoshaphat!" he exclaimed. "The Lord says, 'Don't be afraid! Don't be paralyzed by this mighty army! For the battle is not yours, but God's! 16Tomorrow, go down and attack them! You will find them coming up the slopes of Ziz at the end of the valley that opens into the wilderness of Jeruel. 17But you will not need to fight! Take your places; stand quietly and see the incredible rescue operation God will perform for you, O people of Judah and Jerusalem! Don't be afraid or discouraged! Go out there tomorrow, for the Lord is with you!' "

18Then King Jehoshaphat fell to the ground with his face to the earth, and all the people of Judah and the people of Jerusalem did the same, worshiping the Lord. 19Then the Levites of the Kohath clan and the Korah clan stood to praise the Lord God of Israel with songs of praise that rang out strong and clear.

20Early the next morning the army of Judah went out into the wilderness of Tekoa. On the way Jehoshaphat stopped and called them to attention. "Listen to me, O people of Judah and Jerusalem," he said. "Believe in the Lord your God, and you shall have success! Believe his prophets, and everything will be all right!"

21After consultation with the leaders of the people, he determined that there should be a choir leading the march, clothed in sanctified garments and singing the song "His Lovingkindness Is Forever" as they walked along praising and thanking the Lord! 22And at the moment they began to sing and to praise, the Lord caused the armies of Ammon, Moab, and Mount Seir to begin fighting among themselves, and they destroyed each other! 23For the Ammonites and Moabites turned against their allies from Mount Seir and killed every one of them. And when they had finished that job, they turned against each other! 24So, when the army of Judah arrived at the watchtower that looks out over the wilderness, as far as they could look there were dead bodies lying on the ground—not a single one of the enemy had escaped. 25King Jehoshaphat and his people went out to plunder the bodies and came away loaded with money, garments, and jewels stripped from the corpses—so much that it took them three days to cart it all away! 26On the fourth day they gathered in the Valley of Blessing, as it is called today, and how they praised the Lord! 27Then they returned to Jerusalem, with Jehoshaphat leading them, full of joy that the Lord had given them this marvelous rescue from their enemies.

28They marched into Jerusalem accompanied by a band of harps, lyres, and trumpets and proceeded to the Temple. 29And as had happened before, when the surrounding kingdoms heard that the Lord himself had fought against the enemies of Israel, the fear of God fell upon them. 30So Jehoshaphat's kingdom was quiet, for his God had given him rest.

31A thumbnail sketch of King Jehoshaphat: He became king of Judah when he was thirty-five years old, and reigned twenty-five years, in Jerusalem. His mother's name was Azubah, the daughter of Shilhi. 32He was a good king, just as his father Asa was. He continually tried to follow the Lord, 33with the exception that he did not destroy the idol shrines on the hills, nor had the people as yet really decided to follow the God of their ancestors.

34The details of Jehoshaphat's reign from first to last are written in the history of Jehu the son of Hanani, which is inserted in *The Annals of the Kings of Israel.*

35But at the close of his life, Jehoshaphat, king of Judah, went into partnership with Ahaziah, king of Israel, who was a very wicked man. 36They made ships in Ezion-geber to sail to Tarshish. 37Then Eliezer, son of Dodavahu from Mareshah, prophesied against Jehoshaphat, telling him, "Because you have allied yourself with King Ahaziah, the Lord has destroyed your work." So the ships met disaster and never arrived at Tarshish.

ROMANS 10:13—11:12

ANYONE who calls upon the name of the Lord will be saved.
14But how shall they ask him to save them unless they believe in him? And how can they believe in him if they have never heard about him? And how can they hear about him unless someone tells them? 15And how will anyone go and tell them unless someone sends him? That is what the Scriptures are talking about when they say, "How beautiful are the feet of those who preach the Gospel

of peace with God and bring glad tidings of good things." In other words, how welcome are those who come preaching God's Good News!

16But not everyone who hears the Good News has welcomed it, for Isaiah the prophet said, "Lord, who has believed me when I told them?" 17Yet faith comes from listening to this Good News—the Good News about Christ.

18But what about the Jews? Have they heard God's Word? Yes, for it has gone wherever they are; the Good News has been told to the ends of the earth. 19And did they understand [that God would give his salvation to others if they refused to take it]? Yes, for even back in the time of Moses, God had said that he would make his people jealous and try to wake them up by giving his salvation to the foolish heathen nations. 20And later on Isaiah said boldly that God would be found by people who weren't even looking for him. 21In the meantime, he keeps on reaching out his hands to the Jews, but they keep arguing and refusing to come.

I ask then, has God rejected and deserted his people the Jews? Oh no, not at all. Remember that I myself am a Jew, a descendant of Abraham and a member of Benjamin's family.

2,3No, God has not discarded his own people whom he chose from the very beginning. Do you remember what the Scriptures say about this? Elijah the prophet was complaining to God about the Jews, telling God how they had killed the prophets and torn down God's altars; Elijah claimed that he was the only one left in all the land who still loved God, and now they were trying to kill him too.

4And do you remember how God replied? God said, "No, you are not the only one left. I have seven thousand others besides you who still love me and have not bowed down to idols!"

5It is the same today. Not all the Jews have turned away from God; there are a few being saved as a result of God's kindness in choosing them. 6And if it is by God's kindness, then it is not by their being good enough. For in that case the free gift would no longer be free—it isn't free when it is earned.

7So this is the situation: Most of the Jews have not found the favor of God they are looking for. A few have—the ones God has picked out—but the eyes of the others have been blinded. 8This is what our Scriptures refer to when they say that God has put them to sleep, shutting their eyes and ears so that they do not understand what we are talking about when we tell them of Christ. And so it is to this very day.

9King David spoke of this same thing when he said, "Let their good food and other blessings trap them into thinking all is well between themselves and God. Let these good things boomerang on them and fall back upon their heads to justly crush them. 10Let their eyes be dim," he said, "so that they cannot see, and let them walk bent-backed forever with a heavy load."

11Does this mean that God has rejected his Jewish people forever? Of course not! His purpose was to make his salvation available to the Gentiles, and then the Jews would be jealous and begin to want God's salvation for themselves. 12Now if the whole world became rich as a result of God's offer of salvation, when the Jews stumbled over it and turned it down, think how much greater a blessing the world will share in later on when the Jews, too, come to Christ.

PSALM 21:1–13

How the king rejoices in your strength, O Lord! How he exults in your salvation. 2For you have given him his heart's desire, everything he asks you for!

3You welcomed him to the throne with success and prosperity. You set a royal crown of solid gold upon his head. 4He asked for a long, good life, and you have granted his request; the days of his life stretch on and on forever. 5You have given him fame and honor. You have clothed him with splendor and majesty. 6You have endowed him with eternal happiness. You have given him the unquenchable joy of your presence. 7And because the king trusts in the Lord, he will never stumble, never fall; for he depends upon the steadfast love of the God who is above all gods.

8Your hand, O Lord, will find your enemies, all who hate you. 9,10When you appear, they will be destroyed in the fierce fire of your presence. The Lord will destroy them and their children. 11For these men plot against you, Lord, but they cannot possibly succeed. 12They will turn and flee when they see your arrows aimed straight at them.

13Accept our praise, O Lord, for all your glorious power. We will write songs to celebrate your mighty acts!

PROVERBS FOR TODAY/ 20:4–6

If you won't plow in the cold, you won't eat at the harvest. Though good advice lies deep within a counselor's heart, the wise man will draw it out. Most people will tell you what loyal friends they are, but are they telling the truth?

JULY 28

2 CHRONICLES 21:1—23:21

WHEN Jehoshaphat died, he was buried in the cemetery of the kings in Jerusalem, and his son Jehoram became the new ruler of Judah. 2His brothers—other sons of Jehoshaphat—were Azariah, Jehiel, Zechariah, Azariah, Michael, and Shephatiah. 3,4Their father had given each of them valuable gifts of money and jewels, also the ownership of some of the fortified cities of Judah. However, he gave the kingship to Jehoram because he was the oldest. But when Jehoram had become solidly established as king, he killed all of his brothers and many other leaders of Israel. 5He was thirty-two years old when he began to reign, and he reigned eight years, in Jerusalem. 6But he was as wicked as the kings who were over in Israel. Yes, as wicked as Ahab, for Jehoram had married one of the daughters of Ahab, and his whole life was one constant binge of doing evil. 7However, the Lord was unwilling to end the dynasty of David, for he had made a covenant with David always to have one of his descendants upon the throne.

8At that time the king of Edom revolted, declaring his independence of Judah. 9Jehoram attacked him with his full army and with all of his chariots, marching by night, and almost managed to subdue him. 10But to this day Edom has been successful in throwing off the yoke of Judah. Libnah revolted too, because Jehoram had turned away from the Lord God of his fathers. 11What's more, Jehoram constructed idol shrines in the mountains of Judah, and led the people of Jerusalem in worshiping idols; in fact, he compelled his people to worship them.

12Then Elijah the prophet wrote him this letter: "The Lord God of your ancestor David says that because you have not followed in the good ways of your father Jehoshaphat, nor the good ways of King Asa, 13but you have been as evil as the kings over in Israel, and have made the people of Jerusalem and Judah worship idols just as in the times of King Ahab, and because you have killed your brothers who were better than you, [14]now the Lord will destroy your nation with a great plague. You, your children, your wives, and all that you have will be struck down. [15]You will be stricken with an intestinal disease and your bowels will rot away."

[16]Then the Lord stirred up the Philistines and the Arabs living next to the Ethiopians to attack Jehoram. [17]They marched against Judah, broke across the border, and carried away everything of value in the king's palace, including his sons and his wives; only his youngest son, Jehoahaz, escaped.

[18]It was after this that Jehovah struck him down with the incurable bowel disease. [19]In the process of time, at the end of two years, his intestines came out and he died in terrible suffering. (The customary pomp and ceremony was omitted at his funeral.) [20]He was thirty-two years old when he began to reign and he reigned in Jerusalem eight years, and died unmourned. He was buried in Jerusalem, but not in the royal cemetery.

THEN the people of Jerusalem chose Ahaziah, his youngest son, as their new king (for the marauding bands of Arabs had killed his older sons). [2]Ahaziah was twenty-two years old when he began to reign, and he reigned one year, in Jerusalem. His mother's name was Athaliah, granddaughter of Omri. [3]He, too, walked in the evil ways of Ahab, for his mother encouraged him in doing wrong. [4]Yes, he was as evil as Ahab, for Ahab's family became his advisors after his father's death, and they led him on to ruin.

[5]Following their evil advice, Ahaziah made an alliance with King Joram of Israel (the son of Ahab), who was at war with King Hazael of Syria at Ramoth-gilead. Ahaziah led his army there to join the battle. King Joram of Israel was wounded, [6]and returned to Jezreel to recover. Ahaziah went to visit him, [7]but this turned out to be a fatal mistake; for God had decided to punish Ahaziah for his alliance with Joram. It was during this visit that Ahaziah went out with

Joram to challenge Jehu (son of Nimshi), whom the Lord had appointed to end the dynasty of Ahab.

[8]While Jehu was hunting down and killing the family and friends of Ahab, he met King Ahaziah's nephews, the princes of Judah, and killed them. [9]As he and his men were searching for Ahaziah, they found him hiding in the city of Samaria, and brought him to Jehu, who killed him. Even so, Ahaziah was given a royal burial because he was the grandson of King Jehoshaphat—a man who enthusiastically served the Lord. None of his sons, however, except for Joash, lived to succeed him as king, [10]for their grandmother Athaliah killed them when she heard the news of her son Ahaziah's death.

[11]Joash was rescued by his Aunt Jehoshabeath, who was King Ahaziah's sister, and was hidden away in a storage room in the Temple. She was a daughter of King Jehoram, and the wife of Jehoiada the priest. [12]Joash remained hidden in the Temple for six years while Athaliah reigned as queen. He was cared for by his nurse and by his aunt and uncle.

IN the seventh year of the reign of Queen Athaliah, Jehoiada the priest got up his courage and took some of the army officers into his confidence: Azariah (son of Jeroham), Ishmael (son of Jehohanan), Azariah (son of Obed), Maaseiah (son of Adaiah), and Elishaphat (son of Zichri). [2,3]These men traveled out across the nation secretly, to tell the Levites and clan leaders about his plans and to summon them to Jerusalem. On arrival they swore allegiance to the young king, who was still in hiding at the Temple.

"At last the time has come for the king's son to reign!" Jehoiada exclaimed. "The Lord's promise—that a descendant of King David shall be our king—will be true again. [4]This is how we'll proceed: A third of you priests and Levites who come off duty on the Sabbath will stay at the entrance as guards. [5,6]Another third will go over to the palace, and a third will be at the Lower Gate. Everyone else must stay in the outer courts of the

Temple, as required by God's laws. For only the priests and Levites on duty may enter the Temple itself, for they are sanctified. 7You Levites, form a bodyguard for the king, weapons in hand, and kill any unauthorized person entering the Temple. Stay right beside the king."

8So all the arrangements were made. Each of the three leaders led a third of the priests arriving for duty that Sabbath, and a third of those whose week's work was done and were going off duty—for Jehoiada the chief priest didn't release them to go home. 9Then Jehoiada issued spears and shields to all the army officers. These had once belonged to King David and were stored in the Temple. 10These officers, fully armed, formed a line from one side to the other in front of the Temple and around the altar in the outer court. 11Then they brought out the little prince and placed the crown upon his head and handed him a copy of the law of God, and proclaimed him king.

A great shout went up, "Long live the king!" as Jehoiada and his sons anointed him.

12When Queen Athaliah heard all the noise and commotion, and the shouts of praise to the king, she rushed over to the Temple to see what was going on— and there stood the king by his pillar at the entrance, with the army officers and the trumpeters surrounding him, and people from all over the land rejoicing and blowing trumpets, and the singers singing, accompanied by an orchestra leading the people in a great psalm of praise.

Athaliah ripped her clothes and screamed, "Treason! Treason!"

13,14"Take her out and kill her," Jehoiada the priest shouted to the army officers. "Don't do it here at the Temple. And kill anyone who tries to help her."

15,16,17So the crowd opened up for them to take her out and they killed her at the palace stables.

Then Jehoiada made a solemn contract that he and the king and the people would be the Lord's. And all the people rushed over to the temple of Baal and knocked it down, and broke up the altars and knocked down the idols, and killed Mattan the priest of Baal before his altar. 18Jehoiada now appointed the Levite priests as guards, and to sacrifice the burnt offering to the Lord as prescribed in the law of Moses. He made the identical assignments of the Levite clans that King David had. They sang with joy as they worked. 19The guards at the Temple gates kept out everything that was not consecrated and all unauthorized personnel.

20Then the army officers, nobles, governors, and all the people escorted the king from the Temple, wending their way from the Upper Gate to the palace, and seated the king upon his throne. 21So all the people of the land rejoiced, and the city was quiet and peaceful because Queen Athaliah was dead.

ROMANS 11:13–36

As you know, God has appointed me as a special messenger to you Gentiles. I lay great stress on this and remind the Jews about it as often as I can, 14so that if possible I can make them want what you Gentiles have and in that way save some of them. 15And how wonderful it will be when they become Christians! When God turned away from them it meant that he turned to the rest of the world to offer his salvation; and now it is even more wonderful when the Jews come to Christ. It will be like dead people coming back to life. 16And since Abraham and the prophets are God's people, their children will be too. For if the roots of the tree are holy, the branches will be too.

17But some of these branches from Abraham's tree, some of the Jews, have been broken off. And you Gentiles who were branches from, we might say, a wild olive tree, were grafted in. So now you, too, receive the blessing God has promised Abraham and his children, sharing in God's rich nourishment of his own special olive tree.

18But you must be careful not to brag about being put in to replace the branches that were broken off. Remember that you are important only because you are now a part of God's tree; you are just a branch, not a root.

19"Well," you may be saying, "those branches were broken off to make room for me so I must be pretty good."

20Watch out! Remember that those branches, the Jews, were broken off because they didn't believe God, and you are there only because you do. Do not be proud; be humble and grateful—and careful. 21For if God did not spare the branches he put there in the first place, he won't spare you either.

22Notice how God is both kind and severe. He is very hard on those who disobey, but very good to you if you continue to love and trust him. But if you don't, you too will be cut off. 23On the other hand, if the Jews leave their unbelief behind them and come back to God, God will graft them back into the tree again. He has the power to do it.

24For if God was willing to take you who were so far away from him—being part of a wild olive tree—and graft you into his own good tree—a very unusual thing to do—don't you see that he will be far more ready to put the Jews back again, who were there in the first place?

25I want you to know about this truth from God, dear brothers, so that you will not feel proud and start bragging. Yes, it is true that some of the Jews have set themselves against the Gospel now, but this will last only until all of you Gentiles have come to Christ—those of you who will. 26And then all Israel will be saved.

Do you remember what the prophets said about this? "There shall come out of Zion a Deliverer, and he shall turn the Jews from all ungodliness. 27At that time I will take away their sins, just as I promised."

28Now many of the Jews are enemies of the Gospel. They hate it. But this has been a benefit to you, for it has resulted in God's giving his gifts to you Gentiles. Yet the Jews are still beloved of God because of his promises to Abraham, Isaac, and Jacob. 29For God's gifts and his call can never be withdrawn; he will never go back on his promises. 30Once you were rebels against God, but when the Jews refused his gifts God was merciful to you instead. 31And now the Jews are the rebels, but some day they, too, will share in God's mercy upon you. 32For God has given them all up to sin so that he could have mercy upon all alike.

33Oh, what a wonderful God we have! How great are his wisdom and knowledge and riches! How impossible it is for us to understand his decisions and his methods! 34For who among us can know the mind of the Lord? Who knows enough to be his counselor and guide? 35And who could ever offer to the Lord enough to induce him to act? 36For everything comes from God alone. Everything lives by his power, and everything is for his glory. To him be glory evermore.

PSALM 22:1–18

MY God, my God, why have you forsaken me? Why do you refuse to help me or even to listen to my groans? 2Day and night I keep on weeping, crying for your help, but there is no reply— 3,4for *you are holy.*

The praises of our fathers surrounded your throne; they trusted you and you delivered them. 5You heard their cries for help and saved them; they were never disappointed when they sought your aid.

6But I am a worm, not a man, scorned and despised by my own people and by all mankind. 7Everyone who sees me mocks and sneers and shrugs. 8"Is this the one who rolled his burden on the Lord?" they laugh. "Is this the one who claims the Lord delights in him? We'll believe it when we see God rescue him!"

9,10,11Lord, how you have helped me before! You took me safely from my mother's womb and brought me through the years of infancy. I have depended upon you since birth; you have always been my God. Don't leave me now, for trouble is near and no one else can possibly help.

12I am surrounded by fearsome enemies, strong as the giant bulls from Bashan. 13They come at me with open jaws, like roaring lions attacking their prey. 14My strength has drained away like water, and all my bones are out of joint. My heart melts like wax; 15my strength has dried up like sun-baked clay; my tongue sticks to my mouth, for you have laid me in the dust of death. 16The enemy, this gang of evil men, circles me like a pack of dogs; they have pierced my hands and feet. 17I can count every bone in my body. See these men of evil gloat and stare; 18they divide my clothes among themselves by a toss of the dice.

PROVERBS FOR TODAY/ 20:7

It is a wonderful heritage to have an honest father.

JULY 29

2 CHRONICLES 24:1—25:28

JOASH was seven years old when he became king, and he reigned forty years, in Jerusalem. His mother's name was Zibiah, from Beer-sheba. 2Joash tried hard to please the Lord all during the lifetime of Jehoiada the priest. 3Jehoiada arranged two marriages for him, and he had sons and daughters.

4Later on, Joash decided to repair and recondition the Temple. 5He summoned the priests and Levites and gave them these instructions:

"Go to all the cities of Judah and collect offerings for the building fund, so that we can maintain the Temple in good repair. Get at it right away. Don't delay." But the Levites took their time.

6So the king called for Jehoiada, the High Priest, and asked him, "Why haven't you demanded that the Levites go out and collect the Temple taxes from the cities of Judah, and from Jerusalem? The tax law enacted by Moses the servant of the Lord must be enforced so that the Temple can be repaired."

7,8(The followers of wicked Athaliah had ravaged the Temple, and everything dedicated to the worship of God had been removed to the temple of Baalim.) So now the king instructed that a chest be made and set outside the Temple gate. 9Then a proclamation was sent to all the cities of Judah and throughout Jerusalem telling the people to bring to the Lord the tax that Moses the servant of God had assessed upon Israel. 10And all the leaders and the people were glad, and brought the money and placed it in the chest until it was full.

11Then the Levites carried the chest to the king's accounting office where the recording secretary and the representative of the High Priest counted the money, and took the chest back to the Temple again. This went on day after day, and money continued to pour in. 12The king and Jehoiada gave the money to the building superintendents, who hired masons and carpenters to restore the Temple; and to foundrymen who made articles of iron and brass. 13So the work went forward, and finally the Temple was in much better condition than before. 14When all was finished, the remaining money was brought to the king and Jehoiada, and it was agreed to use it for making the gold and silver spoons and bowls used for incense, and for making the instruments used in the sacrifices and offerings.

Burnt offerings were sacrificed continually during the lifetime of Jehoiada the priest. ¹⁵He lived to a very old age, finally dying at 130. ¹⁶He was buried in the City of David among the kings, because he had done so much good for Israel, for God, and for the Temple.

¹⁷,¹⁸But after his death the leaders of Judah came to King Joash and induced him to abandon the Temple of the God of their ancestors, and to worship shame-idols instead! So the wrath of God came down upon Judah and Jerusalem again. ¹⁹God sent prophets to bring them back to the Lord, but the people wouldn't listen.

²⁰Then the Spirit of God came upon Zechariah, Jehoiada's son. He called a meeting of all the people. Standing before them upon a platform, he said to them, "God wants to know why you are disobeying his commandments. For when you do, everything you try fails. You have forsaken the Lord, and now he has forsaken you."

²¹Then the leaders plotted to kill Zechariah, and finally King Joash himself ordered him executed in the court of the Temple. ²²That was how King Joash repaid Jehoiada for his love and loyalty—by killing his son. Zechariah's last words as he died were, "Lord, see what they are doing and pay them back."

²³A few months later the Syrian army arrived and conquered Judah and Jerusalem, killing all the leaders of the nation and sending back great quantities of booty to the king of Damascus. ²⁴It was a great triumph for the tiny Syrian army, but the Lord let the great army of Judah be conquered by them because they had forsaken the Lord God of their ancestors. In that way God executed judgment upon Joash. ²⁵When the Syrians left—leaving Joash severely wounded—his own officials decided to kill him for murdering the son of Jehoiada the priest. They assassinated him as he lay in bed, and buried him in the City of David, but not in the cemetery of the kings. ²⁶The conspir-

ators were Zabad, whose mother was Shime-ath, a woman from Ammon; and Jehozabad, whose mother was Shimrith, a woman from Moab.

²⁷If you want to read about the sons of Joash, and the curses laid upon Joash, and about the restoration of the Temple, see *The Annals of the Kings.*

When Joash died, his son Amaziah became the new king.

AMAZIAH was twenty-five years old when he became king, and he reigned twenty-nine years, in Jerusalem. His mother's name was Jeho-addan, a native of Jerusalem. ²He did what was right, but sometimes resented it! ³When he was well established as the new king, he executed the men who had assassinated his father. ⁴However, he didn't kill their children but followed the command of the Lord written in the law of Moses, that the fathers shall not die for the children's sins, nor the children for the father's sins. No, everyone must pay for his own sins.

⁵,⁶Another thing Amaziah did was to organize the army, assigning leaders to each clan from Judah and Benjamin. Then he took a census and found that he had an army of 300,000 men twenty years old and older, all trained and highly skilled in the use of spear and sword. He also paid $200,000 to hire 100,000 experienced mercenaries from Israel.

⁷But a prophet arrived with this message from the Lord: "Sir, do not hire troops from Israel, for the Lord is not with them. ⁸If you let them go with your troops to battle, you will be defeated no matter how well you fight; for God has power to help or to frustrate."

⁹"But the money!" Amaziah whined. "What shall I do about that?"

And the prophet replied, "The Lord is able to give you much more than this!"

¹⁰So Amaziah sent them home again to Ephraim, which made them very angry and insulted. ¹¹Then Amaziah took courage and led his army to the Valley of Salt, and there killed 10,000 men from Seir. ¹²Another 10,000 were taken alive to the top of a cliff and thrown over,

so that they were crushed upon the rocks below.

13Meanwhile, the army of Israel that had been sent home raided several of the cities of Judah in the vicinity of Beth-horon, toward Samaria, killing 3,000 people and carrying off great quantities of booty.

14When King Amaziah returned from this slaughter of the Edomites, he brought with him idols taken from the people of Seir, and set them up as gods, and bowed before them, and burned incense to them! 15This made the Lord very angry and he sent a prophet to demand, "Why have you worshiped gods who couldn't even save their own people from you?"

16"Since when have I asked your advice?" the king retorted. "Be quiet now, before I have you killed."

The prophet left with this parting warning: "I know that God has determined to destroy you because you have worshiped these idols, and have not accepted my counsel."

17King Amaziah of Judah now took the advice of his counselors and declared war on King Joash of Israel (son of Jehoahaz, grandson of Jehu).

18King Joash replied with this parable: "Out in the Lebanon mountains a thistle demanded of a cedar tree, 'Give your daughter in marriage to my son.' Just then a wild animal came by and stepped on the thistle, crushing it! 19You are very proud about your conquest of Edom, but my advice is to stay home and don't meddle with me, lest you and all Judah get badly hurt."

20But Amaziah wouldn't listen, for God was arranging to destroy him for worshiping the gods of Edom. 21The armies met at Beth-shemesh, in Judah, 22and Judah was defeated, and its army fled home. 23King Joash of Israel captured the defeated King Amaziah of Judah and took him as a prisoner to Jerusalem. Then King Joash ordered two hundred yards of the walls of Jerusalem dismantled, from the gate of Ephraim to the Corner Gate. 24He carried off all the treasures

and gold bowls from the Temple, as well as the treasures from the palace; and he took hostages, including Obed-edom, and returned to Samaria.

25However, King Amaziah of Judah lived on for fifteen years after the death of King Joash of Israel. 26The complete biography of King Amaziah is written in *The Annals of the Kings of Judah and Israel.* 27This account includes a report of Amaziah's turning away from God, and how his people conspired against him in Jerusalem, and how he fled to Lachish—but they went after him and killed him there. 28And they brought him back on horses to Jerusalem and buried him in the royal cemetery.

ROMANS 12:1–21

AND so, dear brothers, I plead with you to give your bodies to God. Let them be a living sacrifice, holy—the kind he can accept. When you think of what he has done for you, is this too much to ask? 2Don't copy the behavior and customs of this world, but be a new and different person with a fresh newness in all you do and think. Then you will learn from your own experience how his ways will really satisfy you.

3As God's messenger I give each of you God's warning: Be honest in your estimate of yourselves, measuring your value by how much faith God has given you. 4,5Just as there are many parts to our bodies, so it is with Christ's body. We are all parts of it, and it takes every one of us to make it complete, for we each have different work to do. So we belong to each other, and each needs all the others.

6God has given each of us the ability to do certain things well. So if God has given you the ability to prophesy, then prophesy whenever you can—as often as your faith is strong enough to receive a message from God. 7If your gift is that of serving others, serve them well. If you are a teacher, do a good job of teaching. 8If you are a preacher, see to it that your sermons are strong and helpful. If God has given you money, be generous in helping others with it. If God has given you administrative ability and put you in charge of the work of others, take the responsibility seriously. Those who offer comfort to the sorrowing should do so with Christian cheer.

9Don't just pretend that you love others: really love them. Hate what is wrong. Stand on the side of the good. 10Love each other with brotherly affection and take delight in honoring each other. 11Never be lazy in your work but serve the Lord enthusiastically.

12Be glad for all God is planning for you. Be patient in trouble, and prayerful always. 13When God's children are in need, you be the one to help them out. And get into the habit of inviting guests home for dinner or, if they need lodging, for the night.

14If someone mistreats you because you are a Christian, don't curse him; pray that God will bless him. 15When others are happy, be happy with them. If they are sad, share their sorrow. 16Work happily together. Don't try to act big. Don't try to get into the good graces of important people, but enjoy the company of ordinary folks. And don't think you know it all!

17Never pay back evil for evil. Do things in such a way that everyone can see you are honest clear through. 18Don't quarrel with anyone. Be at peace with everyone, just as much as possible.

19Dear friends, never avenge yourselves. Leave that to God, for he has said that he will repay those who deserve it. [Don't take the law into your own hands.] 20Instead, feed your enemy if he is hungry. If he is thirsty give him something to drink and you will be "heaping coals of fire on his head." In other words, he will feel ashamed of himself for what he has done to you. 21Don't let evil get the upper hand but conquer evil by doing good.

PSALM 22:19–31

O Lord, don't stay away. O God my Strength, hurry to my aid. 20Rescue me from death; spare my precious life from all these evil men. 21Save me from these lions' jaws and from the horns of these wild oxen. Yes, God will answer me and rescue me.

22I will praise you to all my brothers; I will stand up before the congregation and testify of the wonderful things you have done. 23"Praise the Lord, each one of you who fears him," I will say. "Each of you must fear and reverence his name. Let all Israel sing his praises, 24for he has not despised my cries of deep despair; he has not turned and walked away. When I cried to him, he heard and came."

25Yes, I will stand and praise you before all the people. I will publicly fulfill my vows in the presence of all who reverence your name.

26The poor shall eat and be satisfied; all who seek the Lord shall find him and shall praise his name. Their hearts shall rejoice with everlasting joy. 27The whole earth shall see it and return to the Lord; the people of every nation shall worship him.

28For the Lord is King and rules the nations. 29Both proud and humble together, all who are mortal—born to die—shall worship him. 30Our children too shall serve him, for they shall hear from us about the wonders of the Lord; 31generations yet unborn shall hear of all the miracles he did for us.

PROVERBS FOR TODAY/ 20:8–10

A king sitting as judge weighs all the evidence carefully, distinguishing the true from false. Who can ever say, "I have cleansed my heart; I am sinless"? The Lord despises every kind of cheating.

2 CHRONICLES 26:1—28:27

THE people of Judah now crowned sixteen-year-old Uzziah as their new king. 2After his father's death, he rebuilt the city of Eloth and restored it to Judah. 3In all, he reigned fifty-two years, in Jerusalem. His mother's name was Jecoliah, from Jerusalem. 4He followed in the footsteps of his father Amaziah, and was, in general, a good king in the Lord's sight.

5While Zechariah was alive Uzziah was always eager to please God. Zechariah was a man who had special revelations from God. And as long as the king followed the paths of God, he prospered, for God blessed him.

6He declared war on the Philistines and captured the city of Gath and broke down its walls, also those of Jabneh and Ashdod. Then he built new cities in the Ashdod area and in other parts of the Philistine country. 7God helped him not only with his wars against the Philistines but also in his battles with the Arabs of Gurbaal and in his wars with the Meunites. 8The Ammonites paid annual tribute to him, and his fame spread even to Egypt, for he was very powerful.

9He built fortified towers in Jerusalem at the Corner Gate, and the Valley Gate, and at the turning of the wall. 10He also constructed forts in the Negeb, and made many water reservoirs, for he had great herds of cattle out in the valleys and on the plains. He was a man who loved the soil and had many farms and vineyards, both on the hillsides and in the fertile valleys.

11He organized his army into regiments to which men were drafted under quotas set by Je-iel, the secretary of the army, and his assistant, Ma-aseiah. The commander-in-chief was General Hananiah. 12Twenty-six hundred brave clan leaders commanded these regiments. 13The army consisted of 307,500 men, all elite troops. 14Uzziah issued to them shields, spears, helmets, coats of mail, bows, and slingstones. 15And he produced engines of war manufactured in Jerusalem, invented by brilliant men to shoot arrows and huge stones from the towers and battlements. So he became very famous, for the Lord helped him wonderfully until he was very powerful.

16But at that point he became proud— and corrupt. He sinned against the Lord his God by entering the forbidden sanctuary of the Temple and personally burning incense upon the altar. 17,18Azariah the High Priest went in after him with eighty other priests, all brave men, and demanded that he get out.

"It is not for you, Uzziah, to burn incense," they declared. "That is the work of the priests alone, the sons of Aaron who are consecrated to this work. Get out, for you have trespassed, and the Lord is not going to honor you for this!"

19Uzziah was furious, and refused to set down the incense burner he was holding. But look! Suddenly—leprosy appeared in his forehead! 20When Azariah and the others saw it, they rushed him out; in fact, he himself was as anxious to get out as they were to get him out, because the Lord had struck him.

21So King Uzziah was a leper until the day of his death and lived in isolation, cut off from his people and from the Temple. His son Jotham became vice-regent, in charge of the king's affairs and of the judging of the people of the land.

22The other details of Uzziah's reign from first to last are recorded by the prophet Isaiah (son of Amoz). 23When Uzziah died, he was buried in the royal cemetery even though he was a leper, and his son Jotham became the new king.

JOTHAM was twenty-five years old at the time he became king, and he reigned sixteen years, in Jerusalem. His mother was

Jerushah, daughter of Zadok. ²He followed the generally good example of his father Uzziah—who had, however, sinned by invading the Temple—but even so his people became very corrupt.

³He built the Upper Gate of the Temple, and also did extensive rebuilding of the walls on the hill where the Temple was situated. ⁴And he built cities in the hill country of Judah, and erected fortresses and towers on the wooded hills.

⁵His war against the Ammonites was successful, so that for the next three years he received from them an annual tribute of $200,000 in silver, 10,000 sacks of wheat, and 10,000 sacks of barley. ⁶King Jotham became powerful because he was careful to follow the path of the Lord his God.

⁷The remainder of his history, including his wars and other activities, is written in *The Annals of the Kings of Israel and Judah.* ⁸In summary, then, he was twenty-five years old when he began to reign and he reigned sixteen years, in Jerusalem. ⁹When he died, he was buried in Jerusalem, and his son Ahaz became the new king.

AHAZ was twenty years old when he became king and he reigned sixteen years, in Jerusalem. But he was an evil king, unlike his ancestor King David. ²For he followed the example of the kings over in Israel and worshiped the idols of Baal. ³He even went out to the Valley of Hinnom, and it was not just to burn incense to the idols, for he even sacrificed his own children in the fire, just like the heathen nations that were thrown out of the land by the Lord to make room for Israel. ⁴Yes, he sacrificed and burned incense at the idol shrines on the hills and under every green tree.

⁵That is why the Lord God allowed the king of Syria to defeat him and deport large numbers of his people to Damascus. The armies from Israel also slaughtered great numbers of his troops. ⁶On a single day, Pekah, the son of Rema-

liah, killed 120,000 of his bravest soldiers because they had turned away from the Lord God of their fathers. ⁷Then Zichri, a great warrior from Ephraim, killed the king's son Ma-aseiah, and the king's administrator Azrikam, and the king's second-in-command Elkanah. ⁸The armies from Israel also captured 200,000 Judean women and children, and tremendous amounts of booty which they took to Samaria.

⁹But Oded, a prophet of the Lord, was there in Samaria and he went out to meet the returning army.

"Look!" he exclaimed. "The Lord God of your fathers was angry with Judah and let you capture them, but you have butchered them without mercy, and all heaven is disturbed. ¹⁰And now are you going to make slaves of these people from Judah and Jerusalem? What about your own sins against the Lord your God? ¹¹Listen to me and return these relatives of yours to their homes, for now the fierce anger of the Lord is upon *you.*"

¹²Some of the top leaders of Ephraim also added their opposition. These men were Azariah the son of Johanan, Berechiah the son of Meshillemoth, Jehizkiah the son of Shallum, and Amasa the son of Hadlai.

¹³"You must not bring the captives here!" they declared. "If you do, the Lord will be angry, and this sin will be added to our many others. We are in enough trouble with God as it is."

¹⁴So the army officers turned over the captives and booty to the political leaders to decide what to do. ¹⁵Then the four men already mentioned distributed captured stores of clothing to the women and children who needed it, and gave them shoes, food, and wine, and put those who were sick and old on donkeys, and took them back to their families in Jericho, the City of Palm Trees. Then their escorts returned to Samaria.

¹⁶About that time King Ahaz of Judah asked the king of Assyria to be his ally in his war against the armies of Edom. For Edom was invading Judah and capturing many people as slaves. ¹⁷,¹⁸Mean-

while, the Philistines had invaded the lowland cities and the Negeb and had already captured Beth-shemesh, Aijalon, Gederoth, Soco, Timnah, and Gimzo with their surrounding villages, and were living there. ¹⁹For the Lord brought Judah very low on account of the evil deeds of King Ahaz of Israel, for he had destroyed the spiritual fiber of Judah and had been faithless to the Lord. ²⁰But when Tilgath-pilneser, king of Assyria, arrived, he caused trouble for King Ahaz instead of helping him. ²¹So even though Ahaz had given him the Temple gold and the palace treasures, it did no good.

²²In this time of deep trial, King Ahaz collapsed spiritually. ²³He sacrificed to the gods of the people of Damascus who had defeated him, for he felt that since these gods had helped the kings of Syria, they would help him too if he sacrificed to them. But instead, they were his ruin, and that of all his people. ²⁴The king took the gold bowls from the Temple and slashed them to pieces, and nailed the door of the Temple shut so that no one could worship there, and made altars to the heathen gods in every corner of Jerusalem. ²⁵And he did the same in every city of Judah, thus angering the Lord God of his fathers.

²⁶The other details of his life and activities are recorded in *The Annals of the Kings of Judah and Israel.* ²⁷When King Ahaz died, he was buried in Jerusalem but not in the royal tombs, and his son Hezekiah became the new king.

ROMANS 13:1–14

O BEY the government, for God is the one who has put it there. There is no government anywhere that God has not placed in power. ²So those who refuse to obey the laws of the land are refusing to obey God, and punishment will follow. ³For the policeman does not frighten people who are doing right; but those doing evil will always fear him. So if you don't want to be afraid, keep the laws and you will get along well. ⁴The policeman is sent by God to help you. But if you are doing something wrong, of course you should be afraid, for he will have you punished. He is sent by God for that very purpose. ⁵Obey the laws, then, for two reasons: first, to keep from being punished, and second, just because you know you should.

⁶Pay your taxes too, for these same two reasons. For government workers need to be paid so that they can keep on doing God's work, serving you. ⁷Pay everyone whatever he ought to have: pay your taxes and import duties gladly, obey those over you, and give honor and respect to all those to whom it is due.

⁸Pay all your debts except the debt of love for others—never finish paying that! For if you love them, you will be obeying all of God's laws, fulfilling all his requirements. ⁹If you love your neighbor as much as you love yourself you will not want to harm or cheat him, or kill him or steal from him. And you won't sin with his wife or want what is his, or do anything else the Ten Commandments say is wrong. All ten are wrapped up in this one, to love your neighbor as you love yourself. ¹⁰Love does no wrong to anyone. That's why it fully satisfies all of God's requirements. It is the only law you need.

¹¹Another reason for right living is this: you know how late it is; time is running out. Wake up, for the coming of the Lord is nearer now than when we first believed. ¹²,¹³The night is far gone, the day of his return will soon be here. So quit the evil deeds of darkness and put on the armor of right living, as we who live in the daylight should! Be decent and true in everything you do so that all can approve your behavior. Don't spend your time in wild parties and getting drunk or in adultery and lust, or fighting, or jealousy. ¹⁴But ask the Lord Jesus Christ to help you live as you should, and don't make plans to enjoy evil.

PSALM 23:1–6

BECAUSE the Lord is my Shepherd, I have everything I need! 2,3He lets me rest in the meadow grass and leads me beside the quiet streams. He gives me new strength. He helps me do what honors him the most.

4Even when walking through the dark valley of death I will not be afraid, for you are close beside me, guarding, guiding all the way.

5You provide delicious food for me in the presence of my enemies. You have welcomed me as your guest; blessings overflow!

6Your goodness and unfailing kindness shall be with me all of my life, and afterwards I will live with you forever in your home.

PROVERBS FOR TODAY/ 20:11

The character of even a child can be known by the way he acts—whether what he does is pure and right.

JULY 31

2 CHRONICLES 29:1–36

HEZEKIAH was twenty-five years old when he became the king of Judah, and he reigned twenty-nine years, in Jerusalem. His mother's name was Abijah, the daughter of Zechariah. 2His reign was generally good in the Lord's sight, just as his ancestor David's had been.

3In the very first month of the first year of his reign, he reopened the doors of the Temple and repaired them. 4,5He summoned the priests and Levites to meet him at the open space east of the Temple, and addressed them thus:

"Listen to me, you Levites. Sanctify yourselves and sanctify the Temple of the Lord God of your ancestors—clean all the debris from the holy place. 6For our fathers have committed a deep sin before the Lord our God; they abandoned the Lord and his Temple and turned their backs on it. 7The doors have been shut tight, the perpetual flame has been put out, and the incense and burnt offerings have not been offered. 8Therefore the wrath of the Lord has been upon Judah and Jerusalem. He has caused us to be objects of horror, amazement, and contempt, as you see us today. 9Our fathers have been killed in war, and our sons and daughters and wives are in captivity because of this.

10"But now I want to make a covenant with the Lord God of Israel so that his fierce anger will turn away from us. 11My children, don't neglect your duties any longer, for the Lord has chosen you to minister to him and to burn incense."

12,13,14Then the Levites went into action:

From the Kohath clan, Mahath (son of Amasai) and Joel (son of Azariah);

From the Merari clan, Kish (son of Abdi) and Azariah (son of Jehallelel);

From the Gershon clan, Joah (son of Zimmah) and Eden (son of Joah).

From the Elizaphan clan, Shimri and Jeuel;

From the Asaph clan, Zechariah and Mattaniah;

From the Hemanite clan, Jehuel and Shime-i;

From the Jeduthun clan, Shemaiah and Uzziel.

15They in turn summoned their fellow Levites and sanctified themselves, and began to clean up and sanctify the Temple, as the king (who was speaking for the Lord) had commanded them. ¹⁶The priests cleaned up the inner room of the Temple, and brought out into the court all the filth and decay they found there. The Levites then carted it out to the brook Kidron. ¹⁷This all began on the first day of April, and by the eighth day they had reached the outer court, which took eight days to clean up, so the entire job was completed in sixteen days.

¹⁸Then they went back to the palace and reported to King Hezekiah, "We have completed the cleansing of the Temple and of the altar of burnt offerings and of its accessories, also the table of the Bread of the Presence and its equipment. ¹⁹What's more, we have recovered and sanctified all the utensils thrown away by King Ahaz when he closed the Temple. They are beside the altar of the Lord."

²⁰Early the next morning, King Hezekiah went to the Temple with the city officials, ²¹taking seven young bulls, seven rams, seven lambs, and seven male goats for a sin offering for the nation and for the Temple.

He instructed the priests, the sons of Aaron, to sacrifice them on the altar of the Lord. ²²So they killed the young bulls, and the priests took the blood and sprinkled it on the altar, and they killed the rams and sprinkled their blood upon the altar, and did the same with the lambs. ²³The male goats for the sin offering were then brought before the king and his officials, who laid their hands upon them. ²⁴Then the priests killed the animals and made a sin offering with their blood upon the altar, to make atonement for all Israel as the king had commanded—for the king had specified that the burnt offering and sin offering must be sacrificed for the entire nation.

²⁵,²⁶He organized Levites at the Temple into an orchestral group, using cymbals, psalteries, and harps. This was in accordance with the directions of David and the prophets Gad and Nathan—who had received their instructions from the

Lord. The priests formed a trumpet corps. ²⁷Then Hezekiah ordered the burnt offering to be placed upon the altar, and as the sacrifice began, the instruments of music began to play the songs of the Lord, accompanied by the trumpets. ²⁸Throughout the entire ceremony everyone worshiped the Lord as the singers sang and the trumpets blew. ²⁹Afterwards the king and his aides bowed low before the Lord in worship. ³⁰Then King Hezekiah ordered the Levites to sing before the Lord some of the psalms of David and of the prophet Asaph, which they gladly did, and bowed their heads and worshiped.

³¹"The consecration ceremony is now ended," Hezekiah said. "Now bring your sacrifices and thank offerings." So the people from every part of the nation brought their sacrifices and thank offerings, and those who wished to, brought burnt offerings too. ³²,³³In all, there were 70 young bulls for burnt offerings, 100 rams, and 200 lambs. In addition, 600 oxen and 3,000 sheep were brought as holy gifts. ³⁴But there were too few priests to prepare the burnt offerings, so their brothers the Levites helped them until the work was finished—and until more priests had reported to work—for the Levites were much more ready to sanctify themselves than the priests were. ³⁵There was an abundance of burnt offerings, and the usual drink offering with each, and many peace offerings. So it was that the Temple was restored to service, and the sacrifices offered again. ³⁶And Hezekiah and all the people were very happy because of what God had accomplished so quickly.

ROMANS 14:1-23

GIVE a warm welcome to any brother who wants to join you, even though his faith is weak. Don't criticize him for having different ideas from yours about what is right and wrong. ²For instance, don't argue with him about whether or not to eat meat that has been offered to idols. You may believe there is no harm in this, but the faith of others is weaker; they think it is wrong, and will go without any meat at all and eat vegetables rather than eat that kind of meat. 3Those who think it is all right to eat such meat must not look down on those who won't. And if you are one of those who won't, don't find fault with those who do. For God has accepted them to be his children. 4They are God's servants, not yours. They are responsible to him, not to you. Let him tell them whether they are right or wrong. And God is able to make them do as they should.

5Some think that Christians should observe the Jewish holidays as special days to worship God, but others say it is wrong and foolish to go to all that trouble, for every day alike belongs to God. On questions of this kind everyone must decide for himself. 6If you have special days for worshiping the Lord, you are trying to honor him; you are doing a good thing. So is the person who eats meat that has been offered to idols; he is thankful to the Lord for it; he is doing right. And the person who won't touch such meat, he, too, is anxious to please the Lord, and is thankful. 7We are not our own bosses to live or die as we ourselves might choose. 8Living or dying we follow the Lord. Either way we are his. 9Christ died and rose again for this very purpose, so that he can be our Lord both while we live and when we die.

10You have no right to criticize your brother or look down on him. Remember, each of us will stand personally before the Judgment Seat of God. 11For it is written, "As I live," says the Lord, "every knee shall bow to me and every tongue confess to God." 12Yes, each of us will give an account of himself to God.

13So don't criticize each other any more. Try instead to live in such a way that you will never make your brother stumble by letting him see you doing something he thinks is wrong.

14As for myself, I am perfectly sure on the authority of the Lord Jesus that there is nothing really wrong with eating meat that has been offered to idols. But if someone believes it is wrong, then he shouldn't do it because for him it is wrong. 15And if your brother is bothered by what you eat, you are not acting in love if you go ahead and eat it. Don't let your eating ruin someone for whom Christ died. 16Don't do anything that will cause criticism against yourself even though you know that what you do is right.

17For, after all, the important thing for us as Christians is not what we eat or drink but stirring up goodness and peace and joy from the Holy Spirit. 18If you let Christ be Lord in these affairs, God will be glad; and so will others. 19In this way aim for harmony in the church and try to build each other up.

20Don't undo the work of God for a chunk of meat. Remember, there is nothing wrong with the meat, but it is wrong to eat it if it makes another stumble. 21The right thing to do is to quit eating meat or drinking wine or doing anything else that offends your brother or makes him sin. 22You may know that there is nothing wrong with what you do, even from God's point of view, but keep it to yourself; don't flaunt your faith in front of others who might be hurt by it. In this situation, happy is the man who does not sin by doing what he knows is right. 23But anyone who believes that something he wants to do is wrong shouldn't do it. He sins if he does, for he thinks it is wrong, and so for him it *is* wrong. Anything that is done apart from what he feels is right is sin.

PSALM 24:1–10

THE earth belongs to God! Everything in all the world is his! 2He is the one who pushed the oceans back to let dry land appear.

3Who may climb the mountain of the Lord and enter where he lives? Who may stand before the Lord? 4Only those with pure hands and hearts, who do not practice dishonesty and lying. 5They will receive God's own goodness as their blessing from him, planted in their lives by God himself, their Savior. 6These are the ones who are allowed to stand before the Lord and worship the God of Jacob.

7Open up, O ancient gates, and let the King of Glory in. 8Who is this King of Glory? The Lord, strong and mighty, invincible in battle. 9Yes, open wide the gates and let the King of Glory in.

10Who is this King of Glory? The Commander of all of heaven's armies!

PROVERBS FOR TODAY/ 20:12

If you have good eyesight and good hearing, thank God who gave them to you.

AUGUST 1

2 CHRONICLES 30:1—31:21

KING Hezekiah now sent letters throughout all of Israel, Judah, Ephraim, and Manasseh, inviting everyone to come to the Temple at Jerusalem for the annual Passover celebration. 2,3The king, his aides, and all the assembly of Jerusalem had voted to celebrate the Passover in May this time, rather than at the normal time in April, because not enough priests were sanctified at the earlier date, and there wasn't enough time to get notices out. 4The king and his advisors were in complete agreement in this matter, 5so they sent a Passover proclamation throughout Israel, from Dan to Beer-sheba, inviting everyone. They had not kept it in great numbers as prescribed.

6"Come back to the Lord God of Abraham, Isaac, and Israel," the king's letter said, "so that he will return to us who have escaped from the power of the kings of Assyria. 7Do not be like your fathers and brothers who sinned against the Lord God of their fathers and were destroyed. 8Do not be stubborn, as they were, but yield yourselves to the Lord and come to his Temple which he has sanctified forever, and worship the Lord your God so that his fierce anger will turn away from you. 9For if you turn to the Lord again, your brothers and your children will be treated mercifully by their captors,

and they will be able to return to this land. For the Lord your God is full of kindness and mercy and will not continue to turn away his face from you if you return to him."

10So the messengers went from city to city throughout Ephraim and Manasseh and as far as Zebulun. But for the most part they were received with laughter and scorn! 11However, some from the tribes of Asher, Manasseh, and Zebulun turned to God and came to Jerusalem. 12But in Judah the entire nation felt a strong, God-given desire to obey the Lord's direction as commanded by the king and his officers. 13And so it was that a very large crowd assembled at Jerusalem in the month of May for the Passover celebration. 14They set to work and destroyed the heathen altars in Jerusalem, and knocked down all the incense altars, and threw them into Kidron Brook.

15On the first day of May the people killed their Passover lambs. Then the priests and Levites became ashamed of themselves for not taking a more active part, so they sanctified themselves and brought burnt offerings into the Temple. 16They stood at their posts as instructed by the law of Moses the man of God; and the priests sprinkled the blood received from the Levites.

17,18,19Since many of the people arriving from Ephraim, Manasseh, Issachar, and Zebulun were ceremonially impure because they had not undergone the purification rites, the Levites killed their Passover lambs for them, to sanctify them. Then King Hezekiah prayed for them and they were permitted to eat the Passover anyway, even though this was contrary to God's rules. But Hezekiah said, "May the good Lord pardon everyone who determines to follow the Lord God of his fathers, even though he is not properly sanctified for the ceremony." 20And the Lord listened to Hezekiah's prayer and did not destroy them.

21So the people of Israel celebrated the Passover at Jerusalem for seven days with great joy.

Meanwhile the Levites and priests praised the Lord with music and cymbals day after day. 22(King Hezekiah spoke very appreciatively to the Levites of their excellent music.)

So, for seven days the observance continued, and peace offerings were sacrificed, and the people confessed their sins to the Lord God of their fathers. 23The enthusiasm continued, so it was unanimously decided to continue the observance for another seven days. 24King Hezekiah gave the people 1,000 young bulls for offerings, and 7,000 sheep; and the princes donated 1,000 young bulls and 10,000 sheep. And at this time another large group of priests stepped forward and sanctified themselves.

25Then the people of Judah, together with the priests, the Levites, the foreign residents, and the visitors from Israel, were filled with deep joy. 26For Jerusalem hadn't seen a celebration like this one since the days of King David's son Solomon. 27Then the priests and Levites stood and blessed the people, and the Lord heard their prayers from his holy temple in heaven.

AFTERWARDS a massive campaign against idol worship was begun. Those who were at Jerusalem for the Passover went out to the cities of Judah, Benjamin, Ephraim, and Manasseh and tore down the idol altars, the obelisks, shame-images, and other heathen centers of worship. Then the people who had come to the Passover from the northern tribes returned again to their own homes.

2Hezekiah now organized the priests and Levites into service corps to offer the burnt offerings and peace offerings, and to worship and give thanks and praise to the Lord. 3He also made a personal contribution of animals for the daily morning and evening burnt offerings, as well as for the weekly Sabbath and monthly new moon festivals, and for the other annual feasts as required in the law of God.

4In addition, he required the people in Jerusalem to bring their tithes to the priests and Levites, so that they wouldn't need other employment but could apply themselves fully to their duties as required in the law of God. 5,6The people responded immediately and generously with the first of their crops and grain, new wine, olive oil, money, and everything else—a tithe of all they owned, as required by law to be given to the Lord their God. Everything was laid out in great piles. The people who had moved to Judah from the northern tribes and the people of Judah living in the provinces also brought in the tithes of their cattle and sheep, and brought a tithe of the dedicated things to give to the Lord and piled them up in great heaps. 7,8The first of these tithes arrived in June, and the piles continued to grow until October. When Hezekiah and his officials came and saw these huge piles, how they blessed the Lord and praised his people!

9"Where did all this come from?" Hezekiah asked the priests and Levites.

10And Azariah the High Priest from the clan of Zadok replied, "These are tithes! We have been eating from these stores of food for many weeks, but all this is left over, for the Lord has blessed his people."

11Hezekiah decided to prepare storerooms in the Temple. 12,13All the dedicated supplies were brought into the

Lord's house. Conaniah, the Levite, was put in charge, assisted by his brother Shime-i and the following aides:

Jehiel, Azaziah, Nahath, Asahel, Jerimoth, Jozabad, Eliel, Ismachiah, Mahath, Benaiah.

These appointments were made by King Hezekiah and Azariah the High Priest.

14,15Kore (son of Imnah, the Levite), who was the gatekeeper at the East Gate, was put in charge of distributing the offerings to the priests. His faithful assistants were Eden, Miniamin, Jeshua, Shemaiah, Amariah, and Shecaniah. They distributed the gifts to the clans of priests in their cities, dividing it to young and old alike. 16However, the priests on duty at the Temple and their families were supplied directly from there, so they were not included in this distribution. 17,18The priests were listed in the genealogical register by clans, and the Levites twenty years old and older were listed under the names of their work corps. A regular food allotment was given to all families of properly registered priests, for they had no other source of income because their time and energies were devoted to the service of the Temple. 19One of the priests was appointed in each of the cities of the priests to issue food and other supplies to all priests in the area, and to all registered Levites. 20In this way King Hezekiah handled the distribution throughout all Judah, doing what was just and fair in the sight of the Lord his God. 21He worked very hard to encourage respect for the Temple, the law, and godly living, and was very successful.

ROMANS 15:1–22

EVEN if we believe that it makes no difference to the Lord whether we do these things, still we cannot just go ahead and do them to please ourselves; for we must bear the "burden" of being considerate of the doubts and fears of others—of those who feel these things are wrong. Let's please the other fellow, not ourselves, and do what is for his good and thus build him up in the Lord. 3Christ didn't please himself. As the Psalmist said, "He came for the very purpose of suffering under the insults of those who were against the Lord." 4These things that were written in the Scriptures so long ago are to teach us patience and to encourage us, so that we will look forward expectantly to the time when God will conquer sin and death.

5May God who gives patience, steadiness, and encouragement help you to live in complete harmony with each other—each with the attitude of Christ toward the other. 6And then all of us can praise the Lord together with one voice, giving glory to God, the Father of our Lord Jesus Christ.

7So, warmly welcome each other into the church, just as Christ has warmly welcomed you; then God will be glorified. 8Remember that Jesus Christ came to show that God is true to his promises and to help the Jews. 9And remember that he came also that the Gentiles might be saved and give glory to God for his mercies to them. That is what the Psalmist meant when he wrote: "I will praise you among the Gentiles, and sing to your name."

10And in another place, "Be glad, O you Gentiles, along with his people the Jews."

11And yet again, "Praise the Lord, O you Gentiles, let everyone praise him."

12And the prophet Isaiah said, "There shall be an Heir in the house of Jesse, and he will be King over the Gentiles; they will pin their hopes on him alone."

13So I pray for you Gentiles that God who gives you hope will keep you happy and full of peace as you believe in him. I pray that God will help you overflow with hope in him through the Holy Spirit's power within you.

14I know that you are wise and good, my brothers, and that you know these things so well that you are able to teach others all about them. 15,16But even so I have been bold enough to emphasize some of these points, knowing that all you need is this reminder from me; for I am, by God's grace, a special messenger from Jesus Christ to you Gentiles, bringing you the Gospel and offering you up as a fragrant sacrifice to God; for you have been made pure and pleasing to him by the Holy Spirit. 17So it is right for me to be a little proud of all Christ Jesus has done through me. 18I dare not judge how effectively he has used others, but I know this: he has used me to win the Gentiles to God. 19I have won them by my message and by the good way I have lived before them, and by the miracles done through me as signs from God—all by the Holy Spirit's power. In this way I have preached the full Gospel of Christ all the way from Jerusalem clear over into Illyricum.

20But all the while my ambition has been to go still farther, preaching where the name of Christ has never yet been heard, rather than where a church has already been started by someone else. 21I have been following the plan spoken of in the Scriptures where Isaiah says that those who have never heard the name of Christ before will see and understand. 22In fact that is the very reason I have been so long in coming to visit you.

PSALM 25:1–11

TO you, O Lord, I pray. 2Don't fail me, Lord, for I am trusting you. Don't let my enemies succeed. Don't give them victory over me. 3None of those who have faith in God will ever be disgraced for trusting him. But all who harm the innocent shall be defeated.

4Show me the path where I should go, O Lord; point out the right road for me to walk. 5Lead me; teach me; for you are the God who gives me salvation. I have no hope except in you. 6,7Overlook my youthful sins, O Lord! Look at me instead through eyes of mercy and forgiveness, through eyes of everlasting love and kindness.

8The Lord is good and glad to teach the proper path to all who go astray; 9he will teach the ways that are right and best to those who humbly turn to him. 10And when we obey him, every path he guides us on is fragrant with his lovingkindness and his truth.

11But Lord, my sins! How many they are. Oh, pardon them for the honor of your name.

PROVERBS FOR TODAY/ 20:13–15

If you love sleep, you will end in poverty. Stay awake, work hard, and there will be plenty to eat! "Utterly worthless!" says the buyer as he haggles over the price. But afterwards he brags about his bargain! Good sense is far more valuable than gold or precious jewels.

AUGUST 2

2 CHRONICLES 32:1—33:13

SOME time later, after this good work of King Hezekiah, King Sennacherib of Assyria invaded Judah and laid siege to the fortified cities, planning to place them under tribute. 2When it was clear that Sennacherib was intending to attack Jerusalem, 3Hezekiah summoned his princes and officers for a council of war, and it was decided to plug the springs outside the city. 4They organized a huge work crew to block them, and to cut off the brook running through the fields.

"Why should the king of Assyria come and find water?" they asked.

⁵Then Hezekiah further strengthened his defenses by repairing the wall wherever it was broken down and by adding to the fortifications, and constructing a second wall outside it. He also reinforced Fort Millo in the City of David, and manufactured large numbers of weapons and shields. ⁶He recruited an army and appointed officers and summoned them to the plains before the city, and encouraged them with this address:

⁷"Be strong, be brave, and do not be afraid of the king of Assyria or his mighty army, for there is someone with us who is far greater than he is! ⁸He has a great army, but they are all mere men, while we have the Lord our God to fight our battles for us!" This greatly encouraged them.

⁹Then King Sennacherib of Assyria, while still besieging the city of Lachish, sent ambassadors with this message to King Hezekiah and the citizens of Jerusalem:

¹⁰"King Sennacherib of Assyria asks, 'Do you think you can survive my siege of Jerusalem? ¹¹King Hezekiah is trying to persuade you to commit suicide by staying there—to die by famine and thirst—while he promises that "the Lord our God will deliver us from the king of Assyria"! ¹²Don't you realize that Hezekiah is the very person who destroyed all the idols, and commanded Judah and Jerusalem to use only the one altar at the Temple, and to burn incense upon it alone? ¹³Don't you realize that I and the other kings of Assyria before me have never yet failed to conquer a nation we attacked? The gods of those nations weren't able to do a thing to save their lands! ¹⁴Name just one time when anyone, anywhere, was able to resist us successfully. What makes you think your God can do any better? ¹⁵Don't let Hezekiah fool you! Don't believe him. I say it again—no god of any nation has ever yet been able to rescue his people from me or my ancestors; how much less your God!' " ¹⁶Thus the ambassador mocked the Lord God and God's servant Hezekiah, heaping up insults.

¹⁷King Sennacherib also sent letters scorning the Lord God of Israel.

"The gods of all the other nations failed to save their people from my hand, and the God of Hezekiah will fail, too," he wrote.

¹⁸The messengers who brought the letters shouted threats in the Jewish language to the people gathered on the walls of the city, trying to frighten and dishearten them. ¹⁹These messengers talked about the God of Jerusalem just as though he were one of the heathen gods—a handmade idol!

²⁰Then King Hezekiah and Isaiah the prophet (son of Amoz) cried out in prayer to God in heaven, ²¹and the Lord sent an angel who destroyed the Assyrian army with all its officers and generals! So Sennacherib returned home in deep shame to his own land. And when he arrived at the temple of his god, some of his own sons killed him there. ²²That is how the Lord saved Hezekiah and the people of Jerusalem. And now there was peace at last throughout his realm.

²³From then on King Hezekiah became immensely respected among the surrounding nations, and many gifts for the Lord arrived at Jerusalem, with valuable presents for King Hezekiah, too.

²⁴But about that time Hezekiah became deathly sick, and he prayed to the Lord, and the Lord replied with a miracle. ²⁵However, Hezekiah didn't respond with true thanksgiving and praise, for he had become proud, and so the anger of God was upon him and upon Judah and Jerusalem. ²⁶But finally Hezekiah and the residents of Jerusalem humbled themselves, so the wrath of the Lord did not fall upon them during Hezekiah's lifetime.

²⁷So Hezekiah became very wealthy and was highly honored. He had to construct special treasury buildings for his silver, gold, precious stones, and spices, and for his shields and gold bowls.

²⁸,²⁹He also built many storehouses for his grain, new wine, and olive oil, with many stalls for his animals, and folds for the great flocks of sheep and goats he purchased; and he acquired many towns, for God had given him great wealth. ³⁰He dammed up the Upper Spring of Gihon and brought the water down through an aqueduct to the west side of the City of David sector in Jerusalem. He prospered in everything he did.

³¹However, when ambassadors arrived from Babylon to find out about the miracle of his being healed, God left him to himself in order to test him and to see what he was really like.

³²The rest of the story of Hezekiah and all of the good things he did are written in *The Book of Isaiah* (the prophet, the son of Amoz), and in *The Annals of the Kings of Judah and Israel.* ³³When Hezekiah died he was buried in the royal hillside cemetery among the other kings, and all Judah and Jerusalem honored him at his death. Then his son Manasseh became the new king.

MANASSEH was only twelve years old when he became king, and he reigned fifty-five years, in Jerusalem. ²But it was an evil reign, for he encouraged his people to worship the idols of the heathen nations destroyed by the Lord when the people of Israel entered the land. ³He rebuilt the heathen altars his father Hezekiah had destroyed—the altars of Baal, and of the shame-images, and of the sun, moon, and stars. ⁴,⁵He even constructed heathen altars in both courts of the Temple of the Lord, for worshiping the sun, moon and stars—in the very place where the Lord had said that he would be honored forever. ⁶And Manasseh sacrificed his own children as burnt offerings in the Valley of Hinnom. He consulted spirit-mediums, too, and fortune-tellers and sorcerers, and encouraged every sort of evil, making the Lord very angry.

⁷Think of it! He placed an idol in the very Temple of God, where God had told David and his son Solomon, "I will be honored here in this Temple, and in Jerusalem—the city I have chosen to be honored forever above all the other cities of Israel. ⁸And if you will only obey my commands—all the laws and instructions given to you by Moses—I won't ever again exile Israel from this land which I gave your ancestors."

⁹But Manasseh encouraged the people of Judah and Jerusalem to do even more evil than the nations the Lord destroyed when Israel entered the land. ¹⁰Warnings from the Lord were ignored by both Manasseh and his people. ¹¹So God sent the Assyrian armies, and they seized him with hooks and bound him with bronze chains and carted him away to Babylon. ¹²Then at last he came to his senses and cried out humbly to God for help. ¹³And the Lord listened, and answered his plea by returning him to Jerusalem and to his kingdom! At that point Manasseh finally realized that the Lord was really God!

ROMANS 15:23—16:7

BUT now at last I am through with my work here, and I am ready to come after all these long years of waiting. ²⁴For I am planning to take a trip to Spain, and when I do, I will stop off there in Rome; and after we have had a good time together for a little while, you can send me on my way again.

²⁵But before I come, I must go down to Jerusalem to take a gift to the Jewish Christians there. ²⁶For you see, the Christians in Macedonia and Achaia have taken up an offering for those in Jerusalem who are going through such hard times. ²⁷They were very glad to do this, for they feel that they owe a real debt to the Jerusalem Christians. Why? Because the news about Christ came to these Gentiles from the church in Jerusalem. And since they received this wonderful spiritual gift of the Gospel from there, they feel that the least they can do in return is to give some material aid. ²⁸As soon as I have delivered this money and completed this good deed of

theirs, I will come to see you on my way to Spain. 29And I am sure that when I come the Lord will give me a great blessing for you.

30Will you be my prayer partners? For the Lord Jesus Christ's sake, and because of your love for me—given to you by the Holy Spirit—pray much with me for my work. 31Pray that I will be protected in Jerusalem from those who are not Christians. Pray also that the Christians there will be willing to accept the money I am bringing them. 32Then I will be able to come to you with a happy heart by the will of God, and we can refresh each other.

33And now may our God, who gives peace, be with you all. Amen.

PHOEBE, a dear Christian woman from the town of Cenchreae, will be coming to see you soon. She has worked hard in the church there. Receive her as your sister in the Lord, giving her a warm Christian welcome. Help her in every way you can, for she has helped many in their needs, including me. 3Tell Priscilla and Aquila "hello." They have been my fellow workers in the affairs of Christ Jesus. 4In fact, they risked their lives for me; and I am not the only one who is thankful to them: so are all the Gentile churches.

5Please give my greetings to all those who meet to worship in their home. Greet my good friend Epaenetus. He was the very first person to become a Christian in Asia. 6Remember me to Mary, too, who has worked so hard to help us. 7Then there are Andronicus and Junias, my relatives who were in prison with me. They are respected by the apostles, and became Christians before I did. Please give them my greetings.

PSALM 25:12–22

WHERE is the man who fears the Lord? God will teach him how to choose the best.

13He shall live within God's circle of blessing, and his children shall inherit the earth.

14Friendship with God is reserved for those who reverence him. With them alone he shares the secrets of his promises.

15My eyes are ever looking to the Lord for help, for he alone can rescue me. 16Come, Lord, and show me your mercy, for I am helpless, overwhelmed, in deep distress; 17my problems go from bad to worse. Oh, save me from them all! 18See my sorrows; feel my pain; forgive my sins. 19See how many enemies I have and how viciously they hate me! 20Save me from them! Deliver my life from their power! Oh, let it never be said that I trusted you in vain!

21Assign me Godliness and Integrity as my bodyguards, for I expect you to protect me 22and to ransom Israel from all her troubles.

PROVERBS FOR TODAY/ 20:16–18

It is risky to make loans to strangers! Some men enjoy cheating, but the cake they buy with such ill-gotten gain will turn to gravel in their mouths. Don't go ahead with your plans without the advice of others; don't go to war until they agree.

AUGUST 3

IT was after this that he rebuilt the outer wall of the City of David and the wall from west of the Spring of Gihon in the Kidron Valley, and then to the Fish Gate, and around Citadel Hill, where it was built very high. And he stationed his army generals in all of the fortified cities of Judah. 15He also removed the foreign gods from the hills and took his idol from the Temple and tore down the altars he had built on the mountain where the Temple stood, and the altars that were in Jerusalem, and dumped them outside the city. 16Then he rebuilt the altar of the Lord and offered sacrifices upon it—peace offerings and thanksgiving offerings—and demanded that the people of Judah worship the Lord God of Israel. 17However, the people still sacrificed upon the altars on the hills, but only to the Lord their God.

18The rest of Manasseh's deeds, and his prayer to God, and God's reply through the prophets—this is all written in *The Annals of the Kings of Israel.* 19His prayer, and the way God answered, and a frank account of his sins and errors, including a list of the locations where he built idols on the hills and set up shame-idols and graven images (this of course was before the great change in his attitude) is recorded in *The Annals of the Prophets.*

20,21When Manasseh died he was buried beneath his own palace, and his son Amon became the new king. Amon was twenty-two years old when he began to reign in Jerusalem, but he lasted for only two years. 22It was an evil reign like the early years of his father Manasseh; for Amon sacrificed to all the idols just as his father had. 23But he didn't change as his father did; instead he sinned more and more. 24At last his own officers assassinated him in his palace. 25But some public-spirited citizens killed all of those who assassinated him, and declared his son Josiah to be the new king.

JOSIAH was only eight years old when he became king. He reigned thirty-one years, in Jerusalem. 2His was a good reign, as he carefully followed the good example of his ancestor King David. 3For when he was sixteen years old, in the eighth year of his reign, he began to search for the God of his ancestor David; and four years later he began to clean up Judah and Jerusalem, destroying the heathen altars and the shame-idols on the hills. 4He went out personally to watch as the altars of Baal were knocked apart, the obelisks above the altars chopped down, and the shame-idols ground into dust and scattered over the graves of those who had sacrificed to them. 5Then he burned the bones of the heathen priests upon their own altars, feeling that this action would clear the people of Judah and Jerusalem from the guilt of their sin of idol-worship.

6Then he went to the cities of Manasseh, Ephraim, and Simeon, even to distant Naphtali, and did the same thing there. 7He broke down the heathen altars, ground to powder the shame-idols, and chopped down the obelisks. He did this everywhere throughout the whole land of Israel before returning to Jerusalem.

8During the eighteenth year of his reign, after he had purged the land and cleaned up the situation at the Temple, he appointed Shaphan (son of Azaliah) and Ma-aseiah, governor of Jerusalem, and Joah (son of Joahaz), the city treasurer, to repair the Temple. 9They set up a collection system for gifts for the Temple. The money was collected at the Temple gates by the Levites on guard duty there. Gifts were brought by the people coming from Manasseh, Ephraim, and other parts of the remnant of Israel, as well as from the people of Jerusalem. The money was taken to Hilkiah the High Priest for accounting, 10,11and then used by the Levites to pay the carpenters and stonemasons, and to purchase building materials—stone building blocks, timber, lumber, and beams. He now rebuilt what earlier kings of Judah had torn down.

12The workmen were energetic under the leadership of Jahath and Obadiah, Levites of the subclan of Merari. Zechariah and Meshullam, of the subclan of Kohath, were the building superintendents. The Levites who were skilled musicians played background music while the work progressed. 13Other Levites superintended the unskilled laborers who carried in the materials to the workmen. Still others assisted as accountants, supervisors, and carriers.

14One day when Hilkiah, the High Priest, was at the Temple recording the money collected at the gates, he found an old scroll which turned out to be the laws of God as given to Moses!

15,16"Look!" Hilkiah exclaimed to Shaphan, the king's secretary. "See what I have found in the Temple! These are the laws of God!" Hilkiah gave the scroll to Shaphan, and Shaphan took it to the king, along with his report that there was good progress being made in the reconstruction of the Temple.

17"The money chests have been opened and counted, and the money has been put into the hand of the overseers and workmen," he said to the king.

18Then he mentioned the scroll, and how Hilkiah had discovered it. So he read it to the king. 19When the king heard what these laws required of God's people, he ripped his clothing in despair, 20and summoned Hilkiah, Ahikam (son of Shaphan), Abdon (son of Micah), Shaphan the treasurer, and Asaiah, the king's personal aide.

21"Go to the Temple and plead with the Lord for me!" the king told them. "Pray for all the remnant of Israel and Judah! For this scroll says that the reason the Lord's great anger has been poured out upon us is that our ancestors have not obeyed these laws that are written here."

22So the men went to Huldah the prophetess, the wife of Shallum (son of Tokhath, son of Hasrah). (Shallum was the king's tailor, living in the second ward.) When they told her of the king's trouble, 23she replied, "The Lord God of Israel says, Tell the man who sent you,

24" 'Yes, the Lord will destroy this city and its people. All the curses written in the scroll will come true. 25For my people have forsaken me and have worshiped heathen gods, and I am very angry with them for their deeds. Therefore, my unquenchable wrath is poured out upon this place.'

26"But the Lord also says this to the king of Judah who sent you to ask me about this: Tell him, the Lord God of Israel says, 27'Because you are sorry and have humbled yourself before God when you heard my words against this city and its people, and have ripped your clothing in despair and wept before me— I have heard you, says the Lord, 28and I will not send the promised evil upon this city and its people until after your death.' " So they brought back to the king this word from the Lord. 29Then the king summoned all the elders of Judah and Jerusalem, 30and the priests and Levites and all the people great and small, to accompany him to the Temple. There the king read the scroll to them—the covenant of God that was found in the Temple. 31As the king stood before them, he made a pledge to the Lord to follow his commandments with all his heart and soul, and to do what was written in the scroll. 32And he required everyone in Jerusalem and Benjamin to subscribe to this pact with God, and all of them did.

33So Josiah removed all idols from the areas occupied by the Jews, and required all of them to worship Jehovah their God. And throughout the remainder of his lifetime they continued serving Jehovah, the God of their ancestors.

SAY "hello" to Ampliatus, whom I love as one of God's own children, [9]and Urbanus, our fellow worker, and beloved Stachys.

[10]Then there is Apelles, a good man whom the Lord approves; greet him for me. And give my best regards to those working at the house of Aristobulus. [11]Remember me to Herodion my relative. Remember me to the Christian slaves over at Narcissus House. [12]Say "hello" to Tryphaena and Tryphosa, the Lord's workers, and to dear Persis, who has worked so hard for the Lord. [13]Greet Rufus for me, whom the Lord picked out to be his very own; and also his dear mother who has been such a mother to me. [14]And please give my greetings to Asyncritus, Phlegon, Hermes, Patrobas, Hermas, and the other brothers who are with them. [15]Give my love to Philologus, Julia, Nereus and his sister, and to Olympas, and all the Christians who are with them. [16]Shake hands warmly with each other. All the churches here send you their greetings.

[17]And now there is one more thing to say before I end this letter. Stay away from those who cause divisions and are upsetting people's faith, teaching things about Christ that are contrary to what you have been taught. [18]Such teachers are not working for our Lord Jesus, but only want gain for themselves. They are good speakers, and simple-minded people are often fooled by them. [19]But everyone knows that you stand loyal and true. This makes me very happy. I want you always to remain very clear about what is right, and to stay innocent of any wrong. [20]The God of peace will soon crush Satan under your feet. The blessings from our Lord Jesus Christ be upon you.

[21]Timothy my fellow-worker, and Lucius and Jason and Sosipater, my relatives, send you their good wishes. [22]I, Tertius, the one who is writing this letter for Paul, send my greetings too, as a Christian brother. [23]Gaius says to say "hello" to you for him. I am his guest, and the church meets here in his home. Erastus, the city treasurer, sends you his greetings and so does Quartus, a Christian brother. [24]Goodbye. May the grace of our Lord Jesus Christ be with you all.

[25,26,27]I commit you to God, who is able to make you strong and steady in the Lord, just as the Gospel says, and just as I have told you. This is God's plan of salvation for you Gentiles, kept secret from the beginning of time. But now as the prophets foretold and as God commands, this message is being preached everywhere, so that people all around the world will have faith in Christ and obey him. To God, who alone is wise, be the glory forever through Jesus Christ our Lord. Amen.

Sincerely,
Paul

PSALM 26:1–12

DISMISS all the charges against me, Lord, for I have tried to keep your laws and have trusted you without wavering. [2]Cross-examine me, O Lord, and see that this is so; test my motives and affections too. [3]For I have taken your lovingkindness and your truth as my ideals. [4]I do not have fellowship with tricky, two-faced men; they are false and hypocritical. [5]I hate the sinners' hangouts and refuse to enter them. [6]I wash my hands to prove my innocence and come before your altar, [7]singing a song of thanksgiving and telling about your miracles.

[8]Lord, I love your home, this shrine where the brilliant, dazzling splendor of your presence lives.

[9,10]Don't treat me as a common sinner or murderer who plots against the innocent and demands bribes.

[11]No, I am not like that, O Lord; I try to walk a straight and narrow path of doing what is right; therefore in mercy save me.

[12]I publicly praise the Lord for keeping me from slipping and falling.

AUGUST 4

2 CHRONICLES 35:1—36:23

THEN Josiah announced that the Passover would be celebrated on the first day of April, in Jerusalem. The Passover lambs were slain that evening. 2He also reestablished the priests in their duties, and encouraged them to begin their work at the Temple again. 3He issued this order to the sanctified Levites, the religious teachers in Israel:

"Since the Ark is now in Solomon's Temple and you don't need to carry it back and forth upon your shoulders, spend your time ministering to the Lord and to his people. 4,5Form yourselves into the traditional service corps of your ancestors, as first organized by King David of Israel and by his son Solomon. Each corps will assist particular clans of the people who bring in their offerings to the Temple. 6Kill the Passover lambs and sanctify yourselves and prepare to assist the people who come. Follow all of the instructions of the Lord through Moses."

7Then the king contributed 30,000 lambs and young goats for the people's Passover offerings, and 3,000 young bulls. 8The king's officials made willing contributions to the priests and Levites. Hilkiah, Zechariah, and Jehiel, the overseers of the Temple, gave the priests 2,600 sheep and goats, and 300 oxen as Passover offerings. 9The Levite leaders—Conaniah, Shemaiah, and Nethanel, and his brothers Hashabiah, Je-iel, and Jozabad—gave 5,000 sheep and goats and 500 oxen to the Levites for their Passover offerings.

10When everything was organized, and the priests were standing in their places, and the Levites were formed into service corps as the king had instructed, 11then the Levites killed the Passover lambs and presented the blood to the priests, who sprinkled it upon the altar as the Levites removed the skins. 12They piled up the carcasses for each tribe to present its own burnt sacrifices to the Lord, as it is written in the law of Moses. They did the same with the oxen. 13Then, as directed by the laws of Moses, they roasted the Passover lambs and boiled the holy offerings in pots, kettles, and pans, and hurried them out to the people to eat. 14Afterwards the Levites prepared a meal for themselves and for the priests, for they had been busy from morning till night offering the fat of the burnt offerings.

15The singers (the sons of Asaph) were in their places, following directions issued centuries earlier by King David, Asaph, Heman, and Jeduthun the king's prophet. The gatekeepers guarded the gates, and didn't need to leave their posts of duty, for their meals were brought to them by their Levite brothers. 16The entire Passover ceremony was completed in that one day. All the burnt offerings were sacrificed upon the altar of the Lord, as Josiah had instructed.

17Everyone present in Jerusalem took part in the Passover observance, and this was followed by the Feast of Unleavened Bread for the next seven days. 18Never since the time of Samuel the prophet had there been such a Passover—not one of the kings of Israel could vie with King Josiah in this respect, involving so many of the priests, Levites, and people from Jerusalem and from all parts of Judah, and from over in Israel. 19This all happened in the eighteenth year of the reign of Josiah.

20Afterwards King Neco of Egypt led his army at Carchemish on the Euphrates River, and Josiah declared war on him.

21But King Neco sent ambassadors to Josiah with this message: "I don't want a fight with you, O king of Judah! I have come only to fight the power with which I am at war. Leave me alone! God has told me to hurry! Don't meddle with God or he will destroy you, for he is with me."

22But Josiah refused to turn back. Instead he led his army into the battle at the Valley of Megiddo. (He laid aside his royal robes so that the enemy wouldn't recognize him.) Josiah refused to believe that Neco's message was from God. 23The enemy archers struck King Josiah with their arrows and fatally wounded him.

"Take me out of the battle," he exclaimed to his aides.

24,25So they lifted him out of his chariot and placed him in his second chariot and brought him back to Jerusalem where he died. He was buried there, in the royal cemetery. And all Judah and Jerusalem, including even Jeremiah the prophet, mourned for him, as did the Temple choirs. To this day they still sing sad songs about his death, for these songs of sorrow were recorded among the official lamentations.

26The other activities of Josiah, and his good deeds, and how he followed the laws of the Lord, 27all are written in *The Annals of the Kings of Israel and Judah.*

JOSIAH'S son Jehoahaz was selected as the new king. 2He was twenty-three years old when he began to reign, but lasted only three months. 3Then he was deposed by the king of Egypt, who demanded an annual tribute from Judah of $230,000.

4The king of Egypt now appointed Eliakim, the brother of Jehoahaz, as the new king of Judah. (Eliakim's name was changed to Jehoiakim.) Jehoahaz was taken to Egypt as a prisoner. 5Jehoiakim was twenty-five years old when he became king, and he reigned eleven years, in Jerusalem; but his reign was an evil one. 6Finally Nebuchadnezzar king of Babylon conquered Jerusalem, and took away the king in chains to Babylon. 7Nebuchadnezzar also took some of the gold bowls and other items from the Temple, placing them in his own temple in Babylon. 8The rest of the deeds of Jehoiakim, and all the evil he did, are written in *The Annals of the Kings of Judah;* and his son Jehoiachin became the new king.

9Jehoiachin was eighteen years old when he ascended the throne. But he lasted only three months and ten days, and it was an evil reign as far as the Lord was concerned. 10The following spring he was summoned to Babylon by King Nebuchadnezzar. Many treasures from the Temple were taken away to Babylon at that time, and King Nebuchadnezzar appointed Jehoiachin's brother Zedekiah as the new king of Judah and Jerusalem.

11Zedekiah was twenty-one years old when he became king and he reigned eleven years, in Jerusalem. 12His reign, too, was evil so far as the Lord was concerned, for he refused to take the counsel of Jeremiah the prophet, who gave him messages from the Lord. 13He rebelled against King Nebuchadnezzar, even though he had taken an oath of loyalty. Zedekiah was a hard and stubborn man so far as obeying the Lord God of Israel was concerned, for he refused to follow him.

14All the important people of the nation, including the High Priests, worshiped the heathen idols of the surrounding nations, thus polluting the Temple of the Lord in Jerusalem. 15Jehovah the God of their fathers sent his prophets again and again to warn them, for he had compassion on his people and on his Temple. 16But the people mocked these messengers of God and despised their words, scoffing at the prophets until the anger of the Lord could no longer be restrained, and there was no longer any remedy.

17Then the Lord brought the king of Babylon against them and killed their young men, even going after them right into the Temple, and had no pity upon them, killing even young girls and old men. The Lord used the king of Babylon to destroy them completely. 18He also took home with him all the items, great and small, used in the Temple, and treasures from both the Temple and the palace, and took with him all the royal princes. 19Then his army burned the Temple and broke down the walls of Jerusalem and burned all the palaces and destroyed all the valuable Temple utensils. 20Those who survived were taken away to Babylon as slaves to the king and his sons until the kingdom of Persia conquered Babylon.

21Thus the word of the Lord spoken through Jeremiah came true, that the land must rest for seventy years to make up for the years when the people refused to observe the Sabbath.

22,23But in the first year of King Cyrus of Persia, the Lord stirred up the spirit of Cyrus to make this proclamation throughout his kingdom, putting it into writing:

"All the kingdoms of the earth have been given to me by the Lord God of heaven, and he has instructed me to build him a Temple in Jerusalem, in the land of Judah. All among you who are the Lord's people, return to Israel for this task, and the Lord be with you."

This also fulfilled the prediction of Jeremiah the prophet.

1 CORINTHIANS 1:1–17

FROM: Paul, chosen by God to be Jesus Christ's missionary, and from brother Sosthenes.

2*To:* The Christians in Corinth, invited by God to be his people and made acceptable to him by Christ Jesus. *And to:* All Christians everywhere—whoever calls upon the name of Jesus Christ, our Lord and theirs.

3May God our Father and the Lord Jesus Christ give you all of his blessings, and great peace of heart and mind.

4I can never stop thanking God for all the wonderful gifts he has given you, now that you are Christ's: 5he has enriched your whole life. He has helped you speak out for him and has given you a full understanding of the truth; 6what I told you Christ could do for you has happened! 7Now you have every grace and blessing; every spiritual gift and power for doing his will are yours during this time of waiting for the return of our Lord Jesus Christ. 8And he guarantees right up to the end that you will be counted free from all sin and guilt on that day when he returns. 9God will surely do this for you, for he always does just what he says, and he is the one who invited you into this wonderful friendship with his Son, even Christ our Lord.

10But, dear brothers, I beg you in the name of the Lord Jesus Christ to stop arguing among yourselves. Let there be real harmony so that there won't be splits in the church. I plead with you to be of one mind, united in thought and purpose. 11For some of those who live at Chloe's house have told me of your arguments and quarrels, dear brothers. 12Some of you are saying, "I am a follower of Paul"; and others say that they are for Apollos or for Peter; and some that they alone are the true followers of Christ. 13And so, in effect, you have broken Christ into many pieces.

But did I, Paul, die for your sins? Were any of you baptized in my name? 14I am so thankful now that I didn't baptize any of you except Crispus and Gaius. 15For now no one can think that I have been trying to start something new, beginning a "Church of Paul." 16Oh, yes, and I baptized the family of Stephanas. I don't remember ever baptizing anyone else. 17For Christ didn't send me to baptize, but to preach the Gospel; and even my preaching sounds poor, for I do not fill my sermons with profound words and high sounding ideas, for fear of diluting the mighty power there is in the simple message of the cross of Christ.

PSALM 27:1-7

THE Lord is my light and my salvation; he protects me from danger—whom shall I fear? ²When evil men come to destroy me, they will stumble and fall! ³Yes, though a mighty army marches against me, my heart shall know no fear! I am confident that God will save me.

⁴The one thing I want from God, the thing I seek most of all, is the privilege of meditating in his Temple, living in his presence every day of my life, delighting in his incomparable perfections and glory. ⁵There I'll be when troubles come. He will hide me. He will set me on a high rock ⁶out of reach of all my enemies. Then I will bring him sacrifices and sing his praises with much joy.

⁷Listen to my pleading, Lord! Be merciful and send the help I need.

PROVERBS FOR TODAY/ 20:20-21
God puts out the light of the man who curses his father or mother. Quick wealth is not a blessing in the end.

AUGUST 5

EZRA 1:1—2:70

DURING the first year of the reign of King Cyrus of Persia, the Lord fulfilled Jeremiah's prophecy by giving King Cyrus the desire to send this proclamation throughout his empire (he also put it into the permanent records of the realm):

²"Cyrus, king of Persia, hereby announces that Jehovah, the God of heaven who gave me my vast empire, has now given me the responsibility of building him a Temple in Jerusalem, in the land of Judah. ³All Jews throughout the kingdom may now return to Jerusalem to rebuild this Temple of Jehovah, who is the God of Israel and of Jerusalem. May his blessings rest upon you. ⁴Those Jews who do not go should contribute toward the expenses of those who do, and also supply them with clothing, transportation, supplies for the journey, and a freewill offering for the Temple."

⁵Then God gave a great desire to the leaders of the tribes of Judah and Benjamin, and to the priests and Levites, to return to Jerusalem at once to rebuild the Temple. ⁶And all the Jewish exiles who chose to remain in Persia gave them whatever assistance they could, as well as gifts for the Temple.

⁷King Cyrus himself donated the gold bowls and other valuable items which King Nebuchadnezzar had taken from the Temple at Jerusalem and had placed in the temple of his own gods. ⁸He instructed Mithredath, the treasurer of Persia, to present these gifts to Sheshbazzar, the leader of the exiles returning to Judah.

⁹,¹⁰The items Cyrus donated included:
1,000 gold trays,
1,000 silver trays,
29 censers,
30 bowls of solid gold,
2,410 silver bowls (of various designs),
1,000 miscellaneous items.

[11]In all there were 5,469 gold and silver items turned over to Shesh-bazzar to take back to Jerusalem.

HERE is the list of the Jewish exiles who now returned to Jerusalem and to the other cities of Judah, from which their parents had been deported to Babylon by King Nebuchadnezzar.

[2]The leaders were:

Zerubbabel, Jeshua, Nehemiah, Seraiah, Re-el-aiah, Mordecai, Bilshan, Mispar, Bigvai, Rehum, Baanah.

Here is a census of those who returned (listed by subclans):

[3-35]From the subclan of Parosh, 2,172;
From the subclan of Shephatiah, 372;
From the subclan of Arah, 775;
From the subclan of Pahath-moab (the descendants of Jeshua and Joab), 2,812;
From the subclan of Elam, 1,254;
From the subclan of Zattu, 945;
From the subclan of Zaccai, 760;
From the subclan of Bani, 642;
From the subclan of Bebai, 623;
From the subclan of Azgad, 1,222;
From the subclan of Adonikam, 666;
From the subclan of Bigvai, 2,056;
From the subclan of Adin, 454;
From the subclan of Ater (the descendants of Hezekiah), 98;
From the subclan of Bezai, 323;
From the subclan of Jorah, 112;
From the subclan of Hashum, 223;
From the subclan of Gibbar, 95;
From the subclan of Bethlehem, 123;
From the subclan of Netophah, 56;
From the subclan of Anathoth, 128;
From the subclan of Azmaveth, 42;
From the subclans of Kiriatharim, Chephirah, and Be-eroth, 743;
From the subclans of Ramah and Geba, 621;
From the subclan of Michmas, 122;
From the subclans of Bethel and Ai, 223;
From the subclan of Nebo, 52;
From the subclan of Magbish, 156;
From the subclan of Elam, 1,254;
From the subclan of Harim, 320;

From the subclans of Lod, Hadid, and Ono, 725;
From the subclan of Jericho, 345;
From the subclan of Senaah, 3,630.

[36-39]Here are the statistics concerning the returning priests:

From the families of Jedaiah of the subclan of Jeshua, 973;
From the subclan of Immer, 1,052;
From the subclan of Pashhur, 1,247;
From the subclan of Harim, 1,017.

[40,41,42]Here are the statistics concerning the Levites who returned:

From the families of Jeshua and Kedmi-el of the subclan of Hodaviah, 74;
The choir members from the clan of Asaph, 128;
From the descendants of the gatekeepers (the families of Shallum, Ater, Talmon, Akkub, Hatita, and Shobai), 139.

[43-54]The following families of the Temple assistants were represented:

Ziha, Hasupha, Tabbaoth, Keros, Siaha, Padon, Lebanah, Hagabah, Akkub, Hagab, Shamlai, Hanan, Giddel, Gahar, Re-aiah, Rezin, Nekoda, Gazzam, Uzza, Paseah, Besai, Asnah, Me-unim, Nephisim, Bakbuk, Hakupha, Harhur, Bazluth, Mehida, Harsha, Barkos, Sisera, Temah, Neziah, Hatipha.

[55,56,57]Those who made the trip also included the descendants of King Solomon's officials:

Sotai, Hassophereth, Peruda, Jaalah, Darkon, Giddel, Shephatiah, Hattil, Pochereth-hazzebaim, Ami.

[58]The Temple assistants and the descendants of Solomon's officers numbered 392.

[59]Another group returned to Jerusalem at this time from the Persian cities of Telmelah, Tel-harsha, Cherub, Addan, and Immer. However, they had lost their genealogies and could not prove that they were really Israelites. [60]This group included the subclans of Delaiah, Tobiah, and Nekoda—a total of 652.

[61]Three subclans of priests—Habaiah, Hakkoz, and Barzillai (he married one of the daughters of Barzillai the Gileadite

and took her family name)—also returned to Jerusalem. 62,63But they too had lost their genealogies, so the leaders refused to allow them to continue as priests; they would not even allow them to eat the priests' share of food from the sacrifices until the Urim and Thummim could be consulted, to find out from God whether they actually were descendants of priests or not.

64,65So a total of 42,360 persons returned to Judah; in addition to 7,337 slaves and 200 choir members, both men and women. 66,67They took with them 736 horses, 245 mules, 435 camels, and 6,720 donkeys.

68Some of the leaders were able to give generously toward the rebuilding of the Temple, 69and each gave as much as he could. The total value of their gifts amounted to $300,000 of gold, $170,000 of silver, and 100 robes for the priests.

70So the priests and Levites and some of the common people settled in Jerusalem and its nearby villages; and the singers, the gatekeepers, the Temple workers, and the rest of the people returned to the other cities of Judah from which they had come.

1 CORINTHIANS 1:18—2:5

I know very well how foolish it sounds to those who are lost, when they hear that Jesus died to save them. But we who are saved recognize this message as the very power of God. 19For God says, "I will destroy all human plans of salvation no matter how wise they seem to be, and ignore the best ideas of men, even the most brilliant of them."

20So what about these wise men, these scholars, these brilliant debaters of this world's great affairs? God has made them all look foolish, and shown their wisdom to be useless nonsense. 21For God in his wisdom saw to it that the world would never find God through human brilliance, and then he stepped in and saved all those who believed his message, which the world calls foolish and silly. 22It seems foolish to the Jews because they want a sign from heaven as proof that what is preached is true; and it is foolish to the Gentiles because they believe only what agrees with their philosophy and seems wise to them. 23So when we preach about Christ dying to save them, the Jews are offended and the Gentiles say it's all nonsense. 24But God has opened the eyes of those called to salvation, both Jews and Gentiles, to see that Christ is the mighty power of God to save them; Christ himself is the center of God's wise plan for their salvation. 25This so-called "foolish" plan of God is far wiser than the wisest plan of the wisest man, and God in his weakness— Christ dying on the cross—is far stronger than any man.

26Notice among yourselves, dear brothers, that few of you who follow Christ have big names or power or wealth. 27Instead, God has deliberately chosen to use ideas the world considers foolish and of little worth in order to shame those people considered by the world as wise and great. 28He has chosen a plan despised by the world, counted as nothing at all, and used it to bring down to nothing those the world considers great, 29so that no one anywhere can ever brag in the presence of God.

30For it is from God alone that you have your life through Christ Jesus. He showed us God's plan of salvation; he was the one who made us acceptable to God; he made us pure and holy and gave himself to purchase our salvation. 31As it says in the Scriptures, "If anyone is going to boast, let him boast only of what the Lord has done."

DEAR brothers, even when I first came to you I didn't use lofty words and brilliant ideas to tell you God's message. 2For I decided that I would speak only of Jesus Christ and his death on the cross. 3I came to you in weakness—timid and trembling. 4And my preaching was very plain, not with a lot of oratory and human wisdom, but the Holy Spirit's power was in my words, proving to those who heard them that the message was from God. 5I did this because I wanted your faith to stand firmly upon God, not on man's great ideas.

PSALM 27:8–14

My heart has heard you say, "Come and talk with me, O my people." And my heart responds, "Lord, I am coming."

9Oh, do not hide yourself when I am trying to find you. Do not angrily reject your servant. You have been my help in all my trials before; don't leave me now. Don't forsake me, O God of my salvation. 10For if my father and mother should abandon me, you would welcome and comfort me.

11Tell me what to do, O Lord, and make it plain because I am surrounded by waiting enemies. 12Don't let them get me, Lord! Don't let me fall into their hands! For they accuse me of things I never did, and all the while are plotting cruelty. 13I am expecting the Lord to rescue me again, so that once again I will see his goodness to me here in the land of the living.

14Don't be impatient. Wait for the Lord, and he will come and save you! Be brave, stouthearted and courageous. Yes, wait and he will help you.

PROVERBS FOR TODAY/ 20:22–23

Don't repay evil for evil. Wait for the Lord to handle the matter. □ *The Lord loathes all cheating and dishonesty.*

AUGUST 6

EZRA 3:1—4:24

During the month of September everyone who had returned to Judah came to Jerusalem from their homes in the other towns. Then Jeshua (son of Jozadak) with his fellow priests, and Zerubbabel (son of Shealtiel) and his clan, rebuilt the altar of the God of Israel; and sacrificed burnt offerings upon it, as instructed in the laws of Moses, the man of God. 3The altar was rebuilt on its old site, and it was used immediately to sacrifice morning and evening burnt offerings to the Lord; for the people were fearful of attack.

4And they celebrated the Feast of Tabernacles as prescribed in the laws of Moses, sacrificing the burnt offerings specified for each day of the feast. 5They also offered the special sacrifices required for the Sabbaths, the new moon celebrations, and the other regular annual feasts of the Lord. Voluntary offerings of the people were also sacrificed. 6It was on the fifteenth day of September that the priests began sacrificing the burnt offerings to the Lord. (This was before they began building the foundation of the Temple.)

7Then they hired masons and carpenters, and bought cedar logs from the people of Tyre and Sidon, paying for them with food, wine, and olive oil. The logs were brought down from the Lebanon mountains and floated along the coast of the Mediterranean Sea to Joppa, for King Cyrus had included this provision in his grant.

8The actual construction of the Temple began in June of the second year of their arrival at Jerusalem. The work force was made up of all those who had returned, and they were under the direction of Zerubbabel (son of Shealtiel), Jeshua (son of Jozadak), and their fellow priests and the Levites. The Levites who were twenty years old or older were appointed to supervise the workmen. 9The supervision of the entire project was given to Jeshua, Kadmi-el, Henadad, and their sons and relatives, all of whom were Levites.

10When the builders completed the foundation of the Temple, the priests put on their official robes and blew their trumpets; and the descendants of Asaph crashed their cymbals to praise the Lord in the manner ordained by King David. 11They sang rounds of praise and thanks to God, singing this song: "He is good, and his love and mercy toward Israel will last forever." Then all the people gave a great shout, praising God because the foundation of the Temple had been laid.

12But many of the priests and Levites and other leaders—the old men who remembered Solomon's beautiful Temple—wept aloud, while others were shouting for joy! 13So the shouting and the weeping mingled together in a loud commotion that could be heard from far away!

WHEN the enemies of Judah and Benjamin heard that the exiles had returned and were rebuilding the Temple, 2they approached Zerubbabel and the other leaders and suggested, "Let us work with you, for we are just as interested in your God as you are; we have sacrificed to him ever since King Esarhaddon of Assyria brought us here."

3But Zerubbabel and Jeshua and the other Jewish leaders replied, "No, you may have no part in this work. The Temple of the God of Israel must be built by the Israelis, just as King Cyrus has commanded."

4,5Then the local residents tried to discourage and frighten them by sending agents to tell lies about them to King Cyrus. This went on during his entire reign and lasted until King Darius took the throne.

6And afterwards, when King Ahasuerus began to reign, they wrote him a letter of accusation against the people of Judah and Jerusalem, 7and did the same thing during the reign of Artaxerxes. Bishlam, Mithredath, and Tabe-el and their associates wrote a letter to him in the Aramaic language, and it was translated to him. 8,9Others who participated were Governor Rehum, Shimshai (a scribe), several judges and other local leaders, the Persians, the Babylonians, the men of Erech and Susa, 10and men from several other nations. (They had been taken from their own lands by the great and noble Osnappar and relocated in Jerusalem, Samaria, and throughout the neighboring lands west of the Euphrates River.)

11Here is the text of the letter they sent to King Artaxerxes:

"Sir: Greetings from your loyal subjects west of the Euphrates River. 12Please be informed that the Jews sent to Jerusalem from Babylon are rebuilding this historically rebellious and evil city; they have already rebuilt its walls and have repaired the foundations of the Temple. 13But we wish you to know that if this city is rebuilt, it will be much to your disadvantage, for the Jews will then refuse to pay their taxes to you.

14"Since we are grateful to you as our patron, and we do not want to see you taken advantage of and dishonored in this way, we have decided to send you this information. 15We suggest that you search the ancient records to discover what a rebellious city this has been in the past; in fact, it was destroyed because of its long history of sedition against the kings and countries who attempted to control it. 16We wish to declare that if this city is rebuilt and the walls finished, you might as well forget about this part of your empire beyond the Euphrates, for it will be lost to you."

17Then the king made this reply to Governor Rehum and Shimshai the scribe, and to their companions living in Samaria and throughout the area west of the Euphrates River:

18"Gentlemen: Greetings! The letter

you sent has been translated and read to me. 19I have ordered a search made of the records and have indeed found that Jerusalem has in times past been a hotbed of insurrection against many kings; in fact, rebellion and sedition are normal there! 20I find, moreover, that there have been some very great kings in Jerusalem who have ruled the entire land beyond the Euphrates River and have received vast tribute, custom, and toll. 21Therefore, I command that these men must stop their work until I have investigated the matter more thoroughly. 22Do not delay, for we must not permit the situation to get out of control!"

23When this letter from King Artaxerxes was read to Rehum and Shimshai, they hurried to Jerusalem and forced the Jews to stop building. 24So the work ended until the second year of the reign of King Darius of Persia.

1 CORINTHIANS 2:6—3:4

Y ET when I am among mature Christians I do speak with words of great wisdom, but not the kind that comes from here on earth, and not the kind that appeals to the great men of this world, who are doomed to fall. 7Our words are wise because they are from God, telling of God's wise plan to bring us into the glories of heaven. This plan was hidden in former times, though it was made for our benefit before the world began. 8But the great men of the world have not understood it; if they had, they never would have crucified the Lord of Glory.

9That is what is meant by the Scriptures which say that no mere man has ever seen, heard or even imagined what wonderful things God has ready for those who love the Lord. 10But we know about these things because God has sent his Spirit to tell us, and his Spirit searches out and shows us all of God's deepest secrets. 11No one can really know what anyone else is thinking, or what he is really like, except that person himself.

And no one can know God's thoughts except God's own Spirit. 12And God has actually given us his Spirit (not the world's spirit) to tell us about the wonderful free gifts of grace and blessing that God has given us. 13In telling you about these gifts we have even used the very words given to us by the Holy Spirit, not words that we as men might choose. So we use the Holy Spirit's words to explain the Holy Spirit's facts. 14But the man who isn't a Christian can't understand and can't accept these thoughts from God, which the Holy Spirit teaches us. They sound foolish to him, because only those who have the Holy Spirit within them can understand what the Holy Spirit means. Others just can't take it in. 15But the spiritual man has insight into everything, and that bothers and baffles the man of the world, who can't understand him at all. 16How could he? For certainly he has never been one to know the Lord's thoughts, or to discuss them with him, or to move the hands of God by prayer. But, strange as it seems, we Christians actually do have within us a portion of the very thoughts and mind of Christ.

DEAR brothers, I have been talking to you as though you were still just babies in the Christian life, who are not following the Lord, but your own desires; I cannot talk to you as I would to healthy Christians, who are filled with the Spirit. 2I have had to feed you with milk and not with solid food, because you couldn't digest anything stronger. And even now you still have to be fed on milk. 3For you are still only baby Christians, controlled by your own desires, not God's. When you are jealous of one another and divide up into quarreling groups, doesn't that prove you are still babies, wanting your own way? In fact, you are acting like people who don't belong to the Lord at all. 4There you are, quarreling about whether I am greater than Apollos, and dividing the church. Doesn't this show how little you have grown in the Lord?

PSALM 28:1–9

I plead with you to help me, Lord, for you are my Rock of safety. If you refuse to answer me, I might as well give up and die. ²Lord, I lift my hands to heaven and implore your help. Oh, listen to my cry.

³Don't punish me with all the wicked ones who speak so sweetly to their neighbors while planning to murder them. ⁴Give them the punishment they so richly deserve! Measure it out to them in proportion to their wickedness; pay them back for all their evil deeds. ⁵They care nothing for God or what he has done or what he has made; therefore God will dismantle them like old buildings, never to be rebuilt again.

⁶Oh, praise the Lord, for he has listened to my pleadings! ⁷He is my strength, my shield from every danger. I trusted in him, and he helped me. Joy rises in my heart until I burst out in songs of praise to him. ⁸The Lord protects his people and gives victory to his anointed king.

⁹Defend your people, Lord; defend and bless your chosen ones. Lead them like a shepherd and carry them forever in your arms.

PROVERBS FOR TODAY/ 20:24–25

Since the Lord is directing our steps, why try to understand everything that happens along the way? □ *It is foolish and rash to make a promise to the Lord before counting the cost.*

AUGUST 7

EZRA 5:1—6:22

B UT there were prophets in Jerusalem and Judah at that time— Haggai, and Zechariah (the son of Iddo)—who brought messages from the God of Israel to Zerubbabel (son of Shealtiel) and Jeshua (son of Jozadak), encouraging them to begin building again! So they did and the prophets helped them.

³But Tattenai, the governor of the lands west of the Euphrates, and Shethar-bozenai, and their companions soon arrived in Jerusalem and demanded, "Who gave you permission to rebuild this Temple and finish these walls?" ⁴They also asked for a list of the names of all the men who were working on the Temple. ⁵But because the Lord was overseeing the entire situation, our enemies did not force us to stop building, but let us continue while King Darius looked into the matter and returned his decision.

⁶Following is the letter which Governors Tattenai and Shethar-bozenai, and the other officials sent to King Darius:

⁷"To King Darius:

"Greetings!

⁸"We wish to inform you that we went to the construction site of the Temple of the great God of Judah. It is being built with huge stones, and timber is being laid in the city walls. The work is going forward with great energy and success. ⁹We asked the leaders, 'Who has given you permission to do this?' ¹⁰And we demanded their names so that we could notify you. ¹¹Their answer was, 'We are the servants of the God of heaven and earth and we are rebuilding the Temple that was constructed here many centuries ago by a great king of Israel. ¹²But afterwards our ancestors angered the God of heaven, and he aban-

doned them and let King Nebuchadnezzar destroy this Temple and exile the people to Babylonia.'

13"But they insist that King Cyrus of Babylon, during the first year of his reign, issued a decree that the Temple should be rebuilt, 14and they say King Cyrus returned the gold and silver bowls which Nebuchadnezzar had taken from the Temple in Jerusalem and had placed in the temple of Babylon. They say these items were delivered into the safekeeping of a man named Shesh-bazzar, whom King Cyrus appointed as governor of Judah. 15The king instructed him to return the bowls to Jerusalem and to let the Temple of God be built there as before. 16So Shesh-bazzar came and laid the foundations of the Temple at Jerusalem; and the people have been working on it ever since, though it is not yet completed. 17We request that you search in the royal library of Babylon to discover whether King Cyrus ever made such a decree; and then let us know your pleasure in this matter."

So King Darius issued orders that a search be made in the Babylonian archives, where documents were stored. 2Eventually the record was found in the palace at Ecbatana, in the province of Media. This is what it said:

3"In this first year of the reign of King Cyrus, a decree has been sent out concerning the Temple of God at Jerusalem where the Jews offer sacrifices. It is to be rebuilt, and the foundations are to be strongly laid. The height will be ninety feet and the width will be ninety feet. 4There will be three layers of huge stones in the foundation, topped with a layer of new timber. All expenses will be paid by the king. 5And the gold and silver bowls which were taken from the Temple of God by Nebuchadnezzar shall be taken back to Jerusalem and put into the Temple as they were before."

6So King Darius II sent this message to Governor Shethar-bozenai, and the other officials west of the Euphrates:

"Do not disturb the construction of the Temple. Let it be rebuilt on its former site, 7and don't molest the governor of Judah and the other leaders in their work. 8Moreover, I decree that you are to pay the full construction costs without delay from my taxes collected in your territory. 9Give the priests in Jerusalem young bulls, rams, and lambs for burnt offerings to the God of heaven; and give them wheat, wine, salt, and olive oil each day without fail. 10Then they will be able to offer acceptable sacrifices to the God of heaven, and to pray for me and my sons. 11Anyone who attempts to change this message in any way shall have the beams pulled from his house and built into a gallows on which he will be hanged; and his house shall be reduced to a pile of rubble. 12The God who has chosen the city of Jerusalem will destroy any king and any nation that alters this commandment and destroys this Temple. I, Darius, have issued this decree; let it be obeyed with all diligence."

13Governors Tattenai and Shethar-bozenai, and their companions complied at once with the command of King Darius.

14So the Jewish leaders continued in their work, and they were greatly encouraged by the preaching of the prophets Haggai and Zechariah (son of Iddo).

The Temple was finally finished, as had been commanded by God and decreed by Cyrus, Darius, and Artaxerxes, the kings of Persia. 15The completion date was February 18 in the sixth year of the reign of King Darius II.

16The Temple was then dedicated with great joy by the priests, the Levites, and all the people. 17During the dedication celebration 100 young bulls, 200 rams, and 400 lambs were sacrificed; and twelve male goats were presented as a sin offering for the twelve tribes of Israel. 18Then the priests and Levites were divided into their various service corps, to do the work of God as instructed in the laws of Moses.

19The Passover was celebrated on the first day of April. 20For by that time many of the priests and Levites had consecrated themselves. 21,22And some of the heathen people who had been relocated in Judah turned from their immoral customs and joined the Israelis in worshiping the Lord God. They, with the entire nation, ate the Passover feast and celebrated the Feast of Unleavened Bread for seven days. There was great joy throughout the land because the Lord had caused the king of Assyria to be generous to Israel and to assist in the construction of the Temple.

1 CORINTHIANS 3:5–23

WHO am I, and who is Apollos, that we should be the cause of a quarrel? Why, we're just God's servants, each of us with certain special abilities, and with our help you believed. 6My work was to plant the seed in your hearts, and Apollos' work was to water it, but it was God, not we, who made the garden grow in your hearts. 7The person who does the planting or watering isn't very important, but God is important because he is the one who makes things grow. 8Apollos and I are working as a team, with the same aim, though each of us will be rewarded for his own hard work. 9We are only God's co-workers. You are *God's* garden, not ours; you are *God's* building, not ours.

10God, in his kindness, has taught me how to be an expert builder. I have laid the foundation and Apollos has built on it. But he who builds on the foundation must be very careful. 11And no one can ever lay any other real foundation than that one we already have—Jesus Christ. 12But there are various kinds of materials that can be used to build on that foundation. Some use gold and silver and jewels; and some build with sticks, and hay, or even straw! 13There is going to come a time of testing at Christ's Judgment Day to see what kind of material each builder has used. Everyone's work will be put through the fire so that all can see whether or not it keeps its value, and what was really accomplished. 14Then every workman who has built on the foundation with the right materials, and whose work still stands, will get his pay. 15But if the house he has built burns up, he will have a great loss. He himself will be saved, but like a man escaping through a wall of flames.

16Don't you realize that all of you together are the house of God, and that the Spirit of God lives among you in his house? 17If anyone defiles and spoils God's home, God will destroy him. For God's home is holy and clean, and you are that home.

18Stop fooling yourselves. If you count yourself above average in intelligence, as judged by this world's standards, you had better put this all aside and be a fool rather than let it hold you back from the true wisdom from above. 19For the wisdom of this world is foolishness to God. As it says in the book of Job, God uses man's own brilliance to trap him; he stumbles over his own "wisdom" and falls. 20And again, in the book of Psalms, we are told that the Lord knows full well how the human mind reasons, and how foolish and futile it is.

21So don't be proud of following the wise men of this world. For God has already given you everything you need. 22He has given you Paul and Apollos and Peter as your helpers. He has given you the whole world to use, and life and even death are your servants. He has given you all of the present and all of the future. All are yours, 23and you belong to Christ, and Christ is God's.

PSALM 29:1–11

PRAISE the Lord, you angels of his; praise his glory and his strength. 2Praise him for his majestic glory, the glory of his name. Come before him clothed in sacred garments.

3The voice of the Lord echoes from the clouds. The God of glory thunders through the skies. 4So powerful is his voice; so full of majesty. 5,6It breaks down the cedars. It splits the giant trees of Lebanon. It shakes Mount Lebanon and Mount Sirion. They leap and skip before him like young calves! 7The voice of the Lord thunders through the lightning. 8It resounds through the deserts and shakes the wilderness of Kadesh. 9The voice of the Lord spins and topples the mighty oaks. It strips the forests bare. They whirl and sway beneath the blast. But in his temple all are praising, "Glory, glory to the Lord."

10At the Flood, the Lord showed his control of all creation. Now he continues to unveil his power. 11He will give his people strength. He will bless them with peace.

PROVERBS FOR TODAY/ 20:26–27

A wise king stamps out crime by severe punishment. A man's conscience is the Lord's searchlight exposing his hidden motives.

AUGUST 8

EZRA 7:1—8:20

HERE is the genealogy of Ezra, who traveled from Babylon to Jerusalem during the reign of King Artaxerxes of Persia:
Ezra was the son of Seriah;
Seriah was the son of Azariah;
Azariah was the son of Hilkiah;
Hilkiah was the son of Shallum;
Shallum was the son of Zadok;
Zadok was the son of Ahitub;
Ahitub was the son of Amariah;
Amariah was the son of Meraioth;
Meraioth was the son of Zerahiah;
Zerahiah was the son of Uzzi;
Uzzi was the son of Bukki;
Bukki was the son of Abishu-a;
Abishu-a was the son of Phinehas;
Phinehas was the son of Eleazar;
Eleazar was the son of Aaron, the chief priest.

6As a Jewish religious leader, Ezra was well versed in Jehovah's laws which Moses had given to the people of Israel. He asked to be allowed to return to Jerusalem, and the king granted his request; for the Lord his God was blessing him. 7,8,9Many ordinary people as well as priests, Levites, singers, gatekeepers, and Temple workers traveled with him. They left Babylon in the middle of March in the seventh year of the reign of Artaxerxes and arrived at Jerusalem in the month of August; for the Lord gave them a good trip. 10This was because Ezra had determined to study and obey the laws of the Lord and to become a Bible teacher, teaching those laws to the people of Israel.

11King Artaxerxes presented this letter to Ezra the priest, the student of God's commands:

12"From: Artaxerxes, the king of kings.

"To: Ezra, the priest, the teacher of the laws of the God of heaven.

13"I decree that any Jew in my realm, including the priests and Levites, may return to Jerusalem with you. 14I and my Council of Seven hereby instruct you to take a copy of God's laws to Judah and Jerusalem and to send back a report of the religious progress being made there. 15We also commission you to take with you to Jerusalem the silver and gold which we are presenting as an offering to the God of Israel.

16"Moreover, you are to collect voluntary Temple offerings of silver and gold from the Jews and their priests in all of the provinces of Babylon. 17These funds are to be used primarily for the purchase of oxen, rams, lambs, grain offerings, and drink offerings, all of which will be offered upon the altar of your Temple when you arrive in Jerusalem.

¹⁸The money that is left over may be used in whatever way you and your brothers feel is the will of your God. ¹⁹And take with you the gold bowls and other items we are giving you for the Temple of your God at Jerusalem. ²⁰If you run short of money for the construction of the Temple or for any similar needs, you may requisition funds from the royal treasury.

²¹"I, Artaxerxes the king, send this decree to all the treasurers in the provinces west of the Euphrates River: 'You are to give Ezra whatever he requests of you (for he is a priest and teacher of the laws of the God of heaven), ²²up to $200,000 in silver; 1,225 bushels of wheat; 990 gallons of wine; any amount of salt; ²³and whatever else the God of heaven demands for his Temple; for why should we risk God's wrath against the king and his sons? ²⁴I also decree that no priest, Levite, choir member, gatekeeper, Temple attendant, or other worker in the Temple shall be required to pay taxes of any kind.'

²⁵"And you, Ezra, are to use the wisdom God has given you to select and appoint judges and other officials to govern all the people west of the Euphrates River; if they are not familiar with the laws of your God, you are to teach them. ²⁶Anyone refusing to obey the law of your God and the law of the king shall be punished immediately by death, banishment, confiscation of goods, or imprisonment."

²⁷Well, praise the Lord God of our ancestors, who made the king want to beautify the Temple of the Lord in Jerusalem! ²⁸And praise God for demonstrating such lovingkindness to me by honoring me before the king and his Council of Seven and before all of his mighty princes! I was given great status because the Lord my God was with me; and I persuaded some of the leaders of Israel to return with me to Jerusalem.

THESE are the names and genealogies of the leaders who accompanied me from Babylon during the reign of King Artaxerxes:

²⁻¹⁴From the clan of Phinehas—Gershom;

From the clan of Ithamar—Daniel;

From the subclan of David of the clan of Shecaniah—Hattush;

From the clan of Parosh—Zechariah, and 150 other men;

From the clan of Pahath-moab—Elie-ho-enai (son of Zerahiah), and 200 other men;

From the clan of Shecaniah—the son of Jahaziel, and 300 other men;

From the clan of Adin—Ebed (son of Jonathan), and 50 other men;

From the clan of Elam—Jeshaiah (son of Athaliah), and 70 other men;

From the clan of Shephatiah—Zebadiah (son of Michael), and 80 other men;

From the clan of Joab—Obadiah (son of Jehiel), and 218 other men;

From the clan of Bani—Shelomith (son of Josiphiah), and 160 other men;

From the clan of Bebai—Zechariah (son of Bebai), and 28 other men;

From the clan of Azgad—Johanan (son of Hakkatan), and 110 other men;

From the clan of Adonikam—Eliphelet, Jeuel, Shemaiah, and 60 other men (they arrived at a later time);

From the clan of Bigvai—Uthai, Zaccur, and 70 other men.

¹⁵We assembled at the Ahava River and camped there for three days while I went over the lists of the people and the priests who had arrived; and I found that not one Levite had volunteered! ¹⁶So I sent for Eliezer, Ari-el, Shemaiah, Elnathan, Jarib, Elnathan, Nathan, Zechariah, and Meshullam, the Levite leaders; I also sent for Joiarib and Elnathan, who were very wise men. ¹⁷I sent them to Iddo, the leader of the Jews at Casiphia, to ask him and his brothers and the Temple attendants to send us priests for the Temple of God at Jerusalem. ¹⁸And God was good! He sent us an outstanding man named Sherebiah, along with eighteen of his sons and brothers; he was

a very astute man and a descendant of Mahli, the son of Levi and grandson of Israel. 19God also sent Hashabiah; and Jeshaiah (the son of Merari), with twenty of his sons and brothers; 20and 220 Temple attendants. (The Temple attendants were assistants to the Levites—a job classification of Temple employees first instituted by King David.) These 220 men were all listed by name.

1 CORINTHIANS 4:1–21

SO Apollos and I should be looked upon as Christ's servants who distribute God's blessings by explaining God's secrets. 2Now the most important thing about a servant is that he does just what his master tells him to. 3What about me? Have I been a good servant? Well, I don't worry over what you think about this, or what anyone else thinks. I don't even trust my own judgment on this point. 4My conscience is clear, but even that isn't final proof. It is the Lord himself who must examine me and decide.

5So be careful not to jump to conclusions before the Lord returns as to whether someone is a good servant or not. When the Lord comes, he will turn on the light so that everyone can see exactly what each one of us is really like, deep down in our hearts. Then everyone will know why we have been doing the Lord's work. At that time God will give to each one whatever praise is coming to him.

6I have used Apollos and myself as examples to illustrate what I have been saying: that you must not have favorites. You must not be proud of one of God's teachers more than another. 7What are you so puffed up about? What do you have that God hasn't given you? And if all you have is from God, why act as though you are so great, and as though you have accomplished something on your own?

8You seem to think you already have all the spiritual food you need. You are full and spiritually contented, rich kings on your thrones, leaving us far behind! I wish you really were already on your thrones, for when that time comes you can be sure that we will be there, too, reigning with you. 9Sometimes I think God has put us apostles at the very end of the line, like prisoners soon to be killed, put on display at the end of a victor's parade, to be stared at by men and angels alike.

10Religion has made us foolish, you say, but of course you are all such wise and sensible Christians! We are weak, but not you! You are well thought of, while we are laughed at. 11To this very hour we have gone hungry and thirsty, without even enough clothes to keep us warm. We have been kicked around without homes of our own. 12We have worked wearily with our hands to earn our living. We have blessed those who cursed us. We have been patient with those who injured us. 13We have replied quietly when evil things have been said about us. Yet right up to the present moment we are like dirt under foot, like garbage.

14I am not writing about these things to make you ashamed, but to warn and counsel you as beloved children. 15For although you may have ten thousand others to teach you about Christ, remember that you have only me as your father. For I was the one who brought you to Christ when I preached the Gospel to you. 16So I beg you to follow my example, and do as I do.

17That is the very reason why I am sending Timothy—to help you do this. For he is one of those I won to Christ, a beloved and trustworthy child in the Lord. He will remind you of what I teach in all the churches wherever I go.

18I know that some of you will have become proud, thinking that I am afraid to come to deal with you. 19But I will come, and soon, if the Lord will let me, and then I'll find out whether these proud men are just big talkers or whether they really have God's power. 20The Kingdom of God is not just talking; it is living by God's power. 21Which do you choose?

Shall I come with punishment and scolding, or shall I come with quiet love and gentleness?

PSALM 30:1–12

I will praise you, Lord, for you have saved me from my enemies. You refuse to let them triumph over me. 2O Lord my God, I pleaded with you, and you gave me my health again. 3You brought me back from the brink of the grave, from death itself, and here I am alive!

4Oh, sing to him you saints of his; give thanks to his holy name. 5His anger lasts a moment; his favor lasts for life! Weeping may go on all night, but in the morning there is joy.

6,7In my prosperity I said, "This is forever; nothing can stop me now! The Lord has shown me his favor. He has made me steady as a mountain." Then, Lord, you turned your face away from me and cut off your river of blessings. Suddenly my courage was gone; I was terrified and panic-stricken. 8I cried to you, O Lord; oh, how I pled: 9"What will you gain, O Lord, from killing me? How can I praise you then to all my friends? How can my dust in the grave speak out and tell the world about your faithfulness? 10Hear me, Lord; oh, have pity and help me." 11Then he turned my sorrow into joy! He took away my clothes of mourning and clothed me with joy 12so that I might sing glad praises to the Lord instead of lying in silence in the grave. O Lord my God, I will keep on thanking you forever!

PROVERBS FOR TODAY/ 20:28–30

If a king is kind, honest and fair, his kingdom stands secure. The glory of young men is their strength; of old men, their experience. Punishment that hurts chases evil from the heart.

AUGUST 9

EZRA 8:21—9:15

THEN I declared a fast while we were at the Ahava River so that we would humble ourselves before our God; and we prayed that he would give us a good journey and protect us, our children, and our goods as we traveled. 22For I was ashamed to ask the king for soldiers and cavalry to accompany us and protect us from the enemies along the way. After all, we had told the king that our God would protect all those who worshiped him, and that disaster could come only to those who had forsaken him! 23So we fasted and begged God to take care of us. And he did.

24I appointed twelve leaders of the priests—Sherebiah, Hashabiah, and ten other priests— 25to be in charge of transporting the silver, gold, the gold bowls, and the other items which the king and his council and the leaders and people of Israel had presented to the Temple of God. 26,27I weighed the money as I gave it to them and found it to total $1,300,000 in silver; $200,000 in silver utensils; many millions in gold; and twenty gold bowls worth a total of $100,000. There were also two beautiful pieces of brass which were as precious as gold. 28I consecrated these men to the Lord, and then consecrated the treasures—the equipment and money and bowls which had been given as free-will offerings to the Lord God of our fathers.

29"Guard these treasures well!" I told them; "present them without a penny lost to the priests and the Levite leaders and the elders of Israel at Jerusalem, where they are to be placed in the treasury of the Temple."

30So the priests and the Levites accepted the responsibility of taking it to God's Temple in Jerusalem. 31We broke camp at the Ahava River at the end of March and started off to Jerusalem; and God protected us and saved us from enemies and bandits along the way. 32So at last we arrived safely at Jerusalem.

33On the fourth day after our arrival the silver, gold, and other valuables were weighed in the Temple by Meremoth (the son of Uriah the priest), Eleazar (son of Phinehas), Jozabad (son of Jeshua), and Noadiah (son of Binnui)—all of whom were Levites. 34A receipt was given for each item, and the weight of the gold and silver was noted.

35Then everyone in our party sacrificed burnt offerings to the God of Israel—twelve oxen for the nation of Israel; ninety-six rams; seventy-seven lambs; and twelve goats as a sin offering. 36The king's decrees were delivered to his lieutenants and the governors of all the provinces west of the Euphrates River, and of course they then cooperated in the rebuilding of the Temple of God.

BUT then the Jewish leaders came to tell me that many of the Jewish people and even some of the priests and Levites had taken up the horrible customs of the heathen people who lived in the land— the Canaanites, Hittites, Perizzites, Jebusites, Ammonites, Moabites, Egyptians, and Amorites. 2The men of Israel had married girls from these heathen nations, and had taken them as wives for their sons. So the holy people of God were being polluted by these mixed marriages, and the political leaders were some of the worst offenders.

3When I heard this, I tore my clothing and pulled hair from my head and beard and sat down utterly baffled. 4Then many who feared the God of Israel because of this sin of his people came and sat with me until the time of the evening burnt offering.

5Finally I stood before the Lord in great embarrassment; then I fell to my knees and lifted my hands to the Lord, 6and cried out, "O my God, I am ashamed; I blush to lift up my face to you, for our sins are piled higher than our heads and our guilt is as boundless as the heavens. 7Our whole history has been one of sin; that is why we and our kings and our priests were slain by the heathen kings—we were captured, robbed, and disgraced, just as we are today. 8But now we have been given a moment of peace, for you have permitted a few of us to return to Jerusalem from our exile. You have given us a moment of joy and new life in our slavery. 9For we were slaves, but in your love and mercy you did not abandon us to slavery; instead you caused the kings of Persia to be favorable to us. They have even given us their assistance in rebuilding the Temple of our God and in giving us Jerusalem as a walled city in Judah.

10"And now, O God, what can we say after all of this? For once again we have abandoned you and broken your laws! 11The prophets warned us that the land we would possess was totally defiled by the horrible practices of the people living there. From one end to the other it is filled with corruption. 12You told us not to let our daughters marry their sons, and not to let our sons marry their daughters, and not to help those nations in any way. You warned us that only if we followed this rule could we become a prosperous nation and forever leave that prosperity to our children as an inheritance. 13And now, even after our punishment in exile because of our wickedness (and we have been punished far less than we deserved), and even though you have let some of us return, 14we have broken your commandments again and intermarried with people who do these awful things. Surely your anger will destroy us now until not even this little remnant escapes. 15O Lord God of Israel, you are a just God; what hope can we have if you give us justice as we stand here before you in our wickedness?"

1 CORINTHIANS 5:1-13

EVERYONE is talking about the terrible thing that has happened there among you, something so evil that even the heathen don't do it: you have a man in your church who is living in sin with his father's wife. 2And are you still so conceited, so "spiritual"? Why aren't you mourning in sorrow and shame, and seeing to it that this man is removed from your membership?

3,4Although I am not there with you, I have been thinking a lot about this, and in the name of the Lord Jesus Christ I have already decided what to do, just as though I were there. You are to call a meeting of the church—and the power of the Lord Jesus will be with you as you meet, and I will be there in spirit— 5and cast out this man from the fellowship of the church and into Satan's hands, to punish him, in the hope that his soul will be saved when our Lord Jesus Christ returns.

6What a terrible thing it is that you are boasting about your purity, and yet you let this sort of thing go on. Don't you realize that if even one person is allowed to go on sinning, soon all will be affected? 7Remove this evil cancer— this wicked person—from among you, so that you can stay pure. Christ, God's Lamb, has been slain for us. 8So let us feast upon him and grow strong in the Christian life, leaving entirely behind us the cancerous old life with all its hatreds and wickedness. Let us feast instead upon the pure bread of honor and sincerity and truth.

9When I wrote to you before I said not to mix with evil people. 10But when I said that I wasn't talking about unbelievers who live in sexual sin, or are greedy cheats and thieves and idol worshipers. For you can't live in this world without being with people like that. 11What I meant was that you are not to keep company with anyone who claims to be a brother Christian but indulges in sexual sins, or is greedy, or is a swindler, or worships idols, or is a drunkard, or is abusive. Don't even eat lunch with such a person.

12It isn't our job to judge outsiders. But it certainly is our job to judge and deal strongly with those who are members of the church, and who are sinning in these ways. 13God alone is the Judge of those on the outside. But you yourselves must deal with this man and put him out of your church.

PSALM 31:1-8

LORD, I trust in you alone. Don't let my enemies defeat me. Rescue me because you are the God who always does what is right. 2Answer quickly when I cry to you; bend low and hear my whispered plea. Be for me a great Rock of safety from my foes. 3Yes, you are my Rock and my fortress; honor your name by leading me out of this peril. 4Pull me from the trap my enemies have set for me. For you alone are strong enough. 5,6Into your hand I commit my spirit.

You have rescued me, O God who keeps his promises. I worship only you; how you hate all those who worship idols, those imitation gods. 7I am radiant with joy because of your mercy, for you have listened to my troubles and have seen the crisis in my soul. 8You have not handed me over to my enemy, but have given me open ground in which to maneuver.

PROVERBS FOR TODAY/ 21:1-2

Just as water is turned into irrigation ditches, so the Lord directs the king's thoughts. He turns them wherever he wants to. We can justify our every deed but God looks at our motives.

AUGUST 10

EZRA 10:1–44

A S I lay on the ground in front of the Temple, weeping and praying and making this confession, a large crowd of men, women, and children gathered around and cried with me.

2Then Shecaniah (the son of Jehiel of the clan of Elam) said to me, "We acknowledge our sin against our God, for we have married these heathen women. But there is hope for Israel in spite of this. 3For we agree before our God to divorce our heathen wives and to send them away with our children; we will follow your commands, and the commands of the others who fear our God. We will obey the laws of God. 4Take courage and tell us how to proceed in setting things straight, and we will fully cooperate."

5So I stood up and demanded that the leaders of the priests and the Levites and all the people of Israel swear that they would do as Shecaniah had said; and they all agreed. 6Then I went into the room of Jehohanan in the Temple and refused all food and drink; for I was mourning because of the sin of the returned exiles.

7,8Then a proclamation was made throughout Judah and Jerusalem that everyone should appear at Jerusalem within three days and that the leaders and elders had decided that anyone who refused to come would be disinherited and excommunicated from Israel. 9Within three days, on the fifth day of December, all the men of Judah and Benjamin had arrived and were sitting in the open space before the Temple; and they were trembling because of the seriousness of the matter and because of the heavy rainfall. 10Then I, Ezra the priest, arose and addressed them:

"You have sinned, for you have married heathen women; now we are even more deeply under God's condemnation than we were before. 11Confess your sin

to the Lord God of your fathers and do what he demands: separate yourselves from the heathen people about you and from these women."

12Then all the men spoke up and said, "We will do what you have said. 13But this isn't something that can be done in a day or two, for there are many of us involved in this sinful affair. And it is raining so hard that we can't stay out here much longer. 14Let our leaders arrange trials for us. Everyone who has a heathen wife will come at the scheduled time with the elders and judges of his city; then each case will be decided and the situation will be cleared up and the fierce wrath of our God will be turned away from us."

15Only Jonathan (son of Asahel), Jahzeiah (son of Tikvah), Meshullam, and Shabbethai the Levite opposed this course of action.

16-19So this was the plan that was followed: Some of the clan leaders and I were designated as judges; we began our work on December 15, and finished by March 15.

Following is the list of priests who had married heathen wives (they vowed to divorce their wives and acknowledged their guilt by offering rams as sacrifices):

Ma-aseiah, Eliezer, Jarib, Gedaliah.

20The sons of Immer:

Hanani, Zebadiah.

21The sons of Harim:

Ma-aseiah, Elijah, Shemaiah, Jehiel, Uzziah.

22The sons of Pashhur:

Eli-o-enai, Ma-aseiah, Ishmael, Nethanel, Jozabad, Elasah.

23The Levites who were guilty:

Jozabad, Shime-i, Kelaiah (also called Kelita), Petha-haiah, Judah, Eliezer.

24Of the singers, there was Eliashib. Of the gatekeepers, Shallum, Telem, and Uri.

25Here is the list of ordinary citizens who were declared guilty:

From the clan of Parosh:
Ramiah, Izziah, Malchijah, Mijamin, Eleazar, Hashabiah, Benaiah.

26From the clan of Elam:
Mattaniah, Zechariah, Jehiel, Abdi, Jeremoth, Elijah.

27From the clan of Zattu:
Eli-o-enai, Eliashib, Mattaniah, Jeremoth, Zabad, Aziza.

28From the clan of Bebai:
Jeho-hanan, Hananiah, Zabbai, Athlai.

29From the clan of Bani:
Meshullam, Malluch, Adaiah, Jashub, Sheal, Jeremoth.

30From the clan of Pahath-moab:
Adna, Chelal, Benaiah, Ma-aseiah, Mattaniah, Bezalel, Binnui, Manasseh.

31,32From the clan of Harim:
Eliezer, Isshijah, Malchijah, Shemaiah, Shime-on, Benjamin, Malluch, Shemariah.

33From the clan of Hashum:
Mattenai, Mattattah, Zabad, Eliphelet, Jeremai, Manasseh, Shime-i.

34-42From the clan of Bani:
Ma-adai, Amram, Uel, Banaiah, Bedeiah, Cheluhi, Vaniah, Meremoth, Eliashib, Mattaniah, Mattenai, Jaasu, Bani, Binnui, Shime-i, Shelemiah, Nathan, Adaiah, Machnadebai, Shashai, Sharai, Azarel, Shelemiah, Shemariah, Shallum, Amariah, Joseph.

43From the clan of Nebo:
Je-iel, Mattithiah, Zabad, Zebina, Jaddai, Joel, Benaiah.

44Each of these men had heathen wives, and many had children by these wives.

1 CORINTHIANS 6:1-20

How is it that when you have something against another Christian, you "go to law" and ask a heathen court to decide the matter instead of taking it to other Christians to decide which of you is right? 2Don't you know that some day we Christians are going to judge and govern the world? So why can't you decide even these little things among yourselves? 3Don't you realize that we Christians will judge and

reward the very angels in heaven? So you should be able to decide your problems down here on earth easily enough. 4Why then go to outside judges who are not even Christians? 5I am trying to make you ashamed. Isn't there anyone in all the church who is wise enough to decide these arguments? 6But, instead, one Christian sues another and accuses his Christian brother in front of unbelievers.

7To have such lawsuits at all is a real defeat for you as Christians. Why not just accept mistreatment and leave it at that? It would be far more honoring to the Lord to let yourselves be cheated. 8But, instead, you yourselves are the ones who do wrong, cheating others, even your own brothers.

9,10Don't you know that those doing such things have no share in the Kingdom of God? Don't fool yourselves. Those who live immoral lives, who are idol worshipers, adulterers or homosexuals—will have no share in his Kingdom. Neither will thieves or greedy people, drunkards, slanderers, or robbers. 11There was a time when some of you were just like that but now your sins are washed away, and you are set apart for God, and he has accepted you because of what the Lord Jesus Christ and the Spirit of our God have done for you.

12I can do anything I want to if Christ has not said no, but some of these things aren't good for me. Even if I am allowed to do them, I'll refuse to if I think they might get such a grip on me that I can't easily stop when I want to. 13For instance, take the matter of eating. God has given us an appetite for food and stomachs to digest it. But that doesn't mean we should eat more than we need. Don't think of eating as important, because some day God will do away with both stomachs and food.

But sexual sin is never right: our bodies were not made for that, but for the Lord, and the Lord wants to fill our bodies with himself. 14And God is going to raise our bodies from the dead by his power just as he raised up the Lord Jesus Christ. 15Don't you realize that your bodies are actually parts and members of Christ? So should I take part of Christ and join him to a prostitute? Never! 16And don't you know that if a man joins himself to a prostitute she becomes a part of him and he becomes a part of her? For God tells us in the Scripture that in his sight the two become one person. 17But if you give yourself to the Lord, you and Christ are joined together as one person.

18That is why I say to run from sex sin. No other sin affects the body as this one does. When you sin this sin it is against your own body. 19Haven't you yet learned that your body is the home of the Holy Spirit God gave you, and that he lives within you? Your own body does not belong to you. 20For God has bought you with a great price. So use every part of your body to give glory back to God, because he owns it.

PSALM 31:9–18

O Lord, have mercy on me in my anguish. My eyes are red from weeping; my health is broken from sorrow. I am pining away with grief;

my years are shortened, drained away because of sadness. My sins have sapped my strength; I stoop with sorrow and with shame. 11I am scorned by all my enemies and even more by my neighbors and friends. They dread meeting me and look the other way when I go by. 12I am forgotten like a dead man, like a broken and discarded pot. 13I heard the lies about me, the slanders of my enemies. Everywhere I looked I was afraid, for they were plotting against my life.

14,15But I am trusting you, O Lord. I said, "You alone are my God; my times are in your hands. Rescue me from those who hunt me down relentlessly. 16Let your favor shine again upon your servant; save me just because you are so kind! 17Don't disgrace me, Lord, by not replying when I call to you for aid. But let the wicked be shamed by what they trust in; let them lie silently in their graves, 18their lying lips quieted at last—the lips of these arrogant men who are accusing honest men of evil deeds."

PROVERBS FOR TODAY/ 21:3

God is more pleased when we are just and fair than when we give him gifts.

AUGUST 11

NEHEMIAH 1:1—3:14

THE autobiography of *Nehemiah, the son of Hecaliah:*
In December of the twentieth year of the reign of King Artaxerxes of Persia, when I was at the palace at Shushan, 2one of my fellow Jews named Hanani came to visit me with some men who had arrived from Judah. I took the opportunity to inquire about how things were going in Jerusalem.

"How are they getting along?" I asked.

"—the Jews who returned to Jerusalem from their exile here?"

3"Well," they replied, "things are not good; the wall of Jerusalem is still torn down, and the gates are burned."

4When I heard this, I sat down and cried. In fact, I refused to eat for several days, for I spent the time in prayer to the God of heaven.

5"O Lord God," I cried out; "O great and awesome God who keeps his promises and is so loving and kind to those who love and obey him! Hear my prayer! 6,7Listen carefully to what I say! Look down and see me praying night and day for your people Israel. I confess that we have sinned against you; yes, I and my people have committed the horrible sin of not obeying the commandments you gave us through your servant Moses. 8Oh, please remember what you told Moses! You said,

" 'If you sin, I will scatter you among the nations; 9but if you return to me and obey my laws, even though you are exiled to the farthest corners of the universe, I will bring you back to Jerusalem. For Jerusalem is the place in which I have chosen to live.'

10"We are your servants, the people you rescued by your great power. 11O Lord, please hear my prayer! Heed the prayers of those of us who delight to honor you. Please help me now as I go in and ask the king for a great favor—put it into his heart to be kind to me." (I was the king's cupbearer.)

ONE day in April, four months later, as I was serving the king his wine he asked me, "Why so sad? You aren't sick, are you? You look like a man with deep troubles." (For until then I had always been cheerful when I was with him.) I was badly frightened, 3but I replied, "Sir, why shouldn't I be sad? For the city where my ancestors are buried is in ruins, and the gates have been burned down."

4"Well, what should be done?" the king asked.

With a quick prayer to the God of heaven, I replied, "If it please Your Majesty and if you look upon me with your royal favor, send me to Judah to rebuild the city of my fathers!"

5,6The king replied, with the queen sitting beside him, "How long will you be gone? When will you return?"

So it was agreed! And I set a time for my departure!

7Then I added this to my request: "If it please the king, give me letters to the governors west of the Euphrates River instructing them to let me travel through their countries on my way to Judah; 8also a letter to Asaph, the manager of the king's forest, instructing him to give me timber for the beams and for the gates of the fortress near the Temple, and for the city walls, and for a house for myself."

And the king granted these requests, for God was being gracious to me.

9When I arrived in the provinces west of the Euphrates River, I delivered the king's letters to the governors there. (The king, I should add, had sent along army officers and troops to protect me!) 10But when Sanballat (the Horonite) and Tobiah (an Ammonite who was a government official) heard of my arrival, they were very angry that anyone was interested in helping Israel.

11,12Three days after my arrival at Jerusalem I stole out during the night, taking only a few men with me; for I hadn't told a soul about the plans for Jerusalem which God had put into my heart. I was mounted on my donkey and the others were on foot, 13and we went out through the Valley Gate toward the Jackal's Well and over to the Dung Gate to see the broken walls and burned gates. 14,15Then we went to the Fountain Gate and to the King's Pool, but my donkey couldn't get through the rubble. So we circled the city, and I followed the brook, inspecting the wall, and entered again at the Valley Gate.

16The city officials did not know I had been out there, or why, for as yet I had said nothing to anyone about my plans—not to the political or religious leaders, or even to those who would be doing the work.

17But now I told them, "You know full well the tragedy of our city; it lies in ruins and its gates are burned. Let us rebuild the wall of Jerusalem and rid ourselves of this disgrace!"

18Then I told them about the desire God had put into my heart, and of my conversation with the king, and the plan to which he had agreed.

They replied at once, "Good! Let's rebuild the wall!" And so the work began.

¹⁹But when Sanballat and Tobiah and Geshem the Arab heard of our plan, they scoffed and said, "What are you doing, rebelling against the king like this?"

²⁰But I replied, "The God of heaven will help us, and we, his servants, will rebuild this wall; but you may have no part in this affair."

THEN Eliashib the High Priest and the other priests rebuilt the wall as far as the Tower of the Hundred and the Tower of Hananel; then they rebuilt the Sheep Gate, hung its doors, and dedicated it. ²Men from the city of Jericho worked next to them, and beyond them was the work crew led by Zaccur (son of Imri).

³The Fish Gate was built by the sons of Hassenaah; they did the whole thing—cut the beams, hung the doors, and made the bolts and bars. ⁴Meremoth (son of Uriah, son of Hakkoz) repaired the next section of wall, and beyond him were Meshullam (son of Berechiah, son of Meshezabel) and Zadok (son of Baana). ⁵Next were the men from Tekoa, but their leaders were lazy and didn't help.

⁶The Old Gate was repaired by Joiada (son of Paseah) and Meshullam (son of Besodeiah). They laid the beams, set up the doors, and installed the bolts and bars. ⁷Next to them were Melatiah from Gibeon; Jadon from Meronoth; and men from Gibeon and Mizpah, who were citizens of the province. ⁸Uzziel (son of Harhaiah) was a goldsmith by trade, but he too worked on the wall. Beyond him was Hananiah, a manufacturer of perfumes. Repairs were not needed from there to the Broad Wall.

⁹Rephaiah (son of Hur), the mayor of half of Jerusalem, was next down the wall from them. ¹⁰Jedaiah (son of Harumaph) repaired the wall beside his own house, and next to him was Hattush (son of Hashabneiah). ¹¹Then came Malchijah (son of Harim) and Hasshub (son of Pahath-moab), who repaired the Furnace Tower in addition to a section of the wall. ¹²Shallum (son of Hallohesh) and his daughters repaired the next section.

He was the mayor of the other half of Jerusalem.

¹³The people from Zanoah, led by Hanun, built the Valley Gate, hung the doors, and installed the bolts and bars; then they repaired the 1,500 feet of wall to the Dung Gate.

¹⁴The Dung Gate was repaired by Malchijah (son of Rechab), the mayor of the Beth-haccherem area; and after building it, he hung the doors and installed the bolts and bars.

1 CORINTHIANS 7:1–19

NOW about those questions you asked in your last letter: my answer is that if you do not marry, it is good. ²But usually it is best to be married, each man having his own wife, and each woman having her own husband, because otherwise you might fall back into sin.

³The man should give his wife all that is her right as a married woman, and the wife should do the same for her husband: ⁴for a girl who marries no longer has full right to her own body, for her husband then has his rights to it, too; and in the same way the husband no longer has full right to his own body, for it belongs also to his wife. ⁵So do not refuse these rights to each other. The only exception to this rule would be the agreement of both husband and wife to refrain from the rights of marriage for a limited time, so that they can give themselves more completely to prayer. Afterwards, they should come together again so that Satan won't be able to tempt them because of their lack of self-control.

⁶I'm not saying you *must* marry; but you certainly *may* if you wish. ⁷I wish everyone could get along without marrying, just as I do. But we are not all the same. God gives some the gift of a husband or wife, and others he gives the gift of being able to stay happily unmarried. ⁸So I say to those who aren't married, and to widows—better to stay unmarried if you can, just as I am. ⁹But if you can't control yourselves, go

ahead and marry. It is better to marry than to burn with lust.

10Now, for those who are married I have a command, not just a suggestion. And it is not a command from me, for this is what the Lord himself has said: A wife must not leave her husband. 11But if she is separated from him, let her remain single or else go back to him. And the husband must not divorce his wife.

12Here I want to add some suggestions of my own. These are not direct commands from the Lord, but they seem right to me: If a Christian has a wife who is not a Christian, but she wants to stay with him anyway, he must not leave her or divorce her. 13And if a Christian woman has a husband who isn't a Christian, and he wants her to stay with him, she must not leave him. 14For perhaps the husband who isn't a Christian may become a Christian with the help of his Christian wife. And the wife who isn't a Christian may become a Christian with the help of her Christian husband. Otherwise, if the family separates, the children might never come to know the Lord; whereas a united family may, in God's plan, result in the children's salvation.

15But if the husband or wife who isn't a Christian is eager to leave, it is permitted. In such cases the Christian husband or wife should not insist that the other stay, for God wants his children to live in peace and harmony. 16For, after all, there is no assurance to you wives that your husbands will be converted if they stay; and the same may be said to you husbands concerning your wives.

PROVERBS FOR TODAY/ 21:4
Pride, lust, and evil actions are all sin.

17But be sure in deciding these matters that you are living as God intended, marrying or not marrying in accordance with God's direction and help, and accepting whatever situation God has put you into. This is my rule for all the churches.

18For instance, a man who already has gone through the Jewish ceremony of circumcision before he became a Christian shouldn't worry about it; and if he hasn't been circumcised, he shouldn't do it now. 19For it doesn't make any difference at all whether a Christian has gone through this ceremony or not. But it makes a lot of difference whether he is pleasing God and keeping God's commandments. That is the important thing.

PSALM 31:19–24

OH, how great is your goodness to those who publicly declare that you will rescue them. For you have stored up great blessings for those who trust and reverence you.

20Hide your loved ones in the shelter of your presence, safe beneath your hand, safe from all conspiring men. 21Blessed is the Lord, for he has shown me that his never-failing love protects me like the walls of a fort! 22I spoke too hastily when I said, "The Lord has deserted me," for you listened to my plea and answered me.

23Oh, love the Lord, all of you who are his people; for the Lord protects those who are loyal to him, but harshly punishes all who haughtily reject him. 24So cheer up! Take courage if you are depending on the Lord.

AUGUST 12

NEHEMIAH 3:15—5:13

SHALLUM (son of Colhozeh), the mayor of the Mizpah district, repaired the Fountain Gate. He rebuilt it, roofed it, hung its doors, and installed its locks and bars. Then he repaired the wall from the Pool of Siloam to the king's garden and the stairs that descend from the City of David section of Jerusalem. 16Next to him was Nehemiah (son of Azbuk), the mayor of half the Bethzur district; he built as far as the royal cemetery, the water reservoir, and the old Officers' Club building. 17Next was a group of Levites working under the supervision of Rehum (son of Bani). Then came Hashabiah, the mayor of half the Keilah district, who supervised the building of the wall in his own district. 18Next down the line were his clan brothers led by Bavvai (son of Henadad), the mayor of the other half of the Keilah district.

19Next to them the workers were led by Ezer (son of Jeshua), the mayor of another part of Mizpah; they also worked on the section of wall across from the Armory, where the wall turns. 20Next to him was Baruch (son of Zabbai), who built from the turn in the wall to the home of Eliashib the High Priest. 21Meremoth (son of Uriah, son of Hakkoz) built a section of the wall extending from a point opposite the door of Eliashib's house to the side of the house.

22Then came the priests from the plains outside the city. 23Benjamin, Hasshub, and Azariah (son of Ma-aseiah, son of Ananiah) repaired the sections next to their own houses. 24Next was Binnui (son of Henadad), who built the portion of the wall from Azariah's house to the corner. 25Palal (son of Uzai) carried on the work from the corner to the foundations of the upper tower of the king's castle beside the prison yard. Next was Pedaiah (son of Parosh).

26The Temple attendants living in Ophel repaired the wall as far as the East Water Gate and the Projecting Tower. 27Then came the Tekoites, who repaired the section opposite the Castle Tower and over to the wall of Ophel. 28The priests repaired the wall beyond the Horse Gate, each one doing the section immediately opposite his own house. 29Zadok (son of Immer) also rebuilt the wall next to his own house, and beyond him was Shemaiah (son of Shecaniah), the gatekeeper of the East Gate. 30Next was Hananiah (son of Shelemiah); Hanun (the sixth son of Zalaph); and Meshullam (son of Berechiah), who built next to his own house. 31Malchijah, one of the goldsmiths, repaired as far as the Temple attendants' and merchants' Guild Hall, opposite the Muster Gate; then to the upper room at the corner. 32The other goldsmiths and merchants completed the wall from that corner to the Sheep Gate.

SANBALLAT was very angry when he learned that we were rebuilding the wall. He flew into a rage, and insulted and mocked us and laughed at us, and so did his friends and the Samaritan army officers. "What does this bunch of poor, feeble Jews think they are doing?" he scoffed. "Do they think they can build the wall in a day if they offer enough sacrifices? And look at those charred stones they are pulling out of the rubbish and using again!"

3Tobiah, who was standing beside him, remarked, "If even a fox walked along the top of their wall, it would collapse!"

4Then I prayed, "Hear us, O Lord God, for we are being mocked. May their scoffing fall back upon their own heads, and may they themselves become captives in a foreign land! 5Do not ignore their sin. Do not blot it out, for they have despised you in despising us who are building your wall."

6At last the wall was completed to half

its original height around the entire city—for the workers worked hard.

7But when Sanballat and Tobiah and the Arabians, Ammonites, and Ashdodites heard that the work was going right ahead and that the breaks in the wall were being repaired, they became furious. 8They plotted to lead an army against Jerusalem to bring about riots and confusion. 9But we prayed to our God and guarded the city day and night to protect ourselves.

10Then some of the leaders began complaining that the workmen were becoming tired; and there was so much rubble to be removed that we could never get it done by ourselves. 11Meanwhile, our enemies were planning to swoop down upon us and kill us, thus ending our work. 12And whenever the workers who lived in the nearby cities went home for a visit, our enemies tried to talk them out of returning to Jerusalem. 13So I placed armed guards from each family in the cleared spaces behind the walls.

14Then as I looked over the situation, I called together the leaders and the people and said to them, "Don't be afraid! Remember the Lord who is great and glorious; fight for your friends, your families, and your homes!"

15Our enemies learned that we knew of their plot, and that God had exposed and frustrated their plan. Now we all returned to our work on the wall; 16but from then on, only half worked while the other half stood guard behind them. 17And the masons and laborers worked with weapons within easy reach beside them, 18or with swords belted to their sides. The trumpeter stayed with me to sound the alarm.

19"The work is so spread out," I explained to them, "and we are separated so widely from each other, that when you hear the trumpet blow you must rush to where I am; and God will fight for us."

20,21We worked early and late, from sunrise to sunset; and half the men were always on guard. 22I told everyone living outside the walls to move into Jerusalem so that their servants could go on guard duty as well as work during the day. 23During this period none of us—I, nor my brothers, nor the servants, nor the guards who were with me—ever took off our clothes except for washing. And we carried our weapons with us at all times.

ABOUT this time there was a great outcry of protest from parents against some of the rich Jews who were profiteering on them. 2,3,4What was happening was that families who ran out of money for food had to sell their children or mortgage their fields, vineyards, and homes to these rich men; and some couldn't even do that, for they already had borrowed to the limit to pay their taxes.

5"We are their brothers, and our children are just like theirs," the people protested. "Yet we must sell our children into slavery to get enough money to live. We have already sold some of our daughters, and we are helpless to redeem them, for our fields, too, are mortgaged to these men."

6I was very angry when I heard this; 7so after thinking about it I spoke out against these rich government officials.

"What is this you are doing?" I demanded. "How dare you demand a mortgage as a condition for helping another Israelite?"

Then I called a public trial to deal with them.

8At the trial I shouted at them, "The rest of us are doing all we can to *help* our Jewish brothers who have returned from exile as slaves in distant lands, but you are forcing them right back into slavery again. How often must we redeem them?"

And they had nothing to say in their own defense.

9Then I pressed further. "What you are doing is very evil," I exclaimed. "Should you not walk in the fear of our God? Don't we have enough enemies among the nations around us who are trying to destroy us? 10The rest of us are lending money and grain to our fellow-Jews without any interest. I beg you, gentlemen, stop this business of usury. [11]Restore their fields, vineyards, olive-yards, and homes to them this very day and drop your claims against them."

[12]So they agreed to do it and said that they would assist their brothers without requiring them to mortgage their lands and sell them their children. Then I summoned the priests and made these men formally vow to carry out their promises. [13]And I invoked the curse of God upon any of them who refused.

"May God destroy your homes and livelihood if you fail to keep this promise," I declared.

And all the people shouted, "Amen," and praised the Lord. And the rich men did as they had promised.

1 CORINTHIANS 7:20–40

USUALLY a person should keep on with the work he was doing when God called him. [21]Are you a slave? Don't let that worry you—but of course, if you get a chance to be free, take it. [22]If the Lord calls you, and you are a slave, remember that Christ has set you free from the awful power of sin; and if he has called you and you are free, remember that you are now a slave of Christ. [23]You have been bought and paid for by Christ, so you belong to him—be free now from all these earthly prides and fears. [24]So, dear brothers, whatever situation a person is in when he becomes a Christian, let him stay there, for now the Lord is there to help him.

[25]Now I will try to answer your other question. What about girls who are not yet married? Should they be permitted to do so? In answer to this question, I have no special command for them from the Lord. But the Lord in his kindness has given me wisdom that can be trusted, and I will be glad to tell you what I think. [26]Here is the problem: We Christians are facing great dangers to our lives at present. In times like these I think it is best for a person to remain unmarried.

[27]Of course, if you already are married, don't separate because of this. But if you aren't, don't rush into it at this time. [28]But if you men decide to go ahead anyway and get married now, it is all right; and if a girl gets married in times like these, it is no sin. However, marriage will bring extra problems that I wish you didn't have to face right now.

[29]The important thing to remember is that our remaining time is very short, [and so are our opportunities for doing the Lord's work]. For that reason those who have wives should stay as free as possible for the Lord; [30]happiness or sadness or wealth should not keep anyone from doing God's work. [31]Those in frequent contact with the exciting things the world offers should make good use of their opportunities without stopping to enjoy them; for the world in its present form will soon be gone.

[32]In all you do, I want you to be free from worry. An unmarried man can spend his time doing the Lord's work and thinking how to please him. [33]But a married man can't do that so well; he has to think about his earthly responsibilities and how to please his wife. [34]His interests are divided. It is the same with a girl who marries. She faces the same problem. A girl who is not married is anxious to please the Lord in all she is and does. But a married woman must consider other things such as housekeeping and the likes and dislikes of her husband.

[35]I am saying this to help you, not to try to keep you from marrying. I want you to do whatever will help you serve the Lord best, with as few other things as possible to distract your attention from him.

[36]But if anyone feels he ought to marry because he has trouble controlling his passions, it is all right, it is not a sin; let him marry. [37]But if a man has the willpower not to marry and decides that he doesn't need to and won't, he has made a wise decision. [38]So the person who marries does well, and the person who doesn't marry does even better.

39The wife is part of her husband as long as he lives; if her husband dies, then she may marry again, but only if she marries a Christian. 40But in my opinion she will be happier if she doesn't marry again; and I think I am giving you counsel from God's Spirit when I say this.

PSALM 32:1–11

WHAT happiness for those whose guilt has been forgiven! What joys when sins are covered over! What relief for those who have confessed their sins and God has cleared their record.

3There was a time when I wouldn't admit what a sinner I was. But my dishonesty made me miserable and filled my days with frustration. 4All day and all night your hand was heavy on me. My strength evaporated like water on a sunny day 5until I finally admitted all my sins to you and stopped trying to hide them. I said to myself, "I will confess them to the Lord." And you forgave me! All my guilt is gone.

6Now I say that each believer should confess his sins to God when he is aware of them, while there is time to be forgiven. Judgment will not touch him if he does.

7You are my hiding place from every storm of life; you even keep me from getting into trouble! You surround me with songs of victory. 8I will instruct you (says the Lord) and guide you along the best pathway for your life; I will advise you and watch your progress. 9Don't be like a senseless horse or mule that has to have a bit in its mouth to keep it in line!

10Many sorrows come to the wicked, but abiding love surrounds those who trust in the Lord. 11So rejoice in him, all those who are his, and shout for joy, all those who try to obey him.

PROVERBS FOR TODAY/ 21:5–7

Steady plodding brings prosperity; hasty speculation brings poverty. Dishonest gain will never last, so why take the risk? Because the wicked are unfair, their violence boomerangs and destroys them.

AUGUST 13

NEHEMIAH 5:14—7:60

I would like to mention that for the entire twelve years that I was governor of Judah—from the twentieth until the thirty-second year of the reign of King Artaxerxes—my aides and I accepted no salaries or other assistance from the people of Israel. 15This was quite a contrast to the former governors who had demanded food and wine and $100 a day in cash, and had put the population at the mercy of their aides, who tyrannized them; but I obeyed God and did not act that way. 16I stayed at work on the wall and refused to speculate in land; I also required my officials to spend time on the wall. 17All this despite the fact that I regularly fed 150 Jewish officials at my table, besides visitors from other countries! 18The provisions required for each day were one ox, six fat sheep, and a large number of domestic fowls; and we needed a huge supply of all kinds of wines every ten days. Yet I refused to make a special levy against the people, for they were already having a difficult time. 19O my God, please keep in mind all that I've done for these people and bless me for it.

WHEN Sanballat, Tobiah, Geshem the Arab, and the rest of our enemies found out that we had almost completed the rebuilding of the wall—though we had not yet hung all the doors of the gates—²they sent me a message asking me to meet them in one of the villages in the Plain of Ono. But I realized they were plotting to kill me, ³so I replied by sending back this message to them:

"I am doing a great work! Why should I stop to come and visit with you?"

⁴Four times they sent the same message, and each time I gave the same reply. ⁵,⁶The fifth time, Sanballat's servant came with an open letter in his hand and this is what it said:

"Geshem tells me that everywhere he goes he hears that the Jews are planning to rebel, and that is why you are building the wall. He claims you plan to be their king—that is what is being said. ⁷He also reports that you have appointed prophets to campaign for you at Jerusalem by saying, 'Look! Nehemiah is just the man we need!'

"You can be very sure that I am going to pass along these interesting comments to King Artaxerxes! I suggest that you come and talk it over with me—for that is the only way you can save yourself!"

⁸My reply was, "You know you are lying. There isn't one bit of truth to the whole story. ⁹You're just trying to scare us into stopping our work." (O Lord God, please strengthen me!)

¹⁰A few days later I went to visit Shemaiah (son of Delaiah, who was the son of Mehetabel), for he said he was receiving a message from God.

"Let us hide in the Temple and bolt the door," he exclaimed, "for they are coming tonight to kill you."

¹¹But I replied, "Should I, the governor, run away from danger? And if I go into the Temple, not being a priest, I would forfeit my life. No, I won't do it!"

¹²,¹³Then I realized that God had not spoken to him, but Tobiah and Sanballat had hired him to scare me and make me sin by fleeing to the Temple; and then they would be able to accuse me.

¹⁴"O my God," I prayed, "don't forget all the evil of Tobiah, Sanballat, No-adiah the prophetess, and all the other prophets who have tried to discourage me."

¹⁵The wall was finally finished in early September—just fifty-two days after we had begun!

¹⁶When our enemies and the surrounding nations heard about it, they were frightened and humiliated, and they realized that the work had been done with the help of our God. ¹⁷During those fifty-two days many letters went back and forth between Tobiah and the wealthy politicians of Judah. ¹⁸For many in Judah had sworn allegiance to him because his father-in-law was Shecaniah (son of Arah) and because his son Jehohanan was married to the daughter of Meshullam (son of Berechiah). ¹⁹They all told me what a wonderful man Tobiah was, and then they told him everything I had said; and Tobiah sent many threatening letters to frighten me.

AFTER the wall was finished and we had hung the doors in the gates and had appointed the gatekeepers, singers, and Levites, ²I gave the responsibility of governing Jerusalem to my brother Hanani and to Hananiah, the commander of the fortress—a very faithful man who revered God more than most people do. ³I issued instructions to them not to open the Jerusalem gates until well after sunrise, and to close and lock them while the guards were still on duty. I also directed that the guards be residents of Jerusalem, and that they must be on duty at regular times, and that each homeowner who lived near the wall must guard the section of wall next to his own home. ⁴For the city was large, but the population was small; and only a few houses were scattered throughout the city.

⁵Then the Lord told me to call together all the leaders of the city, along with the ordinary citizens, for registration. For I had found the record of the genealogies of those who had returned to Judah be-

fore, and this is what was written in it:

6"The following is a list of the names of the Jews who returned to Judah after being exiled by King Nebuchadnezzar of Babylon.

7"Their leaders were:

Zerubbabel, Jeshua, Nehemiah, Azariah, Ra-amiah, Nahamani, Mordecai, Bilshan, Mispereth, Bigvai, Nehum, Baanah.

"The others who returned at that time were:

8-38From the subclan of Parosh, 2,172;
From the subclan of Shephatiah, 372;
From the subclan of Arah, 652;
From the families of Jeshua and Joab of the subclan of Pahath-moab, 2,818;
From the subclan of Elam, 1,254;
From the subclan of Zattu, 845;
From the subclan of Zaccai, 760;
From the subclan of Binnui, 648;
From the subclan of Bebai, 628;
From the subclan of Azgad, 2,322;
From the subclan of Adonikam, 667;
From the subclan of Bigvai, 2,067;
From the subclan of Adin, 655;
From the family of Hezekiah of the subclan of Ater, 98;
From the subclan of Hashum, 328;
From the subclan of Bezai, 324;
From the subclan of Hariph, 112;
From the subclan of Gibeon, 95;
From the subclans of Bethlehem and Netophah, 188;
From the subclan of Anathoth, 128;
From the subclan of Beth-azmaveth, 42;
From the subclans of Kiriath-jearim, Chephirah, and Be-eroth, 743;
From the subclans of Ramah and Geba, 621;
From the subclan of Michmas, 122;
From the subclans of Bethel and Ai, 123;
From the subclan of Nebo, 52;
From the subclan of Elam, 1,254;
From the subclan of Harim, 320;
From the subclan of Jericho, 345;
From the subclans of Lod, Hadid, and Ono, 721;
From the subclan of Senaah, 3,930.

39-42"Here are the statistics concerning the returning priests:

From the family of Jeshua of the subclan of Jedaiah, 973;
From the subclan of Immer, 1,052;
From the subclan of Pashhur, 1,247;
From the subclan of Harim, 1,017.

43,44,45"Here are the statistics concerning the Levites:

From the family of Kadmi-el of the subclan of Hodevah of the clan of Jeshua, 74;
The choir members from the clan of Asaph, 148;
From the clans of Shallum, (all of whom were gatekeepers), 138.

46-56"Of the Temple assistants, the following subclans were represented:

Ziha, Hasupha, Tabbaoth, Keros, Sia, Padon, Lebana, Hagaba, Shalmai, Hanan, Giddel, Gahar, Re-aiah, Rezin, Nekoda, Gazzam, Uzza, Paseah, Besai, Asnah, Me-unim, Nephushesim, Bakbuk, Hakupha, Harhur, Bazlith, Mehida, Harsha, Barkos, Sisera, Temah, Neziah, Hatipha.

57,58,59"Following is a list of the descendants of Solomon's officials who returned to Judah:

Sotai, Sophereth, Perida, Jaala, Darkon, Giddel, Shephatiah, Hattil, Pochereth-hazzebaim, Amon.

60"In all, the Temple assistants and the descendants of Solomon's officers numbered 392."

1 CORINTHIANS 8:1–13

NEXT is your question about eating food that has been sacrificed to idols. On this question everyone feels that only his answer is the right one! But although being a "know-it-all" makes us feel important, what is really needed to build the church is love. 2If anyone thinks he knows all the answers, he is just showing his ignorance. 3But the person who truly loves God is the one who is open to God's knowledge.

4So now, what about it? Should we eat meat that has been sacrificed to idols?

Well, we all know that an idol is not really a god, and that there is only one God, and no other. 5According to some people, there are a great many gods, both in heaven and on earth. 6But we know that there is only one God, the Father, who created all things and made us to be his own; and one Lord Jesus Christ, who made everything and gives us life.

7However, some Christians don't realize this. All their lives they have been used to thinking of idols as alive, and have believed that food offered to the idols is really being offered to actual gods. So when they eat such food it bothers them and hurts their tender consciences. 8Just remember that God doesn't care whether we eat it or not. We are no worse off if we don't eat it, and no better off if we do. 9But be careful not to use your freedom to eat it, lest you cause some Christian brother to sin whose conscience is weaker than yours.

10You see, this is what may happen: Someone who thinks it is wrong to eat this food will see you eating at a temple restaurant, for you know there is no harm in it. Then he will become bold enough to do it too, although all the time he still feels it is wrong. 11So because you "know it is all right to do it," you will be responsible for causing great spiritual damage to a brother with a tender conscience for whom Christ died. 12And it

is a sin against Christ to sin against your brother by encouraging him to do something he thinks is wrong. 13So if eating meat offered to idols is going to make my brother sin, I'll not eat any of it as long as I live, because I don't want to do this to him.

PSALM 33:1–11

LET all the joys of the godly well up in praise to the Lord, for it is right to praise him. 2Play joyous melodies of praise upon the lyre and on the harp. 3Compose new songs of praise to him, accompanied skillfully on the harp; sing joyfully.

4For all God's words are right, and everything he does is worthy of our trust. 5He loves whatever is just and good; the earth is filled with his tender love. 6He merely spoke, and the heavens were formed, and all the galaxies of stars. 7He made the oceans, pouring them into his vast reservoirs.

8Let everyone in all the world—men, women and children—fear the Lord and stand in awe of him. 9For when he but spoke, the world began! It appeared at his command! 10And with a breath he can scatter the plans of all the nations who oppose him, 11but his own plan stands forever. His intentions are the same for every generation.

PROVERBS FOR TODAY/ 21:8–10

A man is known by his actions. An evil man lives an evil life; a good man lives a godly life. It is better to live in the corner of an attic than with a crabby woman in a lovely home. An evil man loves to harm others; being a good neighbor is out of his line.

AUGUST 14

NEHEMIAH 7:61—9:21

ANOTHER group returned to Jerusalem at that time from the Persian cities of Telmelah, Telharsha, Cherub, Addon, and Immer. But

they had lost their genealogies and could not prove their Jewish ancestry; 62these were the subclans of Delaiah, Tobiah, and Nekoda—a total of 642.

63There were also several subclans of

priests named after Habaiah, Hakkoz, and Barzillai (he married one of the daughters of Barzillai the Gileadite and took her family name), 64,65whose genealogies had been lost. So they were not allowed to continue as priests or even to receive the priests' share of food from the sacrifices until the Urim and Thummim had been consulted to find out from God whether or not they actually were descendants of priests.

66There was a total of 42,360 citizens who returned to Judah at that time; 67also, 7,337 slaves and 245 choir members, both men and women. 68,69They took with them 736 horses, 245 mules, 435 camels, and 6,720 donkeys.

70Some of their leaders gave gifts for the work. The governor gave $5,000 in gold, 50 gold bowls, and 530 sets of clothing for the priests. 71The other leaders gave a total of $100,000 in gold and $77,000 in silver; 72and the common people gave $100,000 in gold, $70,000 in silver, and sixty-seven sets of clothing for the priests.

73The priests, the Levites, the gatekeepers, the choir members, the Temple attendants, and the rest of the people now returned home to their own towns and villages throughout Judah. But during the month of September, they came back to Jerusalem.

Now, in mid-September, all the people assembled at the plaza in front of the Water Gate and requested Ezra, their religious leader, to read to them the law of God which he had given to Moses.

So Ezra the priest brought out to them the scroll of Moses' laws. He stood on a wooden stand made especially for the occasion so that everyone could see him as he read. He faced the square in front of the Water Gate, and read from early morning until noon. Everyone stood up as he opened the scroll. And all who were old enough to understand paid close attention. To his right stood Mattithiah, Shema, Anaiah, Uriah, Hilkiah, and Maaseiah. To his left were Pedaiah, Mi-

sha-el, Malchijah, Hashum, Hash-baddenah, Zechariah, and Meshullam.

6Then Ezra blessed the Lord, the great God, and all the people said, "Amen," and lifted their hands toward heaven; then they bowed and worshiped the Lord with their faces toward the ground.

7,8As Ezra read from the scroll, Jeshua, Bani, Sherebiah, Jamin, Akkub, Shabbethai, Hodiah, Ma-aseiah, Kelita, Azariah, Jozabad, Hanan, Pelaiah, and the Levites went among the people and explained the meaning of the passage that was being read. 9All the people began sobbing when they heard the commands of the law.

Then Ezra the priest, and I as governor, and the Levites who were assisting me, said to them, "Don't cry on such a day as this! For today is a sacred day before the Lord your God— 10it is a time to celebrate with a hearty meal, and to send presents to those in need, for the joy of the Lord is your strength. You must not be dejected and sad!"

11And the Levites, too, quieted the people, telling them, "That's right! Don't weep! For this is a day of holy joy, not of sadness."

12So the people went away to eat a festive meal and to send presents; it was a time of great and joyful celebration because they could hear and understand God's words.

13The next day the clan leaders and the priests and Levites met with Ezra to go over the law in greater detail. 14As they studied it, they noted that Jehovah had told Moses that the people of Israel should live in tents during the Festival of Tabernacles to be held that month. 15He had said also that a proclamation should be made throughout the cities of the land, especially in Jerusalem, telling the people to go to the hills to get branches from olive, myrtle, palm, and fig trees and to make huts in which to live for the duration of the feast.

16So the people went out and cut branches and used them to build huts on the roofs of their houses, or in their courtyards, or in the court of the Temple, or on the plaza beside the Water Gate, or at the Ephraim Gate Plaza. 17They lived in these huts for the seven days of the feast, and everyone was filled with joy! (This procedure had not been carried out since the days of Joshua.) 18Ezra read from the scroll on each of the seven days of the feast, and on the eighth day there was a solemn closing service as required by the laws of Moses.

ON October 10 the people returned for another observance; this time they fasted and clothed themselves with sackcloth and sprinkled dirt in their hair. And the Israelis separated themselves from all foreigners. 3The laws of God were read aloud to them for two or three hours, and for several more hours they took turns confessing their own sins and those of their ancestors. And everyone worshiped the Lord their God. 4Some of the Levites were on the platform praising the Lord God with songs of joy. These men were Jeshua, Kadmi-el, Bani, Shebaniah, Bunni, Sherebiah, Bani, and Chenani.

5Then the Levite leaders called out to the people, "Stand up and praise the Lord your God, for he lives from everlasting to everlasting. Praise his glorious name! It is far greater than we can think or say."

The leaders in this part of the service were Jeshua, Kadmi-el, Bani, Hashabneiah, Sherebiah, Hodiah, Shebaniah, and Pethahiah.

6Then Ezra prayed, "You alone are God. You have made the skies and the heavens, the earth and the seas, and everything in them. You preserve it all; and all the angels of heaven worship you.

7"You are the Lord God who chose Abram and brought him from Ur of the Chaldeans and renamed him Abraham. 8When he was faithful to you, you made a contract with him to forever give him and his descendants the land of the Canaanites, Hittites, Amorites, Perizzites, Jebusites, and Girgashites; and now you have done what you promised, for you are always true to your word.

9"You saw the troubles and sorrows of our ancestors in Egypt, and you heard their cries from beside the Red Sea. 10You displayed great miracles against Pharaoh and his people, for you knew how brutally the Egyptians were treating them; you have a glorious reputation because of those never-to-be-forgotten deeds. 11You divided the sea for your people so they could go through on dry land! And then you destroyed their enemies in the depths of the sea; they sank like stones beneath the mighty waters. 12You led our ancestors by a pillar of cloud during the day and a pillar of fire at night so that they could find their way.

13"You came down upon Mount Sinai and spoke with them from heaven and gave them good laws and true commandments, 14including the laws about the holy Sabbath; and you commanded them, through Moses your servant, to obey them all.

15"You gave them bread from heaven when they were hungry and water from the rock when they were thirsty. You commanded them to go in and conquer the land you had sworn to give them; 16but our ancestors were a proud and stubborn lot, and they refused to listen to your commandments.

17"They refused to obey and didn't pay any attention to the miracles you did for them; instead, they rebelled and appointed a leader to take them back into slavery in Egypt! But you are a God of forgiveness, always ready to pardon, gracious and merciful, slow to become angry, and full of love and mercy; you didn't abandon them, 18even though they made a calf-idol and proclaimed, 'This is our God! He brought us out of Egypt!' They sinned in so many ways, 19but in your great mercy you didn't abandon them to die in the wilderness! The pillar of cloud led them forward day by day, and the pillar of fire showed them the way through the night. 20You sent your good Spirit to instruct them, and you did not stop giving them bread from heaven or water for their thirst. 21For forty years you sustained them in the wilderness;

they lacked nothing in all that time. Their clothes didn't wear out and their feet didn't swell!

1 CORINTHIANS 9:1–19

I am an apostle, God's messenger, responsible to no mere man. I am one who has actually seen Jesus our Lord with my own eyes. And your changed lives are the result of my hard work for him. 2If in the opinion of others, I am not an apostle, I certainly am to you, for you have been won to Christ through me. 3This is my answer to those who question my rights.

4Or don't I have any rights at all? Can't I claim the same privilege the other apostles have of being a guest in your homes? 5If I had a wife, and if she were a believer, couldn't I bring her along on these trips just as the other disciples do, and as the Lord's brothers do, and as Peter does? 6And must Barnabas and I alone keep working for our living, while you supply these others? 7What soldier in the army has to pay his own expenses? And have you ever heard of a farmer who harvests his crop and doesn't have the right to eat some of it? What shepherd takes care of a flock of sheep and goats and isn't allowed to drink some of the milk? 8And I'm not merely quoting the opinions of men as to what is right. I'm telling you what God's law says. 9For in the law God gave to Moses he said that you must not put a muzzle on an ox to keep it from eating when it is treading out the wheat. Do you suppose God was thinking only about oxen when he said this? 10Wasn't he also thinking about us? Of course he was. He said this to show us that Christian workers should be paid by those they help. Those who do the plowing and threshing should expect some share of the harvest.

11We have planted good spiritual seed in your souls. Is it too much to ask, in return, for mere food and clothing? 12You give them to others who preach to you, and you should. But shouldn't we have an even greater right to them?

Yet we have *never* used this right, but supply our own needs without your help. We have never demanded payment of any kind for fear that, if we did, you might be less interested in our message to you from Christ.

13Don't you realize that God told those working in his temple to take for their own needs some of the food brought there as gifts to him? And those who work at the altar of God get a share of the food that is brought by those offering it to the Lord. 14In the same way the Lord has given orders that those who preach the Gospel should be supported by those who accept it.

15Yet I have never asked you for one penny. And I am not writing this to hint that I would like to start now. In fact, I would rather die of hunger than lose the satisfaction I get from preaching to you without charge. 16For just preaching the Gospel isn't any special credit to me—I couldn't keep from preaching it if I wanted to. I would be utterly miserable. Woe unto me if I don't.

17If I were volunteering my services of my own free will, then the Lord would give me a special reward; but that is not the situation, for God has picked me out and given me this sacred trust and I have no choice. 18Under this circumstance, what is my pay? It is the special joy I get from preaching the Good News without expense to anyone, never demanding my rights.

19And this has a real advantage: I am not bound to obey anyone just because he pays my salary; yet I have freely and happily become a servant of any and all so that I can win them to Christ.

PSALM 33:12–22

BLESSED is the nation whose God is the Lord, whose people he has chosen as his own. 13,14,15The Lord gazes down upon mankind from heaven where he lives. He has made their hearts and closely watches everything they do.

16,17The best-equipped army cannot

save a king—for great strength is not enough to save anyone. A war horse is a poor risk for winning victories—it is strong but it cannot save.

18,19But the eyes of the Lord are watching over those who fear him, who rely upon his steady love. He will keep them from death even in times of famine!

20We depend upon the Lord alone to save us. Only he can help us; he protects us like a shield. 21No wonder we are happy in the Lord! For we are trusting him. We trust his holy name. 22Yes, Lord, let your constant love surround us, for our hopes are in you alone.

PROVERBS FOR TODAY/ 21:11–12

The wise man learns by listening; the simpleton can learn only by seeing scorners punished. God, the Righteous One, knows what is going on in the homes of the wicked, and will bring the wicked to judgment.

AUGUST 15

NEHEMIAH 9:22—10:39

THEN you helped them conquer great kingdoms and many nations, and you placed your people in every corner of the land; they completely took over the land of King Sihon of Heshbon and King Og of Bashan. 23You caused a population explosion among the Israelis and brought them into the land you had promised to their ancestors. 24You subdued whole nations before them—even the kings and the people of the Canaanites were powerless! 25Your people captured fortified cities and fertile land; they took over houses full of good things, with cisterns and vineyards and oliveyards and many, many fruit trees; so they ate and were full and enjoyed themselves in all your blessings.

26"But despite all this they were disobedient and rebelled against you. They threw away your law, killed the prophets who told them to return to you, and they did many other terrible things. 27So you gave them to their enemies. But in their time of trouble they cried to you and you heard them from heaven, and in great mercy you sent them saviors who delivered them from their enemies. 28But when all was going well, your people turned to sin again, and once more you

let their enemies conquer them. Yet whenever your people returned to you and cried to you for help, once more you listened from heaven, and in your wonderful mercy delivered them! 29You punished them in order to turn them toward your laws; but even though they should have obeyed them, they were proud and wouldn't listen, and continued to sin. 30You were patient with them for many years. You sent your prophets to warn them about their sins, but still they wouldn't listen. So once again you allowed the heathen nations to conquer them. 31But in your great mercy you did not destroy them completely or abandon them forever. What a gracious and merciful God you are!

32"And now, O great and awesome God, you who keep your promises of love and kindness—do not let all the hardships we have gone through become as nothing to you. Great trouble has come upon us and upon our kings and princes and priests and prophets and ancestors from the days when the kings of Assyria first triumphed over us until now. 33Every time you punished us you were being perfectly fair; we have sinned so greatly that you gave us only what we deserved. 34Our kings, princes, priests, and ancestors didn't obey your laws or listen to your warnings. 35They did not worship you despite the wonderful things you did for them and the great goodness you showered upon them. You gave them a large, fat land, but they refused to turn from their wickedness.

36"So now we are slaves here in the land of plenty which you gave to our ancestors! Slaves among all this abundance! 37The lush yield of this land passes into the hands of the kings whom you have allowed to conquer us because of our sins. They have power over our bodies and our cattle, and we serve them at their pleasure and are in great misery. 38Because of all this, we again promise to serve the Lord! And we and our princes and Levites and priests put our names to this covenant."

I, Nehemiah the governor, signed the covenant. The others who signed it were: Zedekiah, Seraiah, Azariah, Jeremiah, Pashhur, Amariah, Malchijah, Hattush, Shebaniah, Malluch, Harim, Meremoth, Obadiah, Daniel, Ginnethon, Baruch, Meshullam, Abijah, Mija-min, Ma-aziah, Bilgai, Shemaiah. (All those listed above were priests.)

9-13These were the Levites who signed:

Jeshua (son of Azaniah), Binnui (son of Henadad), Kadmi-el, Shebaniah, Hodiah, Kelita, Pelaiah, Hanan, Mica, Rehob, Hashabiah, Zaccur, Sherebiah, Shebaniah, Hodiah, Bani, Beninu.

14-27The political leaders who signed: Parosh, Pahath-moab, Elam, Zattu, Bani, Bunni, Azgad, Bebai, Adonijah, Bigvai, Adin, Ater, Hezekiah, Azzur, Hodiah, Hashum, Bezai, Hariph, Anathoth, Nebai, Magpiash, Meshullam, Hezir, Meshezabel, Zadok, Jaddu-a, Pelatiah, Hanan, Anaiah, Hoshea, Hananiah, Hasshub, Hallohesh, Pilha, Shobek, Rehum, Hashabnah, Ma-aseiah, Ahiah, Hanan, Anan, Malluch, Harim, Baanah.

28These men signed on behalf of the entire nation—for the common people; the priests; the Levites; the gatekeepers; the choir members; the Temple servants; and all the rest who, with their wives and sons and daughters who were old enough to understand, had separated themselves from the heathen people of the land in order to serve God. 29For we all heartily agreed to this oath and vowed to accept the curse of God unless we obeyed God's laws as issued by his servant Moses.

30We also agreed not to let our daughters marry non-Jewish men and not to let our sons marry non-Jewish girls.

31We further agreed that if the heathen people in the land should bring any grain or other produce to be sold on the Sabbath or on any other holy day, we would refuse to buy it. And we agreed not to do any work every seventh year and to forgive and cancel the debts of our brother Jews.

32We also agreed to charge ourselves annually with a Temple tax so that there would be enough money to care for the Temple of our God; 33for we needed supplies of the special Bread of the Presence, as well as grain offerings and burnt offerings for the Sabbaths, the new moon feasts, and the annual feasts. We also needed to purchase the other items necessary for the work of the Temple and for the atonement of Israel.

34Then we tossed a coin to determine when—at regular times each year—the families of the priests, Levites, and leaders should supply the wood for the burnt offerings at the Temple as required in the law.

35We also agreed always to bring the first part of every crop to the Temple— whether it be a ground crop or from our fruit and olive trees.

36We agreed to give to God our oldest sons and the firstborn of all our cattle, herds, and flocks, just as the law requires; we presented them to the priests who minister in the Temple of our God. 37They stored the produce in the Temple of our God—the best of our grain crops, and other contributions, the first of our fruit, and the first of the new wine and olive oil. And we promised to bring to the Levites a tenth of everything our land produced, for the Levites were responsible to collect the tithes in all our rural towns. 38A priest—a descendant of Aaron—would be with the Levites as they received these tithes, and a tenth of all that was collected as tithes was delivered to the Temple and placed in the storage areas. 39The people and the Levites were required by law to bring these offerings of grain, new wine, and olive oil to the Temple and place them in the sacred containers for use by the ministering priests, the gatekeepers, and the choir singers.

So we agreed together not to neglect the Temple of our God.

1 CORINTHIANS 9:20—10:14

WHEN I am with the Jews I seem as one of them so that they will listen to the Gospel and I can win them to Christ. When I am with Gentiles who follow Jewish customs and ceremonies I don't argue, even though I don't agree, because I want to help them. 21When with the heathen I agree with them as much as I can, except of course that I must always do what is right as a Christian. And so, by agreeing, I can win their confidence and help them too.

22When I am with those whose consciences bother them easily, I don't act as though I know it all and don't say they are foolish; the result is that they are willing to let me help them. Yes, whatever a person is like, I try to find common ground with him so that he will let me tell him about Christ and let Christ save him. 23I do this to get the Gospel to them and also for the blessing I myself receive when I see them come to Christ.

24In a race, everyone runs but only one person gets first prize. So run your race to win. 25To win the contest you must deny yourselves many things that would keep you from doing your best. An athlete goes to all this trouble just to win a blue ribbon or a silver cup, but we do it for a heavenly reward that never disappears. 26So I run straight to the goal with purpose in every step. I fight to win. I'm not just shadow-boxing or playing around. 27Like an athlete I punish my body, treating it roughly, training it to do what it should, not what it wants to. Otherwise I fear that after enlisting others for the race, I myself might be declared unfit and ordered to stand aside.

FOR we must never forget, dear brothers, what happened to our people in the wilderness long ago. God guided them by sending a cloud that moved along ahead of them; and he brought them all safely through the waters of the Red Sea. 2This might be called their "baptism"—baptized both in sea and cloud!—as followers of Moses—their commitment to him as their leader. 3,4And by a miracle God sent them food to eat and water to drink there in the desert; they drank the water that Christ gave them. He was there with them as a mighty Rock of spiritual refreshment. 5Yet after all this most of them did not obey God, and he destroyed them in the wilderness.

6From this lesson we are warned that we must not desire evil things as they did, 7nor worship idols as they did. (The Scriptures tell us, "The people sat down to eat and drink and then got up to dance" in worship of the golden calf.)

8Another lesson for us is what happened when some of them sinned with other men's wives, and 23,000 fell dead in one day. 9And don't try the Lord's patience—they did, and died from snake bites. 10And don't murmur against God and his dealings with you, as some of them did, for that is why God sent his Angel to destroy them.

11All these things happened to them as examples—as object lessons to us—to warn us against doing the same things; they were written down so that we could read about them and learn from them in these last days as the world nears its end.

12So be careful. If you are thinking, "Oh, I would never behave like that"—let this be a warning to you. For you too may fall into sin. 13But remember this—the wrong desires that come into your life aren't anything new and different. Many others have faced exactly the same problems before you. And no temptation is irresistible. You can trust God to keep the temptation from becoming so strong that you can't stand up against it, for he has promised this and will do what he says. He will show you how to escape temptation's power so that you can bear up patiently against it.

14So, dear friends, carefully avoid idol-worship of every kind.

PSALM 34:1–10

I will praise the Lord no matter what happens. I will constantly speak of his glories and grace. 2I will boast of all his kindness to me. Let all who are discouraged take heart. 3Let us praise the Lord together, and exalt his name.

4For I cried to him and he answered me! He freed me from all my fears. 5Others too were radiant at what he did for them. Theirs was no downcast look of rejection! 6This poor man cried to the Lord—and the Lord heard him and saved him out of his troubles. 7For the Angel of the Lord guards and rescues all who reverence him.

8Oh, put God to the test and see how kind he is! See for yourself the way his mercies shower down on all who trust in him. 9If you belong to the Lord, reverence him; for everyone who does this has everything he needs. 10Even strong young lions sometimes go hungry, but those of us who reverence the Lord will never lack any good thing.

PROVERBS FOR TODAY/ 21:13

He who shuts his ears to the cries of the poor will be ignored in his own time of need.

AUGUST 16

NEHEMIAH 11:1—12:26

THE Israeli officials were living in Jerusalem, the Holy City, at this time; but now a tenth of the people from the other cities and towns of Judah and Benjamin were selected by lot to live there too. 2Some who moved to Jerusalem at this time were volunteers, and they were highly honored.

3Following is a list of the names of the provincial officials who came to Jerusalem (though most of the leaders, the priests, the Levites, the Temple assistants, and the descendants of Solomon's servants continued to live in their own homes in the various cities of Judah).

4,5,6Leaders from the tribe of Judah:
Athaiah (son of Uzziah, son of Zechariah, son of Amariah, son of Shephatiah, son of Mahalalel, a descendant of Perez);

Ma-aseiah (son of Baruch, son of Colhozeh, son of Hazaiah, son of Adaiah, son of Joiarib, son of Zechariah, son of the Shilonite).

These were the 468 stalwart descendants of Perez who lived in Jerusalem.

7,8,9Leaders from the tribe of Benjamin:
Sallu (son of Meshullam, son of Joed, son of Pedaiah, son of Kolaiah, son of Ma-aseiah, son of Ithi-el, son of Jeshaiah).

The 968 descendants of Gabbai and Sallai. Their chief was Joel, son of Zichri, who was assisted by Judah, son of Hassenu-ah.

10-14Leaders from among the priests:
Jedaiah (son of Joiarib);
Jachin;
Seraiah (son of Hilkiah, son of Meshullam, son of Zadok, son of

Meraioth, son of Ahitub the chief priest).

In all, there were 822 priests doing the work at the Temple under the leadership of these men. And there were 242 priests under the leadership of Adaiah (son of Jeroham, son of Pelaliah, son of Amzi, son of Zechariah, son of Pashhur, son of Malchijah).

There were also 128 stalwart men under the leadership of Amashsai (son of Azarel, son of Ahzai, son of Meshillemoth, son of Immer); who was assisted by Zabdiel (son of Haggedolim).

15,16,17Levite leaders:

Shemaiah (son of Hasshub, son of Azrikam, son of Hashabiah, son of Bunni);

Shabbethai and Jozabad, who were in charge of the work outside the Temple;

Mattaniah (son of Mica, son of Zabdi, son of Asaph) was the one who began the thanksgiving services with prayer;

Bakbukiah and Abda (son of Shammua, son of Galal, son of Jeduthun) were his assistants.

18In all, there were 284 Levites in Jerusalem.

19There were also 172 gatekeepers, led by Akkub, Talmon, and others of their clan. 20The other priests, Levites, and people lived wherever their family inheritance was located. 21However, the Temple workers (whose leaders were Ziha and Gishpa) all lived in Ophel.

22,23The supervisor of the Levites in Jerusalem and of those serving at the Temple was Uzzi (son of Bani, son of Hashabiah, son of Mattaniah, son of Mica), a descendant of Asaph, whose clan became the Tabernacle singers. He was appointed by King David, who also set the pay scale of the singers.

24Pethahiah (son of Meshezabel, a descendant of Zerah, a son of Judah) assisted in all matters of public administration.

25-30Some of the towns where the people of Judah lived were:

Kiriath-arba, Dibon, Jekabzeel (and

their surrounding villages), Jeshua, Moladah, Beth-pelet, Hazar-shual, Beer-sheba (and its surrounding villages), Ziklag, Meconah and its villages, En-rimmon, Zorah, Jarmuth, Zanoah, Adullam (and their surrounding villages), Lachish and its nearby fields, Azekah and its towns.

So the people spread from Beer-sheba to the valley of Hinnom.

31-35The people of the tribe of Benjamin lived at:

Geba, Michmash, Aija, Bethel (and its surrounding villages), Anathoth, Nob, Ananiah, Hazor, Ramah, Gittaim, Hadid, Zeboim, Neballat, Lod, Ono (the Valley of the Craftsmen).

36Some of the Levites who lived in Judah were sent to live with the tribe of Benjamin.

HERE is a list of the priests who accompanied Zerubbabel (son of Shealtiel) and Jeshua:

Seraiah, Jeremiah, Ezra, Amariah, Malluch, Hattush, Shecaniah, Rehum, Meremoth, Iddo, Ginnethoi, Abijah, Mijamin, Ma-adiah, Bilgah, Shemaiah, Joiarib, Jedaiah, Sallu, Amok, Hilkiah, Jedaiah.

8The Levites who went with them were: Jeshua, Binnui, Kadmi-el,

Sherebiah, Judah, Mattaniah—who was the one in charge of the thanksgiving service.

9Bakbukiah and Unno, their fellow clansmen, helped them during the service.

10,11Jeshua was the father of Joiakim;

Joiakim was the father of Eliashib;

Eliashib was the father of Joiada;

Joiada was the father of Jonathan;

Jonathan was the father of Jaddu-a.

12-21The following were the clan leaders of the priests who served under the High Priest Joiakim:

Meraiah, leader of the Seraiah clan;

Hananiah, leader of the Jeremiah clan;

Meshullam, leader of the Ezra clan;

Jehohanan, leader of the Amariah clan;

Jonathan, leader of the Malluchi clan;

Joseph, leader of the Shebaniah clan;

Adna, leader of the Harim clan;

Helkai, leader of the Meraioth clan;

Zechariah, leader of the Iddo clan;

Meshullam, leader of the Ginnethon clan;

Zichri, leader of the Abijah clan;

Piltai, leader of the Moadiah and Miniamin clans;

Shammu-a, leader of the Bilgah clan;

Jehonathan, leader of the Shemaiah clan;

Mattenai, leader of the Joiarib clan;

Uzzi, leader of the Jedaiah clan;

Kallai, leader of the Sallai clan;

Eber, leader of the Amok clan;

Hashabiah, leader of the Hilkiah clan;

Nethanel, leader of the Jedaiah clan.

22A genealogical record of the heads of the clans of the priests and Levites was compiled during the reign of King Darius of Persia, in the days of Eliashib, Joiada, Johanan, and Jaddu-a—all of whom were Levites. 23In *The Book of the Chronicles* the Levite names were recorded down to the days of Johanan, the son of Eliashib.

24These were the chiefs of the Levites at that time:

Hashabiah, Sherebiah, and Jeshua (son of Kadmi-el).

Their fellow-clansmen helped them during the ceremonies of praise and thanksgiving, just as commanded by David, the man of God.

25The gatekeepers who had charge of the collection centers at the gates were:

Mattaniah, Bakbukiah, Obadiah, Meshullam, Talmon, Akkub.

26These were the men who were active in the time of Joiakim (son of Jeshua, son of Jozadak), and when I was the governor, and when Ezra was the priest and teacher of religion.

1 CORINTHIANS 10:15—11:2

YOU are intelligent people. Look now and see for yourselves whether what I am about to say is true. 16When we ask the Lord's blessing upon our drinking from the cup of wine at the Lord's Table, this means, doesn't it, that all who drink it are sharing together the blessing of Christ's blood? And when we break off pieces of the bread from the loaf to eat there together, this shows that we are sharing together in the benefits of his body. 17No matter how many of us there are, we all eat from the same loaf, showing that we are all parts of the one body of Christ. 18And the Jewish people, all who eat the sacrifices, are united by that act.

19What am I trying to say? Am I saying that the idols to whom the heathen bring sacrifices are really alive and are real gods, and that these sacrifices are of some value? No, not at all. 20What I am saying is that those who offer food to these idols are united together in sacrificing to demons, certainly not to God. And I don't want any of you to be partners with demons when you eat the same food, along with the heathen, that has been offered to these idols. 21You cannot drink from the cup at the Lord's Table and at Satan's table, too. You cannot eat bread both at the Lord's Table and at Satan's table.

22What? Are you tempting the Lord to be angry with you? Are you stronger than he is?

23You are certainly free to eat food offered to idols if you want to; it's not against God's laws to eat such meat, but that doesn't mean that you should go ahead and do it. It may be perfectly legal, but it may not be best and helpful. 24Don't think only of yourself. Try to think of the other fellow, too, and what is best for him.

25Here's what you should do. Take any meat you want that is sold at the market. Don't ask whether or not it was offered to idols, lest the answer hurt your conscience. 26For the earth and every good thing in it belongs to the Lord and is yours to enjoy.

27If someone who isn't a Christian asks you out to dinner, go ahead; accept the invitation if you want to. Eat whatever is on the table and don't ask any questions about it. Then you won't know whether or not it has been used as a sacrifice to idols, and you won't risk having a bad conscience over eating it. 28But if someone warns you that this meat has been offered to idols, then don't eat it for the sake of the man who told you, and of his conscience. 29In this case *his* feeling about it is the important thing, not yours.

But why, you may ask, must I be guided and limited by what someone else thinks? 30If I can thank God for the food and enjoy it, why let someone spoil everything just because he thinks I am wrong? 31Well, I'll tell you why. It is because you must do everything for the glory of God, even your eating and drinking. 32So don't be a stumbling block to anyone, whether they are Jews or Gentiles or Christians. 33That is the plan I follow, too. I try to please everyone in everything I do, not doing what I like or what is best for me, but what is best for them, so that they may be saved.

AND you should follow my example, just as I follow Christ's.

2I am so glad, dear brothers, that you have been remembering and doing everything I taught you.

PSALM 34:11–22

SONS and daughters, come and listen and let me teach you the importance of trusting and fearing the Lord. 12Do you want a long, good life? 13Then watch your tongue! Keep your lips from lying. 14Turn from all known sin and spend your time in doing good. Try to live in peace with everyone; work hard at it.

15For the eyes of the Lord are intently watching all who live good lives, and he gives attention when they cry to him. 16But the Lord has made up his mind to wipe out even the memory of evil men from the earth. 17Yes, the Lord hears the good man when he calls to him for help, and saves him out of all his troubles.

18The Lord is close to those whose hearts are breaking; he rescues those who are humbly sorry for their sins. 19The good man does not escape all troubles—he has them too. But the Lord helps him in each and every one. 20Not one of his bones is broken.

21Calamity will surely overtake the wicked; heavy penalties are meted out to those who hate the good. 22But as for those who serve the Lord, he will redeem them; everyone who takes refuge in him will be freely pardoned.

PROVERBS FOR TODAY/ 21:14–16

An angry man is silenced by giving him a gift! A good man loves justice, but it is a calamity to evil-doers. The man who strays away from common sense will end up dead!

AUGUST 17

NEHEMIAH 12:27—13:31

DURING the dedication of the new Jerusalem wall, all the Levites throughout the land came to Jerusalem to assist in the ceremonies and to take part in the joyous occasion with their thanksgiving, cymbals, psaltries, and harps. 28The choir members also came to Jerusalem from the surrounding villages and from the villages of the Netophathites; 29they also came from Bethgilgal and the area of Geba and Azmaveth, for the singers had built their own villages as suburbs of Jerusalem.

30The priests and Levites first dedicated themselves, then the people, the gates, and the wall.

31,32I led the Judean leaders to the top of the wall and divided them into two long lines to walk in opposite directions along the top of the wall, giving thanks as they went. The group which went to the right toward the Dung Gate consisted of half of the leaders of Judah, 33including Hoshaiah, Azariah, Ezra, Meshullam, 34Judah, Benjamin, Shemaiah, and Jeremiah.

35,36The priests who played the trumpets were Zechariah (son of Jonathan, son of Shemaiah, son of Mattaniah, son of Micaiah, son of Zaccur, son of Asaph), Shemaiah, Azarel, Milalai, Gilalai, Maai, Nethanel, Judah, and Hanani. (They used the original musical instruments of King David.) Ezra the priest led this procession. 37When they arrived at the Fountain Gate they went straight ahead and climbed the stairs which go up beside the castle to the old City of David; then they went to the Water Gate on the east.

38The other group, of which I was a member, went around the other way to meet them. We walked from the Tower of Furnaces to the Broad Wall, 39then from the Ephraim Gate to the Old Gate, passed the Fish Gate and the Tower of Hananel, and went on to the gate of the Tower of the Hundred; then we continued on to the Sheep Gate and stopped at the Prison Gate.

40,41Both choirs then proceeded to the Temple. Those with me were joined by the trumpet-playing priests—Eliakim, Ma-aseiah, Miniamin, Micaiah, Eli-o-enai, Zechariah, and Hananiah, 42and by the singers—Ma-aseiah, Shemaiah, Eleazar, Uzzi, Jehohanan, Malchijah, Elam and Ezer.

They sang loudly and clearly under the direction of Jezrahiah the choirmaster.

43Many sacrifices were offered on that joyous day, for God had given us cause for great joy. The women and children rejoiced too, and the joy of the people of Jerusalem was heard far away!

44On that day men were appointed to be in charge of the treasuries, the wave offerings, the tithes, and first-of-the-harvest offerings, and to collect these from the farms as decreed by the laws of Moses. These offerings were assigned to the priests and Levites, for the people of Judah appreciated the priests and Levites and their ministry. 45They also appreciated the work of the singers and gatekeepers, who assisted them in worshiping God and performing the purification ceremonies as required by the laws of David and his son Solomon. 46(It was in the days of David and Asaph that the custom began of having choir directors to lead the choirs in hymns of praise and thanks to God.) 47So now, in the days of Zerubbabel and Nehemiah, the people brought a daily supply of food for the members of the choir, the gatekeepers, and the Levites. The Levites, in turn, gave a portion of what they received to the priests.

ON that same day, as the laws of Moses were being read, the people found a statement which said that the Ammonites and Moabites should never be permitted to worship at the Temple. 2For they had not been friendly to the people of Israel. Instead, they had hired Balaam to curse them—although God turned the curse into a blessing. 3When this rule was read, all the foreigners were immediately expelled from the assembly.

4Before this had happened, Eliashib the priest, who had been appointed as custodian of the Temple storerooms and who was also a good friend of Tobiah, 5had converted a storage room into a beautiful guest room for Tobiah. The room had previously been used for storing the grain offerings, frankincense, bowls, and tithes of grain, new wine, and olive oil. Moses had decreed that these offerings belonged to the priests, Levites, the members of the choir, and the gatekeepers.

6I was not in Jerusalem at the time, for I had returned to Babylon in the thirty-second year of the reign of King

Artaxerxes (though I later received his permission to go back again to Jerusalem). 7When I arrived back in Jerusalem and learned of this evil deed of Eliashib—that he had prepared a guest room in the Temple for Tobiah— 8I was very upset and threw out all of his belongings from the room. 9Then I demanded that the room be thoroughly cleaned, and I brought back the Temple bowls, the grain offerings, and frankincense.

10I also learned that the Levites had not been given what was due them, so they and the choir singers who were supposed to conduct the worship services had returned to their farms. 11I immediately confronted the leaders and demanded, "Why has the Temple been forsaken?" Then I called all the Levites back again and restored them to their proper duties. 12And once more all the people of Judah began bringing their tithes of grain, new wine, and olive oil to the Temple treasury.

13I put Shelemiah the priest, Zadok the scribe, and Pedaiah the Levite in charge of the administration of the storehouses; and I appointed Hanan (son of Zaccur, son of Mattaniah) as their assistant. These men had an excellent reputation, and their job was to make an honest distribution to their fellow-Levites.

14O my God, remember this good deed and do not forget all that I have done for the Temple.

15One day I was on a farm and saw some men treading winepresses on the Sabbath, hauling in sheaves, and loading their donkeys with wine, grapes, figs, and all sorts of produce which they took that day into Jerusalem. So I opposed them publicly. 16There were also some men from Tyre bringing in fish and all sorts of wares and selling them on the Sabbath to the people of Jerusalem.

17Then I asked the leaders of Judah, "Why are you profaning the Sabbath? 18Wasn't it enough that your fathers did this sort of thing and brought the present evil days upon us and upon our city? And now you are bringing more wrath upon the people of Israel by permitting the Sabbath to be desecrated in this way."

19So from then on I commanded that the gates of the city be shut as darkness fell on Friday evenings and not be opened until the Sabbath had ended; and I sent some of my servants to guard the gates so that no merchandise could be brought in on the Sabbath day. 20The merchants and tradesmen camped outside Jerusalem once or twice, 21but I spoke sharply to them and said, "What are you doing out here, camping around the wall? If you do this again, I will arrest you." And that was the last time they came on the Sabbath.

22Then I commanded the Levites to purify themselves and to guard the gates in order to preserve the sanctity of the Sabbath. Remember this good deed, O my God! Have compassion upon me in accordance with your great goodness.

23About the same time I realized that some of the Jews had married women from Ashdod, Ammon, and Moab, 24and that many of their children spoke in the language of Ashdod and couldn't speak the language of Judah at all. 25So I confronted these parents and cursed them and punched a few of them and knocked them around and pulled out their hair; and they vowed before God that they would not let their children intermarry with non-Jews.

26"Wasn't this exactly King Solomon's problem?" I demanded. "There was no king who could compare with him, and God loved him and made him the king over all Israel; but even so he was led into idolatry by foreign women. 27Do you think that we will let you get away with this sinful deed?"

28One of the sons of Jehoiada (the son of Eliashib the High Priest) was a son-in-law of Sanballat the Horonite, so I chased him out of the Temple. 29Remember them, O my God, for they have defiled the priesthood and the promises and vows of the priests and Levites. 30So I purged out the foreigners, and assigned tasks to the priests and Levites, making certain that each knew his work.

31They supplied wood for the altar at the proper times and cared for the sacrifices and the first offerings of every harvest. Remember me, my God, with your kindness.

1 CORINTHIANS 11:3–16

BUT there is one matter I want to remind you about: that a wife is responsible to her husband, her husband is responsible to Christ, and Christ is responsible to God. 4That is why, if a man refuses to remove his hat while praying or preaching, he dishonors Christ. 5And that is why a woman who publicly prays or prophesies without a covering on her head dishonors her husband [for her covering is a sign of her subjection to him]. 6Yes, if she refuses to wear a head covering, then she should cut off all her hair. And if it is shameful for a woman to have her head shaved, then she should wear a covering. 7But a man should not wear anything on his head [when worshiping, for his hat is a sign of subjection to men].

God's glory is man made in his image, and man's glory is the woman. 8The first man didn't come from woman, but the first woman came out of man. 9And Adam, the first man, was not made for Eve's benefit, but Eve was made for Adam. 10So a woman should wear a covering on her head as a sign that she is under man's authority, a fact for all the angels to notice and rejoice in.

11But remember that in God's plan men and women need each other. 12For although the first woman came out of man, all men have been born from women ever since, and both men and women come from God their Creator.

13What do you yourselves really think about this? Is it right for a woman to pray in public without covering her head? 14,15Doesn't even instinct itself teach us that women's heads should be covered? For women are proud of their long hair, while a man with long hair tends to be ashamed. 16But if anyone wants to argue about this, all I can say is that we never teach anything else than this—that a woman should wear a covering when prophesying or praying publicly in the church, and all the churches feel the same way about it.

PSALM 35:1–16

O Lord, fight those fighting me; declare war on them for their attacks on me. 2Put on your armor, take your shield and protect me by standing in front. 3Lift your spear in my defense, for my pursuers are getting very close. Let me hear you say that you will save me from them. 4Dishonor those who are trying to kill me. Turn them back and confuse them. 5Blow them away like chaff in the wind—wind sent by the Angel of the Lord. 6Make their path dark and slippery before them, with the Angel of the Lord pursuing them. 7For though I did them no wrong, yet they laid a trap for me and dug a pitfall in my path. 8Let them be overtaken by sudden ruin, caught in their own net, and destroyed.

9But I will rejoice in the Lord. He shall rescue me! 10From the bottom of my heart praise rises to him. Where is his equal in all of heaven and earth? Who else protects the weak and helpless from the strong, and the poor and needy from those who would rob them?

11These evil men swear to a lie. They accuse me of things I have never even heard about. 12I do them good, but they return me harm. I am sinking down to death. 13When they were ill, I mourned before the Lord in sackcloth, asking him to make them well; I refused to eat; I prayed for them with utmost earnestness, but God did not listen. 14I went about sadly as though it were my mother, friend or brother who was sick and nearing death. 15But now that I am in trouble they are glad; they come together in meetings filled with slander against me— I didn't even know some of those who were there. 16For they gather with the worthless fellows of the town and spend their time cursing me.

A man who loves pleasure becomes poor; wine and luxury are not the way to riches! The wicked will finally lose; the righteous will finally win.

AUGUST 18

ESTHER 1:1—3:15

IT was the third year of the reign of King Ahasuerus, emperor of vast Media-Persia, with its 127 provinces stretching from India to Ethiopia. This was the year of the great celebration at Shushan Palace, to which the emperor invited all his governors, aides, and army officers, bringing them in from every part of Media-Persia for the occasion. 4The celebration lasted six months, a tremendous display of the wealth and glory of his empire.

5When it was all over, the king gave a special party for the palace servants and officials—janitors and cabinet officials alike—for seven days of revelry, held in the courtyard of the palace garden. 6The decorations were green, white, and blue, fastened with purple ribbons tied to silver rings imbedded in marble pillars. Gold and silver benches stood on pavements of black, red, white, and yellow marble. 7Drinks were served in gold goblets of many designs, and there was an abundance of royal wine, for the king was feeling very generous. 8The only restriction on the drinking was that no one should be compelled to take more than he wanted, but those who wished could have as much as they pleased. For the king had instructed his officers to let everyone decide this matter for himself.

9Queen Vashti gave a party for the women of the palace at the same time.

10On the final day, when the king was feeling high, half drunk from wine, he told the seven eunuchs who were his personal aides—Mehuman, Biztha, Harbona, Bigtha, Abagtha, Zethar, and Car-

kas— 11to bring Queen Vashti to him with the royal crown upon her head so that all the men could gaze upon her beauty—for she was a very beautiful woman. 12But when they conveyed the emperor's order to Queen Vashti, she refused to come. The king was furious 13,14,15but first consulted his lawyers, for he did nothing without their advice. They were men of wisdom who knew the temper of the times as well as Persian law and justice, and the king trusted their judgment. These men were Carshena, Shethar, Admatha, Tarshish, Meres, Marsena, and Memucan—seven high officials of Media-Persia. They were his personal friends as well as being the chief officers of the government.

"What shall we do about this situation?" he asked them. "What penalty does the law provide for a queen who refuses to obey the king's orders, properly sent through his aides?"

16Memucan answered for the others, "Queen Vashti has wronged not only the king but every official and citizen of your empire. 17For women everywhere will begin to disobey their husbands when they learn what Queen Vashti has done. 18And before this day is out, the wife of every one of us officials throughout your empire will hear what the queen did and will start talking to us husbands the same way, and there will be contempt and anger throughout your realm. 19We suggest that, subject to your agreement, you issue a royal edict, a law of the Medes and Persians that can never be changed, that Queen Vashti be forever banished from your presence and that you choose another queen more worthy than she. 20When this decree is published throughout your great kingdom, husbands everywhere, whatever their rank, will be respected by their wives!"

21The king and all his aides thought this made good sense, so he followed Memucan's counsel, 22and sent letters to all of his provinces, in all the local languages, stressing that every man should rule his home, and should assert his authority.

BUT after King Ahasuerus' anger had cooled, he began brooding over the loss of Vashti, realizing that he would never see her again.

2So his aides suggested, "Let us go and find the most beautiful girls in the empire and bring them to the king for his pleasure. 3We will appoint agents in each province to select young lovelies for the royal harem. Hegai, the eunuch in charge, will see that they are given beauty treatments, 4and after that, the girl who pleases you most shall be the queen instead of Vashti."

This suggestion naturally pleased the king very much, and he put the plan into immediate effect.

5Now there was a certain Jew at the palace named Mordecai (son of Jair, son of Shime-i, son of Kish, a Benjaminite). 6He had been captured when Jerusalem was destroyed by King Nebuchadnezzar, and had been exiled to Babylon along with King Jeconiah of Judah and many others. 7This man had a beautiful and lovely young cousin, Hadassah (also called Esther), whose father and mother were dead, and whom he had adopted into his family and raised as his own daughter. 8So now, as a result of the king's decree, Esther was brought to the king's harem at Shushan Palace, along with many other young girls. 9Hegai, who was responsible for the harem, was very much impressed with her, and did his best to make her happy; he ordered a special menu for her, favored her for the beauty treatments, gave her seven girls from the palace as her maids, and gave

her the most luxurious apartment in the harem. 10Esther hadn't told anyone that she was a Jewess, for Mordecai had said not to. 11He came daily to the court of the harem to ask about Esther and to find out what was happening to her.

12,13,14The instructions concerning these girls were that before being taken to the king's bed, each would be given six months of beauty treatments with oil of myrrh, followed by six months with special perfumes and ointments. Then, as each girl's turn came for spending the night with King Ahasuerus, she was given her choice of clothing or jewelry she wished, to enhance her beauty. She was taken to the king's apartment in the evening and the next morning returned to the second harem where the king's wives lived. There she was under the care of Shaashgaz, another of the king's eunuchs, and lived there the rest of her life, never seeing the king again unless he had especially enjoyed her, and called for her by name.

15When it was Esther's turn to go to the king, she accepted the advice of Hegai, the eunuch in charge of the harem, dressing according to his instructions. And all the other girls exclaimed with delight when they saw her. 16So Esther was taken to the palace of the king in January of the seventh year of his reign. 17Well, the king loved Esther more than any of the other girls. He was so delighted with her that he set the royal crown on her head and declared her queen instead of Vashti. 18To celebrate the occasion, he threw another big party for all his officials and servants, giving generous gifts to everyone and making grants to the provinces in the form of remission of taxes.

19Later, the king demanded a second bevy of beautiful girls. By that time Mordecai had become a government official. 20Esther still hadn't told anyone she was a Jewess, for she was still following Mordecai's orders, just as she had in his home.

21One day, as Mordecai was on duty at the palace, two of the king's eunuchs,

Bigthan and Teresh—who were guards at the palace gate—became angry at the king and plotted to assassinate him. ²²Mordecai heard about it and passed on the information to Queen Esther, who told the king, crediting Mordecai with the information. ²³An investigation was made, the two men found guilty, and impaled alive. This was all duly recorded in the book of the history of King Ahasuerus' reign.

SOON afterwards King Ahasuerus appointed Haman (son of Hammedatha the Agagite), as prime minister. He was the most powerful official in the empire next to the king himself. ²Now all the king's officials bowed before him in deep reverence whenever he passed by, for so the king had commanded. But Mordecai refused to bow.

³,⁴"Why are you disobeying the king's commandment?" the others demanded day after day, but he still refused. Finally they spoke to Haman about it, to see whether Mordecai could get away with it because of his being a Jew, which was the excuse he had given them. ⁵,⁶Haman was furious, but decided not to lay hands on Mordecai alone, but to move against all of Mordecai's people, the Jews, and destroy all of them throughout the whole kingdom of Ahasuerus.

⁷The most propitious time for this action was determined by throwing dice. This was done in April of the twelfth year of the reign of Ahasuerus, and February of the following year was the date indicated.

⁸Haman now approached the king about the matter. "There is a certain race of people scattered through all the provinces of your kingdom," he began, "and their laws are different from those of any other nation, and they refuse to obey the king's laws; therefore, it is not in the king's interest to let them live. ⁹If it please the king, issue a decree that they be destroyed, and I will pay $20,-000,000 into the royal treasury for the expenses involved in this purge."

¹⁰The king agreed, confirming his deci-

sion by removing his ring from his finger and giving it to Haman, telling him, ¹¹"Keep the money, but go ahead and do as you like with these people—whatever you think best."

¹²Two or three weeks later, Haman called in the king's secretaries and dictated letters to the governors and officials throughout the empire, to each province in its own languages and dialects; these letters were signed in the name of King Ahasuerus and sealed with his ring.

¹³They were then sent by messengers into all the provinces of the empire, decreeing that the Jews—young and old, women and children—must all be killed on the 28th day of February of the following year, and their property given to those who killed them. ¹⁴"A copy of this edict," the letter stated, "must be proclaimed as law in every province, and made known to all your people, so that they will be ready to do their duty on the appointed day." ¹⁵The edict went out by the king's speediest couriers, after being first proclaimed in the city of Shushan. Then the king and Haman sat down for a drinking spree as the city fell into confusion and panic.

1 CORINTHIANS 11:17–34

NEXT on my list of items to write you about is something else I cannot agree with. For it sounds as if more harm than good is done when you meet together for your communion services. ¹⁸Everyone keeps telling me about the arguing that goes on in these meetings, and the divisions developing among you, and I can just about believe it. ¹⁹But I suppose you feel this is necessary so that you who are always right will become known and recognized!

²⁰When you come together to eat, it isn't the Lord's Supper you are eating, ²¹but your own. For I am told that everyone hastily gobbles all the food he can without waiting to share with the others, so that one doesn't get enough and goes hungry while another has too much to drink and gets drunk. ²²What? Is this re-

"Be strong and steady, always abounding in the Lord's work."
    1 Corinthians 15:58

THE
LORD
IS COUNTING
ON YOU

"Let him have all your worries and cares, for he is always thinking about you and watching everything that concerns you."

   1 Peter 5:7

"I will praise you with music, telling of your faithfulness to all your promises, O Holy One of Israel."

Psalm 71:22

ally true? Can't you do your eating and drinking at home, to avoid disgracing the church and shaming those who are poor and can bring no food? What am I supposed to say about these things? Do you want me to praise you? Well, I certainly do not!

23For this is what the Lord himself has said about his Table, and I have passed it on to you before: That on the night when Judas betrayed him, the Lord Jesus took bread, 24and when he had given thanks to God for it, he broke it and gave it to his disciples and said, "Take this and eat it. This is my body, which is given for you. Do this to remember me." 25In the same way, he took the cup of wine after supper, saying, "This cup is the new agreement between God and you that has been established and set in motion by my blood. Do this in remembrance of me whenever you drink it." 26For every time you eat this bread and drink this cup you are re-telling the message of the Lord's death, that he has died for you. Do this until he comes again.

27So if anyone eats this bread and drinks from this cup of the Lord in an unworthy manner, he is guilty of sin against the body and the blood of the Lord. 28That is why a man should examine himself carefully before eating the bread and drinking from the cup. 29For if he eats the bread and drinks from the cup unworthily, not thinking about the body of Christ and what it means, he is eating and drinking God's judgment upon himself; for he is trifling with the death of Christ. 30That is why many of you are weak and sick, and some have even died.

31But if you carefully examine yourselves before eating you will not need to be judged and punished. 32Yet, when we are judged and punished by the Lord, it is so that we will not be condemned with the rest of the world. 33So, dear brothers, when you gather for the Lord's Supper—the communion service—wait for each other; 34if anyone is really hungry he should eat at home so that he won't bring punishment upon himself when you meet together.

I'll talk to you about the other matters after I arrive.

PSALM 35:17–28

LORD, how long will you stand there, doing nothing? Act now and rescue me, for I have but one life and these young lions are out to get it. 18Save me, and I will thank you publicly before the entire congregation, before the largest crowd I can find.

19Don't give victory to those who fight me without any reason! Don't let them rejoice at my fall—let them die. 20They don't talk of peace and doing good, but of plots against innocent men who are minding their own business. 21They shout that they have seen *me* doing wrong! "Aha!" they say. "With our own eyes we saw him do it." 22Lord, you know all about it. Don't stay silent! Don't desert me now!

23Rise up, O Lord my God; vindicate me. 24Declare me "not guilty," for you are just. Don't let my enemies rejoice over me in my troubles. 25Don't let them say, "Aha! Our dearest wish against him will soon be fulfilled!" and, "At last we have him!" 26Shame them; let these who boast against me and who rejoice at my troubles be themselves overcome by misfortune that strips them bare of everything they own. Bare them to dishonor. 27But give great joy to all who wish me well. Let them shout with delight, "Great is the Lord who enjoys helping his child!" 28And I will tell everyone how great and good you are; I will praise you all day long.

PROVERBS FOR TODAY/ 21:19–20

Better to live in the desert than with a quarrelsome, complaining woman. The wise man saves for the future, but the foolish man spends whatever he gets.

AUGUST 19

ESTHER 4:1—7:10

WHEN Mordecai learned what had been done, he tore his clothes and put on sackcloth and ashes, and went out into the city, crying with a loud and bitter wail. 2Then he stood outside the gate of the palace, for no one was permitted to enter in mourning clothes. 3And throughout all the provinces there was great mourning among the Jews, fasting, weeping, and despair at the king's decree; and many lay in sackcloth and ashes.

4When Esther's maids and eunuchs came and told her about Mordecai, she was deeply distressed and sent clothing to him to replace the sackcloth, but he refused it. 5Then Esther sent for Hathach, one of the king's eunuchs who had been appointed as her attendant, and told him to go out to Mordecai and find out what the trouble was, and why he was acting like that. 6So Hathach went out to the city square, and found Mordecai just outside the palace gates, 7and heard the whole story from him; and about the $20,000,000 Haman had promised to pay into the king's treasury for the destruction of the Jews. 8Mordecai also gave Hathach a copy of the king's decree dooming all Jews, and told him to show it to Esther and to tell her what was happening, and that she should go to the king to plead for her people. 9So Hathach returned to Esther with Mordecai's message. 10Esther told Hathach to go back and say to Mordecai,

11"All the world knows that anyone, whether man or woman, who goes into the king's inner court without his summons is doomed to die unless the king holds out his gold scepter; and the king has not called for me to come to him in more than a month."

12So Hathach gave Esther's message to Mordecai.

13This was Mordecai's reply to Esther: "Do you think you will escape there in the palace, when all other Jews are killed? 14If you keep quiet at a time like this, God will deliver the Jews from some other source, but you and your relatives will die; what's more, who can say but that God has brought you into the palace for just such a time as this?"

15Then Esther said to tell Mordecai: 16"Go and gather together all the Jews of Shushan and fast for me; do not eat or drink for three days, night or day; and I and my maids will do the same; and then, though it is strictly forbidden, I will go in to see the king; and if I perish, I perish."

17So Mordecai did as Esther told him to.

THREE days later Esther put on her royal robes and entered the inner court just beyond the royal hall of the palace, where the king was sitting upon his royal throne. 2And when he saw Queen Esther standing there in the inner court, he welcomed her, holding out the golden scepter to her. So Esther approached and touched its tip.

3Then the king asked her, "What do you wish, Queen Esther? What is your request? I will give it to you, even if it is half the kingdom!"

4And Esther replied, "If it please Your Majesty, I want you and Haman to come to a banquet I have prepared for you today."

5The king turned to his aides. "Tell Haman to hurry!" he said. So the king and Haman came to Esther's banquet.

6During the wine course the king said to Esther, "Now tell me what you really want, and I will give it to you, even if it is half of the kingdom!"

7,8Esther replied, "My request, my deepest wish, is that if Your Majesty loves me, and wants to grant my request, that you come again with Haman tomorrow to the banquet I shall prepare for you. And tomorrow I will explain what this is all about."

9What a happy man was Haman as he left the banquet! But when he saw Mordecai there at the gate, not standing up or trembling before him, he was furious. 10However, he restrained himself and went on home and gathered together his friends and Zeresh his wife, 11and boasted to them about his wealth, and his many children, and promotions the king had given him, and how he had become the greatest man in the kingdom next to the king himself.

12Then he delivered his punch line: "Yes, and Esther the queen invited only me and the king himself to the banquet she prepared for us; and tomorrow we are invited again! 13But yet," he added, "all this is nothing when I see Mordecai the Jew just sitting there in front of the king's gate, refusing to bow to me."

14"Well," suggested Zeresh his wife and all his friends, "get ready a 75-foot-high gallows, and in the morning ask the king to let you hang Mordecai on it; and when this is done you can go on your merry way with the king to the banquet." This pleased Haman immensely and he ordered the gallows built.

THAT night the king had trouble sleeping and decided to read awhile. He ordered the historical records of his kingdom from the library, and in them he came across the item telling how Mordecai had exposed the plot of Bigthana and Teresh, two of the king's eunuchs, watchmen at the palace gates, who had plotted to assassinate him.

3"What reward did we ever give Mordecai for this?" the king asked.

His courtiers replied, "Nothing!"

4"Who is on duty in the outer court?" the king inquired. Now, as it happened, Haman had just arrived in the outer court of the palace to ask the king to hang Mordecai from the gallows he was building.

5So the courtiers replied to the king, "Haman is out there."

"Bring him in," the king ordered.

6So Haman came in and the king said to him, "What should I do to honor a man who truly pleases me?"

Haman thought to himself, "Whom would he want to honor more than me?" 7,8So he replied, "Bring out some of the royal robes the king himself has worn, and the king's own horse, and the royal crown, 9and instruct one of the king's most noble princes to robe the man and to lead him through the streets on the king's own horse, shouting before him, 'This is the way the king honors those who truly please him!' "

10"Excellent!" the king said to Haman. "Hurry and take these robes and my horse, and do just as you have said— to Mordecai the Jew, who works at the Chancellery. Follow every detail you have suggested."

11So Haman took the robes and put them on Mordecai and mounted him on the king's own steed, and led him through the streets of the city, shouting, "This is the way the king honors those he delights in."

12Afterwards Mordecai returned to his job, but Haman hurried home utterly humiliated. 13When Haman told Zeresh his wife and all his friends what had happened, they said, "If Mordecai is a Jew, you will never succeed in your plans against him; to continue to oppose him will be fatal."

14While they were still discussing it with him, the king's messengers arrived to conduct Haman quickly to the banquet Esther had prepared.

So the king and Haman came to Esther's banquet. 2Again, during the wine course, the king asked her, "What is your petition, Queen Esther? What do you wish? Whatever it is, I will give it to you, even if it is half of my kingdom!"

3And at last Queen Esther replied, "If I have won your favor, O king, and if it please Your Majesty, save my life and the lives of my people. 4For I and my people have been sold to those who will destroy us. We are doomed to destruction and slaughter. If we were only to be sold as slaves, perhaps I could remain quiet, though even then there would be incalculable damage to the king that no amount of money could begin to cover."

5"What are you talking about?" King Ahasuerus demanded. "Who would dare touch you?"

6Esther replied, "This wicked Haman is our enemy."

Then Haman grew pale with fright before the king and queen. 7The king jumped to his feet and went out into the palace garden as Haman stood up to plead for his life to Queen Esther, for he knew that he was doomed. 8In despair he fell upon the couch where Queen Esther was reclining, just as the king returned from the palace garden.

"Will he even rape the queen right here in the palace, before my very eyes?" the king roared. Instantly the death veil was placed over Haman's face.

9Then Harbona, one of the king's aides, said, "Sir, Haman has just ordered a 75-foot gallows constructed, to hang Mordecai, the man who saved the king from assassination! It stands in Haman's courtyard."

"Hang Haman on it," the king ordered.

10So they did, and the king's wrath was pacified.

1 CORINTHIANS 12:1–26

AND now, brothers, I want to write about the special abilities the Holy Spirit gives to each of you, for I don't want any misunderstanding about them. 2You will remember that before you became Christians you went around from one idol to another, not one of which could speak a single word. 3But now you are meeting people who claim to speak messages from the Spirit of God. How can you know whether they are really inspired by God or whether they are fakes? Here is the test: no one speaking by the power of the Spirit of God can curse Jesus, and no one can say, "Jesus is Lord," and really mean it, unless the Holy Spirit is helping him.

4Now God gives us many kinds of special abilities, but it is the same Holy Spirit who is the source of them all. 5There are different kinds of service to God, but it is the same Lord we are serving. 6There are many ways in which God works in our lives, but it is the same God who does the work in and through all of us who are his. 7The Holy Spirit displays God's power through each of us as a means of helping the entire church.

8To one person the Spirit gives the ability to give wise advice; someone else may be especially good at studying and teaching, and this is his gift from the same Spirit. 9He gives special faith to another, and to someone else the power to heal the sick. 10He gives power for doing miracles to some, and to others power to prophesy and preach. He gives someone else the power to know whether evil spirits are speaking through those who claim to be giving God's messages—or whether it is really the Spirit of God who is speaking. Still another person is able to speak in languages he never learned; and others, who do not know the language either, are given power to understand what he is saying. 11It is the same and only Holy Spirit who gives all these gifts and powers, deciding which each one of us should have.

12Our bodies have many parts, but the many parts make up only one body when they are all put together. So it is with the "body" of Christ. 13Each of us is a part of the one body of Christ. Some of us are Jews, some are Gentiles, some are slaves and some are free. But the Holy Spirit has fitted us all together into one body. We have been baptized into Christ's body by the one Spirit, and have all been given that same Holy Spirit.

14Yes, the body has many parts, not just one part. 15If the foot says, "I am not a part of the body because I am not a hand," that does not make it any less a part of the body. 16And what would you think if you heard an ear say, "I am not part of the body because I am only an ear, and not an eye"? Would that make it any less a part of the body? 17Suppose the whole body were an eye— then how would you hear? Or if your whole body were just one big ear, how could you smell anything?

18But that isn't the way God has made us. He has made many parts for our bodies and has put each part just where he wants it. 19What a strange thing a body would be if it had only one part! 20So he has made many parts, but still there is only one body.

21The eye can never say to the hand, "I don't need you." The head can't say to the feet, "I don't need you."

22And some of the parts that seem weakest and least important are really the most necessary. 23Yes, we are especially glad to have some parts that seem rather odd! And we carefully protect from the eyes of others those parts that should not be seen, 24while of course the parts that may be seen do not require this special care. So God has put the body together in such a way that extra honor and care are given to those parts that might otherwise seem less important. 25This makes for happiness among the parts, so that the parts have the same care for each other that they do for themselves. 26If one part suffers, all parts suffer with it, and if one part is honored, all the parts are glad.

PSALM 36:1–12

SIN lurks deep in the hearts of the wicked, forever urging them on to evil deeds. They have no fear of God to hold them back. 2Instead, in their conceit, they think they can hide their evil deeds and not get caught. 3Everything they say is crooked and deceitful; they are no longer wise and good. 4They lie awake at night to hatch their evil plots, instead of planning how to keep away from wrong.

5Your steadfast love, O Lord, is as great as all the heavens. Your faithfulness reaches beyond the clouds. 6Your justice is as solid as God's mountains. Your decisions are as full of wisdom as the oceans are with water. You are concerned for men and animals alike. 7How precious is your constant love, O God! All humanity takes refuge in the shadow of your wings. 8You feed them with blessings from your own table and let them drink from your rivers of delight.

9For you are the Fountain of life; our light is from your Light. 10Pour out your unfailing love on those who know you! Never stop giving your blessings to those who long to do your will.

11Don't let these proud men trample me. Don't let their wicked hands push me around. 12Look! They have fallen. They are thrown down and will not rise again.

PROVERBS FOR TODAY/ 21:21–22

The man who tries to be good, loving, and kind finds life, righteousness, and honor. The wise man conquers the strong man and levels his defenses.

AUGUST 20

ESTHER 8:1—10:3

ON that same day King Ahasuerus gave the estate of Haman, the Jews' enemy, to Queen Esther. Then Mordecai was brought before the king, for Esther had told the king that he was her cousin and foster father. 2The king took off his ring—which he had taken back from Haman—and gave it to Mordecai [appointing him Prime Minister]; and Esther appointed Mordecai to be in charge of Haman's estate.

3And now once more Esther came before the king, falling down at his feet and begging him with tears to stop Haman's plot against the Jews. 4And again the king held out the golden scepter to Esther. So she arose and stood before him, 5and said, "If it please Your Majesty, and if you love me, send out a decree reversing Haman's order to destroy the Jews throughout the king's provinces. 6For how can I endure it, to see my people butchered and destroyed?"

7Then King Ahasuerus said to Queen Esther and Mordecai the Jew, "I have given Esther the palace of Haman and he has been hanged upon the gallows because he tried to destroy you. 8Now go ahead and send a message to the Jews, telling them whatever you want to in the king's name, and seal it with the king's ring, so that it can never be reversed."

9,10Immediately the king's secretaries were called in—it was now the 23rd day of the month of July—and they wrote as Mordecai dictated—a decree to the Jews and to the officials, governors, and princes of all the provinces from India to Ethiopia, 127 in all: the decree was translated into the languages and dialects of all the people of the kingdom. Mordecai wrote in the name of King Ahasuerus and sealed the message with the king's ring and sent the letters by swift carriers—riders on camels, mules, and young dromedaries used in the king's service. 11This decree gave the Jews everywhere permission to unite in the defense of their lives and their families, to destroy all the forces opposed to them, and to take their property. 12The day chosen for this throughout all the provinces of King Ahasuerus was the 28th day of February! 13It further stated that a copy of this decree, which must be recognized everywhere as law, must be broadcast to all the people so that the Jews would be ready and prepared to overcome their enemies. 14So the mail went out swiftly, carried by the king's couriers and speeded by the king's commandment.

The same decree was also issued at Shushan Palace.

15Then Mordecai put on the royal robes of blue and white and the great crown of gold, with an outer cloak of fine linen and purple, and went out from the presence of the king through the city streets filled with shouting people. 16And the Jews had joy and gladness, and were honored everywhere. 17And in every city and province, as the king's decree arrived, the Jews were filled with joy and had a great celebration and declared a holiday. And many of the people of the land pretended to be Jews, for they feared what the Jews might do to them.

So on the 28th day of February, the day the two decrees of the king were to be put into effect—the day the Jews' enemies had hoped to vanquish them, though it turned out quite to the contrary—the Jews gathered in their cities throughout all the king's provinces to defend themselves against any who might try to harm them; but no one tried, for they were greatly feared. 3And all the rulers of the provinces—the governors, officials, and aides—helped the Jews for fear of Mordecai; 4for Mordecai was a mighty name in the king's palace and his fame was known throughout all the provinces, for he had become more and more powerful.

5But the Jews went ahead on that appointed day and slaughtered their enemies. 6They even killed 500 men in Shushan. 7–10They also killed the ten sons of Haman (son of Hammedatha), the Jews' enemy—

Parshandatha, Dalphon, Aspatha, Poratha, Adalia, Aridatha, Parmashta, Arisai, Aridai, and Vaizatha.

But they did not try to take Haman's property.

11Late that evening, when the king was informed of the number of those slain in Shushan, 12he called for Queen Esther. "The Jews have killed 500 men in Shushan alone," he exclaimed, "and also Haman's ten sons. If they have done that here, I wonder what has happened in the rest of the provinces! But now, what more do you want? It will be granted to you. Tell me and I will do it."

13And Esther said, "If it please Your Majesty, let the Jews who are here at Shushan do again tomorrow as they have done today, and let Haman's ten sons be hanged upon the gallows."

14So the king agreed, and the decree was announced at Shushan, and they hung up the bodies of Haman's ten sons. 15Then the Jews at Shushan gathered together the next day also and killed 300 more men, though again they took no property.

16Meanwhile, the other Jews throughout the king's provinces had gathered together and stood for their lives and destroyed all their enemies, killing 75,000 of those who hated them; but they did not take their goods. 17Throughout the provinces this was done on the 28th day of February, and the next day they rested, celebrating their victory with feasting and gladness. 18But the Jews at Shushan went on killing their enemies the second day also, and rested the next day, with feasting and gladness. 19And so it is that the Jews in the unwalled villages throughout Israel to this day have an annual celebration on the second day, when they rejoice and send gifts to each other.

20Mordecai wrote a history of all these events, and sent letters to the Jews near and far, throughout all the king's provinces, 21encouraging them to declare an annual holiday on the last two days of the month, 22to celebrate with feasting, gladness, and the giving of gifts these historic days when the Jews were saved from their enemies, when their sorrow was turned to gladness and their mourning into happiness.

23So the Jews adopted Mordecai's suggestion and began this annual custom, 24,25as a reminder of the time when Haman (son of Hammedatha the Agagite), the enemy of all the Jews, had plotted to destroy them at the time determined by a throw of the dice; and to remind them that when the matter came before the king, he issued a decree causing Haman's plot to boomerang, and he and his sons were hanged on the gallows. 26That is why this celebration is called "Purim," because the word for "throwing dice" in Persian is "pur." 27All the Jews throughout the realm agreed to inaugurate this tradition and to pass it on to their descendants and to all who became Jews; they declared they would never fail to celebrate these two days at the appointed time each year. 28It would be an annual event from generation to generation, celebrated by every family throughout the countryside and cities of the empire, so that the memory of what had happened would never perish from the Jewish race.

29,30,31Meanwhile, Queen Esther (daughter of Abihail and later adopted by Mordecai the Jew) had written a letter throwing her full support behind Mordecai's letter inaugurating his annual Feast of Purim. In addition, letters were sent to all the Jews throughout the 127 provinces of the kingdom of Ahasuerus with messages of good will, and encouragement to confirm these two days annually as the Feast of Purim, decreed by both Mordecai the Jew and by Queen Esther; indeed, the Jews themselves had decided upon this tradition as a remembrance of the time of their national fasting and prayer. 32So the commandment of Esther confirmed these dates and it was recorded as law.

KING Ahasuerus not only laid tribute upon the mainland, but even on the islands of the sea. 2His great deeds, and also the full account of the greatness of Mordecai and the honors given him by the king, are written in *The Book of the Chronicles of the Kings of Media and Persia.* 3Mordecai the Jew was the Prime Minister, with authority next to that of King Ahasuerus himself. He was, of course, very great among the Jews, and respected by all his countrymen because he did his best for his people, and was a friend at court for all of them.

NOW here is what I am trying to say: All of you together are the one body of Christ and each one of you is a separate and necessary part of it. 28Here is a list of some of the parts he has placed in his Church, which is his body:

Apostles,
Prophets—those who preach God's Word,
Teachers,
Those who do miracles,
Those who have the gift of healing;
Those who can help others,
Those who can get others to work together,
Those who speak in languages they have never learned.

29Is everyone an apostle? Of course not. Is everyone a preacher? No. Are all teachers? Does everyone have the power to do miracles? 30Can everyone heal the sick? Of course not. Does God give all of us the ability to speak in languages we've never learned? Can just anyone understand and translate what those are saying who have that gift of foreign speech? 31No, but try your best to have the more important of these gifts.

First, however, let me tell you about something else that is better than any of them!

IF I had the gift of being able to speak in other languages without learning them, and could speak in every language there is in all of heaven and earth, but didn't love others, I would only be making noise. 2If I had the gift of prophecy and knew all about what is going to happen in the future, knew everything about *everything,* but didn't love others, what good would it do? Even if I had the gift of faith so that I could speak to a mountain and make it move, I would still be worth nothing at all without love. 3If I gave everything I have to poor people, and if I were burned alive for preaching the Gospel but didn't love others, it would be of no value whatever.

4Love is very patient and kind, never jealous or envious, never boastful or proud, 5never haughty or selfish or rude. Love does not demand its own way. It is not irritable or touchy. It does not hold grudges and will hardly even notice when others do it wrong. 6It is never glad about injustice, but rejoices whenever truth wins out. 7If you love someone you will be loyal to him no matter what the cost. You will always believe in him, always expect the best of him, and always stand your ground in defending him.

8All the special gifts and powers from God will someday come to an end, but love goes on forever. Someday prophecy, and speaking in unknown languages, and special knowledge—these gifts will disappear. 9Now we know so little, even with our special gifts, and the preaching of those most gifted is still so poor. 10But when we have been made perfect and complete, then the need for these inadequate special gifts will come to an end, and they will disappear.

11It's like this: when I was a child I spoke and thought and reasoned as a child does. But when I became a man my thoughts grew far beyond those of my childhood, and now I have put away the childish things. 12In the same way, we can see and understand only a little about God now, as if we were peering at his reflection in a poor mirror; but someday we are going to see him in his completeness, face to face. Now all that I know is hazy and blurred, but then I will see everything clearly, just as clearly as God sees into my heart right now.

13There are three things that remain—faith, hope, and love—and the greatest of these is love.

PSALM 37:1–11

NEVER envy the wicked! 2Soon they fade away like grass and disappear. 3Trust in the Lord instead. Be kind and good to others; then you will live safely here in the land and prosper, feeding in safety.

4Be delighted with the Lord. Then he

will give you all your heart's desires. 5Commit everything you do to the Lord. Trust him to help you do it and he will. 6Your innocence will be clear to everyone. He will vindicate you with the blazing light of justice shining down as from the noonday sun.

7Rest in the Lord; wait patiently for him to act. Don't be envious of evil men who prosper.

8Stop your anger! Turn off your wrath. Don't fret and worry—it only leads to harm. 9For the wicked shall be destroyed, but those who trust the Lord shall be given every blessing. 10Only a little while and the wicked shall disappear. You will look for them in vain. 11But all who humble themselves before the Lord shall be given every blessing, and shall have wonderful peace.

PROVERBS FOR TODAY/ 21:23-24

Keep your mouth closed and you'll stay out of trouble. Mockers are proud, haughty and arrogant.

AUGUST 21

JOB 1:1—3:26

THERE lived in the land of Uz a man named Job—a good man who feared God and stayed away from evil. 2,3He had a large family of seven sons and three daughters, and was immensely wealthy, for he owned 7,000 sheep, 3,000 camels, 500 teams of oxen, 500 female donkeys, and employed many servants. He was, in fact, the richest cattleman in that entire area.

4Every year when Job's sons had birthdays, they invited their brothers and sisters to their homes for a celebration. On these occasions they would eat and drink with great merriment. 5When these birthday parties ended—and sometimes they lasted several days—Job would summon his children to him and sanctify them, getting up early in the morning and offering a burnt offering for each of them. For Job said, "Perhaps my sons have sinned and turned away from God in their hearts." This was Job's regular practice.

6One day as the angels came to present themselves before the Lord, Satan, the Accuser, came with them.

7"Where have you come from?" the Lord asked Satan.

And Satan replied, "From Earth,

where I've been watching everything that's going on."

8Then the Lord asked Satan, "Have you noticed my servant Job? He is the finest man in all the earth—a good man who fears God and will have nothing to do with evil."

9"Why shouldn't he, when you pay him so well?" Satan scoffed. 10"You have always protected him and his home and his property from all harm. You have prospered everything he does—look how rich he is! No wonder he 'worships' you! 11But just take away his wealth, and you'll see him curse you to your face!"

12,13And the Lord replied to Satan, "You may do anything you like with his wealth, but don't harm him physically."

So Satan went away; and sure enough, not long afterwards when Job's sons and daughters were dining at the oldest brother's house, tragedy struck.

14,15A messenger rushed to Job's home with this news: "Your oxen were plowing, with the donkeys feeding beside them, when the Sabeans raided us, drove away the animals and killed all the farmhands except me. I am the only one left."

16While this messenger was still speaking, another arrived with more bad news:

"The fire of God has fallen from heaven and burned up your sheep and all the herdsmen, and I alone have escaped to tell you."

17Before this man finished, still another messenger rushed in: "Three bands of Chaldeans have driven off your camels and killed your servants, and I alone have escaped to tell you."

18As he was still speaking, another arrived to say, "Your sons and daughters were feasting in their oldest brother's home, 19when suddenly a mighty wind swept in from the desert, and engulfed the house so that the roof fell in on them and all are dead; and I alone escaped to tell you."

20Then Job stood up and tore his robe in grief and fell down upon the ground before God. 21"I came naked from my mother's womb," he said, "and I shall have nothing when I die. The Lord gave me everything I had, and they were his to take away. Blessed be the name of the Lord."

22In all of this, Job did not sin or revile God.

NOW the angels came again to present themselves before the Lord, and Satan with them.

2"Where have you come from?" the Lord asked Satan.

"From Earth, where I've been watching everything that's going on," Satan replied.

3"Well, have you noticed my servant Job?" the Lord asked. "He is the finest man in all the earth—a good man who fears God and turns away from all evil. And he has kept his faith in me despite the fact that you persuaded me to let you harm him without any cause."

4,5"Skin for skin," Satan replied. "A man will give anything to save his life. Touch his body with sickness and he will curse you to your face!"

6"Do with him as you please," the Lord replied; "only spare his life."

7So Satan went out from the presence of the Lord and struck Job with a terrible case of boils from head to foot. 8Then Job took a broken piece of pottery to scrape himself, and sat among the ashes.

9His wife said to him, "Are you still trying to be godly when God has done all this to you? Curse him and die."

10But he replied, "You talk like some heathen woman. What? Shall we receive only pleasant things from the hand of God and never anything unpleasant?" So in all this Job said nothing wrong.

11When three of Job's friends heard of all the tragedy that had befallen him, they got in touch with each other and traveled from their homes to comfort and console him. Their names were Eliphaz the Temanite, Bildad the Shuhite, and Zophar the Naamathite. 12Job was so changed that they could scarcely recognize him. Wailing loudly in despair, they tore their robes and threw dust into the air and put earth on their heads to demonstrate their sorrow. 13Then they sat upon the ground with him silently for seven days and nights, no one speaking a word; for they saw that his suffering was too great for words.

AT last Job spoke, and cursed the day of his birth.

2,3"Let the day of my birth be cursed," he said, "and the night when I was conceived. 4Let that day be forever forgotten. Let it be lost even to God, shrouded in eternal darkness. 5Yes, let the darkness claim it for its own, and may a black cloud overshadow it. 6May it be blotted off the calendar, never again to be counted among the days of the month of that year. 7Let that night be bleak and joyless. 8Let those who are experts at cursing curse it. 9Let the stars of the night disappear. Let it long for light, but never see it, never see the morning light. 10Curse it for its failure to shut my mother's womb, for letting me be born to come to all this trouble.

11"Why didn't I die at birth? 12Why did the midwife let me live? Why did she nurse me at her breasts? 13For if only I had died at birth, then I would be quiet now, asleep and at rest, 14,15along with prime ministers and kings with all their pomp, and wealthy princes whose castles are full of rich treasures. 16Oh, to have been still-born!—to have never breathed or seen the light. 17For there in death the wicked cease from troubling, and there the weary are at rest. 18There even prisoners are at ease, with no brutal jailer to curse them. 19Both rich and poor alike are there, and the slave is free at last from his master.

20,21"Oh, why should light and life be given to those in misery and bitterness, who long for death, and it won't come; who search for death as others search for food or money? 22What blessed relief when at last they die! 23Why is a man allowed to be born if God is only going to give him a hopeless life of uselessness and frustration? 24I cannot eat for sighing; my groans pour out like water. 25What I always feared has happened to me. 26I was not fat and lazy, yet trouble struck me down."

1 CORINTHIANS 14:1–17

LET love be your greatest aim; nevertheless, ask also for the special abilities the Holy Spirit gives, and especially the gift of prophecy, being able to preach the messages of God.

2But if your gift is that of being able to "speak in tongues," that is, to speak in languages you haven't learned, you will be talking to God but not to others, since they won't be able to understand you. You will be speaking by the power of the Spirit but it will all be a secret. 3But one who prophesies, preaching the messages of God, is helping others grow in the Lord, encouraging and comforting them. 4So a person "speaking in tongues" helps himself grow spiritually, but one who prophesies, preaching messages from God, helps the entire church grow in holiness and happiness.

5I wish you all had the gift of "speaking in tongues" but, even more, I wish you were all able to prophesy, preaching God's messages, for that is a greater and more useful power than to speak in unknown languages—unless, of course,

you can tell everyone afterwards what you were saying, so that they can get some good out of it too.

6Dear friends, even if I myself should come to you talking in some language you don't understand, how would that help you? But if I speak plainly what God has revealed to me, and tell you the things I know, and what is going to happen, and the great truths of God's Word—that is what you need; that is what will help you. 7Even musical instruments—the flute, for instance, or the harp—are examples of the need for speaking in plain, simple English rather than in unknown languages. For no one will recognize the tune the flute is playing unless each note is sounded clearly. 8And if the army bugler doesn't play the right notes, how will the soldiers know that they are being called to battle? 9In the same way, if you talk to a person in some language he doesn't understand, how will he know what you mean? You might as well be talking to an empty room.

10I suppose that there are hundreds of different languages in the world, and all are excellent for those who understand them, 11but to me they mean nothing. A person talking to me in one of these languages will be a stranger to me and I will be a stranger to him. 12Since you are so anxious to have special gifts from the Holy Spirit, ask him for the very best, for those that will be of real help to the whole church.

13If someone is given the gift of speaking in unknown tongues, he should pray also for the gift of knowing what he has said, so that he can tell people afterwards, plainly. 14For if I pray in a language I don't understand, my spirit is praying but I don't know what I am saying.

15Well, then, what shall I do? I will do both. I will pray in unknown tongues and also in ordinary language that everyone understands. I will sing in unknown tongues and also in ordinary language, so that I can understand the praise I am giving; 16for if you praise and thank God with the spirit alone, speaking in another language, how can those who don't understand you be praising God along with you? How can they join you in giving thanks when they don't know what you are saying? 17You will be giving thanks very nicely, no doubt, but the other people present won't be helped.

PSALM 37:12–28

THE Lord is laughing at those who plot against the godly, for he knows their judgment day is coming. 14Evil men take aim to slay the poor; they are ready to butcher those who do right. 15But their swords will be plunged into their own hearts and all their weapons will be broken.

16It is better to have little and be godly than to own an evil man's wealth; 17for the strength of evil men shall be broken, but the Lord takes care of those he has forgiven.

18Day by day the Lord observes the good deeds done by godly men, and gives them eternal rewards. 19He cares for them when times are hard; even in fam-

ine, they will have enough. 20But evil men shall perish. These enemies of God will wither like grass, and disappear like smoke. 21Evil men borrow and "cannot pay it back"! But the good man returns what he owes with some extra besides. 22Those blessed by the Lord shall inherit the earth, but those cursed by him shall die.

23The steps of good men are directed by the Lord. He delights in each step they take. 24If they fall it isn't fatal, for the Lord holds them with his hand.

25I have been young and now I am old. And in all my years I have never seen the Lord forsake a man who loves him; nor have I seen the children of the godly go hungry. 26Instead, the godly are able to be generous with their gifts and loans to others, and their children are a blessing.

27So if you want an eternal home, leave your evil, low-down ways and live good lives. 28For the Lord loves justice and fairness; he will never abandon his people. They will be kept safe forever; but all who love wickedness shall perish.

PROVERBS FOR TODAY/ 21:25–26

The lazy man longs for many things but his hands refuse to work. He is greedy to get, while the godly love to give!

AUGUST 22

JOB 4:1—7:21

A reply to Job from Eliphaz the Temanite:
2"Will you let me say a word? For who could keep from speaking out? 3,4In the past you have told many a troubled soul to trust in God and have encouraged those who are weak or falling, or lie crushed upon the ground or are tempted to despair. 5But now, when trouble strikes, you faint and are broken.

6"At such a time as this should not trust in God still be your confidence? Shouldn't you believe that God will care for those who are good? 7,8Stop and think! Have you ever known a truly good and innocent person who was punished? Experience teaches that it is those who sow sin and trouble who harvest the same. 9They die beneath the hand of God. 10Though they are fierce as young lions, they shall all be broken and destroyed. 11Like aged, helpless lions they shall starve, and all their children shall be scattered.

12"This truth was given me in secret, as though whispered in my ear. 13It came in a nighttime vision as others slept. 14Suddenly, fear gripped me; I trembled and shook with terror, 15as a spirit passed before my face—my hair stood up on end. 16I felt the spirit's presence, but couldn't see it standing there. Then out of the dreadful silence came this voice:

17" 'Is mere man more just than God? More pure than his Creator?'

18,19"If God cannot trust his own messengers (for even angels make mistakes), how much less men made of dust, who are crushed to death as easily as moths! 20They are alive in the morning, but by evening they are dead, gone forever with hardly a thought from anyone. 21Their candle of life is snuffed out. They die and no one cares.

"THEY cry for help but no one listens; they turn to their gods, but none gives them aid. 2They die in helpless frustration, overcome by their own anger. 3Those who turn from God may be successful for the moment, but then comes sudden disaster. 4Their children are cheated, with no one to defend them. 5Their harvests are stolen and their wealth slakes the thirst of many others, not themselves! 6Misery comes upon them to punish them for sowing seeds of sin. 7Mankind heads for sin and misery as predictably as flames shoot upwards from a fire.

8"My advice to you is this: Go to God and confess your sins to him. 9For he does wonderful miracles, marvels without number. 10He sends the rain upon the earth to water the fields, 11and gives prosperity to the poor and humble, and takes sufferers to safety.

12"He frustrates the plans of crafty men. 13They are caught in their own traps; he thwarts their schemes. 14They grope like blind men in the daylight; they see no better in the daytime than at night.

15"God saves the fatherless and the poor from the grasp of these oppressors. 16And so at last the poor have hope, and the fangs of the wicked are broken.

17"How enviable the man whom God corrects! Oh, do not despise the chastening of the Lord when you sin. 18For though he wounds, he binds and heals again. 19He will deliver you again and again, so that no evil can touch you.

20"He will keep you from death in famine, and from the power of the sword in time of war.

21"You will be safe from slander; no need to fear the future.

22"You shall laugh at war and famine; wild animals will leave you alone. 23Dangerous animals will be at peace with you.

24"You need not worry about your home while you are gone; nothing shall be stolen from your barns.

25"Your sons shall become important men; your descendants shall be as numerous as grass! 26You shall live a long, good life; like standing grain, you'll not be harvested until it's time! 27I have found from experience that all of this is true. For your own good, listen to my counsel."

JOB'S reply:

2"Oh, that my sadness and troubles were weighed. 3For they are heavier than the sand of a thousand seashores. That is why I spoke so rashly. 4For the Lord has struck me down with his arrows; he has sent his poisoned arrows deep within my heart. All God's terrors are arrayed against me. 5,6,7When wild donkeys bray, it is because their grass is gone; oxen do not low when they have food; a man complains when there is no salt in his food. And how tasteless is the uncooked white of an egg—my appetite is gone when I look at it; I gag at the thought of eating it!

8,9"Oh, that God would grant the thing I long for most—to die beneath his hand, and be freed from his painful grip. 10This, at least, gives me comfort despite all the pain—that I have not denied the words of the holy God. 11Oh, why does my strength sustain me? How can I be patient till I die? 12Am I unfeeling, like stone? Is my flesh made of brass? 13For I am utterly helpless, without any hope.

14"One should be kind to a fainting friend, but you have accused me without the slightest fear of God. 15–18My brother, you have proved as unreliable as a brook; it floods when there is ice and snow, but in hot weather, disappears. The caravans turn aside to be refreshed, but there is nothing there to drink, and so they perish. 19,20,21When caravans from Tema and from Sheba stop for water there, their hopes are dashed. And so my hopes in you are dashed—you turn away from me in terror and refuse to help. 22But why? Have I ever asked you for one slightest thing? Have I begged you for a present? 23Have I ever asked your help? 24All I want is a reasonable answer—then I will keep quiet. Tell me, what have I done wrong?

25,26"It is wonderful to speak the truth, but your criticisms are not based on fact. Are you going to condemn me just because I impulsively cried out in desperation? 27That would be like injuring a helpless orphan, or selling a friend. 28Look at me! Would I lie to your face? 29Stop assuming my guilt, for I am righteous. Don't be so unjust. 30Don't I know the difference between right and wrong? Would I not admit it if I had sinned?

"How mankind must struggle. A man's life is long and hard, like that of a slave. 2How he longs for the day to end. How he grinds on to the end of the week and his wages. 3And so to me also have been allotted months of frustration, these long and weary nights. 4When I go to bed I think, 'Oh, that it were morning,' and then I toss till dawn.

5"My skin is filled with worms and blackness. My flesh breaks open, full of pus. 6My life drags by—day after hopeless day. 7My life is but a breath, and nothing good is left. 8You see me now, but not for long. Soon you'll look upon me dead. 9As a cloud disperses and vanishes, so those who die shall go away forever— 10gone forever from their family and their home—never to be seen again. 11Ah, let me express my anguish. Let me be free to speak out of the bitterness of my soul.

12"O God, am I some monster, that you never let me alone? 13,14Even when I try to forget my misery in sleep, you terrify with nightmares. 15I would rather die of strangulation than go on and on like this. 16I hate my life. Oh, let me alone for these few remaining days. 17What is mere man that you should spend your time persecuting him? 18Must you be his inquisitor every morning, and test him every moment of the day? 19Why won't you let me alone—even long enough to spit?

20"Has my sin harmed you, O God, Watcher of mankind? Why have you made me your target, and made my life so heavy a burden to me? 21Why not just pardon my sin and take it all away? For all too soon I'll lie down in the dust and die, and when you look for me, I shall be gone."

1 CORINTHIANS 14:18–40

I thank God that I "speak in tongues" privately more than any of the rest of you. 19But in public worship I would much rather speak five words that people can understand and be helped by, than ten thousand words while "speaking in tongues" in an unknown language.

20Dear brothers, don't be childish in your understanding of these things. Be innocent babies when it comes to planning evil, but be men of intelligence in understanding matters of this kind. 21We are told in the ancient Scriptures that God would send men from other lands to speak in foreign languages to his people, but even then they would not listen. 22So you see that being able to "speak in tongues" is not a sign to God's children concerning his power, but is a sign to the unsaved. However, prophecy (preaching the deep truths of God) is what the Christians need, and unbelievers aren't yet ready for it. 23Even so, if an unsaved person, or someone who doesn't have these gifts, comes to church and hears you all talking in other languages, he is likely to think you are crazy. 24But if you prophesy, preaching God's Word, [even though such preaching is mostly for believers] and an unsaved person or a new Christian comes in who does not understand about these things, all these sermons will convince him of the fact that he is a sinner, and his conscience will be pricked by everything he hears. 25As he listens, his secret thoughts will be laid bare and he will fall down on his knees and worship God, declaring that God is really there among you.

26Well, my brothers, let's add up what I am saying. When you meet together some will sing, another will teach, or tell some special information God has given him, or speak in an unknown language, or tell what someone else is saying who is speaking in the unknown language, but everything that is done must be useful to all, and build them up in the Lord. 27No more than two or three should speak in an unknown language, and they must speak one at a time, and someone must be ready to interpret what they are saying. 28But if no one is present who can interpret, they must not speak out loud. They must talk silently to themselves and to God in the unknown language but not publicly.

29,30Two or three may prophesy, one at a time, if they have the gift, while all the others listen. But if, while someone is prophesying, someone else receives a message or idea from the Lord, the one who is speaking should stop. 31In this way all who have the gift of prophecy can speak, one after the other, and everyone will learn and be encouraged and helped. 32Remember that a person who has a message from God has the power to stop himself or wait his turn. 33God is not one who likes things to be disorderly and upset. He likes harmony, and he finds it in all the other churches.

34Women should be silent during the church meetings. They are not to take part in the discussion, for they are subordinate to men as the Scriptures also declare. 35If they have any questions to ask, let them ask their husbands at home, for it is improper for women to express their opinions in church meetings.

36You disagree? And do you think that the knowledge of God's will begins and ends with you Corinthians? Well, you are mistaken! 37You who claim to have the gift of prophecy or any other special ability from the Holy Spirit should be the first to realize that what I am saying is a commandment from the Lord himself. 38But if anyone still disagrees—well, we will leave him in his ignorance.

39So, my fellow believers, long to be prophets so that you can preach God's message plainly; and never say it is wrong to "speak in tongues"; 40however, be sure that everything is done properly in a good and orderly way.

PSALM 37:29–40

THE godly shall be firmly planted in the land, and live there forever. 30,31The godly man is a good counselor because he is just and fair and knows right from wrong.

32Evil men spy on the godly, waiting for an excuse to accuse them and then demanding their death. 33But the Lord will not let these evil men succeed, nor let the godly be condemned when they are brought before the judge.

34Don't be impatient for the Lord to act! Keep traveling steadily along his pathway and in due season he will honor you with every blessing, and you will see the wicked destroyed. 35,36I myself have seen it happen: a proud and evil man, towering like a cedar of Lebanon, but when I looked again, he was gone! I searched but could not find him! 37But the good man—what a different story! For the good man—the blameless, the upright, the man of peace—he has a wonderful future ahead of him. For him there is a happy ending. 38But evil men shall be destroyed, and their posterity shall be cut off.

39The Lord saves the godly! He is their salvation and their refuge when trouble comes. 40Because they trust in him, he helps them and delivers them from the plots of evil men.

PROVERBS FOR TODAY/ 21:27

God loathes the gifts of evil men, especially if they are trying to bribe him!

AUGUST 23

JOB 8:1—11:20

BILDAD the Shuhite replies to Job: 2"How long will you go on like this, Job, blowing words around like wind? 3Does God twist justice? 4If your children sinned against him, and he punished them, 5and you begged Almighty God for them— 6if you were pure and good, he would hear your prayer, and answer you, and bless you with a happy home. 7And though you started with little, you would end with much.

8"Read the history books and see— 9for we were born but yesterday and know so little; our days here on earth are as transient as shadows. 10But the wisdom of the past will teach you. The experience of others will speak to you, reminding you that 11,12,13those who forget God have no hope. They are like rushes without any mire to grow in; or grass without water to keep it alive. Suddenly it begins to wither, even before it is cut. 14A man without God is trusting in a spider's web. Everything he counts on will collapse. 15If he counts on his home for security, it won't last. 16At dawn he seems so strong and virile, like a green plant; his branches spread across the garden. 17His roots are in the stream, down among the stones. 18But when he disappears, he isn't even missed! 19That is all he can look forward to! And others spring up from the earth to replace him!

20"But look! God will not cast away a good man, nor prosper evildoers. 21He will yet fill your mouth with laughter and your lips with shouts of joy. 22Those who hate you shall be clothed with shame, and the wicked destroyed."

JOB'S reply:

2"Yes, I know all that. You're not telling me anything new. But how can a man be truly good in the eyes of God? 3If God decides to argue with him, can a man answer even one question of a thousand he asks? 4For God is so wise and so mighty. Who has ever opposed him successfully?

5"Suddenly he moves the mountains, overturning them in his anger. 6He shakes the earth to its foundations. 7The sun won't rise, the stars won't shine, if he commands it so! 8Only he has stretched the heavens out and stalked along the seas. 9He made the Bear, Orion and the Pleiades, and the constellations of the southern Zodiac.

10"He does incredible miracles, too many to count. 11He passes by, invisible; he moves along, but I don't see him go. 12When he sends death to snatch a man away, who can stop him? Who dares to ask him, 'What are you doing?'

13"And God does not abate his anger. The pride of man collapses before him. 14And who am I that I should try to argue with Almighty God, or even reason with him? 15Even if I were sinless I wouldn't say a word. I would only plead for mercy. 16And even if my prayers were answered I could scarce believe that he had heard my cry. [17]For he is the one who destroys, and multiplies my wounds without a cause. [18]He will not let me breathe, but fills me with bitter sorrows. [19]He alone is strong and just.

[20]"But I? Am I righteous? My own mouth says no. Even if I were perfect, God would prove me wicked. [21]And even if I am utterly innocent, I dare not think of it. I despise what I am. [22]Innocent or evil, it is all the same to him, for he destroys both kinds. [23]He will laugh when calamity crushes the innocent. [24]The whole earth is in the hands of the wicked. God blinds the eyes of the judges and lets them be unfair. If not he, then who?

[25]"My life passes swiftly away, filled with tragedy. [26]My years disappear like swift ships, like the eagle that swoops upon its prey.

[27]"If I decided to forget my complaints against God, to end my sadness and be cheerful, [28]then he would pour even greater sorrows upon me. For I know that you will not hold me innocent, O God, [29]but will condemn me. So what's the use of trying? [30]Even if I were to wash myself with purest water and cleanse my hands with lye to make them utterly clean, [31]even so you would plunge me into the ditch and mud; and even my clothing would be less filthy than you consider me to be!

[32,33]"And I cannot defend myself, for you are no mere man as I am. If you were, then we could discuss it fairly, but there is no umpire between us, no middle man, no mediator to bring us together. [34]Oh, let him stop beating me, so that I need no longer live in terror of his punishment. [35]Then I could speak without fear to him, and tell him boldly that I am not guilty.

"I am weary of living. Let me complain freely. I will speak in my sorrow and bitterness. [2]I will say to God, 'Don't just condemn me—tell me *why* you are doing it. [3]Does it really seem right to you to oppress and despise me, a man you have made; and to send joy and prosperity

to the wicked? [4-7]Are you unjust like men? Is your life so short that you must hound me for sins you know full well I've not committed? Is it because you know no one can save me from your hand?

[8]"'You have made me, and yet you destroy me. [9]Oh, please remember that I'm made of dust—will you change me back again to dust so soon? [10]You have already poured me from bottle to bottle like milk, and curdled me like cheese. [11]You gave me skin and flesh and knit together bones and sinews. [12]You gave me life and were so kind and loving to me, and I was preserved by your care.

[13,14]"'Yet all the time your real motive in making me was to destroy me if I sinned; and to refuse to forgive my iniquity. [15]Just the slightest wickedness, and I am done for. And if I'm good, that doesn't count. I am filled with frustration. [16]If I start to get up off the ground, you leap upon me like a lion and quickly finish me off. [17]Again and again you witness against me and pour out an ever-increasing volume of wrath upon me and bring fresh armies against me.

[18]"'Why then did you even let me be born? Why didn't you let me die at birth? [19]Then I would have been spared this miserable existence. I would have gone directly from the womb to the grave. [20,21]Can't you see how little time I have left? Oh, let me alone that I may have a little moment of comfort before I leave for the land of darkness and the shadow of death, never to return— [22]a land as dark as midnight, a land of the shadow of death where only confusion reigns, and where the brightest light is dark as midnight.'"

ZOPHAR the Naamathite replies to Job:

[2]"Shouldn't someone stem this torrent of words? Is a man proved right by all this talk? [3]Should I remain silent while you boast? When you mock God, shouldn't someone make you ashamed? [4]You claim you are pure in the eyes of God! [5]Oh, that God would speak and tell you what he thinks! [6]Oh, that he would

make you truly see yourself, for he knows everything you've done. Listen! God is doubtless punishing you far less than you deserve!

7"Do you know the mind and purposes of God? Will long searching make them known to you? Are you qualified to judge the Almighty? 8He is as faultless as heaven is high—but who are you? His mind is fathomless—what can you know in comparison? 9His Spirit is broader than the earth and wider than the sea. 10If he rushes in and makes an arrest, and calls the court to order, who is going to stop him? 11For he knows perfectly all the faults and sins of mankind; he sees all sin without searching.

12"Mere man is as likely to be wise, as a wild donkey's colt is likely to be born a man!

13,14"Before you turn to God and stretch out your hands to him, get rid of your sins and leave all iniquity behind you. 15Only then, without the spots of sin to defile you, can you walk steadily forward to God without fear. 16Only then can you forget your misery. It will all be in the past. 17And your life will be cloudless; any darkness will be as bright as morning!

18"You will have courage because you will have hope. You will take your time, and rest in safety. 19You will lie down unafraid and many will look to you for help. 20But the wicked shall find no way to escape; their only hope is death."

1 CORINTHIANS 15:1–28

NOW let me remind you, brothers, of what the Gospel really is, for it has not changed—it is the same Good News I preached to you before. You welcomed it then and still do now, for your faith is squarely built upon this wonderful message; 2and it is this Good News that saves you if you still firmly believe it, unless of course you never really believed it in the first place.

3I passed on to you right from the first what had been told to me, that Christ died for our sins just as the Scriptures

said he would, 4and that he was buried, and that three days afterwards he arose from the grave just as the prophets foretold. 5He was seen by Peter and later by the rest of "the Twelve." 6After that he was seen by more than five hundred Christian brothers at one time, most of whom are still alive, though some have died by now. 7Then James saw him and later all the apostles. 8Last of all I saw him too, long after the others, as though I had been born almost too late for this. 9For I am the least worthy of all the apostles, and I shouldn't even be called an apostle at all after the way I treated the church of God.

10But whatever I am now it is all because God poured out such kindness and grace upon me—and not without results: for I have worked harder than all the other apostles, yet actually I wasn't doing it, but God working in me, to bless me. 11It makes no difference who worked the hardest, I or they; the important thing is that we preached the Gospel to you, and you believed it.

12But tell me this! Since you believe what we preach, that *Christ* rose from the dead, why are some of you saying that dead people will never come back to life again? 13For if there is no resurrection of the dead, then Christ must still be dead. 14And if he is still dead, then all our preaching is useless and your trust in God is empty, worthless, hopeless; 15and we apostles are all liars because we have said that God raised Christ from the grave, and of course that isn't true if the dead do not come back to life again. 16If they don't, then Christ is still dead, 17and you are very foolish to keep on trusting God to save you, and you are still under condemnation for your sins; 18in that case all Christians who have died are lost! 19And if being a Christian is of value to us only now in this life, we are the most miserable of creatures.

20But the fact is that Christ did actually rise from the dead, and has become the first of millions who will come back to life again some day.

21Death came into the world because

of what one man (Adam) did, and it is because of what this other man (Christ) has done that now there is the resurrection from the dead. ²²Everyone dies because all of us are related to Adam, being members of his sinful race, and wherever there is sin, death results. But all who are related to Christ will rise again. ²³Each, however, in his own turn: Christ rose first; then when Christ comes back, all his people will become alive again.

²⁴After that the end will come when he will turn the Kingdom over to God the Father, having put down all enemies of every kind. ²⁵For Christ will be King until he has defeated all his enemies, ²⁶including the last enemy—death. This too must be defeated and ended. ²⁷For the rule and authority over all things has been given to Christ by his Father; except, of course, Christ does not rule over the Father himself, who gave him this power to rule. ²⁸When Christ has finally won the battle against all his enemies, then he, the Son of God, will put himself also under his Father's orders, so that God who has given him the victory over everything else will be utterly supreme.

PSALM 38:1–22

O Lord, don't punish me while you are angry! ²Your arrows have struck deep; your blows are crushing me. ³,⁴Because of your anger my body is sick, my health is broken beneath my sins. They are like a flood, higher than my head; they are a burden too heavy to bear. ⁵,⁶My wounds are festering and full of pus. Because of my sins I am bent and racked with pain. My days are filled with anguish. ⁷My loins burn with inflammation and my whole body is diseased. ⁸I am exhausted and crushed; I groan in despair.

⁹Lord, you know how I long for my health once more. You hear my every sigh. ¹⁰My heart beats wildly, my strength fails, and I am going blind. ¹¹My loved ones and friends stay away, fearing my disease. Even my own family stands at a distance.

¹²Meanwhile my enemies are trying to kill me. They plot my ruin and spend all their waking hours planning treachery. ¹³,¹⁴But I am deaf to all their threats; I am silent before them as a man who cannot speak. I have nothing to say. ¹⁵For I am waiting for you, O Lord my God. Come and protect me. ¹⁶Put an end to their arrogance, these who gloat when I am cast down!

¹⁷How constantly I find myself upon the verge of sin; this source of sorrow always stares me in the face. ¹⁸I confess my sins; I am sorry for what I have done. ¹⁹But my enemies persecute with vigor, and continue to hate me—though I have done nothing against them to deserve it. ²⁰They repay me evil for good and hate me for standing for the right.

²¹Don't leave me, Lord; don't go away! ²²Come quickly! Help me, O my Savior.

PROVERBS FOR TODAY/ 21:28–29

No one believes a liar, but everyone respects the words of an honest man. An evil man is stubborn, but a godly man will reconsider.

JOB 12:1—15:35

JOB'S reply:
²"Yes, I realize you know everything! All wisdom will die with you! ³Well, I know a few things myself—you are no better than I am. And who doesn't know these things you've been saying? ⁴I, the man who begged God for help, and God answered him, have become a laughingstock to my neighbors. Yes, I, a righteous man, am now the man they scoff at. ⁵Meanwhile, the rich mock those in trouble and are quick to despise all those in need. ⁶For robbers prosper. Go ahead and provoke God—it makes no difference! He will supply your every need anyway!

⁷,⁸,⁹"Who doesn't know that the Lord does things like that? Ask the dumbest beast—he knows that it is so; ask the birds—they will tell you; or let the earth teach you, or the fish of the sea. ¹⁰For the soul of every living thing is in the hand of God, and the breath of all mankind. ¹¹Just as my mouth can taste good food, so my mind tastes truth when I hear it. ¹²And as you say, older men like me are wise. They understand. ¹³But true wisdom and power are God's. He alone knows what we should do; he understands.

¹⁴"And how great is his might! What he destroys can't be rebuilt. When he closes in on a man, there is no escape. ¹⁵He withholds the rain, and the earth becomes a desert; he sends the storms, and floods the ground. ¹⁶Yes, with him is strength and wisdom. Deceivers and deceived are both his slaves.

¹⁷"He makes fools of counselors and judges. ¹⁸He reduces kings to slaves and frees their servants. ¹⁹Priests are led away as slaves. He overthrows the mighty. ²⁰He takes away the voice of orators, and the insight of the elders. ²¹He pours contempt upon princes, and weakens the strong. ²²He floods the darkness with light, even the dark shadow of death. ²³He raises up a nation and then destroys it. He makes it great, and then reduces it to nothing. ²⁴,²⁵He takes away the understanding of presidents and kings, and leaves them wandering, lost and groping, without a guiding light.

"LOOK, I have seen many instances such as you describe. I understand what you are saying. ²I know as much as you do. I'm not stupid. ³Oh, how I long to speak directly to the Almighty. I want to talk this over with God himself. ⁴For you are misinterpreting the whole thing. You are doctors who don't know what they are doing. ⁵Oh, please be quiet! That would be your highest wisdom.

⁶"Listen to me now, to my reasons for what I think, and to my pleadings. ⁷"Must you go on 'speaking for God' when he never once has said the things that you are putting in his mouth? ⁸Does God want your help if you are going to twist the truth for him? ⁹Be careful that he doesn't find out what you are doing! Or do you think you can fool God as well as men? ¹⁰No, you will be in serious trouble with him if you use lies to try to help him out. ¹¹Doesn't his majesty strike terror to your heart? How can you do this thing? ¹²These tremendous statements you have made have about as much value as ashes. Your defense of God is as fragile as a clay vase!

¹³"Be silent now and let me alone, that I may speak—and I am willing to face the consequences. ¹⁴Yes, I will take my life in my hand and say what I really think. ¹⁵God may kill me for saying this— in fact, I expect him to. Nevertheless I am going to argue my case with him. ¹⁶This at least will be in my favor, that I am not godless, to be rejected instantly from his presence. ¹⁷Listen

closely to what I am about to say. Hear me out.

18"This is my case: *I know that I am righteous.* 19Who can argue with me over this? If you could prove me wrong I would stop defending myself and die.

20"O God, there are two things I beg you not to do to me; only then will I be able to face you. 21Don't abandon me. And don't terrify me with your awesome presence. 22Call to me to come—how quickly I will answer! Or let me speak to you, and you reply. 23Tell me, what have I done wrong? Help me! Point out my sin to me. 24Why do you turn away from me? Why hand me over to my enemy? 25Would you blame a leaf that is blown about by the wind? Will you chase dry, useless straws?

26"You write bitter things against me and bring up all the follies of my youth. 27,28You send me to prison and shut me in on every side. I am like a fallen, rotten tree, like a moth-eaten coat.

"HOW frail is man, how few his days, how full of trouble! 2He blossoms for a moment like a flower—and withers; as the shadow of a passing cloud, he quickly disappears. 3Must you be so harsh with frail men, and demand an accounting from them? 4How can you demand purity in one born impure? 5You have set mankind so brief a span of life—months is all you give him! Not one bit longer may he live. 6So give him a little rest, won't you? Turn away your angry gaze and let him have a few moments of relief before he dies.

7"For there is hope for a tree—if it's cut down it sprouts again, and grows tender, new branches. 8,9Though its roots have grown old in the earth, and its stump decays, it may sprout and bud again at the touch of water, like a new seedling. 10But when a man dies and is buried, where does his spirit go? 11,12As water evaporates from a lake, as a river disappears in drought, so a man lies down for the last time, and does not rise again until the heavens are no more; he shall not awaken, nor be roused from his sleep. 13Oh, that you would hide me with the dead, and forget me there until your anger ends; but mark your calendar to think of me again!

14"If a man dies, shall he live again? This thought gives me hope, so that in all my anguish I eagerly await sweet death! 15You would call and I would come, and you would reward all I do. 16But now, instead, you give me so few steps upon the stage of life, and notice every mistake I make. 17You bundle them all together as evidence against me.

18,19"Mountains wear away and disappear. Water grinds the stones to sand. Torrents tear away the soil. So every hope of man is worn away. 20,21Always you are against him, and then he passes off the scene. You make him old and wrinkled, then send him away. He never knows it if his sons are honored; or they may fail and face disaster, but he knows it not. 22For him there is only sorrow and pain."

THE answer of Eliphaz the Temanite:

2"You are supposed to be a wise man, and yet you give us all this foolish talk. You are nothing but a windbag. 3It isn't right to speak so foolishly. What good do such words do? 4,5Have you no fear of God? No reverence for him? Your sins are telling your mouth what to say! Your words are based on clever deception, 6but why should I condemn you? Your own mouth does!

7,8"Are you the wisest man alive? Were you born before the hills were made? Have you heard the secret counsel of God? Are you called into his counsel room? Do you have a monopoly on wisdom? 9What do you know more than we do? What do you understand that we don't? 10On our side are aged men much older than your father! 11Is God's comfort too little for you? Is his gentleness too rough?

12"What is this you are doing, getting

carried away by your anger, with flashing eyes? 13And you turn against God and say all these evil things against him. 14What man in all the earth can be as pure and righteous as you claim to be? 15Why, God doesn't even trust the angels! Even the heavens can't be absolutely pure compared with him! 16How much less someone like you, who is corrupt and sinful, drinking in sin as a sponge soaks up water!

17,18,19"Listen, and I will answer you from my own experience, confirmed by the experience of wise men who have been told this same thing from their fathers—our ancestors to whom alone the land was given—and they have passed this wisdom to us:

20"A wicked man is always in trouble throughout his life. 21He is surrounded by terrors, and if there are good days they will soon be gone. 22He dares not go out into the darkness, lest he be murdered. 23,24He wanders around begging for food. He lives in fear, distress, and anguish. His enemies conquer him as a king defeats his foes. 25,26Armed with his tin shield, he clenches his fist against God, defying the Almighty, stubbornly assaulting him.

27,28"This wicked man is fat and rich, and has lived in conquered cities after killing off their citizens. 29But he will not continue to be rich, or to extend his possessions. 30No, darkness shall overtake him forever; the breath of God shall destroy him; the flames shall burn up all he has.

31"Let him no longer trust in foolish riches; let him no longer deceive himself, for the money he trusts in will be his only reward. 32Before he dies, all this futility will become evident to him. For all he counted on will disappear, 33and fall to the ground like a withered grape. How little will come of his hopes! 34For the godless are barren: they can produce nothing truly good. God's fire consumes them with all their possessions. 35The only thing they can 'conceive' is sin, and their hearts give birth only to wickedness."

IF the dead will not come back to life again, then what point is there in people being baptized for those who are gone? Why do it unless you believe that the dead will some day rise again?

30And why should we ourselves be continually risking our lives, facing death hour by hour? 31For it is a fact that I face death daily; that is as true as my pride in your growth in the Lord. 32And what value was there in fighting wild beasts—those men of Ephesus—if it was only for what I gain in this life down here? If we will never live again after we die, then we might as well go and have ourselves a good time: let us eat, drink, and be merry. What's the difference? For tomorrow we die, and that ends everything!

33Don't be fooled by those who say such things. If you listen to them you will start acting like them. 34Get some sense and quit your sinning. For to your shame I say it, some of you are not even Christians at all and have never really known God.

35But someone may ask, "How will the dead be brought back to life again? What kind of bodies will they have?" 36What a foolish question! You will find the answer in your own garden! When you put a seed into the ground it doesn't grow into a plant unless it "dies" first. 37And when the green shoot comes up out of the seed, it is very different from the seed you first planted. For all you put into the ground is a dry little seed of wheat, or whatever it is you are planting, 38then God gives it a beautiful new body—just the kind he wants it to have; a different kind of plant grows from each kind of seed. 39And just as there are different kinds of seeds and plants, so also there are different kinds of flesh. Humans, animals, fish, and birds are all different.

40The angels in heaven have bodies far different from ours, and the beauty and the glory of their bodies is different from the beauty and the glory of ours. 41The sun has one kind of glory while the moon and stars have another kind. And the stars differ from each other in their beauty and brightness.

42In the same way, our earthly bodies which die and decay are different from the bodies we shall have when we come back to life again, for they will never die. 43The bodies we have now embarrass us for they become sick and die; but they will be full of glory when we come back to life again. Yes, they are weak, dying bodies now, but when we live again they will be full of strength. 44They are just human bodies at death, but when they come back to life they will be superhuman bodies. For just as there are natural, human bodies, there are also supernatural, spiritual bodies.

45The Scriptures tell us that the first man, Adam, was given a natural, human body but Christ is more than that, for he was life-giving Spirit.

46First, then, we have these human bodies and later on God gives us spiritual, heavenly bodies. 47Adam was made from the dust of the earth, but Christ came from heaven above. 48Every human being has a body just like Adam's, made of dust, but all who become Christ's will have the same kind of body as his—a body from heaven. 49Just as each of us now has a body like Adam's, so we shall some day have a body like Christ's.

50I tell you this, my brothers: an earthly body made of flesh and blood cannot get into God's Kingdom. These perishable bodies of ours are not the right kind to live forever.

51But I am telling you this strange and wonderful secret: we shall not all die, but we shall all be given new bodies! 52It will all happen in a moment, in the twinkling of an eye, when the last trumpet is blown. For there will be a trumpet blast from the sky and all the Christians who have died will suddenly become alive, with new bodies that will never, never die; and then we who are still alive shall suddenly have new bodies too. 53For our earthly bodies, the ones we

have now that can die, must be transformed into heavenly bodies that cannot perish but will live forever.

54When this happens, then at last this Scripture will come true—"Death is swallowed up in victory." 55,56O death, where then your victory? Where then your sting? For sin—the sting that causes death—will all be gone; and the law, which reveals our sins, will no longer be our judge. 57How we thank God for all of this! It is he who makes us victorious through Jesus Christ our Lord!

58So, my dear brothers, since future victory is sure, be strong and steady, always abounding in the Lord's work, for you know that nothing you do for the Lord is ever wasted as it would be if there were no resurrection.

PSALM 39:1–13

I said to myself, I'm going to quit complaining! I'll keep quiet, especially when the ungodly are around me. 2,3But as I stood there silently the turmoil within me grew to the bursting point. The more I mused, the hotter the fires inside. Then at last I spoke, and pled with God: 4Lord, help me to realize how brief my time on earth will be. Help me to know that I am here for but a moment more. 5,6My life is no longer than my hand! My whole lifetime is but a moment to you. Proud man! Frail as breath! A shadow! And all his busy rushing ends in nothing. He heaps up riches for someone else to spend. 7And so, Lord, my only hope is in you.

8Save me from being overpowered by my sins, for even fools will mock me then.

9Lord, I am speechless before you. I will not open my mouth to speak one word of complaint, for my punishment is from you.

10Lord, don't hit me anymore—I am exhausted beneath your hand. 11When you punish a man for his sins, he is destroyed, for he is as fragile as a moth-infested cloth; yes, man is frail as breath.

12Hear my prayer, O Lord; listen to

my cry! Don't sit back, unmindful of my tears. For I am your guest. I am a traveler passing through the earth, as all my fathers were.

13Spare me, Lord! Let me recover and be filled with happiness again before my death.

PROVERBS FOR TODAY/ 21:30–31
No one, regardless of how shrewd or well-advised he is, can stand against the Lord. Go ahead and prepare for the conflict, but victory comes from God.

AUGUST 25

JOB 16:1—19:29

JOB'S reply:
2"I have heard all this before. What miserable comforters all of you are. 3Won't you ever stop your flow of foolish words? What have I said that makes you speak so endlessly? 4But perhaps I'd sermonize the same as you— if you were I and I were you. I would spout off my criticisms against you and shake my head at you. 5But no! I would speak in such a way that it would help you. I would try to take away your grief.

6"But now my grief remains no matter how I defend myself; nor does it help if I refuse to speak. 7For God has ground me down, and taken away my family. 8O God, you have turned me to skin and bones—as a proof, they say, of my sins. 9God hates me and angrily tears at my flesh; he has gnashed upon me with his teeth, and watched to snuff out any sign of life. 10These 'comforters' have gaping jaws to swallow me; they slap my cheek. My enemies gather themselves against me. 11And God has delivered me over to sinners, into the hands of the wicked.

12"I was living quietly until he broke me apart. He has taken me by the neck and dashed me to pieces, then hung me up as his target. 13His archers surround me, letting fly their arrows, so that the ground is wet from my blood. 14Again and again he attacks me, running upon me like a giant. 15Here I sit in sackcloth; and have laid all hope in the dust.

16My eyes are red with weeping and on my eyelids is the shadow of death.

17"Yet I am innocent, and my prayer is pure. 18O earth, do not conceal my blood. Let it protest on my behalf.

19"Yet even now the Witness to my innocence is there in heaven; my Advocate is there on high. 20My friends scoff at me, but I pour out my tears to God, 21pleading that he will listen as a man would listen to his neighbor. 22For all too soon I must go down that road from which I shall never return.

"I am sick and near to death; the grave is ready to receive me. 2I am surrounded by mockers. I see them everywhere. 3,4Will no one anywhere confirm my innocence? But you, O God, have kept them back from understanding this. Oh, do not let them triumph. 5If they accept bribes to denounce their friends, their children shall go blind.

6"He has made me a mockery among the people; they spit in my face. 7My eyes are dim with weeping and I am but a shadow of my former self. 8Fair-minded men are astonished when they see me.

"Yet, finally, the innocent shall come out on top, above the godless; 9the righteous shall move onward and forward; those with pure hearts shall become stronger and stronger.

10"As for you—all of you please go

away; for I do not find a wise man among you. 11My good days are in the past. My hopes have disappeared. My heart's desires are broken. 12They say that night is day and day is night; how they pervert the truth!

13,14"If I die, I go out into darkness, and call the grave my father, and the worm my mother and my sister. 15Where then is my hope? Can anyone find any? 16No, my hope will go down with me to the grave. We shall rest together in the dust!"

THE further reply of Bildad the Shuhite:

2"Who are you trying to fool? Speak some sense if you want us to answer! 3Have we become like animals to you, stupid and dumb? 4Just because you tear your clothes in anger, is this going to start an earthquake? Shall we all go and hide?

5"The truth remains that if you do not prosper, it is because you are wicked. And your bright flame shall be put out. 6There will be darkness in every home where there is wickedness.

7"The confident stride of the wicked man will be shortened; he will realize his failing strength. 8,9He walks into traps, and robbers will ambush him. 10There is a booby-trap in every path he takes. 11He has good cause for fear—his enemy is close behind him!

12"His vigor is depleted by hunger; calamity stands ready to pounce upon him. 13His skin is eaten by disease. Death shall devour him. 14The wealth he trusted in shall reject him, and he shall be brought down to the King of Terrors. 15His home shall disappear beneath a fiery barrage of brimstone. 16He shall die from the roots up, and all his branches will be lopped off.

17"All memory of his existence will perish from the earth; no one will remember him. 18He will be driven out from the kingdom of light into darkness, and chased out of the world. 19He will have neither son nor grandson left, nor any other relatives. 20Old and young alike will be horrified by his fate. 21Yes, that is what happens to sinners, to those rejecting God."

THE reply of Job:

2"How long are you going to trouble me, and try to break me with your words? 3Ten times now you have declared I am a sinner. Why aren't you ashamed to deal with me so harshly? 4And if indeed I was wrong, you have yet to prove it. 5You think yourselves so great? Then prove my guilt!

6"The fact of the matter is that God has overthrown me and caught me in his net. 7I scream for help and no one hears me. I shriek, but get no justice. 8God has blocked my path and turned my light to darkness. 9He has stripped me of my glory and removed the crown from my head. 10He has broken me down on every side, and I am done for. He has destroyed all hope. 11His fury burns against me; he counts me as an enemy. 12He sends his troops to surround my tent.

13"He has sent away my brothers, and my friends. 14My relatives have failed me; my friends have all forsaken me. 15Those living in my home, even my servants, regard me as a stranger. I am like a foreigner to them. 16I call my servant, but he doesn't come; I even beg him! 17My own wife and brothers refuse to recognize me. 18Even young children despise me. When I stand to speak, they mock.

19"My best friends abhor me. Those I loved have turned against me. 20I am skin and bones and have escaped death by the skin of my teeth.

21"Oh, my friends, pity me, for the angry hand of God has touched me. 22Why must you persecute me as God does? Why aren't you satisfied with my anguish? 23,24Oh, that I could write my plea with an iron pen in the rock forever.

25"But as for me, I know that my Redeemer lives, and that he will stand upon the earth at last. 26And I know that after this body has decayed, this body shall see God! 27Then he will be on *my* side! Yes, I shall see him, not as a stranger, but as a friend! What a glorious hope! 28"How dare you go on persecuting me, as though I were proven guilty? 29I warn you, you yourselves are in danger of punishment for your attitude."

1 CORINTHIANS 16:1–24

NOW here are the directions about the money you are collecting to send to the Christians in Jerusalem; (and, by the way, these are the same directions I gave to the churches in Galatia). 2On every Lord's Day each of you should put aside something from what you have earned during the week, and use it for this offering. The amount depends on how much the Lord has helped you earn. Don't wait until I get there and then try to collect it all at once. 3When I come I will send your loving gift with a letter to Jerusalem, to be taken there by trustworthy messengers you yourselves will choose. 4And if it seems wise for me to go along too, then we can travel together.

5I am coming to visit you after I have been to Macedonia first, but I will be staying there only for a little while. 6It could be that I will stay longer with you, perhaps all winter, and then you can send me on to my next destination. 7This time I don't want to make just a passing visit and then go right on; I want to come and stay awhile, if the Lord will let me. 8I will be staying here at Ephesus until the holiday of Pentecost, 9for there is a wide open door for me to preach and teach here. So much is happening, but there are many enemies.

10If Timothy comes make him feel at home, for he is doing the Lord's work just as I am. 11Don't let anyone despise or ignore him [because he is young], but send him back to me happy with his time among you; I am looking forward to seeing him soon, along with the others who are returning.

12I begged Apollos to visit you along with the others, but he thought that it was not at all God's will for him to go now; he will be seeing you later on when he has the opportunity.

13Keep your eyes open for spiritual danger; stand true to the Lord; act like men; be strong; 14and whatever you do, do it with kindness and love.

15Do you remember Stephanas and his family? They were the first to become Christians in Greece and they are spending their lives helping and serving Christians everywhere. 16Please follow their instructions and do everything you can to help them as well as all others like them who work hard at your side with such real devotion. 17I am so glad that Stephanas, Fortunatus, and Achaicus have arrived here for a visit. They have been making up for the help you aren't here to give me. 18They have cheered me greatly and have been a wonderful encouragement to me, as I am sure they were to you, too. I hope you properly appreciate the work of such men as these.

19The churches here in Asia send you their loving greetings. Aquila and Priscilla send you their love and so do all the others who meet in their home for their church service. 20All the friends here have asked me to say "hello" to you for them. And give each other a loving handshake when you meet.

21I will write these final words of this letter with my own hand: 22if anyone does not love the Lord, that person is cursed. Lord Jesus, come! 23May the love and favor of the Lord Jesus Christ rest upon you. 24My love to all of you, for we all belong to Christ Jesus.

Sincerely,
Paul

PSALM 40:1–10

I waited patiently for God to help me; then he listened and heard my cry. 2He lifted me out of the pit of despair, out from the bog and the mire, and set my feet on a hard, firm path and steadied me as I walked along. 3He has given me a new song to sing, of praises to our God. Now many will hear of the glorious things he did for me, and stand in awe before the Lord, and put their trust in him. 4Many blessings are given to those who trust the Lord, and have no confidence in those who are proud, or who trust in idols.

5O Lord my God, many and many a time you have done great miracles for us and we are ever in your thoughts. Who else can do such glorious things? No one else can be compared with you. There isn't time to tell of all your wonderful deeds.

6It isn't sacrifices and offerings which you really want from your people. Burnt animals bring no special joy to your heart. But you have accepted the offer of my life-long service. 7Then I said, "See, I have come, just as all the prophets foretold. 8And I delight to do your will, my God, for your law is written upon my heart!"

9I have told everyone the Good News that you forgive people's sins. I have not been timid about it, as you well know, O Lord. 10I have not kept this Good News hidden in my heart, but have proclaimed your lovingkindness and truth to all the congregation.

PROVERBS FOR TODAY/ 22:1

If you must choose, take a good name rather than great riches; for to be held in loving esteem is better than silver and gold.

AUGUST 26

JOB 20:1—22:30

THE speech of Zophar the Naamathite:

2"I hasten to reply, for I have the answer for you. 3You have tried to make me feel ashamed of myself for calling you a sinner, but my spirit won't let me stop.

4"Don't you realize that ever since man was first placed upon the earth, 5the triumph of the wicked has been short-lived, and the joy of the godless but for a moment? 6Though the godless be proud as the heavens, and walk with his nose in the air, 7yet he shall perish forever, cast away like his own dung. Those who knew him will wonder where he is gone. 8He will fade like a dream. 9Neither his friends nor his family will ever see him again.

10"His children shall beg from the poor, their hard labor shall repay his debts. 11Though still a young man, his bones shall lie in the dust.

12"He enjoyed the taste of his wickedness, letting it melt in his mouth, 13sipping it slowly, lest it disappear. 14But suddenly the food he has eaten turns sour within him. 15He will vomit the plunder he gorged. God won't let him keep it down. 16It is like poison and death to him. 17He shall not enjoy the goods he stole; they will not be butter and honey to him after all. 18His labors shall not be rewarded; wealth will give him no joy. 19For he has oppressed the poor and foreclosed their homes; he will never recover. 20Though he was always greedy, now he has nothing; of all the things he dreamed of—none remain. 21Because he stole at every opportunity, his prosperity shall not continue.

22"He shall run into trouble at the peak of his powers; all the wicked shall destroy him. 23Just as he is about to fill his belly, God will rain down wrath upon him. 24He will be chased and struck down. 25The arrow is pulled from his body—

and the glittering point comes out from his gall. The terrors of death are upon him.

26"His treasures will be lost in deepest darkness. A raging fire will devour his goods, consuming all he has left. 27The heavens will reveal his sins, and the earth will give testimony against him. 28His wealth will disappear beneath the wrath of God. 29This is what awaits the wicked man, for God prepares it for him."

JOB'S reply:

2,3"Listen to me; let me speak, and afterwards, mock on.

4"I am complaining about God, not man; no wonder my spirit is so troubled. 5Look at me in horror, and lay your hand upon your mouth. 6Even I am frightened when I see myself. Horror takes hold upon me and I shudder.

7"The truth is that the wicked live on to a good old age, and become great and powerful. 8They live to see their children grow to maturity around them, and their grandchildren, too. 9Their homes are safe from every fear, and God does not punish them. 10Their cattle are productive, 11they have many happy children, 12,13they spend their time singing and dancing. They are wealthy and need deny themselves nothing; they are prosperous to the end. 14All this despite the fact that they ordered God away and wanted no part of him and his ways.

15" 'Who is Almighty God?' they scoff. 'Why should we obey him? What good will it do us?'

16"Look, everything the wicked touch has turned to gold! But I refuse even to deal with people like that. 17Yet the wicked get away with it every time. They never have trouble, and God skips them when he distributes his sorrows and anger. 18Are they driven before the wind like straw? Are they carried away by the storm? Not at all!

19" 'Well,' you say, 'at least God will punish their children!' But I say that God should punish the man who sins, not his children! Let him feel the penalty himself.

20Yes, let him be destroyed for his iniquity. Let him drink deeply of the anger of the Almighty. 21For when he is dead, then he will never again be able to enjoy his family.

22"But who can rebuke God, the supreme Judge? 23,24He destroys those who are healthy, wealthy, fat, and prosperous; 25God also destroys those in deep and grinding poverty who have never known anything good. 26Both alike are buried in the same dust, both eaten by the same worms.

27"I know what you are going to say— 28you will tell me of rich and wicked men who came to disaster because of their sins. 29But I reply, Ask anyone who has been around and he can tell you the truth, 30,31,32that the evil man is usually spared in the day of calamity, and allowed to escape. No one rebukes him openly. No one repays him for what he has done. And an honor guard keeps watch at his grave. 33A great funeral procession precedes and follows him as the soft earth covers him. 34How can you comfort me when your whole premise is so wrong?"

ANOTHER address from Eliphaz:

2"Is mere man of any worth to God? Even the wisest is of value only to himself! 3Is it any pleasure to the Almighty if you are righteous? Would it be any gain to him if you were perfect? 4Is it because you are good that he is punishing you? 5Not at all! It is because of your wickedness! Your sins are endless!

6"For instance, you must have refused to loan money to needy friends unless they gave you all their clothing as a pledge—yes, you must have stripped them to the bone. 7You must have refused water to the thirsty, and bread to the starving. 8But no doubt you gave men of importance anything they wanted, and let the wealthy live wherever they chose. 9You sent widows away without helping them, and broke the arms of orphans. 10,11That is why you are now surrounded by traps and sudden fears, and darkness and waves of horror.

12"God is so great—higher than the heavens, higher than the stars. 13But you reply, 'That is why he can't see what I am doing! How can he judge through the thick darkness? 14For thick clouds swirl about him so that he cannot see us. He is way up there, walking on the vault of heaven.'

15,16"Don't you realize that those treading the ancient paths of sin are snatched away in youth, and the foundations of their lives washed out forever? 17For they said to God, 'Go away, God! What can you do for us?' 18(God forbid that I should say a thing like that.) Yet they forgot that he had filled their homes with good things. 19And now the righteous shall see them destroyed; the innocent shall laugh the wicked to scorn. 20'See,' they will say, 'the last of our enemies have been destroyed in the fire.'

21"Quit quarreling with God! Agree with him and you will have peace at last! His favor will surround you if you will only admit that you were wrong. 22Listen to his instructions and store them in your heart. 23If you return to God and put right all the wrong in your home, then you will be restored. 24If you give up your lust for money, and throw your gold away, 25then the Almighty himself shall be your treasure; he will be your precious silver!

26"Then you will delight yourself in the Lord, and look up to God. 27You will pray to him, and he will hear you, and you will fulfill all your promises to him. 28Whatever you wish will happen! And the light of heaven will shine upon the road ahead of you. 29If you are attacked and knocked down, you will know that there is someone who will lift you up again. Yes, he will save the humble, 30and help even sinners by your pure hands."

2 CORINTHIANS 1:1-11

DEAR friends, This letter is from me, Paul, appointed by God to be Jesus Christ's messenger; and from our dear brother Timothy. We are writing to all of you Christians there in Corinth and throughout Greece. 2May God our Father and the Lord Jesus Christ mightily bless each one of you, and give you peace.

3,4What a wonderful God we have—he is the Father of our Lord Jesus Christ, the source of every mercy, and the one who so wonderfully comforts and strengthens us in our hardships and trials. And why does he do this? So that when others are troubled, needing our sympathy and encouragement, we can pass on to them this same help and comfort God has given us. 5You can be sure that the more we undergo sufferings for Christ, the more he will shower us with his comfort and encouragement. 6,7We are in deep trouble for bringing you God's comfort and salvation. But in our trouble God has comforted us—and this, too, to help you: to show you from our personal experience how God will tenderly comfort you when you undergo these same sufferings. He will give you the strength to endure.

8I think you ought to know, dear brothers, about the hard time we went through in Asia. We were really crushed and overwhelmed, and feared we would never live through it. 9We felt we were doomed to die and saw how powerless we were to help ourselves; but that was good, for then we put everything into the hands of God, who alone could save us, for he can even raise the dead. 10And he did help us, and saved us from a terrible death; yes, and we expect him to do it again and again. 11But you must help us too, by praying for us. For much thanks and praise will go to God from you who see his wonderful answers to your prayers for our safety!

PSALM 40:11-17

O Lord, don't hold back your tender mercies from me! My only hope is in your love and faithfulness. 12Otherwise I perish, for problems far too big for me to solve are piled higher than my head. Meanwhile my sins, too many to count, have all caught up with me and I am ashamed to look up. My heart quails within me.

¹³Please, Lord, rescue me! Quick! Come and help me! ¹⁴,¹⁵Confuse them! Turn them around and send them sprawling—all these who are trying to destroy me. Disgrace these scoffers with their utter failure!

¹⁶But may the joy of the Lord be given to everyone who loves him and his salvation. May they constantly exclaim, "How great God is!"

¹⁷I am poor and weak, yet the Lord is thinking about me right now! O my God, you are my helper. You are my Savior; come quickly, and save me. Please don't delay!

PROVERBS FOR TODAY/ 22:2–4

The rich and the poor are alike before the Lord who made them all. A prudent man foresees the difficulties ahead and prepares for them; the simpleton goes blindly on and suffers the consequences. True humility and respect for the Lord lead a man to riches, honor, and long life.

AUGUST 27

JOB 23:1—27:23

THE reply of Job:

²"My complaint today is still a bitter one, and my punishment far more severe than my fault deserves. ³Oh, that I knew where to find God—that I could go to his throne and talk with him there. ⁴,⁵I would tell him all about my side of this argument, and listen to his reply, and understand what he wants. ⁶Would he merely overpower me with his greatness? No, he would listen with sympathy. ⁷Fair and honest men could reason with him, and be acquitted by my Judge.

⁸"But I search in vain. I seek him here, I seek him there, and cannot find him. ⁹I seek him in his workshop in the North, but cannot find him there; nor can I find him in the South; there, too, he hides himself. ¹⁰But he knows every detail of what is happening to me; and when he has examined me, he will pronounce me completely innocent—as pure as solid gold!

¹¹"I have stayed in God's paths, following his steps. I have not turned aside. ¹²I have not refused his commandments but have enjoyed them more than my daily food. ¹³Nevertheless, his mind concerning me remains unchanged, and who can turn him from his purposes? Whatever he wants to do, he does. ¹⁴So he will do to me all he has planned, and there is more ahead.

¹⁵"No wonder I am so terrified in his presence. When I think of it, terror grips me. ¹⁶,¹⁷God has given me a fainting heart; he, the Almighty, has terrified me with darkness all around me, thick, impenetrable darkness everywhere.

"WHY doesn't God open the court and listen to my case? Why must the godly wait for him in vain? ²For a crime wave has engulfed us—landmarks are moved, flocks of sheep are stolen, ³and even the donkeys of the poor and fatherless are taken. Poor widows must surrender the little they have as a pledge to get a loan. ⁴The needy are kicked aside; they must get out of the way. ⁵Like the wild donkeys in the desert, the poor must spend all their time just getting barely enough to keep soul and body together. They are sent into the desert to search for food for their children. 6They eat what they find that grows wild, and must even glean the vineyards of the wicked. 7All night they lie naked in the cold, without clothing or covering. 8They are wet with the showers of the mountains and live in caves for want of a home.

9"The wicked snatch fatherless children from their mother's breasts, and take a poor man's baby as a pledge before they will loan him any money or grain. 10That is why they must go about naked, without clothing, and are forced to carry food while they are starving. 11They are forced to press out the olive oil without tasting it, and to tread out the grape juice as they suffer from thirst. 12The bones of the dying cry from the city; the wounded cry for help; yet God does not respond to their moaning.

13"The wicked rebel against the light and are not acquainted with the right and the good. 14,15They are murderers who rise in the early dawn to kill the poor and needy; at night they are thieves and adulterers, waiting for the twilight 'when no one will see me,' they say. They mask their faces so no one will know them. 16They break into houses at night and sleep in the daytime—they are not acquainted with the light. 17The black night is their morning; they ally themselves with the terrors of the darkness.

18"But how quickly they disappear from the face of the earth. Everything they own is cursed. They leave no property for their children. 19Death consumes sinners as drought and heat consume snow. 20Even the sinner's own mother shall forget him. Worms shall feed sweetly on him. No one will remember him any more. For wicked men are broken like a tree in the storm. 21For they have taken advantage of the childless who have no protecting sons. They refuse to help the needy widows.

22,23"Yet sometimes it seems as though God preserves the rich by his power, and restores them to life when anyone else would die. God gives them confidence and strength, and helps them in many ways. 24But though they are very great now, yet in a moment they shall be gone like all others, cut off like heads of grain. 25Can anyone claim otherwise? Who can prove me a liar and claim that I am wrong?"

THE further reply of Bildad the Shuhite:

2"God is powerful and dreadful. He enforces peace in heaven. 3Who is able to number his hosts of angels? And his light shines down on all the earth. 4How can mere man stand before God and claim to be righteous? Who in all the earth can boast that he is clean? 5God is so glorious that even the moon and stars are less than nothing as compared to him. 6How much less is man, who is but a worm in his sight?"

JOB'S reply:

2"What wonderful helpers you all are! And how you have encouraged me in my great need! 3How you have enlightened my stupidity! What wise things you have said! 4How did you ever think of all these brilliant comments?

5,6"The dead stand naked, trembling before God in the place where they go. 7God stretches out heaven over empty space, and hangs the earth upon nothing. 8He wraps the rain in his thick clouds and the clouds are not split by the weight. 9He shrouds his throne with his clouds. 10He sets a boundary for the ocean, yes, and a boundary for the day and for the night. 11The pillars of heaven tremble at his rebuke. 12And by his power the sea grows calm; he is skilled at crushing its pride! 13The heavens are made beautiful by his Spirit; he pierces the swiftly gliding serpent.

14"These are some of the minor things he does, merely a whisper of his power. Who then can withstand his thunder?"

JOB'S final defense:

2"I vow by the living God, who has taken away my rights, even the Almighty God who has embittered my soul, 3that as long as I live, while I have breath from God, 4my lips shall speak no evil, my tongue shall speak no lies. 5I will never, never agree that you are right; until I die I will vow my innocence. 6I am *not* a sinner—I repeat it again and again. My conscience is clear for as long as I live. 7Those who declare otherwise are my wicked enemies. They are evil men.

8"But what hope has the godless when God cuts him off and takes away his life? 9Will God listen to his cry when trouble comes upon him? 10For he does not delight himself in the Almighty or pay any attention to God except in times of crisis.

11"I will teach you about God— 12but really, I don't need to, for you yourselves know as much about him as I do; yet you are saying all these useless things to me.

13"This is the fate awaiting the wicked from the hand of the Almighty: 14If he has a multitude of children, it is so that they will die in war, or starve to death. 15Those who survive shall be brought down to the grave by disease and plague, with no one to mourn them, not even their wives.

16"The evil man may accumulate money like dust, with closets jammed full of clothing— 17yes, he may order them made by his tailor, but the innocent shall wear that clothing, and shall divide his silver among them. 18Every house built by the wicked is as fragile as a spider web, as full of cracks as a leafy booth!

19"He goes to bed rich, but wakes up to find that all his wealth is gone. 20Terror overwhelms him, and he is blown away in the storms of the night. 21The east wind carries him away, and he is gone. It sweeps him into eternity. 22For God shall hurl at him unsparingly. He longs to flee from God. 23Everyone will cheer at his death, and boo him into eternity.

2 CORINTHIANS 1:12—2:8

WE are so glad that we can say with utter honesty that in all our dealings we have been pure and sincere, quietly depending upon the Lord for his help, and not on our own skills. And that is even more true, if possible, about the way we have acted toward you. 13,14My letters have been straightforward and sincere; nothing is written between the lines! And even though you don't know me very well (I hope someday you will), I want you to try to accept me and be proud of me, as you already are to some extent; just as I shall be of you on that day when our Lord Jesus comes back again.

15,16It was because I was so sure of your understanding and trust that I planned to stop and see you on my way to Macedonia, as well as afterwards when I returned, so that I could be a double blessing to you and so that you could send me on my way to Judea.

17Then why, you may be asking, did I change my plan? Hadn't I really made up my mind yet? Or am I like a man of the world who says "yes" when he really means "no"? 18Never! As surely as God is true, I am not that sort of person. My "yes" means "yes."

19Timothy and Silvanus and I have been telling you about Jesus Christ the Son of God. He isn't one to say "yes" when he means "no." He always does exactly what he says. 20He carries out and fulfills all of God's promises, no matter how many of them there are; and we have told everyone how faithful he is, giving glory to his name. 21It is this God who has made you and me into faithful Christians and commissioned us apostles to preach the Good News. 22He has put his brand upon us—his mark of ownership—and given us his Holy Spirit in our hearts as guarantee that we belong to him, and as the first installment of all that he is going to give us.

23I call upon this God to witness against me if I am not telling the absolute truth: the reason I haven't come to visit you yet is that I don't want to sadden you with a severe rebuke. 24When I come, although I can't do much to help your faith, for it is strong already, I want to be able to do something about your joy: I want to make you happy, not sad.

"No," I said to myself, "I won't do it. I'll not make them unhappy with another painful visit." 2For if I make you sad, who is going to make me happy? You are the ones to do it, and how can you if I cause you pain? 3That is why I wrote as I did in my last letter, so that you will get things straightened out before I come. Then, when I do come, I will not be made sad by the very ones who ought to give me greatest joy. I felt sure that your happiness was so bound up in mine that you would not be happy either, unless I came with joy.

4Oh, how I hated to write that letter! It almost broke my heart and I tell you honestly that I cried over it. I didn't want to hurt you, but I had to show you how very much I loved you and cared about what was happening to you.

5,6Remember that the man I wrote about, who caused all the trouble, has not caused sorrow to me as much as to all the rest of you—though I certainly have my share in it too. I don't want to be harder on him than I should. He has been punished enough by your united disapproval. 7Now it is time to forgive him and comfort him. Otherwise he may become so bitter and discouraged that he won't be able to recover. 8Please show him now that you still do love him very much.

PSALM 41:1–13

GOD blesses those who are kind to the poor. He helps them out of their troubles. 2He protects them and keeps them alive; he publicly honors them and destroys the power of their enemies. 3He nurses them when they are sick, and soothes their pains and worries.

4"O Lord," I prayed, "be kind and heal me, for I have confessed my sins." 5But my enemies say, "May he soon die and be forgotten!" 6They act so friendly when they come to visit me while I am sick; but all the time they hate me and are glad that I am lying there upon my bed of pain. And when they leave, they laugh and mock. 7They whisper together about what they will do when I am dead. 8"It's fatal, whatever it is," they say. "He'll never get out of that bed!"

9Even my best friend has turned against me—a man I completely trusted; how often we ate together. 10Lord, don't you desert me! Be gracious, Lord, and make me well again so I can pay them back! 11I know you are pleased with me because you haven't let my enemies triumph over me. 12You have preserved me because I was honest; you have admitted me forever to your presence.

13Bless the Lord, the God of Israel, who exists from everlasting ages past—and on into everlasting eternity ahead. Amen and amen!

PROVERBS FOR TODAY/ 22:5–6

The rebel walks a thorny, treacherous road; the man who values his soul will stay away. Teach a child to choose the right path, and when he is older he will remain upon it.

AUGUST 28

JOB 28:1—30:31

MEN know how to mine silver and refine gold, ²to dig iron from the earth and melt copper from stone. 3,4Men know how to put light into darkness so that a mine shaft can be sunk into the earth, and the earth searched and its deep secrets explored. Into the black rock, shadowed by death, men descend on ropes, swinging back and forth.

5"Men know how to obtain food from the surface of the earth, while underneath there is fire.

6"They know how to find sapphires and gold dust— 7treasures that no bird of prey can see, no eagle's eye observe— 8for they are deep within the mines. No wild animal has ever walked upon those treasures; no lion has set his paw there. 9Men know how to tear apart flinty rocks and how to overturn the roots of mountains. 10They drill tunnels in the rocks and lay bare precious stones. 11They dam up streams of water and pan the gold.

12"But though men can do all these things, they don't know where to find wisdom and understanding. 13They not only don't know how to get it, but, in fact, it is not to be found among the living.

14" 'It's not here,' the oceans say; and the seas reply, 'Nor is it here.'

15"It cannot be bought for gold or silver, 16nor for all the gold of Ophir or precious onyx stones or sapphires. 17Wisdom is far more valuable than gold and glass. It cannot be bought for jewels mounted in fine gold. 18Coral or crystal is worthless in trying to get it; its price is far above rubies. 19Topaz from Ethiopia cannot purchase it, nor even the purest gold.

20"Then where can we get it? Where can it be found? 21For it is hid from the eyes of all mankind; even the sharp-eyed birds in the sky cannot discover it.

22"But Destruction and Death speak of knowing something about it! 23,24And God surely knows where it is to be found, for he looks throughout the whole earth, under all the heavens. 25He makes the winds blow and sets the boundaries of the oceans. 26He makes the laws of the rain and a path for the lightning. 27He knows where wisdom is and declares it to all who will listen. He established it and examined it thoroughly. 28And this is what he says to all mankind: 'Look, to fear the Lord is true wisdom; to forsake evil is real understanding.' "

JOB continues:

2"Oh, for the years gone by when God took care of me, 3when he lighted the way before me and I walked safely through the darkness; 4yes, in my early years, when the friendship of God was felt in my home; 5when the Almighty was still with me and my children were around me; 6when my projects prospered, and even the rock poured out streams of olive oil to me!

7"Those were the days when I went out to the city gate and took my place among the honored elders. 8The young saw me and stepped aside, and even the aged rose and stood up in respect at my coming. 9The princes stood in silence and laid their hands upon their mouths. 10The highest officials of the city stood in quietness. 11All rejoiced in what I said. All who saw me spoke well of me.

12"For I, as an honest judge, helped the poor in their need, and the fatherless who had no one to help them. 13I helped those who were ready to perish and they blessed me. And I caused the widows' hearts to sing for joy. 14All I did was just and honest, for righteousness was my clothing! 15I served as eyes for the blind and feet for the lame. 16I was as a father to the poor, and saw to it that even strangers received a fair trial. 17I knocked out the fangs of the godless oppressors and made them drop their victims.

18"I thought, 'Surely I shall die quietly in my nest after a long, good life.' 19For everything I did prospered; the dew lay all night upon my fields and watered them. 20Fresh honors were constantly given me, and my abilities were constantly refreshed and renewed. 21Everyone listened to me and valued my advice, and was silent until I spoke. 22And after I spoke, they spoke no more, for my counsel satisfied them. 23They longed for me to speak as those in drought-time long for rain. They waited eagerly with open mouths. 24When they were discouraged, I smiled and that encouraged them, and lightened their spirits. 25I told them what they should do, and corrected them as their chief, or as a king instructs his army, and as one who comforts those who mourn.

"BUT now those younger than I deride me—young men whose fathers are less than my dogs. 2Oh, they have strong backs all right, but they are useless, stupid fools. 3They are gaunt with famine and have been cast out into deserts and the wastelands, desolate and gloomy. 4They eat roots and leaves, 5having been driven from civilization. Men shouted after them as after thieves. 6So now they live in frightening ravines, and in caves, and among the rocks. 7They sound like animals among the bushes, huddling together for shelter beneath the nettles. 8These sons of theirs have also turned out to be fools, yes, children of no name, outcasts of civilization.

9"And now I have become the subject of their ribald song! I am a joke among *them!* 10They despise me and won't come near me, and don't mind spitting in my face. 11For God has placed my life in jeopardy. These young men, having humbled me, now cast off all restraint before me. 12This rabble trip me and lay traps in my path. 13They block my road and do everything they can to hasten my calamity, knowing full well that I have no one to help me. 14They come at me from all directions. They rush upon me when I am down.

15"I live in terror now. They hold me in contempt and my prosperity has vanished as a cloud before a strong wind. 16My heart is broken. Depression haunts my days. 17My weary nights are filled with pain as though something were relentlessly gnawing at my bones. 18All night long I toss and turn, and my garments bind about me. 19God has thrown me into the mud. I have become as dust and ashes.

20"I cry to you, O God, but you don't answer me. I stand before you and you don't bother to look. 21You have become cruel toward me, and persecute me with great power and effect. 22You throw me into the whirlwind and dissolve me in the storm. 23And I know that your purpose for me is death. 24I expected my fall to be broken, just as one who falls stretches out his hand or cries for help in his calamity.

25"And did I not weep for those in trouble? Wasn't I deeply grieved for the needy? 26I therefore looked for good to come. Evil came instead. I waited for the light. Darkness came. 27My heart is troubled and restless. Waves of affliction have come upon me. 28,29I am black, but not from sunburn. I stand up and cry to the assembly for help. [But I might as well save my breath,] for I am considered a brother to jackals and a companion to ostriches. 30My skin is black and peeling. My bones burn with fever. 31The voice of joy and gladness has turned to mourning.

2 CORINTHIANS 2:9–17

I wrote to you as I did so that I could find out how far you would go in obeying me. 10When you forgive anyone, I do too. And whatever I have forgiven (to the extent that this affected me too) has been by Christ's authority, and for your good. 11A further reason for forgiveness is to keep from being outsmarted by Satan; for we know what he is trying to do.

12Well, when I got as far as the city of Troas, the Lord gave me tremendous opportunities to preach the Gospel. ¹³But Titus, my dear brother, wasn't there to meet me and I couldn't rest, wondering where he was and what had happened to him. So I said good-bye and went right on to Macedonia to try to find him.

¹⁴But thanks be to God! For through what Christ has done, he has triumphed over us so that now wherever we go he uses us to tell others about the Lord and to spread the Gospel like a sweet perfume. ¹⁵As far as God is concerned there is a sweet, wholesome fragrance in our lives. It is the fragrance of Christ within us, an aroma to both the saved and the unsaved all around us. ¹⁶To those who are not being saved, we seem a fearful smell of death and doom, while to those who know Christ we are a life-giving perfume. But who is adequate for such a task as this? ¹⁷Only those who, like ourselves, are men of integrity, sent by God, speaking with Christ's power, with God's eye upon us. We are not like those hucksters—and there are many of them—whose idea in getting out the Gospel is to make a good living out of it.

PSALM 42:1–11

AS the deer pants for water, so I long for you, O God. ²I thirst for God, the living God. Where can I find him to come and stand before him? ³Day and night I weep for his help, and all the while my enemies taunt me. "Where is this God of yours?" they scoff.

⁴,⁵Take courage, my soul! Do you remember those times (but how could you ever forget them!) when you led a great procession to the Temple on festival days, singing with joy, praising the Lord? Why then be downcast? Why be discouraged and sad? Hope in God! I shall yet praise him again. Yes, I shall again praise him for his help.

⁶Yet I am standing here depressed and gloomy, but I will meditate upon your kindness to this lovely land where the Jordan River flows and where Mount Hermon and Mount Mizar stand. ⁷All your waves and billows have gone over me, and floods of sorrow pour upon me like a thundering cataract.

⁸Yet day by day the Lord also pours out his steadfast love upon me, and through the night I sing his songs and pray to God who gives me life.

⁹"O God my Rock," I cry, "why have you forsaken me? Why must I suffer these attacks from my enemies?" ¹⁰Their taunts pierce me like a fatal wound; again and again they scoff, "Where is that God of yours?" ¹¹But O my soul, don't be discouraged. Don't be upset. Expect God to act! For I know that I shall again have plenty of reason to praise him for all that he will do. He is my help! He is my God!

PROVERBS FOR TODAY/ 22:7

Just as the rich rule the poor, so the borrower is servant to the lender.

AUGUST 29

JOB 31:1—33:33

I made a covenant with my eyes not to look with lust upon a girl. ²,³I know full well that Almighty God above sends calamity on those who do.

⁴He sees everything I do, and every step I take.

⁵"If I have lied and deceived— ⁶but God knows that I am innocent— ⁷,⁸or if I have stepped off God's pathway,

or if my heart has lusted for what my eyes have seen, or if I am guilty of any other sin, then let someone else reap the crops I have sown and let all that I have planted be rooted out.

⁹"Or if I have longed for another man's wife, ¹⁰then may I die, and may my wife be in another man's home, and someone else become her husband. ¹¹For lust is a shameful sin, a crime that should be punished. ¹²It is a devastating fire that destroys to hell, and would root out all I have planted.

¹³"If I have been unfair to my servants, ¹⁴how could I face God? What could I say when he questioned me about it? ¹⁵For God made me, and made my servant too. He created us both.

¹⁶"If I have hurt the poor or caused widows to weep, ¹⁷or refused food to hungry orphans— ¹⁸(but we have always cared for orphans in our home, treating them as our own children)— ¹⁹,²⁰or if I have seen anyone freezing and not given him clothing, or fleece from my sheep to keep him warm, ²¹or if I have taken advantage of an orphan because I thought I could get away with it— ²²if I have done any of these things, then let my arm be torn from its socket! Let my shoulder be wrenched out of place! ²³Rather that than face the judgment sent by God; that I dread more than anything else. For if the majesty of God opposes me, what hope is there?

²⁴"If I have put my trust in money, ²⁵if my happiness depends on wealth, ²⁶or if I have looked at the sun shining in the skies, or the moon walking down her silver pathway, ²⁷and my heart has been secretly enticed, and I have worshiped them by kissing my hand to them, ²⁸this, too, must be punished by the judges. For if I had done such things, it would mean that I denied the God of heaven.

²⁹"If I have rejoiced at harm to an enemy— ³⁰(but actually I have never cursed anyone nor asked for revenge)— ³¹or if any of my servants have ever gone hungry— ³²(actually I have never turned away even a stranger but have opened my doors to all)— ³³or if, like Adam, I have tried to hide my sins, ³⁴fearing the crowd and its contempt, so that I refused to acknowledge my sin and do not go out of my way to help others— ³⁵(oh, that there were someone who would listen to me and try to see my side of this argument. Look, I will sign my signature to my defense; now let the Almighty show me that I am wrong; let *him* approve the indictments made against me by my enemies. ³⁶I would treasure it like a crown. ³⁷Then I would tell him exactly what I have done and why, presenting my defense as one he listens to).

³⁸,³⁹"Or if my land accuses me because I stole the fruit it bears, or if I have murdered its owners to get their land for myself, ⁴⁰then let thistles grow on that land instead of wheat, and weeds instead of barley."

Job's words are ended.

THE three men refused to reply further to Job because he kept insisting on his innocence.

²Then Elihu (son of Barachel, the Buzite, of the Clan of Ram) became angry because Job refused to admit he had sinned and to acknowledge that God had just cause for punishing him. ³But he was also angry with Job's three friends because they had been unable to answer Job's arguments and yet had condemned him. ⁴Elihu had waited until now to speak because the others were older than he.

⁵But when he saw that they had no further reply, he spoke out angrily, ⁶and said, "I am young and you are old, so I held back and did not dare to tell you what I think, ⁷for those who are older are said to be wiser; ⁸,⁹but it is not mere age that makes men wise. Rather, it is the spirit in a man, the breath of the Almighty which makes him intelligent. ¹⁰So listen to me awhile and let me express my opinion.

¹¹,¹²"I have waited all this time, listening very carefully to your arguments, but not one of them has convinced Job that he is a sinner, or has proved that he is. ¹³And don't give me that line about

'only God can convince the sinner of his sin.' 14If Job had been arguing with me, I would not answer with that kind of logic!

15"You sit there baffled, with no further replies. 16Shall I then continue to wait when you are silent? 17No, I will give my answer too. 18For I am pent up and full of words, and the spirit within me urges me on. 19I am like a wine cask without a vent! My words are ready to burst out! 20I must speak to find relief, so let me give my answers. 21,22Don't insist that I be cautious lest I insult someone, and don't make me flatter anyone. Let me be frank, lest God should strike me dead.

"PLEASE listen, Job, to what I have to say. 2I have begun to speak; now let me continue. 3I will speak the truth with all sincerity. 4For the Spirit of God has made me, and the breath of the Almighty gives me life. 5Don't hesitate to answer me if you can.

6"Look, I am the one you were wishing for, someone to stand between you and God and to be both his representative and yours. 7You need not be frightened of me. I am not some person of renown to make you nervous and afraid. I, too, am made of common clay.

8"You have said it in my hearing, yes, you've said it again and again— 9'I am pure, I am innocent; I have not sinned.' 10You say God is using a fine-toothed comb to try to find a single fault, and so to count you as his enemy. 11'And he puts my feet in the stocks,' you say, 'and watches every move I make.'

12"All right, here is my reply: In this very thing, you have sinned by speaking of God that way. For God is greater than man. 13Why should you fight against him just because he does not give account to you of what he does?

14"For God speaks again and again, 15in dreams, in visions of the night when deep sleep falls on men as they lie on their beds. 16He opens their ears in times like that, and gives them wisdom and instruction, 17,18causing them to change their minds, and keeping them from pride, and warning them of the penalties of sin, and keeping them from falling into some trap.

19"Or, God sends sickness and pain, even though no bone is broken, 20so that a man loses all taste and appetite for food and doesn't care for even the daintiest dessert. 21He becomes thin, mere skin and bones, 22and draws near to death.

23,24"But if a messenger from heaven is there to intercede for him as a friend, to show him what is right, then God pities him and says, 'Set him free. Do not make him die, for I have found a substitute.' 25Then his body will become as healthy as a child's, firm and youthful again. 26And when he prays to God, God will hear and answer and receive him with joy, and return him to his duties. 27And he will declare to his friends, 'I sinned, but God let me go. 28He did not let me die. I will go on living in the realm of light.'

29"Yes, God often does these things for man— 30brings back his soul from the pit, so that he may live in the light of the living. 31Mark this well, O Job. Listen to me, and let me say more. 32But if you have anything to say at this point, go ahead. I want to hear it, for I am anxious to justify you. 33But if not, then listen to me. Keep silence and I will teach you wisdom!"

2 CORINTHIANS 3:1–18

ARE we beginning to be like those false teachers of yours who must tell you all about themselves and bring long letters of recommendation with them? I think you hardly need someone's letter to tell you about us, do you? And we don't need a recommendation from you, either! 2The only letter I need is you yourselves! By looking at the good change in your hearts, everyone can see that we have done a good work among you. 3They can see that you are a letter from Christ, written by us. It is not a letter written with pen and ink, but by the Spirit of the living God; not one carved on stone, but in human hearts.

4We dare to say these good things about ourselves only because of our great trust in God through Christ, that he will help us to be true to what we say, 5and not because we think we can do anything of lasting value by ourselves. Our only power and success comes from God. 6He is the one who has helped us tell others about his new agreement to save them. We do not tell them that they must obey every law of God or die; but we tell them there is life for them from the Holy Spirit. The old way, trying to be saved by keeping the Ten Commandments, ends in death; in the new way, the Holy Spirit gives them life.

7Yet that old system of law that led to death began with such glory that people could not bear to look at Moses' face. For as he gave them God's law to obey, his face shone out with the very glory of God—though the brightness was already fading away. 8Shall we not expect far greater glory in these days when the Holy Spirit is giving life? 9If the plan that leads to doom was glorious, much more glorious is the plan that makes men right with God. 10In fact, that first glory as it shone from Moses' face is worth nothing at all in comparison with the overwhelming glory of the new agreement. 11So if the old system that faded into nothing was full of heavenly glory, the glory of God's new plan for our salvation is certainly far greater, for it is eternal.

12Since we know that this new glory will never go away, we can preach with great boldness, 13and not as Moses did, who put a veil over his face so that the Israelis could not see the glory fade away. 14Not only Moses' face was veiled, but

his people's minds and understanding were veiled and blinded too. Even now when the Scripture is read it seems as though Jewish hearts and minds are covered by a thick veil, because they cannot see and understand the real meaning of the Scriptures. For this veil of misunderstanding can be removed only by believing in Christ. 15Yes, even today when they read Moses' writings their hearts are blind and they think that obeying the Ten Commandments is the way to be saved.

16But whenever anyone turns to the Lord from his sins, then the veil is taken away. 17The Lord is the Spirit who gives them life, and where he is there is freedom [from trying to be saved by keeping the laws of God]. 18But we Christians have no veil over our faces; we can be mirrors that brightly reflect the glory of the Lord. And as the Spirit of the Lord works within us, we become more and more like him.

PSALM 43:1–5

O God, defend me from the charges of these merciless, deceitful men. 2For you are God, my only place of refuge. Why have you tossed me aside? Why must I mourn at the oppression of my enemies?

3Oh, send out your light and your truth—let them lead me. Let them lead me to your Temple on your holy mountain, Zion. 4There I will go to the altar of God my exceeding joy, and praise him with my harp. O God—my God! 5O my soul, why be so gloomy and discouraged? Trust in God! I shall again praise him for his wondrous help; he will make me smile again, *for he is my God!*

PROVERBS FOR TODAY/ 22:8–9

The unjust tyrant will reap disaster and his reign of terror shall end. Happy is the generous man, the one who feeds the poor.

AUGUST 30

JOB 34:1—36:33

ELIHU continued:

2"Listen to me, you wise men. 3We can choose the sounds we want to listen to; we can choose the taste we want in food, 4and we should choose to follow what is right. But first of all we must define among ourselves what is good. 5For Job has said, 'I am innocent, but God says I'm not. 6I am called a liar, even though I am innocent. I am horribly punished, even though I have not sinned.'

7,8"Who else is as arrogant as Job? He must have spent much time with evil men, 9for he said, 'Why waste time trying to please God?'

10"Listen to me, you with understanding. Surely everyone knows that *God doesn't sin!* 11Rather, he punishes the sinners. 12There is no truer statement than this: *God is never wicked or unjust.* 13He alone has authority over the earth and dispenses justice for the world. 14If God were to withdraw his Spirit, 15all life would disappear and mankind would turn again to dust.

16"Listen now and try to understand. 17Could God govern if he hated justice? Are you going to condemn the Almighty Judge? 18Are you going to condemn this God who says to kings and nobles, 'You are wicked and unjust'? 19For he doesn't care how great a man may be, and doesn't pay any more attention to the rich than to the poor. He made them all. 20In a moment they die, and at midnight great and small shall suddenly pass away, removed by no human hand.

21"For God carefully watches the goings on of all mankind; he sees them all. 22No darkness is thick enough to hide evil men from his eyes, 23so there is no need to wait for some great crime before a man is called before God in judgment. 24Without making a big issue over it, God simply shatters the greatest of men, and puts others in their places. 25He watches

what they do and in a single night he overturns them, destroying them, 26or openly strikes them down as wicked men. 27For they turned aside from following him, 28causing the cry of the poor to come to the attention of God. Yes, he hears the cries of those being oppressed. 29,30Yet when he chooses not to speak, who can criticize? Again, he may prevent a vile man from ruling, thus saving a nation from ruin, and he can depose an entire nation just as easily.

31"Why don't people exclaim to their God, 'We have sinned, but we will stop'? 32Or, 'We know not what evil we have done; only tell us, and we will cease at once.'

33"Must God tailor his justice to your demands? Must he change the order of the universe to suit your whims? The answer must be obvious even to you! 34,35Anyone even half bright will agree with me that you, Job, are speaking like a fool. 36You should be given the maximum penalty for the wicked way you have talked about God. 37For now you have added rebellion, arrogance and blasphemy to your other sins."

ELIHU continued:

2,3"Do you think it is right for you to claim, 'I haven't sinned, but I'm no better off before God than if I had'?

4"I will answer you, and all your friends too. 5Look up there into the sky, high above you. 6If you sin, does that shake the heavens and knock God from his throne? Even if you sin again and again, what effect will it have upon him? 7Or if you are good, is this some great gift to him? 8Your sins may hurt another man, or your good deeds may profit him. 9,10The oppressed may shriek beneath their wrongs and groan beneath the power of the rich; yet none of them cry to God, asking, 'Where is God my Maker who gives songs in the night, 11and makes us a little wiser than the animals and birds?'

12"But when anyone does cry out this question to him, he never replies by instant punishment of the tyrants. 13But it is false to say he doesn't hear those cries; 14,15and it is even more false to say that he doesn't see what is going on. He *does* bring about justice at last, if you will only wait. But do you cry out against him because he does not instantly respond in anger? 16Job, you have spoken like a fool."

ELIHU continued:

2"Let me go on and I will show you the truth of what I am saying. For I have not finished defending God! 3I will give you many illustrations of the righteousness of my Maker. 4I am telling you the honest truth, for I am a man of well-rounded knowledge.

5"God is almighty and yet does not despise anyone! And he is perfect in his understanding. 6He does not reward the wicked with his blessings, but gives them their full share of punishment. 7He does not ignore the good men but honors them by placing them upon eternal, kingly thrones. 8If troubles come upon them, and they are enslaved and afflicted, 9then he takes the trouble to point out to them the reason, what they have done that is wrong, or how they have behaved proudly. 10He helps them hear his instruction to turn away from their sin.

11"If they listen and obey him, then they will be blessed with prosperity throughout their lives. 12If they won't listen to him, they shall perish in battle and die because of their lack of good sense. 13But the godless reap his anger. They do not even return to him when he punishes them. 14They die young after lives of dissipation and depravity. 15He delivers by distress! This makes them listen to him!

16"How he wanted to lure you away from danger into a wide and pleasant valley and to prosper you there. 17But you are too preoccupied with your imagined grievances against others. 18Watch out!

Don't let your anger at others lead you into scoffing at God! Don't let your suffering embitter you at the only one who can deliver you. 19Do you really think that if you shout loudly enough against God, he will be ashamed and repent? Will this put an end to your chastisement?

20"Do not desire the nighttime, with its opportunities for crime. 21Turn back from evil, for it was to prevent you from getting into a life of evil that God sent this suffering.

22"Look, God is all-powerful. Who is a teacher like him? 23Who can say that what he does is absurd or evil? 24Instead, glorify him for his mighty works for which he is so famous. 25Everyone has seen these things from a distance.

26"God is so great that we cannot begin to know him. No one can begin to understand eternity. 27He draws up the water vapor and then distills it into rain, 28which the skies pour down. 29Can anyone really understand the spreading of the clouds, and the thunders within? 30See how he spreads the lightning around him, and blankets the tops of the mountains. 31By his fantastic powers in nature he punishes or blesses the people, giving them food in abundance. 32He fills his hands with lightning bolts. He hurls each at its target. 33We feel his presence in the thunder. Even the cattle know when a storm is coming.

2 CORINTHIANS 4:1–12

IT is God himself, in his mercy, who has given us this wonderful work [of telling his Good News to others], and so we never give up. 2We do not try to trick people into believing—we are not interested in fooling anyone. We never try to get anyone to believe that the Bible teaches what it doesn't. All such shameful methods we forego. We stand in the presence of God as we speak and so we tell the truth, as all who know us will agree.

3If the Good News we preach is hidden to anyone, it is hidden from the one who is on the road to eternal death. 4Satan, who is the god of this evil world, has made him blind, unable to see the glorious light of the Gospel that is shining upon him, or to understand the amazing message we preach about the glory of Christ, who is God. 5We don't go around preaching about ourselves, but about Christ Jesus as Lord. All we say of ourselves is that we are your slaves because of what Jesus has done for us. 6For God, who said, "Let there be light in the darkness," has made us understand that it is the brightness of his glory that is seen in the face of Jesus Christ.

7But this precious treasure—this light and power that now shine within us—is held in a perishable container, that is, in our weak bodies. Everyone can see that the glorious power within must be from God and is not our own.

8We are pressed on every side by troubles, but not crushed and broken. We are perplexed because we don't know why things happen as they do, but we don't give up and quit. 9We are hunted down, but God never abandons us. We get knocked down, but we get up again and keep going. 10These bodies of ours are constantly facing death just as Jesus did; so it is clear to all that it is only

the living Christ within [who keeps us safe].

11Yes, we live under constant danger to our lives because we serve the Lord, but this gives us constant opportunities to show forth the power of Jesus Christ within our dying bodies. 12Because of our preaching we face death, but it has resulted in eternal life for you.

PSALM 44:1–7

O God, we have heard of the glorious miracles you did in the days of long ago. Our forefathers have told us how you drove the heathen nations from this land and gave it all to us, spreading Israel from one end of the country to the other. 3They did not conquer by their own strength and skill, but by your mighty power and because you smiled upon them and favored them.

4You are my King and my God. Decree victories for your people. 5For it is only by your power and through your name that we tread down our enemies; 6I do not trust my weapons. They could never save me. 7Only you can give us the victory over those who hate us.

PROVERBS FOR TODAY/ 22:10–12

Throw out the mocker, and you will be rid of tension, fighting, and quarrels. He who values grace and truth is the king's friend. The Lord preserves the upright but ruins the plans of the wicked.

AUGUST 31

JOB 37:1—39:30

MY heart trembles at this. 2Listen, listen to the thunder of his voice. 3It rolls across the heavens and his lightning flashes out in every direction. 4Afterwards comes the roaring of the thunder—the tremendous voice of his majesty. 5His voice is glorious in the thunder. We cannot compre-

hend the greatness of his power. 6For he directs the snow, the showers, and storm to fall upon the earth. 7Man's work stops at such a time, so that all men everywhere may recognize his power. 8The wild animals hide in the rocks or in their dens.

9"From the south comes the rain; from the north, the cold. 10God blows upon the rivers, and even the widest torrents freeze. 11He loads the clouds with moisture and they send forth his lightning. 12The lightning bolts are directed by his hand, and do whatever he commands throughout the earth. 13He sends the storms as punishment, or, in his lovingkindness, to encourage.

14"Listen, O Job, stop and consider the wonderful miracles of God. 15Do you know how God controls all nature, and causes the lightning to flash forth from the clouds? 16,17Do you understand the balancing of the clouds with wonderful perfection and skill? Do you know why you become warm when the south wind is blowing and everything is still? 18Can you spread out the gigantic mirror of the skies as he does?

19,20"You who think you know so much, teach the rest of us how we should approach God. For we are too dull to know! With your wisdom, would we then dare to approach him? Well, does a man wish to be swallowed alive? 21For as we cannot look at the sun for its brightness when the winds have cleared away the clouds, 22neither can we gaze at the terrible majesty of God breaking forth upon us from heaven, clothed in dazzling splendor. 23We cannot imagine the power of the Almighty, and yet he is so just and merciful that he does not destroy us. 24No wonder men everywhere fear him! For he is not impressed by the world's wisest men!"

THEN the Lord answered Job from the whirlwind:

2"Why are you using your ignorance to deny my providence? 3Now get ready to fight, for I am going to demand some answers from you, and you must reply.

4"Where were you when I laid the foundations of the earth? Tell me, if you know so much. 5Do you know how its dimensions were determined, and who did the surveying? 6,7What supports its foundations, and who laid its cornerstone, as the morning stars sang together and all the angels shouted for joy? 8,9"Who decreed the boundaries of the seas when they gushed from the depths? Who clothed them with clouds and thick darkness, 10and barred them by limiting their shores, 11and said, 'Thus far and no farther shall you come, and here shall your proud waves stop!'?

12"Have you ever once commanded the morning to appear, and caused the dawn to rise in the east? 13Have you ever told the daylight to spread to the ends of the earth, to end the night's wickedness? 14Have you ever robed the dawn in red, 15and disturbed the haunts of wicked men and stopped the arm raised to strike?

16"Have you explored the springs from which the seas come, or walked in the sources of their depths? 17,18Has the location of the gates of Death been revealed to you? Do you realize the extent of the earth? Tell me about it if you know! 19Where does the light come from, and how do you get there? Or tell me about the darkness. Where does it come from? 20Can you find its boundaries, or go to its source? 21But of course you know all this! For you were born before it was all created, and you are so very experienced!

22,23"Have you visited the treasuries of the snow, or seen where hail is made and stored? For I have reserved it for the time when I will need it in war. 24Where is the path to the distribution point of light? Where is the home of the east wind? 25,26,27Who dug the valleys for the torrents of rain? Who laid out the path for the lightning, causing the rain to fall upon the barren deserts, so that the parched and barren ground is satisfied with water, and tender grass springs up?

28"Has the rain a father? Where does dew come from? 29Who is the mother of the ice and frost? 30For the water changes and turns to ice, as hard as rock.

31"Can you hold back the stars? Can you restrain Orion or Pleiades? 32Can you ensure the proper sequence of the seasons, or guide the constellation of the Bear with her satellites across the heavens? 33Do you know the laws of the universe and how the heavens influence the earth? 34Can you shout to the clouds and make it rain? 35Can you make lightning appear and cause it to strike as you direct it?

36"Who gives intuition and instinct? 37,38Who is wise enough to number all the clouds? Who can tilt the water jars of heaven, when everything is dust and clods? 39,40Can you stalk prey like a lioness, to satisfy the young lions' appetites as they lie in their dens, or lie in wait in the jungle? 41Who provides for the ravens when their young cry out to God as they try to struggle up from their nest in hunger?

"Do you know how mountain goats give birth? Have you ever seen them giving birth to their young? 2,3Do you know how many months of pregnancy they have before they bow themselves to give birth to their young, and carry their burden no longer? 4Their young grow up in the open field, then leave their parents and return to them no more.

5"Who makes the wild donkeys wild? 6I have placed them in the wilderness and given them salt plains to live in. 7For they hate the noise of the city and want no drivers shouting at them! 8The mountain ranges are their pastureland; there they search for every blade of grass.

9"Will the wild ox be your happy servant? Will he stay beside your feeding crib? 10Can you use a wild ox to plow with? Will he pull the harrow for you? 11Because he is so strong, will you trust him? Will you let him decide where to work? 12Can you send him out to bring in the grain from the threshing-floor?

13"The ostrich flaps her wings grandly, but has no true motherly love. 14She lays her eggs on top of the earth, to warm them in the dust. 15She forgets that someone may step on them and crush them, or the wild animals destroy them. 16She ignores her young as though they weren't her own, and is unconcerned though they die, 17for God has deprived her of wisdom. 18But whenever she jumps up to run, she passes the swiftest horse with its rider.

19"Have you given the horse strength, or clothed his neck with a quivering mane? 20Have you made him able to leap forward like a locust? His majestic snorting is something to hear! 21,22,23He paws the earth and rejoices in his strength, and when he goes to war, he is unafraid and does not run away though the arrows rattle against him, or the flashing spear and javelin. 24Fiercely he paws the ground and rushes forward into battle when the trumpet blows. 25At the sound of the bugle he shouts, 'Aha!' He smells the battle when far away. He rejoices at the shouts of battle and the roar of the captain's commands.

26"Do you know how a hawk soars and spreads her wings to the south? 27Is it at your command that the eagle rises high upon the cliffs to make her nest? 28She lives upon the cliffs, making her home in her mountain fortress. 29From there she spies her prey, from a very great distance. 30Her nestlings gulp down blood, for she goes wherever the slain are."

2 CORINTHIANS 4:13—5:11

WE boldly say what we believe [trusting God to care for us], just as the Psalm writer did when he said, "I believe and therefore I speak." 14We know that the same God who brought the Lord Jesus back from death will also bring us back to life again with Jesus, and present us to him along with you. 15These sufferings of ours are for your benefit. And the more of you who are won to Christ, the more there are to thank him for his great kindness, and the more the Lord is glorified.

16That is why we never give up. Though our bodies are dying, our inner strength in the Lord is growing every day. 17These troubles and sufferings of ours are, after all, quite small and won't last very long. Yet this short time of distress will result in God's richest blessing upon us forever and ever! 18So we do not look at what we can see right now, the troubles all around us, but we look forward to the joys in heaven which we have not yet seen. The troubles will soon be over, but the joys to come will last forever.

For we know that when this tent we live in now is taken down—when we die and leave these bodies—we will have wonderful new bodies in heaven, homes that will be ours forevermore, made for us by God himself, and not by human hands. 2How weary we grow of our present bodies. That is why we look forward eagerly to the day when we shall have heavenly bodies which we shall put on like new clothes. 3For we shall not be merely spirits without bodies. 4These earthly bodies make us groan and sigh, but we wouldn't like to think of dying and having no bodies at all. We want to slip into our new bodies so that these dying bodies will, as it were, be swallowed up by everlasting life. 5This is what God has prepared for us and, as a guarantee, he has given us his Holy Spirit.

6Now we look forward with confidence to our heavenly bodies, realizing that every moment we spend in these earthly bodies is time spent away from our eternal home in heaven with Jesus. 7We know these things are true by believing, not by seeing. 8And we are not afraid, but are quite content to die, for then we will be at home with the Lord. 9So our aim is to please him always in everything we do, whether we are here in this body or away from this body and with him in heaven. 10For we must all stand before Christ to be judged and have our lives laid bare—before him. Each of us will receive whatever he deserves for the good or bad things he has done in his earthly body.

11It is because of this solemn fear of the Lord, which is ever present in our minds, that we work so hard to win others. God knows our hearts, that they are pure in this matter, and I hope that, deep within, you really know it too.

PSALM 44:8–26

MY constant boast is God. I can never thank you enough! 9And yet for a time, O Lord, you have tossed us aside in dishonor, and have not helped us in our battles. 10You have actually fought against us and defeated us before our foes. Our enemies have invaded our land and pillaged the countryside. 11You have treated us like sheep in a slaughter pen, and scattered us among the nations. 12You sold us for a pittance. You valued us at nothing at all. 13The neighboring nations laugh and mock at us because of all the evil you have sent. 14You have made the word "Jew" a byword of contempt and shame among the nations, disliked by all. 15,16I am constantly despised, mocked, taunted and cursed by my vengeful enemies.

17And all this has happened, Lord, despite our loyalty to you. We have not violated your covenant. 18Our hearts have not deserted you! We have not left your path by a single step. 19If we had, we could understand your punishing us in the barren wilderness and sending us into darkness and death. 20If we had turned away from worshiping our God, and were worshiping idols, 21would God not know it? Yes, he knows the secrets of every heart. 22But that is not our case. For we are facing death threats constantly because of serving you! We are like sheep awaiting slaughter.

23Waken! Rouse yourself! Don't sleep, O Lord! Are we cast off forever? 24Why do you look the other way? Why do you ignore our sorrows and oppression? 25We lie face downward in the dust. 26Rise up, O Lord, and come and help us. Save us by your constant love.

PROVERBS FOR TODAY/ 22:13

The lazy man is full of excuses. "I can't go to work!" he says. "If I go outside I might meet a lion in the street and be killed!"

SEPTEMBER 1

JOB 40:1—42:17

THE Lord went on: 2"Do you still want to argue with the Almighty? Or will you yield? Do you—God's critic—have the answers?"

3*Then Job replied to God:*

4"I am nothing—how could I ever find the answers? I lay my hand upon my mouth in silence. 5I have said too much already."

6*Then the Lord spoke to Job again from the whirlwind:*

7"Stand up like a man and brace yourself for battle. Let me ask you a question, and give me the answer. 8Are you going to discredit my justice and condemn me, so that you can say you are right? 9Are you as strong as God, and can you shout as loudly as he? 10All right then, put on your robes of state, your majesty and splendor. 11Give vent to your anger. Let it overflow against the proud. 12Humiliate the haughty with a glance; tread down the wicked where they stand. 13Knock them into the dust, stone-faced in death. 14If you can do that, then I'll agree with you that your own strength can save you.

15"Take a look at the hippopotamus! I made him, too, just as I made you! He eats grass like an ox. 16See his powerful loins and the muscles of his belly. 17His tail is as straight as a cedar. The sinews of his thighs are tightly knit together. 18His vertebrae lie straight as a tube of brass. His ribs are like iron bars. 19How ferocious he is among all of God's creation, so let whoever hopes to master him bring a sharp sword! 20The mountains offer their best food to him—the other wild animals on which he preys. 21He lies down under the lotus plants, hidden by the reeds, 22covered by their shade among the willows there beside the stream. 23He is not disturbed by raging rivers, not even when the swelling Jordan rushes down upon him. 24No one

can catch him off guard or put a ring in his nose and lead him away.

"CAN you catch a crocodile with a hook and line? Or put a noose around his tongue? 2Can you tie him with a rope through the nose, or pierce his jaw with a spike? 3Will he beg you to desist or try to flatter you from your intentions? 4Will he agree to let you make him your slave for life? 5Can you make a pet of him like a bird, or give him to your little girls to play with? 6Do fishing partners sell him to the fishmongers? 7Will his hide be hurt by darts, or his head with a harpoon?

8"If you lay your hands upon him, you will long remember the battle that ensues, and you will never try it again! 9No, it's useless to try to capture him. It is frightening even to think about it! 10No one dares to stir *him* up, let alone try to conquer him. And if no one can stand before *him,* who can stand before *me?* 11I owe no one anything. Everything under the heaven is mine.

12"I should mention, too, the tremendous strength in his limbs, and throughout his enormous frame. 13Who can penetrate his hide, or who dares come within reach of his jaws? 14For his teeth are terrible. 15,16,17His overlapping scales are his pride, making a tight seal, so no air can get between them, and nothing can penetrate.

18"When he sneezes, the sunlight sparkles like lightning across the vapor droplets. His eyes glow like sparks. 19Fire leaps from his mouth. 20Smoke flows from his nostrils, like steam from a boiling pot that is fired by dry rushes. 21Yes, his breath would kindle coals—flames leap from his mouth.

22"The tremendous strength in his neck strikes terror wherever he goes. 23His flesh is hard and firm, not soft and fat. 24His heart is hard as rock, just like a millstone. 25When he stands up, the strongest are afraid. Terror grips them. 26No sword can stop him, nor spear nor dart nor pointed shaft. 27,28Iron is nothing but straw to him, and brass is rotten wood. Arrows cannot make him flee. Slingstones are as ineffective as straw. 29Clubs do no good, and he laughs at the javelins hurled at him. 30His belly is covered with scales as sharp as shards; they tear up the ground as he drags through the mud.

31,32"He makes the water boil with his commotion. He churns the depths. He leaves a shining wake of froth behind him. One would think the sea was made of frost! 33There is nothing else so fearless anywhere on earth. 34Of all the beasts, he is the proudest—monarch of all that he sees."

THEN Job replied to God:

2"I know that you can do anything and that no one can stop you. 3You ask who it is who has so foolishly denied your providence. It is I. I was talking about things I knew nothing about and did not understand, things far too wonderful for me.

4"[You said,] 'Listen and I will speak! Let me put the questions to you! See if you can answer them!'

5"[But now I say,] 'I had heard about you before, but now I have seen you, 6and I loathe myself and repent in dust and ashes.' "

7*After the Lord had finished speaking with Job, he said to Eliphaz the Temanite:*

"I am angry with you and with your two friends, for you have not been right in what you have said about me, as my servant Job was. 8Now take seven young bulls and seven rams and go to my servant Job and offer a burnt offering for yourselves; and my servant Job will pray for you, and I will accept his prayer on your behalf, and won't destroy you as I should because of your sin, your failure to speak rightly concerning my servant Job."

9So Eliphaz the Temanite, and Bildad the Shuhite, and Zophar the Naamathite did as the Lord commanded them, and the Lord accepted Job's prayer on their behalf. 10Then, when Job prayed for his friends, the Lord restored his wealth and happiness! In fact, the Lord gave him twice as much as before! 11Then all of his brothers, sisters, and former friends arrived and feasted with him in his home, consoling him for all his sorrow, and comforting him because of all the trials the Lord had brought upon him. And each of them brought him a gift of money, and a gold ring.

12So the Lord blessed Job at the end of his life more than at the beginning. For now he had 14,000 sheep, 6,000 camels, 1,000 teams of oxen, and 1,000 female donkeys.

13,14God also gave him seven more sons and three more daughters.

These were the names of his daughters: Jemima, Kezia, Keren.

15And in all the land there were no other girls as lovely as the daughters of Job; and their father put them into his will along with their brothers.

16Job lived 140 years after that, living to see his grandchildren and great-grandchildren too. 17Then at last he died, an old, old man, after living a long, good life.

2 CORINTHIANS 5:12-21

ARE we trying to pat ourselves on the back again? No, I am giving you some good ammunition! You can use this on those preachers of yours who brag about how well they look and preach, but don't have true and honest hearts. You can boast about us that we, at least, are well intentioned and honest.

13,14Are we insane [to say such things about ourselves]? If so, it is to bring glory to God. And if we are in our right minds, it is for your benefit. Whatever we do, it is certainly not for our own profit, but because Christ's love controls us now. Since we believe that Christ died for all of us, we should also believe that we have died to the old life we used to live. 15He died for all so that all who live—

having received eternal life from him—might live no longer for themselves, to please themselves, but to spend their lives pleasing Christ who died and rose again for them. 16So stop evaluating Christians by what the world thinks about them or by what they seem to be like on the outside. Once I mistakenly thought of Christ that way, merely as a human being like myself. How differently I feel now! 17When someone becomes a Christian he becomes a brand new person inside. He is not the same any more. A new life has begun!

18All these new things are from God who brought us back to himself through what Christ Jesus did. And God has given us the privilege of urging everyone to come into his favor and be reconciled to him. 19For God was in Christ, restoring the world to himself, no longer counting men's sins against them but blotting them out. This is the wonderful message he has given us to tell others. 20We are Christ's ambassadors. God is using us to speak to you: we beg you, as though Christ himself were here pleading with you, receive the love he offers you—be reconciled to God. 21For God took the sinless Christ and poured into him our sins. Then, in exchange, he poured God's goodness into us!

PSALM 45:1–17

MY heart is overflowing with a beautiful thought! I will write a lovely poem to the King, for I am as full of words as the speediest writer pouring out his story.

2You are the fairest of all;
Your words are filled with grace;
God himself is blessing you forever.
3Arm yourself, O Mighty One,
So glorious, so majestic!
4And in your majesty
Go on to victory,
Defending truth, humility, and justice.
Go forth to awe-inspiring deeds!
5Your arrows are sharp
In your enemies' hearts;
They fall before you.
6Your throne, O God, endures forever.
Justice is your royal scepter.
7You love what is good
And hate what is wrong.
Therefore God, your God,
Has given you more gladness
Than anyone else.

8Your robes are perfumed with myrrh, aloes and cassia. In your palaces of inlaid ivory, lovely music is being played for your enjoyment. 9Kings' daughters are among your concubines. Standing beside you is the queen, wearing jewelry of finest gold from Ophir.

10,11"I advise you, O daughter, not to fret about your parents in your homeland far away. Your royal husband delights in your beauty. Reverence him, for he is your lord. 12The people of Tyre, the richest people of our day, will shower you with gifts and entreat your favors."

13The bride, a princess, waits within her chamber, robed in beautiful clothing woven with gold. 14Lovely she is, led beside her maids of honor to the king! 15What a joyful, glad procession as they enter in the palace gates! 16"Your sons will some day be kings like their father. They shall sit on thrones around the world!

17"I will cause your name to be honored in all generations; the nations of the earth will praise you forever."

PROVERBS FOR TODAY/ 22:14

A prostitute is a dangerous trap; those cursed of God are caught in it.

ECCLESIASTES 1:1—3:22

T HE author: Solomon of Jerusalem, King David's son, "The Preacher."

2In my opinion, nothing is worthwhile; everything is futile. 3-7For what does a man get for all his hard work?

Generations come and go but it makes no difference. The sun rises and sets and hurries around to rise again. The wind blows south and north, here and there, twisting back and forth, getting nowhere. The rivers run into the sea but the sea is never full, and the water returns again to the rivers, and flows again to the sea . . . 8-11everything is unutterably weary and tiresome. No matter how much we see, we are never satisfied; no matter how much we hear, we are not content.

History merely repeats itself. Nothing is truly new; it has all been done or said before. What can you point to that is new? How do you know it didn't exist long ages ago? We don't remember what happened in those former times, and in the future generations no one will remember what we have done back here.

12-15I, the Preacher, was king of Israel, living in Jerusalem. And I applied myself to search for understanding about everything in the universe. I discovered that the lot of man, which God has dealt to him, is not a happy one. It is all foolishness, chasing the wind. What is wrong cannot be righted; it is water over the dam; and there is no use thinking of what might have been.

16,17,18I said to myself, "Look, I am better educated than any of the kings before me in Jerusalem. I have greater wisdom and knowledge." So I worked hard to be wise instead of foolish—but now I realize that even this was like chasing the wind. For the more my wisdom, the more my grief; to increase knowledge only increases distress.

I said to myself, "Come now, be merry; enjoy yourself to the full." But I found that this, too, was futile. For it is silly to be laughing all the time; what good does it do?

3So, after a lot of thinking, I decided to try the road of drink, while still holding steadily to my course of seeking wisdom.

Next I changed my course again and followed the path of folly, so that I could experience the only happiness most men have throughout their lives.

4,5,6Then I tried to find fulfillment by inaugurating a great public works program: homes, vineyards, gardens, parks and orchards for myself, and reservoirs to hold the water to irrigate my plantations.

7,8Next I bought slaves, both men and women, and others were born within my household. I also bred great herds and flocks, more than any of the kings before me. I collected silver and gold as taxes from many kings and provinces.

In the cultural arts, I organized men's and women's choirs and orchestras.

And then there were my many beautiful concubines.

9So I became greater than any of the kings in Jerusalem before me, and with it all I remained clear-eyed, so that I could evaluate all these things. 10Anything I wanted, I took, and did not restrain myself from any joy. I even found great pleasure in hard work. This pleasure was, indeed, my only reward for all my labors.

11But as I looked at everything I had tried, it was all so useless, a chasing of the wind, and there was nothing really worthwhile anywhere.

12Now I began a study of the comparative virtues of wisdom and folly, and anyone else would come to the same conclusion I did— 13,14that wisdom is of more value than foolishness, just as light is better than darkness; for the wise man sees, while the fool is blind. And yet I noticed that there was one thing that hap-

pened to wise and foolish alike—
15just as the fool will die, so will I. So
of what value is all my wisdom? Then
I realized that even wisdom is futile.
16For the wise and fool both die, and
in the days to come both will be long
forgotten. 17So now I hate life because
it is all so irrational; all is foolishness,
chasing the wind.

18And I am disgusted about this, that
I must leave the fruits of all my hard
work to others. 19And who can tell
whether my son will be a wise man or
a fool? And yet all I have will be given
to him—how discouraging!

20-23So I turned in despair from hard
work as the answer to my search for
satisfaction. For though I spend my life
searching for wisdom, knowledge, and
skill, I must leave all of it to someone
who hasn't done a day's work in his life;
he inherits all my efforts, free of charge.
This is not only foolish, but unfair. So
what does a man get for all his hard
work? Days full of sorrow and grief, and
restless, bitter nights. It is all utterly ridiculous.

24,25,26So I decided that there was nothing better for a man to do than to enjoy
his food and drink, and his job. Then I
realized that even this pleasure is from
the hand of God. For who can eat or
enjoy apart from him? For God gives
those who please him wisdom, knowledge, and joy; but if a sinner becomes
wealthy, God takes the wealth away
from him and gives it to those who
please him. So here, too, we see an
example of foolishly chasing the
wind.

THERE is a right time for everything:
2A time to be born;
A time to die;
A time to plant;
A time to harvest;
3A time to kill;
A time to heal;
A time to destroy;
A time to rebuild;
4A time to cry;

A time to laugh;
A time to grieve;
A time to dance;
5A time for scattering stones;
A time for gathering stones;
A time to hug;
A time not to hug;
6A time to find;
A time to lose;
A time for keeping;
A time for throwing away;
7A time to tear;
A time to repair;
A time to be quiet;
A time to speak up;
8A time for loving;
A time for hating;
A time for war;
A time for peace.

9What does one really get from hard
work?

10I have thought about this in connection with all the various kinds of work
God has given to mankind. 11Everything
is appropriate in its own time. But though
God has planted eternity in the hearts
of men, even so, many cannot see the
whole scope of God's work from beginning to end. 12So I conclude that, first,
there is nothing better for a man than
to be happy and to enjoy himself as long
as he can; 13and second, that he should
eat and drink and enjoy the fruits of
his labors, for these are gifts from
God.

14And I know this, that whatever God
does is final—nothing can be added or
taken from it; God's purpose in this is
that man should fear the all-powerful
God.

15Whatever is, has been long ago; and
whatever is going to be has been before;
God brings to pass again what was in
the distant past and disappeared.

16Moreover, I notice that throughout
the earth justice is giving way to crime
and even the police courts are corrupt.
17I said to myself, "In due season God
will judge everything man does, both
good and bad."

18And then I realized that God is letting
the world go on its sinful way so that

he can test mankind, and so that men themselves will see that they are no better than beasts. 19For men and animals both breathe the same air, and both die. So mankind has no real advantage over the beasts; what an absurdity! 20All go to one place—the dust from which they came and to which they must return. 21For who can prove that the spirit of man goes upward and the spirit of animals goes downward into dust? 22So I saw that there is nothing better for men than that they should be happy in their work, for that is what they are here for, and no one can bring them back to life to enjoy what will be in the future, so let them enjoy it now.

2 CORINTHIANS 6:1–13

AS God's partners we beg you not to toss aside this marvelous message of God's great kindness. 2For God says, "Your cry came to me at a favorable time, when the doors of welcome were wide open. I helped you on a day when salvation was being offered." Right now God is ready to welcome you. Today he is ready to save you.

3We try to live in such a way that no one will ever be offended or kept back from finding the Lord by the way we act, so that no one can find fault with us and blame it on the Lord. 4In fact, in everything we do we try to show that we are true ministers of God.

We patiently endure suffering and hardship and trouble of every kind. 5We have been beaten, put in jail, faced angry mobs, worked to exhaustion, stayed awake through sleepless nights of watching, and gone without food. 6We have proved ourselves to be what we claim by our wholesome lives and by our understanding of the Gospel and by our patience. We have been kind and truly loving and filled with the Holy Spirit. 7We have been truthful, with God's power helping us in all we do. All of the godly man's arsenal—weapons

of defense, and weapons of attack—have been ours.

8We stand true to the Lord whether others honor us or despise us, whether they criticize us or commend us. We are honest, but they call us liars.

9The world ignores us, but we are known to God; we live close to death, but here we are, still very much alive. We have been injured but kept from death. 10Our hearts ache, but at the same time we have the joy of the Lord. We are poor, but we give rich spiritual gifts to others. We own nothing, and yet we enjoy everything.

11Oh, my dear Corinthian friends! I have told you all my feelings; I love you with all my heart. 12Any coldness still between us is not because of any lack of love on my part, but because your love is too small and does not reach out to me and draw me in. 13I am talking to you now as if you truly were my very own children. Open your hearts to us! Return our love!

PSALM 46:1–11

GOD is our refuge and strength, a tested help in times of trouble. 2And so we need not fear even if the world blows up, and the mountains crumble into the sea. 3Let the oceans roar and foam; let the mountains tremble!

4There is a river of joy flowing through the City of our God—the sacred home of the God above all gods. 5God himself is living in that City; therefore it stands unmoved despite the turmoil everywhere. He will not delay his help. 6The nations rant and rave in anger—but when God speaks, the earth melts in submission and kingdoms totter into ruin.

7The Commander of the armies of heaven is here among us. He, the God of Jacob, has come to rescue us.

8Come, see the glorious things that our God does, how he brings ruin upon the world, 9and causes wars to end throughout the earth, breaking and burning every weapon. 10"Stand silent! Know that I am God! I will be honored by every nation in the world!"

11The Commander of the heavenly armies is here among *us!* He, the God of Jacob, has come to rescue *us!*

PROVERBS FOR TODAY/ 22:15

A youngster's heart is filled with rebellion, but punishment will drive it out of him.

SEPTEMBER 3

ECCLESIASTES 4:1—6:12

NEXT I observed all the oppression and sadness throughout the earth—the tears of the oppressed, and no one helping them, while on the side of their oppressors were powerful allies. 2So I felt that the dead were better off than the living. 3And most fortunate of all are those who have never been born, and have never seen all the evil and crime throughout the earth.

4Then I observed that the basic motive for success is the driving force of envy and jealousy! But this, too, is foolishness, chasing the wind. 5,6The fool won't work and almost starves, but feels that it is better to be lazy and barely get by, than to work hard when, in the long run, it is all so futile.

7I also observed another piece of foolishness around the earth. 8This is the case of a man who is quite alone, without a son or brother, yet he works hard to keep gaining more riches, and to whom will he leave it all? And why is he giving up so much now? It is all so pointless and depressing.

9Two can accomplish more than twice as much as one, for the results can be much better. 10If one falls, the other pulls him up; but if a man falls when he is alone, he's in trouble.

11Also, on a cold night, two under the same blanket gain warmth from each other, but how can one be warm alone?

12And one standing alone can be attacked and defeated, but two can stand back-to-back and conquer; three is even better, for a triple-braided cord is not easily broken.

13It is better to be a poor but wise youth than to be an old and foolish king who refuses all advice. 14Such a lad could come from prison and succeed. He might even become king, though born in poverty. 15Everyone is eager to help a youth like that, even to help him usurp the throne. 16He can become the leader of millions of people, and be very popular. But, then, the younger generation grows up around him and rejects him! So again, it is all foolishness, chasing the wind.

As you enter the Temple, keep your ears open and your mouth shut! Don't be a fool who doesn't even realize it is sinful to make rash promises to God, for he is in heaven and you are only here on earth, so let your words be few. Just as being too busy gives you nightmares, so being a fool makes you a blabbermouth. 4So when you talk to God and vow to him that you will do something, don't delay in doing it, for God has no pleasure in fools. Keep your promise to him. 5It is far better not to say you'll do something than to say you will and then not do it. 6,7In that case, your mouth is making you sin. Don't try to defend yourself by telling the messenger from God that it was all a mistake [to make the vow]. That would make God very angry; and he might destroy your prosperity. Dreaming instead of doing is foolishness, and there is ruin in a flood of empty words; fear God instead.

8If you see some poor man being oppressed by the rich, with miscarriage of justice anywhere throughout the land, don't be surprised! For every official is under orders from higher up, and the higher officials look up to their superiors. And so the matter is lost in red tape and bureaucracy. 9And over them all is the king. Oh, for a king who is devoted to his country! Only he can bring order from this chaos.

10He who loves money shall never have enough. The foolishness of thinking that wealth brings happiness! 11The more you have, the more you spend, right up to the limits of your income, so what is the advantage of wealth—except perhaps to watch it as it runs through your fingers! 12The man who works hard sleeps well whether he eats little or much, but the rich must worry and suffer insomnia.

13,14There is another serious problem I have seen everywhere—savings are put into risky investments that turn sour, and soon there is nothing left to pass on to one's son. 15The man who speculates is soon back to where he began—with nothing. 16This, as I said, is a very serious problem, for all his hard work has been for nothing; he has been working for the wind. It is all swept away. 17All the rest of his life he is under a cloud—gloomy, discouraged, frustrated, and angry.

18Well, one thing, at least, is good: It is for a man to eat well, drink a good glass of wine, accept his position in life, and enjoy his work whatever his job may be, for however long the Lord may let him live. 19,20And, of course, it is very good if a man has received wealth from the Lord, and the good health to enjoy it. To enjoy your work and to accept your lot in life—that is indeed a gift from God. The person who does that will not need to look back with sorrow on his past, for God gives him joy.

Yes, but there is a very serious evil which I have seen everywhere— 2God has given to some men very great wealth and honor, so that they can have everything they want but he doesn't give them the health to enjoy it, and they die and others get it all! This is absurd, a hollow mockery, and a serious fault.

3Even if a man has a hundred sons and as many daughters and lives to be very old, but leaves so little money at his death that his children can't even give him a decent burial—I say that he would be better off born dead. 4For though his birth would then be futile and end in darkness, without even a name, 5never seeing the sun or even knowing its existence, yet that is better than to be an old, unhappy man. 6Though a man lives a thousand years twice over, but doesn't find contentment—well, what's the use?

7,8Wise men and fools alike spend their lives scratching for food, and never seem to get enough. Both have the same problem, yet the poor man who is wise lives a far better life. 9A bird in the hand is worth two in the bush; mere dreaming of nice things is foolish; it's chasing the wind.

10All things are decided by fate; it was known long ago what each man would be. So there's no use arguing with God about your destiny.

11The more words you speak, the less they mean, so why bother to speak at all?

12In these few days of our empty lifetimes, who can say how one's days can best be spent? Who can know what will prove best for the future after he is gone? For who knows the future?

2 CORINTHIANS 6:14—7:7

DON'T be teamed with those who do not love the Lord, for what do the people of God have in common with the people of sin? How can light live with darkness? 15And what harmony can there be between Christ and the devil? How can a Christian be a partner with one who doesn't believe? 16And what union can there be between God's temple and idols? For you are God's temple, the home of the living God, and God has said of you, "I will live in them and walk among them, and I will be their God and they shall be my people." 17That is why the Lord has said, "Leave them; separate yourselves from them; don't touch their filthy things, and I will welcome you, 18and be a Father to you, and you will be my sons and daughters."

HAVING such great promises as these, dear friends, let us turn away from everything wrong, whether of body or spirit, and purify ourselves, living in the wholesome fear of God, giving ourselves to him alone. 2Please open your hearts to us again, for not one of you has suffered any wrong from us. Not one of you was led astray. We have cheated no one nor taken advantage of anyone. 3I'm not saying this to scold or blame you, for, as I have said before, you are in my heart forever and I live and die with you. 4I have the highest confidence in you, and my pride in you is great. You have greatly encouraged me; you have made me so happy in spite of all my suffering.

5When we arrived in Macedonia there was no rest for us; outside, trouble was on every hand and all around us; within us, our hearts were full of dread and fear. 6Then God who cheers those who are discouraged refreshed us by the arrival of Titus. 7Not only was his presence a joy, but also the news that he brought of the wonderful time he had with you. When he told me how much you were looking forward to my visit, and how sorry you were about what had happened, and about your loyalty and warm love for me, well, I overflowed with joy!

PSALM 47:1–9

COME, everyone, and clap for joy! Shout triumphant praises to the Lord! 2For the Lord, the God above all gods, is awesome beyond words; he is the great King of all the earth. 3He subdues the nations before us, 4and will personally select his choicest blessings for his Jewish people—the very best for those he loves.

5God has ascended with a mighty shout, with trumpets blaring. 6,7Sing out your praises to our God, our King. Yes, sing your highest praises to our King, the King of all the earth. Sing thoughtful praises! 8He reigns above the nations, sitting on his holy throne. 9The Gentile rulers of the world have joined with us in praising him—praising the God of Abraham—for the battle shields of all the armies of the world are his trophies. He is highly honored everywhere.

PROVERBS FOR TODAY/ 22:16

He who gains by oppressing the poor or by bribing the rich shall end in poverty.

SEPTEMBER 4

ECCLESIASTES 7:1—9:18

A good reputation is more valuable than the most expensive perfume. The day one dies is better than the day he is born! 2It is better to spend your time at funerals than at festivals. For you are going to die and it is a good thing to think about it while there is still time. 3Sorrow is better than laughter, for sadness has a refining influence on us. 4Yes, a wise man thinks much of death, while the fool thinks only of having a good time now.

5It is better to be criticized by a wise man than to be praised by a fool! 6For a fool's compliment is as quickly gone as paper in fire, and it is silly to be impressed by it.

7The wise man is turned into a fool by a bribe; it destroys his understanding.

8Finishing is better than starting! Patience is better than pride! 9Don't be quick-tempered—that is being a fool.

10Don't long for "the good old days," for you don't know whether they were any better than these!

11To be wise is as good as being rich; in fact, it is better. 12You can get anything by either wisdom or money, but being wise has many advantages.

13[See the way God does things and fall into line. Don't fight the facts of nature.] Who can straighten what he has made crooked? 14Enjoy prosperity whenever you can, and when hard times strike, realize that God gives one as well as the other—so that everyone will realize that nothing is certain in this life.

15,16,17In this silly life I have seen everything, including the fact that some of the good die young and some of the wicked live on and on. So don't be too good or too wise! Why destroy yourself? On the other hand, don't be too wicked either—don't be a fool! Why should you die before your time?

18Tackle every task that comes along, and if you fear God you can expect his blessing.

19A wise man is stronger than the mayors of ten big cities! 20And there is not a single man in all the earth who is always good and never sins.

21,22Don't eavesdrop! You may hear your servant cursing you! For you know how often you yourself curse others!

23I have tried my best to be wise. I declared, "I *will* be wise," but it didn't work. 24Wisdom is far away, and very difficult to find. 25I searched everywhere, determined to find wisdom and the reason for things, and to prove to myself the wickedness of folly, and that foolishness is madness.

26A prostitute is more bitter than death. May it please God that you escape from her, but sinners don't evade her snares.

27,28This is my conclusion, says the Preacher. Step by step I came to this result after researching in every direction: One tenth of one percent of the men I interviewed could be said to be wise, but not one woman!

29And I found that though God has made men upright, each has turned away to follow his own downward road.

HOW wonderful to be wise, to understand things, to be able to analyze them and interpret them. Wisdom lights up a man's face, softening its hardness.

2,3Obey the king as you have vowed to do. Don't always be trying to get out of doing your duty, even when it's unpleasant. For the king punishes those who disobey. 4The king's command is backed by great power, and no one can withstand it or question it. 5Those who obey him will not be punished. The wise man will find a time and a way to do what he says. 6,7Yes, there is a time and a way for everything, though man's trouble lies heavy upon him; for how can he avoid what he doesn't know is going to happen?

8No one can hold back his spirit from departing; no one has the power to prevent his day of death, for there is no discharge from that obligation and that dark battle. Certainly a man's wickedness is not going to help him then.

9,10I have thought deeply about all that goes on here in the world, where people have the power of injuring each other. I have seen wicked men buried and as their friends returned from the cemetery, having forgotten all the dead man's evil deeds, these men were praised in the very city where they had committed their many crimes! How odd! 11Because God does not punish sinners instantly, people feel it is safe to do wrong. 12But though a man sins a hundred times and still lives, I know very well that those who fear God will be better off, [13]unlike the wicked, who will not live long, good lives—their days shall pass away as quickly as shadows because they don't fear God.

[14]There is a strange thing happening here upon the earth: Providence seems to treat some good men as though they were wicked, and some wicked men as though they were good. This is all very vexing and troublesome!

[15]Then I decided to spend my time having fun, because I felt that there was nothing better in all the earth than that a man should eat, drink, and be merry, with the hope that this happiness would stick with him in all the hard work which God gives to mankind everywhere.

[16,17]In my search for wisdom I observed all that was going on everywhere across the earth—ceaseless activity, day and night. (Of course, only God can see everything, and even the wisest man who says he knows everything, doesn't!)

THIS, too, I carefully explored—that godly and wise men are in God's will; no one knows whether he will favor them or not. All is chance! [2,3]The same providence confronts everyone, whether good or bad, religious or irreligious, profane or godly. It seems so unfair, that one fate comes to all. That is why men are not more careful to be good, but instead choose their own mad course, for they have no hope—there is nothing but death ahead anyway.

[4]There is hope only for the living. "It is better to be a live dog than a dead lion!" [5]For the living at least know that they will die! But the dead know nothing; they don't even have their memories. [6]Whatever they did in their lifetimes— loving, hating, envying—is long gone, and they have no part in anything here on earth any more. [7]So go ahead, eat, drink, and be merry, for it makes no difference to God! [8]Wear fine clothes—with a dash of cologne! [9]Live happily with the woman you love through the fleeting days of life, for the wife God gives you is your best reward down here for all your earthly toil. [10]Whatever you do, do well, for in death, where you are going, there is no working or planning, or knowing, or understanding.

[11]Again I looked throughout the earth and saw that the swiftest person does not always win the race, nor the strongest man the battle, and that wise men are often poor, and skillful men are not necessarily famous; but it is all by chance, by happening to be at the right place at the right time. [12]A man never knows when he is going to run into bad luck. He is like a fish caught in a net, or a bird caught in a snare.

[13]Here is another thing that has made a deep impression on me as I have watched human affairs: [14]There was a small city with only a few people living in it, and a great king came with his army and besieged it. [15]There was in the city a wise man, very poor, and he knew what to do to save the city, and so it was rescued. But afterwards no one thought any more about him. [16]Then I realized that though wisdom is better than strength, nevertheless, if the wise man is poor, he will be despised, and what he says will not be appreciated. [17]But even so, the quiet words of a wise man are better than the shout of a king of fools. [18]Wisdom is better than weapons of war, but one rotten apple can spoil a barrelful.

2 CORINTHIANS 7:8–16

I am no longer sorry that I sent that letter to you, though I was very sorry for a time, realizing how painful it would be to you. But it hurt you only for a little while. [9]Now I am glad I sent it, not because it hurt you, but because the pain turned you to God. It was a good kind of sorrow you felt, the kind of sorrow God wants his people to have, so that I need not come to you with harshness. [10]For God sometimes uses sorrow in our lives to help us turn away from sin and seek eternal life. We should never regret his sending it. But the sorrow of the man who is not a Christian is not the sorrow of true repentance and does not prevent eternal death.

11Just see how much good this grief from the Lord did for you! You no longer shrugged your shoulders, but became earnest and sincere, and very anxious to get rid of the sin that I wrote you about. You became frightened about what had happened, and longed for me to come and help. You went right to work on the problem and cleared it up [punishing the man who sinned]. You have done everything you could to make it right.

12I wrote as I did so the Lord could show how much you really do care for us. That was my purpose even more than to help the man who sinned, or his father to whom he did the wrong.

13In addition to the encouragement you gave us by your love, we were made happier still by Titus' joy when you gave him such a fine welcome and set his mind at ease. 14I told him how it would be—told him before he left me of my pride in you—and you didn't disappoint me. I have always told you the truth and now my boasting to Titus has also proved true! 15He loves you more than ever when he remembers the way you listened to him so willingly and received him so anxiously and with such deep concern. 16How happy this makes me, now that I am sure all is well between us again. Once again I can have perfect confidence in you.

PSALM 48:1–14

How great is the Lord! How much we should praise him. He lives upon Mount Zion in Jerusalem. 2What a glorious sight! See Mount Zion rising north of the city high above the plains for all to see—Mount Zion, joy of all the earth, the residence of the great King.

3God himself is the defender of Jerusalem. 4The kings of the earth have arrived together to inspect the city. 5They marvel at the sight and hurry home again, 6afraid of what they have seen; they are filled with panic like a woman in travail! 7For God destroys the mightiest warships with a breath of wind. 8We have heard of the city's glory—the city of our God, the Commander of the armies of heaven. And now we see it for ourselves! God has established Jerusalem forever.

9Lord, here in your Temple we meditate upon your kindness and your love. 10Your name is known throughout the earth, O God. You are praised everywhere for the salvation you have scattered throughout the world. 11O Jerusalem, rejoice! O people of Judah, rejoice! For God will see to it that you are finally treated fairly. 12Go, inspect the city! Walk around and count her many towers! 13Note her walls and tour her palaces, so that you can tell your children.

14For this great God is our God forever and ever. He will be our guide until we die.

PROVERBS FOR TODAY/ 22:17–19

Listen to this wise advice; follow it closely, for it will do you good, and you can pass it on to others: Trust in the Lord.

SEPTEMBER 5

ECCLESIASTES 10:1—12:14

DEAD flies will cause even a bottle of perfume to stink! Yes, a small mistake can outweigh much wisdom and honor. ²A wise man's heart leads him to do right, and a fool's heart leads him to do evil. ³You can identify a fool just by the way he walks down the street!

⁴If the boss is angry with you, don't quit! A quiet spirit will quiet his bad temper.

⁵There is another evil I have seen as I have watched the world go by, a sad situation concerning kings and rulers: ⁶For I have seen foolish men given great authority, and rich men not given their rightful place of dignity! ⁷I have even seen servants riding, while princes walk like servants!

⁸,⁹Dig a well—and fall into it! Demolish an old wall—and be bitten by a snake! When working in a quarry, stones will fall and crush you! There is risk in each stroke of your axe!

¹⁰A dull axe requires great strength; be wise and sharpen the blade.

¹¹When the horse is stolen, it is too late to lock the barn.

¹²,¹³It is pleasant to listen to wise words, but a fool's speech brings him to ruin. Since he begins with a foolish premise, his conclusion is sheer madness. ¹⁴A fool knows all about the future and tells everyone in detail! But who can really know what is going to happen? ¹⁵A fool is so upset by a little work that he has no strength for the simplest matter.

¹⁶,¹⁷Woe to the land whose king is a child and whose leaders are already drunk in the morning. Happy the land whose king is a nobleman, and whose leaders work hard before they feast and drink, and then only to strengthen themselves for the tasks ahead! ¹⁸Laziness lets the roof leak, and soon the rafters begin to rot. ¹⁹A party gives laughter, and wine gives happiness, and money gives everything! ²⁰Never curse the king, not even in your thoughts; nor the rich man, either; for a little bird will tell them what you've said.

GIVE generously, for your gifts will return to you later. ²Divide your gifts among many, for in the days ahead you yourself may need much help.

³When the clouds are heavy, the rains come down; when a tree falls, whether south or north, the die is cast, for there it lies. ⁴If you wait for perfect conditions, you will never get anything done. ⁵God's ways are as mysterious as the pathway of the wind, and as the manner in which a human spirit is infused into the little body of a baby while it is yet in its mother's womb. ⁶Keep on sowing your seed, for you never know which will grow—perhaps it all will.

⁷It is a wonderful thing to be alive! ⁸If a person lives to be very old, let him rejoice in every day of life, but let him also remember that eternity is far longer, and that everything down here is futile in comparison.

⁹Young man, it's wonderful to be young! Enjoy every minute of it! Do all you want to; take in everything, but realize that you must account to God for everything you do. ¹⁰So banish grief and pain, but remember that youth, with a whole life before it, can make serious mistakes.

DON'T let the excitement of being young cause you to forget about your Creator. Honor him in your youth before the evil years come—when you'll no longer enjoy living. ²It will be too late then to try to remember him, when the sun and light and moon and stars are dim to your old eyes, and there is no silver lining left among your clouds. ³For there will come a time when your limbs will tremble with age, and your strong legs will become weak, and your teeth will be too few to do their work, and there will be blindness, too. 4Then let your lips be tightly closed while eating, when your teeth are gone! And you will waken at dawn with the first note of the birds; but you yourself will be deaf and tuneless, with quavering voice. 5You will be afraid of heights and of falling—a white-haired, withered old man, dragging himself along: without sexual desire, standing at death's door, and nearing his everlasting home as the mourners go along the streets.

6Yes, remember your Creator now while you are young, before the silver cord of life snaps, and the gold bowl is broken, and the pitcher is broken at the fountain, and the wheel is broken at the cistern; 7and the dust returns to the earth as it was, and the spirit returns to God who gave it. 8All is futile, says the Preacher; utterly futile.

9But then, because the Preacher was wise, he went on teaching the people all he knew; and he collected proverbs and classified them. 10For the Preacher was not only a wise man, but a good teacher; he not only taught what he knew to the people, but taught them in an interesting manner. 11The wise man's words are like goads that spur to action. They nail down important truths. Students are wise who master what their teachers tell them.

12But, my son, be warned: there is no end of opinions ready to be expressed. Studying them can go on forever, and become very exhausting!

13Here is my final conclusion: fear God and obey his commandments, for this is the entire duty of man. 14For God will judge us for everything we do, including every hidden thing, good or bad.

2 CORINTHIANS 8:1–15

NOW I want to tell you what God in his grace has done for the churches in Macedonia.
2Though they have been going through much trouble and hard times, they have mixed their wonderful joy with their deep poverty, and the result has been an overflow of giving to others. 3They gave not only what they could afford, but far more; and I can testify that they did it because they wanted to, and not because of nagging on my part. 4They begged us to take the money so they could share in the joy of helping the Christians in Jerusalem. 5Best of all, they went beyond our highest hopes, for their first action was to dedicate themselves to the Lord and to us, for whatever directions God might give to them through us. 6They were so enthusiastic about it that we have urged Titus, who encouraged your giving in the first place, to visit you and encourage you to complete your share in this ministry of giving. 7You people there are leaders in so many ways—you have so much faith, so many good preachers, so much learning, so much enthusiasm, so much love for us. Now I want you to be leaders also in the spirit of cheerful giving.

8I am not giving you an order; I am not saying you must do it, but others are eager for it. This is one way to prove that your love is real, that it goes beyond mere words.

9You know how full of love and kindness our Lord Jesus was: though he was so very rich, yet to help you he became so very poor, so that by being poor he could make you rich.

10I want to suggest that you finish what you started to do a year ago, for you were not only the first to propose this idea, but the first to begin doing something about it. 11Having started the ball rolling so enthusiastically, you should carry this project through to completion just as gladly, giving whatever you can out of whatever you have. Let your enthusiastic idea at the start be equalled by your realistic action now. 12If you are really eager to give, then it isn't important how much you have to give. God wants you to give what you have, not what you haven't.

13Of course, I don't mean that those who receive your gifts should have an easy time of it at your expense, 14but you should divide with them. Right now you have plenty and can help them; then at some other time they can share with you when you need it. In this way each will have as much as he needs. 15Do you remember what the Scriptures say about this? "He that gathered much had nothing left over, and he that gathered little had enough." So you also should share with those in need.

PSALM 49:1–20

LISTEN, everyone! High and low, rich and poor, all around the world—listen to my words, 3for they are wise and filled with insight.

4I will tell in song accompanied by harps the answer to one of life's most perplexing problems:

5 *There is no need to fear when times of trouble come,* even though surrounded by enemies! 6They trust in their wealth and boast about how rich they are, 7yet not one of them, though rich as kings, can ransom his own brother from the penalty of sin! For God's forgiveness does not come that way. 8,9For a soul is far too precious to be ransomed by mere earthly wealth. There is not enough of it in all the earth to buy eternal life for just one soul, to keep it out of hell.

10Rich man! Proud man! Wise man! You must die like all the rest! You have no greater lease on life than foolish, stupid men. You must leave your wealth to others. 11You name your estates after yourselves as though your lands could be forever yours, and you could live on them eternally. 12But man with all his pomp must die like any animal. 13Such is the folly of these men, though after they die they will be quoted as having great wisdom.

14Death is the shepherd of all mankind. And "in the morning" those who are evil will be the slaves of those who are good. For the power of their wealth is gone when they die; they cannot take it with them.

15But as for me, God will redeem my soul from the power of death, for he will receive me. 16So do not be dismayed when evil men grow rich and build their lovely homes. 17For when they die they carry nothing with them! Their honors will not follow them. 18Though a man calls himself happy all through his life— and the world loudly applauds success— 19yet in the end he dies like everyone else, and enters eternal darkness.

20For man with all his pomp must die like any animal.

PROVERBS FOR TODAY/ 22:20–21

In the past, haven't I been right? Then believe what I am telling you now, and share it with others.

SEPTEMBER 6

SONG OF SOLOMON 1:1—4:16

THIS song of songs, more wonderful than any other, was composed by King Solomon:

The Girl: 2"Kiss me again and again, for your love is sweeter than wine. 3How fragrant your cologne, and how

great your name! No wonder all the young girls love you! 4Take me with you; come, let's run!"

The Girl: "The king has brought me into his palace. How happy we will be! Your love is better than wine. No wonder all the young girls love you!"

The Girl: 5"I am dark but beautiful, O girls of Jerusalem, tanned as the dark tents of Kedar."

King Solomon: "But lovely as the silken tents of Solomon!"

The Girl: 6"Don't look down on me, you city girls, just because my complexion is so dark—the sun has tanned me. My brothers were angry with me and sent me out into the sun to tend the vineyards, but see what it has done to me!"

The Girl: 7"Tell me, O one I love, where are you leading your flock today? Where will you be at noon? For I will come and join you there instead of wandering like a vagabond among the flocks of your companions."

King Solomon: 8"If you don't know, O most beautiful woman in all the world, follow the trail of my flock to the shepherds' tents, and there feed your sheep and their lambs. 9What a lovely filly you are, my love! 10How lovely your cheeks are, with your hair falling down upon them! How stately your neck with that long string of jewels. 11We shall make you gold earrings and silver beads."

The Girl: 12"The king lies on his bed, enchanted by the fragrance of my perfume. 13My beloved one is a sachet of myrrh lying between my breasts."

King Solomon: 14"My beloved is a bouquet of flowers in the gardens of Engedi. 15How beautiful you are, my love, how beautiful! Your eyes are soft as doves'. 16What a lovely, pleasant thing you are, lying here upon the grass, 17shaded by the cedar trees and firs."

THE Girl: "I am the rose of Sharon, the lily of the valley."

King Solomon: 2"Yes, a lily among thorns, so is my beloved as compared with any other girls."

The Girl: 3"My lover is an apple tree, the finest in the orchard as compared with any of the other youths. I am seated in his much-desired shade and his fruit is lovely to eat. 4He brings me to the banquet hall and everyone can see how much he loves me. 5Oh, feed me with your love—your 'raisins' and your 'apples'—for I am utterly lovesick. 6His left hand is under my head and with his right hand he embraces me. 7O girls of Jerusalem, I adjure you by the gazelles and deer in the park, that you do not awaken my lover. Let him sleep!"

The Girl: 8"Ah, I hear him—my beloved! Here he comes, leaping upon the mountains and bounding over the hills. 9My beloved is like a gazelle or young deer. Look, there he is behind the wall, now looking in at the windows.

10"My beloved said to me, 'Rise up, my love, my fair one, and come away. 11For the winter is past, the rain is over and gone. 12The flowers are springing up and the time of the singing of birds has come. Yes, spring is here. 13The leaves are coming out and the grape vines are in blossom. How delicious they smell! Arise, my love, my fair one, and come away.'

14"My dove is hiding behind some rocks, behind an outcrop of the cliff. Call to me and let me hear your lovely voice and see your handsome face.

15"The little foxes are ruining the vineyards. Catch them, for the grapes are all in blossom.

16"My beloved is mine and I am his. He is feeding among the lilies! 17Before the dawn comes and the shadows flee away, come to me, my beloved, and be like a gazelle or a young stag on the mountains of spices."

THE Girl: "One night my lover was missing from my bed. I got up to look for him but couldn't find him. 2I went out into the streets of the city and the roads to seek him, but I searched in vain. 3The police stopped me and I said to them, 'Have you seen him anywhere, this one I love so much?' 4It was only a little while afterwards that I found him and held him and would not let him go until I had brought him into my childhood home, into my mother's old bedroom. 5I adjure you, O women of Jerusalem, by the gazelles and deer of the park, not to awake my lover. Let him sleep."

The Young Women of Jerusalem: 6"Who is this sweeping in from the deserts like a cloud of smoke along the ground, smelling of myrrh and frankincense and every other spice that can be bought? 7Look, it is the chariot of Solomon with sixty of the mightiest men of his army surrounding it. 8They are all skilled swordsmen and experienced bodyguards. Each one has his sword upon his thigh to defend his king against any onslaught in the night. 9For King Solomon made himself a chariot from the wood of Lebanon. 10Its posts are silver, its canopy gold, the seat is purple; and the back is inlaid with these words: 'With love from the girls of Jerusalem!' "

The Girl: 11"Go out and see King Solomon, O young women of Zion; see the crown with which his mother crowned him on his wedding day, his day of gladness."

KING Solomon: "How beautiful you are, my love, how beautiful! Your eyes are those of doves. Your hair falls across your face like flocks of goats that frisk across the slopes of Gilead. 2Your teeth are white as sheep's wool, newly shorn and washed; perfectly matched, without one missing. 3Your lips are like a thread of scarlet—and how beautiful your mouth. Your cheeks are matched loveliness behind your locks. 4Your neck is stately as the tower of David, jeweled with a thousand heroes' shields. 5Your breasts are like twin fawns of a gazelle, feeding among the lilies. 6Until the morning dawns and the shadows flee away, I will go to the mountain of myrrh and to the hill of frankincense. 7You are so beautiful, my love, in every part of you.

8"Come with me from Lebanon, my bride. We will look down from the summit of the mountain, from the top of Mount Hermon, where the lions have their dens, and panthers prowl. 9You have ravished my heart, my lovely one, my bride; I am overcome by one glance of your eyes, by a single bead of your necklace. 10How sweet is your love, my darling, my bride. How much better it is than mere wine. The perfume of your love is more fragrant than all the richest spices. 11Your lips, my dear, are made of honey. Yes, honey and cream are under your tongue, and the scent of your garments is like the scent of the mountains and cedars of Lebanon.

12"My darling bride is like a private garden, a spring that no one else can have, a fountain of my own. 13,14You are like a lovely orchard bearing precious fruit, with the rarest of perfumes; nard and saffron, calamus and cinnamon, and perfume from every other incense tree, as well as myrrh and aloes, and every other lovely spice. 15You are a garden fountain, a well of living water, refreshing as the streams from the Lebanon mountains."

The Girl: 16"Come, north wind, awaken; come, south wind, blow upon my garden and waft its lovely perfume to my beloved. Let him come into his garden and eat its choicest fruits."

2 CORINTHIANS 8:16–24

I am thankful to God that he has given Titus the same real concern for you that I have. 17He is glad to follow my suggestion that he visit you again—but I think he would have come anyway, for he is very eager to see you! 18I am sending another well-known brother with him, who is highly praised as a preacher of the Good News in all the churches. 19In fact, this man was elected by the churches to travel with me to take the gift to Jerusalem. This will glorify the Lord and show our eagerness to help each other. 20By traveling together we will guard against any suspicion, for we are anxious that no one should find fault with the way we are handling this large gift. 21God knows we are honest, but I want everyone else to know it too. That is why we have made this arrangement.

22And I am sending you still another brother, whom we know from experience to be an earnest Christian. He is especially interested, as he looks forward to this trip, because I have told him all about your eagerness to help.

23If anyone asks who Titus is, say that he is my partner, my helper in helping you, and you can also say that the other two brothers represent the assemblies here and are splendid examples of those who belong to the Lord.

24Please show your love for me to these men and do for them all that I have publicly boasted you would.

PSALM 50:1–23

THE mighty God, the Lord, has summoned all mankind from east to west!

2God's glory-light shines from the beautiful Temple on Mount Zion. 3He comes with the noise of thunder, surrounded by devastating fire; a great storm rages round about him. 4He has come to judge his people. To heaven and earth he shouts, 5"Gather together my own people who by their sacrifice upon my altar have promised to obey me." 6God will judge them with complete fairness, for all heaven declares that he is just.

7O my people, listen! For I am your God. Listen! Here are my charges against you: 8I have no complaint about the sacrifices you bring to my altar, for you bring them regularly. 9But it isn't sacrificial bullocks and goats that I really want from you. 10,11For all the animals of field and forest are mine! The cattle on a thousand hills! And all the birds upon the mountains! 12If I were hungry, I would not mention it to you—for all the world is mine, and everything in it. 13No, I don't need your sacrifices of flesh and blood. 14,15What I want from you is your true thanks; I want your promises fulfilled. *I want you to trust me in your times of trouble, so I can rescue you, and you can give me glory.*

16But God says to evil men: Recite my laws no longer, and stop claiming my promises, 17for you have refused my discipline, disregarding my laws. 18You see a thief and help him, and spend your time with evil and immoral men. 19You curse and lie, and vile language streams from your mouths. 20You slander your own brother. 21I remained silent— you thought I didn't care—but now your time of punishment has come, and I list all the above charges against you. 22This is the last chance for all of you who have forgotten God, before I tear you apart—and no one can help you then.

23But true praise is a worthy sacrifice; this really honors me. Those who walk my paths will receive salvation from the Lord.

PROVERBS FOR TODAY/ 22:22–23

Don't rob the poor and sick! For the Lord is their defender. If you injure them he will punish you.

SEPTEMBER 7

SONG OF SOLOMON 5:1—8:14

KING Solomon: "I am here in my garden, my darling, my bride! I gather my myrrh with my spices and eat my honeycomb with my honey. I drink my wine with my milk."

The Young Women of Jerusalem: "Oh, lover and beloved, eat and drink! Yes, drink deeply!"

The Girl: 2"One night as I was sleeping, my heart awakened in a dream. I heard the voice of my beloved; he was knocking at my bedroom door. 'Open to me, my darling, my lover, my lovely dove,' he said, 'for I have been out in the night and am covered with dew.'

³"But I said, 'I have disrobed. Shall I get dressed again? I have washed my feet, and should I get them soiled?'

⁴"My beloved tried to unlatch the door and my heart was thrilled within me. ⁵I jumped up to open it and my hands dripped with perfume, my fingers with lovely myrrh as I pulled back the bolt. ⁶I opened to my beloved, but he was gone. My heart stopped. I searched for him but couldn't find him anywhere. I called to him, but there was no reply. ⁷The guards found me and struck and wounded me. The watchman on the wall tore off my veil. ⁸I adjure you, O women of Jerusalem, if you find my beloved one, tell him that I am sick with love."

The Young Women of Jerusalem: ⁹"O woman of rare beauty, what is it about your loved one that is better than any other, that you command us this?"

The Girl: ¹⁰"My beloved one is tanned and handsome, better than ten thousand others! ¹¹His head is purest gold, and he has wavy, raven hair. ¹²His eyes are like doves beside the water brooks, deep and quiet. ¹³His cheeks are like sweetly scented beds of spices. His lips are perfumed lilies, his breath like myrrh. ¹⁴His arms are round bars of gold set with topaz; his body is bright ivory encrusted with jewels. ¹⁵His legs are as pillars of marble set in sockets of finest gold, like cedars of Lebanon; none can rival him. ¹⁶His mouth is altogether sweet, lovable in every way. Such, O women of Jerusalem, is my beloved, my friend."

THE Young Women of Jerusalem: "O rarest of beautiful women, where has your loved one gone? We will help you find him."

The Girl: ²"He has gone down to his garden, to his spice beds, to pasture his flock and to gather the lilies. ³I am my beloved's and my beloved is mine. He pastures his flock among the lilies!"

King Solomon: ⁴"O my beloved, you are as beautiful as the lovely land of Tirzah, yes, beautiful as Jerusalem, and how you capture my heart. ⁵Look the other way, for your eyes have overcome me! Your hair, as it falls across your face, is like a flock of goats frisking down the slopes of Gilead. ⁶Your teeth are white as freshly washed ewes, perfectly matched and not one missing. ⁷Your cheeks are matched loveliness behind your hair. ⁸I have sixty other wives, all queens, and eighty concubines, and unnumbered virgins available to me; ⁹but you, my dove, my perfect one, are the only one among them all, without an equal! The women of Jerusalem were delighted when they saw you and even the queens and concubines praise you. ¹⁰'Who is this,' they ask, 'arising as the dawn, fair as the moon, pure as the sun, so utterly captivating?' "

The Girl: ¹¹"I went down into the orchard of nuts and out to the valley to see the springtime there, to see whether the grape vines were budding or the pomegranates were blossoming yet. ¹²Before I realized it I was stricken with terrible homesickness and wanted to be back among my own people."

The Young Women of Jerusalem: ¹³"Return, return to us, O maid of Shulam. Come back, come back, that we may see you once again."

The Girl: "Why should you seek a mere Shulammite?"

King Solomon: "Because you dance so beautifully."

KING Solomon: "How beautiful your tripping feet, O queenly maiden. Your rounded thighs are like jewels, the work of the most skilled of craftsmen. ²Your navel is lovely as a goblet filled with wine. Your waist is like a heap of wheat set about with lilies. ³Your two breasts are like two fawns, yes, lovely twins. 4Your neck is stately as an ivory tower, your eyes as limpid pools in Heshbon by the gate of Bathrabbim. Your nose is shapely like the tower of Lebanon overlooking Damascus.

5"As Mount Carmel crowns the mountains, so your hair is your crown. The king is held captive in your queenly tresses.

6"Oh, how delightful you are; how pleasant, O love, for utter delight! 7You are tall and slim like a palm tree, and your breasts are like its clusters of dates. 8I said, I will climb up into the palm tree and take hold of its branches. Now may your breasts be like grape clusters, and the scent of your breath like apples, 9and your kisses as exciting as the best of wine, smooth and sweet, causing the lips of those who are asleep to speak."

The Girl: 10"I am my beloved's and I am the one he desires. 11Come, my beloved, let us go out into the fields and stay in the villages. 12Let us get up early and go out to the vineyards and see whether the vines have budded and whether the blossoms have opened and whether the pomegranates are in flower. And there I will give you my love. 13There the mandrakes give forth their fragrance and the rarest fruits are at our doors, the new as well as old, for I have stored them up for my beloved."

THE Girl: "Oh, if only you were my brother; then I could kiss you no matter who was watching, and no one would laugh at me. 2I would bring you to my childhood home, and there you would teach me. I would give you spiced wine to drink, sweet pomegranate wine. 3His left hand would be under my head and his right hand would embrace me. 4I adjure you, O women of Jerusalem, not to awaken him until he please."

The Young Women of Jerusalem: 5"Who is this coming up from the desert, leaning on her beloved?"

King Solomon: "Under the apple tree where your mother gave birth to you in her travail, there I awakened your love."

The Girl: 6"Seal me in your heart with permanent betrothal, for love is strong as death and jealousy is as cruel as Sheol. It flashes fire, the very flame of Jehovah. 7Many waters cannot quench the flame of love, neither can the floods drown it. If a man tried to buy it with everything he owned, he couldn't do it."

The Girl's Brothers: 8"We have a little sister too young for breasts. What shall we do if someone asks to marry her?"

King Solomon: 9"If she has no breasts we will build upon her a battlement of silver, and if she is a door we will enclose her with cedar boards."

The Girl: 10"I am slim, tall, and fullbreasted and I have found favor in my lover's eyes. 11Solomon had a vineyard at Baal-hamon which he rented out to some farmers there, the rent being one thousand pieces of silver from each. 12But as for my own vineyard, you, O Solomon, shall have my thousand pieces of silver and I will give two hundred pieces to those who care for it. 13O my beloved, living in the gardens, how wonderful that your companions may listen to your voice; let me hear it too. 14Come quickly, my beloved, and be like a gazelle or young deer upon the mountains of spices."

2 CORINTHIANS 9:1–15

I realize that I really don't even need to mention this to you, about helping God's people. 2For I know how eager you are to do it, and I have boasted to the friends in Macedonia that you were ready to send an offering a year ago. In fact, it was this enthusiasm of yours that stirred up many of them to begin helping. 3But I am sending these men just to be sure that you really are ready, as I told them you would be, with your money all collected; I don't want it to turn out that this time I was wrong in my boasting about you. 4I would be very much ashamed—and so would you—if some of these Macedonian people come with me, only to find that you still aren't ready after all I have told them!

5So I have asked these other brothers to arrive ahead of me to see that the gift you promised is on hand and waiting. I want it to be a real gift and not look as if it were being given under pressure.

6But remember this—if you give little, you will get little. A farmer who plants just a few seeds will get only a small crop, but if he plants much, he will reap much. 7Every one must make up his own mind as to how much he should give. Don't force anyone to give more than he really wants to, for cheerful givers are the ones God prizes. 8God is able to make it up to you by giving you everything you need and more, so that there will not only be enough for your own needs, but plenty left over to give joyfully to others. 9It is as the Scriptures say: "The godly man gives generously to the poor. His good deeds will be an honor to him forever."

10For God, who gives seed to the farmer to plant, and later on, good crops to harvest and eat, will give you more and more seed to plant and will make it grow so that you can give away more and more fruit from your harvest.

11Yes, God will give you much so that you can give away much, and when we take your gifts to those who need them they will break out into thanksgiving and praise to God for your help. 12So, two good things happen as a result of your gifts—those in need are helped, and they overflow with thanks to God. 13Those you help will be glad not only because of your generous gifts to themselves and to others, but they will praise God for this proof that your deeds are as good as your doctrine. 14And they will pray for you with deep fervor and feeling because of the wonderful grace of God shown through you.

15Thank God for his Son—his Gift too wonderful for words.

O loving and kind God, have mercy. Have pity upon me and take away the awful stain of my transgressions. 2Oh, wash me, cleanse me from this guilt. Let me be pure again. 3For I admit my shameful deed—it haunts me day and night. 4It is against you and you alone I sinned, and did this terrible thing. You saw it all, and your sentence against me is just. 5But I was born a sinner, yes, from the moment my mother conceived me. 6You deserve honesty from the heart; yes, utter sincerity and truthfulness. Oh, give me this wisdom.

7Sprinkle me with the cleansing blood and I shall be clean again. Wash me and I shall be whiter than snow. 8And after you have punished me, give me back my joy again. 9Don't keep looking at my sins—erase them from your sight. 10Create in me a new, clean heart, O God, filled with clean thoughts and right desires. 11Don't toss me aside, banished forever from your presence. Don't take your Holy Spirit from me. 12Restore to me again the joy of your salvation, and make me willing to obey you. 13Then I will teach your ways to other sinners, and they—guilty like me—will repent and return to you. 14,15Don't sentence me to death. O my God, you alone can rescue me. Then I will sing of your forgiveness, for my lips will be unsealed—oh, how I will praise you.

16You don't want penance; if you did, how gladly I would do it! You aren't interested in offerings burned before you on the altar. 17It is a broken spirit you want—remorse and penitence. A broken and a contrite heart, O God, you will not ignore.

18And Lord, don't punish Israel for my sins—help your people and protect Jerusalem.

19And when my heart is right, then you will rejoice in the good that I do and in the bullocks I bring to sacrifice upon your altar.

Keep away from angry, short-tempered men, lest you learn to be like them and endanger your soul.

SEPTEMBER 8

ISAIAH 1:1—2:22

THESE *are the messages that came to Isaiah, son of Amoz, in the visions he saw during the reigns of King Uzziah, King Jotham, King Ahaz and King Hezekiah—all kings of Judah. In these messages God showed him what was going to happen to Judah and Jerusalem in the days ahead.*

2Listen, O heaven and earth, to what the Lord is saying:

The children I raised and cared for so long and tenderly have turned against me. 3Even the animals—the donkey and the ox—know their owner and appreciate his care for them, but not my people Israel. No matter what I do for them, they still don't care. 4Oh, what a sinful nation they are! They walk bent-backed beneath their load of guilt. Their fathers before them were evil too. Born to be bad, they have turned their backs upon the Lord, and have despised the Holy One of Israel. They have cut themselves off from my help.

5,6Oh, my people, haven't you had enough of punishment? Why will you force me to whip you again and again? Must you forever rebel? From head to foot you are sick and weak and faint, covered with bruises and welts and infected wounds, unanointed and unbound. 7Your country lies in ruins; your cities are burned; while you watch, foreigners are destroying and plundering everything they see. 8You stand there helpless and abandoned like a watchman's shanty in the field when the harvest time is over—or when the crop is stripped and robbed.

9If the Lord Almighty had not stepped in to save a few of us, we would have been wiped out as Sodom and Gomorrah were. 10An apt comparison! Listen, you leaders of Israel, you men of Sodom and Gomorrah, as I call you now. Listen to the Lord. Hear what he is telling you! 11I am sick of your sacrifices. Don't bring me any more of them. I don't want your fat rams; I don't want to see the blood from your offerings. 12,13Who wants your sacrifices when you have no sorrow for your sins? The incense you bring me is a stench in my nostrils. Your holy celebrations of the new moon and the Sabbath, and your special days for fasting— even your most pious meetings—all are frauds! I want nothing more to do with them. 14I hate them all; I can't stand the sight of them. 15From now on, when you pray with your hands stretched out to heaven, I won't look or listen. Even though you make many prayers, I will not hear, for your hands are those of murderers; they are covered with the blood of your innocent victims.

16Oh, wash yourselves! Be clean! Let me no longer see you doing all these wicked things; quit your evil ways. 17Learn to do good, to be fair and to help the poor, the fatherless, and widows.

18Come, let's talk this over! says the Lord; no matter how deep the stain of your sins, I can take it out and make you as clean as freshly fallen snow. Even if you are stained as red as crimson, I can make you white as wool! 19If you will only let me help you, if you will only obey, then I will make you rich!

20But if you keep on turning your backs and refusing to listen to me, you will be killed by your enemies; I, the Lord, have spoken.

21Jerusalem, once my faithful wife! And now a prostitute! Running after other gods! Once "The City of Fair Play," but now a gang of murderers. 22Once like sterling silver; now mixed with worthless alloy! Once so pure, but now diluted like watered-down wine! 23Your leaders are rebels, companions of thieves; all of them take bribes and won't defend the widows and orphans. 24Therefore the Lord, the Mighty One of Israel, says: I will pour out my anger on you, my enemies! 25I myself will melt you in a smelting pot, and skim off your slag.

26And afterwards I will give you good judges and wise counselors like those you used to have. Then your city shall again be called "The City of Justice," and "The Faithful Town." 27Those who return to the Lord, who are just and good, shall be redeemed.

28(But all sinners shall utterly perish, for they refuse to come to me.) 29Shame will cover you, and you will blush to think of all those times you sacrificed to idols in your groves of "sacred" oaks. 30You will perish like a withered tree or a garden without water. 31The strongest among you will disappear like burning straw; your evil deeds are the spark that sets the straw on fire, and no one will be able to put it out.

THIS is another message to Isaiah from the Lord concerning Judah and Jerusalem:

2In the last days Jerusalem and the Temple of the Lord will become the world's greatest attraction, and people from many lands will flow there to worship the Lord.

3"Come," everyone will say, "let us go up the mountain of the Lord, to the Temple of the God of Israel; there he will teach us his laws, and we will obey them." For in those days the world will be ruled from Jerusalem. 4The Lord will settle international disputes; all the nations will convert their weapons of war into implements of peace. Then at the last all wars will stop and all military training will end. 5O Israel, come, let us walk in the light of the Lord, and be obedient to his laws!

6The Lord has rejected you because you welcome foreigners from the East who practice magic and communicate with evil spirits, as the Philistines do.

7Israel has vast treasures of silver and gold, and great numbers of horses and chariots 8and idols—the land is full of them! They are man-made, and yet you *worship* them! 9Small and great, all bow before them; God will not forgive you for this sin.

10Crawl into the caves in the rocks and hide in terror from his glorious majesty, 11for the day is coming when your proud looks will be brought low; the Lord alone will be exalted. 12On that day the Lord Almighty will move against the proud and haughty and bring them to the dust. 13All the tall cedars of Lebanon and all the mighty oaks of Bashan shall bend low, 14and all the high mountains and hills, 15and every high tower and wall, 16and all the proud ocean ships and trim harbor craft—*all* shall be crushed before the Lord that day. 17All the glory of mankind will bow low; the pride of men will lie in the dust, and the Lord alone will be exalted. 18And all idols will be utterly abolished and destroyed.

19When the Lord stands up from his throne to shake up the earth, his enemies will crawl with fear into the holes in the rocks and into the caves because of the glory of his majesty. 20Then at last they will abandon their gold and silver idols to the moles and bats, 21and crawl into the caverns to hide among the jagged rocks at the tops of the cliffs to try to get away from the terror of the Lord and the glory of his majesty when he rises to terrify the earth. 22Puny man! Frail as his breath! Don't ever put your trust in him!

I plead with you—yes, I, Paul—and I plead gently, as Christ himself would do. Yet some of you are saying, "Paul's letters are bold enough when he is far away, but when he gets here he will be afraid to raise his voice!"

2I hope I won't need to show you when I come how harsh and rough I can be. I don't want to carry out my present plans against some of you who seem to think my deeds and words are merely those of an ordinary man. 3It is true that I am an ordinary, weak human being, but I don't use human plans and methods to win my battles. 4I use God's mighty weapons, not those made by men, to knock down the devil's strongholds. 5These weapons can break down every proud argument against God and every wall that can be built to keep men from finding him. With these weapons I can capture rebels and bring them back to God, and change them into men whose hearts' desire is obedience to Christ. 6I will use these weapons against every rebel who remains after I have first used them on you yourselves, and you surrender to Christ.

7The trouble with you is that you look at me and I seem weak and powerless, but you don't look beneath the surface. Yet if anyone can claim the power and authority of Christ, I certainly can. 8I may seem to be boasting more than I should about my authority over you—authority to help you, not to hurt you—but I shall make good every claim. 9I say this so that you will not think I am just blustering when I scold you in my letters.

10"Don't bother about his letters," some say. "He sounds big, but it's all noise. When he gets here you will see that there is nothing great about him, and you have never heard a worse preacher!" 11This time my personal presence is going to be just as rough on you as my letters are!

12Oh, don't worry, I wouldn't dare say that I am as wonderful as these other men who tell you how good they are! Their trouble is that they are only comparing themselves with each other, and measuring themselves against their own little ideas. What stupidity!

13But we will not boast of authority we do not have. Our goal is to measure up to God's plan for us, and this plan includes our working there with you. 14We are not going too far when we claim authority over you, for we were the first to come to you with the Good News concerning Christ. 15It is not as though we were trying to claim credit for the work someone else has done among you. Instead, we hope that your faith will grow and that, still within the limits set for us, our work among you will be greatly enlarged.

16After that, we will be able to preach the Good News to other cities that are far beyond you, where no one else is working; then there will be no question about being in someone else's field. 17As the Scriptures say, "If anyone is going to boast, let him boast about what the Lord has done and not about himself." 18When someone boasts about himself and how well he has done, it doesn't count for much. But when the Lord commends him, that's different!

PSALM 52:1-9

YOU call yourself a *hero,* do you? You *boast* about this evil deed of yours against God's people. 2You are sharp as a tack in plotting your evil tricks. 3How you love wickedness—far more than good! And lying more than truth! 4You love to slander—you love to say anything that will do harm, O man with the lying tongue.

5But God will strike you down and pull you from your home, and drag you away from the land of the living. 6The followers of God will see it happen. They will watch in awe. Then they will laugh and say, 7"See what happens to those who despise God and trust in their wealth, and become ever more bold in their wickedness."

8But I am like a sheltered olive tree protected by the Lord himself. I trust in the mercy of God forever and ever. 9O Lord, I will praise you forever and ever for your punishment. And I will wait for your mercies—for everyone knows what a merciful God you are.

PROVERBS FOR TODAY/ 22:26–27

Unless you have the extra cash on hand, don't countersign a note. Why risk everything you own? They'll even take your bed!

SEPTEMBER 9

ISAIAH 3:1—5:30

THE Lord will cut off Jerusalem's and Judah's food and water supplies 2and kill her leaders; he will destroy her armies, judges, prophets, elders, 3army officers, businessmen, lawyers, magicians and politicians. 4Israel's kings will be like babies, ruling childishly. 5And the worst sort of anarchy will prevail—everyone stepping on someone else, neighbors fighting neighbors, youths revolting against authority, criminals sneering at honorable men.

6In those days a man will say to his brother, "You have some extra clothing, so you be our king and take care of this mess."

7"No!" he will reply. "I cannot be of any help! I have no extra food or clothes. Don't get me involved!"

8Israel's civil government will be in utter ruin because the Jews have spoken out against their Lord and will not worship him; they offend his glory. 9The very look on their faces gives them away and shows their guilt. And they boast that their sin is equal to the sin of Sodom; they are not even ashamed. What a catastrophe! They have doomed themselves.

10But all is well for the godly man. Tell him, "What a reward you are going to get!" 11But say to the wicked, "Your doom is sure. You too shall get your just deserts. Your well-earned punishment is on the way."

12O my people! Can't you see what fools your rulers are? Weak as women! Foolish as little children playing king. True leaders? No, misleaders! Leading you down the garden path to destruction.

13The Lord stands up! He is the great Prosecuting Attorney presenting his case against his people! 14First to feel his wrath will be the elders and the princes, for they have defrauded the poor. They have filled their barns with grain extorted from the helpless peasants.

15"How dare you grind my people in the dust like that?" the Lord Almighty will demand of them.

16Next, he will judge the haughty Jewish women, who mince along, noses in the air, tinkling bracelets on their ankles, with wanton eyes that rove among the crowds to catch the glances of the men. 17The Lord will send a plague of scabs to ornament their heads! He will expose their nakedness for all to see. 18No longer shall they tinkle with self-assurance as they walk. For the Lord will strip away their artful beauty and their ornaments, 19their necklaces and bracelets and veils of shimmering gauze. 20Gone shall be their scarves and ankle chains, headbands, earrings, and perfumes; 21their rings and jewels, 22and party clothes and negligees and capes and ornate combs and purses; 23their mirrors, lovely lingerie, beautiful dresses and veils. 24Instead of smelling of sweet perfume, they'll stink; for sashes they'll use ropes; their well-set hair will all fall out; they'll wear sacks instead of robes.

All their beauty will be gone; all that will be left to them is shame and disgrace. 25,26Their husbands shall die in battle; the women, ravaged, shall sit crying on the ground.

AT that time so few men will be left alive that seven women will fight over each of them and say, "Let us all marry you! We will furnish our own food and clothing; only let us be called by your name so that we won't be mocked as old maids."

2,3,4Those whose names are written down to escape the destruction of Jerusalem will be washed and rinsed of all their moral filth by the horrors and the fire. They will be God's holy people. And the land will produce for them its lushest bounty and its richest fruit. 5Then the Lord will provide shade on all Jerusalem—over every home and all its public grounds—a canopy of smoke and cloud throughout the day, and clouds of fire at night, covering the Glorious Land, 6protecting it from daytime heat and from rains and storms.

NOW I will sing a song about his vineyard to the one I love. *My Beloved has a vineyard on a very fertile hill. 2He plowed it and took out all the rocks and planted his vineyard with the choicest vines. He built a watchtower and cut a winepress in the rocks. Then he waited for the harvest, but the grapes that grew were wild and sour and not at all the sweet ones he expected.*

3Now, men of Jerusalem and Judah, you have heard the case! You be the judges! 4What more could I have done? Why did my vineyard give me wild grapes instead of sweet? 5I will tear down the fences and let my vineyard go to pasture to be trampled by cattle and sheep. 6I won't prune it or hoe it, but let it be overgrown with briars and thorns. I will command the clouds not to rain on it any more.

7I have given you the story of God's people. They are the vineyard that I spoke about. Israel and Judah are his pleasant acreage! He expected them to yield a crop of justice, but found bloodshed instead. He expected righteousness, but the cries of deep oppression met his ears. 8You buy up property so others have no place to live. Your homes are built on great estates so you can be alone in the midst of the earth! 9But the Lord Almighty has sworn your awful fate—with my own ears I heard him say, "Many a beautiful home will lie deserted, their owners killed or gone." 10An acre of vineyard will not produce a gallon of juice! Ten bushels of seed will yield a one-bushel crop!

11Woe to you who get up early in the morning to go on long drinking bouts that last till late at night—woe to you drunken bums. 12You furnish lovely music at your grand parties; the orchestras are superb! But for the Lord you have no thought or care. 13Therefore I will send you into exile far away because you neither know nor care that I have done so much for you. Your great and honored men will starve, and the common people will die of thirst.

14Hell is licking its chops in anticipation of this delicious morsel, Jerusalem. Her great and small shall be swallowed up, and all her drunken throngs. 15In that day the haughty shall be brought down to the dust; the proud shall be humbled; 16but the Lord Almighty is exalted above all, for he alone is holy, just and good. 17In those days flocks will feed among the ruins. Lambs and calves and kids will pasture there!

18Woe to those who drag their sins behind them like a bullock on a rope. 19They even mock the Holy One of Israel and dare the Lord to punish them. "Hurry up and punish us, O Lord," they say. "We want to see what you can do!" 20They say that what is right is wrong, and what is wrong is right; that black is white and white is black; bitter is sweet and sweet is bitter.

21Woe to those who are wise and

shrewd in their own eyes! 22Woe to those who are "heroes" when it comes to drinking, and boast about the liquor they can hold. 23They take bribes to pervert justice, letting the wicked go free and putting innocent men in jail. 24Therefore God will deal with them and burn them. They will disappear like straw on fire. Their roots will rot and their flowers wither, for they have thrown away the laws of God and despised the Word of the Holy One of Israel. 25That is why the anger of the Lord is hot against his people; that is why he has reached out his hand to smash them. The hills will tremble, and the rotting bodies of his people will be thrown as refuse in the streets. But even so, his anger is not ended; his hand is heavy on them still.

26He will send a signal to the nations far away, whistling to those at the ends of the earth, and they will come racing toward Jerusalem. 27They never weary, never stumble, never stop; their belts are tight, their bootstraps strong; they run without stopping for rest or for sleep. 28Their arrows are sharp; their bows are bent; sparks fly from their horses' hoofs, and the wheels of their chariots spin like the wind. 29They roar like lions and pounce upon the prey. They seize my people and carry them off into captivity with none to rescue them. 30They growl over their victims like the roaring of the sea. Over all Israel lies a pall of darkness and sorrow and the heavens are black.

2 CORINTHIANS 11:1–15

I hope you will be patient with me as I keep on talking like a fool. Do bear with me and let me say what is on my heart. 2I am anxious for you with the deep concern of God himself—anxious that your love should be for Christ alone, just as a pure maiden saves her love for one man only, for the one who will be her husband. 3But I am frightened, fearing that in some way you will be led away from your pure and simple devotion to our Lord, just as Eve was deceived by Satan in the Garden of Eden.

4You seem so gullible: you believe whatever anyone tells you even if he is preaching about another Jesus than the one we preach, or a different spirit than the Holy Spirit you received, or shows you a different way to be saved. You swallow it all.

5Yet I don't feel that these marvelous "messengers from God," as they call themselves, are any better than I am. 6If I am a poor speaker, at least I know what I am talking about, as I think you realize by now, for we have proved it again and again.

7Did I do wrong and cheapen myself and make you look down on me because I preached God's Good News to you without charging you anything? 8,9Instead I "robbed" other churches by taking what they sent me, and using it up while I was with you, so that I could serve you without cost. And when that was gone and I was getting hungry I still didn't ask you for anything, for the Christians from Macedonia brought me another gift. I have never yet asked you for one cent, and I never will. 10I promise this with every ounce of truth I possess—that I will tell everyone in Greece about it! 11Why? Because I don't love you? God knows I do. 12But I will do it to cut out the ground from under the feet of those who boast that they are doing God's work in just the same way we are.

13God never sent those men at all; they are "phonies" who have fooled you into thinking they are Christ's apostles. 14Yet I am not surprised! Satan can change himself into an angel of light, 15so it is no wonder his servants can do it too, and seem like godly ministers. In the end they will get every bit of punishment their wicked deeds deserve.

PSALM 53:1–6

O NLY a fool would say to himself, "There is no God." And why does he say it? Because of his wicked heart, his dark and evil deeds. His life is corroded with sin.

²God looks down from heaven, searching among all mankind to see if there is a single one who does right and really seeks for God. ³But all have turned their backs on him; they are filthy with sin—corrupt and rotten through and through. Not one is good, not one! ⁴How can this be? Can't they understand anything? For they devour my people like bread and refuse to come to God. ⁵But soon unheard-of terror will fall on them. God will scatter the bones of these, your enemies. They are doomed, for God has rejected them.

⁶Oh, that God would come from Zion now and save Israel! Only when the Lord himself restores them can they ever be really happy again.

PROVERBS FOR TODAY/ 22:28–29

Do not move the ancient boundary marks. That is stealing. Do you know a hardworking man? He shall be successful and stand before kings!

SEPTEMBER 10

ISAIAH 6:1—7:25

THE year King Uzziah died I saw the Lord! He was sitting on a lofty throne, and the Temple was filled with his glory. ²Hovering about him were mighty, six-winged angels of fire. With two of their wings they covered their faces; with two others they covered their feet, and with two they flew. ³In a great antiphonal chorus they sang, "Holy, holy, holy is the Lord Almighty; the whole earth is filled with his glory." ⁴Such singing it was! It shook the Temple to its foundations, and suddenly the entire sanctuary was filled with smoke.

⁵Then I said, "My doom is sealed, for I am a foul-mouthed sinner, a member of a sinful, foul-mouthed race; and I have looked upon the King, the Lord of heaven's armies."

⁶Then one of the mighty angels flew over to the altar and with a pair of tongs picked out a burning coal. ⁷He touched my lips with it and said, "Now you are pronounced 'Not guilty' because this coal has touched your lips. Your sins are all forgiven."

⁸Then I heard the Lord asking, "Whom shall I send as a messenger to my people? Who will go?"

And I said, "Lord, I'll go! Send *me.*"

⁹And he said, "Yes, go. But tell my people this: 'Though you hear my words repeatedly, you won't understand them. Though you watch and watch as I perform my miracles, still you won't know what they mean.' ¹⁰Dull their understanding, close their ears and shut their eyes. I don't want them to see or to hear or to understand, or to turn to me to heal them."

¹¹Then I said, "Lord, how long will it be before they are ready to listen?"

And he replied, "Not until their cities are destroyed—without a person left—and the whole country is an utter wasteland, ¹²and they are all taken away as slaves to other countries far away, and all the land of Israel lies deserted! ¹³Yet a tenth—a remnant—will survive; and though Israel is invaded again and again and destroyed, yet Israel will be like a tree cut down, whose stump still lives to grow again."

DURING the reign of Ahaz (the son of Jotham and grandson of Uzziah), Jerusalem was attacked by King Rezin of Syria and King Pekah of Israel (the son of Remaliah). But it was not taken; the city stood. ²However, when the news came to the royal court, "Syria is allied with Israel against us!" the hearts of the king and his people trembled with fear as the trees of a forest shake in a storm.

³Then the Lord said to Isaiah, "Go out to meet King Ahaz, you and Shear-jashub, your son. You will find him at the end of the aqueduct which leads from Gihon Spring to the upper reservoir, near the road that leads down to the bleaching field. ⁴Tell him to quit worrying. Tell him he needn't be frightened by the fierce anger of those two has-beens, Rezin and Pekah. ⁵Yes, the kings of Syria and Israel are coming against you.

"They say, ⁶'We will invade Judah and throw her people into panic. Then we'll fight our way into Jerusalem and install the son of Tabeel as their king.'

⁷"But the Lord God says, This plan will not succeed, ⁸for Damascus will remain the capital of Syria alone, and King Rezin's kingdom will not increase its boundaries. And within sixty-five years Ephraim, too, will be crushed and broken. ⁹Samaria is the capital of Ephraim alone and King Pekah's power will not increase. You don't believe me? If you want me to protect you, you must learn to believe what I say."

¹⁰Not long after this, the Lord sent this further message to King Ahaz:

¹¹"Ask me for a sign, Ahaz, to prove that I will indeed crush your enemies as I have said. Ask anything you like, in heaven or on earth."

¹²But the king refused. "No," he said, "I'll not bother the Lord with anything like that." ¹³Then Isaiah said, O House of David, you aren't satisfied to exhaust *my* patience; you exhaust the Lord's as well! ¹⁴All right then, the Lord himself will choose the sign—a child shall be born to a virgin! And she shall call him Immanuel (meaning, "God is with us"). ¹⁵,¹⁶By the time this child is weaned and knows right from wrong, the two kings you fear so much—the kings of Israel and Syria—will both be dead.

¹⁷But later on, the Lord will bring a terrible curse on you and on your nation and your family. There will be terror, such as has not been known since the division of Solomon's empire into Israel and Judah—the mighty king of Assyria will come with his great army! ¹⁸At that time the Lord will whistle for the army of Upper Egypt, and of Assyria too, to swarm down upon you like flies and destroy you, like bees to sting and to kill. ¹⁹They will come in vast hordes, spreading across the whole land, even into the desolate valleys and caves and thorny parts, as well as to all your fertile acres. ²⁰In that day the Lord will take this "razor"—these Assyrians you have hired to save you—and use it on you to shave off everything you have: your land, your crops, your people.

²¹,²²When they finally stop plundering, the whole nation will be a pastureland; whole flocks and herds will be destroyed, and a farmer will be fortunate to have a cow and two sheep left. But the abundant pastureland will yield plenty of milk, and everyone left will live on curds and wild honey. ²³At that time the lush vineyards will become patches of briars. ²⁴All the land will be one vast thornfield, a hunting ground overrun by wildlife. ²⁵No one will go to the fertile hillsides where once the gardens grew, for thorns will cover them; cattle, sheep and goats will graze there.

2 CORINTHIANS 11:16–33

AGAIN I plead, don't think that I have lost my wits to talk like this; but even if you do, listen to me anyway—a witless man, a fool—while I also boast a little as they do. ¹⁷Such bragging isn't something the Lord commanded me to do, for I am acting like a brainless fool. ¹⁸Yet those other men keep telling you how wonderful they are, so here I go: ¹⁹,²⁰(You think you are so wise—yet you listen gladly to those fools; you don't mind at all when they make you their slaves and take everything you have, and take advantage of you, and put on airs, and slap you in the face. 21I'm ashamed to say that I'm not strong and daring like that!

But whatever they can boast about—I'm talking like a fool again—I can boast about it, too.)

22They brag that they are Hebrews, do they? Well, so am I. And they say that they are Israelites, God's chosen people? So am I. And they are descendants of Abraham? Well, I am too.

23They say they serve Christ? But I have served him far more! (Have I gone mad to boast like this?) I have worked harder, been put in jail oftener, been whipped times without number, and faced death again and again and again. 24Five different times the Jews gave me their terrible thirty-nine lashes. 25Three times I was beaten with rods. Once I was stoned. Three times I was shipwrecked. Once I was in the open sea all night and the whole next day. 26I have traveled many weary miles and have been often in great danger from flooded rivers, and from robbers, and from my own people, the Jews, as well as from the hands of the Gentiles. I have faced grave dangers from mobs in the cities and from death in the deserts and in the stormy seas and from men who claim to be brothers in Christ but are not. 27I have lived with weariness and pain and sleepless nights. Often I have been hungry and thirsty and have gone without food; often I have shivered with cold, without enough clothing to keep me warm.

28Then, besides all this, I have the constant worry of how the churches are getting along: 29Who makes a mistake and I do not feel his sadness? Who falls without my longing to help him? Who is spiritually hurt without my fury rising against the one who hurt him?

30But if I must brag, I would rather brag about the things that show how weak I am. 31God, the Father of our Lord Jesus Christ, who is to be praised forever and ever, knows I tell the truth. 32For instance, in Damascus the governor under King Aretas kept guards at the city gates to catch me; 33but I was let down by rope and basket from a hole in the city wall, and so I got away! [What popularity!]

PSALM 54:1–7

COME with great power, O God, and save me! Defend me with your might! 2Oh, listen to my prayer. 3For violent men have risen against me—ruthless men who care nothing for God are seeking my life.

4But God is my helper. He is a friend of mine! 5He will cause the evil deeds of my enemies to boomerang upon them. Do as you promised and put an end to these wicked men, O God. 6Gladly I bring my sacrifices to you; I will praise your name, O Lord, for it is good.

7God has rescued me from all my trouble, and triumphed over my enemies.

PROVERBS FOR TODAY/ 23:1–3

When dining with a rich man, be on your guard and don't stuff yourself, though it all tastes so good; for he is trying to bribe you, and no good is going to come of his invitation.

ISAIAH 8:1—9:21

AGAIN the Lord sent me a message: "Make a large signboard and write on it the birth announcement of the son I am going to give you. Use capital letters! His name will be Maher-shalal-hash-baz, which means 'Your enemies will soon be destroyed.' " 2I asked Uriah the priest and Zechariah the son of Jeberechiah, both known as honest men, to watch me as I wrote so they could testify that I had written it [before the child was even on the way]. 3Then I had sexual intercourse with my wife and she conceived, and bore me a son, and the Lord said, "Call him Maher-shalal-hash-baz. 4This name prophesies that within a couple of years, before this child is even old enough to say 'Daddy' or 'Mommy,' the king of Assyria will invade both Damascus and Samaria and carry away their riches."

5Then the Lord spoke to me again and said:

6"Since the people of Jerusalem are planning to refuse my gentle care and are enthusiastic about asking King Rezin and King Pekah to come and aid them, 7,8therefore I will overwhelm my people with Euphrates' mighty flood; the king of Assyria and all his mighty armies will rage against them. This flood will overflow all its channels and sweep into your land of Judah, O Immanuel, submerging it from end to end."

9,10Do your worst, O Syria and Israel, our enemies, but you will not succeed—you will be shattered. Listen to me, all you enemies of ours: Prepare for war against us—and perish! Yes! Perish! Call your councils of war, develop your strategies, prepare your plans of attacking us, and perish! For God is with us.

11The Lord has said in strongest terms: Do not under any circumstances go along with the plans of Judah to surrender to Syria and Israel. 12Don't let people call you a traitor for staying true

to God. Don't you panic as so many of your neighbors are doing when they think of Syria and Israel attacking you. 13Don't fear anything except the Lord of the armies of heaven! If you fear him, you need fear nothing else. 14,15He will be your safety; but Israel and Judah have refused his care and thereby stumbled against the Rock of their salvation and lie fallen and crushed beneath it: God's presence among them has endangered them! 16Write down all these things I am going to do, says the Lord, and seal it up for the future. Entrust it to some godly man to pass on down to godly men of future generations.

17I will wait for the Lord to help us, though he is hiding now. My only hope is in him. 18I and the children God has given me have symbolic names that reveal the plans of the Lord of heaven's armies for his people: Isaiah means "Jehovah will save (his people)," Shear-jashub means "A remnant shall return," and Maher-shalal-hash-baz means "Your enemies will soon be destroyed." 19So why are you trying to find out the future by consulting witches and mediums? Don't listen to their whisperings and mutterings. Can the living find out the future from the dead? Why not ask your God?

20"Check these witches' words against the Word of God!" he says. "If their messages are different than mine, it is because I have not sent them; for they have no light or truth in them. 21My people will be led away captive, stumbling, weary and hungry. And because they are hungry they will rave and shake their fists at heaven and curse their King and their God. 22Wherever they look there will be trouble and anguish and dark despair. And they will be thrust out into the darkness."

NEVERTHELESS, that time of darkness and despair shall not go on forever. Though soon the land of Zebulun and Naphtali will be under God's contempt and judgment, yet in the future these very lands, Galilee and Northern Transjordan, where lies the road to the sea, will be filled with glory. ²The people who walk in darkness shall see a great Light—a Light that will shine on all those who live in the land of the shadow of death. ³For Israel will again be great, filled with joy like that of reapers when the harvest time has come, and like that of men dividing up the plunder they have won. ⁴For God will break the chains that bind his people and the whip that scourges them, just as he did when he destroyed the vast host of the Midianites by Gideon's little band. ⁵In that glorious day of peace there will no longer be the issuing of battle gear; no more the blood-stained uniforms of war; all such will be burned.

⁶For unto us a Child is born; unto us a Son is given; and the government shall be upon his shoulder. These will be his royal titles: "Wonderful," "Counselor," "The Mighty God," "The Everlasting Father," "The Prince of Peace." ⁷His ever-expanding, peaceful government will never end. He will rule with perfect fairness and justice from the throne of his father David. He will bring true justice and peace to all the nations of the world. This is going to happen because the Lord of heaven's armies has dedicated himself to do it!

⁸,⁹,¹⁰The Lord has spoken out against that braggart Israel who says that though our land lies in ruins now, we will rebuild it better than before. The sycamore trees are cut down, but we will replace them with cedars! ¹¹,¹²The Lord's reply to your bragging is to bring your enemies against you—the Syrians on the east and the Philistines on the west. With bared fangs they will devour Israel. And even then the Lord's anger against you will not be satisfied—his fist will still be poised to smash you. ¹³For after all this punishment you will not repent and turn to him, the Lord of heaven's armies. ¹⁴,¹⁵Therefore the Lord, in one day, will destroy the leaders of Israel and the lying prophets. ¹⁶For the leaders of his people have led them down the paths of ruin.

¹⁷That is why the Lord has no joy in their young men, and no mercy upon even the widows and orphans, for they are all filthy-mouthed, wicked liars. That is why his anger is not yet satisfied, but his fist is still poised to smash them all. ¹⁸He will burn up all this wickedness, these thorns and briars; and the flames will consume the forests, too, and send a vast cloud of smoke billowing up from their burning. ¹⁹,²⁰The land is blackened by that fire, by the wrath of the Lord of heaven's armies. The people are fuel for the fire. Each fights against his brother to steal his food, but will never have enough. Finally they will even eat their own children! ²¹Manasseh against Ephraim and Ephraim against Manasseh—and both against Judah. Yet even after all of this, God's anger is not yet satisfied. His hand is still heavy upon them, to crush them.

2 CORINTHIANS 12:1–10

THIS boasting is all so foolish, but let me go on. Let me tell about the visions I've had, and revelations from the Lord.

²,³Fourteen years ago I was taken up to heaven for a visit. Don't ask me whether my body was there or just my spirit, for I don't know; only God can answer that. But anyway, there I was in paradise, ⁴and heard things so astounding that they are beyond a man's power to describe or put in words (and anyway I am not allowed to tell them to others). ⁵That experience is something worth bragging about, but I am not going to do it. I am going to boast only about how weak I am and how great God is to use such weakness for his glory. ⁶I have plenty to boast about and would be no fool in doing it, but I don't want anyone to think more highly of me than he should from what he can actually see in my life and my message.

⁷I will say this: because these experiences I had were so tremendous, God

was afraid I might be puffed up by them; so I was given a physical condition which has been a thorn in my flesh, a messenger from Satan to hurt and bother me, and prick my pride. 8Three different times I begged God to make me well again.

9Each time he said, "No. But I am with you; that is all you need. My power shows up best in weak people." Now I am glad to boast about how weak I am; I am glad to be a living demonstration of Christ's power, instead of showing off my own power and abilities. 10Since I know it is all for Christ's good, I am quite happy about "the thorn," and about insults and hardships, persecutions and difficulties; for when I am weak, then I am strong—the less I have, the more I depend on him.

PSALM 55:1–23

LISTEN to my prayer, O God; don't hide yourself when I cry to you. 2Hear me, Lord! Listen to me! For I groan and weep beneath my burden of woe.

3My enemies shout against me and threaten me with death. They surround me with terror and plot to kill me. Their fury and hatred rise to engulf me. 4My heart is in anguish within me. Stark fear overpowers me. 5Trembling and horror overwhelm me. 6Oh, for wings like a dove, to fly away and rest! 7I would fly to the far-off deserts and stay there. 8I would flee to some refuge from all this storm.

9O Lord, make these enemies begin to quarrel among themselves—destroy them with their own violence and strife.

10Though they patrol their walls night and day against invaders, their real problem is internal—wickedness and dishonesty are entrenched in the heart of the city. 11There is murder and robbery there, and cheating in the markets and wherever you look.

12It was not an enemy who taunted me—then I could have borne it; I could have hidden and escaped. 13But it was you, a man like myself, my companion and my friend. 14What fellowship we had, what wonderful discussions as we walked together to the Temple of the Lord on holy days.

15Let death seize them and cut them down in their prime, for there is sin in their homes, and they are polluted to the depths of their souls.

16But I will call upon the Lord to save me—and he will. 17I will pray morning, noon, and night, pleading aloud with God; and he will hear and answer. 18Though the tide of battle runs strongly against me, for so many are fighting me, yet he will rescue me. 19God himself—God from everlasting ages past—will answer them! For they refuse to fear him or even honor his commands.

20This friend of mine betrayed me— I who was at peace with him. He broke his promises. 21His words were oily smooth, but in his heart was war. His words were sweet, but underneath were daggers.

22Give your burdens to the Lord. He will carry them. He will not permit the godly to slip or fall. 23He will send my enemies to the pit of destruction. Murderers and liars will not live out half their days. But I am trusting you to save me.

PROVERBS FOR TODAY/ 23:4–5

Don't weary yourself trying to get rich. Why waste your time? For riches can disappear as though they had the wings of a bird!

SEPTEMBER 12

WOE to unjust judges and to those who issue unfair laws, says the Lord, ²so that there is no justice for the poor, the widows and orphans. Yes, it is true that they even rob the widows and fatherless children.

³Oh, what will you do when I visit you in that day when I send desolation upon you from a distant land? To whom will you turn then for your help? Where will your treasures be safe? ⁴I will not help you; you will stumble along as prisoners or lie among the slain. And even then my anger will not be satisfied, but my fist will still be poised to strike you. ⁵,⁶Assyria is the whip of my anger; his military strength is my weapon upon this godless nation, doomed and damned; he will enslave them and plunder them and trample them like dirt beneath his feet. ⁷But the king of Assyria will not know that it is I who sent him. He will merely think he is attacking my people as part of his plan to conquer the world. ⁸He will declare that every one of his princes will soon be a king, ruling a conquered land.

⁹"We will destroy Calno just as we did Carchemish," he will say, "and Hamath will go down before us as Arpad did; and we will destroy Samaria just as we did Damascus. ¹⁰Yes, we have finished off many a kingdom whose idols were far greater than those in Jerusalem and Samaria, ¹¹so when we have defeated Samaria and her idols we will destroy Jerusalem with hers."

¹²After the Lord has used the king of Assyria to accomplish his purpose, then he will turn upon the Assyrians and punish them too—for they are proud and haughty men.

¹³They boast, "We in our own power and wisdom have won these wars. We are great and wise. By our own strength we broke down the walls and destroyed the people and carried off their treasures. ¹⁴In our greatness we have robbed their nests of riches and gathered up kingdoms as a farmer gathers eggs, and no one can move a finger or open his mouth to peep against us!"

¹⁵But the Lord says, "Shall the axe boast greater power than the man who uses it? Is the saw greater than the man who saws? Can a rod strike unless a hand is moving it? Can a cane walk by itself?"

¹⁶Because of all your evil boasting, O king of Assyria, the Lord of Hosts will send a plague among your proud troops, and strike them down. ¹⁷God, the Light and Holy One of Israel, will be the fire and flame that will destroy them. In a single night he will burn those thorns and briars, the Assyrians who destroyed the land of Israel. ¹⁸Assyria's vast army is like a glorious forest, yet it will be destroyed. The Lord will destroy them, soul and body, as when a sick man wastes away. ¹⁹Only a few from all that mighty army will be left; so few a child could count them!

²⁰Then at last, those left in Israel and in Judah will trust the Lord, the Holy One of Israel, instead of fearing the Assyrians. ²¹A remnant of them will return to the mighty God. ²²But though Israel be now as many as the sands along the shore, yet only a few of them will be left to return at that time; God has rightly decided to destroy his people. ²³Yes, it has already been decided by the Lord God to consume them.

²⁴Therefore the Lord God says, "O my people in Jerusalem, don't be afraid of the Assyrians when they oppress you just as the Egyptians did long ago. ²⁵It will not last very long; in a little while my anger against you will end, and then it will rise against them to destroy them."

²⁶The Lord Almighty will send his angel to slay them in a mighty slaughter like the time when Gideon triumphed over Midian at the rock of Oreb or the

time God drowned the Egyptian armies in the sea. 27On that day God will end the bondage of his people. He will break the slave-yoke off their necks, and destroy it as decreed.

28,29Look, the mighty armies of Assyria are coming! Now they are at Aiath, now at Migron; they are storing some of their equipment at Michmash and crossing over the pass; they are staying overnight at Geba. Fear strikes the city of Ramah; all the people of Gibeah—the city of Saul—are running for their lives. 30Well may you scream in terror, O people of Gallim. Shout out a warning to Laish, for the mighty army comes. O poor Anathoth, what a fate is yours! 31There go the people of Madmenah, all fleeing, and the citizens of Gebim are preparing to run. 32But the enemy stops at Nob for the remainder of that day. He shakes his fist at Jerusalem on Mount Zion.

33Then, look, look! The Lord, the Lord of the armies of heaven, is chopping down the mighty tree! He is destroying all of that vast army, great and small alike, both officers and men. 34He, the Mighty One, will cut down the enemy as a woodsman's axe cuts down the forest trees in Lebanon.

THE royal line of David will be cut off, chopped down like a tree; but from the stump will grow a Shoot—yes, a new Branch from the old root. 2And the Spirit of the Lord shall rest upon him, the Spirit of wisdom, understanding, counsel and might; the Spirit of knowledge and of the fear of the Lord. 3His delight will be obedience to the Lord. He will not judge by appearance, false evidence, or hearsay, 4but will defend the poor and the exploited. He will rule against the wicked who oppress them. 5For he will be clothed with fairness and with truth.

6In that day the wolf and the lamb will lie down together, and the leopard and goats will be at peace. Calves and fat cattle will be safe among lions, and a little child shall lead them all. 7The cows will graze among bears; cubs and calves

will lie down together, and lions will eat grass like the cows. 8Babies will crawl safely among poisonous snakes, and a little child who puts his hand in a nest of deadly adders will pull it out unharmed. 9Nothing will hurt or destroy in all my holy mountain, for as the waters fill the sea, so shall the earth be full of the knowledge of the Lord.

10In that day he who created the royal dynasty of David will be a banner of salvation to all the world. The nations will rally to him, for the land where he lives will be a glorious place. 11At that time the Lord will bring back a remnant of his people for the second time, returning them to the land of Israel from Assyria, Upper and Lower Egypt, Ethiopia, Elam, Babylonia, Hamath and all the distant coastal lands. 12He will raise a flag among the nations for them to rally to; he will gather the scattered Israelites from the ends of the earth. 13Then, at last, the jealousy between Israel and Judah will end; they will not fight each other any more. 14Together they will fly against the nations possessing their land on the east and on the west, uniting forces to destroy them, and they will occupy the nations of Edom and Moab and Ammon.

15The Lord will dry a path through the Red Sea, and wave his hand over the Euphrates, sending a mighty wind to divide it into seven streams that can easily be crossed. 16He will make a highway from Assyria for the remnant there, just as he did for all of Israel long ago when they returned from Egypt.

2 CORINTHIANS 12:11–21

YOU have made me act like a fool—boasting like this—for you people ought to be writing about me and not making me write about myself. There isn't a single thing these other marvelous fellows have that I don't have too, even though I am really worth nothing at all. 12When I was there I certainly gave you every proof that I was truly an apostle, sent to you by God himself: for I patiently did many wonders and signs and mighty works among you. 13The only thing I didn't do for you, that I do everywhere else in all other churches, was to become a burden to you—I didn't ask you to give me food to eat and a place to stay. Please forgive me for this wrong!

14Now I am coming to you again, the third time; and it is still not going to cost you anything, for I don't want your money. I want *you!* And anyway, you are my children, and little children don't pay for their father's and mother's food—it's the other way around; parents supply food for their children. 15I am glad to give you myself and all I have for your spiritual good, even though it seems that the more I love you, the less you love me.

16Some of you are saying, "It's true that his visits didn't seem to cost us anything, but he is a sneaky fellow, that Paul, and he fooled us. As sure as anything he must have made money from us some way."

17But how? Did any of the men I sent to you take advantage of you? 18When I urged Titus to visit you, and sent our other brother with him, did they make any profit? No, of course not. For we have the same Holy Spirit, and walk in each other's steps, doing things the same way.

19I suppose you think I am saying all this to get back into your good graces. That isn't it at all. I tell you, with God listening as I say it, that I have said this to help *you,* dear friends—to build you up spiritually and not to help myself. 20For I am afraid that when I come to visit you I won't like what I find, and then you won't like the way I will have to act. I am afraid that I will find you quarreling, and envying each other, and being angry with each other, and acting big, and saying wicked things about each other and whispering behind each other's backs, filled with conceit and disunity. 21Yes, I am afraid that when I come God will humble me before you and I will be sad and mourn because many of you have sinned before and don't even care about the wicked, impure things you have done: your lust and immorality, and the taking of other men's wives.

PSALM 56:1–13

LORD, have mercy on me; all day long the enemy troops press in. So many are proud to fight against me; how they long to conquer me.

3,4But when I am afraid, I will put my confidence in you. Yes, I will trust the promises of God. And since I am trusting him, what can mere man do to me? 5They are always twisting what I say. All their thoughts are how to harm me. 6They meet together to perfect their plans; they hide beside the trail, listening for my steps, waiting to kill me 7They expect to get away with it. Don't let them, Lord. In anger cast them to the ground.

8You have seen me tossing and turning through the night. You have collected all my tears and preserved them in your bottle! You have recorded every one in your book.

9The very day I call for help, the tide of battle turns. My enemies flee! This one thing I *know: God is for me!* 10,11I am trusting God—oh, praise his promises! I am not afraid of anything mere man can do to me! Yes, praise his promises. 12I will surely do what I have promised, Lord, and thank you for your help. 13For you have saved me from death and my feet from slipping, so that I can walk before the Lord in the land of the living.

PROVERBS FOR TODAY/ 23:6–8

Don't associate with evil men; don't long for their favors and gifts. Their kindness is a trick; they want to use you as their pawn. The delicious food they serve will turn sour in your stomach and you will vomit it, and have to take back your words of appreciation for their "kindness."

SEPTEMBER 13

ISAIAH 12:1—14:32

O N that day you will say, "Praise the Lord! He was angry with me, but now he comforts me. ²See, God has come to save me! I will trust and not be afraid, for the Lord is my strength and song; he is my salvation. ³Oh, the joy of drinking deeply from the Fountain of Salvation!"

⁴In that wonderful day you will say, "Thank the Lord! Praise his name! Tell the world about his wondrous love. How mighty he is!" ⁵Sing to the Lord, for he has done wonderful things. Make known his praise around the world. ⁶Let all the people of Jerusalem shout his praise with joy. For great and mighty is the Holy One of Israel, who lives among you.

THIS is the vision God showed Isaiah (son of Amoz) concerning Babylon's doom.

²See the flags waving as their enemy attacks. Shout to them, O Israel, and wave them on as they march against Babylon to destroy the palaces of the rich and mighty. ³I, the Lord, have set apart these armies for this task; I have called those rejoicing in their strength to do this work, to satisfy my anger. ⁴Hear the tumult on the mountains! Listen as the armies march! It is the tumult and the shout of many nations. The Lord Almighty has brought them here, ⁵from countries far away. They are his weapons against you, O Babylon. They carry his anger with them and will destroy your whole land.

⁶Scream in terror, for the Lord's time has come, the time for the Almighty to crush you. ⁷Your arms lie paralyzed with fear; the strongest hearts melt, ⁸and are afraid. Fear grips you with terrible pangs, like those of a woman in labor. You look at one another, helpless, as the flames of the burning city reflect upon your pallid faces. ⁹For see, the day of the Lord is coming, the terrible day of his wrath

and fierce anger. The land shall be destroyed, and all the sinners with it. ¹⁰The heavens will be black above them. No light will shine from stars or sun or moon.

¹¹And I will punish the world for its evil, the wicked for their sin; I will crush the arrogance of the proud man and the haughtiness of the rich. ¹²Few will live when I have finished up my work.

Men will be as scarce as gold—of greater value than the gold of Ophir. ¹³For I will shake the heavens in my wrath and fierce anger, and the earth will move from its place in the skies.

¹⁴The armies of Babylon will run until exhausted, fleeing back to their own land like deer chased by dogs, wandering like sheep deserted by their shepherd. ¹⁵Those who don't run will be butchered. ¹⁶Their little children will be dashed to death against the pavement right before their eyes; their homes will be sacked, and their wives raped by the attacking hordes. ¹⁷For I will stir up the Medes against Babylon, and no amount of silver or gold will buy them off. ¹⁸The attacking armies will have no mercy on the young people of Babylon or the babies or the children.

¹⁹And so Babylon, the most glorious of kingdoms, the flower of Chaldean culture, will be as utterly destroyed as Sodom and Gomorrah were when God sent fire from heaven; ²⁰Babylon will never rise again. Generation after generation will come and go, but the land will never again be lived in. The nomads will not even camp there. The shepherds won't let their sheep stay overnight. ²¹The wild animals of the desert will make it their home. The houses will be haunted by howling creatures. Ostriches will live there, and the demons will come there to dance. ²²Hyenas and jackals will den within the palaces. Babylon's days are numbered; her time of doom will soon be here.

BUT the Lord will have mercy on the Israelis; they are still his special ones. He will bring them back to settle once again in the land of Israel. And many nationalities will come and join them there and be their loyal allies. 2The nations of the world will help them to return, and those coming to live in their land will serve them. Those enslaving Israel will be enslaved—Israel shall rule her enemies!

3In that wonderful day when the Lord gives his people rest from sorrow and fear, from slavery and chains, 4you will jeer at the king of Babylon and say, "You bully, you! At last you have what was coming to you! 5For the Lord has crushed your wicked power, and broken your evil rule." 6You persecuted my people with unceasing blows of rage and held the nations in your angry grip. You were unrestrained in tyranny. 7But at last the whole earth is at rest and is quiet! All the world begins to sing! 8Even the trees of the woods—the fir trees and cedars of Lebanon—sing out this joyous song: "Your power is broken; no one will bother us now; at last we have peace."

9The denizens of hell crowd to meet you as you enter their domain. World leaders and earth's mightiest kings, long dead, are there to see you. 10With one voice they all cry out, "Now you are as weak as we are!" 11Your might and power are gone; they are buried with you. All the pleasant music in your palace has ceased; now maggots are your sheet, worms your blanket!

12How you are fallen from heaven, O Lucifer, son of the morning! How you are cut down to the ground—mighty though you were against the nations of the world. 13For you said to yourself, "I will ascend to heaven and rule the angels. I will take the highest throne. I will preside on the Mount of Assembly far away in the north. 14I will climb to the highest heavens and be like the Most High." 15But instead, you will be brought down to the pit of hell, down to its lowest depths. 16Everyone there will stare at you and ask, "Can this be the one who shook

the earth and the kingdoms of the world? 17Can this be the one who destroyed the world and made it into a shambles and demolished its greatest cities and had no mercy on his prisoners?"

18The kings of the nations lie in stately glory in their graves, 19but your body is thrown out like a broken branch; it lies in an open grave, covered with the dead bodies of those slain in battle. It lies as a carcass in the road, trampled and mangled by horses' hoofs. 20No monument will be given you, for you have destroyed your nation and slain your people. Your son will not succeed you as the king. 21Slay the children of this sinner. Do not let them rise and conquer the land nor rebuild the cities of the world.

22I, myself, have risen against him, says the Lord of heaven's armies, and will cut off his children and his children's children from ever sitting on his throne. 23I will make Babylon into a desolate land of porcupines, full of swamps and marshes. I will sweep the land with the broom of destruction, says the Lord of the armies of heaven. 24He has taken an oath to do it! For this is his purpose and plan. 25I have decided to break the Assyrian army when they are in Israel and to crush them on my mountains; my people shall no longer be their slaves. 26This is my plan for the whole earth— I will do it by my mighty power that reaches everywhere around the world. 27The Lord, the God of battle, has spoken—who can change his plans? When his hand moves, who can stop him?

28This is the message that came to me the year King Ahaz died:

29Don't rejoice, Philistines, that the king who smote you is dead. That rod is broken, yes; but his son will be a greater scourge to you than his father ever was! From the snake will be born an adder, a fiery serpent to destroy you! 30I will shepherd the poor of my people; they shall graze in my pasture! The needy shall lie down in peace. But as for you— I will wipe you out with famine and the sword. 31Weep, Philistine cities—you are doomed. All your nation is doomed. For a perfectly trained army is coming down from the north against you. 32What then shall we tell the reporters? Tell them that the Lord has founded Jerusalem and is determined that the poor of his people will find a refuge within her walls.

2 CORINTHIANS 13:1–14

THIS is the third time I am coming to visit you. The Scriptures tell us that if two or three have seen a wrong, it must be punished. [Well, this is my third warning, as I come now for this visit.] 2I have already warned those who had been sinning when I was there last; now I warn them again, and all others, just as I did then, that this time I come ready to punish severely and I will not spare them.

3I will give you all the proof you want that Christ speaks through me. Christ is not weak in his dealings with you, but is a mighty power within you. 4His weak, human body died on the cross, but now he lives by the mighty power of God. We, too, are weak in our bodies, as he was, but now we live and are strong, as he is, and have all of God's power to use in dealing with you.

5Check up on yourselves. Are you really Christians? Do you pass the test? Do you feel Christ's presence and power more and more within you? Or are you just pretending to be Christians when actually you aren't at all? 6I hope you can agree that I have stood that test and truly belong to the Lord.

7I pray that you will live good lives, not because that will be a feather in our caps, proving that what we teach is right; no, for we want you to do right even if we ourselves are despised. 8Our responsibility is to encourage the right at all times, not to hope for evil. 9We are glad to be weak and despised if you are really strong. Our greatest wish and prayer is that you will become mature Christians.

10I am writing this to you now in the hope that I won't need to scold and punish when I come; for I want to use the Lord's authority which he has given me, not to punish you but to make you strong.

11I close my letter with these last words:

Be happy.
Grow in Christ.
Pay attention to what I have said.
Live in harmony and peace.

And may the God of love and peace be with you.

12Greet each other warmly in the Lord. 13All the Christians here send you their best regards. 14May the grace of our Lord Jesus Christ be with you all. May God's love and the Holy Spirit's friendship be yours.

Paul

PSALM 57:1–11

O God, have pity, for I am trusting you! I will hide beneath the shadow of your wings until this storm is past. 2I will cry to the God of heaven who does such wonders for me. 3He will send down help from heaven to save me, because of his love and his faithfulness. He will rescue me from these liars who are so intent upon destroying me. 4I am surrounded by fierce lions—hotheads whose teeth are sharp as spears and arrows. Their tongues are like swords. 5Lord, be exalted above the highest heavens! Show your glory high above the earth. 6My enemies have set a trap for me. Frantic fear grips me. They have dug a pitfall in my path. But look! They themselves have fallen into it!

7O God, my heart is quiet and confident. No wonder I can sing your praises! 8Rouse yourself, my soul! Arise, O harp and lyre! Let us greet the dawn with song! 9I will thank you publicly throughout the land. I will sing your praises among the nations. 10Your kindness and love are as vast as the heavens. Your faithfulness is higher than the skies.

11Yes, be exalted, O God, above the heavens. May your glory shine throughout the earth.

Don't waste your breath on a rebel. He will despise the wisest advice. Don't steal the land of defenseless orphans by moving their ancient boundary marks, for their Redeemer is strong; he himself will accuse you.

SEPTEMBER 14

ISAIAH 15:1—18:7

HERE is God's message to Moab: In one night your cities of Ar and Kir will be destroyed. ²Your people in Dibon go mourning to their temples to weep for the fate of Nebo and Medeba; they shave their heads in sorrow and cut off their beards. ³They wear sackcloth through the streets, and from every home comes the sound of weeping. ⁴The cries from the cities of Heshbon and Elealeh are heard far away, even in Jahaz. The bravest warriors of Moab cry in utter terror.

⁵My heart weeps for Moab! His people flee to Zoar and Eglath. Weeping, they climb the upward road to Luhith, and their crying will be heard all along the road to Horonaim. ⁶Even Nimrim River is desolate! The grassy banks are dried up and the tender plants are gone. ⁷The desperate refugees take only the possessions they can carry, and flee across the Brook of Willows. ⁸The whole land of Moab is a land of weeping, from one end to the other. ⁹The stream near Dibon will run red with blood, but I am not through with Dibon yet! Lions will hunt down the survivors, both those who escape and those who remain.

MOAB'S refugees at Sela send lambs as a token of alliance with the king of Judah. ²The women of Moab are left at the fords of the Arnon River like homeless birds. ³[The ambassadors, who accompany the gift to Jerusalem] plead for advice and help. "Give us sanctuary. Protect us. Do

not turn us over to our foes. ⁴,⁵Let our outcasts stay among you; hide them from our enemies! God will reward you for your kindness to us. If you let Moab's fugitives settle among you, then, when the terror is past, God will establish David's throne forever, and on that throne he will place a just and righteous King."

⁶Is this proud Moab, concerning which we heard so much? His arrogance and insolence are all gone now! ⁷Therefore all Moab weeps. Yes, Moab, you will mourn for stricken Kir-hareseth, ⁸and for the abandoned farms of Heshbon and the vineyards at Sibmah. The enemy war-lords have cut down the best of the grape vines; their armies spread out as far as Jazer in the deserts, and even down to the sea. ⁹So I wail and lament for Jazer and the vineyards of Sibmah. My tears shall flow for Heshbon and Elealeh, for destruction has come upon their summer fruits and harvests. ¹⁰Gone now is the gladness, gone the joy of harvest. The happy singing in the vineyards will be heard no more; the treading out of the grapes in the wine presses has ceased forever. I have ended all their harvest joys.

¹¹I will weep, weep, weep, for Moab; and my sorrow for Kir-haresh will be very great. ¹²The people of Moab will pray in anguish to their idols at the tops of the hills, but it will do no good; they will cry to their gods in their idol temples, but none will come to save them. ¹³,¹⁴All this concerning Moab has been said before; but now the Lord says that within three years, without fail, the glory

of Moab shall be ended, and few of all its people will be left alive.

THIS is God's message to Damascus, capital of Syria:

Look, Damascus is gone! It is no longer a city—it has become a heap of ruins! 2The cities of Aroer are deserted. Sheep pasture there, lying quiet and unafraid, with no one to chase them away. 3The strength of Israel and the power of Damascus will end, and the remnant of Syria shall be destroyed. For as Israel's glory departed, so theirs, too, will disappear, declares the Lord Almighty. 4Yes, the glory of Israel will be very dim when poverty stalks the land. 5Israel will be as abandoned as the harvested grain fields in the Valley of Rephaim. 6Oh, a very few of her people will be left, just as a few stray olives are left on the trees when the harvest is ended, two or three in the highest branches, four or five out on the tips of the limbs. That is how it will be in Damascus and Israel—stripped bare of people except for a few of the poor who remain.

7Then at last they will think of God their Creator and have respect for the Holy One of Israel. 8They will no longer ask their idols for help in that day, neither will they worship what their hands have made! They will no longer have respect for the images of Ashtaroth and the sun-idols.

9Their largest cities will be as deserted as the distant wooded hills and mountain tops and become like the abandoned cities of the Amorites, deserted when the Israelites approached (so long ago). 10Why? Because you have turned from the God who can save you—the Rock who can hide you; therefore, even though you plant a wonderful, rare crop of greatest value, 11and though it grows so well that it will blossom on the very morning that you plant it, yet you will never harvest it—your only harvest will be a pile of grief and incurable pain.

12Look, see the armies thundering toward God's land. 13But though they roar like breakers rolling upon a beach, God will silence them. They will flee, scattered like chaff by the wind, like whirling dust before a storm. 14In the evening Israel waits in terror, but by dawn her enemies are dead. This is the just reward of those who plunder and destroy the people of God.

AH, land beyond the upper reaches of the Nile, where winged sailboats glide along the river! 2Land that sends ambassadors in fast boats down the Nile! Let swift messengers return to you, O strong and supple nation feared far and wide, a conquering, destroying nation whose land the upper Nile divides. And this is the message sent to you:

3When I raise my battle flag upon the mountain, let all the world take notice! When I blow the trumpet, listen! 4For the Lord has told me this: Let your mighty army now advance against the land of Israel. God will watch quietly from his Temple in Jerusalem—serene as on a pleasant summer day or a lovely autumn morning during harvest time. 5But before you have begun the attack, and while your plans are ripening like grapes, he will cut you off as though with pruning shears. He will snip the spreading tendrils. 6Your mighty army will be left dead on the field for the mountain birds and wild animals to eat; the vultures will tear bodies all summer, and the wild animals will gnaw bones all winter. 7But the time will come when that strong and mighty nation, a terror to all both far and near, that conquering, destroying nation whose land the rivers divide, will bring gifts to the Lord Almighty in Jerusalem, where he has placed his name.

GALATIANS 1:1–24

FROM: Paul the missionary and all the other Christians here.

To: The churches of Galatia.

I was not called to be a missionary by any group or agency. My call is from Jesus Christ himself, and from God the Father who raised him from the dead.

3May peace and blessing be yours from God the Father and from the Lord Jesus Christ. 4He died for our sins just as God our Father planned, and rescued us from this evil world in which we live. 5All glory to God through all the ages of eternity. Amen.

6I am amazed that you are turning away so soon from God who, in his love and mercy, invited you to share the eternal life he gives through Christ; you are already following a different "way to heaven," which really doesn't go to heaven at all. 7For there is no other way than the one we showed you; you are being fooled by those who twist and change the truth concerning Christ.

8Let God's curses fall on anyone, including myself, who preaches any other way to be saved than the one we told you about; yes, if an angel comes from heaven and preaches any other message, let him be forever cursed. 9I will say it again: if anyone preaches any other Gospel than the one you welcomed, let God's curse fall upon him.

10You can see that I am not trying to please you by sweet talk and flattery; no, I am trying to please God. If I were still trying to please men I could not be Christ's servant.

11Dear friends, I solemnly swear that the way to heaven which I preach is not based on some mere human whim or dream. 12For my message comes from no less a person than Jesus Christ himself, who told me what to say. No one else has taught me.

13You know what I was like when I followed the Jewish religion—how I went after the Christians mercilessly, hunting them down and doing my best to get rid of them all. 14I was one of the most religious Jews of my own age in the whole country, and tried as hard as I possibly could to follow all the old, traditional rules of my religion.

15But then something happened! For even before I was born God had chosen me to be his, and called me—what kindness and grace— 16to reveal his Son within me so that I could go to the Gentiles and show them the Good News about Jesus.

When all this happened to me I didn't go at once and talk it over with anyone else; 17I didn't go up to Jerusalem to consult with those who were apostles before I was. No, I went away into the deserts of Arabia, and then came back to the city of Damascus. 18It was not until three years later that I finally went to Jerusalem for a visit with Peter, and stayed there with him for fifteen days. 19And the only other apostle I met at that time was James, our Lord's brother. 20(Listen to what I am saying, for I am telling you this in the very presence of God. This is exactly what happened—I am not lying to you.) 21Then after this visit I went to Syria and Cilicia. 22And still the Christians in Judea didn't even know what I looked like. 23All they knew was what people were saying, that "our former enemy is now preaching the very faith he tried to wreck." 24And they gave glory to God because of me.

PSALM 58:1–11

JUSTICE? You high and mighty politicians don't even know the meaning of the word! Fairness? Which of you has any left? Not one! All your dealings are crooked: you give "justice" in exchange for bribes. 3These men are born sinners, lying from their earliest words! 4,5They are poisonous as deadly snakes, cobras that close their ears to the most expert of charmers.

6O God, break off their fangs. Tear out the teeth of these young lions, Lord. 7Let them disappear like water into thirsty ground. Make their weapons useless in their hands. 8Let them be as snails that dissolve into slime; and as those who die at birth, who never see the sun. 9God will sweep away both old and young. He will destroy them more quickly than a cooking pot can feel the blazing fire of thorns beneath it.

10The godly shall rejoice in the triumph of right; they shall walk the blood-stained fields of slaughtered, wicked men. ¹¹Then at last everyone will know that good is rewarded, and that there is a God who judges justly here on earth.

PROVERBS FOR TODAY/ 23:12
Don't refuse to accept criticism; get all the help you can.

SEPTEMBER 15

ISAIAH 19:1—21:17

T HIS is God's message concerning Egypt:
Look, the Lord is coming against Egypt, riding on a swift cloud; the idols of Egypt tremble; the hearts of the Egyptians melt with fear. ²I will set them to fighting against each other—brother against brother, neighbor against neighbor, city against city, province against province. ³Her wise counselors are all at their wits' ends to know what to do; they plead with their idols for wisdom, and call upon mediums, wizards and witches to show them what to do.

⁴I will hand over Egypt to a hard, cruel master, to a vicious king, says the Lord Almighty. ⁵And the waters of the Nile will fail to rise and flood the fields; the ditches will be parched and dry, ⁶their channels fouled with rotting reeds. ⁷All green things along the river bank will wither and blow away. All crops will perish; everything will die. ⁸The fishermen will weep for lack of work; those who fish with hooks and those who use the nets will all be unemployed. ⁹The weavers will have no flax or cotton, for the crops will fail. ¹⁰Great men and small—all will be crushed and broken.

¹¹What fools the counselors of Zoan are! Their best counsel to the king of Egypt is utterly stupid and wrong. Will they still boast of their wisdom? Will they dare tell Pharaoh about the long line of wise men they have come from? ¹²What has happened to your "wise counselors," O Pharaoh? Where has their wis-

dom gone? If they are wise, let them tell you what the Lord is going to do to Egypt. ¹³The "wise men" from Zoan are also fools, and those from Memphis are utterly deluded. They are the best you can find, but they have ruined Egypt with their foolish counsel. ¹⁴The Lord has sent a spirit of foolishness on them, so that all their suggestions are wrong; they make Egypt stagger like a sick drunkard. ¹⁵Egypt cannot be saved by anything or anybody—no one can show her the way.

¹⁶In that day the Egyptians will be as weak as women, cowering in fear beneath the upraised fist of God. ¹⁷Just to speak the name of Israel will strike deep terror in their hearts, for the Lord Almighty has laid his plans against them.

¹⁸At that time five of the cities of Egypt will follow the Lord Almighty and will begin to speak the Hebrew language. One of these will be Heliopolis, "The City of the Sun." ¹⁹And there will be an altar to the Lord in the heart of Egypt in those days, and a monument to the Lord at its border. ²⁰This will be for a sign of loyalty to the Lord Almighty; then when they cry to the Lord for help against those who oppress them, he will send them a Savior—and he shall deliver them.

²¹In that day the Lord will make himself known to the Egyptians. Yes, they will know the Lord and give their sacrifices and offerings to him; they will make promises to God and keep them. ²²The Lord will smite Egypt and then restore her! For the Egyptians will turn

to the Lord and he will listen to their plea and heal them.

23In that day Egypt and Iraq will be connected by a highway, and the Egyptians and the Iraqi will move freely back and forth between their lands, and they shall worship the same God. 24And Israel will be their ally; the three will be together, and Israel will be a blessing to them. 25For the Lord will bless Egypt and Iraq because of their friendship with Israel. He will say, "Blessed be Egypt, my people; blessed be Iraq, the land I have made; blessed be Israel, my inheritance!"

IN the year when Sargon, king of Assyria, sent the commander-in-chief of his army against the Philistine city of Ashdod and captured it, 2the Lord told Isaiah, the son of Amoz, to take off his clothing, including his shoes, and to walk around naked and barefoot. And Isaiah did as he was told.

3Then the Lord said, My servant Isaiah, who has been walking naked and barefoot for the last three years, is a symbol of the terrible troubles I will bring upon Egypt and Ethiopia. 4For the king of Assyria will take away the Egyptians and Ethiopians as prisoners, making them walk naked and barefoot, both young and old, their buttocks uncovered, to the shame of Egypt. 5,6Then how dismayed the Philistines will be, who counted on "Ethiopia's power" and their "glorious ally," Egypt! And they will say, "If this can happen to Egypt, what chance have we?"

THIS is God's message concerning Babylon:

Disaster is roaring down upon you from the terrible desert, like a whirlwind sweeping from the Negeb. 2I see an awesome vision: oh, the horror of it all! God is telling me what he is going to do. I see you plundered and destroyed. Elamites and Medes will take part in the siege. Babylon will fall, and the groaning of all the nations she enslaved will end. 3My stomach constricts and burns with pain; sharp pangs of horror are upon me, like the pangs of a woman giving birth to a child. I faint when I hear what God is planning; I am terrified, blinded with dismay. 4My mind reels; my heart races; I am gripped by awful fear. All rest at night—so pleasant once—is gone; I lie awake, trembling.

5Look! They are preparing a great banquet! They load the tables with food; they pull up their chairs to eat. . . . Quick, quick, grab your shields and prepare for battle! You are being attacked!

6,7Meanwhile (in my vision) the Lord had told me, "Put a watchman on the city wall to shout out what he sees. When he sees riders in pairs on donkeys and camels, tell him, 'This is it!' "

8,9So I put the watchman on the wall, and at last he shouted, "Sir, day after day and night after night I have been here at my post. Now at last—look! Here come riders in pairs!"

Then I heard a Voice shout out, "Babylon is fallen, is fallen; and all the idols of Babylon lie broken on the ground."

10O my people, threshed and winnowed, I have told you all that the Lord Almighty, the God of Israel, has said.

11This is God's message to Edom:

Someone from among you keeps calling, calling to me: "Watchman, what of the night? Watchman, what of the night? How much time is left?" 12The watchman replies, "Your judgment day is dawning now. Turn again to God, so that I can give you better news. Seek for him, then come and ask again!"

13This is God's message concerning Arabia:

O caravans from Dedan, you will hide in the deserts of Arabia. 14O people of Tema, bring food and water to these weary fugitives! 15They have fled from drawn swords and sharp arrows and the terrors of war! 16"But a long year from now," says the Lord, "the great power of their enemy, the mighty tribe of Kedar, will end. 17Only a few of its stalwart archers will survive." The Lord, the God of Israel, has spoken.

THEN fourteen years later I went back to Jerusalem again, this time with Barnabas; and Titus came along too. [2]I went there with definite orders from God to confer with the brothers there about the message I was preaching to the Gentiles. I talked privately to the leaders of the church so that they would all understand just what I had been teaching and, I hoped, agree that it was right. [3]And they did agree; they did not even demand that Titus, my companion, should be circumcised, though he was a Gentile.

[4]Even that question wouldn't have come up except for some so-called "Christians" there—false ones, really—who came to spy on us and see what freedom we enjoyed in Christ Jesus, as to whether we obeyed the Jewish laws or not. They tried to get us all tied up in their rules, like slaves in chains. [5]But we did not listen to them for a single moment, for we did not want to confuse you into thinking that salvation can be earned by being circumcised and by obeying Jewish laws.

[6]And the great leaders of the church who were there had nothing to add to what I was preaching. (By the way, their being great leaders made no difference to me, for all are the same to God.) [7,8,9]In fact, when Peter, James, and John, who were known as the pillars of the church, saw how greatly God had used me in winning the Gentiles, just as Peter had been blessed so greatly in his preaching to the Jews—for the same God gave us each our special gifts—they shook hands with Barnabas and me and encouraged us to keep right on with our preaching to the Gentiles while they continued their work with the Jews. [10]The only thing they did suggest was that we must always remember to help the poor, and I, too, was eager for that.

[11]But when Peter came to Antioch I had to oppose him publicly, speaking strongly against what he was doing for it was very wrong. [12]For when he first arrived he ate with the Gentile Christians [who don't bother with circumcision and the many other Jewish laws]. But afterwards when some Jewish friends of James came, he wouldn't eat with the Gentiles anymore because he was afraid of what these Jewish legalists, who insisted that circumcision was necessary for salvation, would say; [13]and then all the other Jewish Christians and even Barnabas became hypocrites too, following Peter's example, though they certainly knew better. [14]When I saw what was happening and that they weren't being honest about what they really believed, and weren't following the truth of the Gospel, I said to Peter in front of all the others, "Though you are a Jew by birth, you have long since discarded the Jewish laws; so why, all of a sudden, are you trying to make these Gentiles obey them? [15]You and I are Jews by birth, not mere Gentile sinners, [16]and yet we Jewish Christians know very well that we cannot become right with God by obeying our Jewish laws, but only by faith in Jesus Christ to take away our sins. And so we, too, have trusted Jesus Christ, that we might be accepted by God because of faith—and not because we have obeyed the Jewish laws. For no one will ever be saved by obeying them."

PSALM 59:1–17

O my God, save me from my enemies. Protect me from these who have come to destroy me. [2]Preserve me from these criminals, these murderers. [3]They lurk in ambush for my life. Strong men are out there waiting. And not, O Lord, because I've done them wrong. [4]Yet they prepare to kill me. Lord, waken! See what is happening! Help me! [5](And O Jehovah, God of heaven's armies, God of Israel, arise and punish the heathen nations surrounding us.) Do not spare these evil, treacherous men. [6]At evening they come to spy, slinking around like dogs that prowl the city. [7]I hear them shouting insults and cursing

God, for "No one will hear us," they think. 8Lord, laugh at them! (And scoff at these surrounding nations too.)

9O God my Strength! I will sing your praises, for you are my place of safety. 10My God is changeless in his love for me and he will come and help me. He will let me see my wish come true upon my enemies. 11Don't kill them—for my people soon forget such lessons—but stagger them with your power and bring them to their knees. Bring them to the dust, O Lord our shield. 12,13They are proud, cursing liars. Angrily destroy them. Wipe them out. (And let the nations find out too that God rules in Israel and will reign throughout the world.) 14,15Let these evil men slink back at evening, and prowl the city all night before they are satisfied, howling like dogs and searching for food.

16But as for me, I will sing each morning about your power and mercy. For you have been my high tower of refuge, a place of safety in the day of my distress. 17O my Strength, to you I sing my praises; for you are my high tower of safety, my God of mercy.

PROVERBS FOR TODAY/ 23:13–14

Don't fail to correct your children; discipline won't hurt them! They won't die if you use a stick on them! Punishment will keep them out of hell.

SEPTEMBER 16

ISAIAH 22:1—24:23

THIS is God's message concerning Jerusalem:

What is happening? Where is everyone going? Why are they running to the rooftops? What are they looking at? 2The whole city is in terrible uproar. What's the trouble in this busy, happy city? Bodies! Lying everywhere, slain by plague and not by sword. 3All your leaders flee; they surrender without resistance. The people slip away but they are captured, too. 4Let me alone to weep. Don't try to comfort me—let me cry for my people as I watch them being destroyed. 5Oh, what a day of crushing trouble! What a day of confusion and terror from the Lord God of heaven's armies! The walls of Jerusalem are breached and the cry of death echoes from the mountainsides. 6,7Elamites are the archers; Syrians drive the chariots; the men of Kir hold up the shields. They fill your choicest valleys and crowd against your gates.

8God has removed his protecting care. You run to the armory for your weapons! 9,10,11You inspect the walls of Jerusalem to see what needs repair! You check over the houses and tear some down for stone for fixing walls. Between the city walls, you build a reservoir for water from the lower pool! But all your feverish plans will not avail, for you never ask for help from God, who lets this come upon you. He is the one who planned it long ago. 12The Lord God called you to repent, to weep and mourn and shave your heads in sorrow for your sins, and to wear clothes made of sackcloth to show your remorse. 13But instead, you sing and dance and play, and feast and drink. "Let us eat, drink, and be merry," you say: "What's the difference, for tomorrow we die." 14The Lord Almighty has revealed to me that this sin will never be forgiven you until the day you die.

15,16Furthermore, the same Lord God of the armies of heaven has told me this: Go and say to Shebna, the palace administrator: "And who do you think you are, building this beautiful sepulchre in the rock for yourself? 17For the Lord who allowed you to be clothed so gorgeously will hurl you away, sending you into captivity, O strong man! 18He will wad you up in his hands like a ball and toss you away into a distant, barren land; there you will die, O glorious one—you who disgrace your nation!

19"Yes, I will drive you out of office," says the Lord, "and pull you down from your high position. 20And then I will call my servant Eliakim, the son of Hilkiah, to replace you. 21He shall have your uniform and title and authority, and he will be a father to the people of Jerusalem and all Judah. 22I will give him responsibility over all my people; whatever he says will be done; none will be able to stop him. 23,24I will make of him a strong and steady peg to support my people; they will load him with responsibility, and he will be an honor to his family name." 25But the Lord will pull out that other peg that seems to be so firmly fastened to the wall! It will come out and fall to the ground, and everything it supports will fall with it, for the Lord has spoken.

THIS is God's message to Tyre:

Weep, O ships of Tyre, returning home from distant lands! Weep for your harbor, for it is gone! The rumors that you heard in Cyprus are all true. 2,3Deathly silence is everywhere. Stillness reigns where once your hustling port was full of ships from Sidon, bringing merchandise from far across the ocean, from Egypt and along the Nile. You were the merchandise mart of the world. 4Be ashamed, O Sidon, stronghold of the sea. For you are childless now! 5When Egypt hears the news, there will be great sorrow. 6Flee to Tarshish, men of Tyre, weeping as you go. 7This silent ruin is all that's left of your once joyous land. What a history was yours! Think of all the colonists you sent to distant lands!

8Who has brought this disaster on Tyre, empire builder and top trader of the world? 9The Commander of the armies of heaven has done it to destroy your pride and show his contempt for all the greatness of mankind. 10Sail on, O ships of Tarshish, for your harbor is gone. 11The Lord holds out his hand over the seas; he shakes the kingdoms of the earth; he has spoken out against this great merchant city, to destroy its strength.

12He says, "Never again, O dishonored virgin, daughter of Sidon, will you rejoice, will you be strong. Even if you flee to Cyprus, you will find no rest."

13It will be the Babylonians, not the Assyrians, who consign Tyre to the wild beasts. They will lay siege to it, raze its palaces and make it a heap of ruins. 14Wail, you ships that ply the oceans, for your home port is destroyed!

15,16For seventy years Tyre will be forgotten. Then, in the days of another king, the city will come back to life again; she will sing sweet songs as a harlot sings who, long absent from her lovers, walks the streets to look for them again and is remembered. 17Yes, after seventy years, the Lord will revive Tyre, but she will be no different than she was before; she will return again to all her evil ways around the world. 18Yet [the distant time will come when] her businesses will give their profits to the Lord! They will not be hoarded but used for good food and fine clothes for the priests of the Lord!

LOOK! The Lord is overturning the land of Judah and making it a vast wasteland of destruction. See how he is emptying out all its people and scattering them over the face of the earth. 2Priests and people, servants and masters, slave girls and mistresses, buyers and sellers, lenders and borrowers, bankers and debtors—none will be spared. 3The land will be completely emptied and looted. The Lord has spoken. 4,5The land suffers for the sins of its people. The earth languishes, the crops wither, the skies refuse their rain. The land is defiled by crime; the people have twisted the laws of God and broken his everlasting commands. 6Therefore the curse of God is upon them; they are left desolate, destroyed by the drought. Few will be left alive.

7All the joys of life will go: the grape harvest will fail, the wine will be gone, the merrymakers will sigh and mourn. 8The melodious chords of the harp and timbrel are heard no more; the happy days are ended. 9No more are the joys of wine and song; strong drink turns bitter in the mouth.

10The city lies in chaos; every home and shop is locked up tight to keep out looters. 11Mobs form in the streets, crying for wine; joy has reached its lowest ebb; gladness has been banished from the land. 12The city is left in ruins; its gates are battered down. 13Throughout the land the story is the same—only a remnant is left.

14But all who are left will shout and sing for joy; those in the west will praise the majesty of God, 15,16and those in the east will respond with praise. Hear them singing to the Lord from the ends of the earth, singing glory to the Righteous One!

But my heart is heavy with grief, for evil still prevails and treachery is everywhere. 17Terror and the captivity of hell are still your lot, O men of the world. 18When you flee in terror you will fall into a pit, and if you escape from the pit you will step into a trap, for destruction falls from the heavens upon you; the world is shaken beneath you. 19The earth has broken down in utter collapse; everything is lost, abandoned and confused. 20The world staggers like a drunkard; it shakes like a tent in a storm. It falls and will not rise again, for the sins of the earth are very great.

21On that day the Lord will punish the fallen angels in the heavens, and the proud rulers of the nations on earth. 22They will be rounded up like prisoners and imprisoned in a dungeon until they are tried and condemned. 23Then the Lord of heaven's armies will mount his throne in Zion and rule gloriously in Jerusalem, in the sight of all the elders of

his people. Such glory there will be that all the brightness of the sun and moon will seem to fade away.

GALATIANS 2:17—3:7

BUT what if we trust Christ to save us and then find that we are wrong, and that we cannot be saved without being circumcised and obeying all the other Jewish laws? Wouldn't we need to say that faith in Christ had ruined us? God forbid that anyone should dare to think such things about our Lord. 18Rather, we are sinners if we start rebuilding the old systems I have been destroying, of trying to be saved by keeping Jewish laws, 19for it was through reading the Scripture that I came to realize that I could never find God's favor by trying—and failing—to obey the laws. I came to realize that acceptance with God comes by believing in Christ.

20I have been crucified with Christ: and I myself no longer live, but Christ lives in me. And the real life I now have within this body is a result of my trusting in the Son of God, who loved me and gave himself for me. 21I am not one of those who treats Christ's death as meaningless. For if we could be saved by keeping Jewish laws, then there was no need for Christ to die.

OH, foolish Galatians! What magician has hypnotized you and cast an evil spell upon you? For you used to see the meaning of Jesus Christ's death as clearly as though I had waved a placard before you with a picture on it of Christ dying on the cross. 2Let me ask you this one question: Did you receive the Holy Spirit by trying to keep the Jewish laws? Of course not, for the Holy Spirit came upon you only after you heard about Christ and trusted him to save you. 3Then have you gone completely crazy? For if trying to obey the Jewish laws never gave you spiritual life in the first place, why do you think that trying to obey them now will make you stronger Christians?

4You have suffered so much for the Gospel. Now are you going to just throw it all overboard? I can hardly believe it!

5I ask you again, does God give you the power of the Holy Spirit and work miracles among you as a result of your trying to obey the Jewish laws? No, of course not. It is when you believe in Christ and fully trust him.

6Abraham had the same experience—God declared him fit for heaven only because he believed God's promises. 7You can see from this that the real children of Abraham are all the men of faith who truly trust in God.

PSALM 60:1–12

O God, you have rejected us and broken our defenses; you have become angry and deserted us. Lord, restore us again to your favor. 2You have caused this nation to tremble in fear; you have torn it apart. Lord, heal it now, for it is shaken to its depths. 3You have been very hard on us and made us reel beneath your blows.

4,5But you have given us a banner to rally to; all who love truth will rally to it; then you can deliver your beloved people. Use your strong right arm to rescue us. 6,7God has promised to help us. He has vowed it by his holiness! No wonder I exult! "Shechem, Succoth, Gilead, Manasseh—still are mine!" he says. "Judah shall continue to produce kings, and Ephraim great warriors. 8Moab shall become my lowly servant, and Edom my slave. And I will shout in triumph over the Philistines."

9,10Who will bring me in triumph into Edom's strong cities? God will! He who cast us off! He who abandoned us to our foes! 11Yes, Lord, help us against our enemies, for man's help is useless.

12With God's help we shall do mighty things, for he will trample down our foes.

PROVERBS FOR TODAY/ 23:15–16

My son, how I will rejoice if you become a man of common sense. Yes, my heart will thrill to your thoughtful, wise words.

SEPTEMBER 17

ISAIAH 25:1—28:13

O Lord, I will honor and praise your name, for you are my God; you do such wonderful things! You planned them long ago, and now you have accomplished them, just as you said! 2You turn mighty cities into heaps of ruins. The strongest forts are turned to rubble. Beautiful palaces in distant lands disappear and will never be rebuilt. 3Therefore strong nations will shake with fear before you; ruthless nations will obey and glorify your name.

4But to the poor, O Lord, you are a refuge from the storm, a shadow from the heat, a shelter from merciless men who are like a driving rain that melts down an earthen wall. 5As a hot, dry land is cooled by clouds, you will cool the pride of ruthless nations. 6Here on Mount Zion in Jerusalem, the Lord Almighty will spread a wondrous feast for everyone around the world—a delicious feast of good food, with clear, well-aged wine and choice beef. 7At that time he will remove the cloud of gloom, the pall of death that hangs over the earth; 8he will swallow up death forever. The Lord God will wipe away all tears and take away forever all insults and mockery against his land and people. The Lord has spoken—he will surely do it!

9In that day the people will proclaim, "This is our God, in whom we trust, for whom we waited. Now at last he is here." What a day of rejoicing! 10For the Lord's good hand will rest upon Jerusalem, and Moab will be crushed as straw beneath his feet and left to rot. 11God will push them down just as a swimmer pushes down the water with his hands. He will end their pride and all their evil works. 12The high walls of Moab will be demolished and brought to dust.

LISTEN to them singing! In that day the whole land of Judah will sing this song: "Our city is strong! We are surrounded by the walls of his salvation!" 2Open the gates to everyone, for all may enter in who love the Lord. 3He will keep in perfect peace all those who trust in him, whose thoughts turn often to the Lord! 4Trust in the Lord God always, for in the Lord Jehovah is your everlasting strength. 5He humbles the proud and brings the haughty city to the dust; its walls come crashing down. 6He presents it to the poor and needy for their use.

7But for good men the path is not uphill and rough! God does not give them a rough and treacherous path, but smooths the road before them. 8O Lord, we love to do your will! Our hearts' desire is to glorify your name. 9All night long I search for you; earnestly I seek for God; for only when you come in judgment on the earth to punish it will people turn away from wickedness and do what is right.

10Your kindness to the wicked doesn't make them good; they keep on doing wrong and take no notice of your majesty. 11They do not listen when you threaten; they will not look to see your upraised fist. Show them how much you love your people. Perhaps then they will be ashamed! Yes, let them be burned up by the fire reserved for your enemies.

12Lord, grant us peace; for all we have and are has come from you. 13O Lord our God, once we worshiped other gods; but now we worship you alone. 14Those we served before are dead and gone; never again will they return. You came against them and destroyed them, and they are long forgotten. 15O praise the Lord! He has made our nation very great. He has widened the boundaries of our land!

16Lord, in their distress they sought for you. When your punishment was on them, they poured forth a whispered prayer. 17How we missed your presence, Lord! We suffered as a woman giving birth, who cries and writhes in pain. 18We too have writhed in agony, but all to no avail. No deliverance has come from all our efforts. 19Yet we have this assurance: Those who belong to God shall live again. Their bodies shall rise again! Those who dwell in the dust shall awake and sing for joy! For God's light of life will fall like dew upon them!

20Go home, my people, and lock the doors! Hide for a little while until the Lord's wrath against your enemies has passed. 21Look! The Lord is coming from the heavens to punish the people of the earth for their sins. The earth will no longer hide the murderers. The guilty will be found.

IN that day the Lord will take his terrible, swift sword and punish leviathan, the swiftly moving serpent, the coiling, writhing serpent, the dragon of the sea.

2In that day [of Israel's freedom] let this anthem be their song:

3Israel is my vineyard; I, the Lord, will tend the fruitful vines; every day I'll water them, and day and night I'll watch to keep all enemies away. 4,5My anger against Israel is gone. If I find thorns and briars bothering her, I will burn them up, unless these enemies of mine surrender and beg for peace and my protection. 6The time will come when Israel will take root and bud and blossom and fill the whole earth with her fruit!

7,8Has God punished Israel as much as he has punished her enemies? No, for he has devastated her enemies, while he has punished Israel but a little, exiling her far from her own land as though blown away in a storm from the east. 9And why did God do it? It was to purge away her sins, to rid her of all her idol altars and her idols. They will never be worshiped again. 10Her walled cities will be silent and empty, houses abandoned, streets grown up with grass, cows grazing through the city munching on twigs and branches.

11My people are like the dead branches of a tree, broken off and used to burn beneath the pots. They are a foolish nation, a witless, stupid people, for they turn away from God. Therefore, he who made them will not have pity on them or show them his mercy. 12Yet the time will come when the Lord will gather them together one by one like handpicked grain, selecting them here and there from his great threshing floor that reaches all the way from the Euphrates River to the Egyptian boundary. 13In that day the great trumpet will be blown, and many about to perish among their enemies, Assyria and Egypt, will be rescued and brought back to Jerusalem to worship the Lord in his holy mountain.

WOE to the city of Samaria, surrounded by her rich valley—Samaria, the pride and delight of the drunkards of Israel! Woe to her fading beauty, the crowning glory of a nation of men lying drunk in the streets! 2For the Lord will send a mighty army (the Assyrians) against you; like a mighty hailstorm he will burst upon you and dash you to the ground. 3The proud city of Samaria—yes, the joy and delight of the drunkards of Israel—will be hurled to the ground and trampled beneath the enemies' feet. 4Once glorious, her fading beauty surrounded by a fertile valley will suddenly be gone, greedily snatched away as an early fig is hungrily snatched and gobbled up!

5Then at last the Lord Almighty himself will be their crowning glory, the diadem of beauty to his people who are left. 6He will give a longing for justice to your judges and great courage to your soldiers who are battling to the last be-

fore your gates. 7But Jerusalem is now led by drunks! Her priests and prophets reel and stagger, making stupid errors and mistakes. 8Their tables are covered with vomit; filth is everywhere.

9"Who does Isaiah think he is," the people say, "to speak to us like this! Are we little children, barely old enough to talk? 10He tells us everything over and over again, a line at a time and in such simple words!"

11But they won't listen; the only language they can understand is punishment! So God will punish them by sending against them foreigners who speak strange gibberish! Only then will they listen to him! 12They could have rest in their own land if they would obey him, if they were kind and good. He told them that, but they wouldn't listen to him. 13So the Lord will spell it out for them again, repeating it over and over in simple words whenever he can; yet over this simple, straightforward message they will stumble and fall and be broken, trapped and captured.

GALATIANS 3:8–22

WHAT'S more, the Scriptures looked forward to this time when God would save the Gentiles also, through their faith. God told Abraham about this long ago when he said, "I will bless those in every nation who trust in me as you do." And so it is: all who trust in Christ share the same blessing Abraham received.

10Yes, and those who depend on the Jewish laws to save them are under God's curse, for the Scriptures point out very clearly, "Cursed is everyone who at any time breaks a single one of these laws that are written in God's Book of the Law." 11Consequently, it is clear that no one can ever win God's favor by trying to keep the Jewish laws, because God has said that the only way we can be right in his sight is by faith. As the prophet Habakkuk says it, "The man who finds life will find it through trusting God." 12How different from this way of faith is the way of law which says that a man is saved by obeying every law of God, without one slip. 13But Christ has bought us out from under the doom of that impossible system by taking the curse for our wrongdoing upon himself. For it is written in the Scripture, "Anyone who is hanged on a tree is cursed" [as Jesus was hung upon a wooden cross].

14Now God can bless the Gentiles, too, with this same blessing he promised to Abraham; and all of us as Christians can have the promised Holy Spirit through this faith.

15Dear brothers, even in everyday life a promise made by one man to another, if it is written down and signed, cannot be changed. He cannot decide afterward to do something else instead.

16Now, God gave some promises to Abraham and his Child. And notice that it doesn't say the promises were to his *children,* as it would if all his sons—all the Jews—were being spoken of, but to his *Child*—and that, of course, means Christ. 17Here's what I am trying to say: God's promise to save through faith—and God wrote this promise down and signed it—could not be canceled or changed four hundred and thirty years later when God gave the Ten Commandments. 18If *obeying those laws* could save us, then it is obvious that this would be a different way of gaining God's favor than Abraham's way, for he simply accepted God's promise.

19Well then, why were the laws given? They were added after the promise was given, to show men how guilty they are of breaking God's laws. But this system of law was to last only until the coming of Christ, the Child to whom God's promise was made. (And there is this further difference. God gave his laws to angels to give to Moses, who then gave them to the people; 20but when God gave his promise to Abraham, he did it by himself alone, without angels or Moses as go-betweens.)

21,22Well then, are God's laws and God's promises against each other? Of course not! If we could be saved by his laws, then God would not have had to give us a different way to get out of the grip of sin—for the Scriptures insist we are all its prisoners. The only way out is through faith in Jesus Christ; the way of escape is open to all who believe him.

PSALM 61:1–8

O God, listen to me! Hear my prayer! 2For wherever I am, though far away at the ends of the earth, I will cry to you for help. When my heart is faint and overwhelmed, lead me to the mighty, towering Rock of safety. 3For you are my refuge, a high tower where my enemies can never reach me. 4I shall live forever in your tabernacle; oh, to be safe beneath the shelter of your wings! 5For you have heard my vows, O God, to praise you every day, and you have given me the blessings you reserve for those who reverence your name.

6You will give me added years of life, as rich and full as those of many generations, all packed into one. 7And I shall live before the Lord forever. Oh, send your lovingkindness and truth to guard and watch over me, 8and I will praise your name continually, fulfilling my vow of praising you each day.

PROVERBS FOR TODAY/ 23:17–18

Don't envy evil men but continue to reverence the Lord all the time, for surely you have a wonderful future ahead of you. There is hope for you yet!

SEPTEMBER 18

ISAIAH 28:14—30:11

THEREFORE hear the word of the Lord, you scoffing rulers in Jerusalem:

15You have struck a bargain with Death, you say, and sold yourselves to the devil in exchange for his protection against the Assyrians. "They can never touch us," you say, "for we are under the care of one who will deceive and fool them."

16But the Lord God says, See, I am placing a Foundation Stone in Zion—a firm, tested, precious Cornerstone that is safe to build on. He who believes need never run away again. 17I will take the line and plummet of justice to check the foundation wall you built; it looks so fine, but it is so weak a storm of hail will knock it down! The enemy will come like a flood and sweep it away, and you will be drowned. 18I will cancel your agreement of compromise with Death and the devil, so when the terrible enemy floods in, you will be trampled into the ground. 19Again and again that flood will come and carry you off, until at last the unmixed horror of the truth of my warnings will finally dawn on you.

20The bed you have made is far too short to lie on; the blankets are too narrow to cover you. 21The Lord will come suddenly and in anger, as at Mount Perazim and Gibeon, to do a strange, unusual thing—to destroy his own people! 22So scoff no more, lest your punishment be made even greater, for the Lord God has plainly told me that he is determined to crush you.

23,24Listen to me, listen as I plead: Does a farmer always plow and never sow? Is he forever harrowing the soil and never planting it? 25Does he not finally plant his many kinds of grain, each in its own section of his land? 26He knows just what to do, for God has made him see and understand. 27He doesn't thresh all grains the same. A sledge is never used on dill, but it is beaten with a stick. A threshing wheel is never rolled on cummin, but it is beaten softly with a flail. 28Bread grain is easily crushed, so he doesn't keep on pounding it. 29The Lord Almighty is a wonderful teacher and gives the farmer wisdom.

WOE to Jerusalem, the city of David. Year after year you make your many offerings, 2but I will send heavy judgment upon you and there will be weeping and sorrow. For Jerusalem shall become as her name "Ariel" means—an altar covered with blood. 3I will be your enemy. I will surround Jerusalem and lay siege against it, and build forts around it to destroy it. 4Your voice will whisper like a ghost from the earth where you lie buried.

5But suddenly your ruthless enemies will be driven away like chaff before the wind. 6In an instant, I, the Lord of Hosts, will come upon them with thunder, earthquake, whirlwind and fire. 7And all the nations fighting Jerusalem will vanish like a dream! 8As a hungry man dreams of eating, but is still hungry, and as a thirsty man dreams of drinking, but is still faint from thirst when he wakes up, so your enemies will dream of victorious conquest, but all to no avail.

9You are amazed, incredulous? You don't believe it? Then go ahead and be blind if you must! You are stupid—and not from drinking, either! Stagger, and not from wine! 10For the Lord has poured out upon you a spirit of deep sleep. He has closed the eyes of your prophets and seers, 11so all of these future events are a sealed book to them. When you give it to one who can read, he says, "I can't, for it's sealed." 12When you give it to another, he says, "Sorry, I can't read."

13And so the Lord says, "Since these people say they are mine but they do not obey me, and since their worship amounts to mere words learned by rote, 14therefore I will take awesome vengeance on these hypocrites, and make their wisest counselors as fools."

15Woe to those who try to hide their plans from God, who try to keep him in the dark concerning what they do! "God can't see us," they say to themselves. "He doesn't know what is going on!" 16How stupid can they be! Isn't he, the Potter, greater than you, the jars he makes? Will you say to him, "He didn't make us"? Does a machine call its inventor dumb?

17Soon—and it will not be very long—the wilderness of Lebanon will be a fruitful field again, a lush and fertile forest. 18In that day the deaf will hear the words of a book, and out of their gloom and darkness the blind will see my plans. 19The meek will be filled with fresh joy from the Lord, and the poor shall exult in the Holy One of Israel. 20Bullies will vanish and scoffers will cease, and all those plotting evil will be killed— 21the violent man who fights at the drop of a hat, the man who waits in hiding to beat up the judge who sentenced him, and the men who use any excuse to be unfair.

22That is why the Lord who redeemed Abraham says: My people will no longer pale with fear, or be ashamed. 23For when they see the surging birth rate and the expanding economy, then they will fear and rejoice in my name, and praise the Holy One of Israel, and stand in awe of him. 24Those in error will believe the truth, and complainers will be willing to be taught!

WOE to my rebellious children, says the Lord; you ask advice from everyone but me, and decide to do what I don't want you to do. You yoke yourselves with unbelievers, thus piling up your sins. 2For without consulting me you have gone down to Egypt to find aid and have put your trust in Pharaoh for his protection. 3But in trusting Pharaoh, you will be disappointed, humiliated and disgraced, for he can't deliver on his promises to save you. 4For though his power extends to Zoan and Hanes, 5yet it will

all turn out to your shame—he won't help one little bit!

6See them moving slowly across the terrible desert to Egypt—donkeys and camels laden down with treasure to pay for Egypt's aid. On through the badlands they go, where lions and swift venomous snakes live—and Egypt will give you nothing in return! 7For Egypt's promises are worthless! "The Reluctant Dragon," I call her!

8Now go and write down this word of mine concerning Egypt, so that it will stand until the end of time, forever and forever, as an indictment of Israel's unbelief. 9For if you don't write it, they will claim I never warned them. "Oh, no," they'll say, "you never told us that!"

For they are stubborn rebels. 10,11They tell my prophets, "Shut up—we don't want any more of your reports!" Or they say, "Don't tell us the truth; tell us nice things; tell us lies. Forget all this gloom; we've heard more than enough about your 'Holy One of Israel' and all he says."

GALATIANS 3:23—4:31

UNTIL Christ came we were guarded by the law, kept in protective custody, so to speak, until we could believe in the coming Savior. 24Let me put it another way. The Jewish laws were our teacher and guide until Christ came to give us right standing with God through our faith. 25But now that Christ has come, we don't need those laws any longer to guard us and lead us to him. 26For now we are all children of God through faith in Jesus Christ, 27and we who have been baptized into union with Christ are enveloped by him. 28We are no longer Jews or Greeks or slaves or free men or even merely men or women, but we are all the same—we are Christians; we are one in Christ Jesus. 29And now that we are Christ's we are the true descendants of Abraham, and all of God's promises to him belong to us.

BUT remember this, that if a father dies and leaves great wealth for his little son, that child is not much better off than a slave until he grows up, even though he actually owns everything his father had. 2He has to do what his guardians and managers tell him to, until he reaches whatever age his father set.

3And that is the way it was with us before Christ came. We were slaves to Jewish laws and rituals for we thought they could save us. 4But when the right time came, the time God decided on, he sent his Son, born of a woman, born as a Jew, 5to buy freedom for us who were slaves to the law so that he could adopt us as his very own sons. 6And because we are his sons God has sent the Spirit of his Son into our hearts, so now we can rightly speak of God as our dear Father. 7Now we are no longer slaves, but God's own sons. And since we are his sons, everything he has belongs to us, for that is the way God planned.

8Before you Gentiles knew God you were slaves to so-called gods that did not even exist. 9And now that you have found God (or I should say, now that God has found you) how can it be that you want to go back again and become slaves once more to another poor, weak, useless religion of trying to get to heaven by obeying God's laws? 10You are trying to find favor with God by what you do or don't do on certain days or months or seasons or years. 11I fear for you. I am afraid that all my hard work for you was worth nothing.

12Dear brothers, please feel as I do about these things, for I am as free from these chains as you used to be. You did not despise me then when I first preached to you, 13even though I was sick when I first brought you the Good News of Christ. 14But even though my sickness was revolting to you, you didn't reject me and turn me away. No, you took me in and cared for me as though I were an angel from God, or even Jesus Christ himself.

15Where is that happy spirit that we felt together then? For in those days I know you would gladly have taken out your own eyes and given them to replace mine if that would have helped me.

16And now have I become your enemy because I tell you the truth?

17Those false teachers who are so anxious to win your favor are not doing it for your good. What they are trying to do is to shut you off from me so that you will pay more attention to them. 18It is a fine thing when people are nice to you with good motives and sincere hearts, especially if they aren't doing it just when I am with you! 19Oh, my children, how you are hurting me! I am once again suffering for you the pains of a mother waiting for her child to be born—longing for the time when you will finally be filled with Christ. 20How I wish I could be there with you right now and not have to reason with you like this, for at this distance I frankly don't know what to do.

21Listen to me, you friends who think you have to obey the Jewish laws to be saved: Why don't you find out what those laws really mean? 22For it is written that Abraham had two sons, one from his slavewife and one from his freeborn wife. 23There was nothing unusual about the birth of the slave-wife's baby. But the baby of the freeborn wife was born only after God had especially promised he would come.

24,25Now this true story is an illustration of God's two ways of helping people. One way was by giving them his laws to obey. He did this on Mount Sinai, when he gave the Ten Commandments to Moses. Mount Sinai, by the way, is called "Mount Hagar" by the Arabs—and in my illustration Abraham's slave-wife Hagar represents Jerusalem, the mother-city of the Jews, the center of that system of trying to please God by trying to obey the Commandments; and the Jews, who try to follow that system, are her slave children. 26But our mother-city is the heavenly Jerusalem, and she is not a slave to Jewish laws.

27That is what Isaiah meant when he

prophesied, "Now you can rejoice, O childless woman; you can shout with joy though you never before had a child. For I am going to give you many children— more children than the slave-wife has."

28You and I, dear brothers, are the children that God promised, just as Isaac was. 29And so we who are born of the Holy Spirit are persecuted now by those who want us to keep the Jewish laws, just as Isaac the child of promise was persecuted by Ishmael the slave-wife's son.

30But the Scriptures say that God told Abraham to send away the slave-wife and her son, for the slave-wife's son could not inherit Abraham's home and lands along with the free woman's son. 31Dear brothers, we are not slave children, obligated to the Jewish laws, but children of the free woman, acceptable to God because of our faith.

PSALM 62:1–12

I stand silently before the Lord, waiting for him to rescue me. For salvation comes from him alone. 2Yes, he alone is my Rock, my rescuer, defense and fortress. Why then should

I be tense with fear when troubles come?

3,4But what is this? They pick on me at a time when my throne is tottering; they plot my death and use lies and deceit to try to force me from the throne. They are so friendly to my face while cursing in their hearts!

5But I stand silently before the Lord, waiting for him to rescue me. For salvation comes from him alone. 6Yes, he alone is my Rock, my rescuer, defense and fortress—why then should I be tense with fear when troubles come?

7My protection and success come from God alone. He is my refuge, a Rock where no enemy can reach me. 8O my people, trust him all the time. Pour out your longings before him, for he can help! 9The greatest of men, or the lowest—both alike are nothing in his sight. They weigh less than air on scales.

10-12Don't become rich by extortion and robbery; if your riches increase, don't be proud. God has said it many times, that power belongs to him; (and also, O Lord, steadfast love belongs to you). He rewards each one of us according to what our works deserve.

PROVERBS FOR TODAY/ 23:19–21

O my son, be wise and stay in God's paths; don't carouse with drunkards and gluttons, for they are on their way to poverty. And remember that too much sleep clothes a man with rags.

SEPTEMBER 19

ISAIAH 30:12—33:12

THIS is the reply of the Holy One of Israel:
Because you despise what I tell you and trust instead in frauds and lies and won't repent, 13therefore calamity will come upon you suddenly, as upon a bulging wall that bursts and falls; in

one moment it comes crashing down. 14God will smash you like a broken dish; he will not act sparingly. Not a piece will be left large enough to use for carrying coals from the hearth, or a little water from the well. 15For the Lord God, the Holy One of Israel, says: Only in returning to me and waiting for me will you be saved; in quietness and confidence is your strength; but you'll have none of this.

16"No," you say. "We will get our help from Egypt; they will give us swift horses for riding to battle." But the only swiftness you are going to see is the swiftness of your enemies chasing you! 17One of them will chase a thousand of you! Five of them will scatter you until not two of you are left together. You will be like lonely trees on the distant mountain tops. 18Yet the Lord still waits for you to come to him, so he can show you his love; he will conquer you to bless you, just as he said. For the Lord is faithful to his promises. Blessed are all those who wait for him to help them.

19O my people in Jerusalem, you shall weep no more, for he will surely be gracious to you at the sound of your cry. He will answer you. 20Though he give you the bread of adversity and water of affliction, yet he will be with you to teach you—with your own eyes you will see your Teacher. 21And if you leave God's paths and go astray, you will hear a Voice behind you say, "No, this is the way; walk here." 22And you will destroy all your silver idols and gold images and cast them out like filthy things you hate to touch. "Ugh!" you'll say to them. "Be gone!"

23Then God will bless you with rain at planting time and with wonderful harvests and with ample pastures for your cows. 24The oxen and young donkeys that till the ground will eat grain, its chaff blown away by the wind. 25In that day when God steps in to destroy your enemies, he will give you streams of water flowing down each mountain and every hill. 26The moon will be as bright as the sun, and the sunlight brighter than seven days! So it will be when the Lord begins to heal his people and to cure the wounds he gave them.

27See, the Lord comes from afar, aflame with wrath, surrounded by thick rising smoke. His lips are filled with fury; his words consume like fire. 28His wrath pours out like floods upon them all, to sweep them all away. He will sift out the proud nations and bridle them and lead them off to their doom.

29But the people of God will sing a song of solemn joy, like songs in the night when holy feasts are held; his people will have gladness of heart, as when a flutist leads a pilgrim band to Jerusalem to the Mountain of the Lord, the Rock of Israel. 30And the Lord shall cause his majestic voice to be heard and shall crush down his mighty arm upon his enemies with angry indignation and with devouring flames and tornados and terrible storms and huge hailstones. 31The voice of the Lord shall punish the Assyrians, who had been his rod of punishment. 32And when the Lord smites them, his people will rejoice with music and song. 33The funeral pyre has long been ready, prepared for Molech, the Assyrian god; it is piled high with wood. The breath of the Lord, like fire from a volcano, will set it all on fire.

WOE to those who run to Egypt for help, trusting their mighty cavalry and chariots instead of looking to the Holy One of Israel and consulting him. 2In his wisdom, he will send great evil on his people and will not change his mind. He will rise against them for the evil they have done, and crush their allies too. 3For these Egyptians are mere men, not God! Their horses are puny flesh, not mighty spirits! When the Lord clenches his fist against them, they will stumble and fall among those they are trying to help. All will fail together.

4,5But the Lord has told me this: When a lion, even a young one, kills a sheep, he pays no attention to the shepherd's shouts and noise. He goes right on and eats. In such manner the Lord will come and fight upon Mount Zion. He will not be frightened away! He, the Lord Almighty, will hover over Jerusalem as birds hover round their nests, and he will defend the city and deliver it.

6Therefore, O my people, though you are such wicked rebels, come, return to God. 7I know the glorious day will come when every one of you will throw away his gold idols and silver images—which in your sinfulness you have made. 8And the Assyrians will be destroyed, but not by swords of men. The "sword of God" will smite them. They will panic and flee, and the strong young Assyrians will be taken away as slaves. 9Even their generals will quake with terror and flee when they see the battle flags of Israel, says the Lord. For the flame of God burns brightly in Jerusalem.

LOOK, a righteous King is coming, with honest princes! 2He will shelter Israel from the storm and wind. He will refresh her as a river in the desert and as the cooling shadow of a mighty rock within a hot and weary land. 3Then at last the eyes of Israel will open wide to God; his people will listen to his voice. 4Even the hotheads among them will be full of sense and understanding, and those who stammer in uncertainty will speak out plainly.

5In those days the ungodly, the atheists, will not be heroes! Wealthy cheaters will not be spoken of as generous, outstanding men! 6Everyone will recognize an evil man when he sees him, and hypocrites will fool no one at all. Their lies about God and their cheating of the hungry will be plain for all to see. 7The smooth tricks of evil men will be exposed, as will all the lies they use to oppress the poor in the courts. 8But good men will be generous to others and will be blessed of God for all they do.

9Listen, you women who loll around in lazy ease; listen to me and I will tell you your reward: 10In a short time—in just a little more than a year—suddenly you'll care, O careless ones. For the crops of fruit will fail; the harvest will not take place. 11Tremble, O women of ease; throw off your unconcern. Strip off your pretty clothes—wear sackcloth for your grief. 12Beat your breasts in sorrow for those bountiful farms of yours that will soon be gone, and for those fruitful vines of other years. 13For your lands will thrive with thorns and briars; your joyous homes and happy cities will be gone. 14Palaces and mansions will all be deserted, the crowded cities empty. Wild herds of donkeys and goats will graze upon the mountains where the watchtowers are, 15until at last the Spirit is poured down on us from heaven. Then once again enormous crops will come. 16Then justice will rule through all the land, 17and out of justice, peace. Quietness and confidence will reign forever more.

18My people will live in safety, quietly at home, 19but the Assyrians will be destroyed and their cities laid low. 20And God will greatly bless his people. Wherever they plant, bountiful crops will spring up, and their flocks and herds will graze in green pastures.

WOE to you, Assyrians, who have destroyed everything around you but have never felt destruction for yourselves. You expect others to respect their promises to you, while you betray them! Now you, too, will be betrayed and destroyed.

2But to us, O Lord, be merciful, for we have waited for you. Be our strength each day and our salvation in the time of trouble. 3The enemy runs at the sound of your voice. When you stand up, the nations flee. 4Just as locusts strip the fields and vines, so Jerusalem will strip the fallen army of Assyria!

5The Lord is very great, and lives in heaven. He will make Jerusalem the home of justice and goodness and righteousness. 6An abundance of salvation is stored up for Judah in a safe place, along with wisdom and knowledge and reverence for God.

7But now your ambassadors weep in bitter disappointment, for Assyria has refused their cry for peace. 8Your roads lie in ruins; travelers detour on back roads. The Assyrians have broken their peace pact and care nothing for the promises they made in the presence of witnesses—they have no respect for anyone. 9All the land of Israel is in trouble; Lebanon has been destroyed; Sharon has become a wilderness; Bashan and Carmel are plundered.

¹⁰But the Lord says, I will stand up and show my power and might. ¹¹You Assyrians will gain nothing by all your efforts. Your own breath will turn to fire and kill you. ¹²Your armies will be burned to lime, like thorns cut down and tossed in the fire.

GALATIANS 5:1–12

SO Christ has made us free. Now make sure that you stay free and don't get all tied up again in the chains of slavery to Jewish laws and ceremonies. ²Listen to me, for this is serious: *if you are counting on circumcision and keeping the Jewish laws to make you right with God, then Christ cannot save you.* ³I'll say it again. Anyone trying to find favor with God by being circumcised must always obey every other Jewish law or perish. ⁴Christ is useless to you if you are counting on clearing your debt to God by keeping those laws; you are lost from God's grace.

⁵But we by the help of the Holy Spirit are counting on Christ's death to clear away our sins and make us right with God. ⁶And we to whom Christ has given eternal life don't need to worry about whether we have been circumcised or not, or whether we are obeying the Jewish ceremonies or not; for all we need is faith working through love.

⁷You were getting along so well. Who has interfered with you to hold you back from following the truth? ⁸It certainly isn't God who has done it, for he is the one who has called you to freedom in Christ. ⁹But it takes only one wrong person among you to infect all the others.

¹⁰I am trusting the Lord to bring you back to believing as I do about these things. God will deal with that person, whoever he is, who has been troubling and confusing you.

¹¹Some people even say that I myself am preaching that circumcision and Jewish laws are necessary to the plan of salvation. Well, if I preached that, I would be persecuted no more—for that message doesn't offend anyone. The fact that I am still being persecuted proves that I am still preaching salvation through faith in the cross of Christ alone.

¹²I only wish these teachers who want you to cut yourselves by being circumcised would cut themselves off from you and leave you alone!

PSALM 63:1–11

O God, my God! How I search for you! How I thirst for you in this parched and weary land where there is no water. How I long to find you! ²How I wish I could go into your sanctuary to see your strength and glory, ³for your love and kindness are better to me than life itself. How I praise you! ⁴I will bless you as long as I live, lifting up my hands to you in prayer. ⁵At last I shall be fully satisfied; I will praise you with great joy.

⁶I lie awake at night thinking of you— ⁷of how much you have helped me—and how I rejoice through the night beneath the protecting shadow of your wings. ⁸I follow close behind you, protected by your strong right arm. ⁹But those plotting to destroy me shall go down to the depths of hell. ¹⁰They are doomed to die by the sword, to become the food of jackals. ¹¹But I will rejoice in God. All who trust in him exult, while liars shall be silenced.

PROVERBS FOR TODAY/ 23:22

Listen to your father's advice and don't despise an old mother's experience.

SEPTEMBER 20

ISAIAH 33:13—36:22

LISTEN to what I have done, O nations far away! And you that are near, acknowledge my might! 14The sinners among my people shake with fear. "Which one of us," they cry, "can live here in the presence of this all-consuming, Everlasting Fire?" 15I will tell you who can live here: All who are honest and fair, who reject making profit by fraud, who hold back their hands from taking bribes, who refuse to listen to those who plot murder, who shut their eyes to all enticement to do wrong. 16Such as these shall dwell on high. The rocks of the mountains will be their fortress of safety; food will be supplied to them and they will have all the water they need.

17Your eyes will see the King in his beauty, and the highlands of heaven far away. 18Your mind will think back to this time of terror when the Assyrian officers outside your walls are counting your towers and estimating how much they will get from your fallen city. 19But soon they will all be gone. These fierce, violent people, with a strange, jabbering language you can't understand, will disappear.

20Instead you will see Jerusalem at peace, a place where God is worshiped, a city quiet and unmoved. 21The glorious Lord will be to us as a wide river of protection, and no enemy can cross. 22For the Lord is our Judge, our Lawgiver and our King; he will care for us and save us. 23The enemies' sails hang loose on broken masts with useless tackle. Their treasure will be divided by the people of God; even the lame will win their share. 24The people of Israel will no longer say, "We are sick and helpless," for the Lord will forgive them their sins and bless them.

COME here and listen, O nations of the earth; let the world and everything in it hear my words. 2For the Lord is enraged against the nations; his fury is against their armies. He will utterly destroy them and deliver them to slaughter. 3Their dead will be left unburied, and the stench of rotting bodies will fill the land, and the mountains will flow with their blood. 4At that time the heavens above will melt away and disappear just like a rolled-up scroll, and the stars will fall as leaves, as ripe fruit from the trees.

5And when my sword has finished its work in the heavens, then watch, for it will fall upon Edom, the people I have doomed. 6The sword of the Lord is sated with blood; it is gorged with flesh as though used for slaying lambs and goats for sacrifice. For the Lord will slay a great sacrifice in Edom and make a mighty slaughter there. 7The strongest will perish, young boys and veterans too. The land will be soaked with blood, and the soil made rich with fat. 8For it is the day of vengeance, the year of recompense for what Edom has done to Israel. 9The streams of Edom will be filled with burning pitch, and the ground will be covered with fire.

10This judgment on Edom will never end. Its smoke will rise up forever. The land will lie deserted from generation to generation; no one will live there anymore. 11There the hawks and porcupines will live, and owls and ravens. For God will observe that land and find it worthy of destruction. He will test its nobles and find them worthy of death. 12It will be called "The Land of Nothing," and its princes soon will all be gone. 13Thorns will overrun the palaces, and nettles will grow in its forts, and it will become the haunt of jackals and a home for ostriches. 14The wild animals of the desert will mingle there with wolves and hyenas. Their howls will fill the night. There the night-monsters will scream at each other, and the demons will come there to rest. 15There the owl will make her nest and lay her eggs and hatch her young and nestle them beneath her wings, and the kites will come, each one with its mate.

16Search the Book of the Lord and see all that he will do; not one detail will he miss; not one kite will be there without a mate, for the Lord has said it, and his Spirit will make it all come true. 17He has surveyed and subdivided the land and deeded it to those doleful creatures; they shall possess it forever, from generation to generation.

EVEN the wilderness and desert will rejoice in those days; the desert will blossom with flowers. 2Yes, there will be an abundance of flowers and singing and joy! The deserts will become as green as the Lebanon mountains, as lovely as Mount Carmel's pastures and Sharon's meadows; for the Lord will display his glory there, the excellency of our God.

3With this news bring cheer to all discouraged ones. 4Encourage those who are afraid. Tell them, "Be strong, fear not, for your God is coming to destroy your enemies. He is coming to save you." 5And when he comes, he will open the eyes of the blind, and unstop the ears of the deaf. 6The lame man will leap up like a deer, and those who could not speak will shout and sing! Springs will burst forth in the wilderness, and streams in the desert. 7The parched ground will become a pool, with springs of water in the thirsty land. Where desert jackals lived, there will be reeds and rushes!

8And a main road will go through that once-deserted land; it will be named "The Holy Highway." No evil-hearted men may walk upon it. God will walk there with you; even the most stupid cannot miss the way. 9No lion will lurk along its course, nor will there be any other dangers; only the redeemed will travel there. 10These, the ransomed of the Lord, will go home along that road to Zion, singing the songs of everlasting joy. For them all sorrow and all sighing will be gone forever; only joy and gladness will be there.

So in the fourteenth year of King Hezekiah's reign, Sennacherib, king of Assyria, came to fight against the walled cities of Judah and conquered them. 2Then he sent his personal representative with a great army from Lachish to confer with King Hezekiah in Jerusalem. He camped near the outlet of the upper pool, along the road going past the field where cloth is bleached.

3Then Eliakim, Hilkiah's son, who was the prime minister of Israel, and Shebna, the king's scribe, and Joah (Asaph's son), the royal secretary, formed a truce team and went out of the city to meet with him. 4The Assyrian ambassador told them to go and say to Hezekiah, "The mighty king of Assyria says you are a fool to think that the king of Egypt will help you. 5What are the Pharaoh's promises worth? Mere words won't substitute for strength, yet you rely on him for help, and have rebelled against me! 6Egypt is a dangerous ally. She is a sharpened stick that will pierce your hand if you lean on it. That is the experience of everyone who has ever looked to her for help. 7But perhaps you say, 'We are trusting in the Lord our God!' Oh? Isn't he the one your king insulted, tearing down his temples and altars in the hills and making everyone in Judah worship only at the altars here in Jerusalem? 8,9My master, the king of Assyria, wants to make a little bet with you!—that you don't have 2,000 men left in your entire army! If you do, he will give you 2,000 horses for them to ride on! With that tiny army, how can you think of proceeding against even the smallest and worst contingent of my master's troops? For you'll get no help from Egypt. 10What's more, do you think I have come here without the Lord's telling me to take this land? The Lord said to me, 'Go and destroy it!' "

11Then Eliakim and Shebna and Joah said to him, "Please talk to us in Aramaic for we understand it quite well. Don't speak in Hebrew, for the people on the wall will hear."

12But he replied, "My master wants everyone in Jerusalem to hear this, not just you. He wants them to know that if you don't surrender, this city will be put under siege until everyone is so hungry and thirsty that he will eat his own dung and drink his own urine."

13Then he shouted in Hebrew to the Jews listening on the wall, "Hear the words of the great king, the king of Assyria:

14"Don't let Hezekiah fool you—nothing he can do will save you. 15Don't let him talk you into trusting in the Lord by telling you the Lord won't let you be conquered by the king of Assyria. 16Don't listen to Hezekiah, for here is the king of Assyria's offer to you: Give me a present as a token of surrender; open the gates and come out, and I will let you each have your own farm and garden and water, 17until I can arrange to take you to a country very similar to this one—a country where there are bountiful harvests of grain and grapes, a land of plenty. 18Don't let Hezekiah deprive you of all this by saying the Lord will deliver you from my armies. Have any other nation's gods ever gained victory over the armies of the king of Assyria? 19Don't you remember what I did to Hamath and Arpad? Did their gods save them? And what about Sepharvaim and Samaria? Where are their gods now? 20Of all the gods of these lands, which one has ever delivered their people from my power? Name just one! And do you think this God of yours can deliver Jerusalem from me? Don't be ridiculous!"

21But the people were silent and answered not a word, for Hezekiah had told them to say nothing in reply. 22Then Eliakim (son of Hilkiah), the prime minister, and Shebna, the royal scribe, and Joah (son of Asaph), the royal secretary, went back to Hezekiah with clothes ripped to shreds as a sign of their despair and told him all that had happened.

GALATIANS 5:13–26

FOR, dear brothers, you have been given freedom: not freedom to do wrong, but freedom to love and serve each other. 14For the whole Law can be summed up in this one command: "Love others as you love yourself." 15But if instead of showing love among yourselves you are always critical and catty, watch out! Beware of ruining each other.

16I advise you to obey only the Holy Spirit's instructions. He will tell you where to go and what to do, and then you won't always be doing the wrong things your evil nature wants you to. 17For we naturally love to do evil things that are just the opposite from the things that the Holy Spirit tells us to do; and the good things we want to do when the Spirit has his way with us are just the opposite of our natural desires. These two forces within us are constantly fighting each other to win control over us, and our wishes are never free from their pressures. 18When you are guided by the Holy Spirit you need no longer force yourself to obey Jewish laws.

19But when you follow your own wrong inclinations your lives will produce these evil results: impure thoughts, eagerness for lustful pleasure, 20idolatry, spiritism (that is, encouraging the activity of demons), hatred and fighting, jealousy and anger, constant effort to get the best for yourself, complaints and criticisms, the feeling that everyone else is wrong except those in your own little group— and there will be wrong doctrine, 21envy, murder, drunkenness, wild parties, and all that sort of thing. Let me tell you again as I have before, that anyone living that sort of life will not inherit the Kingdom of God.

22But when the Holy Spirit controls our lives he will produce this kind of fruit in us: love, joy, peace, patience, kindness, goodness, faithfulness, 23gentleness and self-control; and here there is no conflict with Jewish laws.

24Those who belong to Christ have

nailed their natural evil desires to his cross and crucified them there.

25If we are living now by the Holy Spirit's power, let us follow the Holy Spirit's leading in every part of our lives. 26Then we won't need to look for honors and popularity, which lead to jealousy and hard feelings.

PSALM 64:1–10

LORD, listen to my complaint: Oh, preserve my life from the conspiracy of these wicked men, these gangs of criminals. 3They cut me down with sharpened tongues; they aim their bitter words like arrows straight at my heart. 4They shoot from ambush at the innocent. Suddenly the deed is done, yet they are not afraid. 5They encourage each other to do evil. They meet in secret to set their traps. "He will never notice them here," they say. 6They keep a sharp lookout for opportunities of crime. They spend long hours with all their endless evil thoughts and plans.

7But God himself will shoot them down. Suddenly his arrow will pierce them. 8They will stagger backward, destroyed by those they spoke against. All who see it happening will scoff at them. 9Then everyone shall stand in awe and confess the greatness of the miracles of God; at last they will realize what amazing things he does. 10And the godly shall rejoice in the Lord, and trust and praise him.

PROVERBS FOR TODAY/ 23:23

Get the facts at any price, and hold on tightly to all the good sense you can get.

SEPTEMBER 21

ISAIAH 37:1—38:22

WHEN King Hezekiah heard the results of the meeting, he tore his robes and wound himself in coarse cloth used for making sacks, as a sign of humility and mourning, and went over to the Temple to pray. 2Meanwhile he sent Eliakim his prime minister, and Shebna his royal scribe, and the older priests—all dressed in sackcloth—to Isaiah the prophet, son of Amoz. 3They brought him this message from Hezekiah:

"This is a day of trouble and frustration and blasphemy; it is a serious time, as when a woman is in heavy labor trying to give birth, and the child does not come. 4But perhaps the Lord your God heard the blasphemy of the king of Assyria's representative as he scoffed at the Living God. Surely God won't let him get away with this. Surely God will rebuke him for those words. Oh, Isaiah, pray for us who are left!"

5So they took the king's message to Isaiah.

6Then Isaiah replied, "Tell King Hezekiah that the Lord says, Don't be disturbed by this speech from the servant of the king of Assyria, and his blasphemy. 7For a report from Assyria will reach the king that he is needed at home at once, and he will return to his own land, where I will have him killed."

8,9Now the Assyrian envoy left Jerusalem and went to consult his king, who had left Lachish and was besieging Libnah. But at this point the Assyrian king received word that Tirhakah, crown prince of Ethiopia, was leading an army against him [from the south]. Upon hearing this, he sent messengers back to Jerusalem to Hezekiah with this message:

¹⁰"Don't let this God you trust in fool you by promising that Jerusalem will not be captured by the king of Assyria! ¹¹Just remember what has happened wherever the kings of Assyria have gone, for they have crushed everyone who has opposed them. Do you think you will be any different? ¹²Did their gods save the cities of Gozan, Haran, or Rezeph, or the people of Eden in Telassar? No, the Assyrian kings completely destroyed them! ¹³And don't forget what happened to the king of Hamath, to the king of Arpad, and to the kings of the cities of Sepharvaim, Hena, and Ivvah."

¹⁴As soon as King Hezekiah had read this letter, he went over to the Temple and spread it out before the Lord, ¹⁵and prayed, saying, ¹⁶,¹⁷"O Lord, Almighty God of Israel enthroned between the Guardian Angels, *you alone* are God of all the kingdoms of the earth. You alone made heaven and earth. Listen as I plead; see me as I pray. Look at this letter from King Sennacherib, for he has mocked the Living God. ¹⁸It is true, O Lord, that the kings of Assyria have destroyed all those nations, just as the letter says, ¹⁹and thrown their gods into the fire; for they weren't gods at all, but merely idols, carved by men from wood and stone. Of course the Assyrians could destroy them. ²⁰O Lord our God, save us so that all the kingdoms of the earth will know that you are God, and you alone."

²¹Then Isaiah, the son of Amoz, sent this message to King Hezekiah: "The Lord God of Israel says, This is my answer to your prayer against Sennacherib, Assyria's king.

²²"The Lord says to him: My people—the helpless virgin daughter of Zion—laughs at you and scoffs and shakes her head at you in scorn. ²³Who is it you scoffed against and mocked? Whom did you revile? At whom did you direct your violence and pride? It was against the Holy One of Israel! ²⁴You have sent your messengers to mock the Lord. You boast, 'I came with my mighty army

against the nations of the west. I cut down the tallest cedars and choicest cypress trees. I conquered their highest mountains and destroyed their thickest forests.'

²⁵"You boast of wells you've dug in many a conquered land, and Egypt with all its armies is no obstacle to you! ²⁶But do you not yet know that it was I who decided all this long ago? That it was I who gave you all this power from ancient times? I have caused all this to happen as I planned—that you should crush walled cities into ruined heaps. ²⁷That's why their people had so little power, and were such easy prey for you. They were as helpless as the grass, as tender plants you trample down beneath your feet, as grass upon the housetops, burnt yellow by the sun. ²⁸But I know you well—your comings and goings and all you do—and the way you have raged against me. ²⁹Because of your anger against the Lord—and I heard it all!—I have put a hook in your nose and a bit in your mouth and led you back to your own land by the same road you came."

³⁰Then God said to Hezekiah, "Here is the proof that I am the one who is delivering this city from the king of Assyria: This year he will abandon his siege. Although it is too late now to plant your crops, and you will have only volunteer grain this fall, still it will give you enough seed for a small harvest next year, and two years from now you will be living in luxury again. ³¹And you who are left in Judah will take root again in your own soil and flourish and multiply. ³²For a remnant shall go out from Jerusalem to repopulate the land; the power of the Lord Almighty will cause all this to come to pass.

³³"As for the king of Assyria, his armies shall not enter Jerusalem, nor shoot their arrows there, nor march outside its gates, nor build up an earthen bank against its walls. ³⁴He will return to his own country by the road he came on, and will not enter this city, says the Lord. ³⁵For my own honor I will defend it, and in memory of my servant David."

36That night the Angel of the Lord went out to the camp of the Assyrians and killed 185,000 soldiers; when the living wakened the next morning, all these lay dead before them. 37Then Sennacherib, king of Assyria, returned to his own country, to Nineveh. 38And one day while he was worshiping in the temple of Nisroch his god, his sons Adrammelech and Sharezer killed him with their swords; then they escaped into the land of Ararat, and Esar-haddon his son became king.

It was just before all this that Hezekiah became deathly sick and Isaiah the prophet (Amoz' son) went to visit him and gave him this message from the Lord:

"Set your affairs in order, for you are going to die; you will not recover from this illness."

2When Hezekiah heard this, he turned his face to the wall and prayed:

3"O Lord, don't you remember how true I've been to you and how I've always tried to obey you in everything you said?" Then he broke down with great sobs.

4So the Lord sent another message to Isaiah:

5"Go and tell Hezekiah that the Lord God of your forefather David hears you praying and sees your tears and will let you live fifteen more years. 6He will deliver you and this city from the king of Assyria. I will defend you, says the Lord, 7and here is my guarantee: 8I will send the sun backwards ten degrees as measured on Ahaz' sundial!"

So the sun retraced ten degrees that it had gone down!

9When King Hezekiah was well again, he wrote this poem about his experience:

10"My life is but half done and I must leave it all. I am robbed of my normal years, and now I must enter the gates of Sheol. 11Never again will I see the Lord in the land of the living. Never again will I see my friends in this world. 12My life is blown away like a shepherd's tent; it is cut short as when a weaver stops his working at the loom. In one short day my life hangs by a thread.

13"All night I moaned; it was like being torn apart by lions. 14Delirious, I chattered like a swallow and mourned like a dove; my eyes grew weary of looking up for help. 'O God,' I cried, 'I am in trouble—help me.' 15But what can I say? For he himself has sent this sickness. All my sleep has fled because of my soul's bitterness. 16O Lord, your discipline is good and leads to life and health. Oh, heal me and make me live!

17"Yes, now I see it all—it was good for me to undergo this bitterness, for you have lovingly delivered me from death; you have forgiven all my sins. 18For dead men cannot praise you. They cannot be filled with hope and joy. 19The living, only the living, can praise you as I do today. One generation makes known your faithfulness to the next. 20Think of it! The Lord healed me! Every day of my life from now on I will sing my songs of praise in the Temple, accompanied by the orchestra."

21(For Isaiah had told Hezekiah's servants, "Make an ointment of figs and spread it over the boil, and he will get well again."

22And then Hezekiah had asked, "What sign will the Lord give me to prove that he will heal me?")

GALATIANS 6:1-18

DEAR brothers, if a Christian is overcome by some sin, you who are godly should gently and humbly help him back onto the right path, remembering that next time it might be one of you who is in the wrong. 2Share each other's troubles and problems, and so obey our Lord's command. 3If anyone thinks he is too great to stoop to this, he is fooling himself. He is really a nobody.

4Let everyone be sure that he is doing his very best, for then he will have the personal satisfaction of work well done, and won't need to compare himself with someone else. 5Each of us must bear some faults and burdens of his own. For none of us is perfect!

6Those who are taught the Word of God should help their teachers by paying them.

7Don't be misled; remember that you can't ignore God and get away with it: a man will always reap just the kind of crop he sows! 8If he sows to please his own wrong desires, he will be planting seeds of evil and he will surely reap a harvest of spiritual decay and death; but if he plants the good things of the Spirit, he will reap the everlasting life which the Holy Spirit gives him. 9And let us not get tired of doing what is right, for after a while we will reap a harvest of blessing if we don't get discouraged and give up. 10That's why whenever we can we should always be kind to everyone, and especially to our Christian brothers.

11I will write these closing words in my own handwriting. See how large I have to make the letters! 12Those teachers of yours who are trying to convince you to be circumcised are doing it for just one reason: so that they can be popular and avoid the persecution they would get if they admitted that the cross of Christ alone can save. 13And even those teachers who submit to circumcision don't try to keep the other Jewish laws; but they want you to be circumcised in order that they can boast that you are their disciples.

14As for me, God forbid that I should boast about anything except the cross of our Lord Jesus Christ. Because of that cross my interest in all the attractive things of the world was killed long ago, and the world's interest in me is also long dead. 15It doesn't make any difference now whether we have been circumcised or not; what counts is whether we really have been changed into new and different people.

16May God's mercy and peace be upon all of you who live by this principle and upon those everywhere who are really God's own.

17From now on please don't argue with me about these things, for I carry on my body the scars of the whippings and wounds from Jesus' enemies that mark me as his slave.

18Dear brothers, may the grace of our Lord Jesus Christ be with you all.

Sincerely,
Paul

PSALM 65:1–13

O God in Zion, we wait before you in silent praise, and thus fulfill our vow. And because you answer prayer, all mankind will come to you with their requests. 3Though sins fill our hearts, you forgive them all. 4How greatly to be envied are those you have chosen to come and live with you within the holy tabernacle courts! What joys await us among all the good things there. 5With dread deeds and awesome power you will defend us from our enemies, O God who saves us. You are the only hope of all mankind throughout the world and far away upon the sea.

6He formed the mountains by his mighty strength. 7He quiets the raging oceans and all the world's clamor. 8In the farthest corners of the earth the glorious acts of God shall startle everyone. The dawn and sunset shout for joy! 9He waters the earth to make it fertile. The rivers of God will not run dry! He prepares the earth for his people and sends them rich harvests of grain. 10He waters the furrows with abundant rain. Showers soften the earth, melting the clods and causing seeds to sprout across the land. 11,12Then he crowns it all with green, lush pastures in the wilderness; hillsides blossom with joy. 13The pastures are filled with flocks of sheep, and the valleys are carpeted with grain. All the world shouts with joy, and sings.

PROVERBS FOR TODAY/ 23:24, 25

The father of a godly man has cause for joy—what pleasure a wise son is! So give your parents joy!

SEPTEMBER 22

ISAIAH 39:1—41:16

SOON afterwards, the king of Babylon (Merodach-baladan, the son of Baladan) sent Hezekiah a present and his best wishes, for he had heard that Hezekiah had been very sick and now was well again. 2Hezekiah appreciated this and took the envoys from Babylon on a tour of the palace, showing them his treasure house full of silver, gold, spices and perfumes. He took them into his jewel rooms, too, and opened to them all his treasures—everything.

3Then Isaiah the prophet came to the king and said, "What did they say? Where are they from?"

"From far away in Babylon," Hezekiah replied.

4"How much have they seen?" asked Isaiah.

And Hezekiah replied, "I showed them everything I own, all my priceless treasures."

5Then Isaiah said to him, "Listen to this message from the Lord Almighty: 6"The time is coming when everything you have—all the treasures stored up by your fathers—will be carried off to Babylon. Nothing will be left. 7And some of your own sons will become slaves, yes, eunuchs, in the palace of the king of Babylon."

8"All right," Hezekiah replied. "Whatever the Lord says is good. At least there will be peace during my lifetime!"

COMFORT, yes, comfort my people, says your God. 2Speak tenderly to Jerusalem and tell her that her sad days are gone. Her sins are pardoned, and I have punished her in full for all her sins.

3Listen! I hear the voice of someone shouting, "Make a road for the Lord through the wilderness; make him a straight, smooth road through the desert. 4Fill the valleys; level the hills; straighten out the crooked paths and smooth off the rough spots in the road. 5The glory of the Lord will be seen by all mankind together." The Lord has spoken—it shall be.

6The voice says, "Shout!"

"What shall I shout?" I asked.

"Shout that man is like the grass that dies away, and all his beauty fades like dying flowers. 7The grass withers, the flower fades beneath the breath of God. And so it is with fragile man. 8The grass withers, the flowers fade, but the Word of our God shall stand forever."

9O Crier of Good News, shout to Jerusalem from the mountain tops! Shout louder—don't be afraid—tell the cities of Judah, "Your God is coming!" 10Yes, the Lord God is coming with mighty power; he will rule with awesome strength. See, his reward is with him, to each as he has done. 11He will feed his flock like a shepherd; he will carry the lambs in his arms and gently lead the ewes with young.

12Who else has held the oceans in his hands and measured off the heavens with his ruler? Who else knows the weight of all the earth and weighs the mountains and the hills? 13Who can advise the Spirit of the Lord or be his teacher or give him counsel? 14Has he ever needed anyone's advice? Did he need instruction as to what is right and best? 15No, for all the peoples of the world are nothing in comparison with him—they are but a drop in the bucket, dust on the scales. He picks up the islands as though they had no weight at all. 16All of Lebanon's forests do not contain sufficient fuel to consume a sacrifice large enough to honor him, nor are all its animals enough to offer to our God. 17All the nations are as nothing to him; in his eyes they are less than nothing—mere emptiness and froth.

18How can we describe God? With what can we compare him? 19With an idol? An idol, made from a mold, overlaid with gold, and with silver chains around its neck? 20The man too poor to buy expensive gods like that will find a tree free from rot and hire a man to carve a face on it, and that's his god—a god that cannot even move!

21Are you so ignorant? Are you so deaf to the words of God—the words he gave before the world began? Have you never heard nor understood? 22It is God who sits above the circle of the earth. (The people below must seem to him like grasshoppers!) He is the one who stretches out the heavens like a curtain and makes his tent from them. 23He dooms the great men of the world and brings them all to naught. 24They hardly get started, barely take root, when he blows on them and their work withers and the wind carries them off like straw.

25"With whom will you compare me? Who is my equal?" asks the Holy One.

26Look up into the heavens! Who created all these stars? As a shepherd leads his sheep, calling each by its pet name, and counts them to see that none are lost or strayed, so God does with stars and planets!

27O Jacob, O Israel, how can you say that the Lord doesn't see your troubles and isn't being fair? 28Don't you yet understand? Don't you know by now that the everlasting God, the Creator of the farthest parts of the earth, never grows faint or weary? No one can fathom the depths of his understanding. 29He gives power to the tired and worn out, and strength to the weak. 30Even the youths shall be exhausted, and the young men will all give up. 31But they that wait upon the Lord shall renew their strength. They shall mount up with wings like eagles; they shall run and not be weary; they shall walk and not faint.

LISTEN in silence before me, O lands beyond the sea. Bring your strongest arguments. Come now and speak. The court is ready for your case.

2Who has stirred up this one from the east, whom victory meets at every step? Who, indeed, but the Lord? God has given him victory over many nations and permitted him to trample kings underfoot and to put entire armies to the sword. 3He chases them away and goes on safely, though the paths he treads are new. 4Who has done such mighty deeds, directing the affairs of generations of mankind as they march by? It is I, the Lord, the First and Last; I alone am he.

5The lands beyond the sea watch in fear and wait for word of Cyrus' new campaigns. Remote lands tremble and mobilize for war. 6,7The craftsmen encourage each other as they rush to make new idols to protect them. The carver hurries the goldsmith, and the molder helps at the anvil. "Good," they say. "It's coming along fine. Now we can solder on the arms." Carefully they join the parts together, and then fasten the thing in place so it won't fall over!

8But as for you, O Israel, you are mine, my chosen ones; for you are Abraham's family, and he was my friend. 9I have called you back from the ends of the earth and said that you must serve but me alone, for I have chosen you and will not throw you away. 10Fear not, for I am with you. Do not be dismayed. I am your God. I will strengthen you; I will help you; I will uphold you with my victorious right hand.

11See, all your angry enemies lie confused and shattered. Anyone opposing you will die. 12You will look for them in vain—they will all be gone. 13I am holding you by your right hand—I, the Lord your God—and I say to you, Don't be afraid; I am here to help you. 14Despised though you are, fear not, O Israel; for I will help you. I am the Lord, your Redeemer; I am the Holy One of Israel. 15You shall be a new and sharp-toothed threshing instrument to tear all enemies apart, making chaff of mountains. 16You shall toss them in the air; the wind shall blow them all away; whirlwinds shall scatter them. And the joy of the Lord shall fill you full; you shall glory in the God of Israel.

DEAR Christian friends at Ephesus, ever loyal to the Lord: This is Paul writing to you, chosen by God to be Jesus Christ's messenger. ²May his blessings and peace be yours, sent to you from God our Father and Jesus Christ our Lord.

³How we praise God, the Father of our Lord Jesus Christ, who has blessed us with every blessing in heaven because we belong to Christ.

⁴Long ago, even before he made the world, God chose us to be his very own, through what Christ would do for us; he decided then to make us holy in his eyes, without a single fault—we who stand before him covered with his love. ⁵His unchanging plan has always been to adopt us into his own family by sending Jesus Christ to die for us. And he did this because he wanted to!

⁶Now all praise to God for his wonderful kindness to us and his favor that he has poured out upon us, because we belong to his dearly loved Son. ⁷So overflowing is his kindness toward us that he took away all our sins through the blood of his Son, by whom we are saved; ⁸and he has showered down upon us the richness of his grace—for how well he understands us and knows what is best for us at all times.

⁹God has told us his secret reason for sending Christ, a plan he decided on in mercy long ago; ¹⁰and this was his purpose: that when the time is ripe he will gather us all together from wherever we are—in heaven or on earth—to be with him in Christ, forever. ¹¹Moreover, because of what Christ has done we have become gifts to God that he delights in, for as part of God's sovereign plan we were chosen from the beginning to be his, and all things happen just as he decided long ago. ¹²God's purpose in this was that we should praise God and give glory to him for doing these mighty things for us, who were the first to trust in Christ.

¹³And because of what Christ did, all you others too, who heard the Good News about how to be saved, and trusted Christ, were marked as belonging to Christ by the Holy Spirit, who long ago had been promised to all of us Christians. ¹⁴His presence within us is God's guarantee that he really will give us all that he promised; and the Spirit's seal upon us means that God has already purchased us and that he guarantees to bring us to himself. This is just one more reason for us to praise our glorious God.

¹⁵That is why, ever since I heard of your strong faith in the Lord Jesus and of the love you have for Christians everywhere, ¹⁶,¹⁷I have never stopped thanking God for you. I pray for you constantly, asking God, the glorious Father of our Lord Jesus Christ, to give us wisdom to see clearly and really understand who Christ is and all that he has done for you. ¹⁸I pray that your hearts will be flooded with light so that you can see something of the future he has called you to share. I want you to realize that God has been made rich because we who are Christ's have been given to him! ¹⁹I pray that you will begin to understand how incredibly great his power is to help those who believe him. It is that same mighty power ²⁰that raised Christ from the dead and seated him in the place of honor at God's right hand in heaven, ²¹far, far above any other king or ruler or dictator or leader. Yes, his honor is far more glorious than that of anyone else either in this world or in the world to come. ²²And God has put all things under his feet and made him the supreme Head of the Church— ²³which is his body, filled with himself, the Author and Giver of everything everywhere.

PSALM 66:1–20

SING to the Lord, all the earth! ²Sing of his glorious name! Tell the world how wonderful he is.

³How awe-inspiring are your deeds, O God! How great your power! No wonder your enemies surrender! ⁴All the

earth shall worship you and sing of your glories. 5Come, see the glorious things God has done. What marvelous miracles happen to his people! 6He made a dry road through the sea for them. They went across on foot. What excitement and joy there was that day!

7Because of his great power he rules forever. He watches every movement of the nations. O rebel lands, he will deflate your pride.

8Let everyone bless God and sing his praises, 9for he holds our lives in his hands. And he holds our feet to the path. 10You have purified us with fire, O Lord, like silver in a crucible. 11You captured us in your net and laid great burdens on our backs. 12You sent troops to ride across our broken bodies. We went through fire and flood. But in the end, you brought us into wealth and great abundance.

13Now I have come to your Temple with burnt offerings to pay my vows. 14For when I was in trouble I promised you many offerings. 15That is why I am bringing you these fat male goats, rams and calves. The smoke of their sacrifice shall rise before you.

16Come and hear, all of you who reverence the Lord, and I will tell you what he did for me: 17For I cried to him for help, with praises ready on my tongue. 18He would not have listened if I had not confessed my sins. 19But he listened! He heard my prayer! He paid attention to it!

20Blessed be God who didn't turn away when I was praying, and didn't refuse me his kindness and love.

PROVERBS FOR TODAY/ 23:26–28

O my son, trust my advice—stay away from prostitutes. For a prostitute is a deep and narrow grave. Like a robber, she waits for her victims as one after another become unfaithful to their wives.

SEPTEMBER 23

ISAIAH 41:17—43:13

WHEN the poor and needy seek water and there is none and their tongues are parched from thirst, then I will answer when they cry to me. I, Israel's God, will not ever forsake them. 18I will open up rivers for them on high plateaus! I will give them fountains of water in the valleys! In the deserts will be pools of water, and rivers fed by springs shall flow across the dry, parched ground. 19I will plant trees—cedars, myrtle, olive trees, the cypress, fir and pine—on barren land. 20Everyone will see this miracle and understand that it is God who did it, Israel's Holy One.

21Can your idols make such claims as these? Let them come and show what they can do! says God, the King of Israel. 22Let them try to tell us what occurred in years gone by, or what the future holds. 23Yes, that's it! If you are gods, tell what will happen in the days ahead! Or do some mighty miracle that makes us stare, amazed. 24But no! You are less than nothing, and can do nothing at all. Anyone who chooses you needs to have his head examined!

25But I have stirred up (Cyrus) from the north and east; he will come against the nations and call on my name, and I will give him victory over kings and princes. He will tread them as a potter tramples clay.

26Who but I have told you this would happen? Who else predicted this, making you admit that he was right? No one else! None other said one word!

27I was the first to tell Jerusalem, "Look! Look! Help is on the way!" 28Not one of your idols told you this. Not one gave any answer when I asked. 29See, they are all foolish, worthless things; your idols are all as empty as the wind.

SEE my servant, whom I uphold; my Chosen One, in whom I delight. I have put my Spirit upon him; he will reveal justice to the nations of the world. 2He will be gentle—he will not shout nor quarrel in the streets. 3He will not break the bruised reed, nor quench the dimly burning flame. He will encourage the fainthearted, those tempted to despair. He will see full justice given to all who have been wronged. 4He won't be satisfied until truth and righteousness prevail throughout the earth, nor until even distant lands beyond the seas have put their trust in him.

5The Lord God who created the heavens and stretched them out and created the earth and everything in it, and gives life and breath and spirit to everyone in all the world, he is the one who says [to his Servant, the Messiah],

6"I the Lord have called you to demonstrate my righteousness. I will guard and support you, for I have given you to my people as the personal confirmation of my covenant with them. You shall also be a light to guide the nations unto me. 7You will open the eyes of the blind, and release those who sit in prison darkness and despair. 8I am the Lord! That is my name, and I will not give my glory to anyone else; I will not share my praise with carved idols. 9Everything I prophesied came true, and now I will prophesy again. I will tell you the future before it happens."

10Sing a new song to the Lord; sing his praises, all you who live in earth's remotest corners! Sing, O sea! Sing, all you who live in distant lands beyond the sea! 11Join in the chorus, you desert cities—Kedar and Sela! And you, too, dwellers in the mountain tops. 12Let the western coastlands glorify the Lord and sing his mighty power.

13The Lord will be a mighty warrior, full of fury toward his foes. He will give a great shout and prevail. 14Long has he been silent; he has restrained himself. But now he will give full vent to his wrath; he will groan and cry like a woman delivering her child. 15He will level the mountains and hills and blight their greenery. He will dry up the rivers and pools. 16He will bring blind Israel along a path they have not seen before. He will make the darkness bright before them and smooth and straighten out the road ahead. He will not forsake them. 17But those who trust in idols and call them gods will be greatly disappointed; they will be turned away.

18Oh, how blind and deaf you are towards God! Why won't you listen? Why won't you see? 19Who in all the world is as blind as my own people, who are designed to be my messengers of truth? Who is so blind as my "dedicated one," the "servant of the Lord"? 20You see and understand what is right but won't heed nor do it; you hear but you won't listen.

21The Lord has magnified his law and made it truly glorious. Through it he had planned to show the world that he is righteous. 22But what a sight his people are—these who were to demonstrate to all the world the glory of his law; for they are robbed, enslaved, imprisoned, trapped, fair game for all, with no one to protect them. 23Won't even one of you apply these lessons from the past and see the ruin that awaits you up ahead? 24Who let Israel be robbed and hurt? Did not the Lord? It is the Lord they sinned against, for they would not go where he sent them nor listen to his laws. 25That is why God poured out such fury and wrath on his people and destroyed them in battle. Yet, though set on fire and burned, they will not understand the reason why—that it is God, wanting them to repent.

BUT now the Lord who created you, O Israel, says, Don't be afraid, for I have ransomed you; I have called you by name; you are mine. 2When you go through deep waters and great trouble, I will be with you. When you go through rivers of difficulty, you will not drown! When you walk through the fire of oppression, you will not be burned up—the flames will not consume you. ³For I am the Lord your God, your Savior, the Holy One of Israel. I gave Egypt and Ethiopia and Seba [to Cyrus] in exchange for your freedom, as your ransom. ⁴Others died that you might live; I traded their lives for yours because you are precious to me and honored, and I love you.

⁵Don't be afraid, for I am with you. I will gather you from east and west, ⁶from north and south. I will bring my sons and daughters back to Israel from the farthest corners of the earth. ⁷All who claim me as their God will come, for I have made them for my glory; I created them. ⁸Bring them back to me—blind as they are and deaf when I call (although they see and hear!).

⁹Gather the nations together! Which of all their idols ever has foretold such things? Which can predict a single day ahead? Where are the witnesses of anything they said? If there are no witnesses, then they must confess that only God can prophesy.

¹⁰But I have witnesses, O Israel, says the Lord! You are my witnesses and my servants, chosen to know and to believe me and to understand that I alone am God. There is no other God; there never was and never will be. ¹¹I am the Lord, and there is no other Savior. ¹²Whenever you have thrown away your idols, I have shown you my power. With one word I have saved you. You have seen me do it; you are my witnesses that it is true. ¹³From eternity to eternity I am God. No one can oppose what I do.

EPHESIANS 2:1–22

ONCE you were under God's curse, doomed forever for your sins. ²You went along with the crowd and were just like all the others, full of sin, obeying Satan, the mighty prince of the power of the air, who is at work right now in the hearts of those who are against the Lord. ³All of us used to be just as they are, our lives expressing the evil within us, doing every wicked thing that our passions or our evil thoughts might lead us into. We started out bad, being born with evil natures, and were under God's anger just like everyone else.

⁴But God is so rich in mercy; he loved us so much ⁵that even though we were spiritually dead and doomed by our sins, he gave us back our lives again when he raised Christ from the dead—only by his undeserved favor have we ever been saved— ⁶and lifted us up from the grave into glory along with Christ, where we sit with him in the heavenly realms—all because of what Christ Jesus did. ⁷And now God can always point to us as examples of how very, very rich his kindness is, as shown in all he has done for us through Jesus Christ.

⁸Because of his kindness you have been saved through trusting Christ. And even trusting is not of yourselves; it too is a gift from God. ⁹Salvation is not a reward for the good we have done, so none of us can take any credit for it. ¹⁰It is God himself who has made us what we are and given us new lives from Christ Jesus; and long ages ago he planned that we should spend these lives in helping others.

¹¹Never forget that once you were heathen, and that you were called godless and "unclean" by the Jews. (But their hearts, too, were still unclean, even though they were going through the ceremonies and rituals of the godly, for they circumcised themselves as a sign of godliness.) ¹²Remember that in those days you were living utterly apart from Christ; you were enemies of God's children and he had promised you no help. You were lost, without God, without hope.

¹³But now you belong to Christ Jesus, and though you once were far away from God, now you have been brought very near to him because of what Jesus Christ has done for you with his blood.

14For Christ himself is our way of peace. He has made peace between us Jews and you Gentiles by making us all one family, breaking down the wall of contempt that used to separate us. 15By his death he ended the angry resentment between us, caused by the Jewish laws which favored the Jews and excluded the Gentiles, for he died to annul that whole system of Jewish laws. Then he took the two groups that had been opposed to each other and made them parts of himself; thus he fused us together to become one new person, and at last there was peace. 16As parts of the same body, our anger against each other has disappeared, for both of us have been reconciled to God. And so the feud ended at last at the cross. 17And he has brought this Good News of peace to you Gentiles who were very far away from him, and to us Jews who were near. 18Now all of us, whether Jews or Gentiles, may come to God the Father with the Holy Spirit's help because of what Christ has done for us.

19Now you are no longer strangers to God and foreigners to heaven, but you are members of God's very own family, citizens of God's country, and you belong in God's household with every other Christian.

20What a foundation you stand on now: the apostles and the prophets; and the cornerstone of the building is Jesus Christ himself! 21We who believe are carefully joined together with Christ as parts of a beautiful, constantly growing temple for God. 22And you also are joined with him and with each other by the Spirit, and are part of this dwelling place of God.

PSALM 67:1–7

O God, in mercy bless us; let your face beam with joy as you look down at us.

2Send us around the world with the news of your saving power and your eternal plan for all mankind. 3How everyone throughout the earth will praise the Lord! 4How glad the nations will be, singing for joy because you are their King and will give true justice to their people! 5Praise God, O world! May all the peoples of the earth give thanks to you. 6,7For the earth has yielded abundant harvests. God, even our own God, will bless us. And peoples from remotest lands will worship him.

PROVERBS FOR TODAY/ 23:29–35

Whose heart is filled with anguish and sorrow? Who is always fighting and quarreling? Who is the man with bloodshot eyes and many wounds? It is the one who spends long hours in the taverns, trying out new mixtures. Don't let the sparkle and the smooth taste of strong wine deceive you. For in the end it bites like a poisonous serpent; it stings like an adder. You will see hallucinations and have delirium tremens, and you will say foolish, silly things that would embarrass you no end when sober. You will stagger like a sailor tossed at sea, clinging to a swaying mast. And afterwards you will say, "I didn't even know it when they beat me up. . . . Let's go and have another drink!"

SEPTEMBER 24

ISAIAH 43:14—45:10

THE Lord, your Redeemer, the Holy One of Israel, says:

For your sakes I will send an invading army against Babylon that will walk in, almost unscathed. The boasts of the Babylonians will turn to cries of fear. 15I am the Lord, your Holy One, Israel's Creator and King. 16I am the Lord, who opened a way through the waters, making a path right through the sea. 17I called forth the mighty army of Egypt with all its chariots and horses, to lie beneath the waves, dead, their lives snuffed out like candlewicks.

18But forget all that—it is nothing compared to what I'm going to do! 19For I'm going to do a brand new thing. See, I have already begun! Don't you see it? I will make a road through the wilderness of the world for my people to go home, and create rivers for them in the desert! 20The wild animals in the fields will thank me, the jackals and ostriches too, for giving them water in the wilderness, yes, springs in the desert, so that my people, my chosen ones, can be refreshed. 21I have made Israel for myself, and these my people will some day honor me before the world.

22But O my people, you won't ask my help; you have grown tired of me! 23You have not brought me the lambs for burnt offerings; you have not honored me with sacrifices. Yet my requests for offerings and incense have been very few! I have not treated you as slaves. 24You have brought me no sweet-smelling incense nor pleased me with the sacrificial fat. No, you have presented me only with sins, and wearied me with all your faults.

25I, yes, I alone am he who blots away your sins for my own sake and will never think of them again. 26Oh, remind me of this promise of forgiveness, for we must talk about your sins. Plead your case for my forgiving you. 27From the very first your ancestors sinned against me—all your forebears transgressed my law. 28That is why I have deposed your priests and destroyed Israel, leaving her to shame.

LISTEN to me, O my servant Israel, O my chosen ones:

2The Lord who made you, who will help you, says, O servant of mine, don't be afraid. O Jerusalem, my chosen ones, don't be afraid. 3For I will give you abundant water for your thirst and for your parched fields. And I will pour out my Spirit and my blessings on your children. 4They shall thrive like watered grass, like willows on a river bank. 5"I am the Lord's," they'll proudly say, or, "I am a Jew," and tattoo upon their hands the name of God or the honored name of Israel.

6The Lord, the King of Israel, says—yes, it is Israel's Redeemer, the Lord Almighty, who says it—I am the First and Last; there is no other God. 7Who else can tell you what is going to happen in the days ahead? Let them tell you if they can, and prove their power. Let them do as I have done since ancient times. 8Don't, don't be afraid. Haven't I proclaimed from ages past [that I would save you]? You are my witnesses—is there any other God? No! None that I know about! There is no other Rock!

9What fools they are who manufacture idols for their gods. Their hopes remain unanswered. They themselves are witnesses that this is so, for their idols neither see nor know. No wonder those who worship them are so ashamed. 10Who but a fool would make his own god—an idol that can help him not one whit! 11All that worship these will stand before the Lord in shame, along with all these carpenters—mere men—who claim that they have made a god. Together they will stand in terror. 12The metalsmith stands at his forge to make an axe, pounding on it with all his might. He grows hungry and thirsty, weak and faint. 13Then the woodcarver takes the axe and uses it to make an idol. He measures and marks out a block of wood and carves the figure of a man. Now he has a wonderful idol that can't so much as move from where it is placed. 14He cuts down cedars, he selects the cypress and the oak, he plants the ash in the forest to be nourished by the rain. 15And after his care, he uses part of the wood to make a fire to warm himself and bake his bread, and then—he really does—he takes the rest of it and makes himself a god—a god for men to worship! An idol to fall down before and praise! 16Part of the tree he burns to roast his meat and to keep him warm and fed and well content, 17and with what's left he makes his god: a carved idol! He falls down before it and worships it and prays to it. "Deliver me," he says. "You are my god!"

18Such stupidity and ignorance! God has shut their eyes so that they cannot see, and closed their minds from understanding. 19The man never stops to think or figure out, "Why, it's just a block of wood! I've burned it for heat and used it to bake my bread and roast my meat. How can the rest of it be a god? Should I fall down before a chunk of wood?" 20The poor, deluded fool feeds on ashes; he is trusting what can never give him any help at all. Yet he cannot bring himself to ask, "Is this thing, this idol that I'm holding in my hand, a lie?"

21Pay attention, Israel, for you are my servant; I made you, and I will not forget to help you. 22I've blotted out your sins; they are gone like morning mist at noon! Oh, return to me, for I have paid the price to set you free.

23Sing, O heavens, for the Lord has done this wondrous thing. Shout, O earth; break forth into song, O mountains and forests, yes, and every tree; for the Lord redeemed Jacob and is glorified in Israel! 24The Lord, your Redeemer who made you, says, All things were made by me; I alone stretched out the heavens. By myself I made the earth and everything in it.

25I am the one who shows what liars all false prophets are, by causing something else to happen than the things they say. I make wise men give opposite advice to what they should, and make them into fools. 26But what my prophets say, I do; when they say Jerusalem will be delivered and the cities of Judah lived in once again—it shall be done! 27When I speak to the rivers and say, "Be dry!" they shall be dry. 28When I say of Cyrus, "He is my shepherd," he will certainly do as I say; and Jerusalem will be rebuilt and the Temple restored, for I have spoken it.

THIS is Jehovah's message to Cyrus, God's anointed, whom he has chosen to conquer many lands. God shall empower his right hand and he shall crush the strength of mighty kings. God shall open the gates of Babylon to him; the gates shall not be shut against him any more. 2I will go before you, Cyrus, and level the mountains and smash down the city gates of brass and iron bars. 3And I will give you treasures hidden in the darkness, secret riches; and you will know that I am doing this—I, the Lord, the God of Israel, the one who calls you by your name.

4And why have I named you for this work? For the sake of Jacob, my servant—Israel, my chosen. I called you by name when you didn't know me. 5I am Jehovah; there is no other God. I will strengthen you and send you out to victory even though you don't know me, 6and all the world from east to west will know there is no other God. I am Jehovah and there is no one else. I alone am God. 7I form the light and make the dark. I send good times and bad. I, Jehovah, am he who does these things. 8Open up, O heavens. Let the skies pour out their righteousness. Let salvation and righteousness sprout up together from the earth. I, Jehovah, created them.

9Woe to the man who fights with his

Creator. Does the pot argue with its maker? Does the clay dispute with him who forms it, saying, "Stop, you're doing it wrong!" or the pot exclaim, "How clumsy can you be!"? 10Woe to the baby just being born who squalls to his father and mother, "Why have you produced me? Can't you do anything right at all?"

EPHESIANS 3:1–21

I Paul, the servant of Christ, am here in jail because of you—for preaching that you Gentiles are a part of God's house. 2,3No doubt you already know that God has given me this special work of showing God's favor to you Gentiles, as I briefly mentioned before in one of my letters. God himself showed me this secret plan of his, that the Gentiles, too, are included in his kindness. 4I say this to explain to you how I know about these things. 5In olden times God did not share this plan with his people, but now he has revealed it by the Holy Spirit to his apostles and prophets.

6And this is the secret: that the Gentiles will have their full share with the Jews in all the riches inherited by God's sons; both are invited to belong to his Church, and all of God's promises of mighty blessings through Christ apply to them both when they accept the Good News about Christ and what he has done for them. 7God has given me the wonderful privilege of telling everyone about this plan of his; and he has given me his power and special ability to do it well.

8Just think! Though I did nothing to deserve it, and though I am the most useless Christian there is, yet I was the one chosen for this special joy of telling the Gentiles the Glad News of the endless treasures available to them in Christ; 9and to explain to everyone that God is the Savior of the Gentiles too, just as he who made all things had secretly planned from the very beginning.

10And his reason? To show to all the rulers in heaven how perfectly wise he is when all of his family—Jews and Gentiles alike—are seen to be joined together in his Church, 11in just the way he had always planned it through Jesus Christ our Lord.

12Now we can come fearlessly right into God's presence, assured of his glad welcome when we come with Christ and trust in him.

13So please don't lose heart at what they are doing to me here. It is for you I am suffering and you should feel honored and encouraged.

14,15When I think of the wisdom and scope of his plan I fall down on my knees and pray to the Father of all the great family of God—some of them already in heaven and some down here on earth— 16that out of his glorious, unlimited resources he will give you the mighty inner strengthening of his Holy Spirit. 17And I pray that Christ will be more and more at home in your hearts, living within you as you trust in him. May your roots go down deep into the soil of God's marvelous love; 18,19and may you be able to feel and understand, as all God's children should, how long, how wide, how deep, and how high his love really is; and to experience this love for yourselves, though it is so great that you will never see the end of it or fully know or understand it. And so at last you will be filled up with God himself.

20Now glory be to God who by his mighty power at work within us is able to do far more than we would ever dare to ask or even dream of—infinitely beyond our highest prayers, desires, thoughts, or hopes. 21May he be given glory forever and ever through endless ages because of his master plan of salvation for the Church through Jesus Christ.

PSALM 68:1–18

A RISE, O God, and scatter all your enemies! Chase them away! 2Drive them off like smoke before the wind; melt them like wax in fire! So let the wicked perish at the presence of God.

3But may the godly man exult. May he rejoice and be merry. 4Sing praises to the Lord! Raise your voice in song to him who rides upon the clouds! Jehovah is his name—oh, rejoice in his presence. 5He is a father to the fatherless; he gives justice to the widows, for he is holy. 6He gives families to the lonely, and releases prisoners from jail, singing with joy! But for rebels there is famine and distress.

7O God, when you led your people through the wilderness, 8the earth trembled and the heavens shook. Mount Sinai quailed before you—the God of Israel. 9,10You sent abundant rain upon your land, O God, to refresh it in its weariness! There your people lived, for you gave them this home when they were destitute.

11,12,13The Lord speaks. The enemy flees. The women at home cry out the happy news: "The armies that came to destroy us have fled!" Now all the women of Israel are dividing the booty. See them sparkle with jewels of silver and gold, covered all over as wings cover doves! 14God scattered their enemies like snowflakes melting in the forests of Zalmon.

15,16O mighty mountains in Bashan! O splendid many-peaked ranges! Well may you look with envy at Mount Zion, the mount where God has chosen to live forever. 17Surrounded by unnumbered chariots, the Lord moves on from Mount Sinai and comes to his holy temple high upon Mount Zion. 18He ascends the heights, leading many captives in his train. He receives gifts for men, even those who once were rebels. God will live among us here.

PROVERBS FOR TODAY/ 24:1–2

Don't envy godless men; don't even enjoy their company. For they spend their days plotting violence and cheating.

SEPTEMBER 25

ISAIAH 45:11—48:11

JEHOVAH, the Holy One of Israel, Israel's Creator, says: What right have you to question what I do? Who are you to command me concerning the work of my hands? 12I have made the earth and created man upon it. With my hands I have stretched out the heavens and commanded all the vast myriads of stars. 13I have raised up Cyrus to fulfill my righteous purpose, and I will direct all his paths. He shall restore my city and free my captive people—and not for a reward!

14Jehovah says: The Egyptians, Ethiopians and Sabeans shall be subject to you. They shall come to you with all their merchandise and it shall all be yours. They shall follow you as prisoners in chains, and fall down on their knees before you and say, "The only God there is, is your God!"

15Truly, O God of Israel, Savior, you work in strange, mysterious ways. 16All who worship idols shall be disappointed and ashamed. 17But Israel shall be saved by Jehovah with eternal salvation; they shall never be disappointed in their God through all eternity. 18For Jehovah created the heavens and earth and put everything in place, and he made the world to be lived in, not to be an empty chaos. I am Jehovah, he says, and there is no other! 19I publicly proclaim bold promises; I do not whisper obscurities in some dark corner so that no one can know what I mean. And I didn't tell Israel to ask me for what I didn't plan to give!

No, for I, Jehovah, speak only truth and righteousness.

20Gather together and come, you nations that escape from Cyrus' hand. What fools they are who carry around the wooden idols and pray to gods that cannot save! 21Consult together, argue your case and state your proofs that idol-worship pays! Who but God has said that these things concerning Cyrus would come true? What idol ever told you they would happen? For there is no other God but me—a just God and a Savior—no, not one! 22Let all the world look to me for salvation! For I am God; there is no other. 23I have sworn by myself and I will never go back on my word, for it is true—that every knee in all the world shall bow to me, and every tongue shall swear allegiance to my name.

24"In Jehovah is all my righteousness and strength," the people shall declare. And all who were angry with him shall come to him and be ashamed. 25In Jehovah all the generations of Israel shall be justified, triumphant.

THE idols of Babylon, Bel and Nebo, are being hauled away on ox carts! But look! The beasts are stumbling! The cart is turning over! The gods are falling out onto the ground! Is that the best that they can do? If they cannot even save themselves from such a fall, how can they save their worshipers from Cyrus?

3"Listen to me, all Israel who are left; I have created you and cared for you since you were born. 4I will be your God through all your lifetime, yes, even when your hair is white with age. I made you and I will care for you. I will carry you along and be your Savior.

5"With what in all of heaven and earth do I compare? Whom can you find who equals me? 6Will you compare me with an idol made lavishly with silver and with gold? They hire a goldsmith to take your wealth and make a god from it! Then they fall down and worship it! 7They carry it around on their shoulders, and when they set it down it stays there, for it cannot move! And when someone prays to it there is no answer, for it cannot get him out of his trouble.

8"Don't forget this, O guilty ones. 9And don't forget the many times I clearly told you what was going to happen in the future. For I am God—I only—and there is no other like me 10who can tell you what is going to happen. All I say will come to pass, for I do whatever I wish. 11I will call that swift bird of prey from the east—that man Cyrus from far away. And he will come and do my bidding. I have said I would do it and I will. 12Listen to me, you stubborn, evil men! 13For I am offering you my deliverance; not in the distant future, but right now! I am ready to save you, and I will restore Jerusalem, and Israel, who is my glory.

O Babylon, the unconquered, come sit in the dust; for your days of glory, pomp and honor are ended. O daughter of Chaldea, never again will you be the lovely princess, tender and delicate. 2Take heavy millstones and grind the corn; remove your veil; strip off your robe; expose yourself to public view. 3You shall be in nakedness and shame. I will take vengeance upon you and will not repent."

4So speaks our Redeemer, who will save Israel from Babylon's mighty power; the Lord Almighty is his name, the Holy One of Israel.

5Sit in darkness and silence, O Babylon; never again will you be called "The Queen of Kingdoms." 6For I was angry with my people Israel and began to punish them a little by letting them fall into your hands, O Babylon. But you showed them no mercy. You have made even the old folks carry heavy burdens. 7You thought your reign would never end, Queen Kingdom of the world. You didn't care a whit about my people or think about the fate of those who do them harm.

8O pleasure-mad kingdom, living at ease, bragging as the greatest in the world—listen to the sentence of my court upon your sins. You say, "I alone am God! I'll never be a widow; I'll never lose my children." 9Well, those two things shall come upon you in one moment, in full measure in one day: widowhood and the loss of your children, despite all your witchcraft and magic.

10You felt secure in all your wickedness. "No one sees me," you said. Your "wisdom" and "knowledge" have caused you to turn away from me and claim that you yourself are Jehovah. 11That is why disaster shall overtake you suddenly—so suddenly that you won't know where it comes from. And there will be no atonement then to cleanse away your sins.

12Call out the demon hordes you've worshiped all these years. Call on them to help you strike deep terror into many hearts again. 13You have advisors by the ton—your astrologers and stargazers, who try to tell you what the future holds. 14But they are as useless as dried grass burning in the fire. They cannot even deliver themselves! You'll get no help from them at all. Theirs is no fire to sit beside to make you warm! 15And all your friends of childhood days shall slip away and disappear, unable to help.

HEAR me, my people: you swear allegiance to the Lord without meaning a word of it, when you boast of living in the Holy City and brag about depending on the God of Israel. 3Time and again I told you what was going to happen in the future. My words were scarcely spoken when suddenly I did just what I said. 4I knew how hard and obstinate you are. Your necks are as unbending as iron; you are as hardheaded as brass. 5That is why I told you ahead of time what I was going to do, so that you could never say, "My idol did it; my carved image commanded it to happen!" 6You have heard my predictions and seen them fulfilled, but you refuse to agree it is so. Now I will tell you new things I haven't mentioned before, secrets you haven't heard.

7Then you can't say, "We knew that all the time!"

8Yes, I'll tell you things entirely new, for I know so well what traitors you are, rebels from earliest childhood, rotten through and through. 9Yet for my own sake and for the honor of my name I will hold back my anger and not wipe you out. 10I refined you in the furnace of affliction, but found no silver there. You are worthless, with nothing good in you at all. 11Yet for my own sake— yes, *for my own sake*—I will save you from my anger and not destroy you lest the heathen say their gods have conquered me. I will not let them have my glory.

EPHESIANS 4:1–16

I beg you—I, a prisoner here in jail for serving the Lord—to live and act in a way worthy of those who have been chosen for such wonderful blessings as these. 2Be humble and gentle. Be patient with each other, making allowance for each other's faults because of your love. 3Try always to be led along together by the Holy Spirit, and so be at peace with one another.

4We are all parts of one body, we have the same Spirit, and we have all been called to the same glorious future. 5For us there is only one Lord, one faith, one baptism, 6and we all have the same God and Father who is over us all and in us all, and living through every part of us. 7However, Christ has given each of us special abilities—whatever he wants us to have out of his rich storehouse of gifts.

8The Psalmist tells about this, for he says that when Christ returned triumphantly to heaven after his resurrection and victory over Satan, he gave generous gifts to men. 9Notice that it says he returned to heaven. This means that he had first come down from the heights of heaven, far down to the lowest parts of the earth. 10The same one who came down is the one who went back up, that he might fill all things everywhere with himself, from the very lowest to the very highest.

11Some of us have been given special

ability as apostles; to others he has given the gift of being able to preach well; some have special ability in winning people to Christ, helping them to trust him as their Savior; still others have a gift for caring for God's people as a shepherd does his sheep, leading and teaching them in the ways of God.

12Why is it that he gives us these special abilities to do certain things best? It is that God's people will be equipped to do better work for him, building up the Church, the body of Christ, to a position of strength and maturity; 13until finally we all believe alike about our salvation and about our Savior, God's Son, and all become full-grown in the Lord—yes, to the point of being filled full with Christ.

14Then we will no longer be like children, forever changing our minds about what we believe because someone has told us something different, or has cleverly lied to us and made the lie sound like the truth. 15,16Instead, we will lovingly follow the truth at all times—speaking truly, dealing truly, living truly—and so become more and more in every way like Christ who is the Head of his body, the Church. Under his direction the whole body is fitted together perfectly, and each part in its own special way helps the other parts, so that the whole body is healthy and growing and full of love.

PSALM 68:19–35

WHAT a glorious Lord! He who daily bears our burdens also gives us our salvation. 20He frees us! He rescues us from death. 21But he will crush his enemies, for they refuse to leave their guilty, stubborn ways. 22The Lord says, "Come," to all his people's enemies; they are hiding on Mount Hermon's highest slopes and deep within the sea! 23His people must destroy them. Cover your feet with their blood; dogs will eat them.

24The procession of God my King moves onward to the sanctuary— 25singers in front, musicians behind, girls playing the timbrels in between. 26Let all the people of Israel praise the Lord, who is Israel's fountain. 27The little tribe of Benjamin leads the way. The princes and elders of Judah, and the princes of Zebulun and Naphtali are right behind. 28Summon your might; display your strength, O God, for you have done such mighty things for us.

29The kings of the earth are bringing their gifts to your temple in Jerusalem. 30Rebuke our enemies, O Lord. Bring them—submissive, tax in hand. Scatter all who delight in war. 31Egypt will send gifts of precious metals. Ethiopia will stretch out her hands to God in adoration. 32Sing to the Lord, O kingdoms of the earth—sing praises to the Lord, 33to him who rides upon the ancient heavens, whose mighty voice thunders from the sky.

34Power belongs to God! His majesty shines down on Israel; his strength is mighty in the heavens. 35What awe we feel, kneeling here before him in the sanctuary. The God of Israel gives strength and mighty power to his people. Blessed be God!

PROVERBS FOR TODAY/ 24:3–4

Any enterprise is built by wise planning, becomes strong through common sense, and profits wonderfully by keeping abreast of the facts.

SEPTEMBER 26

ISAIAH 48:12—50:11

LISTEN to me, my people, my chosen ones! I alone am God. I am the First; I am the Last. 13It was my hand that laid the foundations of the earth; the palm of my right hand spread out the heavens above; I spoke and they came into being.

14Come, all of you, and listen. Among all your idols, which one has ever told you this: "The Lord loves Cyrus. He will use him to put an end to the empire of Babylonia. He will utterly rout the armies of the Chaldeans"? 15But I am saying it. I have called Cyrus; I have sent him on this errand and I will prosper him.

16Come closer and listen. I have always told you plainly what would happen, so that you could clearly understand. And now the Lord God and his Spirit have sent me (with this message):

17The Lord, your Redeemer, the Holy One of Israel, says, I am the Lord your God, who punishes you for your own good and leads you along the paths that you should follow.

18Oh, that you had listened to my laws! Then you would have had peace flowing like a gentle river, and great waves of righteousness. 19Then you would have become as numerous as the sands along the seashores of the world, too many to count, and there would have been no need for your destruction.

20Yet even now, be free from your captivity! Leave Babylon, singing as you go; shout to the ends of the earth that the Lord has redeemed his servants, the Jews. 21They were not thirsty when he led them through the deserts; he divided the rock, and water gushed out for them to drink. 22But there is no peace, says the Lord, for the wicked.

LISTEN to me, all of you in far-off lands: The Lord called me before my birth. From within the womb he called me by my name. 2God will make my words of judgment sharp as swords. He has hidden me in the shadow of his hand; I am like a sharp arrow in his quiver.

3He said to me: "You are my Servant, a Prince of Power with God, and you shall bring me glory."

4I replied, "But my work for them seems all in vain; I have spent my strength for them without response. Yet I leave it all with God for my reward."

5"And now," said the Lord—the Lord who formed me from my mother's womb to serve him who commissioned me to restore to him his people Israel, who has given me the strength to perform this task and honored me for doing it!— 6"you shall do more than restore Israel to me. I will make you a Light to the nations of the world to bring my salvation to them too."

7The Lord, the Redeemer and Holy One of Israel, says to the one who is despised, rejected by mankind, and kept beneath the heel of the world's rulers: "Kings shall stand at attention when you pass by; princes shall bow low because the Lord has chosen you; he, the faithful Lord, the Holy One of Israel, chooses you."

8,9The Lord says, "Your request has come at a favorable time. I will keep you from harm and give you as a token and pledge to Israel, proof that I will reestablish the land of Israel and reassign it to its own people again. Through you I am saying to the prisoners of darkness, 'Come out! I am giving you your freedom!' They will be my sheep, grazing in green pastures and on the grassy hills. 10They shall neither hunger nor thirst; the searing sun and scorching desert winds will not reach them any more. For the Lord in his mercy will lead them beside the cool waters. 11And I will make my mountains into level paths for them; the highways shall be raised above the valleys. 12See, my people shall return from far away, from north and west and south."

13Sing for joy, O heavens; shout, O earth. Break forth with song, O mountains, for the Lord has comforted his people, and will have compassion upon them in their sorrow.

14Yet they say, "My Lord deserted us; he has forgotten us."

15"Never! Can a mother forget her little child and not have love for her own son? Yet even if that should be, I will not forget you. 16See, I have tattooed your name upon my palm and ever before me is a picture of Jerusalem's walls in ruins. 17Soon your rebuilders shall come and chase away all those destroying you. 18Look and see, for the Lord has vowed that all your enemies shall come and be your slaves. They will be as jewels to display, as bridal ornaments.

19"Even the most desolate parts of your abandoned land shall soon be crowded with your people, and your enemies who enslaved you shall be far away. 20The generations born in exile shall return and say, 'We need more room! It's crowded here!' 21Then you will think to yourself, 'Who has given me all these? For most of my children were killed and the rest were carried away into exile, leaving me here alone. Who bore these? Who raised them for me?' "

22The Lord God says, "See, I will give a signal to the Gentiles and they shall carry your little sons back to you in their arms, and your daughters on their shoulders. 23Kings and queens shall serve you; they shall care for all your needs. They shall bow to the earth before you, and lick the dust from off your feet; then you shall know I am the Lord. Those who wait for me shall never be ashamed."

24Who can snatch the prey from the hands of a mighty man? Who can demand that a tyrant let his captives go? 25But the Lord says, "Even the captives of the most mighty and most terrible shall all be freed; for I will fight those who fight you, and I will save your children. 26I will feed your enemies with their own flesh and they shall be drunk with rivers of their own blood. All the world shall know that I, the Lord, am your Savior and Redeemer, the Mighty One of Israel."

THE Lord asks, Did I sell you to my creditors? Is that why you aren't here? Is your mother gone because I divorced her and sent her away? No, you went away as captives because of your sins. And your mother, too, was taken in payment for your sins. 2Was I too weak to save you? Is that why the house is silent and empty when I come home? Have I no longer power to deliver? No, that is not the reason! For I can rebuke the sea and make it dry! I can turn the rivers into deserts, covered with dying fish. 3I am the one who sends the darkness out across the skies.

4The Lord God has given me his words of wisdom so that I may know what I should say to all these weary ones. Morning by morning he wakens me and opens my understanding to his will. 5The Lord God has spoken to me and I have listened; I do not rebel nor turn away. 6I give my back to the whip, and my cheeks to those who pull out the beard. I do not hide from shame—they spit in my face.

7Because the Lord God helps me, I will not be dismayed; therefore, I have set my face like flint to do his will, and I know that I will triumph. 8He who gives me justice is near. Who will dare to fight against me now? Where are my enemies? Let them appear! 9See, the Lord God is for me! Who shall declare me guilty? All my enemies shall be destroyed like old clothes eaten up by moths!

10Who among you fears the Lord and obeys his Servant? If such men walk in darkness, without one ray of light, let them trust the Lord, let them rely upon their God. 11But see here, you who live in your own light, and warm yourselves from your own fires and not from God's; you will live among sorrows.

EPHESIANS 4:17-32

LET me say this, then, speaking for the Lord: Live no longer as the unsaved do, for they are blinded and confused. Their closed hearts are full of darkness; they are far away from the life of God because they have shut their minds against him, and they cannot understand his ways. 19They don't care anymore about right and wrong and have given themselves over to impure ways. They stop at nothing, being driven by their evil minds and reckless lusts.

20But that isn't the way Christ taught you! 21If you have really heard his voice and learned from him the truths concerning himself, 22then throw off your old evil nature—the old you that was a partner in your evil ways—rotten through and through, full of lust and sham.

23Now your attitudes and thoughts must all be constantly changing for the better. 24Yes, you must be a new and different person, holy and good. Clothe yourself with this new nature.

25Stop lying to each other; tell the truth, for we are parts of each other and when we lie to each other we are hurting ourselves. 26If you are angry, don't sin by nursing your grudge. Don't let the sun go down with you still angry—get over it quickly; 27for when you are angry you give a mighty foothold to the devil.

28If anyone is stealing he must stop it and begin using those hands of his for honest work so he can give to others in need. 29Don't use bad language. Say only what is good and helpful to those you are talking to, and what will give them a blessing.

30Don't cause the Holy Spirit sorrow by the way you live. Remember, he is the one who marks you to be present on that day when salvation from sin will be complete.

31Stop being mean, bad-tempered and angry. Quarreling, harsh words, and dislike of others should have no place in your lives. 32Instead, be kind to each other, tenderhearted, forgiving one another, just as God has forgiven you because you belong to Christ.

PSALM 69:1-14

SAVE me, O my God. The floods have risen. Deeper and deeper I sink in the mire; the waters rise around me. 3I have wept until I am exhausted; my throat is dry and hoarse; my eyes are swollen with weeping, waiting for my God to act. 4I cannot even count all those who hate me without cause. They are influential men, these who plot to kill me though I am innocent. They demand that I be punished for what I didn't do.

5O God, you know so well how stupid I am, and you know all my sins. 6O Lord God of the armies of heaven, don't let me be a stumbling block to those who trust in you. O God of Israel, don't let me cause them to be confused, 7though I am mocked and cursed and shamed for your sake. 8Even my own brothers pretend they don't know me! 9My zeal for God and his work burns hot within me. And because I advocate your cause, your enemies insult me even as they insult you. 10How they scoff and mock me when I mourn and fast before the Lord! 11How they talk about me when I wear sackcloth to show my humiliation and sorrow for my sins! 12I am the talk of the town and the song of the drunkards. 13But I keep right on praying to you, Lord. For now is the time—you are bending down to hear! You are ready with a plentiful supply of love and kindness. Now answer my prayer and rescue me as you promised. 14Pull me out of this mire. Don't let me sink in. Rescue me from those who hate me, and from these deep waters I am in.

PROVERBS FOR TODAY/ 24:5-6

A wise man is mightier than a strong man. Wisdom is mightier than strength. Don't go to war without wise guidance; there is safety in many counselors.

"The Lord is God! He made
us—we are his people,
the sheep of his pasture."
Psalm 100:3

"Children are a gift from God."
  Psalm 127:3

SEPTEMBER 27

ISAIAH 51:1—53:12

LISTEN to me, all who hope for deliverance, who seek the Lord! Consider the quarry from which you were mined, the rock from which you were cut! Yes, think about your ancestors Abraham and Sarah, from whom you came. You worry at being so small and few, but Abraham was only *one* when I called him. But when I blessed him, he became a great nation. 3And the Lord will bless Israel again, and make her deserts blossom; her barren wilderness will become as beautiful as the Garden of Eden. Joy and gladness will be found there, thanksgiving and lovely songs.

4Listen to me, my people; listen, O Israel, for I will see that right prevails. 5My mercy and justice are coming soon; your salvation is on the way. I will rule the nations; they shall wait for me and long for me to come. 6Look high in the skies and watch the earth beneath, for the skies shall disappear like smoke, the earth shall wear out like a garment, and the people of the earth shall die like flies. But my salvation lasts forever; my righteous rule will never die nor end.

7Listen to me, you who know the right from wrong and cherish my laws in your hearts: don't be afraid of people's scorn or their slanderous talk. 8For the moth shall destroy them like garments; the worm shall eat them like wool; but my justice and mercy shall last forever, and my salvation from generation to generation.

9Awake, O Lord! Rise up and robe yourself with strength. Rouse yourself as in the days of old when you slew Egypt, the dragon of the Nile. 10Are you not the same today, the mighty God who dried up the sea, making a path right through it for your ransomed ones? 11The time will come when God's redeemed will all come home again. They shall come with singing to Jerusalem, filled with joy and everlasting gladness; sorrow and mourning will all disappear.

12I, even I, am he who comforts you and gives you all this joy. So what right have you to fear mere mortal men, who wither like the grass and disappear? 13And yet you have no fear of God, your Maker—you have forgotten him, the one who spread the stars throughout the skies and made the earth. Will you be in constant dread of men's oppression, and fear their anger all day long? 14Soon, soon you slaves shall be released; dungeon, starvation and death are not your fate. 15For I am the Lord your God, the Lord Almighty, who dried a path for you right through the sea, between the roaring waves. 16And I have put my words in your mouth and hidden you safe within my hand. I planted the stars in place and molded all the earth. I am the one who says to Israel, "You are mine."

17Wake up, wake up, Jerusalem! You have drunk enough from the cup of the fury of the Lord. You have drunk to the dregs the cup of terror and squeezed out the last drops. 18Not one of her sons is left alive to help or tell her what to do. 19These two things have been your lot: desolation and destruction. Yes, famine and the sword. And who is left to sympathize? Who is left to comfort you? 20For your sons have fainted and lie in the streets, helpless as wild goats caught in a net. The Lord has poured out his fury and rebuke upon them. 21But listen now to this, afflicted ones—full of troubles and in a stupor (but not from being drunk)— 22this is what the Lord says, the Lord your God who cares for his people: "See, I take from your hands the terrible cup; you shall drink no more of my fury; it is gone at last. 23But I will put that terrible cup into the hands of those who tormented you and trampled your souls to the dust and walked upon your backs."

WAKE up, wake up, Jerusalem, and clothe yourselves with strength [from God]. Put on your beautiful clothes, O Zion, Holy City; for sinners—those who turn from God—will no longer enter your gates. ²Rise from the dust, Jerusalem; take off the slave bands from your neck, O captive daughter of Zion. ³For the Lord says, When I sold you into exile I asked no fee from your oppressors; now I can take you back again and owe them not a cent! ⁴My people were tyrannized without cause by Egypt and Assyria, and I delivered them.

⁵And now, what is this? asks the Lord. Why are my people enslaved again, and oppressed without excuse? Those who rule them shout in exultation, and my name is constantly blasphemed, day by day. ⁶Therefore I will reveal my name to my people and they shall know the power in that name. Then at last they will recognize that it is I, yes, I, who speaks to them.

⁷How beautiful upon the mountains are the feet of those who bring the happy news of peace and salvation, the news that the God of Israel reigns. ⁸The watchmen shout and sing with joy, for right before their eyes they see the Lord God bring his people home again. ⁹Let the ruins of Jerusalem break into joyous song, for the Lord has comforted his people; he has redeemed Jerusalem. ¹⁰The Lord has bared his holy arm before the eyes of all the nations; the ends of the earth shall see the salvation of our God.

¹¹Go now, leave your bonds and slavery. Put Babylon and all it represents far behind you—it is unclean to you. You are the holy people of the Lord; purify yourselves, all you who carry home the vessels of the Lord. ¹²You shall not leave in haste, running for your lives; for the Lord will go ahead of you, and he, the God of Israel, will protect you from behind.

¹³See, my Servant shall prosper; he shall be highly exalted. ¹⁴,¹⁵Yet many shall be amazed when they see him—yes, even far-off foreign nations and their kings; they shall stand dumbfounded, speechless in his presence. For they shall see and understand what they had not been told before. They shall see my Servant beaten and bloodied, so disfigured one would scarcely know it was a person standing there. So shall he cleanse many nations.

BUT, oh, how few believe it! Who will listen? To whom will God reveal his saving power? ²In God's eyes he was like a tender green shoot, sprouting from a root in dry and sterile ground. But in our eyes there was no attractiveness at all, nothing to make us want him. ³We despised him and rejected him—a man of sorrows, acquainted with bitterest grief. We turned our backs on him and looked the other way when he went by. He was despised and we didn't care.

⁴Yet it was *our* grief he bore, *our* sorrows that weighed him down. And we thought his troubles were a punishment from God, for his *own* sins! ⁵But he was wounded and bruised for *our* sins. He was beaten that we might have peace; he was lashed—and we were healed! ⁶*We*—every one of us—have strayed away like sheep! *We,* who left God's paths to follow our own. Yet God laid on *him* the guilt and sins of every one of us!

⁷He was oppressed and he was afflicted, yet he never said a word. He was brought as a lamb to the slaughter; and as a sheep before her shearers is dumb, so he stood silent before the ones condemning him. ⁸From prison and trial they led him away to his death. But who among the people of that day realized it was their sins that he was dying for— that he was suffering their punishment? ⁹He was buried like a criminal, but in a rich man's grave; but he had done no wrong, and had never spoken an evil word.

¹⁰But it was the Lord's good plan to bruise him and fill him with grief. However when his soul has been made an offering for sin, then he shall have a multitude of children, many heirs. He shall

live again and God's program shall prosper in his hands. ¹¹And when he sees all that is accomplished by the anguish of his soul, he shall be satisfied; and because of what he has experienced, my righteous Servant shall make many to be counted righteous before God, for he shall bear all their sins. ¹²Therefore I will give him the honors of one who is mighty and great, because he has poured out his soul unto death. He was counted as a sinner, and he bore the sins of many, and he pled with God for sinners.

EPHESIANS 5:1–33

FOLLOW God's example in everything you do just as a much loved child imitates his father. ²Be full of love for others, following the example of Christ who loved you and gave himself to God as a sacrifice to take away your sins. And God was pleased, for Christ's love for you was like sweet perfume to him.

³Let there be no sex sin, impurity or greed among you. Let no one be able to accuse you of any such things. ⁴Dirty stories, foul talk and coarse jokes—these are not for you. Instead, remind each other of God's goodness and be thankful.

⁵You can be sure of this: The Kingdom of Christ and of God will never belong to anyone who is impure or greedy, for a greedy person is really an idol worshiper—he loves and worships the good things of this life more than God. ⁶Don't be fooled by those who try to excuse these sins, for the terrible wrath of God is upon all those who do them. ⁷Don't even associate with such people. ⁸For though once your heart was full of darkness, now it is full of light from the Lord, and your behavior should show it! ⁹Because of this light within you, you should do only what is good and right and true.

¹⁰Learn as you go along what pleases the Lord. ¹¹Take no part in the worthless pleasures of evil and darkness, but instead, rebuke and expose them. ¹²It would be shameful even to mention here those pleasures of darkness which the ungodly do. ¹³But when you expose them, the light shines in upon their sin and shows it up, and when they see how wrong they really are, some of them may even become children of light! ¹⁴That is why God says in the Scriptures, "Awake, O sleeper, and rise up from the dead; and Christ shall give you light."

¹⁵,¹⁶So be careful how you act; these are difficult days. Don't be fools; be wise: make the most of every opportunity you have for doing good. ¹⁷Don't act thoughtlessly, but try to find out and do whatever the Lord wants you to. ¹⁸Don't drink too much wine, for many evils lie along that path; be filled instead with the Holy Spirit, and controlled by him.

¹⁹Talk with each other much about the Lord, quoting psalms and hymns and singing sacred songs, making music in your hearts to the Lord. ²⁰Always give thanks for everything to our God and Father in the name of our Lord Jesus Christ.

²¹Honor Christ by submitting to each other. ²²You wives must submit to your husbands' leadership in the same way you submit to the Lord. ²³For a husband is in charge of his wife in the same way Christ is in charge of his body the Church. (He gave his very life to take care of it and be its Savior!) ²⁴So you wives must willingly obey your husbands in everything, just as the Church obeys Christ.

²⁵And you husbands, show the same kind of love to your wives as Christ showed to the Church when he died for her, ²⁶to make her holy and clean, washed by baptism and God's Word; ²⁷so that he could give her to himself as a glorious Church without a single spot or wrinkle or any other blemish, being holy and without a single fault. ²⁸That is how husbands should treat their wives, loving them as parts of themselves. For since a man and his wife are now one, a man is really doing himself a favor and loving himself when he loves his wife! ²⁹,³⁰No one hates his own body but lov-

ingly cares for it, just as Christ cares for his body the Church, of which we are parts. 31(That the husband and wife are one body is proved by the Scripture which says, "A man must leave his father and mother when he marries, so that he can be perfectly joined to his wife, and the two shall be one.") 32I know this is hard to understand, but it is an illustration of the way we are parts of the body of Christ.

33So again I say, a man must love his wife as a part of himself; and the wife must see to it that she deeply respects her husband—obeying, praising and honoring him.

PSALM 69:15–36

DON'T let the floods overwhelm me, or the ocean swallow me; save me from the pit that threatens me. 16O Jehovah, answer my prayers, for your lovingkindness is wonderful; your mercy is so plentiful, so tender and so kind. 17Don't hide from me, for I am in deep trouble. Quick! Come and save me. 18Come, Lord, and rescue me. Ransom me from all my enemies. 19You know how they talk about me, and how they so shamefully dishonor me. You see them all and know what each has said.

20Their contempt has broken my heart; my spirit is heavy within me. If even one would show some pity, if even one would comfort me! 21For food they gave me gall; for my awful thirst they offered vinegar. 22Let their joys turn to ashes and their peace disappear; 23let darkness, blindness and great feebleness be theirs. 24Pour out your fury upon them; consume them with the fierceness of your anger. 25Let their homes be desolate and abandoned. 26For they persecute the one you have smitten, and scoff at the pain of the one you have pierced. 27Pile their sins high and do not overlook them. 28Let these men be blotted from the list of the living; do not give them the joys of life with the righteous.

29But rescue me, O God, from my poverty and pain. 30Then I will praise God with my singing! My thanks will be his praise— 31that will please him more than sacrificing a bullock or an ox. 32The humble shall see their God at work for them. No wonder they will be so glad! All who seek for God shall live in joy. 33For Jehovah hears the cries of his needy ones, and does not look the other way.

34Praise him, all heaven and earth! Praise him, all the seas and everything in them! 35For God will save Jerusalem; he rebuilds the cities of Judah. His people shall live in them and not be dispossessed. 36Their children shall inherit the land; all who love his name shall live there safely.

PROVERBS FOR TODAY/ 24:7

Wisdom is too much for a rebel. He'll not be chosen as a counselor!

SEPTEMBER 28

ISAIAH 54:1—57:14

SING, O childless woman! Break out into loud and joyful song, Jerusalem, for she who was abandoned has more blessings now than she whose husband stayed! 2Enlarge your house; build on additions; spread out your home! 3For you will soon be bursting at the seams! And your descendants will possess the cities left behind during the exile, and rule the nations that took their lands.

4Fear not; you will no longer live in shame. The shame of your youth and the sorrows of widowhood will be remembered no more, 5for your Creator will be your "husband." The Lord Almighty is his name; he is your Redeemer, the Holy One of Israel, the God of all the earth. 6For the Lord has called you back from your grief—a young wife abandoned by her husband. 7For a brief moment I abandoned you. But with great compassion I will take you back. 8In a moment of anger I turned my face a little while; but with everlasting love I will have pity on you, says the Lord, your Redeemer.

9Just as in the time of Noah I swore that I would never again permit the waters of a flood to cover the earth and destroy its life, so now I swear that I will never again pour out my anger on you. 10For the mountains may depart and the hills disappear, but my kindness shall not leave you. My promise of peace for you will never be broken, says the Lord who has mercy upon you.

11O my afflicted people, tempest-tossed and troubled, I will rebuild you on a foundation of sapphires and make the walls of your houses from precious jewels. 12I will make your towers of sparkling agate, and your gates and walls of shining gems. 13And all your citizens shall be taught by me, and their prosperity shall be great. 14You will live under a government that is just and fair. Your enemies will stay far away; you will live in peace. Terror shall not come near. 15If any nation comes to fight you, it will not be sent by me to punish you. Therefore it will be routed, for I am on your side. 16I have created the smith who blows the coals beneath the forge and makes the weapons of destruction. And I have created the armies that destroy. 17But in that coming day, no weapon turned against you shall succeed, and you will have justice against every courtroom lie. This is the heritage of the servants of the Lord. This is the blessing I have given you, says the Lord.

SAY there! Is anyone thirsty? Come and drink—even if you have no money! Come, take your choice of wine and milk—it's all free! 2Why spend your money on food that doesn't give you strength? Why pay for groceries that do you no good? Listen and I'll tell you where to get good food that fattens up the soul!

3Come to me with your ears wide open. Listen, for the life of your soul is at stake. I am ready to make an everlasting covenant with you, to give you all the unfailing mercies and love that I had for King David. 4He proved my power by conquering foreign nations. 5You also will command the nations and they will come running to obey, not because of your own power or virtue but because I, the Lord your God, have glorified you.

6Seek the Lord while you can find him. Call upon him now while he is near. 7Let men cast off their wicked deeds; let them banish from their minds the very thought of doing wrong! Let them turn to the Lord that he may have mercy upon them, and to our God, for he will abundantly pardon! 8This plan of mine is not what you would work out, neither are my thoughts the same as yours! 9For just as the heavens are higher than the earth, so are my ways higher than yours, and my thoughts than yours.

10As the rain and snow come down from heaven and stay upon the ground to water the earth, and cause the grain to grow and to produce seed for the farmer and bread for the hungry, 11so also is my Word. I send it out and it always produces fruit. It shall accomplish all I want it to, and prosper everywhere I send it. 12You will live in joy and peace. The mountains and hills, the trees of the field—all the world around you—will rejoice. 13Where once were thorns, fir trees will grow; where briars grew, the myrtle trees will sprout up. This miracle will make the Lord's name very great and be an everlasting sign [of God's power and love].

BE just and fair to all, the Lord God says. Do what's right and good, for I am coming soon to rescue you. ²Blessed is the man who refuses to work during my Sabbath days of rest, but honors them; and blessed is the man who checks himself from doing wrong.

³And my blessings are for Gentiles, too, when they accept the Lord; don't let them think that I will make them second-class citizens. And this is for the eunuchs too. They can be as much mine as anyone. ⁴For I say this to the eunuchs who keep my Sabbaths holy and choose the things that please me, and obey my laws: ⁵I will give them—in my house, within my walls—a name far greater than the honor they would receive from having sons and daughters. For the name that I will give them is an everlasting one; it will never disappear.

⁶As for the Gentiles, the outsiders who join the people of the Lord and serve him and love his name, and are his servants and don't desecrate the Sabbath, and have accepted his covenant and promises, ⁷I will bring them also to my holy mountain of Jerusalem, and make them full of joy within my House of Prayer.

I will accept their sacrifices and offerings, for my Temple shall be called "A House of Prayer for All People"! ⁸For the Lord God who brings back the outcasts of Israel says, I will bring others too besides my people Israel.

⁹Come, wild animals of the field; come, tear apart the sheep; come, wild animals of the forest, devour my people. ¹⁰For the leaders of my people—the Lord's watchmen, his shepherds—are all blind to every danger. They are feather-brained and give no warning when danger comes. They love to lie there, love to sleep, to dream. ¹¹And they are as greedy as dogs, never satisfied; they are stupid shepherds who only look after their own interest, each trying to get as much as he can for himself from every possible source.

¹²"Come," they say. "We'll get some wine and have a party; let's all get drunk. This is really living; let it go on and on, and tomorrow will be even better!"

THE good men perish; the godly die before their time and no one seems to care or wonder why. No one seems to realize that God is taking them away from evil days ahead. ²For the godly who die shall rest in peace.

³But you—come here, you witches' sons, you offspring of adulterers and harlots! ⁴Who is it you mock, making faces and sticking out your tongues? You children of sinners and liars! ⁵You worship your idols with great zeal beneath the shade of every tree, and slay your children as human sacrifices down in the valleys, under overhanging rocks. ⁶Your gods are the smooth stones in the valleys. You worship them and they, not I, are your inheritance. Does all this make me happy? ⁷,⁸You have committed adultery on the tops of the mountains, for you worship idols there, deserting me. Behind closed doors you set your idols up and worship someone other than me. This is adultery, for you are giving these idols your love, instead of loving me. ⁹You have taken pleasant incense and perfume to Molech as your gift. You have traveled far, even to hell itself, to find new gods to love. ¹⁰You grew weary in your search, but you never gave up. You strengthened yourself and went on. ¹¹Why were you more afraid of them than of me? How is it that you gave not even a second thought to me? Is it because I've been too gentle, that you have no fear of me?

¹²And then there is your "righteousness" and your "good works"—none of which will save you. ¹³Let's see if the whole collection of your idols can help you when you cry to them to save you! They are so weak that the wind can carry them off! A breath can puff them away. But he who trusts in me shall possess the land and inherit my Holy Mountain. ¹⁴I will say, Rebuild the road! Clear away the rocks and stones. Prepare a glorious highway for my people's return from captivity.

CHILDREN, obey your parents; this is the right thing to do because God has placed them in authority over you. 2Honor your father and mother. This is the first of God's Ten Commandments that ends with a promise. 3And this is the promise: that if you honor your father and mother, yours will be a long life, full of blessing.

4And now a word to you parents. Don't keep on scolding and nagging your children, making them angry and resentful. Rather, bring them up with the loving discipline the Lord himself approves, with suggestions and godly advice.

5Slaves, obey your masters; be eager to give them your very best. Serve them as you would Christ. 6,7Don't work hard only when your master is watching and then shirk when he isn't looking; work hard and with gladness all the time, as though working for Christ, doing the will of God with all your hearts. 8Remember, the Lord will pay you for each good thing you do, whether you are slave or free.

9And you slave owners must treat your slaves right, just as I have told them to treat you. Don't keep threatening them; remember, you yourselves are slaves to Christ; you have the same Master they do, and he has no favorites.

10Last of all I want to remind you that your strength must come from the Lord's mighty power within you. 11Put on all of God's armor so that you will be able to stand safe against all strategies and tricks of Satan. 12For we are not fighting against people made of flesh and blood, but against persons without bodies—the evil rulers of the unseen world, those mighty satanic beings and great evil princes of darkness who rule this world; and against huge numbers of wicked spirits in the spirit world.

13So use every piece of God's armor to resist the enemy whenever he attacks, and when it is all over, you will still be standing up.

14But to do this, you will need the strong belt of truth and the breastplate of God's approval. 15Wear shoes that are able to speed you on as you preach the Good News of peace with God. 16In every battle you will need faith as your shield to stop the fiery arrows aimed at you by Satan. 17And you will need the helmet of salvation and the sword of the Spirit—which is the Word of God.

18Pray all the time. Ask God for anything in line with the Holy Spirit's wishes. Plead with him, reminding him of your needs, and keep praying earnestly for all Christians everywhere. 19Pray for me, too, and ask God to give me the right words as I boldly tell others about the Lord, and as I explain to them that his salvation is for the Gentiles too. 20I am in chains now for preaching this message from God. But pray that I will keep on speaking out boldly for him even here in prison, as I should.

21Tychicus, who is a much loved brother and faithful helper in the Lord's work, will tell you all about how I am getting along. 22I am sending him to you for just this purpose, to let you know how we are and be encouraged by his report.

23May God give peace to you, my Christian brothers, and love, with faith from God the Father and the Lord Jesus Christ. 24May God's grace and blessing be upon all who sincerely love our Lord Jesus Christ.

Sincerely,
Paul

PSALM 70:1–5

RESCUE me, O God! Lord, hurry to my aid! 2,3They are after my life, and delight in hurting me. Confuse them! Shame them! Stop them! Don't let them keep on mocking me! 4But fill the followers of God with joy. Let those who love your salvation exclaim, "What a wonderful God he is!" 5But I am in deep trouble. Rush to my aid, for only you can help and save me. O Lord, don't delay.

SEPTEMBER 29

ISAIAH 57:15—59:21

THE high and lofty one who inhabits eternity, the Holy One, says this: I live in that high and holy place where those with contrite, humble spirits dwell; and I refresh the humble and give new courage to those with repentant hearts. 16For I will not fight against you forever, nor always show my wrath; if I did, all mankind would perish—the very souls that I have made. 17I was angry and smote these greedy men. But they went right on sinning, doing everything their evil hearts desired. 18I have seen what they do, but I will heal them anyway! I will lead them and comfort them, helping them to mourn and to confess their sins. 19Peace, peace to them, both near and far, for I will heal them all. 20But those who still reject me are like the restless sea, which is never still, but always churns up mire and dirt. 21There is no peace, says my God, for them!

SHOUT with the voice of a trumpet blast; tell my people of their sins! 2Yet they act so pious! They come to the Temple every day and are so delighted to hear the reading of my laws—just as though they would obey them—just as though they don't despise the commandments of their God! How anxious they are to worship correctly; oh, how they love the Temple services! 3"We have fasted before you," they say. "Why aren't you impressed? Why don't you see our sacrifices? Why don't you hear our prayers? We have done much penance, and you don't even notice it!" I'll tell you why! Because you are living in evil pleasure even while you are fasting, and you keep right on oppressing your workers. 4Look, what good is fasting when you keep on fighting and quarreling? This kind of fasting will never get you anywhere with me. 5Is this what I want—this doing of penance and bowing like reeds in the wind and putting on sackcloth and covering yourselves with ashes? Is this what you call fasting?

6No, the kind of fast I want is that you stop oppressing those who work for you and treat them fairly and give them what they earn. 7I want you to share your food with the hungry and bring right into your own homes those who are helpless, poor and destitute. Clothe those who are cold and don't hide from relatives who need your help.

8If you do these things, God will shed his own glorious light upon you. He will heal you; your godliness will lead you forward, and goodness will be a shield before you, and the glory of the Lord will protect you from behind. 9Then, when you call, the Lord will answer. "Yes, I am here," he will quickly reply. All you need to do is to stop oppressing the weak, and to stop making false accusations and spreading vicious rumors!

10Feed the hungry! Help those in trouble! Then your light will shine out from the darkness, and the darkness around you shall be as bright as day. 11And the Lord will guide you continually, and satisfy you with all good things, and keep you healthy too; and you will be like a well-watered garden, like an ever-flowing spring. 12Your sons will rebuild the long-deserted ruins of your cities, and you will be known as "The People Who Rebuild Their Walls and Cities."

13If you keep the Sabbath holy, not having your own fun and business on that day, but enjoying the Sabbath and speaking of it with delight as the Lord's holy day, and honoring the Lord in what you do, not following your own desires and pleasure, nor talking idly— 14then the Lord will be your delight, and I will see to it that you ride high, and get your full share of the blessings I promised to Jacob, your father. The Lord has spoken.

LISTEN now! The Lord isn't too weak to save you. And he isn't getting deaf! He can hear you when you call! 2But the trouble is that your sins have cut you off from God. Because of sin he has turned his face away from you and will not listen anymore. 3For your hands are those of murderers and your fingers are filthy with sin. You lie and grumble and oppose the good. 4No one cares about being fair and true. Your lawsuits are based on lies; you spend your time plotting evil deeds and doing them. 5You spend your time and energy in spinning evil plans which end up in deadly actions. 6You cheat and shortchange everyone. Everything you do is filled with sin; violence is your trademark. 7Your feet run to do evil and rush to murder; your thoughts are only of sinning, and wherever you go you leave behind a trail of misery and death. 8You don't know what true peace is, nor what it means to be just and good; you continually do wrong and those who follow you won't experience any peace, either.

9It is because of all this evil that you aren't finding God's blessings; that's why he doesn't punish those who injure you. No wonder you are in darkness when you expected light. No wonder you are walking in the gloom. 10No wonder you grope like blind men and stumble along in broad daylight, yes, even at brightest noontime, as though it were the darkest night! No wonder you are like corpses when compared with vigorous young men! 11You roar like hungry bears; you moan with mournful cries like doves. You look for God to keep you, but he doesn't. He has turned away. 12For your sins keep piling up before the righteous God, and testify against you.

Yes, we know what sinners we are. 13We know our disobedience; we have denied the Lord our God. We know what rebels we are and how unfair we are, for we carefully plan our lies. 14Our courts oppose the righteous man; fairness is unknown. Truth falls dead in the streets, and justice is outlawed.

15Yes, truth is gone, and anyone who tries a better life is soon attacked. The Lord saw all the evil and was displeased to find no steps taken against sin. 16He saw no one was helping you, and wondered that no one intervened. Therefore he himself stepped in to save you through his mighty power and justice. 17He put on righteousness as armor, and the helmet of salvation on his head. He clothed himself with robes of vengeance and of godly fury. 18He will repay his enemies for their evil deeds—fury for his foes in distant lands. 19Then at last they will reverence and glorify the name of God from west to east. For he will come like a flood-tide driven by Jehovah's breath. 20He will come as a Redeemer to those in Zion who have turned away from sin.

21"As for me, this is my promise to them," says the Lord: "My Holy Spirit shall not leave them, and they shall want the good and hate the wrong—they and their children and their children's children forever."

PHILIPPIANS 1:1–26

FROM: Paul and Timothy, slaves of Jesus Christ.
To: The pastors and deacons and all the Christians in the city of Philippi.

2May God bless you all. Yes, I pray that God our Father and the Lord Jesus Christ will give each of you his fullest blessings, and his peace in your hearts and your lives. 3All my prayers for you are full of praise to God! 4When I pray for you, my heart is full of joy, 5because of all your wonderful help in making known the Good News about Christ from the time you first heard it until now. 6And I am sure that God who began the good work within you will keep right on helping you grow in his grace until his task within you is finally finished on that day when Jesus Christ returns.

7How natural it is that I should feel as I do about you, for you have a very special place in my heart. We have shared together the blessings of God, both when I was in prison and when I was out, defending the truth and telling others about Christ. 8Only God knows how deep is my love and longing for you—with the tenderness of Jesus Christ. 9My prayer for you is that you will overflow more and more with love for others, and at the same time keep on growing in spiritual knowledge and insight, 10for I want you always to see clearly the difference between right and wrong, and to be inwardly clean, no one being able to criticize you from now until our Lord returns. 11May you always be doing those good, kind things which show that you are a child of God, for this will bring much praise and glory to the Lord.

12And I want you to know this, dear brothers: Everything that has happened to me here has been a great boost in getting out the Good News concerning Christ. 13For everyone around here, including all the soldiers over at the barracks, knows that I am in chains simply because I am a Christian. 14And because of my imprisonment many of the Christians here seem to have lost their fear of chains! Somehow my patience has encouraged them and they have become more and more bold in telling others about Christ.

15Some, of course, are preaching the Good News because they are jealous of the way God has used me. They want reputations as fearless preachers! But others have purer motives, 16,17preaching because they love me, for they know that

the Lord has brought me here to use me to defend the Truth. And some preach to make me jealous, thinking that their success will add to my sorrows here in jail! 18But whatever their motive for doing it, the fact remains that the Good News about Christ is being preached and I am glad.

19I am going to keep on being glad, for I know that as you pray for me, and as the Holy Spirit helps me, this is all going to turn out for my good. 20For I live in eager expectation and hope that I will never do anything that will cause me to be ashamed of myself but that I will always be ready to speak out boldly for Christ while I am going through all these trials here, just as I have in the past; and that I will always be an honor to Christ, whether I live or whether I must die. 21For to me, living means opportunities for Christ, and dying—well, that's better yet! 22But if living will give me more opportunities to win people to Christ, then I really don't know which is better, to live or die! 23Sometimes I want to live and at other times I don't, for I long to go and be with Christ. How much happier for *me* than being here! 24But the fact is that I can be of more help to *you* by staying!

25Yes, I am still needed down here and so I feel certain I will be staying on earth a little longer, to help you grow and become happy in your faith; 26my staying will make you glad and give you reason to glorify Christ Jesus for keeping me safe, when I return to visit you again.

PSALM 71:1–24

LORD, you are my refuge! Don't let me down! 2Save me from my enemies, for you are just! Rescue me! Bend down your ear and listen to my plea and save me. 3Be to me a great protecting Rock, where I am always welcome, safe from all attacks. For you have issued the order to save me. 4Rescue me, O God, from these unjust and cruel men. 5O Lord, you alone are my hope;

I've trusted you from childhood. 6Yes, you have been with me from birth and have helped me constantly—no wonder I am always praising you! 7My success—at which so many stand amazed—is because you are my mighty protector. 8All day long I'll praise and honor you, O God, for all that you have done for me.

9And now, in my old age, don't set me aside. Don't forsake me now when my strength is failing. 10My enemies are whispering, 11"God has forsaken him! Now we can get him. There is no one to help him now!" 12O God, don't stay away! Come quickly! Help! 13Destroy them! Cover them with failure and disgrace—these enemies of mine.

14I will keep on expecting you to help me. I praise you more and more. 15I cannot count the times when you have faithfully rescued me from danger. I will tell everyone how good you are, and of your constant, daily care. 16I walk in the strength of the Lord God. I tell everyone that you alone are just and good. 17O God, you have helped me from my earliest childhood—and I have constantly testified to others of the wonderful things you do. 18And now that I am old and gray, don't forsake me. Give me time to tell this new generation (and their children too) about all your mighty miracles. 19Your power and goodness, Lord, reach to the highest heavens. You have done such wonderful things. Where is there another God like you? 20You have let me sink down deep in desperate problems. But you will bring me back to life again, up from the depths of the earth. 21You will give me greater honor than before, and turn again and comfort me.

22I will praise you with music, telling of your faithfulness to all your promises, O Holy One of Israel. 23I will shout and sing your praises for redeeming me. 24I will talk to others all day long about your justice and your goodness. For all who tried to hurt me have been disgraced and dishonored.

PROVERBS FOR TODAY/ 24:9–10

The rebel's schemes are sinful, and the mocker is the scourge of all mankind. You are a poor specimen if you can't stand the pressure of adversity.

SEPTEMBER 30

ISAIAH 60:1—62:6

ARISE, my people! Let your light shine for all the nations to see! For the glory of the Lord is streaming from you. 2Darkness as black as night shall cover all the peoples of the earth, but the glory of the Lord will shine from you. 3All nations will come to your light; mighty kings will come to see the glory of the Lord upon you.

4Lift up your eyes and see! For your sons and daughters are coming home to you from distant lands. 5Your eyes will shine with joy, your hearts will thrill, for merchants from around the world will flow to you, bringing you the wealth of many lands. 6Vast droves of camels will converge upon you, dromedaries from Midian and Sheba and Ephah, too, bringing gold and incense to add to the praise of God. 7The flocks of Kedar shall be given you, and the rams of Nabaioth for my altars, and I will glorify my glorious Temple in that day.

8And who are these who fly like a cloud to Israel, like doves to their nests? 9I have reserved the ships of many lands, the very best, to bring the sons of Israel home again from far away, bringing their wealth with them. For the Holy One of Israel, known around the world, has glorified you in the eyes of all.

¹⁰Foreigners will come and build your cities. Presidents and kings will send you aid. For though I destroyed you in my anger, I will have mercy on you through my grace. ¹¹Your gates will stay wide open around the clock to receive the wealth of many lands. The kings of the world will cater to you. ¹²For the nations refusing to be your allies will perish; they shall be destroyed. ¹³The glory of Lebanon will be yours—the forests of firs and pines, and box trees—to beautify my sanctuary. My Temple will be glorious.

¹⁴The sons of anti-Semites will come and bow before you! They will kiss your feet! They will call Jerusalem "The City of the Lord" and "The Glorious Mountain of the Holy One of Israel."

¹⁵Though once despised and hated and rebuffed by all, you will be beautiful forever, a joy for all the generations of the world, for I will make you so. ¹⁶Powerful kings and mighty nations shall provide you with the choicest of their goods to satisfy your every need, and you will know at last and really understand that I, the Lord, am your Savior and Redeemer, the Mighty One of Israel. ¹⁷I will exchange your brass for gold, your iron for silver, your wood for brass, your stones for iron. Peace and righteousness shall be your taskmasters! ¹⁸Violence will disappear out of your land—all war will end. Your walls will be "Salvation" and your gates "Praise."

¹⁹No longer will you need the sun or moon to give you light, for the Lord your God will be your everlasting light, and he will be your glory. ²⁰Your sun shall never set; the moon shall not go down—for the Lord will be your everlasting light; your days of mourning all will end. ²¹All your people will be good. They will possess their land forever, for I will plant them there with my own hands; this will bring me glory. ²²The smallest family shall multiply into a clan; the tiny group

shall be a mighty nation. I, the Lord, will bring it all to pass when it is time.

THE Spirit of the Lord God is upon me, because the Lord has anointed me to bring good news to the suffering and afflicted. He has sent me to comfort the broken-hearted, to announce liberty to captives and to open the eyes of the blind. ²He has sent me to tell those who mourn that the time of God's favor to them has come, and the day of his wrath to their enemies. ³To all who mourn in Israel he will give:

Beauty for ashes;
Joy instead of mourning;
Praise instead of heaviness.

For God has planted them like strong and graceful oaks for his own glory.

⁴And they shall rebuild the ancient ruins, repairing cities long ago destroyed, reviving them though they have lain there many generations. ⁵Foreigners shall be your servants; they shall feed your flocks and plow your fields and tend your vineyards. ⁶You shall be called priests of the Lord, ministers of our God. You shall be fed with the treasures of the nations and shall glory in their riches. ⁷Instead of shame and dishonor, you shall have a double portion of prosperity and everlasting joy.

⁸For I, the Lord, love justice; I hate robbery and wrong. I will faithfully reward my people for their suffering and make an everlasting covenant with them. ⁹Their descendants shall be known and honored among the nations; all shall realize that they are a people God has blessed.

¹⁰Let me tell you how happy God has made me! For he has clothed me with garments of salvation and draped about me the robe of righteousness. I am like a bridegroom in his wedding suit or a bride with her jewels. ¹¹The Lord will show the nations of the world his justice; all will praise him. His righteousness shall be like a budding tree, or like a garden in early spring, full of young plants springing up everywhere.

BECAUSE I love Zion, because my heart yearns for Jerusalem, I will not cease to pray for her or to cry out to God on her behalf until she shines forth in his righteousness and is glorious in his salvation. ²The nations shall see your righteousness. Kings shall be blinded by your glory; and God will confer on you a new name. ³He will hold you aloft in his hands for all to see—a splendid crown for the King of kings. ⁴Never again shall you be called "The God-forsaken Land" or the "Land that God Forgot." Your new name will be "The Land of God's Delight" and "The Bride," for the Lord delights in you and will claim you as his own. ⁵Your children will care for you, O Jerusalem, with joy like that of a young man who marries a virgin; and God will rejoice over you as a bridegroom with his bride.

⁶O Jerusalem, I have set intercessors on your walls who shall cry to God all day and all night for the fulfillment of his promises.

PHILIPPIANS 1:27—2:18

BUT whatever happens to me, remember always to live as Christians should, so that, whether I ever see you again or not, I will keep on hearing good reports that you are standing side by side with one strong purpose—to tell the Good News ²⁸fearlessly, no matter what your enemies may do. They will see this as a sign of their downfall, but for you it will be a clear sign from God that he is with you, and that he has given you eternal life with him. ²⁹For to you has been given the privilege not only of trusting him but also of suffering for him. ³⁰We are in this fight together. You have seen me suffer for him in the past; and I am still in the midst of a great and terrible struggle now, as you know so well.

Is there any such thing as Christians cheering each other up? Do you love me enough to want to help me? Does it mean anything to you that we are brothers in the Lord, sharing the same Spirit? Are your hearts tender and sympathetic at all? ²Then make me truly happy by loving each other and agreeing wholeheartedly with each other, working together with one heart and mind and purpose.

³Don't be selfish; don't live to make a good impression on others. Be humble, thinking of others as better than yourself. ⁴Don't just think about your own affairs, but be interested in others, too, and in what they are doing.

⁵Your attitude should be the kind that was shown us by Jesus Christ, ⁶who, though he was God, did not demand and cling to his rights as God, ⁷but laid aside his mighty power and glory, taking the disguise of a slave and becoming like men. ⁸And he humbled himself even further, going so far as to actually to die a criminal's death on a cross.

⁹Yet it was because of this that God raised him up to the heights of heaven and gave him a name which is above every other name, ¹⁰that at the name of Jesus every knee shall bow in heaven and on earth and under the earth, ¹¹and every tongue shall confess that Jesus Christ is Lord, to the glory of God the Father.

¹²Dearest friends, when I was there with you, you were always so careful to follow my instructions. And now that I am away you must be even more careful to do the good things that result from being saved, obeying God with deep reverence, shrinking back from all that might displease him. ¹³For God is at work within you, helping you want to obey him, and then helping you do what he wants.

¹⁴In everything you do, stay away from complaining and arguing, ¹⁵so that no one can speak a word of blame against you. You are to live clean, innocent lives as children of God in a dark world full of people who are crooked and stubborn. Shine out among them like beacon lights, ¹⁶holding out to them the Word of Life.

Then when Christ returns how glad I will be that my work among you was so worthwhile. 17And if my lifeblood is, so to speak, to be poured out over your faith which I am offering up to God as a sacrifice—that is, if I am to die for you—even then I will be glad, and will share my joy with each of you. 18For you should be happy about this, too, and rejoice with me for having this privilege of dying for you.

PSALM 72:1–20

O God, help the king to judge as you would, and help his son to walk in godliness. 2Help him to give justice to your people, even to the poor. 3May the mountains and hills flourish in prosperity because of his good reign. 4Help him to defend the poor and needy and to crush their oppressors. 5May the poor and needy revere you constantly, as long as sun and moon continue in the skies! Yes, forever!

6May the reign of this son of mine be as gentle and fruitful as the springtime rains upon the grass—like showers that water the earth! 7May all good men flourish in his reign, with abundance of peace to the end of time.

8Let him reign from sea to sea, and from the Euphrates River to the ends of the earth. 9The desert nomads shall bow before him; his enemies shall fall face downward in the dust. 10Kings along the Mediterranean coast—the kings of Tarshish and the islands—and those from Sheba and from Seba—all will bring their gifts. 11Yes, kings from everywhere! All will bow before him! All will serve him!

12He will take care of the helpless and poor when they cry to him; for they have no one else to defend them. 13He feels pity for the weak and needy, and will rescue them. 14He will save them from oppression and from violence, for their lives are precious to him.

15And he shall live; and to him will be given the gold of Sheba, and there will be constant praise for him. His people will bless him all day long. 16Bless us with abundant crops throughout the land, even on the highland plains; may there be fruit like that of Lebanon; may the cities be as full of people as the fields are of grass. 17His name will be honored forever; it will continue as the sun; and all will be blessed in him; all nations will praise him.

18Blessed be Jehovah God, the God of Israel, who only does wonderful things! 19Blessed be his glorious name forever! Let the whole earth be filled with his glory. Amen, and amen!

20(This ends the psalms of David, son of Jesse.)

PROVERBS FOR TODAY/ 24:11–12

Rescue those who are unjustly sentenced to death; don't stand back and let them die. Don't try to disclaim responsibility by saying you didn't know about it. For God, who knows all hearts, knows yours, and he knows you knew! And he will reward everyone according to his deeds.

OCTOBER 1

ISAIAH 62:7—65:25

TAKE no rest, all you who pray, and give God no rest until he establishes Jerusalem and makes her respected and admired throughout the earth. 8The Lord has sworn to Jerusalem with all his integrity: "I will never again give you to your enemies; never again shall foreign soldiers come and take away your grain and wine.

⁹You raised it; you shall keep it, praising God. Within the Temple courts you yourselves shall drink the wine you pressed.

¹⁰"Go out! Go out! Prepare the roadway for my people to return! Build the roads, pull out the boulders, raise the flag of Israel."

¹¹See, the Lord has sent his messengers to every land and said, "Tell my people, I, the Lord your God, am coming to save you and will bring you many gifts." ¹²And they shall be called "The Holy People" and "The Lord's Redeemed," and Jerusalem shall be called "The Land of Desire" and "The City God Has Blessed."

WHO is this who comes from Edom, from the city of Bozrah, with his magnificent garments of crimson? Who is this in royal robes, marching in the greatness of his strength?

"It is I, the Lord, announcing your salvation; I, the Lord, the one who is mighty to save!"

²"Why are your clothes so red, as from treading out the grapes?"

³"I have trodden the winepress alone. No one was there to help me. In my wrath I have trodden my enemies like grapes. In my fury I trampled my foes. It is their blood you see upon my clothes. ⁴For the time has come for me to avenge my people, to redeem them from the hands of their oppressors. ⁵I looked but no one came to help them; I was amazed and appalled. So I executed vengeance alone; unaided, I meted out judgment. ⁶I crushed the heathen nations in my anger and made them stagger and fall to the ground."

⁷I will tell of the lovingkindnesses of God. I will praise him for all he has done; I will rejoice in his great goodness to Israel, which he has granted in accordance with his mercy and love. ⁸He said, "They are my very own; surely they will not be false again." And he became their Savior. ⁹In all their affliction he was afflicted, and he personally saved them. In his love and pity he redeemed them and lifted them up and carried them through all the years.

¹⁰But they rebelled against him and grieved his Holy Spirit. That is why he became their enemy and personally fought against them. ¹¹Then they remembered those days of old when Moses, God's servant, led his people out of Egypt and they cried out, "Where is the one who brought Israel through the sea, with Moses as their shepherd? Where is the God who sent his Holy Spirit to be among his people? ¹²Where is he whose mighty power divided the sea before them when Moses lifted up his hand, and established his reputation forever? ¹³Who led them through the bottom of the sea? Like fine stallions racing through the desert, they never stumbled. ¹⁴Like cattle grazing in the valleys, so the Spirit of the Lord gave them rest. Thus he gave himself a magnificent reputation."

¹⁵O Lord, look down from heaven and see us from your holy, glorious home; where is the love for us you used to show—your power, your mercy and your compassion? Where are they now? ¹⁶Surely you are still our Father! Even if Abraham and Jacob would disown us, still you would be our Father, our Redeemer from ages past. ¹⁷O Lord, why have you hardened our hearts and made us sin and turn against you? Return and help us, for we who belong to you need you so. ¹⁸How briefly we possessed Jerusalem! And now our enemies have destroyed her. ¹⁹O God, why do you treat us as though we weren't your people, as though we were a heathen nation that never called you "Lord"?

OH, that you would burst forth from the skies and come down! How the mountains would quake in your presence! ²The consuming fire of your glory would burn down the forests and boil the oceans dry. The nations would tremble before you; then your enemies would learn the reason for your fame! ³So it was before when you came down, for you did awesome things beyond our highest expectations, and how the mountains quaked! 4For since the world began no one has seen or heard of such a God as ours, who works for those who wait for him! 5You welcome those who cheerfully do good, who follow godly ways.

But we are not godly; we are constant sinners and have been all our lives. Therefore your wrath is heavy on us. How can such as we be saved? 6We are all infected and impure with sin. When we put on our prized robes of righteousness we find they are but filthy rags. Like autumn leaves we fade, wither and fall. And our sins, like the wind, sweep us away. 7Yet no one calls upon your name or pleads with you for mercy. Therefore you have turned away from us and turned us over to our sins.

8And yet, O Lord, you are our Father. We are the clay and you are the Potter. We are all formed by your hand. 9Oh, be not so angry with us, Lord, nor forever remember our sins. Oh, look and see that we are all your people.

10Your holy cities are destroyed; Jerusalem is a desolate wilderness. 11Our holy, beautiful Temple where our fathers praised you is burned down, and all the things of beauty are destroyed. 12After all of this, must you still refuse to help us, Lord? Will you stand silent and still punish us?

THE Lord says, People who never before inquired about me are now seeking me out. Nations who never before searched for me are finding me.

2But my own people—though I have been spreading out my arms to welcome them all day long—have rebelled; they follow their own evil paths and thoughts. 3All day long they insult me to my face by worshiping idols in many gardens and burning incense on the rooftops of their homes. 4At night they go out among the graves and caves to worship evil spirits, and they eat pork and other forbidden foods. 5Yet they say to one another, "Don't come too close, you'll defile me! For I am holier than you!" They stifle me. Day in and day out they infuriate me.

6See, here is my decree all written out before me: *I will not stand silent; I will repay. Yes, I will repay them—* 7not only for their own sins but for those of their fathers too, says the Lord, for they also burned incense on the mountains and insulted me upon the hills. I will pay them back in full.

8But I will not destroy them all, says the Lord; for just as good grapes are found among a cluster of bad ones (and someone will say, "Don't throw them all away—there are some good grapes there!") so I will not destroy all Israel, for I have true servants there. 9I will preserve a remnant of my people to possess the land of Israel; those I select will inherit it and serve me there. 10As for my people who have sought me, the plains of Sharon shall again be filled with flocks, and the valley of Achor shall be a place to pasture herds.

11But because the rest of you have forsaken the Lord and his Temple and worship gods of "Fate" and "Destiny," 12therefore I will "destine" you to the sword, and your "fate" shall be a dark one; for when I called, you didn't answer; when I spoke, you wouldn't listen. You deliberately sinned before my very eyes, choosing to do what you know I despise. 13Therefore the Lord God says, You shall starve, but my servants shall eat; you shall be thirsty while they drink; you shall be sad and ashamed, but they shall rejoice. 14You shall cry in sorrow and vexation and despair, while they sing for joy. 15Your name shall be a curse word among my people, for the Lord God will slay you and call his true servants by another name.

16And yet, the days will come when all who invoke a blessing or take an oath shall swear by the God of Truth; for I will put aside my anger and forget the evil that you did. 17For see, I am creating new heavens and a new earth—so wonderful that no one will even think about the old ones anymore. 18Be glad; rejoice forever in my creation. Look! I will recreate Jerusalem as a place of happiness, and her people shall be a joy! 19And I will rejoice in Jerusalem, and in my people; and the voice of weeping and crying shall not be heard there any more.

20No longer will babies die when only a few days old; no longer will men be considered old at 100! Only sinners will die that young! 21,22In those days, when a man builds a house, he will keep on living in it—it will not be destroyed by invading armies as in the past. My people will plant vineyards and eat the fruit themselves—their enemies will not confiscate it. For my people will live as long as trees and will long enjoy their hard-won gains. 23Their harvests will not be eaten by their enemies; their children will not be born to be cannon fodder. For they are the children of those the Lord has blessed; and their children, too, shall be blessed. 24I will answer them before they even call to me. While they are still talking to me about their needs, I will go ahead and answer their prayers! 25The wolf and lamb shall feed together, the lion shall eat straw as the ox does, and poisonous snakes shall strike no more! In those days nothing and no one shall be hurt or destroyed in all my Holy Mountain, says the Lord.

PHILIPPIANS 2:19—3:3

IF the Lord is willing, I will send Timothy to see you soon. Then when he comes back he can cheer me up by telling me all about you and how you are getting along. 20There is no one like Timothy for having a real interest in you; 21everyone else seems to be worrying about his own plans and not those of Jesus Christ. 22But you know Timothy. He has been just like a son to me in helping me preach the Good News. 23I hope to send him to you just as soon as I find out what is going to happen to me here. 24And I am trusting the Lord that soon I myself may come to see you.

25Meanwhile, I thought I ought to send Epaphroditus back to you. You sent him

to help me in my need; well, he and I have been real brothers, working and battling side by side. 26Now I am sending him home again, for he has been homesick for all of you and upset because you heard that he was ill. 27And he surely was; in fact, he almost died. But God had mercy on him, and on me too, not allowing me to have this sorrow on top of everything else.

28So I am all the more anxious to get him back to you again, for I know how thankful you will be to see him, and that will make me happy and lighten all my cares. 29Welcome him in the Lord with great joy, and show your appreciation, 30for he risked his life for the work of Christ and was at the point of death while trying to do for me the things you couldn't do because you were far away.

WHATEVER happens, dear friends, be glad in the Lord. I never get tired of telling you this and it is good for you to hear it again and again.

2Watch out for those wicked men— dangerous dogs, I call them—who say you must be circumcised to be saved. 3For it isn't the *cutting of our bodies* that makes us children of God; it is *worshiping him with our spirits.* That is the only true "circumcision." We Christians glory in what Christ Jesus has done for us and realize that we are helpless to save ourselves.

PSALM 73:1–28

HOW good God is to Israel—to those whose hearts are pure. 2But as for me, I came *so* close to the edge of the cliff! My feet were slipping and I was almost gone. 3For I was envious of the prosperity of the proud and wicked. 4Yes, all through life their road is smooth! They grow sleek and fat. 5They aren't always in trouble and plagued with problems like everyone else, 6so their pride sparkles like a jeweled necklace, and their clothing is woven of cruelty! 7These fat cats have everything their hearts could ever wish for!

8They scoff at God and threaten his people. How proudly they speak! 9They boast against the very heavens, and their words strut through the earth.

10And so God's people are dismayed and confused, and drink it all in. 11"Does God realize what is going on?" they ask. 12"Look at these men of arrogance; they never have to lift a finger—theirs is a life of ease; and all the time their riches multiply."

13Have I been wasting my time? Why take the trouble to be pure? 14All I get out of it is trouble and woe—every day and all day long! 15If I had really said that, I would have been a traitor to your people. 16Yet it is so hard to explain it—this prosperity of those who hate the Lord. 17Then one day I went into God's sanctuary to meditate, and thought about the future of these evil men. 18What a slippery path they are on—suddenly God will send them sliding over the edge of the cliff and down to their destruction: 19an instant end to all their happiness, an eternity of terror. 20Their present life is only a dream! They will awaken to the truth as one awakens from a dream of things that never really were!

21When I saw this, what turmoil filled my heart! 22I saw myself so stupid and so ignorant; I must seem like an animal to you, O God. 23But even so, you love me! You are holding my right hand! 24You will keep on guiding me all my life with your wisdom and counsel; and afterwards receive me into the glories of heaven! 25Whom have I in heaven but you? And I desire no one on earth as much as you! 26My health fails; my spirits droop, yet God remains! He is the strength of my heart; he is mine forever!

27But those refusing to worship God will perish, for he destroys those serving other gods.

28But as for me, I get as close to him as I can! I have chosen him and I will tell everyone about the wonderful ways he rescues me.

PROVERBS FOR TODAY/ 24:13–14

My son, honey whets the appetite, and so does wisdom! When you enjoy becoming wise, there is hope for you! A bright future lies ahead!

OCTOBER 2

ISAIAH 66:1–24

HEAVEN is my throne and the earth is my footstool: What Temple can you build for me as good as that? 2My hand has made both earth and skies, and they are mine. Yet I will look with pity on the man who has a humble and a contrite heart, who trembles at my word.

3But those who choose their own ways, delighting in their sins, are cursed. God will not accept their offerings. When such men sacrifice an ox on the altar of God, it is no more acceptable to him than human sacrifice. If they sacrifice a lamb, or bring an offering of grain, it is as loathsome to God as putting a dog or the blood of a swine on his altar! When they burn incense to him, he counts it the same as though they blessed an idol. 4I will send great troubles upon them—all the things they feared, for when I called them, they refused to answer, and when I spoke to them, they would not hear. Instead, they did wrong before my eyes, and chose what they knew I despised.

5Hear the words of God, all you who

fear him, and tremble at his words: Your brethren hate you and cast you out for being loyal to my name. "Glory to God," they scoff. "Be happy in the Lord!" But they shall be put to shame.

6What is all the commotion in the city? What is that terrible noise from the Temple? It is the voice of the Lord taking vengeance upon his enemies.

7,8Who has heard or seen anything as strange as this? For in one day, suddenly, a nation, Israel, shall be born, even before the birth pains come. In a moment, just as Israel's anguish starts, the baby is born; the nation begins. 9Shall I bring to the point of birth and then not deliver? asks the Lord your God. No! Never!

10Rejoice with Jerusalem; be glad with her, all you who love her, you who mourned for her. 11Delight in Jerusalem; drink deep of her glory even as an infant at a mother's generous breasts. 12Prosperity shall overflow Jerusalem like a river, says the Lord, for I will send it; the riches of the Gentiles will flow to her. Her children shall be nursed at her breasts, carried on her hips and dandled on her knees. 13I will comfort you there as a little one is comforted by its mother. 14When you see Jerusalem, your heart will rejoice; vigorous health will be yours. All the world will see the good hand of God upon his people, and his wrath upon his enemies.

15For see, the Lord will come with fire and with swift chariots of doom to pour out the fury of his anger and his hot rebuke with flames of fire. 16For the Lord will punish the world by fire and by his sword, and the slain of the Lord shall be many! 17Those who worship idols that are hidden behind a tree in the garden, feasting there on pork and mouse and all forbidden meat—they will come to an evil end, says Jehovah. 18I see full well what they are doing; I know what they are thinking, so I will gather together all nations and people against Jerusalem, where they shall see my glory. 19I will perform a mighty miracle against them, and I will send those who escape, as missionaries to the nations—to Tarshish, Put, Lud, Meshech, Rosh, Tubal, Javan, and to the lands beyond the sea that have not heard my fame nor seen my glory. There they shall declare my glory to the Gentiles. 20And they shall bring back all your brethren from every nation as a gift to the Lord, transporting them gently on horses and in chariots, and in litters, and on mules and camels, to my holy mountain, to Jerusalem, says the Lord. It will be like offerings flowing into the Temple of the Lord at harvest time, carried in vessels consecrated to the Lord. 21And I will appoint some of those returning to be my priests and Levites, says the Lord.

22As surely as my new heavens and earth shall remain, so surely shall you always be my people, with a name that shall never disappear. 23All mankind shall come to worship me from week to week and month to month. 24And they shall go out and look at the dead bodies of those who have rebelled against me, for their worm shall never die; their fire shall not be quenched, and they shall be a disgusting sight to all mankind.

PHILIPPIANS 3:4–21

YET if anyone ever had reason to hope that he could save himself, it would be I. If others could be saved by what they are, certainly I could! 5For I went through the Jewish initiation ceremony when I was eight days old, having been born into a pure-blooded Jewish home that was a branch of the old original Benjamin family. So I was a real Jew if there ever was one! What's more, I was a member of the Pharisees who demand the strictest obedience to every Jewish law and custom. 6And sincere? Yes, so much so that I greatly persecuted the Church; and I tried to obey every Jewish rule and regulation right down to the very last point.

7But all these things that I once thought very worthwhile—now I've thrown them all away so that I can put my trust and hope in Christ alone.

8Yes, everything else is worthless when compared with the priceless gain of knowing Christ Jesus my Lord. I have put aside all else, counting it worth less than nothing, in order that I can have Christ, 9and become one with him, no longer counting on being saved by being good enough or by obeying God's laws, but by trusting Christ to save me; for God's way of making us right with himself depends on faith—counting on Christ alone. 10Now I have given up everything else—I have found it to be the only way to really know Christ and to experience the mighty power that brought him back to life again, and to find out what it means to suffer and to die with him. 11So, whatever it takes, I will be one who lives in the fresh newness of life of those who are alive from the dead.

12I don't mean to say I am perfect. I haven't learned all I should even yet, but I keep working toward that day when I will finally be all that Christ saved me for and wants me to be.

13No, dear brothers, I am still not all I should be but I am bringing all my energies to bear on this one thing: Forgetting the past and looking forward to what lies ahead, 14I strain to reach the end of the race and receive the prize for which God is calling us up to heaven because of what Christ Jesus did for us.

15I hope all of you who are mature Christians will see eye-to-eye with me on these things, and if you disagree on some point, I believe that God will make it plain to you— 16if you fully obey the truth you have.

17Dear brothers, pattern your lives after mine and notice who else lives up to my example. 18For I have told you often before, and I say it again now with tears in my eyes, there are many who walk along the Christian road who are really enemies of the cross of Christ. 19Their future is eternal loss, for their god is their appetite: they are proud of what they should be ashamed of; and all they think about is this life here on earth. 20But our homeland is in heaven, where our Savior the Lord Jesus Christ is; and we are looking forward to his return from there. 21When he comes back he will take these dying bodies of ours and change them into glorious bodies like his own, using the same mighty power that he will use to conquer all else everywhere.

PSALM 74:1–23

O God, why have you cast us away forever? Why is your anger hot against us—the sheep of your own pasture? 2Remember that we are your people—the ones you chose in ancient times from slavery and made the choicest of your possessions. You chose Jerusalem as your home on earth!

3Walk through the awful ruins of the city, and see what the enemy has done to your sanctuary. 4There they shouted their battle cry and erected their idols to flaunt their victory. 5,6Everything lies in shambles like a forest chopped to the ground. They came with their axes and sledgehammers and smashed and chopped the carved paneling, 7and set the sanctuary on fire, and razed it to the ground—your sanctuary, Lord. 8"Let's wipe out every trace of God," they said, and went through the entire country burning down the assembly places where we worshiped you.

9,10There is nothing left to show that we are your people. The prophets are gone, and who can say when it all will end? How long, O God, will you allow our enemies to dishonor your name? Will you let them get away with this forever? 11Why do you delay? Why hold back your power? Unleash your fist and give them a final blow.

12God is my King from ages past; you have been actively helping me everywhere throughout the land. 13,14You divided the Red Sea with your strength; you crushed the sea-god's heads! You gave him to the desert tribes to eat! 15At your command the springs burst forth to give your people water; and then you dried a path for them across the ever-flowing Jordan. 16Day and night alike belong to you; you made the starlight and the sun. 17All nature is within your hands; you make the summer and the winter too. 18Lord, see how these enemies scoff at you. O Jehovah, an arrogant nation has blasphemed your name.

19O Lord, save me! Protect your turtle-dove from the hawks. Save your beloved people from these beasts. 20Remember your promise! For the land is full of darkness and cruel men. 21O Lord, don't let your downtrodden people be constantly insulted. Give cause for these poor and needy ones to praise your name! 22Arise, O God, and state your case against our enemies. Remember the insults these rebels have hurled against you all day long. 23Don't overlook the cursing of these enemies of yours; it grows louder and louder.

PROVERBS FOR TODAY/ 24:15–16

O evil man, leave the upright man alone, and quit trying to cheat him out of his rights. Don't you know that this good man, though you trip him up seven times, will each time rise again? But one calamity is enough to lay you low.

OCTOBER 3

JEREMIAH 1:1—2:30

THESE are God's messages to Jeremiah the priest (the son of Hilkiah) who lived in the town of Anathoth in the land of Benjamin. The first of these messages came to him in the thirteenth year of the reign of Amon's son Josiah, king of Judah. 3Others came during the reign of Josiah's son Jehoiakim, king of Judah, and at various other times until July of the eleventh year of the reign of Josiah's son Zedekiah, king of Judah, when Jerusalem was captured and the people were taken away as slaves.

4The Lord said to me, 5"I knew you before you were formed within your mother's womb; before you were born I sanctified you and appointed you as my spokesman to the world."

6"O Lord God," I said, "I can't do that! I'm far too young! I'm only a youth!"

7"Don't say that," he replied, "for you will go wherever I send you and speak whatever I tell you to. 8And don't be afraid of the people, for I, the Lord, will be with you and see you through."

9Then he touched my mouth and said, "See, I have put my words in your mouth! 10Today your work begins, to warn the nations and the kingdoms of the world. In accord with my words spoken through your mouth I will tear down some and destroy them, and plant others and nurture them and make them strong and great."

11Then the Lord said to me, "Look, Jeremiah! What do you see?"

And I replied, "I see a whip made from the branch of an almond tree."

12And the Lord replied, "That's right, and it means that I will surely carry out my threats of punishment."

13Then the Lord asked me, "What do you see now?"

And I replied, "I see a pot of boiling water, tipping southward, spilling over Judah."

14"Yes," he said, "for terror from the north will boil out upon all the people of this land. 15I am calling the armies of the kingdoms of the north to come to Jerusalem and set their thrones at the gates of the city and all along its walls, and in all the other cities of Judah.

16This is the way I will punish my people for deserting me and for worshiping other gods—yes, idols they themselves have made! 17Get up and dress and go out and tell them whatever I tell you to say. Don't be afraid of them, or else I will make a fool of you in front of them. 18For see, today I have made you impervious to their attacks. They cannot harm you. You are strong like a fortified city that cannot be captured, like an iron pillar and heavy gates of brass. All the kings of Judah and its officers and priests and people will not be able to prevail against you. 19They will try, but they will fail. For I am with you," says the Lord. "I will deliver you."

AGAIN the Lord spoke to me and said: 2Go and shout this in Jerusalem's streets: The Lord says, I remember how eager you were to please me as a young bride long ago and how you loved me and followed me even through the barren deserts. 3In those days Israel was a holy people, the first of my children. All who harmed them were counted deeply guilty, and great evil fell on anyone who touched them.

4,5O Israel, says the Lord, why did your fathers desert me? What sin did they find in me that turned them away and changed them into fools who worship idols? 6They ignore the fact that it was I, the Lord, who brought them safely out of Egypt and led them through the barren wilderness, a land of deserts and rocks, of drought and death, where no one lives or even travels. 7And I brought them into a fruitful land, to eat of its bounty and goodness, but they made it into a land of sin and corruption and turned my inheritance into an evil thing. 8Even their priests cared nothing for the Lord, and their judges ignored me; their rulers turned against me, and their prophets worshiped Baal and wasted their time on nonsense.

9But I will not give you up—I will plead for you to return to me, and will keep on pleading; yes, even with your children's children in the years to come!

10,11Look around you and see if you can find another nation anywhere that has traded in its old gods for new ones— even though their gods are nothing. Send to the west to the island of Cyprus; send to the east to the deserts of Kedar. See if anyone there has ever heard so strange a thing as this. And yet my people have given up their glorious God for silly idols! 12The heavens are shocked at such a thing and shrink back in horror and dismay. 13For my people have done two evil things: They have forsaken me, the Fountain of Life-giving Water; and they have built for themselves broken cisterns that can't hold water!

14Why has Israel become a nation of slaves? Why is she captured and led far away?

15I see great armies marching on Jerusalem with mighty shouts to destroy her and leave her cities in ruins, burned and desolate. 16I see the armies of Egypt rising against her, marching from their cities of Memphis and Tahpanhes to utterly destroy Israel's glory and power. 17And you have brought this on yourselves by rebelling against the Lord your God when he wanted to lead you and show you the way!

18What have you gained by your alliances with Egypt and with Assyria? 19Your own wickedness will punish you. You will see what an evil, bitter thing it is to rebel against the Lord your God, fearlessly forsaking him, says the Lord Almighty. 20Long ago you shook off my yoke and broke away from my ties. Defiant, you would not obey me. On every hill and under every tree you've bowed low before idols.

21How could this happen? How could this be? For when I planted you, I chose my seed so carefully—the very best. Why have you become this degenerate race of evil men? 22No amount of soap or lye can make you clean. You are stained with guilt that cannot ever be washed away. I see it always before me, the Lord God says. 23You say it isn't so, that you haven't worshiped idols? How can you say a thing like that? Go and look in any valley in the land! Face the awful sins that you have done, O restless female camel, seeking for a male! 24You are a wild donkey, sniffing the wind at mating time. (Who can restrain your lust?) Any jack wanting you need not search, for you come running to him! 25Why don't you turn from all this weary running after other gods? But you say, "Don't waste your breath. I've fallen in love with these strangers and I can't stop loving them now!"

26,27Like a thief, the only shame that Israel knows is getting caught. Kings, princes, priests and prophets—all are alike in this. They call a carved-up wooden post their father, and for their mother they have an idol chiseled out from stone. Yet in time of trouble they cry to me to save them! 28Why don't you call on these gods you have made? When danger comes, let *them* go out and save you if they can! For you have as many gods as there are cities in Judah. 29Don't come to me—you are all rebels, says the Lord. 30I have punished your children but it did them no good; they still will not obey. And you yourselves have killed my prophets as a lion kills its prey.

PHILIPPIANS 4:1–23

DEAR brother Christians, I love you and long to see you, for you are my joy and my reward for my work. My beloved friends, stay true to the Lord.

2And now I want to plead with those two dear women, Euodias and Syntyche. Please, please, with the Lord's help, quarrel no more—be friends again. 3And I ask you, my true teammate, to help these women, for they worked side by side with me in telling the Good News to others; and they worked with Clement, too, and the rest of my fellow workers whose names are written in the Book of Life.

4Always be full of joy in the Lord; I say it again, rejoice! 5Let everyone see that you are unselfish and considerate in all you do. Remember that the Lord is coming soon. 6Don't worry about anything; instead, pray about everything; tell God your needs and don't forget to thank him for his answers. 7If you do this you will experience God's peace, which is far more wonderful than the human mind can understand. His peace will keep your thoughts and your hearts quiet and at rest as you trust in Christ Jesus.

8And now, brothers, as I close this letter let me say this one more thing: Fix your thoughts on what is true and good and right. Think about things that are pure and lovely, and dwell on the fine, good things in others. Think about all you can praise God for and be glad about. 9Keep putting into practice all you learned from me and saw me doing, and the God of peace will be with you.

10How grateful I am and how I praise the Lord that you are helping me again. I know you have always been anxious to send what you could, but for a while you didn't have the chance. 11Not that I was ever in need, for I have learned how to get along happily whether I have much or little. 12I know how to live on almost nothing or with everything. I have learned the secret of contentment in every situation, whether it be a full stomach or hunger, plenty or want; 13for I can do everything God asks me to with the help of Christ who gives me the strength and power. 14But even so, you have done right in helping me in my present difficulty.

15As you well know, when I first brought the Gospel to you and then went on my way, leaving Macedonia, only you Philippians became my partners in giving and receiving. No other church did this. 16Even when I was over in Thessalonica you sent help twice. 17But though I appreciate your gifts, what makes me happiest is the well-earned reward you will have because of your kindness.

18At the moment I have all I need—more than I need! I am generously supplied with the gifts you sent me when Epaphroditus came. They are a sweet-smelling sacrifice that pleases God well.

¹⁹And it is he who will supply all your needs from his riches in glory, because of what Christ Jesus has done for us. ²⁰Now unto God our Father be glory forever and ever. Amen.

Sincerely,
Paul

P.S.

²¹Say "hello" for me to all the Christians there; the brothers with me send their greetings too. ²²And all the other Christians here want to be remembered to you, especially those who work in Caesar's palace. ²³The blessings of our Lord Jesus Christ be upon your spirits.

PSALM 75:1–10

How we thank you, Lord! Your mighty miracles give proof that you care. ²"Yes," the Lord replies, "and when I am ready, I will punish the wicked! ³Though the earth shakes and all its people live in turmoil, yet its pillars are firm, for I have set them in place!"

⁴I warned the proud to cease their arrogance! I told the wicked to lower their insolent gaze, ⁵and to stop being stubborn and proud. ^{6,7}For promotion and power come from nowhere on earth, but only from God. He promotes one and deposes another. ⁸In Jehovah's hand there is a cup of pale and sparkling wine. It is his judgment, poured out upon the wicked of the earth. They must drain that cup to the dregs.

⁹But as for me, I shall forever declare the praises of the God of Jacob. ¹⁰"I will cut off the strength of evil men," says the Lord, "and increase the power of good men in their place."

PROVERBS FOR TODAY/ 24:17–20

Do not rejoice when your enemy meets trouble. Let there be no gladness when he falls—for the Lord may be displeased with you and stop punishing him! Don't envy the wicked. Don't covet his riches. For the evil man has no future; his light will be snuffed out.

OCTOBER 4

JEREMIAH 2:31—4:18

O my people, listen to the words of God: Have I been unjust to Israel? Have I been to them a land of darkness and of evil? Why then do my people say, "At last we are free from God; we won't have anything to do with him again!" ³²How can you disown your God like that? Can a girl forget her jewels? What bride will seek to hide her wedding dress? Yet for years on end my people have forgotten me—the most precious of their treasures.

³³How you plot and scheme to win your lovers. The most experienced harlot could learn a lot from you! ³⁴Your clothing is stained with the blood of the innocent and the poor. Brazenly you murder without a cause. ³⁵And yet you say, "I haven't done a thing to anger God. I'm sure he isn't angry!" I will punish you severely because you say, "I haven't sinned!"

³⁶First here, then there, you flit about, going from one ally to another for their help; but it's all no good—your new friends in Egypt will forsake you as Assyria did before. ³⁷You will be left in despair, and cover your face with your hands, for the Lord has rejected the ones

that you trust. You will not succeed despite their aid.

THERE is a law that if a man divorces a woman who then remarries, he is not to take her back again, for she has become corrupted. But though you have left me and married many lovers, yet I have invited you to come to me again, the Lord says. ²Is there a single spot in all the land where you haven't been defiled by your adulteries—your worshiping these other gods? You sit like a prostitute beside the road waiting for a client! You sit alone like a Bedouin in the desert. You have polluted the land with your vile prostitution. ³That is why even the springtime rains have failed. For you are a prostitute, and completely unashamed. ⁴,⁵And yet you say to me, "O Father, you have always been my Friend; surely you won't be angry about such a little thing! Surely you will just forget it?" So you talk, and keep right on doing all the evil that you can.

⁶This message from the Lord came to me during the reign of King Josiah:

Have you seen what Israel does? Like a wanton wife who gives herself to other men at every chance, so Israel has worshiped other gods on every hill, beneath every shady tree. ⁷I thought that someday she would return to me and once again be mine; but she didn't come back. And her faithless sister Judah saw the continued rebellion of Israel. ⁸Yet she paid no attention, even though she saw that I divorced faithless Israel. But now Judah too has left me and given herself to prostitution, for she has gone to other gods to worship them. ⁹She treated it all so lightly—to her it was nothing at all that she should worship idols made of wood and stone. And so the land was greatly polluted and defiled. ¹⁰Then, afterwards, this faithless one "returned" to me, but her "sorrow" was only faked, the Lord God says. ¹¹In fact, faithless Israel is less guilty than treacherous Judah!

¹²Therefore go and say to Israel, O Israel, my sinful people, come home to me again, for I am merciful; I will not be forever angry with you. ¹³Only acknowledge your guilt; admit that you rebelled against the Lord your God and committed adultery against him by worshiping idols under every tree; confess that you refused to follow me. ¹⁴O sinful children, come home, for I am your Master and I will bring you again to the land of Israel—one from here and two from there, wherever you are scattered. ¹⁵And I will give you leaders after my own heart, who will guide you with wisdom and understanding.

¹⁶Then, when your land is once more filled with people, says the Lord, you will no longer wish for "the good old days of long ago" when you possessed the Ark of God's covenant. Those days will not be missed or even thought about, and the Ark will not be reconstructed, ¹⁷for the Lord himself will be among you, and the whole city of Jerusalem will be known as the throne of the Lord, and all nations will come to him there and no longer stubbornly follow their evil desires. ¹⁸At that time the people of Judah and of Israel will return together from their exile in the north, to the land I gave their fathers as an inheritance forever. ¹⁹And I thought how wonderful it would be for you to be here among my children. I planned to give you part of this beautiful land, the finest in the world. I looked forward to your calling me "Father," and thought that you would never turn away from me again. ²⁰But you have betrayed me; you have gone off and given yourself to a host of foreign gods; you have been like a faithless wife who leaves her husband.

²¹I hear voices high upon the windswept mountains, crying, crying. It is the sons of Israel who have turned their backs on God and wandered far away. ²²O my rebellious children, come back to me again and I will heal you from your sins.

And they reply, Yes, we will come, for you are the Lord our God. ²³We are weary of worshiping idols on the hills and of having orgies on the mountains.

It is all a farce. Only in the Lord our God can Israel ever find her help and her salvation. 24From our childhood we have seen everything our fathers had—flocks and herds and sons and daughters—squandered on priests and idols. 25We lie in shame and in dishonor, for we and our fathers have sinned from childhood against the Lord our God; we have not obeyed him.

O Israel, if you will truly return to me and absolutely discard your idols, 2and if you will swear by me alone, the living God, and begin to live good, honest, clean lives, then you will be a testimony to the nations of the world and they will come to me and glorify my name.

3The Lord is saying to the men of Judah and Jerusalem, Plow up the hardness of your hearts; otherwise the good seed will be wasted among the thorns. 4Cleanse your minds and hearts, not just your bodies, or else my anger will burn you to a crisp because of all your sins. And no one will be able to put the fire out.

5Shout to Jerusalem and to all Judea, telling them to sound the alarm throughout the land. "Run for your lives! Flee to the fortified cities!" 6Send a signal from Jerusalem: "Flee now, don't delay!" For I the Lord am bringing vast destruction on you from the north. 7A lion—a destroyer of nations—stalks from his lair; and he is headed for your land. Your cities will lie in ruin without inhabitant. 8Put on clothes of mourning and weep with broken hearts, for the fierce anger of the Lord has not stopped yet. 9In that day, says the Lord, the king and the princes will tremble in fear; and the priests and the prophets will be stricken with horror.

10(Then I said, "But Lord, the people have been deceived by what you said, for you promised great blessings on Jerusalem. Yet the sword is even now poised to strike them dead!")

11,12At that time he will send a burning wind from the desert upon them—not in little gusts but in a roaring blast—and he will pronounce their doom. 13The enemy shall roll down upon us like a storm wind; his chariots are like a whirlwind; his steeds are swifter than eagles. Woe, woe upon us, for we are doomed.

14O Jerusalem, cleanse your hearts while there is time. You can yet be saved by casting out your evil thoughts. 15From Dan and from Mount Ephraim your doom has been announced. 16Warn the other nations that the enemy is coming from a distant land and they shout against Jerusalem and the cities of Judah. 17They surround Jerusalem like shepherds moving in on some wild animal! For my people have rebelled against me, says the Lord. 18Your ways have brought this down upon you; it is a bitter dose of your own medicine, striking deep within your hearts.

COLOSSIANS 1:1–19

FROM: Paul, chosen by God to be Jesus Christ's messenger, and from Brother Timothy.

2To: The faithful Christian brothers—God's people—in the city of Colosse.

May God our Father shower you with blessings and fill you with his great peace.

3Whenever we pray for you we always begin by giving thanks to God the Father of our Lord Jesus Christ, 4for we have heard how much you trust the Lord, and how much you love his people. 5And you are looking forward to the joys of heaven, and have been ever since the Gospel first was preached to you. 6The same Good News that came to you is going out all over the world and changing lives everywhere, just as it changed yours that very first day you heard it and understood about God's great kindness to sinners.

7Epaphras, our much-loved fellow worker, was the one who brought you this Good News. He is Jesus Christ's faithful slave, here to help us in your place. 8And he is the one who has told us about the great love for others which the Holy Spirit has given you.

9So ever since we first heard about you we have kept on praying and asking God to help you understand what he wants you to do; asking him to make you wise about spiritual things; 10and asking that the way you live will always please the Lord and honor him, so that you will always be doing good, kind things for others, while all the time you are learning to know God better and better.

11We are praying, too, that you will be filled with his mighty, glorious strength so that you can keep going no matter what happens—always full of the joy of the Lord, 12and always thankful to the Father who has made us fit to share all the wonderful things that belong to those who live in the Kingdom of light. 13For he has rescued us out of the darkness and gloom of Satan's kingdom and brought us into the Kingdom of his dear Son, 14who bought our freedom with his blood and forgave us all our sins.

15Christ is the exact likeness of the unseen God. He existed before God made anything at all, and, in fact, 16Christ himself is the Creator who made everything in heaven and earth, the things we can see and the things we can't; the spirit world with its kings and kingdoms, its rulers and authorities; all were made by Christ for his own use and glory. 17He was before all else began and it is his power that holds everything together.

18He is the Head of the body made up of his people—that is, his Church—which he began; and he is the Leader of all those who arise from the dead, so that he is first in everything; 19for God wanted all of himself to be in his Son.

PSALM 76:1–12

GOD'S reputation is very great in Judah and in Israel. 2His home is in Jerusalem. He lives upon Mount Zion. 3There he breaks the weapons of our enemies.

4The everlasting mountains cannot compare with you in glory! 5The mightiest of our enemies are conquered. They lie before us in the sleep of death; not one can lift a hand against us. 6When you rebuked them, God of Jacob, steeds and riders fell. 7No wonder you are greatly feared! Who can stand before an angry God? 8You pronounce sentence on them from heaven; the earth trembles and stands silently before you. 9You stand up to punish the evil-doers and to defend the meek of the earth. 10Man's futile wrath will bring you glory. You will use it as an ornament!

11Fulfill all your vows that you have made to Jehovah your God. Let everyone bring him presents. He should be reverenced and feared, 12for he cuts down princes and does awesome things to the kings of the earth.

PROVERBS FOR TODAY/ 24:21–22

My son, watch your step before the Lord and the king, and don't associate with radicals. For you will go down with them to sudden disaster, and who knows where it all will end?

OCTOBER 5

JEREMIAH 4:19—6:14

MY heart, my heart—I writhe in pain; my heart pounds within me. I cannot be still because I have heard, O my soul, the blast of the enemies' trumpets and the enemies' battle cries. 20Wave upon wave of destruction rolls over the land, until it lies in utter ruin; suddenly, in a moment, every house is crushed. 21How long must this go on? How long must I see war and death surrounding me?

22"Until my people leave their foolishness, for they refuse to listen to me; they are dull, retarded children who have no understanding. They are smart enough at doing wrong, but for doing right they have no talent, none at all."

23I looked down upon their land and as far as I could see in all directions everything was ruins. And all the heavens were dark. 24I looked at the mountains and saw that they trembled and shook. 25I looked, and mankind was gone and the birds of the heavens had fled.

26The fertile valleys were wilderness and all the cities were broken down before the presence of the Lord, and crushed by his fierce anger. 27The Lord's decree of desolation covers all the land.

"Yet," he says, "there will be a little remnant of my people left. 28The earth shall mourn, the heavens shall be draped with black, because of my decree against my people, but I have made up my mind and I will not change it."

29All the cities flee in terror at the noise of marching armies coming near. The people hide in the bushes and flee to the mountains. All the cities are abandoned—all have fled in terror. 30Why do you put on your most beautiful clothing and jewelry and brighten your eyes with mascara? It will do you no good! Your allies despise you and will kill you.

31I have heard great crying like that of a woman giving birth to her first child; it is the cry of my people gasping for breath, pleading for help, prostrate before their murderers.

RUN up and down through every street in all Jerusalem; search high and low and see if you can find even one person who is fair and honest! Search every square, and if you find just one, I'll not destroy the city! 2Even under oath, they all lie. 3O Lord, you are looking for faithfulness. You have tried to get them to be honest, for you have punished them, but they won't change! You have destroyed them but they refuse to turn from their sins. They are determined, with faces hard as rock, not to repent.

4Then I said, "But what can we expect from the poor and ignorant? They don't know the ways of God. How can they obey him?"

5I will go now to their leaders, the men of importance, and speak to them, for they know the ways of the Lord and the judgment that follows sin. But they too had utterly rejected their God.

6So I will send upon them the wild fury of the "lion from the forest"; the "desert wolves" shall pounce upon them, and a "leopard" shall lurk around their cities so that all who go out shall be torn apart. For their sins are very many; their rebellion against me is great.

7How can I pardon you? For even your children have turned away, and worship gods that are not gods at all. I fed my people until they were fully satisfied, and their thanks was to commit adultery wholesale and to gang up at the city's brothels. 8They are well-fed, lusty stallions, each neighing for his neighbor's mate. 9Shall I not punish them for this? Shall I not send my vengeance on such a nation as this? 10Go down the rows of the vineyards and destroy them! But leave a scattered few to live. Strip the branches from each vine, for they are not the Lord's.

11For the people of Israel and Judah

are full of treachery against me, says the Lord. 12They have lied and said, "He won't bother us! No evil will come upon us! There will be neither famine nor war! 13God's prophets," they say, "are windbags full of words with no divine authority. Their claims of doom will fall upon themselves, not us!"

14Therefore this is what the Lord God of Hosts says to his prophets: Because of talk like this I'll take your words and prophecies and turn them into raging fire and burn up these people like kindling wood. 15See, I will bring a distant nation against you, O Israel, says the Lord—a mighty nation, an ancient nation whose language you don't understand. 16Their weapons are deadly; the men are all mighty. 17And they shall eat your harvest and your children's bread, and your flocks of sheep and herds of cattle, yes, and your grapes and figs; and they shall sack your walled cities that you think are safe.

18But I will not completely blot you out. So says the Lord.

19And when your people ask, "Why is it that the Lord is doing this to us?" then you shall say, "You rejected him and gave yourselves to other gods while in your land; now you must be slaves to foreigners in their lands."

20Make this announcement to Judah and to Israel:

21Listen, O foolish, senseless people— you with the eyes that do not see and the ears that do not listen— 22have you no respect at all for me? the Lord God asks. How can it be that you don't even tremble in my presence? I set the shorelines of the world by perpetual decrees, so that the oceans, though they toss and roar, can never pass those bounds. Isn't such a God to be feared and worshiped?

23,24But my people have rebellious hearts; they have turned against me and gone off into idolatry. Though I am the one who gives them rain each year in spring and fall and sends the harvest times, yet they have no respect or fear for me. 25And so I have taken away these wondrous blessings from them. This sin has robbed them of all of these good things.

26Among my people are wicked men who lurk for victims like a hunter hiding in a blind. They set their traps for men. 27Like a coop full of chickens their homes are full of evil plots. And the result? Now they are great and rich, 28and well fed and well groomed, and there is no limit to their wicked deeds. They refuse justice to orphans and the rights of the poor. 29Should I sit back and act as though nothing is going on? the Lord God asks. Shouldn't I punish a nation such as this?

30A horrible thing has happened in this land— 31the priests are ruled by false prophets, and my people like it so! But your doom is certain.

RUN, people of Benjamin, run for your lives! Flee from Jerusalem! Sound the alarm in Tekoa; send up a smoke signal at Beth-haccherem; warn everyone that a powerful army is on the way from the north, coming to destroy this nation! 2Helpless as a girl, you are beautiful and delicate—and doomed. 3Evil shepherds shall surround you. They shall set up camp around the city, and divide your pastures for their flocks. 4See them prepare for battle. At noon it has begun. All afternoon it rages, until the evening shadows fall. 5"Come," they say. "Let us attack by night and destroy her palaces!"

6For the Lord Almighty has said to them, Cut down her trees for battering rams; smash down the walls of Jerusalem. This is the city to be punished, for she is vile through and through. 7She spouts evil like a fountain! Her streets echo with the sounds of violence; her sickness and wounds are ever before me.

8This is your last warning, O Jerusalem. If you don't listen, I will empty the land. 9Disaster on disaster shall befall you. Even the few who remain in Israel shall be gleaned again, the Lord Almighty has said; for as a grape-gatherer checks each vine to pick what he has missed, so the remnant of my people shall be destroyed again. 10But who will listen when I warn them? Their ears are closed and they refuse to hear. The word of God has angered them; they don't want it at all.

¹¹For all this I am full of the wrath of God against them. I am weary of holding it in. I will pour it out over Jerusalem, even upon the children playing in the streets, upon the gatherings of young men, and on husbands and wives and grandparents. ¹²Their enemies shall live in their homes and take their fields and wives. For I will punish the people of this land, the Lord has said. ¹³They are swindlers and liars, from the least of them right to the top! Yes, even my prophets and priests! ¹⁴You can't heal a wound by saying it's not there! Yet the priests and prophets give assurances of peace when all is war.

COLOSSIANS 1:20—2:7

IT was through what his Son did that God cleared a path for everything to come to him—all things in heaven and on earth—for Christ's death on the cross has made peace with God for all by his blood. ²¹This includes you who were once so far away from God. You were his enemies and hated him and were separated from him by your evil thoughts and actions, yet now he has brought you back as his friends. ²²He has done this through the death on the cross of his own human body, and now as a result Christ has brought you into the very presence of God, and you are standing there before him with nothing left against you—nothing left that he could even chide you for; ²³the only condition is that you fully believe the Truth, standing in it steadfast and firm, strong in the Lord, convinced of the Good News that Jesus died for you, and never shifting from trusting him to save you. This is the wonderful news that came to each of you and is now spreading all over the world. And I, Paul, have the joy of telling it to others.

²⁴But part of my work is to suffer for you; and I am glad, for I am helping to finish up the remainder of Christ's sufferings for his body, the Church.

²⁵God has sent me to help his Church and to tell his secret plan to you Gentiles. ²⁶,²⁷He has kept this secret for centuries and generations past, but now at last it has pleased him to tell it to those who love him and live for him, and the riches and glory of his plan are for you Gentiles too. And this is the secret: *that Christ in your hearts is your only hope of glory.*

²⁸So everywhere we go we talk about Christ to all who will listen, warning them and teaching them as well as we know how. We want to be able to present each one to God, perfect because of what Christ has done for each of them. ²⁹This is my work, and I can do it only because Christ's mighty energy is at work within me.

I wish you could know how much I have struggled in prayer for you and for the church at Laodicea, and for my many other friends who have never known me personally. ²This is what I have asked of God for you: that you will be encouraged and knit together by strong ties of love, and that you will have the rich experience of knowing Christ with real certainty and clear understanding. *For God's secret plan, now at last made known, is Christ himself.* ³In him lie hidden all the mighty, untapped treasures of wisdom and knowledge.

⁴I am saying this because I am afraid that someone may fool you with smooth talk. ⁵For though I am far away from you my heart is with you, happy because you are getting along so well, happy because of your strong faith in Christ. ⁶And now just as you trusted Christ to save you, trust him, too, for each day's problems; live in vital union with him. ⁷Let your roots grow down into him and draw up nourishment from him. See that you go on growing in the Lord, and become strong and vigorous in the truth you were taught. Let your lives overflow with joy and thanksgiving for all he has done.

PSALM 77:1–20

I cry to the Lord; I call and call to him. Oh, that he would listen. ²I am in deep trouble and I need his help so much. All night long I pray, lifting my hands to heaven, pleading. There can be no joy for me until he acts. ³I think of God and moan, overwhelmed with longing for his help. ⁴I cannot sleep until you act. I am too distressed even to pray!

⁵I keep thinking of the good old days of the past, long since ended. ⁶Then my nights were filled with joyous songs. I search my soul and meditate upon the difference now. ⁷Has the Lord rejected me forever? Will he never again be favorable? ⁸Is his lovingkindness gone forever? Has his promise failed? ⁹Has he forgotten to be kind to one so undeserving? Has he slammed the door in anger on his love? ¹⁰And I said: This is my fate, that the blessings of God have changed to hate. ¹¹I recall the many miracles he did for me so long ago. ¹²Those wonderful deeds are constantly in my thoughts. I cannot stop thinking about them.

¹³O God, your ways are holy. Where is there any other as mighty as you? ¹⁴You are the God of miracles and wonders! You still demonstrate your awesome power.

¹⁵You have redeemed us who are the sons of Jacob and of Joseph by your might. ¹⁶When the Red Sea saw you, how it feared! It trembled to its depths! ¹⁷The clouds poured down their rain, the thunder rolled and crackled in the sky. Your lightning flashed. ¹⁸There was thunder in the whirlwind; the lightning lighted up the world! The earth trembled and shook.

¹⁹Your road led by a pathway through the sea—a pathway no one knew was there! ²⁰You led your people along that road like a flock of sheep, with Moses and Aaron as their shepherds.

PROVERBS FOR TODAY/ 24:23–25

It is wrong to sentence the poor, and let the rich go free. He who says to the wicked, "You are innocent," shall be cursed by many people of many nations; but blessings shall be showered on those who rebuke sin fearlessly.

OCTOBER 6

JEREMIAH 6:15—8:7

WERE my people ashamed when they worshiped idols? No, not at all—they didn't even blush. Therefore they shall lie among the slain. They shall die beneath my anger.

¹⁶Yet the Lord pleads with you still: Ask where the good road is, the godly paths you used to walk in, in the days of long ago. Travel there, and you will find rest for your souls. But you reply, "No, that is not the road we want!" ¹⁷I set watchmen over you who warned you: "Listen for the sound of the trumpet! It will let you know when trouble comes." But you said, "No! We won't pay any attention!"

¹⁸,¹⁹This, then, is my decree against my people: (Listen to it, distant lands; listen to it, O my people in Jerusalem; listen to it, all the earth!) I will bring evil upon this people; it will be the fruit of their own sin, because they will not listen to me. They reject my law. ²⁰There is no use now in burning sweet incense from Sheba before me! Keep your expensive perfumes! I cannot accept your offerings; they have no sweet

fragrance for me. 21I will make an obstacle course of the pathway of my people; fathers and sons shall be frustrated; neighbors and friends shall collapse together. 22The Lord God says, See the armies marching from the north—a great nation is rising against you. 23They are a cruel, merciless people, fully armed, mounted for war. The noise of their army is like a roaring sea.

24We have heard the fame of their armies and we are weak with fright. Fright and pain have gripped us like that of women in travail. 25Don't go out to the fields! Don't travel the roads! For the enemy is everywhere, ready to kill; we are terrorized at every turn.

26O Jerusalem, pride of my people, put on mourning clothes and sit in ashes and weep bitterly as for an only son. For suddenly the destroying armies will be upon you.

27Jeremiah, I have made you an assayer of metals, that you may test this my people and determine their value. Listen to what they are saying and watch what they are doing. 28Are they not the worst of rebels, full of evil talk against the Lord? They are insolent as brass, hard and cruel as iron. 29The bellows blow fiercely; the refining fire grows hotter, but it can never cleanse them, for there is no pureness in them to bring out. Why continue the process longer? All is dross. No matter how hot the fire, they continue in their wicked ways. 30I must label them "Impure, Rejected Silver," and I have discarded them.

THEN the Lord said to Jeremiah:

2Go over to the entrance of the Temple of the Lord and give this message to the people: O Judah, listen to this message from God. Listen to it, all of you who worship here. 3The Lord, the God of Israel says: Even yet, if you quit your evil ways I will let you stay in your own land. 4But don't be fooled by those who lie to you and say that since the Temple of the Lord is here, God will never let Jerusalem be destroyed. 5You may re-

main under these conditions only: If you stop your wicked thoughts and deeds, and are fair to others, 6and stop exploiting orphans, widows and foreigners. And stop your murdering. And stop worshiping idols as you do now to your hurt. 7Then, and only then, will I let you stay in this land that I gave to your fathers to keep forever.

8You think that because the Temple is here, you will never suffer? Don't fool yourselves! 9Do you really think that you can steal, murder, commit adultery, lie, and worship Baal and all of those new gods of yours, 10and then come here and stand before me in my Temple and chant, "We are saved!"—only to go right back to all these evil things again? 11Is my Temple but a den of robbers in your eyes? For I see all the evil going on in there.

12Go to Shiloh, the city I first honored with my name, and see what I did to her because of all the wickedness of my people Israel. 13,14And now, says the Lord, I will do the same thing here because of all this evil you have done. Again and again I spoke to you about it, rising up early and calling, but you refused to hear or answer. Yes, I will destroy this Temple, as I did in Shiloh—this Temple called by my name, which you trust for help, and this place I gave to you and to your fathers. 15And I will send you into exile, just as I did your brothers, the people of Ephraim.

16Pray no more for these people, Jeremiah. Neither weep for them nor pray nor beg that I should help them, for I will not listen. 17Don't you see what they are doing throughout the cities of Judah and in the streets of Jerusalem? 18No wonder my anger is great! Watch how the children gather wood and the fathers build fires, and the women knead dough and make cakes to offer to "The Queen of Heaven" and to their other idol-gods! 19Am I the one that they are hurting? asks the Lord. Most of all they hurt themselves, to their own shame. 20So the Lord God says, I will pour out my anger, yes, my fury on this place—people, animals, trees and plants will be consumed by the unquenchable fire of my anger.

21The Lord, the God of Israel says, Away with your offerings and sacrifices! 22It wasn't offerings and sacrifices I wanted from your fathers when I led them out of Egypt. That was not the point of my command. 23But what I told them was: *Obey* me and I will be your God and you shall be my people; only do as I say and all shall be well!

24But they wouldn't listen; they kept on doing whatever they wanted to, following their own stubborn, evil thoughts. They went backward instead of forward. 25Ever since the day your fathers left Egypt until now, I have kept on sending them my prophets, day after day. 26But they wouldn't listen to them or even try to hear. They are hard and stubborn and rebellious—worse even than their fathers were.

27Tell them everything that I will do to them, but don't expect them to listen. Cry out your warnings, but don't expect them to respond. 28Say to them: This is the nation that refuses to obey the Lord its God, and refuses to be taught. She continues to live a lie.

29O Jerusalem, shave your head in shame and weep alone upon the mountains; for the Lord has rejected and forsaken this people of his wrath. 30For the people of Judah have sinned before my very eyes, says the Lord. They have set up their idols right in my own Temple, polluting it. 31They have built the altar called Topheth in the Valley of Ben-Hinnom, and there they burn to death their little sons and daughters as sacrifices to their gods—a deed so horrible I've never even thought of it, let alone commanded it to be done. 32The time is coming, says the Lord, when that valley's name will be changed from "Topheth," or the "Valley of Ben-Hinnom," to the "Valley of Slaughter"; for there will be so many slain to bury that there won't be room enough for all the graves and they will dump the bodies in that valley.

33The bodies of my people shall be food for the birds and animals, and no one shall be left to scare them away. 34I will end the happy singing and laughter in the streets of Jerusalem and in the cities of Judah, and the joyous voices of the bridegrooms and brides. For the land shall lie in desolation.

THEN, says the Lord, the enemy shall break open the graves of the kings of Judah and of the princes and priests and prophets and people, 2and dig out their bones and spread them out on the ground before the sun and moon and stars—the gods of my people!—whom they have loved and worshiped. Their bones shall not be gathered up again nor buried but shall be scattered like dung upon the ground. 3And those of this evil nation who are still left alive shall long to die, rather than live where I will scatter them, says the Lord Almighty.

4,5Once again give them this message from the Lord: When a person falls, he jumps up again; when he is on the wrong road and discovers his mistake, he goes back to the fork where he made the wrong turn. But these people keep on along their evil path, even though I warn them. 6I listen to their conversation and what do I hear? Is anyone sorry for sin? Does anyone say, "What a terrible thing I have done?" No, all are rushing pell-mell down the path of sin as swiftly as a horse rushing to the battle! 7The stork knows the time of her migration, as does the turtledove, and the crane, and the swallow. They all return at God's appointed time each year; but not my people! They don't accept the laws of God.

COLOSSIANS 2:8–23

DON'T let others spoil your faith and joy with their philosophies, their wrong and shallow answers built on men's thoughts and ideas, instead of on what Christ has said. 9For in Christ there is all of God in a human body; 10*so you have everything when you have Christ,* and you are filled with God through your union with Christ.

He is the highest Ruler, with authority over every other power.

11When you came to Christ he set you free from your evil desires, not by a bodily operation of circumcision but by a spiritual operation, the baptism of your souls. 12For in baptism you see how your old, evil nature died with him and was buried with him; and then you came up out of death with him into a new life because you trusted the Word of the mighty God who raised Christ from the dead.

13You were dead in sins, and your sinful desires were not yet cut away. Then he gave you a share in the very life of Christ, for he forgave all your sins, 14and blotted out the charges proved against you, the list of his commandments which you had not obeyed. He took this list of sins and destroyed it by nailing it to Christ's cross. 15In this way God took away Satan's power to accuse you of sin, and God openly displayed to the whole world Christ's triumph at the cross where your sins were all taken away.

16So don't let anyone criticize you for what you eat or drink, or for not celebrating Jewish holidays and feasts or new moon ceremonies or Sabbaths. 17For these were only temporary rules that ended when Christ came. They were only shadows of the real thing—of Christ himself. 18Don't let anyone declare you lost when you refuse to worship angels, as they say you must. They have seen a vision, they say, and know you should. These proud men (though they claim to be so humble) have a very clever imagination. 19But they are not connected to Christ, the Head to which all of us who are his body are joined; for we are joined together by his strong sinews and we grow only as we get our nourishment and strength from God.

20Since you died, as it were, with Christ and this has set you free from following the world's ideas of how to be saved—by doing good and obeying various rules—why do you keep right on following them anyway, still bound by such rules as 21not eating, tasting, or even touching certain foods? 22Such rules are mere human teachings, for food was made to be eaten and used up. 23These rules may seem good, for rules of this kind require strong devotion and are humiliating and hard on the body, but they have no effect when it comes to conquering a person's evil thoughts and desires. They only make him proud.

PSALM 78:1–25

O my people, listen to my teaching. Open your ears to what I am saying. 2,3For I will show you lessons from our history, stories handed down to us from former generations. 4I will reveal these truths to you so that you can describe these glorious deeds of Jehovah to your children, and tell them about the mighty miracles he did. 5For he gave his laws to Israel, and commanded our fathers to teach them to their children, 6so that they in turn could teach their children too. Thus his laws pass down from generation to generation. 7In this way each generation has been able to obey his laws and to set its hope anew on God and not forget his glorious miracles. 8Thus they did not need to be as their fathers were—stubborn, rebellious, unfaithful, refusing to give their hearts to God.

9The people of Ephraim, though fully armed, turned their backs and fled when the day of battle came, 10because they didn't obey his laws. They refused to follow his ways. 11,12And they forgot about the wonderful miracles God had done for them, and for their fathers in Egypt. 13For he divided the sea before them and led them through! The water stood banked up along both sides of them! 14In the daytime he led them by a cloud, and at night by a pillar of fire. 15He split open the rocks in the wilderness to give them plenty of water, as though gushing from a spring. 16Streams poured from the rock, flowing like a river!

17Yet they kept on with their rebellion,

sinning against the God who is above all gods. 18They murmured and complained, demanding other food than God was giving them. 19,20They even spoke against God himself. "Why can't he give us decent food as well as water?" they grumbled. 21Jehovah heard them and was angry; the fire of his wrath burned against Israel, 22because they didn't believe in God or trust in him to care for them, 23even though he commanded the skies to open—he opened the windows of heaven— 24and rained down manna for their food. He gave them bread from heaven! 25They ate angels' food! He gave them all they could hold.

PROVERBS 24:26
It is an honor to receive a frank reply.

OCTOBER 7

JEREMIAH 8:8—9:26

HOW can you say, "We understand his laws," when your teachers have twisted them up to mean a thing I never said? 9These wise teachers of yours will be shamed by exile for this sin, for they have rejected the word of the Lord. Are they then so wise? 10I will give their wives and their farms to others; for all of them, great and small, prophet and priest, have one purpose in mind—to get what isn't theirs. 11They give useless medicine for my people's grievous wounds, for they assure them all is well when that isn't so at all! 12Are they ashamed because they worship idols? No, not in the least; they don't even know how to blush! That is why I will see to it that they lie among the fallen. I will visit them with death. 13Their figs and grapes will disappear, their fruit trees will die, and all the good things I prepared for them will soon be gone.

14Then the people will say, "Why should we wait here to die? Come, let us go to the walled cities and perish there. For the Lord our God has decreed our doom and given us a cup of poison to drink because of all our sins. 15We expected peace, but no peace came; we looked for health but there was only terror."

16The noise of war resounds from the northern border. The whole land trembles at the approach of the terrible army, for the enemy is coming, and is devouring the land and everything in it—the cities and people alike. 17For I will send these enemy troops among you like poisonous snakes which you cannot charm. No matter what you do, they will bite you and you shall die.

18My grief is beyond healing; my heart is broken. 19Listen to the weeping of my people all across the land.

"Where is the Lord?" they ask. "Has God deserted us?"

"Oh, why have they angered me with their carved idols and strange evil rites?" the Lord replies.

20"The harvest is finished; the summer is over and we are not saved."

21I weep for the hurt of my people; I stand amazed, silent, dumb with grief. 22Is there no medicine in Gilead? Is there no physician there? Why doesn't God do something? Why doesn't he help?

OH, that my eyes were a fountain of tears; I would weep forever; I would sob day and night for the slain of my people! 2Oh, that I could go away and forget them and live in some wayside shack in the desert, for they are all adulterous, treacherous men.

3"They bend their tongues like bows to shoot their arrows of untruth. They care nothing for right and go from bad to worse; they care nothing for me," says the Lord.

4Beware of your neighbor! Beware of your brother! All take advantage of one another and spread their slanderous lies. 5With practiced tongues they fool and defraud each other; they wear themselves out with all their sinning.

6"They pile evil upon evil, lie upon lie, and utterly refuse to come to me," says the Lord.

7Therefore the Lord Almighty says this: "See, I will melt them in a crucible of affliction. I will refine them and test them like metal. What else can I do with them? 8For their tongues aim lies like poisoned spears. They speak cleverly to their neighbors while planning to kill them. 9Should not I punish them for such things as this?" asks the Lord. "Shall not my soul be avenged on such a nation as this?"

10Sobbing and weeping, I point to their mountains and pastures, for now they are desolate, without a living soul. Gone is the lowing of cattle, gone the birds and wild animals. All have fled.

11"And I will turn Jerusalem into heaps of ruined houses where only jackals have their dens. The cities of Judah shall be ghost towns, with no one living in them."

12Who is wise enough to understand all this? Where is the Lord's messenger to explain it? Why is the land a wilderness so that no one dares even to travel through?

13"Because," the Lord replies, "my people have forsaken my commandments and not obeyed my laws. 14Instead they have done whatever they pleased and worshiped the idols of Baal, as their fathers told them to. 15Therefore this is what the Lord, the God of Israel, says: Look! I will feed them with bitterness and give them poison to drink. 16I will scatter them around the world, to be strangers in distant lands; and even there the sword of destruction shall chase them until I have utterly destroyed them.

17,18"The Lord Almighty says: Send for the mourners! Quick! Begin your crying! Let the tears flow from your eyes. 19Hear Jerusalem weeping in despair. 'We are ruined! Disaster has befallen us! We must leave our land and homes!'" 20Listen to the words of God, O women who wail. Teach your daughters to wail and your neighbors too. 21For death has crept in through your windows into your homes. He has killed off the flower of your youth. Children no longer play in the streets; the young men gather no more in the squares.

22Tell them this, says the Lord: Bodies shall be scattered across the fields like manure, like sheaves after the mower, and no one will bury them.

23The Lord says: Let not the wise man bask in his wisdom, nor the mighty man in his might, nor the rich man in his riches. 24Let them boast in this alone: That they truly know me, and understand that I am the Lord of justice and of righteousness whose love is steadfast; and that I love to be this way.

25,26A time is coming, says the Lord, when I will punish all those who are circumcised in body but not in spirit—the Egyptians, Edomites, Ammonites, Moabites, Arabs, and yes, even you people of Judah. For all these pagan nations also circumcise themselves. Unless you circumcise your hearts by loving me, your circumcision is only a heathen rite like theirs, and nothing more.

COLOSSIANS 3:1–17

SINCE you became alive again, so to speak, when Christ arose from the dead, now set your sights on the rich treasures and joys of heaven where he sits beside God in the place of honor and power. 2Let heaven fill your thoughts; don't spend your time worrying about things down here. 3You should have as little desire for this world as a dead person does. Your real life is in heaven with Christ and God. 4And when Christ who is our real life comes back again, you will shine with him and share in all his glories.

5Away then with sinful, earthly things; deaden the evil desires lurking within you; have nothing to do with sexual sin, impurity, lust and shameful desires; don't worship the good things of life, for that is idolatry. 6God's terrible anger is upon those who do such things. 7You used to do them when your life was still part of this world; 8but now is the time to cast off and throw away all these rotten garments of anger, hatred, cursing, and dirty language.

9Don't tell lies to each other; it was your old life with all its wickedness that did that sort of thing; now it is dead and gone. 10You are living a brand new kind of life that is continually learning more and more of what is right, and trying constantly to be more and more like Christ who created this new life within you. 11In this new life one's nationality or race or education or social position is unimportant; such things mean nothing. Whether a person has Christ is what matters, and he is equally available to all.

12Since you have been chosen by God who has given you this new kind of life, and because of his deep love and concern for you, you should practice tender-hearted mercy and kindness to others. Don't worry about making a good impression on them but be ready to suffer quietly and patiently. 13Be gentle and ready to forgive; never hold grudges. Remember, the Lord forgave you, so you must forgive others.

14Most of all, let love guide your life, for then the whole church will stay together in perfect harmony. 15Let the peace of heart which comes from Christ be always present in your hearts and lives, for this is your responsibility and privilege as members of his body. And always be thankful.

16Remember what Christ taught and let his words enrich your lives and make you wise; teach them to each other and sing them out in psalms and hymns and spiritual songs, singing to the Lord with

thankful hearts. 17And whatever you do or say, let it be as a representative of the Lord Jesus, and come with him into the presence of God the Father to give him your thanks.

PSALM 78:26–58

AND he led forth the east wind and guided the south wind by his mighty power. 27He rained down birds as thick as dust, clouds of them like sands along the shore! 28He caused the birds to fall to the ground among the tents. 29The people ate their fill. He gave them what they asked for. 30But they had hardly finished eating, and the meat was yet in their mouths, 31when the anger of the Lord rose against them and killed the finest of Israel's young men. 32Yet even so the people kept on sinning and refused to believe in miracles. 33So he cut their lives short and gave them years of terror and disaster.

34Then at last, when he had ruined them, they walked awhile behind him; how earnestly they turned around and followed him! 35Then they remembered that God was their Rock—that their Savior was the God above all gods. 36But it was only with their words they followed him, not with their hearts; 37their hearts were far away. They did not keep their promises. 38Yet he was merciful and forgave their sins and didn't destroy them all. Many and many a time he held back his anger. 39For he remembered that they were merely mortal men, gone in a moment like a breath of wind.

40Oh, how often they rebelled against him in those desert years and grieved his heart. 41Again and again they turned away and tempted God to kill them, and limited the Holy One of Israel from giving them his blessings. 42They forgot his power and love, and how he had rescued them from their enemies; 43they forgot the plagues he sent upon the Egyptians in Tanis— 44how he turned their rivers into blood, so that no one could drink, 45and how he sent vast swarms of flies to fill the land, and how the frogs had covered all of Egypt! 46He gave their crops to caterpillars. Their harvest was consumed by locusts. 47He destroyed their grapevines and their sycamores with hail. 48Their cattle died in the fields, mortally wounded by huge hailstones from heaven. Their sheep were killed by lightning. 49He loosed on them the fierceness of his anger, sending sorrow and trouble. He dispatched against them a band of destroying angels. 50He gave free course to his anger and did not spare the Egyptians' lives, but handed them over to plagues and sickness. 51Then he killed the eldest son in each Egyptian family—he who was the beginning of its strength and joy.

52But he led forth his own people like a flock, guiding them safely through the wilderness. 53He kept them safe, so they were not afraid. But the Sea closed in upon their enemies and overwhelmed them. 54He brought them to the border of his land of blessing, to this land of hills he made for them. 55He drove out the nations occupying the land, and gave each tribe of Israel its apportioned place as its home.

56Yet though he did all this for them, they still rebelled against the God above all gods, and refused to follow his commands. 57They turned back from entering the Promised Land and disobeyed as their fathers had. Like a crooked arrow, they missed the target of God's will. 58They made him angry by erecting idols and altars to other gods.

PROVERBS 24:27

Develop your business first before building your house.

OCTOBER 8

JEREMIAH 10:1—11:23

HEAR the word of the Lord, O Israel:

2,3Don't act like the people who make horoscopes and try to read their fate and future in the stars! Don't be frightened by predictions such as theirs, for it is all a pack of lies. Their ways are futile and foolish. They cut down a tree and carve an idol, 4and decorate it with gold and silver and fasten it securely in place with hammer and nails, so that it won't fall over, 5and there stands their god like a helpless scarecrow in a garden! It cannot speak, and it must be carried, for it cannot walk. Don't be afraid of such a god for it can neither harm nor help, nor do you any good.

6O Lord, there is no other god like you. For you are great and your name is full of power. 7Who would not fear you, O King of nations? (And that title belongs to you alone!) Among all the wise men of the earth and in all the kingdoms of the world there isn't anyone like you.

8The wisest of men who worship idols are altogether stupid and foolish. 9They bring beaten sheets of silver from Tarshish and gold from Uphaz, and give them to skillful goldsmiths who make their idols; then they clothe these gods in royal purple robes that expert tailors make.

10But the Lord is the only true God, the living God, the everlasting King. The whole earth shall tremble at his anger; the world shall hide before his displeasure.

11Say this to those who worship other gods: Your so-called gods, who have not made the heavens and earth, shall vanish from the earth, 12but our God formed the earth by his power and wisdom, and by his intelligence he hung the stars in space and stretched out the heavens. 13It is his voice that echoes in the thunder of the storm clouds. He causes mist to rise upon the earth; he sends the lightning and brings the rain, and from his treasuries he brings the wind.

14But foolish men without knowledge of God bow before their idols. It is a shameful business that these men are in, for what they make are frauds, gods without life or power in them. 15All are worthless, silly; they will be crushed when their makers perish. 16But the God of Jacob is not like these foolish idols. He is the Creator of all, and Israel is his chosen nation. The Lord Almighty is his name.

17Pack your bags, he says. Get ready now to leave; the siege will soon begin. 18For suddenly I'll fling you from this land and pour great troubles down; at last you shall feel my wrath.

19*Desperate is my wound. My grief is great. My sickness is incurable, but I must bear it. 20My home is gone; my children have been taken away and I will never see them again. There is no one left to help me rebuild my home.* 21The shepherds of my people have lost their senses; they no longer follow God nor ask his will. Therefore they perish and their flocks are scattered. 22Listen! Hear the terrible sound of great armies coming from the north. The cities of Judah shall become dens of jackals.

23O Lord, I know it is not within the power of man to map his life and plan his course— 24so you correct me, Lord; but please be gentle. Don't do it in your anger, for I would die. 25Pour out your fury on the nations who don't obey the Lord, for they have destroyed Israel and made a wasteland of this entire country.

THEN the Lord spoke to Jeremiah once again and said:

Remind the men of Judah and all the people of Jerusalem that I made a contract with their fathers—and cursed is the man who does not heed it! 4For I told them at the time I brought them out of slavery in Egypt that if they would obey me and do whatever I commanded them, then they and all their children would be mine and I would be their God. 5And now, Israel, obey me, says the Lord, so that I can do for you the wonderful things I swore I would if you obeyed. I want to give you a land that "flows with milk and honey," as it is today. Then I replied, "So be it, Lord!"

6Then the Lord said: Broadcast this message in Jerusalem's streets—go from city to city throughout the land and say, Remember this agreement that your fathers made with God, and do all the things they promised him they would. 7For I solemnly said to your fathers when I brought them out of Egypt—and have kept on saying it over and over again until this day: Obey my every command! 8But your fathers didn't do it. They wouldn't even listen. Each followed his own stubborn will and his proud heart. Because they refused to obey, I did to them all the evils stated in the contract.

9Again the Lord spoke to me and said: I have discovered a conspiracy against me among the men of Judah and Jerusalem. 10They have returned to the sins of their fathers, refusing to listen to me and worshiping idols. The agreement I made with their fathers is broken and canceled. 11Therefore, the Lord says, I am going to bring calamity down upon them and they shall not escape. Though they cry for mercy, I will not listen to their pleas. 12Then they will pray to their idols and burn incense before them, but that cannot save them from their time of anguish and despair. 13O my people, you have as many gods as there are cities, and your altars of shame (your altars to burn incense to Baal) are along every street in Jerusalem.

14Therefore, Jeremiah, pray no longer for this people, neither weep nor plead for them; for I will not listen to them when they are finally desperate enough to beg me for help. 15What right do my beloved people have to come any more to my Temple? For you have been unfaithful and worshiped other gods. Can promises and sacrifices now avert your doom and give you life and joy again? 16The Lord used to call you his green olive tree, beautiful to see and full of good fruit; but now he has sent the fury of your enemies to burn you up and leave you broken and charred. 17It is because of the wickedness of Israel and Judah in offering incense to Baal that the Lord Almighty who planted the tree has ordered it destroyed.

18Then the Lord told me all about their plans and showed me their evil plots. 19I had been as unsuspecting as a lamb or ox on the way to slaughter. I didn't know that they were planning to kill me! "Let's destroy this man and all his messages," they said. "Let's kill him so that his name will be forever forgotten."

20O Lord Almighty, you are just. See the hearts and motives of these men. Repay them for all that they have planned! I look to you for justice.

21,22And the Lord replied, The men of the city of Anathoth shall be punished for planning to kill you. They will tell you not to prophesy in God's name on pain of death. And so their young men shall die in battle; their boys and girls shall starve. 23Not one of these plotters of Anathoth shall survive, for I will bring a great disaster upon them. Their time has come.

COLOSSIANS 3:18—4:18

Y OU wives, submit yourselves to your husbands, for that is what the Lord has planned for you. 19And you husbands must be loving and kind to your wives and not bitter against them, nor harsh.

20You children must always obey your fathers and mothers, for that pleases the Lord. 21Fathers, don't scold your children so much that they become discouraged and quit trying.

22You slaves must always obey your earthly masters, not only trying to please them when they are watching you but all the time; obey them willingly because of your love for the Lord and because you want to please him. 23Work hard and cheerfully at all you do, just as though you were working for the Lord and not merely for your masters, 24remembering that it is the Lord Christ who is going to pay you, giving you your full portion of all he owns. He is the one you are really working for. 25And if you don't do your best for him, he will pay you in a way that you won't like—for he has no special favorites who can get away with shirking.

YOU slave owners must be just and fair to all your slaves. Always remember that you, too, have a Master in heaven who is closely watching you.

2Don't be weary in prayer; keep at it; watch for God's answers and remember to be thankful when they come. 3Don't forget to pray for us too, that God will give us many chances to preach the Good News of Christ for which I am here in jail. 4Pray that I will be bold enough to tell it freely and fully, and make it plain, as, of course, I should.

5Make the most of your chances to tell others the Good News. Be wise in all your contacts with them. 6Let your conversation be gracious as well as sensible, for then you will have the right answer for everyone.

7Tychicus, our much loved brother, will tell you how I am getting along. He is a hard worker and serves the Lord with me. 8I have sent him on this special trip just to see how you are, and to comfort and encourage you. 9I am also sending Onesimus, a faithful and much loved brother, one of your own people. He and Tychicus will give you all the latest news.

10Aristarchus, who is with me here as a prisoner, sends you his love, and so does Mark, a relative of Barnabas. And as I said before, give Mark a hearty welcome if he comes your way. 11Jesus Justus also sends his love. These are the only Jewish Christians working with me here, and what a comfort they have been!

12Epaphras, from your city, a servant of Christ Jesus, sends you his love. He is always earnestly praying for you, asking God to make you strong and perfect and to help you know his will in everything you do. 13I can assure you that he has worked hard for you with his prayers, and also for the Christians in Laodicea and Hierapolis.

14Dear doctor Luke sends his love, and so does Demas.

15Please give my greeting to the Christian friends at Laodicea, and to Nymphas, and to those who meet in his home. 16By the way, after you have read this letter will you pass it on to the church at Laodicea? And read the letter I wrote to them. 17And say to Archippus, "Be sure that you do all the Lord has told you to."

18Here is my own greeting in my own handwriting: Remember me here in jail. May God's blessings surround you.

Sincerely,
Paul

PSALM 78:59–72

WHEN God saw their deeds, his wrath was strong and he despised his people. 60Then he abandoned his Tabernacle at Shiloh, where he had lived among mankind, 61and allowed his Ark to be captured; he surrendered his glory into enemy hands. 62He caused his people to be butchered because his anger was intense. 63Their young men were killed by fire and their girls died before they were old enough to sing their wedding songs. 64The priests were slaughtered and their widows died before they could even begin their lament. 65Then the Lord rose up as though awakening from sleep, and like a mighty man aroused by wine, 66he routed his enemies and drove them back and sent them to eternal shame. 67But he rejected Joseph's family, the tribe of Ephraim, 68and chose the tribe of Judah—and Mount Zion which he loved. 69There he built his towering temple, solid and enduring as the heavens and the earth. 70He chose his servant David, taking him from feeding sheep, 71,72and from following the ewes with lambs; God presented David to his people as their shepherd and he cared for them with a true heart and skillful hands.

PROVERBS FOR TODAY/ 24:28–29

Don't testify spitefully against an innocent neighbor. Why lie about him? Don't say, "Now I can pay him back for all his meanness to me!"

OCTOBER 9

JEREMIAH 12:1—14:10

O Lord, you always give me justice when I bring a case before you to decide. Now let me bring you this complaint: Why are the wicked so prosperous? Why are evil men so happy? 2You plant them. They take root and their business grows. Their profits multiply, and they are rich. They say, "Thank God!" But in their hearts they give no credit to you. 3But as for me—Lord, you know my heart—you know how much it longs for you. (And I am poor, O Lord!) Lord, drag them off like helpless sheep to the slaughter. Judge them, O God! ⁴How long must this land of yours put up with all their goings on? Even the grass of the field groans and weeps over their wicked deeds! The wild animals and birds have moved away, leaving the land deserted. Yet the people say, "God won't bring judgment on us. We're perfectly safe!"

⁵The Lord replied to me: If racing with mere men—these men of Anathoth—has wearied you, how will you race against horses, against the king, his court and all his evil priests? If you stumble and fall on open ground, what will you do in Jordan's jungles? ⁶Even your own brothers, your own family, have turned against you. They have plotted to call for a mob to lynch you. Don't trust them, no matter how pleasantly they speak. Don't believe them.

⁷Then the Lord said: I have abandoned my people, my inheritance; I have surrendered my dearest ones to their enemies. ⁸My people have roared at me like a lion of the forest, so I have treated them as though I hated them. ⁹My people have fallen. I will bring upon them swarms of vultures and wild animals to pick the flesh from their corpses.

¹⁰Many foreign rulers have ravaged my vineyard, trampling down the vines, and turning all its beauty into barren wilderness. ¹¹They have made it desolate; I hear its mournful cry. The whole land is desolate and no one cares. ¹²Destroying armies plunder the land; the sword of the Lord devours from one end of the nation to the other; nothing shall escape. ¹³My people have sown wheat but reaped thorns; they have worked hard but it does them no good. They shall harvest a crop of shame, for the fierce anger of the Lord is upon them.

¹⁴And now the Lord says this to the evil nations, the nations surrounding the land God gave his people Israel: See, I will force you from your land just as Judah will be forced from hers; ¹⁵but afterwards I will return and have compassion on all of you, and will bring you home to your own land again, each man to his inheritance. ¹⁶And if these heathen nations quickly learn my people's ways and claim me as their God instead of Baal (whom they taught my people to worship), then they shall be strong among my people. ¹⁷But any nation refusing to obey me will be expelled again and finished, says the Lord.

THE Lord said to me, Go and buy a linen loincloth and wear it, but don't wash it—don't put it in water at all. ²So I bought the loincloth and put it on. ³Then the Lord's message came to me again. This time he said, ⁴Take the loincloth out to the Euphrates River and hide it in a hole in the rocks.

⁵So I did; I hid it as the Lord had told me to. ⁶Then, a long time afterwards, the Lord said: Go out to the river again and get the loincloth. ⁷And I did; I dug it out of the hole where I had hidden it. But now it was mildewed and falling apart. It was utterly useless!

⁸,⁹Then the Lord said: This illustrates the way that I will rot the pride of Judah and Jerusalem. ¹⁰This evil nation refuses to listen to me, and follows its own evil desires and worships idols; therefore it shall become as this loincloth—good for nothing. ¹¹Even as a loincloth clings to a man's loins, so I made Judah and Israel to cling to me, says the Lord. They were my people, an honor to my name. But then they turned away.

¹²Tell them this: The Lord God of Israel says, All your wine jugs will be full of wine. And they will reply, Of course, you don't need to tell us how prosperous we will be! ¹³Then tell them: That's not what I mean. I mean that I will fill everyone living in this land with helpless bewilderment—from the king sitting on David's throne, and the priests and the prophets right on down to all the people. ¹⁴And I will smash fathers and sons against each other, says the Lord. I will not let pity nor mercy spare them from utter destruction.

¹⁵Oh, that you were not so proud and stubborn! Then you would listen to the Lord, for he has spoken. ¹⁶Give glory

to the Lord your God before it is too late, before he causes deep, impenetrable darkness to fall upon you so that you stumble and fall upon the dark mountains; then, when you look for light, you will find only terrible darkness. 17Do you still refuse to listen? Then in loneliness my breaking heart shall mourn because of your pride. My eyes will overflow with tears because the Lord's flock shall be carried away as slaves.

18Say to the king and queen-mother, Come down from your thrones and sit in the dust, for your glorious crowns are removed from your heads. They are no longer yours. 19The cities of the Negeb to the south of Jerusalem have closed their gates against the enemy. They must defend themselves, for Jerusalem cannot help; and all Judah shall be taken away as slaves. 20See the armies marching from the north! Where is your flock, Jerusalem, your beautiful flock I gave you to take care of? 21How will you feel when I set your allies over you as your rulers? You will writhe in pain like a woman having a child. 22And if you ask yourself, Why is all this happening to me? It is because of the grossness of your sins; that is why you have been raped and destroyed by the invading army.

23Can the Ethiopian change the color of his skin? or a leopard take away his spots? Nor can you who are so used to doing evil now start being good. 24,25Because you have put me out of your mind and put your trust in false gods, I will scatter you as chaff is scattered by the fierce winds off the desert. This then is your allotment, that which is due you, which I have measured out especially for you. 26I myself will expose you to utter shame. 27I am keenly aware of your apostasy, your faithlessness to me, and your abominable idol worship in the fields and on the hills. Woe upon you, O Jerusalem! How long before you will be pure?

THIS message came to Jeremiah from the Lord, explaining why he was holding back the rain:

2Judah mourns; business has ground to a halt; all the people prostrate themselves to the earth and a great cry rises from Jerusalem. 3The nobles send servants for water from the wells, but the wells are dry. The servants return, baffled and desperate, and cover their heads in grief. 4The ground is parched and cracked for lack of rain; the farmers are afraid. 5The deer deserts her fawn because there is no grass. 6The wild donkeys stand upon the bare hills panting like thirsty jackals. They strain their eyes looking for grass to eat, but there is none to be found.

7O Lord, we have sinned against you grievously, yet help us for the sake of your own reputation! 8O Hope of Israel, our Savior in times of trouble, why are you as a stranger to us, as one passing through the land who is merely stopping for the night? 9Are you also baffled? Are you helpless to save us? O Lord, you are right here among us, and we carry your name; we are known as your people. O Lord, don't desert us now!

10But the Lord replies: You have loved to wander far from me and have not tried to follow in my paths. Now I will no longer accept you as my people; now I will remember all the evil you have done, and punish your sins.

1 THESSALONIANS 1:1—2:8

FROM: Paul, Silas and Timothy.
    To: The Church at Thessalonica—to you who belong to God the Father and the Lord Jesus Christ: May blessing and peace of heart be your rich gifts from God our Father, and from Jesus Christ our Lord.

2We always thank God for you and pray for you constantly. 3We never forget your loving deeds as we talk to our God and Father about you, and your strong faith and steady looking forward to the return of our Lord Jesus Christ.

4We know that God has chosen you, dear brothers, much beloved of God. 5For when we brought you the Good News, it was not just meaningless chatter to you; no, you listened with great interest. What we told you produced a powerful effect upon you, for the Holy Spirit gave you great and full assurance that what we said was true. And you know how our very lives were further proof to you of the truth of our message. 6So you became our followers and the Lord's; for you received our message with joy from the Holy Spirit in spite of the trials and sorrows it brought you.

7Then you yourselves became an example to all the other Christians in Greece. 8And now the Word of the Lord has spread out from you to others everywhere, far beyond your boundaries, for wherever we go we find people telling us about your remarkable faith in God. We don't need to tell *them* about it, 9for *they* keep telling *us* about the wonderful welcome you gave us, and how you turned away from your idols to God so that now the living and true God only is your Master. 10And they speak of how you are looking forward to the return of God's Son from heaven—Jesus, whom God brought back to life—and he is our only Savior from God's terrible anger against sin.

YOU yourselves know, dear brothers, how worthwhile that visit was. 2You know how badly we had been treated at Philippi just before we came to you, and how much we suffered there. Yet God gave us the courage to boldly repeat the same message to you, even though we were surrounded by enemies. 3So you can see that we were not preaching with any false motives or evil purposes in mind; we were perfectly straightforward and sincere.

4For we speak as messengers from God, trusted by him to tell the truth; we change his message not one bit to suit the taste of those who hear it; for we serve God alone, who examines our hearts' deepest thoughts. 5Never once did we try to win you with flattery, as you very well know, and God knows we were not just pretending to be your friends so that you would give us money! 6As for praise, we have never asked for it from you or anyone else, although as apostles of Christ we certainly had a right to some honor from you. 7But we were as gentle among you as a mother feeding and caring for her own children. 8We loved you dearly—so dearly that we gave you not only God's message, but our own lives too.

PSALM 79:1–13

O God, your land has been conquered by the heathen nations. Your Temple is defiled and Jerusalem is a heap of ruins. 2The bodies of your people lie exposed—food for birds and animals. 3The enemy has butchered the entire population of Jerusalem; blood has flowed like water. No one is left even to bury them. 4The nations all around us scoff. They heap contempt on us.

5O Jehovah, how long will you be angry with us? Forever? Will your jealousy burn till every hope is gone? 6Pour out your wrath upon the godless nations, not on us! And on kingdoms that refuse to pray, that will not call upon your name! 7For they have destroyed your people Israel, invading every home. 8Oh, do not hold us guilty for our former sins! Let your tenderhearted mercies meet our needs, for we are brought low to the dust. 9Help us, God of our salvation! Help us for the honor of your name. Oh, save us and forgive our sins. 10Why should the heathen nations be allowed to scoff, "Where is their God?" Publicly avenge this slaughter of your people! 11Listen to the sighing of the prisoners and those condemned to die. Demonstrate the greatness of your power by saving them. 12O Lord, take sevenfold vengeance on these nations scorning you.

13Then we your people, the sheep of your pasture, will thank you forever and forever, praising your greatness from generation to generation.

I walked by the field of a certain lazy fellow and saw that it was overgrown with thorns, and covered with weeds; and its walls were broken down. Then, as I looked, I learned this lesson: "A little extra sleep, A little more slumber, A little folding of the hands to rest" means that poverty will break in upon you suddenly like a robber, and violently like a bandit.

OCTOBER 10

JEREMIAH 14:11—16:15

THE Lord told me again: Don't ask me any more to bless this people. Don't pray for them any more. 12When they fast, I will not pay any attention; when they present their offerings and sacrifices to me, I will not accept them. What I will give them in return is war and famine and disease.

13Then I said, O Lord God, their prophets are telling them that all is well—that no war or famine will come. They tell the people you will surely send them peace, that you will bless them. 14Then the Lord said: The prophets are telling lies in my name. I didn't send them or tell them to speak or give them any message. They prophesy of visions and revelations they have never seen nor heard; they speak foolishness concocted out of their own lying hearts. 15Therefore, the Lord says, I will punish these lying prophets who have spoken in my name though I did not send them, who say no war shall come nor famine. By war and famine they themselves shall die! 16And the people to whom they prophesy—their bodies shall be thrown out into the streets of Jerusalem, victims of famine and war; there shall be no one to bury them. Husbands, wives, sons and daughters—all will be gone. For I will pour out terrible punishment upon them for their sins.

17Therefore, tell them this: Night and day my eyes shall overflow with tears; I cannot stop my crying, for my people have been run through with a sword and lie mortally wounded on the ground. 18If I go out in the fields, there lie the bodies of those the sword has killed; and if I walk in the streets, there lie those dead from starvation and disease. And yet the prophets and priests alike have made it their business to travel through the whole country, reassuring everyone that all is well, speaking of things they know nothing about.

19"O Lord," the people will cry, "have you completely rejected Judah? Do you abhor Jerusalem? Even after punishment, will there be no peace? We thought, Now at last he will heal us and bind our wounds. But no peace has come and there is only trouble and terror everywhere. 20O Lord, we confess our wickedness, and that of our fathers too. 21Do not hate us, Lord, for the sake of your own name. Do not disgrace yourself and the throne of your glory by forsaking your promise to bless us! 22What heathen god can give us rain? Who but you alone, O Lord our God, can do such things as this? Therefore we will wait for you to help us."

THEN the Lord said to me, Even if Moses and Samuel stood before me pleading for these people, even then I wouldn't help them—away with them! Get them out of my sight! 2And if they say to you, But where can we go? tell them the Lord says: Those who are destined for death, to death; those who must die by the sword, to the sword; those doomed to starvation, to famine; and those for captivity, to captivity. 3I will appoint over them four kinds of destroyers, says the Lord—the sword to kill, the dogs to tear, and the vultures and wild animals to finish up what's left. 4Because of the wicked things Manasseh, son of Hezekiah, king of Judah, did in Jerusalem, I will punish you so severely that your fate will horrify the peoples of the world.

5Who will feel sorry for you, Jerusalem? Who will weep for you? Who will even bother to ask how you are? 6You have forsaken me and turned your backs upon me. Therefore I will clench my fists against you to destroy you. I am tired of always giving you another chance. 7I will sift you at the gates of your cities and take from you all that you hold dear, and I will destroy my own people because they refuse to turn back to me from all their evil ways. 8There shall be countless widows; at noon time I will bring death to the young men and sorrow to their mothers. I will cause anguish and terror to fall upon them suddenly. 9The mother of seven sickens and faints, for all her sons are dead. Her sun is gone down while it is yet day. She sits childless now, disgraced, for all her children have been killed.

10Then Jeremiah said, "What sadness is mine, my mother; oh, that I had died at birth. For I am hated everywhere I go. I am neither a creditor soon to foreclose nor a debtor refusing to pay—yet they all curse me. 11Well, let them curse! Lord, you know how I have pled with you on their behalf—how I have begged you to spare these enemies of mine."

12,13Can a man break bars of northern iron or bronze? This people's stubborn will can't be broken either. So, because of all your sins against me, I will deliver your wealth and treasures as loot to the enemy. 14I will have your enemies take you as slaves to a land where you have never been before, for my anger burns like fire, and it shall consume you.

15Then Jeremiah replied, "Lord, you know it is for your sake that I am suffering. They are persecuting me because I have proclaimed your word to them. Don't let them kill me! Rescue me from their clutches, and give them what they deserve! 16Your words are what sustain me; they are food to my hungry soul. They bring joy to my sorrowing heart and delight me. How proud I am to bear your name, O Lord. 17,18I have not joined the people in their merry feasts. I sit alone beneath the hand of God. I burst with indignation at their sins. Yet you have failed me in my time of need! You have let them keep right on with all their persecutions. Will they never stop hurting me? Your help is as uncertain as a seasonal mountain brook—sometimes a flood, sometimes as dry as a bone."

19The Lord replied: "Stop this foolishness and talk some sense! Only if you return to trusting me will I let you continue as my spokesman. You are to influence *them,* not let them influence *you!* 20They will fight against you like a besieging army against a high city wall. But they will not conquer you for I am with you to protect and deliver you, says the Lord. 21Yes, I will certainly deliver you from these wicked men and rescue you from their ruthless hands."

ON yet another occasion God spoke to me, and said:

2You must not marry and have children here. 3For the children born in this city, and their mothers and fathers, 4shall die from terrible diseases. No one shall mourn for them or bury them, but their bodies shall lie on the ground to rot and fertilize the soil. They shall die from war and famine, and their bodies shall be picked apart by vultures and wild animals. 5Do not mourn or weep for them, for I have removed my protection and my peace from them—taken away my lovingkindness and my mercies. 6Both great and small shall die in this land, unburied and unmourned, and their friends shall not cut themselves nor shave their heads as signs of sorrow (as is their heathen custom). 7No one shall comfort the mourners with a meal, or send them a cup of wine expressing grief for their parents' death.

8As a sign to them of these sad days ahead, don't you join them any more in their feasts and parties—don't even eat a meal with them. 9For the Lord Almighty, the God of Israel, says: In your own lifetime, before your very eyes, I will end all laughter in this land—the happy songs, the marriage feasts, the songs of bridegrooms and of brides.

10And when you tell the people all these things and they ask, "Why has the Lord decreed such terrible things against us? What have we done to merit such treatment? What is our sin against the Lord our God?" 11tell them the Lord's reply is this: Because your fathers forsook me. They worshiped other gods and served them; they did not keep my laws, 12*and you have been worse than your fathers were!* You follow evil to your hearts' content and refuse to listen to me. 13Therefore I will throw you out of this land and chase you into a foreign land where neither you nor your fathers have been before, and there you can go ahead and worship your idols all you like—and I will grant you no favors!

14,15But there will come a glorious day, says the Lord, when the whole topic of conversation will be that God is bringing his people home from a nation in the north, and from many other lands where he had scattered them. You will look back no longer to the time when I rescued you from your slavery in Egypt. That mighty miracle will scarcely be mentioned any more. Yes, I will bring you back again, says the Lord, to this same land I gave your fathers.

1 THESSALONIANS 2:9—3:13

DON'T you remember, dear brothers, how hard we worked among you? Night and day we toiled and sweated to earn enough to live on so that our expenses would not be a burden to anyone there, as we preached God's Good News among you. 10You yourselves are our witnesses—as is God—

that we have been pure and honest and faultless toward every one of you. 11We talked to you as a father to his own children—don't you remember?—pleading with you, encouraging you and even demanding 12that your daily lives should not embarrass God, but bring joy to him who invited you into his Kingdom to share his glory.

13And we will never stop thanking God for this: that when we preached to you, you didn't think of the words we spoke as being just our own, but you accepted what we said as the very Word of God—which, of course, it was—and it changed your lives when you believed it.

14And then, dear brothers, you suffered what the churches in Judea did, persecution from your own countrymen, just as they suffered from their own people the Jews. 15After they had killed their own prophets, they even executed the Lord Jesus; and now they have brutally persecuted us and driven us out. They are against both God and man, 16trying to keep us from preaching to the Gentiles for fear some might be saved; and so their sins continue to grow. But the anger of God has caught up with them at last.

17Dear brothers, after we left you and had been away from you but a very little while (though our hearts never left you), we tried hard to come back to see you once more. 18We wanted very much to come and I, Paul, tried again and again, but Satan stopped us. 19For what is it we live for, that gives us hope and joy and is our proud reward and crown? It is you! Yes, you will bring us much joy as we stand together before our Lord Jesus Christ when he comes back again. 20For you are our trophy and joy.

FINALLY, when I could stand it no longer, I decided to stay alone in Athens 2,3and send Timothy, our brother and fellow worker, God's minister, to visit you to strengthen your faith and encourage you, and to keep you from becoming fainthearted in all the troubles you were going through. (But of course you know that such troubles are a part of God's plan for us Christians. 4Even while we were still with you we warned you ahead of time that suffering would soon come—and it did.)

5As I was saying, when I could bear the suspense no longer I sent Timothy to find out whether your faith was still strong. I was afraid that perhaps Satan had gotten the best of you and that all our work had been useless. 6And now Timothy has just returned and brings the welcome news that your faith and love are as strong as ever, and that you remember our visit with joy and want to see us just as much as we want to see you. 7So we are greatly comforted, dear brothers, in all of our own crushing troubles and suffering here, now that we know you are standing true to the Lord. 8We can bear anything as long as we know that you remain strong in him.

9How can we thank God enough for you and for the joy and delight you have given us in our praying for you? 10For night and day we pray on and on for you, asking God to let us see you again, to fill up any little cracks there may yet be in your faith.

11May God our Father himself and our Lord Jesus send us back to you again. 12And may the Lord make your love to grow and overflow to each other and to everyone else, just as our love does toward you. 13This will result in your hearts being made strong, sinless and holy by God our Father, so that you may stand before him guiltless on that day when our Lord Jesus Christ returns with all those who belong to him.

PSALM 80:1–19

O Shepherd of Israel who leads Israel like a flock; O God enthroned above the Guardian Angels, bend down your ear and listen as I plead. Display your power and radiant glory. 2Let Ephraim, Benjamin and Manasseh see you rouse yourself and use your mighty power to rescue us.

3Turn us again to yourself, O God. Look down on us in joy and love; only then shall we be saved.

4O Jehovah, God of heaven's armies, how long will you be angry and reject our prayers? 5You have fed us with sorrow and tears, 6and have made us the scorn of the neighboring nations. They laugh among themselves.

7Turn us again to yourself, O God of Hosts. Look down on us in joy and love; only then shall we be saved. 8You brought us from Egypt as though we were a tender vine and drove away the heathen from your land and planted us. 9You cleared the ground and tilled the soil and we took root and filled the land. 10The mountains were covered with our shadow; we were like the mighty cedar trees, 11covering the entire land from the Mediterranean Sea to the Euphrates River. 12But now you have broken down our walls, leaving us without protection. 13The boar from the forest roots around us, and the wild animals feed on us.

14Come back, we beg of you, O God of the armies of heaven, and bless us. Look down from heaven and see our plight and care for this your vine! 15Protect what you yourself have planted, this son you have raised for yourself. 16For we are chopped and burned by our enemies. May they perish at your frown. 17Strengthen the man you love, the son of your choice, 18and we will never forsake you again. Revive us to trust in you.

19Turn us again to yourself, O God of the armies of heaven. Look down on us, your face aglow with joy and love—only then shall we be saved.

PROVERBS FOR TODAY/ 25:1–5

These proverbs of Solomon were discovered and copied by the aides of King Hezekiah of Judah: It is God's privilege to conceal things, and the king's privilege to discover and invent. You cannot understand the height of heaven, the size of the earth, or all that goes on in the king's mind! When you remove dross from silver, you have sterling ready for the silversmith. When you remove corrupt men from the king's court, his reign will be just and fair.

OCTOBER 11

JEREMIAH 16:16—18:23

NOW I am sending for many fishermen to fish you from the deeps where you are hiding from my wrath. I am sending for hunters to chase you down like deer in the forests or mountain goats on inaccessible crags. Wherever you run to escape my judgment, I will find you and punish you. 17For I am closely watching you and I see every sin. You cannot hope to hide from me.

18And I will punish you doubly for all your sins because you have defiled my land with your detestable idols, and filled it up with all your evil deeds.

19O Lord, my Strength and Fortress, my Refuge in the day of trouble, nations from around the world will come to you saying, "Our fathers have been foolish, for they have worshiped worthless idols! 20Can men make God? The gods they made are not real gods at all." 21And when they come in that spirit, I will show them my power and might and make them understand at last that I alone am God.

MY people sin as though commanded to, as though their evil were laws chiseled with an iron pen or diamond point upon their stony hearts or on the corners of their altars. 2,3Their youths do not forget to sin, worshiping idols beneath each tree, high in the mountains or in the open country down below. And so I will give all your treasures to your enemies as the price that you must pay for all your sins. 4And the wonderful heritage I reserved for you will slip out of your hand,

and I will send you away as slaves to your enemies in distant lands. For you have kindled a fire of my anger that shall burn forever.

5The Lord says: Cursed is the man who puts his trust in mortal man and turns his heart away from God. 6He is like a stunted shrub in the desert, with no hope for the future; he lives on the salt-encrusted plains in the barren wilderness; good times pass him by forever.

7But blessed is the man who trusts in the Lord and has made the Lord his hope and confidence. 8He is like a tree planted along a riverbank, with its roots reaching deep into the water—a tree not bothered by the heat nor worried by long months of drought. Its leaves stay green and it goes right on producing all its luscious fruit.

9The heart is the most deceitful thing there is, and desperately wicked. No one can really know how bad it is! 10Only the Lord knows! He searches all hearts and examines deepest motives so he can give to each person his right reward, according to his deeds—how he has lived.

11Like a bird that fills her nest with young she has not hatched and which will soon desert her and fly away, so is the man who gets his wealth by unjust means. Sooner or later he will lose his riches and at the end of his life become a poor old fool.

12But our refuge is your throne, eternal, high and glorious. 13O Lord, the Hope of Israel, all who turn away from you shall be disgraced and shamed; they are registered for earth and not for glory, for they have forsaken the Lord, the Fountain of living waters. 14Lord, you alone can heal me, you alone can save, and my praises are for you alone.

15Men scoff at me and say, "What is this word of the Lord you keep talking about? If these threats of yours are really from God, why don't they come true?"

16Lord, I don't want the people crushed by terrible calamity. The plan is yours, not mine. It is *your* message I've given them, not my own. *I* don't want them doomed! 17Lord, don't desert me now! You alone are my hope. 18Bring confusion and trouble on all who persecute me, but give me peace. Yes, bring double destruction upon them!

19Then the Lord said to me, Go and stand in the gates of Jerusalem, first at the gate where the king goes out, and then at each of the other gates, 20and say to all the people: Hear the word of the Lord, kings of Judah and all the people of this nation, and all you citizens of Jerusalem. 21,22The Lord says: Take warning and live; do no unnecessary work on the Sabbath day but make it a holy day. I gave this commandment to your fathers, 23but they didn't listen or obey. They stubbornly refused to pay attention and be taught.

24But if you obey me, says the Lord, and refuse to work on the Sabbath day and keep it separate, special and holy, 25then this nation shall continue forever. There shall always be descendants of David sitting on the throne here in Jerusalem; there shall always be kings and princes riding in pomp and splendor among the people, and this city shall remain forever. 26And from all around Jerusalem and from the cities of Judah and Benjamin, and from the Negeb and from the lowlands west of Judah, the people shall come with their burnt offerings and grain offerings and incense, bringing their sacrifices to praise the Lord in his Temple.

27But if you will not listen to me, if you refuse to keep the Sabbath holy, if on the Sabbath you bring in loads of merchandise through these gates of Jerusalem, just as on other days, then I will set fire to these gates. The fire shall spread to the palaces and utterly destroy them, and no one shall be able to put out the raging flames.

HERE is another message to Jeremiah from the Lord:

2Go down to the shop where clay pots and jars are made and I will talk to you there. 3I did as he told me, and found the potter working at his wheel. 4But the jar that he was forming didn't turn out as he wished, so he kneaded it into a lump and started again.

5Then the Lord said:

6O Israel, can't I do to you as this potter has done to his clay? As the clay is in the potter's hand, so are you in my hand. 7Whenever I announce that a certain nation or kingdom is to be taken up and destroyed, 8then if that nation renounces its evil ways, I will not destroy it as I had planned. 9And if I announce that I will make a certain nation strong and great, 10but then that nation changes its mind and turns to evil and refuses to obey me, then I too will change my mind and not bless that nation as I had said I would.

11Therefore go and warn all Judah and Jerusalem, saying: Hear the word of the Lord. I am planning evil against you now instead of good; turn back from your evil paths and do what is right.

12But they replied, "Don't waste your breath. We have no intention whatever of doing what God says. We will continue to live as we want to, free from any restraint, full of stubbornness and wickedness!"

13Then the Lord said: Even among the heathen, no one has ever heard of such a thing! My people have done something too horrible to understand. 14The snow never melts high up in the Lebanon mountains. The cold, flowing streams from the crags of Mount Hermon never run dry. 15These can be counted on. But not my people! For they have deserted me and turned to foolish idols. They have turned away from the ancient highways of good, and walk the muddy paths of sin. 16Therefore their land shall become desolate, so that all who pass by will gasp and shake their heads in amazement at its utter desolation. 17I will scatter my people before their enemies as the east wind scatters dust; and in all their trouble I will turn my back on them and refuse to notice their distress.

18Then the people said, "Come, let's get rid of Jeremiah. We have our own priests and wise men and prophets—we don't need his advice. Let's silence him that he may speak no more against us, nor bother us again."

19*O Lord, help me! See what they are planning to do to me!* 20Should they repay evil for good? They have set a trap to kill me, yet I spoke well of them to you and tried to defend them from your anger. 21Now, Lord, let their children starve to death and let the sword pour out their blood! Let their wives be widows and be bereft of all their children! Let their men die in epidemics and their youths die in battle! 22Let screaming be heard from their homes as troops of soldiers come suddenly upon them, for they have dug a pit for me to fall in, and they have hidden traps along my path. 23Lord, you know all their murderous plots against me. Don't forgive them, don't blot out their sin, but let them perish before you; deal with them in your anger.

1 THESSALONIANS 4:1—5:2a

LET me add this, dear brothers: You already know how to please God in your daily living, for you know the commands we gave you from the Lord Jesus himself. Now we beg you—yes, we demand of you in the name of the Lord Jesus—that you live more and more closely to that ideal. 3,4For God wants you to be holy and pure, and to keep clear of all sexual sin so that each of you will marry in holiness and honor— 5not in lustful passion as the heathen do, in their ignorance of God and his ways.

6And this also is God's will: that you never cheat in this matter by taking another man's wife, because the Lord will punish you terribly for this, as we have solemnly told you before. 7For God has not called us to be dirty-minded and full of lust, but to be holy and clean. 8If anyone refuses to live by these rules he is not disobeying the rules of men but of God who gives his *Holy* Spirit to you.

9But concerning the pure brotherly love that there should be among God's people, I don't need to say very much, I'm sure! For God himself is teaching you to love one another. 10Indeed, your love is already strong toward all the Christian brothers throughout your whole nation. Even so, dear friends, we beg you to love them more and more. 11This should be your ambition: to live a quiet life, minding your own business and doing your own work, just as we told you before. 12As a result, people who are not Christians will trust and respect you, and you will not need to depend on others for enough money to pay your bills.

13And now, dear brothers, I want you to know what happens to a Christian when he dies so that when it happens, you will not be full of sorrow, as those are who have no hope. 14For since we believe that Jesus died and then came back to life again, we can also believe that when Jesus returns, God will bring back with him all the Christians who have died.

15I can tell you this directly from the Lord: that we who are still living when the Lord returns will not rise to meet him ahead of those who are in their graves. 16For the Lord himself will come down from heaven with a mighty shout and with the soul-stirring cry of the archangel and the great trumpet-call of God. And the believers who are dead will be the first to rise to meet the Lord. 17Then we who are still alive and remain on the earth will be caught up with them in the clouds to meet the Lord in the air and remain with him forever. 18So comfort and encourage each other with this news.

WHEN is all this going to happen? I really don't need to say anything about that, dear brothers, 2for you know perfectly well that no one knows.

PSALM 81:1–16

THE Lord makes us strong! Sing praises! Sing to Israel's God! 2Sing, accompanied by drums; pluck the sweet lyre and harp. 3Sound the trumpet! Come to the joyous celebrations at full moon, new moon and all the other holidays. 4For God has given us these times of joy; they are scheduled in the laws of Israel. 5He gave them as reminders of his war against Egypt where we were slaves on foreign soil.

I heard an unknown voice that said, 6"Now I will relieve your shoulder of its burden; I will free your hands from their heavy tasks." 7He said, "You cried to me in trouble and I saved you; I answered from Mount Sinai where the thunder hides. I tested your faith at Meri-bah, when you complained there was no water. 8Listen to me, O my people, while I give you stern warnings. O Israel, if you will only listen! 9*You must never worship any other god,* nor ever have an idol in your home. 10For it was I, Jehovah your God, who brought you out of the land of Egypt. Only test me! Open your mouth wide and see if I won't fill it. You will receive every blessing you can use!

11"But no, my people won't listen. Israel doesn't want me around. 12So I am letting them go their blind and stubborn way, living according to their own desires.

13"But oh, that my people would listen to me! Oh, that Israel would follow me, walking in my paths! 14How quickly then I would subdue her enemies! How soon my hands would be upon her foes! 15Those who hate the Lord would cringe before him; their desolation would last forever. 16But he would feed you with the choicest foods. He would satisfy you with honey for the taking."

PROVERBS FOR TODAY/ 25:6–7

Don't demand an audience with the king as though you were some powerful prince. It is better to wait for an invitation rather than to be sent back to the end of the line, publicly disgraced!

OCTOBER 12

JEREMIAH 19:1—21:14

THE Lord said, Buy a clay jar and take it out into the valley of Ben-Hinnom by the east gate of the city. Take some of the elders of the people and some of the older priests with you, and speak to them whatever words I give you.

3Then the Lord spoke to them and said: Listen to the word of the Lord, kings of Judah and citizens of Jerusalem! The Lord Almighty, the God of Israel, says, I will bring terrible evil upon this place, so terrible that the ears of those who hear it will prickle. 4For Israel has forsaken me and turned this valley into a place of shame and wickedness. The people burn incense to idols—idols that neither this generation nor their forefathers nor the kings of Judah have worshiped before—and they have filled this place with the blood of innocent children. 5They have built high altars to Baal and there they burn their sons in sacrifice—

a thing I never commanded them nor even thought of!

⁶The day is coming, says the Lord, when this valley shall no longer be called "Topheth" or "Ben-Hinnom Valley," but "The Valley of Slaughter." ⁷For I will upset the battle plans of Judah and Jerusalem and I will let invading armies kill you here and leave your dead bodies for vultures and wild animals to feed upon. ⁸And I will wipe Jerusalem off the earth, so that everyone going by will gasp with astonishment at all that I have done to her. ⁹I will see to it that your enemies lay siege to the city until all food is gone, and those trapped inside begin to eat their own children and friends.

¹⁰And now, Jeremiah, as these men watch, smash the jar you brought with you, ¹¹and say to them, This is the message to you from the Lord Almighty: As this jar lies shattered, so I will shatter the people of Jerusalem; and as this jar cannot be mended, neither can they. The slaughter shall be so great that there won't be room enough for decent burial anywhere, and their bodies shall be heaped in this valley. ¹²And as it will be in this valley, so it will be in Jerusalem. For I will fill Jerusalem with dead bodies too. ¹³And I will defile all the homes in Jerusalem, including the palace of the kings of Judah—wherever incense has been burned upon the roofs to your star-gods, and libations poured out to them.

¹⁴As Jeremiah returned from Topheth where he had delivered this message, he stopped in front of the Temple of the Lord and said to all the people, ¹⁵The Lord Almighty, the God of Israel, says: I will bring upon this city and her surrounding towns all the evil I have promised, because you have stubbornly refused to listen to the Lord.

NOW when Pashhur (son of Immer), the priest in charge of the Temple of the Lord, heard what Jeremiah was saying, ²he arrested Jeremiah and had him whipped and put in the stocks at Benjamin Gate near the Temple. ³He left him there all night.

The next day when Pashhur finally released him, Jeremiah said, "Pashhur, the Lord has changed your name. He says from now on to call you 'The Man Who Lives in Terror.' ⁴For the Lord will send terror on you and all your friends, and you will see them die by the swords of their enemies. I will hand over Judah to the king of Babylon, says the Lord, and he shall take away these people as slaves to Babylon and kill them. ⁵And I will let your enemies loot Jerusalem. All the famed treasures of the city, with the precious jewels and gold and silver of your kings, shall be carried off to Babylon. ⁶And as for you, Pashhur, you and all your family and household shall become slaves in Babylon and die there—you and those to whom you lied when you prophesied that everything would be all right."

⁷Then I said, O Lord, you deceived me when you promised me your help. I have to give them your messages because you are stronger than I am, but now I am the laughingstock of the city, mocked by all. ⁸You have never once let me speak a word of kindness to them; always it is disaster and horror and destruction. No wonder they scoff and mock and make my name a household joke. ⁹And I can't quit! For if I say I'll never again mention the Lord—never more speak in his name—then his word in my heart is like fire that burns in my bones, and I can't hold it in any longer. ¹⁰Yet on every side I hear their whispered threats, and am afraid. "We will report," they say. Even those who were my friends are watching me, waiting for a fatal slip. "He will trap himself," they say, "and then we will get our revenge on him."

¹¹But the Lord stands beside me like a great warrior, and before him, the Mighty, Terrible One, they shall stumble. They cannot defeat me; they shall be shamed and thoroughly humiliated, and they shall have a stigma upon them forever. ¹²O Lord Almighty, who knows those who are righteous and examines the deepest thoughts of hearts and minds, let me see your vengeance on

them. For I have committed my cause to you. 13Therefore I will sing out in thanks to the Lord! Praise him! For he has delivered me, poor and needy, from my oppressors.

14Yet, cursed be the day that I was born! 15Cursed be the man who brought my father the news that a son was born. 16Let that messenger be destroyed like the cities of old which God overthrew without mercy. Terrify him all day long with battle shouts, 17because he did not kill me at my birth! Oh, that I had died within my mother's womb, that it had been my grave! 18Why was I ever born? For my life has been but trouble and sorrow and shame.

THEN King Zedekiah sent Pashhur (son of Malchiah) and Zephaniah the priest (son of Ma-aseiah) to Jeremiah, and begged, "Ask the Lord to help us, for Nebuchadnezzar, king of Babylon, has declared war on us! 2Perhaps the Lord will be gracious to us and do a mighty miracle as in olden times and force Nebuchadnezzar to withdraw his forces."

3,4Jeremiah replied, "Go back to King Zedekiah and tell him the Lord God of Israel says, I will make all your weapons useless against the king of Babylon and the Chaldeans besieging you. In fact, I will bring your enemies right into the heart of this city, 5and I myself will fight against you, for I am very angry. 6And I will send a terrible plague on this city, and both men and animals shall die. 7And finally I will deliver King Zedekiah himself and all the remnant left in the city into the hands of King Nebuchadnezzar of Babylon, to slaughter them without pity or mercy.

8"Tell these people, the Lord says: Take your choice of life or death! 9Stay here in Jerusalem and die—slaughtered by your enemies, killed by starvation and disease—or go out and surrender to the Chaldean army and live. 10For I have set my face against this city; I will be its enemy and not its friend, says the Lord. It shall be captured by the king of Babylon and he shall reduce it to ashes.

11"And to the king of Judah, the Lord says: 12I am ready to judge you because of all the evil you are doing. Quick! Give justice to these you judge! Begin doing what is right before my burning fury flashes out upon you like a fire no man can quench. 13I will fight against this city of Jerusalem, which boasts, 'We are safe; no one can touch us here!' 14And I myself will destroy you for your sinfulness, says the Lord. I will light a fire in the forests that will burn up everything in its path."

1 THESSALONIANS 5:2b–28

THAT day of the Lord will come unexpectedly like a thief in the night.

3When people are saying, "All is well, everything is quiet and peaceful"—then, all of a sudden, disaster will fall upon them as suddenly as a woman's birth pains begin when her child is born. And these people will not be able to get away anywhere—there will be no place to hide.

4But, dear brothers, you are not in the dark about these things, and you won't be surprised as by a thief when that day of the Lord comes. 5For you are all children of the light and of the day, and do not belong to darkness and night. 6So be on your guard, not asleep like the others. Watch for his return and stay sober. 7Night is the time for sleep and the time when people get drunk. 8But let us who live in the light keep sober, protected by the armor of faith and love, and wearing as our helmet the happy hope of salvation.

9For God has not chosen to pour out his anger upon us, but to save us through our Lord Jesus Christ; 10he died for us so that we can live with him forever, whether we are dead or alive at the time of his return. 11So encourage each other to build each other up, just as you are already doing.

12Dear brothers, honor the officers of your church who work hard among you and warn you against all that is wrong.

13Think highly of them and give them your wholehearted love because they are straining to help you. And remember, no quarreling among yourselves.

14Dear brothers, warn those who are lazy; comfort those who are frightened; take tender care of those who are weak; and be patient with everyone. 15See that no one pays back evil for evil, but always try to do good to each other and to everyone else. 16Always be joyful. 17Always keep on praying. 18No matter what happens, always be thankful, for this is God's will for you who belong to Christ Jesus.

19Do not smother the Holy Spirit. 20Do not scoff at those who prophesy, 21but test everything that is said to be sure it is true, and if it is, then accept it. 22Keep away from every kind of evil. 23May the God of peace himself make you entirely pure and devoted to God; and may your spirit and soul and body be kept strong and blameless until that day when our Lord Jesus Christ comes back again. 24God, who called you to become his child, will do all this for you, just as he promised. 25Dear brothers, pray for us. 26Shake hands for me with all the brothers there. 27I command you in the name of the Lord to read this letter to all the Christians. 28And may rich blessings from our Lord Jesus Christ be with you, every one.

Sincerely,
Paul

PSALM 82:1–8

GOD stands up to open heaven's court. He pronounces judgment on the judges. 2How long will you judges refuse to listen to the evidence? How long will you shower special favors on the wicked? 3Give fair judgment to the poor man, the afflicted, the fatherless, the destitute. 4Rescue the poor and helpless from the grasp of evil men. 5But you are so foolish and so ignorant! Because you are in darkness, all the foundations of society are shaken to the core. 6I have called you all "gods" and "sons of the Most High." 7But in death you are mere men. You will fall as any prince—for all must die.

8Stand up, O God, and judge the earth. For all of it belongs to you. All nations are in your hands.

PROVERBS FOR TODAY/ 25:8–10

Don't be hot-headed and rush to court! You may start something you can't finish and go down before your neighbor in shameful defeat. So discuss the matter with him privately. Don't tell anyone else, lest he accuse you of slander and you can't withdraw what you said.

OCTOBER 13

JEREMIAH 22:1—23:20

THEN the Lord said to me: Go over and speak directly to the king of Judah and say, 2Listen to this message from God, O king of Judah, sitting on David's throne; and let your servants and your people listen too.

3The Lord says: Be fair-minded. Do what is right! Help those in need of justice! Quit your evil deeds! Protect the rights of aliens and immigrants, orphans and widows; stop murdering the innocent! 4If you put an end to all these terrible deeds you are doing, then I will deliver this nation and once more give kings to sit on David's throne, and there shall be prosperity for all.

5But if you refuse to pay attention to this warning, I swear by my own name, says the Lord, that this palace shall become a shambles. 6For this is the Lord's message concerning the palace: You are as beloved to me as fruitful Gilead and the green forests of Lebanon; but I will destroy you and leave you deserted and uninhabited. 7I will call for a wrecking crew to bring out its tools to dismantle you. They will tear out all of your fine cedar beams and throw them on the fire. 8Men from many nations will pass by the ruins of this city and say to one another, "Why did the Lord do it? Why did he destroy such a great city?" 9And the answer will be, "Because the people living here forgot the Lord their God and violated his agreement with them, for they worshiped idols."

10Don't weep for the dead! Instead weep for the captives led away! For they will never return to see their native land again. 11For the Lord says this about Jehoahaz who succeeded his father King Josiah, and was taken away as a captive: 12He shall die in a distant land and never again see his own country.

13And woe to you, King Jehoiakim, for you are building your great palace with forced labor. By not paying wages you are building injustice into its walls and oppression into its doorframes and ceilings. 14You say, "I will build a magnificent palace with huge rooms and many windows, paneled throughout with fragrant cedar and painted a lovely red." 15But a beautiful palace does not make a great king! Why did your father Josiah reign so long? Because he was just and fair in all his dealings. That is why God blessed him. 16He saw to it that justice and help were given the poor and the needy and all went well for him. This is how a man lives close to God. 17But you! You are full of selfish greed and all dishonesty! You murder the innocent, oppress the poor and reign with ruthlessness.

18Therefore this is God's decree of punishment against King Jehoiakim, who succeeded his father Josiah on the throne: His family will not weep for him when he dies. His subjects will not even care that he is dead. 19He shall be buried like a dead donkey—dragged out of Jerusalem and thrown on the garbage dump beyond the gate! 20Weep, for your allies are gone. Search for them in Lebanon; shout for them at Bashan; seek them at the fording points of Jordan. See, they are all destroyed. Not one is left to help you! 21When you were prosperous I warned you, but you replied, "Don't bother me." Since childhood you have been that way—you just won't listen! 22And now all your allies have disappeared with a puff of wind; all your friends are taken off as slaves. Surely at last you will see your wickedness and be ashamed. 23It's very nice to live graciously in a beautiful palace among the cedars of Lebanon, but soon you will cry and groan in anguish—anguish as of a woman in labor.

24,25And as for you, Coniah, son of Jehoiakim king of Judah—even if you were the signet ring on my right hand, I would pull you off and give you to those who seek to kill you, of whom you are so desperately afraid—to Nebuchadnezzar, king of Babylon, and his mighty army. 26I will throw you and your mother out of this country, and you shall die in a foreign land. 27You will never again return to the land of your desire. 28This man Coniah is like a discarded, broken dish. He and his children will be exiled to distant lands.

29O earth, earth, earth! Hear the word of the Lord! 30The Lord says:

Record this man Coniah as childless, for none of his children shall ever sit upon the throne of David or rule in Judah. His life will amount to nothing.

THE Lord declares:

I will send disaster upon the leaders of my people—the shepherds of my sheep—for they have destroyed and scattered the very ones they were to care for. ²Instead of leading my flock to safety, you have deserted them and driven them to destruction. And now I will pour out judgment upon you for the evil you have done to them. ³And I will gather together the remnant of my flock from wherever I have sent them, and bring them back into their own fold, and they shall be fruitful and increase. ⁴And I will appoint responsible shepherds to care for them, and they shall not need to be afraid again; all of them shall be accounted for continually.

⁵,⁶For the time is coming, says the Lord, when I will place a righteous Branch upon King David's throne. He shall be a King who shall rule with wisdom and justice and cause righteousness to prevail everywhere throughout the earth. And this is his name: *The Lord Our Righteousness.* At that time Judah will be saved and Israel will live in peace.

⁷In that day people will no longer say when taking an oath, "As the Lord lives who rescued the people of Israel from the land of Egypt," ⁸but they will say, "As the Lord lives who brought the Jews back to their own land of Israel from the countries to which he had exiled them."

⁹My heart is broken for the false prophets, full of deceit. I awake with fear and stagger as a drunkard does from wine, because of the awful fate awaiting them, for God has decreed holy words of judgment against them. ¹⁰For the land is full of adultery and the curse of God is on it. The land itself is mourning—the pastures are dried up—for the prophets do evil and their power is used wrongly. ¹¹And the priests are like the prophets, all ungodly, wicked men. I have seen their despicable acts right here in my own Temple, says the Lord. ¹²Therefore their paths will be dark and slippery; they will be chased down dark and treacherous trails, and fall. For I will bring evil upon them and see to it, when their time has come, that they pay their penalty in full for all their sins.

¹³I knew the prophets of Samaria were unbelievably evil, for they prophesied by Baal and led my people Israel into sin; ¹⁴but the prophets of Jerusalem are even worse! The things they do are horrible; they commit adultery and love dishonesty. They encourage and compliment those who are doing evil, instead of turning them back from their sins. These prophets are as thoroughly depraved as the men of Sodom and Gomorrah were.

¹⁵Therefore the Lord Almighty says: I will feed them with bitterness and give them poison to drink. For it is because of them that wickedness fills this land. ¹⁶This is my warning to my people, says the Lord Almighty. Don't listen to these false prophets when they prophesy to you, filling you with futile hopes. They are making up everything they say. They do not speak for me! ¹⁷They keep saying to these rebels who despise me, "Don't worry! All is well"; and to those who live the way they want to, "The Lord has said you shall have peace!"

¹⁸But can you name even one of these prophets who lives close enough to God to hear what he is saying? Has even one of them cared enough to listen? ¹⁹See, the Lord is sending a furious whirlwind to sweep away these wicked men. ²⁰The terrible anger of the Lord will not abate until it has carried out the full penalty he decrees against them. Later, when Jerusalem has fallen, you will see what I mean.

2 THESSALONIANS 1:1–12

FROM: Paul, Silas and Timothy.
To: The church of Thessalonica—kept safe in God our Father and in the Lord Jesus Christ.

²May God the Father and the Lord Jesus Christ give you rich blessings and peace-filled hearts and minds.

³Dear brothers, giving thanks to God for you is not only the right thing to

do, but it is our duty to God, because of the really wonderful way your faith has grown, and because of your growing love for each other. 4We are happy to tell other churches about your patience and complete faith in God, in spite of all the crushing troubles and hardships you are going through.

5This is only one example of the fair, just way God does things, for he is using your sufferings to make you ready for his Kingdom, 6while at the same time he is preparing judgment and punishment for those who are hurting you.

7And so I would say to you who are suffering, God will give you rest along with us when the Lord Jesus appears suddenly from heaven in flaming fire with his mighty angels, 8bringing judgment on those who do not wish to know God, and who refuse to accept his plan to save them through our Lord Jesus Christ. 9They will be punished in everlasting hell, forever separated from the Lord, never to see the glory of his power, 10when he comes to receive praise and admiration because of all he has done for his people, his saints. And you will be among those praising him, because you have believed what we told you about him.

11And so we keep on praying for you that our God will make you the kind of children he wants to have—will make you as good as you wish you could be!—rewarding your faith with his power. 12Then everyone will be praising the name of the Lord Jesus Christ because of the results they see in you; and your greatest glory will be that you belong to him. The tender mercy of our God and of the Lord Jesus Christ has made all this possible for you.

PSALM 83:1–18

O God, don't sit idly by, silent and inactive when we pray. Answer us! Deliver us!

2Don't you hear the tumult and commotion of your enemies? Don't you see what they are doing, these proud men who hate the Lord? 3They are full of craftiness and plot against your people, laying plans to slay your precious ones. 4"Come," they say, "and let us wipe out Israel as a nation—we will destroy the very memory of her existence." 5This was their unanimous decision at their summit conference—they signed a treaty to ally themselves against Almighty God— 6these Ishmaelites and Edomites and Moabites and Hagrites; 7people from the lands of Gebal, Ammon, Amalek, Philistia and Tyre; 8Assyria has joined them too, and is allied with the descendants of Lot.

9Do to them as once you did to Midian, or as you did to Sisera and Jabin at the river Kishon, 10and as you did to your enemies at Endor, whose decaying corpses fertilized the soil. 11Make their mighty nobles die as Oreb did, and Zeeb; let all their princes die like Zebah and Zalmunna, 12who said, "Let us seize for our own use these pasturelands of God!"

13O my God, blow them away like dust; like chaff before the wind— 14as a forest fire that roars across a mountain. 15Chase them with your fiery storms, tempests and tornados. 16Utterly disgrace them until they recognize your power and name, O Lord. 17Make them failures in everything they do; let them be ashamed and terrified 18until they learn that you alone, Jehovah, are the God above all gods in supreme charge of all the earth.

PROVERBS FOR TODAY/ 25:11–14

Timely advice is as lovely as gold apples in a silver basket. It is a badge of honor to accept valid criticism. A faithful employee is as refreshing as a cool day in the hot summertime. One who doesn't give the gift he promised is like a cloud blowing over a desert without dropping any rain.

OCTOBER 14

JEREMIAH 23:21—25:38

I have not sent these prophets, yet they claim to speak for me; I gave them no message, yet they say their words are mine. 22If they were mine, they would try to turn my people from their evil ways. 23Am I a God who is only in one place and cannot see what they are doing? 24Can anyone hide from me? Am I not everywhere in all of heaven and earth?

25"Listen to the dream I had from God last night," they say. And then they proceed to lie in my name. 26How long will this continue? If they are "prophets," they are prophets of deceit, inventing everything they say. 27By telling these false dreams they are trying to get my people to forget me in the same way as their fathers did, who turned away to the idols of Baal. 28Let these false prophets tell their dreams and let my true messengers faithfully proclaim my every word. There is a difference between chaff and wheat! 29Does not my word burn like fire? asks the Lord. Is it not like a mighty hammer that smashed the rock to pieces? 30,31So I stand against these "prophets" who get their messages from each other—these smooth-tongued prophets who say, "This message is from God!" 32Their made-up dreams are flagrant lies that lead my people into sin. I did not send them and they have no message at all for my people, says the Lord.

33When one of the people or one of their "prophets" or priests asks you, "Well, Jeremiah, what is the sad news from the Lord today?" you shall reply, "What sad news? You are the sad news, for the Lord has cast you away!" 34And as for the false prophets and priests and people who joke about "today's sad news from God," I will punish them and their families for saying this. 35You can ask each other, "What is God's message? What is he saying?" 36But stop using this term, "God's sad news." For

what is sad is you and your lying. You are twisting my words and inventing "messages from God" that I didn't speak. 37You may respectfully ask Jeremiah, "What is the Lord's message? What has he said to you?" 38,39But if you ask him about "today's sad news from God," when I have warned you not to mock like that, then I, the Lord God, will unburden myself of the burden you are to me. I will cast you out of my presence, you and this city I gave to you and your fathers. 40And I will bring reproach upon you and your name shall be infamous through the ages.

AFTER Nebuchadnezzar, king of Babylon, had captured and enslaved Jeconiah (son of Jehoiakim), king of Judah, and exiled him to Babylon along with the princes of Judah and the skilled tradesmen—the carpenters and blacksmiths—the Lord gave me this vision. 2I saw two baskets of figs placed in front of the Temple in Jerusalem. In one basket there were fresh, just-ripened figs, but in the other the figs were spoiled and moldy—too rotten to eat. 3Then the Lord said to me, "What do you see, Jeremiah?"

I replied, "Figs, some very good and some very bad."

4,5Then the Lord said: "The good figs represent the exiles sent to Babylon. I have done it for their good. 6I will see that they are well treated and I will bring them back here again. I will help them and not hurt them; I will plant them and not pull them up. 7I will give them hearts that respond to me. They shall be my people and I will be their God, for they shall return to me with great joy.

8"But the rotten figs represent Zedekiah, king of Judah, his officials and all the others of Jerusalem left here in this land; those too who live in Egypt. I will treat them like spoiled figs, too bad to use. 9I will make them repulsive to every nation of the earth, and they shall be mocked and taunted and cursed wherever I compel them to go. 10And I will send massacre and famine and disease among them until they are destroyed from the land of Israel, which I gave to them and to their fathers."

THIS message for all the people of Judah came from the Lord to Jeremiah during the fourth year of the reign of King Jehoiakim of Judah (son of Josiah). This was the year Nebuchadnezzar, king of Babylon, began his reign.

2,3For the past twenty-three years, Jeremiah said, from the thirteenth year of the reign of Josiah (son of Amon) king of Judah, until now, God has been sending me his messages. I have faithfully passed them on to you, but you haven't listened. 4Again and again down through the years, God has sent you his prophets, but you have refused to hear. 5Each time the message was this: Turn from the evil road you are traveling and from the evil things you are doing. Only then can you continue to live here in this land which the Lord gave to you and to your ancestors forever. 6*Don't anger me by worshiping idols; but if you are true to me, then I'll not harm you.* 7But you won't listen; you have gone ahead and made me furious with your idols. So you have brought upon yourselves all the evil that has come your way.

8,9And now the Lord God says, Because you have not listened to me, I will gather together all the armies of the north under Nebuchadnezzar, king of Babylon (I have appointed him as my deputy), and I will bring them all against this land and its people and against the other nations near you, and I will utterly destroy you and make you a byword of contempt forever. 10I will take away your joy, your gladness and your wedding feasts; your businesses shall fail and all your homes shall lie in silent darkness. 11This entire land shall become a desolate wasteland; all the world will be shocked at the disaster that befalls you. Israel and her neighboring lands shall serve the king of Babylon for seventy years.

12Then, after these years of slavery are ended, I will punish the king of Babylon and his people for their sins; I will make the land of Chaldea an everlasting waste. 13I will bring upon them all the terrors I have promised in this book—all the penalties announced by Jeremiah against the nations. 14For many nations and great kings shall enslave the Chaldeans, just as they enslaved my people; I will punish them in proportion to their treatment of my people.

15For the Lord God said to me: "Take from my hand this wine cup filled to the brim with my fury, and make all the nations to whom I send you drink from it. 16They shall drink from it and reel, crazed by the death blows I rain upon them."

17So I took the cup of fury from the Lord and made all the nations drink from it—every nation God had sent me to; 18I went to Jerusalem and to the cities of Judah, and their kings and princes drank of the cup so that from that day until this they have been desolate, hated and cursed, just as they are today. 19,20I went to Egypt, and Pharaoh and his servants, the princes and the people—they too drank from that terrible cup, along with all the foreign population living in his land. So did all the kings of the land of Uz and the kings of the Philistine cities: Ashkelon, Gaza, Ekron, and what remains of Ashdod, 21and I visited the nations of Edom, Moab and Ammon; 22and all the kings of Tyre and Sidon, and the kings of the regions across the sea; 23Dedan and Tema and Buz, and the other heathen there; 24and all the kings of Arabia and of the nomadic tribes of the desert; 25and all the kings of Zimri, Elam and Media; 26and all the kings of the northern countries, far and near, one after the other; and all the kingdoms of the world. And finally, the king of Babylon himself drank from this cup of God's wrath.

27Tell them, "The Lord of heaven's armies, the God of Israel, says, Drink from this cup of my wrath until you are drunk and vomit and fall and rise no more, for I am sending terrible wars upon you." 28And if they refuse to accept the cup, tell them, "The Lord of heaven's armies says you *must* drink it! You cannot escape! 29I have begun to punish my own people, so should you go free? No, you shall not evade punishment. I will call for war against all the peoples of the earth."

30Therefore prophesy against them. Tell them the Lord will shout against his own from his holy temple in heaven, and against all those living on the earth. He will shout as the harvesters do who tread the juice from the grapes. 31That cry of judgment will reach the farthest ends of the earth, for the Lord has a case against all the nations—all mankind. He will slaughter all the wicked. 32See, declares the Lord Almighty, the punishment shall go from nation to nation—a great whirlwind of wrath shall rise against the farthest corners of the earth. 33On that day those the Lord has slain shall fill the earth from one end to the other. No one shall mourn for them nor gather up the bodies to bury them; they shall fertilize the earth.

34Weep and moan, O evil shepherds; let the leaders of mankind beat their heads upon the stones, for their time has come to be slaughtered and scattered; they shall fall like fragile women. 35And you will find no place to hide, no way to escape.

36Listen to the frantic cries of the shepherds and to the leaders shouting in despair, for the Lord has spoiled their pastures. 37People now living undisturbed will be cut down by the fierceness of the anger of the Lord. 38He has left his lair like a lion seeking prey; their land has been laid waste by warring armies—because of the fierce anger of the Lord.

2 THESSALONIANS 2:1–17

AND now, what about the coming again of our Lord Jesus Christ, and our being gathered together to meet him? Please don't be upset and excited, dear brothers, by the rumor that this day of the Lord has already begun. If you hear of people having visions and special messages from God about this, or letters that are supposed to have come from me, don't believe them. 3Don't be carried away and deceived regardless of what they say.

For that day will not come until two things happen: first, there will be a time of great rebellion against God, and then the man of rebellion will come—the son of hell. 4He will defy every god there is, and tear down every other object of adoration and worship. He will go in and sit as God in the temple of God, claiming that he himself is God. 5Don't you remember that I told you this when I was with you? 6And you know what is keeping him from being here already; for he can come only when his time is ready.

7As for the work this man of rebellion and hell will do when he comes, it is already going on, but he himself will not come until the one who is holding him back steps out of the way. 8Then this wicked one will appear, whom the Lord Jesus will burn up with the breath of his mouth and destroy by his presence when he returns. 9This man of sin will come as Satan's tool, full of satanic power, and will trick everyone with strange demonstrations, and will do great miracles. 10He will completely fool those who are on their way to hell because they have said "no" to the Truth; they have refused to believe it and love it, and let it save them, 11so God will allow them to believe lies with all their hearts, 12and all of them will be justly judged for believing falsehood, refusing the Truth, and enjoying their sins. 13But we must forever give thanks to God for you, our brothers loved by the Lord, because God chose from the very first to give you salvation, cleansing you by the work of the Holy Spirit and by your trusting in the Truth. 14Through us he told you the Good News. Through us he called you to share in the glory of our Lord Jesus Christ.

15With all these things in mind, dear brothers, stand firm and keep a strong grip on the truth that we taught you in our letters and during the time we were with you.

16May our Lord Jesus Christ himself and God our Father, who has loved us and given us everlasting comfort and hope which we don't deserve, 17comfort your hearts with all comfort, and help you in every good thing you say and do.

PSALM 84:1–12

How lovely is your Temple, O Lord of the armies of heaven. 2I long, yes, faint with longing to be able to enter your courtyard and come near to the Living God. 3Even the sparrows and swallows are welcome to come and nest among your altars and there have their young, O Lord of heaven's armies, my King and my God! 4How happy are those who can live in your Temple, singing your praises.

5Happy are those who are strong in the Lord, who want above all else to follow your steps. 6When they walk through the Valley of Weeping it will become a place of springs where pools of blessing and refreshment collect after rains! 7They will grow constantly in strength and each of them is invited to meet with the Lord in Zion.

8O Jehovah, God of the heavenly armies, hear my prayer! Listen, God of Israel. 9O God, our Defender and our Shield, have mercy on the one you have anointed as your king.

10A single day spent in your Temple is better than a thousand anywhere else! I would rather be a doorman of the Temple of my God than live in palaces of wickedness. 11For Jehovah God is our Light and our Protector. He gives us grace and glory. No good thing will he withhold from those who walk along his paths.

12O Lord of the armies of heaven, blessed are those who trust in you.

PROVERBS FOR TODAY/ 25:15
Be patient and you will finally win, for a soft tongue can break hard bones.

OCTOBER 15

JEREMIAH 26:1—27:22

THIS message came to Jeremiah from the Lord during the first year of the reign of Jehoiakim (son of Josiah), king of Judah:

2Stand out in front of the Temple of the Lord and make an announcement to all the people who have come there to worship from many parts of Judah. Give them the entire message; don't leave out one word of all I have for them to hear. 3For perhaps they will listen and turn from their evil ways, and then I can withhold all the punishment I am ready to pour out upon them because of their evil

deeds. 4Tell them the Lord says: If you will not listen to me and obey the laws I have given you, 5and if you will not listen to my servants, the prophets—for I sent them again and again to warn you, but you would not listen to them— 6then I will destroy this Temple as I destroyed the Tabernacle at Shiloh, and I will make Jerusalem a curse word in every nation of the earth.

7,8When Jeremiah had finished his message, saying everything the Lord had told him to, the priests and false prophets and all the people in the Temple mobbed him, shouting, "Kill him! Kill him! ⁹What right do you have to say the Lord will destroy this Temple like the one at Shiloh?" they yelled. "What do you mean—Jerusalem destroyed and not one survivor?"

¹⁰When the high officials of Judah heard what was going on, they rushed over from the palace and sat down at the door of the Temple to hold court. ¹¹Then the priests and the false prophets presented their accusations to the officials and the people. "This man should die!" they said. "You have heard with your own ears what a traitor he is, for he has prophesied against this city."

¹²Then Jeremiah spoke in his defense. "The Lord sent me," he said, "to prophesy against this Temple and this city. He gave me every word of all that I have spoken. ¹³But if you stop your sinning and begin obeying the Lord your God, he will cancel all the punishment he has announced against you. ¹⁴As for me, I am helpless and in your power—do with me as you think best. ¹⁵But there is one thing sure, if you kill me, you will be killing an innocent man and the responsibility will lie upon you and upon this city and upon every person living in it; for it is absolutely true that the Lord sent me to speak every word that you have heard from me."

¹⁶Then the officials and people said to the priests and false prophets, "This man does not deserve the death sentence, for he has spoken to us in the name of the Lord our God."

¹⁷Then some of the wise old men stood and spoke to all the people standing around and said:

¹⁸"The decision is right; for back in the days when Micah the Morasthite prophesied in the days of King Hezekiah of Judah, he told the people that God said: 'This hill shall be plowed like an open field and this city of Jerusalem razed into heaps of stone, and a forest shall grow at the top where the great Temple now stands!' ¹⁹But did King Hezekiah

and the people kill him for saying this? No, they turned from their wickedness and worshiped the Lord and begged the Lord to have mercy upon them; and the Lord held back the terrible punishment he had pronounced against them. If we kill Jeremiah for giving us the messages of God, who knows what God will do to us!"

²⁰Another true prophet of the Lord, Uriah (son of Shemaiah) from Kiriathjearim, was also denouncing the city and the nation at the same time as Jeremiah was. ²¹But when King Jehoiakim and the army officers and officials heard what he was saying, the king sent to kill him. Uriah heard about it and fled to Egypt. ²²Then King Jehoiakim sent Elnathan (son of Achbor) to Egypt along with several other men to capture Uriah. ²³They took him prisoner and brought him back to King Jehoiakim, who butchered him with a sword and had him buried in an unmarked grave.

²⁴But Ahikam (son of Shaphan), the royal secretary, stood with Jeremiah and persuaded the court not to turn him over to the mob to kill him.

THIS message came to Jeremiah from the Lord at the beginning of the reign of Jehoiakim (son of Josiah), king of Judah:

²Make a yoke and fasten it on your neck with leather thongs as you would strap a yoke on a plow-ox. ³Then send messages to the kings of Edom, Moab, Ammon, Tyre and Sidon, through their ambassadors in Jerusalem, ⁴saying, Tell your masters that the Lord, the God of Israel, sends you this message:

⁵"By my great power I have made the earth and all mankind and every animal; and I give these things of mine to anyone I want to. ⁶So now I have given all your countries to King Nebuchadnezzar of Babylon, who is my deputy. And I have handed over to him all your cattle for his use. ⁷All the nations shall serve him and his son and his grandson until his time is up, and then many nations and

great kings shall conquer Babylon and make him their slave. 8Submit to him and serve him—put your neck under Babylon's yoke! I will punish any nation refusing to be his slave; I will send war, famine and disease upon that nation until he has conquered it.

9"Do not listen to your false prophets, fortune-tellers, dreamers, mediums and magicians who say the king of Babylon will not enslave you. 10For they are all liars, and if you follow their advice and refuse to submit to the king of Babylon, I will drive you out of your land and send you far away to perish. 11But the people of any nation submitting to the king of Babylon will be permitted to stay in their own country and farm the land as usual."

12Jeremiah repeated all these prophecies to Zedekiah, king of Judah. "If you want to live, submit to the king of Babylon," he said. 13"Why do you insist on dying—you and your people? Why should you choose war and famine and disease, which the Lord has promised to every nation that will not submit to Babylon's king? 14Don't listen to the false prophets who keep telling you the king of Babylon will not conquer you, for they are liars. 15I have not sent them, says the Lord, and they are telling you lies in my name. If you insist on heeding them, I must drive you from this land to die—you and all these 'prophets' too."

16I spoke again and again to the priests and all the people and told them: "The Lord says, Don't listen to your prophets who are telling you that soon the gold dishes taken from the Temple will be returned from Babylon. It is all a lie. 17Don't listen to them. Surrender to the king of Babylon and live, for otherwise this whole city will be destroyed. 18If they are really God's prophets, then let them pray to the Lord Almighty that the gold dishes still here in the Temple, left from before; and that those in the palace of the king of Judah and in the palaces in Jerusalem will not be carried away with you to Babylon!

19,20,21"For the Lord Almighty says, The pillars of bronze standing before the Temple, and the great bronze basin in the Temple court, and the metal stands and all the other ceremonial articles left here by Nebuchadnezzar, king of Babylon, when he exiled all the important people of Judah and Jerusalem to Babylon, along with Jeconiah (son of Jehoiakim), king of Judah, 22will all yet be carried away to Babylon and will stay there until I send for them. Then I will bring them all back to Jerusalem again."

2 THESSALONIANS 3:1–18

FINALLY, dear brothers, as I come to the end of this letter I ask you to pray for us. Pray first that the Lord's message will spread rapidly and triumph wherever it goes, winning converts everywhere as it did when it came to you. 2Pray too that we will be saved out of the clutches of evil men, for not everyone loves the Lord. 3But the Lord is faithful; he will make you strong and guard you from satanic attacks of every kind. 4And we trust the Lord that you are putting into practice the things we taught you, and that you always will. 5May the Lord bring you into an ever deeper understanding of the love of God and of the patience that comes from Christ.

6Now here is a command, dear brothers, given in the name of our Lord Jesus Christ by his authority: Stay away from any Christian who spends his days in laziness and does not follow the ideal of hard work we set up for you. 7For you well know that you ought to follow our example: you never saw us loafing; 8we never accepted food from anyone without buying it; we worked hard day and night for the money we needed to live on, in order that we would not be a burden to any of you. 9It wasn't that we didn't have the right to ask you to feed us, but we wanted to show you, firsthand, how you should work for your

"The Word of the Lord will last forever. And his message is the Good News that was preached to you."

1 Peter 1:25

"Happy are the kind and merciful, for they shall be shown mercy."
Matthew 5:7

living. 10Even while we were still there with you we gave you this rule: "He who does not work shall not eat."

11Yet we hear that some of you are living in laziness, refusing to work, and wasting your time in gossiping. 12In the name of the Lord Jesus Christ we appeal to such people—we command them—to quiet down, get to work, and earn their own living. 13And to the rest of you I say, dear brothers, never be tired of doing right.

14If anyone refuses to obey what we say in this letter, notice who he is and stay away from him, that he may be ashamed of himself. 15Don't think of him as an enemy, but speak to him as you would to a brother who needs to be warned.

16May the Lord of peace himself give you his peace no matter what happens. The Lord be with you all.

17Now here is my greeting which I am writing with my own hand, as I do at the end of all my letters, for proof that it really is from me. This is in my own handwriting. 18May the blessing of our Lord Jesus Christ be upon you all.

Sincerely,
Paul

PSALM 85:1–13

LORD, you have poured out amazing blessings on this land! You have restored the fortunes of Israel, 2and forgiven the sins of your people—yes, covered over each one, 3so that all your wrath, your blazing anger, is now ended.

4Now bring us back to loving you, O Lord, so that your anger will never need rise against us again. 5(Or will you be always angry—on and on to distant generations?) 6Oh, revive us! Then your people can rejoice in you again. 7Pour out your love and kindness on us, Lord, and grant us your salvation.

8I am listening carefully to all the Lord is saying—for he speaks peace to his people, his saints, if they will only stop their sinning. 9Surely his salvation is near to those who reverence him; our land will be filled with his glory.

10Mercy and truth have met together. Grim justice and peace have kissed! 11Truth rises from the earth and righteousness smiles down from heaven.

12Yes, the Lord pours down his blessings on the land and it yields its bountiful crops. 13Justice goes before him to make a pathway for his steps.

PROVERBS FOR TODAY/ 25:16

Do you like honey? Don't eat too much of it, or it will make you sick!

OCTOBER 16

JEREMIAH 28:1—29:32

ON a December day in that same year—the fourth year of the reign of Zedekiah, king of Judah—Hananiah (son of Azzur), a false prophet from Gibeon, addressed me publicly in the Temple while all the priests and people listened. He said:

2"The Lord of Hosts, the God of Israel, declares: I have removed the yoke of the king of Babylon from your necks. 3Within two years I will bring back all the Temple treasures that Nebuchadnezzar carried off to Babylon, 4and I will bring back King Jeconiah, son of Jehoiakim, king of Judah, and all the other captives exiled to Babylon, says the Lord. I will surely remove the yoke put on your necks by the king of Babylon."

5Then Jeremiah said to Hananiah, in

front of all the priests and people, 6"Amen! May your prophecies come true! I hope the Lord will do everything you say and bring back from Babylon the treasures of this Temple, with all our loved ones. 7But listen now to the solemn words I speak to you in the presence of all these people. 8The ancient prophets who preceded you and me spoke against many nations, always warning of *war, famine* and *plague.* 9So a prophet who foretells *peace* has the burden of proof on him to prove that God has really sent him. Only when his message comes true can it be known that he really is from God."

10Then Hananiah, the false prophet, took the yoke off Jeremiah's neck and broke it. 11And Hananiah said again to the crowd that had gathered, "The Lord has promised that within two years he will release all the nations now in slavery to King Nebuchadnezzar of Babylon." At that point Jeremiah walked out.

12Soon afterwards, the Lord gave this message to Jeremiah:

13Go and tell Hananiah that the Lord says, You have broken a wooden yoke but these people have yokes of iron on their necks. 14The Lord, the God of Israel, says: I have put a yoke of iron on the necks of all these nations, forcing them into slavery to Nebuchadnezzar, king of Babylon. And nothing will change this decree, for I have even given him all your flocks and herds.

15Then Jeremiah said to Hananiah, the false prophet, "Listen, Hananiah, the Lord has not sent you, and the people are believing your lies. 16Therefore the Lord says you must die. This very year your life will end because you have rebelled against the Lord."

17And sure enough, two months later Hananiah died.

AFTER Jeconiah the king, and the queen-mother, and the court officials, and the tribal officers and craftsmen had been deported to Babylon by Nebuchadnezzar, Jeremiah wrote them a letter from Jerusalem, addressing it to the Jewish elders and priests and prophets, and to all the people. 3He sent the letter with Elasah (son of Shaphan) and Gemariah (son of Hilkiah) when they went to Babylon as King Zedekiah's ambassadors to Nebuchadnezzar. And this is what the letter said:

4The Lord Almighty, the God of Israel, sends this message to all the captives he has exiled to Babylon from Jerusalem:

5Build homes and plan to stay; plant vineyards, for you will be there many years. 6Marry and have children, and then find mates for them and have many grandchildren. Multiply! Don't dwindle away! 7And work for the peace and prosperity of Babylon. Pray for her, for if Babylon has peace, so will you.

8The Lord Almighty, the God of Israel, says: Don't let the false prophets and mediums who are there among you fool you. Don't listen to the dreams that they invent, 9for they prophesy lies in my name. I have not sent them, says the Lord. 10The truth is this: You will be in Babylon for seventy years. But then I will come and do for you all the good things I have promised, and bring you home again. 11For I know the plans I have for you, says the Lord. They are plans for good and not for evil, to give you a future and a hope. 12In those days when you pray, I will listen. 13You will find me when you seek me, if you look for me in earnest.

14Yes, says the Lord, I will be found by you, and I will end your slavery and restore your fortunes, and gather you out of the nations where I sent you and bring you back home again to your own land.

15But now, because you accept the false prophets among you and say the Lord has sent them, 16,17I will send war, famine and plague upon the people left here in Jerusalem—on your relatives who were not exiled to Babylon, and on the king who sits on David's throne—and make them like rotting figs, too bad to eat. 18And I will scatter them around the world. And in every nation where I place them they will be cursed and hissed and mocked, 19for they refuse to listen to me though I spoke to them again and again through my prophets.

20Therefore listen to the word of God, all you Jewish captives over there in Babylon. 21The Lord Almighty, the God of Israel, says this about your false prophets, Ahab (son of Kolaiah) and Zedekiah (son of Maaseiah), who are declaring lies to you in my name: Look, I am turning them over to Nebuchadnezzar to execute publicly. 22Their fate shall become proverbial of all evil, so that whenever anyone wants to curse someone he will say, "The Lord make you like Zedekiah and Ahab whom the king of Babylon burned alive!" 23For these men have done a terrible thing among my people. They have committed adultery with their neighbors' wives and have lied in my name. I know, for I have seen everything they do, says the Lord. 24And say this to Shemaiah the dreamer:

25The Lord, the God of Israel, says: You have written a letter to Zephaniah (son of Ma-aseiah) the priest, and sent copies to all the other priests and to everyone in Jerusalem. 26And in this letter you have said to Zephaniah, "The Lord has appointed you to replace Jehoiada as priest in Jerusalem. And it is your responsibility to arrest any madman who claims to be a prophet, and to put him in the stocks and collar. 27Why haven't you done something about this false prophet Jeremiah of Anathoth? 28For he has written to us here in Babylon saying that our captivity will be long, and that we should build permanent homes and plan to stay many years, that we should plant fruit trees, for we will be here to eat the fruit from them for a long time to come."

29Zephaniah took the letter over to Jeremiah and read it to him! 30Then the Lord gave this message to Jeremiah:

31Send an open letter to all the exiles in Babylon and tell them this: The Lord says that because Shemaiah the Nehelamite has "prophesied" to you when I didn't send him, and has fooled you into believing his lies, 32I will punish him and his family. None of his descendants shall see the good I have waiting for my people, for he has taught you to rebel against the Lord.

1 TIMOTHY 1:1–20

FROM: Paul, a missionary of Jesus Christ, sent out by the direct command of God our Savior and by Jesus Christ our Lord—our only hope. 2To: Timothy.

Timothy, you are like a son to me in the things of the Lord. May God our Father and Jesus Christ our Lord show you his kindness and mercy and give you great peace of heart and mind.

3,4As I said when I left for Macedonia, please stay there in Ephesus and try to stop the men who are teaching such wrong doctrine. Put an end to their myths and fables, and their idea of being saved by finding favor with an endless chain of angels leading up to God—wild ideas that stir up questions and arguments instead of helping people accept God's plan of faith. 5What I am eager for is that all the Christians there will be filled with love that comes from pure hearts, and that their minds will be clean and their faith strong.

6But these teachers have missed this whole idea and spend their time arguing and talking foolishness. 7They want to become famous as teachers of the laws of Moses when they haven't the slightest idea what those laws really show us. 8Those laws are good when used as God intended. 9But they were not made for us, whom God has saved; they are for sinners who hate God, have rebellious hearts, curse and swear, attack their fathers and mothers, and murder. 10,11Yes, these laws are made to identify as sinners all who are immoral and impure: homosexuals, kidnappers, liars, and all others who do things that contradict the glorious Good News of our blessed God, whose messenger I am.

12How thankful I am to Christ Jesus our Lord for choosing me as one of his messengers, and giving me the strength to be faithful to him, 13even though I used to scoff at the name of Christ. I hunted down his people, harming them in every way I could. But God had mercy on me because I didn't know what I was doing, for I didn't know Christ at that time. 14Oh, how kind our Lord was, for he showed me how to trust him and become full of the love of Christ Jesus.

15How true it is, and how I long that everyone should know it, that Christ Jesus came into the world to save sinners—and I was the greatest of them all. 16But God had mercy on me so that Christ Jesus could use me as an example to show everyone how patient he is with even the worst sinners, so that others will realize that they, too, can have everlasting life. 17Glory and honor to God forever and ever. He is the King of the ages, the unseen one who never dies; he alone is God, and full of wisdom. Amen.

18Now, Timothy, my son, here is my command to you: Fight well in the Lord's battles, just as the Lord told us through his prophets that you would. 19Cling tightly to your faith in Christ and always keep your conscience clear, doing what you know is right. For some people have disobeyed their consciences and have deliberately done what they knew was wrong. It isn't surprising that soon they lost their faith in Christ after defying God like that. 20Hymenaeus and Alexander are two examples of this. I had to give them over to Satan to punish them until they could learn not to bring shame to the name of Christ.

PSALM 86:1–17

BEND down and hear my prayer, O Lord, and answer me, for I am deep in trouble.

2Protect me from death, for I try to follow all your laws. Save me, for I am serving you and trusting you. 3Be merciful, O Lord, for I am looking up to you in constant hope. 4Give me happiness, O Lord, for I worship only you. 5O Lord, you are so good and kind, so ready to forgive; so full of mercy for all who ask your aid.

6Listen closely to my prayer, O God. Hear my urgent cry. 7I will call to you whenever trouble strikes, and you will help me.

8Where among the heathen gods is there a god like you? Where are their miracles? 9All the nations—and you made each one—will come and bow before you, Lord, and praise your great and holy name. 10For you are great, and do great miracles. You alone are God.

11Tell me where you want me to go and I will go there. May every fiber of my being unite in reverence to your name. 12With all my heart I will praise you. I will give glory to your name forever, 13for you love me so much! You are constantly so kind! You have rescued me from deepest hell.

14O God, proud and insolent men defy me; violent, godless men are trying to kill me. 15But you are merciful and gentle, Lord, slow in getting angry, full of constant lovingkindness and of truth; 16so look down in pity and grant strength to your servant and save me. 17Send me a sign of your favor. When those who hate me see it they will lose face because you help and comfort me.

PROVERBS FOR TODAY/ 25:17

Don't visit your neighbor too often, or you will outwear your welcome!

OCTOBER 17

JEREMIAH 30:1—31:26

THIS is another of the Lord's messages to Jeremiah:
²The Lord God of Israel says, Write down for the record all that I have said to you. ³For the time is coming when I will restore the fortunes of my people, Israel and Judah, and I will bring them home to this land that I gave to their fathers; they shall possess it and live here again.

⁴And write this also concerning Israel and Judah:

⁵"Where shall we find peace?" they cry. "There is only fear and trembling. ⁶Do men give birth? Then why do they stand there, ashen-faced, hands pressed against their sides like women in labor?"

⁷Alas, in all history when has there ever been a time of terror such as in that coming day? It is a time of trouble for my people—for Jacob—such as they have never known before. Yet God will rescue them! ⁸For on that day, says the Lord Almighty, I will break the yoke from their necks and snap their chains, and foreigners shall no longer be their masters! ⁹For they shall serve the Lord their God, and David their King, whom I will raise up for them, says the Lord.

¹⁰So don't be afraid, O Jacob my servant; don't be dismayed, O Israel; for I will bring you home again from distant lands, and your children from their exile. They shall have rest and quiet in their own land, and no one shall make them afraid. ¹¹For I am with you and I will save you, says the Lord. Even if I utterly destroy the nations where I scatter you, I will not exterminate you; I will punish you, yes—you will not go unpunished.

¹²For your sin is an incurable bruise, a terrible wound. ¹³There is no one to help you or to bind up your wound and no medicine does any good. ¹⁴All your lovers have left you and don't care anything about you any more; for I have wounded you cruelly, as though I were

your enemy; mercilessly, as though I were an implacable foe; for your sins are so many, your guilt is so great.

¹⁵Why do you protest your punishment? Your sin is so scandalous that your sorrow should never end! It is because your guilt is great that I have had to punish you so much.

¹⁶But in that coming day, all who are destroying you shall be destroyed, and all your enemies shall be slaves. Those who rob you shall be robbed; and those attacking you shall be attacked. ¹⁷I will give you back your health again and heal your wounds. Now you are called "The Outcast" and "Jerusalem, the Place Nobody Wants."

¹⁸But, says the Lord, when I bring you home again from your captivity and restore your fortunes, Jerusalem will be rebuilt upon her ruins; the palace will be reconstructed as it was before. ¹⁹The cities will be filled with joy and great thanksgiving, and I will multiply my people and make of them a great and honored nation. ²⁰Their children shall prosper as in David's reign; their nations shall be established before me, and I will punish anyone who hurts them. ²¹They will have their own ruler again. He will not be a foreigner. And I will invite him to be a priest at my altars, and he shall approach me, for who would dare to come unless invited. ²²And you shall be my people and I will be your God.

²³Suddenly the devastating whirlwind of the Lord roars with fury; it shall burst upon the heads of the wicked. ²⁴The Lord will not call off the fierceness of his wrath until it has finished all the terrible destruction he has planned. Later on you will understand what I am telling you.

AT that time, says the Lord, all the families of Israel shall recognize me as the Lord; they shall act like my people. ²I will care for them as I did those who escaped from Egypt, to whom I showed my mercies in the wilderness, when Israel sought for rest. 3For long ago the Lord had said to Israel: I have loved you, O my people, with an everlasting love; with loving-kindness I have drawn you to me. 4I will rebuild your nation, O virgin of Israel. You will again be happy and dance merrily with the timbrels. 5Again you will plant your vineyards upon the mountains of Samaria and eat from your own gardens there.

6The day shall come when watchmen on the hills of Ephraim will call out and say, "Arise, and let us go up to Zion to the Lord our God." 7For the Lord says, Sing with joy for all that I will do for Israel, the greatest of the nations! Shout out with praise and joy: "The Lord has saved his people, the remnant of Israel." 8For I will bring them from the north and from earth's farthest ends, not forgetting their blind and lame, young mothers with their little ones, those ready to give birth. It will be a great company who comes. 9Tears of joy shall stream down their faces, and I will lead them home with great care. They shall walk beside the quiet streams and not stumble. For I am a Father to Israel, and Ephraim is my oldest child.

10Listen to this message from the Lord, you nations of the world, and publish it abroad: The Lord who scattered his people will gather them back together again and watch over them as a shepherd does his flock. 11He will save Israel from those who are too strong for them! 12They shall come home and sing songs of joy upon the hills of Zion, and shall be radiant over the goodness of the Lord—the good crops, the wheat and the wine and the oil, and the healthy flocks and herds. Their life shall be like a watered garden, and all their sorrows shall be gone. 13The young girls will dance for joy, and men folk—old and young—will take their part in all the fun; for I will turn their mourning into joy and I will comfort them and make them rejoice, for their captivity with all its sorrows will be behind them. 14I will feast the priests with the abundance of offerings brought to them at the Temple; I will satisfy my people with my bounty, says the Lord.

15The Lord spoke to me again, saying: In Ramah there is bitter weeping—Rachel weeping for her children and cannot be comforted, for they are gone. 16But the Lord says: Don't cry any longer, for I have heard your prayers and you will see them again; they will come back to you from the distant land of the enemy. 17There is hope for your future, says the Lord, and your children will come again to their own land.

18I have heard Ephraim's groans: "You have punished me greatly; but I needed it all, as a calf must be trained for the yoke. Turn me again to you and restore me, for you alone are the Lord, my God. 19I turned away from God but I was sorry afterwards. I kicked myself for my stupidity. I was thoroughly ashamed of all I did in younger days."

20And the Lord replies: Ephraim is still my son, my darling child. I had to punish him, but I still love him. I long for him and surely will have mercy on him.

21As you travel into exile, set up road signs pointing back to Israel. Mark your pathway well. For you shall return again, O virgin Israel, to your cities here. 22How long will you vacillate, O wayward daughter? For the Lord will cause something new and different to happen—Israel will search for God.

23The Lord, the God of Israel, says: When I bring them back again they shall say in Judah and her cities, "The Lord bless you, O center of righteousness, O holy hill!" 24And city dwellers and farmers and shepherds alike shall live together in peace and happiness. 25For I have given rest to the weary and joy to all the sorrowing.

26(Then Jeremiah wakened. "Such sleep is very sweet!" he said.)

1 TIMOTHY 2:1–15

HERE are my directions: Pray much for others; plead for God's mercy upon them; give thanks for all he is going to do for them.

2Pray in this way for kings and all others who are in authority over us, or are in places of high responsibility, so that we can live in peace and quietness, spending our time in godly living and thinking much about the Lord. 3This is good and pleases God our Savior, 4for he longs for all to be saved and to understand this truth: 5*That God is on one side and all the people on the other side, and Christ Jesus, himself man, is between them to bring them together, 6by giving his life for all mankind.*

This is the message which at the proper time God gave to the world. 7And I have been chosen—this is the absolute truth—as God's minister and missionary to teach this truth to the Gentiles, and to show them God's plan of salvation through faith.

8So I want men everywhere to pray with holy hands lifted up to God, free from sin and anger and resentment. 9,10And the women should be the same way, quiet and sensible in manner and clothing. Christian women should be noticed for being kind and good, not for the way they fix their hair or because of their jewels or fancy clothes. 11Women should listen and learn quietly and humbly.

12I never let women teach men or lord it over them. Let them be silent in your church meetings. 13Why? Because God made Adam first, and afterwards he made Eve. 14And it was not Adam who was fooled by Satan, but Eve, and sin was the result. 15So God sent pain and suffering to women when their children are born, but he will save their souls if they trust in him, living quiet, good, and loving lives.

PSALM 87:1–7

HIGH on his holy mountain stands Jerusalem, the city of God, the city he loves more than any other!

3O city of God, what wondrous tales are told of you! 4Nowadays when I mention among my friends the names of Egypt and Babylonia, Philistia and Tyre, or even distant Ethiopia, someone boasts that he was born in one or another of those countries. 5But someday the highest honor will be to be a native of Jerusalem! For the God above all gods will personally bless this city. 6When he registers her citizens he will place a checkmark beside the names of those who were born here. 7And in the festivals they'll sing, "All my heart is in Jerusalem."

PROVERBS FOR TODAY/ 25:18–19

Telling lies about someone is as harmful as hitting him with an axe, or wounding him with a sword, or shooting him with a sharp arrow. Putting confidence in an unreliable man is like chewing with a sore tooth, or trying to run on a broken foot.

OCTOBER 18

JEREMIAH 31:27—32:44

THE Lord says: The time will come when I will greatly increase the population and multiply the number of cattle here in Israel. 28In the past I painstakingly destroyed the nation but now I will carefully build it up. 29The people shall no longer quote this proverb—"Children pay for their fathers' sins." 30For everyone shall die for his own sins—the person eating sour grapes is the one whose teeth are set on edge.

31The day will come, says the Lord, when I will make a new contract with the people of Israel and Judah. 32It won't be like the one I made with their fathers when I took them by the hand to bring them out of the land of Egypt—a contract they broke, forcing me to reject them, says the Lord. 33But this is the new contract I will make with them: I will inscribe my laws upon their hearts, so that they shall want to honor me; then they shall truly be my people and I will be their God. 34At that time it will no longer be necessary to admonish one another to know the Lord. For everyone, both great and small, shall really know me then, says the Lord, and I will forgive and forget their sins.

35The Lord who gives us sunlight in the daytime and the moon and stars to light the night, and who stirs the sea to make the roaring waves—his name is Lord Almighty—says this:

36I am as likely to reject my people Israel as I am to do away with these laws of nature! 37Not until the heavens can be measured and the foundations of the earth explored, will I consider casting them away forever for their sins!

38,39For the time is coming, says the Lord, when all Jerusalem shall be rebuilt for the Lord, from the Tower of Hananel at the northeast corner, to the Corner Gate at the northwest; and from the Hill of Gareb at the southwest, across to Goah on the southeast. 40And the entire city including the graveyard and ash dump in the valley shall be holy to the Lord, and so shall all the fields out to the brook of Kidron, and from there to the Horse Gate on the east side of the city; it shall never again be captured or destroyed.

THE following message came to Jeremiah from the Lord in the tenth year of the reign of Zedekiah, king of Judah (which was the eighteenth year of Nebuchadnezzar's reign). 2At this time Jeremiah was imprisoned in the dungeon beneath the palace, while the Babylonian army was besieging Jerusalem. 3King Zedekiah had put him there for continuing to prophesy that the city would be conquered by the king of Babylon, 4and that King Zedekiah would be caught and taken as a prisoner before the king of Babylon for trial and sentencing.

5"He shall take you to Babylon and imprison you there for many years until you die. Why fight the facts? You can't win! Surrender now!" Jeremiah had told him again and again.

6,7Then this message from the Lord came to Jeremiah: Your cousin Hanamel (son of Shallum) will soon arrive to ask you to buy the farm he owns in Anathoth, for by law you have a chance to buy before it is offered to anyone else. 8So Hanamel came, as the Lord had said he would, and visited me in the prison. "Buy my field in Anathoth, in the land of Benjamin," he said, "for the law gives you the first right to purchase it." Then I knew for sure that the message I had heard was really from the Lord.

9So I bought the field, paying Hanamel seventeen pieces of silver. 10I signed and sealed the deed of purchase before witnesses, and weighed out the silver and paid him. 11Then I took the sealed deed containing the terms and conditions, and also the unsealed copy, 12and publicly, in the presence of my cousin Hanamel and the witnesses who had signed the deed, and as the prison guards watched, I handed the papers to Baruch (son of Neriah, who was the son of Mahseiah). 13And I said to him as they all listened:

14"The Lord, God of Israel, says: Take both this sealed deed and the copy and put them into a pottery jar to preserve them for a long time. 15For the Lord, God of Israel, says, In the future these papers will be valuable. Someday people will again own property here in this country and will be buying and selling houses and vineyards and fields."

16Then after I had given the papers to Baruch I prayed:

17"O Lord God! You have made the

heavens and earth by your great power; nothing is too hard for you! 18You are loving and kind to thousands, yet children suffer for their fathers' sins; you are the great and mighty God, the Lord Almighty. 19You have all wisdom and do great and mighty miracles; for your eyes are open to all the ways of men, and you reward everyone according to his life and deeds. 20You have done incredible things in the land of Egypt—things still remembered to this day. And you have continued to do great miracles in Israel and all around the world. You have made your name very great, as it is today.

21"You brought Israel out of Egypt with mighty miracles and great power and terror. 22You gave Israel this land that you promised their fathers long ago—a wonderful land that 'flows with milk and honey.' 23Our fathers came and conquered it and lived in it, but they refused to obey you or to follow your laws; they have hardly done one thing you told them to. That is why you have sent all this terrible evil upon them. 24See how the siege mounds have been built against the city walls, and the Babylonians shall conquer the city by sword, famine and disease. Everything has happened just as you said—as you determined it should! 25And yet you say to buy the field—paying good money for it before these witnesses—even though the city will belong to our enemies."

26Then this message came to Jeremiah:

27I am the Lord, the God of all mankind; is there anything too hard for me? 28Yes, I will give this city to the Babylonians and to Nebuchadnezzar, king of Babylon; he shall conquer it. 29And the Babylonians outside the walls shall come in and set fire to the city and burn down all these houses where the roofs have been used to offer incense to Baal, and to pour out libations to other gods, causing my fury to rise! 30For Israel and Judah have done nothing but wrong since their earliest days; they have infuriated me with all their evil deeds. 31From the time this city was built until now it has done nothing but anger me; so I am determined to be rid of it.

32The sins of Israel and Judah—the sins of the people, of their kings, officers, priests and prophets—stir me up. 33They have turned their backs upon me and refused to return; day after day, year after year, I taught them right from wrong, but they would not listen or obey. 34They have even defiled my own Temple by worshiping their abominable idols there. 35And they have built high altars to Baal in the Valley of Hinnom. There they have burnt their children as sacrifices to Molech—something I never commanded, and cannot imagine suggesting. What an incredible evil, causing Judah to sin so greatly!

36Now therefore the Lord God of Israel says concerning this city that it will fall to the king of Babylon through warfare, famine and disease, 37but I will bring my people back again from all the countries where in my fury I will scatter them. I will bring them back to this very city, and make them live in peace and safety. 38And they shall be my people and I will be their God. 39And I will give them one heart and mind to worship me forever, for their own good and for the good of all their descendants.

40And I will make an everlasting covenant with them, promising never again to desert them, but only to do them good. I will put a desire into their hearts to worship me, and they shall never leave me. 41I will rejoice to do them good and will replant them in this land, with great joy. 42Just as I have sent all these terrors and evils upon them, so will I do all the good I have promised them.

43Fields will again be bought and sold in this land, now ravaged by the Babylonians, where men and animals alike have disappeared. 44Yes, fields shall once again be bought and sold—deeds signed and sealed and witnessed—in the country of Benjamin and here in Jerusalem, in the cities of Judah and in the hill country, in the Philistine plain and in the Negeb too, for some day I will restore prosperity to them.

IT is a true saying that if a man wants to be a pastor he has a good ambition. 2For a pastor must be a good man whose life cannot be spoken against. He must have only one wife, and he must be hard working and thoughtful, orderly, and full of good deeds. He must enjoy having guests in his home, and must be a good Bible teacher. 3He must not be a drinker or quarrelsome, but he must be gentle and kind, and not be one who loves money. 4He must have a well-behaved family, with children who obey quickly and quietly. 5For if a man can't make his own little family behave, how can he help the whole church?

6The pastor must not be a new Christian, because he might be proud of being chosen so soon, and pride comes before a fall. (Satan's downfall is an example.) 7Also, he must be well spoken of by people outside the church—those who aren't Christians—so that Satan can't trap him with many accusations, and leave him without freedom to lead his flock.

8The deacons must be the same sort of good, steady men as the pastors. They must not be heavy drinkers and must not be greedy for money. 9They must be earnest, wholehearted followers of Christ who is the hidden Source of their faith. 10Before they are asked to be deacons they should be given other jobs in the church as a test of their character and ability, and if they do well, then they may be chosen as deacons.

11Their wives must be thoughtful, not heavy drinkers, not gossipers, but faithful in everything they do. 12Deacons should have only one wife and they should have happy, obedient families. 13Those who do well as deacons will be well rewarded both by respect from others and also by developing their own confidence and bold trust in the Lord.

14I am writing these things to you now, even though I hope to be with you soon, 15so that if I don't come for awhile you will know what kind of men you should choose as officers for the church of the living God, which contains and holds high the truth of God.

16It is quite true that the way to live a godly life is not an easy matter. But the answer lies in Christ, who came to earth as a man, was proved spotless and pure in his Spirit, was served by angels, was preached among the nations, was accepted by men everywhere and was received up again to his glory in heaven.

PSALM 88:1–18

OJehovah, God of my salvation, I have wept before you day and night. 2Now hear my prayers; oh, listen to my cry, 3for my life is full of troubles, and death draws near. 4They say my life is ebbing out—a hopeless case. 5They have left me here to die, like those slain on battlefields, from whom your mercies are removed.

6You have thrust me down to the darkest depths. 7Your wrath lies heavy on me; wave after wave engulfs me. 8You have made my friends to loathe me, and they have gone away. I am in a trap with no way out. 9My eyes grow dim with weeping. Each day I beg your help; O Lord, I reach my pleading hands to you for mercy.

10Soon it will be too late! Of what use are your miracles when I am in the grave? How can I praise you then? 11Can those in the grave declare your lovingkindness? Can they proclaim your faithfulness? 12Can the darkness speak of your miracles? Can anyone in the Land of Forgetfulness talk about your help?

13O Lord, I plead for my life and will keep on pleading day by day. 14O Jehovah, why have you thrown my life away? Why are you turning your face from me, and looking the other way?

15From my youth I have been sickly and ready to die. I stand helpless before your terrors. 16Your fierce wrath has overwhelmed me. Your terrors have cut me off. 17They flow around me all day long. 18Lover, friend, acquaintance—all are gone. There is only darkness everywhere.

Being happy-go-lucky around a person whose heart is heavy is as bad as stealing his jacket in cold weather, or rubbing salt in his wounds. If your enemy is hungry, give him food! If he is thirsty, give him something to drink! This will make him feel ashamed of himself, and God will reward you.

OCTOBER 19

JEREMIAH 33:1—34:22

WHILE Jeremiah was still in jail, the Lord sent him this second message:

2The Lord, the Maker of heaven and earth—Jehovah is his name—says this:

3Ask me and I will tell you some remarkable secrets about what is going to happen here. 4For though you have torn down the houses of this city, and the king's palace too, for materials to strengthen the walls against the siege weapons of the enemy, 5yet the Babylonians will enter, and the men of this city are already as good as dead, for I have determined to destroy them in my furious anger. I have abandoned them because of all their wickedness, and I will not pity them when they cry for help.

6Nevertheless the time will come when I will heal Jerusalem's damage and give her prosperity and peace. 7I will rebuild the cities of both Judah and Israel and restore their fortunes. 8And I will cleanse away all their sins against me, and pardon them. 9Then this city will be an honor to me, and it will give me joy and be a source of praise and glory to me before all the nations of the earth! The people of the world will see the good I do for my people and will tremble with awe!

10,11The Lord declares that the happy voices of bridegrooms and of brides, and the joyous song of those bringing thanksgiving offerings to the Lord will be heard again in this doomed land. The people will sing: "Praise the Lord! For he is good and his mercy endures forever!" For I will make this land happier and more prosperous than it has ever been before. 12This land—though every man and animal and city is doomed—will once more see shepherds leading sheep and lambs. 13Once again their flocks will prosper in the mountain villages and in the cities east of the Philistine plain, in all the cities of the Negeb, in the land of Benjamin, in the vicinity of Jerusalem and in all the cities of Judah. 14Yes, the day will come, says the Lord, when I will do for Israel and Judah all the good I promised them.

15At that time I will bring to the throne the true Son of David, and he shall rule justly. 16In that day the people of Judah and Jerusalem shall live in safety and their motto will be, "The Lord is our righteousness!" 17For the Lord declares that from then on, David shall forever have an heir sitting on the throne of Israel. 18And there shall always be Levites to offer burnt offerings and meal offerings and sacrifices to the Lord.

19Then this message came to Jeremiah from the Lord:

20,21If you can break my covenant with the day and with the night so that day and night don't come on their usual schedule, only then will my covenant with David, my servant, be broken so that he shall not have a son to reign upon his throne; and my covenant with the Levite priests, my ministers, is noncancelable. 22And as the stars cannot be counted nor the sand upon the seashores measured, so the descendants of David my servant and the line of the Levites who minister to me will be multiplied.

23The Lord spoke to Jeremiah again and said:

24Have you heard what people are saying?—that the Lord chose Judah and Israel and then abandoned them! They are sneering and saying that Israel isn't worthy to be counted as a nation. 25,26But this is the Lord's reply: I would no more reject my people than I would change my laws of night and day, of earth and sky. I will never abandon the Jews, or David my servant, or change the plan that his Child will someday rule these descendants of Abraham, Isaac and Jacob. Instead I will restore their prosperity and have mercy on them.

THIS is the message that came to Jeremiah from the Lord when Nebuchadnezzar, king of Babylon, and all his armies from all the kingdoms he ruled, came and fought against Jerusalem and the cities of Judah:

2Go tell Zedekiah, king of Judah, that the Lord says this: I will give this city to the king of Babylon and he shall burn it. 3You shall not escape; you shall be captured and taken before the king of Babylon and he shall pronounce sentence against you and you shall be exiled to Babylon. 4But listen to this, O Zedekiah, king of Judah: God says you won't be killed in war and carnage, 5but that you will die quietly among your people, and they will burn incense in your memory, just as they did for your fathers. They will weep for you and say, "Alas, our king is dead!" This I have decreed, says the Lord.

6So Jeremiah delivered the message to King Zedekiah. 7At this time the Babylonian army was besieging Jerusalem, Lachish and Azekah—the only walled cities of Judah still standing.

8This is the message that came to Jeremiah from the Lord after King Zedekiah of Judah had freed all the slaves in Jerusalem— 9(for King Zedekiah had ordered everyone to free his Hebrew slaves, both men and women. He had said that no Jew should be the master of another Jew for all were brothers. 10The princes and all the people had obeyed the king's command and freed their slaves, but the action was only temporary. 11They changed their minds and made their servants slaves again. 12That is why the Lord gave the following message to Jerusalem.)

13The Lord, the God of Israel, says:

I made a covenant with your fathers long ago when I brought them from their slavery in Egypt. 14I told them that every Hebrew slave must be freed after serving six years. But this was not done. 15Recently you began doing what was right, as I commanded you, and freed your slaves. You had solemnly promised me in my Temple that you would do it. 16But now you refuse and have defiled my name by shrugging off your oath and have made them slaves again.

17Therefore, says the Lord, because you will not listen to me and release them, I will release you to the power of death by war and famine and disease. And I will scatter you over all the world as exiles. 18,19Because you have refused the terms of our contract I will cut you apart just as you cut apart the calf when you walked between its halves to solemnize your vows. Yes, I will butcher you, whether you are princes, court officials, priests or people—for you have broken your oath. 20I will give you to your enemies and they shall kill you. I will feed your dead bodies to the vultures and wild animals. 21And I will surrender Zedekiah, king of Judah, and his officials to the army of the king of Babylon, though he has departed from the city for a little while. 22I will summon the Babylonian armies back again and they will fight against it and capture this city and burn it. And I will see to it that the cities of Judah are completely destroyed and left desolate without a living soul.

1 TIMOTHY 4:1–16

BUT the Holy Spirit tells us clearly that in the last times some in the church will turn away from Christ and become eager followers of teachers with devil-inspired ideas. 2These teachers will tell lies with straight faces and do it so often that their consciences won't even bother them.

³They will say it is wrong to be married and wrong to eat meat, even though God gave these things to well-taught Christians to enjoy and be thankful for. ⁴For everything God made is good, and we may eat it gladly if we are thankful for it, ⁵and if we ask God to bless it, for it is made good by the Word of God and prayer.

⁶If you explain this to the others you will be doing your duty as a worthy pastor who is fed by faith and by the true teaching you have followed.

⁷Don't waste time arguing over foolish ideas and silly myths and legends. Spend your time and energy in the exercise of keeping spiritually fit. ⁸Bodily exercise is all right, but spiritual exercise is much more important and is a tonic for all you do. So exercise yourself spiritually and practice being a better Christian, because that will help you not only now in this life, but in the next life too. ⁹,¹⁰This is the truth and everyone should accept it. We work hard and suffer much in order that people will believe it, for our hope is in the living God who died for all, and particularly for those who have accepted his salvation.

¹¹Teach these things and make sure everyone learns them well. ¹²Don't let anyone think little of you because you are young. Be their ideal; let them follow the way you teach and live; be a pattern for them in your love, your faith, and your clean thoughts. ¹³Until I get there, read and explain the Scriptures to the church; preach God's Word.

¹⁴Be sure to use the abilities God has given you through his prophets when the elders of the church laid their hands upon your head. ¹⁵Put these abilities to work; throw yourself into your tasks so that everyone may notice your improvement and progress. ¹⁶Keep a close watch on all you do and think. Stay true to what is right and God will bless you and use you to help others.

PSALM 89:1–13

FOREVER and ever I will sing about the tender kindness of the Lord! Young and old shall hear about your blessings. ²Your love and kindness are forever; your truth is as enduring as the heavens.

³,⁴The Lord God says, "I have made a solemn agreement with my chosen servant David. I have taken an oath to establish his descendants as kings forever on his throne, from now until eternity!"

⁵All heaven shall praise your miracles, O Lord; myriads of angels will praise you for your faithfulness. ⁶For who in all of heaven can be compared with God? What mightiest angel is anything like him? ⁷The highest of angelic powers stand in dread and awe of him. Who is as revered as he by those surrounding him? ⁸O Jehovah, Commander of the heavenly armies, where is there any other Mighty One like you? Faithfulness is your very character.

⁹You rule the oceans when their waves arise in fearful storms; you speak, and they lie still. ¹⁰You have cut haughty Egypt to pieces. Your enemies are scattered by your awesome power. ¹¹The heavens are yours, the world, everything—for you created them all. ¹²You created north and south! Mount Tabor and Mount Hermon rejoice to be signed by your name as their maker! ¹³Strong is your arm! Strong is your hand! Your right hand is lifted high in glorious strength.

PROVERBS 25:23–24

As surely as a wind from the north brings cold, just as surely a retort causes anger! It is better to live in a corner of an attic than in a beautiful home with a cranky, quarrelsome woman.

OCTOBER 20

JEREMIAH 35:1—36:32

THIS is the message the Lord gave Jeremiah when Jehoiakim (son of Josiah) was the king of Judah:

2Go to the settlement where the families of the Rechabites live and invite them to the Temple. Take them into one of the inner rooms and offer them a drink of wine.

3So I went over to see Ja-azaniah (son of Jeremiah, who was the son of Habazziniah), and brought him and all his brothers and sons—representing all the Rechab families— 4to the Temple, into the room assigned for the use of the sons of Hanan the prophet (the son of Igdaliah). This room was located next to the one used by the palace official, directly above the room of Ma-aseiah (son of Shallum), who was the temple doorman. 5I set cups and jugs of wine before them and invited them to have a drink, 6but they refused.

"No," they said. "We don't drink, for Jonadab our father (son of Rechab) commanded that none of us should ever drink, neither we nor our children forever. 7He also told us not to build houses or plant crops or vineyards and not to own farms, but always to live in tents; and that if we obeyed we would live long, good lives in our own land. 8And we have obeyed him in all these things. We have never had a drink of wine since then, nor our wives or our sons or daughters either. 9We haven't built houses or owned farms or planted crops. 10We have lived in tents and have fully obeyed everything that Jonadab our father commanded us. 11But when Nebuchadnezzar, king of Babylon, arrived in this country, we were afraid and decided to move to Jerusalem. That's why we are here."

12Then the Lord gave this message to Jeremiah:

13The Lord, the God of Israel, says: Go and say to Judah and Jerusalem, Won't you learn a lesson from the families of Rechab? 14They don't drink, because their father told them not to. But I have spoken to you again and again and you won't listen or obey. 15I have sent you prophet after prophet to tell you to turn back from your wicked ways and to stop worshiping other gods and that if you obeyed, then I would let you live in peace here in the land I gave to you and your fathers. But you wouldn't listen or obey. 16The families of Rechab have obeyed their father completely, but you have refused to listen to me. 17Therefore the Lord Almighty, the God of Israel, says: Because you refuse to listen or answer when I call, I will send upon Judah and Jerusalem all the evil I have ever threatened.

18,19Then Jeremiah turned to the Rechabites and said: "The Lord, the God of Israel, says that because you have obeyed your father in every respect, he shall always have descendants who will worship me."

IN the fourth year of the reign of King Jehoiakim of Judah (son of Josiah) the Lord gave this message to Jeremiah:

2"Get a scroll and write down all my messages against Israel, Judah and the other nations. Begin with the first message back in the days of Josiah, and write down every one of them. 3Perhaps when the people of Judah see in writing all the terrible things I will do to them, they will repent. And then I can forgive them."

4So Jeremiah sent for Baruch (son of Neriah), and as Jeremiah dictated, Baruch wrote down all the prophecies.

5When all was finished, Jeremiah said to Baruch, "Since I am a prisoner here, 6you read the scroll in the Temple on the next Day of Fasting, for on that day people will be there from all over Judah. 7Perhaps even yet they will turn from their evil ways and ask the Lord to forgive them before it is too late, even though these curses of God have been pronounced upon them."

8Baruch did as Jeremiah told him to, and read all these messages to the people at the Temple. 9This occurred on the Day of Fasting held in December of the fifth year of the reign of King Jehoiakim (son of Josiah). People came from all over Judah to attend the services at the Temple that day. 10Baruch went to the office of Gemariah the Scribe (son of Shaphan) to read the scroll. (This room was just off the upper assembly hall of the Temple, near the door of the New Gate.)

11When Micaiah (son of Gemariah, son of Shaphan) heard the messages from God, 12he went down to the palace to the conference room where the administrative officials were meeting. Elishama (the scribe) was there, as well as Delaiah (son of Shamaiah), Elnathan (son of Achbor), Gemariah (son of Shaphan), Zedekiah (son of Hananiah), and all the others with similar responsibilities. 13When Micaiah told them about the messages Baruch was reading to the people, 14,15the officials sent Jehudi (son of Nethaniah, son of Shelemiah, son of Cushi) to ask Baruch to come and read the messages to them too, and Baruch did.

16By the time he finished they were badly frightened. "We must tell the king," they said. 17"But first, tell us how you got these messages. Did Jeremiah himself dictate them to you?" 18So Baruch explained that Jeremiah had dictated them to him word by word, and he had written them down in ink upon the scroll. 19"You and Jeremiah both hide," the officials said to Baruch. "Don't tell a soul where you are!" 20Then the officials hid the scroll in the room of Elishama the scribe and went to tell the king.

21The king sent Jehudi to get the scroll. Jehudi brought it from Elishama the scribe and read it to the king as all his officials stood by. 22The king was in a winterized part of the palace at the time, sitting in front of a fireplace, for it was December, and cold. 23And whenever Jehudi finished reading three or four columns, the king would take his knife, and

slit off the section and throw it into the fire, until the whole scroll was destroyed. 24,25And no one protested except Elnathan, Delaiah and Gemariah. They pled with the king not to burn the scroll, but he wouldn't listen to them. Not another of the king's officials showed any signs of fear or anger at what he had done.

26Then the king commanded Jerahmeel (a member of the royal family) and Seraiah (son of Azri-el) and Shelemiah (son of Abdeel) to arrest Baruch and Jeremiah. But the Lord hid them!

27After the king had burned the scroll, the Lord said to Jeremiah:

28Get another scroll and write everything again just as you did before, 29and say this to the king: "The Lord says, You burned the scroll because it said the king of Babylon would destroy this country and everything in it. 30And now the Lord adds this concerning you, Jehoiakim, king of Judah: He shall have no one to sit upon the throne of David. His dead body shall be thrown out to the hot sun and frosty nights, 31and I will punish him and his family and his officials because of their sins. I will pour out upon them all the evil I promised—upon them and upon all the people of Judah and Jerusalem, for they wouldn't listen to my warnings."

32Then Jeremiah took another scroll and dictated again to Baruch all he had written before, only this time the Lord added a lot more!

1 TIMOTHY 5:1–25

NEVER speak sharply to an older man, but plead with him respectfully just as though he were your own father. Talk to the younger men as you would to much loved brothers. 2Treat the older women as mothers, and the girls as your sisters, thinking only pure thoughts about them.

3The church should take loving care of women whose husbands have died, if they don't have anyone else to help them. 4But if they have children or grandchildren, these are the ones who should take the responsibility, for kindness should begin at home, supporting needy parents. This is something that pleases God very much.

5The church should care for widows who are poor and alone in the world, if they are looking to God for his help and spending much time in prayer; 6but not if they are spending their time running around gossiping, seeking only pleasure and thus ruining their souls. 7This should be your church rule so that the Christians will know and do what is right.

8But anyone who won't care for his own relatives when they need help, especially those living in his own family, has no right to say he is a Christian. Such a person is worse than the heathen.

9A widow who wants to become one of the special church workers should be at least sixty years old and have been married only once. 10She must be well thought of by everyone because of the good she has done. Has she brought up her children well? Has she been kind to strangers as well as to other Christians? Has she helped those who are sick and hurt? Is she always ready to show kindness?

11The younger widows should not become members of this special group because after awhile they are likely to disregard their vow to Christ and marry again. 12And so they will stand condemned because they broke their first promise. 13Besides, they are likely to be lazy and spend their time gossiping around from house to house, getting into other people's business. 14So I think it is better for these younger widows to marry again and have children, and take care of their own homes; then no one will be able to say anything against them. 15For I am afraid that some of them have already turned away from the church and been led astray by Satan.

16Let me remind you again that a widow's relatives must take care of her, and not leave this to the church to do. Then the church can spend its money for the care of widows who are all alone and have nowhere else to turn.

17Pastors who do their work well should be paid well and should be highly appreciated, especially those who work hard at both preaching and teaching. 18For the Scriptures say, "Never tie up the mouth of an ox when it is treading out the grain—let him eat as he goes along!" And in another place, "Those who work deserve their pay!"

19Don't listen to complaints against the pastor unless there are two or three witnesses to accuse him. 20If he has really sinned, then he should be rebuked in front of the whole church so that no one else will follow his example.

21I solemnly command you in the presence of God and the Lord Jesus Christ and of the holy angels to do this whether the pastor is a special friend of yours or not. All must be treated exactly the same. 22Never be in a hurry about choosing a pastor; you may overlook his sins and it will look as if you approve of them. Be sure that you yourself stay away from all sin. 23(By the way, this doesn't mean you should completely give up drinking wine. You ought to take a little sometimes as medicine for your stomach because you are sick so often.)

24Remember that some men, even pastors, lead sinful lives and everyone knows it. In such situations you can do something about it. But in other cases only the judgment day will reveal the terrible truth. 25In the same way, everyone knows how much good some pastors do, but sometimes their good deeds aren't known until long afterward.

PSALM 89:14–37

YOUR throne is founded on two strong pillars—the one is Justice and the other Righteousness. Mercy and Truth walk before you as your attendants. Blessed are those who hear the joyful blast of the trumpet, for they shall walk in the light of your presence. 16They rejoice all day long in your wonderful reputation and in your perfect righteousness. 17You are their strength. What glory! Our power is based on your favor!

18Yes, our protection is from the Lord himself and he, the Holy One of Israel, has given us our king.

19In a vision you spoke to your prophet and said, "I have chosen a splendid young man from the common people to be the king— 20he is my servant David! I have anointed him with my holy oil. 21I will steady him and make him strong. 22His enemies shall not outwit him, nor shall the wicked overpower him. 23I will beat down his adversaries before him, and destroy those who hate him. 24I will protect and bless him constantly and surround him with my love; he will be great because of me. 25He will hold sway from the Euphrates River to the Mediterranean Sea. 26And he will cry to me, 'You are my Father, my God, and my Rock of Salvation.'

27"I will treat him as my firstborn son, and make him the mightiest king in all the earth. 28I will love him forever, and be kind to him always; my covenant with him will never end. 29He will always have an heir; his throne will be as endless as the days of heaven. 30,31,32If his children forsake my laws and don't obey them, then I will punish them, 33but I will never completely take away my lovingkindness from them, nor let my promise fail. 34No, I will not break my covenant; I will not take back one word of what I said. 35,36For I have sworn to David (and a holy God can never lie), that his dynasty will go on forever, and his throne will continue to the end of time. 37It shall be eternal as the moon, my faithful witness in the sky!"

PROVERBS 25:25–27

Good news from far away is like cold water to the thirsty. If a godly man compromises with the wicked, it is like polluting a fountain or muddying a spring. Just as it is harmful to eat too much honey, so also it is bad for men to think about all the honors they deserve!

OCTOBER 21

JEREMIAH 37:1—38:28

NEBUCHADNEZZAR, King of Babylon, did not appoint Coniah (King Jehoiakim's son) to be the new king of Judah. Instead he chose Zedekiah (son of Josiah). 2But neither King Zedekiah nor his officials nor the people who were left in the land listened to what the Lord said through Jeremiah. 3Nevertheless, King Zedekiah sent Jehucal (son of Shelemiah) and Zephaniah the priest (son of Ma-aseiah) to ask Jeremiah to pray for them. 4(Jeremiah had not been imprisoned yet, so he could go and come as he pleased.)

5When the army of Pharaoh Hophra of Egypt appeared at the southern border of Judah to relieve the besieged city of Jerusalem, the Babylonian army withdrew from Jerusalem to fight the Egyptians.

6Then the Lord sent this message to Jeremiah:

7"The Lord, the God of Israel, says: Tell the king of Judah, who sent you to ask me what is going to happen, that Pharaoh's army, though it came here to help you, is about to return in flight to Egypt! The Babylonians shall defeat them and send them scurrying home. 8These Babylonians shall capture this city and burn it to the ground. 9Don't fool yourselves that the Babylonians are gone for good. They aren't! 10Even if you destroyed the entire Babylonian army until there was only a handful of survivors and they lay wounded in their tents, yet they would stagger out and defeat you and put this city to the torch!"

11When the Babylonian army set out from Jerusalem to engage Pharaoh's army in battle, 12Jeremiah started to leave the city to go to the land of Benjamin, to see the property he had bought. 13But as he was walking through the Benjamin Gate, a sentry arrested him as a traitor, claiming he was defecting to the Babylonians. The guard making the arrest was Irijah (son of Shelemiah, grandson of Hananiah).

14"That's not true," Jeremiah said. "I have no intention whatever of doing any such thing!"

But Irijah wouldn't listen; he took Jeremiah before the city officials. 15,16They were incensed with Jeremiah and had him flogged and put into the dungeon under the house of Jonathan the scribe, which had been converted into a prison. Jeremiah was kept there for several days, 17but eventually King Zedekiah sent for him to come to the palace secretly. The king asked him if there was any recent message from the Lord. "Yes," said Jeremiah, "there is! You shall be defeated by the king of Babylon!"

18Then Jeremiah broached the subject of his imprisonment. "What have I ever done to deserve this?" he asked the king. "What crime have I committed? Tell me what I have done against you or your officials or the people? 19Where are those prophets now who told you that the king of Babylon would not come? 20Listen, O my lord the king: I beg you, don't send me back to that dungeon, for I'll die there."

21Then King Zedekiah commanded that Jeremiah not be returned to the dungeon, but be placed in the palace prison instead, and that he be given a small loaf of fresh bread every day as long as there was any left in the city. So Jeremiah was kept in the palace prison.

BUT when Shephatiah (son of Mattan) and Gedaliah (son of Pashhur) and Jucal (son of Shelemiah) and Pashhur (son of Malchiah) heard what Jeremiah had been telling the people— 2that everyone remaining in Jerusalem would die by sword, starvation or disease, but anyone surrendering to the Babylonians would live, 3and that the city of Jerusalem would surely be captured by the king of Babylon— 4they went to the king and said: "Sir, this fellow must die. That kind of talk will undermine the morale of the few soldiers we have left, and of all the people too. This man is a traitor."

5So King Zedekiah agreed. "All right," he said. "Do as you like—I can't stop you."

6They took Jeremiah from his cell and lowered him by ropes into an empty cistern in the prison yard. (It belonged to Malchiah, a member of the royal family.) There was no water in it, but there was a thick layer of mire at the bottom, and Jeremiah sank down into it.

7When Ebed-melech the Ethiopian, an important palace official, heard that Jeremiah was in the cistern, 8he rushed out to the Gate of Benjamin where the king was holding court.

9"My lord the king," he said, "these men have done a very evil thing in putting Jeremiah into the cistern. He will die of hunger, for almost all the bread in the city is gone."

10Then the king commanded Ebed-melech to take thirty men with him and pull Jeremiah out before he died. 11So Ebed-melech took thirty men and went to a palace depot for discarded supplies where used clothing was kept. There he found some old rags and discarded garments which he took to the cistern and lowered to Jeremiah on a rope. 12Ebed-melech called down to Jeremiah, "Use these rags under your armpits to protect you from the ropes." Then, when Jeremiah was ready, 13they pulled him out and returned him to the palace prison, where he remained.

14One day King Zedekiah sent for Jeremiah to meet him at the side entrance of the Temple.

"I want to ask you something," the

king said, "and don't try to hide the truth."

15Jeremiah said, "If I tell you the truth, you will kill me. And you won't listen to me anyway."

16So King Zedekiah swore before Almighty God his Creator that he would not kill Jeremiah or give him to the men who were after his life.

17Then Jeremiah said to Zedekiah, "The Almighty Lord, the God of Israel, says: If you will surrender to Babylon, you and your family shall live and the city will not be burned. 18If you refuse to surrender, this city shall be set afire by the Babylonian army and you will not escape."

19"But I am afraid to surrender," the king said, "for the Babylonians will hand me over to the Jews who have defected to them, and who knows what they will do to me?"

20Jeremiah replied, "You won't get into their hands if only you will obey the Lord; your life will be spared and all will go well for you. 21,22But if you refuse to surrender, the Lord has said that all the women left in your palace will be brought out and given to the officers of the Babylonian army; and these women will taunt you with bitterness. 'Fine friends you have,' they'll say, 'those Egyptians. They have betrayed you and left you to your fate!' 23All your wives and children will be led out to the Babylonians, and you will not escape. You will be seized by the king of Babylon, and this city will be burned."

24Then Zedekiah said to Jeremiah, "On pain of death, don't tell anyone you told me this! 25And if my officials hear that I talked with you and they threaten you with death unless you tell them what we discussed, 26just say that you begged me not to send you back to the dungeon in Jonathan's house, for you would die there."

27And sure enough, it wasn't long before all the city officials came to Jeremiah and asked him why the king had called for him. So he said what the king had told him to, and they left without finding

out the truth, for the conversation had not been overheard by anyone. 28And Jeremiah remained confined to the prison yard until the day Jerusalem was captured.

1 TIMOTHY 6:1–21

CHRISTIAN slaves should work hard for their owners and respect them; never let it be said that Christ's people are poor workers. Don't let the name of God or his teaching be laughed at because of this. 2If their owner is a Christian, that is no excuse for slowing down; rather they should work all the harder because a brother in the faith is being helped by their efforts.

Teach these truths, Timothy, and encourage all to obey them.

3Some may deny these things, but they are the sound, wholesome teachings of the Lord Jesus Christ and are the foundation for a godly life. 4Anyone who says anything different is both proud and stupid. He is quibbling over the meaning of Christ's words and stirring up arguments ending in jealousy and anger, which only lead to name-calling, accusations, and evil suspicions. 5These arguers—their minds warped by sin—don't know how to tell the truth; to them the Good News is just a means of making money. Keep away from them.

6Do you want to be truly rich? You already are if you are happy and good. 7After all, we didn't bring any money with us when we came into the world, and we can't carry away a single penny when we die. 8So we should be well satisfied without money if we have enough food and clothing. 9But people who long to be rich soon begin to do all kinds of wrong things to get money, things that hurt them and make them evil-minded and finally send them to hell itself. 10For the love of money is the first step toward all kinds of sin. Some people have even turned away from God because of their love for it, and as a result have pierced themselves with many sorrows. ¹¹Oh, Timothy, you are God's man. Run from all these evil things and work instead at what is right and good, learning to trust him and love others, and to be patient and gentle. ¹²Fight on for God. Hold tightly to the eternal life which God has given you, and which you have confessed with such a ringing confession before many witnesses.

¹³I command you before God who gives life to all, and before Christ Jesus who gave a fearless testimony before Pontius Pilate, ¹⁴that you fulfill all he has told you to do, so that no one can find fault with you from now until our Lord Jesus Christ returns. ¹⁵For in due season Christ will be revealed from heaven by the blessed and only Almighty God, the King of kings and Lord of lords, ¹⁶who alone can never die, who lives in light so terrible that no human being can approach him. No mere man has ever seen him, nor ever will. Unto him be honor and everlasting power and dominion forever and ever. Amen.

¹⁷Tell those who are rich not to be proud and not to trust in their money, which will soon be gone, but their pride and trust should be in the living God who always richly gives us all we need for our enjoyment. ¹⁸Tell them to use their money to do good. They should be rich in good works and should give happily to those in need, always being ready to share with others whatever God has given them. ¹⁹By doing this they will be storing up real treasure for themselves in heaven—it is the only safe investment for eternity! And they will be living a fruitful Christian life down here as well.

²⁰Oh, Timothy, don't fail to do these things that God entrusted to you. Keep out of foolish arguments with those who

boast of their "knowledge" and thus prove their lack of it. ²¹Some of these people have missed the most important thing in life—they don't know God. May God's mercy be upon you.

Sincerely,
Paul

PSALM 89:38–52

THEN why cast me off, rejected? Why be so angry with the one you chose as king? ³⁹Have you renounced your covenant with him? For you have thrown his crown in the dust. ⁴⁰You have broken down the walls protecting him and laid in ruins every fort defending him. ⁴¹Everyone who comes along has robbed him while his neighbors mock. ⁴²You have strengthened his enemies against him and made them rejoice. ⁴³You have struck down his sword and refused to help him in battle. ⁴⁴You have ended his splendor and overturned his throne. ⁴⁵You have made him old before his time and publicly disgraced him.

⁴⁶O Jehovah, how long will this go on? Will you hide yourself from me forever? How long will your wrath burn like fire? ⁴⁷Oh, remember how short you have made man's lifespan. Is it an empty, futile life you give the sons of men? ⁴⁸No man can live forever. All will die. Who can rescue his life from the power of the grave?

⁴⁹Lord, where is the love you used to have for me? Where is your kindness that you promised to David with a faithful pledge? ⁵⁰Lord, see how all the people are despising me. ⁵¹Your enemies joke about me, the one you anointed as their king.

⁵²And yet—blessed be the Lord forever! Amen and amen!

PROVERBS FOR TODAY/ 25:28

A man without self-control is as defenseless as a city with broken-down walls.

OCTOBER 22

JEREMIAH 39:1—41:18

I T was in January of the ninth year of the reign of King Zedekiah of Judah, that King Nebuchadnezzar and all his army came against Jerusalem again and besieged it. 2Two years later, in the month of July, they breached the wall, and the city fell, 3and all the officers of the Babylonian army came in and sat in triumph at the middle gate. Nergal-sharezer was there, and Samgar-nebo and Sarsechim and Nergal-sharezer the king's chief assistant, and many others.

4When King Zedekiah and his soldiers realized that the city was lost, they fled during the night, going out through the gate between the two walls back of the palace garden and across the fields toward the Jordan valley. 5But the Babylonians chased the king and caught him on the plains of Jericho and brought him to Nebuchadnezzar, king of Babylon who was at Riblah, in the land of Hamath, where he pronounced judgment upon him. 6The king of Babylon made Zedekiah watch as they killed his children and all the nobles of Judah. 7Then he gouged out Zedekiah's eyes and bound him in chains to send him away to Babylon as a slave.

8Meanwhile the army burned Jerusalem, including the palace, and tore down the walls of the city. 9Then Nebuzaradan, the captain of the guard, and his men sent the remnant of the population and all those who had defected to him to Babylon. 10But throughout the land of Judah he left a few people, the very poor, and gave them fields and vineyards.

11,12Meanwhile King Nebuchadnezzar had told Nebuzaradan to find Jeremiah. "See that he isn't hurt," he said. "Look after him well and give him anything he wants." 13So Nebuzaradan, the captain of the guard, and Nebushazban, the chief of the eunuchs, and Nergal-sharezer, the king's advisor, and all the officials took steps to do as the king had commanded.

14They sent soldiers to bring Jeremiah out of the prison, and put him into the care of Gedaliah (son of Ahikam, son of Shaphan), to take him back to his home. And Jeremiah lived there among his people who were left in the land.

15The Lord gave the following message to Jeremiah before the Babylonians arrived, while he was still in prison:

16"Send this word to Ebed-melech the Ethiopian: The Lord, the God of Israel, says: I will do to this city everything I threatened; I will destroy it before your eyes, 17but I will deliver you. You shall not be killed by those you fear so much. 18As a reward for trusting me, I will preserve your life and keep you safe."

NEBUZARADAN, captain of the guard, took Jeremiah to Ramah along with all the exiled people of Jerusalem and Judah who were being sent to Babylon, but then released him.

2,3The captain called for Jeremiah and said, "The Lord your God has brought this disaster on this land, just as he said he would. For these people have sinned against the Lord. That is why it happened. 4Now I am going to take off your chains and let you go. If you want to come with me to Babylon, fine; I will see that you are well cared for. But if you don't want to come, don't. The world is before you—go where you like. 5If you decide to stay, then return to Gedaliah, who has been appointed as governor of Judah by the king of Babylon, and stay with the remnant he rules. But it's up to you; go where you like."

Then Nebuzaradan gave Jeremiah some food and money and let him go. 6So Jeremiah returned to Gedaliah and lived in Judah with the people left in the land.

7Now when the leaders of the Jewish guerrilla bands in the countryside heard that the king of Babylon had appointed

Gedaliah as governor over the poor of the land who were left behind, and had not exiled everyone to Babylon, 8they came to see Gedaliah at Mizpah, where his headquarters were. These are the names of the leaders who came: Ishmael (son of Nethaniah), Johanan and Jonathan (sons of Kareah), Seraiah (son of Tanhumeth), the sons of Ephai (the Netophathite), Jezaniah (son of a Ma-acathite), and their men. 9And Gedaliah assured them that it would be safe to surrender to the Babylonians.

"Stay here and serve the king of Babylon," he said, "and all will go well for you. 10As for me, I will stay at Mizpah and intercede for you with the Babylonians who will come here to oversee my administration. Settle in any city you wish and live off the land. Harvest the grapes and summer fruits and olives and store them away."

11When the Jews in Moab and among the Ammonites and in Edom and the other nearby countries heard that a few people were still left in Judah, and that the king of Babylon had not taken them all away, and that Gedaliah was the governor, 12they all began to return to Judah from the many places to which they had fled. They stopped at Mizpah to discuss their plans with Gedaliah and then went out to the deserted farms and gathered a great harvest of wine grapes and other crops.

13,14But soon afterwards Johanan (son of Kareah) and the other guerrilla leaders came to Mizpah to warn Gedaliah that Baalis, king of the Ammonites, had sent Ishmael (son of Nethaniah) to assassinate him. But Gedaliah wouldn't believe them. 15Then Johanan had a private conference with Gedaliah. Johanan volunteered to kill Ishmael secretly.

"Why should we let him come and murder you?" Johanan asked. "What will happen then to the Jews who have returned? Why should this remnant be scattered and lost?"

16But Gedaliah said, "I forbid you to do any such thing, for you are lying about Ishmael."

BUT in October, Ishmael (son of Nethaniah, son of Elishama), who was a member of the royal family and one of the king's top officials, arrived in Mizpah, accompanied by ten men. Gedaliah invited them to dinner. 2While they were eating, Ishmael and the ten men in league with him suddenly jumped up, pulled out their swords and killed Gedaliah. 3Then they went out and slaughtered all the Jewish officials and Babylonian soldiers who were in Mizpah with Gedaliah.

4The next day, before the outside world knew what had happened, 5eighty men approached Mizpah from Shechem, Shiloh and Samaria, to worship at the Temple of the Lord. They had shaved off their beards, torn their clothes and cut themselves, and were bringing offerings and incense. 6Ishmael went out from the city to meet them, crying as he went. When he faced them he said, "Oh, come and see what has happened to Gedaliah!"

7Then, when they were all inside the city, Ishmael and his men killed all but ten of them and threw their bodies into a cistern. 8The ten had talked Ishmael into letting them go by promising to bring him their treasures of wheat, barley, oil and honey they had hidden away. 9The cistern where Ishmael dumped the bodies of the men he murdered was the large one constructed by King Asa when he fortified Mizpah to protect himself against Baasha, king of Israel.

10Ishmael made captives of the king's daughters and of the people who had been left under Gedaliah's care in Mizpah by Nebuzaradan, captain of the guard. Soon after he took them with him when he headed toward the country of the Ammonites.

11But when Johanan (son of Kareah) and the rest of the guerrilla leaders heard what Ishmael had done, 12they took all their men and set out to stop him. They caught up with him at the pool near Gibeon. 13,14The people with Ishmael shouted for joy when they saw Johanan and his men, and ran to meet them.

15Meanwhile Ishmael escaped with

eight of his men into the land of the Ammonites.

16,17Then Johanan and his men went to the village of Geruth Chimham, near Bethlehem, taking with them all those they had rescued—soldiers, women, children and eunuchs, to prepare to leave for Egypt. 18For they were afraid of what the Babylonians would do when the news reached them that Ishmael had killed Gedaliah the governor, for he had been chosen and appointed by the Babylonian emperor.

2 TIMOTHY 1:1–18

FROM: Paul, Jesus Christ's missionary, sent out by God to tell men and women everywhere about the eternal life he has promised them through faith in Jesus Christ.

2*To:* Timothy, my dear son. May God the Father and Christ Jesus our Lord shower you with his kindness, mercy and peace.

3How I thank God for you, Timothy. I pray for you every day, and many times during the long nights I beg my God to bless you richly. He is my fathers' God, and mine, and my only purpose in life is to please him.

4How I long to see you again. How happy I would be, for I remember your tears as we left each other.

5I know how much you trust the Lord, just as your mother Eunice and your grandmother Lois do; and I feel sure you are still trusting him as much as ever.

6This being so, I want to remind you to stir into flame the strength and boldness that is in you, that entered into you when I laid my hands upon your head and blessed you. 7For the Holy Spirit, God's gift, does not want you to be afraid of people, but to be wise and strong, and to love them and enjoy being with them.

8If you will stir up this inner power, you will never be afraid to tell others about our Lord, or to let them know that I am your friend even though I am here in jail for Christ's sake. You will

be ready to suffer with me for the Lord, for he will give you strength in suffering.

9It is he who saved us and chose us for his holy work, not because we deserved it but because that was his plan long before the world began—to show his love and kindness to us through Christ. 10And now he has made all of this plain to us by the coming of our Savior Jesus Christ, who broke the power of death and showed us the way of everlasting life through trusting him. 11And God has chosen me to be his missionary, to preach to the Gentiles and teach them.

12That is why I am suffering here in jail and I am certainly not ashamed of it, for I know the one in whom I trust, and I am sure that he is able to safely guard all that I have given him until the day of his return.

13Hold tightly to the pattern of truth I taught you, especially concerning the faith and love Christ Jesus offers you. 14Guard well the splendid, God-given ability you received as a gift from the Holy Spirit who lives within you.

15As you know, all the Christians who came here from Asia have deserted me; even Phygellus and Hermogenes are gone. 16May the Lord bless Onesiphorus and all his family, because he visited me and encouraged me often. His visits revived me like a breath of fresh air, and he was never ashamed of my being in jail. 17In fact, when he came to Rome he searched everywhere trying to find me, and finally did. 18May the Lord give him a special blessing at the day of Christ's return. And you know better than I can tell you how much he helped me at Ephesus.

PSALM 90:1—91:16

LORD, through all the generations you have been our home! 2Before the mountains were created, before the earth was formed, you are God without beginning or end.

3You speak, and man turns back to dust. 4A thousand years are but as yesterday to you! They are like a single hour! 5,6We glide along the tides of time as swiftly as a racing river, and vanish as quickly as a dream. We are like grass that is green in the morning but mowed down and withered before the evening shadows fall. 7We die beneath your anger; we are overwhelmed by your wrath. 8You spread out our sins before you— our secret sins—and see them all. 9No wonder the years are long and heavy here beneath your wrath. All our days are filled with sighing.

10Seventy years are given us! And some may even live to eighty. But even the best of these years are often emptiness and pain; soon they disappear, and we are gone. 11Who can realize the terrors of your anger? Which of us can fear you as he should?

12Teach us to number our days and recognize how few they are; help us to spend them as we should.

13O Jehovah, come and bless us! How long will you delay? Turn away your anger from us. 14Satisfy us in our earliest youth with your lovingkindness, giving us constant joy to the end of our lives. 15Give us gladness in proportion to our former misery! Replace the evil years with good. 16Let us see your miracles again; let our children see glorious things, the kind you used to do, 17and let the Lord our God favor us and give us success. May he give permanence to all we do.

WE live within the shadow of the Almighty, sheltered by the God who is above all gods.

2This I declare, that he alone is my refuge, my place of safety; he is my God, and I am trusting him. 3For he rescues you from every trap, and protects you from the fatal plague. 4He will shield you with his wings! They will shelter you. His faithful promises are your armor. 5Now you don't need to be afraid of the dark any more, nor fear the dangers of the day; 6nor dread the plagues of darkness, nor disasters in the morning.

7Though a thousand fall at my side, though ten thousand are dying around me, the evil will not touch me. 8I will see how the wicked are punished but I will not share it. 9For Jehovah is my refuge! I choose the God above all gods to shelter me. 10How then can evil overtake me or any plague come near? 11For he orders his angels to protect you wherever you go. 12They will steady you with their hands to keep you from stumbling against the rocks on the trail. 13You can safely meet a lion or step on poisonous snakes, yes, even trample them beneath your feet!

14For the Lord says, "Because he loves me, I will rescue him; I will make him great because he trusts in my name. 15When he calls on me I will answer; I will be with him in trouble, and rescue him and honor him. 16I will satisfy him with a full life and give him my salvation."

PROVERBS FOR TODAY/ 26:1–2

Honor doesn't go with fools any more than snow with summertime or rain with harvest time! An undeserved curse has no effect. Its intended victim will be no more harmed by it than by a sparrow or swallow flitting through the sky.

OCTOBER 23

JEREMIAH 42:1—44:23

THEN Johanan and the army captains and all the people, great and small, came to Jeremiah 2and said, "Please pray for us to the Lord your God, for as you know so well, we are only a tiny remnant of what we were before. 3Beg the Lord your God to show us what to do and where to go."

4"All right," Jeremiah replied. "I will ask him and I will tell you what he says. I will hide nothing from you."

5Then they said to Jeremiah, "May the curse of God be on us if we refuse to obey whatever he says we should do! 6Whether we like it or not, we will obey the Lord our God, to whom we send you with our plea. For if we obey him, everything will turn out well for us."

7Ten days later the Lord gave his reply to Jeremiah. 8So he called for Johanan and the captains of his forces, and for all the people, great and small, 9and said to them: "You sent me to the Lord, the God of Israel, with your request, and this is his reply:

10"Stay here in this land. If you do, I will bless you and no one will harm you. For I am sorry for all the punishment I have had to give to you. 11Don't fear the king of Babylon any more, for I am with you to save you and to deliver you from his hand. 12And I will be merciful to you by making him kind so that he will not kill you or make slaves of you but will let you stay here in your land. 13,14"But if you refuse to obey the Lord and say, 'We will not stay here,'—and insist on going to Egypt where you think you will be free from war and hunger and alarms, 15then this is what the Lord replies, O remnant of Judah: The Lord Almighty, the God of Israel, says: If you insist on going to Egypt, 16the war and famine you fear will follow close behind you and you will perish there. 17That is the fate awaiting every one of you who insists on going to live in Egypt. Yes, you will die from sword, famine and disease. None of you will escape from the evil I will bring upon you there.

18"For the Lord, the God of Israel, says: Just as my anger and fury were poured out upon the people of Jerusalem, so it will be poured out on you when you enter Egypt. You will be received with disgust and with hatred—you will be cursed and reviled. And you will never again see your own land. 19For the Lord has said: O remnant of Judah, do not go to Egypt!"

Jeremiah concluded: "Never forget the warning I have given you today. 20If you go, it will be at the cost of your lives. For you were deceitful when you sent me to pray for you and said, 'Just tell us what God says and we will do it!' 21And today I have told you exactly what he said, but you will not obey any more now than you did the other times. 22Therefore know for a certainty that you will die by sword, famine and disease in Egypt, where you insist on going."

WHEN Jeremiah had finished giving this message from God to all the people, 2,3Azariah (son of Hoshaiah) and Johanan (son of Kareah) and all the other proud men, said to Jeremiah, "You lie! The Lord our God hasn't told you to tell us not to go to Egypt! Baruch (son of Neriah) has plotted against us and told you to say this so that we will stay here and be killed by the Babylonians or carried off to Babylon as slaves."

4So Johanan and all the guerrilla leaders and all the people refused to obey the Lord and stay in Judah. 5All of them, including all those who had returned from the nearby countries where they had fled, now started off for Egypt with Johanan and the other captains in command. 6In the crowd were men, women and children, the king's daughters and all those whom Nebuzaradan, the captain of the guard, had left with Gedaliah. They even forced Jeremiah and Baruch to go with them too. ⁷And so they arrived in Egypt at the city of Tahpanhes, for they would not obey the Lord.

⁸Then at Tahpanhes, the Lord spoke to Jeremiah again and said:

⁹"Call together the men of Judah and, as they watch you, bury large rocks between the pavement stones at the entrance of Pharaoh's palace here in Tahpanhes, ¹⁰and tell the men of Judah this: The Lord Almighty, the God of Israel, says: I will surely bring Nebuchadnezzar, king of Babylon, here to Egypt, for he is my servant. I will set his throne upon these stones that I have hidden. He shall spread his royal canopy over them. ¹¹And when he comes he shall destroy the land of Egypt, killing all those I want killed, and capturing those I want captured, and many shall die of plague. ¹²He will set fire to the temples of the gods of Egypt and burn the idols and carry off the people as his captives. And he shall plunder the land of Egypt as a shepherd picks fleas from his cloak! And he himself shall leave unharmed. ¹³And he shall break down the obelisks standing in the city of Heliopolis, and burn down the temples of the gods of Egypt."

THIS is the message God gave to Jeremiah concerning all the Jews who were living in the north of Egypt in the cities of Migdol, Tahpanhes and Memphis, and throughout southern Egypt as well:

2,3The Lord Almighty, the God of Israel, says: You saw what I did to Jerusalem and to all the cities of Judah. Because of all their wickedness they lie in heaps and ashes, without a living soul. For my anger rose high against them for worshiping other gods—"gods" that neither they nor you nor any of your fathers have ever known.

⁴I sent my servants, the prophets, to protest over and over again and to plead with them not to do this horrible thing I hate, ⁵but they wouldn't listen and wouldn't turn back from their wicked ways; they have kept right on with their sacrifices to these "gods." ⁶And so my fury and anger boiled over and fell as fire upon the cities of Judah and into the streets of Jerusalem, and there is desolation until this day.

⁷And now the Lord, the Lord Almighty, the God of Israel, asks you: Why are you destroying yourselves? For not one of you shall live—not a man, woman or child among you who has come here from Judah, not even the babies in arms. ⁸For you are rousing my anger with the idols you have made and worshiped here in Egypt, burning incense to them, and causing me to destroy you completely and to make you a curse and a stench in the nostrils of all the nations of the earth. ⁹Have you forgotten the sins of your fathers, and the sins of the kings and queens of Judah, and your own sins, and the sins of your wives in Judah and Jerusalem? ¹⁰And even until this very hour there has been no apology; no one has wanted to return to me, or follow the laws I gave you and your fathers before you.

¹¹Therefore the Lord, the God of Israel, says: There is fury in my face and I will destroy every one of you! ¹²I will take this remnant of Judah that insisted on coming here to Egypt and I will consume them. They shall fall here in Egypt, killed by famine and sword; all shall die, from the least important to the greatest. They shall be despised and loathed, cursed and hated. ¹³I will punish them in Egypt just as I punished them in Jerusalem, by sword, famine and disease. ¹⁴Not one of them shall escape from my wrath except those who repent of their coming and escape from the others by returning again to their own land.

¹⁵Then all the women present and all the men who knew that their wives had burned incense to idols (it was a great crowd of all the Jews in southern Egypt) answered Jeremiah:

¹⁶"We will not listen to your false 'Messages from God'! ¹⁷We will do whatever we want to. We will burn incense to the 'Queen of Heaven' and sacrifice to her just as much as we like—just as

we and our fathers before us, and our kings and princes have always done in the cities of Judah and in the streets of Jerusalem; for in those days we had plenty to eat and we were well off and happy! 18But ever since we quit burning incense to the 'Queen of Heaven' and stopped worshiping her we have been in great trouble and have been destroyed by sword and famine."

19"And," the women added, "do you suppose that we were worshiping the 'Queen of Heaven' and pouring out our libations to her and making cakes for her with her image on them, without our husbands knowing it and helping us? Of course not!"

20Then Jeremiah said to all of them, men and women alike, who had given him that answer:

21"Do you think the Lord didn't know that you and your fathers and your kings and princes and all the people were burning incense to idols in the cities of Judah and in the streets of Jerusalem? 22It was because he could no longer bear all the evil things you were doing that he made your land desolate, an incredible ruin, cursed, without an inhabitant, as it is today. 23The very reason all these terrible things have befallen you is because you have burned incense and sinned against the Lord and refused to obey him."

2 TIMOTHY 2:1–21

OH, Timothy, my son, be strong with the strength Christ Jesus gives you. 2For you must teach others those things you and many others have heard me speak about. Teach these great truths to trustworthy men who will, in turn, pass them on to others.

3Take your share of suffering as a good soldier of Jesus Christ, just as I do, 4and as Christ's soldier do not let yourself become tied up in worldly affairs, for then you cannot satisfy the one who has enlisted you in his army. 5Follow the Lord's rules for doing his work, just as an athlete either follows the rules or is disqualified and wins no prize. 6Work hard, like a farmer who gets paid well if he raises a large crop. 7Think over these three illustrations, and may the Lord help you to understand how they apply to you.

8Don't ever forget the wonderful fact that Jesus Christ was a Man, born into King David's family; and that he was God, as shown by the fact that he rose again from the dead. 9It is because I have preached these great truths that I am in trouble here and have been put in jail like a criminal. But the Word of God is not chained, even though I am. 10I am more than willing to suffer if that will bring salvation and eternal glory in Christ Jesus to those God has chosen.

11I am comforted by this truth, that when we suffer and die for Christ it only means that we will begin living with him in heaven. 12And if we think that our present service for him is hard, just remember that some day we are going to sit with him and rule with him. But if we give up when we suffer, and turn against Christ, then he must turn against us. 13Even when we are too weak to have any faith left, he remains faithful to us and will help us, for he cannot disown us who are part of himself, and he will always carry out his promises to us.

14Remind your people of these great facts, and command them in the name of the Lord not to argue over unimportant things. Such arguments are confusing and useless, and even harmful. 15Work hard so God can say to you, "Well done." Be a good workman, one who does not need to be ashamed when God examines your work. Know what his Word says and means. 16Steer clear of foolish discussions which lead people into the sin of anger with each other. 17Things will be said that will burn and hurt for a long time to come. Hymenaeus and Philetus, in their love of argument, are men like that. 18They have left the path of truth, preaching the lie that the resurrection of the dead has already occurred; and they have weakened the faith of some who believe them.

19But God's truth stands firm like a

great rock, and nothing can shake it. It is a foundation stone with these words written on it: "The Lord knows those who are really his," and "A person who calls himself a Christian should not be doing things that are wrong."

20In a wealthy home there are dishes made of gold and silver as well as some made from wood and clay. The expensive dishes are used for guests, and the cheap ones are used in the kitchen or to put garbage in. 21If you stay away from sin you will be like one of these dishes made of purest gold—the very best in the house—so that Christ himself can use you for his highest purposes.

PSALM 92:1—93:5

IT is good to say, "Thank you" to the Lord, to sing praises to the God who is above all gods. 2Every morning tell him, "Thank you for your kindness," and every evening rejoice in all his faithfulness. 3Sing his praises, accompanied by music from the harp and lute and lyre. 4You have done so much for me, O Lord. No wonder I am glad! I sing for joy.

5O Lord, what miracles you do! And how deep are your thoughts! 6Unthinking people do not understand them! No fool can comprehend this: 7that although the wicked flourish like weeds, there is only eternal destruction ahead of them. 8But the Lord continues forever, exalted in the heavens, 9while his enemies—all evil-doers—shall be scattered.

10But you have made me as strong as a wild bull. How refreshed I am by your blessings! 11I have heard the doom of my enemies announced and seen them destroyed. 12But the godly shall flourish like palm trees, and grow tall as the cedars of Lebanon. 13For they are transplanted into the Lord's own garden, and are under his personal care. 14Even in old age they will still produce fruit and be vital and green. 15This honors the Lord, and exhibits his faithful care. He is my shelter. There is nothing but goodness in him!

JEHOVAH is King! He is robed in majesty and strength. The world is his throne. 2O Lord, you have reigned from prehistoric times, from the everlasting past. 3The mighty oceans thunder your praise. 4You are mightier than all the breakers pounding on the seashores of the world! 5Your royal decrees cannot be changed. Holiness is forever the keynote of your reign.

PROVERBS FOR TODAY/ 26:3–5

Guide a horse with a whip, a donkey with a bridle, and a rebel with a rod to his back! When arguing with a rebel, don't use foolish arguments as he does, or you will become as foolish as he is! Prick his conceit with silly replies!

OCTOBER 24

JEREMIAH 44:24—47:7

THEN Jeremiah said to them all, including the women: "Listen to the word of the Lord, all you citizens of Judah who are here in Egypt! 25The Lord, the God of Israel, says: Both you and your wives have said that you will never give up your devotion and sacrifices to the 'Queen of Heaven,' and you have proved it by your actions. Then go ahead and carry out your promises and vows to her! 26But listen to the word of the Lord, all you Jews who are living in the land of Egypt: I have sworn by my great name, says the Lord, that it will do you no good to seek my help and blessing any more, saying, 'O Lord our God, help us!' 27For I will watch over you, but *not* for good! I will see to it that evil befalls you, and you shall be destroyed by war and famine until all of you are dead.

28"Only those who return to Judah (it will be but a tiny remnant) shall escape my wrath, but all who refuse to go back—who insist on living in Egypt—shall find out who tells the truth, I or they! 29And this is the proof I give you that all I have threatened will happen to you, and that I will punish you here: 30I will turn Pharaoh Hophra, king of Egypt, over to those who seek his life, just as I turned Zedekiah, king of Judah, over to Nebuchadnezzar, king of Babylon."

THIS is the message Jeremiah gave to Baruch in the fourth year of the reign of King Jehoiakim (son of Josiah), after Baruch had written down all God's messages as Jeremiah was dictating them to him:

2O Baruch, the Lord God of Israel says this to you:

3You have said, Woe is me! Don't I have troubles enough already? And now the Lord has added more! I am weary of my own sighing and I find no rest. 4But tell Baruch this, The Lord says: I will destroy this nation that I built; I will wipe out what I established. 5Are you seeking great things for yourself? Don't do it! For though I will bring great evil upon all these people, I will protect you wherever you go, as your reward.

HERE are the messages given to Jeremiah concerning foreign nations.

The Egyptians

2This message was given against! Egypt at the occasion of the battle of Carchemish when Pharaoh Necho, king of Egypt, and his army were defeated beside the Euphrates River by Nebuchadnezzar, king of Babylon, in the fourth year of the reign of Jehoiakim (son of Josiah), king of Judah:

3Buckle on your armor, you Egyptians and advance to battle! 4Harness the horses and prepare to mount them—don your helmets, sharpen your spears, put on your armor. 5But look! The Egyptian army flees in terror; the mightiest of its soldiers run without a backward glance. Yes, terror shall surround them on every side, says the Lord. 6The swift will not escape, nor the mightiest of warriors. In the north, by the river Euphrates, they have stumbled and fallen.

7What is this mighty army, rising like the Nile at flood time, overflowing all the land? 8It is the Egyptian army, boasting that it will cover the earth like a flood, destroying every foe. 9Then come, O horses and chariots and mighty soldiers of Egypt! Come, all of you from Cush and Put and Lud who handle the shield and bend the bow! 10For this is the day of the Lord, the Lord Almighty, a day of vengeance upon his enemies. The sword shall devour until it is sated, yes, drunk with your blood, for the Lord, the Lord Almighty will receive a sacrifice today in the north country beside the river Euphrates! 11Go up to Gilead for medicine, O virgin daughter of Egypt! Yet there is no cure for your wounds. Though you have used many medicines, there is no healing for you. 12The nations have heard of your shame. The earth is filled with your cry of despair and defeat; your mightiest soldiers will stumble across each other and fall together.

13Then God gave Jeremiah this message concerning the coming of Nebuchadnezzar, king of Babylon, to attack Egypt:

14Shout it out in Egypt; publish it in the cities of Migdol, Memphis and Tahpanhes! Mobilize for battle, for the sword of destruction shall devour all around you. 15Why has Apis, your bull god, fled in terror? Because the Lord knocked him down before your enemies. 16Vast multitudes fall in heaps. (Then the remnant of the Jews will say, "Come, let us return again to Judah where we were born and get away from all this slaughter here!")

17Rename Pharaoh Hophra and call him "The Man with No Power But with Plenty of Noise!"

18As I live, says the King, the Lord of Hosts, one is coming against Egypt who is as tall as Mount Tabor or Mount Carmel by the sea! 19Pack up; get ready to leave for exile, you citizens of Egypt, for the city of Memphis shall be utterly destroyed, and left without a soul alive. 20,21Egypt is sleek as a heifer, but a gadfly sends her running—a gadfly from the north! Even her famed mercenaries have become like frightened calves. They turn and run, for it is the day of great calamity for Egypt, a time of great punishment. 22,23Silent as a serpent gliding away, Egypt flees; the invading army marches in. The numberless soldiers cut down your people like woodsmen who clear a forest of its trees. 24Egypt is as helpless as a girl before these men from the north.

25The Lord, the God of Israel, says: I will punish Amon, god of Thebes, and all the other gods of Egypt. I will punish Pharaoh too, and all who trust in him. 26I will deliver them into the hands of those who want them killed—into the hands of Nebuchadnezzar, king of Babylon, and his army. But afterwards the land shall recover from the ravages of war.

27But don't you be afraid, O my people who return to your own land, don't be dismayed; for I will save you from far away and bring your children from a distant land. Yes, Israel shall return and be at rest and nothing shall make her afraid. 28Fear not, O Jacob, my servant, says the Lord, for I am with you. I will destroy all the nations to which I have exiled you, but I will not destroy you. I will punish you, but only enough to correct you.

The Philistines

THIS is God's message to Jeremiah concerning the Philistines of Gaza, before the city was captured by the Egyptian army.

2The Lord says: A flood is coming from the north to overflow the land of the Philistines; it will destroy their cities and everything in them. Strong men will scream in terror and all the land will weep. 3Hear the clattering hoofs and rumbling wheels as the chariots go rushing by; fathers flee without a backward glance at their helpless children, 4for the time has come when all the Philistines and their allies from Tyre and Sidon will be destroyed. For the Lord is destroying the Philistines, those colonists from Caphtor. 5The cities of Gaza and Ashkelon will be razed to the ground and lie in ruins. O descendants of the Anakim, how you will lament and mourn!

6O sword of the Lord, when will you be at rest again? Go back into your scabbard; rest and be still! 7But how can it be still when the Lord has sent it on an errand? For the city of Ashkelon and those living along the sea must be destroyed.

2 TIMOTHY 2:22—3:17

RUN from anything that gives you the evil thoughts that young men often have, but stay close to anything that makes you want to do right. Have faith and love, and enjoy the companionship of those who love the Lord and have pure hearts.

23Again I say, don't get involved in foolish arguments which only upset people and make them angry. 24God's people must not be quarrelsome; they must be gentle, patient teachers of those who are wrong. 25Be humble when you are trying to teach those who are mixed up concerning the truth. For if you talk meekly and courteously to them they are more likely, with God's help, to turn away from their wrong ideas and believe what is true. 26Then they will come to their senses and escape from Satan's trap of slavery to sin which he uses to catch them whenever he likes, and then they can begin doing the will of God.

YOU may as well know this too, Timothy, that in the last days it is going to be very difficult to be a Christian. 2For people will love only themselves and their money; they will be proud and boastful, sneering at God, disobedient to their parents, ungrateful to them, and thoroughly bad. 3They will be hardheaded and never give in to others; they will be constant liars and troublemakers and will think nothing of immorality. They will be rough and cruel, and sneer at those who try to be good. 4They will betray their friends; they will be hotheaded, puffed up with pride, and prefer good times to worshiping God. 5They will go to church, yes, but they won't really believe anything they hear. Don't be taken in by people like that.

6They are the kind who craftily sneak into other people's homes and make friendships with silly, sin-burdened women and teach them their new doctrines. 7Women of that kind are forever following new teachers, but they never understand the truth. 8And these teachers fight truth just as Jannes and Jambres fought against Moses. They have dirty minds, warped and twisted, and have turned against the Christian faith.

9But they won't get away with all this forever. Some day their deceit will be well known to everyone, as was the sin of Jannes and Jambres.

10But you know from watching me that I am not that kind of person. You know what I believe and the way I live and what I want. You know my faith in Christ and how I have suffered. You know my love for you, and my patience. 11You know how many troubles I have had as a result of my preaching the Good News. You know about all that was done to me while I was visiting in Antioch, Iconium and Lystra, but the Lord delivered me. 12Yes, and those who decide to please Christ Jesus by living godly lives will suffer at the hands of those who hate him. 13In fact, evil men and false teachers will become worse and worse, deceiving many, they themselves having been deceived by Satan.

14But you must keep on believing the things you have been taught. You know

they are true for you know that you can trust those of us who have taught you. 15You know how, when you were a small child, you were taught the holy Scriptures; and it is these that make you wise to accept God's salvation by trusting in Christ Jesus. 16The whole Bible was given to us by inspiration from God and is useful to teach us what is true and to make us realize what is wrong in our lives; it straightens us out and helps us do what is right. 17It is God's way of making us well prepared at every point, fully equipped to do good to everyone.

PSALM 94:1–23

LORD God, to whom vengeance belongs, let your glory shine out. Arise and judge the earth; sentence the proud to the penalties they deserve. 3Lord, how long shall the wicked be allowed to triumph and exult? 4Hear their insolence! See their arrogance! How these men of evil boast! 5See them oppressing your people, O Lord, afflicting those you love. 6,7They murder widows, immigrants, and orphans, for "The Lord isn't looking," they say, "and besides, he doesn't care."

8Fools! 9Is God deaf and blind—he who makes ears and eyes? 10He punishes the nations—won't he also punish you? He knows everything—doesn't he also know what you are doing?

11The Lord is fully aware of how limited and futile the thoughts of mankind are, 12,13so he helps us by punishing us. This makes us follow his paths, and gives us respite from our enemies while God traps them and destroys them. 14The Lord will not forsake his people, for they are his prize. 15Judgment will again be just and all the upright will rejoice.

16Who will protect me from the wicked? Who will be my shield? 17I would have died unless the Lord had helped me. 18I screamed, "I'm slipping, Lord!" and he was kind and saved me.

19Lord, when doubts fill my mind, when my heart is in turmoil, quiet me and give me renewed hope and cheer.

²⁰Will you permit a corrupt government to rule under your protection—a government permitting wrong to defeat right? ²¹,²²Do you approve of those who condemn the innocent to death? No! The Lord my God is my fortress—the mighty Rock where I can hide. ²³God has made the sins of evil men to boomerang upon them! He will destroy them by their own plans. Jehovah our God will cut them off.

PROVERBS FOR TODAY/ 26:6–8

To trust a rebel to convey a message is as foolish as cutting off your feet and drinking poison! In the mouth of a fool a proverb becomes as useless as a paralyzed leg. Honoring a rebel will backfire like a stone tied to a slingshot!

OCTOBER 25

JEREMIAH 48:1—49:22

The Moabites

THIS is the message of the Lord of Hosts, the God of Israel, against Moab:

Woe to the city of Nebo, for it shall lie in ruins. The city of Kiriathaim and its forts are overwhelmed and captured. ²,³,⁴No one will ever brag about Moab any more, for there is a plot against her life. In Heshbon, plans have been completed to destroy her. "Come," they say, "we will cut her off from being a nation." In Madmen all is silent. And then the roar of battle will surge against Horonaim, for all Moab is being destroyed. Her crying will be heard as far away as Zoar. ⁵Her refugees will climb the hills of Luhith, weeping bitterly, while cries of terror rise from the city below. ⁶Flee for your lives; hide in the wilderness! ⁷For you trusted in your wealth and skill; therefore you shall perish. Your god Chemosh, with his priests and princes, shall be taken away to distant lands!

⁸All the villages and cities, whether they be on the plateaus or in the valleys, shall be destroyed, for the Lord has said it. ⁹Oh, for wings for Moab that she could fly away, for her cities shall be left without a living soul. ¹⁰Cursed be those withholding their swords from your blood, refusing to do the work that God has given them!

¹¹From her earliest history Moab has lived there undisturbed from all invasions. She is like wine that has not been poured from flask to flask, and is fragrant and smooth. But now she shall have the pouring out of exile! ¹²The time is coming soon, the Lord has said, when he will send troublemakers to spill her out from jar to jar and then shatter the jars! ¹³Then at last Moab shall be ashamed of her idol Chemosh, as Israel was of her calf-idol at Bethel.

¹⁴Do you remember that boast of yours: "We are heroes, mighty men of war"? ¹⁵But now Moab is to be destroyed; her destroyer is on the way; her choicest youth are doomed to slaughter, says the King, the Lord Almighty. ¹⁶Calamity is coming fast to Moab.

¹⁷O friends of Moab, weep for her and cry! See how the strong, the beautiful is shattered! ¹⁸Come down from your glory and sit in the dust, O people of Dibon, for those destroying Moab shall shatter Dibon too, and tear down all her towers. ¹⁹Those in Aroer stand anxiously beside the road to watch, and shout to those who flee from Moab, "What has happened there?"

20And they reply, "Moab lies in ruins; weep and wail. Tell it by the banks of the Arnon, that Moab is destroyed."

21All the cities of the tableland lie in ruins too, for God's judgment has been poured out upon them all—on Holon and Jahzah and Mepha-ath, 22and Dibon and Nebo and Beth-diblathaim, 23and Kiria-thaim and Beth-gamul and Beth-meon, 24and Keri-oth and Bozrah—and all the cities of the land of Moab, far and near.

25The strength of Moab is ended—her horns are cut off; her arms are broken. 26Let her stagger and fall like a drunkard, for she has rebelled against the Lord. Moab shall wallow in her vomit, scorned by all. 27For you scorned Israel and robbed her, and were happy at her fall.

28O people of Moab, flee from your cities and live in the caves like doves that nest in the clefts of the rocks. 29We have all heard of the pride of Moab, for it is very great. We know your lofti-ness, your arrogance and your haughty heart. 30I know her insolence, the Lord has said, but her boasts are false—her helplessness is great. 31Yes, I wail for Moab, my heart is broken for the men of Kir-heres.

32O men of Sibmah, rich in vineyards, I weep for you even more than for Jazer. For the destroyer has cut off your spreading tendrils and harvested your grapes and summer fruits. He has plucked you bare! 33Joy and gladness are gone from fruitful Moab. The presses yield no wine; no one treads the grapes with shouts of joy. There is shouting, yes, but not the shouting of joy. 34Instead the awful cries of terror and pain rise from all over the land—from Heshbon clear across to Elealeh and to Jahaz; from Zoar to Horonaim and to Eglath-she-lishiyah. The pastures of Nim-rim are deserted now.

35For the Lord says: I have put a stop to Moab's worshiping false gods and burning incense to idols. 36Sad sings my heart for Moab and Kir-heres, for all their wealth has disappeared. 37They shave their heads and beards in anguish, and slash their hands and put on clothes of sackcloth. 38Crying and sorrow will be in every Moabite home and on the streets; for I have smashed and shattered Moab like an old, unwanted bottle. 39How it is broken! Hear the wails! See the shame of Moab! For she is a sign of horror and of scoffing to her neighbors now.

40A vulture circles ominously above the land of Moab, says the Lord. 41Her cities are fallen; her strongholds are seized. The hearts of her mightiest warriors fail with fear like women in the pains of giving birth. 42Moab shall no longer be a nation, for she has boasted against the Lord. 43Fear and traps and treachery shall be your lot, O Moab, says the Lord. 44He who flees shall fall in a trap and he who escapes from the trap shall run into a snare. I will see to it that you do not get away, for the time of your judgment has come. 45They flee to Heshbon, unable to go farther. But a fire comes from Heshbon—Sihon's an-cestral home—and devours the land from end to end with all its rebellious people.

46Woe to you, O Moab; the people of the god Chemosh are destroyed, and your sons and daughters are taken away as slaves. 47But in the latter days, says the Lord, I will reestablish Moab.

(Here the prophecy concerning Moab ends.)

The Ammonites

WHAT is this you are doing? Why are you living in the cities of the Jews? Aren't there Jews enough to fill them up? Didn't they inherit them from me? Why then have you, who worship Milcom, taken over Gad and all its cities? 2I will punish you for this, the Lord declares, by de-stroying your city of Rabbah. It shall become a desolate heap, and the neigh-boring towns shall be burned. Then Israel shall come and take back her land from you again. She shall dispossess those who dispossessed her, says the Lord.

3Cry out, O Heshbon, for Ai is de-stroyed! Weep, daughter of Rabbah! Put on garments of mourning; weep and wail, hiding in the hedges, for your god Milcom shall be exiled along with his princes and priests. 4You are proud of your fertile valleys, but they will soon be ruined. O wicked daughter, you trusted in your wealth and thought no one could ever harm you. 5But see, I will bring terror upon you, says the Lord, the Lord Almighty. For all your neighbors shall drive you from your land and none shall help your exiles as they flee. 6But afterward I will restore the fortunes of the Ammonites, says the Lord.

The Edomites

7The Lord says: Where are all your wise men of days gone by? Is there not one left in all of Teman? 8Flee to the remotest parts of the desert, O people of Dedan; for when I punish Edom, I will punish you! 9,10Those who gather grapes leave a few for the poor, and even thieves don't take everything, but I will strip bare the land of Esau, and there will be no place to hide. Her children, her brothers, her neighbors—all will be destroyed—and she herself will perish too. 11(But I will preserve your fatherless children who remain, and let your widows depend upon me.)

12The Lord says to Edom: If the innocent must suffer, how much more must you! You shall not go unpunished! You must drink this cup of judgment! 13For I have sworn by my own name, says the Lord, that Bozrah shall become heaps of ruins, cursed and mocked; and her cities shall be eternal wastes.

14I have heard this message from the Lord:

He has sent a messenger to call the nations to form a coalition against Edom and destroy her. 15I will make her weak among the nations and despised by all, says the Lord. 16You have been fooled by your fame and your pride, living there in the mountains of Petra, in the clefts of the rocks. But though you live among the peaks with the eagles, I will bring you down, says the Lord.

17The fate of Edom will be horrible; all who go by will be appalled, and gasp at the sight. 18Your cities will become as silent as Sodom and Gomorrah and their neighboring towns, says the Lord. No one will live there anymore. 19I will send against them one who will come like a lion from the wilds of Jordan stalking the sheep in the fold. Suddenly Edom shall be destroyed, and I will appoint over the Edomites the person of my choice. For who is like me and who can call me to account? 20What shepherd can defy me? Take note: The Lord will certainly do this to Edom and also the people of Teman—even little children will be dragged away as slaves! It will be a shocking thing to see.

21The earth shakes with the noise of Edom's fall; the cry of the people is heard as far away as the Red Sea. 22The one who will come will fly as swift as a vulture and will spread his wings against Bozrah. Then the courage of the mightiest warriors will disappear like that of women in labor.

2 TIMOTHY 4:1–22

AND so I solemnly urge you before God and before Christ Jesus— who will some day judge the living and the dead when he appears to set up his Kingdom— 2to preach the Word of God urgently at all times, whenever you get the chance, in season and out, when it is convenient and when it is not. Correct and rebuke your people when they need it, encourage them to do right, and all the time be feeding them patiently with God's Word.

3For there is going to come a time when people won't listen to the truth, but will go around looking for teachers who will tell them just what they want to hear. 4They won't listen to what the Bible says but will blithely follow their own misguided ideas.

5Stand steady, and don't be afraid of suffering for the Lord. Bring others to Christ. Leave nothing undone that you ought to do.

6I say this because I won't be around to help you very much longer. My time has almost run out. Very soon now I will be on my way to heaven. 7I have fought long and hard for my Lord, and through it all I have kept true to him. And now the time has come for me to stop fighting and rest. 8In heaven a crown is waiting for me which the Lord, the righteous Judge, will give me on that great day of his return. And not just to me, but to all those whose lives show that they are eagerly looking forward to his coming back again.

9Please come as soon as you can, 10for Demas has left me. He loved the good things of this life and went to Thessalonica. Crescens has gone to Galatia, Titus to Dalmatia. 11Only Luke is with me. Bring Mark with you when you come, for I need him. 12(Tychicus is gone too, as I sent him to Ephesus.) 13When you come, be sure to bring the coat I left at Troas with Brother Carpus, and also the books, but especially the parchments.

14Alexander the coppersmith has done me much harm. The Lord will punish him, 15but be careful of him, for he fought against everything we said.

16The first time I was brought before the judge no one was here to help me. Everyone had run away. I hope that they will not be blamed for it. 17But the Lord stood with me and gave me the opportunity to boldly preach a whole sermon for all the world to hear. And he saved me from being thrown to the lions. 18Yes, and the Lord will always deliver me from all evil and will bring me into his heavenly Kingdom. To God be the glory forever and ever. Amen.

19Please say "hello" for me to Priscilla and Aquila and those living at the home of Onesiphorus. 20Erastus stayed at Corinth, and I left Trophimus sick at Miletus.

21Do try to be here before winter. Eubulus sends you greetings, and so do Pudens, Linus, Claudia, and all the others. 22May the Lord Jesus Christ be with your spirit.

Farewell,
Paul

OH, come, let us sing to the Lord! Give a joyous shout in honor of the Rock of our salvation! 2Come before him with thankful hearts. Let us sing him psalms of praise. 3For the Lord is a great God, the great King of all gods. 4He controls the formation of the depths of the earth and the mightiest mountains; all are his. 5He made the sea and formed the land; they too are his. 6Come, kneel before the Lord our Maker, 7for he is our God. We are his sheep and he is our Shepherd. Oh, that you would hear him calling you today and come to him!

8Don't harden your hearts as Israel did in the wilderness at Meribah and Massah. 9For there your fathers doubted me, though they had seen so many of my miracles before. My patience was severely tried by their complaints. 10"For forty years I watched them in disgust," the Lord God says. "They were a nation whose thoughts and heart were far away from me. They refused to accept my laws. 11Therefore in mighty wrath I swore that they would never enter the Promised Land, the place of rest I planned for them."

SING a new song to the Lord! Sing it everywhere around the world! 2Sing out his praises! Bless his name. Each day tell someone that he saves.

3Publish his glorious acts throughout the earth. Tell everyone about the amazing things he does. 4For the Lord is great beyond description, and greatly to be praised. Worship only him among the gods! 5For the gods of other nations are merely idols, but our God made the heavens! 6Honor and majesty surround him; strength and beauty are in his Temple.

7O nations of the world, confess that God alone is glorious and strong. 8Give him the glory he deserves! Bring your offering and come to worship him. 9Worship the Lord with the beauty of holy lives. Let the earth tremble before him. 10Tell the nations that Jehovah reigns! He rules the world. His power can never be overthrown. He will judge all nations fairly.

¹¹Let the heavens be glad, the earth rejoice; let the vastness of the roaring seas demonstrate his glory. ¹²Praise him for the growing fields, for they display his greatness. Let the trees of the forest rustle with praise. ¹³For the Lord is coming to judge the earth; he will judge the nations fairly and with truth!

PROVERBS FOR TODAY/ 26:9–12

A rebel will misapply an illustration so that its point will no more be felt than a thorn in the hand of a drunkard. The master may get better work from an untrained apprentice than from a skilled rebel! As a dog returns to his vomit, so a fool repeats his folly. There is one thing worse than a fool, and that is a man who is conceited.

OCTOBER 26

JEREMIAH 49:23—50:46

Damascus

THE cities of Hamath and Arpad are stricken with fear, for they have heard the news of their doom. Their hearts are troubled like a wild sea in a raging storm. ²⁴Damascus has become feeble and all her people turn to flee. Fear, anguish and sorrow have gripped her as they do women in labor. ²⁵O famous city, city of joy, how you are forsaken now! ²⁶Your young men lie dead in the streets; your entire army shall be destroyed in one day, says the Lord Almighty. ²⁷And I will start a fire at the edge of Damascus that shall burn up the palaces of Benhadad.

Kedar and Hazor

²⁸This prophecy is about Kedar and the kingdoms of Hazor, which are going to be destroyed by Nebuchadnezzar, king of Babylon, for the Lord will send him to destroy them. ²⁹Their flocks and their tents will be captured, says the Lord, with all their household goods. Their camels will be taken away, and all around will be the shouts of panic, "We are surrounded and doomed!" ³⁰Flee for your lives, says the Lord. Go deep into the deserts, O people of Hazor, for Nebuchadnezzar, king of Babylon, has plotted against you and is preparing to destroy you.

³¹"Go," said the Lord to King Nebuchadnezzar. "Attack those wealthy Bedouin tribes living alone in the desert without a care in the world, boasting that they are self-sufficient—that they need neither walls nor gates. ³²Their camels and cattle shall all be yours, and I will scatter these heathen to the winds. From all directions I will bring calamity upon them."

³³Hazor shall be a home for wild animals of the desert. No one shall ever live there again. It shall be desolate forever.

Elam

³⁴God's message against Elam came to Jeremiah in the beginning of the reign of Zedekiah, king of Judah:

³⁵The Lord says: I will destroy the army of Elam, ³⁶and I will scatter the people of Elam to the four winds; they shall be exiled to countries throughout the world. ³⁷My fierce anger will bring great evil upon Elam, says the Lord, and I will cause her enemies to wipe her out.

³⁸And I will set my throne in Elam, says the Lord. I will destroy her king and princes. ³⁹But in the latter days I will bring the people back, says the Lord.

Babylon

THIS is the message from the Lord against Babylon and the Chaldeans, spoken by Jeremiah the prophet:

²Tell all the world that Babylon will be destroyed; her god Marduk will be utterly disgraced! ³For a nation shall come down upon her from the north with such destruction that no one shall live in her again; all shall be gone—both men and animals shall flee.

⁴Then the people of Israel and Judah shall join together, weeping and seeking the Lord their God. ⁵They shall ask the way to Zion and start back home again. "Come," they will say, "let us be united to the Lord with an eternal pledge that will never be broken again."

⁶My people have been lost sheep. Their shepherds led them astray and then turned them loose in the mountains. They lost their way and didn't remember how to get back to the fold. ⁷All who found them devoured them and said, "We are permitted to attack them freely, for they have sinned against the Lord, the God of justice, the hope of their fathers."

⁸But now, flee from Babylon, the land of the Chaldeans; lead my people home again, ⁹for see, I am raising up an army of great nations from the north and I will bring them against Babylon to attack her, and she shall be destroyed. The enemies' arrows go straight to the mark; they do not miss! ¹⁰And Babylon shall be sacked until everyone is sated with loot, says the Lord.

¹¹Though you were glad, O Chaldeans, plunderers of my people, and are fat as cows that feed in lush pastures, and neigh like stallions, ¹²yet your mother shall be overwhelmed with shame, for you shall become the least of the nations—a wilderness, a dry and desert land. ¹³Because of the anger of the Lord, Babylon shall become deserted wasteland, and all who pass by shall be appalled and shall mock at her for all her wounds.

¹⁴Yes, prepare to fight with Babylon, all you nations round about; let the archers shoot at her; spare no arrows, for she has sinned against the Lord. ¹⁵Shout against her from every side. Look! She surrenders! Her walls have fallen. The Lord has taken vengeance. Do to her as she has done! ¹⁶Let the farm hands all depart. Let them rush back to their own lands as the enemies advance.

¹⁷The Israelites are like sheep the lions chase. First the king of Assyria ate them up; then Nebuchadnezzar, the king of Babylon, crunched their bones. ¹⁸Therefore the Lord, the God of Israel, says: Now I will punish the king of Babylon and his land as I punished the king of Assyria. ¹⁹And I will bring Israel home again to her own land, to feed in the fields of Carmel and Bashan and to be happy once more on Mount Ephraim and Mount Gilead. ²⁰In those days, says the Lord, no sin shall be found in Israel or in Judah, for I will pardon the remnant I preserve.

²¹Go up, O my warriors, against the land of Merathaim and against the people of Pekod. Yes, march against Babylon, the land of rebels, a land that I will judge! Annihilate them, as I have commanded you. ²²Let there be the shout of battle in the land, a shout of great destruction. ²³Babylon, the mightiest hammer in all the earth, lies broken and shattered. Babylon is desolate among the nations! ²⁴O Babylon, I have set a trap for you and you are caught, for you have fought against the Lord.

²⁵The Lord has opened his armory and brought out weapons to explode his wrath upon his enemies. The terror that befalls Babylon will be the work of the Lord God. ²⁶Yes, come against her from distant lands; break open her granaries; knock down her walls and houses into heaps of ruins and utterly destroy her; let nothing be left. ²⁷Not even her cattle—woe to them, too! Kill them all! For the time has come for Babylon to be devastated.

28But my people will flee; they will escape back to their own country to tell how the Lord their God has broken forth in fury upon those who destroyed his Temple.

29Send out a call for archers to come to Babylon; surround the city so that none can escape. Do to her as she has done to others, for she has haughtily defied the Lord, the Holy One of Israel. 30Her young men will fall in the streets and die; her warriors will all be killed. 31For see, I am against you, O people so proud; and now your day of reckoning has come. 32Land of pride, you will stumble and fall and no one will raise you up, for the Lord will light a fire in the cities of Babylon that will burn everything around them.

33The Lord says: The people of Israel and Judah have been wronged. Their captors hold them and refuse to let them go. 34But their Redeemer is strong. His name is the Lord Almighty. He will plead for them and see that they are freed to live again in quietness in Israel.

As for the people of Babylon—there is no rest for them! 35The sword of destruction shall smite the Chaldeans, says the Lord. It shall smite the people of Babylon—her princes and wise men too. 36All her wise counselors shall become fools! Panic shall seize her mightiest warriors! 37War shall devour her horses and chariots, and her allies from other lands shall become as weak as women. Her treasures shall all be robbed; 38even her water supply will fail. And why? Because the whole land is full of images, and the people are madly in love with their idols.

39Therefore this city of Babylon shall become inhabited by ostriches and jackals; it shall be a home for the wild animals of the desert. Never again shall it be lived in by human beings; it shall lie desolate forever. 40The Lord declares that he will destroy Babylon just as he destroyed Sodom and Gomorrah and their neighboring towns. No one has lived in them since, and no one will live again in Babylon.

41See them coming! A great army from the north! It is accompanied by many kings called by God from many lands. 42They are fully armed for slaughter; they are cruel and show no mercy; their battle cry roars like the surf against the shoreline. O Babylon, they ride against you fully ready for the battle.

43When the king of Babylon received the dispatch, his hands fell helpless at his sides; pangs of terror gripped him like the pangs of a woman in labor.

44*I will send against them an invader who will come upon them suddenly, like a lion from the jungles of Jordan that leaps upon the grazing sheep. I will put her defenders to flight and appoint over them whomsoever I please. For who is like me? What ruler can oppose my will? Who can call me to account?* 45*Listen to the plan of the Lord against Babylon, the land of the Chaldeans. For even little children shall be dragged away as slaves; oh, the horror; oh, the terror.* 46The whole earth shall shake at Babylon's fall, and her cry of despair shall be heard around the world.

TITUS 1:1–16

FROM: Paul, the slave of God and the messenger of Jesus Christ.

I have been sent to bring faith to those God has chosen and to teach them to know God's truth—the kind of truth that changes lives—so that they can have eternal life, which God promised them before the world began—and he cannot lie. 3And now in his own good time he has revealed this Good News and permits me to tell it to everyone. By command of God our Savior I have been trusted to do this work for him.

4*To:* Titus, who is truly my son in the affairs of the Lord.

May God the Father and Christ Jesus our Savior give you his blessings and his peace.

5I left you there on the island of Crete so that you could do whatever was needed to help strengthen each of its churches, and I asked you to appoint pastors in every city who would follow the instructions I gave you. 6The men you choose must be well thought of for their good lives; they must have only one wife and their children must love the Lord and not have a reputation for being wild or disobedient to their parents.

7These pastors must be men of blameless lives because they are God's ministers. They must not be proud or impatient; they must not be drunkards or fighters or greedy for money. 8They must enjoy having guests in their homes and must love all that is good. They must be sensible men, and fair. They must be clean minded and level headed. 9Their belief in the truth which they have been taught must be strong and steadfast, so that they will be able to teach it to others and show those who disagree with them where they are wrong.

10For there are many who refuse to obey; this is especially true among those who say that all Christians must obey the Jewish laws. But this is foolish talk; it blinds people to the truth, 11and it must be stopped. Already whole families have been turned away from the grace of God. Such teachers are only after your money. 12One of their own men, a prophet from Crete, has said about them, "These men of Crete are all liars; they are like lazy animals, living only to satisfy their stomachs." 13And this is true. So speak to the Christians there as sternly as necessary to make them strong in the faith, 14and to stop them from listening to Jewish folk tales and the demands of men who have turned their backs on the truth.

15A person who is pure of heart sees goodness and purity in everything; but a person whose own heart is evil and untrusting finds evil in everything, for his dirty mind and rebellious heart color all he sees and hears. 16Such persons claim they know God, but from seeing the way they act, one knows they don't. They are rotten and disobedient, worthless so far as doing anything good is concerned.

JEHOVAH is King! Let all the earth rejoice! Tell the farthest islands to be glad. 2Clouds and darkness surround him. Righteousness and justice are the foundation of his throne. 3Fire goes forth before him and burns up all his foes. 4His lightning flashes out across the world. The earth sees and trembles. 5The mountains melt like wax before the Lord of all the earth. 6The heavens declare his perfect righteousness; every nation sees his glory.

7Let those who worship idols be disgraced—all who brag about their worthless gods—for every god must bow to him! 8,9Jerusalem and all the cities of Judah have heard of your justice, Lord, and are glad that you reign in majesty over the entire earth and are far greater than these other gods.

10The Lord loves those who hate evil; he protects the lives of his people, and rescues them from the wicked. 11Light is sown for the godly and joy for the good. 12May all who are godly be happy in the Lord and crown him, our holy God.

SING a new song to the Lord telling about his mighty deeds! For he has won a mighty victory by his power and holiness. 2,3He has announced this victory and revealed it to every nation by fulfilling his promise to be kind to Israel. The whole earth has seen God's salvation of his people. 4That is why the earth breaks out in praise to God, and sings for utter joy!

5Sing your praise accompanied by music from the harp. 6Let the cornets and trumpets shout! Make a joyful symphony before the Lord, the King! 7Let the sea in all its vastness roar with praise! Let the earth and all those living on it shout, "Glory to the Lord."

8,9Let the waves clap their hands in glee, and the hills sing out their songs of joy before the Lord, for he is coming to judge the world with perfect justice.

The lazy man won't go out and work. "There might be a lion outside!" he says. He sticks to his bed like a door to its hinges! He is too tired even to lift his food from his dish to his mouth! Yet in his own opinion he is smarter than seven wise men.

OCTOBER 27

JEREMIAH 51:1–53

THE Lord says: I will stir up a destroyer against Babylon, against that whole land of the Chaldeans, and destroy it. ²Winnowers shall come and winnow her and blow her away; they shall come from every side to rise against her in her day of trouble. ³The arrows of the enemy shall strike down the bowmen of Babylon and pierce her warriors in their coats of mail. No one shall be spared; both young and old alike shall be destroyed. ⁴They shall fall down slain in the land of the Chaldeans, slashed to death in her streets. ⁵For the Lord Almighty has not forsaken Israel and Judah. He is still their God, but the land of the Chaldeans is filled with sin against the Holy One of Israel.

⁶Flee from Babylon! Save yourselves! Don't get trapped! If you stay, you will be destroyed when God takes his vengeance on all of Babylon's sins. ⁷Babylon has been as a gold cup in the Lord's hands, a cup from which he made the whole earth drink and go mad. ⁸But now, suddenly Babylon too has fallen. Weep for her; give her medicine; perhaps she can yet be healed. ⁹We would help her if we could, but nothing can save her now. Let her go. Abandon her and return to your own land, for God is judging her from heaven. ¹⁰The Lord has vindicated us. Come, let us declare in Jerusalem all the Lord our God has done.

¹¹Sharpen the arrows! Lift up the shields! For the Lord has stirred up the spirit of the kings of the Medes to march on Babylon and destroy her. This is his vengeance on those who wronged his people and desecrated his Temple. ¹²Prepare your defenses, Babylon! Set many watchmen on your walls; send out an ambush, for the Lord will do all he has said he would concerning Babylon. ¹³O wealthy port, great center of commerce, your end has come; the thread of your life is cut. ¹⁴The Lord Almighty has taken this vow, and sworn to it in his own name: Your cities shall be filled with enemies, like fields filled with locusts in a plague, and they shall lift to the skies their mighty shouts of victory.

¹⁵God made the earth by his power and wisdom. He stretched out the heavens by his understanding. ¹⁶When he speaks there is thunder in the heavens and he causes the vapors to rise around the world; he brings the lightning with the rain and the winds from his treasuries. ¹⁷Compared to him, all men are stupid beasts. They have no wisdom—none at all! The silversmith is dulled by the images he makes, for in making them he lies; for he calls them gods, when there is not a breath of life in them at all! ¹⁸Idols are nothing! They are lies! And the time is coming when God will come and see, and shall destroy them all. ¹⁹But the God of Israel is no idol! For he made everything there is, and Israel is his nation; the Lord Almighty is his name.

²⁰Cyrus is God's battleaxe and sword. I will use you, says the Lord, to break nations in pieces and to destroy many

kingdoms. 21With you I will crush armies, destroying the horse and his rider, the chariot and the charioteer— 22yes, and the civilians too, both old and young, young men and maidens, 23shepherds and flocks, farmers and oxen, captains and rulers; 24before your eyes I will repay Babylon and all the Chaldeans for all the evil they have done to my people, says the Lord.

25For see, I am against you, O mighty mountain, Babylon, destroyer of the earth! I will lift my hand against you and roll you down from your heights and leave you, a burnt-out mountain. 26You shall be desolate forever; even your stones shall never be used for building again. You shall be completely wiped out.

27Signal many nations to mobilize for war on Babylon. Sound the battle cry; bring out the armies of Ararat, Minni, and Ashkenaz. Appoint a leader; bring a multitude of horses! 28Bring against her the armies of the kings of the Medes and their generals, and the armies of all the countries they rule.

29Babylon trembles and writhes in pain, for all that the Lord has planned against her stands unchanged. Babylon will be left desolate without a living soul. 30Her mightiest soldiers no longer fight; they stay in their barracks. Their courage is gone; they have become as women. The invaders have burned the houses and broken down the city gates. 31Messengers from every side come running to the king to tell him all is lost! 32All the escape routes are blocked; the fortifications are burning and the army is in panic.

33For the Lord, the God of Israel, says: Babylon is like the wheat upon a threshing floor; in just a little while the flailing will begin.

34,35The Jews in Babylon say, "Nebuchadnezzar, king of Babylon, has eaten and crushed us and emptied out our strength; he has swallowed us like a great monster and filled his belly with our riches and cast us out of our own country. May Babylon be repaid for all she did to us! May she be paid in full for all our blood she spilled!"

36And the Lord replies: I will be your lawyer; I will plead your case; I will avenge you. I will dry up her river, her water supply, 37and Babylon shall become a heap of ruins, haunted by jackals, a land horrible to see, incredible, without a living soul. 38In their drunken feasts, the men of Babylon roar like lions. 39And while they lie inflamed with all their wine, I will prepare a different kind of feast for them, and make them drink until they fall unconscious to the floor, to sleep forever, never to waken again, says the Lord. 40I will bring them like lambs to the slaughter, like rams and goats.

41How Babylon is fallen—great Babylon, lauded by all the earth! The world can scarcely believe its eyes at Babylon's fall! 42The sea has risen upon Babylon; she is covered by its waves. 43Her cities lie in ruins—she is a dry wilderness where no one lives nor even travelers pass by. 44And I will punish Bel, the god of Babylon, and pull from his mouth what he has taken. The nations shall no longer come and worship him; the wall of Babylon has fallen.

45O my people, flee from Babylon; save yourselves from the fierce anger of the Lord. 46But don't panic when you hear the first rumor of approaching forces. For rumors will keep coming year by year. Then there will be a time of civil war as the governors of Babylon fight against each other. 47For the time is surely coming when I will punish this great city and all her idols; her dead shall lie in the streets. 48Heaven and earth shall rejoice, for out of the north shall come destroying armies against Babylon, says the Lord. 49Just as Babylon killed the people of Israel, so must she be killed. 50Go, you who escaped the sword! Don't stand and watch—flee while you can! Remember the Lord and return to Jerusalem far away!

51*"We are ashamed because the Temple of the Lord has been defiled by foreigners from Babylon."*

52Yes, says the Lord. But the time is

coming for the destruction of the idols of Babylon. All through the land will be heard the groans of the wounded. ⁵³Though Babylon be as powerful as heaven, though she increase her strength immeasurably, she shall die, says the Lord.

TITUS 2:1–15

BUT as for you, speak up for the right living that goes along with true Christianity. ²Teach the older men to be serious and unruffled; they must be sensible, knowing and believing the truth and doing everything with love and patience.

³Teach the older women to be quiet and respectful in everything they do. They must not go around speaking evil of others and must not be heavy drinkers, but they should be teachers of goodness. ⁴These older women must train the younger women to live quietly, to love their husbands and their children, ⁵and to be sensible and clean minded, spending their time in their own homes, being kind and obedient to their husbands, so that the Christian faith can't be spoken against by those who know them.

⁶In the same way, urge the young men to behave carefully, taking life seriously. ⁷And here you yourself must be an example to them of good deeds of every kind. Let everything you do reflect your love of the truth and the fact that you are in dead earnest about it. ⁸Your conversation should be so sensible and logical that anyone who wants to argue will be ashamed of himself because there won't be anything to criticize in anything you say!

⁹Urge slaves to obey their masters and to try their best to satisfy them. They must not talk back, ¹⁰nor steal, but must show themselves to be entirely trustworthy. In this way they will make people want to believe in our Savior and God.

¹¹For the free gift of eternal salvation is now being offered to everyone; ¹²and along with this gift comes the realization that God wants us to turn from godless living and sinful pleasures and to live good, God-fearing lives day after day, ¹³looking forward to that wonderful time we've been expecting, when his glory shall be seen—the glory of our great God and Savior Jesus Christ. ¹⁴He died under God's judgment against our sins, so that he could rescue us from constant falling into sin and make us his very own people, with cleansed hearts and real enthusiasm for doing kind things for others. ¹⁵You must teach these things and encourage your people to do them, correcting them when necessary as one who has every right to do so. Don't let anyone think that what you say is not important.

PSALM 99:1–9

JEHOVAH is King! Let the nations tremble! He is enthroned between the Guardian Angels. Let the whole earth shake.

²Jehovah sits in majesty in Zion, supreme above all rulers of the earth. ³Let them reverence your great and holy name.

⁴This mighty King is determined to give justice. Fairness is the touchstone of everything he does. He gives justice throughout Israel. ⁵Exalt the Lord our holy God! Bow low before his feet.

⁶When Moses and Aaron and Samuel, his prophet, cried to him for help, he answered them. ⁷He spoke to them from the pillar of cloud and they followed his instructions. ⁸O Jehovah our God! You answered them and forgave their sins, yet punished them when they went wrong.

⁹Exalt the Lord our God, and worship at his holy mountain in Jerusalem, for he is holy.

PROVERBS FOR TODAY/ 26:17

Yanking a dog's ears is no more foolish than interfering in an argument that isn't any of your business.

JEREMIAH 51:54—52:34

LISTEN! Hear the cry of great destruction out of Babylon, the land the Chaldeans rule! 55For the Lord is destroying Babylon; her mighty voice is stilled as the waves roar in upon her. 56Destroying armies come and slay her mighty men; all her weapons break in her hands, for the Lord God gives just punishment and is giving Babylon all her due. 57I will make drunk her princes, wise men, rulers, captains, warriors. They shall sleep and not wake up again! So says the King, the Lord Almighty. 58For the wide walls of Babylon shall be leveled to the ground and her high gates shall be burned; the builders from many lands have worked in vain—their work shall be destroyed by fire!

59During the fourth year of Zedekiah's reign, this message came to Jeremiah to give to Seraiah (son of Neriah, son of Mahseiah), concerning Seraiah's capture and exile to Babylon along with Zedekiah, king of Judah. (Seraiah was quartermaster of Zedekiah's army.) 60Jeremiah wrote on a scroll all the terrible things God had scheduled against Babylon—all the words written above— 61,62and gave the scroll to Seraiah and said to him, "When you get to Babylon, read what I have written and say, 'Lord, you have said that you will destroy Babylon so that not a living creature will remain, and it will be abandoned forever.' 63Then, when you have finished reading the scroll, tie a rock to it and throw it into the Euphrates River, 64and say, 'So shall Babylon sink, never more to rise, because of the evil I am bringing upon her.' "

(This ends Jeremiah's messages.)

ZEDEKIAH was twenty-one years old when he became king, and he reigned eleven years in Jerusalem. His mother's name was Hamutal (daughter of Jeremiah of Libnah). 2But he was a wicked king, just as Jehoiakim had been. 3Things be-

came so bad at last that the Lord, in his anger, saw to it that Zedekiah rebelled against the king of Babylon until he and the people of Israel were ejected from the Lord's presence in Jerusalem and Judah, and were taken away as captives to Babylon.

4In the ninth year of Zedekiah's reign, on the tenth day of the tenth month, Nebuchadnezzar, king of Babylon, came with all his army against Jerusalem and built forts around it, 5and laid siege to the city for two years. 6Then finally, on the ninth day of the fourth month, when the famine in the city was very serious, with the last of the food entirely gone, 7the people in the city tore a hole in the city wall and all the soldiers fled from the city during the night, going out by the gate between the two walls near the king's gardens (for the city was surrounded by the Chaldeans), and made a dash for it across the fields, toward Arabah.

8But the Chaldean soldiers chased them and caught King Zedekiah in some fields near Jericho—for all his army was scattered from him. 9They brought him to the king of Babylon who was staying in the city of Riblah in the kingdom of Hamath, and there judgment was passed upon him. 10He made Zedekiah watch while his sons and all the princes of Judah were killed before his eyes, 11and then his eyes were gouged out and he was taken in chains to Babylon and put in prison for the rest of his life.

12On the tenth day of the fifth month during the nineteenth year of the reign of Nebuchadnezzar, king of Babylon, Nebuzaradan, captain of the guard, arrived in Jerusalem, 13and burned the Temple and the palace and all the larger homes, 14and set the Chaldean army to work tearing down the walls of the city. 15Then he took to Babylon, as captives, some of the poorest of the people—along with those who survived the city's destruction, and those who had deserted Zedekiah and had come over to the Babylonian army, and the tradesmen who were left. ¹⁶But he left some of the poorest people to care for the crops as vinedressers and plowmen.

¹⁷The Babylonians dismantled the two large bronze pillars that stood at the entrance of the Temple, and the bronze laver and bronze bulls on which it stood, and carted them off to Babylon. ¹⁸And he took along all the bronze pots and kettles, and ash shovels used at the altar, and the snuffers, spoons, bowls, and all the other items used in the Temple. ¹⁹He also took the firepans and the solid gold and silver candlesticks and cups and bowls.

²⁰The weight of the two enormous pillars and the laver and twelve bulls was tremendous. They had no way of estimating it. (They had been made in the days of King Solomon.) ²¹For the pillars were each twenty-seven feet high and eighteen feet in circumference, hollow, with three-inch walls. ²²The top 7½ feet of each column had bronze carvings, a network of bronze pomegranates. ²³There were ninety-six pomegranates on the sides, and on the network round about there were a hundred more.

²⁴,²⁵The captain of the guard took along with him, as his prisoners, Seraiah the chief priest, and Zephaniah his assistant, the three chief Temple guards, one of the commanding officers of the army, seven of the king's special counselors discovered in the city, and the secretary of the general-in-chief of the Jewish army (who was in charge of recruitment) and sixty other men of importance found hiding. ²⁶He took them to the king of Babylon at Riblah, ²⁷where the king killed them all.

So it was that Judah's exile was accomplished.

²⁸The number of captives taken to Babylon in the seventh year of Nebuchadnezzar's reign was 3,023. ²⁹Then, eleven years later, he took 832 more; ³⁰five years after that he sent Nebuzaradan, his captain of the guard, and took 745—a total of 4,600 captives in all.

³¹On February 25, of the 37th year of the imprisonment in Babylon of Jehoiachin, king of Judah, Evil-merodach, who became king of Babylon that year, was kind to King Jehoiachin and brought him out of prison, ³²and spoke pleasantly to him and gave him preference over all the other kings in Babylon, ³³and gave him new clothes and fed him from the king's kitchen as long as he lived. ³⁴And he was given a regular allowance to cover his daily needs until the day of his death.

TITUS 3:1-15

REMIND your people to obey the government and its officers, and always to be obedient and ready for any honest work. ²They must not speak evil of anyone, nor quarrel, but be gentle and truly courteous to all.

³Once we, too, were foolish and disobedient; we were misled by others and became slaves to many evil pleasures and wicked desires. Our lives were full of resentment and envy. We hated others and they hated us.

⁴But when the time came for the kindness and love of God our Savior to appear, ⁵then he saved us—not because we were good enough to be saved, but because of his kindness and pity—by washing away our sins and giving us the new joy of the indwelling Holy Spirit ⁶whom he poured out upon us with wonderful fullness—and all because of what Jesus Christ our Savior did ⁷so that he could declare us good in God's eyes—all because of his great kindness; and now we can share in the wealth of the eternal life he gives us, and we are eagerly looking forward to receiving it. ⁸These things I have told you are all true. Insist on them so that Christians will be careful to do good deeds all the time, for this is not only right, but it brings results.

⁹Don't get involved in arguing over unanswerable questions and controver-

sial theological ideas; keep out of arguments and quarrels about obedience to Jewish laws, for this kind of thing isn't worthwhile; it only does harm. 10If anyone is causing divisions among you, he should be given a first and second warning. After that have nothing more to do with him, 11for such a person has a wrong sense of values. He is sinning, and he knows it.

12I am planning to send either Artemas or Tychicus to you. As soon as one of them arrives, please try to meet me at Nicopolis as quickly as you can, for I have decided to stay there for the winter. 13Do everything you can to help Zenas the lawyer and Apollos with their trip; see that they are given everything they need. 14For our people must learn to help all who need their assistance, that their lives will be fruitful.

15Everybody here sends greetings. Please say "hello" to all of the Christian friends there. May God's blessings be with you all.

Sincerely,
Paul

PSALM 100:1–5

SHOUT with joy before the Lord, O earth! 2Obey him gladly; come before him, singing with joy.

3Try to realize what this means—the Lord is God! He made us—we are his people, the sheep of his pasture.

4Go through his open gates with great thanksgiving; enter his courts with praise. Give thanks to him and bless his name. 5For the Lord is always good. He is always loving and kind, and his faithfulness goes on and on to each succeeding generation.

PROVERBS FOR TODAY/ 26:18–19

A man who is caught lying to his neighbor and says, "I was just fooling," is like a madman throwing around firebrands, arrows, and death!

OCTOBER 29

LAMENTATIONS 1:1—2:19

JERUSALEM'S streets, once thronged with people, are silent now. Like a widow broken with grief, she sits alone in her mourning. She, once queen of nations, is now a slave.

2She sobs through the night; tears run down her cheeks. Among all her lovers, there is none to help her. All her friends are now her enemies.

3Why is Judah led away, a slave? Because of all the wrong she did to others, making them her slaves. Now she sits in exile far away. There is no rest, for those she persecuted have turned and conquered her.

4The roads to Zion mourn, no longer filled with joyous throngs who come to celebrate the Temple feasts; the city gates are silent, her priests groan, her virgins have been dragged away. Bitterly she weeps.

5Her enemies prosper, for the Lord has punished Jerusalem for all her many sins; her young children are captured and taken far away as slaves.

6All her beauty and her majesty are gone; her princes are like starving deer that search for pasture—helpless game too weak to keep on running from their foes.

7And now in the midst of all Jerusalem's sadness she remembers happy bygone days. She thinks of all the precious joys she had before her mocking enemy struck her down—and there was no one to give her aid.

8For Jerusalem sinned so horribly; therefore she is tossed away like dirty rags. All who honored her despise her now, for they have seen her stripped naked and humiliated. She groans and hides her face.

9She indulged herself in immorality, and refused to face the fact that punishment was sure to come. Now she lies in the gutter with no one left to lift her out. "O Lord," she cries, "see my plight. The enemy has triumphed."

10Her enemies have plundered her completely, taking everything precious she owns. She has seen foreign nations violate her sacred Temple—foreigners you had forbidden even to enter.

11Her people groan and cry for bread; they have sold all they have for food to give a little strength. "Look, O Lord," she prays, "and see how I'm despised."

12Is it nothing to you, all you who pass by? Look and see if there is any sorrow like my sorrow, because of all the Lord has done to me in the day of his fierce wrath.

13He has sent fire from heaven that burns within my bones; he has placed a pitfall in my path and turned me back. He has left me sick and desolate the whole day through.

14He wove my sins into ropes to hitch me to a yoke of slavery. He sapped my strength and gave me to my enemies; I am helpless in their hands.

15The Lord has trampled all my mighty men. A great army has come at his command to crush the noblest youth. The Lord has trampled his beloved city as grapes in a winepress.

16For all these things I weep; tears flow down my cheeks. My Comforter is far away—he who alone could help me. My children have no future; we are a conquered land.

17Jerusalem pleads for help but no one comforts her. For the Lord has spoken: "Let her neighbors be her foes! Let her be thrown out like filthy rags!"

18And the Lord is right, for we rebelled. And yet, O people everywhere, behold and see my anguish and despair, for my sons and daughters are taken far away as slaves to distant lands.

19I begged my allies for their help. False hope—they could not help at all. Nor could my priests and elders—they were starving in the streets while searching through the garbage dumps for bread.

20*See, O Lord, my anguish;* my heart is broken and my soul despairs, for I have terribly rebelled. In the streets the sword awaits me; at home, disease and death.

21*Hear my groans!* And there is no one anywhere to help. All my enemies have heard my troubles and they are glad to see what you have done. And yet, O Lord, the time will surely come—for you have promised it—when you will do to them as you have done to me.

22Look also on their sins, O Lord, and punish them as you have punished me, for my sighs are many and my heart is faint.

A cloud of anger from the Lord has overcast Jerusalem; the fairest city of Israel lies in the dust of the earth, cast from the heights of heaven at his command. In his day of awesome fury he has shown no mercy even to his Temple.

2The Lord without mercy has destroyed every home in Israel. In his wrath he has broken every fortress, every wall. He has brought the kingdom to dust, with all its rulers.

3All the strength of Israel vanishes beneath his wrath. He has withdrawn his protection as the enemy attacks. God burns across the land of Israel like a raging fire.

4He bends his bow against his people as though he were an enemy. His strength is used against them to kill their finest youth. His fury is poured out like fire upon them.

5Yes, the Lord has vanquished Israel like an enemy. He has destroyed her forts and palaces. Sorrows and tears are his portion for Jerusalem.

6He has violently broken down his Temple as though it were a booth of leaves and branches in a garden! No longer can the people celebrate their holy feasts and Sabbaths. Kings and priests together fall before his wrath.

7The Lord has rejected his own altar, for he despises the false "worship" of his people; he has given their palaces to their enemies, who carouse in the Temple as Israel used to do on days of holy feasts!

8The Lord determined to destroy Jerusalem. He laid out an unalterable line of destruction. Therefore the ramparts and walls fell down before him.

9Jerusalem's gates are useless. All their locks and bars are broken, for he has crushed them. Her kings and princes are enslaved in far-off lands, without a temple, without a divine law to govern them, or prophetic vision to guide them.

10The elders of Jerusalem sit upon the ground in silence, clothed in sackcloth; they throw dust upon their heads in sorrow and despair. The virgins of Jerusalem hang their heads in shame.

11I have cried until the tears no longer come; my heart is broken, my spirit poured out, as I see what has happened to my people; little children and tiny babies are fainting and dying in the streets.

12"Mama, Mama, we want food," they cry, and then collapse upon their mothers' shrunken breasts. Their lives ebb away like those wounded in battle.

13In all the world has there ever been such sorrow? O Jerusalem, what can I compare your anguish to? How can I comfort you? For your wound is deep as the sea. Who can heal you?

14Your "prophets" have said so many foolish things, false to the core. They have not tried to hold you back from slavery by pointing out your sins. They lied and said that all was well.

15All who pass by scoff and shake their heads and say, "Is this the city called 'Most Beautiful in All the World,' and 'Joy of All the Earth'?"

16All your enemies deride you. They hiss and grind their teeth and say, "We have destroyed her at last! Long have we waited for this hour and it is finally here! With our own eyes we've seen her fall."

17But it is the Lord who did it, just as he had warned. He has fulfilled the promises of doom he made so long ago. He has destroyed Jerusalem without mercy and caused her enemies to rejoice over her and boast of their power.

18Then the people wept before the Lord. O walls of Jerusalem, let tears fall down upon you like a river; give yourselves no rest from weeping day or night.

19Rise in the night and cry to your God. Pour out your hearts like water to the Lord; lift up your hands to him; plead for your children as they faint with hunger in the streets.

PHILEMON 1:1–25

FROM: Paul, in jail for preaching the Good News about Jesus Christ, and from Brother Timothy.

To: Philemon, our much loved fellow worker, and to the church that meets in your home, and to Apphia our sister, and to Archippus who like myself is a soldier of the cross.

3May God our Father and the Lord Jesus Christ give you his blessings and his peace.

4I always thank God when I am praying for you, dear Philemon, 5because I keep hearing of your love and trust in the Lord Jesus and in his people. 6And I pray that as you share your faith with others it will grip their lives too, as they see the wealth of good things in you that come from Christ Jesus. 7I myself have gained much joy and comfort from your love, my brother, because your kindness has so often refreshed the hearts of God's people.

8,9Now I want to ask a favor of you. I could demand it of you in the name of Christ because it is the right thing for you to do, but I love you and prefer just to ask you—I, Paul, an old man now, here in jail for the sake of Jesus Christ. 10My plea is that you show kindness to my child Onesimus, whom I won to the Lord while here in my chains. 11Onesimus (whose name means "Useful") hasn't been of much use to you in the past, but now he is going to be of real use to both of us. 12I am sending him back to you, and with him comes my own heart.

13I really wanted to keep him here with me while I am in these chains for preaching the Good News, and you would have been helping me through him, 14but I didn't want to do it without your consent. I didn't want you to be kind because you had to but because you wanted to. 15Perhaps you could think of it this way: that he ran away from you for a little while so that now he can be yours forever, 16no longer only a slave, but something much better—a beloved brother, especially to me. Now he will mean much more to you too, because he is not only a servant but also your brother in Christ.

17If I am really your friend, give him the same welcome you would give to me if I were the one who was coming. 18If he has harmed you in any way or stolen anything from you, charge me for it. 19I will pay it back (I, Paul, personally guarantee this by writing it here with my own hand) but I won't mention how much you owe me! The fact is, you even owe me your very soul! 20Yes, dear brother, give me joy with this loving act and my weary heart will praise the Lord.

21I've written you this letter because I am positive that you will do what I ask and even more!

22Please keep a guest room ready for me, for I am hoping that God will answer your prayers and let me come to you soon.

23Epaphras my fellow prisoner, who is also here for preaching Christ Jesus, sends you his greetings. 24So do Mark, Aristarchus, Demas and Luke, my fellow workers.

25The blessings of our Lord Jesus Christ be upon your spirit.

Paul

PSALM 101:1–8

I will sing about your lovingkindness and your justice, Lord. I will sing your praises!

2I will try to walk a blameless path, but how I need your help, especially in my own home, where I long to act as I should.

3Help me to refuse the low and vulgar things; help me to abhor all crooked deals of every kind, to have no part in them. 4I will reject all selfishness and stay away from every evil. 5I will not tolerate anyone who secretly slanders his neighbors; I will not permit conceit and pride. 6I will make the godly of the land my heroes, and invite them to my home. Only those who are truly good shall be my servants. 7But I will not allow those who deceive and lie to stay in my house. 8My daily task will be to ferret out criminals and free the city of God from their grip.

PROVERBS FOR TODAY/ 26:20
Fire goes out for lack of fuel, and tensions disappear when gossip stops.

OCTOBER 30

LAMENTATIONS 2:20—3:66

O Lord, think! These are your own people to whom you are doing this. Shall mothers eat their little children, those they bounced upon their knees? Shall priests and prophets die within the Temple of the Lord?

21See them lying in the streets—old and young, boys and girls, killed by the enemies' swords. You have killed them, Lord, in your anger; you have killed them without mercy.

22You have deliberately called for this destruction; in the day of your anger none escaped or remained. All my little children lie dead upon the streets before the enemy.

I am the man who has seen the afflictions that come from the rod of God's wrath. 2He has brought me into deepest darkness, shutting out all light. 3He has turned against me. Day and night his hand is heavy on me. 4He has made me old and has broken my bones.

5He has built forts against me and surrounded me with anguish and distress. 6He buried me in dark places, like those long dead. 7He has walled me in; I cannot escape; he has fastened me with heavy chains. 8And though I cry and shout, he will not hear my prayers! 9He has shut me into a place of high, smooth walls; he has filled my path with detours.

10He lurks like a bear, like a lion, waiting to attack me. 11He has dragged me into the underbrush and torn me with his claws, and left me bleeding and desolate.

12He has bent his bow and aimed it squarely at me, 13and sent his arrows deep within my heart.

14My own people laugh at me; all day long they sing their ribald songs.

15He has filled me with bitterness, and given me a cup of deepest sorrows to drink. 16He has made me eat gravel and broken my teeth; he has rolled me in ashes and dirt. 17O Lord, all peace and all prosperity have long since gone, for you have taken them away. I have forgotten what enjoyment is. 18All hope is gone; my strength has turned to water, for the Lord has left me. 19Oh, remember the bitterness and suffering you have dealt to me! 20For I can never forget these awful years; always my soul will live in utter shame.

21*Yet there is one ray of hope:* 22*his compassion never ends.* It is only the Lord's mercies that have kept us from complete destruction. 23Great is his faithfulness; his lovingkindness begins afresh each day. 24My soul claims the Lord as my inheritance; therefore I will hope in him. 25The Lord is wonderfully good to those who wait for him, to those who seek for him. 26It is good both to hope and wait quietly for the salvation of the Lord.

27It is good for a young man to be under discipline, 28for it causes him to sit apart in silence beneath the Lord's demands, 29to lie face downward in the dust; then at last there is hope for him. 30Let him turn the other cheek to those who strike him, and accept their awful insults, 31for the Lord will not abandon him forever. 32Although God gives him grief, yet he will show compassion too, according to the greatness of his lovingkindness. 33For he does not enjoy afflicting men and causing sorrow.

34,35,36But you have trampled and crushed beneath your feet the lowly of the world, and deprived men of their God-given rights, and refused them justice. No wonder the Lord has had to deal with you! 37For who can act against you without the Lord's permission? 38It is the Lord who helps one and harms another.

39Why then should we, mere humans as we are, murmur and complain when punished for our sins? 40Let us examine ourselves instead, and repent and turn again to the Lord. 41Let us lift our hearts and hands to him in heaven, 42for we have sinned; we have rebelled against the Lord, and he has not forgotten it.

43You have engulfed us by your anger, Lord, and slain us without mercy. 44You have veiled yourself as with a cloud so that our prayers do not reach through. 45You have made us as refuse and garbage among the nations. 46All our enemies have spoken out against us. 47We are filled with fear, for we are trapped and desolate, destroyed.

48,49My eyes flow day and night with never-ending streams of tears because of the destruction of my people. 50Oh, that the Lord might look down from heaven and respond to my cry! 51My heart is breaking over what is happening to the young girls of Jerusalem.

52My enemies, whom I have never harmed, chased me as though I were a bird. 53They threw me in a well and capped it with a rock. 54The water flowed above my head. I thought, This is the end! 55But I called upon your name, O Lord, from deep within the well, 56and you heard me! You listened to my pleading; you heard my weeping! 57Yes, you came at my despairing cry and told me not to fear.

58O Lord, you are my lawyer! Plead my case! For you have redeemed my life. 59You have seen the wrong they did to me; be my Judge, to prove me right. 60You have seen the plots my foes have laid against me. 61You have heard the vile names they have called me, 62and all they say about me and their whispered plans. 63See how they laugh and sing with glee, preparing my doom.

64O Lord, repay them well for all the evil they have done. 65Harden their hearts and curse them, Lord. 66Go after them in fierce pursuit and wipe them off the earth, beneath the heavens of the Lord.

HEBREWS 1:1–14

LONG ago God spoke in many different ways to our fathers through the prophets [in visions, dreams, and even face to face], telling them little by little about his plans.

2But now in these days he has spoken to us through his Son to whom he has given everything, and through whom he made the world and everything there is.

3God's Son shines out with God's glory, and all that God's Son is and does marks him as God. He regulates the universe by the mighty power of his command. He is the one who died to cleanse us and clear our record of all sin, and then sat down in highest honor beside the great God of heaven.

4Thus he became far greater than the angels, as proved by the fact that his name "Son of God," which was passed on to him from his Father, is far greater than the names and titles of the angels. 5,6For God never said to any angel, "You are my Son, and today I have given you the honor that goes with that name." But God said it about Jesus. Another time he said, "I am his Father and he is my Son." And still another time—when his firstborn Son came to earth—God said, "Let all the angels of God worship him."

7God speaks of his angels as messengers swift as the wind and as servants made of flaming fire; 8but of his Son he says, "Your Kingdom, O God, will last forever and ever; its commands are always just and right. 9You love right and hate wrong; so God, even your God, has poured out more gladness upon you than on anyone else."

10God also called him "Lord" when he said, "Lord, in the beginning you made the earth, and the heavens are the work of your hands. 11They will disappear into nothingness, but you will remain forever. They will become worn out like old clothes, 12and some day you will fold them up and replace them. But you yourself will never change, and your years will never end."

13And did God ever say to an angel, as he does to his Son, "Sit here beside me in honor until I crush all your enemies beneath your feet"? 14No, for the angels are only spirit-messengers sent out to help and care for those who are to receive his salvation.

LORD, hear my prayer! Listen to my plea! 2Don't turn away from me in this time of my distress. Bend down your ear and give me speedy answers, 3,4for my days disappear like smoke. My health is broken and my heart is sick; it is trampled like grass and is withered. My food is tasteless, and I have lost my appetite. 5I am reduced to skin and bones because of all my groaning and despair. 6I am like a vulture in a far-off wilderness, or like an owl alone in the desert. 7I lie awake, lonely as a solitary sparrow on the roof.

8My enemies taunt me day after day and curse at me. 9,10I eat ashes instead of bread. My tears run down into my drink because of your anger against me, because of your wrath. For you have rejected me and thrown me out. 11My life is passing swiftly as the evening shadows. I am withering like grass, 12while you, Lord, are a famous King forever. Your fame will endure to every generation.

13I know that you will come and have mercy on Jerusalem—and now is the time to pity her—the time you promised help. 14For your people love every stone in her walls and feel sympathy for every grain of dust in her streets. 15Now let the nations and their rulers tremble before the Lord, before his glory. 16For Jehovah will rebuild Jerusalem! He will appear in his glory!

17He will listen to the prayers of the destitute, for he is never too busy to heed their requests. 18I am recording this so that future generations will also praise the Lord for all that he has done. And a people that shall be created shall praise the Lord. 19Tell them that God looked down from his temple in heaven, 20and heard the groans of his people in slavery—they were children of death—and released them, 21,22so that multitudes would stream to the Temple in Jerusalem to praise him, and his praises were sung throughout the city; and many rulers throughout the earth came to worship him.

23He has cut me down in middle life, shortening my days. 24But I cried to him, "O God, you live forever and forever! Don't let me die half through my years! 25In ages past you laid the foundations of the earth, and made the heavens with your hands! 26They shall perish, but you go on forever. They will grow old, like worn-out clothing, and you will change them like a man putting on a new shirt and throwing away the old one! 27But you yourself never grow old. You are forever, and your years never end.

28"But our families will continue; generation after generation will be preserved by your protection."

PROVERBS FOR TODAY/ 26:21–22

A quarrelsome man starts fights as easily as a match sets fire to paper. Gossip is a dainty morsel eaten with great relish.

OCTOBER 31

LAMENTATIONS 4:1—5:22

HOW the finest gold has lost its luster! For the inlaid Temple walls are scattered in the streets! 2The cream of our youth—the finest of the gold—are treated as earthenware pots. 3,4Even the jackals feed their young, but not my people, Israel. They are like cruel desert ostriches, heedless of their babies' cries. The children's tongues stick to the roofs of their mouths for thirst, for there is not a drop of water left. Babies cry for bread but no one can give them any. 5Those who used to eat fastidiously are begging in the streets for anything at all. Those brought up in palaces now scratch in garbage pits for food. 6For the sin of my people is greater than that of Sodom, where utter disaster struck in a moment without the hand of man.

7Our princes were lean and tanned, the finest specimens of men; 8but now their faces are as black as soot. No one can recognize them. Their skin sticks to their bones; it is dry and hard and withered. 9Those killed by the sword are far better off than those who die of slow starvation. 10Tenderhearted women have cooked and eaten their own children; thus they survived the siege.

11But now at last the anger of the Lord is satisfied; his fiercest anger has been poured out. He started a fire in Jerusalem that burned it down to its foundations. 12Not a king in all the earth—no one in all the world—would have believed an enemy could enter through Jerusalem's gates! 13Yet God permitted it because of the sins of her prophets and priests, who defiled the city by shedding innocent blood. 14Now these same men are blindly staggering through the streets, covered with blood, defiling everything they touch.

15"Get away!" the people shout at them. "You are defiled!" They flee to distant lands and wander there among the foreigners; but none will let them stay. 16The Lord himself has dealt with them; he no longer helps them, for they persecuted the priests and elders who stayed true to God.

17We look for our allies to come and save us, but we look in vain. The nation we expected most to help us makes no move at all.

18We can't go into the streets without danger to our lives. Our end is near— our days are numbered. We are doomed. 19Our enemies are swifter than the eagles; if we flee to the mountains they find us. If we hide in the wilderness, they are waiting for us there. 20Our king— the life of our life, the Lord's anointed— was captured in their snares. Yes, even our mighty king, about whom we had boasted that under his protection we could hold our own against any nation on earth!

21Do you rejoice, O people of Edom, in the land of Uz? But you too will feel the awful anger of the Lord. 22Israel's exile for her sins will end at last, but Edom's never.

O Lord, remember all that has befallen us; see what sorrows we must bear! 2Our homes, our nation, now are filled with foreigners. 3We are orphans—our fathers dead, our mothers widowed. 4We must even pay for water to drink; our fuel is sold to us at the highest of prices. 5We bow our necks beneath the victors' feet; unending work is now our lot. 6We beg for bread from Egypt, and Assyria too.

7Our fathers sinned but died before the hand of judgment fell. We have borne the blow that they deserved!

8Our former servants have become our masters; there is no one left to save us. 9We went into the wilderness to hunt for food, risking death from enemies. 10Our skin was black from famine. 11They rape the women of Jerusalem and the girls in Judah's cities. 12Our princes are hanged by their thumbs. Even aged men are treated with contempt. 13They take away the young men to grind their grain and the little children stagger beneath their heavy loads.

14The old men sit no longer in the city gates; the young no longer dance and sing. 15The joy of our hearts has ended; our dance has turned to death. 16Our glory is gone. The crown is fallen from our head. Woe upon us for our sins. 17Our hearts are faint and weary; our eyes grow dim. 18Jerusalem and the Temple of the Lord are desolate, deserted by all but wild animals lurking in the ruins.

19O Lord, forever you remain the

same! Your throne continues from generation to generation. 20Why do you forget us forever? Why do you forsake us for so long? 21Turn us around and bring us back to you again! That is our only hope! Give us back the joys we used to have! *22Or have you utterly rejected us? Are you angry with us still?*

HEBREWS 2:1–18

So we must listen very carefully to the truths we have heard, or we may drift away from them. 2For since the messages from angels have always proved true and people have always been punished for disobeying them, 3what makes us think that we can escape if we are indifferent to this great salvation announced by the Lord Jesus himself, and passed on to us by those who heard him speak?

4God always has shown us that these messages are true by signs and wonders and various miracles and by giving certain special abilities from the Holy Spirit to those who believe; yes, God has assigned such gifts to each of us.

5And the future world we are talking about will not be controlled by angels. 6No, for in the book of Psalms David says to God, "What is mere man that you are so concerned about him? And who is this Son of Man you honor so highly? 7For though you made him lower than the angels for a little while, now you have crowned him with glory and honor. 8And you have put him in complete charge of everything there is. Nothing is left out."

We have not yet seen all of this take place, 9but we do see Jesus—who for awhile was a little lower than the angels—crowned now by God with glory and honor because he suffered death for us. Yes, because of God's great kindness, Jesus tasted death for everyone in all the world.

10And it was right and proper that God, who made everything for his own glory, should allow Jesus to suffer, for in doing this he was bringing vast multitudes of God's people to heaven; for his suffering made Jesus a perfect Leader, one fit to bring them into their salvation.

11We who have been made holy by Jesus, now have the same Father he has. That is why Jesus is not ashamed to call us his brothers. 12For he says in the book of Psalms, "I will talk to my brothers about God my Father, and together we will sing his praises." 13At another time he said, "I will put my trust in God along with my brothers." And at still another time, "See, here am I and the children God gave me."

14Since we, God's children, are human beings—made of flesh and blood—he became flesh and blood too by being born in human form; for only as a human being could he die and in dying break the power of the devil who had the power of death. 15Only in that way could he deliver those who through fear of death have been living all their lives as slaves to constant dread.

16We all know he did not come as an angel but as a human being—yes, a Jew. 17And it was necessary for Jesus to be like us, his brothers, so that he could be our merciful and faithful High Priest before God, a Priest who would be both merciful to us and faithful to God in dealing with the sins of the people. 18For since he himself has now been through suffering and temptation, he knows what it is like when we suffer and are tempted, and he is wonderfully able to help us.

PSALM 103:1–22

I bless the holy name of God with all my heart. 2Yes, I will bless the Lord and not forget the glorious things he does for me.

3He forgives all my sins. He heals me. 4He ransoms me from hell. He surrounds me with lovingkindness and tender mercies. 5He fills my life with good things! My youth is renewed like the eagle's! 6He gives justice to all who are treated unfairly. 7He revealed his will and nature to Moses and the people of Israel.

8He is merciful and tender toward

those who don't deserve it; he is slow to get angry and full of kindness and love. 9He never bears a grudge, nor remains angry forever. 10He has not punished us as we deserve for all our sins, 11for his mercy toward those who fear and honor him is as great as the height of the heavens above the earth. 12He has removed our sins as far away from us as the east is from the west. 13He is like a father to us, tender and sympathetic to those who reverence him. 14For he knows we are but dust, 15and that our days are few and brief, like grass, like flowers, 16blown by the wind and gone forever.

17,18But the lovingkindness of the Lord is from everlasting to everlasting, to those who reverence him; his salvation is to children's children of those who are faithful to his covenant and remember to obey him!

19The Lord has made the heavens his throne; from there he rules over everything there is. 20Bless the Lord, you mighty angels of his who carry out his orders, listening for each of his commands. 21Yes, bless the Lord, you armies of his angels who serve him constantly.

22Let everything everywhere bless the Lord. And how I bless him too!

PROVERBS FOR TODAY/ 26:23

Pretty words may hide a wicked heart, just as a pretty glaze covers a common clay pot.

NOVEMBER 1

EZEKIEL 1:1—3:15

EZEKIEL *was a priest (the son of Buzi) who lived with the Jewish exiles beside the Chebar Canal in Babylon.*

One day late in June, when I was thirty years old, the heavens were suddenly opened to me and I saw visions from God. 4I saw, in this vision, a great storm coming toward me from the north, driving before it a huge cloud glowing with fire, with a mass of fire inside that flashed continually; and in the fire there was something that shone like polished brass.

5Then from the center of the cloud, four strange forms appeared that looked like men, 6except that each had four faces and two pairs of wings! 7Their legs were like those of men, but their feet were cloven like calves' feet, and shone like burnished brass. 8And beneath each of their wings I could see human hands.

9The four living beings were joined wing to wing, and they flew straight forward without turning. 10Each had the face of a man [in front], with a lion's face on the right side [of his head], and the face of an ox on the left side, and the face of an eagle at the back! 11Each had two pairs of wings spreading out from the middle of his back. One pair stretched out to attach to the wings of the living beings on each side, and the other pair covered his body. 12Wherever their spirit went they went, going straight forward without turning.

13Going up and down among them were other forms that glowed like bright coals of fire or brilliant torches, and it was from these the lightning flashed. 14The living beings darted to and fro, swift as lightning.

15As I stared at all of this, I saw four wheels on the ground beneath them, one wheel belonging to each. 16The wheels looked as if they were made of polished amber and each wheel was constructed with a second wheel crosswise inside. ¹⁷They could go in any of the four directions without having to face around. ¹⁸The four wheels had rims and spokes, and the rims were filled with eyes around their edges.

¹⁹,²⁰,²¹When the four living beings flew forward, the wheels moved forward with them. When they flew upwards, the wheels went up too. When the living beings stopped, the wheels stopped. For the spirit of the four living beings was in the wheels; so wherever their spirit went, the wheels and the living beings went there too.

²²The sky spreading out above them looked as though it were made of crystal; it was inexpressibly beautiful.

²³The wings of each stretched straight out to touch the others' wings, and each had two wings covering his body. ²⁴And as they flew, their wings roared like waves against the shore, or like the voice of God, or like the shouting of a mighty army. When they stopped they let down their wings. ²⁵And every time they stopped, there came a voice from the crystal sky above them.

²⁶For high in the sky above them was what looked like a throne made of beautiful blue sapphire stones, and upon it sat someone who appeared to be a Man.

²⁷,²⁸From his waist up, he seemed to be all glowing bronze, dazzling like fire; and from his waist down he seemed to be entirely flame, and there was a glowing halo like a rainbow all around him. That was the way the glory of the Lord appeared to me. And when I saw it, I fell face downward on the ground, and heard the voice of someone speaking to me:

AND he said to me: "Stand up, son of dust, and I will talk to you."

²And the Spirit entered into me as he spoke, and set me on my feet.

³"Son of dust," he said, "I am sending you to the nation of Israel, to a nation rebelling against me. They and their fathers have kept on sinning against me

until this very hour. ⁴For they are a hardhearted, stiff-necked people. But I am sending you to give them my messages—the messages of the Lord God. ⁵And whether they listen or not (for remember, they are rebels), they will at least know they have had a prophet among them.

⁶"Son of dust, don't be afraid of them; don't be frightened even though their threats are sharp and barbed and sting like scorpions. Don't be dismayed by their dark scowls. For remember, they are rebels! ⁷You must give them my messages whether they listen or not (but they won't, for they are utter rebels). ⁸Listen, son of dust, to what I say to you. Don't you be a rebel too! Open your mouth and eat what I give you."

⁹,¹⁰Then I looked and saw a hand holding out to me a scroll, with writing on both sides. He unrolled it, and I saw that it was full of warnings and sorrows and pronouncements of doom.

AND he said to me: "Son of dust, eat what I am giving you—eat this scroll! Then go and give its message to the people of Israel."

²So I took the scroll.

³"Eat it all," he said. And when I ate it, it tasted sweet as honey.

⁴Then he said: "Son of dust, I am sending you to the people of Israel with my messages. ⁵I am not sending you to some far-off foreign land where you can't understand the language— ⁶no, not to tribes with strange, difficult tongues. (If I did, they would listen!) ⁷I am sending you to the people of Israel, and they won't listen to you any more than they listen to me! For the whole lot of them are hard, impudent and stubborn. ⁸But see, I have made you hard and stubborn too—as tough as they are. ⁹I have made your forehead as hard as rock. So don't be afraid of them, or fear their sullen, angry looks, even though they are such rebels."

¹⁰Then he added: "Son of dust, let all my words sink deep into your own heart first; listen to them carefully for yourself.

11Then, afterward, go to your people in exile, and whether or not they will listen, tell them: This is what the Lord God says!"

12Then the Spirit lifted me up and the glory of the Lord began to move away, accompanied by the sound of a great earthquake. 13It was the noise of the wings of the living beings as they touched against each other, and the sound of their wheels beside them.

14,15The Spirit lifted me up and took me away to Tel Abib, another colony of Jewish exiles beside the Chebar River. I went in bitterness and anger, but the hand of the Lord was strong upon me. And I sat among them, overwhelmed, for seven days.

HEBREWS 3:1–19

THEREFORE, dear brothers whom God has set apart for himself— you who are chosen for heaven— I want you to think now about this Jesus who is God's Messenger and the High Priest of our faith.

2For Jesus was faithful to God who appointed him High Priest, just as Moses also faithfully served in God's house. 3But Jesus has far more glory than Moses, just as a man who builds a fine house gets more praise than his house does. 4And many people can build houses, but only God made everything.

5Well, Moses did a fine job working in God's house, but he was only a servant; and his work was mostly to illustrate and suggest those things that would happen later on. 6But Christ, God's faithful Son, is in complete charge of God's house. And we Christians are God's house—he lives in us!—if we keep up our courage firm to the end, and our joy and our trust in the Lord.

7,8And since Christ is so much superior, the Holy Spirit warns us to listen to him, to be careful to hear his voice today and not let our hearts become set against him, as the people of Israel did. They steeled themselves against his love and complained against him in the desert while he was testing them. 9But God was patient with them forty years, though they tried his patience sorely; he kept right on doing his mighty miracles for them to see. 10"But," God says, "I was very angry with them, for their hearts were always looking somewhere else instead of up to me, and they never found the paths I wanted them to follow."

11Then God, full of this anger against them, bound himself with an oath that he would never let them come to his place of rest.

12Beware then of your own hearts, dear brothers, lest you find that they, too, are evil and unbelieving and are leading you away from the living God. 13Speak to each other about these things every day while there is still time, so that none of you will become hardened against God, being blinded by the glamor of sin. 14For if we are faithful to the end, trusting God just as we did when we first became Christians, we will share in all that belongs to Christ.

15But now is the time. Never forget the warning, "Today if you hear God's voice speaking to you, do not harden your hearts against him, as the people of Israel did when they rebelled against him in the desert."

16And who were those people I speak of, who heard God's voice speaking to them but then rebelled against him? They were the ones who came out of Egypt with Moses their leader. 17And who was it who made God angry for all those forty years? These same people who sinned and as a result died in the wilderness. 18And to whom was God speaking when he swore with an oath that they could never go into the land he had promised his people? He was speaking to all those who disobeyed him. 19And why couldn't they go in? Because they didn't trust him.

PSALM 104:1–24

I bless the Lord: O Lord my God, how great you are! You are robed with honor and with majesty and light! You stretched out the starry curtain of the heavens, 3and hollowed out the surface of the earth to form the seas. The clouds are his chariots. He rides upon the wings of the wind. 4The angels are his messengers—his servants of fire!

5You bound the world together so that it would never fall apart. 6You clothed the earth with floods of waters covering up the mountains. 7,8You spoke, and at the sound of your shout the water collected into its vast ocean beds, and mountains rose and valleys sank to the levels you decreed. 9And then you set a boundary for the seas, so that they would never again cover the earth.

10He placed springs in the valleys, and streams that gush from the mountains. 11They give water for all the animals to drink. There the wild donkeys quench their thirst, 12and the birds nest beside the streams and sing among the branches of the trees. 13He sends rain upon the mountains and fills the earth with fruit. 14The tender grass grows up at his command to feed the cattle, and there are fruit trees, vegetables and grain for man to cultivate, 15and wine to make him glad, and olive oil as lotion for his skin, and bread to give him strength. 16The Lord planted the cedars of Lebanon. They are tall and flourishing. 17There the birds make their nests, the storks in the firs. 18High in the mountains are pastures for the wild goats, and rock-badgers burrow in among the rocks and find protection there.

19He assigned the moon to mark the months, and the sun to mark the days. 20He sends the night and darkness, when all the forest folk come out. 21Then the young lions roar for their food, but they are dependent on the Lord. 22At dawn they slink back into their dens to rest, 23and men go off to work until the evening shadows fall again. 24O Lord, what a variety you have made! And in wisdom you have made them all! The earth is full of your riches.

PROVERBS 26:24–26

A man with hate in his heart may sound pleasant enough, but don't believe him; for he is cursing you in his heart. Though he pretends to be so kind, his hatred will finally come to light for all to see.

NOVEMBER 2

EZEKIEL 3:16—6:14

AT the end of the seven days, the Lord said to me:

17"Son of dust, I have appointed you as a watchman for Israel; whenever I send my people a warning, pass it on to them at once. 18If you refuse to warn the wicked when I want you to tell them, you are under the penalty of death, therefore repent and save your life—they will die in their sins, but I will punish you. I will demand your blood for theirs. 19But if you warn them and they keep on sinning, and refuse to repent, they will die in their sins, but you are blameless—you have done all you could. 20And if a good man becomes bad, and you refuse to warn him of the consequences, and the Lord destroys him, his previous good deeds won't help him— he shall die in his sin. But I will hold you responsible for his death, and punish you. 21But if you warn him and he repents, he shall live and you have saved your own life too."

22I was helpless in the hand of God, and when he said to me, "Go out into the valley and I will talk to you there"—

23I arose and went, and oh, I saw the glory of the Lord there, just as in my first vision! And I fell to the ground on my face.

24Then the Spirit entered into me and set me on my feet. He talked to me and said: "Go, imprison yourself in your house, 25and I will paralyze you so you can't leave; 26and I will make your tongue stick to the roof of your mouth so that you can't reprove them; for they are rebels. 27But whenever I give you a message, then I will loosen your tongue and let you speak, and you shall say to them: The Lord God says, Let anyone listen who wants to, and let anyone refuse who wants to, for they are rebels.

"AND now, son of dust, take a large brick and lay it before you and draw a map of the city of Jerusalem on it. Draw a picture of siege mounds being built against the city, and enemy camps around it, and battering rams surrounding the walls. 3And put an iron plate between you and the city, like a wall of iron. Demonstrate how an enemy army will capture Jerusalem!

"There is special meaning in each detail of what I have told you to do. For it is a warning to the people of Israel. 4,5"Now lie on your left side for 390 days, to show that Israel will be punished for 390 years by captivity and doom. Each day you lie there represents a year of punishment ahead for Israel. 6Afterwards, turn over and lie on your right side for forty days, to signify the years of Judah's punishment. Each day will represent one year.

7"Meanwhile continue your demonstration of the siege of Jerusalem; lie there with your arm bared [to signify great strength and power in the attack against her]. This will prophesy her doom. 8And I will paralyze you so that you can't turn over from one side to the other until you have completed all the days of your siege.

9"During the first 390 days eat bread made of flour mixed from wheat, barley, beans, lentils, and spelt. Mix the various kinds of flour together in a jar. 10You are to ration this out to yourself at the rate of eight ounces at a time, one meal a day. 11And use one quart of water a day; don't use more than that. 12Each day take flour from the barrel and prepare it as you would barley cakes. While all the people are watching, bake it over a fire, using dried human dung as fuel, and eat it. 13For the Lord declares, Israel shall eat defiled bread in the Gentile lands to which I exile them!"

14Then I said, "O Lord God, must I be defiled by using dung? For I have never been defiled before in all my life. From the time I was a child until now I have never eaten any animal that died of sickness or that I found injured or dead; and I have never eaten any of the kinds of animals our law forbids."

15Then the Lord said, "All right, you may use cow dung instead of human dung."

16Then he told me, "Son of dust, bread will be tightly rationed in Jerusalem. It will be weighed out with great care and eaten fearfully. And the water will be portioned out in driblets, and the people will drink it with dismay. 17I will cause the people to lack both bread and water, and to look at one another in frantic terror, and to waste away beneath their punishment.

"SON of dust, take a sharp sword and use it as a barber's razor to shave your head and beard; use balances to weigh the hair into three equal parts. 2Place a third of it at the center of your map of Jerusalem. After your siege, burn it there. Scatter another third across your map and slash at it with a knife. Scatter the last third to the wind, for I will chase my people with the sword. 3Keep just a bit of the hair and tie it up in your robe; 4then take a few hairs out and throw them into the fire, for a fire shall come from this remnant and destroy all Israel."

5,6,7The Lord God says, "This illustrates what will happen to Jerusalem, for she has turned away from my laws and has been even more wicked than the nations surrounding her." 8Therefore the Lord God says, I, even I, am against you and will punish you publicly while all the nations watch. 9Because of the terrible sins you have committed, I will punish you more terribly than I have ever done before or ever will again. 10Fathers will eat their own sons, and sons will eat their fathers; and those who survive will be scattered into all the world.

11"For I promise you: Because you have defiled my Temple with idols and evil sacrifices, therefore I will not spare you nor pity you at all. 12One-third of you will die from famine and disease; one-third will be slaughtered by the enemy; and one-third I will scatter to the winds, sending the sword of the enemy chasing after you. 13Then at last my anger will be appeased. And all Israel will know that what I threaten, I do.

14"So I will make a public example of you before all the surrounding nations and before everyone traveling past the ruins of your land. 15You will become a laughingstock to the world and an awesome example to everyone, for all to see what happens when the Lord turns against an entire nation in furious rebuke. I, the Lord, have spoken it!

16"I will shower you with deadly arrows of famine to destroy you. The famine will become more and more serious until every bit of bread is gone. 17And not only famine will come, but wild animals will attack you and kill you and your families; disease and war will stalk your land, and the sword of the enemy will slay you; I, the Lord, have spoken it!"

AGAIN a message came from the Lord: 2"Son of dust, look over toward the mountains of Israel and prophesy against them. 3Say to them, O mountains of Israel, hear the message of the Lord God against you and against the rivers and valleys. I, even I the Lord, will bring war upon you to destroy your idols. 4-7All your cities will be smashed and burned, and the idol altars abandoned. Your gods will be shattered; the bones of their worshipers will lie scattered among the altars. Then at last you will know I am the Lord.

8"But I will let a few of my people escape—to be scattered among the nations of the world. 9Then when they are exiled among the nations, they will remember me, for I will take away their adulterous hearts—their love of idols— and I will blind their lecherous eyes that long for other gods. Then at last they will loathe themselves for all this wickedness. 10They will realize that I alone am God, and that I wasn't fooling when I told them that all this would happen to them.

11"The Lord God says: Raise your hands in horror and shake your head with deep remorse and say, Alas for all the evil we have done! For you are going to perish from war and famine and disease. 12Disease will strike down those in exile; war will destroy those in the land of Israel; and any who remain will die by famine and siege. So at last I will expend my fury on you. 13When your slain lie scattered among your idols and altars on every hill and mountain and under every green tree and great oak where they offered incense to their gods—you will realize that I alone am God. 14I will crush you and make your cities desolate from the wilderness in the south to Riblah in the north. Then you will know I am the Lord."

HEBREWS 4:1–16

ALTHOUGH God's promise still stands—his promise that all may enter his place of rest—we ought to tremble with fear because some of you may be on the verge of failing to get there after all. 2For this wonderful news—the message that God wants to save us—has been given to us just as it was to those who lived in the time of Moses. But it didn't do them any good because they didn't believe it. They didn't mix it with faith. 3For only we who believe God can enter into his place of rest. He has said, "I have sworn in my anger that those who don't believe me will never get in," even though he has been ready and waiting for them since the world began.

4We know he is ready and waiting because it is written that God rested on the seventh day of creation, having finished all that he had planned to make. 5Even so they didn't get in, for God finally said, "They shall never enter my rest." 6Yet the promise remains and some get in—but not those who had the first chance, for they disobeyed God and failed to enter.

7But he has set another time for coming in, and that time is now. He announced this through King David long years after man's first failure to enter, saying in the words already quoted, "Today when you hear him calling, do not harden your hearts against him."

8This new place of rest he is talking about does not mean the land of Israel that Joshua led them into. If that were what God meant, he would not have spoken long afterwards about "today" being the time to get in. 9So there is a full complete rest *still waiting* for the people of God. 10Christ has already entered there. He is resting from his work, just as God did after the creation. 11Let us do our best to go into that place of rest, too, being careful not to disobey God as the children of Israel did, thus failing to get in.

12For whatever God says to us is full of living power: it is sharper than the sharpest dagger, cutting swift and deep into our innermost thoughts and desires with all their parts, exposing us for what we really are. 13He knows about everyone, everywhere. Everything about us is bare and wide open to the all-seeing eyes of our living God; nothing can be hidden from him to whom we must explain all that we have done.

14But Jesus the Son of God is our great High Priest who has gone to heaven itself to help us; therefore let us never stop trusting him. 15This High Priest of ours understands our weaknesses, since he had the same temptations we do, though he never once gave way to them and sinned. 16So let us come boldly to the very throne of God and stay there to receive his mercy and to find grace to help us in our times of need.

PSALM 104:25–35

THERE before me lies the mighty ocean, teeming with life of every kind, both great and small. 26And look! See the ships! And over there, the whale you made to play in the sea. 27Every one of these depends on you to give them daily food. 28You supply it, and they gather it. You open wide your hand to feed them and they are satisfied with all your bountiful provision.

29But if you turn away from them, then all is lost. And when you gather up their breath, they die and turn again to dust. 30Then you send your Spirit, and new life is born to replenish all the living of the earth. 31Praise God forever! How he must rejoice in all his work! 32The earth trembles at his glance; the mountains burst into flame at his touch.

33I will sing to the Lord as long as I live. I will praise God to my last breath! 34May he be pleased by all these thoughts about him, for he is the source of all my joy. 35Let all sinners perish—all who refuse to praise him. But I will praise him. Hallelujah!

PROVERBS FOR TODAY/ 26:27

The man who sets a trap for others will get caught in it himself. Roll a boulder down on someone, and it will roll back and crush you.

NOVEMBER 3

EZEKIEL 7:1—9:11

THIS further message came to me from God:

2"Tell Israel, Wherever you look—east, west, north or south—your land is finished. 3No hope remains, for I will loose my anger on you for your worshiping of idols. 4I will turn my eyes away and show no pity; I will repay you in full, and you shall know I am the Lord."

5,6The Lord God says: "With one blow after another I will finish you. The end has come; your final doom is waiting. 7O Israel, the day of your damnation dawns; the time has come; the day of trouble nears. It is a day of shouts of anguish, not shouts of joy! 8,9Soon I will pour out my fury and let it finish its work of punishing you for all your evil deeds. I will not spare nor pity you, and you will know that I, the Lord, am doing it. 10,11The day of judgment has come; the morning dawns, for your wickedness and pride have run their course and reached their climax—none of these rich and wicked men of pride shall live. All your boasting will die away, and no one will be left to bewail your fate.

12"Yes, the time has come; the day draws near. There will be nothing to buy or sell, for the wrath of God is on the land. 13And even if a merchant lives, his business will be gone, for God has spoken against all the people of Israel; all will be destroyed. Not one of those whose lives are filled with sin will recover.

14"The trumpets shout to Israel's army, 'Mobilize!' but no one listens, for my wrath is on them all. 15If you go outside the walls, there stands the enemy to kill you. If you stay inside, famine and disease will devour you. 16Any who escape will be lonely as mourning doves hiding on the mountains, each weeping for his sins. 17All hands shall be feeble, and all knees as weak as water. 18You shall clothe yourselves with sackcloth,

and horror and shame shall cover you; you shall shave your heads in sorrow and remorse.

19"Throw away your money! Toss it out like worthless rubbish, for it will have no value in that day of wrath. It will neither satisfy nor feed you, for your love of money is the reason for your sin. 20I gave you gold to use in decorating the Temple, and you used it instead to make idols! Therefore I will take it all away from you. 21I will give it to foreigners and to wicked men as booty. They shall defile my Temple. 22I will not look when they defile it, nor will I stop them. Like robbers, they will loot the treasures and leave the Temple in ruins.

23"Prepare chains for my people, for the land is full of bloody crimes. Jerusalem is filled with violence, so I will enslave her people. 24I will crush your pride by bringing to Jerusalem the worst of the nations to occupy your homes, break down your fortifications you are so proud of, and defile your Temple. 25For the time has come for the cutting off of Israel. You will sue for peace, but you won't get it. 26,27Calamity upon calamity will befall you; woe upon woe, disaster upon disaster! You will long for a prophet to guide you, but the priests and elders and the kings and princes will stand helpless, weeping in despair. The people will tremble with fear, for I will do to them the evil they have done, and give them all their just deserts. They shall learn that I am the Lord."

THEN, late in August of the sixth year of King Jehoiachin's captivity, as I was talking with the elders of Judah in my home, the power of the Lord God fell upon me. 2I saw what appeared to be a Man; from his waist down, he was made of fire; from his waist up, he was all amber-colored brightness. 3He put out what seemed to be a hand and took me by the hair. And the Spirit lifted me up into the sky and seemed to transport me to Jerusalem, to the entrance of the north gate, where the large idol was that had made the Lord so angry. 4Suddenly the glory of the God of Israel was there, just as I had seen it before in the valley.

5He said to me, "Son of dust, look toward the north." So I looked and, sure enough, north of the altar gate, in the entrance, stood the idol.

6And he said: "Son of dust, do you see what they are doing? Do you see what great sins the people of Israel are doing here, to push me from my Temple? But come, and I will show you greater sins than these!"

7Then he brought me to the door of the Temple court, where I could see an opening in the wall.

8"Now dig into the wall," he said. I did, and uncovered a door to a hidden room.

9"Go in," he said, "and see the wickedness going on in there!"

10So I went in. The walls were covered with pictures of all kinds of snakes, lizards and hideous creatures, besides all the various idols worshiped by the people of Israel. 11Seventy elders of Israel were standing there along with Ja-azaniah (son of Shaphan) worshiping the pictures. Each of them held a censer of burning incense, so there was a thick cloud of smoke above their heads.

12Then the Lord said to me: "Son of dust, have you seen what the elders of Israel are doing in their minds? For they say, 'The Lord doesn't see us; he has gone away!'" 13Then he added, "Come, and I will show you greater sins than these!"

14He brought me to the north gate of the Temple, and there sat women weeping for Tammuz, their god.

15"Have you seen this?" he asked. "But I will show you greater evils than these!"

16Then he brought me into the inner court of the Temple and there at the door, between the porch and the bronze altar, were about twenty-five men standing with their backs to the Temple of the Lord, facing east, worshiping the sun!

17"Have you seen this?" he asked. "Is it nothing to the people of Judah that they commit these terrible sins, leading the whole nation into idolatry, thumbing their noses at me and arousing my fury against them? 18Therefore I will deal with them in fury. I will neither pity nor spare. And though they scream for mercy, I will not listen."

THEN he thundered, "Call those to whom I have given the city! Tell them to bring their weapons with them!"

2Six men appeared at his call, coming from the upper north gate, each one with his sword. One of them wore linen clothing and carried a writer's case strapped to his side. They all went into the Temple and stood beside the bronze altar. 3And the glory of the God of Israel rose from between the Guardian Angels where it had rested and stood above the entrance to the Temple.

And the Lord called to the man with the writer's case, 4and said to him, "Walk through the streets of Jerusalem and put a mark on the foreheads of the men who weep and sigh because of all the sins they see around them."

5Then I heard the Lord tell the other men: "Follow him through the city and kill everyone whose forehead isn't marked. Spare not nor pity them— 6kill them all—old and young, girls, women and little children; but don't touch anyone with the mark. And begin right here at the Temple." And so they began by killing the seventy elders.

7And he said, "Defile the Temple! Fill its courts with the bodies of those you kill! Go!" And they went out through the city and did as they were told.

8While they were fulfilling their orders, I was alone. I fell to the ground on my face and cried out: "O Lord God! Will your fury against Jerusalem wipe out everyone left in Israel?"

9But he said to me, "The sins of the people of Israel and Judah are very great and all the land is full of murder and injustice, for they say, 'The Lord doesn't see it! He has gone away!' 10And so I will not spare them nor have any pity on them, and I will fully repay them for all that they have done."

11Just then the man in linen clothing, carrying the writer's case, reported back and said, "I have finished the work you gave me to do."

HEBREWS 5:1–14

THE Jewish high priest is merely a man like anyone else, but he is chosen to speak for all other men in their dealings with God. He presents their gifts to God and offers to him the blood of animals that are sacrificed to cover the sins of the people and his own sins too. And because he is a man he can deal gently with other men, though they are foolish and ignorant, for he, too, is surrounded with the same temptations and understands their problems very well.

4Another thing to remember is that no one can be a high priest just because he wants to be. He has to be called by God for this work in the same way God chose Aaron.

5That is why Christ did not elect himself to the honor of being High Priest; no, he was chosen by God. God said to him, "My Son, today I have honored you." 6And another time God said to him, "You have been chosen to be a priest forever, with the same rank as Melchizedek."

7Yet while Christ was here on earth he pleaded with God, praying with tears and agony of soul to the only one who would save him from [premature] death. And God heard his prayers because of his strong desire to obey God at all times.

8And even though Jesus was God's Son, he had to learn from experience what it was like to obey, when obeying meant suffering. 9It was after he had proved himself perfect in this experience that Jesus became the Giver of eternal salvation to all those who obey him. 10For remember that God has chosen him to be a High Priest with the same rank as Melchizedek.

11There is much more I would like to say along these lines, but you don't seem to listen, so it's hard to make you understand.

12,13You have been Christians a long time now, and you ought to be teaching others, but instead you have dropped back to the place where you need someone to teach you all over again the very first principles in God's Word. You are like babies who can drink only milk, not old enough for solid food. And when a person is still living on milk it shows he isn't very far along in the Christian life, and doesn't know much about the difference between right and wrong. He is still a baby-Christian! 14You will never be able to eat solid spiritual food and understand the deeper things of God's Word until you become better Christians and learn right from wrong by practicing doing right.

PSALM 105:1–15

THANK the Lord for all the glorious things he does; proclaim them to the nations. 2Sing his praises and tell everyone about his miracles. 3Glory in the Lord; O worshipers of God, rejoice.

4Search for him and for his strength, and keep on searching!

5,6Think of the mighty deeds he did for us, his chosen ones—descendants of God's servant Abraham, and of Jacob. Remember how he destroyed our enemies. 7He is the Lord our God. His goodness is seen everywhere throughout the land. 8,9Though a thousand generations pass he never forgets his promise, his covenant with Abraham and Isaac, 10,11and confirmed with Jacob. This is his never-ending treaty with the people of Israel: *"I will give you the land of Canaan as your inheritance."* 12He said this when they were but few in number, very few, and were only visitors in Canaan. 13Later they were dispersed among the nations, and were driven from one kingdom to another; 14but through it all he would not let one thing be done to them apart from his decision. He destroyed many a king who tried! 15"Touch not these chosen ones of mine," he warned, "and do not hurt my prophets."

PROVERBS 26:28
Flattery is a form of hatred and wounds cruelly.

NOVEMBER 4

EZEKIEL 10:1—11:25

SUDDENLY a throne of beautiful blue sapphire appeared in the sky above the heads of the Guardian Angels.

2Then the Lord spoke to the man in linen clothing and said: "Go in between the whirling wheels beneath the Guardian Angels, and take a handful of glowing coals and scatter them over the city." He did so while I watched. 3The Guardian Angels were standing at the south end of the Temple when the man went in. And the cloud of glory filled the inner court. 4Then the glory of the Lord rose from above the Guardian Angels and went over to the door of the Temple. The Temple was filled with the cloud of glory, and the court of the Temple was filled with the brightness of the glory of the Lord. 5And the sound of the wings of the Guardian Angels was as the voice of Almighty God when he speaks and could be heard clear out in the outer court.

6When the Lord told the man in linen clothing to go between the Guardian Angels and take some burning coals from between the wheels, the man went in and stood beside one of the wheels, 7,8and one of the Guardian Angels reached out his hand (for each of the mighty angels had, beneath his wings, what looked like human hands) and took some live coals from the flames between the Angels and put them into the hands

of the man in linen clothes, who took them and went out.

9-13Each of the four Guardian Angels had a wheel beside him—"The Whirl-Wheels," as I heard them called, for each one had a second wheel crosswise within—sparkling like chrysolite, giving off a greenish-yellow glow. Because of the construction of these wheels, the Angels could go straight forward in each of four directions; they did not turn when they changed direction but could go in any of the four ways their faces looked. Each of the four wheels was covered with eyes, including the rims and spokes. 14Each of the four Guardian Angels had four faces—the first was that of an ox; the second, a man's; the third, a lion's; and the fourth, an eagle's.

15,16These were the same beings I had seen beside the Chebar Canal, and when they rose into the air the wheels rose with them, and stayed beside them as they flew. 17When the Guardian Angels stood still, so did the wheels, for the spirit of the Guardian Angels was in the wheels.

18Then the glory of the Lord moved from the door of the Temple and stood above the Guardian Angels. 19And as I watched, the Guardian Angels flew with their wheels beside them to the east gate of the Temple. And the glory of the God of Israel was above them.

20These were the living beings I had seen beneath the God of Israel beside the Chebar Canal. I knew they were the same, 21for each had four faces and four wings, with what looked like human hands under their wings. 22Their faces too were identical to the faces of those I had seen at the Canal, and they traveled straight ahead, just as the others did.

THEN the Spirit lifted me and brought me over to the east gate of the Temple, where I saw twenty-five of the most prominent men of the city, including two officers, Ja-azaniah (son of Azzur) and Pelatiah (son of Benaiah).

Then the Spirit said to me, "Son of dust, these are the men who are responsible for all of the wicked counsel being given out in this city. 3For they say to the people, 'It is time to rebuild Jerusalem, for our city is an iron shield and will protect us from all harm.' 4Therefore, son of dust, prophesy against them loudly and clearly."

5Then the Spirit of the Lord came upon me and told me to say: "The Lord says to the people of Israel: Is that what you are saying? Yes, I know it is, for I know everything you think—every thought that comes into your minds. 6You have murdered endlessly and filled your streets with the dead.

7"Therefore the Lord God says: You think this city is an iron shield? No, it isn't! It will not protect you. Your slain will lie within it, but you will be dragged out and slaughtered. 8I will expose you to the war you have so greatly feared, says the Lord God, 9and I will take you from Jerusalem and hand you over to foreigners who will carry out my judgments against you. 10You will be slaughtered all the way to the borders of Israel, and you will know I am the Lord. 11No, this city will not be an iron shield for you, and you safe within. I will chase you even to the borders of Israel, 12and you will know I am the Lord— you who have not obeyed me, but rather have copied the nations all around you."

13While I was still speaking and telling them this, Pelatiah (son of Benaiah) suddenly died. Then I fell to the ground on my face and cried out: "O Lord God, are you going to kill everyone in all Israel?"

14Again a message came from the Lord:

15"Son of dust, the remnant left in Jerusalem are saying about your brother exiles: 'It is because they were so wicked that the Lord has deported them. Now the Lord has given us their land!'

16"But tell the exiles that the Lord God says: Although I have scattered you in the countries of the world, yet I will be a sanctuary to you for the time that you are there, 17and I will gather you back from the nations where you are scattered and give you the land of Israel again. 18And when you return you will remove every trace of all this idol worship. 19I will give you one heart and a new spirit; I will take from you your hearts of stone and give you tender hearts of love for God, 20so that you can obey my laws and be my people, and I will be your God. 21But as for those now in Jerusalem, who long for idols, I will repay them fully for their sins," the Lord God says.

22Then the Guardian Angels lifted their wings and rose into the air with their wheels beside them, and the glory of the God of Israel stood above them. 23Then the glory of the Lord rose from over the city and stood above the mountain on the east side.

24Afterwards the Spirit of God carried me back again to Babylon, to the Jews in exile there. And so ended the vision of my visit to Jerusalem. 25And I told the exiles everything the Lord had shown me.

HEBREWS 6:1–20

LET us stop going over the same old ground again and again, always teaching those first lessons about Christ. Let us go on instead to other things and become mature in our understanding, as strong Christians ought to be. Surely we don't need to speak further about the foolishness of trying to be saved by being good, or about the necessity of faith in God; 2you don't need further instruction about baptism and spiritual gifts and the resurrection of the dead and eternal judgment.

3The Lord willing, we will go on now to other things.

4There is no use trying to bring you back to the Lord again if you have once understood the Good News and tasted for yourself the good things of heaven and shared in the Holy Spirit, 5and know how good the Word of God is, and felt the mighty powers of the world to come, 6and then have turned against God. You cannot bring yourself to repent again if you have nailed the Son of God to the cross again by rejecting him, holding him up to mocking and to public shame.

7When a farmer's land has had many showers upon it and good crops come up, that land has experienced God's blessing upon it. 8But if it keeps on having crops of thistles and thorns, the land is considered no good and is ready for condemnation and burning off.

9Dear friends, even though I am talking like this I really don't believe that what I am saying applies to you. I am confident you are producing the good fruit that comes along with your salvation. 10For God is not unfair. How can he forget your hard work for him, or forget the way you used to show your love for him—and still do—by helping his children? 11And we are anxious that you keep right on loving others as long as life lasts, so that you will get your full reward.

12Then, knowing what lies ahead for you, you won't become bored with being a Christian, nor become spiritually dull and indifferent, but you will be anxious to follow the example of those who receive all that God has promised them because of their strong faith and patience.

13For instance, there was God's promise to Abraham: God took an oath in his own name, since there was no one greater to swear by, 14that he would bless Abraham again and again, and give him a son and make him the father of a great nation of people. 15Then Abraham waited patiently until finally God gave him a son, Isaac, just as he had promised.

16When a man takes an oath, he is calling upon someone greater than himself to force him to do what he has promised, or to punish him if he later refuses to do it; the oath ends all argument about it. 17God also bound himself with an oath, so that those he promised to help would be perfectly sure and never need to wonder whether he might change his plans.

18He has given us both his promise and his oath, two things we can completely count on, for it is impossible for God to tell a lie. Now all those who flee to him to save them can take new courage when they hear such assurances from God; now they can know without doubt that he will give them the salvation he has promised them.

19This certain hope of being saved is a strong and trustworthy anchor for our souls, connecting us with God himself behind the sacred curtains of heaven, 20where Christ has gone ahead to plead for us from his position as our High Priest, with the honor and rank of Melchizedek.

PSALM 105:16–38

HE called for a famine on the land of Canaan, cutting off its food supply. 17Then he sent Joseph as a slave to Egypt to save his people from starvation. 18There in prison they hurt his feet with fetters, and placed his neck in an iron collar, 19until God's time finally came—how God tested his patience! 20Then the king sent for him and set him free. 21He was put in charge of all the king's possessions. 22At his pleasure he could imprison the king's aides and teach the king's advisors.

23Then Jacob (Israel) arrived in Egypt and lived there with his sons. 24In the years that followed, the people of Israel multiplied explosively, until they were a greater nation than their rulers. 25At that point God turned the Egyptians against the Israelis; they hated and enslaved them.

²⁶But God sent Moses as his representative, and Aaron with him, ²⁷to call down miracles of terror upon the land of Egypt. ²⁸They followed his instructions and he sent thick darkness through the land, ²⁹and turned the nation's water into blood, poisoning the fish. ³⁰Then frogs invaded in enormous numbers; they were found even in the king's private rooms. ³¹When Moses spoke, the flies and other insects swarmed in vast clouds from one end of Egypt to the other. ³²Instead of rain he sent down murderous hail, and lightning flashes overwhelmed the nation. ³³Their grape vines and fig trees were ruined; all the trees lay broken on the ground. ³⁴He spoke, and hordes of locusts came, ³⁵and ate up everything green, destroying all the crops. ³⁶Then he killed the oldest child in each Egyptian home, their pride and joy— ³⁷and brought his people safely out from Egypt, loaded with silver and gold; there were no sick and feeble folk among them then. ³⁸Egypt was glad when they were gone, for the dread of them was great.

PROVERBS 27:1–2

Don't brag about your plans for tomorrow—wait and see what happens. Don't praise yourself; let others do it!

NOVEMBER 5

EZEKIEL 12:1—14:11

A GAIN a message came to me from the Lord:

²"Son of dust," he said, "you live among rebels who could know the truth if they wanted to, but they don't want to; they could hear me if they would listen, but they won't, ³for they are rebels. So now put on a demonstration, to show them what being exiled will be like. Pack whatever you can carry on your back and leave your home—go somewhere else. Go in the daylight so they can see, for perhaps even yet they will consider what this means, even though they are such rebels. ⁴Bring your baggage outside your house during the daylight so they can watch. Then leave the house at night, just as captives do when they begin their long march to distant lands. ⁵Dig a tunnel through the city wall while they are observing and carry your possessions out through the hole. ⁶As they watch, lift your pack to your shoulders and walk away into the night; muffle your face and don't gaze around. All this is a sign to the people of Israel of the evil that will come upon Jerusalem."

⁷So I did as I was told. I brought my pack outside in the daylight—all I could take into exile—and in the evening I dug through the wall with my hands. I went out into the darkness with my pack on my shoulder while the people looked on. ⁸The next morning this message came to me from the Lord:

⁹"Son of dust, these rebels, the people of Israel, have asked what all this means. ¹⁰Tell them the Lord God says it is a message to King Zedekiah in Jerusalem and to all the people of Israel. ¹¹Explain that what you did was a demonstration of what is going to happen to them, for they shall be driven out of their homes and sent away into exile.

¹²"Even King Zedekiah shall go out at night through a hole in the wall, taking only what he can carry with him, with muffled face, for he won't be able to see.

13I will capture him in my net and bring him to Babylon, the land of the Chaldeans; but he shall not see it, and he shall die there. 14I will scatter his servants and guards to the four winds and send the sword after them. 15And when I scatter them among the nations, then they shall know I am the Lord. 16But I will spare a few of them from death by war and famine and disease. I will save them to confess to the nations how wicked they have been, and they shall know I am the Lord."

17Then this message came to me from the Lord:

18"Son of dust, tremble as you eat your meals; ration out your water as though it were your last, 19and say to the people, the Lord God says that the people of Israel and Jerusalem shall ration their food with utmost care and sip their tiny portions of water in utter despair because of all their sins. 20Your cities shall be destroyed and your farmlands deserted, and you shall know I am the Lord."

21Again a message came to me from the Lord:

22"Son of dust, what is that proverb they quote in Israel—'The days as they pass make liars out of every prophet.' 23The Lord God says, I will put an end to this proverb and they will soon stop saying it. Give them this one instead: 'The time has come for all these prophecies to be fulfilled.'

24"Then you will see what becomes of all the false predictions of safety and security for Jerusalem. 25For I am the Lord! What I threaten always happens. There will be no more delays, O rebels of Israel! I will do it in your own lifetime!" says the Lord God.

26Then this message came:

27"Son of dust, the people of Israel say, 'His visions won't come true for a long, long time.' 28Therefore say to them: 'The Lord God says, All delay has ended! I will do it now!'"

THEN this message came to me:

2,3"Son of dust, prophesy against the false prophets of Israel who are inventing their own visions and claiming to have messages from me when I have never told them anything at all. Woe upon them!

4"O Israel, these 'prophets' of yours are as useless as foxes for rebuilding your walls! 5O evil prophets, what have you ever done to strengthen the walls of Israel against her enemies—by strengthening Israel in the Lord? 6Instead you have lied when you said, 'My message is from God!' God did not send you. And yet you expect him to fulfill your prophecies. 7Can you deny that you have claimed to see 'visions' you never saw, and that you have said, 'This message is from God,' when I never spoke to you at all?

8"Therefore the Lord God says: I will destroy you for these 'visions' and lies. 9My hand shall be against you, and you shall be cut off from among the leaders of Israel; I will blot out your names and you will never see your own country again. And you shall know I am the Lord. 10For these evil men deceive my people by saying, 'God will send peace,' when that is not my plan at all! My people build a flimsy wall and these prophets praise them for it—and cover it with whitewash!

11"Tell these evil builders that their wall will fall. A heavy rainstorm will undermine it; great hailstones and mighty winds will knock it down. 12And when the wall falls, the people will cry out, 'Why didn't you tell us that it wasn't good enough? Why did you whitewash it and cover up its faults?' 13Yes, it will surely fall. The Lord God says: I will sweep it away with a storm of indignation and with a great flood of anger and with hailstones of wrath. 14I will break down your whitewashed wall, and it will fall on you and crush you, and you shall know I am the Lord. 15Then at last my wrath against the wall will be completed; and concerning those who praised it, I will say: The wall and its builders both are gone. 16For they were lying prophets, claiming Jerusalem will have peace when there is no peace, says the Lord God. 17"Son of dust, speak out against the women prophets too who pretend the Lord has given them his messages. 18Tell them the Lord God says: Woe to these women who are damning the souls of my people, of both young and old alike, by tying magic charms on their wrists and furnishing them with magic veils and selling them indulgences. They refuse to even offer help unless they get a profit from it. 19For the sake of a few paltry handfuls of barley or a piece of bread will you turn away my people from me? You have led those to death who should not die! And you have promised life to those who should not live, by lying to my people—and how they love it!

20"And so the Lord says: I will crush you because you hunt my people's souls with all your magic charms. I will tear off the charms and set my people free like birds from cages. 21I will tear off the magic veils and save my people from you; they will no longer be your victims, and you shall know I am the Lord. 22Your lies have discouraged the righteous, when I didn't want it so. And you have encouraged the wicked by promising life, though they continue in their sins. 23But you will lie no more; no longer will you talk of seeing 'visions' that you never saw, nor practice your magic, for I will deliver my people out of your hands by destroying you, and you shall know I am the Lord."

THEN some of the elders of Israel visited me, to ask me for a message from the Lord, 2and this is the message that came to me to give to them:

3"Son of dust, these men worship idols in their hearts—should I let them ask me anything? 4Tell them, the Lord God says: I the Lord will personally deal with anyone in Israel who worships idols and then comes to ask my help. 5For I will punish the minds and hearts of those who turn from me to idols.

6,7"Therefore warn them that the Lord God says: Repent and destroy your idols, and stop worshiping them in your hearts. I the Lord will personally punish everyone, whether people of Israel or the for-eigners living among you, who rejects me for idols, and then comes to a prophet to ask for my help and advice. 8I will turn upon him and make a terrible example of him, destroying him; and you shall know I am the Lord. 9And if one of the false prophets gives him a message anyway, it is a lie. His prophecy will not come true, and I will stand against that 'prophet' and destroy him from among my people Israel. 10False prophets and hypocrites—evil people who say they want my words—all will be punished for their sins, 11so that the people of Israel will learn not to desert me and not to be polluted any longer with sin, but to be my people and I their God. So says the Lord."

HEBREWS 7:1–17

THIS Melchizedek was king of the city of Salem, and also a priest of the Most High God. When Abraham was returning home after winning a great battle against many kings, Melchizedek met him and blessed him; 2then Abraham took a tenth of all he had won in the battle and gave it to Melchize-dek.

Melchizedek's name means "Justice," so he is the King of Justice; and he is also the King of Peace because of the name of his city, Salem, which means "Peace." 3Melchizedek had no father or mother and there is no record of any of his ancestors. He was never born and he never died but his life is like that of the Son of God—a priest forever.

4See then how great this Melchizedek is:

(a)Even Abraham, the first and most honored of all God's chosen people, gave Melchizedek a tenth of the spoils he took from the kings he had been fighting. 5One could understand why Abraham would do this if Melchizedek had been a Jewish priest, for later on God's people were required by law to give gifts to help their priests because the priests were their relatives. 6But Melchizedek was not a relative, and yet Abraham paid him.

(b)Melchizedek placed a blessing upon mighty Abraham, 7and as everyone knows, a person who has the power to bless is always greater than the person he blesses.

8(c) The Jewish priests, though mortal, received tithes; but we are told that Melchizedek lives on.

9(d) One might even say that Levi himself (the ancestor of all Jewish priests, of all who receive tithes), paid tithes to Melchizedek through Abraham. 10For although Levi wasn't born yet, the seed from which he came was in Abraham when Abraham paid the tithes to Melchizedek.

11(e) If the Jewish priests and their laws had been able to save us, why then did God need to send Christ as a priest with the rank of Melchizedek, instead of sending someone with the rank of Aaron—the same rank all other priests had?

12,13,14And when God sends a new kind of priest, his law must be changed to permit it. As we all know, Christ did not belong to the priest-tribe of Levi, but came from the tribe of Judah, which had not been chosen for priesthood; Moses had never given them that work. 15So we can plainly see that God's method changed, for Christ, the new High Priest who came with the rank of Melchizedek, 16did not become a priest by meeting the old requirement of belonging to the tribe of Levi, but on the basis of power flowing from a life that cannot end. 17And the Psalmist points this out when he says of Christ, "You are a priest forever with the rank of Melchizedek."

PSALM 105:39–45

HE spread out a cloud above them to shield them from the burning sun, and gave them a pillar of flame at night to give them light. 40They asked for meat and he sent them quail, and gave them manna—bread from heaven. 41He opened up a rock, and water gushed out to form a river through the dry and barren land; 42for he remembered his sacred promises to Abraham his servant.

43So he brought his chosen ones singing into the Promised Land. 44He gave them the lands of the Gentiles, complete with their growing crops; they ate what others planted. 45This was done to make them faithful and obedient to his laws. Hallelujah!

PROVERBS FOR TODAY/ 27:3
A rebel's frustrations are heavier than sand and rocks.

NOVEMBER 6

EZEKIEL 14:12—16:42

THEN this message of the Lord came to me:
13"Son of dust, when the people of this land sin against me, then I will crush them with my fist and break off their food supply and send famine to destroy both man and beast. 14If Noah, Daniel and Job were here today, they alone would be saved by their righteousness, and I would destroy the remainder of Israel, says the Lord God.

15"When I send an invasion of dangerous wild animals into the land to devastate the land, 16even if these three men were here, the Lord God swears that it would do no good—it would not save the people from their doom. Those three only would be saved, but the land would be devastated.

17"Or when I bring war against that land and tell the armies of the enemy to come and destroy everything, 18even if these three men were in the land, the Lord God declares that they alone would be saved.

19"And when I pour out my fury by sending an epidemic of disease into the land, and the plague kills man and beast alike, 20though Noah, Daniel and Job were living there, the Lord God says that only they would be saved, because of their righteousness.

21"And the Lord says: Four great punishments await Jerusalem to destroy all life: war, famine, ferocious beasts, plague. 22If there are survivors and they come here to join you as exiles in Babylon, you will see with your own eyes how wicked they are, and you will know it was right for me to destroy Jerusalem. 23You will agree, when you meet them, that it is not without cause that all these things are being done to Israel."

THEN this message came to me from the Lord:

2"Son of dust, what good are vines from the forest? Are they as useful as trees? Are they even as valuable as a single branch? 3No, for vines can't be used even for making pegs to hang up pots and pans! 4All they are good for is fuel—and even so, they burn but poorly! 5,6So they are useless both before and after being put in the fire!

"This is what I mean, the Lord God says: The people of Jerusalem are like the vines of the forest—useless before being burned and certainly useless afterwards! 7And I will set myself against them to see to it that if they escape from one fire, they will fall into another; and then you shall know I am the Lord. 8And I will make the land desolate because they worship idols," says the Lord God.

THEN again a message came to me from the Lord.

2"Son of dust," he said, "speak to Jerusalem about her loathsome sins. 3Tell her, the Lord God says: You are no better than the people of Canaan—your father must have been an Amorite and your mother a Hittite! 4When you were born, no one cared for you. When I first saw you, your umbilical cord was uncut, and you had been neither washed nor rubbed with salt nor clothed. 5No one had the slightest interest in you; no one pitied you or cared for you. On that day when you were born, you were dumped out into a field and left to die, unwanted.

6,7"But I came by and saw you there, covered with your own blood, and I said, 'Live! Thrive like a plant in the field!' And you did! You grew up and became tall, slender and supple, a jewel among jewels. And when you reached the age of maidenhood your breasts were full-formed and your pubic hair had grown; yet you were naked.

8"Later, when I passed by and saw you again, you were old enough for marriage; and I wrapped my cloak around you to legally declare my marriage vow. I signed a covenant with you, and you became mine. 9,10Then, when the marriage had taken place, I gave you beautiful clothes of linens and silk, embroidered, and sandals made of dolphin hide. 11I gave you lovely ornaments, bracelets and beautiful necklaces, 12a ring for your nose and two more for your ears, and a lovely tiara for your head. 13And so you were made beautiful with gold and silver, and your clothes were silk and linen and beautifully embroidered. You ate the finest foods and became more beautiful than ever. You looked like a queen, and so you were! 14Your reputation was great among the nations for your beauty; it was perfect because of all the gifts I gave you, says the Lord God.

15"But you thought you could get along without me—you trusted in your beauty instead; and you gave yourself as a prostitute to every man who came along. Your beauty was his for the asking. 16You used the lovely things I gave you for making idol shrines and to decorate your bed of prostitution. Unbelievable! There has never been anything like it before! 17You took the very jewels and gold and silver ornaments I gave to you and made statues of men and worshiped them, which is adultery against me. 18You used the beautifully embroidered clothes I gave you—to cover your idols! And used my oil and incense to worship *them!* 19You set before them—imagine it—the fine flour and oil and honey I gave you; you used it as a lovely sacrifice to *them!* 20And you took my sons and daughters you had borne to me, and sacrificed them to your gods; and they are gone. Wasn't it enough that you should be a prostitute? 21Must you also slay my children by sacrificing them to idols?

22"And in all these years of adultery and sin you have not thought of those days long ago when you were naked and covered with blood.

23"And then, in addition to all your other wickedness—woe, woe upon you, says the Lord God— 24you built a spacious brothel for your lovers, and idol altars on every street, 25and there you offered your beauty to every man who came by, in an endless stream of prostitution. 26And you added lustful Egypt to your prostitutions by your alliance with her. My anger is great.

27"Therefore I have crushed you with my fist; I have reduced your boundaries and delivered you into the hands of those who hate you—the Philistines—and even they are ashamed of you.

28"You have committed adultery with the Assyrians too [by making them your allies and worshiping their gods]; it seems that you can never find enough new gods. After your adultery there, you still weren't satisfied, 29so you worshiped the gods of that great merchant land of Babylon—and you still weren't satisfied. 30What a filthy heart you have, says the Lord God, to do such things as these; you are a brazen prostitute, 31building your idol altars, your brothels, on every street. You have been worse than a prostitute, so eager for sin that you have not even charged for your love! 32Yes, you are an adulterous wife who lives with other men instead of her own husband. 33,34Prostitutes charge for their services—men pay with many gifts. But not you, you give *them* gifts, bribing them to come to you! So you are different from other prostitutes. But you had to pay them, for no one wanted you.

35"O prostitute, hear the word of the Lord:

36"The Lord God says: Because I see your filthy sins, your adultery with your lovers—your worshiping of idols—and the slaying of your children as sacrifices to your gods, 37this is what I am going to do: I will gather together all your allies—these lovers of yours you have sinned with, both those you loved and those you hated—and I will make you naked before them, that they may see you. 38I will punish you as a murderess is punished and as a woman breaking wedlock living with other men. 39I will give you to your lovers—these many nations—to destroy, and they will knock down your brothels and idol altars, and strip you and take your beautiful jewels and leave you naked and ashamed. 40,41They will burn your homes, punishing you before the eyes of many women. And I will see to it that you stop your adulteries with other gods and end your payments to your allies for their love.

42"Then at last my fury against you will die away; my jealousy against you will end, and I will be quiet and not be angry with you anymore.

HEBREWS 7:18–28

YES, the old system of priesthood based on family lines was canceled because it didn't work. It was weak and useless for saving people. 19It never made anyone really right with God. But now we have a far better hope, for Christ makes us acceptable to God, and now we may draw near to him.

20God took an oath that Christ would

always be a Priest, 21although he never said that of other priests. Only to Christ he said, "The Lord has sworn and will never change his mind: You are a Priest forever, with the rank of Melchizedek." 22Because of God's oath, Christ can guarantee forever the success of this new and better arrangement.

23Under the old arrangement there had to be many priests, so that when the older ones died off, the system could still be carried on by others who took their places.

24But Jesus lives forever and continues to be a Priest so that no one else is needed. 25He is able to save completely all who come to God through him. Since he will live forever, he will always be there to remind God that he has paid for their sins with his blood.

26He is, therefore, exactly the kind of High Priest we need; for he is holy and blameless, unstained by sin, undefiled by sinners, and to him has been given the place of honor in heaven. 27He never needs the daily blood of animal sacrifices, as other priests did, to cover over first their own sins and then the sins of the people; for he finished all sacrifices, once and for all, when he sacrificed himself on the cross. 28Under the old system, even the high priests were weak and sinful men who could not keep from doing wrong, but later God appointed by his oath his Son who is perfect forever.

PSALM 106:1–12

HALLELUJAH! Thank you, Lord! How good you are! Your love for us continues on forever. 2Who can ever list the glorious miracles of God? Who can ever praise him half enough?

3Happiness comes to those who are fair to others and are always just and good.

4Remember me too, O Lord, while you are blessing and saving your people. 5Let me share in your chosen ones' prosperity and rejoice in all their joys, and receive the glory you give to them.

6Both we and our fathers have sinned so much. 7They weren't impressed by the wonder of your miracles in Egypt, and soon forgot your many acts of kindness to them. Instead they rebelled against you at the Red Sea. 8Even so you saved them—to defend the honor of your name and demonstrate your power to all the world. 9You commanded the Red Sea to divide, forming a dry road across its bottom. Yes, as dry as any desert! 10Thus you rescued them from their enemies. 11Then the water returned and covered the road and drowned their foes; not one survived.

12Then at last his people believed him. Then they finally sang his praise.

PROVERBS 27:4–6

Jealousy is more dangerous and cruel than anger. Open rebuke is better than hidden love! Wounds from a friend are better than kisses from an enemy!

NOVEMBER 7

EZEKIEL 16:43—17:24

BUT first, because you have not remembered your youth, but have angered me by all these evil things you do, I will fully repay you for

all of your sins, says the Lord. For you are thankless in addition to all your other faults.

44" 'Like mother, like daughter'—that is what everyone will say of you.

45For your mother loathed her husband and her children, and you do too. And you are exactly like your sisters, for they despised their husbands and their children. Truly, your mother must have been a Hittite and your father an Amorite.

46"Your older sister is Samaria, living with her daughters north of you; your younger sister is Sodom and her daughters, in the south. 47You have not merely sinned as they do—no, that was nothing to you; in a very short time you far surpassed them.

48"As I live, the Lord God says, Sodom and her daughters have never been as wicked as you and your daughters. 49Your sister Sodom's sins were pride and laziness and too much food, while the poor and needy suffered outside her door. 50She insolently worshiped many idols as I watched. Therefore I crushed her.

51"Even Samaria has not committed half your sins. You have worshiped idols far more than your sisters have; they seem almost righteous in comparison with you! 52Don't be surprised then by the lighter punishment they get. For your sins are so awful that in comparison with you, your sisters seem innocent! 53(But someday I will restore the fortunes of Sodom and Samaria again, and those of Judah too.) 54Your terrible punishment will be a consolation to them, for it will be greater than theirs.

55"Yes, your sisters, Sodom and Samaria, and all their people will be restored again, and Judah too will prosper in that day. 56In your proud days you held Sodom in unspeakable contempt. 57But now your greater wickedness has been exposed to all the world, and you are the one who is scorned—by Edom and all her neighbors and by all the Philistines. 58This is part of your punishment for all your sins, says the Lord.

59,60"For the Lord God says: I will repay you for your broken promises. You lightly broke your solemn vows to me, yet I will keep the pledge I made to you when you were young. I will establish an everlasting covenant with you forever, 61and you will remember with shame all the evil you have done; and you will be overcome by my favor when I take your sisters, Samaria and Sodom, and make them your daughters, for you to rule over. You will know you don't deserve this gracious act, for you did not keep my covenant. 62I will reaffirm my covenant with you, and you will know I am the Lord. 63Despite all you have done, I will be kind to you again; you will cover your mouth in silence and in shame when I forgive you all that you have done, says the Lord God."

THEN this message came to me from the Lord:

2"Son of dust, give this riddle to the people of Israel:

3,4"A great eagle with broad wings full of many-colored feathers came to Lebanon and plucked off the shoot at the top of the tallest cedar tree and carried it into a city filled with merchants. 5There he planted it in fertile ground beside a broad river, where it would grow as quickly as a willow tree. 6It took root and grew and became a low but spreading vine that turned toward the eagle and produced strong branches and luxuriant leaves. 7But when another great, broadwinged, full-feathered eagle came along, this tree sent its roots and branches out toward him instead, 8even though it was already in good soil with plenty of water to become a splendid vine, producing leaves and fruit.

9"The Lord God asks: Shall I let this tree grow and prosper? No! I will pull it out, roots and all! I will cut off its branches and let its leaves wither and die. It will pull out easily enough—it won't take a big crew or a lot of equipment to do that. 10Though the vine began so well, will it thrive? No, it will wither away completely when the east wind touches it, dying in the same choice soil where it had grown so well."

11Then this message came to me from the Lord:

12,13"Ask these rebels of Israel: Don't you understand what this riddle of the eagles means? I will tell you. Nebuchadnezzar, king of Babylon [the first of the two eagles], came to Jerusalem and took away her king and princes [her topmost buds and shoots] and brought them to Babylon. Nebuchadnezzar made a covenant with a member of the royal family [Zedekiah], and made him take an oath of loyalty. He took a seedling and planted it in fertile ground beside a broad river and he exiled the top men of Israel's government, [14]so that Israel would not be strong again and revolt. But by keeping her promises, Israel could be respected and maintain her identity.

[15]"Nevertheless, Zedekiah rebelled against Babylon, sending ambassadors to Egypt to seek for a great army and many horses to fight against Nebuchadnezzar. But will Israel prosper after breaking all her promises like that? Will she succeed? [16]No! For as I live, says the Lord, the king of Israel shall die. (Nebuchadnezzar will pull out the tree, roots and all!) Zedekiah shall die in Babylon, where the king lives who gave him his power, and whose covenant he despised and broke. [17]Pharaoh and all his mighty army shall fail to help Israel when the king of Babylon lays siege to Jerusalem again and slaughters many lives. [18]For the king of Israel broke his promise after swearing to obey; therefore he shall not escape.

[19]"The Lord God says: As I live, surely I will punish him for despising the solemn oath he made in my name. [20]I will throw my net over him and he shall be captured in my snare, and I will bring him to Babylon and deal with him there for this treason against me. [21]And all the best soldiers of Israel will be killed by the sword, and those remaining in the city will be scattered to the four winds. Then you will know that I, the Lord, have spoken these words.

[22,23]"The Lord God says: I will take a tender sprout from the top of a tall cedar, and I will plant it on the top of Israel's highest mountain. It shall become a noble cedar, bringing forth branches and bearing seed. Animals of every sort will gather under it; its branches will shelter every kind of bird. [24]And everyone shall know that it is I, the Lord, who cuts down the high trees and exalts the low, that I make the green tree wither and the dead tree grow. I, the Lord, have said that I would do it, and I will."

HEBREWS 8:1–13

WHAT we are saying is this: Christ, whose priesthood we have just described, is our High Priest, and is in heaven at the place of greatest honor next to God himself. [2]He ministers in the temple in heaven, the true place of worship built by the Lord and not by human hands.

[3]And since every high priest is appointed to offer gifts and sacrifices, Christ must make an offering too. [4]The sacrifice he offers is far better than those offered by the earthly priests. (But even so, if he were here on earth he wouldn't even be permitted to be a priest, because down here the priests still follow the old Jewish system of sacrifices.) [5]Their work is connected with a mere earthly model of the real tabernacle in heaven; for when Moses was getting ready to build the tabernacle, God warned him to follow exactly the pattern of the heavenly tabernacle as shown to him on Mount Sinai. [6]But Christ, as a Minister in heaven, has been rewarded with a far more important work than those who serve under the old laws, because the new agreement which he passes on to us from God contains far more wonderful promises.

[7]The old agreement didn't even work. If it had, there would have been no need for another to replace it. [8]But God himself found fault with the old one, for he said, "The day will come when I will make a new agreement with the people of Israel and the people of Judah. [9]This new agreement will not be like the old one I gave to their fathers on the day when I took them by the hand to lead them out of the land of Egypt; they did not keep their part in that agreement, so I had to cancel it. [10]But this is the

new agreement I will make with the people of Israel, says the Lord: I will write my laws in their minds so that they will know what I want them to do without my even telling them, and these laws will be in their hearts so that they will want to obey them, and I will be their God and they shall be my people. 11And no one then will need to speak to his friend or neighbor or brother, saying, 'You, too, should know the Lord,' because everyone, great and small, will know me already. 12And I will be merciful to them in their wrongdoings, and I will remember their sins no more."

13God speaks of these new promises, of this new agreement, as taking the place of the old one; for the old one is out of date now and has been put aside forever.

PSALM 106:13–31

YET how quickly they forgot again! They wouldn't wait for him to act, 14but demanded better food, testing God's patience to the breaking point. 15So he gave them their demands, but sent them leanness in their souls. 16They were envious of Moses; yes, and Aaron, too, the man anointed by God as his priest. 17Because of this the earth opened and swallowed Dathan, Abiram and his friends; 18and fire fell from heaven to consume these wicked men. 19,20For they preferred a statue of an ox that eats grass, to the glorious presence of God himself. 21,22Thus they despised their Savior who had done such mighty miracles in Egypt and at the Sea. 23So the Lord declared he would destroy them. But Moses, his chosen one, stepped into the breach between the people and their God and begged him to turn from his wrath, and not destroy them.

24They refused to enter the Promised Land, for they wouldn't believe his solemn oath to care for them. 25Instead, they pouted in their tents and mourned and despised his command. 26Therefore he swore that he would kill them in the wilderness 27and send their children away to distant lands as exiles. 28Then our fathers joined the worshipers of Baal at Peor and even offered sacrifices to the dead! 29With all these things they angered him—and so a plague broke out upon them 30and continued until Phineas executed those whose sins had caused the plague to start. 31(For this good deed Phineas will be remembered forever.)

PROVERBS 27:7–9

Even honey seems tasteless to a man who is full; but if he is hungry, he'll eat anything! A man who strays from home is like a bird that wanders from its nest. Friendly suggestions are as pleasant as perfume.

NOVEMBER 8

EZEKIEL 18:1—19:14

THEN the Lord's message came to me again.
2"Why do people use this proverb about the land of Israel: The children are punished for their fathers' sins? 3As I live, says the Lord God, you will not use this proverb any more in Israel, 4for all souls are mine to judge—fathers and sons alike—and my rule is this: It is for a man's own sins that he will die.

5"But if a man is just and does what is lawful and right, 6and has not gone out to the mountains to feast before the idols of Israel and worship them, and does not commit adultery, nor lie with any woman during the time of her menstruation, 7and is a merciful creditor, not holding on to the items given to him in pledge by poor debtors, and is no robber, but gives food to the hungry and clothes to those in need, 8and grants loans without interest, and stays away from sin, and is honest and fair when judging others, 9and obeys my laws—that man is just, says the Lord, and he shall surely live.

10"But if that man has a son who is a robber or murderer and who fulfills none of his responsibilities, 11who refuses to obey the laws of God, but worships idols on the mountains and commits adultery, 12and oppresses the poor and helpless, and robs his debtors by refusing to let them redeem what they have given him in pledge, and loves idols and worships them, 13and loans out his money at interest—shall that man live? No! He shall surely die, and it is his own fault.

14"But if this sinful man has, in turn, a son who sees all his father's wickedness, so that he fears God and decides against that kind of life, 15and doesn't go up on the mountains to feast before the idols and worship them, and does not commit adultery, 16and is fair to those who borrow from him and doesn't rob them, but feeds the hungry and clothes the needy, 17and helps the poor and does not loan money at interest, and obeys my laws—he shall not die because of his father's sins; he shall surely live. 18But his father shall die for his own sins because he is cruel and robs and does wrong.

19" 'What?' you ask. 'Doesn't the son pay for his father's sins?' No! For if the son does what is right and keeps my laws, he shall surely live. 20The one who sins is the one who dies. The son shall not be punished for his father's sins, nor the father for his son's. The righteous person will be rewarded for his own goodness and the wicked person for his wickedness. 21But if a wicked person

turns away from all his sins and begins to obey my laws and do what is just and right, he shall surely live and not die. 22All his past sins will be forgotten, and he shall live because of his goodness.

23"Do you think I like to see the wicked die? asks the Lord. Of course not! I only want him to turn from his wicked ways and live. 24However, if a righteous person turns to sinning and acts like any other sinner, should he be allowed to live? No, of course not. All his previous goodness will be forgotten and he shall die for his sins.

25"Yet you say: The Lord isn't being fair! Listen to me, O people of Israel. Am I the one who is unfair, or is it you? 26When a good man turns away from being good and begins sinning and dies in his sins, he dies for the evil he has done. 27And if a wicked person turns away from his wickedness and obeys the law, and does right, he shall save his soul, 28for he has thought it over and decided to turn from his sins and live a good life. He shall surely live—he shall not die.

29"And yet the people of Israel keep saying: 'The Lord is unfair!' O people of Israel, it is you who are unfair, not I. 30I will judge each of you, O Israel, and punish or reward each according to your own actions. Oh, turn from your sins while there is yet time. 31Put them behind you and receive a new heart and a new spirit. For why will you die, O Israel? 32I do not enjoy seeing you die, the Lord God says. Turn, turn and live!

SING this death dirge for the leaders of Israel: 2What a woman your mother was—like a lioness! Her children were like lion's cubs! 3One of her cubs [King Jehoahaz] grew into a strong young lion, and learned to catch prey and became a man-eater. 4Then the nations called out their hunters and trapped him in a pit and brought him in chains to Egypt.

5"When Israel, the mother lion, saw that all her hopes for him were gone, she took another of her cubs [King Jehoiachin] and taught him to be 'king of the beasts.' 6He became a leader among the lions and learned to catch prey, and he too became a man-eater. 7He demolished the palaces of the surrounding nations and ruined their cities; their farms were desolated, their crops destroyed; everyone in the land shook with terror when they heard him roar. 8Then the armies of the nations surrounded him, coming from every side, and trapped him in a pit and captured him. 9They prodded him into a cage and brought him before the king of Babylon. He was held in captivity so that his voice could never again be heard upon the mountains of Israel.

10"Your mother was like a vine beside an irrigation ditch, with lush, green foliage because of all the water. 11Its strongest branch became a ruler's scepter and it was very great, towering above the others and noticed from far away. 12But the vine was uprooted in fury and thrown down to the ground. Its branches were broken and withered by a strong wind from the east; the fruit was destroyed by fire. 13Now the vine is planted in the wilderness where the ground is hard and dry. 14It is decaying from within; no strong branch remains. The fulfillment of this sad prophecy has already begun, and there is more ahead."

HEBREWS 9:1–12

NOW in that first agreement between God and his people there were rules for worship and there was a sacred tent down here on earth. Inside this place of worship there were two rooms. The first one contained the golden candlestick and a table with special loaves of holy bread upon it; this part was called the Holy Place. 3Then there was a curtain and behind the curtain was a room called the Holy of Holies. 4In that room there were a golden incense-altar and the golden chest, called the ark of the covenant, completely covered on all sides with pure gold. Inside the ark were the tablets of stone with the Ten Commandments written on them, and a golden jar with some manna

in it, and Aaron's wooden cane that budded. 5Above the golden chest were statues of angels called the cherubim— the guardians of God's glory—with their wings stretched out over the ark's golden cover, called the mercy seat. But enough of such details.

6Well, when all was ready the priests went in and out of the first room whenever they wanted to, doing their work. 7But only the high priest went into the inner room, and then only once a year, all alone, and always with blood which he sprinkled on the mercy seat as an offering to God to cover his own mistakes and sins, and the mistakes and sins of all the people.

8And the Holy Spirit uses all this to point out to us that under the old system the common people could not go into the Holy of Holies as long as the outer room and the entire system it represents were still in use.

9This has an important lesson for us today. For under the old system, gifts and sacrifices were offered, but these failed to cleanse the hearts of the people who brought them. 10For the old system dealt only with certain rituals—what foods to eat and drink, rules for washing themselves, and rules about this and that. The people had to keep these rules to tide them over until Christ came with God's new and better way.

11He came as High Priest of this better system which we now have. He went into that greater, perfect tabernacle in heaven, not made by men nor part of this world, 12and once for all took blood into that inner room, the Holy of Holies, and sprinkled it on the mercy seat; but it was not the blood of goats and calves. No, he took his own blood, and with it he, by himself, made sure of our eternal salvation.

PSALM 106:32–48

AT Meribah, too, Israel angered God, causing Moses serious trouble, 33for he became angry and spoke foolishly.

³⁴Nor did Israel destroy the nations in the land as God had told them to, ³⁵but mingled in among the heathen and learned their evil ways, ³⁶sacrificing to their idols, and were led away from God. ³⁷,³⁸They even sacrificed their little children to the demons—the idols of Canaan—shedding innocent blood and polluting the land with murder. ³⁹Their evil deeds defiled them, for their love of idols was adultery in the sight of God. ⁴⁰That is why Jehovah's anger burned against his people, and he abhorred them. ⁴¹,⁴²That is why he let the heathen nations crush them. They were ruled by those who hated them and oppressed by their enemies.

⁴³Again and again he delivered them from their slavery, but they continued to rebel against him, and were finally destroyed by their sin. ⁴⁴Yet, even so, he listened to their cries and heeded their distress; ⁴⁵he remembered his promises to them and relented because of his great love, ⁴⁶and caused even their enemies who captured them to pity them.

⁴⁷O Lord God, save us! Regather us from the nations so we can thank your holy name and rejoice and praise you.

⁴⁸Blessed be the Lord, the God of Israel, from everlasting to everlasting. Let all the people say, "Amen!" Hallelujah!

PROVERBS FOR TODAY/ 27:10

Never abandon a friend—either yours or your father's. Then you won't need to go to a distant relative for help in your time of need.

NOVEMBER 9

EZEKIEL 20:1–49

LATE in July, six years after King Jeconiah was captured, some of the elders of Israel came to ask instructions from the Lord, and sat before me awaiting his reply.

²Then the Lord gave me this message:

³"Son of dust, say to the elders of Israel: The Lord God says: How dare you come to ask my help? I swear that I will tell you nothing. ⁴Judge them, son of dust; condemn them; tell them of all the sins of this nation from the times of their fathers until now. ⁵,⁶Tell them the Lord God says: When I chose Israel and revealed myself to her in Egypt, I swore to her and her descendants that I would bring them out of Egypt to a land I had discovered and explored for them—a good land, flowing as it were with milk and honey, the best of all lands anywhere.

⁷"Then I said to them: Get rid of every idol; do not defile yourselves with the Egyptian gods, for I am the Lord your God. ⁸But they rebelled against me and would not listen. They didn't get rid of their idols, nor forsake the gods of Egypt. Then I thought, I will pour out my fury upon them and fulfill my anger against them while they are still in Egypt.

⁹,¹⁰"But I didn't do it, for I acted to protect the honor of my name, lest the Egyptians laugh at Israel's God who couldn't keep them back from harm. So I brought my people out of Egypt right before the Egyptians' eyes, and led them into the wilderness. ¹¹There I gave them my laws so they could live by keeping them. If anyone keeps them, he shall live. ¹²And I gave them the Sabbath—a day of rest every seventh day—as a symbol between them and me, to remind them

that it is I, the Lord, who sanctifies them, that they are truly my people.

13"But Israel rebelled against me. There in the wilderness they refused my laws. They would not obey my rules even though obeying them means life. And they misused my Sabbaths. Then I thought, I will pour out my fury upon them and utterly consume them in the desert.

14"But again I refrained in order to protect the honor of my name, lest the nations who saw me bring them out of Egypt would say that it was because I couldn't care for them that I destroyed them. 15But I swore to them in the wilderness that I would not bring them into the land I had given them, a land full of milk and honey, the choicest spot on earth, 16because they laughed at my laws, ignored my wishes, and violated my Sabbaths—their hearts were with their idols! 17Nevertheless, I spared them. I didn't finish them off in the wilderness.

18"Then I spoke to their children and said: Don't follow your fathers' footsteps. Don't defile yourselves with their idols, 19for I am the Lord your God. Follow my laws; keep my ordinances; 20hallow my Sabbaths; for they are a symbol of the contract between us to help you remember that I am the Lord your God.

21"But their children too rebelled against me. They refused my laws—the laws that, if a person keeps them, he shall live. And they defiled my Sabbaths. So then I said: Now at last I will pour out my fury upon you in the wilderness.

22"Nevertheless, again I withdrew my judgment against them to protect my name among the nations who had seen my power in bringing them out of Egypt. 23,24But I took a solemn oath against them while they were in the wilderness that I would scatter them, dispersing them to the ends of the earth because they did not obey my laws but scorned them and violated my Sabbaths and longed for their fathers' idols. 25I let them adopt customs and laws which were worthless. Through the keeping of them they could not attain life. 26In the hope that they

would draw back in horror, and know that I alone am God, I let them pollute themselves with the very gifts I gave them. They burnt their firstborn children as offerings to their gods!

27,28"Son of dust, tell them that the Lord God says: Your fathers continued to blaspheme and betray me when I brought them into the land I promised them, for they offered sacrifices and incense on every high hill and under every tree! They roused my fury as they offered up their sacrifices to those 'gods.' They brought their perfumes and incense and poured out their drink offerings to them! 29I said to them: 'What is this place of sacrifice where you go?' And so it is still called 'The Place of Sacrifice'—that is how it got its name.

30"The Lord God wants to know whether you are going to pollute yourselves just as your fathers did, and keep on worshiping idols? 31For when you offer gifts to them and give your little sons to be burned to ashes as you do even today, shall I listen to you or help you, Israel? As I live, the Lord God says, I will not give you any message, though you have come to me to ask.

32"What you have in mind will not be done—to be like the nations all around you, serving gods of wood and stone. 33I will rule you with an iron fist and in great anger and with power. 34With might and fury I will bring you out from the lands where you are scattered, 35,36and will bring you into my desert judgment hall. I will judge you there, and get rid of the rebels, just as I did in the wilderness after I brought you out of Egypt. 37I will count you carefully and let only a small quota return. 38And the others—the rebels and all those who sin against me—I will purge from among you. They shall not enter Israel, but I will bring them out of the countries where they are in exile. And when that happens, you will know I am the Lord.

39"O Israel, the Lord God says: If you insist on worshiping your idols, go right ahead, but then don't bring your gifts to me as well! Such desecration of my holy name must stop!

40"For at Jerusalem in my holy mountain, says the Lord, all Israel shall worship me. There I will accept you, and require you to bring me your offerings and the finest of your gifts. 41You will be to me as an offering of perfumed incense when I bring you back from exile, and the nations will see the great change in your hearts. 42Then, when I have brought you home to the land I promised your fathers, you will know I am the Lord. 43Then you will look back at all your sins and loathe yourselves because of the evil you have done. 44And when I have honored my name by blessing you despite your wickedness, then, O Israel, you will know I am the Lord."

45Then this message came to me from the Lord:

46"Son of dust, look toward Jerusalem and speak out against it and the forest lands of the Negeb. 47Prophesy to it and say: Hear the word of the Lord. I will set you on fire, O forest, and every tree will die, green and dry alike. The terrible flames will not be quenched and they will scorch the world. 48And all the world will see that I, the Lord, have set the fire. It shall not be put out."

49Then I said, "O Lord God, they say of me, 'He only talks in riddles!' "

HEBREWS 9:13–28

AND if under the old system the blood of bulls and goats and the ashes of young cows could cleanse men's bodies from sin, 14just think how much more surely the blood of Christ will transform our lives and hearts. His sacrifice frees us from the worry of having to obey the old rules, and makes us want to serve the living God. For by the help of the eternal Holy Spirit, Christ willingly gave himself to God to die for our sins—he being perfect, without a single sin or fault. 15Christ came with this new agreement so that all who are invited may come and have forever all the wonders God has prom-

ised them. For Christ died to rescue them from the penalty of the sins they had committed while still under that old system.

16Now, if someone dies and leaves a will—a list of things to be given away to certain people when he dies—no one gets anything until it is proved that the person who wrote the will is dead. 17The will goes into effect only after the death of the person who wrote it. While he is still alive no one can use it to get any of those things he has promised them.

18That is why blood was sprinkled [as proof of Christ's death] before even the first agreement could go into effect. 19For after Moses had given the people all of God's laws, he took the blood of calves and goats, along with water, and sprinkled the blood over the book of God's laws and over all the people, using branches of hyssop bushes and scarlet wool to sprinkle with. 20Then he said, "This is the blood that marks the beginning of the agreement between you and God, the agreement God commanded me to make with you." 21And in the same way he sprinkled blood on the sacred tent and on whatever instruments were used for worship. 22In fact we can say that under the old agreement almost everything was cleansed by sprinkling it with blood, and without the shedding of blood there is no forgiveness of sins.

23That is why the sacred tent down here on earth, and everything in it—all copied from things in heaven—all had to be made pure by Moses in this way, by being sprinkled with the blood of animals. But the real things in heaven, of which these down here are copies, were made pure with far more precious offerings.

24For Christ has entered into heaven itself, to appear now before God as our Friend. It was not in the earthly place of worship that he did this, for that was merely a copy of the real temple in heaven. 25Nor has he offered himself again and again, as the high priest down here on earth offers animal blood in the

Holy of Holies each year. 26If that had been necessary, then he would have had to die again and again, ever since the world began. But no! He came once for all, at the end of the age, to put away the power of sin forever by dying for us.

27And just as it is destined that men die only once, and after that comes judgment, 28so also Christ died only once as an offering for the sins of many people; and he will come again, but not to deal again with our sins.

This time he will come bringing salvation to all those who are eagerly and patiently waiting for him.

PSALM 107:1–43

SAY "Thank you" to the Lord for being so good, for always being so loving and kind. 2Has the Lord redeemed you? Then speak out! Tell others he has saved you from your enemies.

3He brought the exiles back from the farthest corners of the earth. 4They were wandering homeless in the desert, 5hungry and thirsty and faint. 6"Lord, help!" they cried, and he did! 7He led them straight to safety and a place to live. 8Oh, that these men would praise the Lord for his loving-kindness, and for all of his wonderful deeds! 9For he satisfies the thirsty soul and fills the hungry soul with good.

10Who are these who sit in darkness, in the shadow of death, crushed by misery and slavery? 11They rebelled against the Lord, scorning him who is the God above all gods. 12That is why he broke them with hard labor; they fell and none could help them rise again. 13Then they cried to the Lord in their troubles, and he rescued them! 14He led them from the darkness and shadow of death and snapped their chains. 15Oh, that these men would praise the Lord for his loving-kindness and for all of his wonderful deeds! 16For he broke down their prison gates of brass and cut apart their iron bars.

17Others, the fools, were ill because of their sinful ways. 18Their appetites were gone and death was near. 19Then they cried to the Lord in their troubles, and he helped them and delivered them. 20He spoke, and they were healed—snatched from the door of death. 21Oh, that these men would praise the Lord for his lovingkindness and for all of his wonderful deeds! 22Let them tell him "Thank you" as their sacrifice, and sing about his glorious deeds.

23And then there are the sailors sailing the seven seas, plying the trade routes of the world. 24They, too, observe the power of God in action. 25He calls to the storm winds; the waves rise high. 26Their ships are tossed to the heavens and sink again to the depths; the sailors cringe in terror. 27They reel and stagger like drunkards and are at their wit's end. 28Then they cry to the Lord in their trouble, and he saves them. 29He calms the storm and stills the waves. 30What a blessing is that stillness, as he brings them safely into harbor! 31Oh, that these men would praise the Lord for his lovingkindness and for all of his wonderful deeds! 32Let them praise him publicly before the congregation, and before the leaders of the nation.

33He dries up rivers, 34and turns the good land of the wicked into deserts of salt. 35Again, he turns deserts into fertile, watered valleys. 36He brings the hungry to settle there and build their cities, 37to sow their fields and plant their vineyards, and reap their bumper crops! 38How he blesses them! They raise big families there, and many cattle.

39But others become poor through oppression, trouble and sorrow. 40For God pours contempt upon the haughty and causes princes to wander among ruins; 41but he rescues the poor who are godly and gives them many children and much prosperity. 42Good men everywhere will see it and be glad, while evil men are stricken silent.

43Listen, if you are wise, to what I am saying. Think about the lovingkindness of the Lord!

My son, how happy I will be if you turn out to be sensible! It will be a public honor to me.

NOVEMBER 10

EZEKIEL 21:1—22:31

THEN this message came to me from the Lord:

2"Son of dust, face toward Jerusalem and prophesy against Israel and against my Temple! 3For the Lord says: I am against you, Israel. I will unsheath my sword and destroy your people, good and bad alike— 4I will not spare even the righteous. I will make a clean sweep throughout the land from the Negeb to your northern borders. 5All the world shall know that it is I, the Lord. His sword is in his hand, and it will not return to its sheath again until its work is finished.

6"Sigh and groan before the people, son of dust, in your bitter anguish; sigh with grief and broken heart. 7When they ask you why, tell them: Because of the fearsome news that God has given me. When it comes true, the boldest heart will melt with fear; all strength will disappear. Every spirit will faint; strong knees will tremble and become as weak as water. And the Lord God says: Your doom is on the way; my judgments will be fulfilled!"

8Then again this message came to me from God:

9,10,11"Son of dust, tell them this: A sword is being sharpened and polished for terrible slaughter. Now will you laugh? For those far stronger than you have perished beneath its power. It is ready now to hand to the executioner. 12Son of dust, with sobbing, beat upon your thigh, for that sword shall slay my people and all their leaders. All alike shall die. 13It will put them all to the test—

and what chance do they have? the Lord God asks.

14"Prophesy to them in this way: Clap your hands vigorously, then take a sword and brandish it twice, thrice, to symbolize the great massacre they face! 15Let their hearts melt with terror, for a sword glitters at every gate; it flashes like lightning; it is razor-edged for slaughter. 16O sword, slash to the right and slash to the left, wherever you will, wherever you want. 17And you have prophesied with clapping hands that I, the Lord, will smite Jerusalem and satisfy my fury."

18Then this message came to me. The Lord said:

19,20"Son of dust, make a map and on it trace two routes for the king of Babylon to follow—one to Jerusalem and the other to Rabbah in Trans-Jordan. And put a signpost at the fork in the road from Babylon. 21For the king of Babylon stands at a fork, uncertain whether to attack Jerusalem or Rabbah. He will call his magicians to use divination; they will cast lots by shaking arrows from the quiver; they will sacrifice to idols and inspect the liver of their sacrifice. 22They will decide to turn toward Jerusalem! With battering rams they will go against the gates, shouting for the kill; they will build siege towers and make a hill against the walls to reach the top. 23Jerusalem won't understand this treachery; how could the diviners make this terrible mistake? For Babylon is Judah's ally and has sworn to defend Jerusalem! But (the king of Babylon) will think only of the times the people rebelled. He will attack and defeat them.

24"The Lord God says: Again and again your guilt cries out against you, for your sins are open and unashamed. Wherever you go, whatever you do, all is filled with sin. And now the time of punishment has come.

25"O King Zedekiah, evil prince of Israel, your final day of reckoning is here. 26Take off your jeweled crown, the Lord God says. The old order changes. Now the poor are exalted, and the rich brought very low. 27I will overturn, overturn, overturn the kingdom, so that even the new order that emerges will not succeed until the Man appears who has a right to it. And I will give it all to him.

28"Son of dust, prophesy to the Ammonites too, for they mocked my people in their woe. Tell them this:

"Against you also my glittering sword is drawn from its sheath; it is sharpened and polished and flashed like lightning. 29Your magicians and false prophets have told you lies of safety and success—that your gods will save you from the king of Babylon. Thus they have caused your death along with all the other wicked, for when the day of final reckoning has come you will be wounded unto death. 30Shall I return my sword to its sheath before I deal with you? No, I will destroy you in your own country where you were born. 31I will pour out my fury upon you and blow upon the fire of my wrath until it becomes a roaring conflagration, and I will deliver you into the hands of cruel men skilled in destruction. 32You are the fuel for the fire; your blood will be spilled in your own country and you will be utterly wiped out, your memory lost in history. For I, the Lord, have spoken it."

Now another message came from the Lord. He said:

2"Son of dust, indict Jerusalem as the City of Murder. Publicly denounce her terrible deeds. 3City of Murder, doomed and damned—City of Idols, filthy and foul— 4you are guilty both of murder and idolatry. Now comes your day of doom. You have reached the limit of your years. I will make you a laughingstock and a reproach to all the nations of the world. 5Near and far they will mock you, a city of infamous rebels.

6"Every leader in Israel who lives within your walls is bent on murder. 7Fathers and mothers are contemptuously ignored; immigrants and visitors are forced to pay you for your 'protection'; orphans and widows are wronged and oppressed. 8The things of God are all despised; my Sabbaths are ignored. 9Prisoners are falsely accused and sent to their death. Every mountain top is filled with idols; lewdness is everywhere. 10There are men who commit adultery with their fathers' wives and lie with menstruous women. 11Adultery with a neighbor's wife, a daughter-in-law, a half sister—this is common. 12Hired murderers, loan racketeers and extortioners are everywhere. You never even think of me and my commands, the Lord God says.

13"But now I snap my fingers and call a halt to your dishonest gain and bloodshed. 14How strong and courageous will you be then, in my day of reckoning? For I, the Lord, have spoken, and I will do all that I have said. 15I will scatter you throughout the world and burn out the wickedness within you. 16You will be dishonored among the nations, and you shall know I am the Lord."

17Then the Lord said this:

18,19,20"Son of dust, the people of Israel are the worthless slag left when silver is smelted. They are the dross, compounded from the brass, the tin, the iron and the lead. Therefore the Lord God says: Because you are worthless dross, I will bring you to my crucible in Jerusalem, to smelt you with the heat of my wrath. 21I will blow the fire of my wrath upon you, 22and you will melt like silver in fierce heat, and you will know that I, the Lord, have poured my wrath upon you."

23Again the message of the Lord came to me, saying:

24"Son of dust, say to the people of Israel: In the day of my indignation you shall be like an uncleared wilderness, or a desert without rain. 25Your 'prophets' have plotted against you like lions stalking prey. They devour many lives; they seize treasures and extort wealth; they multiply the widows in the land. 26Your priests have violated my laws and defiled my Temple and my holiness. To them the things of God are no more important than any daily task. They have not taught my people the difference between right and wrong, and they disregard my Sabbaths, so my holy name is greatly defiled among them. 27Your leaders are like wolves, who tear apart their victims, and they destroy lives for profit. 28Your 'prophets' describe false visions and speak false messages they claim are from God, when he hasn't spoken one word to them at all. Thus they repair the walls with whitewash! 29Even the common people oppress and rob the poor and needy and cruelly extort from aliens.

30"I looked in vain for anyone who would build again the wall of righteousness that guards the land, who could stand in the gap and defend you from my just attacks, but I found not one. 31And so the Lord God says: I will pour out my anger upon you; I will consume you with the fire of my wrath. I have heaped upon you the full penalty for all your sins."

HEBREWS 10:1–17

THE old system of Jewish laws gave only a dim foretaste of the good things Christ would do for us. The sacrifices under the old system were repeated again and again, year after year, but even so they could never save those who lived under their rules. 2If they could have, one offering would have been enough; the worshipers would have been cleansed once for all, and their feeling of guilt would be gone.

3But just the opposite happened: those yearly sacrifices reminded them of their disobedience and guilt instead of relieving their minds. 4For it is not possible for the blood of bulls and goats really to take away sins.

5That is why Christ said, as he came into the world, "O God, the blood of bulls and goats cannot satisfy you, so you have made ready this body of mine for me to lay as a sacrifice upon your altar. 6You were not satisfied with the animal sacrifices, slain and burnt before you as offerings for sin. 7Then I said, 'See, I have come to do your will, to lay down my life, just as the Scriptures said that I would.' "

8After Christ said this, about not being satisfied with the various sacrifices and offerings required under the old system, 9he then added, "Here I am. I have come to give my life."

He cancels the first system in favor of a far better one. 10Under this new plan we have been forgiven and made clean by Christ's dying for us once and for all.

11Under the old agreement the priests stood before the altar day after day offering sacrifices that could never take away our sins. 12But Christ gave himself to God for our sins as one sacrifice for all time, and then sat down in the place of highest honor at God's right hand, 13waiting for his enemies to be laid under his feet. 14For by that one offering he made forever perfect in the sight of God all those whom he is making holy.

15And the Holy Spirit testifies that this is so, for he has said, 16"This is the agreement I will make with the people of Israel, though they broke their first agreement: I will write my laws into their minds so that they will always know my will, and I will put my laws in their hearts so that they will want to obey them." 17And then he adds, "I will never again remember their sins and lawless deeds."

PSALM 108:1–13

O God, my heart is ready to praise you! I will sing and rejoice before you.

2Wake up, O harp and lyre! We will meet the dawn with song. 3I will praise you everywhere around the world, in every nation. ⁴For your lovingkindness is great beyond measure, high as the heavens. Your faithfulness reaches the skies. ⁵His glory is far more vast than the heavens. It towers above the earth. ⁶Hear the cry of your beloved child—come with mighty power and rescue me.

⁷God has given sacred promises; no wonder I exult! He has promised to give us all the land of Shechem, and also Succoth Valley. ⁸"Gilead is mine to give to you," he says, "and Manasseh as well;

the land of Ephraim is the helmet on my head. Judah is my scepter. ⁹But Moab and Edom are despised; and I will shout in triumph over the Philistines."

¹⁰Who but God can give me strength to conquer these fortified cities? Who else can lead me into Edom?

¹¹Lord, have you thrown us away? Have you deserted our army? ¹²Oh, help us fight against our enemies, for men are useless allies. ¹³But with the help of God we shall do mighty acts of valor. For he treads down our foes.

PROVERBS FOR TODAY/ 27:12

A sensible man watches for problems ahead and prepares to meet them. The simpleton never looks, and suffers the consequences.

NOVEMBER 11

EZEKIEL 23:1–49

THE Lord's message came to me again, saying:

2,3"Son of dust, there were two sisters who as young girls became prostitutes in Egypt.

4,5"The older girl was named Oholah; her sister was Oholibah. (I am speaking of Samaria and Jerusalem!) I married them, and they bore me sons and daughters. But then Oholah turned to other gods instead of me, and gave her love to the Assyrians, her neighbors, ⁶for they were all attractive young men, captains and commanders, in handsome blue, dashing about on their horses. ⁷And so she sinned with them—the choicest men of Assyria—worshiping their idols, defiling herself. ⁸For when she left Egypt, she did not leave her spirit of prostitution behind, but was still as lewd as in her youth, when the Egyptians poured out their lusts upon her and robbed her of her virginity.

⁹"And so I delivered her into the evil clutches of the Assyrians whose gods

she loved so much. ¹⁰They stripped her and killed her and took away her children as their slaves. Her name was known to every woman in the land as a sinner who had received what she deserved.

¹¹"But when Oholibah (Jerusalem) saw what had happened to her sister she went right ahead in the same way, and sinned even more than her sister. ¹²She fawned over her Assyrian neighbors, those handsome young men on fine steeds, those army officers in handsome uniforms—all of them desirable. ¹³I saw the way she was going, following right along behind her older sister.

14,15"She was in fact more debased than Samaria, for she fell in love with pictures she saw painted on a wall! They were pictures of Babylonian military officers, outfitted in striking red uniforms, with handsome belts, and flowing turbans on their heads. ¹⁶When she saw these paintings she longed to give herself to the men pictured, so she sent messengers to Chaldea to invite them to come to her. ¹⁷And they came and committed adultery with her, defiling her in the bed of love, but afterward she hated them and broke off all relations with them.

18"And I despised her just as I despised her sister, because she flaunted herself before them and gave herself to their lust. 19,20But that didn't bother her. She turned to even greater prostitution, sinning with the lustful men she remembered from her youth when she was a prostitute in Egypt. 21And thus you celebrated those former days when as a young girl you gave your virginity to those from Egypt.

22"And now the Lord God says that he will raise against you, O Oholibah (Jerusalem), those very nations from which you turned away, disgusted. 23For the Babylonians will come, and all the Chaldeans from Pekod and Shoa and Koa; and all the Assyrians with them—handsome young men of high rank, riding their steeds. 24They will come against you from the north with chariots and wagons and a great army fully prepared for attack. They will surround you on every side with armored men and I will let them at you, to do with you as they wish. 25And I will send my jealousy against you and deal furiously with you, and cut off your nose and ears; your survivors will be killed; your children will be taken away as slaves, and everything left will be burned. 26They will strip you of your beautiful clothes and jewels.

27"And so I will put a stop to your lewdness and prostitution brought from the land of Egypt; you will no more long for Egypt and her gods. 28For the Lord God says: I will surely deliver you over to your enemies, to those you loathe. 29They will deal with you in hatred, and rob you of all you own, leaving you naked and bare. And the shame of your prostitution shall be exposed to all the world.

30"You brought all this upon yourself by worshiping the gods of other nations, defiling yourself with all their idols. 31You have followed in your sister's footsteps, so I will punish you with the same terrors that destroyed her. 32Yes, the terrors that fell upon her will fall upon you—

and the cup from which she drank was full and large. And all the world will mock you for your woe. 33You will reel like a drunkard beneath the awful blows of sorrow and distress, just as your sister Samaria did. 34In deep anguish you will drain that cup of terror to the very bottom and will lick the inside to get every drop. For I have spoken, says the Lord. 35Because you have forgotten me and turned your backs upon me, therefore you must bear the consequence of all your sin.

36"Son of dust, you must accuse Jerusalem and Samaria of all their awful deeds. 37For they have committed both adultery and murder; they have worshiped idols and murdered my children whom they bore to me, burning them as sacrifices on their altars. 38On the same day they defiled my Temple and ignored my Sabbaths, 39for when they had murdered their children in front of their idols, then even that same day they actually came into my Temple to worship! That is how much regard they have for me!

40"You even sent away to distant lands for priests to come with other gods for you to serve, and they have come and been welcomed! You bathed yourself, painted your eyelids, and put on your finest jewels for them. 41You sat together on a beautifully embroidered bed and put my incense and my oil upon a table spread before you. 42From your apartment came the sound of many men carousing—lewd men and drunkards from the wilderness, who put bracelets on your wrists and beautiful crowns upon your head. 43Will they commit adultery with these who have become old harlot hags? 44Yet that is what they did. They went in to them—to Samaria and Jerusalem, these shameless harlots—with all the zest of lustful men who visit prostitutes. 45But just persons everywhere will judge them for what they really are— adulteresses and murderers. They will mete out to them the sentences the law demands.

46"The Lord God says: Bring an army

against them and hand them out to be crushed and despised. 47For their enemies will stone them and kill them with swords; they will butcher their sons and daughters and burn their homes. 48Thus will I make lewdness and idolatry to cease from the land. My judgment will be a lesson against idolatry for all to see. 49For you will be fully repaid for all your harlotry, your worshiping of idols. You will suffer the full penalty, and you will know that I alone am God."

HEBREWS 10:18–39

NOW, when sins have once been forever forgiven and forgotten, there is no need to offer more sacrifices to get rid of them.

19And so, dear brothers, now we may walk right into the very Holy of Holies where God is, because of the blood of Jesus. 20This is the fresh, new, life-giving way which Christ has opened up for us by tearing the curtain—his human body—to let us into the holy presence of God.

21And since this great High Priest of ours rules over God's household, 22let us go right in, to God himself, with true hearts fully trusting him to receive us, because we have been sprinkled with Christ's blood to make us clean, and because our bodies have been washed with pure water.

23Now we can look forward to the salvation God has promised us. There is no longer any room for doubt, and we can tell others that salvation is ours, for there is no question that he will do what he says.

24In response to all he has done for us, let us outdo each other in being helpful and kind to each other and in doing good.

25Let us not neglect our church meetings, as some people do, but encourage and warn each other, especially now that the day of his coming back again is drawing near.

26If anyone sins deliberately by reject-ing the Savior after knowing the truth of forgiveness, this sin is not covered by Christ's death; there is no way to get rid of it. 27There will be nothing to look forward to but the terrible punishment of God's awful anger which will consume all his enemies. 28A man who refused to obey the laws given by Moses was killed without mercy if there were two or three witnesses to his sin. 29Think how much more terrible the punishment will be for those who have trampled underfoot the Son of God and treated his cleansing blood as though it were common and unhallowed, and insulted and outraged the Holy Spirit who brings God's mercy to his people.

30For we know him who said, "Justice belongs to me; I will repay them"; who also said, "The Lord himself will handle these cases." 31It is a fearful thing to fall into the hands of the living God.

32Don't ever forget those wonderful days when you first learned about Christ. Remember how you kept right on with the Lord even though it meant terrible suffering. 33Sometimes you were laughed at and beaten, and sometimes you watched and sympathized with others suffering the same things. 34You suffered with those thrown into jail, and you were actually joyful when all you owned was taken from you, knowing that better things were awaiting you in heaven, things that would be yours forever.

35Do not let this happy trust in the Lord die away, no matter what happens. Remember your reward! 36You need to keep on patiently doing God's will if you want him to do for you all that he has promised. 37His coming will not be delayed much longer. 38And those whose faith has made them good in God's sight must live by faith, trusting him in everything. Otherwise, if they shrink back, God will have no pleasure in them.

39But we have never turned our backs on God and sealed our fate. No, our faith in him assures our souls' salvation.

PSALM 109:1–31

O God of my praise, don't stand silent and aloof 2while the wicked slander me and tell their lies. 3They have no reason to hate and fight me, yet they do! 4I love them, but even while I am praying for them, they are trying to destroy me. 5They return evil for good, and hatred for love.

6Show him how it feels! Let lies be told about him, and bring him to court before an unfair judge. 7When his case is called for judgment, let him be pronounced guilty. Count his prayers as sins. 8Let his years be few and brief; let others step forward to replace him. 9,10May his children become fatherless and his wife a widow; may they be evicted from the ruins of their home. 11May creditors seize his entire estate and strangers take all he has earned. 12,13Let no one be kind to him; let no one pity his fatherless children. May they die. May his family name be blotted out in a single generation. 14Punish the sins of his father and mother. Don't overlook them. 15Think constantly about the evil things he has done, and cut off his name from the memory of man.

16For he refused all kindness to others, and persecuted those in need, and hounded brokenhearted ones to death. 17He loved to curse others; now you curse him. He never blessed others; now don't you bless him. 18Cursing is as much a part of him as his clothing, or as the water he drinks, or the rich food he eats.

19Now may those curses return and cling to him like his clothing or his belt. 20This is the Lord's punishment upon my enemies who tell lies about me and threaten me with death.

21But as for me, O Lord, deal with me as your child, as one who bears your name! Because you are so kind, O Lord, deliver me.

22,23I am slipping down the hill to death; I am shaken off from life as easily as a man brushes a grasshopper from his arm. 24My knees are weak from fasting and I am skin and bones. 25I am a symbol of failure to all mankind; when they see me they shake their heads.

26Help me, O Lord my God! Save me because you are loving and kind. 27Do it publicly, so all will see that you yourself have done it. 28Then let them curse me if they like—I won't mind that if you are blessing me! For then all their efforts to destroy me will fail, and I shall go right on rejoicing!

29Make them fail in everything they do. Clothe them with disgrace. 30But I will give repeated thanks to the Lord, praising him to everyone. 31For he stands beside the poor and hungry to save them from their enemies.

PROVERBS FOR TODAY/ 27:13

The world's poorest credit risk is the man who agrees to pay a stranger's debts.

NOVEMBER 12

EZEKIEL 24:1—26:21

O NE day late in December of the ninth year (of King Jehoiachin's captivity), another message came to me from the Lord.

2"Son of dust," he said, "write down this date, for today the king of Babylon has attacked Jerusalem. 3And now give this parable to these rebels, Israel; tell them the Lord God says: Put a pot of water on the fire to boil. 4Fill it with choicest mutton, the rump and shoulder and all the most tender cuts. 5Use only the best sheep from the flock, and heap fuel on the fire beneath the pot. Boil the meat well, until the flesh falls off the bones.

6"For the Lord God says: Woe to Jerusalem, City of Murderers; you are a pot that is pitted with rust and with wickedness. So take out the meat chunk by chunk in whatever order it comes—for none is better than any other. 7For her wickedness is evident to all—she boldly murders, leaving blood upon the rocks in open view for all to see; she does not even try to cover it. 8And I have left it there, uncovered, to shout to me against her and arouse my wrath and vengeance.

9"Woe to Jerusalem, City of Murderers. I will pile on the fuel beneath her. 10Heap on the wood; let the fire roar and the pot boil. Cook the meat well and then empty the pot and burn the bones. 11Now set it empty on the coals to scorch away the rust and corruption. 12But all for naught—it all remains despite the hottest fire. 13It is the rust and corruption of your filthy lewdness, of worshiping your idols. And now, because I wanted to cleanse you and you refused, remain filthy until my fury has accomplished all its terrors upon you! 14I, the Lord, have spoken it; it shall come to pass and I will do it."

15Again a message came to me from the Lord, saying:

16"Son of dust, I am going to take away your lovely wife. Suddenly, she will die. Yet you must show no sorrow. Do not weep; let there be no tears. 17You may sigh, but only quietly. Let there be no wailing at her grave; don't bare your head nor feet, and don't accept the food brought to you by consoling friends."

18I proclaimed this to the people in the morning, and in the evening my wife died. The next morning I did all the Lord had told me to.

19Then the people said: "What does all this mean? What are you trying to tell us?"

20,21And I answered, "The Lord told me to say to the people of Israel: I will destroy my lovely, beautiful Temple, the strength of your nation. And your sons and daughters in Judea will be slaughtered by the sword. 22And you will do as I have done; you may not mourn in public or console yourself by eating the food brought to you by sympathetic friends. 23Your head and feet shall not be bared; you shall not mourn or weep. But you will sorrow to one another for your sins, and mourn privately for all the evil you have done. 24Ezekiel is an example to you, the Lord God says. You will do as he has done. And when that time comes, then you will know I am the Lord."

25"Son of dust, on the day I finish taking from them in Jerusalem the joy of their hearts and their glory and joys— their wives and their sons and their daughters— 26on that day a refugee from Jerusalem will start on a journey to come to you in Babylon to tell you what has happened. 27And on the day of his arrival, your voice will suddenly return to you so that you can talk with him; and you will be a symbol for these people and they shall know I am the Lord."

THEN the Lord's message came to me again. He said:

2"Son of dust, look toward the land of Ammon and prophesy against its people. 3Tell them: Listen to what the Lord God says. Because you scoffed when my Temple was destroyed, and mocked Israel in her anguish, and laughed at Judah when she was marched away captive, 4therefore I will let the Bedouins from the desert to the east of you overrun your land. They will set up their encampments among you. They will harvest all your fruit and steal your dairy cattle. 5And I will turn the city of Rabbah into a pasture for camels and all the country of the Ammonites into a waste land where flocks of sheep can graze. Then you will know I am the Lord.

6"For the Lord God says: Because you clapped and stamped and cheered with glee at the destruction of my people,

7therefore I will lay my hand heavily upon you, delivering you to many nations for devastation. I will cut you off from being a nation any more. I will destroy you; then you shall know I am the Lord.

8"And the Lord God says: Because the Moabites have said that Judah is no better off than any other nation, 9,10therefore I will open up the eastern flank of Moab, wiping out her frontier cities, the glory of the nation—Beth-jesh-imoth, Baal-meon and Kiriathaim. And Bedouin tribes from the desert to the east will pour in upon her, just as they will upon Ammon. And Moab will no longer be counted among the nations. 11Thus I will bring down my judgment upon the Moabites, and they shall know I am the Lord.

12"And the Lord God says: Because the people of Edom have sinned so greatly by avenging themselves upon the people of Judah, 13I will smash Edom with my fist and wipe out her people, her cattle and her flocks. The sword will destroy everything from Teman to De-dan. 14By the hand of my people, Israel, this shall be done. They will carry out my furious vengeance.

15"And the Lord God says: Because the Philistines have acted against Judah out of revenge and long-standing hatred, 16I will shake my fist over the land of the Philistines, and I will wipe out the Cherithites and utterly destroy those along the sea coast. 17I will execute terrible vengeance upon them to rebuke them for what they have done. And when all this happens, then they shall know I am the Lord."

ANOTHER message came to me from the Lord on the first day of the month, in the eleventh year (after King Jehoiachin was taken away to captivity).

2"Son of dust, Tyre has rejoiced over the fall of Jerusalem, saying, 'Ha! She who controlled the lucrative north-south trade routes along the coast and along the course of the Jordan River has been broken, and I have fallen heir! Because she has been laid waste, I shall become wealthy!'

3"Therefore the Lord God says: I stand against you, Tyre, and I will bring nations against you like ocean waves. 4They will destroy the walls of Tyre and tear down her towers. I will scrape away her soil and make her a bare rock! 5Her island shall become uninhabited, a place for fishermen to spread their nets, for I have spoken it, says the Lord God. Tyre shall become the prey of many nations, 6and her mainland city shall perish by the sword. Then they shall know I am the Lord.

7"For the Lord God says: I will bring Nebuchadnezzar, king of Babylon—the king of kings from the north—against Tyre with a great army and cavalry and chariots. 8First he will destroy your sub-urbs; then he will attack your mainland city by building a siege wall and raising a roof of shields against it. 9He will set up battering rams against your walls and with sledge hammers demolish your forts. 10The hoofs of his cavalry will choke the city with dust, and your walls will shake as the horses gallop through your broken gates, pulling chariots be-hind them. 11Horsemen will occupy every street in the city; they will butcher your people, and your famous, huge pillars will topple.

12"They will plunder all your riches and merchandise and break down your walls. They will destroy your lovely homes and dump your stones and timber and even your dust into the sea. 13I will stop the music of your songs. No more will there be the sound of harps among you. 14I will make your island a bare rock, a place for fishermen to spread their nets. You will never be rebuilt, for I, the Lord, have spoken it. So says the Lord. 15The whole country will shake with your fall; the wounded will scream as the slaughter goes on.

16"Then all the seaport rulers shall come down from their thrones and lay aside their robes and beautiful garments and sit on the ground shaking with fear at what they have seen. 17And they shall wail for you, singing this dirge: 'O mighty island city, with your naval power that terrorized the mainland, how you have vanished from the seas! 18How the islands tremble at your fall! They watch dismayed.'

19"For the Lord God says: I will destroy Tyre to the ground. You will sink beneath the terrible waves of enemy attack. Great seas shall swallow you. 20I will send you to the pit of hell to lie there with those of long ago. Your city will lie in ruins, dead, like the bodies of those in the underworld who entered long ago the nether world of the dead. Never again will you be inhabited or be given beauty here in the land of those who live. 21I will bring you to a dreadful end; no search will be enough to find you, says the Lord."

HEBREWS 11:1–16

WHAT is faith? It is the confident assurance that something we want is going to happen. It is the certainty that what we hope for is waiting for us, even though we cannot see it up ahead. 2Men of God in days of old were famous for their faith.

3By faith—by believing God—we know that the world and the stars—in fact, all things—were made at God's command; and that they were all made from things that can't be seen.

4It was by faith that Abel obeyed God and brought an offering that pleased God more than Cain's offering did. God accepted Abel and proved it by accepting his gift; and though Abel is long dead, we can still learn lessons from him about trusting God.

5Enoch trusted God too, and that is why God took him away to heaven without dying; suddenly he was gone because God took him. Before this happened God had said how pleased he was with Enoch. 6You can never please God without faith, without depending on him. Anyone who wants to come to God must believe that there is a God and that he rewards those who sincerely look for him.

7Noah was another who trusted God. When he heard God's warning about the future, Noah believed him even though there was then no sign of a flood, and wasting no time, he built the ark and saved his family. Noah's belief in God was in direct contrast to the sin and disbelief of the rest of the world—which refused to obey—and because of his faith he became one of those whom God has accepted.

8Abraham trusted God, and when God told him to leave home and go far away to another land which he promised to give him, Abraham obeyed. Away he went, not even knowing where he was going. 9And even when he reached God's promised land, he lived in tents like a mere visitor, as did Isaac and Jacob, to whom God gave the same promise. 10Abraham did this because he was confidently waiting for God to bring him to that strong heavenly city whose designer and builder is God.

11Sarah, too, had faith, and because of this she was able to become a mother in spite of her old age, for she realized that God, who gave her his promise, would certainly do what he said. 12And so a whole nation came from Abraham, who was too old to have even one child—a nation with so many millions of people that, like the stars of the sky and the sand on the ocean shores, there is no way to count them.

13These men of faith I have mentioned died without ever receiving all that God had promised them; but they saw it all awaiting them on ahead and were glad, for they agreed that this earth was not their real home but that they were just strangers visiting down here. 14And quite obviously when they talked like that, they were looking forward to their real home in heaven.

15If they had wanted to, they could have gone back to the good things of this world. 16But they didn't want to. They were living for heaven. And now God is not ashamed to be called their God, for he has made a heavenly city for them.

PSALM 110:1–7

JEHOVAH said to my Lord the Messiah, "Rule as my regent—I will subdue your enemies and make them bow low before you."

2Jehovah has established your throne in Jerusalem to rule over your enemies. 3In that day of your power your people shall come to you willingly, dressed in holy altar robes. And your strength shall be renewed day by day like morning dew. 4Jehovah has taken oath, and will not rescind his vow, that you are a priest forever like Melchizedek. 5God stands beside you to protect you. He will strike down many kings in the day of his anger. 6He will punish the nations, and fill them with their dead. He will crush many heads. 7But he himself shall be refreshed from springs along the way.

PROVERBS FOR TODAY/ 27:14

If you shout a pleasant greeting to a friend too early in the morning, he will count it as a curse!

NOVEMBER 13

EZEKIEL 27:1—28:26

THEN this message came to me from the Lord. He said:

2"Son of dust, sing this sad dirge for Tyre:

3"O mighty seaport city, merchant center of the world, the Lord God speaks. You say, 'I am the most beautiful city in all the world.' 4You have extended your boundaries out into the sea; your architects have made you glorious. 5You are like a ship built of finest fir from Senir. They took a cedar from Lebanon to make a mast for you. 6They made your oars from oaks of Bashan. The walls of your cabin are of cypress from the southern coast of Cyprus. 7Your sails are made of Egypt's finest linens; you stand beneath awnings bright with purple and scarlet dyes from eastern Cyprus.

8"Your sailors come from Sidon and Arvad; your helmsmen are skilled men from Zemer. 9Wise old craftsmen from Gebal do the calking. Ships come from every land with all their goods to barter for your trade.

10"Your army includes men from far-off Paras, Lud and Put. They serve you—it is a feather in your cap to have their shields hang upon your walls; it is the ultimate of honor. 11Men from Arvad and from Helech are the sentinels upon your walls; your towers are manned by men from Gamad. Their shields hang row on row upon the walls, perfecting your glory.

12"From Tarshish come all kinds of riches to your markets—silver, iron, tin and lead. 13Merchants from Javan, Tubal and Meshech bring slaves and bronze dishes, 14while from Togarmah come chariot horses, steeds and mules.

15"Merchants come to you from Rhodes, and many coastlands are your captive markets, giving payment in ebony and ivory. 16Edom sends her traders to buy your many wares. They bring emeralds, purple dyes, embroidery, fine linen, and jewelry of coral and agate. 17Judah and the cities in what was once the kingdom of Israel send merchants with wheat from Minnith and Pannag, and with honey, oil and balm. 18Damascus comes. She brings wines from Helbon, and white Syrian wool to trade for all the rich variety of goods you make. 19Vedan and Javan bring Arabian yarn, wrought iron, cassia and calamus, 20while Dedan brings expensive saddlecloths for riding.

21"The Arabians, and Kedar's wealthy merchant princes bring you lambs and rams and goats. 22The merchants of Sheba and Raamah come with all kinds of spices, jewels and gold. 23Haran and Canneh, Eden, Asshur and Chilmad all send their wares. 24They bring choice fabrics to trade—blue cloth, embroidery and many-colored carpets bound with cords and made secure. 25The ships of Tarshish are your ocean caravans; your island warehouse is filled to the brim!

26"But now your statesmen bring your ship of state into a hurricane! Your mighty vessel flounders in the heavy eastern gale, and you are wrecked in the heart of the seas! 27Everything is lost. Your riches and wares, your sailors and pilots, your shipwrights and merchants and soldiers and all the people sink into the sea on the day of your vast ruin.

28"The surrounding cities quake at the sound as your pilots scream with fright. 29All your sailors out at sea come to land and watch upon the mainland shore, 30weeping bitterly and casting dust upon their heads and wallowing in ashes. 31They shave their heads in grief and put on sackcloth and weep for you with bitterness of heart and deep mourning.

32"And this is the song of their sorrow: 'Where in all the world was there ever such a wondrous city as Tyre, destroyed in the midst of the sea? 33Your merchandise satisfied the desires of many nations. Kings at the ends of the earth rejoiced in the riches you sent them. 34Now you lie broken beneath the sea; all your merchandise and all your crew have perished with you. 35All who live along the coastlands watch, incredulous. Their kings are horribly afraid and look on with twisted faces. 36The merchants of the nations shake their heads, for your fate is dreadful; you have forever perished.' "

HERE is another message given to me from the Lord:

2,3"Son of dust, say to the prince of Tyre: The Lord God says: You are so proud you think you are God, sitting on the throne of a god on your island home in the midst of the seas. But you are only a man, and not a god, though you boast yourself to be like God. You are wiser than Daniel, for no secret is hidden from you. 4You have used your wisdom and understanding to get great wealth—gold and silver and many treasures. 5Yes, your wisdom has made you very rich and very proud.

6"Therefore the Lord God says: Because you claim that you are as wise as God, 7an enemy army, the terror of the nations, shall suddenly draw their swords against your marvelous wisdom and defile your splendor! 8They will bring you to the pit of hell and you shall die as those pierced with many wounds, there on your island in the heart of the seas. 9Then will you boast as a god? At least to these invaders you will be no god, but merely man! 10You will die like an outcast at the hands of foreigners. For I have spoken it, the Lord God says."

11Then this further message came to me from the Lord:

12"Son of dust, weep for the king of Tyre. Tell him, the Lord God says: You were the perfection of wisdom and beauty. 13You were in Eden, the garden of God; your clothing was bejeweled with every precious stone—ruby, topaz, diamond, chrysolite, onyx, jasper, sapphire, carbuncle, and emerald—all in beautiful settings of finest gold. They were given to you on the day you were created. 14I appointed you to be the anointed Guardian Angel. You had access to the holy mountain of God. You walked among the stones of fire.

15"You were perfect in all you did from the day you were created until that time when wrong was found in you. 16Your great wealth filled you with internal turmoil and you sinned. Therefore, I cast you out of the mountain of God like a common sinner. I destroyed you, O Guardian Angel, from the midst of the stones of fire. 17Your heart was filled with pride because of all your beauty; you corrupted your wisdom for the sake of your splendor. Therefore I have cast you down to the ground and exposed you helpless before the curious gaze of kings. 18You defiled your holiness with lust for gain; therefore I brought forth fire from your own actions and let it burn you to ashes upon the earth in the sight of all those watching you. 19All who know you are appalled at your fate; you are an example of horror; you are destroyed forever."

20Then another message came to me from the Lord:

21"Son of dust, look toward the city of Sidon and prophesy against it. Say to it:

22"The Lord God says: I am your enemy, O Sidon, and I will reveal my power over you. When I destroy you and show forth my holiness upon you then all who see shall know I am the Lord. 23I will send an epidemic of disease and an army to destroy; the wounded shall be slain in your streets by troops on every side. Then you will know I am the Lord. 24No longer shall you and Israel's other neighbor nations prick and tear at Israel like thorns and briars, though they formerly despised her and treated her with great contempt.

25"The people of Israel will once more live in their own land, the land I gave their father Jacob. For I will gather them back again from distant lands where I have scattered them and I will show the nations of the world my holiness among my people. 26They will live safely in Israel, and build their homes and plant their vineyards. When I punish all the bordering nations that treated them with such contempt, then they shall know I am the Lord their God."

HEBREWS 11:17–31

WHILE God was testing him, Abraham still trusted in God and his promises, and so he offered up his son Isaac, and was ready to slay him on the altar of sacrifice; 18yes, to slay even Isaac, through whom

God had promised to give Abraham a whole nation of descendants!

19He believed that if Isaac died God would bring him back to life again; and that is just about what happened, for as far as Abraham was concerned, Isaac was doomed to death, but he came back again alive! 20It was by faith that Isaac knew God would give future blessings to his two sons, Jacob and Esau.

21By faith Jacob, when he was old and dying, blessed each of Joseph's two sons as he stood and prayed, leaning on the top of his cane.

22And it was by faith that Joseph, as he neared the end of his life, confidently spoke of God bringing the people of Israel out of Egypt; and he was so sure of it that he made them promise to carry his bones with them when they left!

23Moses' parents had faith too. When they saw that God had given them an unusual child, they trusted that God would save him from the death the king commanded, and they hid him for three months, and were not afraid.

24,25It was by faith that Moses, when he grew up, refused to be treated as the grandson of the king, but chose to share ill-treatment with God's people instead of enjoying the fleeting pleasures of sin. 26He thought that it was better to suffer for the promised Christ than to own all the treasures of Egypt, for he was looking forward to the great reward that God would give him. 27And it was because he trusted God that he left the land of Egypt and wasn't afraid of the king's anger. Moses kept right on going; it seemed as though he could see God right there with him. 28And it was because he believed God would save his people that he commanded them to kill a lamb as God had told them to and sprinkle the blood on the doorposts of their homes, so that God's terrible Angel of Death could not touch the oldest child in those homes, as he did among the Egyptians.

29The people of Israel trusted God and went right through the Red Sea as though they were on dry ground. But when the

Egyptians chasing them tried it, they all were drowned.

30It was faith that brought the walls of Jericho tumbling down after the people of Israel had walked around them seven days, as God had commanded them. 31By faith—because she believed in God and his power—Rahab the harlot did not die with all the others in her city when they refused to obey God, for she gave a friendly welcome to the spies.

PSALM 111:1–10

HALLELUJAH! I want to express publicly before his people my heartfelt thanks to God for his mighty miracles. All who are thankful should ponder them with me. 3For his

miracles demonstrate his honor, majesty, and eternal goodness.

4Who can forget the wonders he performs—deeds of mercy and of grace? 5He gives food to those who trust him; he never forgets his promises. 6He has shown his great power to his people by giving them the land of Israel, though it was the home of many nations living there. 7All he does is just and good, and all his laws are right, 8for they are formed from truth and goodness, and stand firm forever. 9He has paid a full ransom for his people; now they are always free to come to Jehovah (what a holy, awe-inspiring name that is).

10How can men be wise? The only way to begin is by reverence for God. For growth in wisdom comes from obeying his laws. Praise his name forever.

PROVERBS FOR TODAY/ 27:15, 16

A constant dripping on a rainy day and a cranky woman are much alike! You can no more stop her complaints than you can stop the wind or hold onto anything with oil-slick hands.

NOVEMBER 14

EZEKIEL 29:1—30:26

LATE in December of the tenth year (of the imprisonment of King Jehoiachin), this message came to me from the Lord:

2"Son of dust, face toward Egypt and prophesy against Pharaoh her king and all her people. 3Tell them that the Lord God says: I am your enemy, Pharaoh, king of Egypt—mighty dragon lying in the middle of your rivers. For you have said, 'The Nile is mine; I have made it for myself!' 4I will put hooks into your jaws and drag you out onto the land with fish sticking to your scales. 5And I will leave you and all the fish stranded in the desert to die, and you won't be buried, for I have given you as food to the wild animals and birds.

6"Because of the way your might col-

lapsed when Israel called on you for aid [instead of trusting me], all of you shall know I am the Lord. 7Israel leaned on you but, like a cracked staff, you snapped beneath her hand and wrenched her shoulder out of joint and made her stagger with the pain. 8Therefore the Lord God says: I will bring an army against you, O Egypt, and destroy both men and herds. 9The land of Egypt shall become a desolate wasteland, and the Egyptians will know that I, the Lord, have done it.

10"Because you said: 'The Nile is mine! I made it!' therefore I am against you and your river and I will utterly destroy the land of Egypt, from Migdol to Syene, as far south as the border of Ethiopia. 11For forty years not a soul will pass that way, neither men nor animals. It will be completely uninhabited. ¹²I will make Egypt desolate, surrounded by desolate nations, and her cities will lie as wastelands for forty years. I will exile the Egyptians to other lands.

¹³"But the Lord God says that at the end of the forty years he will bring the Egyptians home again from the nations to which they will be banished. ¹⁴And I will restore the fortunes of Egypt and bring her people back to the land of Pathros in southern Egypt where they were born, but she will be an unimportant, minor kingdom. ¹⁵She will be the lowliest of all the nations; never again will she raise herself above the other nations; never again will Egypt be great enough for that.

¹⁶"Israel will no longer expect any help from Egypt. Whenever she thinks of asking for it, then she will remember her sin in seeking it before. Then Israel will know that I alone am God."

¹⁷In the twenty-seventh year of King Jehoiachin's captivity, around the middle of March, this message came to me from the Lord:

¹⁸"Son of dust, the army of King Nebuchadnezzar of Babylon fought hard against Tyre. The soldiers' heads were bald (from carrying heavy basketfuls of earth); their shoulders were raw and blistered (from burdens of stones for the siege). And Nebuchadnezzar received no compensation and could not pay the army for all this work. ¹⁹Therefore, the Lord God says, I will give the land of Egypt to Nebuchadnezzar, king of Babylon, and he will carry off her wealth, plundering everything she has, for his army. ²⁰Yes, I have given him the land of Egypt for his salary, because he was working for me during those thirteen years at Tyre, says the Lord. ²¹And the day will come when I will cause the ancient glory of Israel to revive, and then at last her words will be respected, and Egypt shall know I am the Lord."

ANOTHER message from the Lord!

²,³"Son of dust, prophesy and say: The Lord God says, Weep, for the terrible day is almost here; the day of the Lord; a day of clouds and gloom; a day of despair for the nations! ⁴A sword shall fall on Egypt; the slain shall cover the ground. Her wealth is taken away, her foundations destroyed. The land of Cush has been ravished. ⁵For Cush and Put and Lud, Arabia and Libya and all the countries leagued with them shall perish in that war.

⁶"For the Lord says: All Egypt's allies shall fall, and the pride of her power shall end. From Migdol to Syene they shall perish by the sword. ⁷She shall be desolate, surrounded by desolate nations, and her cities shall be in ruins, surrounded by other ruined cities. ⁸And they will know I am the Lord when I have set Egypt on fire and destroyed her allies. ⁹At that time I will send swift messengers to bring panic to the Ethiopians; great terror shall befall them at that time of Egypt's doom. This will all come true.

¹⁰"For the Lord God says: Nebuchadnezzar, king of Babylon, will destroy the multitudes of Egypt. ¹¹He and his armies—the terror of the nations—are sent to demolish the land. They shall war against Egypt and cover the ground with the slain. ¹²I will dry up the Nile and sell the whole land to wicked men. I will destroy Egypt and everything in it, using foreigners to do it. I, the Lord, have spoken it.

¹³"And I will smash the idols of Egypt and the images at Memphis, and there will be no king in Egypt; anarchy shall reign!

¹⁴"The cities of Pathros [along the upper Nile], and Zoan and Thebes shall lie in ruins by my hand. ¹⁵And I will pour out my fury upon Pelusium, the strongest fortress of Egypt, and I will stamp out the people of Thebes. ¹⁶Yes, I will set fire to Egypt, Pelusium will be racked with pain, Thebes will be torn apart, Memphis will be in daily terror. ¹⁷The young men of Heliopolis and Bubastis shall die by the sword and the women will be taken away as slaves. ¹⁸When I come to break the power of Egypt it will be a dark day for Tehaphnehes too;

a dark cloud will cover her, and her daughters will be taken away as captives. ¹⁹And so I will greatly punish Egypt and they shall know I am the Lord."

²⁰A year later, around the middle of March of the eleventh year of King Jehoiachin's captivity, this message came to me:

²¹"Son of dust, I have broken the arm of Pharaoh, king of Egypt, and it has not been set nor put into a cast to make it strong enough to hold a sword again. ²²For, the Lord God says, I am against Pharaoh, king of Egypt, and I will break both his arms—the strong one and the one that was broken before, and I will make his sword clatter to the ground. ²³And I will banish the Egyptians to many lands. ²⁴And I will strengthen the arms of the king of Babylon and place my sword in his hand. But I will break the arms of Pharaoh, king of Egypt, and he shall groan before the king of Babylon as one who has been wounded unto death. ²⁵I will strengthen the hands of the king of Babylon, while the arms of Pharaoh fall useless to his sides. Yes, when I place my sword into the hand of the king of Babylon, and he swings it over the land of Egypt, Egypt shall know I am the Lord. ²⁶I will scatter the Egyptians among the nations; then they shall know I am the Lord."

HEBREWS 11:32—12:13

WELL, how much more do I need to say? It would take too long to recount the stories of the faith of Gideon and Barak and Samson and Jephthah and David and Samuel and all the other prophets. ³³These people all trusted God and as a result won battles, overthrew kingdoms, ruled their people well, and received what God had promised them; they were kept from harm in a den of lions, ³⁴and in a fiery furnace. Some, through their faith, escaped death by the sword. Some were made strong again after they had been weak or sick. Others were given great power in battle; they made whole armies turn and run away. ³⁵And some women, through faith, received their loved ones back again from death. But others trusted God and were beaten to death, preferring to die rather than turn from God and be free—trusting that they would rise to a better life afterwards.

³⁶Some were laughed at and their backs cut open with whips, and others were chained in dungeons. ³⁷,³⁸Some died by stoning and some by being sawed in two; others were promised freedom if they would renounce their faith, then were killed with the sword. Some went about in skins of sheep and goats, wandering over deserts and mountains, hiding in dens and caves. They were hungry and sick and ill-treated—too good for this world. ³⁹And these men of faith, though they trusted God and won his approval, none of them received all that God had promised them; ⁴⁰for God wanted them to wait and share the even better rewards that were prepared for us.

SINCE we have such a huge crowd of men of faith watching us from the grandstands, let us strip off anything that slows us down or holds us back, and especially those sins that wrap themselves so tightly around our feet and trip us up; and let us run with patience the particular race that God has set before us.

²Keep your eyes on Jesus, our leader and instructor. He was willing to die a shameful death on the cross because of the joy he knew would be his afterwards; and now he sits in the place of honor by the throne of God.

³If you want to keep from becoming fainthearted and weary, think about his patience as sinful men did such terrible things to him. ⁴After all, you have never yet struggled against sin and temptation until you sweat great drops of blood.

⁵And have you quite forgotten the encouraging words God spoke to you, his child? He said, "My son, don't be angry when the Lord punishes you. Don't be discouraged when he has to show you where you are wrong. ⁶For when he pun-

ishes you, it proves that he loves you. When he whips you it proves you are really his child."

7Let God train you, for he is doing what any loving father does for his children. Whoever heard of a son who was never corrected? 8If God doesn't punish you when you need it, as other fathers punish their sons, then it means that you aren't really God's son at all—that you don't really belong in his family. 9Since we respect our fathers here on earth, though they punish us, should we not all the more cheerfully submit to God's training so that we can begin really to live?

10Our earthly fathers trained us for a few brief years, doing the best for us that they knew how, but God's correction is always right and for our best good, that we may share his holiness. 11Being punished isn't enjoyable while it is happening—it hurts! But afterwards we can see the result, a quiet growth in grace and character.

12So take a new grip with your tired hands, stand firm on your shaky legs, 13and mark out a straight, smooth path for your feet so that those who follow you, though weak and lame, will not fall and hurt themselves, but become strong.

PSALM 112:1–10

PRAISE the Lord! For all who fear God and trust in him are blessed beyond expression. Yes, happy is the man who delights in doing his commands.

2His children shall be honored everywhere, for good men's sons have a special heritage. 3He himself shall be wealthy, and his good deeds will never be forgotten. 4When darkness overtakes him, light will come bursting in. He is kind and merciful— 5and all goes well for the generous man who conducts his business fairly.

6Such a man will not be overthrown by evil circumstances. God's constant care of him will make a deep impression on all who see it. 7He does not fear bad news, nor live in dread of what may happen. For he is settled in his mind that Jehovah will take care of him. 8That is why he is not afraid, but can calmly face his foes. 9He gives generously to those in need. His deeds will never be forgotten. He shall have influence and honor.

10Evil-minded men will be infuriated when they see all this; they will gnash their teeth in anger and slink away, their hopes thwarted.

PROVERBS FOR TODAY/ 27:17

A friendly discussion is as stimulating as the sparks that fly when iron strikes iron.

NOVEMBER 15

EZEKIEL 31:1—32:32

IN mid-May of the eleventh year of King Jehoiachin's captivity, this message came to me from the Lord: 2,3"Son of dust, tell Pharaoh, king of Egypt, and all his people: You are as Assyria was—a great and mighty nation— like a cedar of Lebanon, full of thick branches and forest shade, with its head high up among the clouds. 4Its roots went deep into the moist earth. It grew luxuriantly and gave streamlets of water to all the trees around. 5It towered above all the other trees. It prospered and grew long thick branches because of all the water at its roots. 6The birds nested in its branches, and in its shade the flocks and herds gave birth to young. All the great nations of the world lived beneath its shadow. 7It was strong and beautiful, for its roots went deep to water. 8This tree was taller than any other in the garden of God; no cypress had branches equal to it; none had boughs to compare; none equaled it in beauty. 9Because of the magnificence that I gave it, it was the envy of all the other trees of Eden.

10"But Egypt has become proud and arrogant, the Lord God says. Therefore because she has set herself so high above the others, reaching to the clouds, 11I will deliver her into the hands of a mighty nation, to destroy her as her wickedness deserves. I, myself, will cut her down. 12A foreign army (from Babylon)—the terror of the nations—will invade her land and cut her down and leave her fallen on the ground. Her branches will be scattered across the mountains and valleys and rivers of the land. All those who live beneath her shade will go away and leave her lying there. 13The birds will pluck off her twigs and the wild animals will lie among her branches; 14let no other nation exult with pride for its own prosperity, though it be higher than the clouds, for all are doomed and they will land in hell, along with all the proud men of the world.

15"The Lord God says: When she fell I made the oceans mourn for her and restrained their tides. I clothed Lebanon in black and caused the trees of Lebanon to weep. 16I made the nations shake with fear at the sound of her fall, for I threw her down to hell with all the others like her. And all the other proud trees of Eden, the choicest and the best of Lebanon, the ones whose roots went deep into the water, are comforted to find her there with them in hell. 17Her allies too are all destroyed and perish with her. They went down with her to the nether world—those nations that had lived beneath her shade.

18"O Egypt, you are great and glorious among the trees of Eden—the nations of the world. And you will be brought down to the pit of hell with all these other nations. You will be among the nations you despise, killed by the sword. This is the fate of Pharaoh and all his teeming masses, says the Lord."

IN mid-February of the twelfth year of King Jehoiachin's captivity, this message came to me from the Lord:

2"Son of dust, mourn for Pharaoh, king of Egypt, and say to him: You think of yourself as a strong young lion among the nations, but you are merely a crocodile along the banks of the Nile, making bubbles and muddying the stream.

3"The Lord God says: I will send a great army to catch you with my net. I will haul you out, 4and leave you stranded on the land to die. And all the birds of the heavens will light upon you and the wild animals of the whole earth will devour you until they are glutted and full. 5And I will cover the hills with your flesh and fill the valleys with your bones. 6And I will drench the earth with your gushing blood, filling the ravines to the tops of the mountains. 7I will blot you out, and I will veil the heavens and darken the stars. I will cover the sun with a cloud, and the moon shall not give you her light. 8Yes, darkness will be everywhere across your land—even the bright stars will be dark above you.

9"And when I destroy you, grief will be in many hearts among the distant nations you have never seen. 10Yes, terror shall strike in many lands, and their kings shall be terribly afraid because of all I do to you. They shall shudder with terror when I brandish my sword before them. They shall greatly tremble for their lives on the day of your fall.

11"For the Lord God says: The sword of the king of Babylon shall come upon you. 12I will destroy you with Babylon's mighty army—the terror of the nations. It will smash the pride of Egypt and all her people; all will perish. 13I will destroy all your flocks and herds that graze beside the streams, and neither man nor animal will disturb those waters any more. ¹⁴Therefore the waters of Egypt will be as clear and flow as smoothly as olive oil, the Lord God says. ¹⁵And when I destroy Egypt and wipe out everything she has, then she shall know that I, the Lord, have done it. ¹⁶Yes, cry for the sorrows of Egypt. Let all the nations weep for her and for her people, says the Lord."

¹⁷Two weeks later, another message came to me from the Lord. He said:

¹⁸"Son of dust, weep for the people of Egypt and for the other mighty nations. Send them down to the nether world among the denizens of death. ¹⁹What nation is as beautiful as you, O Egypt? Yet your doom is the pit; you will be laid beside the people you despise. ²⁰The Egyptians will die with the multitudes slain by the sword, for the sword is drawn against the land of Egypt. She will be drawn down to judgment. ²¹The mighty warriors in the nether world will welcome her as she arrives with all her friends, to lie there beside the nations she despised, all victims of the sword.

²²"The princes of Assyria lie there surrounded by the graves of all her people, those the sword has slain. ²³Their graves are in the depths of hell, surrounded by their allies. All these mighty men who once struck terror into the hearts of everyone are now dead at the hands of their foes.

²⁴"Great kings of Elam lie there with their people. They scourged the nations while they lived, and now they lie undone in hell; their fate is the same as that of ordinary men. ²⁵They have a resting place among the slain, surrounded by the graves of all their people. Yes, they terrorized the nations while they lived, but now they lie in shame in the pit, slain by the sword.

²⁶"The princes of Meshech and Tubal are there, surrounded by the graves of all their armies—all of them idolaters— who once struck terror to the hearts of all; now they lie dead. ²⁷They are buried in a common grave, and not as the fallen lords who are buried in great honor with their weapons beside them, with their shields covering them and their swords beneath their heads. They were a terror to all while they lived. ²⁸Now you will lie crushed and broken among the idolaters, among those who are slain by the sword.

²⁹"Edom is there with her kings and her princes; mighty as they were, they too lie among the others whom the sword has slain, with the idolaters who have gone down to the pit. ³⁰All the princes of the north are there, and the Sidonians, all slain. Once a terror, now they lie in shame; they lie in ignominy with all the other slain who go down to the pit.

³¹"When Pharaoh arrives, he will be comforted to find that he is not alone in having all his army slain, says the Lord God. ³²For I have caused my terror to fall upon all the living. And Pharaoh and his army shall lie among the idolaters who are slain by the sword."

HEBREWS 12:14–29

TRY to stay out of all quarrels and seek to live a clean and holy life, for one who is not holy will not see the Lord. ¹⁵Look after each other so that not one of you will fail to find God's best blessings. Watch out that no bitterness takes root among you, for as it springs up it causes deep trouble, hurting many in their spiritual lives. ¹⁶Watch out that no one becomes involved in sexual sin or becomes careless about God as Esau did: he traded his rights as the oldest son for a single meal. ¹⁷And afterwards, when he wanted those rights back again, it was too late, even though he wept bitter tears of repentance. So remember, and be careful.

¹⁸You have not had to stand face to face with terror, flaming fire, gloom, darkness and a terrible storm, as the Israelites did at Mount Sinai when God gave them his laws. ¹⁹For there was an awesome trumpet blast, and a voice with a

message so terrible that the people begged God to stop speaking. ²⁰They staggered back under God's command that if even an animal touched the mountain it must die. ²¹Moses himself was so frightened at the sight that he shook with terrible fear.

²²But you have come right up into Mount Zion, to the city of the living God, the heavenly Jerusalem, and to the gathering of countless happy angels; ²³and to the church, composed of all those registered in heaven; and to God who is Judge of all; and to the spirits of the redeemed in heaven, already made perfect; ²⁴and to Jesus himself, who has brought us his wonderful new agreement; and to the sprinkled blood which graciously forgives instead of crying out for vengeance as the blood of Abel did.

²⁵So see to it that you obey him who is speaking to you. For if the people of Israel did not escape when they refused to listen to Moses, the earthly messenger, how terrible our danger if we refuse to listen to God who speaks to us from heaven! ²⁶When he spoke from Mount Sinai his voice shook the earth, but, "Next time," he says, "I will not only shake the earth, but the heavens too." ²⁷By this he means that he will sift out everything without solid foundations, so that only unshakable things will be left.

²⁸Since we have a Kingdom nothing can destroy, let us please God by serving him with thankful hearts, and with holy fear and awe. ²⁹For our God is a consuming fire.

PSALM 113:1—114:8

HALLELUJAH! O servants of Jehovah, praise his name. ²Blessed is his name forever and forever. ³Praise him from sunrise to sunset! ⁴For he is high above the nations; his glory is far greater than the heavens.

⁵Who can be compared with God enthroned on high? ⁶Far below him are the heavens and the earth; he stoops to look, ⁷and lifts the poor from the dirt, and the hungry from the garbage dump, ⁸and sets them among princes! ⁹He gives children to the childless wife, so that she becomes a happy mother.

Hallelujah! Praise the Lord.

LONG ago when the Israelis escaped from Egypt, from that land of foreign tongue, ²then the lands of Judah and of Israel became God's new home and kingdom.

³The Red Sea saw them coming and quickly broke apart before them. The Jordan River opened up a path for them to cross. ⁴The mountains skipped like rams, the little hills like lambs! ⁵What's wrong, Red Sea, that made you cut yourself in two? What happened, Jordan River, to your waters? Why were they held back? ⁶Why, mountains, did you skip like rams? Why, little hills, like lambs?

⁷Tremble, O earth, at the presence of the Lord, the God of Jacob. ⁸For he caused gushing streams to burst from flinty rock.

PROVERBS FOR TODAY/ 27:18–20

A workman may eat from the orchard he tends; anyone should be rewarded who protects another's interests. A mirror reflects a man's face, but what he is really like is shown by the kind of friends he chooses. Ambition and death are alike in this: neither is ever satisfied.

NOVEMBER 16

ONCE again a message came to me from the Lord. He said:

2"Son of dust, tell your people: When I bring an army against a country, and the people of that land choose a watchman, 3and when he sees the army coming, and blows the alarm to warn them, 4then anyone who hears the alarm and refuses to heed it—well, if he dies the fault is his own. 5For he heard the warning and wouldn't listen; the fault is his. If he had heeded the warning, he would have saved his life. 6But if the watchman sees the enemy coming and doesn't sound the alarm and warn the people, he is responsible for their deaths. They will die in their sins, but I will charge the watchman with their deaths.

7"So with you, son of dust. I have appointed you as a watchman for the people of Israel; therefore listen to what I say and warn them for me. 8When I say to the wicked, 'O wicked man, you will die!' and you don't tell him what I say, so that he does not repent—that wicked person will die in his sins, but I will hold you responsible for his death. 9But if you warn him to repent and he doesn't, he will die in his sin, and you will not be responsible.

10"O people of Israel, you are saying: 'Our sins are heavy upon us; we pine away with guilt. How can we live?' 11Tell them: As I live, says the Lord God, I have no pleasure in the death of the wicked; *I desire that the wicked turn from his evil ways and live.* Turn, turn from your wickedness, for why will you die, O Israel? 12For the good works of a righteous man will not save him if he turns to sin; and the sins of an evil man will not destroy him if he repents and turns from his sins.

13"I have said the good man will live. But if he sins, expecting his past goodness to save him, then none of his good deeds will be remembered. I will destroy

him for his sins. 14And when I tell the wicked he will die and then he turns from his sins and does what is fair and right— 15if he gives back the borrower's pledge and returns what he has stolen and walks along the paths of right, not doing evil— he shall surely live. He shall not die. 16None of his past sins shall be brought up against him, for he has turned to the good and shall surely live.

17"And yet your people are saying the Lord isn't fair. The trouble is *they* aren't fair. 18For again I say, when the good man turns to evil, he shall die. 19But if the wicked turns from his wickedness and does what's fair and just, he shall live. 20Yet you are saying the Lord isn't fair. But I will judge each of you in accordance with his deeds."

21In the eleventh year of our exile, late in December, one of those who escaped from Jerusalem arrived to tell me, "The city has fallen!" 22Now the hand of the Lord had been upon me the previous evening, and he had healed me so that I could speak again by the time the man arrived.

23Then this message came to me:

24"Son of dust, the scattered remnants of Judah living among the ruined cities keep saying, 'Abraham was only one man and yet he got possession of the whole country! We are many, so we should certainly be able to get it back!' 25But the Lord God says: You are powerless, for you do evil! You eat meat with the blood; you worship idols, and murder. Do you suppose I'll let you have the land? 26Murderers! Idolators! Adulterers! Should you possess the land?

27"Tell them: The Lord God says: As I live, surely those living in the ruins shall die by the sword. Those living in the open fields shall be eaten by wild animals, and those in the forts and caves shall die of disease. 28I will desolate the land and her pride, and her power shall come to an end. And the mountain villages of Israel shall be so ruined that no one will even travel through them. ²⁹When I have ruined the land because of their sins, then they shall know I am the Lord.

³⁰"Son of dust, your people are whispering behind your back. They talk about you in their houses and whisper about you at the doors, saying, 'Come on, let's have some fun! Let's go hear him tell us what the Lord is saying!' ³¹So they come as though they are sincere and sit before you listening. But they have no intention of doing what I tell them to; they talk very sweetly about loving the Lord, but with their hearts they are loving their money. ³²You are very entertaining to them, like someone who sings lovely songs with a beautiful voice or plays well on an instrument. They hear what you say but don't pay any attention to it! ³³But when all these terrible things happen to them—as they will—then they will know a prophet has been among them."

THEN this message came to me from the Lord:

²"Son of dust, prophesy against the shepherds, the leaders of Israel, and say to them: The Lord God says to you: Woe to the shepherds who feed themselves instead of their flocks. Shouldn't shepherds feed the sheep? ³You eat the best food and wear the finest clothes, but you let your flocks starve. ⁴You haven't taken care of the weak nor tended the sick nor bound up the broken bones nor gone looking for those who have wandered away and are lost. Instead you have ruled them with force and cruelty. ⁵So they were scattered, without a shepherd. They have become a prey to every animal that comes along. ⁶My sheep wandered through the mountains and hills and over the face of the earth, and there was no one to search for them or care about them.

⁷"Therefore, O shepherds, hear the word of the Lord:

⁸"As I live, says the Lord God, you abandoned my flock, leaving them to be attacked and destroyed, and you were no real shepherds at all, for you didn't search for them. You fed yourselves and let them starve; ⁹,¹⁰therefore I am against the shepherds, and I will hold them responsible for what has happened to my flock. I will take away their right to feed the flock—and take away their right to eat. I will save my flock from being taken for their food.

¹¹"For the Lord God says: I will search and find my sheep. ¹²I will be like a shepherd looking for his flock. I will find my sheep and rescue them from all the places they were scattered in that dark and cloudy day. ¹³And I will bring them back from among the people and nations where they were, back home to their own land of Israel, and I will feed them upon the mountains of Israel and by the rivers where the land is fertile and good. ¹⁴Yes, I will give them good pasture on the high hills of Israel. There they will lie down in peace and feed in luscious mountain pastures. ¹⁵,¹⁶I myself will be the Shepherd of my sheep, and cause them to lie down in peace, the Lord God says. I will seek my lost ones, those who strayed away, and bring them safely home again. I will put splints and bandages upon their broken limbs and heal the sick. And I will destroy the powerful, fat shepherds; I will feed them, yes—feed them punishment!

¹⁷"And as for you, O my flock—my people—the Lord God says, I will judge you and separate good from bad, sheep from goats.

¹⁸"Is it a small thing to you, O evil shepherds, that you not only keep the best of the pastures for yourselves, but trample down the rest? That you take the best water for yourselves, and muddy the rest with your feet? ¹⁹All that's left for my flock is what you've trampled down; all they have to drink is water that you've fouled.

²⁰"Therefore the Lord God says: I will surely judge between these fat shepherds and their scrawny sheep. ²¹For these

shepherds push and butt and crowd my sick and hungry flock until they're scattered far away. ²²So I myself will save my flock; no more will they be picked on and destroyed. And I will notice which is plump and which is thin, and why!

²³"And I will set one Shepherd over all my people, even my Servant, David. He shall feed them and be a Shepherd to them.

²⁴"And I, the Lord, will be their God, and my Servant David shall be a Prince among my people. I, the Lord, have spoken it.

²⁵"I will make a peace pact with them, and drive away the dangerous animals from the land so that my people can safely camp in the wildest places and sleep safely in the woods. ²⁶I will make my people and their homes around my hill a blessing. And there shall be showers, showers of blessing, for I will not shut off the rains but send them in their seasons. ²⁷Their fruit trees and fields will yield bumper crops, and everyone will live in safety. When I have broken off their chains of slavery and delivered them from those who profiteered at their expense, they shall know I am the Lord. ²⁸No more will other nations conquer them nor wild animals attack. They shall live in safety and no one shall make them afraid.

²⁹"And I will raise up a notable Vine [the Messiah], in Israel so that my people will never again go hungry nor be shamed by heathen conquest. ³⁰In this way they will know that I, the Lord their God, am with them, and that they, the people of Israel, are my people, says the Lord God. ³¹You are my flock, the sheep of my pasture. You are my men and I am your God, so says the Lord."

HEBREWS 13:1–25

CONTINUE to love each other with true brotherly love. ²Don't forget to be kind to strangers, for some who have done this have entertained angels without realizing it! ³Don't forget about those in jail. Suffer with them as though you were there yourself. Share the sorrow of those being mistreated, for you know what they are going through.

⁴Honor your marriage and its vows, and be pure; for God will surely punish all those who are immoral or commit adultery.

⁵Stay away from the love of money; be satisfied with what you have. For God has said, "I will never, *never* fail you nor forsake you." ⁶That is why we can say without any doubt or fear, "The Lord is my Helper and I am not afraid of anything that mere man can do to me."

⁷Remember your leaders who have taught you the Word of God. Think of all the good that has come from their lives, and try to trust the Lord as they do.

⁸Jesus Christ is the same yesterday, today, and forever. ⁹So do not be attracted by strange, new ideas. Your spiritual strength comes as a gift from God, not from ceremonial rules about eating certain foods—a method which, by the way, hasn't helped those who have tried it!

¹⁰We have an altar—the cross where Christ was sacrificed—where those who continue to seek salvation by obeying Jewish laws can never be helped. ¹¹Under the system of Jewish laws the high priest brought the blood of the slain animals into the sanctuary as a sacrifice for sin, and then the bodies of the animals were burned outside the city. ¹²That is why Jesus suffered and died outside the city, where his blood washed our sins away.

¹³So let us go out to him beyond the city walls [that is, outside the interests of this world, being willing to be despised] to suffer with him there, bearing his shame. ¹⁴For this world is not our home; we are looking forward to our everlasting home in heaven.

¹⁵With Jesus' help we will continually offer our sacrifice of praise to God by telling others of the glory of his name.

16Don't forget to do good and to share what you have with those in need, for such sacrifices are very pleasing to him. 17Obey your spiritual leaders and be willing to do what they say. For their work is to watch over your souls, and God will judge them on how well they do this. Give them reason to report joyfully about you to the Lord and not with sorrow, for then you will suffer for it too.

18Pray for us, for our conscience is clear and we want to keep it that way. 19I especially need your prayers right now so that I can come back to you sooner.

20,21And now may the God of peace, who brought again from the dead our Lord Jesus, equip you with all you need for doing his will. May he who became the great Shepherd of the sheep by an everlasting agreement between God and you, signed with his blood, produce in you through the power of Christ all that is pleasing to him. To him be glory forever and ever. Amen.

22Brethren, please listen patiently to what I have said in this letter, for it is a short one. 23I want you to know that Brother Timothy is now out of jail; if he comes here soon, I will come with him to see you. 24,25Give my greetings to all your leaders and to the other believers there. The Christians from Italy who are here with me send you their love. God's grace be with you all.

Good-bye.

PSALM 115:1–18

GLORIFY your name, not ours, O Lord! Cause everyone to praise your lovingkindness and your truth. 2Why let the nations say, "Their God is dead!"

3For he is in the heavens, and does as he wishes. 4Their gods are merely manmade things of silver and of gold. 5They can't talk or see, despite their eyes and mouths! 6Nor can they hear, nor smell, 7nor use their hands or feet! Nor speak! 8And those who make and worship them are just as foolish as their idols are.

9O Israel, trust the Lord! He is your helper. He is your shield. 10O priests of Aaron, trust the Lord! He is your helper; he is your shield. 11All of you, his people, trust in him. He is your helper; he is your shield.

12Jehovah is constantly thinking about us and he will surely bless us. He will bless the people of Israel and the priests of Aaron, 13and all, both great and small, who reverence him.

14May the Lord richly bless both you and your children. 15Yes, Jehovah who made heaven and earth will personally bless you! 16The heavens belong to the Lord, but he has given the earth to all mankind.

17The dead cannot sing praises to Jehovah here on earth, 18but we can! We praise him forever! Hallelujah! Praise the Lord!

PROVERBS FOR TODAY/ 27:21–22

The purity of silver and gold can be tested in a crucible, but a man is tested by his reaction to men's praise. You can't separate a rebel from his foolishness though you crush him to powder.

NOVEMBER 17

EZEKIEL 35:1—36:38

AGAIN a message came from the Lord. He said:

2"Son of dust, face toward Mount Seir and prophesy against the people saying:

3"The Lord God says: I am against you and I will smash you with my fist and utterly destroy you. 4,5Because you hate my people Israel, I will demolish your cities and make you desolate, and then you shall know I am the Lord. You butchered my people when they were helpless, when I had punished them for all their sins. 6As I live, the Lord God says, since you enjoy blood so much, I will give you a blood bath—your turn has come! 7I will utterly wipe out the people of Mount Seir, killing off all those who try to escape and all those who return. 8I will fill your mountains with the dead—your hills, your valleys and your rivers will be filled with those the sword has killed. 9Never again will you revive. You will be abandoned forever; your cities will never be rebuilt. Then you shall know I am the Lord.

10"For you said, 'Both Israel and Judah shall be mine. We will take possession of them. What do we care that God is there!' 11Therefore as I live, the Lord God says, I will pay back your angry deeds with mine—I will punish you for all your acts of envy and of hate. And I will honor my name in Israel by what I do to you. 12And you shall know that I have heard each evil word you spoke against the Lord, saying, 'His people are helpless; they are food for us to eat!' 13Saying that, you boasted great words against the Lord. And I have heard them all!

14"The whole world will rejoice when I make you desolate. 15You rejoiced at Israel's fearful fate. Now I will rejoice at yours! You will be wiped out, O people of Mount Seir and all who live in Edom! And then you will know I am the Lord!

SON of dust, prophesy to Israel's mountains. Tell them: Listen to this message from the Lord.

2"Your enemies have sneered at you and claimed your ancient heights as theirs, 3and destroyed you on every side and sent you away as slaves to many lands. You are mocked and slandered. 4Therefore, O mountains of Israel, hear the word of the Lord God. He says to the hills and mountains, dales and valleys, and to the ruined farms and the long-deserted cities, destroyed and mocked by heathen nations all around: 5My anger is afire against these nations, especially Edom, for grabbing my land with relish, in utter contempt for me, to take it for themselves.

6"Therefore prophesy and say to the hills and mountains, dales and valleys of Israel: The Lord God says, I am full of fury because you suffered shame before the surrounding nations. 7Therefore I have sworn with hand held high, that those nations are going to have their turn of being covered with shame, 8but for Israel, good times will return. There will be heavy crops of fruit to prepare for my people's return—and they will be coming home again soon! 9See, I am for you, and I will come and help you as you prepare the ground and sow your crops. 10I will greatly increase your population throughout all Israel, and the ruined cities will be rebuilt and filled with people. 11Not only the people, but your flocks and herds will also greatly multiply. O mountains of Israel, again you will be filled with homes. I will do even more for you than I did before. Then you shall know I am the Lord. 12My people will walk upon you once again, and you will belong to them again; and you will no longer be a place for burning their children on idol altars.

13"The Lord God says: Now the other nations taunt you, saying, 'Israel is a land that devours her people!' 14But they will not say this any more. Your birth rate will rise and your infant mortality rate will drop off sharply, says the Lord. 15No longer will those heathen nations sneer, for you will no longer be a nation of sinners, the Lord God says."

16Then this further word came to me from the Lord:

17"Son of dust, when the people of Israel were living in their own country, they defiled it by their evil deeds; to me their worship was as foul as filthy rags. 18They polluted the land with murder and with the worshiping of idols, so I poured out my fury upon them. 19And I exiled them to many lands; that is how I punished them for the evil way they lived. 20But when they were scattered out among the nations, then they were a blight upon my holy name because the nations said, 'These are the people of God and he couldn't protect them from harm!' 21I am concerned about my reputation that was ruined by my people throughout the world.

22"Therefore say to the people of Israel: The Lord God says, I am bringing you back again, but not because you deserve it; I am doing it to protect my holy name which you tarnished among the nations. 23I will honor my great name that you defiled, and the people of the world shall know I am the Lord. I will be honored before their eyes by delivering you from exile among them. 24For I will bring you back home again to the land of Israel.

25"Then it will be as though I had sprinkled clean water on you, for you will be clean—your filthiness will be washed away, your idol worship gone. 26And I will give you a new heart—I will give you new and right desires—and put a new spirit within you. I will take out your stony hearts of sin and give you new hearts of love. 27And I will put my Spirit within you so that you will obey my laws and do whatever I command.

28"And you shall live in Israel, the land which I gave your fathers long ago. And you shall be my people and I will be your God. 29I will cleanse away your sins. I will abolish crop failures and famine. 30I will give you huge harvests from your fruit trees and fields, and never again will the surrounding nations be able to scoff at your land for its famines. 31Then you will remember your past sins and loathe yourselves for all the evils you did. 32But always remember this: It is not for your own sakes that I will do this, but for mine. O my people Israel, be utterly ashamed of all that you have done!

33"The Lord God says: When I cleanse you from your sins, I will bring you home again to Israel, and rebuild the ruins. 34Acreage will be cultivated again that through the years of exile lay empty as a barren wilderness; all who passed by were shocked to see the extent of ruin in your land. 35But when I bring you back they will say, 'This God-forsaken land has become like Eden's garden! The ruined cities are rebuilt and walled and filled with people!' 36Then the nations all around—all those still left—will know that I, the Lord, rebuilt the ruins and planted lush crops in the wilderness. For I, the Lord, have promised it, and I will do it.

37,38"The Lord God says: I am ready to hear Israel's prayers for these blessings, and to grant them their requests. Let them but ask and I will multiply them like the flocks that fill Jerusalem's streets at time of sacrifice. The ruined cities will be crowded once more, and everyone will know I am the Lord."

JAMES 1:1–18

FROM: James, a servant of God and of the Lord Jesus Christ.

To: Jewish Christians scattered everywhere. Greetings!

2Dear brothers, is your life full of difficulties and temptations? Then be happy, 3for when the way is rough, your patience has a chance to grow. 4So let it grow, and don't try to squirm out of your problems. For when your patience is finally in full bloom, then you will be ready for anything, strong in character, full and complete.

5If you want to know what God wants you to do, ask him, and he will gladly tell you, for he is always ready to give a bountiful supply of wisdom to all who ask him; he will not resent it. 6But when you ask him, be sure that you really expect him to tell you, for a doubtful mind will be as unsettled as a wave of the sea that is driven and tossed by the wind; 7,8and every decision you then make will be uncertain, as you turn first this way, and then that. If you don't ask with faith, don't expect the Lord to give you any solid answer.

9A Christian who doesn't amount to much in this world should be glad, for he is great in the Lord's sight. 10,11But a rich man should be glad that his riches mean nothing to the Lord, for he will soon be gone, like a flower that has lost its beauty and fades away, withered— killed by the scorching summer sun. So it is with rich men. They will soon die and leave behind all their busy activities.

12Happy is the man who doesn't give in and do wrong when he is tempted, for afterwards he will get as his reward the crown of life that God has promised those who love him. 13And remember, when someone wants to do wrong it is never God who is tempting him, for God never wants to do wrong and never tempts anyone else to do it. 14Temptation is the pull of man's own evil thoughts and wishes. 15These evil thoughts lead to evil actions and afterwards to the death penalty from God. 16So don't be misled, dear brothers.

17But whatever is good and perfect comes to us from God, the Creator of all light, and he shines forever without change or shadow. 18And it was a happy day for him when he gave us our new lives, through the truth of his Word, and we became, as it were, the first children in his new family.

PSALM 116:1–19

I love the Lord because he hears my prayers and answers them. 2Because he bends down and listens, I will pray as long as I breathe!

3Death stared me in the face—I was frightened and sad. 4Then I cried, "Lord, save me!" 5How kind he is! How good he is! So merciful, this God of ours! 6The Lord protects the simple and the childlike; I was facing death and then he saved me. 7Now I can relax. For the Lord has done this wonderful miracle for me. 8He has saved me from death, my eyes from tears, my feet from stumbling. 9I shall live! Yes, in his presence—here on earth!

10,11In my discouragement I thought, "They are lying when they say I will recover." 12But now what can I offer Jehovah for all he has done for me? 13I will bring him an offering of wine and praise his name for saving me. 14I will publicly bring him the sacrifice I vowed I would. 15His loved ones are very precious to him and he does not lightly let them die.

16O Lord, you have freed me from my bonds and I will serve you forever. 17I will worship you and offer you a sacrifice of thanksgiving. 18,19Here in the courts of the Temple in Jerusalem, before all the people, I will pay everything I vowed to the Lord. Praise the Lord.

PROVERBS FOR TODAY/ 27:23–27

Riches can disappear fast. And the king's crown doesn't stay in his family forever— so watch your business interests closely. Know the state of your flocks and your herds; then there will be lamb's wool enough for clothing, and goat's milk enough for food for all your household after the hay is harvested, and the new crop appears, and the mountain grasses are gathered in.

NOVEMBER 18

EZEKIEL 37:1—38:23

THE power of the Lord was upon me and I was carried away by the Spirit of the Lord to a valley full of old, dry bones that were scattered everywhere across the ground. He led me around among them, 3and then he said to me:

"Son of dust, can these bones become people again?"

I replied, "Lord, you alone know the answer to that."

4Then he told me to speak to the bones and say: "O dry bones, listen to the words of God, 5for the Lord God says, See! I am going to make you live and breathe again! 6I will replace the flesh and muscles on you and cover you with skin. I will put breath into you, and you shall live and know I am the Lord."

7So I spoke these words from God, just as he told me to; and suddenly there was a rattling noise from all across the valley, and the bones of each body came together and attached to each other as they used to be. 8Then, as I watched, the muscles and flesh formed over the bones, and skin covered them, but the bodies had no breath. 9Then he told me to call to the wind and say: "The Lord God says: Come from the four winds, O Spirit, and breathe upon these slain bodies, that they may live again." 10So I spoke to the winds as he commanded me and the bodies began breathing; they lived, and stood up—a very great army.

11Then he told me what the vision meant: "These bones," he said, "represent all the people of Israel. They say: 'We have become a heap of dried-out bones—all hope is gone.' 12But tell them, the Lord God says: My people, I will open your graves of exile and cause you to rise again and return to the land of Israel. 13And, then at last, O my people, you will know I am the Lord. 14I will

put my Spirit into you, and you shall live and return home again to your own land. Then you will know that I, the Lord, have done just what I promised you."

15Again a message from the Lord came to me, saying:

16"Take a stick and carve on it these words: 'This stick represents Judah and her allied tribes.' Then take another stick and carve these words on it: 'This stick represents all the other tribes of Israel.' 17Now hold them together in your hand as one stick. 18,19,20Tell these people (holding the sticks so they can see what you are doing), the Lord God says: I will take the tribes of Israel and join them to Judah and make them one stick in my hand.

21"For the Lord God says: I am gathering the people of Israel from among the nations, and bringing them home from around the world to their own land, 22to unify them into one nation. One king shall be king of them all; no longer shall they be divided into two nations. 23They shall stop polluting themselves with idols and their other sins, for I will save them from all this foulness. Then they shall truly be my people and I their God.

24"And David, my Servant—the Messiah—shall be their King, their only Shepherd; and they shall obey my laws and all my wishes. 25They shall live in the land of Israel where their fathers lived, the land I gave my servant Jacob. They and their children after them shall live there, and their grandchildren, for all generations. And my Servant David, their Messiah, shall be their Prince forever. 26And I will make a covenant of peace with them, an everlasting pact. I will bless them and multiply them and put my Temple among them forever. 27And I will make my home among them. Yes, I will be their God and they shall be my people. 28And when my Temple remains among them forever, then the nations will know that I, the Lord, have chosen Israel as my very own."

HERE is another message to me from the Lord:

2,3"Son of dust, face northward toward the land of Magog, and prophesy against Gog king of Meshech and Tubal. Tell him that the Lord God says: I am against you, Gog. 4I will put hooks into your jaws and pull you to your doom. I will mobilize your troops and armored cavalry, and make you a mighty host, all fully armed. 5Peras, Cush and Put shall join you too with all their weaponry, 6and so shall Gomer and all his hordes and the armies of Togarmah from the distant north, as well as many others. 7Be prepared! Stay mobilized. You are their leader, Gog!

8"A long time from now you will be called to action. In distant years you will swoop down onto the land of Israel, that will be lying in peace after the return of its people from many lands. 9You and all your allies—a vast and awesome army—will roll down upon them like a storm and cover the land like a cloud. 10For at that time an evil thought will have come to your mind. 11You will have said, 'Israel is an unprotected land of unwalled villages! I will march against her and destroy these people living in such confidence! 12I will go to those once-desolate cities that are now filled with people again—those who have returned from all the nations—and I will capture vast amounts of loot and many slaves. For the people are rich with cattle now, and the whole earth revolves around them!'

13"But Sheba and Dedan and the merchant princes of Tarshish with whom she trades will ask, 'Who are you to rob them of silver and gold and drive away their cattle and seize their goods and make them poor?'

14"The Lord God says to Gog: When my people are living in peace in their land, then you will rouse yourself. 15,16You will come from all over the north with your vast host of cavalry and cover the land like a cloud. This will happen

in the distant future—in the latter years of history. I will bring you against my land, and my holiness will be vindicated in your terrible destruction before their eyes, so that all the nations will know that I am God.

17"The Lord God says: You are the one I spoke of long ago through the prophets of Israel, saying that after many years had passed, I would bring you against my people. 18But when you come to destroy the land of Israel, my fury will rise! 19For in my jealousy and blazing wrath, I promise a mighty shaking in the land of Israel on that day. 20All living things shall quake in terror at my presence; mountains shall be thrown down; cliffs shall tumble; walls shall crumble to the earth. 21I will summon every kind of terror against you, says the Lord God, and you will fight against yourselves in mortal combat! 22I will fight you with sword, disease, torrential floods, great hailstones, fire and brimstone! 23Thus will I show my greatness and bring honor upon my name, and all the nations of the world will hear what I have done, and know that I am God!

JAMES 1:19—2:17

DEAR brothers, don't ever forget that it is best to listen much, speak little, and not become angry; 20for anger doesn't make us good, as God demands that we must be.

21So get rid of all that is wrong in your life, both inside and outside, and humbly be glad for the wonderful message we have received, for it is able to save our souls as it takes hold of our hearts.

22And remember, it is a message to obey, not just to listen to. So don't fool yourselves. 23For if a person just listens and doesn't obey, he is like a man looking at his face in a mirror; 24as soon as he walks away, he can't see himself anymore or remember what he looks like. 25But if anyone keeps looking steadily into God's law for free men, he will not only remember it but he will do what it says, and God will greatly bless him in everything he does.

26Anyone who says he is a Christian but doesn't control his sharp tongue is just fooling himself, and his religion isn't worth much. 27The Christian who is pure and without fault, from God the Father's point of view, is the one who takes care of orphans and widows, and who remains true to the Lord—not soiled and dirtied by his contacts with the world.

DEAR brothers, how can you claim that you belong to the Lord Jesus Christ, the Lord of glory, if you show favoritism to rich people and look down on poor people?

2If a man comes into your church dressed in expensive clothes and with valuable gold rings on his fingers, and at the same moment another man comes in who is poor and dressed in threadbare clothes, 3and you make a lot of fuss over the rich man and give him the best seat in the house and say to the poor man, "You can stand over there if you like, or else sit on the floor"—well, 4judging a man by his wealth shows that you are guided by wrong motives.

5Listen to me, dear brothers: God has chosen poor people to be rich in faith, and the Kingdom of Heaven is theirs, for that is the gift God has promised to all those who love him. 6And yet, of the two strangers, you have despised the poor man. Don't you realize that it is usually the rich men who pick on you and drag you into court? 7And all too often they are the ones who laugh at Jesus Christ, whose noble name you bear.

8Yes indeed, it is good when you truly obey our Lord's command, "You must love and help your neighbors just as much as you love and take care of your-self." 9But you are breaking this law of our Lord's when you favor the rich and fawn over them; it is sin.

10And the person who keeps every law of God, but makes one little slip, is just as guilty as the person who has broken every law there is. 11For the God who said you must not marry a woman who already has a husband, also said you must not murder, so even though you have not broken the marriage laws by committing adultery, but have murdered someone, you have entirely broken God's laws and stand utterly guilty before him.

12You will be judged on whether or not you are doing what Christ wants you to. So watch what you do and what you think; 13for there will be no mercy to those who have shown no mercy. But if you have been merciful, then God's mercy toward you will win out over his judgment against you.

14Dear brothers, what's the use of saying that you have faith and are Christians if you aren't proving it by helping others? Will *that* kind of faith save anyone? 15If you have a friend who is in need of food and clothing, 16and you say to him, "Well, good-bye and God bless you; stay warm and eat hearty," and then don't give him clothes or food, what good does that do?

17So you see, it isn't enough just to have faith. You must also do good to prove that you have it. Faith that doesn't show itself by good works is no faith at all—it is dead and useless.

PSALM 117:1–2

PRAISE the Lord, all nations everywhere. Praise him, all the peoples of the earth. 2For he loves us very dearly, and his truth endures. Praise the Lord.

PROVERBS FOR TODAY/ 28:1

The wicked flee when no one is chasing them! But the godly are bold as lions!

NOVEMBER 19

EZEKIEL 39:1—40:27

SON of dust, prophesy this also against Gog. Tell him:

I stand against you, Gog, leader of Meshech and Tubal. 2I will turn you and drive you toward the mountains of Israel, bringing you from the distant north. And I will destroy 85 percent of your army in the mountains. 3I will knock your weapons from your hands and leave you helpless. 4You and all your vast armies will die upon the mountains. I will give you to the vultures and wild animals to devour you. 5You will never reach the cities—you will fall upon the open fields; for I have spoken, the Lord God says. 6And I will rain down fire on Magog and on all your allies who live safely on the coasts, and they shall know I am the Lord.

7"Thus I will make known my holy name among my people Israel; I will not let it be mocked at anymore. And the nations too shall know I am the Lord, the Holy One of Israel. 8That day of judgment will come; everything will happen just as I have declared it.

9"The people of the cities of Israel will go out and pick up your shields and bucklers, bows and arrows, javelins and spears, to use for fuel—enough to last them seven years. 10For seven years they will need nothing else for their fires. They won't cut wood from the fields or forests, for these weapons will give them all they need. They will use the possessions of those who abused them.

11"And I will make a vast graveyard for Gog and his armies in the Valley of the Travelers, east of the Dead Sea. It will block the path of the travelers. There Gog and all his armies will be buried. And they will change the name of the place to 'The Valley of Gog's Army.' 12It will take seven months for the people of Israel to bury the bodies. 13Everyone in Israel will help, for it will be a glorious victory for Israel on that day when I dem-

onstrate my glory, says the Lord. 14At the end of the seven months, they will appoint men to search the land systematically for any skeletons left and bury them, so that the land will be cleansed. 15,16Whenever anyone sees some bones, he will put up a marker beside them so that the buriers will see them and take them to the Valley of Gog's Army to bury them. A city named 'Multitude' is there! And so the land will finally be cleansed.

17"And now, son of dust, call all the birds and animals and say to them: Gather together for a mighty sacrificial feast. Come from far and near to the mountains of Israel. Come, eat the flesh and drink the blood! 18Eat the flesh of mighty men and drink the blood of princes—they are the rams, the lambs, the goats and the fat young bulls of Bashan for my feast! 19Gorge yourselves with flesh until you are glutted, drink blood until you are drunk; this is the sacrificial feast I have prepared for you. 20Feast at my banquet table—feast on horses, riders and valiant warriors, says the Lord God. 21Thus I will demonstrate my glory among the nations; all shall see the punishment of Gog and know that I have done it.

22"And from that time onward, the people of Israel will know I am the Lord their God. 23And the nations will know why Israel was sent away to exile—it was punishment for sin, for they acted in treachery against their God. Therefore I turned my face away from them and let their enemies destroy them. 24I turned my face away and punished them in proportion to the vileness of their sins.

25"But now, the Lord God says, I will end the captivity of my people and have mercy upon them and restore their fortunes, for I am concerned about my reputation! 26Their time of treachery and shame will all be in the past; they will be home again, in peace and safety in their own land, with no one bothering them or making them afraid. 27I will bring them home from the lands of their enemies—and my glory shall be evident to all the nations when I do it. Through them I will vindicate my holiness before the nations. 28Then my people will know I am the Lord their God—responsible for sending them away to exile, and responsible for bringing them home. I will leave none of them remaining among the nations. 29And I will never hide my face from them again, for I will pour out my Spirit upon them, says the Lord God."

EARLY in April of the twenty-fifth year of our exile—the fourteenth year after Jerusalem was captured—the hand of the Lord was upon me, 2and in a vision he took me to the land of Israel and set me down on a high mountain where I saw what appeared to be a city opposite me. 3Going nearer, I saw a man whose face shone like bronze, standing beside the Temple gate, holding in his hand a measuring tape and a measuring stick.

4He said to me: "Son of dust, watch and listen and take to heart everything I show you, for you have been brought here so I can show you many things; and then you are to return to the people of Israel to tell them all you have seen." 5The man began to measure the wall around the outside of the Temple area with his measuring stick, which was 10½ feet long. He told me, "This wall is 10½ feet high and 10½ feet wide." 6Then he took me over to the passageway that goes through the eastern wall. We climbed the seven steps into the entrance and he measured the entry hall of the passage; it was 10½ feet wide.

7-12Walking on through the passageway I saw that there were three guardrooms on each side; each of these rooms was 10½ feet square, with a distance of 8¾ feet along the wall between them. In front of these rooms was a low barrier eighteen inches high and eighteen inches wide. Beyond the guardrooms was a 10½-foot doorway opening into a 14-foot hall with 3½-foot columns. Beyond this hall, at the inner end of the passageway was a vestibule 22¾ feet wide and 17½ feet long.

13Then he measured the entire outside width of the passageway, measuring across the roof from the outside doors of the guardrooms; this distance was 43¾ feet. 14Then he estimated the pillars on each side of the porch to be about 100 feet high. 15The full length of the entrance passage was 87½ feet from one end to the other. 16There were windows that narrowed inward through the walls along both sides of the passageway and along the guardroom walls. The windows were also in the exit and in the entrance halls. The pillars were decorated with palm tree decorations.

17And so we passed through the passageway to the court inside. A stone pavement ran around the inside of the walls, and thirty rooms were built against the walls, opening onto this pavement. 18This was called "the lower pavement." It extended out from the walls into the court the same distance as the passageway did.

19Then he measured across to the wall on the other side of this court (which was called "the outer court" of the Temple) and found that the distance was 175 feet. 20As I followed, he left the eastern passageway and went over to the passage through the northern wall and measured it. 21Here too there were three guardrooms on each side, and all the measurements were the same as for the east passageway—87½ feet long and 43¾ feet from side to side across the top of the guardrooms. 22There were windows, an entry hall and the palm tree decorations just the same as on the east side. And there were seven steps leading up to the doorway to the entry hall inside.

23Here at the north entry, just as at the east, if one walked through the passageway into the court, and straight across it, he came to an inner wall and a passageway through it to an inner court. The distance between the two passageways was 175 feet. 24Then he took me around to the south gate and measured the various sections of its passageway and found they were just the same as in the others. 25It had windows along the walls as the others did, and an entry hall. And like the others, it was 87½ feet long and 43¾ feet wide. 26It too had a stairway of seven steps leading up to it, and there were palm tree decorations along the walls. 27And here again, if one walked through the passageway into the court and straight across it, he came to the inner wall and a passageway through it to the inner court. And the distance between the passageways was 175 feet.

JAMES 2:18—3:18

BUT someone may well argue, "You say the way to God is by faith alone, plus nothing; well, I say that good works are important too, for without good works you can't prove whether you have faith or not; but anyone can see that I have faith by the way I act."

19Are there still some among you who hold that "only believing" is enough? Believing in one God? Well, remember that the demons believe this too—so strongly that they tremble in terror! 20Fool! When will you ever learn that "believing" is useless without *doing* what God wants you to? Faith that does not result in good deeds is not real faith.

21Don't you remember that even our father Abraham was declared good because of what he *did,* when he was willing to obey God, even if it meant offering his son Isaac to die on the altar? 22You see, he was trusting God so much that he was willing to do whatever God told him to; his faith was made complete by what he did, by his actions, his good deeds. 23And so it happened just as the Scriptures say, that Abraham trusted God, and the Lord declared him good in God's sight, and he was even called "the friend of God." 24So you see, a man is saved by what he does, as well as by what he believes.

25Rahab, the prostitute, is another example of this. She was saved because of what she did when she hid those messengers and sent them safely away by a different road. 26Just as the body is dead when there is no spirit in it, so faith is dead if it is not the kind that results in good deeds.

DEAR brothers, don't be too eager to tell others their faults, for we all make many mistakes; and when we teachers of religion, who should know better, do wrong, our punishment will be greater than it would be for others.

If anyone can control his tongue, it proves that he has perfect control over himself in every other way. 3We can make a large horse turn around and go wherever we want by means of a small bit in his mouth. 4And a tiny rudder makes a huge ship turn wherever the pilot wants it to go, even though the winds are strong.

5So also the tongue is a small thing, but what enormous damage it can do. A great forest can be set on fire by one tiny spark. 6And the tongue is a flame of fire. It is full of wickedness, and poisons every part of the body. And the tongue is set on fire by hell itself, and can turn our whole lives into a blazing flame of destruction and disaster.

7Men have trained, or can train, every kind of animal or bird that lives and every kind of reptile and fish, 8but no human being can tame the tongue. It is always ready to pour out its deadly poison. 9Sometimes it praises our heavenly Father, and sometimes it breaks out into curses against men who are made like God. 10And so blessing and cursing come pouring out of the same mouth. Dear brothers, surely this is not right! 11Does a spring of water bubble out first with fresh water and then with bitter water? 12Can you pick olives from a fig tree, or figs from a grape vine? No, and you can't draw fresh water from a salty pool.

13If you are wise, live a life of steady goodness, so that only good deeds will pour forth. And if you don't brag about them, then you will be truly wise! 14And by all means don't brag about being wise and good if you are bitter and jealous and selfish; that is the worst sort of lie. 15For jealousy and selfishness are not God's kind of wisdom. Such things are earthly, unspiritual, inspired by the devil. 16For wherever there is jealousy or selfish ambition, there will be disorder and every other kind of evil.

17But the wisdom that comes from heaven is first of all pure and full of quiet gentleness. Then it is peace-loving and courteous. It allows discussion and is willing to yield to others; it is full of mercy and good deeds. It is wholehearted and straightforward and sincere. 18And those who are peacemakers will plant seeds of peace and reap a harvest of goodness.

PSALM 118:1–18

OH, thank the Lord, for he's so good! His lovingkindness is forever.

2Let the congregation of Israel praise him with these same words: "His lovingkindness is forever." 3And let the priests of Aaron chant, "His lovingkindness is forever." 4Let the Gentile converts chant, "His lovingkindness is forever."

PROVERBS 28:2

When there is moral rot within a nation, its government topples easily; but with honest, sensible leaders there is stability.

5In my distress I prayed to the Lord and he answered me and rescued me. 6He is for me! How can I be afraid? What can mere man do to me? 7The Lord is on my side, he will help me. Let those who hate me beware.

8It is better to trust the Lord than to put confidence in men. 9It is better to take refuge in him than in the mightiest king!

10Though all the nations of the world attack me, I will march out behind his banner and destroy them. 11Yes, they surround and attack me; but with his flag flying above me I will cut them off. 12They swarm around me like bees; they blaze against me like a roaring flame. Yet beneath his flag I shall destroy them. 13You did your best to kill me, O my enemy, but the Lord helped me. 14He is my strength and song in the heat of battle, and now he has given me the victory. 15,16Songs of joy at the news of our rescue are sung in the homes of the godly. The strong arm of the Lord has done glorious things! 17I shall not die, but live to tell of all his deeds. 18The Lord has punished me, but not handed me over to death.

NOVEMBER 20

EZEKIEL 40:28—41:26

THEN he took me over to the inner wall and its south passageway. He measured this passageway and found that it had the same measurements as the passageways of the outer wall. 29,30Its guardrooms, pillars and entrance and exit hall were identical to all the others, and so were the windows along its

walls and entry. And, like the others, it was 87½ feet long by 43¾ feet wide. 31The only difference was that it had eight steps leading up to it instead of seven. It had palm tree decorations on the pillars, just as the others.

32Then he took me along the court to the eastern entrance of the inner wall, and measured it. It too had the same measurements as the others. ³³Its guard-rooms, pillars and entrance hall were the same size as those of the other passageways, and there were windows along the walls and in the entry hall; and it was 87½ feet long by 43¾ feet wide. ³⁴Its entry hall faced the outer court and there were palm tree decorations on its columns, but there were eight steps instead of seven going up to the entrance.

³⁵Then he took me around to the north gate of the inner wall, and the measurements there were just like the others: ³⁶The guardrooms, pillars and entry hall of this passageway were the same as the others, with a length of 87½ feet and a width of 43¾ feet. ³⁷Its entry hall faced toward the outer court, and it had palm tree decorations on the walls of each side of the passageway, and there were eight steps leading up to the entrance.

³⁸But a door led from its entry hall into a side room where the flesh of the sacrifices was washed before being taken to the altar; ³⁹on each side of the entry hall of the passageway there were two tables where the animals for sacrifice were slaughtered for the burnt offerings, sin offerings and guilt offerings to be presented in the Temple. ⁴⁰Outside the entry hall, on each side of the stairs going up to the north entrance, there were two more tables. ⁴¹So, in all, there were eight tables, four inside and four outside, where the sacrifices were cut up and prepared. ⁴²There were also four stone tables where the butchering knives and other implements were laid. These tables were about 2⅝ feet square and 1¾ feet high. ⁴³There were hooks, three or four inches long, fastened along the walls of the entry hall, and on the tables the flesh of the offering was to be laid.

⁴⁴In the inner court, there were two one-room buildings, one beside the northern entrance, facing south, and one beside the southern entrance, facing north.

⁴⁵And he said to me: "The building beside the inner northern gate is for the priests who supervise the maintenance. ⁴⁶The building beside the inner southern entrance is for the priests in charge of the altar—the descendants of Zadok—for they alone of all the Levites may come near to the Lord to minister to him."

⁴⁷Then he measured the inner court [in front of the Temple] and found it to be 175 feet square, and there was an altar in the court, standing in front of the Temple. ⁴⁸,⁴⁹Then he brought me to the entrance hall of the Temple. Ten steps led up to it from the inner court. Its walls extended up on either side to form two pillars, each of them 8¾ feet thick. The entrance was 24½ feet wide with 5¼-foot walls. Thus the entry hall was 35 feet wide and 19¼ feet long.

AFTERWARD he brought me into the nave, the large main room of the Temple, and measured the pillars that formed its doorway. They were 10½ feet square. ²The entrance hall was 17½ feet wide and 8¾ feet deep. The nave itself was seventy feet long by thirty-five feet.

³Then he went into the inner room at the end of the nave and measured the columns at the entrance and found them to be 3½ feet thick; its doorway was 10½ feet wide, with a hallway 12¼ feet deep behind it. ⁴The inner room was thirty-five feet square. "This," he told me, "is the Most Holy Place."

⁵Then he measured the wall of the Temple and found that it was 10½ feet thick, with a row of rooms along the outside. Each room was seven feet wide. ⁶These rooms were in three tiers, one above the other, with thirty rooms in each tier. The whole structure was supported by girders and not attached to the Temple wall for support. ⁷Each tier was wider than the one below it, corresponding to the narrowing of the Temple wall as it rose higher. A stairway at the side of the Temple led up from floor to floor.

⁸I noticed that the Temple was built on a terrace and that the bottom row of rooms extended out 10½ feet onto

the terrace. 9The outer wall of these rooms was 8¾ feet thick, leaving a free space of 8¾ feet out to the edge of the terrace, the same on both sides.

10Thirty-five feet away from the terrace, on both sides of the Temple, was another row of rooms down in the inner court. 11Two doors opened from the tiers of rooms to the terrace yard, which was 8¾ feet wide; one door faced north and the other south.

12A large building stood on the west, facing the Temple yard, measuring 122½ feet wide by 157½ feet long. Its walls were 8¾ feet thick. 13Then he measured the Temple and its immediately surrounding yards. The area was 175 feet square. 14The inner court at the east of the Temple was also 175 feet wide, 15,16and so was the building west of the Temple, including its two walls.

The nave of the Temple and the Holy of Holies and the entry hall were paneled, and all three had recessed windows. The inner walls of the Temple were paneled with wood above and below the windows. 17,18The space above the door leading into the Holy of Holies was also paneled. The walls were decorated with carvings of Guardian Angels, each with two faces, and of palm trees alternating with the Guardian Angels. 19,20One face—that of a man—looked toward the palm tree on one side, and the other face—that of a young lion—looked toward the palm tree on the other side. And so it was, all around the inner wall of the Temple.

21There were square doorposts at the doors of the nave, and in front of the Holy of Holies was what appeared to be an altar, but it was made of wood. 22This altar was 3½ feet square, and 5¼ feet high; its corners, base and sides were all of wood. "This," he told me, "is the Table of the Lord."

23Both the nave and the Holy of Holies had double doors, 24each with two swinging sections. 25The doors leading into the nave were decorated with cherubim and palm trees, just as on the walls. And there was a wooden canopy over the entry hall. 26There were recessed windows and carved palm trees on both sides of the entry hall, the hallways beside the Temple, and on the canopy over the entrance.

JAMES 4:1–17

WHAT is causing the quarrels and fights among you? Isn't it because there is a whole army of evil desires within you? 2You want what you don't have, so you kill to get it. You long for what others have, and can't afford it, so you start a fight to take it away from them. And yet the reason you don't have what you want is that you don't ask God for it. 3And even when you do ask you don't get it because your whole aim is wrong—you want only what will give *you* pleasure.

4You are like an unfaithful wife who loves her husband's enemies. Don't you realize that making friends with God's enemies—the evil pleasures of this world—makes you an enemy of God? I say it again, that if your aim is to enjoy the evil pleasure of the unsaved world, you cannot also be a friend of God. 5Or what do you think the Scripture means when it says that the Holy Spirit, whom God has placed within us, watches over us with tender jealousy? 6But he gives us more and more strength to stand against all such evil longings. As the Scripture says, God gives strength to the humble, but sets himself against the proud and haughty.

7So give yourselves humbly to God. Resist the devil and he will flee from you. 8And when you draw close to God, God will draw close to you. Wash your hands, you sinners, and let your hearts be filled with God alone to make them pure and true to him. 9Let there be tears for the wrong things you have done. Let there be sorrow and sincere grief. Let there be sadness instead of laughter, and gloom instead of joy. 10Then when you realize your worthlessness before the Lord, he will lift you up, encourage and help you.

11Don't criticize and speak evil about

each other, dear brothers. If you do, you will be fighting against God's law of loving one another, declaring it is wrong. But your job is not to decide whether this law is right or wrong, but to obey it. 12Only he who made the law can rightly judge among us. He alone decides to save us or destroy. So what right do you have to judge or criticize others?

13Look here, you people who say, "Today or tomorrow we are going to such and such a town, stay there a year, and open up a profitable business." 14How do you know what is going to happen tomorrow? For the length of your lives is as uncertain as the morning fog—now you see it; soon it is gone. 15What you ought to say is, "If the Lord wants us to, we shall live and do this or that." 16Otherwise you will be bragging about your own plans, and such self-confidence never pleases God.

17Remember, too, that knowing what is right to do and then not doing it is sin.

PSALM 118:19–29

OPEN the gates of the Temple—I will go in and give him my thanks. 20Those gates are the way into the presence of the Lord, and the godly enter there. 21O Lord, thank you so much for answering my prayer and saving me.

22The stone rejected by the builders has now become the capstone of the arch! 23This is the Lord's doing, and it is marvelous to see! 24This is the day the Lord has made. We will rejoice and be glad in it. 25O Lord, please help us. Save us. Give us success. 26Blessed is the one who is coming, the one sent by the Lord. We bless you from the Temple. 27,28Jehovah God is our light. I present to him my sacrifice upon the altar, for you are my God, and I shall give you this thanks and this praise. 29Oh, give thanks to the Lord, for he is so good! For his lovingkindness is forever.

PROVERBS FOR TODAY/ 28:3–5

When a poor man oppresses those even poorer, he is like an unexpected flood sweeping away their last hope. To complain about the law is to praise wickedness. To obey the law is to fight evil. Evil men don't understand the importance of justice, but those who follow the Lord are much concerned about it.

NOVEMBER 21

EZEKIEL 42:1—43:27

THEN he led me out of the Temple, back into the inner court to the rooms north of the Temple yard, and to another building. 2This group of structures was 175 feet long by 87½ feet wide. 3The rows of rooms behind this building were the inner wall of the court. The rooms were in three tiers, overlooking the outer court on one side, and having a 35-foot strip of inner court on the other. 4A 17½-foot walk ran between the

building and the tiers of rooms, extending the entire length, with the doors of the building facing north. 5The upper two tiers of rooms were not as wide as the lower one, because the upper tiers had wider walkways beside them. 6And since the building was not built with girders as those in the outer court were, the upper stories were set back from the ground floor.

7,8The north tiers, next to the outer court, were 87½ feet long—only half as long as the inner wing that faced the Temple court, which was 175 feet long. But a wall extended from the end of the shorter wing, parallel to the longer wing. 9,10And there was an entrance from the outer court to these rooms from the east. On the opposite side of the Temple a similar building composed of two units of tiers was on the south side of the inner court, between the Temple and the outer court, arranged the same as the other. 11There was a walk between the two wings of the building, the same as in the other building across the court—the same length and width and the same exits and doors—they were identical units. 12And there was a door from the outer court at the east.

13Then he told me: "These north and south tiers of rooms facing the Temple yard are holy; there the priests who offer up the sacrifices to the Lord shall eat of the most holy offerings and store them—the cereal offerings, sin offerings, and guilt offerings, for these rooms are holy. 14When the priests leave the Holy Place—the nave of the Temple—they must change their clothes before going out to the outer court. The special robes in which they have been ministering must first be removed, for these robes are holy. They must put on other clothes before entering the parts of the building open to the public."

15When he had finished making these measurements, he led me out through the east passageway to measure the entire Temple area. 16–20He found that it was in the form of a square, 875 feet long on each side, with a wall all around it to separate the restricted area from the public places.

AFTERWARD he brought me out again to the passageway through the outer wall leading to the east. 2And suddenly the glory of the God of Israel appeared from the east. The sound of his coming was like the roar of rushing waters and the whole landscape lighted up with his glory. 3It was just as I had seen it in the other visions, first by the Chebar Ca-nal, and then later at Jerusalem when he came to destroy the city. And I fell down before him with my face in the dust. 4And the glory of the Lord came into the Temple through the eastern passageway.

5Then the Spirit took me up and brought me into the inner court; and the glory of the Lord filled the Temple. 6And I heard the Lord speaking to me from within the Temple (the man who had been measuring was still standing beside me).

7And the Lord said to me:

"Son of dust, this is the place of my throne, and my footstool, where I shall remain, living among the people of Israel forever. They and their kings will not defile my holy name any longer through the adulterous worship of other gods or by worshiping the totem poles erected by their kings. 8They built their idol temples beside mine, with only a wall between, and worshiped their idols. Because they sullied my holy name by such wickedness, I consumed them in my anger. 9Now let them put away their idols and the totem poles erected by their kings, and I will live among them forever.

10"Son of dust, describe the Temple I have shown you to the people of Israel. Tell them its appearance and its plan so they will be ashamed of all their sins. 11And if they are truly ashamed of what they have done, then explain to them the details of its construction—its doors and entrances—and everything about it. Write out all the directions and the rules for them to keep. 12And this is the basic law of the Temple: *Holiness!* The entire top of the hill where the Temple is built is *holy*. Yes, this is the primary law concerning it.

13"And these are the measurements of the altar: The base is twenty-one inches high, with a nine-inch rim around its edge, and it extends twenty-one inches beyond the altar on all sides. 14The first stage of the altar is a stone platform 3½ feet high. This platform is twenty-one inches narrower than the base block on all sides. Rising from this is a narrower platform, twenty-one inches narrower on all sides, and seven feet high. 15From it a still narrower platform rises seven feet, and this is the top of the altar, with four horns projecting twenty-one inches up from the corners. 16This top platform of the altar is twenty-one feet square. 17The platform beneath it is 24½ feet square with a 10½-inch curb around the edges. The entire platform extends out from the top twenty-one inches on all sides. On the east side are steps to climb the altar."

18And he said to me:

"Son of dust, the Lord God says: These are the measurements of the altar to be made in the future, when it is erected for the burning of offerings and the sprinkling of blood upon it. 19At that time the Zadok family of the Levite tribe, who are my ministers, are to be given a bullock for a sin offering. 20You shall take some of its blood and smear it on the four horns of the altar and on the four corners of the top platform and in the curb around it. This will cleanse and make atonement for the altar. 21Then take the bullock for the sin offering and burn it at the appointed place outside the Temple area.

22"The second day, sacrifice a young male goat without any defects—without sickness, deformities, cuts or scars—for a sin offering. Thus the altar shall be cleansed, as it was by the bullock. 23When you have finished this cleansing ceremony, offer another perfect bullock and a perfect ram from the flock. 24Present them before the Lord, and the priests shall sprinkle salt upon them as a burnt offering.

25"Every day for seven days a male goat, a bullock and a ram from the flock shall be sacrificed as a sin offering. None are to have any defects or unhealthiness of any kind. 26Do this each day for seven days to cleanse and make atonement for the altar, thus consecrating it. 27On the eighth day, and on each day afterward, the priests will sacrifice on the altar the burnt offerings and thank offerings of the people, and I will accept you, says the Lord God."

JAMES 5:1-20

LOOK here, you rich men, now is the time to cry and groan with anguished grief because of all the terrible troubles ahead of you. 2Your wealth is even now rotting away, and your fine clothes are becoming mere moth-eaten rags. 3The value of your gold and silver is dropping fast, yet it will stand as evidence against you, and eat your flesh like fire. That is what you have stored up for yourselves, to receive on that coming day of judgment. 4For listen! Hear the cries of the field workers whom you have cheated of their pay. Their cries have reached the ears of the Lord of Hosts.

5You have spent your years here on earth having fun, satisfying your every whim, and now your fat hearts are ready for the slaughter. 6You have condemned and killed good men who had no power to defend themselves against you.

7Now as for you, dear brothers who are waiting for the Lord's return, be patient, like a farmer who waits until the autumn for his precious harvest to ripen. 8Yes, be patient. And take courage, for the coming of the Lord is near.

9Don't grumble about each other, brothers. Are you yourselves above criticism? For see! The great Judge is coming. He is almost here. [Let him do whatever criticizing must be done.]

10For examples of patience in suffering, look at the Lord's prophets. 11We know how happy they are now because they stayed true to him then, even though they suffered greatly for it. Job is an example of a man who continued to trust the Lord in sorrow; from his experiences we can see how the Lord's plan finally ended in good, for he is full of tenderness and mercy.

12But most of all, dear brothers, do not swear either by heaven or earth or anything else; just say a simple yes or no, so that you will not sin and be condemned for it.

¹³Is anyone among you suffering? He should keep on praying about it. And those who have reason to be thankful should continually be singing praises to the Lord.

¹⁴Is anyone sick? He should call for the elders of the church and they should pray over him and pour a little oil upon him, calling on the Lord to heal him. ¹⁵And their prayer, if offered in faith, will heal him, for the Lord will make him well; and if his sickness was caused by some sin, the Lord will forgive him.

¹⁶Admit your faults to one another and pray for each other so that you may be healed. The earnest prayer of a righteous man has great power and wonderful results. ¹⁷Elijah was as completely human as we are, and yet when he prayed earnestly that no rain would fall, none fell for the next three and one half years! ¹⁸Then he prayed again, this time that it *would* rain, and down it poured and the grass turned green and the gardens began to grow again.

¹⁹Dear brothers, if anyone has slipped away from God and no longer trusts the Lord and someone helps him understand the Truth again, ²⁰that person who brings him back to God will have saved a wandering soul from death, bringing about the forgiveness of his many sins.

Sincerely,
James

PSALM 119:1–16

HAPPY are all who perfectly follow the laws of God. ²Happy are all who search for God, and always do his will, ³rejecting compromise with evil, and walking only in his paths. ⁴You have given us your laws to obey—⁵oh, how I want to follow them consistently. ⁶Then I will not be disgraced, for I will have a clean record.

⁷After you have corrected me I will thank you by living as I should! ⁸I *will* obey! Oh, don't forsake me and let me slip back into sin again.

⁹How can a young man stay pure? By reading your Word and following its rules. ¹⁰I have tried my best to find you—don't let me wander off from your instructions. ¹¹I have thought much about your words, and stored them in my heart so that they would hold me back from sin.

¹²Blessed Lord, teach me your rules. ¹³I have recited your laws, ¹⁴and rejoiced in them more than in riches. ¹⁵I will meditate upon them and give them my full respect. ¹⁶I will delight in them and not forget them.

PROVERBS 28:6–7

Better to be poor and honest than rich and a cheater. Young men who are wise obey the law; a son who is a member of a lawless gang is a shame to his father.

NOVEMBER 22

EZEKIEL 44:1—45:12

THEN the Lord brought me back to the outer wall's eastern passageway, but it was closed. ²And he said to me:

"This gate shall remain closed; it shall never be opened. No man shall pass through it; for the Lord, the God of Israel, entered here and so it shall remain shut. ³Only the prince—because he is the prince—may sit inside the passageway to feast there before the Lord. But he shall go and come only through the entry hall of the passage."

⁴Then he brought me through the north passageway to the front of the Temple. I looked and saw that the glory of the Lord filled the Temple of the Lord, and I fell to the ground with my face in the dust.

⁵And the Lord said to me:

"Son of dust, notice carefully; use your eyes and ears. Listen to all I tell you about the laws and rules of the Temple of the Lord. Note carefully who may be admitted to the Temple, and who is to be excluded from it. ⁶And say to these rebels, the people of Israel, The Lord God says: O Israel, you have sinned greatly, ⁷by letting the uncircumcised into my sanctuary—those who have no heart for God—when you offer me my food, the fat and the blood. Thus you have broken my covenant in addition to all your other sins. ⁸You have not kept the laws I gave you concerning these holy affairs, for you have hired foreigners to take charge of my sanctuary.

⁹"The Lord God says: No foreigner of all the many among you shall enter my sanctuary if he has not been circumcised and does not love the Lord. ¹⁰And the men of the tribe of Levi who abandoned me when Israel strayed away from God to idols must be punished for their unfaithfulness. ¹¹They may be Temple guards and gatemen; they may slay the animals brought for burnt offerings and be present to help the people. ¹²But because they encouraged the people to worship other gods, causing Israel to fall into deep sin, I have raised my hand and taken oath, says the Lord God, that they must be punished. ¹³They shall not come near me to minister as priests; they may not touch any of my holy things, for they must bear their shame for all the sins they have committed. ¹⁴They are the Temple caretakers, to do maintenance work and to assist the people in a general way.

¹⁵"However, the sons of Zadok, of the tribe of Levi, continued as my priests in the Temple when Israel abandoned me for idols. These men shall be my ministers; they shall stand before me to offer the fat and blood of the sacrifices, says the Lord God. ¹⁶They shall enter my sanctuary and come to my Table to minister to me; they shall fulfill my requirements.

¹⁷"They must wear only linen clothing when they enter the passageway to the inner court, for they must wear no wool while on duty in the inner court or in the Temple. ¹⁸They must wear linen turbans and linen trousers; they must not wear anything that would cause them to perspire. ¹⁹When they return to the outer court, they must take off the clothes they wear while ministering to me, leaving them in the sacred chambers, and put on other clothes lest they harm the people by touching them with this clothing.

²⁰"They must not let their hair grow too long, nor shave it off. Regular, moderate haircuts are all they are allowed. ²¹No priest may drink wine before coming to the inner court. ²²He may marry only a Jewish maiden, or the widow of a priest; he may not marry a divorced woman.

²³"He shall teach my people the difference between what is holy and what is secular, what is right and what is wrong.

²⁴"They will serve as judges to resolve any disagreements among my people. Their decisions must be based upon my laws. And the priests themselves shall obey my rules and regulations at all the sacred festivals, and they shall see to it that the Sabbath is kept a sacred day.

²⁵"A priest must not defile himself by being in the presence of a dead person, unless it is his father, mother, child, brother or unmarried sister. In such cases it is all right. ²⁶But afterward he must wait seven days before he is cleansed and able to perform his Temple duties again. ²⁷The first day he returns to work and enters the inner court and the sanctuary, he must offer a sin offering for himself, the Lord God says.

²⁸"As to property, they shall not own

any, for I am their heritage! That is enough!

29"Their food shall be the gifts and sacrifices brought to the Temple by the people—the cereal offerings, the sin offerings and the guilt offerings. Whatever anyone gives to the Lord shall be the priests'. 30The first of the first-ripe fruits and all the gifts for the Lord shall go to the priests. The first samples of each harvest of grain shall be donated to the priests too, so that the Lord will bless your homes. 31Priests may never eat meat from any bird or animal that dies a natural death or that dies after being attacked by other animals.

"WHEN you divide the land among the tribes of Israel, you shall first give a section of it to the Lord as his holy portion. This piece shall be 8⅓ miles long and 6⅔ miles wide. It shall all be holy ground.

2"A section of this land, 875 feet square, shall be designated for the Temple. An additional 87½-foot strip all around is to be left empty. 3The Temple shall be built within the area which is 8⅓ miles long and 3⅓ miles wide. 4All this section shall be holy land; it will be used by the priests, who minister in the sanctuary, for their homes and for my Temple.

5"The strip next to it, 8⅓ miles long and 3⅓ miles wide, shall be the residence area for the Levites who work at the Temple. 6Adjacent to the holy lands will be a section 8⅓ miles by 1⅔ miles for a city open to everyone in Israel.

7"Two special sections of land shall be set apart for the prince—one on each side of the holy lands and city; it is contiguous with them in length, and its eastern and western boundaries are the same as those of the tribal sections. 8This shall be his allotment. My princes shall no longer oppress and rob my people, but shall assign all the remainder of the land to the people, giving a portion to each tribe. 9For the Sovereign Lord says to the rulers: Quit robbing and cheating my people out of their land, and expelling them from their homes. Always be fair and honest.

10"You must use honest scales, honest bushels, honest gallons. 11A homer [about five bushels] shall be your standard unit of measurement for both liquid and dry measure. Smaller units shall be the ephah [about one half bushel] for dry measure, and the bath [about seventeen quarts] for liquid. 12The unit of weight shall be the silver shekel [about half an ounce]; it must always be exchanged for twenty gerahs, no less; five shekels shall be valued at five shekels, no less; and ten shekels at ten shekels! Fifty shekels shall always equal one mina.

1 PETER 1:1-13

FROM: Peter, Jesus Christ's missionary.

To: The Jewish Christians driven out of Jerusalem and scattered throughout Pontus, Galatia, Cappadocia, Asia Minor, and Bithynia.

2Dear friends, God the Father chose you long ago and knew you would become his children. And the Holy Spirit has been at work in your hearts, cleansing you with the blood of Jesus Christ and making you to please him. May God bless you richly and grant you increasing freedom from all anxiety and fear.

3All honor to God, the God and Father of our Lord Jesus Christ; for it is his boundless mercy that has given us the privilege of being born again, so that we are now members of God's own family. Now we live in the hope of eternal life because Christ rose again from the dead. 4And God has reserved for his children the priceless gift of eternal life; it is kept in heaven for you, pure and undefiled, beyond the reach of change and decay. 5And God, in his mighty power, will make sure that you get there safely to receive it, because you are trusting him. It will be yours in that coming last day for all to see. 6So be truly glad! There is wonderful joy ahead, even though the going is rough for a while down here.

7These trials are only to test your faith,

to see whether or not it is strong and pure. It is being tested as fire tests gold and purifies it—and your faith is far more precious to God than mere gold; so if your faith remains strong after being tried in the test tube of fiery trials, it will bring you much praise and glory and honor on the day of his return.

8You love him even though you have never seen him; though not seeing him, you trust him; and even now you are happy with the inexpressible joy that comes from heaven itself. 9And your further reward for trusting him will be the salvation of your souls.

10This salvation was something the prophets did not fully understand. Though they wrote about it, they had many questions as to what it all could mean. 11They wondered what the Spirit of Christ within them was talking about, for he told them to write down the events which, since then, have happened to Christ: his suffering, and his great glory afterwards. And they wondered when and to whom all this would happen.

12They were finally told that these things would not occur during their lifetime, but long years later, during yours. And now at last this Good News has been plainly announced to all of us. It was preached to us in the power of the same heaven-sent Holy Spirit who spoke to them; and it is all so strange and wonderful that even the angels in heaven would give a great deal to know more about it.

13So now you can look forward soberly and intelligently to more of God's kindness to you when Jesus Christ returns.

PSALM 119:17–35

BLESS me with life so that I can continue to obey you. 18Open my eyes to see wonderful things in your Word. 19I am but a pilgrim here on earth: how I need a map—and your commands are my chart and guide. 20I long for your instructions more than I can tell.

21You rebuke those cursed proud ones who refuse your commands— 22don't let them scorn me for obeying you. 23For even princes sit and talk against me, but I will continue in your plans. 24Your laws are both my light and my counselors.

25I am completely discouraged—I lie in the dust. Revive me by your Word. 26I told you my plans and you replied. Now give me your instructions. 27Make me understand what you want; for then I shall see your miracles.

28I weep with grief; my heart is heavy with sorrow; encourage and cheer me with your words. 29,30Keep me far from every wrong; help me, undeserving as I am, to obey your laws, for I have chosen to do right. 31I cling to your commands and follow them as closely as I can. Lord, don't let me make a mess of things. 32If you will only help me to want your will, then I will follow your laws even more closely.

33,34Just tell me what to do and I will do it, Lord. As long as I live I'll wholeheartedly obey. 35Make me walk along the right paths for I know how delightful they really are.

PROVERBS 28:8–10

Income from exploiting the poor will end up in the hands of someone who pities them. God doesn't listen to the prayers of those who flout the law. A curse on those who lead astray the godly. But men who encourage the upright to do good shall be given a worthwhile reward.

EZEKIEL 45:13—46:24

THIS is the tax you must give to the prince: a bushel of wheat or barley for every sixty you reap; 14and one per cent of your olive oil; 15from each 200 sheep in all your flocks in Israel, give him one sheep. These are the meal offerings, burnt offerings and thank offerings to make atonement for those who bring them, says the Lord God. 16All the people of Israel shall bring their offerings to the prince.

17"The prince shall be required to furnish the people with sacrifices for public worship—sin offerings, burnt offerings, meal offerings, drink offerings and thank offerings—to make reconciliation for the people of Israel. This shall be done at the time of the religious feasts, the new moon ceremonies, the Sabbaths and all other similar occasions.

18"The Lord God says: On each New Year's Day sacrifice a young bull with no blemishes, to purify the Temple. 19The priest shall take some of the blood of this sin offering and put it on the door posts of the Temple and upon the four corners of the base of the altar and upon the walls at the entry of the inner court. 20Do this also on the seventh day of that month for anyone who has sinned through error or ignorance, and so the Temple will be cleansed.

21"On the fourteenth day of the same month, you shall celebrate the Passover. It will be a seven-day feast. Only bread without yeast shall be eaten during those days. 22On the day of Passover the prince shall provide a young bull for a sin offering for himself and all the people of Israel. 23On each of the seven days of the feast he shall prepare a burnt offering to the Lord. This daily offering will consist of seven young bulls and seven rams without blemish. A male goat shall also be given each day for a sin offering. 24And the prince shall provide one half bushel of grain with each bullock and ram for a meal offering, and three quarts of olive oil.

25"Early in October, during each of the seven days of the annual festival of shelters, he shall provide these same sacrifices for the sin offering, burnt offering, meal offering and oil offering.

"THE Lord God says, the inner wall's eastern entrance shall be closed during the six work days but open on the Sabbath and on the days of the new moon celebrations. 2The prince shall enter the outside entry hall of the passageway and proceed to the inner wall at the other end while the priest offers his burnt offering and peace offering. He shall worship inside the passageway and then return back to the entrance, which shall not be closed until evening. 3The people shall worship the Lord in front of this passageway on the Sabbaths and on the days of the new moon celebrations.

4"The burnt offering which the prince sacrifices to the Lord on the Sabbath days shall be six lambs and a ram, all unblemished. 5He shall present a meal offering of one half bushel of flour to go with the ram, and whatever amount he is willing for, to go with each lamb. And he shall bring three quarts of olive oil for each half bushel of flour. 6At the new moon celebration, he shall bring one young bull, in perfect condition; six lambs and one ram, all without any blemish. 7With the young bull, he must bring one half bushel of flour for a meal offering. With the ram, he must bring one half bushel of flour. With the lamb, he is to bring whatever he is willing to give. With each half bushel of grain he is to bring three quarts of olive oil.

8"The prince shall go in at the entry hall of the passageway and out the same way; 9but when the people come in through the north passageway to sacrifice during the religious feasts, they must go out through the south passageway.

Those coming in from the south must go out by the north. They must never go out the same way they come in, but must always use the opposite passageway. 10The prince shall enter and leave with the common people on these occasions.

11"To summarize: At the special feasts and sacred festivals the meal offering shall be one half bushel with the young bull; one half bushel with the ram; as much as the prince is willing to give with each lamb; and three quarts of oil with each half bushel of grain. 12Whenever the prince offers an extra burnt offering or peace offering to be sacrificed to the Lord, the inner eastern gate shall be opened up for him to enter and he shall offer his sacrifices just as on the Sabbaths. Then he shall turn around and go out, and the passage shall be shut behind him.

13"Each morning a yearling lamb must be sacrificed as a burnt offering to the Lord. 14,15And there must be a meal offering each morning—five pounds of flour with one quart of oil with which to mix it. This is a permanent ordinance—the lamb, the grain offering and the olive oil shall be provided every morning for the daily sacrifice.

16"The Sovereign Lord says: If the prince gives a gift of land to one of his sons, it will belong to him forever. 17But if he gives a gift of land to one of his servants, the servant may keep it only until the Year of Release (every seventh year) when he is set free; then the land returns to the prince. Only gifts to his sons are permanent. 18And the prince may never take anyone's property by force. If he gives property to his sons, it must be from his own land, for I don't want my people losing their property and having to move away."

19,20After that, using the door through the wall at the side of the main passageway, he led me through the entrance to the block of sacred chambers that faced north. There, at the extreme west end of these rooms, I saw a place where, my guide told me, the priests boil the meat of the trespass offering and sin offering and bake the flour of the flour offerings into bread. They do it here to avoid the necessity of carrying the sacrifices through the outer court, in case they harm the people.

21,22Then he brought me out to the outer court again and led me to each of the four corners of the court. I saw that in each corner there was a room 70 feet long by 52½ feet wide, enclosed by walls. 23Around the inside of these walls there ran a line of brick boiling vats, with ovens underneath. 24He said these rooms were where the Temple assistants—the Levites—boil the sacrifices the people offer.

1 PETER 1:14—2:10

OBEY God because you are his children; don't slip back into your old ways—doing evil because you knew no better. 15But be holy now in everything you do, just as the Lord is holy, who invited you to be his child. 16He himself has said, "You must be holy, for I am holy."

17And remember that your heavenly Father to whom you pray has no favorites when he judges. He will judge you with perfect justice for everything you do; so act in reverent fear of him from now on until you get to heaven. 18God paid a ransom to save you from the impossible road to heaven which your fathers tried to take, and the ransom he paid was not mere gold or silver, as you very well know. 19But he paid for you with the precious lifeblood of Christ, the sinless, spotless Lamb of God. 20God chose him for this purpose long before the world began, but only recently was he brought into public view, in these last days, as a blessing to you.

21Because of this, your trust can be in God who raised Christ from the dead and gave him great glory. Now your faith and hope can rest in him alone. 22Now you can have real love for everyone because your souls have been cleansed from selfishness and hatred when you trusted Christ to save you; so see to it that you really do love each other warmly, with all your hearts.

23For you have a new life. It was not passed on to you from your parents, for the life they gave you will fade away. This new one will last forever, for it comes from Christ, God's ever-living Message to men. 24Yes, our natural lives will fade as grass does when it becomes all brown and dry. All our greatness is like a flower that droops and falls; 25but the Word of the Lord will last forever. And his message is the Good News that was preached to you.

So get rid of your feelings of hatred. Don't just pretend to be good! Be done with dishonesty and jealousy and talking about others behind their backs. 2,3Now that you realize how kind the Lord has been to you, put away all evil, deception, envy, and fraud. Long to grow up into the fullness of your salvation; cry for this as a baby cries for his milk.

4Come to Christ, who is the living Foundation of Rock upon which God builds; though men have spurned him, he is very precious to God who has chosen him above all others.

5And now you have become living building-stones for God's use in building his house. What's more, you are his holy priests; so come to him—[you who are acceptable to him because of Jesus Christ]—and offer to God those things that please him. 6As the Scriptures express it, "See, I am sending Christ to be the carefully chosen, precious Cornerstone of my church, and I will never disappoint those who trust in him."

7Yes, he is very precious to you who believe; and to those who reject him, well—"The same Stone that was rejected by the builders has become the Cornerstone, the most honored and important part of the building." 8And the Scriptures also say, "He is the Stone that some will stumble over, and the Rock that will make them fall." They will stumble because they will not listen to God's Word,

nor obey it, and so this punishment must follow—that they will fall.

9But you are not like that, for you have been chosen by God himself—you are priests of the King, you are holy and pure, you are God's very own—all this so that you may show to others how God called you out of the darkness into his wonderful light. 10Once you were less than nothing; now you are God's own. Once you knew very little of God's kindness; now your very lives have been changed by it.

PSALM 119:36–52

HELP me to prefer obedience to making money! 37Turn me away from wanting any other plan than yours. Revive my heart toward you. 38Reassure me that your promises are for me, for I trust and revere you.

39How I dread being mocked for obeying, for your laws are right and good. 40,41,42I long to obey them! Therefore in fairness renew my life, for this was your promise—yes, Lord, to save me! Now spare me by your kindness and your love. Then I will have an answer for those who taunt me, for I trust your promises.

43May I never forget your words; for they are my only hope. 44,45,46Therefore I will keep on obeying you forever and forever, free within the limits of your laws. I will speak to kings about their value, and they will listen with interest and respect.

47How I love your laws! How I enjoy your commands! 48"Come, come to me," I call to them, for I love them and will let them fill my life.

49,50Never forget your promises to me your servant, for they are my only hope. They give me strength in all my troubles; how they refresh and revive me! 51Proud men hold me in contempt for obedience to God, but I stand unmoved. 52From my earliest youth I have tried to obey you; your Word has been my comfort.

"The Spirit of the Lord . . . has sent me to heal the brokenhearted."
  Luke 4:18-19

"May you be given more and more of God's kindness, peace, and love."
    Jude 1:2

Brook of Egypt (Wadi el-Arish) to the Mediterranean.

20"On the west side, the Mediterranean itself will be your boundary, from the southern boundary to the point where the northern boundary begins.

21"Divide the land within these boundaries among the tribes of Israel. 22Distribute the land as an inheritance for yourselves and for the foreigners who live among you with their families. All children born in the land—whether or not their parents are foreigners—are to be considered citizens and have the same rights your own children have. 23All these immigrants are to be given land according to the tribe where they now live.

"HERE is the list of the tribes and the territory each is to get. For Dan: From the northwest boundary at the Mediterranean, across to Hethlon, then to Labweh, and then on to Hazar-enon on the border between Damascus to the south and Hamath to the north. Those are the eastern and western limits of the land. 2Asher's territory lies south of Dan's and has the same east and west boundaries. 3Naphtali's land lies south of Asher's, with the same boundary lines on the east and the west. 4Then comes Manasseh, south of Naphtali, with the same eastern and western boundary lines. 5,6,7Next, to the south, is Ephraim, and then Reuben and then Judah, all with the same boundaries on the east and the west.

8"South of Judah is the land set aside for the Temple. It has the same eastern and western boundaries as the tribal units, with the Temple in the center. 9This Temple area will be 8⅓ miles long and 6⅔ miles wide.

10"A strip of land measuring 8⅓ miles long by 3⅓ miles wide, north to south, surrounds the Temple. 11It is for the priests, that is, the sons of Zadok who obeyed me and didn't go into sin when the people of Israel and the rest of their tribe of Levi did. 12It is their special portion when the land is distributed, the most sacred land of all. Next to it lies the area where the other Levites will live.

13It will be of the same size and shape as the first. Together they measure 8⅓ miles by 6⅔ miles. 14None of this special land shall ever be sold or traded or used by others, for it belongs to the Lord; it is holy.

15"The strip of land 8⅓ miles long by 1⅔ miles wide, south of the Temple section, is for public use—homes, pasture and parks, with a city in the center. 16The city itself is to be 1½ miles square. 17Open land for pastures shall surround the city for approximately a tenth of a mile. 18Outside the city, stretching east and west for three miles alongside the holy grounds, is garden area belonging to the city, for public use. 19It is open to anyone working in the city, no matter where he comes from in Israel.

20"The entire area—including sacred lands and city lands—is 8⅓ miles square.

21,22"The land on both sides of this area, extending clear out to the eastern and western boundaries of Israel, shall belong to the prince. This land, lying between the sections alloted to Judah and Benjamin, is 8⅓ miles square on each side of the sacred and city lands.

23"The sections given to the remaining tribes are as follows: Benjamin's section extends across the entire country of Israel, from its eastern border clear across to the western border. 24South of Benjamin's area lies that of Simeon, also extending out to these same eastern and western borders. 25Next is Issachar, with the same boundaries. 26Then comes Zebulun, also extending all the way across. 27,28Then Gad, with the same borders on east and west, while its south border runs from Tamar to the Spring at Meribathkadesh, and then follows the Brook of Egypt (Wadi el-Arish) to the Mediterranean. 29These are the allotments to be made to each tribe, says the Lord God.

30,31"Each city gate will be named in honor of one of the tribes of Israel. On the north side, with its 1½-mile wall, there will be three gates, one named for Reuben, one for Judah and one for Levi. 32On the east side, with its 1½-mile wall, the gates will be named for Joseph, Benja-

NOVEMBER 24

EZEKIEL 47:1—48:35

THEN he brought me back to the door of the Temple. I saw a stream flowing eastward from beneath the Temple and passing to the right of the altar, that is, on its south side. 2Then he brought me outside the wall through the north passageway and around to the eastern entrance, where I saw the stream flowing along on the south side [of the eastern passageway]. 3Measuring as he went, he took me 1,500 feet east along the stream and told me to go across. At that point the water was up to my ankles. 4He measured off another 1,500 feet and told me to cross again. This time the water was up to my knees. 5Fifteen hundred feet after that it was up to my waist. Another 1,500 feet and it had become a river so deep I wouldn't be able to get across unless I were to swim. It was too deep to cross on foot.

6He told me to keep in mind what I had seen, then led me back along the bank. 7And now, to my surprise, many trees were growing on both sides of the river!

8He told me: "This river flows east through the desert and the Jordan Valley to the Dead Sea, where it will heal the salty waters and make them fresh and pure. 9Everything touching the water of this river shall live. Fish will abound in the Dead Sea, for its waters will be healed. Wherever this water flows, everything will live. 10Fishermen will stand along the shores of the Dead Sea, fishing all the way from En-gedi to En-eglaim. The shores will be filled with nets drying in the sun. Fish of every kind will fill the Dead Sea just as they do the Mediterranean! 11But the marshes and swamps will not be healed; they will still be salty. 12All kinds of fruit trees will grow along the river banks. The leaves will never turn brown and fall, and there will always be fruit. There will be a new crop every month—without fail! For they are watered by the river flowing from the Temple. The fruit will be for food and the leaves for medicine.

13"The Lord God says: Here are the instructions for dividing the land to the twelve tribes of Israel: The tribe of Joseph (Ephraim and Manasseh) shall be given two sections. 14Otherwise, each tribe will have an equal share. I promised with hand raised in oath of truth to give the land to your fathers, and you shall inherit it now.

15"The northern boundary will run from the Mediterranean toward Hethlon, then on through Labweh to Zedad; 16then to Berothah and Sibraim, which are on the border between Damascus and Hamath, and finally to Hazer-hatticon, on the border of Hauran. 17So the northern border will be from the Mediterranean to Hazar-enon, on the border with Hamath to the north and Damascus to the south.

18"The eastern border will run south from Hazar-enon to Mount Hauran, where it will bend westward to the Jordan at the southern tip of the Sea of Galilee, and down along the Jordan River separating Israel from Gilead, past the Dead Sea to Tamar.

19"The southern border will go west from Tamar to the springs at Meribath-kadesh and then follow the course of the min and Dan. 33The south wall, also the same length, will have the gates of Simeon, Issachar and Zebulun; 34on the 1½ miles of the west side, they will be named for Gad, Asher and Naphtali.

35"The entire circumference of the city is six miles. And the name of the city will be 'The City of God.' "

1 PETER 2:11—3:9

DEAR brothers, you are only visitors here. Since your real home is in heaven I beg you to keep away from the evil pleasures of this world; they are not for you, for they fight against your very souls.

12Be careful how you behave among your unsaved neighbors; for then, even if they are suspicious of you and talk against you, they will end up praising God for your good works when Christ returns.

13For the Lord's sake, obey every law of your government: those of the king as head of the state, 14and those of the king's officers, for he has sent them to punish all who do wrong, and to honor those who do right.

15It is God's will that your good lives should silence those who foolishly condemn the Gospel without knowing what it can do for them, having never experienced its power. 16You are free from the law, but that doesn't mean you are free to do wrong. Live as those who are free to do only God's will at all times.

17Show respect for everyone. Love Christians everywhere. Fear God and honor the government.

18Servants, you must respect your masters and do whatever they tell you—not only if they are kind and reasonable, but even if they are tough and cruel. 19Praise the Lord if you are punished for doing right! 20Of course, you get no credit for being patient if you are beaten for doing wrong; but if you do right and suffer for it, and are patient beneath the blows, God is well pleased.

21This suffering is all part of the work God has given you. Christ, who suffered for you, is your example. Follow in his steps: 22He never sinned, never told a lie, 23never answered back when insulted; when he suffered he did not threaten to get even; he left his case in the hands of God who always judges fairly. 24He personally carried the load of our sins in his own body when he died on the cross, so that we can be finished with sin and live a good life from now on. For his wounds have healed ours! 25Like sheep you wandered away from God, but now you have returned to your Shepherd, the Guardian of your souls who keeps you safe from all attacks.

WIVES, fit in with your husbands' plans; for then if they refuse to listen when you talk to them about the Lord, they will be won by your respectful, pure behavior. Your godly lives will speak to them better than any words.

3Don't be concerned about the outward beauty that depends on jewelry, or beautiful clothes, or hair arrangement. 4Be beautiful inside, in your hearts, with the lasting charm of a gentle and quiet spirit which is so precious to God. 5That kind of deep beauty was seen in the saintly women of old, who trusted God and fitted in with their husbands' plans.

6Sarah, for instance, obeyed her husband Abraham, honoring him as head of the house. And if you do the same, you will be following in her steps like good daughters and doing what is right; then you will not need to fear [offending your husbands].

7You husbands must be careful of your wives, being thoughtful of their needs and honoring them as the weaker sex. Remember that you and your wife are partners in receiving God's blessings, and if you don't treat her as you should, your prayers will not get ready answers.

8And now this word to all of you: You should be like one big happy family, full of sympathy toward each other, loving one another with tender hearts and humble minds. 9Don't repay evil for evil. Don't snap back at those who say unkind things about you. Instead, pray for God's help for them, for we are to be kind to others, and God will bless us for it.

PSALM 119:53–70

I am very angry with those who spurn your commands. ⁵⁴For these laws of yours have been my source of joy and singing through all these years of my earthly pilgrimage. ⁵⁵I obey them even at night and keep my thoughts, O Lord, on you. ⁵⁶What a blessing this has been to me—to constantly obey.

⁵⁷Jehovah is mine! And I promise to obey! ⁵⁸With all my heart I want your blessings. Be merciful just as you promised. ⁵⁹,⁶⁰I thought about the wrong direction in which I was headed, and turned around and came running back to you. ⁶¹Evil men have tried to drag me into sin, but I am firmly anchored to your laws.

⁶²At midnight I will rise to give my thanks to you for your good laws. ⁶³Anyone is my brother who fears and trusts the Lord and obeys him. ⁶⁴O Lord, the earth is full of your lovingkindness! Teach me your good paths.

⁶⁵Lord, I am overflowing with your blessings, just as you promised. ⁶⁶Now teach me good judgment as well as knowledge. For your laws are my guide. ⁶⁷I used to wander off until you punished me; now I closely follow all you say. ⁶⁸You are good and do only good; make me follow your lead.

⁶⁹Proud men have made up lies about me, but the truth is that I obey your laws with all my heart. ⁷⁰Their minds are dull and stupid, but I have sense enough to follow you.

PROVERBS 28:12–13

When the godly are successful, everyone is glad. When the wicked succeed, everyone is sad. A man who refuses to admit his mistakes can never be successful. But if he confesses and forsakes them, he gets another chance.

NOVEMBER 25

DANIEL 1:1—2:23

THREE years after King Jehoiakim began to rule in Judah, Babylon's King Nebuchadnezzar attacked Jerusalem with his armies, and the Lord gave him victory over Jehoiakim. When he returned to Babylon, he took along some of the sacred cups from the Temple of God, and placed them in the treasury of his god in the land of Shinar.

³,⁴Then he ordered Ashpenaz, who was in charge of his palace personnel, to select some of the Jewish youths brought back as captives—young men of the royal family and nobility of Judah— and to teach them the Chaldean language and literature. "Pick strong, healthy, good-looking lads," he said; "those who have read widely in many fields, are well informed, alert and sensible, and have enough poise to look good around the palace."

⁵The king assigned them the best of food and wine from his own kitchen during their three-year training period, planning to make them his counselors when they graduated.

⁶Daniel, Hananiah, Misha-el, and Azariah were four of the young men chosen, all from the tribe of Judah. ⁷However, their superintendent gave them Babylonian names, as follows:

Daniel was called Belteshazzar;
Hananiah was called Shadrach;

Misha-el was called Meshach;
Azariah was called Abednego.

8But Daniel made up his mind not to eat the food and wine given to them by the king. He asked the superintendent for permission to eat other things instead. 9Now as it happened, God had given the superintendent a special appreciation for Daniel, and sympathy for his predicament. 10But he was alarmed by Daniel's suggestion.

"I'm afraid you will become pale and thin compared with the other youths your age," he said, "and then the king will behead me for neglecting my responsibilities."

11Daniel talked it over with the steward who was appointed by the superintendent to look after Daniel, Hananiah, Misha-el, and Azariah, 12and suggested a ten-day diet of only vegetables and water; 13then, at the end of this trial period the steward could see how they looked in comparison with the other fellows who ate the king's rich food, and decide whether or not to let them continue their diet.

14The steward finally agreed to the test. 15Well, at the end of the ten days, Daniel and his three friends looked healthier and better nourished than the youths who had been eating the food supplied by the king! 16So after that the steward fed them only vegetables and water, without the rich foods and wines!

17God gave these four youths great ability to learn and they soon mastered all the literature and science of the time, and God gave to Daniel special ability in understanding the meanings of dreams and visions.

18,19When the three-year training period was completed, the superintendent brought all the young men to the king for oral exams, as he had been ordered to do. King Nebuchadnezzar had long talks with each of them, and none of them impressed him as much as Daniel, Hananiah, Misha-el, and Azariah. So they were put on his regular staff of advisors. 20And in all matters requiring information and balanced judgment, the king found these young men's advice ten times better than that of all the skilled magicians and wise astrologers in his realm.

21Daniel held this appointment as the king's counselor until the first year of the reign of King Cyrus.

ONE night in the second year of his reign, Nebuchadnezzar had a terrifying nightmare, and awoke trembling with fear. And to make matters worse, he couldn't remember his dream! He immediately called in all his magicians, incantationists, sorcerers, and astrologers, and demanded that they tell him what his dream had been.

"I've had a terrible nightmare," he said as they stood before him, "and I can't remember what it was. Tell me, for I fear some tragedy awaits me."

4Then the astrologers (speaking in Aramaic) said to the king, "Sir, tell us the dream and then we can tell you what it means."

5But the king replied, "I tell you, the dream is gone—I can't remember it. And if you won't tell me what it was and what it means, I'll have you torn limb from limb and your houses made into heaps of rubble! 6But I will give you many wonderful gifts and honors if you tell me what the dream was and what it means. So, begin!"

7They said again, "How can we tell you what the dream means unless you tell us what it was?"

8,9The king retorted, "I can see your trick! You're trying to stall for time until the calamity befalls me that the dream foretells. But if you don't tell me the dream, you certainly can't expect me to believe your interpretation!"

10The astrologers replied to the king, "There isn't a man alive who can tell others what they have dreamed! And there isn't a king in all the world who would ask such a thing! 11This is an impossible thing the king requires. No one except the gods can tell you your dream, and they are not here to help."

12Upon hearing this, the king was furious, and sent out orders to execute all the wise men of Babylon. 13And Daniel and his companions were rounded up with the others to be killed.

14But when Ari-och, the chief executioner, came to kill them, Daniel handled the situation with great wisdom by asking, 15"Why is the king so angry? What is the matter?"

Then Ari-och told him all that had happened.

16So Daniel went in to see the king. "Give me a little time," he said, "and I will tell you the dream and what it means."

17Then he went home and told Hananiah, Misha-el, and Azariah, his companions. 18They asked the God of heaven to show them his mercy by telling them the secret, so they would not die with the others. 19And that night in a vision God told Daniel what the king had dreamed.

Then Daniel praised the God of heaven, 20saying, "Blessed be the name of God forever and ever, for he alone has all wisdom and all power. 21World events are under his control. He removes kings and sets others on their thrones. He gives wise men their wisdom, and scholars their intelligence. 22He reveals profound mysteries beyond man's understanding. He knows all hidden things, for he is light, and darkness is no obstacle to him. 23I thank and praise you, O God of my fathers, for you have given me wisdom and glowing health, and now, even this vision of the king's dream, and the understanding of what it means."

1 PETER 3:10—4:6

IF you want a happy, good life, keep control of your tongue, and guard your lips from telling lies. 11Turn away from evil and do good. Try to live in peace even if you must run after it to catch and hold it! 12For the Lord is watching his children, listening to their prayers; but the Lord's face is hard against those who do evil.

13Usually no one will hurt you for wanting to do good. 14But even if they

should, you are to be envied, for God will reward you for it. 15Quietly trust yourself to Christ your Lord and if anybody asks why you believe as you do, be ready to tell him, and do it in a gentle and respectful way.

16Do what is right; then if men speak against you, calling you evil names, they will become ashamed of themselves for falsely accusing you when you have only done what is good. 17Remember, if God wants you to suffer, it is better to suffer for doing good than for doing wrong!

18Christ also suffered. He died once for the sins of all us guilty sinners, although he himself was innocent of any sin at any time, that he might bring us safely home to God. But though his body died, his spirit lived on, 19and it was in the spirit that he visited the spirits in prison, and preached to them— 20spirits of those who, long before in the days of Noah, had refused to listen to God, though he waited patiently for them while Noah was building the ark. Yet only eight persons were saved from drowning in that terrible flood. 21(That, by the way, is what baptism pictures for us: In baptism we show that we have been saved from death and doom by the resurrection of Christ; not because our bodies are washed clean by the water, but because in being baptized we are turning to God and asking him to cleanse our *hearts* from sin.) 22And now Christ is in heaven, sitting in the place of honor next to God the Father, with all the angels and powers of heaven bowing before him and obeying him.

SINCE Christ suffered and underwent pain, you must have the same attitude he did; you must be ready to suffer, too. For remember, when your body suffers, sin loses its power, 2and you won't be spending the rest of your life chasing after evil desires, but will be anxious to do the will of God. 3You have had enough in the past of the evil things the godless enjoy—sex sin, lust, getting drunk, wild parties, drinking bouts, and the worship of idols, and other terrible sins.

⁴Of course, your former friends will be very surprised when you don't eagerly join them any more in the wicked things they do, and they will laugh at you in contempt and scorn. ⁵But just remember that they must face the Judge of all, living and dead; they will be punished for the way they have lived. ⁶That is why the Good News was preached even to those who were dead—killed by the flood—so that although their bodies were punished with death, they could still live in their spirits as God lives.

PSALM 119:71–80

THE punishment you gave me was the best thing that could have happened to me, for it taught me to pay attention to your laws. They are more valuable to me than millions in silver and gold!

⁷³You made my body, Lord; now give me sense to heed your laws. ⁷⁴All those who fear and trust in you will welcome me because I too am trusting in your Word.

⁷⁵,⁷⁶,⁷⁷I know, O Lord, that your decisions are right and that your punishment was right and did me good. Now let your lovingkindness comfort me, just as you promised. Surround me with your tender mercies, that I may live. For your law is my delight.

⁷⁸Let the proud be disgraced, for they have cut me down with all their lies. But I will concentrate my thoughts upon your laws.

⁷⁹Let all others join me, who trust and fear you, and we will discuss your laws. ⁸⁰Help me to love your every wish; then I will never have to be ashamed of myself.

PROVERBS 28:14

Blessed is the man who reveres God, but the man who doesn't care is headed for serious trouble.

NOVEMBER 26

DANIEL 2:24—3:30

THEN Daniel went in to see Ari-och, who had been ordered to execute the wise men of Babylon, and said, "Don't kill them. Take me to the king and I will tell him what he wants to know."

²⁵Then Ari-och hurried Daniel in to the king and said, "I've found one of the Jewish captives who will tell you your dream!"

²⁶The king said to Daniel, "Is this true? Can you tell me what my dream was and what it means?"

²⁷Daniel replied, "No wise man, astrologer, magician, or wizard can tell the king such things, ²⁸but there is a God in heaven who reveals secrets, and he

has told you in your dream what will happen in the future. This was your dream:

²⁹"You dreamed of coming events. He who reveals secrets was speaking to you. ³⁰(But remember, it's not because I am wiser than any living person that I know this secret of your dream, for God showed it to me for your benefit.)

³¹"O king, you saw a huge and powerful statue of a man, shining brilliantly, frightening and terrible. ³²The head of the statue was made of purest gold, its chest and arms were of silver, its belly and thighs of brass, ³³its legs of iron, its feet part iron and part clay. ³⁴But as you watched, a Rock was cut from the

mountainside by supernatural means. It came hurtling toward the statue and crushed the feet of iron and clay, smashing them to bits. ³⁵Then the whole statue collapsed into a heap of iron, clay, brass, silver, and gold; its pieces were crushed as small as chaff, and the wind blew them all away. But the Rock that knocked the statue down became a great mountain that covered the whole earth.

³⁶"That was the dream; now for its meaning:

³⁷"Your Majesty, you are a king over many kings, for the God of heaven has given you your kingdom, power, strength and glory. ³⁸You rule the farthest provinces, and even animals and birds are under your control, as God decreed. You are that head of gold.

³⁹"But after your kingdom has come to an end, another world power will arise to take your place. This empire will be inferior to yours. And after that kingdom has fallen, yet a third great power—represented by the bronze belly of the statue—will rise to rule the world. ⁴⁰Following it, the fourth kingdom will be strong as iron—smashing, bruising, and conquering. ⁴¹,⁴²The feet and toes you saw—part iron and part clay—show that later on, this kingdom will be divided. Some parts of it will be as strong as iron, and some as weak as clay. ⁴³This mixture of iron with clay also shows that these kingdoms will try to strengthen themselves by forming alliances with each other through intermarriage of their rulers; but this will not succeed, for iron and clay don't mix.

⁴⁴"During the reigns of those kings, the God of heaven will set up a kingdom that will never be destroyed; no one will ever conquer it. It will shatter all these kingdoms into nothingness, but it shall stand forever, indestructible. ⁴⁵That is the meaning of the Rock cut from the mountain without human hands—the Rock that crushed to powder all the iron and brass, the clay, the silver, and the gold.

"Thus the great God has shown what will happen in the future, and this interpretation of your dream is as sure and certain as my description of it."

⁴⁶Then Nebuchadnezzar fell to the ground before Daniel and worshiped him, and commanded his people to offer sacrifices and burn sweet incense before him.

⁴⁷"Truly, O Daniel," the king said, "your God is the God of gods, Ruler of kings, the Revealer of mysteries, because he has told you this secret."

⁴⁸Then the king made Daniel very great; he gave him many valuable gifts, and appointed him to be ruler over the whole province of Babylon, as well as chief over all his wise men.

⁴⁹Then, at Daniel's request, the king appointed Shadrach, Meshach, and Abednego as Daniel's assistants, to be in charge of all the affairs of the province of Babylon; Daniel served as chief magistrate in the king's court.

KING Nebuchadnezzar made a gold statue ninety feet high and nine feet wide and set it up on the Plain of Dura, in the province of Babylon; ²then he sent messages to all the princes, governors, captains, judges, treasurers, counselors, sheriffs, and rulers of all the provinces of his empire, to come to the dedication of his statue. ³When they had all arrived and were standing before the monument, ⁴a herald shouted out, "O people of all nations and languages, this is the king's command:

⁵"When the band strikes up, you are to fall flat on the ground to worship King Nebuchadnezzar's gold statue; ⁶anyone who refuses to obey will immediately be thrown into a flaming furnace."

⁷So when the band began to play, everyone—whatever his nation, language, or religion—fell to the ground and worshiped the statue.

⁸But some officials went to the king and accused some of the Jews of refusing to worship!

⁹"Your Majesty," they said to him, ¹⁰"you made a law that everyone must fall down and worship the gold statue when the band begins to play, ¹¹and that anyone who refuses will be thrown into

a flaming furnace. 12But there are some Jews out there—Shadrach, Meshach, and Abednego, whom you have put in charge of Babylonian affairs—who have defied you, refusing to serve your gods or to worship the gold statue you set up."

13Then Nebuchadnezzar, in a terrible rage, ordered Shadrach, Meshach, and Abednego to be brought in before him. 14"Is it true, O Shadrach, Meshach, and Abednego," he demanded, "that you are refusing to serve my gods or to worship the gold statue I set up? 15I'll give you one more chance. When the music plays, if you fall down and worship the statue, all will be well. But if you refuse, you will be thrown into a flaming furnace within the hour. And what god can deliver you out of my hands then?"

16Shadrach, Meshach, and Abednego replied, "O Nebuchadnezzar, we are not worried about what will happen to us. 17If we are thrown into the flaming furnace, our God is able to deliver us; and he will deliver us out of your hand, Your Majesty. 18But if he doesn't, please understand, sir, that even then we will never under any circumstance serve your gods or worship the gold statue you have erected." 19Then Nebuchadnezzar was filled with fury and his face became dark with anger at Shadrach, Meshach, and Abednego. He commanded that the furnace be heated up seven times hotter than usual, 20and called for some of the strongest men of his army to bind Shadrach, Meshach, and Abednego, and throw them into the fire.

21So they bound them tight with ropes and threw them into the furnace, fully clothed. 22And because the king, in his anger, had demanded such a hot fire in the furnace, the flames leaped out and killed the soldiers as they threw them in! 23So Shadrach, Meshach, and Abednego fell down bound into the roaring flames.

24But suddenly, as he was watching, Nebuchadnezzar jumped up in amazement and exclaimed to his advisors, "Didn't we throw three men into the furnace?"

"Yes," they said, "we did indeed, Your Majesty."

25"Well, look!" Nebuchadnezzar shouted. "I see *four* men, unbound, walking around in the fire, and they aren't even hurt by the flames! And the fourth looks like a god!"

26Then Nebuchadnezzar came as close as he could to the open door of the flaming furnace and yelled: "Shadrach, Meshach, and Abednego, servants of the Most High God! Come out! Come here!" So they stepped out of the fire.

27Then the princes, governors, captains, and counselors crowded around them and saw that the fire hadn't touched them—not a hair of their heads was singed; their coats were unscorched, and they didn't even smell of smoke!

28Then Nebuchadnezzar said, "Blessed be the God of Shadrach, Meshach, and Abednego, for he sent his angel to deliver his trusting servants when they defied the king's commandment, and were willing to die rather than serve or worship any god except their own. 29Therefore, I make this decree, that any person of any nation, language, or religion who speaks a word against the God of Shadrach, Meshach, and Abednego shall be torn limb from limb and his house knocked into a heap of rubble. For no other God can do what this one does."

30Then the king gave promotions to Shadrach, Meshach, and Abednego, so that they prospered greatly there in the province of Babylon.

1 PETER 4:7—5:14

THE end of the world is coming soon. Therefore be earnest, thoughtful men of prayer. 8Most important of all, continue to show deep love for each other, for love makes up for many of your faults. 9Cheerfully share your home with those who need a meal or a place to stay for the night.

10God has given each of you some special abilities; be sure to use them to help each other, passing on to others God's many kinds of blessings. 11Are you called to preach? Then preach as though God himself were speaking through you. Are you called to help others? Do it with all the strength and energy that God supplies, so that God will be glorified through Jesus Christ—to him be glory and power forever and ever. Amen.

12Dear friends, don't be bewildered or surprised when you go through the fiery trials ahead, for this is no strange, unusual thing that is going to happen to you. 13Instead, be really glad—because these trials will make you partners with Christ in his suffering, and afterwards you will have the wonderful joy of sharing his glory in that coming day when it will be displayed.

14Be happy if you are cursed and insulted for being a Christian, for when that happens the Spirit of God will come upon you with great glory. 15Don't let me hear of your suffering for murdering or stealing or making trouble or being a busybody and prying into other people's affairs. 16But it is no shame to suffer for being a Christian. Praise God for the privilege of being in Christ's family and being called by his wonderful name! 17For the time has come for judgment, and it must begin first among God's own children. And if even we who are Christians must be judged, what terrible fate awaits those who have never believed in the Lord? 18If the righteous are barely saved, what chance will the godless have?

19So if you are suffering according to God's will, keep on doing what is right and trust yourself to the God who made you, for he will never fail you.

AND now, a word to you elders of the church. I, too, am an elder; with my own eyes I saw Christ dying on the cross; and I, too, will share his glory and his honor when he returns. Fellow elders, this is my plea to you: 2Feed the flock of God; care for it willingly, not grudgingly; not for what you will get out of it, but because you are eager to serve the Lord. 3Don't be tyrants, but lead them by your good example, 4and when the Head Shepherd comes, your reward will be a never-ending share in his glory and honor.

5You younger men, follow the leadership of those who are older. And all of you serve each other with humble spirits, for God gives special blessings to those who are humble, but sets himself against those who are proud. 6If you will humble yourselves under the mighty hand of God, in his good time he will lift you up.

7Let him have all your worries and cares, for he is always thinking about you and watching everything that concerns you.

8Be careful—watch out for attacks from Satan, your great enemy. He prowls around like a hungry, roaring lion, looking for some victim to tear apart. 9Stand firm when he attacks. Trust the Lord; and remember that other Christians all around the world are going through these sufferings too.

10After you have suffered a little while, our God, who is full of kindness through Christ, will give you his eternal glory. He personally will come and pick you up, and set you firmly in place, and make you stronger than ever. 11To him be all power over all things, forever and ever. Amen.

12I am sending this note to you through the courtesy of Silvanus who is, in my opinion, a very faithful brother. I hope I have encouraged you by this letter for I have given you a true statement of the way God blesses. What I have told you here should help you to stand firmly in his love.

13The church here in Rome—she is your sister in the Lord—sends you her greetings; so does my son Mark. 14Give each other the handshake of Christian love. Peace be to all of you who are in Christ.

PSALM 119:81–95

I faint for your salvation; but I expect your help, for you have promised it. 82My eyes are straining to see your promises come true. When will you comfort me with your help? 83I am shriveled like a wineskin in the smoke, exhausted with waiting. But still I cling to your laws and obey them. 84How long must I wait before you punish those who persecute me? 85,86These proud men who hate your truth and laws have dug deep pits for me to fall in. Their lies have brought me into deep trouble. Help me, for you love only truth. 87They had almost finished me off, yet I refused to yield and disobey your laws. 88In your kindness, spare my life; then I can continue to obey you.

89Forever, O Lord, your Word stands firm in heaven. 90,91Your faithfulness extends to every generation, like the earth you created; it endures by your decree, for everything serves your plans.

92I would have despaired and perished unless your laws had been my deepest delight. 93I will never lay aside your laws, for you have used them to restore my joy and health. 94I am yours! Save me! For I have tried to live according to your desires. 95Though the wicked hide along the way to kill me, I will quietly keep my mind upon your promises.

PROVERBS 28:15–16

A wicked ruler is as dangerous to the poor as a lion or bear attacking them. Only a stupid prince will oppress his people, but a king will have a long reign if he hates dishonesty and bribes.

NOVEMBER 27

DANIEL 4:1–37

THIS is the proclamation of Nebuchadnezzar the king, which he sent to people of every language in every nation of the world:

Greetings:

2I want you all to know about the strange thing that the Most High God did to me. 3It was incredible—a mighty miracle! And now I know for sure that his kingdom is everlasting; he reigns forever and ever.

4I, Nebuchadnezzar, was living in peace and prosperity, 5when one night I had a dream that greatly frightened me. 6I called in all the wise men of Babylon to tell me the meaning of my dream, 7but when they came—the magicians, astrologers, fortunetellers, and wizards—and I told them the dream, they couldn't interpret it. 8At last Daniel came in—the man I named Belteshazzar after my god—the man in whom is the spirit of the holy gods, and I told him the dream.

9"O Belteshazzar, master magician," I said, "I know that the spirit of the holy gods is in you and no mystery is too great for you to solve. Tell me what my dream means:

10,11"I saw a very tall tree out in a field, growing higher and higher into the sky until it could be seen by everyone in all the world. 12Its leaves were fresh and green, and its branches were weighted down with fruit, enough for everyone to eat. Wild animals rested beneath its shade and birds sheltered in its branches, and all the world was fed from it. 13Then as I lay there dreaming, I saw one of God's angels coming down from heaven.

14"He shouted, 'Cut down the tree; lop off its branches; shake off its leaves, and scatter its fruit. Get the animals out from under it and the birds from its branches, 15but leave its stump and roots in the ground, banded with a chain of iron and brass, surrounded by the tender grass.

Let the dews of heaven drench him and let him eat grass with the wild animals! 16For seven years let him have the mind of an animal instead of a man. 17For this has been decreed by the Watchers, demanded by the Holy Ones. The purpose of this decree is that all the world may understand that the Most High dominates the kingdoms of the world, and gives them to anyone he wants to, even the lowliest of men!'

18"O Belteshazzar, that was my dream; now tell me what it means. For no one else can help me; all the wisest men of my kingdom have failed me. But you can tell me, for the spirit of the holy gods is in you."

19Then Daniel sat there stunned and silent for an hour, aghast at the meaning of the dream. Finally the king said to him: "Belteshazzar, don't be afraid to tell me what it means."

Daniel replied: "Oh, that the events foreshadowed in this dream would happen to your enemies, my lord, and not to you! 20For the tree you saw growing so tall, reaching high into the heavens for all the world to see, 21with its fresh green leaves, loaded with fruit for all to eat, the wild animals living in its shade, with its branches full of birds— 22that tree, Your Majesty, is you. For you have grown strong and great; your greatness reaches up to heaven, and your rule to the ends of the earth.

23"Then you saw God's angel coming down from heaven and saying, 'Cut down the tree and destroy it, but leave the stump and the roots in the earth surrounded by tender grass, banded with a chain of iron and brass. Let him be wet with the dew of heaven. For seven years let him eat grass with the animals of the field.'

24"Your Majesty, the Most High God has decreed—and it will surely happen— 25that your people will chase you from your palace, and you will live in the fields like an animal, eating grass like a cow, your back wet with dew from heaven. For seven years this will be your life, until you learn that the Most High God

dominates the kingdoms of men, and gives power to anyone he chooses. 26But the stump and the roots were left in the ground! This means that you will get your kingdom back again, when you have learned that heaven rules.

27"O King Nebuchadnezzar, listen to me—stop sinning; do what you know is right; be merciful to the poor. Perhaps even yet God will spare you."

28But all these things happened to Nebuchadnezzar. 29Twelve months after this dream, he was strolling on the roof of the royal palace in Babylon, 30and saying, "I, by my own mighty power, have built this beautiful city as my royal residence, and as the capital of my empire."

31While he was still speaking these words, a voice called down from heaven, "O King Nebuchadnezzar, this message is for you: You are no longer ruler of this kingdom. 32You will be forced out of the palace to live with the animals in the fields, and to eat grass like the cows for seven years until you finally realize that God parcels out the kingdoms of men and gives them to anyone he chooses."

33That very same hour this prophecy was fulfilled. Nebuchadnezzar was chased from his palace and ate grass like the cows, and his body was wet with dew; his hair grew as long as eagles' feathers, and his nails were like birds' claws.

34"At the end of seven years I, Nebuchadnezzar, looked up to heaven, and my sanity returned, and I praised and worshiped the Most High God and honored him who lives forever, whose rule is everlasting, his kingdom evermore. 35All the people of the earth are nothing when compared to him; he does whatever he thinks best among the angels of heaven, as well as here on earth. No one can stop him or challenge him, saying, 'What do you mean by doing these things?' 36When my mind returned to me, so did my honor and glory and kingdom. My counselors and officers came back to me and I was reestablished as head of my kingdom, with even greater honor than before.

37"Now, I, Nebuchadnezzar, praise and glorify and honor the King of Heaven, the Judge of all, whose every act is right and good; for he is able to take those who walk proudly and push them into the dust!"

2 PETER 1:1–21

FROM: Simon Peter, a servant and missionary of Jesus Christ.

To: all of you who have our kind of faith. The faith I speak of is the kind that Jesus Christ our God and Savior gives to us. How precious it is, and how just and good he is to give this same faith to each of us.

2Do you want more and more of God's kindness and peace? Then learn to know him better and better. 3For as you know him better, he will give you, through his great power, everything you need for living a truly good life: he even shares his own glory and his own goodness with us! 4And by that same mighty power he has given us all the other rich and wonderful blessings he promised; for instance, the promise to save us from the lust and rottenness all around us, and to give us his own character.

5But to obtain these gifts, you need more than faith; you must also work hard to be good, and even that is not enough. For then you must learn to know God better and discover what he wants you to do. 6Next, learn to put aside your own desires so that you will become patient and godly, gladly letting God have his way with you. 7This will make possible the next step, which is for you to enjoy other people and to like them, and finally you will grow to love them deeply. 8The more you go on in this way, the more you will grow strong spiritually and become fruitful and useful to our Lord Jesus Christ. 9But anyone who fails to go after these additions to faith is blind indeed, or at least very shortsighted, and has forgotten that God delivered him from the old life of sin so that now he can live a strong, good life for the Lord. 10So, dear brothers, work hard to prove that you really are among those God has called and chosen, and then you will never stumble or fall away. 11And God will open wide the gates of heaven for you to enter into the eternal kingdom of our Lord and Savior Jesus Christ.

12I plan to keep on reminding you of these things even though you already know them and are really getting along quite well! 13,14But the Lord Jesus Christ has showed me that my days here on earth are numbered, and I am soon to die. As long as I am still here I intend to keep sending these reminders to you, 15hoping to impress them so clearly upon you that you will remember them long after I have gone.

16For we have not been telling you fairy tales when we explained to you the power of our Lord Jesus Christ and his coming again. My own eyes have seen his splendor and his glory: 17,18I was there on the holy mountain when he shone out with honor given him by God his Father; I heard that glorious, majestic voice calling down from heaven, saying, "This is my much-loved Son; I am well pleased with him."

19So we have seen and proved that what the prophets said came true. You will do well to pay close attention to everything they have written, for, like lights shining into dark corners, their words help us to understand many things that otherwise would be dark and difficult. But when you consider the wonderful truth of the prophets' words, then the light will dawn in your souls and Christ the Morning Star will shine in your hearts. 20,21For no prophecy recorded in Scripture was ever thought up by the prophet himself. It was the Holy Spirit within these godly men who gave them true messages from God.

PSALM 119:96–112

NOTHING is perfect except your words. 97Oh, how I love them. I think about them all day long. 98They make me wiser than my enemies, because they are my constant guide.

99Yes, wiser than my teachers, for I am ever thinking of your rules. 100They make me even wiser than the aged.

101I have refused to walk the paths of evil for I will remain obedient to your Word. 102,103No, I haven't turned away from what you taught me; your words are sweeter than honey. 104And since only your rules can give me wisdom and understanding, no wonder I hate every false teaching.

105Your words are a flashlight to light the path ahead of me, and keep me from stumbling. 106I've said it once and I'll say it again and again: I will obey these wonderful laws of yours.

107I am close to death at the hands of my enemies; oh, give me back my life again, just as you promised me. 108Accept my grateful thanks and teach me your desires. 109My life hangs in the balance, but I will not give up obedience to your laws. 110The wicked have set their traps for me along your path, but I will not turn aside. 111Your laws are my joyous treasure forever. 112I am determined to obey you until I die.

PROVERBS 28:17–18

A murderer's conscience will drive him into hell. Don't stop him! Good men will be rescued from harm, but cheaters will be destroyed.

NOVEMBER 28

DANIEL 5:1–31

BELSHAZZAR the king invited a thousand of his officers to a great feast where the wine flowed freely. 2,3,4While Belshazzar was drinking he was reminded of the gold and silver cups taken long before from the Temple in Jerusalem during Nebuchadnezzar's reign, and brought to Babylon. Belshazzar ordered that these sacred cups be brought in to the feast, and when they arrived he and his princes, wives, and concubines drank toasts from them to their idols made of gold and silver, brass and iron, wood and stone.

5Suddenly, as they were drinking from these cups, they saw the fingers of a man's hand writing on the plaster of the wall opposite the lampstand. The king himself saw the fingers as they wrote. 6His face blanched with fear, and such terror gripped him that his knees knocked together and his legs gave way beneath him.

7"Bring the magicians and astrologers!" he screamed. "Bring the Chaldeans! Whoever reads that writing on the wall, and tells me what it means, will be dressed in purple robes of royal honor with a gold chain around his neck, and become the third ruler in the kingdom!"

8But when they came, none of them could understand the writing or tell him what it meant.

9The king grew more and more hysterical; his face reflected the terror he felt, and his officers too were shaken. 10But when the queen-mother heard what was happening, she rushed to the banquet hall and said to Belshazzar, "Calm yourself, Your Majesty, don't be so pale and frightened over this. 11For there is a man in your kingdom who has within him the spirit of the holy gods. In the days of your father this man was found to be as full of wisdom and understanding as though he were himself a god. And in the reign of King Nebuchadnezzar, he was made chief of all the magicians, astrologers, Chaldeans and soothsayers of

Babylon. 12Call for this man, Daniel—or Belteshazzar, as the king called him—for his mind is filled with divine knowledge and understanding. He can interpret dreams, explain riddles, and solve knotty problems. He will tell you what the writing means."

13So Daniel was rushed in to see the king. The king asked him, "Are you the Daniel brought from Israel as a captive by King Nebuchadnezzar? 14I have heard that you have the spirit of the gods within you and that you are filled with enlightenment and wisdom. 15My wise men and astrologers have tried to read that writing on the wall, and tell me what it means, but they can't. 16I am told you can solve all kinds of mysteries. If you can tell me the meaning of those words, I will clothe you in purple robes, with a gold chain around your neck, and make you the third ruler in the kingdom."

17Daniel answered, "Keep your gifts, or give them to someone else, but I will tell you what the writing means. 18Your Majesty, the Most High God gave Nebuchadnezzar, who long ago preceded you, a kingdom and majesty and glory and honor. 19He gave him such majesty that all the nations of the world trembled before him in fear. He killed any who offended him, and spared any he liked. At his whim they rose or fell. 20But when his heart and mind were hardened in pride, God removed him from his royal throne and took away his glory, 21and he was chased out of his palace into the fields. His thoughts and feelings became those of an animal, and he lived among the wild donkeys; he ate grass like the cows and his body was wet with the dew of heaven, until at last he knew that the Most High overrules the kingdoms of men, and that he appoints anyone he desires to reign over them.

22"And you, his successor, O Belshazzar—you knew all this, yet you have not been humble. 23For you have defied the Lord of Heaven, and brought here these cups from his Temple; and you and your officers and wives and concubines have been drinking wine from them while praising gods of silver, gold, brass, iron, wood, and stone—gods that neither see nor hear, nor know anything at all. But you have not praised the God who gives you the breath of life and controls your destiny! 24,25And so God sent those fingers to write this message: 'Mene,' 'Mene,' 'Tekel,' 'Parsin.'

26"This is what it means:

"Mene means 'numbered'—God has numbered the days of your reign, and they are ended.

27"Tekel means 'weighed'—you have been weighed in God's balances and have failed the test.

28"Parsin means 'divided'—your kingdom will be divided and given to the Medes and Persians."

29Then at Belshazzar's command, Daniel was robed in purple, and a gold chain was hung around his neck, and he was proclaimed third ruler in the kingdom.

30That very night Belshazzar, the Chaldean king, was killed, 31and Darius the Mede entered the city and began reigning at the age of sixty-two.

2 PETER 2:1–22

BUT there were false prophets, too, in those days, just as there will be false teachers among you. They will cleverly tell their lies about God, turning against even their Master who bought them; but theirs will be a swift and terrible end. 2Many will follow their evil teaching that there is nothing wrong with sexual sin. And because of them Christ and his way will be scoffed at.

3These teachers in their greed will tell you anything to get hold of your money. But God condemned them long ago and their destruction is on the way. 4For God did not spare even the angels who sinned, but threw them into hell, chained in gloomy caves and darkness until the judgment day. 5And he did not spare any of the people who lived in ancient times before the flood except Noah, the one man who spoke up for God, and his family of seven. At that time God completely destroyed the whole world of ungodly men with the vast flood. 6Later, he turned the cities of Sodom and Gomorrah into heaps of ashes and blotted them off the face of the earth, making them an example for all the ungodly in the future to look back upon and fear.

7,8But at the same time the Lord rescued Lot out of Sodom because he was a good man, sick of the terrible wickedness he saw everywhere around him day after day. 9So also the Lord can rescue you and me from the temptations that surround us, and continue to punish the ungodly until the day of final judgment comes. 10He is especially hard on those who follow their own evil, lustful thoughts, and those who are proud and willful, daring even to scoff at the Glorious Ones without so much as trembling, 11although the angels in heaven who stand in the very presence of the Lord, and are far greater in power and strength than these false teachers, never speak out disrespectfully against these evil Mighty Ones.

12But false teachers are fools—no better than animals. They do whatever they feel like; born only to be caught and killed, they laugh at the terrifying powers of the underworld which they know so little about; and they will be destroyed along with all the demons and powers of hell.

13That is the pay these teachers will have for their sin. For they live in evil pleasures day after day. They are a disgrace and a stain among you, deceiving you by living in foul sin on the side while they join your love feasts as though they were honest men. 14No woman can escape their sinful stare, and of adultery they never have enough. They make a game of luring unstable women. They train themselves to be greedy; and are doomed and cursed. 15They have gone off the road and become lost like Balaam, the son of Beor, who fell in love with the money he could make by doing wrong; 16but Balaam was stopped from his mad course when his donkey spoke

to him with a human voice, scolding and rebuking him.

17These men are as useless as dried-up springs of water, promising much and delivering nothing; they are as unstable as clouds driven by the storm winds. They are doomed to the eternal pits of darkness. 18They proudly boast about their sins and conquests, and, using lust as their bait, they lure back into sin those who have just escaped from such wicked living.

19"You aren't saved by being good," they say, "so you might as well be bad. Do what you like, be free."

But these very teachers who offer this "freedom" from law are themselves slaves to sin and destruction. For a man is a slave to whatever controls him. 20And when a person has escaped from the wicked ways of the world by learning about our Lord and Savior Jesus Christ, and then gets tangled up with sin and becomes its slave again, he is worse off than he was before. 21It would be better if he had never known about Christ at all than to learn of him and then afterwards turn his back on the holy commandments that were given to him. 22There is an old saying that "A dog comes back to what he has vomited, and a pig is washed only to come back and wallow in the mud again." That is the way it is with those who turn again to their sin.

PSALM 119:113–131

I hate those who are undecided whether or not to obey you; but my choice is clear—I love your law. 114You are my refuge and my shield, and your promises are my only source of hope. 115Begone, you evil-minded men. Don't try to stop me from obeying God's commands. 116Lord, you promised to let me live! Never let it be said that God failed me. 117Hold me safe above the heads of all my enemies; then I can continue to obey your laws.

118But you have rejected all who reject your laws. They are only fooling themselves. ¹¹⁹The wicked are the scum you skim off and throw away; no wonder I love to obey your laws! ¹²⁰I tremble in fear of you; I fear your punishments.

¹²¹Don't leave me to the mercy of my enemies, for I have done what is right; I've been perfectly fair. ¹²²Commit yourself to bless me! Don't let the proud oppress me! ¹²³My eyes grow dim with longing for you to fulfill your wonderful promise to rescue me. ¹²⁴Lord, deal with me in lovingkindness, and teach me, your servant, to obey; ¹²⁵for I am your servant; therefore give me common sense to apply your rules to everything I do.

¹²⁶Lord, it is time for you to act. For these evil men have violated your laws, ¹²⁷while I love your commandments more than the finest gold. ¹²⁸Every law of God is right, whatever it concerns. I hate every other way.

¹²⁹Your laws are wonderful; no wonder I obey them. ¹³⁰As your plan unfolds, even the simple can understand it. ¹³¹No wonder I wait expectantly for each of your commands.

PROVERBS 28:19–20

Hard work brings prosperity; playing around brings poverty. The man who wants to do right will get a rich reward. But the man who wants to get rich quick will quickly fail.

NOVEMBER 29

DANIEL 6:1–28

DARIUS divided the kingdom into 120 provinces, each under a governor. ²The governors were accountable to three presidents (Daniel was one of them) so the king could administer the kingdom efficiently.

³Daniel soon proved himself more capable than all the other presidents and governors, for he had great ability, and the king began to think of placing him over the entire empire as his administrative officer.

⁴This made the other presidents and governors very jealous, and they began searching for some fault in the way Daniel was handling his affairs so that they could complain to the king about him. But they couldn't find anything to criticize! He was faithful and honest, and made no mistakes. ⁵So they concluded, "Our only chance is his religion!"

⁶They decided to go to the king and say, "King Darius, live forever! ⁷We presidents, governors, counselors and deputies have unanimously decided that you should make a law, irrevocable under any circumstance, that for the next thirty days anyone who asks a favor of God or man—except from you, Your Majesty—shall be thrown to the lions. ⁸Your Majesty, we request your signature on this law; sign it so that it cannot be canceled or changed; it will be a 'law of the Medes and Persians' that cannot be revoked."

⁹So King Darius signed the law.

¹⁰But though Daniel knew about it, he went home and knelt down as usual in his upstairs bedroom, with its windows open toward Jerusalem, and prayed three times a day, just as he always had, giving thanks to his God.

¹¹Then the men thronged to Daniel's house and found him praying there, asking favors of his God. ¹²They rushed back to the king and reminded him about his law. "Haven't you signed a decree," they demanded, "that permits no petitions to any God or man—except you—for thirty days? And anyone disobeying will be thrown to the lions?"

"Yes," the king replied, "it is 'a law of the Medes and Persians,' that cannot be altered or revoked."

¹³Then they told the king, "That fellow Daniel, one of the Jewish captives, is paying no attention to you or your law. He is asking favors of his God three times a day."

¹⁴Hearing this, the king was very angry with himself for signing the law, and determined to save Daniel. He spent the rest of the day trying to think of some way to get Daniel out of this predicament.

¹⁵In the evening the men came again to the king and said, "Your Majesty, there is nothing you can do. You signed the law and it cannot be changed."

¹⁶So at last the king gave the order for Daniel's arrest, and he was taken to the den of lions. The king said to him, "May your God, whom you worship continually, deliver you." And then they threw him in. ¹⁷A stone was brought and placed over the mouth of the den; and the king sealed it with his own signet ring, and that of his government, so that no one could rescue Daniel from the lions.

¹⁸Then the king returned to his palace and went to bed without dinner. He refused his usual entertainment and didn't sleep all night. ¹⁹Very early the next morning he hurried out to the lions' den, ²⁰and called out in anguish, "O Daniel, servant of the Living God, was your God, whom you worship continually, able to deliver you from the lions?"

²¹Then he heard a voice! "Your Majesty, live forever!" It was Daniel! ²²"My God has sent his angel," he said, "to shut the lions' mouths so that they can't touch me; for I am innocent before God, nor, sir, have I wronged you."

²³The king was beside himself with joy and ordered Daniel lifted from the den. And not a scratch was found on him, because he believed in his God.

²⁴Then the king issued a command to bring the men who had accused Daniel, and throw them into the den along with their children and wives, and the lions leaped upon them and tore them apart

before they even hit the bottom of the den.

²⁵,²⁶Afterward King Darius wrote this message addressed to everyone in his empire:

"Greetings! I decree that everyone shall tremble and fear before the God of Daniel in every part of my kingdom. For his God is the living, unchanging God whose kingdom shall never be destroyed and whose power shall never end. ²⁷He delivers his people, preserving them from harm; he does great miracles in heaven and earth; it is he who delivered Daniel from the power of the lions."

²⁸So Daniel prospered in the reign of Darius, and in the reign of Cyrus the Persian.

2 PETER 3:1–18

THIS is my second letter to you, dear brothers, and in both of them I have tried to remind you—if you will let me—about facts you already know: facts you learned from the holy prophets and from us apostles who brought you the words of our Lord and Savior.

³First, I want to remind you that in the last days there will come scoffers who will do every wrong they can think of, and laugh at the truth. ⁴This will be their line of argument: "So Jesus promised to come back, did he? Then where is he? He'll never come! Why, as far back as anyone can remember everything has remained exactly as it was since the first day of creation."

⁵,⁶They deliberately forget this fact: that God did destroy the world with a mighty flood, long after he had made the heavens by the word of his command, and had used the waters to form the earth and surround it. ⁷And God has commanded that the earth and the heavens be stored away for a great bonfire at the judgment day, when all ungodly men will perish.

⁸But don't forget this, dear friends, that a day or a thousand years from now

is like tomorrow to the Lord. 9He isn't really being slow about his promised return, even though it sometimes seems that way. But he is waiting, for the good reason that he is not willing that any should perish, and he is giving more time for sinners to repent. 10The day of the Lord is surely coming, as unexpectedly as a thief, and then the heavens will pass away with a terrible noise and the heavenly bodies will disappear in fire, and the earth and everything on it will be burned up.

11And so since everything around us is going to melt away, what holy, godly lives we should be living! 12You should look forward to that day and hurry it along—the day when God will set the heavens on fire, and the heavenly bodies will melt and disappear in flames. 13But we are looking forward to God's promise of new heavens and a new earth afterwards, where there will be only goodness.

14Dear friends, while you are waiting for these things to happen and for him to come, try hard to live without sinning; and be at peace with everyone so that he will be pleased with you when he returns.

15,16And remember why he is waiting. He is giving us time to get his message of salvation out to others. Our wise and beloved brother Paul has talked about these same things in many of his letters. Some of his comments are not easy to understand, and there are people who are deliberately stupid, and always demand some unusual interpretation—they have twisted his letters around to mean something quite different from what he meant, just as they do the other parts of the Scripture—and the result is disaster for them.

17I am warning you ahead of time, dear brothers, so that you can watch out and not be carried away by the mistakes of these wicked men, lest you yourselves become mixed up too. 18But grow in spiritual strength and become better acquainted with our Lord and Savior Jesus Christ. To him be all glory and splendid honor, both now and forevermore. Goodbye.

Peter

PSALM 119:132–155

COME and have mercy on me as is your way with those who love you. 133Guide me with your laws so that I will not be overcome by evil. 134Rescue me from the oppression of evil men; then I can obey you. 135Look down in love upon me and teach me all your laws. 136I weep because your laws are disobeyed.

137O Lord, you are just and your punishments are fair. 138Your demands are just and right. 139I am indignant and angry because of the way my enemies have disregarded your laws. 140I have thoroughly tested your promises and that is why I love them so much. 141I am worthless and despised, but I don't despise your laws.

142Your justice is eternal for your laws are perfectly fair. 143In my distress and anguish, your commandments comfort me. 144Your laws are always fair; help me to understand them and I shall live.

145I am praying with great earnestness; answer me, O Lord, and I will obey your laws. 146"Save me," I cry, "for I am obeying." 147Early in the morning, before the sun is up, I am praying and pointing out how much I trust in you. 148I stay awake through the night to think about your promises. 149Because you are so loving and kind, listen to me and make me well again.

150Here come these lawless men to attack me; 151but you are near, O Lord; all your commandments are based on truth. 152I have known from earliest days that your will never changes.

153Look down upon my sorrows and rescue me, for I am obeying your commands. 154Yes, rescue me and give me back my life again just as you have promised. 155The wicked are far from salvation for they do not care for your laws.

Giving preferred treatment to rich people is a clear case of selling one's soul for a piece of bread. Trying to get rich quick is evil and leads to poverty.

NOVEMBER 30

DANIEL 7:1–28

ONE night during the first year of Belshazzar's reign over the Babylonian empire, Daniel had a dream and he wrote it down. This is his description of what he saw:

2In my dream I saw a great storm on a mighty ocean, with strong winds blowing from every direction. 3Then four huge animals came up out of the water, each different from the other. 4The first was like a lion, but it had eagle's wings! And as I watched, its wings were pulled off so that it could no longer fly, and it was left standing on the ground, on two feet, like a man; and a man's mind was given to it. 5The second animal looked like a bear with its paw raised, ready to strike. It held three ribs between its teeth, and I heard a voice saying to it, "Get up! Devour many people!" 6The third of these strange animals looked like a leopard, but on its back it had wings like those of birds, and it had four heads! And great power was given to it over all mankind.

7Then, as I watched in my dream, a fourth animal rose up out of the ocean, too dreadful to describe and incredibly strong. It devoured some of its victims by tearing them apart with its huge iron teeth, and others it crushed beneath its feet. It was far more brutal and vicious than any of the other animals, and it had ten horns.

8As I was looking at the horns, suddenly another small horn appeared among them, and three of the first ones were yanked out, roots and all, to give it room; this little horn had a man's eyes and a bragging mouth.

9I watched as thrones were put in place and the Ancient of Days—the Almighty God—sat down to judge. His clothing was as white as snow, his hair like whitest wool. He sat upon a fiery throne brought in on flaming wheels, and 10a river of fire flowed from before him. Millions of angels ministered to him and hundreds of millions of people stood before him, waiting to be judged. Then the court began its session and The Books were opened.

11As I watched, the brutal fourth animal was killed and its body handed over to be burned because of its arrogance against Almighty God, and the boasting of its little horn. 12As for the other three animals, their kingdoms were taken from them, but they were allowed to live a short time longer.

13Next I saw the arrival of a Man— or so he seemed to be—brought there on clouds from heaven; he approached the Ancient of Days and was presented to him. 14He was given the ruling power and glory over all the nations of the world, so that all people of every language must obey him. His power is eternal—it will never end; his government shall never fall.

15I was confused and disturbed by all I had seen [Daniel wrote in his report], 16so I approached one of those standing beside the throne and asked him the meaning of all these things, and he explained them to me.

17"These four huge animals," he said, "represent four kings who will someday rule the earth. 18But in the end the people of the Most High God shall rule the governments of the world forever and forever."

19Then I asked about the fourth animal, the one so brutal and shocking, with its iron teeth and brass claws that tore men apart and that stamped others to death with its feet. 20I asked, too, about the ten horns and the little horn that came up afterward and destroyed three of the others—the horn with the eyes, and the loud, bragging mouth, the one which was stronger than the others. 21For I had seen this horn warring against God's people and winning, 22until the Ancient of Days came and opened his court and vindicated his people, giving them worldwide powers of government.

23"This fourth animal," he told me, "is the fourth world power that will rule the earth. It will be more brutal than any of the others; it will devour the whole world, destroying everything before it. 24His ten horns are ten kings that will rise out of his empire; then another king will arise, more brutal than the other ten, and will destroy three of them. 25He will defy the Most High God, and wear down the saints with persecution, and try to change all laws, morals, and customs. God's people will be helpless in his hands for three and a half years.

26"But then the Ancient of Days will come and open his court of justice and take all power from this vicious king, to consume and destroy it until the end. 27Then every nation under heaven, and all their power, shall be given to the people of God; they shall rule all things forever, and all rulers shall serve and obey them."

28That was the end of the dream. When I awoke, I was greatly disturbed, and my face was pale with fright, but I told no one what I had seen.

1 JOHN 1:1–10

CHRIST was alive when the world began, yet I myself have seen him with my own eyes and listened to him speak. I have touched him with my own hands. He is God's message of life. 2This one who is life from God has been shown to us and we guarantee that we have seen him; I am speaking of Christ, who is eternal Life. He was with the Father and then was shown to us. 3Again I say, we are telling you about what we ourselves have actually seen and heard, so that you may share the fellowship and the joys we have with the Father and with Jesus Christ his son. 4And if you do as I say in this letter, then you, too, will be full of joy, and so will we.

5This is the message God has given us to pass on to you: that God is Light and in him is no darkness at all. 6So if we say we are his friends, but go on living in spiritual darkness and sin, we are lying. 7But if we are living in the light of God's presence, just as Christ does, then we have wonderful fellowship and joy with each other, and the blood of Jesus his Son cleanses us from every sin.

8If we say that we have no sin, we are only fooling ourselves, and refusing to accept the truth. 9But if we confess our sins to him, he can be depended on to forgive us and to cleanse us from every wrong. [And it is perfectly proper for God to do this for us because Christ died to wash away our sins.] 10If we claim we have not sinned, we are lying and calling God a liar, *for he says we have sinned.*

PSALM 119:156–176

LORD, how great is your mercy; oh, give me back my life again. 157My enemies are so many. They try to make me disobey, but I have not swerved from your will. 158I loathe these traitors because they care nothing for your laws. 159Lord, see how much I really love your demands. Now give me back my life and health because you are so kind. 160There is utter truth in all your laws; your decrees are eternal.

161Great men have persecuted me, though they have no reason to, but I stand in awe of only your words. 162I rejoice in your laws like one who finds a great treasure. 163How I hate all falsehood but how I love your laws. 164I will praise you seven times a day because of your wonderful laws.

165Those who love your laws have great peace of heart and mind and do not stumble. 166I long for your salvation, Lord, and so I have obeyed your laws. 167I have looked for your commandments and I love them very much; 168yes, I have searched for them. You know this because everything I do is known to you.

169O Lord, listen to my prayers; give me the common sense you promised.

170Hear my prayers; rescue me as you said you would. 171I praise you for letting me learn your laws. 172I will sing about their wonder, for each of them is just. 173Stand ready to help me because I have chosen to follow your will. 174O Lord, I have longed for your salvation, and your law is my delight. 175If you will let me live, I will praise you; let your laws assist me.

176I have wandered away like a lost sheep; come and find me for I have not turned away from your commandments.

PROVERBS FOR TODAY/ 28:23–24

In the end, people appreciate frankness more than flattery. A man who robs his parents and says, "What's wrong with that?" is no better than a murderer.

DECEMBER 1

DANIEL 8:1–27

IN the third year of the reign of King Belshazzar, I had another dream similar to the first.

2This time I was at Susa, the capital in the province of Elam, standing beside the Ulai River. 3As I was looking around, I saw a ram with two long horns standing on the river bank; and as I watched, one of these horns began to grow, so that it was longer than the other. 4The ram butted everything out of its way and no one could stand against it or help its victims. It did as it pleased and became very great.

5While I was wondering what this could mean, suddenly a buck goat appeared from the west, so swiftly that it didn't even touch the ground. This goat, which had one very large horn between its eyes, 6rushed furiously at the two-horned ram. 7And the closer he came, the angrier he was. He charged into the ram and broke off both his horns. Now the ram was helpless and the buck goat

knocked him down and trampled him, for there was no one to rescue him.

8The victor became both proud and powerful, but suddenly, at the height of his power, his horn was broken, and in its place grew four good-sized horns pointing in four directions. 9One of these, growing slowly at first, soon became very strong and attacked the south and east, and warred against the land of Israel. 10He fought against the people of God and defeated some of their leaders. 11He even challenged the Commander of the army of heaven by canceling the daily sacrifices offered to him, and by defiling his Temple. 12But the army of heaven was restrained from destroying him for this transgression. As a result, truth and righteousness perished, and evil triumphed and prospered.

13Then I heard two of the holy angels talking to each other. One of them said, "How long will it be until the daily sacrifice is restored again? How long until the destruction of the Temple is avenged and God's people triumph?"

¹⁴The other replied, "Twenty-three hundred days must first go by."

¹⁵As I was trying to understand the meaning of this vision, suddenly a man was standing in front of me—or at least he looked like a man— ¹⁶and I heard a man's voice calling from across the river, "Gabriel, tell Daniel the meaning of his dream."

¹⁷So Gabriel started toward me. But as he approached, I was too frightened to stand, and fell down with my face to the ground. "Son of man," he said, "you must understand that the events you have seen in your vision will not take place until the end times come."

¹⁸Then I fainted, lying face downward on the ground. But he roused me with a touch, and helped me to my feet. ¹⁹"I am here," he said, "to tell you what is going to happen in the last days of the coming time of terror—for what you have seen pertains to that final event in history.

²⁰"The two horns of the ram you saw are the kings of Media and Persia; ²¹the shaggy-haired goat is the nation of Greece, and its long horn represents the first great king of that country. ²²When you saw the horn break off, and four smaller horns replace it, this meant that the Grecian Empire will break into four sections with four kings, none of them as great as the first.

²³"Toward the end of their kingdoms, when they have become morally rotten, an angry king shall rise to power with great shrewdness and intelligence. ²⁴His power shall be mighty, but it will be satanic strength and not his own. Prospering wherever he turns, he will destroy all who oppose him, though their armies be mighty, and he will devastate God's people.

²⁵"He will be a master of deception, defeating many by catching them off guard as they bask in false security. Without warning he will destroy them. So great will he fancy himself to be that he will even take on the Prince of Princes

in battle; but in so doing he will seal his own doom, for he shall be broken by the hand of God, though no human means could overpower him.

²⁶"And then in your vision you heard about the twenty-three hundred days to pass before the rights of worship are restored. This number is literal, and means just that. But none of these things will happen for a long time, so don't tell anyone about them yet."

²⁷Then I grew faint and was sick for several days. Afterward I was up and around again and performed my duties for the king, but I was greatly distressed by the dream and did not understand it.

1 JOHN 2:1–17

MY little children, I am telling you this so that you will stay away from sin. But if you sin, there is someone to plead for you before the Father. His name is Jesus Christ, the one who is all that is good and who pleases God completely. ²He is the one who took God's wrath against our sins upon himself, and brought us into fellowship with God; and he is the forgiveness for our sins, and not only ours but all the world's.

³And how can we be sure that we belong to him? By looking within ourselves: are we really trying to do what he wants us to?

⁴Someone may say, "I am a Christian; I am on my way to heaven; I belong to Christ." But if he doesn't do what Christ tells him to, he is a liar. ⁵But those who do what Christ tells them to will learn to love God more and more. That is the way to know whether or not you are a Christian. ⁶Anyone who says he is a Christian should live as Christ did.

⁷Dear brothers, I am not writing out a new rule for you to obey, for it is an old one you have always had, right from the start. You have heard it all before. ⁸Yet it is always new, and works for you just as it did for Christ; and as we obey this commandment, *to love one another,* the darkness in our lives disappears and the new light of life in Christ shines in.

⁹Anyone who says he is walking in the light of Christ but dislikes his fellow man, is still in darkness. ¹⁰But whoever loves his fellow man is "walking in the light" and can see his way without stumbling around in darkness and sin. ¹¹For he who dislikes his brother is wandering in spiritual darkness and doesn't know where he is going, for the darkness has made him blind so that he cannot see the way.

¹²I am writing these things to all of you, my little children, because your sins have been forgiven in the name of Jesus our Savior. ¹³I am saying these things to you older men because you really know Christ, the one who has been alive from the beginning. And you young men, I am talking to you because you have won your battle with Satan. And I am writing to you younger boys and girls because you, too, have learned to know God our Father.

¹⁴And so I say to you fathers who know the eternal God, and to you young men who are strong, with God's Word in your hearts, and have won your struggle against Satan: ¹⁵Stop loving this evil world and all that it offers you, for when you love these things you show that you do not really love God; ¹⁶for all these worldly things, these evil desires—the craze for sex, the ambition to buy everything that appeals to you, and the pride that comes from wealth and importance—these are not from God. They are from this evil world itself. ¹⁷And this world is fading away, and these evil, forbidden things will go with it, but whoever keeps doing the will of God will live forever.

PSALM 120:1–7

IN my troubles I pled with God to help me and he did!

²Deliver me, O Lord, from liars. ³O lying tongue, what shall be your fate? ⁴You shall be pierced with sharp arrows and burned with glowing coals.

⁵,⁶My troubles pile high among these haters of the Lord, these men of Meshech and Kedar. I am tired of being here among these men who hate peace. ⁷I am for peace, but they are for war, and my voice goes unheeded in their councils.

PROVERBS FOR TODAY/ 28:25–26

Greed causes fighting; trusting God leads to prosperity. A man is a fool to trust himself! But those who use God's wisdom are safe.

DECEMBER 2

DANIEL 9:1—10:21

IT was now the first year of the reign of King Darius, the son of Ahasuerus. (Darius was a Mede but became king of the Chaldeans.) ²In that first year of his reign, I, Daniel, learned from the book of Jeremiah the prophet, that Jerusalem must lie desolate for seventy years. ³So I earnestly pleaded with the Lord God [to end our captivity and send us back to our own land].

As I prayed, I fasted, and wore rough sackcloth, and sprinkled myself with ashes, ⁴and confessed my sins and those of my people.

"O Lord," I prayed, "you are a great and awesome God; you always fulfill your promises of mercy to those who love you and who keep your laws. ⁵But we have sinned so much; we have rebelled against you and scorned your commands. ⁶We have refused to listen to your servants the prophets, whom you sent again and again down through the years, with your messages to our kings and princes and to all the people.

7"O Lord, you are righteous; but as for us, we are always shamefaced with sin, just as you see us now; yes, all of us—the men of Judah, the people of Jerusalem, and all Israel, scattered near and far wherever you have driven us because of our disloyalty to you. 8O Lord, we and our kings and princes and fathers are weighted down with shame because of all our sins.

9"But the Lord our God is merciful, and pardons even those who have rebelled against him.

10"O Lord our God, we have disobeyed you; we have flouted all the laws you gave us through your servants, the prophets. 11All Israel has disobeyed; we have turned away from you and haven't listened to your voice. And so the awesome curse of God has crushed us—the curse written in the law of Moses your servant. 12And you have done exactly as you warned us you would do, for never in all history has there been a disaster like what happened at Jerusalem to us and our rulers. 13Every curse against us written in the law of Moses has come true; all the evils he predicted—all have come. But even so we still refuse to satisfy the Lord our God by turning from our sins and doing right.

14"And so the Lord deliberately crushed us with the calamity he prepared; he is fair in everything he does, but we would not obey. 15O Lord our God, you brought lasting honor to your name by removing your people from Egypt in a great display of power. Lord, do it again! Though we have sinned so much and are full of wickedness, 16yet because of all your faithful mercies, Lord, please turn away your furious anger from Jerusalem, your own city, your holy mountain. For the heathen mock at you because your city lies in ruins for our sins.

17"O our God, hear your servant's prayer! Listen as I plead! Let your face shine again with peace and joy upon your desolate sanctuary—for your own glory, Lord.

18"O my God, bend down your ear and listen to my plea. Open your eyes and see our wretchedness, how your city lies in ruins—for everyone knows that it is yours. We don't ask because we merit help, but because you are so merciful despite our grievous sins.

19"O Lord, hear; O Lord, forgive. O Lord, listen to me and act! Don't delay—for your own sake, O my God, because your people and your city bear your name."

20Even while I was praying and confessing my sin and the sins of my people, and desperately pleading with the Lord my God for Jerusalem, his holy mountain, 21Gabriel, whom I had seen in the earlier vision, flew swiftly to me at the time of the evening sacrifice, 22and said to me, "Daniel, I am here to help you understand God's plans. 23The moment you began praying, a command was given. I am here to tell you what it was, for God loves you very much. Listen, and try to understand the meaning of the vision that you saw!

24"The Lord has commanded 490 years of further punishment upon Jerusalem and your people. Then at last they will learn to stay away from sin, and their guilt will be cleansed; then the kingdom of everlasting righteousness will begin, and the Most Holy Place (in the Temple) will be rededicated, as the prophets have declared. 25Now listen! It will be forty-nine years plus 434 years from the time the command is given to rebuild Jerusalem, until the Anointed One comes! Jerusalem's streets and walls will be rebuilt despite the perilous times.

26"After this period of 434 years, the Anointed One will be killed, his kingdom still unrealized . . . and a king will arise whose armies will destroy the city and the Temple. They will be overwhelmed as with a flood, and war and its miseries are decreed from that time to the very end. 27This king will make a seven-year treaty with the people, but after half that time, he will break his pledge and stop the Jews from all their sacrifices and their offerings; then, as a climax to all his terrible deeds, the Enemy shall utterly defile the sanctuary of God. But in God's time and plan, his judgment will be poured out upon this Evil One."

IN the third year of the reign of Cyrus, king of Persia, Daniel (also called Belteshazzar) had another vision. It concerned events certain to happen in the future: times of great tribulation—wars and sorrows, and this time he understood what the vision meant.

2When this vision came to me (Daniel said later) I had been in mourning for three full weeks. 3All that time I tasted neither wine nor meat, and of course I went without desserts. I neither washed nor shaved nor combed my hair.

4Then one day early in April, as I was standing beside the great Tigris River, 5,6I looked up and suddenly there before me stood a person robed in linen garments, with a belt of purest gold around his waist, and glowing, lustrous skin! From his face came blinding flashes like lightning, and his eyes were pools of fire; his arms and feet shone like polished brass, and his voice was like the roaring of a vast multitude of people.

7I, Daniel, alone saw this great vision; the men with me saw nothing, but they were suddenly filled with unreasoning terror and ran to hide, 8and I was left alone. When I saw this frightening vision my strength left me, and I grew pale and weak with fright.

9Then he spoke to me, and I fell to the ground face downward in a deep faint. 10But a hand touched me and lifted me, still trembling, to my hands and knees. 11And I heard his voice—"O Daniel, greatly beloved of God," he said, "stand up and listen carefully to what I have to say to you, for God has sent me to you." So I stood up, still trembling with fear.

12Then he said, "Don't be frightened, Daniel, for your request has been heard in heaven and was answered the very first day you began to fast before the Lord and pray for understanding; that very day I was sent here to meet you. 13But for twenty-one days the mighty Evil Spirit who overrules the kingdom of Persia blocked my way. Then Michael, one of the top officers of the heavenly army, came to help me, so that I was able to break through these spirit rulers of Persia. 14Now I am here to tell you what will happen to your people, the Jews, at the end times—for the fulfillment of this prophecy is many years away."

15All this time I was looking down, unable to speak a word. 16Then someone—he looked like a man—touched my lips and I could talk again, and I said to the messenger from heaven, "Sir, I am terrified by your appearance and have no strength. 17How can such a person as I even talk to you? For my strength is gone and I can hardly breathe."

18Then the one who seemed to be a man touched me again, and I felt my strength returning. 19"God loves you very much," he said; "don't be afraid! Calm yourself; be strong—yes, strong!"

Suddenly, as he spoke these words, I felt stronger and said to him, "Now you can go ahead and speak, sir, for you have strengthened me."

20,21He replied, "Do you know why I have come? I am here to tell you what is written in the 'Book of the Future.' Then, when I leave, I will go again to fight my way back, past the prince of Persia; and after him, the prince of Greece. Only Michael, the angel who guards your people Israel, will be there to help me.

1 JOHN 2:18—3:6

DEAR children, this world's last hour has come. You have heard about the Antichrist who is coming—the one who is against Christ—and already many such persons have appeared. This makes us all the more certain that the end of the world is near. 19These "against-Christ" people used to be members of our churches, but they never really belonged with us or else they would have stayed. When they left us it proved that they were not of us at all.

20But you are not like that, for the Holy Spirit has come upon you, and you know the truth. 21So I am not writing to you as to those who need to know the truth, but I warn you as those who can discern the difference between true and false.

22And who is the greatest liar? The one who says that Jesus is not Christ. Such a person is antichrist, for he does not believe in God the Father and in his Son. 23For a person who doesn't believe in Christ, God's Son, can't have God the Father either. But he who has Christ, God's Son, has God the Father also.

24So keep on believing what you have been taught from the beginning. If you do, you will always be in close fellowship with both God the Father and his Son. 25And he himself has promised us this: *eternal life.*

26These remarks of mine about the Antichrist are pointed at those who would dearly love to blindfold you and lead you astray. 27But you have received the Holy Spirit and he lives within you, in your hearts, so that you don't need anyone to teach you what is right. For he teaches you all things, and he is the Truth, and no liar; and so, just as he has said, you must live in Christ, never to depart from him.

28And now, my little children, stay in happy fellowship with the Lord so that when he comes you will be sure that all is well, and will not have to be ashamed and shrink back from meeting him. 29Since we know that God is always good and does only right, we may rightly assume that all those who do right are his children.

SEE how very much our heavenly Father loves us, for he allows us to be called his children—think of it—and we really *are!* But since most people don't know God, naturally they don't understand that we are his children. 2Yes, dear friends, we are already God's children, right now, and we can't even imagine what it is going to be like later on. But we do know this, that when he comes we will be like him, as a result of seeing him as he really is. 3And everyone who really believes this will try to stay pure because Christ is pure.

4But those who keep on sinning are against God, for every sin is done against the will of God. 5And you know that he became a man so that he could take away our sins, and that there is no sin in him, no missing of God's will at any time in any way. 6So if we stay close to him, obedient to him, we won't be sinning either; but as for those who keep on sinning, they should realize this: They sin because they have never really known him or become his.

PSALM 121:1–8

SHALL I look to the mountain gods for help? 2No! My help is from Jehovah who made the mountains! And the heavens too! 3,4He will never let me stumble, slip or fall. For he is always watching, never sleeping.

5Jehovah himself is caring for you! He is your defender. 6He protects you day and night. 7He keeps you from all evil, and preserves your life. 8He keeps his eye upon you as you come and go, and always guards you.

PROVERBS FOR TODAY/ 28:27–28

If you give to the poor, your needs will be supplied! But a curse upon those who close their eyes to poverty. When the wicked prosper, good men go away; when the wicked meet disaster, good men return.

DANIEL 11:1–34

I was the one sent to strengthen and help Darius the Mede in the first year of his reign. ²But now I will show you what the future holds. Three more Persian kings will reign, to be succeeded by a fourth, far richer than the others. Using his wealth for political advantage, he will plan total war against Greece.

³"Then a mighty king will rise in Greece, a king who will rule a vast kingdom and accomplish everything he sets out to do. ⁴But at the zenith of his power, his kingdom will break apart and be divided into four weaker nations, not even ruled by his sons. For his empire will be torn apart and given to others. ⁵One of them, the king of Egypt, will increase in power, but this king's own officials will rebel against him and take away his kingdom and make it still more powerful.

⁶"Several years later an alliance will be formed between the king of Syria and the king of Egypt. The daughter of the king of Egypt will be given in marriage to the king of Syria as a gesture of peace, but she will lose her influence over him and not only will her hopes be blighted, but those of her father, the king of Egypt, and of her ambassador and child. ⁷But when her brother takes over as king of Egypt, he will raise an army against the king of Syria, and march against him and defeat him. ⁸When he returns again to Egypt he will carry back their idols with him, along with priceless gold and silver dishes and for many years afterward he will leave the Syrian king alone.

⁹"Meanwhile the king of Syria will invade Egypt briefly, but will soon return again to his own land. ¹⁰,¹¹However, the sons of this Syrian king will assemble a mighty army that will overflow across Israel into Egypt, to a fortress there. Then the king of Egypt, in great anger, will rally against the vast forces of Syria and defeat them. ¹²Filled with pride after this great victory, he will have many thousands of his enemies killed, but his success will be short-lived.

¹³"A few years later the Syrian king will return with a fully-equipped army far greater than the one he lost, ¹⁴and other nations will join him in a crusade against Egypt. Insurgents among your own people, the Jews, will join them, thus fulfilling prophecy, but they will not succeed. ¹⁵Then the Syrian king and his allies will come and lay siege to a fortified city of Egypt and capture it, and the proud armies of Egypt will go down to defeat.

¹⁶"The Syrian king will march onward unopposed; none will be able to stop him. And he will also enter 'The Glorious Land' of Israel, and pillage it. ¹⁷This will be his plot for conquering all Egypt: he too will form an alliance with the Egyptian king, giving him a daughter in marriage, so that she can work for him from within. But the plan will fail.

¹⁸"After this he will turn his attention to the coastal cities and conquer many. But a general will stop him and cause him to retreat in shame. ¹⁹He will turn homeward again, but will have trouble on the way, and disappear.

²⁰"His successor will be remembered as the king who sent a tax collector into Israel, but after a very brief reign, he will die mysteriously, neither in battle nor in riot.

²¹"Next to come to power will be an evil man not directly in line for royal succession. But during a crisis he will take over the kingdom by flattery and intrigue. ²²Then all opposition will be swept away before him, including a leader of the priests. ²³His promises will be worthless. From the first his method will be deceit; with a mere handful of followers, he will become strong. ²⁴He will en-

ter the richest areas of the land without warning and do something never done before: he will take the property and wealth of the rich and scatter it out among the people. With great success he will besiege and capture powerful strongholds throughout his dominions, but this will last for only a short while. 25Then he will stir up his courage and raise a great army against Egypt; and Egypt, too, will raise a mighty army, but to no avail, for plots against him will succeed.

26"Those of his own household will bring his downfall; his army will desert, and many be killed.

27"Both these kings will be plotting against each other at the conference table, attempting to deceive each other. But it will make no difference, for neither can succeed until God's appointed time has come.

28"The Syrian king will then return home with great riches, first marching through Israel and destroying it. 29Then, at the predestined time, he will once again turn his armies southward, as he had threatened, but now it will be a very different story from those first two occasions. 30,31For Roman warships will scare him off, and he will withdraw and return home. Angered by having to retreat, the Syrian king will again pillage Jerusalem and pollute the sanctuary, putting a stop to the daily sacrifices, and worshiping idols inside the Temple. He will leave godless Jews in power when he leaves—men who have abandoned their fathers' faith. 32He will flatter those who hate the things of God, and win them over to his side. But the people who know their God shall be strong and do great things.

33"Those with spiritual understanding will have a wide ministry of teaching in those days. But they will be in constant danger, many of them dying by fire and sword, or being jailed and robbed. 34Eventually these pressures will subside, and some ungodly men will come, pretending to offer a helping hand, only to take advantage of them.

OH, dear children, don't let anyone deceive you about this: if you are constantly doing what is good, it is because you *are* good, even as he is. 8But if you keep on sinning, it shows that you belong to Satan, who since he first began to sin has kept steadily at it. But the Son of God came to destroy these works of the devil. 9The person who has been born into God's family does not make a practice of sinning, because now God's life is in him; so he can't keep on sinning, for this new life has been born into him and controls him—he has been *born again.*

10So now we can tell who is a child of God and who belongs to Satan. Whoever is living a life of sin and doesn't love his brother shows that he is not in God's family; 11for the message to us from the beginning has been that we should love one another.

12We are not to be like Cain, who belonged to Satan and killed his brother. Why did he kill him? Because Cain had been doing wrong and he knew very well that his brother's life was better than his. 13So don't be surprised, dear friends, if the world hates you.

14If we love other Christians it proves that we have been delivered from hell and given eternal life. But a person who doesn't have love for others is headed for eternal death. 15Anyone who hates his Christian brother is really a murderer at heart; and you know that no one wanting to murder has eternal life within. 16We know what real love is from Christ's example in dying for us. And so we also ought to lay down our lives for our Christian brothers.

17But if someone who is supposed to be a Christian has money enough to live well, and sees a brother in need, and won't help him—how can God's love be within *him?* 18Little children, let us stop just *saying* we love people; let us *really* love them, and *show it* by our *actions.* 19Then we will know for sure, by our actions, that we are on God's side, and our consciences will be clear, even when we stand before the Lord. ²⁰But if we have bad consciences and feel that we have done wrong, the Lord will surely feel it even more, for he knows everything we do.

²¹But, dearly loved friends, if our consciences are clear, we can come to the Lord with perfect assurance and trust, ²²and get whatever we ask for because we are obeying him and doing the things that please him. ²³And this is what God says we must do: Believe on the name of his Son Jesus Christ, and love one another. ²⁴Those who do what God says—they are living with God and he with them. We know this is true because the Holy Spirit he has given us tells us so.

PSALM 122:1–9

I was glad for the suggestion of going to Jerusalem, to the Temple of the Lord. ²,³Now we are standing here inside the crowded city. ⁴All Israel—Jehovah's people—have come to worship as the law requires, to thank and praise the Lord. ⁵Look! There are the judges holding court beside the city gates, deciding all the people's arguments.

⁶Pray for the peace of Jerusalem. May all who love this city prosper. ⁷O Jerusalem, may there be peace within your walls and prosperity in your palaces. ⁸This I ask for the sake of all my brothers and my friends who live here; ⁹and may there be peace as a protection to the Temple of the Lord.

PROVERBS FOR TODAY/ 29:1

The man who is often reproved but refuses to accept criticism will suddenly be broken and never have another chance.

DECEMBER 4

DANIEL 11:35—12:13

A ND some who are most gifted in the things of God will stumble in those days and fall, but this will only refine and cleanse them and make them pure until the final end of all their trials, at God's appointed time.

³⁶"The king will do exactly as he pleases, claiming to be greater than every god there is, even blaspheming the God of gods, and prospering—until his time is up. For God's plans are unshakable. ³⁷He will have no regard for the gods of his fathers, nor for the god beloved of women, nor any other god, for he will boast that he is greater than them all. ³⁸Instead of these he will worship the Fortress god—a god his fathers never knew—and lavish on him costly gifts! ³⁹Claiming his help he will have

great success against the strongest fortresses. He will honor those who submit to him, appointing them to positions of authority and dividing the land to them as their reward.

⁴⁰"Then at the time of the end, the king of the south will attack him again, and the northern king will react with the strength and fury of a whirlwind; his vast army and navy will rush out to bury him with their might. ⁴¹He will invade various lands on the way, including Israel, the Pleasant Land, and overthrow the governments of many nations. Moab, Edom, and most of Ammon will escape, ⁴²but Egypt and many other lands will be occupied. ⁴³He will capture all the treasures of Egypt, and the Libyans and Ethiopians shall be his servants.

⁴⁴"But then news from the east and

north will alarm him and he will return in great anger to destroy as he goes. 45He will halt between Jerusalem and the sea, and there pitch his royal tents, but while he is there his time will suddenly run out and there will be no one to help him.

AT that time Michael, the mighty angelic prince who stands guard over your nation, will stand up [and fight for you in heaven against satanic forces], and there will be a time of anguish for the Jews greater than any previous suffering in Jewish history. And yet every one of your people whose names are written in the Book will endure it.

2"And many of those whose bodies lie dead and buried will rise up, some to everlasting life and some to shame and everlasting contempt.

3"And those who are wise—the people of God—shall shine as brightly as the sun's brilliance, and those who turn many to righteousness will glitter like stars forever.

4"But Daniel, keep this prophecy a secret; seal it up so that it will not be understood until the end times, when travel and education shall be vastly increased!"

5Then I, Daniel, looked and saw two men on each bank of a river. 6And one of them asked the man in linen robes who was standing now above the river, "How long will it be until all these terrors end?"

7He replied, with both hands lifted to heaven, taking oath by him who lives forever and ever, that they will not end until three and a half years after the power of God's people has been crushed.

8I heard what he said but I didn't understand what he meant, so I said, "Sir, how will all this finally end?"

9But he said, "Go now, Daniel, for what I have said is not to be understood until the time of the end. 10Many shall be purified by great trials and persecutions. But the wicked shall continue in their wickedness, and none of them will understand. Only those who are willing to learn will know what it means.

11"From the time the daily sacrifice is taken away and the Horrible Thing is set up to be worshiped, there will be 1,290 days. 12And blessed are those who wait and remain until the 1335th day!

13"But go on now to the end of your life and your rest; for you will rise again and have your full share of those last days."

1 JOHN 4:1–21

DEARLY loved friends, don't always believe everything you hear just because someone says it is a message from God: test it first to see if it really is. For there are many false teachers around, 2and the way to find out if their message is from the Holy Spirit is to ask: Does it really agree that Jesus Christ, God's Son, actually became man with a human body? If so, then the message is from God. 3If not, the message is not from God but from one who is against Christ, like the "Antichrist" you have heard about who is going to come, and his attitude of enmity against Christ is already abroad in the world.

4Dear young friends, you belong to God and have already won your fight with those who are against Christ, because there is someone in your hearts who is stronger than any evil teacher in this wicked world. 5These men belong to this world, so, quite naturally, they are concerned about worldly affairs and the world pays attention to them. 6But we are children of God; that is why only those who have walked and talked with God will listen to us. Others won't. That is another way to know whether a message is really from God; for if it is, the world won't listen to it.

7Dear friends, let us practice loving each other, for love comes from God and those who are loving and kind show that they are the children of God, and that they are getting to know him better. 8But if a person isn't loving and kind, it shows that he doesn't know God— for God is love.

9God showed how much he loved us by sending his only Son into this wicked world to bring to us eternal life through his death. 10In this act we see what real love is: it is not our love for God, but his love for us when he sent his Son to satisfy God's anger against our sins.

11Dear friends, since God loved us as much as that, we surely ought to love each other too. 12For though we have never yet seen God, when we love each other God lives in us and his love within us grows ever stronger. 13And he has put his own Holy Spirit into our hearts as a proof to us that we are living with him and he with us. 14And furthermore, we have seen with our own eyes and now tell all the world that God sent his Son to be their Savior. 15Anyone who believes and says that Jesus is the Son of God has God living in him, and he is living with God.

16We know how much God loves us because we have felt his love and because we believe him when he tells us that he loves us dearly. God is love, and anyone who lives in love is living with God and God is living in him. 17And as we live with Christ, our love grows more perfect and complete; so we will not be ashamed and embarrassed at the day of judgment, but can face him with confidence and joy, because he loves us and we love him too.

18We need have no fear of someone who loves us perfectly; his perfect love for us eliminates all dread of what he might do to us. If we are afraid, it is for fear of what he might do to us, and shows that we are not fully convinced that he really loves us. 19So you see, our love for him comes as a result of his loving us first.

20If anyone says "I love God," but keeps on hating his brother, he is a liar; for if he doesn't love his brother who is right there in front of him, how can he love God whom he has never seen? 21And God himself has said that one must love not only God, but his brother too.

PSALM 123:1–4

O God enthroned in heaven, I lift my eyes to you. 2We look to Jehovah our God for his mercy and kindness just as a servant keeps his eyes upon his master or a slave girl watches her mistress for the slightest signal.

3,4Have mercy on us, Lord, have mercy. For we have had our fill of contempt and of the scoffing of the rich and proud.

PROVERBS FOR TODAY/ 29:2–4

With good men in authority, the people rejoice; but with the wicked in power, they groan. A wise son makes his father happy, but a lad who hangs around with prostitutes disgraces him. A just king gives stability to his nation, but one who demands bribes destroys it.

DECEMBER 5

HOSEA 1:1—3:5

THESE are the messages from the Lord to Hosea, son of Beeri, during the reigns of these four kings of Judah:

Uzziah, Jotham, Ahaz, and Hezekiah; and one of the kings of Israel, Jeroboam, son of Joash.

2Here is the first message:

The Lord said to Hosea, "Go and

marry a girl who is a prostitute, so that some of her children will be born to you from other men. This will illustrate the way my people have been untrue to me, committing open adultery against me by worshiping other gods."

3So Hosea married Gomer, daughter of Diblaim, and she conceived and bore him a son.

4,5And the Lord said, "Name the child Jezreel, for in the Valley of Jezreel I am about to punish King Jehu's dynasty to avenge the murders he committed; in fact, I will put an end to Israel as an independent kingdom, breaking the power of the nation in the Valley of Jezreel."

6Soon Gomer had another child—this one a daughter. And God said to Hosea, "Name her Lo-ruhamah (meaning 'No more mercy') for I will have no more mercy upon Israel, to forgive her again. 7But I *will* have mercy on the tribe of Judah. I will personally free her from her enemies without any help from her armies or her weapons."

8After Gomer had weaned Lo-ru-hamah, she again conceived and this time gave birth to a son. 9And God said, "Call him Lo-ammi (meaning 'Not mine'), for Israel is not mine and I am not her God.

10"Yet the time will come when Israel shall prosper and become a great nation; in that day her people will be too numerous to count—like sand along a seashore! Then, instead of saying to them, 'You are not my people,' I will tell them, 'You are my sons, children of the Living God.' 11Then the people of Judah and Israel will unite and have one leader; they will return from exile together; what a day that will be—the day when God will sow his people in the fertile soil of their own land again."

O Jezreel, rename your brother and sister. Call your brother Ammi (which means "Now you are mine"); name your sister Ruhamah ("Pitied"), for now God will have mercy upon her!

2Plead with your mother, for she has become another man's wife—I am no longer her husband. Beg her to stop her harlotry, to quit giving herself to others. 3If she doesn't, I will strip her as naked as the day she was born, and cause her to waste away and die of thirst as in a land riddled with famine and drought. 4And I will not give special favors to her children as I would to my own, for they are not my children; they belong to other men.

5For their mother has committed adultery. She did a shameful thing when she said, "I'll run after other men and sell myself to them for food and drinks and clothes."

6But I will fence her in with briars and thornbushes; I'll block the road before her to make her lose her way, so that 7when she runs after her lovers she will not catch up with them. She will search for them but not find them. Then she will think, "I might as well return to my husband, for I was better off with him than I am now."

8She doesn't realize that all she has, has come from me. It was I who gave her all the gold and silver she used in worshiping Baal, her god!

9But now I will take back the wine and ripened corn I constantly supplied, and the clothes I gave her to cover her nakedness—I will no longer give her rich harvests of grain in its season, or wine at the time of the grape harvest. 10Now I will expose her nakedness in public for all her lovers to see, and no one will be able to rescue her from my hand.

11I will put an end to all her joys, her parties, holidays, and feasts. 12I will destroy her vineyards and her orchards—gifts she claims her lovers gave her—and let them grow into a jungle; wild animals will eat their fruit.

13For all the incense she burned to Baal her idol and for the times when she put on her earrings and jewels and went out looking for her lovers, and deserted me: for all these things I will punish her, says the Lord.

14But I will court her again, and bring her into the wilderness, and speak to her tenderly there. ¹⁵There I will give back her vineyards to her, and transform her Valley of Troubles into a Door of Hope. She will respond to me there, singing with joy as in days long ago in her youth, after I had freed her from captivity in Egypt.

¹⁶In that coming day, says the Lord, she will call me "My Husband" instead of "My Master." ¹⁷O Israel, I will cause you to forget your idols, and their names will not be spoken anymore.

¹⁸At that time I will make a treaty between you and the wild animals, birds, and snakes, not to fear each other any more; and I will destroy all weapons, and all wars will end.

Then you will lie down in peace and safety, unafraid; ¹⁹and I will bind you to me forever with chains of righteousness and justice and love and mercy. ²⁰I will betroth you to me in faithfulness and love, and you will really know me then as you never have before.

²¹,²²In that day, says the Lord, I will answer the pleading of the sky for clouds, to pour down water on the earth in answer to its cry for rain. Then the earth can answer the parched cry of the grain, the grapes, and the olive trees for moisture and for dew—and the whole grand chorus shall sing together that "God sows!" He has given all!

²³At that time I will sow a crop of Israelites and raise them for myself! I will pity those who are "not pitied," and I will say to those who are "not my people," "Now you are my people"; and they will reply, "You are our God!"

THEN the Lord said to me, "Go, and get your wife again and bring her back to you and love her, even though she loves adultery. For the Lord still loves Israel though she has turned to other gods and offered them choice gifts."

²So I bought her [back from her slavery] for a couple of dollars and eight bushels of barley, ³and I said to her, "You must live alone for many days; do not go out with other men nor be a prostitute, and I will wait for you."

⁴This illustrates the fact that Israel will be a long time without a king or prince, and without an altar, temple, priests, or even idols!

⁵Afterward they will return to the Lord their God, and to the Messiah, their King, and they shall come trembling, submissive to the Lord and to his blessings, in the end times.

1 JOHN 5:1–21

IF you believe that Jesus is the Christ—that he is God's Son and your Savior—then you are a child of God. And all who love the Father love his children too. ²So you can find out how much you love God's children—your brothers and sisters in the Lord—by how much you love and obey God. ³Loving God means doing what he tells us to do, and really, that isn't hard at all; ⁴for every child of God can obey him, defeating sin and evil pleasure by trusting Christ to help him.

⁵But who could possibly fight and win this battle except by believing that Jesus is truly the Son of God? ⁶,⁷,⁸And we know he is, because God said so with a voice from heaven when Jesus was baptized, and again as he was facing death—yes, not only at his baptism but also as he faced death. And the Holy Spirit, forever truthful, says it too. So we have these three witnesses: the voice of the Holy Spirit in our hearts, the voice from heaven at Christ's baptism, and the voice before he died. And they all say the same thing: that Jesus Christ is the Son of God. ⁹We believe men who witness in our courts, and so surely we can believe whatever God declares. And God declares that Jesus is his Son. ¹⁰All who believe this know in their hearts that it is true. If anyone doesn't believe this, he is actually calling God a liar, because he doesn't believe what God has said about his Son.

¹¹And what is it that God has said? That he has given us eternal life, and that this life is in his Son. ¹²So whoever

has God's Son has life; whoever does not have his Son, does not have life.

¹³I have written this to you who believe in the Son of God so that you may know you have eternal life. ¹⁴And we are sure of this, that he will listen to us whenever we ask him for anything in line with his will. ¹⁵And if we really know he is listening when we talk to him and make our requests, then we can be sure that he will answer us.

¹⁶If you see a Christian sinning in a way that does not end in death, you should ask God to forgive him and God will give him life, unless he has sinned that one fatal sin. But there is that one sin which ends in death and if he has done that, there is no use praying for him. ¹⁷Every wrong is a sin, of course. I'm not talking about these ordinary sins; I am speaking of that one that ends in death.

¹⁸No one who has become part of God's family makes a practice of sinning, for Christ, God's Son, holds him securely and the devil cannot get his hands on him. ¹⁹We know that we are children of God and that all the rest of the world around us is under Satan's power and control. ²⁰And we know that Christ, God's Son, has come to help us understand and find the true God. And now we are in God because we are in Jesus Christ his Son, who is the only true God; and he is eternal Life.

²¹Dear children, keep away from anything that might take God's place in your hearts. Amen.

Sincerely,
John

PSALM 124:1–8

I F the Lord had not been on our side (let all Israel admit it), if the Lord had not been on our side, ²,³we would have been swallowed alive by our enemies, destroyed by theiranger. ⁴,⁵We would have drowned beneath the flood of these men's fury and pride.

⁶Blessed be Jehovah who has not let them devour us. ⁷We have escaped with our lives as a bird from a hunter's snare. The snare is broken and we are free!

⁸Our help is from the Lord who made heaven and earth.

PROVERBS FOR TODAY/ 29:5–8

Flattery is a trap; evil men are caught in it, but good men stay away and sing for joy. The good man knows the poor man's rights; the godless don't care. Fools start fights everywhere while wise men try to keep peace.

DECEMBER 6

HOSEA 4:1—5:15

H EAR the word of the Lord, O people of Israel. The Lord has filed a lawsuit against you listing the following charges: There is no faithfulness, no kindness, no knowledge of God in your land. ²You swear and lie and kill and steal and commit adultery. There is violence everywhere, with one murder after another.

³That is why your land is not producing; it is filled with sadness, and all living things grow sick and die; the animals, the birds, and even the fish begin to disappear.

⁴Don't point your finger at someone else, and try to pass the blame to him! Look, priest, I am pointing my finger at *you*. ⁵As a sentence for your crimes, you priests will stumble in broad daylight

as well as in the night, and so will your false "prophets" too; and I will destroy your mother, Israel. ⁶My people are destroyed because they don't know me, and it is all your fault, you priests, for you yourselves refuse to know me; therefore I refuse to recognize you as my priests. Since you have forgotten my laws, I will "forget" to bless your children. ⁷The more my people multiplied, the more they sinned against me. They exchanged the glory of God for the disgrace of idols.

⁸The priests rejoice in the sins of the people; they lap it up and lick their lips for more! ⁹And thus it is: "Like priests, like people"—because the priests are wicked, the people are too. Therefore, I will punish both priests and people for all their wicked deeds. ¹⁰They will eat and still be hungry. Though they do a big business as prostitutes, they shall have no children, for they have deserted me and turned to other gods.

¹¹Wine, women, and song have robbed my people of their brains. ¹²For they are asking a piece of wood to tell them what to do. "Divine Truth" comes to them through tea leaves! Longing after idols has made them foolish. For they have played the harlot, serving other gods, deserting me. ¹³They sacrifice to idols on the tops of mountains; they go up into the hills to burn incense in the pleasant shade of oaks and poplars and sumac trees.

There your daughters turn to prostitution and your brides commit adultery. ¹⁴But why should I punish them? For you men are doing the same thing, sinning with harlots and temple prostitutes. Fools! Your doom is sealed, for you refuse to understand.

¹⁵But though Israel is a prostitute, may Judah stay far from such a life. O Judah, do not join with those who insincerely worship me at Gilgal and at Bethel. Their worship is mere pretense. ¹⁶Don't be like Israel, stubborn as a heifer, resisting the Lord's attempts to lead her in green pastures. ¹⁷Stay away from her, for she is wedded to idolatry.

¹⁸The men of Israel finish up their drinking bouts, and off they go to find some whores. Their love for shame is greater than for honor.

¹⁹Therefore, a mighty wind shall sweep them away; they shall die in shame, because they sacrifice to idols.

LISTEN to this, you priests and all of Israel's leaders; listen, all you men of the royal family: You are doomed! For you have deluded the people with idols at Mizpah and Tabor, ²and dug a deep pit to trap them at Acacia. But never forget—I will settle up with all of you for what you've done.

³I have seen your evil deeds: Israel, you have left me as a prostitute leaves her husband; you are utterly defiled. ⁴Your deeds won't let you come to God again, for the spirit of adultery is deep within you, and you cannot know the Lord.

⁵The very arrogance of Israel testifies against her in my court. She will stumble under her load of guilt, and Judah, too, shall fall. ⁶Then at last, they will come with their flocks and herds to sacrifice to God, but it will be too late—they will not find him. He has withdrawn from them and they are left alone.

⁷For they have betrayed the honor of the Lord, bearing children that aren't his. Suddenly they and all their wealth will disappear. ⁸Sound the alarm! Warn with trumpet blasts in Gibeah and Ramah, and on over to Beth-aven; tremble, land of Benjamin! ⁹Hear this announcement, Israel: When your day of punishment comes, you will become a heap of rubble.

¹⁰The leaders of Judah have become the lowest sort of thieves. Therefore, I will pour my anger down upon them like a waterfall, ¹¹and Ephraim will be crushed and broken by my sentence because she is determined to follow idols. ¹²I will destroy her as a moth does wool; I will sap away the strength of Judah like dry rot.

¹³When Ephraim and Judah see how sick they are, Ephraim will turn to Assyria, to the great king there, but he can neither help nor cure.

14I will tear Ephraim and Judah as a lion rips apart its prey; I will carry them off and chase all rescuers away.

15I will abandon them and return to my home until they admit their guilt and look to me for help again, for as soon as trouble comes, they will search for me and say:

2 JOHN 1:1–13

FROM: John, the old Elder of the church.
    To: That dear woman Cyria, one of God's very own, and to her children whom I love so much, as does everyone else in the church. 2Since the Truth is in our hearts forever, 3God the Father and Jesus Christ his Son will bless us with great mercy and much peace, and with truth and love.

4How happy I am to find some of your children here, and to see that they are living as they should, following the Truth, obeying God's command.

5And now I want to urgently remind you, dear friends, of the old rule God gave us right from the beginning, that Christians should love one another. 6If we love God, we will do whatever he tells us to. And he has told us from the very first to love each other.

7Watch out for the false leaders—and there are many of them around—who don't believe that Jesus Christ came to earth as a human being with a body like ours. Such people are against the truth and against Christ. 8Beware of being like them, and losing the prize that you and I have been working so hard to get. See to it that you win your full reward from the Lord. 9For if you wander beyond the teaching of Christ, you will leave God behind; while if you are loyal to Christ's teachings, you will have God too. Then you will have both the Father and the Son.

10If anyone comes to teach you, and he doesn't believe what Christ taught, don't even invite him into your home. Don't encourage him in any way. 11If you do you will be a partner with him in his wickedness.

12Well, I would like to say much more, but I don't want to say it in this letter, for I hope to come to see you soon and then we can talk over these things together and have a joyous time.

13Greetings from the children of your sister—another choice child of God.

Sincerely,
John

PSALM 125:1–5

THOSE who trust in the Lord are steady as Mount Zion, unmoved by any circumstance.
2Just as the mountains surround and protect Jerusalem, so the Lord surrounds and protects his people. 3For the wicked shall not rule the godly, lest the godly be forced to do wrong. 4O Lord, do good to those who are good, whose hearts are right with the Lord; 5but lead evil men to execution. And let Israel have quietness and peace.

PROVERBS FOR TODAY/ 29:9–11

There's no use arguing with a fool. He only rages and scoffs, and tempers flare. The godly pray for those who long to kill them. A rebel shouts in anger; a wise man holds his temper in and cools it.

DECEMBER 7

HOSEA 6:1—9:17

COME, let us return to the Lord; it is he who has torn us—he will heal us. He has wounded—he will bind us up. 2In just a couple of days, or three at the most, he will set us on our feet again, to live in his kindness! 3Oh, that we might know the Lord! Let us press on to know him, and he will respond to us as surely as the coming of dawn or the rain of early spring."

4O Ephraim and Judah, what shall I do with you? For your love vanishes like morning clouds, and disappears like dew. 5I sent my prophets to warn you of your doom; I have slain you with the words of my mouth, threatening you with death. Suddenly, without warning, my judgment will strike you as surely as day follows night.

6I don't want your sacrifices—I want your love; I don't want your offerings—I want you to know me.

7But like Adam, you broke my covenant; you refused my love. 8Gilead is a city of sinners, tracked with footprints of blood. 9Her citizens are gangs of robbers, lying in ambush for their victims; packs of priests murder along the road to Shechem and practice every kind of sin. 10Yes, I have seen a horrible thing in Israel—Ephraim chasing other gods, Israel utterly defiled.

11O Judah, for you also there is a plentiful harvest of punishment waiting—and I wanted so much to bless you!

I wanted to forgive Israel, but her sins were far too great—no one can even live in Samaria without being a liar, thief, and bandit!

2Her people never seem to recognize that I am watching them. Their sinful deeds give them away on every side; I see them all. 3The king is glad about their wickedness; the princes laugh about their lies. 4They are all adulterers; as a baker's oven is constantly aflame—except after he kneads the dough and waits for it to rise again—so are these people constantly aflame with lust.

5On the king's birthday, the princes get him drunk; he makes a fool of himself and drinks with those who mock him. 6Their hearts blaze like a furnace with intrigue. Their plot smolders through the night, and in the morning it flames forth like raging fire.

7They kill their kings one after another, and none cries out to me for help.

8My people mingle with the heathen, picking up their evil ways; thus they become as good-for-nothing as a half-baked cake!

9Worshiping foreign gods has sapped their strength, but they don't know it. Ephraim's hair is turning gray, and he doesn't even realize how weak and old he is. 10His pride in other gods has openly condemned him; yet he doesn't return to his God, nor even try to find him.

11Ephraim is a silly, witless dove, calling to Egypt, flying to Assyria. 12But as she flies, I throw my net over her and bring her down like a bird from the sky; I will punish her for all her evil ways.

13Woe to my people for deserting me; let them perish, for they have sinned against me. I wanted to redeem them but their hard hearts would not accept the truth. 14They lie there sleepless with anxiety, but won't ask my help. Instead, they worship heathen gods, asking them for crops and for prosperity.

15I have helped them, and made them strong, yet now they turn against me.

16They look everywhere except to heaven, to the Most High God. They are like a crooked bow that always misses targets; their leaders will perish by the sword of the enemy for their insolence to me. And all Egypt will laugh at them.

SOUND the alarm! They are coming! Like a vulture, the enemy descends upon the people of God because they have broken my treaty and revolted against my laws.

2Now Israel pleads with me and says, "Help us, for you are our God!" 3But it is too late! Israel has thrown away her chance with contempt, and now her enemies will chase her. 4She has appointed kings and princes, but not with my consent. They have cut themselves off from my help by worshiping the idols that they made from their silver and gold.

5O Samaria, I reject this calf—this idol you have made. My fury burns against you. How long will it be before one honest man is found among you? 6When will you admit this calf you worship was made by human hands! It is not God! Therefore, it must be smashed to bits.

7They have sown the wind and they will reap the whirlwind. Their cornstalks stand there barren, withered, sickly, with no grain; if it has any, foreigners will eat it.

8Israel is destroyed; she lies among the nations as a broken pot. 9She is a lonely, wandering wild ass. The only friends she has are those she hires; Assyria is one of them.

10But though she hires "friends" from many lands, I will send her off to exile. Then for a while at least she will be free of the burden of her wonderful king! 11Ephraim has built many altars, but they are not to worship me! They are altars of sin! 12Even if I gave her ten thousand laws, she'd say they weren't for her—that they applied to someone far away. 13Her people love the ritual of their sacrifice, but to me it is meaningless! I will call for an accounting of their sins and punish them; they shall return to Egypt.

14Israel has built great palaces; Judah has constructed great defenses for her cities, but they have forgotten their Maker. Therefore, I will send down fire upon those palaces and burn those fortresses.

O Israel, rejoice no more as others do, for you have deserted your God and sacrificed to other gods on every threshing floor.

2Therefore your harvests will be small; your grapes will blight upon the vine.

3You may no longer stay here in this land of God; you will be carried off to Egypt and Assyria, and live there on scraps of food. 4There, far from home, you are not allowed to pour out wine for sacrifice to God. For no sacrifice that is offered there can please him; it is polluted, just as food of mourners is; all who eat such sacrifices are defiled. They may eat this food to feed themselves, but may not offer it to God. 5What then will you do on holy days, on days of feasting to the Lord, 6when you are carried off to Assyria as slaves? Who will inherit your possessions left behind? Egypt will! She will gather your dead; Memphis will bury them. And thorns and thistles will grow up among the ruins.

7The time of Israel's punishment has come; the day of recompense is almost here and soon Israel will know it all too well. "The prophets are crazy"; "The inspired men are mad." Yes, so they mock, for the nation is weighted with sin, and shows only hatred for those who love God.

8I appointed the prophets to guard my people, but the people have blocked them at every turn and publicly declared their hatred, even in the Temple of the Lord. 9The things my people do are as depraved as what they did in Gibeah long ago. The Lord does not forget. He will surely punish them.

10O Israel, how well I remember those first delightful days when I led you through the wilderness! How refreshing was your love! How satisfying, like the early figs of summer in their first season! But then you deserted me for Baal-peor, to give yourselves to other gods, and soon you were as foul as they. 11The glory of Israel flies away like a bird, for your children will die at birth, or perish in the womb, or never even be conceived.

12And if your children grow, I will take them from you; all are doomed. Yes, it will be a sad day when I turn away and leave you alone.

13In my vision I have seen the sons of Israel doomed. The fathers are forced to lead their sons to slaughter. 14O Lord, what shall I ask for your people? I will ask for wombs that don't give birth, for breasts that cannot nourish.

15All their wickedness began at Gilgal; there I began to hate them. I will drive them from my land because of their idolatry. I will love them no more, for all their leaders are rebels. 16Ephraim is doomed. The roots of Israel are dried up; she shall bear no more fruit. And if she gives birth, I will slay even her beloved child.

17My God will destroy the people of Israel because they will not listen or obey. They will be wandering Jews, homeless among the nations.

3 JOHN 1:1–15

FROM: John, the Elder.
   To: Dear Gaius, whom I truly love.

2Dear friend, I am praying that all is well with you and that your body is as healthy as I know your soul is. 3Some of the brothers traveling by have made me very happy by telling me that your life stays clean and true, and that you are living by the standards of the Gospel. 4I could have no greater joy than to hear such things about my children.

5Dear friend, you are doing a good work for God in taking care of the traveling teachers and missionaries who are passing through. 6They have told the church here of your friendship and your loving deeds. I am glad when you send them on their way with a generous gift. 7For they are traveling for the Lord, and take neither food, clothing, shelter, nor money from those who are not Christians, even though they have preached to them. 8So we ourselves shou'd take care of them in order that we may become partners with them in the Lord's work.

9I sent a brief letter to the church about this, but proud Diotrephes, who loves to push himself forward as the leader of the Christians there, does not admit my authority over him and refuses to listen to me. 10When I come I will tell you some of the things he is doing and what wicked things he is saying about me and what insulting language he is using. He not only refuses to welcome the missionary travelers himself, but tells others not to, and when they do he tries to put them out of the church.

11Dear friend, don't let this bad example influence you. Follow only what is good. Remember that those who do what is right prove that they are God's children; and those who continue in evil prove that they are far from God. 12But everyone, including Truth itself, speaks highly of Demetrius. I myself can say the same for him, and you know I speak the truth.

13I have much to say but I don't want to write it, 14for I hope to see you soon and then we will have much to talk about together. 15So good-bye for now. Friends here send their love, and please give each of the folks there a special greeting from me.

Sincerely,
John

PSALM 126:1–6

WHEN Jehovah brought back his exiles to Jerusalem, it was like a dream! 2How we laughed and sang for joy. And the other nations said, "What amazing things the Lord has done for them."

3Yes, glorious things! What wonder! What joy! 4May we be refreshed as by streams in the desert.

5Those who sow tears shall reap joy. 6Yes, they go out weeping, carrying seed for sowing, and return singing, carrying their sheaves.

A wicked ruler will have wicked aides on his staff. Rich and poor are alike in this: each depends on God for light. A king who is fair to the poor shall have a long reign.

DECEMBER 8

HOSEA 10:1—14:9

HOW prosperous Israel is—a luxuriant vine all filled with fruit! But the more wealth I give her, the more she pours it on the altars of her heathen gods; the richer the harvests I give her, the more beautiful the statues and idols she erects. ²The hearts of her people are false toward God. They are guilty and must be punished. God will break down their heathen altars and smash their idols. ³Then they will say, "We deserted the Lord and he took away our king. But what's the difference? We don't need one anyway!"

⁴They make promises they don't intend to keep. Therefore punishment will spring up among them like poisonous weeds in the furrows of the field. ⁵The people of Samaria tremble lest their calf-god idols at Beth-aven should be hurt; the priests and people, too, mourn over the departed honor of their shattered gods. ⁶This idol—this calf-god thing—will be carted with them when they go as slaves to Assyria, a present to the great king there. Ephraim will be laughed at for trusting in this idol; Israel will be put to shame. ⁷As for Samaria, her king shall disappear like a chip of wood upon an ocean wave. ⁸And the idol altars of Aven at Bethel where Israel sinned will crumble. Thorns and thistles will grow up to surround them. And the people will cry to the mountains and hills to fall upon them and crush them.

⁹O Israel, ever since that awful night in Gibeah, there has been only sin, sin, sin! You have made no progress whatever. Was it not right that the men of Gibeah were wiped out? ¹⁰I will come against you for your disobedience; I will gather the armies of the nations against you to punish you for your heaped-up sins.

¹¹Ephraim is accustomed to treading out the grain—an easy job she loves. I have never put her under a heavy yoke before; I have spared her tender neck. But now I will harness her to the plow and harrow. Her days of ease are gone.

¹²Plant the good seeds of righteousness and you will reap a crop of my love; plow the hard ground of your hearts, for now is the time to seek the Lord, that he may come and shower salvation upon you.

¹³But you have cultivated wickedness and raised a thriving crop of sins. You have earned the full reward of trusting in a lie—believing that military might and great armies can make a nation safe!

¹⁴Therefore the terrors of war shall rise among your people, and all your forts will fall, just as at Beth-arbel, which Shalman destroyed; even mothers and children were dashed to death there. ¹⁵That will be your fate, too, you people of Israel, because of your great wickedness. In one morning the king of Israel shall be destroyed.

WHEN Israel was a child I loved him as a son and brought him out of Egypt. ²But the more I called to him, the more he rebelled, sacrificing to Baal and burning incense to idols. ³I trained him from infancy, I taught him to walk, I held him in my arms. But he doesn't know or even care that it was I who raised him.

4As a man would lead his favorite ox, so I led Israel with my ropes of love. I loosened his muzzle so he could eat. I myself have stooped and fed him. 5But my people shall return to Egypt and Assyria because they won't return to me.

6War will swirl through their cities; their enemies will crash through their gates and trap them in their own fortresses. 7For my people are determined to desert me. And so I have sentenced them to slavery, and no one shall set them free.

8Oh, how can I give you up, my Ephraim? How can I let you go? How can I forsake you like Admah and Zeboiim? My heart cries out within me; how I long to help you! 9No, I will not punish you as much as my fierce anger tells me to. This is the last time I will destroy Ephraim. For I am God and not man; I am the Holy One living among you, and I did not come to destroy.

10For the people shall walk after the Lord. I shall roar as a lion [at their enemies] and my people shall return trembling from the west. 11Like a flock of birds, they will come from Egypt—like doves flying from Assyria. And I will bring them home again; it is a promise from the Lord.

12Israel surrounds me with lies and deceit, but Judah still trusts in God and is faithful to the Holy One.

ISRAEL is chasing the wind, yes, shepherding a whirlwind—a dangerous game! For she has given gifts to Egypt and Assyria to get their help, and in return she gets their worthless promises.

2But the Lord is bringing a lawsuit against Judah. Jacob will be justly punished for his ways. 3When he was born, he struggled with his brother; when he became a man, he even fought with God. 4Yes, he wrestled with the Angel and prevailed. He wept and pleaded for a blessing from him. He met God there at Bethel face to face. God spoke to

him— 5the Lord, the God of heaven's armies—Jehovah is his name.

6Oh, come back to God. Live by the principles of love and justice, and always be expecting much from him, your God.

7But no, my people are like crafty merchants selling from dishonest scales—they love to cheat. 8Ephraim boasts, "I am so rich! I have gotten it all by myself!" But riches can't make up for sin.

9I am the same Lord, the same God, who delivered you from slavery in Egypt, and I am the one who will consign you to living in tents again, as you do each year at the Tabernacle Feast. 10I sent my prophets to warn you with many a vision and many a parable and dream. 11But the sins of Gilgal flourish just the same. Row on row of altars—like furrows in a field—are used for sacrifices to your idols. And Gilead, too, is full of fools who worship idols. 12Jacob fled to Syria and earned a wife by tending sheep. 13Then the Lord led his people out of Egypt by a prophet, who guided and protected them. 14But Ephraim has bitterly provoked the Lord. The Lord will sentence him to death as payment for his sins.

IT used to be when Israel spoke, the nations shook with fear, for he was a mighty prince; but he worshiped Baal and sealed his doom.

2And now the people disobey more and more. They melt their silver to mold into idols, formed with skill by the hands of men. "Sacrifice to these!" they say—men kissing calves! 3They shall disappear like morning mist, like dew that quickly dries away, like chaff blown by the wind, like a cloud of smoke.

4I alone am God, your Lord, and have been ever since I brought you out from Egypt. You have no God but me, for there is no other Savior. 5I took care of you in the wilderness, in that dry and thirsty land. 6But when you had eaten and were satisfied, then you became proud and forgot me. 7So I will come upon you like a lion, or a leopard lurking along the road. 8I will rip you to pieces like a bear whose cubs have been taken away, and like a lion I will devour you.

9O Israel, if I destroy you, who can save you? 10Where is your king? Why don't you call on him for help? Where are all the leaders of the land? You asked for them, now let them save you! 11I gave you kings in my anger, and I took them away in my wrath. 12Ephraim's sins are harvested and stored away for punishment.

13New birth is offered him, but he is like a child resisting in the womb—how stubborn! how foolish! 14Shall I ransom him from hell? Shall I redeem him from Death? O Death, bring forth your terrors for his tasting! O Grave, demonstrate your plagues! For I will not relent!

15He was called the most fruitful of all his brothers, but the east wind—a wind of the Lord from the desert—will blow hard upon him and dry up his land. All his flowing springs and green oases will dry away, and he will die of thirst. 16Samaria must bear her guilt, for she rebelled against her God. Her people will be killed by the invading army, her babies dashed to death against the ground, her pregnant women ripped open with a sword.

O Israel, return to the Lord, your God, for you have been crushed by your sins. 2Bring your petition. Come to the Lord and say, "O Lord, take away our sins; be gracious to us and receive us, and we will offer you the sacrifice of praise. 3Assyria cannot save us, nor can our strength in battle; never again will we call the idols we have made 'our gods'; for in you alone, O Lord, the fatherless find mercy."

4Then I will cure you of idolatry and faithlessness, and my love will know no bounds, for my anger will be forever gone! 5I will refresh Israel like the dew from heaven; she will blossom as the lily and root deeply in the soil like cedars in Lebanon. 6Her branches will spread out, as beautiful as olive trees, fragrant as the forests of Lebanon. 7Her people will return from exile far away and rest beneath my shadow. They will be a watered garden and blossom like grapes and be as fragrant as the wines of Lebanon.

8O Ephraim! Stay away from idols! I am living and strong! I look after you and care for you. I am like an evergreen tree, yielding my fruit to you throughout the year. My mercies never fail.

9Whoever is wise, let him understand these things. Whoever is intelligent, let him listen. For the paths of the Lord are true and right, and good men walk along them. But sinners trying it will fail.

JUDE 1:1–25

FROM: Jude, a servant of Jesus Christ, and a brother of James. *To:* Christians everywhere— beloved of God and chosen by him. 2May you be given more and more of God's kindness, peace, and love.

3Dearly loved friends, I had been planning to write you some thoughts about the salvation God has given us, but now I find I must write of something else instead, urging you to stoutly defend the truth which God gave, once for all, to his people to keep without change through the years. 4I say this because some godless teachers have wormed their way in among you, saying that after we become Christians we can do just as we like without fear of God's punishment. The fate of such people was written long ago, for they have turned against our only Master and Lord, Jesus Christ.

5My answer to them is: Remember this fact—which you know already—that the Lord saved a whole nation of people out of the land of Egypt, and then killed every one of them who did not trust and obey him. 6And I remind you of those angels who were once pure and holy, but turned to a life of sin. Now God has them chained up in prisons of darkness, waiting for the judgment day. 7And don't forget the cities of Sodom and Gomorrah and their neighboring towns, all full of lust of every kind including lust of men for other men. Those cities were destroyed by fire and continue to be a warning to us that there is a hell in which sinners are punished.

8Yet these false teachers carelessly go right on living their evil, immoral lives, degrading their bodies and laughing at those in authority over them, even scoffing at the Glorious Ones. 9Yet Michael, one of the mightiest of the angels, when he was arguing with Satan about Moses' body, did not dare to accuse even Satan, or jeer at him, but simply said, "The Lord rebuke you." 10But these men mock and curse at anything they do not understand, and, like animals, they do whatever they feel like, thereby ruining their souls.

11Woe upon them! For they follow the example of Cain who killed his brother; and, like Balaam, they will do anything for money; and like Korah, they have disobeyed God and will die under his curse.

12When these men join you at the love feasts of the church, they are evil smears among you, laughing and carrying on, gorging and stuffing themselves without a thought for others. They are like clouds blowing over dry land without giving rain, promising much, but producing nothing. They are like fruit trees without any fruit at picking time. They are not only dead, but doubly dead, for they have been pulled out, roots and all, to be burned.

13All they leave behind them is shame and disgrace like the dirty foam left along the beach by the wild waves. They wander around looking as bright as stars, but ahead of them is the everlasting gloom and darkness that God has prepared for them.

14Enoch, who lived seven generations after Adam, knew about these men and said this about them: "See, the Lord is coming with millions of his holy ones. 15He will bring the people of the world before him in judgment, to receive just punishment, and to prove the terrible things they have done in rebellion against God, revealing all they have said against him." 16These men are constant gripers, never satisfied, doing whatever evil they feel like; they are loudmouthed "show-offs," and when they show respect for others, it is only to get something from them in return.

17Dear friends, remember what the apostles of our Lord Jesus Christ told you, 18that in the last times there would come these scoffers whose whole purpose in life is to enjoy themselves in every evil way imaginable. 19They stir up arguments; they love the evil things of the world; they do not have the Holy Spirit living in them.

20But you, dear friends, must build up your lives ever more strongly upon the foundation of our holy faith, learning to pray in the power and strength of the Holy Spirit.

21Stay always within the boundaries where God's love can reach and bless you. Wait patiently for the eternal life that our Lord Jesus Christ in his mercy is going to give you. 22Try to help those who argue against you. Be merciful to those who doubt. 23Save some by snatching them as from the very flames of hell itself. And as for others, help them to find the Lord by being kind to them, but be careful that you yourselves aren't pulled along into their sins. Hate every trace of their sin while being merciful to them as sinners.

24,25And now—all glory to him who alone is God, who saves us through Jesus Christ our Lord; yes, splendor and majesty, all power and authority are his from the beginning; his they are and his they evermore shall be. And he is able to keep you from slipping and falling away, and to bring you, sinless and perfect, into his glorious presence with mighty shouts of everlasting joy. Amen.

Jude

PSALM 127:1–5

UNLESS the Lord builds a house, the builders' work is useless. Unless the Lord protects a city, sentries do no good. 2It is senseless for you to work so hard from early morning until late at night, fearing you will starve to death; for God wants his loved ones to get their proper rest.

³Children are a gift from God; they are his reward. ⁴Children born to a young man are like sharp arrows to defend him.

⁵Happy is the man who has his quiver full of them. That man shall have the help he needs when arguing with his enemies.

PROVERBS FOR TODAY/ 29:15–17

Scolding and spanking a child helps him to learn. Left to himself, he brings shame to his mother. When rulers are wicked, their people are too; but good men will live to see the tyrant's downfall. Discipline your son and he will give you happiness and peace of mind.

DECEMBER 9

JOEL 1:1—3:21

THIS message came from the Lord to Joel, son of Pethuel:

²Listen, you aged men of Israel! Everyone, listen! In all your lifetime, yes, in all your history, have you ever heard of such a thing as I am going to tell you? ³In years to come, tell your children about it; pass the awful story down from generation to generation. ⁴After the cutter-locusts finish eating your crops, the swarmer-locusts will take what's left! After them will come the hopper-locusts! And then the stripper-locusts, too!

⁵Wake up and weep, you drunkards, for all the grapes are ruined and all your wine is gone! ⁶A vast army of locusts covers the land. It is a terrible army too numerous to count, with teeth as sharp as those of lions! ⁷They have ruined my vines and stripped the bark from the fig trees, leaving trunks and branches white and bare.

⁸Weep with sorrow, as a virgin weeps whose fiancé is dead. ⁹Gone are the offerings of grain and wine to bring to the Temple of the Lord; the priests are starving. Hear the crying of these ministers of God. ¹⁰The fields are bare of crops. Sorrow and sadness are everywhere. The grain, the grapes, the olive oil are gone.

¹¹Well may you farmers stand so shocked and stricken; well may you vinedressers weep. Weep for the wheat and the barley too, for they are gone. ¹²The grapevines are dead; the fig trees are dying; the pomegranates wither; the apples shrivel on the trees; all joy has withered with them.

¹³O priests, robe yourselves in sackcloth. O ministers of my God, lie all night before the altar, weeping. For there are no more offerings of grain and wine for you. ¹⁴Announce a fast; call a solemn meeting. Gather the elders and all the people into the Temple of the Lord your God, and weep before him there.

¹⁵Alas, this terrible day of punishment is on the way. Destruction from the Almighty is almost here! ¹⁶Our food will disappear before our eyes; all joy and gladness will be ended in the Temple of our God. ¹⁷The seed rots in the ground; the barns and granaries are empty; the grain has dried up in the fields. ¹⁸The cattle groan with hunger; the herds stand perplexed for there is no pasture for them; the sheep bleat in misery.

¹⁹Lord, help us! For the heat has withered the pastures and burned up all the trees. ²⁰Even the wild animals cry to you for help, for there is no water for them.

The creeks are dry and the pastures are scorched.

SOUND the alarm in Jerusalem! Let the blast of the warning trumpet be heard upon my holy mountain! Let everyone tremble in fear, for the day of the Lord's judgment approaches.

2It is a day of darkness and gloom, of black clouds and thick darkness. What a mighty army! It covers the mountains like night! How great, how powerful these "people" are! The likes of them have not been seen before, and never will again throughout the generations of the world! 3Fire goes before them and follows them on every side! Ahead of them the land lies fair as Eden's Garden in all its beauty, but they destroy it to the ground; not one thing escapes. 4They look like tiny horses, and they run as fast. 5Look at them leaping along the tops of the mountain! Listen to the noise they make, like the rumbling of chariots, or the roar of fire sweeping across a field, and like a mighty army moving into battle.

6Fear grips the waiting people; their faces grow pale with fright. 7These "soldiers" charge like infantry; they scale the walls like picked and trained commandos. Straight forward they march, never breaking ranks. 8They never crowd each other. Each is right in place. No weapon can stop them. 9They swarm upon the city; they run upon the walls; they climb up into the houses, coming like thieves through the windows. 10The earth quakes before them and the heavens tremble. The sun and moon are obscured and the stars are hid.

11The Lord leads them with a shout. This is his mighty army and they follow his orders. The day of the judgment of the Lord is an awesome, terrible thing. Who can endure it?

12That is why the Lord says, "Turn to me now, while there is time. Give me all your hearts. Come with fasting, weeping, mourning. 13Let your remorse tear at your hearts and not your gar-ments." Return to the Lord your God, for he is gracious and merciful. He is not easily angered; he is full of kindness, and anxious not to punish you.

14Who knows? Perhaps even yet he will decide to let you alone and give you a blessing instead of his terrible curse. Perhaps he will give you so much that you can offer your grain and wine to the Lord as before!

15Sound the trumpet in Zion! Call a fast and gather all the people together for a solemn meeting. 16Bring every-one—the elders, the children, and even the babies. Call the bridegroom from his quarters and the bride from her privacy.

17The priests, the ministers of God, will stand between the people and the altar, weeping; and they will pray, "Spare your people, O our God; don't let the heathen rule them, for they belong to you. Don't let them be disgraced by the taunts of the heathen who say, 'Where is this God of theirs? How weak and helpless he must be!' "

18Then the Lord will pity his people and be indignant for the honor of his land! 19He will reply, "See, I am sending you much corn and wine and oil, to fully satisfy your need. No longer will I make you a laughingstock among the nations. 20I will remove these armies from the north and send them far away; I will turn them back into the parched wastelands where they will die; half shall be driven into the Dead Sea and the rest into the Mediterranean, and then their rotting stench will rise upon the land. The Lord has done a mighty miracle for you."

21Fear not, my people; be glad now and rejoice, for he has done amazing things for you.

22"Let the flocks and herds forget their hunger; the pastures will turn green again. The trees will bear their fruit; the fig trees and grape vines will flourish once more.

23"Rejoice, O people of Jerusalem, re-joice in the Lord your God! For the rains he sends are tokens of forgiveness. Once more the autumn rains will come, as well as those of spring. 24The threshing floors will pile high again with wheat, and the presses overflow with olive oil and wine. 25And I will give you back the crops the locusts ate!—my great destroying army that I sent against you. 26Once again you will have all the food you want.

"Praise the Lord, who does these miracles for you. Never again will my people experience disaster such as this. 27And you will know that I am here among my people Israel, and that I alone am the Lord, your God. And my people shall never again be dealt a blow like this.

28"After I have poured out my rains again, I will pour out my Spirit upon all of you! Your sons and daughters will prophesy; your old men will dream dreams, and your young men see visions. 29And I will pour out my Spirit even on your slaves, men and women alike, 30and put strange symbols in the earth and sky—blood and fire and pillars of smoke.

31"The sun will be turned into darkness and the moon to blood before the great and terrible Day of the Lord shall come.

32"Everyone who calls upon the name of the Lord will be saved; even in Jerusalem some will escape, just as the Lord has promised, for he has chosen some to survive.

"AT that time, when I restore the prosperity of Judah and Jerusalem," says the Lord, 2"I will gather the armies of the world into the 'Valley Where Jehovah Judges' and punish them there for harming my people, for scattering my inheritance among the nations and dividing up my land.

3"They divided up my people as their slaves; they traded a young lad for a prostitute, and a little girl for wine enough to get drunk. 4Tyre and Sidon, don't you try to interfere! Are you trying to take revenge on me, you cities of Philistia? Beware, for I will strike back swiftly, and return the harm to your own heads.

5"You have taken my silver and gold and all my precious treasures and carried them off to your heathen temples. 6You have sold the people of Judah and Jerusalem to the Greeks, who took them far from their own land. 7But I will bring them back again from all these places you have sold them to, and I will pay you back for all that you have done. 8I will sell your sons and daughters to the people of Judah and they will sell them to the Sabeans far away. This is a promise from the Lord."

9Announce this far and wide: Get ready for war! Conscript your best soldiers; collect all your armies. 10Melt your plowshares into swords and beat your pruning hooks into spears. Let the weak be strong. 11Gather together and come, all nations everywhere.

And now, O Lord, bring down your warriors! 12Collect the nations; bring them to the Valley of Jehoshaphat, for there I will sit to pronounce judgment on them all. 13Now let the sickle do its work; the harvest is ripe and waiting. Tread the winepress, for it is full to overflowing with the wickedness of these men.

14Multitudes, multitudes waiting in the valley for the verdict of their doom! For the Day of the Lord is near, in the Valley of Judgment.

15The sun and moon will be darkened and the stars withdraw their light. 16The Lord shouts from his Temple in Jerusalem and the earth and sky begin to shake. But to his people Israel, the Lord will be very gentle. He is their Refuge and Strength. 17"Then you shall know at last that I am the Lord your God in Zion, my holy mountain. Jerusalem shall be mine forever; the time will come when no foreign armies will pass through her any more.

18"Sweet wine will drip from the mountains, and the hills shall flow with milk. Water will fill the dry stream beds of Judah, and a fountain will burst forth from the Temple of the Lord to water Acacia Valley. 19Egypt will be destroyed, and Edom too, because of their violence against the Jews, for they killed innocent people in those nations.

20"But Israel will prosper forever, and Jerusalem will thrive as generations pass. 21For I will avenge the blood of my people; I will not clear their oppressors of guilt. For my home is in Jerusalem with my people."

REVELATION 1:1–20

THIS book unveils some of the future activities soon to occur in the life of Jesus Christ. God permitted him to reveal these things to his servant John in a vision; and then an angel was sent from heaven to explain the vision's meaning. 2John wrote it all down—the words of God and Jesus Christ and everything he heard and saw.

3If you read this prophecy aloud to the church, you will receive a special blessing from the Lord. Those who listen to it being read and do what it says will also be blessed. For the time is near when these things will all come true.

4*From:* John

To: The seven churches in Turkey.
Dear Friends:

May you have grace and peace from God who is, and was, and is to come! and from the seven-fold Spirit before his throne; 5and from Jesus Christ who faithfully reveals all truth to us. He was the first to rise from death, to die no more. He is far greater than any king in all the earth. All praise to him who always loves us and who set us free from our sins by pouring out his lifeblood for us. 6He has gathered us into his Kingdom and made us priests of God his Father. Give to him everlasting glory! He rules forever! Amen!

7See! He is arriving, surrounded by clouds; and every eye shall see him— yes, and those who pierced him. And the nations will weep in sorrow and in terror when he comes. Yes! Amen! Let it be so!

8"I am the A and the Z, the Beginning and the Ending of all things," says God, who is the Lord, the All Powerful One who is, and was, and is coming again!

9It is I, your brother John, a fellow sufferer for the Lord's sake, who am writing this letter to you. I, too, have shared the patience Jesus gives, and we shall share his Kingdom!

I was on the island of Patmos, exiled there for preaching the Word of God, and for telling what I knew about Jesus Christ. 10It was the Lord's Day and I was worshiping, when suddenly I heard a loud voice behind me, a voice that sounded like a trumpet blast, 11saying, "I am A and Z, the First and Last!" And then I heard him say, "Write down everything you see, and send your letter to the seven churches in Turkey: to the church in Ephesus, the one in Smyrna, and those in Pergamos, Thyatira, Sardis, Philadelphia, and Laodicea."

12When I turned to see who was speaking, there behind me were seven candlesticks of gold. 13And standing among them was one who looked like Jesus who called himself the Son of Man, wearing a long robe circled with a golden band across his chest. 14His hair was white as wool or snow, and his eyes penetrated like flames of fire. 15His feet gleamed like burnished bronze, and his voice thundered like the waves against the shore. 16He held seven stars in his right hand and a sharp, double-bladed sword in his mouth, and his face shone like the power of the sun in unclouded brilliance.

17,18When I saw him, I fell at his feet as dead; but he laid his right hand on me and said, "Don't be afraid! Though I am the First and Last, the Living One who died, who is now alive forevermore, who has the keys of hell and death— don't be afraid! 19Write down what you have just seen, and what will soon be shown to you. 20This is the meaning of the seven stars you saw in my right hand, and the seven golden candlesticks: The seven stars are the leaders of the seven churches, and the seven candlesticks are the churches themselves.

BLESSINGS on all who reverence and trust the Lord—on all who obey him!

2Their reward shall be prosperity and happiness. 3Your wife shall be contented in your home. And look at all those children! There they sit around the dinner table as vigorous and healthy as young olive trees. 4That is God's reward to those who reverence and trust him.

5May the Lord continually bless you with heaven's blessings as well as with human joys. 6May you live to enjoy your grandchildren! And may God bless Israel!

PROVERBS FOR TODAY/ 29:18

Where there is ignorance of God, crime runs wild; but what a wonderful thing it is for a nation to know and keep his laws.

DECEMBER 10

AMOS 1:1—3:15

AMOS was a herdsman living in the village of Tekoa. [All day long he sat on the hillsides watching the sheep, keeping them from straying.]

2One day, in a vision, God told him some of the things that were going to happen to his nation, Israel. This vision came to him at the time Uzziah was king of Judah, and while Jeroboam (son of Joash) was king of Israel—two years before the earthquake.

This is his report of what he saw and heard: The Lord roared—like a ferocious lion from his lair—from his Temple on Mount Zion. And suddenly the lush pastures of Mount Carmel withered and dried, and all the shepherds mourned.

3The Lord says, "The people of Damascus have sinned again and again, and I will not forget it. I will not leave her unpunished any more. For they have threshed my people in Gilead as grain is threshed with iron rods. 4So I will set fire to King Hazael's palace, destroying the strong fortress of Ben-hadad. 5I will snap the bars that locked the gates of Damascus, and kill her people as far away as the plain of Aven, and the people of Syria shall return to Kir as slaves." The Lord has spoken.

6The Lord says, "Gaza has sinned again and again, and I will not forget it. I will not leave her unpunished any more. For she sent my people into exile, selling them as slaves in Edom. 7So I will set fire to the walls of Gaza, and all her forts shall be destroyed. 8I will kill the people of Ashdod, and destroy Ekron and the king of Ashkelon; all Philistines left will perish." The Lord has spoken.

9The Lord says, "The people of Tyre have sinned again and again and I will not forget it. I will not leave them unpunished any more. For they broke their treaty with their brother, Israel; they attacked and conquered him, and led him into slavery to Edom. 10So I will set fire to the walls of Tyre, and it will burn down all his forts and palaces."

11The Lord says, "Edom has sinned again and again, and I will not forget it. I will not leave him unpunished any more. For he chased his brother, Israel, with the sword; he was pitiless in unrelenting anger. 12So I will set fire to Teman, and it will burn down all the forts of Bozrah."

13The Lord says, "The people of Ammon have sinned again and again, and I will not forget it. I will not leave them unpunished any more. For in their wars in Gilead to enlarge their borders, they committed cruel crimes, ripping open pregnant women with their swords.

14"So I will set fire to the walls of Rabbah, and it will burn down their forts and palaces; there will be wild shouts of battle like a whirlwind in a mighty storm. 15And their king and his princes will go into exile together." The Lord has spoken.

THE Lord says, "The people of Moab have sinned again and again, and I will not forget it. I will not leave them unpunished any more. For they desecrated the tombs of the kings of Edom, with no respect for the dead. 2Now in return I will send fire upon Moab, and it will destroy all the palaces in Kerioth. Moab shall go down in tumult as the warriors shout and trumpets blare. 3And I will destroy their king and slay all the leaders under him." The Lord has spoken.

4The Lord says, "The people of Judah have sinned again and again, and I will not forget it. I will not leave them unpunished any more. For they have rejected the laws of God, refusing to obey him. They have hardened their hearts and sinned as their fathers did. 5So I will destroy Judah with fire, and burn down all Jerusalem's palaces and forts."

6The Lord says, "The people of Israel have sinned again and again, and I will not forget it. I will not leave them unpunished any more. For they have perverted justice by accepting bribes, and sold into slavery the poor who can't repay their debts; they trade them for a pair of shoes. 7They trample the poor in the dust and kick aside the meek.

"And a man and his father defile the same temple-girl, corrupting my holy name. 8At their religious feasts they lounge in clothing stolen from their debtors, and in my own Temple they offer sacrifices of wine they purchased with stolen money.

9"Yet think of all I did for them! I cleared the land of the Amorites before them—the Amorites, as tall as cedar trees, and strong as oaks! But I lopped off their fruit and cut their roots. 10And I brought you out from Egypt and led you through the desert forty years, to possess the land of the Amorites. 11And I chose your sons to be Nazirites and prophets—can you deny this, Israel?" asks the Lord. 12"But you caused the Nazirites to sin by urging them to drink your wine, and you silenced my prophets, telling them, 'Shut up!'

13"Therefore I will make you groan as a wagon groans that is loaded with sheaves. 14Your swiftest warriors will stumble in flight. The strong will all be weak, and the great ones can no longer save themselves. 15The archer's aim will fail, the swiftest runners won't be fast enough to flee, and even the best of horsemen can't outrun the danger then. 16The most courageous of your mighty men will drop their weapons and run for their lives that day." The Lord God has spoken.

LISTEN! This is your doom! It is spoken by the Lord against both Israel and Judah—against the entire family I brought from Egypt:

2"Of all the peoples of the earth, I have chosen you alone. That is why I must punish you the more for all your sins. 3For how can we walk together with your sins between us?

4"Would I be roaring as a lion unless I had a reason? The fact is, I am getting ready to destroy you. Even a young lion, when it growls, shows it is ready for its food. 5A trap doesn't snap shut unless it is stepped on; your punishment is well deserved. 6The alarm has sounded—listen and fear! For I, the Lord, am sending disaster into your land.

7"But always, first of all, I warn you through my prophets. This I now have done."

8The Lion has roared—tremble in fear. The Lord God has sounded your doom— I dare not refuse to proclaim it.

9Call together the Assyrian and Egyptian leaders, saying, "Take your seats now on the mountains of Samaria to witness the scandalous spectacle of all Israel's crimes. 10My people have forgotten what it means to do right," says the Lord. "Their beautiful homes are full of the loot from their thefts and banditry. ¹¹Therefore," the Lord God says, "an enemy is coming! He is surrounding them and will shatter their forts and plunder those beautiful homes."

¹²The Lord says, "A shepherd tried to rescue his sheep from a lion, but it was too late; he snatched from the lion's mouth two legs and a piece of ear. So it will be when the Israelites in Samaria are finally rescued—all they will have left is half a chair and a tattered pillow.

¹³"Listen to this announcement, and publish it throughout all Israel," says the Lord, the Lord Almighty: ¹⁴"On the same day that I punish Israel for her sins, I will also destroy the idol altars at Bethel. The horns of the altar will be cut off and fall to the ground.

¹⁵"And I will destroy the beautiful homes of the wealthy—their winter mansions and their summer houses, too—and demolish their ivory palaces."

REVELATION 2:1–17

WRITE *a letter to the leader of the church at Ephesus and tell him this:*

"I write to inform you of a message from him who walks among the churches and holds their leaders in his right hand.

"He says to you: ²I know how many good things you are doing. I have watched your hard work and your patience; I know you don't tolerate sin among your members, and you have carefully examined the claims of those who say they are apostles but aren't. You have found out how they lie. ³You have patiently suffered for me without quitting.

⁴"Yet there is one thing wrong; you don't love me as at first! ⁵Think about those times of your first love (how different now!) and turn back to me again and work as you did before; or else I will come and remove your candlestick from its place among the churches.

⁶"But there is this about you that is

good: You hate the deeds of the licentious Nicolaitans, just as I do.

⁷"Let this message sink into the ears of anyone who listens to what the Spirit is saying to the churches: To everyone who is victorious, I will give fruit from the Tree of Life in the Paradise of God.

⁸*"To the leader of the church in Smyrna write this letter:*

"This message is from him who is the First and Last, who was dead and then came back to life.

⁹"I know how much you suffer for the Lord, and I know all about your poverty (but you have heavenly riches!). I know the slander of those opposing you, who say that they are Jews—the children of God—but they aren't, for they support the cause of Satan. ¹⁰Stop being afraid of what you are about to suffer—for the devil will soon throw some of you into prison to test you. You will be persecuted for 'ten days.' Remain faithful even when facing death and I will give you the crown of life—an unending, glorious future. ¹¹Let everyone who can hear, listen to what the Spirit is saying to the churches: He who is victorious shall not be hurt by the Second Death.

¹²*"Write this letter to the leader of the church in Pergamos:*

"This message is from him who wields the sharp and double-bladed sword. ¹³I am fully aware that you live in the city where Satan's throne is, at the center of satanic worship; and yet you have remained loyal to me, and refused to deny me, even when Antipas, my faithful witness, was martyred among you by Satan's devotees.

¹⁴"And yet I have a few things against you. You tolerate some among you who do as Balaam did when he taught Balak how to ruin the people of Israel by involving them in sexual sin and encouraging them to go to idol feasts. ¹⁵Yes, you have some of these very same followers of Balaam among you!

¹⁶"Change your mind and attitude, or else I will come to you suddenly and fight against them with the sword of my mouth.

¹⁷"Let everyone who can hear, listen to what the Spirit is saying to the churches: Every one who is victorious shall eat of the hidden manna, the secret nourishment from heaven; and I will give to each a white stone, and on the stone will be engraved a new name that no one else knows except the one receiving it.

PSALM 129:1–8

Persecuted from my earliest youth (Israel is speaking), ²and faced with never-ending discrimination—but not destroyed! My enemies have never been able to finish me off!

³,⁴Though my back is cut to ribbons with their whips, the Lord is good. For he has snapped the chains that evil men had bound me with.

⁵May all who hate the Jews be brought to ignominious defeat. ⁶,⁷May they be as grass in shallow soil, turning sere and yellow when half grown, ignored by the reaper, despised by the binder. ⁸And may those passing by refuse to bless them by saying, "Jehovah's blessings be upon you; we bless you in Jehovah's name."

PROVERBS FOR TODAY/ 29:19–20

Sometimes mere words are not enough—discipline is needed. For the words may not be heeded. There is more hope for a fool than for a man of quick temper.

DECEMBER 11

AMOS 4:1—6:14

Listen to me, you "fat cows" of Bashan living in Samaria—you women who encourage your husbands to rob the poor and crush the needy—you who never have enough to drink! ²The Lord God has sworn by his holiness that the time will come when he will put hooks in your noses and lead you away like the cattle you are; they will drag the last of you away with fishhooks! ³You will be hauled from your beautiful homes and tossed out through the nearest breach in the wall. The Lord has said it.

⁴Go ahead and sacrifice to idols at Bethel and Gilgal. Keep disobeying—your sins are mounting up. Sacrifice each morning and bring your tithes twice a week! ⁵Go through all your proper forms and give extra offerings. How you pride yourselves and crow about it everywhere!

⁶"I sent you hunger," says the Lord, "but it did no good; you still would not return to me. ⁷I ruined your crops by holding back the rain three months before the harvest. I sent rain on one city, but not another. While rain fell on one field, another was dry and withered. ⁸People from two or three cities would make their weary journey for a drink of water to a city that had rain, but there wasn't ever enough. Yet you wouldn't return to me," says the Lord.

⁹"I sent blight and mildew on your farms and your vineyards; the locusts ate your figs and olive trees. And still you wouldn't return to me," says the Lord. ¹⁰"I sent you plagues like those of Egypt long ago. I killed your lads in war and drove away your horses. The stench of death was terrible to smell. And yet you refused to come. ¹¹I destroyed some of your cities, as I did Sodom and Gomorrah; those left are like

half-burned firebrands snatched away from fire. And still you won't return to me," says the Lord.

12"Therefore I will bring upon you all these further evils I have spoken of. Prepare to meet your God in judgment, Israel. 13For you are dealing with the one who formed the mountains and made the winds, and knows your every thought; he turns the morning to darkness and crushes down the mountains underneath his feet: Jehovah, the Lord, the Lord Almighty, is his name."

SADLY I sing this song of grief for you, O Israel:

2"Beautiful Israel lies broken and crushed upon the ground and cannot rise. No one will help her. She is left alone to die." 3For the Lord God says, "The city that sends a thousand men to battle, a hundred will return. The city that sends a hundred, only ten will come back alive."

4The Lord says to the people of Israel, "Seek me—and live. 5Don't seek the idols of Bethel, Gilgal, or Beer-sheba; for the people of Gilgal will be carried off to exile, and those of Bethel shall surely come to grief."

6Seek the Lord and live, or else he will sweep like fire through Israel and consume her, and none of the idols in Bethel can put it out.

7O evil men, you make "justice" a bitter pill for the poor and oppressed. "Righteousness" and "fair play" are meaningless fictions to you!

8Seek him who created the Seven Stars and the constellation Orion, who turns darkness into morning, and day into night, who calls forth the water from the ocean and pours it out as rain upon the land. The Lord, Jehovah, is his name. 9With blinding speed and violence he brings destruction on the strong, breaking all defenses.

10How you hate honest judges! How you despise people who tell the truth! 11You trample the poor and steal their smallest crumb by all your taxes, fines, and usury; therefore you will never live in the beautiful stone houses you are building, nor drink the wine from the lush vineyards you are planting.

12For many and great are your sins. I know them all so well. You are the enemies of everything good; you take bribes; you refuse justice to the poor. 13Therefore those who are wise will not try to interfere with the Lord in the dread day of your punishment.

14Be good, flee evil—and live! Then the Lord, the Lord Almighty, will truly be your Helper, as you have claimed he is. 15Hate evil and love the good; remodel your courts into true halls of justice. Perhaps even yet the Lord God of Hosts will have mercy on his people who remain.

16Therefore the Lord God says this: "There will be crying in all the streets and every road. Call for the farmers to weep with you, too; call for professional mourners to wail and lament. 17There will be sorrow and crying in every vineyard, for I will pass through and destroy. 18You say, 'If only the Day of the Lord were here, for then God would deliver us from all our foes.' But you have no idea what you ask. For that day will *not* be light and prosperity, but darkness and doom! How terrible the darkness will be for you; not a ray of joy or hope will shine. 19In that day you will be as a man who is chased by a lion—and met by a bear, or a man in a dark room who leans against a wall—and puts his hand on a snake. 20Yes, that will be a dark and hopeless day for you.

21"I hate your show and pretense— your hypocrisy of 'honoring' me with your religious feasts and solemn assemblies. 22I will not accept your burnt offerings and thank offerings. I will not look at your offerings of peace. 23Away with your hymns of praise—they are mere noise to my ears. I will not listen to your music, no matter how lovely it is.

24"I want to see a mighty flood of justice—a torrent of doing good.

25,26,27"You sacrificed to me for forty years while you were in the desert, Israel—but always your real interest has been in your heathen gods—in Sakkuth your king, and in Kaiwan, your god of the stars, and in all the images of them you made. So I will send them into captivity with you far to the east of Damascus," says the Lord, the Lord Almighty.

WOE to those lounging in luxury at Jerusalem and Samaria, so famous and popular among the people of Israel. 2Go over to Calneh and see what happened there; then go to great Hamath and down to Gath in the Philistines' land. Once they were better and greater than you, but look at them now. 3You push away all thought of punishment awaiting you, but by your deeds you bring the Day of Judgment near.

4You lie on ivory beds surrounded with luxury, eating the meat of the tenderest lambs and the choicest calves. 5You sing idle songs to the sound of the harp, and fancy yourselves to be as great musicians as King David was.

6You drink wine by the bucketful and perfume yourselves with sweet ointments, caring nothing at all that your brothers need your help. 7Therefore you will be the first to be taken as slaves; suddenly your revelry will end.

8Jehovah the Almighty Lord has sworn by his own name, "I despise the pride and false glory of Israel, and hate their beautiful homes. I will turn over this city and everything in it to her enemies."

9If there are as few as ten of them left, and even one house, they too will perish. 10A man's uncle will be the only one left to bury him, and when he goes in to carry his body from the house, he will ask the only one still alive inside, "Are any others left?" And the answer will be, "No," and he will add, "Shhh . . . don't mention the name of the Lord—he might hear you."

11For the Lord commanded this: That homes both great and small should be smashed to pieces. 12Can horses run on rocks? Can oxen plow the sea? Stupid even to ask, but no more stupid than what you do when you make a mockery of justice, and corrupt and sour all that should be good and right. 13And just as

stupid is your rejoicing in how great you are, when you are less than nothing! And priding yourselves on your own tiny power!

14"O Israel, I will bring against you a nation that will bitterly oppress you from your northern boundary to your southern tip, all the way from Hamath to the brook of Arabah," says the Lord, the Lord Almighty.

REVELATION 2:18—3:6

WRITE this letter to the leader of the church in Thyatira:

"This is a message from the Son of God, whose eyes penetrate like flames of fire, whose feet are like glowing brass.

19"I am aware of all your good deeds—your kindness to the poor, your gifts and service to them; also I know your love and faith and patience, and I can see your constant improvement in all these things.

20"Yet I have this against you: You are permitting that woman Jezebel, who calls herself a prophetess, to teach my servants that sex sin is not a serious matter; she urges them to practice immorality and to eat meat that has been sacrificed to idols. 21I gave her time to change her mind and attitude, but she refused. 22Pay attention now to what I am saying: I will lay her upon a sickbed of intense affliction, along with all her immoral followers, unless they turn again to me, repenting of their sin with her; 23and I will strike her children dead. And all the churches shall know that I am he who searches deep within men's hearts, and minds; I will give to each of you whatever you deserve.

24,25"As for the rest of you in Thyatira who have not followed this false teaching ('deeper truths,' as they call them—depths of Satan, really), I will ask nothing further of you; only hold tightly to what you have until I come.

26"To every one who overcomes—who to the very end keeps on doing things that please me—I will give power over the nations. 27You will rule them with a rod of iron just as my Father gave me the authority to rule them; they will be shattered like a pot of clay that is broken into tiny pieces. 28And I will give you the Morning Star!

29"Let all who can hear, listen to what the Spirit says to the churches.

To the leader of the church in Sardis write this letter:

"This message is sent to you by the one who has the seven-fold Spirit of God and the seven stars.

"I know your reputation as a live and active church, but you are dead. 2Now wake up! Strengthen what little remains—for even what is left is at the point of death. Your deeds are far from right in the sight of God. 3Go back to what you heard and believed at first; hold to it firmly and turn to me again. Unless you do, I will come suddenly upon you, unexpected as a thief, and punish you.

4"Yet even there in Sardis some haven't soiled their garments with the world's filth; they shall walk with me in white, for they are worthy. 5Everyone who conquers will be clothed in white, and I will not erase his name from the Book of Life, but I will announce before my Father and his angels that he is mine.

6"Let all who can hear, listen to what the Spirit is saying to the churches.

PSALM 130:1–8

O Lord, from the depths of despair I cry for your help: 2"Hear me! Answer! Help me!"

3,4Lord, if you keep in mind our sins then who can ever get an answer to his prayers? But you forgive! What an awesome thing this is! 5That is why I wait expectantly, trusting God to help, for he has promised. 6I long for him more than sentinels long for the dawn.

7O Israel, hope in the Lord; for he is loving and kind, and comes to us with armloads of salvation. 8He himself shall ransom Israel from her slavery to sin.

PROVERBS FOR TODAY/ 29:21–22

Pamper a servant from childhood, and he will expect you to treat him as a son! A hot-tempered man starts fights and gets into all kinds of trouble.

DECEMBER 12

AMOS 7:1—9:15

THIS is what the Lord God showed me in a vision: He was preparing a vast swarm of locusts to destroy all the main crop that sprang up after the first mowing, which went as taxes to the king. 2They ate everything in sight. Then I said, "O Lord God, please forgive your people! Don't send them this plague! If you turn against Israel, what hope is there? For Israel is so small!" 3So the Lord relented, and did not fulfill the vision. "I won't do it," he told me.

4Then the Lord God showed me a great fire he had prepared to punish them; it had burned up the waters and was devouring the entire land.

5Then I said, "O Lord God, please don't do it. If you turn against them, what hope is there? For Israel is so small!"

6Then the Lord turned from this plan too, and said, "I won't do that either."

7Then he showed me this: The Lord was standing beside a wall built with a plumbline, checking it with a plumbline to see if it was straight. 8And the Lord said to me, "Amos, what do you see?"

I answered, "A plumbline."

And he replied, "I will test my people with a plumbline. I will no longer turn away from punishing. 9The idol altars and temples of Israel will be destroyed, and I will destroy the dynasty of King Jeroboam by the sword."

10But when Amaziah, the priest of Bethel, heard what Amos was saying, he rushed a message to Jeroboam, the king: "Amos is a traitor to our nation and is plotting your death. This is intolerable. It will lead to rebellion all across the land. 11He says you will be killed, and Israel will be sent far away into exile and slavery."

12Then Amaziah sent orders to Amos, "Get out of here, you prophet, you! Flee to the land of Judah and do your prophesying there! 13Don't bother us here with your visions, not here in the capital, where the king's chapel is!"

14But Amos replied, "I am not really one of the prophets. I do not come from a family of prophets. I am just a herdsman and fruit picker. 15But the Lord took me from caring for the flocks and told me, 'Go and prophesy to my people Israel.'

16"Now therefore listen to this message to you from the Lord. You say, 'Don't prophesy against Israel.' 17The Lord's reply is this: 'Because of your interference, your wife will become a prostitute in this city, and your sons and daughters will be killed and your land divided up. You yourself will die in a heathen land, and the people of Israel will certainly become slaves in exile, far from their land.' "

THEN the Lord God showed me, in a vision, a basket full of ripe fruit.

2"What do you see, Amos?" he asked.
I replied, "A basket full of ripe fruit."
Then the Lord said, "This fruit represents my people Israel—ripe for punishment. I will not defer their punishment again. 3The riotous sound of singing in the Temple will turn to weeping then. Dead bodies will be scattered everywhere. They will be carried out of the city in silence." The Lord has spoken.

4Listen, you merchants who rob the poor, trampling on the needy; 5you who long for the Sabbath to end and the religious holidays to be over, so you can get out and start cheating again—using your weighted scales and under-sized measures; 6you who make slaves of the poor, buying them for their debt of a piece of silver or a pair of shoes, or selling them your moldy wheat— 7the Lord, the Pride of Israel, has sworn: "I won't forget your deeds! 8The land will tremble as it awaits its doom, and everyone will mourn. It will rise up like the river Nile at floodtime, toss about, and sink again. 9At that time I will make the sun go down at noon and darken the earth in the daytime.

10"And I will turn your parties into times of mourning, and your songs of joy will be turned to cries of despair. You will wear funeral clothes and shave your heads as signs of sorrow, as if your only son had died; bitter, bitter will be that day. 11The time is surely coming," says the Lord God, "when I will send a famine on the land—not a famine of bread or water, but of hearing the words of the Lord. 12Men will wander everywhere from sea to sea, seeking the Word of the Lord, searching, running here and going there, but will not find it.

13"Beautiful girls and fine young men alike will grow faint and weary, thirsting for the Word of God. 14And those who worship the idols of Samaria, Dan, and Beersheba shall fall and never rise again."

I saw the Lord standing beside the altar, saying, "Smash the tops of the pillars and shake the Temple until the pillars crumble and the roof crashes down upon the people below. Though they run, they will not escape; they all will be killed.

2"Though they dig down to Sheol, I will reach down and pull them up; though they climb into the heavens, I will bring them down. 3Though they hide among the rocks at the top of Carmel, I will search them out and capture them. Though they hide at the bottom of the ocean, I will send the sea-serpent after them to bite and destroy them. 4Though they volunteer for exile, I will command the sword to kill them there. I will see to it that they receive evil and not good."

5The Lord Almighty touches the land and it melts, and all its people mourn. It rises like the river Nile in Egypt, and then sinks again. 6The upper stories of his home are in the heavens, the first floor on the earth. He calls for the vapor to rise from the ocean and pours it down as rain upon the ground. Jehovah, the Lord, is his name.

7"O people of Israel, are you any more to me than the Ethiopians are? Have not I, who brought you out of Egypt, done as much for other people, too? I brought the Philistines from Caphtor and the Syrians out of Kir.

8"The eyes of the Lord God are watching Israel, that sinful nation, and I will root her up and scatter her across the world. *Yet I have promised that this rooting out will not be permanent.* 9For I have commanded that Israel be sifted by the other nations as grain is sifted in a sieve, yet not one true kernel will be lost. 10But all these sinners who say, 'God will not touch us,' will die by the sword.

11"Then, at that time I will rebuild the City of David, which is now lying in ruins, and return it to its former glory, 12and Israel will possess what is left of Edom, and of all the nations that belong to me." For so the Lord, who plans it all, has said.

13"The time will come when there will be such abundance of crops, that the harvest time will scarcely end before the farmer starts again to sow another crop, and the terraces of grapes upon the hills of Israel will drip sweet wine! 14I will restore the fortunes of my people Israel, and they shall rebuild their ruined cities, and live in them again, and they shall plant vineyards and gardens and eat their crops and drink their wine. 15I will firmly plant them there upon the land that I have given them; they shall not be pulled up again," says the Lord your God.

WRITE *this letter to the leader of the church in Philadelphia.*

"This message is sent to you by the one who is holy and true, and has the key of David to open what no one can shut and to shut what no one can open.

8"I know you well; you aren't strong, but you have tried to obey and have not denied my Name. Therefore I have opened a door to you that no one can shut.

9"Note this: I will force those supporting the causes of Satan while claiming to be mine (but they aren't—they are lying) to fall at your feet and acknowledge that you are the ones I love.

10"Because you have patiently obeyed me despite the persecution, therefore I will protect you from the time of Great Tribulation and temptation, which will come upon the world to test everyone alive. 11Look, I am coming soon! Hold tightly to the little strength you have—so that no one will take away your crown.

12"As for the one who conquers, I will make him a pillar in the temple of my God; he will be secure, and will go out no more; and I will write my God's Name on him, and he will be a citizen in the city of my God—the New Jerusalem, coming down from heaven from my God; and he will have my new Name inscribed upon him.

13"Let all who can hear, listen to what the Spirit is saying to the churches.

14 *Write this letter to the leader of the church in Laodicea:*

"This message is from the one who stands firm, the faithful and true Witness [of all that is or was or evermore shall be], the primeval source of God's creation:

15"I know you well—you are neither hot nor cold; I wish you were one or the other! 16But since you are merely lukewarm, I will spit you out of my mouth!

17"You say, 'I am rich, with everything I want; I don't need a thing!' And you don't realize that spiritually you are wretched and miserable and poor and blind and naked.

18"My advice to you is to buy pure gold from me, gold purified by fire—only then will you truly be rich. And to purchase from me white garments, clean and pure, so you won't be naked and ashamed; and to get medicine from me to heal your eyes and give you back your sight. 19I continually discipline and punish everyone I love; so I must punish you, unless you turn from your indifference and become enthusiastic about the things of God.

20"Look! I have been standing at the door and I am constantly knocking. If anyone hears me calling him and opens the door, I will come in and fellowship with him and he with me. 21I will let every one who conquers sit beside me on my throne, just as I took my place with my Father on his throne when I had conquered. 22Let those who can hear, listen to what the Spirit is saying to the churches."

PSALM 131:1–3

LORD, I am not proud and haughty. I don't think myself better than others. I don't pretend to "know it all." 2I am quiet now before the Lord, just as a child who is weaned from the breast. Yes, my begging has been stilled.

3O Israel, you too should quietly trust in the Lord—now, and always.

PROVERBS FOR TODAY/ 29:23

Pride ends in a fall, while humility brings honor.

DECEMBER 13

OBADIAH 1:1–21

IN a vision the Lord God showed Obadiah the future of the land of Edom.

"A report has come from the Lord," he said, "that God has sent an ambassador to the nations with this message: 'Attention! You are to send your armies against Edom and destroy her!' "

2I will cut you down to size among the nations, Edom, making you small and despised.

3You are proud because you live in those high, inaccessible cliffs. "Who can ever reach us way up here!" you boast. Don't fool yourselves! 4Though you soar as high as eagles, and build your nest among the stars, I will bring you plummeting down, says the Lord.

5Far better it would be for you if thieves had come at night to plunder you—for they would not take everything! Or if your vineyards were robbed of all their fruit—for at least the gleanings would be left! 6Every nook and cranny will be searched and robbed, and every treasure found and taken.

7All your allies will turn against you and help to push you out of your land. They will promise peace while plotting your destruction. Your trusted friends will set traps for you and all your counterstrategy will fail. 8In that day not one wise man will be left in all of Edom! says the Lord. For I will fill the wise men of Edom with stupidity. 9The mightiest soldiers of Teman will be confused, and helpless to prevent the slaughter.

10And why? Because of what you did to your brother Israel. Now your sins will be exposed for all to see; ashamed and defenseless, you will be cut off forever. 11For you deserted Israel in his time of need. You stood aloof, refusing to lift a finger to help him when invaders carried off his wealth and divided Jerusalem among them by lot; you were as one of his enemies.

12You should not have done it. You should not have gloated when they took him far away to foreign lands; you should not have rejoiced in the day of his misfortune; you should not have mocked in his time of need. 13You yourselves went into the land of Israel in the day of his calamity and looted him. You made yourselves rich at his expense. 14You stood at the crossroads and killed those trying to escape; you captured the survivors and returned them to their enemies in that terrible time of his distress.

15The Lord's vengeance will soon fall upon all Gentile nations. As you have done to Israel, so will it be done to you. Your acts will boomerang upon your heads. 16You drank my cup of punishment upon my holy mountain, and the nations round about will drink it, too; yes, drink and stagger back and disappear from history, no longer nations any more.

17But Jerusalem will become a refuge, a way of escape. Israel will reoccupy the land. 18Israel will be a fire that sets the dry fields of Edom aflame. There will be no survivors, for the Lord has spoken.

19Then my people who live in the Negeb shall occupy the hill country of Edom; those living in Judean lowlands shall possess the Philistine plains, and repossess the fields of Ephraim and Samaria. And the people of Benjamin shall possess Gilead.

20The Israeli exiles shall return and occupy the Phoenician coastal strip as far north as Zarephath. Those exiled in Asia Minor shall return to their homeland and conquer the Negeb's outlying villages. 21For deliverers will come to Jerusalem and rule all Edom. And the Lord shall be King!

spoke to me and said, "Come up here and I will show you what must happen in the future!"

2And instantly I was, in spirit, there in heaven and saw—oh, the glory of it!—a throne and someone sitting on it! 3Great bursts of light flashed forth from him as from a glittering diamond, or from a shining ruby, and a rainbow glowing like an emerald encircled his throne. 4Twenty-four smaller thrones surrounded his, with twenty-four Elders sitting on them; all were clothed in white, with golden crowns upon their heads. 5Lightning and thunder issued from the throne, and there were voices in the thunder. Directly in front of his throne were seven lighted lamps representing the seven-fold Spirit of God. 6Spread out before it was a shiny crystal sea. Four Living Beings, dotted front and back with eyes, stood at the throne's four sides. 7The first of these Living Beings was in the form of a lion; the second looked like an ox; the third had the face of a man; and the fourth, the form of an eagle, with wings spread out as though in flight. 8Each of these Living Beings had six wings, and the central sections of their wings were covered with eyes. Day after day and night after night they kept on saying, "Holy, holy, holy, Lord God Almighty—the one who was, and is, and is to come."

9And when the Living Beings gave glory and honor and thanks to the one sitting on the throne, who lives forever and ever, 10the twenty-four Elders fell down before him and worshiped him, the Eternal Living One, and cast their crowns before the throne, singing, 11"O Lord, you are worthy to receive the glory and the honor and the power, for you have created all things. They were created and called into being by your act of will."

REVELATION 4:1–11

THEN as I looked, I saw a door standing open in heaven, and the same voice I had heard before, that sounded like a mighty trumpet blast,

PSALM 132:1–18

LORD, do you remember that time when my heart was so filled with turmoil? 2-5I couldn't rest, I couldn't sleep, thinking how I ought to build a permanent home for the Ark of the Lord, a Temple for the mighty one of Israel. Then I vowed that I would do it; I made a solemn promise to the Lord.

⁶First the Ark was in Ephrathah, then in the distant countryside of Jaar. ⁷But now it will be settled in the Temple, in God's permanent home here on earth. That is where we will go to worship him. ⁸Arise, O Lord, and enter your Temple with the Ark, the symbol of your power.

⁹We will clothe the priests in white, the symbol of all purity. May our nation shout for joy.

¹⁰Do not reject your servant David— the king you chose for your people. ¹¹For you promised me that my son would sit on my throne and succeed me. And surely you will never go back on a promise! ¹²You also promised that if my descendants will obey the terms of your contract with me, then the dynasty of David shall never end.

¹³O Lord, you have chosen Jerusalem as your home: ¹⁴"This is my permanent home where I shall live," you said, "for I have always wanted it this way. ¹⁵I will make this city prosperous and satisfy her poor with food. ¹⁶I will clothe her priests with salvation; her saints shall shout for joy. ¹⁷David's power shall grow, for I have decreed for him a mighty Son. ¹⁸I'll clothe his enemies with shame, but he shall be a glorious King."

PROVERBS FOR TODAY/ 29:24–25

A man who assists a thief must really hate himself! For he knows the consequence but does it anyway. Fear of man is a dangerous trap, but to trust in God means safety.

DECEMBER 14

JONAH 1:1—4:11

THE Lord sent this message to Jonah, the son of Amittai:

²"Go to the great city of Nineveh, and give them this announcement from the Lord: 'I am going to destroy you, for your wickedness rises before me; it smells to highest heaven.' "

³But Jonah was afraid to go and ran away from the Lord. He went down to the seacoast, to the port of Joppa, where he found a ship leaving for Tarshish. He bought a ticket, went on board, and climbed down into the dark hold of the ship to hide there from the Lord.

⁴But as the ship was sailing along, suddenly the Lord flung a terrific wind over the sea, causing a great storm that threatened to send them to the bottom. ⁵Fearing for their lives, the desperate sailors shouted to their gods for help and threw the cargo overboard to lighten the ship. And all this time Jonah was sound asleep down in the hold.

⁶So the captain went down after him. "What do you mean," he roared, "sleeping at a time like this? Get up and cry to your god, and see if he will have mercy on us and save us!"

⁷Then the crew decided to draw straws to see which of them had offended the gods and caused this terrible storm; and Jonah drew the short one.

⁸"What have you done," they asked, "to bring this awful storm upon us? Who are you? What is your work? What country are you from? What is your nationality?"

⁹,¹⁰And he said, "I am a Jew; I worship Jehovah, the God of heaven, who made the earth and sea." Then he told them he was running away from the Lord.

The men were terribly frightened when they heard this. "Oh, why did you do it?" they shouted. ¹¹"What should we do to you to stop the storm?" For it was getting worse and worse.

¹²"Throw me out into the sea," he said, "and it will become calm again. For I know this terrible storm has come because of me."

¹³They tried harder to row the boat ashore, but couldn't make it. The storm was too fierce to fight against. ¹⁴Then they shouted out a prayer to Jehovah, Jonah's God. "O Jehovah," they pleaded, "don't make us die for this man's sin, and don't hold us responsible for his death, for it is not our fault—you have sent this storm upon him for your own good reasons."

¹⁵Then they picked up Jonah and threw him overboard into the raging sea—and the storm stopped!

¹⁶The men stood there in awe before Jehovah, and sacrificed to him and vowed to serve him.

¹⁷Now the Lord had arranged for a great fish to swallow Jonah. And Jonah was inside the fish three days and three nights.

THEN Jonah prayed to the Lord his God from inside the fish:

²"In my great trouble I cried to the Lord and he answered me; from the depths of death I called, and Lord, you heard me! ³You threw me into the ocean depths; I sank down into the floods of waters and was covered by your wild and stormy waves. ⁴Then I said, 'O Lord, you have rejected me and cast me away. How shall I ever again see your holy Temple?'

⁵"I sank beneath the waves, and death was very near. The waters closed above me; the seaweed wrapped itself around my head. ⁶I went down to the bottoms of the mountains that rise from off the ocean floor. I was locked out of life and imprisoned in the land of death. But, O Lord my God, you have snatched me from the yawning jaws of death!

⁷"When I had lost all hope, I turned my thoughts once more to the Lord. And my earnest prayer went to you in your holy Temple. ⁸(Those who worship false gods have turned their backs on all the mercies waiting for them from the Lord!)

⁹"I will never worship anyone but you! For how can I thank you enough for all you have done? I will surely fulfill my promises. For my deliverance comes from the Lord alone."

¹⁰And the Lord ordered the fish to spit up Jonah on the beach, and it did.

THEN the Lord spoke to Jonah again: "Go to that great city, Nineveh," he said, "and warn them of their doom, as I told you to before!"

³So Jonah obeyed, and went to Nineveh. Now Nineveh was a very large city, with many villages around it—so large that it would take three days to walk through it.

⁴·⁵But the very first day when Jonah entered the city and began to preach, the people repented. Jonah shouted to the crowds that gathered around him, "Forty days from now Nineveh will be destroyed!" And they believed him and declared a fast; from the king on down, everyone put on sackcloth—the rough, coarse garments worn at times of mourning.

⁶For when the king of Nineveh heard what Jonah was saying, he stepped down from his throne and laid aside his royal robes and put on sackcloth and sat in ashes. ⁷And the king and his nobles sent this message throughout the city: "Let no one, not even the animals, eat anything at all, nor even drink any water. ⁸Everyone must wear sackcloth and cry mightily to God, and let everyone turn from his evil ways, from his violence and robbing. ⁹Who can tell? Perhaps even yet God will decide to let us live, and will hold back his fierce anger from destroying us."

¹⁰And when God saw that they had put a stop to their evil ways, he aban-

doned his plan to destroy them, and didn't carry it through.

THIS change of plans made Jonah very angry. ²He complained to the Lord about it: "This is exactly what I thought you'd do, Lord, when I was there in my own country and you first told me to come here. That's why I ran away to Tarshish. For I knew you were a gracious God, merciful, slow to get angry, and full of kindness; I knew how easily you could cancel your plans for destroying these people.

³"Please kill me, Lord; I'd rather be dead than alive [when nothing that I told them happens]."

⁴Then the Lord said, "Is it right to be *angry* about *this?*"

⁵So Jonah went out and sat sulking on the east side of the city, and he made a leafy shelter to shade him as he waited there to see if anything would happen to the city. ⁶And when the leaves of the shelter withered in the heat, the Lord arranged for a vine to grow up quickly and spread its broad leaves over Jonah's head to shade him. This made him comfortable and very grateful.

⁷But God also prepared a worm! The next morning the worm ate through the stem of the plant, so that it withered away and died.

⁸Then, when the sun was hot, God ordered a scorching east wind to blow on Jonah, and the sun beat down upon his head until he grew faint and wished to die. For he said, "Death is better than this!"

⁹And God said to Jonah, "Is it right for you to be angry because the plant died?"

"Yes," Jonah said, "it is; it is right for me to be angry enough to die!"

¹⁰Then the Lord said, "You feel sorry for yourself when your shelter is destroyed, though you did no work to put it there, and it is, at best, short-lived. ¹¹And why shouldn't I feel sorry for a great city like Nineveh with its 120,000 people in utter spiritual darkness, and all its cattle?"

AND I saw a scroll in the right hand of the one who was sitting on the throne, a scroll with writing on the inside and on the back, and sealed with seven seals. ²A mighty angel with a loud voice was shouting out this question: "Who is worthy to break the seals on this scroll, and to unroll it?" ³But no one in all heaven or earth or from among the dead was permitted to open and read it.

⁴Then I wept with disappointment because no one anywhere was worthy; no one could tell us what it said.

⁵But one of the twenty-four Elders said to me, "Stop crying, for look! The Lion of the tribe of Judah, the Root of David, has conquered, and proved himself worthy to open the scroll and to break its seven seals."

⁶I looked and saw a Lamb standing there before the twenty-four Elders, in front of the throne and the Living Beings, and on the Lamb were wounds that once had caused his death. He had seven horns and seven eyes, which represent the seven-fold Spirit of God, sent out into every part of the world. ⁷He stepped forward and took the scroll from the right hand of the one sitting upon the throne. ⁸And as he took the scroll, the twenty-four Elders fell down before the Lamb, each with a harp and golden vials filled with incense—the prayers of God's people!

⁹They were singing him a new song with these words: "You are worthy to take the scroll and break its seals and open it; for you were slain, and your blood has bought people from every nation as gifts for God. ¹⁰And you have gathered them into a kingdom and made them priests of our God; they shall reign upon the earth."

¹¹Then in my vision I heard the singing of millions of angels surrounding the throne and the Living Beings and the Elders: ¹²"The Lamb is worthy" (loudly they sang it!) "—the Lamb who was slain. He is worthy to receive the power,

and the riches, and the wisdom, and the strength, and the honor, and the glory, and the blessing."

13And then I heard everyone in heaven and earth, and from the dead beneath the earth and in the sea, exclaiming, "The blessing and the honor and the glory and the power belong to the one sitting on the throne, and to the Lamb forever and ever." 14And the four Living Beings kept saying, "Amen!" And the twenty-four Elders fell down and worshiped him.

PSALM 133:1–3

HOW wonderful it is, how pleasant, when brothers live in harmony! 2For harmony is as precious as the fragrant anointing oil that was poured over Aaron's head, and ran down onto his beard, and onto the border of his robe. 3Harmony is as refreshing as the dew on Mount Hermon, on the mountains of Israel. And God has pronounced this eternal blessing on Jerusalem, even life forevermore.

PROVERBS FOR TODAY/ 29:26–27

Do you want justice? Don't fawn on the judge, but ask the Lord for it! The good hate the badness of the wicked. The wicked hate the goodness of the good.

DECEMBER 15

MICAH 1:1—4:13

THESE *are messages from the Lord to Micah, who lived in the town of Moresheth during the reigns of King Jotham, King Ahaz, and King Hezekiah, all kings of Judah. The messages were addressed to both Samaria and Judah, and came to Micah in the form of visions.*

2Attention! Let all the peoples of the world listen. For the Lord in his holy Temple has made accusations against you!

3Look! He is coming! He leaves his throne in heaven and comes to earth, walking on the mountaintops. 4They melt beneath his feet, and flow into the valleys like wax in fire, like water pouring down a hill.

5And why is this happening? Because of the sins of Israel and Judah. What sins? The idolatry and oppression centering in the capital cities, Samaria and Jerusalem!

6Therefore the entire city of Samaria will crumble into a heap of rubble, and become an open field, her streets plowed up for planting grapes! The Lord will tear down her wall and her forts, exposing their foundations, and pour their stones into the valleys below. 7All her carved images will be smashed to pieces; her ornate idol temples, built with the gifts of worshipers, will all be burned.

8I will wail and lament, howling as a jackal, mournful as an ostrich crying across the desert sands at night. I will walk naked and barefoot in sorrow and shame; 9for my people's wound is far too deep to heal. The Lord stands ready at Jerusalem's gates to punish her. 10Woe to the city of Gath. Weep, men of Bakah. In Beth-le-aphrah roll in the dust in your anguish and shame. 11There go the people of Shaphir, led away as slaves—stripped, naked and ashamed. The people of Zaanan dare not show themselves outside their walls. The foundations of Beth-ezel are swept away—the very ground on which it stood. 12The people of Maroth vainly hope for better days, but only bitterness awaits them as the Lord stands poised against Jerusalem.

¹³Quick! Use your swiftest chariots and flee, O people of Lachish, for you were the first of the cities of Judah to follow Israel in her sin of idol worship. Then all the cities of the south began to follow your example.

¹⁴Write off Moresheth of Gath; there is no hope of saving her. The town of Achzib has deceived the kings of Israel, for she promised help she cannot give. ¹⁵You people of Mareshah will be a prize to your enemies. They will penetrate to Adullum, the "Pride of Israel."

¹⁶Weep, weep for your little ones. For they are snatched away and you will never see them again. They have gone as slaves to distant lands. Shave your heads in sorrow.

WOE to you who lie awake at night, plotting wickedness; you rise at dawn to carry out your schemes; because you can, you do. ²You want a certain piece of land, or someone else's house (though it is all he has); you take it by fraud and threats and violence.

³But the Lord God says, I will reward your evil with evil; nothing can stop me; never again will you be proud and haughty after I am through with you. ⁴Then your enemies will taunt you and mock your dirge of despair: "We are finished, ruined. God has confiscated our land and sent us far away, and given what is ours to others." ⁵Others will set your boundaries then. "The People of the Lord" will live where they are sent.

⁶"Don't say such things," the people say. "Don't harp on things like that. It's disgraceful, that sort of talk. Such evils surely will not come our way."

⁷Is that the right reply for you to make, O House of Jacob? Do you think the Spirit of the Lord likes to talk to you so roughly? No! His threats are for your good, to get you on the path again.

⁸Yet to this very hour my people rise against me. For you steal the shirts right off the backs of those who trusted you, who walk in peace.

⁹You have driven out the widows from their homes, and stripped their children of every God-given right. ¹⁰Up! Begone! This is no more your land and home, for you have filled it with sin and it will vomit you out.

¹¹"I'll preach to you the joys of wine and drink"—that is the kind of drunken, lying prophet that you like!

¹²The time will come, O Israel, when I will gather you—all that are left—and bring you together again like sheep in a fold, like a flock in a pasture—a noisy, happy crowd. ¹³The Messiah will lead you out of exile and bring you through the gates of your cities of captivity, back to your own land. Your King will go before you—the Lord leads on.

LISTEN, you leaders of Israel—you are supposed to know right from wrong, ²yet you are the very ones who hate good and love evil; you skin my people and strip them to the bone.

³You devour them, flog them, break their bones, and chop them up like meat for the cooking pot— ⁴and then you plead with the Lord for his help in times of trouble! Do you really expect him to listen? He will look the other way! ⁵You false prophets! You who lead his people astray! You who cry "Peace" to those who give you food, and threaten those who will not pay!

This is God's message to you: ⁶The night will close about you and cut off all your visions; darkness will cover you, with never a word from God. The sun will go down upon you, and your day will end. ⁷Then at last you will cover your faces in shame, and admit that your messages were not from God.

⁸But as for me, I am filled with power, with the Spirit of the Lord, fearlessly announcing God's punishment on Israel for her sins.

⁹Listen to me, you leaders of Israel who hate justice and love unfairness, ¹⁰and fill Jerusalem with murder and sin of every kind— ¹¹you leaders who take bribes; you priests and prophets who won't preach and prophesy until you're paid. (And yet you fawn upon the Lord and say, "All is well—the Lord is here

*"The Savior—yes, the Messiah, the Lord—
has been born tonight in Bethlehem!"*
   Luke 2:11

"Let the heavens be glad, the earth rejoice."
    Psalm 96:11

"I will praise you, my God and King, and bless your name each day and forever."
Psalm 145:1-2

among us. No harm can come to us.")
¹²It is because of you that Jerusalem will be plowed like a field, and become a heap of rubble; the mountaintop where the Temple stands will be overgrown with brush.

BUT in the last days Mount Zion will be the most renowned of all the mountains of the world, praised by all nations; people from all over the world will make pilgrimages there.

²"Come," they will say to one another, "let us visit the mountain of the Lord, and see the Temple of the God of Israel; he will tell us what to do, and we will do it." For in those days the whole world will be ruled by the Lord from Jerusalem! He will issue his laws and announce his decrees from there.

³He will arbitrate among the nations, and dictate to strong nations far away. They will beat their swords into plowshares and their spears into pruninghooks; nations shall no longer fight each other, for all war will end. There will be universal peace, and all the military academies and training camps will be closed down.

⁴Everyone will live quietly in his own home in peace and prosperity, for there will be nothing to fear. The Lord himself has promised this. ⁵(Therefore we will follow the Lord our God forever and ever, even though all the nations around us worship idols!)

⁶In that coming day, the Lord says that he will bring back his punished people—sick and lame and dispossessed— ⁷and make them strong again in their own land, a mighty nation, and the Lord himself shall be their King from Mount Zion forever. ⁸O Jerusalem—the Watchtower of God's people—your royal might and power will come back to you again, just as before.

⁹But for now, now you scream in terror. Where is your king to lead you? He is dead! Where are your wise men? All are gone! Pain has gripped you like a woman in labor. ¹⁰Writhe and groan in your terrible pain, O people of Zion, for you must leave this city and live in the fields; you will be sent far away into exile in Babylon. But there I will rescue you and free you from the grip of your enemies.

¹¹True, many nations have gathered together against you, calling for your blood, eager to destroy you. ¹²But they do not know my thoughts nor understand my plan, for the time will come when the Lord will gather together the enemies of his people like sheaves upon the threshing floor, ¹³helpless before Israel.

Rise, thresh, O daughter of Zion; I will give you horns of iron and hoofs of brass and you will trample to pieces many people, and you will give their wealth as offerings to the Lord, the Lord of all the earth.

REVELATION 6:1–17

AS I watched, the Lamb broke the first seal and began to unroll the scroll. Then one of the four Living Beings, with a voice that sounded like thunder, said, "Come!"

²I looked, and there in front of me was a white horse. Its rider carried a bow, and a crown was placed upon his head; he rode out to conquer in many battles and win the war.

³Then he unrolled the scroll to the second seal, and broke it open too. And I heard the second Living Being say, "Come!"

⁴This time a red horse rode out. Its rider was given a long sword and the authority to banish peace and bring anarchy to the earth; war and killing broke out everywhere.

⁵When he had broken the third seal, I heard the third Living Being say, "Come!" And I saw a black horse, with its rider holding a pair of balances in his hand. ⁶And a voice from among the four Living Beings said, "A loaf of bread for $20, or three pounds of barley flour, but there is no olive oil or wine."

⁷And when the fourth seal was broken, I heard the fourth Living Being say, "Come!" ⁸And now I saw a pale horse,

and its rider's name was Death. And there followed after him another horse whose rider's name was Hell. They were given control of one-fourth of the earth, to kill with war and famine and disease and wild animals.

9And when he broke open the fifth seal, I saw an altar, and underneath it all the souls of those who had been martyred for preaching the Word of God and for being faithful in their witnessing. 10They called loudly to the Lord and said, "O Sovereign Lord, holy and true, how long will it be before you judge the people of the earth for what they've done to us? When will you avenge our blood against those living on the earth?" 11White robes were given to each of them, and they were told to rest a little longer until their other brothers, fellow servants of Jesus, had been martyred on the earth and joined them.

12I watched as he broke the sixth seal, and there was a vast earthquake; and the sun became dark like black cloth, and the moon was blood-red. 13Then the stars of heaven appeared to be falling to earth—like green fruit from fig trees buffeted by mighty winds. 14And the starry heavens disappeared as though rolled up like a scroll and taken away; and every mountain and island shook and shifted. 15The kings of the earth, and world leaders and rich men, and high-ranking military officers, and all men great and small, slave and free, hid themselves in the caves and rocks of the mountains, 16and cried to the mountains to crush them. "Fall on us," they pleaded, "and hide us from the face of the one sitting on the throne, and from the anger of the Lamb, 17because the great day of their anger has come, and who can survive it?"

PSALM 134:1–3

O H, bless the Lord, you who serve him as watchmen in the Temple every night. 2Lift your hands in holiness and bless the Lord.

3The Lord bless you from Zion—the Lord who made heaven and earth.

PROVERBS FOR TODAY/ 30:1–4

These are the messages of Agur, son of Jakeh addressed to Ithiel and Ucal: *I am tired out, O God, and ready to die. I am too stupid even to call myself a human being! I cannot understand man, let alone God. Who else but God goes back and forth to heaven? Who else holds the wind in his fists, and wraps up the oceans in his cloak? Who but God has created the world? If there is any other, what is his name—and his Son's name—if you know it?*

DECEMBER 16

MICAH 5:1—7:20

M OBILIZE! The enemy lays siege to Jerusalem! With a rod they shall strike the Judge of Israel on the face.

2O Bethlehem Ephrathah, you are but a small Judean village, yet you will be the birthplace of my King who is alive from everlasting ages past! 3God will abandon his people to their enemies until she who is to give birth has her son; then at last his fellow countrymen—the exile remnants of Israel—will rejoin their brethren in their own land.

4And he shall stand and feed his flock in the strength of the Lord, in the majesty of the name of the Lord his God, and his people shall remain there undisturbed, for he will be greatly honored all around the world. 5He will be our Peace. And when the Assyrian invades our land and marches across our hills, he will appoint seven shepherds to watch over us, eight princes to lead us. 6They will rule Assyria with drawn swords and enter the gates of the land of Nimrod. He will deliver us from the Assyrians when they invade our land.

7Then the nation of Israel will refresh the world like a gentle dew or the welcome showers of rain, 8and Israel will be as strong as a lion. The nations will be like helpless sheep before her! 9She will stand up to her foes; all her enemies will be wiped out.

10At that same time, says the Lord, I will destroy all the weapons you depend on, 11and tear down your walls and demolish the defenses of your cities. 12I will put an end to all witchcraft—there will be no more fortune-tellers to consult— 13and destroy all your idols. Never again will you worship what you have made, 14and I will abolish the heathen shrines from among you, and destroy the cities where your idol temples stand.

15And I will pour out my vengeance upon the nations who refuse to obey me.

LISTEN to what the Lord is saying to his people:

Stand up and state your case against me. Let the mountains and hills be called to witness your complaint.

2And now, O mountains, listen to the Lord's complaint! For he has a case against his people Israel! He will prosecute them to the full. 3O my people, what have I done that makes you turn away from me? Tell me why your patience is exhausted! Answer me! 4For I brought you out of Egypt, and cut your chains of slavery. I gave you Moses, Aaron, and Miriam to help you.

5Don't you remember, O my people, how Balak, king of Moab, tried to destroy you through the curse of Balaam, son of Beor, but I made him bless you in-

stead? That is the kindness I showed you again and again. Have you no memory at all of what happened at Acacia and Gilgal, and how I blessed you there?

6"How can we make up to you for what we've done?" you ask. "Shall we bow before the Lord with offerings of yearling calves?"

Oh, no! 7For if you offered him thousands of rams and ten thousands of rivers of olive oil—would that please him? Would he be satisfied? If you sacrificed your oldest child, would that make him glad? Then would he forgive your sins? Of course not!

8No, he has told you what he wants, and this is all it is: *to be fair and just and merciful, and to walk humbly with your God.* 9The Lord's voice calls out to all Jerusalem—listen to the Lord if you are wise! The armies of destruction are coming; the Lord is sending them.

10For your sins are very great—is there to be no end of getting rich by cheating? The homes of the wicked are full of ungodly treasures and lying scales. 11Shall I say "Good!" to all your merchants with their bags of false, deceitful weights? How could God be just while saying that? 12Your rich men are wealthy through extortion and violence; your citizens are so used to lying that their tongues can't tell the truth!

13Therefore I will wound you! I will make your hearts miserable for all your sins. 14You will eat but never have enough; hunger pangs and emptiness will still remain. And though you try and try to save your money, it will come to nothing at the end, and what little you succeed in storing up I'll give to those who conquer you! 15You will plant crops but not harvest them; you will press out the oil from the olives, and not get enough to anoint yourself! You will trample the grapes, but get no juice to make your wine.

16The only commands you keep are those of Omri; the only example you follow is that of Ahab! Therefore I will make an awesome example of you—I will destroy you. I will make you the laughingstock of the world; all who see you will snicker and sneer!

WOE is me! It is as hard to find an honest man as grapes and figs when harvest days are over. Not a cluster to eat, not a single early fig, however much I long for it! The good men have disappeared from the earth; not one fairminded man is left. They are all murderers, turning against even their own brothers. ³They go at their evil deeds with both hands, and how skilled they are in using them! The governor and judge alike demand bribes. The rich man pays them off and tells them whom to ruin. Justice is twisted between them. ⁴Even the best of them are prickly as briars; the straightest is more crooked than a hedge of thorns. But your judgment day is coming swiftly now; your time of punishment is almost here; confusion, destruction, and terror will be yours.

⁵Don't trust anyone, not your best friend—not even your wife! ⁶For the son despises his father; the daughter defies her mother; the bride curses her mother-in-law. Yes, a man's enemies will be found in his own home.

⁷As for me, I look to the Lord for his help; I wait for God to save me; he will hear me. ⁸Do not rejoice against me, O my enemy, for though I fall, I will rise again! When I sit in darkness, the Lord himself will be my Light. ⁹I will be patient while the Lord punishes me, for I have sinned against him; then he will defend me from my enemies, and punish them for all the evil they have done to me. God will bring me out of my darkness into the light, and I will see his goodness. ¹⁰Then my enemy will see that God is for me, and be ashamed for taunting me, "Where is that God of yours?" Now with my own eyes I see them trampled down like mud in the street.

¹¹Your cities, people of God, will be rebuilt, much larger and more prosperous than before. ¹²Citizens of many lands will come and honor you—from Assyria to Egypt, and from Egypt to the Eu-

phrates, from sea to sea and from distant hills and mountains.

¹³But first comes terrible destruction to Israel for the great wickedness of her people. ¹⁴O Lord, come and rule your people; lead your flock; make them live in peace and prosperity; let them enjoy the fertile pastures of Bashan and Gilead as they did long ago.

¹⁵"Yes," replies the Lord, "I will do mighty miracles for you, like those when I brought you out of slavery in Egypt. ¹⁶All the world will stand amazed at what I will do for you, and be embarrassed at their puny might. They will stand in silent awe, deaf to all around them." ¹⁷They will see what snakes they are, lowly as worms crawling from their holes. They will come trembling out from their fortresses to meet the Lord our God. They will fear him; they will stand in awe.

¹⁸Where is another God like you, who pardons the sins of the survivors among his people? You cannot stay angry with your people, for you love to be merciful. ¹⁹Once again you will have compassion on us. You will tread our sins beneath your feet; you will throw them into the depths of the ocean! ²⁰You will bless us as you promised Jacob long ago. You will set your love upon us, as you promised our father Abraham!

REVELATION 7:1–17

THEN I saw four angels standing at the four corners of the earth, holding back the four winds from blowing, so that not a leaf rustled in the trees, and the ocean became as smooth as glass. ²And I saw another angel coming from the east, carrying the Great Seal of the Living God. And he shouted out to those four angels who had been given power to injure earth and sea, ³"Wait! Don't do anything yet—hurt neither earth nor sea nor trees—until we have placed the Seal of God upon the foreheads of his servants."

⁴⁻⁸How many were given this mark? I heard the number—it was 144,000; out

of all twelve tribes of Israel, as listed here:

Judah	12,000
Reuben	12,000
Gad	12,000
Asher	12,000
Naphtali	12,000
Manasseh	12,000
Simeon	12,000
Levi	12,000
Issachar	12,000
Zebulun	12,000
Joseph	12,000
Benjamin	12,000

9After this I saw a vast crowd, too great to count, from all nations and provinces and languages, standing in front of the throne and before the Lamb, clothed in white, with palm branches in their hands. 10And they were shouting with a mighty shout, "Salvation comes from our God upon the throne, and from the Lamb."

11And now all the angels were crowding around the throne and around the Elders and the four Living Beings, and falling face down before the throne and worshiping God. 12"Amen!" they said. "Blessing, and glory, and wisdom, and thanksgiving, and honor, and power, and might, be to our God forever and forever. Amen!"

13Then one of the twenty-four Elders asked me, "Do you know who these are, who are clothed in white, and where they come from?"

14"No, sir," I replied. "Please tell me."

"These are the ones coming out of the Great Tribulation," he said; "they washed their robes and whitened them by the blood of the Lamb. 15That is why they are here before the throne of God, serving him day and night in his temple. The one sitting on the throne will shelter them; 16they will never be hungry again, nor thirsty, and they will be fully protected from the scorching noontime heat. 17For the Lamb standing in front of the throne will feed them and be their Shepherd and lead them to the springs of the Water of Life. And God will wipe their tears away."

PSALM 135:1–21

Hallelujah! 2Yes, let his people praise him as they stand in his Temple courts. 3Praise the Lord because he is so good; sing to his wonderful name. 4For the Lord has chosen Israel as his personal possession.

5I know the greatness of the Lord— that he is greater far than any other god. 6He does whatever pleases him throughout all of heaven and earth, and in the deepest seas. 7He makes mists rise throughout the earth and sends the lightning to bring down the rain; and sends the winds from his treasuries. 8He destroyed the eldest child in each Egyptian home, along with the firstborn of the flocks. 9He did great miracles in Egypt before Pharaoh and all his people. 10He smote great nations, slaying mighty kings— 11Sihon, king of Amorites; and Og, the king of Bashan; and the kings of Canaan— 12and gave their land as an eternal gift to his people Israel.

13O Jehovah, your name endures forever; your fame is known to every generation. 14For Jehovah will vindicate his people, and have compassion on his servants.

15The heathen worship idols of gold and silver, made by men— 16idols with speechless mouths and sightless eyes 17and ears that cannot hear; they cannot even breathe. 18Those who make them become like them! And so do all who trust in them!

19O Israel, bless Jehovah! High priests of Aaron, bless his name. 20O Levite priests, bless the Lord Jehovah! Oh, bless his name, all of you who trust and reverence him. 21All people of Jerusalem, praise the Lord, for he lives here in Jerusalem. Hallelujah!

PROVERBS FOR TODAY/ 30:5–6

Every word of God proves true. He defends all who come to him for protection. Do not add to his words, lest he rebuke you, and you be found a liar.

NAHUM 1:1—3:19

THIS is the vision God gave to Nahum, who lived in Elkosh, concerning the impending doom of Nineveh:

2God is jealous over those he loves; that is why he takes vengeance on those who hurt them. He furiously destroys their enemies. 3He is slow in getting angry, but when aroused, his power is incredible, and he does not easily forgive. He shows his power in the terrors of the cyclone and the raging storms; clouds are billowing dust beneath his feet! 4At his command the oceans and rivers become dry sand; the lush pastures of Bashan and Carmel fade away; the green forests of Lebanon wilt. 5In his presence mountains quake and hills melt; the earth crumbles and its people are destroyed.

6Who can stand before an angry God? His fury is like fire; the mountains tumble down before his anger.

7The Lord is good. When trouble comes, he is the place to go! And he knows everyone who trusts in him! 8But he sweeps away his enemies with an overwhelming flood; he pursues them all night long.

9What are you thinking of, Nineveh, to defy the Lord? He will stop you with one blow; he won't need to strike again. 10He tosses his enemies into the fire like a tangled mass of thorns. They burst into flames like straw. 11Who is this king of yours who dares to plot against the Lord? 12But the Lord is not afraid of him! "Though he build his army millions strong," the Lord declares, "it will vanish.

"O my people, I have punished you enough! 13Now I will break your chains and release you from the yoke of slavery to this Assyrian king." 14And to the king he says, "I have ordered an end to your dynasty; your sons will never sit upon your throne. And I will destroy your gods and temples, and I will bury you! For how you stink with sin!"

15See, the messengers come running down the mountains with glad news: "The invaders have been wiped out and we are safe!" O Judah, proclaim a day of thanksgiving, and worship only the Lord, as you have vowed. For this enemy from Nineveh will never come again. He is cut off forever; he will never be seen again.

NINEVEH, you are finished! You are already surrounded by enemy armies! Sound the alarm! Man the ramparts! Muster your defenses, full force, and keep a sharp watch for the enemy attack to begin! 2For the land of the people of God lies empty and broken after your attacks but the Lord will restore their honor and power again!

3Shields flash red in the sunlight! The attack begins! See their scarlet uniforms! See their glittering chariots moving forward side by side, pulled by prancing steeds! 4Your own chariots race recklessly along the streets and through the squares, darting like lightning, gleaming like torches. 5The king shouts for his officers; they stumble in their haste, rushing to the walls to set up their defenses. 6But too late! The river gates are open! The enemy has entered! The palace is in panic!

7The queen of Nineveh is brought out naked to the streets, and led away, a slave, with all her maidens weeping after her; listen to them mourn like doves, and beat their breasts! 8Nineveh is like a leaking water tank! Her soldiers slip away, deserting her; she cannot hold them back. "Stop, stop," she shouts, but they keep on running.

9Loot the silver! Loot the gold! There seems to be no end of treasures. Her vast, uncounted wealth is stripped away. 10Soon the city is an empty shambles; hearts melt in horror; knees quake; her people stand aghast, pale-faced and trembling.

11Where now is that great Nineveh, lion of the nations, full of fight and boldness, where even the old and feeble, as well as the young and tender, lived unafraid?

12O Nineveh, once mighty lion! You crushed your enemies to feed your children and your wives, and filled your city and your homes with captured goods and slaves.

13But now the Lord Almighty has turned against you. He destroys your weapons. Your chariots stand there, silent and unused. Your finest youth lie dead. Never again will you bring back slaves from conquered nations; never again will you rule the earth.

WOE to Nineveh, City of Blood, full of lies, crammed with plunder. 2Listen! Hear the crack of the whips as the chariots rush forward against her, wheels rumbling, horses' hoofs pounding, and chariots clattering as they bump wildly through the streets! 3See the flashing swords and glittering spears in the upraised arms of the cavalry! The dead are lying in the streets—bodies, heaps of bodies, everywhere. Men stumble over them, scramble to their feet, and fall again.

4All this because Nineveh sold herself to the enemies of God. The beautiful and faithless city, mistress of deadly charms, enticed the nations with her beauty, then taught them all to worship her false gods, bewitching people everywhere.

5"No wonder I stand against you," says the Lord Almighty; "and now all the earth will see your nakedness and shame. 6I will cover you with filth and show the world how really vile you are." 7All who see you will shrink back in horror: "Nineveh lies in utter ruin." Yet no one anywhere regrets your fate!

8Are you any better than Thebes, straddling the Nile, protected on all sides by the river? 9Ethiopia and the whole land of Egypt were her mighty allies, and she could call on them for infinite assistance, as well as Put and Libya. 10Yet Thebes fell and her people were led off as slaves; her babies were dashed to death against the stones of the streets. Soldiers drew straws to see who would get her officers as servants. All her leaders were bound in chains.

11Nineveh, too, will stagger like a drunkard and hide herself in fear. 12All your forts will fall. They will be devoured like first-ripe figs that fall into the mouths of those who shake the trees. 13Your troops will be weak and helpless as women. The gates of your land will be opened wide to the enemy and set on fire and burned. 14Get ready for the siege! Store up water! Strengthen the forts! Prepare many bricks for repairing your walls! Go into the pits to trample the clay, and pack it in the molds!

15But in the middle of your preparations, the fire will devour you; the sword will cut you down; the enemy will consume you like young locusts that eat up everything before them. There is no escape, though you multiply like grasshoppers. 16Merchants, numerous as stars, filled your city with vast wealth, but your enemies swarm like locusts and carry it away. 17Your princes and officials crowd together like grasshoppers in the hedges in the cold, but all of them will flee away and disappear, like locusts when the sun comes up and warms the earth.

18O Assyrian king, your princes lie dead in the dust; your people are scattered across the mountains; there is no shepherd now to gather them. 19There is no healing for your wound—it is far too deep to cure. All who hear your fate will clap their hands for joy, for where can one be found who has not suffered from your cruelty?

REVELATION 8:1–13

WHEN the Lamb had broken the seventh seal, there was silence throughout all heaven for what seemed like half an hour. 2And I saw the seven angels that stand before God, and they were given seven trumpets.

3Then another angel with a golden censer came and stood at the altar; and a great quantity of incense was given to him to mix with the prayers of God's people, to offer upon the golden altar before the throne. 4And the perfume of the incense mixed with prayers ascended up to God from the altar where the angel had poured them out.

5Then the angel filled the censer with fire from the altar and threw it down upon the earth; and thunder crashed and rumbled, lightning flashed, and there was a terrible earthquake.

6Then the seven angels with the seven trumpets prepared to blow their mighty blasts.

7The first angel blew his trumpet, and hail and fire mixed with blood were thrown down upon the earth. One-third of the earth was set on fire so that one-third of the trees were burned, and all the green grass.

8,9Then the second angel blew his trumpet, and what appeared to be a huge burning mountain was thrown into the sea, destroying a third of all the ships; and a third of the sea turned red as blood; and a third of the fish were killed.

10The third angel blew, and a great flaming star fell from heaven upon a third of the rivers and springs. 11The star was called "Bitterness" because it poisoned a third of all the water on the earth and many people died.

12The fourth angel blew his trumpet and immediately a third of the sun was blighted and darkened, and a third of the moon and the stars, so that the daylight was dimmed by a third, and the nighttime darkness deepened. 13As I watched, I saw a solitary eagle flying through the heavens crying loudly, "Woe, woe, woe to the people of the earth because of the terrible things that will soon happen when the three remaining angels blow their trumpets."

OH, give thanks to the Lord, for he is good; his lovingkindness continues forever.

2Give thanks to the God of gods, for his lovingkindness continues forever. 3Give thanks to the Lord of lords, for his lovingkindness continues forever. 4Praise him who alone does mighty miracles, for his lovingkindness continues forever. 5Praise him who made the heavens, for his lovingkindness continues forever. 6Praise him who planted the water within the earth, for his lovingkindness continues forever. 7Praise him who made the heavenly lights, for his lovingkindness continues forever: 8the sun to rule the day, for his lovingkindness continues forever; 9and the moon and stars at night, for his lovingkindness continues forever. 10Praise the God who smote the firstborn of Egypt, for his lovingkindness to Israel continues forever.

11,12He brought them out with mighty power and upraised fist to strike their enemies, for his lovingkindness to Israel continues forever. 13Praise the Lord who opened the Red Sea to make a path before them, for his lovingkindness continues forever, 14and led them safely through, for his lovingkindness continues forever— 15but drowned Pharaoh's army in the sea, for his lovingkindness to Israel continues forever.

16Praise him who led his people through the wilderness, for his lovingkindness continues forever. 17Praise him who saved his people from the power of mighty kings, for his lovingkindness continues forever, 18and killed famous kings who were their enemies, for his lovingkindness to Israel continues forever: 19Sihon, king of Amorites—for God's lovingkindness to Israel continues forever— 20and Og, king of Bashan—for his lovingkindness to Israel continues forever. 21God gave the land of these kings to Israel as a gift forever, for his lovingkindness to Israel continues forever; 22yes, a permanent gift to his servant Israel, for his lovingkindness continues forever.

²³He remembered our utter weakness, for his lovingkindness continues forever. ²⁴And saved us from our foes, for his lovingkindness continues forever.

²⁵He gives food to every living thing, for his lovingkindness continues forever. ²⁶Oh, give thanks to the God of heaven, for his lovingkindness continues forever.

PROVERBS FOR TODAY/ 30:7–9

O God, I beg two favors from you before I die: First, help me never to tell a lie. Second, give me neither poverty nor riches! Give me just enough to satisfy my needs! For if I grow rich, I may become content without God. And if I am too poor, I may steal, and thus insult God's holy name.

DECEMBER 18

HABAKKUK 1:1—3:19

THIS is the message that came to the prophet Habakkuk in a vision from God:

²O Lord, how long must I call for help before you will listen? I shout to you in vain; there is no answer. "Help! Murder!" I cry, but no one comes to save. ³Must I forever see this sin and sadness all around me?

Wherever I look there is oppression and bribery and men who love to argue and to fight. ⁴The law is not enforced and there is no justice given in the courts, for the wicked far outnumber the righteous, and bribes and trickery prevail.

⁵The Lord replied: "Look, and be amazed! You will be astounded at what I am about to do! For I am going to do something in your own lifetime that you will have to see to believe. ⁶I am raising a new force on the world scene, the Chaldeans, a cruel and violent nation who will march across the world and conquer it. ⁷They are notorious for their cruelty. They do as they like, and no one can interfere. ⁸Their horses are swifter than leopards. They are a fierce people, more fierce than wolves at dusk.

Their cavalry move proudly forward from a distant land; like eagles they come swooping down to pounce upon their prey. ⁹All opposition melts away before the terror of their presence. They collect captives like sand.

¹⁰"They scoff at kings and princes, and scorn their forts. They simply heap up dirt against their walls and capture them! ¹¹They sweep past like wind and are gone, but their guilt is deep, for they claim their power is from their gods."

¹²O Lord my God, my Holy One, you who are eternal—is your plan in all of this to wipe us out? Surely not! O God our Rock, you have decreed the rise of these Chaldeans to chasten and correct us for our awful sins. ¹³We are wicked, but they far more! Will you, who cannot allow sin in any form, stand idly by while they swallow us up? Should you be silent while the wicked destroy those who are better than they?

¹⁴Are we but fish, to be caught and killed? Are we but creeping things that have no leader to defend them from their foes? ¹⁵Must we be strung up on their hooks and dragged out in their nets, while they rejoice? ¹⁶Then they will wor-

ship their nets and burn incense before them! "These are the gods who make us rich," they'll say.

17Will you let them get away with this forever? Will they succeed forever in their heartless wars?

I will climb my watchtower now, and wait to see what answer God will give to my complaint.

2And the Lord said to me, "Write my answer on a billboard, large and clear, so that anyone can read it at a glance and rush to tell the others. 3But these things I plan won't happen right away. Slowly, steadily, surely, the time approaches when the vision will be fulfilled. If it seems slow, do not despair, for these things will surely come to pass. Just be patient! They will not be overdue a single day!

4"Note this: Wicked men trust themselves alone [as these Chaldeans do], and fail; but the righteous man trusts in me, and lives! 5What's more, these arrogant Chaldeans are betrayed by all their wine, for it is treacherous. In their greed they have collected many nations, but like death and hell, they are never satisfied. 6The time is coming when all their captives will taunt them, saying: 'You robbers! At last justice has caught up with you! Now you will get your just deserts for your oppression and extortion!'

7"Suddenly your debtors will rise up in anger and turn on you and take all you have, while you stand trembling and helpless. 8You have ruined many nations; now they will ruin you. You murderers! You have filled the countryside with lawlessness and all the cities too.

9"Woe to you for getting rich by evil means, attempting to live beyond the reach of danger. 10By the murders you commit, you have shamed your name and forfeited your lives. 11The very stones in the walls of your homes cry out against you, and the beams in the ceilings echo what they say.

12"Woe to you who build cities with money gained from murdering and robbery! 13Has not the Lord decreed that godless nations' gains will turn to ashes in their hands? They work so hard, but all in vain!

14("The time will come when all the earth is filled, as the waters fill the sea, with an awareness of the glory of the Lord.)

15"Woe to you for making your neighboring lands reel and stagger like drunkards beneath your blows, and then gloating over their nakedness and shame. 16Soon your own glory will be replaced by shame. Drink down God's judgment on yourselves. Stagger and fall! 17You cut down the forests of Lebanon—now you will be cut down! You terrified the wild animals you caught in your traps—now terror will strike you because of all your murdering and violence in cities everywhere.

18"What profit was there in worshiping all your man-made idols? What a foolish lie that they could help! What fools you were to trust what you yourselves had made. 19Woe to those who command their lifeless wooden idols to arise and save them, who call out to the speechless stone to tell them what to do. Can images speak for God? They are overlaid with gold and silver, but there is no breath at all inside!

20"But the Lord is in his holy Temple; let all the earth be silent before him."

THIS is the prayer of triumph that Habakkuk sang before the Lord:

2O Lord, now I have heard your report, and I worship you in awe for the fearful things you are going to do. In this time of our deep need, begin again to help us, as you did in years gone by. Show us your power to save us. In your wrath, remember mercy.

3I see God moving across the deserts from Mount Sinai. His brilliant splendor fills the earth and sky; his glory fills the heavens, and the earth is full of his praise! What a wonderful God he is! 4From his hands flash rays of brilliant light. He rejoices in his awesome power. 5Pestilence marches before him; plague follows close behind. 6He stops; he stands still for a moment, gazing at the earth. Then he shakes the nations, scattering the everlasting mountains and leveling the hills. His power is just the same as always! 7I see the people of Cushan and of Midian in mortal fear.

8,9Was it in anger, Lord, you smote the rivers and parted the sea? Were you displeased with them? No, you were sending your chariots of salvation! All saw your power! Then springs burst forth upon the earth at your command! 10The mountains watched and trembled. Onward swept the raging water. The mighty deep cried out, announcing its surrender to the Lord. 11The lofty sun and moon began to fade, obscured by brilliance from your arrows and the flashing of your glittering spear.

12You marched across the land in awesome anger, and trampled down the nations in your wrath. 13You went out to save your chosen people. You crushed the head of the wicked and laid bare his bones from head to toe. 14You destroyed with their own weapons those who came out like a whirlwind, thinking Israel would be an easy prey.

15Your horsemen marched across the sea; the mighty waters piled high. 16I tremble when I hear all this; my lips quiver with fear. My legs give way beneath me and I shake in terror. I will quietly wait for the day of trouble to come upon the people who invade us.

17Even though the fig trees are all destroyed, and there is neither blossom left nor fruit, and though the olive crops all fail, and the fields lie barren; even if the flocks die in the fields and the cattle barns are empty, 18yet I will rejoice in the Lord; I will be happy in the God of my salvation. 19The Lord God is my Strength, and he will give me the speed of a deer and bring me safely over the mountains.

(*A note to the choir director: When singing this ode, the choir is to be accompanied by stringed instruments.*)

REVELATION 9:1–21

THEN the fifth angel blew his trumpet and I saw one who was fallen to earth from heaven, and to him was given the key to the bottomless pit. 2When he opened it, smoke poured out as though from some huge furnace, and the sun and air were darkened by the smoke.

3Then locusts came from the smoke and descended onto the earth and were given power to sting like scorpions. 4They were told not to hurt the grass or plants or trees, but to attack those people who did not have the mark of God on their foreheads. 5They were not to kill them, but to torture them for five months with agony like the pain of scorpion stings. 6In those days men will try to kill themselves but won't be able to—death will not come. They will long to die—but death will flee away!

7The locusts looked like horses armored for battle. They had what looked like golden crowns on their heads, and their faces looked like men's. 8Their hair was long like women's, and their teeth were those of lions. 9They wore breastplates that seemed to be of iron, and their wings roared like an army of chariots rushing into battle. 10They had stinging tails like scorpions, and their power to hurt, given to them for five months, was in their tails. 11Their king is the Prince of the bottomless pit whose name in Hebrew is Abaddon, and in Greek, Apollyon [and in English, the Destroyer]

12One terror now ends, but there are two more coming!

13The sixth angel blew his trumpet and I heard a voice speaking from the four horns of the golden altar that stands before the throne of God, 14saying to the sixth angel, "Release the four mighty demons held bound at the great River Euphrates." 15They had been kept in readiness for that year and month and day and hour, and now they were turned loose to kill a third of all mankind. 16They led an army of 200,000,000 warriors—I heard an announcement of how many there were.

17,18I saw their horses spread out before me in my vision; their riders wore fiery-red breastplates, though some were sky-blue and others yellow. The horses' heads looked much like lions', and smoke and fire and flaming sulphur billowed from their mouths, killing one-third of all mankind. 19Their power of death was not only in their mouths, but in their tails as well, for their tails were similar to serpents' heads that struck and bit with fatal wounds.

20But the men left alive after these plagues *still refused to worship God!* They would not renounce their demon-worship, nor their idols made of gold and silver, brass, stone, and wood—which neither see nor hear nor walk! 21Neither did they change their mind and attitude about all their murders and witchcraft, their immorality and theft.

PSALM 137:1–9

WEEPING, we sat beside the rivers of Babylon thinking of Jerusalem. 2We have put away our lyres, hanging them upon the branches of the willow trees, 3,4for how can we sing? Yet our captors, our tormentors, demand that we sing for them the happy songs of Zion! 5,6If I forget you, O Jerusalem, let my right hand forget its skill upon the harp. If I fail to love her more than my highest joy, let me never sing again.

7O Jehovah, do not forget what these Edomites did on that day when the armies of Babylon captured Jerusalem. "Raze her to the ground!" they yelled. 8O Babylon, evil beast, you shall be destroyed. Blessed is the man who destroys you as you have destroyed us. 9Blessed is the man who takes your babies and smashes them against the rocks!

PROVERBS FOR TODAY/ 30:10

Never falsely accuse a man to his employer, lest he curse you for your sin.

DECEMBER 19

ZEPHANIAH 1:1—3:20

SUBJECT: a message from the Lord. *To:* Zephaniah (son of Cushi, grandson of Gedaliah, great-grandson of Amariah, and great-great-grandson of Hezekiah). *When:* During the reign of Josiah (son of Amon) king of Judah.

2"I will sweep away everything in all your land," says the Lord. "I will destroy it to the ground. 3I will sweep away both men and animals alike. Mankind and all the idols that he worships—all will vanish. Even the birds of the air and the fish in the sea will perish. 4I will crush Judah and Jerusalem with my fist, and destroy every remnant of those who worship Baal; I will put an end to their idolatrous priests, so that even the memory of them will disappear. 5They go up on their roofs and bow to the sun, moon and stars. They 'follow the Lord,' but worship Molech, too! I will destroy them. 6And I will destroy those who formerly worshiped the Lord, but now no longer do, and those who never loved him and never wanted to."

7Stand in silence in the presence of the Lord. For the awesome Day of his Judgment has come; he has prepared a great slaughter of his people and has chosen their executioners. 8"On that Day of Judgment I will punish the leaders and princes of Judah, and all others wearing heathen clothing. 9Yes, I will punish those who follow heathen customs and who rob and kill to fill their masters' homes with evil gain of violence and fraud. 10A cry of alarm will begin at the farthest gate of Jerusalem, coming closer and closer until the noise of the advancing army reaches the very top of the hill where the city is built.

11"Wail in sorrow, you people of Jerusalem. All your greedy businessmen, all your loan sharks—all will die.

12"I will search with lanterns in Jerusalem's darkest corners to find and punish those who sit contented in their sins, indifferent to God, thinking he will let them alone. 13They are the very ones whose property will be plundered by the enemy, whose homes will be ransacked; they will never have a chance to live in the new homes they have built. They will never drink wine from the vineyards they have planted."

14"That terrible day is near. Swiftly it comes—a day when strong men will weep bitterly. 15It is a day of the wrath of God poured out; it is a day of terrible distress and anguish, a day of ruin and desolation, of darkness, gloom, clouds, blackness, 16trumpet calls and battle cries; down go the walled cities and strongest battlements!

17"I will make you as helpless as a blind man searching for a path, because you have sinned against the Lord; therefore your blood will be poured out into the dust and your bodies will lie there rotting on the ground."

18Your silver and gold will be of no use to you in that day of the Lord's wrath. You cannot ransom yourselves with it. For the whole land will be devoured by the fire of his jealousy. He will make a speedy riddance of all the people of Judah.

GATHER together and pray, you shameless nation, 2while there still is time—before judgment begins, and your opportunity is blown away like chaff; before the fierce anger of the Lord falls and the terrible day of his wrath begins. 3Beg him to save you, all who are humble—all who have tried to obey.

Walk humbly and do what is right; perhaps even yet the Lord will protect you from his wrath in that day of doom.

4Gaza, Ashkelon, Ashdod, Ekron—these Philistine cities, too, will be rooted out and left in desolation. 5And woe to you Philistines living on the coast and in the land of Canaan, for the judgment is against you, too. The Lord will destroy you until not one of you is left. 6The coastland will become a pasture, a place of shepherd camps and folds for sheep.

7There the little remnant of the tribe of Judah will be pastured. They will lie down to rest in the abandoned houses in Ashkelon. For the Lord God will visit his people in kindness and restore their prosperity again.

8"I have heard the taunts of the people of Moab and Ammon, mocking my people and invading their land. 9Therefore as I live," says the Lord Almighty, God of Israel, "Moab and Ammon will be destroyed like Sodom and Gomorrah, and become a place of stinging nettles and salt pits and eternal desolation; those of my people who are left will plunder and possess them." 10They will receive the wages of their pride, for they have scoffed at the people of the Lord Almighty. 11The Lord will do terrible things to them. He will starve out all those gods of foreign powers, and everyone shall worship him, each in his own land throughout the world.

12You Ethiopians, too, will be slain by his sword, 13and so will the lands of the north; he will destroy Assyria and make its great capital Nineveh a desolate wasteland like a wilderness. 14That once proud city will become a pastureland for sheep. All sorts of wild animals will have their homes in her. Hedgehogs will burrow there; the vultures and the owls will live among the ruins of her palaces, hooting from the gaping windows; the ravens will croak from her doors. All her cedar paneling will lie open to the wind and weather.

15This is the fate of that vast, prosperous city that lived in such security, that said to herself, "In all the world there is no city as great as I." But now—see how she has become a place of utter ruins, a place for animals to live! Everyone passing that way will mock, or shake his head in disbelief.

WOE to filthy, sinful Jerusalem, city of violence and crime. ²In her pride she won't listen even to the voice of God. No one can tell her anything; she refuses all correction. She does not trust the Lord, nor seek for God.

³Her leaders are like roaring lions hunting for their victims—out for everything that they can get. Her judges are like ravenous wolves at evening time, who by dawn have left no trace of their prey.

⁴Her "prophets" are liars seeking their own gain; her priests defile the Temple by their disobedience to God's laws.

⁵But the Lord is there within the city, and he does no wrong. Day by day his justice is more evident, but no one heeds—the wicked know no shame.

⁶"I have cut off many nations, laying them waste to their farthest borders; I have left their streets in silent ruin and their cities deserted without a single survivor to remember what happened. ⁷I thought, 'Surely they will listen to me now—surely they will heed my warnings, so that I'll not need to strike again.' But no; however much I punish them, they continue all their evil ways from dawn to dusk and dusk to dawn." ⁸But the Lord says, "Be patient; the time is coming soon when I will stand up and accuse these evil nations. For it is my decision to gather together the kingdoms of the earth, and pour out my fiercest anger and wrath upon them. All the earth shall be devoured with the fire of my jealousy.

⁹"At that time I will change the speech of my returning people to pure Hebrew so that all can worship the Lord together. ¹⁰My scattered people who live in the Sudan, beyond the rivers of Ethiopia, will come with their offerings, asking me to be their God again. ¹¹And then you will no longer need to be ashamed of yourselves, for you will no longer be rebels against me. I will remove all your proud and arrogant people from among you; there will be no pride or haughtiness on my holy mountain. ¹²Those who are left will be the poor and the humble, and they will trust in the name of the Lord. ¹³They will not be sinners, full of lies and deceit. They will live quietly, in peace, and lie down in safety, and no one will make them afraid."

¹⁴Sing, O daughter of Zion; shout, O Israel; be glad and rejoice with all your heart, O daughter of Jerusalem. ¹⁵For the Lord will remove his hand of judgment, and disperse the armies of your enemy. And the Lord himself, the King of Israel, will live among you! At last your troubles will be over—you need fear no more.

¹⁶On that day the announcement to Jerusalem will be, "Cheer up, don't be afraid. ¹⁷,¹⁸For the Lord your God has arrived to live among you. He is a mighty Savior. He will give you victory. He will rejoice over you in great gladness; he will love you and not accuse you." Is that a joyous choir I hear? No, it is the Lord himself exulting over you in happy song:

"I have gathered your wounded and taken away your reproach. ¹⁹And I will deal severely with all who have oppressed you. I will save the weak and helpless ones, and bring together those who were chased away. I will give glory to my former exiles, mocked and shamed.

²⁰"At that time, I will gather you together and bring you home again, and give you a good name, a name of distinction among all the peoples of the earth, and they will praise you when I restore your fortunes before your very eyes," says the Lord.

REVELATION 10:1–11

THEN I saw another mighty angel coming down from heaven, surrounded by a cloud, with a rainbow over his head; his face shone like the sun and his feet flashed with fire. 2And he held open in his hand a small scroll. He set his right foot on the sea and his left foot on the earth, 3and gave a great shout—it was like the roar of a lion—and the seven thunders crashed their reply.

4I was about to write what the thunders said when a voice from heaven called to me, "Don't do it. Their words are not to be revealed."

5Then the mighty angel standing on the sea and land lifted his right hand to heaven, 6and swore by him who lives forever and ever, who created heaven and everything in it and the earth and all that it contains and the sea and its inhabitants, that there should be no more delay, 7but that when the seventh angel blew his trumpet, then God's veiled plan—mysterious through the ages ever since it was announced by his servants the prophets—would be fulfilled.

8Then the voice from heaven spoke to me again, "Go and get the unrolled scroll from the mighty angel standing there upon the sea and land."

9So I approached him and asked him to give me the scroll. "Yes, take it and eat it," he said. "At first it will taste like honey, but when you swallow it, it will make your stomach sour!" 10So I took it from his hand, and ate it! And just as he had said, it was sweet in my mouth but it gave me a stomach ache when I swallowed it.

11Then he told me, "You must prophesy further about many peoples, nations, tribes, and kings."

PSALM 138:1–8

LORD, with all my heart I thank you. I will sing your praises before the armies of angels. 2I face your Temple as I worship, giving thanks to you for all your lovingkindness and your faithfulness, for your promises are backed by all the honor of your name. 3When I pray, you answer me, and encourage me by giving me the strength I need.

4Every king in all the earth shall give you thanks, O Lord, for all of them shall hear your voice. 5Yes, they shall sing about Jehovah's glorious ways, for his glory is very great. 6Yet though he is so great, he respects the humble, but proud men must keep their distance. 7Though I am surrounded by troubles, you will bring me safely through them. You will clench your fist against my angry enemies! Your power will save me. 8The Lord will work out his plans for my life—for your lovingkindness, Lord, continues forever. Don't abandon me— for you made me.

PROVERBS FOR TODAY/ 30:11–14

There are those who curse their father and mother, and feel themselves faultless despite their many sins. They are proud beyond description, arrogant, disdainful. They devour the poor with teeth as sharp as knives!

DECEMBER 20

HAGGAI 1:1—2:23

SUBJECT: a message from the Lord. *To:* Haggai the prophet, who delivered it to Zerubbabel (son of She-alti-el), governor of Judah; and to Joshua (son of Josedech), the High Priest—for it was addressed to them.

When: In late August of the second year of the reign of King Darius I.

2"Why is everyone saying it is not the right time for rebuilding my Temple?" asks the Lord.

³,⁴His reply to them is this: "Is it then the right time for you to live in luxurious homes, when the Temple lies in ruins? ⁵Look at the result: ⁶You plant much but harvest little. You have scarcely enough to eat or drink, and not enough clothes to keep you warm. Your income disappears, as though you were putting it into pockets filled with holes!

⁷"Think it over," says the Lord Almighty. "Consider how you have acted, and what has happened as a result! ⁸Then go up into the mountains and bring down timber, and rebuild my Temple, and I will be pleased with it and appear there in my glory," says the Lord.

⁹"You hope for much but get so little. And when you bring it home, I blow it away—it doesn't last at all. Why? Because my Temple lies in ruins and you don't care. Your only concern is your own fine homes. ¹⁰That is why I am holding back the rains from heaven and giving you such scant crops. ¹¹In fact, I have called for a drought upon the land, yes, and in the highlands, too; a drought to wither the grain and grapes and olives and all your other crops, a drought to starve both you and all your cattle, and ruin everything you have worked so hard to get."

¹²Then Zerubbabel (son of She-alti-el), the governor of Judah, and Joshua (son of Josedech), the High Priest, and the few people remaining in the land obeyed Haggai's message from the Lord their God; they began to worship him in earnest.

¹³Then the Lord told them (again sending the message through Haggai, his messenger), "I am with you; I will bless you." ¹⁴,¹⁵And the Lord gave them a desire to rebuild his Temple; so they all gathered in early September of the second year of King Darius' reign, and volunteered their help.

IN early October of the same year, the Lord sent them this message through Haggai:

²Ask this question of the governor and High Priest and everyone left in the land:

³"Who among you can remember the Temple as it was before? How glorious it was! In comparison, it is nothing now, is it? ⁴But take courage, O Zerubbabel and Joshua and all the people; take courage and work, for 'I am with you,' says the Lord Almighty. ⁵'For I promised when you left Egypt that my Spirit would remain among you; so don't be afraid.'

⁶"For the Lord Almighty says, 'In just a little while I will begin to shake the heavens and earth—and the oceans, too, and the dry land— ⁷I will shake all nations, and the Desire of All Nations shall come to this Temple, and I will fill this place with my glory,' says the Lord Almighty. ⁸,⁹'The future splendor of this Temple will be greater than the splendor of the first one! For I have plenty of silver and gold to do it! And here I will give peace,' says the Lord."

¹⁰In early December, in the second year of the reign of King Darius, this message came from the Lord through Haggai the prophet:

¹¹Ask the priests this question about the law: ¹²"If one of you is carrying a holy sacrifice in his robes, and happens to brush against some bread or wine or meat, will it too become holy?"

"No," the priests replied. "Holiness does not pass to other things that way."

¹³Then Haggai asked, "But if someone touches a dead person, and so becomes ceremonially impure, and then brushes against something, does it become contaminated?"

And the priests answered, "Yes."

¹⁴Haggai then made his meaning clear. "You people," he said (speaking for the Lord), "were contaminating your sacrifices by living with selfish attitudes and evil hearts—and not only your sacrifices, but everything else that you did as a 'service' to me. ¹⁵And so everything you did went wrong. But all is different now, because you have begun to build the Temple. ¹⁶,¹⁷Before, when you expected a twenty-bushel crop, there were only ten. When you came to draw fifty gallons from the olive press, there were only twenty. I rewarded all your labor with

rust and mildew and hail. Yet, even so, you refused to return to me," says the Lord.

18,19"But now note this: From today, this 24th day of the month, as the foundation of the Lord's Temple is finished, and from this day onward, I will bless you. Notice, I am giving you this promise now before you have even begun to rebuild the Temple structure, and before you have harvested your grain, and before the grapes and figs and pomegranates and olives have produced their next crops: *From this day I will bless you.*"

20Another message came to Haggai from the Lord that same day:

21Tell Zerubbabel, the governor of Judah, "I am about to shake the heavens and the earth, 22and to overthrow thrones and destroy the strength of the kingdoms of the nations. I will overthrow their armed might, and brothers and companions will kill each other. 23But when that happens, I will take you, O Zerubbabel my servant, and honor you like a signet ring upon my finger; for I have specially chosen you," says the Lord Almighty.

REVELATION 11:1–19

NOW I was given a measuring stick and told to go and measure the temple of God, including the inner court where the altar stands, and to count the number of worshipers. 2"But do not measure the outer court," I was told, "for it has been turned over to the nations. They will trample the Holy City for forty-two months. 3And I will give power to my two witnesses to prophesy 1,260 days clothed in sackcloth."

4These two prophets are the two olive trees, and two candlesticks standing before the God of all the earth. 5Anyone trying to harm them will be killed by bursts of fire shooting from their mouths. 6They have power to shut the skies so that no rain will fall during the three and a half years they prophesy, and to turn rivers and oceans to blood, and to send every kind of plague upon the earth as often as they wish.

7When they complete the three and a half years of their solemn testimony, the tyrant who comes out of the bottomless pit will declare war against them and conquer and kill them; 8,9and for three and a half days their bodies will be exposed in the streets of Jerusalem (the city fittingly described as "Sodom" or "Egypt")—the very place where their Lord was crucified. No one will be allowed to bury them, and people from many nations will crowd around to gaze at them. 10And there will be a worldwide holiday—people everywhere will rejoice and give presents to each other and throw parties to celebrate the death of the two prophets who had tormented them so much!

11But after three and a half days, the spirit of life from God will enter them and they will stand up! And great fear will fall on everyone. 12Then a loud voice will shout from heaven, "Come up!" And they will rise to heaven in a cloud as their enemies watch.

13The same hour there will be a terrible earthquake that levels a tenth of the city, leaving 7,000 dead. Then everyone left will, in their terror, give glory to the God of heaven.

14The second woe is past, but the third quickly follows:

15For just then the seventh angel blew his trumpet, and there were loud voices shouting down from heaven, "The Kingdom of this world now belongs to our Lord, and to his Christ; and he shall reign forever and ever."

16And the twenty-four Elders sitting on their thrones before God threw themselves down in worship, saying, 17"We give thanks, Lord God Almighty, who is and was, for now you have assumed your great power and have begun to reign. 18The nations were angry with you, but now it is your turn to be angry with them. It is time to judge the dead, and reward your servants—prophets and people alike, all who fear your Name, both great and small—and to destroy those who have caused destruction upon the earth."

[19]Then, in heaven, the temple of God was opened and the ark of his covenant could be seen inside. Lightning flashed and thunder crashed and roared, and there was a great hailstorm and the world was shaken by a mighty earthquake.

PSALM 139:1–24

O Lord, you have examined my heart and know everything about me. [2]You know when I sit or stand. When far away you know my every thought. [3]You chart the path ahead of me, and tell me where to stop and rest. Every moment, you know where I am. [4]You know what I am going to say before I even say it. [5]You both precede and follow me, and place your hand of blessing on my head.

[6]This is too glorious, too wonderful to believe! [7]I can *never* be lost to your Spirit! I can *never* get away from my God! [8]If I go up to heaven, you are there; if I go down to the place of the dead, you are there. [9]If I ride the morning winds to the farthest oceans, [10]even there your hand will guide me, your strength will support me. [11]If I try to hide in the darkness, the night becomes light around me. [12]For even darkness cannot hide from God; to you the night shines as bright as day. Darkness and light are both alike to you.

[13]You made all the delicate, inner parts of my body, and knit them together in my mother's womb. [14]Thank you for making me so wonderfully complex! It is amazing to think about. Your workmanship is marvelous—and how well I know it. [15]You were there while I was being formed in utter seclusion! [16]You saw me before I was born and scheduled each day of my life before I began to breathe. Every day was recorded in your Book!

[17,18]How precious it is, Lord, to realize that you are thinking about me constantly! I can't even count how many times a day your thoughts turn towards me. And when I waken in the morning, you are still thinking of me!

[19]Surely you will slay the wicked, Lord! Away, bloodthirsty men! Begone! [20]They blaspheme your name and stand in arrogance against you—how silly can they be? [21]O Lord, shouldn't I hate those who hate you? Shouldn't I be grieved with them? [22]Yes, I hate them, for your enemies are my enemies too.

[23]Search me, O God, and know my heart; test my thoughts. [24]Point out anything you find in me that makes you sad, and lead me along the path of everlasting life.

PROVERBS FOR TODAY/ 30:15–16

There are two things never satisfied, like a leech forever craving more: no, three things! no, four! Hell. The barren womb. A barren desert. Fire.

DECEMBER 21

ZECHARIAH 1:1–21

SUBJECT: *messages from the Lord. These messages from the Lord were given to Zechariah (son of Berechiah, and grandson of Iddo the prophet) in early November of the second year of the reign of King Darius.*

[2]The Lord Almighty was very angry with your fathers. [3]But he will turn again and favor you if only you return to him. [4]Don't be like your fathers were! The earlier prophets pled in vain with them to turn from all their evil ways.

"Come, return to me," the Lord God

said. But no, they wouldn't listen; they paid no attention at all.

5,6Your fathers and their prophets are now long dead, but remember the lesson they learned, that *God's Word endures!* It caught up with them and punished them. Then at last they repented.

"We have gotten what we deserved from God," they said. "He has done just what he warned us he would."

7The following February, still in the second year of the reign of King Darius, another message from the Lord came to Zechariah (son of Berechiah and grandson of Iddo the prophet), in a vision in the night: 8I saw a Man sitting on a red horse that was standing among the myrtle trees beside a river. Behind him were other horses, red and bay and white, each with its rider.

9An angel stood beside me, and I asked him, "Sir, what are all those horses for?"

"I'll tell you," he replied.

10Then the rider on the red horse—he was the Angel of the Lord—answered me, "The Lord has sent them to patrol the earth for him."

11Then the other riders reported to the Angel of the Lord, "We have patrolled the whole earth, and everywhere there is prosperity and peace."

12Upon hearing this, the Angel of the Lord prayed this prayer: "O Lord Almighty, for seventy years your anger has raged against Jerusalem and the cities of Judah. How long will it be until you again show mercy to them?"

13And the Lord answered the angel who stood beside me, speaking words of comfort and assurance.

14Then the angel said, "Shout out this message from the Lord Almighty: Don't you think I care about what has happened to Judah and Jerusalem? I am as jealous as a husband for his captive wife. 15I am very angry with the heathen nations sitting around at ease, for I was only a little displeased with my people, but the nations afflicted them far beyond my intentions. 16Therefore the Lord declares: I have returned to Jerusalem filled with mercy; my Temple will be rebuilt,

says the Lord Almighty, and so will all Jerusalem. 17Say it again: The Lord Almighty declares that the cities of Israel will again overflow with prosperity, and the Lord will again comfort Jerusalem and bless her and live in her."

18Then I looked and saw four animal horns!

19"What are these?" I asked the angel.

He replied, "They represent the four world powers that have scattered Judah, Israel, and Jerusalem."

20Then the Lord showed me four blacksmiths.

21"What have these men come to do?" I asked.

The angel replied, "They have come to take hold of the four horns that scattered Judah so terribly, and to pound them on the anvil and throw them away."

REVELATION 12:1–17

THEN a great pageant appeared in heaven, portraying things to come. I saw a woman clothed with the sun, with the moon beneath her feet, and a crown of twelve stars on her head. 2She was pregnant and screamed in the pain of her labor, awaiting her delivery.

3Suddenly a red Dragon appeared, with seven heads and ten horns, and seven crowns on his heads. 4His tail drew along behind him a third of the stars, which he plunged to the earth. He stood before the woman as she was about to give birth to her child, ready to eat the baby as soon as it was born.

5She gave birth to a boy who was to rule all nations with a heavy hand, and he was caught up to God and to his throne. 6The woman fled into the wilderness, where God had prepared a place for her, to take care of her for 1,260 days.

7Then there was war in heaven; Michael and the angels under his command fought the Dragon and his hosts of fallen angels. 8And the Dragon lost the battle and was forced from heaven. 9This great Dragon—the ancient serpent called the devil, or Satan, the one deceiving the whole world—was thrown down onto the earth with all his army.

¹⁰Then I heard a loud voice shouting across the heavens, "It has happened at last! God's salvation and the power and the rule, and the authority of his Christ are finally here; for the Accuser of our brothers has been thrown down from heaven onto earth—he accused them day and night before our God. ¹¹They defeated him by the blood of the Lamb, and by their testimony; for they did not love their lives but laid them down for him. ¹²Rejoice, O heavens! You citizens of heaven, rejoice! Be glad! But woe to you people of the world, for the devil has come down to you in great anger, knowing that he has little time."

¹³And when the Dragon found himself cast down to earth, he persecuted the woman who had given birth to the child. ¹⁴But she was given two wings like those of a great eagle, to fly into the wilderness to the place prepared for her, where she was cared for and protected from the Serpent, the Dragon, for three and a half years.

¹⁵And from the Serpent's mouth a vast flood of water gushed out and swept toward the woman in an effort to get rid of her; ¹⁶but the earth helped her by opening its mouth and swallowing the flood! ¹⁷Then the furious Dragon set out to at-

tack the rest of her children—all who were keeping God's commandments and confessing that they belong to Jesus. He stood waiting on an ocean beach.

PSALM 140:1–13

O Lord, deliver me from evil men. Preserve me from the violent, ²who plot and stir up trouble all day long. ³Their words sting like poisonous snakes. ⁴Keep me out of their power. Preserve me from their violence, for they are plotting against me. ⁵These proud men have set a trap to catch me, a noose to yank me up and leave me dangling in the air; they wait in ambush with a net to throw over and hold me helpless in its meshes.

⁶,⁷,⁸O Jehovah, my Lord and Savior, my God and my shield—hear me as I pray! Don't let these wicked men succeed; don't let them prosper and be proud. ⁹Let their plots boomerang! Let them be destroyed by the very evil they have planned for me. ¹⁰Let burning coals fall down upon their heads, or throw them into the fire, or into deep pits from which they can't escape.

¹¹Don't let liars prosper here in our land; quickly punish them. ¹²But the Lord will surely help those they persecute; he will maintain the rights of the poor. ¹³Surely the godly are thanking you, for they shall live in your presence.

PROVERBS FOR TODAY/ 30:17

A man who mocks his father and despises his mother shall have his eye plucked out by ravens and eaten by vultures.

DECEMBER 22

ZECHARIAH 2:1—3:10

WHEN I looked around me again, I saw a man carrying a yardstick in his hand.

²"Where are you going?" I asked.

"To measure Jerusalem," he said. "I

want to see whether it is big enough for all the people!"

³Then the angel who was talking to me went over to meet another angel coming toward him.

⁴"Go tell this young man," said the

other angel, "that Jerusalem will some day be so full of people that she won't have room enough for all! Many will live outside the city walls, with all their many cattle—and yet they will be safe. ⁵For the Lord himself will be a wall of fire protecting them and all Jerusalem; he will be the glory of the city.

6,7" 'Come, flee from the land of the north, from Babylon,' says the Lord to all his exiles there; 'I scattered you to the winds but I will bring you back again. Escape, escape to Zion now!' says the Lord.

⁸"The Lord of Glory has sent me against the nations that oppressed you, for he who harms you sticks his finger in Jehovah's eye!

⁹" 'I will smash them with my fist and their slaves will be their rulers! *Then you will know it was the Lord Almighty who sent me.* ¹⁰Sing, Jerusalem, and rejoice! For I have come to live among you,' says the Lord. ¹¹,¹²'At that time many nations will be converted to the Lord, and they too shall be my people; I will live among them all. *Then you will know it was the Lord Almighty who sent me to you.* And Judah shall be the Lord's inheritance in the Holy Land, for God shall once more choose to bless Jerusalem.'

¹³"Be silent, all mankind, before the Lord, for he has come to earth from heaven, from his holy home."

THEN the Angel showed me (in my vision) Joshua the High Priest standing before the Angel of the Lord; and Satan was there too, at the Angel's right hand, accusing Joshua of many things.

²And the Lord said to Satan, "I reject your accusations, Satan; yes, I, the Lord, for I have decided to be merciful to Jerusalem—I rebuke you. I have decreed mercy to Joshua and his nation; they are like a burning stick pulled out of the fire."

³Joshua's clothing was filthy as he stood before the Angel of the Lord. ⁴Then the Angel said to the others standing there, "Remove his filthy cloth-

ing." And turning to Joshua he said, "See, I have taken away your sins, and now I am giving you these fine new clothes."

⁵,⁶Then I said, "Please, could he also have a clean turban on his head?" So they gave him one.

Then the Angel of the Lord spoke very solemnly to Joshua and said, ⁷"The Lord Almighty declares: 'If you will follow the paths I set for you and do all I tell you to, then I will put you in charge of my Temple, to keep it holy; and I will let you walk in and out of my presence with these angels. ⁸Listen to me, O Joshua the High Priest, and all you other priests, you are illustrations of the good things to come. Don't you see?—Joshua represents my servant the Branch whom I will send. ⁹He will be the Foundation Stone of the Temple that Joshua is standing beside, and I will engrave this inscription on it seven times: *I will remove the sins of this land in a single day.* ¹⁰And after that,' the Lord Almighty declares, 'you will all live in peace and prosperity and each of you will own a home of your own where you can invite your neighbors.' "

REVELATION 13:1–18

AND now, in my vision, I saw a strange Creature rising up out of the sea. It had seven heads and ten horns, and ten crowns upon its horns. And written on each head were blasphemous names, each one defying and insulting God. ²This Creature looked like a leopard but had bear's feet and a lion's mouth! And the Dragon gave him his own power and throne and great authority.

³I saw that one of his heads seemed wounded beyond recovery—but the fatal wound was healed! All the world marveled at this miracle and followed the Creature in awe. ⁴They worshiped the Dragon for giving him such power, and they worshiped the strange Creature. "Where is there anyone as great as he?" they exclaimed. "Who is able to fight against him?"

5Then the Dragon encouraged the Creature to speak great blasphemies against the Lord; and gave him authority to control the earth for forty-two months. 6All that time he blasphemed God's Name and his temple and all those living in heaven. 7The Dragon gave him power to fight against God's people and to overcome them, and to rule over all nations and language groups throughout the world. 8And all mankind—whose names were not written down before the founding of the world in the slain Lamb's Book of Life—worshiped the evil Creature.

9Anyone who can hear, listen carefully: 10The people of God who are destined for prison will be arrested and taken away; those destined for death will be killed. But do not be dismayed, for here is your opportunity for endurance and confidence.

11Then I saw another strange animal, this one coming up out of the earth, with two little horns like those of a lamb but a fearsome voice like the Dragon's. 12He exercised all the authority of the Creature whose death-wound had been healed, whom he required all the world to worship. 13He did unbelievable miracles such as making fire flame down to earth from the skies while everyone was watching. 14By doing these miracles, he was deceiving people everywhere. He could do these marvelous things whenever the first Creature was there to watch him. And he ordered the people of the world to make a great statue of the first Creature, who was fatally wounded and then came back to life. 15He was permitted to give breath to this statue and even make it speak! Then the statue ordered that anyone refusing to worship it must die!

16He required everyone—great and small, rich and poor, slave and free—to be tattooed with a certain mark on the right hand or on the forehead. 17And no one could get a job or even buy in any store without the permit of that mark, which was either the name of the Creature or the code number of his name. 18Here is a puzzle that calls for careful thought to solve it. Let those who are able, interpret this code: the numerical values of the letters in his name add to 666!

PSALM 141:1–10

QUICK, Lord, answer me—for I have prayed. Listen when I cry to you for help! 2Regard my prayer as my evening sacrifice and as incense wafting up to you.

3Help me, Lord, to keep my mouth shut and my lips sealed. 4Take away my lust for evil things; don't let me want to be with sinners, doing what they do, sharing their delicacies. 5Let the godly smite me! It will be a kindness! If they reprove me, it is medicine! Don't let me refuse it. But I am in constant prayer against the wicked and their deeds. 6,7When their leaders are condemned, and their bones are strewn across the ground, then these men will finally listen to me and know that I am trying to help them.

8I look to you for help, O Lord God. You are my refuge. Don't let them slay me. 9Keep me out of their traps. 10Let them fall into their own snares, while I escape.

PROVERBS FOR TODAY/ 30:18–20

There are three things too wonderful for me to understand—no, four! How an eagle glides through the sky. How a serpent crawls upon a rock. How a ship finds its way across the heaving ocean. The growth of love between a man and a girl. There is another thing too: how a prostitute can sin and then say, "What's wrong with that?"

DECEMBER 23

ZECHARIAH 4:1—5:11

THEN the angel who had been talking with me woke me, as though I had been asleep.

2"What do you see now?" he asked.

I answered, "I see a gold lampstand holding seven lamps, and at the top there is a reservoir for the olive oil that feeds the lamps, flowing into them through seven tubes. 3And I see two olive trees carved upon the lampstand, one on each side of the reservoir. 4What is it, sir?" I asked. "What does this mean?"

5"Don't you really know?" the angel asked.

"No, sir," I said, "I don't."

6Then he said, "This is God's message to Zerubbabel: 'Not by might, nor by power, but by my Spirit, says the Lord Almighty—you will succeed because of my Spirit, though you are few and weak.' 7Therefore no mountain, however high, can stand before Zerubbabel! For it will flatten out before him! And Zerubbabel will finish building this Temple with mighty shouts of thanksgiving for God's mercy, declaring that all was done by grace alone."

8Another message that I received from the Lord said:

9"Zerubbabel laid the foundation of this Temple, and he will complete it. (Then you will know these messages are from God, the Lord Almighty.) 10Do not despise this small beginning, for the eyes of the Lord rejoice to see the work begin, to see the plumbline in the hand of Zerubbabel. For these seven lamps represent the eyes of the Lord that see everywhere around the world."

11Then I asked him about the two olive trees on each side of the lampstand, 12and about the two olive branches that emptied oil into gold bowls through two gold tubes.

13"Don't you know?" he asked.

"No, sir," I said.

14Then he told me, "They represent the two anointed ones who assist the Lord of all the earth."

I looked up again and saw a scroll flying through the air.

2"What do you see?" he asked.

"A flying scroll!" I replied. "It appears to be about thirty feet long and fifteen feet wide!"

3"This scroll," he told me, "represents the words of God's curse going out over the entire land. It says that all who steal and lie have been judged and sentenced to death."

4"I am sending this curse into the home of every thief and everyone who swears falsely by my name," says the Lord Almighty. "And my curse shall remain upon his home and completely destroy it."

5Then the angel left me for awhile, but he returned and said, "Look up! Something is traveling through the sky!"

6"What is it?" I asked.

He replied, "It is a bushel basket filled with the sin prevailing everywhere throughout the land."

7Suddenly the heavy lead cover on the basket was lifted off, and I could see a woman sitting inside the basket!

8He said, "She represents wickedness," and he pushed her back into the basket and clamped down the heavy lid again.

9Then I saw two women flying toward us, with wings like those of a stork. And they took the bushel basket and flew off with it, high in the sky.

10"Where are they taking her?" I asked the angel.

11He replied, "To Babylon where they will build a temple for the basket, to worship it!"

THEN I saw a Lamb standing on Mount Zion in Jerusalem, and with him were 144,000 who had his Name and his Father's Name written on their foreheads. 2And I heard a sound from heaven like the roaring of a great waterfall or the rolling of mighty thunder. It was the singing of a choir accompanied by harps.

3This tremendous choir—144,000 strong—sang a wonderful new song in front of the throne of God and before the four Living Beings and the twenty-four Elders; and no one could sing this song except those 144,000 who had been redeemed from the earth. 4For they are spiritually undefiled, pure as virgins, following the Lamb wherever he goes. They have been purchased from among the men on the earth as a consecrated offering to God and the Lamb. 5No falsehood can be charged against them; they are blameless.

6And I saw another angel flying through the heavens, carrying the everlasting Good News to preach to those on earth—to every nation, tribe, language and people.

7"Fear God," he shouted, "and extol his greatness. For the time has come when he will sit as Judge. Worship him who made the heaven and the earth, the sea and all its sources."

8Then another angel followed him through the skies, saying, "Babylon is fallen, is fallen—that great city—because she seduced the nations of the world and made them share the wine of her intense impurity and sin."

9Then a third angel followed them shouting, "Anyone worshiping the Creature from the sea and his statue and accepting his mark on the forehead or the hand, 10must drink the wine of the anger of God; it is poured out undiluted into God's cup of wrath. And they will be tormented with fire and burning sulphur in the presence of the holy angels and the Lamb. 11The smoke of their torture rises forever and ever, and they will have no relief day or night, for they have worshiped the Creature and his statue, and have been tattooed with the code of his name. 12Let this encourage God's people to endure patiently every trial and persecution, for they are his saints who remain firm to the end in obedience to his commands and trust in Jesus."

13And I heard a voice in the heavens above me saying, "Write this down: At last the time has come for his martyrs to enter into their full reward. Yes, says the Spirit, they are blest indeed, for now they shall rest from all their toils and trials; for their good deeds follow them to heaven!" 14Then the scene changed and I saw a white cloud, and someone sitting on it who looked like Jesus, who was called "The Son of Man," with a crown of solid gold upon his head and a sharp sickle in his hand.

15Then an angel came from the temple and called out to him, "Begin to use the sickle, for the time has come for you to reap; the harvest is ripe on the earth." 16So the one sitting on the cloud swung his sickle over the earth, and the harvest was gathered in. 17After that another angel came from the temple in heaven, and he also had a sharp sickle.

18Just then the angel who has power to destroy the world with fire, shouted to the angel with the sickle, "Use your sickle now to cut off the clusters of grapes from the vines of the earth, for they are fully ripe for judgment." 19So the angel swung his sickle on the earth and loaded the grapes into the great winepress of God's wrath. 20And the grapes were trodden in the winepress outside the city, and blood flowed out in a stream 200 miles long and as high as a horse's bridle.

PSALM 142:1–7

HOW I plead with God, how I implore his mercy, pouring out my troubles before him. 3For I am overwhelmed and desperate, and you alone know which way I ought to turn to miss the traps my enemies have set for me. 4(There's one—just over there to the right!) No one gives me a passing thought. No one will help me; no one cares a bit what happens to me. 5Then I prayed to Jehovah. "Lord," I pled, "you are my only place of refuge. Only you can keep me safe.

6"Hear my cry, for I am very low. Rescue me from my persecutors, for they are too strong for me. 7Bring me out of prison, so that I can thank you. The godly will rejoice with me for all your help."

PROVERBS FOR TODAY/ 30:21–23

There are three things that make the earth tremble—no, four it cannot stand: A slave who becomes a king. A rebel who prospers. A bitter woman when she finally marries. A servant girl who marries her mistress' husband.

DECEMBER 24

ZECHARIAH 6:1—7:14

THEN I looked up again and saw four chariots coming from between what looked like two mountains made of brass. 2The first chariot was pulled by red horses, the second by black ones, 3the third by white horses and the fourth by dappled-greys.

4"And what are these, sir?" I asked the angel.

5He replied, "These are the four heavenly spirits who stand before the Lord of all the earth; they are going out to do his work. 6The chariot pulled by the black horses will go north, and the one pulled by white horses will follow it there, while the dappled-greys will go south."

7The red horses were impatient to be off, to patrol back and forth across the earth, so the Lord said, "Go. Begin your patrol." So they left at once.

8Then the Lord summoned me and said, "Those who went north have executed my judgment and quieted my anger there."

9In another message the Lord said:

10,11"Heldai, Tobijah, and Jedaiah will bring gifts of silver and gold from the Jews exiled in Babylon. The same day they arrive, meet them at the home of Josiah (son of Zephaniah), where they will stay. Accept their gifts and make from them a crown from the silver and gold. Then put the crown on the head of Joshua (son of Josedech) the High Priest. 12Tell him that the Lord Almighty says, 'You represent the Man who will come, whose name is "The Branch"— he will grow up from himself—and will build the Temple of the Lord. 13To him belongs the royal title. He will rule both as King and as Priest, with perfect harmony between the two!'

14"Then put the crown in the Temple of the Lord, to honor those who gave it—Heldai, Tobijah, Jedaiah, and also Josiah. 15These three who have come from so far away represent many others who will some day come from distant lands to rebuild the Temple of the Lord. And when this happens you will know my messages have been from God, the Lord Almighty. But none of this will happen unless you carefully obey the commandments of the Lord your God."

ANOTHER message came to me from the Lord in late November of the fourth year of the reign of King Darius.

²The Jews of the city of Bethel had sent a group of men headed by Sharezer, the chief administrative officer of the king, and Regem-melech, to the Lord's Temple at Jerusalem, to seek his blessing, ³and to speak with the priests and prophets about whether they must continue their traditional custom of fasting and mourning during the month of August each year, as they had been doing so long.

⁴This was the Lord's reply:

⁵"When you return to Bethel, say to all your people and your priests, 'During those seventy years of exile when you fasted and mourned in August and October, were you really in earnest about leaving your sins behind, and coming back to me? No, not at all! ⁶And even now in your holy feasts to God, you don't think of me, but only of the food and fellowship and fun. ⁷Long years ago, when Jerusalem was prosperous and her southern suburbs out along the plain were filled with people, the prophets warned them that this attitude would surely lead to ruin, as it has.'"

⁸,⁹Then this message from the Lord came to Zechariah. "Tell them to be honest and fair—and not to take bribes—and to be merciful and kind to everyone. ¹⁰Tell them to stop oppressing widows and orphans, foreigners and poor people, and to stop plotting evil against each other. ¹¹Your fathers would not listen to this message. They turned stubbornly away and put their fingers in their ears to keep from hearing me. ¹²They hardened their hearts like flint, afraid to hear the words that God, the Lord Almighty, commanded them—the laws he had revealed to them by his Spirit through the early prophets. That is why such great wrath came down on them from God. ¹³I called but they refused to listen, so when they cried to me, I turned away. ¹⁴I scattered them as with a whirlwind among the far-off nations. Their land became desolate; no one even traveled through it; the Pleasant Land lay bare and blighted."

REVELATION 15:1–8

AND I saw in heaven another mighty pageant showing things to come: Seven angels were assigned to carry down to earth the seven last plagues—and then at last God's anger will be finished.

²Spread out before me was what seemed to be an ocean of fire and glass, and on it stood all those who had been victorious over the Evil Creature and his statue and his mark and number. All were holding harps of God, ³,⁴and they were singing the song of Moses, the servant of God, and the song of the Lamb:

"Great and marvelous
Are your doings,
Lord God Almighty.
Just and true
Are your ways,
O King of Ages.
Who shall not fear,
O Lord,
And glorify your Name?
For you alone are holy.
All nations will come
And worship before you,
For your righteous deeds
Have been disclosed."

⁵Then I looked and saw that the Holy of Holies of the temple in heaven was thrown wide open!

⁶The seven angels who were assigned to pour out the seven plagues then came from the temple, clothed in spotlessly white linen, with golden belts across their chests. ⁷And one of the four Living Beings handed each of them a golden flask filled with the terrible wrath of the Living God who lives forever and forever. ⁸The temple was filled with smoke from his glory and power; and no one could enter until the seven angels had completed pouring out the seven plagues.

PSALM 143:1–12

HEAR my prayer, O Lord; answer my plea, because you are faithful to your promises. ²Don't bring me to trial! For as compared with you, no one is perfect.

³My enemies chased and caught me. They have knocked me to the ground. They force me to live in the darkness like those in the grave. ⁴I am losing all hope; I am paralyzed with fear.

⁵I remember the glorious miracles you did in days of long ago. ⁶I reach out for you. I thirst for you as parched land thirsts for rain. ⁷Come quickly, Lord, and answer me, for my depression deepens; don't turn away from me or I shall die. ⁸Let me see your kindness to me in the morning, for I am trusting you. Show me where to walk, for my prayer is sincere. ⁹Save me from my enemies. O Lord, I run to you to hide me. ¹⁰Help me to do your will, for you are my God. Lead me in good paths, for your Spirit is good.

¹¹Lord, saving me will bring glory to your name. Bring me out of all this trouble because you are true to your promises. ¹²And because you are loving and kind to me, cut off all my enemies and destroy those who are trying to harm me; for I am your servant.

PROVERBS FOR TODAY/ 30:24–28

There are four things that are small but unusually wise: Ants: they aren't strong, but store up food for the winter. Cliff badgers: delicate little animals who protect themselves by living among the rocks. The locusts: though they have no leader, they stay together in swarms. The lizards: they are easy to catch and kill, yet are found even in king's palaces!

DECEMBER 25

ZECHARIAH 8:1–23

AGAIN the Lord's message came to me:
²"The Lord Almighty says, I am greatly concerned—yes, furiously angry—because of all that Jerusalem's enemies have done to her. ³Now I am going to return to my land and I, myself, will live within Jerusalem, and Jerusalem shall be called 'The Faithful City,' and 'The Holy Mountain,' and 'The Mountain of the Lord Almighty.' "

⁴The Lord Almighty declares that Jerusalem will have peace and prosperity so long that there will once again be aged men and women hobbling through her streets on canes, ⁵and the streets will be filled with boys and girls at play.

⁶The Lord says, "This seems unbelievable to you—a remnant, small, discouraged as you are—but it is no great thing for me. ⁷You can be sure that I will rescue my people from east and west, wherever they are scattered. ⁸I will bring them home again to live safely in Jerusalem, and they will be my people, and I will be their God, just and true and yet forgiving them their sins!"

⁹The Lord Almighty says, "Get on with the job and finish it! You have been listening long enough! For since you began laying the foundation of the Temple, the prophets have been telling you about the blessings that await you when it's finished. ¹⁰Before the work began there were no jobs, no wages, no security; if you left the city, there was no assurance you would ever return, for crime was rampant.

¹¹"But it is all so different now!" says the Lord Almighty. ¹²"For I am sowing peace and prosperity among you. Your crops will prosper; the grapevines will be weighted down with fruit; the ground will be fertile, with plenty of rain; all these blessings will be given to the people left

in the land. 13"May you be as poor as Judah,' the heathen used to say to those they cursed! But no longer! For now 'Judah' is a word of blessing, not a curse. 'May you be as prosperous and happy as Judah is,' they'll say. So don't be afraid or discouraged! Get on with rebuilding the Temple! 14,15If you do, I will certainly bless you. And don't think that I might change my mind. I did what I said I would when your fathers angered me and I promised to punish them, and I won't change this decision of mine to bless you. 16Here is your part: Tell the truth. Be fair. Live at peace with everyone. 17Don't plot harm to others; don't swear that something is true when it isn't! How I hate all that sort of thing!" says the Lord.

18Here is another message that came to me from the Lord Almighty:

19"The traditional fasts and times of mourning you have kept in July, August, October, and January are ended. They will be changed to joyous festivals if you love truth and peace! 20,21People from around the world will come on pilgrimages and pour into Jerusalem from many foreign cities to attend these celebrations. People will write their friends in other cities and say, 'Let's go to Jerusalem to ask the Lord to bless us, and be merciful to us. I'm going! Please come with me. Let's go now!' 22Yes, many people, even strong nations, will come to the Lord Almighty in Jerusalem to ask for his blessing and help. 23In those days ten men from ten different nations will clutch at the coat sleeves of one Jew and say, 'Please be my friend, for I know that God is with you.'"

REVELATION 16:1–21

AND I heard a mighty voice shouting from the temple to the seven angels, "Now go your ways and empty out the seven flasks of the wrath of God upon the earth."

2So the first angel left the temple and poured out his flask over the earth, and horrible, malignant sores broke out on everyone who had the mark of the Creature and was worshiping his statue.

3The second angel poured out his flask upon the oceans, and they became like the watery blood of a dead man; and everything in all the oceans died.

4The third angel poured out his flask upon the rivers and springs and they became blood. 5And I heard this angel of the waters declaring, "You are just in sending this judgment, O Holy One, who is and was, 6for your saints and prophets have been martyred and their blood poured out upon the earth; and now, in turn, you have poured out the blood of those who murdered them; it is their just reward."

7And I heard the angel of the altar say, "Yes, Lord God Almighty, your punishments are just and true."

8Then the fourth angel poured out his flask upon the sun, causing it to scorch all men with its fire. 9Everyone was burned by this blast of heat, and they cursed the name of God who sent the plagues—they did not change their mind and attitude to give him glory.

10Then the fifth angel poured out his flask upon the throne of the Creature from the sea, and his kingdom was plunged into darkness. And his subjects gnawed their tongues in anguish, 11and cursed the God of heaven for their pains and sores, but they refused to repent of all their evil deeds.

12The sixth angel poured out his flask upon the great River Euphrates and it dried up so that the kings from the east could march their armies westward without hindrance. 13And I saw three evil spirits disguised as frogs leap from the mouth of the Dragon, the Creature, and his False Prophet. 14These miracle-working demons conferred with all the rulers of the world to gather them for battle against the Lord on that great coming Judgment Day of God Almighty.

15"Take note: I will come as unexpectedly as a thief! Blessed are all who are awaiting me, who keep their robes in readiness and will not need to walk naked and ashamed."

16And they gathered all the armies of the world near a place called, in Hebrew, Armageddon—the Mountain of Megiddo.

17Then the seventh angel poured out his flask into the air; and a mighty shout came from the throne of the temple in heaven, saying, "It is finished!" 18Then the thunder crashed and rolled, and lightning flashed; and there was a great earthquake of a magnitude unprecedented in human history. 19The great city of "Babylon" split into three sections, and cities around the world fell in heaps of rubble; and so all of "Babylon's" sins were remembered in God's thoughts, and she was punished to the last drop of anger in the cup of the wine of the fierceness of his wrath. 20And islands vanished, and mountains flattened out, 21and there was an incredible hailstorm from heaven; hailstones weighing a hundred pounds fell from the sky onto the people below, and they cursed God because of the terrible hail.

PSALM 144:1–15

BLESS the Lord who is my immovable Rock. He gives me strength and skill in battle. 2He is always kind and loving to me; he is my fortress, my tower of strength and safety, my deliverer. He stands before me as a shield. He subdues my people under me.

3O Lord, what is man that you even notice him? Why bother at all with the human race? 4For man is but a breath; his days are like a passing shadow.

5Bend down the heavens, Lord, and come. The mountains smoke beneath your touch.

6Let loose your lightning bolts, your arrows, Lord, upon your enemies, and scatter them.

7Reach down from heaven and rescue me; deliver me from deep waters, from the power of my enemies. 8Their mouths are filled with lies; they swear to the truth of what is false.

9I will sing you a new song, O God, with a ten-stringed harp. 10For you grant victory to kings! You are the one who will rescue your servant David from the fatal sword. 11Save me! Deliver me from these enemies, these liars, these treacherous men.

12-15Here is my description of a truly happy land where Jehovah is God:

Sons vigorous and tall as growing plants.

Daughters of graceful beauty like the pillars of a palace wall.

Barns full to the brim with crops of every kind.

Sheep by the thousands out in our fields.

Oxen loaded down with produce.

No enemy attacking the walls, but peace everywhere.

No crime in our streets.

Yes, happy are those whose God is Jehovah.

PROVERBS FOR TODAY/ 30:29–31

There are three stately monarchs in the earth—no, four: The lion, king of the animals. He won't turn aside for anyone. The peacock. The male goat. A king as he leads his army.

DECEMBER 26

ZECHARIAH 9:1–17

THIS is the message concerning God's curse on the lands of Hadrach and Damascus, for the Lord is closely watching all mankind, as well as Israel.

2"Doomed is Hamath, near Damascus, and Tyre, and Zidon, too, shrewd though they be. 3Though Tyre has armed herself to the hilt, and become so rich that silver is like dirt to her, and fine gold like dust in the streets, 4yet the Lord will dispossess her, and hurl her fortifications into the sea; and she shall be set on fire and burned to the ground.

5"Ashkelon will see it happen and be filled with fear; Gaza will huddle in desperation and Ekron will shake with terror, for their hopes that Tyre would stop the enemies' advance will all be dashed. Gaza will be conquered, her king killed, and Ashkelon will be completely destroyed.

6"Foreigners will take over the city of Ashdod, the rich city of the Philistines. 7I will yank her idolatry out of her mouth, and pull from her teeth her sacrifices that she eats with blood. Everyone left will worship God and be adopted into Israel as a new clan: the Philistines of Ekron will intermarry with the Jews, just as the Jebusites did so long ago. 8And I will surround my Temple like a guard to keep invading armies from entering Israel. I am closely watching their movements and I will keep them away; no foreign oppressors will again overrun my people's land.

9"Rejoice greatly, O my people! Shout with joy! For look—your King is coming! He is the Righteous One, the Victor! Yet he is lowly, riding on a donkey's colt! 10I will disarm all peoples of the earth, including my people in Israel, and he shall bring peace among the nations. His realm shall stretch from sea to sea, from the river to the ends of the earth.

11"I have delivered you from death in a waterless pit because of the covenant I made with you, sealed with blood. 12Come to the place of safety, all you prisoners, for there is yet hope! I promise right now, I will repay you two mercies for each of your woes! 13Judah, you are my bow! Ephraim, you are my arrow! Both of you will be my sword, like the sword of a mighty soldier brandished against the sons of Greece."

14The Lord shall lead his people as they fight! His arrows shall fly like lightning; the Lord God shall sound the trumpet call and go out against his enemies like a whirlwind off the desert from the south. 15He will defend his people and they will subdue their enemies, treading them beneath their feet. They will taste victory and shout with triumph. They will slaughter their foes, leaving horrible carnage everywhere. 16,17The Lord their God will save his people in that day, as a Shepherd caring for his sheep. They shall shine in his land as glittering jewels in a crown. How wonderful and beautiful all shall be! The abundance of grain and grapes will make the young men and girls flourish; they will be radiant with health and happiness.

REVELATION 17:1–18

ONE of the seven angels who had poured out the plagues came over and talked with me. "Come with me," he said, "and I will show you what is going to happen to the Notorious Prostitute, who sits upon the many waters of the world. 2The kings of the world have had immoral relations with her, and the people of the earth have been made drunk by the wine of her immorality."

3So the angel took me in spirit into the wilderness. There I saw a woman sitting on a scarlet animal that had seven heads and ten horns, written all over with blasphemies against God. 4The woman wore purple and scarlet clothing and beautiful jewelry made of gold and precious gems and pearls, and held in her hand a golden goblet full of obscenities:

5A mysterious caption was written on her forehead: "Babylon the Great, Mother of Prostitutes and of Idol Worship Everywhere around the World."

6I could see that she was drunk— drunk with the blood of the martyrs of Jesus she had killed. I stared at her in horror.

7"Why are you so surprised?" the angel asked. "I'll tell you who she is and what the animal she is riding represents. 8He was alive but isn't now. And yet, soon he will come up out of the bottomless pit and go to eternal destruction; and the people of earth, whose names have not been written in the Book of Life before the world began, will be dumbfounded at his reappearance after being dead.

9"And now think hard: his seven heads represent a certain city built on seven hills where this woman has her residence. 10They also represent seven kings. Five have already fallen, the sixth now reigns, and the seventh is yet to come, but his reign will be brief. 11The scarlet animal that died is the eighth king, having reigned before as one of the seven; after his second reign, he too, will go to his doom. 12His ten horns are ten kings who have not yet risen to power; they will be appointed to their kingdoms for one brief moment, to reign with him. 13They will all sign a treaty giving their power and strength to him. 14Together they will wage war against the Lamb, and the Lamb will conquer them; for he is Lord over all lords, and King of kings, and his people are the called and chosen and faithful ones.

15"The oceans, lakes and rivers that the woman is sitting on represent masses of people of every race and nation.

16"The scarlet animal and his ten horns—which represent ten kings who will reign with him—all hate the woman, and will attack her and leave her naked and ravaged by fire. 17For God will put a plan into their minds, a plan that will carry out his purposes: They will mutually agree to give their authority to the scarlet animal, so that the words of God will be fulfilled. 18And this woman you saw in your vision represents the great city that rules over the kings of the earth."

PSALM 145:1–21

I will praise you, my God and King, and bless your name each day and forever.

3Great is Jehovah! Greatly praise him! His greatness is beyond discovery! 4Let each generation tell its children what glorious things he does. 5I will meditate about your glory, splendor, majesty and miracles. 6Your awe-inspiring deeds shall be on every tongue; I will proclaim your greatness. 7Everyone will tell about how good you are, and sing about your righteousness.

8Jehovah is kind and merciful, slow to get angry, full of love. 9He is good to everyone, and his compassion is intertwined with everything he does. 10All living things shall thank you, Lord, and your people will bless you. 11They will talk together about the glory of your kingdom and mention examples of your power. 12They will tell about your miracles and about the majesty and glory of your reign. 13For your kingdom never ends. You rule generation after generation.

14The Lord lifts the fallen and those bent beneath their loads. 15The eyes of all mankind look up to you for help; you give them their food as they need it. 16You constantly satisfy the hunger and thirst of every living thing.

17The Lord is fair in everything he does, and full of kindness. 18He is close to all who call on him sincerely. 19He fulfills the desires of those who reverence and trust him; he hears their cries for help and rescues them. 20He protects all those who love him, but destroys the wicked.

21I will praise the Lord and call on all men everywhere to bless his holy name forever and forever.

If you have been a fool by being proud or plotting evil, don't brag about it—cover your mouth with your hand in shame.

DECEMBER 27

ZECHARIAH 10:1—11:17

ASK the Lord for rain in the springtime, and he will answer with lightning and showers. Every field will become a lush pasture. 2How foolish to ask the idols for anything like that! Fortune-tellers' predictions are all a bunch of silly lies; what comfort is there in promises that don't come true? Judah and Israel have been led astray and wander like lost sheep; everyone attacks them, for they have no shepherd to protect them.

3"My anger burns against your 'shepherds'—your leaders—and I will punish them—these goats. For the Lord Almighty has arrived to help his flock of Judah. I will make them strong and glorious like a proud steed in battle. 4From them will come the Cornerstone, the Peg on which all hope hangs, the Bow that wins the battle, the Ruler over all the earth. 5They will be mighty warriors for God, grinding their enemies' faces into the dust beneath their feet. The Lord is with them as they fight; their enemy is doomed.

6"I will strengthen Judah, yes, and Israel too; I will re-establish them because I love them. It will be as though I had never cast them all away, for I, the Lord their God, will hear their cries. 7They shall be like mighty warriors. They shall be happy as with wine. Their children, too, shall see the mercies of the Lord and be glad. Their hearts shall rejoice in the Lord. 8When I whistle to them, they'll come running, for I have bought them back again. From the few that are left, their population will grow again to former size. 9Though I have scattered them like seeds among the nations, still they will remember me and return again to God; with all their children, they will come home again to Israel. 10I will bring them back from Egypt and Assyria, and resettle them in Israel—in Gilead and Lebanon; there will scarcely be room for all of them! 11They shall pass safely through the sea of distress, for the waves will be held back. The Nile will become dry—the rule of Assyria and Egypt over my people will end."

12The Lord says, "I will make my people strong with power from me! They will go wherever they wish, and wherever they go, they will be under my personal care."

OPEN your doors, O Lebanon, to judgment. You will be destroyed as though by fire raging through your forests. 2Weep, O cypress trees, for all the ruined cedars; the tallest and most beautiful of them are fallen. Cry in fear, you oaks of Bashan, as you watch the thickest forests felled. 3Listen to the wailing of Israel's leaders—all these evil shepherds—for their wealth is gone. Hear the young lions roaring—the princes are weeping, for their glorious Jordan valley lies in ruins.

4Then said the Lord my God to me, "Go and take a job as shepherd of a flock being fattened for the butcher. 5This will illustrate the way my people have been bought and slain by wicked leaders, who go unpunished. 'Thank God, now I am rich!' say those who have betrayed them—their own shepherds have sold them without mercy. 6And I won't spare them either," says the Lord, "for I will let them fall into the clutches of their own wicked leaders, and they will slay them. They shall turn the land into a wilderness and I will not protect it from them."

7So I took two shepherd's staffs, naming one "Grace" and the other "Union," and I fed the flock as I had been told to do. 8And I got rid of their three evil shepherds in a single month. But I became impatient with these sheep—this nation—and they hated me too.

9So I told them, "I won't be your shepherd any longer. If you die, you die; if you are killed, I don't care. Go ahead and destroy yourselves!"

10And I took my staff called "Grace" and snapped it in two, showing that I had broken my contract to lead and protect them. 11That was the end of the agreement. Then those who bought and sold sheep, who were watching, realized that God was telling them something through what I did.

12And I said to their leaders, "If you like, give me my pay, whatever I am worth; but only if you want to."

So they counted out thirty little silver coins as my wages.

13And the Lord told me, "Use it to buy a field from the pottery makers—this magnificent sum they value you at!"

So I took the thirty coins and threw them into the Temple for the pottery makers. 14Then I broke my other staff, "Union," to show that the bond of unity between Judah and Israel was broken.

15Then the Lord told me to go again and get a job as a shepherd; this time I was to act the part of a worthless, wicked shepherd.

16And he said to me, "This illustrates how I will give this nation a shepherd who will not care for the dying ones, nor look after the young, nor heal the broken bones, nor feed the healthy ones, nor carry the lame that cannot walk; instead, he will eat the fat ones, even tearing off their feet. 17Woe to this worthless shepherd who doesn't care for the flock.

God's sword will cut his arm and pierce through his right eye; his arm will become useless and his right eye blinded."

REVELATION 18:1–24

AFTER all this I saw another angel come down from heaven with great authority, and the earth grew bright with his splendor.

2He gave a mighty shout, "Babylon the Great is fallen, is fallen; she has become a den of demons, a haunt of devils and every kind of evil spirit. 3For all the nations have drunk the fatal wine of her intense immorality. The rulers of earth have enjoyed themselves with her, and businessmen throughout the world have grown rich from all her luxurious living."

4Then I heard another voice calling from heaven, "Come away from her, my people; do not take part in her sins, or you will be punished with her. 5For her sins are piled as high as heaven and God is ready to judge her for her crimes. 6Do to her as she has done to you, and more—give double penalty for all her evil deeds. She brewed many a cup of woe for others—give twice as much to her. 7She has lived in luxury and pleasure—match it now with torments and with sorrows. She boasts, 'I am queen upon my throne. I am no helpless widow. I will not experience sorrow.' 8Therefore the sorrows of death and mourning and famine shall overtake her in a single day, and she shall be utterly consumed by fire; for mighty is the Lord who judges her."

9And the world leaders, who took part in her immoral acts and enjoyed her favors, will mourn for her as they see the smoke rising from her charred remains. 10They will stand far off, trembling with fear and crying out, "Alas, Babylon, that mighty city! In one moment her judgment fell."

11The merchants of the earth will weep and mourn for her, for there is no one left to buy their goods. 12She was their biggest customer for gold and silver, precious stones, pearls, finest linens, purple silks, and scarlet; and every kind of perfumed wood, and ivory goods and most expensive wooden carvings, and brass and iron and marble; 13and spices and perfumes and incense, ointment and frankincense, wine, olive oil, and fine flour; wheat, cattle, sheep, horses, chariots, and slaves—and even the souls of men.

14"All the fancy things you loved so much are gone," they cry. "The dainty luxuries and splendor that you prized so much will never be yours again. They are gone forever."

15And so the merchants who have become wealthy by selling her these things shall stand at a distance, fearing danger to themselves, weeping and crying, 16"Alas, that great city, so beautiful—like a woman clothed in finest purple and scarlet linens, decked out with gold and precious stones and pearls! 17In one moment, all the wealth of the city is gone!"

And all the shipowners and captains of the merchant ships and crews will stand a long way off, 18crying as they watch the smoke ascend, and saying, "Where in all the world is there another city such as this?" 19And they will throw dust on their heads in their sorrow and say, "Alas, alas, for that great city! She made us all rich from her great wealth. And now in a single hour all is gone. . . ."

20But you, O heaven, rejoice over her fate; and you, O children of God and the prophets and the apostles! For at last God has given judgment against her for you.

21Then a mighty angel picked up a boulder shaped like a millstone and threw it into the ocean and shouted, "Babylon, that great city, shall be thrown away as I have thrown away this stone, and she

shall disappear forever. 22Never again will the sound of music be there—no more pianos, saxophones, and trumpets. No industry of any kind will ever again exist there, and there will be no more milling of the grain. 23Dark, dark will be her nights; not even a lamp in a window will ever be seen again. No more joyous wedding bells and happy voices of the bridegrooms and the brides. Her businessmen were known around the world and she deceived all nations with her sorceries. 24And she was responsible for the blood of all the martyred prophets and the saints."

PSALM 146:1–10

PRAISE the Lord! Yes, really praise him! 2I will praise him as long as I live, yes, even with my dying breath.

3Don't look to men for help; their greatest leaders fail; 4for every man must die. His breathing stops, life ends, and in a moment all he planned for himself is ended. 5But happy is the man who has the God of Jacob as his helper, whose hope is in the Lord his God— 6the God who made both earth and heaven, the seas and everything in them. He is the God who keeps every promise, 7and gives justice to the poor and oppressed, and food to the hungry. He frees the prisoners, 8and opens the eyes of the blind; he lifts the burdens from those bent down beneath their loads. For the Lord loves good men. 9He protects the immigrants, and cares for the orphans and widows. But he turns topsy-turvy the plans of the wicked.

10The Lord will reign forever. O Jerusalem, your God is King in every generation! Hallelujah! Praise the Lord!

PROVERBS FOR TODAY/ 30:33

As the churning of cream yields butter, and a blow to the nose causes bleeding, so anger causes quarrels.

DECEMBER 28

ZECHARIAH 12:1—13:9

THIS is the fate of Israel, as pronounced by the Lord, who stretched out the heavens and laid the foundation of the earth, and formed the spirit of man within him:

2"I will make Jerusalem and Judah like a cup of poison to all the nearby nations that send their armies to surround Jerusalem. 3Jerusalem will be a heavy stone burdening the world. And though all the nations of the earth unite in an attempt to move her, they will all be crushed.

4"In that day," says the Lord, "I will bewilder the armies drawn up against her, and make fools of them, for I will watch over the people of Judah, but blind all her enemies.

5"And the clans of Judah shall say to themselves, 'The people of Jerusalem have found strength in the Lord Almighty, their God.'

6"In that day I will make the clans of Judah like a little fire that sets the forest aflame—like a burning match among the sheaves; they will burn up all the neighboring nations right and left, while Jerusalem stands unmoved. 7The Lord will give victory to the rest of Judah first, before Jerusalem, so that the people of Jerusalem and the royal line of David won't be filled with pride at their success.

8"The Lord will defend the people of Jerusalem; the weakest among them will be as mighty as King David! And the royal line will be as God, like the Angel of the Lord who goes before them! 9For my plan is to destroy all the nations that come against Jerusalem.

10"Then I will pour out the spirit of grace and prayer on all the people of Jerusalem, and they will look on him they pierced, and mourn for him as for an only son, and grieve bitterly for him as for an oldest child who died. 11The sorrow and mourning in Jerusalem at that time will be even greater than the grievous mourning for the godly King Josiah, who was killed in the valley of Megiddo.

12,13,14"All of Israel will weep in profound sorrow. The whole nation will be bowed down with universal grief—king, prophet, priest, and people. Each family will go into private mourning, husbands and wives apart, to face their sorrow alone.

"AT that time a Fountain will be opened to the people of Israel and Jerusalem, a Fountain to cleanse them from all their sins and defilement."

2And the Lord Almighty declares, "In that day I will get rid of every vestige of idol worship throughout the land, so that even the names of the idols will be forgotten. All false prophets and fortunetellers will be wiped out, 3and if anyone begins false prophecy again, his own father and mother will slay him! 'You must die,' they will tell him, 'for you are prophesying lies in the name of the Lord.'

4"No one will be boasting then of his prophetic gift! No one will wear prophet's clothes to try to fool the people then.

5" 'No,' he will say. 'I am not a prophet; I am a farmer. The soil has been my livelihood from my earliest youth.'

6"And if someone asks, 'Then what are these scars on your chest and your back?' he will say, 'I got into a brawl at the home of a friend!'

7"Awake, O sword, against my Shepherd, the man who is my associate and equal," says the Lord Almighty. "Strike down the Shepherd and the sheep will scatter, but I will come back and comfort and care for the lambs. 8Two-thirds of all the nation of Israel will be cut off and die, but a third will be left in the land. 9I will bring the third that remain through the fire and make them pure, as gold and silver are refined and purified by fire. They will call upon my name and I will hear them; I will say, 'These are my people,' and they will say, 'The Lord is our God.' "

REVELATION 19:1-21

AFTER this I heard the shouting of a vast crowd in heaven, "Hallelujah! Praise the Lord! Salvation is from our God. Honor and authority belong to him alone; 2for his judgments are just and true. He has punished the Great Prostitute who corrupted the earth with her sin; and he has avenged the murder of his servants."

3Again and again their voices rang, "Praise the Lord! The smoke from her burning ascends forever and forever!"

4Then the twenty-four Elders and four Living Beings fell down and worshiped God, who was sitting upon the throne, and said, "Amen! Hallelujah! Praise the Lord!"

5And out of the throne came a voice that said, "Praise our God, all you his servants, small and great, who fear him."

6Then I heard again what sounded like the shouting of a huge crowd, or like the waves of a hundred oceans crashing on the shore, or like the mighty rolling of great thunder, "Praise the Lord. For the Lord our God, the Almighty, reigns. 7Let us be glad and rejoice and honor him; for the time has come for the wedding banquet of the Lamb, and his bride has prepared herself. 8She is permitted to wear the cleanest and whitest and finest of linens." (Fine linen represents the good deeds done by the people of God.)

9And the angel dictated this sentence to me: "Blessed are those who are invited to the wedding feast of the Lamb." And he added, "God himself has stated this."

10Then I fell down at his feet to worship him, but he said, "No! Don't! For I am a servant of God just as you are, and as your brother Christians are, who testify of their faith in Jesus. Worship God. The purpose of all prophecy and of all I have shown you is to tell about Jesus."

11Then I saw heaven opened and a white horse standing there; and the one sitting on the horse was named "Faithful and True"—the one who justly punishes and makes war. 12His eyes were like flames, and on his head were many crowns. A name was written on his forehead, and only he knew its meaning. 13He was clothed with garments dipped in blood, and his title was "The Word of God." 14The armies of heaven, dressed in finest linen, white and clean, followed him on white horses.

15In his mouth he held a sharp sword to strike down the nations; he ruled them with an iron grip; and he trod the winepress of the fierceness of the wrath of Almighty God. 16On his robe and thigh was written this title: "King of Kings and Lord of Lords."

17Then I saw an angel standing in the sunshine, shouting loudly to the birds, "Come! Gather together for the supper of the Great God! 18Come and eat the flesh of kings, and captains, and great generals; of horses and riders; and of all humanity, both great and small, slave and free."

19Then I saw the Evil Creature gathering the governments of the earth and their armies to fight against the one sitting on the horse and his army. 20And the Evil Creature was captured, and with him the False Prophet, who could do mighty miracles when the Evil Creature was present—miracles that deceived all who had accepted the Evil Creature's mark, and who worshiped his statue. Both of them—the Evil Creature and his False Prophet—were thrown alive into the Lake of Fire that burns with sulphur. 21And their entire army was killed with the sharp sword in the mouth of the one riding the white horse, and all the birds of heaven were gorged with their flesh.

PSALM 147:1-20

HALLELUJAH! Yes, praise the Lord! How good it is to sing his praises! How delightful, and how right!

2He is rebuilding Jerusalem and bringing back the exiles. 3He heals the brokenhearted, binding up their wounds. 4He counts the stars and calls them all by name. ⁵How great he is! His power is absolute! His understanding is unlimited. ⁶The Lord supports the humble, but brings the wicked into the dust.

⁷Sing out your thanks to him; sing praises to our God, accompanied by harps. ⁸He covers the heavens with clouds, sends down the showers and makes the green grass grow in mountain pastures. ⁹He feeds the wild animals and the young ravens cry to him for food. ¹⁰The speed of a horse is nothing to him. How puny in his sight is the strength of a man. ¹¹But his joy is in those who reverence him, those who expect him to be loving and kind.

¹²Praise him, O Jerusalem! Praise your God, O Zion! ¹³For he has fortified your gates against all enemies, and blessed your children. ¹⁴He sends peace across your nation, and fills your barns with plenty of the finest wheat. ¹⁵He sends his orders to the world. How swiftly his word flies. ¹⁶He sends the snow in all its lovely whiteness, and scatters the frost upon the ground, ¹⁷and hurls the hail upon the earth. Who can stand before his freezing cold? ¹⁸But then he calls for warmer weather, and the spring winds blow and all the river ice is broken. ¹⁹He has made known his laws and ceremonies of worship to Israel— ²⁰something he has not done with any other nation; they have not known his commands.

Hallelujah! Yes, praise the Lord!

PROVERBS FOR TODAY/ 31:1–7

These are the wise sayings of King Lemuel of Massa, taught to him at his mother's knee: *O my son, whom I have dedicated to the Lord, do not spend your time with women—the royal pathway to destruction. And it is not for kings, O Lemuel, to drink wine and whiskey. For if they drink they may forget their duties and be unable to give justice to those who are oppressed. Hard liquor is for sick men at the brink of death, and wine for those in deep depression. Let them drink to forget their poverty and misery.*

DECEMBER 29

ZECHARIAH 14:1–21

WATCH, for the day of the Lord is coming soon! On that day the Lord will gather together the nations to fight Jerusalem; the city will be taken, the houses rifled, the loot divided, the women raped; half the population will be taken away as slaves, and half will be left in what remains of the city.

³Then the Lord will go out fully armed for war, to fight against those nations. ⁴That day his feet will stand upon the Mount of Olives, to the east of Jerusalem, and the Mount of Olives will split apart, making a very wide valley running from east to west, for half the mountain will move toward the north and half toward the south. ⁵You will escape through that valley, for it will reach across to the city gate. Yes, you will escape as your people did long centuries ago from the earthquake in the days of Uzziah, king of Judah, and the Lord my God shall come, and all his saints and angels with him.

⁶The sun and moon and stars will no longer shine, ⁷yet there will be continuous day! Only the Lord knows how! There will be no normal day and night— at evening time it will still be light.

8Life-giving waters will flow out from Jerusalem, half toward the Dead Sea and half toward the Mediterranean, flowing continuously both in winter and in summer.

9And the Lord shall be King over all the earth. In that day there shall be one Lord—his name alone will be worshiped. 10All the land from Geba (the northern border of Judah) to Rimmon (the southern border) will become one vast plain, but Jerusalem will be on an elevated site, covering the area all the way from the Gate of Benjamin over to the site of the old gate, then to the Corner Gate, and from the Tower of Hananel to the king's wine presses. 11And Jerusalem shall be inhabited, safe at last, never again to be cursed and destroyed.

12And the Lord will send a plague on all the people who fought Jerusalem. They will become like walking corpses, their flesh rotting away; their eyes will shrivel in their sockets, and their tongues will decay in their mouths.

13They will be seized with terror, panic-stricken from the Lord, and will fight against each other in hand-to-hand combat. 14All Judah will be fighting at Jerusalem. The wealth of all the neighboring nations will be confiscated—great quantities of gold and silver and fine clothing. 15(This same plague will strike the horses, mules, camels, donkeys, and all the other animals in the enemy camp.)

16In the end, those who survive the plague will go up to Jerusalem each year to worship the King, the Lord Almighty, to celebrate a time of thanksgiving. 17And any nation anywhere in all the world that refuses to come to Jerusalem to worship the King, the Lord Almighty, will have no rain. 18But if Egypt refuses to come, God will punish her with some other plague. 19And so Egypt and the other nations will all be punished if they refuse to come.

20In that day the bells on the horses will have written on them, "These Are Holy Property"; and the trash cans in the Temple of the Lord will be as sacred as the bowls beside the altar. 21In fact, every container in Jerusalem and Judah shall be sacred to the Lord Almighty; all who come to worship may use any of them free of charge to boil their sacrifices in; there will be no more grasping traders in the Temple of the Lord Almighty!

REVELATION 20:1–15

THEN I saw an angel come down from heaven with the key to the bottomless pit and a heavy chain in his hand. 2He seized the Dragon—that old Serpent, the devil, Satan—and bound him in chains for 1,000 years, 3and threw him into the bottomless pit, which he then shut and locked, so that he could not fool the nations any more until the thousand years were finished. Afterwards he would be released again for a little while.

4Then I saw thrones, and sitting on them were those who had been given the right to judge. And I saw the souls of those who had been beheaded for their testimony about Jesus, for proclaiming the Word of God, and who had not worshiped the Creature or his statue, nor accepted his mark on their foreheads or their hands. They had come to life again and now they reigned with Christ for a thousand years.

5This is the First Resurrection. (The rest of the dead did not come back to life until the thousand years had ended.) 6Blessed and holy are those who share in the First Resurrection. For them the Second Death holds no terrors, for they will be priests of God and of Christ, and shall reign with him a thousand years.

7When the thousand years end, Satan will be let out of his prison. 8He will go out to deceive the nations of the world and gather them together, with Gog and Magog, for battle—a mighty host, numberless as sand along the shore. 9They will go up across the broad plain of the earth and surround God's people and the beloved city of Jerusalem on every side. But fire from God in heaven will flash down on the attacking armies and consume them.

10Then the devil who had betrayed them will again be thrown into the Lake of Fire burning with sulphur where the Creature and False Prophet are, and they will be tormented day and night forever and ever.

11And I saw a great white throne and the one who sat upon it, from whose face the earth and sky fled away, but they found no place to hide. 12I saw the dead, great and small, standing before God; and The Books were opened, including the Book of Life. And the dead were judged according to the things written in The Books, each according to the deeds he had done. 13The oceans surrendered the bodies buried in them; and the earth and the underworld gave up the dead in them. Each was judged according to his deeds. 14And Death and Hell were thrown into the Lake of Fire. This is the Second Death—the Lake of Fire. 15And if anyone's name was not found recorded in the Book of Life, he was thrown into the Lake of Fire.

PSALM 148:1–14

PRAISE the Lord, O heavens! Praise him from the skies! 2Praise him, all his angels, all the armies of heaven. 3Praise him, sun and moon, and all you twinkling stars. 4Praise him, skies above. Praise him, vapors high above the clouds.

5Let everything he has made give praise to him. For he issued his command, and they came into being; 6he established them forever and forever. His orders will never be revoked.

7And praise him down here on earth, you creatures of the ocean depths. 8Let fire and hail, snow, rain, wind and weather, all obey. 9Let the mountains and hills, the fruit trees and cedars, 10the wild animals and cattle, the snakes and birds, 11the kings and all the people with their rulers and their judges, 12young men and maidens, old men and children— 13all praise the Lord together. For he alone is worthy. His glory is far greater than all of earth and heaven. 14He has made his people strong, honoring his godly ones—the people of Israel, the people closest to him.

Hallelujah! Yes, praise the Lord!

PROVERBS FOR TODAY/ 31:8–9

You should defend those who cannot help themselves. Yes, speak up for the poor and helpless, and see that they get justice.

DECEMBER 30

MALACHI 1:1—2:17

HERE is the Lord's message to Israel, given through the prophet Malachi:

2,3"I have loved you very deeply," says the Lord.

But you retort, "Really? When was this?"

And the Lord replies, "I showed my love for you by loving your father, Jacob. I didn't need to. I even rejected his very own brother, Esau, and destroyed Esau's mountains and inheritance, to give it to the jackals of the desert. 4And if his descendants should say, 'We will rebuild the ruins,' then the Lord Almighty will say, 'Try to if you like, but I will destroy it again,' for their country is named 'The

Land of Wickedness' and their people are called 'Those Whom God Does Not Forgive.' "

5O Israel, lift your eyes to see what God is doing all around the world; then you will say, "Truly, the Lord's great power goes far beyond our borders!"

6"A son honors his father, a servant honors his master. I am your Father and Master, yet you don't honor me, O priests, but you despise my name."

"Who? Us?" you say. "When did we ever despise your name?"

7"When you offer polluted sacrifices on my altar."

"Polluted sacrifices? When have we ever done a thing like that?"

"Every time you say, 'Don't bother bringing anything very valuable to offer to God!' 8You tell the people, 'Lame animals are all right to offer on the altar of the Lord—yes, even the sick and the blind ones.' And you claim this isn't evil? Try it on your governor sometime—give him gifts like that—and see how pleased he is!

9" 'God have mercy on us,' you recite; 'God be gracious to us!' But when you bring that kind of gift, why should he show you any favor at all?

10"Oh, to find one priest among you who would shut the doors and refuse this kind of sacrifice. I have no pleasure in you," says the Lord Almighty, "and I will not accept your offerings.

11"But my name will be honored by the Gentiles from morning till night. All around the world they will offer sweet incense and pure offerings in honor of my name. For my name shall be great among the nations," says the Lord Almighty. 12"But you dishonor it, saying that my altar is not important, and encouraging people to bring cheap, sick animals to offer to me on it.

13"You say, 'Oh, it's too difficult to serve the Lord and do what he asks.' And you turn up your noses at the rules he has given you to obey. Think of it! Stolen animals, lame and sick—as offerings to God! Should I accept such offerings as these?" asks the Lord. 14"Cursed is that man who promises a fine ram from his flock, and substitutes a sick one to sacrifice to God. For I am a Great King," says the Lord Almighty, "and my name is to be mightily revered among the Gentiles."

LISTEN, you priests, to this warning from the Lord Almighty:

"If you don't change your ways and give glory to my name, then I will send terrible punishment upon you, and instead of giving you blessings as I would like to, I will turn on you with curses. Indeed, I have cursed you already because you haven't taken seriously the things that are most important to me.

3"Take note that I will rebuke your children and I will spread on your faces the manure of these animals you offer me, and throw you out like dung. 4Then at last you will know it was I who sent you this warning to return to the laws I gave your father Levi," says the Lord Almighty. 5"The purpose of these laws was to give him life and peace, to be a means of showing his respect and awe for me, by keeping them. 6He passed on to the people all the truth he got from me. He did not lie or cheat; he walked with me, living a good and righteous life, and turned many from their lives of sin.

7"Priests' lips should flow with the knowledge of God so the people will learn God's laws. The priests are the messengers of the Lord Almighty, and men should come to them for guidance. 8But not to you! For you have left God's paths. Your 'guidance' has caused many to stumble in sin. You have distorted the covenant of Levi, and made it into a grotesque parody," says the Lord Almighty. 9"Therefore I have made you contemptible in the eyes of all the people; for you have not obeyed me, but you let your favorites break the law without rebuke."

10We are children of the same father, Abraham, all created by the same God. And yet we are faithless to each other, violating the covenant of our fathers! 11In Judah, in Israel, and in Jerusalem, there is treachery, for the men of Judah have defiled God's holy and beloved Temple by marrying heathen women who worship idols. 12May the Lord cut off from his covenant every last man, whether priest or layman, who has done this thing!

13Yet you cover the altar with your tears because the Lord doesn't pay attention to your offerings anymore, and you receive no blessing from him. 14"Why has God abandoned us?" you cry. I'll tell you why; it is because the Lord has seen your treachery in divorcing your wives who have been faithful to you through the years, the companions you promised to care for and keep. 15You were united to your wife by the Lord. In God's wise plan, when you married, the two of you became one person in his sight. And what does he want? Godly children from your union. Therefore guard your passions! Keep faith with the wife of your youth.

16For the Lord, the God of Israel, says he hates divorce and cruel men. Therefore control your passions—let there be no divorcing of your wives.

17You have wearied the Lord with your words.

"Wearied him?" you ask in fake surprise. "How have we wearied him?"

By saying that evil is good, that it pleases the Lord! Or by saying that God won't punish us—he doesn't care.

REVELATION 21:1–27

THEN I saw a new earth (with no oceans!) and a new sky, for the present earth and sky had disappeared. 2And I, John, saw the Holy City, the new Jerusalem, coming down from God out of heaven. It was a glorious sight, beautiful as a bride at her wedding.

3I heard a loud shout from the throne saying, "Look, the home of God is now among men, and he will live with them and they will be his people; yes, God himself will be among them. 4He will wipe away all tears from their eyes, and there shall be no more death, nor sorrow, nor crying, nor pain. All of that has gone forever."

5And the one sitting on the throne said, "See, I am making all things new!" And then he said to me, "Write this down, for what I tell you is trustworthy and true: 6It is finished! I am the A and the Z—the Beginning and the End. I will give to the thirsty the springs of the Water of Life—as a gift! 7Everyone who conquers will inherit all these blessings, and I will be his God and he will be my son. 8But cowards who turn back from following me, and those who are unfaithful to me, and the corrupt, and murderers, and the immoral, and those conversing with demons, and idol worshipers and all liars—their doom is in the Lake that burns with fire and sulphur. This is the Second Death."

9Then one of the seven angels, who had emptied the flasks containing the seven last plagues, came and said to me, "Come with me and I will show you the bride, the Lamb's wife."

10In a vision he took me to a towering mountain peak and from there I watched that wondrous city, the holy Jerusalem, descending out of the skies from God. 11It was filled with the glory of God, and flashed and glowed like a precious gem, crystal clear like jasper. 12Its walls were broad and high, with twelve gates guarded by twelve angels. And the names of the twelve tribes of Israel were written on the gates. 13There were three gates on each side—north, south, east, and west. 14The walls had twelve foundation stones, and on them were written the names of the twelve apostles of the Lamb.

15The angel held in his hand a golden measuring stick to measure the city and its gates and walls. 16When he measured it, he found it was a square as wide as it was long; in fact it was in the form of a cube, for its height was exactly the same as its other dimensions—1,500 miles each way. 17Then he measured the thickness of the walls and found them to be 216 feet across (the angel called out these measurements to me, using standard units).

18,19,20The city itself was pure, transparent gold like glass! The wall was made of jasper, and was built on twelve layers of foundation stones inlaid with gems:

The first layer with jasper;
The second with sapphire;
The third with chalcedony;
The fourth with emerald;
The fifth with sardonyx;
The sixth layer with sardus;
The seventh with chrysolite;
The eighth with beryl;
The ninth with topaz;
The tenth with chrysoprase;
The eleventh with jacinth;
The twelfth with amethyst.

21The twelve gates were made of pearls—each gate from a single pearl! And the main street was pure, transparent gold, like glass.

22No temple could be seen in the city, for the Lord God Almighty and the Lamb are worshiped in it everywhere. 23And the city has no need of sun or moon to light it, for the glory of God and of the Lamb illuminate it. 24Its light will light the nations of the earth, and the rulers of the world will come and bring their glory to it. 25Its gates never close; they stay open all day long—and there is no night! 26And the glory and honor of all the nations shall be brought into it. 27Nothing evil will be permitted in it—no one immoral or dishonest—but only those whose names are written in the Lamb's Book of Life.

PSALM 149:1–9

HALLELUJAH! Yes, praise the Lord! Sing him a new song. Sing his praises, all his people.

2O Israel, rejoice in your Maker. O people of Jerusalem, exult in your King. 3Praise his name with dancing, accompanied by drums and lyre.

4,5For Jehovah enjoys his people; he will save the humble. Let his people rejoice in this honor. Let them sing for joy as they lie upon their beds.

6,7Adore him, O his people! And take a double-edged sword to execute his punishment upon the nations. 8Bind their kings and leaders with iron chains, 9and execute their sentences.

He is the glory of his people. Hallelujah! Praise him!

PROVERBS FOR TODAY/ 31:10–24

If you can find a truly good wife, she is worth more than precious gems! Her husband can trust her, and she will richly satisfy his needs. She will not hinder him, but help him all her life. She finds wool and flax and busily spins it. She buys imported foods, brought by ship from distant ports. She gets up before dawn to prepare breakfast for her household, and plans the day's work for her servant girls. She goes out to inspect a field, and buys it; with her own hands she plants a vineyard. She is energetic, a hard worker, and watches for bargains. She works far into the night! She sews for the poor, and generously helps those in need. She has no fear of winter for her household, for she has made warm clothes for all of them. She also upholsters with finest tapestry; her own clothing is beautifully made— a purple gown of pure linen. Her husband is well known, for he sits in the council chamber with the other civic leaders. She makes belted linen garments to sell to the merchants.

DECEMBER 31

MALACHI 3:1—4:6

LISTEN: I will send my messenger before me to prepare the way. And then the one you are looking for will come suddenly to his Temple—the Messenger of God's promises, to bring you great joy. Yes, he is surely coming," says the Lord Almighty. 2"But who can live when he appears? Who can endure his coming? For he is like a blazing fire refining precious metal and he can bleach the dirtiest garments! 3Like a refiner of silver he will sit and closely watch as the dross is burned away. He will purify the Levites, the ministers of God, refining them like gold or silver, so that they will do their work for God with pure hearts. 4Then once more the Lord will enjoy the offerings brought to him by the people of Judah and Jerusalem, as he did before. 5At that time my punishments will be quick and certain; I will move swiftly against wicked men who trick the innocent, against adulterers, and liars, against all those who cheat their hired hands, or oppress widows and orphans, or defraud strangers, and do not fear me," says the Lord Almighty.

6"For I am the Lord—I do not change. That is why you are not already utterly destroyed [for my mercy endures forever].

7"Though you have scorned my laws from earliest time, yet you may still return to me," says the Lord Almighty. "Come and I will forgive you.

"But you say, 'We have never even gone away!'

8"Will a man rob God? Surely not! And yet you have robbed me.

" 'What do you mean? When did we ever rob you?'

"You have robbed me of the tithes and offerings due to me. 9And so the awesome curse of God is cursing you, for your whole nation has been robbing me. 10Bring all the tithes into the storehouse so that there will be food enough in my Temple; if you do, I will open up the windows of heaven for you and pour out a blessing so great you won't have room enough to take it in!

"Try it! Let me prove it to you! 11Your crops will be large, for I will guard them from insects and plagues. Your grapes won't shrivel away before they ripen," says the Lord Almighty. 12"And all nations will call you blessed, for you will be a land sparkling with happiness. These are the promises of the Lord Almighty.

13"Your attitude toward me has been proud and arrogant," says the Lord.

"But you say, 'What do you mean? What have we said that we shouldn't?'

14,15"Listen; you have said, 'It is foolish to worship God and obey him. What good does it do to obey his laws, and to sorrow and mourn for our sins? From now on, as far as we're concerned, "Blessed are the arrogant." For those who do evil shall prosper, and those who dare God to punish them shall get off scot-free.' "

16Then those who feared and loved the Lord spoke often of him to each other. And he had a Book of Remembrance drawn up in which he recorded the names of those who feared him and loved to think about him.

17"They shall be mine," says the Lord Almighty, "in that day when I make up my jewels. And I will spare them as a man spares an obedient and dutiful son. 18Then you will see the difference between God's treatment of good men and bad, between those who serve him and those who don't.

"WATCH now," the Lord Almighty declares, "the day of judgment is coming, burning like a furnace. The proud and wicked will be burned up like straw; like a tree, they will be consumed—roots and all.

2"But for you who fear my name, the Sun of Righteousness will rise with healing in his wings. And you will go free, leaping with joy like calves let out to pasture. 3Then you will tread upon the wicked as ashes underfoot," says the Lord Almighty. 4"Remember to obey the laws I gave all Israel through Moses my servant on Mount Horeb.

5"See, I will send you another prophet like Elijah before the coming of the great and dreadful judgment day of God. 6His preaching will bring fathers and children together again, to be of one mind and heart, for they will know that if they do not repent, I will come and utterly destroy their land."

REVELATION 22:1-21

AND he pointed out to me a river of pure Water of Life, clear as crystal, flowing from the throne of God and the Lamb, 2coursing down the center of the main street. On each side of the river grew Trees of Life, bearing twelve crops of fruit, with a fresh crop each month; the leaves were used for medicine to heal the nations.

3There shall be nothing in the city which is evil; for the throne of God and of the Lamb will be there, and his servants will worship him. 4And they shall see his face; and his name shall be written on their foreheads. 5And there will be no night there—no need for lamps or sun—for the Lord God will be their light; and they shall reign forever and ever.

6,7Then the angel said to me, "These words are trustworthy and true: 'I am coming soon!' God, who tells his prophets what the future holds, has sent his angel to tell you this will happen soon. Blessed are those who believe it and all else written in the scroll."

8I, John, saw and heard all these things, and fell down to worship the angel who showed them to me; 9but again he said,

"No, don't do anything like that. I, too, am a servant of Jesus as you are, and as your brothers the prophets are, as well as all those who heed the truth stated in this Book. Worship God alone."

10Then he instructed me, "Do not seal up what you have written, for the time of fulfillment is near. 11And when that time comes, all doing wrong will do it more and more; the vile will become more vile; good men will be better; those who are holy will continue on in greater holiness."

12"See, I am coming soon, and my reward is with me, to repay everyone according to the deeds he has done. 13I am the A and the Z, the Beginning and the End, the First and Last. 14Blessed forever are all who are washing their robes, to have the right to enter in through the gates of the city, and to eat the fruit from the Tree of Life.

15"Outside the city are those who have strayed away from God, and the sorcerers and the immoral and murderers and idolaters, and all who love to lie, and do so.

16"I, Jesus, have sent my angel to you to tell the churches all these things. I am both David's Root and his Descendant. I am the bright Morning Star. 17The Spirit and the bride say, 'Come.' Let each one who hears them say the same, 'Come.' Let the thirsty one come—anyone who wants to; let him come and drink the Water of Life without charge. 18And I solemnly declare to everyone who reads this book: If anyone adds anything to what is written here, God shall add to him the plagues described in this book. 19And if anyone subtracts any part of these prophecies, God shall take away his share in the Tree of Life, and in the Holy City just described.

20"He who has said all these things declares: Yes, I am coming soon!"

Amen! Come, Lord Jesus!

21The grace of our Lord Jesus Christ be with you all. Amen!

PSALM 150:1–6

HALLELUJAH! Yes, praise the Lord!

Praise him in his Temple, and in the heavens he made with mighty power. ²Praise him for his mighty works. Praise his unequaled greatness. ³Praise him with the trumpet and with lute and harp. ⁴Praise him with the drums and dancing. Praise him with stringed instruments and horns. ⁵Praise him with the cymbals, yes, loud clanging cymbals.

⁶Let everything alive give praises to the Lord! *You* praise him!

Hallelujah!

PROVERBS FOR TODAY/ 31:25–31

She is a woman of strength and dignity, and has no fear of old age. When she speaks, her words are wise, and kindness is the rule for everything she says. She watches carefully all that goes on throughout her household, and is never lazy. Her children stand and bless her; so does her husband. He praises her with these words: "There are many fine women in the world, but you are the best of them all!" Charm can be deceptive and beauty doesn't last, but a woman who fears and reverences God shall be greatly praised. Praise her for the many fine things she does. These good deeds of hers shall bring her honor and recognition from people of importance.